Under the surface

On the face of it a calm sea, but under the surface a cruel environment. Barr & Stroud submarine periscopes have a pedigree which is more than a match for the harsh conditions these vital equipments have to withstand. Every area of operation is served, from the Equator to the Polar icecap, from periscope depth to deep dive. Every class of submarine can be equipped, from midget to nuclear.

BARR AND STROUD

Glasgow and London

Plessey Marine is the principal sonar contractor to the Royal Navy —and to navies around the world.

- ☐ Frigate and Corvette sonars
- ☐ Submarine sonars
- ☐ Helicopter sonars
- ☐ Minehunting sonars
- ☐ Passive sonars

PLESSEY
electronic systems

PLESSEY MARINE
Ilford Essex United Kingdom IG2 6BB
Telephone: London (01) 478 3040

608 PO51 A

JANE'S FIGHTING SHIPS

Edited by **Captain John E. Moore**
RN, FRGS

Order of Contents

World Sales Distribution

Jane's Yearbooks,
Paulton House, 8 Shepherdess Walk
London N1 7LW, England

All the World
except

United States of America and Canada:
Franklin Watts Inc
730 Fifth Avenue
New York, NY 10019, USA

Editorial communication to:

The Editor, Jane's Fighting Ships
Jane's Yearbooks, Paulton House, 8 Shepherdess Walk
London N1 7LW, England
Telephone 01-251 1666

Advertisement communication to:

The Advertisement Manager
Jane's Yearbooks, Paulton House, 8 Shepherdess Walk
London N1 7LW, England
Telephone 01-251 1666

*Classified List of Advertisers
The various products available from the advertisers in this edition are listed alphabetically in about 350 different headings.

Pilot Boats for safety in the sea

[2]

JANE'S FIGHTING SHIPS
ALPHABETICAL LIST OF ADVERTISERS
1976/77 EDITION

Page   Page

Sonar systems
for surface and underwater vessels

Graseby market the following Sonar Systems complete from Dome and Hull Outfit to Computer Interface equipment.

G1750 — A multi-purpose, all-round scanning Sonar for Corvettes and Frigates and above. Active/passive capability of a very high order with consistently accurate auto-tracking, producing close tolerance digital data input to weapon control computers. Incorporates solid-state electronics and is based on the type 184 manufactured by Graseby and fitted to all RN ASW Ships.

G1768 — Sonar derived from the 750 family for use in smaller ships but with many of the features and advantages including auto-tracking.

G1738 — A towed system using modern techniques for decoying active and passive torpedos. Deck machinery is of novel lightweight construction.

G1777 — A small compact Sonar System complete, designed for patrol craft down to 100 tons. Particular emphasis is placed on Display/Operator Interface technology to optimise performance of both equipment and operator.

G1780 — A passive Sonar specially designed to meet the requirements and limitations of very small submarines. Again the latest display technologies have been used to convey information from the equipment to the operator.

UNDERWATER SURVEILLANCE — All types and sizes designed and manufactured, based on unequalled expertise in transducer/hydrophone design and manufacture as well as electronic processing systems.

G1732 — A ship-mounted, modernised version of the RN Throughwater Communications System type 185. Capable of handling high-speed data transmissions from Ship to Submarines and between Submarines.

G1720 — Diver-to-diver and diver-to-surface ship throughwater communications equipment, built to Defence standards and fits neatly onto diver with no impairment of working ability.

G1733 — (S.L.U.T.T.) Ship Launched Underwater Transponder Target used for Sonar/Radar/Visual alignment checks and as a training aid. Electrical frequencies and electronics especially designed to suit a wide range and variety of Sonar transmission characteristics. In quantity production for RN.

These equipments are in volume production for several important Navies.

800 Series — A new development project embracing a family of Sonars of modular construction to provide commonality across the total underwater electro-acoustic spectrum. The very latest concepts of ASW requirements are being used as well as the most uptodate engineering techniques. This project is still on the Secret List.

GRASEBY INSTRUMENTS LIMITED
Kingston-By-Pass, Surbiton, Surrey, Great Britain, KT6 7LR
Telephone: 01-397 5311   Telex: 262795

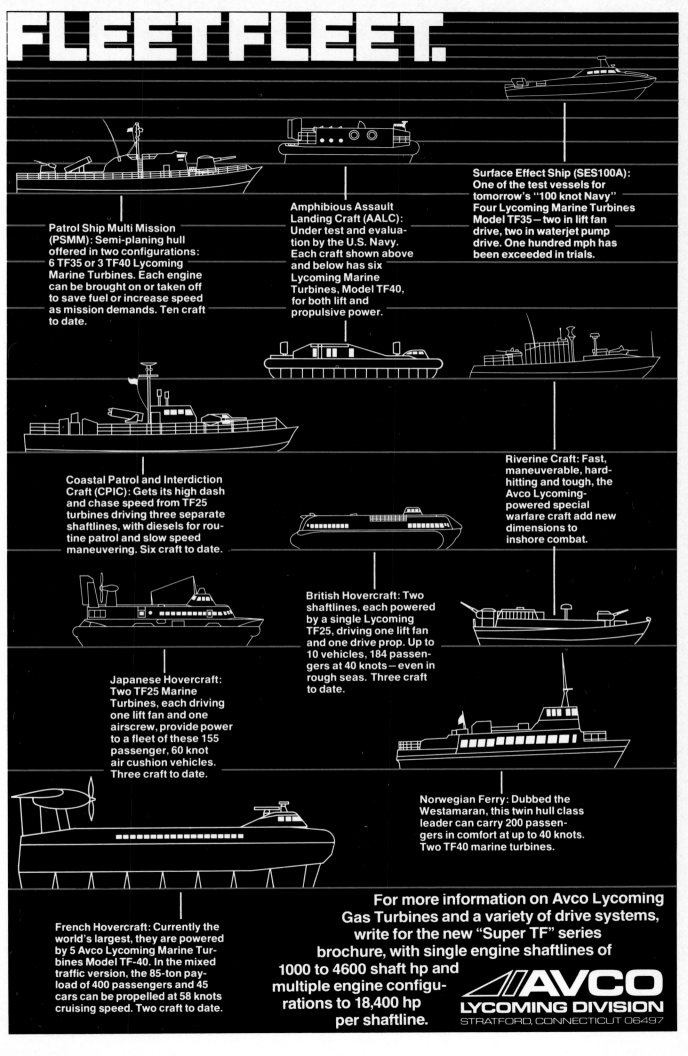

FLEET FLEET.

Patrol Ship Multi Mission (PSMM): Semi-planing hull offered in two configurations: 6 TF35 or 3 TF40 Lycoming Marine Turbines. Each engine can be brought on or taken off to save fuel or increase speed as mission demands. Ten craft to date.

Amphibious Assault Landing Craft (AALC): Under test and evaluation by the U.S. Navy. Each craft shown above and below has six Lycoming Marine Turbines, Model TF40, for both lift and propulsive power.

Surface Effect Ship (SES100A): One of the test vessels for tomorrow's "100 knot Navy." Four Lycoming Marine Turbines Model TF35—two in lift fan drive, two in waterjet pump drive. One hundred mph has been exceeded in trials.

Coastal Patrol and Interdiction Craft (CPIC): Gets its high dash and chase speed from TF25 turbines driving three separate shaftlines, with diesels for routine patrol and slow speed maneuvering. Six craft to date.

Riverine Craft: Fast, maneuverable, hard-hitting and tough, the Avco Lycoming-powered special warfare craft add new dimensions to inshore combat.

Japanese Hovercraft: Two TF25 Marine Turbines, each driving one lift fan and one airscrew, provide power to a fleet of these 155 passenger, 60 knot air cushion vehicles. Three craft to date.

British Hovercraft: Two shaftlines, each powered by a single Lycoming TF25, driving one lift fan and one drive prop. Up to 10 vehicles, 184 passengers at 40 knots—even in rough seas. Three craft to date.

Norwegian Ferry: Dubbed the Westamaran, this twin hull class leader can carry 200 passengers in comfort at up to 40 knots. Two TF40 marine turbines.

French Hovercraft: Currently the world's largest, they are powered by 5 Avco Lycoming Marine Turbines Model TF-40. In the mixed traffic version, the 85-ton payload of 400 passengers and 45 cars can be propelled at 58 knots cruising speed. Two craft to date.

For more information on Avco Lycoming Gas Turbines and a variety of drive systems, write for the new "Super TF" series brochure, with single engine shaftlines of 1000 to 4600 shaft hp and multiple engine configurations to 18,400 hp per shaftline.

AVCO LYCOMING DIVISION
STRATFORD, CONNECTICUT 06497

airconditioned by Kaeser

We produce and supply airconditioning systems for destroyers, frigates, corvettes, minehunters, fast patrol boats, minesweepers, submarines and hydrofoils.

Our reputation as experts in the field of marine airconditioning is world-wide. Our extensive experience and our ability to adapt to individual conditions enable us to develop and install airconditioning systems designed to meet specific demands (for instance, spacesaving units, lightweight units, shock and vibration proof units or intermagnetic models of our airconditioning equipment and systems).

In this respect we have up to now installed airconditioning for 371 navy-vessels for over 50 different international customers.

Our airconditioning experts are ready for a new challenge. Contact us personally or ask for our brochure "Marine Airconditioning".

JANE'S FIGHTING SHIPS
CLASSIFIED LIST OF ADVERTISERS
1977-78 EDITION

The companies advertising in this publication have informed us
that they are involved in the fields of manufacture indicated
below:

ACTIVE INFORMATION SYSTEMS
D.T.C.N.
Ferranti
Plessey Radar
S.M.A.
Vickers

ACTIVE INFORMATION TRAINERS
Ferranti

AIR COMPRESSORS
CIT Alcatel
Fincantieri

AIRCRAFT, ANTI-SUBMARINE PATROL
Hawker Siddeley
Rinaldo Piaggio

AIRCRAFT ARRESTING GEAR
Aérospatiale
MacTaggart Scott

AIRCRAFT CARRIERS
Cantieri Navali Riuniti
Fincantieri
Vickers
Vosper Thornycroft

AIRCRAFT COUNTERMEASURE DISPENSER SYSTEMS
Hycor/Miscota

AIRCRAFT INSTRUMENTS
Cossor
D.T.C.N.
Edo
Ferranti
Rolex
Sperry Gyroscope

AIRCRAFT, MARITIME RECONNAISSANCE
D.T.C.N.
Hawker Siddeley
Rinaldo Piaggio

AIR CUSHION VEHICLES
Bell Aerospace Canada
British Hovercraft Corporation
D.T.C.N.
Vosper Thornycroft

AIRFRAME MANUFACTURERS
Aérospatiale
Agusta
British Hovercraft Corporation
Hawker Siddeley Aviation
Rinaldo Piaggio

ALIGNMENT EQUIPMENT
British Aircraft Corporation

ALTERNATORS
D.T.C.N.

AMMUNITION
Bofors
D.T.C.N.
Oerlikon-Buhrle
Snia Viscosa

AMMUNITION FUSES
Borletti Fratelli
D.T.C.N.
Oerlikon-Buhrle
Snia-Viscosa

AMMUNITION HOISTS
Blohm & Voss
D.T.C.N.
MacTaggart Scott
Oto Melara
Vickers

ANTENNAE
Aeromaritime
British Aircraft Corporation
S.G. Brown Communications
Cossor
D.T.C.N.
Hollandse Signaalapparaten
Marconi
Philips Elektronikindustrier

ANTI-SHIP MISSILE DEFENCE SYSTEMS
Hycor/Miscota

ANTI-SUBMARINE LAUNCHERS
Brooke Marine
D.T.C.N.
Plessey Marine
Vickers
Yarrow (Shipbuilders)

ANTI-SUBMARINE ROCKET LAUNCHERS
Bofors
D.T.C.N.
Vickers

ANTI-SUBMARINE ROCKETS
Bofors
CIT Alcatel
D.T.C.N.

ASSAULT CRAFT
Ailsa Shipbuilding
Bell Aerospace Canada
Blohm & Voss
British Hovercraft Corporation
Brooke Marine
Cantieri Baglietto
Cantieri di Pisa
Crestitalia
Fairey Marine
Fincantieri
Lambie (Boats)
S.F.C.N.
Vosper Thorneycroft

ASSAULT SHIPS
Blohm & Voss
Brooke Marine
Cantieri Navali Riuniti
Fincantieri
S.F.C.N.
Vickers
Vosper Thornycroft
Yarrow (Shipbuilders)

ASW WEAPON CONTROL SYSTEMS
D.T.C.N.
Ferranti
Graseby Instruments
Hollandse Signaalapparaten
Philips Elektronikindustrier
S.E.P.A.
Singer Librascope

AUDIO ANCILLARY TEST SETS
S.G. Brown Communications

AUTOMATIC CONTROL SYSTEMS
CIT Alcatel
D.T.C.N.
Ferranti
Motoren-und Turbin'en-Union
S.E.P.A.
Singer Librascope
Sperry Gyroscope
Thomson CSF

AUTOMATIC STEERING
Sperry Gyroscope

AUXILIARY MACHINERY
Blohm & Voss
D.T.C.N.
Fincantieri
Motoren-und Turbinen-Union

BINOCULARS
Barr & Stroud
British Aircraft Corporation
D.T.C.N.
Fincantieri
Officine Galileo

BOILERS
Blohm & Voss
Bremer Vulkan
Howaldtswerke-Deutsche Werft
Ruston Paxman Diesels
Yarrow (Shipbuilders)

BOOKS (NAVAL)
D.T.C.N.
Vosper Thornycroft

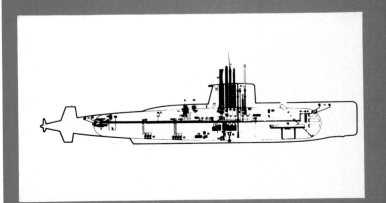

BULK CARRIERS
Ailsa Shipbuilding
Blohm & Voss
Bremer Vulkan
Cantieri Navali Riuniti
Dubigeon-Normandie
Fincantieri
Howaldtswerke-Deutsche Werft
Italcantieri
Lürssen Werft
Sippican
Vickers

B-OSS IN STERNFRAME
Italsider

CAPSTANS AND WINDLASSES
Fincantieri
MacTaggart Scott
Riva Calzoni

CAR FERRIES
Ailsa Shipbuilding
Bell Aerospace Canada
Blohm & Voss
Bremer Vulkan
British Hovercraft Corporation
Brooke Marine
Cantieri Navali Riuniti
C.N.I.M.
D.T.C.N.
Dubigeon-Normandie
Fincantieri
Italcantieri
Lürssen Werft
Vickers
Yarrow (Shipbuilders)

CARGO HANDLING EQUIPMENT
Blohm & Voss
Bremer Vulkan
D.T.C.N.
MacTaggart Scott
S.E.P.A.

CARGO SHIPS
Ailsa Shipbuilding
Blohm & Voss
Bremer Vulkan
Brooke Marine
Cantieri Navali Riuniti
D.T.C.N.
Dubigeon-Normandie
Fincantieri
Howaldtswerke-Deutsche Werft
Italcantieri
Lürssen Werft
Vickers

CASTINGS, ALUMINIUM/BRONZE
Barr & Stroud
LIPS
Vickers

CASTINGS, HIGH DUTY IRON
Bremer Vulkan

CASTINGS, NON-FERROUS
Vickers

CASTINGS, SHELL MOULDED
Bremer Vulkan
Ferranti

CASTINGS, S.G. IRON
Bremer Vulkan
Ferranti

CASTINGS, STEEL
Bremer Vulkan
Italsider

CATHODIC PROTECTION EQUIPMENT
Marconi
Thomson CSF
Vickers

CENTRALISED AND AUTOMATIC CONTROL
CIT Alcatel
C.S.E.E.
S.E.P.A.
Thomson CSF

CHAFF
Hycor/Miscota

COASTAL AND INSHORE MINESWEEPERS
Ailsa Shipbuilding
Bell Aerospace Canada
British Hovercraft Corporation
Brooke Marine
Cantieri Baglietto
Cantieri Navali Riuniti
D.C.T.N.
Fincantieri
Italcantieri
Netherlands United Shipbuilders
Vickers
Vosper Thornycroft
Yarrow (Shipbuilders)

COMMAND/CONTROL/COMMUNICATIONS SYSTEMS
Aeromaritime
D.T.C.N.
Ferranti
Graseby Instruments
Hollandse Signaalapparaten
Marconi
Oerlikon-Buhrle
Philips Elektronikindustrier
Singer Librascope
Vosper Thornycroft

COMMAND/CONTROL REAL-TIME DISPLAYS
Ferranti
Hollandse Signaalapparaten
Philips Elektronikindustrier
Singer Librascope

COMPRESSED AIR STARTERS FOR GAS TURBINES AND DIESEL ENGINES
D.T.C.N.
Fincantieri
Hatch & Kirk

COMPRESSORS
CIT Alcatel
D.T.C.N.
Fincantieri

COMPUTER SERVICES
Ferranti
S.E.P.A.
Thomson CSF
Vickers
Yarrow (Shipbuilders)

COMPUTERS
CIT Alcatel
Ferranti
Hollandse Signaalapparaten
Oto Melara
Philips Elektronikindustrier
S.E.P.A.
Sperry Gyroscope
Thomson CSF

CONDENSER TUBES
Fincantieri

CONDENSERS
Blohm & Voss
Bremer Vulkan
Fincantieri

CONTAINER SHIPS
Ailsa Shipbuilding
Blohm & Voss
Bremer Vulkan
Brooke Marine
Cantieri Navali Riuniti
D.T.C.N.
Dubigeon-Normandie
Fincantieri
Howaldtswerke-Deutsche Werft
Italcantieri
Vickers

CONTROL DESKS (ELECTRIC)
Lürssen Werft
S.E.P.A.
Vosper Thornycroft
Whipp & Bourne

CONTROL GEAR
Fincantieri
Philips Elektronikindustrier
Ruston Paxman Diesels
Vosper Thornycroft

CORVETTES
Blohm & Voss
Bremer Vulkan
Brooke Marine
Cantieri Navali Riuniti
Crestitalia
C.S.E.E.
D.T.C.N.
Dubigeon-Normandie
Fincantieri
Howaldtswerke-Deutsche Werft
I.N.M.A.
Italcantieri
Lürssen Werft
Netherlands United Shipbuilders
Sofrexan
Vickers
Vosper Thornycroft
Yarrow (Shipbuilders)

331/396

538

652

956

400 to 6000 horses mtu diesel power

mtu Motoren- und Turbinen-Union Friedrichshafen GmbH · M.A.N. Maybach Mercedes-Benz · 799 Friedrichshafen · W.-Germany

[13]

CRANES, SHIPS'
D.T.C.N.
Dubigeon-Normandie

CRANKSHAFTS FOR LOW-SPEED DIESEL ENGINES
Italsider

CRANKSHAFTS IN CONTINUOUS-GRAIN-FLOW FOR MEDIUM SPEED ENGINES
Italsider

CRUISERS
Brooke Marine
Cantieri di Pisa
Cantieri Navali Riuniti
Crestitalia
Dubigeon-Normandie
Fincantieri
Netherlands United Shipbuilders
Vickers
Vosper Thornycroft
Yarrow (Shipbuilders)

CYLINDER COVERS FORGED AND CAST
Italsider

DATA RECORDING SYSTEMS
S.G. Brown Communications
Decca Navigator/Radar
S.E.P.A.

DECK MACHINERY
Cantieri Navali Riuniti
Fincantieri
MacTaggart Scott

DESTROYERS
Blohm & Voss
Brooke Marine
Cantieri Navali Riuniti
D.T.C.N.
Dubigeon-Normandie
Fincantieri
Italcantieri
Netherlands United Shipbuilders
Sofrexan
Vickers
Vosper Thornycroft
Yarrow (Shipbuilders)

DIESEL ENGINES, AUXILIARY
Blohm & Voss
Bremer Vulkan
D.T.C.N.
Fincantieri
Grandi Motori Trieste
Isotta Fraschini
Korody-Colyer
Motoren-und Turbinen-Union
Ruston Paxman Diesels
S.A.C.M.
Vickers

DIESEL ENGINES, MAIN PROPULSION
Alsthom Atlantique
Blohm & Voss
Bremer Vulkan
C.R.M.
D.T.C.N.
Fincantieri
Grandi Motori Trieste
Isotta Fraschini
Korody-Colyer
Motoren-und Turbinen-Union
Ruston Paxman Diesels
S.A.C.M.
Vickers

DIESEL ENGINE SPARE PARTS
Blohm & Voss
Bremer Vulkan
Cantieri Navali Riuniti
C.R.M.
Grandi Motori Trieste
Fincantieri
Hatch & Kirk
Korody-Colyer
Motoren-und Turbinen-Union
Ruston Paxman Diesels
Vickers

DIESEL—FUEL-INJECTION EQUIPMENT
Hatch & Kirk
Korody-Colyer

DISPLAY SYSTEMS
Decca Navigator/Radar
Hollandse Signaalapparaten
Philips Elektronikindustrier
Plessey Radar
S.E.P.A.

DIVING EQUIPMENT
D.T.C.N.
Graseby Instruments
Officine Panerai
Rolex

DOCK GATES
Bremer Vulkan
Dubigeon-Normandie
Fincantieri
Vickers

DREDGERS
Ailsa Shipbuilding
Brooke Marine
Dubigeon-Normandie
Fincantieri
S.F.C.N.

DRY CARGO VESSELS
Ailsa Shipbuilding
Blohm & Voss
Bremer Vulkan
Brooke Marine
Cantieri Navali Riuniti
D.T.C.N.
Dubigeon-Normandie
Fincantieri
Howaldtswerke-Deutsche Werft
Italcantieri
Lürssen Werft
Vickers

DRY DOCK PROPRIETORS
Ailsa Shipbuilding
Blohm & Voss
CIT Alcatel
Fincantieri

DYNAMIC POSITIONING
British Hovercraft Corporation
LIPS
Thomson CSF

ECHO SOUNDERS
Graseby Instruments
Marconi
Thomson CSF

ELECTRIC CABLES
British Hovercraft Corporation
Standard Telephones & Cables

ELECTRIC COUNTERMEASURES
Bofors
British Aircraft Corporation
Decca Navigator/Radar
Sperry Gyroscope
Thomson CSF

ELECTRICAL AUXILIARIES
D.T.C.N.
S.E.P.A.

ELECTRICAL EQUIPMENT
D.T.C.N.
Officine Panerai

ELECTRICAL FITTINGS
D.T.C.N.

ELECTRICAL INSTALLATIONS AND REPAIRS
Bremer Vulkan
D.T.C.N.
Vickers

ELECTRICAL SWITCHGEAR
Lürssen Werft
Thomson CSF
Vosper Thornycroft
Whipp & Bourne

ELECTRO-HYDRAULIC AUXILIARIES
D.T.C.N.
Fincantieri
MacTaggart Scott
Vosper Thornycroft

ELECTRONIC COUNTERMEASURES
Cossor Electronic
Decca Navigator/Radar
D.T.C.N.
Philips Elektronikindustrier
Plessey Radar

ELECTRONIC ENGINE ROOM TELEGRAPH
Officine Panerai
S.E.P.A.
Vosper Thornycroft

ELECTRONIC EQUIPMENT
Aeromaritime
British Aircraft Corporation
S.G. Brown Communications
CIT Alcatel
Decca Navigator/Radar
D.T.C.N.
Edo Corporation
Ferranti
Marconi
Montadel
Motoren-und Turbinen-Union
Oto Melara
Plessey Marine
Plessey Radar
Philips Elektronikindustrier
S.E.P.A.
Sippican
S.M.A.
Sperry Gyroscope
Thomson CSF
USEA
Vickers
Vosper Thornycroft

ELECTRONIC EQUIPMENT REFITS
D.T.C.N.
Ferranti
Marconi
Philips Elektronikindustrier
Plessey Marine
Plessey Radar
Sperry Gyroscope
Vosper Thornycroft

ENGINE MONITORS AND DATA LOGGERS
Decca Navigator/Radar
S.E.P.A.
Vosper Thornycroft

ENGINE PARTS, DIESEL
Bremer Vulkan
C.R.M.
Fincantieri
Grandi Motori Trieste
Hatch & Kirk
Vickers

ENGINE SPEED CONTROLS
S.E.P.A.
Vosper Thornycroft

ENGINE START AND SHUT-DOWN CONTROLS
S.E.P.A.
Vosper Thornycroft

ENGINES, AIRCRAFT
Avco Lycoming
FIAT
Motoren-und Turbinen-Union
Rinaldo Piaggio

ENGINES, DIESEL
Alsthom Atlantique
Blohm & Voss
Bremer Vulkan
C.R.M.
Fincantieri
Isotta Fraschini
Motoren-und Turbinen-Union
Ruston Paxman Diesels
S.A.C.M.

ENGINES, GAS TURBINE
Avco Lycoming
CIT Alcatel
FIAT
Motoren-und Turbinen-Union
Rinaldo Piaggio
S.A.C.M.
Yarrow (Shipbuilders)

ENGINES, STEAM TURBINE
Blohm & Voss
Bremer Vulkan
Cantieri Navali Riuniti
Fincantieri
Yarrow (Shipbuilders)

EPICYCLIC GEARS
British Hovercraft Corporation
Fincantieri
Vickers

EQUIPMENT FOR HELICOPTER NIGHT DECK LANDING
D.T.C.N.
Officine Panerai

ESCORT VESSELS
Blohm & Voss
Bremer Vulkan
Brooke Marine
Cantieri Navali Riuniti
D.T.C.N.
Fairey Marine
Fincantieri
Italcantieri
Lürssen Werft
Netherlands United Shipbuilders
S.F.C.N.
Sofrexan
Vickers
Vosper Thornycroft
Yarrow (Shipbuilders)

FAST PATROL CRAFT
Ailsa Shipbuilding
Bell Aerospace Canada
Bianchi & Cecchi
British Hovercraft Corporation
Brooke Marine
Cantieri Baglietto
Cantieri di Pisa
Cantieri Navali Riuniti
Crestitalia
C.S.E.E.
D.T.C.N.
Fairey Marine
Fincantieri
I.N.M.A.
Lambie (Boats)
Lürssen Werft
Netherlands United Shipbuilders
S.F.C.N.
Sofrexan
Supramar
Vosper Thornycroft
Yarrow (Shipbuilders)

FAST WARSHIP DESIGN SERVICE
Brooke Marine
British Hovercraft Corporation
Cantieri Navali Riuniti
D.T.C.N.
Fincantieri
Lüssen Werft
Supramar
Vickers
Vosper Thornycroft

FEED WATER HEATERS
Blohm & Voss
D.T.C.N.
Fincantieri

FERRIES
Ailsa Shipbuilding
Bell Aerospace Canada
Bremer Vulkan
British Hovercraft Corporation
Brooke Marine
Cantieri Navali Riuniti
D.T.C.N.
Dubigeon-Normandie
Fincantieri
Hawaldtswerke-Deutsche Werft
Italcantieri
S.F.C.N.
Vickers
Yarrow (Shipbuilders)

FIBRE OPTICS
Barr & Stroud
D.T.C.N.
Plessey Radar

FIBREGLASS VESSELS AND OTHER PRODUCTS
Crestitalia
D.T.C.N.
Fairey Marine
Lürssen Werft
Vickers
Vosper Thornycroft

FILTERS, ELECTRIC
Barr & Stroud*
Fincantieri

FIRE AND SALVAGE VESSELS
Bell Aerospace Canada
Brooke Marine
Cantieri Navali Riuniti
Crestitalia
Fincantieri
S.F.C.N.

FIRE CONTROL AND GUNNERY EQUIPMENT
Bofors
C.S.E.E.
D.T.C.N.
Ferranti
Hollandse Signaalapparaten
Oerlikon-Buhrle
Oto Melara
Philips Elektronikindustrier
Plessey Marine
Singer Librascope
Sperry Gyroscope
Thomson CSF
Vickers

EMERLEC·30

THE MODERN MOUNT TO MEET TOTAL FLEET NEEDS

- LAND TARGETS
- SEA TARGETS
- AIR TARGETS

FOR SMALL BOATS, SURFACE SKIMMERS OR LARGE SHIPS

The EMERLEC-30, the most modern gun mount available, offers a lightweight versatile solution to your armament needs. Now in use by many countries, this 30mm flexible system features a high rate-of-fire using local or remote control.

An on-mount battery allows firing a full complement of ammunition even without ship's power. Built-in heating and ventilating systems afford maximum operator comfort.

Caliber: 30mm
Elevation: −15° to 80°
Traverse: +360°
Rate of fire: 600 rounds/barrel/min
Ready rounds: 950 rounds/gun
Projectile weight: 0.35kg
Maximum range: 8km

FOR ADDITIONAL INFORMATION CONTACT MARKETING MANAGER, NAVAL SURFACE ARMAMENT EMERSON ELECTRIC CO., 8100W FLORISSANT AVENUE, ST. LOUIS, MISSOURI 63136, USA TELEPHONE (314) 553-2133 TELEX 44-879

EMERSON

OTO MELARA

OTO MELARA S.p.A. 19100 - La Spezia (Italy) 15, Via Valdilocchi Tel. 504041 - Telex 27368 OTO

OTO Melara was established in 1905 to manufacture guns for the Italian Army and Navy. Since then, except for brief periods immediately following the two world wars, it has continued to be one of the most important suppliers of weapons to the Italian Armed Forces and to more than 30 countries throughout the world.

35 mm OE/OTO TWIN MOUNTING

Rate of fire: 1,100 rds/min
Crew: none. Automatic fire: 800 rds
Training: unlimited
Weight (w/out ammo): 4,900 kg
Versions: remote control, local control, integrated F.C.S.
(Private venture OTO Melara-Oerlikon)

OTO 76/62 COMPACT MOUNTING (3-INCH)

Rate of fire: 85 rds/min
Crew: none. Automatic fire: 80 rds
Training: unlimited
Weight (w/out ammo): 7,350 kg
Versions: remote control, local control, integrated F.C.S.

OTO 127/54 COMPACT MOUNTING (5-INCH)

Rate of fire: 45 rds/min
Crew: none. Automatic fire: 66 rds
Training: 350°
Weight (w/out ammo): 32,500 kg
Versions: remote control, local control.

- Navy small and medium caliber automatic rapid fire guns. Remote control systems for naval armament. Anti-ship missiles. Research and development of army and naval ammunition.

- Handling and launching equipment for naval anti-ship and anti-aircraft medium and long range missiles. Army missiles handling and transport equipments.

105/14 PACK HOWITZER

Ammunition: US M1
Shell weight: 14,9 kg
Range: max 10,575 m
Elevation: −5° to + 65°
Traverse: 36°
Total weight: 1,290 kg

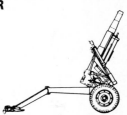

INFANTRY ARMOURED FIGHTING VEHICLE

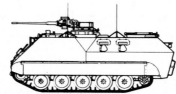

Crew: 9
Weight: 11,560 kg
Road speed: 64 km/h
Range: 550 km
Armament:
12.7 mm machine gun or 20 mm rapid fire gun.

6616 ARMOURED CAR

Crew: 3
Weight: 7,400 kg
Road speed: over 95 km/h
Range: 750 km
Armament:
20 mm, 7.62 mm guns;
40 mm grenade launcher.

- Mono-propellant and bi-propellant auxiliary propulsion systems for attitude and orbital control of artificial satellites.

- Tanks production. Track floating personnel carrier vehicles production, and special armed versions. Armament of self-propelled howitzers.

- Army medium caliber artillery. Automatic loading devices for field medium caliber guns and tanks.

OTOMAT ANTI-SHIP MISSILE SYSTEM

Speed: 0.9 mach.
Warhead: 250 kg
Effective range: > 80 km
Guidance: - target approach: inertial preset at launch
        - target attack: active homing
Attacking path: dive on target unaffected by sea state conditions.
(Private venture OTO Melara-Engins Matra).

LEOPARD MAIN BATTLE TANK

Crew: 4
Weight: 40 tons
Gun: 105/51
Road speed: 65 km/h
Range: 600 km
(Under licence)

ALBATROS SYSTEM S/A MISSILE LAUNCHER

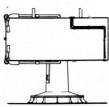

Training: ± 165°
Elevation: −5° to +65°
Weight: (without missiles) 7 tons
Missiles on launcher:
8 (Sparrow III)

SELF PROPELLED HOWITZER - SP70

Crew: 5
Weight: 44 tons
Road speed: 67 km/h
Range: 450 km
Armament: 155/39 howitzer automatic loading system;
cal. 7.62 mm gun.

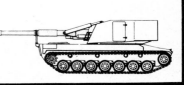

FIRE RESISTANT LIFEBOATS
Bianchi & Cecchi
Lambie (Boats)

FITTINGS, SHIPS
Fincantieri

FLARES
Hycor/Miscota

FLIGHT DECK COATINGS
Preferred Products

FORGINGS, STEEL
Italsider

FRIGATES
Blohm & Voss
Bremer Vulkan
Brooke Marine
Cantieri Navali Riuniti
C.S.E.E.
D.T.C.N.
Dubigeon-Normandie
Fincantieri
Italcantieri
Netherlands United Shipbuilders
Sofrexan
Vickers
Vosper Thornycroft
Yarrow (Shipbuilders)

FUEL FILTRATION EQUIPMENT
Fincantieri
Vickers

GAS TURBINE BOATS
Avco Lycoming
Bell Aerospace Canada
Blohm & Voss
Cantieri Baglietto
Cantieri Navali Riuniti
D.T.C.N.
Fincantieri
Vickers
Vosper Thornycroft
Yarrow (Shipbuilders)

GAS TURBINES
Avco Lycoming
CIT Alcatel
D.T.C.N.
FIAT
Motoren-und Turbinen-Union
S.A.C.M.

GEAR CASINGS
Bremer Vulkan
Fincantieri
Vickers

GEARS
Isotta Fraschini

GEARS AND GEARING
FIAT
British Hovercraft Corporation
Fincantieri
Howaldtswerke-Deutsche Werft
Vickers
Vosper Thornycroft

GEARS, HYPOID
Fincantieri

GEARS, SPIRAL BEVEL
Fincantieri

GEARS, REVERSE-REDUCTION
C.R.M.
Fincantieri
Isotta Fraschini
Motoren-und Turbinen-Union
Vickers
Zahnradfabrik

GEARS, SPUR
Fincantieri

GEARS, VEE DRIVE
C.R.M.
Vosper Thornycroft
Isotta Fraschini
Zahnradfabrik

GENERATORS, ELECTRIC
Avco Lycoming
Ferranti

GOVERNORS
Fincantieri
Hatch & Kirk
S.E.P.A.

GOVERNORS, ENGINE SPEED
Fincantieri
Hatch & Kirk
S.E.P.A.

GUIDED MISSILE SERVICING EQUIPMENT
Aérospatiale
British Aircraft Corporation
Oto Melara
Thomson CSF

GUIDED MISSILE SHIPS
Blohm & Voss
Bremer Vulkan
Brooke Marine
Cantieri Navali Riuniti
D.T.C.N.
Fincantieri
Italcantieri
Lürssen Werft
Netherlands United Shipbuilders
S.F.C.N.
Supramar
Vickers
Vosper Thornycroft
Yarrow (Shipbuilders)

GUIDED MISSILES
Aérospatiale
Bofors
British Aircraft Corporation
D.T.C.N.
Oto Melara
Sistel-Sistemi Elettronici
S.M.A.
Sperry Gyroscope

GUN BOATS
Ailsa Shipbuilding
Bell Aerospace Canada
Brooke Marine
Cantieri Baglietto
Cantieri Navali Riuniti
Crestitalia
D.T.C.N.
Fairey Marine
Fincantieri
I.N.M.A.
Netherlands United Shipbuilders
S.F.C.N.
Vosper Thornycroft
Yarrow (Shipbuilders)

GUNS & MOUNTINGS
Bofors
Breda Meccanica Bresciana
Oerlikon-Buhrle
Oto Melara
Vickers

GUN MOUNTS
Bofors
Emerson Electric
Oerlikon-Buhrle
Oto Melara
Vickers

GUN-SIGHTING APPARATUS AND HEIGHT FINDERS
Oerlikon-Buhrle
Officine Galileo
Philips Elektronikindustrier
Thomson CSF
Vickers

GYROSCOPIC COMPASSES
British Aircraft Corporation
Decca Navigator/Radar
D.T.C.N.
Sperry Gyroscope
Thomson CSF

HANDSETS
S.G. Brown Communications

HEADPHONES
S.G. Brown Communications
D.T.C.N.
Marconi

HEADSETS
S.G. Brown Communications

HEAT EXCHANGERS
Blohm & Voss
Bremer Vulkan
Fincantieri
Howaldtswerke-Deutsche Werft
Yarrow (Shipbuilders)

HEAVY DUTY MOORING MOTORBOATS
Bianchi & Cecchi
Fincantieri

HIGH LEVEL LIQUID ALARM SYSTEMS
Officine Panerai
S.E.P.A.

Now-small ship displays get mini computers to speed tactical data

New Plessey A10/CIC systems for command and control.

Faster decision-making is aided by this entirely new concept from Plessey Radar; naval autonomous displays with individual minicomputers. These processors, with their firmware programs, enable the tactical picture to be compiled rapidly, then distributed and presented in the action information system. Integration of sensors and weapons is achieved without the need for a large central computer complex. And the firmware removes all on-board program handling problems, whilst retaining the ability to evolve new tactics and procedures.

Contact us at the address below for further information.

PLESSEY *electronic systems*

PLESSEY RADAR
Addlestone Surrey England KT15 2PW
Telephone: Weybridge (0932) 47282

603 P166A

HOVERCRAFT
Aérospatiale
Bell Aerospace Canada
British Hovercraft Corporation
D.T.C.N.
Vosper Thornycroft

HYDRAULIC EQUIPMENT
D.T.C.N.
Fincantieri
MacTaggart Scott
Officine Galileo
Oto Melara
Riva Calzoni
Vickers
Vosper Thornycroft

HYDRAULIC MACHINERY
Cantieri Navali Riuniti
D.T.C.N.
Fincantieri
MacTaggart Scott
Riva Calzoni
Vickers
Vosper Thornycroft

HYDRAULIC PLANT
Aerimpianti SpA
Fincantieri
MacTaggart Scott
Riva Calzoni
Vosper Thornycroft

HYDROFOILS
Aérospatiale
Blohm & Voss
Cantiere Navaltecnica
Cantieri Navali Riuniti
D.T.C.N.
Edo
Fincantieri
Supramar
Vosper Thornycroft

**HYDROGRAPHIC SURVEY
EQUIPMENT**
D.T.C.N.
Edo

I.F.F. RADAR
Aeromaritime
Bell Aerospace Canada
Cossor
D.T.C.N.
Hollandse Signaalapparaten
Italtel
Philips Elektronikindustrier
Plessey Radar
Thomson CSF

I.F.F. Mk 10 SYSTEMS
Aeromaritime
Cossor
D.T.C.N.
Italtel
Plessey Radar
Thomson CSF

INDICATORS, ELECTRIC
D.T.C.N.
Thomson CSF

INERTIAL NAVIGATION SYSTEMS
D.T.C.N.
Ferranti
Sperry Gyroscope

**INFRA-RED COUNTERMEASURE
SYSTEMS**
Hycor/Miscota

INFRA-RED MATERIALS
Barr & Stroud
D.T.C.N.
Thomson CSF

INFRA-RED SYSTEMS
Barr & Stroud
D.T.C.N.
Hollandse Signaalapparaten
Officine Galileo
Vickers

**INSTRUMENT CALIBRATION
SERVICES**
Vickers

**INSTRUMENT COMPONENTS
(MECHANICAL)**
Thomson CSF

INSTRUMENTS, ELECTRONIC
Bofors
S.G. Brown Communications
Decca Navigator/Radio
Ferranti
Howaldtswerke-Deutsche Werft
S.E.P.A.
Sperry Gyroscope
Thomson CSF

INSTRUMENTS, NAUTICAL
Sippican Oceanographic Systems
Sperry Gyroscope

INSTRUMENT PANELS
Ferranti
Lürssen Werft
S.E.P.A.
Thomson CSF
Vosper Thornycroft

INSTRUMENTS, PRECISION
D.T.C.N.
Ferranti
Sperry Gyroscope

**INTERIOR DESIGN AND FURNISHING
FOR SHIPS**
Blohm & Voss
Bremer Vulkan
Brooke Marine
Fincantieri
Vickers
Vosper Thornycroft

INVERTERS AND BATTERY CHARGERS
Ferranti

LANDING CRAFT
Ailsa Shipbuilding
Bell Aerospace Canada
Bremer Vulkan
British Hovercraft Corporation
Brooke Marine
Cantieri Baglietto
C.N.I.M.
D.T.C.N.
I.N.M.A.
Lambie (Boats)
Lürssen Werft
Netherlands United Shipbuilders
S.F.C.N.
Vosper Thornycroft
Yarrow (Shipbuilders)

LASER RANGEFINDERS
Barr & Stroud
Bofors
D.T.C.N.
Ferranti
Hollandse Signaalapparaten
Thomson CSF

LASER SYSTEMS
Barr & Stroud
D.T.C.N.
Ferranti
Officine Galileo
Thomson CSF
Vickers

LIFEBOATS
Bianchi & Cecchi
Brooke Marine
Crestitalia
D.T.C.N.
Fairey Marine
Fincantieri
Lambie (Boats)
S.F.C.N.
Vosper Thornycroft

LIFTS, HYDRAULIC
MacTaggart Scott

LIGHTS AND LIGHTING
Officine Panerai

**LIQUID PETROLEUM
GAS CARRIERS**
Bremer Vulkan
C.N.I.M.
Dubigeon-Normandie
Fincantieri
Italcantieri
S.F.C.N.
Vickers

exocet
mm 38

am 39

for sea-power

18 countries today have made the choice of an incomparable weapon - EXOCET - the missile which evades all enemy defences.
Its autonomy and sea-skimming flight make it virtually invulnerable. The range, speed, accuracy and hitting power of EXOCET weapon systems provide tactical superiority to those navies which adopt them.
In production or under development are:
☐ MM 38 already operational in 9 navies and which is suitable for all types of surface vessels from patrol-boat to cruiser,
☐ AM 39 fired from helicopters and assault or maritime patrol aircraft,
☐ MM 40 with a range of more than 35 nautical miles for over-the-horizon engagement of surface targets,
capable of being fitted in quadruple mounts in the smallest types of naval craft.
MM 38 and 40 can also be installed on shore as fixed or mobile coastal batteries.

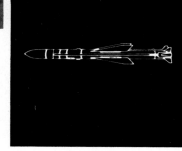

MM 38

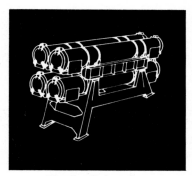

Quadruple launcher
MM 40

Exocet mobile
Coastal battery MM 40

  aerospatiale

division engins tactiques
2, rue Béranger - Châtillon 92320 FRANCE

AEROSPATIALE MISSILES Ltd., 178 Piccadilly, LONDON W1V OBA

Publicité aerospatiale

LOUDSPEAKER EQUIPMENT
Thomson CSF

MACHINED PARTS, FERROUS
Blohm & Voss
Bremer Vulkan
Vickers

MACHINED PARTS, NON-FERROUS
Blohm & Voss
Vickers

MAINTENANCE AND REPAIR SHIPS
Bremer Vulkan
Brooke Marine
Cantiere Navaltecnica
D.T.C.N.
Dubigeon-Normandie
Fincantieri
Vickers
Vosper Thornycroft

MARINE ARCHITECTS
A.B.M.T.M.
Bremer Vulkan
British Hovercraft Corporation
Brooke Marine
D.T.C.N.
Fincantieri
Ingenieurkontor Lübeck
Lürssen Werft
Netherlands United Shipbuilders
Vickers
Vosper Thornycroft

MARINE CONSULTANTS
A.B.M.T.M.

**MARINE ENGINE MONITORING
AND DATA RECORDING SYSTEMS**
Decca Navigator/Radar
Hatch & Kirk
S.E.P.A.
Vosper Thornycroft

MARINE RADAR
Cossor Electronics
Decca Navigator/Radar
D.T.C.N.
Ferranti
Hollandse Signaalapparaten
Graseby Instruments
Marconi
Oerlikon-Buhrle
Philips Elektronikindustrier
S.M.A.
Thomson CSF

MATERIALS HANDLING EQUIPMENT
D.T.C.N.
MacTaggart Scott

MARKET INTELLIGENCE REPORTS
D.M.S.

MERCHANT SHIPS
Ailsa Shipbuilding
Blohm & Voss
Bremer Vulkan
Brooke Marine
Cantieri Navali Riuniti
D.T.C.N.
Dubigeon-Normandie
Fincantieri
Italcantieri
Lürssen Werft
S.F.C.N.
Vickers

MICROPHONE EQUIPMENT
S.G. Brown Communications
Thomson CSF

MINE COUNTERMEASURES
British Hovercraft Corporation
CIT Alcatel
Decca Navigator/Radar
D.T.C.N.
Fairey Marine
Philips Elektronikindustrier
Plessey Marine
S.M.A.
Sperry Gyroscope

MINELAYERS
Blohm & Voss
Bremer Vulkan
British Hovercraft Corporation
Brooke Marine
Cantieri Navali Riuniti
D.T.C.N.
Dubigeon-Normandie
Fincantieri
Netherlands United Shipbuilders
Vickers
Vosper Thornycroft
Yarrow (Shipbuilders)

MINESWEEPERS
Ailsa Shipbuilding
Blohm & Voss
British Hovercraft Corporation
Brooke Marine
Cantieri Baglietto
Cantieri Navali Riuniti
D.T.C.N.
Dubigeon-Normandie
Fincantieri
Italcantieri
Netherlands United Shipbuilders
Thomson CSF
Vickers
Vosper Thornycroft
Yarrow (Shipbuilders)

MINESWEEPING EQUIPMENT
Edo

MISSILE CONTROL SYSTEMS
Aérospatiale
CIT Alcatel
D.T.C.N.
Ferranti
Oerlikon-Buhrle
Officine Galileo
Oto Melara
Philips Elektronikindustrier
Sistel-Sistemi Elettronici
Sperry Gyroscope
Thomson CSF
Vickers

MISSILE INSTALLATIONS
Aérospatiale
D.T.C.N.
Oto Melara
Sistel-Sistemi Elettronici
Thomson CSF
Vickers

MISSILE LAUNCHING SYSTEMS
Aérospatiale
British Hovercraft Corporation
CIT Alcatel
D.T.C.N.
Ferranti
Oto Melara
Sistel-Sistemi Elettronici
Vickers

MISSILE SHIPS
Blohm & Voss
Bremer Vulkan
British Hovercraft Corporation
Brooke Marine
Cantiere Navaltecnica
Cantieri Baglietto
Cantieri Navali Riuniti
D.T.C.N.
Fincantieri
Italcantieri
Lürssen Werft
Netherlands United Shipbuilders
Sofrexan
Vickers
Vosper Thornycroft
Yarrow (Shipbuilders)

MODEL MAKERS AND DESIGNERS
Ailsa Shipbuilding
British Hovercraft Corporation
D.T.C.N.
Fincantieri
Ingenieurkontor Lübeck
Netherlands United Shipbuilders
Vickers
Vosper Thornycroft
Yarrow (Shipbuilders)

**MODEL TEST TOWING
TANK SERVICE**
British Hovercraft Corporation
Vickers

MOTOR CONTROL GEAR
Bremer Vulkan
Thomson CSF

MOTOR STARTERS
Thomson CSF

MOTOR TORPEDO BOATS
Brooke Marine
Cantieri Baglietto
Cantieri Navali Riuniti
D.T.C.N.
Dubigeon-Normandie
Fincantieri
I.N.M.A.
Lürssen Werft
Netherlands United Shipbuilders
S.F.C.N.
Thomson CSF
Vosper Thornycroft
Yarrow (Shipbuilders)

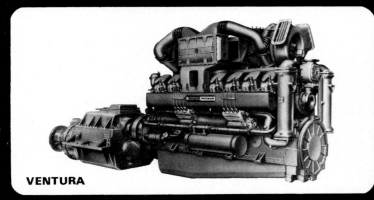
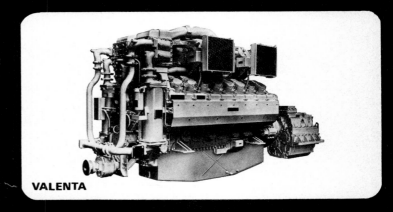

PORTABLE EQUIPMENT FOR AIRCRAFT LANDING
Officine Panerai

PRESSURE VESSELS
Bremer Vulkan
D.T.C.N.
Fincantieri
Vickers
Yarrow (Shipbuilders)

PROPELLANTS
Bofors
Snia Viscosa

PROPELLER SHAFT COUPLINGS, FLEXIBLE
Vickers

PROPELLER SHAFTS AND INTERMEDIATE SHAFTS
Italsider

PROPELLERS, SHIPS'
Fincantieri
LIPS
Vickers
Vosper Thornycroft

PROPELLERS, SHIPS' RESEARCH
Fincantieri
LIPS
Vosper Thornycroft

PROPULSION MACHINERY
Avco Lycoming
Blohm & Voss
Bremer Vulkan
Cantieri Navali Riuniti
Fincantieri
Motoren-und Turbinen-Union
Ruston Paxman Diesels
S.A.C.M.
Vickers

PUMPS
CIT Alcatel
Fincantieri
Termomeccanica Italiana
MacTaggart Scott
Vickers

PUMPS, COMPONENTS PARTS
Fincantieri
Termomeccanica Italiana

PUBLISHERS
DMS
Macdonald & Jane's

RADAR AERIALS
Aeromaritime
British Aircraft Corporation
Cossor
Decca Navigator/Radar
D.T.C.N.
Hollandse Signaalapparaten
Marconi
Philips Elektronikindustrier
Plessey Radar
S.M.A.
Thomson CSF

RADAR COUNTERMEASURES
Hycor/Miscota
Cossor Electronics

RADAR FOR FIRE CONTROL
D.T.C.N.
Ferranti
Hollandse Signaalapparaten
Marconi
Oerlikon-Buhrle
Philips Elektronikindustrier
Plessey Radar
S.M.A.
Sperry Gyroscope
Thomson CSF

RADAR FOR HARBOUR SUPERVISION
Decca Navigator/Radar
D.T.C.N.
Hollandse Signaalapparaten
S.M.A.
Thomson CSF

RADAR FOR NAVIGATION WARNING INTERCEPTION
Decca Navigator/Radar
D.T.C.N.
Hollandse Signaalapparaten
Marconi
Philips Elektronikindustrier
S.M.A.
Thomson CSF

RADIO, AIR
Thomson CSF

RADIO, DIRECTION FINDING
Marconi

RADIO EQUIPMENT
S.G. Brown Communications
Cossor
Marconi
Montedel
Thomson CSF

RADIO TRANSMITTERS AND RECEIVERS
S.G. Brown Communications
Cossor
Ferranti
Italtel
Marconi
Montedel
Philips Elektronikindustrier
Thomson CSF

RADOMES
British Aircraft Corporation
British Hovercraft Corporation
D.T.C.N.
Hollandse Signaalapparaten
Lürssen Werft
Thomson CSF
Vickers

RAMJETS
Aerospatiale

RANGEFINDERS
Barr & Stroud
S.M.A.
Thomson CSF

REFRIGERATION PLANTS
Termomeccanica Italiana

RELOCALISATION DEVICES
CIT Alcatel
D.T.C.N.

REMOTE CONTROLS
Italtel
LIPS
Oerlikon-Buhrle
Oto Melara
S.E.P.A.
Thomson CSF

REMOTE LEVEL INDICATOR EQUIPMENT FOR SUBMARINE TRIM TANKS
Officine Panerai

REPLACEMENT PARTS FOR DIESEL ENGINES
Blohm & Voss
Bremer Vulkan
Fincantieri
MacTaggart Scott
Vickers

RESEARCH SHIPS
Ailsa Shipbuilding
Bell Aerospace Canada
Bremer Vulkan
Brooke Marine
Cantieri Navali Riuniti
D.T.C.N.
Dubigeon-Normandie
Fincantieri
Lürssen Werft
Netherlands United Shipbuilders
S.F.C.N.
Vickers
Yarrow (Shipbuilders)

REVERSE REDUCTION GEARS, OIL OPERATED
Fincantieri
Isotta Fraschini
Vickers

REVERSING GEARS
C.R.M.
Fincantieri
Isotta Fraschini
Vickers

See in the dark
without flares, searchlights, scanners or monitors, or things that go bleep in the night.

Rank's image intensifying night sights give you daylight viewing in pitch blackness, starlight or battle flash. They contain their own power packs and need no artificial lighting to give your position away. They're fully sealed units, weather-proof and waterproof. They're all portable and some of them can be fitted to weapons.

They're ideal for both detection and detailed identification. They can also be used on gun directors. Their range varies up to 10 kms.

The two sights most favoured for maritime use are the Twiggy sight SS32 and the Individual Weapon Sight SS20.

Without question they perform better than any other kind of passive night vision equipment in the world. Talk to Rank for full details.

Individual Weapon Sight SS20

Twiggy night sight SS32

ROCKET LAUNCHERS
Bofors
Breda Meccanica Bresciana
C.N.I.M.
D.T.C.N.
Oto Melara
Snia Viscosa
Vickers

ROLL DAMPING FINS
Blohm & Voss
Vickers
Vosper Thornycroft

RUDDERS
Ailsa Shipbuilding
Bremer Vulkan
Brooke Marine
Fincantieri
Howaldtswerke-Deutsche Werft
Vosper Thornycroft
Yarrow (Shipbuilders)

RUDDERSTOCKS
Italsider

RUNNING GEARS/FORGINGS
Italsider

SALVAGE VESSELS
Ailsa Shipbuilding
Brooke Marine
Crestitalia
Fincantieri
I.N.M.A.
S.F.C.N.

SALVAGE AND BOOM VESSELS
Ailsa Shipbuilding
Bremer Vulkan
Brooke Marine
Cantiere Navaltecnica
Cantieri Navali Riuniti
Crestitalia
Fincantieri
Lambie (Boats)
Netherlands United Shipbuilders
Yarrow (Shipbuilders)

SCIENTIFIC INSTRUMENTS
D.T.C.N.
Ferranti
Thomson CSF
Vickers

SHIP BUILDERS AND SHIP REPAIRERS
Ailsa Shipbuilding
Blohm & Voss
Bremer Vulkan
Brooke Marine
Cantiere Navaltecnica
Cantieri Navali Riuniti
D.T.C.N.
Dubigeon-Normandie
Fairey Marine
Fincantieri
Howaldtswerke-Deutsche Werft
Italcantieri
Lürssen Werft
Netherlands United Shipbuilders
S.F.C.N.
Sofrexan
Vickers
Vosper Thornycroft
Yarrow (Shipbuilders)

SHIP DEFENCE SYSTEMS
Hycor/Miscota

SHIP AND SUBMARINE DESIGN
Ailsa Shipbuilding
Cantieri Navali Riuniti
D.T.C.N.
Dubigeon-Normandie
Fincantieri
Ingenieurkontor Lübeck
Netherlands United Shipbuilders
Vickers
Vosper Thornycroft
Yarrow (Shipbuilders)

SHIP MACHINERY
Alsthom Atlantique
Blohm & Voss
Bremer Vulkan
Cantieri Navali Riuniti
D.T.C.N.
Fincantieri
Motoren-und Turbinen-Union
Vickers
Yarrow (Shipbuilders)

SHIPBOARD AIR CONDITIONING AND VENTILATING PLANT
Aerimpianti SpA
Kaesar Klimatechnik

SHIPS MAGNETIC COMPASS TEST TABLES
Barr & Stroud

SHIP STABILISERS
Blohm & Voss
Cantieri Navali Riuniti
D.T.C.N.
Fincantieri
Howaldtswerke-Deutsche Werft
Supramar
Vickers
Vosper Thornycroft

SHIP SYSTEMS ENGINEERING
Cantiere Navaltecnica
Cantieri Navali Riuniti
C.S.E.E.
D.T.C.N.
Fincantieri
LIPS
Netherlands United Shipbuilders
Vickers

SHIPS BRASS FOUNDRY FOR SONAR AND RADAR
D.T.C.N.

SHIPS MAGNETIC COMPASS TEST TABLE
D.T.C.N.

SIGNALS
Hycor/Miscota

SIMULATORS
CIT Alcatel
Ferranti
Philips Elektronikindustrier
S.E.P.A.
Vickers

SMOKE INDICATORS
Barr & Stroud

SOCKETS AND PLUGS, ELECTRIC WATERTIGHT
Standard Telephones & Cables
Thomson CSF

SOCKETS AND PLUGS, MULTI-PIN PATTERNS
Thomson CSF

SOCKET TERMINATIONS
Thomson CSF

SONAR EQUIPMENT
British Aircraft Corporation
CIT Alcatel
D.T.C.N.
Emerson Electric
Ferranti
Graseby Instruments
Hollandse Signaalapparaten
Marconi
Plessey Marine
Sippican Oceanographic Systems
Thomson CSF
U.S.E.A.

SONAR EQUIPMENT (PASSIVE ACTIVE-INTERCEPT)
CIT Alcatel
D.T.C.N.
Edo
Graseby Instruments
Hollandse Signaalapparaten
Plessey Marine
Thomson CSF
U.S.E.A.

SONAR EQUIPMENT, HULL FITINGS AND HYDRAULICS
CIT Alcatel
D.T.C.N.
Edo
Graseby Instruments
Hollandse Signaalapparaten
Plessey Marine
U.S.E.A.

SONAR RANGES (DESIGN AND INSTALLATION)
Graseby Instruments

SPARE PARTS FOR DIESEL ENGINES
Blohm & Voss
Bremer Vulkan
C.R.M.
Fincantieri
Grandi Motori Trieste
Vickers

SPEED BOATS
Bell Aerospace Canada
Cantieri Baglietto
Crestitalia
D.T.C.N.
Fairey Marine
Fincantieri
S.F.C.N.
Vosper Thornycroft

STABILISING EQUIPMENT
Blohm & Voss
D.T.C.N.
Ferranti
Hollandse Signaalapparaten
S.E.P.A.
Vickers
Vosper Thornycroft

STABILISING EQUIPMENT FOR FIRE CONTROL
D.T.C.N.
Ferranti
Vickers

STEAM-RAISING PLANT, CONVENTIONAL
Blohm & Voss
Bremer Vulkan
Fincantieri
Yarrow (Shipbuilders)

STEAM-RAISING PLANT, NUCLEAR
Vickers
Yarrow (Shipbuilders)

STEAM TURBINES
Blohm & Voss
Bremer Vulkan
Cantieri Navali Riuniti
D.T.C.N.
Fincantieri
Howaldtswerke-Deutsche Werft

STEEL, ALLOY AND SPECIAL STEEL FORGINGS, PLATES AND SECTIONS, STAMPINGS
Bofors
D.T.C.N.

STEEL MANGANESE, WEAR-RESISTING
Bofors

STEERING GEAR
Fincantieri
Vickers
Vosper Thornycroft

STERNFRAMES
Italsider

STRESS RELIEVING
Bremer Vulkan
Fincantieri
Vickers
Yarrow (Shipbuilders)

SUBMARINE DISTRESS BUOY
Barr & Stroud
D.T.C.N.
Sofrexan
Thomson CSF

SUBMARINE FIRE CONTROL
CIT Alcatel
D.T.C.N.
Ferranti
Hollandse Signaalapparaten
Philips Elektronikindustrier
S.E.P.A.
Singer Librascope
Sperry Gyroscope
Vickers

SUBMARINE PERISCOPES
Barr & Stroud
D.T.C.N.
Thomson CSF

SUBMARINES
D.T.C.N.
Fincantieri
Howaldtswerke-Deutsche Werft
Ingenieurkontor Lübeck
Italcantieri
Netherlands United Shipbuilders
Vickers

SUBMARINES (CONVENTIONAL)
D.T.C.N.
Dubigeon-Normandie
Fincantieri
Ingenieurkontor Lübeck
Netherlands United Shipbuilders
Vickers

SUBMERSIBLES (WET)
D.T.C.N.
Fincantieri
Vickers
Yarrow (Shipbuilders)

SUPPORT SERVICES
Blohm & Voss
Bremer Vulkan
Brooke Marine
Cofras
Fincantieri
Vickers
Vosper Thornycroft

SURVEY EQUIPMENT
D.T.C.N.

SURVEYS/MARKET INTELLIGENCE
D.M.S.

SWITCHBOARDS
Blohm & Voss
D.T.C.N.
Lürssen Werft
Vosper Thornycroft
Whipp & Bourne

SWITCHBOARDS AND SWITCHGEAR
Lürssen Werft
Vosper Thornycroft
Whipp & Bourne

TACTICAL TRAINING SIMULATORS
British Hovercraft Corporation
Ferranti
Marconi
Oerlikon-Buhrle
Sofrexan
Vickers

TANKERS
Blohm & Voss
Bremer Vulkan
Cantieri Navali Riuniti
D.T.C.N.
Fincantieri
Howaldtswerke-Deutsche Werft
Italcantieri
Netherlands United Shipbuilders
S.F.C.N.
Vickers
Yarrow (Shipbuilders)

TANKERS (SMALL)
Bremer Vulkan
Cantieri Navali Riuniti
D.T.C.N.
Dubigeon-Normandie
Fincantieri
Italcantieri
Lürssen Werft
Yarow (Shipbuilders)

TANKS, OIL AND WATER STORAGE
Bremer Vulkan
Fincantieri
Howaldtswerke-Deutsche Werft

TECHNICAL PUBLICATIONS
Vickers
Vosper Thornycroft

TELECOMMUNICATION EQUIPMENT
Aeromaritime
S.G. Brown Communications
CIT Alcatel
Cossor Electronics
D.T.C.N.
Ferranti
Italtel
Marconi
Montedel
Thomson CSF

TELEGRAPH SYSTEMS
Montedel
Thomson CSF

TELEMOTORS
MacTaggart Scott

TENDERS
Ailsa Shipbuilding
Blohm & Voss
Bremer Vulkan
Brooke Marine
Howaldtswerke-Deutsche Werft
Lambie (Boats)
Netherlands United Shipbuilders
Yarrow (Shipbuilders)

TEST EQUIPMENT FOR FIRE CONTROL SYSTEMS
CIT Alcatel
C.S.E.E.
D.T.C.N.
Philips Elektronikindustrier
S.E.P.A.
Singer Librascope
Thomson CSF

THERMAL IMAGING SYSTEMS
Barr & Stroud

TIMERS
Borletti Fratelli

TORPEDO CONTROL SYSTEMS
CIT Alcatel
D.T.C.N.
Ferranti
Philips Elektronikindustrier
Plessey Marine
S.E.P.A.
Sperry Gyroscope
Thomson CSF
Vickers

TORPEDO DEPTH AND ROLL RECORDERS
D.T.C.N.

TORPEDO ORDER AND DEFLECTION CONTROL
CIT Alcatel
D.T.C.N.
S.E.P.A.
Vickers

TORPEDO SIDE-LAUNCHERS
D.T.C.N.

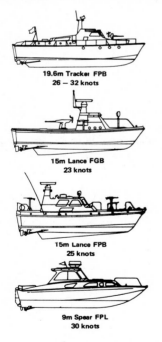
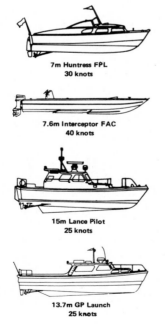
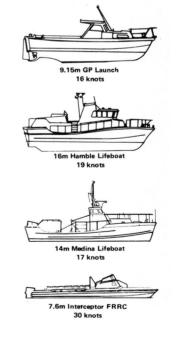

TORPEDOES AND TORPEDO TUBES
CIT Alcatel
D.T.C.N.
Plessey Marine
Vickers

TRAINING EQUIPMENT
A.B.M.T.M.
CIT Alcatel
C.S.E.E.
D.T.C.N.
Ferranti
Fincantieri
Graseby Instruments
Oerlikon-Buhrle
Philips Elektronikindustrier
S.E.P.A.
Vickers

TRAINING PROGRAMMES
A.B.M.T.M.

TRAWLERS
Brooke Marine
Crestitalia
D.T.C.N.
Dubigeon-Normandie
Fincantieri
Howaldtswerke-Deutsche Werft
Lambie (Boats)
S.F.C.N.
Yarrow (Shipbuilders)

TUGS
Ailsa Shipbuilding
Ameeco (Hydrospace)
Brooke Marine
Crestitalia
Dubigeon-Normandie
Fincantieri
Lambie (Boats)
S.F.C.N.
Yarrow (Shipbuilders)

TURBINE GEARS
Bremer Vulkan
Cantieri Navali Riuniti
CIT Alcatel
D.T.C.N.
Fincantieri
Vickers

TURBINES
Avco Lycoming
Blohm & Voss
Bremer Vulkan
Cantieri Navali Riuniti
D.T.C.N.
Fiat
Fincantieri
Hatch & Kirk
S.A.C.M.
Yarrow (Shipbuilders)

TURBINES, EXHAUST
Avco Lycoming
Bremer Vulkan
Cantieri Navali Riuniti
D.T.C.N.
Fincantieri

TURBINES, GAS MARINE
Avco Lycoming
D.T.C.N.
S.A.C.M.
Yarrow (Shipbuilders)

TURBINES, STEAM MARINE
Blohm & Voss
Cantieri Navali Riuniti
D.T.C.N.
Fincantieri
Yarrow (Shipbuilders)

UNDERWATER ACOUSTIC SYSTEMS
Singer Librascope

UNDERWATER COMMUNICATION
Marconi

UNDERWATER LIGHTS
D.T.C.N.
Officine Panerai

UNDERWATER TELEVISION EQUIPMENT
D.T.C.N.
Edo
Sofrexan
Thomson CSF

VALVES AND COCKS, HYDRAULICS
MacTaggart Scott

V/STOL AIRCRAFT
Hawker Siddeley

VOLTAGE REGULATORS, AUTOMATIC
Ferranti

WARSHIP REPAIRERS
Bremer Vulkan
Brooke Marine
Cantieri Navali Riuniti
D.T.C.N.
Fincantieri
Howaldtswerke-Deutsche Werft
Lürssen Werft
Netherlands United Shipbuilders
Vosper Thornycroft
Yarrow (Shipbuilders)

WARSHIPS
Blohm & Voss
Brooke Marine
Cantieri Navali Riuniti
D.T.C.N.
Dubigeon-Normandie
Fincantieri
Lürssen Werft
Netherlands United Shipbuilders
S.F.C.N.
Sofrexan
Vickers
Vosper Thornycroft
Yarrow (Shipbuilders)

WATER TUBE BOILERS
Bremer Vulkan
Fincantieri
Yarrow (Shipbuilders)

WEAPON CONTROL SYSTEMS
Singer Librascope

WEAPON SYSTEMS
Aérospatiale
Bofors
C.S.E.E.
D.T.C.N.
Ferranti
Oerlikon-Buhrle
Officine Galileo
Oto Melara
Philips Elektronikindustrier
Plessey Marine
Plessey Radar
Sippican Oceanographic Systems
Sistel-Sistemi Elettronici
Snia Viscosa
Sofrexan
Sperry Gyroscope
Thomson CSF
Vickers
Vosper Thornycroft

WEAPON SYSTEMS (SONAR COMPONENTS)
CIT Alcatel
D.T.C.N.
Edo
Graseby Instruments
Oerlikon-Buhrle
Plessey Marine
Thomson CSF
Vosper Thornycroft

WELDING, ARC, ARGON ARC OR GAS
Fincantieri
Lürssen Werft
Vickers
Yarrow (Shipbuilders)

WINCHES
D.T.C.N.
Standard Telephones & Cables
Vickers

WRIST COMPASSES AND DEPTH METERS FOR UNDERWATER OPERATORS
D.T.C.N.
Officine Panerai
Rolex

X-RAY WORK
D.T.C.N.
Lürssen Werft
Vickers

YACHTS (POWERED)
Ailsa Shipbuilding
Brooke Marine
Cantiere Navaltecnica
Cantieri Baglietto
Crestitalia
D.T.C.N.
Dubigeon-Normandie
Fairey Marine
Fincantieri
Lürssen Werft
Vosper Thornycroft
Yarrow (Shipbuilders)

CANTIERE NAVALTECNICA S.p.A.

MILITARY HYDROFOILS

are the right answer to
the new trends of the world's navies
as regards coast defence and attack

MAFIUS 600

—A NEW WORLD IN THE FIELDS OF FAST LIGHT MILITARY SHIPS

—THE RIGHT HIGH/SPEED WARSHIP FOR TODAY'S AND TOMORROW'S NEEDS

—EQUIPPED WITH A HELICOPTER AND PARTICULARLY QUALIFIED FOR MISSILE ATTACK,
PATROLLING, LONG RANGE MISSIONS, ASW, RECONNAISSANCE AND OTHER TASKS

CANTIERE NAVALTECNICA S.p.A.
22, Via S. Ranieri - 98100 MESSINA (ITALY) - Phone (090) 774862

Cable: NAVALTECNICA MESSINA - Telex: 98030 RODRIKEZ

Marine Limited

AND CONSULTING NAVAL ARCHITECTS

ESTABLISHED 1874

Designers and builders of specialised ships and naval vessels for British, Commonwealth and Foreign navies

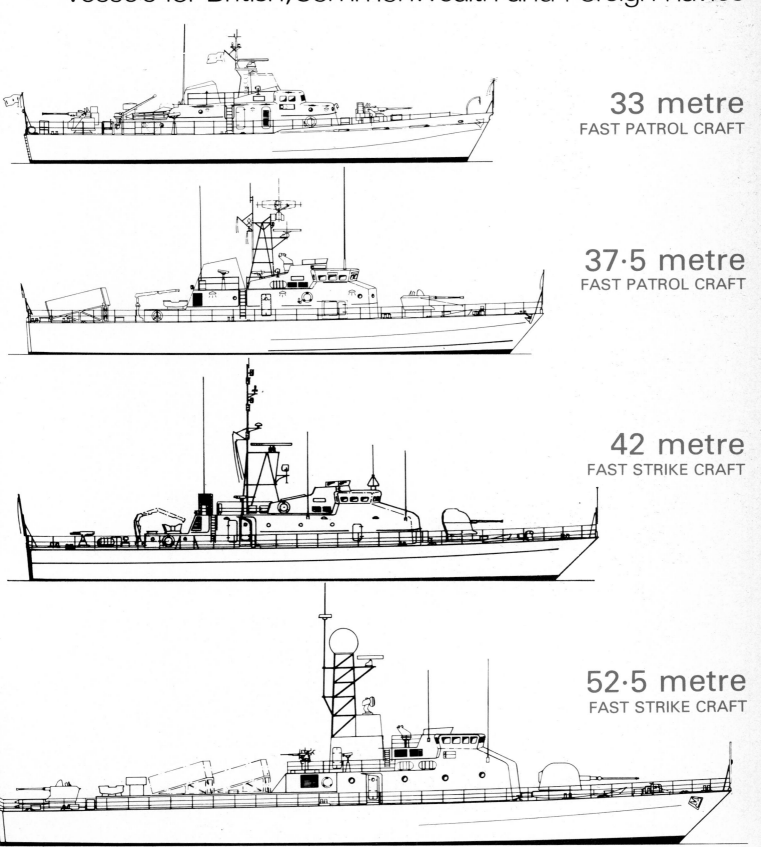

33 metre
FAST PATROL CRAFT

37·5 metre
FAST PATROL CRAFT

42 metre
FAST STRIKE CRAFT

52·5 metre
FAST STRIKE CRAFT

On target– Raytheon's new ASW sonar.

You're looking at a target being tracked on the digital display of Raytheon's new ASW sonar–the system for the 1980's that's ready for duty today.

The DE1160B has been selected by the Spanish and Italian Navies for frigate class vessels. A version, AN/SQS-56, has been procured by the U.S. Navy for the new guided missile frigate.

 The new sonar performs directional as well as omni-directional active and passive detection of submarines and torpedoes, and determines precise range and bearing for weapon control and guidance. High reliability, compact size, and reduced weight result from the system's modern, yet proven, solid state design. An advanced digital display linked to an integral computer provides fast and accurate target identification and tracking. And, built-in fault-sensing circuits simplify maintenance.

The DE1160B is just one model in Raytheon's DE1160+ series of sonar systems. All are ready to go aboard any vessel in the free world.

For further details on the entire range of Raytheon's ASW sonar systems, write Raytheon Company, Government Marketing, 141 Spring Street, Lexington, Massachusetts 02173.

TGT1   TGT2
BRG   075   201
RNG   5500   9636
500

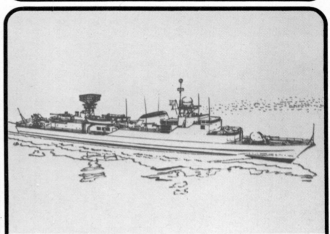

Now you'll carrier when you

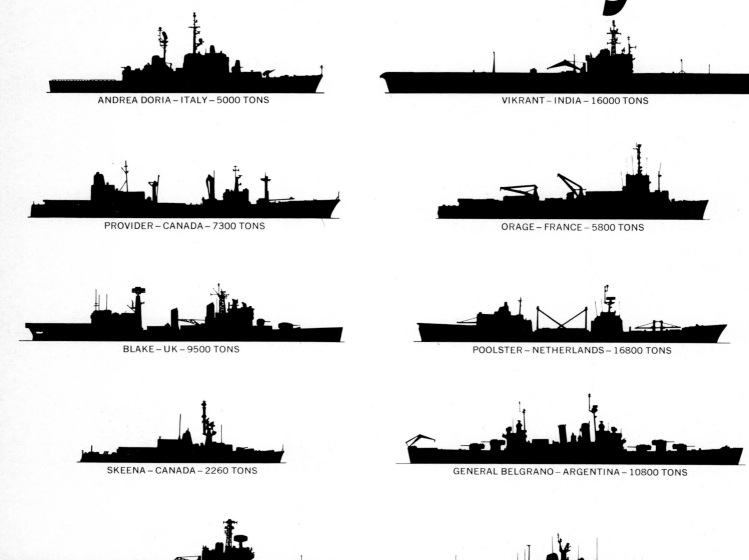

ANDREA DORIA – ITALY – 5000 TONS

VIKRANT – INDIA – 16000 TONS

PROVIDER – CANADA – 7300 TONS

ORAGE – FRANCE – 5800 TONS

BLAKE – UK – 9500 TONS

POOLSTER – NETHERLANDS – 16800 TONS

SKEENA – CANADA – 2260 TONS

GENERAL BELGRANO – ARGENTINA – 10800 TONS

MELBOURNE – AUSTRALIA – 16000 TONS

KATORI – JAPAN – 3372 TONS

Huge, expensive, often vulnerable, the modern jet aircraft carrier is today giving way to the Harrier Carrier – any ship, large or small, with deck-space enough to operate one or more V/STOL Sea Harrier strike aircraft.

The implications are enormous.

For the Harrier alone can instantly transform a whole range of mobile, pad-equipped ships into the naval equivalent of dispersed strike-jet air-fields – giving unparalleled flexibility to naval air operations.

And, most important of all, even small navies, with vessels of only a few thousand tons, can now reap the operational advantages of their own organic seaborne jet strike force, large or small.

The Sea Harrier has changed everything.

know an aircraft see one.

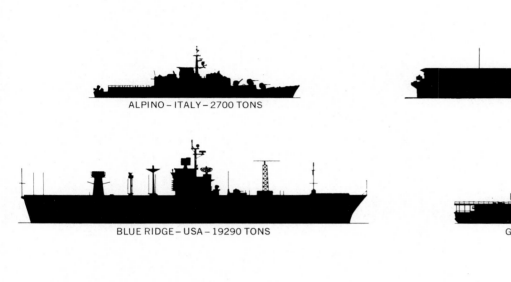

ALPINO – ITALY – 2700 TONS

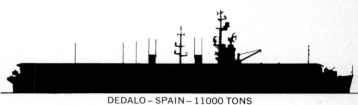
DEDALO – SPAIN – 11000 TONS

BLUE RIDGE – USA – 19290 TONS

GREEN ROVER – UK – 3185 TONS

STALWART – AUSTRALIA – 10000 TONS

LA SALLE – USA – 8040 TONS

HARUNA – JAPAN – 4700 TONS

JEANNE D'ARC – FRANCE – 10000 TONS

MINAS GERAIS – BRAZIL – 15890 TONS

VITTORIO VENETO – ITALY – 7500 TONS

Fast, powerfully armed and equipped with dual-mode radar, it can take off either vertically from heli-pad type decks on small vessels, or – with greater range and armament loads – make short take offs from through-deck cruisers or from small or older carriers.

Now that the Sea Harrier is here, naval tactics will never be the same again.

The unique Sea Harrier by Hawker Siddeley Aviation, ordered for the Royal Navy.

[39]

Sippican helps you sample a changing ocean.

TB 76 PROXIMITY FUZE

The TB 76 Proximity fuze, specially developed for the Oto Melara 76/62 naval gun system, is provided with proximity, percussion and self-destruction functions and incorporates antiwave circuits. Its burst area complies with the optimum fragmentation effect of the OS shell.

publinter wpt 2/77

cantiere navale breda

construction of: tankers up to 250,000 tdw; ore-oil carriers and bulkcarriers up to 175,000 tdw; ore-bulk-oil carriers, completely double-skinned, up to 150,000 tdw; product carriers up to 80,000 tdw; liquid gas carriers up to 80,000 tdw; container-ships of all types and dimensions; general dry cargo and multipurpose vessels of all types and dimensions; merchant and/or passenger/merchant ferry boats; navy crafts: guided missile gun boats, corvettes, minesweepers. great jumboizing works. construction of industrial plants: refining towers, heat exchangers, electrical power station condensers.

design stefano fiorentino roma italy

230 T Standard displacement
260 T full load displacement

Guided missile gunboat

Dimensions	Max Engine Output	Speed	
49.80×7.50 (m)	20,000 HP	max	42 knots
		max continuous	40 knots
		cruising	20 knots

Crew		Endurance	
35 men		at 40 knots	500 miles
		at 20 knots	2,000 miles

Armament

4 missiles on fixed launching ramps

1 76/62 OTO MELARA compact gun

1 40/70 BREDA BOFORS twin gun

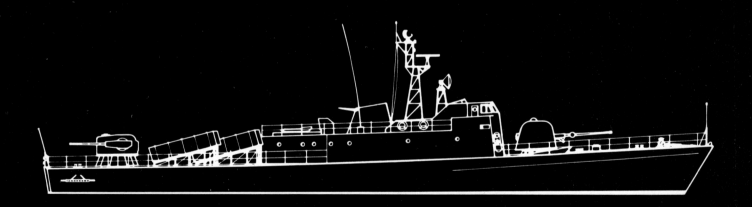

cantiere navale breda spa

venice marghera italy
via delle industrie 18
phone (041) 59860
telex 41106 bredanav
cables cantbreda venice
postal address
p.o.b. 1043 (succ. 1) 30170 mestre

LIBRASCOPE

specialist in naval electronic systems.

For more than 30 years Librascope pioneered technological advances in all areas of Antisubmarine Warfare weapon control. We've had in-depth experience in the evolutionary process of four generations of hardware technologies—from mechanical analog to electro-mechanical analog to hybrid electromechancial analog/digital to the all-digital electronic systems now deployed aboard the latest surface ships and submarines of the U.S. Navy and others.

Total involvement in all disciplines of ASW weapon control qualifies Librascope as expert in system concept and design, manufacture, software development, documentation, test, installation, system integration, spares provisioning and field service.

The broad technology base developed during these three decades has provided the experience necessary to pioneer in related fields such as acoustic warfare.

International inquiries are welcome. Please contact your Embassy or write to Singer, Librascope Division, 833 Sonora Ave., Glendale, Calif., 91201, U.S.A., telephone (213) 245-8711. Our Washington Office is located at 1828 L Street N.W., Suite 402, Washington, D.C. 20036, telephone (202) 223-4100.

SINGER
AEROSPACE & MARINE SYSTEMS

Oerlikon

Modern and efficient automatic naval guns with appropriate ammunition against air-and surface-targets.

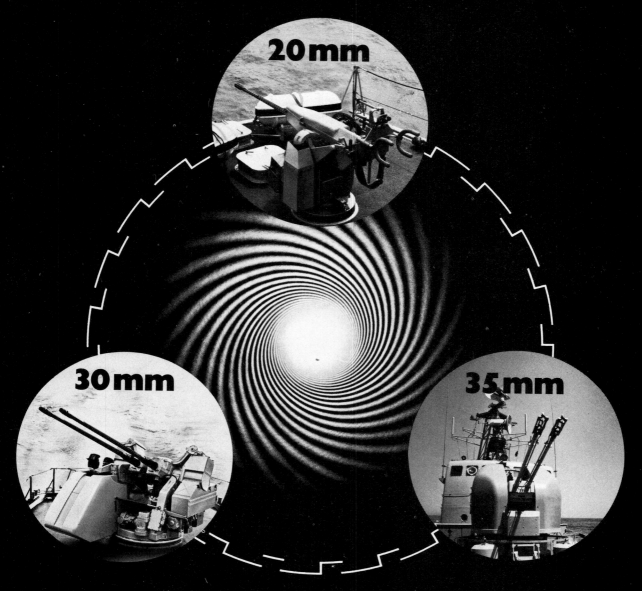

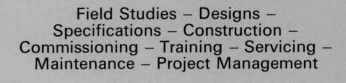

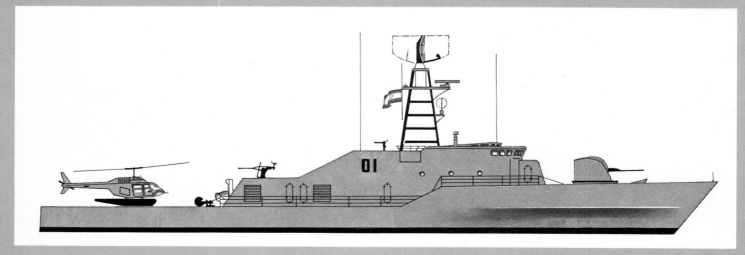
[48]

Breda 40 L 70 Twin Mounting "Compact"

● High rate of fire, (600 rds/min) ● Considerable quantities of ready use ammunition immediately available, (444 or 736, depending on magazine type) ● Maximum reliability ● Advanced design resulting in complete automation, readiness for operation and low maintenance requirements ● Complete remote control and high servo-system performance ● Maximum accuracy during firing and low reaction time ● Capability of employment with proximity fused ammunition.

Breda Automatic Feeding Devices for 40 mm. L/70 Naval Mountings.

Breda 105 mm. Multipurpose Rocket Launcher.

BREDA MECCANICA BRESCIANA S.p.A.
VIA LUNGA. 2 / 25100 BRESCIA / ITALY – TELEX: 30056 BREDARMI

CANTIERI NAVALI RIUNITI

Head Office:

Via Cipro 11 - 16129 Genova (Italy) - Telex: CANTGE 27168 - Tel. 010-59951

Shipyards:

RIVA TRIGOSO - ANCONA - PALERMO

Repair Works:

GENOVA - PALERMO

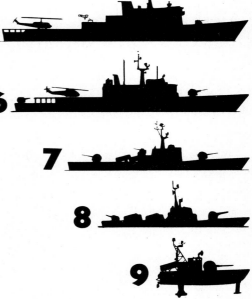

1) 17.000 ton
SEA CONTROL AND ASSAULT SHIP

2) 6.000 ton
TRAINING, COMMAND AND ASSAULT SHIP

3) FLEET SUPPORT SHIP "STROMBOLI"

4) 2.400 ton GUIDED MISSILE FRIGATE

5) 1.700 ton HYDROGRAPHIC SURVEY SHIP

6) 1.000 ton CORVETTE

7) 550 ton GUIDED MISSILE CORVETTE

8) 280 ton MISSILE FAST PATROL BOAT

9) 60 ton MISSILE HYDROFOIL "SPARVIERO"

FINCANTIERI GROUP

CN
R

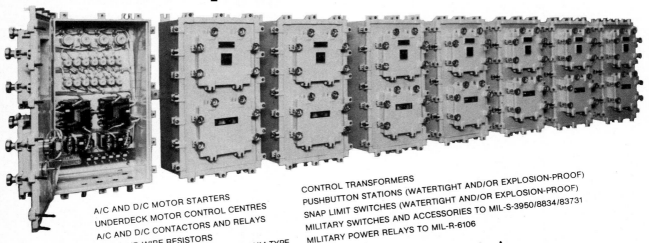

a.s.w.

CIT-ALCATEL
DIVISION MARINE

Anti-submarine warfare
French specialist

systems • equipment • armaments
for surface ships • submarines
and aircrafts

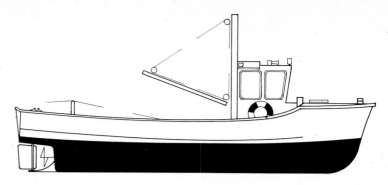
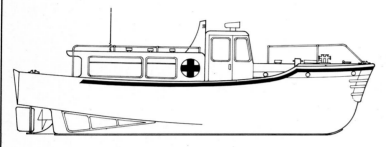

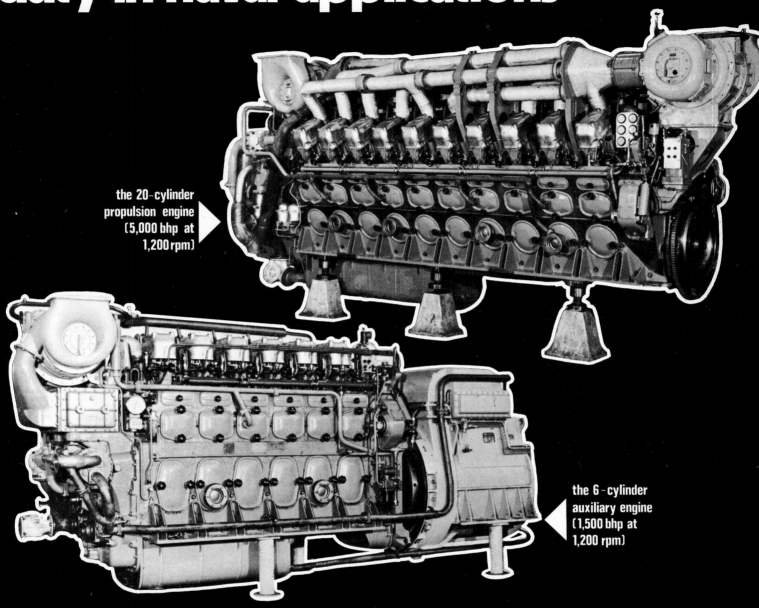

Newbuilding, Repair, Modernisation and Refitting
of Surface Naval Vessels

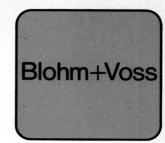

Zeiträume zwischen Kiellegung und Indienststellung, sowie der Instandsetzung, Umrüstung und Nachrüstung

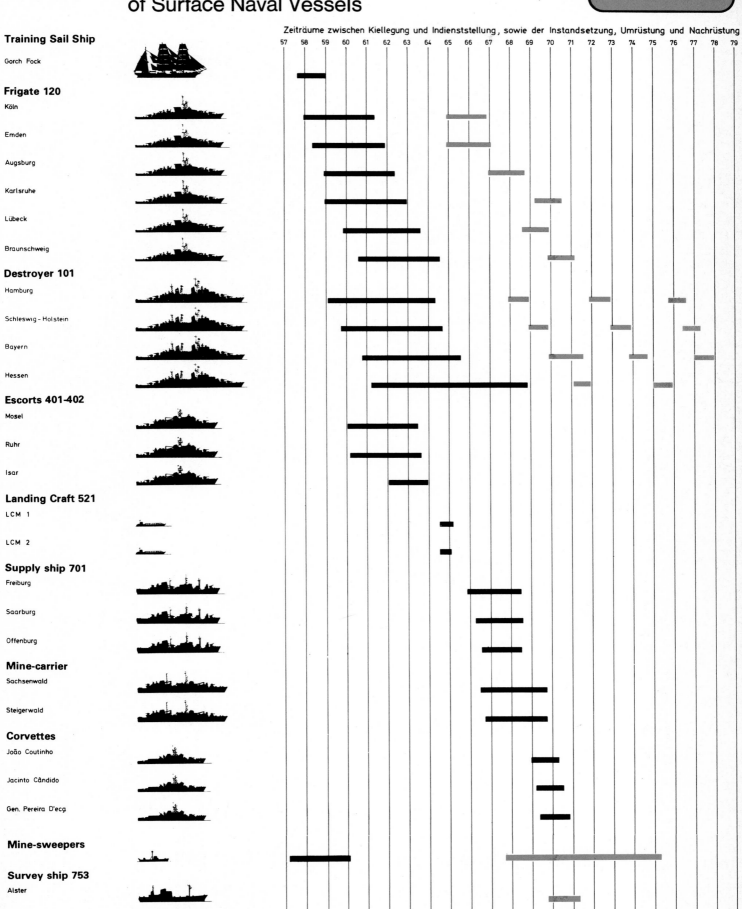

Training Sail Ship
Gorch Fock

Frigate 120
Köln
Emden
Augsburg
Karlsruhe
Lübeck
Braunschweig

Destroyer 101
Hamburg
Schleswig - Holstein
Bayern
Hessen

Escorts 401-402
Mosel
Ruhr
Isar

Landing Craft 521
LCM 1
LCM 2

Supply ship 701
Freiburg
Saarburg
Offenburg

Mine-carrier
Sachsenwald
Steigerwald

Corvettes
João Coutinho
Jacinto Cândido
Gen. Pereira D'eça

Mine-sweepers

Survey ship 753
Alster
Oker

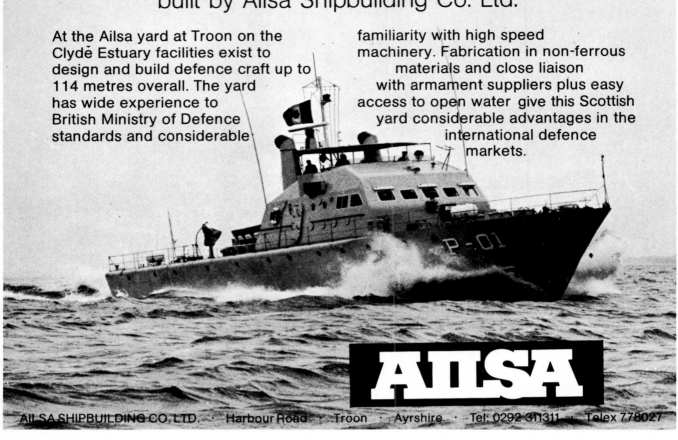
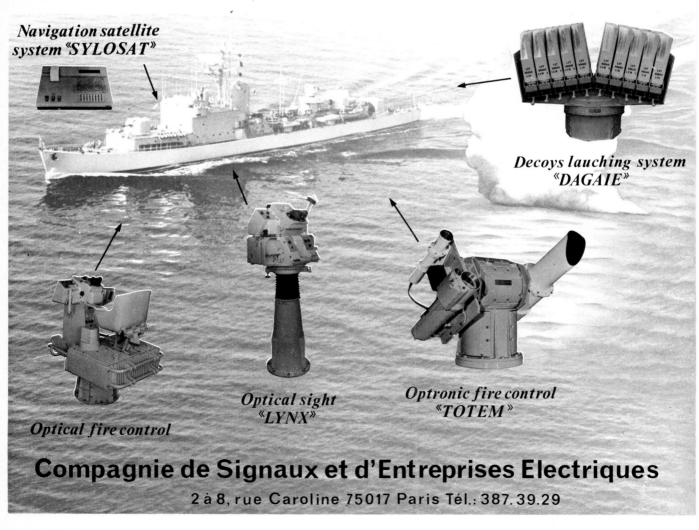

THE LARGEST SHIPBUILDING
AND SHIPREPAIRING GROUP
IN THE MEDITERRANEAN

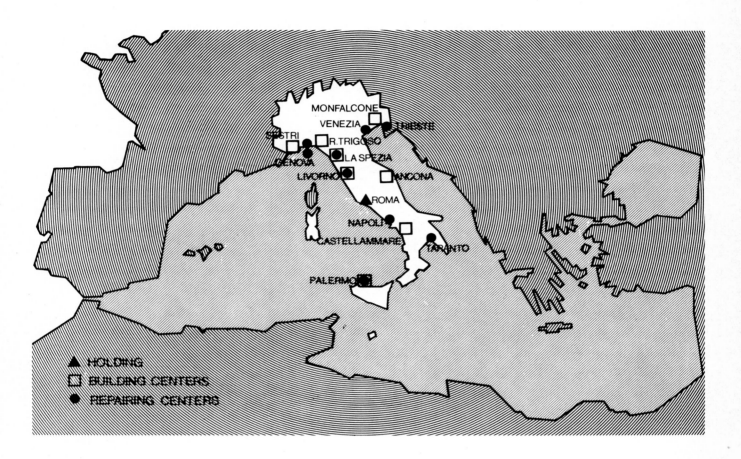

Shipbuilding system

8 yards with an annual production capacity of about
1 million grt. for any kind of ship up to over 300,000
dwt. Each yard is specialized in building the
ships most suitable for its own lay-out, equipment,
skills and traditions.

Shiprepairing system

9 yards with 26 graving docks for ships up to
350,000 dwt. (3 new graving docks for v.l.c.c. up
to 400,000 dwt. under construction), 10 floating
docks for ships up to 160,000 dwt. and about 15
kilometres of outfitting quays.

Mechanical products

3 factories for the production of main and auxiliary
Diesel engines, main and auxiliary turbines,
deck and E.R. machinery and marine propellers.

GROUP'S COMPANIES

ITALCANTIERI (Trieste)
CANTIERI NAVALI RIUNITI "C.N.R." (Genova)
CANTIERE NAVALE MUGGIANO (La Spezia)
CANTIERE NAVALE LUIGI ORLANDO "C.N.L.O."(Livorno)
**OFFICINE ALLESTIMENTO E RIPARAZIONE NAVI
"O.A.R.N." (Genova)**
**SOCIETÀ ESERCIZIO BACINI NAPOLETANI
"S.E.B.N." (Napoli)**
STABILIMENTI NAVALI (Taranto)
**CANTIERI NAVALI E OFFICINE MECCANICHE DI
VENEZIA "C.N.O.M.V." (Venezia)**
ARSENALE TRIESTINO S. MARCO (Trieste)
LIPS ITALIANA (Livorno)
GRANDI MOTORI TRIESTE "G.M.T." (Trieste)

FINCANTIERI

Società Finanziaria Cantieri Navali
via Sardegna n. 40 Roma
phone (06) 482241
telex 61180 FINCANT.

ITALCANTIERI
A LARGE SHIPBUILDING CONCERN FOR ALL TYPES OF VESSELS

Submarine **1077** type
500 - ton class

4,400 SHIPS BUILT FOR ALL FLAGS of which **1,870** naval vessels

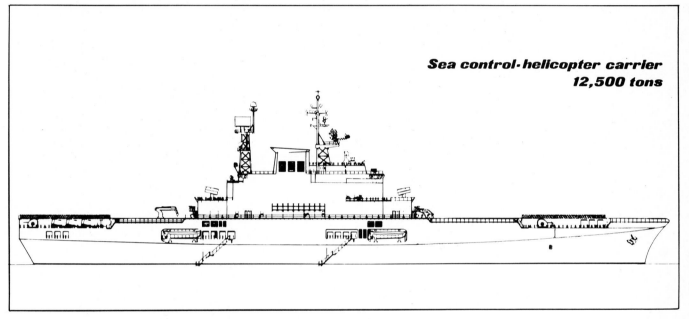

Sea control - helicopter carrier
12,500 tons

SUBMARINE **1081** TYPE
SAURO CLASS
Surface displacement: 1,450 tons

You are on the right course, when you see these symbols

Your partner not only for sophisticated navy ships,
but also for almost all types of merchant ships
up to 320,000 tdw, for repairs, drydockings and conversions.
Also the main propulsion plant for your new ship
would come from our works.
Benifit from our long experience as the
leading containership builder in the world.

Please contact:

BREMER VULKAN
SCHIFFBAU UND MASCHINENFABRIK

Telex: 024 4858 · Telegr.: Bremer Vulkan, Bremen
P.O.Box 700220/240 · 282 Bremen 70 · Tel.: (04 21) 6 60 31

italsider

steel forgings
and castings
for the marine industry

propellers and intermediate shafts, also hollow bored
rudderstocks
sternframes
crankshafts
running gears for low-speed Diesel engines

italsider
high quality
production

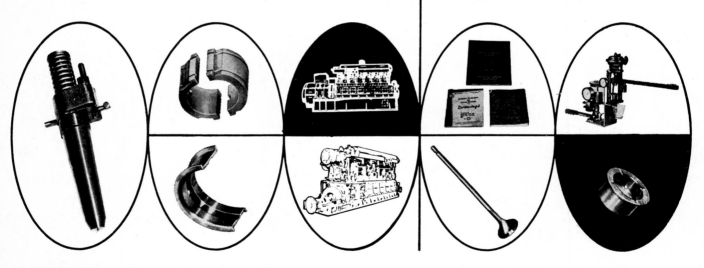

P.166-DL3 : the versatile round-the-clock performer

Powered by two Avco Lycoming LTP-101-600,

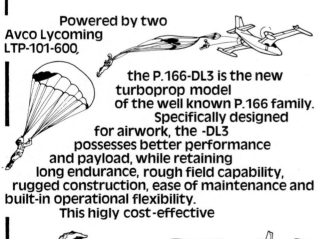

the P.166-DL3 is the new turboprop model of the well known P.166 family. Specifically designed for airwork, the -DL3 possesses better performance and payload, while retaining long endurance, rough field capability, rugged construction, ease of maintenance and built-in operational flexibility. This higly cost-effective

and reliable aircraft is an ideal tool for a variety of military and commercial missions. Maritime patrol SAR, light tactical transport, air command post, paratroop-dropping and ambulance

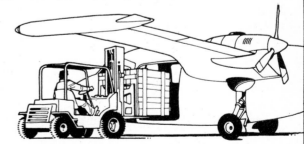

are just a few of the various tasks which have been field-proven by the P.166 family and which will be even better performed by this new turboprop.

RINALDO PIAGGIO
Via Brigata Bisagno 14 - Genova - Italy - Telex 27695

CANTIERI NAVALI DI PISA

56100 PISA - VIA AURELIA KM. 334 DARSENA PISANA - TEL. (050) 22072 - 22073
TELEGRAMMI: CNIPAM - PISA TELEX 58635 CANTPISA

TWO OF OUR FAST PATROL BOATS IN SERVICE

- **FAST PATROL BOAT of m. 46**
- Equipped with 3 engines MTU type MB20V538TB91 (HP 4500 x 3) knots 40

- **COAST-GUARD of m. 27**
- Equipped with 2 engines MTU type MB20V672TY (HP 3500 x 2) knots 42
- Equipped with 4 engines MTU type MB12V331TC81 (HP 1350 x 4) knots 35
- Equipped with 3 engines MTU type MB12V331TC81 (HP 1350 x 3) knots 30

- **COAST-GUARD of m. 23**
- Equipped with 3 engines MTU type MB12V331TC81 (HP 1350 x 3) knots 38
- Equipped with 2 engines MTU type MB12V331TC81 (HP 1350 x 2) knots 30

- **COAST-GUARD of m. 16,60**
- Equipped with 2 engines MTU type MB8V331TC80 (HP 900 x 2) knots 38
- Equipped with 2 engines MTU type 6V331TC80 (HP 675 x 2) knots 31
- Equipped with 2 engines G.M. type 12V71TI (HP 650 x 2) knots 30

- **COAST-GUARD of m. 14,00**
- Equipped with 2 engines G.M. type 8V71N (HP 350 x 2) knots 25
- Equipped with 2 engines G.M. type 8V71TI (HP 435 x 2) knots 30
- Equipped with 2 engines G.M. type 12V71TI (HP 675 x 2) knots 38

FOR SWIFT INTERVENTIONS ON WATER

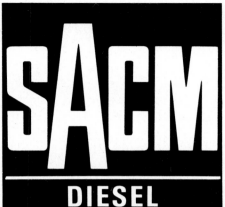

SACM
DIESEL

From 150 to 8 000 hp

Our range includes top high performance light weight engines to suit the requirements of the newest military fast patrol crafts.
SACM main engines and generating sets cover every aspect of power for naval applications.

SACM
MULHOUSE

H+H Conseil

SOCIÉTÉ ALSACIENNE DE CONSTRUCTIONS MÉCANIQUES DE MULHOUSE
1, rue de la Fonderie / BP 1319 / 68054 Mulhouse Cedex (France) / Tél. (89) 42.99.08 / Télex N° 881699 Mécalsa Mulhs

Crestitalia S.p.A.

21 METRES HIGH-SPEED PATROL BOAT

CRESTITALIA builds a wide selection of g.r.p. fast patrol boats ranging from 7 to 21 metres.
The high speed patrol boat shown above is one of the most modern, efficient and rational boats yet built in the field of open sea planing hulls.
The main features of the vessel are the hydrodynamic hull shape, the robustness of the hull and its proportions as well as the proportions and the reliability of the essential equipment (In particular the power plant and the control equipment) the stability, the safety, the manoeuvrability and, finally, the combination of the logistic, styling and functional characteristics.

The Deep-Vee hull has been developed from the well proven "CLIPPER 37" and "SENECA" line of power boats.

Open sea tests carried out on the prototype only served to confirm the parameters characteristic of this series and high-lighted the low water resistance, the very best performance in heavy seas even at low speed and when in a displacement condition, the excellent qualities of manoeuvrability and directional stability.

MAIN SPECIFICATION

LOA overall lenght	mts.	21
LWL stationary width	mts.	5,3
displacement, unloaded and dry ..	tons.	32,6
maximum speed, at full power with full load plus four (4) persons, in still water and calm air	Knots	35
cruising speed	Knots	30
engines: Isotta Fraschini Breda mod. ID 36 SS 12 V	HP	2x1.400

This boat can be equipped also with diesel engines: CRM, GM, Caterpillar, M.T.U.

CRESTITALIA S.p.A. - Head office: 20151 Milano - Via Gallarate, 36 - tel. 3271873 - telegr. Crestitalia-Milano
Yard: 19031 Ameglia (La Spezia) tel. 65746 - 65583 - 65584 - telex: Savid 38201

Some of the other ships that are or are to be equipped with 9 LV 200 weapon control systems

Swedish Navy FPB JÄGAREN

A trial ship that has been evaluated for the coming series of Swedish Navy FPBs. Despite its small dimensions — displacement 140 tons, length 36 m — it is armed with one 57 mm Bofors dual-purpose gun which is controlled by a PEAB 9 LV 200 system.

Royal Danish Navy TB 68

This series of ships, which is now being delivered to the Royal Danish Navy, has a full load displacement of 240 tons and a length of 42 m. Armament consists of 53 cm torpedoes, and a 76 mm OTO-Melara dual-purpose gun. These weapons are controlled by PEAB TORCI 204 and 9 LV 200 fire control systems.

Swedish Navy FPB

The coming series of FPBs will be equipped with the PEAB 9 LV 200 Mk 2 fire control system. This system will control the dual-purpose 57 mm gun as well as the six PENGUIN sea-to-sea guided missiles.

9 LV 200 naval weapon control systems

The 9 LV 200 weapon control system, in various versions, is today in operation in the navies of several countries. Operational testing on sea-going units over a number of years has demonstrated the dependability and high performance capabilities of the system for controlling dual-purpose guns and sea-to-sea missiles.

The frequency agility radar, which is used for tracking as well as surveillance, contributes considerably to the unique firing accuracy of the system.

Another feature that helps to improve performance and reduce weight and space is the use of special hydraulic motors for angular control of the surveillance antenna and the director.

The 9 LV 200 Mk 2, which is soon to be delivered in series is even lighter and smaller than the earlier version, as well as having improved performance.

Philips Elektronikindustrier AB

Defence Electronics
Fack
S-175 20 JÄRFÄLLA 1, Sweden
Tel.Nat. 0758/100 00
Tel.Int. +46758100 00
Telex: 11505 peab S

PHILIPS

NEW COSSOR IFF 850 INTERROGATOR

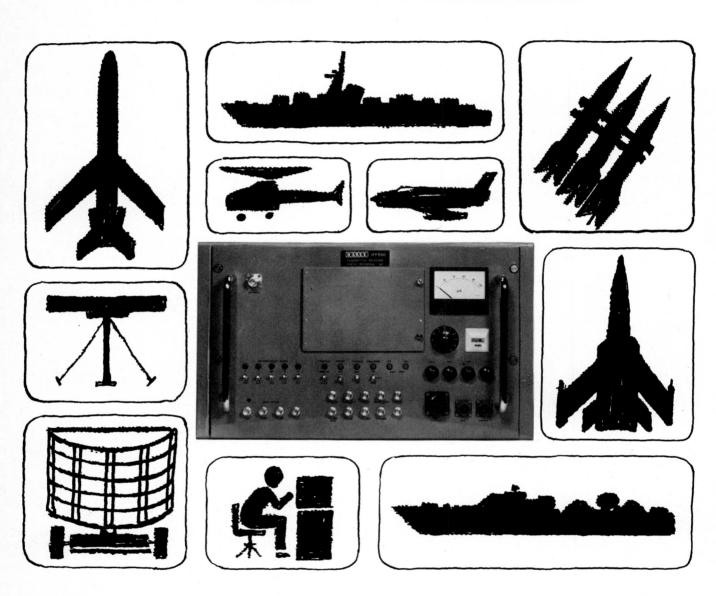

the heart of flexible systems

Engineered to meet the IFF requirements of
* Long Range Static & Mobile Radar Systems
* Medium Range Static & Mobile Radar Systems
* All classes of Shipborne Radar Systems

The use of a single type IFF 850 Interrogator for all systems reduced the cost and complexity of stores holding and maintenance requirements. Cossor provide Antennas – Video Processing and Display equipment to complement the new IFF 850 Interrogator.

Cossor Electronics Limited
The Pinnacles • Harlow • Essex
Telephone: Harlow 26862 • Telex: 81228

INMA presents its constructions:

- **fast patrol boat**
- **training ship**
- **landing ship**
- **fleet support ship**

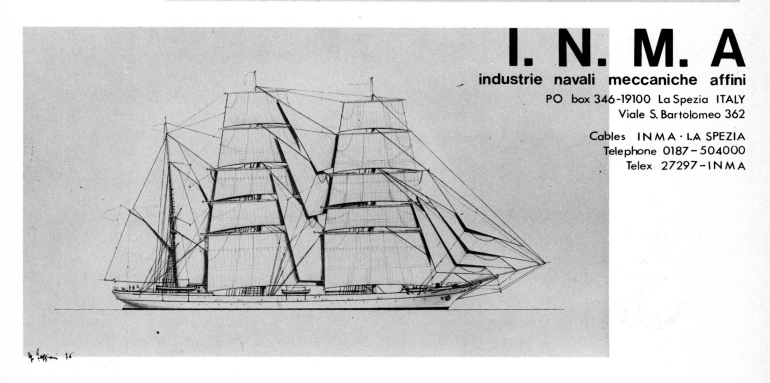

I. N. M. A

industrie navali meccaniche affini

PO box 346-19100 La Spezia ITALY
Viale S. Bartolomeo 362

Cables INMA · LA SPEZIA
Telephone 0187 – 504000
Telex 27297 – INMA

[75]

III/32

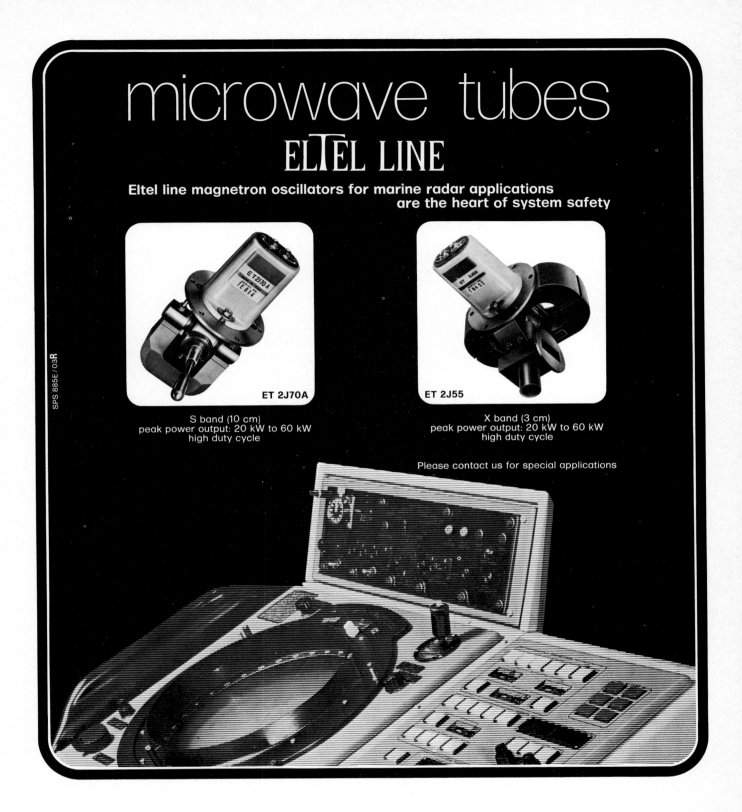

[77]

Propelled and climatised by Marelli.

The Italian Navy's new Sauro class submarines rely on high performance systems and components

Aermarelli environment

Aermarelli has designed and supplied the air filtration purification and ventilation systems.

These comprise two independent air conditioning refrigerating plants with changeover facility.

All equipment has been optimised by Aermarelli to completely overcome thermal shock conditions.

Ercole Marelli propulsion.

Ercole Marelli has supplied the propulsion motor and the three 720 kW generators.

The main characteristics of the motor are:
- continuous rating of 2 x 2,100 kW at 225 rpm
- sprint rating of 2 x 1,750 kW at 244 rpm
- waterproof up to shaft height
- cooling by four independent fans in conjunction with two sea-water coolers
- infinitely controllable from 0 to 244 rpm

Front-line engineering: front-line products.

Ercole Marelli Group

Aermarelli
Viale V. Lancetti, 43 - 20158 Milan - Italy
Tel. (02) 6998 - Telex: Aermarel 36004

TNC 45

TNC 51

FPB 57

FPB 57

FR. LÜRSSEN WERFT

FED. REPUBLIC OF GERMANY

2820 BREMEN 70
P.O. BOX 70 05 60
TELEPHONE 04 21 / 6 60 41
TELEX 02 44 484

CANTIERI NAVALI RIUNITI

GENOVA
via Cipro 11   telex   2716

 GRANDI MOTORI TRIESTE

TRIESTE
via Cavour 1   telex   462

 FIAT AVIATION DIVISION
SEPA

TORINO
via Nizza 312   telex   2132
TORINO
lungo Stura Lazio 45   telex   2152

 OTO MELARA

LA SPEZIA
via Valdilocchi 15   telex   2736

 BREDA
MECCANICA BRESCIANA

BRESCIA
via Lunga 2   telex   3005

 SELENIA
ELETTRONICA SAN GIORGIO
NAVAL SYSTEMS DIVISION

ROMA
via Tiburtina Km 12.400   telex   6110
GENOVA-SESTRI
via Hermada 6   telex   2766

ELETTRONICA

ROMA
via Tiburtina Km 13.700   telex   6202

MONTEDEL
ELMER division MONTEDEL
ELMER DIVISION

POMEZIA (ROMA)
viale Industria 4   telex   6111

Sea control and assault ship

Training command and assault ship

Fleet support schip

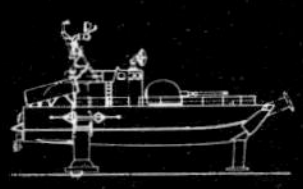

Missile Hydro foil

2400 ton guided missile frigate

Hydrographic survey ship

1000 ton Corvette

550 ton guided missile Corvette

280 ton missile fast patrol boat

MELARA CLUB

-MELARA CLUB- MAY BE IDENTIFIED AS A GROUP OF FIRMS FORMING THE BACKBONE OF THE ITALIAN SHIPBUILDING INDUSTRY FOR THE NAVY.

WITH THE DIRECT POSITIVE AID OF THE ITALIAN NAVY, THIS GROUP CAN, ON A WORLDWIDE SCALE, PROVIDE FOR COMPLETE SHIPS, ITALIAN-MADE THROUGHOUT, AS WELL AS REFITTING PROJECTS AND CONNECTED LOGISTIC SUPPORT

C.N.R. SHIPYARD

LAUNCHING OF THE -LUPO- CLASS FRIGATE OF THE ITALIAN NAVY

OFFICINE PANERAI SRL

has elaborated for over a century an activity of research, design and production of optical, mechanical and electronic equipment, apparatus and devices.

Panerai precision devices, such as compasses, pressure gauges, depth-meters, watches, depth-recorders and watertight flashlights were used underwater by the first frog-men, honour and pride of the Italian Military Navy. The main headline of this activity has always been the quality of produced materials, made in small and medium series for special uses. Herein are some characteristic items of the present, non-classified production of the company, in use by the Italian Armed Forces:

- Equipment for helicopters night deck landing
- Portable equipment for aircraft landing
- Remote level indicator equipment for submarines trim tanks
- High level water (or liquid in general) alarm systems
- Electronic engine room telegraph
- Fixed and portable optical apparatus, for naval and land uses
- Wrist compasses and depth-meters for underwater operators.

The production and studies of the company include also the field of weapons, devices and fixtures for special troops, which, owing to their top secret nature, cannot be desclosed to the public, but for which the company may give direct and exact information to parties concerned, except when, in very particular productions, the release of these information requires the permission of the Italian Military Navy.

The accurate performance and high reliability of Panerai production have always obtained the widest acknowledgement and also the personal and warm thanks of many Commanders for whom the availability of Panerai equipment, at the right place and time, has been the resolutive factor in the aims achievement.

OFFICINE PANERAI S.R.L.
2 Piazza G. Ferraris
50131 FIRENZE

Phone: 055/579304
Cable: PANERAI FIRENZE

We are specialists in the design, production and installation of underwater and marine equipment.

The Company's products include the following:-

Cable Penetrators and Connectors for Pressure Hull and Equipment Applications

Umbilical Cable Terminations

Cable Jointing Equipment

Hydrophones

Towed Seismic Arrays

Torsionmeters for propulsion Shafts

Complete Underwater Electrical and Electroacoustic Systems

Designed and manufactured to the highest standards of reliability for all underwater and marine applications.

ameeco
(Hydrospace Limited)

Bilton Road, Erith, Kent
Telephone: Erith 46821 Telex: 896230

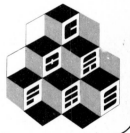

COFRAS
specialised assistance

Our "NAVY" Department

brings to buyers of French equipment, (Surface boats, submarines, navy airpatrol, coastal defence) cmplete or partial assistance towards the solution of problems such as:—

* Training of Personnel

* Extensive research and studies have also been made to ensure that the most favourable environments are available for the best use and functioning of theirequipment.

COFRAS

compagnie française d'assistance spécialisée
32 rue de lisbonne 75008 paris
tel: 292 31 50 - télex 660449 F

ELMER division of
MONTEDEL
the instinct for communication

The most comprehensive range of:

- Multi-purpose radio communication equipment
- Advanced radio communication systems
- Integrated radio communication systems
for ground, naval and airborne
military applications

**RADIO COMMUNICATION SYSTEMS
AND EQUIPMENTS
WITH A VERY ADVANCED TECHNOLOGY**

MONTEDEL -ELMER division

Viale dell'Industria, 4 - 00040 POMEZIA (ITALY) - P.O. Box 189
Telex 61112 ELMER - Phone (06) 9121706 - 9121707 - 9121741/2/3

GRUPPO MONTEDISON

MONTEDISON
SISTEMI

Tomorrow we'll be facing a different sea.

Our image of the sea may change any moment. This requires alertness and possibly action, which means a need of new ships. Here we come in to help find the best solution.

The first step is to produce the design and specifications, to make a contract for the delivery of ships and their main systems.

The next step is to provide the drawings for the actual construction, assembly and outfitting as well as the technical preparations for the purchase of materials and components.

And finally we can advise on supervision, training of personnel and logistic support.

Don't hesitate to contact Nevesbu when you want to anticipate at new naval tasks. We have a briefing team available at short notice.

Nevesbu

P.O. Box 289 – 2501 CG – The Hague – The Netherlands
Telephone (+31 70) 602813 – Telex 31640 genuf nl.

SEARCH RADARS	RAN 3L	early warning radar for cruisers, destroyers and large frigates.
	RAN 10S	combined air and surface surveillance coded radar for medium tonnage warships.
	RAN 11L/X	Dual purpose, dual frequency integrated radar system for air and surface search for application on small warships, or, as complementary sensor, on large vessels.
COAST SURVEILLANCE RADARS	RAT 8S	Transportable radars for coastal surveillance.
	RAT 10S	Long range, high resolution radar for fixed installations.
TRACKING RADARS	ORION SERIES	Multirole acquisition and tracking radars for missile and gun fire control.
WEAPON CONTROL SYSTEMS	NA10 mod. 2	fire control system for small and medium calibre guns and S/A missiles (Albatros system) used on frigates, destroyers and cruisers.
	NA10 mod. 3	fire control system for light naval vessels (hydrofoil and fast patrol boats).
	ALBATROS SYSTEM	combined missile and gun weapon system to counter the air threat both in the self-defence and mutual defence roles, and to perform conventional gunfire actions.
	DARDO SYSTEM	for short range defence.
	SCLAR	multi-role rockets launching system.
	ANTISUBMARINE SYSTEMS	for A/S bomb and torpedo launching control.
DATA HANDLING	IPN10 SERIES	Computer assisted display systems for command and control functions.
INTEGRATED SHIPBORNE SYSTEMS		Design and Engineering activities for Combat system integration.

NAVAL SYSTEMS DIVISION

SELENIA
INDUSTRIE ELETTRONICHE ASSOCIATE
S p.A.

via Tiburtina km 12.400
00131 ROMA (Italy)

ELETTRONICA SAN GIORGIO
ELSAG   S p.A.
via Hermada, 6
16154 GENOVA-SESTRI (Italy)

SOCIÉTÉ FRANÇAISE DE CONSTRUCTIONS NAVALES | FOR HIGH SPEED MISSILED LONG RANGE STRIKE CRAFTS

sfcn

Société Française de
Constructions Navales
66, quai Alfred Sisley
92390 Villeneuve-la-Garenne
Tél. 752.18.20
Télex : 610998 F FRACONA

P.R. 72

Some things ...like Edo excellence ...never change

In 1935 Edo floats crossed Antarctica with Bernt Balchen on Lincoln Ellsworth's Polar Star. Today, Edo sonar routinely dives under the Polar ice cap aboard the nuclear submarines of the U.S. Navy. In 46 years our standard of excellence has never been lowered...in Edo systems developed for antisubmarine warfare, oceanography, mine countermeasures, strike warfare, airborne navigation, hydrodynamics and airframes, command and control. And speaking of sonar, sonar designed and built by Edo is standard equipment aboard all the nuclear-powered submarines of the U.S. Navy and many of our modern destroyers.

EDO Corporation
College Point, N.Y. 11356

Why the Rolex Sea Dweller never gets the bends.

Divers are not the only ones to experience decompression sickness, or 'the bends'. Watches, as well as people, can suffer in much the same way.

When diving to depths in excess of 300 feet a diver must rely on a breathing mixture containing a high percentage of helium.

T. Walker Lloyd, one of the world's leading scuba and saturation divers, takes up the story:

"Helium molecules are so small that no substance known to man can contain or inhibit this gas under pressure—even the Rolex Oyster case! When decompressing, this gas is unable to escape quickly enough from an ordinary watch case.

"I've actually known watches to explode as a result."

The Rolex Sea Dweller, however, is fitted with a patented gas escape valve. As the Oceanographic Consultant for Rolex, T. Walker Lloyd has kept in touch with the development of this unique feature since its conception.

"The operation of the valve is a masterpiece of simplicity. It is a spring-loaded one-way valve. When pressure within the watch becomes greater than ambient pressure, the valve simply opens allowing the trapped gas to equalise.

"In effect, this means that the watch decompresses with the diver."

T. Walker Lloyd has worked as diving supervisor for Dr. George Bass, when excavating a 4th-century Roman wreck in the Agean Sea.

He was also a member of the first team to saturate on 95% nitrogen and 5% oxygen at a depth of 100 feet. During the experiment, the team made working dives of up 265 feet on compressed air. So he understands better than most the importance of highly accurate and reliable equipment.

The Rolex Sea Dweller is certainly a remarkable watch. And yet apart from the gas escape valve and a specially strengthened case, it is made in exactly the same way as any other Rolex Oyster.

Which means that if T. Walker Lloyd ever gets tired of underwater exploration, his watch will be equally at home in the frozen Arctic, the heat of the Sahara Desert, or at the top of Mount Everest.

♛ ROLEX
of Geneva

Pictured: The Rolex Sea Dweller Chronometer. Available only in stainless steel, with matching bracelet.

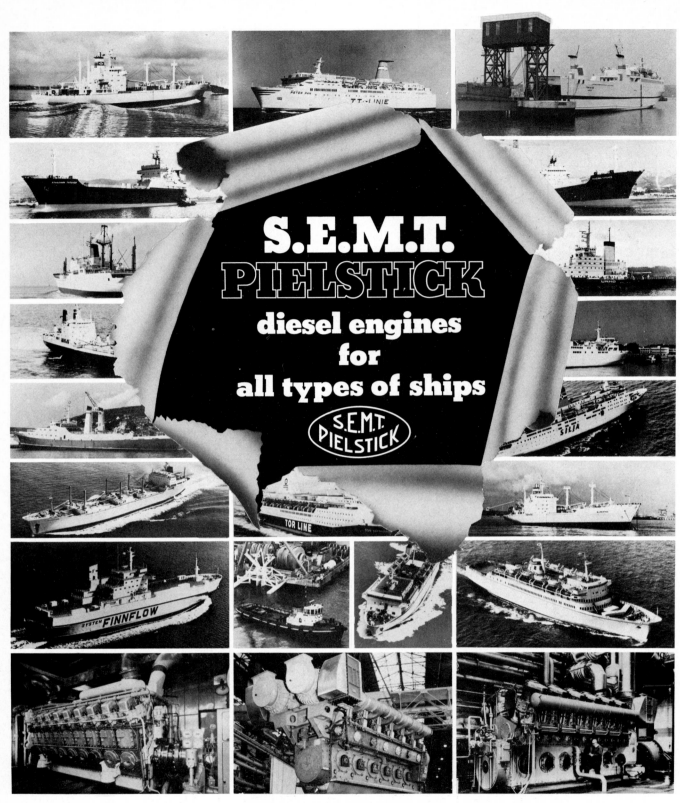

Nowadays manœuvring a warship can be as easy as pressing a button...

... with SEPA military systems

- ☐ Entirely electronic, making wide use of militarized original SEPA mini and microcomputers
- ☐ Simple to be operated and maintained

- ☐ Modular in construction easily adaptable to any propulsion configuration
- ☐ Highly reliable with great availability factor

Our experience covers

- ☐ Propulsion plant automation including gas turbine, diesel and mixed
- ☐ Electrical generation and distribution automation
- ☐ Control systems for special purpose military vessels
- ☐ Governor units and instrumentation for gas turbines

- ☐ Hydrofoils automatic depth and attitude control
- ☐ Torpedo guidance and home controls
- ☐ Multiple fire stations controls
- ☐ Shipborne system trainers
- ☐ Mathematical simulation of ship systems
- ☐ Automatic test equipments

Società di Elettronica per l' Automazione S.p.A.
Lungo Stura Lazio 45 - 10156 Torino (Italy)
Tel. (011) 262.3333 (5 linee r.a.) Telex: 23527 Sepa

User size electronics

dolci italia

[95]

CANTIERI BAGLIETTO SpA
17019 VARAZZE — ITALIA

GEMINI II   fast strike&coast guard patrol craft

MANGUSTA 30 coast guard patrol&missile craft

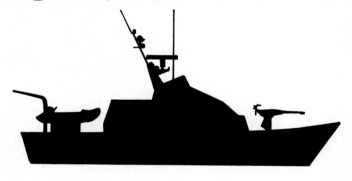

20 GC   coast   guard fast patrol boat

18 GC   coastal   patrol boat

BAGLIETTO VARAZZE
☎ (019) 95901 - 95902 - 95903
TX 28214 CANABAG

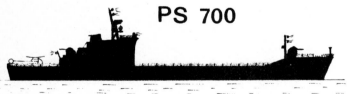

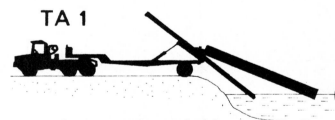
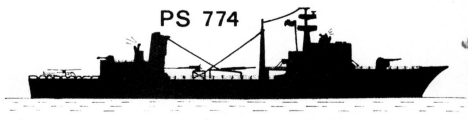
[98]

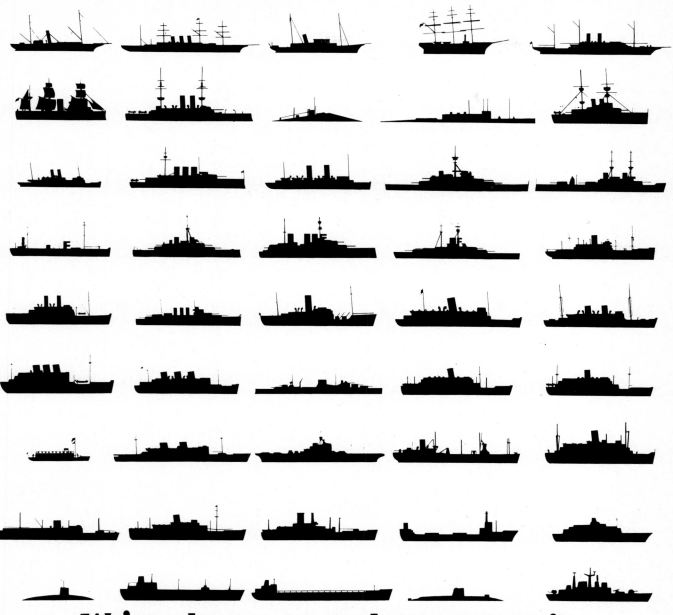

We've always earned our reputation as shipbuilders

It's one thing to be a great shipbuilder, but another to make profits as well.

Year in, year out, since the 1890s Vickers have built famous ships of every conceivable kind and built them profitably.

We built the first submarine to go into service with the Royal Navy before the turn of the century. And the first British nuclear submarine in the 1960s.

We built the first all-welded passenger liner and also the biggest liner ever built in England.

We built Europe's first 100,000 ton tanker and the first liquid petroleum gas carrier and we are now fitting-out Invincible, the Royal Navy's first anti-submarine cruiser recently launched by HM The Queen.

Just a few examples from Vickers long record of shipbuilding achievement.

The Shipbuilding Group has a consistent record of profitability. Today its yard at Barrow is busy, and export orders have long held a significant place in the order book. Whatever the future may hold, the accent is on continuity and growth.

Vickers Limited Shipbuilding Group Barrow-in-Furness Cumbria

...History already

G/C GUGLIELMI
2 motori 18 D/S-2

G/C RUSSO
2 motori 18 D/S-2

G/C ZARA
2 motori 18 D/S-2

G/C CICALESE
2 motori 18 D/S-2

G/C IGNESTI
2 motori 18 D/S-2

G/C DE TURRIS
2 motori 18 D/S-2

G/C D'AGOSTINO
2 motori 18 D/S-2

G/C CAVATORTO
2 motori 18 D/S-2

G/C CHIARAMIDA
2 motori 18 D/S-2

G/C DI SESSA
2 motori 18 D/S-2

G/C CAVALIERI D'ORO
2 motori 18 D/S-2

G/C PREITE
2 motori 18 D/S-2

G/C FUSCO
2 motori 18 D/S-2

G/C MAZZEO
2 motori 18 D/S-2

G/C BIANCA
2 motori 18 D/S-2

G/C GABRIELE
3 motori 18 D/2

G/C GRASSO
3 motori 18 D/2

G/C GL. 432
2 motori 12 D/S-2

G/C GL. 433
2 motori 12 D/S-2

G/C VITALI
2 motori 18 D/S

G/C INZUCCHI
2 motori 18 D/S

G/C URSO
2 motori 18 D/S

G/C RAMACI
2 motori 18 D/S-2

G/C RD 36
2 motori 18 D/S-2

G/C GORI
2 motori 18 D/S-2

G/C STERI
2 motori 18 D/S-2

G/C GIANNOTTI
2 motori 18 D/S-2

G/C COTUGNO
2 motori 18 D/S-2

G/C CARRUBBA
2 motori 18 D/S-2

G/C NUVOLETTA
2 motori 18 D/S-2

History on the seas is made by men, by winds, by vessels, by CRM motors. To become aware of that, one just has to read some very important documents of daily chronicle, such as the log-books of the Customs' patrol-boats, or those of the most important competition boats. Everything started approximately 30 years ago, just after the war, when also the Navy was among the many things to be re-built.

The demand of motors for patrol-boats could promptly be satisfied by CRM. Those were tough times and the working conditions were extremely uncomfortable: patched-up sheds and recovered instruments were the elements by which a first group of very skilled CRM specialists started manufacturing the first motors, thus writing the first pages of History. Since then, a lot of things

happened: today our factory in Castellanza covers an area of 20.000 square meters; our labour force rose from the initial 20 persons, up to a great, highly specialized group; our working plants are equipped with the most up-to-date machinery. By adding up all the Horse Powers produced until now, we reached 500.000 units, including petrol engines during the first years and diesel engines since 1961.

made its choice

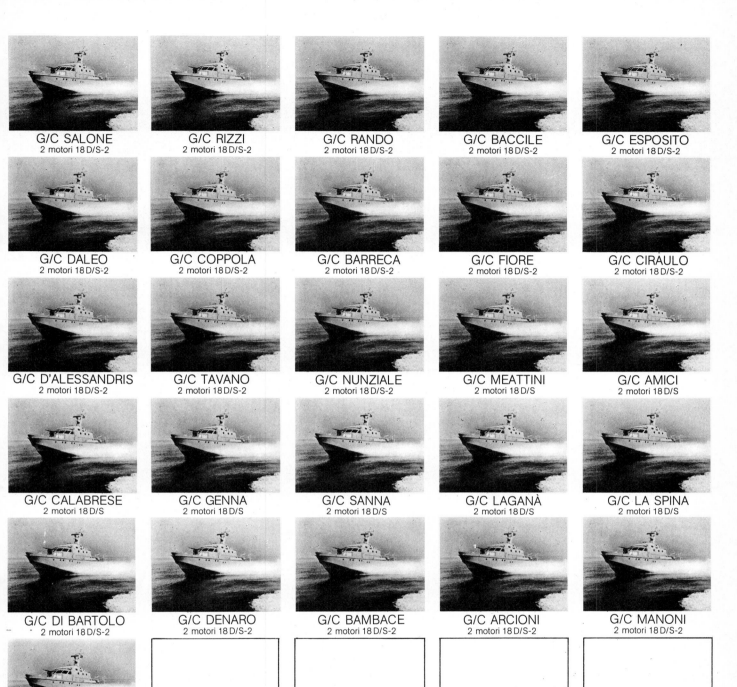

G/C SALONE 2 motori 18 D/S-2	**G/C RIZZI** 2 motori 18 D/S-2	**G/C RANDO** 2 motori 18 D/S-2	**G/C BACCILE** 2 motori 18 D/S-2	**G/C ESPOSITO** 2 motori 18 D/S-2
G/C DALEO 2 motori 18 D/S-2	**G/C COPPOLA** 2 motori 18 D/S-2	**G/C BARRECA** 2 motori 18 D/S-2	**G/C FIORE** 2 motori 18 D/S-2	**G/C CIRAULO** 2 motori 18 D/S-2
G/C D'ALESSANDRIS 2 motori 18 D/S-2	**G/C TAVANO** 2 motori 18 D/S-2	**G/C NUNZIALE** 2 motori 18 D/S-2	**G/C MEATTINI** 2 motori 18 D/S	**G/C AMICI** 2 motori 18 D/S
G/C CALABRESE 2 motori 18 D/S	**G/C GENNA** 2 motori 18 D/S	**G/C SANNA** 2 motori 18 D/S	**G/C LAGANÀ** 2 motori 18 D/S	**G/C LA SPINA** 2 motori 18 D/S
G/C DI BARTOLO 2 motori 18 D/S-2	**G/C DENARO** 2 motori 18 D/S-2	**G/C BAMBACE** 2 motori 18 D/S-2	**G/C ARCIONI** 2 motori 18 D/S-2	**G/C MANONI** 2 motori 18 D/S-2
G/C PREVITE 2 motori 18 D/S-2				

Our CRM motors are writing History at a speed exceeding 30 knots for normal watercrafts, and at much higher speeds for high-performance boats. These are the results of a basic concept that identified in the ratio between weight and power the problem to be solved; the fact that 1 CRM diesel H.P. weighs less than 2 Kg. means a lot of things. We were saying that History on the seas is made by water, by winds, by vessels, by men, by CRM motors: please, remember that when you will read or hear about the brilliant fights of the Customs' motor-boats against smugglers, the rescues made by the Navy's patrol-boats, or the most exciting sporting records.

the most important pages of the sea

JANE'S

JANE'S ALL THE WORLD'S AIRCRAFT

Edited by John W. R. Taylor,
Fellow, Royal Historical Society,
Associate Fellow, Royal Aeronautical Society.

JANE'S FIGHTING SHIPS

Edited by Captain J. E. Moore, Royal Navy

JANE'S WEAPON SYSTEMS

Edited by Ronald Pretty

JANE'S INFANTRY WEAPONS

Edited by Denis H. R. Archer

JANE'S SURFACE SKIMMERS

Edited by Roy McLeavy

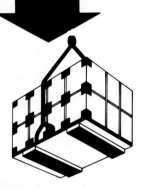

JANE'S OCEAN TECHNOLOGY

Edited by Robert L. Trillo

JANE'S FREIGHT CONTAINERS

Edited by Patrick Finlay

JANE'S WORLD RAILWAYS

Edited by Paul Goldsack

JANE'S MAJOR COMPANIES OF EUROPE

Edited by Jonathan Love

DECCA ELECTRONICS
The choice of the world's navies
Standard marine radar for navigational and tactical roles–Special displays–Navigation and Action Information Systems–EW Systems–Marine automation systems–Coastal surveillance and harbour radar.

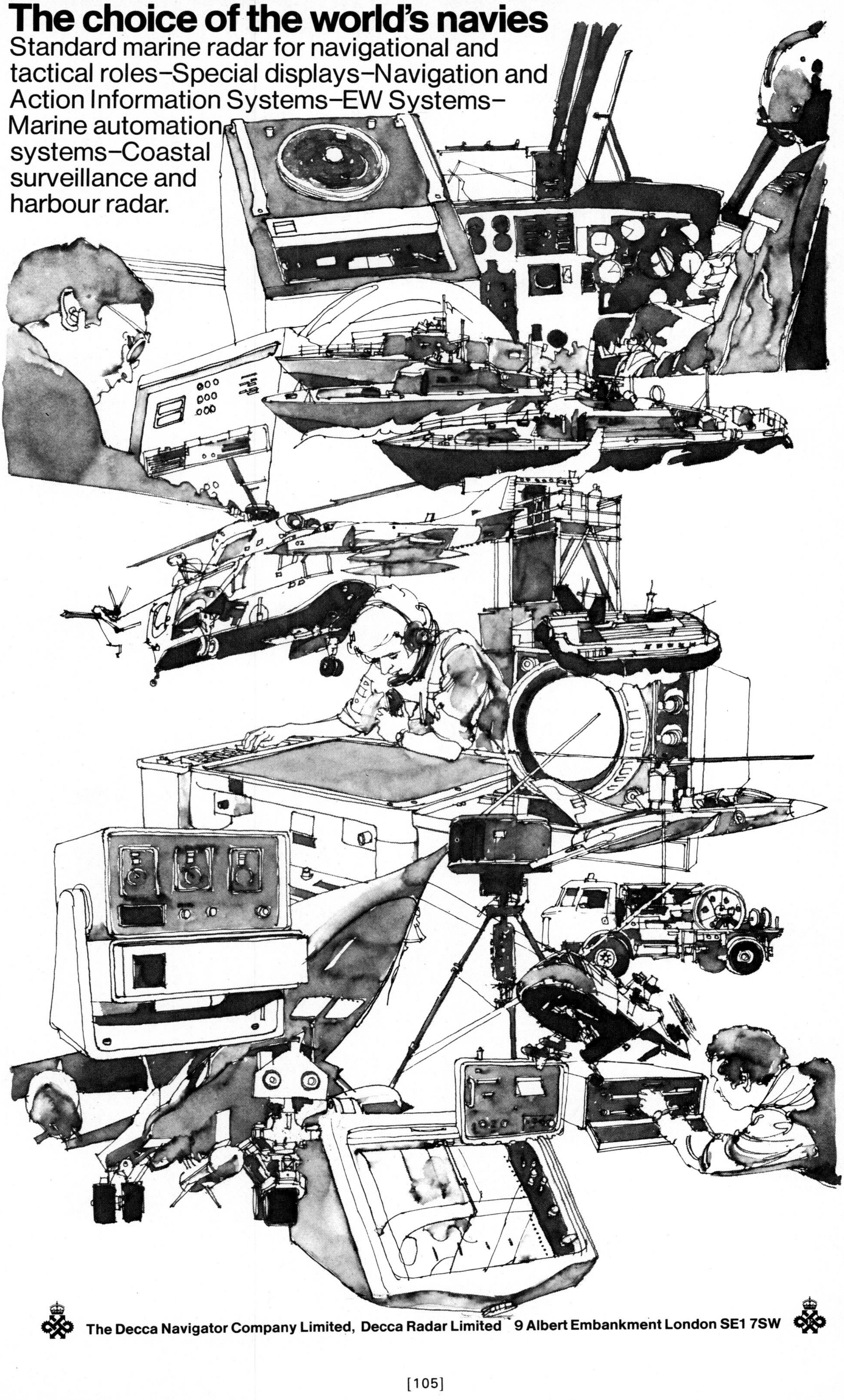

The Decca Navigator Company Limited, Decca Radar Limited   9 Albert Embankment London SE1 7SW

Judge us by the company we keep!

Some of the biggest names place their trust in Whipp & Bourne Switchgear–organisations like British Rail, The Central Electricity Generating Board, the Ministry of Defence, the British Steel Corporation; international companies like Shell, Mobil, Rio Tinto Zinc, Selection Trust. They know for heavy situations where reliability is essential, the reputation of Whipp & Bourne stands supreme. Rigorously tested to the most exacting standards, Whipp & Bourne equipment is specified with absolute confidence for applications in power, chemicals, steel, oil, traction, water, shipping and indeed throughout the whole of industry.

Write for technical literature:-
Switchgear · Switchboards · Switches · Circuit Breakers

Whipp & Bourne (1975) ltd

Castleton, Rochdale, England. Tel: Rochdale 32051 (10 lines)
Telex: 63442 (Whipborn, Casltn.)
Member of Babcock & Wilcox Ltd. (Electrical Group).

AB 212ASW
the self-contained killer that only needs the deck of a ship

Many Navies throughout the World have been looking out for an anti-submarine/anti-ship helicopter for immediate use, completely self-contained, and requiring only the minimum maintenance normally available aboard light vessels.

Agusta, with its long experience in designing naval helicopters, meets this requirement with its twin-engined AB 212ASW, which has a rugged, well-proven airframe and sophisticated avionics equipment optimized to provide a genuinely all-weather weapon system.

The AB 212ASW has integrated equipment for navigation, piloting, target acquisition, as well as for the transport and launching of missiles, torpedoes and sonobuoys over a wide radius.

AGUSTA

Cascina Costa - Gallarate - Italy - Telex 39569

Jubilee Year launching of **HMS Invincible** by HM Queen Elizabeth II

May 1977, MoD(N)

JANE'S
FIGHTING SHIPS

FOUNDED IN 1897 BY FRED T. JANE

EDITED BY
CAPTAIN JOHN E. MOORE RN, FRGS

1977-78

I.S.B.N. 0 531 03277-9

L. of C. Cat. No. 75 15172

JANE'S YEARBOOKS

FRANKLIN WATTS INC.
NEW YORK

JANE'S FIGHTING SHIPS 1977-78

EDITED BY

CAPTAIN JOHN E. MOORE

CONTENTS

[111]

INTRODUCTION

by

His Royal Highness The Prince of Wales K.G., K.T., G.C.B.

Buckingham Palace

I must admit that I am somewhat amazed, and indeed honoured, that I should have been singled out to contribute the introduction to this splendid yearbook. Perhaps the editor of this notable publication has in fact made a dreadful mistake and has simply been unable to correct it . . .

Jane's "Fighting Ships" is surely a wardroom name to every naval officer. Every good bridge should have one of these books in a prominent position for the Officer of the Watch to grab at the first opportunity. Last year, when I was commanding the minehunter H.M.S. BRONINGTON, a 1976 copy was sent to me by some generous donor who must have known that minesweepers and minehunters rarely if ever, possess one. I am not sure if this is for reasons of economy or for the simple lack of storage space, but whatever the case the book was greatly valued and used continuously throughout my period in command. I daresay it is still being used by my successor.

Of course, one of the most important functions of Jane's is to assist ship recognition at sea and this is where it is invaluable. Personally, I believe that fast and accurate recognition at sea is absolutely vital. Some people might be excused for thinking that eyeball recognition is of far less importance than it used to be because of modern electronic developments and sophisticated radar systems, but electronic countermeasures are a feature of operations at sea and in the air and, as such, could conceivably reduce warfare to the absolute basics where qualities like rapid recognition and the seaman's eye become vital.

With increasing numbers of ships of many different types going to sea each year it is not an easy task to keep up to date, but it is surely part of the professionalism of any naval officer to recognise friend from foe, particularly when belonging to a multi-national alliance, such as N.A.T.O., with a host of widely differing ship types. Jane's therefore, provides an essential service to all who go about their business on the sea and unlike this introduction, the editorial provides a useful insight into present day naval developments all over the world.

I have absolutely no need to recommend this book - but I cannot resist it.

Charles.

You sometimes have to look beneath the surface to see our achievements.

STC Hydrospace Division has designed, developed and produced many types of cable and associated equipment for marine defence systems all over the world and is a major supplier to the British Ministry of Defence.

ELECTRICAL AND ELECTRO-MECHANICAL CABLES for:
Helicopter dipping and variable depth sonars
Sonobuoys and torpedoes
Towing and diving
Surveillance and tracking
Minesweeping-acoustic and magnetic
Submersibles and seafloor vehicles
Fixed underwater installations
Buoyant and neutrally buoyant systems

ELECTRICAL GLANDS AND PENETRATORS for:
Submarines and submersibles
Diving units
Underwater equipment housings
ELECTRICAL CONNECTORS for underwater connection and disconnection of low power and communications circuits.

SHIPBOARD CABLE HANDLING SYSTEMS AND RELATED EQUIPMENT for:
Towing and diving
Seafloor cable installation, including trans-oceanic systems
Oceanography and deep sea coring.

Look into STC for a proper *under*standing of what goes on below.
Standard Telephones and Cables Ltd., Hydrospace Division, Dept: J4, Christchurch Way, Greenwich, London SE10 0AG. Telephone: 01-858 3291. Telex: 23687

Standard Telephones and Cables Limited

A British Company of ITT

FOREWORD

Amongst the great number of constructive comments, both verbal and written, which resulted from last year's edition of this book were certain criticisms which were neither constructive nor objective. These ranged from the "Imperialist lackey" sally from Moscow to the views of certain extremists of both the Right and Left in Europe who were incensed that an attempt had been made to place the world's fleets in a political context.

On 22 January 1941 Winston Churchill rounded on his critics in the House of Commons with the disarming remark, "I do not resent criticism even when, for the sake of emphasis, it parts for the time with reality." It is worthwhile considering where those with these extreme views have parted with reality in this case.

Seapower has been an adjunct of politics since the days of Themistocles and the Battle of Salamis in 480 BC. Before that, ships had been merely a means of trading — from that time onwards navies became, increasingly, a part of the story of the expanding world. The Punic Wars, Rome's invasion of Britain, the Norsemen's advance, the depredations of the Normans — all were precursors of modern maritime strategy, all were linked to internal problems and external ambitions. Today, in a world increasingly fragmented under the banner of Nationalism yet ever more interdependent in an age of advanced technology, the sea continues to maintain an unchallenged place as the main commercial link and an area where maritime strategy can achieve a supreme position. The lessons of the past 50 years are there to be learned — unfortunately they are too frequently ignored, particularly at times of economic stress.

Expansionist aims, "Imperialism" to those who have not had the opportunity to benefit from them in the past, are becoming increasingly prevalent in today's world. The majority of countries with such aims are possessed of a seaboard and the changes in Naval patterns are fequently symptomatic of alterations in political intentions. Increasing portions of many countries' budgets are channelled towards defence and yet it is a subject which receives scant attention beyond the offices of those immediately involved. Defence is an amalgam of so many factors that no one of them can be considered in isolation unless spurious and misleading conclusions are to be drawn. The armed forces of a country take a long time to assemble, much longer to train — the intentions of their political leaders may change overnight due to death, election or a hundred other reasons.

Therefore, if the place of the world's fighting ships in this total picture is to be understood with any clarity by those most affected, the ordinary citizens, naval forces must be displayed against a background of the political currents and undercurrents which control their possible employment. Seapower remains, as it has over the centuries, a vital element in the maintenance of peace. Despite the enormous technical advances of the last fifty years, over ninety-five per cent by weight of mankind's commerce depends on sea-lanes. The transport of armies requires the essential support of ships whilst only a maritime strategy can supply the long-term waiting game which could well influence the final outcome of a political crisis. Even in the era of supersonic flight, ships will remain for many years to come an essential part of man's economy and it will continue to be the duty of governments to defend those ships.

The need for this defence, the proportions of each element of seapower required, must vary with individual countries. Some are great carriers, others possess minimal merchant fleets and rely on others for their transport — some have problems with the smuggling of humans and contraband, others have to protect their fisheries and off-shore installations. A few are faced with a combination of all these problems. Japan relies almost entirely on imports and has a huge merchant marine to provide them. The USA has import/export figures that have nearly trebled in five years while those of the USSR have more than doubled despite her very slight reliance on external raw materials. The Soviet merchant marine at just over twenty million tons is a third again the size of that of the USA.

The problems that confront those who are charged with the design and building of the world's fighting ships are concerned not only with the immediate future but with long-range planning, sometimes a quarter of a century ahead. It must be remembered that the conception, design and building of a ship is a very lengthy process, sometimes requiring up to ten years lead-time. From first commissioning that ship may well be in service for at least twenty-five years, a period in this rapidly advancing technical world which may see a great number of changes in armament, sensors and propulsion, apart from those changes that take place between conception and com-

missioning. So the naval planner must try to combine the qualities of mystic, technical forecaster and paper-shuffler, producing the best possible answer in the span of a 2½ − 3 year appointment. When Winston Churchill first set up the Admiralty's Naval Staff in London in 1912 he demanded that there should be a gathering of officers with time to think. This time is hard to find in a life over-loaded with dockets and papers — "The Silent Service was not mute because it was absorbed in thought and study, but because it was weighed down by its daily routine and by its ever-complicating and diversifying technique." Except in certain special cases this is as true today as it was when Churchill wrote those words in "The World Crisis." The naval planner must have support from without, whatever country he may work for.

The first necessity is a clear political directive — a glimpse of the country's future plans as they affect his element. Here lies the first problem in Western states, where an election, a Defense Review or a shift in governmental power may change the whole pattern. Is a country to rely on overseas bases or on afloat support? Will its policy be in support of its friends abroad or confined to the home base? These and many other factors are of prime concern in designing the particular type of ship required and it is in this respect that dictatorial states have time on their side insofar as their external policies remain unchanging.

The general requirements having been agreed, the next step is the design of the ship and here continuity is of the utmost value. A constructor may have just arrived from the managerial position with little previous design experience or, as in the Soviet Union, be part of a long-term team. The benefits of the latter system are obvious and are demonstrated in a steady progression from class to class in the Soviet Fleet. The decisions as to what equipment is to be fitted must also be the result of experience. The desire for nothing but the very best may cause other factors to be ignored — penalties of cost, weight and development time — when, in truth, the "very best" may be too good for the job in hand. Western committee methods are very inclined to provide ships in which everybody has his say, too little control is evident and the result either prices itself out of the market or fails to meet the anticipated need. Too often ships are provided at great expense in which it is obvious that some particular elements of technology have received overemphasis at the expense of others of equal importance and the navy in question is being called on to fry an egg in a platinum-plated pan when a non-stick lining would have been more efficient.

Time is so precious in a short-term environment that pressing needs and a comparatively free economy often result in prodigious waste. Once again a comparison between the Warsaw Pact with its Soviet-dominated procurement system and the NATO line-up is disturbing for Western observers. Here again politics is the main element in the arena. In the USSR the economy is directed primarily towards military spending, possibly up to as much as 13-15 per cent of the GNP and rising by 5 per cent per year. The result is a large body of production designed to supply the armed forces of the Warsaw Pact on a continuing basis, working to a long-term plan.

NATO, on the other hand, is a loose gathering of nations, each with its own economic problems and political aims. In time of peace the requirements of the Alliance's commanders are met only within this framework and, at present, with little co-ordination of research, development and construction. At the same time the research which is carried out on behalf of an individual country's armed forces frequently has a civilian application which, in a competitive economy, is advantageous to that country's industry. From the domestic political point-of-view employment engenders votes and this is of great importance to candidates whose opposite numbers in the one-party states are not similarly troubled. So each country strives for its own ends while the NATO commands, weighed down by a massive committee-system frequently dominated by national requirements, must base their planning as much on hope as on promises. Few enough are the occasions on which NATO's commanders' requests for forces are fully met and, even then, the time factor for assembly is as out-of-joint as the widely-differing equipment is disparate. Although the year-old Independent European Programme Group is attempting to co-ordinate their military requirements, nearly a quarter of a century has been lost in havering. The appalling rise in costs of modern weapon systems may soon force the NATO countries into further and more productive collaboration but until that takes place the watchword appears to be "interoperability".

Two unique Royal Navy answers to missile attack on warships

...at close range

Seawolf is the only ship-borne point defence missile system with proven anti-missile as well as anti-aircraft capability – and missiles, not aircraft, are the real threat to today's warships. No comparable system has demonstrated the ability to intercept and destroy small, supersonic, anti-ship missiles. Successful sea trials on the British frigate HMS Penelope have cleared the way for Seawolf's service with entry into the Royal Navy in the late 1970s. The standard version is fully automatic and all-weather. Lighter-weight "blindfire", "darkfire" and "visual-only" variants are suitable for ships from 400–2,000 tons.

...at long range

Sea Skua is the only helicopter launched lightweight weapon which has been developed to counter the threat from missile-carrying fast patrol craft, launching their attacks from over the horizon. The combination of the wide radius of action of modern helicopters and Sea Skua's own considerable range ensures that the threat can be neutralised before the attacking craft can approach within effective missile-launching distance. Already at an advanced stage of development, Sea Skua will be widely used on frigate-borne Lynx helicopters of the Royal Navy from the late 1970s onwards.

Seawolf

Ship-borne anti-missile and anti-aircraft system

Sea Skua

Lightweight helicopter borne anti-ship system

 BRITISH AIRCRAFT CORPORATION

Guided Weapons Division, Stevenage, Herts, England.

GWN 12

This nasty piece of jargon means that countries will use the same fuel, the same ammunition and, where possible, mutually adaptable spares, a policy which, from the naval point of view, could notably reduce the volume of fleet support required, with a consequent easing of the problems of escorts and, believe it or not, real estate. At NATO's birth the USA was the prime contractor for the Alliance's hardware. Over the years this balance has changed to a huge collection of individually produced weapon systems and propulsors. Until the balance is redressed to provide a reasonable mix between dependence and independence NATO cannot fail to be the loser with its defensive capabilities notably reduced. Since the early days of the Alliance peace of a sort has been maintained because NATO has possessed sufficient strength to make the success of any opponent's adventure problematical. As many in the West cry for further cuts in defence spending so does the balance swing against NATO. Weakness begets attack and subsequent defeat; it begets blackmail and surrender to threats.

USSR

Against the background of endless arguments over defence-spending in the NATO countries the steady advance of Soviet forces in both quantity and quality has continued during the past year. Bearing in mind that the Kremlin has made no secret of the fact that it views détente as a period in which to accelerate the shift of foreign relationships, "the correlation of world forces," in its favour, this was hardly suprising. Increasing land and air forces in Europe would ensure not only stability within the Warsaw Pact area but would divert the West's energy and attention from happenings abroad.

From the naval point-of-view 1976-77 has seen a continuation in both building programmes and the introduction of new weapons, although the former must be set against the fact of the large number of ships built in the 1950s which are increasingly becoming obsolete. The overall numbers probably reached a maximum figure in the early 1970s, a figure limited by the number of men that can be trained in a year. The introduction of aircraft carriers is inevitably a considerable drain on resources both of manpower and finances and so too is the commissioning of large numbers of ballistic missile submarines (SSBNs). However, the quality of the ships and submarines is being steadily improved and it is amongst the shorter range ships specifically designed for defence in home waters that new designs of an improved standard may be expected — new frigates, new missile craft.

SOVIET SUBMARINES

The submarine programme has continued at the rate of some twelve a year, six SSBNs being of the "Delta I" and huge "Delta II" (16 000 tons) classes. An improved version of their basic missile, the SS-N-8, was launched in November 1976 to a range of 5600 nautical miles, allowing a coverage of nearly half the world from a firing position off northern Soviet bases. At the same time trials of a new missile, SS-NX-18, were carried out to a range of 4600 nautical miles. This liquid fuelled rocket with a triple warhead is being deployed in the "Delta" class during 1977. Nor have the 34 SSBNs of the "Yankee" class been forgotten: it appears probable that their 1300 nautical mile SS-N-6 missiles will be replaced this year by the new SS-NX-17, a solid fuelled weapon with a range of 2400 nautical miles, although so far used with only a single head. Although there has been no further evidence of the SS-NX-13 at sea this is yet another item in the inventory which may represent a future threat to task forces at sea.

The remainder of the submarine programme continues to provide a regular reinforcement of the forces aimed at anti-surface and anti-submarine operations. Variations on a theme are evident in both cruise-missile and attack nuclear submarines. With "Charlie II", "Victor II," "Papa" and "Alpha" classes at sea it would be surprising if a new design for the next generation of such submarines, benefitting in propulsion and sound-reduction from lessons already learned was not already on the drawing-boards. It is of interest that not only is the new "Tango" class of diesel-electric submarine building but that a "Foxtrot" class building stream has been opened up to provide for Libyan requirements.

SURFACE SHIPS

Most dramatic of unveilings in the year was undoubtedly that of *Kiev,* an aircraft carrier in all but her Soviet class-name of "anti-submarine cruiser". Differing in many ways from her Western predecessors she is the first of a class of at least three and possibly four. Armed with eight surface-to-surface missile launchers, both anti-air and anti-submarine missiles, as well as more conventional gun and A/S armament, she has both hull and towed sonar and can carry a mixed aircraft complement of VTOL and helicopters. That ships of this class will be of advantage in an anti-submarine war is undoubted but their peacetime role, either alone or with a task-force, deserves reflection. It is worth remembering that designs for the USN's VSS (VSTOL support ship) included an allowance for 500 troops for limited periods. It is not impossible, bearing in mind the austere conditions under which Soviet sailors live, that a similar allowance has been made in this design. If this is not so the attendance of LSTs which could embark their troops at any of the increasing number of air-ferry stations now available to the USSR around the world could provide the same answer. However it is done, the result would be the same—a powerful intervention force, should the use of surrogate troops in a crisis, real or engineered, be impracticable or inefficient.

The backing, should it be needed, of other surface forces would result from the continuing construction of a couple of cruisers and four destroyers a year to add to thirty-five cruisers and over a hundred destroyers already available, as well as a continuing programme of 23 000-ton fleet replenishment ships and a fleet of sixty-five depot and repair ships.

NAVAL AIR FORCE AND NAVAL INFANTRY

Some of the air-ferry stations referred to can also provide operational bases for the long-range aircraft of the Soviet Navy equipped as they are for strike, reconnaissance, ASW and electronic warfare. Their operations abroad in support of the fleet were a notable part of Exercise Okean II in 1975 and since then the additional deployment of the Backfire bomber to the navy has increased this capability. A study of the disposition of Soviet-inclined states suggests that re-fuelling should cause no problems, irrespective of the area of operation. The Naval Infantry has kept up with the times with an ever-increasing use of air-cushion vehicles and this small but elite force is also being provided with new and improved landing ships.

SOVIET NAVY—GENERAL

The overall picture is of a very powerful and well-knit navy whose capabilities, if not numbers, are increasing month by month. Deadly though the weapons may be there are still many problems which beset Admiral Gorshkov as its C-in-C. Lucky though he has been in the efforts of the eleven shipyards which serve his fleet he has still the inevitable problem of manning the ships with conscript junior ratings and officers who are forced into a departmental approach which would be distressing for a Western commander. A tendency to conduct a ship's affairs by committee has been commented on before but there is continuing evidence of centralised control which must inhibit initiative and which relies on that vulnerable necessity, naval wireless communications.

This reliance is brought into focus when the operations of the Soviet fleet over the last year are considered. The Mediterranean has remained the main centre of "out-of-area" operations with an average of 60 ships of all kinds, the majority being support ships, present at any time. The westward movement observed during the Angolan "civil war" was reversed and West African waters saw only the two or three ships and the small contingent of naval infantry which has become the standard Soviet force centred on Conakry, whence both raw material sources and air base facilities need to be assured.

Further afield, visits to Cuba, Guinea Bissau, Nigeria, Angola, Mauritius, Aden, Iraq, India and Canada complemented half-a-dozen calls at European and Mediterranean ports. Several lengthy cruises passed across the Indian Ocean where a steady presence of about five ships was maintained and, East again, the Pacific fleet was more active than usual in the Japanese area.

Assured anchorages and berthing facilities remain available in Cuba, Guinea, Somalia, the Yemens and Iraq to which must now be added Angola and possibly Mozambique. Having obtained flight facilities—officially to relieve trawler crews—at Mauritius, similar facilities were sought in Tonga and Western Samoa in return for airfield construction. Unconfirmed reports of mooring rights in the Maldives should be added to the already existing open-water anchorages off the Seychelles, Chagos and Socotra. All in all the Soviets now have a capability to deploy in security to all the major strategical maritime areas.

Accurate information on all these activities, essential for the proper analysis of Soviet operations and capabilities, relies to a large extent on surveillance by ships and aircraft. While the Soviets operate a fleet of 54 specialised intelligence collectors, backed by merchant and fishing vessels, the number of Western facilities and areas available for this purpose has been dramatically reduced over the last few years, Western intelligence services' capabilities being correspondingly reduced.

In sum the Soviet naval capabilities in mid-1977 are considerable, although they suffer from manpower problems and rely heavily on centralised control. In the event of a nuclear exchange, although some 80 per cent of their ICBM capability is land-based, they have a sea-borne armoury of around 250 mis-

siles with ranges between 4 200 and 5 600 nautical miles, 544 with a 1 300 nautical mile range which may be extended to 2 400 in the fairly near future, and 90 other missiles in the 400-500 mile range which, if SALT-I is adhered to, must be phased out as further building continues. Because of the very long range of the missiles in the "Delta" class it is not possible to determine what proportion is on station at any moment but it should be possible to deploy at least 70 per cent in a crisis—probably more.

The surface ship force has an increasing A/S and missile potential and is already more than strong enough to exercise sea control in selected areas in both peace and war while making diversionary moves in other theatres. For close-in defence the numbers available are more than adequate although of declining efficiency.

Of the 380 general-purpose submarines listed this year probably only 250-270, of which 80 are nuclear propelled, would be available for operations. Thus approximately 200 could be put to sea if hostilities were imminent. Remembering that the reinforcement of Europe from the USA in these circumstances could take as much as two months the following quotation is of interest: "A total of 175-200 submarines will be used to prevent or impair landings and to reduce the forces conveyed and their stores and armour and to attack the Atlantic convoys necessary to maintain the build-up and renewal of men." This is part of a British Naval Intelligence appreciation of January 1944 when the Royal Navy alone had over 800 major escorts available as compared with the current strength of 67.

U.S.A.

However, it is not to the Royal Navy that NATO looks today for the main bulk of its naval support but to the USA and it is here that, according to the last Secretary of Defence, Donald H. Rumsfeld, there were congressional cuts of the President's recommended Defence Budgets of an average of about $5 billion per year between 1965-75. Considering the size of vote this compares favourably with the British defence cuts of $14 billion for ten years following 1973-74. President Carter's election campaign emphasized a $5-7 billion reduction in the Defence Budget although it has subsequently been emphasized that these are long-range aims.

The immediate results on naval appropriations are not entirely clear but it does seem that the nuclear strike-cruiser programme is likely to be deleted for the time being, submarine programmes are being adjusted and the hydrofoil programme has been cancelled at one craft. At the same time the characteristics of the next class of aircraft carriers show a return to conventional propulsion for ships designed to carry about 60 aircraft, a change of policy advocated in this book four years ago. The new cruisers of the "Virginia" and "California" classes are, however, nuclear powered and the costs of the former have, for many reasons, almost trebled over the years. Is the return on over $300 million really cost-effective for a ship whose only surface-to-surface capability is currently a pair of 5-inch guns? Admittedly *Virginia* can carry two helicopters and is to receive Harpoon but there is no space for aircraft in *California*, nor is there any rumour of the future fitting of surface-to-surface missiles. The chase after long-legs does not seem to have been complemented by the hunt for hitting power although, should the very versatile and advanced Tomahawk cruise-missile be put into service, such deficiencies could be overcome at comparatively low cost.

Another class that is now being commissioned, this time without any missile system at all, is the "Spruance". On 7 300 tons it seems remarkable that space has been found for only two 5-inch guns, an Asroc, two triple torpedo mountings and two LAMPS helicopters. The FFG17 class at half the tonnage has a relatively more impressive armament although some criticise her single screw. Despite all such carping the plain fact is that, after a slump in building, available numbers in the active fleet are rising and this is vital for a navy with world-wide commitments. Grossly misleading comparisons can be made between the USN and other fleets—one US Representative has chosen to add up the total tonnage of the fleets of the USA and the USSR. What this was designed to prove is not readily apparent but what it can obscure is that 91 400 tons of *Nimitz* can be in only one place at a time, despite the range of her aircraft, whilst eighteen 5 000-ton ships can be in eighteen places. There is an undoubted role for both types of ship but no useful purpose is served by such obscurantist statements. The habit continues, too, of adding up numbers of ships as a measure of a fleet's capability. This attitude has been castigated in this book for at least five years but repetition should not dim the truth. Only when capabilities, training and a dozen other factors are included in the argument is there any hope of making a sensible comparison. Let us get off the adding machine and think about

men. It is here that the all-volunteer USN has the edge on so many rivals despite recurrent problems in certain spheres.

Other new construction programmes include the "Ohio" class SSBNs to be armed with the new Trident I missile and the "Los Angeles" class SSNs, while in the near future are twelve ocean surveillance ships to operate the Surface Towed Array Surveillance System (STASS). This new method of submarine detection will, however, be of little use against the Soviet "Delta" class with their long range SS-N-8s which in 1976 outranged by 1 600 miles the Trident I system which is due to enter service in 1979. STASS will be of immense value for surveillance of normal submarine operations—other and more sophisticated means are needed to keep tabs on an SSBN which can hit San Diego, California, Quito, Recife, Mozambique, Indonesia and Hawaii from the haven of the Kola Inlet.

THE REST OF NATO

The May 1977 meetings of the heads of the NATO countries suggested a more urgent approach to the increasing Soviet threat which has been advertised in this book over the years. Often, as in successive British Defence White Papers, the assessment of a major threat to peace from this direction has been followed by a notable reduction in forces. A. H. Clough foresaw this attitude more than a century ago:

"Swear not at all, for for thy curse
Thine enemy is none the worse."

The Royal Navy will, before very long, be a "small-ship" navy with the backing of one, later, two, maybe three medium sized ships. The current nuclear submarine building programme could produce twelve SSNs by 1980. The cost of the new MCM ships will so limit their numbers that only two or three major ports could be dealt with at one time. The offshore patrol ships are so lacking in speed and air capability that any major crisis will necessitate the call-up of fleet units and helicopters.

This is all that Great Britain can afford, we are told. Is it? Is available design capability being fully exploited? Over twenty years since the first hovercraft was built in England there is no major programme to utilise its superior speed and other abilities. While the "Invincible" class moves on its majestic way, only one design of frigate allows for two helicopters and no further mention has been made of the "Harrier-Carrier" concept. New designs of helicopter-carrying corvettes have been given in support and the enormous improvements in modern diesel-electric submarines have not been reflected in the Fleet. If the main weight of the Royal Navy is to be deployed in the North-East Atlantic, including UK Home Waters, the use of fast attack craft with missiles would seem logical, yet none is even scheduled in the building programme. All these classes would be less costly than current construction, all would fill a need and, even with the vicious inroads made upon defence spending over the recent years, more hulls would result.

Other NATO countries have felt the impact of inflation and financial stringency and there is little to add to last year's comments. Canada has no new building programme while Norway and Denmark continue with modest programmes and Germany's new Type 122 frigate is now approved with a possible programme of twelve ships. A similar number of their near sisters of the "Kortenaer" class are building in the Netherlands to become part of a well-planned and balanced fleet.

Belgium has opted for a less expensive version in her E-71 class frigates but Italy is now moving ahead with the export-worthy "Lupos" to be followed by the "Maestrales" which will be concurrent with new designs of helicopter cruiser and destroyers.

Greece and Turkey are both building powerful forces of fast attack craft backed by modern submarines. The latter is well-stocked with amphibious forces, so necessary for the support of the First Army in Thrace. Two thousand miles to the West, Portugal has had little opportunity to do more than pare her fleet to a state consistent with the removal of her African commitments.

Lastly in this list, although "with" but not "of" the NATO military line-up, is France. Here is a fleet of several contradictions. Backed by brilliant designers she has built up a home-planned navy where ships, missiles, sensors, submarines and aircraft all come from French drawing boards. This and the high quality resulting are her major strengths but this quality is somewhat undermined by too-frequent political problems and the high proportion of conscripts amongst the junior ratings. The lack of sufficient afloat-support for a navy which is, with the USA and USSR, one of three able to claim a truly world-wide deployment is being remedied in part and this fleet could, given adequate backing in political circles, be a major force in maritime affairs. Already its capabilities have been recognised abroad in the considerable orders for French ships and craft from other navies.

BOFORS
a modern company specialized in weapons technology

57 mm All-purpose Naval Gun

- The Bofors 57 mm all-purpose gun is specially intended for installation on small and medium-sized ships.

- With its proximity-fuzed ammunition, the gun can be used for combatting all kinds of aerial targets, with the same effect as guns intended strictly for anti-aircraft use.

- The penetrating shell with delayed burst gives an effect in surface targets comparable to that of guns with considerably larger calibres.

- Low weight, high rate of fire, and alternative types of ammunition for aerial and surface targets, make the Bofors 57 mm gun system a highly effective weapon.

BOFORS ORDNANCE

AB BOFORS Ordnance Division   Box 500   S-690 20 BOFORS, Sweden
Telephone: 0586-360 00 Cables: Boforsco, Bofors Telex: 73210 bofors s

NON-NATO EUROPE

One of these countries is Spain who, with her own thriving ship-building industry, has benefitted from French skill in submarine matters. But the new helicopter ship and the new frigates will derive help from American advice and more help has come from Germany for her patrol craft. This is a navy in which the problems presented by coasts facing both the Atlantic and the Mediterranean have been clearly realised as they are in the French Naval staff.

The last three naval powers, Sweden, Finland and Yugoslavia have interesting and home-designed building programmes. The Scandinavians have a long history of both design and building and it is the Yugoslavian arrival on the scene which is of particular importance.

THE MEDITERRANEAN

The balance amongst the remaining Mediterranean countries has not so far changed much over the year but several indicators point to matters of moment in the near future. Egypt is turning more to Western suppliers as the Soviet fount runs dry while Israel continues her own programmes of both ships and missiles, exporting both as her capability grows. But westward lie the clouds of uncertainty. Libya, the unpredictable, is now receiving from East and West. The first submarine and missile craft of an expanding programme have arrived in Libyan waters from the USSR—new missile ships are building for her in France and Italy. What this portends at a vital strategic point in the Mediterranean can only be surmised. Part history and the recent utterances of Colonel Qadaffi must make these sombre ones.

In the Red Sea and the Persian Gulf the build-up continues. Sudan retains her independence and operates a small naval group. The reinforcement of Ethiopia by the USSR must be expected though how this will affect Somalia remains uncertain. Uncertain, too, is how far Saudi and Kuwaiti pressure will affect the two Yemens. What is clear is that in the Gulf itself growing forces flank the sea-routes. Oman is introducing ship-borne missiles, the states of the UAE are under a single command while Qatar, Bahrain, Saudi Arabia and Kuwait are becoming increasingly aware of the sea. With Iran building up a fleet of major proportions Iraq remains the only committed supporter of the USSR having apparently sold her birth-right in August 1976 for the promise of friendship, support, military re-equipment and ten "missile frigates."

THE ORIENT

The future further East continues split, apparently, between Western suppliers and the Communist countries and clouded by political uncertainties: Pakistan has received "Hai Nan" patrol craft from China and destroyers from the USA; India is receiving "Nanuchkas" from the USSR while completing British "Leanders" at Bombay; Sri Lanka is reported to be seeking British craft to add to her Chinese and Soviet acquisitions.

There is an ambivalence here which is not repeated in South-East Asia. Burma has no programme apparently but to her south both Malaysia and Singapore are very conscious of their sea frontiers and are reinforcing them with Western designs. The former with a new frigate, six new attack craft and four missile craft under construction lines up alongside Singapore who has recently acquired minesweepers and amphibious forces. Their neighbours, Indonesia and Thailand, are increasing their building rates and operating at sea, a form of training denied the Cambodian and Vietnamese navies where the liquidation of a large proportion of the experienced officers, lack of fuel and insufficient spares have made their considerable squadrons largely inoperative.

Quite how the Philippines are finding sufficient trained men for their much-expanded fleet is not clear. Martial law could provide the men but not the experience. In Taiwan enthusiasm is a bonus which may well be helping raise the efficiency of a navy which, having only recently accepted submarines, has now added missiles to its inventory. Further north the two Koreas may snarl at each other with fleets growing in numbers and capability but here the enthusiasm may be less spontaneous.

As the counter-balance to Soviet influence in the North-West Pacific China herself still continues her defensive posture. A new class of frigates has been added to the steadily increasing order-of-battle which has placed her submarine fleet third in world ranking whilst her growing force of fast attack craft includes well over a third of the entire world total. Large numbers of small amphibious craft further point the fact that this is a fleet designed for home waters — designed for local defence and not for expansion into seas and oceans where others are already fishing. All the information available suggests that the Chinese navy is well-found, well-trained, efficient and well-organised.

These advantages are shared by the Japanese Maritime Self-Defence Force who could operate to the mutual advantage of the two countries were the Japanese to restrict their overseas trade routes by finding their raw materials in the vast cornucopia of China's hinterland. The Japanese designs now being translated into ships are imaginative and workmanlike, designed for their purpose with greater objectivity than the fleets of the pre-1941 era.

THE ANTIPODES AND SOUTH AFRICA

Watching all these developments and vitally affected by the current Soviet Grab-for-Africa are the Australians, the New Zealanders and the South Africans. The former have emerged from a period of belief in man's good nature to plan a navy capable of defending their 16,000 miles of coastline (·5517241 that of the Soviet Union). New Zealand, with a third of the Australians' length of coastline and well under a quarter of the population of her neighbour has a naval strength of considerably less than a fifth of that controlled by Canberra. Perhaps figures are less relevant to the South African problem but here, in a position strategically vital to the Western world and potentially threatened by Soviet pressure from Angola, Mozambique and Mauritius, their fleet is being reinforced by imports from France and Israel. As Western idealism in this case supports Eastern imperialism the government in Pretoria is seeking salvation in its own shipyards — new vessels from Durban will soon add to its strength.

SOUTH AMERICA

Lastly, South America. Here there is little change in strengths although the overall, if unfounded, fear of the giant Brazil is a general factor. The giant has, admittedly, an increasing aircraft industry which could make use of her position as the largest aircraft carrier in the South Atlantic. But there is no indication of her intervention in the possible access of Bolivia to the sea through the disputed Chilean-Peruvian border. Both the latter powers are increasing their naval forces and, where the USSR has lost footing in the former, it is clear it has advanced in the latter in all areas but the naval, where the fleet is now being reinforced from the Netherlands and Italy.

South and Central America are a disturbing melange. Some states are being honeycombed by the KGB of Cuba, some are violent dictatorships, some are striving for affiliation with the democracies of the West. But their naval capabilities, irrespective of their leanings, are increasing and these forces, lying athwart major trade routes, should be considered as an important factor in this sector.

THE FUTURE

If the happenings of 1976 and early-1977 are to be used as guides certain assumptions are possible:—

(a) The external policies of the USSR will continue to provide support for "wars of national liberation" in any countries she may choose.

(b) This fact, the alteration of the "correlation of forces" abroad and increasing Soviet armed capability could well affect the availability of raw materials and markets for the West.

(c) Western economic problems will continue to limit defence budgets — over-spending could adversely affect the present precarious balance.

(d) Within the lifetime of ships now building the provision of oil products, even allowing for widely differing forecasts, will become further attenuated and increasingly expensive.

(e) This will have a marked effect not only on overall economics but also on two important aspects in the naval sphere — ships' propulsion and the ability of currently oil-rich countries to subscribe to the order-books and, hence, the research and development budgets, of foreign suppliers.

(f) The cost of modern weapon systems will continue to rise sharply.

(g) Advances in the capabilities of satellite-reconnaissance will affect deployments and increase the vulnerability of surface forces.

(h) Increasing central control of forces will put greater strain on communications while advances in electronic warfare will make it essential to develop new tactics.

(i) Despite the possibility of limits being placed on strategic nuclear weapons these will remain, probably as the ultimate blackmail, while the importance of non-nuclear arsenals increases as the awesome results of modern nuclear warfare make that event less likely.

The results of an amalgam of all these assumptions suggest certain necessary courses of action:—

(a) The need for NATO and the West generally to look much further than the former's current artificial boundaries to defend their interests and lifelines.

(b) The requirement for an urgent programme to investigate new forms of propulsion.

Minefields

Move in fast. Sweep in safety. Moored mines can't reach you. Your very low acoustic and magnetic signatures below the surface provide maximum immunity. No submerged hull, no propellers- just a shock-absorbing air cushion. The perfect minesweeper **British Hovercraft.**

(c) The provision of less expensive hulls with increased range.

(d) A ruthless programme to ensure that ships' components are tailored to needs rather than a hypothetical all-round excellence.

(e) Continuing attention to the need for reducing ships' companies which, in the West, can absorb over half the total cost of a ship during her life.

(f) Cost-sharing developments of new systems with stress being placed on inter-operability where standardisation is not possible due to time or economic factors.

(g) The continuing need for a deep study of both strategy and

tactics to ensure that not only is the greatest value extracted from modern technology but also that people are encouraged to use their own initiative.

(h) That a proper balance is struck between the costs of strategic nuclear systems, tactical nuclear systems and conventional forces.

Our future peace depends on the solution of problems such as these — we may all pray that it is not too late.

John E. Moore

ACKNOWLEDGEMENTS

This edition, continued and up-dated in the same format as last year, owes a great deal to the great number of people who have written to me over the year. It has been impossible to keep up-to-date with acknowledgements for all this help and for that I apologise. My only reason is, once again, that to compile this book successfully my wife and I have to concentrate very much on producing the copy on time for the publishers and this leaves little over for other things until publication date is reached.

Also this year, as Mr. Norman Polmar has left the staff after nine invaluable years for which we are all most grateful, I have also had to care for the sections on South Korea, the Philippines and the USA. This would have been impossible had it not been for the unstinting aid given by Mr. Samuel L. Morison and the support of Rear Admiral David M. Cooney and his staff in the office of Naval Information, particularly Mr. Robert Carlisle. New additions are the revised section of silhouettes and the pennant list of the majority of the world's major ships other than those of the Soviet bloc and some whose numbers change frequently. These two sections would have been impossible to produce without the aid of Mr. Robert Abernethy and his staff in Washington.

With facts and photographs the following have given me every support, not only in revising the last year's copy but in keeping matters up-to-date: Contre Amiral M. J. Adam CVO CBE, Dr. Giorgio Arra, Lieutenant-Commander Erminio Bagnasco, Herr Siegfried Breyer, Mr. John Callas, Commander A. Fracaroli, Lieutenant-Commander A. Hague VRD, Mr. G. K. Jacobs, Captain F. de Blocq van Kuffeler, Mr. M. C. J. Lennon, Mr. John Mortimer, Mr. S. L. Morison, Mr. J. S. Rowe, Mr. A. J. R. Risseeuw, Mr. C. W. E. Richardson, Senor J. Taibo, Mr. and Mrs. C. Taylor, Mr. R. Winfield. Mr. Graeme Andrews has given invaluable help with the editing of the Australian and New Zealand sections. Mr. Jack Wood and his artists have greatly assisted in providing new line-drawings. To all of them and to the many who are not mentioned by name, my very grateful thanks. This book could not have been produced without the continual help of my wife and Mr. and Mrs. Jean Parsons.

So far as timing is concerned I would remind people of the old staff aim of "the safe and timely arrival of the convoy". Items may reach me safely but if not "timely" (i.e. before 1st December) may not be available for inclusion. November and December are the period of Jane's main harvest.

What leaves my desk is dealt with most sympathetically by Macdonald and Janes where Mr. Stuart Bannerman and the production team under the overall supervision of Mr. Ken Harris are ever ready to help. Glynis Long and the Paulton House girls have worked miracles with my copy while Brenda Perfect and the editorial team have kept me on the straight path of grammar

and, where necessary, political ideology.

In the long-run it all descends on Netherwood, Dalton & Co. Ltd. who have to print it — they have worked wonders and should one day qualify for cryptographic training.

The collection of data for the USA section has been the responsibility of Mr. Samuel Morison. He has been greatly helped by: Rear Admiral David M. Cooney, USN, Chief, Office of Naval Information, Captain William Blanchard, Mr. Robert Carlisle, Miss Anna Urband, Journalist William Lane and LTJG Ed Zesk of his staff; Commander David Rogers, Security Assistance Division, Office of Chief of Naval Operations; Captains R. E. Groder, W. Test, T. Morse, Commander Byers, Mr. Walt Dailey of the Ships Maintenance and Logistics Division, Office of Chief of Naval Operations; Mr. Sranley Krol of the Navy Shipbuilding and Scheduling office, Naval Sea Systems Command; Mr. Christopher Wright, Naval Systems Division, Pentagon; Mrs. Jeanne Koontz, Miss Barbara Gilmore and Mr. Charles Haberlain of the Naval Historical Center; Mr. John S. Rowe co-editor of the 10th edition of *Ships and Aircraft of the U.S. Fleet;* Mr. Larry Manning of the Military Sealift Command; Captain Edmund Kope, Public Affairs Officer, United States Coast Guard, Lt. Tom Philpot, Mr. Robert Scheina, the Coast Guard Historian, Mr. Truman Strobridge, the former Coast Guard Historian and last but not least Miss Elizabeth Segedi, Head, Photo Branch, U.S. Coast Guard. The layout of this section has been my responsibility in order to bring it approximately into line with the listings in the rest of the book.

Finally to the editors of the other naval annuals I send my thanks for the part they have played; *Almanacco Navale* edited by Dr. Giorgio Giorgerini and Signor Augusto Nani, *Flottentaschenbuch* edited by Herr Gerhard Albrecht, *Flottes de Combat* edited by M. J. Labayle-Couhat, and *Marinkalender* edited by Captain Allan Kull.

No illustrations from this book may be reproduced without the publishers' permission but the Press may reproduce information and governmental photographs provided JANE'S FIGHTING SHIPS is acknowledged as the source. Photographs credited to other than official organisations must not be reproduced without permission from the originator.

Contributions for the next edition, which is already in preparation, should be sent as soon as possible to:

Captain J. E. Moore, RN,
Editor, Jane's Fighting Ships,
Elmhurst,
Rickney,
Hailsham,
Sussex BN27 1SF,
England.

LM 2500

a marine gas turbine for navy
applications jointly developed
by Fiat and General Electric Co.

.low fuel consumption
.low weight
.reduced volume
.long life

The LACV-30

Where in the world can't it travel?

The new LACV-30 (lighter, amphibian air cushion vehicle, 30-ton payload) has been specially developed by Bell Aerospace Textron to carry larger, heavier loads faster, farther and across more difficult terrain than any amphibious re-supply vehicle now in operation. Over water, marginal areas, beaches, ice and snow, the LACV-30 has been clocked at speeds of up to 56 mph at 59½ tons gross weight, 70 mph with lighter loads. Able to transport wheeled and tracked vehicles and engineer equipment, as well as the 8 x 8 x 20-foot military and commercial cargo containers now most commonly used, the LACV-30 is de-signed for combat service support missions including search and rescue and medical evacuation. This high-speed successor to the U.S. Army's LARC-5 and LARC-15 marks another first from Bell Aerospace Textron, first in air cushion vehicle technology.

Bell Aerospace TEXTRON

Division of Textron Inc.

Grand Bend, Ontario, Canada

Buffalo, New York 14240 U.S.A.

MAJOR MATTERS

ANGOLA
Since independence in Nov 1975 a naval force has been built up, largely from Portugal—four large patrol craft, six coastal patrol craft, two LCTs. Also acquired—five ex-Soviet LCUs and up to eight merchant ships.

ARGENTINA
Six Type 21 frigates are to be built at AFNE with assistance from Vosper Thornycroft. No further news. In addition the first Type 42 destroyer has commissioned and Two Type 209 submarines are projected.

AUSTRALIA
Two new frigates. To enter service in 1981. New patrol craft, an amphibious heavy liftship, a replenishment ship, a research ship and new MCM vessels are being programmed.

BAHRAIN
Three new coastal patrol craft.

BANGLADESH
HMS *Llandaff* taken over Dec 1976 and renamed *Umar Farooq.*

BELGIUM
The first two "E71" frigates commissioned.

BRAZIL
Minas Gerais undergoing major refit. *Niteroi* commissioned Nov 1976, *Defensora* April 1977. Last two "Oberon" class submarines commissioned.

BRUNEI
Two LCUs acquired.

BULGARIA
Two "Whiskey" class submarines deleted. Three ex-Soviet "Poti" class acquired.

CHINA
1 "Luta" class destroyer, six new "Romeo" class submarines, ten new "Osa" class and ten new "Komar/Hoku" class missile craft and 10 "Shanghai" class have been built. A new frigate class—"Kiang Hu"—now completing.

CUBA
Three "Osa II" class acquired from USSR.

DENMARK
Three "KV72" corvettes being laid down in 1977. First new minelayer commissioning.

DOMINICAN REPUBLIC
Three Ex-US "Cohoes" class transferred for surveying.

ECUADOR
Two more Type 209 submarines reported ordered. Three missile craft commissioned.

EQUATORIAL GUINEA
New force with one ex-Soviet "P6" and a "Poluchat".

FIJI
Surveying ship acquired from Marine Department.

FINLAND
New construction programme of two frigates, five "Osa" class, one minelayer, four minesweepers and three coastguard craft.

FRANCE
Sixth SSBN (SNLE) delayed until 1982. Two "Agosta" class submarines completed. Nuclear helicopter carrier delayed until 1980-81. *Georges Leygues* launched. Five Type A69 avisos completed—two transferred to South Africa. Six large missile craft to be built. Twelve new minehunters planned. *La Durance* (Replenishment Tanker) commissioned—sister *(Meuse)* building.

GERMANY (FEDERAL REPUBLIC)
Possibly Twelve Type 122 frigates planned. "Hamburg" class being fitted with Exocet. All ten Type 143 missile craft in service. Status of hydrofoil order doubtful.

GERMANY (DEMOCRATIC REPUBLIC)
Series production of "Libelle" class fast attack craft.

GREECE
Extra Ex-US "Gearing" class destroyer transferred. Fourth new Type 209 submarine ordered. Four "La Combattante III" class missile craft commissioned. Two Ex-US "Asheville" class PGs and two Ex-US LSTs transferred. Local building increasing.

GUATEMALA
New Halter "Broadsword" class.

GUINEA
Six "Shanghai" class are now in service.

GUINEA BISSAU
This navy is newly founded, with a number of river craft and LCUs.

GUYANA
Vosper 103 ft large patrol craft *Peccari* commissioned March 1977.

ICELAND
Vessels taken up from research etc for "Cod War" being returned.

INDIA
Despite India's refusal to admit to any increase in her fleet it is clear that all six "Leander" class will soon be completed, that up to six ex-Soviet "Nanuchka" class corvettes with SS-N-2 missiles have been ordered of which three are probably in service, that another eight ex-Soviet "Osa" class missile craft have been delivered, that four of an improved "Abhay" class patrol craft have been delivered with four more to come and eight ordered for the customs and that a new survey ship is in hand at Garden Reach.

INDONESIA
Whilst numbers of ex-Soviet craft fall new orders exist for four PSSM Mk 5 missile craft from South Korea two type 209(?) class submarines, while at least six coastal patrol craft have been obtained from De Havilland with the possibility of six more "Attack" class from Australia.

IRAN
Four "Spruance" class (modified) on order from US with three "Tang" class submarines earmarked First of French "La Combattante (Kaman)" class soon to be in service. Third Fleet supply ship building with reports of extra three Landing Ships (Logistic).

IRAQ
Three ex-Soviet "Yevgenya" minesweepers transferred with reports of "Ten missile frigates" to come from USSR as part of August 1976 Treaty.

IRELAND
New training ship, *Setanta*, acquired 1976.

ISRAEL
A building programme of "Reshef" and "Dabur" classes is continuing. First type 206 submarine *Gal* reached Haifa from UK Dec 1976. Second launched 25 Oct 1976.

ITALY
New helicopter cruiser, possible *Giuseppe Garibaldi,* may be ordered 1980. Two "Improved Audace" class destroyers to be ordered and first four of eight "Maestrale" class "Improved Lupos", to be ordered late 1977. First "Sauro" class submarine launched 9 Oct 1976 and second April 1977. Thirteen more missile hydrofoils to be built and new 6 000 ton LPH (to double as training ship in place of *San Giorgio)* due in late 1970s.

JAPAN
The MSDF has requested one DDG, one DD, one PCE, one ARC, one SS and two MSC in 1977 programme. With three frigates deleted the first "Tachikaze" class has commissioned and the first "Improved Haruna" class has been laid down. The eleventh "Chikugo" class frigate has commissioned as have two more LSTs and the first new MSC. The last "Uzushio" class submarine is building with the first of a new and larger class to commission in 1979.

KOREA, NORTH
"Romeo" class submarines are being constructed locally, in addition to "Najin" class frigates and "P6" class patrol craft.

KOREA, SOUTH
A further two "Gearing" class and one LSD were transferred by the USA. Seven "PSMM5" type missile craft will be completed in 1977. Eight fast attack craft are completing and four 1 600 ton frigates are planned.

LIBYA
The first of possibly six "Foxtrot" submarines and the first group of possibly twenty-four "Osa" class missile craft were delivered in late 1976. Western contributions to this navy include four 550 ton missile corvettes now building in Italy, four "La Combattante IIG" missile craft and two "PS700" class LCTs building in France. New naval ports are planned.

MALAWI
One Fairey-Marine "Spear" acquired.

MALAYSIA
HMS *Mermaid* transferred. Six fast attack craft added. Four Swedish "Spica M" class on order. New survey ship due in 1977.

MEXICO
Eight more "Azteca" class are under construction with eighty as the possible target.

MOROCCO
A programme of two more "PR72" type corvettes in addition to the pair now delivered and twelve "P32" class patrol craft has been agreed. Three "Batral" type delivered.

NETHERLANDS
Twelve "Kortenaer" class frigates being built with Harpoon missiles which are also being fitted in "Van Speijk" class. A new submarine design is in hand, a minehunter programme is under study with France and Belgium. New survey ship *Tydeman* commissioned Nov 1976.

NIGERIA
First of two Vosper Mk 9 corvettes launched Jan 1977. New survey ship *Lana* completed Sept 1976.

NORWAY
New construction programme consists of fourteen "Hauk" class missile craft and two minelayers as well as a depot ship and seven patrol craft for the newly created Coastguard. A design for Type 210 submarines is in hand with the Federal German Republic.

OMAN
Four large patrol craft delivered 1966-67. Three others to be fitted with Exocet in 1977.

PAKISTAN
Two ex-US "Gearing" class transferred 1977. Fourth "Daphne" class submarine transferred from Portugal after refit. Two more "Shanghai" class transferred. Two "Hai Nan" class transferred 1976.

PERU
De Zeven Provincien (cruiser) transferred by Netherlands under reconstruction as helicopter cruiser. Two "Daring" class and two "Fletcher" class refitted with helicopter platforms. Two "Maestrale" class and four modified "Lupo" class frigates, two Type 209 submarines to join the present pair, one 25 000-ton tanker and one 10 000-ton tanker are on order or building as well as six 150 ton patrol craft for the Coast Guard.

PHILIPPINES
Strength of navy almost doubled by transfers from S. Vietnam and Japan. In addition some seventy patrol craft under construction.

PORTUGAL
New oceanographic ship building.

QATAR
Ten more Fairey Marine "Spears" delivered, bringing total to twenty-five.

ROMANIA
A programme of local variants of "Shanghai" and "Hu-chwan" classes continues in addition to locally built river patrol craft.

SAUDI ARABIA
Six missile corvettes, four "MSC 322", up to nine fast attack craft—missile and three training ships on order from USA with considerable training programme provided by USN.

SENEGAL
Fairey Marine "Lance" delivered.

SHARJAH
Four coastal patrol craft on order.

SINGAPORE
Two Ex-US MSCs transferred with five LSTs.

SOMALIA
Three "Osa II" class were transferred by the USSR.

SOUTH AFRICA
With paying off of a destroyer and three frigates, two A69 corvettes bought from France with two "Agosta" class submarines building. Six "Reshef" class missile craft building, three in Israel and three in Durban.

SPAIN
Plans continue for *Dedalo's* replacement. First four "Descubierta" class frigates building with four "Agosta" class submarines ordered—delivery 1980 onwards. All twelve large patrol craft will be delivered by mid-1978.

SURINAM
Three patrol craft on order in Netherlands.

SWEDEN
A construction programme of three submarines (with new design under consideration), three corvettes, sixteen missile craft (the first has been completed), one minelayer, nine minehunters and twenty-five LCUs is in hand or projected.

TAIWAN
Two extra ex-US "Gearing" class destroyers acquired. Gabriel missiles fitted in several destroyers. Fifteen PSMM5 missile craft building.

THAILAND
Transfer of two ex-US MSOs cancelled.

TOGO
Two coastal patrol craft delivered from France.

TUNISIA
First of two Vosper Thornycroft 103 ft patrol craft delivered.

TURKEY
Two Type 209 submarines to be built at Gölcuk. Four missile craft delivered by 1978. "Nasty" class under construction. Fourteen SAR 33 large patrol craft on order for Gendarmerie.

UNITED KINGDOM
Hermes completed modification as an A/S carrier. *Invincible* launched 3 May 1977, *Illustrious* under construction. *Superb* commissioned—first of new class SSN to be ordered. Three Type 42 destroyers completed—six more on order. Seven Type 21 frigates completed—one building. Three Type 22 frigates building. Various "Leander" conversions continue. Two "Hunt" class MCMVs ordered. All five offshore patrol craft to commission by end 1977, as do all four "Bird" class large patrol craft. First new Fleet replenishment ship to commission 1977, second in 1978.

USA
Building programme of four SSBNs ("Ohio" class), twenty seven SSNs, two nuclear aircraft carriers, three nuclear cruisers, twenty-five destroyers, ten missile frigates and four LHAs. The programme is under review by the new administration which has already deleted the strike cruiser and patrol hydrofoil programmes although the first order for a 3 000 ton surface effect ship has been confirmed. Considerable deletions have been made from the Service Forces.

USSR
At least two more of the "Kiev" class aircraft carriers are building. A programme of "Delta II" "Charlie" and "Charlie II", "Victor" and "Victor II" and "Tango" classes of submarines, "Kara" and "Kresta II" class cruisers. "Krivak" class destroyers, "Grisha" and "Nanuchka" class corvettes, "Ropucha" class LSTs, "Turya" and "Zhuk" classes of light forces, "Sonya" and "Natya" class minesweepers, "Amur", "Ugra", "Boris Chilikin" and several smaller classes in the support section is continuing.

VENEZUELA
Both Type 209 submarines now completed. Six "Lupo" class frigates have been ordered.

YUGOSLAVIA
A home based programme of at least two 964-ton submarines, ten missile craft and at least one 3,000-ton LST with GRP hulled LCAs is underway.

WSA 400 Series. The weapon systems that give small ships big-ship accuracy.

It began with WSA 4, the Ferranti gun and missile control system specially developed for Royal Navy Type 21 frigates and now proved at sea.

Now that much smaller ships such as fast patrol boats are carrying sophisticated weapons it's natural that variants of WSA 4 should be chosen to control them.

With one or other of the WSA 400 Series you can control any gun in ship-to-ship or ship-to-air attack, or any shipbourne missile used against aircraft, submarines or other ships. Three of the Series are already in production for the Brazilian Navy's Niteroi class frigates.

Ferranti WSA 400 systems have high accuracy, very fast reaction time, a two-channel capability and minimum crew requirement—one weapon one controller.
Ferranti Limited, Digital Systems Division, Bracknell, Berkshire RG12 1RA Telephone: 0344 3232 Telex: 848117

FERRANTI
Total Systems Capability

DS 67

SHIP DESIGNATIONS

In an effort to standardise the type designations in the various navies, despite somewhat idiosyncratic listing in some fleets, a regular formula has been used wherever possible in the majority of sections. This has caused some queries and comments, therefore a list is given below.

TYPE DESIGNATIONS

AIRCRAFT CARRIERS
Attack Carriers (Large)	Over 50,000 tons (all US ships)
Attack Carriers (Medium and Light)	*Essex, Ark Royal,* two French *et al*
Helicopter Carriers/ Cruisers	*Kiev* and *Moskva*

MAJOR SURFACE SHIPS
A/S Cruisers	"Invincible" class
Cruisers	Pre 1960 cruisers, including missile conversions
Light Cruisers	Above 5,000 tons
Destroyers	3,000 tons and over, plus original conventional destroyers
Frigates	1,100 to 3,000 tons
Corvettes	500 to 1,100 tons

LIGHT FORCES
Fast Attack Craft 25 and above 25 knots	FAC (Missile) FAC (Gun) FAC (Torpedo) FAC (Patrol)
Patrol Craft Below 25 knots	Large Patrol Craft (100 to 500 tons) Coastal Patrol Craft (below 100 tons)

SUBMARINES
Strategic Missile	Nuclear propelled and conventionally propelled
Fleet Submarines	Nuclear propelled
Patrol Submarines	Conventionally propelled

AMPHIBIOUS FORCES
Command Ships
Assault Ships
Landing Ships
Landing Craft
Transports

MINE WARFARE FORCES
Mine Layers
MCM Support Ships
Mine Sweepers (Ocean)
Mine Hunters
Mine Sweepers (Coastal)
Mine Sweepers (Inshore)
Mine Sweeping Boats

SURVEYING VESSELS
Surveying Ships
Coastal Surveying Craft
Inshore Surveying Craft

THE USE OF JANE'S FIGHTING SHIPS

All deletions are now listed at the head of each country's section and the data on a navy is now placed above these in a similar order, where this is possible without undue pedantry throughout. Pennant lists are now provided for major navies and the line drawings, at a standard scale of 1 : 1200, are largely new entries. Again, so far as possible, tonnages are included in both standard and full-load displacements—that of "standard" because it is the usage of international documents (eg. The London Naval Treaty of March 1936 and the Montreux Convention of July 1936) and is defined as "the displacement of the vessel, complete, fully manned, engined and equipped ready for sea—but without fuel or reserve feed-water on board". Unless otherwise stated the lengths given are overall.

The major matters relating to the fleets of the world are included after the foreword to relieve that section of the necessity for quantities of figures. Also intended as relief from such complexities, details of radar, sonars, torpedoes and guns have been added at the end in addition to the tables of missiles and aircraft.

A new section of silhouettes has been provided. These are arranged in groups rather than countries to assist recognition. For the same purpose a world pennant list of major surface ships has been added. No attempt has been made to include Soviet ships, whose pennant numbers change frequently.

IDENTIFICATION SILHOUETTES

The following silhouettes are not to scale but are arranged in an order which is designed to make it easier to differentiate between the various classes; eg. ships with two funnels, ships with an island and no visible funnels, ships with one funnel and massive bridge-structure.

IDENTIFICATION SILHOUETTES

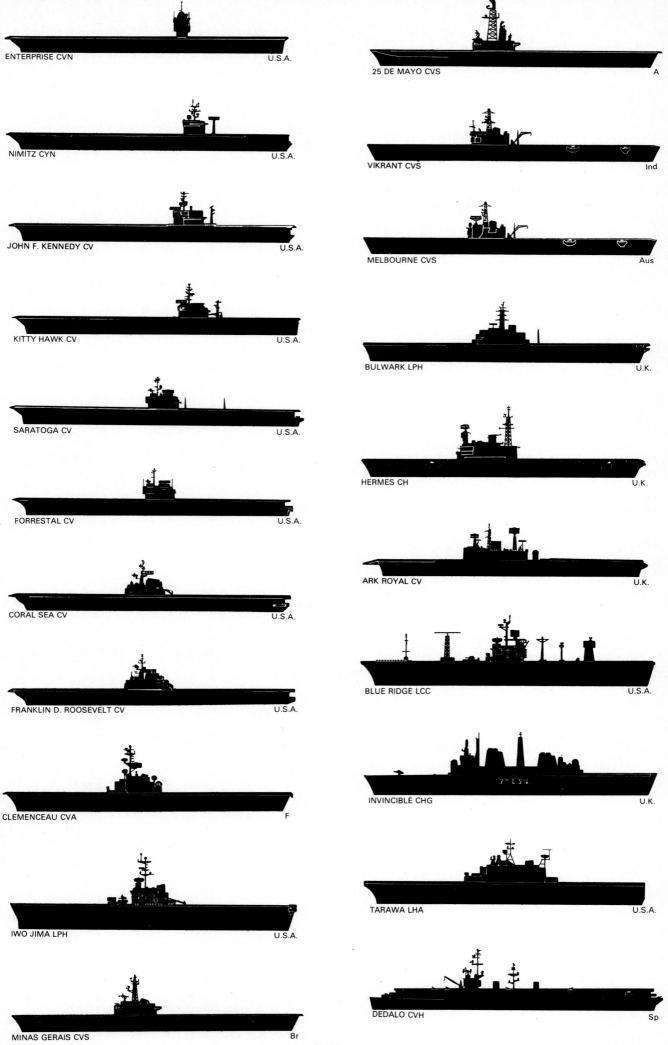

ENTERPRISE CVN — U.S.A.

NIMITZ CYN — U.S.A.

JOHN F. KENNEDY CV — U.S.A.

KITTY HAWK CV — U.S.A.

SARATOGA CV — U.S.A.

FORRESTAL CV — U.S.A.

CORAL SEA CV — U.S.A.

FRANKLIN D. ROOSEVELT CV — U.S.A.

CLEMENCEAU CVA — F

IWO JIMA LPH — U.S.A.

MINAS GERAIS CVS — Br

25 DE MAYO CVS — A

VIKRANT CVS — Ind

MELBOURNE CVS — Aus

BULWARK LPH — U.K.

HERMES CH — U.K.

ARK ROYAL CV — U.K.

BLUE RIDGE LCC — U.S.A.

INVINCIBLE CHG — U.K.

TARAWA LHA — U.S.A.

DEDALO CVH — Sp

[135]

IDENTIFICATION SILHOUETTES

KIEV CHG   Rus

ASHLAND LSD   T

MOSKVA CHG   Rus

JEANNE D'ARC CVH   F

VITTORIO VENETO CHG   I

CASA GRANDE/CABILDO LSD   Gr, Sp, T, U.S.A.

NEWPORT LST   U.S.A.

FEARLESS LPD   U.K.

THOMASTON LSD   U.S.A.

ANCHORAGE LSD   U.S.A.

AUSTIN LPD   U.S.A.

RALEIGH LPD   U.S.A.

IDENTIFICATION SILHOUETTES

LONG BEACH   U.S.A.

TRUXTUN CGN   U.S.A.

KRESTA II CLGM   Rus

GEORGE LEYGUES DEG   F

KRESTA I CLGM   Rus

ALBANY CG   U.S.A.

CALIFORNIA CGN   U.S.A.

WAINWRIGHT CG   U.S.A.

VIRGINIA CGN   U.S.A.

BELKNAP CG   U.S.A.

TOURVILLE DDGSH   F

LEAHY CG   U.S.A.

SUFFREN DLG   F

TAKATSUKI DD   J

KNOX FF (unmodifed)   U.S.A.

AUDACE DDG   I

ACONIT DE   F

LUTJENS DDG   Ger

BAINBRIDGE CGN   U.S.A.

IDENTIFICATION SILHOUETTES

SALISBURY DE, DER, DERP   U.K.
Chichester has no main radar.

PROVIDENCE CG   U.S.A.

HALLAND DDGS   Sw

LITTLE ROCK CG   U.S.A.

TAMANDARE CL   Br

HALLAND MOD DD   Col

ALMIRANTE WILLIAMS DDGSP   Chi

GEARING FRAM II DD   Tur

TIGER CLH   U.K.

HERBERT J. THOMAS DD   T

FERRE DDGS   P

ALLEN M. SUMNER FRAM DDGS   Ir

COLONY MOD CL   In, P

ALLEN M. SUMNER FRAM DD, DDGS   A, Br, Col, Gr, Kor, T, T, Ven

FRIESLAND DD   N

IMPETUOSO DD   I

HOLLAND DD   N

TYPE 47 (ASW) DD   Fr

GEARING FRAM I DD   Br, Sp, T, U.S.A.

IDENTIFICATION SILHOUETTES

GEARING FRAM II DD   Arg, Gr, Kor

GEARING FRAM I DD   Br, Gr, Sp, Tu, Tw

BROOKLYN CL   Arg, Chi

DIDO MOD CL   Pak

KIROV CA   Rus

AYANAMI DD   J

SAMADIKUN DE   Ind

KYNDA CLGM   Rus

ANDREA DORIA DLG

BRISTOL DLG   U.K.

COUNTY DLGMH   U.K.

COUNTY DLGH   U.K.

PEDER SKRAM DE   D

OSTERGOTLAND DDP   Sw

KANIN DDG   Rus

KOTLIN DDG   Po, Rus

KRUPNY DDGS   Rus

[139]

IDENTIFICATION SILHOUETTES

FARRAGUT DDG U.S.A.

DECATUR DDG U.S.A.

MITSCHER DDG U.S.A.

MAHAN DDG U.S.A.

KASHIN DLG Rus

YAMAGUMO DD J

KASHIN DLGM Rus

KILDIN MOD DDGS Rus

TYPE 47 DDG F

KILDIN DDGS Rus

SPRUANCE DD U.S.A.

DARING DD Aus

HAMBURG DD Ger

BARRY DD U.S.A.

TYPE 53 DDG F

KOTLIN DD Rus

MURASAME DD J

KOTLIN MOD DD Rus

IMPAVIDO DDG I

KOLA DE Rus

IDENTIFICATION SILHOUETTES

CHAPAYEV CL — Rus

TALLIN DD — Rus

ALMIRANTE GRAU CL — P

ALMIRANTE LATORRE CL — Chi

AKIZUKI DD — J

SAN GIORGIO DL — I

SVERDLOV CL — Rus

MANLEY DD — U.S.A.

SVERDLOV CLG — Rus

JONAS INGRAHAM DD — U.S.A.

SVERDLOV CLCP — Rus

CARPENTER DD — U.S.A.

GEARING FRAM II DD — Ger, T

LUTA DDG — C

SKORY DD — Eg, Fin, Po, Rus

AKEBONO DE — J

SKORY MOD DD — Eg, Rus

IDENTIFICATION SILHOUETTES

AMATSUKAZE DDG   J

LA GALISSIONIERE DDH   F

AUDAZ DE   Sp

VISBY DE   Sw

DUPERRÉ DD   Fr

TRIBAL DEHP   U.K.

ALAVA DD   Sp

FANTE DE   I

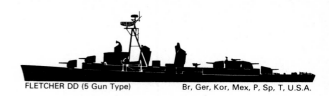

FLETCHER DD (5 Gun Type)   Br, Ger, Kor, Mex, P, Sp, T, U.S.A.

FLETCHER DD (4 Gun Type)   A, Br, Chi, Col, I, Ger, Gr, P, Sp, U.S.A.

ALLEN M. SUMNER DD   A, Br, Col, T, Ven

ROGER DE LAURIA DD   Sp

HARUKAZE DD   J

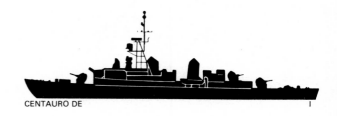

CENTAURO DE   I

CHARLES F. ADAMS DDG   Aus, U.S.A.

[142]

IDENTIFICATION SILHOUETTES

TROMP DDGH   N

ARTEMIZ DDGSP   Ir

KATORI AGDE   J

NITEROL DDH (GP version)   Br

MERMAID FR   M

DAT-ASSAWARI DEP   Lib

LEANDER DE. DEGH   U.K.

BROADSWORD DEGMH   U.K.

SWAN DE   Aus

LEANDER DEGSH   U.K.

RAHMAT DEP   M.

LEANDER DEGSH   U.K.

MAKUT RAJAKUMARN DEP   Th

ALMIRANTE CONDELL DEG   Chi

SAAM DEGSP   Ir

SHEFFIELD DDGH   A, U.K.

PRESIDENT KRUGER DE   S.A.

[143]

IDENTIFICATION SILHOUETTES

ROTHESAY MOD DEPH — In, U.K.

MACKENZIE DD — Can

TORQUAY DE — U.K.

BLACKWOOD DE — In, U.K.

EASTBOURNE DE — U.K.

OLIVER HAZARD PERRY FFG — U.S.A.

OTAGO DE — N.Z.

KRIVAK DDGSP — Rus

TALWAR DE, DEP — In

KIANGTUNG DEG — C

AMAZON DEP, DEGSP — U.K.

ISUZU DE — J

KARA CLGM — Rus

EL FATEH DD — Eg

FRASER DDH — Can

DEUTSCHLAND CLT/AG — Ger

CHAUDIERE DD — Can

COLBERT CLG — F

IDENTIFICATION SILHOUETTES

LEOPARD DE   In, U.K.

Note: Other RIVER Class units differ in after mast configuration

STUART DEP   Aus

MINEGUMO DD   J

CHIKUGO DE   J

GORDY DDG   C

NIGERIA DE   Nig

SPLIT DD   Y

EDSALL/SAVAGE DE/DER   Mex, T, U.S.A.

JUPITER DE   Sp

DELHI CL   In

LE NORMAND DE   F

LE CORSE DE   F

CROSLEY PF   Col, Kor, Mex, T

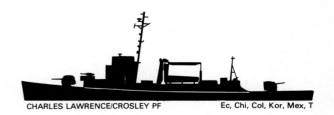

CHARLES LAWRENCE/CROSLEY PF   Ec, Chi, Col, Kor, Mex, T

[145]

IDENTIFICATION SILHOUETTES

GARCIA FF   U.S.A.

GARCIA FF (with Lamps)   U.S.A.

GLOVER AGFF   U.S.A.

BROOKE FFG   U.S.A.

TALBOT FFG   U.S.A.

BRONSTEIN FF   U.S.A.

KNOX FF   U.S.A.

KNOX FF (Improved)   U.S.A.

BALEARES DEG   Sp

BERGAMINI DE   I

HARUNA DDH   J

IDENTIFICATION SILHOUETTES

ALPINO DE   I

PETYA II DE   Rus

PIETRO DE CRISTOFARO PF   I

MIRKA DE   Rus

OLAND DD   Sw

PETYA IA DE   Ur

SAGUENAY DDH   Can

IROQUOIS DDHP   Can

ANNAPOLIS DDH   Can

COMMANDANTE RIVIERE DE   Por

EXMOUTH DE   U.K.

RIGA DE   Bu, C, Ge, Ind, Rus

KOLN DE   Ger

RIGA DE   Fi

PETYA 1 DE   In, Rus

NUEVA ESPARTA DD, DDP   Ven

[147]

IDENTIFICATION SILHOUETTES

ALAMGIR DD
Pak

PIZARRO MOD
Sp

TARIK DE
Eg

ATREVIDA DE
Sp

KISTNA DE
In

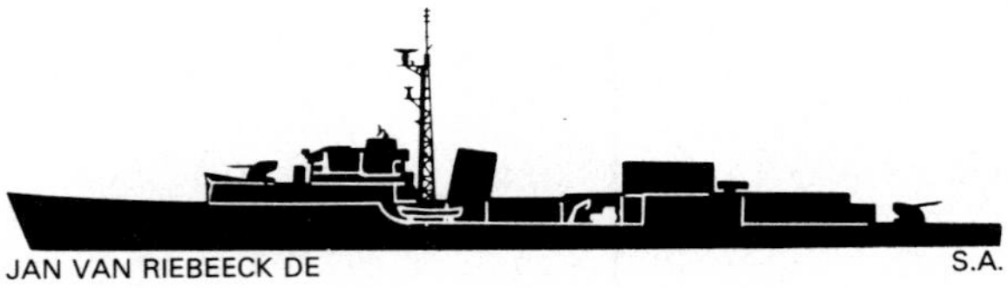

JAN VAN RIEBEECK DE
S.A.

SHAH JAHAN DD
Pak

DEALEY DE
Por, Ur

COURTNEY DE
Col

MATTI KURKI DE
Fin

LOCH PF
S.A.

PERO ESCOBAR DE
Por

GATINEAU DD
Can

ALMIRANTE CLEMENTE DE
Ven

TIPPU SULTAN DE
Pak

JOAO COUNTINHO DE
Por

IDENTIFICATION SILHOUETTES

KIANGNAN DE   C

ALBATROS PF   I, D, Ind

RUDDEROW DE   Kor, T

OSLO DE, DEGSP   Nor

HUNT DE   Ec, Eg, In

BERK DE   T

BAYANDOR PF   Ir

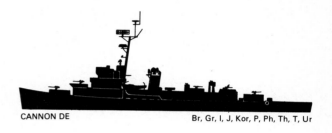

CANNON DE   Br, Gr, I, J, Kor, P, Ph, Th, T, Ur

IKAZUCHI DE   J

MAJOR SURFACE SHIPS
PENNANT LIST

LIST OF COUNTRY ABBREVIATIONS

A	Argentina	Et	Ethiopia	Lib	Libya	Sin	Singapore
Aus	Australia	Fin	Finland	Ma	Malagasy	S.A.	South Africa
Ba	Bangladesh	F	France	M	Malaysia	Sp	Spain
Bel	Belgium	Ger	Germany (Federal Republic)	Mex	Mexico	Sri	Sri Lanka
Br	Brazil	Gh	Ghana	Mor	Morocco	Sw	Sweden
Can	Canada	Gr	Greece	N	Netherlands	T	Taiwan
Chi	Chile	Gu	Guatemala	N.Z.	New Zealand	Th	Thailand
C	China (People's Republic)	In	India	Nic	Nicaragua	T	Turkey
Col	Colombia	Ind	Indonesia	Nig	Nigeria	U.K.	United Kingdom
Cu	Cuba	Ir	Iran	Nor	Norway	U.S.A.	United States of America
D	Denmark	Is	Israel	Pak	Pakistan	Ur	Uruguay
Dom	Dominican Republic	I	Italy	P	Peru	Ven	Venezuela
Ec	Ecuador	J	Japan	Ph	Philippines	V	Vietnam
Eg	Egypt	Kor	Korea (Republic of)	Por	Portugal	Y	Yugoslavia

Pennant No.	Ship Name	Type	Country	Pennant No.	Ship Name	Type	Country
1	Phosamton	MSF	Th.	6	Julius A. Furer	FFG	U.S.A.
1	Tahchin	PF	Th.	6	Barney	DDG	U.S.A.
1	Brooke	FFG	U.S.A.	6	Providence	CG	U.S.A.
1	Glover	AGFF	U.S.A.	B 6	Usumacinta	PF	Mex.
1	Raleigh	LPD	U.S.A.	06	Condell	DEG	Chi.
1	Tarawa	LHA	U.S.A.	06	Siete De Agosto	DD	Col.
B 1	Durango	PF	Mex.	06	Aspis	DD	Gr.
F 1	Cuauthemoc	DD	Mex.	TA06	Manuel Azueta	DE	Mex.
D 1	25 De Julio	PF	Ec.	7	Makut Rajakumarn	FF	Th.
D 1	Samadikun	DE	Ind.	7	Cleveland	LPD	U.S.A.
De 1	Uruguay	DE	Ur.	7	Henry B. Wilson	DDG	U.S.A.
PF 1	Montevideo	PF	Ur.	7	Springfield	CG	U.S.A.
F 01	Dat Assawari	DEG	Lib.	7	Guadalcanal	LPH	U.S.A.
01	Hercules	DDGH	A.	7	Oliver Hazard Perry	FFG	U.S.A.
01	Aetos	DE	Gr.	C 7	Guanajuato	PF	Mex.
PH 01	Dedalo	CVH	Sp.	D 7	Babr	DDGS	Ir.
2	Prasae	PF	Th.	E 7	President Bourguiba	DER	Tu.
2	Ramsey	FFG	U.S.A.	07	Lynch	DEG	Chi.
2	Charles F. Adams	DDG	U.S.A.	8	Dubuque	LPD	U.S.A.
2	Iwo Jima	LPH	U.S.A.	8	Lynde McCormick	DDG	U.S.A.
2	Vancouver	LPD	U.S.A.	B 8	Chihuahua	PF	Mex.
2	Saipan	LHA	U.S.A.	C 8	Queretaro	PF	Mex.
V 2	25 De Mayo	CVS	A.	R 08	Bulwark	LPH	U.K.
B 2	Coahuila	PF	Mex.	08	Vendetta	DD	Aus.
F 2	Cuitlahuac	DD	Mex.	9	Denver	LPD	U.S.A.
D 2	Presidente Alfaro	DE	Ec.	9	Towers	DDG	U.S.A.
D 2	Martadinata	DE	Ind.	9	Long Beach	CGN	U.S.A.
DE 2	Artigas	DE	Ur.	C 9	Potosi	PF	Mex.
D 02	Caldas	DD	Col.	D 9	Palang	DDGS	Ir.
D 02	Devonshire	DLGH	U.K.	R 09	Ark Royal	CV	U.K.
02	Santissima Trinidad	DDGH	A.	10	Albany	CG	U.S.A.
02	O'Higgins	CL	Chi.	10	Juneau	LPD	U.S.A.
3	Pin Klao	DE	Th.	10	Sampson	DDG	U.S.A.
3	Maeklong	PF	Th.	10	Tripoli	LPH	U.S.A.
3	Schofield	FFG	U.S.A.	D 10	Acre	DD	Br.
3	John King	DDG	U.S.A.	F 10	Aurora	FFGH	U.K.
3	Okinawa	LPH	U.S.A.	L 10	Fearless	LPD	U.K.
D 3	Pres. Velasco Ibarra	DE	Ec.	11	Vampire	DD	Aus.
D 3	Ngurah Rai	DE	Ind.	11	Port Said	DE	Eg.
DE 3	18 De Julio	DE	Ur.	11	Matti Kurki	DE	Fin.
LHA3	Belleau Wood	LHA	U.S.A.	11	Chicago	CG	U.S.A.
03	Pratt	CL	Chi.	11	Coronado	LPD	U.S.A.
4	General Belgrano	CL	A.	11	Sellers	DDG	U.S.A.
4	Austin	LPD	U.S.A.	11	New Orleans	LPH	U.S.A.
4	Talbot	FFG	U.S.A.	11	Split	DD	Y.
4	Lawrence	DDG	U.S.A.	A 11	Minas Gerais	CVS	Br.
B 4	Papaloapan	PF	Mex.	D 11	Nueva Esparta	DD	Ven.
D 4	Monginsidi	FF	Ind.	F 11	Visby	DD	Sw.
LHA4	Nassau	LHA	U.S.A.	L 11	Intrepid	LPD	U.K.
04	Lattore	CL	Chi.	R 11	Vikrant	CVS	In.
04	Almirante Tono	DT	Col.	12	Columbus	CG	U.S.A.
5	Nueve de Julio	CL	A.	12	Shreveport	LPD	U.S.A.
5	Tapi	FF	Th.	12	Robison	DDG	U.S.A.
5	Ogden	LPD	U.S.A.	12	Inchon	LPH	U.S.A.
5	Richard L. Page	FFG	U.S.A.	C 12	Tamandare	CL	Br.
5	Claude V. Ricketts	DDG	U.S.A.	D 12	Kent	DLGH	U.K.
5	Oklahoma City	CG	U.S.A.	D 12	Almirante Clemente	DE	Ven.
5	Da Nang	LHA	U.S.A.	DE12	Saam	DE	Ir.
B 5	Tehuantepec	PF	Mex.	F 12	Vulcano	DE	Sp.
D 5	Artemiz	DDGS	Ir.	F 12	Sundsval	DD	Sw.
05	Veinte De Julio	DD	Col.	F 12	Achilles	FFGH	U.K.
6	Khirirat	FF	Th.	R 12	Hermes	LPH	U.K.
6	Duluth	LPD	U.S.A.	13	Nashville	LPD	U.S.A.

Pennant No.	Ship Name	Type	Country	Pennant No.	Ship Name	Type	Country
13	Hoel	DDG	U.S.A.	25	Bainbridge	CGN	U.S.A.
D 13	G. Juan Jose Flores	DE	Ven.	D 25	Marcilio Diaz	DD	Br.
F 13	Halsingborg	DE	Sw.	D 25	Jorge Juan	DD	Sp.
14	Blanco Encalada	DD	Chi.	F 25	Bayandor	PF	Ir.
14	Trenton	LPD	U.S.A.	26	Bouchard	DD	A.
14	Buchanan	DDG	U.S.A.	26	Serrano	PF	Chi.
DE14	Zaal	DE	Ir.	26	Belknap	CG	U.S.A.
F 14	Kalmar	DE	Sw.	26	Tortuga	LSD	U.S.A.
F 14	Leopard	FF	U.K.	D 26	Mariz E. Barros	DD	Br.
15	Cochrane	DD	Chi.	F 26	Naghdi	PF	Ir.
15	Cordoba	DT	Col.	27	Py	DD	A.
15	Ponce	LPD	U.S.A.	27	Orella	PF	Chi.
15	Berkeley	DDG	U.S.A.	27	Josephus Daniels	CG	U.S.A.
F 15	Euryalus	FFGH	U.K.	27	Whetstone	LSD	U.S.A.
16	Boyaca	DE	Col.	D 27	Para	DD	Br.
16	Velos	DD	Gr.	F 27	Lynx	DE	U.K.
16	Cabildo	LSD	U.S.A.	28	Riquelme	PF	Chi.
16	Joseph Strauss	DDG	U.S.A.	28	Thyella	DD	Gr.
16	Lexington	CVT	U.S.A.	28	Wainwright	CG	U.S.A.
16	Leahy	CG	U.S.A.	28	Thomaston	LSD	U.S.A.
D 16	London	DLGH	U.K.	D 28	Paraiba	DD	Br.
DE16	Rostam	DE	Ir.	F 28	Kahnamuie	PF	Ir.
F 16	Diomede	FFGH	U.K.	F 28	Cleopatra	FFGH	U.K.
F 16	Umar Farooq	DE	Ba.	29	Uribe	PF	Chi.
J 16	Oland	DD	Sw.	29	Jouett	CG	U.S.A.
17	Conyngham	DDG	U.S.A.	29	Plymouth Rock	LSD	U.S.A.
17	Harry E. Yarnell	CG	U.S.A.	D 29	Parana	DD	Br.
J 17	Uppland	DD	Sw.	30	Horne	CG	U.S.A.
18	Almirante Riveros	DDG	Chi.	30	Fort Snelling	LSD	U.S.A.
18	Colonial	LSD	U.S.A.	D 30	Pernambuco	DD	Br.
18	Semmes	DDG	U.S.A.	31	Ierax	DE	Gr.
18	Worden	CG	U.S.A.	31	Galicia	LSD	Sp.
D 18	Antrim	DLGH	U.K.	31	Sterett	CG	U.S.A.
DE18	Faramaz	DE	Ir.	31	Decatur	DDG	U.S.A.
F 18	Galatea	FFGH	U.K.	31	Point Defiance	LSD	U.S.A.
J 18	Halland	DD	Sw.	D 31	Audaz	DE	Sp.
19	Almirante Williams	DDG	Chi.	F 31	Brahamaputra	DE	In.
19	Blue Ridge	LCC	U.S.A.	32	William H. Standley	CG	U.S.A.
19	Comstock	LSD	U.S.A.	32	John Paul Jones	DDG	U.S.A.
19	Tattnall	DDG	U.S.A.	32	Spiegel Grove	LSD	U.S.A.
19	Dale	CG	U.S.A.	D 32	General Jose De Austria	DE	Ven.
D 19	Glamorgan	DLGH	U.K.	F 32	Salisbury	DER	U.K.
J 19	Småland	DD	Sw.	33	Fox	CG	U.S.A.
20	Almirante Brown	DD	A.	33	Parsons	DDG	U.S.A.
20	Mount Whitney	LCC	U.S.A.	33	Alamo	LSD	U.S.A.
20	Donner	LSD	U.S.A..	D 33	Maranhao	DD	Br.
20	Goldsborough	DDG	U.S.A.	D 33	Almirante Jose Garcia	DE	Ven.
20	Richmond K. Turner	CG	U.S.A.	34	Biddle	CG	U.S.A.
C 20	Tiger	CL	U.K.	34	Somers	DDG	U.S.A.
D 20	Fife	DLGH	U.K.	34	Oriskany	CV	U.S.A.
J 20	Ostergotland	DD	Sw.	34	Hermitage	LSD	U.S.A.
21	Espora	DD	A.	D 34	Mato Grosso	DD	Br.
21	Melbourne	CVS	Aus.	35	Mitscher	DDG	U.S.A.
21	Cochrane	DDG	U.S.A.	35	Monticello	LSD	U.S.A.
21	Gridley	CG	U.S.A.	35	Truxtun	CGN	U.S.A.
D 21	Inhauma	DD	Br.	D 35	Alagoas	DD	Br.
D 21	Lepanto	DD	Sp.	36	Anchorage	LSD	U.S.A.
D 21	Norfolk	DLGH	U.K.	36	California	CGN	U.S.A.
D 21	Falcon	DD	Ven.	36	John S. McCain	DDG	U.S.A.
D 21	Zulia	DD	Ven.	D 36	Sergipe	DD	Br.
J 21	Sodermanland	DD	Sw.	F 36	Whitby	DE	U.K.
22	Rosales	DD	A.	37	Portland	LSD	U.S.A.
22	Benjamin Stoddert	DDG	U.S.A.	37	South Carolina	CGN	U.S.A.
22	England	CG	U.S.A.	37	Farragut	DDG	U.S.A.
D 22	Jaceguay	DD	Br.	D 37	Rio Grande Do Norte	DD	Br.
D 22	Almirante Ferrandiz	DD	Sp.	F 37	Jaguar	DE	U.K.
D 22	G. Jose Trinidad Moran	DE	Ven.	38	Perth	DDG	Aus.
23	Almirante Domecq Garcia	DD	A.	38	Pensacola	LSD	U.S.A.
J 22	Gastrikland	DD	Sw.	38	Luce	DDG	U.S.A.
23	Richard E. Byrd	DDG	U.S.A.	38	Virginia	CGN	U.S.A.
23	Halsey	CG	U.S.A.	D 38	Espirito Santo	DD	Br.
D 23	Frontin	DD	Br.	D 38	Intrepido	DE	Sp.
D 23	Almirante Valdes	DD	Sp.	F 38	Arethusa	FFGH	U.K.
D 23	Bristol	DLG	U.K.	39	Hobart	DDG	Aus.
D 23	Almirante Brion	DE	Ven.	39	Mount Vernon	LSD	U.S.A.
J 23	Halsingland	DD	Sw.	39	Macdonough	DDG	U.S.A.
24	Almirante Storni	DD	A.	39	Texas	CGN	U.S.A.
24	Waddell	DDG	U.S.A.	F 39	Naiad	FFGH	U.K.
24	Reeves	CG	U.S.A.	40	Fort Fisher	LSD	U.S.A.
D 24	Greenhalgh	DD	Br.	40	Coontz	DDG	U.S.A.
D 24	Alcala Galiano	DD	Sp.	40	Mississippi	CGN	U.S.A.
F 24	Rahmat	DE	M.	F 40	Niteroi	DDH	Br.
25	Segui	DD	A.	F 40	Sirius	FFGH	U.K.

Pennant No.	Ship Name	Type	Country	Pennant No.	Ship Name	Type	Country
41	Brisbane	DDG	Aus.	72	Kang Won	DE	Kor.
41	King	DDG	U.S.A.	72	Guise	DD	P.
41	Midway	CV	U.S.A.	F 72	Andalucia	DEG	Sp.
D 41	Oquendo	DD	Sp.	F 72	Ariadne	FFGH	U.K.
D 41	Caraboba	DD	Ven.	73	Chung Nam	DE	Kor.
F 41	Defensora	DDH	Br.	73	Palacios	DDGS	P.
F41	Vincent Yanez Pinzon	PF	Sp.	F 73	Cataluña	DEG	Sp.
42	Tarik	DE	Eg.	F 73	Eastbourne	DE	U.K.
42	Mahan	DDG	U.S.A.	P 73	Anjadip	FFL	In.
42	Franklin D. Roosevelt	CV	U.S.A.	74	Ferre	DDGS	P.
D 42	Roger De Lauria	DD	Sp.	C 74	Delhi	CL	In.
F 42	Independencia	DDH	Br.	F 74	Asturias	DEG	Sp.
F 42	Legazpi	PF	Sp.	P 74	Andaman	FFL	In.
F 42	Phoebe	FFGH	U.K.	F 75	Extremadura	DEG	Sp.
43	Rashid	DE	Eg.	F 75	Charybdis	FFGH	U.K.
43	Dahlgren	DDG	U.S.A.	P 75	Amini	FFL	In.
43	Coral Sea	CV	U.S.A.	76	Datu Kalantiaw	DE	Ph.
D 43	Marques De La Ensenada	DD	Sp.	P 77	Kamorta	FFL	In.
F 43	Uniao	DDH	Br.	F 78	Blackwood	DE	U.K.
F 43	Torquay	DE	U.K.	P 78	Kadmatt	FFL	In.
44	William V. Pratt	DDG	U.S.A.	P 79	Kiltan	FFL	In.
F 44	Constituciao	DDH	Br.	D 80	Sheffield	DDGH	U.K.
45	Yarra	DE	Aus.	F 80	Duncan	DE	U.K.
45	Dewey	DDG	U.S.A.	P 80	Kavaratti	FFL	In.
F 45	Liberal	DDH	Br.	81	Kyong Nam	PF	Kor.
F 45	Minerva	FFGH	U.K.	81	Almirante Grau	CL	P.
46	Parramatta	DE	Aus.	F 81	Descubierta	FF	Sp.
46	Preble	DDG	U.S.A.	P 81	Katchal	FFL	In.
F 46	Kistna	FF	In.	82	Ah San	PF	Kor.
F 47	Danae	FFGH	U.K	82	Coronel Bolognesi	CL	P.
48	Stuart	DE	Aus.	83	Ung Po	PF	Kor.
F 48	Dundas	DE	U.K.	83	Capitan Quiñones	CL	P.
49	Derwent	DE	Aus.	84	Babur	CL	Pak.
50	Swan	DE	Aus.	F 84	Exmouth	DE	U.K.
D 51	Liniers	DD	Sp.	85	Sfendoni	DD	Gr.
D 52	Alava	DD	Sp.	85	Kyong Puk	PF	Kor.
F 52	Juno	FFGH	U.K.	F 85	Keppel	DE	U.K.
53	Torrens	DE	Aus.	86	Jonnam	PF	Kor.
54	Leon	DE	Gr.	D 86	Birmingham	DDGH	U.K.
F 54	Hardy	DE	U.K.	87	Chi Ju	PF	Kor.
F 55	Waikato	FFGH	N.Z.	D 87	Newcastle	DDGH	U.K.
56	Lonchi	DD	Gr.	F 87	Nigeria	DE	Nig.
F 56	Argonaut	FFGH	U.K.	D 88	Glasgow	DDGH	U.K.
F 57	Andromeda	FFGH	U.K.	91	Chung Mu	DD	Kor.
F 58	Hermione	FFGH	U.K.	92	Seoul	DD	Kor.
59	Forrestal	CV	U.S.A.	D 92	Godavari	DE	In.
A 59	Deutschland	CLT	Ger.	93	Pusan	DD	Kor.
F 59	Chichester	DE	U.K.	95	Chung Buk	DD	Kor.
60	Saratoga	CV	U.S.A.	96	Jeong Buk	DD	Kor.
C 60	Mysore	CL	In.	97	Dae Gu	DD	Kor.
F 60	Jupiter	FFGH	U.K.	F 97	Russell	DE	U.K.
61	Castilla	DE	P.	R 97	Jeanne D'Arc	CHV	F.
61	Ranger	CV	U.S.A.	98	In Cheon	DD	Kor.
D 61	Churruca	DD	Sp.	R 98	Clemenceau	CVS	F.
F 61	Atrevida	DE	Sp.	C 99	Blake	CL	U.K.
62	Independence	CV	U.S.A.	F 99	Lincoln	DER	U.K.
D 62	Gravina	DD	Sp.	R 99	Foch	CVS	F.
F 62	Princesa	DE	Sp.	F 101	Yarmouth	DEH	U.K.
63	Navarinon	DD	Gr.	101	Harukaze	DD	J.
63	Rodriquez	BE	P.	102	Yukikaze	DD	J.
63	Kitty Hawk	CV	U.S.A.	103	Ayanami	DD	J.
D 63	Mendez Nunez	DD	Sp.	F 103	Lowestoft	DEH	U.K.
64	Constellation	CV	U.S.A.	104	Isonami	DD	J.
D 64	Langara	DD	Sp.	F 104	Dido	FFGH	U.K.
F 64	Nautilus	DE	Sp.	105	Uranami	DD	J.
65	Enterprise	CVN	U.S.A.	106	Shikinami	DD	J.
D 65	Blas De Lezo	DD	Sp.	F 106	Brighton	DEH	U.K.
F 65	Villa Bilbao	DE	Sp.	107	Murasame	DD	J.
66	America	CV	U.S.A.	F 107	Rothesay	DEH	U.K.
67	Panthir	DE	Gr.	108	Yudachi	DD	J.
67	John F. Kennedy	CV	U.S.A.	D 108	Cardiff	DDGH	U.K.
68	Nimitz	CVN	U.S.A.	F 108	Londonderry	DEH	U.K.
P 68	Arnala	FFL	In.	109	Harusame	DD	J.
69	Dwight D. Eisenhower	CVN	U.S.A.	F 109	Leander	FFGH	U.K.
F 69	Bacchante	FFGH	U.K.	110	Takanami	DD	J.
P 69	Androth	FFL	In.	F 110	Kaveri	FF	In.
70	Carl Vinson	CVN	U.S.A.	111	Oanami	DD	J.
F 70	Apollo	FFGH	U.K.	F 111	Otago	DE	N.Z.
71	Kyong Ki	DE	Kor.	112	Makinami	DD	J.
71	Villar	DD	P.	113	Yamagumo	DD	J.
F 71	Baleares	DEG	Sp.	F 113	Falmouth	DEH	U.K.
F 71	Scylla	FFGH	U.K.	114	Makigumo	DD	J.

Pennant No.	Ship Name	Type	Country	Pennant No.	Ship Name	Type	Country
F 114	Ajax	FFGH	U.K.	F 217	Milanian	PF	Ir.
115	Asagumo	DD	J.	218	Tokachi	DE	J.
F 115	Berwick	DEH	U.K.	219	Iwase	DE	J.
116	Minegumo	DD	J.	220	Chitose	DE	J.
117	Natsugumo	DD	J.	F 220	Köln	DE	Ger.
F 117	Ashanti	DEH	U.K.	221	Niyodo	DE	J.
118	Murakumo	DD	J.	F 221	Emden	DE	Ger.
D 118	Coventry	DDGH	U.K.	222	Teshio	DE	J.
119	Aokumo	DD	J.	F 222	Augsburg	DE	Ger.
F 119	Eskimo	DEH	U.K.	223	Yoshino	DE	J.
F 122	Gurkha	DEH	U.K.	F 223	Karlsruhe	DE	Ger.
F 124	Zulu	DEH	U.K.	224	Kumano	DE	J.
F 125	Mohawk	DEH	U.K.	F 224	Lübek	DE	Ger.
F 126	Plymouth	DEH	U.K.	F 225	Braunschweig	DE	Ger.
F 127	Penelope	FFGH	U.K.	229	Ottawa	DDH	Can.
F 129	Rhyl	DEH	U.K.	230	Margaree	DDH	Can.
F 131	Nubian	DEH	U.K.	233	Fraser	DDH	Can.
F 133	Tartar	DEH	U.K.	F 233	Nilgiri	FFGH	In.
F 137	Beas	DE	In.	234	Assiniboine	DDH	Can.
F 139	Betwa	DE	In.	F 234	Himgiri	FFGH	In.
F 140	Talwar	DE	In.	236	Gatineau	DDE	Can.
141	Haruna	DDH	J.	D 237	Simon Van Der Stel	DE	S.A.
142	Hiei	DDH	J.	250	Iman Bondjol	PF	Ind.
F 143	Trishul	DE	In.	251	Surapati	PF	Ind.
F 144	Kirpan	DE	In.	252	Pattimura	PF	Ind.
F 145	President Pretorius	DE	S.A.	253	Sultan Hasanudin	PF	Ind.
F 146	Kuthar	DE	In.	F 256	Tir	FF	Ind.
F 147	President Steyn	DE	S.A.	257	Restigouche	DDE	Can.
F 148	Taranaki	DE	N.Z.	258	Kootenay	DDE	Can.
F 150	President Kruger	DE	S.A.	259	Terra Nova	DDE	Can.
L 153	Nafkratoussa	LSD	Gr.	260	Tippu Sultan	DE	Pak.
154	Duchess	DD	Aus.	261	Mackenzie	DD	Can.
F 157	Vrystaat	FF	S.A.	261	Tughril	DE	Pak.
160	Alamgir	DD	Pak.	262	Saskatchewan	DD	Can.
161	Akizuki	DD	J.	263	Yukon	DD	Can.
161	Badr	DD	Pak.	264	Qu 'Appelle	DD	Can.
162	Teruzuki	DD	J.	265	Annapolis	DDH	Can.
162	Jahangir	DD	Pak.	266	Nipigon	DDH	Can.
163	Amatsukaze	DDG	J.	273	Grom	DD	Po.
164	Takatsuki	DD	J.	274	Wicher	DD	Po.
164	Shah Jahan	DD	Pak.	275	Warszawa	DDG	Po.
165	Kikuzuki	DD	J.	D 278	Jan Van Riebeeck	DE	S.A.
166	Mochizuki	DD	J.	280	Iroquois	DDH	Can.
167	Nagatsuki	DD	J.	281	Huron	DDH	Can.
168	Tachikaze	DDG	J.	282	Athabaskan	DDH	Can.
169	—	DDG	J.	283	Algonquin	DDH	Can.
F 169	Amazon	DE	U.K.	M 291	Pietermaritzburg	FF	S.A.
F 170	Antelope	DE	U.K.	F 300	Oslo	DE	Nor.
D 171	Z 2	DD	Ger.	F 301	Bergen	DE	Nor.
F 171	Active	DE	U.K.	F 302	Trondheim	DE	Nor.
D 172	Z 3	DD	Ger.	F 303	Stavanger	DE	Nor.
F 172	Ambuscade	DE	U.K.	F 304	Narvik	DE	Nor.
F 173	Arrow	DE	U.K.	F 335	Pero Escobar	DE	Por.
F 174	Alacrity	DE	U.K.	D 340	Istanbul	DD	T.
F 175	Ardent	DE	U.K.	F 340	Beskytteren	FFH	D.
F 176	Avenger	DE	U.K.	D 341	Izmir	DD	T.
D 178	Z 4	DD	Ger.	F 341	Samadikun	DE	Ind.
D 179	Z 5	DD	Ger.	D 342	Izmit	DD	T.
D 181	Hamburg	DD	Ger.	F 342	Martadinata	DE	Ind.
D 182	Schleswig Holstein	DD	Ger.	D 343	Iskenderun	DD	T.
D 183	Bayern	DD	Ger.	F 343	Mongisidi	DE	Ind.
D 184	Hessen	DD	Ger.	D 344	Içel	DD	T.
D 185	Lütjens	DDG	Ger.	F 344	Bellona	PF	D.
D 186	Mölders	DDG	Ger.	F 344	Ngurah Rai	DE	Ind.
D 187	Rommel	DDG	Ger.	F 345	Diana	PF	D.
201	Akebono	DE	J.	F 346	Flora	PF	D.
202	Ikazuchi	DE	J.	F 347	Triton	PF	D.
203	Inazuma	DE	J.	F 348	Hvidbjornen	FFH	D.
205	St. Laurent	DDH	Can.	F 349	Vaedderen	FFH	D.
206	Saguenay	DDH	Can.	F 350	Ingolf	FFH	D.
207	Skeena	DDH	Can.	351	Jos Sudarso	DE	Ind.
210	Themistocles	DD	Gr.	F 351	Fylla	FFH	D.
211	Isuzu	DE	J.	D 352	Gayret	DD	T.
212	Kanaris	DD	Gr.	F 352	Peder Skram	DE	D.
212	Mogami	DE	J.	D 353	Adatepe	DD	T.
213	Kontouriotis	DD	Gr.	F 353	Herluf Trolle	DE	D.
213	Kitakami	DE	J.	D 355	Tinaztepe	DD	T.
214	Sachtouris	DD	Gr.	D 356	Zafer	DD	T.
214	Ooi	DE	J.	D 357	Muavenet	DD	T.
215	Chikugo	DE	J.	D 358	Berk	DE	T.
216	Ayase	DE	J.	359	Kakiali	DE	Ind.
217	Mikuma	DE	J.	D 359	Peyk	DE	T.

Pennant No.	Ship Name	Type	Country	Pennant No.	Ship Name	Type	Country
360	Nuku	DE	Ind.	F 733	Commandant Riviére	FF	F.
F 421	Canterbury	DEGH	N.Z.	F 740	Commandant Bourdais	FF	F.
F 433	Hang Tuah	PF	M.	743	Sutherland	DD	U.S.A.
462	Hayase	AM	J.	F 748	Protet	DE	F.
F 471	Antonio Enes	DE	Por.	F 749	Enseigne Henry	DE	F.
F 472	Alm. Da Silva	DE	Por.	763	William C. Lawe	DD	U.S.A.
F 473	Alm. Coutinho	DE	Por.	F 763	Le Boulonnais	DE	F.
F 474	Alm. Correa	DE	Por.	F 765	Le Normand	DE	F.
F 475	Joao Coutinho	DE	Por.	F 766	Le Picard	DE	F.
F 476	Jacinto Candido	DE	Por.	F 767	Le Gascon	DE	F.
F 477	Gen. Pereira D'Eca	DE	Por.	F 768	Le Lorrain	DE	F.
F 480	Com. Belo	DE	Por.	F 769	Le Bourguignon	DE	F.
F 481	Com. Capelo	DE	Por.	F 770	Le Champenois	DE	F.
F 482	Com. Ivens	DE	Por.	F 771	Le Savoyard	DE	F.
F 483	Com. Cabral	DE	Por.	F 772	Le Breton	DE	F.
F 484	De Castilho	DE	Por.	F 773	Le Basque	DE	F.
F 487	Joao Roby	DE	Por.	F 774	L'Agenais	DE	F.
F 488	Afonso Cerqueira	DE	Por.	F 775	Le Béarnais	DE	F.
F 489	Oliveira E. Carmo	DE	Por.	F 776	L'Alsacien	DE	F.
F 490	Baptista De Andrade	DE	Por.	F 777	Le Provencal	DE	F.
F 540	Pietro De Cristofaro	PF	I.	F 778	Le Vendeen	DE	F.
F 541	Umberto Grosso	PF	I.	F 781	D'Estienne D'Orves	FF	F.
F 542	Aquila	PF	I.	F 782	Amyot D'Inville	FF	F.
F 543	Albatros	PF	I.	F 783	Drogou	FF	F.
F 544	Alcione	PF	I.	784	McKean	DD	U.S.A.
F 545	Airone	PF	I.	F 784	Detroyat	FF	F.
F 546	Licio Visintini	PF	I.	785	Henderson	DD	U.S.A.
550	Vittorio Veneto	DLGH	I.	F 785	Jean Moulin	FF	F.
D 550	Ardito	DDG	I.	F 786	Quartier Maitre Anquetil	FF	F.
F 550	Salvatore Todaro	PF	I.	F 787	Com De Pimodan	FF	F.
D 551	Audace	DDG	I.	788	Hollister	DD	U.S.A.
F 551	Canopo	DE	I.	F 788	Seconde Maitre Le Bihan	FF	F.
553	Andrea Doria	DLGH	I.	F 790	Lieut. Lavallée	FF	F.
F 553	Castore	DE	I.	F 792	Premier Maitre L'Her	FF	F.
554	Caio Duilio	DLGH	I.	F 793	Comblaison	FF	F.
F 554	Centauro	DE	I.	F 794	Enseigne Jacoubet	FF	F.
F 555	Cigno	DE	I.	F 801	Tromp	DDG	N.
D 558	Impetuoso	DD	I.	F 802	Van Speijk	FFGH	N.
D 559	Indomito	DD	I.	F 803	Van Galen	FFGH	N.
D 561	Fante	DD	I.	F 804	Tjerk Hiddes	FFGH	N.
D 562	San Giorgio	DD	I.	F 805	Van Nes	FFGH	N.
D 570	Impavido	DDG	I.	805	Higbee	DD	U.S.A.
D 571	Intrepido	DDG	I.	F 806	De Ruyter	DDG	N.
F 580	Alpino	DE	I.	D 808	Holland	DDH	N.
F 581	Carabiniere	DE	I.	D 809	Zeeland	DDH	N.
F 590	Aldebaran	DE	I.	D 812	Friesland	DD	N.
F 593	Carlo Bergamini	DE	I.	D 813	Gröningen	DD	N.
F 594	Virginio Fasan	DE	I.	D 814	Limburg	DD	N.
F 595	Carlo Margottini	DE	I.	F 814	Isaac Sweers	FFGH	N.
F 596	Luigi Rizzo	DE	I.	D 815	Overijssel	DD	N.
D 602	Suffren	DLG	F.	F 815	Evertsen	FFGH	N.
D 603	Duquesne	DLG	F.	D 816	Drenthe	DD	N.
D 609	Aconit	DD	F.	817	Corry	DD	U.S.A.
D 610	Tourville	DDG	F.	D 817	Utrecht	DD	N.
C 611	Colbert	CLG	F.	D 818	Rotterdam	DD	N.
D 611	Duguay-Trouin	DDG	F.	D 819	Amsterdam	DD	N.
D 612	De Grasse	DDG	F.	820	Rich	DD	U.S.A.
D 622	Kersaint	DDG	F.	821	Johnston	DD	U.S.A.
D 624	Bouvet	DDG	F.	822	Robert H. McCard	DD	U.S.A.
D 625	Du Petit Thouars	DDG	F.	824	Basilone	DD	U.S.A.
D 627	Maille Brezé	DDG	F.	825	Carpenter	DD	U.S.A.
D 628	Vauquelin	DDG	F.	826	Agerholm	DD	U.S.A.
D 629	D'Estrées	DDG	F.	827	Robert A. Owens	DD	U.S.A.
D 630	Du Chayla	DDG	F.	829	Myles C. Fox	DD	U.S.A.
D 631	Casabianca	DDG	F.	835	Charles P. Cecil	DD	U.S.A.
D 632	Guépratte	DDG	F.	837	Sarsfield	DD	U.S.A.
D 633	Duperré	DDG	F.	839	Power	DD	U.S.A.
D 634	La Bourdonnais	DDG	F.	842	Fiske	DD	U.S.A.
D 635	Forbin	DDG	F.	862	Vogelgesang	DD	U.S.A.
D 636	Tartu	DDG	F.	863	Steinaker	DD	U.S.A.
D 637	Jauréguiberry	DDG	F.	864	Harold J. Ellison	DD	U.S.A.
D 638	La Galissoniere	DD	F.	865	Cone	DD	U.S.A.
D 640	Georges Leygues	DGH	F.	867	Stribling	DD	U.S.A.
D 641	Dupleix	DGH	F.	871	Damato	DD	U.S.A.
D 642	Montcalm	DGH	F.	873	Hawkins	DD	U.S.A.
714	William R. Rush	DD	U.S.A.	876	Rogers	DD	U.S.A.
718	Hamner	DD	U.S.A.	880	Dyess	DD	U.S.A.
F 725	Victor Schoelcher	FF	F.	883	Newman K. Perry	DD	U.S.A.
F 726	Commandant Bory	FF	F.	885	John R. Craig	DD	U.S.A.
F 727	Admiral Charner	FF	F.	886	Orleck	DD	U.S.A.
F 728	Doudart de Lagrée	FF	F.	890	Meredith	DD	U.S.A.
F 729	Balny	FF	F.	F 910	Wielingen	FF	Bel.

Pennant No.	Ship Name	Type	Country	Pennant No.	Ship Name	Type	Country
F 911	Westdiep	FF	Bel.	1065	Stein	FF	U.S.A.
F 912	Wanderlaar	FF	Bel.	1066	Marvin Shields	FF	U.S.A.
F 913	Westhinder	FF	Bel.	1067	Francis Hammond	FF	U.S.A.
931	Forrest Sherman	DD	U.S.A.	1068	Vreeland	FF	U.S.A.
933	Barry	DD	U.S.A.	1069	Bagley	FF	U.S.A.
937	Davis	DD	U.S.A.	1070	Downes	FF	U.S.A.
938	Jonas Ingram	DD	U.S.A.	1071	Badger	FF	U.S.A.
940	Manley	DD	U.S.A.	1072	Blakely	FF	U.S.A.
941	Du Pont	DD	U.S.A.	1073	Robert E. Peary	FF	U.S.A.
942	Bigelow	DD	U.S.A.	1074	Harold E. Holt	FF	U.S.A.
943	Blandy	DD	U.S.A.	1075	Trippe	FF	U.S.A.
944	Mullinnix	DD	U.S.A.	1076	Fanning	FF	U.S.A.
945	Hull	DD	U.S.A.	1077	Ouellet	FF	U.S.A.
946	Edson	DD	U.S.A.	1078	Joseph Hewes	FF	U.S.A.
948	Morton	DD	U.S.A.	1079	Bowan	FF	U.S.A.
950	Richard S. Edwards	DD	U.S.A.	1080	Paul	FF	U.S.A.
951	Turner Joy	DD	U.S.A.	1081	Aylwin	FF	U.S.A.
951	Souya	ML	J	1082	Elmer Montgomery	FF	U.S.A.
963	Spruance	DD	U.S.A.	1083	Cook	FF	U.S.A.
964	Paul F. Foster	DD	U.S.A.	1084	McCandless	FF	U.S.A.
965	Kincaid	DD	U.S.A.	1085	Donald B. Beary	FF	U.S.A.
966	Hewitt	DD	U.S.A.	1086	Brewton	FF	U.S.A.
967	Elliott	DD	U.S.A.	1087	Kirk	FF	U.S.A.
968	Arthur W. Radford	DD	U.S.A.	1088	Barbey	FF	U.S.A.
969	Peterson	DD	U.S.A.	1089	Jesse L. Brown	FF	U.S.A.
970	Caron	DD	U.S.A.	1090	Ainsworth	FF	U.S.A.
971	David R Ray	DD	U.S.A.	1091	Miller	FF	U.S.A.
972	Oldendorf	DD	U.S.A.	1092	Thomas S. Hart	FF	U.S.A.
973	John Young	DD	U.S.A.	1093	Capodanno	FF	U.S.A.
974	Comte De Grasse	DD	U.S.A.	1094	Pharris	FF	U.S.A.
1037	Bronstein	FF	U.S.A.	1095	Truett	FF	U.S.A.
1038	McCloy	FF	U.S.A.	1096	Valdez	FF	U.S.A.
1040	Garcia	FF	U.S.A.	1097	Moinester	FF	U.S.A.
1041	Bradley	FF	U.S.A.	1179	Newport	LST	U.S.A.
1043	Edward McDonnell	FF	U.S.A.	1180	Manitowoc	LST	U.S.A.
1044	Brumby	FF	U.S.A.	1181	Sumter	LST	U.S.A.
1045	Davidson	FF	U.S.A.	1182	Fresno	LST	U.S.A.
1047	Voge	FF	U.S.A.	1183	Peoria	LST	U.S.A.
1048	Sample	FF	U.S.A.	1184	Frederick	LST	U.S.A.
1049	Koelsch	FF	U.S.A.	1185	Schenectady	LST	U.S.A.
1050	Albert David	FF	U.S.A.	1186	Cayuga	LST	U.S.A.
1051	O'Callahan	FF	U.S.A.	1187	Tuscaloosa	LST	U.S.A.
1052	Knox	FF	U.S.A.	1188	Saginaw	LST	U.S.A.
1053	Roark	FF	U.S.A.	1189	San Bernardino	LST	U.S.A.
1054	Gray	FF	U.S.A.	1190	Boulder	LST	U.S.A.
1055	Hepburn	FF	U.S.A.	1191	Racine	LST	U.S.A.
1056	Connole	FF	U.S.A.	1192	Spartanburg County	LST	U.S.A.
1057	Rathburne	FF	U.S.A.	1193	Fairfax County	LST	U.S.A.
1058	Meyerkord	FF	U.S.A.	1194	La Moure County	LST	U.S.A.
1059	W. S. Sims	FF	U.S.A.	1195	Barbour County	LST	U.S.A.
1060	Lang	FF	U.S.A.	1196	Harlan County	LST	U.S.A.
1061	Patterson	FF	U.S.A.	1197	Barnstable County	LST	U.S.A.
1062	Whipple	FF	U.S.A.	1198	Bristol County	LST	U.S.A.
1063	Reasoner	FF	U.S.A.	3501	Katori	AGDE	J.
1064	Lockwood	FF	U.S.A.	4201	Azuma	ATS	J.

SHIP REFERENCE SECTION

ABU DHABI

(see United Arab Emirates)

Senior Officer

Commander of the Navy: Commander G. A. St G. Poole

Personnel

(a) 1977: 627 (113 officers, 514 ratings)
(b) Voluntary service

The Naval Force of Abu Dhabi was formed in March 1968. The Force's function was to patrol territorial waters and oil installations in the UAE Marine Areas. Now called the United Arab Emirates Naval Force.

Ports

Abu Dhabi, Murban.

LIGHT FORCES

6 VOSPER THORNYCROFT TYPE (LARGE PATROL CRAFT)

Name	No.	Builders	Commissioned
ARDHANA	1101	Vosper Thornycroft	24 June 1975
ZURARA	1102	Vosper Thornycroft	14 Aug 1975
MURBAN	1103	Vosper Thornycroft	16 Sep 1975
AL GHULLAN	1104	Vosper Thornycroft	16 Sep 1975
RADOOM	1105	Vosper Thornycroft	1 July 1976
GHANADHAH	1106	Vosper Thornycroft	1 July 1976

Displacement, tons: 110 standard; 175 full load
Dimensions, feet (metres): 110 oa × 21 × 6·6 *(33·5 × 6·4 × 1·7)*
Guns: 2—30 mm A32 (twin); 1—20 mm A41A
Main engines: 2 Paxman Valenta diesels; 5 400 hp = 30 knots
Range, miles: 1 800 at 14 knots
Complement: 26

A class of round bilge steel hull craft. 1101-2 and 1105-6 transported to Abu Dhabi by heavy-lift ships. 1103 and 1104 were sailed out.

MURBAN   9/1975, John G. Callis

3 KEITH NELSON TYPE (COASTAL PATROL CRAFT)

Name	No.	Builders	Commissioned
BANI YAS	P563	Keith Nelson, Bembridge	27 Dec 1969
KAWKAB	P561	Keith Nelson, Bembridge	7 Mar 1969
THOABAN	P562	Keith Nelson, Bembridge	7 Mar 1969

Displacement, tons: 32
Dimensions, feet (metres): 57 × 16·5 × 4·5 *(17·4 × 5·1 × 1·4)*
Guns: 2—20 mm (single)
Main engines: 2 Caterpillar diesels. 750 bhp = 19 knots
Range, miles: 445 at 15 knots
Complement: 11 (2 officers, 9 men)

Of glass fibre hull construction.

BANI YAS   11/1976, UAE Armed Forces

6 "DHAFEER" CLASS (COASTAL PATROL CRAFT)

Name	No.	Builders	Commissioned
DHAFEER	P401	Keith Nelson, Bembridge	1 July 1968
DURGHAM	P404	Keith Nelson, Bembridge	7 June 1969
GHADUNFAR	P402	Keith Nelson, Bembridge	1 July 1968
HAZZA	P403	Keith Nelson, Bembridge	1 July 1968
MURAYJIB	P406	Keith Nelson, Bembridge	7 June 1970
TIMSAH	P405	Keith Nelson, Bembridge	1 June 1969

Displacement, tons: 10
Dimensions, feet (metres): 40·3 × 11 × 3·5 *(12·3 × 3·4 × 1·1)*
Guns: 2—7·62 mm MG
Main engines: 2 Cummins diesels; 370 bhp = 19 knots
Range, miles: 350 at 15 knots
Complement: 6 (1 officer, 5 men)

Of glass fibre hull construction.

TIMSAH   11/1976, UAE Armed Forces

2 27 FT CHEVERTON TYPE (COASTAL PATROL CRAFT)

A 271   A 272

Of 3 tons and 10 knots. Acquired from Chevertons, Cowes, Isle of Wight in 1975.

POLICE CRAFT

5 FAIREY MARINE "SPEAR" CLASS (COASTAL PATROL CRAFT)

Dimensions, feet (metres): 29·8 × 9·2 × 2·6 *(9·1 × 2·8 × ·8)*
Guns: 2—7·62 mm MGs
Main engines: 2 Perkins diesels of 290 hp = 25 knots
Complement: 3

Order placed in Feb 1974. Craft delivered between July 1974 and Jan 1975.

"SPEAR" Class   *1974, Faireys*

ALBANIA

Ministerial

Minister of Defence: Mehmet Shehu

Personnel

(a) 1977: Total 3 000 including 300 coastal frontier guards.
(b) Ratings on 3 years military service.

Bases

Durazzo (Durresi) and Valona (Vlora)

Mercantile Marine

Lloyd's Register of Shipping:
    20 vessels of 57 368 tons gross.

Strength of the Fleet

Corvettes	4
Submarines	4
Fast Attack Craft (Torpedo)	42
Fast Attack Craft (Gun)	4
Minesweepers—Ocean	2
Minesweepers—Inshore	6
MSB	10
Tankers	4
Small Auxiliaries	approx 20

CORVETTES

4 Ex-SOVIET "KRONSHTADT" CLASS

Displacement, tons: 310 standard; 380 full load
Dimensions, feet (metres): 170·6 × 21·5 × 9·0 *(52·0 × 6·5 × 2·7)*
Guns: 1—3·5 in *(85 mm);* 2—37 mm (single); 6—12·7 MG (3 vertical twin)
A/S weapons: 2 depth charge projectors; 2 DC rails; 2—5-tube rocket launchers
Main engines: 3 Diesels; 3 shafts; 3 300 bhp = 24 knots
Range, miles: 1 500 at 12 knots
Complement: 65

Equipped for minelaying: 2 rails; about 8 mines. Four were transferred from the USSR in 1958. Albania sent two for A/S updating in 1960 and two others in 1961.

Radar: Surface search—Ball Gun. Navigation—Neptun. IFF—High Pole.

"KRONSHTADT" Class

SUBMARINES

4 Ex-SOVIET "WHISKEY" CLASS

Displacement, tons: 1 030 surfaced; 1 350 dived
Length, feet (metres): 249·3 *(76)*
Beam, feet (metres): 22·0 *(6·7)*
Draught, feet (metres): 15·0 *(4·6)*
Torpedo tubes: 6—21 in (4 bow, 2 stern); 18 torpedoes or 40 mines
Main machinery: Diesels; 4 000 bhp; 2 shafts = 17 knots surfaced
    Electric motors; 2 500 hp = 15 knots dived
Range, miles: 13 000 at 8 knots surfaced
Complement: 60

Three of the four "Whiskey" class submarines are operational and one is now used as a harbour training boat. All are based at Vlora. Two were transferred from the USSR in 1960, and two others were reportedly seized from the USSR in mid-1961 upon the withdrawal of Soviet ships from their Albanian base.

Radar: Snoop Plate.

"WHISKEY" Class

LIGHT FORCES

32 Ex-CHINESE "HU CHWAN" CLASS (FAST ATTACK HYDROFOIL—TORPEDO)

Displacement, tons: 45
Dimensions, feet (metres): 71 × 14·5 × 3·1 *(21·8 × 4·5 × 0·9)*
Guns: 2—14·5 mm (twin vertical)
Torpedo tubes: 2—21 inch
Main engines: 3 M50 Diesels; 2 shafts; 3 600 hp = 55 knots

Built in Shanghai and transferred as follows: 6 in 1968, 15 in 1969, 2 in 1970 and 7 in 1971

Construction: Have foils forward while the stern planes on the surface.

Radar: Skinhead.

HU CHWAN   1972

4 Ex-CHINESE "SHANGHAI II" CLASS

Displacement, tons: 120 standard; 155 full load
Dimensions, feet (metres): 128 × 18 × 5·6 *(39 × 5·5 × 1·7)*
Guns: 4—37 mm (twins); 4—25 mm (twins)
A/S armament: 8 DCs
Mines: Minerails can be fitted; probably only 10 mines
Main engines: 4 Diesels; 4 800 bhp = 30 knots
Complement: 25

Transferred in mid-1974.

Radar: Skinhead.

"SHANGHAI II" Class

12 Ex-SOVIET "P-4" CLASS (FAST ATTACK CRAFT—TORPEDO)

111   115   304   +9

Displacement, tons: 22
Dimensions, feet (metres): 62·3 × 11·5 × 5·6 *(19·0 × 3·5 × 1·7)*
Guns: (See notes)
Torpedo tubes: 2—18 in *(450 mm)*
Main engines: 2 M50 Diesels; 2 Shafts; 2 200 bhp = 50 knots

Six were transferred from the USSR in 1956 (with radar and 2-12·7 mm MG) and six from China, three in April 1965 and three in Sep 1965, without radar and with 4—12·7 mm MG (2 twin). Radar now fitted.

"P4" Class

MINE WARFARE FORCES

2 Ex-SOVIET "T 43" CLASS (MINESWEEPERS, OCEAN)

Displacement, tons: 500 standard; 610 full load
Dimensions, feet (metres): 190·2 × 28·2 × 6·9 *(58·0 × 8·6 × 2·1)*
Guns: 4—37 mm (2 twin); 8—12·7 mm MG
A/S weapons: 2 DCT
Main engines: 2 Type 9D diesels; 2 shafts; 2 000 bhp = 17 knots
Range, miles: 1 600 at 10 knots
Complement: 40

Transferred in Aug 1960.

"T 43" Class

10 Ex-SOVIET "PO 2" CLASS (MSB)

Displacement, tons: 40 to 45 standard; 45 to 50 full load
Dimensions, feet (metres): 70·0 × 16·7 × 5·6 *(21·3 × 5·1 × 1·7)*
Gun: 1—12·7 mm MG
Main engines: Diesels = 39 knots

There are reports of some 10 "PO 2" class in service and possibly 3 ex-Italian "MS 501" class. The "PO 2" class, though primarily minesweeping boats, are also general utility craft. They were transferred as follows: 3 in 1957, 3 in 1958-59, 4 in 1960.

6 Ex-SOVIET "T 301" CLASS (MINESWEEPERS—INSHORE)

343   344   +4
Displacement, tons: 150 standard; 180 full load
Dimensions, feet (metres): 128·0 × 18·0 × 4·9 *(39·0 × 5·5 × 1·5)*
Guns: 2—37 mm; 4—12·7 mm (twins)
Main engines: 3 diesels; 3 shafts; 1 440 bhp = 9 knots
Range, miles: 2 200 at 9 knots
Complement: 25

Transferred from USSR—two in 1957, two in 1959 and two in 1960.

"T 301" Class

DEGAUSSING SHIP

1 Ex-SOVIET "SEKSTAN" CLASS

354

Dimensions, feet (metres): 134·0 × 40·0 × 14·0 *(40·9 × 12·2 × 4·3)*
Main engines: Diesels; 400 bhp = 11 knots
Complement: 35

Built in Finland in 1956. Transferred from the USSR in 1960.

TANKERS

2 Ex- SOVIET "KHOBI" CLASS (PETROL TANKERS)

PATOS   SEMANI

Displacement, tons: 2 200
Measurement, tons: 1 600 deadweight; 1 500 oil
Dimensions, feet (metres): 220·0 × 33·0 × 15·0 *(67·1 × 10·1 × 4·6)*
Main engines: 2 diesels; 1 600 bhp = 12 knots

Launched in 1956. Transferred from the USSR in Sep 1958 and Feb 1959. *Semani* may be ex-Soviet M/V *Linda.*

Radar: Neptun.

"KHOBI" Class

1 Ex-SOVIET "TOPLIVO 1" CLASS (YARD TANKER)

Displacement, tons: 280

Transferred from the USSR in March 1960. Similar to "Khobi" class in appearance though smaller.

1 Ex-SOVIET "TOPLIVO 3" CLASS (YARD TANKER)

Displacement, tons: 275

Transferred from the USSR in 1960.

MISCELLANEOUS

1 Ex-SOVIET "POLUCHAT I" CLASS

SKENDERBEU A641

Displacement, tons: 86 standard; 91 full load
Dimensions, feet (metres): 98·0 pp × 15·0 × 4·8 *(29·9 × 4·6 × 1·5)*
Guns: 2—14·5 mm
Main engines: 2 M50 Diesels; 2 Shafts; 2 400 bhp = 18 knots
Range, miles: 460 at 17 knots
Complement: 16

Probably used for torpedo recovery. Transferred in 1968.

TUGS

Several small tugs are employed in local duties or harbour service.

DIVING TENDER

1 Ex-SOVIET "NYRYAT" CLASS

There are reported to be a dozen or so harbour and port tenders including a water carrier and two small transports. The "Atrek" class submarine tender transferred from USSR in 1961 as a depot ship was converted into a merchant ship. With large lakes on both the Yugoslav and Greek borders a number of small patrol craft are stationed on these lakes.

ALGERIA

Ministerial

Minister of Defence: Col. Houari Boumediene (President)

Personnel

(a) 1977: Total 3 800 (300 officers and cadets and 3 500 men)
(b) Voluntary service

Bases

Algiers, Annaba, Mers el Kebir

Mercantile Marine

Lloyd's Register of Shipping:
    78 vessels of 246 432 tons gross

Strength of the Fleet

Large Patrol Craft	6
Fast Attack Craft (Missile)	9
Fast Attack Craft (Torpedo)	10
Minesweepers—Ocean	2
Training Ship	1

Disposal

1976 *Sidi Fradj* (training ship)

LIGHT FORCES

6 Ex-SOVIET "SO I" CLASS (LARGE PATROL CRAFT)

P651-656

Displacement, tons: 215 light; 250 full load
Dimensions, feet (metres): 138·6 × 20·0 × 9·2 *(42·3 × 6·1 × 2·8)*
Guns: 4—25 mm (2 twin mounts)
A/S weapons: 4 MBU 1800 rocket launchers
Main engines: 3 diesels; 6 000 bhp = 29 knots
Range, miles: 1 100 at 13 knots
Complement: 30

Delivered by USSR on 7 and 8 Oct 1967, first two, and the other four since 1968.

"SO I" Class

3 Ex-SOVIET "OSA I" CLASS (FAST ATTACK CRAFT—MISSILE)

R167   R267   R367

Displacement, tons: 165 standard; 200 full load
Dimensions, feet (metres): 128·7 × 25·1 × 5·9 *(39·3 × 7·7 × 1·8)*
Missiles: 4 SS-N-2 (Styx)
Guns: 4—30 mm (2 twin)
Main engines: 3 diesels; 13 000 bhp = 32 knots
Range, miles: 800 at 25 knots
Complement: 25

One boat was delivered by USSR on 7 Oct 1967. Two others transferred later in same year.

"OSA I" Class

6 Ex-SOVIET "KOMAR" CLASS (FAST ATTACK CRAFT—MISSILE)

671-676

Displacement, tons: 70 standard; 80 full load
Dimensions, feet (metres): 84·2 × 21·1 × 5·0 *(25·7 × 6·4 × 1·5)*
Missiles: 2 SS-N-2 (Styx)
Guns: 2—25 mm (twin)
Main engines: 4 diesels, 4 shafts, 4 800 bhp = 40 knots
Range, miles: 400 at 30 knots
Complement: 20

Acquired in 1967 from USSR.

10 Ex-SOVIET "P6" CLASS (FAST ATTACK CRAFT—TORPEDO)

621-630

Displacement, tons: 66 standard; 75 full load
Dimensions, feet (metres): 84·2 × 20·0 × 5·0 *(25·7 × 6·1 × 1·5)*
Guns: 4—25 mm (twin)
Torpedo tubes: 2—21 inch (or mines or depth charges)
Main engines: 4 diesels, 4 shafts, 4 800 bhp = 43 knots
Range, miles: 450 at 30 knots
Complement: 25

Acquired from the USSR between 1963 and 1966. Four retain their original armament whilst the remainder, with tubes removed, are used for coast-guard duties. Two deleted 1975.

MINE WARFARE FORCES

2 Ex-SOVIET "T 43" CLASS (MINESWEEPERS, OCEAN)

M221 M222

Displacement, tons: 500 standard; 610 full load
Dimensions, feet (metres): 190·2 × 28·2 × 6·9 *(58·0 × 8·6 × 2·1)*
Guns: 4—37 mm (twins); 8—12·7 mm (twins)
A/S weapons: 2 DCT
Main engines: 2 Type 9D diesels; 2 shafts; 2 200 bhp = 17 knots
Range, miles: 1 600 at 10 knots
Complement: 40

Transferred in 1968.

"T 43" Class

MISCELLANEOUS

1 Ex-SOVIET "POLUCHAT" CLASS

A641
Operates as TRV.

1 Ex-SOVIET "SEKSTAN" CLASS

VASOUYA A640

Transferred in 1964. Operates as survey ship.

1 HARBOUR TUG

YAVDEZAN VP650

Completed in 1965.

2 FISHERY PROTECTION CRAFT

JEBEL ANTAR   **JEBEL HONDA**

ANGOLA

Independence was granted to Angola by Portugal on 11 Nov 1975. The civil war of 1975-76 saw Agostinho Neto and his Soviet and Cuban backed MPLA take over power. A number of Portuguese ships were transferred at the time of independence and it is reported that these have been reinforced by ex-Soviet landing craft and ships taken up from trade. Angolan names are not known—the details given are in all cases Portuguese.

Ministerial

Minister of Defence: Major Enrique Carreira

Personnel

(a) 1977: Approx. 600
(b) Voluntary

Ports and Bases

Luanda, Lobito, Moçamedes. (A number of other good harbours are available on the 1 000 mile coastline).

Mercantile Marine

Lloyds Register of Shipping: 7 vessels of 4 056 tons gross.

LIGHT FORCES

4 Ex-PORTUGUESE "ARGOS" CLASS (LARGE PATROL CRAFT)

Name	No.	Builders	Commissioned (Portugal)
Ex-**CENTAURO**	P1130	Arsenal do Alfeite, Lisbon	1965
Ex-**ESCORPIAO**	P 375	Arsenal do Alfeite, Lisbon	1964
Ex-**LIRA**	P 361	Estaleiros Navais de Viano do Castelo	1963
Ex-**PEGASO**	P 362	Estaleiros Navais de Viano do Castelo	1963

Displacement, tons: 180 standard; 210 full load
Dimensions, feet (metres): 136·8 oa × 20·5 × 7 *(41·6 × 6·2 × 2·2)*
Guns: 2—40 mm
Main engines: 2 Maybach (MTU) diesels; 1 200 bhp = 17 knots
Oil fuel, tons: 16
Complement: 24

Argos, Dragao and *Orion* of same class transferred, reportedly, for spares.

"ARGOS" Class   *Portuguese Navy*

2 Ex-PORTUGUESE "JUPITER" CLASS (COASTAL PATROL CRAFT)

Name	No.	Builders	Commissioned (Portugal)
Ex-**JUPITER**	P 1132	Estaleiros Navais do Mondego	1964
Ex-**VENUS**	P 1133	Estaleiros Navais do Mondego	1965

Displacement, tons: 32 standard; 43·5 full load
Dimensions, feet (metres): 69 oa × 16·5 × 4·3 *(21 × 5 × 1·3)*
Gun: 1—20 mm Oerlikon
Main engines: 2 Cummins diesels; 1 270 bhp = 20 knots
Complement: 8

Ex-JUPITER   *Portuguese Navy*

4 Ex-PORTUGUESE "BELLATRIX" CLASS (COASTAL PATROL CRAFT)

Name	No.	Builders	Commissioned (Portugal)
Ex-**ALTAIR**	P 377	Beyerische Schiffbaugesellschaft	1962
Ex-**ESPIGA**	P 366	Beyerische Schiffbaugesellschaft	1961
Ex-**POLLUX**	P 368	Beyerische Schiffbaugesellschaft	1961
Ex-**RIGEL**	P 378	Beyerische Schiffbaugesellschaft	1962

"BELLATRIX" Class   Portuguese Navy

Displacement, tons: 23 standard; 27·6 full load
Dimensions, feet (metres): 68 oa × 16·2 × 4 *(20·7 × 5·1 × 1·2)*
Gun: 1—20 mm Oerlikon
Main engines: 2 Cummins diesels; 470 bhp = 15 knots
Complement: 7

AMPHIBIOUS FORCES

Note: In addition to those below 5 ex-Soviet LCUs reported transferred in 1976.

2 Ex-PORTUGUESE "ALFANGE" CLASS (LCT)

Name	No.	Builders	Commissioned (Portugal)
Ex-**ALFANGE**	LDG 101	Estaleiros Navais do Mondego	1965
Ex-**ARIETE**(?)	LDG 102	Estaleiros Navais do Mondego	1965

Ex-ALFANGE   Portuguese Navy

Displacement, tons: 500
Dimensions, feet (metres): 187 × 39 × 6·2 *(57 × 12 × 1·9)*
Main engines: 2 diesels; 1 000 bhp = 11 knots
Complement: 20

MISCELLANEOUS

Also reported that up to 8 merchant ships have been acquired from local shipping.

ANGUILLA

1 FAIREY MARINE "HUNTSMAN" CLASS

A 28 ft launch supplied in 1974. She is unarmed and used for anti-smuggling operations and for Air-Sea Rescue. Belongs to the Royal St. Christopher, Nevis and Anguilla Police Force being based at Basseterre, St. Kitts under the supervision of Superintendent W. Galloway.

ARGENTINA

Headquarters Appointments

Commander of the Navy and Chief of Naval Operations:
Rear Admiral E. E. Massera
Chief of Naval Staff:
Rear Admiral A. Lambruschini

Diplomatic Representation

Head of Argentinian Training Mission Asunción, Paraguay:
Captain Jorge E. Bocaccio
Naval Attaché in Bogota:
Captain Luis Santiago Martella
Naval Attaché in Brasilia:
Captain Mario E. Olrnos
Naval Attaché in Cape Town:
Captain Eldo Buzzo
Naval Attaché in London and The Hague and Head of the Argentine Naval Mission in Europe:
Rear Admiral Jorge I. Anaya
Naval Attaché in Lima:
Captain Horacio M. Goñi
Naval Attaché in Madrid:
Captain Isidro A. Paradelo
Naval Attaché in Montevideo:
Captain Pedro H. Dimenna
Naval Attaché in Paris:
Captain J. C. Malugani
Naval Attaché in Rome:
Captain Mario F. Robles
Naval Attaché in Santiago:
Captain Niceto E. Ayerra
Naval Attaché in Tokyo:
Captain Rafael J. Serra
Naval Attaché in Washington:
Rear Admiral Antonio Vanek

Personnel

(a) 1977: 32 900 (2 890 officers, 18 010 petty officers and ratings and 12 000 conscripts)
Marine Corps: 6 000 officers and men
(b) Volunteers plus 14 months national service

Note. Corpo de Infanteria de Marina (Marine Corps)
1st Marine Force: (3 battalions)
2nd Marine Force: (1 field artillery battalion, 1 air defence battalion, 1 anti-tank company, communication and amphibious craft units)
Based at or near naval bases and installations. Equipped with 20 LVTP-7, 15 LARC-5, 10 "Tigercat" SAM, 155 mm and 105 mm how., 30 mm guns, "Bantam" A-T missiles, 105 mm recoilless rifles.

Naval Bases

Buenos Aires (Darsena Norte): Dockyard, 2 Dry Docks, 3 Floating Docks, 1 Floating Crane, Schools.
Rio Santiago (La Plata): Naval Base, Schools, Naval shipbuilding yard (AFNE), 1 Slipway, 1 Floating Crane.
Mar de Plata: Submarine base with slipway, 1 Floating Crane.
Puerto Belgrano: Main Naval Base, Schools, 2 Dry Docks, 1 Floating Dock, 1 Floating Crane.
Ushaia: Small naval base.

Naval Aviation

15   A-4Q Skyhawk*
12   Aermacchi MB 326 GB
6   S-2A Tracker*

3   HU-16B Albatross maritime patrol
4   P2-H Neptune
—   PBY-5A Catalina

4   Alouette III Helicopter
6   Bell 47 (Sioux) (2 with PNA)
6   Hughes 500M (Cayuse) (PNA)
4   Sikorsky S-61D (Sea King)
2   Sikorsky S-61 NR
2   Sea Lynx
5   Sikorsky S-55 (Chickasaw)

3   DHC Beaver Transport
8   C-47 Dakota/Skytrain
3   C-54 Skymaster
1   FMA IA 50 GII
1   HS 125 Srs. 400A
3   Lockheed L-188 Electra
5   Short Skyvan (PNA)
30   T-28 Fennec Trainer
1   DHC-6 Twin Otter
2   Beech Super King Air 200
3   Fairchild-Hiller Porter
6   Beech C45-H/AT 11
10   North American SNJ-5C/T-6

*Carrier-based.

Prefectura Naval Argentina (PNA)

PNA is responsible for coastguard and rescue duties. It also administers the Merchant Navy School at Buenos Aires.

Prefix to Ships' Names

ARA

Mercantile Marine

Lloyd's Register of Shipping:
379 vessels of 1 469 754 tons gross

Strength of the Fleet

Type	Active	Building
Attack Carrier (Medium)	1	—
Cruisers	2	—
Destroyers	9	1
Frigates	—	(6)*
Corvettes	12	—
Patrol Submarines	4	(2)**
Landing Ships (Tank)	4	1
Landing Craft (Tank)	1	—
Minor Landing Craft	19	—
Fast Attack Craft (Missile)	—	2
Fast Attack Craft (Gun)	2	—
Fast Attack Craft (Torpedo)	2	—
Large Patrol Craft	5	—
Minesweepers (Coastal)	4	—
Minehunters	2	—
Survey Ships	5	2
Survey Launches	2	—
Transports	2	—
Tankers (Fleet Support)	3	—
Icebreaker	1	1
Training Ship	1	—
Tugs	14	—

*Preliminary agreement was reached with Vosper Thornycroft in May 1975 for building at AFNE of six Type 21 Frigates.
**2 Type 209 projected for building in Argentine yards.

DELETIONS

Attack Carrier (medium)

1971 *Independencia*

Cruiser

1973 *La Argentina*

Destroyers

1971 *Buenos Aires, Misiones, San Luis*
1973 *Entre Rios, San Juan, Santa Cruz*

Frigates

1973 *Juan B Azopardo, Piedrabuena, Azopardo*

Minesweeper Support Ship

1971 *Corrientes* (to Paraguay)

Submarines

1972 *Santa Fe (ex-Lamprey) Santiago del Estero (ex-Macabi)*, scrapped for spares

Amphibious Forces

1971 *BDI 4, BDI 15, BDM 1, Cabo San Bartolome*
1973 *EDVP 4, 5, 6, 11, 20, 22, 27*

Survey Ships

1970 *Commodoro Augusto Lasserre*
1972 *Capitan Canepa* (scrap)
1973 *Ushuia* sunk in collision

Transports

1971 *La Pataia* (sold)
1973 *Bahia Thetis*
1975 *San Julian*

Tankers

1971 *Punta Rasa, Punta Lara*

Salvage Ship

1974 *Guardiamarina Zicari*

Tugs

1971 *Querendi*
1974 *Mataco*

PENNANT LIST

Aircraft Carrier

| V | 2 | 25 de Mayo |

Cruisers

| C | 4 | Belgrano |
| C | 5 | 9 de Julio |

Destroyers

D	20	Almirante Brown
D	21	Espora
D	22	Rosales
D	23	Almirante Domecq Garcia
D	24	Almirante Storni
D	25	Segui
D	26	Bouchard
D	27	Py
D	28	Hercules
D	29	Santissima Trinidad

Corvettes

P	20	Murature
P	21	King
A	1	Com. G. Irigoyen
A	2	Com. G. Zapiola
A	3	Francisco de Churruca
A	4	Thompson
A	5	Diaguita
A	6	Yamana
A	7	Chiriguano
A	8	Sanavirón
A	9	Alferez Sobral
A	10	Comodoro Somellera

Submarines

S	21	Santa Fe
S	22	Santiago del Estero
S	31	Salta
S	32	San Luis

Mine Warfare Forces

M	1	Neuquen
M	2	Rio Negro
M	3	Chubut
M	4	Tierra del Fuego
M	5	Chaco
M	6	Formosa

Light Forces

P	55	Surubi
P	82	Alakush
P	84	Towara
P	85	Intrepida
P	86	Indomita
GC	21	Lynch
GC	22	Toll
GC	23	Erezcano
GC	31	—

Amphibious Forces

Q	42	Cabo San Antonio
Q	43	Candido De Lasala
Q	44	Cabo San Gonzalo
Q	46	Cabo San Isidro
Q	50	Cabo San Pio
Q	56	BDI

Miscellaneous

B	2	Bahia Aguirre
B	6	Bahia Buen Suceso
B	12	Punta Alta
B	16	Punta Delgada
B	1	Punta Médanos
Q	2	Libertad
Q	4	General San Martin
Q	7	El Austral
Q	9	Islas Orcadas
Q	15	Cormoran
R	3	Mataco
R	4	Toba
R	5	Mocovi
R	6	Calchaqui
R	10	Huarpe
R	12	Huarpe
R	16	Capayan
R	18	Chiquillan
R	19	Morcoyan
R	29	Pehuenche
R	30	Tonocote
R	32	Quilmes
R	33	Guaycuru

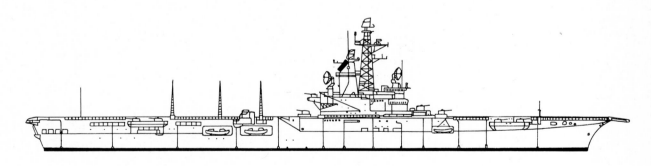

VEINTICINCO DE MAYO

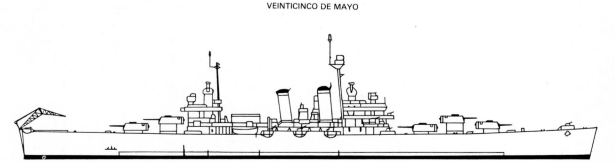

"BROOKLYN" Class

AIRCRAFT CARRIER
1 Ex-BRITISH "COLOSSUS" CLASS

Name	No.	Builders	Laid down	Launched	Commissioned
VEINTICINCO DE MAYO	V 2	Cammell Laird & Co. Ltd., Birkenhead	3 Dec 1942	30 Dec 1943	17 Jan 1945
(ex-*HNMS Karel Doorman*, ex-*HMS Venerable*)					

Displacement, tons: 15 892 standard; 19 896 full load
Length, feet (metres): 630 *(192·0)* pp 693·2 *(211·3)* oa
Beam, feet (metres): 80 *(24·4)*
Draught, feet (metres): 25 *(7·6)*
Width, feet (metres): 121·3 *(37·0)* oa
Hangar:
  Length, feet (metres): 455 *(138·7)*
  Width, feet (metres): 52 *(15·8)*
  Height, feet (metres): 17·5 *(5·3)*
Aircraft: Capacity 21; operates with variable complement of S-2A Trackers, A-4Q Skyhawks and S-61D Sea King ASW helicopters
Guns: 9—40 mm (single Bofors 40/70)
Main engines: Parsons geared turbines; 40 000 shp; 2 shafts
Boilers: 4 three-drum; working pressure 400 psi *(28·1 kg/cm²)*; Superheat 700°F *(371°C)*
Speed, knots: 24·25
Oil fuel, tons: 3 200
Range, miles: 12 000 at 14 knots, 6 200 at 23 knots
Complement: 1 500

25 DE MAYO

1969, Argentine Navy

Purchased from Great Britain on 1 Apr 1948 and commissioned in the Royal Netherlands Navy on 28 May 1948.   Damaged by boiler fire on 29 Apr 1968.   Sold to Argentina on 15 Oct 1968 and refitted at Rotterdam by N. V. Dok en Werf Mij Wilton Fijenoord.   Commissioned in the Argentine Navy on 12 Mar 1969.   Completed refit on 22 Aug 1969 and sailed for Argentina on 1 Sep 1969.   With modified island superstructure and bridge lattice tripod radar mast, and tall raked funnel, she differs considerably from her former appearance and from her original sister ships in the British, Australian, Brazilian, French and Indian navies.

Electronics: Fitted with Ferranti CAAIS with Plessey Super-CAAIS displays.   The system has been modified to provide control of carrier based aircraft and will be capable of direct computer-to-computer radio data links with the new Type 42 destroyers.

Engineering: The turbine sets and boilers are arranged *en echelon,* the two propelling-machinery spaces having two boilers and one set of turbines in each space, on the unit

system. She was reboiled in 1965-1966 with boilers removed from HMS *Leviathan*. During refit for Argentina in 1968-1969 she received new turbines, also from HMS *Leviathan*.

Radar: Search: Two Philips LWO series early warning radars with associated height finders of VI series for air interception. Tactical: One DAO 2 and one LWO 8 tactical and navigation radars.

Reconstruction: Underwent extensive refit modernisation in 1955-1958 including angled flight deck and steam catapult, rebuilt island, mirror sight landing system, and new anti-aircraft battery of ten 40 mm guns, at the Wilton-Fijenoord Shipyard, at a cost of 25 million guilders. Conversion completed in July 1958.

25 DE MAYO

1974, Argentine Navy

CRUISERS

2 Ex-US "BROOKLYN" CLASS

No.	Builders	Laid down	Launched	Commissioned
C 4	New York S.B. Corp, Camden	15 Apr 1935	12 Mar 1938	18 Mar 1939
C 5	Newport News S.B. & D.D. Co.	1 Apr 1935	3 Dec 1936	1 Feb 1939

Name
GENERAL BELGRANO (ex-*17 de Octubre*, ex-*Phoenix*, CL 46)
NUEVE DE JULIO (ex-*Boise*, CL 47)

Displacement, tons: *Gen. Belgrano:* 10 800 standard; 13 645 full load. *Nueve de Julio:* 10 500 standard; 13 645 full load
Length, feet (metres): 608·3 *(185·4)* oa
Beam, feet (metres): 69 *(21·0)*
Draught, feet (metres): 24 *(7·3)*
Aircraft: 2 helicopters
Missiles: 2 quadruple Sea Cat launchers (*General Belgrano* only)
Guns: *Gen. Belgrano:* 15—6 in *(153 mm)* 47 cal; 8—5 in *(127 mm)* 25 cal; 2 Twin—40 mm; 4—47 mm (saluting)
Nueve de Julio: 15—6 in *(153 mm)* 47 cal; 6—5 in *(127 mm)* 25 cal; 4 Twin—40 mm; 4—47 mm (saluting)
Armour:
Belt 4 in—1½ in *(102–38 mm)*
Decks 3 in—2 in *(76–51 mm)*
Turrets 5 in—3 in *(127–76 mm)*
Conning Tower 8 in *(203 mm)*
Main engines: Parsons geared turbines; 100 000 shp; 4 shafts
Boilers: 8 Babcock & Wilcox Express type
Speed, knots: 32·5 (when new)
Range, miles: 7 600 at 15 knots
Oil fuel, tons: 2 200
Complement: 1 200

GENERAL BELGRANO   *1973, Argentine Navy*

Superstructure was reduced, bulges added, beam increased, and mainmast derricks and catapults removed before transfer. Purchased from the United States in 1951 at a cost of $7 800 000 and transferred to the Argentine Navy on 12 Apr 1951. *General Belgrano* was commissioned under the name *17 de Octubre* at Philadelphia on 17 Oct 1951. *9 de Julio* was commissioned into the Argentine Navy at Philadelphia on 11 Mar 1952. *9 de Julio* refers to 9 July 1816, when the Argentine provinces signed the Declaration of Independence. *17 de Octubre* was renamed *General Belgrano* in 1956 following the overthrow of President Peron the year before.

Gunnery: FCS 33 (2) (1 in *Belgrano*), FCS 34 (1), FCS 57 (2), FCS 63 (2), FCS NA9-D1 (1 in *Belgrano*), TDS (1)

Hangar: The hangar in the hull right aft accommodates two helicopters together with engine spares and duplicate parts, though 4 aircraft was the original complement.

Radar: Search: LWO and DA Series (Signaal).

9 DE JULIO   *1971, Argentine Navy*

DESTROYERS

1 + 1 BRITISH TYPE 42

No.	Builders	Laid down	Launched	Commissioned
D 28	Vickers, Barrow-in-Furness	16 June 1971	24 Oct 1972	10 June 1976
D 29	AFNE, Rio Santiago	11 Oct 1971	9 Nov 1974	1977 (?)

Name
HERCULES
SANTISSIMA TRINIDAD

Displacement, tons: 3 150 standard; 3 500 full load
Length, feet (metres): 392·0 *(119·5)* wl; 410·0 *(125·0)* oa
Beam, feet (metres): 48 *(14·6)*
Draught, feet (metres): 17 *(5·2)*
Missile launchers: 1 Sea Dart (twin)
Aircraft: 1 Lynx helicopter
Guns: 1—4·5 in automatic; 2—20 mm Oerlikon
A/S weapons: 6—Mk 32 (2 triple) torpedo tubes
Main engines: Rolls Royce Olympus gas turbines for full power; Rolls Royce Tyne gas turbines for cruising; 2 shafts; 50 000 shp
Speed, knots: 30
Range, miles: 4 000 at 18 knots
Complement: 300

These two destroyers are of the British Type 42. On 18 May 1970 the signing of a contract between the Argentine Government and Vickers Ltd, Barrow-in-Furness was announced. This provided for the construction of these two ships, one to be built at Barrow-in-Furness and the second at Rio Santiago with British assistance and overseeing. *Santissima Trinidad* was sabotaged on 22 Aug 1975 whilst fitting-out and subsequently placed in floating-dock at AFNE. Completion date remains uncertain.

Electronics: ADAWS-4 for co-ordination of action information by Plessey-Ferranti.

Radar: Search: One Type 965 with double AKE2 array and IFF Surveillance and Target Indication: One Type 992Q.
Sea Dart fire control: Two Type 909.
Navigation, HDWS and helicopter control: One Type 1006.

Sonar: Type 184 hull-mounted. Type 162 classification.

HERCULES   *12/1976, Michael D. J. Lennon*

5 Ex-US "FLETCHER" CLASS

Name		No.	Builders	Laid down	Launched	Commissioned
ALMIRANTE BROWN (ex-USS *Heermann*, DD 532)		D 20	Bethlehem Steel Co, San Francisco	8 May 1942	5 Dec 1942	6 July 1943
ESPORA (ex-USS *Dortch*, DD 670)		D 21	Federal S.B. & D.D. Co, Port Newark	2 Mar 1943	20 June 1943	7 Aug 1943
ROSALES (ex-USS *Stembel*, DD 644)		D 22	Bath Iron Works Corporation, Bath, Maine	21 Dec 1942	8 May 1943	16 July 1943
ALMIRANTE DOMECQ GARCIA (ex-USS *Braine*, DD 630)		D 23	Bath Iron Works Corporation, Bath, Maine	12 Oct 1942	7 Mar 1943	11 May 1943
ALMIRANTE STORNI (ex-USS *Cowell*, DD 547)		D 24	Bethlehem Steel Co, San Pedro	7 Sep 1942	18 Mar 1943	23 Aug 1943

Displacement, tons: 2 100 standard; 3 050 full load
Length, feet (metres): 376·5 *(114·8)* oa
Beam, feet (metres): 39·5 *(12·0)*
Draught, feet (metres): 18 *(5·5)*
Guns: 4—5 in *(127 mm)* 38 cal; 6—3 in *(76 mm)* 50 cal; 2—40 mm (D20-22)
Torpedo tubes: 4—21 in *(533 mm)* quad (20, 21, 22); 6—Mk 32 (Triples) (23, 24)
A/S weapons: 2 fixed Hedgehogs; 1 DC rack (Mk 3); 2 side-launching torpedo racks (D20-22)
Main engines: 2 sets GE or AC geared turbines 60 000 shp; 2 shafts
Boilers: 4 Babcock & Wilcox
Speed, knots: 35
Range, miles: 6 000 at 15 knots
Oil fuel, tons: 650
Complement: 300

First three transferred to the Argentine Navy on 1 Aug 1961. *Espora* is of the later "Fletcher" class. Last pair transferred 17 Aug 1971. *Almirante Brown* is division leader.

A/S: All fitted with FCS 105.

Missiles: To be fitted with Exocet.

Radar: Search: SPS 6.
Tactical: SPS 10.
Fire Control: Mk 37 director with Mk 25 radar; Mk 56 director with Mk 35 radar; Mk 63 director with Mk 34 radar (40 mm).

Sonar: 1 SQS 4.

ESPORA

1974, Argentine Navy

2 Ex-US "ALLEN M. SUMNER" CLASS

Name		No.	Builders	Laid down	Launched	Commissioned
BOUCHARD (ex-USS *Borie* DD 704)		D 26	Federal SB & DD Co.	—	4 July 1944	21 Sep 1944
SEGUI (ex-USS *Hank* DD 702)		D 25	Federal SB & DD Co.	—	21 May 1944	28 Aug 1944

Displacement, tons: 2 200 standard; 3 320 full load
Length, feet (metres): 376·5 *(114·8)* oa
Beam, feet (metres): 40·9 *(12·5)*
Draught, feet (metres): 19 *(5·8)*
Guns: 6—5 in *(127 mm)* 38 cal; 8; DP (twin); 4—3 in *(Segui* only)
A/S Weapons: 6—Mk 32 (Triple); 2 ahead-firing Hedgehogs; Facilities for small helicopter
Main engines: 2 geared turbines; 60 000 shp; 2 shafts
Boilers: 4
Speed, knots: 34
Range, miles: 3 865 at 11 knots; 990 at 31 knots
Complement: *Bouchard* 291; *Segui* 331

Transferred to Argentina 1 July 1972. *Bouchard* has been modernised with VDS, helicopter facilities and hangar. Two units, ex-USS *Mansfield* DD 728 and ex-USS *Collet* DD 730, transferred June 1974 and Apr 1974 respectively for spares.

A/S: Fitted with FCS 105.

Missiles: To be fitted with Exocet.

Radar: Search: SPS 6.
Tactical: SPS 10.
Fire control: Mk 37 director with Mk 25 radar. Mk 56 director with Mk 35 radar *(Segui)*.

Sonar: *(Bouchard)*. SQS 30, SQA 10 (VDS). *(Segui)* SQS 30.

BOUCHARD (as USS BORIE)

1 Ex-US "GEARING" CLASS (FRAM II)

Name		No.	Builders	Laid down	Launched	Commissioned
PY (ex-USS *Perkins* DD 877)		D 27	Consolidated Steel Corpn.	7 Dec 1944	—	5 Apr 1945

Displacement, tons: 2 425 standard; approx 3 500 full load
Length, feet (metres): 390·5 *(119·0)*
Beam, feet (metres): 40·9 *(12·4)*
Draught, feet (metres): 19·0 *(5·8)*
Guns: 6—5 inch *(127 mm)*, 38 cal. DP (twins)
A/S weapons: 2 Fixed Hedgehogs; 6—Mk 32 (triple). Facilities for small helicopter
Main engines: 2 geared Westinghouse turbines
Boilers: 4 Babcock & Wilcox
Speed, knots: 31·5
Range, miles: 6 150 at 11 knots; 1 475 at 30 knots
Complement: 275

Transferred by sale 15 Jan 1973.

A/S: Fitted with FCS 105.

Gunnery: FCS 37 (1).

Radar: SPS 37.

Sonar: SQS 29.

PY (as USS PERI

FRIGATES

Discussions in progress with Vosper Thornycroft Ltd for the construction of 6 Type 21 frigates at AFNE, Rio Santiago.

CORVETTES

2 "KING" CLASS

Name	No.	Builders	Commissioned
KING	P 21	Astillero Nav. Rio Santiago	28 July 1946
MURATURE	P 20	Astillero Nav. Rio Santiago	18 Nov 1946

Displacement, tons: 913 standard; 1 000 normal; 1 032 full load
Length, feet (metres): 252·7 (77·0)
Beam, feet (metres): 29 (8·8)
Draught, feet (metres): 7·5 (2·3)
Guns: 3—4·1 (105 mm); 4—40 mm Bofors; 2—MG
A/S: 4—DCT
Main engines: 2—Werkspoor 4-stroke diesels; 2 500 bhp; 2 shafts
Speed, knots: 18
Oil fuel (tons): 90
Range, miles: 6 000 at 12 knots
Complement: 130

Named after Captain John King, an Irish follower of Admiral Brown, who distinguished himself in the war with Brazil, 1826-28; and Captain Murature, who performed conspicuous service against the Paraguayans at the Battle of Cuevas on Aug 6 1865. Used for cadet training.

MURATURE   1974, Argentine Navy

6 Ex-US ATA TYPE

Name	No.	Builders	Commissioned
ALFEREZ SOBRAL	A 9	Levingstone	1944
(ex-USS *Catawba*, ATA 210)		Sb Co, Orange	
CHIRIGUANO (ex-US ATA 227)	A 7	,,	1945
COMODORO SOMELLERA	A 10	,,	1945
(ex-USS *Salish* ATA 187)			
DIAGUITA (ex-US ATA 124)	A 5	,,	1945
SANAVIRON (ex-US ATA 228)	A 8	,,	1945
YAMANA (ex-US ATA 126)	A 6	,,	1945

Displacement, tons: 689 standard; 800 full load
Dimensions, feet (metres): 134·5 wl; 143 oa × 34 × 12 (43·4 × 10·4 × 3·6)
Gun: 1—40/60 mm
Main engines: Diesel-electric; 1 500 bhp = 12·5 knots
Oil fuel (tons): 154
Range, miles: 16 500 at 8 knots
Complement: 49

Former US auxiliary ocean tugs. *Diaguita* and *Yamana* are fitted as rescue ships. A 5, A 6, A 7 and A 8 which were acquired in 1947 bear names of South American Indian tribes. Classified as ocean salvage tugs until 1966 when they were re-rated as patrol vessels. A 9 and A 10 were transferred on 10 Feb 1972. A 10 operated by Coast Guard.

YAMANA   1969, Argentine Navy

3 Ex-US ATF TYPE

Name	No.	Builders	Commissioned
COMMANDANTE GENERAL IRIGOYEN	A 1	Charleston	10 Mar 1945
(ex-USS *Cahuilla* ATF 152)		SB and DD Co.	
COMMANDANTE GENERAL ZAPIOLA	A 2	Charleston	20 Jan 1943
(ex-USS *Arapaho* ATF 68)		SB and DD Co.	
FRANCISCO DE CHURRUCA	A 3	Charleston	17 Mar 1945
(ex-USS *Luiseno* ATF 156)		SB and DD Co.	(launched)

Displacement, tons: 1 235 standard; 1 675 full load
Dimensions, feet (metres): 195 wl; 205 oa × 38·2 × 15·3 (62·5 × 11·6 × 4·7)
Guns: 6—40/60 mm (2 twin; 2 single)
Main engines: 4 sets diesels with electric drive; 3 000 bhp = 16 knots
Complement: 85

Former US fleet ocean tugs of the "Apache" class. Fitted with powerful pumps and other salvage equipment. First two transferred to Argentina at San Diego, California, in 1961. Classified as tugs until 1966 when they were re-rated as patrol vessels. *Francisco De Churruca* transferred 1 July 1975 by sale.

FRANCISCO DE CHURRUCA (as LUISENO)   USN

1 "BOUCHARD" CLASS

Name	No.	Builders	Commissioned
SPIRO	GC 12	Rio Santiago	1938

Displacement, tons: 560 normal; 650 full load
Dimensions, feet (metres): 197 oa × 24 × 11·5 (60·1 × 7·3 × 3·5)
Guns: 4—40 mm
Main engines: 2 MAN Diesels; 2 000 bhp = 13 knots
Range, miles: 3 000 at 10 knots
Complement: 77

Former minesweeper of the "Bouchard" class, now operated by the Prefectura Naval Argentina. Sister ships *Bouchard*, *Py*, *Parker* and *Seaver* were transferred to the Paraguayan Navy in 1964-67. This class, originally of 9, were the first warships built in Argentine yards.

SPIRO   1969, Argentine Navy

SUBMARINES
2 +(2) "SALTA" CLASS (TYPE 209)

Name	No.	Builders	Laid down	Launched	Commissioned
SALTA	S 31	Howaldtswerke, Kiel	—	22 Nov 1972	May 1974
SAN LUIS	S 32	Howaldtswerke, Kiel	—	2 May 1973	May 1974

Displacement, tons: 980 surfaced; 1 230 dived
Length, feet (metres): 183·4 *(55·9)*
Beam, feet (metres): 20·5 *(6·25)*
Draught, feet (metres): 17·9 *(5·4)*
Torpedo tubes: 8—21 in; bow tubes (with reloads)
Main machinery: Diesel electric; MTU Diesels, 4 generators; 1 shaft; 5 000 hp
Speed knots: 10 surfaced, 22 dived
Complement: 32

Built in sections by Howaldtswerke Deutsche Werft AG, Kiel from the IK 68 design of Ingenieurkontor, Lübeck. Sections were shipped to Argentina for assembly at Tandanor, Buenos Aires.

Future Programme: Two more projected for building in Argentina.

SALTA   *1973, Argentine Navy*

2 "GUPPY (IA and II)" CLASS

Name	No.	Builders	Laid down	Launched	Commissioned
SANTE FE (ex-USS *Catfish* SS 339)	S 21	Electric Boat Co.	—	19 Nov 1944	19 Mar 1945
SANTIAGO DEL ESTERO (ex-USS *Chivo* SS 341)	S 22	Electric Boat Co.	—	14 Jan 1945	28 Apr 1945

Displacement, tons: 1 870 surfaced; 2 420 *(Santa Fe)*; 2 540 *(Santiago)* dived
Length, feet (metres): 307·5 *(93·8)* oa
Beam, feet (metres): 27·2 *(8·3)*
Draught, feet (metres): 18·0 *(5·5)* *(Santa Fe)*; 17·0 *(5·2)* *(Santiago)*
Torpedo tubes: 10—21 in *(533 mm)*; 6 fwd, 4 aft
Main machinery: 3 diesels; 4 800 shp; 2 electric motors; 5 400 shp; 2 shafts
Speed, knots: 18 surfaced; 15 dived
Oil fuel, tons: 300
Range, miles: 12 000 at 10 knots
Complement: 82-84

SANTA FE   *1972, Argentine Navy*

Both of the "Balao" class. *Catfish* was modified under the Guppy II programme (1948-50) and *Chivo* under the Guppy 1A programme (1951). Both transferred to Argentina at Mare Island on 7 Jan 1971 by sale.

AMPHIBIOUS FORCES
1 Ex-US LANDING SHIP (DOCK)

Name	No.	Builders	Commissioned
CANDIDO DE LASALA (ex-USS *Gunston Hall* LSD 5)	Q 43	Moor Dry Dock Co, Oakland	10 Nov 1943

Displacement, tons: 5 480 standard; 9 375 full load
Dimensions, feet (metres): 457·8 oa × 72·2 × 18·0 *(139·6 × 22 × 6·3)*
Guns: 12—40 mm
Main engines: 2 Skinner Unaflow; 2 shafts; 7 400 shp = 15·4 knots
Boilers: 2 Two drum
Range, miles: 8 000 at 15 knots
Complement: Accommodation for 326 (17 officers and 309 men)

CANDIDO DE LASALA   *1973, Argentine Navy*

Arcticized in 1948/9. Transferred from the US Navy on 1 May 1970. Carries 14 LCA and has helicopter facilities. Used as light forces tender.

1 LANDING SHIP (TANK)

Name	No.	Builders	Commissioned
CABO SAN ANTONIO	Q 42	AFNE, Rio Santiago	1976

Displacement, tons: 4 300 light; 8 000 full load
Dimensions, feet (metres): 445 oa × 62 × 16·5 *(135·7 × 18·9 × 5)*
Guns: 12—40/60 mm (3 quad)
Main engines: Diesels; 2 shafts; 13 700 bhp = 16 knots
Complement: 124

Designed to carry a helicopter and two landing craft. Launched 1968. Completion delayed—fitting out continuing early 1976. Modified US "De Soto" Class—principal difference being the fitting of Stülcken heavy-lift gear.

Radar: Plessey AWS-1.

CABO SAN ANTONIO   *1974, Argentine Navy*

3 Ex-US LST TYPE

Name	No.	Builders	Commissioned
CABO SAN GONZALO (ex-USS LST 872)	Q 44	Puget Sound B and D Co, Seattle	1944
CABO SAN ISIDRO (ex-USS LST 919)	Q 46	Puget Sound B and D Co, Seattle	1944
CABO SAN PIO (ex-USS LST 1044)	Q 50	Puget Sound B and D Co, Seattle	1944

Displacement, tons: 2 366 beaching; 4 080 full load
Dimensions, feet (metres): 328 oa × 50 × 14 *(100 × 15·3 × 4·3)*
Main engines: 2 diesels; 2 shafts; 1 800 bhp = 11 knots
Oil fuel, tons: 700
Range, miles: 9 500 at 9 knots
Complement: 80

Transferred 1946-47.

1 Ex-US LCT TYPE

BDI (ex-USS *LCIL* 583) Q 56

Displacement, tons: 230 light; 387 full load
Dimensions, feet (metres): 159 oa × 23·2 × 5 *(48·5 × 7·1 × 1·5)*
Guns: 2—20 mm
Main engines: 8 sets diesels; 3 200 bhp = 14 knots. Two reversible propellers
Oil fuel, tons: 110
Range, miles: 6 000 at 12 knots
Complement: 30

Used for training.

27 MINOR LANDING CRAFT

EDM 1, 2, 3, 4

It was stated in Jan 1971 that four LCMs of 195 tons and 11 knots built in the USA had been incorporated in the Fleet.

EDVP 1, 3, 7, 8, 9, 10, 12, 13, 17, 19, 21, 24, 28, 29, 30

Displacement, tons: 12
Dimensions, feet (metres): 39·5 × 10·5 × 5·5 *(12·1 × 3·2 × 1·7)*
Main engines: Diesels, 9 knots

Ex-USN LCVPs. Transferred 1946.

8 Ex-US LCVPs

Dimensions, feet (metres): 63 × 14·1 × —*(19·2 × 4·3 ×—)*
Main engines: 1 diesel; approx 250 hp

Incorporated at the end of 1970. Numbers not known.

LIGHT FORCES

2 GERMAN TYPE 148 (FAST ATTACK CRAFT—MISSILE)

Displacement, tons: 234 standard; 265 full load
Dimensions, feet (metres): 154·2 × 23·0 × 5·9 *(47 × 7 × 2)*
Missiles: Triple launcher for Gabriel missiles
Guns: 1—76 mm; 1—40 mm
Torpedo tubes: 2—21 in (or 8 mines)
Main engines: 4 Diesels= 38 knots
Range, miles: 600 at 30 knots
Complement: 30

Building in Argentina.

GERMAN TYPE 148   *1974, Federal German Navy*

2 "COMBATTANTE II" CLASS (FAST ATTACK CRAFT—GUN)

Name	No.	Builders	Commissioned
INTREPIDA	P 85	Lürssen, Vegesack	20 July 1974
INDOMITA	P 86	Lürssen, Vegesack	Dec 1974

Displacement, tons: 240
Dimensions, feet (metres): 164 × 24 × 8·2 *(50 × 7·3 × 2·5)*
Guns: 1—3 in *(76 mm)* OTO Melara; 2—40 mm
Rocket launcher: One Oerlikon twin 81 mm
Torpedo tubes: 2—21 inch for wire-guided torpedoes
Main engines: 4 Diesels; 4 shafts; 12 000 hp = 40 knots
Complement: 35

These two vessels were ordered in 1970.

Radar: Fire control: Hollandse Signaal M20.

INTREPIDA   *4/1974, Stefan Terzibaschitsch*

3 "LYNCH" CLASS (LARGE PATROL CRAFT)

Name	No.	Builders	Commissioned
EREZCANO	GC 23	AFNE Rio Santiago	1967
LYNCH	GC 21	AFNE Rio Santiago	1964
TOLL	GC 22	AFNE Rio Santiago	1965

Displacement, tons: 100 normal; 117 full load
Dimensions, feet (metres): 90 × 19 × 6 *(27·5 × 5·8 × 1·8)*
Gun: 1—20 mm
Main engines: 2 Maybach Diesels; 2 700 bhp = 22 knots
Complement: 16

Patrol craft operated by the Prefectura Naval Argentina.

LYNCH   *1969, Argentine Navy*

1 LARGE PATROL CRAFT

Name	No.	Builders	Commissioned
SURUBI	P 55	Ast. Nav. del Estero	1951

Displacement, tons: 100
Guns: 2—20 mm
Speed, knots: 20

1 Ex-US 63 ft AVR (LARGE PATROL CRAFT)

GC 31

Dimensions as for US 63 ft AVR class but of slightly different silhouette.

GC 31   1971

2 EX-US "HIGGINS" CLASS (FAST ATTACK CRAFT—TORPEDO)

Name	No.	Builders	Commissioned
ALAKUSH	P 82	New Orleans SB	1946
TOWORA	P 84	New Orleans SB	1946

Displacement, tons: 45 standard; 50 full load
Dimensions, feet (metres): 78·7 × 9·8 × 4·6 *(24 × 3 × 1·4)*
Guns: 2—40/60 mm; 4—MG
Torpedo launchers: 4—21 inch racks
Rocket launchers: 2 sextuple sets 12·7 cm
Main engines: 3 Packard (Petrol); 4 500 hp = 42 knots
Range, miles: 1 000 at 20 knots
Complement: 12

The last of a class of nine. Given names in 1972.

Note. In addition the following are listed as operated by PNA: *Delfin* of 1 000 tons and 15 knots, *Robalo, Mandubi, Adhara, Albatross, Dorado,* LT 1 and 8, PAV 1, 2 and 3. PAM 1, 2 and 3, V 2 and 6, GN 1, 4, 38 and 42, PF 17, P 2, 5, 13, 22, 26, 39 and 41.

MINE WARFARE FORCES

6 Ex-BRITISH "TON" CLASS
(MINESWEEPERS—COASTAL and MINEHUNTERS)

Name	No.	Builders	Launched
CHACO (ex-HMS *Rennington*)	M 5	Richards	27 Nov 1958
CHUBUT (ex-HMS *Santon*)	M 3	Fleetlands	18 Aug 1955
FORMOSA (ex-HMS *Ilmington*)	M 6	Camper, Nicholson	8 Mar 1954
NEUQUEN (ex-HMS *Hickleton*)	M 1	Thornycroft	26 Jan 1955
RIO NEGRO (ex-HMS *Tarlton*)	M 2	Doig	10 Nov 1954
TIERRA DEL FUEGO (ex- HMS *Bevington*)	M 4	Whites	17 Mar 1953

Displacement, tons: 360 standard; 425 full load
Dimensions, feet (metres): 140 pp; 153 oa × 28·8 × 8·2 *(46·3 × 8·8 × 2·5)*
Gun: 1—40/60 mm
Main engines: 2 Diesels; 2 shafts; 3 000 bhp = 15 knots
Oil fuel, tons: 45
Range, miles: 2 300 at 13 knots; 3 000 at 8 knots
Complement: Minesweepers 27; Minehunters 36

Former British coastal minesweepers of the "Ton" class. Of composite wooden and non-magnetic metal construction. Purchased in 1967. In 1968 *Chaco* and *Formosa* were converted into minehunters in HM Dockyard, Portsmouth, and the other four were refitted and modernised as minesweepers by the Vosper Thornycroft Group with Vosper activated-fin stabiliser equipment.

NEUQUEN (SWEEPER)   1974, Argentine Navy

SURVEY AND OCEANOGRAPHICAL SHIPS

1 NEW CONSTRUCTION OCEANOGRAPHICAL SHIP

Displacement, tons: 1 960 standard

Laid down in 1974 at Alianza, Avellaneda.

1 NEW CONSTRUCTION RESEARCH SHIP

Displacement, tons: 2 100 standard
Dimensions, feet (metres): 249 × 43·4 × 14·9 *(75·9 × 13·2 × 4·5)*
Main engine: 1 Diesel; 2 600 hp = 12 knots

Laid down at Astarsa, San Fernando in 1974 for Consejo Nacional de Investigaciones Tecnicas y Scientificas. Civilian manned.

2 Ex-US TYPE V4 TUGS

Name	No.	Builders	Commissioned
GOYENA (ex-USS *Dry Tortuga*)	Q 17 (ex-A 3)	Pendleton SY, New Orleans	1943
THOMPSON (ex-USS *Sombrero Key*)	A 4	Pendleton SY, New Orleans	1943

Displacement, tons: 1 863 full load
Dimensions, feet (metres): 191·3 × 37 × 18 *(58·3 × 11·3 × 5·5)*
Guns: 2—40 mm Bofors (twin); 2—20 mm (single)
Main engines: 2 Enterprise Diesels; 2 250 bhp = 12 knots
Oil fuel, tons: 532
Complement: 62

Leased to Argentina in 1965. Temporarily used as survey ships.

THOMPSON   1973, Argentine Navy

Name	No.	Builders	Commissioned
ISLAS ORCADAS	Q 9	Avondale, New Orleans	2 Aug 1957
(ex-USS *Eltanin*, T-AGOR 8)			

Displacement, tons: 2 036 light; 4 942 full load
Dimensions, feet (metres): 262·2 oa × 51·5 × 18·7 *(80 × 15·7 × 5·7)*
Main engines: Diesel electric; 3 200 bhp; 2 shafts = 12 knots
Complement: 12 officers, 36 men, 38 scientists

Converted for Antarctic Research 1961. Operated in conjunction by Argentine Navy, US National Science Foundation and Argentine National Directorate of the Antarctic.

1 AUXILIARY SAILING SHIP

Name	No.	Builders	Commissioned
EL AUSTRAL (ex-*Atlantis*)	Q 7	Burmeister and Wain, Copenhagen	1931

Displacement, tons: 571
Dimensions, feet (metres): 110 pp; 141 oa × 27 × 20 *(33·6; 43 × 8·2 × 6·1)*
Main engines: Diesels; 400 bhp
Oil fuel, tons: 22
Complement: 19

Incorporated into the Argentine Navy on 30 April, 1966. Acquired from USA. (Wood's Hole 'nstitute).

Name	No.	Builders	Commissioned
COMODORO RIVADAVIA	Q —	Mestrina, Tigre	Sept 1976

Displacement, tons: 609 standard; 667 full load
Dimensions, feet (metres): 167 × 28·9 × 8·5 *(50·9 × 8·8 × 2·6)*
Main engines: 2 Werkspoor Diesels = 12 knots
Complement: 27

Laid down 17 July 1971, launched 2 Dec 1972. Completion ex-trials Dec 1974.

CORMORAN Q 15

Coastal survey launch of 102 tons with complement of 19, built in 1963. Speed 13 knots.

PETREL

Coastal survey launch of 50 tons with complement of 9, built in 1965.

TRANSPORTS

Name	No.	Builders	Commissioned
BAHIA AGUIRRE	B 2	Canadian Vickers, Halifax	1950
BAHIA BUEN SUCESO	B 6	Canadian Vickers, Halifax	June 1950

Displacement, tons: 3 100 standard; 5 000 full load
Dimensions, feet (metres): 334·7 × 47 × 13·8 *(95·1 × 14·3 × 7·9)*
Main engines: 2 sets Nordberg diesels; 2 shafts; 3 750 bhp = 16 knots
Oil fuel, tons: 442 (B 6); 355 (B 2)
Complement: 100

Survivors of class of three.

BAHIA BUEN SUCESO   *1974, Argentine Navy*

3 "COSTA SUR" CLASS

Measurement, tons: 4 600 gross; 5 800 deadweight
Dimensions, feet (metres): 390·3 × 57·4 × 21 *(119 × 17·5 × 6·4)*
Main engines: 2 diesels; 3 200 hp = 15 knots

Ordered 1975 from Ast. Principe Menghi y Penco Ga, Avellaneda. To replace 3 ex-US LSTs *(Cabo san Gonzalo)*. Delivery 1978-79.

TANKERS

1 LARGE FLEET TANKER (FLEET SUPPORT)

Name	No.	Builders	Commissioned
PUNTA MEDANOS	B 18	Swan Hunter	10 Oct 1950

Displacement, tons: 14 352 standard; 16 331 full load
Measurement, tons: 8 250 deadweight
Dimensions, feet (metres): 470 pp; 502 oa × 62 × 28·5 *(143·4; 153·1 × 18·9 × 8·7)*
Main engines: Double reduction geared turbines. 2 shafts; 9 500 shp = 18 knots
Boilers: 2 Babcock & Wilcox two-drum integral furnace water-tube
Oil fuel, tons: 1 500
Range, miles: 13 700 at 15 knots
Complement: 99

Available as a training vessel. Boilers built under licence by the Wallsend Slipway & Engineering Company. Steam conditions of 400 lb per sq in pressure and 750 deg F.

PUNTA MEDANOS   *1973, Argentine Navy*

1 Ex-US MS TYPE (FLEET SUPPORT)

Name	No.	Builders	Commissioned
PUNTA DELGADA	B 16	St. Johns River SB, Jacksonville	1945
(ex-USS *Sugarland*, ex-*Nanticoke* AOG 66)			

Displacement, tons: 5 930 standard; 6 090 full load
Dimensions, feet (metres): 325 × 48·2 × 20 *(99·1 × 14·7 × 6·1)*
Main engines: Westinghouse diesel; 1 shaft; 1 400 bhp = 11·5 knots
Oil fuel, tons: 150
Range, miles: 9 000 at 11 knots
Complement: 72

USMS type T1-M-BT1. Launched on 7 Apr 1945.

1 TANKER (FLEET SUPPORT)

Name	No.	Builder	Commissioned
PUNTA ALTA	B 12	Puerto Belgrano	1938

Displacement, tons: 1 600 standard; 1 900 full load
Measurement, tons: 800 deadweight
Dimensions, feet (metres): 210 × 33·8 × 12·5 *(64 × 10·3 × 3·8)*
Main engines: Diesel; 1 shaft; 1 850 bhp = 8 knots
Oil fuel, tons: 146

TRAINING SHIP

Name	No.	Builders	Commissioned
LIBERTAD	Q 2	AFNE, Rio Santiago	1962

Displacement, tons: 3 025 standard; 3 765 full load
Dimensions, feet (metres): 262 wl; 301 oa × 47 × 21·8 *(92, 94·5 × 13·8 × 6·8)*
Guns: 1—3 in; 4—40 mm; 4—47 mm saluting
Main engines: 2 Sulzer diesels; 2 400 bhp = 13·5 knots
Complement: 370 (crew) plus 150 cadets

Launched on 20 June 1956. She is the largest sail training ship in the world and set up the fastest crossing of the N. Atlantic under sail in 1966, a record which still stands.

LIBERTAD   *10/1973, Reiner Nerlich*

ICEBREAKERS

1 NEW CONSTRUCTION WÄRTSILA TYPE

Dimensions, feet (metres):392 × 82 × 31·2 *(119 × 25 × 9·5)*
Main engines: Diesel electric; 16 200 shp (4 Wärtsila-SEMT Pielstick 8PC2-5L diesels); 2 shafts
Speed, knots: 16·5
Complement: 133 ship's company; 100 passengers

Contract signed on 17 Dec 1975 with Wärtsila (Helsinki) delivery to be in Autumn 1978. The ship is designed for Antarctic support operations and will be able to remain in the polar regions throughout the winter with 210 people aboard. Fitted for helicopters and landing craft with two 16 ton cranes. Will have fin stabilisers, Wärtsila bubbling system and a 60 ton towing winch.

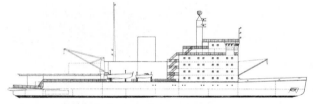

New Construction Wärtsila Icebreaker   *1975*

Name	No.	Builders	Commissioned
GENERAL SAN MARTIN	Q 4	Seebeck Yd-Weser AG	Oct 1954

Displacement, tons: 4 854 standard; 5 301 full load
Measurement, tons: 1 600 deadweight
Dimensions, feet (metres): 279 × 61 × 21 *(85·1 × 18·6 × 6·4)*
Aircraft: 1 reconnaissance aircraft and 1 helicopter
Guns: 2—40 mm Bofors
Main engines: 4 diesel-electric; 2 shafts; 7 100 hp = 16 knots
Oil fuel, tons: 1 100
Range, miles: 35 000 at 10 knots
Complement: 160

Launched on 24 June 1954. Fitted for research. New second radar mast fitted on after end of the hangar in late 1972.

GENERAL SAN MARTIN   *1970, Argentine Navy*
(2nd radar mast now fitted and 4 in gun removed)

TUGS

GUAYCURU R 33   **QUILMES** R 32

Displacement, tons: 368 full load
Dimensions, feet (metres): 107·2 × 24·4 × 12·5 *(32·7 × 7·4 × 3·8)*
Main engines: Skinner Unaflow engines; 645 ihp = 9 knots
Boilers: Cylindrical
Oil fuel, tons: 52
Range, miles: 2 200 at 7 knots
Complement: 14

"Quilmes" class tugs built at Rio Santiago Naval Yard. Laid down on 23 Aug and 15 Mar 1956 respectively, launched on 27 Dec 1959 and 8 July 1957 and completed on 29 July and 30 Mar 1960.

PEHUENCHE R 29   **TONOCOTE** R 30

Displacement, tons: 330
Dimensions, feet (metres): 105 × 24·7 × 12·5 *(32 × 7·5 × 3·8)*
Main engines: Triple expansion; 600 ihp = 11 knots
Boilers: 2
Oil fuel, tons: 36
Range, miles: 1 200 at 9 knots
Complement: 13

Both built in Rio Santiago Naval Yard. Commissioned for service in 1954.

TOBA R 4

Displacement, tons: 600
Measurement, tons: 339 gross
Dimensions, feet (metres): 139 oa × 28.5 × 11.5 *(42·4 × 8·7 × 3·5)*
Main engines: Triple expansion; 2 shafts; 1 200 ihp = 12 knots
Boilers: 2
Oil fuel, tons: 95
Range, miles: 3 900 at 10 knots
Complement: 34

Built by Hawthorn Leslie, Ltd, Hebburn-on-Tyne. Launched on 23 Dec 1927 and completed in Mar 1928.

HUARPE R 12

Displacement, tons: 370
Dimensions, feet (metres): 107 × 27·2 × 12 *(32·2 × 8·3 × 3·7)*
Main engines: Triple expansion; 800 ihp
Boilers: 1 cylindrical (Howaldtwerke)
Oil fuel, tons: 58
Complement: 13

Built by Howaldtwerke in 1927. Entered service in the Argentine Navy in 1942.

CALCHAQUI	R 6 (ex-US YTL 445)	**CHULUPI**	R 10 (ex-US YTL 426)
CAPAYAN	R 16 (ex-US YTL 443)	**MOCOVI**	R 5 (ex-US YTL 441)
CHIQUILLAN	R 18 (ex-US YTL 444)	**MORCOYAN**	R 19 (ex-US YTL 448)

Displacement, tons: 70
Dimensions, feet (metres): 67 × 14 × 13 *(20·4 × 4·3 × 4)*
Main engines: Diesel; 310 bhp = 10 knots
Oil fuel, tons: 8·7
Complement: 5

YTL Type built in USA and transferred on lease in Mar 1965 R (16, 18 and 19), remainder in Mar 1969

Note. Two harbour tugs built by Vicente Forte entered service in 1974.

FLOATING DOCKS

Number	Dimensions, feet (metres)	Capacity, tons
Y 1 (ex-ARD 23)	492 × 88·6 × 56 *(150 × 27 × 17·1)*	3 500
2	300·1 × 60 × 41 *(91·5 × 18·3 × 12·5)*	1 000
ASD 40	215·8 × 46 × 45·5 *(65·8 × 14 × 13·7)*	750
—	215·8 × 46 × 45·5 *(65·8 × 14 × 13·7)*	750

First three are at Darsena Norte, Buenos Aires and the fourth at Puerto Belgrano.

MISCELLANEOUS

Two naval sail-training ships, *Fortuna* and *Juana* built by Tandanor, Buenos Aires.
Two auxiliaries, *E 6,* and *Itati* listed.
The ex-training ship *Presidente Sarmiento* is retained at Buenos Aires as a museum ship, as also is the 1874 Corvette *Uruguay*.

FLOATING CRANES

At least four—at Darsena Norte, Rio Santiago, Mar de Plata and Puerto Belgrano.

AUSTRALIA

Administration

Minister for Defence (and Navy):
Hon. D. J. Killen, MP

Chief of Defence Force Staff:
General Sir Francis Hassett, AC, KBE, CB, DSO, MVO

Headquarters Appointments

Chief of Naval Staff:
Vice-Admiral A. M. Synnott, AO, CBE
Chief of Naval Personnel:
Rear-Admiral R. G. Griffiths, DSO, DSC
Chief of Naval Technical Services:
Rear-Admiral M. P. Reed
Chief of Naval Materiel:
Rear Admiral P. H. Doyle, OBE
Deputy Chief of the Naval Staff:
Rear-Admiral B. S. Murray

Senior Appointments

Flag Officer Commanding Australian Fleet:
Rear-Admiral G. V. Gladstone, AO, DSC*
Flag Officer Commanding East Australian Area:
Rear-Admiral N. E. McDonald

Diplomatic Representation

Naval Representative in London:
Commodore G. J. H. Woolrych
Naval Attaché in Washington:
Commodore R. G. Loosli, CBE
Naval Attaché in Tokyo:
Captain P. E. M. Holloway
Naval Attaché in Jakarta:
Captain R. J. Whitten
Defence Adviser in Port Moresby:
Captain J. A. Matthew, MBE

Personnel

1 January 1973: 17 128 officers and sailors
1 January 1974: 16 743 officers and sailors
1 January 1975: 15 811 officers and sailors
1 January 1976: 15 909 officers and sailors
1 January 1977: 16 000 officers and sailors (app)
(including 850 WRANS)

Navy Estimates

$A
1972-73: 293 094 000*
1973-74: 319 994 000*
1974-75: 375 014 000
1975-76: 428 879 000
1976-77: 539 808 000
(*Includes United States Credits)

Naval Bases

FOCEA—Sydney and Jervis Bay
NOC Queensland—Brisbane and Cairns (PCs and LCHs)
NOC Northern Territory—Darwin (PCs)
NOC W. Australia—Cockburn Sound (estimated completion 1978-79)

Naval Shipyards

Building at Williamstown (Melbourne) and Cockatoo Island (Sydney). Refits at both and Garden Island (Sydney).

Fleet Air Arm

Squadron	Aircraft
HC-723	Iroquois, Wessex 31B (Utility) and Bell 206B-1 helos (Utility, SAR and FRU)
VC-724	A4G and TA4G Skyhawks, Macchi Trainers (Training, FRU and Trials)
VF-805	A4G Skyhawks (Front line fighter/strike)
VS-816	S2E Trackers (Front line A/S)
HS-817	Sea King Mk 50 helos (Front line A/S)
VC-851	S2E Trackers, HS 748 (Training, communications and FRU)

Note: On 5th Dec 1976 twelve of thirteen S2E Trackers were destroyed by fire at NAS Nowra. Action in hand to hasten 6 Trackers on order and to investigate other replacements

Prefix to Ships' Names

HMAS.   Her Majesty's Australian Ship

Mercantile Marine

Lloyd's Register of Shipping:
424 vessels of 1 247 172 tons gross

Army Craft

Army watercraft squadrons have been much reduced and, responsibility for larger vessels has been absorbed into the RAN. Two tugs, several work-boats, LCVPs and LCM8s and other small craft are still in Army use.

Strength of the Fleet

Type	Active	Building
Attack Carrier (Medium)	1	—
Destroyers	5 (3DDG)	—
Frigates (GM)	—	2
Frigates	6	—
Patrol Submarines	4	2
MCM Vessels	3	—
Large Patrol Craft	12	—
Survey Ships	4	1
Fleet Tanker	1	—
Destroyer Tender	1	—
Landing Craft (Heavy)	6	—
Training Ship	1	—

Naval Procurement and Modernisation

In February 1976 the Australian Government accepted a letter of offer from the United States Navy for two guided missile frigates of the "Oliver Hazard Perry" (FFG 7) class. These ships will enter service in the RAN in 1981. In a White Paper on Australian defence tabled in November 1976 the Government stated that consideration was being given to ordering a third FFG. The acquisition of this ship would raise the strength of the destroyer fleet from 11 to 12. The White Paper also stated that investigations were being made into the concepts, characteristics, and cost of "follow-on" destroyers, preferably for construction in Australia. These investigations would be in con-

junction with those of missile armed patrol boats.
A decision is expected early in 1977 on the design of a new class of patrol boat. Two craft—the Brooke Marine PCF 420 and a variant of the Lürssen Werft FPB 45—were selected for project definition in May 1976 and the two companies were contracted to complete funded studies by the end of 1976. $A115 million (at January 1976 prices) has been earmarked for 15 new patrol boats; all, with the possible exception of the lead craft, will be built in Australia. The new boats are expected to begin entering service in the late 1970s.
Work on a new Amphibious Heavy Lift Ship (AHLS), HMAS *Tobruk*, is expected to begin in mid-1977. HMAS *Tobruk* will be an improved version of the British "Sir Bedivere" class, displacing about 6 000 tonnes, and capable of carrying a squadron of Leopard tanks, large numbers of wheeled vehicles, and between 300 and 500 troops all of which it will be able to land across a beach. The ship will operate Wessex 31B utility helicopters.
An underway replenishment ship is due to enter service by 1980 when the Fleet Tanker, HMAS *Supply*, is due to retire. Two European designs are under consideration at the time of writing and a decision is expected early in 1977. Consideration is also being given to acquisition of a second ship of this class.
It is planned to acquire a new purpose-built training ship to replace HMAS *Duchess* in the early 1980s. However the Department of Defence is also investigating the possibility of acquiring the former Australian National Line roll-on roll-off ship, *Australian Trader*, which could be employed in a training and logistics role.
The RAN is proceeding with initial prototype design and acquisition of long-lead items for two prototype MCM vessels. These ships, which will be the first of a class intended to replace the ageing "Ton" class ships now in service, will feature a GRP catamaran hull. The new class is due to enter service in the first half of the 1980s.
A new oceanographic ship, HMAS *Cook*, is being constructed to replace HMAS *Diamantina*, and a new trials and research ship to replace HMAS *Kimbla* in the early 1980s is also contemplated. The White Paper announced an intention to construct a further two hydrographic ships and six large survey launches. The first of the new ships would probably be similar to HMAS *Flinders*.
Two new "Oberon" class submarines building in UK are due to be commissioned in 1977.
Other procurement and modernisation proposals referred to in the White Paper include:
Limited acquisition of anti-shipping missiles (e.g. Harpoon, Exocet) for destroyers and submarines.
Six additional S2E Tracker ASW aircraft to be acquired in the US in 1977 at a cost of $A1 million. (See note in Fleet Air Arm section).
New fire control and combat data processing systems to be fitted from 1977 onwards, and an improved attack/intercept submarine sonar for "Oberon" class submarines.
"Perth" class DDGs are being progressively modernised by installation of new gun mounts, naval combat data systems, and "Standard" SAM systems.
Three of the older "River" class DEs will be modernised, and a fourth, HMAS *Yarra* began a half-life refit in 1976. When this work is completed in 1981 it is planned to start modernisation of HMAS *Swan* and HMAS *Torrens*.

Papua-New Guinea Defence Force

The RAN base in the Admiralty Islands, HMAS *Tarangau*, was decommissioned 14.11.74 and handed over to the PNG Defence Force. It is now the PNG Defence Force Base, Lombrum. Five RAN "Attack" class patrol boats, *Aitape*, *Ladava*, *Lae*, *Madang* and *Samarai*, plus two LCHs *Buna* and *Salamaua* have been re-commissioned as PNG Ships and are fully or partially manned by PNG personnel with some RAN personnel as technical advisers.

DELETIONS

Landing Craft (Heavy)

Buna	To Papua New Guinea
Salamaua	Defence Force 14.11.74

MCM Vessels

Hawk	Sold 1975
Gull	Sold 1975
Teal	Awaiting Disposal

Large Patrol Craft

Archer and *Bandolier*	To Indonesia 21.10.74 & 16.11.73
Arrow	Sunk Darwin (Cyclone Tracy) 25.12.74
Aitape, Ladava, Lae, Madang, Samarai	To Papua New Guinea Defence Force 16.9.75

Ex-Carrier

Sydney	For disposal 20.7.73. Left Sydney for South Korean breakers 23.12.75

Destroyers

Arunta	Sank under tow to breaker 13.2.69
Tobruk	Left Sydney for Taiwan 10.4.72
Anzac	Left Sydney for Hong Kong 30.12.75

Frigates

Barcoo	Left Sydney for Taiwan 17.3.72
Culgoa	Left Sydney for Taiwan 17.3.72
Quickmatch	Left Sydney for Japan 10.4.72
Quiberon	Left Sydney for Japan 6.7.72
Gascoyne	Left Sydney for Taiwan 6.7.72
Queenborough	Left Sydney for Hong Kong 12.5.75

Miscellaneous

SDB 1321	1972
Kara Kara	Base Ship sunk as target 30.1.73
Paluma	Sold Commercial 1974
Otter	Sold as fishing boat 1974
Tortoise and *Turtle*	Sold Commercial 1975
Bronzewing (tug)	Awaiting Disposal
Tug 503	To PNGDF 1974

PENNANT LIST

Aircraft Carrier

21	Melbourne

Submarines

57	Oxley
59	Otway
60	Onslow
61	Orion
62	Otama
70	Ovens

Destroyers

08	Vendetta
11	Vampire
38	Perth
39	Hobart
41	Brisbane

Frigates

45	Yarra
46	Parramatta
48	Stuart
49	Derwent
50	Swan
53	Torrens

Minehunters

1102	Snipe
1121	Curlew

Minesweeper (Coastal)

1183	Ibis

Training Ship

154	Duchess

Large Patrol Craft

81	Acute
82	Adroit
83	Advance
87	Ardent
89	Assail
90	Attack
91	Aware
97	Barbette
98	Barricade
99	Bombard
100	Buccaneer
101	Bayonet

Amphibious Heavy Lift Ship

L50	Tobruk

Landing Craft

L126	Balikpapan
L127	Brunei
L128	Labuan
L129	Tarakan
L130	Wewak
L133	Betano

General Purpose Ships

A244	Banks
A247	Bass

Survey Ships

GS 73	Moresby
GOR266	Diamantina
GS312	Flinders
GDR314	Kimbla

Fleet Tanker

O195	Supply

Destroyer Tender

D215	Stalwart

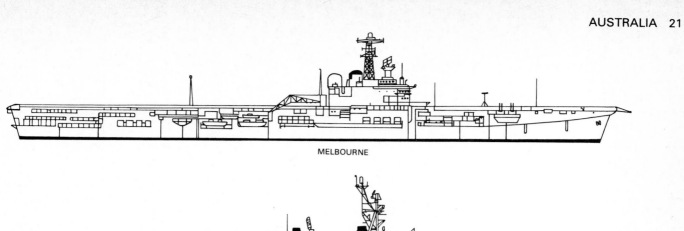

MELBOURNE

"PERTH" Class

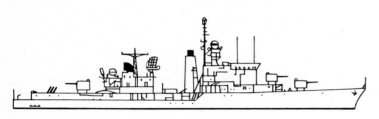

VAMPIRE and VENDETTA

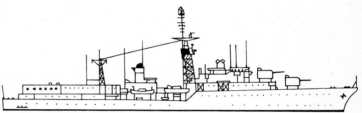

DUCHESS

PARRAMATTA and YARRA

SWAN and TORRENS

DERWENT and STUART

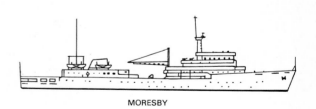

MORESBY

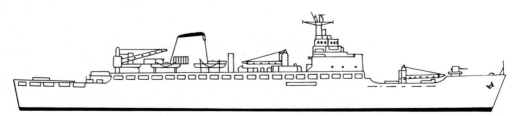

STALWART

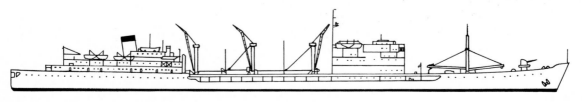

SUPPLY

AIRCRAFT CARRIER

1 MODIFIED "MAJESTIC" CLASS

Name	No.	Builders	Laid down	Launched	Commissioned
MELBOURNE (ex-Majestic)	21	Vickers-Armstrong, Barrow-in-Furness	15 Apr 1943	28 Feb 1945	28 Oct 1955

Displacement, tons: 16 000 standard; 19 966 full load
Length, feet (metres): 650·0 (198·1) wl; 701·5 (213·8) oa
Beam, feet (metres): 80·2 (24·5) hull
Draught, feet (metres): 25·5 (7·8)
Width, feet (metres): 80·0 (24·4) flight deck
126·0 (38·4) oa including 6 deg angled deck and mirrors
Hangar, feet (metres): 444 × 52 × 17·5 (135·3 × 15·8 × 5·3)
Aircraft: A mix of A4G Skyhawk jet fighters, S2E Tracker A/S aircraft and Sea King Mk 50 A/S helicopters (see Aircraft notes)
Guns: 12—40 mm (4 twin, 4 single) Bofors
Boilers: 4 Admiralty 3-drum type
Main engines: Parsons single reduction geared turbines; 2 shafts; 42 000 shp
Speed, knots: 23
Range, miles: 12 000 at 14 knots; 6 200 àt 23 knots
Complement: 1 335 (includes 347 Carrier Air Group personnel); 1 070 (75 officers and 995 sailors) as Flagship

At the end of the Second World War, when she was still incomplete, work on this ship was brought to a standstill pending a decision as to future naval requirements. When full-scale work was resumed during 1949-55, and after her design had been re-cast several times, she underwent reconstruction and modernisation in Great Britain, including the fitting of the angled deck, steam catapult and mirror deck landing sights, and was transferred to the RAN on completion. She was commissioned and renamed at Barrow-in-Furness on 28 Oct 1955, sailed from Portsmouth on 5 Mar 1956, and arrived at Fremantle, Australia, on 23 April 1956. She became flagship of the Royal Australian Navy at Sydney on 14 May 1956. She cost £A8 309 000.

Aircraft: The aircraft complement formerly comprised 8 Sea Venom Mk 53 jet fighters, 16 Gannet Mk 1 turbo-prop A/S aircraft and 2 Sycamore helicopters. The complement changed twice before 1967 to 10 Sea Venoms, 10 Gannets, 2 Sycamores and finally 4 Sea Venoms, 6 Gannets and 10 Wessex Mk 31 A/S helicopters. Fourteen S2E Tracker A/S aircraft, eight A4G Skyhawk fighter/strike aircraft and two TA4G Skyhawk trainer aircraft were delivered from the USA in 1967 at a cost of about $A46,000,000, Squadrons first embarked in Melbourne in 1969. Another eight A4G and two TA4G Skyhawk aircraft were delivered in 1971. HS-817 Squadron recommissioned in February 1976 with Sea King Mk 50 A/S helicopters. A general purpose complement embarked in Melbourne is 8 Skyhawks, 4 Trackers and 5 Sea Kings which can be varied to meet various other roles.

Electronics: Plessey tactical displays.

Modernisation: Melbourne completed her extended refit during 1969 at a cost of over $A8 750 000 to enable her to operate with S2E Tracker and A4G Skyhawk aircraft, and to improve habitability. In 1971 the catapult was rebuilt and a bridle-catcher fitted, and the flight deck was strengthened. Under refit from November 1972 to July 1973.
On completion of a major refit in 1976 it was announced that Melbourne could remain operational until 1985.

Radar: Search: Philips LWO series early warning and associated height finders for aircraft direction.
Tactical: Type 293 Target Indication and surface warning.
EW: Electronic intelligence and warfare equipment also fitted.
Carrier controlled approach Radar. (Dome on island).

MELBOURNE (with DERWENT and VENDETTA entering Sydney)   1976, Royal Australian Navy

MELBOURNE   1974, John Mortimer

MELBOURNE   1974, Royal Australian Navy

DESTROYERS

3 "PERTH" CLASS (DDGs)

Name	No.	Builders	Laid down	Launched	Commissioned
BRISBANE	41	Defoe Shipbuilding Co, Bay City, Mich.	15 Feb 1965	5 May 1966	16 Dec 1967
HOBART	39	Defoe Shipbuilding Co, Bay City, Mich.	26 Oct 1962	9 Jan 1964	18 Dec 1965
PERTH	38	Defoe Shipbuilding Co, Bay City, Mich.	21 Sep 1962	26 Sep 1963	17 July 1965

Displacement, tons: 3 370 standard; 4 618 full load
Length, feet (metres): 431·0 *(131·4)* wl; 437·0 *(132·2)* oa
Beam, feet (metres): 47·1 *(14·3)*
Draught, feet (metres): 20·1 *(6·1)*
Missile launchers: 1 single for Tartar (see Modernisation note)
Guns: 2—5 in *(127 mm)* 54 cal. dp, single-mount
A/S weapons: 2 single launchers for Ikara system
Torpedo tubes: 6 (2 triple) for A/S torpedoes
Main engines: 2 GE double reduction turbines, 2 shafts; 70 000 shp
Boilers: 4 Foster Wheeler "D" type, 1 200 psi; 950°F
Speed, knots: 35
Range, miles: 4 500 at 15 knots; 2 000 at 30 knots
Complement: 333 (21 officers, 312 sailors)

On 6 Jan 1962, in Washington, US defence representatives and Australian military officials (on behalf of the Royal Australian Navy) and executives of the Defoe Shipbuilding Company, of Bay City, Michigan, signed a $A25 726 700 contract for the construction of two guided-missile destroyers (shipbuilding cost only). On 22 Jan 1963 it was announced by the Navy Minister in Canberra, Australia, that a third guided-missile destroyer was to be built in USA for Australia. The first of their kind for the Australian Navy, they constitute the 1st Destroyer Squadron, RAN. All three ships saw action off Vietnam where they served with the US 7th fleet.
These are technically of "Charles F. Adams" class.
Cost: Original estimate $A12 800 000 to $A14 000 000 each (with missiles and electronics $A40 000 000 each). The total cost of *Perth* was reported to be $A50 000 000.

Design: Generally similar to the US "Charles F. Adams" class, but they differ by the addition of a broad deckhouse between the funnels enclosing the Ikara anti-submarine torpedo-carrying missile system, and the mounting of a single-arm launcher, instead of a twin, for the Tartar surface-to-air guided missiles. They have a new hull design with aluminium super-structures. The most recent habitability improvements have been incorporated into their construction, including air-conditioning of all living spaces.

Modernisation: *Perth* started a modernisation at the Long Beach Naval Shipyard on 3 Sep 1974, completing 2 Jan 1975. The work included the installation of a Naval Combat Data System, updating of the Tartar missile fire control system, replacing 5-inch gun mounts and modernising radars. *Hobart* and *Brisbane* will receive similar modernisations in Australia at Garden Island Dockyard. *Hobart's* modernisation started in Nov 1976 and *Brisbane's* will start late-1977. *Hobart's* gun mounts were replaced in the USA in 1972 and *Brisbane's* replacement was completed at Garden Island in Oct 1976. This gunnery alteration includes deletion of local surface fire control with increased reliability.

Radar: Three dimensional: SPS 52.
Air and surface search: SPS 10 and 40.

Sonar: SQS 23F; AN/UQC 1D/E; Type 189.

Weapons: Ikara launcher temporarily removed from *Perth* after modification in USA.

BRISBANE   *1976, Royal Australian Navy*

PERTH   *1976, Royal Australian Navy*

BRISBANE   *11/1975, John Mortimer*

3 "DARING" CLASS (DD)

Name	No.	Builders	Laid down	Launched	Commissioned
VAMPIRE	11	Cockatoo Island Dockyard, Sydney	1 July 1952	27 Oct 1956	23 June1959
VENDETTA	08	HMA Naval Dockyard, Williamstown	4 July 1949	3 May 1954	26 Nov 1958
DUCHESS	154	John I. Thornycroft & Co, Southampton	2 July 1948	9 Apr 1951	23 Oct 1952

Displacement, tons: 2 800 standard; 3 600 full load; 3 580 (Duchess)
Length, feet (metres): 366 (111·3) pp; 388·5 (118·4) oa
Beam, feet (metres): 43 (13·1)
Draught, feet (metres): 12·8 (3·9)
Guns: 6—4·5 in (115 mm) in 3 twin turrets, two forward and one aft (4 forward guns only in Duchess); 6—40 mm (2—40 mm in Duchess)
A/S weapons: 1 3-barrelled Limbo mortar (not Duchess) (see Design notes)
Main engines: English Electric geared turbines; 2 shafts; 54 000 shp
Boilers: 2 Foster Wheeler; 650 psi; 850°F
Speed, knots: 30·5
Range, miles: 3 700 at 20 knots; 3 000 at 20 knots (Duchess)
Oil fuel, tons: 584
Complement: 320 (14 officers, 306 sailors); 260 (Duchess, including Trainees)

Vampire and Vendetta, constitute the 2nd Destroyer Squadron, RAN, and are the largest destroyers ever built in Australia. They were ordered in 1946. Their sister ship, Voyager, the prototype of the class, collided with the aircraft carrier Melbourne and sank off the southern coast of New South Wales on the night of 10 Feb 1964. She was replaced by the British destroyer Duchess, lent to Australia by the United Kingdom for four years on 8 May 1964, later extended to 1971 and purchased by RAN in 1972.
Four large destroyers of this type were originally projected, to have been named after the Royal Australian Navy's famous "Scrap Iron Flotilla" of destroyers during the Second World War, but Waterhen was cancelled in 1954.

Design: Vampire and Vendetta were of similar design, including all welded construction, to that of the "Daring" class, built in Great Britain, but were modified to suit Australian conditions and have "Limbo" instead of "Squid" anti-submarine mortars. The superstructure is of light alloy, instead of steel, to reduce weight.

Modernisation: Vampire completed in Dec 1971. Vendetta completed May 1973. The $A20 million programme for both ships included new Mk 22 fire-control systems, new LW-02 air-warning and navigation radars, new action-information centre, modernised communications, fitting modernised turrets, improved habitability, the fitting of an enclosed bridge and new funnels. The work was carried out by Williamstown Dockyard. These alterations afford an interesting comparison with the Peruvian "Darings" (ex-Decoy and Diana) with their eight Exocet SSMs and rebuilt forefunnel and radar.

Radar: Philips LW-02 early warning, 8GR301 and M22 (not Duchess).

Note: Duchess has been converted for training purposes, including the removal of X-turret and Squid to make way for new upper-deck classrooms. She retains her forward battery, radar (Type 293 and I-band fire control) and sonar (in maintenance). Completed November 1974.

Sonar: Types 162, 170, 174 and 185 (Vendetta and Vampire). Types 147, 162, 164, 174 and 185 (Duchess).

VAMPIRE — 1974, Graeme Andrews

DUCHESS — 1976, Royal Australian Navy

VENDETTA — 1976, Royal Australian Navy

VAMPIRE — 1976, Royal Australian Navy

FRIGATES
0 + 2 + 1(?) US "FFG 7" CLASS

Displacement, tons: 3 605 full load
Length, feet (metres): 445 *(135·6)*
Beam, feet (metres): 45 *(13·7)*
Draught, feet (metres): 24·5 *(7·5)*
Missile launcher: 1 Mk 13 Mod 4 (US) for Standard/Harpoon missiles
Gun: 1—76 mm OTO-Melara; provision for point defence weapon system
A/S weapons: 2 helicopters (to be selected); 6 (2 triple) Mk 32 torpedo tubes
Main engines: 2 GE LM 2 500 gas turbines; 40 000 shp; 1 shaft (cp propeller)
Speed: 28+
Range, miles: 4 500 at 20 knots
Complement: 185/190

Two ordered from USA in Feb 1976 for delivery 1981. Consideration being given to order for a third.

Fire Control: Mk 92/STIR gun and missile control.

Radar: Long range air search and early warning: AN SPS 49. Search and navigation: AN SPS 55.

Sonar: Australian Mulloka

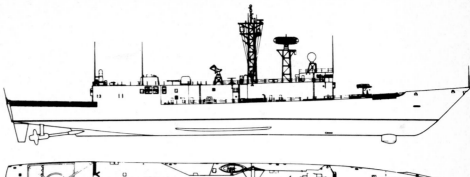

"FFG 7" Class   *1976, Royal Australian Navy*

6 "RIVER" CLASS

Name	No.	Builders	Laid down	Launched	Commissioned
YARRA	45	Williamstown Naval Dockyard, Melbourne	9 Apr 1957	30 Sep 1958	27 July 1961
PARRAMATTA	46	Cockatoo Island Dockyard, Sydney	3 Jan 1957	31 Jan 1959	4 July 1961
STUART	48	Cockatoo Island Dockyard, Sydney	20 Mar 1959	8 Apr 1961	28 June1963
DERWENT	49	Williamstown Naval Dockyard, Melbourne	16 June1958	17 Apr 1961	30 Apr 1964
SWAN	50	Williamstown Naval Dockyard, Melbourne	18 Aug 1965	16 Dec 1967	20 Jan 1970
TORRENS	53	Cockatoo Island Dockyard, Sydney	18 Aug 1965	28 Sep 1968	19 Jan 1971

Displacement, tons: 2 100 standard; 2 700 full load
Length, feet (metres): 360·0 *(109·7)* pp; 370·0 *(112·8)* oa
Beam, feet (metres): 41·0 *(12·5)*
Draught, feet (metres): 17·3 *(5·3)*
Missile launchers: 1 quadruple for Seacat
Guns: 2—4·5 in *(115 mm)*
A/S weapons: 1 launcher for Ikara system; 1 Limbo 3-barrelled DC mortar
Main engines: 2 double reduction geared turbines; 2 shafts; 30 000 shp
Boilers: 2 Babcock & Wilcox; 550 psi; 850°F
Speed, knots: 30
Range, miles: 3 400 at 12 knots
Complement: 247 (13 officers, 234 sailors) in *Swan* and *Torrens;* 250 (13 officers, 237 sailors) in other four ships

The design of the first four is basically similar to that of British "Type 12", the last pair to that of the "Leander" frigates. All are modified by the Royal Australian Navy to incorporate improvements in equipment and habitability. *Stuart* was the first ship fitted with the Ikara anti-submarine guided missile; (trial ship for the system). *Derwent* was the first RAN ship to be fitted with Seacat. The variable depth sonar has been removed from *Derwent* and *Stuart.* Note difference in silhouette between *Swan* and *Torrens* and the earlier ships of the class, the former pair having a straight-run upper deck.

Modernisation: *Parramatta, Stuart* and *Derwent* to begin half-life refits and modernisation in 1977 at Williamstown. These will include improved accommodation consequent on reduction in complement, installation of M22 gunnery direction system, the fitting of Australian Mulloka sonar (provided the set goes into production), the conversion of the boilers to burn diesel fuel, installation of Mk 32 torpedo tubes in lieu of Limbo mortar and new navigation radar. *Yarra* has been fitted with Mulloka sonar, trials beginning in April 1975. In Oct 1976 she started a half-life refit at Cockatoo Island Dockyard and is due to rejoin the Fleet in Dec 1977.
The whole modernisation programme is due to be completed by 1981.

Radar: Search: All ships fitted with Philips LWO series of C Band early warning radars. Type 293 combined air and surface warning, except *Swan* and *Torrens* which have Philips/HSA I Band radar. Fire Control: MRS 3 or HSA systems, I Band radar.

Sonar: Types 162, 170, 177m, 185 and 189 *(Swan and Torrens)*

YARRA (PARRAMATTA similar)   *11/1975, John Mortimer*

STUART (DERWENT similar)   *10/1976, Graeme Andrews*

SWAN (TORRENS similar)   *1976, Michael D. J. Lennon*

SUBMARINES

6 "OXLEY" CLASS (BRITISH "OBERON" CLASS)

Name	No.	Builders	Laid down	Launched	Commissioned
ONSLOW	60	Scotts' Shipbuilding & Eng Co Ltd, Greenock	4 Dec 1967	3 Dec 1968	22 Dec 1969
OTWAY	59	Scotts' Shipbuilding & Eng Co Ltd, Greenock	29 June1965	29 Nov 1966	23 Apr 1968
OVENS	70	Scotts' Shipbuilding & Eng Co Ltd, Greenock	17 June1966	4 Dec 1967	18 Apr 1969
OXLEY	57	Scotts' Shipbuilding & Eng Co Ltd, Greenock	2 July 1964	24 Sep 1965	18 Apr 1967
ORION	61	Scotts' Shipbuilding & Eng Co Ltd, Greenock	6 Oct 1972	16 Sep 1974	May 1977
OTAMA	62	Scotts' Shipbuilding & Eng Co Ltd, Greenock	25 May 1973	3 Dec 1975	late 1977

Displacement, tons: 1 610 standard; 2 196 surfaced; 2 417 dived
Length, feet (metres): 241 (73·5) pp; 295·5 (90·1) oa
Beam, feet (metres): 26·5 (8·1)
Draught, feet (metres): 18 (5·5)
Torpedo tubes: 8—21 in (533 mm) (6 bow, 2 stern)
Main machinery: 2 Admiralty Standard Range Diesels; 3 600 bhp; 2 shafts; 2 electric motors; 6 000 shp; electric drive
Speed, knots: 16 surfaced; 18 dived
Oil fuel, tons: 300
Range, miles: 12 000 at 10 knots
Complement: 62 (7 officers, 55 sailors)

It was announced by the Minister for the Navy on 22 Jan 1963 that four submarines of the "Oberon" class were to be built in British shipyards under Admiralty supervision at an overall cost of £A5 000 000 each. These were to constitute the 1st Submarine Squadron RAN based at HMAS Platypus, Neutral Bay, Sydney. Subsequently two more were ordered in October 1971 for delivery in 1975-76 later extended to 1977.

Dock: Slave Dock (Sydney) was first used in 1974, allowing submarine dockings to be carried out without occupying graving docks.

Modernisation: All submarines are to be fitted with a passive-ranging sonar built by Sperry Corporation, a new attack sonar from Krupp-Atlas of Germany and an advanced fire control system being developed with Singer-Librascope Corporation. Advanced torpedoes are to be acquired together with, possibly, Harpoon missiles from the USA. In addition modern radar is being fitted in all submarines.

Names: *Oxley* and *Otway* are named after two earlier RAN submarines, completed in 1927. *Otama* is the Queensland aboriginal word for Dolphin, *Onslow* is a town in Western Australia, *Ovens* was an early explorer and *Orion* is named after the constellation.

R.N. Squadron: The last unit of the Fourth Submarine Squadron of the Royal Navy, *Trump,* was withdrawn from Balmoral, Sydney in Jan 1969.
Odin arrived in Australian waters in Dec 1972 for attachment to the RAN, leaving on 16 Sep 1975.

Radar: Type 1006

Sonar: Attack: Type 187C
Intercept: Type 197.
Torpedo warning: Type 719
Long range Passive Search: Type 2007

OXLEY

1975, Royal Australian Navy

OVENS

1976, John Mortimer

MINE WARFARE SHIPS

Note: A new class of MCMV is planned (see Naval Procurement notes on lead page)

3 BRITISH "TON" CLASS (MODIFIED)

Name	No.	Builders	Laid down	Launched	Commissioned
CURLEW (ex-HMS *Chediston*)	1121	Montrose SY	1952	6 Oct 1953	1954
IBIS (ex-HMS *Singleton*)	1183	Montrose SY	1952	23 Nov 1955	1956
SNIPE (ex-HMS *Alcaston*)	1102	Thornycroft	1952	5 Jan 1953	1953

Displacement, tons: 375 standard; 445 full load
Dimensions, feet (metres): 140 pp; 152 oa × 28·8 × 8·2 *(42·7; 46·4 × 8·8 × 2·5)*
Guns: *Ibis* 2—40 mm; *Curlew* and *Snipe* 1—40 mm
Main engines: Napier Deltic diesels; 2 shafts; 3 000 bhp = 16 knots
Range, miles: 2 300 at 13 knots; 3 500 at 8 knots
Complement: *Ibis* 34 (4 officers; 30 sailors); *Curlew* and *Snipe* 38 (3 officers, 35 sailors)

"Ton" class coastal minesweepers. Six purchased from the United Kingdom in 1961, and modified in British Dockyards to suit Australian conditions. Turned over to the Royal Australian Navy, commissioned and re-named on 21 Aug, 7 Sep and 11 Sep 1962, respectively. Mirlees diesels were replaced by Napier Deltic, and ships air-conditioned and fitted with stabilisers. Sailed from Portsmouth to Australia on 1 Oct 1962. Constitute the 1st Mine Countermeasures Squadron. *Curlew* and *Snipe* have been converted into minehunters—*Curlew* 26 June 1967 to 13 Dec 1968 and *Snipe* 10 Apr 1969 to 18 Dec 1970.

Radar: Type 975 I-band.

Sonar: Type 193 (except *Ibis*)

SNIPE

8/1976, Graeme Andrews

LIGHT FORCES

Note: A new class is planned to complement and eventually replace the "Attack" class (see Naval Procurement notes on lead page).

12 "ATTACK" CLASS (LARGE PATROL CRAFT)

Name	No.	Builders	Laid down	Launched	Commissioned
ACUTE	81	Evans Deakin Ltd.	April 1967	26 Aug 1967	26 April 1968
ADROIT	82	Evans Deakin Ltd.	Aug 1967	3 Feb 1968	17 Aug 1968
ADVANCE	83	Walkers Ltd.	Mar 1967	16 Aug 1967	24 Jan 1968
ARDENT	87	Evans Deakin Ltd.	Oct 1967	27 April 1968	26 Oct 1968
ASSAIL	89	Evans Deakin Ltd.	Aug 1967	18 Nov 1967	12 July 1968
ATTACK	90	Evans Deakin Ltd.	Sep 1966	8 April 1967	17 Nov 1967
AWARE	91	Evans Deakin Ltd.	July 1967	7 Oct 1967	21 June 1968
BARBETTE	97	Walkers Ltd.	Nov 1967	10 April 1968	16 Aug 1968
BARRICADE	98	Evans Deakin Ltd.	Dec 1967	29 June 1968	26 Oct 1968
BOMBARD	99	Walkers Ltd.	April 1968	6 July 1968	5 Nov 1968
BUCCANEER	100	Evans Deakin Ltd.	June 1968	14 Sep 1968	11 Jan 1969
BAYONET	101	Walkers Ltd.	Oct 1968	6 Nov 1968	22 Feb 1969

Displacement, tons: 146 full load
Dimensions, feet (metres): 107·5 oa × 20 × 7·3 *(32·8 × 6·1 × 2·2)*
Guns: 1—40 mm; 2 medium MG (no guns in *Aware*)
Main engines: Paxman 16 YJCM Diesels 3 500 hp; 2 shafts = 21-24 knots
Range, miles: 1 220 at 13 knots
Complement: 19 (3 officers, 16 sailors)

Steel construction. Ordered in Nov 1965. First vessel was originally scheduled for delivery in Aug 1966, but was not launched until Mar 1967. Cost $A800 000 each. *Aware* does not carry armament but all have been employed in fishery protection and search and rescue off North Australia. These craft are expected to be replaced by a new class by 1980.

Disposals: *Bandolier* transferred to Indonesia after refit 16 Nov 1973. *Archer* transferred 21 Oct 1974. *Aitape, Ladava, Lae, Madang, Samarai* transferred to Papua-New Guinea Defence Force 16 Sep 1975.

Darwin Cyclone: On 25 Dec 1974 *Arrow* was lost during Cyclone Tracy at Darwin. *Attack* was beached and badly damaged at the same time but was salved and towed to Cairns for repairs.

Radar: Type 975 I band to be replaced by RM916

BUCCANEER

10/1976, Graeme Andrews

OCEANOGRAPHIC AND SURVEY SHIPS

1 NEW CONSTRUCTION

Name	No.	Builders	Laid down	Launched	Commissioned
COOK	291	Williamstown Naval DY	30 Sep 1974	1976	?

Displacement, tons: 1 910 standard; 2 650 full load
Length, feet (metres): 317·5 *(91·2)*
Beam, feet (metres): 44·0 *(13·4)*
Draught, feet (metres): 15·1 *(4·6)*
Main engines: Diesels; 2 shafts; 3 400 bhp
Speed, knots: 17
Oil fuel, tons: 640
Range, miles: 11 000 at 14 knots
Complement: 150 including 13 scientists

Intended to replace HMAS *Diamantina*. She will have dual hydrographic and oceanographic roles. The after part of the ship will contain research equipment and facilities. Accommodation for 13 scientists. One survey launch. Specialised oceanographic gear will include a data logger, 3 oceanographic winches, a stabilised narrow-beam echo sounder, wet laboratory, dry laboratory, magnetometer and gravimeter. No helicopter.

Radar: TM 829.

Sonar: Simrad SU2.

COOK

1972, Official, revised artist's impression

Name	No.	Builders	Laid down	Launched	Commissioned
MORESBY	73	State Dockyard, Newcastle NSW	June 1961	7 Sep 1963	6 Mar 1964

Displacement, tons: 1 714 standard; 2 351 full load
Length, feet (metres): 284·5 (86·7) pp; 314·0 (95·7) oa
Beam, feet (metres): 42·0 (12·8)
Draught, feet (metres): 15·0 (4·6)
Aircraft: 1 Bell 206B-1 (Kiowa) helicopter
Guns: 2—40 mm Bofors (single) (removed)
Main engines: Diesel-electric; 3 diesels; 3 990 bhp; 2 electric
  motors; 2 shafts; 5 000 shp = 19 knots
Complement: 135

The Royal Australian Navy's first specifically designed survey
ship. Built at a cost of £A2 000 000 ($A4 000 000). Guns are not
currently embarked.

Refit: During refit from 13 Aug 1973 to 18 Jan 1974 *Moresby's*
funnel was heightened, her 40 mm guns removed and an
exhaust outlet fitted on her forecastle.

Radar: TM 829

Sonar: Simrad SU2.

MORESBY (new funnel cap—no guns)   1974, Royal Australian Navy

Name	No.	Builders	Laid down	Launched	Commissioned
DIAMANTINA	266 (ex-F 377)	Walkers Ltd, Maryborough, Queensland	12 Apr 1943	6 Apr 1944	27 Apr 1945

Displacement, tons: 1 340 standard; 2 127 full load
Length, feet (metres): 283 (86·3) pp; 301·3 (91·8) oa
Beam, feet (metres): 36·7 (11·2)
Draught, feet (metres): 12·5 (3·8)
Gun: 1—40 mm
Main engines: Triple expansion 5 500 ihp; 2 shafts
Boilers: 2 Admiralty 3-drum
Speed, knots: 19·5
Range, miles: 7 700 at 12 knots
Complement: 125 (6 officers, 119 sailors)

Frigate converted in 1959-60 for survey and completed conversion for oceanographic research in June 1969. The conversion
included the provision of special laboratories. Sister ship *Lachlan* was sold to the Royal New Zealand Navy, and was finally
paid off in 1975. *Diamantina* is to be replaced by *Cook* in 1978.

Armament: The two 4-inch guns and two "Squid" A/S mortars
in "B" position were removed.

Radar: Type 975

Sonar: Type 144

DIAMANTINA   1974, John Mortimer

Name	No.	Builders	Laid down	Launched	Commissioned
FLINDERS	312	Williamstown Naval Dockyard	11 June1971	29 July 1972	27 Apr 1973

Displacement, tons: 750
Dimensions, feet (metres): 161 × 33 × 12 (49·1 × 10 × 3·7)
Main engines: 2 Paxman Ventura Diesels, bhp 1 680
Speed, knots: 13·5
Range, miles: 5 000 at 9 knots
Complement: 38 (4 officers, 34 sailors)

Similar in design to *Atyimba* built for the Philippines, she
replaced *Paluma* in April 1973, the latter having been running
steadily since her conversion from stores tender in 1959. *Flinders* is based at Cairns, with her primary responsibility in the
Barrier Reef area.

Radar: TM 829.

Sonar: Simrad SU2.

FLINDERS   1976, Royal Australian Navy

Name	No.	Builders	Laid down	Launched	Commissioned
KIMBLA	A314	Walkers Ltd, Maryborough, Queensland	4 Nov 1953	23 Mar 1955	26 Mar 1956

Displacement, tons: 762 standard; 1 021 full load
Dimensions, feet (metres): 150 pp; 179 oa × 32 × 12 (45·8; 54·6
  × 9·8 × 3·7)
Main engines: Triple expansion; 1 shaft; 350 ihp
Speed, knots: 9·5
Complement: 40 (4 officers, 36 sailors)

Built as a boom defence vessel. Converted to trials vessel in
1959. Guns were removed (1—40 mm; 2—20 mm). Expected to
continue in service until about 1980.

Radar: Type 975.

Sonar: Simrad SU2.

KIMBLA   1976, Royal Australian Navy

SERVICE FORCES

1 DESTROYER TENDER

Name STALWART	No. 215

Displacement, tons: 10 000 standard; 15 500 full load
Length, feet (metres): 515·5 *(157·1)* oa
Beam, feet (metres): 67·5 *(20·6)*
Draught, feet (metres): 29·5 *(9·0)*
Missiles: Provision for Seacat
Guns: 4—40 mm (2 twin)
Main engines: 2 Scott-Sulzer 6-cyl diesels 2 shafts; 14 400 bhp
Speed, knots: 20+
Range, miles: 12 000 at 12 knots
Complement: 396 (23 officers and 373 sailors)

Largest naval vessel designed and built in Australia. Ordered on 11 Sep 1963. Designed to maintain destroyers and frigates, and advanced weapons systems, including guided missiles. She has a helicopter flight deck and a hangar, being capable of operating two Wossex 31B or two Sea King Mk 50 helicopters. High standard of habitability. Formerly rated as Escort Maintenance Ship. Redesignated Destroyer Tender in 1968. Cost officially estimated at just under $A15 000 000.

Builders Cockatoo Island DY, Sydney	Laid down June 1964	Launched 7 Oct 1966	Commissioned 9 Feb 1968

STALWART   *1976, Royal Australian Navy*

1 FLEET TANKER

Name SUPPLY (ex-*Tide Austral*)	No. 195

Displacement, tons: 15 000 standard; 25 941 full load
Measurement, tons: 17 600 deadweight; 11 200 gross
Dimensions, feet (metres): 550 pp; 583 oa × 71 × 32 *(167·8; 177·8 × 21·7 × 9·8)*
Guns: 6—40 mm (2 twin, 2 single)
Main engines: Double reduction geared turbines; 15 000 shp
Speed, knots: 17·25
Range, miles: 8 500 at 13 knots
Complement: 205

British "Tide" Class. Lent to Great Britain until 1 Sep 1962, when *Tide Austral* was re-named HMAS *Supply* and commissioned in the Royal Australian Navy at Portsmouth 15 Aug 1962. Sailed for Australia 1 Oct 1962. Bridge was rebuilt in 1973-74.

Radar: Type 975 (to be replaced by RM 16).

Replacement: An underway replenishment ship of a new class is planned for 1980. Consideration is being given to the construction of a second ship of the class.

Builders Harland and Wolff, Belfast	Laid down 5 Aug 1952	Launched 1 Sep 1954	Commissioned Mar 1955

SUPPLY   *1976, Royal Australian Navy*

AMPHIBIOUS FORCES

0 + 1 HEAVY LIFT SHIP

TOBRUK L50

Displacement, tons: 6 000
Length, feet (metres): 425 *(300)* approx
Aircraft: Wessex 31B helicopters
Guns: Possibly 2—40 mm
Main engines: 2 diesels = 17 knots (?)
Complement: 130 approx

In Aug 1976 it was announced that tenders had been called for for this ship, planned to replace the lift capability lost when *Sydney* paid off in 1973. The design is based on the British "Sir Bedivere" class, has a bow door and stern ramp and considerable helicopter facilities. A pontoon bridge will be carried. Full capacity, in addition to a quantity of helicopters, will be a squadron of Leopard tanks, many wheeled vehicles and 300-500 troops. Full communication fit and minor hospital facilities will be fitted. Work is planned to start in mid-1977 with completion in 1980.

TOBRUK   *1976, Royal Australian Navy Drawing*

6 LANDING CRAFT (HEAVY) (LCH)

Name	No.	Builders	Laid down	Launched	Commissioned
BALIKPAPAN	L 126	Walkers Ltd.	May 1971	15 Aug 1971	8 Dec 1971
BRUNEI	L 127	Walkers Ltd.	July 1971	15 Oct 1971	5 Jan 1973
LABUAN	L 128	Walkers Ltd.	Oct 1971	29 Dec 1971	9 Mar 1973
TARAKAN	L 129	Walkers Ltd.	Dec 1971	16 Mar 1972	15 June 1973
WEWAK	L 130	Walkers Ltd.	Mar 1972	18 May 1972	10 Aug 1973
BETANO	L 133	Walkers Ltd.	Sep 1972	5 Dec 1972	8 Feb 1974

Displacement, tons: 310 light; 503 full load
Dimensions, feet (metres): 146 × 33 × 6·5 *(44·5 × 10·1 × 1·9)*
Guns: 2—0·5 in MG
Main engines: 2 GM Diesels; twin screw = 10 knots
Range, miles: 3 000 at 10 knots
Complement: 13 (2 officers, 11 sailors)

Originally this class was ordered for the Army with whom *Balikpapan* remained until June 1974 being commissioned for naval service on 27 Sep 1974. All now transferred to RAN. Can carry three medium tanks.

PNGDF: *Buna* and *Salamaua* transferred to Papua-New Guinea Defence Force in Nov 1974.

Radar: Decca 101 (to be replaced by RM 916).

BALIKPAPAN   *1976, Royal Australian Navy*

GENERAL PURPOSE VESSELS

Name	No.	Builders	Commissioned
BANKS	A 244	Walkers, Maryborough	16 Feb 1960
BASS	A 247	Walkers, Maryborough	25 May 1960

Displacement, tons: 207 standard; 255 and 260 full load respectively
Dimensions, feet (metres): 90 pp; 101 oa × 22 × 8 *(27·5; 30·8 × 6·7 × 2·4)*
Main engines: Diesels; speed = 10 knots
Complement: 14 (2 officers, 12 sailors)

"Explorer" class. Of all steel construction. *Banks* was fitted for fishery surveillance and *Bass* for surveying, but both are used for other duties, including reserve training. *Banks* based in Port Adelaide, *Bass* in Hobart. Minor differences—*Bass* has a higher flying bridge with consequent raising of her radar pedestal. Ventilators differ.

BASS   *1976, Royal Australian Navy*

TORPEDO RECOVERY VESSELS

TRV 801   802   803

Displacement, tons: 91·6
Dimensions, feet (metres): 88·5 × 20·9 × 4·5 *(27 × 6·4 × 1·4)*
Main engines: 3 GM diesels; 890 hp; triple screws = 13 knots.
Complement: 9 (1 officer, 8 men)

All built at Williamstown—completed between Jan 1970 and Apr 1971. TRV 802 used as diving tender.

TRV 803   *11/1976, Graeme Andrews*

AUSTRALIA 31

DIVING TENDERS

Name	No.	Builders	Launched
PORPOISE (ex-HMS *Neasham*)	Y280	White, Cowes	14 Mar 1956
SEAL (ex-HMS *Wintringham*)	Y298	White, Cowes	24 May 1955

Displacement, tons: 120 standard; 159 full load
Dimensions, feet (metres): 100 pp × 22 × 5·8 *(30·7 × 6·7 × 1·8)*
Main engines: 2 Paxman diesels; 1 100 bhp = 14 knots
Range, miles: 2 000 at 9 knots; 1 500 at 12 knots
Complement: 7 (can accommodate 14 divers)

Purchased from the Royal Navy in 1966-67, these ex-inshore Minesweepers were converted to Diving Tenders and attached to the Diving School at Sydney. HMS *Popham* (Vospers, launched 11 Jan 1955) also purchased and renamed *Otter* but not converted and was sold in 1974. *Porpoise* and *Seal* carry recompression chambers.

PORPOISE *7/1976, Graeme Andrews*

TUGS

BRONZEWING DT 932

Built in 1946—of 132 tons gross. Laid up and awaiting disposal.

501 **502** **504**

Displacement, tons: 47·5
Dimensions, feet (metres): 50 × 15 × — *(15·4 × 4·6 × —)*
Main engines: 2 GM Diesels; 340 bhp = 8-9 knots
Complement: 3

First pair with bipod mast funnel built by Stannard Bros, Sydney in 1969 and second pair with conventional funnel by Perrin Engineering, Brisbane in 1972.

Transfer: Tug 503 transferred to Papua New Guinea in 1974.

504 *1976, Royal Australian Navy*

2 Ex-US ARMY TYPE

SARDIUS TB9 — TB1536

Of 29 tons GRT (app 60 tons, full load), 45 ft long with 240 hp Hercules diesel, capable of 10 knots. Complement 4. *Sardius* employed in Sydney as ammunition-lighter tug, TB1536 at HMAS *Cerberus* (Victoria). Wooden hulled.

SARDIUS

MISCELLANEOUS

1 TANK CLEANING VESSEL

Name	No.	Builders	Launched
COLAC	—	Mort's Dock Sydney	13 Aug 1941

Originally 1 025 ton "Bathurst" class minesweeper. Now a dumb craft, painted black, based in Sydney. Sister ship *Castlemaine,* given by D of D as museum ship to Melbourne in 1973.

1 AIR SEA RESCUE CRAFT

Name	No.	Builders	Commissioned
AIR SPRITE	Y256	Halvorsen, Sydney	1960

Displacement, tons: 23·5 standard
Dimensions, feet (metres): 63 × 15·5 × 3·3 *(19·2 × 4·7 × 1)*
Main engines: Two Scott Hall Defender (Petrol) = 25 knots
Complement: Up to 8

Used as rescue craft from Jervis Bay with TRV 253 and AWL 304. Other similar craft are operated by the RAAF.

AIR SPRITE *Royal Australian Navy*

4 MOTOR WATER LIGHTERS

GAYUNDAH (MRL 253), MWL 254, 256, 257

Displacement, tons: 300 standard; 600 (app) full load.
Draught, feet (metres): 120 × 24 × — (36·5 × 7·3 × —).
Main engines: 2 Ruston and Hornsby diesels; 440 bhp=9·5 knots

Sisters of the earlier survey ship *Paluma*; used for carrying water and stores.

1 AIRCRAFT LIGHTER—CATAMARAN

AWL 304

Dimensions, feet (metres): 77·8 × 32 × 6·6 (23·7 × 9·8 × 2)

Built at Cockatoo Dockyard 1967-68. Coastal craft. Capacity one S2E Tracker or two A4D Skyhawks.

3 CRANE STORES LIGHTERS

CSL 01   02   03

Based on design of AWL 304 but with crane and after superstructure. Built from 1972.

CSL 01   *1973, Graeme Andrews*

2 Ex ASR CRAFT

38101   38102

38 ft Bertram craft of little value except in harbour.

WORK BOATS

AM 400-415 +5

More than 20 are in use all built to a basic 40 ft (12·2 m) design.

ARMY WATERCRAFT

11 Ex-US LCM(8) CLASS

AB 1050-1053   1055-1061

Displacement, tons: 116 full load
Dimensions, feet (metres): 73·5 × 21 × 3·3 (22·4 × 6·4 × 1)
Main engines: 2 GM diesels; 600 hp = 9 knots
Range, miles: 140 at 9 knots

Can carry 60 tons of cargo.

AB 1052   *Australian Army*

6 LCVP

AB 751   752   755   756   758   759

Of 56 ft. Can carry 120 people.

2 TUGS

JOE MANN   THE LUKE

Built in 1964. Of 60 tons with a range of 5 700 miles and fitted for firefighting, the first at Sydney, the second at Brisbane.

JOE MANN   *Australian Army*

AUSTRIA

Commanding Officer

Major Walter Slovacek

Diplomatic Representation

Defence Attaché in London:
Brigadier General H. Wingelbauer

Personnel

1977: a) 1 officer, 13 NCOs, 13 ratings (cadre personnel and national service), plus a small shipyard unit
b) 6 months national service plus 2 months a year for 12 years

Base

Marinekaserne Tegetthof, Wien-Kuchelau (under command of Austrian School of Military Engineering)

Mercantile Marine

Lloyd's Register of Shipping:
15 vessels of 3 670 tons gross

RIVERINE PATROL CRAFT

Name	No.	Builders	Commissioned
NIEDERÖSTERREICH	A604	Korneuberg Werft AG	April 1970

Displacement, tons: 75
Dimensions, feet (metres): 96·8 × 17·8 × 3·6 *(29·4 × 5·4 × 1·1)*
Guns: 1—20 mm SPz Mk 66 Oerlikon in a turret; 1—12·7 mm MG; 1—Mk 42 MG; 2—8·4 cm PAR 66 "Carl Gustav" AT rifles
Main engines: 2 V 16 Diesels (turbo engines); 1 600 hp = 22 knots
Complement: 9

Fully welded. Only one built of a projected class of twelve. Engines by MWM, Munich.

NIEDERÖSTERREICH   *1975, Austrian Government*

Name	No.	Builders	Commissioned
OBERST BRECHT	A 601	Korneuberg Werft AG	—

Displacement, tons: 10
Dimensions, feet (metres): 40·3 × 8·2 × 2·5 *(12·3 × 2·5 × 0·75)*
Gun: 1—12·7 mm MG
Main engines: 2 Diesels; 214 bhp = 10 knots
Complement: 5

Welded hull. Engines by Gräf and Stift, Vienna.

OBERST BRECHT   *1974, Heeres Film*

10 Ex-US "M3" PATROL CRAFT

	No.	Builders	Commissioned
4 M3B Type	—	Highway Products and Marine Corp USA	1965
6 M3D Type	—	Aluminium Co of America	1976

Displacement, tons: 2·9
Dimensions, feet (metres): 27·2 × 8·2 × 6·5 *(8·3 × 2·5 × 2)*
Main engines: M3B—2 Gray Parol (petrol); 204 hp =18 knots
M3D—2 GM diesels; 184 hp = 18 knots

Unarmed, they form part of the military floating bridge equipment.

"M3" Class   *1976, Heeres Film*

BAHAMAS

Senior Officers

Assistant Commissioner:
L. W. Major
Deputy Superintendent:
Leon L. Smith
Assistant Superintendent:
E. K. Andrews

Base

Bay Shore Marina, Nassau

New Construction

Reported that several new craft are contemplated.

Mercantile Marine

Lloyd's Register of Shipping:
119 vessels of 189 890 tons gross

PATROL CRAFT

4 60 ft GRP TYPE

Name	No.	Builders	Commissioned
ACKLINS	4	Vosper Thornycroft	5 Mar 1971
ANDROS	—	Vosper Thornycroft	5 Mar 1971
ELEVTHERA	—	Vosper Thornycroft	5 Mar 1971
SAN SALVADOR	—	Vosper Thornycroft	5 Mar 1971

Displacement, tons: 30 standard
Dimensions, feet (metres): 62·0 × 15·8 × 4·6 *(18·9 × 4·8 × 1·4)*
Guns: 1 MG forward; 2 LMG on bridge
Main engines: 2 Caterpillar diesels = 20 knots
Complement: 11

"60 ft" Keith Nelson patrol craft in glass reinforced plastic, delivered as the first four units of the Bahamas Police Marine Division. With air-conditioned living spaces, these craft are designed for patrol amongst the many islands of the Bahamas Group. The foredeck is specially strengthened for a 20 mm MG with light MGs in sockets either side of the bridge.

ACKLINS   *1976, Bahamas Police, Marine Division*

BAHRAIN

Ministerial

Minister of the Interior:
  Muhammad ibn Khalifa ibn Hamid Al Khalifa

Personnel

a) 1977: About 150.
b) Voluntary.

Mercantile Marine

Lloyd's Register of Shipping:
  15 vessels of 3 670 tons

Coastguard

This unit is under the direction of the Ministry of the Interior and not Defence.

1 FAIREY MARINE "TRACKER" CLASS

Displacement, tons: 26
Dimensions, feet (metres): 64 × 16 × 5 *(19·5 × 4·9 × 1·5)*
Gun: 1—20 mm
Main engines: 2 diesels; 1 120 bhp = 28 knots

Purchased 1974.

"TRACKER" Class   *1974, Fairey Marine*

2 FAIREY MARINE "INTERCEPTOR" CLASS

25 ft *(7·6 metres)* craft with catamaran hull. Can carry eight 25-man liferafts (as shown) or a platoon of soldiers. Powered by twin 135 hp outboard motors for a speed of 30 knots.

"INTERCEPTOR" Class   *1975, Fairey Marine*

2 FAIREY MARINE "SPEAR" CLASS

Dimensions, feet (metres): 29·8 × 9·2 × 2·6 *(9·1 × 2·8 × ·8)*
Guns: 2 MG
Main engines: 2 Perkins diesels, 290 hp = 26 knots
Complement: 3

Purchased 1974.

1 50ft CHEVERTON TYPE (COASTAL PATROL CRAFT)

Purchased 1976.

2 PATROL CRAFT

HOWAR   JIDA

Displacement, tons: 15
Dimensions, feet (metres): 45·5 × 12 × 3 *(13·9 × 3·7 × 0·9)*
Main engines: 2 Diesels; 1 080 bhp = 23 knots

3 27ft CHEVERTON TYPE (COASTAL PATROL CRAFT)

Displacement, tons: 3·5
Dimensions, feet (metres): 27 × 9 × 2·8 *(8·2 × 2·7 × 0·8)*
Main engines: Twin diesels = 15 knots

Purchased 1976.

AMPHIBIOUS CRAFT

1 60ft CHEVERTON "LOADMASTER"

Measurement, tons: 60 deadweight
Dimensions, feet (metres): 60 oa × 20 × 3·5 *(18·3 × 6·1 × 1·1)*
Main engines: 2 120 hp diesels =8·5 knots

Purchased 1976.

BANGLADESH

Headquarters Appointments

Chief of Naval Staff:
  Rear Admiral Mosharraf Hussain Khan psn
Assistant Chief of Naval Staff (Ops) and Administrative Authority, Dacca:
  Commodore Mahbub Ali Khan psn
Assistant Chief of Naval Staff (Material):
  Captain K. M. J. Akbar
Assistant Chief of Naval Staff (Logistics):
  Captain F. Ahmed

Senior Appointments

Commodore Chittagong:
  Captain Sultan Ahmad
NOIC Khulna:
  Captain Mujibur Rahman

Naval Bases

Chittagong (BNS Issa Khan), Dacca (BNS Haji Mohsin), Khulna (BNS Titumir), Kaptai (BNS Shaheed Moazzam), Juldia, Chittagong (Marine Academy)

Prefix to Ships' Names

BNS

Personnel:

a) 1977: 3 500 (200 officers, 3 300 ratings)
b) Voluntary

Mercantile Marine

Lloyd's Register of Shipping:
  120 vessels of 133 016 tons gross

Formation

The Bangladesh Navy was the last of the three services to be formed, Commander Nurul Huq being appointed Chief of Staff at the end of March 1972. The first ship was commissioned by General Osmani on 12 June 1972 as P101. Rear Admiral Khan took over on 6 Nov 1975.

Strength of the Fleet

Frigate	1
Large Patrol Craft	4
Riverine Patrol Craft	5
Training Ship	1

FRIGATE

1 Ex-BRITISH "SALISBURY" CLASS (TYPE 61)

Name	No.	Builders	Laid down	Launched	Commissioned
UMAR FAROOQ (ex-HMS *Llandaff*)	F 16	Hawthorn Leslie Ltd, Hebburn-on-Tyne	27 Aug 1953	30 Nov 1955	11 Apr 1958

UMAR FAROOQ   *1977, Michael E. G. Lennon*

Displacement, tons: 2 170 standard; 2 408 full load
Length, feet (metres): 320 *(97·5)* pp; 339·8 *(103·6)* oa
Beam, feet (metres): 40 *(12·2)*
Draught, feet (metres): 15·5 *(4·7)*
Guns: 2—4·5 in *(115 mm)*; 2—40 mm
A/S weapons: 1 Squid Triple-barrelled DC mortar
Main engines: 8 ASR 1 diesels in three engine rooms; 2 shafts; 14 400 bhp
Speed, knots: 24
Oil fuel, tons: 230
Range, miles: 2 300 at full power; 7 500 at 16 knots
Complement: 237 (14 officers, 223 ratings)

Ordered by RN on 28 June 1951. All welded. Transferred to Bangladesh at Royal Albert Dock, London on 10 Dec 1976 for work-up and passage.

Radar: Long-range surveillance: One Type 965 with double AKE 2 array.
Combined warning: One Type 993.
Height finder: One Type 277Q.
Target Indication: One Type 982.
Fire Control; Mk 6m director with Type 275.
Navigation: One Type 975.

Sonar: Types 174 and 170B.

LIGHT FORCES

2 Ex-YUGOSLAV "KRALJEVICA" CLASS (LARGE PATROL CRAFT)

Name	No.	Builders	Commissioned
KARNAPHULI (ex-*PBR 502*)	P301	Yugoslavia	1956
TISTA (ex-*PBR 505*)	P302	Yugoslavia	1956

Displacement, tons: 190 standard; 202 full load
Dimensions, feet (metres): 134·5 × 20·7 × 7·2 *(41 × 6·3 × 2·2)*
Guns: 1—128 mm rocket launcher; 1—40/60 mm
Main engines: MAN W8V 30/38 diesels; 2 shafts; 3 300 bhp = 18 knots
Range, miles: 1 000 at 12 knots
Complement: 44 (4 officers, 40 ratings)

Transferred and commissioned on 6 June 1975.

Radar: Decca-45.

Sonar: QCU-2.

TISTA   *1975, Bangladesh Navy*

2 Ex-INDIAN "AKSHAY" CLASS (LARGE PATROL CRAFT)

Name	No.	Builders	Commissioned
PADMA (ex-*INS Akshay*)	P 201	Hooghly D & E Co, Calcutta	1962
SURMA (ex-*INS Ajay*)	P 202	Hooghly D & E Co, Calcutta	1962

Displacement, tons: 120 standard; 150 full load
Dimensions, feet (metres): 117·2 × 20 × 5·5 *(35·7 × 6·1 × 1·7)*
Gun: 1—40/60 mm
Main engines: 2 Paxman diesels = 12·5 knots
Range, miles: 5 000 at 10 knots
Complement: 35 (3 officers, 32 ratings)

Generally similar to Royal Navy's "Ford" class. Transferred and commissioned on 12 Apr 1973 and 26 July 1974 respectively.

SURMA   *1975, Bangladesh Navy*

5 "PABNA" CLASS (RIVERINE PATROL CRAFT)

Name	No.	Builders	Commissioned
BOGRA	P104	DEW Narayangonj, Dacca	June 1977
NOAKHALI	P102	DEW Narayangonj, Dacca	8 July 1972
PABNA	P101	DEW Narayangonj, Dacca	12 June 1972
PATUAKHALI	P103	DEW Narayangonj, Dacca	7 Nov 1974
RANGAMATI	P105	DEW Narayangonj, Dacca	June 1977

Displacement, tons: 69·5
Dimensions, feet (metres): 75 × 20 × 3·5 *(22·9 × 6·1 × 1·1)*
Gun: 1—40/60 Bofors
Main engines: Cummins diesel = 10·8 knots
Range, miles: 700
Complement: 33 (3 officers, 30 ratings)

The first indigenous naval craft built in Bangladesh.

Radar: Decca Navigational.

PATUAKHALI   *1975, Bangladesh Navy*

TRAINING SHIP

SHAHEED RUHUL AMIN *(ex-MS Anticosti)*

Displacement, tons: 710 full load
Dimensions, feet (metres):155·8 × 36·5 × 10 *(47·5 × 11·1 × 3·1)*
Gun: 1—40/60 mm Bofors
Main engines: Caterpillar diesel; 1 shaft = 11·5 knots
Range, miles: 4 000
Complement: 80 (8 officers, 72 ratings)

After use in relief work was handed over to BN in 1972, modified at Khulna and commissioned 10 Dec 1974.

SHAHEED RUHUL AMIN   *1976, Bangladesh Navy*

BARBADOS

Senior Officer

CO Barbados Coast Guard: Major C. A. McConney

Coastguard

This was formed early in 1973.

Prefix to Ships' Names

BCGS

Personnel

(a) 1977: 61 (4 officers, 57 other ranks).
(b) Voluntary.

Base

Christ Church, Barbados

Mercantile Marine

Lloyd's Register of Shipping: 30 vessels of 3 897 tons gross

1 20 Metre "GUARDIAN " CLASS (COASTAL PATROL CRAFT)

Name	No.	Builders	Commissioned
GEORGE FERGUSON	CG 601	Halmatic/Aquarius UK	Dec 1974

Displacement, tons: 30
Dimensions, feet (metres): 65·6 × 17·4 × 4·3 *(20 × 5·3 × 1·3)*
Guns: 2—76 mm MG (provision for—not fitted)
Main engines: 2 GM 12V 71 TI diesels; 1 300 hp = 24 knots
Range, miles: 560 at 18 knots
Complement: 10

GRP hull. Air conditioned and designed for coastguard/SAR duties. Launched 16 Oct 1974 for delivery in December.

3 12 Metre "GUARDIAN" CLASS (COASTAL PATROL CRAFT)

Name	No.	Builders	Commissioned
COMMANDER MARSHALL	CG 402	Halmatic/Aquarius UK	Dec 1973
J. T. C. RAMSEY	CG 404	Halmatic/Aquarius UK	Nov 1974
T. T. LEWIS	CG 403	Halmatic/Aquarius UK	Feb 1974

Displacement, tons: 11
Dimensions, feet (metres): 41 × 12·1 × 3·3 *(12·5 × 3·7 × 1)*
Gun: 1—76 mm MG (Provision for—not fitted)
Main engines: 2 Caterpillar Diesels; 580 hp = 24 knots
Complement: 4

GRP Hulls. Designed for coastal patrol/SAR duties.

MISCELLANEOUS

The ex-US LST *Kemper County* was transferred to Barbadian commerical interests 6 Jan 1976.

BELGIUM

Headquarters Appointment

Chief of Naval Staff:

Vice Admiral J. P. L. van Dyck

Diplomatic Representation

Naval, Military and Air Attaché in Bonn:
Colonel AF Derille (Army)
Naval, Military and Air Attaché in The Hague:
Lieutenant-Colonel de Brouchoven de Bergeyck
Naval, Military and Air Attaché in London:
Colonel K. Dewulf (Army)
Naval, Military and Air Attaché in Paris:
Colonel J. A. L. Joseph (Air Force)
Naval, Military and Air Attaché in Washington:
Brigadier-General CA de Wilde (Army)

Personnel

(a) 1977; 4 457 (1 150 National Service)
(b) 11 months National Service

Naval Aviation

3 Alouette III helicopters
2 Sikorsky S58 helicopters

New Construction

It is planned to build new minehunters to replace ex-US MSOs and MSCs, the first unit to be completed in 1981.

Strength of the Fleet

Type	Active	Building
Frigates	2	2
Minehunters (Ocean)	7	—
Minehunters (Coastal)	2	—
Minesweepers (Coastal)	4	—
Minesweepers (Inshore)	14	—
Support Ships	2	—
River Patrol Boats	6	—
Research Ships	2	—
Auxiliary and Service Craft	12	—

Mercantile Marine

Lloyd's Register of Shipping:
258 vessels of 1 499 431 tons gross

Bases

Ostend: Main base for support ships, 1 MSO Squadron, 1 MSC Squadron.
Nieuwpoort: 1 MSI Squadron, reserve MSCs.
Kallo: River patrol boats, 1 MSI Squadron, reserve MSIs.
Zeebrugge: Frigates.
Koksijde: Naval aviation.

Disposal

1976 *Knokke* (MSO)

PENNANT LIST

Frigates

F 910	Wielingen
F 911	Westdiep
F 912	Wandelaar
F 913	Westhinder

Minewarfare Forces

M 471	Hasselt
M 472	Kortryk
M 473	Lokeren
M 474	Turnhout
M 475	Tongeren
M 476	Merksem
M 477	Oudenaarde
M 478	Herstal
M 479	Huy
M 480	Seraing
M 482	Vise

Minewarfare Forces *(Cont)*

M 483	Ougrée
M 484	Dinant
M 485	Andenne
M 902	Haverbeke
M 903	Dufour
M 904	De Brouwer
M 906	Breydel
M 907	Artevelde
M 908	Truffaut
M 909	Bovesse
M 927	Spa
M 928	Stavelot
M 929	Heyst
M 930	Rochefort
M 931	Knokke
M 932	Nieuwport
M 933	Koksijde
M 934	Verviers
M 935	Veurne

Support Ships and Auxiliaries

A 950	Valcke
A 951	Hommel
A 952	Wesp
A 953	Bij
A 956	Krekel
A 958	Zenobe Gramme
A 959	Mier
A 960	Godetia
A 961	Zinnia
A 962	Mechelen

River Patrol Boats

P 901	Leie
P 902	Liberation
P 903	Meuse
P 904	Sambre
P 905	Schelde
P 906	Semois

FRIGATES

2 + 2 "E-71" CLASS

Name	No.	Builders	Laid down	Launched	Commissioning
WIELINGEN	F 910	Boelwerf, Temse	5 Mar 1974	30 Mar 1976	Mar 1976
WESTDIEP	F 911	Cockerill, Hoboken	2 Sep 1974	8 Dec 1975	June1977
WANDELAAR	F 912	Boelwerf, Temse	1 Apr 1975	1 Mar 1977	Dec 1977
WESTHINDER	F 913	Cockerill, Hoboken	8 Dec 1975	28 Jan 1977	June1978

Displacement, tons: 1 940 light; 2 430 full load
Length, feet (metres): 347·7 *(106)*
Beam, feet (metres): 40·3 *(12·3)*
Draught, feet (metres): 18·8 *(5·6)*
Guns: 1—3·9 in *(100 mm)* 1 CIWS
Missiles: 1 NATO Sea Sparrow SAM, (8 cells); 4 Exocet SSM
Torpedo launchers: 2 for L-5 torpedos
A/S rocket launchers: 1—6 × 375 mm LR Bofors
Rocket launchers: 2—8 barrelled Corvus dual-purpose Chaff/flare launchers
Main engines: CODOG—1 Rolls Royce Olympus TM3 gas turbine, 28 000 bhp; 2 Cockerill CO-240 diesels; 6 000 bhp. Twin vp propellers
Speed, knots: 28 (15 on 1 diesel, 18 on 2 diesels)
Range, miles: 4 500 at 18 knots
Complement: 14 officers; 146 men

This compact, well-armed class of frigate is the first class fully designed by the Belgian Navy and built in Belgian yards. All to be fitted with hull-mounted sonar and fin stabilisers.

Electronics: Fully integrated and automated weapons command and control system of HSA (SEWACO 4). ECM capability.

Missiles: Sea Sparrow RIM 7H-2. Exocet MM 38.

Radar: Air and surface warning and target indication radar with Control System (HSA). Navigation radar by Raytheon.

Sonar: SQS 505A (Westinghouse).

WIELINGEN   *1977, Royal Belgian Navy*

WIELINGEN   *1977, Michael D. J. Lennon*

MINE WARFARE FORCES

7 Ex-U.S. MSO (Ex-AM) TYPE 498 (MINEHUNTERS)

Name	No.	Builders	Laid down	Launched	Commissioned
A. F. DUFOUR (ex-*Lagen* M 950, ex-MSO 498)	M 903	Bellingham Shipyard Inc, Wash.	1954	13 Aug 1954	27 Sep 1955
ARTEVELDE (ex-MSO 503, ex-AM 503)	M 907	Tacoma Boatbuilding Co, Tacoma, Wash.	1953	19 June1954	15 Dec 1955
BREYDEL (ex-MSO 504, ex-AM 504)	M 906	Tacoma Boatbuilding Co, Tacoma, Wash.	1954	25 Mar 1955	24 Jan 1956
DE BROUWER (ex-*Nansen,* M 951, ex-MSO 499)	M 904	Bellingham Shipyard Inc, Wash.	1954	15 Oct 1954	1 Nov 1955
F. BOVESSE (ex-MSO 516, ex-AM 516)	M 909	Tampa Shipbuilding Co, Inc. Tampa, Fla.	1954	8 Feb 1956	21 Dec 1956
G. TRUFFAUT (ex-MSO 515, ex-AM 515)	M 908	Tampa Shipbuilding Co, Inc, Tampa, Fla.	1955	1 Nov 1955	21 Sep 1956
VAN HAVERBEKE (ex-MSO 522)	M 902	Petersen Builders Inc, Sturgeon Bay, Wisc.	1959	25 Oct 1959	7 Nov 1960

Displacement, tons: 720 standard; 780 full load
Length, feet (metres): 165·0 *(50·3)* wl; 172·5 *(52·6)* oa
Beam, feet (metres): 35·0 *(10·7)*
Draught, feet (metres): 11·0 *(3·4)*
Gun: 1—40 mm (except *De Brouwer* and *Dufour)*
Main engines: 2 GM diesels; 2 shafts; 1 600 bhp
Speed, knots: 14
Oil fuel, tons: 50
Range, miles: 2 400 at 12 knots; 3 000 at 20 knots
Complement: 72 (5 officers, 67 men)

Wooden hulls and non-magnetic structure. Capable of sweeping mines of all types. Diesels of non-magnetic stainless steel alloy. Controllable pitch propellers.

Dufour and *De Brouwer* originally served in Royal Norwegian Navy (1955-66). *Artevelde* converted to Diving Vessel in 1974 but retains minehunting capability.

Sonar: SQQ 14 (GE) (except *Artevelde).*

Transfer dates: M 902 9 Dec 1960, M 903 14 Apr 1966, M 904 14 Apr 1966, M 906 15 Feb 1956, M 907 16 Dec 1955, M 908 12 Oct 1956, M 909 25 Jan 1957.

BREYDEL   *12/1974, C. and S. Taylor*

MINE WARFARE FORCES

8 Ex-US MSC (ex-AMS) TYPE 60 (MINESWEEPERS/HUNTERS—COASTAL)

Name	No.	Builders	Commissioned	
HEIST	M 929	Boelwerf, Temse	Nov	1955
KOKSIJDE	M 933	Beliard, Ostend	Nov	1955
NIEUWPOORT	M 932	Beliard, Ostend	May	1955
ROCHEFORT	M 930	Beliard, Ostend	Feb	1955
SPA	M 927	Boelwerf, Temse	Mar	1955
STAVELOT	M 928	Boelwerf, Temse	July	1955
VERVIERS (ex-MSC 259)	M 934	Boston, USA	1956	
VEURNE (ex-MSC 260)	M 935	Boston, USA	1956	

VERVIERS (before conversion)   1976, Royal Belgian Navy

Displacement, tons: 330 light; 390 full load
Dimensions, feet (metres): 139 pp; 144 oa × 27·9 × 8 *(42·4; 44·0 × 8·5 × 2·6)*
Gun: 1—40 mm
Main engines: 2 GM diesels; 2 shafts (Voigt-Schneider propellers); 880 bhp = 13·5 knots
Oil fuel, tons: 28
Range, miles: 3 000 at economical speed (10·5 knots)
Complement: 39

Wooden hulls and constructed throughout of materials with the lowest possible magnetic signature. M 934 and 935 were built in USA, under MDAP, and M 926-933 of same type were built in Belgium with machinery and equipment from USA. M 934 (ex-MSC 259) transferred 19 June 1956, M 935 (ex-MSC 260) was transferred on 7 Sep 1956. *Verviers* and *Veurne* converted to minehunters with Voith-Schneider propellers.

Reclassification: *Mechelen*, M 926, former coastal minesweeper of this class, was re-rated as a research ship in 1964 and re-numbered A 962 in 1966 (see next page). *Spa* and *Heist* to be used as auxiliaries 1977-78 (new numbers A 963 and A 964 respectively).

Sonar: Type 193 (Plessey).

14 "HERSTAL" CLASS (MINESWEEPERS—INSHORE)

Name	No.	Builders	Launched
ANDENNE	M 485 (ex-MSI 97)	Mercantile Marine Yard, Kruibeke	May 1958
DINANT	M 484 (ex-MSI 96)	Mercantile Marine Yard, Kruibeke	5 Apr 1958
HASSELT	M 471	Mercantile Marine Yard, Kruibeke	Mar 1958
HERSTAL	M 478 (ex-MSI 90)	Mercantile Marine Yard, Kruibeke	6 Aug 1956
HUY	M 479 (ex-MSI 91)	Mercantile Marine Yard, Kruibeke	17 Nov 1956
KORTRYK	M 472	Mercantile Marine Yard, Kruibeke	May 1957
LOKEREN	M 473	Mercantile Marine Yard, Kruibeke	18 May 1957
MERKSEM	M 476	Mercantile Marine Yard, Kruibeke	5 April 1958
OUDENAARDE	M 477	Mercantile Marine Yard, Kruibeke	May 1958
OUGREE	M 483 (ex-MSI 95)	Mercantile Marine Yard, Kruibeke	16 Nov 1957
SERAING	M 480 (ex-MSI 92)	Mercantile Marine Yard, Kruibeke	Mar 1957
TONGEREN	M 475	Mercantile Marine Yard, Kruibeke	16 Nov 1957
TURNHOUT	M 474	Mercantile Marine Yard, Kruibeke	7 Sep 1957
VISÉ	M 482 (ex-MSI 94)	Mercantile Marine Yard, Kruibeke	7 Sep 1957

VISE   7/1975, JLM van der Burg

Displacement, tons: 160 light; 190 full load
Dimensions, feet (metres): 106·7 pp; 113·2 oa × 22·3 × 6 *(32·5; 34·5 × 6·9 × 1·8)*
Guns: 2 — ·5 (Twin)
Main engines: 2 diesels; 2 shafts; 1 260 bhp = 15 knots
Oil fuel, tons: 18
Range, miles: 2 300 at 10 knots
Complement: 17

Modified AMI "100-foot" class. Originally a class of sixteen. The first MSI *Herstal* was completed in June 1957 the last pair being completed in 1959.

The first group of eight (M 478 to 485) was a United States "off shore order", the remaining eight (M 470 to 477) being financed under the Belgian Navy Estimates.

SUPPORT SHIPS

Name	No.	Builders	Commissioned
ZINNIA	A 961	Cockerill, Hoboken	5 Sep 1967

Displacement, tons: 1 705 light; 2 685 full load
Length, feet (metres): 299·2 *(91·2)* pp; 309 *(94·2)* wl; 326·4 *(99·5)* oa
Beam, feet (metres): 49·9 *(14·0)*
Draught, feet (metres): 11·8 *(3·6)*
Guns: 3—40 mm (single)
Aircraft: 1 helicopter
Main engines: 2 Cockerill V 12 RT 240 CO diesels; 5 000 bhp; 1 Shaft
Speed, knots: 20
Oil fuel, tons: 500
Range, miles: 14 000 at 12·5 knots
Complement: 125

ZINNIA   7/1975, J. L. M. van der Burg

Launched on 6 May 1967. Controllable pitch propeller. Design includes a platform and a retractable hangar for one light liaison-helicopter. Rated as Command and Logistic Support Ship.

Name	No.	Builders	Commissioned
GODETIA	A 960	Boelwerf, Temse	23 May 1966

Displacement, tons: 1 700 light; 2 500 full load
Dimensions, feet (metres): 289 wl; 301 oa × 46 × 11·5 *(88·0; 91·8 × 14 × 3·5)*
Guns: 2—40 mm (twin)
Main engines: 4 ACEC—MAN diesels; 2 shafts; 5 400 bhp = 19 knots
Oil fuel, tons: 294
Range, miles: 8 700 at 12·5 knots
Complement: 100 plus 35 spare billets

Laid down on 15 Feb 1965, launched on 7 Dec 1965. Controllable pitch propellers. Provided with a platform which can take a light liaison-helicopter.

GODETIA   10/1974, Reiner Nerlich

RIVER PATROL BOATS

LEIE P 901	**MEUSE** P 903	**SCHELDE** P 905
LIBERATION P 902	**SAMBRE** P 904	**SEMOIS** P 906

Displacement, tons: 25 light; 27·5 full load
Dimensions, feet (metres): 75·5 pp; 82 oa × 12·5 × 3 (23·0; 25·0 × 3·8 × 0·9)
 Liberation 85·5 × 13·1 × 3·2 (26·0 × 4·0 × 1·0)
Guns: 2—13 mm (·50) MG
Main engines: 2 diesels; 2 shafts; 440 bhp = 19 knots
Complement: 7

Built by Hitzler, Regensburg, Germany, in 1953, except *Liberation* in 1954. *Semois* acts as base ship for divers.

MEUSE

1974, Belgian Navy

RESEARCH SHIPS

ZENOBE GRAMME A 958

Displacement, tons: 149
Dimensions, feet (metres): 92 × 22·5 × 7 (28·2 × 6·8 × 2·1)
Main engines: 1 MWM diesel; 1 shaft; 200 bhp = 10 knots
Complement: 14

Auxiliary sail ketch. Built by Boelwerf, Temse, Belgium, commissioned 23 Oct 1961. Designed for scientific research.

MECHELEN (ex-M 926) A962

Displacement, tons: 330 light; 390 full load
Dimensions, feet (metres): 139 pp; 144 oa × 27·9 × 7·5 (42·4; 44·0 × 8·5 × 2·3)
Main engines: 2 GM diesels; 2 shafts; 880 bhp = 13·5 knots
Oil fuel, tons: 28
Range, miles: 3 000 at economical speed (10·5 knots)
Complement: 39

Former coastal minesweeper built by Boelwerf, Temse and commissioned in Dec 1954. Used as a research ship since 1964 being renumbered as A 962 in 1966.

MECHELEN

1974, Neptunus, Ostend

TUGS

O/Lt VALCKE (ex-AT 1) A 950

Displacement, tons: 110
Dimensions, feet (metres): 78·8 pp; 95 oa × 21 × 5·5 (24·0; 29·0 × 6·4 × 1·7)
Main engines: 1 diesel; 1 shaft; 600 bhp = 12 knots
Complement: 14

Built by Holland Nautic NV, Haarlem, Netherlands in 1951 and served as Dutch mercantile tug *Elis* until purchased by Belgian Navy in 1953.

BIJ A 953　　**KREKEL** A 956

Harbour tugs with fire-fighting facilities. Of 71 tons and twin shafts; 400 hp with Voith-Schneider propellers. *Bij* built by Akerboom 1959, *Krekel* by Ch. Navals de Rupelmonde 1961.

HOMMEL A 951　　**WESP** A 952

Harbour tugs of 22 tons, 300 bhp diesels with Voith-Schneider propellers. Both built by Voith, Heidenheim in 1953.

MIER A 959

Harbour tug of 17·5 tons with 90 bhp diesel. Built Liége 1962.

MISCELLANEOUS

Harbour craft: There are three barges, namely **FN 4, FN 5** and **FN 6,** displacement 300 tons, length 105 feet, built by Plaquet, Peronne-lez-Antoing in 1957; the ammunition ship *Ekster,* displacement 140 tons, length 118 feet, built at Niel (Germany) in 1953; a diving cutter **ZM 4,** displacement 8 tons, length 33 feet, built at Ostend in 1954; and the harbour transport cutter *Spin,* displacement 32 tons, length 47·8 feet, with 250 bhp diesels = 8 knots and Voith-Schneider propeller, built in the Netherlands in 1958.

BELIZE

Personnel

(a) 50 approx
(b) Voluntary

Base

Belize

Mercantile Marine

Lloyd's Register of Shipping: 3 vessels of 620 tons gross

2 COASTAL PATROL CRAFT

Name	No.	Builders	Commissioned
BELIZE	PBM 01	Brooke Marine, Lowestoft	1972
BELMOPAN	PBM 02	Brooke Marine, Lowestoft	1972

Displacement, tons: 15
Dimensions, feet (metres): 40 × 12 × 2 (12·2 × 3·6 × 0·6)
Guns: 3 MG
Main engines: 2 Diesels; 370 hp × 22 knots

BOLIVIA

Headquarters Appointment

Commander-in-Chief: Vice Admiral Gutemberg Barroso Hurtado

Personnel

(a) 1977: 1 500 officers and men (including marines)
(b) 12 months selective military service

A small navy used for patrolling Lake Titicaca and the Beni River system. Most of the training of officers and senior ratings is carried out in Argentina.

Base

Tiquina

Prefix to Ships' Names

FNB

1 TRANSPORT

CORONEL ABAROA M 08

16 PATROL CRAFT

Of various sizes.

BRAZIL

Headquarters Appointments

Chief of Naval Staff:
  Admiral Gualter Maria Menezes de Magalhães
Chief of Naval Material:
  Admiral Sylvio de Magalhães Figueiredo
Chief of Naval Personnel:
  Admiral Eddy Sampaio Espellet

Diplomatic Representation

Naval Attaché in Asunción:
  Captain Luiz Fernando da Silva e Souza
Naval and Defence Attaché in Athens:
  Captain Gerson Fleischauer
Naval and Defence Attaché in Buenos Aires:
  Captain Odilon Lima Cardoso
Naval and Defence Attaché in Lima:
  Captain Luis Carlos de Freitas
Naval Attaché in La Paz:
  Captain Paulo Demaria Serôa da Motta
Naval and Defence Attaché in Lisbon and Madrid:
  Captain Valbert Lisieux Medeiros de Figueiredo
Naval Attaché in London:
  Captain Mauricio Henrique Bittencourt de Carvalho
Naval Attaché in Paris:
  Captain Henrique Octávio Aché Pillar
Naval and Defence Attaché in Santiago:
  Captain Francisco Lafayette de Moraes
Naval and Defence Attaché in Tokyo:
  Captain Luiz Augusto Paraguassu de Sá
Naval Attaché in Washington:
  Rear Admiral Rafael de Azevedo Branco

Personnel

(a)
1972: 42 125 (3 264 officers and 38 861 men)
1973: 44 337 (3 591 officers and 40 746 men)
1974: 49 600 (3 887 officers and 45 713 men)
1975: 43 100 (3 800 officers and 39 300 men)
1976: 45 300 (3 800 officers and 41 500 men)
Figures include marines and auxiliary corps

(b) 1 years National service

Naval Bases

Rio de Janeiro (main base with 3 dry docks and 1 floating dock)
Aratu (Bahia) (major naval yard with 1 dry dock and 1 floating dock)
Belém (naval base and repair yard with 1 dry dock)
Recife (naval base and repair yard)
Natal (small naval base and repair yard with 1 floating dock)
Ladario (river base of *Mato Grosso* flotilla)
Sao Pedro (naval air station)

Maritime Aviation

A Fleet Air Arm was formed on 26 January 1965.

Navy

  6 Sikorsky SH-3D
  3 Westland Whirlwind (UH-5)
  3 Westland Wasp HAS-1 (UH-2)
18 Bell 206B Jetrangers
  9 Westland Lynx WG 13 to be provided for "Niteroi" class

Air Force (Comando Costeira)

  8 Grumman S-2E Trackers (ASW).
12 Grumman HU-16A Albatross (SAR)
  5 Grumman S-2A Trackers (to be replaced by S-2E)
  3 Lockheed RC-130E Hercules (SAR/PR)
  6 Convair PBY-5A Catalinas (Transport)
16 EMB-111 (on order—delivery from 1978)
  4 EMB-110B (PR)
15 Neiva T25 Universal I (liaison)
  5 Bell SH-1D (SAR helicopters)
  2 Bell 476 (SAR helicopters)

Prefix to Ships' Names

These vary, indicating the type of ship e.g. N Ae L = Aircraft Carrier; CT = Destroyer.

Mercantile Marine

Lloyd's Register of Shipping:
  520 vessels of 3 096 293 tons gross

Strength of the Fleet

Type	Active	Building
Attack Carrier (medium)	1	—
Destroyers	12	6
Submarines (Patrol)	8	2
Landing Ships	2	—
Monitor and Gunboats	9	—
River Patrol Ships	5	—
Minesweepers (Coastal)	8	2
Survey Ships	6	—
Survey Launches	11	—
S/M Rescue Ships	1	—
Repair Ship	1	—
Tankers	2 (1 small)	—
Transports	4	—
Tugs	3	—
Floating Docks	3	—

New Construction

A revised plan is being developed

DELETIONS

Cruisers

1973 *Barroso*
1975 *Tamandaré* offered for auction (September)
      (both ex-US "St Louis" class)

Destroyers

1973 *Amazonas, Mariz E. Barros*
1974 *Acre, Araguaia, Araguari*—(auction July for scrap)
      (All Brazilian built 1949-51)

Frigates

1973 *Baependi, Bracui*
1975 *Benevente, Bocaina* (auction Feb for scrap)
      (All ex-US "Bostwick" class)

Submarines

1972 *Rio Grande do Sul* (ex-*Sandlance*) sold for scrap June
      1975
      Bahia (ex-*Plaice*) sold to Brazilian Museum of Naval
      Technology, Santos by USA as a memorial

Mine Warfare Forces

1974 *Jutai, Juruena* (paid off in Aug)
      (ex-US AMS)

Patrol Forces

1971 *Piraju, Piranha*
1972 *Paraguaçu*
1973 *Pirague*

PENNANT LIST

Aircraft Carrier

A	11	Minas Gerais

Destroyers

F	40	Niteroi
F	41	Defensora
F	42	Independencia
F	43	União
F	44	Constituição
F	45	Liberal
D	25	Marcilio Dias
D	26	Mariz E. Barros
D	27	Para
D	28	Paraiba
D	29	Parana
D	30	Pernambuco
D	33	Maranhão
D	34	Mato Grosso
D	35	Sergipe
D	36	Alagoas
D	37	Rio Grande Do Norte
D	38	Espirito Santo

Submarines

S	10	Guanabara
S	11	Rio Grande Do Sul
S	12	Bahia
S	13	Rio De Janeiro
S	14	Ceara
S	15	Goiaz
S	16	Amazonas
S	20	Humaita
S	21	Tonelero
S	22	Riachuelo

Amphibious Forces

G	26	Duque De Caxias
G	28	Garcia D'Avila

Patrol Forces

P	20	Pedro Teixeira
P	21	Raposo Tavares
P	30	Roraima
P	31	Rondonia
P	32	Amapa
U	17	Parnaiba
V	15	Imperial Marinheiro
V	16	Iguatemi
V	17	Ipiranga
V	18	Forte De Coimbra
V	19	Cabocla
V	20	Angostura
V	21	Baiana
V	22	Mearim
V	23	Purus
V	24	Solimoes

Light Forces

P	10	Piratini
P	11	Piraja
P	12	Pampeiro
P	13	Parati
P	14	Penedo
P	15	Poti
R	54	Anchova
R	55	Arenque
R	56	Atum
R	57	Acara
R	58	Agulha
R	59	Aruana

Mine Warfare Forces

M	15	Aratu
M	16	Anhatomirim
M	17	Atalaia
M	18	Aracatuba
M	19	Abrolhos
M	20	Albardão

Survey Vessels and Tenders

H	11	Paraibano
H	12	Rio Branco
H	13	Mestre João Dos Santos
H	14	Nogueira Da Gama
H	15	Itacurussa
H	16	Camocim
H	17	Caravelas
H	21	Sirius
H	22	Canopus
H	24	Castelhanos
H	27	Faroleiro Areas
H	28	Faroleiro Santana
H	30	Faroleiro Nascimento
H	31	Argus
H	32	Orion
H	33	Taurus
H	34	Graça Aranha
H	41	Almirante Camara
U	10	Almirante Saldanha

Miscellaneous

G	15	Paraguassu
G	16	Barroso Pereira
G	17	Potengi
G	21	Ary Parreiras
G	22	Soares Dutra
G	24	Belmonte
G	25	Afonso Pena
G	26	Am. Jeronimo Gonçalves
G	27	Marajó
K	10	Gastao Moutinho
M	11	Javari
M	13	Jurua
R	21	Tritão
R	22	Tridente
R	23	Triunfo
U	20	Rio Doce
U	21	Rio Das Contas
U	22	Rio Formoso
U	23	Rio Real
U	24	Rio Turvo
U	25	Rio Verde
U	26	Custodio De Mello
U	40	Rio Pardo
U	41	Rio Negro
U	42	Rio Chui
U	43	Rio Oiapoque

AIRCRAFT CARRIER

1 Ex-BRITISH "COLOSSUS" CLASS

Name	No.	Builders	Laid down	Launched	Commissioned
MINAS GERAIS (ex-HMS *Vengeance*)	A 11	Swan, Hunter & Wigham Richardson, Ltd, Wallsend on Tyne	16 Nov 1942	23 Feb 1944	15 Jan 1945

Displacement, tons: 15 890 standard; 17 500 normal;
  19 890 full load (see *Displacement* note)
Length, feet (metres): 630 *(192·0)* pp; 695 *(211·8)* oa
Beam, feet (metres): 80 *(24·4)*
Draught, feet (metres): 24·5 *(7·5)*
Flight deck,
  Length, feet (metres): 690 *(210·3)*
  Width, feet (metres): 121 *(37·0)* oa as reconstructed
  Height, feet (metres): 39 *(11·9)* above water line
Catapults: 1 steam
Aircraft: 20 aircraft including 7 S2A Trackers, 4 Sea Kings
Guns: 10—40 mm (2 quadruple, 1 twin), 2—47 mm (saluting)
Main engines: Parsons geared turbines; 2 shafts; 40 000 shp
Boilers: 4 Admiralty 3-drum type; Working pressure 400 psi *(28
  kg/cm²);* max superheat 700°F *(371°C)*
Speed, knots: 24; 25·3 on trials after reconstruction
Oil fuel, tons: 3 200
Range, miles: 12 000 at 14 knots; 6 200 at 23 knots
Complement: 1 000 (1 300 with air group)

MINAS GERAIS

1971, Brazilian Navy

Served in the Royal Navy from 1945 onwards. Fitted out in late 1948 to early 1949 for experimental cruise to the Arctic. Lent to the Royal Australian Navy early in 1953, returned to the Royal Navy in Aug 1955. Purchased by the Brazilian Government on 14 Dec 1956. Reconstructed at Verolme Dock, Rotterdam from summer 1957 to Dec 1960. The conversion and overhaul included the installation of the angled deck, steam catapult, mirror-sight deck landing system, armament fire control and radar equipment. The ship was purchased for $9 000 000 and the reconstruction cost $27 000 000. Commissioned in the Brazilian Navy at Rotterdam on 6 Dec 1960. Left Rotterdam for Rio de Janeiro on 13 Jan 1961. Used primarily for anti-submarine aircraft and helicopters. Currently under refit 1976-78.

Displacement: Before reconstruction: 13 190 tons standard; 18 010 tons full load.

Engineering: The two units each have one set of turbines and two boilers installed side by side. Maximum speed at 120 rpm. Steam capacity was increased when the boilers were retubed during reconstruction in 1957-60.

Electrical: During reconstruction an alternating current system was installed with a total of 2 500 kW supplied by four turbo-generators and one diesel generator.

Hangar: Dimensions: length, 445 feet; width, 52 feet; clear depth, 17·5 feet. Aircraft lifts: 45 feet by 34 feet. During reconstruction in 1957-60 new lifts replaced the original units.

Radar: Air Surveillance SPS 12; Surface Search SPS 4; Fighter Direction SPS 8B; Air Control SPS 8A; Fire Control SPG 34; Navigation MP 1402.

Operational: Single track catapult for launching, and arrester wires for recovering, 30 000 lb aircraft at 60 knots. Catapult accelerator gear port side forward.

MINAS GERAIS

1972, Brazilian Navy

MINAS GERAIS

1972, Brazilian Navy

DESTROYERS

6 "NITEROI" CLASS

Name	No.	Builders	Laid down	Launched	Commissioning
CONSTITUIÇÃO	F 44	Vosper Thornycroft Ltd.	13 Mar 1974	Apr 1976	Feb 1978
DEFENSORA	F 41	Vosper Thornycroft Ltd.	14 Dec 1972	27 Mar 1975	April 1977
INDEPENDENCIA	F 42	Arsenal de Marinho, Rio de Janeiro	11 June 1972	2 Sep 1974	Mar 1978
LIBERAL	F 45	Vosper Thornycroft Ltd.	2 May 1975	7 Feb 1977	Aug 1978
NITEROI	F 40	Vosper Thornycroft Ltd.	8 June 1972	8 Feb 1974	20 Nov 1976
UNIÃO	F 43	Arsenal de Marinho, Rio de Janeiro	11 June 1972	14 Mar 1975	Oct 1978

Displacement, tons: 3 200 standard; 3 800 full load
Length, feet (metres): 400 *(121·9)* wl; 424 *(129·2)* oa
Beam, feet (metres): 44·2 *(13·5)*
Draught, feet (metres): 18·2 *(5·5)*
Aircraft: One WG 13 Lynx helicopter
Missile launchers: 2 twin Exocet MM 38 surface-to-surface in General Purpose version; 2 triple Seacat; Ikara in Anti-Submarine version
Guns: 2—4·5 inch Mark 8 in General Purpose version; 1—4·5 inch Mark 8 in Anti-Submarine version; 2—40 mm
A/S weapons: One Bofors 375 mm twin tube A/S rocket launcher; Two triple Mark 32 torpedo tubes; 1 DC rail
Main engines: CODOG system; 2 Rolls Royce Olympus gas turbines = 56 000 bhp; 4 MTU diesels = 18 000 shp
Speed, knots: 30 on gas turbines; 22 on diesels
Range, miles: 5 300 at 17 knots (2 diesels); 4 200 at 19 knots (4 diesels); 1 300 at 28 knots (gas turbine)
Endurance: 45 days stores; 60 days provisions
Complement: 200

A very interesting design of handsome appearance—Vosper Thornycroft Mark 10. The moulded depth is 28½ feet *(8·8 metres)*. Exceptionally economical in personnel, amounting to a fifty per cent reduction of manpower in relation to previous warships of this size and complexity. Require 100 fewer men than the British Type 42 of approximately similar characteristics. *Niteroi* started trials in Jan 1976. *Defensora* launched 17 Apr 1975 and started trials Oct 1976.

Class: F 40, 41, 44 and 45 are of the A/S configuration. F 42 and 43 are General Purpose design.

Contract: A contract announced on 29 Sep 1970, valued at about £100 000 000, was signed between the Brazilian Government and Vosper Thornycroft Ltd, Portsmouth, England for the design and building of these six Vosper Thornycroft Mark 10 frigates comparable with the British Type 42 guided missile destroyers being built for the Royal Navy.

Construction: Materials, equipment and lead-yard services supplied by Vosper Thornycroft at Arsenal de Marinho.

Electronics: CAAIS equipment by Ferranti (FM 1600B computers). ECM by Decca.

Names: The names of the six ships as originally allocated in 1971 were: *Campista, Constituição, Defensora, Imperatriz, Isabel* and *Niteroi.*

Radar:
Air Warning: 1 Plessey AWS-2 with Mk 10 IFF.
Surface Warning: 1 Signaal ZWO-6.
Weapon Control and Tracking: 2 Selenia RTN-10X.
Ikara Tracker: 1 set in A/S ships only.

Sonar: 1 EDO 610E medium range.
1 EDO 700E VDS (A/S ships only).

NITEROI   1/1976, Michael D. J. Lennon

DEFENSORA on trials   10/1976, Michael D. J. Lennon

NITEROI   2/1976, Michael D. J. Lennon

5 Ex-US "FLETCHER" CLASS

Name	No.	Builders	Laid down	Launched	Commissioned
PARA (ex-USS *Guest,* DD 472)	D 27	Boston Navy Yard	27 Sep 1941	20 Feb 1942	15 Dec 1942
PARAIBA (ex-USS *Bennett,* DD 473)	D 28	Boston Navy Yard	10 Dec 1941	16 Apr 1942	9 Feb 1943
PARAÑA (ex-USS *Cushing,* DD 797)	D 29	Bethlehem Steel Co (Staten Island)	3 May 1943	30 Sep 1943	17 Jan 1944
PERNAMBUCO (ex-USS *Hailey,* DD 556)	D 30	Seattle-Tacoma S.B. Corpn, (Seattle)	1 Apr 1942	9 Mar 1943	30 Sep 1943
MARANHAO (ex-USS *Shields,* DD 596)	D 33	Puget Sound Navy Yard	10 Aug 1943	25 Sep 1944	8 Feb 1945

Displacement, tons: 2 050 standard; 3 050 full load
Length, feet (metres): 376·5 *(114·8)* oa
Beam, feet (metres): 39·3 *(12·0)*
Draught, feet (metres): 18 *(5·5)*
Missiles: 1 quadruple Seacat *(Maranhao only)*
Guns: 5—5 in *(127 mm)* 38 cal (except *Pernambuco:* 4—5 in);
  6—3 in *(76 mm)* 50 cal (3 twin) *(Pernambuco only)*;
  10—40 mm *(2 quad, 1 twin) (Paraiba, Paraña and Maranhão)*;
  6—40 mm (3 twin) *(Para)*
Torpedo tubes: 5—21 in *(533 mm)* (not in *Maranhao)*
A/S weapons: 2 Hedgehogs;
  1 DC rack;
  2 side launching torpedo racks (not in *Maranhao)*;
  2 triple Mk 32 torpedo launchers *(Maranhao only)*
Main engines: 2 GE geared turbines; 2 shafts; 60 000 shp
Boilers: 4 Babcock & Wilcox
Speed, knots: 35
Oil fuel, tons: 650
Range, miles: 5 000 at 15 knots; 1 260 at 30 knots
Complement: 260

Para was transferred on loan 5 June 1959; *Paraiba* on loan 15 Dec 1959 and subsequently by sale 1 Aug 1973. *Parana* on loan 20 July 1961 and subsequently by sale 8 Jan 1973; *Pernambuco* on loan 20 July 1961 and *Maranhao* by sale 1 July 1972. *Piaui* (ex-*Lewis Hancock* DD 675) was transferred on loan 2 Aug 1967 whilst *Santa Catarina* (ex-*Irwin* DD 794) was transferred on loan 10 May 1968, and both by sale 11 April 1973, being used subsequently for spare parts.

Radar: Search: SPS 6. Tactical: SPS 10. Fire Control: I Band.

PERNAMBUCO (four 5 inch guns)   *1974, Brazilian Navy*

PARAÑA (five 5 inch guns)   *1970, Captain A. M. de Silva*

1 Ex-US "ALLEN M. SUMNER" and 4 Ex-US "ALLEN M. SUMNER FRAM II" CLASSES

Name	No.	Builders	Laid down	Launched	Commissioned
ALAGOAS (ex-USS *Buck* DD 761)	D 36	Bethlehem (San Francisco)	—	11 Mar 1945	28 June1946
ESPIRITO SANTO (ex-USS *Lowry* DD 770)	D 38	Bethlehem (San Pedro)	—	6 Feb 1944	23 July 1944
RIO GRANDE DO NORTE (ex-USS *Strong* DD 758)	D 37	Bethlehem (San Francisco)	—	23 Apr 1944	8 Mar 1945
SERGIPE (ex-USS *James C. Owens* DD 776)	D 35	Bethlehem (San Pedro)	—	1 Oct 1944	17 Feb 1945
MATO GROSSO (ex-USS *Compton,* DD 705)	D 34	Federal S.B. & D.D. Co.	—	17 Sep 1944	4 Nov 1944

Displacement, tons: 2 200 standard; 3 320 full load
Length, feet (metres): 376·5 *(114·8)* oa
Beam, feet (metres): 40·9 *(12·4)*
Draught, feet (metres): 19 *(5·8)*
Missiles: Sea Cat system *(Mato Grosso only)*
Guns: 6—5 in *(127 mm)* 38 cal (twins)
A/S weapons: 2 triple torpedo launchers; 2 ahead-firing Hedgehogs; facilities for small helicopter (Fram II).
  Depth charges *(Mato Grosso)*
Main engines: 2 geared turbines; 60 000 shp; 2 shafts
Boilers: 4
Speed, knots: 34
Range, miles: 4 600 at 15 knots, 1 260 at 30 knots
Complement: 274

Transferred to Brazil as follows: *Mato Grosso* 27 Sep 1972, *Sergipe* and *Alagoas* 16 July 1973, *Espirito Santo* 29 Oct 1973, *Rio Grande do Norte* 31 Oct 1973, the last four being FRAM II conversions, *Mato Grosso* being of the original "Sumner" class.

Gunnery: 3 inch guns in *Mato Grosso* removed before transfer.

Missiles: Sea Cat system transferred to *Mato Grosso* from deleted *Mariz E Barros* of "Marcilio Dias" class.

MATO GROSSO   *1974, Brazilian Navy*

Radar: SPS 6 and 10 and Mk 20 director *(Mato Grosso).* SPS 10 and 37 *(Espirito Santo).* SPS 10 and 40 (remainder).   **Sonar:** SQS 31 *(Mato Grosso).* SQA 10 and SQS 40 (remainder).

2 Ex-US "GEARING" (FRAM I) CLASS

Name	No.	Builders	Laid down	Launched	Commissioned
MARCILIO DIAS (ex-USS *Henry W. Tucker* DD 875)	D 25	Consolidated Steel	1944	8 Nov 1944	12 Mar 1945
MARIZ E. BARROS (ex-USS *Brinkley Bass* D 887)	D 26	Consolidated Steel	1944	26 May 1945	1 Oct 1945

Displacement, tons: 2 425 standard; 3 500 full load
Length, feet (metres): 390·5 *(119·0)*
Beam, feet (metres): 40·9 *(12·4)*
Draught, feet (metres): 19 *(5·8)*
Guns: 4—5 inch *(127 mm)* 38 cal (twin)
A/S weapons: 1 Asroc 8-tube launcher; 2 triple Mk 32 torpedo launchers; facilities for small helicopter
Main engines: 2 GE geared turbines; 60 000 shp; 2 shafts
Boilers: 4 Babcock & Wilcox
Speed, knots: 34
Range, miles: 5 800 at 15 knots
Complement: 274 (14 officers, 260 men)

Enlarged "Allen M. Sumner" class—14 feet longer.
Fitted with VDS. Transferred 3 Dec 1973.

"GEARING" (FRAM I) Class

Radar: SPS-10 and SPS-40.   **Sonar:** SQS-23.

SUBMARINES

3 BRITISH "OBERON" CLASS

Name	No.	Builders	Laid down	Launched	Commissioned
HUMAITA	S 20	Vickers, Barrow	3 Nov 1970	5 Oct 1971	18 June1973
TONELERO	S 21	Vickers, Barrow	18 Nov 1971	22 Nov 1972	? 1977
RIACHUELO	S 22	Vickers, Barrow	26 May 1973	6 Sep 1975	Early 1977

Displacement, tons: 1 610 standard;
2 030 surfaced; 2 410 dived
Length, feet (metres): 295·5 (90·1) oa
Beam, feet (metres): 26·5 (8·1)
Draught, feet (metres): 18·0 (5·5)
Tubes: 8—21 in (533 mm) (6 bow and 2 stern)
Main machinery: 2 Admiralty Standard Range 1 16-cyl diesels;
3 680 bhp; 2 electric motors; 6 000 shp; 2 shafts; electric
drive
Speed, knots: 12 surfaced, 17 dived
Complement: 70 (6 officers and 64 men)

In 1969 it was announced that two submarines of the British
"Oberon" class were ordered from Vickers, Barrow. The third
boat was ordered in 1972. Completion of *Tonelero* has been
much delayed by a serious fire on board. She spent a period in
Chatham Dockyard, having been towed from Barrow, return-
ing in January 1976. Completion unlikely before early 1977.
Whilst in Chatham the centre 60 ft was replaced. Diesels by
Vickers Shipbuilding Group. Electric Motors by AEI-English
Electric. Sonar, modern navigational aids and provision for
modern fire control system developed by Vickers.

HUMAITA   1973, Vickers

2 Ex-US GUPPY III TYPE

Name	No.	Builders	Laid down	Launched	Commissioned
AMAZONAS (ex-USS *Greenfish* SS 351)	S 16	Electric Boat Co	29 June1944	21 Dec 1945	7 June1946
GOIÀZ (ex-USS *Trumpetfish* SS 425)	S 15	Cramp SB Co	23 Aug 1943	13 May 1945	29 Jan 1946

Displacement, tons: 1 975 standard; 2 450 dived
Length, feet (metres): 326·5 (99·4)
Beam, feet (metres): 27 (8·2)
Draught, feet (metres): 17 (5·2)
Torpedo tubes: 10—21 in; 6 bow 4 stern
Main machinery: 4 diesels; 6 400 hp; 2 electric motors;
5 400 hp; 2 shafts
Speed, knots: 20 surfaced; 15 dived
Complement: 85

Converted in 1960-62. *Goiàz* transferred by sale 15 Oct 1973
and *Amazonas* by sale 19 Dec 1973.

Sonar: BQR-2 array, BQG-4 (PUFFS) fire control sonar (fins on
casing).

AMAZONAS   1969, USN

5 Ex-US GUPPY II TYPE

Name	No.	Builders	Laid down	Launched	Commissioned
GUANABARA (ex-USS *Dogfish* SS 350)	S 10	Electric Boat Co	22 June1944	27 Oct 1945	29 Apr 1946
RIO GRANDE DO SUL (ex-USS *Grampus* SS 523)	S 11	Boston Navy Yard	8 Feb 1944	15 Dec 1944	26 Oct 1946
BAHIA (ex-USS *Sea Leopard* SS 483)	S 12	Portsmouth Navy Yard	7 Nov 1944	2 Mar 1945	11 June1945
RIO DE JANEIRO (ex-*Guanabara*, ex-USS *Odax* SS 484)	S 13	Portsmouth Navy Yard	4 Dec 1944	10 Apr 1945	11 July 1945
CEARÁ (ex-USS *Amberjack* SS 522)	S 14	Boston Navy Yard	8 Feb 1944	15 Dec 1944	4 Mar 1946

Displacement, tons: 1 870 standard; 2 420 dived
Length, feet (metres): 307·5 (93·8) oa
Beam, feet (metres): 27·2 (8·3)
Draught, feet (metres): 18 (5·5)
Torpedo tubes: 10—21 in (6 bow, 4 stern)
Main machinery: 3 diesels, 4 800 shp; 2 motors; 5 400 shp;
2 shafts
Speed, knots: 18 surfaced; 15 dived
Range, miles: 12 000 at 10 knots (surfaced)
Complement: 82

Modernised under Guppy II programme 1948-50 except *Rio de
Janeiro* which was first modernised to Guppy I standards and
later to Guppy II. Transferred 13 May 1972 (*Rio Grande do Sul*),
8 July 1972 (*Rio de Janeiro*), 28 July 1972 (*Guanabara*), 27 Mar
1973 (*Bahia*), 17 Oct 1973 (*Ceara*). All by sale.

RIO GRANDE DO SUL   1972, Brazilian Navy

AMPHIBIOUS FORCES

1 Ex-US TANK LANDING SHIP

Name	No.	Builders	Commissioned
GARCIA D'AVILA	G 28	—	17 Apr 1945
(ex-USS *Outagamie County* LST 1073)			

Displacement, tons: 1 653 standard; 2 366 beaching; 4 080 full load
Dimensions, feet (metres): 328 oa × 50 × 14 *(100 × 15·3 × 3·4)*
Guns: 8—40 mm (2 twin, 4 single)
Main engines: GM diesels; 2 shafts; 1 700 bhp = 11·6 knots
Complement: 119
Troops: 147

Of LST 511-1152 Series. Transferred on loan to Brazil by USN 21 May 1971, purchased 1 Dec 1973.

GARCIA D'AVILA   1973, Brazilian Navy

1 Ex-US TANK LANDING SHIP

Name	No.	Builders	Commissioned
DUQUE DE CAXAIS	G 26	Avondale, New Orleans	8 Nov 1957
(ex-USS *Grant County* LST 1174)			

Displacement, tons: 3 828 light; 7 804 full load
Dimensions, feet (metres): 445 oa × 62 × 16·9 *(135·7 × 18·9 × 5·2)*
Guns: 2—3 in 50 cal (twins)
Main engines: Diesels; 13 700 shp; 2 shafts; CP propellers = 17·2 knots
Complement: 175 (11 officers, 164 men)
Troops: App. 575

"De Soto County" Class. Launched 12 Oct 1956 and transferred 15 Jan 1973. On lease.

28 LCV (P)

Built in Japan 1959-60.

7 EDVP

Fitted with Saab-Skania Diesels of 153 hp. 37 ft long and with glass-fibre hulls. Built in Brazil in 1971-73. Can carry 36 men or equivalent amount of equipment.

4 LCU TYPE

CAMBORIÁ   **GUARAPARI**   **TIMBAN**   **TRAMANDAI**

Built in Rio de Janeiro 1974-75 by Arsenal de Marinha.

9 LCM (6)

Also reported but not confirmed.

PATROL FORCES

Note: 6-12 750 ton corvettes are projected.

10 "IMPERIAL MARINHEIRO" CLASS

Name	No.	Builders	Commissioned
IMPERIAL MARINHEIRO	V 15	Netherlands	1954
IGUATEMI	V 16	Netherlands	1954
IPIRANGA	V 17	Netherlands	1954
FORTE DE COIMBRA	V 18	Netherlands	1954
CABACLA	V 19	Netherlands	1954
ANGOSTURA	V 20	Netherlands	1955
BAIANA	V 21	Netherlands	1955
MEARIM	V 22	Netherlands	1955
PURUS	V 23	Netherlands	1955
SOLIMOES	V 24	Netherlands	1955

Displacement, tons: 911 standard
Dimensions, feet (metres): 184 × 30·5 × 11·7 *(55·7 × 9·6 × 4·6)*
Guns: 1—3 in 50 cal; 4—20 mm
Main engines: 2 Sulzer diesels; 2 160 bhp = 16 knots
Oil fuel, tons: 135
Complement: 60

SOLIMOES   1972, Brazilian Navy

Actually fleet tugs classed as corvettes. Equipped for fire fighting. *Imperial Marinheiro* employed as submarine support ship.

2 "PEDRO TEIXEIRA" CLASS (RIVER PATROL SHIPS)

Name	No.	Builders	Commissioned
PEDRO TEIXEIRA	P 20	Arsenal de Marinha, Rio de Janeiro	17 Dec 1973
RAPOSO TAVARES	P 21	Arsenal de Marinha, Rio de Janeiro	17 Dec 1973

Displacement, tons: 700 standard
Dimensions, feet (metres): 203·4 × 30·7 × 6·3 *(62 × 9·4 ×1·7)*
Guns: 1—40 mm; 2—81 mm mortars 6—50 cal MG
Main engines: 4 diesels; 2 shafts = 16 knots

Helicopter platform and hangar fitted. Carry one LCVP. *Pedro Teixeira* launched 14 Oct 1970—*Raposo Tavares* 11 June 1972. Belong to Amazon Flotilla.

PEDRO TEIXEIRA   1974, Brazilian Navy

1 THORNYCROFT TYPE (RIVER MONITOR)

Name	No.	Builders	Commissioned
PARNAIBA	U 17 (ex-P 2)	Arsenal de Marinha, Rio de Janeiro	Nov 1937

Displacement, tons: 620 standard; 720 full load
Dimensions, feet (metres):180·5 oa × 33·3 × 5·1 *(54·5 × 10·2 × 1·5)*
Guns: 1—3 in, 50 cal; 2—47 mm; 2—40 mm, 6—20 mm
Armour: 3 in side and partial deck protection
Main engines: 2 Thornycroft triple expansion; 2 shafts; 1 300 ihp = 12 knots
Boilers: 2 three drum type, working pressure 250 psi
Oil fuel, tons: 70
Range, miles: 1 350 at 10 knots
Complement: 90

Laid down on 11 June 1936. Launched on 2 Sep 1937. In Mato Grosso Flotilla. Rearmed with the above guns in 1960.

PARNAIBA   *1971, Brazilian Navy*

3 "RORAIMA" CLASS (RIVER PATROL SHIPS)

Name	No	Builders	Commissioned
RORAIMA	P 30	Maclaren, Niteroi	Mar 1974
RONDONIA	P 31	Maclaren, Niteroi	1974
AMAPA	P 32	Maclaren, Niteroi	1975

Displacement, tons: 340 standard; 365 full load
Dimensions, feet (metres): 147·6 × 27·7 × 4·2 *(45 × 8·5 × 1·4)*
Guns: 1—40 mm; 2—81 mm mortars; 6—50 cal MGs
Main engines: Diesels; 2 shafts = 14·5 knots

Rondônia launched 10 Jan 1973, *Amapa* 9 Mar 1973. Belong to Amazon Flotilla.

RORAIMA   *1975, Brazilian Navy*

LIGHT FORCES
Note: A new class of Fast Attack Craft is projected.

6 "PIRATINI" CLASS (LARGE PATROL CRAFT)

Name	No.	Builders	Commissioned
PIRATINI (ex-PGM 109)	P 10	Arsenal de Marinha, Rio de Janeiro	Nov 1970
PIRAJA (ex-PGM 110)	P 11	Arsenal de Marinha, Rio de Janeiro	Mar 1971
PAMPEIRO (ex-PGM 118)	P 12	Arsenal de Marinha, Rio de Janeiro	May 1971
PARATI (ex-PGM 119)	P 13	Arsenal de Marinha, Rio de Janeiro	July 1971
PENEDO (ex-PGM 120)	P 14	Arsenal de Marinha, Rio de Janeiro	Sept 1971
POTI (ex-PGM 121)	P 15	Arsenal de Marinha, Rio de Janeiro	Oct 1971

Displacement, tons: 105 standard
Dimensions, feet (metres): 95 × 19 × 6·5 *(30·5 × 6·1 ×1·9)*
Guns: 3—·50 cal MG; 1—81 mm mortar
Main engines: 4 diesels; 1 100 bhp = 17 knots
Range, miles: 1 700 at 12 knots
Complement: 15 officers and men

Built under offshore agreement with the USA.

POTI   *1972, Brazilian Navy*

6 "ANCHOVA" CLASS (RIVER PATROL CRAFT)

Name	No.	Builders	Commissioned
ANCHOVA	R 54	Brazil	1965
ARENQUE	R 55	Brazil	1965
ATUM	R 56	Brazil	1966
ACARA	R 57	Brazil	1966
AGULHA	R 58	Brazil	1967
ARUANA	R 59	Brazil	1967

Displacement, tons: 11
Dimensions, feet (metres): 42·6 × 12·5 × 3·9 *(13 × 3·8 ×1·2)*
Main engines: 2 Diesels; 280 hp = 25 knots
Range, miles: 400 at 20 knots
Complement: 3 plus 12 passengers

4 RIVER PATROL CRAFT

Built in 1968. Of about 30 tons and 45 feet *(13·7 metres)* in length. Capable of 17 knots and with a range of 1 400 miles at 10 knots. Operate on the Upper Amazon.

MINE WARFARE FORCES

6 "ARATU" CLASS (MINESWEEPERS—COASTAL)

Name	No.	Builders	Commissioned
ARATU	M 15	Abeking and Rasmussen	5 May 1971
ANHATOMIRIM	M 16	Abeking and Rasmussen	30 Nov 1971
ATALAIA	M 17	Abeking and Rasmussen	13 Dec 1972
ARACATUBA	M 18	Abeking and Rasmussen	13 Dec 1972
ABROLHOS	M 19	Abeking and Rasmussen	16 Apr 1975
ALBARDÃO	M 20	Abeking and Rasmussen	21 July 1975

Displacement, tons: 230 standard; 280 full load
Dimensions, feet (metres): 154·9 × 23·6 × 6·9 *(47·2 × 7·2 × 2·1)*
Gun: 1—40 mm
Main engines: 4 Maybach diesels; 2 shafts; 4 500 bhp = 24 knots
Range, miles: 710 at 20 knots
Complement: 39

Wooden hulled. First four ordered in April 1969 and another pair in Nov 1973. Same design as W. German "Schütze" class.

ABROLHOS   *4/1975, Reiner Nerlich*

SURVEY SHIPS

ALVARO ALBERTO

Dimensions, feet (metres): 196·8 × 3·7 × 14·1 *(60 × 12 × 4·3)*
Complement: 26 plus 17 scientists

A new oceanographic research ship ordered in 1973.

1 Ex-US "CONRAD" CLASS

Name	No.	Builders	Commissioned
ALMIRANTE CÀMARA	H 41	Marietta Co, Point Pleasant	8 Feb 1965
(ex-USNS *Sands* T-AGOR 6)		West Va.	

Displacement, tons: 1 200 standard; 1 380 full load
Dimensions, feet (metres): 208·9 oa × 37·4 × 15·3 *(63·7 × 11·4 × 4·7)*
Main engines: Diesel electric; Caterpillar Tractor Co diesels; 10 000 bhp; 1 shaft = 13·5 knots
Range, miles: 12 000 at 12 knots
Complement: 26 (+15 scientists)

Built specifically for oceanographic research. Equipped for gravimetric, magnetic and geological research. Has bow thruster, 10 ton crane and 620 hp gas turbine for providing "quiet power". Transferred 1 July 1974.

ALMIRANTE CÀMARA (as USNS *Sands*)　　　　　USN

2 "SIRIUS" CLASS

Name	No.	Builders	Commissioned
CANOPUS	H 22	Ishikawajima Co Ltd, Tokyo	15 Mar 1958
SIRIUS	H 21	Ishikawajima Co Ltd, Tokyo	1 Jan 1958

Displacement, tons: 1 463 standard; 1 800 full load
Dimensions, feet (metres): 255·7 oa × 39·3 × 12·2 *(78 × 12 × 3·7)*
Guns: 1—3 in; 4—20 mm MG
Main engines: 2 Sulzer diesels; 2 shafts; 2 700 bhp = 15·75 knots
Range, miles: 12 000 at cruising speed of 11 knots
Complement: 116

Laid down 1955-56. Helicopter platform aft. Special surveying apparatus, echo sounders, Raydist equipment, sounding machines installed, and helicopter, landing craft (LCVP), jeep, and survey launches carried. All living and working spaces are air-conditioned. Controllable pitch propellers.

SIRIUS　　　　　1970, Brazilian Navy

3 "ARGUS" CLASS

Name	No.	Builders	Commissioned
ARGUS	H 31	Arsenal da Marinha, Rio de Janeiro	29 Jan 1959
ORION	H 32	Arsenal da Marinha, Rio de Janeiro	11 June1959
TAURUS	H 33	Arsenal da Marinha, Rio de Janeiro	23 Apr 1959

Displacement, tons: 250 standard; 343 full load
Dimensions, feet (metres): 147·7 oa × 20 × 6·6 *(45 × 6·1 × 2)*
Guns: 2—20 mm
Main engines: 2 diesels coupled to two shafts; 1 200 bhp = 15 knots
Oil fuel, tons: 35
Range, miles: 1 200 at 15 knots
Complement: 42

All laid down in 1955 and launched Dec 1957—Feb 1958.

TAURUS　　　　　1972, Brazilian Navy

Name	No.	Builders	Launched
ALMIRANTE SALDANHA	U 10 (ex-NE I)	Vickers Armstrong Ltd	19 Dec 1933

Displacement, tons: 3 325 standard; 3 825 full load
Dimensions, feet (metres): 307·2 oa × 52 × 18·2 *(93·7 × 15·9 × 5·6)*
Main engines: Diesel; 1 400 bhp = 11 knots
Range, miles: 12 000 at 10 knots
Complement: 218

Former training ship with a total sail area of 25 990 sq ft and armed with four 4-inch guns, one 3-inch AA gun and four 3-pounders. Cost £314 500. Instructional minelaying gear was included in equipment. The single 21-inch torpedo tube was removed. Re-classified as an Oceanographic Ship (NOc) Aug 1959, and completely remodelled by 1964. A photograph as sailing ship appears in the 1952-53 to 1959-60 editions.

ALMIRANTE SALDANHA　　　　　1972, Brazilian Navy

1 LIGHTHOUSE TENDER

Name	No.	Builders	Commissioned
GRAÇA ARANHA	H 34	Elbin, Niteroi	Dec 1974

Displacement, tons: 1 250
Dimensions, feet (metres): 247·6 × 42·6 × 12·1 *(75·5 × 13 × 3·7)*
Aircraft: 1 Helicopter
Main engines: 1 Diesel; 2 000 hp; 1 shaft = 14 knots
Complement: 95

Laid down in 1971 and launched 23 May 1974. Fitted with collapsible helo-hangar.

SURVEY LAUNCHES

CAMOCIM H 16
CARAVELAS H 17
ITACURUSSA H 15

NOGUEIRA DA GAMA (ex-*Jaceguai*) H 14
PARAIBANO H 11
RIO BRANCO H 12

Displacement, tons: 32 standard; 50 full load
Dimensions, feet (metres): 52·5 × 15·1 × 4·3 *(16 × 4·6 × 1·3)*
Main engines: 1 diesel; 165 bhp = 11 knots
Range, miles: 600 at 11 knots
Complement: 11

First four launched 1968—last pair in 1972. Built by Bormann, Rio de Janeiro.

PARAIBANO　　　　　　　　　　　　　　*1974, Brazilian Navy*

CASTELHANOS H 24
FAROLEIRO AREAS H 27
FAROLEIRO NASCIMENTO H 25

FAROLEIRO SANTANA H 28
MESTRE JOÀO DOS SANTOS H 13

Buoy Tenders. Taken over 1973.

CASTELHANOS　　　　　　　　　　　　*1974, Brazilian Navy*

2 "JAVARI" CLASS (BUOY TENDERS)

JAVARI (ex-USS *Cardinal*) M 11
JURUA (ex-USS *Jackdaw*) M 13

Displacement, tons: 270 standard; 350 full load
Dimensions, feet (metres): 136 × 24·5 × 8 *(41·5 × 7·5 × 2·5)*
Guns: 4—20 mm in two twin mountings
A/S weapons: 2 DCT
Main engines: 2 GM diesels; 2 shafts; 1 000 bhp = 15 knots
Oil fuel, tons: 16
Range, miles: 2 300 at 8·5 knots
Complement: 50

Of wooden construction, launched in 1942-43. Originally known in USA as Auxiliary Motor minesweepers (AMS). *Javari* was transferred to Brazil by USA at Charleston Naval Shipyard on 15 Aug 1960. *Juruá* was transferred in Jan 1963 and will probably be disposed of in 1976.

SUBMARINE RESCUE SHIP

Name	No.	Builders	Launched
GASTÀO MOUTINHO (ex-USS *Skylark* ASR 20)	K 10	Charleston SB & DD Co.	19 Mar 1946

Displacement, tons: 1 235 standard; 1 740 full load
Dimensions, feet (metres): 205 oa × 38·5 × 15·3 *(62·5 × 11·7 × 4·7)*
Main engines: Diesel electric; 1 shaft; 3 000 bhp = 14 knots
Complement: 85

Converted to present form in 1947. Fitted with special pumps, compressors and submarine rescue chamber. Fitted for oxy-helium diving. Transferred 30 June 1973.

GASTÀO MOUTINHO　　　　　　　　　　*1975, Brazilian Navy*

REPAIR AND SUPPORT SHIPS

Name	No.	Builders	Commissioned
BELMONTE (ex-USS *Helios* ARB 12, ex-LST 1127)	G 24	Maryland DD Co, Baltimore	26 Feb 1945

Displacement, tons: 1 625 light; 2 030 standard; 4 100 full load
Dimensions, feet (metres): 328 oa × 50 × 11 *(98·4 × 15·3 × 3·4)*
Guns: 8—40 mm
Main engines: GM diesels; 2 shafts; 1 800 bhp = 11·6 knots
Oil fuel, tons: 1 000
Range, miles: 6 000 at 9 knots

Former United States battle damage repair ship (ex LST). Laid down on 23 Nov 1944. Launched on 14 Feb 1945. Loaned to Brazil by USA in Jan 1962 under MAP.

BAURU (ex-USS *McAnn* DE 179) U 28

An ex-US "Bostwick" class DE, last of eight transferred in 1944. Of 1 900 tons full load used as support vessel in Guanabara Bay.

TANKERS

Name	No.	Builders	Commissioned
MARAJO	G 27	Ishikawajima do Brasil-Estaleisos SA	22 Oct 1968

Measurements, tons: 10 500 deadweight
Dimensions, feet (metres): 440·7 × 63·3 × 24 *(134·4 × 19·3 × 7·3)*
Main engines: Diesel; one shaft = 13·6 knots
Capacity, (cu metres): 14 200
Range, miles: 9 200 at 13 knots
Complement: 80

Laid down on 13 Dec 1966 and launched on 31 Jan 1968.

MARAJO   *1972, Brazilian Navy*

Name	No.	Builders	Launched
POTENGI	G 17	Papendrecht, Netherlands	16 Mar 1938

Displacement, tons: 600
Dimensions, feet (metres): 178·8 oa × 24·5 × 6 *(54·5 × 7·5 × 1·8)*
Main engines: Diesels; 2 shafts ; 550 bhp = 10 knots
Oil fuel, tons: 450
Complement: 19

Employed in the Mato Grosso Flotilla on river service.

MARTINS DE OLIVEIRA (Ex-*Gastao Moutinho*) R 11

Displacement, tons: 588
Dimensions, feet (metres): 162 × 23·1 × 7·9 *(49·4 × 7 × 2·4)*
Speed, knots: 10·3

Taken over 1973.

TRANSPORTS

4 "PEREIRA" CLASS

Name	No.	Builders	Commissioned
ARY PARREIRAS	G 21	Ishikawajima Co Ltd, Tokyo	29 Dec 1956
BARROSO PEREIRA	G 16	Ishikawajima Co Ltd, Tokyo	1 Dec 1954
CUSTÒDIO DE MELLO	U 26	Ishikawajima Co Ltd, Tokyo	30 Dec 1954
SOARES DUTRA	G 22	Ishikawajima Co Ltd, Tokyo	23 Mar 1957

Displacement, tons: 4 800 standard; 7 300 full load
Measurement, tons: 4 200 deadweight; 4 879 gross (Panama)
Dimensions, feet (metres): 362 pp; 391·8 oa × 52·5 × 20·5 *(110·4; 119·5 × 16 × 6·3)*
Guns: 4—3 in (U 26); 2—3 in (others); 2/4—20 mm
Main engines: Ishikawajima double reduction geared turbines; 2 shafts; 4 800 shp = 17·67 knots (sea speed 15 knots)
Boilers: 2 Ishikawajima two drum water tube type, oil fuel
Complement: 127 (Troop capacity 497)

Transports and cargo vessels. Helicopter landing platform aft. Troop carrying capacity for 497, with commensurate medical, hospital and dental facilities. Working and living quarters are mechanically ventilated with partial air conditioning. Refrigerated cargo space 15 500 cubic feet. Can carry 4 000 tons of cargo. *Custòdio de Mello* has been classified as a training ship since July 1961.

CUSTODIO DE MELLO   *5/1975, C and S. Taylor*

6 "RIO DOCE" CLASS (HARBOUR TRANSPORTS)

Name	No.	Builders	Commissioned
RIO DOCE	U 20	Netherlands	1954
RIO DAS CONTAS	U 21	Netherlands	1954
RIO FORMOSO	U 22	Netherlands	1954
RIO REAL	U 23	Netherlands	1955
RIO TURVO	U 24	Netherlands	1955
RIO VERDE	U 25	Netherlands	1955

Displacement, tons: 150
Dimensions, feet (metres): 120 oa × 21·3 × 6·2 *(36·6 oa × 6·5 × 1·9)*
Main engines: 2 Sulzer 6-TD24; 900 bhp = 14 knots

Can carry 600 passengers. *Rio Doce* in collision in Rio Bay 13 Jan 1976.

4 NEW CONSTRUCTION (HARBOUR TRANSPORTS)

RIO PARDO U 40   **RIO NEGRO** U 41   **RIO CHUI** U 42   **RIO OIAPOQUE** U 43

Displacement, tons: 150
Dimensions, feet (metres): 116·8 × 21·3 × 6·2 *(35·4 × 6·5 × 1·9)*
Main engines: 2 Diesels = 14 knots

Capable of carrying 600 passengers. Completed by Inconav de Niteroi 1975-76.

PARAGUASSU (ex-*Guarapunava*) G 15 (RIVER TRANSPORT)

Displacement, tons: 285
Dimensions, feet (metres): 131·2 × 23 × 3·9 *(40 × 7 × 1·2)*
Speed knots: 12
Range, miles: 2 500 at 10 knots

FLOATING DOCKS

3 FLOATING DOCKS

CIDADE DE NATAL (ex-AFDL 39)

Displacement, tons: 7 600
Length, feet (metres): 390·3 *(119)*
Beam, feet (metres): 86·9 *(26·5)*
Capacity, tons: 2 800

Concrete floating dock loaned to Brazil by USN, 10 Nov 1966.

ALMIRANTE JERONIMO GONCALVES
(ex-*Goiaz* AFDL 4 ex-G 26)
Displacement, tons: 3 000
Length, feet (metres): 200 *(61)*
Beam, feet (metres): 44 *(13·4)*
Capacity, tons: 1 000

Steel floating dock sold to Brazil by USN, 10 Nov 1966.

AFONSO PENA (ex-*Ceara*, ex-ARD 14) G 25

Displacement, tons: 5 200
Dimensions, feet (metres): 402·0 × 81·0 *(122·6 × 24·7)*

Transferred from the US Navy to the Brazilian Navy in 1963.

TUGS

3 Ex-US ATA TYPE

TRIDENTE (ex-ATA 235) R 22   **TRITÀO** (ex-ATA 234) R 21   **TRIUNFO** (ex-ATA 236 R 23

Displacement, tons: 534 standard; 835 full load
Dimensions, feet (metres): 143 oa × 33 × 13·2 *(43·6 × 10 × 4)*
Guns: 2—20 mm
Main engines: GM diesel-electric; 1 500 hp = 13 knots

All built by Gulfport Boiler & Welding Works, Inc, Port Arthur, Texas, and launched in 1944. Sold to Brazil 1947.

ISLAS DE NORONHA

Of 200 tons. Built 1972.

2 COASTAL TUGS

DNOG   **LAHMEYER**

Of 100 tons and 105 ft long, built in Brazil in 1972. Based at Aratu.

LAURINDO PITTA R 14

514 tons. Vickers 1910. Reconstructed 1969.

WANDENKOLK R 20

350 tons. UK 1910.

ANTONIO JOA R 26

80 tons. Built Rio. Mato Grosso flotilla.

STORE TRANSPORTS

TENENTE FABIO **TENENTE RAUL**

Displacement, tons: 55 tons
Dimensions, feet (metres): 66·6 × 16·7 × 3·9 (20·3 × 5·10 × 1·20)
Main engines: Diesel 135 hp = 10 knots

1969. 2 ton derrick.

MUNITIONS TRANSPORTS

SAN FRANCISCO DOS SANTOS

1964.

UBIRAJARA DOS SANTOS **OPERARIO LUIS LEAL**

1968.

TORPEDO TRANSPORTS

MIGUEL DOS SANTOS **APRENDIZ LEDIO CONCEIÇAO**

1968.

TANKER

ANITA GARIBALDI

TUGS

AUDAZ R 31 **LAMEGO** R 34
CENTAURO R 32 **PASSO da PATRIA** R 35
GUARANI R 33 **VOLUNTARIO** R 36

Displacement, tons: 130 tons
Dimensions, feet (metres): 90·5 oa × 23·6 × 10·2 (27·6 × 7·2 × 3·1)
Main engines: Womag diesel of 765 hp = 11 knots
Complement: 12

Built by Holland Nautic Yard, Netherlands in 1953.

RAIMUNDO NONATO **ETCHBARNE** R 28 **GRUMETE** (1961)

WATER BOATS

PAULO AFONSO R 43 **ITAPURA** R 42

Displacement, tons: 485·3
Dimensions, feet (metres): 140·5 × 23 × 8 (42·8 × 7 × 2·5)
Main engines: Diesel

Capacity 389 tons. Launched 1957.

BUOY TENDERS/SURVEY CRAFT

FAROLEIRO WANDERLEY H 29 **PRATICO JUVENCIO** H 26
GETULIO LIMA H 23 **FAROL. N. SANTOS** H 30

MISCELLANEOUS

IGUASSU R 41 **MARIA QUITERIA** R 44 **ALMIRANTE BRASIL** R 13
DR. GONDIM R 38 **GUAIRIA** R 40 **A. BARBOSA** R 27
RIO PARDO R 30   **MARISCO**
RIO NEGRO R 37 Renamed or deleted? **TENENTE CLAUDIO**
TONELEROS R 18   **DHN-225**

BRUNEI

(Askar Melayu Diraja Brunei (Royal Brunei Malay Regiment) Flotilla)

Commanding Officer:
  Commander David Wright RN

Personnel

(a) 1977: 292 (22 officers and 270 ratings)
(b) Voluntary

Base

Muara Marine Base

Prefix to Ships' Names

KDB (Kapal Di-Raja Brunei)

Mercantile Marine

Lloyd's Register of Shipping:
  2 vessels of 899 tons gross

LIGHT FORCES

1 "PAHLAWAN" CLASS (FAST ATTACK CRAFT—MISSILE)

Name	No.	Builders	Commissioned
PAHLAWAN	P 01	Vosper (UK)	19 Oct 1967

Displacement, tons: 95 standard; 114 full load
Dimensions, feet (metres): 99·0 oa × 25·2 × 7·0 (30·3 × 7·3 × 2·2)
Missiles: 8—SS 12 on 2 launchers
Guns: 1—40 mm; 1—20 mm Hispano Suiza
Main engines: 3 Bristol Siddeley Proteus gas turbines; 3 shafts; 12 750 bhp = 57 knots;
  2 diesels for cruising and manoeuvring
Range, miles: 450 at full speed; 2 300 at 10 knots
Complement: 20

Ordered from Vosper Ltd, Portsmouth, England, on 10 Dec 1965. Launched on 5 Dec 1966. Constructed of resin bonded timber with aluminium alloy superstructure. Missile launchers fitted in May 1972.

Radar: Decca TM 616.

PAHLAWAN *1976, Royal Brunei Malay Regiment*

3 "PERWIRA" CLASS (COASTAL PATROL CRAFT)

Name	No.	Builders	Commissioned
PERWIRA	P 14	Vosper Thornycroft (Singapore)	9 Sept 1974
PEMBURU	P 15	Vosper Thornycroft (Singapore)	April 1975
PENYARANG	P 16	Vosper Thornycroft (Singapore)	April 1975

Displacement, tons: 30
Dimensions, feet (metres): 71 × 20 × 5 *(21·7 × 6·1 × 1·2)*
Guns: 2—20 mm Hispano Suiza; 2—7·62 MG
Main engines: 2 MTU MB 12V 331 TC81 Diesels; 2 450 bhp
Speed, knots: 32
Range, miles: 600 at 22 knots; 1 000 miles cruising
Complement: 12

Perwira launched 9 May 1974. Other two ordered June 1974. Of all wooden construction on laminated frames. Fitted with enclosed bridges—modified July 1976.

Radar: Decca 916.

PERWIRA 1974, Royal Brunei Malay Regiment

3 "RAJA ISTERI" CLASS (COASTAL PATROL CRAFT)

Name	No.	Builders	Commissioned
MASNA	P 12	Vosper Thornycroft (Singapore)	1972
NORAIN	P 13	Vosper Thornycroft (Singapore)	Aug 1972
SALEHA	P 11	Vosper Thornycroft (Singapore)	1972

Displacement, tons: 25
Dimensions, feet (metres): 62·0 × 16·0 × 4·5 *(18·9 × 4·8 × 1·4)*
Guns: 2—20 mm Hispano-Suiza; 2 MG
Main engines: 2 GM 71 16 cylinder diesels; 1 250 bhp = 26 knots
Range, miles: 600 at 23 knots
Complement: 8

Fitted with Decca 202 radar. Named after Brunei princesses.

NORAIN 1974, Royal Brunei Malay Regiment

3 PATROL CRAFT (RIVERINE)

Name	No.	Conversion
BENDAHARA	P 21	1974
KEMAINDERA	P 23	1975
MAHARAJALELA	P 22	1975

Displacement, tons: 10
Dimensions, feet (metres): 47·0 × 12·0 × 3·0 *(14·3 × 3·6 × 0·9)*
Guns: 2 twin MG 42, 7·62 cal
Main engines: 2 GM diesels; 334 bhp = 20 knots
Range, miles: 200
Complement: 6

Fitted with Decca 202 radar.

Conversion: *Kemaindera* was converted in July 1974 for riverine duties. Other pair were similarly converted during 1975.

BENDAHARA 1976, Royal Brunei Malay Regiment

AMPHIBIOUS FORCES

2 CHEVERTON "LOADMASTERS"

DAMUAN L31 + **1**

Displacement, tons: 60
Dimensions, feet (metres): 65 × 20 × 3·6 *(19·8 × 6·1 × 1·1)*
Main engines: 2 GM V 71 6 cylinder diesels = 9 knots
Range, miles: 1 000
Complement: 13

Damuan commissioned May 1976, second in Feb 1977.

Radar: Decca RM 1216.

DAMUAN 1976, Royal Brunei Malay Regiment

24 FAST ASSAULT BOATS

Rigid Raider type with 1 MG and two 50 hp outboards.

BULGARIA

Ministerial

Minister of National Defence:
General Dobri Dzhurov

Headquarters Appointment

Commander-in-Chief, Navy:
Vice-Admiral VG Yanakiev

Diplomatic Representation

Naval, Military and Air Attaché in London:
Colonel Dimitar Toskov

Personnel

(a) 1977: 10 000 officers and ratings
(b) 3 years national service (6 000)

Bases

Varna, Burgas, Sozopol

Naval Aviation

2 Mi1 Helicopters
6 Mi4 (Hound) Helicopters

Strength of the Fleet

No building programme available

Type	Active
Frigates	2
Corvettes	9
Patrol Submarines	2
Fast Attack Craft (Missile)	4
Fast Attack Craft (Torpedo)	8
Minesweepers (Ocean)	2
Minesweepers (Coastal)	4
Minesweeping Boats	24
Landing Craft	18
Auxiliaries	several

Mercantile Marine

Lloyd's Register of Shipping:
176 vessels of 933 361 tons gross

DELETIONS

Submarines

1972 2 "Whiskey" Class (names transferred to "Romeo" class)

Corvettes

1975 2 "Kronshstadt" class (numbers transferred to "Poti" class)

Light Forces

1975 4 "P4" class

Minewarfare Forces

1974 3 "T301" class
1975 1 "T301" class

FRIGATES
2 Ex-SOVIET "RIGA" CLASS

DRUZKI 31   **SMELI** 32

Displacement, tons: 1 200 standard; 1 600 full load
Length, feet (metres): 298·8 *(91·0)*
Beam, feet (metres): 33·7 *(10·2)*
Draught, feet (metres): 11·0 *(3·4)*
Guns: 3—3·9 in *(100 mm)*; 4—37 mm
A/S Weapons: 4 MBU 1 800 (5 tubed), 4 DCT
Torpedo tubes: 3—21 in *(533 mm)*
Main engines: Geared turbines; 2 shafts; 25 000 shp
Speed, knots: 28
Range, miles: 2 500 at 15 knots
Complement: 150

Transferred from USSR in 1957-8.

Radar: Search; Slim Net. Navigation; Neptune.
IFF; Highpole A. Fire Control; Wasphead/Sunvisor A.

"RIGA" Class

SUBMARINES (PATROL)
2 Ex-SOVIET "ROMEO" CLASS

POBEDA   **SLAVA**

Displacement, tons: 1 000 surfaced; 1 600 dived
Length, feet (metres): 249·3 *(76)*
Beam, feet (metres): 24 *(7·3)*
Draught, feet (metres): 14·5 *(4·4)*
Torpedo tubes: 6—21 in *(533 mm)* (bow)
Main machinery: 2 Diesels; 4 000 hp; 2 main motors; 4 000 hp; 2 shafts
Speed, knots: 17 surfaced, 14 dived
Complement: 65

Transferred in 1972-73 as replacements for "Whiskey", whose names they took over.

Radar. Snoop Plate.

"ROMEO" Class

1974

CORVETTES

3 Ex-SOVIET "POTI" CLASS

33   34   35

Displacement, tons: 550 standard; 600 full load
Dimensions, feet (metres): 193·5 × 26·2 × 9·2 *(59 × 8 × 2·8)*
Guns: 2—57 mm (twin)
Torpedo tubes: 4—16 in A/S
A/S weapons: 2 MBU 2 500 A
Main engines: 2 gas turbines; 2 diesels; 4 shafts; total 20 000 hp = 28 knots

Transferred Dec 1975. Built 1961-68.

Radar: Strut Curve, Muff Cob and Don.

Soviet "POTI" Class   1975

LIGHT FORCES

6 Ex-SOVIET "SO I" CLASS

41 to 46

Displacement, tons: 215 light; 250 full load
Length, feet (metres): 138·6 *(42·3)*
Beam, feet (metres): 20 *(6·1)*
Draught, feet (metres): 9·2 *(2·8)*
Guns: 4—25 mm (2 twin)
A/S weapons: 4 five-barrelled MBU 1800 launchers; DCs
Main engines: 3 diesels; 6 000 bhp = 26 knots
Range, miles: 1 100 at 13 knots
Complement: 30

Steel hulled vessels transferred from USSR in 1963.

Radar: Pot Head.

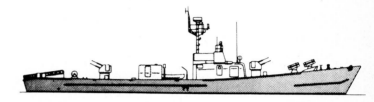

"SO 1" Class

4 Ex-SOVIET "OSA I" CLASS (FAST ATTACK CRAFT—MISSILE)

21   22   23   24

Displacement, tons: 165 standard; 200 full load
Dimensions, feet (metres): 128·7 × 25·1 × 5·9 *(39·3 × 7·7 × 1·8)*
Missile launchers: 4 in two pairs abreast for SSN-2 system
Guns: 4—30 mm (2 twin, 1 forward, 1 aft)
Main engines: 3 diesels; 13 000 bhp = 36 knots
Range, miles: 800 at 25 knots
Complement: 25

Reported to have been transferred from USSR in 1970-71.

Radar: Drum Tilt and Square Tie.

"OSA 1" Class

4 Ex-SOVIET "SHERSHEN" CLASS (FAST ATTACK CRAFT—TORPEDO)

27   28   29   30

Displacement, tons: 150 standard; 160 full load
Dimensions, feet (metres): 115·5 × 23·1 × 5·0 *(35·2 × 7·1 × 1·5)*
Guns: 4—30 mm (2 twin)
Tubes: 4—21 in (single)
A/S armament: 12 DCs
Main engines: 3 diesels; 3 shafts; 13 000 bhp = 41 knots
Range, miles: 700 at 20 knots
Complement: 25

Transferred from USSR in 1970.

Radar: Pot Drum, Drum Tilt. IFF; High Pole A.

"SHERSHEN" Class

4 Ex-SOVIET "P 4" CLASS (FAST ATTACK CRAFT—TORPEDO)

Displacement, tons: 22 full load
Dimensions, feet (metres): 62·7 × 11·6 × 5·6 *(19·1 × 3·5 × 1·7)*
Guns: 2—15 mm
Torpedo tubes: 2—18 in
Main engines: 2 diesels; 2 shafts; 2 200 bhp = 50 knots
Complement: 12

Transferred from USSR in 1956. Will soon be deleted.

"P 4" Class

MINE WARFARE FORCES

2 Ex-SOVIET "T 43" CLASS (MINESWEEPERS—OCEAN)

Displacement, tons: 500 standard; 610 full load
Dimensions, feet (metres): 190·2 × 28·2 × 6·9 (58·0 × 8·6 × 2·1)
Guns: 4—37 mm (twin); 4—12·7 mm (twins)
Main engines: 2 Diesels; 2 shafts; 2 000 hp = 17 knots
Range, miles: 1 600 at 10 knots
Complement: 40

Three were transferred from USSR in 1953—One scrapped for spares. These are the only short-hulled, low bridge, tripod mast T43s in existance.

4 Ex-SOVIET "VANYA" CLASS (MINESWEEPERS—COASTAL)

36	37	38	39

Displacement, tons: 250 standard; 275 full load
Dimensions, feet (metres): 130·7 × 24 × 6·9 (39·9 × 7·3 × 2·1)
Guns—2—30 mm (twin)
Main engines: 2 Diesels; 2 200 bhp = 18 knots
Complement: 30

Transferred from USSR in 1971-72.

24 "PO 2" CLASS (MSB)

Built in Bulgaria—first units completed in 1957 and last in early 1960s.

AMPHIBIOUS FORCES

10 Ex-SOVIET "VYDRA" CLASS

Displacement, tons: 300 standard; 500 full load
Dimensions, feet (metres): 157·4 × 24·6 × 7·2 (48 × 7·5 × 2·2)
Main engines: 2 diesels; 2 shafts; 400 bhp = 15 knots

Transferred from USSR in 1970.

"VYDRA" Class   1971

10 MFP TYPE

Dimensions, feet (metres): 164·0 oa × 20·0 × 6·6 (50 × 6·1 × 2·0)
Guns: 1—37 mm or none

Built in Bulgaria in 1954. Based on a German Second World War MFP design.

AUXILIARIES

3 Coastal Tankers, 5 Tugs, 2 "Varna" class Survey Ships (built in Bulgaria in 1959), 2 Salvage Craft and up to another 12 auxiliaries have been reported.

BURMA

Ministerial

Minister of Defence:
Kyaw Htin

Headquarters Appointment

Vice-Chief of Staff, Defence Services (Navy):
Commodore Thaung Tin

Diplomatic Representation

Naval, Military and Air Attaché in London:
Lieutenant-Colonel Than Lwin

Naval, Military and Air Attaché in Washington:
Colonel Tin Htut

Strength of the Fleet

Type	Active	Building
Frigates	2	—
Corvettes	4	—
River Patrol Craft	35	—
Gunboats	36	—
Survey Vessels	2	—
Auxiliaries	10	—

Bases

Bassein, Mergui, Moulmein, Seikyi, Sinmalaik, Sittwo.

Personnel

(a) 1977: 7 000 including 800 marines
(b) Voluntary

Mercantile Marine

Lloyd's Register of Shipping:
39 vessels of 68 867 tons gross

DELETIONS

Light Forces

1975   T201-205—Saunders-Roe convertibles

Gunboats

1976   *Indaw* sold commercially.

Transport

1971   *Pyi Daw Aye* scrapped.

FRIGATES

1 Ex-BRITISH "RIVER" CLASS

Name	No.	Builders	Laid down	Launched	Commissioned
MAYU (ex-HMS *Fal*)	–	Smiths Dock Co Ltd, South Bank-on-Tees, Middlesbrough, England	20 May 1942	9 Nov 1942	2 July 1943

Displacement, tons: 1 460 standard; 2 170 full load
Length, feet (metres): 283 *(86·3)* pp; 301·3 *(91·8)* oa
Beam, feet (metres): 36·7 *(11·3)*
Draught, feet (metres): 12 *(3·7)*
Guns: 1—4 in *(102 mm)*; 4—40 mm
Main engines: Triple expansion 5 500 ihp; 2 shafts
Boilers: 2—three drum type
Speed, knots: 19
Oil fuel, tons: 440
Range, miles: 4 200 at 12 knots
Complement: 140

"River" class frigate. Acquired from Great Britain and renamed in March 1948.

Radar: British Type 974.

MAYU   *Burmese Navy*

1 Ex-BRITISH "ALGERINE" CLASS

Name	No.	Builders	Laid down	Launched	Commissioned
YAN MYO AUNG (ex-HMS *Mariner*, ex-*Kincardine*)	–	Port Arthur Shipyards, Canada	26 Aug 1943	9 May 1944	23 May 1945

Displacement, tons: 1 040 standard; 1 335 full load
Length, feet (metres): 225 *(68·6)* pp; 235 *(71·6)* oa
Beam, feet (metres): 35·5 *(19·8)*
Draught, feet (metres): 11·5 *(3·5)*
Guns: 1—4 in *(102 mm)*; 4—40 mm
Main engines: Triple expansion; 2 000 ihp; 2 shafts
Boilers: 2 three-drum type
Speed, knots: 16·5
Range, miles: 4 000 at 12 knots
Complement: 140

Former ocean minesweeper in the British Navy, used as escort vessel. Handed over to Burma in London and renamed *Yan Myo Aung*, on 18 Apr 1958. Fitted for minelaying and can carry 16 mines, eight on each side.

Radar: Decca Type 202.

Sonar: British Type 144.

YAN MYO AUNG   *1964, Burmese Navy*

CORVETTES

1 Ex-US "PCE 827" CLASS

Name	No.	Builders	Commissioned
YAN TAING AUNG (ex-USS *Farmington* PCE 894)	PCE 41	Willamette Iron & Steel Co, Portland, Oregon	10 Aug 1943

Displacement, tons: 640 standard; 903 full load
Dimensions, feet (metres): 180 wl; 184 oa × 33 × 9·5 *(56 × 10·1 × 2·9)*
Guns: 1—3 in 50 cal dp; 2—40 mm (1 twin); 8—20 mm (4 twin)
A/S weapons: 1 hedgehog; 2 DCT; 2 DC racks
Main engines: GM diesels; 2 shafts; 1 800 bhp = 15 knots

Laid down on 7 Dec 1942, launched on 15 May 1943. Transferred on 18 June 1965.

1 Ex-US "ADMIRABLE" CLASS

Name	No.	Builders	Commissioned
YAN GYI AUNG (ex-USS *Craddock* MSF 356)	PCE 42	Willamette Iron & Steel Co, Portland, Oregon	1944

Displacement, tons: 650 standard; 945 full load
Dimensions, feet (metres): 180 wl; 184·5 oa × 33 × 9·8 *(56× 10·1 × 2·8)*
Guns: 1—3 in 50 cal single forward; 4—40 mm (2 twin); 4—20 mm (2 twin)
A/S weapons: 1 US Hedgehog; 2 DCT; 2 DC Racks
Main engines: Diesels; 2 shafts; 1 710 shp = 14·8 knots
Range, miles: 4 300 at 10 knots

Laid down on 10 Nov 1943 and launched on 22 July 1944. Transferred at San Diego on 31 Mar 1967.

2 "NAWARAT" CLASS

Name	No.	Builders	Commissioned
NAGAKYAY	—	Government Dockyard, Dawbon, Rangoon	3 Dec 1960
NAWARAT	—	Government Dockyard, Dawbon, Rangoon	26 Apr 1960

Displacement, tons: 400 standard; 450 full load
Dimensions, feet (metres): 163 × 26·8 × 5·8 *(49·7 × 8·2 × 1·8)*
Guns: 2—25 pdr QF; 2—40 mm
Main engines: 2 Paxman-Ricardo turbo-charged diesels; 2 shafts; 1 160 bhp = 12 knots
Complement: 43

NAGAKYAY   *1962, Burmese Navy*

LIGHT FORCES

10 BURMESE-BUILT RIVER PATROL CRAFT

Small craft, 50 feet long, built in Burma in 1951-52.

25 YUGOSLAV-BUILT RIVER PATROL CRAFT

Small craft, 52 feet long, acquired from Yugoslavia in 1965.

GUNBOATS

3 Ex-BRITISH LCG (M) TYPE

INLAY   INMA   INYA

Displacement, tons: 381
Dimensions, feet (metres): 154 oa × 22·5 × 7·8 *(47·1 × 6·8 × 2·4)*
Guns: 2—25 pdr; 2—2 pdr
Main engines: Paxman Ricardo diesels; 2 shafts; 1 000 bhp = 13 knots
Complement: 39

Former British landing craft, gun (medium) LCG (M). Employed as gunboats.

Radar: British Type 974.

INMA   *Burmese Navy*

10 "Y 301" CLASS

Y 301   Y 302   Y 303   Y 304   Y 305   Y 306   Y 307   Y 308   Y 309   Y 310

Displacement, tons: 120
Dimensions, feet (metres): 100 pp; 104·8 oa × 24 × 3 *(32 × 7·3 × 0·9)*
Guns: 2—40 mm; 1—2 pdr
Main engines: 2 Mercedes-Benz (MTU) diesels; 2 shafts; 1 000 bhp = 13 knots
Complement: 29

All ten of these boats were completed in 1958 at the Uljanik Shipyard, Pula, Yugoslavia.

Y 310   *1964, Burmese Navy*

2 IMPROVED "Y 301" CLASS

Y 311   Y 312

Guns: 2—40 mm (single); 4—20 mm (single).

Dimensions approximately as "Y 301" Class. Built in Burma 1969.

8 GUNBOATS (Ex-TRANSPORTS)

SABAN   SEINDA   SETYAHAT   SHWETHIDA
SAGU   SETKAYA   SHWEPAZUN   SINMIN

Displacement, tons: 98
Dimensions, feet (metres): 94·5 × 22 × 4·5 *(28·8 × 6·7 × 1·4)*
Guns: 1—40 mm, 3—20 mm
Main engines: Crossley ERL—6 diesel; 160 bhp = 12 knots
Complement: 32

SHWEPAZUN   *1971, Burmese Navy*

6 Ex-US PGM TYPE

PGM 401   PGM 402   PGM 403   PGM 404   PGM 405   PGM 406

Displacement, tons: 141
Dimensions, feet (metres): 101 × 21·1 × 7·5 *(30·0 × 6·5 × 2·3)*
Guns: 1—40 mm 2—20 mm (twin); 2—50 Cal MG
Main engines: 8 GM 6-71 diesels; 2 shafts; 2 040 bhp = 17 knots
Range, miles: 1 000 cruising
Complement: 17

Built by the Marinette Marine Corporation, USA. Ex-US PGM 43-46, 51 and 52 respectively. Machinery comprises 2-stroke, 6-cylinder, tandem geared twin diesel propulsion unit—1 LH and 1 RH; 500 bhp per unit.

Radar: Raytheon 1 500 in PGM 405-6; EDO 320 in PGM 401-4.

PGM 401   *1962, Burmese Navy*

7 Ex-US CGC TYPE

MGB 101   MGB 102   MGB 104   MGB 105   MGB 106   MGB 108   MGB 110

Displacement, tons: 49 standard; 66 full load
Dimensions, feet (metres): 78 pp; 83 oa × 16 × 5·5 *(25·3 × 4·9 × 1·7)*
Guns: 1—40 mm; 1—20 mm
Main engines: 4 GM diesels; 2 shafts; 800 bhp = 11 knots
Complement: 16

Ex-USCG 83-ft type cutters with new hulls built in Burma. Completed in 1960. Three of this class are reported to have been sunk.

MGB 102   *1962, Burmese Navy*

SURVEY VESSELS

1 OCEAN SURVEY SHIP

Name	No.	Builders	Commissioned
THU TAY THI	—	Yugoslavia	1965

Displacement, tons: 1 059
Length, feet (metres): 204 oa *(62·2)*
Complement: 99

Fitted with helicopter platform. The Burmese Air Force operates Alouette III, Husky and Sioux helicopters.

1 COASTAL SURVEY SHIP

Name	No.	Builders	Commissioned
YAY BO	UBHL 807	Netherlands	1957

Displacement, tons: 108
Complement: 25

SUPPORT SHIP
YAN LON AUNG

Light forces support ship of 520 tons, acquired from Japan in 1967.

TRANSPORTS

1 Ex-US LCU TYPE

AIYAR LULIN (ex-USS LCU 1626) 603

Displacement, tons: 200 light; 342 full load
Dimensions, feet (metres): 135·2 oa × 29 × 5·5 *(41·2 × 8·8 × 1·7)*
Main engines: 4 GM 12007 T Diesels; 2 shafts (Kort nozzles); 1 000 bhp = 11 knots

US type utility landing craft 603 completed in Rangoon 1966. Two transferred as Grant aid in Oct 1967. Used as transport. Cargo capacity 168 tons.

8 Ex-US LCM 3 TYPE

LCM 701   LCM 702   LCM 703   LCM 704   LCM 705   LCM 706   LCM 707   LCM 708

Displacement, tons: 52 tons full load
Dimensions, feet (metres): 50 × 14 × 4 *(15·2 × 4·3 × 1·2)*
Guns: 2—20 mm single
Main engines: 2 Gray Marine diesels; 450 bhp = 9 knots

US-built LCM type landing craft. Used as local transports for stores and personnel. Cargo capacity 30 tons.

CAMEROON

Ministerial

Minister of Armed Forces:
 Daoudou Sadou

Personnel

1977: 300 officers and men

Base

Douala

Mercantile Marine

Lloyd's Register of Shipping:
 23 vessels of 19 045 tons gross

DELETIONS

1975   French VC Type—*Vigilant* (ex-VC 6), *Audacieux* (ex VC-8)

LIGHT FORCES

1 LARGE PATROL CRAFT

Displacement, tons: 250 full load
Dimensions, feet (metres): 157·5 × 23·3 × 7·5 *(48 × 7·1 × 2·3)*
Guns: 2—40 mm
Main engines: 2 AGO Diesels; 4 000 hp = 20 knots
Range, miles: 2 000 at 16 knots

Ordered from Soc. Français Construction Naval in Sep 1974 for delivery in 1976. Similar to "Bizerte" class in Tunisia.

1 LARGE PATROL CRAFT

Name	No.	Builders	Commissioned
QUARTIER MAÎTRE ALFRED MOTTO	—	At. et Ch. de l'Afrique Equatoriale Libreville, Gabon	1974

Displacement, tons: 96
Dimensions, feet (metres): 95·4 × 20·3 × 6·3 *(29·1 × 6·2 × 1·9)*
Guns: 2—20 mm; 2 MG
Main engines: 2 Baudoin diesels; 1 290 bhp = 15·5 knots
Complement: 17

ALFRED MOTTO   *1973, Y. Betrand*

Name	No.	Builders	Commissioned
BRIGADIER M'BONGA TOUNDA	—	Ch. Navals d l'Esterel	1967

Displacement, tons: 20 full load
Dimensions, feet (metres): 60 × 13·5 × 4 *(18·3 × 4·1 × 1·2)*
Gun: 1—12·7 mm MG
Main engines: Caterpillar Diesel; 2 shafts; 540 bhp = 22·5 knots
Complement: 8

Customs duties. Sister of Mauritanian *Imrag 'ni.*

Name	No.	Builders	Commissioned
LE VALEUREUX	—	Ch. Navals de l'Esterel	1970

Displacement, tons: 45 full load
Dimensions, feet (metres): 78·1 × 16·3 × 5·1 *(26·8 × 5·0 × 1·6)*
Guns: 2—20 mm
Main engines: 2 diesels; 2 shafts; 960 hp = 25 knots
Complement: 9

2 HARBOUR LAUNCHES

SANAGA   BIMBIA

Of 10 tons.

5 LCVP

INDÉPENDANCE   REUNIFICATION   SOUELLABA   MACHTIGAL   MANOKA

Built by Ateliers et Chantiers de l'Afrique Equatoriale, Libreville, Gabon. Of 11 tons and 10 knots.

1 LCM

BAKASI

Built by Carena, Abidjan, Ivory Coast. Of 57 tons and 56 feet long. 9 knots on 2 Baudoin diesels.

MISCELLANEOUS

Tornade and *Ouragan*—Built in 1966. *St. Sylvestre*—Built in 1967.
Three small outboard craft.
Mungo operated by Transport Ministry. *Dr. Jamot* operated by Health Ministry.

CANADA

Ministerial

Minister of National Defence:
  The Hon. Barney Danson MP

Headquarters Appointments

Chief of Maritime Doctrine and Operations:
  Rear Admiral D. N. Mainguy CD

Senior Appointments

Commander, Maritime Command:
  Vice-Admiral D. S. Boyle, CD
Commander, Maritime Forces, Pacific:
  Rear-Admiral A. L. Collier DSC, CD

Diplomatic Representation

Senior Liaison Officer (Maritime) London:
  Captain (N) H. O. Arnsdorf, CD
Canadian Forces Attaché and Maritime Liaison Officer, Washington:
  Commodore M. A. Martin, CD
Canadian Forces Attaché (Naval) Moscow:
  Commander H. R. Waddell, CD
Canadian Forces Attaché (Naval) Oslo, Stockholm and Copenhagen:
  Captain (N) J. W. Mason, CD

Establishment

The Royal Canadian Navy was officially established on 4 May 1910, when Royal Assent was given to the Naval Service Act. On 1 February 1968 the Canadian Forces Reorganisation Act unified the three branches of the Canadian Forces and the title "Royal Canadian Navy" was dropped.

Personnel

(a) 1971: 16 906 (2 379 officers, 14 527 men and women)
    1972: 15 223 (2 590 officers, 12 633 men and women)
    1973: 16 003 (1 985 officers, 14 018 men and women)
    1974: 14 000 (2 000 officers, 12 000 men and women)
Note: Canada no longer accounts for separate services in a unified command. Total armed forces 78 000

(b) Voluntary Service

Defence Estimates (Naval)

1971-72: $348 000 000
1972-73: $363 000 000
1973-74: $394 300 000
1975-76: $472 268 000
1976-77: $712 000 000

Note: Canada no longer accounts for separate services in a unified command.

Bases

Halifax and Esquimalt

Air Arm

In an integrated force there is no specific Fleet Air Arm, but two squadrons of Sea King helicopters provide for ships' needs.

Prefix to Ships' Names

HMCS

Mercantile Marine

Lloyd's Register of Shipping:
  1 269 vessels of 2 638 692 tons gross

Strength of the Fleet

Type	Active	Building
Destroyers (DDH)	4	—
Frigates (some with helicopters)	16	—
Patrol Submarines	3	—
Replenishment Ships	3	—
Small Tankers	2	—
Patrol Escorts (Small)	7	—
Patrol Craft	6	—
Research Ships	5	—
Diving Support Ships and Tenders	3	—
Gate Vessels	5	—
Tugs: Ocean	2	—
Large	1	—
Medium	2	—
Coastal	5	—
Small	5	—
	(6 NRU)	
Police Patrol Vessels	32	—

Reserve (Cat. C)

Frigates

1974 *Columbia, St. Croix, Chaudiere*

Hydrofoil

1971 *Bras D'Or*

DELETIONS

Frigates

1974 *Granby*
1975 *St. Laurent.* Break-up at Halifax

Submarine

1974 *Rainbow* broken up at Esquimalt

Maintenance Ships

1972 *Cape Breton* and *Cape Scott* decommissioned but remain in alongside service

Research Vessels

1972 *Fort Frances* scrapped in Spain
1976 *Kapuskasing*

Tugs

1975 *Glendyne* sunk for diver training, *Heatherton* transferred to DPW (Canada)
1976 *Clifton, Glenbrook, Glenlivet, Mannville, Parksville, Merrickville*

Attack Carrier (medium)

1970 *Bonaventure* paid off 1 April, towed to Taiwan for scrap, leaving Halifax 27 October.

Destroyers

1971 *Algonquin* left Victoria BC for Taiwan 21 April, *Crescent* left Victoria BC for Taiwan 21 May

TRANSFERS

Patrol Escorts (Small)

1973 *Fort Steele* from RCMP to DND
1975 *PBLs 191, 192, 193, 194, 195* from RCMP to DND
1976 *PBL 196* from RCMP to DND

Gate Vessels

1974 *Porte Dauphine* from MOT to DND

PENNANT NUMBERS

Destroyers

280	Iroquois
281	Huron
282	Athabaskan
283	Algonquin

Frigates

206	Saguenay
207	Skeena
229	Ottawa
230	Margaree
233	Fraser
234	Assiniboine
235	*Chaudiere
236	Gatineau
256	*St. Croix
257	Restigouche
258	Kootenay
259	Terra Nova
260	*Columbia
261	Mackenzie
262	Saskatchewan
263	Yukon
264	Qu'Appelle
265	Annapolis
266	Nipigon

Submarines

72	Ojibwa
73	Onondaga
74	Okanagan
75	*Rainbow

Replenishment Ships

AOR 508	Provider
AOR 509	Protecteur
AOR 510	Preserver
AOC 501	Dundalk
AOC 502	Dundurn

Research Vessels

AGOR 113	Sackville
AGOR 114	Bluethroat
AGOR 171	Endeavour
AGOR 172	Quest
AGOR 516	Laymore

Patrol Escort (PFL)

140	Fort Steele
159	Fundy
160	Chignecto
161	Thunder
162	Cowichan
163	Miramichi
164	Chaleur

Gate Vessels

180	Porte St. Jean
183	Porte St. Louis
184	Porte de la Reine
185	Porte Quebec
186	Porte Dauphine

Patrol Craft (PBLs ex-RCMP)

191	Adversus
192	Detector
193	Captor
194	Acadian
195	Sidney
196	Nicholson

Tugs

ATA 528	Riverton
ATA 531	St. Anthony
ATA 533	St. Charles
ATA 640	Glendyne
ATA 641	Glendale
ATA 642	Glenevis
ATA 643	Glenbrook
ATA 644	Glenside
YMT 550	Eastwood
YMT 553	Wildwood
YTS 582	Burrard
YTS 583	Beamsville
YTS 584	Cree
YTS 586	Queensville
YTS 587	Plainsville
YTS 588	Youville
YTS 589	Loganville
YTS 590	Lawrenceville
YTS 591	Parksville
YTS 592	Listerville
YTS 593	Merrickville
YTS 594	Marysville

*Cat C Reserve 1974.

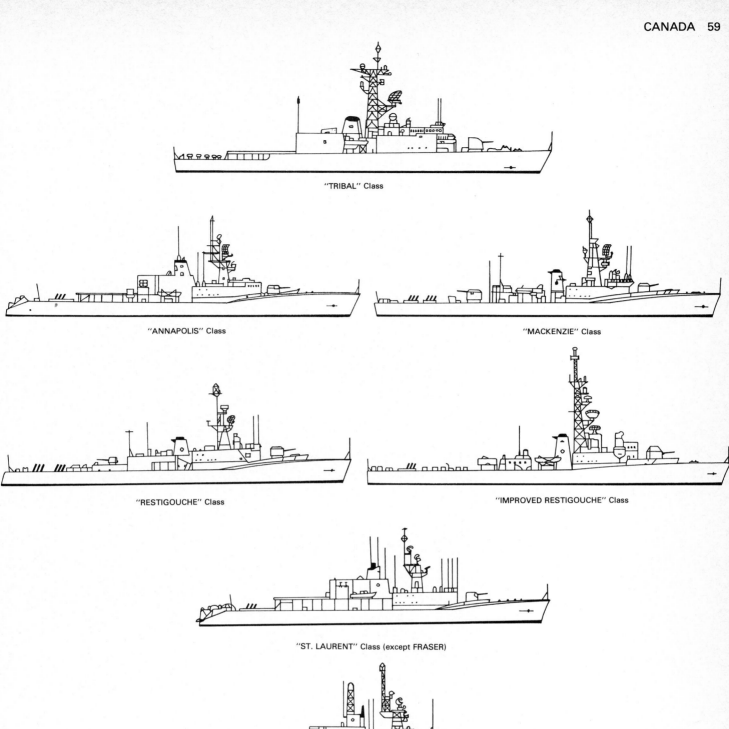

"TRIBAL" Class

"ANNAPOLIS" Class

"MACKENZIE" Class

"RESTIGOUCHE" Class

"IMPROVED RESTIGOUCHE" Class

"ST. LAURENT" Class (except FRASER)

FRASER

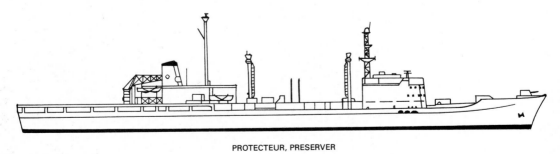

PROTECTEUR, PRESERVER

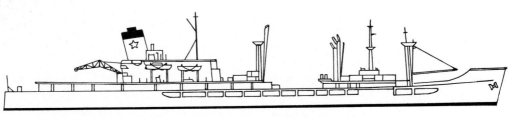

PROVIDER

DESTROYERS (DDH)

4 "TRIBAL" CLASS

Name	No.	Builders	Laid down	Launched	Commissioned
ALGONQUIN	283	Davie SB Co, Lauzon	1 Sep 1969	23 Apr 1971	30 Sep 1973
ATHABASKAN	282	Davie SB Co, Lauzon	1 June1969	27 Nov 1970	30 Nov 1972
HURON	281	Marine Industries Ltd, Sorel	15 Jan 1969	3 Apr 1971	16 Dec 1972
IROQUOIS	280	Marine Industries Ltd, Sorel	15 Jan 1969	28 Nov 1970	29 July 1972

Displacement, tons: 4 200 full load
Length, feet (metres): 398 *(121·3)* pp; 426 *(129·8)* oa
Beam, feet (metres): 50 *(15·2)*
Draught, feet (metres): 14·5 *(4·4)*
Aircraft: 2 "Sea King" CHSS-2 A/S Helicopters
Missiles: (see note)
Gun: 1—5 in *(127 mm)* 54 cal single Oto-Melara
A/S: 1 Mk 10 Limbo
Torpedo tubes: 2 triple Mk 32 for A/S homing torpedoes
Main engines: Gas turbine; 2 Pratt & Whitney FT4A2 50 000 shp; 2 Pratt & Whitney FT12AH3 7 400 shp for cruising; 2 shafts
Speed, knots: 29 +
Range, miles: 4 500 at 20 knots
Complement: 245 (20 officers, 225 men) plus air unit, (7 officers + 33 men)

These ships have the same hull design, dimensions and basic characteristics as the large general purpose frigates cancelled at the end of 1963 (see particulars and illustration in the 1963-64 edition). Designed as anti-submarine ships, they are fitted with variable depth and hull sonar, landing deck equipped with double hauldown and Beartrap, flume type anti-rolling tanks to stabilise the ships at low speed, pre-wetting system to counter radio-active fallout, enclosed citadel, and bridge control of machinery.

Engineering: The gas turbines feed through a Swiss double reduction gearbox to two five bladed CP propellers.

Electronics: Mk 22 Weapon System Control by Hollandse Signaal. CSS 280.

Missiles: Launch system (GMLS) by Raytheon for Mk III Sea Sparrow missiles. Two quadruple launchers in forward end of the superstructure.

Radar: Surface warning and navigation; SPQ 2D.
Long range Warning; SPS 501 (SPS 12). Fire Control; M 22.

Sonar: Hull mounted; SQS 505 in 14 ft dome. VDS; 18 ft towed body aft. Bottomed target classification; SQS 501.

Torpedoes: The Mk 32 tubes are to be used with Mk 46 torpedoes.

ALGONQUIN — 1975, Reiner Nerlich

HURON — 1975, Canadian Forces

ATHABASKAN — 9/1975, Dr Giorgio Arra

FRIGATES

2 "ANNAPOLIS" CLASS

Name	No.	Builders	Laid down	Launched	Commissioned
ANNAPOLIS	265	Halifax Shipyards Ltd, Halifax	July 1960	27 Apr 1963	19 Dec 1964
NIPIGON	266	Marine Industries Ltd, Sorel	Apr 1960	10 Dec 1961	30 May 1964

Displacement, tons: 2 400 standard; 3 000 full load
Length, feet (metres): 371·0 (113·1) oa
Beam, feet (metres): 42·0 (12·8)
Draught, feet (metres): 14·4 (4·4)
Aircraft: 1 CHSS-2 Sea King helicopter
Guns: 2—3 in (76 mm) 50 cal (1 twin)
A/S weapons: 1 Mk 10 Limbo in after well; 6 (2 triple) Mk 32 A/S torpedo tubes
Main engines: Geared turbines; 2 shafts; 30 000 shp
Boilers: 2 water tube
Speed, knots: 28 (30 on trials)
Range, miles: 4 570 at 14 knots
Complement: 210 (11 0fficers, 199 ratings)

These two ships represented the logical development of the original "St. Laurent" class, through the "Restigouche" and "Mackenzie" designs. Due to the erection of a helicopter hangar and flight deck, and Variable Depth Sonar only one Limbo mounting could be installed. Also the 50 cal 3 inch mounting had to be moved forward to replace the 70 cal mounting in the original design.

Classification: Officially classified as DDH.

Construction: As these are largely prefabricated no firm laying down date is officially given. Work on hull units started under cover long before components were laid on the slip.

Electronics: Tacan (AN/URN-22) aerial fitted above funnel.

Radar: Search: SPS 12. **Tactical:** SPS 10. **Fire Control:** I Band.

Sonar: Types 501, 502, 503, 504, 505. SQS 10/11.

ANNAPOLIS   6/1974, J. L. M. van der Burg

4 "MACKENZIE" CLASS

Name	No.	Builders	Laid down	Launched	Commissioned
MACKENZIE	261	Canadian Vickers Ltd, Montreal	15 Dec 1958	25 May 1961	6 Oct 1962
QU'APPELLE	264	Davie Shipbuilding & Repairing	14 Jan 1960	2 May 1962	14 Sep 1963
*SASKATCHEWAN	262	Victoria Machinery (and Yarrow)	16 July 1959	1 Feb 1961	16 Feb 1963
YUKON	263	Burrard DD & Shipbuilding	25 Oct 1959	27 July 1961	25 May 1963

Displacement, tons: 2 380 standard; 2 880 full load
Length, feet (metres): 366·0 (111·5) oa
Beam, feet (metres): 42·0 (12·8)
Draught, feet (metres): 13·5 (4·1)
Guns: 4—3 in (76 mm) (2 twin) (UK 70 cal fwd, US Mk 33 50 cal aft); (Qu'Appelle 2—3 in 50 cal (twin))
A/S weapons: 2 Mk 10 Limbo in well aft; side launchers for Mk 43 torpedoes
Main engines: Geared turbines; 2 shafts; 30 000 shp
Boilers: 2 water tube
Speed, knots: 28
Range, miles: 4 750 at 14 knots
Complement: 210 (11 officers, 199 ratings)

Classification: Officially classified as DDE.

Fire Control: US Gunnar system.

Radar: Search: SPS 12. **Tactical:** SPS 10. **Fire Control:** I Band.

Sonar: 501, 502, 503, SQS 10/11.

*Saskatchewan was launched by Victoria Machinery Depot Co Ltd, but completed by Yarrow's Ltd.

YUKON   5/1974, John G. Callis

3 "RESTIGOUCHE" CLASS

Name	No.	Builders	Laid down	Launched	Commissioned
CHAUDIERE	235	Halifax Shipyards Ltd	30 July 1953	13 Nov 1957	14 Nov 1959
COLUMBIA	260	Burrard DD and Shipbuilding	11 June1953	1 Nov 1956	7 Nov 1959
ST. CROIX	256	Marine Industries Ltd, Sorel	15 Oct 1954	17 Nov 1957	4 Oct 1958

Displacement, tons: 2 370 standard; 2 880 full load
Length, feet (metres): 366·0 (111·5) oa
Beam, feet (metres): 42·0 (12·8)
Draught, feet (metres): 13·5 (4·1)
Guns: 4—3 in (76 mm) (2 twin)
A/S weapons: 2 Mk 10 Limbo in well aft; side launchers for Mk 43 torpedoes
Main engines: Geared turbines; 2 shafts; 30 000 shp
Boilers: 2 water tube
Speed, knots: 28
Range, miles: 4 750 at 14 knots
Complement: 248 (12 officers, 236 ratings)

All three declared surplus and paid off into Category C Reserve in 1974.

Classification: Officially classified as DDE.

Radar: Search: SPS 12. **Tactical:** SPS 10. **Fire Control:** SPG 48.

Sonar: 501, 502, 503, SQS 10/11.

CHAUDIERE   1970, Canadian Forces

4 "IMPROVED RESTIGOUCHE"

Name	No.	Builders	Laid down	Launched	Commissioned
GATINEAU	236	Davie Shipbuilding & Repairing	30 Apr 1953	3 June 1957	17 Feb 1959
KOOTENAY	258	Burrard DD & Shipbuilding	21 Aug 1952	15 June 1954	7 Mar 1959
RESTIGOUCHE	257	Canadian Vickers, Montreal	15 July 1953	22 Nov 1954	7 June 1958
TERRA NOVA	259	Victoria Machinery Depot Co.	14 Nov 1952	21 June 1955	6 June 1959

Displacement, tons: 2 390 standard; 2 900 full load
Length, feet (metres): 371·0 *(113·1)*
Beam, feet (metres): 42·0 *(12·8)*
Draught, feet (metres): 14·1 *(4·3)*
Guns: 2—3 in *(76 mm)* 70 cal (twin forward)
A/S weapons: ASROC aft and 1 Mk 10 Limbo in after well
Main engines: Geared turbines; 2 shafts; 30 000 shp
Boilers: 2 water tube
Speed, knots: 28 plus
Range, miles: 4 750 at 14 knots
Complement: 214 (13 officers, 201 ratings)

Classification: Officially classified as DDE.

Conversion: These four ships were refitted with ASROC aft and lattice foremast. Work included removing the after 3 inch 50 cal twin gun mounting and one Limbo A/S Mk 10 triple mortar, to make way for ASROC and Variable Depth Sonar. Dates of refits *Terra Nova* was completed on 18 Oct 1968: *Gatineau* completed in 1972 and *Kootenay* and *Restigouche* in 1973. Refit also included improvements to communications fit.

Radar: Search: SPS 12. Tactical: SPS 10. Fire Control: SPG 48. Navigation: Sperry Mk II.

Sonar: 501, 505, 505 VDS.

GATINEAU　　　　　　　　　　　　　　　　　1972, Canadian Forces

6 "ST. LAURENT" CLASS

Name	No.	Builders	Laid down	Launched	Commissioned
SAGUENAY	206	Halifax Shipyards Ltd, Halifax	4 Apr 1951	30 July 1953	15 Dec 1956
SKEENA	207	Burrard Dry Dock & Shipbuilding	1 June 1951	19 Aug 1952	30 Mar 1957
OTTAWA	229	Canadian Vickers Ltd, Montreal	8 June 1951	29 Apr 1953	10 Nov 1956
MARGAREE	230	Halifax Shipyards Ltd, Halifax	12 Sep 1951	29 Mar 1956	5 Oct 1957
*FRASER	233	Yarrows Ltd, Esquimalt, B.C.	11 Dec 1951	19 Feb 1953	28 June 1957
ASSINIBOINE	234	Marine Industries Ltd, Sorel, Quebec	19 May 1952	12 Feb 1954	16 Aug 1956

Displacement, tons: 2 260 standard; 2 858 full load
Length, feet (metres): 366·0 *(111·5)* oa
Beam, feet (metres): 42·0 *(12·8)*
Draught, feet (metres): 13·2 *(4·0)*
Aircraft: 1 CHSS-2 "Sea King" helicopter
Guns: 2—3 in *(76 mm)* 50 cal (1 twin)
A/S weapons: 1 Mk 10 Limbo in after well; 2 triple Mk 32 torpedo tubes
Main engines: English Electric geared turbines; 2 shafts; 30 000 shp
Boilers: 2 water tube
Speed, knots: 28·5
Range, miles: 4 570 at 12 knots
Complement: 208 (11 officers, 197 ratings) (plus air unit of 7 officers and 13 ratings)

The first major warships to be designed in Canada. In design, much assistance was received from the Royal Navy (propelling machinery of British design) and the US Navy.
St. Laurent declared surplus in 1974.

*Fraser was launched by Burrard Dry Dock & Shipbuilding but completed by Yarrows Ltd.

Classification: Officially classified as DDH.

Gunnery: Original armament was 4—3 inch, .50 cal (2 twin), 2—40 mm (single), and 2 Limbo mortars.

Radars: Search: SPS 12. Tactical: SPS 10. Nav: Sperry Mk II. Fire Control: SPG 48.

Reconstruction: All have helicopter platforms and VDS. Twin funnels were fitted to permit forward extension of the helicopter hangar.
Gunhouses are of glass fibre. In providing helicopter platforms and hangars it was possible to retain only one three barrelled Limbo mortar and only one twin 3-inch gun mounting. Dates of recommissioning after conversion: *Assiniboine* 28 June 1963, *St. Laurent* 4 Oct 1963, *Ottawa* 21 Oct 1964, *Saguenay* 14 May 1965, *Skeena* 15 Aug 1965, *Margaree* 15 Oct 1965, *Fraser* 31 Aug 1966.
Fraser has lattice radar-mast by the funnels for Tacan aerial.

Sonar: 501, 502, SQS 502, 503, 504.

SKEENA　　　　　　　　　　　　　　　　　1975, Canadian Forces

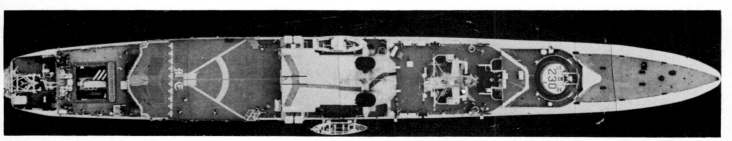

MARGAREE　　　　　　　　　　　　　　　1975, Commander R. E. George

SUBMARINES

3 "OBERON" CLASS (PATROL SUBMARINES)

Name	No.	Builders	Laid down	Launched	Commissioned
OJIBWA (ex-*Onyx*)	72	HM Dockyard, Chatham	27 Sep 1962	29 Feb 1964	23 Sep 1965
OKANAGAN	74	HM Dockyard, Chatham	25 Mar 1965	17 Sep 1966	22 June1968
ONONDAGA	73	HM Dockyard, Chatham	18 June1964	25 Sep 1965	22 June1967

Displacement, tons: 2 060 full bouyancy surface;
2 200 normal surfaced; 2 420 dived
Length, feet (metres): 294·2 *(90·0)* oa
Beam, feet (metres): 26·5 *(8·1)*
Draught, feet (metres): 18 *(5·5)*
Torpedo tubes: 8—21 in *(533 mm)*, 6 bow and 2 stern
Main machinery: 2 Admiralty Standard Range diesels;
3 680 bhp; 2 shafts; 2 electric motors; 6 000 hp
Speed, knots: 12 surfaced; 17 dived
Complement: 65 (7 officers, 58 ratings)

On 11 April 1962 the Ministry of National Defence announced that Canada was to buy three "Oberon" class submarines in UK. The first of these patrol submarines was obtained by the Canadian Government from the Royal Navy construction programme. She was laid down as *Onyx* but launched as *Ojibwa*. The other two were specific Canadian orders. There were some design changes to meet specific new needs including installation of RCN communications equipment and increase of air-conditioning capacity to meet the wide extremes of climate encountered in Canadian operating areas.

Nomenclature: The name *Ojibwa* is that of a tribe of North American Indians now widely dispersed in Canada and the USA and one of the largest remnants of aboriginal population. *Okanagan* and *Onondaga* are also Canadian Indian tribes.

Radar: Type 1006.

Sonar: Attack: Type 187.
Intercept: Type 197.
Torpedo Warning: Type 719
Long Range Passive Search: Type 2007.

OKANAGAN   *6/1973, Wright and Logan*

OJIBWA   *10/1975, Dr. Giorgio Arra*

REPLENISHMENT SHIPS

Name	No.	Builders	Laid down	Launched	Commissioned
PRESERVER	AOR 510	Saint John Dry Dock Co Ltd, N.B.	17 Oct 1967	29 May 1969	30 July 1970
PROTECTEUR	AOR 509	Saint John Dry Dock Co Ltd, N.B.	17 Oct 1967	18 July 1968	30 Aug 1969

Displacement, tons: 8 380 light; 24 700 full load
Measurement, tons: 22 100 gross; 13 250 deadweight
Length, feet (metres): 564 *(172)* oa
Beam, feet (metres): 76 *(23·2)*
Draught, feet (metres): 30 *(9·1)*
Aircraft: 3 CHSS-2 "Sea King" helicopters
Guns: 2—3 in *(76 mm)*
A/S launcher: 1 Sea Sparrow to be fitted
Main engines: Geared turbine; 21 000 shp; 1 shaft
Boilers: 2 forced draught water tube
Range, miles: 4 100 at 20, 7 500 at 11·5 knots
Complement: 227 (15 officers, 212 ratings)

Contract price $47 500 000 for both ships. In design they are an improvement on that of the prototype *Provider*. They could carry spare anti-submarine helicopters, military vehicles and bulk equipment for sealift purposes. 13 100 tons FFO, 600 tons diesel, 400 tons aviation fuel, 1 048 tons dry cargo and 1 250 tons of ammunition.

Electronics: Tacan aerial.

Radar: Decca 969, Sperry Mk II.

Sonar: SQS 505.

PROTECTEUR   *9/1974, Reiner Nerlich*

Name	No.	Builders	Laid down	Launched	Commissioned
PROVIDER	AOR 508	Davie Shipbuilding Ltd, Lauzon	1 May 1961	5 July 1962	28 Sep 1963

Displacement, tons: 7 300 light; 22 000 full load
Measurement, tons: 20 000 gross; 14 700 deadweight
Length, feet (metres): 523 (159·4) pp; 555 (169·2) oa
Beam, feet (metres): 76 (23·2)
Draught, feet (metres): 32 (9·8)
Aircraft: 3 CHSS-2 "Sea King" helicopters
Main engines: Double reduction geared turbine 21 000 shp;
  1 shaft
Boilers: 2 water tube
Speed, knots: 20
Oil fuel, tons: 12 000
Range, miles: 3 600 at 20 knots
Complement: 166 (15 officers, 151 ratings)

Preliminary construction work was begun in September 1960.
Cost $15 700 000.
The helicopter flight deck is aft with the hangar at the same
level and immediately below the funnel. 3 Sea King Helicopters
can be accommodated in the hangar. The flight deck can
receive the largest and heaviest helicopters. A total of 20
electro-hydraulic winches are fitted on deck for ship-to-ship
movements of cargo and supplies, as well as shore-to-ship
requirements when alongside.

PROVIDER   1975, Canadian Forces

2 "DUN" CLASS TANKERS

DUNDALK AOC 501 **DUNDURN** AOC 502

Displacement, tons: 950
Dimensions, feet (metres): 178·8 × 32·2 × 13 (54·5 × 9·8 × 3·9)
Main engines: Diesel; 700 bhp = 10 knots
Complement: 24.

Small tankers, classed as fleet auxiliaries.

DUNDURN   1969

MAINTENANCE SHIPS

2 "CAPE" CLASS

Name	No.	Builders	Laid down	Launched	Commissioned
CAPE BRETON	100	Burrard Dry Dock Co, Vancouver, BC	5 July 1944	7 Oct 1944	25 Apr 1945
CAPE SCOTT	101	Burrard Dry Dock Co, Vancouver, BC	8 June 1944	27 Sep 1944	20 Mar 1945

Displacement, tons: 8 580 standard; 10 000 full load
Dimensions, feet (metres): 441·5 × 57 × 20 (134·7 × 17·4 × 6·1)

Alongside Base Ships for FMUs on each coast. They are
decommissioned and no further operational role is planned.
These ships, with a number of sisters, were originally built in
Canada for the R.N. Purchased back 1951.

CAPE BRETON   Canadian Forces

RESEARCH VESSELS

Name	No.	Builders	Commissioned
BLUETHROAT	AGOR 114	Geo. T. Davie & Sons Ltd, Lauzon	28 Nov 1955

Displacement, tons: 785 standard; 870 full load
Dimensions, feet (metres): 157 oa × 33 × 10 *(47 × 9·9 × 3)*
Main engines: Diesel; 2 shafts; 1 200 bhp = 13 knots

Authorised under 1951 Programme. Laid down on 31 Oct 1952. Launched on 15 Sep 1955. Completed on 28 Nov 1955 as Mine and Loop Layer. In 1957 she was rated Controlled Minelayer, NPC 114. Redesignated as Cable Layer (ALC) in 1959, and as Research Vessel (AGOR) and GP craft in 1964.

BLUETHROAT   *1975, Canadian Forces*

Name	No.	Builders	Commissioned
SACKVILLE	AGOR 113	St John Dry Dock Co.	30 Dec 1941

Displacement, tons: 1 085 standard; 1 350 full load
Dimensions, feet (metres): 205 oa × 33 × 14·5 *(62·5 × 10·1 × 6·4)*
Main engines: Triple expansion; 2 750 ihp = 16 knots
Boilers: 2 SE

Ex-"Flower" class corvette completed 30 Dec 1941. Later converted to loop layer. Designated AN 113—rated cable layer in 1959 (ALC). Redesignated as research vessel 1964. Employed by Naval Research Laboratories for oceanographic work.

SACKVILLE   *1976, Michael D. J. Lemon*

Name	No.	Builders	Commissioned
QUEST	AGOR 172	Burrard Dry Dock Co, Vancouver	21 Aug 1969

Displacement, tons: 2 130
Dimensions, feet (metres): 235 oa × 42 × 15·5 *(77·2 × 12·8 × 4·6)*
Aircraft: Light helicopter
Main engines: Diesel electric; 2 shafts; 2 950 shp = 16 knots; bow thruster propeller
Range, miles: 10 000 at 12 knots
Complement: 55

Built for the Naval Research Establishment of the Defence Research Board for acoustic, hydrographic and general oceanographic work. Capable of operating in heavy ice in the company of an icebreaker. Construction began in 1967. Launched on 9 July 1968. Completed on 21 Aug 1969. Based at Halifax.

QUEST   *1972, Canadian Maritime Command*

Name	No.	Builders	Commissioned
ENDEAVOUR	AGOR 171	Yarrows Ltd, Esquimalt, B.C.	9 Mar 1965

Displacement, tons: 1 560
Dimensions, feet (metres): 236 oa × 38·5 × 13 *(71·9 × 11·7 × 4)*
Aircraft: 1 light helicopter
Main engines: Diesel electric; 2 shafts; 2 960 shp = 16 knots
Range, miles: 10 000 at 12 knots
Complement: 50 (10 officers, 13 scientists, 25 ratings plus helicopter pilot and engineer)

A naval research ship designed primarily for anti-submarine research. Flight deck 48 by 31 feet. Stiffened for operating in ice-covered areas. She is able to turn in 2·5 times her own length. Two 9-ton Austin-Weston telescopic cranes are fitted. There are two oceanographical winches each holding 5 000 fathoms of wire, two bathythermograph winches and a deep-sea anchoring and coring winch. She has acoustic insulation in her machinery spaces.

ENDEAVOUR   *1970, Canadian Maritime Command*

LAYMORE AGOR 516 (ex-AKS 516)

Measurement, tons: 560 gross, 262 net
Dimensions, feet (metres): 76·5 × 32 × 8 *(53·6 × 9·8 × 2·5)*
Main engines: GM diesels; 1 000 bhp = 10·8 knots

Former coastal supply vessel, rated as fleet auxiliary and designated AKS. Converted to research vessel 2 Aug 1965 to Mar 1966 and reclassified AGOR.

1 ANTI-SUBMARINE HYDROFOIL (FHE)

BRAS D'OR FHE 400

Displacement, tons: 180
Dimensions, feet (metres): 150·8 × 21·5 × 15 (hull depth) *(46 × 6·6 × 5·1)* = *(7·5 (2·3)* (60 knots) draught on foils) Foil base 90
Main engines: Pratt & Whitney FT4A-2 gas turbine on foils; 22 000 shp = 50-60 knots
Davey Paxman Diesel when hull borne; 2 000 shp = 12-15 knots
Pratt and Whitney ST 6A gas-turbine for hull-borne boost and foil-borne auxiliary power—390 shp

A prototype craft designed by De Havilland Aircraft (Canada). After very successful trials she was laid up ashore at Halifax in 1971 for 5 years, a period now extended.

BRAS D'OR   *1971, Canadian Forces*

PATROL CRAFT

ADVERSUS PBL 191		**DETECTOR** PBL 192	
CAPTOR PBL 193		**ACADIAN** PBL 194	
SIDNEY PBL 195		**NICHOLSON** PBL 195	

All transferred from RCMP in 1975, except *Nicholson* (75 ft) in 1976.

TRAINING SHIPS

6 "BAY" CLASS Ex-MSC (PFL)

Name	No.	Builders	Commissioned
CHALEUR	164	Marine Industries Ltd, Sorel	12 Sep 1957
CHIGNECTO	160	Davie Shipbuilding Co, Lauzon	1 Aug 1957
COWICHAN	162	Yarrows Ltd, Esquimalt	19 Dec 1957
FUNDY	159	Davie Shipbuilding Co, Lauzon	27 Nov 1956
MIRAMICHI	163	Victoria Machinery Depot Co	28 Oct 1957
THUNDER	161	Port Arthur SB Co	3 Oct 1957

Displacement, tons: 390 standard; 464 full load
Dimensions, feet (metres): 152·0 oa × 28·0 × 7·0 *(50 × 9·2 × 2·8)*
Main engines: 2 GM V-12 diesels; 2 shafts; 2 400 bhp = 16 knots
Oil fuel, tons: 52
Range, miles: 3 290 at 12 knots
Complement: 18+ (2 officers, 16 ratings + trainees)

Extensively built of aluminium, including frames and decks. There were originally 14 vessels of this class of which four were transferred to Turkey and four sold commercially. Named after Canadian straits and bays. Designation changed from AMC to MCB in 1954. They were redesignated as Patrol Escorts (small) (PFL) in 1972 being used as training ships.

MIRAMICHI *1975, Canadian Forces*

1 "FORT" CLASS PATROL ESCORT (PFL)

Name	No.	Builders	Commissioned
FORT STEELE	AGOR 140	Canadian SB and Eng. Co	Nov 1955

Displacement, tons: 85
Dimensions, feet (metres): 118 oa × 21 × 7 *(36× 6·4 × 2·1)*
Main engines: 2 Paxman Ventura 12 YJCM diesels; 2 shafts; Kamewa cp propellers; 2 800 bhp = 18 knots
Complement: 16

Steel hull aluminium superstructure. Twin rudders. Acquired by DND in 1973 from RCMP—acts as Reserve Training ship based on Halifax.

FORT STEELE *1975, Canadian Forces*

5 "PORTE" CLASS (GATE VESSELS)

Name	No.	Builders	Commissioned
PORTE DE LA REINE	184	Victoria Machinery	19 Sep 1952
PORTE QUEBEC	185	Burrard Dry Dock	7 Oct 1952
PORTE ST. JEAN	180	Geo T. Davie	4 June 1952
PORTE ST. LOUIS	183	Geo T. Davie	28 Aug 1952
PORTE DAUPHINE	186	Ferguson Ind.	12 Dec 1952

Displacement, tons: 429 full load
Dimensions, feet (metres): 125·5 × 26·3 × 13 *(38 × 8·5 × 3·9)*
Main engines: Diesel; A/C Electric; 1 shaft; 600 bhp = 11 knots
Complement: 23 (3 officers, 20 ratings)

Of trawler design. Multi-purpose vessels used for operating gates in A/S booms, fleet auxiliaries, anti-submarine netlayers for entrances to defended harbours. Can be fitted for minesweeping. Designation changed from YNG to YMG in 1954. First four used during summer for training Reserves. *Porte Dauphine* was reacquired from MOT in 1974 and employed in Reserve Training in Great Lakes area.

Note: Ex-Diving Tender YMT2 of 46 ft is used for sea-cadet training and the yacht *Oriole* QW3 has been used for officer cadet training since 1953.

PORTE ST. LOUIS *1972, Canadian Forces*

DIVING SHIP AND TENDERS

1 FLEET DIVING SUPPORT SHIP

ASXL 20 (ex-*Aspa Quarto*)

Displacement, tons: 2 500
Dimensions, feet (metres): 236 × 39 × 16·5 *(72 × 11·9 × 5)*
Main engines: Diesel electric = 14 knots

Ex-Italian stern trawler bought in 1975 for conversion. When operational she will carry, launch and recover the Canadian submersible SDL/1, and support saturation diving operations.

2 DIVING TENDERS

Name	No.	Builders	Commissioned
YMT 11	—	Ferguson, Picton, NS	Jan 1962
YMT 12	—	Ferguson, Picton, NS	7 Aug 1963

Displacement, tons: 110
Dimensions, feet (metres): 125·5 × 26·3 × 13 *(38·3 × 8 × 4)*
Main engines: GM diesels; 228 bhp = 10·75 knots
Complement: 23 (3 officers, 20 ratings)

Can operate 4 divers at a time to 250 ft. Recompression chamber.

7 "VILLE" CLASS (OLD)

Name	No.	Builders	Commissioned
BURRARD (ex-*Lawrenceville*)	YTS 582	Russell Bros	1944
CREE (ex-*Adamsville*)	YTS 584	Russell Bros	1944
BEAMSVILLE	YTS 583	Russell Bros	1944
QUEENSVILLE	YTS 586	Russell Bros	1944
PLAINSVILLE	YTS 587	Russell Bros	1944
YOUVILLE	YTS 588	Russell Bros	1944
LOGANVILLE	YTS 589	Russell Bros	1944

Dimensions, feet (metres): 40 × 10·5 × 4·8 *(12·2 × 3·2 × 1·5)*
Main engines: Diesel; 1 shaft; 150 bhp

Small harbour tugs now used for Reserve training.

There are small diving tenders YMT 6, YMT 8, YMT 9 and YMT 10, 70 tons, 75 × 18·5 × 8·5 feet, 2 diesels 165 bhp. YMT 1 (46 ft) was transferred to the Naval Research Establishment as a yard craft. Two new diving tenders, YSD 1 and YSD 2, entered service in 1965.

TUGS

2 "SAINT" CLASS

Name	No.	Builders	Commissioned
SAINT ANTHONY	ATA 531	St. John Dry Dock Co.	22 Feb 1957
SAINT CHARLES	ATA 533	St. John Dry Dock Co.	7 June1957

Displacement, tons: 840 full load
Dimensions, feet (metres): 151·5 × 33 × 17 (46·2 × 10 × 5·2)
Main engine: Diesel; 1 shaft; 1 920 bhp = 14 knots
Complement: 21

Ocean tugs. Authorised under the 1951 Programme. Originally class of three.

ST. CHARLES
1975, Canadian Forces

1 "NORTON" CLASS

Name	No.	Builders	Commissioned
RIVERTON	ATA 528	—	Late 1944

Displacement, tons: 462
Dimensions, feet (metres): 111·2 oa × 28 × 11 (33·9 × 8·5 × 3·4)
Main engine: Dominion Sulzer diesel; 1 000 bhp = 11 knots
Complement: 17

Large harbour tug.

5 "GLEN" CLASS (HARBOUR/COASTAL)

Name	No.	Builders	Commissioned
GLENDYNE	ATA 640	Yarrows, Esquimalt	1975
GLENDALE	ATA 641	Yarrows, Esquimalt	1975
GLENEVIS	ATA 642	Georgetown Sy. PEI	1976
GLENBROOK	ATA 643	Georgetown Sy. PEI	1977
GLENSIDE	ATA 644	Georgetown Sy. PEI	1977

Displacement, tons: 255
Dimensions, feet (metres): 92·5 × 28 × 14·5 (28·2 × 8·5 × 4·4)
Main engines: 2 diesels with Voith-Schneider propellers = 11·5 knots
Complement: 6

2 "WOOD" CLASS

Name	No.	Builders	Commissioned
EASTWOOD	YMT 550	Le Blanc SB	1944
WILDWOOD	YMT 553	Falconer Marine	1944

Displacement, tons: 65
Dimensions, feet (metres): 60 oa × 16 × 5 (18·3 × 4·9 × 1·5)
Main engines: Diesel; 250 hp = 10 knots
Complement: 3

Medium harbour tugs. Used as A/S Target Towing Vessels.

Other medium harbour tugs are:
FT1, FT2. Employed as fire tugs, hull numbers YMT 556 and 557 respectively.

5 "VILLE" CLASS (NEW)

Name	No.	Builders	Commissioned
LAWRENCEVILLE	YTS 590	Vito Steel & Barge Co.	1974
PARKSVILLE	YTS 591	Vito Steel & Barge Co.	1974
LISTERVILLE	YTS 592	Georgetown SY PEI	1974
MERRICKVILLE	YTS 593	Georgetown SY PEI	1974
MARYSVILLE	YTS 594	Georgetown SY PEI	1974

Dimensions, feet (metres): 64 × 15·5 × 9 (19·5 × 4·7 × 2·7)
Main engines: Diesel; 1 shaft; 365 bhp = 9·8 knots

Small harbour tugs employed at Esquimalt and Halifax.

PARKSVILLE
1974, Canadian Forces

2 TORPEDO RECOVERY VESSELS

Name	No.	Builders	Commissioned
SONGHEE	YMR 1	Falconer Marine	1944
NIMPKISH	YMR 120	Falconer Marine	1944

Displacement, tons: 162
Length, feet (metres): 94·5 (22·8)
Main engines: 400 bhp
Complement: 7

R.C.M.P. MARINE DIVISION

2 75 ft "DETACHMENT" CLASS

STAND OFF   **CENTENNIAL**

Displacement, tons: 69
Dimensions, feet (metres): 75 oa × 17 × 6·5 *(22·9 × 5·2 × 2)*
Main engines: 2 diesels; 1 018 bhp = 16 knots
Complement: 5

Of wood construction. First pair built by Smith and Rhuland Shipyard of Lunenburg, NS and completed in 1967 and 1968 respectively. *Centennial* built by A. F. Therault and Sons Meteghan River NS. Intended for service on the Atlantic coast.

STAND OFF   *1973, RCMP*

2 65 ft "DETACHMENT" CLASS

TOFINO   **GANGES**

Displacement, tons: 48
Dimensions, feet (metres): 65 × 15 × 4 *(19·8 × 4·6 × 1·2)*
Main engines: 1 Cummins diesel; 1 shaft; 410 bhp = 12 knots

Coastal patrol police boats for service on the east and west coasts.

2 52 ft PATROL VESSELS

RIVETT-CARNAC   **PEARKES**

Displacement, tons: 34
Dimensions, feet (metres): 52 × 14·75 × 3 *(15·9 × 4·5 × ·9)*
Main engines: 2 Cummins 903 (320 hp each); twin shafts = 20 knots

RIVETT-CARNAC   *1974, RCMP*

1 50 ft "DETACHMENT" CLASS

MOOSOMIN II

Dimensions, feet (metres): 50 × 13 × 3 *(15·3 × 4·1 × ·9)*
Main engines: 2 diesels; 600 bhp = over 17 knots

In service on the Great Lakes.

Valleyfield II, Outlook, Whitehorse, Yellowknife, Fort MacLeod and *Brule,* patrol craft varying from 26 to 41 ft in length, operate on the Great Lakes. *Advance, McLennan, Harvison* and *Mayberries* are located on the West coast together with *Duncan* (28 ft), *Dufferin* (41 ft) and *Regina* (41 ft).

CANADIAN COAST GUARD

Administration

Minister of Transport:
    Hon. Otto Lang, MP, PC
Deputy Minister of Transport:
    Mr. Sylvain Cloutier
Administrator, Marine Transportation Administration:
    Mr. R. Illing
Commissioner Canadian Coast Guard:
    Mr. W. A. O'Neil

Establishment

In January 1962 all ships owned and operated by the Federal Department of Transport with the exception of pilotage and canal craft, were amalgamated into the Canadian Coast Guard, a civilian service.

Ships

The Canadian Coast Guard comprises 146 ships and craft of all types (including 63 barges). They operate in Canadian waters from the Great Lakes to the northernmost reaches of the Arctic Archipelago.
There are heavy icebreakers, icebreaking ships for tending buoys and lighthouses, marine survey craft, weather-oceanographic ships, and many specialised vessels for tasks such as search and rescue, cable lifting and repair, marine research and shallow-draft operations in areas such as the Mackenzie River system and some parts of the Arctic.
The Ship Building and Heavy Equipment Branch of the Department of Defence Productions arranges for the design, construction and repair of Coast Guard ships and also provides this service for a number of other Canadian Government departments.
Principle bases for the ships are the department's 11 District offices, located at— St. John's, Newfoundland; Dartmouth, N.S.; Saint John, N.B.; Charlottetown, P.E.I.; Quebec and Sorel, Que; Prescott and Parry Sound, Ont.; Victoria and Prince Rupert, B.C.; and at Hay River, on Great Slave Lake.

Flag

The Canadian Coast Guard has its own distinctive jack, a red maple leaf on a white ground at the hoist and two gold dolphins on a blue ground at the fly.
Canadian Coast Guard vessels have white funnels with a red band at the top and the red maple leaf against the white.

Missions

The Canadian Coast Guard carries out the following missions:
1. Icebreaking and Escort. Icebreaking is carried out in the Gulf of St. Lawrence and River St. Lawrence and the Great Lakes in winter to assist shipping and for flood control, and in Arctic waters in summer.
2. Icebreaker-Aids to Navigation Tenders. Installation, supply and maintenance of fixed and floating aids-to-navigation in Canadian waters.
3. Organise and provide icebreaker support and some cargo vessels for the annual Northern sealift which supplies bases and settlements in the Canadian Arctic and Hudson Bay.
4. Provide and operate special patrol cutters and lifeboats for marine search and rescue.
5. Provide and operate survey and sounding vessels for the St. Lawrence River Ship Channel.
6. Provide and operate weatherships for Ocean Station "Papa" in the Pacific.
7. Provide and operate vessel for the repairing of undersea cables.
8. Provide and operate vessel for Marine Traffic Control on the St. Lawrence river.
9. Operate a small fleet of aircraft primarily for aids to navigation, ice reconnaissance, and pollution control work.

Fleet Strength

Weather ships	2
Cable ship	1
Heavy Icebreakers	5
Medium Icebreaker	1
Medium Icebreaking aid-to-navigation vessels	8
Light Icebreaking aid-to-navigation vessels	7
Ice strengthened aid-to-navigation vessels	4
Aid-to-navigation vessels	7
Offshore patrol cutters	2
Great Lakes Patrol Cutters	3
R Class cutters	5
Lifeboats	14
Hovercraft	1
Launches	6
St. Lawrence River vessels	4
Training vessels	2
Survey and sounding vessels	6
Mackenzie River navigation craft	5
Total	83

Aircraft

Fixed wing	1
Helicopters	33

New Construction

A new class of large icebreakers is under construction by Burrards, the first being launched in 1975. There are discussions under way concerning a large nuclear-propelled icebreaker.

WEATHER SHIPS

Name	No.	Builders	Commissioned
QUADRA	—	Burrard Dry Dock Co Ltd	Mar 1967
VANCOUVER	—	Burrard Dry Dock Co Ltd	4 July 1966

Displacement, tons: 5 600 full load
Dimensions, feet (metres): 404·2 oa × 50 × 17·5 *(121 × 15·5 × 5·3)*
Aircraft: 1 helicopter
Main engines: Turbo-electric; 2 shafts; 7 500 shp = 18 knots
Boilers: 2 automatic Babcock & Wilcox D type
Range, miles: 10 400 at 14 knots
Complement: 96

Turbo-electric twin screw weather and oceanographic vessels for Pacific Ocean service. *Quadra* laid down Feb 1965, launched 4 July 1966. *Vancouver* laid down Mar 1964, launched 29 June 1965. They have bow water jet reaction system to assist steering at slow speeds. Flume stabilisation systems are fitted. They are turbo-electric powered, with oil-fired boilers to provide the quiet operation needed for vessels housing much scientific equipment. Their complement includes 15 technical officers such as meteorologists, oceanographers and electronics technicians.

VANCOUVER

1975, Canadian Ministry of Transport

CABLE SHIP

Name	No.	Builders	Commissioned
JOHN CABOT	—	Canadian Vickers Ltd, Montreal	July 1965

Displacement, tons: 6 375 full load
Dimensions, feet (metres): 313·3 × 60 × 21·5 (95·6 × 18·3 × 6·6)
Aircraft: 1 helicopter
Main engines: Diesel-electric; 2 shafts; 9 000 shp = 15 knots
Range, miles: 10 000 at 12 knots
Complement: 85 officers and men

Laid down May 1963 and launched 15 April 1964. Combination cable repair ship and icebreaker. Designed to repair and lay cable over the bow only. For use in East Coast and Arctic waters. Bow water jet reaction manoeuvring system, heeling tanks and Flume stabilisation system. Three circular storage holds handle a total of 400 miles of submarine cable. Personnel include technicians and helicopter pilots.

JOHN CABOT   1975, Canadian Ministry of Transport

ICEBREAKERS

Notes: (a) A new class is under construction by Burrards—the first launched in 1975.
(b) Discussions continuing into construction of large nuclear icebreaker.

Name	No.	Builders	Commissioned
LOUIS ST. LAURENT	—	Canadian Vickers Ltd, Montreal	Oct 1969

Displacement, tons: 13 800 full load
Dimensions, feet (metres): 366·5 oa × 80 × 31 (111·8 × 24·4 × 9·5)
Aircraft: 2 helicopters
Main engines: Turbo-electric; 3 shafts; 24 000 shp = 17·75 knots
Range, miles: 16 000 miles at 13 knots cruising speed
Complement: Total accommodation for 216

She is larger than any of the former Coast Guard icebreakers. She has a helicopter hangar below the flight deck, with an elevator to raise the two helicopters to the deck when required. She was launched on 3 Dec 1966. She is officially rated as a heavy icebreaker.

LOUIS ST. LAURENT   1971, Canadian Coast Guard

Name	No.	Builders	Commissioned
NORMAN McLEOD ROGERS	—	Canadian Vickers Ltd, Montreal	Oct 1969

Displacement, tons: 6 320 full load
Dimensions, feet (metres): 295 oa × 62·5 × 20 (90 × 19·5 × 6·1)
Aircraft: 1 helicopter
Landing craft: 2
Main engines: 4 diesels and 2 gas turbines powering 2 electric motors; 2 shafts; 12 000 shp = 15 knots
Complement: 55

Built for use in the Gulf of St. Lawrence and East Coast waters. This is the world's first application of gas turbine/electric propulsion in an icebreaker. Officially rated as a heavy icebreaker.

NORMAN McLEOD ROGERS   1975, Canadian Coastguard

Name	No.	Builders	Commissioned
JOHN A. MACDONALD	—	Davie Shipbuilding Ltd, Lauzon	Sep 1960

Displacement, tons: 9 160 full load
Measurement, tons: 6 186 gross
Dimensions, feet (metres): 315 × 70 × 28 (96 × 21·3 × 8·6)
Aircraft: 2 helicopters
Main engines: Diesel-electric; 15 000 shp = 15·5 knots

Officially rated as a heavy icebreaker. Launched 3 Oct 1959.

JOHN A. MACDONALD   1975, Canadian Coastguard

Name	No.	Builders	Commissioned
MONTCALM	—	Davie Shipbuilding Ltd, Lauzon	June 1957
WOLFE	—	Canadian Vickers Ltd, Montreal	Nov 1959

Displacement, tons: 3 005 full load
Measurement, tons: 2 022 gross
Dimensions, feet (metres): 220 × 48 × 16 (72·7 × 14·6 × 4·9)
Aircraft: 1 helicopter
Main engines: Steam reciprocating; 4 000 ihp = 13 knots

Montcalm launched 23 Oct 1956. Officially rated as Medium Icebreaking Aid to Navigation Vessels.

WOLFE   1975, Canadian Coastguard

Name	No.	Builders	Commissioned
LABRADOR	—	Marine Industries Ltd, Sorel	8 July 1954

Displacement, tons: 6 490 full load
Measurement, tons: 3 823 gross
Dimensions, feet (metres): 290·0 oa × 63·5 × 29·0 *(88·5 × 19·4 × 8·8)*
Aircraft: Provision for 2 helicopters
Main engines: Diesel-electric; 10 000 shp = 16 knots

Ordered in Feb 1949, laid down on 18 Nov 1949, launched on 14 Dec 1951 and completed for the Royal Canadian Navy but transferred to the Department of Transport in Feb 1958. Officially rated as a Heavy Icebreaker. She was the first naval vessel to traverse the North West passage and circumnavigate North America, when she was Canada's largest and most modern icebreaker.

LABRADOR   *1975, Dept. of Transport*

Name	No.	Builders	Commissioned
D'IBERVILLE	—	Davie Shipbuilding Ltd, Lauzon	May 1953

Displacement, tons: 9 930 full load
Measurement, tons: 5 678 gross
Dimensions, feet (metres): 310 × 66·5 × 30·2 *(94·6 × 20·3 × 9·2)*
Main engines: Steam reciprocating; 10 800 ihp = 15 knots

Officially rated as a Heavy Icebreaker.

D'IBERVILLE   *1975 Canadian Coast Guard*

AID TO NAVIGATION VESSELS

Name	No.	Builders	Commissioned
CAMSELL	—	Burrard Dry Dock Co Ltd	Oct 1959

Displacement, tons: 3 072 full load
Measurement, tons: 2 020 gross
Dimensions, feet (metres): 223·5 × 48 × 16 *(68·2 × 14·6 × 4·9)*
Main engines: Diesel-electric; 4 250 shp = 13 knots

Launched 17 Feb 1959. Officially rated as Medium Icebreaking Aid to Navigation Vessel.

CAMSELL   *1975, Canadian Coast Guard*

Name	No.	Builders	Commissioned
SIR HUMPHREY GILBERT	—	Davie Shipbuilding Ltd, Lauzon	June 1959

Displacement, tons: 3 000 full load
Measurement, tons: 1 930 gross
Dimensions, feet (metres): 220 × 48 × 16·3 *(68 × 14·6 × 5·0)*
Main engines: Diesel-electric; 4 250 shp = 13 knots

Officially rated as Medium Icebreaking Aid to Navigation Vessel.

SIR HUMPHREY GILBERT   *1970, Canadian Coast Guard*

Name	No.	Builders	Commissioned
ERNEST LAPOINTE	—	Davie Shipbuilding Ltd, Lauzon	Feb 1941

Displacement, tons: 1 675 full load
Measurement, tons: 1 179 gross
Dimensions, feet (metres): 184 × 36 × 15·5 *(56·1 × 11 × 4·7)*
Main engines: Steam reciprocating; 2 000 ihp = 13 knots

Officially rated as St. Lawrence Ship Channel Icebreaking Survey and Sounding Vessel.

Name	No.	Builders	Commissioned
SIR WILLIAM ALEXANDER	—	Halifax Shipyards Ltd	June 1959

Displacement, tons: 3 555 full load
Measurements, tons: 2 153 gross
Dimensions, feet (metres): 227·5 × 45 × 17·5 *(69·4 × 13·7 × 5·3)*
Main engines: Diesel electric; 4 250 shp = 15 knots

Launched 13 Dec 1958. Equipped with Flume Stabilisation System. Officially rated as a Medium Icebreaking Aid to Navigation Vessel.

SIR WILLIAM ALEXANDER   *1975, Dept. of Transport*

Name	No.	Builders	Commissioned
GRIFFON	—	Davie Shipbuilding Ltd, Lauzon	Dec 1970

Displacement, tons: 3 096
Dimensions, feet (metres): 234 × 49 × 15·5 *(71·4 × 14·9 × 4·7)*
Main engines: Diesel; 4 000 bhp; 13·5 knots

Officially rated as Medium Icebreaking Aid to Navigation Vessel.

GRIFFON   *1975, Canadian Coast Guard*

Name	No.	Builders	Commissioned
N. B. McLEAN	—	Halifax S.Y. Ltd	1930

Displacement, tons: 5 034 full load
Measurements, tons: 3 254 gross
Dimensions, feet (metres): 277 × 60·5 × 24·0 *(90 × 19·5 × 6·1)*
Main engines: Steam reciprocating; 6 500 ihp = 13 knots

Officially rated as Medium Icebreaker.

Name	No.	Builders	Commissioned
J. E. BERNIER	—	Davie Shipbuilding Ltd, Lauzon	Aug 1967

Displacement, tons: 3 096
Dimensions, feet (metres): 231 × 49 × 16 *(70·5 × 14·9 × 4·9)*
Aircraft: 1 helicopter
Main engines: Diesel Electric; 4 250 bhp = 13·5 knots (trial speed)

Officially rated as Medium Icebreaking Aid to Navigation Vessel.

J. E. BERNIER   *1975, Ministry of Transport*

Name	No.	Builders	Commissioned
ALEXANDER HENRY	—	Port Arthur SB Ltd	July 1959

Displacement, tons: 2 497 full load
Measurements, tons: 1 647 gross
Dimensions, feet (metres): 210 × 43·5 × 16 *(64 × 13·3 × 4·9)*
Main engines: Diesel; 3 550 bhp = 13 knots

Launched 18 July 1958. Officially rated as a Medium Icebreaking Aid to Navigation Vessel.

Name	No.	Builders	Commissioned
SIMON FRASER	—	Burrard D. Y. Co. Ltd	Feb 1960
TUPPER	—	Marine Industries Ltd	Dec 1959

Displacement, tons: 1 876 full load
Measurements, tons: 1 357 gross
Dimensions, feet (metres): 204·5 × 42 × 14 *(62·4 × 12·8 × 4·3)*
Main engines: Diesel-electric; 2 900 shp = 13·5 knots

Simon Fraser was launched 18 Aug 1959. Both officially rated as Light Icebreaking Aid to Navigation Vessels.

Name	No.	Builders	Commissioned
THOMAS CARLETON	—	St. John Dry Dock Ltd	1960

Displacement, tons: 1 532 full load
Dimensions, feet (metres): 180 × 42 × 13 *(54·9 × 12·8 × 4)*
Main engines: Diesel; 2 000 bhp = 12 knots

Officially rated as Light Icebreaking Aid to Navigation Vessel.

Name	No.	Builder	Commissioned
EDWARD CORNWALLIS	—	Canadian Vickers Ltd, Montreal	Dec 1949

Displacement, tons: 3 700 full load
Measurement, tons: 1 965 gross
Dimensions, feet (metres): 259 × 43·5 × 18 *(79 × 13·3 × 5·5)*
Main engines: Steam reciprocating; 2 800 ihp = 13·5 knots

Launched 5 Aug 1949. In reserve . Officially rated as a Light Icebreaking Aid to Navigation Vessel.

EDWARD CORNWALLIS   *1971, Canadian Coast Guard*

Name	No.	Builders	Commissioned
TRACY	—	Port Weller Drydocks	1968

Displacement, tons: 1 300
Dimensions, feet (metres): 251·5 × 42 × 12 *(76·7 × 12·8 × 3·7)*
Main engines: Diesel; 2 000 bhp = 11 knots

Officially rated as Light Icebreaking Aid to Navigation Vessel.

Name	No.	Builders	Commissioned
WALTER E. FOSTER	—	Canadian Vickers Ltd, Montreal	Dec 1954

Displacement, tons: 2 715 full load
Measurement, tons: 1 672 gross
Dimensions, feet (metres): 229·2 × 42·5 × 16 *(69·9 × 12·9 × 4·9)*
Main engines: Steam reciprocating; 2 000 ihp = 12·5 knots

Officially rated as a Light Icebreaking Aid to Navigation Vessel.

WALTER E. FOSTER   1975, Canadian Coast Guard

Name	No.	Builders	Commissioned
NARWHAL	—	Canadian Vickers Ltd, Montreal	July 1963

Measurement, tons: 2 064 gross
Dimensions, feet (metres): 251·5 × 42·0 × 12·0 *(76·7 × 12·8 × 3·7)*
Main engines: Diesel; 2 000 bhp
Range, miles: 9 200 cruising
Complement: 32

Originally rated as Sealift Stevedore Depot Vessel, now re-rated as Light Icebreaking Aid to Navigation Vessel.

NARWHAL   1975, Canadian Coast Guard

Name	No.	Builders	Commissioned
SIMCOE	—	Canadian Vickers Ltd, Montreal	1962

Displacement, tons: 1 300 full load
Dimensions, feet (metres): 179·5 × 38 × 12 *(54·7 × 11·6 × 3·7)*
Main engines: Diesel-electric; 2 000 shp = 12 knots

Officially rated as Ice Strengthened Aid to Navigation Vessel.

Name	No.	Builders	Commissioned
BARTLETT	—	—	1970
PROVO WALLIS	—	—	1970

Displacement, tons: 1 620
Dimensions, feet (metres): 189·3 × 42·5 × 12·5 *(57·7 × 13 × 3·8)*
Main engines: Diesel; 1 760 bhp = 12 knots

Classed as Ice Strengthened Aid to Navigation Vessels.

BARTLETT   1975, Ministry of Transport

Name	No.	Builders	Commissioned
MONTMORENCY	—	Davie Shipbuilding Ltd, Lauzon	Aug 1957

Displacement, tons: 1 006 full load
Measurement, tons: 750 gross
Dimensions, feet (metres): 163× 34 × 11 *(49·7 × 10·2 × 3·4)*
Main engines: Diesel; 1 200 bhp

Officially rated as an Ice Strengthened Aid to Navigation Vessel.

MONTMORENCY   *1975, Canadian Coast Guard*

Name	No.	Builders	Commissioned
MONTMAGNY	—	Russel Bros, Owen Sound	May 1963

Displacement, tons: 565 full load
Dimensions, feet (metres): 148·0 × 29·0 × 8·0 *(45·1 × 10·2 × 2·4)*
Main engines: Diesels; 1 000 bhp

Officially rated as Aid to Navigation Tender.

MONTMAGNY   *1970, Canadian Coast Guard*

Name	No.	Builders	Commissioned
VERENDRYE	—	Davie Shipbuilding Ltd, Lauzon	Oct 1959

Displacement, tons: 400 full load
Dimensions, feet (metres): 125·0 × 26·0 × 7·0 *(38·1 × 7·9 × 2·1)*
Main engines: Diesels; 760 bhp

Officially rated as Aid to Navigation Tender.

Name	No.	Builders	Commissioned
ROBERT FOULIS	—	St John Drydock	1969

Displacement, tons: 260
Dimensions, feet (metres): 104 × 25 × 7 *(31·7 × 7·6 × 2·1)*
Main engines: Diesel; 960 bhp = 10 knots

Officially rated as Aid to Navigation Tender.

KENOKI

Displacement, tons: 270
Dimensions, feet (metres): 108 × 36 × 5 *(32·9 × 11 × 1·5)*
Main engines: Diesel; 940 bhp = 10 knots

Officially rated as Aid to Navigation Tender.

Name	No.	Builders	Commissioned
ALEXANDER MACKENZIE	—	Burrard Dry Dock Ltd	1950
SIR JAMES DOUGLAS	—	Burrard Dry Dock Ltd	Nov 1956

Displacement, tons: 720 full load
Dimensions, feet (metres): 150·0 × 30·0 × 10·3 *(45·8 × 9 × 3·1)*
Main engines: Diesels; 1 000 bhp

Officially rated as Aid to Navigation Tenders.

NOKOMIS

Displacement, tons: 64
Dimensions, feet (metres): 66 × 17 × 7 *(20·1 × 5·2 × 2·1)*
Main engines: Diesel; 120 bhp

Officially rated as Aid to Navigation Tender.

SEARCH AND RESCUE CUTTERS

Name	No.	Builders	Commissioned
ALERT	—	Davie Shipbuilding Ltd, Lauzon	Dec 1969

Displacement, tons: 2 025
Dimensions, feet (metres): 234·3 × 39·9 × 15·1 *(71·5 × 12·2 × 4·6)*
Aircraft: 1 helicopter
Main engines: Diesel electric; 7 716 hp = 18·75 knots
Range, miles: 6 000

Officially rated as Offshore Patrol Cutter.

ALERT   *1975, Canadian Coast Guard*

Name	No.	Builders	Commissioned
DARING (ex-*Wood*, MP 17)	—	Davie Shipbuilding Ltd, Lauzon	July 1958

Displacement, tons: 600 standard
Dimensions, feet (metres): 178 oa × 29 × 9·8 *(54·3 × 8·8 × 3·0)*
Main engines: 2 Fairbanks-Morse diesels; 2 shafts; 2 660 bhp = 16 knots

Used for patrol on the east coast of Canada, this ship is built of steel, strengthened against ice, with aluminium superstructure. Transferred from the Royal Canadian Mounted Police Marine Division to the Ministry of Transport in 1971, and renamed *Daring*. Offshore Patrol Cutter.

DARING (as *Wood*)   1966, Director of Marine Services

CG 101-109   CG 114-118

Displacement, tons: 18
Dimensions, feet (metres): 44 × 12 × 3 *(13·4 × 3·7 × 0·9)*
Main engines: Diesel; 294 bhp = 14 knots
Range, miles: 150

Lifeboats shore-based at Coast Guard Stations on both coasts.

Name	No.	Builders	Commissioned
RACER	—	Yarrows Ltd, Esquimalt	1963
RALLY	—	Davie Shipbuilding Ltd	1963
RAPID	—	Ferguson Industries, Picton	1963
READY	—	Burrard Dry Dock	1963
RELAY	—	Kingston Shipyard	1963
RIDER	—	—	1963

Measurement, tons: 153 gross
Dimensions, feet (metres): 95·2 × 20 × 6·5 *(29 × 6·1 × 2)*
Main engines: Diesel; 2 400 bhp = 20 knots designed

Rider, completed for the Dept. of Fisheries, was taken over by the Coast Guard in Mar 1969. *Relay* rerated as St. Lawrence River Marine Traffic Control Vessel.

RELAY   1975, Ministry of Transport

Name	No.	Builders	Commissioned
SPINDRIFT	—	Cliff Richardson Ltd, Meaford	1963
SPRAY	—	J. J. Taylor & Sons Ltd, Toronto	1963
SPUME	—	Grew Ltd, Penetanguishene	1964

Measurement, tons: 57 gross
Dimensions, feet (metres): 70 × 16·8 × 4·7 *(21·4 × 5·1 × 1·4)*
Main engines: 2 diesels; 1 050 bhp = 19 knots

Employed on Great Lakes Patrol.

Note. For search and rescue and patrol duties: six launches *(Mallard, Moorhen,* CG 110-113) and one Hovercraft (CG 021).

SPINDRIFT   1975, Canadian Coast Guard

NORTHERN SUPPLY VESSELS

2 FORMER TANK LANDING CRAFT (LCT 8)

Name	No.	Builders	Commissioned
EIDER	—	Sir Wm Arrol & Co	1946
SKUA	—	Harland & Wolff	1946

Measurement, tons: 1 083 to 1 104 gross
Dimensions, feet (metres): 231·2 oa × 38 × 7 *(70·5 × 11·6 × 2·1)*
Main engines: Diesel; 1 000 shp = 9 knots

Converted LCT (8)s, acquired from Great Britain in 1957-61.

SKUA   Canadian Coast Guard

1 FORMER TANK LANDING CRAFT (LCT 4)

Name	No.	Builders	Commissioned
MINK	—	—	1944

Displacement, tons: 586 full load
Dimensions, feet (metres): 187·2 × 33·8 × 4 *(57·1 × 10·3 × 1·2)*
Main engines: Diesel; 920 shp = 8 knots

Converted LCT (4) acquired from Great Britain in 1958. Formerly officially rated as Steel Landing Craft for Northern Service, now re-rated as Aids to Navigation Tender, in reserve.

MINK   1963, Canadian Coast Guard

SURVEY AND SOUNDING VESSELS

BEAUPORT

Displacement, tons: 767 full load
Dimensions, feet (metres): 167·5 × 24·0 × 9·0 *(51·1 × 7·3 × 2·7)*
Main engines: Diesels; 1 280 bhp

Completed in 1960.

DETECTOR

Displacement, tons: 584 full load
Dimensions, feet (metres): 140·0 × 35·0 × 10·0 *(42·7 × 10·7 × 3·1)*
Main engines: Steam reciprocating

NICOLET

Displacement, tons: 935 full load
Dimensions, feet (metres): 166·5 × 35·0 × 9·6 *(50·8 × 10·7 × 2·9)*
Main engines: Diesels; 1 350 bhp

VILLE MARIE

Displacement, tons: 493 full load
Dimensions, feet (metres): 134·0 × 28·0 × 9·5 *(40·9 × 8·5 × 2·9)*
Main engines: Diesel electric; 1 000 hp

Completed in 1960.

There are also two smaller vessels *Glendada* and *Jean Bourdon* for the St. Lawrence Ship Channel.

SHORE-BASED CRAFT

DUMIT   **ECKALOO**   **MISKANAW**   **TEMBAH**   **NAHIDIK**

Assist navigation in Mackenzie River operations. Small tug/buoy tender type.

TRAINING SHIPS

MIKULA

Displacement, tons: 617
Dimensions, feet (metres): 128 × 30 × 11 *(39 × 9·2 × 3·4)*
Main engines: Diesel; 150 bhp = 9 knots

Converted Light Vessel.

SKIDEGATE

Displacement, tons: 200
Dimensions, feet (metres): 87 × 22·× 8 *(26·5 × 6·7 × 2·4)*
Main engines: Diesel; 640 bhp = 11 knots

Formerly an Aid to Navigation Tender.

CHILE

Ministerial

Minister of National Defence:
Major General

Headquarters Appointments

Commander-in-Chief of the Navy:
Admiral José Toribio Merino Castro
Chief of the Naval Staff:
Rear-Admiral Carlos A. Le May Délano

Diplomatic Representation

Naval Attaché in Brasilia:
Captain Reinaldo Rivas
Naval Attaché in Buenos Aires and Montevideo:
Captain Eri Solis
Naval Attaché in Lima:
Captain Jorge Contreras
Naval Attaché in London, Paris, The Hague and Stockholm:
Rear Admiral Maurice Poisson
Naval Attaché in Madrid:
Captain Guillermo Aldoney
Naval Attaché in Quito:
Captain Franklin Gonzalez
Naval Attaché in Tokyo:
Commander Ernesto Huber
Naval Attaché in Washington:
Rear Admiral Ronald McIntyre

Personnel

(a) 1977: 23 000 (1 320 officers, 19 000 ratings, 3 680 marines)
(b) 1 year National Service

Naval Bases

Talcahuano. Main Naval Base, Schools, major repair yard, (2 dry docks, 2 floating docks) 2 floating cranes.
Valparaiso. Naval Base, Schools, major repair yard.
Puerto Monti. Small naval base.
Punta Arenas. Small naval base. Repair yard with slipway.
Puerto Williams. Small naval base.

Maritime Air

Personnel—500

4 Bell 206 A JetRangers
2 Bell 47
4 Lockheed SP-2E Neptunes (Air Force)
5 Grumman HU-16B Albatross (Air force)
3 Convair PBY-6A Catalina (SAR)
5 Douglas C 47
5 Beech C-45/D18s
1 Piper PA-31-310 Navajo
6 Beech T-34B Mentor
3 EMB-110 Bandeirante

There is a requirement for 12 new maritime patrol aircraft but the UK and Netherlands Governments have vetoed the supply of HS. 748 or Fokker/VFW F.27 MP aircraft. It is possible that Brazilian EMB-111 may be bought instead.

Infanteria de Marina

1 Brigade and Coast Defence units (2 680 marines).
Four bases at Iquique, Punta Arenas, Talcahuano and Valparaiso in addition to an embarked battalion.

Strength of the Fleet

Type	Active	Building
Cruisers	2	—
Destroyers	6	—
Frigates	5	—
Corvettes	3	—
Patrol Submarines	3	—
Landing Ships (Tank)	4	—
Landing Craft	3	—
Fast Attack Craft (Torpedo)	4	—
Large Patrol Craft	3	—
Coastal Patrol Craft	3	—
Survey Ship	1	—
Sail Training Ship	1	—
Transports	4	—
Tankers	3	1
Floating Docks	2	—
Tugs	7	—

Mercantile Marine

Lloyd's Register of Shipping:
142 vessels of 409 756 tons gross

DELETIONS

Cruiser

1975 *O'Higgins* ("Brooklyn" Class) grounded in Aug 1974. Subsequently used as alongside accommodation ship.

Submarine

1973 *Thomson* (ex-US "Balao" Class)

Frigate

1973 *Riquelme* (ex-US "Charles Lawrence" Class)

Landing Craft

1971 *Bolados* (LCU 95)
1973 *Grumete Tellez* (withdrawn from service)

Tugs

1971 *Cabrales, Ugarte*

PENNANT LIST

Cruisers

03 Prat
04 Latorre

Destroyers/Frigates

06 Condell
07 Lynch
14 Blanco Encalada
15 Cochrane
16 Ministero Zenteno
17 Ministero Portales
18 Almirante Riveros
19 Almirante Williams
26 Serrano
27 Orella
29 Uribe

Submarines

21 Simpson
22 O'Brien
23 Hyatt

Corvettes

60 Lientul
62 Lautaro
63 Sergento Aldea

Light Forces

37 Papudo
75 Marinero Fuentealba
76 Cabo Odger
79 Contramaestre Ortiz
80 Guacolda
81 Fresia
82 Quidora
83 Tegualda

Survey Ship

64 Yelcho

Training Ship

43 Esmeralda

Amphibious Forces

88 Comandante Hemmerdinger
89 Comandante Araya
90 Elicura
91 Aguila
92 Aspirante Morel
94 Orompello
96 Grumete Diaz
97 Comandante Toro

Transports

45 Piloto Pardo
47 Aquiles
110 Meteoro
111 Cirujano Videla

Tankers

52 Al Jorge Montt
53 Araucano
54 Beagle

Tugs

63 S. Aldea
73 Colocolo
104 Ancud
105 Monreal
120 Reyes
127 Caupolican
128 Cortez

LATORRE

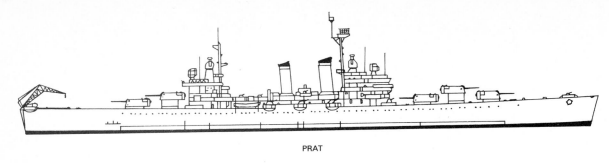

PRAT

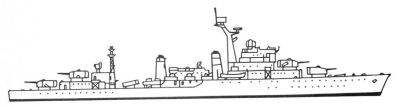

"ALMIRANTE" Class

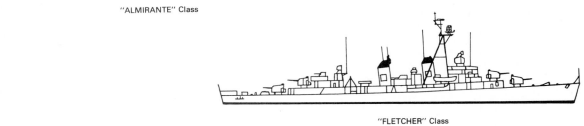

"FLETCHER" Class

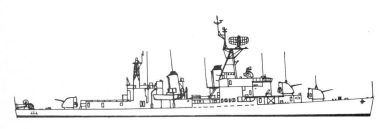

"ALLEN M. SUMNER" Class

CRUISERS

1 Ex-SWEDISH "GOTA LEJON" CLASS

Name	No.	Builders	Laid down	Launched	Commissioned
LATORRE (ex-*Göta Lejon*)	04	Eriksberg Mekaniska Verkstad, Göteborg	27 Sep 1943	17 Nov 1945	15 Dec 1947

Displacement, tons: 8 200 standard; 9 200 full load
Length, feet (metres): 590·5 *(180·0)* wl; 597 *(182·0)* oa
Beam, feet (metres): 54 *(16·5)*
Draught, feet (metres): 21·5 *(6·6)*
Guns: 7—6 in *(150 mm)* 53 cal. 4—57 mm; 11—40 mm
Tubes: 6—21 inch
Armour: 3 in—5 in *(75—125 mm)*
Main engines: 2 sets De Laval geared turbines; 100 000 shp;
  2 shafts
Boilers: 4 Swedish 4-drum type
Speed, knots: 33
Complement: 610

Radar control arrangements were installed for 6-inch guns. Fitted for minelaying with a capacity of 120 mines. Reconstructed in 1951-52, modernised in 1958, with new radar, 57 mm guns etc.

Gunnery: The 6 inch guns are high angle automatic anti-aircraft weapons with an elevation of 70 degrees.

Radar: Search: LW-03, Type 227. Tactical: Type 293. Fire Control: I band.

Transfer: Purchased by Chile from Sweden July 1971. Commissioned in Chilean Navy 18 Sep 1971.

LATORRE   *1973, Chilean Navy*

1 Ex-US "BROOKLYN" CLASS

Name	No.	Builders	Laid down	Launched	Commissioned
PRAT (ex-USS *Nashville* CL 43)	03	New York S.B. Corp.	24 Jan 1935	2 Oct 1937	25 Nov 1938

Displacement, tons: 10 000 standard; 13 500 full load
Length, feet (metres): 608·3 *(185·4)* oa
Beam, feet (metres): 69 *(21·0)*
Draught, feet (metres): 24 *(7·3)*
Aircraft: 1 Bell helicopter
Guns: 15—6 in *(153 mm)* 47 cal (5 triple); 8—5 in *(127 mm)*
25 cal (single); 28—40 mm; 24—20 mm
Armour, inches (mm):
Belt 4 in—1½ in *(102—38)*;
Decks 3 in—2 in *(76—51)*;
Turrets 5 in—3 in *(127—76)*; C.T. 8 in *(203)*
Main engines: Parsons geared turbines 100 000 shp; 4 shafts
Boilers: 8 Babcock & Wilcox Express type
Oil fuel, tons: 2 100
Speed, knots: 32·5
Range, miles: 14 500 at 15 knots
Complement: 888 to 975 (peace)

Former cruiser of the US "Brooklyn" Class. Purchased from the United States in 1951 at a price representing 10 per cent of original cost ($37 000 000) plus the expense of reconditioning. Again refitted in USA 1957-58.

Class: *O'Higgins* (ex-USS *Brooklyn*) was damaged by grounding in August 1974. She has subsequently been used as an alongside accommodation ship and is no longer considered operational.

Hangar: The hangar in the hull right aft could accommodate 6 aircraft if necessary together with engine spares and duplicate parts, though 4 aircraft was the normal capacity. Above the hangar two catapults were mounted as far outboard as possible, and a revolving crane was placed at the stern extremity overhanging the aircraft hatch.

Radar: Search: SPS 12. Tactical: SPS 10.

PRAT   *1974, Chilean Navy*

DESTROYERS

2 "ALMIRANTE" CLASS

Name	No.	Builders	Laid down	Launched	Commissioned
ALMIRANTE RIVEROS	18	Vickers-Armstrong Ltd, Barrow	12 Apr 1957	12 Dec 1958	31 Dec 1960
ALMIRANTE WILLIAMS	19	Vickers-Armstrong Ltd, Barrow	20 June1956	5 May 1958	26 Mar 1960

Displacement, tons: 2 730 standard; 3 300 full load
Length, feet (metres): 402 *(122·5)* oa
Beam, feet (metres): 43 *(13·1)*
Draught, feet (metres): 13·3 *(4·0)*
Missiles: 4 Exocet MM 38 Launchers;
2 Quadruple launchers for Seacat
Guns: 4—4 in *(102 mm)*; 4—40 mm (singles)
A/S weapons: 2 Squid 3-barrelled DC mortars;
6 (2 triple) Mk 32 torpedo tubes (Mk 44 torpedoes)
Main engines: Parsons Pametrada geared turbines;
54 000 shp; 2 shafts
Boilers: 2 Babcock & Wilcox
Speed, knots: 34·5
Range, miles: 6 000 at 16 knots
Complement: 266

Ordered in May 1955. Layout and general arrangements are conventional. Bunks fitted for entire crew. Both modernised by Swan Hunter, *Almirante Williams* in 1971-74 and *Almirante Riveros* in 1973-75.

Electrical: The electrical system is on alternating current. Galleys are all electric. There is widespread use of fluorescent lighting. Degaussing cables are fitted.

Gunnery: The four inch guns are in four single mountings, two superimposed forward and two aft. They are automatic with a range of 12 500 yards *(11 400 metres)* and an elevation of 75 degrees.

Missiles: British Seacat surface-to-air installations were fitted at the Chilean Navy Yard at Talcahuano in 1964. Exocet MM 38 fitted during modernisations.

Operational: The operations room and similar spaces are air-conditioned. Twin rudders. Ventilation and heating system designed to suit Chilean conditions, extending from the tropics to the Antarctic.

Radar: Plessey AWS-I and Target Indication radar with AIO autonomous displays being fitted at refits.

ALMIRANTE RIVEROS   *1974, Swan Hunter*

ALMIRANTE WILLIAMS   *1974, Swan Hunter*

2 Ex-US "FLETCHER" CLASS

Name	No.	Builders	Laid down	Launched	Commissioned
BLANCO ENCALADA (ex-USS *Wadleigh DD 689*)	14	Bath Iron Works Corpn, Bath	Mar 1943	7 Aug 1943	19 Oct 1943
COCHRANE (ex-USS *Rooks DD 804*)	15	Todd Pacific Shipyards	Jan 1944	6 June1944	2 Sep 1944

Displacement, tons: 2 100 standard; 2 750 full load
Length, feet (metres): 376·5 *(110·5)* oa
Beam, feet (metres): 39·5 *(12·0)*
Draught, feet (metres): 18 *(5·5)*
Guns: 4—5 in *(127 mm)* 38 cal; 6—3 in *(76 mm)* 50 cal
Torpedo tubes: 5—21 in (quintupled)
A/S weapons: 2 Hedgehogs; 2 side launching torpedo racks; 1 DC rack; 6 "K" DCT
Main engines: 2 Westinghouse geared turbines; 60 000 shp; 2 shafts
Boilers: 4 Babcock & Wilcox
Speed, knots: 35
Oil fuel, tons: 650
Range, miles: 5 000 at 15 knots; 1 260 at 30 knots
Complement: 250 (14 officers, 236 men). Accommodation for 324 (24 officers, 300 men)

Transferred to Chile under the Military Aid Programme in 1963. Three more destroyers were scheduled for transfer from the United States Navy to the Chilean Navy under a new transfer law signed by the President of the United States in 1966. The ships were to have been refitted and modernised and adapted to Chilean requirements before transfer to the new flag, but the four Frigates of the US "Charles Lawrence" Class were transferred instead.

Radar: Search: SPS 6. Tactical: SPS 10. Fire control: I Band.

COCHRANE   *1972, Chilean Navy*

2 Ex-US "ALLEN M. SUMNER FRAM II" CLASS

Name	No.	Builders	Laid down	Launched	Commissioned
MINISTRO PORTALES (ex-USS *Douglas H. Fox, DD 779*)	17	Federal SB and DD Co.	1943	13 Mar 1944	17 May 1944
MINISTRO ZENTENO (ex-USS *Charles S. Sperry, DD 697*)	16	Todd (Pacific) Shipyards	1944	30 Sep 1944	26 Dec 1944

Displacement, tons: 2 200 standard; 3 320 full load
Length, feet (metres): 376·5 *(114·8)* oa
Beam, feet (metres): 40·9 *(12·4)*
Draught, feet (metres): 19 *(5·8)*
Guns: 6—5 in *(127 mm)* 38 cal
A/S weapons: 2 triple Mk 32 launchers; 2 Hedgehogs; Facilities for small helicopter
Main engines: 2 Geared Turbines; 60 000 shp; 2 shafts
Boilers: 4
Speed, knots: 34
Range, miles: 4 600 at 15 knots
Complement: 274

Transferred 8 Jan 1974.

Radar: Search; SPS 37 *(Zenteno)*, SPS 40 *(Portales)*. Tactical; SPS 10.

Sonar: SQS 40.

MINISTRO ZENTENO   *1976, Chilean Navy*

MINISTRO PORTALES   *1975*

FRIGATES

2 BRITISH "LEANDER" CLASS

Name	No.
CONDELL	06
ALMIRANTE LYNCH	07

Builders	Laid down	Launched	Commissioned
Yarrow & Co. Ltd.	5 June 1971	12 June 1972	21 Dec 1973
Yarrow & Co. Ltd.	6 Dec 1971	6 Dec 1972	25 May 1974

Displacement, tons: 2 500 standard; 2 962 full load
Length, feet (metres): 360·0 *(109·7)* wl; 372·0 *(113·4)* oa
Beam, feet (metres): 43·0 *(13·1)*
Draught, feet (metres): 18·0 *(5·5)*
Aircraft: 1 light helicopter
Missiles: 4 Exocet launchers; 1 quadruple Seacat
Guns: 2—4·5 in (1 twin); 2—20 mm
A/S weapons: 6 (2 triple) Mk 32 torpedo tubes
Main engines: 2 geared turbines; 30 000 shp
Boilers: 2
Speed, knots: 30
Range, miles: 4 500 at 12 knots
Complement: 263

Ordered from Yarrow & Co Ltd, Scotstoun in the modernisation programme of the Chilean Navy. Until the Swedish cruiser was acquired, *Condell*, laid down on 5 June 1971, was to have been named *Latorre*. Renamed 1971. Both arrived in Chilean waters by February 1975.

Appearance: Have slightly taller foremasts than British "Leanders". No Limbo or VDS.

Missiles: The Exocet launchers are placed on the quarter-deck thus, as opposed to the British conversion, allowing the retention of the 4·5 in turret.

Radar: Surveillance, Target Indication; Type 992Q.
Air search; Type 965.
Navigation; Type 975.
Seacat/Gunnery; GWS 22/MRS3.

Sonar: Type 162, 170 and 177.

ALMIRANTE LYNCH   10/1974, C. and S. Taylor

3 Ex-US "CHARLES LAWRENCE" CLASS

Name
SERRANO (ex-USS *Odum*, APD 71, ex-DE 670)
ORELLA (ex-USS *Jack C. Robinson*, APD 72, ex-DE 671)
URIBE (ex-USS *Daniel Griffin*, APD 38, ex-DE 54)

No.	Builders	Laid down	Launched	Commissioned
26	Consolidated Steel, Orange	15 Oct 1943	19 Jan 1944	12 Jan 1945
27	Consolidated Steel, Orange	10 Nov 1943	8 Jan 1944	2 Feb 1945
29	Bethlehem, Hingham	7 Sep 1942	25 Feb 1943	9 June 1943

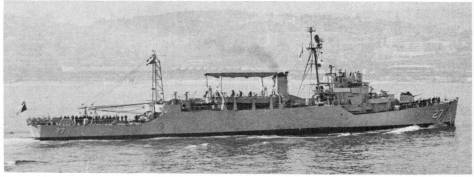

Displacement, tons: 1 400 standard; 2 130 full load
Length, feet (metres): 300·0 *(91·4)* wl; 306·0 *(93·3)* oa
Beam, feet (metres): 37·0 *(11·3)*
Draught, feet (metres): 12·6 *(3·8)*
Guns: 1—5 in 38 cal; 6—40 mm
A/S weapons: 2 Hedgehogs (some); 2 DC racks
Main engines: GE turbo-electric; 2 shafts; 12 000 shp = 23·6 knots; 2 turbines 6 000 hp each; 2 generators 4 500 kW each
Boilers: 2 Foster Wheeler "D" type
Range, miles: 5 000 at 15 knots; 2 000 at 23 knots
Complement: 209

These former high speed transports (APD) were purchased from the USA, transferred at Orange, Texas 25 Nov 1966 (first two) and Norfolk Va 1 Dec 1966 *(Uribe)*. They have been modernised, *Riquelme* was also transferred but was used for provision of spare parts. Deleted 1973.

Radar: Combined search; AN/SPS-4.
Navigation; commercial (no gunnery control by radar).

ORELLA   1974, Chilean Navy

SUBMARINES

2 BRITISH "OBERON" CLASS

Name	No.
O'BRIEN	22
HYATT (ex-*Condell*)	23

Builders	Laid down	Launched	Commissioned
Scott-Lithgow	17 Jan 1971	21 Dec 1972	April 1976
Scott-Lithgow	10 Jan 1972	26 Sep 1973	31 Aug 1976

Displacement, tons: 1 610 standard; 2 030 surfaced; 2 410 dived
Length, feet (metres): 241·0 *(73·5)* pp; 295·2 *(90·0)* oa
Beam, feet (metres): 26·5 *(8·1)*
Draught, feet (metres): 18·1 *(5·5)*
Torpedo tubes: 8—21 in *(533 mm)*
Main machinery: 2 diesels 3 680 bhp; 2 electric motors 6 000 shp; 2 shafts, electric drive
Speed, knots: 12 surfaced; 17 dived

Ordered from Scott's Shipbuilding & Engineering Co Ltd, Greenock, late 1969. Both have suffered delays in fitting out due to re-cabling and a minor explosion in *Hyatt* in Jan 1976. Original completion was due in July 1974 and Apr 1975 (see new commissioning dates above). *O'Brien* arrived in Chile July 1976, *Hyatt* Sep 1976.

O'BRIEN   1974, W. Ralston

1 Ex-US "BALAO" CLASS

Name	No.	Builders	Laid down	Launched	Commissioned
SIMPSON (ex-USS *Spot*, SS413)	SS 21	Mare Island Navy Yard	1943	20 May 1944	3 Aug 1944

Displacement, tons: 1 816 surfaced; 2 425 dived
Length, feet (metres): 311·6 *(95)*
Beam, feet (metres): 27 *(8·2)*
Draught, feet (metres): 17 *(5·2)*
Torpedo Tubes: 10—21 in *(533 mm)* (6 bow, 4 stern)
Main machinery: 4 GM diesels; 6 500 hp; 2 electric motors; 4 610 bhp
Speed, knots: 20 surfaced; 10 dived
Complement: 80

Transferred end of 1961. Paid off 1975. Reactivated 1977.

SIMPSON   *1972, Chilean Navy*

CORVETTES
2 Ex-US "SOTOYOMO" CLASS

Name	No.	Builders	Commissioned
LAUTARO (ex-USS *ATA 122)*	62	Levingstone SB Co, Orange	1943
LIENTUR (ex-USS *ATA 177)*	60	Levingstone SB Co, Orange	1944

Displacement, tons: 534 standard; 835 full load
Dimensions, feet (metres): 134·5 wl; 143 oa × 33 × 13·2 *(43·6 × 10·1 × 4)*
Guns: 1—3 in; 2—20 mm
Main engines: GM diesel-electric; 1 500 shp = 12·5 knots
Oil fuel, tons: 187
Complement: 33

Launched—*Lautaro* 27 Nov 1942, *Lientur* 5 June 1944. Originally ocean rescue tugs (ATRs), transferred to the Chilean Navy and reslassified as patrol vessels.

LAUTARO   *1969, Chilean Navy*

1 Ex-US "CHEROKEE" CLASS

Name	No.	Builders	Commissioned
SERGENTO ALDEA (ex-USS *Arikara*, ATF 98)	63	Charleston SB & DD Co.	5 Jan 1944

Displacement, tons: 1 235 standard; 1 675 full load
Dimensions, feet (metres): 195·0 wl; 205·0 oa × 38·5 × 15·5 *(62·5 × 11·7 × 4·7)*
Gun: 1—3 in 50 cal
Main engines: Diesel Electric; 1 shaft; 3 000 bhp = 15 knots
Complement: 85

Launched on 22 June 1943. Transferred on 1 July 1971.

SERGENTO ALDEA   *1976, Chilean Navy*

LIGHT FORCES
4 LÜRSSEN TYPE (FAST ATTACK CRAFT—TORPEDO)

Name	No.	Builders	Commissioned
GUACOLDA	80	Bazan, Cadiz	30 July 1965
FRESIA	81	Bazan, Cadiz	9 Dec 1965
QUIDORA	82	Bazan, Cadiz	1966
TEGUALDA	83	Bazan, Cadiz	1966

Displacement, tons: 134
Dimensions, feet (metres): 118·1 × 18·4 × 7·2 *(36 × 5·6 × 2·2)*
Guns: 2—40 mm
Tubes: 4—21 in
Main engines: Diesels; 2 shafts; 4 800 bhp = 32 knots
Range, miles: 1 500 at 15 knots
Complement: 20

Built to German Lürssen design.

QUIDORA (*Tegualda* and *Guacolda* behind)   *1976, Chilean Navy*

1 US "PC-1644 CLASS" (LARGE PATROL CRAFT)

Name	No.	Builders	Commissioned
PAPUDO (ex-US PC 1646)	37	Asmar, Talcahuano	27 Nov 1971

PAPUDO   1976, Chilean Navy

Displacement, tons: 450 full load
Dimensions, feet (metres): 173·0 × 23·0 × 10·2 *(52·8 × 7 × 3·1)*
Guns: 1—40 mm; 4—20 mm (twins)
A/S weapons: 1 Mk 15 Trainable Hedgehog; 2 "K" DCT; 4 DC racks
Main engines: 2 diesels; 2 shafts; 2 800 bhp = 19 knots
Complement: 69 (4 officers, 65 men)

Of similar design to the Turkish "Hisar" class built to the US PC plan.

2 LARGE PATROL CRAFT

Name	No.	Builders	Commissioned
MARINERO FUENTEALBAS	75	Asmar, Talcahuano	22 July 1966
CABO ODGER	76	Asmar, Talcahuano	21 Apr 1967

Displacement, tons: 215
Dimensions, feet (metres): 80 × 21 × 9 *(24·4 × 6·4 × 2·7)*
Guns: 2—20 mm; 2—12·7 mm MG
Main engines: One Cummins diesel 340 hp = 9 knots
Range, miles: 2 600 at 9 knots
Complement: 19

MARINERO FUENTEALBAS   1972, Chilean Navy

1 COASTAL PATROL CRAFT

CONTRAMAESTRO ORTIZ 79

Displacement, tons: 33
Length, feet (metres): 59·4 *(18·1)*
Guns: 2—20 mm
Speed, knots: 15

2 COASTAL PATROL CRAFT

Two 32 ft Equity Standard Craft delivered in 1968. Diesel; 400 hp = 35 knots.

AMPHIBIOUS FORCES
4 Ex-US LANDING SHIPS (TANK)

Name	No.	Builders	Commissioned
COMANDANTE HEMMERDINGER (ex-USS *New London County*, LST 1066)	88	Bethlehem Steel, Hingham	20 Mar 1945
COMANDANTE ARAYA (ex-USS *Nye County*, LST 1067)	89	Bethlehem Steel, Hingham	24 Mar 1945
AGUILA (ex-USS *Aventinus ARVE 3*, ex-LST 1092)	91	American Bridge Co, Ambridge	19 May 1945
COMANDANTE TORO (ex-USS LST 277)	97	American Bridge Co, Ambridge	1 Oct 1943

Displacement, tons: 1 653 standard; 4 080 full load
Dimensions, feet (metres): 328 × 50 × 14 *(100 × 15·3 × 4·3)*
Guns: Fitted for 8—40 mm
Main engines: GM Diesels; 1 700 shp; 2 shafts = 11·6 knots
Complement: approx 110

Nos 88 and 89 transferred 29 Aug 1973. No 91 was a conversion to Aircraft Repair Ship and was transferred to Chile in 1963 under MAP. No. 97 was transferred 2 Feb 1973. After various employments all are now available for amphibious duties.

Name	No.	Builders	Commissioned
ASPIRANTE MOREL (ex-USS *Aloto*, LSM 444)	92	Dravo Corpn, Wilmington	12 May 1945

Displacement, tons: 743 standard; 1 095 full load
Dimensions, feet (metres): 196·5 wl; 203·5 oa × 34·5 × 7·3 *(62·1 × 10·5 × 2·2)*
Main engines: Diesel; 2 shafts; 2 800 bhp = 12 knots
Oil fuel (tons): 60
Range, miles: 2 500 at 9 knots
Complement: 60

Former United States medium landing ship launched in 1945. *Aspirante Morel* (ex-*Aloto*) was leased to Chile on 2 Sep 1960 at Pearl Harbour to replace the older LSM of the same name. Now non-operational.

ASPIRANTE MOREL   1972, Chilean Navy

1 Ex-US LANDING CRAFT (TANK)

Name	No.	Builders	Commissioned
GRUMETE DIAZ (ex-LCU 1396)	96	Mount Vernon Bridge Co.	19 Oct 1944

Displacement, tons: 143 to 160 light; 329 full load
Dimensions, feet (metres): 105 wl; 119 oa × 32·7 × 5 *(36·3 × 10 × 1·5)*
Main engines: Diesels; 3 shafts; 675 bhp = 10 knots
Oil fuel (tons): 11
Range, miles: 700 at 7 knots
Complement: 12

Former United States tank landing craft of the LCT (6) type. Transferred by sale June 1970, in use as harbour craft.

2 CHILEAN LANDING CRAFT

Name	No.	Builders	Commissioned
ELICURA	90	Talcahuano	10 Dec 1968
OROMPELLO	94	Dade Dry Dock Co, Miami	15 Sep 1964

Displacement, tons: 290 light; 750 full load
Dimensions, feet (metres): 138 wl; 145 oa × 34 × 12·8 *(44·2 × 10·4 × 3·9)*
Guns: 3—20 mm *(Elicura)*
Main engines: Diesels; 2 shafts; 900 bhp = 10·5 knots
Oil fuel (tons): 77
Range, miles: 2 900 at 9 knots
Complement: 20

Orompello was built for the Chilean Government in Miami, *Elicura* was launched on 21 April 1967.

OROMPELLO　　　　　　　　　　　　1971, Chilean Navy

SURVEY SHIP

1 Ex-US "CHEROKEE" CLASS

Name	No.	Builders	Commissioned
YELCHO	64	Commercial Iron Works,	16 Aug 1943
(ex-USS *Tekesta, ATF 93)*		Portland, Oregon	

Displacement, tons: 1 235 standard; 1 675 full load
Dimensions, feet (metres): 195 wl; 205 oa × 38·5 × 15·3 *(62·5 × 11·7 × 4·7)*
Guns: 2—40 mm
Main engines: 4 diesels/Diesel electric; 1 shaft; 3 000 bhp = 16 knots
Complement: 85

Fitted with powerful pumps and other salvage equipment. *Yelcho* was laid down on 7 Sep 1942, launched on 20 Mar 1943 and loaned to Chile by the USA on 15 May 1960, having since been employed as Antarctic research ship and surveying vessel.

YELCHO　　　　　　　　　　　　1972, Chilean Navy

TRAINING SHIP

Name	No.	Builders	Commissioned
ESMERALDA (ex-*Don John de Austria)*	43	Echevarietta, Cadiz	1952

Displacement, tons: 3 040 standard; 3 673 full load
Dimensions, feet (metres): 308·8 oa × 43 × 23 *(94· 2 × 13·1 ×7)*
Guns: 2—57 mm (saluting)
Sail area: Total 26 910 sq feet
Main engines: 1 Fiat Auxiliary diesel; 1 shaft; 1 400 bhp = 11 knots
Range, miles: 8 000 at 8 knots
Complement: 271 plus 80 cadets

Four-masted schooner originally intended for the Spanish Navy. Transferred to Chile on 12 May 1953. Near sister ship of *Juan Sebastian de Elcano* in the Spanish Navy. Replaced transport *Presidente Pinto* as training ship.

ESMERALDA　　　　　　　　　　　　1974, Chilean Navy

TRANSPORTS

Name	No.	Builders	Commissioned
AQUILES (ex-*Tjaldur)*	47	Aalborg Vaerft, Denmark	1953

Measurement, tons: 2 660 registered; 1 462 net; 1 395 dw
Dimensions, feet (metres): 288 × 44 × 17 *(87·8 × 13·4 × 5·2)*
Main engines: 1 Slow Burmeister and Wain Diesel; 3 600 bhp = 16 knots
Range, miles: 5 500 at 16 knots
Complement: 60 crew plus 447 troops

Ex-Danish MV *Tjaldur* bought by Chile in 1967.

AQUILES　　　　　　　　　　　　1976, Chilean Navy

Name	No.	Builders	Commissioned
PILOTO PARDO	45	Haarlemsche Scheepsbouw, Netherlands	1959

Displacement, tons: 1 250 light; 2 000 standard; 3 000 full load
Dimensions, feet (metres): 269 × 39 × 15 *(82 × 11·9 × 4·6)*
Aircraft: 1 helicopter
Guns: 1—101 mm 50 cal; 2—20 mm
Main engines: 2 diesel-electric; 2 000 hp = 14 knots
Range, miles: 6 000 at 10 knots
Complement: 44 (plus 24 passengers)

Antarctic patrol ship, transport and research vessel with reinforced hull to navigate in ice. Launched 11 June 1958.

PILOTO PARDO　　　　　　　　　　　　1974, Chilean Navy

Name	No.	Builders	Commissioned
METEORO	110	Asmar, Talcahuano	1967

Displacement, tons: 205
Main engines: Diesel = 8 knots

Ferry—capacity 220.

Name	No.	Builders	Commissioned
CIRUJANO VIDELA	111	Asmar, Talcahuano	1964

Displacement, tons: 140
Dimensions, feet (metres): 101·7 × 21·3 × 6·6 (*31 × 6·5 × 2)*
Main engines: Diesel; 700 hp = 14 knots

Hospital and dental facilities are fitted. A modified version of US PGM 59 design with larger superstructure and less power.

TANKERS
1 Ex-US "PATAPSCO" CLASS

Name	No.	Builders	Commissioned
BEAGLE (ex-USS *Genesee, AOG 8)*	54	Cargill Inc., Savage, Minn.	27 May 1944

Displacement, tons: 4 240 standard
Dimensions, feet (metres): 310 × 48·7 × 16 *(94·6 × 14·9 × 4·9)*
Guns: 2—3 inch 50 cal; 4—20 mm
Range, miles: 6 690 at 10 knots

Transferred on loan 5 July 1972.

BEAGLE 1972, Chilean Navy

Name	No.	Builders	Commissioned
ARAUCANO	53	Burmeister & Wain, Copenhagen	10 Jan 1967

Displacement, tons: 17 300
Measurement, tons: 18 030 deadweight
Dimensions, feet (metres): 497·6 × 74·9 × 28·8 *(151·8 × 22·8 × 8·8)*
Guns: 8—40 mm (twin)
Main engines: B and W diesels; 10 800 bhp = 15·5 knots (17 on trial)
Range, miles: 12 000 at 15·5 knots

Launched on 21 June 1966.

ARAUCANO 1972, U.S. Navy

Name	No.	Builders	Commissioned
ALMIRANTE JORGE MONTT	52	Ateliers et Chantiers de la Seine Maritime, Le Trait	Mar 1956

Displacement, tons: 9 000 standard; 17 500 full load
Measurement, tons: 11 800 gross; 17 750 deadweight
Dimensions, feet (metres): 548 × 67·5 × 30 *(167·1 × 20·6 × 9·2)*
Guns: 4—40 mm; 6—20 mm
Main engines: Rateau Bretagne geared turbine; 1 shaft; 6 300 shp = 14 knots
Boilers: 2 Babcock & Wilcox
Range, miles: 16 500 at 14 knots

Laid down in 1954. Launched on 14 Jan 1956. Used as storage hulk since 1975.

ALMIRANTE JORGE MONTT 1969, Chilean Navy

1 NEW CONSTRUCTION

Measurement, tons: 19 500 deadweight
Dimensions, feet (metres): 579·6 × 83·6 × — *(176·7 × 25·5 × —)*
Main engines: 18 300 hp

Ordered late 1976 from ASMAR, Talcahuano.

FLOATING DOCKS
2 Ex-US ARD

MUTILLA (ex-US *ARD 32)* 132   **INGENIERO MERY** (ex-US *ARD 25)* 131

Displacement, tons: 5 200
Capacity, tons: 3 000
Dimensions, feet (metres): 492 × 84 × 5·7 to 33·2 *(150·1 × 25·6 × 1·7 to 10·1)*

Mutilla leased to Chile 15 Dec 1960, *Ingeniero Mery* transferred 20 Aug 1973.

2 Floating Cranes of 30 and 180 tons lift are at Talcahuano.

TUGS

Name	No.	Builders	Commissioned
COLOCOLO	73	Bow, McLachlan & Co, Paisley	1930

Displacement, tons: 790
Dimensions, feet (metres): 126·5 × 27·0 × 12·0 *(38·6 × 8·2 × 3·7)*
Main engines: Triple expansion; 1 050 ihp = 11 knots
Oil fuel, tons: 155

Formerly classed as coastguard vessel. Rebuilt in 1962-63. Last of class of five.

Name	No.	Builders	Commissioned
GALVEZ	—	Southern Shipbuilders Ltd, Faversham, England	June 1975

Measurement, tons: 112 gross
Dimensions, feet (metres): 83·6 × 24 × 9·2 *(25·5 × 7·3 × 2·8)*

Dockyard tug in Talcahuano.

ANCUD 104   **CORTEZ** 128   **REYES** 120
CAUPOLICAN 127   **MONREAL** 105

Note: Tug HMS *Samson* was reported sold to Chile in 1974 but is still laid up in Portsmouth.

MISCELLANEOUS

Notes: (a) *Huascar,* completed 1865, previously Peruvian, now harbour flagship at Talcahuano.
(b) Two new ships, *Castor* and *Sobenes,* now listed.

CHINA (People's Republic)

Administration

Minister of National Defence:
Yeh Chien-ying

Headquarters Appointments

Commander-in-Chief of the Navy:
Hsiao Ching Kuang
1st Political Commissar:
Su Chen-Hua
2nd Political Commissar:
Wang Hung-K'un
Chief of Staff:
P'an Yen

Fleet Commanders

North Sea Fleet:
Ma Chung-Ch'uan
East Sea Fleet:
Mei Chia-Sheng
South Sea Fleet:
Kuei Shao-Pin

Diplomatic Representation

Defence and Naval Attaché in London:
Fang Wen

Personnel

(a) 1977: 172 000 officers and men, including 20 000 naval air force and 38 000 marines.

(b) 6 years National Service.

Training

Carried out at following schools/academies:
Shanghai:
  Officer Training School
  Naval Aviation School
  Coastal Artillery School
  Supply School
  Radar School
  School of Naval Architecture
  Fleet Training Centre (Ratings)
Dairen:
  Naval Academy
  Mining School
Nanking:
  War College
  Ratings Training School
Tsingtao:
  Naval Aviation School
  Main Ratings Training School
  Submarine School
Lushua:
  Submarine School
Yulin:
  Submarine School

Minor ratings' schools at Wei Hai Wee, An' Ching, Foochow, Chusan and Hangchow.

Bases

North Sea Fleet: Tsingtao (HQ), Lu Shun, Wei Hai Hui, Ching San, Luta, Hu Lu Tao, Hsiao Ping Tao
East Sea Fleet: Shanghai (HQ), Chusan, Tai Shan, Ta Hsieh Tao, Hsia Men, Wen Chou, Hai Men, Ma Wei, Fu Chou
South Sea Fleet: Chan Chiang (HQ), Yu Lin, Hai Kou, Huang Pu/Canton, Shan Tou, Pei Hai
(The fleet is split with the main emphasis on the North Sea Fleet).

Strength of the Fleet

Type	Active	Building
Destroyers (DDG)	9	2
Frigates	12	2
Corvettes	40	4
Fleet Submarines	1	?
Missile Firing Submarines	1	—
Patrol Submarines	65	6
Fast Attack Craft (Missile)	140	20
Fast Attack Craft (Gun)	438	?10
Fast Attack Craft (Torpedo)	240	?10
Coastal Patrol Craft	40+	?
Minesweepers (Ocean)	18	—
Landing Ships (LST)	15	—
LSMs	15	—
LSILs	6	—
LCTs	17	—
LCMs—LCUs	450	—
Survey & Research Ships	11	—
Supply Ships	14 (+?12)	—
Tankers (small)	10	—
Boom Defence Vessels	6	—
Escorts (old)	16	—
Repair Ship	1	—
Misc. Small Craft	375	—

DELETIONS

1976 10 "P4" class, 1 "Shantung" class, 10 "Swatow" class, 5 "Whampoa" class, 4 ex-US YMS, 2 ex-Japanese AMS.
(Where other alterations of numbers occur this is as a result of more up-to-date information).

Mercantile Marine

Lloyd's Register of Shipping:
  551 vessels of 3 588 726 tons gross

The Chinese Navy

While studying this section it must be remembered that not only is there a steady building programme of all classes in the modernised Chinese Yards but also the Chinese have an advanced nuclear and missile capability. This combination will make the Chinese navy, already more than twice as strong in manpower as the Royal Navy, an important element in the future balance of power East of Suez.

Recently there has been evidence of delays in all the new building programmes except Submarines and Light Forces. Whether this is due to problems of weapon production, faults discovered in new construction ships or a straight political decision is not known. It is of interest that these delays appear to date from 1972, shortly after the flight and death of Lin Piao, the Defence Minister under whom the programmes were presumably generated. This may be coincidence but the plain fact is that the main emphasis today is on defensive units rather than the long-range forces whose design must have started in the mid or early 1960s.

Naval Air Force

With 30 000 officers and men and over 450 aircraft, this is a considerable land-based naval air force. Equipped with about 300 MIG 17 and 19 (and possibly MIG 21) fighter aircraft and SA2-SAM, with 100 IL 28 Torpedo bombers, Tu-2 bombers, Madge flying boats, Hound M14 helicopters and transport and communication aircraft this is primarily a defensive force.

Naval Radars

Code Name	Frequency	Function	Fitting
Ball End	E/F	Surface Warning	Kaibokan and other escorts
Ball Gun	E/F	Surface Warning	Kronshtadt, T 43
Cross Bird	G	Early Warning	Gordy
Cross Slot		Early Warning	Luta, Chang Ch'iang
Decca 707	I	Surface Search	Corvettes, Light Forces
Drum Tilt	I	Armament Control	Osa
High Pole A	G	IFF	General
Mina	I	Fire Control	Gordy 130mm
Neptun	I	Navigation	General
Post Lamp	I	Fire Control	Luta
Pot Head	I	Surface Search	Hai Nan, Kronshtadt, Light Forces
Skinhead	I	Surface Search	Light Forces
Ski Pole	G	IFF	Gordy
Slim Net	E/F	Surface Warning	Riga
Square Tie	I	Fire Control	Gordy, Luta, Riga, Osa
Sun Visor	I	Fire Control	Kiangnan, Riga

"LUTA" Class

"GORDY" Class

"KIANGNAN" Class

"KRONSHTADT" Class

"RIGA" Class

DESTROYERS

5 + 2 "LUTA" CLASS (DDG)

Name	No.	Builders	Laid down	Launched	Commissioned
—	240	Dairen (Luta)	—	—	1971
—	241	Dairen (Luta)	—	—	1972
—	242	Dairen (Luta)	—	—	1972
—	243	Dairen (Luta)	—	—	1973
—	244	Dairen (Luta)	—	—	1975
—	—	Dairen (Luta)	—	—	—
—	—	Dairen (Luta)	—	—	—

Displacement, tons: 3 250 standard; 3 750 full load
Dimensions, feet (metres): 450 × 45 × 15 *(137·3 × 13·7 × 4·6)*
Missile launchers: 2 Triple SS-N-2 type
Guns: 4—130 mm (2 twins) 8—57 mm or 37 mm; 8—25 mm
A/S weapons: 2—A/S rocket launchers
Main engines: Geared turbines; 60 000 shp
Speed: 32+
Range, miles (estimated): 4 000 at 15 knots
Complement (approx): 300

The first Chinese-designed destroyers of such a capability to be built. The programme has been much retarded since 1971 which, possibly coincidentally, marked the death of Lin Piao. Although capable of foreign deployment none so far reported.

Gunnery: Some mount 57 mm secondary armament although the majority carry 37 mm.

Radar: Air search: Cross Slot.
Fire control, guns: Wasphead, Post Lamp.
Fire control, missiles: Square Tie.
Navigation: Neptun.

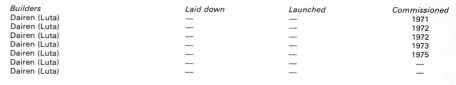
"LUTA" Class   *1972, Chinese*

"LUTA" Class

"LUTA" Class   *1973*

4 Ex-SOVIET "GORDY" CLASS

Name	No.	Builders	Laid down	Launched	Commissioned
ANSHAN	—	USSR	—	1936-41	1939-43
CHANG CHUN	—	USSR	—	1936-41	1939-43
CHI LIN	—	USSR	—	1936-41	1939-43
FU CHUN	—	USSR	—	1936-41	1939-43

Displacement, tons: 1 657 standard; 2 040 full load
Length, feet (metres): 357·7 *(109·0)* pp; 370 *(112·8)* oa
Beam, feet (metres): 33·5 *(10·2)*
Draught, feet (metres): 13 *(4·0)*
Missile launchers: 2 twin SS-N-2 type
Guns: 4—5·1 in *(130 mm)*; 8—37 mm (twins)
A/S weapons: 2 DC racks
Main engines: Tosi geared turbines; 48 000 shp; 2 shafts
Boilers: 3-drum type
Speed, knots: 36
Oil fuel, tons: 540
Range, miles: 800 at 36 knots; 2 600 at 19 knots
Complement: 250

CHANG CHUN (before conversion)   *Hajime Fukaya*

Gordy Type 7 of Odero-Terni-Orlando design. Fitted for minelaying. Two transferred in Dec 1954 and two in July 1955.

Conversion: All converted between 1971 and 1974. The alterations consist of the replacement of the torpedo tubes by a pair of twin SS-N-2 launchers and the fitting of twin 37 mm mounts in place of the original singles.

Radar: Air Search: Cross Bird.
Fire Control: Square Tie.
Navigation: Neptune.
IFF: Ski Pole.

FRIGATES
2 + 1 "KIANG HU" CLASS

Displacement, tons: 1 800 approx
Dimensions, feet (metres): 350 × 40 approx *(106 × 21)*
Missiles: 2 twin SS-N-2 type
Guns: 4—3·9 in *(100 mm)* (twins); 8/12-37 mm

First ship probably launched 1975, completing trials in 1976.
Second ship launched 1976. Appears to be a modification of
"Kiangtung" class.

1 + 1(?) "KIANGTUNG" CLASS

Name	No.	Builders	Laid down	Launched	Commissioned
CHUNG TUNG	—	Hutang-Shanghai	1971	1973	1977

Displacement, tons: 1 800 tons standard
Dimensions, feet (metres): 350 × 40 approx *(106 × 12)*
Missiles: 2 twin SAM
Guns: 4—3·9 in *(100 mm)* twin; 12—37 mm (twins)
A/S weapons: 2 MBU 1 800; 2 DCT
Main engines: Diesel = ? 28 knots

There have apparently been no further additions to this
class—further evidence of the delays in new construction of
major surface ships. It is reported that first of class is not yet
operational which may suggest problems with the first
Chinese-designed naval SAM system.

5 "KIANGNAN" CLASS

Name	No.	Builders	Laid down	Launched	Commissioned
—	209	Canton/Shanghai	1965	—	1967
—	214	Canton/Shanghai	1965	—	1967
—	231	Canton/Shanghai	1966	—	1968
—	232	Canton/Shanghai	1966	—	1968
—	233	Canton/Shanghai	1967	—	1969

Displacement, tons: 1 350 standard; 1 600 full load
Length, feet (metres): 298 *(90·8)*
Beam, feet (metres): 33·5 *(10·2)*
Draught, feet (metres): 11 *(3·4)*
Guns: 3—3·9 in *(100 mm)* 56 cal, 1 fwd, 2 aft;
6—37 mm (twin); 4—12·7 mm (twin)
A/S weapons: 2 MBU 1 800; 4 DCT; 2 DC racks
Main engines: Diesels; 24 000 shp
Speed, knots: 28
Complement: 175

The Chinese Navy embarked on a new building programme in
1965 of which this class was the first. One of this class was
reported as engaged with South Vietnam forces on 19-20
January 1974.

Radar: Fire Control: Sun Visor.

"KIANGNAN" Class   1973

4 "RIGA" CLASS

Name	No.	Builders	Laid down	Launched	Commissioned
CH'ENG TU	204	Hutang, Shanghai	1954	28 Apr 1956	1958
KUEI LIN	205	—	1955	26 Sept 1956	1958
KUEI YANG	206	Hutang, Shanghai	—	1957	1959
K'UN MING	207	—	—	1957	1959

Displacement, tons: 1 200 standard; 1 600 full load
Length, feet (metres): 298·8 *(91)* oa
Beam, feet (metres): 33·7 *(10·2)*
Draught, feet (metres): 10 *(3·0)*
Missile launchers: 1 twin SS-N-2 type
Guns: 3—3·9 in *(100 mm)* (single); 4—37 mm
A/S weapons: 4 DC projectors
Mines: 50 capacity, fitted with rails
Main engines: Geared turbines; 2 shafts; 25 000 shp
Boilers: 2
Speed, knots: 28
Oil fuel, tons: 300
Range, miles: 2 000 at 10 knots
Complement: 150

All had light tripod mast and high superstructure, but later
converted with heavier mast and larger bridge. Similar to the
Soviet "Riga" class frigates. Two were redesigned with modified superstructure.

Conversion: Two started conversion in 1971 for the replacement of the torpedo tubes by a twin SS-N-2 launcher. All now
converted.

Radar: Surface warning: Slim Net.
Fire Control: Sun Visor for Guns, Square Tie for missiles.
Navigation: Neptune.

"RIGA" Class (before conversion)   1971

SUBMARINES

Note: In 1973 the visit to West Germany from Peking of a party led by Professor Chang Wei highlighted Chinese interest in nuclear propulsion for ships. It also suggests that the Chinese may be meeting design problems as such visits are rare events.

However, reports suggest the construction of at least one nuclear submarine. This combined with the known Chinese capability to build liquid-fuelled rockets of the MRBM, IRBM and

ICBM types and the completion of a solid-propellant factory, suggests that the forecast of a Chinese ballistic-missile nuclear submarine in the early 1980s may not be out of the question.

1 "HAN" CLASS

This is the first possible Chinese nuclear submarine. With an Albacore hull the first of this class was probably laid down in

1971-72. Its construction may have been delayed if the problems mentioned in the note above have been encountered, but

it appears to have run trials in 1974. Existence of a second "Han" class is reported but not confirmed. Built at Luta.

Displacement, tons: Possibly about 1 500 tons standard
Length, feet: Possibly about 250 feet
Armament: Possibly 6—21 in tubes
Main machinery: Probably diesels and main motors

2 "MING" CLASS

First believed to have been laid down in 1971-72 which would give an operational date around late 1974 or 1975.

1 SOVIET "GOLF" CLASS

(BALLISTIC MISSILE TYPE)

Displacement, tons: 2 350 surfaced; 2 800 dived
Length, feet (metres): 320·0 *(97·5)*
Beam, feet (metres): 25·1 *(7·6)*
Draught, feet (metres): 22·0 *(6·7)*
Missile launchers: 3 vertical tubes
Torpedo tubes: 10—21 in *(533 mm)* bow
Main machinery: 3 diesels, total 6 000 hp; 3 shafts
 3 electric motors, total 6 000 hp
Speed, knots: 20 surfaced; 17 dived
Range, miles: 22 700 surfaced; cruising
Complement: 86 (1 officers, 74 men)

Ballistic missile submarine similar to the Soviet "Golf" class. Built at Dairen in 1964. The missile tubes are fitted in the conning tower. It is not known whether this boat has been fitted with missiles, although it is possible in the future and well within Chinese technical capability (see note above concerning SLBMs).

"GOLF" Class   *1972*

42 Ex-SOVIET AND CHINESE "ROMEO" CLASS (PATROL TYPE)

Displacement, tons: 1 100 surfaced; 1 600 dived
Length, feet (metres): 246·0 *(75·0)*
Beam, feet (metres): 24 *(7·3)*
Draught, feet (metres): 14·5 *(4·4)*
Torpedo tubes: 6—21 in (bow) 18 torpedoes
Main machinery: 2 diesels; total 4 000 hp; 2 Electric motors;
 total 4 000 hp; 2 shafts
Speed, knots: 17 surfaced; 14 dived
Complement: 65

The Chinese are now building their own Soviet designed "Romeo" class submarines possibly at a rate of 6 a year at Kuang Chou/Canton, Kiangnan/Shanghai and Wu Chang. Above details are for Soviet "Romeo" of which possibly four were transferred in early 1960. It is reliably reported that the Chinese variant is larger—1 400 tons surfaced/1 800 dived, 6 feet longer, armed with 8 torpedo tubes and capable of carrying 36 mines in lieu of torpedoes.

"ROMEO" Class   *1975*

21 SOVIET "WHISKEY" CLASS (PATROL TYPE)

Displacement, tons: 1 030 surfaced; 1 180 dived
Length, feet (metres): 240 *(73·2)*
Beam, feet (metres): 22 *(6·7)*
Draught, feet (metres): 15 *(4·6)*
Guns: 2—25 mm (twin) in some at base of fin
Torpedo tubes: 6—21 in *(533 mm)*; 4 bow 2 stern (20 torpedoes
 or 40 mines)
Main machinery: Diesel-electric; 2 shafts; 4 000 bhp diesels;
 2 500 hp electric motors
Speed, knots: 17 surfaced; 15 dived
Range, miles: 13 000 at 8 knots surfaced
Complement: 60

Equipped with snort. Assembled from Soviet components in Chinese yards between 1956 and 1964.

"WHISKEY" Class   *1972*

1 Ex-SOVIET "S-1" CLASS (PATROL TYPE)

Displacement, tons: 840 surfaced; 1 050 dived
Torpedo tubes: 6—21 in *(533 mm)*
Main machinery: 4 200 hp diesels; 2 200 hp electric motors

Launched in 1939. Transferred from the USSR in 1955. One deleted. Last of class now harbour training boat.

ESCORTS

Note: It is reported that the majority of these escorts are, in fact, not only still in commission but have been refitted and rearmed.

Class	Total	Names	No.	Displacement tons, standard	Speed (knots)	Guns	Launched	Range, miles	Complement
Ex-Japanese "Kamishima"	1	—	391	766	16	2—3 in 6—37 mm	1945	2 400 at 11 knots	130 (est)
Ex-Japanese "Ukuru"	1	HUI AN (ex-*Shisaka*)	218	940	19·5	3—3·9 in 6—37 mm	1943	5 000 at 16 knots	—
Ex-Japanese "Etorofu"	1	CHANG PI (ex-*Oki*)	—	870	19	3—3·9 in 3—37 mm	1942	8 000 at 16 knots	—
Ex-Japanese "Hashidate"	1	NAN CHANG (ex-*Uji II*)	—	999	19·5	2—5·1 in 6—37 mm	1940	3 460 at 14 knots	—
Ex-Japanese "C"/Kaibokan I	2	— (ex-*Shen Yang*) — (ex-*Chi-An*)	— —	745	15·5	2—3·9 in 6—37 mm (single) 4/8—25 mm	1945	6 500 at 14 knots	145
Ex-Japanese "D"/Kaibokan II	5	TUNG AN (ex-*Jap 192*) CHIANG SHA (ex-*Chieh 12*) CHI NAN (ex-*Chieh 6*) HSI AN (ex-*Chieh 14*) WU CHANG (ex-*Chieh 5*)	215 216 217 219 220	740	17·5	2—3 in or 8—37 mm (single) 4/8—25 mm	1944 to 1945	4 500 at 14 knots	145
Ex-British "Castle"	1	KUANG CHOU (ex-HMS *Hever Castle*, ex-HMCS *Koppercliff*)	602	1 100	16·5	2—3·9 in 10—37 mm	1944	5 400 at 9·5 knots	120
Ex-British "Flower"	2	KAI FENG (ex-HMS *Clover*)	211						
		LIN I (ex-HMS *Heliotrope*)	213	1 020	16	2—3·9 in 4—37 mm	1941	—	—
Ex-Australian "Bathurst"	1	LOYANG (ex-HMAS *Bendigo*)	—	815	15	2—3·9 in 4—37 mm	1941	4 300 at 10 knots	100
—	1	CHANG CHIANG (ex-*Hsien Nin*)	53/219	418	17	4—37 mm (twin)	1928	—	50?

HUI AN   1974

LIGHT FORCES

Note: There are numerous reports, stemming from a film sequence, of a new class of Fast Attack Craft (Missile). An examination of this design which is credited with gas turbines and at least six missile tubes suggests that it is either an experimental craft or a film prop. The top weight problem is enormous and there is no clear evidence of the air-intakes for gas turbines although one report speaks of a "large funnel". If not designed for the cinema this could be a test-bed for new missiles and for propulsion systems. It can certainly steam, and steam fast, in a calm sea.

20 "KRONSHTADT" CLASS

Nos. 251 252 253 261 262 263 264 265 266 286 + 10

Displacement, tons: 310 standard; 380 full load
Dimensions, feet (metres): 170·6 × 21·5 × 9 *(52 × 6·5 × 2·7)*
Guns: 1—3·5 in; 2—37 mm; 6—12·7 mm
A/S weapons: 2 Rocket launchers; 2 DC racks
Mines: 2 rails for 8-10 mines
Main engines: Diesels; 2 shafts; 3 300 shp = 24 knots
Range, miles: 1 500 at 12 knots
Complement: 65

Six built in 1950-53 were received from USSR in 1956-57. Remainder were built at Shanghai and Canton, with 12 completed in 1956. The last was completed in 1957.

Radar: Ball Gun.

"KRONSHTADT" Class firing Rocket Launchers   1972

19 "HAINAN" CLASS

Nos. 267—285

Displacement, tons: 360 standard, 400 full load
Dimensions, feet (metres): 197 oa × 24 × 6·1 *(60 × 7·4 × 2·1)*
Guns: 2—3 in (fore and aft); 4—25 mm (twins)
A/S weapons: 4—MBU 1 800; 2 DCT; 2 DC racks
Mines: Rails fitted
Main engines: Diesels; 8 000 shp
Speed, knots: 28
Range, miles: 1 000 at 10 knots (est)
Complement: 60 (est)

Chinese built. Low freeboard. The 25 mm guns are abaft the bridge. Programme started 1963-64 and continues—probably 4 per year.

Radar: Pothead in most ships, Skinhead in others.

1 Ex-US 170 ft TYPE

Displacement, tons: 280 standard; 450 full load
Dimensions, feet (metres): 173·5 × 23 × 10·8 *(52·9 × 7 × 3·3)*
Guns: 2—3 in *(76 mm)* (single); 3—37 mm (single)
A/S weapons: 2 DC racks; 1 DC rail
Main engines: 2 Diesels; 2 880 bhp; 2 shafts = 20 knots
Range, miles: 3 000 at 15 knots
Complement: 70

Transferred 1947. Partially rearmed in 1950s. Used for training in South Sea Fleet.

70 SOVIET and CHINESE "OSA" CLASS (FAST ATTACK CRAFT—MISSILE)

Displacement, tons: 165 standard; 200 full load
Dimensions, feet (metres): 128·7 × 25·1 × 5·9 *(39·3 × 7·7 × 1·8)*
Missiles: 4 SS-N-2 system launchers in two pairs abreast aft
Guns: 4—25 mm (2 twin, 1 forward and 1 aft) (30 mm in first four)
Main engines: 3 Diesels; 13 000 bhp = 32 knots
Range, miles: 800 at 25 knots
Complement: 25

It was reported in Jan 1965 that one "Osa" class guided missile patrol boat had joined the Navy from the USSR. Four more were acquired in 1966-67, and two in 1968. A building programme of 10 boats a year in China is assumed. The only boat of the "Hola" class, a Chinese variant of the "Osa", has now joined the fleet. The chief differences are the fitting of a radome aft, (this may be a dummy), no guns, slightly larger dimensions, and a folding mast.

Radar: Square Tie and Drum Tilt in "Osas".

"OSA" Class   1972

4 + 66 SOVIET "KOMAR" and CHINESE "HOKU" CLASS (FAST ATTACK CRAFT—MISSILE)

Displacement, tons: 70 standard; 80 full load
Dimensions, feet (metres): 83·7 oa × 19·8 × 5 *(25·5 × 6 × 1·5)*
Missiles: 2 SS-N-2 system launchers
Guns: 2—25 mm (1 twin forward)
Main engines: Diesels; 2 shafts; 4 800 bhp = 40 knots

One "Komar" class was reported as joining the fleet from the USSR in 1965. Two or three more were delivered in 1967. A building programme of 10 a year is assumed of the "Hoku" class a Chinese variant of the "Komar" with a steel hull instead of wooden. The chief external difference is the siting of the launchers clear of the bridge and further inboard, eliminating sponsons and use of pole instead of lattice mast. A hydrofoil variant has also been reported.

"KOMAR" Class   1972

25 "SHANGHAI" CLASS TYPE I (FAST ATTACK CRAFT—GUN)

Displacement, tons: 100 full load
Dimensions, feet (metres): 115 × 18 × 5·5 *(35·1 × 5·5 × 1·7)*
Guns: 1—57 mm (forward); 2—37 mm (twin, aft)
Torpedo tubes: Twin 18 in (originally in some—now removed)
A/S armament: 8 DCs
Mines: Minerails can be fitted
Main engines: 4 diesels; 4 800 bhp = 28 knots
Complement: 25

The prototype of these boats appeared in 1959. Main difference from successors is lack of midships guns.

Radar: Skinhead.

330 "SHANGHAI" CLASS TYPE II (FAST ATTACK CRAFT—GUN)

Displacement, tons: 120 standard; 155 full load
Dimensions, feet (metres): 128 × 18 × 5·6 *(39 × 5·5 × 1·7)*
Guns: 4—37 mm (twin); 4—25 mm (twin)
 Note: In some boats a twin 75 mm recoilless rifle is mounted forward
A/S weapons: 8 DCs
Mines: Minerails can be fitted but probably for no more than 10 mines
Main engines: 4 Diesels; 4 800 bhp = 30 knots
Complement: 25

"SHANGHAI II" Class (with 75 mm forward)

Construction continues at Shanghai and other yards at rate of about 10 a year.

Appearance: The three types vary slightly in the outline of their bridges.

Radar: Skinhead.

Transfers: 4 to Albania, 3 to Congo, 4 to Guinea, 15 to North Korea, 12 to Pakistan, 5 to Sri Lanka in 1972, 2 to Sierra Leone in 1973, 6 to Tanzania in 1970-71, 4 to North Vietnam in May 1966. + Romanian craft of indigenous construction.

"SHANGHAI II" Class   1970

6 "HAI KOU" CLASS (FAST ATTACK CRAFT—GUN)

Displacement, tons: 160 standard; 175 full load (est)
Dimensions, feet (metres): 150 × 21 × 7 (est) *(45·5 × 6·4 × 2·1)*
Guns: 4—37 mm (twin); 4—25 mm (twin, vertical)
Main engines: Diesel = 30 knots (?)
Range, miles: 850 at 20 knots (est)

Believed built in 1960s on enlarged "Shanghai" hull.

40 "SWATOW" CLASS (FAST ATTACK CRAFT—GUN)

Displacement, tons: 80 full load
Dimensions, feet (metres): 83·5 × 19 × 6·5 *(25·5 × 5·8 × 2)*
Guns: 4—37 mm, in twin mountings; 2—12·7 mm (some boats mount a twin 75 mm recoilless rifle forward)
A/S weapons: 8 DC
Main engines: 4 diesels; 3 000 bhp = 28 knots
Range, miles: 500 at 28 knots; 750 at 15 knots
Complement: 17

From 1958 constructed at Dairen, Canton, and Shanghai. Now obsolescent and being deleted.

Transfers: 12 to North Vietnam.

110 "HU CHWAN" CLASS (FAST ATTACK CRAFT—TORPEDO)

Displacement, tons: 45
Dimensions, feet (metres): 70 × 16·6 oa × 7·9 (hullborne) (21·3 × 5 × 2·5)
Guns: 4—12·7 mm (2 twins)
Torpedo tubes: 2—21 inch
Main engines: 3 M50 12 cylinder Diesels; 2 shafts; 3 600 hp = 50+ knots in calm conditions
Range, miles: 500 cruising

"HU CHWAN" Class

Hydrofoils designed and built by China, in the Hutang yard, Shanghai. Construction started in 1956. At least 25 hydrofoils were reported to be in the South China Fleet in 1968. Of all-metal construction with a bridge well forward and a low super-structure extending aft. The guns are mounted one pair on the main deck and one on the superstructure. Forward pair of foils can apparently be withdrawn into recesses in the hull. A continuing programme at possibly 10 per year.

Transfers: 30 to Albania, 4 to Pakistan, + Romanian craft of indigenous construction.

70 "P 6" CLASS (FAST ATTACK CRAFT—TORPEDO)

Displacement, tons: 66 standard; 75 full load
Dimensions, feet (metres): 84 × 20 × 6 (25·7 × 6·1 × 1·8)
Guns: 4—25 mm
Torpedo tubes: 2—21 in (or mines or DCs)
Main engines: 4 M50 diesels; 4 800 bhp = 43 knots
Range, miles: 450 at 30 knots
Complement: 25

"P 6" Class

This class has wooden hulls. Some were constructed in Chinese yards. Most built prior to 1966.

Radar: Pothead or Skinhead.

Transfers: 6 to North Vietnam in 1967.

50 "P 4" CLASS (FAST ATTACK CRAFT—TORPEDO)

Displacement, tons: 25
Dimensions, feet (metres): 62·7 × 11·6 × 5·6 (19·1 × 3·5 × 1·7)
Guns: 2—14·5 mm
Torpedo tubes: 2—18 in
Main engines: 2 Diesels; 2 200 bhp; 2 shafts = 50 knots

"P 4" Class

This class has aluminium hulls. Numbers decreasing.

35 "WHAMPOA" CLASS (FAST ATTACK CRAFT—GUN)

Displacement, tons: 42 standard; 50 full load
Length, feet (metres): 75·5 × 13 × 5 (27 × 4 × 1·5)
Guns: 2—37 mm (singles); 2 MG (single)
Main engines: 2 Diesels; 600 hp = 12 knots
Range, miles: 400 at 9 knots
Complement: 25

Built in Canton and Shanghai 1950-55 probably for riverine duties. Underpowered with low freeboard. Now probably decreasing in numbers.

"YU LIN" CLASS (COASTAL PATROL CRAFT)

Displacement, tons: 10
Dimensions, feet (metres): 40 × 9·5 × 3·5 (13 × 2·9 × 1·1)
Guns: 2—14·5 mm (twin); 2—12·7 mm
Main engines: 1 Diesel; 300 bhp; 1 shaft = 20-24 knots
Complement: 10

Built in Shanghai 1964-68.

Transfers: 4 to Congo (1966), 3 to Khmers, 4 to Tanzania.

4 "TAI SHAN" CLASS (COASTAL PATROL CRAFT)

2 "SHANTUNG" CLASS (FAST ATTACK HYDROFOIL—GUN)

Displacement, tons: 75-85
Dimensions, feet (metres): 80 × 16 × 6 (24·4 × 4·9 × 1·8)
Guns: 4—37 mm (twins)
Speed, knots: 40

An unsuccessful hydrofoil design. Numbers decreasing.

1 "FUKIEN" CLASS (FAST ATTACK CRAFT—GUN)

"YING KOU" CLASS (COASTAL PATROL CRAFT)

Displacement, tons: 20 (est)
Dimensions, feet (metres): 70 × 12 × 3 (21·3 × 3·7 × 0·8)
Guns: 2—12·7 mm (single)
Main engines: 1 Diesel; 300 bhp; 1 shaft = 16 knots

Built in early 1960s.

30 "WU HSI/PEI HAI" CLASS (COASTAL PATROL CRAFT)

MINE WARFARE FORCES

Note: (a) 1 ship of "Wu Sung" class (MSC) built in 1970-72. Apparently unsuccessful. Reported transferred to N. Vietnam 1974.
(b) There are also some 60 auxiliary minesweepers of various types including trawlers.

18 SOVIET "T 43" CLASS (MINESWEEPERS—OCEAN)

Nos. 377, 386, 396 + 15

Displacement, tons: 500 standard; 610 full load
Dimensions, feet (metres): 196·8 × 28·2 × 6·9 (60 × 8·6 × 2·1)
Guns: 4—37 mm (2 twin); 4—25 mm (2 twin); 4—14·5 mm (twin—in most ships)
A/S weapons: 2 DCT
Main engines: 2 diesels; 2 shafts; 2 000 bhp = 17 knots
Range, miles: 1 600 at 10 knots
Complement: 40

"T 43" Class 1972

Four were acquired from USSR in 1954-55. Two being returned 1960. Twenty-one more were built in Chinese shipyards, the first two in 1956. The construction of "T 43" class fleet mine-sweepers was stopped at Wuchang, but continued at Canton. 3 converted for surveying 3 transferred as civilian research ships. Most of the Chinese variant are of the 60 m "Long hull" design.

Radar: Ballgun.

AMPHIBIOUS WARFARE FORCES

15 Ex-US LST 511-1152 SERIES

CHANG PAI SHAN
CH'ING KANG SHAN
I MENG SHAN (ex-*Chung 106*, ex-US *LST 589*)
TA PIEH SHAN
TAI HSING SHAN
SZU CH'ING SHAN
Ex-CHUNG 100 (ex-US *LST 355*)
Ex-CHUNG 101 (ex-US *LST 804*)

Ex-CHUNG 102
Ex-CHUNG 107 (ex-US *LST 1027*)
Ex-CHUNG 110
Ex-CHUNG 111 (ex/US *LST 805*)
Ex-CHUNG 116 (ex-US *LST 406*)
Ex-CHUNG 122 (ex-*Ch'ing Ling*)
Ex-CHUNG 125

Displacement, tons: 1 653 standard; 4 080 full load
Dimensions, feet (metres): 316 wl; 328 oa × 50 × x4 *(96·4; 100 × 15·3 × 4·4)*
Guns: 2/3—76·2 mm; 6/8—40 mm
Mines: All capable of minelaying
Main engines: Diesel; 2 shafts; 1 700 bhp = 11 knots

Two transferred to N. Vietnam as tankers. Some other ex-US LSTs are in the merchant service.

US LST

1968, USN

13 Ex-US LSM TYPE

Ex-HUA 201 (ex-US *LSM 112*)
Ex-HUA 202 (ex-US *LSM 248*)
Ex-HUA 204 (ex-US *LSM 430*)
Ex-HUA 205 (ex-US *LSM 336*)
Ex-HUA 207 (ex-US *LSM 282*)
Ex-HUA 208 (ex-US *LSM 42*)
Ex-HUA 209 (ex-US *LSM 153*)

Ex-HUA 211
Ex-HUA 212
Ex-CHUAN SHIH SHUI
Ex-HUAI HO (ex-Chinese *Wan Fu*)
Ex-HUANG HO (ex-Chinese *Mei Sheng* ex-US *LSM 433*)
Ex-YUN HO (ex-Chinese *Wang Chung*)

Displacement, tons: 743 beaching; 1 095 full load
Dimensions, feet (metres): 196·5 wl; 203·5 oa × 34·5 × 8·8 *(59·9; 62·1 × 10·5 × 2·7)*
Guns: 4—37 mm (twins)
Main engines: Diesel; 2 shafts; 2 800 hp = 12 knots

Built in USA in 1944-45. Some were converted for minelaying and as support ships. Armament varies. Up to ten of these may be transferred temporarily to commercial operations.

15 Ex-US LSIL TYPE

| MIN 301 | 306 | 312 | 319 |
| 303 | 311 | 313 | 321 | +7 |

Displacement, tons: 230 light; 387 full load
Dimensions, feet (metres): 159 × 23·7 × 5·7 *(48·5 × 7·2 × 1·7)*
Guns: 4—20 or 25 mm
Main engines: Diesel; 2 shafts; 1 320 bhp = 14 knots

Built in USA in 1943-45. Reported to be fitted with rocket launchers. Some are fitted as minesweepers. Armament varies.

17 Ex-US or BRITISH LCU (ex-LCT) TYPE

Displacement, tons: 160 light; 320 full load
Dimensions, feet (metres): 119 oa × 33 × 5 *(36·3 × 10 × 1·5)*
Main engines: Diesel; 3 shafts; 475 bhp = 10 knots
Oil fuel (tons): 80

Former United States Navy Tank Landing Craft later reclassified as Utility Landing Craft. There are reported to be eleven utility landing craft comprising two of the ex-British LCT (3) class and eight of the ex-US LCT (5) and LCT (6) class. Used for logistic support and carry auxiliary pennants.

1 "YU LING" CLASS (LSM)

250 ft *(76·3 metres)*—1 500 ton LSM built in China since 1971. Continuing programme.

LCMs—LCUs

At least 450 of these types are employed on logistic support.

300 "YNNAN" CLASS

Built in China 1968-72.

About 150 Ex-BRITISH/US LCMs

SUBMARINE SUPPORT SHIP

TA CHIH

Displacement, tons: 5 to 6 000
Dimensions, feet (metres): 350 × 50 × 20 *(106·8 × 15·3 × 6·1)*
Guns: 4—37 mm (twins); 4—25 mm (twins)

Reported in 1973.

REPAIR SHIP

TAKU SHAN (ex-*Hsing An*, ex-USS *Achilles, ARL 41*, ex-*LST 455*)

Displacement, tons: 1 625 light; 4 100 full load
Dimensions, feet (metres): 328 oa × 50 × 11 *(100 × 15·3 × 3·4)*
Guns: 12—37 mm (twins)
Main engines: Diesel-electric; 2 shafts; 1 800 bhp = 11 knots

Launched on 17 Oct 1942. Burned and grounded in 1949, salvaged and refitted.

SURVEY AND RESEARCH SHIPS

2 "SHIH JIAN" CLASS (RESEARCH SHIPS)

SHIH JIAN   TUNG FAN HUNG 02

Of about 400 feet. Completed 1974. Civilian manned.

SHIH JIAN

1973

1 "YEN HSI" CLASS

HSIANG YANG HUNG WU

Completed Poland 1971-72. An environmental research ship.
Civilian manned. Stationed at Canton.

HSIANG YANG HUNG WU   *1974*

HSIANG YANG HUNG SAN +**2** others, maybe more

These ships, of varying tonnage but all of an ocean-going size, operate in conjunction with the
Academy of Science.

2 "HA T'SE" CLASS (SURVEY SHIPS)

HAI SHENG 701   **HAI SHENG** 702

Displacement, tons: 400 standard
Dimensions, feet (metres): 125 × 25 × 11 (est) *(38 × 7·6 × 3·4)*
Guns: 4—25 mm (vertical twins)
Main engines: 1 Diesel; 4 600 bhp = 12 knots (est)

Possibly built in 1960s. Certainly operational in 1971 off Paraul Islands.

1 "YEN LUN" CLASS (RESEARCH SHIP)

YEN LUN

Completed in 1965, possibly at Shanghai. Similar to Soviet 3 000-ton "Zubov" class.

1 Ex-JAPANESE "KAIBOKAN" CLASS

Displacement, tons: 740
Speed, knots: 17·5

Believed built in 1945.

3 "SHU KUANG" CLASS (ex T-43)

SHU KUANG 1-3

For details see under Mine Warfare Forces. Converted from Minesweepers for use as Survey
Ships, in late 1960s. All painted white.

1 COASTAL SURVEY CRAFT

Ex-CHUNG NING (ex-Japanese *Takebu Maru*)

Displacement, tons: 200 standard
Dimensions, feet (metres): 115 × 16 × 6 *(35 × 4·9 × 1·8)*
Speed, knots: 10

Former Japanese. Employed for hydrographic and general purpose duties.

1 COASTAL SURVEY CRAFT

Ex-FUTING

Displacement, tons: 160 standard
Dimensions, feet (metres): 90 × 20 × 8 *(27 × 6·1 × 2·4)*
Speed, knots: 11

BOOM DEFENCE VESSELS

1 Ex-BRITISH "BAR" CLASS

— (Ex-Japanese No. 101, ex-HMS *Barlight*)

Displacement, tons: 750 standard; 1 000 full load
Dimensions, feet (metres): 173·8 oa × 32·2 × 9·5 *(53 × 9·8 × 2·9)*
Guns: 1—3 in; 6 MG
Main engines: Triple expansion; 850 ihp = 11·75 knots
Boilers: 2 single-ended

Built by Lobnitz & Co Ltd, Renfrew. Launched on 10 Sep 1938. Captured by Japanese in 1941.
Acquired by China in 1945.

5 Ex-US "TREE" CLASS

Displacement, tons: 560 standard; 805 full load
Dimensions, feet (metres): 163 oa × 30·5 × 11·8 *(49·7 × 9·3 × 3·6)*
Gun: 1—3 in
Main engines: Diesel-electric; 800 bhp = 13 knots

SUPPLY SHIPS

5 Ex-US ARMY FS 330 TYPE

Ex-US Army FS 146 (ex-*Clover*)
Ex-US Army FS 155 (ex-*Violet*)   +**3**

Displacement, tons: 1 000 standard
Dimensions, feet (metres): 175 oa × 32 × 10 *(53·4 × 9·9 × 2)*
Main engines: GM diesels; 1 000 bhp = 12 knots

Built in USA in 1944-45. Two are reported to be employed as fast attack craft.

2 "GALATI" CLASS (AK)

HAI YUN 318   **HAI CHIU** 600

From Romania.

2 Ex-US ARMY FS 330 TYPE

1 "AN TUNG" CLASS

Chinese built AF.

2 or 3 "TAN LIN" CLASS

1 500 ton AK.

There may be another 12 coastal merchant ships operating under naval control.

TANKERS

14 + "FU CHOU" CLASS

Small tankers of approximately 1 400 tons.

3 "LEI CHOU" CLASS

LEI CHOU   FOU CHOU   + 1 (?)

Ships of 1 000 to 1 500 tons, the number in the class not yet being confirmed.

2 Ex-US "MATTAWEE" CLASS

Originally petrol tankers.

1 Ex-JAPANESE "TM" CLASS

An emergency class which was handed over to USSR in 1945 and transferred to China 1950 in Shanghai.

1 Ex-BRITISH "EBONOL" CLASS

2 200 tons. Built in 1917. As an RFA scuttled in Hong Kong, salved, renamed *Enoshima Maru*, recovered in 1945 at Batavia, sold in 1947.

ICEBREAKERS

2 "HAI PING" CLASS

101   102

Displacement, tons: 3 000
Dimensions, feet (metres): 275 × 50 × 16 *(83·8 × 15·3 × 4·9)*
Guns: 8—37 mm (twins)
Main engines: 3 000 hp; 1 shaft = 15 knots

Built in 1969-73 at Shanghai. Employed as icebreaking tugs in Po Hai Gulf for port clearance.

1 "YEN HANG" CLASS (AGBL)

REPAIR SHIPS

1 Ex-US ARL TYPE

TAKU SHAN

Converted AK.

1 "GALATI" CLASS

TUGS

10 "GROMOVOY" CLASS (SALVAGE TUGS)

Chinese built.

2 Ex-SOVIET "ROSLAVL" CLASS (SALVAGE TUGS)

2 Ex-US 149' ATA

2 Ex-US 143' ATA

5 Ex-US ARMY 75' YTL

SERVICE CRAFT

There are also reported to be 125 armed motor junks, 100 armed motor launches and 150 services craft and miscellaneous boats.

COLOMBIA

Ministerial

Minister of National Defence:
  General Abraham Varon Valencia

Headquarters Appointments

Fleet Commander:
  Admiral Jaime Barrera Larrarte
Chief of Naval Operations:
  Vice Admiral Alfonso Diaz Osorio
Chief of Naval Staff:
  Rear Admiral Héctor Calderón Salazar

Diplomatic Representative

Naval Attaché in Washington:
  Captain Rafael Grau Arano

Personnel

(a) 1977: 700 officers and 6 500 men and 1 500 marines
(b) 2 years' national service

Destroyer

1973 *Antioquia* ("Fletcher" class) (paid off 20 Dec)

Frigates

1972 *Almirante Brion* (ex-US APD type)
1973 *Almirante Padilla* (ex-US APD type)

Bases

Cartagena. Main naval base (floating dock, 1 slipway), schools.
Buenaventura. Small Pacific base.

Maritime Air Force

The Colombian Air Force with 50 helicopters and a number of attack/reconnaissance aircraft provides any support required by the navy.

Naval Infantry

Corpo de Infanteria de Marina is one battalion based at Cartagena, Buenaventura and Barranquilla.

Prefix to Ships' Names

ARC (Armada Republica de Colombia)

DELETIONS

Light Forces

1974 *Gen. Rafael Reyes, Alberto Restrepo, Independiente, Palace, Tormentosa, Triunfante, Valerosa, Voladora*

Survey Ship

1974 *Bocas de Ceniza*

Strength of the Fleet

Type	Active	Building
Destroyers	4	—
Frigates	3	—
Submarines	2 + 4 (70 tons)	—
Coastal Patrol Craft	25	—
Survey Vessels	4	—
Transports	5	—
Tanker	1	—
Training Ship	1	—
Tugs	12	—
Floating Docks	3	—
Floating Workshop	1	—

Mercantile Marine

Lloyd's Register of Shipping:
  53 vessels of 211 961 tons gross

Transport

1974 *Bell Salter, Rafael Martinez*

Tankers

1970 *Tumaco, Barran Cabermeja*
1974 *Covenas, Mamonal, Sancho Jimeno*

Tug

1975 *Bahia Honda* (grounded and scrapped 13 Feb)

DESTROYERS

2 MODIFIED "HALLAND" CLASS

Name	No.	Builders	Laid down	Launched	Commissioned
SIETE DE AGOSTO	D 06	Götaverken, Göteborg	Nov 1955	19 June 1956	31 Oct 1958
VEINTE DE JULIO	D 05	Kockums Mek Verkstads A/B, Malmo	Oct 1955	26 June 1956	15 June 1958

Displacement, tons: 2 650 standard; 3 300 full load
Length, feet (metres): 380·5 (116·0) pp; 397·2 (121·1) oa
Beam, feet (metres): 40·7 (12·4)
Draught, feet (metres): 15·4 (4·7)
Guns: 6—4·7 in (120 mm) (3 twin turrets); 4—40 mm (single
Torpedo tubes: 4—21 in (533 mm)
A/S weapons: 1 Bofors 375 mm A/S rocket launcher
Main engines: De Laval double reduction geared turbines; 2 shafts; 55 000 shp
Boilers: 2 Penhöet, Motala Verkstad; 568 psi; 840°F
Speed, knots: 25 (16 economical)
Oil fuel, tons: 524
Range, miles: 445 at full power
Complement: 260 (20 officers, 240 men)

SIETE DE AGOSTO

1971, Colombian Navy

Ordered in 1954. The hull and machinery are similar to the Swedish class but they have different armament (six 4·7 inch instead of four, no 57 mm guns, four 40 mm guns instead of six, and four torpedo tubes instead of eight) and different accommodation arrangements. They have an anti-submarine rocket projector, more radar and communication equipment, and air-conditioned living spaces, having been designed for the tropics. One is reported to be due for deletion.

Engineering: Although the designed speed was 35 knots, it is officially stated that the maximum sustained speed does not exceed 25 knots.

Radar: Search: HSA, LW-03/SGR 114.
Tactical: HSA DA-02/SGR 105.
Fire Control: I band, probably HSA M20 series.

Refit: *Siete de Agosto* returned to Colombia in 1975 after a lengthy refit in USA during which her engines were extensively overhauled.

SIETE DE AGOSTO

1975, Dhr. J. van der Woude

1 Ex-US "ALLEN M. SUMNER" CLASS, 1 Ex-US "ALLEN M. SUMNER FRAM II" CLASS

Name	No.	Builders	Laid down	Launched	Commissioned
CALDAS (ex-USS Willard Keith, DD 775)	D 02	Bethlehem (San Pedro)	—	29 Aug 1944	27 Dec 1944
SANTANDER (ex-USS Waldron, DD 699)	D 03	Federal SB Co	—	26 Mar 1944	8 June 1944

Displacement, tons: 2 200 standard; 3 320 full load
Length, feet (metres): 376 (114·8) oa
Beam, feet (metres): 40·9 (12·4)
Draught, feet (metres): 19 (5·8)
Guns: 6—5 in (127 mm) 38 cal (twins); 4—3 in (twins) (Caldas only)
A/S weapons: 2 Fixed Hedgehogs; 2 triple torpedo tubes (Mk 32); Facilities for small helicopter (Santander only)
Main engines: 2 geared turbines; 2 shafts; 60 000 shp
Boilers: 4
Speed, knots: 34
Range, miles: 2 400 at 25 knots; 4 800 at 15 knots
Complement: 274

Caldas, an unmodified "Allen M. Sumner" class, was transferred on 1 July 1972 by sale.
Santander was modernised under the Fram II programme and transferred by sale on 30 Oct 1973.

Radar:
Caldas; SPS 6 and 10 Mk 25 gun fire control radar on Mk 37 director.
Santander; As above but SPS 40 in place of SPS 6.

Sonar: VDS removed from *Santander* before transfer.

CALDAS

1974

SANTANDER

1975, Dhr. J. van der Woude

FRIGATES

2 Ex-US APD TYPE

Name	No.	Builders	Commissioned
ALMIRANTE TONO	DT 04	Consolidated Steel Co,	23 Feb 1945
(ex-USS *Basset APD 73*, ex-*DE 672*)		Orange	
CORDOBA (ex-USS *Ruchamkin LPR 89*,	DT 15	Philadelphia Navy Yard	June 1945
ex-*APD 89*, ex-*DE 228*)			

Displacement, tons: 1 400 standard; 2 130 full load
Dimensions, feet (metres): 306 oa × 37 × 12·6 *(93·3 × 11·3 × 3·8)*
Guns: 1—5 in 38 cal; 4—40 mm
A/S weapons: 2 Mk 32 launchers *(Cordoba only)*
Main engines: GEC Turbines with electric drive; 2 shafts; 12 000 shp = 23 knots
Boilers: 2 "D" Express
Range, miles: 5 500 at 15 knots
Complement: 204 (plus accommodation for 162 troops)

Almirante Tono was laid down on 28 Nov 1943, launched on 15 Jan 1944, and transferred at Boston, Mass, on 6 Sep 1968. *Cordoba* was laid down on 14 Feb 1944, launched on 15 June 1944 and transferred on 24 Nov 1969.
Modernised to Fram II standards. *(Cordoba* only).

CORDOBA   1974

1 Ex-US "COURTNEY" CLASS

Name	No.	Builders	Commissioned
BOYACA (ex-USS *Hartley DE 1029*)	DE 16	New York SB Corpn.	26 Jan 1957

Displacement, tons: 1 450 standard; 1 914 full load
Dimensions, feet (metres): 314·5 oa × 36·8 × 13·6 *(95·9 × 11·2 × 4·1)*
Guns: 2—3 in; 50 cal (twin)
A/S weapons: 2 triple Mk 32 torpedo tubes; 1 DC rack
Main engines: 1 De Laval geared turbine; 20 000 shp; 1 shaft
Boilers: 2 Foster Wheeler
Speed, knots: 25
Complement: 165

Transferred 8 July 1972, by sale. Helicopter platform in X position.

Radar: SPS 6 and 10.

BOYACA   1974

SUBMARINES

2 TYPE 209 PATROL SUBMARINES

Name	No.	Builders	Commissioned
PIJAO	SS 28	Howaldtswerke, Kiel	17 Apr 1975
TAYRONA	SS 29	Howaldtswerke, Kiel	18 July 1975

Displacement, tons: 1 000 surfaced; 1 290 dived
Length, feet (metres): 183·4 *(55·9)*
Beam, feet (metres): 20·5 *(6·25)*
Torpedo tubes: 8—21 in bow with reloads
Main machinery: Diesel electric; 1 shaft; 5 000 hp
Speed, knots: 22 dived

Ordered in 1971.

PIJAO   1975, Dhr J. van der Woude

4 TYPE SX-506 SUBMARINES

Name	No.	Builders	Commissioned
INTREPIDO	SS 20	Cosmos Livorno	1972
INDOMABLE	SS 21	Cosmos Livorno	1972
RONCADOR	SS 23	Cosmos Livorno	1974
QUITA SUENO	SS 24	Cosmos Livorno	1974

Displacement, tons: 58 surfaced; 70 dived
Dimensions, feet (metres): 75·4 × 6·6 × 13·2 *(23 × 2 × 4)*
Main machinery: Diesel-electric; 300 bhp
Speed, knots: 8 surfaced; 6 dived; 7 snorting
Range, miles: 1 200 at 7 knots
Complement: 5

Delivered in sections for assembly in Cartagena. Can carry 8 attack swimmers with 2 tons of explosives, as well as two swimmer-delivery-vehicles (SDVs). Diving depth 330 ft *(100 m)*.

LIGHT FORCES

Name	No.	Builders	Commissioned
GENERAL VASQUES COBO	AN 202	Lürssen	1955

Displacement, tons: 146
Dimensions, feet (metres): 124·7 oa × 23 × 5 *(38 × 7 × 1·5)*
Gun: 1—40 mm
Main engines: 2 Maybach (MTU) diesels; 2 500 bhp = 18 knots

Launched on 27 Sep 1955.

Name	No.	Builders	Commissioned
CARLOS ALBAN	—	Finland	1971
JORGE SOTO DEL CORVAL	—	Finland	1971
NITO RESTREPO	—	Finland	1971

Displacement, tons: 100
Dimensions, feet (metres): 108 × 18 × 6 *(33 × 5·5 × 1·8)*
Guns: 2—20 mm
Main engines: 2 (MTU) Diesels; 2 450 bhp = 17 knots

Near sisters to Finnish "Ruissalo" class.

CARLOS ALBAN   1971, Colombian Navy

Name	No.	Builders	Commissioned
PEDRO GUAL	AN 204	Schurenstedt KG Barden Fleth	1964
ESTEBAN JARAMILLO	AN 205	Schurenstedt KG Barden Fleth	1964
CARLOS E. RESTREPO	AN 206	Schurenstedt KG Barden Fleth	1964

Displacement, tons: 85
Dimensions, feet (metres): 107·8 pp × 18 × 6 *(32·9 × 5·5 × 1·8)*
Gun: 1—20 mm
Main engines: 2 Maybach (MTU) diesels; 2 450 bhp = 26 knots

PEDRO GUAL   *1965, Colombian Navy*

3 "ARAUCA" CLASS GUNBOATS

Name	No.	Builders	Commissioned
RIOHACHA	CF 35	Union Industrial de Barranquilla	1956
LETICIA	CF 36	Union Industrial de Barranquilla	1956
ARAUCA	CF 37	Union Industrial de Barranquilla	1956

Displacement, tons: 184 full load
Dimensions, feet (metres): 163·5 oa × 23·5 × 2·8 *(49·9 × 7·2 × 0·9)*
Guns: 2—3 in, 50 cal; 4—20 mm
Main engines: 2 Caterpillar diesels; 916 bhp = 14 knots
Range, miles: 1 890 at 14 knots
Complement: 43 (*Leticia* 39 and 6 orderlies)

Launched in 1955. *Leticia* has been equipped as a hospital ship with 6 beds.

RIOHACHA   *1966, Colombian Navy*

1 "BARRANQUILLA" CLASS GUNBOAT

Name	No.	Builders	Commissioned
CARTAGENA	CF 33	Yarrow & Co Ltd, Scotstoun	1930

Displacement, tons: 142
Dimensions, feet (metres): 137·8 oa × 23·5 × 2·8 *(42 × 7·2 × 0·9)*
Guns: 2—3 in; 1—20 mm; 4 MG
Main engines: 2 Gardner semi-diesels; 2 shafts working in tunnels; 600 hp = 15·5 knots
Oil fuel (tons): 24
Complement: 39

Launched on 22 Mar 1930. Sister ships *Santa Marta*, CF 32, withdrawn from service in Dec 1962, and *Barranquilla* in 1970.

CARTAGENA   *1971, Colombian Navy*

Name	No.	Builders	Commissioned
OLAYA HERRERA	AN 203	Ast. Magdalena Barranquilla	1960

Displacement, tons: 40
Dimensions, feet (metres): 68·8 pp × 12·8 × 3·5 *(21 × 3·9 × 1·1)*
Gun: 1—50 mm Browning
Main engines: 2 Merbens diesels; 570 bhp = 20 knots

Name	No.	Builders	Commissioned
ESPARTANA	GC 100	Ast. Naval, Cartagena	1950

Displacement, tons: 50
Dimensions, feet (metres): 96 oa × 13·5 × 4 *(29·3 × 4·1 × 1·2)*
Gun: 1—20 mm
Main engines: 2 diesels; 300 bhp = 13·5 knots

Name	No.	Builders	Commissioned
CAPITAN R. D. BINNEY	GC 101	Ast. Naval, Cartagena	1947

Displacement, tons: 23
Dimensions, feet (metres): 67 × 10·7 × 3·5 *(20·4 × 3·3 × 1·1)*
Main engines: Diesels; 115 bhp = 13 knots

Buoy and lighthouse inspection boat. Named after first head of Colombian Naval Academy, Lt-Commander Ralph Douglas Binney, RN.

Name	No.	Builders	Commissioned
CARLOS GALINDO	LR 128	Ast. Naval, Cartagena	1954
HUMBERTO CORTES	LR 126	Ast. Naval, Cartagena	1953
JUAN LUCIO	LR 122	Ast. Naval, Cartagena	1953

Displacement, tons: 35
Dimensions, feet (metres): 81·8 oa × 12 × 2·8 *(24·6 × 3·7 × 0·8)*
Guns: 1—20 mm; 4 MG
Main engines: 2 GM diesels; 260 bhp = 13 knots
Complement: 13

Originally class of four.

Name	No.	Builders	Commissioned
ALFONSO VARGAS	LR 123	Ast. Naval, Cartagena	1952
FRITZ HAGALE	LR 124	Ast. Naval, Cartagena	1952

Displacement, tons: 33
Dimensions, feet (metres): 76 oa × 12 × 2·8 *(23·2 × 3·7 × 0·8)*
Guns: 1—20 mm; 4 MG
Main engines: 2 GM diesels 280 bhp = 13 knots
Complement: 10

Designed for operations on rivers. Named after naval officers.

Name	No.	Builders	Commissioned
DILIGENTE	LR 138	Ast. Naval, Cartagena	1952
VENGADORA	LR 139	Ast. Naval, Cartagena	1954

Originally a class of eight.

1 40 ft CGB

Name	No.	Builders	Commissioned
RODRIGUEZ	AN 1	—	—

SURVEY VESSELS

Name	No.	Builders	Commissioned
SAN ANDRES (ex-USS *Rockville, PCER 851*)	BO 151	Pullman Standard Car Co, Chicago	15 May 1944

Displacement, tons: 674 standard; 968 full load
Dimensions, feet (metres): 184·5 oa × 33·6 × 7·0 *(56·3 × 10·2 × 2·1)*
Main engines: 2 diesels; 2 shafts; 1 800 bhp = 15 knots
Complement: 50

Former US patrol rescue escort vessel. Laid down on 18 Oct 1943, launched on 22 Feb 1944. Acquired on 5 June 1969 for conversion to a surveying vessel.

Name	No.	Builders	Commissioned
GORGONA	FB 161	Lidingoverken, Sweden	1955

Displacement, tons: 574
Dimensions, feet (metres): 135 × 29·5 × 9·3 *(41·2 × 9 × 2·8)*
Main engines: 2 Nohab diesels; 910 bhp = 13 knots
Complement: 45

Formerly classified as a tender.

GORGONA   *1971, Colombian Navy*

Name	No.	Builders	Commissioned
QUINDIO (ex-US *YPR 443*)	BO 153	—	1943

Displacement, tons: 380 light; 600 full load
Dimensions, feet (metres): 131 × 29·8 × 9 *(40 × 9·1 × 2·7)*
Main engines: 2 diesels; 300 hp = 10 knots
Complement: 17

Transferred by lease July 1964.

TANKER

1 Ex-US "PATAPSCO" CLASS (AOG)

Name	No.	Builders	Commissioned
TUMACO (ex-USS *Chewaucan, AOG 50*)	BT 67	Cargill Inc, Savage, Minn.	19 Feb 1945

Displacement, tons: 1 850 light; 4 570
Dimensions, feet (metres): 310·8 × 48·5 × 16 *(94·8 × 14·8 × 4·9)*
Guns: 2—3 in *(76 mm)*
Main engines: Diesel electric; 2 shafts; 3 840 bhp = 15 knots
Range, miles: 4 740 at 15 knots; 8 350 at 11·5 knots
Complement: 95

Transferred 1975.

TUMACO (As USS *Chewaucan*)   *1970, A. and J. Pavia*

TRANSPORTS

Name	No.	Builders	Commissioned
CIUDAD DE QUIBDO (ex-*Shamrock*)	TM 43	Gebr Sander Deltzijl	1953 (see note)

Displacement, tons: 633
Dimensions, feet (metres): 165 × 23·5 × 9 *(49·9 × 7·2 × 2·7)*
Main engines: 1 MAN diesel; 1 shaft; 390 bhp = 11 knots
Oil fuel, tons: 32
Complement: 12

Ex-Dutch coaster *Shamrock* sold to Colombia by commercial firm in Mar 1953.

CIUDAD DE QUIBDO   *1971, Colombian Navy*

Name	No.	Builders	Commissioned
MARIO SERPA	TF 51	Ast. Naval Cartagena	1954
HERNANDO GUTIERREZ	TF 52	Ast. Naval Cartagena	1955
SOCORRO (ex-*Alberto Gomez*)	BD 33	Ast. Naval Cartagena	1956

Displacement, tons: 70
Dimensions, feet (metres): 82 × 18 × 2·8 *(25 × 5·5 × 0·9)*
Main engines: 2 GM diesels; 260 bhp = 9 knots
Oil fuel, tons: 4
Range, miles: 650 at 9 knots
Complement: 12 (berths for 48 troops and medical staff)

River transports. Named after Army officers. *Socorro* was converted in July 1967 into a floating surgery. *Hernando Gutierrez* and *Mario Serpa* were converted into dispensary ships in 1970.

TRAINING SHIP

Name	No.	Builders	Commissioned
GLORIA	—	Bilbao	1968

Displacement, tons: 1 300
Dimensions, feet (metres): 212 × 34·8 × 21·7 *(64·7 × 10·6 × 6·6)*
Main engines: Auxiliary diesel; 500 bhp = 10·5 knots

Sail training ship. Barque rigged. Hull is entirely welded.
Sail area: 1 675 sq yards *(1 400 sq metres).*

GLORIA   *1971, Colombian Navy*

PEDRO DE HEREDIA (ex-USS *Choctaw, ATF 70*) RM 72

Displacement, tons: 1 235 standard; 1 764 full load
Dimensions, feet (metres): 205 oa × 38·5 × 15·5 *(62·5 × 11·7 × 4·7)*
Main engines: 4 diesels; electric drive; 3 000 bhp = 16·5 knots

Former United States ocean tug of the "Cherokee" class. Launched on 18 Oct 1942. Transferred 1961.

TUGS

PEDRO DE HEREDIA   8/1975, S. Terzibaschitsch

BAHIA UTRIA (ex-USS *Kalmia* ATA 184) RM 75

Displacement, tons: 534 standard; 858 full load
Dimensions, feet (metres): 143·0 oa × 33·9 × 8·0 *(43·6 × 10·3 × 2·4)*
Gun: 1—3 in
Main engines: 2 GM diesel-electric; 1 shaft; 1 500 bhp = 13 knots
Complement: 45

Launched 29 Aug 1944. Transferred from the United States Navy on 1 July 1971 on lease.

CANDIDO LEGUIZAMO RR 82	**CAPITAN RIGOBERTO GIRALDO** RR 86
CAPITAN ALVARO RUIZ RR 84	**CAPITAN VLADIMIR VALEK** RR 87
CAPITAN CASTRO RR 81	**JOVES FIALLO** RR 90
	TENIENTE LUIS BERNAL RR 88

Displacement, tons: 50
Dimensions, feet (metres): 63 × 14 × 2·5 *(19·2 × 4·3 × 0·8)*
Main engines: 2 GM diesels; 260 bhp = 9 knots

ANDAGOYA RM 71

Measurement, tons: 117 gross
Dimensions, feet (metres): 92·6 × 20 × 10 *(28·2 × 6·1 × 3·05)*
Main engines: Caterpillar diesel; 400 bhp = 10 knots

Launched in 1928. Re-engined in 1955.

TENIENTE SORZANO RM 73

Displacement, tons: 54
Dimensions, feet (metres): 65·7 oa × 17·5 × 9 *(20 × 5·3 × 2·7)*
Main engines: 6-cylinder diesel; 240 bhp

Former US tug.

ABADIA MENDEZ

Displacement, tons: 39
Dimensions, feet (metres): 52·5 × 11 × 4 *((16 × 3·4 × 1·2)*
Main engines: Caterpillar diesel; 80 bhp = 8 knots

Built in Germany in 1924. Harbour tug. Existence now doubtful.

TENIENTE MIGUEL SILVA RR 89

Dimensions, feet (metres): 73·3 × 17·5 × 3 *(22·4 × 5·3 × 0·9)*
Main engines: 2 diesels; 260 bhp = 9 knots

River tug. Built by Union Industrial (Unial) of Barranquilla.

FLOATING DOCK

MAYOR ARIAS

Displacement, tons: 700
Capacity, tons: 165
Length, feet (metres): 140 *(42·7)*

Note: It is reported that the 6 700 ton *Rodriguez Zamora* (ex-ARD 28), the small floating dock *Manuel Lara*, the floating workshop *Mantilla* (ex-YR 66) and the repair craft *Victor Cubillos* are probably under civil contract.

CONGO

The Republic of Congo, which became independent on 15 Aug 1960, formed a naval service, but the patrol vessel *Reine N' Galifowou* (ex-French P 754) which was transferred 16 Nov 1962 was returned to France on 18 Feb 1965 and then re-transferred to Senegal as *Siné Saloum*.

Ministerial

Minister of Defence:
  Major Marien N'gouabi

Personnel

(a) 1977: 200 officers and men
(b) Voluntary service

Base

Pointe-Noire.

Mercantile Marine

Lloyd's Register of Shipping:
  13 vessels of 2 453 tons gross

3 Ex-CHINESE "SHANGHAI" CLASS

Displacement, tons: 120 standard; 155 full load
Dimensions, feet (metres): 128 × 18 × 5·6 *(39 × 5·5 × 1·7)*
Guns: 4—37 mm (twin); 2—25 mm (twin)
A/S armament: 8 DCs (may be removed)
Mines: Mine rails can be fitted for up to 10 mines
Main engines: 4 Diesels; 4 800 hp = 30 knots
Complement: 25

Probably transferred in 1974.

"SHANGHAI" Class

4 RIVER PATROL CRAFT

Reported as about 10 tons, transferred by China.

MISCELLANEOUS

It is reported that up to 12 small craft with outboard motors are employed on river patrol.

COSTA RICA

Personnel

(a) 1977: 50 officers and men
(b) Voluntary

Ports

Limon, Golfito, Puntarenas

Mercantile Marine

Lloyd's Register of Shipping:
  15 vessels of 6 257 tons gross

3 COASTAL PATROL CRAFT

401   402   403

Displacement, tons: 10
Dimensions, feet (metres): 41 × 10 × 2·3 *(12·5 × 3·1 × 0·7)*
Gun: 1 MG

Built in mid-1950s. Of US Coastguard 40 ft type.
An armed tug is also reported.

CUBA

Ministerial

Minister of the Revolutionary Armed Forces:
  Raul Castro Ruz

Senior Appointment

Commander in Chief:
  Commodore Aldo Santamaria

Personnel

(a) 1977: 6 000 (380 officers, 220 petty officers and 5 400 men)
(b) 3 years national service

Standard of Efficiency

The US embargo on exports to Cuba has been running for over a decade. As a result all ex-USN ships in the Cuban Navy must be suffering from lack of spares, though some may have been stripped to provide for others. Cuba has the highest estimated defence expenditure in Central America and the Caribbean at about £120 million, a fair proportion of this being on Soviet aid. The navy is the smallest of the three services but, with an adequate budget and Soviet assistance in training, must be assessed as having a reasonable level of tactical and material efficiency.

Naval Establishments

Naval Academy:
  At Mariel, for officers and cadets

Naval School:
  At Morro Castle, for petty officers and men

Naval Bases:
  Cabanas, Cienfuegos, Havana, Mariel, Varadero plus at least four more in preparation.

Maritime Airforce

A helicopter force of 25 Mi-4 (Hound) and 30 Mi-1 (Hare) from USSR is in existence although these are probably all operated by the Air Force.

Strength of the Fleet

	Active	Building or (Reserve)
Frigates	—	(1)
Large Patrol Craft	18	—
Fast Attack Craft (Missile)	26	—
Fast Attack Craft (Torpedo)	24	—
Fast Attack Craft (Patrol)	7	—
Coastal Patrol Craft	22	—
LCMs	7	—
Survey Vessels	6	—
Miscellaneous	9	—

Mercantile Marine

Lloyd's Register of Shipping:
  294 vessels of 603 750 tons gross

DELETIONS

Cruiser (so called)

1972 *Cuba* (built 1911—of 2 000 tons)

Frigates

1975 *Antonio Maceo, Jose Marti* (ex-US PF Type) sunk as targets.

Corvettes

1973 *Sibony* (ex-US PCER)
1976 *Caribe* (ex-US PCER)

Light Forces

1973 *Donotivo, Matanzas*

Tug

1976 *Diez de Octubre*

FRIGATES

One of the three ex-US frigates of the PF type—believed to be *Maximo Gomez*—which was completed in 1944 and acquired in 1947 is still in existence as harbour hulk but has no operational value.

LIGHT FORCES

12 Ex-SOVIET "SO I" CLASS

Displacement, tons: 215 standard; 250 full load
Dimensions, feet (metres): 138·6 × 20 × 9·2 *(42·3 × 6·1 × 2·8)*
Guns: 4—25 mm (2 twin)
A/S weapons: 4 five-barrelled rocket launchers
Main engines: 3 diesels; 6 000 bhp = 29 knots
Range, miles: 1 100 at 13 knots
Complement: 30

Six were transferred from the USSR by Sep 1964, and six more in 1967.

"SO I" Class   *1970, USN*

6 Ex-SOVIET "KRONSHTADT" CLASS

Displacement, tons: 310 standard; 380 full load
Dimensions, feet (metres): 170·6 × 21·3 × 9 *(52·0 × 6·5 × 2·7)*
Guns: 1—3·5 in; 2—37 mm; 6—12·7 mm (twins)
A/S weapons: 2 MBU 1800A; 2 DCT; 2 DC racks
Mines: 6 on two racks at the stern
Main engines: 3 diesels; 3 shafts; 3 030 hp = 24 knots
Range, miles: 1 500 at 12 knots
Complement: 65

Transferred from the USSR in 1962.

Radar: Surface: Ballgun. Navigation: Don. IFF; High Pole A.

Soviet "KRONSHTADT" Class

18 Ex-SOVIET "KOMAR" CLASS (FAST ATTACK CRAFT—MISSILE)

Displacement, tons: 70 standard; 80 full load
Dimensions, feet (metres): 83·4 × 21·1 × 5·0 *(25·4 × 6·4 × 1·5)*
Missiles: 2 SS-N-2 launchers
Guns: 2—25 mm
Main engines: 4 diesels; 4 shafts; 4 800 bhp = 40 knots
Range, miles: 400 at 30 knots

First twelve transferred in 1962. Last pair arrived in Dec 1966.

"KOMAR" Class   *1970, USN*

5 Ex-SOVIET "OSA I" AND 3 "OSA II" CLASS (FAST ATTACK CRAFT—MISSILE)

Displacement, tons: 165 standard; 200 full load
Dimensions, feet (metres): 128·7 × 25·1 × 5·9 *(39·3 × 7·7 × 1·8)*
Missiles: 4 SS-N-2 launchers in two pairs
Guns: 4—30 mm (2 twin, 1 forward, 1 aft)
Main engines: 3 diesels; 13 000 bhp = 35 knots
Range, miles: 800 at 25 knots
Complement: 25

Two boats of this class were transferred to Cuba from the USSR in January 1972 and three in 1973. These were followed by two "Osa II" in mid 1976 and one in Dec 1976. With the obvious rundown of the ex-USN ships in the Cuban Navy and the determination of the Cuban Government to maintain an independent Naval presence in the Caribbean, these could be the forerunners of further reinforcements. With the "Komar" class units there are now twenty-six hulls mounting 68 of the proven and effective Styx missiles in a highly sensitive area.

"OSA I" Class

12 Ex-SOVIET "P 6" CLASS (FAST ATTACK CRAFT—TORPEDO)

Nos. 80-92

Displacement, tons: 66 standard; 75 full load
Dimensions, feet (metres): 83·4 × 20 × 6 *(25·4 × 6·1 × 1·5)*
Guns: 4—25 mm (two twin)
Torpedo tubes: 2—21 in (two single)
Main engines: 4 diesels; 4 shafts; 4 800 hp = 43 knots
Range, miles: 450 at 30 knots
Complement: 25

Transferred in 1962. Pot Head or Skin Head Radar. Can carry mines or depth charges in place of torpedo tubes.

"P 6" Class   *1970, USN*

12 Ex-SOVIET "P 4" CLASS (FAST ATTACK CRAFT—TORPEDO)

Displacement, tons: 25
Dimensions, feet (metres): 62·7 × 11·6 × 5·6 *(19·1 × 3·5 × 1·7)*
Guns: 2—25 mm
Torpedo tubes: 2—18 in
Main engines: 2 diesels; 2 200 bhp; 2 shafts = 50 knots
Complement: 12

Transferred from the USSR in 1962-64.

"P 4" Class   *1971*

5 Ex-SOVIET "ZHUK" CLASS (FAST ATTACK CRAFT—PATROL)

Displacement, tons: 60
Dimensions, feet (metres): 75 × 16 × 5 *(22·9 × 4·9 × 1·5)*
Guns: 4—14·5 mm (twin)
Main engines: Diesels = 34 knots (28 knots normal)
Complement: 18?

Transferred 1975.

"ZHUK" Class

2 Ex-US PT TYPE (FAST ATTACK CRAFT—PATROL)

R 41 (ex-PT 715)   **R 42** (ex-PT 716)

Displacement, tons: 35
Dimensions, feet (metres): 71 × 19·2 × 5 *(21·7 × 5·9 × 1·5)*
Guns: 2 MG
Main engines: 2 Packard petrol engines; 3 shafts; 3 600 bhp = 35 knots

Former US motor torpedo boats of the PT type. Built in the USA by Annapolis Yacht Yard Inc, Annapolis, Md. Launched on 9 July 1945 (R 41) and 17 July 1945 (R 42). Sunk during a hurricane on 5 Oct 1948, but were salvaged and put into service primarily as fast rescue craft. May have been deleted.

4 Ex-US COASTAL PATROL CRAFT

HABANA (ex-SC 1291) GC 107   **ORIENTE** (ex-SC 1000) GC 104
LAS VILLAS (ex-SC 1290) GC 106   **PINAR DEL RIO** (ex-SC 1301) GC 108

Displacement, tons: 95
Dimensions, feet (metres): 107·5 wl; 111 oa × 17 × 6·6 *(33·7 × 5·7 × 2)*
Guns: 2—20 mm
Main engines: 2 GM diesels; 2 shafts; 1 000 bhp = 15 knots
Complement: 25

Built in the United States by Dingle Boat Works *(Oriente),* W. A. Robinson, Inc, Ipswich, Mass. *(Havana* and *Las Villas),* and Perkins & Vaughn Inc, Wickford, RI *(Pinar del Rio)* in 1942/43.

HABANA   *Cuban Navy*

1 COASTAL PATROL CRAFT

LEONCIO PRADO GC 101

Displacement, tons: 80
Dimensions, feet (metres): 110 × 17·7 × 6·2 *(33·5 × 5·4 × 1·9)*
Gun: 1—20 mm
Main engines: 2 8-cycle, 2 stroke diesels; 1 000 bhp = 15 knots
Oil fuel: 2 232 gallons

Built at Havana. Launched in 1946. Of wooden hulled construction.

LEONCIO PRADO   *1966, Cuban Navy*

3 Ex-US CG 56 ft TYPE (COASTAL PATROL CRAFT)

GC 32 (ex-USCGC 56191)   **GC 33** (ex-USCGC 56190)   **GC 34** (ex-USCGC 56192)

Length, feet (metres): 56 *(17·1)*
Gun: 1—20 mm
Main engines: 2 superior diesels; 460 bhp = 12 knots

Transferred 1943

3 Ex-US CG 83 ft TYPE (COASTAL PATROL CRAFT)

GC 11 (ex-USCGC 83351)   **GC 13** (ex-USCGC 83385)   **GC 14** (ex-USCGC 83395)

Displacement, tons: 45
Dimensions, feet (metres): 83 × 16 × 4·5 *(25·3 × 4·9 × 1·4)*
Gun: 1—20 mm
Main engines: 2 Sterling Viking petrol motors; 1 200 hp = 18 knots
Complement: 12

Built in USA. Ex-Coast Guard Cutters. Launched in 1942-43. Of wooden hulled construction. Received from US Navy in March 1943.

6 COASTAL PATROL CRAFT

SV 7   **SV 8**   **SV 9**   **SV 10**   **SV 12**   **SV 14**

Length, feet (metres): 40 *(12·2)*
Gun: 1—50 cal MG
Main engines: 2 GM diesels = 25 knots

Later boats of the SV type equipped with radar. Completed 1958.

6 COASTAL PATROL CRAFT

SV 1   **SV 2**   **SV 3**   **SV 4**   **SV 5**   **SV 6**

Displacement, tons: 6·15
Dimensions, feet (metres): 32 × 10 × 2·8 *(9·8 × 3·1 × ·8)*
Main engines: 2 Chrysler Crown, 230 bhp = 18 knots

Auxiliary patrol boats for port patrol, launched in 1953.

AMPHIBIOUS FORCES

7 "T4" CLASS LCMs

Obtained 1967-74. Mainly employed as Harbour Craft.

SURVEY VESSELS

6 Ex-SOVIET "NYRYAT 1" CLASS

H 91   **H 92**   **H 93**   **H 94**   **H 95**   **H 96**

Displacement, tons: 145
Main engines: Diesels = 12·5 knots
Complement: 15

All-purpose craft reportedly used for surveying.

MISCELLANEOUS

1 TRAINING SHIP

H 101

Measurement, tons: 530

An ex-fishing trawler/buoy tender now used for cadet training.

2 LIGHTHOUSE TENDERS

ENRIQUE COLLAZO (ex-*Joaquin Godoy*)

Displacement, tons: 815
Dimensions, feet (metres): 211 × 24 × 9 *(64 × 10·5 × 2·8)*
Main engines: Triple expansion; 2 shafts; 672 ihp = 8 knots

Built at Paisley, Scotland. Launched in 1906. Acquired in 1950 from Cuban Mercantile Marine.

BERTHA SF 10

Displacement, tons: 98
Dimensions, feet (metres): 104 × 19 × 11 *(31·5 × 5·8 × 3·4)*
Main engines: 2 Gray Marine diesels; 450 bhp = 10 knots

Launched in 1944.

1 Ex-SOVIET "QKHTENSKY" CLASS (OCEAN TUG)

CARIBE

Displacement, tons: 835
Dimensions, feet (metres): 143 oa × 34 × 15 *(43·6 × 10·4 × 4·6)*
Guns: 1—3 in *(76 mm)*; 2—20 mm.
Main engines: 2 BM diesels; 2 electric motors; 2 shafts; 1 875 bhp = 14 knots
Oil fuel, tons: 187
Complement: 34

Transferred in 1976 to replace *Diez de Octubre*. Name taken from deleted corvette.

GRANMA A 11

Yacht which reached Cuba on 2 Dec 1956 with Dr Fidel Castro and the men who began the liberation war. Historic vessel incorporated into the Navy as an Auxiliary.

3 HARBOUR AUXILIARIES

A1   **A2**   **A3**

Displacement, tons: 60
Dimensions, feet (metres): 74 × 15 × 5 *(22·6 × 4·6 × 1·5)*
Gun: 1 MG
Main engines: 2 diesels

Built in USA 1949.

CYPRUS

Personnel

1977: 330 officers and men

Mercantile Marine

Lloyd's Register of Shipping:
  765 vessels of 3 114 263 tons gross

New Construction

Two Fast Attack Craft (Missile) ordered from Chantiers Navals de l'Esterel were not taken up and were transferred to Greece as *Kelefstis Stamou* and *Diopos Antionio*.

LIGHT FORCES

6 Ex-SOVIET "P 4" CLASS

Displacement, tons: 25
Dimensions, feet (metres): 62·7 × 11·6 × 6·5 *(19·1 × 3·5 × 1·7)*
Guns: 2—14·5 mm
Torpedo tubes: 2—18 in
Main engines: 2 diesels; 2 200 bhp; 2 shafts = 50 knots
Complement: 12

Four of these were transferred by USSR in Oct 1964 and two in Feb 1965. Also reported that two extra engines have been supplied since that time.

Radar: Skin Head.

"P 4" Class

2 Ex-GERMAN "R" CLASS

Displacement, tons: 125
Dimensions, feet (metres): 124 × 19 × 4·5 *(37·8 × 5·8 × 1·4)*
Guns: 1—40 mm; 2—20 mm
Main engines: 2 MAN (MTU) diesels; 1 800 bhp = 18 knots

Built in 1943.

Originally three of this class were taken up from mercantile use and re-armed. One was destroyed by Turkish air attack on 8 Aug 1964 at Xeros.

It is reported that there are 10 small craft of about 50 tons, armed with one or two 20 mm guns.

"R" Class

1972, Dr. Giorgio Arra

CZECHOSLOVAKIA

Although a navy as such does not exist there is a river patrol force, the personnel of which wear naval-type uniforms.

DENMARK

Ministerial

Minister of Defence:
 H. Orla Moller

Headquarters Appointment

Commander-in-Chief:
 Vice-Admiral S. Thostrup
Flag Officer Denmark:
 Rear-Admiral H. M. Petersen

Diplomatic Representation

Defence Attaché, Bonn
 Colonel P. E. M. O. Gruner
Defence Attaché, London:
 Colonel H. H. Prince Georg of Denmark, KCVO
Assistant Defence Attaché, London:
 Commander I. E. Eriksen, MVO
Defence Attaché, Washington:
 Colonel P. B. Nissen

Personnel

(a) 1977: 5 800 officers and men
    (Reserves of 3 100 Naval Home Guard)
(b) 9 months National Service

Navy Estimates

1973-74: 583 600 000 Kr.
1974-75: 638 500 000 Kr.
1975-76: 729 900 000 Kr.

Naval Bases

Copenhagen, Korsør, Frederikshavn,
Grønnedal (Greenland)

Farvands Direktoratet

This Directorate of Waters (under the MOD) now controls the
Pilot Service. Lighthouse Service, and Lifeboat Service.

Naval Air Arm

8 Alouette III helicopters

Prefix to Ships' Names

HDMS

Strength of the Fleet

Type	Active	Building or Projected
Frigates	7	—
Corvettes	3	3
Submarines (Patrol)	6	—
Fast Attack Craft (Missile)	4	6
Fast Attack Craft (Torpedo)	10	—
Large Patrol Craft	23	—
Coastal Patrol Craft	23	—
Minelayers	4	2
Minesweepers (Coastal)	8	—
Tankers (Small)	2	—
Icebreakers	3	—
Royal Yacht	1	—

Mercantile Marine

Lloyd's Register of Shipping:
 1 371 vessels of 4 478 112 tons gross

New Construction

Programme includes 3 Corvettes, 2 Minelayers, 6 Fast Attack
Craft.

DELETIONS

Corvette

1974 *Diana* ("Triton" class)

Fast Attack Craft

1974 6 "Flyvefisken" Class (scrapped May 1976)

Large Patrol Craft

1972 *Alholm*

Coastal Patrol Craft

1975 Y 354, Y 359, *Ertholm, Lindholm*
1976 *Faeno*

Mine Warfare Forces

1974 2 "Lougen" Class Minelayers
      4 "Vig" Class Inshore Minesweepers

Tenders

1970 *Hollaenderdybet, Kongedybet*
1973 *Hjaelperen* (laid up)
1974 *Henrik Gerner*

Icebreakers

1972 *Lillebjørn*
1975 *Storebjørn*

PENNANT LIST

Frigates and Corvettes

F 340	Beskytteren
F 344	Bellona
F 346	Flora
F 347	Triton
F 348	Hvidbjørnen
F 349	Vaedderen
F 350	Ingolf
F 351	Fylla
F 352	Peder Skram
F 353	Herluf Trolle

Submarines

S 320	Nahrvalen
S 321	Nordkaperen
S 326	Delfinen
S 327	Spaekhuggeren
S 328	Tumleren
S 329	Springeren

Light Forces

P 506	Falken
P 507	Glenten
P 508	Gribben
P 509	Høgen
P 510	Søløven
P 511	Søridderen
P 512	Søbjørnen
P 513	Søhesten
P 514	Søhunden
P 515	Søulven
P 530	Daphne
P 531	Dryaden
P 532	Havmanden
P 533	Havfruen
P 534	Najaden
P 535	Nymfen
P 536	Neptun
P 537	Ran
P 538	Rota
P 540	Bille

Light Forces

P 541	Bredal
P 542	Hammer
P 543	Huitfeldt
P 544	Krieger
P 545	Norby
P 546	Rodsteen
P 547	Sehested
P 548	Suenson
P 549	Willemoes
Y 300	Barsø
Y 301	Drejø
Y 302	Romsø
Y 303	Samsø
Y 304	Thurø
Y 305	Vejrø
Y 306	Farø
Y 307	Laesø
Y 308	Rømø

Light Forces

Y 383	Tejsten
Y 384	Maagen
Y 385	Mallemukken
Y 386	Agdleq
Y 387	Agpa

Minewarfare Forces

N 80	Falster
N 81	Fyen
N 82	Møen
N 83	Sjaelland
M 571	Aarøsund
M 572	Alssund
M 573	Egernsund
M 574	Grønsund
M 575	Guldborgsund
M 576	Omøsund
M 577	Ulvsund
M 578	Wilsund

Auxiliaries

A 540	Dannebrog
A 568	Rimfaxe
A 569	Skinfaxe

Naval Home Guard

MHV 53	
MHV 64	
MHV 70	
MHV 71	
MHV 72	
MHV 81	Askø
MHV 82	Enø
MHV 83	Manø
MHV 84	Baagø
MHV 85	Hjortø
MHV 86	Lyø
MHV 90	
MHV 91	
MHV 92	
MHV 93	
MHV 94	
MHV 95	

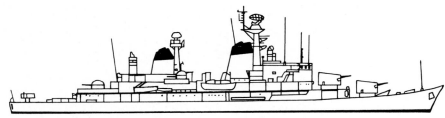

"PEDER SKRAM" Class

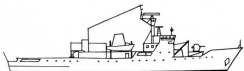

BESKYTTEREN

"FALSTER" Class

"HVIDBJORNEN" Class

FRIGATES

2 "PEDER SKRAM" CLASS

Name	No.	Builders	Laid down	Launched	Commissioned
HERLUF TROLLE	F 353	Helsingörs J. & M.	18 Dec 1964	8 Sep 1965	16 Apr 1967
PEDER SKRAM	F 352	Helsingörs J. & M.	25 Sep 1964	20 May 1965	30 June 1966

Displacement, tons: 2 030 standard; 2 720 full load
Length, feet (metres): 354·3 (108) pp; 396·5 (112·6) oa
Beam, feet (metres): 39·5 (12)
Draught, feet (metres): 11·8 (3·6)
Missiles: 1 Sea Sparrow (4 cell) on quarter-deck (see Missile note)
Guns: 4—5 in (127 mm) 38 cal (twins); 4—40 mm
Torpedo tubes: 4—21 in for wire-guided and A/S torpedoes
A/S weapons: DCs
Main engines: CODOG:—2 GM 16-567 D diesels; 4 800 hp; 2 Pratt & Whitney PWA GG 4A-3 gas turbines; 44 000 hp total output; 2 shafts
Speed, knots: 30, 18 economical
Complement: 200

PEDER SKRAM   1974, Royal Danish Navy

Danish design. In addition to other armament they were originally designed for three 21 inch torpedo tubes and the Terne anti-submarine weapon. But the latter has been dropped in favour of Sea Sparrow and two twin 21 in mountings fitted on the beams.

Conversion: Mid-life conversion in 1976-77.

Missiles: Sea Sparrow fitted in *Herluf Trolle* Oct 1976 later for *Peder Skram. Herluf Trolle* being fitted for 8 Harpoon missiles in place of B turret.

Radar: Combined warning: Two CWS 3.
Fire control: Three CGS-1.
Tactical: One NWS-1.
Navigation: One NWS-2.

Sonar: PMS 26 to be fitted during conversion.

4 "HVIDBJØRNEN" CLASS

Name	No.	Builders	Laid down	Launched	Commissioned
FYLLA	F 351	Aalborg Vaerft	27 June 1962	18 Dec 1962	10 July 1963
HVIDBJØRNEN	F 348	Aarhus Flydedok	4 June 1961	23 Nov 1961	15 Dec 1962
INGOLF	F 350	Svendborg Vaerft	5 Dec 1961	27 July 1962	27 July 1963
VAEDDEREN	F 349	Aalborg Vaerft	30 Oct 1961	6 Apr 1962	19 Mar 1963

Displacement, tons: 1 345 standard; 1 650 full load
Length, feet (metres): 219·8 (67·0) pp; 238·2 (72·6) oa
Beam, feet (metres): 38·0 (11·6)
Draught, feet (metres): 16 (4·9)
Aircraft: 1 Alouette III helicopter
Gun: 1—3 in (76 mm)
Main engines: 4 GM 16—567C diesels; 6 400 bhp; 1 shaft
Speed, knots: 18
Range, miles: 6 000 at 13 knots
Complement: 75

Ordered in 1960-61. Of frigate type for fishery protection and surveying duties in the North Sea, Faroe Islands and Greenland waters. They are equipped with a helicopter platform aft.

Radar: Search: One AWS 1/CWS 2.
Tactical: One NWS 1.

Sonar: PMS 26.

INGOLF   1974, Royal Danish Navy

1 MODIFIED "HVIDBJØRNEN" CLASS

Name	No.	Builders	Laid down	Launched	Commissioned
BESKYTTEREN	F 340	Aalborg Vaerft	15 Dec 1974	27 May 1975 (Delayed)	27 Feb 1976

Displacement, tons: 1 970 full load
Length, feet (metres): 244 (74·4) oa
Beam, feet (metres): 39 (11·8)
Draught, feet (metres): 15 (4·5)
Aircraft: 1 Alouette III helicopter
Gun: 1—76 mm OTO Melara
Main engines: 3 B.W. Alpha diesels; 7 440 bhp; 1 shaft
Speed, knots: 18
Range, miles: 4 500 at 16 knots on 2 engines; 6 000 at 13 knots on 1 engine
Complement: 60

Cost approx £5 million. Strengthened for navigation in ice. Designed for similar duties as *Hvidbjørnen.*

Radar: Search; One AWS 1/CWS 2.
Tactical: One NWS 1.
Navigation: One NWS 2.

Sonar: PMS 26.

BESKYTTEREN   1976, Royal Danish Navy

CORVETTES

3 NEW CONSTRUCTION "KV 72" CLASS

Displacement, tons: 1 320 full load
Length, feet (metres): 275 oa (84)
Beam, feet (metres): 33·8 (10·3)
Draught, feet (metres): 10·1 (3·1)
Missiles: Sea Sparrow; (8 cell); 8 Harpoon (2 quad by funnel)
Gun: 1—76 mm OTO Melara
A/S weapons: Uncertain
Mines: Have laying capability
Main engines: CODOG 1 Rolls Royce Olympus; 25 400 hp; 2 MTU 20 V—956 diesels; 4 800 hp at 1 500 revs, 6 000 for short periods; SSS clutches; GEC gearbox; 2 shafts.
Speed, knots: 28
Complement: 90

First of a class which is planned eventually to reach a total of 6. Designed to replace "Triton" class and, possibly, "Peder Skram" class.
YARD Glasgow designed the class to Danish order. Three Danish shipyards were asked to tender in early 1975 (Helsingør, Lindø and Aalborg). On 5 Dec 1975 announced that first three would be built by Aalborg Vaerft. Long lead items ordered immediately for keel laying in early 1977.

Radar: Plessey AWS 5.

"KV 72" Class

3 "TRITON" CLASS

Name	No.	Builders	Laid down	Launched	Commissioned
BELLONA	F 344	Naval Meccanica, Castellammare	1954	9 Jan 1955	31 Jan 1957
FLORA	F 346	Cantiere del Tirreno, Riva Trigoso	1953	25 June 1955	28 Aug 1956
TRITON	F 347	Cantiere Navali di Taranto	1953	12 Sep 1954	10 Aug 1955

Displacement, tons: 760 standard; 873 full load
Length, feet (metres): 242·8 (74·0) pp; 250·3 (76·3) oa
Beam, feet (metres): 31·5 (9·6)
Draught, feet (metres): 9 (2·7)
Guns: 2—3 in (76 mm); 1—40 mm
A/S: 2 hedgehogs; 4 DCT
Main engines: 2 Ansaldo Fiat 409T diesels, 4 400 bhp; 2 shafts
Speed, knots: 20
Range, miles: 3 000 at 18 knots
Complement: 110

These were built in Italy for the Danish Navy under the United States "offshore" account. Sisters of the Italian "Albatros" class. Diana deleted 1974.

Classification: Officially classified as corvettes in 1954, but have "F" pennant numbers.

Radar: Search: Plessey AWS 1. Navigation: E Band.

Sonar: QCU-2.

FLORA   1974, Royal Danish Navy

SUBMARINES

Note: Denmark is planning to build six new submarines. It is likely that these will eventually be of the same design as the German/Norwegian Type 210 of about 750 tons. First informal contacts have already been made.

2 "NARHVALEN" CLASS

Name	No.	Builders	Laid down	Launched	Commissioned
NARHVALEN	S 320	Royal Dockyard, Copenhagen	16 Feb 1965	10 Sep 1968	27 Feb 1970
NORDKAPEREN	S 321	Royal Dockyard, Copenhagen	20 Jan 1966	18 Dec 1969	22 Dec 1970

Displacement, tons: 370 surfaced; 450 dived
Length, feet (metres): 144·4 (44·3)
Beam, feet (metres): 15 (4·6)
Draught, feet (metres): 12·5 (3·8)
Torpedo tubes: 8—21 in (533 mm) bow
Main machinery: 2 MB Diesels; 1 500 bhp surfaced; 2 electric motors; 1 500 bhp dived
Speed, knots: 12 surfaced; 17 dived
Complement: 22

These coastal submarines are similar to the German Improved Type 205 and were built under licence at the Royal Dockyard, Copenhagen with modifications for Danish needs. Active and passive sonar.

NARHVALEN   1974, Royal Danish Navy

4 "DELFINEN" CLASS

Name	No.	Builders	Laid down	Launched	Commissioned
DELFINEN	S 326	Royal Dockyard, Copenhagen	1 July 1954	4 May 1956	16 Sep 1958
SPAEKHUGGEREN	S 327	Royal Dockyard, Copenhagen	1 Dec 1954	20 Feb 1957	27 June 1959
TUMLEREN	S 328	Royal Dockyard, Copenhagen	22 May 1956	22 May 1958	15 Jan 1960
SPRINGEREN	S 329	Royal Dockyard, Copenhagen	3 Jan 1961	26 Apr 1963	22 Oct 1964

Displacement, tons: 550 standard; 595 surfaced; 643 dived
Length, feet (metres): 117·2 (54·0)
Beam, feet (metres): 15·4 (4·7)
Draught, feet (metres): 13·1 (4·0)
Torpedo tubes: 4—21 in (533 mm)
Main machinery: 2 Burmeister & Wain diesels; 1 200 bhp surfaced; electric motors; 1 200 hp dived
Speed, knots: 15 surfaced and dived
Range, miles: 4 000 at 8 knots
Complement: 33

Active and passive sonar.

TUMLEREN   1975, Royal Danish Navy

LIGHT FORCES

10 "WILLEMOES" CLASS (FAST ATTACK CRAFT—MISSILE)

Name	No.	Builders	Commissioned
BILLE	P 540	Frederikshavn V and F	Mar 1976
BREDAL	P 541	Frederikshavn V and F	Late 1976
HAMMER	P 542	Frederikshavn V and F	1976
HUITFELDE	P 543	Frederikshavn V and F	—
KRIEGER	P 544	Frederikshavn V and F	—
NORBY	P 545	Frederikshavn V and F	—
RODSTEEN	P 546	Frederikshavn V and F	—
SEHESTED	P 547	Frederikshavn V and F	—
SUENSON	P 548	Frederikshavn V and F	—
WILLEMOES	P 549	Frederikshavn V and F	7 Oct 1975 (trials)

WILLEMOES   1975, Royal Danish Navy

Displacement, tons: 240 full load
Dimensions, feet (metres): 151 × 24 × 8 *(46 × 7·4 × 2·4)*
Missiles: 4 or 8 Harpoon (in place of after torpedo tubes)
Gun: 1—76 mm OTO Melara
Torpedo tubes: 2 or 4—21 in (see notes)
Main engines: CODAG arrangement of 3 Rolls Royce Proteus gas turbines; 12 000 hp; diesels for cruising on wing shafts; 8000 hp; Cp propellers.
Speed, knots: 40 (12 on diesels).
Complement: 24 (6 officers, 18 ratings).

Designed by Lürssen to Danish order. Very similar to Swedish "Spica II" class (also Lürssen). Original order to Frederikshavn for 4 boats, increased to 8 and finally 10. Total of 24 is planned. Building dates: *Willemoes* (prototype) laid down 20 July 1974, launched 5 Oct 1974 and completed for trials (with 4 torpedo tubes and no missiles) in 7 Oct 1975. Series production with *Bille* in 1974. She was launched 26 Mar 1976. Further boats laid down 12 Oct 1974, 14 Dec 1974 (?) and 17 Feb 1975. If this rate was maintained all should have been laid down by Mid 1976.

Missiles: The total of Harpoon launchers fitted is not certain.

Radar: Warning combined: One.
Fire control: One.
Navigation: One NWS 3.

6 "SØLØVEN" CLASS (FAST ATTACK CRAFT—TORPEDO)

Name	No.	Builders	Commissioned
SØLØVEN	P 510	Vosper	12 Feb 1965
SØRIDDEREN	P 511	Vosper	10 Feb 1965
SØBJORNEN	P 512	R. Dockyard, Copenhagen	Sep 1965
SØHESTEN	P 513	R. Dockyard, Copenhagen	June 1966
SØHUNDEN	P 514	R. Dockyard, Copenhagen	Dec 1966
SØULVEN	P 515	R. Dockyard, Copenhagen	Mar 1967

SØHUNDEN   1974, Royal Danish Navy

Displacement, tons: 95 standard; 114 full load
Dimensions, feet (metres): 90 pp; 96 wl; 99 oa × 25·5 × 7 *(30·3 × 7·3 × 2·2)*
Guns: 2—40 mm Bofors
Torpedo tubes: 4—21 in
Main engines: 3 Bristol Siddeley Proteus gas turbines; 3 shafts; 12 750 bhp = 54 knots GM diesels on wing shafts for cruising = 10 knots
Range, miles: 400 at 46 knots
Complement: 29

The design is a combination of the Vosper "Brave" class hull form and "Ferocity" type construction. *Søløven* and *Søridderen* were both completed in June 1964 and handed over to the RDN after 6 month's trials.

Radar: One NWS 1.

4 "FALKEN" CLASS (FAST ATTACK CRAFT—TORPEDO)

Name	No.	Builders	Commissioned
FALKEN	P 506	R. Dockyard, Copenhagen	4 Oct 1962
GLENTEN	P 507	R. Dockyard, Copenhagen	15 Dec 1962
GRIBBEN	P 508	R. Dockyard, Copenhagen	26 Apr 1963
HØGEN	P 509	R. Dockyard, Copenhagen	6 June 1963

HØGEN   1974, Royal Danish Navy

Displacement, tons: 119
Dimensions, feet (metres): 118 × 17·8 × 6 *(35·9 × 5·4 × 1·8)*
Guns: 1—40 mm; 1—20 mm
Torpedo tubes: 4—21 in
Main engines: 3 MTU diesels; 3 shafts; 9 000 bhp = 40 knots
Complement: 23

Ordered under US offshore procurement in the Military Aid Programme. All laid down in 1961-62.

Radar: One NSW 1.

9 "DAPHNE" CLASS (LARGE PATROL CRAFT)

Name	No.	Builders	Commissioned
DAPHNE	P 530	R. Dockyard, Copenhagen	19 Dec 1961
DRYADEN	P 531	R. Dockyard, Copenhagen	4 Apr 1962
HAVFRUEN	P 533	R. Dockyard, Copenhagen	20 Dec 1962
HAVMANDEN	P 532	R. Dockyard, Copenhagen	30 Aug 1962
NAJADEN	P 534	R. Dockyard, Copenhagen	26 Apr 1963
NEPTUN	P 536	R. Dockyard, Copenhagen	18 Dec 1963
NYMFEN	P 535	R. Dockyard, Copenhagen	4 Oct 1963
RAN	P 537	R. Dockyard, Copenhagen	15 May 1964
ROTA	P 538	R. Dockyard, Copenhagen	20 Jan 1965

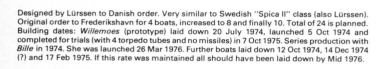

Displacement, tons: 170
Dimensions, feet (metres): 121·3 × 20 × 6·5 *(38 × 6·8 × 2)* (P 530-533)
Gun: 1—40 mm plus 2—51 mm flare launchers
A/S weapons: DCs
Main engines: 2 FD6 Foden diesels; 2 shafts; 2 600 bhp = 20 knots (plus 1 cruising engine; 100 bhp)
Complement: 23

4 were built under US offshore programme. Some have been disarmed.

Design: P 530-533 have a rounded stern and P 534-538 have a straight stern.

Radar: One NWS 3.

Sonar: PMS 26.

NEPTUN   1974, Royal Danish Navy

2 "AGDLEQ" CLASS (LARGE PATROL CRAFT)

Name	No.	Builders	Commissioned
AGDLEQ	Y 386	Svendborg Vaerft	12 Mar 1974
AGPA	Y 387	Svendborg Vaerft	14 May 1974

Displacement, tons: 300
Dimensions, feet (metres): 101·7 × 25·3 × 10·9 *(31 × 7·7 × 3·3)*
Guns: 2—20 mm
Speed, knots: 12
Complement: 15

Designed for service off Greenland.

Radar: Navigation: Two NWS 3.

AGDLEQ   1974, Royal Danish Navy

9 "BARSØ" CLASS (LARGE PATROL CRAFT)

Name	No.	Builders	Commissioned
BARSØ	Y 300	Svendborg Vaerft	1969
DREJØ	Y 301	Svendborg Vaerft	1969
ROMSØ	Y 302	Svendborg Vaerft	1969
SAMSØ	Y 303	Svendborg Vaerft	1969
THURØ	Y 304	Svendborg Vaerft	1969
VEJRØ	Y 305	Svendborg Vaerft	1969
FARØ	Y 306	Svendborg Vaerft	1972
LAESØ	Y 307	Svendborg Vaerft	1973
ROMØ	Y 308	Svendborg Vaerft	1973

Displacement, tons: 155
Dimensions, feet (metres): 83·7 × 19·7 × 9·8 *(25·5 × 6 × 2·8)*
Guns: 2—20 mm
Speed: 11 knots

Rated as patrol cutters.

Radar: One NWS 3.

DREJØ   1974, Royal Danish Navy

2 "MAAGEN" CLASS (LARGE PATROL CRAFT)

Name	No.	Builders	Commissioned
MAAGEN	Y 384	Helsingør Dockyard	May 1960
MALLEMUKKEN	Y 385	Helsingør Dockyard	May 1960

Displacement, tons: 190
Dimensions, feet (metres): 88·5 × 21·7 × 9·5 *(37 × 6·6 × 2·9)*
Gun: 1—40 mm
Main engines: 385 hp; 1 shaft = 11 knots

Of steel construction. Laid down 15 Jan 1960.

Radar: Two NWS 3.

MAAGEN   1976, Royal Danish Navy

1 "TEJSTEN" CLASS (LARGE PATROL CRAFT)

Name	No.	Builders	Commissioned
TEJSTEN	Y 383	Holbaek Skibsbyggeri	1951

Displacement, tons: 130
Dimensions, feet (metres): 82 × 20·7 × 9·4 *(25 × 6·1 × 2·9)*
Main engines: Alfa Diesel; 180 bhp = 9 knots

Auxiliary ketch of wooden construction. Based in Faeroe Is.

2 LARGE BOTVED TYPE (COASTAL PATROL CRAFT)

Y 375   Y 376

Displacement, tons: 12
Dimensions, feet (metres): 42·9 × 14·8 × 3·7 *(13·3 × 4·5 × 1·1)*
Main engines: Diesel; 2 shafts; 680 hp = 26 knots

Built in 1974 by Botved Boats

Radar: One NWS 3.

Y 376   1975, Royal Danish Navy

3 SMALL BOTVED TYPE (COASTAL PATROL CRAFT)

Y 377   **Y 378**   **Y 379**

Displacement, tons: 9
Dimensions, feet (metres): 32·1 × 10·4 × 3·1 *(9·8 × 3·3 × 0·9)*
Main engines: Diesels; 2 shafts; 500 hp = 27 knots

Built in 1975 by Botved Boats.

Radar: One NWS 3.

Small BOTVED Type   *1975, Royal Danish Navy*

3 Y TYPE (COASTAL PATROL CRAFT)

Y 338   **Y 339**   **Y 343**

Miscellaneous patrol cutters (ex-fishing vessels) all built in 1944-45.

6 "MHV 90" CLASS (COASTAL PATROL CRAFT)

MHV 90   **MHV 91**   **MHV 92**   **MHV 93**   **MHV 94**   **MHV 95**

Displacement, tons: 90
Dimensions, feet (metres): 64·9 × 18·7 × 8·2 *(19·8 × 5·7 × 2·5)*
Gun: 1—20 mm
Main engines: Diesel; 1 shaft = 10 knots

Built in 1975. Manned by Naval Home Guard.

Radar: One NWS 3.

MHV 93   *1975, Royal Danish Navy*

6 "MHV 80" CLASS (COASTAL PATROL CRAFT)

Name	No.	Builders	Commissioned
ASKØ (ex-Y 386, ex-M 560, ex-MS 2)	MHV 81	Denmark	1941
BAAGØ (ex-Y 387, ex-M 561, ex-MS 3)	MHV 84	Denmark	1941
ENØ (ex-Y 388, ex-M 562, ex-MS 5)	MHV 82	Denmark	1941
HJORTØ (ex-Y 389, ex-M 564, ex- MS 7)	MHV 85	Denmark	1941
LYØ (ex-Y 390, ex-M 565, ex-MS 8)	MHV 86	Denmark	1941
MANØ (ex-Y 391, ex-M 566, ex-MS 9)	MHV 83	Denmark	1941

Displacement, tons: 74
Dimensions, feet (metres): 78·8 × 21 × 5 *(24·4 × 4·9 × 1·6)*
Gun: 1—20 mm
Main engines: Diesel; 1 shaft; 350 bhp = 11 knots

Of wooden construction. All launched in 1941. Former inshore minesweepers. Manned by the Naval Home Guard.

Radar: One NWS 3.

"MHV 80" Class   *1974, Royal Danish Navy*

3 "MHV 70" CLASS (COASTAL PATROL CRAFT)

Name	No.	Builders	Commissioned
MHV 70	—	R. Dockyard, Copenhagen	1958
MHV 71	—	R. Dockyard, Copenhagen	1958
MHV 72	—	R. Dockyard, Copenhagen	1958

Displacement, tons: 76
Dimensions, feet (metres): 65·9 × 16·7 × 8·2 *(20·1 × 5·1 × 2·5)*
Gun: 1—20 mm
Main engines: 200 bhp = 10 knots

Patrol boats and training craft for the Naval Home Guard. Formerly designated DMH, but allocated MHV numbers in 1969.

Radar: One NWS 3.

In addition there are some 20 small vessels of the trawler and other types—including MHV 53 and 64.

MHV 71   *1974, Royal Danish Navy*

MINE WARFARE FORCES

4 "FALSTER" CLASS MINELAYERS

Name	No.	Builders	Commissioned
FALSTER	N 80	Nakskov Skibsvaerft	7 Nov 1963
FYEN	N 81	Frederikshavn Vaerft	18 Sep 1963
MØEN	N 82	Frederikshavn Vaerft	29 Apr 1964
SJAELLAND	N 83	Nakskov Skibsvaerft	7 July 1964

Displacement, tons: 1 900 full load
Length, feet (metres): 238 *(72·5)* pp; 252·6 *(77·0)* oa
Beam, feet (metres): 41 *(12·5)*
Draught, feet (metres): 10 *(3·0)*
Missiles: Seasparrow
Guns: 4—3 in *(76 mm)*, (twin US Mk 35)
Mines: 400
Main engines: 2 GM—567D 3 diesels; 4 800 shp; 2 shafts
Speed, knots: 17
Complement: 120

FALSTER   *1972, Royal Danish Navy*

Ordered in 1960-61 and launched 1962-63. All are named after Danish islands. The steel hull is flush-decked with a raking stem, a full stern and a prominent knuckle forward. The hull has been specially strengthened for ice navigation. Similar to Turkish *Nusret*.

Conversion: *Sjaelland* converted in 1976 to act as depôt ship for submarines and FAC in place of *Henrik Gerner*.

Gunnery: All mountings now fitted with shields.

Radar: Warning Combined: One CWS 2.
Fire Control: One CGS 1.
Tactical: One NWS 1.
Navigation: One NWS 2.

2 NEW CONSTRUCTION MINELAYERS "LINDORMEN" CLASS

Name	No.	Builders	Commissioned
LINDORMEN	N 43	Svendborg Vaerft	1977
LOSSEN	N 44	Svendborg Vaerft	1978

Displacement, tons: 570
Dimensions, feet (metres): 147·6 × 29·5 × 8·9 *(45 × 9 × 2·7)*
Guns: 2—20 mm
Main engines: Diesels; 1 600 hp = 14 knots
Complement: 27

Replacements for "Lougen" Class. Controlled Minelayers.

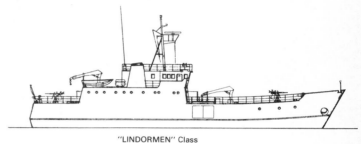

"LINDORMEN" Class

1 "LANGELAND" CLASS (COASTAL MINELAYER)

Name	No.	Builders	Commissioned
LANGELAND	N 42	Royal Dockyard, Copenhagen	1951

Displacement, tons: 310 standard; 332 full load
Dimensions, feet (metres): 133·5 oa; 128·2 pp × 23·7 × 7·2 *(40·7; 39·1 × 7·2 × 2·1)*
Guns: 2—40 mm; 2—20 mm Madsen
Main engines: Diesel; 2 shafts; 385 bhp = 11·6 knots
Complement: 37

Laid down in 1950. Launched on 17 May 1950.

LANGELAND   *1973, Royal Danish Navy*

8 "SUND" CLASS (MINESWEEPERS—COASTAL)

AARØSUND (ex-*MSC* 127) M 571		GULDBORGSUND (ex-*MSC* 257) M 575	
ALSSUND (ex-*MSC* 128) M 572		OMØSUND (ex-*MSC* 221) M 576	
EGERNSUND (ex-*MSC* 129) M 573		ULVSUND (ex-*MSC* 263) M 577	
GRØNSUND (ex-*MSC* 256) M 574		VILSUND (ex-*MSC* 264) M 578	

Displacement, tons: 350 standard; 376 full load
Dimensions, feet (metres): 138 pp; 144 oa × 27 × 8·5 *(41·5; 43 × 8 × 2·6)*
Guns: 1—40 mm or 2—20 mm
Main engines: Diesels; 2 shafts; 1 200 bhp = 13 knots
Range, miles: 2 500 at 10 knots
Complement: 35

MSC (ex-AMS) 60 class NATO coastal minesweepers all built in USA. Completed in 1954-56. *Aarøsund* was transferred on 24 Jan 1955, *Alssund* on 5 Apr 1955, *Egernsund* on 3 Aug 1955, *Grønsund* on 21 Sep 1956, *Guldborgsund* on 11 Nov 1956, *Omøsund* on 20 June 1956, *Ulvsund* on 20 Sep 1956 and *Vilsund* on 15 Nov 1956, *Guldborgsund* has been fitted with a charthouse between bridge and funnel and is employed on surveying duties.

Radar: One NWS 3.

ULVSUND   *1975, Reiner Nerlich*

SLEIPNER A 558

A 200 ton torpedo recovery/transporter.

SERVICE FORCES

TANKERS

Name	No.	Builders	Commissioned
RIMFAXE (ex-US *YO 226*)	A 568	USA	1945
SKINFAXE (ex-US *YO 229*)	A 569	USA	1945

Displacement, tons: 422 light; 1 390 full load
Dimensions, feet (metres): 174 oa × 32 × 13·2 *(53·1 × 9·8 × 4)*
Main engines: 1 GM diesel; 560 bhp = 10 knots
Complement: 23

Transferred to the Royal Danish Navy from the USA on 2 Aug 1962.

RIMFAXE   *1971, Royal Danish Navy*

ICEBREAKERS

Note: Icebreakers are controlled by the Ministry of Trade and Shipping, but are maintained by RDN at Frederikshavn in summer.

Name	No.	Builders	Commissioned
DANBJØRN	—	Lindø Vaerft	1965
ISBJØRN	—	Lindø Vaerft	1956

Displacement, tons: 3 685
Dimensions, feet (metres): 252 × 56 × 20 *(75·6 × 16·8 × 6)*
Main engines: Diesels; electric drive; 11 890 bhp = 14 knots
Complement: 34

DANBJØRN   *1976, Royal Danish Navy*

Name	No.	Builders	Commissioned
ELBJØRN	—	Frederikshavn Vaerft	1953

Displacement, tons: 893 standard; 1.400 full load
Dimensions, feet (metres): 156·5 × 40·3 × 14·5 *(47 × 12·1 × 4·4)*
Main engines: Diesels; electric drive; 3 600 bhp = 12 knots

Recently used by RDN for surveying in summer.

ROYAL YACHT

Name	No.	Builders	Commissioned
DANNEBROG	A 540	R. Dockyard, Copenhagen	1932

Displacement, tons: 1 130
Dimensions, feet (metres): 246 oa × 34 × 11·2 *(75 × 10·4 × 3·4)*
Guns: 2—37 mm
Main engines: 2 sets Burmeister & Wain 8 cylinder; 2 cycle diesels; 1 800 bhp = 14 knots
Complement: 57

Launched on 10 Oct 1931.

DANNEBROG   *1976, Royal Danish Navy*

DOMINICAN REPUBLIC

Ministerial

Minister of the Armed Forces:
  Juan Rene Beauchamps Javier

Headquarters Appointments

Chief of Naval Staff:
  Commodore Francisco J. Rivera Caminero
Vice-Chief of Naval Staff:
  Captain Francisco Ant. Marte Victoria

Personnel

(a) 1977: 3 800 officers and men
(b) Selective Military Service

Mercantile Marine

Lloyd's Register of Shipping:
  20 vessels of 8 469 tons gross

Maritime Air
(All operated by Dominican Air Force)

2 PBY-5A Catalinas
3 Alouette II/III helicopters
2 H-19 Chickasaws
7 OH-6A Cayuse
2 Hiller 12-E Ravens

Naval Bases

"Las Calderas": HQ of CNS. Naval School. Marine Training.
Haina: Naval Dockyard (Ast. Navales Dominicanos), Naval Training Centre, Supply Base and 750-ton lift marine elevator.
San Pedro de Macoris.

Strength of the Fleet

Type	Active	Projected
Frigates	3	—
Corvettes	7	—
Large Patrol Craft	2	—
Coastal Patrol Craft	13	—
LSM	1	—
LCU	1	1
Survey Vessel	1	—
Tankers (Small)	2	—
Tugs (Large)	2	—
Tugs (Harbour)	6	—

Note: Although listed as "Active" several of the major units are reported as non-operational.

DELETIONS

Destroyer

1972 *Duarte* (ex-HMS *Hotspur*)

Corvettes

1972 *Gerardo Jansen, Juan Bautista Cambiaso, Juan Bautista Maggiola* (all ex-Canadian "Flower" class)

Light Forces

1975 *Maymyon, Puerto Hemosa*

Amphibious Craft

1975 *Enriquillo*

Survey Craft

1972 *Caonobo*

Tugs

1975 *Consuelo, Haina, Santana*

FRIGATES

2 Ex-US "TACOMA" CLASS

Name
CAP. GENERAL PEDRO SANTANA
(ex-*Presidente Peynado*, ex-USS *Knoxville, PF 64*)
GREGORIO LUPERON
(ex-*Presidente Troncoso*, ex-USS *Pueblo, PF 13*)

No.	Builders	Laid down	Launched	Commissioned
453 (ex-F 104)	Kaiser S.Y. Richmond, Cal.	14 Nov 1943	20 Jan 1944	27 May 1944
452 (ex-F 103)	Leatham D. Smith S.B. Co. Wis.	15 April 1943	10 July 1943	29 April 1944

Displacement, tons: 1 430 standard; 2 415 full load
Length, feet (metres): 298·0 *(90·8)* wl; 304·0 *(92·7)* oa
Beam, feet (metres): 37·5 *(11·4)*
Draught, feet (metres): 13·7 *(4·2)*
Guns: 3—3 in *(76 mm)* single; 4—40 mm (2 twin);
   6—20 mm; 4—0·5 in *(12·7 mm)* MG (2 twin)
Main engines: Triple expansion; 2 shafts; 5 500 ihp
Boilers: 2 of three-drum type
Speed, knots: 19
Oil fuel, tons: 760
Range, miles: 9 500 at 12 knots
Complement: 140

Formerly United States patrol frigates, PF of the "Tacoma"
class similar to the contemporary British frigates of the "River"
class. Transferred from the US Navy to the Dominican Republic
Navy in July 1946 (453) and Sept 1947 (452). Renamed in 1962.

GREGORIO LUPERON   *1972, Dominican Navy*

1 Ex-CANADIAN "RIVER" CLASS

Name
MELLA (ex-*Presidente Trujillo*, ex-HMCS *Carlplace*)

No.	Builders	Laid down	Launched	Commissioned
451	Davies SB & Repairing Co., Lauzon, Canada	—	6 July 1944	1944

Displacement, tons: 1 400 standard; 2 125 full load
Length, feet (metres): 310·5 *(91·9)*
Beam, feet (metres): 36·7 *(11·2)*
Draught, feet (metres): 12·0 *(3·7)*
Guns: 1—4 in; 2—47 mm; 1—40 mm; 4—20 mm (2 twin)
Main engines: Triple expansion; 2 shafts; 5 500 ihp
Boilers: 2 of three-drum type
Speed, knots: 20
Oil fuel, tons: 645
Range, miles: 4 200 at 12 knots
Complement: 195 (15 officers, 130 ratings, 50 midshipmen)

Transferred to the Dominican Navy in 1946. Modified for use as
Presidential yacht with extra accommodation and deck-houses
built up aft. Pennant number as a frigate was F 101, but as the
Presidential yacht it was no longer worn. Now carries pennant
number 451 as training ship. Renamed *Mella* in 1962. Used for
training midshipmen.

MELLA   *1972, Dominican Navy*

CORVETTES

2 Ex-CANADIAN "FLOWER" CLASS

Name
CRISTOBAL COLON (ex-HMCS *Lachute*)
JUAN ALEJANDRO ACOSTA (ex-HMCS *Louisburg*)

No.	Builders	Laid down	Launched	Commissioned
401 (ex-C 101)	Morton Ltd, Quebec City, P.Q.	—	9 June 1944	24 Oct 1944
402 (ex-C 102)	Morton Ltd, Quebec City, P.Q.	—	13 July 1943	13 Dec 1943

Displacement, tons: 1 060 standard; 1 350 full load
Length, feet (metres): 193·0 *(58·8)* pp; 208·0 *(63·4)* oa
Beam, feet (metres): 33·0 *(10·0)*
Draught, feet (metres): 13·3 *(4·0)*
Guns: 1—4 in *(102 mm)*
  C. Colon: 2—40 mm (twin); 6—20 mm; 4—0·5 in MG (2 twin)
  J. A. Acosta: 1—40 mm; 6—20 mm; 2—0·5 in MG
Main engines: Triple expansion; 2 750 ihp
Boilers: 2 of three-drum type
Speed, knots: 16
Oil fuel, tons: 282
Range, miles: 2 900 at 15 knots
Complement: 53

Built in Canadian shipyards under the emergency construction
programme during the Second World War. Five were transferred to the Dominican Navy in 1947. Pennant numbers were
changed in 1968.

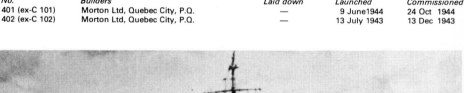

JUAN ALEJANDRO ACOSTA   *1972, Dominican Navy*

2 Ex-US "ADMIRABLE" CLASS

Name	No.	Builders	Commissioned
PRESTOL BOTELLO (ex-*Separacion*, ex-USS *Skirmish, MSF 303*)	BM 454	Associated SB	16 Aug 1943
TORTUGERO (ex-USS *Signet, MSF 302*)	BM 455	Associated SB	16 Aug 1943

Displacement, tons: 650 standard; 900 full load
Dimensions, feet (metres): 180·0 wl; 184·5 oa × 33·0 × 14·5 *(56·3 × 9·9 × 4·4)*
Guns: 1—3 in; 2—40 mm; 6—20 mm
Main engines: 2 diesels; 2 shafts; 1 710 bhp = 14 knots
Range, miles: 5 600 at 9 knots
Complement: 90 (8 officers, 82 men)

Former US fleet minesweepers. Purchased on 13 Jan 1965. *Prestol Botello* renamed early 1976.

PRESTOL BOTELLO   *USN*

3 Ex-USCG 165 ft TYPE

Name	No.	Builders	Commissioned
INDEPENDENCIA (ex-USCGC *Icarus*)	204 (ex-*P 105*)	Bath Ironworks	1932
LIBERTAD (ex-*Rafael Atoa*, ex-USCGC *Thetis*)	205 (ex-*P 106*)	—	—
RESTAURACION (ex-USCGC *Galathea*)	203 (ex-*P 104*)	John H. Machis & Co, Camden, N.J.	1933

Displacement, tons: 337 standard
Dimensions, feet (metres): 165·0 × 25·2 × 9·5 *(50·3 × 7·7 × 2·9)*
Guns: 1—3 in; 1—40 mm; 1—20 mm
Main engines: 2 Diesels; 1 280 bhp = 15 knots
Range, miles: 1 300 at 15 knots
Complement: 49 (5 officers, 44 men)

Ex-US Coastguard Cutters. All in reserve.

RESTAURACION   *1972, Dominican Navy*

LIGHT FORCES

1 US PGM TYPE (LARGE PATROL CRAFT)

Name	No.	Builders	Commissioned
BETELGEUSE (ex-US *PGM 77*)	GC 102	Peterson, USA	1966

Displacement, tons: 145·5
Dimensions, feet (metres): 101·5 × 21·0 × 5·0 *(30·9 × 6·4 × 1·5)*
Guns: 1—40 mm; 4—20 mm (2 twin); 2—0·5 in 50 cal MG
Main engines: 8 GM6-71 diesels; 2 shafts; 2 200 bhp = 21 knots
Range, miles: 1 500 at 10 knots
Complement: 20

Built in the USA and transferred to the Dominican Republic under the Military Aid Programme on 14 Jan 1966.

BETELGEUSE   *1972, Dominican Navy*

1 LARGE PATROL CRAFT

Name	No.	Builders	Commissioned
CAPITAN ALSINA (ex-*RL 101*)	GC 105	—	1944

Displacement, tons: 100 standard
Dimensions, feet (metres): 92·0 wl; 104·8 oa × 19·2 × 5·8 *(32 × 5·9 × 1·8)*
Guns: 2—20 mm
Main engines: 2 GM diesels; 2 shafts; 1 000 hp = 17 knots
Complement: 20

Of wooden construction. Launched in 1944. Named as above in 1957.

CAPITAN ALSINA

1 "ATLANTIDA" CLASS (COASTAL PATROL CRAFT)

ATLANTIDA BA 8

Probably employed on surveying duties.

4 "BELLATRIX" CLASS (COASTAL PATROL CRAFT)

Name	No.	Builders	Commissioned
BELLATRIX	GC 106	Sewart Seacraft Inc, Berwick, La.	1967
PROCYON	GC 103	Sewart Seacraft Inc, Berwick, La.	1967
CAPELLA	GC 108	Sewart Seacraft Inc, Berwick, La.	1968
ALDEBARÁN	GC 104	Sewart Seacraft Inc, Berwick, La.	1972

Displacement, tons: 60
Dimensions, feet (metres): 85 × 18 × 5 *(25·9 × 5·5 × 1·5)*
Guns: 3—5 MG
Main engines: 2 GM Diesels; 500 bhp = 18·7 knots

Transferred to the Dominican Navy by USA, *Bellatrix* on 18 Aug 1967, *Procyon* on 1 May 1967, *Capella* on 15 Oct 1968 and *Aldebarán* in May 1972.

BELLATRIX   *1970, Dominican Navy*

1 COASTAL PATROL CRAFT

Name	No.	Builders	Commissioned
RIGEL (ex-US AVR)	GC 101		1953

Displacement, tons: 27 standard; 32·2 full load
Dimensions, feet (metres): 63·0 × 15·5 × 5·0 (19·2 × 4·7 × 1·5)
Guns: 2—50 cal MG
Main engines: General Motors V8—71 diesels = 18·5 knots
Complement: 9

Originally built in 1953. Reconditioned by NAUSTA, Key West, USA.

6 COASTAL PATROL CRAFT

Name	No.	Builders	Commissioned
CARITE	—	Ast. Navales Dominicanos	1975
ALBACORA	—	Ast. Navales Dominicanos	1975
BONITO	—	Ast. Navales Dominicanos	1975
ATÚN	—	Ast. Navales Dominicanos	1975
PICÚA	—	Ast. Navales Dominicanas	1975
MERO	—	Ast. Navales Dominicanos	1975

Displacement, tons: Approx 30
Dimensions, feet (metres): 45 × 13 × 6 (13·7 × 4 × 1·8)
Gun: 1—30 mm
Main engines: GM Diesels; 200 hp

AMPHIBIOUS FORCES

1 LCT

Name	No.	Builders	Commissioned
SAMANA (ex-LA 2)	LDM 302	Ast. Navales Dominicanos	1958

Displacement, tons: 150 standard; 310 full load
Dimensions, feet (metres): 105 wl; 119·5 oa × 36 × 3 (36·4 × 11 × 0·9)
Gun: 1—50 cal MG
Main engines: 3 General Motors diesels; 441 bhp = 8 knots
Oil fuel, tons: 80
Complement: 17

Similar characteristics to US LCT 5 Type although slightly larger.

SAMANA   1972, Dominican Navy

1 LCM

Name	No.	Builders	Commissioned
OCOA	LDM 303	Ast. Navales Dominicanos	1976

Displacement, tons: 55 full load
Dimensions, feet (metres): 56·2 × 14 × 3·9 (17·1 × 4·3 × 1·2)
Main engines: 2—6 cyl Diesels; 450 bhp = 9 knots
Range, miles: 130 at 9 knots

Capacity about 30 tons.
Same characteristics as US LCM 6 Type.

SURVEY VESSELS

(See also Atlantida under Light Forces)

3 Ex-US "COHOES" CLASS

Name	No.	Builders	Commissioned
– (ex-USS Etlah, AN 79)	P 201	Commercial Ironworks	1945
– (ex-USS Passaconaway, AN 86)	P 202	Marine SB Co	1944
– (ex-USS Passaic, AN 87)	P 206	Leatham D Smith SB Co	1944

Displacement, tons: 650 standard; 785 full load
Dimensions, feet (metres): 168·5 × 33 × 10·8 (51·4 × 10 × 3·3)
Guns: 1—3 in (76 mm); 3—20 in
Main engines: Busch Sulzer diesel-electric; 1 200 shp = 12 knots
Complement: 48

Ex-netlayers in reserve in USA since 1963. Transferred by sale 29 Sep 1976.

Name	No.	Builders	Commissioned
CAPOTILLO (ex-Camillia)	FB 1	—	—

Displacement, tons: 337
Dimensions, feet (metres): 117 × 24 × 7·8 (35·7 × 7·3 × 2·4)
Main engines: 2 Diesels; 880 bhp = 10 knots
Complement: 29

Built in the United States in 1911. Acquired from the United States Coast Guard in 1949. Underwent a major refit in Dominican Republic in 1970.

Name	No.	Builders	Commissioned
NEPTUNO (ex-Toro)	BA 10	John H. Mathis Co, New Jersey	Feb 1954

Measurement, tons: 67·1 (net)
Dimensions, feet (metres): 64 × 18·7 × 8 (19·5 × 5·7 × 2·4)
Main engines: 2 Diesels = 12·5 knots

NEPTUNO   1975, Dominican Navy

TANKERS

2 Ex-US OIL BARGES

Name	No.	Builders	Commissioned
CAPITAN W. ARVELO (ex-US YO 213)	—	Ira S. Bushey Inc, Brooklyn	1943
CAPITAN BEOTEGUI (ex-US YO 215)	—	Ira S. Bushey Inc, Brooklyn	1945

Displacement, tons: 1 076 full load
Dimensions, feet (metres): 156·3 × 30 × 13·0 (47·7 × 9·1 × 4)
Gun: 1—20 mm
Main engines: 2 Union diesels; 525 bhp = 8 knots
Capacity: 6 071 barrels
Complement: 27

Former United States self-propelled fuel oil barges. Lent by the USA in April 1964.

TUGS

1 Ex-US "CHEROKEE" CLASS

Name	No.	Builders	Commissioned
MACORIX (ex-USS *Kiowa ATF 72*)	RM 21	—	1942

Displacement, tons: 1 235 standard; 1 675 full load
Dimensions, feet (metres): 195 wl; 205 oa × 38·5 × 15·5 *(62·5 × 11·7 × 4·7)*
Gun: 1—3 in 50 cal
Main engines: Diesel-electric; 1 shaft; 3 000 bhp = 15 knots
Complement: 85

Carries additional salvage equipment. Transferred 16 Oct 1972.

Radar: AN/SPS-5D.

MACORIX　　　　　　　　　　　　　　　　1975, Dominican Navy

1 Ex-US "SOTOYOMO" CLASS

Name	No.	Builders	Commissioned
CAONABO (ex-USS *Sagamore ATA 208*)	RM 18	—	1944

Displacement, tons: 534 standard; 835 full load
Dimensions, feet (metres): 143 oa × 33·9 × 13 *(43·6 × 10·3 × 4)*
Main engines: 2 GM diesel-electric; 1 shaft; 1 500 bhp = 13 knots

Transferred 1 Feb 1972.

Radar: AN/SPS-5D.

CAONABO　　　　　　　　　　　　　　　　1975, Dominican Navy

2 "HERCULES" CLASS

Name	No.	Builders	Commissioned
HERCULES (ex-*R 2*)	RP 12	Ast. Navales Dominicanos	1960
GUACANAGARIX (ex-*R 5*)	RP 13	Ast. Navales Dominicanos	1960

Displacement, tons: 200 (approx)
Dimensions, feet (metres): 70·0 × 15·6 × 9·0 *(21·4 × 4·8 × 2·7)*
Main engines: 1 Caterpillar motor; 500 hp; 1 225 rpm
Complement: 8 to 11

4 HARBOUR TUGS

BOHECHIO RP 16　　　　　　**MAGUANA** (ex-*R 10*) RP 14
CALDERAS RP 19　　　　　　**ISABELA** (ex-*R 1*) RP 20

Small tugs for harbour and coastal use. Not all of uniform type and dimensions. *Bohechio* of US YTL 600 type, transferred Jan 1971.

MISCELLANEOUS

1 Ex-US LSM

Name	No.	Builders	Commissioned
SIRIO (ex-US *LSM 483*)	BDM 301 (ex-*BA 104*)	Brown SB Co, Houston	13 April 1945

Displacement, tons: 734 standard; 1 100 full load
Dimensions, feet (metres): 196 wl; 203·5 oa × 34 × 10 *(62·1 × 10·4 × 3·1)*
Main engines: 2 General Motors diesels; 2 shafts; 1 800 bhp = 14 knots
Oil fuel, tons: 164
Complement: 30

Laid down on 17 Feb 1945, launched on 10 Mar 1945. Transferred to the Dominican Navy in Mar 1958. Refitted in Dominican Republic in 1970. Now decked over and used for commercial logistic service. Included because of capability in emergency.

SIRIO　　　　　　　　　　　　　　　　1968, Dominican Navy

DUBAI

(See United Arab Emirates)
These craft operate with the Union Coast Guard (Border Guard)

1 FAIREY MARINE "SPEAR" CLASS (MK 1)
(COASTAL PATROL CRAFT)

Dimensions, feet (metres): 29·8 × 9·2 × 2·6 *(9·1 × 2·8 × 0·8)*
Guns: 2—7·62 mm MGs
Main engines: 2 Perkins diesels; 290 hp = 25 knots
Complement: 3

Delivered Nov 1974.

1 FAIREY MARINE "INTERCEPTOR" CLASS

25 ft *(7·6 metres)* craft with catamaran hull. Powered by twin 135 hp outboard motors—speed 3 knots. Can carry a platoon of soldiers or 8 life-rafts.

ECUADOR

Ministerial

Minister of Defence:
  General Andres Arrata Macias

Headquarters Appointment

Commander-in-Chief of the Navy:
  Vice Admiral Alfredo Poveda Burbano

Diplomatic Representation

Naval Attaché in Bonn:
  Captain Ethiel Rodriguez
Naval and Air Attaché in London:
  Colonel Alfonso Villagomez
Naval Attaché in Washington:
  Captain Fausto Cevallos V

Personnel

a) 1977. Total 3 800 (300 officers and 3 500 men)
b) Two years selective National Service

Naval Bases

Guayaquil (main naval base).
San Lorenzo and Galapagos Island (small bases).

Establishments

The Naval Academy is in Guayaquil

Maritime Air

Air Force planes working with the Navy.

2 Alouette III helicopters
1 IAI Arava
1 Cessna 320E
1 Cessna 177
2 Cessna T 337 F/G
2 Cessna T-41D/172H

Naval Infantry

A small force of naval infantry (700 men) exists of which a detachment is based on the Galapagos Islands and in the Eastern area.

Prefix to Ships' Names

BAE

Strength of the Fleet

Type	Active	Building
Frigates	3	—
Corvettes	2	—
Patrol Submarines	—	2
Fast Attack Craft (Missile)	3	—
Fast Attack Craft (Torpedo)	3	—
Large Patrol Craft	2	—
Coastal Patrol Craft	5	—
LSMs	2	—
Survey Vessels	2	—
Tugs	4	—
Supply Ship (Small)	1	—
Floating Dock	1	—
Miscellaneous	4	—
Sail Training Ship	1	—

New Construction

The Ecuadorian Navy, after considering the purchase of two "Whitby" class frigates from UK is now investigating new construction frigates.

Mercantile Marine

Lloyd's Register of Shipping:
  46 vessels of 180 623 tons gross

DELETIONS

Frigate

1972 *Guayas* (ex-US PF Type)

Light Forces

1976 LSP 4, 5 and 6

PENNANT LIST

Frigates

D 01	Morán Valverde
D 02	Presidente Alfaro
D 03	Presidente Velasco Ibarra

Corvettes

| P 21 | Esmeraldas |
| P 23 | Manabi |

Submarines

| S 11 | Shiry |
| S 12 | Huancavilca |

Light Forces

LC 61	24 De Mayo
LC 62	25 De Julio
LM 31	Quito
LM 32	Guayaquil
LM 33	Cuenca
LP 81	10 De Agosto
LP 82	9 De Octubre
LP 83	3 De Noviembre
LT 41	Manta
LT 42	Tulcan
LT 43	Nuevo Rocafuerte

Amphibious Forces

| T 51 | Jambeli |
| T 52 | Tarqui |

Survey Vessels

| O 111 | Orion |
| O 112 | Rigel |

Tugs

R 101	Cayambe
R 102	Sangay
R 103	Cotopaxi
R 104	Antizana

Miscellaneous

BE 01	Guayas
DF 121	Amazonas
BT 123	Putumayo
T 53	Calicuchima
T 62	Atahualpa
UT 111	Isla de la Plata
UT 112	Isla Puná

FRIGATES

1 Ex-US "CHARLES LAWRENCE" CLASS

Name	No.	Builders	Laid down	Launched	Commissioned
MORAN VALVERDE (ex-USS *Enright*, APD 66, ex-*DE 216*, ex-*Veinticinco de Julio*)	D 01 (ex-E 12)	Philadelphia Navy Yard	22 Feb 1943	29 May 1943	21 Sep 1943

Displacement, tons: 1 400 standard; 2 130 full load
Dimensions, feet (metres): 306·0 oa × 37·0 × 12·6 *(93·3 × 11·3 × 3·8)*
Guns: 1—5 in 38 cal; 4—40 mm
A/S weapons: DC racks
Main engines: GE geared turbines with electric drive; 2 shafts; 12 000 shp = 23 knots
Boilers: 2 "D" Express
Range, miles: 2 000 at 23 knots
Complement: 204

Former US high speed transport (APD, modified destroyer escort). Transferred to Ecuador on 14 July 1967 under MAP. Can carry 162 troops.

Radar: AN/SPS 6 and SPS 10.

MORAN VALVERDE (Now D 01)

1968, Ecuadorian Navy

2 Ex-BRITISH "HUNT" CLASS (TYPE 1)

Name	No.	Builders	Laid down	Launched	Commissione
PRESIDENTE ALFARO (ex-HMS *Quantock*)	D 02 (ex-D 01)	Scotts S.B. & Eng Co Ltd, Greenock	26 July 1939	22 Apr 1940	6 Feb 1941
PRESIDENTE VELASCO IBARRA (ex-HMS *Meynell*)	D 03 (ex-D 02)	Swan Hunter & Wigham Richardson, Wallsend	10 Aug 1939	7 June1940	30 Dec 1940

Displacement, tons: 1 000 standard; 1 490 full load
Length, feet (metres): 272·3 *(83·0)* pp; 280 *(85·4)* oa
Beam, feet (metres): 29 *(8·8)*
Draught, feet (metres): 14 *(4·3)*
Guns: 4—4 in *(102 mm)*; 2—40 mm (twin); 2—20 mm
A/S weapons: DC throwers, DC racks
Main engines: Parsons geared turbines (by Wallsend Slipway in *Presidente Velasco Ibarra*); 19 000 shp; 2 shafts
Boilers: 2 Admiralty 3-drum
Speed, knots: 23
Oil fuel, tons: 280
Range, miles: 2 000 at 12 knots
Complement: 146

"Hunt" class. Type 1, purchased by Ecuador from Great Britain on 18 Oct 1954, and refitted by J. Samuel White & Co. Ltd, Cowes, Isle of Wight. *Quantock* was taken over by the Ecuadorian Navy in Portsmouth Dockyard on 16 Aug 1955, when she was renamed *Presidente Alfaro*. Sister ship *Meynell* was transferred to the Ecuadorian Navy and renamed *Presidente Velasco Ibarra* in Aug 1955.
Due for disposal

PRESIDENTE ALFARO (now D 02)　　　　　　　　　　1970, Ecuadorian Nav

CORVETTES

2 Ex-US PCE TYPE

Name	No.	Builders	Laid down	Launched	Commissione
ESMERALDAS (ex-USS *Eunice*, PCE 846)	P 22 (ex-E 22, ex-E 03)	USA	—	—	4 Mar 1944
MANABI (ex-USS *Pascagoula*, PCE 874)	P 23 (ex-E 23, ex-E 02)	USA	—	—	31 Dec 1943

Displacement, tons: 640 standard; 903 full load
Dimensions, feet (metres): 180 wl; 184·5 oa × 33 × 9·5 *(56·3 × 10 × 2·9)*
Guns: 1—3 in; 6—40 mm
A/S weapons: 4 DCT; 2 DC Racks; hedgehog
Main engines: GM diesels; 2 shafts; 1 800 bhp = 15·4 knots
Range, miles: 4 300 at 10 knots
Complement: 100 officers and men

Former United States patrol vessels (180 ft Escorts). Transferred on 29 Nov and 5 Dec 1960 respectively.

MANABI　　　　　　　　　　　　　　　　　　　　　197

SUBMARINES

2 TYPE 209

Name	No.	Builders	Laid down	Launched	Commissione
SHYRI	S 11	Howaldtswerke, Kiel	1975	8 Oct 1976	1977
HUANCAVILCA	S 12	Howaldtswerke, Kiel	1975	—	1977

Displacement, tons: 980 surfaced; 1 356 dived
Dimensions, feet (metres): 183·4 × 20·5 × 17·9 *(55·9 × 6·3 × 5·4)*
Torpedo tubes: 8—21 in (bow) with reloads
Main machinery: Diesel-electric; MTU diesels; 4 generators; 1 shaft; 5 000 shp
Speed, knots: 10 surfaced; 22 dived
Complement: 32

Ordered in 1974. Two more reported ordered.

LIGHT FORCES

3 LÜRSSEN TYPE (FAST ATTACK CRAFT—MISSILE)

Name	No.	Builders	Commissioned
QUITO	LM 31	Lürssen, Vegesack	Aug 1976
GUAYAQUIL	LM 32	Lürssen, Vegesack	Dec 1976
CUENCA	LM 33	Lürssen, Vegesack	Mar 1976

Displacement, tons: 255
Dimensions, feet (metres): 147·6 × 23 × 12·8 *(45 × 7 × 3·9)*
Missiles: 4—MM 38 Exocet
Guns: 1—76 mm; 2—35 mm
Main engines: 4 MTU Diesels; 14 000 hp; 4 shafts = 40 knots
Range, miles: 700 at 40 knots; 1 800 at 16 knots
Complement: 35

Launched—*Quito*, 20 Nov 1975; *Guayaquil* and *Cuenca* 1976.

3 "MANTA" CLASS (FAST ATTACK CRAFT—TORPEDO)

Name	No.	Builders	Commissioned
MANTA	LT 41	Lürssen, Vegesack	11 June1971
TULCAN	LT 42	Lürssen, Vegesack	2 Apr 1971
NUEVO ROCAFUERTE	LT 43	Lürssen, Vegesack	23 June1971

Displacement, tons: 119 standard; 134 full load
Dimensions, feet (metres): 119·4 × 19·1 × 6·0 *(36 × 5·8 × 1·7)*
Guns: 1—40 mm; 1—twin Oerlikon unguided rocket launcher
Torpedo tubes: 2—21 inch
Main engines: 3 MTU diesels; 3 shafts; 9 000 bhp = 35 knots
Range, miles: 700 at 30 knots; 1 500 at 15 knots
Complement: 19

Similar design to the Chilean "Guacoida" Class with an extra diesel—3 knots faster. *Manta* launched 8 Sep 1970.

MANTA (old Pennant number) 1972, Ecuadorian Navy

2 US "PGM-71" CLASS (LARGE PATROL CRAFT)

Name	No.	Builders	Commissioned
25 DE JULIO (ex-*Guayaquil*, ex-US PGM 76)	LC 62	Peterson, USA	1965
24 DE MAYO (ex-US *Quito* ex-US PGM 75)	LC 61	Peterson, USA	1965

Displacement, tons: 130 standard; 145·5 full load
Dimensions, feet (metres): 101·5 oa × 21 × 5 *(30·9 × 6·4 × 1·5)*
Guns: 1—40 mm; 4—20 mm (twin); 2—0·5 cal MGs
Main engines: 8 GM 6-71 diesels; 2 shafts; 2 200 bhp = 21 knots
Range, miles: 1 500 at cruising speed
Complement: 15

Transferred to the Ecuadorian Navy under MAP on 30 Nov 1965. Original names transferred to missile craft

25 DE JULIO (old pennant number) 1967, Ecuadorian Navy

3 COASTAL PATROL CRAFT

Name	No.	Builders	Commissioned
10 DE AGOSTO	LP 81	Schurenstedt, Bardenfleth	Aug 1954
9 DE OCTUBRE	LP 82	Schurenstedt, Bardenfleth	Aug 1954
3 DE NOVIEMBRE	LP 83	Schurenstedt, Bardenfleth	1955

Displacement, tons: 45 standard; 64 full load
Dimensions, feet (metres): 76·8 × 13·5 × 6·3 *(23·4 × 4·6 × 1·8)*
Guns: Light MGs
Main engines: Bohn & Kähler diesel; 2 shafts; 1 200 bhp = 22 knots
Range, miles: 550 at 16 knots
Complement: 9

Ordered in 1954.

LP Class 1963, Ecuadorian Navy

1 US 65 ft COASTAL PATROL CRAFT

Built by Halter Marine, New Orleans. Delivered 1976.

1 US 40 ft COASTAL PATROL CRAFT

Transferred 1971.

AMPHIBIOUS SHIPS

Note: ex-USS *Sutter County* (LST 1150) taken over in 1975-76.

2 Ex-US "LSM-1" CLASS

Name	No.	Builders	Commissioned
JAMBELI (ex-USS *LSM 539*)	T 51	Brown S.B. Co, Houston	1945
TARQUI (ex-USS *LSM 555*)	T 52	Charleston Navy Yard	1945

Displacement, tons: 743 beaching; 1 095 full load
Dimensions, feet (metres): 196·5 wl; 203·0 oa × 34·0 × 7·9 *(61·9 × 10·3 × 2·4)*
Guns: 2—40 mm
Range, miles: 2 500 at 12 knots
Main engines: Diesels; 2 shafts; 2 800 bhp = 12·5 knots

Jambeli was laid down on 10 May 1945, *Tarqui* was laid down on 3 Mar 1945 and launched on 22 Mar 1945. Transferred to the Ecuadorian Navy at Green Cove Springs, Florida in Nov 1958.

JAMBELI (old pennant number) 1967, Ecuadorian Navy

SURVEY VESSELS

1 Ex-US "ALOE" CLASS

Name	No.	Builders	Commissioned
ORION	O 111	Commercial Iron Works,	1941
(ex-USS *Mulberry, AN 27)*	(ex-*A 101)*	Portland, Oregon	

Displacement, tons: 560 standard; 805 full load
Dimensions, feet (metres): 146 wl; 163 oa × 30·5 × 11·8 *(49·7 × 9·3 × 3·6)*
Gun: 1—3 in
Main engines: Diesel-electric; 800 bhp = 13 knots
Complement: 35

Former United States netlayer. Launched on 26 Mar 1941. Transferred to Ecuador in Nov 1965 as loan.

RIGEL O 112

Of 50 tons, launched in 1975. Complement 10.

TUGS

1 Ex-US "CHEROKEE" CLASS

Name	No.	Builders	Commissioned
CAYAMBE	R 101	Charleston SB & DD Co	1945
(ex-USS *Cusabo, ATF 155)*	(ex-*R 51,* ex-*R 01)*		

Displacement, tons: 1 235 standard; 1 675 full load
Dimensions, feet (metres): 195 wl; 205 oa × 38·5 × 15·5 *(62·5 × 11·7 × 4·7)*
Guns: 1—3 in; 2—40 mm; 2—20 mm
Main engines: 4 diesels with electric drive; 3 000 bhp = 16·5 knots
Complement: 85

Launched on 26 Feb 1945. Fitted with powerful pumps and other salvage equipment. Transferred to Ecuador by lease on 2 Nov 1960 and renamed *Los Rios.* Again renamed *Cayambe* in 1966.

CAYAMBE (old pennant number)   *1970, Ecuadorian Navy*

Name	No.	Builders	Commissioned
SANGAY (ex-*Loja)*	R 102 (ex-*R 53)*	—	1952

Displacement, tons: 295 light; 390 full load
Dimensions, feet (metres): 107 × 26 × 14 *(32·6 × 7·9 × 4·3)*
Main engines: Fairbanks Morse diesel; speed = 12 knots

Acquired by the Ecuadorian Navy in 1964. Renamed in 1966.

Name	No.	Builders	Commissioned
COTOPAXI (ex-USS *R. T. Ellis)*	R 103 (ex-*R 52)*	Equitable Building Corpn.	1945

Displacement, tons: 150
Dimensions, feet (metres): 82 × 21 × 8 *(25 × 6·4 × 2·4)*
Main engines: Diesel; 1 shaft; 650 bhp = 9 knots

Purchased from the United States in 1947.

ANTIZANA R 104

MISCELLANEOUS

TRAINING SHIP

Name	No.	Builders	Commissioned
GUAYAS	BE 01	Ast. Celaya, Spain	Mar 1977

Measurement, tons: 934 gross
Dimensions, feet (metres): 249·9 × 34·8 × 13·4 *(76·2 × 10·6 × 4·2)*
Main engines: General Motors; 700 bhp = 10 knots

Sail training ship. Launched 23 Sep 1976.

1 Ex-US SUPPLY SHIP

Name	No.	Builders	Commissioned
CALICUCHIMA (ex-US *FS 525)*	T 53 (ex-*T 34,* ex-*T 42)*	USA	1944

Displacement, tons: 650 light; 950 full load
Dimensions, feet (metres): 176 × 32 × 14 *(53·7 × 9·8 × 4·3)*
Main engines: Diesels; 2 shafts; 500 bhp = 11 knots

Former United States small cargo ship of the Army FS type. Leased to Ecuador on 8 Apr 1963 and purchased in April 1969. Provides service to the Galapagos Islands.

2 Ex-US YP TYPE

Name	No.	Builders	Commissioned
ISLA DE LA PLATA	UT 111	USA	—
ISLA PUNA	UT 112	USA	—

Displacement, tons: 650 light; 14
Dimensions, feet (metres): 42 *(12·8)*
Main engines: One diesel

Transferred 1962. Coastguard utility boats.

1 Ex-US YR TYPE

Name	No.	Builders	Commissioned
PUTUMAYO (ex-US *YR 34)*	BT 123 (ex-*BT 62)*	USA	—

Repair barge leased July 1962.

1 Ex-US "YW" CLASS WATER CARRIER

Name	No.	Builders	Commissioned
ATAHUALPA	T 62	Leatham D. Smith SB Co.	1945
(ex-US *YW 131)*	(ex-*T 33,* ex-*T 41,* ex-*A 01)*		

Displacement, tons: 415 light; 1 235 full load
Dimensions, feet (metres): 174·0 × 32·0 × 15·0 *(53·1 × 9·8 × 4·6)*
Main engines: GM diesels; 750 bhp = 11·5 knots

Acquired by the Ecuadorian Navy on 2 May 1963.

1 Ex-US "ARD 12" CLASS FLOATING DOCK

Name	No.	Builders	Commissioned
AMAZONAS (ex-US *ARD 17)*	DF 121	USA	1944

Measurement, tons: 3 500 lifting capacity
Dimensions, feet (metres): 491·7 oa × 81·0 oa × 32·9 *(149·9 × 24·7 × 10)*

Transferred on loan on 7 Jan 1961. Suitable for docking destroyers and landing ships. Dry dock companion craft YFND 20 was leased on 2 Nov 1961.

EGYPT

Ministerial

Minister of War:
Muhammad Abd al-Ghani Jamasi

Administrative

Armed Forces Chief of Staff:
General Mohammad Ali Fahmi

Headquarters Appointment

Commander Naval Forces:
Vice-Admiral Fuad Zikry

Diplomatic Representation

Defence Attaché in London:
Brigadier M. Lotfy Abou el Kheir

Light Forces

1975 4 ''P 6'' Class
      4 ''108'' Class

Personnel

(a) 1977: 17 500 officers and men, including the Coast Guard. (Reserves of about 12 000)
(b) 3 years National Service

Bases

Alexandria, Port Said, Mersa Matru, Port Tewfik and Berenice (Ras Banas) on the Red Sea.

Coastal Defences

The Samlet missiles employed for Coastal Defence are Naval-manned.

Mercantile Marine

Lloyd's Register of Shipping:
157 vessels of 376 066 tons gross

Strength of the Fleet

Type	Active	Building
Destroyers	5	—
Frigates	3	—
Submarines (Patrol)	12	—
Fast Attack Craft (Missile)	16	—
Fast Attack Craft (Torpedo)	30	—
Large Patrol Craft	15	—
Coastal Patrol Craft	20	—
LCTs	3	—
LCUs	11	—
Minesweepers (Ocean)	10	—
Minesweepers (Inshore)	2	—
Training Ships	2	—
Tugs	2	—
Hovercraft	3	—

DELETIONS

Auxiliary

1972(?) *Nasr* (ex-HMS *Bude*) sunk as Styx target

EL FATEH

DESTROYERS

4 Ex-SOVIET ''SKORY'' CLASS

SUEZ	DIAMIETTE
AL ZAFFER	**6 OCTOBER** (ex-*Al Nasser*)

Displacement, tons: 2 600 standard; 3 500 full load
Length, feet (metres): 395·2 *(120·5)*
Beam, feet (metres): 38·7 *(11·8)*
Draught, feet (metres): 15·1 *(4·6)*
Guns: 4—5·1 in *(130 mm)* 50 cal; 2—3·4 in *(88 mm);*
8—37 mm; 4—25 mm (twins) (unmodified);
4—57 mm (quad); 4—37 mm (twins);
4—25 mm (twins) (modified)
A/S weapons: 2 DCT; 2 DC racks (unmodified)
2—12 barrelled RBU 2500;
2 DCT; 2 DC racks (modified)
Torpedo tubes: 10—21 in *(533 mm)* (quins)
Mines: 80 can be carried
Main engines: Geared turbines; 2 shafts; 60 000 shp
Boilers: 3
Speed, knots: 35
Range, miles: 4 000 at 15 knots
Complement: 260

''SKORY'' Class   1966

Launched in 1951. *Al Nasser* and *Al Zaffer* were delivered to the Egyptian Navy on 11 June 1956 at Alexandria. *Damiette* and *Suez* were delivered at Alexandria in Jan 1962. In April 1967 the original *Al Nasser* and *Damiette* were exchanged for ships with modified secondary and A/S armament which took the same names. *Al Nasser* was later renamed *6 October* to commemo-rate the Egyptian crossing of the Suez Canal in the 1973 Israeli war.

Radar: Search: Probably E/F Band.
Tactical: Probably G Band.
Fire Control: Hawk Screech.

1 Ex-BRITISH ''Z'' CLASS

Name	No.	Builders	Laid down	Launched	Commissioned
EL FATEH (ex-HMS *Zenith*)	—	Wm. Denny & Bros, Dumbarton	19 May 1942	5 June 1944	22 Dec 1944

Displacement, tons: 1 730 standard; 2 575 full load
Length, feet (metres): 350 *(106·8)* wl; 362·8 *(110·6)* oa
Beam, feet (metres): 35·7 *(10·9)*
Draught, feet (metres): 17·1 *(5·2)*
Guns: 4—4·5 in *(115 mm)*; 6—40 mm
A/S weapons: 4 DCT
Main engines: Parsons geared turbines; 2 shafts; 40 000 shp
Boilers: 2 Admiralty 3-drum
Speed, knots: 31
Oil fuel, tons: 580
Range, miles: 2 800 at 20 knots
Complement: 250

Purchased from Great Britain in 1955. Before being taken over by Egypt, *El Fateh* was refitted by John I. Thornycroft & Co Ltd, Woolston, Southampton in July 1956, subsequently moder-nised by J. S. White & Co Ltd, Cowes, completing July 1964.

Radar: Search: Type 960 Metric wavelength.
Tactical: Type 293. E/F Band. Fire Control: I Band.

EL FATEH

FRIGATES

1 Ex-BRITISH "BLACK SWAN" CLASS

Name	No.	Builders	Laid down	Launched	Commissioned
TARIQ (ex-*Malek Farouq*, ex-HMS *Whimbrel*)	555 (ex-42)	Yarrow & Co Ltd, Glasgow	31 Oct 1941	25 Aug 1942	13 Jan 1943

Displacement, tons: 1 490 standard; 1 925 full load
Length, feet (metres): 283 *(86·3)* pp; 299·5 *(91·3)* oa
Beam, feet (metres): 38·5 *(11·7)*
Draught, feet (metres): 14·0 *(4·3)*
Guns: 6—4 in *(102 mm)*; 4—40 mm; 2—20 mm
A/S weapons: 4 DCT
Main engines: Geared turbines; 2 shafts; 4 300 shp
Boilers: 2 three-drum type
Speed, knots: 19·75
Oil fuel, tons: 370
Range, miles: 4 500 at 12 knots
Complement: 180

Transferred from Great Britain in Nov 1949. Was recently to have been converted as a submarine tender—decision deferred.

TARIQ   1976, Michael D. J. Lennon

1 Ex-BRITISH "RIVER" CLASS

Name	No.	Builders	Laid down	Launched	Commissioned
RASHID (ex-HMS *Spey*)	43	Smith's Dock Co Ltd	18 July 1941	10 Dec 1941	19 May 1942

Displacement, tons: 1 490 standard; 2 216 full load
Length, feet (metres): 283 *(86·3)* pp; 301·5 *(91·9)* oa
Beam, feet (metres): 36·7 *(11·2)*
Draught, feet (metres): 14·1 *(4·3)*
Guns: 1—4 in *(102 mm)*; 2—40 mm; 6—20 mm
A/S weapons: 4 DCT
Main engines: Triple expansion; 2 shafts; 5 500 ihp
Boilers: 2 Admiralty 3-drum type
Speed, knots: 18
Range, miles: 7 700 at 12 knots
Oil fuel, tons: 640
Complement: 180

Purchased in Dec 1949. Has been operated as Submarine Support Ship.

Appearance: Was fitted with large deck-house aft.

RASHID

1 Ex-BRITISH "HUNT" CLASS

Name	No.	Builders	Laid down	Launched	Commissioned
PORT SAID (ex-*Mohamed Ali*, ex-*Ibrahim el Awal*, ex-HMS *Cottesmore*)	525 (ex-11)	Yarrow & Co Ltd, Scotstoun, Glasgow	12 Dec 1939	5 Sep 1940	29 Dec 1940

Displacement, tons: 1 000 standard; 1 490 full load
Length, feet (metres): 273 *(83·2)* wl; 280 *(85·3)* oa
Beam, feet (metres): 29 *(8·8)*
Draught, feet (metres): 15·1 *(4·3)*
Guns: 4—4 in *(103 mm)* 2—37 mm; 2—25 mm (twin); 2—·50 cal MG (twin)
A/S weapons: 2DCT
Main engines: Parsons geared turbines; 2 shafts; 19 000 shp
Boilers: 2 three-drum type
Speed, knots: 25
Range, miles: 2 000 at 12 knots
Oil fuel, tons: 280
Complement: 146

PORT SAID (ex-*Mohamed Ali*) (old pennant number)

Transferred from the Royal Navy to the Egyptian Navy in July 1950: sailed for Egypt in April 1951, after a nine months refit by J. Samuel White & Co Ltd, Cowes.

SUBMARINES

6 Ex-SOVIET "ROMEO" CLASS

744   745   765   766   +2
Displacement, tons: 1 000 surfaced; 1 600 dived
Length, feet (metres): 249·3 *(76·0)*
Beam, feet (metres): 24·0 *(7·3)*
Draught, feet (metres): 14·5 *(4·4)*
Torpedo tubes: 6—21 in *(533 mm)* bow
Main machinery: 2 Diesels; 4 000 bhp; 2 electric motors; 4 000 hp; 2 shafts
Speed, knots: 17 surfaced; 14 dived
Complement: 65

One "Romeo" was transferred to Egypt in Feb 1966. Two more replaced "Whiskeys" in May 1966 and another pair was delivered later that year. The sixth boat joined in 1969.

"ROMEO" Class   *1968, Skyfotos*

6 Ex-SOVIET "WHISKEY" CLASS

415   418   421   455   +2

Displacement, tons: 1 030 surface; 1 350 dived
Length, feet (metres): 249·6 *(76)* oa
Beam, feet (metres): 22 *(6·7)*
Draught, feet (metres): 15 *(4·6)*
Torpedo tubes: 6—21 in *(533 mm)*; 4 bow, 2 stern; 18 torpedoes or 40 mines
Main machinery: 2 diesels; 4 000 bhp; 2 electric motors; 2 500 hp
Speed, knots: 17 surfaced; 15 dived
Range, miles: 13 000 at 8 knots surfaced
Complement: 60

The first four "Whiskey" class were transferred from the Soviet Navy to the Egyptian Navy in June 1957. Three more arrived at Alexandria on 24 Jan 1958. Another was transferred to Egypt at Alexandria in Jan 1962. Two were replaced by "Romeos" in Feb 1966.
Two "Whiskey" class sailed from Alexandria to Leningrad in late 1971 under escort, being replaced the following year.

"WHISKEY" Class   *1974*

LIGHT FORCES

6 Ex-SOVIET "OSA I" CLASS (FAST ATTACK CRAFT—MISSILE)

312   324   378   +3

Displacement, tons: 165 standard; 200 full load
Dimensions, feet (metres): 128·7 × 25·1 × 5·9 *(39·3 × 7·7 × 1·8)*
Missiles: 4 launchers in two pairs abreast for SS-N-2 system
Guns: 4—30 mm (2 twin, 1 forward, 1 aft) (+2 MG in refitted craft)
Main engines: 3 diesels; 13 000 bhp = 35 knots (Italian CRM diesels in refitted craft)
Complement: 25

Reported to have been delivered to Egypt by the Soviet Navy in 1966. Four reported sunk during the Israeli War October 1973. At least four have been refitted as above.

Missiles: Some carry SA-7 Grail.

Radar: Recently refitted craft carry a new Kelvin Hughes 1006 surveillance radar and a Decca navigation radar.

"OSA I" Class   *1974, USN*

4 Ex-SOVIET "KOMAR" CLASS (FAST ATTACK CRAFT—MISSILE)

Displacement, tons: 70 standard; 80 full load
Dimensions, feet (metres): 83·7 × 19·8 × 5·0 *(25·5 × 6 × 1·5)*
Missiles: 2 launchers for SS-N-2 system
Guns: 2—25 mm
Main engines: 4 diesels; 4 shafts; 4 800 hp = 40 knots
Range, miles: 400 at 30 knots
Complement: 20

Transferred from the USSR in 1962 to 1967. One of this type was sunk by Israeli jets on 16 May 1970. Two reported sunk in Israeli War October 1973.

"KOMAR" Class   *1966, Col. Bjorn Borg*

6 EGYPTIAN "KOMAR" TYPE (FAST ATTACK CRAFT—MISSILE)

Displacement, tons: 80 full load
Dimensions, feet (metres): 84 × 20 × 5 *(25·6 × 6 × 1·5)*
Missiles: ? Otomat
Guns: ? Twin 25 mm
Main engines: 4 diesels; 4 shafts; 4 800 hp = 40 knots
Range, miles: 400 at 30 knots
Complement: ? 20

Built in Alexandria 1975—76. Hull of same design as Soviet "Komar" class and fitted with Soviet diesels. The armament is of West European manufacture.

12 Ex-SOVIET "SO I" CLASS (LARGE PATROL CRAFT)

211   217   222   229   233   236   244   255   +4

Displacement, tons: 215 light; 250 full load
Dimensions, feet (metres): 138·6 × 20 × 9·2 *(42·3 × 6·1 × 2·8)*
Guns: 4—25 mm (2 twin mountings)
A/S weapons: 4 five-barrelled MBU 1800
Main engines: 3 diesel; 6 000 bhp = 29 knots
Range, miles: 1 100 at 13 knots
Complement: 30

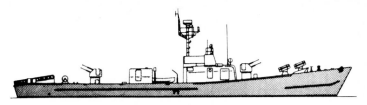

Eight reported to have been transferred by the USSR to Egypt in 1962 to 1967 and four others later.
Reported as carrying SA-7 Grail missiles in some units and 2—21 inch torpedo tubes in others.

"SO I" Class

6 Ex-SOVIET "SHERSHEN" CLASS
(FAST ATTACK CRAFT—TORPEDO)

332   343   354   356   +2

Displacement, tons: 150 standard; 160 full load
Dimensions, feet (metres): 115·5 × 23 × 5 *(35·2 × 7·1 × 1·5)*
Guns: 4—30 mm (2 twin)
Rocket launchers: 40 tube; 122 mm (see notes)
Torpedo tubes: 4—21 in (single)
A/S weapons: 12 DC
Main engines: 3 diesels; 3 shafts; 13 000 hp = 41 knots
Complement: 16

One delivered from USSR in Feb 1967, two more in Oct 1967, and three since. Four have had their guns and tubes removed to make way for multiple rocket-launchers and one SA-7 Grail.

"SHERSHEN" Class   1974, USN

20 Ex-SOVIET "P 6" CLASS (FAST ATTACK CRAFT—TORPEDO)

Displacement, tons: 66 standard; 75 full load
Dimensions, feet (metres): 84·2 × 20 × 6 *(25·7 × 6·1 × 1·8)*
Guns: 2 or 4—25 mm (some have forward guns replaced by 122 mm 8-barrelled rocket launcher)
Torpedo tubes: 2—21 in (4—21 in in two boats)
Main engines: 4 diesels; 4 shafts; 4 800 hp = 43 knots
Range, miles: 450 at 30 knots
Complement: 25

The first twelve boats arrived at Alexandria on 19 Apr 1956, 6 more in 1960. Two were destroyed by British naval aircraft on 4 Nov 1956, two were sunk by the Israeli destroyer *Elath* off Sinai on 12 July 1967, two by Israeli MTBs off Sinai coast on 11 July 1967, two by Israeli air attacks in 1969, and two in the Red Sea on 22 Jan 1970.
Further reinforcements have been sent by USSR—none since Oct 1973. Several have been built at Alexandria.

Radar: Decca in most craft.

"P 4" Class with 8-barrelled rocket launcher   10/1974

3 LARGE PATROL CRAFT

NISR 1, 2 and 3

Displacement, tons: 110
Gun: 1—20 mm

Built by Castro, Port Said and launched in May 1963.

4 Ex-SOVIET/SYRIAN "P 4" CLASS
(FAST ATTACK CRAFT—TORPEDO)

Transferred by Syria in 1970. Now armed with 8 barrelled 122 mm rocket launcher forward and twin 14·5 mm aft. Decca radar is now fitted.

20 BERTRAM TYPE (COASTAL PATROL CRAFT)

Displacement, tons: 8 approx
Length, feet (metres): 28 *(8·5)*
Guns: 2—12·7 mm MG
Rocket launchers: 4—122 mm

GRP hulls. Built in Miami, Florida

Now in service probably with the coastguard.

BERTRAM Type   10/1974

2 Ex-YUGOSLAVIAN "108" CLASS (FAST TARGET CRAFT)

Displacement, tons: 55 standard; 60 full load
Dimensions, feet (metres): 69 pp; 78 oa × 21·3 × 7·8 *(23·8 oa × 6·5 × 2·4)*
Main engines: 3 Packard motors; 3 shafts; 5 000 bhp = 36 knots
Complement: 14

Purchased from Yugoslavia in 1956. Similar to the boats of the US "Higgins" class. Originally a class of six. Remaining pair now fitted with reflectors and used as targets.

AMPHIBIOUS FORCES

3 Ex-SOVIET "POLNOCNY" CLASS (LCT)

Displacement, tons: 800 full load
Dimensions, feet (metres): 239·4 × 29·5 × 9·8 *(73 × 9 × 3)*
Guns: 2—25 mm (twin)
Rocket launchers: 2—18 barrelled 140 mm launchers
Main engines: 2 diesels; 5 000 bhp = 18 knots

Can carry 6 tanks. Transferred early 1970s.

Soviet "POLNOCNY" Class

10 Ex-SOVIET "VYDRA" CLASS (LCU)

Displacement, tons: 300 standard; 500 full load
Dimensions, feet (metres): 157·4 × 24·6 × 7·2 *(48 × 7·5 × 2·2)*
Main engines: 2 3D 12 diesels; 2 shafts; 600 bhp = 15 knots

Can carry and land up to 250 tons of military equipment and stores. For a period after the "October War" several were fitted with rocket launchers and 2—37 or 40 mm guns all of which have now been removed.

10 LCMs

Generally used as harbour-craft.

1 Ex-SOVIET "SMB 1" CLASS (LCU)

Displacement, tons: 200 standard; 420 full load
Dimensions, feet (metres): 157·5 × 21·3 × 5·6 *(48 × 6·5 × 1·7)*
Main engines: 2 diesels; 2 shafts; 400 hp = 11 knots

Delivered to the Egyptian Navy in 1965. Can carry 150 tons of military equipment.

MINEWARFARE FORCES

6 Ex-SOVIET "T 43" CLASS (MINESWEEPERS—OCEAN)

ASSIUT	**CHARKIEH**	**GHARBIA**
BAHAIRA	**DAKHLA**	**SINAI**

Displacement, tons: 500 standard; 610 full load
Dimensions, feet (metres): 190·2 × 28·2 × 6·9 *(58·0 × 8·6 × 2·1)*
Guns: 4—37 mm (twins); 8—14·5 mm (twins)
Main engines: 2 diesels; 2 shafts; 2 000 hp = 17 knots
Range, miles: 1 600 at 10 knots
Complement: 40

Three were transferred from the Soviet Navy and delivered to Egypt 1956-59, and three since 1970. *Miniya* was sunk by Israeli air attack in the Gulf of Suez on 6 Feb 1970 but was later replaced.

Soviet "T 43" Class — *1967, USN*

4 Ex-SOVIET "YURKA" CLASS (MINESWEEPERS—OCEAN)

ASWAN 695	**GIZA** 690	**SOHAG** 699	**QENA** 696

Displacement, tons: 500 standard; 550 full load
Dimensions, feet (metres): 172 × 31 × 8·9 *(52·5 × 9·5 × 2·7)*
Guns: 4—30 mm (2 twin)
Main engines: 2 diesels; 4 000 bhp = 18 knots

Steel-hulled minesweepers transferred from USSR 1970-71.

Appearance: Egyptian "Yurka" class do not carry Drum Tilt radar and have a number of ship's-side scuttles.

Soviet "YURKA" Class — *S. Breyer*

2 Ex-SOVIET "T 301" CLASS (MINESWEEPERS—INSHORE)

Displacement, tons: 130 standard; 180 full load
Dimensions, feet (metres): 124·6 × 19·7 × 4·9 *(39 × 5·5 × 1·5)*
Guns: 2—37 mm; 2—MG
Main engines: 3 diesels; 1 440 hp = 9 knots
Complement: 30

Reported to have been transferred by the USSR to Egypt in 1962; a third ship may have been transferred later.

Ex-SOVIET "K 4" CLASS
(MINESWEEPERS—INSHORE)

Several transferred but used mainly as harbour craft.

MISCELLANEOUS

3 WINCHESTER (SRN 6) HOVERCRAFT

Displacement, tons: 10 normal gross weight
Dimensions, feet (metres): 48·4 × 25·3 × 15·9 (height) *(14·8 × 7·7 × 4·8)*
Main engines: 1 Gnome Model 1050 gas turbine = 58 knots

Purchased in 1975 as refitted second-hand craft.

2 TRAINING SHIPS

EL HORRIYA (ex-*Mahroussa*)

Of 4 560 tons, built by Sanuda, Poplar in 1865 and once the Egyptian Royal Yacht, has been completely refitted and is used as a training ship.

INTISHAT

A smaller training ship.

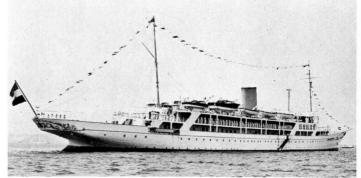

EL HORRIYA — *1976, USN*

2 Ex-SOVIET "OKHTENSKY" CLASS TUGS

AL MAKAS   **ANTAR**

Two transferred to the Egyptian Navy in 1966—assembled in Egypt.

1 Ex-SOVIET "SEKSTAN" CLASS

160 tons. Used as cadet training ship.

SWIMMER DELIVERY VEHICLES

There is a strong underwater team in the Egyptian navy who use, amongst other equipment, the 2-man SDVs shown here. Range could be 4 hours at 3-4 knots.

SDV   *10/1974*

EL SALVADOR

Personnel

(a) 1977: 130 officers and men
(b) Voluntary Service

Ports

Acajutla, La Libertad, La Union

Mercantile Marine

Lloyd's Register of Shipping:
   3 vessels of 2 128 tons gross

DELETION

1975 GC 1

PATROL BOATS

1 Ex-BRITISH HDML

Name	No.	Builders	Commissioned
GC 2 (ex-*Nohaba*)	—	UK	1942

Displacement, tons: 46
Dimensions, feet (metres): 72 oa × 16 × 5·5 *(21·9 × 4·9 × 1·7)*
Gun: 1—20 mm
Main engines: 2 diesels; 2 shafts = 12 knots
Complement: 16

Purchased from commercial sources in 1959.

2 Ex-US CG TYPE

Name	No.	Builders	Commissioned
GC 3	—	USA	1950
GC 4	—	USA	1950

Displacement, tons: 14

1 SEWART 65 ft TYPE

Name	No.	Builders	Commissioned
GC 5	—	Sewart, USA	1967

Displacement, tons: 33
Dimensions, feet (metres): 65 × 16·3 × 5·0 *(19·8 × 4·9 × 1·5)*
Guns: 3 MG
Main engines: GM Diesels; 1 600 hp = 25 knots

Transferred Sep 1967.

EQUATORIAL GUINEA

Ministerial

President and Minister of Peoples Armed Forces:
   Francisco Macias Nguema

Ports

Santa Isabel (Fernando Po), Bata (Rio Muni).

LIGHT FORCES

1 Ex-SOVIET "P6" CLASS (FAST ATTACK CRAFT—TORPEDO)

Displacement, tons: 66 standard; 75 full load
Dimensions, feet (metres): 84·2 × 20 × 6 *(25·7 × 6·1 × 1·8)*
Guns: 4—25 mm
Torpedo tubes: 2—21 in
Main engines: 4 Diesels; 4 shafts; 4 800 hp = 43 knots
Range, miles: 450 at 30 knots
Complement: 25

1 Ex-SOVIET "POLUCHAT" CLASS

Displacement, tons: 86 standard; 91 full load
Dimensions, feet (metres): 98 pp × 15 × 4·8 *(29·9 × 4·6 × 1·5)*
Guns: 2—14·5 mm (twin)
Main engines: 2 diesels; 2 shafts; 1 200 bhp = 18 knots
Range, miles: 460 at 17 knots
Complement: 16

Doubtful if the torpedo armament is operational. Up to four of this class reported but unconfirmed.

ETHIOPIA

Personnel

(a) 1977: 1 500 officers and men
(b) Voluntary service

Naval Establishments

Massawa: Naval Base and College, established in 1956.
Embaticalla: Marine Commando Training School.
Assab: Naval Base, expanding to include a ship repair facility.

Mercantile Marine

Lloyd's Register of Shipping:
   23 vessels of 24 953 tons gross

New Construction

Reported that eight 32 metre Large Patrol Craft with 2—20 mm guns were ordered in 1976 in Morgan City, Louisiana.

MINESWEEPER (COASTAL)

1 Ex-NETHERLANDS "WILDERVANK" CLASS

Name	No.	Builders	Commissioned
MS 41 (ex-*Elst, M 829)*	—	Netherlands	1956

Displacement, tons: 373 standard; 417 full load
Dimensions, feet (metres): 149·8 oa × 28·0 × 7·5 *(46·6 × 8·8 × 2·3)*
Guns: 2—40 mm
Main engines: 2 Werkspoor diesels; 2 shafts; 2 500 bhp = 14 knots
Oil fuel, tons: 25 tons
Range, miles: 2 500 at 10 knots
Complement: 38

Launched 21 Mar 1956. Purchased by Ethiopia and transferred from the Royal Netherlands Navy in 1971.

Missiles: It has been reported that MS 41 has been fitted for launching SS-12 missiles.

MS 41 (as *Elst)*

TRAINING SHIP

1 Ex-US "BARNEGAT" CLASS

Name	No.	Builders	Commissioned
ETHIOPIA (ex-USS *Orca*, AVP 49)	A 01	Lake Washington SY	23 Jan 1944

Displacement, tons: 1 766 standard; 2 800 full load
Dimensions, feet (metres): 310·8 oa × 41 × 13·5 *(94·7 × 12·5 × 3·7)*
Guns: 1—5 in 38 cal; 5—40 mm
Main engines: 2 sets diesels; 2 shafts; 6 080 bhp = 18·2 knots
Complement: 215

Former United States small seaplane tender of "Barnegat" class. Laid down 13 July 1942, launched on 4 Oct 1942. Transferred from the US Navy in Jan 1962.

ETHIOPIA   *1972, Imperial Ethiopian Navy*

LIGHT FORCES

5 PGM TYPE (LARGE PATROL CRAFT)

Name	No.	Builders	Commissioned
PC 11 (ex-US CG WVP 95304)	—	Petersen, USA	1958
PC 12 (ex-US CG WVP 95310)	—	Petersen, USA	1958
PC 13 (ex-USN PGM 53)	—	Petersen, USA	1961
PC 14 (ex-USN PGM 54)	—	Petersen, USA	1961
PC 15 (ex-USN PGM 58)	—	Petersen, USA	1962

Displacement, tons: 145·5 full load
Dimensions, feet (metres): 95 × 19 × 5·2 *(28·8 × 5·8 × 1·6)*
Guns: 1—40 mm; 1—50 cal MG
A/S weapons: 1 Mousetrap
Main engines: 4 diesels; 2 shafts; 2 200 bhp = 21 knots
Range, miles: 1 500 at cruising speed
Complement: 20

PC 12   *1970, Imperial Ethiopian Navy*

1 Ex-YUGOSLAV "KRALJEVICA" CLASS (LARGE PATROL CRAFT)

Name	No.	Builders	Commissioned
— (ex-509)	—	Yugoslavia	1953

Displacement, tons: 190·5 standard; 202 full load
Dimensions, feet (metres): 134·5 × 20·7 × 7·2 *(41 × 6·3 × 2·2)*
Guns: 1—3 in; 1—40 mm; 4—20 mm
A/S weapons: DCs
Main engines: MAN diesels; 2 shafts; 3 300 bhp = 18 knots

Transferred 1975.

4 "SEWART" CLASS (COASTAL PATROL CRAFT)

Name	No.	Builders	Commissioned
GB 21	—	Sewart Inc, Berwick	1966
GB 22	—	Sewart Inc, Berwick	1966
GB 23	—	Sewart Inc, Berwick	1967
GB 24	—	Sewart Inc, Berwick	1967

Displacement, tons: 15
Length, feet (metres): 40 *(12·2)*
Guns: 2—50 calibre machine guns
Speed, knots: 20
Complement: 7

GB 21   *1970, Imperial Ethiopian Navy*

LANDING CRAFT

There are 2 of the US LCM type and 2 of the US LCVP type. Two were bought in 1962 and two in 1971.

FIJI

On 12 June 1974 the Royal Fiji Military Forces were authorised to raise a Naval Squadron to carry out Fishery Protection, Surveillance, Hydrographic Surveying and Coastguard duties. The RFMF is under the authority of the Minister for Home Affairs. In addition to its normal tasks the Naval Squadron runs an all-conquering Rugby Team.

Ministerial

Minister for Home Affairs:
  Ratu Sir Penaia Ganilau KBE CMG CVO DSO

Commanding Officers

RFMF:
  Colonel P. F. Manueli OBE

Naval Squadron:
  Commander S. B. Brown MBE VRD

Personnel

1977: 159 (19 officers, 140 sailors)

Base

HMFS *Viti,* Suva.

Prefix to Ships' Names

HMFS.

3 Ex-US "REDWING" CLASS (MINESWEEPERS—COASTAL)

Name	No.	Builders	Commissioned
KULA (ex-USS *Vireo, MSC 205*)	205	Bellingham SY, USA	7 June 1955
KIRO (ex-USS *Warbler, MSC 206*)	206	Bellingham SY, USA	23 July 1955
KIKAU (ex-USS *Woodpecker, MSC 209*)	204	Bellingham SY, USA	3 Feb 1956

Displacement, tons: 370 full load
Dimensions, feet (metres): 144 oa × 28 × 8·5 *(43·9 × 8·5 × 2·6)*
Guns: 1—20 mm; 2—0·5 MG
Main engines: 2 GM Diesels; 2 shafts; 880 bhp = 13 knots
Range, miles: 2 500 at 10 knots
Complement: 39

First pair transferred 14 Oct 1975 and the third in June 1976. *Kiro* and *Kula* have been refitted for removal of magnetic MS equipment.

KIRO   1976, RFMF

RUVE (ex-*Volasiga*, ex-*Marinetta*)

Dimensions, feet (metres): 94 oa × 17·5 × 7·5 *(28·7 × 5·3 × 2·3)*

Transferred from Fiji Marine Department, June 1976. Used for Surveying.

FINLAND

Headquarters Appointment

Commander-in-Chief Finnish Navy:
  Rear-Admiral S. O. Wikberg

Diplomatic Representation

Naval Attaché in London:
  Lieutenant-Colonel Pertti E. Nykänen

Naval Attaché in Moscow:
  Colonel E. Pallasvirta

Naval Attaché in Paris:
  Lieutenant-Colonel Sami Sihvo

Naval Attaché in Washington:
  Colonel Erkki Kaira

Treaty Limitations

The Finnish Navy is limited by the Treaty of Paris (1947) to 10 000 tons of ships and 4 500 personnel. Submarines and motor torpedo boats are prohibited.

Personnel

(a) 1972: 2 000 (150 officers and 1 850 ratings)
     1973: 2 500 (200 officers and 2 300 ratings)
     1974: 2 500 (200 officers and 2 300 ratings)
     1975: 2 500 (200 officers and 2 300 ratings)
     1976: 2 500 (200 officers and 2 300 ratings)
(b) 8-11 months National Service

Hydrographic Department

This office and the survey ships come under the Ministry of Trade and Industry.

Coast Guard

All Coast Guard vessels come under the Ministry of the Interior.

Icebreakers

All these ships work for the Board of Navigation.

Mercantile Marine

Lloyd's Register of Shipping:
  350 vessels of 2 115 322 tons gross

Strength of the Fleet

Type	Active	Building (Planned)
Frigates	2	—
Corvettes	2	(2)
Fast Attack Craft (Missile)	4+1	(9)
Fast Attack Craft (Gun)	15	—
Large Patrol Craft	5	—
Minelayer	1	(1)
Minesweepers	6	(10 inshore)
HQ Ships	2	—
Transports (LCUs)	11	—
Tugs	3	—
Support Ships	3	—
Transport Craft	57	—
Cable Ship	1	—
Icebreakers	9+1	—

Coastguard

Large Patrol Craft	5	3
Training Ship	1	—
Supply Ship	1	—
Coastal Patrol Craft	97	—

New Construction

Staff studies begun on 2 new frigates. Additional Fast Attack Craft (Missile) to bring total up to nine by addition of five "Tuima" class. Design of one new minelayer completed mid-1976 for construction 1977-79—also to act as training ship. Four more "Kuha" class minesweepers to be built. Three more patrol craft, first ordered 24 June 1975, of improved "Valpas" class for coastguard.

DELETIONS

Frigates
1975 *Matti Kurki* (ex-British "Bay" Class)

Light Forces
1975 *Tursas* (Large Patrol Craft)

Minewarfare Forces
1975 *Ruotsinsalmi*

Coastguard Vessels
1970 VMV 11, 13, 19 and 20
1971 *Aura*

"UUSIMAA" Class

"TURUNMAA" Class

FRIGATES

2 Ex-SOVIET "RIGA" CLASS

HÄMEENMAA   **UUSIMAA**

Displacement, tons: 1 200 standard; 1 600 full load
Length, feet (metres): 298·8 *(91)*
Beam, feet (metres): 33·7 *(10·2)*
Draught, feet (metres): 11 *(3·4)*
Guns: 3—3·9 in *(100 mm)* single; 2—40 mm;
 2—30 mm (twin) (in bow)
A/S weapons: 1 hedgehog; 4 DC projectors
Torpedo tubes: 3—21 in *(533 mm)*
Mines: 50 (capacity)
Main engines: Geared turbines; 2 shafts; 25 000 shp
Speed, knots: 28
Boilers: 2
Range, miles: 2 000 at 10 knots
Complement: 150

Built in USSR—*Uusimaa* in 1955 and *Hämeenmaa* in 1957. Purchased from the USSR and transferred to the Finnish Navy on 29 April 1964 and 14 May 1964, respectively. Armament modified in 1971 with extra 30 mm.

Radar: Search: Slim Net.
Fire control: Sun Visor A (with Wasphead fire control system).
Navigation: Decca.
IFF: Ski Pole and Yard Rake.

Sonar: Hull mounted.

UUSIMAA   *1974, Finnish Navy–SA Kuva*

CORVETTES

2 "TURUNMAA" CLASS

Name	No.	Builders	Laid down	Launched	Commissioned
KARJALA	—	Wärtsilä, Helsinki	Mar 1967	16 Aug 1967	21 Oct 1968
TURUNMAA	—	Wärtsilä, Helsinki	Mar 1967	11 July 1967	29 Aug 1968

Displacement, tons: 660 standard; 770 full load
Dimensions, feet (metres): 243·1 × 25·6 × 7·9 *(74·1 × 7·8 × 2·4)*
Guns: 1—4·7 in *(120 mm)* Bofors forward; 2—40 mm; 2—30 mm (1 twin) aft
A/S weapons: 2 DCT; 2 DC racks
Main engines: CODOG. 3 Mercedes-Benz (MTU) diesels; 3 000 bhp; 1 Rolls Royce Olympus gas turbine; 22 000 hp = 35 knots. On diesels = 17 knots
Complement: 70

Ordered on 18 Feb 1965 from Wärtsilä, Helsinki. Flush decked. Rocket flare guide rails on sides of 4·7 in turret. Fitted with Vosper Thornycroft fin stabiliser equipment.

Radar: Search and Tactical: H/I Band. (HSA).

KARJALA   *1975, Finnish Navy*

LIGHT FORCES

4 "TUIMA" CLASS (FAST ATTACK CRAFT—MISSILE)

TUIMA   **TUULI**   **TUISKU**   **TYRSKY**

Displacement, tons: 165 standard; 200 full load
Dimensions, feet (metres): 128·7 × 25·1 × 5·9 *(39·3 × 7·7 × 1·8)*
Missiles: 4—SS-N-2 system launchers
Guns: 4—30 mm (twin)
Main engines: 3 Diesels; 13 000 hp
Speed, knots: 36
Range, miles: 800 at 25 knots
Complement: 25

Ex-Soviet "Osa" class purchased from USSR. 1974—75. New construction but with Finnish electronics. Five more planned.

TUIMA   *1975, Finnish Navy*

1 EXPERIMENTAL CRAFT—MISSILE

Name	No.	Builders	Commissioned
ISKU	—	Reposaaron, Konepaja	1970

Displacement, tons: 140 full load
Dimensions, feet (metres): 86·5 × 28·6 × 6·4 *(26 × 8·7 × 1·8)*
Missile launchers: 4 SS-N-2 system launchers
Guns: 2—30 mm (1 twin)
Main engines: 4 Soviet M50 diesels; 3 600 bhp = 15 knots
Complement: 25

Guided missile craft of novel design built for training and experimental work. The construction combines a missile boat armament on a landing craft hull. Laid down Nov 1968 and launched 4 Dec 1969.

ISKU   *1976, Finnish Navy*

13 "NUOLI" CLASS (FAST ATTACK CRAFT—GUN)

Name	No.	Builders	Commissioned
NUOLI 1—13	1—13	Laivateollisuus, Turku	1961—6

Displacement, tons: 40 standard
Dimensions, feet (metres): 72·2 × 21·7 × 5·0 *(22 × 6·6 × 1·5)*
Guns: 1—40 mm; 1—20 mm
A/S weapons: 4 DCs
Main engines: 3 Soviet M50 diesels; 2 700 bhp = 40 knots
Complement: 15

Designed by Laivateollisuus, Turku. Delivery dates— 14 Sep 1961, 19 Oct 1961, 1 Nov 1961, 21 Nov 1961, 6 July 1962, 3 Aug 1962, 22 Aug 1962, 10 Oct 1962, 27 Oct 1963, 5 May 1964, 5 May 1964, 30 Nov 1964, 12 Oct 1966. This class is split into two: Nuoli 1 (1-9) and Nuoli 2 (10-13). The main difference is a lower superstructure in Nuoli 2.

Radar: I-band Decca.

"NUOLI" Class   1976, Finnish Navy

2 "VASAMA" CLASS (FAST ATTACK CRAFT—GUN)

Name	No.	Builders	Commissioned
VASAMA I	1	Saunders Roe (Anglesey) Ltd	1 Apr 1957
VASAMA 2	2	Saunders Roe (Anglesey) Ltd	1 May 1957

Displacement, tons: 50 standard; 70 full load
Dimensions, feet (metres): 67·0 pp; 71·5 oa × 19·8 × 6·1 *(21·8 oa × 5·9 × 1·8)*
Guns: 2—40 mm
A/S weapons: 4 DCT
Main engines: 2 Napier Deltic diesels; 5 000 bhp = 40 knots
Complement: 20

British "Dark" class.

VASAMA 2   1976, Finnish Navy

3 "RUISSALO" CLASS (LARGE PATROL CRAFT)

Name	No.	Builders	Commissioned
RAISIO	4	Laivatteollisuus, Turku	12 Sep 1959
RÖYTTA	5	Laivatteollisuus, Turku	14 Oct 1959
RUISSALO	3	Laivatteollisuus, Turku	11 Aug 1959

Displacement, tons: 110 standard; 130 full load
Dimensions, feet (metres): 111·5 × 19·8 × 5·9 *(33 × 6 × 1·8)*
Guns: 1—40 mm; 1—20 mm; 2 MG
A/S weapons: 1 Squid mortar
Mines: Can lay mines
Main engines: 2 Mercedes-Benz (MTU) diesels; 2 500 bhp = 18 knots
Complement: 20

Ordered in Jan 1958. Launched on 16 June, 2 July and 2 June 1959.

Radar: Decca.

Sonar: One hull-mounted.

RAISIO   1975, Finnish Navy

2 "RIHTNIEMI" CLASS (LARGE PATROL CRAFT)

Name	No.	Builders	Commissioned
RIHTNIEMI	1	Rauma-Repola, Rauma	21 Feb 1957
RYMÄTTYLÄ	2	Rauma-Repola, Rauma	20 May 1957

Displacement, tons: 90 standard; 110 full load
Dimensions, feet (metres): 101·7 × 18·7 × 5·9 *(31 × 5·6 × 1·8)*
Guns: 1—40 mm; 1—20 mm; 2 MG
A/S weapons: 2 DC racks
Mines: Can lay mines
Main engines: 2 Mercedes-Benz (MTU) diesels; 1 400 bhp = 15 knots
Complement: 20

Ordered in June 1955, launched in 1956. Controllable pitch propellers.

RIHTNIEMI   1976, Finnish Navy

MINE WARFARE FORCES

Note: Design of new construction Minelayer/Training Ship completed 1976—construction 1977-79—approx 800 tons, 230 ft *(70 metres)*.

1 MINELAYER

Name	No.	Builders	Commissioned
KEIHÄSSALMI	—	Valmet, Helsinki	1957

Displacement, tons: 360
Dimensions, feet (metres): 168× 23 × 6 *(52 × 7 × 1·9)*
Guns: 4—30 mm (twins); 2—20 mm
Mines: Up to 100 capacity
Main engines: 2 Wärtsilä diesels; 2 shafts; 2 000 bhp = 15 knots
Complement: 60

Of improved "Ruotsinsalmi" Class. Contract dated June 1955. Launched on 16 Mar 1957. Armament modified in 1972.

Radar: Search and Tactical; I band. Decca.

KEIHÄSSALMI   *1974, Finnish Navy*

6 "KUHA" CLASS (MINESWEEPERS—INSHORE)

Name	No.	Builders	Commissioned
KUHA 21—26	21—26	Laivatteollisuus, Turku	1974—75

Displacement, tons: 90
Dimensions, feet (metres): 87·2 × 23 *(26·6 × 7)*
Guns: 1 or 2—20 mm
Main engines: 2 Diesels; 600 shp; 1 shaft (cp) = 12 knots
Complement: 15

All ordered 1972. Fitted for magnetic, acoustic and pressure-mine sweeping. Have active rudders.
Kuha 21 completed 28 June 1974. *Kuha 26* in late 1975. Hulls are of Glass Reinforced Plastic (GRP). Funds for further 8 craft provided.

Radar: Decca.

KUHA 22   *1974, Finnish Navy—SA Kuva*

MISCELLANEOUS

KORSHOLM (ex-*Korsholm III*, ex-*Öland*) (HQ SHIP)

Displacement, tons: 650
Dimensions, feet (metres): 157·4 × 27·9 × 9·5 *(48 × 8·5 × 2·9)*
Guns: 2—20 mm
Main engine: Steam; 865 hp = 11 knots

Converted car ferry. Built in 1931 in Sweden. Bought by Rederi Ab Vaasa-Umea in 1958. Sold to Navy in 1967.

1 Ex-ICEBREAKER (HQ SHIP)

Name	No.	Builders	Commissioned
LOUHI (ex-*Sisu*)	—	Wärtsilä, Helsinki	1939

Displacement, tons: 2 075
Dimensions, feet (metres): 210·2 oa × 46·5 × 16·8 *(64·1 × 14·2 × 5·1)*
Guns: 2—3·9 in
Main engines: 2 sets Atlas Polar Diesels with electric drive; 2 shafts and a bow propeller; 4 000 hp = 16 knots
Complement: 28

Launched on 24 Sep 1938. Used as submarine depot ship 1939—45. Converted 1975 to be HQ and Logistics ship.

6 "KALA" CLASS (LCU TRANSPORTS)

KALA 1—6

Displacement, tons: 60
Dimensions, feet (metres): 88·6 × 26·2 × 6 *(27 × 8 × 1·8)*
Gun: 1—20 mm
Mines: 34
Main engines: 2 Valmet diesels; 360 bhp = 9 knots
Complement: 10

Completed between 20 June 1956 *(Kala 1)* and 4 Dec 1959 *(Kala 6)*. Can be used as transports, amphibious craft, minelayers or for shore support. Armament can be changed to suit role.

KALA 2   *7/1974, Dittmair*

5 "KAVE" CLASS (LCU TRANSPORTS)

KAVE 1—4 and 6

Displacement, tons: 27
Dimensions, feet (metres): 59 × 16·4 × 4·3 *(18 × 5 × 1·3)*
Gun: 1—20 mm
Main engines: 2 Valmet diesels; 360 hp = 9 knots
Complement: 3

Completed between 16 Nov 1956 *(Kave 1)* and 1960 *(Kave 6* on 19 Dec 1960). Built by Haminan Korepaja Oy *(Kave 1)*—remainder by F. W. Hollming, Rauma. *Kave 5* lost in tow 15 Dec 1960.

KAVE 4   *1961, Finnish Navy*

3 "PUKKIO" CLASS (SUPPORT SHIPS)

PANSIO   PORKKALA   PUKKIO

Displacement, tons: 162 standard
Dimensions, feet (metres): 93·4 × 19·2 × 9·0 *(28·5 × 6·0 × 2·7)*
Guns: 1—40 mm; 1—20 mm·
Mines: 20
Main engines: Diesels; 300 bhp = 9 knots

Built by Valmet, Turku. Delivered 25 May 1947, 1940 and 1939 respectively. Vessels of the tug type used as transports, minesweeping tenders, minelayers and patrol vessels.

3 "PIRTTISAARI" CLASS

PIRTTISAARI (ex-DR 7)   **PYHTÄA** (ex-DR 2)   **PURHA** (ex-DR 10)

Displacement, tons: 150
Dimensions, feet (metres): 69 × 20 × 8·5 *(21 × 6·1 × 2·6)*
Gun: 1—20 mm
Main engine: 1 diesel; 400 bhp = 8 knots
Complement: 10

Former US Army Tugs. Launched in 1943-44. General purpose vessels used as minesweepers, minelayers, patrol vessels, tenders, tugs or personnel transports. *Pyhtää* belongs to the Coast Artillery.

PIRTTISAARI   *1970, Finnish Navy*

PUTSAARI (CABLE SHIP)

Displacement, tons: 430
Dimensions, feet (metres): 149·2 × 29·2 × 7·5 *(45·5 × 8·9 × 2·3)*
Main engine: 1 Wärtsilä diesel; 450 bhp = 10 knots
Complement: 10

Built by Rauma Repola, Rauma. Ordered 11 Nov 1963. Launched in Dec 1965. Fitted with bow-thruster and active rudder, two 10 ton cable winches and accommodation for 20. Strengthened for ice operations.

TRANSPORT CRAFT

Class	Nos.	Tonnage	Speed	Commissioned
K	1-24	16	9	1957-66
Fabian Wrede	2	20	10	1915
Y	1-10	8	7	1960
L	1-7	1·5	11	1960-68
YM 1	1&2	0·7 (GRP)	7	1970-71
YM 4	4 & 5	2	7	1947
YM 22	22	2	11	—
YM 55	55, 60, 63	6·5	8	1942-57
H	1-6	34	10	1960

ICEBREAKERS

Controlled by Board of Navigation.

2 "URHO" CLASS

Name	No.	Builders	Commissioned
URHO	—	Wärtsilä, Helsinki	5 Mar 1975
SISU	—	Wärtsilä, Helsinki	28 Jan 1976

Displacement, tons: 7 900 standard; 9 500 full load
Dimensions, feet (metres): 337·8 × 77·1 × 24·6 *(104·6 × 23·8 × 8·3)*
Aircraft: 1 helicopter
Main engines: Diesel-electric; 5 Wärtsilä-SEMT Pielstick diesels 25 000 bhp. Electric Motors; 22 000 shp; 2 shafts forward, 2 aft; = 18 knots
Complement: 57

Ordered on 11 Dec 1970 and 10 May 1971 respectively. Fitted with two screws aft, taking 60% of available power and two forward, taking the remainder. Sisters to Swedish "Atle" class.

URHO   *1975, Wärtsilä*

3 "TARMO" CLASS

Name	No.	Builders	Commissioned
TARMO	—	Wärtsilä, Helsinki	1963
VARMA	—	Wärtsilä, Helsinki	1968
APU	—	Wärtsilä, Helsinki	25 Nov 1970

Displacement, tons: 4 890
Dimensions, feet (metres): 281·0 × 71·0 × 22·5 *(85·7 × 21·7 × 6·8)*
Aircraft: 1 helicopter
Main engines: Wärtsilä-Sulzer diesels; electric drive; 4 shafts (2 screws forward 2 screws aft); 12 000 bhp = 17 knots

VARMA   *1975, Finnish Navy*

3 "KARHU" CLASS

Name	No.	Builders	Commissioned
KARHU	—	Wärtsilä, Helsinki	Dec 1958
MURTAJA	—	Wärtsilä, Helsinki	1959
SAMPO	—	Wärtsilä, Helsinki	1960

Displacement, tons: 3 540
Dimensions, feet (metres): 243·2 × 57 × 21 *(74·2 × 17·4 × 6·4)*
Main engines: Diesel-electric; 4 shafts; 7 500 bhp = 16 knots

Karhu was launched on 22 Oct 1957, *Murtaja* was launched on 23 Sep 1958.

KARHU   *1975, Finnish Navy*

1 "VOIMA" CLASS

Name	No.	Builders	Commissioned
VOIMA	—	Wärtsilä, Helsinki	1953

Displacement, tons: 4 415
Dimensions, feet (metres): 274 oa × 63·7 × 22·5 *(83·6 × 19·4 ʹ× 6·8)*
Main engines: Diesels with electric drive; 4 shafts; 14 000 bhp = 16·5 knots
Oil fuel, tons: 740

Launched in 1953. Two propellers forward and aft.

There is also the West German owned, Finnish manned, icebreaker *Hansa,* of the "Karhu" class, completed on 25 Nov 1966, which operates off Germany in winter and off Finland at other times.

VOIMA · 1975, Finnish Navy

COASTGUARD

Controlled by Ministry of the Interior.

1 LARGE PATROL CRAFT

Name	No.	Builders	Commissioned
VALPAS	—	Laivateollisuus, Turku	21 July 1971

Displacement, tons: 545
Dimensions, feet (metres): 159·1 × 27·9 × 12·5 *(48·5 × 8·5 × 3·8)*
Gun: 1—20 mm
Main engine: 1 Werkspoor diesel; 2 000 bhp = 15 knots
Complement: 22

An improvement on the *Silmä* design. Ordered 14 July 1969—launched 22 Dec 1970. First coastguard ship with sonar. Ice strengthened.

Sonar: Hull mounted set.

VALPAS · 1975, Finnish Navy

1 LARGE PATROL CRAFT

Name	No.	Builders	Commissioned
SILMÄ	—	Laivateollisuus, Turku	19 Aug 1963

Displacement, tons: 530
Dimensions, feet (metres): 154·5 × 27·2 × 14·1 *(48·3 × 8·3 × 4·3)*
Gun: 1—20 mm
Main engine: 1 Werkspoor diesel; 1 800 hp = 15 knots
Complement: 22

Improved *Uisko* design. Ordered 21 Feb 1962, launched 25 Mar 1963.

SILMA · 1975, Finnish Navy

1 LARGE PATROL CRAFT

Name	No.	Builders	Commissioned
UISKO	—	Valmet, Helsinki	1959

Displacement, tons: 370
Dimensions, feet (metres): 141 × 24 × 12·8 *(43 × 7·3 × 3·9)*
Gun: 1—20 mm
Main engine: 1 Werkspoor diesel; 1 800 hp = 15 knots
Complement: 21

Coast Guard vessel. Launched in 1958.

UISKO · 1975, Finnish Navy

1 LARGE PATROL CRAFT

Name	No.	Builders	Commissioned
VIIMA	—	Laivatteollisuus, Turku	1964

Displacement, tons: 135
Dimensions, feet (metres): 118·1 × 21·7 × 7·5 *(36 × 6·6 × 2·3)*
Gun: 1—20 mm
Main engines: 3 Mercedes-Benz diesels; 4 050 bhp = 25 knots
Complement: 13

Launched 20 July 1964.

VIIMA · 1974, Finnish Navy

8 "TELKKA/KOSKELO" CLASS (COASTAL PATROL CRAFT)

KAAKKURI**	KOSKELO*	KUIKKA**	TAVI*
KIISLA*	KUOVI*	KURKI*	TELKKA

(*"Koskelo" class, **Unmodified craft)

Displacement, tons: 92 *(Telkka);* 95 *(Koskelo)* full load
Dimensions, feet (metres): 95·1 × 16·4 × 4·9 *(29 × 5 × 1·5)*
Gun: 1—20 mm (see notes)
Main engines: 2 Mercedes-Benz (MTU) diesels; 2 shafts; 2 700 bhp = 23 knots (modified). 2 Mercedes-Benz diesels; 1 000 hp = 15 knots (unmodified)
Complement: 9 *(Telkka),* 11 *(Koskelo)*

TELKKA   1975, Finnish Navy

Built of steel and strengthened against ice. between 1955 *(Koskelo)* and 1960 *(Tavi).* Originally of much lower horsepower. *Telkka* modernised in 1970 and "Koskelo"s in 1972-74 by Laivatteol- lisuss. New internal arrangements, new decking and new engines increasing their speed by 8 knots. Can all mount a 40 mm on quarter-deck.

1 LARGE PATROL CRAFT

Name	No.	Builders	Commissioned
TURSAS	—	Tensche, Belgium	1938

Displacement, tons: 380
Dimensions, feet (metres): 133·5 × 23·6 × 14·4 *(40·7 × 7·2 × 4·4)*
Gun: 1—20 mm
Main engine: 950 hp = 13 knots
Complement: 20

Was bought from Belgium in 1939 with her sister *Uisko* who was lost by enemy action in 1943.

1 TRAINING SHIP

Name	No.	Builders	Commissioned
OCKERO	—	Kone and Silta	1954

Displacement, tons: 55
Dimensions, feet (metres): 70·2 × 13·1 × 6·2 *(21·4 × 4 × 1·9)*
Main engine: Mercedes-Benz diesel; 445 hp = 10 knots

Former customs vessel now used for coastguard training.

1 SUPPLY SHIP

Name	No.	Builders	Commissioned
TURJA	—	Hietalahden, Helsinki	1928

Displacement, tons: 65
Dimensions, feet (metres): 74·1 × 14·8 × 8·2 *(22·6 × 4·5 × 2·5)*
Main engine: Mercedes-Benz diesel; 225 hp = 11 knots

Former coastal patrol ship at Petsamo 1929-45. Then a customs vessel. Converted as supply ship in 1973.

COASTAL PATROL CRAFT

Class	Nos.	Tonnage	Speed	Commissioned
RV 1	1	10	9	1933
RV 4	4 & 5	12	9	1951
RV 6	6 & 7	15	9	1953
RV 8	8	10	10	1958
RV 9	9-17	12	10	1959-60
RV 10	18-28	18	10	1961-63
RV 30	30-36	19	10	1973-74
RV 41	41	17	10	1965
RV 97	97, 102-105 108, 121; 144, 145, 160, 162	10	9	1934-49
NV 11	11-12	3	35	1966
NV 13	13-14	4	33	1969
NV 15	15-22	4	34	1972-74
NV 24	24	1·6	45	1960
NV 30	30-35	1·1	35	1974
NV 101	Hydrofoil 101	1·8	33	1972 from USSR
PV 1	1, 3, 4-7, 9	2	19	1957-59
PV 11	11-12	2 (GRP)	13	1959
PV 21	21-26	4 (GRP)	21	1963
PV 27	27-34	4	21	1965-66
PV 32	32	4	26	1965
PV 51	51	5	21	1966
KR 3 (ice-riders)	3-9	1	?	1972-74

FRANCE

Ministerial

Minister of Defence:
  M. Yvon Bourges

Headquarters Appointments

Conseil Supérieur de la Marine:
  Amiraux Lannuzel and Le Franc
  Vice-Amiraux d'Escadre, Banuls, Tardy
  Vice-Amiraux Wacrenier and Sabarvin

Senior Appointments

Préfet Maritime de la Première Région (PREMAR UN):
  Vice-Amiral Wacrenier
C in C Atlantic Theatre (CECLANT) and Préfet Maritime de la Deuxième Région (PREMAR DEUX):
  Vice-Amiral d'Escadre Coulondier
C in C Mediterranean Theatre (CECMED) and Préfet Maritime de la Troisième Région (PREMAR TROIS):
  Vice-Amiral d'Escadre Tardy
C in C French Naval Forces, Polynesia:
  Contre-Amiral de Castelbajac
C in C Atlantic Fleet:
  Vice-Amiral de Gaulle
C in C Mediterranean Fleet:
  Vice-Amiral de Bigault de Cazanove

Diplomatic Representation

Naval Attaché in Algiers:
  Capitaine de Vaisseau Le Bars
Naval Attaché in Bonne:
  Capitaine de Frégate Faivre
Naval Attaché in Brasilia:
  Capitaine de Corvette de Gentile Duquesne
Naval Attaché in the Hague:
  Capitaine de Vaisseau Fabre
Naval Attaché in Lisbon:
  Capitaine de Frégate Rambourg
Naval Attaché in London (& Defence Attaché):
  Contre-Amiral François Flohic
Naval Attaché in Madrid:
  Capitaine de Vaisseau d'Illices
Naval Attaché in Moscow:
  Capitaine de Vaisseau Large
Naval Attaché in Oslo:
  Capitaine de Vaisseau Bigot
Naval Attaché in Rome:
  Capitaine de Vaisseau de Seynes
Naval Attaché in Santiago:
  Capitaine de Frégate Tourrel
Naval Attaché in Tokyo:
  Capitaine de Vaisseau Lemaire
Naval Attaché in Washington:
  Contre-Amiral Chaline
Naval Attaché in Wellington:
  Capitaine de Frégate Bouver

Personnel

(a) 1971: 68 586 (4 732 officers, 63 854 ratings)
     1972: 68 308 (4 604 officers, 63 704 ratings)
     1973: 67 600 (4 400 officers, 63 200 ratings)
     1974: 67 700 (4 500 officers, 63 200 ratings)
     1975: 68 000 (4 550 officers, 63 450 ratings)
     1976: 68 315 (4 550 officers, 63 765 ratings)

(personnel to be increased by 5 000 under the 15-year re-equipment plan)

(b) National Service 12 months
     (providing approx 16 000 ratings)

Bases

Cherbourg: Atlantic Fleet base. Prémar Un
Brest: Main Atlantic base. SSBN base. Prémar Deux
Lorient: Atlantic submarine base
Toulon: Main Mediterranean Fleet base. Prémar Trois

Fleet Dispositions

Atlantic: *Colbert,* all new destroyers, frigates and one tanker. All SSBNs and 8 submarines
Mediterranean: *Foch, Clemenceau, Duquesne, Suffren,* older destroyers and frigates, one tanker and 11 submarines

Mercantile Marine

Lloyd's Register of Shipping:
  1 388 vessels of 11 278 016 tons gross

Strength of the Fleet

Type	Active	Building or (Projected)
Attack Carriers (Medium)	2	—
Helicopter VSTOL Carrier (Nuclear)	—	(1)
Cruisers	2	—
Destroyers	21	3
Frigates	29	6 (2)
Submarines (Strat Missile)	4	1 (1)
	1 (Diesel powered)	
Submarines (Fleet)	—	1 (1)
Submarines (Patrol)	22	1
Fast Attack Craft (Missile)	5	— (6)
Large Patrol Craft	28	—
Coastal Patrol Craft	6	—
LPD	2	—
LST	5	—
LCT	13	—
LCM	16	—
Batral	2	—
Minesweepers (Ocean)	8	—
Minesweepers (Coastal)	31	—
Minehunters	10	—
Surveying Ships	5	—
Coastal Survey Ships	4	—
Inshore Survey Craft	1	—
Tankers (UR)	5	1
Tankers (Support)	5	—
Maintenance Ships	2	—
Depot Ships	5	—
Repair Ships (ex-LCT)	2	—
Trials Ships	9	—
Boom Defence Vessels	14	—
Torpedo Recovery Vessels	2	—
Victualling Stores Ship	1	—
Stores Ship	1	—
Supply Tenders	4	—
Small Transports	13	2
Tenders	13	—
Tugs	109	10
Training Ships	8	—

Naval Air Stations

St. Raphael, Lann Bihoue, Nimes Garon, Lanveox Poulmic, Dax, Aspretto, Landvisiau, Hyères, St. Mandrier.

Shipyards (Naval)

Cherbourg: Submarines and Fast Attack Craft
Brest: Major warships and refitting
Lorient: Destroyers, frigates and avisos

Submarine Service

Known as Force Océanique Stratégique (FOST) with HQ at Houilles near Paris. SSBN *(SNLE)* force based at Ile Longue Brest with a training base at Roche-Douvres and VLFW/T station at Rosay. Patrol submarines are based at Lorient and Toulon. Plans for nuclear fleet submarines are included in the 15 year plan, with the first being laid down in 1976.

15-Year Re-equipment Plan

Note: All submarines laid down from 1976 onwards are to be nuclear-powered.

This programme ("Plan Bleu") was approved by l'Assemblé on 29 Feb 1972 and provided for the following fleet by 1985:

  2 Aircraft Carriers
  2 Helicopter Carriers
 30 Frigates or Corvettes
 35 Avisos
  6 SSBN
 20 Patrol Submarines (or Fleet)
 30 Fast Attack Craft
 36 MHC and MSC
  5 Replenishment Tankers
    Logistic Support and Maintenance Ships
  2 Assault Ships
    Landing Ships and Craft
    Transports
 50 LRMP aircraft
    Carrier borne craft
    Helicopters

1971-75 New Construction Plan

Financial problems have necessitated the addition of an extra year to this plan. Financial allowance made for construction of ships listed below as well as a second Fleet Replenishment Ship, 1 Fleet Submarine (SSN), and the first new minehunter.

  1 Helicopter Carrier (PH 75)
  3 Guided Missile Destroyers ("Corvettes") "C 70" Type
  3 Guided Missile Destroyers ("Corvettes") "C 67" Type
 14 Escorts (officially rated as *Avisos*) "A 69" Type
  3 Nuclear Powered Ballistic Missile Submarines
  4 Patrol Submarines
  4 Patrol Boats (for overseas service)
  1 Fleet Support & Repair Ship (major conversion)
  1 Fleet Replenishment Ship
  2 Medium Landing Ships (Transports)

1977-81 New Construction Plan

This plan allows for:
  1 Nuclear-propelled carrier (PA 75) (new designation of planned helicopter/VSTOL carrier)
  3 C 70 ASM destroyers ("Georges Leygues" class)
  3 C 70 AA destroyers ("Georges Leygues" class)
  4 SSN Fleet submarines (3 sisters to SNA 72 and 1 advanced type)
  1 SSBN (L'Inflexible) postponed until 1982
 12 Minehunters (in collaboration with Belgium and Netherlands)
  6 Large Patrol Vessels (250-350 tons)

DELETIONS

Helicopter Carrier
1974 *Arromanches*

Cruiser
1973 *De Grasse*

Destroyers
1974 *Chevalier Paul, Cassard*
1976 *La Bourdonnais*

Frigates
1974 *Le Bordelais, Le Corse* (Type E 50)
1975 *Le Brestois* (Type E 50)
1976 *Le Henaff* and *L'Herminier* (Type A 69) transferred to South Africa

Light Forces
1974 M 691, VC 2, VC 10, P 9785, P 9786
1975 *Le Fougueux, L'Opiniatre* and *L'Agile* ("Le Fougueux" class)

Minewarfare Forces
1974 *Begonia,* and *Glaieul* deleted; *Aries* ("Sirius" class) (To Morocco)
1975 *Bellatrix, Dénébola, Pégase* ("Sirius" class) deleted; *Jacinthe, Liseron* and *Magnolia* ("Adjutant" class) as diving base ships.
1976 *Bleuér* and *Chrysanthéme* ("Adjutant" class)

Amphibious Forces
1974 LCT 9099 deleted; LCT 9095 to Senegal

Survey Ships
1973 *La Coquille*
1975 *La Découverte* (for use as target)

Service Forces
1972 *Lac Chambon, Lac Tchad* (small Tankers)
1973 *Médoc* (Supply Ship)
1974 *Oasis* (Water Carrier)
1975 *Maurienne* (Fleet Support Ship)

L 9082 and 9083 (Repair Ships)
Tréberon (ex-German Transport)
Cataracte (Water Carrier)

Trials Ship
1975 *Arago*

BDV
1972 *Tarantule*
1974 *Scorpion, Locuste, Persistante*
1976 *Araignée*

Miscellaneous
1974 M691 (ex-*SC 525),* FNRS 3
1975 *Belier, Pachyderme, Infatigable, Peuplier* (Tugs)
1975 *Belouga* (Tender)

Transport
1976 *Falleron* (Jan)

PENNANT LIST

R Aircraft and Helicopter Carriers

97	Jeanne d'Arc
98	Clemenceau
99	Foch

C Cruiser

611	Colbert

D Destroyers

602	Suffren
603	Duquesne
609	Aconit
610	Tourville
611	Duguay-Trouin
612	De Grasse
622	Kersaint
624	Bouvet
625	Dupetit Thouars
627	Maillé Brézé
628	Vauquelin
629	D'Estrées
630	Du Chayla
631	Casablanca
632	Guépratte
633	Duperré
635	Forbin
636	Tartu
637	Jauréguiberry
638	La Galissonniere
640	Georges Leygues
641	Dupleix
642	Montcalm

S Submarines

610	Le Foudroyant
611	Le Redoutable
612	Le Terrible
613	L'Indomptable
614	Le Tonnant
620	Agosta
621	Bévéziers
622	La Praya
623	Ouessant
631	Narval
632	Marsouin
633	Dauphin
634	Requin
635	Aréthuse
636	Argonaute
637	Espadon
638	Morse
639	Amazone
640	Ariane
641	Daphné
642	Diane
643	Doris
645	Flore
646	Galatée
648	Junon
649	Venus
650	Psyche
651	Sirène
655	Gymnote

F Frigates and Corvettes

725	Victor Schoelcher
726	Commandant Bory
727	Amiral Charner
728	Doudart de Lagrée
729	Balny
733	Commandant Rivière
740	Commandant Bourdais
748	Protet
749	Enseigne de Vaisseau Henry
763	Le Boulonnais
765	Le Normand
766	Le Picard
767	Le Gascon
768	Le Lorrain
769	Le Bourguignon
770	Le Champenois
771	Le Savoyard
772	Le Breton
773	Le Basque
774	L'Agenais
775	Le Béarnais
776	L'Alsacien
777	Le Provençal
778	Le Vendéen
781	D'Estienne d'Orves
782	Amyot d'Inville
783	Drogou
784	Detroyat
785	Jean Moulin
786	Quartier Maitre Anquetil
787	Commandant de Pimodan
788	Seconde Maitre Le Bihan
790	Lieutenant de Vâisseau Lavallée
792	Premier Maitre l'Her
793	Commandant Blaison
794	Enseigne de Vaisseau Jacoubet

M Minewarfare Forces

609	Narvik
610	Ouistreham
612	Alençon
613	Berneval
615	Cantho
616	Dompaire
617	Garigliano
618	Mytho
619	Vinh-long
620	Berlaimont
622	Autun
623	Baccarat
624	Colmar
632	Pervenche
633	Pivoine
635	Résèda
638	Acacia
639	Acanthe
640	Marjolaine
668	Azalée
671	Camélia
674	Cyclamen
675	Eglantine
677	Giroflée
679	Glycine
681	Laurier
682	Lilas
684	Lobelia
687	Mimosa
688	Muguet
703	Antares
704	Algol
707	Véga
712	Cybele
713	Calliope
714	Clio
715	Circe
716	Ceres
737	Capricorne
740	Cassiopée
741	Eridan
743	Sagittaire
747	Bételgeuse
749	Phénix
755	Capella
756	Céphée
757	Verseau
759	Lyre
765	Mercure

P Light Forces

630	L'Intrépide
635	L'Ardent
637	L'Etourdi
638	L'Effronté
639	Le Frondeur
640	Le Fringant
644	L'Adroit
645	L'Alerte
646	L'Attentif
647	L'Enjoué
648	Le Hardi
650	Arcturus
651	La Malouine
652	La Lorientaise
653	La Dunkerquoise
654	La Bayonnaise
655	La Dieppoise
656	Altair
657	La Paimpolaise
658	Croix du Sud
659	Canopus
660	Etoile Polaire
661	Jasmin
662	Petunia
670	Trident
671	Glaive
672	Epée
673	Pertuisane
730	La Combattante
770	PB
771	PB
772	PB
774	PB
784	Geranium
787	Jonquille
788	Violette

L Amphibious Forces

9003	Argens
9004	Bidassoa
9007	Trieux
9008	Dives
9009	Blavet
9021	Ouragan
9022	Orage
9030	Champlain
9031	Francis Garnier
9061	LCT
9070	LCT
9071	LCT
9072	LCT
9073	LCT
9074	LCT

L Amphibious Forces

9081	Workshop
9082	LCT
9083	LCT
9084	Workshop
9091	LCT
9092	LCT
9093	LCT
9094	LCT
9096	LCT
(CTM	LCMs 1-16)

A Auxiliaries and Support Ships

603	Henry Poincaré
608	Moselle
610	Ile d'Oléron
615	Loire
617	Garonne
618	Rance
619	Aber Wrach
620	Jules Verne
621	Rhin
622	Rhône
625	Papenoo
626	La Charente
627	La Seine
628	La Sâone
629	La Durance
630	Lac Tonlé Sap
632	Punaruu
638	Sahel
640	Origny
643	Aunis
644	Berry
646	Triton
648	Archimède
649	L'Etoile
650	La Belle Poule
652	Mutin
653	La Grande Hermine
660	Hippopotame
664	Malabar
665	Goliath
666	Eléphant
667	Hercules
668	Rhinocéros
669	Tenace
671	Le Fort
672	Utile
673	Lutteur
674	Centaure
675	Isère
682	Alidade
683	Octant
684	Coolie
685	Robuste
686	Actif
687	Laborieux
688	Valeureux
692	Travailleur
694	Efficace
695	Acharne
698	Petrel
699	Pelican
701	Ajonc
706	Courageux
710	Myosotis
711	Gardénia
716	Oiseau des Iles
722	Poseidon
723	Liseron 730 Libellule
731	Tianée
733	Saintonge
735	Hibiscus
736	Dahlia
737	Tulipe
738	Capucine
739	Oeillet
740	Hortensia
741	Armoise
742	Paquerette
755	Commandant Robert Giraud
756	Espérance
757	D'Entrecasteaux
758	La Recherche
759	Marcel Le Bihan
760	Cigale
761	Criquet
762	Fourmi
763	Grillon
764	Scarabée
766	Estafette
767	Chamois
768	Elan
770	Magnolia
772	Engageante
773	Vigilante
774	Chevreul
775	Gazelle
777	Luciole
780	L'Astrolabe
781	Boussole
789	Archéonaute
794	Corail

Y Auxiliaries

601	Acajou
602	Aigrette
604	Ariel
607	Balsa
608	Bambou
611	Bengali
612	Bouleau
613	Faune
616	Canari
617	Mouette
618	Cascade
620	Chataigner
621	Mésange
623	Charme
624	Chêne
628	Colibri
629	Cormier
630	Bonite
631	Courlis
632	Cygne
633	Délange
634	Rouget
635	Equeurdibille
636	Martinet
637	Fauvette
640	Fontaine
641	Forméne
644	Fréne
645	Gave
646	Geyser
647	Giens
648	Goeland
649	Grive
651	Hanneton
652	Haut Barr
653	Heron
654	Hétre
655	Hévéat
657	Hirondelle
659	Jonque
661	Korrigan
662	Dryade
663	Latanier
664	Lutin
666	Manguier
667	Tupa
668	Méléze
669	Merisier
670	Merle
671	Morgane
673	Moineau
675	Martin Pecheur
678	Moule
680	Muréne
682	Okoume
683	Ondée
684	Oued
685	Oursin
686	Palétuvier
687	Passereau
688	Peuplier
689	Pin
690	Pingouin
691	Pinson
694	Pivert
695	Platane
696	Alphée
699	Poulpé
702	Rascasse
704	Rossignol
706	Chimère
708	Saule
709	Sycamore
710	Sylphe
711	Farfadet
717	Ébene
718	Erable
719	Olivier
720	Santal
721	Alouette
722	Vauneau
723	Engoulevent
724	Surcelle
725	Marabout
726	Toucan
727	Macreuse
728	Grand Duc
729	Eider
730	Ara
735	Merlin
736	Mélusine
738	Marronier
739	Noyer
740	Papayer
741	Elfe
743	Palangrin
745	Aiguiére
746	Embrun
747	Loriot
748	Gelinotte
749	La Prudente
750	La Perséverante
751	La Fidèle
760	PB

NAVAL AIR ARM

Squadron Number	Base	Aircraft	Task
Embarked Squadrons			
4F	Lann Bihoue	BR1050 "Alize"	Patrol & A/S
6F	Nimes Garons	BR1050 "Alize"	Patrol & A/S
11F	Landivisiau	ETD IV M	Fighter Bomber
12F	Landivisiau	F8E "Crusader"	Interceptors
14F	Landivisiau	F8E "Crusader"	Interceptors
16F	Landivisiau	ETD IV P	Reconnaissance
17F	Hyeres	ETD IV M	Fighter Bomber
31F	St. Mandrier	HSS 1	A/S
32F	Lanveoc Poulmic	Super-Frelon	A/S
33F	St. Mandrier	HSS 1	Assault
J. d'Arc	J. d'Arc or St. Mandrier	HSS 1	Training
SRL	Landivisiau	MS 760 "Paris"	Support
Support Squadrons			
2S	Lann Bihoue	Navajo, Nord 262	Support 1st & 2nd Region
3S	Hyeres	Navajo, Nord 262	Support 3rd Region
10S	St. Raphael	Nord 2504, BR1050 Navajo, MS 733	Trials CEPA
20S	St. Raphael	AL 11, AL 111 AL 111 ASM HSS 1, Super Frelon	Trials CEPA
22S	Lanveoc Poulmic	AL 11, AL 111 AL 111 VSV	Support 2nd Region, SAR
23S	St. Mandrier	AL 11, AL 111	Support 3rd Region, SAR
SSD	Dugny	C 54, Nord 262 Navajo	Support

Squadron Number	Base	Aircraft	Task
Maritime Patrol Squadrons			
21F	Nimes Garons	BR 1150 "Atlantic"	MP
22F	Nimes Garons	BR 1150 "Atlantic"	MP
23F	Lann Bihoue	BR 1150 "Atlantic"	MP
24F	Lann Bihoue	BR 1150 "Atlantic"	MP
25F	Lann Bihoue	Neptune P2H	MP
Training Squadrons			
55S	Aspretto	Nord 262, SNB 5	Twin-engine conversion
56S	Nimes Garons	C 47	Flying School
59S	Hyeres	ET IV, BR 1050 CM 175 "Zephyr"	Fighter School
SVS	Lanveoc Poulmic	MS 733	Naval School Recreational
Esalat Dax	Dax	AL 11	Helicopter School
Overseas Detachments			
New Caledonia	Tontouta	C 54, C 47	Support and Liaison
Malagasy	Diego Suarez	C 47	Support and Liaison
CEP Formations			
Sectal Pac.	Hao	AL 111	Support
27S	Hao	Super-Frelon	Support
12S	Papeete	Neptune P2H	MP

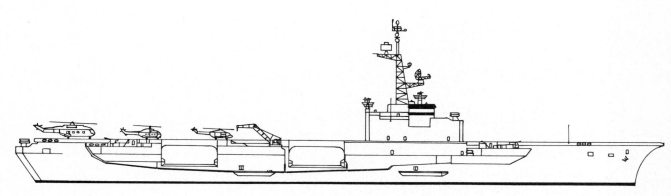

PA 75

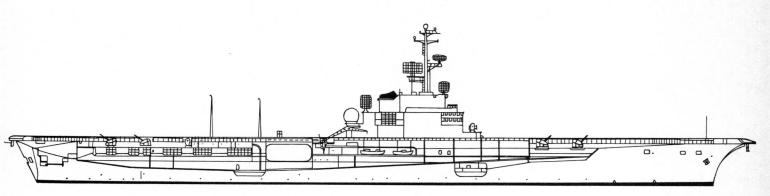

"CLEMENCEAU" Class

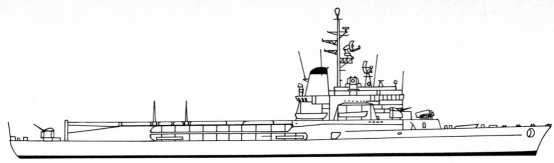

JEANNE D'ARC

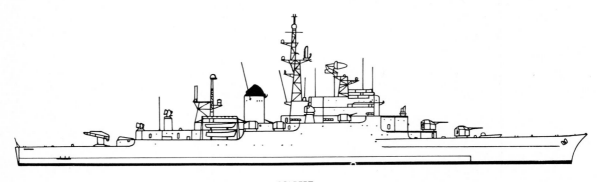

COLBERT

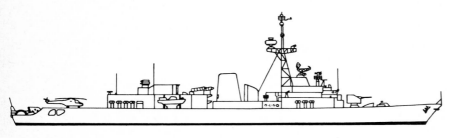

TYPE C70

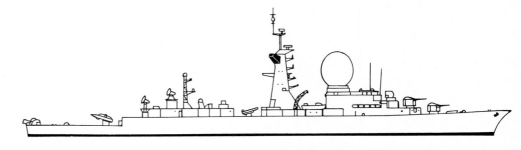

"SUFFREN" Class

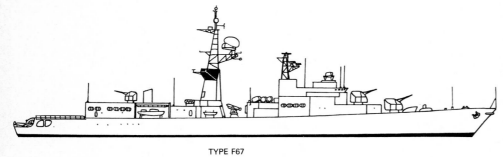

TYPE F67

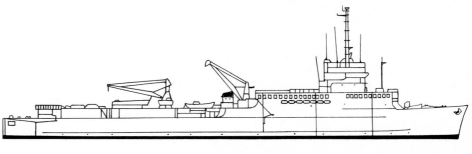

OURAGAN and ORAGE

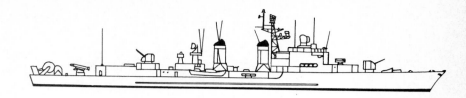

TYPE 47 (DDG)

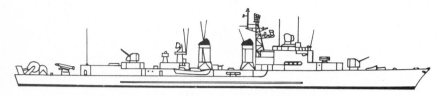

TYPE 47 (ASW)

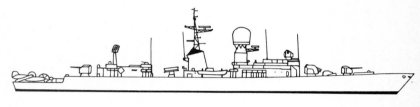

ACONIT

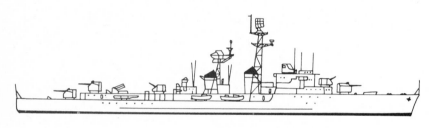

TYPE 53

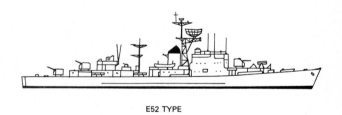

E52 TYPE

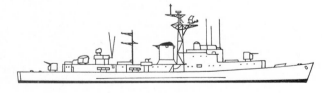

E52B TYPE

E50 TYPE

A69 TYPE

SUBMARINES

5 + NUCLEAR POWERED BALLISTIC MISSILE TYPE (SNLE)

Name	No.	Builders	Laid down	Launched	Trials	Operational
LE REDOUTABLE	S 611	Cherbourg Naval Dockyard	30 Mar 1964	29 Mar 1967	July 1969	1 Dec 1971
LE TERRIBLE	S 612	Cherbourg Naval Dockyard	24 June1967	12 Dec 1969	1971	1 Jan 1973
LE FOUDROYANT	S 610	Cherbourg Naval Dockyard	12 Dec 1969	4 Dec 1971	May 1973	6 July 1974
L'INDOMPTABLE	S 613	Cherbourg Naval Dockyard	4 Dec 1971	17 Aug 1974	Dec 1975	Jan 1977
LE TONNANT	S 614	Cherbourg Naval Dockyard	Oct 1974	1975	1976	April 1979
L'INFLEXIBLE (see note)	— (Q 260)	Cherbourg Naval Dockyard	—	—	—	—

Displacement, tons: 7 500 surfaced; 9 000 dived
Length, feet (metres): 420 *(128·0)*
Beam, feet (metres): 34·8 *(10·6)*
Draught, feet (metres): 32·8 *(10·0)*
Missile launchers: 16 tubes amidships for MSBS
Torpedo tubes: 4—21·7 inch (18 torpedoes)
Nuclear reactor: 1 pressurised water-cooled
Main machinery: 2 turbo-alternators; 1 electric motor;
  15 000 hp; 1 shaft
Auxiliary propulsion: 1 diesel; 2 670 hp; fuel for 5 000 miles
Speed, knots: 20 surfaced; 25 dived
Complement: Two alternating crews each of 135 (15 officers,
  120 men)
Diving depth: Over 700 ft

Le Redoutable was the first French nuclear-powered, ballistic
missile armed submarine and the prototype of the *"Force de
dissuasion"* of six such vessels which the Navy plans to have in
the early 1980s. The decision to build a fourth unit of this class
was announced on 7 Dec 1967, the fifth in Feb 1972 and the
sixth on 30 April 1974. The construction of *L'Inflexible* delayed
by 4th 5 Year Plan until 1982. She may then be lead-ship of an
improved class.

Missiles: First boats armed with MSBS M-1 of 18 tons launch
weight. *Le Foudroyant* is armed with MSBS M-2 of 19·9 tons
with a 1 300 n. mile range carrying a 500 KT head. *Le Redoutable* is being fitted with M-2 at her first refit (started early 1976).
L'Indomptable has the M-20 system with 1 500 n. mile range
missiles carrying a megaton reinforced head. All of this class
will later receive the M-4 system with a range reportedly in the
3 000 mile bracket and carrying MIRV warheads.

Radar: *Le Redoutable* is equipped with Calypso I Band radar for
navigation and attack. Has passive ECM and DF systems.

Reactor: The reactor is a natural-water-cooled type running on
enriched uranium, feeding twin turbines and two turbo-
alternators.

Subroc: Possibility of acquisition being investigated.

LE REDOUTABLE   *1975, French Navy*

LE REDOUTABLE, LE TERRIBLE, LE FOUDROYANT   *1973, French Navy*

1 EXPERIMENTAL MISSILE TYPE

Name	No.	Builders	Laid down	Launched	Commissioned
GYMNOTE	S 655	Cherbourg Naval Dockyard	17 Mar 1963 (see **Hull** Note)	17 Mar 1964	17 Oct 1966

Displacement, tons: 3 000 surfaced; 3 250 dived
Length, feet (metres): 275·6 *(84·0)*
Beam, feet (metres): 34·7 *(10·6)*
Draught, feet (metres): 25 *(7·6)*
Missile launchers: 2 tubes for MSBS
Main machinery: 4 sets 620 kW diesel electric; 2 electric motors; 2 shafts; 2 600 hp
Speed, knots: 11 surface; 10 dived
Complement: 78 (8 officers, 70 men)

An experimental submarine for testing ballistic missiles for the French nuclear-powered SSBNs, and for use as an underwater laboratory to prove equipment and arms for nuclear-powered submarines.

Started conversion in early 1977 (completion early 1978) for trial firings of M 4 Missiles. These will require tubes of greater diameter.

Hull: *Gymnote* was the hull laid down in 1958 as the nuclear-powered submarine Q 244 which was cancelled in 1959. The hull was still available when a trials vessel for the French MSBS type missiles was required and was completed as *Gymnote*. Has fixed bow-planes.

GYMNOTE   *1970, French Navy*

FLEET SUBMARINES

1 NEW CONSTRUCTION FLEET SUBMARINE

Name	No.	Builders	Laid down	Launched	Commissioned
—	S 616	Cherbourg Naval Dockyard	10 Dec 1976	—	1981

Displacement, tons: 2 385 surfaced; 2 670 dived
Dimensions, feet (metres): 236·5 × 24·9 × 21 *(72·1 × 7·6 × 6·4)*
Torpedo tubes: 4—21 in *(533 mm)* (14 torpedoes or mines)
Main machinery: 1 nuclear reactor; 48 MW; 2 turbo alternators; 1 main motor; 1 shaft 6 400 hp (?)
Auxiliary machinery: 1 set diesel-electric
Speed, knots: 25
Complement: 66 (9 officers, 35 petty officers, 22 junior ratings)

A prototype for a new class of fleet-submarines included in the 1974 programme. The armament, sonar and fire control equipment will be similar to the "Agosta" class.

Future: Two squadrons of these submarines are forecast, one to be stationed at Brest and the other at Toulon. Under the 4th Five Year Plan three sisters to S 616 are planned as well as a fourth of an improved type.

Machinery: Studies of the machinery are in progress at Cadaraché.

Name: The well-known name "Rubis" has been mentioned as a possible choice.

PATROL SUBMARINES

4 "AGOSTA" CLASS

Name	No.	Builders	Laid down (see note)	Launched	Commissioned
AGOSTA	S 620	Cherbourg Naval Dockyard	1 Nov 1972	19 Oct 1974	1977
BÉVÉZIERS	S 621	Cherbourg Naval Dockyard	17 May 1973	14 June 1975	1977
LA PRAYA	S 622	Cherbourg Naval Dockyard	1974	15 May 1976	1978
OUESSANT	S 623	Cherbourg Naval Dockyard	1974	Jan 1976	1978

Displacement, tons: 1 200 standard; 1 450 surfaced; 1 725 dived
Length, feet (metres): 221·7 *(67·6)*
Beam, feet (metres): 22·3 *(6·8)*
Draught, feet (metres): 17·7 *(5·2)*
Torpedo tubes: 4—21·7 in *(550 mm)* 20 reload torpedoes
Main machinery: Diesel-electric; 2 SEMT Pielstick 16 PA4 diesels 3 600 hp; 1 main motor (3 500 kW) 4 600 hp; 1 cruising motor (23 kW); 1 shaft
Speed, knots: 12 surfaced; 20 dived
Range, miles: 8 500 at 9 knots (snorting); 350 at 3·5 knots (dived)
Endurance: 45 days
Complement: 50 (7 officers, 43 men)

Building of this class was announced in 1970 under the third five-year new construction plan 1971-75. Considerable efforts have been made to improve the silencing of this class, including a clean casing and the damping of internal noise.

Laid down dates: Those given are for the placing of the first prefabricated section in the building dock. Prefabrication of *Agosta* started 7 Feb 1972 and of *Beveziers* Dec 1972.

Radar: Possibly I Band Calypso Th D 1030 or 1031 for search/navigation.

Sonar: DUUA 2 active sonar with transducers forward and aft; DSUV passive sonar with 36 hydrophones; passive ranging; intercept set.

Torpedo tubes: A new design allowing for torpedo discharge at all speeds and down to full diving depth. Rapid reloading fitted.

Foreign orders: Four to be built at Cartagena for Spanish Navy and two for South Africa by Dubigeon.

AGOSTA   *1977, French Navy*

9 "DAPHNÉ" CLASS

Name	No.
DAPHNÉ	S 641
DIANE	S 642
DORIS	S 643
FLORE	S 645
GALATÉE	S 646
JUNON	S 648
VENUS	S 649
PSYCHÉ	S 650
SIRÈNE	S 651

Builders	Laid down	Launched	Commissioned
Dubigeon	Mar 1958	20 June 1959	1 June 1964
Dubigeon	July 1958	4 Oct 1960	20 June 1964
Cherbourg Naval Dockyard	Sep 1958	14 May 1960	26 Aug 1964
Cherbourg Naval Dockyard	Sep 1958	21 Dec 1960	21 May 1964
Cherbourg Naval Dockyard	Sep 1958	22 Sep 1961	25 July 1964
Cherbourg Naval Dockyard	July 1961	11 May 1964	25 Feb 1966
Cherbourg Naval Dockyard	Aug 1961	24 Sep 1964	1 Jan 1966
Brest Naval Dockyard	May 1965	28 June 1967	1 July 1969
Brest Naval Dockyard	May 1965	28 June 1967	1 Mar 1970

Displacement, tons: 869 surfaced; 1 043 dived
Length, feet (metres): 189·6 *(57·8)*
Beam, feet (metres): 22·3 *(6·8)*
Draught, feet (metres): 15·1 *(4·6)*
Torpedo tubes: 12—21·7 in *(550 mm)* 8 bow 4 stern
Main machinery: SEMT-Pielstick diesel-electric;
 1 300 bhp surfaced; 1 600 bhp motors dived; 2 shafts
Range, miles: 2 700 at 12·5 knots (surfaced); 4 500 at 5 knots
 (snorting); 3 000 at 7 knots (snorting)
Speed, knots: 13·5 surfaced; 16 dived
Complement: 45 (6 officers, 39 men)

Improved "Aréthuse" class with diving depth about 1 000 ft
(300 metres). *Sirène* sank at Lorient in 1972, and was subsequently salved.

Modernisation: In hand from 1971 to improve sonar and armament.

Radar: I Band Calypso II for search/navigation.

Sonar: DUUA 2 active sonar with transducers forward and aft;
passive ranging; intercept set.

Foreign orders: South Africa (1967) (3), Pakistan (1966) (3),
Portugal (1964) (4), Spain (built in Spain) (1965) (4), Libya (built
in Spain) (1976 on) (4).

PSYCHÉ
11/1976, Michael D. J. Lennon

DIANE
1975, Wright and Logan

4 "ARÉTHUSE" CLASS

Name	No.
AMAZONE	S 639
ARÉTHUSE	S 635
ARGONAUTE	S 636
ARIANE	S 640

Builders	Laid down	Launched	Commissioned
Cherbourg Naval Dockyard	Dec 1955	3 April 1958	1 July 1959
Cherbourg Naval Dockyard	Mar 1955	9 Nov 1957	23 Oct 1958
Cherbourg Naval Dockyard	Mar 1955	29 June 1957	11 Feb 1959
Cherbourg Naval Dockyard	Dec 1955	12 Sep 1958	16 Mar 1960

Displacement, tons: 400 standard; 543 surfaced;
 669 dived
Length, feet (metres): 162·7 *(49·6)*
Beam, feet (metres): 19 *(5·8)*
Draught, feet (metres): 13·1 *(4·0)*
Torpedo tubes: 4—21·7 in *(550 mm)* bow, 4 reloads
Main machinery: 12-cyl SEMT-Pielstick diesel-electric;
 1 060 bhp surfaced; 1 300 hp motors dived; 1 shaft
Speed, knots: 12·5 surfaced; 16 dived
Complement: 40 (6 officers, 34 men)

An excellent class of small submarines with a minimum
number of ballast tanks and a diving depth of about 600 feet.

Sonar: DUUA 2.

ARÉTHUSE
6/1976, Dr. Giorgio Arra

6 "NARVAL" CLASS

Name	No.
NARVAL	S 631
MARSOUIN	S 632
DAUPHIN	S 633
REQUIN	S 634
ESPADON	S 637
MORSE	S 638

Builders	Laid down	Launched	Commissioned
Cherbourg Naval Dockyard	June 1951	11 Dec 1954	1 Dec 1957
Cherbourg Naval Dockyard	Sep 1951	21 May 1955	1 Oct 1957
Cherbourg Naval Dockyard	May 1952	17 Sep 1955	1 Aug 1958
Cherbourg Naval Dockyard	June 1952	3 Dec 1955	1 Aug 1958
Normand	Dec 1955	15 Sep 1958	2 April 1960
Seine Maritime	Feb 1956	10 Dec 1958	2 May 1960

Displacement, tons: 1 320 standard; 1 635 surfaced; 1 910
 dived
Length, feet (metres): 257·2 *(77·6)*
Beam, feet (metres): 25·6 *(7·8)*
Draught, feet (metres): 18·5 *(5·4)*
Torpedo tubes: 6—21·7 in *(550 mm)* bow; 14 reload torpedoes;
 capable of minelaying
Main machinery: Diesel electric, three 12-cyl SEMT-Pielstick
 diesels; two 2 400 hp electric motors; 2 shafts
Speed, knots: 15 surfaced; 18 dived
Range, miles: 15 000 at 8 knots (snorting)
Endurance: 45 days
Complement: 63 (7 officers, 56 men)

Improved versions based on the German Type XXI. *Dauphin,
Marsouin, Narval* and *Requin* were built in seven prefabricated
parts each of 10 metres in length.

Engineering: New main propelling machinery installed on
reconstruction during 1965 to 1970 includes diesel-electric
drive on the surface with SEMT-Pielstick diesels. The original
main machinery was Schneider 4 000 bhp 7 cyl. 2 str. diesels

REQUIN
11/1976, Michael D. J. Lennon

for surface propulsion and 5 000 hp electric motors dived.

Reconstruction: During a five-year reconstruction programme, announced in 1965 and completed by the end of 1970,
these submarines, *Requin* in Spring 1967 and *Espadon* and

Morse in succession at Lorient followed by the other three,
were given a new diesel electric power plant as well as new
weapon and detection equipment.

Sonar: DUUA 1.

AIRCRAFT CARRIERS

1 PA 75 (NUCLEAR-PROPELLED HELICOPTER CARRIER)

Name	No.	Builders	Laid down	Launched	Commissioning
—	PA 75	DCAN, Brest	?1980-81	—	—

Displacement. tons: 16 400 trials; 18 400 full load
Length, feet (metres): 682·2 oa (208)
Length, feet (metres): 662·6 flight deck (202)
Beam, feet (metres): 86·6 wl (26·4)
Beam, feet (metres): 157·4 flight deck (46)
Draught, feet (metres): 21·3 (6·5)
Aircraft: 25 WG 13 Lynx or 10 Super Frelon or 15 Puma helicopters
Missiles: 2 Crotale SAM systems; 4 SAM systems with a sea-skimming capability for anti-missile defence are eventually to replace the guns
Guns: 2—100 mm (singles—forward)
Main engines: 1—CAS 230 reactor to two turbines; 65 000 bhp; two emergency AGO diesels
Speed, knots: 28
Range, miles: Unlimited on reactor; 3 000 at 18 knots (diesels)
Endurance: Stores for 45 days; 30 days for passengers
Complement: 890 (840 ship, 50 staff) plus 1 500 passengers

Coming at a time of financial stringency, this is a bold design showing the French Navy's appreciation of the great and universal value of helicopters in both peace and war. While her wartime role in a force composed of both A/S and A/A ships is clear, she has been designed with an intervention role in mind as well. For peacetime duties in the event of natural disasters, her large passenger and hospital capacity will be of immense value. Although the original plan allowed for her completion in 1980 the new 1977-81 plan states that she will not be laid down until 1980-81, being the first of a class of these ships. However some long-lead items have already been ordered.

Accommodation: A crew of 840 plus 50 staff and Ground Intervention Staff is provided for. Passenger accommodation is available for 1 000, with more austere conditions on portable bunks for an extra 500 in the garage (forward of the hangar).

Aircraft: Although designed primarily for helicopter operations the possibility of VTOL operations was also taken into account.

Electrical supply: A total of 9 400 kW from two turbines each driving a pair of 1 500 kW alternators and four diesel alternators of 850 kW each.

Flight Deck: The flight deck, 662 feet long, is 157 feet wide at its maximum and 102 feet at the island. Four spots are provided for Super Frelon helicopters and eight for Lynx or Puma.

Hangar: One hangar, 275 × 69 × 21 feet, is provided with two lateral lifts to starboard at the rear of the island. Storage for 1 000 cubic metres of TR5 fuel in tanks is available. One fixed crane and one mobile crane are provided.

Hospital: 3 main wards, 1 X-ray ward, 1 intensive care ward, 1 infectious diseases ward, 2 dental surgeries and a laboratory.

Main engines: The CAS 230 reactor of 230 megawatts is being constructed under the supervision of l'Etablissement des Constructions et Armes Navales d'Indret.

Operations Rooms: Normal Operations Room, ASW centre and Communication Offices are supplemented by an Operations Centre with facilities for Ground Intervention Forces and Air Intervention Forces. These include a Warfare Coordinating Centre, an Air Intervention Command Centre and a Helicopter Command Station.

Radar: 1 DRBV 26 long range air search set; 1 DRBV 51C combined search set; 2 Decca systems; 2DRBC 32 for missile guidance.

Replenishment: 1 250 tons of fuel is carried for replenishment of Escorts.

Type: Although originally classified as PH (Porte helicoptères) this has been changed to PA (Porte aeronefs) signifying her V/STOL capability.

Sonar: 1 DUBA 25.

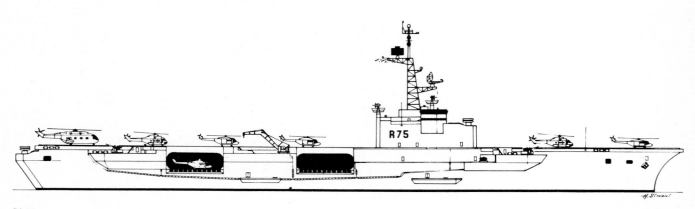

PA 75

1974, French Navy

2 "CLEMENCEAU" CLASS

Name	No.	Builders	Laid down	Launched	Commissioned
CLEMENCEAU	R 98	Brest Dockyard	Nov 1955	21 Dec 1957	22 Nov 1961
FOCH	R 99	Chantiers de l'Atlantique	Feb 1957	28 July 1960	15 July 1963

Displacement, tons: 27 307 normal; 32 780 full load
Length, feet (metres): 780·8 *(238·0)* pp; 869·4 *(265·0)* oa
Beam, feet (metres): 104·1 *(31·7)* hull (with bulges)
Width, feet (metres): 168·0 *(51·2)* oa
Draught, feet (metres): 28·2 *(8·6)*
Aircraft: Capacity 40. Each carries 3 Flights—1 of Etendard IV, 1 of Crusader, 1 of Breguet Alizé
Catapults: 2 Mitchell-Brown steam, Mk BS 5
Guns: 8—3·9 in *(100 mm)* automatic in single turrets
Armour: Flight deck, island superstructure and bridges, hull (over machinery spaces and magazines)
Main engines: 2 sets Parsons geared turbines; 2 shafts; 126 000 shp
Boilers: 6; steam pressure 640 psi *(45 kg/cm²),* superheat 842°F *(450°C)*
Speed, knots: 32
Oil fuel, tons: 3 720
Range, miles: 7 500 at 18 knots; 4 800 at 24 knots; 3 500 at full power
Complement: 1 228 (65 officers, 1 163 men)

First aircraft carriers designed as such and built from the keel to be completed in France. Authorised in 1953 and 1955, respectively. *Clemenceau* ordered from Brest Dockyard on 28 May 1954 and begun in Nov 1955. *Foch* begun at Chantiers de l'Atlantique at St. Nazaire, Penhoet-Loire, in a special dry dock (contract provided for the construction of the hull and propelling machinery) and completed by Brest Dockyard.

Bulges: *Foch* was completed with bulges. These having proved successful, *Clemenceau* was modified similarly on first refit, increasing her beam by 6 feet.

Electronics: Comprehensive DF and ECM equipment. Both fitted with SENIT 4 Tactical data automation system.

Flight Deck: Angled deck, two lifts, measuring 52·5 × 36 feet, one on the starboard deck edge, two steam catapults and two mirror landing aids. The flight deck measures 543 × 96·8 feet and is angled at 8 degrees.
Flight deck letters: F = *Foch,* U = *Clemenceau.*

Gunnery: Originally to have been armed with 24—2·25 inch guns in twin mountings, but the armament was revised to 12—3·9 inch *(100 mm)* in 1956 and to 8—3·9 inch *(100 mm)* in 1958. Rate of fire 60 rounds per minute.

Hangar: Dimensions of the hangar are 590·6 × 78·7 × 23·0 feet *(180 × 24 × 7 metres)*

Radar: One DRBV 20C; one DRBV 23B; two DRBI 10; one DRBV 50; one DRBC 31.

Sonar: One SQS 505.

CLEMENCEAU   7/1976, Dr. Giorgio Arra

FOCH   1974, Dr. Giorgio Arra

CLEMENCEAU   7/1976, Dr. Giorgio Arra

CRUISERS

Name	No.	Builders	Laid down	Launched	Commissioned
JEANNE D'ARC (ex-*La Résolue*)	R 97	Brest Dockyard	7 July 1960	30 Sep 1961	1 July 1963 (trials) 30 June 1964 (service)

Displacement, tons: 10 000 standard; 12 365 full load
Length, feet (metres): 564·2 *(172)* pp; 597·1 *(182·0)* oa
Beam, feet (metres): 78·7 *(24·0)* hull
Draught, feet (metres): 24·0 *(7·3)*
Flight deck, feet (metres): 203·4 × 68·9 *(62·0 × 21·0)*
Aircraft: Heavy A/S helicopters (4 in peace-time as training ship; 8 in wartime)
Missiles: 6—MM38 Exocet
Guns: 4—3·9 in *(100 mm)* single
Main engines: Rateau-Bretagne geared turbines; 2 shafts; 40 000 shp
Boilers: 4; working pressure 640 psi *(45 kg/cm²)*; 842°F *(450°C)*
Speed, knots: 26·5
Oil fuel, tons: 1 360
Range, miles: 6 000 at 15 knots
Complement: 809 (30 officers, 587 ratings and 192 cadets)

Authorised under the 1957 estimates. Used for training officer cadets in peacetime in place of the old training cruiser *Jeanne d'Arc* (which was decommissioned on 28 July 1964 and sold for scrap in Dec 1965 at Brest). In wartime, after rapid modification, she would be used as a commando ship, helicopter carrier or troop transport with commando equipment and a battalion of 700 men. The lift has a capacity of 12 tons. The ship is almost entirely air-conditioned.

Missiles: Due to be fitted with Crotale.

Modifications: Between first steaming trials and completion for operational service the ship was modified with a taller funnel to clear the superstructure and prevent the smoke and exhaust gases swirling on to the bridges.

Radar: One DRBV 22D; one DRBV 50; one DRBN 32; one DRBI 10.

Sonar: One SQS 503.

JEANNE D'ARC   *1975, French Navy*

JEANNE D'ARC   *1975, French Navy*

Name	No.	Builders	Laid down	Launched	Commissioned
COLBERT	C 611	Brest Dockyard	Dec 1953	24 Mar 1956 (floated out of dry dock)	5 May 1959 (trials late 1957)

Displacement, tons: 8 500 standard; 11 300 full load
Length, feet (metres): 593·2 *(180·8)*
Beam, feet (metres): 66·1 *(20·2)*
Draught, feet (metres): 25·2 *(7·7)*
Missile launchers: 1 twin Masurca surface-to-air aft.
    4-MM38 Exocet to be fitted
Guns: 2—3·9 in *(100 mm)* single automatic;
    12—57 mm in 6 twin mountings, 3 on each side
Armour: 50—80 mm belt and 50 mm deck
Main engines: 2 sets CEM-Parsons geared turbines; 2 shafts;
    86 000 shp
Boilers: 4 Indret multitubular; 640 psi *(45 kg/cm²)*; 842°F *(450°C)*
Speed, knots: 31·5
Oil fuel, tons: 1 492
Range, miles: 4 000 at 25 knots
Complement: 560 (24 officers, 536 men)

She was equipped as command ship and for radar control of air strikes.

Electronics: Senit data automation system; radar intercept equipment; wireless intercept equipment; two Knebworth Corvus dual-purpose launchers for CHAFF.

Gunnery: Prior to Apr 1970 the armament comprised sixteen 5 inch *(127 mm)* dual purpose guns in eight twin mountings, and twenty 57 mm Bofors anti-aircraft guns in ten twin mountings.

Missiles: *Colbert* carries 48 Masurca missiles (Mk 2 Mod 3 semi-active radar homing version). 4 Exocet to be shipped at a later refit.

Radar: Navigation: one Decca RM416.
Surveillance: one DRBV 50.
Air surveillance: one DRBV 23C
Warning: one DRBV 20.
Fire control: two DRBR 51; one DRBR 32C; two DRBC 31.
Height finder: one DRBI 10D.

Reconstruction: Between April 1970 and October 1972 she underwent a complete reconstruction and rearmament. The gunnery systems were altered to those given above, the Masurca surface-to-air missile system was fitted and helicopter facilities were installed on the quarter-deck. Reductions in the original armament schedule saved 80 mil francs from the original refit cost of 350 mil francs.

Sonar: Hull mounted set.

COLBERT   7/1976, Dr. Giorgio Arra

COLBERT   3/1976, Reinhard Nerlich

COLBERT   7/1976, Dr. Giorgio Arra

DESTROYERS

3 TYPE C 70

Name	No.	Builders	Laid down	Launched	Commissioned
GEORGES LEYGUES	D 640	Brest Dockyard	16 Sep 1974	18 Dec 1976	1978
DUPLEIX	D 641	Brest Dockyard	17 Oct 1975	—	1979
MONTCALM	D 642	Brest Dockyard	Dec 1975	—	1979

Displacement, tons: 3 800 standard; 4 100 full load
Length, feet (metres): 455·9 oa *(139)*
Beam, feet (metres): 45·9 *(14)*
Draught, feet (metres): 18·7 *(5·7)*
Aircraft: 2WG 13 Lynx helicopters with Mk 44 or 46 torpedoes
Missile launchers: 4 MM 38 Exocet; 1 Crotale
Guns: 1—3·9 in *(100 mm)*; 2—20 mm
Torpedo tubes: 10 tubes in 2 mountings for Mk L5
Main engines: CODOG; 2 Rolls Royce Olympus gas turbines 42 000 bhp; 2 SEMT-Pielstick 16PA6 diesels 10 000 bhp; 2 shafts; VP screws
Speed, knots: 29·75 (19·5 on diesels)
Range, miles: 9 000 at 18 knots on diesels
Complement: 242 (19 officers, 223 ratings)

A new C 70 type of so-called "corvette".
A total of at least 24 is planned for completion by 1985, eighteen being of an A/S version like *G. Leygues* and six of an A/A version. Three more of the A/S version are to be built under the 4th Five Year Plan (1977-81). Three of the Air Defence version are also to be ordered under the same plan to be fitted with Standard/Tartar SM 2 and 1—100 mm gun as well as Exocet with DRBV 13 radar and DUBV 25 sonar. These to be laid down towards end of period of plan.

Electronics: Senit action data automation system.

Helicopter: The Lynx, as well as its A/S role, can have an anti-surface role when armed with 4 AS 12 missiles.

Missiles: AA version to carry Standard SM2 system.

Radar: one DRBV 26; one DRBV 51; one DRBV 32E; two Decca 1226.

Sonar: One DUBV 23 (hull-mounted); one DUBV 43 (VDS).

GEORGES LEYGUES · 1977, French Navy

TYPE C70 · 1976, French Navy

2 "SUFFREN" CLASS

Name	No.	Builders	Laid down	Launched	Commissioned
DUQUESNE	D 603	Brest Dockyard	Nov 1964	12 Feb 1966	Apr 1970
SUFFREN	D 602	Lorient Dockyard	Dec 1962	15 May 1965	July 1967

Displacement, tons: 5 090 standard; 6 090 full load
Length, feet (metres): 517·1 (157·6) oa
Beam, feet (metres): 50·9 (15·5)
Draught, feet (metres): 20·0 (6·1)
Missile launchers: Twin Masurca surface-air (see notes)
Guns: 2—3·9 in (100 mm) (automatic, single)
  2—30 mm (automatic single)
A/S weapons: Malafon single launcher with 13 missiles; 4
  launchers (2 each side) for L5 A/S homing torpedoes
Main engines: Double reduction Rateau geared turbines;
  2 shafts; 72 500 shp
Boilers: 4 automatic; working pressure 640 psi (45 kg/cm²);
  superheat 842°F (450°C)
Speed, knots: 34
Range, miles: 5 100 at 18 knots; 2 400 at 29 knots
Complement: 426 (23 officers, 332 men)

Ordered under the 1960 Programme. Equipped with gyro controlled stabilisers controlling three pairs of non-retractable fins. Air-conditioning of accommodation and operational areas. Excellent sea-boats and weapon platforms.

Electronics: Senit I action data automatic system. Two Syllex.

Missiles: Carry 48 Masurca missiles, a mix of Mk 2 Mod 2 beam riders and Mk 2 Mod 3 semi-active homers. During their 1977 refit 4 Exocet launchers will replace one of the 100 mm gun mountings. *Duquesne* completed Feb 1977.

Radar: Search and navigation: one DRBN 32.
Air surveillance and target designator (radome): one DRBI 23.
Surface surveillance: one DRBV 50.
Masurca fire-control: two DRBR 51.
Gun fire-control: one DRBC 32A.

Sonar: One DUBV 23 hull-mounted set and a DUBV 43 VDS.

SUFFREN   7/1976, Dr. Giorgio Arra

SUFFREN   7/1976, Dr. Giorgio Arra

SUFFREN   11/1975, Dr. Giorgio Arra

3 TYPE F 67 (ex-C-67A)

Name	No.
TOURVILLE	D 610
DUGUAY-TROUIN	D 611
DE GRASSE	D 612

Builders	Laid down	Launched	Commissioned
Lorient Naval Dockyard	16 Mar 1970	13 May 1972	21 June1974
Lorient Naval Dockyard	25 Feb 1971	1 June1973	17 Sep 1975
Lorient Naval Dockyard	1972	30 Nov 1974	July 1976

Displacement, tons: 4 580 standard; 5 745 full load
Length, feet (metres): 510·3 *(152·8)* oa
Beam, feet (metres): 50·2 *(15·3)*
Draught, feet (metres): 18·7 *(5·7)*
Aircraft: 2 WG 13 Lynx ASW helicopters
Missile launchers: 6 MM 38 Exocet;
  1—Crotale SAM *(De Grasse)* (see note)
Guns: 3—3·9 in *(100 mm)* (2 in *De Grasse)*
A/S weapons: 1 Malafon rocket/homing torpedo
  (13 missiles); 2 mountings for Mk L5 torpedoes
Main engines: Rateau geared turbines; 2 shafts; 54 400 shp
Boilers: 4 automatic
Speed, knots: 31
Range, miles: 5 000 at 18 knots
Complement: 303 (25 officers, 278 men)

Developed from the "Aconit" design. Originally rated as "Corvettes" but reclassified as "Frigates" on 8 July 1971 and given "D" pennant numbers like destroyers.

Electronics: Senit action data automatic system. Two Syllex.

Missiles: Octuple Crotale fitted in *De Grasse* in place of after 100 mm gun and to be retro-fitted in first refit of others of class.

Radar: Surface/air surveillance: one DRBV 51
Fire control: one DRBC 32D
Navigation: two Decca type 1226
Air search: one DRBV 26

Sonars: One DUBV 23 hull-mounted; one DUBV 43 VDS.

DUGUAY-TROUIN   *1976, French Navy*

TOURVILLE   *7/1976, Dr. Giorgio Arra*

1 TYPE T 56

Name	No.
LA GALISSONNIÈRE	D 638

Builders	Laid down	Launched	Commissioned
Lorient Naval Dockyard	Nov 1958	12 Mar 1960	July 1962

Displacement, tons: 2 750 standard; 3 740 full load
Length, feet (metres): 435·7 *(132·8)* oa
Beam, feet (metres): 41·7 *(12·7)*
Draught, feet (metres): 21·4 *(6·3)*
Aircraft: 1 A/S helicopter
A/S weapons: 1 Malafon rocket/homing torpedo launcher
Guns: 2—3·9 in *(100 mm)* automatic, single
Torpedo tubes: 6—21·7 in *(550 mm)* ASM, 2 triple for Mks K2
  and L3
Main engines: 2 sets Rateau geared turbines; 2 shafts;
  63 000 shp
Boilers: 4 A & C de B Indret; 500 psi *(35 kg/cm²)*; 617°F (380°C)
Speed, knots: 32
Oil fuel, tons: 800
Range, miles: 5 000 at 18 knots
Complement: 270 (15 officers, 255 men)

Same characteristics as regards hull and machinery as T 47 and T 53 types, but different armament. She has a hangar which hinges outwards and a platform for landing a helicopter. When first commissioned she was used as an experimental ship for new sonars and anti-submarine weapons.

Armament: First French combatant ship to be armed with Malafon. This is the reason for the two 3·9 in *(100 mm)* guns instead of the 3 or 4 previously planned. France's first operational guided missile ship.

Electronics: Tacan beacon and full DF and ECM fit.

Radar: Surface/air surveillance: one DRBV 50
Navigation: one DRBN 32
Air search: one DRBV 22
Gun fire-control: one DRBC 32A

Sonar: One hull mounted DUBV 23; one DUBV 43 VDS.

LA GALISSONIÈRE   *7/1976, Dr. Giorgio Arra*

1 TYPE T 53 (MODIFIED—ASW)

Name	No.	Builders	Laid down	Launched	Commissioned
DUPERRÉ	D 633	Lorient Naval Dockyard	Nov 1954	23 June 1956	8 Oct 1957

Displacement, tons: 2 800 standard; 3 900 full load
Length, feet (metres): 435·7 *(132·8)* oa
Beam, feet (metres): 41·7 *(12·7)*
Draught, feet (metres): 20 *(6·1)*
Aircraft: 1 WG 13 Lynx helicopter
Missiles: 4 MM 38 Exocet
Gun: 1—3·9 in *(100 mm)*
A/S weapons: Launcher for 8 torpedoes (Mk L5)
Main engines: 2 sets Rateau geared turbines; 2 shafts;
  63 000 shp
Boilers: 4 A & C de B Indret; 500 psi *(35 kg/cm²)*; 617°F (380°C)
Speed, knots: 32
Oil fuel, tons: 800
Range, miles: 5 000 at 18 knots
Complement: 272 (15 officers, 257 men)

Originally built with 6—5 in guns.
After serving as trial ship from 1967-71, she was converted at
Brest to her present state in 1972-74. Recommissioned 21 May
1974.

Electronics: One Senit automatic data system; two Syllex.

Gunnery: Appears to lack radar fire-control for 100 mm gun.

Radar: Air search: one DRBV 22A
Navigation: one Decca
Helicopter: one Decca
Fire control: one DRBC 32E
Surface/air surveillance: one DRBV 51

Sonar: DUBV 23 hull-mounted; DUBV 43 VDS.

DUPERRÉ   6/1975, Dr. Giorgio Arra

3 TYPE T 53

Name	No.	Builders	Laid down	Launched	Commissioned
FORBIN	D 635	Brest Naval Dockyard	Aug 1954	15 Oct 1955	1 Feb 1958
TARTU	D 636	At. Chantiers de Bretagne	Nov 1954	2 Dec 1955	5 Feb 1958
JAURÉGUIBERRY	D 637	Gironde	Sep 1954	5 Nov 1955	July 1958

Displacement, tons: 2 750 standard; 3 740 full load
Length, feet (metres): 421·3 *(128·6)*
Beam, feet (metres): 41·7 *(12·7)*
Draught, feet (metres): 18·0 *(5·5)*
Guns: 6—5 in *(127 mm)* (twins); *(Forbin* 4—5 in);
  6—57 mm (twins); 2—20 mm
A/S weapons: 2 triple mountings *(550 mm)* for Mk K2 and L3;
  375 mm Mk 54 projector
Main engines: 2 geared turbines; 63 000 shp; 2 shafts
Boilers: 4 A & C de B Indret
Speed, knots: 32
Oil fuel, tons: 800
Range, miles: 5 000 at 18 knots
Complement: 276 (15 officers, 261 men)

Air-direction ships—*Forbin* has helicopter platform aft in place
of Y mount.
Forbin acts as a training ship for l'École d'Application des
Enseignes de Vaisseau, being part of the *Jeanne d'Arc* group.

Electronics: Senit automatic data system.
Tacan Beacon.

Radar: Three dimensional air search: DRBI 10A
Air search: DRBV 22A
Navigation: DRBV 31

Sonar: One DUBA 1; one DUBV 24.

TARTU   7/1976, Dr. Giorgio Arra

FORBIN (with helo platform)   1973, French Navy

4 TYPE T 47 (DDG)

Name	No.	Builders	Laid down	Launched	Commissioned
KERSAINT	D 622	Lorient Naval Dockyard	June 1951	3 Oct 1953	20 Mar 1956
BOUVET	D 624	Lorient Naval Dockyard	Nov 1951	3 Oct 1953	13 May 1956
DUPETIT THOUARS	D 625	Brest Naval Dockyard	Mar 1952	4 Mar 1954	15 Sep 1956
DU CHAYLA	D 630	Brest Naval Dockyard	July 1953	27 Nov 1954	4 June1957

Displacement, tons: 2 750 standard; 3 740 full load
Length, feet (metres): 421·3 *(128·6)*
Beam, feet (metres): 41·7 *(12·7)*
Draught, feet (metres): 21·4 *(6·3)*
Missiles: Single Mk 13 Tartar launcher (40 missiles—SMI or SMIA)
Guns: 6—57 mm (twins)
A/S weapons: 2 triple mountings *(550 mm)* for Mk K2 and L3; 375 mm Mk 54 projector
Main engines: 2 geared turbines; 63 000 shp; 2 shafts
Boilers: 4 A & C de B Indret
Speed, knots: 32
Oil fuel, tons: 800
Range, miles: 5 000 at 18 knots
Complement: 277 (17 officers, 260 men)

Originally built as all-gun destroyers with 6—5 in guns. Converted into DDGs 1961-65.

Electronics: Senit automatic data system.

Radar: Air-search: one DRBV 20 A
Tartar search (3D): one SPS 39
Tartar control: two SPG 51B
Navigation: one DRBV 31

Sonars: One DUBA 1; one DUBV 24.

KERSAINT   *1976, Michael D. J. Lennon*

KERSAINT   *7/1976, Reinhard Nerlich*

5 TYPE T 47 (ASW)

Name	No.	Builders	Laid down	Launched	Commissioned
MAILLE BRÉZÉ	D 627	Lorient Naval Dockyard	Oct 1953	26 Sep 1954	4 May 1957
VAUQUELIN	D 628	Lorient Naval Dockyard	Mar 1953	26 Sep 1954	3 Nov 1956
D'ESTRÉES	D 629	Brest Naval Dockyard	May 1953	27 Nov 1954	19 Mar 1957
CASABIANCA	D 631	F. C. Gironde	Oct 1953	13 Nov 1954	4 May 1957
GUÉPRATTE	D 632	A. C. Bretagne	Aug 1953	8 Nov 1954	6 June1957

Displacement, tons: 2 750 standard; 3 900 full load
Length, feet (metres): 434·6 *(132·5)*
Beam, feet (metres): 41·7 *(12·7)*
Draught, feet (metres): 21·4 *(6·3)*
Guns: 2—3·9 in *(100 mm)* (singles); 2—20 mm
A/S weapons: 1 Malafon; 1—375 mm Mk 54 projector; two triple mountings *(550 mm)* for Mk K2 and L3
Main engines: 2 geared turbines; 63 000 shp; 2 shafts
Boilers: 4 A & C de B Indret
Speed, knots: 32
Range, miles: 5 000 at 18 knots
Oil fuel, tons: 800
Complement: 260 (15 officers, 245 men)

Originally with 6—5 in guns.
Converted between 1968-71 including air-conditioning of living spaces, replacement of electronic equipment and updating of damage control equipment.

D'ESTRÉES (after last refit with new aerial outfit)   *7/1976, Dr. Giorgio Arra*

Electronics: Senit data handling.
Radar: Navigation: one DRBN 32
Air surveillance: one DRBV 22A

Air/surface search: one DRBV 50
Gun fire control: two DRBC 32A
Sonars: One DUBV 23 hull mounted; one DUBV 43 VDS.

MAILLE BRÉZÉ   *6/1975, Dr. Giorgio Arra*

1 TYPE C 65

Name	No.	Builders	Laid down	Launched	Commissioned
ACONIT	D 609 (ex-*F 703*)	Lorient Naval Dockyard	Jan 1966	7 Mar 1970	30 Mar 1973 (trials 15 May 1971)

Displacement, tons: 3 500 standard; 3 900 full load
Length, feet (metres): 416·7 *127·0)* oa
Beam, feet (metres): 44·0 *(13·4)*
Draught, feet (metres): 18·9 *(5·8)*
Missiles: Malafon rocket/homing torpedo;
  MM 38 Exocet to be fitted
Guns: 2—3·9 in *(100 mm)*
A/S weapons: 1 quadruple 12 in *(305 mm)* mortar;
  2 launchers for Mk L5 torpedoes
Main engines: 1 Rateau geared turbine; 1 shaft; 28 650 shp
Boilers: 2 automatic (450°C)
Speed, knots: 27
Range, miles: 5 000 at 18 knots
Complement: 228 (15 officers, 213 men)

Forerunner of the F67 Type. A one-off class ordered under 1965 programme. Has no helicopter or facilities for such.

Electronics: An early form of centralised data analysis. Two Syllex.

Radar: Pulse Doppler (E/F band surveillance): one DRBV 13
100 mm guns fire-control: one DRBC 32B
Navigation: one DRBN 32
Air surveillance: one DRBV 22A.

Sonar: One hull-mounted DUBV 23; one DUBV 43 VDS.

ACONIT   *3/1976, Reinhard Nerlich*

ACONIT   *6/1975, Dr. Giorgio Arra*

FRIGATES

9 "COMMANDANT RIVIÈRE" CLASS

Name	No.	Builders	Laid down	Launched	Commissioned
AMIRAL CHARNER	F 727	Lorient Naval Dockyard	Nov 1958	Mar 1960	Dec 1962
BALNY	F 729	Lorient Naval Dockyard	Mar 1960	Mar 1962	Feb 1971
COMMANDANT BORY	F 726	Lorient Naval Dockyard	Mar 1958	Oct 1958	Mar 1964
COMMANDANT BOURDAIS	F 740	Lorient Naval Dockyard	April 1959	April 1961	Mar 1963
COMMANDANT RIVIÈRE	F 733	Lorient Naval Dockyard	April 1957	Oct 1958	Dec 1962
DOUDART DE LAGRÉE	F 728	Lorient Naval Dockyard	Mar 1960	April 1961	Mar 1963
ENSEIGNE DE VAISSEAU HENRY	F 749	Lorient Naval Dockyard	Sep 1962	Dec 1963	Jan 1965
PROTET	F 748	Lorient Naval Dockyard	Sep 1961	Dec 1962	May 1964
VICTOR SCHOELCHER	F 725	Lorient Naval Dockyard	Oct 1957	Oct 1958	Dec 1962

Displacement, tons: 1 750 standard; 2 250 full load
  (*Balny* 1 650 standard; 1 950 full load)
Length, feet (metres): 321·5 *(98·0)* pp; 340·3 *(103·7)* oa
Beam, feet (metres): 38·2 *(11·7)*
Draught, feet (metres): 15·7 *(4·8)*
Aircraft: 1 light helicopter can land aft
Missiles: 4 MM 38 Exocet (except *Balny*)
Guns: 2—3·9 in *(100 mm)* automatic, singles; 2—30 mm
A/S weapons: 1—12 in *(305 mm)* quadruple mortar
Torpedo tubes: 6—21 in *(533 mm)* (triple) for Mk K2 and L3
Main engines: 4SEMT-Pielstick diesels; 16 000 bhp; 2 shafts;
  (except *Balny:* CODAG; 2 diesels (16 cyl); one TG Turboméca
  M38; 1 shaft; VP screw)
Speed, knots: 25
Range, miles: 7 500 at 15 knots (*Balny* 8 000 at 12 knots)
Complement: 167 (10 officers, 157 men)

Built for world-wide operations—air-conditioned.

Accommodation: Can carry a senior officer and staff. If necessary a force of 80 soldiers can be carried as well as two 30 ft *(9 m)* LCPs with a capacity of 25 men at 11 knots.

Engines: Experimental CODAG arrangement in *Balny*. *Commandant Bory* was fitted with experimental machinery which was replaced with SEMT-Pielstick diesels in 1974-75.

Helicopter: In 1973 the after 100 mm mounting in *Commandant Bourdais* and *Enseigne Henry* was removed to make way for a helicopter platform. (See "Missile" note).

Missiles: All of this class except *Balny* are to be fitted with 4—MM 38 Exocet in place of X gun. *Bory* was the first to be fitted followed by *Doudart de Lagrée*. At the same time the 100 mm gun is replaced in Y position.

Radar: Navigation: one DRBN 32
Fire control: one DRBC 32A
Air search: one DRBV 22A
Surface/air search: one DRBV 50
Exocet ships: one DRBC 32C.

Sonar: One DUBA 3; one SQS 17.

PROTET (with Exocet)   *7/1976, Dr. Giorgio Arra*

AMIRAL CHARNER   *1975, Wright and Logan*

14 TYPE E 52

Name	No.	Builders	Laid down	Launched	Commissioned
L'AGENAIS	F 774	Lorient Naval Dockyard	Aug 1955	23 June 1956	14 May 1958
L'ALSACIEN	F 776	Lorient Naval Dockyard	July 1956	26 Jan 1957	27 Aug 1960
LE BASQUE	F 773	Lorient Naval Dockyard	Dec 1954	25 Feb 1956	18 Oct 1957
LE BÉARNAIS	F 775	Lorient Naval Dockyard	Dec 1955	23 June 1956	18 Oct 1958
LE BRETON	F 772	Lorient Naval Dockyard	June 1954	2 April 1955	20 Aug 1957
LE BOURGUIGNON	F 769	Penhoet	Jan 1954	28 Jan 1956	11 July 1957
LE CHAMPENOIS	F 770	A. C. Loire	May 1954	12 Mar 1955	1 June 1957
LE GASCON	F 767	A. C. Loire	Feb 1954	23 Oct 1954	29 Mar 1957
LE LORRAIN	F 768	F. Ch. de la Medit	July 1953	13 Feb 1954	3 Nov 1956
LE NORMAND	F 765	F. Ch. de la Medit	July 1953	13 Feb 1954	3 Nov 1956
LE PICARD	F 766	A. C. Loire	Nov 1954	31 May 1954	20 Sep 1956
LE PROVENÇAL	F 777	Lorient Naval Dockyard	Feb 1957	5 Oct 1957	6 Nov 1959
LE SAVOYARD	F 771	F. Ch. de la Medit	Nov 1953	7 May 1955	14 June 1956
LE VENDÉEN	F 778	F. Ch. de la Medit	Mar 1957	27 July 1957	1 Oct 1960

Displacement, tons: 1 250 standard; 1 702 full load
Length, feet (metres): 311·7 (95·0) pp; 325·8 (99·8) oa
Beam, feet (metres): 33·8 (10·3)
Draught, feet (metres): 13·5 (4·1)
Guns: 6—2·25 in (57 mm) in twin mountings (4 only in F 771, 772, 773); 2—20 mm
A/S weapons: Sextuple Bofors ASM mortar forward (except F 776, 777, 778 with 1—12 in (305 mm) quadruple mortar); 2 DC mortars; 1 DC rack; 12 ASM (4 triple mountings aft) for Mk K2 and L3.
Main engines: Parsons or Rateau geared turbines; 20 000 shp
Boilers: 2 Indret; pressure 500 psi (35·2 kg/cm²); superheat 725°F (385°C)
Speed, knots: 27
Range, miles: 4 500 at 15 knots
Oil fuel, tons: 310
Complement: 205 (13 officers, 192 men)

L'Agenais, L'Alsacien, Le Basque, Le Béarnais, Le Breton, Le Provencial and Le Vendéen have a different arrangement of bridges from the remainder. L'Alsacien, Le Provencal and Le Vendéen are of the E 52B type and have the Strombos-Velensi modified funnel cap.

Class: Le Lorrain was disarmed on 31 Dec 1975 and Le Champenois on 4 Aug 1975.
Le Breton and Le Bourguignon to reserve in 1976.

Radar: Navigation: one DRBV 31
Air search: one DRBV 22A
Fire control: one DRBC 31

Sonar: One DUBV 24; one DUBA 1 (except 771, 772, 773; one DUBV 1 and one DUBA 1).

Trials: Le Basque carries experimental fire-control equipment in place of third mounting.
Le Savoyard carries large electronic missile guidance equipment in place of after gun-mounting.

LE BÉARNAIS   1976, Wright and Logan

L'ALSACIEN   1976, Wright and Logan

1 TYPE E 50

Name	No.	Builders	Laid down	Launched	Commissioned
LE BOULONNAIS	F 763	A. C. Loire	Mar 1952	12 May 1953	5 Aug 1955

Displacement, tons: 1 250 standard; 1 528 for trials; 1 702 full load
Length, feet (metres): 311·7 (95·0) pp; 327·3 (99·8) oa
Beam, feet (metres): 33·8 (10·3)
Draught, feet (metres): 13·5 (4·1)
Guns: 6—2·25 in (57 mm) (twins); 2—20 mm
A/S weapons: 1—375 mm Mk 54 rocket launcher;
Torpedo tubes: 12 tubes (four triple mounts forward) for Mk K2 and L3
Main engines: 2 Rateau A & C de B geared turbines; 20 000 shp; 2 shafts
Speed, knots: 27 (29 on trials); economical speed 14
Oil fuel, tons: 292
Range, miles: 4 500 at 15 knots
Complement: 205 (13 officers, 192 men)

Last survivor of a class of four

Radar: Air search: one DRBV 20
Navigation: one DRBN 32
Fire control: one DRBC 31

Sonar: One DUBV 1; one DUBA 1.

LE BOULONNAIS

12 + 2 TYPE A 69

Name	No.	Builders	Laid down	Launched	Commissioned
D'ESTIENNE D'ORVES	F 781	Lorient Naval Dockyard	1 Sep 1972	1 June1973	Nov 1975
AMYOT D'INVILLE	F 782	Lorient Naval Dockyard	Sep 1973	30 Nov 1974	May 1976
DROGOU	F 783	Lorient Naval Dockyard	1 Oct 1973	30 Nov 1974	July 1976
DÉTROYAT	F 784	Lorient Naval Dockyard	15 Dec 1974	31 Jan 1976	Feb 1977
JEAN MOULIN	F 785	Lorient Naval Dockyard	15 Jan 1975	31 Jan 1976	Mar 1977
QUARTIER MAITRE ANQUETIL	F 786	Lorient Naval Dockyard	1 Aug 1975	7 Aug 1976	Sep 1977
COMMANDANT DE PIMODAN	F 787	Lorient Naval Dockyard	1 Sep 1975	7 Aug 1976	Oct 1977
SECOND MAITRE LE BIHAN	F 788	Lorient Naval Dockyard	15 Feb 1976	Mar 1977	Feb 1978
LIEUTENANT DE VAISSEAU LAVALLÉE	F 790	Lorient Naval Dockyard	1 Sep 1976	Sep 1977	Oct 1978
PREMIER MAITRE L'HER	F 792	Lorient Naval Dockyard	15 Mar 1977	April 1978	Mar 1979
COMMANDANT BLAISON	F 793	Lorient Naval Dockyard	15 April 1977	April 1978	April 1979
ENSEIGNE DE VAISSEAU JACOUBET	F 794	Lorient Naval Dockyard	—	—	—

Displacement, tons: 950 standard; 1 170 full load
Length, feet (metres): 262·5 (80·0) oa
Beam, feet (metres): 33·8 (10·3)
Draught, feet (metres): 9·8 (3·0)
Missiles: 2 MM 38 Exocet (see Missile note)
Guns: 1—3·9 in (100 mm); 2—20 mm
A/S weapons: 1—375 mm Mk 54 Rocket launcher; 4 fixed tubes
for Mk L3 and L5 torpedoes
Main engines: 2 SEMT-Pielstick PC2V diesels; 2 shafts;
controllable pitch propellers; 11 000 bhp
Speed, knots: 24
Range, miles: 4 500 at 15 knots
Endurance, days: 15
Complement: 64 (spare berths for extra 29)

Primarily intended for coastal A/S operations—officially classified as "Avisos". Also available for overseas patrols and can carry an extra detachment of 1 officer and 17 men. *D'Estienne d'Orves* commissioned for trials 26 Oct 1974. Construction of *Ens. de V. Jacoubet* has been delayed for financial reasons. 2 additional ships to be built to replace those transferred to South Africa.

Missiles: 2—MM 38 Exocet will be fitted in those ships earmarked for foreign service—either side of the funnel.

Radar: Navigation: one Decca Type 202; one DRBN 32
Surface/air search: one DRBV 51
Fire control: one DRBC 32E

Sonar: One hull mounted sonar DUBA 25.

Transfers: *Lieutenant de Vaisseau Le Henaff* (F 789) and *Commandant l'Herminier* (F 791) sold to South Africa in 1976 whilst under construction.

D'ESTIENNE D'ORVES   4/1976, Dr. Giorgio Arra

D'ESTIENNE D'ORVES   4/1976, Dr. Giorgio Arra

AMYOT D'INVILLE   6/1976, French Navy

NEW CONSTRUCTION TYPE A 70

Although this was originally planned as a separate class with missiles the fitting of Exocet in type A 69 has removed the major difference.

AMPHIBIOUS FORCES

2 LANDING SHIPS (DOCK) (TCD)

Name	No.	Builders	Laid down	Launched	Commissioned
OURAGAN	L 9021	Brest Dockyard	June 1967	9 Nov 1963	June 1965
ORAGE	L 9022	Brest Dockyard	June 1966	22 April1967	Mar 1968

Displacement, tons: 5 800 light; 8 500 full load; 15 000 when
fully immersed
Length, feet (metres): 488·9 *(149·0)*
Beam, feet (metres): 70·5 *(21·5)*
Draught, feet (metres): 16·1 *(4·9)*; 28·5 *(8·7)* (flooded)
Guns: 2—4·7 in *(120 mm)* mortars; 6—30 mm *(Ouragan)*;
6—40 mm *(Orage)*
Main engines: 2 diesels; 2 shafts; 8 640 bhp
Speed, knots: 17
Range, miles: 4 000 at 15 knots
Complement: 201 *(Orage)*; 207 *(Ouragan)*

Ouragan was completed for trials in 1964. Bridge is on the
starboard side. Fitted with a platform for four heavy helicopters
and portable platform aft. Able to carry two EDICs loaded with
eleven light tanks each, or 18 loaded LCMs Type VI. In the
logistic role 1 500 tons of material and equipment can be carried and handled by two 35 ton cranes. *Orage* is allocated to the
Pacific Nuclear Experimental Centre. Can carry 350 troops
normally or 470 for short periods. Have command facilities for
directing amphibious and helicopter operations.

Gunnery: 40 mm guns fitted in *Orage* in 1975-76. She does not
carry mortars.

Sonar: One SQS-17 in *Ouragan*

OURAGAN   1975, Wright and Logan

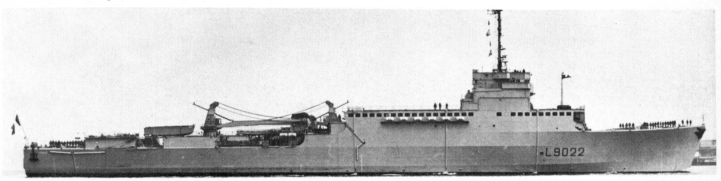

ORAGE   1969, French Navy

2 BATRAL TYPE (LIGHT TRANSPORTS)

Name	No.	Builders	Commissioned
CHAMPLAIN	L 9030	Brest	5 Oct 1974
FRANCIS GARNIER	L 9031	Brest	21 June1974

Displacement, tons: 750 standard; 1 250 full load
Dimensions, feet (metres): 262·4 × 42·6 × 7·5 *(80 × 13 × 2·3)*
Guns: 2—40 mm; 2—81 mm mortars
Main engines: 2 Diesels; 2 shafts; 1 800 hp = 16 knots
Range, miles: 3 500 at 13 knots
Complement: 39

Fitted with bow doors, and stowage for vehicles above and below decks. Helicopter landing
platform. Can carry a landing company (Guépard) of 5 officers and 133 men with 12 vehicles.
Both launched 17 Nov 1973.

CHAMPLAIN   1974, DCAN Brest

5 LANDING SHIPS (TANK) (BDC)

Name	No.	Builders	Commissioned
ARGENS	L 9003	Ch. de Bretagne	1960
BIDASSOA	L 9004	Ch. Seine Maritime	1961
BLAVET	L 9009	Ch. de Bretagne	1960
DIVES	L 9008	Ch. Seine Maritime	1961
TRIEUX	L 9007	Ch. de Bretagne	1960

Displacement, tons: 1 400 standard; 1 765 normal; 4 225 full load
Dimensions, feet (metres): 328 oa × 50 × 14 *(102·1 × 15·5 × 3·2)*
Guns: 2—40 mm; 4—20 mm *(Argens, Trieux)* 1—4·7 in mortar; 3—40 mm *(Bidassoa, Blavet,
Dives)*
Main engines: SEMT-Pielstick diesels; 2 shafts; 2 000 bhp = 11 knots
Range, miles: 18 500 at 10 knots
Complement: 75 (6 officers and 69 men) . Plus 170 troops (normal)

Launched on 7 April 1959, 30 Dec 1960, 15 Jan 1960, 29 June 1960 and 6 Dec 1958, respectively.
Can carry: 4 LCVPs, 1 800 tons of freight, 335 troops under austere conditions (up to 807 in a
brief emergency). *Blavet* and *Trieux* are fitted as light helicopter carriers with a hangar before
the bridge and can carry two Alouette III.

ARGENS   11/1975, Dr. Giorgio Arra

12 LANDING CRAFT (TANK) (EDIC)

L 9070 (30 Mar 1967)	**L 9074** (22 July 1969)	**L 9092** (2 Dec 1958)
L 9071 (4 Nov 1967)	**L 9082** (1964)	**L 9093** (17 April 1958)
L 9072 (1968)	**L 9083** (1964)	**L 9094** (24 July 1958)
L 9073 (1968)	**L 9091** (7 Jan 1958)	**L 9096** (11 Oct 1958)

Displacement, tons: 250 standard; 670 full load
Dimensions, feet (metres):193·5 × 39·2 × 4·5 *(59 × 12 × 1·3)*
Guns: 2—20 mm
Main engines: MGO diesels; 2 shafts; 1 000 bhp = 8 knots
Range, miles: 1 800 at 8 knots
Complement: 16 (1 officer, and 15 men)

Seven were built by C. N. Franco Belges, three by Toulon Dockyard, two by La Perrière. Launch dates above. Can carry 11 lorries or 5 Light Fighting Vehicles.

EDIC L 9092   *1973, Dr. Giorgio Arra*

Transfer: L 9095 transferred to Senegal 1 July 1974 as *La Falence.*

ISSOLE A 734

Displacement, tons: 610 full load
Dimensions, feet (metres): 160·8 × 32 × 7·2 *(49 × 9·7 × 2·2)*
Main engines: 2 diesels; 1 000 bhp = 12 knots

Built at Toulon in 1957-58. LCT type with bow doors and ramp.

ISSOLE   *1974, Michael D. J. Lennon*

16 LCMs

CTM 1 to 16

Displacement, tons: 56 standard; 150 full load
Dimensions, feet (metres): 92·8 × 21 × 3·9 *(28·3 × 6·4 × 1·2)*
Main engines: Hispano diesels; 2 shafts; 225 hp = 9·5 knots
Complement: 6

Can carry up to 90 tons in coastal or protected waters.

20 LCMs

Of varying displacements between 26 and 52 tons.

1 Ex-BRITISH LCT (8)

LCT 9061 (ex-HMS *Buttress, LCT (8) 4099*)

Displacement, tons: 657 standard; 1 000 full load
Dimensions, feet (metres): 231·2 × 39 × 5·9 *(70·5 × 11·9 × 1·8)*
Guns: 2—20 mm; 1—120 mm mortar
Main engines: 4 Paxman diesels; 2 shafts; 1 840 bhp = 9 knots
Complement: 29 (2 officers, 27 men)

Former British landing craft bought in July 1965. Lent to the Comoro Islands.

LIGHT FORCES

4 "TRIDENT" CLASS (FAST ATTACK CRAFT—MISSILE)

Note: 6 more of a larger class (250-350 tons) to be built under 1977-81 programme.

Name	No.	Builders	Commissioned
TRIDENT	P 670	Auroux, Arcachon	17 June 1976
GLAIVE	P 671	Auroux, Arcachon	Nov 1976
EPÉE	P 672	C.M.N. Cherbourg	6 Aug 1976
PERTUISANE	P 673	C.M.N. Cherbourg	Oct 1976

Displacement, tons: 115 standard; 130 full load
Dimensions, feet (metres): 121·4 × 18 × 5·2 *(37 × 5·5 × 1·6)*
Missiles: 6—SS 12
Gun: 1—40 mm
Main engines: 2 AGO diesels; 2 shafts; 4 000 hp = 26 knots
Range, miles: 1 500 at 25 knots
Complement: 18 (1 officer and 17 men)

Trident laid down 3 Dec 1974, launched 31 May 1975; *Glaive,* 16 Jan 1975 and 27 Aug 1975; *Epée* 10 Apr 1975, 31 Mar 1976; *Pertuisane,* 26 Aug 1975 and 2 June 1976. These were intended as lead boats for a class of 30 in "Plan Bleu" of which 16 were to be adapted for overseas service. Trials for *Trident* started 1· Oct 1975.

PERTUISANE   *6/1976, Contre-Amiral M. Adam*

1 LA COMBATTANTE I TYPE (FAST ATTACK CRAFT—MISSILE)

Name	No.	Builders	Commissioned
LA COMBATTANTE	P 730	C.M. de Normandie	1 Mar 1964

Displacement, tons: 180 standard; 202 full load
Dimensions, feet (metres): 147·8 × 24·2 × 6·5 *(45 × 7·4 × 2·5)*
Missiles: 1 quadruple launcher for SS 11
Guns: 2—40 mm
Main engines: 2 SEMT-Pielstick diesels; 2 shafts; controllable pitch propellers; 3 200 bhp = 23 knots
Range, miles: 2 000 at 12 knots
Complement: 25 (3 officers, 22 men)

Authorised under the 1960 Programme. Laid down in April 1962, launched on 20 June 1963. Of wooden and plastic laminated non-magnetic construction. Can carry a raiding force of 80 for a very short run.

Gunnery: Flare launcher aft replaced by 40 mm Mk 3 gun before she left for Indian Ocean in 1975.

LA COMBATTANTE   *1974, Dr. Giorgio Arra*

9 "SIRIUS" CLASS (LARGE PATROL CRAFT)

ALTAIR P 656
ANTARES P 703
ARCTURUS P 650
CANOPUS P 659
CROIX DU SUD P 658

ERIDAN P 741
ÉTOILE POLAIRE P 660
SAGITTAIRE P 743
VEGA P 707

All of "Sirius" class minesweepers (see Minewarfare Section for details) transferred for coastal patrol operations 1973. Minesweeping gear removed. P 703, 707, 741, 743 in reserve.

CANOPUS   1975, J. van der Woude

11 "LE FOUGUEUX" CLASS (LARGE PATROL CRAFT)

L'ADROIT P 644
L'ALERTE P 645
L'ATTENTIF P 646
L'ARDENT P 635
L'EFFRONTÉ P 638
L'ENJOUÉ P 647

L'ÉTOURDI P 637
LE FRINGANT P 640
LE FRONDEUR P 639
LE HARDI P 648
L'INTRÉPIDE P 630

Displacement, tons: 325 standard; 400 full load
Dimensions, feet (metres): 170 pp × 23 × 6·5 *(53 × 7·3 × 3·1)*
Guns: 2—40 mm Bofors
A/S weapons: 1—120 mm A/S mortar; 2 DC mortars; 2 DC racks
Torpedo tubes: *L'Intrepide* has a tube mounted on the stern
Main engines: 4 SEMT-Pielstick diesel engines coupled 2 by 2; 3 240 bhp = 18·6 knots
Range, miles: 3 000 at 12 knots; 2 000 at 15 knots
Complement: 46 (4 officers, 42 men)

Five were built under the 1955 and six under the 1956 estimates. All launched 1957-59. Original 3 of this class of 14 deleted 1975.

Reserve: *L'Intrépide, L'Étourdi, L'Attentif* and *L'Enjoué* to reserve 1976.
L'Alerte, L'Effronté, Le Frondeur, Le Hardi to reserve 1977.

Radar: One set Decca.

Sonar: One QCU2.

Similar classes: "Boavista" class (Portugal), one in Yugoslavia, one in W. Germany, one in Italy.

LE FRONDEUR   7/1976, Dr. Giorgio Arra

5 "LA DUNKERQUOISE" CLASS (LARGE PATROL CRAFT)

Name	No.	Builders	Commissioned
LA DUNKERQUOISE (ex-*Fundy*)	P 653	Canada	1954
LA MALOUINE (ex-*Cowichan*)	P 651	Canada	1954
LA PAIMPOLAISE (ex-*Thunder*)	P 657	Canada	1954
LA DIEPPOISE (ex-*Chaleur*)	P 655	Canada	1954
LA LORIENTAISE (ex-*Miramichi*)	P 652	Canada	1954

Displacement, tons: 370 full load; 470 standard
Dimensions, feet (metres): 140 pp; 152 oa × 28 × 8·7 *(50 × 9·2 × 2·8)*
Gun: 1—40 mm
Main engines: General Motors diesels; 2 shafts; 2 500 bhp = 15 knots
Oil fuel, tons: 52
Range, miles: 4 500 at 11 knots
Complement: 35 (4 officers, 31 men)

La Malouine (launched 12 Nov 1951) and *La Paimpolaise* (launched 17 July 1953) were transferred to the French flag at Halifax on 1 April 1954, *Dunkerquoise* (launched 17 July 1953) on 30 April 1954, and *La Dieppoise* (launched 21 June 1952) and *La Lorientaise* (launched in 1953) on 10 Oct 1954. All similar to the "Bay" class in the Canadian Forces. All transferred from minesweeping to overseas patrol operations 1973. They have been air conditioned.

LA DIEPPOISE (old pennant number)   1971, French Navy

Reserve: *La Malouine* to reserve 1976.

5 Ex-BRITISH "HAM" CLASS (LARGE PATROL CRAFT)

GÉRANIUM (ex-*Tibenham* ex-*M 784*) P784
JONQUILLE (ex-*Sulham*, ex-*M 787*) P 787
VIOLETTE (ex-*Mersham*, ex-*M 773*) P 788
JASMIN (ex-*Stedham*, ex-*M 776*) P 661
PETUNIA (ex-*Pineham*, ex-*M 789*) P 662

Displacement, tons: 140 standard; 170 full load
Dimensions, feet (metres): 100 pp; 106·5 oa × 21·2 × 5·5 *(32·4 × 6·5 × 1·7)*
Gun: 1—20 mm Oerlikon forward
Main engines: 2 Paxman diesels; 550 bhp = 14 knots
Oil fuel, tons: 15
Complement: 12 (2 officers, 10 men)

Former British inshore minesweepers of the "Ham" class transferred to France under the US "off-shore" procurement programme in 1955. Now used as patrol craft, the first three by Gendarmerie Maritime. Of these *Violette* was replaced by *Paquerette* A 742 in 1976, the former taking her place as a tender.

JONQUILLE   11/1975, Dr. Giorgio Arra

1 FAIRMILE ML TYPE (LARGE PATROL CRAFT)

OISEAU DES ILES A 716

Displacement, tons: 140 full load
Dimensions, feet (metres): 111·5 × 18·4 × 4·3 *(34 × 5·6 × 1·3)*
Speed, knots: 11·5

Former Fairmile motor launch used for training frogmen.

4 TECIMAR TYPE (COASTAL PATROL CRAFT)

P 770   P 771   P 772   P 774

Displacement, tons: 30
Dimensions, feet (metres): 43·6 × 13·4 × 3·5 *(13·3 × 4·1 × 1·1)*
Guns: 1—12·7 mm MG; 1—7·5 mm MG
Main engines: 2 GM diesels; 480 bhp = 25 knots

Hulls of moulded polyester. Built for gendarmerie in 1974.

1 COASTAL PATROL CRAFT

Y 760 (ex-*P 9786*)

Displacement, tons: 45
Dimensions, feet (metres): 79·3 × 14·8 × 4·2 *(24·2 × 4·5 × 1·3)*
Guns: 8—0·5 MG (four twin mountings)
Main engines: 2 Daimler-Benz (MTU) diesels; 2 shafts; 1 000 bhp = 18 knots

Built by Bodenwerft-Kressbronn. Completed in 1954.

1 COASTAL PATROL CRAFT

TOURMALINE A 714

Displacement, tons: 45
Dimensions, feet (metres): 88 × 16·8 × 4·8 *(26·8 × 5·1 × 1·5)*
Gun: 1—20 mm
Main engines: 2 diesels; 1 120 hp = 27 knots
Complement: 9

Completed 1974 by Ch. Navals de L'Esterel for training duties.

MINE WARFARE FORCES

Note: 12 new minehunters of an improved "Circe" class are to be built under the 1977-81 Plan in collaboration with Belgium and Netherlands. To be of 500 tons, built of GRP with one screw, two active rudders, one small MHV propeller and fitted with Sonar DUBH-21 and improved PAP.

5 "CIRCE" CLASS (MINEHUNTERS)

Name	No.	Builders	Commissioned
CYBÈLE	M 712	C.M. de Normandie	28 Sep 1972
CIRCE	M 715	C.M. de Normandie	18 May 1972
CALLIOPE	M 713	C.M. de Normandie	28 Sep 1972
CERES	M 716	C.M. de Normandie	8 Mar 1973
CLIO	M 714	C.M. de Normandie	18 May 1972

Displacement, tons: 460 standard; 495 normal; 510 full load
Dimensions, feet (metres): 167 oa × 29·2 × 11·15 *(50·9 × 8·9 × 3·4)*
Gun: 1—20 mm
Main engines: 1 MTU diesel; single axial screw; 1 800 bhp = 15 knots
Range, miles: 3 000 at 12 knots
Complement: 48 (4 officers, 44 men)

Ordered in 1968. *Circe* launched 15 Dec 1970; *Clio* launched 10 June 1971; *Calliope* launched 21 Nov 1971; *Cybèle* launched Jan 1972; *Ceres* launched 10 Aug 1972.

Minehunting: All ships are fitted with DUBM 20 minehunting sonar. The 9 foot long PAP is propelled by two electric motors at 6 knots and is wire-guided to a maximum range of 500 m. Fitted with a television camera, this machine detects the mine and lays its 100 kgm charge nearby. This is then detonated by an ultra-sonic signal.

Minesweeping: These ships carry no normal minesweeping equipment.

CLIO   *1975, Dr. Giorgio Arra*

13 Ex-US "AGGRESSIVE" and "MSO-498" CLASS
(MINESWEEPERS—OCEAN and MINEHUNTERS)

NARVIK (ex-*MSO 512)* M 609
OUISTREHAM (ex-*MSO 513)* M 610
ALENCON (ex-*MSO 453)* M 612
BERNEVAL (ex-*MSO 450)* M 613
CANTHO (ex-*MSO 476)* M 615
DOMPAIRE (ex-*MSO 454)* M 616
GARIGLIANO (ex-*MSO 452)* M 617

MYTHO (ex-*MSO 475)* M 618
VINH LONG (ex-*MSO 477)* M 619
BERLAIMONT (ex-*MSO 500)* M 620
AUTUN (ex-*MSO 502)* M 622
BACCARAT (ex-*MSO 505)* M 623
COLMAR (ex-*MSO 514)* M 624

Displacement, tons: 700 standard; 780 full load
Dimensions, feet (metres): 165 wl; 171 oa × 35 × 10·3 *(50·3 × 10·7 × 3·2)*
Gun: 1—40 mm
Main engines: 2 GM diesels; 2 shafts; V.P. propellers; 1 600 bhp = 13·5 knots
Oil fuel, tons: 47
Range, miles: 3 000 at 10 knots
Complement: 58 (5 officers, 53 men)

The USA transferred these MSOs to France in three batches during 1953. *Bir Hacheim* M 614 (ex-MSO 451) was returned to the US Navy at Brest on 4 Sep 1970 and transferred to Uruguayan navy, being renamed *Maldonado*. *Origny* converted for survey duties in 1960.

Appearance: *Autun, Baccarat, Berlaimont, Colmar, Narvik* and *Ouistreham* have a taller funnel.

Minehunters: *Cantho, Dompaire, Garigliano, Mytho* and *Vinh Long* converted for minehunting between 1975 and 1977. *Dompaire* commissioned as minehunter Jan 1976.
Autun, Baccarat, Berlaimont, Colmar and *Ouistreham* being converted between 1976 and 1 May 1977—Jan 1979. Considerable change in appearance has resulted.

OUISTREHAM (tall funnel)   *12/1974, Wright and Logan*

GARIGLIANO (squat funnel)   *12/1974, Wright and Logan*

9 "SIRIUS" CLASS (MINESWEEPERS—COASTAL)

ALGOL (15 April 1953) M 704
BETELGEUSE (12 July 1954) M 747
CAPELLA (6 Sep 1955) M 755
CAPRICORNE (8 Aug 1956) M 737
CASSIOPÉE (16 Nov 1953) M 740

CÉPHÉE (3 Jan 1956) M 756
LYRE (3 May 1956) M 759
PHÉNIX (23 May 1955) M 749
VERSEAU (26 April 1956) M 757

Displacement, tons: 400 standard; 440 full load
Dimensions, feet (metres): 140 pp; 152 oa × 28 × 8·2 *(42·7; 46·4 × 8·6 × 2·5)*
Guns: 1—40 mm Bofors; 1—20 mm Oerlikon (several have 2—20 mm)
Main engines: SIGMA free piston generators and Alsthom or Rateau-Bretagne gas turbines or SEMT-Pielstick 16-cyl diesels; 2 shafts; 2 000 bhp = 15 knots (11·5 knots when sweeping)
Oil fuel, tons: 48
Range, miles: 3 000 at 10 knots
Complement: 38 (3 officers, 35 men)

Of wooden and aluminium alloy construction. Of same general characteristics as the British "Ton" class, *Bételgeuse, Capella, Capricorne, Céphée, Lyre, Phénix* and *Verseau* have SEMT-Pielstick diesels. Launch dates above.
Algol and *Cassiopée* form a trials squadron.

Reserve: *Lyre* to reserve 1977. *Antares, Eridan, Sagittaire* and *Vega* to reserve as patrol craft 1977.

CASSIOPÉE (40 mm gun)   *7/1974, Wright and Logan*

Transfers: Three of this class, built in France and originally numbered D 25, 26 and 27 (now called *Hrabri, Smeli* and *Slobodni*), were joined by *Snazni* (built in Yugoslavia) after their transfer to Yugoslavia in 1957. *Fomalhaut, Orion, Pollux* and *Procyon* were returned to the USN in 1970, *Achernar* and *Centaure* in 1971. *Aries* (M 758) loaned to Morocco for four years 1975.

16 Ex-US "ADJUTANT" CLASS (MINESWEEPERS—COASTAL)

ACACIA (ex-*MSC 69*) M 638	**LAURIER** (ex-*MSC 86*) M 681
ACANTHE (ex-*MSC 70*) M 639	**LILAS** (ex-*MSC 93*) M 682
AZALÉE (ex-*MSC 67*) M 668	**LOBÉLIA** (ex-*MSC 96*) M 684
CAMÉLIA (ex-*MSC 68*) M 671	**MIMOSA** (ex-*MSC 99*) M 687
CYCLAMEN (ex-*MSC 119*) M 674	**MUGUET** (ex-*MSC 97*) M 688
EGLANTINE (ex-*MSC 117*) M 675	**PERVENCHE** (ex-*MSC 141*) M 632
GIROFLÉE (ex-*MSC 85*) M 677	**PIVOINE** (ex-*MSC 125*) M 633
GLYCINE (ex-*MSC 118*) M 679	**RÉSÉDA** (ex-*MSC 126*) M 635

Displacement, tons: 300 standard; 372 full load
Dimensions, feet (metres): 136·2 pp; 141 oa × 26 × 8·3 *(43 × 8 × 2·6)*
Guns: 2—20 mm
Main engines: 2 GM diesels; 2 shafts; 1 200 bhp = 13 knots (8 sweeping)
Oil fuel, tons: 40
Range, miles: 2 500 at 10 knots
Complement: 38 (3 officers, 35 men)

The USA agreed in Sep 1952 to allocate to France in 1953, 36 new AMS (later redesignated MSC) under the Mutual Defence Assistance Programme, but only 30 were finally transferred to France in 1953.

Deletions:
Bleuét and *Chrysanthème* cannibalized for spares—1976 onwards.

Transfers:
(a) Six of the class were not taken up by France—two (MSC 139 and 143) to Spain; two to Japan (MSC 95, 144) and two retained by USA.
(b) *Marguerite* (ex-*MSC 94*) M 686 returned to USA and transferred to Uruguay as *Rio Negro* 10 Nov 1969.
(c) *Pavot* (ex-*MSC 124*) M 631 and *Renoncule* (ex-*MSC 142*) M 634 returned to USA and transferred to Turkey on 24 Mar 1970 and 19 Nov 1970 respectively.
(d) *Coquelicot* (ex-*MSC 84*) M 673 to Tunisia in 1973.
(e) *Bégonia* (ex-*MSC 83*) M 669 and *Glaieul* (ex-*MSC 120*) M 678 returned to USA 1974.
(f) *Marjolaine* to Tunisia 1977.

ACANTHE   *1976, Wright and Logan*

Change of Task:
(a) *Ajonc* (ex-*M 667*) A 701 to diving training ship—1974.
(b) *Liseron* (ex-*M 683*) A 623 and *Gardénia* (ex-*M 676*) A 711 to clearance-diving base ship. *Magnolia* M 685 to join this task in 1976.
(c) *Jacinthe* M 680 to minelaying duties in 1968.
(d) *Acacia* M 638, *Azalée* M 668 and *Lobélia* M 684 to reserve 1976.

1 SPECIAL TYPE DBI (MINESWEEPER—COASTAL)

Name	No.	Builders	Commissioned
MERCURE	M 765	Mecaniques de Normandie	Dec 1958

Displacement, tons: 333 light; 365 normal; 400 full load
Dimensions, feet (metres): 137·8 pp; 145·5 oa × 27 × 8·5 *(44·4 × 8·3 × 4)*
Guns: 2—20 mm
Main engines: 2 Mercedes-Benz (MTU) diesels; 2 shafts; Kamewa variable pitch propellers; 4 000 bhp = 15 knots
Oil fuel, tons: 48
Range, miles: 3 000 at 15 knots
Complement: 48

Ordered in France under the "off-shore" programme. Laid down in Jan 1955. Launched on 21 Dec 1957. Will be fitted as fishery protection vessel 1977.

Foreign sales: Six built for W. Germany.

MERCURE   *1968, French Navy*

SURVEY SHIPS

Note: (a) Survey ships are painted white. (b) A total of 20 officers and 74 technicians with oceanographic and hydrographic training is employed in addition to the ships' companies listed here. They occupy the extra billets marked as "scientists".

Name	No.	Builders	Commissioned
D'ENTRECASTEAUX	A 757	Brest	10 Oct 1970

Displacement, tons: 2 400 full load
Dimensions, feet (metres): 295·2 × 42·7 × 12·8 *(89 × 13 × 3·9)*
Main engines: 2 diesel-electric; 1 000 kW; 2 controllable pitch propellers; speed: 15 knots
Auxiliary engines: 2 Schottel trainable and retractable
Range, miles: 10 000 at 12 knots
Complement: 79 (6 officers, 73 men plus scientific staff)

This ship was specially designed for oceanographic surveys. Accommodation for 38 scientists. Hangar for Alouette II helicopter. Carries one LCPS and three survey launches.

Radar: two sets.

Sonar: two sets.

D'ENTRECASTEAUX   *1975, Wright and Logan*

Name	No.	Builders	Commissioned
ESPÉRANCE (ex-*Jacques Coeur*)	A 756	Gdynia	see note
ESTAFETTE (ex-*Jacques Cartier*)	A 766	Gdynia	see note

Displacement, tons: 956 standard; 1 360 full load
Dimensions, feet (metres): 196·1 × 32·2 × 14·8 *(63·5 × 9·8 × 5·9)*
Main engines: MAN diesels; 1 850 bhp = 15 knots
Range, miles: 7 500 at 13 knots
Complement: 32 (3 officers, 29 men plus scientists)

Former trawlers built in 1962 at Gdynia and purchased in 1968-69. Adapted as survey ships commissioning in 1969 and 1972. Can carry 14 scientists.

Appearance: *Espérance* has a normal foremast in place of the crane in *Estafette*.

ESPÉRANCE   *4/1976, Michael D. J. Lennon*

Name	No.	Builders	Commissioned
LA RECHERCHE (ex-*Guyane*)	A 758	Chantiers Ziegler, Dunkirk	see note

Displacement, tons: 810 standard; 910 full load
Dimensions, feet (metres): 221·5 oa × 34·2 × 13 *(67·5 × 10·4 × 4·5)*
Main engines: 1 Werkspoor diesel; 1 535 bhp = 13·5 knots
Range, miles: 3 100 at 10 knots
Complement: 23 (2 officers, 21 men) (plus 43 scientists)

Former passenger motor vessel. Launched in April 1951. Purchased in 1960 and converted by Cherbourg Dockyard into a surveying ship. Commissioned into the French Navy in March 1961 and her name changed from *Guyane* to *La Recherche*. To improve stability she was fitted with bulges. Now comes under the Ministry for Overseas Affairs.

LA RECHERCHE   *1975, Dr. Giorgio Arra*

1 "BERNEVAL" CLASS

ORIGNY A 640

Displacement, tons: 700 standard; 795 full load
Dimensions, feet (metres): 171 × 35 × 10·5 *(52·2 × 10·7 × 3·2)*
Gun: 1—40 mm
Main engines: 2 GM diesels; 2 shafts; 1 600 bhp = 13·5 knots
Range, miles: 3 000 at 10 knots
Complement: 52

Launched Feb 1955 as a Minesweeper—Ocean of "Berneval" class. Converted for Oceanographic research 1961-62.

ORIGNY   *1974, Wright and Logan*

Name	No.	Builders	Commissioned
L'ASTROLABE	A 780	Chantiers de la Seine Maritime, Le Trait	1964
BOUSSOLE	A 781	Chantiers de la Seine Maritime, Le Trait	1964

Displacement, tons: 330 standard; 440 full load
Dimensions, feet (metres): 137·8 × 27 × 8·2 *(42·7 × 8·5 × 2·9)*
Guns: 1—40 mm; 2 MG *(L'Astrolabe only)*
Main engines: 2 Baudoin DV.8 diesels; 1 shaft; variable pitch propeller; 800 bhp = 13 knots
Range, miles: 4 000 at 12 knots
Complement: 33 (1 officer, 32 men)

Authorised under the 1961 Programme. Specially designed for surveys in tropical waters. Laid down in 1962, launched on 27 May and 11 April 1963 respectively. Each ship carries a crane on either side of the funnel and has two 4·5 ton wireless-equipped survey craft .

L'ASTROLABE   *3/1976, Michael D. J. Lennon*

ALIDADE (ex-*Evelyne Marie*) A 682   **OCTANT** (ex-*Michel Marie*) A 683

Displacement, tons: 128 standard; 133 full load
Dimensions, feet (metres): 78 × 20 × 10·5 *(24 × 6·1 × 3·2)*
Main engines: 2 diesels; 1 shaft; V.P propeller; 200 bhp = 9 knots
Range, miles: 2 000 at 7 knots
Endurance: 12 days
Complement: 13 (1 officer, 12 men)

Two small fishing trawlers purchased by the Navy and converted into survey craft by the Constructions Mécaniques de Normandie at Cherbourg as tenders to *La Recherche*. Wooden hull and steel upperworks. *Alidade* completed conversion on 15 Nov 1962 and *Octant* on 20 Dec 1962. Commissioned in 1963.

OCTANT   *1973, Dr. Giorgio Arra*

1 INSHORE SURVEY CRAFT

Name	No.	Builders	Commissioned
CORAIL (ex-*Marc Joly*)	A 794	Thuin, Belgium	1967

Displacement, tons: 54·8 light
Dimensions, feet (metres): 58·4 × 16·1 × 5·9 *(17·8 × 4·9 × 1·8)*
Main engines: 1 Caterpillar diesel; 250 bhp = 10·3 knots
Complement: 7

Operating in New Caledonia from 1974.

SERVICE FORCES

2 NEW CONSTRUCTION
(UNDERWAY REPLENISHMENT TANKERS)

Name	No.	Builders	Commissioned
LA DURANCE	A 629	Brest Naval Dockyard	July 1976
MEUSE	—	Brest Naval Dockyard	—

Displacement, tons: 17 800 full load
Dimensions, feet (metres): 515·9 × 69·5 × 28·5 *(157·3 × 21·2 × 8·7)*
Aircraft: 1 WG 13 Lynx helicopter
Guns: 2—40 mm
Main engines: 2 diesels SEMT-Pielstick 16 PC 2·5; 2 shafts; VP propellers 20 000 hp = 19 knots
Oil fuel, tons: 750
Range, miles: 9 000 at 15 knots
Complement: 150 (45 passengers)

La Durance laid down 1973, launched 5 Sep 1975. Beam fuelling both sides as well as astern. Helicopter hangar. Classed as P.R.E. (Pétrolier Ravitailleur d'Escadre). A second of this class, *Meuse* is in the 1976 Estimates.

Capacity: To carry a total of 10 000 tonnes (7 500 FFO; 1 500 diesel, 500 TR5, 130 distilled water, 170 victuals, 150 munitions, 50 naval stores).

LA DURANCE   *1976, French Navy*

1 UNDERWAY REPLENISHMENT TANKER and COMMAND SHIP

LA CHARENTE (ex-*Beaufort*) A 626

Displacement, tons: 7 440 light; 26 000 full load
Dimensions, feet (metres): 587·2 × 72 × 30·3 *(179 × 21·9 × 9·3)*
Guns: 4—40 mm
Main engines: 1 General Electric geared turbine; 1 screw = 17·5 knots
Boilers: 2
Complement: 100 (6 officers, 94 men)

Former Norwegian tanker built by Haldnes Mek. Verksted Tönsberg in 1957. Purchased by the French Navy in May 1964. Now converted for service as flagship of the Flag Officer commanding Indian Ocean forces. Fitted with helicopter platform and hangar and carries LCVP.

LA CHARENTE (after conversion)   *1974, French Navy*

1 UNDERWAY REPLENISHMENT TANKER

Name	No.	Builders	Commissioned
ISÈRE	A 675	Ch. Seine Maritime	see note
(ex-*La Mayenne*, ex-*Caltex Strasbourg*)			

Displacement, tons: 7 440 standard; 26 700 full load
Dimensions, feet (metres): 559 × 71·2 × 30·3 *(170·4 × 21·7 × 9·3)*
Main engines: 1 single geared Parsons turbine; 8 260 shp = 16 knots
Boilers: 2
Complement: 92 (6 officers, 86 men)

Launched on 22 June 1959. Former French tanker. Purchased in 1965. Fitted for beam fuelling as well as stern rig.

ISÈRE   *11/1975, Dr. Giorgio Arra*

1 UNDERWAY REPLENISHMENT TANKER

LA SAONE A 628

Displacement, tons: 8 550 light; 24 200 full load
Dimensions, feet (metres): 525 × 72·5 × 33 *(160 × 22·1 × 10)*
Guns: 3—40 mm
Main engines: Parsons geared turbines; 2 shafts; 15 800 shp = 18 knots
Boilers: 3 Penhoet
Complement: 177 (9 officers, 168 men)

Ordered as fleet tanker. Completed as merchant tanker in 1948. Returned to the French Navy from charter company in Sep 1953. *La Saône* was fitted as a fleet replenishment ship in 1961. Carries 9 000 tons of fuel, 750 tons of diesel fuel, 275 tons of food and wine tanks holding 82 000 litres. Fitted with automatic tensioning.

LA SEINE (*La Saone* Similar)   *11/1975, Dr. Giorgio Arra*

1 SUPPORT TANKER

LAC TONLÉ SAP A 630

Displacement, tons: 800 light; 2 700 full load
Dimensions, feet (metres): 235 × 37 × 15·8 *(71·7 × 11·3 × 4·8)*
Guns: 3—20 mm
Main engines: 2 Fairbanks-Morse diesels; 1 150 bhp = 11 knots
Range, miles: 6 300 at 11 knots
Complement: 37 (2 officers, 35 men)

Ex-US Oil Barge acquired in 1945.

LAC TONLÉ SAP   *1973, French Navy*

2 SUPPORT TANKERS

PAPENOO (ex-Norwegian *Bow Queen*) A 625
PUNARUU (ex-Norwegian *Bow Cecil*) A 632

Displacement, tons: 1 195 standard; 2 927 full load
Dimensions, feet (metres): 272·2 × 45·6 × 18·0 *(83 × 13·9 × 5·5)*
Main engines: 2 diesels; 1 vp screw; 2 050 hp = 12 knots (bow screw in addition)

Two small tankers added to the navy in late 1969. Capacity 2 500 cu. m. (ten tanks).

PUNARUU   *1975, French Navy*

1 SUPPORT TANKER

Name	No.	Builders	Commissioned
ABERWRACH (ex-*CA 1*)	A 619	Cherbourg	1966

Displacement, tons: 1 220 standard; 3 500 full load
Dimensions, feet (metres): 284 oa × 40 × 15·8 *(86·6 × 12·2 × 4·8)*
Gun: 1—40 mm
Main engines: 1 diesel; vp propeller; 3 000 bhp = 12 knots
Range, miles: 5 000 at 12 knots
Complement: 48 (3 officers, 45 men)

Authorised in 1956. Ordered in 1959. Laid down in 1961. The after part with engine room was launched on 24 April 1963. The fore part was built on the vacated slip, launched and welded to the after part. Complete hull floated up on 21 Nov 1963. Carries white oil, lubricating oil and petrol.

ABERWRACH   *1970, French Navy*

5 "RHIN" CLASS (DEPOT SHIPS)

Name	No.	Builders	Commissioned
GARONNE	A 617	Lorient Naval Dockyard	1 Sep 1965
LOIRE	A 615	Lorient Naval Dockyard	10 Oct 1967
RANCE	A 618	Lorient Naval Dockyard	5 Feb 1966
RHIN	A 621	Lorient Naval Dockyard	1 Mar 1964
RHÔNE	A 622	Lorient Naval Dockyard	1 Dec 1964

Displacement, tons: 2 075 standard; 2 445 full load *(Rhin, Rance and Rhône)*
 2 320 standard *(Garonne and Loire)*
Dimensions, feet (metres): 302·0 pp; 331·5 oa × 43·0 × 12·1 *(92·1; 101·1 × 13·1 × 3·7)*
Guns: 3—40 mm (except *Garonne*)
Aircraft: 1 to 3 Alouette helicopters (except *Garonne* and *Loire*)
Landing craft: 2 LCP
Main engines: 2 SEMT-Pielstick diesels (16PA2V in *Rhin* and *Rhône*, 12PA4 in *Rance, Loire* and *Garonne);* 1 shaft; 3 300 bhp = 16·5 knots
Range, miles: 13 000 at 13 knots
Complement: *Rhin* and *Rhône* 148 (6 officers, 142 men); *Rance* 150 (10 officers, 140 men) and about 118 passengers; *Garonne* 221 (10 officers, 211 men); *Loire* 140 (9 officers, 131 men)

Designed for supporting various classes of ships. Have a 5 ton crane, carry two LCPs and have a helicopter platform (except *Garonne*). *Rhin* and *Rhône* have a hangar and carry an Alouette helicopter. *Rance* carries three in her hangar and *Loire* has only the helicopter platform. *Garonne* is designed as a Repair Workshop. *Loire* for minesweeper support, *Rance* for laboratory and radiological services, *Rhin* for electronic maintenance. *Loire* and *Rhône* are currently operating in support of North Atlantic fishery patrols.

Radar: One DRBV 50 (in *Rhin* and *Rhône*).

RHÔNE (RHIN and LOIRE similar)   *11/1976, Michael D. J. Lennon*

GARONNE   *French Navy*   RANCE   *11/1975, Dr. Giorgio Arra*

1 SUPPORT TANKER

Name	No.	Builders	Commissioned
SAHEL	A 638	Chantiers Naval de Caen	Aug 1951

Displacement, tons: 630 light; 1 450 full load
Measurement, tons: 650 deadweight
Dimensions, feet (metres): 176·2 × 29·5 × 14·5 *(53·7 × 9 × 4·5)*
Guns: 2—20 mm
Main engines: 2 diesels; 1 400 bhp = 12 knots

SAHEL   1972, Dr. Giorgio Arra

1 MAINTENANCE SHIP

Name	No.	Builders	Commissioned
MOSELLE (ex-*Foucauld*)	A 608	Swan, Hunter & Wigham Richardson Ltd, Wallsend-on-Tyne	1948

Displacement, tons: 8 200 standard; 8 700 full load
Dimensions, feet (metres): 480 oa × 62 × 22·3 *(146·3 × 18·9 × 6·9)*
Main engines: 2 Doxford diesels; 2 shafts; 8 800 bhp = 15 knots
Complement: 177 (7 officers, 170 men)

Former motor passenger ship of the Chargeurs Réunis (West Africa Coast Service). Launched on 17 July 1947. *Moselle* was converted in 1967. Used as Base Ship in Pacific Trial Centre. Can carry 500 passengers.

MOSELLE   1972, Dr. Giorgio Arra

1 MAINTENANCE and REPAIR SHIP

JULES VERNE (ex-*Achéron*) A 620

Displacement, tons: 6 485 standard; 10 250 full load
Dimensions, feet (metres): 482·2 × 70·5 × 21·3 *(147 × 21·5 × 6·5)*
Aircraft: 2 Helicopters
Guns: 2—40 mm
Main engines: 2 diesels SEMT-Pielstick; 1 shaft; 21 500 hp = 18 knots
Range, miles: 9 500 at 18 knots
Complement: 323 (20 officers, 303 men)

Ordered in 1961 budget, originally as an Armament Supply Ship. Role and design changed—now rated as Engineering and Electrical Maintenance Ship. Launched 30 May 1970. In service March 1976. Currently serving in Indian Ocean.

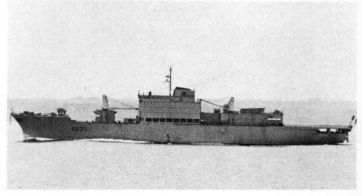

JULES VERNE   3/1976, J. van der Woude

2 REPAIR SHIPS (Ex-LCT)

L 9081   L9084

Displacement, tons: 310 standard; 685 full load
Dimensions, feet (metres): 193·5 × 39 × 5 *(59 × 11·9 × 1·6)*
Main engines: 2 Diesels MGO; 1 000 bhp = 8 knots
Range, miles: 1 800 at 8 knots
Complement: 15

Built in 1964-65 by Ch. N. Franco-Belge. Repair facilities grafted onto LCT hulls. 9081 is fitted with mechanical workshops, and 9084 is primarily an electrical stores ship.

Ex-LCT   1972, Dr. Giorgio Arra

4 SUPPLY TENDERS

Name	No.	Builders	Commissioned
CHAMOIS	A 767	La Perrière, Lorient	30 Apr 1976
ELAN	A 768	La Perrière, Lorient	1976
CHEVREUL	A 774	La Perrière, Lorient	1976
GAZELLE	A 775	La Perrière, Lorient	1976

Displacement, tons: 495 full load
Dimensions, feet (metres): 136·1 × 24·6 × 10·5 *(41·5 × 7·5 × 3·2)*
Main engines: 2 Diesels SACM AGO V-16; 2 VP propellers; 2 200 hp = 14·5 knots
Complement: 10 (4 spare berths)

Similar to the standard FISH oil rig support ships. Fitted with hydraulic crane for torpedo recovery. Can act as tugs, oil pollution vessels, salvage craft (28 ton pull), coastal and harbour controlled minelaying, torpedo recovery, diving tenders and a variety of other tasks. Bow thruster of 80 hp and twin rudders. Five more planned.

1 VICTUALLING STORES SHIP

SAINTONGE (ex-*Santa Maria*) A 733

Measurement, tons: 300 standard; 990 full load
Dimensions, feet (metres): 177 × 28 × 10·5 *(54 × 8·5 × 3·2)*
Main engines: 1 diesel; 1 shaft; 760 bhp = 10 knots
Complement: 15

Built by Chantiers Duchesne et Bossière, Le Havre, for a Norwegian owner under the name of *Sven Germa*. Launched on 12 July 1956. Purchased in April 1965 from the firm of H. Beal & Co, Fort de France for the Pacific Nuclear Experimental Centre.

TRIALS RESEARCH SHIPS

Name	No.	Builders	Commissioned
HENRI POINCARÊ	A 603	Cantieri Riuniti de Adriaticos,	—
(ex-*Maina Marasso*)		Monfalcone	

Displacement, tons: 24 000 full load
Dimensions, feet (metres): 565·0 pp; 590·6 oa × 72·8 × 28·9 *(180 × 22·2 × 9·4)*
Guns: 2—20 mm
Main engines: 1 Parsons geared turbine; 1 shaft; 10 000 shp = 15 knots
Boilers: 2 Foster Wheeler high pressure water tube
Range, miles: 11 800 at 13·5 knots
Complement: 214 + 9 (11 officers, 9 civilians, 203 men)

Launched in Oct 1960. Former Italian tanker. Purchased in Sep 1964. Converted in Brest dockyard from 1 Oct 1964 to 1967. To work with the experimental guided missile station in the Landes (SW France). Named after the mathematician and scientist.

Aircraft: Can land heavy helicopters and has space for two large or five light helicopters in her hangar.

Operations: She is primarily a missile-range-ship and acts as Flagship of Force M, the trials squadron of the French Navy. To enable her to plot the trajectory etc of missiles fired from land or sea she is equipped with three tracking radars, a telemetry station, transit nav-aid, cinetheodolite, infra-red tracking as well as an up-to-date fit of hull-mounted sonar, meteorological and oceanographic equipment.

Radar: One Savoie, two Bearn, one DRBV 22D.

HENRI POINCARÊ   7/1976, Michael D. J. Lennon

ILE D'OLÉRON (ex-*Munchen,* ex-*Mur)* A 610

Displacement, tons: 5 500 standard; 6 500 full load
Dimensions, feet (metres): 350·0 pp; 377·5 × 50·0 × 21·3 *(106·7 pp; 115·2 oa × 15·2 × 6·5)*
Main engines: MAN 6-cylinder diesels; 1 shaft; 3 500 bhp
Speed, knots: 14·5
Oil fuel, tons: 340
Range, miles: 7 200 at 12 knots
Complement: 195 (12 officers, 183 men)

Launched in Germany in 1939. Taken as a war prize. Formerly rated as a transport. Converted to experimental guided missile ship in 1957-58 by Chantiers de Provence and l'Arsenal de Toulon. Commissioned early in 1959. Equipped with stabilisers.

Experimental: When converted, was designed for experiments with two launchers for ship-to-air missiles, the medium range Masurca and the long range Masalca, and one launcher for ship to shore missiles, the Malaface. Latterly fitted with one launcher for target planes. Now fitted for trials on MM 38 Exocet and for Crotale trials from 1977.

Radar: One DRBV 22C, one DRBV 50, one DRBI 10.
The missile system tracking radar operates in G band.

ILE D'OLÉRON   9/1976, Dr. Giorgio Arra

1 TRIALS SHIP

Name	No.	Builders	Commissioned
AUNIS (ex-*Regina Pacis*)	A 643	Roland Werft, Bremen	see note

Displacement, tons: 2 900 full load
Dimensions, feet (metres): 284·5 × 38 × 15 *(86·5 × 11·6 × 4·6)*
Main engines: MAN diesels geared to 1 shaft; 2 400 bhp = 12 knots
Range, miles: 4 500 at 12 knots

Launched on 3 July 1956. Purchased in Nov 1966 from Scotto Ambrosino & Pugliese and converted in Toulon 1972-73. Employed as trials ship in Operation Cormoran with deep sonar. Sonar transferred from *Duperré.*

AUNIS   1975, Wright and Logan

1 TRIALS SHIP

BERRY (ex-M/S *Médoc)* A 644

Displacement, tons: 1 148 standard; 2 700 full load
Dimensions, feet (metres): 284·5 oa × 38 × 15 *(86·7 × 11·6 × 4·6)*
Main engines: 2 MWM diesels coupled on one shaft; 2 400 bhp = 15 knots
Range, miles: 7 000 at 15 knots

Built by Roland Werft, Bremen. Launched on 10 May 1958. Purchased in Oct 1964 and refitted in 1964-66. In 1976-77 converted at Toulon from victualling stores ship to Mediterranean electronic trials ship. Recommissioned Feb 1977.

BERRY   1969, French Navy

1 TRIALS SHIP

Name	No.	Builders	Commissioned
TRITON	A 646	Lorient	1972

Displacement, tons: 1 410 standard; 1 510 full load
Dimensions, feet (metres): 242·7 × 38·9 × 12 *(74 × 11·8 × 3·7)*
Main engines: 2 MGO V Diesels driving a Voith Schneider screw aft; 2 electric motors driving a Voith Schneider forward
Speed, knots: 13
Range, miles: 4 000 at 13 knots
Complement: 65 (4 officers, 44 men + 5 officers and 12 men for diving)

Under sea recovery and trials ship. Equipped with a helicopter platform. Launched on 7 Mar 1970. Support ship for the 2-man submarine *Griffon*.

Operations: Operated by G.E.R.S. (Groupe d'Etude et de Recherches Sousmarins) for trials of submarines and deep-sea diving equipment. Underwater TV, recompression chamber, 4 man diving bell and laboratories are fitted. Available as submarine rescue ship.

Radar: Navigational.

Sonar: Special equipment for deep operations.

Submarine: The submarine *Griffon* is carried amidships on the starboard side of *Triton*. She is 25 feet *(7·8 metres)* long, displaces 16 tons and is driven by an electric motor. Her diving depth is 2 000 feet *(600 metres)* and her endurance 24 miles at 4 knots. Can be used for deep recovery operations.

TRITON (with *Griffon* amidships)　　　　　　　　6/1975, Dr. Giorgio Arra

1 TRIALS SHIP

Name	No.	Builders	Commissioned
MARCEL LE BIHAN (ex-*Greif*)	A 759	Lubecker Flendewerke	1937

Displacement, tons: 800 standard; 1 250 full load
Dimensions, feet (metres): 236·2 × 34·8 × 10·5 *(72 × 10·6 × 3·2)*
Guns: 4—20 mm (twins)
Main engines: 2 GM diesels; 2 shafts; 4 400 bhp = 13 knots
Range, miles: 2 500 at 13 knots
Complement: 50 (3 officers, 47 men), accommodation for 22 extra hands

Former German aircraft tender. Launched in 1936. Transferred by USA in Feb 1948. 4·1 in gun and 2—40 mm removed. Tender for DSV *Archimède*.

MARCEL LE BIHAN　　　　　　　　7/1976, Dr. Giorgio Arra

1 DEEP SUBMERGENCE VEHICLE

ARCHIMÈDE A 648

Built in Toulon. 68·9 feet long with surface displacement of 60 tons. Diving depth 36 000 feet *(11 000 metres)*. *Marcel le Bihan* acts as tender. FNRS 3 deleted 1974.

ARCHIMÈDE　　　　　　　　1974, Wright and Logan

1 ARCHAEOLOGICAL RESEARCH CRAFT

L'ARCHÉONAUTE A 789

Built by Auroux, Arcachon August 1967. 120 tons full load and 96 feet long *(29·3 metres)* with two Baudoin diesels; 600 hp; twin VP propellers; 12 knots. For underwater archaeological research carries a complement of 2 officers, 4 men, 3 archaeologists and 6 divers.

L'ARCHÉONAUTE　　　　　　　　1975, Wright and Logan

1 RADIOLOGICAL RESEARCH CRAFT

PALANGRIN Y 743

Acquired 1969. Of 44 tons with single diesel of 220 hp.

BOOM AND MOORING VESSELS

LA FIDÈLE Y 751   **LA PERSÉVÉRANTE** Y 750   **LA PRUDENTE** Y 749

Displacement, tons: 446 standard; 626 full load
Dimensions, feet (metres): 142·8 × 32·8 × 9·2 *(43·5 × 10 × 2·8)*
Main engines: 2 Baudoin diesels; Diesel-electric; 1 shaft; 620 bhp=10 knots
Range, miles: 4 000 at 10 knots
Complement: 30 (1 officer, 29 men)

Net layers and tenders built by Atel. Ch. La Manche, Dieppe, *(La Fidèle* and *La Prudente)* and
Atel. Ch. La Rochelle *(La Persévérante)*. Launched on 26 Aug 1968 *(La Fidèle)*, 14 May 1968 *(La
Persévérante)* and 13 May 1968 *(La Prudente)*. 25 ton lift.

LA PERSÉVÉRANTE   11/1975 Dr. Giorgio Arra

TIANÉE A 731

Displacement, tons: 842 standard; 905 full load
Dimensions, feet (metres): 178·1 × 34·8 *(54·3 × 10·6)*
Main engines: Diesel-electric; 2 diesels; 1 shaft = 12 knots
Range, miles: 5 200 at 12 knots
Complement: 37 (1 officer, 36 men)

Built at Brest. Launched 17 Nov 1973. For service in the Pacific. Fitted with lateral screws in bow
tunnel.

TIANÉE   1974, French Navy

CIGALE (ex-*AN 98)* A 760   **FOURMI** (ex-*AN 97)* A 762
CRIQUET (ex-*AN 96)* A 761   **GRILLON** (ex-*AN 95)* A 763
                                  SCARABÉE (ex-*AN 94)* A 764

Displacement, tons: 770 standard; 850 full load
Dimensions, feet (metres): 151·9 oa × 33·5 × 10·5 *(46·3 × 10·2 × 3·2)*
Guns: 1—40 mm Bofors; 4—20 mm
Main engines: 2, 4-stroke diesels, electric drive, 1 shaft; 1 600 bhp = 12 knots
Range, miles: 5 200 at 12 knots
Complement: 37 (1 officer, 36 men)

US off-shore order. Sister ship G 6 was allocated to Spain. *Cerberus* transferred to Netherlands
and subsequently to Turkey as AG 6. *Criquet* was launched on 3 June 1954, *Cigale* on 23 Sep
1954, *Fourmi* on 6 July 1954, *Grillon* on 18 Feb 1954 and *Scarabée* on 21 Nov 1953.

GRILLON   10/1976, Michael D. J. Lennon

2 Ex-US AN TYPE NETLAYERS

LIBELLULE (ex-*Rosewood)* A 730
LUCIOLE (ex-*Sandalwood)* A 777

Displacement, tons: 560 standard; 850 full load
Dimensions, feet (metres): 146·0 wl; 163·0 oa × 30·5 × 11·7 *(50 × 9·3 × 4·8)*
Guns: 1—3 in; some MG
Main engines: 2 GM diesels; diesel-electric; 1 shaft; 1 300 bhp = 13 knots
Range, miles: 7 200 at 12 knots
Complement: 39 (2 officers, 37 men)

Launched on 6 Mar 1941, 1 Apr 1941, 6 Mar 1941 respectively. *Luciole* was purchased in 1967,
Libellule in 1969. Both to reserve 1976.

LUCIOLE   1974, Wright and Logan

3 MOORING VESSELS

COMMANDANT ROBERT GIRAUD (ex-*Immelmann)* A 755 (ex-*F 755)*

Displacement, tons: 1 142 standard; 1 220 full load
Length, feet (metres): 239·0 *(72·9)* pp; 256·0 *(78·0)* oa
Beam, feet (metres): 36·0 *(11·0)*
Draught, feet (metres): 12·0 *(3·7)*
Main engines: 4 MAN diesels; 2 shafts; 5 720 bhp
Range, miles: 9 000 at 10 knots
Oil fuel, tons: 236
Complement: 54 (1 officer, 53 men)

Ex-German aircraft tender. Built by Norderwerft, Hamburg. Launched in Dec 1941. Transferred
by Great Britain in Aug 1946. The diesels are coupled two by two with hydraulic transmission on
two shafts. Crane lift 18 tons. To reserve 1976.

COMMANDANT ROBERT GIRAUD   1975, Dr. Giorgio Arra

TUPA Y 667

292 tons with 210 hp diesel.

CALMAR Y 688

Converted for raising moorings.

TORPEDO RECOVERY VESSELS

PÉLICAN (ex-*Kerfany*) A 699

Displacement, tons: 362 standard; 425 full load
Dimensions, feet (metres): 121·4 × 28·0 × 13·1 *(37 × 8·6 × 4)*
Torpedo tube: One
Main engines: 1 Burmeister and Wain diesel; 1 shaft; 650 bhp = 11 knots
Complement: 19

Built in USA in 1951. Purchased in 1965 and converted from tunny fisher into torpedo recovery craft in 1966.

PÉLICAN *11/1975, Dr. Giorgio Arra*

PÉTREL (ex-*Cap Lopez*, ex-*Yvon Loic II*) A 698

Displacement, tons: 277 standard; 318 full load
Dimensions, feet (metres): 98·4 × 25·6 × 11·5 *(30 × 7·8 × 3·5)*
Main engines: 2 Baudoin diesels; 1 vp screw; 600 bhp = 10 knots
Complement: 19

Built by Dubigeon 1960. Purchased 1965 and converted from tunny fisher to torpedo recovery craft.

TRANSPORTS

6 SMALL TRANSPORTS

ALPHÉE Y 696	**DRYADE** Y 662	**FAUNE** Y 613
ARIEL Y 604	**ELFE** Y 741	**KORRIGAN** Y 661

Displacement, tons: 195 standard; 225 full load
Dimensions, feet (metres): 132·8 × 24·5 × 10·8 *(40·5 × 7·5 × 3·3)*
Main engines: 2 diesels; 2 shafts; 1 640 bhp;/1 730 bhp = 15 knots
Complement: 9

Ariel was launched on 27 April 1964. *Korrigan* on 6 March 1964. *Alphée* on 10 June 1969. *Elfe* on 14 April 1970, *Faune* on 8 Sept 1971, *Dryade* in 1973. All built by Societe Française de Construction Naval (ex-Franco-Belge). Can carry 400 passengers (250 seated).

ALPHÉE *1972, Admiral M. Adam*

5 SMALL TRANSPORTS

SYLPHE Y 710

Displacement, tons: 171 standard; 189 full load
Dimensions, feet (metres): 126·5 × 22·7 × 8·2 *(38·5 × 6·9 × 2·5)*
Main engines: One MGO diesel; 1 shaft; 425 bhp = 12 knots
Complement: 9

Small transport for passengers, built by Chantiers Franco-Belge in 1959-60.

LUTIN (ex-*Georges Clemenceau*) Y 664

Displacement, tons: 68
Main engines: 400 hp = 10 knots

Purchased in 1965. Ex-vedette. Detection school, Toulon.

MÉLUSINE Y 736	**MERLIN** Y 735	**MORGANE** Y 671

Displacement, tons: 170
Dimensions, feet (metres): 103·3 × 23·2 × 7·9 *(31·5 × 7·1 × 2·4)*
Main engines: MGO diesels; 2 shafts; 960 bhp = 11 knots

Small transports for 400 passengers built by Chantiers Navals Franco-Belge at Chalon sur Saône (*Mélusine* and *Merlin*) and Ars. de Mourillon *(Morgane)*. Laid down in Dec 1966 and accepted June 1968. Their home port is Toulon.

MORGANE *1975, Wright and Logan*

DIVING TENDERS

4 Ex-US "ADJUTANT" CLASS (MSC)

AJONC (ex-*M 667*) A 701
GARDÉNIA (ex-*M 676*) A 711
LISERON (ex-*M683*) A 723
MAGNOLIA (ex-*M 685*) A 770

Details as in same class under Minewarfare Forces except for complement, now 11. *Ajonc* employed as diving training ship, remainder as clearance-diving base ships. *Magnolia* transferred 1976.

GARDÉNIA   6/1975, Dr. Giorgio Arra

1 Ex-BRITISH "HAM" CLASS (MSI)

MYOSOTIS (ex-*M 788*) A 710

Details as in same class under Light Forces. Employed as diving-tender.

TENDERS

8 Ex-BRITISH "HAM" CLASS (MSI)

ARMOISE (ex-*Vexham*, ex-*M 772*) A 741
CAPUCINE (ex-*Petersham*, ex-*M 782*) A 738
DAHLIA (ex-*Whippingham*, ex-*M 786*) A 736
HIBISCUS (ex-*Sparham*, ex-*M 785*) A 735
HORTENSIA (ex-*Mileham*, ex-*M 783*) A 740
OEILLET (ex-*Isham*, ex-*M 774*) A 739
PAQUERETTE (ex-*Kingham*, ex-*M 775*) A 742
TULIPE (ex-*Frettenham*, ex-*M 771*) A 737

Details as in same class under Light Forces. Now general purpose tenders.

ARMOISE   11/1975, Dr. Giorgio Arra

POSEIDON A 722

Displacement, tons: 220
Dimensions, feet (metres): 132·9 × 23·6 × 7·3 *(40·5 × 7·2 × 2·2)*
Main engines: 1 diesel; 600 bhp = 13 knots
Endurance: 8 days
Complement: 42

Base ships for assault swimmers. Completed 6 Aug 1975.

POSEIDON   1975, French Navy

SSBN TENDER. A 1 200-ton service lighter of 1 000 hp for nuclear fuel elements of SSBNs was launched on 26 Oct 1967 for delivery in May 1968.

TRAINING SHIPS

CHIMÈRE Y 706   **FARFADET** Y 711

Displacement, tons: 100
Main engine: 1 diesel; 200 hp = 11 knots

Auxiliary sail training ships built at Bayonne in 1971. Tenders to the Naval School.

LA GRANDE HERMINE (ex-*La Route Est Belle*, ex-*Ménestral*) A 653

Ex-sailing fishing boat built in 1932. Purchased in 1964 in replacement for *Dolphin* (ex-*Simone Marcelle*) as the Navigation School (E.O.R.) Training ship. Length 46 feet.

ENGAGEANTE (ex-*Cayolle*) A 772   **VIGILANTE** (ex-*Iseran*) A 773

Displacement, tons: 286
Dimensions, feet (metres): 98·4 × 22 × 12·5 *(30 × 6·7 × 3·8)*
Main engine: 1 Deutz diesel; 560 hp; 1 shaft = 11 knots

Ex-motor trawlers built by At. et Ch. de la Rochelle-Pallice in 1964. Bought in 1975 for conversion as training ships for the Petty Officers Navigation School. Decca radar.

LA BELLEPOULE A 650   **L'ÉTOILE** A 649

Displacement, tons: 227
Dimensions, feet (metres): 128 oa × 23·7 × 11·8 *(32·3 × 7 × 3·2)*
Main engines: Sulzer diesels; 125 bhp = 6 knots

Auxiliary sail vessels. Built by Chantiers de Normandie (Fécamp) in 1932. Accommodation for 3 officers, 30 cadets, 5 petty officers, 12 men. Attached to Naval School.

MUTIN A 652

A small 57 ton coastal tender built in 1927. Auxiliary diesel and sails. Attached to the Navigation School.

TUGS

3 OCEAN TUGS

CENTAURE A 674   **MALABAR** A 664   **TENACE** A 669

Displacement, tons: 1 080 light; 1 454 full load
Dimensions, feet (metres): 167·3 oa × 37·8 × 18·6 *(51 × 11·5 × 5·7)*
Main engines: 2 diesels; Kort engines 4 600 hp; 1 shaft = 15 knots
Range, miles: 9 500 at 15 knots
Complement: 42

Malabar and *Tenace* built by J. Oelkers, Hamburg, *Centaure* built at La Pallice 1972-74. *Malabar* commissioned 7 Oct 1975.

TENACE   *1973, Reiner Nerlich*

1 OCEAN TUG

ÉLÉPHANT (ex-*Bar*) A 666

Displacement, tons: 880 standard; 1 180 full load
Main engines: Triple expansion 2 000 ihp = 11 knots

2 OCEAN TUGS

HIPPOPOTAME (ex-*Utrecht*) A 660   **RHINOCEROS** A 668

Displacement, tons: 640 standard; 940 full load
Main engines: Diesel-electric; 1 850 shp = 12 knots

Hippopotame built as USN ATA of "Sotoyomo" class. Former Netherlands civilian ocean tug. Built in 1943. Purchased by the French Navy in Jan 1964 to be used at the Experimental Base in the Pacific. *Rhinoceros* purchased direct from USN.

1 COASTAL TUG

GOLIATH A 665

Displacement, tons: 380
Main engines: 900 hp

1 COASTAL TUG

COOLIE A 684

Displacement, tons: 300
Main engines: 1 000 hp

RHINOCEROS   *7/1976, Dr. Giorgio Arra*

12 COASTAL TUGS

ACHARNÉ A 693	**HERCULE** A 667	**ROBUSTE** A 685
ACTIF A 686	**LE FORT** A 671	**TRAVAILLEUR** A 692
COURAGEUX A 706	**LABORIEUX** A 687	**VALEUREUX** A 688
EFFICACE A 694	**LUTTEUR** A 673	**UTILE** A 672

Displacement, tons: 230
Dimensions, feet (metres): 92 × 26 × 13 *(28·1 × 7·9 × 4)*
Main engines: 1 MGO diesel; 1 050 bhp = 11 knots
Range, miles: 2 400
Complement: 15

Courageux, Hercule, Robuste and *Valeureux* were completed in 1960, four more in 1962-63, two more in late 60s and *Acharné* and *Efficace* in 1974.

HERCULE   *11/1975, Dr. Giorgio Arra*

80 HARBOUR TUGS

Acajou Y 601, *Aigrette* Y 602, *Balsa* Y 607, *Bambou* Y 608, *Bengali* Y 611, *Bouleau* Y 612, *Canari* Y 616, *Mouette* Y 617, *Chataigner* Y 620, *Mésange* Y621, *Charme* Y 623, *Chêne* Y 624, *Colibri* Y 628, *Cormier* Y 629, *Bonite* Y 630, *Courlis* Y 631, *Cygne* Y 632, *Délange* Y 633, *Rouget* Y 634, *Equeurdiville* Y 635, *Martinet* Y 636, *Fauvette* Y 637, *Fontaine* Y 640, *Forméne* Y 641, *Fréne* Y 644, *Giens* Y 647, *Goeland* Y 648, *Grive* Y 649, *Hanneton* Y 651, *Haut-Barr* Y 652, *Heron* Y 653, *Hétre* Y 654, *Hévéat* Y 655, *Hirondelle* Y 657, *Jonque* Y659, *Latanier* Y 663, *Manguier* Y 666, *Tupa* Y 667, *Méléze* Y 668, *Merisier* Y 669, *Merle* Y 670, *Moineau* Y 673, *Martin Pécheur* Y 675, *Moule* Y 678, *Muréne* Y 680, *Okoume* Y 682, *Ondée* Y 683, *Oursin* Y 685, *Palétuvier* Y 686, *Passereau* Y 687, *Pin* Y 689, *Pingouin* Y 690, *Pinson* Y 691, *Pivert* Y 694, *Platane* Y 695, *Calmar* Y 698, *Poulpe* Y 699, *Rascasse* Y 702, *Rossignol* Y 704, *Saule* Y 708, *Sycomore* Y 709, *Ébène* Y 717, *Erable* Y 718, *Olivier* Y 719, *Santal* Y 720, *Alouette* Y 721, *Vauneau* Y 722, *Engoulevent* Y 723, *Sarcelle* Y 724, *Marabout* Y 725, *Toucan* Y 726, *Macreuse* Y 727, *Grand Duc* Y 728, *Eider* Y 729, *Ara* Y 730, *Marronier* Y 738, *Noyer* Y 739, *Papayer* Y 740, *Loriot* Y 747, *Gelinotte* Y 748.

Note: Reported that 10 Water Tractors are under construction and that two other Tugs *Dourade* and *Girelle* are listed.

BAMBOU   *11/1975, Dr. Giorgio Arra*

6 PUMP-TUGS

Aiguière Y 745, *Cascade* Y 618, *Embrun* Y 746, *Gave* Y 645, *Geyser* Y 646, *Oued* Y 684.

GABON

Ministerial

Minister of National Defence:
  President Albert Bernard Bongo

Personnel

(a) 1977: 100 officers and men
(b) Volunteers

Mercantile Marine

Lloyd's Register of Shipping: 14 vessels of 98 285 tons gross

Bases

Libreville, Port Gentil

DELETION

1975 *Bouet-Willaumez (ex-HDML 102)*

LIGHT FORCES

1 FAST ATTACK CRAFT (MISSILE)

Name	No.	Builders	Commissioned
—	—	Chantiers Navals de l'Esterel	1977

Displacement, tons: 155
Dimensions, feet (metres): 137·8 × 25·6 × 6·2 *(42 × 7·8 × 1·9)*
Missiles: 4—SS 12
Guns: 2—40 mm Bofors
Main engines: 2 MTU 16 V 538 TB 91 diesels; 7 200 hp = 33 knots
Range, miles: 1 000 at 18 knots
Complement: 25

Name	No.	Builders	Commissioned
PRESIDENT ALBERT BERNARD BONGO	—	Chantiers Navals de l'Esterel	Mar 1972

Displacement, tons: 80
Dimensions, feet (metres): 104 × 19 × 5 *(32 × 5·8 × 1·5)*
Guns: 2—20 mm
Main engines: 2 MTU diesels; 2 700 hp = 30 knots
Range, miles: 1 500 at 15 knots
Complement: 17 (3 officers, 14 ratings)

Fitted with radar and echo sounder.

PRESIDENT ALBERT BERNARD BONGO   *1972, Chantiers Navals de l'Esterel*

Name	No.	Builders	Commissioned
PRESIDENT LEON M'BA	GCO 1	Gabon	1968

Displacement, tons: 85 standard
Dimensions, feet (metres): 92 × 20·5 × 5 *(28 × 6·3 × 1·5)*
Guns: 1—75 mm; 1—12·7 mm MG
Main engines: Diesel = 12·5 knots
Complement: 16

Launched on 16 Jan 1968.

Name	No.	Builders	Commissioned
N'GUENE	GCO 3	Swiftships, USA	April 1975

Displacement, tons: 118
Dimensions, feet (metres): 105·6 × — × 7·5 *(32·2 × — × 2·3)*
Guns: 2—40 mm (twin); 2—20 mm (twin); 2—12·7 mm MG
Main engines: 3 Diesels; 3 shafts = 27 knots
Range, miles: 825 at 25 knots
Complement: 21

COASTGUARD

6 ARCOA COASTAL PATROL CRAFT

Capable of 15 knots.

1 ARCOA 960 COASTAL PATROL CRAFT

Capable of 25 knots.

THE GAMBIA

Mercantile Marine

Lloyd's Register of Shipping:
  3 vessels of 1 337 tons

Port

Banjul

MANSA KILA IV

Displacement, tons: 40
Dimensions, feet (metres): 74·5 × 19·7 × 5·0 *(22·7 × 6·0 × 1·5)*
Main engines: 2 Cummins diesels; 750 bhp = 20 knots

Built by Camper and Nicholson Ltd, Gosport, England to Keith Nelson 75 ft design for a private order—eventually purchased by The Gambia in 1974.

1 FAIREY MARINE "LANCE" CLASS
(COASTAL PATROL CRAFT)

Displacement, tons: 17
Dimensions, feet (metres): 48·7 × 15·3 × 4·3 *(14·8 × 4·7 × 1·3)*
Guns: 2—7·62 mm
Main engines: 2 GM 8V 71 T1; 850 hp = 23 knots
Complement: 9

Delivered 1976 for the Customs service.

GERMANY (Federal Republic)

Headquarters Appointment

Chief of Naval Staff, Federal German Navy:
Vice-Admiral Gunter Luther

Senior Appointment

Commander-in-Chief of the Fleet:
Vice Admiral H. H. Klose

Diplomatic Representation

Naval Attaché in The Hague:
Commander H. Grande
Defence Attaché in Lisbon:
Commander K. Perlich
Naval Attaché in London:
Rear Admiral Dr. W. Schünemann
Commander P. Laabs (ANA)
Naval Attaché in Oslo (and Stockholm):
Commander H. Komatowsky
Naval Attaché in Paris:
Captain W. Koever
Naval Attaché in Rome:
Commander W. D. Fischer-Mühlen
Naval Attaché in Washington:
Captain K-J. Steindorff

Personnel

(a) 1973: 36 000 (4 550 officers, 31 450 men)
1974: 36 000 (4 550 officers, 31 450 men)
1975: 35 900 (4 775 officers, 31 125 men)
1976: 35 900 (5 100 officers, 30 800 men)
1977: 38 275 (5 600 officers, 32 675 men)

(Includes Naval Air Arm)

(b) 15 months National Service

Bases

Flensburg, Wilhelmshaven, Kiel, Olpenitz.
The administration of these bases is vested in the Naval Support Command at Wilhelmshaven (Rear-Admiral Feindt)

Naval Air Arm

(See Future Developments)

6 000 men total
2 LRMP squadrons (15 Breguet Atlantic)
4 Fighter bomber squadrons (60 F104G)
1 Helicopter squadron (re-equipping with 22 Sea King Mk 41 for SAR.)
20 Liaison aircraft (DO28)

Prefix to Ships' Names

Not normally used but in British waters prefix FGS is used.

Mercantile Marine

Lloyd's Register of Shipping:
1 957 vessels of 9 264 671 tons gross

Future Development

Interest is being shown by the Naval Staff in various and varied projects.
(a) Development of more powerful ship-to-ship missiles.
(b) Development of SAMs and ASMs with the Franco German Kormoran ASM
(c) Construction of 230 ton hydrofoils of USS Pegasus type. (Type 162)
(d) New frigates of 2 500 tons standard, 3 800 tons full load with guided weapons to replace "Köln" Class—12 are planned, first batch similar to Netherlands "Kortenaer" class.
(e) Replacement of F104G aircraft by MRCAs.
(f) Replacement of Breguet Atlantics by S3A Vikings.
(g) Minewarfare forces to be improved by conversion of 12 MSCs to Minehunters and replacement of "Schütze" class by remotely controlled unmanned systems.

Hydrographic Service

This service is under the direction of the Ministry of Transport, is civilian manned with HQ at Hamburg. Survey ships are listed at the end of the section.

Strength of the Fleet

Type	Active	Building (Projected)
Destroyers	11	—
Frigates	6	(12)
Corvettes	6	
Submarines—Patrol	24	—
Fast Attack Craft (Missile)	30	4 (6) (hydrofoils)
Fast Attack Craft (Torpedo)	10	
LCUs	22	—
LCMs	19	—
Minesweepers— Coastal and Minehunter	40	—
Minesweepers—Inshore	18	—
Depot Ships	11	—
Repair Ships	3	—
	(1 small)	
Replenishment Tankers	6	—
Support Tankers	5	—
Support Ships	8	—
Ammunition Transports	2	—
Mine Transports	2	—
Training Ship	1	—
Sail Training Ships	2	—
Survey Ship	1	—
TRVs	13	—
SAR Launch	1	—
Coastal Patrol Craft	7	—
Auxiliaries (some non-naval)	28	—
Tugs—Ocean	8	—
Tugs—Harbour/Coastal	18	—
*Icebreakers	3	—
*Coastguard Craft	8+	—
*Survey Ships	6	—
*Fishery Protection Ships	10	—

*Non-naval

DELETIONS

Destroyers

1972 Z1

Frigates

1972 *Scharnhorst* and *Gneisenau*

Submarines

1974 U4, 5, 6, 7, 8, (Type 205)

Fast Attack Craft (Torpedo)

1972 *Marder*
1973 *Jaguar, Kranich, Leopard, Luchs, Panther*
1974 *Dommel, Elster*
1975 20 "Jaguar" class transferred (*Alk, Fuchs, Häher, Löwe, Pelikan, Pinguin, Reiher, Storch, Tiger* and *Wolf* to Turkey and *Albatros, Bussard, Falke, Geier, Greif, Habicht, Kondor, Kormoran, Seeadler* and *Sperber* to Greece).·

Coastal Patrol Craft

1974 TM 1, KW 2, KW 8, FW 2, FW 3

Minelayers

1972 *Bochum, Bottrop* transferred to Turkey.

Minesweepers Coastal

1972 *Algol* ("Schütze" class) scrapped.
1973 *Capella, Krebs, Mira, Orion, Pegasus, Steinbock, Uranus* ("Schütze" class).
1975 *Vegesack, Hampeln, Siegen, Detmold, Worms* ("Vegesack" class) transferred to Turkey, Sept)

Depot Ships

1975 *Weser* transferred to Greece.
1976 *Ruhr* (transferred to Turkey)

Supply Ships

1972 *Angeln* transferred to Turkey.
1974 *Schwarzwald*
1976 *Dithmarschen* (transferred to Turkey)

Auxiliaries

1975 FW 6 to Turkey, *Karl Kolls* (sold).

PENNANT LIST

Destroyers

D 171	Z 2
D 172	Z 3
D 178	Z 4
D 179	Z 5
D 181	Hamburg
D 182	Schleswig-Holstein
D 183	Bayern
D 184	Hessen
D 185	Lütjens
D 186	Mölders
D 187	Rommel

Frigates

F 220	Köln
F 221	Emden
F 222	Augsburg
F 223	Karlsrühe
F 224	Lübeck
F 225	Braunschweig

Submarines

S 170	U 21
S 171	U 22
S 172	U 23
S 173	U 24
S 174	U 25
S 175	U 26
S 176	U 27
S 177	U 28
S 178	U 29
S 179	U 30
S 180	U 1
S 181	U 2
S 188	U 9
S 189	U 10
S 190	U 11
S 191	U 12
S 192	U 13
S 193	U 14
S 194	U 15
S 195	U 16
S 196	U 17
S 197	U 18

Submarines

S 198	U 19
S 199	U 20

Light Forces

6092	Zobel
6093	Wiesel
6094	Dachs
6095	Hermelin
6096	Nerz
6097	Puma
6098	Gepard
6099	Hyäne
6100	Frettchen
6101	Ozelot
6111	S 61
6112	S 62
6113	S 63
6114	S 64
6115	S 65
6116	S 66
6117	S 67

Light Forces

6118	S 68
6119	S 69
6120	S 70
6141	S 41
6142	S 42
6143	S 43
6144	S 44
6145	S 45
6146	S 46
6147	S 47
6148	S 48
6149	S 49
6150	S 50
6151	S 51
6152	S 52
6153	S 53
6154	S 54
6155	S 55
6156	S 56
6157	S 57
6158	S 58
6159	S 59
6160	S 60

Minewarfare Forces

1051	Castor
1054	Pollux
1055	Sirius
1056	Rigel
1057	Regulus
1058	Mars
1059	Spica
1060	Skorpion.
1062	Schütze
1063	Waage
1064	Deneb
1065	Jupiter
1067	Atair
1069	Wega
1070	Göttingen
1071	Koblenz
1072	Lindau
1073	Schleswig
1074	Tübingen
1075	Wetzlar
1076	Paderborn
1077	Weilheim
1078	Cuxhaven
1079	Düren
1080	Marburg
1081	Konstanz
1082	Wolfburg
1083	Ulm
1084	Flensburg
1085	Minden
1086	Fulda
1087	Völklingen
1090	Perseus
1092	Pluto
1093	Neptun
1094	Widder
1095	Herkilles
1096	Fischer
1097	Gemma
1099	Uranus
2650	Ariadne
2651	Freya
2652	Vineta
2653	Hertha
2654	Nymphe
2655	Nixe
2656	Amazone
2657	Gazelle
2658	Frauenlob
2659	Nautilus
2660	Gefion
2661	Medusa
2662	Undine
2663	Minerva
2664	Diana
2665	Loreley
2666	Atlantis
2667	Acheron

Patrol Craft

P	6052	Thetis
P	6053	Hermes
P	6054	Najade
P	6055	Triton
P	6056	Theseus

Amphibious Forces

L	760	Flunder
L	761	Karpfen
L	762	Lachs
L	763	Plötze
L	764	Rochen
L	765	Schleie
L	766	Stör
L	767	Tümmler
L	768	Wels
L	769	Zander
L	788	Butt
L	789	Brasse
L	790	Barbe
L	791	Delphin
L	792	Dorsch
L	793	Felchen
L	794	Forelle
L	795	Inger
L	796	Makrele
L	797	Mürane
L	798	Renke
L	799	Salm

Support Ships and Auxiliaries

A	50	Alster
A	52	Oste
A	53	Oker
A	54	Isar
A	55	Lahn
A	56	Lech
A	58	Rhein
A	59	Deutschland
A	60	Gorch Fock
A	61	Elbe
A	63	Main
A	65	Saar
A	66	Neckar
A	67	Mosel
A	68	Werra
A	69	Donau
A	512	Odin
A	513	Wotan
A	1401	Eisvogel
A	1402	Eisbär
A	1406	Bodensee
A	1407	Wittensee
A	1411	Lüneburg
A	1412	Coburg
A	1413	Freiburg
A	1414	Glücksburg
A	1415	Saarburg
A	1416	Nienburg
A	1417	Offenburg
A	1418	Meersburg
A	1424	Walchensee
A	1425	Ammersee
A	1426	Tegernsee
A	1427	Westensee
A	1428	Harz
A	1429	Eifel
A	1435	Westerwald
A	1436	Odenwald
A	1437	Sachsenwald
A	1438	Steigerwald
A	1439	Frankenland
A	1440	Emsland
A	1441	Münsterland
A	1449	Hans Bürkner
A	1450	Planet
A	1451	Wangerooge
A	1452	Spiekeroog
A	1453	Langeoog
A	1454	Baltrum
A	1455	Norderney
A	1456	Juist
A	1457	Helgoland
A	1458	Fehmarn
Y	801	Pellworm
Y	802	Plon
Y	803	Blauort
Y	804	Wieland
Y	805	Memmert
Y	806	Hansa
Y	809	Arcona
Y	811	Knurrhahn
Y	812	Lütje Hörn
Y	813	Mellum
Y	814	Knechtsand
Y	815	Schärhorn
Y	816	Vogelsand
Y	817	Nordstrant
Y	818	Trischen
Y	819	Langeness
Y	820	Sylt
Y	821	Föhr
Y	822	Amrum
Y	823	Neuwerk
Y	827	KW 15
Y	829	KW 3
Y	830	KW 16
Y	832	KW 18
Y	833	KW 19
Y	834	Nordwind
Y	836	Holnis
Y	837	SP 1
Y	838	Wilhelm Pullwer
Y	841	Walther van Ledebur
Y	845	KW 17
Y	846	KW 20
Y	847	OT 2
Y	849	Stier
Y	851-56	TF 101-106
Y	857-859	FL 5-7
Y	862	FL 10
Y	863	FL 11
Y	864-69	FW 1-6
Y	871	Heinz Roggenkamp
Y	872-74	TF 106-108
Y	877	H.C. Oersted
Y	878	H. von Helmholtz
Y	880	Wilhelm Bauer
Y	881	Adolf Bestelmeyer
Y	882	Otto Meycke
Y	887	Karl Kolls
Y	888	Friedrich Voge
Y	889	Rudolf Diesel
Y	1641	Förde
Y	1642	Jade
Y	1643	Niobe
Y	1662	Ems
Y	1663	Eider

Coastguard

BG	11	Neustadt
BG	12	Bad Bramstedt
BG	13	Uelzen
BG	14	Duderstadt
BG	15	Eschwege
BG	16	Alsfeld
BG	17	Bayreuth
BG	18	Rosenheim

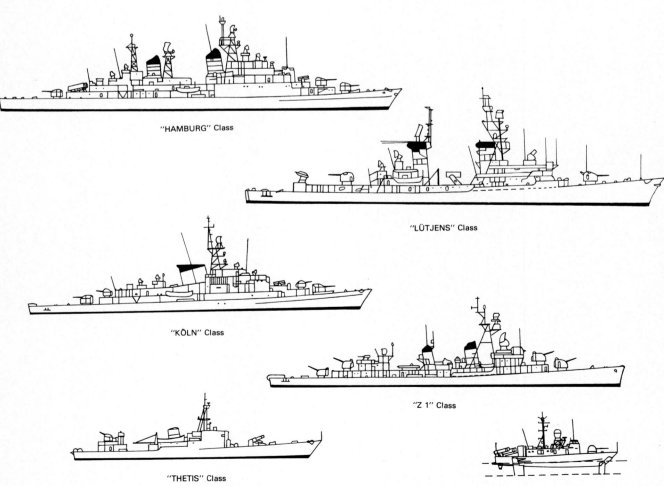

"HAMBURG" Class

"LÜTJENS" Class

"KÖLN" Class

"Z 1" Class

"THETIS" Class

DESTROYERS

3 US "CHARLES F. ADAMS" CLASS (DDGs)

Name	No.	Builders	Laid down	Launched	Commissioned
LÜTJENS (ex-US DDG 28)	D 185	Bath Iron Works Corp	1 Mar 1966	11 Aug 1967	12 Mar 1969
MÖLDERS (ex-US DDG 29)	D 186	Bath Iron Works Corp	12 April 1966	13 April 1968	12 Sep 1969
ROMMEL (ex-US DDG 30)	D 187	Bath Iron Works Corp	22 Aug 1967	1 Feb 1969	24 April 1970

Displacement, tons: 3 370 standard; 4 500 full load
Length, feet (metres): 431 (131·4) wl; 440 (134·1) oa
Beam, feet (metres): 47 (14·3)
Draught, feet (metres): 20 (6·1)
Missile launchers: 1 Tartar single
Guns: 2—5 in (127 mm) single
A/S weapons: Asroc; 2 triple torpedo; 1 DCT
Main engines: Geared steam turbines 70 000 shp; 2 shafts
Boilers: 4 Combustion Engineering; 1 200 psi (84·4 kg cm²)
Speed, knots: 35
Oil fuel, tons: 900
Range, miles: 4 500 at 20 knots
Complement: 340 (21 officers, 319 men)

Modified to suit Federal German requirements and practice.
1965 contract.
Cost $43 754 000 each.

Appearance: Some differences from "Charles F Adams" in W/T aerials.

Electronics: SATIR I (similar to SENIT 2) automatic data system. TACAN beacon.

Radar: Three dimensional air search and target designator: one SPS 52 (after funnel)
Air surveillance: one SPS 40 (main-mast)
Tartar fire control: two SPG 51 (abaft after funnel)
Surface warning: one SPS 10.
Gun fire control: one GFCS 68.

Sonar: One SQS 23.

LÜTJENS   4/1976, Dr Giorgio Arra

LÜTJENS   4/1976, Reinhard Nerlich

LÜTJENS   1976, Michael D. J. Lennon

4 "HAMBURG" CLASS

Name	No.	Builders	Laid down	Launched	Commissioned
BAYERN	D 183	H. C. Stülcken Sohn, Hamburg	1961	14 Aug 1962	6 July 1965
HAMBURG	D 181	H. C. Stülcken Sohn, Hamburg	1959	26 Mar 1960	23 May 1964
HESSEN	D 184	H. C. Stülcken Sohn, Hamburg	1962	4 May 1963	8 Oct 1968
SCHLESWIG-HOLSTEIN	D 182	H. C. Stülcken Sohn, Hamburg	1959	20 Aug 1960	12 Oct 1964

Displacement, tons: 3 400 standard; 4 400 full load
Length, feet (metres): 420 (128) wl; 439·7 (134·0) oa
Beam, feet (metres): 44 (13·4)
Draught, feet (metres): 17 (5·2)
Guns: 4—3·9 in (100 mm) (single); 8—40 mm (4 twin)
A/S weapons: 2 Bofors 4-barrel DC Mortars; 1 DCT
Torpedo tubes: 4—12 in for A/S torpedoes
Boilers: 4 Wahodag; 910 psi (64 kg/cm²), 860°F (460°C)
Main engines: 2 Wahodag dr geared turbines; 68 000 shp; 2 shafts
Speed, knots: 35·8; 18 economical
Range, miles: 6 000 at 13 knots; 920 at 35 knots
Complement: 280 (17 officers, 263 men)

All named after countries of the German Federal Republic. Capable of minelaying.

Electronics: FCS for Bofors A/S launcher, torpedoes and DC from Hollandse Signaalapparaten. ECM fitted.

Modernisation: Plans in hand for replacement of 100 mm in X position by four MM 38 Exocet, replacement of 40 mm Bofors by Bredas and addition of two extra A/S torpedo tubes. Modernisation started in 1975 with *Hessen* to be followed by *Hamburg, Schleswig-Holstein* and *Bayern,* all completing by 1977. *Hessen* completed Nov 1975. *Hamburg* taken in hand by Blöhm and Voss 18 Aug 1975. *Schleswig-Holstein* taken in hand April 1976. *Bayern* started early in 1977.

Radar: All by Hollandse Signaalapparaten.
Navigation/surface warning: one set
Air warning: one LW.02/3
Target designator: one DAO 2
100 mm fire control: two M 45 series
40 mm fire control: two M 45 series

Sonar: One ELAC 1BV hull-mounted.

HESSEN (with Exocet launchers)   4/1976, Reinhard Nerlich

HESSEN (after conversion—MM 38 Exocet not shipped)   10/1975, Reinhard Nerlich

SCHLESWIG-HOLSTEIN   11/1975, Michael D. J. Lennon

4 Ex-US "FLETCHER" CLASS

Name	No.
Z 2 (ex-USS *Ringgold, DD 500)*	D 171
Z 3 (ex-USS *Wadsworth, DD 516)*	D 172
Z 4 (ex-USS *Claxton, DD 571)*	D 178
Z 5 (ex-USS *Dyson, DD 572)*	D 179

Builders	Laid down	Launched	Commissioned
Federal SB & DD Co, Port Newark	25 June1942	11 Nov 1942	24 Dec 1942
Bath Iron Works Corporation, Maine	18 Aug 1942	10 Jan 1943	16 Mar 1943
Consolidated Steel Corporation, Orange	25 June1941	1 April1942	8 Dec 1942
Consolidated Steel Corporation, Orange	25 June1941	15 April1942	30 Dec 1942

Displacement, tons: 2 100 standard; 2 750 full load
Length, feet (metres): 368·4 *(112·3)* wl; 376·5 *(114·8)* oa
Beam, feet (metres): 39·5 *(12)*
Draught, feet (metres): 18 *(5·5)*
Guns: 4—5 in *(127 mm)* 38 cal
  6—3 in *(76 mm)* 50 cal (twins)
A/S weapons: 2 Hedgehogs; 1 DC rack
Torpedo tubes: 5—21 in *(533 mm)* (quintuple); 2 ASW tubes
Main engines: 2 sets GE geared turbines; 60 000 shp; 2 shafts
Boilers: 4 Babcock & Wilcox, 569 psi *(40 kg/cm²)*; 851°F *(455°C)*
Speed, knots: 32; 17 economical
Oil fuel, tons: 540
Range, miles: 6 000 at 15 knots
Complement: 250

Former US "Fletcher" class destroyers. The original loan from the United States of a class of five for five years was extended. First ship arrived at Bremerhaven on 14 April 1958. Commissioned in FGN as follows: Z 2, 14 July 1959; Z 3, 6 Oct 1959; Z 4, 15 Dec 1959; Z 5, 23 Feb 1960. Capable of minelaying.

Gunnery: Z 4 carried out trials of a containerised 3-in *(76 mm)* OTO Melara gun in 1975 in place of after 3-in mounting. On completion of trials OTO Melara mounting was removed but original twin 3-in was not replaced.

Radar: Air and surface search: one SPS 6
Surface surveillance: one SPS 10
Fire control: one GFCS 56 and 68.

Sonar: SQS 29.

Z3 — 4/1976, Dr Giorgio Arra

FRIGATES
0 + 6 + ?6 TYPE 122

Displacement, tons: 3 750 full load (approx)
Dimensions, feet (metres): 419·8 × 48·5 × 19·7 *(128 oa × 14·8 × 6)*
Aircraft: 2 helicopters (? Lynx)
Missiles: 8 Harpoon; 1 8 cell Seasparrow; 2 multiple Stinger launchers
Guns: 1—76 mm 62 cal; Breda 105 mm 20 tube rocket launcher
A/S weapons: 6 Mk 32 torpedo tubes (triples)
Main engines: 2 Rolls Royce Olympus gas-turbines; 53 200 hp; 2 MTU diesels; 16 000 hp; 2 shafts
Speed, knots: 30
Range, miles: 4 000 at 18 knots
Complement: 185

Approval given in early 1976 for six of this class, a modification of the Netherlands "Kortenaer" class. The first is expected in service in 1981 with a possible 6 more to follow.

TYPE 122 — 1976, Federal German Navy

6 "KÖLN" CLASS

Name	No.
AUGSBURG	F 222
BRAUNSCHWEIG	F 225
EMDEN	F 221
KARLSRUHE	F 223
KÖLN	F 220
LÜBECK	F 224

Builders	Laid down	Launched	Commissioned
H. C. Stülcken Sohn, Hamburg	—	15 Aug 1959	7 April 1962
H. C. Stülcken Sohn, Hamburg	—	3 Feb 1962	16 June 1964
H. C. Stülcken Sohn, Hamburg	—	21 Mar 1959	24 Oct 1961
H. C. Stülcken Sohn, Hamburg	—	24 Oct 1959	15 Dec 1962
H. C. Stülcken Sohn, Hamburg	—	6 Dec 1958	15 April 1961
H. C. Stülcken Sohn, Hamburg	—	23 July 1960	6 July 1963

Displacement, tons: 2 100 standard; 2 550 full load
Length, feet (metres): 360·9 *(110)*
Beam, feet (metres): 36·1 *(11·0)*
Draught, feet (metres): 11·2 *(3·4)*
Guns: 2—3.9 in *(100 mm)*
  6—40 mm (2 twin and 2 single)
A/S weapons: 2 Bofors 4-barrel DC mortars (72 charges)
Torpedo tubes: 4—21 in *(533 mm)* (twins) for A/S torpedoes
Mines: Can carry 80
Main engines: Combined diesel and gas turbine plant; 4 MAN 16-cyl diesels; total 12 000 bhp; 2 Brown Boveri gas turbines, 24 000 bhp; total 36 000 bhp; 2 shafts
Speed, knots: 32; 23 economical
Oil fuel, tons: 333
Range, miles: 920 at 32 knots
Complement: 200

Ordered in Mar 1957. All ships of this class are named after towns of West Germany.

Electronics: Hollandse Signaalapparaten FCS for Bofors A/S launchers. M9 torpedo fire control.

Engineering: Each of the two shafts is driven by two diesels coupled and geared to one BBC gas turbine. Controllable pitch propellers. A speed of 32 knots is reported to have been attained on full power trials.

Radar: All by Hollandse Signaalapparaten.
Navigation/surface search: one set.
Target designator: one DA 02.
Fire control *(100 mm)*: two M 45 series.
Fire control *(40 mm)*: two M 45 series.

Sonar: One PAE/CWE M/F set, hull-mounted.

KARLSRUHE — 9/1976, Michael D. J. Lennon

SUBMARINES
TYPE 210

A development project is in hand by the Norwegian and Federal German navies for a 750 ton class to replace the Type 205 (FGN) and Type 207 (Norway) in the 1980s.

18 TYPE 206

Name	No.	Builders	Laid down	Launched	Commissioned
U 13	S 192	Howaldtswerke, Kiel	24 Nov 1969	28 Oct 1971	1973
U 14	S 193	Reinstahl Nordseewerke, Emden	21 Apr 1970	1 Mar 1972	1973
U 15	S 194	Howaldtswerke, Kiel	29 May 1970	15 June1972	1973
U 16	S 195	Reinstahl Nordseewerke, Emden	15 Dec 1970	29 Aug 1972	1973
U 17	S 196	Howaldtswerke, Kiel	19 Oct 1970	10 Oct 1972	1973
U 18	S 197	Reinstahl Nordseewerke, Emden	16 Mar 1971	31 Oct 1972	1973
U 19	S 198	Howaldtswerke, Kiel	15 Jan 1971	15 Dec 1972	1973
U 20	S 199	Reinstahl Nordseewerke, Emden	7 May 1971	16 Jan 1973	1974
U 21	S 170	Howaldtswerke, Kiel	14 Apr 1971	9 Mar 1973	1974
U 22	S 171	Reinstahl Nordseewerke, Emden	7 July 1971	27 Mar 1973	1974
U 23	S 172	Reinstahl Nordseewerke, Emden	26 Apr 1972	22 May 1974	1975
U 24	S 173	Reinstahl Nordseewerke, Emden	1 Sep 1971	24 June1973	1974
U 25	S 174	Howaldtswerke, Kiel	30 June1971	23 May 1973	1974
U 26	S 175	Reinstahl Nordseewerke, Emden	28 Oct 1971	20 Nov 1973	1975
U 27	S 176	Howaldtswerke, Kiel	6 Oct 1971	21 Aug 1973	1975
U 28	S 177	Reinstahl Nordseewerke, Emden	1 Feb 1972	22 Jan 1974	1975
U 29	S 178	Howaldtswerke, Kiel	11 Jan 1972	5 Sep 1973	1975
U 30	S 179	Reinstahl Nordseewerke, Emden	29 Feb 1972	26 Mar 1974	1975

Displacement, tons: 400 surfaced; 600 dived
Length, feet (metres): 159·4 (48·6)
Beam, feet (metres): 15·4 (4·7)
Draught, feet (metres): 13·1 (4·0)
Torpedo tubes: 8—21 in (533 mm) (bow)
Main machinery: MTU diesel-electric; 1 shaft; 1 800 hp
Speed, knots: 10 surfaced; 17 dived
Range, miles: 4 500 at 5 knots (surfaced)
Complement: 22

Authorised on 7 June 1969 from Howaldtswerke Deutsche Werft (8) and Reinstahl Nordseewerke Emden, (10).

Squadrons: First: U 25-30 U 1 and 2, 9-12. Third: U 13-24.

U 28   6/1976, Reinhard Nerlich

6 TYPE 205

Name	No.	Builders	Laid down	Launched	Commissioned
U 1	S 180	Howaldtswerke, Kiel	—	21 Oct 1961	—
U 2	S 181	Howaldtswerke, Kiel	—	25 Jan 1962	—
U 9	S 188	Howaldtswerke, Kiel	—	20 Oct 1966	—
U 10	S 189	Howaldtswerke, Kiel	—	20 July 1967	—
U 11	S 190	Howaldtswerke, Kiel	—	9 Feb 1968	21 June 1968
U 12	S 191	Howaldtswerke, Kiel	—	10 Sep 1968	14 Jan 1969

Displacement, tons: 370 surfaced; 450 dived
Length, feet (metres): 142·7 (43·5) oa
Beam, feet (metres): 15·1 (4·6)
Draught, feet (metres): 12·8 (3·8)
Torpedo tubes: 8—21 in (533 mm) (bow)
Main machinery: 2 Maybach (MTU) diesels; total 1 200 bhp
 2 Siemens electric motors, total 1 700 bhp; single screw
Speed, knots: 10 surfaced; 17 dived
Complement: 21

All built in floating docks. Fitted with snort mast. First submarines designed and built by Germany since the end of the Second World War. U 4-12 were built to a heavier and improved design. U 1 and U 2 were modified accordingly and refloated on 17 Feb 1967 and 15 July 1966 respectively. U 1 was reconstructed late 1963 to 4 Mar 1965. (See original appearance in the 1962-63 and 1963-64 editions.) U 9-12 have hulls of different steel alloys of non-magnetic properties. U 3 of this class lent to Norway on 10 July 1962 and temporarily named Kobben (S 310), was returned to Germany in 1964 and decommissioned on 15 Sep 1967 for disposal.

Radar: French Thomson-CSF Calypso, nav/attack set. Passive DF.

Torpedo equipment: The boats are trimmed by the stern to load through the bow caps. Also fitted for minelaying. Fire control by Hollandse. Mk 8.

U 9   1975, Reinhard Nerlich

1 CONVERTED TYPE XXI

Name	No.	Builders	Laid down	Launched	Commissioned
WILHELM BAUER (ex-U 2540)	Y 880	Blohm and Voss, Hamburg	1943	1944	1944

Displacement, tons: 1 620 surfaced; 1 820 dived
Length, feet (metres): 252·7 (77·0) pp
Beam, feet (metres): 21·7 (6·6)
Draught, feet (metres): 20·3 (6·2)
Torpedo tubes: 4—21 in (533 mm) (bow)
Main machinery: MTU diesel-electric drive;
 2 diesels total 4 200 bhp; 2 electric motors total 5 000 hp
Speed, knots: 15·5 surfaced; 17·5 dived

Scuttled after air attack off Flensburg on 4 May 1945. Raised in 1957. Rebuilt in 1958-59 at Howaldtswerke, Kiel. Commissioned on 1 Sep 1960. Used for experiments on submarine equipment. Conning tower was modified.

WILHELM BAUER   1973, Howaldtswerke, Kiel

CORVETTES

5 "THETIS" CLASS

Name	No.	Builders	Commissioned
HERMES	P 6053	Rolandwerft, Bremen	16 Dec 1961
NAJADE	P 6054	Rolandwerft, Bremen	12 May 1962;
THESEUS	P 6056	Rolandwerft, Bremen	15 Aug 1963
THETIS	P 6052	Rolandwerft, Bremen	1 July 1961
TRITON	P 6055	Rolandwerft, Bremen	10 Nov 1962

Displacement, tons: 564 standard; 650 full load
Dimensions, feet (metres): 229·7 × 27 × 14 (70 × 8·5 × 4·2)
Guns: 2—Breda 40 mm L 70 (twin mounting) (To be replaced by 1—3 in OTO Melara)
A/S weapons: Bofors DC mortar (4 barrelled)
Torpedo tubes: 4—21 in (533 mm)
Main engines: 2 MAN diesels; 2 shafts; 6 800 bhp = 24 knots
Complement: 48

Some have computer house before bridge.

Electronics: HSA M9 series torpedo control.

Radar: Nav/surface warning; KH14; TRS-N.

Sonar: ELAC 1BV.

THETIS (blockbridge type). *1975, Federal German Navy*

NAJADE (forebridge type) *1975, Federal German Navy*

Name	No.	Builders	Commissioned
HANS BÜRKNER	A 1449	Atlaswerke, Bremen	18 May 1963

Displacement, tons: 950 standard; 1 000 full load
Dimensions, feet (metres): 265·2 oa × 30·8 × 10 (81 × 9·4 × 2·8)
A/S weapons: 1 DC mortar (four-barrelled) 2 DC racks
Torpedo tubes: 2—21 in (533 mm)
Main engines: 4 MAN diesels; 2 shafts; 13 600 shp = 24 knots
Complement: 50

Launched on 16 July 1961. Named after designer of German First World War battleships (1909-18). General purpose utility vessel.

Radar: TRS-N; KH14.

Sonar: Has small VDS aft.

HANS BÜRKNER *1975, Federal German Navy*

LIGHT FORCES

4 + (6?) TYPE 162 (FAST ATTACK HYDROFOIL—MISSILE)

Displacement, tons: 202 standard; 235 full load
Dimensions, feet (metres): 131·9 × 29·2 × 6·2 (40·2 × 8·9 × 1·9)
Missiles: 4 launchers for Exocet MM 38
Gun: 1—76 mm
Main engines: Gas turbines; 26 200 bhp; 2—MTU diesels; 1 340 bhp
Speed, knots: 50 on turbines; 12 on diesels
Component: 21

First four ordered from Boeing, Seattle in May 1975. To be similar to USN "Pegasus" class and to replace "Zobel" class in 1980s.

10 TYPE 143 (FAST ATTACK CRAFT—MISSILE)

Name	No.	Builders	Commissioned
S 61	P 6111	Lürssen, Vegesack	1976
S 62	P 6112	Lürssen, Vegesack	1976
S 63	P 6113	Lürssen, Vegesack	1976
S 64	P 6114	Lürssen, Vegesack	1976
S 65	P 6115	Kröger, Rendsburg	1976
S 66	P 6116	Lürssen, Vegesack	1976
S 67	P 6117	Kröger, Rendsburg	1976
S 68	P 6118	Lürssen, Vegesack	1977
S 69	P 6119	Kroger, Rendsburg	1977
S 70	P 6120	Lürssen, Vegesack	1977

Displacement, tons: 295 nominal, 378 full load
Dimensions, feet (metres): 200·0 × 24·6 × 8·5 (57 × 7·8 × 2·4)
Missiles: 4 launchers for Exocet MM 38
Guns: 1—76 mm OTO Melara; 1 Breda 40 mm L 70
Torpedoes: 2—21 in wire guided aft
Main engines: 4 MTU diesels; 16 000 hp; 4 shafts = 38 knots
Range, miles: 1 300 at 30 knots
Complement: 40

S 61 *3/1975, Reinhard Nerlich*

Ordered in 1972 as replacements for last ten boats of the "Jaguar" class from 1976 onwards. Final funds allocated 13 July 1972. First laid down late 1972. The first boat, S 61, started trials in Dec 1974. Wooden-hulled craft. Launch dates—S 61, 22 Oct 1973; S 62, 21 March 1974; S 63, 18 Sep 1974; S 64, 10 Dec 1974; S 65, 10 Dec 1974; S 66, 5 Sep 1975; S 67, 6 March 1975; S 68, —; S 69, 5 June 1975; S 70, —.

Electronics: Believed that data automation system AGIS is being fitted to permit use of Type 143 as control ship for concerted operation as Type 148 boats.

Radar: All by Hollandse Signaal. WM 27 in radome for Exocet, gun and torpedo control.

20 TYPE 148 (FAST ATTACK CRAFT—MISSILE)

Name	No.	Builders (see note re Lürssen)	Commissioned	
S 41	P 6141	C. M. de Normandie, Cherbourg	30 Oct	1972
S 42	P 6142	C. M. de Normandie, Cherbourg	8 Jan	1973
S 43	P 6143	C. M. de Normandie, Cherbourg	9 April	1973
S 44	P 6144	C. M. de Normandie, Cherbourg	14 June	1973
S 45	P 6145	C. M. de Normandie, Cherbourg	21 Aug	1973
S 46	P 6146	C. M. de Normandie, Cherbourg	17 Oct	1973
S 47	P 6147	C. M. de Normandie, Cherbourg	13 Nov	1973
S 48	P 6148	C. M. de Normandie, Cherbourg	9 Jan	1974
S 49	P 6149	C. M. de Normandie, Cherbourg	26 Feb	1974
S 50	P 6150	C. M. de Normandie, Cherbourg	27 Mar	1974
S 51	P 6151	C. M. de Normandie, Cherbourg	12 June	1974
S 52	P 6152	C. M. de Normandie, Cherbourg	17 July	1974
S 53	P 6153	C. M. de Normandie, Cherbourg	24 Sep	1974
S 54	P 6154	C. M. de Normandie, Cherbourg	27 Nov	1974
S 55	P 6155	C. M. de Normandie, Cherbourg	7 Jan	1975
S 56	P 6156	C. M. de Normandie, Cherbourg	12 Feb	1975
S 57	P 6157	C. M. de Normandie, Cherbourg	3 April	1975
S 58	P 6158	C. M. de Normandie, Cherbourg	22 May	1975
S 59	P 6159	C. M. de Normandie, Cherbourg	24 June	1975
S 60	P 6160	C. M. de Normandie, Cherbourg	6 Aug	1975

S 54   *9/1976, Reinhard Nerlich*

Displacement, tons: 234 standard; 265 full load
Dimensions, feet (metres): 154·2 × 23·0 × 5·9 *(47 × 7 × 2)*
Missiles: 4 launchers for Exocet MM 38
Guns: 1—76 mm OTO Melara; 1—40 mm (Bofors)
Main engines: 4 MTU diesels; 4 shafts; 12 000 bhp = 35·5 knots
Oil fuel, tons: 39
Range, miles: 600 at 30 knots
Complement: 30 (4 officers, 26 men)

Ordered in Oct 1970. For completion from 1973 onwards to replace the first 20 of the "Jaguar" class. Eight hulls contracted to Lürssen but all fitted out in France. Steel-hulled craft.
Launch dates: S 41, 27 Sep 1972; S 42, 12 Dec 1972; S 43, 7 Mar 1973; S 44, 5 May 1973; S 45, 3 July 1973; S 46, 21 May 1973; S 47, 20 Sep 1973; S 48, 10 Sep 1973; S 49 11 Jan 1974; S 50, 10 Dec 1973; S 51, 11 June 1974; S 52, 25 May 1974; S 53, 4 July 1974; S 54, 8 July 1974; S 55, 15 Nov 1974; S 56, 30 Oct 1974; S 57, 18 Feb 1975; S 58, 26 Feb 1975; S 59, 15 May 1975; S 60, 26 May 1975.

Electronics: Thomson-CSF, Vega-Pollux PCET control system, controlling missiles, torpedoes and guns.

Radar: Navigation: 3 RM 20.
Air and surface search/target designator: Triton G-band
Tracking: Pollux I band.

Squadrons: Third: S 41-50. Fifth: S 51-60.

S 59   *8/1976, Reinhard Nerlich*

10 "ZOBEL" CLASS (TYPE 142 FAST ATTACK CRAFT—TORPEDO)

Name	No.	Builders	Commissioned
DACHS	P 6094	Lürssen, Vegesack	1962
FRETTCHEN	P 6100	Lürssen, Vegesack	1963
GEPARD	P 6098	Kröger, Rendsburg	1963
HERMELIN	P 6095	Lürssen, Vegesack	1962
HYANE	P 6099	Kröger, Rendsburg	1963
NERZ	P 6096	Lürssen, Vegesack	1963
OZELOT	P 6101	Kröger, Rendsburg	1963
PUMA	P 6097	Lürssen, Vegesack	1962
WIESEL	P 6093	Lürssen, Vegesack	1962
ZOBEL	P 6092	Lürssen, Vegesack	1961

Displacement, tons: 225 full load
Dimensions, feet (metres): 139·4 × 23·4 × 7·9 *(42·5 × 7·2 × 2·4)*
Guns: 2—40 mm Bofors L 70 (single)
Torpedo tubes: 2—21 in for Seal wire-guided torpedoes
Main engines: 4 Mercedes-Benz (MTU) 20 cyl diesels; 4 shafts; 12 000 bhp = 40·5 knots
Complement: 39

Originally units of the "Jaguar" class, but, after conversion, known as the "Zobel" class. Form 7th Squadron.

Radar: Fire control: two M 20 series in radome

HYANE   *8/1976, Reinhard Nerlich*

NERZ   *11/1976, Stefan Terzibaschitsch*

AMPHIBIOUS FORCES

22 TYPE 520 (LCUs)

BARBE L 790	FELCHEN L 793	LACHS L 762	SALM L 799
BRASSE L 789	FLUNDLER L 760	MAKRELE L 796	SCHLEI L 765
BUTT L 788	FORELLE L 794	MURÄNE L 797	STÖR L 766
DELPHIN L 791	INGER L 795	PLOTZE L 763	TÜMMLER L 767
DORSCH L 792	KARPFEN L 761	RENKE L 798	WELS L 768
		ROCHEN L 764	ZANDER L 769

Displacement, tons: 200 light; 403 full load
Dimensions, feet (metres): 136·5 × 28·9 × 6·9 *(41·6 × 8·8 × 2·1)*
Guns: 1 or 2—20 mm (see *Gunnery* notes)
Main engines: GM diesels; 2 shafts; 1 380 bhp = 12 knots
Complement: 17

Similar to the United States LCU (Landing Craft Utility) type. Provided with bow and stern ramp. Built by Howaldtswerke, Hamburg, 1964-67. To carry 160 tons load. *Inge* employed for seamanship training. *Renke* and *Salm* in reserve.

Gunnery: Are being rearmed with two modern 20 mm.

STÖR   *11/1976, Stefan Terzibaschitsch*

19 LCM TYPE 521

LCM 1-19

Displacement, tons: 116 standard; 140 full load
Dimensions, feet (metres): 67·6 wl × 21 × 4·3 *(20·6 × 6·4 × 1·3)*
Main engines: 2 diesels; 1 320 hp = 10 knots

Similar to US LCM 8 type. Built by Blöhm and Voss 1965-67. Can carry 50 tons.

LCM 19   *2/1976, Reinhard Nerlich*

MINE WARFARE FORCES

18 "LINDAU" CLASS (TYPE 320)
(MINESWEEPERS—COASTAL and MINEHUNTERS)

Name	No.	Builders	Commissioned
CUXHAVEN	M 1078	Burmester, Bremen	1959
DÜREN	M 1079	Burmester, Bremen	1959
FLENSBURG	M 1084	Burmester, Bremen	1959
FULDA	M 1086	Burmester, Bremen	1960
GÖTTINGEN	M 1070	Burmester, Bremen	1958
KOBLENZ	M 1071	Burmester, Bremen	1958
KONSTANZ	M 1081	Burmester, Bremen	1959
LINDAU	M 1072	Burmester, Bremen	1958
MARBURG	M 1080	Burmester, Bremen	1959
MINDEN	M 1085	Burmester, Bremen	1960
PADERBORN	M 1076	Burmester, Bremen	1958
SCHLESWIG	M 1073	Burmester, Bremen	1958
TÜBINGEN	M 1074	Burmester, Bremen	1958
ULM	M 1083	Burmester, Bremen	1959
VÖLKLINGEN	M 1087	Burmester, Bremen	1960
WEILHEIM	M 1077	Burmester, Bremen	1959
WETZLAR	M 1075	Burmester, Bremen	1958
WOLFSBURG	M 1082	Burmester, Bremen	1959

Displacement, tons: 370 standard; 420 full load
Dimensions, feet (metres): 137·8 pp; 147·7 oa × 27·2 × 8·5 *(49·7 × 8·3 × 2·5)*
Guns: 1—40 mm; 2—20 mm
Main engines: Maybach (MTU) diesels; 2 shafts; 4 000 bhp = 16·5 knots
Range, miles: 850 at 16·5 knots
Complement: 46

Lindau, first German built vessel for the Federal German Navy since the Second World War, launched on 16 Feb 1957. Basically of NATO WU type but modified for German requirements. The hull is of wooden construction, laminated with plastic glue. The engines are of non-magnetic materials. The first six, *Göttingen, Koblenz, Lindau, Schleswig, Tubingen* and *Wetzlar*, were modified with lower bridges in 1958-59. *Schleswig* was lengthened by 6·8 feet in 1960—all others in 1960-64. *Fulda* and *Flensburg* were converted into minehunters in 1968-69 as part of a total of twelve ships to be so converted, with the second group started in 1975 with *Lindau, Tubingen* and *Minden.* These will be fitted with Plessey sonar and French PAP exploders. The remaining six will be fitted with Troika during 1978-80.

PADERBORN (Sweeper)   *8/1975, C and S Taylor*

FULDA (Hunter)   *6/1975, Reinhard Nerlich*

22 "SCHÜTZE" CLASS (TYPE 340-341)
(MINESWEEPERS—COASTAL (FAST))

Name	No.	Builders	Commissioned
ATAIR	M 1067	Schlichting, Travemünde	1961
CASTOR	M 1051	Abeking and Rasmussen	1962
DENEB	M 1064	Schürenstedt	1961
FISCHE	M 1096	Abeking and Rasmussen	1960
GEMMA	M 1097	Abeking and Rasmussen	1960
HERKULES	M 1095	Schlichting, Travemünde	1960
JUPITER	M 1065	Schürenstedt	1961
MARS	M 1058	Abeking and Rasmussen	1960
NEPTUN	M 1093	Schlichting, Travemünde	1960
PERSEUS	M 1090	Schlichting, Travemünde	1961
POLLUX	M 1054	Abeking and Rasmussen	1961
PLUTO	M 1092	Schürenstedt	1960
REGULUS	M 1057	Abeking and Rasmussen	1962
RIGEL	M 1056	Abeking and Rasmussen	1962
SCHÜTZE	M 1062	Abeking and Rasmussen	1959
SIRIUS	M 1055	Abeking and Rasmussen	1961
SKORPION	M 1060	Abeking and Rasmussen	1963
SPICA	M 1059	Abeking and Rasmussen	1961
STIER	Y 849	Abeking and Rasmussen	1961
WAAGE	M 1063	Abeking and Rasmussen	1962
WEGA	M 1089	Abeking and Rasmussen	1963
WIDDER	M 1094	Schürenstedt	1960

Displacement, tons: 204 standard; 230 full load
Dimensions, feet (metres): 124·7 × 27·2 × 6·6 *(43·8 × 8·2 × 2)*
Gun: 1—40 mm (except *Stier*)
Main engines: MTU diesels = 14 knots
Range, miles: 2 000 at 13 knots
Complement: 24

30 originally built between 1959 and 1964. (Ex-*Uranus* is now German Navy League ship in Trier). The design is a development of the "R" boats of World War II. *Stier*, former number M 1061, carries no weapons, but has a recompression chamber, being a clearance diving vessel. Formerly classified as inshore minesweepers, but re-rated as fast minesweepers in 1966.

Radar: TRS-N.

Transfer: Five transferred to Greece, deleted in 1974.

HERKULES   *1975, Federal German Navy*

STIER (with recompression chamber)   *1975, Federal German Navy*

10 "FRAUENLOB" CLASS (TYPE 394)
(MINESWEEPERS—INSHORE)

Name	No.	Builders	Commissioned
ACHERON	M 2667	Krögerwerft, Rendsburg	1969
ATLANTIS	M 2666	Krögerwerft, Rendsburg	1968
DIANA	M 2664	Krögerwerft, Rendsburg	1967
FRAUENLOB	M 2658	Krögerwerft, Rendsburg	1966
GEFION	M 2660	Krögerwerft, Rendsberg	1967
LORELEY	M 2665	Krögerwerft, Rendsburg	1968
MEDUSA	M 2661	Krögerwerft, Rendsburg	1967
MINERVA	M 2663	Krögerwerft, Rendsburg	1967
NAUTILUS	M 2659	Krögerwerft, Rendsburg	1966
UNDINE	M 2662	Krögerwerft, Rendsburg	1967

Displacement, tons: 230 standard; 280 full load
Dimensions, feet (metres): 154·5 oa × 22·3 × 7·2 *(47·2 × 7·2 × 2·2)*
Gun: 1—40 mm
Mines: Laying capability
Main engines: Maybach (MTU) diesels; 2 shafts; Escher Wyss propellers; 3 600 bhp = 24·5 knots
Complement: 39

Launched in 1965-67. Originally designed coastguard boats with W numbers. Rated as inshore minesweepers in 1968 with the M numbers. All subsequently allocated Y numbers and later reallocated M numbers.

UNDINE   *1976, Federal Germany Navy*

8 "ARIADNE" CLASS (TYPE 393)
(MINESWEEPERS—INSHORE)

Name	No.	Builders	Commissioned
AMAZONE	M 2656	Krögerwerft, Rendsburg	1963
ARIADNE	M 2650	Krögerwerft, Rendsburg	1961
FREYA	M 2651	Krögerwerft, Rendsburg	1962
GAZELLE	M 2657	Krögerwerft, Rendsburg	1963
HERTHA	M 2653	Krögerwerft, Rendsburg	1962
NIXE	M 2655	Krögerwerft, Rendsburg	1963
NYMPHE	M 2654	Krögerwerft, Rendsburg	1963
VINETA	M 2652	Krögerwerft, Rendsburg	1962

Displacement, tons: 184 standard; 210 full load
Dimensions, feet (metres): 124·3 × 27·2 × 6·6 *(37·9 × 8·3 × 2)*
Gun: 1—40 mm
Mines: Laying capability
Main engines: 2 Mercedes-Benz (MTU) diesels; 2 shafts; 2 000 bhp = 14 knots
Range, miles: 740 at 14 knots
Complement: 23

All launched between April 1960 *(Ariadne)* and June 1966 *(Freya)*. All named after cruisers of 1897-1900. Formerly classified as patrol boats but re-rated as inshore minesweepers in 1966, and given new M numbers in Jan 1968, Y numbers in 1970, and M numbers once more in 1974.

VINETA   *11/1976, Stefan Terzibaschitsch*

1 TRIALS MINESWEEPER

Name	No.	Builders	Commissioned
HOLNIS	Y 836 (ex-*M 2651*)	Abeking and Rasmussen	1966

Displacement, tons: 180
Dimensions, feet (metres): 116·8 × 24·3 × 6·9 *(35·6 × 7·4 × 2·1)*
Gun: 1—20 mm
Main engines: 2 Mercedes-Benz (MTU) diesels; 2 shafts; 2 000 bhp = 14·5 knots
Complement: 21

Now serving for trials and evaluation. *Holnis* was launched on 22 May 1965 as the prototype of a new design projected as a class of 20 such vessels but she is the only unit of this type, the other 19 boats having been cancelled. Hull number changed from M 2651 to Y 836 in 1970.

HOLNIS
1975, Federal German Navy

2 "NIOBE" CLASS (MINESWEEPERS—INSHORE)

Name	No.	Builders	Commissioned
HANSA	Y 806	Krögerwerft, Rendsburg	1958
NIOBE	Y 1643	Krögerwerft, Rendsburg	1958

Displacement, tons: 150 standard; 180 full load
Dimensions, feet (metres): 115·2 × 21·3 × 5·6 *(35·1 × 6·5 × 1·7)*
Gun: 1—40 mm
Mines: Laying capability
Main engines: *Hansa:* 1 Mercedes-Benz (MTU) diesel; 1 shaft; 950 bhp = 14 knots
  Niobe: 2 Mercedes-Benz (MTU) diesels; 2 shafts; 1 900 bhp = 16 knots
Range, miles: 1 100 at max speed
Complement: *Hansa* 19; *Niobe* 22

Hansa serves as support ship for clearance divers. *Niobe* is test and trials ship.

HANSA
1975, Federal German Navy

SERVICE FORCES

11 "RHEIN" CLASS (DEPOT SHIPS)

Name	No.	Builders	Commissioned
DONAU	A 69	Schlichting, Travemünde	1964
ELBE	A 61	Schliekerwerft, Hamburg	1962
ISAR	A 54	Blöhm and Voss	1964
LAHN	A 55	Flender, Lübeck	1964
LECH	A 56	Flender, Lübeck	1964
MAIN	A 63	Lindenau, Kiel	1963
MOSEL	A 67	Schliekerwerft, Hamburg	1963
NECKAR	A 66	Lürssen, Vegesack	1963
RHEIN	A 58	Schliekerwerft, Hamburg	1961
SAAR	A 65	Norderwerft, Hamburg	1963
WERRA	A 68	Lindenau, Kiel	1964

Displacement, tons: 2 370 standard; 2 540 full load
  except *Lahn* and *Lech* 2 460 standard; 2 680 full load
Length, feet (metres): 304·5 *(92·8)* wl; 323·5 *(99)* oa
Beam, feet (metres): 38·8 *(11·8)*
Draught, feet (metres): 11·2 *(3·4)*; 12·2 *(3·7)* in *Lahn* and *Lech*
Guns: 2—3·9 in *(100 mm)*; none in *Lahn, Lech*; 4—40 mm
Main engines: 6 Maybach or Daimler (MTU) diesels; Diesel-electric drive in *Isar, Lahn, Lech, Mossel, Saar* 11 400 bhp; 2 shafts
Speed, knots: 20·5, 15 economical
Range, miles: 1 625 at 15 knots
Oil fuel, tons: 334
Complement: 110 (accommodation for 200); 198 *(Lahn* and *Lech)*

Originally a class of 13. Rated as depot ships for minesweepers (*Isar, Mosel, Saar*), submarines (*Lahn, Lech*), Type 206 submarines (*Rhein*), and motor torpedo boats (others) but these ships with their 3·9 in *(100 mm)* guns could obviously be used in lieu of frigates.

Conversion: *Lahn* major conversion in 1975.

Launch dates: *Donau* 26 Nov 1960, *Elbe* 5 May 1960, *Isar* 14 July 1962, *Lahn* 21 Nov 1961, *Lech* 4 May 1962, *Main* 23 July 1960, *Mosel* 15 Dec 1969, *Neckar* 26 June 1961, *Rhein* 10 Feb 1959, *Saar* 11 Mar 1961, *Werra* 26 Mar 1963.

Radar: All by Hollandse. Search: HSA DA 02.
Fire control: Two HSA M 45 for 100 mm and 40 mm.

LECH
5/1976, MOD. London

Status: Five of these comparatively new ships, namely *Donau, Isar, Lahn, Lech* and *Weser* (now deleted) were placed in reserve by July 1968. This was part of the economy programme announced by the Federal German Navy in Sep 1967 but all have subsequently been recommissioned or transferred.

Transfer: *Weser* to Greece 1975. *Rühr* to Turkey 1976.

2 Ex-US "ARISTAEUS" CLASS (REPAIR SHIPS)

ODIN (ex-USS *Diomedes*, ARB 11, ex-*LST 1119*) A 512
WOTAN (ex-USS *Ulysses*, ARB 9, ex-*LST 967*) A 513

Displacement, tons: 1 625 light; 3 455 full load
Dimensions, feet (metres): 328 oa × 50 × 9·2 *(100 × 15·2 × 2·8)*
Guns: 4—20 mm
Main engines: 2 GM diesels, 2 shafts; 1 800 bhp = 11·6 knots
Oil fuel, tons: 600
Range, miles: 2 000 at 9 knots
Complement: 187

Repair ships. Transferred under MAP in June 1961. *Odin* commissioned in Jan 1966 and *Wotan* on 2 Dec 1965. *Wotan* now civilian-manned.

WOTAN
1975, Federal German Navy

MEMMERT Y 805

The small repair ship *Memmert* Y 805 (ex-USN *106*, ex-*India*, ex-*BP 34*), 165 tons and 8 knots, rated as torpedo repair ship, salvage vessel with a derrick.

1 REPLENISHMENT TANKER

Name	No.	Builders	Commissioned
FRANKENLAND	A 1439 (ex-*Y 827*)	Lithgow, Greenock	29 April 1959
(ex-*Münsterland*, ex-*Powell*)			

Displacement, tons: 11 708 standard; 16 060 full load
Dimensions, feet (metres): 521·8 × 70·2 × 37·5 *(167 × 21·4 × 9·1)*
Main engines: Diesels; 5 800 bhp = 13·5 knots

Launched in 1950.

FRANKENLAND   1972

2 "EMSLAND" CLASS (REPLENISHMENT TANKERS)

Name	No.	Builders	Commissioned
EMSLAND	A 1440 (ex-*Y 828*)	CRDA Monfalcone	7 Nov 1961
(ex-*Antonio Zotti*)			
MÜNSTERLAND	A 1441 (ex-*Y 829*)	Ansaldo, Genoa	16 Oct 1961
(ex-*Angela Germona*)			

Displacement, tons: 6 200 gross *(Emsland)*; 6 191 *(Münsterland)*
Dimensions, feet (metres): 461 × 54·2 × 25·8 *(141 × 16·5 × 7·8)*
Main engines: Diesels; CRDA; 4 800 bhp *(Emsland)*; Fiat 5 500 bhp *(Münsterland)* = 12·5 knots
Complement: 53

Both launched in 1943. Completed in 1947 and 1946 respectively. Purchased in 1960 from Italian owners. Converted in 1960-61 by Schliekerwerft, Hamburg, and Howaldtswerke, Hamburg, respectively. Civilian crew.

EMSLAND   1975, Reiner Nerlich

2 "BODENSEE" CLASS (REPLENISHMENT TANKERS)

Name	No.	Builders	Commissioned
BODENSEE (ex-*Unkas*)	A 1406 (ex-*A 54*)	Lindenau, Kiel	26 Mar 1959
WITTENSEE (ex-*Sioux*)	A 1407	Lindenau, Kiel	26 Mar 1959

Measurement, tons: 1 238 deadweight; 985 gross
Dimensions, feet (metres): 208·3 × 32·5 × 15 *(61·2 × 9·8 × 4·3)*
Main engines: Diesels; 1 050—1 250 bhp = 12 knots
Complement: 21

Launched on 19 Nov 1955 and on 23 Sep 1958, respectively.
Details above for *Bodensee—Wittensee* slightly larger.

WITTENSEE   5/1975, Reiner Nerlich

1 REPLENISHMENT TANKER

Name	No.	Builders	Commissioned
EIFEL (ex-*Friedrich Jung*)	A 1429	Norderwerft, Hamburg	27 May 1963

Displacement, tons: 4 720
Dimensions, feet (metres): 334 × 47·2 × 23·3 *(102 × 14·4 × 7·1)*
Main engines: 3 360 hp = 13 knots

Launched on 29 Mar 1958. Purchased in 1963 for service in the Federal German Navy.

EIFEL   1970, Federal German Navy

4 "WALCHENSEE" CLASS (TYPE 703) (SUPPORT TANKERS)

Name	No.	Builders	Commissioned
AMMERSEE	A 1425	Lindenau, Kiel	2 Mar 1967
TEGERNSEE	A 1426	Lindenau, Kiel	23 Mar 1967
WALCHENSEE	A 1424	Lindenau, Kiel	29 June 1966
WESTENSEE	A 1427	Lindenau, Kiel	6 Oct 1967

Displacement, tons: 2 174
Dimensions, feet (metres): 233 × 36·7 × 13·5 *(74·2 × 11·2 × 4·1)*
Main engines: Diesels; 2 shafts; 1 400 bhp = 12·6 knots

Launched on 22 Sep 1966, 22 Oct 1966, 10 July 1965 and 25 Feb 1966 respectively.

WALCHENSEE   1975, Reiner Nerlich

1 SUPPORT TANKER

Name	No.	Builders	Commissioned
HARZ (ex-*Claere Jung*)	A 1428	Norderwerft, Hamburg	27 May 1963 (see note)

Displacement, tons: 3 696 deadweight
Dimensions, feet (metres): 303·2 × 43·5 × 21·7 *(92·4 × 13·2 × 6·6)*
Main engines: 2 520 hp = 12 knots
Complement: 42

Built in 1953 and purchased in 1963 for service as a tanker.

HARZ
1970, Federal German Navy

8 "LÜNEBURG" CLASS (SUPPORT SHIPS)

Name	No.	Builders	Commissioned
COBURG	A 1412	Flensburger Schiffbau	9 July 1968
FREIBURG	A 1413	Blöhm and Voss	27 May 1968
GLÜCKSBURG	A 1414	Flensburger, Schiffbau	9 July 1968
LÜNEBURG	A 1411	Flensburger, Schiffbau	9 July 1968
MEERSBURG	A 1418	Vulkan, Bremen	25 June 1968
NIENBURG	A 1416	Vulkan, Bremen	1 Aug 1968
OFFENBURG	A 1417	Blöhm and Voss	27 May 1968
SAARBURG	A 1415	Blöhm and Voss	30 July 1968

Displacement, tons: 3 254
Dimensions, feet (metres): 341·2 × 43·3 × 13·8 *(104 × 13·2 × 4·2)*
Guns: 4—40 mm (cocooned)
Main engines: 2 Maybach (MTU) diesels; 2 shafts; 5 600 bhp = 17 knots
Complement: 103

Modernisation: Four of this class are being lengthened and modernised to serve the new classes of Fast Attack Craft, including MM 38 Exocet maintenance. *Saarburg* completed 1975—*Lüneburg* 1976.

FREIBURG
10/1976, Wright and Logan

2 "WESTERWALD" CLASS (AMMUNITION TRANSPORTS)

Name	No.	Builders	Commissioned
ODENWALD	A 1436	Lübecker, Masch	23 Mar 1967
WESTERWALD	A 1435	Lübecker, Masch	1 Feb 1967

Displacement, tons: 3 460
Dimensions, feet (metres): 347·8 × 46 × 12·2 *(106 × 14 × 3·7)*
Guns: 4—40 mm
Main engines: MTU diesels; 5 600 bhp = 17 knots
Complement: 60

Odenwald was launched on 5 May 1966 and *Westerwald* was launched on 25 Feb 1966.

WESTERWALD
4/1976, Dr Giorgio Arra

2 "SACHSENWALD" CLASS (MINE TRANSPORTS)

Name	No.	Builders	Commissioned
SACHESENWALD	A 1437	Blöhm and Voss, Hamburg	20 Aug 1969
STEIGERWALD	A 1438	Blöhm and Voss, Hamburg	20 Aug 1969

Displacement, tons: 3 850 full load
Dimensions, feet (metres): 363·5 × 45·6 × 11·2 *(111 × 13·9 × 3·4)*
Guns: 4—40 mm (two twin mountings)
Mines: Laying capacity
Main engines: 2 MTU diesels; 2 shafts; 5 600 hp = 17 knots
Range, miles: 3 500
Complement: 65

Built as mine transports. Laid down on 1 Aug 1966 and 9 May 1966. Launched on 10 Dec 1966 and 10 Mar 1967. Have mine ports in the stern and can be used as minelayers.

SACHSENWALD
1976, German Federal Navy

5 "FW" CLASS (WATER BOATS)

FW 1 Y 864   **FW 2** Y 865   **FW 3** Y 866   **FW 4** Y 867   **FW 5** Y 868

Measurement, tons: 350 deadweight
Dimensions, feet (metres): 144·4 × 25·6 × 8·2 *(44·1 × 7·8 × 2·5)*
Main engines: MWM diesel, 230 bhp = 9·5 knots

Built in pairs by Schiffbarges, Unterweser, Bremerhaven; H. Rancke, Hamburg and Jadewerft, Wilhelmshaven, in 1963-64. *FW 6* to Turkey 1975.

TRAINING SHIPS

1 "DEUTSCHLAND" CLASS

Name	No.	Builders	Commissioned
DEUTSCHLAND	A 59	Nobiskrug, Rendesburg	25 May 1963

Displacement, tons: 4 880 normal; 5 400 full load
Length, feet (metres): 452·8 (138·0) pp; 475·8 (145·0) oa
Beam, feet (metres): 59 (18)
Draught, feet (metres): 15·7 (4·8)
Aircraft: 1 A/S helicopter
Guns: 4—3·9 in (100 mm) (single); 6—40 mm (2 twin and 2 single)
A/S weapons: 2 Bofors 4-barrel rocket launchers
Torpedo tubes: 2—21 in (533 mm) (surface targets); 4—21 in (533 mm) (A/S)
Mines: Laying capacity
Main engines: 6 800 bhp MTU diesels (2 Daimler-Benz and 2 Maybach); 2 shafts with VP propellers; 8 000 shp double reduction MAN geared turbines; 1 shaft
Boilers: 2 Wahodag; 768 psi (54 km/cm²); 870°F (465°C)
Speed, knots: 22 (3 shafts); 17 (2 shafts) 14 economical (1 shaft)
Oil fuel, tons: 230 furnace; 410 diesel
Range, miles: 6 000 at 17 knots
Complement: 554 (33 officers, 271 men, 250 cadets)

DEUTSCHLAND   6/1974, USN

First West German naval ship to exceed the post-war limit of 3 000 tons. Designed with armament and machinery of different types for training purposes. The name originally planned for this ship was *Berlin*. Ordered in 1956. Laid down in 1959 and launched 5 Nov 1960. Carried out her first machinery sea trials on 15 Jan 1963.

Electronics: HSA fire control for Bofors A/S launchers and torpedoes.

Radar: All by Hollandse Signaalapparaten.
Navigation/surface warning: SGR 103, 105, 114.
Air warning: one LW-02/3
Target designator: one DA 02.
Fire control: two M 45 series (M2/2; M4).

Sonar: 1 ELAC 1BV hull-mounted set.

SAIL TRAINING SHIPS

Name	No.	Builders	Commissioned
GORCH FOCK	A 60	Blöhm and Voss, Hamburg	17 Dec 1958

Displacement, tons: 1 760 standard; 1 870 full load
Dimensions, feet (metres): 257 oa × 39·2 × 15·8 (81·3 × 12 × 4·8)
Main engines: Auxiliary MAN diesel; 880 bhp = 11 knots
Sail area, sq ft: 21 141
Range, miles: 1 990 on auxiliary diesel
Complement: 206 (10 officers, 56 ratings, 140 cadets)

Sail training ship of the improved "Horst Wessel" type. Barque rig. Launched on 23 Aug 1958.

GORCH FOCK   10/1975, Reinhard Nerlich

Name	No.	Builders	Commissioned
NORDWIND	Y 834	—	1944

Displacement, tons: 110
Dimensions, feet (metres): 78·8 × 22 × 9 (24 × 6·4 × 2·5)
Main engines: Diesel; 150 bhp = 8 knots (Sail area 2 037·5 sq ft)

Ketch rigged.

There are over 70 other sailing vessels of various types serving for sail training and recreational purposes. *Achat, Alarich, Amsel, Argonaut, Borasco, Brigant, Dankwart, Diamont, Dietrich, Drossel, Dompfaff, Fafnir, Fink, Flibustier, Freibeuter, Gernot, Geiserich, Geuse, Giselher, Gödicke, Gunnar, Gunter, Hadubrand, Hagen, Hartnaut, Hilderbrand, Horand, Hunding, Jaspis, Kaper, Klipper, Korsar, Kuchkuch, Lerche, Likendeeler, Magellan, Michel, Mime, Meise, Mistral, Monsun, Nachtigall, Ortwin, Ostwind, Pampero, Pirol, Ruediger, Samum, Saphir, Schirocco, Seeteufel, Siegfried, Siegmund, Siegura, Smaragd, Star, Stieglitz, Storetbecker, Taifun, Teja, Topas, Tornadon, Totila, Vitalienbrüder, Volker, Walter, Wate, Westwind, Wiking, Wittigo, Zeisig.*

MISCELLANEOUS

1 S.A.R. LAUNCH

Name	No.	Builders	Commissioned
FL 11	Y 863 (ex-D 2766)	Kröger, Rendsburg	1955

Displacement, tons: 70
Dimensions, feet (metres): 95·2 × 15·6 × 4·2 (29 × 5 × 1·3)
Main engines: Maybach (MTU) diesels; 2 shafts; 3 200 bhp = 30 knots
Range, miles: 600 at 25 knots

FL 10 (FL 11 similar)   1972

13 TORPEDO RECOVERY VESSELS

TF 1-6 (Y 851-856)   **TF 101-104** (Y 883-886)   **TF 106-108** (Y 872-874)

All of approximately 30-40 tons. TF 1-6 and 106-108 built in 1966, the remainder a deal older.

TF 108   1974, Reiner Nerlich

7 COASTAL PATROL CRAFT

KW 15 Y 827
KW 16 Y 830
KW 17 Y 845

KW 18 Y 832
KW 19 Y 833
KW 20 Y 846

Displacement, tons: 45 standard; 60 full load
Dimensions, feet (metres): 93·5 oa × 15·5 × 4·0 *(28·9 × 4·9 × 1·5)*
Main engines: 2 Mercedes-Benz (MTU) diesels; 2 000 bhp = 25 knots
Complement: 14

Built in 1951-53.

KW 3 Y 829. Of 112 tons and 8 knots built in 1943.

KW 18   *5/1975, Reiner Nerlich*

TUGS

2 SALVAGE TUGS

Name	No.	Builders	Commissioned
FEHMARN	A 1458	Unterweser, Bremerhaven	1 Feb 1967
HELGOLAND	A 1457	Unterweser, Bremerhaven	8 Mar 1966

Displacement, tons: 1 310 standard; 1 643 full load
Dimensions, feet (metres): 223·1 × 41·7 × 14·4 *(68·0 × 12·7 × 4·4)*
Guns: 2—40 mm
Main engines: Diesel-electric; 4 MWM diesels; 2 shafts; 3 800 hp = 17 knots
Range, miles: 6 000 at 10 knots
Complement: 36-45

Launched on 25 Nov 1965 and 8 April 1965. Carry firefighting equipment.

FEHMARN   *1974, Federal German Navy—Marineamt*

6 SALVAGE TUGS

Name	No.	Builders	Commissioned
BALTRUM	A 1454	Schichau, Bremerhaven	8 Oct 1968
JUIST	A 1456	Schichau, Bremerhaven	1968
LANGEOOG	A 1453	Schichau, Bremerhaven	14 Aug 1968
NORDERNEY	A 1455	Schichau, Bremerhaven	1968
SPIEKEROOG	A 1452	Schichau, Bremerhaven	14 Aug 1968
WANGEROOGE	A 1451	Schichau, Bremerhaven	9 April 1968

Displacement, tons: 854 standard; 1 024 full load
Dimensions, feet (metres): 170·6 × 39·4 × 12·8 *(52·0 × 12·1 × 3·9)*
Gun: 1—40 mm
Main engines: Diesel-electric; 2 shafts; 2 400 hp = 14 knots
Range, miles: 5 000 at 10 knots
Complement: 24-35

Wangerooge, prototype salvage tug, was launched on 4 July 1966, *Baltrum* on 8 Oct 1968. *Baltrum* diving training ship (1974). Pennant numbers believed changed in late 1976.

SPIEKEROOG   *2/1976, Reiner Nerlich*

1 COASTAL TUG

Name	No.	Builders	Commissioned
PELLWORM	Y 801	Schichau, Königsberg	1939

Displacement, tons: 437 standard; 500 full load
Dimensions, feet (metres): 138·7 × 27·9 × 3·6 *(38·7 × 8·5 × 1·2)*
Main engines: 1—MWM-DM Diesel; 1 shaft; 800 hp = 12 knots
Range, miles: 2 900 at 8 knots

4 HARBOUR TUGS

Name	No.	Builders	Commissioned
AMRUM	Y 822	Schichau, Bremerhaven	1963
FÖHR	Y 82 i	Schichau, Bremerhaven	1962
NEUWERK	Y 823	Schichau, Bremerhaven	1963
SYLT	Y 820	Schichau, Bremerhaven	1962

Displacement, tons: 266 standard
Dimensions, feet (metres): 100·7 oa × 25·2 *(30·6 × 7·5)*
Main engines: 1 Deutz diesel 800 bhp = 12 knots
Complement: 10

Launched in 1961.

SYLT   *1974, Federal German Navy*

3 HARBOUR TUGS

Name	No.	Builders	Commissioned
ELLERBEK	Y 1682	Schichau, Bremerhaven	1971
HEPPENS	Y 1681	Schichau, Bremerhaven	1971
NEUENDE	Y 1680	Schichau, Bremerhaven	1971

Displacement, tons: 122
Dimensions, feet (metres): 87·2 × 24·3 × 8·5 (26·6 × 7·4 × 2·6)
Main engines: 1 MWM diesel; 1 shaft; 800 hp
Speed, knots: 12
Complement: 6

ELLERBEK   1975, Federal German Navy

Harbour Type: There are also ten small harbour tugs all completed in 1958-60:— *Blauort* Y 803, *Knechtsand* Y 814, *Langeness* Y 819, *Lütje Horn* Y 812, *Mellum* Y 813, *Nordstrand* Y 817, *Plon* Y 802, *Scharhörn* Y 815, *Trischen* Y 818 and *Vogelsand* Y 816.

ICEBREAKERS

Name	No.	Builders	Commissioned
HANSE	—	Wärtsilä, Helsinki	13 Dec 1966

Displacement, tons: 2 771
Dimensions, feet (metres): 226·6 × 57 × 28·9 (69·1 × 17·4 × 8·8)
Main engines: Diesel-electric; 4 shafts; 7 500 bhp = 16 knots

Laid down on 12 Jan 1965. Launched on 17 Oct 1966. Completed on 25 Nov 1966. Although owned by West Germany she sails under the Finnish flag, manned by a Finnish crew. Only when the winter is so severe that icebreakers are needed in the southern Baltic will she be transferred under the German flag and command. She is of improved "Karhu" class. She does not belong to the Bundesmarine.

Name	No.	Builders	Commissioned
EISBAR	A 1402	J. G. Hitzler, Lauenburg	1 Nov 1961
EISVOGEL	A 1401	J. G. Hitzler, Lauenburg	11 Mar 1961

Displacement, tons: 560 standard
Dimensions, feet (metres): 125·3 × 31·2 × 15·1 (38·2 × 9·5 × 4·6)
Gun: 1—40 mm
Main engines: 2 Maybach diesels; 2 shafts; 2 000 bhp = 14 knots

Launched on 9 June and 28 April 1960 respectively.

EISVOGEL   5/1975, Reiner Nerlich

AUXILIARY SHIPS

1 Ex-BRITISH "ISLES" CLASS (MC TRAINING SHIP)

Name	No.	Builders	Commissioned
EIDER	Y 1663	Davie & Sons	1942
(ex-*Catherine,* ex-*Dochet*)	(ex-*A 50*)	Lauzon, Canada	

Displacement, tons: 480 standard; 750 full load
Dimensions, feet (metres): 164·0 pp; 177·2 oa × 27·5 × 14·0 (53·9 × 8·4 × 4)
Guns: 1—40 mm; 1—20 mm
Main engines: Triple expansion; 1 shaft; 750 ihp = 12 knots
Range, miles: 3 700
Oil fuel, tons: 130
Complement: 45

Employed as a mine clearance training vessel. She has been civilian manned since 1 Jan 1968.

EIDER   5/1975, Reiner Nerlich

1 RADAR TRIALS SHIP

Name	No.	Builders	Commissioned
OSTE (ex-*Puddefjord*, ex-USN *101*)	A 52	Akers Mekaniske V, Oslo	1943

Displacement, tons: 567 gross
Dimensions, feet (metres): 160 × 29·7 × 17 *(48·8 × 9 × 5·2)*
Main engines: 1 Akers diesel; 1 shaft; 1 600 bhp = 12 knots

Taken over from the US Navy. Converted in 1968.

OSTE (as radar testing ship)   1970, Stefan Terzibaschitsch

2 RADAR TRIALS SHIPS

Name	No.	Builders	Commissioned
ALSTE (ex-*Mellum*)	A 50	Unterweser, Bremen	1972
OKER (ex-*Hoheweg*)	A 53	Unterweser, Bremen	1972

Measurement, tons: 1 187
Dimensions, feet (metres): 237·8 × 34·4 × 16·1 *(72·5 × 10·5 × 4·9)*
Main engines: Diesel-electric; 1 screw = 15 knots
Complement: 30

OKER   2/1977, Michael D. J. Lennon

1 DIVING TENDER

Name	No.	Builders	Commissioned
EMS (ex-*Harle*, ex-USN *104*)	Y 1662 (ex-*A 53*)	Kremer, Elmshorn	1941

Measurement, tons: 660 gross
Dimensions, feet (metres): 185·7 oa × 29 × 15·5 *(56·6 × 8·8 × 4·7)*
Guns: 4—20 mm
Main engines: Sulzer diesels; 1 000 bhp = 12 knots
Range, miles: 2 400 at 12 knots

EMS   2/1976, Reinhard Nerlich

1 DEGAUSSING SHIP

Name	No.	Builders	Commissioned
WALTHER VON LEDEBUR	Y 841	Burmester, Bremen	1966

Displacement, tons: 725
Dimensions, feet (metres): 219·8 × 34·8 × 8·9 *(63 × 10·6 × 2·7)*
Main engines: Maybach (MTU) diesels; 2 shafts; 5 000 bhp = 19 knots
Complement: 11 + 10

Wooden hulled vessel. Trials ship. Launched on 30 June 1966.

WALTHER VON LEDEBUR   10/1975, Reinhard Nerlich

5 Ex-COASTAL MINESWEEPERS

ADOLF BESTELMEYER (ex-*BYMS 2213*) Y 881
H.C. OERSTED (ex-*Vinstra*, ex-*NYMS 247*) Y 877
HERMAN VON HELMOLTZ Y 878
RUDOLF DIESEL (ex-*BYMS 2279*) Y 889
OT 2 Y 847

Displacement, tons: 270 standard; 350 full load
Dimensions, feet (metres): 136 × 24·5 × 8 *(41·5 × 7·5 × 2·4)*
Main engines: 2 MTU diesels; 2 shafts; 1 000 bhp = 15 knots

Of US YMS type. Built in 1943. *Adolf Bestelmeyer* and *Rudolf Diesel* are used for gunnery trials.
H. C. Oersted was acquired from the Royal Norwegian Navy and with *Herman von Helmholtz*,
commissioned on 18 Dec 1962, used as degaussing ships.

RUDOLF DIESEL   2/1976, Reinhard Nerlich

PLANET A 1450 of 1 943 tons and 13·5 knots. Built in 1965. Weapons research ship.

WILHELM PULLWER Y 838, **SP 1** Y 837 of 160 tons and 12·5 knots. Built in 1966. Trials ships.

HEINZ ROGGENKAMP Y 871. Of 785 tons and 12 knots. Built in 1952. Trials ship.

FRIEDRICH VOGE Y 888. Of 179 tons. Trials ship.

OTTO MEYCKE Diving Trials.

EF 3 Y 840 of 100 tons and 13·4 knots, ex-FPB built in 1943. Trials ship.

TB 1 Y 1678 of 70 tons and 14 knots. Diving boat built in 1972.

LP 1, 2 and **3**. Battery workshop craft of 180 tons built in 1963-73.

FÖRDE Y 1641   **JADE** Y 1642

Tank cleaning vessels. Of 600 tons, completed in 1967.

FÖRDE   8/1975, Stefan Terzibaschitsch

FRIEDRICH VOGE   1975, Federal German Navy

KNURRHAHN Y 811 of 261 tons.
ARCONA (ex-*Royal Prince*) Y 809

Both accommodation ships. *Arcona* ex-liner.

BARBARA Y 844, lifting ship of 3 500 tons.

GRIEP Y 876, **HIEV** Y 875, Floating cranes.

SURVEY SHIPS

1 "VEGESACK" CLASS

PASSAU

Displacement, tons: 362 standard; 378 full load
Dimensions, feet (metres): 144·3 oa × 26·2 × 9 *(44·2 × 8 × 2·7)*
Main engines: 2 Mercedes-Benz (MTU) diesels; 1 500 hp; 2 shafts; CP propellers = 15 knots.

The last of 6 "Vegesack" class minesweepers built in Cherbourg 1959-60. Converted for oceanographic research. Other five transferred to Turkey.

The following ships operate for the Deutsches Hydrographisches Institut, under the Ministry of Transport.

METEOR (research ship) 3 085 tons, launched 1964, complement 55
KOMET (survey and research) 1 595 tons, launched 1969, complement 42
GAUSS (survey and research) 1 074 tons, launched 1949, complement 40
SÜDEROOG (survey ship) 211 tons, launched 1956, complement 16
ATAIR (survey and wrecks) 148 tons, launched 1962, complement 13
WEGA (survey and wrecks) 148 tons, launched 1962, complement 12

GAUSS   1974, Rèiner Nerlich

COASTGUARD VESSELS

(BUNDESGRENZSCHUTZ—SEE)

Note: This paramilitary force consists of about 1 000 men who operate the craft below as well as helicopters.

8 LARGE PATROL CRAFT

ALSFELD BG 16   **ESCHWEGE** BG 15
BAD BRAMSTEDT BG 12   **NEUSTADT** BG 11
BAYREUTH BG 17   **ROSENHEIM** BG 18
DUDERSTADT BG 14   **UELTZEN** BG 13

Displacement, tons: 203
Length, feet (metres): 127·1 *(38·5)*
Guns: 2—40 mm
Main engines: 3 MTU diesels; 4 500 hp = 30 knots

All built between 1969 and late 1970—BG 13 by Schlichting, Travemünde, the remainder by Lürssen, Vegesack. Form two flotillas: BG 11-14 the 1st and BG 15-18 the 2nd. A third flotilla of smaller craft has been formed.

ROSENHEIM   8/1974, Dittmair

1 TUG

A 600 hp tug was ordered autumn 1975 from Mützelfeldtwerft, Cuxhaven to complete in 1976. Voight-Schneider propeller.

FISHERY PROTECTION SHIPS

Operated by Ministry of Agriculture and Fisheries.

ANTON DOHRN of 1 950 tons and 15 knots
FRITHJOF of 2 150 tons and 15 knots.
MEERKATZE of 1 000 tons and 12 knots.
MINDEN of 973 tons and 16 knots.
NORDENHAM of 975 tons and 16 knots.
POSEIDON of 935 tons and 12 knots.
ROTERSAND of 1 000 tons. Built in 1974.
SOLEA of 340 tons and 12 knots.
UTHÖRN of 110 tons and 9 knots.
WALTHER HERTWIG of 2 500 tons and 15 knots.

GERMANY (Democratic Republic)

Ministerial

Minister of National Defence:
General Heinz Hoffmann

Headquarters Appointments

Commander-in-Chief, Volksmarine:
Vice Admiral Willi Ehm
Chief of Naval Staff:
Rear Admiral Gustav Hesse

Personnel

(a) 1974: 1 750 officers and 15 300 men (including GBK)
    1975: 1 800 officers and 15 500 men (including GBK)
    1976: 1 850 officers and 16 000 men (including GBK)
    1977: 1 800 officers and 15 200 men (including GBK)

(b) 18 months National Service

Mercantile Marine

Lloyd's Register of Shipping:
446 vessels of 1 437 054 tons gross

Bases

Rostock/Gehlsdorf: Navy Headquarters;
Peenemunde: HQ 1st Flotilla;
Warnemunde: HQ 4th Flotilla;
Dranske-Bug: HQ 6th Flotilla;
Sassuitz: Minor base;
Wolgast: Minor base;
Tarnewitz: Minor base.

Naval Air

1 squadron with 8 Mi-4 helicopters

Grenzbrigade Kuste (GBK)

The seaborne branch of the Frontier Guards, this is a force of
about 3 000 men. Their various craft are difficult to disentangle
from those of the Navy, many being taken from that list. Where
possible, mention of this is made in the notes.

Strength of the Fleet

Type	Active	Building
Frigates	2	—
Large Patrol Craft	18	—
Fast Attack Craft—Missile	15	—
Fast Attack Craft—Torpedo	65	—
Fast Attack Craft—Patrol	4 (GBK)	—
Coastal Patrol Craft	18	—
Landing Ships and Craft	20	—
Minesweepers—Coastal	52	3
Intelligence Ships	3	—
Survey Ships	4	—
Supply Ships	4	—
Support Tankers	4	—
Buoy Tenders	17	—
Ice Breakers	3	—
Tugs	13	—
Tenders	4	—
Training Ships and Craft	10	—
Cable Layer	1	—
Torpedo Recovery Vessels	2	—

"HAI" Class

"ILTIS" Class

FRIGATES

2 Ex-SOVIET "RIGA" CLASS

ERNEST THÄLMANN 141   **KARL MARX** 142

Displacement, tons: 1 200 standard; 1 600 full load
Dimensions, feet (metres): 298·8 × 33·7 × 11 *(91 × 10·2 × 3·4)*
Guns: 3—3·9 in (single); 4—37 mm (twin)
Torpedo tubes: 2—21 in (twin)
A/S weapons: 4 depth charge projectors; 4 RBU 1800
Mines: Can carry 50
Main engines: Geared turbines; 2 shafts; 25 000 shp = 28 knots
Oil fuel, tons: 300
Range, miles: 2 500 at 15 knots
Complement: 150

Sister ships *Friedrich Engels* 124 and *Karl Liebnecht* 123 were scrapped in 1971. A fifth ship of
this type was burnt out at the end of 1959 and became a total wreck. Two of these hulks are
beached at Warnemünde.

Radar: Slim Net; Sun Visor; Neptun.

KARL MARX   *1965, Werner Kähling*

LIGHT FORCES

4 Ex-SOVIET "SO-I" CLASS (LARGE PATROL CRAFT)

421   422   423   424

Displacement, tons: 215 standard; 250 full load
Dimensions, feet (metres): 138 × 20 × 9·2 *(42·3 × 6·1 × 2·8)*
Guns: 4—25 mm (2 twin mounts)
A/S weapons: 4 MBU 1 800 5 barrelled launchers; 2 DCT
Main engines: 3 diesels; 6 000 bhp = 29 knots
Range, miles: 1 100 at 13 knots
Complement: 30

Fitted with mine rails. These vessels belonged to the coast guard (GBK) but have now been
returned to the navy.

"SO-I" Class   *1970, Niels Gartig*

14 "HAI" CLASS (LARGE PATROL CRAFT)

BAD DOBERAN	LÜBZ	RIBNITZ-DAMGARTEN
BÜTZOW	LUDWIGSLUST	STERNBERG
GREVESMÜHLEN	PARCHIM	TETEROW
GADEBUSCH	PERLEBERG	WISMAR + 2

Displacement, tons: 300 standard; 370 full load
Dimensions, feet (metres): 174 pp; 187 oa × 19 × 10 *(53·1, 57 × 5·8 × 3·1)*
Guns: 4—30 mm (2 twin)
A/S weapons: 4 RBU 1 800 5 barrelled launchers
Main engines: 2 gas turbines; diesels; 8 000 bhp = 25 knots
Complement: 45

Built by Peenewerft, Wolgast. The prototype vessel was completed in 1963. All were in service by the end of 1969, and the programme is now completed.
Pennant numbers are: 411-414, 431-434, 451-454, V 81 and 1 unknown.

"HAI" Class   1974

"HAI" Class   1974

12 Ex-SOVIET "OSA I" CLASS — 3 "OSA II" CLASS
(FAST ATTACK CRAFT—MISSILE)

ARVID HARNACK	MAX REICHPIETSCH
AUGUST LUTTGENS	OTTO TOST
FRITZ GAST	PAUL EISENSCHNEIDER
HEINRICH DORRENBACH	PAUL WIECZOREK
JOSEF SCHARES	RICHARD SORGE
KARL MESEBERG	RUDOLF EGELHOFER +3

Displacement, tons: 165 standard; 200 full load
Dimensions, feet (metres): 128·7 × 25·1 × 5·9 *(39·3 × 7·7 × 1·8)*
Missiles: 4 mountings in 2 pairs for SS-N-2 system
Guns: 4—30 mm (2 twin, 1 forward, 1 aft)
Main engines: 3 diesels; 13 000 hp = 36 knots

Pennant numbers: 711-714, 731-734, 751-754. 3 "Osa II" transferred 1976.

"OSA I" Class   1965, Reinecke

18 Ex-SOVIET "SHERSHEN" CLASS
(FAST ATTACK CRAFT—TORPEDO)

ADAM KUCKHOFF	FIETE SCHULZE
ANTON SAEFKOW	FRITZ BEHN
ARTHUR BECKER	FRITZ HECKERT
BERNHARD BÄSTLEIN	HANS COPPI
BRUNO KÜHN	HEINZ KAPELLE
EDGAR ANDRÉ	RUDOLF BREITSCHEID
ERNST GRUBE	WILLI BANSCH
ERNST SCHNELLER	+3

Displacement, tons: 150 standard; 160 full load
Dimensions, feet (metres): 115·5 × 23·1 × 5 *(35·2 × 7·1 × 1·5)*
Guns: 4—30 mm (2 twin)
A/S weapons: 12 DC
Torpedo tubes: 4—21 in (single)
Main engines: 3 Diesels; 13 000 bhp; 3 shafts = 41 knots
Complement: 16

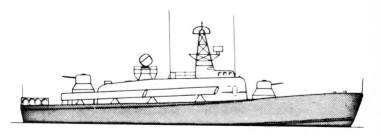

"SHERSHEN" Class

Acquired from the USSR. Four were delivered in 1968-69, the first installment of a flotilla. The last three transferred 1976. They do not differ from the Soviet boats of the class.
Pennant numbers 811-5, 831-5, 851-5.

7 "LIBELLE" CLASS (FAST ATTACK CRAFT—TORPEDO)

Displacement, tons: 20
Dimensions, feet (metres): 52·5 × 11·5 × 3·6 *(16 × 3·5 × 1·1)*
Guns: 2—14·5 mm (twin)
Torpedo tubes: 2—21 inch (stern launching)
Main engines: 3 Diesels; 3 600 hp = 50 knots

A new class first reported in 1975. An improved "Iltis" class. Can be used for minelaying and commando operations. Conversion for new tasks is a speedy job. In series production.

40 "ILTIS" CLASS (FAST ATTACK CRAFT—TORPEDO)

Displacement, tons: 20
Dimensions, feet (metres): 55·8 × 10·5 × 2·5 *(17 × 3·2 × 0·8)*
Torpedo tubes: 2—21 in (torpedoes fired over stern). Some have three tubes (Type 3)
   Mines can be carried in place of torpedo tubes
Main engines: Diesels; 3 000 bhp = 30 knots

No guns. Several different types of this class exist, varying in hull material and silhouette, eg Type 1 are flush-decked and Type 2 have a raised forecastle. With the torpedo tubes removed these boats are used to land frogmen and raiding parties. Displacement and dimensions given are for Type 2. Others vary slightly. Built by Mitteldeutschland, starting in 1962. Some pennant numbers in 970, 980, 990 series.

"ILTIS" Class   *1971, S. Breyer*

4 Ex-SOVIET "P 6" CLASS (FAST ATTACK CRAFT—PATROL)

Displacement, tons: 66 standard; 75 full load
Dimensions, feet (metres): 84·2 × 20 × 6 *(25·7 × 6·1 × 1·8)*
Guns: 4—25 mm (2 twin mountings) (removed in target boats)
Main engines: 4 diesels; 4 800 bhp; 4 shafts = 43 knots
Range, miles: 450 at 30 knots
Complement: 25

Acquired in 1957-60 from the USSR. Originally there were 27. Wooden hull. Most of this class has been scrapped or converted. Four have had their tubes removed and been transferred to the GBK with pennant Nos G81-84. Pot Head radar.

18 "KB 123" CLASS (COASTAL PATROL CRAFT)

Displacement, tons: about 25
Dimensions, feet (metres): 74 × 16·4 × — *(23 × 5 × —)*
Main engines: 2 Diesels = 14 knots

This class (total uncertain) was introduced in 1971 for operations on rivers and inland waterways by the GBK. It appears to be fast and unarmed, though small arms are certainly carried.

"KB 123" Class   *1972*

AMPHIBIOUS FORCES

2 "FRÖSCH" CLASS (LST)

Displacement, tons: 1 950
Dimensions, feet (metres): 298.4 × 39.4 × — *(91 × 12 × –)*
Guns: 2 twin 57 mm: 2 twin 30 mm
Main engines: Diesels

A new class similar but not identical to Soviet "Ropuchka" class. First seen in Baltic in 1976. Continuing programme.

6 "ROBBE" CLASS (LST)

EBERSWALDE	**GRIMMEN**	**LÜBBEN**
ELSENHÜTTENSTADT	**HOYERSWERDA**	**SCHWEDT**

Displacement, tons: 600 standard; 800 full load
Dimensions, feet (metres): 196·8 × 32·8 × 6·6 *(60 × 10 × 2·0)*
Guns: 2—57 mm (1 twin); 4—25 mm (2 twin)
Main engines: Diesels = 12 knots

Launched in 1962-64. Can carry 500 tons stores and vehicles.

"ROBBE" Class   *1971, S. Breyer*

12 "LABO" CLASS (LCT)

GERHARD PRENZLER   HEINZ WILKOWSKI   ROLF PETERS   + 9

Displacement, tons: 150 standard; 200 full load
Dimensions, feet (metres): 131·2 × 27·9 × 5·9 (40·0 × 8·5 × 1·8)
Guns: 4—25 mm (2 twin)
Main engines: Diesels = 10 knots

Built by Peenewerft, Wolgast. Launched in 1961-63.

"LABO" Class   1969, S. Breyer

MINE WARFARE FORCES

52 "KONDOR I" and "II" CLASS
(MINESWEEPERS—COASTAL)

AHRENSHOOP	GUBEN	ROSSLAU
ALTENTREPTOW	GREIFSWALD	SCHÖNEBECK
ANKLAM	KAMENZ	SÖMMERA
BANSIN	KLÜTZ	STRALSUND
BERGEN	KUHLUNGSBORN	STRASBURG
BITTERFELD	KYRITZ	TANGERHÜTTE
BERNAU	NEURUPPIN	TEMPLIN
BOLTENHAGEN	NEUSTRELITZ	UCKERMÜNDE
DEMMIN	ORANIENBURG	VITTE
DESSAU	PASEWALK	WARNEMÜNDE
EILENBURG	PREROW	WEISSWASSER
EISLEBEN	PRITZWALK	WILHELM PIECKSTADT
GENTHIN	RATHENOW	WITTSTOCK
GRAAL-MÜRITZ	RIESA	WOLGAST
GRIMMA	ROBEL	ZEITZ
		ZERBST
		ZINGST
		+5

Displacement, tons: 245 standard; 280 full load
Dimensions, feet (metres): 154·2 × 23·0 × 6·6 (47 × 7 × 2) ("Kondor II" plus 2 metres)
Guns: 2—25 mm ("Kondor I"); 6—25 mm (twins) ("Kondor II")
Main engines: 2 diesels; 2 shafts; 4 000 bhp = 21 knots

Built by Peenewerft Wolgast. Five units were operational in 1970 and 15 by the end of 1971. They replace the small minesweepers of the "Schwalbe" class. Type II has additional length and extra MGs. First appeared in 1971. Production continues.

"KONDOR I" Class   9/1976

PENNANT NUMBERS

These have been changed with some frequency. At present the following is as near as can be offered;

Type I (Total 22)   Prototype-V31. S24-26. Attached to GBK; G11-16. G21-26, G41-46.
Conversion for torpedo recovery—B73 and B74.
Conversion to AGIs Meteor and Komet.

Type II (Total 30)   Prototype—V32. Active minesweepers 311-316, 321-327, 331-336, 341-347. S21-23.

"KONDOR II" Class   9/1976

INTELLIGENCE SHIPS

2 "KONDOR I" CLASS

METEOR   KOMET

Displacement, tons: 245 standard; 280 full load
Dimensions, feet (metres): 154·2 × 23·0 × 6·6 (47 × 7 × 2)
Guns: 2—25 mm
Main engines: 2 diesels; 2 shafts; 4 000 bhp
Speed, knots: 21

Conversions from standard "Kondor" class Coastal Minesweepers.

HYDROGRAPH

Displacement, tons: 500
Dimensions, feet (metres): 167 × 28·8 × — (50·9 × 8·7 ×—)
Main engines: Diesel; 540 hp = 11 knots

Built in 1960 by Volkswerft, Stralsund.

SURVEY SHIPS

KARL F. GAUS

Built on a 280 ton "Kondor" hull in 1976. Unarmed. Carries 4 small survey launches. Naval manned.

PROFESSOR KRÜMMEL

Built in 1954. Of 135 tons and 10 knots. Civilian Research Ship.

JORDAN

Of 100 tons and 9 knots.

FLAGGTIEF

Built in 1953. Of 50 tons and 8 knots.

SERVICE FORCES

1 "BASKUNCHAK" CLASS (SUPPLY SHIP)

USEDOM

Displacement, tons: 2 500
Dimensions, feet (metres): 227 × 29 × 12·3 *(70 × 8·9 × 3·8)*
Speed, knots: 13

Tanker converted to act as supply ship.

USEDOM   *1973, S. Breyer*

3 TYPE 600 (SUPPORT TANKERS)

C 37   — (ex-*Hiddensee*)   **POEL** (ex-*Riems*)

Displacement, tons: 600 DWT
Dimensions, feet (metres): 195 oa × 29·5 × 12·5 *(59·5 × 9·0 × 3·8)*
Guns: 4—25 mm (twin)
Main engines: 2 diesels; 2 800 bhp = 14 knots
Complement: 26

Built by Peenewerft, Wolgast, in 1960-61. Civilian manned. Oil capacity 645 tons.

POEL   *1971, S. Breyer*

5 "KUMO" CLASS

E 18   **E 44**   **RUDEN**   **RUGEN** V 71   **VILM**

Displacement, tons: 400
Dimensions, feet (metres): 118 × 24 × 8·9 *(36 × 7·3 × 2·7)*
Speed, knots: 10

Built in mid-1950s. *Rugen* is a torpedo Trials Ship, *Vilm* a tanker and the other three employed as Supply Ships.

1 Ex-SOVIET "KAMENKA" CLASS (BUOY LAYER)

BUK

Displacement, tons: 1 000 standard
Dimensions, feet (metres): 180·5 × 31·2 × 11·5 *(55 × 9·5 × 3·4)*
Main engines: Diesels = 16 knots

BUK   *1970*

1 CABLE LAYER

DORNBUSCH

Cable layer of 700 tons with bow rollers.

DORNBUSCH   *1967*

2 "KONDOR I" CLASS (TRVs)

B 73   B 74

Details under Minewarfare Forces. Converted for Torpedo Recovery.

LUMME

Small diving tender. Tug type.

FREESENDORF

Built in 1963. Buoy-layer.

4 "TAUCHER" CLASS (DIVING TENDERS)

SATZHAFF (?) +3

Displacement, tons: 310 full load
Dimensions, feet (metres): 98·4 × 21·3 × 9 *(30 × 6·5 × 3)*
Main engines: 2 diesels = 12 knots

Small diving tenders with recompression chamber.

8 BUOY TENDERS

BREITLING	GOLWITZ	LANDTIEFF	RAMZOW
ESPER ORT	GRASS ORT	PALMER ORT	ROSEN ORT

Displacement, tons: 158
Dimensions, feet (metres): 97 × 20·3 × 6·2 *(29;6 × 6·2 × 1·9)*
Main engines: 1 diesel; 580 hp = 11·5 knots

Delivered 1970-72. Civilian manned under the Naval Hydrographic Service.

BREITLING   *1972*

3 BUOY TENDERS

ARKONA   DASSER ORT   STUBBEN KAMMER

Built in 1956. Of 55 tons and 10 knots.

TRAINING SHIPS

WILHELM PIECK

Displacement, tons: 2 000
Dimensions, feet (metres): 239·4 × 39·4 × — *(73 × 12 × —)*
Guns: 2—30 mm (twin); 4—25 mm (twin)
Speed, knots: 17
Complement: 100

Cadets' training ship commissioned 6 July 1976. Built Polish Naval Yard, Gdynia. Sister ship to Polish "Wodnik" class training ships.

3 "KRAKE" CLASS (ex-MINESWEEPERS—OCEAN)

BERLIN   POTSDAM   ROSTOCK

Displacement, tons: 650 standard
Dimensions, feet (metres): 229·7 × 26·5 × 12·2 *(70 × 8·1 × 3·7)*
Guns: 1—3·4 in; 10—25 mm (vertical twins)
A/S weapons: 4 DCT
Mines: Can carry 30
Main engines: Diesels; 2 shafts; 3 400 bhp = 18 knots
Complement: 90

"KRAKE" Class   *1970, Niels Gartig*

Built in 1956-58 by Peenewerft, Wolgast. Of the original ten, four completed in 1958, were originally for Poland. Appearance is different compared with the first type, the squat wide funnel being close to the bridge with lattice mast and radar. Fitted for minelaying. On 1 May 1961 they were given the names of the capitals of districts etc. of East Germany. Pennant numbers are S11-13. All used for training and will probably be deleted before long.

6 "KONDOR I" CLASS

Details in Minewarfare Forces, being part of that total.

ICEBREAKERS

STEPHAN JANTZEN

Of 2 500 tons and 13 knots built in 1965. Of Soviet "Dobrynya Nikitch" class. Civilian manned.

EISBAR   EISVOGEL

Of 550 tons and 12 knots built in 1957. Civilian manned.

TUGS

11 HARBOUR TUGS

Of varying classes.

A 14

Of 800 tons and 12 knots.

WISMAR

Of 700 tons and 14 knots. Possibly civilian manned.

Note: Gesellschaft für Sport und Technik (GST) (Association for Sport and Technical Science) controls several training ships—*Ernst Thälman,* a retired "Habicht I" Class minesweeper; *Ernst Schneller,* "Tummler" class; *Partisan,* and *Pionier* of 80 tons; *Freundschaft* of 200 tons; *F. L. Jahn* of 100 tons; and the sail training ships *Seid Bereil, Jonny Scheer, Max Reichpietsch II* and *Knechtsand II.*

GHANA

Administration

Commander of the Navy: Commodore C. K. Dzang

Personnel

(a) 1977: 2 000
(b) Voluntary Service

Naval Bases

Secondi (Western Naval Command)
Tema, near Accra (Eastern Naval Command)

Deletions

1973: 3 ex-Soviet "Poluchat I" Class Patrol Craft

Mercantile Marine

Lloyd's Register of Shipping: 84 vessels of 183 089 tons gross

CORVETTES

2 "KROMANTSE" CLASS (VOSPER MARK I TYPE)

Name	No.	Builders	Commissioned
KROMANTSE	F 17	Vosper Ltd.	27 July 1964
KETA	F 18	Vickers Ltd (Tyne)	18 May 1965

Displacement, tons: 380 light; 440 standard; 500 full load
Dimensions, feet (metres): 162 wl; 177 oa × 28·5 × 13 (49·4, 54 × 8·7 × 4)
Guns: 1—4 in; 1—40 mm (see notes)
A/S weapons: 1 Squid triple-barrelled depth charge mortar
Main engines: 2 Bristol Siddeley Maybach (MTU) diesels; 2 shafts; 390 rpm; 7 100 bhp = 20 knots
Oil fuel, tons: 60
Range, miles: 2 000 at 16 knots; 2 900 at 14 knots
Complement: 54 (6 + 3 officers, 45 ratings)

Designed by Vosper Ltd, Portsmouth, a joint venture with Vickers-Armstrong's Ltd, one ship being built by each company. Vosper roll damping fins, and air conditioning throughout excepting machinery spaces. Generators 360 kW. The electrical power supply is 440 volts, 60 cycles ac. A very interesting patrol vessel design, an example of what can be achieved on a comparatively small platform to produce an inexpensive and quickly built anti-submarine vessel. *Kromantse* was launched at the Camber Shipyard, Portsmouth, on 5 Sep 1963. *Keta* was launched at Newcastle on 18 Jan 1965.

KROMANTSE   9/1975, Vosper Thornycroft

Radar: Search: Plessey AWS 1.

Refit: Both were fully refitted by Vosper Thornycroft Ltd (a £1·2 million contract) in 1974-75—*Keta* completed in April 1975 and *Kromantse* in Sep 1975.

Sonar: Both fitted with hull-mounted set.

LIGHT FORCES

2 LARGE PATROL CRAFT

Name	No.	Builders	Commissioned
DIELA	P 24	Ruthof Werft, Mainz	1974
SAHENE	P 25	Ruthof Werft, Mainz	1974

Displacement, tons: 160
Dimensions, feet (metres): 115·5 × 21·3 × 5·9 (35·2 × 6·5 × 1·8)
Guns: 2—40 mm

Ordered from Ruthof Werft (Mainz) BRG in 1973 as part of a class of six. Only these two had been delivered when the builders went bankrupt in 1975—no further decisions known.

2 "FORD" CLASS (LARGE PATROL CRAFT)

Name	No.	Builders	Commissioned
ELMINA	P 13	—	—
ROMENDA	P 14	Yarrows, Scotstoun	Dec 1962

Displacement, tons: 120 standard; 142 full load
Dimensions, feet (metres): 110 wl; 117·5 oa × 20 × 7 (33·6; 35·8 × 6·1 × 2·1)
Gun: 1—40 mm, 60 cal Bofors
A/S weapons: Depth charge throwers
Main engines: 2 MTU (Maybach) diesels; type MD 16 V 53 87 B 90: 2 shafts = 3 000 hp at 1 790 rpm
Range, miles: 1 000 at 30 knots
Complement: 32 = 3 officers, 29 ratings

KOMENDA   1969, Ghana Navy

MINEWARFARE FORCES

1 Ex-BRITISH "TON" CLASS (MINESWEEPER—COASTAL)

Name	No.	Builders	Commissioned
EJURA (ex-HMS *Aldington*)	M 16	Camper and Nicholson	1955

Displacement, tons: 360 standard; 425 full load
Dimensions, feet (metres): 140 pp; 153 oa × 28·8 × 8·2 (42·7; 46·7 × 8·6 × 2·4)
Guns: 1—40 mm forward; 2—20 mm aft
Main engines: Deltic diesels; 2 shafts; 3 000 bhp = 15 knots
Oil fuel, tons: 45
Range, miles: 2 300 at 13 knots
Complement: 27

Lent to Ghana by Britain in 1964. Acquired outright in 1974.

2 Ex-BRITISH "HAM" CLASS (MINESWEEPERS—INSHORE)

Name	No.	Builders	Commissioned
AFADZATO (ex-HMS *Ottringham*)	M 12	Ailsa (Clyde)	30 Oct 1959
YOGAGA (ex-HMS *Malham*)	M 11	Fairlie Yacht Co.	2 Oct 1959

Displacement, tons: 120 standard; 159 full load
Dimensions, feet (metres): 100 pp; 107·5 oa × 22 × 5·8 (30·5; 32·8 × 6·7 × 1·8)
Gun: 1—20 mm
Main engines: 2 Paxman diesels; 1 100 bhp = 14 knots
Oil fuel, tons: 15
Range, miles: 2 000 at 9 knots
Complement: 22

Yogaga and *Afadzato* sailed for Ghana on 31 Oct 1959 under original names, and were transferred from the Royal Navy to the Ghana Navy at Takoradi at the end of Nov 1959 and renamed after hills in Ghana. Fitted with funnel.

YOGAGA   1966, Ghana Navy

SERVICE CRAFT

ASUANTSI (ex-*MRC* 1122)

Displacement, tons: 657
Dimensions, feet (metres): 225 pp; 231·3 oa × 39 × 5 (68·6; 70·5 × 11·9 × 1·5)
Main engines: 4 Paxman; 1 840 bhp = 9 knots cruising

Acquired from Britain in 1965 and arrived in Ghana waters in July 1965. Used as a base workshop at Tema Naval Base. Is kept operational, and does a fair amount of seatime in general training and exercise tasks. Converted LCT.

GREECE

Ministerial

Minister of National Defence:
Evangelos Averof

Headquarters Appointments

Chief Hellenic Navy:
Vice-Admiral Konofaos
Deputy Chief:
Rear-Admiral I. Deyiannis

Fleet Command

Commander of the Fleet:
Vice-Admiral N. Andronopoulos

Diplomatic Representation

Naval Attaché in London:
Captain Papas
Naval Attaché in Washington:
Captain O. Kapetos
Naval Attaché in Bonn:
Captain T. Alicampiotis
Naval Attaché in Cairo:
Captain P. Vossos
Naval Attaché in Ankara:
Captain G. Tsakonas

Personnel

(a) 1977: 17 600 (1 900 officers and 15 700 ratings)
(b) 2 years National Service

Naval Bases

Mitilini, Piraeus, Salamis, Salonika, Suda Bay and Valos.

Naval Aviation

1 Squadron Alouette III helicopters with naval crews formed on 7 Aug 1975.
14 HU-16B Albatross are operated under naval command by mixed Air Force and Navy crews.

Harbour Corps

This force is equipped with coastal patrol craft and charged with harbour policing and coast-guard duties.

Prefix to Ships' Names

H.S. (Hellenic Ship)

Mercantile Marine

Lloyd's Register of Shipping:
2 921 vessels of 25 034 585 tons gross

Strength of the Fleet

Type	Active	Building
Destroyers	12	—
Frigates	4	—
Corvettes	5	—
Patrol Submarines	7	4
Fast Attack Craft—Missile	10	—
Fast Attack Craft—Torpedo	19	—
Large Patrol Craft	5	—
Fast Attack Craft—Patrol	10	—
Large Patrol Craft	5	—
Landing Ships	16	—
LCUs	6	—
Minor Landing Craft	47	—
Minelayers—Coastal	2	—
Minesweepers—Coastal	15	—
Survey Vessels	5	—
Depot Ship	1	—
Support Tankers	2	—
Harbour Tankers	4	2
Salvage Ship	1	—
Repair Ship	1	—
Lighthouse Tenders	2	—
Tugs	12	—
Netlayer	1	—
Water Boats	8	—
Auxiliary Transports	2	—

New Construction

It is reported that interest is being shown in the purchase of two A-69 Avisos from France.

DELETIONS

Destroyers

1972 *Doxa, Niki* ("Gleaves" Class)

Submarines

1975 *Poseidon*
1976 *Triaina* returned to USA for disposal.

Light Forces

1971 *Antiploiarkhos Laskos, Ploiarchos Meletopoulos*
1972 *Inionos* ("Nasty" Class)
1976 *Plotarkhis Maridakis, Plotarkhis Vlachavas*

Minesweepers—Coastal

1972 *Paxi*
1973 *Afroessa, Kalymnos, Karteria, Kerkyra, Papalos, Zakynthos*

Amphibious Forces

1971 *Nafkratoussa* (ex-*Hyperion*, ex-*LSD 9*)
1972 *Ipopliarkhos Merlin* (ex-US *LSM 557*) sunk in collision with a supertanker (15 Nov).
1975 *Skopelos* and *Kea* (ex-US *LCT 6*)

Survey Vessel

1973 *Ariadne*

Minesweeper Depot Ship

1973 *Hermes*

Harbour Tanker

1976 *Prometheus* (target)

Tugs

1972 *Aegeus, Adamastos*

Water Boat

1972 *Kaliroe*

Light House Tenders

1976 *St. Lykoudis, Skyros*

PENNANT NUMBERS

Destroyers and Frigates

01	Aetos
06	Aspis
16	Velos
28	Thyella
31	Ierax
54	Leon
56	Lonchi
63	Navarinon
67	Panthir
85	Sfendoni
210	Themistocles
211	Miaoulis
212	Kanaris
213	Kontouriotis
214	Sachtouris

Submarines

86	Triaina
110	Glavkos
111	Nereus
112	Triton
113	Proteus
114	Papanikolis
115	Katsonis

Minelayers

N04	Aktion
N05	Amvrakia

Minesweepers and Corvettes

M12	Armatolos
M58	Mahitis
M64	Navmachos
M74	Polemistis

M202	Atalanti
M205	Antiopi
M206	Faedra
M210	Thalia
M211	Alkyon
M213	Argo
M214	Avra
M240	Pleias
M241	Kichli
M242	Kissa
M245	Doris
M246	Aigli
M247	Dafni
M248	Aedon
M254	Niovi

Light Forces

P14	Arslanoglou
P15	Dolphin
P16	Draken
P17	Polikos
P18	Polidefkis
P19	Aiolos
P20	Astrapi
P21	Andromeda
P22	N.I. Goulandras I
P23	Kastor
P24	Kyknos
P25	Pigassos
P26	Toxotis
P27	Foinix
P28	Kelefstis Stamou

P29	Diopos Antoniou
P50	Antihliarpos Laskos
P51	Plotarhis Blessas
P52	Ipoploiarhos Troupakis
P53	Ipoploiarhos Mikonios
P54	Ipoploiarhos Batsis
P55	Ipoploiarhos Arliotis
P56	Ipoploiarhos Anninos
P57	Ipoploiarhos Konidis
P70	A. Pezopoulos
P96	P. Chadzikonstandis
P196	Esperos
P197	Kataigis
P198	Kentauros
P199	Kyklon
P228	Laieps
P229	Scorpios
P230	Tyfon

Amphibious Forces

L144	Syros
L145	Kassos
L146	Karpathos
L147	Kimonos
L149	Kithnos
L150	Sifnos
L152	Skiathos
L153	Nafkratoussa
L154	Ikaria
L157	Rodos
L158	Limnos
L161	I. Grigoropoulos
L162	I. Tournas
L163	I. Daniolos
L164	I. Roussen
L165	I. Krystalidis
L171	Kriti
L172	Lesbos
L179	Samos
L195	Chios

Service Forces

A215	Aegeon
A307	Thetis
A329	Sakipis
A345	Sirios
A372	Zeus
A373	Kronos
A376	Orion
A377	Arethousa
A384	Sotir
A407	Antaios
A408	Atlas
A409	Achilleus
A410	Atromitos
A413	Hephestos
A414	Ariadni
A415	Pandora
A416	Pandrosos
A418	Romaleos
A421	Minotauros
A427	Patraikos
A429	Perseus
A430	Samson
A431	Titan
A432	Cigas
A467	Volvi
A469	Anemos
A470	Kastoria
A471	Vivies
A472	Stymphalia
A473	Trihonis
A474	Iliki
A476	Pyrpolitis
A478	Naftilos
A481	St. Lykoudis
A485	I. Theophilopoulos Karavoyiannos
	Evros
	Kerkini
	Kalliroe
	Prespa

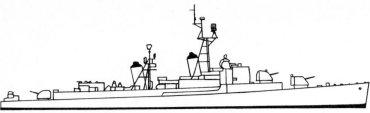

"GEARING FRAM I" Class

"GEARING FRAM II" Class

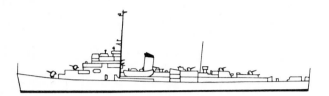

"BOSTWICK" Class

"FLETCHER" Class (4 Guns)

"ALGERINE" Class

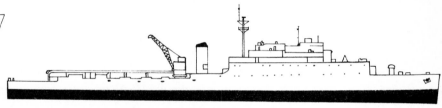

NAFKRATOUSSA

DESTROYERS

1 Ex-US "GEARING FRAM II" CLASS
4 Ex-US "GEARING FRAM I" CLASS

Name	No.	Builders	Laid down	Launched	Commissioned
SACHTOURIS (ex-USS *Arnold J. Isbell, DD 869*)	214	Bethlehem (Staten Island)	14 Mar 1945	6 Aug 1945	5 Jan 1946
KANARIS (ex-USS *Stickell, DD 888*)	212	Consolidated Steel Corp	5 Jan 1945	16 June 1945	26 Sep 1945
KONTOURIOTIS (ex-USS *Rupertus, DD 851*)	213	Bethlehem (Quincy)	2 May 1945	21 Sep 1945	8 Mar 1946
THEMISTOCLES (ex-USS *Frank Knóx, DD 742*)	210	Bath Iron Works	8 May 1944	17 Sep 1944	11 Dec 1944
— (ex-USS *Gurke, DD 783*)	—	Todd Pacific Shipyards	Oct 1944	15 Feb 1945	12 May 1945

Displacement, tons: 2 425 standard; 3 500 full load
Length, feet (metres): 390·5 *(119·0)* oa
Beam, feet (metres): 40·9 *(12·4)*
Draught, feet (metres): 19·0 *(5·8)*
Aircraft: 1 helicopter
Missiles: See *Modernisation* note
Guns: 2—76 mm OTO Melara Compact *(Themistocles)* (See notes); 4—5 in (twin) (remainder) (See notes)
A/S weapons: 2 fixed Hedgehogs, *(Themistocles);* 1 ASROC 8-barrelled launcher and facilities for small helicopter in remainder
Torpedo tubes: 2 triple (Mk 32)
Main engines: 2 Westinghouse geared turbines; 2 shafts; 60 000 shp
Boilers: 4 Babcock & Wilcox
Speed, knots: 34
Range, miles: 4 800 at 15 knots
Complement: 269 (16 officers, 253 men)

Themistocles was a FRAM II Radar Picket conversion, remainder are FRAM I DD conversions.

Modernisation: Cantieri Navali Riuniti is carrying out a series of modernisations: the first, *Themistocles* in 1976. This major work consists of:—
a) Albatros 8-cell BPDM launcher
b) Two 76 mm OTO Melara Compact guns
c) Exocet launchers
d) 2 NA-10 Argo fire control systems
e) Helo deck extended to stern
f) VDS fitted below helo deck
g) Reduction in size of mast and bridge

Transfers: From USA: *Sachtouris,* 4 Dec 1973; *Kanaris,* 1 July 1972; *Kontouriotis,* 10 July 1973; *Themistocles* 30 Jan 1971; ex-USS *Gurke* 1977.

THEMISTOCLES (FRAM II)   *1972, Hellenic Navy*

KANARIS (FRAM I)   *1973, Hellenic Navy*

Name	No.
MIAOULIS (ex-USS *Ingraham, DD 694*)	211

Displacement, tons: 2 200 standard; 3 320 full load
Length, feet (metres): 376·5 (*114·8*) oa
Beam, feet (metres): 40·9 (*12·4*)
Draught, feet (metres): 19·0 (*5·8*)
Guns: 6—5 in (*127 mm*) 38 cal
A/S weapons: 2 triple torpedo launchers, Mk 32;
   2 ahead throwing hedgehogs
Main engines: 2 geared turbines; 2 shafts; 60 000 shp
Boilers: 4
Speed, knots: 34
Range, miles: 4 600 at 15 knots
Complement: 269 (16 officers, 94 POs, 159 men)

Former fleet destroyer of the "Allen M. Sumner" class which had been modernised under the FRAM II programme. Transferred by USA July 1971.

1 Ex-US "ALLEN M. SUMNER" CLASS

Builders	Laid down	Launched	Commissioned
Federal SB & DD Co	4 Aug 1943	16 Jan 1944	10 Mar 1944

MIAOULIS   *1973, Hellenic Navy*

6 Ex-US "FLETCHER" CLASS

Name	No.
ASPIS (ex-USS *Conner, DD 582*)	06
LONCHI ((ex-USS *Hall, DD 583*)	56
NAVARINON (ex-USS *Brown, DD 546*)	63
SFENDONI (ex-USS *Aulick, DD 569*)	85
THYELLA (ex-USS *Bradford, DD 545*)	28
VELOS (ex-USS *Charette, DD 581*)	16

Displacement, tons: 2 100 standard; 3 050 full load
Length, feet (metres): 376·5 (*114·7*) oa
Beam, feet (metres): 39·5 (*12·0*)
Draught, feet (metres): 18 (*5·5*)
Guns: 4—5 in (*127 mm*) 38 cal. in *Aspis, Lonchi, Sfendoni* and
  Velos, 5 in *Navarinon* and *Thyella*
  6—3 in (*76 mm*), 3 twin, in *Aspis, Lonchi, Sfendoni* and *Velos*.
  10—40 mm (2 quadruple, 1 twin) in *Navarinon* and *Thyella*
A/S weapons: Hedgehogs; DCs
Torpedo tubes: 5—21 in (*533 mm*), quintuple bank, in *Aspis,
  Lonchi, Sfendoni* and *Velos*, none in *Navarinon* and *Thyella*
Torpedo racks: Side-launching for A/S torpedoes
Main engines: 2 sets GE geared turbines; 2 shafts; 60 000 shp
Boilers: 4 Babcock & Wilcox; 615 psi (*43·5 km/cm²*) 800°F
  (*427°C*)
Speed, knots: 32
Range, miles: 6 000 at 15 knots; 1 260 at full power
Oil fuel, tons: 506
Complement: 250

Transferred from USA, *Aspis, Lonchi* and *Velos* at Long Beach, Cal, on 15 Sep 1959, 9 Feb 1960 and 15 June 1959, respectively, *Sfendoni* at Philadelphia on 21 Aug 1959, *Navarinon* and *Thyella* at Seattle, Wash, on 27 Sep 1962. All purchased 1976.

Electronics: Reported that whole class has received extensive electronic modernisation.

Radar: Search: SPS 6, SPS 10.
Fire control: GFC 56 and 63 systems.

Builders	Laid down	Launched	Commissioned
Boston Navy Yard	16 Apr 1942	18 July 1942	8 June 1943
Boston Navy Yard	16 Apr 1942	18 July 1942	6 July 1943
Bethlehem (S. Pedro)	27 June1942	22 Feb 1943	10 July 1943
Consolidated Steel Corp. Texas	14 May 1941	2 Mar 1942	27 Oct 1942
Bethlehem (S. Pedro)	28 Apr 1942	12 Dec 1942	12 June 1943
Boston Navy Yard	20 Feb 1941	3 June1942	18 May 1943

VELOS   *1973, Dr Giorgia Arra*

FRIGATES

Note: Depot ship *Aegeon* currently employed on frigate duties.

4 Ex-US "CANNON" CLASS

Name	No.
AETOS (ex-USS *Slater, DE 766*)	01
IERAX (ex-USS *Elbert, DE 768*)	31
LEON (ex-USS *Eldridge, DE 173*)	54
PANTHIR (ex-USS *Garfield Thomas, DE 193*)	67

Displacement, tons: 1 240 standard; 1 900 full load
Length, feet (metres): 306 (*93·3*) oa
Beam, feet (metres): 36·7 (*11·2*)
Draught, feet (metres): 14 (*4·3*)
Guns: 3—3 in (*76 mm*) 50 cal. 6—40 mm, (3 twin)
  14—20 mm (7 twin)
A/S weapons: Hedgehog; 8 DCT; 1 DC rack
Torpedo racks: Side launching for A/S torpedoes
Main engines: 4 sets GM diesel-electric 6 000 bhp; 2 shafts
Speed, knots: 19·25
Oil fuel, tons: 316
Range, miles: 9 000 at 12 knots
Complement: 220

Aetos and *Ierax* were transferred on 15 Mar 1951 and *Leon* and *Panthir* on 15 Jan 1951. Their 3—21 inch torpedo tubes in a triple mount were removed.

Builders	Laid down	Launched	Commissioned
Tampa SB Co.	9 Mar 1943	13 Feb 1944	1 May 1944
Tampa SB Co.	1 Apr 1943	23 May 1944	12 July 1944
Federal SB & DD Co.	22 Feb 1943	25 June1943	27 Aug 1943
Federal SB & DD Co.	23 Sep 1943	12 Dec 1943	24 Jan 1944

LEON   *1972, Hellenic Navy*

CORVETTES

5 Ex-BRITISH "ALGERINE" CLASS

Name	No.	Builders	Laid down	Launched	Commissioned
ARMATOLOS (ex-HMS *Aries*)	.M 12	Redfern Construction Co	23 Mar 1942	19 Sep 1942	17 July 1943
MAHITIS (ex-HMS *Postillion*)	M 58	Redfern Construction Co	17 Nov 1942	18 Mar 1942	25 Nov 1943
NAVMACHOS (ex-HMS *Lightfoot*)	M 64	Redfern Construction Co	18 Aug 1942	14 Nov 1942	19 Oct 1943
POLEMISTIS (ex-HMS *Gozo*)	M 74	Redfern Construction Co	5 Aug 1942	27 Jan 1943	29 Sep 1943
PYRPOLITIS (ex-HMS *Arcturus*)	A 476	Redfern Construction Co	21 Feb 1942	21 Aug 1942	23 Oct 1943

Displacement, tons: 1 030 standard; 1 325 full load
Length, feet (metres): 225 *(68·6)* oa
Beam, feet (metres): 35·5 *(10·8)*
Draught, feet (metres): 11·5 *(3·5)*
Guns: 2—3 in *(76 mm)* (US Mark 21) (1 in *Pyrpolitis*, none in *Polemistis* or *Mahitis*); 4—20 mm (US), 2 MG
A/S weapons: 2 to 4 DCT
Main engines: 2 triple expansion, 2 shafts; 2 700 ihp
Speed, knots: 16
Boilers: 2 Yarrow, 250 psi *(17·6 kg cm²)*
Oil fuel, tons: 235
Range, miles: 5 000 at 10 knots; 2 270 at 14·5 knots
Complement: 85

Former British ocean minesweepers. Acquired from the Executive Committee of Surplus Allied Material. Latterly employed as Corvettes. The armament of *Mahitis* was removed when she became a training ship. *Armatolos* now used as a light house tender and the others as personnel transports—*Pyrpolitis* as training ship for POs School, Poros. One, identity unknown, reported sunk as target.

POLEMISTIS

1974, Hellenic Navy

SUBMARINES

4 + 4 TYPE 209 "GLAVKOS" CLASS

Name	No.	Builders	Laid down	Launched	Commissioned
GLAVKOS	S 110	Howaldtswerke, Kiel	—	Sep 1970	5 Nov 1971
NEREUS	S 111	Howaldtswerke, Kiel	—	Sep 1971	10 Feb 1972
PROTEUS	S 113	Howaldtswerke, Kiel	—	Dec 1971	8 Aug 1972
TRITON	S 112	Howaldtswerke, Kiel	—	1971	23 Nov 1972

Displacement, tons: 990 surfaced; 1 290 dived
Length, feet (metres): 177·1 *(54·0)*
Beam, feet (metres): 20·3 *(6·2)*
Torpedo tubes: 8—21 in (with reloads) bow
Main machinery: Diesel-electric; 4 MTU; Siemens diesel-generators; 1 Siemens electric motor; 1 shaft
Speed, knots: 10 surfaced; 22 dived
Range: 50 days
Complement: 31

Designed by Ingenieurkontor, Lübeck for construction by Howaldtswerke, Kiel and sale by Ferrostaal Essen all acting as a consortium.
A single-hull design with two ballast tanks and forward and after trim tanks. Fitted with snort and remote machinery control. The single screw is slow revving. Very high capacity batteries with GRP lead-acid cells and battery cooling—by Wilh. Hagen and VARTA. Active and passive sonar, sonar detection equipment, sound ranging and underwater telephone. Fitted with two periscopes, radar and Omega receiver.

TRITON

1973, Hellenic Navy

NEW CONSTRUCTION

A further three of this class were ordered from Howaldtswerke in a contract signed 1 Nov 1975 and a fourth in Sep 1976.

1 Ex-US "GUPPY III" CLASS

Name	No.	Builders	Laid down	Launched	Commissioned
KATSONIS (ex-USS *Remora*, SS 487)	S 115	Portsmouth Navy Yard	5 Mar 1945	12 July 1945	3 Jan 1946

Displacement, tons: 1 975 standard; 2 450 dived
Dimensions, feet (metres): 326 × 27 × 17 *(99·4 × 8·2 × 5·2)*
Torpedo tubes: 10—21 in; 6 bow, 4 stern
Main machinery: 4 diesels; 6 400 hp; 2 electric motors; 5 400 shp; 2 shafts
Speed, knots: 20 surfaced; 15 dived
Range, miles: 12 000 at 10 knots (surfaced)
Complement: 85

Originally of the wartime "Tench" class, subsequently converted under the Guppy II programme and, in 1961-62 to Guppy III. Amongst other modifications this involved the fitting of BQG-4 Sonar (Puffs) for dived fire-control, in addition to the BQR-2 array sonar. Transferred 29 Oct 1973.

KATSONIS

1974, Commander Aldo Fraccaroli

1 Ex-US "GUPPY IIA" CLASS

Name	No.	Builders	Laid down	Launched	Commissioned
PAPANIKOLIS (ex-USS *Hardhead, SS 365*)	S 114	Manitowoc SB Co	7 July 1943	12 Dec 1943	April 1944

Displacement, tons: 1 840 standard; 2 445 dived
Length, feet (metres): 306 *(93·2)*
Beam, feet (metres): 27 *(8·3)*
Draught, feet (metres): 17 *(5·2)*
Torpedo tubes: 10—21 inch; 6 bow, 4 stern
Main machinery: 3 diesels; 4 800 shp;
2 Motors, 5 400 shp; 2 shafts
Speed, knots: 17 surfaced; 15 dived
Range, miles: 12 000 at 10 knots (surfaced)
Complement: 84

Transferred 26 July 1972.

PAPANIKOLIS

1973, Hellenic Navy

1 Ex-US "BALAO" CLASS

Name	No.	Builders	Commissioned
TRIAINA (ex-USS *Scabbard Fish SS 397*)	S 86	Portsmouth Navy Yard	29 Apr 1944

Displacement, tons: 1 816 surfaced; 2 425 dived
Length, feet (metres): 311·5 *(94·9)* oa
Beam, feet (metres): 27·0 *(8·2)*
Draught, feet (metres): 17·0 *(5·2)*
Torpedo tubes: 10—21 in *(533 mm)*, 6 bow, 4 stern
Main machinery: 6 500 bhp diesels (surface), 4 610 hp motors
(submerged)
Speed, knots: 20 on surface, 10 submerged
Range, miles: 12 000 at 10 knots (surface)
Complement: 85

Originally one of the wartime "Balao" class later having a
streamlined fin fitted. Transferred 26 Feb 1965.

TRIAINA

1974, Hellenic Navy

LIGHT FORCES

4 "LA COMBATTANTE III" CLASS (FAST ATTACK CRAFT—MISSILE)

Name	No.	Builders	Commissioned
ANTIPLOIARHOS LASKOS	P 50	Construction M. de Normandie	Oct 1976
PLOTARHIS BLESSAS	P 51	Construction M. de Normandie	Jan 1977
IPOPLOIARHOS TROUPAKIS	P 52	Construction M. de Normandie	1977
IPOPLOIARHOS MIKONIOS	P 53	Construction M. de Normandie	1977

Displacement, tons: 385 standard; 425 full load
Dimensions, feet (metres): 184 × 26 × 7 *(56·2 × 8 × 2·1)*
Missiles: 4 MM 38 Exocet
Guns: 2—76 mm Breda; 4—30 mm Emerlec (twins)
Torpedo tubes: 2—21 in *(533 mm)*
Main engines: 4 MTU diesels; 18 000 bhp; 4 shafts (cp propellers) = 35·7 knots
Range, miles: 700 at 32·6 knots; 2 000 at 15 knots
Complement: 42

Ordered in September 1974. *A. Laskos* laid down 28 June 1975, launched 6 July 1976; *P. Blessas*
laid down 5 Nov 1975, launched 10 Nov 1976; *I. Troupakis* laid down 27 Jan 1976, launched Jan
1977.

Radar: Surveillance and navigation: 1 Triton
Fire control: I band

ANTIPLOIARHOS LASKOS

9/1976, CMN

4 + 6 "LA COMBATTANTE II" CLASS (FAST ATTACK CRAFT—MISSILE)

Name	No.	Builders	Commissioned
IPOPLOIARHOS ARLIOTIS	P 55	C. M. de Normandie, Cherbourg	April 1972
IPOPLOIARHOS ANNINOS	P 56	C. M. de Normandie, Cherbourg	June 1972
IPOPLOIARHOS BATSIS	P 54	C. M. de Normandie, Cherbourg	Dec 1971
IPOPLOIARHOS KONIDIS	P 53	C. M. de Normandie, Cherbourg	July 1972

Displacement, tons: 234 standard; 255 full load
Dimensions, feet (metres): 154·2 × 23·3 × 8·2 *(47 × 7·1 × 2·5)*
Missiles: 4 MM 38 Exocet surface-to-surface
Guns: 4—35 mm (2 twin)
Torpedo tubes: 2 aft for wire-guided torpedoes
Main engines: 4 MTU diesels; 4 shafts; 12 000 bhp = 36·5 knots
Oil fuel, tons: 39
Range, miles: 850 at 25 knots
Complement: 40 (4 officers, and 36 men)

Ordered in 1969. Fitted with Thomson CSF Triton radar and Plessey IFF Mk 10. *I. Arliotis*
launched 26 April 1971. *I. Anninos* launched 8 Sep 1971. *I. Batsis* launched 26 Jan 1971. *I. Konidis*
launched 20 Dec 1971. Six more ordered 23 Dec 1976, first pair to be built at Cherbourg,
remainder in Greece.

I. KONIDIS

1973, Hellenic Navy

2 Ex-US "ASHEVILLE" CLASS (LARGE PATROL CRAFT)

Name	No.	Builders	Commissioned
— (ex-USS *Beacon, PG 99)*	—	Peterson Builders	21 Nov 1969
— (ex-USS *Green Bay, PG 101)*	—	Peterson Builders	5 Dec 1969

Displacement, tons: 225 standard; 245 full load
Dimensions, feet (metres): 164·5 × 23·5 × 9·5 *(50·2 × 7·2 × 2 9)*
Guns: 1—3 in *(76 mm)* 50 cal forward; 1—40 mm; 4—50 cal MG
Main engines: Codag; 2 Cummins diesels; 1 450 hp; 2 shafts = 16 knots.
    1 GE gas turbine; 13 300 hp; 2 shafts = 40+ knots
Complement: 27

Transferred 1 April 1977.

Ex-BEACON   9/1975, Dr. Giorgio Arra

5 "SILBERMÖWE" CLASS (FAST ATTACK CRAFT—TORPEDO)

Name	No.	Builders	Commissioned
DOLPHIN (ex-*Sturmmöwe*)	P 15	Lurrsen, Vegesack	1951-1956
DRAKON (ex-*Silbermöwe*)	P 16	Lurssen, Vegesack	1951-1956
FOINIX (ex-*Eismöwe*)	P 27	Lurssen, Vegesack	1951-1956
POLIKOS (ex-*Raubmöwe*)	P 17	Lurssen, Vegesack	1951-1956
POLIDEFKIS (ex-*Wildschwan*)	P 18	Lurssen, Vegesack	1951-1956

Displacement, tons: 119 standard; 155 full load
Dimensions, feet (metres): 116·1 × 16·7 × 5·9 *(35·5 × 5·1 × 1·8)*
Torpedo tubes: 2—21 in
Guns: 1—40 mm; 2—20 mm (1 twin)
Main engines: 3 diesels; 3 shafts; 9 000 bhp = 38 knots

Old S-Boote taken over from Germany 17 Dec 1968. Due for deletion.

2 FAST ATTACK CRAFT (MISSILE)

Name	No.	Builders	Commissioned
KELEFSTIS STAMOU	P 28	Ch. N. de l'Esterel	1975
DIOPOS ANTONIOU	P 29	Ch. N. de l'Esterel	1976

Displacement, tons: 80
Dimensions, feet (metres): 105 × 21 × 5·2 *(32 × 6·4 × 1·6)*
Missiles: 4—SS 12
Guns: 2—20 mm
Main engines: 2 MTU 12V 331 TC81 diesels; 2 700 hp = 30 knots
Range, miles: 1 500 at 15 knots
Complement: 17

Wooden hulls. Originally ordered for Cyprus; later transferred to Greece.

5 "NASTY" CLASS (FAST ATTACK CRAFT—TORPEDO)

Name	No.	Builders	Commissioned
ANDROMEDA	P 21	Mandal, Norway	Feb 1967
KASTOR	P 23	Mandal, Norway	1967
KYKNOS	P 24	Mandal, Norway	1967
PIGASSOS	P 25	Mandal, Norway	1967
TOXOTIS	P 26	Mandal, Norway	1967

Displacement, tons: 69 standard; 76 full load
Dimensions, feet (metres): 75 pp; 80·4 oa × 24·6 × 6·9 *(22·9; 24·5 × 7·5 × 2·1)*
Torpedo tubes: 4—21 in
Guns: 2—40 mm
Main engines: 2 Napier Deltic T 18-37 K diesels; 3 100 bhp = 43 knots
Complement: 22

Andromeda and *Inionos* (deleted 1972) were taken over in Feb 1967 from Mandal, Norway. *Kastor* and *Kyknos,* and the third pair, *Pigassos* and *Toxotis,* were delivered in succession in 1967.

ANDROMEDA   1974, Hellenic Navy

7 Ex-GERMAN "JAGUAR" CLASS
(FAST ATTACK CRAFT—TORPEDO)

Name	No.	Builders	Commissioned
ESPEROS (ex-*Seeadler P 6068*)	P 196	FDR	1958
KATAIGIS (ex-*Falke P 6072*)	P 197	FDR	1958
KENTAUROS (ex-*Habicht P 6075*)	P 198	FDR	1958
KYKLON (ex-*Greif P 6071*)	P 199	FDR	1958
LAIAPS (ex-*Kondor P 6070*)	P 228	FDR	1958
SCORPIOS (ex-*Kormoran P 6077*)	P 229	FDR	1958
TYFON (ex-*Geier P 6073*)	P 230	FDR	1958

Displacement, tons: 160 standard; 190 full load
Dimensions, feet (metres): 139·4 × 23·4 × 7·9 *(42·5 × 7·2 × 2·4)*
Guns: 2—40 mm Bofors L70 (single)
Torpedo tubes: 4—21 inch
Main engines: 4 Diesels; 4 shafts; 12 000 bhp—42 knots
Complement: 39

Transferred 1976-77. First three commissioned in Hellenic Navy 12 Dec 1976. Three others (ex-*Albatros,* ex-*Bussard* and ex-*Sperber*) transferred at same time for spares. Built by Lürssen Vegesack or Kroger Rendsburg.

GEIER (before transfer)   1975, Reiner Nerlich

1 VOSPER "BRAVE" CLASS
(FAST ATTACK CRAFT—TORPEDO)

Name	No.	Builders	Commissioned
ASTRAPI (ex-*Strahl P6194*)	P 20	Vosper, Portsmouth	21 Nov 1962

Displacement, tons: 95 standard; 110 full load
Dimensions, feet (metres): 99 oa × 25 × 7 *(30·2 × 7·6 × 2·1)*
Torpedo chutes: 4—21 in side launching
Guns: 2—40 mm
Main engines: 3 Bristol Siddeley Marine Proteus gas turbines; 3 shafts; 12 750 bhp = 55·5 knots

Launched on 10 Jan 1962. Commissioned in Federal German Navy on 21 Nov 1962. Transferred to Royal Hellenic Navy in Apr 1967. Refitted by Vosper in 1968. Of similar design to British "Brave" class.

ASTRAPI   1972, Hellenic Navy

1 VOSPER "FEROCITY" CLASS
(FAST ATTACK CRAFT—TORPEDO)

Name	No.	Builders	Commissioned
AIOLOS (ex-*Pfeil P 6193*)	P 19	Vosper, Portsmouth	27 June 1962

Displacement, tons: 75 standard; 80 full load
Dimensions, feet (metres): 92 wl; 95 oa × 23·9 × 6·5 *(28·1; 29 × 7·3 × 2)*
Torpedo chutes: 4—21 in side launching
Guns: 2—40 mm
Main engines: 2 Bristol Siddeley Marine Proteus gas turbines; 2 shafts; 8 500 bhp = 50 knots

Launched on 26 Oct 1961. Commissioned in German Navy on 27 June 1962. Transferred to Royal Hellenic Navy in Apr 1967. Refitted by Vosper in 1968. Based on design of Vosper prototype *Ferocity*.

AIOLOS   1972, Hellenic Navy

10 FAST ATTACK CRAFT—PATROL

Displacement, tons: 75
Dimensions, feet (metres): 95·1 × 16·2 × — *(29 × 5 × —)*
Speed, knots: 28
Complement: 20

Ordered from Skaramanga Shipyard in May 1976.

3 Ex-US "PGM-9" CLASS (LARGE PATROL CRAFT)

ANTIPLIARKOS PEZOPOULOS (ex-*PGM 21*, ex-*PC 1552*) P 70
PLOTARKHIS ARSLANOGLOU (ex-*PGM 25*, ex-*PC 1565*) P 14
PLOTARKHIS CHADZIKONSTANDIS (ex-*PGM 29*, ex-*PC 1565*) P 96

Displacement, tons: 335 standard; 439 full load
Dimensions, feet (metres): 170 wl; 174·7 oa × 23 × 10·8 *(51·8; 53·3 × 7 × 3·3)*
Guns: 1—3 in; 6—20 mm
A/S weapons: Hedgehog; side launching torpedo racks; depth charges
Main engines: 2 GM diesels; 2 shafts; 3 600 bhp = 19 knots

All launched in 1943-44. Acquired from USA in Aug 1947. The two 40 mm guns were removed and a Hedgehog was installed in 1963.

ANTIPLIARKOS PEZOPOULOS   1973, Hellenic Navy

3 + ? COASTAL PATROL CRAFT

Name	No.	Builders	Commissioned
N. I. GOULANDRIAS I	P 22	Syros Shipyard	June 25 1975
E. PANAGOPOULOS	—	Syros Shipyard	June 23 1976
N. I. GOULANDRIAS II	—	Syros Shipyard	1977

Displacement, tons: 38·5
Dimensions, feet (metres): 78·7 × 20·3 × 3·4 *(24 × 6·2 × 1·1)*
Speed, knots: 25
Range, miles: 1 600 at cruising speed

The first of these craft was donated to the Hellenic Navy by the wealthy shipowner after whom she is named. She is lead craft of a number of the same type, most of them donated by Greek shipowners.

2 Ex-FDR "KW" CLASS

ARHIKELEFSTIS STASSIS   **ARHIKELEFSTIS MALIOPOULOS**

Transferred 1976.

AMPHIBIOUS FORCES

1 Ex-US "CABILDO" CLASS (LSD)

Name	No.	Builders	Commissioned
NAFKRATOUSSA	L 153	Boston Navy Yard	31 Oct 1945
(ex-USS *Fort Mandan, LSD 21*)			

Displacement, tons: 4 790 light; 9 357 full load
Dimensions, feet (metres): 457·8 oa × 72·2 × 18 *(139·6 × 22 × 5·5)*
Guns: 8—40 mm
Main engines: Geared turbines; 2 shafts; 7 000 shp = 15·4 knots
Boilers: 2

Laid down on 2 Jan 1945. Launched on 22 May 1945. Taken over from USA in 1971 replacing the previous *Nafkratoussa* (ex-*Hyperion*, ex-*LSD 9*) out of service in 1971 as Headquarters ship of Captain, Landing Forces.

NAFKRATOUSSA   1973, Hellenic Navy

2 Ex-US "TERREBONNE PARISH" CLASS (LSTs)

Name	No.	Builders	Commissioned
— (ex-USS *Terrell County, LST 1157*)	—	Bath Iron Works Corpn	19 Mar 1953
— (ex-USS *Whitfield County, LST 1169*)	—	Christy Corpn	14 Sep 1954

Displacement, tons: 2 590 light; 5 800 full load
Dimensions, feet (metres): 384 oa × 55 × 17 *(117·1 × 16·7 × 5·2)*
Guns: 6—3 in 50 cal
Main engines: 4 GM diesels; 6 000 bhp; 2 shafts (cp propellers) = 15 knots
Complement: 115
Troops: 395

Part of class of fifteen—transferred late 1976. Discussions on purchase of second pair.

8 Ex-US LSTs
(2 of 511—1152 series, 6 of 1—510 series)

511—1152 Series

IKARIA (ex-USS *Potter County, LST 1086*) L 154
KRITI (ex-USS *Page County, LST 1076*) L 171

1—510 Series

CHIOS (ex-USS *LST 35*) L 195
LESBOS (ex-USS *Boone County, LST 389*) L 172
LIMNOS (ex-USS *LST 36*) L 158
RODOS (ex-USS *Bowman County, LST 391*) L 157
SAMOS (ex-USS *LST 33*) L 179
SYROS (ex-USS *LST 325*) L 144

Displacement, tons: 1 653 standard; 2 366 beaching; 4 080 full load
Dimensions, feet (metres): 328 × 50 × 14 *(100 × 15·3 × 2·9)*
Guns: 8—40 mm; 6—20 mm *(Rodos 10—40 mm)*
Main engines: 2 GM diesels; 2 shafts; 1 700 bhp = 11·6 knots
Range, miles: 9 500 at 9 knots
Complement: 93 (8 officers, 85 men)

Former United States tank landing ships. Cargo capacity 2 100 tons. *Ikaria*, *Lesbos* and *Rodos* were transferred to the Royal Hellenic Navy on 9 Aug 1960. *Syros* was transferred on 29 May 1964 at Portsmouth, Virginia, under MAP. *Kriti* was transferred in Mar 1971. Others under lease-lend in 1943.

RODOS   1976, Michael D. J. Lennon

5 Ex-US "LSM 1" CLASS

IPOPLIARKHOS KRISTALIDIS (ex-USS *LSM 541*) L 165
IPOPLIARKHOS DANIOLOS (ex-USS *LSM 227*) L 163
IPOPLIARKHOS GRIGOROPOULOS (ex-USS *LSM 45*) L 161
IPOPLIARKHOS ROUSSEN (ex-USS *LSM 399*) L 164
IPOPLIARKHOS TOURNAS (ex-USS *LSM 102*) L 162

Displacement, tons: 743 beaching; 1 095 full load
Dimensions, feet (metres): 196·5 wl; 203·5 oa × 34·2 × 8·3 *(59·9; 62·1 × 10·4 × 2·5)*
Guns: 2—40 mm; 8—20 mm
Main engines: Diesel direct drive; 2 shafts; 3 600 bhp = 13 knots

LSM 541 was handed over to Greece at Salamis on 30 Oct 1958 and *LSM 45, LSM 102, LSM 227* and *LSM 399* at Portsmouth, Virginia on 3 Nov 1958. All were renamed after naval heroes killed during World War 2.

IPOPLIARKHOS KRISTALIDIS   1974, Hellenic Navy

6 Ex-US "LCU 501" CLASS (Ex-LCT 6)

Name	No.	Builders	Commissioned
KARPATHOS (ex-*LCU 1379*)	L 146	—	1944
KASSOS (ex-*LCU 1382*)	L 145	—	1944
KIMONOS (ex-*LCU 971*)	L 147	—	1944
KITHNOS (ex-*LCU 763*)	L 149	—	1944
SIFNOS (ex-*LCU 677*)	L 150	—	1944
SKIATHOS (ex-*LCU 827*)	L 152	—	1944

Displacement, tons: 143 standard; 309 full load
Dimensions, feet (metres): 105 wl; 119 oa × 32·7 × 5 *(32; 36·3 × 10 × 1·5)*
Guns: 2—20 mm
Main engines: Diesel; 3 shafts; 440 bhp = 8 knots
Complement: 13

Former US Utility Landing Craft of the *LCU* (ex-*LCT 6*) type. *Skiathos* acquired in 1959. *Kithnos* and *Sifnos* were transferred from USA in 1961, and *Karpathos, Kassos* and *Kimonos* in 1962.

KITHNOS   1971, Hellenic Navy

13 LCMs

Transferred from USA.

34 LCVPs

Transferred from USA.

MINE WARFARE FORCES

2 COASTAL MINELAYERS

Name	No.	Builders	Commissioned
AKTION (ex-LSM 301, ex-MMC 6)	N 04	Charleston Naval Shipyard	1 Jan 1945
AMVRAKIA (ex-LSM 303, ex-MMC 7)	N 05	Charleston Naval Shipyard	6 Jan 1945

Displacement, tons: 720 standard; 1 100 full load
Dimensions, feet (metres): 203·5 oa × 34·5 × 8·3 (62·1 × 10·5 × 2·5)
Guns: 8—40 mm (4 twin); 6—20 mm (single)
Mines: Capacity 100 to 130
Main engines: 2 diesels; 2 shafts; 3 600 bhp = 12·5 knots
Range, miles: 3 000 at 12 knots
Complement: 65

Former US "LSM 1" Class. Aktion was launched on 1 Jan 1945 and Amvrakia on 14 Nov 1944. Converted in the USA into minelayers for the Royal Hellenic Navy. Underwent extensive rebuilding from the deck up. Twin rudders. Transferred on 1 Dec 1953.

AMVRAKIA *1974, Hellenic Navy*

10 Ex-US "FALCON" CLASS (MINESWEEPERS—COASTAL)

Name	No.	Builders	Commissioned
AEDON (ex-MSC 310)	M 248	Peterson Builders	13 Oct 1964
AIGLI (ex-MSC 299)	M 246	Tacoma, California	4 Jan 1965
ALKYON (ex-MSC 319)	M 211	Peterson Builders	3 Dec 1968
ARGO (ex-MSC 317)	M 213	Peterson Builders	7 Aug 1968
AVRA (ex-MSC 318)	M 214	Peterson Builders	3 Oct 1968
DAFNI (ex-MSC 307)	M 247	Peterson Builders	23 Sep 1964
DORIS (ex-MSC 298)	M 245	Tacoma, California	9 Nov 1964
KICHLI (ex-MSC 308)	M 241	Peterson Builders	14 July 1964
KISSA (ex-MSC 309)	M 242	Peterson Builders	1 Sep 1964
PLEIAS (ex-MSC 314)	M 240	Peterson Builders	22 June 1967

Displacement, tons: 320 standard; 370 full load
Dimensions, feet (metres): 138 pp; 144 oa × 28 × 8·2 (42·1; 43·3 × 8·5 × 2·5)
Guns: 2—20 mm (twin)
Main engines: 2 GM diesels; 2 shafts; 880 bhp = 13 knots
Complement: 39

Built in USA for Greece. Wooden hulls.

AVRA *1974, Hellenic Navy*

5 Ex-US "ADJUTANT" CLASS (MINESWEEPERS—COASTAL)

ANTIOPI (ex-Belgian Herve, M 921, ex-USS MSC 153) M 205
ATALANTI (ex-Belgian St. Truiden, M 919, ex-USS MSC 169) M 202
NIOVI (ex-Belgian Laroche, M 924, ex-USS MSC 171) M 254
FAEDRA (ex-Belgian Malmedy, M 922, ex-USS MSC 154) M 206
THALIA (ex-Belgian Blankenberge, M 923, ex-USS MSC 170) M 210

Displacement, tons: 330 standard; 402 full load
Dimensions, feet (metres): 145·0 oa × 27·9 × 8·0 (44·2 × 8·5 × 2·4)
Guns: 2—20 mm Oerlikon (1 twin)
Main engines: 2 GM diesels; 2 shafts; 900 bhp = 14 knots
Complement: 38 officers and men

Originally supplied to Belgium under MDAP. Subsequently returned to USA and simultaneously transferred to Greece as follows:— 29 July 1969 (Herve and St. Truiden) and 26 Sep 1969 (Laroche, Malmedy and Blankenberge). Atalanti employed on surveying duties.

ANTIOPI *1973, Dr. Giorgio Arra*

SURVEY AND RESEARCH VESSELS

Name	No.	Builders	Commissioned
NAFTILOS	A 478	Annastadiades Tsortanides (Perama)	Mar 1976

Displacement, tons: 1 400
Dimensions, feet (metres): 207 × 38 × 13·3 (63·1 × 11·6 × 4·2)
Main engines: 1 B and W diesel; 2 640 hp = 15 knots
Complement: 74 (8 officers, 66 men)

Launched 19 Nov 1975. Trials Feb 1976.

ATALANTI

Of "Adjutant" class MSCs. For details see Minewarfare Forces.

ANEMOS (ex-German KFK KW7) A 469

Displaces 112 tons, was launched in 1944 and has a complement of 16. Added to the Navy List in 1969.

1 Ex-US "BARNEGAT" CLASS

Name	No.	Builders	Commissioned
HEPHESTOS (ex-USNS Josiah Willard Gibbs, T-AGOR 1, ex-USS San Carlos, AVP 51)	A 413	Lake Washington Shipyard, Houghton, Wash.	21 Mar 1944

Displacement, tons: 1 750 standard; 2 800 full load
Dimensions, feet (metres): 300·0 wl; 310·8 oa × 41·2 × 13·5 (91·5; 94·8 × 12·6 × 4·1)
Main engines: 2 Fairbanks-Morse diesels; 2 shafts; 6 080 bhp = 18 knots
Range, miles: 10 000 at 14 knots
Endurance: 30 days
Complement: 82 (8 officers and 74 men)

Former US seaplane tender converted for oceanographic research. Laid down on 7 Sep 1942, launched on 20 Dec 1942. Transferred to the Hellenic Navy on 7 Dec 1971.

HEPHESTOS *1974, Hellenic Navy*

1 SURVEYING LAUNCH

Of 25 tons, launched in 1940. Complement 9.

SERVICE FORCES

1 NEW CONSTRUCTION TRAINING SHIP

Of 3 200 tons. Laid down in Oct 1976 at Salamis.

1 Ex-FDR DEPOT SHIP

Name	No.	Builders	Commissioned
AEGEON (ex-*Weser A 62*)	A 215	Elsflether Werft	1960

Displacement, tons: 2 370
Dimensions, feet (metres): 323·5 × 38·8 × 11·2 *(99 × 11·8 × 3·4)*
Guns: 2—3·9 in *(100 mm)*; 4—40 mm
Main engines: 6 Diesels; 12 000 hp
Speed, knots: 20·5
Range, miles: 1 625 at 15 knots (economical)
Complement: 110

Transferred 1976. Currently employed on frigate duties.

AEGEON   7/1976, Roland Wiegran

2 Ex-US "PATAPSCO" CLASS (SUPPORT TANKERS)

Name	No.	Builders	Commissioned
ARETHOUSA (ex-USS *Natchaug, AOG 54*)	A 377	Cargill Inc, Savage, Minn.	1945
ARIADNI (ex-USS *Tombigbee, AOG 11*)	A 414	Cargill Inc, Savage, Minn.	12 July 1944

Displacement, tons: 1 850 light; 4 335 full load
Measurement, tons: 2 575 deadweight; cargo capacity 2 040
Dimensions, feet (metres): 292 wl; 310·8 oa × 48·5 × 15·7 *(89·1; 93·2 × 14·8 × 4·8)*
Guns: 4—3 in; 50 cal
Main engines: GM diesels; 2 shafts; 3 300 bhp = 14 knots
Complement: 43 (6 officers, 37 men)

Former US petrol carriers. *Arethousa* laid down on 15 Aug 1944. Launched on 16 Dec 1944. Transferred from the USA to Greece under the Mutual Defense Assistance Program in July 1959 and *Ariadni* transferred 7 July 1972, both at Pearl Harbor.

ARETHOUSA   1972, Hellenic Navy

1 AMMUNITION SHIP

Name	No.	Builders	Commissioned
EVROS (ex-FDR *Schwarzwald* A1400, ex-*Amalthee*)	—	Ch. Dubigeon Nantes	1957

Measurement, tons: 1 667 gross
Dimensions, feet (metres): 263·1 × 39 × 15·1 *(80·2 × 11·9 × 4·6)*
Guns: 4—40 mm Bofors
Main engines: Sulzer diesel; 3 000 bhp = 15 knots

Bought by FDR from Societé Navale Caënnaise in Feb 1960. Transferred to Greece 6 June 1976.

EVROS (as *Schwarzwald*)   1971

2 NEW CONSTRUCTION HARBOUR TANKERS

Announced on 24 June 1976 that two 1 200 ton tankers were under construction.

1 HARBOUR TANKER

VIVIES A 471

Originally a water carrier. Capacity 687 tons.

1 HARBOUR TANKER

KRONOS (ex-*Islay*, ex-*Dresden*) A 373

Displacement, tons: 311
Capacity: 110 tons

ORION (ex-US tanker *Y 126*) A 376

Formerly small United States yard tanker. Capacity 700 tons.

1 HARBOUR TANKER

SIRIOS (ex-*Poseidon*, ex-*Empire Faun*) A 345

Formerly on loan from Great Britain, but purchased outright in 1962. This ship was renamed *Sirios* when the name *Poseidon* was given to the submarine *Lapon* acquired from the USA in 1958. Capacity 850 tons.

1 PETROL CARRIER

ZEUS (ex-*YOG 98*) A 372

Dimensions, feet (metres): 165 × 35 × 10 *(50·3 × 10·2 × 3·2)*

Former US yard petrol carrier. Launched in 1944. Capacity 900 tons.

1 HARBOUR TANKER

ORION   1969, Hellenic Navy

1 YACHT

THESSEUS

Ex-Royal Yacht used for VIP visits.

1 SALVAGE SHIP

SOTIR (ex-*Salventure*) A 384

Displacement, tons: 1 440 standard; 1 700 full load
Measurement, tons: 1 112 gross
Dimensions, feet (metres): 216 oa × 37·8 × 13 *(65·9 × 11·5 × 4)*
Main engines: Triple expansion; 2 shafts; 1 500 ihp = 12 knots
Oil fuel, tons: 310
Complement: 60

Former British Royal Fleet Auxiliary ocean salvage vessel of the "Salv" class. On loan from Great Britain. Equipped with a recompression chamber.

SOTIR   *1972, Dr. Giorgio Arra*

1 REPAIR SHIP

Name	No.	Builders	Commissioned
SAKIPIS (ex-*HNoMS Ellida*, ex-USS *ARB 18*, ex-USS *LST 50*)	A 329	Dravo Corporation, Pittsburgh	27 Nov 1943

Displacement, tons: 3 800 standard; 5 000 full load
Dimensions, feet (metres): 316 wl; 328 oa × 50 × 11 *(96·4; 100 × 15·3 × 3·4)*
Guns: 12—40 mm; 12—20 mm
Main engines: GM diesels; 2 shafts; 1 800 bhp = 10 knots
Complement: 200

Laid down on 29 Aug 1943, launched on 16 Oct 1943. Converted to a repair ship in 1952 by Puget Sound Bridge & Dry Dock Co. Taken over by the Royal Norwegian Navy at Seattle on 14 Nov 1952. Returned to the US Navy on 1 July 1960. Transferred to Greece on 16 Sep 1960 at Bergen.

SAKIPIS   *1972, Hellenic Navy*

1 NETLAYER

Name	No.	Builders	Commissioned
THETIS (ex-USS *AN 103*)	A 307	Krüger, Rendsburg	April 1960

Displacement, tons: 680 standard; 805 full load
Dimensions, feet (metres): 146 wl; 169·5 oa × 33·5 × 11·8 *(44·5; 51·7 × 10·2 × 3·6)*
Guns: 1—40 mm; 4—20 mm
Main engines: MAN diesels; 1 shaft; 1 400 bhp = 12 knots
Complement: 48

US offshore order. Launched in 1959.

THETIS   *1971, Hellenic Navy*

2 AUXILIARY TRANSPORTS

Name	No.	Builders	Commissioned
PANDORA	A 415	Perama Shipyard	1973
PANDROSOS	A 416	Perama Shipyard	1974

Displacement, tons: 350
Length, feet (metres): 212·2 *(64·6)*
Speed, knots: 13

Launched 1972 and 1973. Transport capacity for 500 people.

2 LIGHTHOUSE TENDERS

ST. LYKOUDIS A 481
I. THEOPHILOPOULOS KARAVOYIANNOS A 485

Displacement, tons: 1 350
Length, feet (metres): 207·3 *(63·2)*

Built at Perama Shipyard 1976-77. Have facilities for small helicopter.

12 TUGS

ACCHILEUS (ex-USS *Confident*) A 409
AIAS (ex-USS *Ankachak*, YTM 767)
ANTAIOS (ex-USS *Busy*, YTM 2012) A 407
ATLAS (ex-*F 5*) A 408
ATROMITOS A 410
CIGAS A 432

MINOTAUROS (ex-*Theseus*, ex-*ST 539*) A 421
PATRAIKOS A 427
PERSEUS (ex-*ST 722*) A 429
ROMALEOS A 418
SAMSON (ex-*F 16*) A 430
TITAN A 431

Ankachak transferred on lease 1972.

8 WATER BOATS

ILIKI A 474   **KALLIROE** A —   **TRIHONIS** A 473
KASTORIA A 470   **PRESPA** A —   **VOLVI** A 467
KERKINI (ex-FDR FW)   **STYMFALIA** A 472

Capacity: *Iliki* and *Stymfalia* 120 tons, *Trihonis* 300 tons, *Volvi* 350 tons, *Kastoria* 520 tons. *Kerkini*, of 350 ton DWT transferred by FDR 1976. *Kalliroe* and *Prespa* completed at Perama Shipyard on 13 Dec 1976. (600 tons).

2 + 1 FLOATING CRANES

Two under construction in Greece with another ordered.

GRENADA

Grenada was granted self-government, in association with Great Britain (who was responsible for her defence) on 3 March 1967.
Full self-government was achieved in February 1973.

Mercantile Marine

Lloyd's Register of Shipping: 2 vessels of 226 tons gross

---

1 COASTAL PATROL CRAFT

Displacement, tons: 15
Dimensions, feet (metres): 40 × 12 × 2 *(12·2 × 3·7 × 0·6)*
Guns: 3 MG
Main engines: 2 Diesels; 370 hp = 22 knots

Delivered by Brooke Marine, Lowestoft early in 1972.

GUATEMALA

On 5 Jan 1959 Guatemala announced the establishment of a navy for coastguard work. Subsequently the navy was assigned missions of search and rescue and the support of amphibious operations. The commissioning of a Marine Elevator (Synchrolift) at Santo Tomás on 23 June 1973 (230 ton lift) has greatly improved this navy's repair facilities.

Ministerial

Minister of National Defence:
General D. F. Rubio Coronado

Personnel

(a) 1977: 400 (50 officers and 350 men, including 10 officers and 200 men of the Marines)
(b) 2 years National Service

Bases

Santo Tomás de Castillas (Atlantic); Sipacate (Pacific)

Mercantile Marine

Lloyd's Register of Shipping: 6 vessels of 8 197 tons gross

2 85 ft COASTAL PATROL CRAFT

Name	No.	Builders	Commissioned
USORIO SARAVIA	P 852	Sewart, Louisiana	1972
UTATLAN	P 851	Sewart, Louisiana	May 1967

Displacement, tons: 60
Dimensions, feet (metres): 85 × 18·7 × 3 *(25·9 × 5·7 × 0·9)*
Guns: 2 MG
Main engines: 2 GM Diesels; 2 200 bhp = 23 knots
Range, miles: 400 at 12 knots
Complement: 12 (2 officers, 10 ratings)

Built to "Commercial Cruiser" design.

UTATLAN   *1973, Guatemalan Navy*

? "BROADSWORD" CLASS (COASTAL PATROL CRAFT)

Dimensions, feet (metres): 105 × 20·5 × 6·3 *(32 × 6·3 × 1·9)*
Guns: 1—75 mm recoilless; 1—81 mm mortar; 5—0·50 MG
Main engines: 2 GM diesels = 32 knots
Complement: 20

First delivered by Halter Marine, Louisiana in Autumn 1976. Total number uncertain.

3 65 ft COASTAL PATROL CRAFT

Name	No.	Builders	Commissioned
AZUMANCHE	P 653	Halter, USA	1972
KAIBILBALAM	P 652	Halter, USA	1972
TECUNUMAN	P 651	Halter, USA	1972

Displacement, tons: 32
Dimensions, feet (metres): 64·5 × 17 × 3 *(19·7 × 5·2 × 0·9)*
Guns: 2 MG
Main engines: 2 GM Diesels = 25 knots
Complement: 10 (2 officers, 8 ratings)

2 63 ft COASTAL CRAFT (ex-USCGS)

Name	No.	Builders	Commissioned
CABRAKAN	P 631	USA	—
HUNAHPU	P 632	USA	—

Displacement, tons: 32
Dimensions, feet (metres): 63·3 × 15·4 × 3 *(19·3 × 4·7 × 0·9)*
Guns: 2 MG
Main engines: 2 GM Diesels 8V71 = 25 knots
Complement: 10 (2 officers, 8 men)

Transferred from USA—*Hunahpu,* 1964; *Cabrakan,* 1965.

2 Ex-USCG 40 ft UTILITY BOATS MK IV

TIKAL P 401   IXINCHE P 402

Transferred Aug 1963.

1 Ex-US LCM (6)

CHINALTENANGO 561

Transferred Dec 1965.

6 MOTOR LAUNCHES

Procured in late 1960s. Reported as inboard/outboard craft.

1 Ex-US REPAIR BARGE

Ex-US YR 40. Transferred in 1952.

2 28 ft COASTAL PATROL CRAFT

XUCUXUY P 281   CAMALOTE P 282

Striker Utility Patrol Craft modified for one GM 6-53 Diesel. 28 ft, 6½ tons with 1 MG. Transferred in 1961.

1 TUG

Note: Three other names listed—*Escuintla, Mazatenango, Retalhuleu*—in addition to two yachts—*Mendieta* and one other.

GUINEA

Personnel

a) 1977: 350 officers and men
b) Conscript service—2 years

Bases

Conakry, Kakanda

Mercantile Marine

Lloyd's Register of Shipping: 11 vessels of 15 280 tons gross

---

LIGHT FORCES

6 Ex-CHINESE "SHANGHAI II" CLASS (FAST ATTACK CRAFT—GUN)

P 733   P 734   P 735   P 736   +2

"SHANGHAI" Class

Displacement, tons: 120 standard; 155 full load
Dimensions, feet (metres): 128 × 18 × 5·6 *(39 × 5·5 × 1·7)*
Guns: 4—37 mm (twin); 4—25 mm (twin)
A/S weapons: 8 DCs
Main engines: 4 Diesels; 3 600 hp = 28 knots
Complement: 25

Transferred 1973-74 (first four) and 1976.

4 Ex-SOVIET "P 6" CLASS (FAST ATTACK CRAFT—TORPEDO)

Displacement, tons: 66 standard; 75 full load
Dimensions, feet (metres): 84·2 × 20·0 × 6·0 *(25·7 × 6·1 × 1·8)*
Guns: 4—25 mm
Torpedo tubes: 2—21 in (or mines or depth charges)
Main engines: 4 Diesels; 4 shafts; 4 800 bhp = 43 knots
Range, miles: 450 at 30 knots
Complement: 25

It seems unlikely that the torpedo armament is operational.

2 Ex-SOVIET "POLUCHAT I" CLASS (COASTAL PATROL CRAFT)

Displacement, tons: 86 standard; 91 full load
Dimensions, feet (metres): 98·0 pp × 15·0 × 4·8 *(29·9 × 4·6 × 1·5)*
Guns: 2—14·5 mm (1 twin)
Main engines: 2 diesels; 2 shafts; 1 200 bhp = 18 knots
Oil fuel, tons: 9·25
Range, miles: 460 at 17 knots
Complement: 16 (2 officers, 14 ratings)

2 Ex-SOVIET "MO VI" CLASS (COASTAL PATROL CRAFT)

Displacement, tons: 64 standard; 73 full load
Dimensions, feet (metres): 83·6 × 19·7 × 4·0 *(25·5 × 6 × 1·2)*
Guns: 4—25 mm (twin)
A/S weapons: DC mortars and racks
Main engines: 4 Diesels; 4 shafts; 4 800 hp = 40 knots

Transferred 1972-73. Radar—Pot Head.

LANDING CRAFT

2 SMALL UTILITY TYPE

Recent visits by considerable numbers of Soviet ships may have increased these numbers.

GUINEA BISSAU

Personnel

(a) 1977: 100 officers and men.
(b) Voluntary service.

Base

Bissau.

Mercantile Marine

Lloyd's Register of Shipping: 1 vessel of 219 tons gross

Several river craft and some small LCU type are reported in service rather than the two ex-Soviet craft listed last year.

GUYANA

Ministerial

Premier and Minister of National Security:
  L. F. S. Burnham

Mercantile Marine

Lloyd's Register of Shipping: 69 vessels of 19 105 tons gross

Bases

Georgetown, New Amsterdam

Prefix to Ships' Names

GDFS

1 VOSPER THORNYCROFT 103 ft TYPE
(LARGE PATROL CRAFT)

Name	No.	Builders	Commissioned
PECCARI	—	Vosper Thornycroft	Mar 1977

Displacement, tons: 96 standard; 109 full load
Dimensions, feet (metres): 103 oa × 19·8 × 5·5 *(31·4 × 6·0 × 1·6)*
Guns: 2—40 mm
Main engines: 2 diesels, 3 500 hp = 27 knots
Range, miles: 1 400 at 14 knots
Complement: 22

Trials started 25 Nov 1976.

PECCARI

1977, C. and S. Taylor

3 VOSPER 12·2 METRE TYPE
(COASTAL PATROL CRAFT)

Name	No.	Builders	Commissioned
JAGUAR	—	Vospers	28 April 1971
MARGAY	—	Vospers	21 May 1971
OCELOT	—	Vospers	22 June 1971

Displacement, tons: 10
Dimensions, feet (metres): 40 × 12 × 3·5 *(12·2 × 3·7 × 1·1)*
Gun: 1—7·62 mm MG
Main engines: 2 Cummins diesels; 370 hp = 19 knots
Range, miles: 150 at 12 knots
Complement: 6

They have glass fibre hulls with aluminium superstructures.

1 LIGHTER

YFN 960 transferred from US 1 Aug 1975. Under AIP.

JAGUAR

1971, C. and S. Taylor

HAITI

Ministerial:

Secretary for Interior and National Defence:
  Pierre Biamby

Personnel

(a) 1977: Total 300 (40 officers and 260 men)
(b) Voluntary service

Availability:

It is uncertain how many—if any—of these ships are now in service. Negotiations, so far unsuccessful, for the purchase of up to 26 fast coastal patrol craft in the USA suggest that the majority may be derelict.

Base

Port Au Prince

COAST GUARD VESSELS

1 Ex-US "COHOES" CLASS (ex-NETLAYER)

Name	No.	Builders	Commissioned
JEAN JACQUES DESSALINES (ex-USS *Tonawanda, AN 89*)	GC10	Leatham D. Smith SB Co	1944

Displacement, tons: 650 standard; 785 full load
Dimensions, feet (metres): 168·5 × 33 × 10·8 *(51·4 × 10 × 3·3)*
Guns: 1—76 mm; 3—20 mm
Main engines: Busch-Sulzer diesel-electric; 1 200 shp = 12 knots
Complement: 48

Launched on 14 Nov 1944. Loaned to Haiti in 1960.

1 Ex-US WAGL TYPE

Name	No.	Builders	Commissioned
AMIRAL KILLICK (ex-USCG *Black Rock, WAGL 367*)	GC 7	—	Jan 1956 (Haiti)

Displacement, tons: 160
Length feet (metres): 114 *(35)*

Former buoy tender purchased from the US Coast Guard in 1955, commissioned in Jan 1956.

1 Ex- USCG 95 ft CUTTER

Name	No.	Builders	Commissioned
LA CRETE A PIERROT (ex-USCG *95315*)	GC 8	US Coast Guard Yard, Curtiss Bay, Maryland	—

Displacement, tons: 100
Dimensions, feet (metres): 95 × 19 × 5 *(29 × 5·8 × 1·5)*
Guns: 3—20 mm
Main engines: 4 diesels; 2 shafts; 2 200 bhp = 21 knots
Range, miles: 1 500
Complement: 15

Former US Coast Guard steel cutter. Acquired on 26 Feb 1956.

1 Ex-US SC TYPE

SEIZE AOUT 1946 (ex-*SC 453*) GC 2

Displacement, tons: 110 standard; 138 full load
Dimensions, feet (metres): 110·5 × 18·8 × 6·5 *(33·7 × 5·7 × 2)*
Guns: 2—40 mm; 2—20 mm
Main engines: Diesels; 2 shafts; 1 000 hp = 15 knots

Of the SC type acquired during 1947 from the US Navy. Launched in 1943. Laid up in reserve.

1 Ex-USCG 56 ft CUTTER

Name	No.	Builders	Commissioned
SAVANNAH	GC 1	Wheeler Shipyard,	1944
(ex-USCG 563200)		Brooklyn, USA	

Displacement, tons: 47
Dimensions, feet (metres): 56 × 16 × 4·2 (17·1 × 4·9 × 1·3)
Main engines: Diesels; 2 shafts; 200 bhp = 9 knots
Complement: 12

1 Ex-US LCT

ARTIBONITE (ex-US LCT) GC 5

Displacement, tons: 134 standard; 285 full load
Dimensions, feet (metres): 120·3 oa × 32 × 4·2 (36·7 × 9·8 × 1·3)
Main engines: 3 diesels; 675 bhp = 8 knots
Range, miles: 700 at 7 knots
Complement: 12

Former US tank landing craft. Transferred 1944. Salvaged by Haitian Coast Guard after grounding and converted.

6 Ex-USCG 83 ft CUTTERS

Displacement, tons: 45
Dimensions, feet (metres): 83 × 16 × 4·5 (25·3 × 4·9 × 1·4)
Gun: 1—20 mm
Main engines: 2 Petrol; 1 200 hp = 20 knots

Built in 1942.

1 PRESIDENTIAL YACHT

SANS SOUCI (ex-Captain James Taylor)

Displacement, tons: 161
Main engines: 2 diesels; 2 shafts; 300 bhp × 10 knots

Employed, when required, as the Presidential Yacht. Built in USA.

HONDURAS

Ministerial

Minister of Defence:
Brigadier Gen. M. E. Chinchilla Carcamao

Personnel

(a) 1977: 35
(b) 8 months conscript service

Base

Puerto Cortes

Mercantile Marine

Lloyd's Register of Shipping: 57 vessels of 71 042 tons gross

3 COASTAL PATROL CRAFT

Employed on coastguard duties.

1 HYDROGRAPHIC LAUNCH

Of 56 ft, transferred from USA 1976.

HONG KONG

All the following craft are operated by the Marine District of the Royal Hong Kong Police Force.

Senior officers

District Police Commander:
Mr. Sze-to Che-yan CPM JP

Assistant Commissioner:
Mr. R. J. L. MacDonald

Personnel

(a) 1977: 71 officers, 330 NCOs, 891 constables
(b) Voluntary service

Deletion

1975: Logistic Craft No 24
45 ft Patrol Craft No 5 and 8

Mercantile Marine

Lloyd's Register of Shipping: 98 vessels of 423 218 tons gro

2 COMMAND VESSELS

No. 1   No. 2

Displacement, tons: 222·5
Dimensions, feet (metres): 111·3 × 24 × 10·5 (33·9 × 7·3 × 3·2)
Main engines: 2 diesels of 337 bhp = 11·8 knots
Range, miles: 5 200 at 11·8 knots
Complement: 25

Built at Taikoo 1965 (now Hong Kong United Dockyard). Can carry two platoons in addition to complement. Cost $HK 1 778 550.

POLICE LAUNCH No. 2   1974, RHK

7 78 ft PATROL CRAFT

Nos. 50-56

Displacement, tons: 82
Dimensions, feet (metres): 78·5 oa × 17·2 × 5·6 (23·9 × 5·2 × 1·7)
Gun: 1—·50 cal MG
Main engines: Two Cummins diesels; 1 500 hp = 20·7 knots
Range, miles: 4 000 at 20 knots
Complement: 16

Steel hulled craft built by Vosper Thornycroft Private Ltd, Singapore. Delivered May 1972 to May 1973 to the Royal Hong Kong Police. Can carry an extra Platoon. Cost $HK 1 873 800.

POLICE LAUNCH No. 51   1974, RHK

1 78 ft PATROL CRAFT

No. 4

Displacement, tons: 72
Dimensions, feet (metres): 78 × 15 × 4·5 *(22·8 × 4·6 × 1·4)*
Main engines: 3 diesels of 690 hp = 15·5 knots
Range, miles: 600 at 15·5 knots
Complement: 21

Built by Thornycroft, Singapore in 1958.

9 70 ft PATROL CRAFT

Nos. 26-34

Displacement, tons: 52
Dimensions, feet (metres): 70 × 17 × 5·2 *(24·5 × 5·2 × 1·6)*
Main engines: 2 Diesels of 215 bhp = 10 knots
Range, miles: 1 600 at 10 knots
Complement: 12

Built by Hong Kong SY (26-28) in 1954 and Cheoy Lee SY (29-34 in 1955).

POLICE LAUNCH No. 26   *1976, RHKP*

1 65 ft PATROL CRAFT

No. 6

Displacement, tons: 48
Dimensions, feet (metres): 65 × 14·5 × 5·5 *(19·8 × 4·4 × 1·8)*
Main engines: 1 diesel; 152 bhp = 10·5 knots
Range, miles: 1 400 at 9 knots
Complement: 11

8 45 ft PATROL CRAFT

Nos. 9-16

Displacement, tons: 27·7
Dimensions, feet (metres): 45 × 15 × 7 *(13·7 × 4·6 × 2·1)*
Main engines: 1 diesel; 144 bhp = 9 knots
Range, miles: 1 700 at 8 knots
Complement: 5

Built by Australian Min. of Munitions in 1946.

POLICE LAUNCH No. 12   *1976, RHKP*

3 40 ft PATROL CRAFT

Nos. 20-22

Displacement, tons: 17
Dimensions, feet (metres): 40·3 × 11·6 × 2 *(12·3 × 3·5 × 0·6)*
Main engines: 2 diesels of 370 bhp = 24 knots
Range, miles: 380 at 24 knots
Complement: 5

Built in Choy Lee in 1971.

POLICE LAUNCH No. 22   *1974, RHKP*

1 58 ft LOGISTIC CRAFT

No. 3

Of 37 tons and 16 knots with a range of 240 miles at 15 knots. Complement 8.
Built by Thornycroft Singapore in 1958.

POLICE LAUNCH No. 3   *1976, RHKP*

1 LOGISTIC CRAFT

No. 7

Of 18·5 tons and 23·5 knots. Range 200 miles at 20 knots. Complement of 5—can carry 25 passengers. Built by Hip Hing Cheung Shipyard in 1975.

POLICE LAUNCH No. 7   1976, RHKP

11 22 ft LAUNCHES

Nos. 35-45

Of 4·8 tons and 20 knots with a range of 160 miles at full speed. Built by Choy Lee SY in 1970.

POLICE LAUNCH No. 35   1976, RHKP

HUNGARY

Ministerial

Minister of Defence: Lazos Czinege

Diplomatic Representation

Military and Air Attaché London: Colonel Imry Mózsik

Personnel

(a) 1977: 500 officers and men
(b) 2 years national service

Mercantile Marine

Lloyd's Register of Shipping: 18 vessels of 54 926 tons gross

The Navy was dissolved by 1969 but a maritime wing of the Army is still very active on the Danube.

LIGHT FORCES

10 100 ton PATROL CRAFT

Displacement, tons: 100
Gun: 1—14·7 mm
Main engines: 2 diesels

MINEWARFARE FORCES

Several riverine MCM vessels.

SERVICE FORCES

Several troop transports of up to 1 000 tons.
Five small LCUs.
A number of tugs.
Several river ice-breakers.
Transport barges which can double as landing craft or bridging element.

ICELAND

Ministerial

Minister of Justice:
Olafur Johannesson

Senior Officer

Director of Coastguard:
Pétur Sigurøsson

Personnel

1977: 170 officers and men

Duties

The Coast Guard Service (Landhelgisgaezlan) deals with fishery protection, salvage, rescue, hydrographic research, surveying and lighthouse duties.

New Construction

A programme to expand the Coastguard is under consideration. Enquiries have been made in several countries for varying types of ships including patrol craft from Norway.

Base

Reykjavik

Aircraft

2 Bell helicopter
1 Hughes helicopter
1 Fokker Friendship (1 more on order)

Research Ships

A number of Government Research Ships bearing RE pennant numbers operate off Iceland.

Mercantile Marine

Lloyd's Register of Shipping:
370 vessels of 162 268 tons gross

COAST GUARD PATROL VESSELS

Name	No.	Builders	Commissioned
AEGIR	—	Aalborg Vaerft, Denmark	1968
TYR	—	Aarhus Flyedock AS, Aalborg, Denmark	15 Mar 1975

Displacement, tons: 1 150 *(Tyr 1500)*
Dimensions, feet (metres): 204 × 33 × 14·8 *(62·2 × 10 × 4·6) Aegir*
229·6 × 32·8 × 19 *(70 × 10 × 5·8) Tyr*
Gun: 1—57 mm
Main engines: 2 MAN diesels; 2 shafts; 8 000 bhp = 19 knots (8 600 hp = 20 knots *Tyr)*
Complement: 22

Aegir was the first new construction patrol vessel for the Icelandic Coast Guard Service for about eight years. Projected in Feb 1965. Laid down in May 1967. *Tyr,* basically similar to *Aegir,* but a slightly improved design with higher speed was launched by Aarhus Flyedock AS, Aalborg, Denmark on 10 October 1974. Both have helicopter deck.

Radar: Three search sets.

Sonar: One hull mounted.

AEGIR   *1969, Icelandic Coast Guard*

Name	No.	Builders	Commissioned
ODINN	—	Aalborg Vaerft, Denmark	Jan 1960

Displacement, tons: 1 000
Dimensions, feet (metres): 187 pp × 33 × 13 *(57 × 10 × 4)*
Gun: 1—57 mm
Main engines: 2 B and W diesels; 2 shafts; 5 050 bhp = 18 knots
Complement: 22

Laid down in Jan 1959. Launched in Sep 1959. Refitted in Denmark by Aarhus Flydedock late 1975, with twin funnels and helicopter hangar.

Radar: Two search sets.

Sonar: One hull mounted.

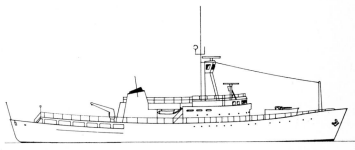

ODINN (after 1975 refit)   *1976, Icelandic Coast Guard*

Name	No.	Builders	Commissioned
THOR	—	Aalborg Vaerft, Denmark	Late 1951

Displacement, tons: 920
Dimensions, feet (metres): 183·3 pp; 206 oa × 31·2 × 13 *(55·8; 62·8 × 9·5 × 4)*
Gun: 1—57 mm
Main engines: 2—6 cyl. MWM diesels; 3 200 bhp = 17 knots
Complement: 22

Launched in 1951. Fitted with helicopter platform during refit in 1972. Now has twin funnels and hangar.

Radar: Two search sets.

Sonar: One hull-mounted set.

THOR   *1975, Icelandic Coast Guard*

Name	No.	Builders	Commissioned
ARVAKUR	—	Bodewes, Netherlands	1962

ARVAKUR   *1976, Icelandic Coast Guard*

Displacement, tons: 716
Dimensions, feet (metres): 106 × 33 × 13 *(32·3 × 10 × 4)*
Gun: 1 MG
Main engine: 1 diesel; 1 000 bhp = 12 knots
Complement: 12

Built as a lighthouse tender in the Netherlands. Acquired by Iceland for duty in the Coast Guard Service in 1969.

Radar: Two search sets.

Name	No.	Builders	Commissioned
ALBERT	—	Stalsmidjan, Reykjavik	Apr 1957

ALBERT   *1975, Icelandic Coast Guard*

Displacement, tons: 200 gross
Dimensions, feet (metres): Length: 111·2 *(33·9)*
Gun: 1—47 mm
Main engines: 1 Nohab diesel; 650 bhp = 12·5 knots
Complement: 15

Launched in 1956. Refitted in 1972.

Radar: Two search sets.

Name	No.	Builders	Commissioned
BALDUR	—	Stoeznia lm. Kommuny Paryskiez, Gdynia, Poland	1974

BALDUR   *2/1976*

Displacement, tons: 740
Dimensions, feet (metres): 201 × 37 × 15 *(62 × 11·3 × 4·6)*
Gun: 1—57 mm
Main engines: 6 cyl Sulzer diesel; 3 000 bhp; 3 000 bhp = 15 knots; single shaft
Complement: 20

Stern trawler taken over on charter in 1975 from Adalsteinn Loftssohn, Dalvik.
Transferred in 1975 from Government Fishery Research to Coastguard. Will return to research duties mid 1977.

Radar: Two search sets.

Sonar: ? Fish sonar.

INDIA

Ministerial

Minister of Defence:
Bansi Lal

Headquarters Appointment

Chief of the Naval Staff:
Admiral J. Cursetji

Senior Appointments

Flag Officer C in C, Western Naval Command:
Vice-Admiral R. L. Pereira
Flag Officer Commanding Western Fleet:
Rear-Admiral M. R. Schunker
Flag Officer C in C Eastern Naval Command:
Vice-Admiral S. Parkash
Flag Officer Commanding Eastern Fleet:
Rear-Admiral D. S. Paintal
Flag Officer, Southern Naval Area:
Rear-Admiral V. E. C. Barboza

Diplomatic Representation

Naval Attaché in Bonn:
Commodore H. Johnson
Naval Adviser, Dacca:
Captain R. B. Mukherjee
Naval Attaché in Djakarta:
Captain R. V. Singh
Naval Adviser in London:
Commodore C. L. Sachdeva
Naval Attaché in Moscow:
Commodore I. J. S. Khurana
Defence Attaché in Washington:
Brigadier Srendra Singh MC

Personnel

(a) 1977: 46 000 officers and ratings (including Naval Air Arm)
(b) Voluntary service

Naval Bases and Establishments

Bombay (C in C Western Fleet, barracks and main Dockyard);
Vishakapatnam (C in C Eastern Command, submarine base, dockyard and barracks);
Cochin (FO Southern Area Naval Air Station, barracks and professional schools);
Lonavala and Jamnagar (professional schools);
Calcutta, Goa and Port Blair (small bases only);
New Delhi (HQ)

Naval Air Arm

Squadron No.	Aircraft	Role
300	Seahawk FGA6 (25)	Strike
310	Alize 1050 (10)	ASW
321	Alouette III (7)	SAR
330	Sea Kings (12)	ASW
331	Alouette III (7)	ASW
550	Alize, Alouette	Training
561	2 Devon	Training
	4 Hughes 300,	
	4 Vampire T-55,	
	7 HJT 16-Kiran	

Note: 5 Britten-Norman Defenders ordered in 1976

Prefix to Ships' Names

IS (Indian Ship)

Mercantile Marine

Lloyd's Register of Shipping:
526 vessels of 5 093 984 tons gross

Strength of the Fleet

Type	Active	Building
Attack Carrier (Medium)	1	—
Cruisers	2	—
Frigates	25	2
Corvettes	—	3
Patrol Submarines	8	—
Fast Attack Craft—Missile	16	—
Large Patrol Craft	1	—
Coastal Patrol Craft	7	—
Landing Ship	1	—
Landing Craft	6	—
Minesweepers—Coastal	4	—
Minesweepers—Inshore	4	—
Survey Ships	3	1
Submarine Tender	1	—
Submarine Rescue Ship	1	—
Replenishment Tankers	2	—
Support Tankers	3	—
Repair Ship	1	—
Ocean Tug	1	—
Harbour Craft	5	—

DELETIONS

Destroyers

1976 *Rana, Rajput, Ranjit* (British "R" Class)

Frigates

1971 *Khukri* sunk in war with Pakistan (9 Dec)
1975 *Ganga* and *Gomati* ("Hunt" Class) paid off.

Survey Ship

1975 *Investigator* ("River" class) paid off.

Light Forces

1974 *Ajay* and *Akshay* to Bangladesh, *Amar* to Mauritius (April).
1975 *Savitri, Sharayu, Subhadra, Suvarna* paid off.

Minewarfare Forces

1973 *Konkan* (last of 6 "Bangor" class) paid off.

Harbour Tankers

1976 *Chilka, Sambhar.*

PENNANT LIST

Aircraft Carrier

R	11	Vikrant

Cruisers

C	60	Mysore
C	74	Delhi

Frigates

D	92	Godavari
F	11	Jamuna (Survey)
F	31	Brahmaputra
F	32	Nilgiri
F	33	Himgiri
F	34	Udaygiri
F	35	Dunagiri
F	36	Taragiri
F	37	Vindhyagiri
F	46	Kistna
F	95	Sutlej
F	110	Kaveri
F	137	Beas
F	139	Betwa
F	40	Talwar
F	43	Trishul
F	144	Kirpan
F	146	Kuthar
F	256	Tir

Corvettes

—	Nanuchka I
—	Nanuchka II
—	Nanuchka III

Submarines

S	40	Vela
S	41	Vagir
S	42	Vagli
S	43	Vagsheer
S	121	Kalvari
S	122	Kanderi
S	123	Karanj
S	124	Karsula

Light Forces
(including "Petya" class)

P	168	Arnala
P	169	Androth
P	173	Anjadip
P	174	Andaman
P	175	Amini
P	177	Kamorta
P	178	Kadmath
P	179	Kiltan
P	180	Kavaratti
P	181	Katchal
P	246	Panvel
P	247	Pamban
P	248	Puri
P	249	Panaji
P	250	Pulicat
P	684	Nashak
P	685	Nirbhik
P	686	Veer
P	690	Nirghat
P	691	Nipat
P	692	Vinash
P	693	Vigeta
P	694	Vidyut
SPB	3132	Sukanya
SPB	3133	Sharada
P	3135	Abhay

Minewarfare Forces

M	89	Bhaktal
M	90	Bulsar
M	1190	Kuddalore
M	1191	Cannanore
M	1197	Karwar
M	1201	Kakinada
M	2705	Bimlipitan
M	2707	Bassein

Amphibious Forces

L	3011	Magar
L	3032	Gharial
L	3033	Guldar
L	3034	Ghorpad
L	3035	Kesari
L	3036	Shardul
L	3037	Sharab

Service Forces

A	14	Amba
A	15	Nistar
A	136	Shakti
A	139	Darshak
A	306	Dharini
A	1750	Deepak

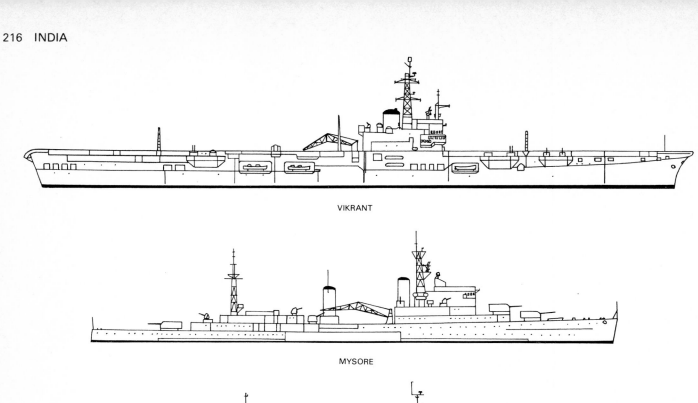

VIKRANT

MYSORE

DELHI

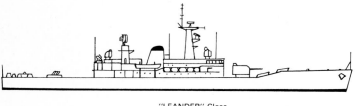
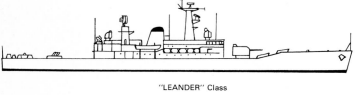

"LEANDER" Class

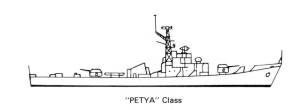

"PETYA" Class

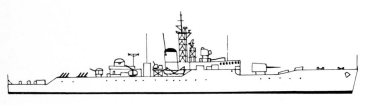

TALWAR, TRISHUL

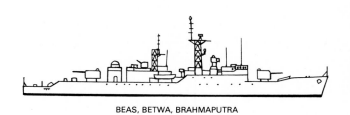

BEAS, BETWA, BRAHMAPUTRA

KIRPAN, KUTHAR

"HUNT" Class

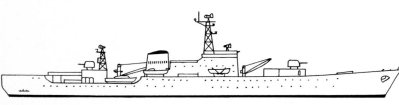

AMBA

AIRCRAFT CARRIER (ATTACK MEDIUM)

1 Ex-BRITISH "MAJESTIC" CLASS

Name	No.	Builders	Laid down	Launched	Commissioned
VIKRANT (ex-HMS *Hercules*)	R 11	Vickers-Armstrong Ltd, Tyne	14 Oct 1943	22 Sep 1945	4 Mar 1961

Displacement, tons: 16 000 standard; 19 500 full load
Length, feet (metres): 630 *(192·0)* pp; 700 *(213·4)* oa
Beam, feet (metres): 80 *(24·4)* hull
Width, feet (metres): 128 *(39·0)*
Draught, feet (metres): 24 *(7·3)*
Aircraft: 22 capacity (18 Seahawk, 4 Alize)
Guns: 15—40 mm (4 twin, 7 single)
Main engines: Parsons single reduction geared turbines;
   40 000 shp; 2 shafts
Boilers: 4 Admiralty 3-drum; 400 psi; 700°F
Speed, knots: 24·5
Oil fuel, tons: 3 200
Range, miles: 12 000 at 14 knots; 6 200 at 23 knots
Complement: 1 075 (peace); 1 345 (war)

Acquired from Great Britain in Jan 1957 after having been suspended in May 1946 when structurally almost complete and 75% fitted out. Taken in hand by Harland & Wolff Ltd, Belfast, in April 1957 for completion in 1961. Commissioned on 4 Mar 1961 and renamed *Vikrant*.
Completed extensive overhaul—1973 to Aug 1974.

Aircraft: Still equipped with Seahawks although re-equipment is planned. Harrier trials in mid-1972 showed promise, but subsequently the IN is understood to have preferred Soviet Yakovlev VTOL aircraft due to problems in purchasing the Harrier.

Engineering: One set of turbines and two boilers are installed side by side in each of the two propelling machinery spaces, on the unit system, so that the starboard propeller shaft is longer than the port.

Flight deck: The aircraft, including strike and anti-submarine aircraft, operate from an angled deck with steam catapult, landing sights and two electrically operated lifts.

Habitability: Partially air-conditioned and insulated for tropical service, the ship's sides being sprayed with asbestos cement instead of being lagged. Separate messes and dining halls.

Radar: Search: Type 960, Type 277.
Tactical: Type 293.
Miscellaneous: Type 963 Carrier Controlled Approach.

VIKRANT

1971, John G. Callis

CRUISERS

1 Ex-BRITISH "FIJI" CLASS

Name	No.	Builders	Laid down	Launched	Commissioned
MYSORE (ex-HMS *Nigeria*)	C 60	Vickers-Armstrong Ltd, Tyne	8 Feb 1938	18 July 1939	23 Sep 1940

Displacement, tons: 8 700 standard; 11 040 full load
Length, feet (metres): 538·0 *(164·0)* pp; 549·0 *(176·3)* wl
   555·5 *(169·3)* oa
Beam, feet (metres): 62·0 *(18·9)*
Draught, feet (metres): 21·0 *(6·4)*
Guns: 9—6 in *(152 mm)*, (3 triple); 8—4 in *(102 mm)*, (4 twin);
   12—40 mm (5 twin, 2 single)
Armour: Side 4½ in—3 in *(114—76 mm)*; Deck 2 in *(51 mm)*;
   Conning tower 4 in *(102 mm)*; Turrets 2 in *(51 mm)*
Main engines: Parsons geared turbines; 4 shafts; 72 500 shp
Boilers: 4 Admiralty 3-drum type
Speed, knots: 31·5
Complement: 800

Flagship at the Battle of Porsanger Fjord Sep 1941. Purchased from Great Britain on 8 April 1954 for £300 000. Extensively refitted and reconstructed by Cammell Laird & Co Ltd, Birkenhead, before commissioning. Formally handed over to the Indian Navy at Birkenhead and renamed *Mysore* on 29 Aug 1957. Involved in two serious collisions, the second in late 1972 with *Beas*, resulting in two months of repairs.

Radar: Search: Type 960, Type 277.
Tactical: Type 293.
Fire control: I Band.

MYSORE

1971, Roland Rodwell

Reconstruction: Ship formerly had tripod masts. During reconstruction the triple 6 inch turret in "X" position and the 6—21 inch torpedo tubes (tripled) were removed, the bridge was modified, two lattice masts were stepped, all electrical equipment was replaced and the engine room and other parts of the ship were refitted.

Name **No.**
DELHI (ex-HMS *Achilles*) C 74

Displacement, tons: 7 114 standard; 9 740 full load
Length, feet (metres): 522·0 *(159·1)* pp; 544·5 *(166·0)* oa
Beam, feet (metres): 55·2 *(16·8)*
Draught, feet (metres): 20·0 *(6·1)*
Guns: 6—6 in *(152 mm)* (3 twins); 10—40 mm (2 twin, 6 single);
4—3 pdr saluting
Armour: 4 in-2 in side; 1 in gunhouses; 1 in bridge; 2 in deck
Main engines: Parsons geared turbines; 4 shafts 72 000 shp
Boilers: 4 Admiralty 3-drum type
Oil fuel, tons: 1 800
Speed, knots: 32
Complement: 800

As HMS *Achilles,* then lent to the Royal New Zealand Navy, this ship, with HMS *Ajax* and HMS *Exeter,* defeated the German battleship *Admiral Graf Spee* in the Battle of the River Plate on 13 Dec 1939. Purchased from Great Britain and delivered on 5 July 1948. Refitted in 1955. Now used for training cadets. Reported as due for deletion.

Gunnery: Eight 4 in guns removed to provide space for deckhouses required for cadet accommodation. 40 mm armament reduced from fourteen to ten.

Radar: Search: Type 960, Type 277.
Tactical: Type 293.
Fire control: Early design.

Torpedo Tubes: In 1958 the original eight 21 inch torpedo tubes, in two quadruple banks, were removed, and the forecastle deck plating was consequently extended aft to the twin 40 mm gun mounting abreast the boat stowage.

1 Ex-BRITISH "LEANDER" CLASS

Builders	Laid down	Launched	Commissioned
Cammell Laird & Co Ltd, Birkenhead	11 June 1931	1 Sep 1932	5 Oct 1933

DELHI
1969, Graeme Andrews

FRIGATES

6 BRITISH "LEANDER" CLASS

Name **No.**
DUNAGIRI F 35
HIMGIRI F 33
NILGIRI F 32
UDAYGIRI F 34
TARAGIRI F 36
VINDHYAGIRI F 37

Displacement, tons: 2 450 standard; 2 800 full load
Length, feet (metres): 360 *(109·7)* wl; 372 *(113·4)* oa
Beam, feet (metres): 43 *(13·1)*
Draught, feet (metres): 18 *(5·5)*
Aircraft: 1 Alouette III helicopter
Missiles: 2 Seacat quadruple launchers (all but *Nilgiri*—one)
Guns: 2—4·5 in *(115 mm)* (1 twin); 2—20 mm
A/S weapons: 1 Limbo 3 barrelled DC mortar
Main engines: 2 geared turbines; 30 000 shp
Boilers: 2
Oil fuel, tons: 460
Speed, knots: 30
Range, miles: 4 500 at 12 knots
Complement: 263

Builders	Laid down	Launched	Commissioned
Mazagon Docks Ltd, Bombay	Jan 1973	9 Mar 1974	1976
Mazagon Docks Ltd, Bombay	1967	6 May 1970	23 Nov 1974
Mazagon Docks Ltd, Bombay	Oct 1966	23 Oct 1968	3 June 1972
Mazagon Docks Ltd, Bombay	14 Sep 1970	24 Oct 1972	1975
Mazagon Docks Ltd, Bombay	—	—	—
Mazagon Docks Ltd, Bombay	—	—	—

First major warships built in Indian yards. Of similar design to later (broad beam) "Leander" class in the Royal Navy. Hangar has been enlarged to take Alouette III helicopter.

Missiles: *Nilgiri* has one Seacat launcher with UK GWS22 control. Remainder have two Seacat launchers with two Dutch M4 directors.

Radar: HSA radars in place of UK types.

NILGIRI
1973, Vickers Ltd

AMINI P 175	**KADMATH** P 178
ANDAMAN P 174	**KAMORTA** P 177
ANDROTH P 169	**KATCHAL** P 181
ANJADIP P 173	**KAVARATTI** P 180
ARNALA P 168	**KILTAN** P 179

Displacement, tons: 950 standard; 1 150 full load
Length, feet (metres): 250·0 *(76·2)* wl; 270 *(82·3)* oa
Beam, feet (metres): 29·9 *(9·1)*
Draught, feet (metres): 10·5 *(3·2)*
Guns: 4—3 in *(76 mm)* (2 twin)
A/S weapons: 4 MBU 2 500 (16 barrelled rocket launchers);
2 internal DC racks
Torpedo tubes: 3—21 in *(533 mm)*
Mines: Have minerails
Main engines: 2 gas turbines; 30 000 hp;
2 diesels; 2 shafts; 6 000 hp
Speed, knots: 30
Complement: 100

Transferred to the Indian Navy since 1969. *Andaman* delivered Mar 1974, *Amini* late 1974. All are of an export version of "Petya II" class with simplified communications.

Radar: Surface Search: Slim Net.

10 Ex-SOVIET "PETYA II" CLASS

KAVARATTI
S. Breyer

2 Ex-BRITISH "WHITBY" CLASS

Name	No.
TALWAR	F 40
TRISHUL	F 43

Builders	Laid down	Launched	Commissioned
Cammell Laird & Co Ltd, Birkenhead	1957	18 July 1958	1960
Harland & Wolff Ltd, Belfast	1957	18 June 1959	1960

Displacement, tons: 2 144 standard;
 2 545 full load (*Talwar*), 2 557 (*Trishul*)
Length, feet (metres): 360 *(109·7)* pp 369·8 *(112·7)* oa
Beam, feet (metres): 41 *(12·5)*
Draught, feet (metres): 17·8 *(5·4)*
Missiles: see note
Guns: 2—4·5 in *(115 mm)* (see missile note);
 4—40 mm (1 twin before Limbos, 2 singles abaft funnel)
A/S weapons: 2 Limbo 3-barrelled DC mortars
Main engines: 2 sets geared turbines; 30 000 shp; 2 shafts
Boilers: 2 Babcock & Wilcox
Oil fuel, tons: 400
Speed, knots: 30
Range, miles: 4 500 at 12 knots
Complement: 231 (11 officers, 220 men)

Generally similar to the British frigates of the "Whitby" class, but slightly modified to suit Indian conditions. *Trishul* acts as Squadron commander.

Missiles: In late 1975 *Talwar* was fitted with three SS-N-2 missile launchers from an "Osa" class in place of the 4·5 inch turret.

Radar: Tactical: Type 293 and 277.
Fire control: I Band. (FPS 6 director).
Missile control *(Talwar):* Square Tie.

TALWAR (after SS-N-2 Mod)   *1976*

3 Ex-BRITISH "LEOPARD" CLASS

Name	No.
BEAS	F 137
BETWA	F 139
BRAHMAPUTRA (ex-*Panther*)	F 31

Builders	Laid down	Launched	Commissioned
Vickers-Armstrong Ltd, Newcastle-on-Tyne	1957	9 Oct 1958	24 May 1960
Vickers-Armstrong Ltd, Newcastle-on-Tyne	1957	15 Sep 1959	8 Dec 1960
John Brown & Co Ltd, Clydebank	1956	15 Mar 1957	28 Mar 1958

Displacement, tons: 2 251 standard; 2 515 full load
Length, feet (metres): 320·0 *(97·5)* pp; 330·0 *(100·6)* wl;
 339·8 *(103·6)* oa
Beam, feet (metres): 40·0 *(12·2)*
Draught, feet (metres): 16·0 *(4·9)*
Guns: 4—4·5 in *(114 mm)* (2 twin); 2—40 mm
A/S weapons: 1 Squid 3-barrelled DC motar
Main engines: Admiralty standard range diesels 2 shafts;
 12 380 bhp
Speed, knots: 25
Range, miles: 7 500 at 16 knots
Complement: 210

Brahmaputra, orignally ordered as *Panther* for the Royal Navy on 28 June 1951, was the first major warship to be built in Great Britain for the Indian Navy since India became independent. All three ships are generally similar to the British frigates of the "Leopard" class, but modified to suit Indian conditions.

Radar: Search: Type 960
Tactical: Type 293.
Fire control: I Band forward and aft.

BRAHMAPUTRA   *1971, Indian Navy*

2 Ex-BRITISH "BLACKWOOD" CLASS

Name	No.
KIRPAN	F 144
KUTHAR	F 146

Builders	Laid down	Launched	Commissioned
Alex Stephen & Sons Ltd, Govan, Glasgow	1957	19 Aug 1958	July 1959
J. Samuel White & Co Ltd, Cowes, Isle of Wight	1957	14 Oct 1958	1959

Displacement, tons: 1 180 standard; 1 456 full load
Length, feet (metres): 300 *(91·4)* pp; 310 *(94·5)* oa
Beam, feet (metres): 33 *(10·0)*
Draught, feet (metres): 15·5 *(4·7)*
Guns: 3—40 mm (single)
A/S weapons: 2 Limbo 3-barrelled DC mortars
Main engines: 1 set geared turbines; 15 000 shp; 1 shaft
Boilers: Babcock & Wilcox
Speed, knots: 27·8
Oil fuel, tons: 300
Range, miles: 4 000 at 12 knots
Complement: 150

Generally similar to the British frigates of the "Blackwood" class, but slightly modified to suit Indian requirements. *Khukri* of this class was sunk in the Pakistan war on 9 Dec 1971.

Radar: Fitted with E Band air and surface surveillance radar.

KHUKRI (*Kirpan* and *Kuthar* similar)   *A & J Pavia*

1 Ex-BRITISH "HUNT" CLASS TYPE II

Name
GODAVARI (ex-HMS *Bedale*, ex-ORP *Slazak*, ex-HMS *Bedale*)

No.	Builders	Laid down	Launched	Commissioned
D 92	R. & W. Hawthorn, Leslie & Co Ltd, Hebburn	25 May 1940	23 July 1941	9 May 1942

Displacement, tons: 1 050 standard; 1 610 full load
Length, feet (metres): 264·2 *(80·5)* pp; 280·0 *(85·3)* oa
Beam, feet (metres): 31·5 *(9·6)*
Draught, feet (metres): 14·0 *(4·3)*
Guns: 6—4 in *(102 mm)* (twins); 4—20 mm
Main engines: Parsons geared turbines; 2 shafts; 19 000 shp
Boilers: 2 Admiralty 3-drum
Oil fuel, tons: 280
Speed, knots: 25
Range, miles: 3 700 at 14 knots
Complement: 150

Lent to Poland Apr 1942—Nov 1946. Transferred from Great Britain in May 1953. Lent to the Indian Navy for three years, subject to extension by agreement. Now used for training. Ran aground in Maldives 1976—subsequently salvaged but may soon be deleted.

GANGA (Godavari similar)   A & J Pavia

2 Ex-BRITISH "BLACK SWAN" CLASS

Name	No.
KAVERI	F 110
KISTNA	F 46

Builders	Laid down	Launched	Commissioned
Yarrow & Co Ltd, Scotstoun, Glasgow	28 Oct 1942	15 June 1943	21 Oct 1943
Yarrow & Co Ltd, Scotstoun, Glasgow	14 July 1942	22 April 1943	23 Aug 1943

Displacement, tons: 1 470 standard; 1 925 full load
Length, feet (metres): 283·0 *(86·3)* pp; 295·5 *(90·1)* wl; 299·5 *(91·3)* oa
Beam, feet (metres): 38·5 *(11·7)*
Draught, feet (metres): 11·2 *(3·4)*
Guns: 4—4 in *(102 mm)*; 4—40 mm
A/S weapons: 2 DCT
Main engines: Parsons geared turbines; 2 shafts; 4 300 shp
Boilers: 2 three-drum type
Speed, knots: 19
Oil fuel, tons: 370
Range, miles: 4 500 at 12 knots
Complement: 210

Former sloops of the British "Black Swan" class built for India and modified to suit Indian conditions. *Cauvery* was renamed *Kaveri* in 1968.

Radar: Fitted with E band air and surface surveillance radar and ranging radar for the gunfire control systems.

KISTNA

1 Ex-BRITISH "RIVER" CLASS

Name	No.
TIR (ex-HMS *Bann)*	F 256

Builders	Laid down	Launched	Commissioned
Charles Hill & Sons Ltd, Bristol	18 June 1942	29 Dec 1942	7 May 1943

Displacement, tons: 1 463 standard; 1 934 full load
Length, feet (metres): 283·0 *(86·3)* pp; 303 *(92·4)* oa
Beam, feet (metres): 37·6 *(11·2)*
Draught, feet (metres): 14·5 *(4·4)*
Guns: 1—4 in *(102 mm)*; 1—40 mm; 2—20 mm
Main engines: Triple expansion; 2 shafts; 5 500 ihp
Boilers: 2 Admiralty 3-drum type
Speed, knots: 18
Oil fuel, tons: 385
Range, miles: 4 200 at 12 knots
Complement: 120

Transferred on 3 Dec 1945. Converted to a Midshipman's Training Frigate by Bombay Dockyard in 1948.

TIR   1971, Indian Navy

CORVETTES

3 + (?3) Ex-SOVIET "NANUCHKA" CLASS

Displacement, tons: 850 full load
Length, feet (metres): 196·8 *(60)*
Beam, feet (metres): 39·6 *(12)*
Draught, feet (metres): 9·9 *(3)*
Missiles: Probably SS-N-2 (Styx)
Guns: 2—57 mm (twin)
Main engines: Diesels; 28 000 shp; 2 shafts
Speed, knots: 30
Complement: 70

A notable addition to Indian capabilities. Delivery 1976-77. Reported that a further three may be expected.

Radar: Search; Slim Net.
Navigation: Don.

SUBMARINES

Note: India is still discussing plans to build her own submarines though no details have been released.

8 Ex-SOVIET "FOXTROT" CLASS

KALVARI S 121	**VELA** S 40
KANDERI S 122	**VAGIR** S 41
KARANJ S 123	**VAGLI** S 42
KURSURA S 124	**VAGSHEER** S 43

Displacement, tons: 2 000 surfaced; 2 300 dived
Length, feet (metres): 296·8 *(90·5)*
Beam, feet (metres): 42·1 *(7·3)*
Draught, feet (metres): 19·0 *(5·8)*
Torpedo tubes: 10—21 in (20 torpedoes carried)
Main machinery: 3 diesels; 3 shafts; 6 000 bhp;
   3 electric motors; 6 000 hp
Speed, knots: 20 surfaced; 15 dived
Complement: 70

Kalvari arrived in India on 16 July 1968, *Kanderi* in Jan 1969.
Karanj in Oct 1970 and *Kursura* in Dec 1970. *Vela* Nov 1973,
Vagir Dec 1973, *Vagli* Sep 1974, *Vagsheer* May 1975.

Additions: There are reports, so far unconfirmed, that a further
pair may be transferred later.

VAGSHEER   *1974, Contre Amiral M. Adam*

LIGHT FORCES

16 Ex-SOVIET "OSA I and II" CLASS (FAST ATTACK CRAFT—MISSILE)

NASHAK P 684	**VEER** P 686	**PRALAYA**
NIPAT P 691	**VIDYUT** P 694	**PRACHAND**
NIRBHIK P 685	**VIJETA** P 693	**PRATAP**
NIRGHAT P 690	**VINASH** P 692	**PRABAL** + 4

Displacement, tons: 165 standard; 200 full load
Dimensions, feet (metres): 128·7 × 25·1 × 5·9 *(37 × 7 × 1·8)*
Missiles: 4 in two pairs for SS-N-2
Guns: 4—30 mm (2 twin)
Main engines: 3 diesels; 3 shafts; 13 000 bhp = 36 knots
Complement: 25

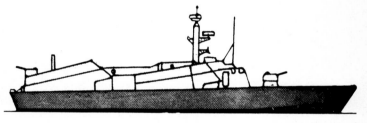

"OSA" Class

Some of these craft took part in a night attack with Styx off Karachi on 4-5 Dec 1971. They sank
the PNS *Khaibar,* damaged *Badr* and a CMS as well as one Panamanian m/s without damage to
themselves.
Further eight delivered Mar-Apr 1976. ("Osa II" class).

Missiles: One craft had three SS-N-2 launchers transferred to I. S. *Talwar* in late 1975.

Radar: Square Tie and Drum Tilt. IFF—Ski Pole.

4 + 4 "IMPROVED ABHAY" CLASS (LARGE PATROL CRAFT)

Of 140 tons with four diesels of 7 500 bhp. 1—40 mm gun.
First launched 1976, three more building at Garden Reach, Calcutta. Four more planned. Indian
Customs Service to purchase eight—"for but not with" armament.

1 "ABHAY" CLASS (LARGE PATROL CRAFT)

Name	*No.*	*Builders*	*Commissioned*
ABHAY	P 3135	Hoogly Docking & Engineering Co Ltd, Calcutta	13 Nov 1961

Displacement, tons: 120 standard; 151 full load
Dimensions, feet (metres): 110 pp; 117·2 oa × 20 × 5 *(33·6; 35·7 × 6·1 × 1·5)*
Gun: 1—40 mm
Main engines: 2 diesels; speed = 18 knots

Generally similar to the "Ford" class in the Royal Navy. Originally a class of six. *Ajay* and *Akshay*
transferred to Bangladesh 1974, *Amar* to Mauritius April 1974.

5 Ex-SOVIET "POLUCHAT" CLASS (COASTAL PATROL CRAFT)

PAMBAN P 247	**PANVEL** P 246	**PURI** P 248
PANAJI P 249	**PULICAT** P 250	

Displacement, tons: 86 standard; 91 full load
Dimensions, feet (metres): 98 × 15 × 4·8 *(29·9 × 4·6 × 1·5)*
Guns: 2—14·5 mm (twin)
Main engines: 2 Diesels; 2 shafts; 1 200 bhp = 18 knots
Range, miles: 460 at 17 knots
Complement: 16

One transferred to Bangladesh in 1973 but returned.

2 "SHARADA" CLASS (COASTAL PATROL CRAFT)

Name	*No.*	*Builders*	*Commissioned*
SHARADA	SPB 3133	Yugoslavia	5 Dec 1959
SUKANYA	SPB 3132	Yugoslavia	5 Dec 1959

Displacement, tons: 86
Dimensions, feet (metres): 103·2 *(31·5)* length
Guns: Small arms
Main engines: 2 MTU diesels

AMPHIBIOUS FORCES

6 Ex-SOVIET "POLNOCNY" CLASS (LCT)

GHARIAL L 3032   **GHORPAD** L 3034   **SHARDUL** L 3036
GULDAR L 3033   **KESARI** L 3035   **SHARAB** L 3037

Displacement, tons: 780 standard; 1 000 full load (3032 and 3033);
1 100 full load (remainder)
Dimensions, feet (metres): 239 × 29·5 × 9·8 *(72·9 × 9 × 3)* (3032 and 3033);
Remainder length 265 ft *(80·8),* beam 31 ft *(9·5)*
Guns: 2—25 mm (twin) (3032 and 3033); 4—30 mm (twins) (remainder)
Rocket launcher: Multi-barrelled 140 mm
Main engines: 2 diesels; 5 000 bhp = 18 knots

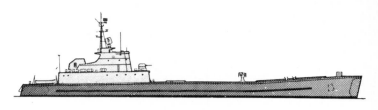

"POLNOCNY" Class

First pair transferred from USSR in 1966, *Ghorpad* in 1975, *Kesari* Sep 1975, *Shardul* Dec 1975 and *Sharab* Mar 1976.

Radar: Drum Tilt removed.

1 Ex-BRITISH LST (3)

MAGAR (ex-HMS *Avenger)* L 3011

Displacement, tons: 2 256 light; 4 980 full load
Dimensions, feet (metres): 347·5 oa × 55·2 × 11·2 *(106 × 16·8 × 3·4)*
Guns: 2—40 mm; 6—20 mm; (2 twin, 2 single)
Main engines: Triple expansion; 2 shafts; 5 500 ihp = 13 knots

There is also LCT 4294 (ex-1294), yard craft of 200 tons, speed 9·5 knots.

MAGAR   *1964, A. & J. Pavia*

MINE WARFARE FORCES

4 Ex-BRITISH "TON" CLASS (MINESWEEPERS—COASTAL)

Name	No.	Builders	Commissioned
CANNANORE	M 1191	Fleetlands Shipyard Ltd, Gosport	1956
(ex-HMS *Whitton)*			
KUDDALORE	M 1190	J. S. Doig Ltd, Grimsby	1955
(ex-HMS *Wennington)*			
KAKINADA	M 1201	Dorset Yacht Co Ltd, Hamworthy	1955
(ex-HMS *Durweston)*			
KARWAR	M 1197	Camper & Nicholson Ltd, Gosport	1956
(ex-HMS *Overton)*			

Displacement, tons: 360 standard; 425 full load
Dimensions, feet (metres): 140·0 pp; 153·0 oa × 28·8 × 8·2 *(46·7 × 8·8 × 2·5)*
Guns: 2—20 mm
Main engines: Napier Deltic diesels; 2 shafts; 1 250 bhp = 15 knots
Oil fuel, tons: 45
Range, miles: 3 000 at 8 knots
Complement: 40

KARWAR   *1971, Wright & Logan*

"Ton" class coastal minesweepers of wooden construction built for the Royal Navy, but transferred from Great Britain to the Indian Navy in 1956. *Cannanore* was launched 30 Jan 1956, *Karwar* was launched 30 Jan 1956. *Kuddalore* and *Kakinada* were taken over in Aug 1956, and sailed for India in Nov-Dec 1956. Named after minor ports in India. Constitute the 18th Mine Counter Measures Squadron, together with the inshore minesweepers.

4 "HAM" CLASS (IMS)

Name	No.	Builders	Commissioned
BASSEIN	M 2707	Brooke Marine Ltd,	1954
(ex-HMS *Littleham)*		Oulton Broad, Lowestoft	
BHAKTAL	M 89	Magazon Dockyard, Bombay	1968
BIMLIPITAN	M 2705	Vosper Ltd, Portsmouth	1954
(ex-HMS *Hildersham)*			
BULSAR	M 90	Magazon Dockyard, Bombay	1970

Displacement, tons: 120 standard; 170 full load
Dimensions, feet (metres): 98·0 pp; 107·0 oa × 22·0 × 6·7 *(32·6 × 6·7 × 1·6)*
Gun: 1—20 mm
Main engines: 2 Paxman diesels; 550 bhp = 14 knots (9 knots sweeping)
Oil fuel, tons: 15
Complement: 16

BASSEIN   *1971, A & J Pavia*

Of wooden construction two of which were built for the Royal Navy but transferred from Great Britain to the Indian Navy in 1955. *Bassein* was launched on 4 May 1954; *Bimlipitan* was launched on 5 Feb 1954. *Bhaktal* was launched in·April 1967, and *Bulsar* on 17 May 1969.

SURVEY SHIPS

Note: New construction survey ship in hand at Garden Reach Dockyard.

Name	No.	Builders	Commissioned
DARSHAK	A 139	Hindustan Shipyard, Vishakapatnam	28 Dec 1964

Displacement, tons: 2 790
Length, feet (metres): 319 *(97·2)* oa
Beam, feet (metres): 49 *(14·9)*
Draught, feet (metres): 28·8 *(8·8)*
Main engines: 2 diesel-electric units; 3 000 bhp
Speed, knots: 16
Complement: 150

First ship built by Hindustan Shipyard for the Navy. Launched on 2 Nov 1959. Provision was made to operate a helicopter. The ship is all welded.

DARSHAK   *1967*

2 "SUTLEJ" CLASS

Name	No.	Builders	Laid down	Launched	Commissioned
JAMUNA (ex-*Jumna*)	F 11	Wm. Denny & Bros Ltd, Dumbarton	20 Feb 1940	16 Nov 1940	13 May 1941
SUTLEJ	F 95	Wm. Denny & Bros Ltd, Dumbarton	4 Jan 1940	10 Oct 1940	23 Apr 1941

Displacement, tons: 1 300 standard; 1 750 full load
Length, feet (metres): 276 *(84·1)* wl; 292·5 *(89·2)* oa
Beam, feet (metres): 37·5 *(11·4)*
Draught, feet (metres): 11·5 *(3·5)*
Main engines: Parsons geared turbines 3 600 shp; 2 shafts
Boilers: 2 Admiralty 3-drum
Speed, knots: 18
Oil fuel, tons: 370
Range, miles: 5 600 at 12 knots
Complement: 150

Former frigates employed as survey ships since 1957 and 1955 respectively. Both ships are generally similar to the former British frigates of the "Egret" class.

JAMUNA   *11/1975, P. Elliott*

SERVICE FORCES

1 Ex-SOVIET "UGRA" CLASS (SUBMARINE TENDER)

AMBA A 14

Displacement, tons: 6 000 light; 9 000 full load
Length, feet (metres): 370 pp; 420 oa × 65 × 20 *(138 × 16·8 × 6·5)*
Guns: 4—3 in *(76 mm)* (twins)
Main engines: Diesels; 2 shafts; 7 000 bhp = 17 knots

Acquired from the USSR in 1968. Provision for helicopter. Can accommodate 750. Two cranes, one of 6 tons and one of 10 tons.

Radar: One Slim Net; two Hawk Screech.

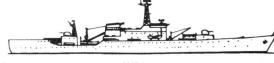

AMBA

1 Ex-SOVIET "T58" (Mod.) CLASS (SUBMARINE RESCUE SHIP)

NISTAR A 15

Displacement, tons: 790 standard; 900 full load
Dimensions, feet (metres): 220·0 × 29·5 × 7·9 *(67·7 × 9·1 × 2·3)*
Main engines: 2 diesels; 2 shafts; 5 000 bhp = 18 knots

Converted from a fleet minesweeper to a submarine rescue ship and transferred from USSR late-1971. Carries diving-bell and recompression chamber.

1 REPAIR SHIP

DHARINI (ex- *La Petite Hermine*) A 306

Displacement, tons: 6 000 (oil capacity 1 000)
Dimensions, feet (metres): 324·7 × 45·6 × 13·3 *(99 × 13·9 × 4)*
Main engines: Triple expansion; 809 ihp = 9 knots
Oil fuel, tons: 621

Cargo ship built by Foundation Maritime Ltd, Canada as *Ketowna Park*. Launched 25 July 1944. Sold to India for commercial use in 1953. Transferred to navy in 1957. Converted and commissioned in May 1960.

DHARINI   *1964, Indian Navy*

2 REPLENISHMENT TANKERS

DEEPAK A 1750   **+ 1**

Displacement, tons: 15 800
Measurement, tons: 12 690·6 GRT
Dimensions, feet (metres): 552·6 oa × 75·5 × 30 *(168·4 × 23 × 9·2)*
Guns: 3—40 mm; 2—20 mm
Main engines: Steam turbines = 20 knots

On charter to Indian Navy from Mogul Lines. Fitted with a helicopter landing platform aft, but no hangar. Automatic tensioning fitted to replenishment gear. Also carries dry cargo.
Deepak built by Bremer-Vulkan in 1972. Second ship launched by Bremer-Vulkan Sep 1975 and completed 31 Dec 1975.

1 SUPPORT TANKER

SHAKTI A 136

Displacement, tons: 3 500
Dimensions, feet (metres): 323 × 44 × 20 *(97 × 13·5 × 6·6)*
Main engines: Diesel; speed = 13 knots

Laid up in reserve, probably for disposal.
Acquired from Italy in Nov 1953.

1 SUPPORT TANKER

LOK ADHAR (ex-*Hooghly*)

Displacement, tons: 9 231

Formerly *Baqir* of Gulf Shipping Corp. Ltd. Acquired in 1972.

1 TUG (OCEAN)

Name	No.	Builders	Commissioned
HATHI	—	Taikoo Dock & Engineering Company, Hong Kong	1933

Displacement, tons: 668
Dimensions, feet (metres): 147·5 × 23·7 × 15 *(45 × 7·2 × 4·6)*
Main engines: Triple expansion; speed = 13 knots

Launched in 1932.

4 Ex-BRITISH HDML TYPE

SPC 3110 (ex-*HDML 1110*)   **SPC 3117** (ex-*HDML 1117*)
SPC 3112 (ex-*HDML 1112*)   **SPC 3118** (ex-*HDML 1118*)

Displacement, tons: 48 standard; 54 full load
Dimensions, feet (metres): 72 oa × 16 × 4·7 *(22 × 4·9 × 1·4)*
Guns: 2—20 mm
Main engines: Diesels; 2 shafts; 320 bhp = 12 knots
Complement: 14

Used as harbour craft.

1 SUPPORT TANKER

DESH DEEP

Measurement, tons: 11 000 DWT

Ex-Japanese merchant tanker taken over in 1972.

A number of harbour tankers (approx 1 000 tons) have been built at Bombay.
A new class of fleet tug (approx 1 200 bhp) has been built recently at Garden Reach.

Barq (ex-*MMS 132*), *MMS 130* and *MMS 154*, former British motor minesweepers of the "105 ft" type of wooden construction, transferred from Great Britain, are employed as yard craft. *MMS 1632* and *MMS 1654* are yard craft in Bombay.

INDONESIA

Ministerial

Minister of Defence and Security:
General Maraden Panggabean

Administration

Chief of the Naval Staff:
Admiral R. Subiyakto
Deputy Chief of the Naval Staff Operations:
Rear-Admiral Wulujo Sugito
Inspector General of the Navy:
Commodore M. Wibowo
Chief for Naval Material:
Commodore Urip Subiyanto
Chief for Naval Personnel:
Commodore Imem Muharam
Commander of Navy Marine Corps:
Major General Moch Anwar
Commander-in-Chief Indonesian Fleet:
Rear-Admiral Rudy Purwana

Diplomatic Representation

Naval Attaché in Bangkok:
Lt. Colonel Purnomo
Naval Attaché in Canberra:
Colonel Eddy Tumengkol
Naval Attaché in Delhi:
Lt. Colonel B. Sumitro
Naval Attaché and Naval Attaché for Air in London:
Colonel Sumarjono
Naval Attaché in Moscow:
Colonel Priyonggo
Naval Attaché in Tokyo:
Colonel Agus Subroto
Naval Attaché and Naval Attaché for Air in Washington:
Colonel Ariffin Roesady

Personnel

(a) 1977: 39 000 including 5 000 Marine Commando Corps and 1 000 Naval Air Arm
(b) Selective National Service

Bases

Gorontalo, Kemajaran (Jakarta), Surabaja

Strength of the Fleet

Type	Active	Building
Frigates	11	3
Patrol Submarines	3	—
Fast Attack Craft—Missile	13	—
Fast Attack Craft—Torpedo	5	—
Large Patrol Craft	19	—
Coastal Patrol Craft	8	—
LSTs	9	—
LCUs	2	—
Minesweepers—Ocean	5	—
Minesweepers—Coastal	2	—
Survey Ships	4	—
Submarine Tenders	2	—
Destroyer Depot Ship	1	—
Repair Ship	1	—
Replenishment Tanker	1	—
Support Tankers	4	—
Harbour Tankers	3	—
Cable Ship	1	—
Tugs	3	—
Training Ship	1	—
Customs	19+	—
Army	23	—
Air Force	6	—

Ex-Soviet Ships

Indonesia obtained 104 ships from the USSR. Of these half have now been deleted and all will have gone in the near future.

Future Plans

It is planned, over the next 20 years, to provide a Navy of some 25 000 seamen and 5 000 marines to man a Fleet including 4 fast A/S Frigates, some Submarines, Light Forces of Fast Attack Craft—Missile and—Torpedo, Minelayers, Minesweepers, a fast HQ ship and a fast Supply Ship. 3 Corvettes/Frigates are being built by the Netherlands.

Naval Air Arm

6—GAF Nomad (MR)
5—HU 16B Albatross (SAR)
6—C 47
3—Alouette II helicopters
3—Alouette III helicopters
4—Bell 47G helicopters
3—Commander

Prefix to Ships' Names

KRI (Kapal di Republik Indonesia)

Mercantile Marine

Lloyd's Register of Shipping:
882 vessels of 1 046 198 tons gross

DELETIONS

Cruiser

1972 *Irian*

Destroyers

1973 *Brawidjaja, Sandjaja, Sultan Babarudin*

Frigates

1973 *Lambung Mangkurat, Slamet Rijadi*
1974 *Ngurah Rai* ("Riga" class)

Submarines

1974 *Alugoro, Hendradjala, Nagarangsang, Tjandrasa, Tjundmani, Trisula, Widjajadanu*
(all "Whiskey" class)

Amphibious Forces

1974 3 ex-Yugoslav LCTs, *Tandjung Nusanive* (ex-US LST); 3 ex-US LCI Type

Minewarfare Forces

1974 4 ex-Dutch CMS, 5 "R" Class
1976 *Pulau Rondo* ("T 43" class), *Rau, Rindja, Rusa* ("R" class), *Pulau Alor, Pulau Anjer, Pulau Antang, Pulau Aru, Pulah Aruan, Pulau Impalasa* ("Falcon" class)

Light Forces

1970 *310, 314, 315, 316* (Kraljevica), *Dorang, Lajang, Rubara*
1974 2 "Jaguar" class, 25 HDMLs, 10 Motor Launches, *Palu, Tenggiri*

1975 14 "P 6" class, 18 "BK" class, *Landjuru, Lapai, Lumba Lumba, Madidihang, Tongkol, Tjutjut* ("Kronshtadt" class)
1976 *Katula, Tohok* ("Kronshtadt" class), *Krapu* ("Kraljevica" class), *Hardadali, Katjabola, Tritusta* ("Komar" class)

Survey Ships

1972 *Hidral*
1973 *Dewa Kembar*

Auxiliaries

1974 2 Transports, 1 Salvage Vessel, 1 Tug, 37 Patrol Craft
1976 *Thamrin* ("Atrek" class), *Pangkalin Brandan, Wono Kromo* ("Uda" class)

PENNANT LIST

Frigates

350	Iman Bondjol
351	Surapati
352	Pattimura
353	Sultan Hasanudin
341	Samadikun
342	Martadinata
343	Mongisidi
344	Ngurah Rai
351	Jos Sudarso
359	Kakiali
360	Nuku

Submarines

403	Nagabanda
410	Pasopati
412	Bramastra

Light Forces

313	Tjakalang
317	Torani
318	Hiu
570	Bentang Kalakuang
571	Bentang Waitatire
572	Bentang Silunkang
602	Anoa
603	Biruang
604	Harimau
605	Matjan Kumbang
607	Serigala
814	Pandrong
815	Sura
816	Kakap
817	Barakuda
830	Sibarau
831	Silinan
?	Momare
?	Sembilang

Amphibious Forces

501	Teluk Langsa
502	Teluk Bajur
504	Teluk Kau
505	Teluk Manado
510	Teluk Saleh
511	Teluk Bone
?	Teluk Tomini
?	Teluk Rati
869	Teluk Amboina

Support Ships

561	Multatuli
?	Ratulangi

Service Forces

901	Tjepu
903	Sambu
904	Bunju
911	Sorong
921	Jaya Widjaja
928	Rakata
934	Lampo Batang
936	Bromo
1006	Purudjulasad

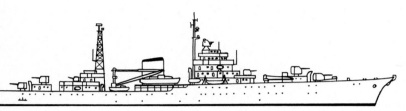

RATULANGI

"RIGA" Class

"CLAUD JONES" Class

"SURAPATI" Class

FRIGATES

3 NEW CONSTRUCTION

Displacement, tons: 1 500
Main engines: CODOG arrangement; 1 Olympus gas turbine; 2

MTU diesels; 4 000 hp;
2 shafts

Building by Wilton Fyenoord, Netherlands. First laid down Autumn 1976. Officially rated as "Corvettes"

4 Ex-US "CLAUD JONES" CLASS

Name	No.	Builders	Laid down	Launched	Commissioned
SAMADIKUN (ex-USS John R. Perry DE 1034)	341	Avondale Marine Ways	1 Oct 1957	29 July 1958	5 May 1959
MARTADINATA (ex-USS Charles Berry DE 1035)	342	American SB Co, Toledo, Ohio	29 Oct 1958	17 Mar 1959	25 Nov 1959
NGURAH RAI (ex-USS McMorris DE 1036)	344	American SB Co, Toledo, Ohio	5 Nov 1958	26 May 1959	4 Mar 1960
MONGISIDI (ex-USS Claud Jones DE 1033)	343	Avondale Marine Ways	1 June 1957	27 May 1958	10 Feb 1959

Displacement, tons: 1 450 standard; 1 750 full load
Length, feet (metres): 310 (95) oa
Beam, feet (metres): 37 (11·3)
Draught, feet (metres): 18 (5·5)
Guns: 1—3 in (76 mm) 50 cal; 2—37 mm (twin); 2—25 mm (twin) (341-342); 2—3 in (76 mm) (single); 2—25 mm (twin) (343-344)
A/S weapons: 2 triple Torpedo Tubes (Mk 32); 2 Hedgehog
Main engines: 4 diesels; 9 200 hp; 1 shaft
Speed, knots: 22
Complement: 175

Samadikun acts as fleet flagship.

Electronics: ECM/ESM gear removed

Gunnery: Fire control system Mk 70 for 3-in. Secondary armament is ex-Soviet artillery.

Radar: SPS 6 and 10.

Sonar: SQS 29-32 series.

Transfer: *Samadikun,* 20 Feb 1973; *Martadinata,* 31 Jan 1974; *Mongisidi* and *Ngurah Rai* 16 Dec 1974.

SAMADIKUN

1975, Indonesian Navy

JOS SUDARSO 351   **NUKU** 360
KAKIALI 359

Displacement, tons: 1 200 standard; 1 600 full load
Length, feet (metres): 298·8 (91)
Beam, feet (metres): 33·7 (10·2)
Draught, feet (metres): 11 (3·4)
Guns: 3—3·9 in (100 mm) (single); 4—37 mm
A/S weapons: 4 DC projectors
Torpedo tubes: 3—21 in (533 mm)
Mines: Fitted with mine rails
Main engines: Geared steam turbines; 2 shafts; 25 000 shp
Boilers: 2
Speed, knots: 28
Range, miles: 2 500 at 15 knots
Complement: 150

Transferred in 1964.

Radar: Slim Net search and warning; Fire control Sun Visor A with Wasp Head director; Navigation Neptun; IFF, High Pole A.

3 Ex-SOVIET "RIGA" CLASS

JOS SUDARSO   1974, John Mortimer

2 "SURAPATI" CLASS

Name	No.	Builders	Laid down	Launched	Commissioned
IMAN BONDJOL	250	Ansaldo, Genoa	8 Jan 1956	5 May 1956	19 May 1958
SURAPATI	251	Ansaldo, Genoa	8 Jan 1956	5 May 1956	28 May 1958

Displacement, tons: 1 150 standard; 1 500 full load
Dimensions, feet (metres): 325 × 36 × 8·5 (99 × 11 × 2·6)
Guns: 4—4 in (102 mm) (twins); 6—30 mm (twins);
   6—20 mm (twins)
A/S weapons: 2 Hedgehogs; 4 DCT
Torpedo tubes: 3—21 in (533 mm)
Boilers: 2 Foster Wheeler
Main engines: 2 sets Parsons geared turbines, 2 shafts;
   24 000 shp
Speed, knots: 32
Oil fuel, tons: 350
Range, miles: 2 800 at 22 knots
Complement: 200

Near sisters of the "Almirante Clemente" class of Venezuela.

IMAN BONDJOL   Dr Ing Luigi Accorsi

2 "PATTIMURA" CLASS

Name	No.	Builders	Laid down	Launched	Commissioned
PATTIMURA	252	Ansaldo, Leghorn	8 Jan 1956	1 July 1956	28 Jan 1958
SULTAN HASANUDIN	253	Ansaldo, Leghorn	8 Jan 1957	24 Mar 1957	8 Mar 1958

Displacement, tons: 950 standard; 1 200 full load
Length, feet (metres): 246 (75·0) pp; 270·2 (82·4) oa
Beam, feet (metres): 34 (10·4)
Draught, feet (metres): 9 (2·7)
Guns: 2—3 in (76 mm) 40 cal. 2—30 mm 70 cal (twin)
A/S weapons: 2 Hedgehogs; 4 DCT
Main engines: 3 Ansaldo-Fiat diesels; 3 shafts; 6 900 bhp
Speed, knots: 22
Range, miles: 2 400 at 18 knots
Oil fuel, tons: 100
Complement: 110

Similar to Italian "Albatros" class.

PATTIMURA   Dr Ing Luigi Accorsi

SUBMARINES

3 Ex-SOVIET "WHISKEY" CLASS

BRAMASTRA 412   **PASOPATI** 410
NAGGA BANDA 403

Displacement, tons: 1 030 surfaced; 1 350 dived
Length, feet (metres): 249·3 (76)
Beam, feet (metres): 22 (6·7)
Draught, feet (metres): 15 (4·6)
Torpedo tubes: 6—21 in (533 mm) 4 forward, 2 aft;
   18 torpedoes carried
Guns: 2—25 mm (403)
Mines: 40 in lieu of torpedoes
Main machinery: 4 000 bhp diesels; 2 500 hp electric motors, diesel-electric drive; 2 shafts
Speed, knots: 17 surfaced; 15 dived
Range, miles: 13 000 at 8 knots surfaced
Complement: 60

"WHISKEY" Class

The four Soviet submarines of the "Whiskey" class, which arrived in Indonesia on 28 June 1962, brought the total number of this class transferred to Indonesia to 14 units, but it was reported that only six would be maintained operational, while six would be kept in reserve and two used for spare parts. Now reduced to three operational boats of which two have been refitted and have received new batteries from UK.

LIGHT FORCES

6 Ex-SOVIET "KRONSHTADT" CLASS (LARGE PATROL CRAFT)

BARAKUDA 817	**MOMARE**	**SEMBILANG**
KAKAP 816	**PANDRONG** 814	**SURA** 815

Displacement, tons: 310 standard; 380 full load
Dimensions, feet (metres): 170·6 × 21·5 × 9 *(52·0 × 6·5 × 2·7)*
Guns: 1—3·5 in *(85 mm)*; 2—37 mm; 6—12·7 mm
A/S weapons: 2 DCT; 2 RBU 1800; 2 dc racks
Mines: 2 mine rails for 10 mines
Main engines: 3 Diesels; 3 shafts; 3 300 bhp = 19 knots
Oil fuel, tons: 20
Range, miles: 1 500 at 12 knots
Complement: 65

Built in 1951-54. Transferred to the Indonesian Navy on 30 Dec 1958.

Radar: Ball Gun or Don 2; IFF, High Pole A

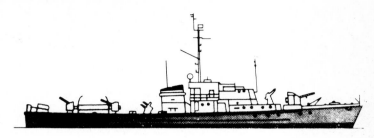

"KRONSHTADT" Class

3 Ex-US "PC-461" CLASS (LARGE PATROL CRAFT)

HIU (ex-USS *Malvern*, PC 580) 318
TJAKALANG (ex-USS *Pierre*, PC 1141) 313
TORANI (ex-USS *Manville*, PC 581) 317

Displacement, tons: 280 standard; 450 full load
Dimensions, feet (metres): 170 wl; 173·7 oa × 23 × 10·8 *(55·7; 53 × 7 × 3·3)*
Guns: 1—37 mm; 4—25 mm (twin)
A/S weapons: 4 DCT
Main engines: 2 GM diesels; 2 shafts; 2 880 bhp = 20 knots
Oil fuel, tons: 60
Range, miles: 5 000 at 10 knots
Complement: 54 (4 officers, 50 men)

Gunnery: Original armament of 1—3 in *(76 mm)*; 1—40 mm; 2—20 mm has been replaced in most ships by armament shown from deleted ex-Soviet ships.

Built in 1942-43. *Pierre* transferred from the US Navy at Pearl Harbor, Hawaii in Oct 1958 and *Malvern* and *Manville* in Mar 1960.

"PC-461" Class

1966, Indonesian Navy

4 PSSM Mark 5 (FAST ATTACK CRAFT—MISSILE)

Displacement, tons: 250 full load
Dimensions, feet (metres): 165 × 24 × 6·6 *(50·3 × 7·3 × 2)*
Missiles: 4 launchers for Standard SSM
Guns: 1—3 in *(76 mm)* 50 cal; 1—40 mm; 2—0·50 cal MG
Main engines: 6 Avco-Lycoming gas turbines; 2 shafts (cp propellers) = 40 knots
Complement: 32

Ordered from Tacoma Boatbuilding Co, Washington for delivery 1976-77.
Building in South Korea.

9 Ex-SOVIET "KOMAR" CLASS
(FAST ATTACK CRAFT—MISSILE)

GUAWIDJAJA	**KELAPLINTAH**	**SUROTAMA**
KALAMISANI	**PULANGGENI**	**SARPAMINA**
KALANADA	**NAGAPASA**	**SARPAWASESA**

Displacement, tons: 70 standard; 80 full load
Dimensions, feet (metres): 83·7 × 19·8 × 5 *(25·5 × 6·0 × 1·8)*
Guns: 2—35 mm (1 twin)
Missiles: 2 launchers for S-SN-2
Main engines: 4 diesels; 4 800 hp = 40 knots
Range, miles: 400 at 30 knots
Complement: 20

Six were transferred to Indonesia in 1961-63, four more in Sep 1964 and two in 1965. Missiles probably of doubtful capability.

Loss: *Hardadali* of this class sank early 1976 after hitting an underwater obstacle.

Indonesian "KOMAR" Class

1967

5 "LURSSEN TNC-45" CLASS
(FAST ATTACK CRAFT—TORPEDO)

Name	No.	Builders	Commissioned
ANOA	602	Singapore	1959
BIRUANG	603	Singapore	1959
HARIMAU	604	Singapore	1960
MATJAN KUMBANG	605	Singapore	1960
SERIGALA	607	Singapore	1960

Displacement, tons: 160 standard; 190 full load
Dimensions, feet (metres): 131 pp; 138 oa × 22 × 7·5 *(42·9; 42·1 × 6·7 × 2·3)*
Guns: 2—40 mm (single)
Torpedo tubes: 4—21 in
Main engines: 4 Daimler-Benz (MTU) diesels; 4 shafts; 12 000 bhp = 42 knots
Complement: 39

The first four boats had wooden hulls. Built to Lürssen design. Similar to German "Jaguar" class.

HARIMAU *Indonesia*

3 Ex-US "PGM 53" CLASS (LARGE PATROL CRAFT)

BENTANG SILUNGKANG (ex-*PGM 55*) 572
BENTANG WAITATIRE (ex-*PGM 56*) 571
BENTANG KALAKUANG (ex-*PGM 57*) 570

Displacement, tons: 122 full load
Dimensions, feet (metres): 100 × 21 × 8·5 *(30·5 × 6·4 × 2·6)*
Guns: 2—20 mm; 2 MG

Main engines: 2 Mercedes-Benz MB 820 dB diesels; 2 shafts = 17 knots

Originally intended as Amphibious Control Craft. Now used for normal patrol duties. All transferred Jan 1962.

Gunnery: Original armament 4—12·7 mm MG (twin)

2 Ex-AUSTRALIAN "ATTACK" CLASS
(LARGE PATROL CRAFT)

SIBARAU (ex-HMAS *Bandolier*) 830
SILINAN (ex-HMAS *Archer*) 831

Displacement, tons: 146 full load
Dimensions, feet (metres): 107·5 × 20 × 7·3 *(32·8 × 6·1 × 2·2)*
Guns: 1—40 mm; 2 medium MGs
Main engines: 2 Paxman diesels; 2 shafts = 21 knots
Complement: 19 (3 officers, 16 men)

Transferred from RAN after refit—*Bandolier* 16 Nov 1973, *Archer* in 1974. It is reported, though not confirmed, that another six may be transferred.

SIBARAU *1973, Graeme Andrews*

5 Ex-YUGOSLAVIAN "KRALJEVICA" CLASS
(LARGE PATROL CRAFT)

BUBARA	LAJANG	TODAK
DORANG	LEMADANG	

Displacement, tons: 190 standard; 245 full load
Dimensions, feet (metres): 134·5 × 20·8 × 7 *(41 × 6·3 × 2·1)*
Guns: 1—3 in; 1—40 mm; 6—20 mm
A/S weapons: DC
Main engines: 2 MAN diesels; 2 shafts; 3 300 bhp = 20 knots
Oil fuel, tons: 15
Range, miles: 1 500 at 12 knots
Complement: 54

Purchased and transferred on 27th Dec 1958.

DORANG *1968, Indonesian Navy*

3 "KELABANG" CLASS (LARGE PATROL CRAFT)

KALAHITAM   **KELABANG**   **KOMPAS**

Displacement, tons: 147
Gun: 1—40/60 mm; 4—12·7 mm MG (twins)
Main engines: 2 MAN diesels = 21 knots

Built in Indonesia in 1966-70.

KALAHITAM   1968, Indonesian Navy

2 FAIREY MARINE "SPEAR" CLASS
(COASTAL PATROL CRAFT)

Dimensions, feet (metres): 29·8 × 9·2 × 2·6 (9·1 × 2·8 × ·8)   Purchased in 1973-74.
Main engines: Twin 180 hp diesels
Speed, knots: 30
Range, miles: 200 at 26 knots

6 (?) AUSTRALIAN DE HAVILLAND TYPE
(COASTAL PATROL CRAFT)

52·5 ft (16 metres). Craft transferred 1976-77. Speed 30 knots. Built by Hawker-De Havilland, Sydney.

AMPHIBIOUS FORCES

8 Ex-US "LST 511" CLASS

Name	No.	Builders	Commissioned
TELUK BAJUR (ex-USS *LST 616*)	502	—	—
TELUK BONE (ex-USS *Iredell County, LST 839*)	511	—	—
TELUK KAU (ex-USS *LST 652*)	504	—	—
TELUK LANGSA (ex-USS *LST 1128*)	501	—	—
TELUK MANADO (ex-USS *LST 657*)	505	—	—
TELUK RATAI	—	—	—
TELUK SALEH (ex-USS *Clark County, LST 601*)	510	—	—
TELUK TOMINI	—	—	—

Displacement, tons: 1 653 standard; 4 080 full load
Dimensions, feet (metres): 316 wl; 328 oa × 50 × 14 (103·6; 100 × 15·3 × 4·3)

Guns: 7—40 mm; 2—20 mm (some); 6—37 mm (remainder)
Main engines: GM diesels; 2 shafts; 1 700 bhp = 11·6 knots
Oil fuel, tons: 600
Range, miles: 7 200 at 10 knots
Cargo capacity: 2 100 tons
Complement: 119 (accommodation for 266)

Gunnery: Older units and later unarmed ships fitted with ex-Soviet 37 mm.

Transfers: 505 in Mar 1960, 502, 510 and 511 in June 1961. 504 and 501 in July 1970.

1 JAPANESE TYPE LST

Name	No.	Builders	Commissioned
TELUK AMBOINA	LST 869	Japan	1961

Displacement, tons: 2 200 standard; 4 800 full load
Dimensions, feet (metres): 327 × 50 × 15 (99·7 × 15·3 × 4·6)
Guns: 4—40 mm; 1—37 mm
Main engines: MAN diesels; 2 shafts; 3 000 bhp = 13·1 knots
Oil fuel, tons: 1 200
Range, miles: 4 000 at 13·1 knots
Complement: 88 (accommodation for 300)

Launched on 17 Mar 1961 and transferred in June 1961. A copy of US "LST 511" class.

2 LCU TYPE

DORE   **AMURANG**

Displacement, tons: 182 standard; 275 full load
Dimensions, feet (metres): 125·7 × 32·8 × 5·9 (38·3 × 10 × 1·8)
Main engines: Diesels; 210 hp = 8 knots
Complement: 17

Built in Austria.

MINE WARFARE FORCES

5 Ex-SOVIET "T 43" CLASS (MINESWEEPERS—OCEAN)

PULAU RANI   **PULAU RATENO**   **PULAU RORBAS**
PULAU RADJA   **PULAU ROON**

Displacement, tons: 500 standard; 610 full load
Dimensions, feet (metres): 190·2 × 28·2 × 6·9 (58 × 8·6 × 2·1)
Guns: 4—37 mm (twin); 8—12·7 mm (twin)
A/S weapons: 2 DCT

Main engines: 2 diesels; 2 shafts; 2 000 bhp = 17 knots
Range, miles: 1 600 at 10 knots
Complement: 40

Transferred to Indonesia by the USSR, four in 1962 and two in 1964. *Pulau Rondo* is in reserve.

2 "R" CLASS (MINESWEEPERS—COASTAL)

Name	No.	Builders	Commissioned
PULAU RENGATI	—	Abeking & Rasmussen Jacht-und Bootswerft, Lemwerder	—
PULAU RUPAT	—	Abeking & Rasmussen Jacht-und Bootswerft, Lemwerder	—

Displacement, tons: 139·4 standard
Dimensions, feet (metres): 129 × 18·7 × 5 (39·3 × 5·7 × 1·5)
Guns: 1—40 mm; 2—20 mm
Main engines: 2 MAN diesels; 12 cyl; 2 800 bhp = 24·6 knots
Complement: 26

Originally a class of ten. These boats have a framework of light metal covered with wood.

"R" Class   Indonesian Navy

SURVEY SHIPS

Name	No.	Builders	Commissioned
BURUDJULASAD	1006	—	1967

Displacement, tons: 2 150 full load
Dimensions, feet (metres): 269·5 × 37·4 × 11·5 *(82·2 × 11·4 × 3·5)*
Main engines: 4 MAN diesels; 2 shafts; 6 850 bhp = 19·1 knots
Complement: 113

Burudjulasad was launched in 1966; her equipment includes laboratories for oceanic and meteorological research, a cartographic room, and a helicopter.

ARIES

Displacement, tons: 35
Dimensions, feet (metres): 68·9 × 12·5 × 6·6 *(21 × 3·8 × 2)*
Main engines: Werkspoor diesel engines; 450 bhp
Complement: 13

Launched 1960.

Name	No.	Builders	Commissioned
BURDJAMHAL	—	Scheepswerf De Waal, Zaltbommel	6 July 1953

Displacement, tons: 1 500 full load
Dimensions, feet (metres): 211·7 oa; 192 pp × 33·2 × 10 *(58·6 × 10·1 × 3·3)*
Main engines: 2 Werkspoor diesels; 1 160 bhp = 10 knots
Complement: 90

Launched on 6 Sep 1952.

JALANIDHI

Displacement, tons: 985
Dimensions, feet (metres): 159·1 × 31·2 × 14·1 *(48·5 × 9·5 × 4·3)*
Speed, knots: 11·5
Complement: 58

Launched in 1962.

COMMAND AND SUPPORT SHIPS

1 SUBMARINE TENDER

Name	No.	Builders	Commissioned
MULTATULI	561	Ishikawajima-Harima Heavy Industries Co Ltd	Aug 1961

Displacement, tons: 3 220
Dimensions, feet (metres): 338 pp; 365·3 oa × 52·5 × 23 *(103; 111·4 × 16 × 7)*
Guns: 8—37 mm (2 twin, 4 single); 4—MG
Aircraft: 1 Alouette II helicopter
Main engines: B & W diesel; 5 500 bhp = 18·5 knots
Oil fuel, tons: 1 400
Range, miles: 6 000 at 16 knots cruising speed
Complement: 134

Built as a submarine tender. Launched on 15 May 1961. Delivered to Indonesia Aug 1961. Flush decker. Capacity for replenishment at sea (fuel oil, fresh water, provisions, ammunition, naval stores and personnel). Medical and hospital facilities. Equipment for supplying compressed air, electric power and distilled water to submarines. Air-conditioning and mechanical ventilation arrangements for all living and working quarters. Now used as fleet flagship.

Reconstruction: After 76 mm mounting replaced by helicopter deck.

1 Ex-SOVIET "DON" CLASS (SUBMARINE TENDER)

RATULANGI

Displacement, tons: 6 700 standard; 9 000 full load
Dimensions, feet (metres): 458·9 × 57·7 × 22·3 *(140 × 17·6 × 6·8)*
Guns: 4—3·9 in; 8—57 mm; 8—25 mm (twins)
Main engines: Diesels; 14 000 bhp = 21 knots
Complement: 300

A submarine support ship, escort vessel and maintenance tender transferred from the USSR to Indonesia in 1962, arriving in Indonesia in July. Fitted with Slim Net search and warning radar and with fire control radar.

RATULANGI   *1968, Indonesian Navy*

SERVICE FORCES

1 Ex-US "ACHELOUS" CLASS (REPAIR SHIP)

JAYA WIDJAJA (ex-USS *Askari 9109*, ex-*ARL 30*, ex-*LST 1131*) 921

Displacement, tons: 1 625 light; 4 100 full load
Dimensions, feet (metres): 316·0 wl; 328·0 oa × 50·0 × 11·0 *(96·4; 100 × 15·3 × 3·4)*
Guns: 8—40 mm (2 quadruple)
Main engines: General Motors diesels; 2 shafts; 1 800 bhp = 11·6 knots
Complement: 280

Of wartime construction this ship was in reserve from 1956-66. She was recommissioned and reached Vietnam in 1967 to support River Assault Flotilla One. She was used by the USN and Vietnamese Navy working up the Mekong in support of the Cambodian operations in May 1970. Transferred on lease to Indonesia at Guam on 31 Aug 1971.

1 Ex-US "SHENANDOAH" CLASS (DESTROYER DEPOT SHIP)

DUMAI (ex-USS *Tidewater* AD31)

Displacement, tons: 8 165 standard; 16 635 full load
Dimensions, feet (metres): 465 wl; 492 oa × 69·5 × 27·2 *(141·8; 150·1 × 21·2 × 8·3)*
Gun: 1—5 in; 38 cal
Main engines: Geared turbines; 1 shaft; 8 500 shp = 18·4 knots
Boilers: 2 Babcock & Wilcox
Complement: 778

Transferred Feb 1971 as destroyer depot ship. No longer operational with most of equipment removed and used as accommodation ship for oil-field personnel.

1 REPLENISHMENT TANKER

SORONG 911

Measurement, tons: 5 100 dead weight
Dimensions, feet (metres): 367·4 × 50·5 × 21·6 *(112 × 15·4 × 6·6)*
Guns: 8—12·7 mm (twins)
Speed, knots: 15 (10 economical)

Built in Yugoslavia in 1965. Has underway replenishment facilities. Capacity 3 000 tons fuel and 300 tons water.

SORONG   *1974, John Mortimer*

2 Ex-SOVIET TYPE (SUPPORT TANKERS)

BUNJU 904   **SAMBU** 903

Displacement, tons: 2 170 standard; 6 170 full lad
Dimensions, feet (metres): 350·5 × 49·2 × 20·2 *(106·9 × 15 × 6·2)*
Guns: 2—20 mm
Main engines: Polar diesel; 1 shaft; 2 650 bhp = 10 knots
Oil fuel, tons: 390
Cargo capacity: 4 739 tons
Complement: 71

Transferred to the Indonesian Navy on 19 June 1959. Both laid up in 1969.

1 Ex-SOVIET "UDA" CLASS (SUPPORT TANKER)

BALIKPAPAN

Displacement, tons: 5 500 standard; 7 200 full load
Dimensions, feet (metres): 400·3 × 51·8 × 20·3 *(122·1 × 15·8 × 6·2)*
Guns: 6—25 mm (twins)
Main engines: Diesels; 2 shafts; 8 000 bhp = 17 knots

1 SUPPORT TANKER

TJEPU (ex-*Scandus*, ex-*Nordhem*) 901

Displacement, tons: 1 372
Measurement, tons: 1 042 gross
Dimensions, feet (metres): 226·5 × 34 × 14·2 *(69·1 × 10·4 × 6·3)*
Main engines: Polar diesel; 1 shaft; 850 bhp = 11 knots

Built in Sweden in 1949. Acquired in 1951. Laid up in 1969.

2 HARBOUR TANKERS

TARAKAN   **BULA**

Displacement, tons: 1 340 full load
Dimensions, feet (metres): 352·0 × 37·7 × 14·8 *(107·4 × 11·5 × 4·5)*
Main engines: Diesels; 1 shaft; 1 500 bhp = 13 knots

1 Ex-SOVIET "KHOBI" CLASS (HARBOUR TANKER)

PAKAN BARU

Displacement, tons: 1 500 full load
Dimensions, feet (metres): 63 × 11·5 × 4·5 *(19·2 × 3·5 × 1·2)*
Main engines: Diesels; 2 shafts; 800 bhp = 11 knots

TRAINING SHIP

Name	No.	Builders	Commissioned
DEWARUTJI	—	H. C. Stülcken & Sohn, Hamburg	9 July 1953

Displacement, tons: 810 standard; 1 500 full load
Dimensions, feet (metres): 136·2 oa, 191·2 pp × 31·2 × 13·9 *(41·5; 58·3 × 9·5 × 4·2)*
Main engines: MAN diesels; 600 bhp = 10·5 knots
Complement: 110 (32 + 78 midshipmen)

Barquentine of steel construction. Sail area, 1 305 sq yds *(1 091 sq metres)*. Launched on 24 Jan 1953.

CABLE SHIP

Name	No.	Builders	Commissioned
BIDUK	—	J & K Smit, Kinderijk	30 July 1952

Displacement, tons: 1 250 standard
Dimensions, feet (metres): 213·2 oa × 39·5 × 11·5 *(65 × 12 × 3·5)*
Main engines: 1 Triple expansion engine; 1 600 ihp = 12 knots
Complement: 66

Cable Layer, Lighthouse Tender, and multi-purpose naval auxiliary. Launched on 30 Oct 1951.

TUGS

RAKATA (ex-USS *Menominee, ATF 73*) 928

Displacement, tons: 1 235 standard; 1 675 full load
Dimensions, feet (metres): 195 wl; 205 oa × 38·5 × 15·5 *(59·5; 62·5 × 11·7 × 4·7)*
Guns: 1—3 in *(76 mm)*; 2—40 mm; 4—25 mm (twins)
Main engines: 4 diesels with electric drive; 3 000 bhp = 16·5 knots
Complement: 85

Former American fleet ocean tug of the "Cherokee" class. Launched on 14 Feb 1942. Transferred from the United States Navy to the Indonesian Navy at San Diego in Mar 1961. Civilian manned.

Name	No.	Builders	Commissioned
LAMPO BATANG	934	Japan	Nov 1961

Displacement, tons: 250
Dimensions, feet (metres): 86·7 pp; 92·3 oa × 23·2 × 11·3 *(26·4; 28·2 × 7·1 × 3·4)*
Main engines: 2 diesels; 1 200 bhp = 11 knots
Oil fuel, tons: 18
Range, miles: 1 000 at 11 knots
Complement: 43

Ocean tug. Launched in April 1961. Delivered in Nov 1961.

Name	No.	Builders	Commissioned
BROMO	936	Japan	Aug 1961

Displacement, tons: 150
Dimensions, feet (metres): 71·7 wl; 79 oa × 21·7 × 9·7 *(21·9; 24·1 × 6·6 × 3)*
Main engines: MAN diesel; 2 shafts; 600 bhp = 10·5 knots
Oil fuel, tons: 9
Range, miles: 690 at 10·5 knots
Complement: 15

Harbour tug. Launched in June 1961. Delivered in Aug 1961.

CUSTOMS PATROL CRAFT

A very large force of which the following are examples.

3 COASTAL PATROL CRAFT

Name	No.	Builders	Commissioned
—	BC 1001	Ch. Navals de l'Esterel	11 Apr 1975
—	BC 1002	Ch. Navals de l'Esterel	23 June 1975
—	BC 1003	Ch. Navals de l'Esterel	25 Sep 1975

Displacement, tons: 55
Dimensions, feet (metres): 91·8 × 17·1 × 5·2 *(28 × 5·2 × 1·6)*
Gun: 1—20 mm
Main engines: 2 MTU 12V 331 TC 81; 2 700 hp = 35 knots
Range, miles: 750 at 15 knots
Complement: 9

BC 1002

1976, Ch. N de l'Esterel

15 DKN TYPE

Name	No.	Builders	Commissioned
—	DKN 901	Lürssen, Vegesack	1958
—	DKN 902	Lürssen, Vegesack	1958
—	DKN 903	Abeking & Rasmussen Lemwerder	1958
—	DKN 904	Lürssen, Vegesack	1959
—	DKN 905	Abeking & Rasmussen Lemwerder	1959
—	DKN 907	Italy	1959
—	DKN 908	Italy	1960
—	DKN 909	Italy	1960
—	DKN 910	Italy	1960
—	DKN 911	Italy	1960
—	DKN 912	Italy	1960
—	DKN 913	Italy	1960
—	DKN 914	Italy	1960
—	DKN 915	Italy	1960
—	DKN 916	Italy	1960

Displacement, tons: 140
Dimensions, feet (metres): 128 × 19 × 5·2 *(39 × 5·8 × 1·6)*
Guns: 4—20 mm
Main engines: Maybach diesels; 2 shafts; 3 000 bhp = 24·5 knots

In addition are DKN 504-13.

6 "PAT" CLASS

PAT 01   PAT 02   PAT 03   PAT 04   PAT 05   PAT 06

Dimensions, feet (metres): 91·9 pp; 100 oa × 17 × 6 *(28; 30·5 × 5·2 × 1·8)*
Main engines: 2 Caterpillar diesels; 340 bhp

ARMY CRAFT

A.D.R.I. operate fourteen 6-8000 GRT transports, two ex-US LSTs, five ex-Soviet "Keyla" class cargo ships *(Karmata, Karimundja, Mentawai, Natuna, Talaud),* ex-Soviet "Okhtensky" class tug *(Tamrau)* and tug *Tambora* (sister to *Bromo* above).

AIR FORCE CRAFT

A.U.R.I. operates six cargo ships (all with bow doors).

IRAN

Ministerial

Minister of War:
General R. Azimi

Headquarters Appointments

Commander-in-Chief Imperial Iranian Navy:
Vice Admiral Habibelahi
Deputy Commander-in-Chief:
Rear-Admiral Biglari

Fleet Command

Commander Fleet
Rear-Admiral Azadhi

Diplomatic Representation

Naval Attaché in London, Brussels and The Hague:
Captain F. Fiuzi
Naval Attaché in Rome and Paris:
Captain H. Keshvardoust
Naval Attaché in Washington and Ottawa:
Captain S. Baharmast

Personnel

(a) 1977: 22 000 officers and men
(b) 2 years National Service

Note: A Marine Battalion is being formed.

Bases

Persian Gulf
  Bandar Abbas (MHQ)
  Booshehr
  Kharg Island
  Khorramshar (Light Forces)
Indian Ocean
  Chah Bahar (under construction)
Caspian Sea
  Bandar—Pahlavi (Training)

Naval Air

7 Sikorsky SH-3D (Sea King) (11 on order)
7 Bell AB-212
2 Lockheed P-3C Orions (Maritime Patrol)
2 Fokker F-27 Mk 400 M (Transport)
6 Aero Commanders (Flag officers)
2 Mk 600 Friendship
5 Agusta—205A helicopters
14 Agusta—206A helicopters
3 RH.53D helicopters (3 on order)

Prefix to Ships' Names

IIS

Mercantile Marine

Lloyd's Register of Shipping:
  168 vessels of 683 329 tons

Strength of the Fleet

Type	Active	Building (Planned)
Destroyers	3	4
Frigates	4	—
Corvettes	4	—
Submarines	—	(3)
Fast Attack Craft (Missile)	—	12
Large Patrol Craft	7	—
Hovercraft	14	—
Landing Ships (L)	2	1 (2 ?)
Landing Craft (U)	1	—
Minesweepers—Coastal	3	—
Minesweepers—Inshore	2	—
Replenishment Tanker	—	1
Supply Ships	2	1
Repair Ship	1	—
Harbour Tanker	1	—
Water Boat	1	—
Tugs	3	—
Yachts	2	—
Floating Dock	1	—
Survey Craft	3	—
Customs Craft	2	—
Coastguard (Coastal Patrol Craft)	30	—

Missile Purchase

222 Harpoon missiles purchased.

DELETIONS

Mine Warfare Forces

1974 *Shahbaz* (ex-US *MSC*) after collision damage.

Service Forces

1974 *Sohrab* (ex-US *ARL 36)* sunk as A/S target.

Coastguard

1975 *Gohar, Shahpar, Shahram* (to Sudan)

PENNANT NUMBERS

Destroyers

51	Artemiz
61	Babr
62	Palang

Frigates

71	Saam
72	Zaal
73	Rostam
74	Faramarz

Corvettes

81	Bayandor
82	Naghdi
83	Milanian
84	Khanamuie

Submarines

101	Kusseh
102	Nahang
103	Dolfin

Light Forces

01-08	"Winchester" class hovercraft
101-106	"Wellington" class hovercraft
201	Kayvan
202	Tiran
203	Mehran
204	Mahan
211	Parvin
212	Bahram
213	Nahid
P 221	Kaman
P 222	Zoubin
P 223	Khadang
P 224	Peykan
P 225	Joshan
P 226	Falakhon
P 227	Shamshir
P 228	Gorz
P 229	Gardouneh
P 230	Khanjar
P 231	Neyzeh
P 232	Tabarzin

Mine Warfare Forces

301	Shahrokh
302	Simorgh
303	Karkas
311	Harischi
312	Riazi

Service and Auxiliary Forces

45	Bahmanshir
98	Kharg
401	Lengeh
402	Hormuz
421	Bandar Abbas
422	Booshehr
441	Chahbahar
501	Quesham
511	Hengam
512	Lerak

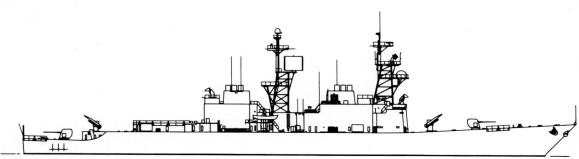

"DD 993" Class

1976, A. D. Baker III

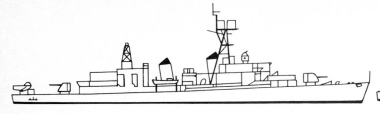

BABR and PALANG

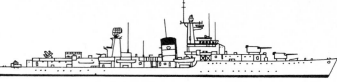

ARTEMIZ

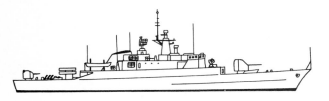

"SAAM" Class

"BAYANDOR" Class

DESTROYERS

4 US "DD 993 (SPRUANCE)" CLASS

Name	No.	Builders	Laid down	Launched	Commissioned
KOUROOSH (ex-US DD 993)	11	Litton Industries, USA	—	—	—
DARYUSH (ex-US DD 994)	12	Litton Industries, USA	—	—	—
ARDESHIR (ex-US DD 995)	13	Litton Industries, USA	—	—	—
NADER (ex-US DD 996)	14	Litton Industries, USA	—	—	—

Displacement, tons: approx 8 500 full load
Dimensions, feet (metres): 563·3 oa × 55 × 29
  (171·1 × 17·6 × 8·8)
Aircraft: 1 helicopter (Sea King)
Missiles: 2 twin Tartar-D launchers for Standard-MR SAM (Mk 26)
Guns: 2—5 in (127 mm) Mk 45, 54 cal
A/S weapons: 2 triple Mk 32 torpedo tubes
Main engines: 4 gas turbines; 80 000 shp; 2 shafts
Speed, knots: 30+
Range, miles: 6 000 at 20 knots
Complement: approx 290

Ordered from Litton Industries, USA, in 1974, first to be delivered in 1980. Original order was for six ships, reduced 2 Mar 1976 with cancellation of *Shapour* and *Anoushiroan.* They are modifications of the "Spruance" design with improved AA capability, better radars, and more powerful air-conditioning.

Radar: Radome; SPQ-9
Search; SPG-60
3-D; SPS-48
Fire control radars

Sonar: SQS 53 (mod) bow-mounted

"DD 993" Class

1975, Imperial Iranian Navy

1 Ex-BRITISH "BATTLE" CLASS

Name	No.	Builders	Laid down	Launched	Commissioned
ARTEMIZ (ex-HMS *Sluys,* D 60)	51	Cammell Laird & Co Ltd, Birkenhead	24 Nov 1943	28 Feb 1945	30 Sep 1946

Displacement, tons: 2 325 standard; 3 360 full load
Length, feet (metres): 355·0 *(108·2)* pp; 379·0 *(115·5)* oa
Beam, feet (metres): 40·5 *(12·3)*
Draught, feet (metres): 17·5 *(5·2)*
Missiles: 4 Standard launchers with 8 missiles; 1 quadruple Seacat aft
Guns: 4—4·5 in *(115 mm)* (2 twin forward); 4—40 mm (single)
A/S weapons: 1 Squid 3-barrelled DC mortar
Main engines: Parsons geared turbines; 2 shafts; 50 000 shp
Boilers: 2 Admiralty 3-drum type
Speed, knots: 35·5
Oil fuel, tons: 680
Range, miles: 3 000 at 20 knots
Complement: 270

Transferred to Iran at Southampton on 26 Jan 1967, and handed over to the Imperial Iranian Navy after a 3-year modernisation refit by the Vosper Thornycroft Group.

Radar: Search: Plessey AWS 1. Air surveillance with on-mounted IFF; Contraves Sea-Hunter fire control; Decca RDL 1 radar intercept; Racal DF equipment.

Refit: At Capetown 1975-76.

ARTEMIZ (old pennant number)

1975, Imperial Iranian Navy

2 Ex-US "ALLEN M. SUMNER" CLASS (FRAM II)

Name	No.
BABR (ex-USS Zellers, DD 777)	61
PALANG (ex-USS Stormes, DD 780)	62

Builders	Laid down	Launched	Commissioned
Todd Pacific Shipyards	—	19 July 1944	25 Oct 1944
Todd Pacific Shipyards	—	4 Nov 1944	27 Jan 1945

Displacement, tons: 2 200 standard; 3 320 full load
Length, feet (metres): 376·5 (114·8) oa
Beam, feet (metres): 40·9 (12·4)
Draught, feet (metres): 19 (5·8)
Aircraft: 1 A/S helicopter
Missiles: 4 Standard launchers with 8 missiles
Guns: 4—5 in (127 mm) 38 calibre (twin)
A/S weapons: 2 fixed Hedgehogs;
  2 triple torpedo launchers (Mk 32)
Main engines: 2 geared turbines; 60 000 shp; 2 shafts
Boilers: 4
Speed, knots: 34
Complement: 274 (14 officers, 260 ratings)

Two "FRAM II" conversion destroyers of the "Allen M. Sumner" class nominally transferred to Iran from the USN in March 1971 for delivery in 1972.

Conversion: Both ships received a full refit as well as conversion at Philadelphia NSY before sailing for Iran. This included a much-improved air-conditioning layout, the removal of B gun-mount with its magazine, altered accommodation, the fitting of a Canadian telescopic hangar, the siting of the four Standard missile launchers athwartships beside the new torpedo stowage between the funnels, the rigging of VDS and fitting of Hedgehogs in B position.

Electronics: Extensive intercept and jamming (ULQ/6) arrays fitted.

Radar: SPS 10 search; SPS 37 air-surveillance with on-mounted IFF; Gun fire control system Mk 37 with radar Mk 25 on director. Navigational; one on bridge.

Sonar: SQS 29 series; VDS (Babr).

Spares: USS Gainard (DD 706) was to have been taken over in Mar 1971, but, being beyond repair, was replaced by USS Stormes (DD 780). Ex-USS Kenneth D. Bailey (DD 713) ("Gearing" class) purchased 13 Jan 1975 for spares.

PALANG (old pennant number)   1975, Imperial Iranian Navy

FRIGATES
4 "SAAM" CLASS

Name	No.
FARAMARZ	74
ROSTAM	73
SAAM	71
ZAAL	72

Builders	Laid down	Launched	Commissioned
Vosper Thornycroft, Woolston	25 July 1968	30 July 1969	28 Feb 1972
Vickers, Newcastle & Barrow	10 Dec 1967	4 Mar 1969	June 1972
Vosper Thornycroft, Woolston	22 May 1967	25 July 1968	20 May 1971
Vickers, Barrow	3 Mar 1968	4 Mar 1969	1 Mar 1971

Displacement, tons: 1 110 standard; 1 290 full load
Length, feet (metres): 310·0 (94·4) oa
Beam, feet (metres): 34·0 (10·4)
Draught, feet (metres): 11·2 (3·4)
Missile launchers: 1 quintuple Seakiller; 1 triple Seacat
Guns: 1—4·5 in (115 mm) Mk 8
  2—35 mm Oerlikon (1 twin)
A/S weapons: 1 Limbo 3-barrelled DC mortar
Main engines: 2 Rolls-Royce "Olympus" gas turbines; 46 000 shp; 2 Paxman diesels; 3 800 shp; 2 shafts
Speed, knots: 40
Complement: 125 (accommodation for 146)

It was announced on 25 Aug 1966 that Vosper Ltd, Portsmouth had received an order for four vessels for the Iranian Navy. Air-conditioned throughout. Fitted with Vosper stabilisers. Rostam was towed to Barrow for completion.

Radar: Plessey AWS 1 air surveillance with on-mounted IFF. Two Contraves Seahunter systems for control of 35 mm, Sea-killers and Seacats. Decca RDL 1 passive DF equipment.

Refit: Saam and Zaal taken in hand by HM Dockyard Devonport July/Aug 1975 for major refit including replacement of Mk 5 4·5 in gun by Mk 8.

SAAM (new 4·5 in gun and pennant number)   1/1977, Michael D. J. Lennon

CORVETTES

4 Ex-US "PF 103" CLASS

Name	No.
BAYANDOR (ex-US PF 103)	81
KAHNAMUIE (ex-US PF 106)	84
MILANIAN (ex-US PF 105)	83
NAGHDI (ex-US PF 104)	82

Builders	Laid down	Launched	Commissioned
Levingstone Shipbuilding Co, Orange, Texas	20 Aug 1962	7 July 1963	18 May 1964
Levingstone Shipbuilding Co, Orange, Texas	12 June 1967	4 April 1968	13 Feb 1969
Levingstone Shipbuilding Co, Orange, Texas	1 May 1967	4 Jan 1968	13 Feb 1969
Levingstone Shipbuilding Co, Orange, Texas	12 Sep 1962	10 Oct 1963	22 July 1964

Displacement, tons: 900 standard; 1 135 full load
Length, feet (metres): 275·0 (83·8) oa
Beam, feet (metres): 33·0 (10·0)
Draught, feet (metres): 10·2 (3·1)
Guns: 2—3 in (76 mm); 2—40 mm (twin)
A/S weapons: 1 Hedgehog; 4 DCT; 2 DC racks
Main engines: F-M diesels; 2 shafts; 6 000 bhp
Speed, knots: 20
Complement: 140

Built as two pairs, five years apart. Transferred from the USA to Iran under the Mutual Assistance programme in 1964 (Bayandor and Naghdi) and 1969 (Kahnamuie and Milanian).

Radar: SPS 6 search.
Navigation; Raytheon.
Fire control; AN/SPG-34 on forward 76 mm (Mk 33) mount. Mk 63 for 76 mm. Mk 51 for 40 mm.

BAYANDOR (old pennant number)   1975, Imperial Iranian Navy

SUBMARINES

(3) Ex-US "TANG" CLASS (PATROL SUBMARINES)

Name	No.	Builders	Laid down	Launched	Commissioned
KUSSEH (ex-USS *Trout, SS 566*)	101	Electric Boat Co, Groton	1 Dec 1949	21 Aug 1951	27 June 1952
NAHANG (ex-USS *Wahoo, SS 565*)	102	Portsmouth Navy Yard	24 Oct 1949	16 Oct 1951	30 May 1952
DOLFIN (ex-USS *Tang, SS 563*)	103	—	—	—	—

Displacement, tons: 2 100 surfaced; 2 700 dived
Dimensions, feet (metres): 287 × 27·3 × 19 *(87·4 × 8·3 × 6·2)*
Torpedo tubes: 8—21 in *(533 mm)* (6 forward, 2 aft)
Main machinery: 3 Diesels; 4 500 bhp;
    2 electric motors; 5 600 shp; 2 shafts
Speed, knots: 16 surfaced; 16 dived
Complement: 87 (8 officers, 79 men)

Agreement on transfer from USN reached in 1975 to provide training for the establishment of a larger submarine force.

Transfer: *Kusseh* Aug 1978; *Nahang* 1979; *Dolfin* 1979-80.

"TANG" Class   1970, USN

LIGHT FORCES

12 "KAMAN" CLASS (FAST ATTACK CRAFT—MISSILE)

Name	No.	Builders	Commissioned
KAMAN	P 221	Construction de Mécanique, Normandie	—
ZOUBIN	P 222	Construction de Mécanique, Normandie	—
KHADANG	P 223	Construction de Mécanique, Normandie	—
PEYKAN	P 224	Construction de Mécanique, Normandie	—
JOSHAN	P 225	Construction de Mécanique, Normandie	—
FALAKHON	P 226	Construction de Mécanique, Normandie	—
SHAMSHIR	P 227	Construction de Mécanique, Normandie	—
GORZ	P 228	Construction de Mécanique, Normandie	—
GARDOUNEH	P 229	Construction de Mécanique, Normandie	—
KHANJAR	P 230	Construction de Mécanique, Normandie	—
NEYZEH	P 231	Construction de Mécanique, Normandie	—
TABARZIN	P 232	Construction de Mécanique, Normandie	—

Displacement, tons: 249 standard; 275 full load
Dimensions, feet (metres): 154·2 × 23·3 × 6·4 *(47 × 7·1 × 1·9)*
Missiles: 2 Twin Harpoon launchers
Guns: 1—76 OTO Melara; 1—40 mm Bofors
Main engines: 4 MTU diesels; 4 shafts; 14 400 bhp = 36 knots
Oil fuel, tons: 41
Range, miles: 700 at 30+ knots
Complement: 30

"KAMAN" Class   1975, Imperial Iranian Navy

Of La Combattante II design. Ordered in Feb 1974. For completion by April 1979. *Kaman* laid down 5 Feb 1975, launched 8 Jan 1976; *Zoubin* laid down 4 April 1975, launched 31 Mar 1976; *Khadang* laid down 20 June 1975, launched 15 July 1976; *Peykan* laid down 15 Oct 1975, launched Oct 1976. *Joshan* laid down 5 Jan 1976, launched Dec 1976; *Falakhon* laid down 15 Mar 1976, launched Feb 1977; *Shamshir* laid down 15 May 1976; *Gorz* laid down 5 Aug 1976.

Radar: Tactical and Fire control: WM 28 (Hollandse Signaalapparaten)

KAMAN   5/1976, Contre Amiral M. Adam

3 IMPROVED "PGM-71" CLASS (LARGE PATROL CRAFT)

Name	No.	Builders	Commissioned
BAHRAAM (ex-US *PGM 112*)	212	Tacoma Boatbuilding Co, Tacoma	1967
NAHID (ex-US *PGM 122*)	213	Tacoma Boatbuilding Co, Tacoma	1968
PARVIN (ex-US *PGM 103*)	211	Peterson Builders Inc, Sturgeon Bay, Wisconsin	1970

Displacement, tons: 105 standard; 146 full load
Dimensions, feet (metres): 100 × 22 × 10 *(30·5 × 6·7 × 3·1)*
Guns: 1—40 mm; 2—20 mm; 2—50 cal MG
Main engines: 8 GM diesels; 2 000 bhp = 15 knots

PARVIN (original number)   1971

4 US COASTGUARD "CAPE" CLASS (LARGE PATROL CRAFT)

Name	No.	Builders	Commissioned
KAYVAN	201	USA	14 Jan 1956
MAHAN	204	USA	1959
TIRAN	202	US Coast Guard, Curtis Bay, Maryland	1957
MEHRAN	203	USA	1959

Displacement, tons: 85 standard; 107 full load
Dimensions, feet (metres): 90 pp; 95 oa × 20·2 × 6·8 *(27·5; 28·9 × 6·2 × 2)*
Gun: 1—40 mm
A/S weapons: 8-barrelled 7·2 in projector, 8—300 lb depth charges
Main engines: 4 Cummins diesels; 2 shafts; 2 200 bhp = 20 knots
Range, miles: 1 500 cruising
Complement: 15

MAHAN   *1975, Imperial Iranian Navy*

6 "WELLINGTON" (BH.7) CLASS (HOVERCRAFT)

Name	No.	Builders	Commissioned
—	101	British Hovercraft Corporation	Nov 1970
—	102	British Hovercraft Corporation	Mar 1971
—	103	British Hovercraft Corporation	Mid 1974
—	104	British Hovercraft Corporation	Mid 1974
—	105	British Hovercraft Corporation	Late 1974
—	106	British Hovercraft Corporation	Early 1975

Displacement, tons: 50 max weight, 33 empty
Dimensions, feet (metres): 76 × 45 ×42 *(23·2 × 13·7 × 12·8)*
Missiles: SSMs in last four (see note)
Guns: 2 Browning MG
Main engines: 1 Proteus 15 M/541 gas turbine = 60 knots
Oil fuel, tons: 10

First pair are BH 7 Mk 4 (delivered Nov 70 and Mar 71) and the next four are Mk 5 craft (two in mid 1974, one in late 1974, and one in early 1975). Mk 5 craft fitted for, but not with, surface-to-surface missiles.

"Wellington" Hovercraft 101   *1975, Imperial Iranian Navy*

8 "WINCHESTER" (SR.N6) CLASS (HOVERCRAFT)

Name	No.	Builders	Commissioned
—	01	British Hovercraft Corporation	1973
—	02	British Hovercraft Corporation	1973
—	03	British Hovercraft Corporation	1973
—	04	British Hovercraft Corporation	1974
—	05	British Hovercraft Corporation	1974
—	06	British Hovercraft Corporation	1975
—	07	British Hovercraft Corporation	1975
—	08	British Hovercraft Corporation	1975

Displacement, tons: 10 normal gross weight (basic weight 14 200 lbs; disposable load 8 200 lbs)
Dimensions, feet (metres): 48·4 × 25·3 × 15·9 (height) *(14·8 × 7·7 × 4·8)*
Guns: 1 or 2 50 cal MGs
Main engines: 1 Gnome Model 1050 gas turbine = 58 knots
1 Peters diesel as auxiliary power unit

Ordered 1970-72. The Imperial Iranian Navy has the world's largest fully operational hovercraft squadron, which is used for coastal defence and logistic duties.

"Winchester" Hovercraft 03   *1971*

LANDING CRAFT

QUESHAM (ex-US *LCU 1431*) 501

Displacement, tons: 160 light; 320 full load
Dimensions, feet (metres): 119 × 32 × 5·7 *(36·3 × 9·8 × 1·7)*
Guns: 2—20 mm
Main engines: Diesels; 675 bhp = 10 knots
Complement: 14

LCU 1431 was transferred to Iran by US in Sep 1964 under the Military Aid Programme.

QUESHAM   *1971*

MINE WARFARE FORCES

3 Ex-US "MSC 292 and 268" CLASS (MINESWEEPERS—COASTAL)

Name	No.	Builders	Commissioned
KARKAS (ex-USS *MSC 292*)	303	Petersen Builders Inc	1959
SHAHROKH (ex-USS *MSC 276*)	301	Bellingham Shipyards Co	1960
SIMORGH (ex-USS *MSC 291*)	302	Tacoma Boatbuilding Co	1962

Displacement, tons: 320 light; 378 full load
Dimensions, feet (metres): 138 pp; 145·8 oa × 28 × 8·3 *(42·1; 44·5 × 8·5 × 2·5)*
Gun: 1—20 mm (double-barrelled)
Main engines: 2 GM diesels; 2 shafts; 890 bhp = 12·8 knots
Oil fuel, tons: 27
Range, miles: 2 400 at 11 knots
Complement: 40 (4 officers, 2 midshipmen, 34 men)

Originally class of four. Of wooden construction. Launched in 1958-61 and transferred from US to Iran under MAP in 1959-62. *Shahrokh* now in the Caspian Sea.

SIMORGH (old pennant number) *1975, Imperial Iranian Navy*

2 US MSI TYPE (MINESWEEPERS—INSHORE)

Name	No.	Builders	Commissioned
HARISCHI (ex-*Kahnamuie*, ex-*MSI 14*)	311	Tacoma Boatbuilding Co	3 Sep 1964
RIAZI (ex-*MSI 13*)	312	Tacoma Boatbuilding Co	15 Oct 1964

Displacement, tons: 180 standard; 235 full load
Dimensions, feet (metres): 111 × 23 × 6 *(33·9 × 7·0 × 1·8)*
Gun: 1 50 cal MG
Main engines: Diesels; 650 bhp = 13 knots
Oil fuel, tons: 20
Range, miles: 1 000 at 9 knots
Complement: 23 (5 officers, 18 men)

Delivered to Iran under MAP. Laid down on 22 June 1962 and 1 Feb 1963, and transferred at Seattle, Washington, on 3 Sep 1964 and 15 Oct 1964, respectively. In Aug 1967 *Kahnamuie* was renamed *Harischi* as the name was required for one of the new US PFs (see Light Forces).

RIAZI (old pennant number) *1975, Imperial Iranian Navy*

SERVICE FORCES

1 REPLENISHMENT TANKER

Name	No.	Builders	Commissioned
KHARG	98	Swan Hunter Ltd, Wallsend	1978

Displacement, tons: 10 890 light; 36 000 full load
Measurement, tons: 25 000 dwt
Dimensions, feet (metres): 648 × 84 × 34 *(197·5 × 25·6 × 10·5)*
Aircraft: 2 helicopters

Main engines: Pametrade double reduction geared turbines; 26 500 shp
Boilers: 2 Babcock and Wilcox
Speed, knots: 19
Complement: 87

Ordered Oct 1974. Laid down Jan 1976.

2 + 1 + (2?) LANDING SHIPS (LOGISTIC)

Name	No.	Builders	Commissioned
HENGAM	511	Yarrow, Clyde	12 Aug 1974
LARAK	512	Yarrow, Clyde	12 Nov 1974
—	—	Yarrow, Clyde	—

Displacement, tons: 2 500
Length, feet (metres): 300 *(91·5)*
Aircraft: 1 helicopter
Guns: 4—40 mm (single)
Main engines: Diesels; 2 shafts; 5 600 bhp
Speed, knots: 16

Similar in many respects to British *Sir Lancelot* but smaller with bridge amidships. Ordered 1972. *Hengam* laid down late 1972, launched 24 Sep 1973. *Larak* laid down 1973, launched 7 May 1974. One under construction. Two more may be ordered.

LARAK (old pennant number) *5/1975, C. & S. Taylor*

2 + 1 FLEET SUPPLY SHIPS

Name	No.	Builders	Commissioned
BANDAR ABBAS	421	C. Lühring Yard, Brake, W. Germany	Apr 1974
BOOSHEHR	422	C. Lühring Yard, Brake, W. Germany	Nov 1974
—	—	C. Lühring Yard, Brake, W. Germany	—

Measurement, tons: 3 250 deadweight
Dimensions, feet (metres): 354·2 × 54·4 × 14·8 *(108 × 16·6 × 4·5)*
Aircraft: 1 helicopter
Guns: 2—40 mm
Main engines: 2 MAN (MTU) diesels; 2 shafts; 6 000 bhp
Speed, knots: 16
Complement: 60

BANDAR ABBAS (old pennant number) *1975, Imperial Iranian Navy*

Combined tankers and store-ships carrying victualling, armament and general stores. *Bandar Abbas* launched 11 Aug 1973, *Booshehr* launched 23 Mar 1974. Third under construction

1 Ex-US "AMPHION" CLASS (REPAIR SHIP)

Name	*No.*	*Builders*	*Commissioned*
CHAHBAHAR (ex-USS *Amphion,* ex-*AR 13*)	441	Tampa Shipbuilding Co	30 Jan 1946

Displacement, tons: 7 826 standard; 14 490 full load
Dimensions, feet (metres): 456·0 wl; 492·0 oa × 70·0 × 27·5 *(139; 150·1 × 21·4 × 8·4)*
Guns: 2—3 in 50 cal
Main engines: Westinghouse turbines; 1 shaft; 8 500 shp = 16·5 knots
Boilers: 2 Foster-Wheeler
Complement: Accommodation for 921

Launched on 15 May 1945. Transferred to IIN on 1 Oct 1971. Based at Bandar Abbas as permanent repair facility, although she does go to sea.

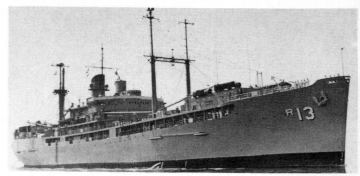

CHAHBAHAR (old pennant number)   *1972, Imperial Iranian Navy*

1 HARBOUR TANKER

Name	*No.*	*Builders*	*Commissioned*
HORMUZ (ex-*YO 247*)	402	Cantiere Castellamàre di Stabia	1956

Displacement, tons: 1 250 standard; 1 700 full load
Dimensions, feet (metres): 171·2 wl; 178·3 oa × 32·2 × 14 *(52·2; 54·4 × 9·8 × 4·3)*
Guns: 2—20 mm
Main engines: 1 Ansaldo Q 370, 4 cycle diesel
Oil fuel, tons: 25

Cargo oil capacity: 5 000 to 6 000 barrels.

HORMUZ   *1970, Imperial Iranian Navy*

1 Ex-US YW TYPE (WATER BOAT)

LENGEH (ex-US *YW 88*) 401

Displacement, tons: 1 250 standard
Dimensions, feet (metres): 178 × 32 × 14 *(54·3 × 9·8 × 4·3)*
Main engines: Diesels; speed = 10 knots

Transferred to Iran by US in 1964. Similar to tanker *Hormuz*

LENGEH (old pennant number)   *1975, Imperial Iranian Navy*

1 TUG

BAHMANSHIR 45

Harbour tug (ex-US Army *ST 1002)*, 150 tons, transferred in 1962.

2 HARBOUR TUGS

No. 1 (ex-German *Karl)*   **No. 2** (ex-German *Ise)*

Sister ships of 134 tons taken over from W. Germany 17 June 1974. Both built 1962-63.

No. 1 and No. 2   *4/1974, Reiner Nerlich*

IMPERIAL YACHTS

Name	No.	Builders	Commissioned
KISH	—	Yacht und Bootswerft, Burmester, Germany	1970

Displacement, tons: 178
Dimensions, feet (metres): 122 × 25 × 7 *(37·2 × 7·6 × 2·1)*
Main engines: 2 MTU diesels; 2 920 hp

A smaller and more modern Imperial. In the Persian Gulf.

KISH   *1971*

Name	No.	Builders	Commissioned
SHAHSAVAR	—	N.V. Boele's Scheepwerven, Bolnes, Netherlands	1936

Displacement, tons: 530
Dimensions, feet (metres): 176 × 25·3 × 10·5 *(53·7 × 7·7 × 3·2)*
Main engines: 2 sets diesels; 1 300 bhp

Launched in 1936. In the Caspian Sea.

SHAHSAVAR   *1971, Imperial Iranian Navy*

FLOATING DOCK

FD 4 (ex-US *ARD 29)*

Dimensions, feet (metres):
Lift: 3 000 tons

Transferred Sep 1971. Of steel construction.

COAST GUARD

24 50 ft TYPE (COASTAL PATROL CRAFT)

Built by Peterson Builders, Wisconsin 1975-76.

6 40 ft SEWART TYPE (COASTAL PATROL CRAFT)

MAHNAVI-HAMRAZ	MAHNAVI-VAHEDI	MORVARID
MAHNAVI-TAHERI	MARDJAN	SADAF

Displacement, tons: 10 standard
Dimensions, feet (metres): 40·0 × 11·0 × 3·7 *(12·2 × 3·4 × 1·1)*
Guns: Light MG
Main engines: 2 General Motors diesels = 30 knots

Small launches for port duties of Sewart (USA) standard 40 ft type. All transferred June 1953. Pennant numbers 5001 and above. Some serve in the Caspian Sea.

CUSTOMS VESSELS

TOUFAN   **TOUSAN**

Built by CN Inmar, La Spezia in 1954-55. Of 65 tons with twin diesels. 22 knots.

SURVEY VESSELS

(Operated by the Ministry of Finance)

MEHR

Of 422 tons. Launched in 1964. Complement 22.

HYDROGRAPH SHAHPOUR

Of 9 tons. Launched in 1965.

HYDROGRAPH PAHLAVI

Of 9 tons. Launched in 1966.

IRAQ

Ministerial

Minister of Defence:
Ahmad Hasan al-Bakr

Administration

Commander-in-Chief:
Rear-Admiral Abd Al Diri
Chief of Staff:
Commander Samad Sat Al Mufti

Personnel

(a) 1977: 3 000 officers and men
(b) 2 years National Service

SOVIET-IRAQI TREATIES

Under the treaty, signed in April 1972, the Soviet fleet would have access to the Iraqi base of Umm Qasr, in return for Soviet assistance to strengthen Iraq's defences. This resulted in the acquisition by Iraq of 10 "Osa" class.

A further treaty signed in August 1976 has been kept secret but it is reported that, from the naval point of view, it includes provision for the Soviet occupation of Umm Qasr in return for the provision of "10 missile frigates" to Iraq. Whether these will be similar to the "Nanuchka" class being sent to India remains to be seen.

Mercantile Marine

Lloyd's Register of Shipping:
87 vessels of 748 774 tons gross

Bases

Basra, Umm Qasr

LIGHT FORCES

3 Ex-SOVIET "SO I" CLASS

Displacement, tons: 215 light; 250 full load
Dimensions, feet (metres): 138·6 × 20 × 9·2 *(42·3 × 6·1 × 2·8)*
Guns: 4—25 mm
A/S weapons: 4 five-barrelled RBU 1200
Main engines: 3 diesels; 7 500 bhp = 29 knots
Complement: 30

Delivered by the USSR to Iraq in 1962.

12 Ex-SOVIET "OSA" CLASS (FAST ATTACK CRAFT—MISSILE)

Displacement, tons: 165 standard; 200 full load
Dimensions, feet (metres): 128·7 × 25·1 × 5·9 *(39·3 × 7·7 × 1·8)*
Missiles: 4 launchers for SS-N-2
Guns: 4—30 mm (twin)
Main engines: 3 Diesels; 13 000 hp = 32 knots
Range, miles: 800 at 25 knots
Complement: 25

A combination of 6 "Osa I" and 4 "Osa II" classes acquired after 1972. This increase in the Iraqi navy must make a major impact on naval affairs in the Persian Gulf. Other navies have shown the effectiveness of the Styx missiles, even in comparatively untrained hands, against unalerted forces. It will be a surprise if this Soviet incursion does not accelerate the build up of high-effectiveness forces in this area. Further pair delivered 1976.

Radar: Drum Tilt.

"OSA I" Class

12 Ex-SOVIET "P 6" CLASS
(FAST ATTACK CRAFT—TORPEDO)

AL IDRISS P220, **GHAZI** P 221, **IBN SAID** P 222, **RAMAZAN, SHULAB, TAMUZ** plus P 217-219

Displacement, tons: 66 standard; 75 full load
Dimensions, feet (metres): 84·2 × 20 × 6 *(25·7 × 6·1 × 1·8)*
Guns: 4—25 mm
Torpedo tubes: 2—21 in
Main engines: Diesels; 4 800 bhp = 45 knots
Complement: 25

Transferred from the USSR. Two were received in 1959, four in Nov 1960, and six in Jan 1961. Some remain non-operational.

2 Ex-SOVIET "POLUCHAT I" CLASS (LARGE PATROL CRAFT)

Displacement, tons: 100 standard
Dimensions, feet (metres): 98·4 × 19·0 × 5·9 *(30·0 × 5·8 × 1·8)*
Guns: 2—25 mm

Transferred by USSR in late 1960s.

4 Ex-SOVIET "ZHUK" CLASS
(COASTAL PATROL CRAFT)

Displacement, tons: 50
Dimensions, feet (metres): 75 × 16 × — *(22·9 × 4·9 × —)*
Guns: 2—14·5 mm MG; 1—12·7 mm MG
Main engines:
Speed, knots: 30

Transferred in 1975.

4 COASTAL PATROL CRAFT

Name	No.	Builders	Commissioned
—	1	John I. Thornycroft & Co Ltd, Woolston, Southampton	1937
—	2	John I. Thornycroft & Co Ltd, Woolston, Southampton	1937
—	3	John I. Thornycroft & Co Ltd, Woolston, Southampton	1937
—	4	John I. Thornycroft & Co Ltd, Woolston, Southampton	1937

Displacement, tons: 67
Dimensions, feet (metres): 100 × 17 × 3 *(30·5 × 5·2 × 0·9)*
Guns: 1—3·7 in howitzer; 2—3 in mortars; 4 MG
Main engines: 2 Thornycroft diesels; 2 shafts; 280 bhp = 12 knots

Protected by bullet-proof plating. All built by John I. Thornycroft & Co Ltd, Woolston, Southampton. All launched, completed and delivered in 1937.

4 THORNYCROFT 21 ft TYPE

Length, feet (metres): 21 *(6·4)*
Main engines: 1 diesel; 40 bhp

Pilot despatch launches built by John I. Thornycroft & Co for the Iraqi Ports.

8 THORNYCROFT 36 ft TYPE

Length, feet (metres): 36 *(11·0)*
Main engines: 1 diesel; 125 bhp

Patrol boats built by John I. Thornycroft & Co for the Iraqi Ports Administration.

4 Ex-SOVIET "NYRYAT II" CLASS (COASTAL PATROL CRAFT)

Length, feet (metres): 70 *(21·3)*
Main engines: 150 bhp

Similar in appearance to "PO 2" class without bulwarks. Multi-purpose craft probably used as a diving craft.

2 Ex-SOVIET "PO 2" CLASS (COASTAL PATROL CRAFT)

Displacement, tons: 50 full load
Dimensions, feet (metres): 82 × 16·7 × 5·6 *(25 × 5·1 × 1·7)*
Guns: 2—25 mm or 2—12·7 mm
Main engines: 2 diesels = 30 knots

MINE WARFARE FORCES

2 Ex-SOVIET "T 43" CLASS (MSO)

No: 465, 475

Transferred early 1970s. See USSR section for details.

3 Ex-SOVIET "YEVGENYA" CLASS
(INSHORE MINESWEEPERS)

Displacement, tons: 90 full load
Length, feet (metres): 88·6 *(27)*
Guns: 2—25 mm (twin)
Main engines: 2 diesels

GRP hulls. Delivered in 1975 under cover-name of "oceanographic craft".

HARBOUR AUTHORITY CRAFT

AL THAWRA (ex-*Malike Aliye*)

Displacement, tons: 746
Main engines: Diesels; 2 shafts; 1 800 shp = 14 knots

Royal Yacht before assassination of King Faisal II in 1958, after which she was renamed *Al Thawra (The Revolution)* instead of *Malike Aliye (Queen Aliyah)*.

AL THAWRA   *1966, Aldo Fraccaroli*

MISCELLANEOUS

A number of customs craft and a large Dutch-built dredger of the Harbour Authority are also listed.

IRELAND (REPUBLIC of)

Minister for Defence: Mr. Liam Cosgrave (Prime Minister)
Commanding Officer and Director Naval Service: Captain P. Kavanagh, NS

The Irish Naval Service is administered from Naval Headquarters, Department of Defence, Dublin, by the Commanding Officer and Director Naval Service. The naval base and dockyard are on Haulbowline island in Cork Harbour.

Personnel

a) 1977: Approximately 650 officers and men
b) Voluntary

DELETIONS

Cliona (ex-HMS *Bellwort*) and *Macha* (ex-HMS *Borage*), both built by George Brown, & Co (Marine) Ltd, Greenock, were sold for breaking up in 1970-71. *Maev* (ex-HMS *Oxlip*) deleted 1972. Tender *Wyndham* sold in 1968 and *General McHardy* in 1971.

Mercantile Marine

Lloyd's Register of Shipping:
   96 vessels of 201 965 tons gross

CORVETTES

Name	No.	Builders	Commissioned
DEIRDRE	FP 20	Verolme, Cork	May 1972
—	FP 21	Verolme, Cork	Nov 1977

Displacement, tons: 972
Dimensions, feet (metres): 184·3 pp × 34·1 × 14·4 *(56·2 × 10·4 × 4·4)*
Gun: 1—40 mm Bofors
Main engines: 2 British Polar diesels coupled to 1 shaft; 4 200 bhp = 18 knots
Oil fuel, tons: 170
Range, miles: 5 000 at 12 knots
Complement: 46 (5 officers, 41 men)

Controllable pitch propeller, stabilisers and sonar. *Deirdre* was the first vessel ever built for the Naval Service in the Republic of Ireland. Launched on 29 Dec 1971. A second vessel of this class has been ordered from Verolme for delivery Nov 1977. Improvements in design will result in an increase of 6·5 ft *(2 metres)* in the overall length of this ship. The starboard life-boat and mainmast are being deleted. She will have SEMT Pielstick diesels in place of Polar giving an additional 2 knots.

Classification: Officially classified as "Patrol Vessel".

DEIRDRE   *7/1976, Irish Naval Service*

COASTAL MINESWEEPERS

3 Ex-BRITISH "TON" CLASS

Name	No.	Builders	Commissioned
BANBA (ex-HMS *Alverton, M 1104*)	CM 11	Camper and Nicholson	1953
FÓLA (ex-HMS *Blaxton, M 1132*)	CM 12	Thornycroft	1956
GRÁINNE (ex-HMS *Oulston, M 1129*)	CM 10	Thornycroft	1955

Displacement, tons: 360 standard; 425 full load
Dimensions, feet (metres): 140·0 pp; 153·0 oa × 28·8 × 8·2 *(42·7; 46·7 × 8·8 × 2·5)*
Guns: 1—40 mm; 2—20 mm
Main engines: 2 diesels; 2 shafts; 3 000 bhp = 15 knots
Oil fuel, tons: 45
Range, miles: 2 300 at 13 knots
Complement: 33

Former British "Ton" class coastal minesweepers. Double mahogany hulls and otherwise constructed of aluminium alloy and other materials with the lowest possible magnetic signature. Purchased from Great Britain in 1971 for fishery protection duties as replacements for previous corvettes.

GRÁINNE   *5/1974, Irish Naval Service*

TRAINING SHIP

Name	No.	Builders	Commissioned
SETANTA (ex-*Isolda*)	A 15	Liffey DY, Dublin	1953

Displacement, tons: 1 173
Dimensions, feet (metres): 208 pp × 38 × 13 *(63·5 × 11·6 × 4)*
Main engines: Steam recip: 1 500 ihp; 2 shafts = 11·5 knots
Oil fuel, tons: 276
Range, miles: 3 500 at 10 knots
Complement: 44

Acquired from the Commissioners of Irish Lights in 1976.

TENDER

Name	No.	Builders	Commissioned
JOHN ADAMS	—	Richard Dunston, Thorne, Yorks.	1934

Measurement, tons: 94 gross
Dimensions, feet (metres): 85 × 18·5 × 7 *(25·9 × 5·6 × 2·1)*
Main engines: Diesel; 216 bhp = 10 knots

Employed on harbour duties. New engine fitted in 1976.

ISRAEL

Headquarters Appointment

Commander in Chief of the Israeli Navy:
Rear Admiral Michael Barkai

Diplomatic Representation

Defence Attaché in London:
Brigadier General R. Sivron
Naval Attaché in Rome:
Captain P. Pinchasi
Naval Attaché in Washington:
Captain M. Tabak

Personnel

(a) 1977: 4 500 (350 officers and 4 150 men, of whom 1 000 are conscripts, including a Naval Commando)
(b) 3 years National Service for Jews and Druses.
Note (An additional 5 000 Reserves available on mobilisation).

Submarines

1975 *Leviathan* (ex-T class)

Bases

Haifa, Ashdod, Sharm-el-Sheikh
A repair base has been built at Eilat where a synchro-lift is installed.

Prefix to Ships' Names

INS (Israeli Naval Ship)

Mercantile Marine

Lloyd's Register of Shipping:
68 vessels of 481 594 tons gross

Strength of the Fleet

Type	Active	Building
Patrol Submarines	2	2
Fast Attack Craft (Missile)	19	5
Coastal Patrol Craft	64	—
"Firefish"	3	
LSMs	3	—
LCTs	6	—
LCMs	3	—
Transports	2	—
Support Ship	1	—
Training Ship	1	—

Deployment

At Sharm-el-Sheikh there are normally 4 "Reshef" class, 2 "Saar" class, some tugs, landing craft and a depot ship.

DELETIONS

Light Forces

1975   12 Bertram Type; 14 Swift Type

SUBMARINES

2 + 1 IKL/VICKERS TYPE 206

Name	No.	Builders	Laid down	Launched	Commissioned
GAL	—	Vickers Ltd, Barrow	2 Dec 1975	—	Jan 1977
GUR	—	Vickers Ltd, Barrow	—	25 Oct 1976	1977
—	—	Vickers Ltd, Barrow	—	—	1978

Displacement, tons: 420 surfaced; 600 dived
Dimensions, feet (metres): 146·7 × 15·4 × 12 *(45·0 × 4·7 × 3·7)*
Torpedo tubes: 8—21 in bow
Main machinery: Diesels; 2 000 hp; Electric motor; 1 800 hp; 1 shaft; diesel-electric
Speed, knots: 11 surfaced; 17 dived
Complement: 22

A contract was signed for the building of these boats by Vickers in April 1972.

GAL

1977, Israeli Navy

1 Ex-BRITISH "T" CLASS (PATROL SUBMARINE)

Name	No.	Builders	Laid down	Launched	Commissioned
DOLPHIN (ex-HMS *Truncheon*)	77	HM Dockyard, Devonport	5 Nov 1942	22 Feb 1944	25 May 1945

Displacement, tons: 1 310 standard; 1 535 surfaced; 1 740 dived
Length, feet (metres): 293·5 *(89·5)* oa
Beam, feet (metres): 26·5 *(8·1)*
Draught, feet (metres): 14·8 *(4·5)*
Torpedo tubes: 6—21 in *(533 mm)* 4 bow, 2 stern
Main machinery: Diesels; 2 500 bhp (surfaced); Electric Motors; 2 900 hp (dived)
Speed, knots: 15·25 surfaced; 15 dived
Complement: 65

Aged "T" class lengthened and modernised during conversion (plus 20 feet). Handed over after extensive refit on 9 Jan 1968. Probably now non-operational.

Loss: Original sister ship *Dakar* (ex-HMS *Totem*), handed over to Israel on 10 Nov 1967, was lost in the Eastern Mediterranean on 25 Jan 1968.

DOLPHIN

1975, Israeli Navy

LIGHT FORCES

7 + 5 "RESHEF" CLASS (FAST ATTACK CRAFT—MISSILE)

Name	No.	Builders	Commissioned
RESHEF	—	Haifa Shipyard	April 1973
KESHET	—	Haifa Shipyard	Oct 1973
ROMAH	—	Haifa Shipyard	Mar 1974
KIDON	—	Haifa Shipyard	Sep 1974
TARSHISH	—	Haifa Shipyard	Mar 1975
YAFFO	—	Haifa Shipyard	April 1975
—	—	Haifa Shipyard	Jan 1977

Displacement, tons: 415 standard
Dimensions, feet (metres): 190·6 × 25 × 8 *(58 × 7·8 × 2·4)*
Missile launchers: 6 Gabriel
Guns: 2—76 mm OTO Melara; 2—20 mm Oerlikon (see Note)
Engines: 4 Maybach (MTU) diesels; 2 670 hp each; 2 screws
Speed, knots: 32
Range, miles: approx 1 500 at 30 knots
Complement: 45

These steel-hulled boats carry Israeli-made missiles and electronics.

Reshef was launched on 19 Feb 1973; *Keshet* 2 Aug 1973. This very interesting class has an extremely long range at cruising speed, two pairs having made the passage from Israel to the Red Sea via the Strait of Gibraltar and Cape of Good Hope, relying entirely on refuelling at sea. This is a great tribute not only to their endurance but also to their sea-keeping qualities. A further illustration of this was the appearance of two "Reshefs" in New York July 1976 (shown right).
The first pair was successfully engaged in the Arab-Israeli War, Oct 1973. The whole class will eventually be equipped with the new 22 mile range Gabriel missiles.
An expansion of the building slips at Haifa Dockyard will allow the more rapid construction of the next six boats ordered in January 1975. These slightly larger with an overall length of 200 ft *(60·9 m)*. First of second batch completed Jan 1977.

Sonar: Fitted in ships deployed in the Red Sea. (ELAC).

Deployment: *Tarshish* and *Yaffo* in Mediterranean. Other four of first six in Red Sea.

Transfers: Six of this class building for South Africa in Haifa and Durban.

RESHEF   *1974, Michael D. J. Lennon*

YAFFO   *7/1976, A. D. Baker III*

12 "SAAR" CLASS (FAST ATTACK CRAFT—MISSILE)

Name	No.	Builders	Commissioned
Group A			
ACCO	—	Ch. de Normandie	1968
EILAT	—	Ch. de Normandie	1968
HAIFA	—	Ch. de Normandie	1968
MISGAV	—	Ch. de Normandie	1968
MIVTACH	—	Ch. de Normandie	1968
MIZNACH	—	Ch. de Normandie	1968
Group B			
GAASH	—	Ch. de Normandie	1969
HANIT	—	Ch. de Normandie	1969
HEREV	—	Ch. de Normandie	1969
HETZ	—	Ch. de Normandie	1969
SAAR	—	Ch. de Normandie	1969
SOUFA	—	Ch. de Normandie	1969

Displacement, tons: 220 standard; 250 full load
Dimensions, feet (metres): 147·6 oa × 23·0 × 8·2 *(45·0 × 7·0 × 2·5)*
Missile launchers: Gabriel surface to surface (see notes)
Guns: 40 mm or 76 mm (see notes)
A/S weapons: 4 US Mk 32 for Mk 46 torpedoes (Group A)
Main engines: 4 Maybach (MTU) diesels; 13 500 bhp; 4 shafts = 40+ knots
Oil fuel, tons: 30
Range, miles: 2 500 at 15 knots; 1 600 at 20 knots; 1 000 at 30 knots
Complement: 35 to 40

Built from designs by Lürssen Werft of Bremen. Political problems caused their building in France instead of Germany—a political embargo kept the last five in France until their journey to Israel began on Christmas Eve 1969. Two batches were built, the first six (Group A) being fitted originally with three 40 mm AA guns and ordered in 1965. The second six (Group B) were ordered in 1966 and fitted with 76 mm OTO Melara guns. Five of these ships were delivered to Israel and two *(Acco* and *Saar)* made the journey on completion of local trials after the 1969 French arms embargo. The last five arrived off Haifa in January 1970 after a much-publicised passage which proved the remarkable endurance of this class.
The first batch was fitted for sonar but this was omitted from the 76 mm gun fitted group. Since their arrival in Israel provision of Gabriel surface to surface missiles has progressed. The first group can mount an armament varying from one 40 mm gun and eight Gabriel missiles (two single fixed mounts forward and two triple trainable mounts amidships) to three 40 mm and guns four torpedo tubes. The second group can mount the two triple Gabriel launchers amidships as well as the 76 mm OTO Melara gun forward.
The Gabriel missile system is controlled by radar and optical sights and launches a low-altitude missile with a 150 lb HE head to a range of 12·5 miles in the first configuration and 22 miles in the later versions.

Sonar: ELAC sonar in Group A.

"SAAR" Class with 76 mm and five Gabriel missiles   *1973*

"SAAR" Class with 40 mm guns and torpedo tubes   *1974*

HANIT with one 40 mm and eight Gabriel missiles   *1971, Israeli Navy*   "SAAR" Class with three 40 mm and torpedo tubes   *1974*

30 "DABUR" CLASS (COASTAL PATROL CRAFT)

Displacement, tons: 35 full load
Dimensions, feet (metres): 64·9 × 19 × 2·6 (19·8 × 5·8 × 0·8)
Guns: 2—20 mm; 2 twin 50 cal MGs (see note)
Main engines: 2 geared diesels; 960 shp; 2 shafts = 25 knots
Complement: 6/9 depending on armament

12 built in USA and remainder by Israel Aircraft Industry. Aluminium hull. There are several variations in their armament. Deployed in the Mediterranean and Red Seas, this being facilitated as these craft have been designed for overland transport. Good rough weather performance. A continuing programme in hand at the IAI plant at Ramta.

Missiles: There are reports that some may carry missiles of an unspecified type.

"DABUR" Class   1975, Israeli Navy

30 Ex-US PBR TYPE (COASTAL PATROL CRAFT)

Dimensions, feet (metres): 32 × 11 × 2·6 (9·8 × 3·4 × 0·8)
Guns: 2—12·7 mm MG
Main engines: 2 geared diesels; waterjets = 25 knots
Complement: 5

Purchased 1974 and subsequently. GRP Hulls.

PBR Type   1976, Israeli Navy

3 FIREFISH MODEL III

Displacement, tons: 6
Dimensions, feet (metres): 28 × 7·5 (8·5 × 2·3)
Main engines: 2 Mercruiser V-8; 430 hp
Speed, knots: 52
Range, miles: 250 cruising; 150 max speed

Built by Sandaire, San Diego. Glass fibre craft, can carry five men. Capable of being radio-controlled for attack missions or minesweeping under ship or aircraft control.

FIREFISH III   1976, Israeli Navy

AMPHIBIOUS FORCES

Note: USS *Casa Grande* reported last year—transaction cancelled.

3 Ex-US "LSM 1" CLASS

Displacement, tons: 1 095 full load
Dimensions, feet (metres): 203·5 oa × 34·5 × 7·3 (62·1 × 10·5 × 2·2)
Guns: 2—40 mm; 4—20 mm
Main engines: Diesels; 2 800 bhp; 2 shafts = 12·5 knots
Complement: 70

Purchased in 1972 from commercial sources.

"LSM 1" Class   1976, Israeli Navy

3 "ASH" CLASS (LCT)

Name	No.	Builders	Commissioned
ASHDOD	61	Israel Shipyards, Haifa	1966
ASHKELON	—	Israel Shipyards, Haifa	1967
ACHZIV	—	Israel Shipyards, Haifa	1967

Displacement, tons: 400 standard; 730 full load
Dimensions, feet (metres): 180·5 pp; 205·5 oa × 32·8 × 5·8 (55·1; 62·7 × 10·0 × 1·8)
Guns: 2—20 mm
Main engines: 3 MWM diesels; 3 shafts; 1 900 bhp = 10·5 knots
Oil fuel, tons: 37
Complement: 20

"ASH" Class (being fitted with helicopter deck aft)   1976, Israeli Navy

3 LC TYPE (LCT)

Name	No.	Builders	Commissioned
ETZION GUEBER	51	Israel Shipyards, Haifa	1965
SHIKOMONA	53	Israel Shipyards, Haifa	1965
—	55	Israel Shipyards, Haifa	1965

Displacement, tons: 182 standard; 230 full load
Dimensions, feet (metres): 120·0 × 23·2 × 4·7 *(Etzion Geuber* of only 90 ft length) *(36·6 × 7·1 × 1·4 (27·5))*
Guns: 2—20 mm
Main engines: 2 diesels; 2 shafts; 1 280 bhp = 10 knots
Complement: 12

LC Type   *1976, Israeli Navy*

3 Ex-US LCM TYPE

Displacement, tons: 22 tons standard; 60 full load
Dimensions, feet (metres): 50 × 14 × 3·2 *(15·3 × 4·3 × 1)*

Main engines: 2 diesels; 450 bhp = 11 knots

LCM Type   *1976, Israeli Navy*

SUPPORT SHIPS

Note: Training ship *'Nogah'* converted from 500 ton coaster.

Name	No.	Builders	Commissioned
MA'OZ	—	Todd Marine, Washington	1976

Displacement, tons: 4 000

Oil-rig tender for use as Light Forces Support ship.

1 "BAT SHEVA" CLASS (TRANSPORT)

Name	No.	Builders	Commissioned
BAT SHEVA	—	Netherlands	1967

Displacement, tons: 900
Dimensions, feet (metres): 311·7 × 36·7 × 26·9 *(95·1 × 11·2 × 8·2)*
Guns: 4—20 mm
Main engines: Diesels; speed = 10 knots
Complement: 26

Purchased from South Africa in 1968.

BAT SHEVA   *1971, Israeli Navy*

1 "BAT YAM" CLASS (TRANSPORT)

Name	No.	Builders	Commissioned
BAT YAM	T 82	Netherlands	—

A small armed merchant ship of 1 200 tons used as a transport. Bought from Netherlands in 1967.

MISCELLANEOUS

1 "YAR" CLASS (TRAINING CRAFT)

Name	No.	Builders	Commissioned
YARDEN	42	Yacht & Bootswerft, Burmester, Bremen	1958

Displacement, tons: 96 standard; 109 full load
Dimensions, feet (metres): 100 × 20 × 6 *(30·5 × 6·1 × 1·8)*
Guns: 2—20 mm
Main engines: MTU diesels; 2 shafts; speed 22 knots
Complement: 16

Has become non-naval training craft.

YARDEN   *Israeli Navy*

4 "KEDMA" CLASS (COASTAL PATROL CRAFT)

Name	No.	Builders	Commissioned
KEDMA	46	Japan	1968
NEGBA	52	Japan	1968
YAMA	48	Japan	1968
ZAFONA	60	Japan	1968

Displacement, tons: 32
Dimensions, feet (metres): 67·0 × 15·0 × 4·8 *(20·4 × 4·6 × 1·5)*
Guns: 2—20 mm
Main engines: 2 diesels; 2 shafts; 1 540 bhp = 25 knots
Complement: 10

Used for coastguard and police work in peace time.

"KEDMA" Class   *1976, Israeli Navy*

ITALY

Headquarters Appointment

Chief of Naval Staff:
  Admiral Gino de Giorgi
Vice Chief of Naval Staff:
  Vice-Admiral Giuliano Martinelli
Chief of Naval Personnel:
  Admiral Giovanni Torrisi

Principal Flag Officers

*Commander, Allied Naval Forces, Southern Europe (Naples)
  and Commander-in-Chief Dipartimento Basso Tirreno:*
  Admiral Aldo Baldini
Commander-in-Chief of Fleet (and Comedcent):
  Admiral Girolano Fantoni
Commander-in-Chief Dipartimento Alto Tirreno:
  Admiral Giuseppe Oriana
Commander-in-Chief Dipartimento Adriatico:
  Admiral Enzo Consolo
*Commander-in-Chief Dipartimento dello Jonio
  e Canale d'Otranto:*
  Admiral Mario Bini
Commander Sicilian Naval Area:
  Vice-Admiral Luigi de Ferrante
Commander 1st Naval Squadron:
  Rear-Admiral Vittorio Marulli
Commander 2nd Naval Squadron:
  Rear-Admiral Vittorio Gioncado
Commander 3rd Naval Squadron:
  Rear-Admiral Massimiliano Marandino
Commander 4th Naval Squadron:
  Rear-Admiral Mario Calzeroni

Diplomatic Representation

Naval Attaché in London:
  Captain Benini
Naval Attaché in Moscow:
  Captain Armando Vigliano
Naval Attaché in Paris:
  Captain P. Della Croce di Dojola
Naval Attaché in Washington:
  Captain Carlo A. Vandini

Personnel

(a) 1977: 42 000 (including Naval Air Arm and an expanding
    Force of Marines)
(b) 1½ years National Service

Bases

Main—La Spezia (Alto Tirreno), Taranto (Jonio e Canale
  d'Otranto), Ancona (Adriatico)
Secondary—Brindisi, Augusta, Messina, La Maddalena,
  Cagliari, Napoli, Venezia

Mercantile Marine

Lloyd's Register of Shipping:
  1 719 vessels of 11 077 549 tons gross

Naval Air Arm

2 LRMP Squadrons—18 Breguet Atlantics (BR 1150)
1 SRMP Squadron—Grumman S2F
2 Shore-based helicopter Squadrons (24 SH 3D)
30 AB 204B (36 more on order) helicopters for ships

Strength of the Fleet

Type	Active	Building (Planned)
Cruisers	3	(1)
Destroyers	9	(2)
Frigates	11	3 (8)
Corvettes	13	—
Submarines	10	2 (2)
Hydrofoil—Missile	1	(13)
Fast Attack Craft	10	—
LSTs	2	—
Minehunters	1	(10)
Minesweepers—Ocean	4	—
Minesweepers—Coastal	30	—
Minesweepers—Inshore	10	—
Survey/Research Vessels	4	—
Replenishment Tankers	1	1
Transport	1	—
Fleet Support Ship	1	—
Coastal Transports	10	—
Transports (LCM)	20	—
Transports (LCVP)	39	—
Sail Training Ships	4	—
Netlayers	2	—
Lighthouse Tenders	4	—
Salvage Ships	1	(1)
Repair Craft	7	—
Water Carriers	15	—
Tugs—Large	29	—
Tugs—Small	31	—

Shipbuilding and Conversion Programme

In 1975 a law (Legge Navale) was approved which provided
1 000 billion lire for the next ten years (1975-84), for the provision of new and converted ships and aircraft over and above
the normal annual expenditure.
The tentative new-construction programme is as follows:
  1   Helicopter Cruiser of about 10 000 tons
  2   Guided Missile Destroyers; "Audace" class
 12   Frigates; 4 "Lupo" and 8 "Maestrale" classes
  4   Submarines; 2 "Sauro" class and 2 of new class
 10   Minehunters
  9   "Sparviero" class Hydrofoils
  4   NATO Hydrofoils
  1   LPD
  1   Replenishment Tanker; sister to *Stromboli* probably
      named *Vesuvio*
  1   Salvage Ship
 17   Tugs
 62   AB212 Helicopters
 12   SH3D Helicopters
The conversion programme (1977-80) is: 9 MSCs to MSHs.

DELETIONS

Cruiser

1971 *Giuseppe Garibaldi*

Destroyers

1971 *San Marco, Artigliere, Lanciere*

Frigates

1971 *Altair* (demolition target)
1975 *Aviere* (target)
1976 *Aldebaran* (ex-US "Cannon" class)

Corvettes

1970-72 12 "Ape" Class

Submarines

1972 *Pietro Calvi*
1973 *Leonardo da Vinci, Enrico Tazzoli*
1975 *Francesco Morosini* ("Balao" Class) (15 Nov)

Minesweepers (Coastal)

1974 *Rovere, Acacia, Betulla, Ciliegio*

Minesweepers (Inshore)

1974 *Arsella, Attinia, Calamaro, Conchiglia, Dromia, Ostrica,
      Paguro, Seppia, Tellina, Totano*

Amphibious Forces

1974 *Anteo, MTM 9903, 9904, 9906, 9921. MTP 9701, 9702,
      9704-6, 9709, 9712, 9717, 9718, 9721, 9722, 9724, 9731*

Light Forces

1974 *MS 472* (ex-*813*)
1975 *MS 452* (ex-*852*) *MS 473* (ex-*813*)

Miscellaneous

1974 *Po, Flegetonte, Isonzo, Sesia, Metauro, Arno, Leno* and
      Sprugola (water carriers). 24 tugs
1975 *Aviere* (experimental ship), *Sterope* (repl. tanker),
      Frigido (water carrier), *MTM 9916-7, Porto Vecchio* (tug)

PENNANT NUMBERS

Cruisers

C550	Vittorio Veneto
C553	Andrea Dorea
C554	Caio Duilio

Destroyers

D550	Ardito
D551	Audace
D555	Geniere
D558	Impetuoso
D559	Indomito
D561	Fante
D562	San Giorgio
D570	Impavido
D571	Intrepido

Frigates

F551	Canopo
F553	Castore
F554	Centauro
F555	Cigno
F564	Lupo
F580	Alpino
F581	Carabiniere
F590	Aldebaran
F593	Carlo Bergamini
F594	Virginio Fasan
F595	Carlo Margottini
F596	Luigi Rizzo

Corvettes

F540	Pietro De Cristofaro
F541	Umberto Grosso
F542	Aquila
F543	Albatros
F544	Alcione
F545	Airone
F546	Licio Visintini
F549	Bombarda
F550	Salvatore Todaro
F569	Chimera
F579	Sfinge
F597	Vedetta

Submarines

S501	Primo Longobardo
S502	Gianfranco Gazzana Priaroggia
S505	Attilio Bagnolini
S506	Enrico Toti
S507	Alfredo Cappellini
S513	Enrico Dandolo
S514	Lazzaro Mocenigo
S515	Livio Piomarta
S516	Romeo Romei

Light Forces

P420	Sparviero
P490	Folgore
P491	Lampo
P492	Baleno
P493	Freccia
P494	Saetta
—	MS441
—	MS443
—	MS453
—	MS474
—	MS481

Minesweepers

M5430	Salmone
M5431	Storione
M5432	Sgombro
M5433	Squalo
M5450	Aragosta
M5452	Astice
M5457	Gambero
M5458	Granchio
M5459	Mitilo
M5462	Pinna
M5463	Polipo
M5464	Porpora
M5465	Riccio
M5466	Scampo
M5501	Abete
M5504	Castagno
M5505	Cedro
M5507	Faggio
M5508	Frassino
M5509	Gelso
M5510	Larice
M5511	Noce
M5512	Olmo
M5513	Ontano
M5514	Pino
M5516	Platano
M5517	Quercia
M5519	Mandorlo
M5521	Bambù
M5522	Ebano
M5523	Mango
M5524	Mogano
M5525	Palma
M5527	Sandalo
M5531	Agave

Minesweepers—continued

M5532	Alloro
M5533	Edera
M5534	Gaggia
M5535	Gelsomino
M5536	Giaggiolo
M5537	Glicine
M5538	Loto
M5540	Timo
M5541	Trifoglio
M5542	Vischio

Amphibious Forces

L9871	Andrea Bafile
L9890	Grado
L9891	Caorle

Service Forces

A5301	Pietro Cavezzale
A5303	Ammiraglio Magnaghi
A5304	Alicudi
A5305	Filicudi
A5306	Mirto
A5307	Pioppo
A5309	Rampino
A5310	Proteo
A5311	Palinuro
A5312	Amerigo Vespucci
A5313	Stella Polare
A5314	Quarto
A5316	Corsaro II

Service Forces—continued

A5319	Ciclope
A5320	Colosso
A5321	Forte
A5322	Gagliardo
A5323	Robusto
A5324	Ustica
A5326	S. Giusto
A5327	Stromboli
A5328	Ape
A5331-5338	MOC 1201-1208
A5354	Piave
A5355	Tevere
A5356	Basento
A5357	Bradano
A5358	Brenta
A5359	Bormida
A5361-5363	MTF 1301-1303
A5366	Volturno
A5369	Adige
A5374	Mincio
A5376	Tanaro
A5377	Ticino
A5378	Porto d'Ischia
A5379	Riva Trigoso
A5381	Caprera
A5382	Pantelleria
A5385	Favignana
A5386	Porto Pisano
A5387	Porto Recanati
A5388	—
A5391	Salvore
A5392	Tino
A5394	Vigoroso
A5396	Pianova
A5397	Levanzo

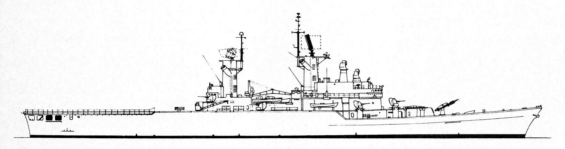

VITTORIO VENETO

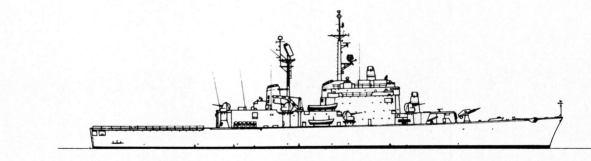

ANDREA DORIA

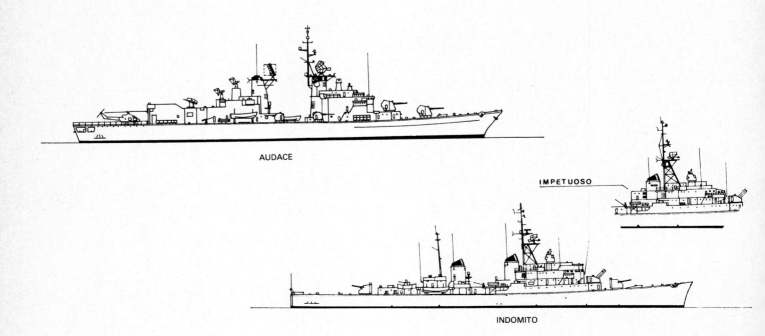

AUDACE

IMPETUOSO

INDOMITO

FANTE

SAN GIORGIO

IMPAVIDO

LUPO

CENTAURO

ALPINO

PIETRO DE CRISTOFARO

ALBATROS

PIETRO CAVEZZALE

AMMIRAGLIO MAGNAGHI

STROMBOLI

Drawings by Lieutenant-Commander Erminio Bagnasco

CRUISERS

1 NEW CONSTRUCTION HELICOPTER CRUISER

GIUSEPPE GARIBALDI

A new through-deck design of 10 000-12 000 tons being developed by Italian Navy in conjunction with Cantieri Navali Riuniti. Approx 574 feet (175 metres). Propulsion to be decided. Speed approx 30 knots. Possible laying down date 1980 to replace "Andrea Doria" class in mid-1980s. Planned to carry helicopters and V/STOL aircraft.

1 HELICOPTER CRUISER

Name	No.	Builders	Laid down	Launched	Commissioned
VITTORIO VENETO	C 550	Navalmeccanica, Castellammare di Stabia	10 June 1965	5 Feb 1967	12 July 1969

Displacement, tons: 7 500 standard; 8 850 full load
Length, feet (metres): 589 (179·6) oa
Beam, feet (metres): 63·6 (19·4)
Draught, feet (metres): 19·7 (6)
Aircraft: 9 AB-204B helicopters
Missiles: 1 Terrier/Asroc twin launcher forward
Guns: 8—3 in (76 mm) 62 cal
Torpedo tubes: 2 triple US Mk 32 for A/S torpedoes
Main engines: 2 Tosi double reduction geared turbines; 73 000 shp; 2 shafts
Boilers: 4 Foster-Wheeler; 711 psi (50 kg/cm²); 842°F (450°C)
Speed, knots: 32
Oil fuel, tons: 1 200
Range, miles: 6 000 at 20 knots
Complement: 560 (60 officers, 500 men)

Developed from the "Andrea Doria" class but with much larger helicopter squadron and improved facilities for anti-submarine operations. Projected under the 1959-60 New Construction Programme, but her design was recast several times. Started trials 30 April 1969. Flagship of C-in-C Fleet.

Electronics: Tacan AN/URN-20 fitted.

Radar: Air search and target designator (3D on fore funnel): one SPS 52.
Long-range search (after funnel): one SPS 40.
Search and navigation: one SMA/SPQ-2.
Terrier fire control: two SPG 55B.
Gun fire control: four Orion radars in Argo/Elsag NA9 systems.

Sonar: One SQS 23.

VITTORIO VENETO   1974, Dr. Giorgio Arra

VITTORIO VENETO   1973, Dr. Giorgio Arra

VITTORIO VENETO   1973, Dr. Giorgio Arra

2 "ANDREA DORIA" CLASS

Name	No.	Builders	Laid down	Launched	Commissioned
ANDREA DORIA	C 553	Cantieri del Tirreno, Riva Trigoso	11 May 1958	27 Feb 1963	23 Feb 1964
CAIO DUILIO	C 554	Navalmeccanica di Stabia	16 May 1958	22 Dec 1962	30 Nov 1964

Displacement, tons: 5 000 standard; 6 500 full load
Length, feet (metres): 489·8 *(149·3)* oa
Beam, feet (metres): 56·4 *(17·2)*
Draught, feet (metres): 16·4 *(5·0)*
Aircraft: 4 AB-204B helicopters
Missiles: 1 Terrier twin launcher forward
Guns: 8—3 in *(76 mm)* 62 cal.
Torpedo tubes: 2 triple for A/S torpedoes
Main engines: 2 double reduction geared turbines 60 000 shp; 2 shafts
Boilers: 4 Foster-Wheeler 711 psi *(50 kg/cm²)*; 842°F *(450°C)*
Speed, knots: 31
Range, miles: 6 000 at 20 knots
Oil fuel, tons: 1 100
Complement: 485 (45 officers, 440 men)

Escort cruisers of novel design with a good helicopter capacity in relation to their size. *Enrico Dandolo* was the name originally allocated to *Andrea Doria.*

Electronics: ECM and DF. Tacan beacon (AN/URN-20).

Gunnery: The anti-aircraft battery includes eight 3-inch fully automatic guns of a new pattern, disposed in single turrets, four on each side amidships abreast the funnels and the bridge.

Helicopter platform: Helicopters operate from a platform aft measuring 98·5 feet by 52·5 feet *(30 by 16 metres).*

Roll damping: Both ships have Gyrofin-Salmoiraghi stabilisers.

Radar: Air surveillance and target designator (3D on mainmast): one SPS 39
Long range search: one SPS 40.
Navigation: one set.
Terrier fire-control: two SPG 55A.
Gun fire control: four Orion radars in Argo/Elsag NA9 systems

Sonar: One SQS 23.

ANDREA DORIA   11/1975, Dr. Giorgio Arra

ANDREA DORIA   1973, Dr. Giorgio Arra

CAIO DUILIO   5/1974, Commander Aldo Fraccarali

DESTROYERS

Note: 2 "Improved Audace" class with COGOG or CODOG machinery to be built under Legge Navale as replacements for "Impetuoso" class

2 "AUDACE" CLASS (DDG)

Name	No.	Builders	Laid down	Launched	Commissioned
ARDITO	D 550	Navalmeccanica, Castellammare	19 July 1968	27 Nov 1971	5 Dec 1973
AUDACE	D 551	Cantieri del Tirreno, Riva Trigoso	27 April 1968	2 Oct 1971	16 Nov 1972

Displacement, tons: 3 600 standard; 4 400 full load
Length, feet (metres): 446·4 *(136·6)*
Beam, feet (metres): 47·1 *(14·5)*
Draught, feet (metres): 15 *(4·6)*
Aircraft: 2 AB-204B helicopters
Missile launcher: 1 Tartar
Guns: 2—5 in *(127 mm)* 54 cal single; 4—3 in *(76 mm)* 62 cal
Torpedo tubes: 6 A/S (two triple) 4 fixed tubes
Main engines: 2 geared turbines; 73 000 shp; 2 shafts
Boilers: 4 Foster Wheeler type
Speed, knots: 33
Complement: 380 (30 officers, 350 men)

It was announced in April 1966 that two new guided missile destroyers would be built. They are basically similar to, but an improvement in design on that of the "Impavido" class.

Aircraft: Originally planned to carry two AB-204B helicopters carrying two A/S torpedoes. These may be replaced by two Sea King SH3Ds.

Radar: Air Surveillance (3D on after funnel): one SPS 52
Tracking and missile guidance: two SPG 51
Surface Search: one SPS 12
Gun fire control: three Orion RTN 10X for Argo 10/Elsag NA 10 systems

Sonar: one CWE 610

SCLAR: fitted with SCLAR control and launch units for 105 mm rockets which can be fitted with chaff dispensers, flares or HE heads and have a range of 7 miles.

Torpedo tubes: The two triple Mk 32 launchers for Mk 44 torpedoes are on either beam amidships. The four fixed torpedo tubes (A 184 System) for A/S or anti-ship torpedoes are built into the transom, a pair being fitted high on either quarter.

AUDACE   6/1976, Commander Aldo Fraccaroli

ARDITO   1974, Commander Aldo Fraccaroli

ARDITO   10/1976, Commander Aldo Fraccaroli

2 "IMPAVIDO" CLASS (DDG)

Name	No.
IMPAVIDO	D 570
INTREPIDO	D 571

Builders	Laid down	Launched	Commissioned
Cantieri del Tirreno, Riva Trigoso	10 June1957	25 May 1962	16 Nov 1963
Ansaldo, Leghorn	16 May 1959	21 Oct 1962	30 Oct 1964

Displacement, tons: 3 201 standard; 3 851 full load
Length, feet (metres): 429·5 *(131·3)*
Beam, feet (metres): 44·7 *(13·6)*
Draught, feet (metres): 14·8 *(4·5)*
Aircraft: 1 AB-204 B helicopter
Missiles: 1 Tartar launcher, aft
Guns: 2—5 in *(127 mm)* 38 cal. forward; 4—3 in *(76 mm)* 62 cal
Torpedo tubes: 2 triple for A/S torpedoes
Boilers: 4 Foster Wheeler; 711 psi *(50 kg/cm²)*; 842°F *(450°C)*
Main engines: 2 double reduction geared turbines 70 000 shp; 2 shafts
Speed, knots: 34
Range, miles: 3 300 at 20 knots; 2 900 at 25 knots
Oil fuel, tons: 650
Complement: 335 (23 officers, 312 men)

Built under the 1956-57 and 1958-59 programmes respectively. Both ships have stabilisers.

Engineering; On first full power trials *Impavido,* at light displacement, reached 34·5 knots (33 knots at normal load).

Modernisation: In 1974-75 *Intrepido* underwent modernisation which included the improvement of the missile system and the replacement of the original gun fire-control system by Argo 10/Elsag NA 10 system. Same modifications carried out in *Impavido* 1975-76.

Radar: Search: SPS 12 and SPS 39 (3-D)
Fire control: SPG 51 for Tartar; Argo 10/Elsag NA 10 for guns.

Sonar: One SQS 23

IMPAVIDO 1975, *Michael D. J. Lennon*

INTREPIDO 6/1975, *Dr Giorgio Arra*

1 "SAN GIORGIO" CLASS (DD)

Name	No.
SAN GIORGIO (ex-*Pompeo Magno*)	D 562

Builders	Laid down	Launched	Commissioned
Cantieri N. Riuniti Ancona	23 Sep 1939	28 Aug 1941	24 June 1943

Displacement, tons: 3 950 standard; 4 350 full load
Length, feet (metres): 455·2 *(138·8)* wl; 466·5 *(142·3)* oa
Beam, feet (metres): 47·2 *(14·4)*
Draught, feet (metres): 21·0 *(4·5)*
Guns: 4—5 in *(127 mm)* 38 cal; 3—3 in *(76 mm)* 62 cal
A/S weapons: 1 three-barrelled mortar (MENON); 2 triple torpedo tubes
Main engines: 2 Tosi Metrovick gas turbines; 15 000 bhp; 4 Fiat diesels; 16 600 hp; 2 shafts
Speed, knots: 20 (diesels), 28 (diesel and gas)
Range, miles: 4 800 at 20 knots
Oil fuel, tons: 500 (diesel oil)
Complement: 295 (15 officers, 280 men) plus 130 cadets

Converted into fleet destroyer in 1951 by Cantieri del Tirreno, Genoa, being completed 1 July 1955. Underwent complete re-construction at the Naval Dockyard, La Spezia, in 1963-65. The modernisation included her adaptation as a Training Ship for 130 cadets of the Accademia Navale. Changes were made in the armament and new machinery was fitted, gas turbines and diesels replacing steam turbines and boilers.

Gunnery: 5 in. control—US Mk 37 with Mk 25 radar.

Radar: Search: SPS 6.
Fire control: Four I Band sets.
Navigation: One set.

Sonar: One SQS 10.

SAN GIORGIO 7/1976, *A. D. Baker III*

Name	No.
IMPETUOSO	D 558
INDOMITO	D 559

2 "IMPETUOSO" CLASS

Builders	Laid down	Launched	Commissioned
Cantieri del Tirreno, Riva Trigosa	7 May 1952	16 Sep 1956	25 Jan 1958
Ansaldo, Leghorn (formerly OTO)	24 April 1952	7 Aug 1955	23 Feb 1958

INDOMITO   1975, Commander Aldo Fraccaroli

Displacement, tons: 2 755 standard; 3 800 full load
Length, feet (metres): 405 (123·4) pp; 418·7 (127·6) oa
Beam, feet (metres): 43·5 (13·3)
Draught, feet (metres): 17·5 (4·5)
Guns: 4—5 in (127 mm) 38 cal. 16—40 mm 56 cal
A/S weapons: 1 three-barrelled mortar; 4 DCT; 1 DC rack 6 (2 triple)
Torpedo tubes: for A/S torpedoes
Main engines: 2 double reduction geared turbines; 2 shafts; 65 000 shp
Boilers: 4 Foster-Wheeler; 711 psi (50 kg/cm²) working pressure; 842°F (450°C) superheat temperature
Speed, knots: 34 (see Engineering notes)
Oil fuel, tons: 650
Range, miles: 3 400 at 20 knots
Complement: 315 (15 officers, 300 men)

Italy's first destroyers built since Second World War. To be relieved in mid-1980s by "Improved Audace" class.

Engineering: On their initial sea trials these ships attained a speed of 35 knots at full load.

Gunnery: For 5 in.—US Mk 37 director with Mk 25 radar. For 40 mm—four mounts have US Mk 34 radars. In addition six US Mk 51 directors.

Radar: Search: one SGS 6B.
Fire Control: one SFS 60.

Sonar: One SQS 4 or 11.

IMPETUOSO   1975, Commander Aldo Fraccaroli

2 Ex-US "FLETCHER' CLASS

Name	No.
FANTE (ex-USS Walker, DD 517)	D 561
GENIERE (ex-USS Pritchett, DD 561)	D 555

Builders	Laid down	Launched	Commissioned
Bath Iron Works Corp.	31 Aug 1942	31 Jan 1943	2 April 1943
Seattle-Tacoma SB Corpn	30 July 1942	31 July 1943	15 Jan 1944

Displacement, tons: 2 080 standard; 2 940 full load
Length, feet (metres): 376·5 (114·3) oa
Beam, feet (metres): 39·5 (12·0)
Draught, feet (metres): 18 (5·5)
Guns: 2—5 inch, 38 cal; 4—3 inch, 50 cal in twin mountings
A/S weapons: 1 DC rack, 2 fixed Hedgehogs; 6 (2 triple) US Mk 32 torpedo tubes
Main engines: GE geared turbines; 2 shafts; 60 000 shp
Boilers: 4 Babcock & Wilcox
Speed, knots: 35
Oil fuel, tons: 650
Range, miles: 6 000 at 15 knots
Complement: 250 (10 officers, 240 men)

Walker was transferred from the United States and commissioned as Fante on 2 July 1969. Pritchett transferred 7 Jan 1970.

Gunnery: For 5 inch—Mk 37 director.
For 3 inch—Mk 56 director.

Radar: Search: SPS 6 and SPS 10.

Sonar: One hull mounted set. SQS-4 series

Torpedo tubes: Original 21 inch torpedo tubes were replaced in 1948 by four fixed A/S tubes, the present armament dating from early 1960s.

FANTE (after removal of weapon Able)   1973, Dr. Giorgio Arra

FRIGATES

8 "MAESTRALE" CLASS

ALISEO	**GRECALE**	**SCIROCCO**
ESPERU	**LIBECCIO**	**ZEFFIRO**
EURO	**MAESTRALE**	

An improved "Lupo" class provided for in Legge Navale. Of approximately 3 000 tons with CODOG machinery and missile armament. First four will probably be ordered late 1977.

4 "LUPO" CLASS

Name	No.	Builders	Laid down	Launched	Commissioned
LUPO	D 564	CNR, Riva Trigoso	11 Oct 1974	29 July 1976	April 1977
SAGITTARIO	—	CNR, Riva Trigoso	4 Feb 1976	April 1977	Jan 1978
PERSEO	—	CNR, Riva Trigoso	Dec 1976	Nov 1977	Aug 1978
ORSA	—	CNR, Riva Trigoso	May 1977	April 1978	April 1979

Displacement, tons: 2 208 standard; 2 500 full load
Length, feet (metres): 355·4 *(108·4)*
Beam, feet (metres): 37·1 *(11·3)*
Draught, feet (metres): 12·1 *(3·7)*
Aircraft: 2 AB 212 helicopters
Missiles: 1—Otomat (OTO-Melara) surface-to-surface system with 4 launchers; 1—Albatros (Selenia) surface-to-air system
Guns: 1—5 in (127/54) OTO-Melara Compact; 4—40 mm 70 cal (Breda) (twin Dardo systems)
Rocket launcher: 1 SCLAR system with 2 multiple, trainable mountings
A/S weapons: 6 (2 triple) Mk 32
Torpedo tubes: For Mk 46 A/S torpedoes
Main engines: CODOG—2 Fiat LM 2 500 gas turbines; 50 000 hp; 2 GMT diesels; 7 800 hp; 2 shafts
Speed, knots: 35 on turbines; 21 on diesels
Range, miles: 4 400 at 16 knots (diesels)
Complement: 185 (16 officers, 169 ratings)

First of class named after the most famous Italian torpedo-boat of 2nd World War.

Aircraft: Although two helicopters can be carried there is hangar space for only one.

Construction: 14 watertight compartments; fixed-fin stablisers; 90 days endurance.

Electronics: Automatic command and control system IPN 10 (Selenia); ECM System (Elettronica); Telecommunications System (Elmer).

Radar: Air search: one Selenia.
Combined search: one RAN 11L/X system (Selenia).
Gun fire control: Orion in Argo 10/Elsag NA10 system.

Sonar: One QMS 32 (Plessey) M/F hull-mounted set.

Foreign sales: Similar ships being built for Peru and Venezuela.

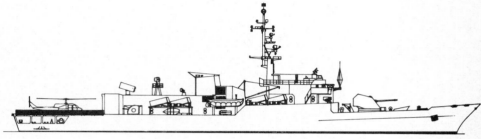

"LUPO" Class   1976, Italian Navy

LUPO at launching   7/1976, Commander Aldo Fraccaroli

2 "ALPINO" CLASS

Name	No.	Builders	Laid down	Launched	Commissioned
ALPINO (ex-*Circe*)	F 580	Cantieri Navali del Tirreno, Riva Trigoso	27 Feb 1963	10 June 1967	14 Jan 1968
CARABINIERE (ex-*Climene*)	F 581	Cantieri Navali del Tirreno, Riva Trigoso	9 Jan 1965	30 Sep 1967	28 April 1968

Displacement, tons: 2 700 full load
Length, feet (metres): 349·0 *(106·4)* pp; 352·0 *(107·3)* wl; 371·7 *(113·3)* oa
Beam, feet (metres): 43·6 *(13·3)*
Draught, feet (metres): 12·7 *(3·9)*
Aircraft: 2 AB-204B helicopters
Guns: 6—3 in *(76 mm)* 62 cal (single)
A/S weapons: 1 single depth charge mortar; 6 (2 triple) Mk 32 A/S torpedo tubes
Main engines: 4 Tosi diesels; 16 800 hp; 2 Tosi Metrovick gas turbines; 15 000 hp; 2 shafts
Speed, knots: 22 (diesel); 29 (diesel and gas)
Oil fuel, tons: 275
Range, miles: 4 200 at 18 knots
Complement: 253 (20 officers, 233 men)

The design is an improved version of that of the "Centauro" class combined with that of the "Bergamini" class.

Gunnery: MAD gunfire control aerial fitted in *Alpino* 1975.

Radar: Combined search: one SPS 12.
Air/surface search/navigation: one SPQ2.
Fire control: 3 Orion radars in Elsag/Argo "O" control systems.
Radar intercept: MM/SPR A.

Sonar: One SQS 29. One SQA 10 VDS.

ALPINO   1976, Dr. Giorgio Arra

Name
CARLO BERGAMINI
CARLO MARGOTTINI
LUIGI RIZZO
VIRGINIO FASAN

No.
F 593
F 595
F 596
F 594

4 "BERGAMINI" CLASS

Builders	Laid down	Launched	Commissioned
San Marco, CRDA Trieste	19 May 1959	16 June 1960	23 June 1962
Navalmeccanica, Castellammare	26 May 1957	12 June 1960	5 May 1962
Navalmeccanica, Castellammare	26 May 1957	6 Mar 1960	15 Dec 1961
Navalmeccanica, Castellammare	6 Mar 1960	9 Oct 1960	10 Oct 1962

Displacement, tons: 1 650 full load
Length, feet (metres): 311·7 *(95·0)* oa
Beam, feet (metres): 37·4 *(11·4)*
Draught, feet (metres): 10·5 *(3·2)*
Aircraft: 1 AB-204B helicopter
Guns: 2—3 in *(76 mm)* 62 cal single
A/S weapons: 1 single depth charge mortar; 6 (2 triple) US Mk 32 for A/S torpedoes
Main engines: 4 diesels (Fiat in *Fasan* and *Margottini*, Tosi in others); 2 shafts; 15 000 bhp
Speed, knots: 24·5
Range, miles: 4 000 at 18 knots
Complement: 158 (19 officers, 139 men)

Modernisation: A slightly enlarged helicopter platform was fitted and a telescopic hangar shipped to allow for embarkation of one AB-204B helicopter. The after 3-inch gun was removed. *Carlo Margottini,* 1968; *Virginio Fasan,* 1969; *Carlo Bergamini,* 1970; *Luigi Rizzo,* 1971.

Radar: Combined search: one SPS 12.
Air/surface search/navigation: one SPQ 2.
Fire control: two Orion radars in Elsag/Argo control systems.
Radar intercept: MM/SPR A.

Roll damping: Two Denny-Brown stabilisers reduce inclination in heavy seas from 20 to 5 degrees.

Sonar: One SQS 11.

CARLO BERGAMINI   5/1974, Commander Aldo Fraccaroli

Name
CANOPO
CASTORE
CENTAURO
CIGNO

No.
F 551 (ex-*D 570*)
F 553 (ex-*D 573*)
F 554 (ex-*D 571*)
F 555 (ex-*D 572*)

4 "CENTAURO" CLASS

Builders	Laid down	Launched	Commissioned
Cantieri Navali di Taranto	15 May 1952	20 Feb 1955	1 April 1958
Cantieri Navali di Taranto	14 Mar 1955	8 July 1956	14 July 1957
Ansaldo, Leghorn	31 May 1952	4 April 1954	5 May 1957
Cantieri Navali di Taranto	10 Feb 1954	20 Mar 1955	7 Mar 1957

Displacement, tons: 1 807 standard; 2 250 full load
Length, feet (metres): 308·4 *(94)* pp; 338·4 *(103·1)* oa
Beam, feet (metres): 39·5 *(12)*
Draught, feet (metres): 12·6 *(3·8)*
Guns: 3—3 in *(76 mm)* 62 cal (single)
A/S weapons: 1 three-barrelled depth charge mortar; 6 (2 triple) US Mk 32 A/S torpedo tubes
Main engines: 2 double reduction geared turbines 2 shafts; 22 000 shp
Boilers: 2 Foster Wheeler; 626 psi *(44 kg/cm²)* working pressure; 842°F *(450°C)* superheat temperature
Speed, knots: 25
Oil fuel, tons: 400
Range, miles: 3 660 at 20 knots
Complement: 225 (16 officers, 209 men)

Built to Italian plans and specifications under the US off-shore programme.

Conversion: Carried out as follows: *Castore*—1966-67, *Canopo*—1968-69, *Centauro*—1970-71, *Cigno*—1972-73. This provided the new 3 in *(76 mm)* armament.

Radar: Search: one SPS 6.
Combined search and navigation: one SMA/SPQ 2.
Fire control: I band.
Radar Intercept: MM/SPR A.

Sonar: SQS-11.

CENTAURO   6/1975, Dr. Giorgio Arra

CORVETTES

4 "DE CRISTOFARO" CLASS

Name
LICIO VISINTINI
PIETRO DE CRISTOFARO
SALVATORE TODARO
UMBERTO GROSSO

No.
F 546
F 540
F 550
F 541

Builders	Laid down	Launched	Commissioned
CRDA Monfalcone	30 Sep 1963	30 May 1965	25 Aug 1966
Cantiere Navali de Tirreno, Riva Trigoso	30 Apr 1963	29 May 1965	19 Dec 1965
Cantiere Ansaldo, Leghorn	21 Oct 1962	24 Oct 1964	25 Apr 1966
Cantiere Ansaldo, Leghorn	21 Oct 1962	12 Dec 1964	25 Apr 1966

Displacement, tons: 850 standard; 1 020 full load
Length, feet (metres): 246 *(75·0)* pp; 263·2 *(80·2)* oa
Beam, feet (metres): 33·7 *(10·3)*
Draught, feet (metres): 9 *(2·7)*
Guns: 2—3 in *(76 mm)* 62 cal, (single)
A/S weapons: 1 single-barrelled DC mortar; 2 triple US Mk 32 A/S torpedo tubes
Main engines: 2 diesels = 8 400 bhp; 2 shafts
Speed, knots: 23·5
Oil fuel, tons: 100
Range, miles: 4 000 at 18 knots
Complement: 131 (8 officers, 123 men)

The design is an improved version of the "Albatros" class.

Radar: Air and surface surveillance radar with antenna mounted at top of foremast. Gunfire control system has director mounted aft, above compass platform, with I band tracker radar.

Sonar: ELSAG DLB-1 fire control system.
SQS 11 (hull-mounted)
SQS 36 (VDS)

LICIO VISINTINI   6/1975, Dr Giorgio Arra

Corvettes—*continued*

4 "ALBATROS" CLASS

Name	No.	Builders	Laid down	Launched	Commissioned
AIRONE	F 545	Navalmeccanica, Castellammare di Stabia	1953	21 Nov 1954	29 Dec 1955
ALBATROS	F 543	Navalmeccanica, Castellammare di Stabia	1953	18 July 1954	1 June 1955
ALCIONE	F 544	Navalmeccanica, Castellammare di Stabia	1953	19 Sep 1954	23 Oct 1955
AQUILA	F 542	Breda Marghera, Mestre, Venezia	25 July 1953	31 July 1954	2 Oct 1956

Displacement, tons: 800 standard; 950 full load
Length, feet (metres): 250·3 *(76·3)* oa
Beam, feet (metres): 31·5 *(9·6)*
Draught, feet (metres): 9·2 *(2·8)*
Guns: 4—40 mm 70 cal Bofors (see *Gunnery*)
A/S weapons: 2 Hedgehogs Mk II; 2 DCT; 1 DC rack; 6 (2 triple) US Mk 32 A/S torpedo tubes
Main engines: 2 Fiat diesels; 2 shafts; 5 200 bhp
Speed, knots: 19
Oil fuel, tons: 100
Range, miles: 3 000 at 18 knots
Complement: 109

ALBATROS 1974, *Dr. Giorgio Arra*

Eight ships of this class were built in Italy under US offshore MDAP orders. 3 for Italy, 4 for Denmark and 1 for the Netherlands. *Aquila,* laid down on 25 July 1953, was transferred to the Italian Navy on 18 Oct 1961 at Den Helder.

Gunnery: The two 3-inch guns originally mounted, one forward and one aft, were temporarily replaced by two 40 mm guns in 1963. The ultimate armament was planned to include two 3-inch (76 mm) OTO Melara guns.

Radar: Combined search and navigation: one SMA/SPQ-2. Fire control: radar control for Elsag NA-2 system.

4 "APE" CLASS

Name	No.	Builders	Laid down	Launched	Commissioned
APE	A 5328	Navalmeccanica, Castellamare	1942	1942	1943
BOMBARDA	F 549	Breda, Venezia	1942	1944	1951
CHIMERA	F 569	—	—	—	1942
SFINGE	F 579	CRDA, Trieste	1942	1942	1943

Displacement, tons: 670 standard; 771 full load
Length, feet (metres): 192·8 *(58·8)* wl; 212·6 *(64·8)* oa
Beam, feet (metres): 28·5 *(8·7)*
Draught, feet (metres): 8·9 *(2·7)*
Guns: 4—40 mm 56 cal (Only 2 in *Ape* and *Chimera);* in addition 2—20 mm 70 cal *(Bombarda* only)
A/S weapons: 1 Hedgehog Mk 10
Main engines: 2 Fiat diesels; 2 shafts; 3 500 bhp
Speed, knots: 15
Oil fuel, tons: 64
Range, miles: 2 450 at 15 knots
Complement: 56 (6 officers, 50 men)

Originally fitted for minesweeping. Modified with navigating bridge. *Ape* is now support ship for frogmen and commandos. Remainder fitted for target work.

Radar: Search: SPS 6 in *Sfinge.*

CHIMERA (with drone catapult) 6/1976, *Dr Giorgio Arra*

APE (Diving support ship) 6/1976, *Dr Giorgio Arra*

1 US PC TYPE

Name	No.	Builders	Laid down	Launched	Commissioned
VEDETTA (ex-*Belay Deress,* ex-US PC 1616)	F 597	Arsenal Naval, Brest	1953	1954	1955

Displacement, tons: 325 standard; 450 full load
Dimensions, feet (metres): 170 pp; 174 oa × 23 × 10 *(51·9; 53·1 × 7 × 3·1)*
Guns: 2—40 mm 56 cal Bofors; 2—20 mm
A/S weapons: 1 Hedgehog; 4 DCT; 2 DC racks
Main engines: 4 diesels; 2 shafts; 3 500 bhp = 19 knots
Range, miles: 6 350 at 12 knots
Complement: 60 (6 officers, 54 men)

Originally allocated to Germany and then to Ethiopia (1957-59). She was sold to Italy, being transferred on 3 Feb 1959. Air-conditioning equipment is installed. Refitted in La Spezia Navy Yard in 1959. Employed as a Fishery Protection Vessel.

VEDETTA 1974, *Dr Giorgio Arra*

SUBMARINES

2 + (2) "SAURO" CLASS (1081 TYPE)

Name	No.	Builders	Laid down	Launched	Commissioned
NAZARIO SAURO	—	CRDA Monfalcone	15 July 1974	9 Oct 1976	Dec 1977
FECIA DI COSSATO	—	CRDA Monfalcone	15 Nov 1975	April 1977	Oct 1978

Displacement, tons: 1 456 surfaced; 1 631 dived
Length, feet (metres): 210 (63·9)
Beam, feet (metres): 22·5 (6·8)
Draught, feet (metres): 18·9 (5·7)
Torpedo tubes: 6—21 in (bow) (6 reloads)
Main machinery: 3 diesel generators; 3 210 bhp; 1 electric motor; 3 650 hp; 1 shaft
Speed, knots: 11 surfaced; 20 dived; 12 (snorting)
Range, miles: 7 000 miles surfaced; 12 500 snorting at 4 knots; 400 miles dived at 4 knots; 20 miles dived at 20 knots
Endurance: 45 days
Complement: 45

Two of this class were originally ordered in 1967 but were cancelled in the following year. Reinstated in the building programme in 1972. Further pair provided for in Legge Navale.

Diving depth: 1 000 feet + (300 metres +).

Electronics: ECM; IFF, full communications fit.

Radar: 1 Search set (periscopic).

Sonar: Active and passive; Velox; Passive ranging; Acoustic ESM.

"SAURO" Class

1976, Italcantieri

4 "TOTI" CLASS (1075 TYPE)

Name	No.	Builders	Laid down	Launched	Commissioned
ATTILIO BAGNOLINI	S 505	CRDA Monfalcone	15 April 1965	26 Aug 1967	16 June 1968
ENRICO DANDOLO	S 513	CRDA Monfalcone	10 Mar 1967	16 Dec 1967	25 Sep 1968
LAZZARO MOCENIGO	S 514	CRDA Monfalcone	12 June 1967	20 April 1968	11 Jan 1969
ENRICO TOTI	S 506	CRDA Monfalcone	15 April 1965	12 Mar 1967	22 Jan 1968

Displacement, tons: 460 standard; 524 surfaced; 582 dived
Length, feet (metres): 151·5 (46·2)
Beam, feet (metres): 15·4 (4·7)
Draught, feet (metres): 13·1 (4·0)
Torpedo tubes: 4—21 in
Main machinery: 2 Fiat MB 820 N/I diesels, 1 electric motor, Diesel-electric drive; 2 200 hp; 1 shaft
Speed, knots: 14 surfaced; 15 dived
Range, miles: 3 000 at 5 knots (surfaced)
Complement: 26 (4 officers, 22 men)

Italy's first indigenously-built submarines since the Second World War. The design was recast several times.

Diving depth: 600 feet (180 metres).

Electronics: WT, HF, UHF and VLF equipment. Computer based fire control.

Radar: Search/nav set. IFF, ECM.

Sonar: Passive set in stem. Active set in bow dome. Passive range finding. Ray path analyzer.

ENRICO DANDOLO

9/1976, Commander Aldo Fraccaroli

2 Ex-US "TANG" CLASS

Name	No.	Builders	Laid down	Launched	Commissioned
ROMEO ROMEI (ex-USS Harder, SS 568)	S 516	General Dynamics (Electric Roat Div)	30 June 1950	14 June 1951	31 Mar 1952
LIVIO PIOMARTA (ex-USS Trigger, SS 564)	S 515	General Dynamics (Electric Boat Div)	24 Feb 1949	3 Dec 1951	19 Aug 1952

Displacement, tons: 2 100 surfaced; 2 700 dived
Length, feet (metres): 287 (87·4)
Beam, feet (metres): 27·3 (8·3)
Draught, feet (metres): 19 (6·2)
Torpedo tubes: 8—21 in; 6 bow, 2 stern
Main machinery: 3 Diesels 4 500 shp; 2 electric motors 5 600 hp
Speed, knots: 20 surfaced; 18 dived
Complement: 83 (8 officers, 75 men)

Transferred as follows: *Romeo Romei* 20 Feb 1974, *Livio Piomarta* 10 July 1973. Subsequently refitted at Philadelphia Navy Yard.

ROMEO ROMEI

11/1975, Dr. Giorgio Arra

2 Ex-US "GUPPY III" CLASS

Name	No.	Builders	Laid down	Launched	Commissioned
GIANFRANCO GAZZANA PRIAROGGIA (ex-USS *Volador, SS 490)*	S 501	Boston Navy Yard	8 Feb 1944	15 Dec 1944	4 April 1949
PRIMO LONGOBARDO (ex-USS *Pickerel, SS 524)*	S 502	Portsmouth Navy Yard	15 June1945	17 Jan 1946	10 Jan 1948

Displacement, tons: 1 975 standard; 2 450 dived
Length, feet (metres): 326·5 *(99·4)* oa
Beam, feet (metres): 27 *(8·2)*
Draught, feet (metres): 17 *(5·2)*
Torpedo tubes: 10—21 in; 6 bow, 4 stern
Main machinery: 4 diesels; 6 400 bhp;
 2 electric motors; 5 400 shp; 2 shafts
Speed, knots: 20 surfaced; 15 dived
Oil fuel, tons: 300
Range, miles: 12 000 at 10 knots (surfaced)
Complement: 85 (10 officers, 75 men)

Both transferred 18 Aug 1972.

GIANFRANCO GAZZANA PRIAROGGIA
1975, Wright and Logan

2 Ex-US "BALAO" CLASS

Name	No.	Builders	Laid down	Launched	Commissioned
ALFREDO CAPPELLINI (ex-USS *Capitaine, SS 336)*	S 507	General Dynamics (Electric Boat Div)	1944	1 Oct 1944	26 Jan 1945
EVANGELISTA TORRICELLI (ex-USS *Lizardfish, SS 373)*	S 512	Manitowoc SB Co, Wisconsin	1944	16 July 1944	30 Dec 1944

Displacement, tons: 1 600 standard; 1 855 surfaced; 2 455
 dived
Length, feet (metres): 311·5 *(95·0)*
Beam, feet (metres): 27 *(8·2)*
Draught, feet (metres): 17 *(5·2)*
Torpedo tubes: 10—21 in *(533 mm)* 6 bow and 4 stern
Main machinery: 4 GM 16/278 diesels; 6 000 hp;
 4 electric motors; 2 750 hp
Speed, knots: 18 surfaced; 10 dived
Oil fuel, tons: 300
Range, miles: 14 000 at 10 knots (surfaced)
Complement: 75 (7 officers, 68 men)

Transferred 5 Mar 1966. *E. Torricelli* now used for training and experimental duties.

ALFREDO CAPPELLINI
1974, Dr. Giorgio Arra

LIGHT FORCES

Note: Construction of four hydrofoils of similar details as USS *Pegasus* planned under Legge Navale.

1 + (9) "SPARVIERO" CLASS (HYDROFOIL—MISSILE)

Name	No.	Builders	Commissioned
SPARVIERO	P 420	Alinavi, La Spezia	15 July 1974

Displacement, tons: 62·5
Dimensions, feet (metres): 80·7 × 39·7 × 14·4 *(24·6 × 12·1 × 4·4)* (length and beam foils
 extended, draught hullborne)
Missile launchers: 2 fixed for Otomat ship-to-ship missiles
Gun: 1 OTO Melara 76 mm automatic anti-aircraft
Main engines: Proteus gas turbine driving waterjet pump; 4 500 bhp; diesel and retractable
 propeller unit for hullborne propulsion
Range, miles: 400 at 45 knots; 1 200 at 8 knots
Speed, knots: 50 max, 42 cruising (sea state 4)
Complement: 10 (2 officers, 8 men)

Completed for trials 9 May 1973. Missiles made by OTO Melara/Matra. Fitted with Elsag NA-10 Mod 1 fire control system with Orion RTN-10X radar. Delivered to the Navy as class prototype on 5 July 1974. Nine more hydrofoils planned of this class in addition to four NATO Type (USS *Pegasus*).

SPARVIERO
1974, Italian Navy

2 "FRECCIA" CLASS (FAST ATTACK CRAFT—CONVERTIBLE)

Name	No.	Builders	Commissioned
FRECCIA (ex-*MC 590)*	P 493	Cantiere del Tirreno, Riva Trigoso	6 July 1965
SAETTA (ex-*MC 591)*	P 494	CRDA, Monfalcone	1966

Displacement, tons: 188 standard; 205 full load
Dimensions, feet (metres): 150 × 23·8 × 5·5 *(45·8 × 7·3 × 1·7)*
Guns: *As Gunboat:* 3—40 mm, 70 cal or 2—40 mm, 70 cal. *As Fast Minelayer:* 1—40 mm with 8
 mines. *As Torpedo Boat:* 2—40 mm, 70 cal
Torpedo tubes: *As Torpedo Boat:* 2—21 in
Main engines: 2 diesels; 7 600 bhp; 1 Bristol Siddeley Proteus gas turbine, 4 250 shp;
 Total hp 11 850 = 40 knots
Complement: 37 (4 officers, 33 men)

Freccia was laid down on 30 Apr 1963 and launched on 9 Jan 1965. *Saetta* was laid down on 11 June 1963, launched on 11 Apr 1965. Can be converted in 24 hours to gunboat, torpedo boat, fast minelayer, or missile boat. Fitted with E band navigation and tactical radar. The gunfire control system has a director with I band tracker radar. *Saetta* has been armed with Sea Killer Mk 1 system with 5 round trainable launcher, Contraves fire control, including target-tracking radar, with TV camera mounted on top.

SAETTA experimentally armed with 5 Sea Killer I missiles
1970, Italian Navy

FRECCIA
1974, Italian Navy

2 "LAMPO" CLASS (FAST ATTACK CRAFT—CONVERTIBLE)

Name	No.	Builders	Commissioned
LAMPO (ex-*MC 491*)	P 491	Arsenale MM, Taranto	July 1963
BALENO (ex-*MC 492*)	P 492	Arsenale MM, Taranto	16 July 1965

Displacement, tons: 170 standard; 196 full load
Dimensions, feet (metres): 131·5 × 21 × 5 *(40·1 × 6·4 × 1·5)*
Guns: *As Gunboat:* 3—40 mm, 70 cal or 2—40 mm, 70 cal; *As Torpedo Boat:* 2—40 mm, 70 cal
Torpedo tubes: *As Torpedo Boat:* 2—21 in
Main engines: 2 Fiat diesels; 1 Metrovick gas turbine; 3 shafts; total 11 700 hp = 39 knots
Complement: 33 (5 officers, 28 men)

Convertible gunboats, improved versions of the *Folgore* prototype. *Lampo* was laid down on 4 Jan 1958 and launched on 22 Nov 1960. *Baleno* was laid-down on the same slip on 22 Nov 1960, launched on 10 May 1964. She has been converted to an improved design.

LAMPO   *6/1975, Dr Giorgio Arra*

1 FAST ATTACK CRAFT—TORPEDO

Name	No.	Builders	Commissioned
FOLGORE (ex-*MC 490*)	P 490	CRDA, Monfalcone	21 July 1955

Displacement, tons: 160 standard; 190 full load
Dimensions, feet (metres): 129·5 × 19·7 × 5 *(39·5 × 6 × 1·5)*
Guns: 2—40 mm
Torpedo tubes: 2—21 in
Main engines: 4 diesels; 4 shafts; 10 000 bhp = 38 knots (accelerating from 20 knots to full speed very rapidly)
Complement: 39 (9 officers, 30 men)

Authorised in Nov 1950, launched on 21 Jan 1954. Two rudders. Probably due for disposal.

FOLGORE   *1972, Dr Giorgio Arra*

3 Ex-US "HIGGINS" CLASS (FAST PATROL CRAFT)

MS 441 (ex-841)   **MS 443** (ex-843)   **MS 453** (ex-853)

Displacement, tons: 64 full load
Dimensions, feet (metres): 78 × 20 × 6 *(23·8 × 6·1 × 1·8)*
Guns: 2—20 mm, 70 cal
Main engines: 3 petrol motors; 3 shafts; 4 500 bhp = 34 knots
Range, miles: 1 000 at 20 knots
Complement: 24 (3 officers, 21 men)

MS 441 and 453 converted for frogmen support with after weapons removed. Refitted in Italy in 1949-53. New radar installed.

M 453 (modified for frogmen support)   *6/1975, Dr Giorgio Arra*

2 FAST ATTACK CRAFT—TORPEDO

Name	No.	Builders	Commissioned
—	MS 474 (ex-*614*)	CRDA, Monfalcone	1942
—	MS 481 (ex-*615*)	CRDA, Monfalcone	1942

Displacement, tons: 72 full load
Dimensions, feet (metres): 92 × 15 × 5 *(28·1 × 4·6 × 1·5)*
Guns: 1 or 2—40 mm, 56 cal
Torpedoes: 2—17·7 in (no tubes)
Main engines: Petrol motors; 3 shafts; 3 450 bhp = 27 knots
Range, miles: 600 at 16 knots
Complement: 24 (3 officers, 21 men)

Converted as MV (motovedette) with no tubes under the Peace Treaty. Reconverted in 1951-53. MS 473 and MS 481 were refitted as convertible boats in 1960 and MS 474 in 1961. Originally class of four. Further refits 1965-69.

MS 481   *1974, Italian Navy*

AMPHIBIOUS FORCES

Note: A new 6 000 ton LPH is to be built under Legge Navale to act as training ship in place of *San Giorgio* in addition to amphibious duties.

2 Ex-US "DE SOTO COUNTY" CLASS (LSTs)

Name	No.	Builders	Commissioned
GRADO (ex-USS De Soto County, LST 1171)	L 9890	Avondale, New Orleans	1957
CAORLE (ex-USS York County, LST 1175)	L 9891	Newport News SB & DD Co.	1957

Displacement, tons: 4 164 light; 8 000 full load
Dimensions, feet (metres): 444 × 62 × 16·5 *(133·4 × 18·9 × 5)*
Guns: 6—3 inch *(76 mm)*
Main engines: Diesels; 1 440 shp; 2 shafts; (CP propellers) = 17·5 knots
Complement: 165 (10 officers, 155 men)
Troops: Approx 575

Both completed 1957 and transferred 17 July 1972.

GRADO · 1974, Dr. Giorgio Arra

1 Ex-US "KENNETH WHITING" CLASS (TRANSPORT)

Name	No.	Builders	Commissioned
ANDREA BAFILE (ex-USS St. George, AV 16, ex-A 5314)	L 9871	—	1944

Displacement, tons: 8 510 standard; 14 000 full load
Dimensions, feet (metres): 492 oa × 69·5 × 26 *(163 × 23 × 8·5)*
Aircraft: 1 or 2 helicopters
Guns: 2—5 in 38 cal
Main engines: Allis-Chalmers geared turbines; 1 shaft; 8 500 shp = 17 knots
Boilers: 2 Foster-Wheeler
Range, miles: 13 400 at 13 knots
Complement: 58 (10 officers, 48 men)

Former USN seaplane tender, launched on 14 Feb 1944. Purchased and commissioned in the Italian Navy on 11 Dec 1968 and modified. Depot ship for "Special Forces". In reserve at Taranto.

ANDREA BAFILE · 1974, Italian Navy

MINE WARFARE FORCES

10 NEW CONSTRUCTION (MINEHUNTERS/SWEEPERS)

Displacement, tons: 470
Dimensions, feet (metres): 163·7 × 30·8 × 8·2 *(49·9 × 9·4 × 2·5)*
Gun: 1—40 mm
Main engines: Passage—1 GMT 230 8 cylinder diesel = 15 knots; Hunting—Hydraulic thrust jets = 0 to 7 knots
Range, miles: 2 500 at 12 knots
Endurance: 10 days
Complement: 39

To be ordered under Legge Navale from Intermarine, La Spezia.

Construction: Of GRP throughout hull, decks and bulkheads.

Electronics: 440 volt, 60 cycle 3 phase AC.

Engineering: All machinery is mounted on vibration dampers.

Minehunting: CGE-Fiart AN/SQQ 14 minehunting sonar; SMA navigation system with data processing; 2 underwater detection/destruction vehicles; diving equipment and recompression chamber.

Minesweeping: Oropesa wire sweep.

Radar: SMA.

Sonar: CGE-Fiart AN/SQQ-14 VDS (lowered from keel forward of bridge).

NEW CONSTRUCTION · · · · · · · · · · · · · · · · · 1976, Intermarine

4 Ex-US "AGILE" CLASS
(MINESWEEPERS—OCEAN)

Name	No.	Builders	Commissioned
SALMONE (ex-MSO 507)	M 5430	Martinolich SB Co	17 June 1956
GOMBRO (ex-MSO 517)	M 5432	—	June 1957
SQUALO (ex-MSO 518)	M 5433	—	June 1957
STORIONE (ex-MSO 506)	M 5431	Martinolich SB Co	23 Feb 1956

Displacement, tons: 665 standard; 750 full load
Dimensions, feet (metres): 173 oa × 35 × 13·6 *(52·7 × 10·7 × 4)*
Gun: 1—40 mm, 56 cal
Main engines: 2 diesels; 2 shafts; 1 600 bhp = 14 knots
Oil fuel, tons: 46
Range, miles: 3 000 at 10 knots
Complement: 51 (7 officers, 44 men)

Wooden hulls and non-magnetic diesels of stainless steel alloy. Controllable pitch propellers. *Storione,* launched on 13 Nov 1954, *Salmone,* launched on 19 Feb 1955 transferred at San Diego, on 17 June 1956.

STORIONE · 6/1976, Dr Giorgio Arra

14 Ex-US "BLUEBIRD" CLASS
(MINESWEEPERS/HUNTERS—COASTAL)

ABETE M 5501	**GELSO** M 5509	**ONTANO** M 5513
CASTAGNO M 5504	**LARICE** M 5510	**PINO** M 5514
CEDRO M 5505	**MANDORLO** M 5519	**PLATANO** M 5516
FAGGIO M 5507	**NOCE** M 5511	**QUERCIA** M 5517
FRASSINO M 5508	**OLMO** M 5512	

Displacement, tons: 378 standard; 405 full load *(Mandorlo* 360)
Dimensions, feet (metres): 138 pp; 144 oa × 26·5 × 8·5 *(42·1; 43·9 × 8·1 × 2·6)*
Gun: 1—20 mm
Main engines: 2 diesels; 2 shafts; 1 200 bhp = 13·5 knots
Oil fuel, tons: 25
Range, miles: 2 500 at 10 knots
Complement: 38 (5 officers, 33 men)

Wooden hulled and constructed throughout of anti-magnetic materials. All transferred by the US in 1953-54. Originally class of 18. *Pioppo* used for surveying. *Mandorlo* now converted for minehunting.

MANDORLO (as minehunter)   9/1976, Commander Aldo Fraccaroli

ONTANO   6/1976, Dr Giorgio Arra

17 "AGAVE" CLASS (MINESWEEPERS—COASTAL)

BAMBU M 5521	**AGAVE** M 5531	**GLICINE** M 5537
EBANO M 5522	**ALLORO** M 5532	**LOTO** M 5538
MANGO M 5523	**EDERA** M 5533	**TIMO** M 5540
MOGANO M 5524	**GAGGIA** M 5534	**TRIFOGLIO** M 5541
PALMA M 5525	**GELSOMINO** M 5535	**VISCHIO** M 5542
SANDALO M 5527	**GIAGGIOLO** M 5536	

Displacement, tons: 375 standard; 405 full load
Dimensions, feet (metres): 144 oa × 25·6 × 8·5 *(43 × 8 × 2·6)*
Guns: 2—20 mm 70 cal
Main engines: 2 diesels; 2 shafts; 1 200 bhp = 13·5 knots
Oil fuel, tons: 25
Range, miles: 2 500 at 10 knots
Complement: 38 (5 officers, 33 men)

Non-magnetic minesweepers of composite wooden and alloy construction similar to those transferred from the US but built in Italian yards. First six were built by CRDA, Monfalcone, and launched in 1956. Originally class of nineteen. *Mirto* now used for surveying.

AGAVE   6/1975, Dr Giorgio Arra

10 "ARAGOSTA" CLASS (MINESWEEPERS—INSHORE)

ARAGOSTA M 5450	**GRANCHIO** M 5458	**POLIPO** M 5463
ASTICE M 5452	**MITILO** M 5459	**PORPORA** M 5464
GAMBERO M 5457	**PINNA** M 5462	**RICCIO** M 5465
		SCAMPO M 5466

Displacement, tons: 188 full load
Dimensions, feet (metres): 106 × 21 × 6 *(32·5 × 6·4 × 1·8)*
Main engines: 2 diesels; 1 000 bhp = 14 knots
Oil fuel, tons: 15
Range, miles: 2 000 at 9 knots
Complement: 16 (4 officers, 12 men)

Similar to the British "Ham" class. All constructed in Italian yards to the order of NATO in 1955-57. All names of small sea creatures. Designed armament of one 20 mm gun mounted. Originally class of twenty.

PORPORA   6/1976, Dr Giorgio Arra

ARAGOSTA (with deckhouse for frogmen support)   6/1976, Dr Giorgio Arra

SURVEY VESSELS

Name	No.	Builders	Commissioned
AMMIRAGLIO MAGNAGHI	A 5303	Cantieri Navali di Tirreno é Riuniti	1975

Displacement, tons: 1 700
Dimensions, feet (metres): 271·3 × 44·9 × 11·5 *(82·7 × 13·7 × 3·5)*
Aircraft: 1—AB 204 helicopter
Gun: 1—40 mm
Main engines: 2 Fiat diesels = 3 000 hp; 1 shaft; Auxiliary electric motor—240 hp = 4 knots
Speed, knots: 16
Range, miles: 6 000 at 12 knots (1 diesel); 4 200 at 16 knots (2 diesels)
Complement: 140 (15 officers, 15 scientists, 110 men)

Ordered under 1972 programme. Laid down 13 June 1973. Launched 11 Oct 1974. Fitted with flight-deck and hangar, bow thruster, full air-conditioning, bridge engine controls, flume-type stabilisers and fully equipped for oceanographical studies.

AMMIRAGLIO MAGNAGHI   6/1976, Dr. Giorgio Arra

MIRTO A 5306   **PIOPPO** A 5307

Mirto of the "Agave" class and *Pioppo* of the "Abete" class (see Minewarfare section for details) have been converted for surveying duties.

MIRTO   1973, Dr. Giorgio Arra

BARBARA

Displacement, tons: 195
Dimensions, feet (metres): 98·4 × 20·7 × 6·6 *(30 × 6·3 × 2)*
Main engines: 2 diesels; 300 hp = 12 knots

A fishing vessel purchased for research work in early 1976.

SERVICE FORCES

1 + 1 REPLENISHMENT TANKERS

Name	No.	Builders	Commissioned
STROMBOLI	A 5327	Cantiere Navali Riuniti, Riva Trigoso	1975
VESUVIO	—	Cantiere Navali Riuniti, Riva Trigoso	1978

Displacement, tons: 3 556 light; 8 706 full load
Dimensions, feet (metres): 403·4 oa × 59 × 21·3 *(123 oa × 18 × 6·5)*
Guns: 1—76 mm/62 cal OTO Melara; 2—40 mm
Main engines: 2 Fiat diesels C428 SS; 11 400 hp; 1 shaft; 4-bladed LIPS propeller
Speed, knots: 20
Complement: 115 (9 officers, 106 men)

Stromboli laid down on 1 Oct 1973. Launched 20 Feb 1975. Second of class ordered mid 1976.

Aircraft: Helicopter flight deck but no hangar.

Capacity: 3 000 tons FFO; 1 000 tons dieso, 400 tons lub oil, 100 tons other stores.

STROMBOLI   10/1975, Commander Aldo Fraccaroli

1 EXPERIMENTAL SHIP

Name	No.	Builders	Commissioned
QUARTO	A 5314	Taranto Naval Shipyard	1967

Displacement, tons: 764 standard; 980 full load
Dimensions, feet (metres): 226·4 × 31·3 × 6 *(69·1 × 9·5 × 1·8)*
Guns: 4—40 mm (2 twin)
Main engines: 3 diesels; 2 300 bhp = 13 knots
Range, miles: 1 300 at 13 knots

Laid down on 19 Mar 1966 and launched on 18 Mar 1967. The design is intermediate between that of LSM and LCT. She is now being used as experimental ship for new weapon-systems trials and evaluation. Currently employed on Otomat trials with 2 launchers forward and requisite aerials on mast and bridge.

QUARTO (fitted for missile trials)   6/1975, Commander Aldo Fraccaroli

1 Ex-US "BARNEGAT" CLASS (SUPPORT SHIP)

Name	No.	Builders	Commissioned
PIETRO CAVEZZALE (ex-USS *Oyster Bay, ex-AGP 6, AVP 28)*	A 5301	Lake Washington Shipyard	1943

Displacement, tons: 1 766 standard; 2 800 full load
Dimensions, feet (metres): 311·8 oa × 41 × 13·5 *(95 × 12·5 × 3·7)*
Guns: 1—76 mm; 2—40 mm, 56 cal
Main engines: 2 sets diesels; 2 shafts; 6 080 bhp = 16 knots
Oil fuel, tons: 400
Range, miles: 10 000 at 11 knots
Complement: 143 (12 officers, 131 men)

Former United States seaplane tender (previously motor torpedo boat tender). Launched on 7 Sep 1942. Transferred to the Italian Navy on 23 Oct 1957 and renamed.

Radar: SPS-6.

PIETRO CAVEZZALE   6/1976, Dr. Giorgio Arra

10 Ex-GERMAN MFP TYPE (COASTAL TRANSPORTS)

MTC 1001	MTC 1004	MTC 1006	MTC 1008	MTC 1010
MTC 1003	MTC 1005	MTC 1007	MTC 1009	MTC 1102

Displacement, tons: 240 standard
Dimensions, feet (metres): 164 × 21·3 × 5·7 *(50 × 6·5 × 1·7)*
Guns: 2 or 3—20 or 37 mm
Main engines: 2 or 3 diesels; 500 bhp = 10 knots
Complement: 19 (1 officer, 18 men)

Moti-Trasporti Costieri, MTC 1001 to 1010 are Italian MZ *(Motozattere).* MTC 1102 ex-German built in Italy.

MTC 1006   1974, Italian Navy

20 Ex-US LCM TYPE

MTM 9901	MTM 9909	MTM 9914	MTM 9920	MTM 9925	**Displacement, tons:** 20 standard
MTM 9902	MTM 9911	MTM 9915	MTM 9922	MTM 9926	**Dimensions, feet (metres):** 49·5 × 14·8 × 4·2 *(15·1 × 4·5 × 1·3)*
MTM 9905	MTM 9912	MTM 9918	MTM 9923	MTM 9927	**Guns:** 2—20 mm
MTM 9908	MTM 9913	MTM 9919	MTM 9924	MTM 9928	**Main engines:** Diesels; speed 10 knots

39 US LCVP TYPE

MTP 9703	MTP 9715	MTP 9730	MTP 9739	MTP 9747	**Displacement, tons:** 10 standard
MTP 9707	MTP 9719	MTP 9732	MTP 9740	MTP 9748	**Dimensions, feet (metres):** 36·5 × 10·8 × 3 *(11·1 × 3·3 × 0·9)*
MYP 9708	MTP 9720	MTP 9733	MTP 9741	MTP 9749	**Guns:** 2 MG
MTP 9710	MTP 9723	MTP 9734	MTP 9742	MTP 9750	**Main engines:** Diesels; Speed 12 knots
MTP 9711	MTP 9726	MTP 9735	MTP 9743	MTP 9751	
MTP 9713	MTP 9727	MTP 9736	MTP 9744	MTP 9752	
MTP 9714	MTP 9728	MTP 9737	MTP 9745	MTP 9753	MTP 9703 to 9723 are former US landing craft of the LCVP type. MTP 9726 and following craft of
	MTP 9729	MTP 9738	MTP 9746	MTP 9754	similar characteristics are of Italian construction.

TRAINING SHIPS

Name	No.	Builders	Commissioned
AMERIGO VESPUCCI	A 5312	Castellammare	1931

Displacement, tons: 3 543 standard; 4 146 full load
Dimensions, feet (metres): 229·5 pp; 270 oa hull; 330 oa bowsprit × 51 × 22 *(70; 82·4; 100 × 15·5 × 7)*
Guns: 4—3 in, 50 cal; 1—20 mm
Main engines: Two Fiat diesels with electric drive to 2 Marelli motors, 1 shaft; 2 000 hp = 10 knots
Sail area: 22 604 square feet
Endurance: 5 450 miles at 6·5 knots
Complement: 67 (7 officers, 60 men)

Launched on 22 March 1930. Hull, masts and yards are of steel. Extensively refitted at La Spezia Naval Dockyard in 1964.

AMERIGO VESPUCCI   1974, Wright and Logan

Name	No.	Builders	Commissioned
PALINURO (ex-*Commandant Louis Richard)*	A 5311	France	1921

Displacement, tons: 1 042 standard; 1 450 full load
Measurement, tons: 858 gross
Dimensions, feet (metres): 204 pp; 226·3 oa × 32 × 18·7 *(59 × 10 × 4·8)*
Main engines: 1 diesel; 1 shaft; 450 bhp = 7·5 knots
Endurance, miles: 5 390 at 7·5 knots
Sail area, square feet: 1 152

Barquentine launched in 1920. Purchased in 1950. Rebuilt and commissioned in Italian Navy on 16 July 1955.

PALINURO   1968, Italian Navy

Name	No.	Builders	Commissioned
CORSARO II	A 5316	Costaguta Yard, Voltri	1960

Measurement, tons: 47
Dimensions, feet (metres): 69 × 15·4 × 9·8 *(21 × 4·7 × 3)*
Sail area, square feet: 2 200
Complement: 13 (7 officers, 6 men)

Special yacht for sail training and oceanic navigation. RORC class.

Name	No.	Builders	Commissioned
STELLA POLARE	A 5313	Sangermani, Chiavari	1965

Measurement, tons: 41
Dimensions, feet (metres): 68·6 × 15·4 × 9·5 *(20·9 × 4·7 × 2·9)*
Auxiliary engines: 1 Mercedes-Benz diesel, 96 bhp
Sail area: 2 117 square feet
Complement: 14 (8 officers, 6 men)

Yawl rigged built as a sail training vessel for the Italian Navy.

NETLAYERS

2 "ALICUDI" CLASS

Name	No.	Builders	Commissioned
ALICUDI (ex-USS *AN 99*)	A 5304	Ansaldo, Leghorn	1955
FILICUDI (ex-USS *AN 100*)	A 5305	Ansaldo, Leghorn	1955

Displacement, tons: 680 standard; 834 full load
Dimensions, feet (metres): 151·8 pp; 165·3 oa × 33·5 × 10·5 *(46·3 × 10·2 × 3·2)*
Guns: 1—40 mm, 70 cal; 4—20 mm, 70 cal
Main engines: Diesel-electric; 1 200 shp = 12 knots
Complement: 51 (5 officers, 46 men)

Built to the order of NATO. Laid down on 22 April 1954 and 19 July 1954, respectively, and launched on 11 July 1954 and 26 Sep 1954.

ALICUDI   6/1975, Dr. Giorgio Arra

LIGHTHOUSE TENDERS

Name	No.	Builders	Commissioned
RAMPINO	A 5309	Osaka	1912

Displacement, tons: 350 standard; 645 full load
Dimensions, feet (metres): 158·8 × 24·2 × 13 *(48·4 × 7·4 × 4)*
Main engines: Triple expansion = 7 knots
Complement: 40 (3 officers, 37 men)

Buoy tender. Of netlayer type.

3 Ex-BRITISH LCT (3) TYPE

MTF 1301 A 5361   **MTF 1302** A 5362   **MTF 1303** A 5363

Displacement, tons: 296 light; 700 full load
Dimensions, feet (metres): 192 × 31 × 7 *(58·6 × 9·5 × 2·1)*
Guns: 1—40 mm, 56 cal; 2—20 mm, 70 cal
Main engines: Diesel; 1 shaft = 8 knots
Complement: 23 (3 officers, 20 men)

Converted to lighthouse stores transports.

MTF 1301   1968, Italian Navy

SALVAGE SHIP

Note: New construction salvage ship ordered from Cantieri Navali Breda-Mestre in mid-1976.

Name	No.	Builders	Commissioned
PROTEO (ex-*Perseo*)	A 5310	Cantieri Navali Riuniti, Ancona	1950

Displacement, tons: 1 865 standard; 2 147 full load
Dimensions, feet (metres): 220·5 pp; 248 oa × 38 × 21 *(67·3; 75·6 × 11·6 × 6·4)*
Gun: 1—3·9 in
Main engines: 2 diesels; 4 800 bhp; single shaft = 16 knots
Range, miles: 7 500 at 13 knots
Complement: 130 (10 officers, 120 men)

Laid down at Cantieri Navali Riuniti, Ancona, in 1943. Suspended in 1944. Seized by Germans and transferred to Trieste. Construction re-started at Cantieri Navali Riuniti, Ancona, in 1949. Formerly mounted one 3·9 inch gun and two 20 mm.

PROTEO   1975, Italian Navy

REPAIR CRAFT

7 Ex-BRITISH LCT 3s

MOC 1201 A 5331   **MOC 1203** A 5333   **MOC 1205** A 5335   **MOC 1208** A 5338
MOC 1202 A 5332   **MOC 1204** A 5334   **MOC 1207** A 5337

Displacement, tons: 350 standard; 640 full load
Dimensions, feet (metres): 192 × 31 × 7 *(58·6 × 9·5 × 2·1)*
Guns: 2—40 mm; 2—20 mm (2 ships have 2—40 mm and 1 ship has 3—20 mm)
Main engines: Diesel = 8 knots
Complement: 24 (3 officers, 21 men)

Originally converted as repair craft. Other duties have been taken over—MOC 1207 and 1208 are ammunition transports and MOC 1201 is used for torpedo trials.

MOC 1201 (with torpedo tube)   6/1976, Dr Giorgio Arra

WATER CARRIERS

PIAVE A 5354   **TEVERE** A 5355

4 973 tons full load—built 1971-73. Complement 55 (7 officers, 48 men).

Guns: 4—40 mm (twins).

PIAVE   1974, Commander Aldo Fraccaroli

Name	No.	Builders	Commissioned
BASENTO	A 5356	Inma di La Spezia	1970
BRADANO	A 5357	Inma di La Spezia	1971
BRENTA	A 5358	Inma di La Spezia	1972

1 914 tons. Laid down in 1969-70. Complement 24 (3 officers, 21 men)

Guns: 2—20 mm

BASENTO   6/1976, Dr Giorgio Arra

ADIGE (ex-*YW 92*) A 5369   **TANARO** (ex-*YW 99*) A 5376
TICINO (ex-*YW 79*) A 5377

Ex-US Army YW type. 1 470 tons full load. Complement 35 (4 officers, 31 men).

TANARO   6/1976, Dr Giorgio Arra

VOLTURNO A 5366

Complement 67 (7 officers, 60 men)

MINCIO A 5374

645 tons. Launched in 1929. Complement 19 (1 officer, 18 men).

BORMIDA A 5359

Complement 11 (1 officer, 10 men)

TIMAVO

645 tons. Built by COMI, Venezia, 1926.

OFANTO

250 tons. Built 1913-14.

SIMETO   **STURA**

Small water carriers of 167 and 126 tons displacement, respectively.

TUGS

CICLOPE A 5319

Displacement, tons: 1 200
Dimensions, feet (metres): 157·5 × 32·5 × 13 *(48 × 9·8 × 4)*
Main engines: Triple expansion; 1 shaft; 1 000 ihp = 8 knots

Launched in 1944.

Name	No.	Builders	Commissioned
ATLANTE	A 5317	Visentini-Donada	14 Aug 1975
PROMETEO	A 5318	Visentini-Donada	14 Aug 1975

Displacement, tons: 750 full load
Dimensions, feet (metres): 116·7 × 28·8 × 14·8 *(39 × 9·6 × 4·1)*
Main engines: Diesel; 1 shaft; cp propeller; 2670 hp

Both launched 1974.

ATLANTE   1975, Dr Luigi Accorsi

COLOSSO (ex-*LT 214*) A 5320   **FORTE** (ex-*LT 159*) A 5321

Displacement, tons: 525 standard; 835 full load
Dimensions, feet (metres): 142·8 × 32·8 × 11 *(43·6 × 10 × 3·4)*
Main engines: 2 diesel-electric; 690 hp = 11 knots

Ex-US Army.

COLOSSO   *6/1976, Dr Giorgio Arra*

SAN GIUSTO A 5326

Displacement, tons: 486 standard
Main engines: 900 hp = 12 knots

ERCOLE A 5388 (1971)   **GAGLIARDO** A 5322 (1938)
ROBUSTO A 5323 (1939)   **VIGOROSO** A 5394 (1971)

Displacement, tons: 389 standard; 506 full load
Main engines: 1 000 ihp = 8 knots

PORTO D'ISCHIA A 5378   **RIVA TRIGOSO** A 5379

Displacement, tons: 296 full load
Dimensions, feet (metres): 83·7 × 23·3 × 10·8 *(25·5 × 7·1 × 3·3)*
Main engines: Diesel; 1 shaft; 850 bhp = 12·1 knots

Both launched in Sep 1969. Controllable pitch propeller.

MISENO   **MONTE CRISTO**

Displacement, tons: 285

Former United States Navy harbour tugs.

CAPRERA A 5381 (1972)   **PORTO PISANO** A 5386 (1937)
LEVANZO A 5397 (1973)   **PORTO RECANATI** A 5387 (1937)
PANTELLERIA A 5382 (1972)   **SALVORE** A 5391 (1927)
PIANOVA A 5396 (1914)   **TINO** A 5392 (1930)

Displacement, tons: 270
Dimensions, feet (metres): 88·8 × 22 × 10 *(27·1 × 6·7 × 3·1)*
Main engines: 600 ihp = 9 knots

Principally employed as harbour tugs.

FAVIGNANA A 5385 (1973)   **USTICA** A 5324 (1973)

Displacement, tons: 270 standard
Dimensions, feet (metres): 114·8 × 29·5 × 13 *(35 × 9 × 4)*
Main engines: 1 200 hp

AUSONIA   **PANARIA**

Displacement, tons: 240

Both launched in 1948. Coastal tugs for general duties.

VENTIMIGLIA

Displacement, tons: 230 standard
Dimensions, feet (metres): 108·2 × 23 × 7·2 *(33 × 7 × 2·2)*
Main engines: 550 hp = 10 knots

PASSERO Y 439 (1934)   **RIZZUTO** Y 473 (1956)   **CIRCEO** Y 433 (1956)

Principally employed as ferry tugs.

ABBAZIA Y 411 (1968)   **MESCO** Y 435 (1933)
ALBENGA Y 412 (1973)   **NISIDA** Y 437 (1943)
ARZACHENA Y 414 (1931)   **PIOMBINO** Y 440 (1969)
ASINARA Y 415 (1933¾)   **POZZI** Y 422 (1912)
BOEO Y 417 (1943)   **SAN BENEDETTO** Y 446 (1941)
CARBONARA Y 419 (1936)   **SPERONE** Y 454 (1965)
CHIOGGIA Y 421 (1919)   **TAVOLARA** Y 455 (1955)
CORDEVOLE Y 423 (1915)   **No 78** Y 469 (1965)
LAMPEDUSA Y 416 (1972)   **No 96** Y 474 (1962)
LINARO Y 430 (1913)

Small tugs for harbour duties.

RP 101 Y 403 (1972)   **RP 105** Y 408 (1974)   **RP 109** Y 456 (1975)
RP 102 Y 404 (1972)   **RP 106** Y 410 (1974)   **RP 110** Y 458 (1975)
RP 103 Y 406 (1974)   **RP 107** Y 413 (1974)   **RP 111** Y 460 (1975)
RP 104 Y 407 (1974)   **RP 108** Y 452 (1975)   **RP 112** Y 462 (1975)

Displacement, tons: 36 standard
Dimensions, feet (metres): 61·6 × 14·6 × 5·9 *(18·8 × 4·5 × 1·8)*
Main engines: 1 diesel; 500 hp

Built by Cantiere Navale Visentini-Donado (Rovigo).

IVORY COAST

Ministerial

Minister of Defence and Civic Services:
  Kouadio M'Bahia Ble

Bases

Use made of ports at Abidjan, Sassandra, Tabou and San Pedro

Personnel

1977: 240 officers and men

Mercantile Marine

Lloyd's Register of Shipping: 53 vessels of 114 191 tons gross

Future Plans

Eventually it is intended to organise the navy into two coastal patrol squadrons.

LIGHT FORCES

2 FRANCO-BELGE TYPE

Name	No.	Builders	Commissioned
VIGILANT	—	SFCN	1968
LE VALEUREUX	—	SFCN	25 Sept 1976

Displacement, tons: 235 standard (250 *Valeureux*)
Dimensions, feet (metres): 149·3 pp; 155·8 oa × 23·6 × 8·2 *(45·5; 47·5 × 7 × 2·6)*
  (*Valeureux* 157·5 feet oa *(48 metres)*)
Missiles: 8—SS12
Guns: 2—40 mm
Main engines: 2 AGO diesels; 2 shafts; 4 220 bhp = 18·5 knots (*Valeureux* 22 knots)
Range, miles: 2 000 at 15 knots
Complement: 25 (3 officers, and 22 men)

Vigilant laid down in Feb 1967. Launched on 23 May 1967. Sister ship to *Malaika* of Malagasy Navy and to *Saint Louis* and *Popenguine* of Senegal and similar craft in Tunisia and Cameroons. *Le Valeureux* ordered Oct 1974, laid down 20 Oct 1975, launched 8 Mar 1976.

1 Ex-FRENCH VC TYPE

Name	No.	Builders	Commissioned
PERSEVERANCE (ex-*VC 9, P 759*)	—	Constructions Mécaniques de Normandie, Cherbourg	25 Feb 1958

Displacement, tons: 75 standard; 82 full load
Dimensions, feet (metres): 104·5 × 15·5 × 5·5 *(31·8 × 4·7 × 1·7)*
Guns: 2—20 mm
Main engines: 2 Mercedes-Benz (MTU) diesels; 2 shafts; 2 700 bhp = 28 knots
Oil fuel, tons: 10
Range, miles: 1 100 at 16·5 knots; 800 at 21 knots
Complement: 15

Former French seaward defence motor launch. Transferred from France to Ivory Coast 26 April 1963. Recently reported as unserviceable.

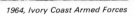

PERSEVERANCE   *1964, Ivory Coast Armed Forces*

5 RIVER PATROL CRAFT

Of varying sizes from 24—34 feet. Used for river and lake patrols.

LANDING CRAFT

1 BATRAL TYPE (LIGHT TRANSPORT)

Name	No.	Builders	Commissioned
ELEPHANT	—	Dubigeon/Normandy Nantes	1976

Displacement, tons: 750 standard; 1 250 full load
Dimensions, feet (metres): 262·4 × 42·6 × 7·5 *(80 × 13 × 2·3)*
Guns: 2—40 mm; 2—81 mm mortars
Main engines: 2 diesels; 2 shafts; 1 800 hp = 16 knots
Range, miles: 3 500 at 13 knots
Complement: 39

Ordered 20 Aug 1974. Laid down 1975.

2 LCVP

Displacement, tons: 7
Guns: 2 MG
Main engines: Mercedes diesels
Speed, knots: 9

Built in Abidjan in 1970.

MISCELLANEOUS

1 SMALL TRANSPORT

Capable of carrying 25 men.

LOKODJO

Displacement, tons: 450

Now used as a training and supply ship. Built in West Germany in 1953 and purchased in 1970. Trawler type.

JAMAICA

Defence Force Coast Guard

Jamaica, which became independent within the Commonwealth on 6 Aug 1962, formed the Coast Guard as the Maritime Arm of the Defence Force. This is Based at HMJS Cagway, Port Royal.

Administration

Officer Commanding Jamaican Defence Force Coast Guard:
Lieutenant-Commander L. E. Scott

Personnel

1977: 18 officers, 115 petty officers and ratings *(Coast Guard Reserve:* 16 officers, 30 men)

Training

a) Officers: BRNC Dartmouth and other RN Establishments, RCN and US Search and Rescue School.
b) Ratings: JMDF Training depot, RN, RCN, US Search and Rescue School and MTU Engineering Germany.

Mercantile Marine

Lloyd's Register of Shipping: 5 vessels of 6 740 tons gross.

LIGHT FORCES

Name	No.	Builders	Commissioned
FORT CHARLES	P 7	Teledyne Sewart Seacraft Inc, Berwick, La, USA	1974

Displacement, tons: 103
Dimensions, feet (metres): 105 × 22 × 7 *(31·5 × 6·6 × 2·1)*
Guns: 1—20 mm; 2—50 cal MG
Main engines: 2 Maybach (MTU) MB 16V 538 TB90 diesels; 7 000 shp = 32 knots
Range, miles: 1 200 at 18 knots
Complement: 16

Of all aluminium construction launched July 1974. Navigation equipment includes Omega Navigator
Accommodation for 24 soldiers and may be used as 24 bed mobile hospital in an emergency.

FORT CHARLES   *1975, Jamaican CG*

Name	No.	Builders	Commissioned
DISCOVERY BAY	P 4	Teledyne Sewart Seacraft Inc, Berwick, La, USA	3 Nov 1966
HOLLAND BAY	P 5	Teledyne Sewart Seacraft Inc, Berwick, La, USA	4 April 1967
MANATEE BAY	P 6	Teledyne Sewart Seacraft Inc, Berwick, La, USA	9 Aug 1967

Displacement, tons: 60
Dimensions, feet (metres): 85 × 18 × 6·0 *(25·9 × 5·7 × 1·8)*
Guns: 3—50 cal Browning
Main engines: 3 GM 12 V71 diesels; 3 shafts; 6 000 shp = 26·5 knots;
(P 4—3 MTU 8V331TC81 diesels, 3 shafts; 6 000 shp = 30 knots)
Oil fuel, tons: 13
Range, miles: 800 at 20 knots
Complement: 10

All aluminium construction. *Discovery Bay*, the prototype was launched in Aug 1966. *Holland Bay* and *Manatee Bay* were supplied under the US Military Assistance programme. All three boats were extensively refitted and modified in 1972-73 by the builders with GM 12V 71 Turbo-injected engines to give greater range, speed and operational flexibility. *Discovery Bay* was again re-engined and refitted late 1975 at Swift Ship Inc, Louisiana, USA.

DISCOVERY BAY   *1973, Jamaica CG*

JAPAN

Naval Board

Chief of the Maritime Staff, Defence Agency:
  Admiral Teiji Nakamura
Commander-in-Chief, Self-Defence Fleet:
  Vice-Admiral Kiyonori Kunishima
Chief, Administration Division, Maritime Staff Office:
  Rear-Admiral Masayuki Akiyama

Diplomatic Representation

Defence (Naval) Attaché in London:
  Captain Hideo Sato
Defence (Naval) Attaché in Washington:
  Captain Tameo Oki
Naval Attaché in Moscow:
  Captain Takao Endo
Defence Attaché in Paris:
  Colonel Yoshiaki Murata

Personnel

1976: 39 000 (including Naval Air)
1977: 42 199 (including Naval Air)

Bases

Naval—Yokosuka, Kure, Sasebo, Maizuru, Oominato
Naval Air—Atsugi, Hachinohe, Iwakuni, Kanoya, Komatsujima, Okinawa, Ozuki, Oominato, Oomura, Shimofusa, Tateyama, Tokushima.

Fleet Air Arm

14 Air ASW Sqns, P2-J, P2V-7, PS-1, S2F-1, HSS-2
4   Air Training Sqns, P2-J, P2V-7, YS-11, B-65, KM-2, Mentor, Bell-47, OH-6, HSS-2
1   Transport Sqn, YS-11
1   MCM Sqn

Names

The practice of painting the ships' names on the broadsides of the hulls was discontinued in 1970. For submarines the painting of pennant numbers on the fins was stopped in Sept 1976.

Mercantile Marine

Lloyd's Register of Shipping:
  9 748 vessels of 41 663 188 tons gross

New Construction Programme

1973   1 DD, 1 DE, 1 SS, 2 MSC, 2 MSB, 1 PT, 1 LST
1974   1 DDK, 2 MSC, 1 LST
1975   1 DDH, 1 SS, 3 MSC, 1 LST
1976   1 DDH, 1 MSC, 1 AGS, 1 AOE
1977   MSDF request for 1 DDG, 1 DD, 1 PCE, 1 ARC, 1 SS, 2 MSC

Defence Plan—New Construction

If programmes are agreed in period 1977-81 the fleet in 1982 will consist of: 60 DD, 16 SS, 40-45 MSC/MSB, 25-30 others, 15 supply ships, LST and special duty ships and 220 aircraft. (White Paper of 30 Oct 1976).
In order to provide 2 DDH for each of four escort groups a further request for 4 DDH may be expected. Similarly 2 extra DDGs may be requested as well as a possible new frigate class of 6-8 ships. Further possible additions are 3 missile hydrofoils, 1 ARC, 1 AS, 1 ATS, 1 AGS and 4-5 500 ton LSMs.
The 1977 MSDF request for new construction as agreed by Dept. of Finance in Jan 1977 was for one 2 900 ton DD, one 1 500 ton frigate, one 2 200 ton submarine, two 440 ton MSC, one 4 500 ton ARC. This deleted one 3 900 ton DDG from the original request.

Strength of the Fleet

Type	Active	Building (Projected)
Destroyers	31	3 (1)
Frigates	15	1
Corvettes	16	—
Submarines—Patrol	15	2
Fast Attack Craft—Torpedo	5	—
Patrol Craft—Coastal	10	—
LSTs	6	—
M/S Support Ships	2	—
Minesweepers—Coastal	29	3
MSBs	6	—
Training Ship	1	—
S/M Rescue Vessels	2	—
Support Tanker	1	(1)
Icebreaker	1	—
Auxiliaries	24	—
Survey Ships	6	(1)
Cable Layer	1	(1)
Training Support Ship	1	—

Maritime Safety Agency (Coast Guard)

10 Large Patrol Vessels
57 Medium Patrol Vessels
19 Smalll Patrol Vessels
209 Patrol Craft
6   Surveying Vessels
21 Surveying Launches
5   Tenders
1   Underwater Research Vessel
50 Utility Launches
11 Fire Fighting Craft

DELETIONS

Note: A number of ships on removal from the active list are classified as YAC (Harbour accommodation ship). As these have no operational value they are included as deletions marked *

Destroyers

1974 *Ariake, Yugure* (Transferred to S. Korea for spares in 1976—scrapped).

Frigates

1972 *Kaya, Bura, Kashi, Moni, Tochi, Ume, Maki, Kusu, Matsu, Nata, Sakura,* (all ex-US PFs). *Wakaba*
1975 *Asahi* and *Hatsuhi* (ex-"Cannon" class) returned to US for disposal
1976 *Inazuma* for disposal. *Ikazuchi*, *Akebono**

Corvettes

1977 *Kari, Kiji, Taka, Washi*

Submarine

1976 *Oyashio* (scrap list 30 Sept)

Light Forces

1972 PT 7, 9; PB 4, 11, 13-16, 18
1973 PB 1, 3, 12, 17; *Kosoku* 3
1974 PT 8; *Kosoku* 2, 4 and 5
1975 PT 10

LSTs

1972 *Hayatomo*
1974 *Oosumi*
1975 *Shimokita*
1976 *Shiretoko* (returned to US in Mar and passed to Philippines)

LSM

1974 3001

Minewarfare Forces

1972 MSB 01, 02
1974 MSB 03, 04, 05, 06 deleted, *Kusu**
1975 Five MSC converted
1976 One MSC converted

Tenders

1973 YAS 49 (ex-PT 2), YAS 52 (ex-PT 3), YAS 53 (ex-PT 4)
1974 YAS 48 (ex-PT 1), YAS 54 (ex-PT 5), YAS 55 (ex-PT 6), YAS 45 (*Suma,* ex-US YTL 749), YAS 59 (*Minho,* ex-US FS 524)
1976 YAS 51 (NAS *Ami* ex-US FS 409), YAS 3 (ex-US YTL 750), YAS 47 (ex-MSC 652)

PENNANT LIST

Destroyers

DD 101	Harukaze
102	Yukikaze
103	Ayanami
104	Isonami
105	Uranami
106	Shikinami
107	Murasame
108	Yudachi
109	Harusame
110	Takanami
111	Oonami
112	Makinami
113	Yamagumo
114	Makigumo
115	Asagumo
116	Minegumo
117	Natsugumo
118	Murakumo
119	Aokumo
120	Akigumo
121	New construction
141	Haruna
142	Hiei
143	New Construction
144	New Construction
161	Akizuki

Destroyers—*cont.*

162	Teruzuki
163	Amatsukaze
164	Takatsuki
165	Kikuzuki
166	Mochizuki
167	Nagatsuki
168	Tachikaze
169	New Construction

Frigates

DE 211	Isuzu
212	Mogami
213	Kitakami
214	Ooi
215	Chikugo
216	Ayase
217	Mikuma
218	Tokachi
219	Iwase
220	Chitose
221	Niyodo
222	Teshio
223	Yoshino
224	Kumano
225	Noshiro

Corvettes

PC 305	Kamome
306	Tsubame
307	Misago
308	Hayabusa
309	Umitaka
310	Otaka
311	Mizutori
312	Yamadori
313	Otori
314	Kasasagi
315	Hatsukari
316	Umidori
317	Wakataka
318	Kumataka
319	Shiratori
320	Hiyodori

PENNANT LIST—continued

Submarines—Patrol

SS 521	Hayashio
522	Wakashio
523	Natsushio
524	Fuyushio
561	Ooshio
562	Asashio
563	Harushio
564	Michishio
565	Arashio
566	Uzushio
567	Makishio
568	Isoshio
569	Narushio
570	Kuroshio
571	Takashio
572	New Construction
573	New Construction

Minesweepers—Coastal

MSC 617	Karato
618	Hario
619	Mutsure
620	Chiburi
621	Ootsu
622	Kudako
623	Rishiri
624	Rebun
625	Amami
626	Urume
627	Minase
628	Ibuki
629	Katsura
630	Takami
631	Iou
632	Miyake
633	Utone
634	Awaji
635	Toushi
636	Teuri
637	Murotsu
638	Tashiro
639	Miyato
640	Takane
641	Muzuki
642	Yokose
643	Sakate
644	Oumi
645	Fukue
646	New Construction
647	New Construction
648	New Construction

Minesweeping Boats

707	Nana-go
708	Hachi-go
709	Kyuu-go
710	Jyuu-go
711	Jyuu-Ichi-go
712	Jyuu-Ni-go

Minesweeper Tender

MST 473	Kouzu

Light Forces

811-815	PT 11-15
919-927	PB 19-27
06	Kosoku 6

MSC Support Ships

MMC 951	Souya
MST 462	Hayase

Amphibious Forces

LST 4101	Atsumi
4102	Motobu
4103	New Construction
4151	Miura
4152	Ozika
4153	Satsuma

Salvage Vessel

41	Shobo

Submarine Rescue Ships

ASR 401	Chihaya
402	Fusimir

Tanker

AO 411	Hamana

Fleet Support Ship

AOE 421	New Construction

Training Ship

TV 3501	Katori

Training Support Ship

ATS 4201	Azuma

Cable Layer

ARC 481	Tsugaru

Icebreaker

AGB 5001	Fuji

Surveying Ships

AGS 5101	Akashi
5111	Ichi-Go
5112	Ni-Go
5113	San-Go
5114	Yon-Go
5115	Go-Go

Tug

YT 55

Tenders

YAS 46	Yashima
56	Atada
57	Itsuki
58	Yashiro
60	Tsushima
61	Toshima
62	Shisaka
63	Koshiki
64	Sakito
65	Kanawa
66	Tsukumi
67	Mikura
68	Sikine
69	Erimo
70	Hotaka
YAS 101-105	

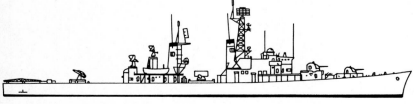

"HARUNA" Class

"TAKATSUKI" Class

"YAMAGUMO" Class

"MINEGUMO" Class

AMATSUKAZE

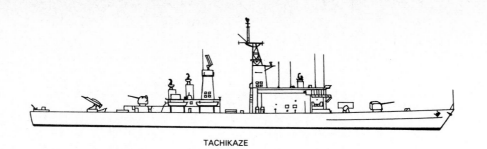

TACHIKAZE

"AKIZUKI" Class

"MURASAME" Class

"AYANAMI" Class

"HARUKAZE" Class

"CHIKUGO" Class

"ISUZU" Class

"MIZUTORI" Class

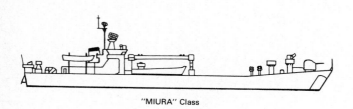

"MIURA" Class

KATORI

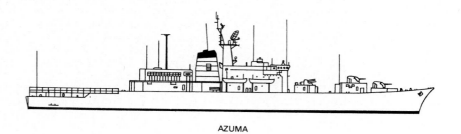

AZUMA

DESTROYERS

NEW CONSTRUCTION

Displacement, tons: 2 900
Aircraft: One A/S helicopter
Missiles: Harpoon; Seasparrow
Main engines: CODOG or COGOG = 30 knots

A new class now under consideration. Possible programme of 6-8 ships by 1981.

2 "TACHIKAZE" CLASS

Name	No.	Builders	Laid down	Launched	Commissioned
TACHIKAZE	DD 168	Mitsubishi Heavy Industry Co, Nagasaki	19 June 1973	7 Dec 1974	26 Mar 1976
—	DD 169	Mitsubishi Heavy Industry Co, Nagasaki	27 May 1976	Nov 1977	Mar 1979

Displacement, tons: 3 900
Dimensions, feet (metres): 443 × 47 × 15 *(143 × 14·3 × 4·6)*
Missiles: 1 Tartar D launcher Mk 13 Mod 3 for Standard RIM 60A SAM
Guns: 2—5 in *(127 mm)* 54 cal (singles)
A/S weapons: 8 tube ASROC and 2 triple (324 mm) A/S torpedo tubes
Main engines: 2 turbines; 2 shafts; 60 000 hp
Speed, knots: 33
Complement: 260

DD 169 ordered 3 March 1975.

Gunnery: GFCS Mk 1.

Radar: 3 D; SPS 52. Tactical: OPS-17.

Sonar: VDS. SQS-35(J).

TACHIKAZE   *1975, Japanese Maritime Self-Defence Force*

2 "HARUNA" CLASS

Name	No.	Builders	Laid down	Launched	Commissioned
HARUNA	DD 141	Mitsubishi, Nagasaki	19 Mar 1970	1 Feb 1972	22 Feb 1973
HIEI	DD 142	Ishikawajima, Tokyo	8 Mar 1972	13 Aug 1973	27 Nov 1974

Displacement, tons: 4 700
Length, feet (metres): 502·0 *(153·0)*
Beam, feet (metres): 57·4 *(17·5)*
Draught, feet (metres): 16·7 *(5·1)*
Aircraft: 3 anti-submarine helicopters
Guns: 2—5 in *(127 mm)* (single)
A/S weapons: Asroc launcher; 6—(2 triple) Mk 32 A/S torpedo tubes
Main engines: 2 turbines; 70 000 shp; 2 shafts
Speed, knots: 32
Complement: 364

Ordered under the third five-year defence programme (from 1967-71).

Gunnery: GFCS Mk 1.

Radar: OPS-11, OPS-17.

Sonar: OQS-3.

HIEI   *5/1976*

2 "IMPROVED HARUNA" CLASS

Name	No.	Builders	Laid down	Launched	Commissioned
—	DD 143	Ishikawajima Harima Jyuko Ltd, Tokyo	25 Feb 1977	Sep 1978	Mar 1980
—	DD 144	—	—	—	1981

Displacement, tons: 5 200
Length, feet (metres): 521 *(158·8)*
Beam, feet (metres): 57·5 *(17·5)*
Draught, feet (metres): 17·5 *(5·3)*
Aircraft: 3 anti-submarine helicopters
Missiles: 1 Sea Sparrow launcher
Guns: 2—5 in *(127 mm)* 54 cal (singles); 2—35 mm
A/S weapons: 1 Asroc launcher; 6—(2 triple) Mk 32 A/S torpedo tubes
Main engines: 2 turbines; 75 000 shp; 2 shafts
Speed, knots: 32
Complement: 370

One in 1975 Programme and one in 1976 Programme. To be twin funnelled.

Radar: OPS-12; OPS-28.

Sonar: OQS-101 (hull-mounted); SQS-35(J) (VDS).

4 "TAKATSUKI" CLASS

Name	No.	Builders	Laid down	Launched	Commissioned
KIKUZUKI	DD 165	Mitsubishi Jyuko Co, Nagasaki	15 Mar 1966	25 Mar 1967	27 Mar 1968
MOCHIZUKI	DD 166	Ishikawajima Jyuko Co, Tokyo	25 Nov 1966	15 Mar 1968	25 Mar 1969
NAGATSUKI	DD 167	Mitsubishi Jyuko Co, Nagasaki	2 Mar 1968	19 Mar 1969	12 Feb 1970
TAKATSUKI	DD 164	Ishikawajima Jyuko Co, Tokyo	8 Oct 1964	7 Jan 1966	15 Mar 1967

Displacement, tons: 3 100
Length, feet (metres): 446·2 *(136·0)* oa
Beam, feet (metres): 44·0 *(13·4)*
Draught, feet (metres): 14·5 *(4·4)*
Aircraft: 2 HSS-2 helicopters
Guns: 2—5 in *(127 mm)* 54 cal (single)
A/S weapons: Octuple Asroc; 1 four barrelled rocket launcher; 6—(2 triple) Mk 32 A/S torpedo tubes
Torpedo tubes: 2 triple for A/S torpedoes
Main engines: 2 Mitsubishi WH geared turbines; 60 000 shp; 2 shafts
Boilers: 2 Mitsubishi CE
Speed, knots: 32
Range, miles: 7 000 at 20 knots
Complement: 270

Takatsuki was provided under the 1963 programme. Equipped with helicopter hangar.

Aircraft: 3 Dash helicopters exchanged for 2 HSS-2 helicopters during 1977.

Radar: Search: OPS-11.
Tactical: OPS-17.
Fire control: GFCS 56 with I Band.

Sonars: VDS; SQS-35(J); *Takatsuki* (1970), *Kikuzuki* (1972). Remainder not so fitted though planned).
Hull: SQS-23 (164-165); OQS-3 (166-167).

NAGATSUKI   7/1976, Stefan Terzibaschitsch

6 "YAMAGUMO" CLASS

Name	No.	Builders	Laid down	Launched	Commissioned
AKIGUMO	DD 120	Sumitomo, Uraga	7 July 1972	23 Oct 1973	24 July 1974
AOKUMO	DD 119	Sumitomo, Uraga	2 Oct 1970	30 Mar 1972	25 Nov 1972
ASAGUMO	DD 115	Maizuru	24 June1965	25 Nov 1966	29 Aug 1967
MAKIGUMO	DD 114	Uraga	10 June1964	26 July 1965	19 Mar 1966
YAMAGUMO	DD 113	Mitsui, Tamano	23 Mar 1964	27 Feb 1965	29 Jan 1966
—	DD 121	Sumitomo Heavy Industries, Uraga	4 Feb 1976	May 1977	Mar 1978

Displacement, tons: 2 100
Length, feet (metres): 377 *(115)*
Beam, feet (metres): 38·7 *(11·8)*
Draught, feet (metres): 13·1 *(4)*
Guns: 4—3 in; 50 cal (2 twin)
A/S weapons: 1 Asroc ; 1 four barrelled rocket launcher; 6—(2 triple) Mk 32 A/S torpedo tubes
Main engines: 6 Diesels; 26 500 bhp; 2 shafts
Speed, knots: 27
Range, miles: 7 000 at 20 knots
Complement: 210

Class: DD 121 is lead ship of an improved class—slightly larger with CODOG machinery giving possibly up to 32 knots.

Radar: Search: OPS-11.
Tactical: OPS-17.
Fire control: I band control of GFCS 56.

Sonar: Hull-mounted: SQS-23 (113-115); OQS-3 (119-121).
VDS: SQS-35(J) (113, 114, 120).

AKIGUMO   1975, Japanese Maritime Self-Defence Force

3 "MINEGUMO" CLASS

Name	No.	Builders	Laid down	Launched	Commissioned
MINEGUMO	DD 116	Mitsui, Tamano	14 Mar 1967	16 Dec 1967	21 Aug 1968
MURAKUMO	DD 118	Maizuru	19 Oct 1968	15 Nov 1969	21 Aug 1970
NATSUGUMO	DD 117	Uraga	26 June1967	25 July 1968	25 April 1969

All details as for "Yamagumo" class except:

Aircraft: 2 Dash helicopter in place of Asroc although this will be reversed during 1977.

Note difference in silhouettes between this and the "Yamagumo" class.

Gunnery: In 1976 *Murakumo* had Y turret removed and replaced by an OTO Melara 76 mm Compact for trials.

Radar: Search: OPS-11.
Tactical: OPS-17.

Sonar: Hull-mounted: OQS 3.
VDS: SQS-35(J) (118).

NATSUGUMO   *1972, Japanese Maritime Self-Defence Force*

1 "AMATSUKAZE" CLASS

Name	No.	Builders	Laid down	Launched	Commissioned
AMATSUKAZE	DD 163	Mitsubishi, Nagasaki	29 Nov 1962	5 Oct 1963	15 Feb 1965

Displacement, tons: 3 050 standard; 4 000 full load
Length, feet (metres): 429·8 *(131·0)*
Beam, feet (metres): 44 *(13·4)*
Draught, feet (metres): 13·8 *(4·2)*
Aircraft: Helicopter
Missile launchers: 1 single Tartar
Guns: 4—3 in *(76 mm)* 50 cal, (2 twin)
A/S weapons: Asroc; 2 Hedgehogs
  6 Short A/S launchers (triples)
Main engines: 2 Ishikawajima GE geared turbines 2 shafts;
  60 000 shp
Boilers: 2 Ishikawajima Foster Wheeler
Speed, knots: 33
Oil fuel, tons: 900
Range, miles: 7 000 at 18 knots
Complement: 290

Ordered under the 1960 programme. Refitted in 1967 when A/S Tubes and new Sonar were fitted.

Radar: Search: SPS 37 and SPS 39 (3 D).
Fire control: SPS 51 for Tartar: I band for guns.

Sonar: SQS 23.

AMATSUKAZE   *1975, Japanese Maritime Self-Defence Force*

2 "AKIZUKI"CLASS

Name	No.	Builders	Laid down	Launched	Commissioned
AKIZUKI	DD 161	Mitsubishi Zoosen Co, Nagasaki	31 July 1958	26 June1959	13 Feb 1960
TERUZUKI	DD 162	Shin Mitsubishi Jyuko Co, Kobe	15 Aug 1958	24 June1959	29 Feb 1960

Displacement, tons: 2 350 standard; 2 890 full load
Length, feet (metres): 387·2 *(118·0)* oa
Beam, feet (metres): 39·4 *(12·0)*
Draught, feet (metres): 13·1 *(4·0)*
Guns: 3—5 in *(127 mm)* 54 cal (single)
  4—3 in *(76 mm)* 50 cal, (2 twin)
A/S weapons: 1—US model Mk 108 rocket launcher; 2 hedgehogs; 2 Short A/S torpedo launchers; (161); 6 A/S tubes (triple); one 4-barrelled Bofors rocket launcher (162) (see note)
Torpedo tubes: 4—21 in *(533 mm)* (quadrupled)
Main engines: 2 geared turbines:— *Akizuki:* Mitsubishi Escher-Weiss. *Teruzuki:* Westinghouse 45 000 shp, 2 shafts
Boilers: 2 Mitsubishi CE type
Speed, knots: 32
Complement: 330

Built under the 1957 Military Aid Programme.

A/S weapons: *Teruzuki* rearmed Sept 1976-Jan 1977.

Radar: Search: SPS 6.
Tactical: SPS 10.
Fire control: I Band.

Refit: *Akikuzuki* expected to refit 1977 with similar change of A/S weapons to *Teruzuki.*

Sonar: Hull mounted: SQS-29.
VDS: OQA-1 (161 (1968)—162 (1967)).

TERUZUKI   *1974, Japanese Maritime Self-Defence Force*

3 "MURASAME" CLASS

Name	No.	Builders	Laid down	Launched	Commissioned
HARUSAME	DD 109	Uraga Dock Co	17 June1958	18 June1959	15 Dec 1959
MURASAME	DD 107	Mitsubishi Zoosen Co, Nagasaki	17 Dec 1957	31 July 1958	28 Feb 1959
YUDACHI	DD 108	Ishikawajima Jyuko Co, Tokyo	16 Dec 1957	29 July 1958	25 Mar 1959

Displacement, tons: 1 800 standard; 2 500 full load
Length, feet (metres): 354·3 *(108·0)* oa
Beam, feet (metres): 36 *(11·0)*
Draught, feet (metres): 12·2 *(3·7)*
Guns: 3—5 in *(127 mm)* 54 cal
  4—3 in *(76 mm)* 50 cal, (2 twin)
A/S weapons: 2 Short A/S torpedo launchers; 1 Hedgehog;
  1 DC rack; 1 Y-gun (see note)
Main engines: 2 sets geared turbines; 30 000 shp; 2 shafts
Boilers: 2 (see *Engineering* notes)
Speed, knots: 30
Range, miles: 6 000 at 18 knots
Complement: 250

Murasame and *Yudachi* were built under the 1956 Programme, *Harusame* 1957 Programme.

A/S weapons: *Murasame* fitted Sep 1975 with two triple tubes in place of those above. DC rack and Y-gun removed.

Engineering: *Murasame* has Mitsubishi Jyuko turbines and Mitsubishi CE boilers; and the other two have Ishikawajima Harima Jyuko turbines and Ishikawajima FW-D boilers.

Radar: Search: SPS 6.
Tactical: SPS 10.
Fire control: I Band—Mk 63 and 57.

Sonar: Hull mounted: SQS 29.
VDS: OQA-1 (109 (1968)).

HARUSAME　　　　　　　　　　1975, Japanese Maritime Self-Defence Force

7 "AYANAMI" CLASS

Name	No.	Builders	Laid down	Launched	Commissioned
AYANAMI	DD 103	Mitsubishi Zoosen Co, Nagasaki	20 Nov 1956	1 June1957	12 Feb 1958
ISONAMI	DD 104	Shin Mitsubishi Jyuko Co, Kobe	14 Dec 1956	30 Sep 1957	14 Mar 1958
MAKINAMI	DD 112	Iino Jyuko Co, Maizuru	20 Mar 1959	25 April1960	30 Oct 1960
OONAMI	DD 111	Ishikawajima Jyuko Co, Tokyo	20 Mar 1959	13 Feb 1960	29 Aug 1960
SHIKINAMI	DD 106	Mitsui Zoosen Co, Tamano	24 Dec 1956	25 Sep 1957	15 Mar 1958
TAKANAMI	DD 110	Mitsui Zoosen Co, Tamano	8 Nov 1958	8 Aug 1959	30 Jan 1960
URANAMI	DD 105	Kawasaki Jyuko Co, Tokyo	1 Feb 1957	29 Aug 1957	27 Feb 1958

Displacement, tons: 1 700 standard; 2 500 full load
Length, feet (metres): 357·6 *(109·0)* oa
Beam, feet (metres): 35·1 *(10·7)*
Draught, feet (metres): 12 *(3·7)*
Guns: 6—3 in *(76 mm)* 50 cal (3 twin)
A/S weapons: 6—(2 triple) A/S torpedo tubes (Mk 32) (103, 104, 105, 106, 112); 2 A/S torpedo launchers (110, 111);
  2 US Mk 15 Hedgehogs
Torpedo tubes: 4—21 in *(533 mm)* (quadruple) (see *Training Ship* note) (103, 105, 110, 111, 112)
  2 Short A/S torpedo launchers
Main engines: 2 Mitsubishi Escher-Weiss geared turbines;
  2 shafts; 35 000 shp
Boilers: 2 (see *Engineering)*
Speed, knots: 32
Range, miles: 6 000 at 18 knots
Complement: 230

Anti-submarine: Trainable Hedgehogs forward of the bridge.

Engineering: Types of boilers installed are as follows: Mitsubishi CE in *Ayanami, Isonami,* and *Uranami.* Hitachi, Babcock & Wilcox in *Oonami, Shikinami* and *Takanami.* Kawasaki Jyuko BD in *Makinami.*

Radar: Search: SPS 12.
Tactical: SPS 10. **Fire control:** I Band.

Training Ships: *Isonami* and *Shikinami* converted 1975-76 to training ships in place of *Asahi* and *Hatsuhi.* 21 inch torpedo tubes removed and lecture hall built in the space.

Sonar: Hull mounted: OQS-12.
VDS: OQA-1 (103, 104, 110)

MAKINAMI　　　　　　　　　　1975, Japanese Maritime Self-Defence Force

2 "HARUKAZE" CLASS

Name	No.
HARUKAZE	DD 101
YUKIKAZE	DD 102

Builders	Laid down	Launched	Commissioned
Mitsubishi Zoosen Co, Nagasaki	15 Dec 1954	20 Sep 1955	26 Apr 1956
Shin Mitsubishi Jyuko Co, Kobe	17 Dec 1954	20 Aug 1955	31 July 1956

Displacement, tons: 1 700 standard; 2 340 full load
Length, feet (metres): 347·8 (106·0) wl; 358·5 (190·3) oa
Beam, feet (metres): 34·5 (10·5)
Draught, feet (metres): 12·0 (3·7)
Guns: 3—5 in (127 mm) 38 cal; 8—40 mm (2 quadruple)
A/S weapons: 2 Short A/S torpedo launchers; 2 Hedgehogs;
4 K-guns; 1 DC rack (see note)
Main engines: 2 sets geared turbines; Harukaze; 2 Mitsubishi
Escher Weiss; Yukikaze; 2 Westinghouse; 2 shafts; 30 000
shp
Boilers: Harukaze: 2 Hitachi-Babcock; Yukikaze: 2 Combustion
Engineering
Speed, knots: 30
Range, miles: 6 000 at 18 knots
Oil fuel, tons: 557
Complement: 240

Authorised under the 1953 programme. First destroyer hulled
vessels built in Japan after the Second World War. Electric
welding was extensively used in hull construction; development of weldable high tension steel in main hull and light alloy
in superstructure were also new.
Nearly all the armament was supplied from the USA under the
MSA clause.

Modifications: Yukikaze has been modified for experimental
duties. 1—5 in (Y gun), 4 K-guns and 1 DC rack removed to
make way for towed passive sonar array.

Radar: Search: L Band.
Tactical: SPS 10.
Fire control: I Band. Mk 57 (101); Contraves (102).

Sonar: SQS-29.

HARUKAZE
1975, Japanese Maritime Self-Defence Force

YUKIKAZE
1972, Toshio Tamura

FRIGATES

6-8 NEW CONSTRUCTION

Displacement, tons: 1 300 (approx)
Missiles: Harpoon
Gun: 1—76 mm OTO Melara
A/S weapons: Asroc (?); Short A/S torpedo launchers
Main engines: COGOG or CODOG = 25 knots (approx)

It is possible that this class will be built 1978-81 with the first
requested in the 1978 programme.

11 "CHIKUGO" CLASS

Name	No.
AYASE	DE 216
CHIKUGO	DE 215
CHITOSE	DE 220
IWASE	DE 219
KUMANO	DE 224
MIKUMA	DE 217
NIYODO	DE 221
NOSHIRO	DE 225
TESHIO	DE 222
TOKACHI	DE 218
YOSHINO	DE 223

Builders	Laid down	Launched	Commissioned
Ishikawajima Harima	5 Dec 1969	16 Sep 1970	20 May 1971
Mitsui Zoosen, Tamano	9 Dec 1968	13 Jan 1970	31 July 1970
Hitachi Zoosen Maizuru	7 Oct 1971	25 Jan 1973	31 Aug 1973
Mitsui Zoosen, Tamano	6 Aug 1971	29 June1972	12 Dec 1972
Hitachi Zoosen, Maizuru	29 May 1974	24 Feb 1975	19 Nov 1975
Mitsui Zoosen, Tamano	17 Mar 1970	16 Feb 1971	26 Aug 1971
Mitsui Zoosen, Tamano	20 Sep 1972	28 Aug 1973	8 Feb 1974
Mitsui Zoosen, Tamano	27 Jan 1976	23 Dec 1976	June 1977
Hitachi Zoosen, Maizuru	11 July 1973	29 May 1974	10 Jan 1975
Mitsui Zoosen, Tamano	11 Dec 1970	25 Nov 1971	17 May 1972
Mitsui Zoosen, Tamano	28 Sep 1973	22 Aug 1974	6 Feb 1975

Displacement, tons: 1 470 (216, 217-219,221); 1 480 (215, 220);
1 500 (222 onwards)
Length, feet (metres): 305·5 (93·0) oa
Beam, feet (metres): 35·5 (10·8)
Draught, feet (metres): 11·5 (3·5)
Guns: 2—3 in (76 mm) 50 cal, (1 twin); 2—40 mm (1 twin)
A/S weapons: 8 tube Asroc; 6 (2 triple) Mk 32 A/S torpedo tubes
Main engines: 4 Mitsui B & W diesels (215, 217, 218, 219, 221,
223, 225); 4 Mitsubishi UEV 30/40 N diesels (remainder); 2
shafts; 16 000 shp
Speed, knots: 25
Complement: 165

Radar: Search: OPS-14; OPS-18.
Tactical: SPS 10.
Fire control: I Band. GFCS Mk 1.

Sonar: Hull mounted: OQS-3.
VDS: SPS-35(J).

KUMANO
1976, Japanese Maritime Self-Defence For

4 "ISUZU" CLASS

Name	No.	Builders	Laid down	Launched	Commissioned
ISUZU	DE 211	Mitsui Zoosen Co, Tamano	16 Apr 1960	17 Jan 1961	29 July 1961
KITAKAMI	DE 213	Ishikawajima-Harima Co, Tokyo	7 June1962	21 June1963	27 Feb 1964
MOGAMI	DE 212	Mitsubishi Zoosen Co, Nagasaki	4 Aug 1960	7 Mar 1961	28 Oct 1961
OOI	DE 214	Maizuru Co.	10 June1962	15 June1963	22 Jan 1964

Displacement, tons: 1 490 standard; 1 700 full load
Length, feet (metres): 309·5 (94) oa
Beam, feet (metres): 34·2 (10·4)
Draught, feet (metres): 11·5 (3·5)
Guns: 4—3 in (76 mm) 50 cal, (2 twin)
A/S weapons: 4 Barrelled Bofors rocket launcher; 2 Triple Short A/S tubes; 1 Y-gun; 1 DC rack (Ooi and Isuzu)
Torpedo tubes: 4—21 in (533 mm) (quadrupled)
Main engines: 4 diesels, Mitsui in Ooi, Isuzu, Mitsubishi in Kitakami, Mogami, 16 000 hp; 2 shafts
Speed, knots: 25
Complement: 180

Modernisation: In 1966 (Mogami) and 1968 (Kitakami) 1 Y-gun and DC racks removed for VDS. Isuzu (1974-75) and Mogami (1974) modified for new Bofors rocket launcher.

Radar: Search: SPS 6
Tactical: SPS 10.

Sonar: Hull mounted: SQS-29.
VDS: OQA-1 (212-213).

KITAKAMI

1975, Japanese Maritime Self-Defence Force

CORVETTES

8 "MIZUTORI" CLASS (PC)

Name	No.	Builders	Laid down	Launched	Commissioned
MATSUKARI	315	Sasebo Shipyard	25 Jan 1960	24 June1960	15 Nov 1960
HIYODORI	320	Sasebo Shipyard	26 Feb 1965	25 Sep 1965	28 Feb 1966
KASASAGI	314	Fujinagata, Osaka	18 Dec 1959	31 May 1960	31 Oct 1960
MIZUTORI	311	Kawasaki, Kobe	13 Mar 1959	22 Sep 1959	27 Feb 1960
OTORI	313	Kure Shipyard	16 Dec 1959	27 May 1960	13 Oct 1960
SHIRATORI	319	Sasebo Shipyard	29 Feb 1964	8 Oct 1964	26 Feb 1965
UMIDORI	316	Sasebo Shipyard	15 Feb 1962	15 Oct 1962	30 Mar 1963
YAMADORI	312	Fujinagata, Osaka	14 Mar 1959	22 Oct 1959	15 Mar 1960

Displacement, tons: 420 to 440 standard
Dimensions, feet (metres): 197·0 × 23·3 × 7·5 (60·1 × 7·1 × 2·3)
Guns: 2—40 mm (1 twin)
A/S weapons: 1 Hedgehog; 1 DC rack; 6 A/S Short torpedo tubes (triple) (316, 319, 320); 2 A/S Short torpedo launchers (remainder)
Main engines: 2 MAN diesels; 2 shafts; 3 800 bhp = 20 knots
Range, miles: 2 000 at 12 knots
Complement: 80

Gunnery: GFCS Mk 63.

Radar: OPS-35 (311-312); OPS-36 (313-316); OPS-16 (319-320).

Sonar: SQS-11A.

SHIRATORI

1975

4 "UMITAKA" CLASS (PC)

Name	No.	Builders	Laid down	Launched	Commissioned
OTAKA	310	Kure Shipyard	18 Mar 1959	3 Sep 1959	14 Jan 1960
UMITAKA	309	Kawasaki, Kobe	13 Mar 1959	25 July 1959	30 Nov 1959
KUMATAKA	318	Fujinagata, Osaka	20 Mar 1963	21 Oct 1963	25 Mar 1964
WAKATAKA	317	Kure Shipyard	5 Mar 1962	13 Nov 1962	30 Mar 1963

Displacement, tons: 440 to 460 standard
Dimensions, feet (metres): 197·0 × 23·3 × 8·0 (60·1 × 7·1 × 2·4)
Guns: 2—40 mm (1 twin)
A/S weapons: 1 Hedgehog, 1 DC rack; 2 triple A/S Short torpedo tubes (317, 318); 2 A/S Short torpedo launchers (309,310)
Main engines: 2 B & W diesels; 2 shafts; 4 000 bhp = 20 knots
Range, miles: 3 000 at 12 knots
Complement: 80

Gunnery: GFCS Mk 63.

Radar: OPS-35 (309-310); OPS-36 (317); OPS-16 (318)

Sonar: SQS-11A.

WAKATAKA

1976, Japanese Maritime Self-Defence Force

1 "HAYABUSA" CLASS (PC)

Name	No.	Builders	Laid down	Launched	Commissioned
HAYABUSA	308	Mitsubishi Shipbuilding & Engineering Co. Ltd, Nagasaki	23 May 1956	20 Nov 1956	10 June 1957

Displacement, tons: 380 standard
Dimensions, feet (metres): 190·2 × 25·7 × 7 (58 × 7·8 × 2·1)
Guns: 2—40 mm (1 twin)
A/S weapons: 1 Hedgehog; 2 Y Guns; 2 DC racks
Main engines: 2 diesels; 4 000 bhp; 2 shafts = 20 knots
Range, miles: 3 000 at 12 knots
Complement: 75

Built under the 1954 fiscal year programme.
A gas turbine was installed in Mar 1962 and removed in 1970.

Gunnery: GFCS Mk 63.

Radar: OPS-37.

Sonar: SQS-11A.

HAYABUSA

1974, Japanese Maritime Self-Defence Force

3 "KAMOME" CLASS (PC)

Name	No.	Builders	Laid down	Launched	Commissioned
KAMOME	305	Uraga	27 Jan 1956	3 Sep 1956	14 Jan 1957
MISAGO	307	Uraga	27 Jan 1956	1 Nov 1956	11 Feb 1957
TSUBAME	306	Kure Shipyard	15 Mar 1956	10 Oct 1956	31 Jan 1957

Displacement, tons: 330 standard
Dimensions, feet (metres): 177·1 × 21·6 × 6·8 *(54 × 6·6 × 2·1)*
Guns: 2—40 mm (1 twin)
A/S weapons: 1 Hedgehog; 2-Y guns; 2 DC racks
Main engines: 2 diesels (Mitsui-Burmeister & Wain). 2 shafts; 4 000 bhp = 20 knots
Oil fuel, tons: 21·5
Range, miles: 2 000 at 12 knots
Complement: 70

Authorised under the 1954 programme. At the time they were an entirely new type of fast patrol vessel, reminiscent of the United States PC type but modified and improved in many ways.

Gunnery: GFCS Mk 63.

Radar: OPS-37.

Sonar: SQS-11A.

KAMOME   1975, Japanese Maritime Self-Defence Force

MISAGO   1970, Japanese Maritime Self Defence Force

SUBMARINES

6 + 2 "UZUSHIO" and "IMPROVED UZUSHIO" CLASS

Name	No.	Builders	Laid down	Launched	Commissioned
UZUSHIO	SS 566	Kawasaki Jyuko, Kobe	25 Sep 1968	11 Mar 1970	21 Jan 1971
MAKISHIO	SS 567	Mitsubishi Jyuko, Kobe	21 June 1969	27 Jan 1971	2 Feb 1972
ISOSHIO	SS 568	Kawasaki Jyuko, Kobe	9 July 1970	18 Mar 1972	25 Nov 1972
NARUSHIO	SS 569	Mitsubishi Jyuko, Kobe	8 May 1971	22 Nov 1972	28 Sep 1973
KUROSHIO	SS 570	Kawasaki Jyuko, Kobe	5 July 1972	22 Feb 1974	27 Nov 1974
TAKASHIO	SS 571	Mitsubishi Jyuko, Kobe	6 July 1973	30 June 1975	30 Jan 1976
—	SS 572	Kawasaki Jyuko, Kobe	14 April 1975	April 1977	Mar 1978
—	SS 573	Mitsubishi Jyuko, Kobe	3 Dec 1976	Mar 1978	1979

Displacement, tons: 1 850 standard
Length, feet (metres): 236·2 *(72·0)*
Beam, feet (metres): 29·5 *(9·0)*
Draught, feet (metres): 24·6 *(7·5)*
Torpedo tubes: 6—21 in *(533 mm)*; amidships
Main machinery: 2 Kawasaki MAN diesels; 3 400 bhp; 1 shaft; 1 electric motor; 7 200 hp
Speed, knots: 12 surfaced; 20 dived
Complement: 80

Of double-hull construction and "tear-drop" form, built of HT steel to increase diving depth. New bow sonar fitted.
An enlarged version of 2 200 tons, 249·3 × 32·5 × 24·6 ft *(76 × 9·9 × 7·5 metres)* and with increased diving depth is to be built. First of "Improved" class is SS 573.

MAKISHIO   1976, Japanese Maritime Self-Defence Force

5 "OOSHIO" CLASS

Name	No.	Builders	Laid down	Launched	Commissioned
ARASHIO	SS 565	Mitsubishi Jyuko, Kobe	5 July 1967	24 Oct 1968	25 July 1969
ASASHIO	SS 562	Kawasaki Jyuko Co, Kobe	5 Oct 1964	27 Nov 1965	13 Oct 1966
HARUSHIO	SS 563	Mitsubishi Jyuko Co, Kobe	12 Oct 1965	25 Feb 1967	1 Dec 1967
MICHISHIO	SS 564	Kawasaki Jyuko, Kobe	26 July 1966	5 Dec 1967	29 Aug 1968
OOSHIO	SS 561	Mitsubishi Jyuko Co, Kobe	29 June 1963	30 April 1964	31 Mar 1965

Displacement, tons: 1 650 standard; *Ooshio* 1 600
Length, feet (metres): 288·7 *(88·0)*
Beam, feet (metres): 26·9 *(8·2)*
Draught, feet (metres): 16·2 *(4·9) Ooshio* 15·4 *(4·7)*
Torpedo tubes: 6—21 in *(533 mm)* (bow); 2—12·7 in A/S torpedoes in swim-out tubes
Main machinery: 2 diesels; 2 900 bhp; 2 shafts; 2 electric motors; 6 300 hp
Speed, knots: 14 surfaced; 18 dived
Complement: 80

Double-hulled boats. A bigger design to obtain improved seaworthiness, a larger torpedo capacity and more comprehensive sonar and electronic devices. *Ooshio* was built under the 1961 programme, *Asashio* 1963. Cost $5 600 000.

ASASHIO   1976, Japanese Maritime Self-Defence For

4 "HAYASHIO" and "NATSUSHIO" CLASS

Name	No.	Builders	Laid down	Launched	Commissioned
FUYUSHIO	SS 524	Kawasaki Jyuko Co, Kobe	6 Dec 1961	14 Dec 1962	17 Sep 1963
HAYASHIO	SS 521	Shin Mitsubishi Jyuko Co, Kobe	6 June1960	31 July 1961	30 June 1962
NATSUSHIO	SS 523	Shin Mitsubishi Jyuko Co, Kobe	5 Dec 1961	18 Sep 1962	29 June 1963
WAKASHIO	SS 522	Kawasaki Jyuko Co, Kobe	7 June1960	28 Aug 1961	17 Aug 1962

Displacement, tons: 750 standard; (SS 521, 522); 790 standard (SS 523, 524)
Length, feet (metres): 193·6 *(59·0)* oa (SS 521, 522); 200·1 *(61·0)* oa (SS 523, 524)
Beam, feet (metres): 21·3 *(6·5)*
Draught, feet (metres): 13·5 *(4·1)*
Torpedo tubes: 3—21 in *(533 mm)* (bow)
Main machinery: 2 diesels; total 900 hp; 2 shafts; 2 electric motors, total 2 300 hp
Speed, knots: 11 surfaced; 15 dived (14 dived "Hayashio" class)
Complement: 40

Very handy and successful boats, with a large safety factor, complete air-conditioning and good habitability.

"Hayashio" class   SS 521-522
"Natsushio" class   SS 523-524

NATSUSHIO   *1976, Japanese Maritime Self-Defence Force*

LIGHT FORCES

Note: Possible new construction of some 3 Missile hydrofoils of 180 tons, 45 knots armed with Harpoon and OTO Melara 76 mm gun.

5 FAST ATTACK CRAFT—TORPEDO

Name	No.	Builders	Commissioned
PT 11	811	Mitsubishi, Shimonoseki	27 Mar 1971
PT 12	812	Mitsubishi, Shimonoseki	28 Mar 1972
PT 13	813	Mitsubishi, Shimonoseki	16 Dec 1972
PT 14	814	Mitsubishi, Shimonoseki	15 Feb 1974
PT 15	815	Mitsubishi, Shimonoseki	10 July 1975

Displacement, tons: 100
Dimensions, feet (metres): 116·4 × 30·2 × 3·9 *(35·5 × 9·2 × 1·2)*
Guns: 2—40 mm
Torpedo tubes: 4—21 inch
Main engines: CODAG 2 Mitsubishi diesels; 2 IHI gas turbines; 3 shafts; 11 000 hp (PT 11; 10 500 hp) = 40 knots
Complement: 26-28

Laid down on 17 Mar 1970, 22 Apr 1971, 28 Mar 1972, 23 Mar 1973, and 23 Apr 1974 respectively.

Radar: OPS-13.

PT 14   *1976, Japanese Maritime Self-Defence Force*

9 COASTAL PATROL CRAFT

Name	No.	Builders	Commissioned
PB 19	919	Ishikawajima, Yokohama	31 Mar 1971
PB 20	920	Ishikawajima, Yokohama	31 Mar 1971
PB 21	921	Ishikawajima, Yokohama	31 Mar 1971
PB 22	922	Ishikawajima, Yokohama	31 Mar 1971
PB 23	923	Ishikawajima, Yokohama	31 Mar 1972
PB 24	924	Ishikawajima, Yokohama	31 Mar 1972
PB 25	925	Ishikawajima, Yokohama	29 Mar 1973
PB 26	926	Ishikawajima, Yokohama	29 Mar 1973
PB 27	927	Ishikawajima, Yokohama	29 Mar 1973

Displacement, tons: 18
Dimensions, feet (metres): 55·8 × 14·1 × 2·7 *(17 × 4·3 × 0·7)*
Gun: 1—20 mm
Main engines: 2 diesels; 760 hp = 20 knots
Complement: 6

GRP hulls.

Radar: OPS-29.

PB 22   *11/1975, Toshio Tamura*

Name	No.	Builders	Commissioned
KOSOKU 6	06	Mitsubishi Shimonoseki	20 Mar 1967

Displacement, tons: 40
Dimensions, feet (metres): 75·9 × 18·2 × 3·3 *(23·1 × 5·6 × 1)*
Main engines: 3 diesels; 2 800 bhp = 30 knots

Of aluminium construction. Laid down on 28 June 1966 under the 1965 Programme. Launched 22 Nov 1966.

Radar: OPS-4C.

KOSOKU 6   *1974, Japanese Maritime Self-Defence Force*

AMPHIBIOUS FORCES

Note: Possible new construction 1978-81 of 4/5 500 ton LSMs.

3 "MIURA" CLASS (LST)

Name	No.	Builders	Commissioned
MIURA	4151	Ishikawajima Harima Heavy Industry Co,Tokyo	29 Jan 1975
OJIKA	4152	Ishikawajima Harima Heavy Industry Co,Tokyo	22 Mar 1976
SATSUMA	4153	Ishikawajima Harima Heavy Industry Co,Tokyo	17 Feb 1977

Displacement, tons: 2 000
Dimensions, feet (metres): 321·4 × 45·9 × 9·8 *(98 × 14 × 3)*
Guns: 2—3 in *(76 mm)* (twin); 2—40 mm (twin)
Main engines: 2 Kawasaki/MAN V8V 22/30 ATL diesels; 2 shafts; 4 400 hp = 14 knots
Complement: 115

Fitted with bow doors. *Miura* laid down 26 Nov 1973, launched 13 Aug 1974. *Ojika* laid down 10 June 1974, launched 2 Sep 1975. *Satsuma* laid down 26 May 1975, launched 12 May 1976. Carry 2 LCMs and 2 LCVPs, 10 type 74 tanks.

Radar: OPS-14; OPS-18.

MIURA   *1976, Japanese Maritime Self-Defence Force*

3 "ATSUMI" CLASS (LST)

Name	No.	Builders	Commissioned
ATSUMI	4101	Sasebo Jyuko Co, Sasebo	27 Nov 1972
MOTOBU	4102	Sasebo Jyuko Co, Sasebo	21 Dec 1973
—	4103	Sasebo Jyuko Co, Sasebo	Oct 1977

Displacement, tons: 1 480 *(Atsumi)*; 1 550 *(Motobu)*; 1 500 (4103)
Dimensions, feet (metres): 291·9 × 42·6 × 8·5 *(89 × 13 × 2·7)*
Guns: 4—40 mm (twins)
Main engines: 2 diesels; 4 400 hp = 13 knots *(Motobu)* = 14 knots *(Atsumi)*
Complement: 100 *(Atsumi)*; 95 *(Motobu)*

Atsumi laid down 7 Dec 1971, launched 13 June 1972. *Motobu* laid down 23 April 1973, launched 3 Aug 1973. 4103 laid down 18 Nov 1976; launched May 1977.

Radar: OPS-9.

MOTOBU   *1974, Japanese Maritime Self-Defence Force*

MINE WARFARE FORCES

1 "SOUYA" CLASS (MINESWEEPER SUPPORT SHIP)

Name	No.	Builders	Laid down	Launched	Commissioned
SOUYA	951	Hitachi Zoosen, Maizuru	9 July 1970	31 Mar 1971	30 Sep 1971

Displacement, tons: 2 150 standard; 3 050 full load
Length, feet (metres): 324·8 *(99·0)*
Beam, feet (metres): 49·5 *(15·0)*
Draught, feet (metres): 13·9 *(4·2)*
Guns: 2—3 in *(76 mm)* 50 cal (1 twin); 2—20 mm
A/S weapons: 6 (2 triple) Mk 32 A/S torpedo tubes
Main engines: 4 diesels; 4 000 bhp; 2 shafts
Speed, knots: 18
Complement: 185

With twin rails can carry 200 buoyant mines. Has helicopter platform aft and acts at times as command ship for MCM forces.

Fire Control: GFCS Mk 1.

Radar: OPS-14; OPS-16.

Sonar: SQS-11A

SOUYA   *1974, Japanese Maritime Self-Defence Force*

1 "HAYASE" CLASS (MINESWEEPER SUPPORT SHIP)

Name	No.	Builders	Commissioned
HAYASE	462	Ishikawajima, Haruna	6 Nov 1971

Displacement, tons: 2 000 standard
Length, feet (metres): 324·8 (99·0)
Beam, feet (metres): 42·7 (13·0)
Draught, feet (metres): 12·5 (3·8)
Guns: 2—3 in (76 mm) 50 cal, (1 twin); 2—20 mm
A/S weapons: 6 (2 triple) Mk 32 A/S torpedo tubes
Main engines: 2 diesels; 4 000 bhp; 2 shafts
Speed, knots: 18
Complement: 185

Laid down 16 Sep 1970, launched 21 June 1971. Has helicopter platform aft.

Radar: OPS-14; OPS-16

Sonar: SQS-11A

HAYASE   1972, Japanese Maritime Self Defence Force

3 NEW CONSTRUCTION (MINESWEEPERS—COASTAL)

Name	No.	Builders	Commissioned
—	MSC 646	Hitachi, Kanagawa	Sep 1977
—	MSC 647	Nippon Steel Tube Co	31 Mar 1978
—	MSC 648	Hitachi, Kanagawa	31 Mar 1978

Displacement, tons: 440 standard
Dimensions, feet (metres): 177·1 × 30·8 × 13·8 (54 × 9·4 × 4·2)
Gun: 1—20 mm
Main engines: 2 diesels; 2 shafts; 1 440 bhp = 14 knots

To be fitted with new S4 mine detonating equipment, a remote-controlled counter-mine charge. First of class ordered under 1976 programme. Laid down dates—646, 26 April 1976; 647, Feb 1977; 648, 20 July 1976.

13 "KASADO" CLASS (MINESWEEPERS—COASTAL)

Name	No.	Builders	Commissioned
AMAMI	MSC 625	Nippon Steel Tube Co.	6 Mar 1967
CHIBURI	MSC 620	Hitachi, Kanagawa	25 Mar 1964
HARIO	MSC 618	Hitachi, Kanagawa	23 Mar 1963
IBUKI	MSC 628	Hitachi, Kanagawa	27 Feb 1968
KARATO	MSC 617	Nippon Steel Tube Co	23 Mar 1963
KATSURA	MSC 629	Nippon Steel Tube Co	15 Feb 1968
KUDAKO	MSC 622	Hitachi, Kanagawa	24 Mar 1965
MINASE	MSC 627	Nippon Steel Tube Co.	25 Mar 1967
MUTSURE	MSC 619	Nippon Steel Tube Co.	24 Mar 1964
OOTSU	MSC 621	Nippon Steel Tube Co.	24 Feb 1965
REBUN	MSC 624	Hitachi, Kanagawa	24 Mar 1966
RISHIRI	MSC 623	Nippon Steel Tube Co	5 Mar 1966
URUME	MSC 626	Hitachi, Kanagawa	30 Jan 1967

Displacement, tons: 330 standard; (380 later ships); 448 full load (later ships)
Dimensions, feet (metres): 150·9 × 28 × 7·5 (46 × 8·5 × 2·3); 171·6 × 28·9 × 7·9 (52·3 × 8·8 × 2·4) later ships
Gun: 1—20 mm
Main engines: 2 diesels; 2 shafts; 1 200 bhp (1 440 later ships) = 14 knots
Complement: 43

Originally a class of 29 ships. Hull is of wooden construction. Otherwise built of non-magnetic materials. Sixteen of this class transferred as MCM support ship (1), survey craft (4), EOD (diving tenders) (3) and tenders (8).

Radar: OPS-9 or OPS-4.

IBUKI   1976, Japanese Maritime Self-Defence Force

16 "TAKAMI" CLASS (MINESWEEPERS—COASTAL)

Name	No.	Builders	Commissioned
AWAJI	MSC 634	Hitachi, Kanagawa	29 Mar 1971
IOU	MSC 631	Nippon Steel Tube Co	22 Jan 1970
MIYAKE	MSC 632	Hitachi, Kanagawa	19 Nov 1970
MIYATO	MSC 639	Nippon Steel Tube Co	24 Aug 1973
MUROTSU	MSC 637	Nippon Steel Tube Co	3 Mar 1972
TAKAMI	MSC 630	Hitachi Kanagawa	15 Dec 1969
TASHIRO	MSC 638	Hitachi Kanagawa	30 July 1973
TEURI	MSC 636	Hitachi Kanagawa	10 Mar 1972
TOUSHI	MSC 635	Nippon Steel Tube Co	18 Mar 1971
UTONE	MSC 633	Nippon Steel Tube Co	3 Sep 1970
TAKANE	MSC 640	Hitachi Kanagawa	28 Aug 1974
MUZUKI	MSC 641	Nippon Steel Tube Co	28 Aug 1974
YOKOSE	MSC 642	Hitachi Kanagawa	15 Dec 1975
SAKATE	MSC 643	Nippon Steel Tube Co	17 Dec 1975
OUMI	MSC 644	Hitachi Kanagawa	18 Nov 1976
FUKUE	MSC 645	Nippon Steel Tube Co	18 Nov 1976

Of similar dimensions to "Kasado" class but of slightly different construction and with a displacement of 380 tons.
As minehunters fitted with mine-detecting sonar and carry four clearance divers.

Radar: OPS-9.

Sonar: ZQS-2.

SAKATE   1976, Japanese Maritime Self-Defence Force

1 "KOUZU" CLASS (MCM SUPPORT SHIP)

KOUZU MST 473 (ex-*MSC 609*)

Similar to "Kasado" class but has had minesweeping gear removed and was fitted as MCM command ship in June 1972.

6 "NANA-GO" CLASS (MSBs)

Name	No.	Builders	Commissioned	
NANA-GO	707	Hitachi, Kanagawa	30 Mar	1973
HACHI-GO	708	Nippon Kokan, Tsurumi	27 Mar	1973
KYUU-GO	709	Hitachi, Kanagawa	28 Mar	1974
JYUU-GO	710	Nippon Kokan, Tsurumi	29 Mar	1974
JYUU-ICHI-GO	711	Hitachi, Kanagawa	10 May	1975
JYUU-NI-GO	712	Nippon Kokan, Tsurumi	22 Apr	1975

Displacement, tons: 53
Dimensions, feet (metres): 73·8 × 17·7 × 3·3 *(22·5 × 5·4 × 1)*
Main engines: 2 Mitsubishi diesels; 2 shafts; 480 hp = 11 knots
Complement: 10

Laid down 26 May 1972, 3 Aug 1972, 5 July 1973, 7 June 1973, 2 July 1974, respectively. 712 launched 27 Jan 1975. No radar.

JYUU-GO

3/1974, Toshio Tamura

SERVICE FORCES

Note: 1 submarine tender to be included in future programmes as well as 1 AOE at Hitachi Zoosen Maizuru.

Name	No.	Builders	Commissioned
AZUMA	ATS 4201	Maizuru Jyuko Co, Maizuru	26 Nov 1969

Displacement, tons: 1 950 standard; 2 500 full load
Length, feet (metres): 323·4 *(98·6)*
Beam, feet (metres): 42·7 *(13·0)*
Draught, feet (metres): 12·5 *(3·8)*
Aircraft: 1 helicopter, 3 jetdrones, 7 propeller drones
Gun: 1—3 in *(76 mm)* 50 cal
A/S weapons: 2 A/S Short Torpedo launchers
Main engines: 2 diesels; 2 shafts; 4 000 bhp
Speed, knots: 18
Complement: 185

Laid down on 15 July 1968, launched on 14 Apr 1969. Has drone hangar amidships and catapult-on flight deck.
Training Support Ship.

Radar: OPS-16; SPS-40

Sonar: SQS-11A

AZUMA

1974, Japanese Maritime Self-Defence Force

Name	No.	Builders	Commissioned
KATORI	3501	Ishikawajima Harima, Tokyo	10 Sep 1969

Displacement, tons: 3 350 standard; 4 000 full load
Length, feet (metres): 422·4 *(128·0)*
Beam, feet (metres): 49·5 *(15·0)*
Draught, feet (metres): 14·6 *(4·3)*
Guns: 4—3 in *(76 mm)* 50 cal
A/S weapons: 1 four barrelled rocket launcher; 6 (2 triple) for A/S torpedoes
Main engines: Geared turbines; 2 shafts; 20 000 shp
Range, miles: 7 000 at 18 knots
Speed, knots: 25
Complement: 460 (295 ship's company and 165 trainees)

Laid down 8 Dec 1967, launched on 19 Nov 1968. Training ship. Provided with a landing deck aft for a helicopter and large auditorium for trainees amidships.

Radar: Search: OPS-17 Tactical: SPS-12

Sonar: SQS-4

KATORI

1976, Michael D. J. Lennon

1 E.O.D. TENDER

Name	No.	Builders	Commissioned
ERIMO	YAS 69 (ex-*AMC 491*)	Uraga Dock Co.	28 Dec 1955

Displacement, tons: 630 standard
Dimensions, feet (metres): 210 × 26 × 8 *(64·1 × 7·9 × 2·4)*
Guns: 2—40 mm; 2—20 mm
A/S weapons: 1 Hedgehog; 2 K-guns; 2 DC racks
Main engines: Diesel; 2 shafts; 2 500 bhp = 18 knots
Complement: 80

Conversion to tender for EOD (mine hunting diver) completed Mar 1976.

ERIMO

1973, Japanese Maritime Self-Defence Force

4 E.O.D. TENDERS

YASHIMA (ex-US *AMS 144*) YAS 46
SAKITO (ex-*MSC 607*) YAS 64
TSUKUMI (e-*MSC 611*) YAS 66
HOTAKA (ex-*MSC 616*) YAS 70

YAS 46, former US AMS of 375 tons, and remainder of "Kasado" class (see Minewarfare Section for details) transferred after conversion to EOD (Mine Hunting diver) duties.

1 SUBMARINE RESCUE SHIP

Name	No.	Builders	Commissioned
FUSIMI	ASR 402	Sumnitorho SB & Machinery Co	10 Feb 1970

Displacement, tons: 1 430 standard
Dimensions, feet (metres): 249·5 × 41 × 12 *(76·1 × 12·5 × 3·7)*
Main engines: 2 diesels; 1 shaft; 3 000 bhp = 16 knots
Complement: 100

Laid down on 5 Nov 1968, launched 10 Sep 1969. Has a rescue chamber and two recompression chambers.

Radar: OPS-9.

Sonar: SQS-11A

FUSIMI   *1976, Japanese Maritime Self-Defence Force*

1 SUBMARINE RESCUE SHIP

Name	No.	Builders	Commissioned
CHIHAYA	ASR 401	Mitsubishi Nippon Heavy Industries Co, Yokohama	15 Mar 1961

Displacement, tons: 1 340 standard
Dimensions, feet (metres): 239·5 × 39·3 × 12·7 *(73 × 12 × 3·9)*
Main engines: Diesels; 2 700 bhp = 15 knots
Complement: 90

Authorised under the 1959 programme. The first vessel of her kind to be built in Japan. Laid down on 15 Mar 1960. Launched on 4 Oct 1960. Has rescue chamber, 2 recompression chambers, four-point mooring equipment and a 12 ton derrick.

Radar: OPS-4.

Sonar: SQS-11A.

CHIHAYA   *1976, Japanese Maritime Self-Defence Force*

1 SALVAGE VESSEL

Note: 1 salvage and rescue ship to be included in future programmes.

Name	No.	Builders	Commissioned
SHOBO	41	Azumo Zoosen, Yokosuka	28 Feb 1964

Displacement, tons: 45
Dimensions, feet (metres): 75 × 18 × 3·3 *(22·9 × 5·5 × 1)*
Main engines: 4 diesels; 3 shafts; Speed = 19 knots
Complement: 8

Four fixed fire hoses fitted.

1 CABLE LAYER

Note: 1 cable repair ship to be included in future programmes.

Name	No.	Builders	Commissioned
TSUGARU	ARC 481	Yokohama Shipyard & Engine Works	15 Dec 1955

Displacement, tons: 2 150 standard
Dimensions, feet (metres): 337·8 × 40·7 × 16 *(103 × 12·4 × 4·9)*
Guns: 2—20 mm
Main engines: 2 diesels; 2 shafts; 3 200 bhp = 13 knots
Complement: 103

Dual purpose cable layer and coastal minelayer. Built under the 1953 programme. Laid down on 18 Dec 1954. Launched on 19 July 1955. Converted to cable-layer 10 July 1969-30 April 1970 by Nippon Steel Tube Co.

TSUGARU   *1972, Toshio Tamura*

1 SUPPORT TANKER

Name	No.	Builders	Commissioned
HAMANA	AO 411	Uraga Dock Co	10 Mar 1962

Displacement, tons: 2 900 light, 7 550 full load
Dimensions, feet (metres): 420 × 51·5 × 20·5 *(128·1 × 15·7 × 6·3)*
Guns: 2—40 mm
Main engines: 1 diesel; 5 000 bhp 1 shaft = 16 knots
Complement: 100

Built under the 1960 programme. Laid down on 17 Apr 1961, launched on 24 Oct 1961.

1 NEW CONSTRUCTION FLEET SUPPORT SHIP

AOE 421

Displacement, tons: 4 500
Dimensions, feet (metres): 459·3 × 62·3 × 35·4 *(140 × 19 × 10·8)*
Main engines: 2 diesels; 2 shafts; 20 000 bhp
Speed, knots: 22
Range, miles: 9 500 at 20 knots
Complement: 131

Merchant type hull. Included in 1976 estimates.

SURVEYING SHIPS

Note: 1 surveying ship to be included in future programmes

1 "AKASHI" CLASS (AGS)

Name	No.	Builders	Commissioned
AKASHI	5101	Nippon Steel Tube Co	25 Oct 1969

Displacement, tons: 1 420
Dimensions, feet (metres): 244·2 × 42·2 × 14·2 (74·0 × 13·0 × 4·3)
Main engines: 2 diesels; 2 shafts; 3 200 bhp
Speed, knots: 16
Range, miles: 16 500 at 14 knots
Complement: 65

Laid down 21 Sep 1968. Launched 30 May 1969.

Radar: OPS-9.

AKASHI   1974, Japanese Maritime Self-Defence Force

1 NEW CONSTRUCTION

Displacement, tons: 2 000
Dimensions, feet (metres): 295·3 × 49·2 × 24·9 (90 × 15 × 7·6)
Main engines: 2 diesels; 2 shafts; 4 400 hp
Speed, knots: 16

Similar (but larger) to "Akashi" class. Building by Mitsubishi Jyuko, Shimonoseki under 1976 estimates.

Radar: OPS-18.

5 Ex-"KASADO" CLASS (AGS)

ICHI-GO (ex-Kasado MSC 604) 5111	SAN-GO (ex-Tatara MSC 610) 5113
NI-GO (ex-Habushi MSC 608) 5112	YON-GO (ex-Hirado MSC 614) 5114
	GO-GO (ex-AMS) 5115

Displacement, tons: 340
Dimensions, feet (metres): 150·9 × 28 × 7·5 (46 × 8·5 × 2·3)
Main engines: 2 diesels; 2 shafts; 1 200 bhp = 14 knots

TENDERS

5 "500 TON" CLASS

Name	Laid down	Launched	Commissioned
YAS 101	10 Oct 1967	18 Jan 1968	30 Mar 1968
YAS 102	25 Sep 1968	20 Dec 1968	31 Mar 1969
YAS 103	2 Apr 1971	24 May 1971	30 Sep 1971
YAS 104	4 Feb 1972	15 June1972	13 Sep 1972
YAS 105	20 Feb 1973	16 July 1973	19 Sep 1973

Displacement, tons: 500
Dimensions, feet (metres): 171·6 × 33·0 × 8·3 (52·3 × 10·1 × 2·5)
Main engines: 2 diesels; 2 shafts; 1 600 bhp = 14 knots

Training support and rescue.

Radar: OPS-19 (105);
OPS-29(104);
OPS-10 (remainder).

YAS 101   1975, Japanese Maritime Self-Defence Force

8 Ex-"KASADO" CLASS

Name	No.	Builders	Commissioned
ATADA(ex-MSC 601)	YAS 56	Hitachi, Kanagawa	30 Apr 1956
ITSUKI (ex-MSC 602)	YAS 57	Hitachi, Kanagawa	20 June 1956
YASHIRO (ex-MSC 603)	YAS 58	Nippon Steel Tube Co	10 July 1956
SHISAKA (ex-MSC 605)	YAS 62	Nippon Steel Tube Co	16 Aug 1958
KOSHIKI (ex-MSC 615)	YAS 63	Nippon Steel Tube Co	29 Jan 1962
KANAWA (ex-MSC 606)	YAS 65	Hitachi, Kanagawa	24 July 1959
MIKURA (ex-MSC 612)	YAS 67	Nippon Steel Tube Co	27 May 1960
SHIKINE (ex-MSC 613)	YAS 68	Nippon Steel Tube Co	15 Nov 1960

Details as for "Kasado" class under Minewarfare Forces.

2 TENDERS

TOSHIMA (ex-USS MSC; ex-AMS 258) YAS 61
TSUSHIMA (ex-USS MSC; ex-AMS 255) YAS 60

Former US auxiliary minesweepers.

ICEBREAKER

Name	No.	Builders	Commissioned
FUJI	5001	Nippon Steel Tube Co	15 July 1965

Displacement, tons: 5 250 standard; 7 760 normal; 8 838 full load
Dimensions, feet (metres): 328 × 72·2 × 29 (100 × 22 × 8·8)
Aircraft: 3 helicopters
Main engines: 4 diesel-electric; 2 shafts; 12 000 bhp = 17 knots
Oil fuel, tons: 1 900
Range, miles: 15 000 at 15 knots
Complement: 200 plus 35 scientists and observers

Antarctic Support Ship. Laid down on 28 Aug 1964, launched on 18 Mar 1965. Hangar and flight deck aft. Can cope with ice up to 8·5 feet (2·5 metres).

Radar: OPS-4; OPS-16.

Sonar: SQS-11A.

FUJI   1975, Japanese Maritime Self-Defence Force

1 TUG

YT 55

Displacement, tons: 195
Dimensions, feet (metres): 84·8 × 23 × 7·5 (25·9 × 7 × 2·3)
Main engines: 2 diesels; 500 hp = 11 knots
Complement: 15

Entered service 22 Aug 1975.

MARITIME SAFETY AGENCY

Establishment

Establis!..:d in May 1948 to carry out patrol and rescue duties as well as hydrographic and navigation aids services.

Commandant: Yasuhiko Sonomura

Personnel:

1977: 11 203

Strength of the Fleet

	Active
Large Patrol Vessels	10
Medium Patrol Vessels	57
Small Patrol Vessels	19
Patrol Craft	209
Survey Vessels	6
Surveying Launches	21
Tenders	5
Underwater Research Vessel	1
Firefighting Craft	11
Utility Launches	50

DELETIONS

1975: *Abukuma, Fuji, Ishikari, Isuzu, Kikuchi, Kuzuryu, Oyodo, Tenryu* ("Fuji", later "Sagami" class small patrol vessels)
Suzunami, Hayanami, Hatagumo, Makigumo, Tatsugumo (Patrol Craft)
CS 57, 58, 115 (harbour patrol craft)
FS 01, 02, 04, 05, 06 (Salvage Craft)

1976: *Sagami, Yoshino, Noshiro, Kiso, Nagara, Tone* (small patrol vessels)
Yaegumo (patrol craft)
CS 105, 117 (harbour patrol craft)
FS 03 (salvage craft)

LARGE PATROL VESSELS

2 "IZU" CLASS

Name	No.	Builders	Commissioned
IZU	PL 31	Hitachi Mukai Shima	July 1967
MIURA	PL 32	Maizuru Jukogyo Ltd	Mar 1969

Displacement, tons: 2 080 normal
Dimensions, feet (metres): 313.3 oa × 38 × 12.8 *(95.6 × 11.6 × 3.9)*
Main engines: 2 diesels; 2 shafts; 10 400 bhp = 21.6 knots
Range, miles: 14 500 at 12.7 knots; 5 000 at 21 knots
Complement: 72

Izu was laid down in Aug 1966, launched in Jan 1967. *Miura* was laid down in May 1968, launched in Oct 1968. Employed in long range rescue and patrol and weather observation duties. Equipped with weather observation radar, various types of marine instruments. Ice strengthened hull.

Radar: One navigation set; one weather set.

MIURA   *1975, Japanese Maritime Safety Agency*

4 "ERIMO" CLASS

Name	No.	Builders	Commissioned
DAIO	PL 15	Hitachi Maizuru	28 Sep 1973
ERIMO	PL 13	Hitachi Zoosen Co Ltd	30 Nov 1965
MUROTO	PL 16	Naikai Zoosen Co Ltd	30 Nov 1974
SATSUMA	PL 14	Hitachi Zoosen Co Ltd	30 July 1966

Displacement, tons: 1 009 normal (1 206 *Daio*)
Dimensions, feet (metres): 251.3 oa × 30.2 × 9.9 (31.5 × 10.7 *Daio*) *(76.6 × 9.2 × 3) (9.6 × 3.3 Daio)*
Guns: 1—3 in 50 cal; 1—20 mm (1—40 mm; 1—20 mm *Daio*)
Main engines: Diesels; 2 shafts; 4 800 bhp = 19.78 knots (7 000 bhp CP propellers = 20 knots, *Daio*)
Range, miles: 5 000 at 17 knots
Complement: 72

Erimo was laid down on 29 Mar 1965 and launched on 14 Aug 1965. Her structure is strengthened against ice. Employed as a patrol vessel off northern Japan. *Satsuma,* is assigned to guard and rescue south of Japan. *Daio* was laid down 18 Oct 1972 and launched 19 June 1973. *Muroto* was laid down 15 Mar 1974 and launched 5 Aug 1974.

Radar: One navigation set.

DAIO   *1973, Japanese Maritime Safety Agency*

Name	No.	Builders	Commissioned
KOJIMA	PL 21	Kure Zoosen	21 May 1964

Displacement, tons: 1 206
Dimensions, feet (metres): 228.3 oa × 33.8 × 10.5 *(69.6 × 10.3 × 3.2)*
Guns: 1—3 in; 1—40 mm; 1—20 mm
Main engines: Diesels; 2 600 hp = 17 knots
Range, miles: 6 000 at 13 knots
Complement: 17 officers, 42 men, 47 cadets

Maritime Safety Agency training ship.

Radar: Two navigation sets.

KOJIMA   *1974, Japanese Maritime Safety Agency*

2 "NOJIMA" CLASS

Name	No.	Builders	Commissioned
NOJIMA	PL 11	Uraga Dock Co Ltd	30 April 1962
OJIKA	PL 12	Uraga Dock Co Ltd	10 June 1963

Displacement, tons: 950 standard; 1 009 normal; 1 113 full load
Dimensions, feet (metres): 208·8 pp; 226·5 oa × 30·2 × 10·5 *(63·7; 69·1 × 9·2 × 3·2)*
Main engines: 2 sets diesels; 3 000 bhp = 17·5 knots
Range, miles: 9 270 at 17 knots
Complement: 51

Nojima laid down on 27 Oct 1961, launched on 12 Feb 1962. Both employed as patrol vessels and weather ships.

Radar: One navigation set.

OJIKA   *1974, Japanese Maritime Safety Agency*

Name	No.	Builders	Commissioned
SOYA	PL 107	Kawanami Zoosen	May 1938

Displacement, tons: 4 364 normal; 4 818 full load
Dimensions, feet (metres): 259·2 wl × 51·9 (including bulge) × 18·9 *(79·1 × 15·8 × 5·8)*
Main engines: 2 sets diesels; 4 800 bhp = 12·5 knots on trials
Range, miles: 10 000 at 12 knots
Complement: 96

Assigned to guard and rescue service.

Radar: Two navigation sets.

SOYA   *1975, Japanese Maritime Safety Agency*

MEDIUM PATROL VESSELS

16 "BIHORO" CLASS

Name	No.	Builders	Commissioned
ABUKUMA	PM 79	Tohoku Zoosen	30 Jan 1976
BIHORO	PM 73	Tohoku Zoosen	28 Feb 1974
FUJI	PM 75	Usuki Tekko	7 Feb 1975
ISHIKARI	PM 78	Tohoku Zoosen	13 Mar 1976
ISUZU	PM 80	Naikai Zoosen	10 Mar 1976
KABASHIMA	PM 76	Usuki Tekko	25 Mar 1975
KIKUCHI	PM 81	Usuki Tekko	6 Feb 1976
KUMA	PM 74	Usuki Tekko	28 Feb 1974
KUZURYU	PM 82	Usuki Tekko	18 Mar 1976
SADO	PM 77	Tohoku Zoosen	1 Feb 1975
HOROBUTSU	PM 83	Tohoku Zoosen	Jan 1977
SHIRAKAMI	PM 84	Tohoku Zoosen	Mar 1977
SAGAMI	PM 85	Naikai Zoosen	Nov 1976
TONE	PM 86	Usuki Tekko	Nov 1976
YOSHINO	PM 87	Usuki Tekko	Jan 1977
KUROBE	PM 88	Shikoku Dock Co Ltd	Feb 1977

Displacement, tons: 636 standard; 657 full load
Dimensions, feet (metres): 208 × 25·6 × 8·3 *(63·4 × 7·8 × 2·5)*
Gun: 1—20 mm
Main engines: Diesels; 2 shafts; 3 000 hp = 18 knots
Range, miles: 3 200 at 18 knots
Complement: 34

Radar: Two navigation sets.

KUMA   *1974, Japanese Maritime Safety Agency*

3 "MIYAKE" CLASS

Name	No.	Builders	Commissioned
AWAJI	PM 71	Usuki Tekko	25 Jan 1973
MIYAKE	PM 70	Tohoku Zoosen	25 Jan 1973
YAEYAMA	PM 72	Usuki Tekko	20 Dec 1972

Displacement, tons: 530 standard; 574 full load
Dimensions, feet (metres): 190·4 oa × 24·2 × 8·2 *(58·1 × 7·4 × 2·5)*
Gun: 1—20 mm
Main engines: Diesels; 2 shafts; cp propellers; 3 200 hp = 17·8 knots
Range, miles: 3 580 at 16 knots
Complement: 36

Of similar hull design to "Kunashiri" class.

Radar: Two Navigation sets.

MIYAKE   *1973, Japanese Maritime Safety Agency*

4 "KUNASHIRI" CLASS

Name	No.	Builders	Commissioned
KAMISHIMA	PM 68	Usuki Tekko	Jan 1972
KUNASHIRI	PM 65	Maizuru Jukogyo Ltd	Mar 1969
MINABE	PM 66	Maizuru Jukogyo Ltd	Mar 1970
SAROBETSO	PM 67	Maizuru Jukogyo Ltd	Mar 1971

Displacement, tons: 498 normal
Dimensions, feet (metres): 190·4 oa × 24·2 × 7·9 *(58·1 × 7·4 × 2·4)*
Gun: 1—20 mm
Main engines: 2 sets diesels; 2 600 bhp = 17·6 knots
Range, miles: 3 000 at 16·9 knots
Complement: 40

Kunashiri was laid down in Oct 1968 and launched in Dec 1968. *Minabe* was laid down in Oct 1969.

Radar: One navigation set.

KUNASHIRI   *1970, Japanese Maritime Safety Agency*

Name	No.	Builders	Commissioned
AMAMI	PM 62	Hitachi Zoosen Co Ltd	29 Mar 1965
KARATSU	PM 64	Hitachi Zoosen Co Ltd	31 Mar 1967
MATSUURA	PM 60	Osaka Shipbuilding Co Ltd	18 Mar 1961
NATORI	PM 63	Hitachi Zoosen Co Ltd	20 Jan 1966
SENDAI	PM 61	Osaka Shipbuilding Co Ltd	21 April 1962

Displacement, tons: 420 standard; 425 normal
Dimensions, feet (metres): 163·3 pp; 181·5 oa × 23 × 7·5 *(49·8; 55·4 × 7 × 2·3)*
Gun: 1—20 mm
Main engines: 2 sets diesels; 1 400 bhp = 16·5 knots *(Matsuura, Sendai);*
 1 800 bhp = 16·8 knots *(Amami, Natori);* 2 600 bhp *(Karatsu)*
Range, miles: 3 500 at 12 knots
Complement: 37

Matsuura was laid down on 16 Oct 1960, launched on 24 Dec 1960. *Sendai* was laid down on 23 Aug 1961, launched on 18 Jan 1962.

Radar: One navigation set

MATSUURA   1975, Japanese Maritime Safety Agency

7 "YAHAGI" CLASS

Name	No.	Builders	Commissioned
CHITOSE	PM 56	Niigata Engineering Co Ltd	30 April 1958
HORONAI	PM 59	Niigata Engineering Co Ltd	4 Feb 1961
OKINAWA	PM 69	Usuki Tekko	1 Oct 1970
SORACHI	PM 57	Niigata Engineering Co Ltd	1 Mar 1959
SUMIDA	PM 55	Niigata Engineering Co Ltd	30 June 1957
YAHAGI	PM 54	Niigata Engineering Co Ltd	31 July 1956
YUBARI	PM 58	Niigata Engineering Co Ltd	15 Mar 1960

Displacement, tons: 333·15 standard; 375·7 normal
Dimensions, feet (metres): 147·3 pp; 164·9 oa × 24 × 7·4 *(44·9; 50·3 × 7·3 × 2·3)*
Gun: 1—40 mm
Main engines: 2 sets diesels; 1 400 bhp = 15·5 knots
Range, miles: 3 500 at 12 knots
Complement: 37

Yahagi was laid down on 9 Dec 1955, launched on 19 May 1956. *Chitose* was laid down on 20 Sep 1957, launched on 24 Feb 1958.

Radar: One navigation set

YAHAGI   1975, Japanese Maritime Safety Agency

Name	No.	Builders	Commissioned
TESIO	PM 53	Uraga Dock Co Ltd	19 Mar 1955

Displacement, tons: 421·5 normal
Dimensions, feet (metres): 149·4 pp; 165 oa × 23 × 8·2 *(45·6; 50·3 × 7 × 2·5)*
Gun: 1—40 mm
Main engines: 2 sets diesels; 1 400 bhp = 15·71 knots
Range, miles: 3 800 at 12 knots
Complement: 37

Laid down on 15 Sep 1954, launched on 12 Jan 1955.

Radar: One navigation set.

TESIO   1975, Japanese Maritime Safety Agency

2 "TOKACHI" CLASS

Name	No.	Builders	Commissioned
TATSUTA	PM 52	Harima Dockyard, Kure	10 Sep 1954
TOKACHI	PM 51	Harima Dockyard, Kure	31 July 1954

Displacement, tons: 336 standard; 381 normal *(Tokachi)*
 324 standard; 369 normal *(Tatsuta)*
Dimensions, feet (metres): 157·5 pp; 164 wl; 170 oa × 21·9 × 11·2 *(48; 50; 51·9 × 6·7 × 3·4)*
Gun: 1—40 mm
Main engines: 2 sets of 4 cycle single acting diesels
 1 500 bhp = 16 knots *(Tokachi)*
 1 400 bhp = 15 knots *(Tatsuta)*
Range, miles: 3 800 at 12 knots
Complement: 37

Tokachi was laid down on 14 Nov 1953, launched on 8 May 1954.

Radar: One navigation set.

TOKACHI   1975, Japanese Maritime Safety Agency

5 "CHIFURI" CLASS

Name	No.	Builders	Commissioned
CHIFURI	PM 18	Nihonkai Jukogyo	April 1952
KOZU	PM 20	Niigata Eng Co Ltd	Dec 1951
SHIKINE	PM 21	Niigata Eng Co Ltd	Jan 1952
DAITO	PM 22	Niigata Eng Co Ltd	Feb 1952
KUROKAMI	PM 19	Nihonkai Jukogyo	Mar 1952

Displacement, tons: 465 standard; 483 normal
Dimensions, feet (metres): 182·7 oa × 25·2 × 8·5 *(55·9 × 7·7 × 2·6)*
Guns: 1—3 in 50 cal; 1—20 mm
Main engines: 2 sets diesels; 1 300 bhp = 15·8 knots
Range, miles: 3 000 at 12 knots
Complement: 45

Radar: One navigation set.

CHIFURI   1975, Japanese Maritime Safety Agency

14 "REBUN" CLASS

Name	No.	Builders	Commissioned
AMAKUSA	PM 09	Nakanihon Jukogyo	Mar 1951
HIRADO	PM 17	Nishinihon Jukogyo	Sep 1951
NOTO	PM 13	Fujinagata Zoosen	Aug 1951
GENKAI	PM 07	Mitsui Tamano	Mar 1951
IKI	PM 05	Hitachi Zoosen	Mar 1951
OKI	PM 06	Mitsui Tamano	Feb 1951
HACHIJO	PM 08	Nakanihon Jukogyo	Mar 1951
KOSHIKI	PM 16	Nishinihon Jukogyo	Aug 1951
OKUSHIRI	PM 10	Hitachi Mukaishima	June 1951
HEKURA	PM 14	Harima Zoosen	June 1951
KUSAKAKI	PM 11	Hitachi Mukaishima	July 1951
REBUN	PM 04	Hitachi Zoosen	Mar 1951
MIKURA	PM 15	Harima Zoosen	July 1951
RISHIRI	PM 12	Fujinagata Zoosen	June 1951

Displacement, tons: 450 standard; 495 normal
Dimensions, feet (metres): 155·2 pp; 164 wl; 171·9 oa × 26·5 × 8·5 *(47·3; 50; 52·4 × 8·1 × 2·6)*
Guns: 1—3 in 50 cal; 1—20 mm
Main engines: 2 sets diesels; 1 300 bhp = 15 knots
Range, miles: 3 000 at 12 knots
Complement: 45

A development of the original "Awaji" class design. All completed in 1951.

Radar: One navigation set.

REBUN   1975, Japanese Maritime Safety Agency

SMALL PATROL VESSELS

1 "NAGARA" CLASS

Name	No.	Builders	Commissioned
KITAKAMI	PS 20	Nippon Kokan Shimizu	Mar 1952

Displacement, tons: 296
Dimensions, feet (metres): 133·4 oa × 23 × 7·2 *(40·7 × 7 × 2·2)*
Gun: 1—40 mm
Main engines: 2 diesels; 2 shafts; 800 bhp = 13·5 knots
Range, miles: 2 000 at 12 knots
Complement: 35

Improved version of the "Sagami" class.

Radar: One navigation set.

KITAKAMI   1975, Japanese Maritime Safety Agency

4 "SAGAMI" CLASS

Name	No.	Builders	Commissioned
CHIKUGO	PS 16	Mitsubishi Shimonoseki	Jan 1952
MOGAMI	PS 11	Ishikawajima H.I.	Sep 1951
SHINANO	PS 15	Mitsubishi Shimonoseki	Dec 1951
KUMANO	PS 17	Mitsubishi Shimonoseki	Feb 1952

Displacement, tons: 258 standard; 275 normal
Dimensions, feet (metres): 122 pp; 126·3 wl; 132·2 oa × 23 × 7·5 *(37·2; 38·5; 40·3 × 7 × 2·3)*
Gun: 1—40 mm
Main engines: 2 sets diesels; 800 bhp = 13·6 knots
Range, miles: 2 000 at 12 knots
Complement: 35

Radar: One navigation set.

MOGAMI   1975, Japanese Maritime Safety Agency

14 "HIDAKA" CLASS

Name	No.	Builders	Commissioned
ASHITAKA	PS 43	Usuki Tekko	Feb 1967
AKIYOSHI	PS 37	Hashihama Zoosen	Feb 1965
HIDAKA	PS 32	Azuma Shipbuilding Co	23 April 1962
HIYAMA	PS 33	Hitachi Shipbuilding Co	Mar 1963
IBUKI	PS 45	Usuki Tekko	Mar 1967
KAMUI	PS 41	Hayashikane Zoosen	Feb 1966
KUNIMI	PS 38	Hayashikane Zoosen	15 Feb 1965
KURAMA	PS 44	Usuki Tekko	Feb 1967
NOBARU	PS 49	Hitachi Mukaishima	Dec 1968
ROKKO	PS 35	Shikuku Dock	Jan 1965
TAKANAWA	PS 36	Hayashikane Zoosen	Jan 1965
TAKATSUKI	PS 39	Kurashima DY	Mar 1966
TOUMI	PS 46	Usuki Tekko	Mar 1968
TSURUGI	PS 34	Hitachi Shipbuilding Co	Mar 1963

Displacement, tons: 166·2 to 164·4 standard; 169·4 normal
Dimensions, feet (metres): 100 pp; 111 oa × 20·8 × 5·5 *(30·5; 33·8 × 6·3 × 1·7)*
Main engines: 1 set diesels; 1 shaft; 690 to 700 bhp = 13·5 knots
Range, miles: 1 200 at 12 knots
Complement: 17

Hidaka was laid down on 4 Oct 1961, launched on 2 Mar 1962. *Kunimi* was built under the 1964 programme, laid down on 15 Nov 1964, launched on 19 Dec 1964.

Radar: One navigation set.

ASHITAKA   *1975, Japanese Maritime Safety Agency*

COASTAL PATROL CRAFT

Name	No.	Builders	Commissioned
TSUKUBA	PS 31	Hitachi Zoosen, Kanagawa	30 May 1962

Displacement, tons: 65
Dimensions, feet (metres): 80·5 × 21·5 × 3·7 *(24·6 × 6·6 × 1·1)*
Main engines: 2 Niigata diesels; 1 800 bhp = 18 knots
Range, miles: 230 at 15 knots
Complement: 19

Radar: One navigation set.

TSUKUBA   *1974, Japanese Maritime Safety Agency*

Name	No.	Builders	Commissioned
ASAMA	PS 47	Shimonoseki Shipyard & Engine Works	Feb 1969
BIZAN	PS 42	Shimonoseki Shipyard & Engine Works	Mar 1966
SHIRAMINE	PS 48	Shimonoseki Shipyard & Engine Works	Dec 1969

Displacement, tons: 40 normal; *Shiramine* 48 normal
Dimensions, feet (metres): 85·3 oa × 18·3 × 2·8 *(26 × 5·6 × 0·9)*
Gun: 1 MG aft
Main engines: 2 Mitsubishi diesels; 1 140 bhp = 21·6 knots. *Shiramine*, 2 Benz (MTU) diesels; 2 200 bhp = 25 knots
Range, miles: 400 at 18 knots; *Shiramine* 250 at 25 knots
Complement: 14

Of light metal construction.

Radar: One navigation set.

BIZAN   *1974, Japanese Maritime Safety Agency*

Name	No.	Builders	Commissioned
AKAGI	PS 40	Hitachi Zoosen, Kanagawa	1965

Displacement, tons: 42
Dimensions, feet (metres): 78·8 oa × 17·8 × 3·2 *(24·0 × 5·4 × 1)*
Main engines: 2 Mercedes Benz diesels; 2 200 bhp = 28 knots
Range, miles: 350 at 21 knots
Complement: 19

Radar: One navigation set.

AKAGI   *1974, Japanese Maritime Safety Agency*

2 "ASAGUMO" CLASS

Name	No.	Builders	Commissioned
ASAGUMO	PC 34	Sumidagawa Zoosen	Mar 1955
MATSUGUMO	PC 35	Sumidagawa Zoosen	Mar 1955

Displacement, tons: 42
Dimensions, feet (metres): 69 × 17·2 × 3·2 (21 × 5·2 × 1)
Main engines: 2 Diesels; 1 400 bhp = 20·5 knots
Complement: 12

Completed in 1954-55. Wooden hulls.

Radar: One navigation set.

3 "HANAYUKI" CLASS

Name	No.	Builders	Commissioned
HANAYUKI	PC 37	Sumidagawa Zoosen	Mar 1959
MINEYUKI	PC 38	Azuma Shipbuilding	Mar 1959
ISOYUKI	PC 39	Sumidagawa Zoosen	Feb 1960

Displacement, tons: 46
Dimensions, feet (metres): 72 oa × 17·6 × 3·2 (22 × 5·4 × 1)
Main engines: 3 diesels; 1 500 bhp = 20·7 knots (Hanayuki)
  2 diesels; 1 800 bhp = 21·3 knots (Isoyuki)
Complement: 13

Of light wooden hulls.

Radar: One navigation set.

8 "AKIZUKI" CLASS

Name	No.	Builders	Commissioned
AKIZUKI	PC 64	Mitsubishi Heavy Industries Co Ltd	28 Feb 1974
HATAGUMO	PC 76	Mitsubishi Heavy Industries Co Ltd	21 Feb 1976
ISEYUKI	PC 73	Mitsubishi Heavy Industries Co Ltd	31 July 1975
MAKIGUMO	PC 75	Mitsubishi Heavy Industries Co Ltd	19 Mar 1976
SHINONOME	PC 65	Mitsubishi Heavy Industries Co Ltd	25 Feb 1974
URAYUKI	PC 72	Mitsubishi Heavy Industries Co Ltd	31 May 1975
HAMAZUKI	PC 77	Mitsubishi Heavy Industries Co Ltd	29 Nov 1976
ISOZUKI	PC 78	Mitsubishi Heavy Industries Co Ltd	18 Mar 1977

Displacement, tons: 74
Dimensions, feet (metres): 83·5 oa × 20·7 × 9·8 (26 × 8·2 × 3)
Main engines: 3 Mitsubishi diesels; 3 000 bhp = 22·1 knots
Range, miles: 220 at 22 knots
Complement: 10

Radar: One navigation set.

AKIZUKI   1974, Japanese Maritime Safety Agency

14 "MATSUYUKI" CLASS

Name	No.	Builders	Commissioned
ASAGIRI	PC 47	Hitachi Kanagawa	Mar 1967
HAMAGIRI	PC 48	Sumidagawa Zoosen	Mar 1968
HAMANAMI	PC 52	Sumidagawa Zoosen	Mar 1970
HAMAYUKI	PC 43	Hitachi Kanagawa	Mar 1965
HAYAGIRI	PC 51	Hitachi Kanagawa	Mar 1969
KOMAYUKI	PC 45	Hitachi Kanagawa	Mar 1966
MATSUNAMI	PC 53	Hitachi Kanagawa	Mar 1970
MATSUYUKI	PC 40	Hitachi Kanagawa	Mar 1964
SAGIRI	PC 49	Hitachi Kanagawa	Mar 1968
SETOGIRI	PC 50	Hitachi Kanagawa	Mar 1969
SHIMAYUKI	PC 41	Hitachi Kanagawa	Jan 1964
TAMAYUKI	PC 42	Hitachi Kanagawa	Feb 1965
UMIGIRI	PC 46	Hitachi Kanagawa	Mar 1967
YAMAYUKI	PC 44	Hitachi Kanagawa	Mar 1966

Displacement, tons: 40-60 tons
Dimensions, feet (metres): 69 oa × 16·6 × 3·2 (21 × 5·1 × 1)
Gun: 1—13 mm
Main engines: 2 Mercedes Benz (MTU) diesels; 2 200 bhp = 26·3 knots;
  PC 48 1 140 bhp = 14·6 knots; PC 52 = 21·8 knots; PC 53 = 20·8 knots
Range, miles: About 300 miles at near maximum speed
Complement: 10

PCs 40-47 and 49-51 were built of light alloy frames with wooden hulls. PCs 48 and 52 were built of steel; PC 53 was built completely of light alloy.

Radar: One navigation set.

MATSUYUKI   1975, Japanese Maritime Safety Agency

17 "SHIKINAMI" CLASS

Name	No.	Builders	Commissioned
ASOYUKI	PC 74	Hitachi Kanagawa	Mar 1975
HARUZUKI	PC 61	Mitsubishi Shimonoseki	Jan 1972
ISENAMI	PC 57	Hitachi Kanagawa	Feb 1972
KIYONAMI	PC 69	Mitsubishi Shimonoseki	Oct 1973
KIYOZUKI	PC 62	Mitsubishi Shimonoseki	Dec 1973
MINEGUMO	PC 68	Mitsubishi Shimonoseki	Nov 1973
MOCHIZUKI	PC 60	Hitachi Kanagawa	Dec 1972
MUTSUKI	PC 59	Hitachi Kanagawa	Dec 1972
OKINAMI	PC 70	Hitachi Kanagawa	Feb 1974
SHIKINAMI	PC 54	Mitsubishi Shimonoseki	Feb 1971
TAKANAMI	PC 58	Mitsubishi Shimonoseki	Nov 1971
TAMANAMI	PC 67	Mitsubishi Shimonoseki	Dec 1973
TOMONAMI	PC 55	Mitsubishi Shimonoseki	Mar 1971
URANAMI	PC 66	Hitachi Kanagawa	Dec 1973
URAZUKI	PC 63	Hitachi Kanagawa	Jan 1973
WAKAGUMO	PC 71	Hitachi Kanagawa	Mar 1974
WAKANAMI	PC 56	Mitsubishi Shimonoseki	Oct 1971

Displacement, tons: 44
Dimensions, feet (metres): 69 oa × 17·4 × 3·2 (21 × 5·3 × 1)
Main engines: 2 Mercedes Benz (MTU) Diesels; 2 200 bhp = 26·5 knots
Range, miles: 280 miles at near maximum speed
Complement: 10

Built completely of light alloy.

Radar: One navigation set.

KIYONAMI   1973, Japanese Maritime Safety Agency

155 15 METRE MOTOR LAUNCH TYPE

CL 21—156, 301—319

Displacement, tons: 20·2 full load
Dimensions, feet (metres): 49·2 × 13·5 × 3·1 *(15 × 4·1 × 1)*
Main engines: Diesels; 2 shafts; 520 bhp = 19 knots
Range, miles: 160 at 15 knots
Complement: 6

For coastal patrol and rescue duties. Since 1971 about 20 of this class, built of high tensile steel, have been delivered each year.

Radar: One navigation set.

CL 127

1973, Japanese Maritime Safety Agency

12 HARBOUR PATROL CRAFT

CS 100, 107, 108, 116, 118—120, 122—126

SURVEYING VESSELS

Name	*No.*	*Builders*	*Commissioned*
SHOYO	HL 01	Hitachi Zoosen, Maizuru	Feb 1972

Displacement, tons: 2 044 standard
Dimensions, feet (metres): 262·4 × 40·3 × 13·8 *(80 × 12·3 × 4·2)*
Main engines: 2 Fuji V-12; 4 800 hp; 1 shaft = 17·4 knots
Range, miles: 8 340 at 16 knots
Complement: 73

Launched 18 Sep 1971. Fully equipped for all types of hydrographic and oceanographic work.

Radar: Two navigation sets.

SHOYO

1973, Japanese Maritime Safety Agency

Name	*No.*	*Builders*	*Commissioned*
TAKUYO	HL 02	Niigata Engineering Co Ltd	March 1957

Displacement, tons: 880 standard
Dimensions, feet (metres): 204·7 oa × 31·2 × 10·7 *(62·4 × 9·5 × 3·3)*
Main engines: 2 sets diesels; 1 300 bhp = 14 knots
Range, miles: 8 000 at 12 knots
Complement: 50

Laid down on 19 May 1956, launched on 19 Dec 1956.

Radar: One navigation set.

TAKUYO

1975, Japanese Maritime Safety Agency

Name	*No.*	*Builders*	*Commissioned*
MEIYO	HL 03	Nagoya Shipbuilding & Engineering Co, Nagoya	15 Mar 1963

Displacement, tons: 486 normal
Measurement, tons: 360 gross
Dimensions, feet (metres): 133 wl; 146 oa × 26·5 × 9·5 *(40·6; 44·5 × 8·1 × 2·9)*
Main engines: 1 set diesel; 700 bhp = 12 knots
Range, miles: 5 000 at 11 knots
Complement: 40

Laid down on 14 Sep 1962, launched 22 Dec 1962. Controllable pitch propeller.

Radar: One navigation set.

MEIYO

1975, Japanese Maritime Safety Agency

Name	*No.*	*Builders*	*Commissioned*
HEIYO	HM 04	Shimuzu Dockyard, Nipponkokan Kabushiki Kaisha	Mar 1955

Displacement, tons: 69
Dimensions, feet (metres): 76·5 oa × 14·5 × 8 *(23·3 × 4·4 × 2·4)*
Main engines: Diesel; 150 bhp = 9 knots
Range, miles: 670 at 9 knots
Complement: 13

Radar: One navigation set.

HEIYO

1975, Japanese Maritime Safety Agency

Name	No.	Builders	Commissioned
TENYO	HM 05	Yokohama Yacht Co	Mar 1961

Displacement, tons: 171
Dimensions, feet (metres): 99·1 oa × 19·2 × 9·2 *(30·2 × 5·9 × 2·8)*
Main engines: Diesels; 230 bhp = 10 knots
Range, miles: 3 160 at 10 knots
Complement: 25

Radar: One navigation set.

TENYO   *1975, Japanese Maritime Safety Agency*

Name	No.	Builders	Commissioned
KAIYO	HM 06	Nagoya Shipbuilding & Engineering Co, Nagoya	14 Mar 1964

Displacement, tons: 378 normal
Dimensions, feet (metres): 132·5 wl; 146 oa × 26·5 × 7·8 *(40·4; 44·5 × 8·1 × 2·4)*
Main engines: 1 set diesels; 450 bhp = 12 knots
Range, miles: 6 100 at 11 knots
Complement: 34

Controllable pitch propeller.

Radar: One navigation set.

KAIYO   *1975, Japanese Maritime Safety Agency*

Note. There are 21 surveying launches of 5-8 tons.

NAVIGATION AID VESSELS

Name	No.	Builders	Commissioned
WAKAKUSA	LL 01	Hitachi Innoshima Dockyard	April 1948

Displacement, tons: 1 760 normal
Dimensions, feet (metres): 226·4 oa × 32·2 × 19·1 *(69·1 × 9·8 × 5·8)*
Main engines: 2 100 hp
Range, miles: 4 800 at 9 knots

Purchased from Osaka Shosen Kaisha in Jan 1956. Rated as Navigation Aid Vessel (Lighthouse Supply Ship).

Radar: One navigation set.

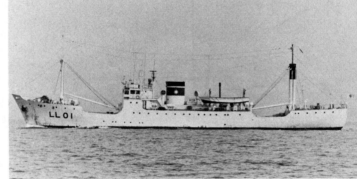

WAKAKUSA   *1971, Japanese Maritime Safety Agency*

Name	No.	Builders	Commissioned
GINGA	LL 12	Osaka Shipbuilding Co Ltd	30 June 1954

Displacement, tons: 500
Dimensions, feet (metres): 135·5 oa × 31·2 × 13·9 *(41·3 × 9·4 × 4·2)*
Main engines: 2 diesels; 420 bhp = 11·26 knots
Range, miles: 2 800 at 10 knots
Complement: 38

Ginga was laid down on 11 Nov 1953 and launched on 6 May 1954. Equipped with 15 ton derrick for laying buoys. Rated as Navigation Aid Vessel (Buoy Tender).

Radar: One navigation set

GINGA   *1971, Japanese Maritime Safety Agency*

Name	No.	Builders	Commissioned
MYOJO	LM 11	Nipponkokan, Tsurumi	Mar 1974

Displacement, tons: 318 normal
Dimensions, feet (metres): 88·6 oa × 39·4 × 8·8 *(27 × 12 × 2·7)*
Main engines: 2 sets diesels; 600 bhp = 11·1 knots
Range, miles: 1 360 at 10 knots
Complement: 49

Completed in Mar 1974 to replace an identical ship of the same name, completed in 1967, which was lost in collision April 1972. Catamaran type buoy tender, propelled by controllable pitch propeller, this ship is employed in maintenance and position adjustment service to floating aids to navigation.

MYOJO   1974, Japanese Maritime Safety Agency

Name	No.	Builders	Commissioned
HOKUTO	LL 11	Kawasaki H.I. Co Ltd	Mar 1952
KAIO	LL 13	Namura Zoosen	Mar 1955

Displacement, tons: 616 standard
Dimensions, feet (metres): 153·8 × 33·8 × 8·9 *(46·9 × 10·3 × 2·7)*
Main engines: Recip; 400 ihp = 10·4 knots
Range, miles: 1 821
Complement: 38

There are also 9 LMs (LM 101 to LM 109) and 15 navigation and buoy tenders for miscellaneous service.

UNDERWATER RESEARCH VESSEL

Name	No.	Builders	Commissioned
SHINKAI	HU 06	Kawasaki Heavy Industries Ltd	Mar 1969

Displacement, tons: 91
Dimensions, feet (metres): 54·2 oa × 18·1 × 13 *(16·5 × 5·5 × 4)*
Main engines: 1 set electric motors; 11 kW
Range, miles: 4·6 at 2·3 knots
Complement: 4

SHINKAI   1970, Japanese Maritime Safety Agency

Laid down in Sep 1967, launched in Mar 1968. An underwater vehicle designed for carrying out research on biological and underground resources of the continental shelves. With a main propeller and two auxiliary ones installed on each side of the hull, this ship can dive to 2 000 feet and stay on the sea bed for sampling, observing and photographing.

FIRE FIGHTING CRAFT

4 "HIRYU" CLASS

Name	No.	Builders	Commissioned
HIRYU	FL 01	Nipponkokan Kabushiki Kaisha, Asano Dockyard	4 Mar 1969
NANRYU	FL 03	Nipponkokan Kabushiki Kaisha, Asano Dockyard	4 Mar 1971
SHORYU	FL 02	Nipponkokan Kabushiki Kaisha, Asano Dockyard	4 Mar 1970
KAIRYU	FL 04	Nipponkokan Tsurumi	4 Mar 1977

Displacement, tons: 251 normal
Dimensions, feet (metres): 90·2 oa × 34·1 × 7·2 *(27·5 × 10·4 × 2·2)*
Main engines: 2 sets diesels; 2 200 bhp = 13·5 knots
Range, miles: 395 at 13·4 knots
Complement: 14

Hiryu, a catamaran type fire boat, was laid down in Oct 1968, launched 21 Jan 1969. Designed and built for firefighting services to large tankers. *Shoryu* was launched on 18 Jan 1970, and *Nanryu* was launched on 16 Jan 1971.

Radar: One navigation set.

HIRYU   1970, Japanese Maritime Safety Agency

7 "NUNOBIKI" CLASS

Name	No.	Builders	Commissioned	
KOTOBIKI	FM 05	Yokohama Yacht Co Ltd	Jan	1976
NACHI	FM 06	Sumidagawa Zoosen	Feb	1976
NUNOBIKI	FM 01	Yokohama Yacht Co Ltd		1974
OTOWA	FM 03	Sumidagawa Zoosen	Dec	1974
SHIRAITO	FM 04	Yokohama Yacht Co Ltd	Feb	1975
YODO	FM 02	Yokohama Yacht Co Ltd	Mar	1975
KEGON	FM 07	Yokohama Yacht Co Ltd	Jan	1977

Displacement, tons: 87
Dimensions, feet (metres): 75·4 oa × 19·7 × 10·5 *(23 × 6 × 3·2)*
Main engines: 1 Mercedes-Benz (MTU) diesel plus 2 Nissan diesels;
   1 100 bhp + 500 bhp = 14 knots
Range, miles: 180 at 14 knots
Complement: 12

Radar: One navigation set.

NUNOBIKI   *1974*

POLLUTION CLEARANCE CRAFT

SOKAI

92 ft long *(28 metres)* with 2 diesels, 1 080 hp = 11 knots; completed Nov 1974. Catamaran

---

UTILITY LAUNCHES

There are 50 local and miscellaneous boats of various sizes and employment.

JORDAN

Ministerial

Minister of Defence:
 Mudar Badran (Premier)

Diplomatic Representation

Defence Attaché in London:
 Brigadier Rm. Khatkhuda

Coastal Guard

It was officially stated in 1969 that Jordan had no naval force known as such, but the Jordan Coastal Guard, sometimes called the Jordan Sea Force, took orders directly from the Director of Operations at General Headquarters. There is no longer a flotilla in the Dead Sea.

Base

Aqaba

Personnel

a) 1977: 300 officers and men
b) Voluntary

Mercantile Marine

Lloyd's Register of Shipping: 1 vessel of 200 tons gross

LIGHT FORCES

HUSSEIN ABDALLAH

Wooden hulled of 40 ft *(12 m)* acquired in Aug 1974.

1 BERTRAM TYPE (COASTAL PATROL CRAFT)

Displacement, tons: 7
Dimensions, feet (metres): 30·4 × 10·8 × 1·6 *(9·2 × 3·3 × 0·5)*
Guns: 1—12·7 mm; 1—7·2 mm
Main engines: Diesels = 24 knots
Complement: 8

Glass fibre hull.

4 25 ft TYPE (COASTAL PATROL CRAFT)

Aluminium hulls.

4 PATROL CRAFT

Wooden-hulled craft of about 18 ft—unarmed.

KAMPUCHEA (CAMBODIA)

The Marine Royale Khmer was established on 1 March 1954 and became Marine Nationale Khmer on 9 October 1970. With the imminent victory of the forces of Khmer Rouge in April-May 1975, several ships (listed in Deletions section) escaped from Khmer waters.
Originally Cambodia, became known as Khmer Rouge Republic and is now variously known by that name, Cambodian Peoples' Republic or Kampuchea (now officially used by Lloyd's).

Ministerial

Deputy Prime Minister for National Defence:
 Son Sen

Personnel

(a) 1975: 11 000 officers and men including Marine Corps (4 000 officers and men) (current situation not known)
(b) 18 months National Service

Mercantile Marine

Lloyd's Register of Shipping:
 2 vessels of 1 208 tons gross

DELETIONS

Corvettes

1975 E 311 to Thailand (16 May), E 312 to Subic Bay, Philippines (2 May). P111 and P112 to Subic Bay (17 Apr) and to Philippine Navy.

Light Forces

1975 VR1 and VR2 (ex-Yugoslav "101" class) believed sunk by US aircraft during *Mayaguez* incident (13 May).

LIGHT FORCES

17 Ex-US "SWIFT" CLASS (COASTAL PATROL CRAFT)

Displacement, tons: 22·5
Dimensions, feet (metres): 50× 13 × 3·5 *(15 × 4 × 1·1)*
Guns: 1—81 mm mortar; 3—50 cal MG
Main engines: 2 diesels; 960 hp; 2 shafts = 28 knots
Complement: 6

Transferred in 1972-73

2 Ex-US AVR TYPE (COASTAL PATROL CRAFT)

VR 3   VR 4

Displacement, tons: 30
Dimensions, feet (metres): 63 × 13 × 4·6 *(19·1 × 4 × 1·4)*
Guns: 4—12·7 mm MG
Main engines: GM Diesel 500 bhp = 15 knots
Complement: 12

65 Ex-US PBR MARK 1 and II (RIVER PATROL CRAFT)

Displacement, tons: 8
Dimensions, feet (metres): 32 × 11 × 2·6 *(9·8 × 3·4 × 0·8)*
Guns: 3—50 cal MG; 1 grenade launcher
Main engines: 2 geared diesels; water jets = 25 knots
Complement: 5

Transferred 1973-74.

PBR Mk II Type   *United States Navy*

3 Ex-CHINESE "YU-LIN" CLASS (COASTAL PATROL CRAFT)

VP 1	VP 2	VP 3

Displacement, tons: 7·7 standard; 9·7 full load
Dimensions, feet (metres): 40 × 9·5 × 3·5 *(13 × 2·9 × 1·1)*
Guns: 2—14·5 mm; 2—12·7 mm
Main engines: Diesel, 300 bhp = 24 knots
Complement: 10

Transferred from the People's Republic of China in Jan 1968. Built in Shanghai.

1 Ex-HDML TYPE (COASTAL PATROL CRAFT)

VP 212 (ex-*VP 748*, ex-*HDML 1223*)

Displacement, tons: 46 standard; 54 full load
Dimensions, feet (metres): 72 oa × 16 × 5·5 *(22 × 4·9 × 1·7)*
Guns: 2—20 mm; 4—7·5 mm MG
Main engines: 2 diesels; 2 shafts; 300 bhp = 10 knots
Complement: 8

Former British harbour defence motor launch of the HDML type. Transferred from the British Navy to the French Navy in 1950 and again transferred from the French Navy to the MNK in 1956.

AMPHIBIOUS VESSELS

1 Ex-US "LCU 1466" CLASS

T 917 (ex-US *YFU*, ex-*LCU 1577*)

Displacement, tons: 320 full load
Dimensions, feet (metres): 119 oa × 32·7 × 5 *(36·3 × 10 × 1·5)*
Guns: 2—20 mm
Main engines: Diesels; 675 bhp; 3 shafts = 10 knots
Complement: 13

Transferred Oct 1969.

US "LCU 1466" Class   *1970, Defoe Shipbuilding*

1 EDIC TYPE

T 916 (ex-*EDIC 606*)

Displacement, tons: 292 standard; 650 full load
Dimensions, feet (metres): 193·5 × 39·2 × 4·5 *(59 × 12 × 1·4)*
Guns: 1—81 mm mortar; 2—12·7 mm MG
Main engines: 2 MGO diesels; 2 shafts; 1 000 bhp = 10 knots
Complement: 16 (1 officer, 15 men)

Completed and transferred from the French Government in Aug 1969.

1 Ex-US YFU TYPE

SKILAK (ex-US *YFU*) T 920

Of approximately 300 tons. Transferred in Nov 1953.

4 Ex-US "LCU 501" CLASS

T 914 (ex-US *LCU 783*)	**T 918** (ex-US *LCU 646*)
T 915 (ex-US *LCU 1421*)	**T 919** (ex-US *LCU 1385*)

Displacement, tons: 180 standard; 360 full load
Dimensions, feet (metres): 115 wl; 119 oa × 34 × 6 *(35·1; 36·3 × 10·4 × 1·8)*
Guns: 2—20 mm
Main engines: 3 diesels; 3 shafts; 675 bhp = 8 knots
Complement: 12

LCU 783 and LCU 1421 were transferred on 31 May 1962. T919 (ex-US *LCU 1577*) was sunk by a mine on 5 May 1970, her number being taken by new T919 transferred in Nov 1972 at same time as T918. Both these had operated as YFU—68 and 56 respectively.

US "LCU 501" Class   *1969, Marine Nat. Khmer*

TUG

PINGOUIE R 911 (ex-US *YTL 556*)

KENYA

Ministerial

Minister of Defence:
Mr James Samuel Gichuru

Establishment

The Kenya Navy was inaugurated on 12 Dec 1964, the first anniversary of Kenya's independence.

Administration

Commander, Kenya Navy: Lieut. Col. J. C. J. Kimaro

Personnel

(a) 1977: 350 officers and men
(b) Volunteers

Mercantile Marine

Lloyd's Register of Shipping: 19 vessels of 15 469 tons gross

Prefix to Ships' Names

KNS

Base

Mombasa

LIGHT FORCES

3 BROOKE MARINE 32·6 metre TYPE
(LARGE PATROL CRAFT)

Name	No.	Builders	Commissioned
MADARAKA	P 3121	Brooke Marine, Lowestoft	16 June 1975
JAMHURI	P 3122	Brooke Marine, Lowestoft	16 June 1975
HARAMBEE	P 3123	Brooke Marine, Lowestoft	22 Aug 1975

Displacement, tons: 120 standard; 145 full load
Dimensions, feet (metres): 107 × 20 × 5·6 *(32·6 × 6·1 × 1·7)*
Guns: 2—40 mm
Main engines: 2 Ruston-Paxman Valenta diesels; 5 400 bhp; 2 shafts = 25·5 knots
Range, miles: 2 500 at 12 knots
Complement: 21 (3 officers, 18 men)

Ordered 10 May 1973. *Madaraka* launched 28 Jan 1975, *Jamhuri* 14 Mar 1975, *Harambe* 2 May 1975.

HARAMBEE

7/1976, Michael D. J. Lennon

BROOKE MARINE 37·5 metre TYPE
(LARGE PATROL CRAFT)

Name	No.	Builders	Commissioned
MAMBA	P 3100	Brooke Marine, Lowestoft	7 Feb 1974

Displacement, tons: 125 standard; 160 full load
Dimensions, feet (metres): 123 × 22·5 × 5·2 *(37·5 × 6·9 × 1·6)*
Guns: 2—40 mm Bofors
Main engines: 2—16 cylinder Rustons diesels; 4 000 hp = 25 knots
Range, miles: 3 300 at 13 knots
Complement: 25 (3 officers, 22 men)

Laid down 17 Feb 1972.

MAMBA

1974

3 VOSPER 31 metre TYPE (LARGE PATROL CRAFT)

Name	No.	Builders	Commissioned
CHUI	P 3112	Vosper Ltd, Portsmouth	7 July 1966
NDOVU	P 3117	Vosper Ltd, Portsmouth	27 July 1966
SIMBA	P 3110	Vosper Ltd, Portsmouth	23 May 1966

Displacement, tons: 96 standard; 109 full load
Dimensions, feet (metres): 95 wl; 103 oa × 19·8 × 5·8 *(28·8; 31·4 × 6 × 1·8)*
Guns: 2—40 mm Bofors
Main engines: 2 Paxman Ventura diesels; 2 800 bhp = 24 knots
Range, miles: 1 000 at economical speed; 1 500 at 16 knots
Complement: 23 (3 officers and 20 ratings)

The first ships specially built for the Kenya Navy. Ordered on 28 Oct 1964. *Simba* was launched on 9 Sep 1965. All three left Portsmouth on 22 Aug 1966 and arrived at their base in Mombasa on 4 Oct 1966. Air-conditioned. Fitted with modern radar communications equipment and roll damping fins.

SIMBA

1973, Kenyan Navy

KOREA (North)

Ministerial

Minister of Peoples Armed Forces:
O Chin-u

Administration

Commander of the Navy: Rear Admiral Yu Chang Kwon

Personnel

(a) 1977: 18 000 officers and men (40 000 reserves)
(b) National Service; 5 years

Strength of the Fleet

Type	Active
Submarines—Patrol	13

Frigates	2
Fast Attack Craft—Missile	18
Fast Attack Craft—Torpedo	157
Fast Attack Craft—Gun	44
Large Patrol Craft	21
Coastal Patrol Craft	30
LCMs	90
Trawlers etc.	105

Bases

Main: Wonsan (East), Chinnampo (West)
Minor: Ch'ongjin, Haeju, Nampo, Najin, Munchon, Pipa-got, Cha-ho, Mayang Do, Sagon-ni.

Mercantile Marine

Lloyd's Register of Shipping:
19 vessels of 89 482 tons gross

SUBMARINES

9 Ex-CHINESE "ROMEO" CLASS (PATROL TYPE)

Displacement, tons: 1 000 surfaced; 1 600 dived
Dimensions, feet (metres): 249·3 × 24 × 14·5 *(76 × 7·3 × 4·4)*
Torpedo tubes: 6—21 in (bow); 18 torpedoes
Main machinery: 2 diesels—4 000 bhp; 2 electric motors—4 000 hp; 2 shafts
Speed, knots: 17 surfaced; 14 dived
Complement: 65

Two transferred from China 1973, two in 1974 and three in 1975. Local building at Mayand Do provided two more in 1976. Continuing programme with slightly different dimensions etc. Stationed on West coast (Yellow Sea).

Chinese "ROMEO" Class

4 Ex-SOVIET "WHISKEY" CLASS (PATROL TYPE)

Displacement, tons: 1 030 surfaced; 1 350 dived
Dimensions, feet (metres): 249·3 × 22 × 15 *(76 × 6·7 × 4·6)*
Torpedo tubes: 6—21 in (4 bow, 2 stern); 18 torpedoes carried normally (or up to 40 mines)
Main machinery: 2 diesels; 4 000 bhp; 2 electric motors; 2 500 hp; 2 shafts
Speed, knots: 17 surfaced; 15 dived
Range, miles: 13 000 at 8 knots
Complement: 60

Stationed on East Coast (Sea of Japan).

"WHISKEY" Class   *1975*

FRIGATES

2 "NAJIN" CLASS

Displacement, tons: 1 800
Dimensions, feet (metres): 330 × 33 × 9 *(100 × 10 × 2·7)*
Guns: 2—3·9 in *(100 mm)*, 56 cal; 4—57 mm (twin); 4—25 mm (twin vertical); 8—14·5 mm
Mines: 30 (estimated)
Main engines: 2 diesels; 5 000 bhp; 2 shafts
Speed, knots: 25 (estimated)
Complement: 90 (estimated)

Built in North Korea. First laid down 1971-72, completed 1973, second completed 1975, third probably to be launched in 1977.

Radar: Surface Search, Skin Head; IFF, Ski Pole.

LIGHT FORCES

1 or 2 Ex-SOVIET "TRAL" CLASS (LARGE PATROL CRAFT)

Displacement, tons: 475
Dimensions, feet (metres): 203·5 × 23·8 × 7·8 *(62 × 7·2 × 2·4)*
Guns: 1—3·9 in *(100 mm)* 56 cal; 3—37 mm (singles); 4—12·7 mm MG
A/S weapons: 2 DC racks
Mines: 30
Main engines: 2 diesels; 2 800 hp; 2 shafts
Speed, knots: 18
Complement: 55

An elderly class of Fleet Minesweepers of which some 4-5 were transferred by USSR in mid 1950s. Used for escort purposes.

Radar: Surface search: Skin Head. IFF: Yard Rake.

"TRAL" Class

3 "SARIWAN" CLASS (LARGE PATROL CRAFT)

Displacement, tons: 475
Dimensions, feet (metres): 203·5 × 24 × 7·8 *(62·1 × 7·3 × 2·4)*
Guns: 1—85 mm; 2—57 mm (twin); 8—14·5 mm
Mines: 30
Main engines: 2 diesels; 3 000 bhp; 2 shafts

Speed, knots: 21 (estimated)
Complement: 65-70

Built in North Korea in the mid 1960s.

Radar: Surface search: Skin Head. IFF: Ski Pole or Yard Rake.

15 SOVIET "SO 1" CLASS (LARGE PATROL CRAFT)

Displacement, tons: 215 light; 250 normal
Dimensions, feet (metres): 138·6 × 20·0 × 9·2 *(42·3 × 6·1 × 2·8)*
Guns: 1—85 mm; 2—37 mm (twin); 4—14·5 mm MG
Main engines: 3 diesels; 6 000 bhp = 29 knots
Range, miles: 1 100 at 13 knots
Complement: 30

6 transferred by USSR in 1957-58. Remainder built in North Korea.

Soviet "SO 1" Class (guns differ in Korean version)   *1972*

8 Ex-SOVIET "OSA I" CLASS (FAST ATTACK CRAFT—MISSILE)

Displacement, tons: 165 standard; 200 full load
Dimensions, feet (metres): 128·7 × 25·1 × 5·9 *(39·3 × 7·7 × 1·8)*
Missile launchers: 4 in two pairs abreast for Styx missiles
Guns: 4—30 mm (1 twin forward, and aft)
Main engines: 3 diesels; 13 000 bhp = 32 knots
Range, miles: 800 at 25
Complement: 25

The combination of the "Osa" flotilla and the "Komar" units both armed with the very potent 23 mile range Styx missile, provides a powerful striking force on the South Korean border and within 250 miles of Japan.

"OSA I" Class   *1970*

10 Ex-SOVIET "KOMAR" CLASS (FAST ATTACK CRAFT—MISSILE)

Displacement, tons: 70 standard; 80 full load
Dimensions, feet (metres): 83·7 × 19·8 × 5·0 *(25·5 × 6·0 × 1·8)*
Missile launchers: 2 for Styx missiles
Guns: 2—25 mm (1 twin forward)
Main engines: 4 diesels; 4 shafts; 4 800 bhp = 40 knots
Range, miles: 400 at 30 knots

See note under "Osa" class above.

"KOMAR" Class

8 Ex-CHINESE "SHANGHAI" CLASS (FAST ATTACK CRAFT—GUN)

Displacement, tons: 120 standard; 155 full load
Dimensions, feet (metres): 128 × 18 × 5·6 *(39 × 5·5 × 1·7)*
Guns: 4—37 mm (twin); 4—25 mm (abaft bridge);
  2—3 in *(75 mm)* recoilless rifles (bow)
A/S weapons: 8 DC
Main engines: 4 diesels; 4 800 bhp = 30 knots
Mines: Rails can be fitted for 10 mines
Range, miles: 800 at 17 knots
Complement: 25

Acquired from China since 1967. Skin Head radar.

"SHANGHAI" Class.

8 Ex-CHINESE "SWATOW" CLASS (FAST ATTACK CRAFT—GUN)

Displacement, tons: 80
Dimensions, feet (metres): 83·5 × 19 × 6·5 *(25·5 × 5·8 × 2)*
Guns: 4—37 mm (twins); 2—12·7 mm
A/S weapons: 8 DC
Main engines: 4 diesels; 3 000 bhp = 28 knots
Range, miles: 500 at 28 knots
Complement: 17

Transferred from China in 1968.

4 "CHODO" CLASS (FAST ATTACK CRAFT—GUN)

Displacement, tons: 130 (estimated)
Dimensions, feet (metres): 140 × 19 × 8·5 *(42·7 × 5·8 × 2·6)*
Guns: 1—3 in *(76 mm)* 50 cal (forward); 3—37 mm (single); 4—25 mm (twin, vertical)
Main engines: Diesels; 2 shafts; 6 000 bhp
Speed, knots: 24 (estimated)
Complement: 40 (estimated)

Built in North Korea in mid 1960s.

Radar. Skin Head.

4 "K-48" CLASS (FAST ATTACK CRAFT—GUN)

Displacement, tons: 110 (estimated)
Dimensions, feet (metres): 125 × 18 × 5 *(38·1 × 5·5 × 1·5)*
Guns: 1—3 in *(76 mm)* 50 cal (forward); 3—37 mm (single);
4/6—14·5 mm MG (twin)
Main engines: Diesels; 4/5 000 bhp; 2 shafts
Speed, knots: 24 (estimated)

May have been built in North Korea in mid 1950s.

Radar: Skin Head.

20 Ex-SOVIET "MO IV" CLASS (FAST ATTACK CRAFT—GUN)

Displacement, tons: 56
Dimensions, feet (metres): 88·5 × 13·2 × 5 *(27 × 4 × 1·5)*
Guns: 1—37 mm; 1/2—14·5 mm MG
Main engines: 2 Skoda diesels; 2 600 hp = 25 knots
Complement: 20

Transferred in 1950s. Built in 1945-47. Wooden hulls.

4 Ex-SOVIET "SHERSHEN" CLASS
(FAST ATTACK CRAFT—TORPEDO)

Displacement, tons: 150 standard; 160 full load
Dimensions, feet (metres): 115·5 × 23 × 5 *(35·2 × 7·1 × 1·5)*
Guns: 4—30 mm (2 twin)
Torpedo tubes: 4—21 (single)
A/S weapons: 12 DC
Main engines: 3 diesels; 3 shafts; 13 000 bhp = 41 knots
Complement: 16

Transferred in 1973-74.

Soviet "SHERSHEN" Class   *1970*

60 Ex-SOVIET "P 6" CLASS
(FAST ATTACK CRAFT—TORPEDO)

Displacement, tons: 66 standard; 75 full load
Dimensions, feet (metres): 84·2 × 20 × 6 *(25·7 × 6·1 × 1·8)*
Guns: 4—25 mm
Torpedo tubes: 2—21 in (or mines or DC)
Main engines: 4 diesels; 4 800 hp; 4 shafts = 43 knots
Range, miles: 450 at 30 knots

There is a growing number of these craft in N. Korea with local building programme in hand.

Radar: Pothead or Skin Head.

"P 6" Class   *1972*

12 Ex-SOVIET "P 4" CLASS (FAST ATTACK CRAFT—TORPEDO)

Displacement, tons: 25
Dimensions, feet (metres): 62·7 × 11·6 × 5·6 *(19·1 × 3·5 × 1·7)*
Guns: 2—MG
Torpedo tubes: 2—18 in
Main engines: 2 diesels; 2 200 bhp = 50 knots.

Built in 1951-57. Aluminium hulls.

"P 4" Class   *1971*

15 "IWON" CLASS (FAST ATTACK CRAFT—TORPEDO)

Displacement, tons: 40
Dimensions, feet (metres): 63 × 12 × 5 *(19·2 × 3·7 × 1·5)*
Guns: 4—25 mm (twin, vertical)
Torpedo tubes: 2—21 in

Built in North Korea in late 1950s. Similar to older Soviet "P 2" class.

Radar: Skin Head.

"CHAHO" CLASS (FAST ATTACK CRAFT—TORPEDO)

Reported as building in North Korea.

6 "AN JU" CLASS (FAST ATTACK CRAFT—TORPEDO)

Displacement, tons: 35
Dimensions, feet (metres): 65 × 12 × 6 *(19·8 × 3·7 × 1·8)*
Guns: 2—25 mm (twin, vertical)
Torpedo tubes: 2—21 in

Built in North Korea in 1960s.

60 "SIN HUNG" and "KOSONG" CLASSES
(FAST ATTACK CRAFT—TORPEDO)

Displacement, tons: 35
Dimensions, feet (metres): 60 × 11 × 5·5 *(18·3 × 3·4 × 1·7)*
Guns: 2—14·5 mm (twin)
Torpedo tubes: 2—18 in or 2—21 in

Built in North Korea mid 1950s to 1970. Frequently operated on South Korean border. All resemble the Soviet "D-3" class of 25 years ago.

1 or 2 Ex-SOVIET "ARTILLERIST" CLASS
(LARGE PATROL CRAFT)

Displacement, tons: 240
Dimensions, feet (metres): 160·8 × 19 × 6·5 *(49 × 5·8 × 2)*
Guns: 1—3·9 in *(100 mm)*; 2—37 mm (singles); 4/6—25 mm (twin, vertical)
Main engines: 2 diesels; 3 300 bhp; 2 shafts
Speed, knots: 25
Complement: 30

Transferred in mid 1950s.

10 Ex-SOVIET "KM 4" CLASS
(COASTAL PATROL CRAFT)

Displacement, tons: 10
Dimensions, feet (metres): 46 × 10·5 × 3 *(14 × 3·2 × ·9)*
Guns: 1—36 mm; 1—14·5 mm MG
Main engines: Petrol; 146 shp; 2 shafts
Complement: 10

20 LIGHT GUNBOATS

Believed to be for inshore patrols. Locally built.

AMPHIBIOUS FORCES

90 LCM now in service with others building in North Korea. Used on South Korean border.

SERVICE FORCES

5-10 Large Trawlers and small cargo vessels used as store ships. Some of the trawlers operate on South Korean border where several have been sunk in the last few years. Some 100 craft in all of various types are employed as support craft with a secondary mission of coastal patrol.

KOREA (REPUBLIC OF)

Ministerial

Minister of National Defence:
So Chong-Ch'ol

Senior Flag Officers

Chief of Naval Operations:

Vice Chief of Naval Operations:

Commander-in-Chief of Fleet:
Rear-Admiral Chong-Yon Hwang

Diplomatic Representation

Naval Attaché in London:
Commander Chang Hyon Paek
Naval Attaché in Paris:
Colonel Ock-Sup Yoon (Army)
Naval Attaché in Washington:
Captain Choong Hah Choi (Navy)

Personnel

a) 1977: 20 000 (approx) Navy, 20 000 (approx) Marine Corps.
b) 3 years (Navy), 33 months (Marines) National Service.

Bases

Major: Chinhae, Inchon, Pusan.
Minor: Cheju, Mokpo, Mukho, Pohang.

Marine Corps

Over 20 000 organised into one division and one brigade plus smaller and support units. Since October 1973 the ROK Marine Force has been placed directly under the ROK Navy command with a Vice Chief of Naval Operations for Marine Affairs replacing the Commandant of Marine Corps.

Naval Aviation

The ROK Navy operates 20+ S-2 Tracker anti-submarine aircraft. Approximately ten utility aircraft and several helicopters are operated by the ROK Marine Corps. Additional Tracker aircraft are being acquired.

Mercantile Marine

Lloyd's Register of Shipping:
936 vessels of 1 796 106 tons gross

Strength of the Fleet

Type	Active	Building (Proposed)
Destroyers	9	—
Frigates	9	(4)
Corvettes	10	—
Fast Attack Craft—Missile	8	—
Fast Attack Craft—Patrol	5	3
Large Patrol Craft	10	—
Coastal Patrol Craft	23	—
MSCs	10	—
MSB	1	—
LSD	1	—
LSTs	8	—
LSMs	12	—
LCU	1	—
Repair Ship	1	—
Supply Ships	6	—
Tankers	4	—
Tugs	2	—
Survey Ships	3	—

DESTROYERS

4 Ex-US "GEARING" CLASS (FRAM I and II)

Name	No.	Builders	Laid down	Launched	Commissioned
CHUNG BUK (ex-USS *Chevalier, DD 805*)	DD 95	Bath Iron Works Corp, Bath, Maine	—	29 Oct 1944	9 Jan 1945
JEONG BUK (ex-USS *Everett F. Larson, DD 830*)	DD 96	Bath Iron Works Corp, Bath, Maine	—	28 Jan 1945	6 April 1945
— (ex-USS *Richard E. Kraus, DD 849*)	—	Bath Iron Works Corp, Bath, Maine	31 July 1945	2 Mar 1946	23 May 1946
— (ex-USS *New, DD 818*)	—	Consolidated Steel Corp	14 April 1945	18 Aug 1945	5 April 1946

Displacement, tons: 2 425 standard; approx 3 500 full load
Length, feet (metres): 383 *(116·7)* wl; 390·5 *(119·0)* oa
Beam, feet (metres): 40·9 *(12·4)*
Draught, feet (metres): 19 *(5·8)*
Guns: 6—5 inch *(127 mm)* 38 cal (twin) (Mk 38); 1—20 mm Vulcan Gatling; 2—30 mm (twin Emerlak) *(Jeong Buk* only)
A/S weapons: 6—(2 triple) Mk 32 A/S torpedo tubes; 2 fixed hedgehogs (Mk 11)
Main engines: 2 geared turbines (General Electric); 60 000 shp; 2 shafts
Boilers: 4 (Babcock & Wilcox)
Speed, knots: 34
Complement: approx 275

These ships were converted to radar picket destroyers (DDR) in 1949; subsequently modernised under the US Navy's Fleet Rehabilitation and Modernisation programme—first pair to Fram II standards, second pair Fram I. Fitted with small helicopter hangar and flight deck. Anti-ship torpedo tubes have been removed.

A/S weapons: 15 inch Mk 32 torpedo tubes are fitted with liners to reduce them to 12·75 inches.

Radar: SPS 10 and 40.

Sonar: SQS 29 series (hull mounted).

Transfers: First pair on 5 July 1972 and 30 Oct 1972 respectively. Second pair in 1977.

JEONG BUK 1973

2 Ex-US "ALLEN M. SUMNER" CLASS (FRAM II)

Name	No.	Builders	Laid down	Launched	Commissioned
DAE GU (ex-USS *Wallace L. Lind, DD 703*)	DD 97	Bath Iron Works Corp, Bath, Maine	April 1944	14 June 1944	8 Sep 1944
IN CHEON (ex-USS *De Haven, DD 727*)	DD 98	Federal SB & DD Co, Kearney, New Jersey	Oct 1943	9 Jan 1944	31 Mar 1944

Displacement, tons: 2 200 standard; 3 320 full load
Length, feet (metres): 376·5 *(114·8)* oa
Beam, feet (metres): 40·9 *(12·4)*
Draught, feet (metres): 19 *(5·8)* (Mk 38)
Guns: 6—5 inch *(127 mm)* 38 calibre (twin) (Mk 38); 1—20 mm Vulcan Gatling
A/S weapons: 6—(2 triple) Mk 32 A/S torpedo tubes; 2 fixed hedgehogs (Mk 11)
Main engines: 2 geared turbines (General Electric); 60 000 shp; 2 shafts
Boilers: 4 (Babcock & Wilcox)
Speed, knots: 34
Complement: approx 275

Both ships were modernised under the US Navy's Fleet Rehabilitation and Modernisation (FRAM II) programme. Fitted with small helicopter deck and hangar.

Radar: SPS 10 and 40 *(Dae Gu).*
SPS 10 and 37 *(In Cheon).*

Sonar: SQS-29 Series (hull-mounted).
SQA-10 (VDS).

Transfers: 3-4 Dec 1973.

DAE GU (as USS *Wallace L. Lind)* 1967, United States Navy

3 Ex-US "FLETCHER" CLASS

Name	No.	Builders	Laid down	Launched	Commissioned
CHUNG MU (ex-USS *Erben, DD 631*)	DD 91	Bath Iron Works, Bath, Maine	28 Oct 1942	21 Mar 1943	28 May 1943
SEOUL (ex-USS *Halsey Powell, DD 686*)	DD 92	Bethlehem Steel, Staten Island, New York	30 June 1943	30 June 1943	25 Oct 1943
PUSAN (ex-USS *Hickox, DD 673*)	DD 93	Federal Shipbuilding, Kearny, New Jersey	4 July 1943	4 July 1943	10 Sep 1943

Displacement, tons: 2 050 standard; 3 050 full load
Length, feet (metres): 360 *(110·3)* wl; 376·5 *(114·8)* oa
Beam, feet (metres): 39·6 *(12·0)*
Draught, feet (metres): 18 *(5·5)*
Guns: 5—5 inch *(127 mm)* 38 cal (single) (Mk 30); 10—40 mm (2 quad, 1 twin) except *Seoul* (none)
A/S weapons: 6—(2 triple) Mk 32 A/S torpedo tubes; 2 hedgehogs (Mk 10/11); depth charges
Main engines: Geared turbines (General Electric) 60 000 shp; 2 shafts
Boilers: 4 (Babcock & Wilcox)
Speed, knots: 35
Complement: approx 250

Radar: SPS-6 and -10.

Transfers: DD 91, 1 May 1963; DD 92, 27 April 1968; DD 93, 15 Nov 1968.

SEOUL

1968, United States Navy

FRIGATES

Note: It is reported that plans exist for the construction of four 1 600 ton frigates in S. Korean yards. These are to carry 1—5 in gun and SSM.

1 Ex-US "RUDDEROW" CLASS

Name	No.	Builders	Laid down	Launched	Commissioned
CHUNG NAM (ex-USS *Holt, DE 706*)	DE 73	Defoe Shipbuilding, Bay City, Michigan	Oct 1943	15 Dec 1943	9 June 1944

Displacement, tons: 1 450 standard; 1 890 full load
Length, feet (metres): 300 *(91·5)* wl; 306 *(83·2)* oa
Beam, feet (metres): 37 *(11·3)*
Draught, feet (metres): 14 *(4·3)*
Guns: 2—5 inch *(127 mm)* 38 cal; 4—40 mm (twin)
A/S weapons: 6—(2 triple) Mk 32 A/S torpedo tubes; 1 hedgehog; depth charges
Main engines: Turbo-electric drive (General Electric geared turbines); 12 000 shp; 2 shafts
Boilers: 2 (Combustion Engineering)
Speed, knots: 24
Complement: approx 210

Former US destroyer escort of the TEV design.

Radar: SPS-5 and 6.

Transfer: 19 June 1963.

CHUNG NAM

1971, Korean Navy

2 Ex-US "CANNON" CLASS

Name	No.	Builders	Laid down	Launched	Commissioned
KYONG KI (ex-USS *Muir, DE 770*)	DE 71	Tampa Shipbuilding, Tampa, Florida	Mar 1944	4 June 1944	30 Aug 1944
KANG WON (ex-USS *Sutton, DE 771*)	DE 72	Tampa Shipbuilding, Tampa, Florida	May 1944	6 Aug 1944	22 Dec 1944

Displacement, tons: 1 265 standard; 1 700 full load
Length, feet (metres): 300 *(91·5)* wl; 306 *(93·3)* oa
Beam, feet (metres): 36·6 *(11·2)*
Draught, feet (metres): 14 *(4·3)*
Guns: 3—3 inch *(76 mm)* 50 cal; 6—40 mm (twin); 4—20 mm (single)
A/S weapons: 6—(2 triple) Mk 32 A/S torpedo tubes; 1 hedgehog; depth charges
Main engines: Diesel-electric (4 General Motors diesels); 6 000 bhp; 2 shafts
Speed, knots: 21
Complement: approx 210

Former US destroyer escorts of DET design. Refitted at Pearl Harbor, Hawaii, in 1964, being provided with tripod masts to support improved radar antennae.

Radar: SPS-5 and 6.

Transfers: Both on 2 Feb 1956.

KYONG KI

Korean Navy

6 Ex-US "CHARLES LAWRENCE" and "CROSSLEY" CLASSES

Name	No.	Builders	Launched	Commissioned	Transferred
KYONG NAM (ex-USS Cavallaro, APD 128)	APD 81	Defoe Shipbuilding Co, Bay City, Michigan	15 June 1944	13 Mar 1945	Oct 1959
AH SAN (ex-USS Harry L. Corl, APD 108)	APD 82	Bethlehem Shipbuilding Co, Higham, Massachusetts	1 Mar 1944	5 June 1945	June 1966
UNG PO (ex-USS Julius A. Raven, APD 110)	APD 83	Bethlehem Shipbuilding Co, Higham, Massachusetts	3 Mar 1944	28 June 1945	June 1966
KYONG PUK (ex-USS Kephart, APD 61)	APD 85	Charleston Navy Yard, South Carolina	6 Sep 1943	7 Jan 1944	Aug 1967
JONNAM (ex-USS Hayter, APD 80)	APD 86	Charleston Navy Yard, South Carolina	11 Nov 1943	16 Mar 1944	Aug 1967
CHR JU (ex-USS William M. Hobby, APD 95)	APD 87	Charleston Navy Yard, South Carolina	11 Feb 1944	4 April 1945	Aug 1967

Displacement, tons: 1 400 standard; 2 130 full load
Length, feet (metres): 300 (91·4) wl; 306 (93·3) oa
Beam, feet (metres): 37 (11·3)
Draught, feet (metres): 12·6 (3·2)
Guns: 1—5 inch (127 mm) 38 cal; 6—40 mm (twin)
A/S weapons: depth charges
Main engines: Turbo-electric (General Electric turbines);
12 000 shp; 2 shafts
Boilers: 2 (Foster Wheeler "D" Express)
Speed, knots: 23·6
Complement: approx 200
Troop capacity: approx 160

All begun as destroyers escorts (DE), but converted during construction or after completion to high-speed transports (APD).
In Korean service four latter ships originally rated as gunboats (PG); changed in 1972 to APD. All are fitted to carry approximately 160 troops. Can carry four LCVPs.
Two different configurations; "Charles Lawrence (APD 37)" class with high bridge and lattice mast supporting 10-ton capacity boom; "Crossley (APD 87)" class with low bridge and tripod mast supporting 10-ton capacity boom.

KYONG NAM

CORVETTES

3 Ex-US "AUK" CLASS

Name	No.	Builders	Launched
SHIN SONG (ex-USS Ptarmigan, MSF 376)	PCE 1001	Savannah Machine & Foundry Co, Savannah, Georgia	15 Jan 1944
SUNCHON (ex-USS Speed, MSF 116)	PCE 1002	American SB Co, Lorain, Ohio	15 Oct 1942
KOJE (ex-USS Dextrous, MSF 341)	PCE 1003	Gulf SB Corp, Madisonville, Texas	8 Sep 1943

Displacement, tons: 890 standard; 1 250 full load
Dimensions, feet (metres): 215 (61·3) wl; 221·2 oa × 32·2 × 10·8 (63·2 × 9·2 × 3)
Guns: 2—3 inch (76 mm) 50 cal (single); 4—40 mm (twin); 4—20 mm (twin)
A/S weapons: 3—(1 triple) Mk 32 A/S torpedo tubes; 1 hedgehog; depth charges
Main engines: Diesel-electric (General Motors diesels); 3 532 bhp; 2 shafts = 18 knots
Complement: approx 110

Former US Navy minesweepers (originally designated AM). PCE 1001 transferred to ROK Navy in July 1963, PCE 1002 in Nov 1967, and PCE 1003 in Dec 1967.
The minesweeping gear was removed prior to transfer and a second 3 inch gun fitted aft; additional anti-submarine weapons also fitted.

A/S weapons: Mk 32 tubes fitted with 12·75 inch liners.

SHIN SONG

7 Ex-US "PCE 827" CLASS

Name	No.	Builders	Commissioned
RO RYANG (ex-USS PCEC 882)	PCEC 51	—	1944
MYONG RYANG (ex-USS PCEC 896)	PCEC 52	—	1943
HAN SAN (ex-USS PCEC 873)	PCEC 53	—	1943
OK PO (ex-USS PCEC 898)	PCEC 55	—	1943
PYOK PA (ex-USS Dania, PCE 870)	PCE 57	—	1943
RYUL PO (ex-USS Somerset, PCE 892)	PCE 58	—	1943
SA CHON (ex-USS Batesburg, PCE 903)	PCE 59	—	1943

Displacement, tons: 640 standard; 950 full load
Dimensions, feet (metres): 180 (51·4) wl; 184·5 oa × 33 × 9·5 (52·7 × 9·4 × 2·7)
Guns: 1—3 inch (76 mm) 50 cal; 6—40 mm (twin); 4 or 8—20 mm (single or twin)
A/S weapons: 1 hedgehog; depth charges
Main engines: Diesels (General Motors); 2 000 bhp; 2 shafts = 15 knots
Complement: approx 100

OK PO   1969

Four units had been modified in US service as "control" ships (PCEC) for operation with landing craft, being fitted with additional communications equipment in an enlarged bridge area.
Ro Ryang and Myong Ryang transferred to South Korea in Feb 1955; Han San and Ok Po in Sep 1955; Pyok Pa, Ryul Po, and Sa Chon in Dec 1961.

LIGHT FORCES

7 TACOMA PSMM 5 TYPE (FAST ATTACK CRAFT—MISSILE)

Name	No.	Builders	Commissioned
PAEK KU 12	102	Tacoma Boatbuilding Co, Tacoma, Washington	14 Mar 1975
PAEK KU 13	103	Tacoma Boatbuilding Co, Tacoma, Washington	14 Mar 1975
PAEK KU 15	105	Tacoma Boatbuilding Co, Tacoma, Washington	1976
PAEK KU 16	106	South Korea	1976-77
PAEK KU 17	107	South Korea	1976-77
PAEK KU 18	108	South Korea	1976-77
PAEK KU 19	109	South Korea	1976-77

Displacement, tons: approx 250 full load
Dimensions, feet (metres): 165 oa × 24 × 9·5 *(50·3 × 7·3 × 2·9)*
Missile launchers: 4 launchers for Standard missiles (1 reload each)
Guns: 1—3 inch *(76 mm)* 50 cal (forward)
    1—40 mm (aft; may have been removed with missile installation)
    2—50 cal MG
Main engines: 6 gas turbines (Avco Lycoming); 16 800 hp; 2 shafts (controllable pitch propellers) = 40+ knots
Complement: 32 (5 officers, 27 enlisted men)

Aluminium hulls. Based on the US Navy's *Asheville* (PG 84) design. Tacoma design designation was PSMM for multi-mission patrol ship. The Korean designation *Paek Ku* means seagull. *Paek Ku 12* launched 17 Feb 1975.

Engineering: The six TF 35 gas turbines turn two propeller shafts; the "Asheville" class ships have combination gas turbine-diesel power plants. In the Korean units one, two, or three turbines can be selected to provide each shaft with a variety of power settings.

PAEK KU 12 (old pennant number)   *1975, Alfred W. Harris*

PAEK KU 12 (old pennant number)   *1975, Alfred W. Harris*

1 Ex-US "ASHEVILLE" CLASS (FAST ATTACK CRAFT—MISSILE)

Name	No.	Builders	Commissioned
PAEK KU 11	PGM 101	Tacoma Boatbuilding Co,	25 Apr 1970
(ex-USS *Benicia, PG 96*)	(ex-*PGM 11*)	Tacoma, Washington	

Displacement, tons: 225 standard; 245 full load
Dimensions, feet (metres): 164·5 oa × 23·8 × 9·5 *(50·1 × 7·3 × 2·9)*
Missiles: Launchers for Standard SSM
Guns: 1—3 inch *(76 mm)* 50 cal (forward); 1—40 mm (aft); 4—50 cal MG (twin)
Main engines: CODAG; 2 diesels (Cummins); 1 450 bhp; 2 shafts = 16 knots; 1 gas turbine (General Electric); 13 300 shp; 2 shafts = 40+ knots
Complement: approx 25

Former US "Asheville" class patrol gunboat. Launched 20 Dec 1969; transferred to ROK Navy on 15 Oct 1971 and arrived in Korea in January 1972. See United States section for design, engineering, and gunnery notes. No anti-submarine sensors or weapons are fitted.

Missiles: During 1971, while in US Navy service, this ship was fitted experimentally with one launcher for the Standard surface-to-surface missile. The box-like container/launcher held two missiles. Launchers fitted in S. Korea 1975-76.

PAEK KU 11 (old pennant number)   *1972*

5 + 3 CPIC TYPE (FAST ATTACK CRAFT—PATROL)

Name	No.	Builders	Commissioned
GIREOGI	PKM 123	Tacoma Boatbuilding Co, Tacoma, Washington	1975
—	PKM 125	S. Korea	1976
—	PKM 126	S. Korea	1976
—	PKM 127	S. Korea	1976
—	PKM 128	S. Korea	1977
—	PKM 129	S. Korea	—
—	PKM 130	S. Korea	—
—	PKM 131	S. Korea	—

Displacement, tons: 71·25 full load
Dimensions, feet (metres): 100 oa × 18·5 × 6 *(30·5 × 5·6 × 1·8)*
Guns: 2—30 mm MG (twin) (Mk 74) (see *Gunnery* notes); 1—20 mm
Main engines: 3 gas turbines (Avco Lycoming); 6 750 shp; 3 shafts = 45 knots; 2 auxiliary diesels (Volvo); 500 bhp
Complement: approx 11 (varies with armament)

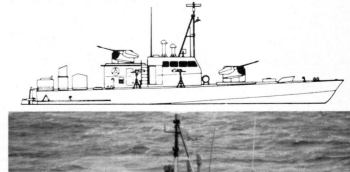

These are high-speed patrol and interdiction craft designed by the US Navy specifically for foreign sales and as a successor to PTFs in the US Navy. The CPIC is capable of operating in rougher waters than PTFs and is more adaptable for cold and hot weather operating areas. Fitted with fin stabilisers.
The lead craft, after extensive Navy trials, was transferred to South Korea on 1 Aug 1975.

Gunnery: The lead craft was completed with a twin rapid-fire 30 mm mount forward of the bridge structure. As shown in the drawing, light machine guns can be fitted along the sides and a second 30 mm gun mount or missile launchers can be installed aft of the bridge. Up to 20 000 pounds of weapons can be carried.

CPIC on trials   *1974, United States Navy*

8 Ex-US COAST GUARD "CAPE" CLASS
(LARGE PATROL CRAFT)

PB 3 (ex-USCGC *Cape Rosier, WPB 95333*)
PB 5 (ex-USCGC *Cape Sable, WPB 95334*)
PB 6 (ex-USCGC *Cape Providence, WPB 95335*)
PB 8 (ex-USCGC *Cape Porpoise, WPB 95327*)
PB 9 (ex-USCGC *Cape Falcon, WPB 95330*)
PB 10 (ex-USCGC *Cape Trinity, WPB 95331*)
PB 11 (ex-USCGC *Cape Darby, WPB 95323*)
PB 12 (ex-USCGC *Cape Kiwanda, WPB 95329*)

Displacement, tons: 98 full load
Dimensions, feet (metres): 95 oa × 19 × 6 *(31·1 × 6·2 × 1·9)*
Guns: 1—50 cal MG; 1—81 mm mortar; several ·30 cal MG
Main engines: 4 diesels (Cummins); 2 200 bhp; 2 shafts = 20 knots
Complement: 13

Former US Coast Guard steel-hulled patrol craft. Built in 1958-1959. Nine units transferred to South Korea in Sep 1968.
Combination machinegun/mortar mount is forward; single light machineguns are mounted aft.
See US Coast Guard listings for additional details.

PB 11

2 100-ft PATROL TYPE (LARGE PATROL CRAFT)

PK 10   **PK 11**

Displacement, tons: 120
Dimensions, feet (metres): 100 oa *(32·7)*
Missiles: 2 Exocet
Guns: 1—40 mm; 1—20 mm
Main engines: Diesels (Mercedes Benz-MTU); 10 200 bhp; 3 shafts = 35 knots

Two patrol craft reported built in Korea in 1971-1972.

10+ "SCHOOLBOY" CLASS (COASTAL PATROL CRAFT)

Displacement, tons: 30
Dimensions, feet (metres): 72 oa × 11·5 × 3·6 *(23·6 × 3·8 × 1·2)*
Guns: 2—20 mm (single)
Main engines: 2 MTU diesels; 1 600 bhp; 2 shafts

At least 10 and possibly as many as 20 patrol craft of this type are being built in Korea, with the first units completed in 1973. Believed to be designated in the PB series.

9 US 65-ft SEWART TYPE (COASTAL PATROL CRAFT)

FB 1   **FB 3**   **FB 6**   **FB 8**   **FB 10**
FB 2   **FB 5**   **FB 7**   **FB 9**

Displacement, tons: 33 full load
Dimensions, feet (metres): 65 oa × 16 *(21·3 × 5·2)*
Guns: 2—20 mm (single)
Main engines: 3 diesels (General Motors); 1 590 bhp; 3 shafts = 25 knots
Complement: 5

These craft were built in the United States by Sewart. The design is adapted from a commercial 65-foot craft. Referred to as "Toksuuri" No. 1 etc. by the South Koreans. Transferred to South Korea in August 1967.

FB 10 on marine railway

4 US 40-ft SEWART TYPE (COASTAL PATROL CRAFT)

SB 1   **SB 2**   **SB 3**   **SB 5**

Displacement, tons: 9·25 full load
Dimensions, feet (metres): 40 oa × 12 × 3 *(13·1 × 3·9 × 0·9)*
Guns: 1—·50 cal MG; 2—·30 cal MG
Main engines: 2 diesels (General Motors); 500 bhp; 2 shafts = 31 knots
Complement: 7

These are aluminium-hulled craft built in the United States by Sewart. Transferred to South Korea in 1964.

MINESWEEPERS

8 Ex-US "MSC 268" and "294" CLASSES

Name	No.	Builders	Commissioned
KUM SAN (ex-US *MSC 284*)	MSC 522	Peterson Builders, Wisconsin	1959
KO HUNG (ex-US *MSC 285*)	MSC 523	Peterson Builders, Wisconsin	1959
KUM KOK (ex-US *MSC 286*)	MSC 525	Peterson Builders, Wisconsin	1959
NAM YANG (ex-US *MSC 295*)	MSC 526	Peterson Builders, Wisconsin	1963
NA DONG (ex-US *MSC 296*)	MSC 527	Peterson Builders, Wisconsin	1963
SAM CHOK (ex-US *MSC 316*)	MSC 528	Peterson Builders, Wisconsin	1968
YONG DONG (ex-US *MSC 320*)	MSC 529	Peterson Builders, Wisconsin	1975
OK CHEON (ex-US *MSC 321*)	MSC 530	Peterson Builders, Wisconsin	1975

Displacement, tons: 320 light; 370 full load
Dimensions, feet (metres): 144 oa × 28 × 8·2 *(117·2 × 9·2 × 2·7)*
Guns: 2—20 mm
Main engines: Diesels; 1 200 bhp; 2 shafts = 14 knots
Complement: approx 40

Built by the United States specifically for transfer under the Military Aid Programme. Wood hulled with non-magnetic metal fittings. *Kum San* transferred to South Korea in June 1959, *Ko Hung* in Sep 1959, *Kum Kok* in Nov 1959, *Nam Yang* in Sep 1963, *Na Dong* in Nov 1963, *Sam Chok* in July 1968, *Yong Dong* and *Ok Cheon* on 1 Oct 1975.

KUM KOK

2 Ex-US "ALBATROSS" CLASS (YMS)

Name	No.
KIM PO (ex-USS *Kite, MSCO 22, ex-AMS 22, ex-YMS 375*)	MSC 520
KO CHANG (ex-USS *Mockingbird, MSCO 27, ex-AMS 27, ex-YMS 419*)	MSC 521

Displacement, tons: 270 standard; 350 full load
Dimensions, feet (metres): 136 oa × 24·5 × 8 *(44·6 × 8·1 × 2·6)*
Guns: 1—40 mm; 2—20 mm
Main engines: Diesels; 1 000 bhp = 15 knots
Complement: approx 50

Former US Navy auxiliary motor minesweepers built in 1941-1942. Wood hulled. *Kim Po,* and *Ko Chang* transferred to South Korea in Jan 1956.

KO CHANG

1969, Korean Navy

1 Ex-US MSB

Name	No.
PI BONG (ex-US *MSB 2*)	MSB 1

Displacement, tons: 30 light; 39 full load
Dimensions, feet (metres): 57·2 oa × 15·3 × 4 *(18·7 × 5 × 1·3)*
Guns: machine guns
Main engines: 2 geared diesels (Packard); 600 bhp; 2 shafts = 12 knots

Transferred on 1 Dec 1961. Wood hulled.

PI BONG

1969, Korean Navy

AMPHIBIOUS FORCES

1 Ex-US "CABILDO" CLASS (LSD)

Name	No.	Builders	Commissioned
– (ex-USS *Fort Marion, LSD 22*)	—	Gulf Shipbuilding Corp, Chickasaw, Alabama	29 Jan 1946

Displacement, tons: 4 790 standard; 9 375 full load
Dimensions, feet (metres): 475·4 oa × 76·2 × 18 *(144·5 × 23·2 × 5·5)*
Guns: 12—40 mm (2 quad, 2 twin)
Main engines: Geared turbines; 9 000 shp; 2 shafts = 15·4 knots
Boilers: 2

Launched on 22 May 1945, and transferred to South Korea in 1976.
Docking well is 392 × 44 feet; can accommodate 3 LCUs or 18 LCMs or 32 LVTs (amphibious tractors) in docking well. Fitted with helicopter platform (which can be used to transport truck or equipment for loading into landing craft).

Ex-USS FORT MARION ballasted down at stern

1969, United States Navy

8 Ex-US "1-510" and "511-1152" CLASSES (LST)

Name	No.	Commissioned
UN PONG (ex-USS *LST 1010*)	LST 807	1944
DUK BONG (ex-USS *LST 227*)	LST 808	1943
BI BONG (ex-USS *LST 218*)	LST 809	1943
KAE BONG (ex-USS *Berkshire County, LST 288*)	LST 810	1944
WEE BONG (ex-USS *Johnson County, LST 849*)	LST 812	1945
SU YONG (ex-USS *Kane County, LST 853*)	LST 813	1945
BUK HAN (ex-USS *Lynn County, LST 900*)	LST 815	1945
HWA SAN (ex-USS *Pender County, LST 1080*)	LST 816	1945

Displacement, tons: 1 653 standard; 2 366 beaching; 4 080 full load
Dimensions, feet (metres): 316 wl; 328 oa × 50 × 14 *(103·6; 107·5 × 16·4 × 4·6)*
Guns: 6 or 8—40 mm
Main engines: Diesels; 1 700 bhp; 2 shafts = 11·6 knots
Complement: approx 110

HWA SAN

Former US Navy tank landing ships. Cargo capacity 2 100 tons. *Un Bong* transferred to South Korea in Feb 1955, *Duk Bong* in Mar 1955, *Bi Bong* in May 1955, *Kae Bong* in Mar 1956, *Wee Bong* in Jan 1959, *Su Yong* and *Buk Han* in Dec 1958, and *Hwa San* in Oct 1958.

Launch dates: 807, 29 Mar 1944; 808, 21 Sep 1943; 809, 20 July 1943; 810, 7 Nov 1943; 812, 30 Dec 1944; 813, 17 Nov 1944; 815, 9 Dec 1944; 816, 2 May 1945.

DUK BONG

1 Ex-US "ELK RIVER" CLASS (LSMR)

Name	No.	Builders
SI HUNG (ex-USS *St Joseph River LSMR 527*)	LSMR 311	Brown Shipbuilding Co, Houston, Texas

Displacement, tons: 944 standard; 1 084 full load
Dimensions, feet (metres): 204·5 wl; 206·2 oa × 34·5 × 10 *(67·1; 67·6 × 11·3 × 3·3)*
Guns: 1—5 inch *(127 mm)* 38 cal; 2—40 mm; 4—20 mm
Rocket launchers: 8 twin Mk 105 launchers for 5 inch rockets
Main engines: 2 diesels (General Motors); 2 800 bhp; 2 shafts = 12·6 knots
Complement: approx 140

Former US Navy landing ship completed as a rocket-firing ship to support amphibious landing operations. Launched on 19 May 1945, transferred to South Korea on 15 Sep 1960. Configuration differs from conventional LSM type with "island" bridge structure and 5 inch gun aft; no bow doors.

SI HUNG

1967, Korean Navy

11 Ex-US "LSM-1" CLASS

Name	No.
AE CHO (ex-USS *LSM 546*)	LSM 601
YO TO (ex-USS *LSM 268*)	LSM 602
A TOK (ex-USS *LSM 462*)	LSM 605
O MUN (ex-USS *LSM 30*)	LSM 606
IAN (ex-USS *LSM 96*)	LSM 607
UNG TO (ex-USS *LSM 54*)	LSM 608
VOL MI (ex-USS *LSM 57*)	LSM 609
RIN (ex-USS *LSM 19*)	LSM 610
UNG RA (ex-USS *LSM 84*)	LSM 611
IN MI (ex-USS *LSM 316*)	LSM 612
L RUNG (ex-USS *LSM 17*)	LSM 613

TYO TO   1969

Displacement, tons: 743 beaching; 1 095 full load
Dimensions, feet (metres): 196·5 wl; 203·5 oa × 34·6 × 8·5 *(64·4; 66·7 × 11·3 × 2·8)*
Guns: 2—40 mm AA (twin); several 20 mm AA
Main engines: 2 diesels (direct drive; Fairbanks Morse except *Tyo To* General Motors); 2 800 bhp; 2 shafts = 12·5 knots
Complement: approx 60

Former US Navy medium landing ships. Built 1944-1945. LSM 601, 602, and 605 transferred to South Korea in 1955; others in 1956. *Sin Mi* served in Indochina as French L 9014 and *Ul Rung* as French L 9017 during 1954-1955; returned to United States in Oct 1955 and retransferred to South Korea in autumn 1956.

Pung To serves as mine force flagship fitted with mine-laying rails and designated LSML. Arrangement of 20 mm guns differs; some ships have two single mounts adjacent to forward 40 mm mount on forecastle; other 20 mm guns along sides of cargo well.

1 Ex-US "LCU 501" CLASS

CU 1 (ex-USS *LCU 531*)

Displacement, tons: 309 full load
Dimensions, feet (metres): 105 wl; 119·1 oa × 32·66 × 5 *(34·4; 39 × 10·7 × 1·6)*
Main engines: Diesels (Gray Marine); 675 bhp; 3 shafts = 10 knots

Former US Navy utility landing craft. Built in 1943 as LCT(6) 531. Transferred to South Korea in Dec 1960. No name assigned.

SERVICE FORCES

1 Ex-US "ACHELOUS" CLASS (LIGHT REPAIR SHIP)

Name	No.	Builders	Commissioned
DUK SU (ex-USS *Minotaur*, ARL 15, ex-LST 645)	ARL 1	Chicago Bridge & Iron Co, Seneca, Illinois	30 Sep 1944

DUK SU

Displacement, tons: 2 366 standard; 4 100 full load
Dimensions, feet (metres): 316 wl; 328 oa × 50 × 11·2 *(103·6; 107·5 × 16·4 × 3·7)*
Guns: 8—40 mm; 12—20 mm
Main engines: Diesels (General Motors); 1 800 bhp; 2 shafts = 11·6 knots
Complement: approx 250

Former US Navy landing craft repair ship. Converted during construction from an LST. Launched on 20 Sep 1944, transferred to South Korea in Oct 1955.

6 Ex-US ARMY FS TYPE (SUPPLY SHIPS)

Name	No.	Builders
CHON (ex-US Army *FS 198*)	AKL 902	Higgins Industries
II NAM PO (ex-US Army *FS 356*)	AKL 905	J. K. Welding
OK PO (ex-USCGC *Trillium*, WAK 170, ex-US Army *FS 397*)	AKL 907	Ingalls, Decatur, Alabama
J SAN (ex-USS *Sharps*, AKL 10, ex-AG 139, ex-US Army *FS 385*)	AKL 908	Ingalls, Decatur, Alabama
A SAN (ex-USS AKL 35, ex-US Army *FS 383*)	AKL 909	Ingalls, Decatur, Alabama
SAN (ex-USS *Brule*, AKL 28, ex-US Army *FS 370*)	AKL 910	Sturgeon Bay

MA SAN   1957

Displacement, tons: approx 700
Dimensions, feet (metres): 176·5 oa × 32·8 × 10 *(57·9 × 10·7 × 3·3)*
Guns: 2—20 mm (single) in most ships
Main engines: Diesel; 1 000 bhp; 1 shaft = 10 knots
Complement: approx 20

Originally US Army freight and supply ships built in World War II for coastal operation. *Chon* and *Chin Nam Po* transferred to South Korea in 1951; *Mok Po, Kin San,* and *Ma San* in 56; *Ul San* on 1 Nov 1971. Many subsequently served in US Navy and Military Sea Transportation Service (later Military Sealift Command). Details and configurations differ.

1 Ex-NORWEGIAN TANKER

Name	No.	Builders	Launched
HUN JI (ex-*Birk*)	AO 2	A/S Berken Mek Verks, Bergen	1951

Displacement, tons: 1 400 standard; 4 160 full load
Dimensions, feet (metres): 297·5 oa × 44·5 × 18·2 *(97·5 × 14·6 × 5·9)*
Guns: 1—40 mm; several 20 mm
Main engines: 2 diesels; 1 800 bhp; 1 shaft = 12 knots
Complement: approx 70

Transferred to South Korea in Sep 1953.

CHUN JI

1 Ex-US 235-ft YO TYPE (HARBOUR TANKER)

Name	No.
HWA CHON (ex-*Paek Yeon AO 5*, ex-USS *Derrick YO 59*)	AO 5

HWA CHON   *1969*

Displacement, tons: 890 standard; 2 700 full load
Dimensions, feet (metres): 235 oa × 37 × 15 *(77 × 12·1 × 4·9)*
Guns: several 20 mm
Main engines: Diesel (Fairbanks Morse); 1 150 bhp; 1 shaft = 10·5 knots
Complement: approx 45

Former US Navy self-propelled fuel barge. Transferred to South Korea on 14 Oct 1955. Capacity 10 000 barrels petroleum. The ship has been laid up in reserve since 1974.

2 Ex-US 174-ft YO TYPE (HARBOUR TANKERS)

KU YONG (ex-USS *YO 118*) AO 1   — (ex-USS *YO 179*) YO 6

Displacement, tons: 1 400 full load
Dimensions, feet (metres): 174 oa × 32 *(57 × 10·5)*
Guns: several 20 mm
Main engines: Diesel (Union); 500 bhp; 1 shaft = 7 knots
Complement: approx 35

Former US Navy self-propelled fuel barges. Transferred to South Korea on 3 Dec 1946 and 13 Sep 1971, respectively. Cargo capacity 6 570 barrels.

2 Ex-US "SOTOYOMO" CLASS (TUGS)

Name	No.	Builders	Launched
YONG MUN (ex-USS *Keosanqua, ATA 198*)	ATA 2	Levingston SB Co, Orange, Texas	17 Jan 1945
DO BONG (ex-USS *Pinola, ATA 206*)	ATA (S) 3	Gulfport Boiler & Welding Works, Port Arthur, Texas	14 Dec 1944

Displacement, tons: 538 standard; 835 full load
Dimensions, feet (metres): 133·66 wl × 143 oa × 33·8 *(43·8; 46·9 × 11·1)*
Guns: 1—3 inch *(76 mm)* 50 cal; 4—20 mm
Main engines: Diesel (General Motors); 1 500 bhp; 1 shaft = 13 knots
Complement: approx 45

Former US Navy auxiliary ocean tugs. Both transferred to South Korea in February 1962. *Do Bong* modified for salvage work.

The South Korean Navy also operates nine small harbour tugs (designated YTL). These include one ex-US Navy craft (YTL 550) and five ex-US Army craft.

SERVICE CRAFT

The South Korean Navy operates approximately 35 small service craft in addition to the YO-type tankers listed above and the harbour tugs noted above. These craft include open lighters, floating cranes, diving tenders, dredgers, ferries, non-self-propelled fuel barges, pontoon barges, and sludge removal barges. Most are former US Navy craft.

HYDROGRAPHIC SERVICE

The following craft are operated by the Korean Hydrographic Service which is responsible to the Ministry of Transportation.

2 Ex-BELGIAN MSI TYPE

SURO 5 (ex-Belgian *Temse*, ex-US *MSI 470*)
SURO 6 (ex-Belgian *Tournai*, ex-US *MSI 481*)

Displacement, tons: 160 light; 190 full load
Dimensions, feet (metres): 113·2 oa × 22·3 × 6 *(37·1 × 7·3 × 1·9)*
Main engines: Diesels; 1 260 bhp; 2 shafts = 15 knots

Former Belgian inshore minesweepers. Built in Belgium, the *Tournai* being financed by United States. Launched on 6 Aug 1956 and 18 May 1957, respectively. Transferred to South Korea in March 1970.

SURO 2

Of 145 tons launched in 1942. Complement 12.

1 Ex-US "YMS-1" CLASS

SURO 3 (ex-USC&GS *Hodgson*)

Displacement, tons: 289 full load
Dimensions, feet (metres): 136 oa × 24·5 × 9·25 *(44·6 × 8·1 × 3)*
Main engines: Diesels; 1 000 bhp; 2 shafts = 15 knots

YMS type transferred to South Korea from US Coast & Geodetic Survey in 1968.

SURO 7   SURO 8

Of 30 tons with complement of 6.

COAST GUARD

The Korean Coast Guard operates about 25 small ships and craft including several tugs and rescue craft.

KUWAIT

Ministerial

Minister of Defence:
  Sa'd al Abdallah al-Sabah

Personnel

(a) 1977: 500 (Coastguard) Administered by Ministry of the Interior
(b) Voluntary

Mercantile Marine

Lloyd's Register of Shipping: 182 vessels of 1 106 816 tons gross

Future Plans

Expansion of this force, including the building of a base, is understood to be under consideration.

LIGHT FORCES

10 THORNYCROFT 78 ft TYPE (COASTAL PATROL CRAFT)

AL SALEMI	AMAN	MASHHOOR	MURSHED
AL SHURTI	INTISAR	MAYMOON	WATHAH
AL MUBARAKI	MARZOOK		

Displacement, tons: 40
Dimensions, feet (metres): 78 oa × 15·5 × 4·5 *(23·8 × 4·7 × 1·4)*
Gun: 1 MG
Main engines: 2 Rolls Royce V8 marine diesels; 1 340 shp at 1 800 rpm; 1 116 shp at 1 700 rpm = 20 knots
Range, miles: 700 at 15 knots
Complement: 12 (5 officers, 7 men)

Two were built by Thornycroft before the merger and eight by Vosper Thornycroft afterwards. *Al Salemi* and *Al Mubaraki* were shipped to Kuwait on 8 Sep 1966.
Hulls are of welded steel construction, with superstructures of aluminium alloy. Twin hydraulically operated rudders, Decca type D 202 radar. The later boats are slightly different in appearance with modified superstructure and no funnel, see photograph of *Intisar*.

INTISAR   *1972, Vosper Thornycroft*

2 VOSPER THORNYCROFT 56 ft TYPE
(COASTAL PATROL CRAFT)

Name	No.	Builders	Commissioned
DASTOOR	—	Vosper Thornycroft Private Ltd, Singapore	June 1974
KASAR	—	Vosper Thornycroft Private Ltd, Singapore	June 1974

Displacement, tons: 25
Length, feet (metres): 56 *(17·8)*
Guns: 1—20 mm; 2 MG
Main engines: 2 MTU MB6 V.331 diesels; 1 350 hp = 26 knots
Range, miles: 320 at 20 knots
Complement: 8 (2 officers, 6 men)

Ordered September 1973. Both laid down 31 Oct 1973. Steel hulls and aluminium superstructure.

KASAR (guns not fitted)   *1974, Vosper Thornycroft*

7 THORNYCROFT 50 ft TYPE (COASTAL PATROL CRAFT)

Built by the Singapore Yard of Thornycroft (Malaysia) Limited, now the Tanjong Rhu, Singapore Yard of Vosper Thornycroft Private Ltd.

1 VOSPER THORNYCROFT 46 ft TYPE (COASTAL PATROL CRAFT)

Name	No.	Builders	Commissioned
MAHROOS	—	Vosper Thornycroft Private Ltd, Singapore	Jan 1976

Length, feet (metres): 46 *(14)*
Guns: Can mount 2—20 mm
Main engines: 2 Rolls-Royce-C8M-410 diesels; 780 hp = 21+ knots
Complement: 5

Ordered in Oct 1974. Hull is of welded steel construction with aluminium superstructure.

8 VOSPER THORNYCROFT 35 ft TYPE
(COASTAL PATROL CRAFT)

Length, feet (metres): 35 *(10·3)*
Main engines: 2 turbocharged Perkins Diesels = 25 knots

Ordered July 1972 from Vosper Thornycroft Private Ltd, Singapore. Built of double-skinned teak with Cascover sheathing. First four delivered late 1972, second four in May 1973.

MAHROOS (guns not fitted)   *1975, Singapore Hilton*

LANDING CRAFT

3 VOSPER THORNYCROFT 88 ft TYPE

Name	No.	Builders	Commissioned
WAHEED	—	Vosper Thornycroft Private Ltd, Singapore	May 1971
FAREED	—	Vosper Thornycroft Private Ltd, Singapore	May 1971
REGGA	—	Vosper Thornycroft Private Ltd, Singapore	Nov 1975

Dimensions, feet (metres): 88 × 22·6 × 4·3 *(27 × 6·9 × 1·3)*
Main engines: 2 Rolls-Royce C8M-410 diesels; 752 bhp = 10 knots
Complement: 9 (can carry 8 passengers)

First pair ordered in 1970 and third in Oct 1974 by Kuwait Ministry of the Interior. Can carry 6 400 gals oil-fuel, 9 400 gals water and 40 tons deck cargo, the last being handled by a 2·5 ton derrick. Used to support landing-parties working on Kuwait's off-shore islands.

WAHEED   *1974, Vosper Thornycroft*

LAOS

The situation in this force is uncertain.

Ministerial

Minister of National Defence:
  Khamtai Siphandon

Personnel

(a) 1977: 550 officers and men
(b) 18 months National Service

RIVER PATROL CRAFT

7	LCM (6) Type	28 tons	4 in commission, 3 in reserve
6	Cabin Type	21 tons	2 in commission, 4 in reserve
2	Chris Craft Type	15 tons	2 in commission
12	11 metre Type	10 tons	5 in commission, 7 in reserve
8	8 metre Type	6 tons	8 in reserve
7	Cargo Transport	50 tons	1 in commission, 6 in reserve

The above craft are formed into four squadrons, although at least half of them must be considered non-operational.

LEBANON

Diplomatic Representation

Naval Military and Air Attaché in London:
  Colonel F. El Hussami

Personnel

1977: 250 officers and men

Mercantile Marine

Lloyd's Register of Shipping:
  136 vessels of 213 572 tons gross

DELETION

1975 Djounieh (ex-*Fairmile B. ML*)

LIGHT FORCES

Note: The 135 ton Large Patrol Craft ordered from Hamelin SY in Jan 1974 has not been delivered due to the internal Lebanese problems. It is reported that Iceland has shown interest in her acquisition.

1 LARGE PATROL CRAFT

Name	No.	Builders	Commissioned
TARABLOUS	31	Ch. Navals de l'Estérel	1959

Displacement, tons: 90
Dimensions, feet (metres): 124·7 × 18 × 5·8 *(38 × 5·6 × 1·6)*
Guns: 2—40 mm; 2—12·7 mm
Main engines: 2 MTU diesels; 2 shafts; 2 700 bhp = 27 knots
Range, miles: 1 500 at 15 knots
Complement: 19 (3 officers, 16 men)

Laid down in June 1958. Launched in June 1959. Completed in 1959.

TARABLOUS   *1975, Chantiers Navals de l'Esterel*

3 "BYBLOS" CLASS (COASTAL PATROL CRAFT)

Name	No.	Builders	Commissioned
BYBLOS	11	Ch. Navals de l'Estérel	1955
SIDON	12	Ch. Navals de l'Estérel	1955
BEYROUTH (ex-*Tir*)	13	Ch. Navals de l'Estérel	1955

Displacement, tons: 28 standard
Dimensions, feet (metres): 66 × 13·5 × 4 *(20·1 × 4·1 × 1·2)*
Guns: 1—20 mm; 2 MG
Main engines: General Motors diesels; 2 Shafts; 530 bhp = 18·5 knots

French built ML type craft. Launched in 1954-55.

LANDING CRAFT

1 Ex-US "LCU 1466" CLASS

SOUR (ex-*LCU 1474*)

Displacement, tons: 180 standard; 360 full load
Dimensions, feet (metres): 115 × 34 × 6 *(35·1 × 10·4 × 1·8)*
Guns: 2—20 mm
Main engines: 3 diesels; 3 shafts; 675 bhp = 10 knots

Built in 1957, transferred in Nov 1958.

LIBERIA

Ministerial

Minister of National Defence:
E. Jonathan Goodridge

Command

This Coastguard force is controlled by a Coastguard Commander who is responsible to the Minister of National Defence.

Personnel

(a) 1977:   about 200 officers and men
(b) Voluntary

Mercantile Marine

Lloyd's Register of Shipping:
2 600 vessels of 73 477 326 tons gross

MOTOR GUNBOAT

1 US "PGM 71" CLASS

ALERT (ex-US *PGM 102*) 102

Displacement, tons: 100
Dimensions, feet (metres): 95 oa × 19 × 5 *(29 × 5·8 × 1·5)*
Gun: 1—40 mm
Main engines: 4 diesels; 2 shafts; 2 200 bhp = 21 knots
Complement: 15

PGM 102 (US number) was built in the United States for transfer under the Military Aid Programme in 1967.

PRESIDENTIAL YACHT

LIBERIAN (ex-*Virginia*)

Measurement, tons: 692·27 gross; 341·6 net
Dimensions, feet (metres): 173 wl; 209 oa × 29·7 × 13·1 *(52·8; 63·7 × 9·1 × 4)*

Motor yacht of 742 tons (yacht measurement) built in 1930 by William Beardmore & Co Ltd, Dalmuir. Purchased by Liberia for use as the Presidential Yacht in 1957. Extensively refitted by Cammell Laird & Co Ltd, Birkenhead, at the end of 1962.

LIBERIAN

1976, Michael D. J. Lennon

PATROL BOATS

ML 4001   **ML 4002**

Displacement, tons: 11·5
Dimensions, feet (metres): 40·5 oa × 11·5 × 3·5 *(12·3 × 3·5 × 1·1)*
Guns: 2 MG
Main engines: 2 GM diesels; 2 shafts; 380 bhp = 23 knots

Coastguard cutters built at the United States Coast Guard Yard, Curtis Bay, Maryland, presented by the USA and transferred during 1957. Civilian manned craft which are probably non-operational.

ML 4002

Dr Giorgio Arra

LANDING CRAFT

Landing craft reported to be used for transport and general utility purposes.

LIBYA

Establishment

The Libyan Navy was established in Nov 1962 when a British Naval Mission was formed and first recruits were trained at HMS *St. Angelo*, Malta. Cadets were also trained at the Britannia Royal Navy College, Dartmouth, and technical ratings at HMS *Sultan*, Gosport, and HMS *Collingwood*, Fareham, England.

Headquarters Appointment

Senior Officer, Libyan Navy: Commander A. Shaksuki

Personnel

(a) 1977: Total 2 000 officers and ratings, including Coast Guard
(b) Voluntary service

Base

Tripoli. Operating Ports at Benghazi, Darna, Tobruk, Burayqah.

Future programmes

In a manner reminiscent of some other countries, such as India, Libya is obtaining naval supplies from both West and East. The final result if all programmes are fulfilled (4 missile corvettes (Italian), 10 missile craft (French) and reportedly 24 (Soviet) plus 4 submarines (French/Spanish) and an unspecified number (Soviet) will be a large and up-to-date fleet at a crucial position in the Mediterranean. While the training task to man this fleet must be formidable the Libyans are also showing keen interest in the procurement of GRP minehunters/sweepers.

Strength of the Fleet

Type	Active	Building (Planned)
Frigate	1	—
Submarines	1	4 (?6)
LSD	1	—
Corvettes	1	4 (missiles)
Fast Attack Craft—Missile	3+?3	10 (?24)
Large Patrol Craft	1C	
Coastal Patrol Craft	1	—
MRC	1	—
LST	1	1

Mining Capability

Although none of the listed Libyan ships is credited with a mining capability the fact that, in June 1973, two minefields were laid off Tripoli harbour, some eight miles out, suggests that a stock of mines is available.

Mercantile Marine

Lloyd's Register of Shipping:
34 vessels of 458 805 tons gross

DELETIONS

Inshore Minesweepers

1973 *Brak* and *Zura* ("Ham" Class)

FRIGATE

1 VOSPER THORNYCROFT MARK 7

Name	No.	Builders	Laid down	Launched	Commissioned
DAT ASSAWARI	F 01	Vosper Thornycroft	27 Sep 1968	Sep 1969	1 Feb 1973

Displacement, tons: 1 325 standard; 1 625 full load
Length, feet (metres): 310·0 (94·5) pp; 330·0 (100·6) oa
Beam, feet (metres): 36·0 (11·0)
Draught, feet (metres): 11·2 (3·4)
A/S weapons: 1 Mortar Mk 10
Missile launchers: 6 (2 triple) Seacat close range ship-to-air
Guns: 1—4·5 in; 2—40 mm (singles); 2—35 mm (twin)
Main engines: CODOG arrangement; 2 shafts; with Kamewa cp propellers; 2 Rolls Royce gas turbines; 23 200 shp = 37·5 knots; 2 Paxman diesels; 3 500 bhp = 17 knots economical cruising speed
Range, miles: 5 700 at 17 knots

Mark 7 Frigate ordered from Vosper Thornycroft on 6 Feb 1968. Generally similar in design to the two Iranian Mark Vs built by this firm, but larger and with different armament. After trials she carried out work-up at Portland, England, reaching Tripoli autumn 1973.

Radar: AWS-1 air surveillance set; fire control radar and RDL-1 radar direction finder.

DAT ASSAWARI　　　　　　　　　　　　　　　　　　1973, John G. Callis

SUBMARINES

4 FRENCH "DAPHNE" CLASS

Displacement, tons: 869 surfaced; 1 043 dived
Dimensions, feet (metres): 189·6 × 22·3 × 15·1 (57·8 × 6·8 × 4·6)
Torpedo tubes: 12—21·7 in (550 mm) (8 forward, 4 aft)
Main machinery: SEMT-Pielstick diesel electric; 2 shafts
Speed, knots: 13·5 surfaced; 16 dived
Range, miles: 2 700 at 12·5 knots (surfaced); 3 000 at 7 knots (snorting)
Complement: 52

Ordered under licence from DTCN Paris from Bazán, Spain in 1976. Delivery could be 1980-81.
Present state of construction uncertain.

"DAPHNE" Class　　　　　　　　　　　　　　　　　1975, Dr Giorgio Arra

? 6 SOVIET "FOXTROT" CLASS

The Libyan government stated in Nov 1975 that submarines of this class would be provided by the USSR. The training of Libyans in the Soviet Union offered confirmation of this. First delivery early 1977, named *Babr*.

LOGISTIC SUPPORT SHIP

1 LSD TYPE

Name	No.	Builders	Laid down	Launched	Commissioned
ZELTIN	—	Vosper Thornycroft, Woolston	1967	29 Feb 1968	23 Jan 1969

Displacement, tons: 2 200 standard; 2 470 full load
Length, feet (metres): 300·0 (91·4) wl; 324·0 (98·8) oa
Beam, feet (metres): 48·0 (14·6)
Draught, feet (metres): 10·2 (3·1); 19·0 (5·8) aft when flooded
Dock:
Length, feet (metres): 135·0 (41·1)
Width, feet (metres): 40·0 (12·2)
Guns: 2—40 mm
Main engines: 2 Paxman 16 cyl diesels; 3 500 bhp; 2 shafts
Speed, knots: 15
Range, miles: 3 000 at 14 knots
Complement: As Senior Officer Ship: 101 (15 officers and 86 ratings)

The ship provides full logistic support, including mobile docking maintenance and repair facilities for the Libyan fleet. Craft up to 120 ft can be docked. Used as tender for Light Forces. The Vosper-Thornycroft Group received the order for this ship in Jan 1967 for delivery in late 1968.
Fitted with accommodation for a flag officer or a senior officer and staff. Operational and administrative base of the squadron.

ZELTIN　　　　　　　　　　　　　　　　　　　　　　1969

Workshops with a total area of approx 4 500 sq ft are situated amidships with ready access to the dock, and there is a 3-ton travelling gantry fitted with outriggers to cover ships berthed alongside up to 200 feet long.

CORVETTES

4 550 TON MISSILE CORVETTES

Displacement, tons: 547 full load
Dimensions, feet (metres): 202·4 oa × 30·5 × 16·3 (61·7 oa × 9·3 × 5)
Missiles: 4 Otomat
Guns: 1—76/62 mm; 2—40 mm 70 cal Breda (twin)
A/S weapons: 6—(2 triple) Mk 32 A/S torpedo tubes
Mines: Can lay mines
Main engines: 4 MTU MA 16 V956 TB91 Diesels; 1 800 hp; 4 shafts = 31 knots
Complement: 54

Ordered from Cantieri Navali del Tirreno e Riuniti in 1974. Completion presumed to be 1977-78. As this corvette can be provided with two, three or four diesels, the performance is very variable. The data given above is basic information for the missile variant (schedule 1).

Electronics: ECM equipment; ELMER telecommunications system.

Radar: Air and surface search: Selenia RAN 11 LX
Navigation: Decca TM 1226. Fire control: Elsag NA 10.

Sonar: An EDO 700E can be fitted.

550 ton Corvette　　　　　　　　　　　　　　　　1975, CNTR

Name	No.	Builders	Commissioned
TOBRUK	—	Vosper Ltd, Portsmouth and Vickers Ltd	20 April 1966

Displacement, tons: 440 standard; 500 full load
Dimensions, feet (metres): 162 wl; 177 oa × 28·5 × 13 *(49·4; 54 × 8·7 × 4)*
Guns: 1—4 in; 4—40 mm (single)
Main engines: 2 Paxman Ventura 16 YJCM diesels; 2 shafts; 3 800 bhp = 18 knots
Range, miles: 2 900 at 14 knots
Complement: 63 (5 officers and 58 ratings)

Launched on 29 July 1965, completed on 30 Mar 1966, commissioned for service at Portsmouth on 20 Apr 1966, and arrived in Tripoli on 15 June 1966. Fitted with surface warning radar, Vosper roll damping fins and air-conditioning. A suite of State apartments is included in the accommodation.

TOBRUK

1971, A. & J. Pavia

LIGHT FORCES

10 "COMBATTANTE II G" CLASS
(FAST ATTACK CRAFT—MISSILE)

Displacement, tons: 311
Dimensions, feet (metres): 160·7 × 24·9 × 7·9 *(49 × 7·6 × 2·4)*
Missiles: 4 MM 38 Exocet
Guns: 1—76 mm OTO Melara (forward); 2—40 mm Bofors Breda (twin)
Main engines: 4 diesels; 20 000 bhp; 4 shafts = 40 knots
Range, miles: 1 600 at 15 knots
Complement: 31

Steel hull with alloy superstructure. Ordered from CMN Cherbourg in 1975. Delivery expected 1977-78.

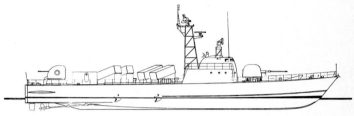

"COMBATTANTE II G"

1976, CMN Cherbourg

? 24 Ex-SOVIET "OSA" CLASS
(FAST ATTACK CRAFT—MISSILE)

It is reliably reported that the USSR is planning to provide up to 24 of this class, the first units having arrived in Libya in October 1976.

3 "SUSA" CLASS (FAST ATTACK CRAFT—MISSILE)

Name	No.	Builders	Commissioned
SEBHA (ex-*Sokna*)	—	Vosper Ltd, Portsmouth	1969
SIRTE	—	Vosper Ltd, Portsmouth	23 Jan 1969
SUSA	—	Vosper Ltd, Portsmouth	23 Jan 1969

Displacement, tons: 95 standard; 114 full load
Dimensions, feet (metres): 90·0 pp; 96·0 wl; 100·0 oa × 25·5 × 7·0 *(27·5; 29·3; 30·5 × 7·8 × 2·1)*
Missiles: 8—SS 12
Guns: 2—40 mm (single)
Main engines: 3 Bristol Siddeley "Proteus" gas turbines; 3 shafts; 12 750 bhp = 54 knots
Complement: 20

The order for these three fast patrol boats was announced on 12 Oct 1966. They are generally similar to the "Soloven" class designed and built by Vosper for the Royal Danish Navy. Fitted with air-conditioning and modern radar and radio equipment. *Suza* was launched on 31 Aug 1967, *Sirte* on 10 Jan 1968 and *Sokna* (renamed *Sebha*) on 29 Feb 1968. First operational vessels

SEBHA

1969, Wright & Logan

in the world to be armed with Nord-Aviation SS 12(M) guided weapons with sighting turret installation and other equipment developed jointly by Vosper and Nord.

4 "GARIAN" CLASS (LARGE PATROL CRAFT)

Name	No.	Builders	Commissioned
KHAWLAN	—	Brooke Marine, Lowestoft	30 Aug 1969
MERAWA	—	Brooke Marine, Lowestoft	early 1970
SABRATHA	—	Brooke Marine, Lowestoft	early 1970
GARIAN	—	Brooke Marine, Lowestoft	30 Aug 1969

Displacement, tons: 120 standard; 159 full load
Dimensions, feet (metres): 100 pp; 106 oa × 21·2 × 5·5 *(30·5; 32·3 × 6·5 × 1·7)*
Guns: 1—40 mm; 1—20 mm
Main engines: 2 Paxman diesels; 2 200 bhp = 24 knots
Range, miles: 1 500 at 12 knots
Complement: 15 to 22

Launched on 21 April 29, May, 25 Oct and 30 Sep 1969, respectively.

KHAWLAN

1970, Brooke Marine

6 THORNYCROFT TYPE (LARGE PATROL CRAFT)

Name	No.	Builders	Commissioned
AKRAMA	—	Vosper Thornycroft	early 1969
AR RAKIB	—	John I. Thornycroft, Woolston	4 May 1967
BENINA	—	Vosper Thornycroft	29 Aug 1968
FARWA	—	John I. Thornycroft, Woolston	4 May 1967
HOMS	—	Vosper Thornycroft	early 1969
MISURATA	—	Vosper Thornycroft	29 Aug 1968

Displacement, tons: 100
Dimensions, feet (metres): 100 × 21 × 5·5 *(30·5 × 6·4 × 1·7)*
Gun: 1—20 mm
Main engines: 3 Rolls-Royce DV8TLM Diesels; 1 740 bhp = 18 knots
Range, miles: 1 800 at 14 knots

Welded steel construction. Slight difference in silhouette between first pair and the remainder.

FARWA

1969, Thornycroft

1 THORNYCROFT TYPE (COASTAL PATROL CRAFT)

Dimensions, feet (metres): 78 × 15 × 4·5 *(23·8 × 4·6 × 1·4)*
Gun: 1 MG
Main engines: 3 Rolls-Royce diesels; 3 shafts; 945 bhp = 22·5 knots
Range, miles: 400 at 15 knots

Built by John I. Thornycroft, Singapore in 1962. Two similar but smaller boats transferred to Malta in 1974.

AMPHIBIOUS FORCES

2 ''PS 700'' CLASS (LST)

Name	No.	Builders	Commissioned
IBN OUF	—	CNIM	May 1977
HARISSA	—	CNIM	Mar 1978

Displacement, tons: 2 800 full load
Dimensions, feet (metres): 326·4 × 51·2 × 8·2 *(99·5 × 15·6 × 2·5)*
Aircraft: Deck for Alouette III
Guns: 2—30 mm
Main engines: 2 SEMT Pielstick diesels; 5 340 hp; 2 shafts (cp propellers) = 15·2 knots
Range, miles: 4 000 at 14 knots
Complement: 34

Can carry 240 troops under normal conditions. Have bow doors and ramp for the 11 tanks carried.
Launch dates: *Ibn Ouf* 22 Oct 1976; *Harissa* Feb 1977.

MAINTENANCE REPAIR CRAFT

ZLEITEN (ex-*MRC 1013*, ex-*LCT*)

Displacement, tons: 657 standard; 900 approx full load
Dimensions, feet (metres): 225·0 pp; 231·3 oa × 39·0 × 5·0 *(68·6; 70·5 × 11·9 × 1·5)*
Main engines: 4 Paxman diesels; 2 shafts; 1 840 bhp × 9 knots cruising

Built in 1944-45. Purchased from Great Britain on 5 Sep 1966. Now a hulk.

MALAWI

1 FAIREY MARINE ''SPEAR'' CLASS

Dimensions, feet (metres): 29·8 × 9·2 × 2·6 *(9·1 × 2·8 × ·8)*
Guns: 2—7·62 mm MG
Main engines: 2 Perkins diesels of 290 hp = 25 knots
Complement: 3

Acquired late 1976.

Three other small patrol-boats are deployed on Lake Nyasa (L. Malawi); the first was bought in 1968.

MALAYSIA

SEE ALSO SABAH

Administration

Minister of Defence:
 Hon. Dato Hussein bin Onn

Headquarters Appointments

Chief of the Naval Staff:
 Rear-Admiral Mohd. Zain bin Mohd. Salleh, KMN
Deputy Chief of the Naval Staff:
 Commodore Abdul Wahab bin Haji Nawi

Senior Commands

Commander Naval Area 1:
 Commodore P. K. Nettur, KMN
Commander Naval Area 2:
 Commodore Aril Fadzullah bin Alaug Ahmad

Diplomatic Representation

Services Adviser in London:
 Colonel M. Shah Bin Yahaya

Personnel

(a) 1977: 6 000 officers and ratings (Reserves about 1 000)
(b) Voluntary service

Bases

KD *Malaya*, Johore Straits; Port Swettenham; Penang; Labuan. (KD *Sri Labuan, Sri Tawau, Sri Rejang, Pelandok*).

Prefix to Ships' Names

The names of Malaysian warships are prefixed by KD, (Kapal Diraja).

Mercantile Marine

Lloyd's Register of Shipping:
 150 vessels of 442 740 tons gross

Strength of the Fleet

Type	Active	Building
Frigates	3	—
Fast Attack Craft—Missile	8	—
Fast Attack Craft—Gun	6	4
Large Patrol Craft	22	—
Minesweepers—Coastal	6	—
Diving Tender	1	—
Survey Vessel	1	—
LSTs	3	—
Police Launches	27	3

DELETIONS

Light Forces

1976 *Sri Kedah, Sri Pahang*

PENNANT LIST

Frigates

F 24	Rahmat
F 433	Hang Tuah

Light Forces

P 34	Kris
P 36	Sundang
P 37	Badek
P 38	Renchong
P 39	Tombak
P 40	Lembing
P 41	Serampang
P 42	Panah
P 43	Kerambit
P 44	Beledau
P 45	Kelewang
P 46	Rentaka
P 47	Sri Perlis
P 49	Sri Johor
P 150	Perkasa

Light Forces—Cont.

P 151	Handalan
P 152	Gempita
P 153	Pendekar
P 3139	Sri Selangor
P 3140	Sri Perak
P 3142	Sri Kelantan
P 3143	Sri Trengganu
P 3144	Sri Sabah
P 3145	Sri Sarawak
P 3146	Sri Negri Sembilan
P 3147	Sri Melaka
P 3501	Perdana
P 3502	Serang
P 3503	Ganas
P 3504	Ganyang
P 3505	Jerong
P 3506	Todak
P 3507	Paus
P 3508	Yu
P 3509	Baung
P 3510	Pari

Minewarfare Forces

M 1127	Mahamiru
M 1134	Kinabalu
M 1143	Ledang
M 1163	Tahan
M 1168	Jerai
M 1172	Brinchang

Support Forces

A 151	Perantau
A 1109	Duyong
A 1500	Sri Langkawi
A 1501	Sri Banggi
A 1502	Rajah Jarom

Police Craft

PX 1-30	Coastal Patrol Craft

FRIGATES

1 YARROW TYPE

Name	No.	Builders	Laid down	Launched	Commissioned
RAHMAT (ex-*Hang Jebat*)	F 24	Yarrow	Feb 1966	18 Dec 1967	Mar 1971

Displacement, tons: 1 250 standard; 1 600 full load
Length, feet (metres): 300·0 *(91·44)* pp; 308 *(93·9)* oa
Beam, feet (metres): 34·1 *(10·4)*
Draught, feet (metres): 14·8 *(4·5)*
Aircraft: Can land helo. on MacGregor hatch on Limbo well
Missile launchers: 1 quadruple Seacat surface-to-air
Guns: 1—4·5 in *(114 mm)*; 2—40 mm
A/S weapon: 1 Limbo three-barrelled mortar
Main engines: 1 Bristol Siddeley Olympus gas turbine; 19 500 shp; Crossley Pielstick Diesel; 3 850 bhp; 2 shafts
Speed, knots: 26 boosted by gas turbine; 16 on diesel alone
Range, miles: 6 000 at 16 knots; 1 000 at 26 knots
Complement: 140

General purpose frigate of new design developed by Yarrow. Fully automatic with saving in complement. Ordered on 11 Feb 1966.

Radar: Air Surveillance: HSA LW 02. Fire control: M 20 with radar in spherical radome for guns; M 44 for Seacat.

RAHMAT   *1972, Wright & Logan*

1 YARROW TYPE

Name	No.	Builders	Laid down	Launched	Commissioned
— (ex-*Mermaid*)	ex-F 76	Yarrow Shipbuilders & Co Ltd	1965	29 Dec 1966	16 May 1973 (see notes)

Displacement, tons: 2 300 standard; 2 520 full load
Dimensions, feet (metres): 320 pp; 330 wl; 339·3 oa × 40 × 12 *(97·6; 100·7; 103·5 × 12·2 × 3·7)*
Guns: 2—4 inch (twin); 2—40 mm
A/S weapons: 1 Squid
Main engines: 8 Diesels; 2 shafts; 2 cp propellers = 24 knots
Oil fuel, tons: 230
Range, miles: 4 800 at 15 knots

Similar in hull and machinery to "Leopard" and "Salisbury" classes. Originally built for Ghana as a display ship for ex-President Nkrumah at a cost of £5m but put up for sale after his departure. She was launched without ceremony on 29 Dec 1966 and completed in 1968. She was transferred to Portsmouth Dockyard in April 1972 being acquired by the Royal Navy. Refit started October 1972 at Chatham. Commissioned in Royal Navy 16 May 1973. She was based at Singapore 1974-75 returning to UK early 1976.

Transfer: To Malaysia April 1977 as replacement for *Hang Tuah*.

Ex-MERMAID

1 Ex-BRITISH "LOCH" CLASS

Name	No.	Builders	Laid down	Launched	Commissioned
HANG TUAH (ex-HMS *Loch Insh*)	F 433	Henry Robb Ltd, Leith	17 Nov 1943	10 May 1944	20 Oct 1944

Displacement, tons: 1 575 standard; 2 400 full load
Length, feet (metres): 297·2 *(90·6)* wl; 307·0 *(93·6)* oa
Beam, feet (metres): 38·5 *(11·7)*
Draught, feet (metres): 14·8 *(4·5)*
Guns: 4—40 mm
Main engines: 2 triple expansion; 5 500 ihp; 2 shafts
Boilers: 2 Admiralty 3-drum
Speed, knots: 19·5
Range, miles: 6 400 at 10 knots
Complement: 140

On transfer, refitted (in Portsmouth Dockyard) with helicopter deck, air-conditioning, modern radar and extra accommodation. Re-commissioned on 12 Oct 1964. Sailed on 12 Nov 1964. Converted into a training ship in April 1971, the two 4-inch guns and the two Squid mortars having been removed. *Hang Tuah* was the name of a Malay Admiral of the 15th century.

Radar: Search: Type 272.

HANG TUAH   *1972, Royal Malaysian Navy*

LIGHT FORCES
6 "JERONG" CLASS (FAST ATTACK CRAFT—GUN)

Name	No.	Builders	Commissioned
BAUNG	3509	Hong-Leong-Lürssen, Butterworth	Jan 1977
JERONG	3505	Hong-Leong-Lürssen, Butterworth	27 Mar 1976
PARI	3510	Hong-Leong-Lürssen, Butterworth	Mar 1977
PAUS	3507	Hong-Leong-Lürssen, Butterworth	16 Aug 1976
TODAK	3506	Hong-Leong-Lürssen, Butterworth	16 June 1976
YU	3508	Hong-Leong-Lürssen, Butterworth	15 Nov 1976

Displacement, tons: 254 full load
Dimensions, feet (metres): 147·3 × 23 × 12·8 *(44·9 × 7 × 3·9)*
Guns: 1—57 mm; 1—40 mm
Main engines: 3 Maybach Mercedes-Benz diesels; 3 300 bhp = 32 knots
Range, miles: 2 000 at 15 knots

Launch dates: *Jerong,* 28 July 1975; *Todak,* 15 Mar 1976; *Paus,* 3 June 1976; *Yu,* 17 July 1976; *Baung,* 5 Oct 1976; *Pari,* Jan 1977.

JERONG   1976, Royal Malaysian Navy

4 "SPICA-M" CLASS (FAST ATTACK CRAFT—TORPEDO)

Displacement, tons: 230
Dimensions, feet (metres): 134·5 × 23·3 × 5·2 *(41 × 7·1 × 1·6)*
Gun: 1—57 mm
Torpedo tubes: 6—21 inch
Main engines: 3 MTU diesels = 38 knots

Ordered from Karlskrona Shipyard in 1976 for delivery in 1979.

4 "PERDANA" CLASS (FAST ATTACK CRAFT—MISSILE)

Name	No.	Builders	Commissioned
PERDANA	P 3501	Constructions Mécaniques de Normandie	Dec 1972
GANAS	P 3503	Constructions Mécaniques de Normandie	28 Feb 1973
SERANG	P 3502	Constructions Mécaniques de Normandie	31 Jan 1973
GANYANG	P 3504	Constructions Mécaniques de Normandie	20 Mar 1973

Displacement, tons: 234 standard; 265 full load
Dimensions, feet (metres): 154·2 × 23·1 × 12·8 *(47·0 × 7·0 × 3·9)*
Missile launchers: 2 MM38 Exocet
Guns: 1—57 mm Bofors; 1—40 mm 70 cal Bofors
Main engines: 4 MTU diesels; 4 shafts; 14 000 bhp = 36·5 knots
Range, miles: 800 at 25 knots

Perdana launched 31 May 1972 and *Ganas* launched 26 Oct 1972, *Serang* launched 22 Dec 1971, and *Ganyang* launched 16 March 1972. All of basic "La Combattante II" design. Left Cherbourg for Malaysia 2 May 1973.

GANAS   4/1973, Wright & Logan

4 "PERKASA" CLASS (FAST ATTACK CRAFT—MISSILE)

Name	No.	Builders	Commissioned
GEMPITA	P 152	Vosper Ltd, Portsmouth	1967
HANDALAN	P 151	Vosper Ltd, Portsmouth	1967
PENDEKAR	P 153	Vosper Ltd, Portsmouth	1967
PERKASA	P 150	Vosper Ltd, Portsmouth	1967

Displacement, tons: 95 standard; 114 full load
Dimensions, feet (metres): 90 pp; 96 wl; 99 oa × 25·5 × 7 *(27·5; 29·3; 30·2 × 7·8 × 2·1)*
Missiles: 8—SS 12 (M) in 2 quadruple launchers
Guns: 1—40 mm; 1—20 mm
Main engines: 3 Rolls Royce Proteus gas turbines; 3 shafts; 12 750 bhp = 54 knots; GM diesels on wing shafts for cruising = 10 knots

The design is a combination of the "Brave" class hull form and Ferocity type construction. Ordered on 22 Oct 1964. They can also operate in the gunboat role or a minelaying role. *Perkasa* (Valiant) was launched on 26 Oct 1965, *Handalan* (Reliant) on 18 Jan 1966, *Gempita* (Thunderer) on 6 Apr 1966 and *Pendekar* (Champion) on 24 June 1966. The hull is entirely of glued laminated wooden construction, with upperworks of aluminium alloy. Equipment includes Rover gas turbine generating sets, full air-conditioning, Decca radar and comprehensive navigation and communications system. The craft were shipped to Malaysia in mid-1967. They were re-armed with eight SS 12 missiles in place of four 21-inch torpedoes in 1971.

GEMPITA (Firing SS 12 missile)   1972, Royal Malaysian Navy

4 "KEDAH" CLASS (LARGE PATROL CRAFT)

Name	No.	Builders	Commissioned
SRI KELANTAN	P 3142	Vosper Ltd, Portsmouth	12 Nov 1963
SRI PERAK	P 3140	Vosper Ltd, Portsmouth	June 1963
SRI SELANGOR	P 3139	Vosper Ltd, Portsmouth	25 Mar 1963
SRI TRENGGANU	P 3143	Vosper Ltd, Portsmouth	16 Dec 1963

4 "SABAH" CLASS (LARGE PATROL CRAFT)

Name	No.	Builders	Commissioned
SRI MELAKA	P 3147	Vosper Ltd, Portsmouth	2 Nov 1964
SRI NEGRI SEMBILAN	P 3146	Vosper Ltd, Portsmouth	28 Sep 1964
SRI SABAH	P 3144	Vosper Ltd, Portsmouth	2 Sep 1964
SRI SARAWAK	P 3145	Vosper Ltd, Portsmouth	30 Sep 1964

14 "KRIS" CLASS (LARGE PATROL CRAFT)

Name	No.	Builders	Commissioned
BADEK	P 37	Vosper Ltd, Portsmouth	15 Dec 1966
BELEDAU	P 44	Vosper Ltd, Portsmouth	12 Sep 1967
KELEWANG	P 45	Vosper Ltd, Portsmouth	4 Oct 1967
KERAMBIT	P 43	Vosper Ltd, Portsmouth	28 July 1967
KRIS	P 34	Vosper Ltd, Portsmouth	1 Jan 1966
LEMBING	P 40	Vosper Ltd, Portsmouth	12 Apr 1967
PANAH	P 42	Vosper Ltd, Portsmouth	27 July 1967
RENCHONG	P 38	Vosper Ltd, Portsmouth	17 Jan 1967
RENTAKA	P 46	Vosper Ltd, Portsmouth	22 Sep 1967
SERAMPANG	P 41	Vosper Ltd, Portsmouth	19 May 1967
SRI JOHOR	P 49	Vosper Ltd, Portsmouth	14 Feb 1968
SRI PERLIS	P 47	Vosper Ltd, Portsmouth	24 Jan 1968
SUNDANG	P 36	Vosper Ltd, Portsmouth	29 Nov 1966
TOMBAK	P 39	Vosper Ltd, Portsmouth	2 Mar 1967

BADEK ("Kris" Class)   1972, Royal Malaysian Navy

Displacement, tons: 96 standard; 109 full load
Dimensions, feet (metres): 95 wl; 103 oa × 19·8 × 5·5 *(29; 31·4 × 6 × 1·7)*
Guns: 2—40 mm; 70 cal
Main engines: 2 Bristol Siddeley/Maybach (MTU) MD 655/18 diesels; 3 500 bhp = 27 knots
Range, miles: 1 400 *(Sabah* class 1 660) at 14 knots
Complement: 22 (3 officers, 19 ratings)

The first six boats, constituting the "Kedah" class were ordered in 1961 for delivery in 1963. The four boats of the "Sabah" class were ordered in 1963 for delivery in 1964. The remaining 14

boats of the "Kris" class were ordered in 1965 for delivery between 1966 and 1968. All are of prefabricated steel construction and are fitted with Decca radar, air-conditioning and Vosper roll damping equipment. The differences between the three classes are minor, the later ones having improved radar, communications, evaporators and engines of Maybach (MTU), as opposed to Bristol Siddeley construction. *Sri Johor,* the last of the 14 boats of the "Kris" class, was launched on 22 June 1967.

MINE WARFARE FORCES

6 Ex-BRITISH "TON" CLASS (MINESWEEPERS—COASTAL)

Name	No.	Builders	Commissioned
BRINCHANG (ex-HMS *Thankerton*)	M 1172	Camper and Nicholson	1957
JERAI (ex-HMS *Dilston*)	M 1168	Cook, Welton and Gemmell	1955
KINABALU (ex-HMS *Essington*)	M 1134	Camper and Nicholson	1955
LEDANG (ex-HMS *Hexton*)	M 1143	Cook, Welton and Gemmell	1954
MAHAMIRU (ex-HMS *Darlaston*)	M 1127	Cook, Welton and Gemmell	1954
TAHAN (ex-HMS *Lullington*)	M 1163	Harland and Wolff	1956

MAHAMIRU   1972, Royal Malaysian Navy

Displacement, tons: 360 standard; 425 full load
Dimensions, feet (metres): 140 pp; 152 oa × 28·8 × 8·2 *(42·7; 46·4 × 8·8 × 2·5)*
Guns: 1 —40 mm forward; 2—20 mm aft
Main engines: 2 Deltic diesels; 2 shafts; 2 500 bhp = 15 knots
Oil fuel, tons: 45
Range, miles: 2 300 at 13 knots
Complement: 39

Mahamiru transferred from the Royal Navy on May 1960. *Ledang,* refitted at Chatham Dockyard before transfer, commissioned for Malaysia in Oct 1963. *Jerai* and *Kinabalu,* refitted in Great Britain, arrived in Malaysia summer 1964. *Brinchang* and *Tahan,* refitted in Singapore, transfer-

red to Malaysian Navy in May and Apr 1966, respectively. All six underwent a 9-month refit by Vosper Thornycroft, Singapore during 1972-73 which will extend their availability by some years.

AMPHIBIOUS FORCES

3 Ex-US "511-1152" CLASS (LSTs)

SRI LANGKAWI (ex-USS *Hunterdon County LST 838, AGP 838*) A 1500
SRI BANGGI (ex-USS *Henry County LST 824*) A 1501
RAJAH JAROM (ex-USS *Sedgewick County LST 1123*) A 1502

SRI LANGKAWI   1972, Royal Malaysian Navy

Displacement, tons: 1 653 standard; 2 366 beaching; 4 080 full load
Dimensions, feet (metres): 316·0 wl; 328·0 oa × 50·0 × 14·0 *(96·4; 100 × 15·3 × 4·3)*
Guns: 8—40 mm (2 twin, 4 single)
Main engines: GM diesels; 2 shafts; 1 700 bhp = 11·6 knots
Complement: 138 (11 officers, 127 ratings)

Built in 1945. *Sri Langkawi* transferred from the US Navy and commissioned in the Royal Malaysian Navy on 1 July 1971. Sold 1 Aug 1974. Other two transferred 7 Oct 1976 and used as cargo support ships. Cargo capacity 2 100 tons.
Sri Langkawi operates as a tender to Light Forces.

SURVEY VESSEL

1 Ex-BRITISH "TON" CLASS

Name	No.	Builders	Commissioned
PERANTAU (ex-HMS *Myrmidon*, ex-HMS *Edderton*)	A 151	Doig	20 July 1964

PERANTAU   1972, Royal Malaysian Navy

Displacement, tons: 360 standard; 420 full load
Dimensions, feet (metres): 152 oa × 28·8 × 8·2 *(46·4 × 8·8 × 2·5)*
Main engines: 2 Mirrlees diesels; 2 shafts; 3 000 bhp = 15 knots
Range, miles: 2 300 at 13 knots
Complement: 35

A former coastal minesweeper of the "Ton" class, converted by the Royal Navy into a survey ship, renamed *Myrmidon* in Apr 1964, and commissioned for service on 20 July 1964. Paid off in 1968 and purchased by Malaysia in 1969. Service in Malaysian waters since 1970.

Replacement: A contract was placed in early 1975 for a replacement new-design survey ship to be built at Hong Leong Lürssen, Butterworth. This ship, KD *Mutiara,* is due for delivery in 1977.

DIVING TENDER

Name	No.	Builders	Commissioned
DUYONG	A 1109	Kall·Teck (Pte) Ltd, Singapore	5 Jan 1971

Displacement, tons: 120 standard; 140 full load
Dimensions, feet (metres): 99·5 wl; 110·0 oa × 21·0 × 5·8 *(30·3; 33·6 × 6·4 × 1·8)*
Gun: 1—20 mm
Main engines: 2 Cummins diesels; 1 900 rpm; 500 bhp = 10 knots
Complement: 23

Launched on 18 Aug 1970 as TRV.

DUYONG   1973

ROYAL MALAYSIAN POLICE

18 PX CLASS

MAHKOTA PX 1	**BENTARA** PX 7	**PEKAN** PX 13
TEMENGGONG PX 2	**PERWIRA** PX 8	**KELANG** PX 14
HULUBALANG PX 3	**PERTANDA** PX 9	**KUALA KANGSAR** PX 15
MAHARAJASETIA 4	**SHAHBANDAR** PX 10	**ARAU** PX 16
MAHARAJALELA PX 5	**SANGSETIA** PX 11	**SRI GUMANTONG** PX 17
PAHLAWAN PX 6	**LAKSAMANA** PX 12	**SRI LABUAN** PX 18

Displacement, tons: 85
Dimensions, feet (metres): 87·5 oa × 19 × 4·8 *(26·7 × 5·8 × 1·5)*
Guns: 2—20 mm
Main engines: 2 Mercedes Benz (MTU) diesels; 2 shafts; 2 700 hp = 25 knots
Range, miles: 700 at 15 knots
Complement: 15

6 IMPROVED PX CLASS

ALOR STAR PX 19	**KUALA TRENGGANU** PX 21	**SRI MENANTI** PX 23
KOTA BAHRU PX 20	**JOHORE BAHRU** PX 22	**KUCHING** PX 24

Displacement, tons: 92
Dimensions, feet (metres): 91 oa *(27·8)*
Guns: 2—20 mm
Main engines: 2 (MTU) diesels; 2 460 hp = 25 knots
Range, miles: 750 at 15 knots
Complement: 18

All 24 boats built by Vosper Thornycroft Private, Singapore; PX class between 1963 and 1970, Improved PX class 1972-73. *Sri Gumantong* and *Sri Labuan* operated by Sabah Government, remainder by Royal Malaysian Police.

SRI MENANTI   *1972, Yam Photos, Singapore*

3 + 3 LÜRSSEN PATROL CRAFT

SRI — PX 25	**SRI KUDAT** PX 26	**SRI TAWAU** PX 27

Of 62·5 tons and 25 knots with 1—20 mm. Completed mid-1973. Three more building.

MALAGASY

Ministerial

Minister of Defence:
Lieutenant-Colonel Mampila Jaona

Personnel

(a) 1977: 600 officers and men (including Marine Company)
(b) 18 months National Service

Mercantile Marine

Lloyd's Register of Shipping: 49 vessels of 49 738 tons gross

Bases and Ports

Diego Suarez, Tamatave, Majunga, Tulear, Nossi-Be, Fort Dauphin, Manakara.

LIGHT FORCES

1 LARGE PATROL CRAFT

Name	No.	Builders	Commissioned
MALAIKA	—	Chantiers Navals Franco-Belges	Dec 1967

Displacement, tons: 235 light
Dimensions, feet (metres): 149·3 pp; 155·8 oa × 23·6 × 8·2 *(45·5; 47·5 × 7·1 × 2·5)*
Guns: 2—40 mm
Main engines: 2 MGO diesels; 2 shafts; 2 400 bhp = 18·5 knots
Range, miles: 4 000 at 18 knots
Complement: 25

Ordered by the French Navy for delivery to Madagascar. Laid down in Nov 1966, launched on 22 Mar 1967.

5 PATROL BOATS

Displacement, tons: 46
Gun: 1—40 mm
Main engines: 2 diesels = 22 knots

Used by the Maritime Police. Built by Küstenwache in 1962.

AMPHIBIOUS FORCE

1 "BATRAM" CLASS

Name	No.	Builders	Commissioned
TOKY	—	Arsenal de Diego Suarez	Oct 1974

Displacement, tons: 810
Dimensions, feet (metres): 217·8 × 41 × 6·2 *(66·4 × 12·5 × 1·9)*
Missiles: 8—SS12
Guns: 2—40 mm
Main engines: 2 MGO diesels; 2 400 hp; 2 shafts = 13 knots
Complement: 27
Range, miles: 3 000 at 12 knots

Bow doors. Can carry 250 tons stores and 30 passengers or 120 troops over short distances. Paid for by the French Government as military assistance.

TRAINING SHIP

Name	No.	Builders	Commissioned
FANANTENANA (ex-*Richelieu*)	—	A. G. Weser, Bremen, Germany	1959

Displacement, tons: 1 040 standard; 1 200 full load
Dimensions, feet (metres): 183·7 pp; 206·4 oa × 30 × 14·8 *(56; 62·9 × 9·2 × 4·5)*
Guns: 2—40 mm
Main engines: 2 Deutz diesels; 1 shaft; 1 060 + 500 bhp = 12 knots

Trawler purchased and converted in 1966-67 to Coast Guard and training ship. 691 tons gross.

TENDER

JASMINE (ex-*D 385,* ex-*D 211,* ex-*YMS 31*)

Displacement, tons: 280 standard; 325 full load
Dimensions, feet (metres): 134·5 × 24·5 × 12 *(41 × 7·5 × 3·7)*
Main engines: 2 diesels; 2 shafts; 1 000 bhp = 12 knots
Oil fuel, tons: 22

Former coastal minesweeper of the ex-US YMS type launched on 10 April 1942 acquired by France in 1954 and Malagasy in 1965.

MALDIVES

A series of widely separated atolls where fishing has been interrupted by foreign craft and the small communities can be reached only by sea.

Mercantile Marine

Lloyd's Register of Shipping: 44 vessels of 121 462 tons gross.

3 Ex-TAIWANESE TRAWLERS

Confiscated for illegal fishing. Fitted with one twin 25 mm (Soviet) gun on foc's'le.

1 FAIREY MARINE 45 ft TYPE

Provided for patrol and intercommunication duties in 1975.

FAIREY 45 ft TYPE·   *1975, Brian Manby*

MALI

Personnel

1977: 50 officers and men

Patrol Craft

A small river patrol service with 3 craft operating on headwaters of the Niger with bases at Bamako, Segou, Mopti and Timbuktu.

MALTA

A coastal patrol force of small craft was formed in 1973. It is manned by the Maltese Regiment and primarily employed as a coastguard.

Mercantile Marine

Lloyd's Register of Shipping: 32 vessels of 39 140 tons gross

2 Ex-US "SWIFT" CLASS

C 23 (ex-US C 6823)   **C 24** (ex-US C 6824)

Displacement, tons: 22·5
Dimensions, feet (metres): 50 × 13 × 3·5 *(15·6 × 4 × 1·2)*
Guns: 3—12·7 cal MG
Main engines: 2 Gray diesels = 25 knots
Endurance: 24 hours
Complement: 6

Built in 1967. Bought in Feb 1971.

C 23 and 24   *1975, D. Bateman*

2 Ex-LIBYAN CUSTOMS LAUNCHES

C 25   **C 26**

Dimensions, feet (metres): 100 *(33)* length
Gun: 1 Light MG
A/S weapons: 2 DCs
Main engines: 2 RR Diesels; 2 shafts; 630 bhp = 21 knots

First transferred 16 Jan 1974.

C 26   *1976, Michael D. J. Lennon*

3 Ex-GERMAN CUSTOMS LAUNCHES

C 27 (ex-*Brunsbuttel*)

Of 90 tons and 104 feet *(31·7 m)*
Gun—1 MG. Built by Buschmann, Hamburg.

C 27   *1976, Michael D. J. Lennon*

C 28 (ex-*Geier*)

Of 115 tons and 92 feet *(28 m)*.
Gun—1 MG.

C 28   *1976, Michael D. J. Lennon*

C 29 (ex-*Kondor*)

Of 100 tons and 92 feet *(28 m)*.
Gun—1 MG. Built by Lürssen, Vegesack 1952.

C 29   *1975, D. Bateman*

1 CUSTOMS LAUNCH

C 21

Built by Malta Drydocks 1969 and purchased 1973.

MAURITANIA

Ministerial

Minister of National Defence:
  Abdullahi Ould Bah

Personnel

(a) 1977: 100 officers and men
(b) Voluntary service

Base

Port Etienne

Mercantile Marine

Lloyd's Register of Shipping: 4 vessels of 1 113 tons gross

PATROL BOATS

Name	No.	Builders	Commissioned
DAR EL BARKA	—	Chantiers Navals de l'Estérel	June 1969
TICHITT	—	Chantiers Navals de l'Estérel	April 1969

Displacement, tons: 75 standard; 80 full load
Dimensions, feet (metres): 105 × 18·9 × 5·2 *(31·4 × 5·8 × 1·6)*
Guns: 2—20 mm
Main engines: 2 Mercedes Maybach (MTU) 12V 331 TC81 diesels; 2 shafts; 2 700 bhp = 30 knots
Range, miles: 1 500 at 15 knots
Complement: 17

DAR EL BARKA   *Chantiers Navals de l'Esterel*

Name	No.	Builders	Commissioned	
IM RAQ NI	—	Chantiers Navals de l'Estérel	Nov 1965	**CHINGUETTI**
SLOUGHI	—	Chantiers Navals de l'Estérel	May 1968	Small patrol craft reaching the end of her life.

Displacement, tons: 20
Dimensions, feet (metres): 59 × 13·5 × 3·8 *(18 × 4·1 × 1·2)*
Gun: 1—12·7 mm
Main engines: 2 GM 671M diesels; 512 bhp = 22·5 knots
Range, miles: 860 at 12 knots; 400 at 15 knots
Complement: 6

MAURITIUS

Ministerial

Minister of National Defence:
Sir Seewoosagur Ramgoolam (Premier)

Mercantile Marine

Lloyd's Register of Shipping: 13 vessels of 35 146 tons gross

1 Ex-INDIAN "ABHAY" CLASS (LARGE PATROL CRAFT)

— (ex-I.S. *Amar*)

Displacement, tons: 120 standard; 151 full load
Dimensions, feet (metres): 110 pp; 117·2 oa × 20 × 5 *(33·6 pp; 35·7 oa × 6·1 × 1·5)*
Gun: 1—40 mm
Main engines: 2 diesels = 18 knots

Built by Hooghly D & E Co, Calcutta 1961. Transferred April 1974.

"ABHAY" Class

MEXICO

Ministerial

Secretary of National Defence:
General Hermenegildo Cuenca Diaz

Headquarters Appointments

Secretary of the Navy:
Admiral C. G. Demn. Luis M. Bravo Carrera
Under-Secretary of the Navy:
Rear-Admiral Ing M. N. Ricardo Chazaro Lara
Commander-in-Chief of the Navy:
Vice-Admiral C. G. Demn. Humberto Uribe Escandon
Chief of the Naval Staff:
Rear-Admiral C. G. Demn. Miguel A. Gomez Ortega
Director Naval Air Services:
Rear Admiral Blanco Peyrefitte
Director of Services:
Rear-Admiral C. G. Demn. Mario Artigas Fernandez

Diplomatic Representation

Naval Attaché in London:
Rear-Admiral C. Lopez Sotelo
Naval Attaché in Washington:
Vice-Admiral Miguel Manzarraga

Personnel

(a) 1977: Total 11 000 officers and men (including Naval Air
     Force and Marines)
(b) Voluntary Service

Mercantile Marine

Lloyd's Register of Shipping:
290 vessels of 593 875 tons gross

Naval Air Force

Naval air bases at Mexico City, Las Bajadas, Puerto Cortes, Isla
Mujeres, Ensenada.

4 Hu-16 Albatros
2 Bell 47G helicopters
1 Bell 47J helicopter
4 Alouette III helicopters
5 Hughes 269A
4 DC 3 (Dakota)
1 Riley Turbo-Rocket
1 Cessna 402B
3 Beechcraft C45H
4 Cessna 150
1 Cessna 180-D
1 Cessna 337
1 Cessna 402B
1 Stearman
3 Mentor T-43B
1 Beech B-55 Baron
2 Beech F-33A Bonanza
1 Learjet 24D

Naval Bases

The Naval Command is split between the Pacific and Gulf areas
and each subdivided into Naval Zones and, subsequently,
Naval Sectors.

Gulf Command: (odd numbered zones):
Veracruz (HQ 3rd Naval Zone and Command HQ)
Tampico (1st Naval Zone)
Ciudad del Carmen (5th Naval Zone)
Isla Mujeres (7th Naval Zone)
Tuxpan, Coatzacoalcos, Progreso, Chetumal (Naval Sector
HQs)

Pacific Command: (even numbered zones):
Acapulco (HQ 8th Naval Zone and Command HQ)
Puerto Cortes (2nd Naval Zone)
Guaymas (4th Naval Zone)
Manzanillo (6th Naval Zone)
Ensenada, La Paz, Mazatlan, Salina Cruz (Naval Sector HQs)

Strength of the Fleet

Type	Active	Building
Destroyers	2	—
Frigates	6	—
Corvettes	35	—
Large Patrol Craft	22	9
Survey Vessel	1	—
Coastal and River Patrol Craft	14	—
Transport	1	—
LSTs (1 repair ship)	3	—
Tankers-Harbour	2	—
Tugs	6	—
Floating Docks	4	—
Training Ship	1	—
Floating Cranes	7	—

DELETIONS

Frigates

1972 *Potosi, Queretaro* ("Guanajato" class). *California* (APD
      type) standard (16 Jan)
1975 *Guanajato*
1976 *Papaloapan* (ex-US APD)

Survey Ships

1973 *Sotavento*
1975 *Virgilio Uribe*

Tug

1974 *R4*

DESTROYERS

2 Ex-US "FLETCHER" CLASS

Name
CUAUTHEMOC (ex-USS *Harrison, DD 573*)
CUITLAHUAC (ex-USS *John Rodgers, DD 574*)

No.	Builders	Laid down	Launched	Commissioned
IE 01 (ex-F 1)	Consolidated Steel	25 July 1941	7 May 1942	25 Jan 1943
IE 02 (ex-F 2)	Consolidated Steel	25 July 1941	7 May 1942	9 Feb 1943

CUAUTHEMOC   *1972, Mexican Navy*

Displacement, tons: 2 100 standard; 3 050 full load
Length, feet (metres): 376·5 *(114·7)* oa
Beam, feet (metres): 39·5 *(12·0)*
Draught, feet (metres): 18·0 *(5·5)*
Guns (original): 5—5 in *(127 mm)*; 10—40 mm; (twin)
Torpedo tubes: 5—21 in *(533 mm)* (quintuple)
Main engines: 2 geared turbines; 2 shafts; 60 000 shp
Boilers: 4
Speed, knots: 36; 14 economical
Oil fuel, tons: 650
Range, miles: 5 000 at 14 knots
Complement: 197

Former US destroyers of the original "Fletcher" class. Transferred to the Mexican Navy in Aug 1970.

Radar and Fire Control:
Mk 12 radar for Mk 37 director: SC and SG1 radars; 1 modern commercial radar; 5—Mk 51 GFCS for 40 mm.

FRIGATES

1 Ex-US "EDSALL" CLASS

Name
COMO MANUEL AZUETA (ex-USS *Hurst, DE 250*)

No.	Builders	Laid down	Launched	Commissioned
IA 06	Brown SB Co, Houston	1942	14 April 1943	30 Aug 1943

"EDSALL" Class   *USN*

Displacement, tons: 1 200 standard; 1 850 full load
Dimensions, feet (metres): 306 × 36·6 × 13 *(93·3 × 11·3 × 4)*
Guns: 3—3 in *(76 mm)*, 50 cal
A/S weapons: Hedgehog; DC racks
Main engines: 4 diesels; 6 000 shp; 2 shafts
Speed, knots: 20; 12 economical
Complement: 149

Transferred to Mexico 1 Oct 1973. Employed as training ship.

1 "DURANGO" CLASS

Name   **No.**
DURANGO   B-1 (ex-128)

Builders	Laid down	Launched	Commissioned
Union Naval de Levante, Valencia	1934	28 June 1935	1936

DURANGO   *1972, Mexican Navy*

Displacement, tons: 1 600 standard; 2 000 full load
Length, feet (metres): 256·5 *(78·2)* oa
Beam, feet (metres): 36·6 *(11·2)*
Draught, feet (metres): 10·5 *(3·1)*
Guns: 2—4 in *(102 mm)*; 2—2·24 in *(57 mm)*; 4—20 mm
Main engines: 2 Enterprise DMR-38 diesels electric drive; 2 shafts; 5 000 bhp
Speed, knots: 18; 12 economical
Oil fuel, tons: 140
Range, miles: 3 000 at 12 knots
Complement: 149 (24 officers and 125 men)

Originally designed primarily as an armed transport with accommodation for 20 officers and 450 men. The two Yarrow boilers and Parsons geared turbines of 6 500 shp installed when first built were replaced with two 2 500 bhp diesels in 1967 when the ship was re-rigged with remodelled funnel.

4 Ex-US "CHARLES LAWRENCE" and "CROSSLEY" CLASSES

Name	No.	Builders	Laid down	Launched	Commissioned
COAHUILA (ex-USS *Rednour*, APD 102, ex-*DE 592*)	IB-08	Bethlehem SB Co, Hingham	9 Jan 1944	1 Mar 1944	15 Mar 1945
CHIHUAHUA (ex-USS *Barber*, LPR, ex-*APD 57*, ex-*DE 161*)	IB-07	Norfolk Navy Yard, Norfolk, Va	27 Apr 1943	20 May 1943	10 Oct 1943
TEHUANTEPEC (ex-USS *Joseph M. Auman*, APD 117, ex-*DE 674*)	IB-05 (ex-H 5)	Consolidated Steel Corp, Orange	8 Nov 1943	5 Feb 1944	25 Apr 1945
USUMACINTA (ex-USS *Don O. Woods*, APD 118, ex-*DE 721*)	IB-06 (ex-H 6)	Consolidated Steel Corp, Orange	1 Dec 1943	19 Feb 1944	28 May 1945

Displacement, tons: 1 400 standard; 2 130 full load
Length, feet (metres): 300·0 *(91·5)* wl; 306·0 *(93·3)* oa
Beam, feet (metres): 37·0 *(11·3)*
Draught, feet (metres): 11·3 *(3·4)*
Guns: 1—5 in *(127 mm)* 38 cal; 6—40 mm (3 twin); 6—20 mm (single)
Main engines: GE turbo-electtic; 2 shafts; 12 000 shp
Speed, knots: 20; 13 economical
Boilers: 2 Foster Wheeler "D" with superheater
Range, miles: 5 000 at 15 knots
Oil fuel, tons: 350
Complement: 204 plus 162 troops

IB 5-6 were purchased by Mexico in December 1963 and IB 7 and 8 on 17 Feb 1969. *California* (ex-USS *Belet* APD 109) stranded and lost 16 Jan 1972 on Bahia Peninsula.

Fire Control: 5 in: local control.
40 mm: 3—Mk 51 GFCS.

Radar: Combined search: SC.
Navigation: Commercial.

TEHUANTEPEC   1975, Mexican Navy

CORVETTES

18 Ex-US "AUK" Class

Name	No.
FRANCISCO ZARCO (ex-USS *Threat*, MSF 124)	IG-13
GUILLERMO PRIETO (ex-USS *Symbol*, MSF 123)	IG-02
GUTIERRIEZ ZAMORA (ex-USS *Scoter*, MSF 381)	IG-16
HERMENEGILDO GALENA (ex-USS *Sage*, MSF 111)	IG-19
IGNACIO ALTAMIRANO (ex-USS *Sway*, MSF 120)	IG-12
IGNACIO L. VALLARTA (ex-USS *Velocity*, MSF 128)	IG-14
IGNACIO DE LA LLAVE (ex-USS *Spear*, MSF 322)	IG-08
JESUS G. ORTEGA (ex-USS *Chief*, MSF 315)	IG-15
JUAN ALDAMA (ex-USS *Pilot*, MSF 104)	IG-18
JUAN N. ALVARES (ex-USS *Ardent*, MSF 340)	IG-09
LEANDRO VALLE (ex-USS *Pioneer*, MSF 105)	IG-01
MANUAL DOBLADO (ex-USS *Defense*, MSF 317)	IG-05
MARIANO ESCOBEDO (ex-USS *Champion*, MSF 314)	IG-03
MELCHOR OCAMPO (ex-USS *Roselle*, MSF 379)	IG-10
PONCIANO ARRIAGA (ex-USS *Competent*, MSF 316)	IG-04
SANTOS DEGOLLADO (ex-USS *Gladiator*, MSF 319)	IG-07
SEBASTIAN L. DE TEJADA (ex-USS *Devastator*, MSF 318)	IG-06
VALENTIN G. FARIAS (ex-USS *Starling*, MSF 64)	IG-11

Displacement, tons: 890 standard; 1 250 full load
Dimensions, feet (metres): 215 wl; 221·2 oa × 32·2 × 10·8 *(65·6; 67·5 × 10 × 3·3)*
Guns: 1—3 in 50 cal; 4—40 mm (twins); 8—20 mm (twins)
Main engines: Diesel electric; 2 shafts; 3 500 bhp
Speed, knots: 17; 10 economical
Complement: 9 officers and 96 ratings

IGNACIO DE LA LLAVE   1975, Mexican Navy

Transferred—6 in Feb 1973, 4 in Apr 1973, 9 in Sep 1973. Employed on patrol duties—*Mariano Matamoros* of this class employed on surveying duties with after armament replaced by large deck-house. (see Survey section)

Radar: SO13 and commercial navigation set.

17 Ex-US "ADMIRABLE" CLASS

Name	No.
DM 01 (ex-USS *Jubilant* AM 255)	ID-01
DM 02 (ex-USS *Hilarity* AM 241)	ID-02
DM 03 (ex-USS *Execute* AM 232)	ID-03
DM 04 (ex-USS *Specter* AM 306)	ID-04
DM 05 (ex-USS *Scuffle* AM 298)	ID-05
DM 06 (ex-USS *Eager* AM 224)	ID-06
DM 10 (ex-USS *Instill* AM 252)	ID-10
DM 11 (ex-USS *Device* AM 220)	ID-11
DM 12 (ex-USS *Ransom* AM 283)	ID-12
DM 13 (ex-USS *Knave* AM 256)	ID-13
DM 14 (ex-USS *Rebel* AM 284)	ID-14
DM 15 (ex-USS *Crag* AM 214)	ID-15
DM 16 (ex-USS *Dour* AM 223)	ID-16
DM 17 (ex-USS *Diploma* AM 221)	ID-17
DM 18 (ex-USS *Invade* AM 254)	ID-18
DM 19 (ex-USS *Intrigue* AM 253)	ID-19
DM 20 (ex-USS *Harlequin* AM 365)	ID-20

Displacement, tons: 650 standard; 945 full load
Dimensions, feet (metres): 184·5 oa × 33 × 9 *(56·3 × 10·1 × 3·1)*
Guns: 1—3 in, 50 cal; 4—40 mm; 6/8—20 mm (see note)
Main engines: 2 diesels; 2 shafts; 1 710 bhp = 15 knots
Range, miles: 4 300 at 10 knots
Complement: 104

Former US steel-hulled fleet minesweepers. All completed in 1943-44.

Gunnery: 20 mm armament varies from 6 (2 twin, 2 single) to 8 (4 twin).

DM 14 (old pennant number)   1975, Mexican Navy

LIGHT FORCES

22 + 9 "AZTECA" CLASS (LARGE PATROL CRAFT)

Name	No.	Builders	Commissioned
ANDRES QUINTANA ROOS	P 01	Ailsa Shipbuilding Co Ltd	1 Nov 1974
MATIAS DE CORDOVA	P 02	Scott & Sons, Bowling	22 Oct 1974
MIGUEL RAMOS ARIZPE	P 03	Ailsa Shipbuilding Co Ltd	23 Dec 1974
JOSE MARIA IZAZGU	P 04	Ailsa Shipbuilding Co Ltd	19 Dec 1974
JUAN BAUTISTA MORALES	P 05	Scott & Sons, Bowling	19 Dec 1974
IGNACIO LOPEZ RAYON	P 06	Ailsa Shipbuilding Co Ltd	19 Dec 1974
MANUEL CRECENCIO REJON	P 07	Ailsa Shipbuilding Co Ltd	4 July 1975
ANTONIO DE LA FUENTE	P 08	Ailsa Shipbuilding Co Ltd	4 July 1975
LEON GUZMAN	P 09	Scott & Sons, Bowling	7 April 1975
IGNACIO RAMIREZ	P 10	Ailsa Shipbuilding Co Ltd	17 July 1975
IGNACIO MARISCAL	P 11	Ailsa Shipbuilding Co Ltd	23 Sep 1975
HERIBERTO JARA CORONA	P 12	Ailsa Shipbuilding Co Ltd	7 Nov 1975
JOSE MARIA MAJA	P 13	J. Lamont & Co Ltd	13 Oct 1975
FELIX ROMERO	P 14	Scott & Sons, Bowling	23 June 1975
FERNANDO LIZARDI	P 15	Ailsa Shipbuilding Co Ltd	24 Dec 1975
FRANCISCO J. MUJICA	P 16	Ailsa Shipbuilding Co Ltd	21 Nov 1975
PASTOR ROUAIX	P 17	Scott & Sons, Bowling	7 Nov 1975
JOSE MARIA DEL CASTILLO VELASCO	P 18	Lamont & Co Ltd	14 Jan 1975
LUIS MANUEL ROJAS	P 19	Lamont & Co Ltd	3 April 1976
JOSE NATIVIDAD MACIAS	P 20	Lamont & Co Ltd	Sept 1976
ESTEBAN BACA CALDERON	P 21	Lamont & Co Ltd	18 June 1976
IGNACIO ZARAGOZA	P 22	Vera Cruz	1 June 1976

Displacement, tons: 130
Dimensions, feet (metres): 111·8 oa × 28·1 × 6·8 *(34·1 × 8·6 × 2·0)*
Guns: 1—40 mm; 1—20 mm
Main engines: 2—12 cyl Paxman Ventura diesels; 3 600 bhp = 24 knots
Range, miles: 2 500 at 12 knots
Complement: 24

JOSE MARIA IZAZGU   *1975, Mexican Navy*

Ordered by Mexico, for Fishery Protection duties, on 27 Mar 1973 from Associated British Machine Tool Makers Ltd.
HM Queen Elizabeth II went to sea in *Andres Quintana Roos* during her visit to Mexico in Mar 1975—an intention to place further orders for this class was announced shortly afterwards. Ten have been ordered for building in Mexican yards with ABMTM assistance (7 at Vera Cruz, 3 at Salina Cruz) and a final total of 80 is planned.

2 "AZUETA" CLASS (COASTAL PATROL CRAFT)

Name	No.	Builders	Commissioned
AZUETA	IF 06 (ex-G 9)	Astilleros de Tampico	1959
VILLAPANDO	IF 07 (ex-G 6)	Astilleros de Tampico	1960

Displacement, tons: 80 standard; 85 full load
Dimensions, feet (metres): 85·3 × 16·4 × 7·0 *(26 × 5 × 2·1)*
Guns: 2—13·2 mm (1 twin)
Main engines: Superior diesels; 600 bhp = 12 knots

Of all steel construction.

4 "POLIMAR" CLASS (COASTAL PATROL CRAFT)

Name	No.	Builders	Commissioned
POLIMAR 1	IF 01 (ex-G 1)	Astilleros de Tampico	1 Oct 1962
POLIMAR 2	IF 02 (ex-G 2)	Icacas Shipyard, Guerrero	1966
POLIMAR 3	IF 03 (ex-G 3)	Icacas Shipyard, Guerrero	1966
POLIMAR 4	IF 04 (ex-G 4)	Astilleros de Tampico	1968

Displacement, tons: 37 standard; 57 full load
Dimensions, feet (metres): 60·1 × 15·1 × 4·0 *(20·1 × 5·3 × 3·3)*
Gun: 1—20 mm
Main engines: 2 diesels; 456 bhp = 11 knots

Of steel construction.

POLIMAR 3   *1972, Mexican Navy*

8 RIVER TYPE (RIVER PATROL CRAFT)

Name	No.	Builders	Commissioned
AM 1	IF 11	Tampico	1960
AM 2	IF 12	Vera Cruz	1960
AM 3	IF 13	Tampico	1961
AM 4	IF 14	Vera Cruz	1961
AM 5	IF 15	Tampico	1961
AM 6	IF 16	Vera Cruz	1962
AM 7	IF 17	Tampico	1962
AM 8	IF 18	Vera Cruz	1962

Displacement, tons: 37
Dimensions, feet (metres): 56·1 × 16·4 × 8·2 *(17·1 × 5 × 2·5)*
Main engines: Diesel; speed = 6 knots

Of steel construction.

TRANSPORT

Name	No.	Builders	Commissioned
ZACATECAS	B 2	Ulua Shipyard, Veracruz	1960

Displacement, tons: 785 standard
Dimensions, feet (metres): 158 × 27·2 × 10 *(48·2 × 8·3 × 2·7)*
Guns: 1—40 mm; 2—20 mm (single)
Main engines: 1 MAN diesel; 560 hp = 8 knots
Complement: 50 (13 officers and 37 men)

Launched in 1959. Cargo ship type. The hull is of welded steel construction. Cargo capacity 400 tons.

SURVEY VESSEL

1 Ex-US "AUK" CLASS

MARIANO METAMOROS (ex-USS *Herald, MSF 101*) IH 01 (ex-*IG 17*)

Details given in "Auk" class under Corvettes. Took over surveying duties from *Virgilio Uribe*. After guns replaced by large deck-house.

SERVICE FORCES

2 Ex-US "511-1152" CLASS (LSTs)

RIO PANUCO (ex-USS *Park County, LST 1077)* IA 01
MANZANILLO (ex-USS *Clearwater County, LST 602)* IA 02

Displacement, tons: 1 653 standard; 2 366 beaching; 4 080 full load
Dimensions, feet (metres): 316 wl; 328 oa × 50 × 14 *(96·4; 100 × 15·3 × 4·3)*
Guns: 6—40 mm (1 twin; 4 singles)
Main engines: 2 GM diesels; 2 shafts; 1 700 bhp = 10·5 knots
Range, miles: 6 000 at 11 knots
Complement: 130
Troop capacity: 147

Transferred to Mexico on 20 Sep 1971 and 25 May 1972 respectively. Both employed as rescue ships.

RIO PANUCO   1975, Mexican Navy

1 Ex-US "FABIUS" CLASS (LIGHT FORCES TENDER)

GENERAL VINCENTE GUERRERO (ex-USS *Megara, ARVA-6)*

Displacement, tons: 1 625 light; 4 100 full load
Dimensions, feet (metres): 328 oa × 50 × 14 *(100 × 15·3 × 4·3)*
Guns: 8—40 mm
Main engines: 2 GM diesels; 2 shafts; 1 800 bhp = 14·6 knots
Range, miles: 10 000 at 10 knots
Complement: 250

Ex-aircraft repair ship sold to Mexico 1 Oct 1973.

2 Ex-US YOG/YO TYPE (HARBOUR TANKERS)

Name	No.	Builders	Commissioned
AGUASCALIENTES	A-5	Geo H. Mathis Co Ltd,	1943
(ex-*YOG 6)*		Camden, N.J.	
TLAXCALA	A-6	Geo Lawley & Son,	1943
(ex-*YO 107)*		Neponset, Mass	

Displacement, tons: 440 light; 1 480 full load
Dimensions, feet (metres): 159·2 × 30 × 8·2 *(48·6 × 9·2 × 2·5)*
Guns: 2—20 mm (singles)
Main engines: Union diesel; 1 shaft; 500 bhp = 8 knots
Capacity: 6 570 barrels
Complement: 26 (5 officers and 21 ratings)

Former US self-propelled fuel oil barges. Purchased in 1964. Entered service in Nov 1964.

AGUASCALIENTES   1975, Mexican Navy

MISCELLANEOUS

4 Ex-US MARITIME ADMINISTRATION "V 4" CLASS (TUGS)

R-1 (ex-*Farallon)* A 11
R-2 (ex-*Montauk)* A 12

R-3 (ex-*Point Vicente)* A 13
R-5 (ex-*Burnt Island)* A 15

Acquired in 1968.

PRAGMAR   PATRON

Tugs acquired in 1973.

4 FLOATING DOCKS

Ex-US ARD 2   Ex-US ARD 11   Ex-US ARD 15

Lift capacity of 3 000 tons. Built of steel. Transferred June 1974.

Ex-US AFDL 28

Lift capacity of 1 000 tons. Built of steel.

7 FLOATING CRANES

Ex-US YDs 156, 157, 179, 180, 183, 194 and 203, transferred Sep 1964 to July 1971.

1 PILE DRIVER

Ex-US YPD 43 leased Aug 1968.

TRAINING SHIP

Spanish merchant ship *Monte Anaga* purchased in late 1973 for conversion into a training ship for merchant navy cadets. Of 6 813 tons and built in 1959.

MONTSERRAT

Senior Officers

Commissioner of Police:
  Mr Galton B St John
CO Base:
  Cpl. Angus Prospere

Marine Police

The following craft is employed on general patrol duties under control of Montserrat Police Force.

Base

Plymouth

Mercantile Marine

Lloyd's Register of Shipping: 3 vessels of 1 130 tons gross

1 BROOKE MARINE 12 metre TYPE

EMERALD STAR

Displacement, tons: 15
Length, feet (metres): 40 *(12)*
Guns: Can mount 3 MGs
Main engines: 2 diesels; 370 hp = 22 knots
Complement: 4

Purchased in 1971.

EMERALD STAR   1975, Montserrat Government

MOROCCO

Diplomatic Representation

Defence Attaché in London:
Colonel Benomar Sbay

Personnel

(a) 1977: 2 000 officers and ratings (including 500 Marines)
(b) 18 months National Service

Bases

Casablanca, Safi, Agadir, Kenitra, Tangier

Mercantile Marine

Lloyd's Register of Shipping:
  53 vessels of 79 863 tons gross

Strength of the Fleet

Type	Active	Building (Projected)
Large Patrol Craft	5	(2)
Coastal Patrol Craft	9	6
MSC	1	—
Landing Craft	4	—
Customs Craft	12	—

New Construction Programme 1973-77

  4—PR 72 Large Patrol Craft
12—32 metre Coastal Patrol Craft
  3—Batral Type Landing Ships (Logistics)

DELETION

Frigate

1975 *Al Maouna*

LIGHT FORCES

2 FRENCH PR 72 TYPE (LARGE PATROL CRAFT)

Name	No.	Builders	Commissioned
OKBA	—	Soc. Francaise de Construction Navale	1976
TRIKI	—	Soc. Francaise de Construction Navale	1977

Displacement, tons: 375 standard; 445 full load
Dimensions, feet (metres): 188·8 × 25 × 7·1 *(57·5 × 7·6 × 2·1)*
Guns: 1—76 mm OTO-Melara; 1—40 mm Breda Bofors
Main engines: 4 AGO V16 diesels; 4 shafts; 11 040 hp
Speed, knots: 28
Range, miles: 2 500 at 16 knots
Complement: 53 (5 officers; 48 ratings)

Ordered June 1973. This type can be fitted with Exocet—as the Vega control system will be installed this would be a simple operation. *Okba* launched 10 Oct 1975, *Triki* 1 Feb 1976. Two more in the New Construction Programme.

1 LARGE PATROL CRAFT

Name	No.	Builders	Commissioned
LIEUTENANT RIFFI	32	Constructions Mécaniques de Normandie, Cherbourg	May 1964

Displacement, tons: 311 standard; 374 full load
Dimensions, feet (metres): 174 × 23 × 6·6 *(53 × 7 × 2)*
Guns: 1—76 mm; 2—40 mm
A/S weapons: 2—A/S mortars
Main engines: 2 SEMT Pielstick diesels; 2 cp propellers; 3 600 bhp = 19 knots
Range, miles: 3 000 at 12 knots
Complement: 49

Of modified "Fougeux" design. Laid down May 1963.

LIEUTENANT RIFFI   CMN

1 LARGE PATROL CRAFT

Name	No.	Builders	Commissioned
AL BACHIR	22 (ex-*12*)	Constructions Mécaniques de Normandie, Cherbourg	30 Mar 1967

Displacement, tons: 125 light; 154 full load
Dimensions, feet (metres): 124·7 pp; 133·2 oa × 20·8 × 4·7 *(38; 40·6 × 6·4 × 1·4)*
Guns: 2—40 mm; 2—MG
Main engines: 2 SEMT-Pielstick diesels; 2 shafts; 3 600 bhp = 25 knots
Oil fuel, tons: 21
Range, miles: 2 000 at 15 knots
Complement: 23

Ordered in 1964. Launched 25 Feb 1967.

AL BACHIR   CMN

1 Ex-FRENCH LARGE PATROL CRAFT

Name	No.	Builders	Commissioned
EL SABIQ (ex-*P 762, VC 12*)	11	Chantiers Navals de l'Estérel	1958

Displacement, tons: 60 standard; 82 full load
Dimensions, feet (metres): 104·5 × 15·5 × 5·5 *(31·8 × 4·7 × 1·7)*
Guns: 2—20 mm
Main engines: 2 Mercedes-Benz diesels; 2 shafts; 2 700 bhp = 28 knots
Range, miles: 1 500 at 15 knots
Complement: 17

Former French seaward defence motor launch of the VC type. Launched on 13 Aug 1957.
Transferred from the French Navy to the Moroccan Navy on 15 Nov 1960 and renamed *El Sabiq.*

6 + (6) P 32 TYPE (COASTAL PATROL CRAFT)

Name	No.	Builders	Commissioned
EL WACIL	—	Constructions Mécaniques de Normandie, Cherbourg	9 Oct 1975
EL JAIL	—	Constructions Mécaniques de Normandie, Cherbourg	3 Dec 1975
EL MIKDAM	—	Constructions Mécaniques de Normandie, Cherbourg	30 Jan 1976
EL HARIS	—	Constructions Mécaniques de Normandie, Cherbourg	30 June 1976
EL KHAFIR	—	Constructions Mécaniques de Normandie, Cherbourg	16 Apr 1976
EL SEHIR	—	Constructions Mécaniques de Normandie, Cherbourg	16 July 1976

Displacement, tons: 90
Dimensions, feet (metres): 105 oa × 17·6 × 9·8 *(32 × 5·3 × 2·9)*
Guns: 2—20 mm
Main engines: 2 MGO-12V BZSHR Diesels; 2 700 bhp; 2 shafts = 29 knots
Range, miles: 1 500 at 15 knots
Complement: 17

Wooden hull sheathed in plastic.
The first six of these patrol craft were ordered in Feb 1974. Launch dates—*El Wacil* 12 June 1975, *El Jail* 10 Oct 1975, *El Mikdam* 26 Nov 1975, *El Haris* 3 Mar 1976, *El Khafir* 1 Jan 1976, *El Sehir* 2 June 1976. Six more in the New Construction Programme.

Radar: 1 set Decca

EL WACIL   1976, CMN

3 COASTAL PATROL CRAFT

Arcor 31 type of 24 knots built by C. N. Arcor, Bordeaux.

MINE WARFARE SHIP

1 MINESWEEPER—COASTAL

TAWFIC (ex-*Aries M 758*)

Displacement, tons: 365 standard; 424 full load
Dimensions, feet (metres): 152 oa × 28 × 8·2 *(46·3 × 8·5 × 2·1)*
Guns: 1—40 mm; 1—20 mm
Main engines: 2 diesels; 2 shafts; 2 000 bhp = 15 knots
Range, miles: 3 000 at 15 knots
Complement: 38

Launched 31 Mar 1956 of the French "Sirius" class. Transferred on loan by France on 28 Nov 1974 for 4 years.

AMPHIBIOUS FORCES

3 BATRAL TYPE

Displacement, tons: 750 standard; 1 250 full load
Dimensions, feet (metres): 262·4 × 42·6 × 7·5 *(80× 13 × 2·3)*
Guns: 2—40 mm; 2—81 mm mortars
Main engines: 2 Diesels; 2 shafts; 1 800 hp = 16 knots
Range, miles: 3 500 at 13 knots
Complement: 37

Fitted with helicopter landing platform and with vehicle-stowage above and below decks. Can carry an extra 140 men and twelve vehicles. Two ordered from Dubigeon on 12 Mar 1975. Third ordered 19 Aug 1975.

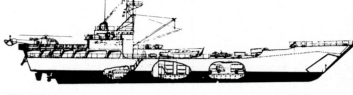

BATRAL TYPE   *1974, French Navy*

Name	No.	Builders	Commissioned
LIEUTENANT MALGHAGH	21	Chantiers Navals Franco-Belges	1964

Displacement, tons: 292 standard; 642 full load
Dimensions, feet (metres): 193·6 × 39·2 × 4·3 *(59 × 12 × 1·3)*
Guns: 2—20 mm; 1—120 mm mortar
Main engines: 2 MGO diesels; 2 shafts; 1 000 bhp = 8 knots
Complement: 16 (1 officer, 15 men)

Ordered early in 1963. Similar to the French landing craft of the EDIC type built at the same yard.

MISCELLANEOUS

There are also the yacht *Essaouira,* 60 tons, from Italy in 1967, used as a training vessel for watchkeepers; and twelve customs boats, four of 40 tons, 82 feet, diesels 940 bhp = 23 knots, and eight 42·7 feet; all built in 1963. The *Murene,* Coast Guard Cutter, has also been reported.

NETHERLANDS

Administration

Minister of Defence and State Secretary of Defence (Equipment):
A. Stemerdink
State Secretary of Defence (Personnel):
C. L. J. van Lent
Chief of the Defence Staff:
Lt-Gen. A. J. W. Wijting R.N.A.F.

Headquarters Appointments

Chief of the Naval Staff:
Vice-Admiral B. Veldkamp
Vice Chief of the Naval Staff:
Rear-Admiral H. L. van Beek
Flag Officer Naval Personnel:
Rear-Admiral J. G. C. van de Lind
Flag Officer Naval Material:
Rear-Admiral J. L. Langenberg

Commands

Admiral Netherlands Home Command:
Rear-Admiral H. E. Rambonnet
Commander Netherlands Task Group:
Rear-Admiral J. H. B. Hulshof
Commandant General Royal Netherlands Marine Corps:
Major-General A. J. Romijn
Flag Officer Netherlands Antilles:
Commodore W. Gonggrijp

Diplomatic Representation

Naval Attaché in Bonn:
Captain R. H. Berts
Naval Attaché in London:
Captain J. R. Roele
Naval Attaché in Paris:
Captain C. J. van Westenbrugge
Naval Attaché in Washington and NLR SACLANT:
Rear-Admiral J. J. Binnendijk

Personnel

(a) 1 January 1977: 17 200 officers and ratings (including the Navy Air Service, Royal Netherlands Marine Corps and about 360 officers and women of the W.R.NI.NS.)
(b) 14-17 months National Service

Bases

Main Base: Den Helder
Minor Bases: Flushing and Curacao
Fleet Air Arm: NAS Valkenburgh (main),
NAS De Kooy (helicopters)
R. Neth. Marines: Rotterdam
Training Bases: Amsterdam and Hilversum

Naval Air Force

Personnel: 1 700

3 MR Squadrons with 8 Atlantics, 15 Neptunes
12 Wasps and 7 AB-204B helicopters
(new MR aircraft by late 70s—6 Lynx replacements in 1977)

Prefix to Ships' Names

HNLMS

Mercantile Marine

Lloyd's Register of Shipping:
1 325 vessels of 5 919 892 tons gross

Strength of the Fleet

	Active	Building (Projected)
Destroyers	12	—
Frigates	6	8 (4)
Corvettes	6	—
Submarines (Patrol)	6	—
MCM Support Ships	4	—
Minehunters	4	(15)
Minesweepers—Coastal	11	—
Diving Ships	3	—
Minesweepers—Inshore	16	—
Large Patrol Craft	5	—
LCAs	11	—
Surveying Vessels	3	—
Combat Support Ships	2	—
Training Ships	2	—
Tugs	13	—
Tenders	6	—

Future New Construction Programme

1 Frigate (Command and Air Defence)
12 Frigates (ASW)
16 Lynx Helicopters

Planned Strength in 1980s

2 ASW Groups each of 6 ASW frigates, 1 DLG, 1 Support Ship (helicopters in all ships) to operate in Eastlant Area
1 ASW Group of 6 ASW frigates and 1 DLG to operate in Channel Approaches
1 ASW Group of 4 frigates to operate in Channel Command
6 Patrol Submarines
21 LRMP Aircraft in 3 squadrons (1 training)
2 MCM Groups of 12 ships each operating off Dutch ports
1 MCM Group of 7 ships for Channel command
2 R. Neth. Marine Commando Groups and 1 Cold Weather Reinforced Company

DELETIONS

Cruisers

Oct 1972 *De Ruyter* to Peru as *Almirante Grau*
Aug 1976 *De Zeven Provincien* to Peru

Destroyers

1973 *Gelderland* for harbour training
1974 *Noord Brabant* (after collision 9 Jan 1974)

Submarines

Nov 1970 *Zeeleuw* (ex-*Hawkbill*)
Nov 1971 *Walrus* (ex-*Icefish*)
returned to US and scrapped

MCM Support Ships

1976 *Onversaagd* (returned to US)

Minesweepers

1972 *Onvermoeid, Bolsward, Breukelen, Bruinisse* returned to USN
1973 *Grijpskerk* for harbour training
1974 *Wildervank, Meppel, Goes, Brummen, Brouwershaven* to disposal
Axel, Aalsmeer to Oman
1975 *Waalwijk, Leersum* ("Wildervank" class)
Beemster, Bedum, Beilen, Borculo, Borne, Blaricum, Brielle, Breskens, Boxtel ("Beemster" class MSC)

Survey Ships

1972 *Luymes* to disposal
1973 *Snellius* as accommodation ship

Amphibious Forces

1975 L 9515, 9521

Storeships

1972 *Woendi*
1973 *Pelikaan*

PENNANT NUMBERS

Destroyers

F	801	Tromp
F	806	De Ruyter
D	808	Holland
D	809	Zeeland
D	812	Friesland
D	813	Groningen
D	814	Limburg
D	815	Overijssel
D	816	Drenthe
D	817	Utrecht
D	818	Rotterdam
D	819	Amsterdam

Frigates

F	802	Van Speijk
F	803	Van Galen
F	804	Tjerk Hiddes
F	805	Van Nes
F	814	Isaac Sweers
F	815	Evertsen

Submarines

S	804	Potvis
S	805	Tonijn
S	806	Zwaardvis
S	807	Tijgerhaai
S	808	Dolfijn
S	809	Zeehond

Corvettes

F	817	Wolf
F	818	Fret
F	819	Hermelijn
F	820	Vos
F	821	Panter
F	822	Jaguar

MCM Command/Support and Escort Ships

A	855	Onbevreesd
A	858	Onvervaard
A	859	Onverdroten

Mine Hunters

M	801	Dokkum
M	818	Drunen
M	828	Staphorst
M	842	Veere

Coastal Minesweepers

M	802	Hoogezand
M	809	Naaldwijk
M	810	Abcoude
M	812	Drachten
M	813	Ommen
M	815	Giethoorn
M	817	Venlo
M	823	Naarden
M	827	Hoogeveen
M	830	Sittard
M	841	Gemert

Inshore Minesweepers

M	868	Alblas
M	869	Bussemaker
M	870	Lacomblé
M	871	Van Hamel
M	872	Van Straelen
M	873	Van Moppes
M	874	Chömpff
M	875	Van Well-Groeneveld
M	876	Schuiling
M	877	Van Versendaal
M	878	Van Der Wel
M	879	Van 't Hoff
M	880	Mahu
M	881	Staverman
M	882	Houtepen
M	883	Zomer

Diving Vessels

M 806 Roermond
M 820 Woerden
M 844 Rhenen

Large Patrol Craft

P 802 Balder
P 803 Bulgia
P 804 Freijer
P 805 Hadda
P 806 Hefring

Amphibious Forces

L 9510-14
L 9516-18
L 9520
L 9522
L 9526

Auxiliary Ships

A 832 Zuiderkruis
A 835 Poolster
A 847 Argus
A 848 Triton
A 849 Nautilus
A 850 Hydra
A 856 Mercuur
A 870 Wamandai
A 871 Wambrau
A 872 Westgat
A 873 Wielingen
A 903 Zeefakkel
A 904 Buyskes
A 905 Blommendal
A 906 Tydeman
A 923 Van Bochove
Y 8014 Harbour Tug
Y 8016 Harbour Tug
Y 8017 Harbour Tug
Y 8020 Dreg IV
Y 8022 Harbour Tug

Auxiliary Ships—*Cont.*

Y 8028 Harbour Tug
Y 8037 Berkel
Y 8038 Dintel
Y 8039 Dommel
Y 8040 Ijssel
Y 8050 Urania

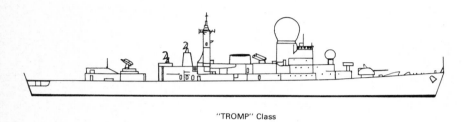

"TROMP" Class

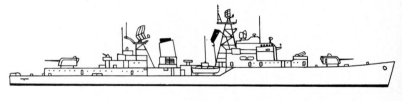

"FRIESLAND" Class

"HOLLAND" Class

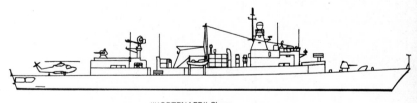

"KORTENAER" Class

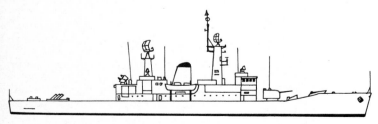

"VAN SPEIJK" Class

"WOLF" Class

"BALDER" Class

DESTROYERS

2 "TROMP" CLASS (DLG)

Name	No.	Builders	Laid down	Launched	Commissioned
DE RUYTER	F 806	Koninklijke Maatschappij De Schelde, Flushing	22 Dec 1971	9 Mar 1974	3 June 1976
TROMP	F 801	Koninklijke Maatschappij De Schelde, Flushing	4 Sep 1971	4 June1973	3 Oct 1975

Displacement, tons: 4 300 standard; 5 400 full load
Length, feet (metres): 429·5 *(130·9)* pp; 454·1 *(138·4)* oa
Beam, feet (metres): 48·6 *(14·8)*
Draught, feet (metres): 15·1 *(4·6)*
Aircraft: 1 Lynx helicopter
Missile launchers: 1 Tartar aft; Seasparrow Point defence missile system; Harpoon (2 quadruple) (8 missiles)
Guns: 2—4·7 in (twin turret)
A/S weapons: 6 (2 triple) Mk 32 ASW torpedo tubes
Main engines: 2 Olympus gas turbines; 50 000 hp;
   2 Tyne cruising gas turbines, 8 000 hp
Speed, knots: 30
Complement: 306

First design allowance was voted for in 1967 estimates. Ordered (announced on 27 July 1970) for laying down in 1971. Hangar and helicopter spot landing platform aft. Fitted as flagships.

ECM: 2 Knebworth Corvus Chaff projectors (and illuminators).

Electronics: SEWACO I automated AIO.

Engineering: Each ship carries 4-1 000 KW Diesel generators by Ruston Paxman, England.

Gunnery: Turrets from *Gelderland* with considerable modifications. Including full automation.

Radar: Search and designator; One HSA 3D in radome. Search, tracker and fire control for Seasparrow and 4·7 in guns; one HSA WM 25.
Tartar control: Two SPG-51.
Navigation: Two Decca.

Sonar: One CWE 610. One Type 162.

Trials: *De Ruyter*—Jan 1976. *Tromp*—Mar 1975.

TROMP   *1975, Royal Netherlands Navy*

DE RUYTER   *11/1976, Michael D. J. Lennon*

DE RUYTER   *11/1976, Michael D. J. Lennon*

8 "FRIESLAND" CLASS

Name	No.	Builders	Laid down	Launched	Commissioned
FRIESLAND	D 812	Nederlandse Dok en Scheepsbouw Mij, Amsterdam	17 Dec 1951	21 Feb 1953	22 Mar 1956
GRONINGEN	D 813	Nederlandse Dok en Scheepsbouw Mij, Amsterdam	21 Feb 1952	9 Jan 1954	12 Sep 1956
LIMBURG	D 814	Koninklijke Maatschappij De Schelde, Flushing	28 Nov 1953	5 Sep 1955	31 Oct 1956
OVERIJSSEL	D 815	Dok-en-Werfmaatschappij Wilton-Fijenoord	15 Oct 1953	8 Aug 1955	4 Oct 1957
DRENTHE	D 816	Nederlandse Dok en Scheepsbouw Mij, Amsterdam	9 Jan 1954	26 Mar 1955	1 Aug 1957
UTRECHT	D 817	Koninklijke Maatschappij De Schelde, Flushing	15 Feb 1954	2 June1956	1 Oct 1957
ROTTERDAM	D 818	Rotterdamse Droogdok Mij, Rotterdam	7 Jan 1954	26 Jan 1956	28 Feb 1957
AMSTERDAM	D 819	Nederlandse Dok en Schepsbouw Mij, Amsterdam	26 Mar 1955	25 Aug 1956	10 Aug 1958

Displacement, tons: 2 497 standard; 3 070 full load
Length, feet (metres): 370 *(112·8)* pp; 380·5 *(116·0)* oa
Beam, feet (metres): 38·5 *(11·7)*
Draught, feet (metres): 17 *(5·2)*
Guns: 4—4·7 in *(120 mm)* (twin turrets) 4—40 mm
A/S weapons: 2 four-barrelled 375 mm. Bofors rocket launchers; 2 DC racks
Main engines: 2 Werkspoor geared turbines, 60 000 shp; 2 shafts
Boilers: 4 Babcock
Speed, knots: 36
Complement: 284

OVERIJSSEL   *11/1975, Dr. Giorgio Arra*

These ships have side armour as well as deck protection. Twin rudders. Propellers 370 rpm. Named after provinces of the Netherlands, and the two principal cities. To be replaced by "Kortenaer" class of frigates.

Gunnery: The 4·7 inch guns are fully automatic with a rate of fire of 42 rounds per minute. All guns are radar controlled. Originally six 40 mm guns were mounted.

Radar: Search: LW 03.
Tactical: DA 05.
Fire Control: HSA M 45 for 4·7 in.
HSA fire control for 40 mm and A/S rockets.

Torpedo tubes: *Utrecht* was equipped with eight 21 inch A/S torpedo tubes (single, four on each side) in 1960 and *Overijssel* in 1961, and the others were to have been, but the project was dropped and tubes already fitted were removed.

LIMBURG   *1976, Michael D. J. Lennon*

2 "HOLLAND" CLASS

Name	No.	Builders	Laid down	Launched	Commissioned
HOLLAND	D 808	Rotterdamse Droogdok Mij, Rotterdam	21 April1950	11 April1953	31 Dec 1954
ZEELAND	D 809	Koninklijke Maatschappij De Schelde, Flushing	12 Jan 1951	27 June1953	1 Mar 1955

Displacement, tons: 2 215 standard; 2 765 full load
Length, feet (metres): 360·5 *(109·9)* pp; 371·1 *(113·1)* oa
Beam, feet (metres): 37·5 *(11·4)*
Draught, feet (metres): 16·8 *(5·1)*
Guns: 4—4·7 in *(120 mm)*; 1—40 mm
A/S weapons: 2 four-barrelled 375 mm, Bofors rocket launchers; 2 DC racks
Main engines: Werkspoor Parsons geared turbines; 2 shafts; 45 000 shp
Boilers: 4 Babcock
Speed, knots: 32
Complement: 247

Two ships of this class were equipped with engines of the pre-war "Callenburgh" class design and the other two with engines of German construction. (The four "Callenburgh" class destroyers were being built in 1940. *Isaac Sweers* was towed to England and completed there, *Tjerk Hiddes* was completed by the Germans as ZH 1. The other two, *Callenburgh* and *Van Almonde,* were too severely damaged for further use and were scrapped, the engines being installed in the "Holland" class).

Gunnery: The 4·7 inch guns are fully automatic with a rate of fire of 42 rounds per minute. All guns are radar controlled.

Radar: Search: LW 03.
Tactical: DA 02.
Fire Control: HSA M 45 for 4·7 in.
HSA fire control for A/S rocket launcher.

Sisterships: *Gelderland* now a harbour-training hulk in Amsterdam. *Noord Brabant* too severely damaged in collision 9 Jan 1974 for repair. To be replaced by "Kortenaer" class.

HOLLAND   *1976, J. A. Verhoog*

FRIGATES

7 + 1 + (4) "KORTENAER" CLASS

Name	No.	Builders	Laid down	Launched	Commissioned
KORTENAER	F 807	Koninklijke Maatschappij De Schelde, Flushing	8 Apr 1975	18 Dec 1976	Autumn 1978
CALLENBURGH	F 808	Koninklijke Maatschappij De Schelde, Flushing	30 June 1975	1977	Autumn 1979
VAN KINSBERGEN	F 809	Koninklijke Maatschappij De Schelde, Flushing	2 Sep 1975	1977	Summer 1980
BANCKERT	F 810	Koninklijke Maatschappij De Schelde, Flushing	25 Feb 1976	1978	Spring 1981
PIET HEYN	F 811	Koninklijke Maatschappij De Schelde, Flushing	1977		Late 1981
PIETER FLORISZ	F 812	Koninklijke Maatschappij De Schelde, Flushing	1977		Autumn 1982
WITTE DE WITH	F 813	Koninklijke Maatschappij De Schelde, Flushing	1977		Summer 1983
ABRAHAM CRIJNSSEN	F 816	Koninklijke Maatschappij De Schelde, Flushing	1978		Spring 1984

Displacement, tons: 3 500
Dimensions, feet (metres): 419·8 × 47·2 × 14·3 *(128 × 14·4 × 4·4)*
Aircraft: 1 Lynx helicopter
Missiles: 8 Harpoon surface-to-surface; NATO Seasparrow PDMS
Guns: 2—76 mm OTO Melara (see notes)
A/S weapons: 6 (2 triple) Mk 32 torpedo tubes for Mk 46 in after deckhouse
Main engines: 2 Rolls Royce Olympus gas turbines = 50 000 shp; 2 Rolls Royce Tyne gas turbines = 8 000 shp; 2 variable pitch propellers
Speed, knots: 30
Range, miles: 4 000 on Tyne cruising turbines
Complement: 185

"KORTENAER" Class   *1974, Royal Netherlands Navy*

First four of class ordered 31 Aug 1974, second four 28 Nov 1974. Third four 29 Dec 1976 (two to built by same constructors as rest of class, two by Wilton-Fijenoord). The thirteenth of class (SAM version) has been delayed. *Kortenaer* to be ready for trials 1 Apr 1978. *Callenburgh* to commission in Autumn 1979 and thereafter at 9 monthly intervals. These ships are to replace the "Holland" and "Friesland" classes. Cost at 1974 prices £37 m.

Complement: Reduced to 185 by adoption of large amount of automation.

Gunnery: Twin 35 mm/90 is to be mounted on top of hangar when system becomes available. Until then second 76 mm will be mounted in lieu.

Radar: Hollandse Signaal for radar and fire-control.

Sonar: SQS 505.

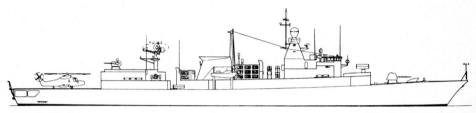

"KORTENAER" Class   *1973, Royal Netherlands Navy*

6 "VAN SPEIJK" CLASS

Name	No.	Builders	Laid down	Launched	Commissioned
EVERTSEN	F 815	Koninklijke Maatschappij De Schelde, Flushing	6 July 1965	18 June 1966	21 Dec 1967
ISAAC SWEERS	F 814	Nederlandse Dok en Scheepsbouw Mij, Amsterdam	5 May 1965	10 Mar 1967	15 May 1968
TJERK HIDDES	F 804	Nederlandse Dok en Scheepsbouw Mij, Amsterdam	1 June 1964	17 Dec 1965	16 Aug 1967
VAN GALEN	F 803	Koninklijke Maatschappij De Schelde, Flushing	25 July 1963	19 June 1965	1 Mar 1967
VAN NES	F 805	Koninklijke Maatschappij De Schelde, Flushing	25 July 1963	26 Mar 1966	9 Aug 1967
VAN SPEIJK	F 802	Nederlandse Dok en Scheepsbouw Mij, Amsterdam	1 Oct 1963	5 Mar 1965	14 Feb 1967

Displacement, tons: 2 200 standard; 2 850 full load
Dimensions, feet (metres): 360 wl, 372 oa × 41 × 18 *(109·8; 113·4 × 12·5 × 5·8)*
Aircraft: 1 Wasp helicopter
Missile: 2 quadruple Seacat anti-aircraft (see note)
Guns: 2—4·5 in (twin turret)
A/S weapons: 1 Limbo three-barrelled depth charge mortar
Main engines: 2 double reduction geared turbines; 2 shafts; 30 000 shp
Boilers: 2 Babcock & Wilcox
Speed, knots: 30
Complement: 254

Four ships were ordered in Oct 1962 and two later.

Design: Although in general these ships are based on the design of the British Improved Type 12 ("Leander" class), there are a number of modifications to suit the requirements of the Royal Netherlands Navy. As far as possible equipment of Netherlands manufacture was installed. This resulted in a number of changes in the ship's superstructure compared with the British "Leander" class. To avoid delay these ships were in some cases fitted with equipment already available, instead of going through long development stages.

Modernisation: This class is undergoing mid-life modernisation at Den Helder. This will take 18 months, one ship being accepted every 6 months from Dec 1976 when *Van Speijk* was taken in hand. This will consist of replacement of 4·5 in turret by one 76 mm OTO Melara, removal of Limbo, fitting of two quadruple Harpoon amidships, fitting of six (two triple) Mk 32 A/S torpedo tubes, conversion of hangar to take Lynx, new electronics, updating of Ops. Room, improved communications, extensive automation with reduction in complement and improved habitability.

Electronics: ECM equipment.

Radar: LW 02 air surveillance on mainmast
DA 05 target indicator on foremast
Kelvin-Hughes Surface-warning/nav set on foremast
1-M45 for 4·5 in guns
2-M44 for Seacat

Sonar: Hull-mounted and VDS.

TJERK HIDDES   *10/1976, Michael D. J. Lennon*

VAN GALEN   *4/1976, J. L. M. van der Burg*

SUBMARINES

Note: A sum was set aside in the 1975 Estimates to start design work on an "Improved Zwaardvis" class to be ordered in 1979.

2 "ZWAARDVIS" CLASS

Name	No.	Builders	Laid down	Launched	Commissioned
TIJGERHAAI	S 807	Rotterdamse Droogdok Mij, Rotterdam	14 July 1966	25 May 1971	20 Oct 1972
ZWAARDVIS	S 806	Rotterdamse Droogdok Mij, Rotterdam	14 July 1966	2 July 1970	18 Aug 1972

Displacement, tons: 2 350 surfaced; 2 640 dived
Length, feet (metres): 217·2 *(66·2)*
Beam, feet (metres): 33·8 *(10·3)*
Draught, feet (metres): 23·3 *(7·1)*
Torpedo tubes: 6—21 in *(533 mm)*
Main machinery: Diesel-electric; 3 diesel generators; 1 shaft
Speed, knots: 13 surfaced; 20 dived
Complement: 67

In the 1964 Navy Estimates a first instalment was approved for the construction of two conventionally powered submarines of tear-drop design. HSA M8 Fire Control.

Radar: Type 1001.

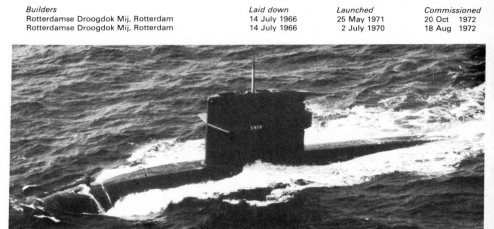

ZWAARDVIS

1972, Royal Netherlands Navy

2 "POTVIS" CLASS
2 "DOLFIJN" CLASS

Name	No.	Builders	Laid down	Launched	Commissioned
POTVIS	S 804	Wilton-Fijenoord, Schiedam	17 Sep 1962	12 Jan 1965	2 Nov 1965
TONIJN	S 805	Wilton-Fijenoord, Schiedam	27 Nov 1962	14 June 1965	24 Feb 1966
DOLFIJN	S 808	Rotterdamse Droogdok Mij, Rotterdam	30 Dec 1954	20 May 1959	16 Dec 1960
ZEEHOND	S 809	Rotterdamse Droogdok Mij, Rotterdam	30 Dec 1954	20 Feb 1960	16 Mar 1961

Displacement, tons: 1 140 standard; 1 494 surfaced; 1 826 dived
Length, feet (metres): 260·9 *(79·5)*
Beam, feet (metres): 25·8 *(7·8)*
Draught, feet (metres): 15·8 *(4·8)*
Torpedo tubes: 8—21 in *(533 mm)*
Main machinery: 2 MAN diesels; 3 100 bhp
Electric motors; 4 200 hp; 2 shafts
Speed, knots: 14·5 surfaced; 17 dived
Complement: 64

These submarines are of a triple-hull design, giving a diving depth 980 feet *(300 metres)*. *Potvis* and *Tonijn*, originally voted for in 1949 with the other pair, but suspended for some years, had several modifications compared with *Dolfijn* and *Zeehond* and were officially considered to be a separate class; but modernisation of both classes has been completed, and all four boats are now almost identical. HSA M8 Fire control.

Construction: The hull consists of three cylinders arranged in a triangular shape. The upper cylinder accommodates the crew, navigational equipment and armament. The lower two cylinders house the propulsion machinery comprising diesel engines, batteries and electric motors, as well as store-rooms.

Radar: Type 1001.

POTVIS

8/1976, Michael D. J. Lennon

CORVETTES

6 "WOLF" CLASS

Name	No.	Builders	Commissioned
FRET (ex-*PCE 1604*)	F 818	General Shipbuilding and Engineering Works, Boston	4 May 1954
HERMELIJN (ex-*PCE 1605*)	F 819	General Shipbuilding and Engineering Works, Boston	5 Aug 1954
JAGUAR (ex-*PCE 1609*)	F 822	Avondale Marine Ways, Inc, New Orleans, Louisiana	11 June 1954
PANTER (ex-*PCE 1608*)	F 821	Avondale Marine Ways, Inc, New Orleans, Louisiana	11 June 1954
VOS (ex-*PCE 1606*)	F 820	General Shipbuilding and Engineering Works, Boston	2 Dec 1954
WOLF (ex-*PCE 1607*)	F 817	Avondale Marine Ways, Inc, New Orleans, Louisiana	26 Mar 1954

Displacement, tons: 870 standard; 975 full load
Dimensions, feet (metres): 180 pp; 184·5 oa × 33 × 14·5 *(54·9; 56·2 × 10 × 4·4)*
Guns: 1—3 in *(76 mm)*; 6—40 mm *(Jaguar, Panter: 4—40 mm)*; 8—20 mm (not mounted)
A/S weapons: 1 Hedgehog; 2 DCT *(Jaguar, Panter:* 4); 2 DC racks
Main engines: 2 GM diesels; 1 800 bhp; 2 shafts
Speed, knots: 15
Range, miles: 4 300 at 10 knots
Complement: 96

Built as part of the US "off-shore" agreement—all laid down 1952-53. 20 mm guns not fitted in peacetime.

Radar: Kelvin Hughes navigation set.

Sonar: One hull mounted set.

HERMELIJN

1976, Michael D. J. Lennon

LIGHT FORCES

5 "BALDER" CLASS (LARGE PATROL CRAFT)

Name	No.	Builders	Commissioned
BALDER	P 802	Rijkswerf Willemsoord	6 Aug 1954
BULGIA	P 803	Rijkswerf Willemsoord	9 Aug 1954
FREYR	P 804	Rijkswerf Willemsoord	1 Dec 1954
HADDA	P 805	Rijkswerf Willemsoord	3 Feb 1955
HEFRING	P 806	Rijkswerf Willemsoord	23 Mar 1955

Displacement, tons: 169 standard; 225 full load
Dimensions, feet (metres): 114·9 pp; 119·1 oa × 20·2 × 5·9 *(35; 36·3 × 6·2 × 1·8)*
Guns: 1—40 mm; 3—20 mm
A/S weapons: Mousetrap
Main engines: Diesels; 2 shafts; 1 300 shp = 15·5 knots
Range, miles: 1 000 at 13 knots
Complement: 27

Built on US "off-shore" account.

Radar: Decca navigation set.

Sonar: One hull mounted.

HADDA   *4/1976, J. L. M. van der Burg*

MINE WARFARE FORCES

Future Construction: Agreement reached with France and Belgium to develop an improved "Circe" class minehunter to be fitted with PAP mine-destructor. Combined planning centre set up in Paris—France will build the lead ship. Fifteen will be built in the Netherlands to replace "Onversaagd" and "Dokkum" classes. To complete mid-1980s. Names: *Alkmaar, Delfzijl, Dordrecht, Haarlem, Harlingen, Hellevoetsluis, Makkum, Middelburg, Scheveningen, Schiedam, Urk, Veer, Vlaardingen, Willemstad* plus one to be named.

4 "ONVERSAAGD" CLASS
(MCM SUPPORT SHIPS, ESCORTS and TORPEDO TENDER)

Name	No.	Builders	Commissioned
MERCUUR (ex-Onvers-chrokken, ex-AM 483)	A 856	Peterson Builders, Wisconsin	22 July 1954
ONBEVREESD (ex-AM 481)	A 855 (ex-M 885)	Astoria Marine Construction Co	21 Sep 1954
ONVERDROTEN (ex-AM 485)	A 859 (ex-M 889)	Peterson Builders, Wisconsin	22 Nov 1954
ONVERVAARD (ex-AM 482)	A 858 (ex-M 888)	Astoria Marine Construction Co	31 Mar 1955

Displacement, tons: 735 standard; 790 full load
Dimensions, feet (metres): 165·0 pp; 172·0 oa × 36·0 × 10·6 *(50·3; 52·5 × 11 × 3·2)*
Gun: 1—40 mm
A/S weapons: 2 DC
Main engines: Diesels; 1 600 bhp = 15·5 knots
Oil fuel, tons: 46
Range, miles: 2 400 at 12 knots
Complement: 70

Built in USA for the Netherlands. Of wooden and non-magnetic construction. Originally designed as Minesweepers—Ocean—reclassified in 1966 and in 1972. *Onbevreesd, Onverdroten* and *Onvervaard* are MCM Command/Support Ships. *Mercuur* (ex-*Onverschrokken*) was converted into a Torpedo Trials Ship in 1972.

ONBEVREESD   *1976, Michael D. J. Lennon*

18 "DOKKUM" CLASS
(MINESWEEPERS, COASTAL and MINEHUNTERS)

ABCOUDE M 810	HOOGEZAND M 802	ROERMOND M 806 (D)
DOKKUM M 801 (H)	HOOGEVEEN M 827	SITTARD M 830
DRACHTEN M 812	NAALDWIJK M 809	STAPHORST M 828 (H)
DRUNEN M 818 (H)	NAARDEN M 823	VEERE M 842 (H)
GEMERT M 841	OMMEN M 813	VENLO M 817
GIETHOORN M 815	RHENEN M 844 (D)	WOERDEN M 820 (D)

Displacement, tons: 373 standard; 453 full load
Dimensions, feet (metres): 149·8 oa × 28 × 6·5 *(45·7 × 8·5 × 2)*
Guns: 2—40 mm
Main engines: 2 diesels; Fijenoord MAN; 2 500 bhp = 16 knots
Range, miles: 2 500 at 10 knots
Complement: 38

Of 32 Western Union type coastal minesweepers built in the Netherlands, 18 were under offshore procurement as the "Dokkum" class, with MAN engines, and 14 on Netherlands account as the "Wildervank" class, with Werkspoor diesels. All launched in 1954-56 and completed in 1955-56.
Of the "Dokkum" class four have been converted to minehunters (H), (1968-73) and three to diving vessels (D) (1962-68). The remaining eleven minesweepers of this class were subject to a fleet rehabilitation and modernisation programme completed by 1977. All "Wildervank" class deleted by 1976.

Sonar: Type 193 in hunters.

HOOGEVEEN (sweeper)   *1976, Michael D. J. Lennon*

DRUNEN (hunter)   4/1975, John G. Callis

ROERMOND (diving vessel)   4/1976, J. L. M. van der Burg

16 "VAN STRAELEN" CLASS (MINESWEEPERS—INSHORE)

Name	No.	Builders	Commissioned
ALBLAS	M 868	Werf de Noord, Albasserdam	12 Mar 1960
BUSSEMAKER	M 869	G. de Vries Lentsch Jr, Amsterdam	1960
CHÖMPFF	M 874	Werf de Noord, Albasserdam	1961
HOUTEPEN	M 882	N.V. de Arnhemse Scheepsbouw Maatschappij	1962
LACOMBLE	M 870	N.V. de Arnhemse Scheepsbouw Maatschappij	1960
MAHU	M 880	Werf de Noord, Albasserdam	1962
SCHUILING	M 876	G. de Vries Lentsch Jr, Amsterdam	1961
STAVERMAN	M 881	G. de Vries Lentsch Jr, Amsterdam	1962
VAN DER WEL	M 878	G. de Vries Lentsch Jr, Amsterdam	1961
VAN HAMEL	M 871	G. de Vries Lentsch Jr, Amsterdam	1960
VAN 'T HOFF	M 879	Werf de Noord, Albasserdam	1961
VAN MOPPES	M 873	Werf de Noord, Albasserdam	1960
VAN STRAELEN	M 872	N.V. de Arnhemse Scheepsbouw Maatschappij	1960
VAN VERSENDAAL	M 877	Werf de Noord, Albasserdam	1961
VAN WELL GROENVELD	M 875	N.V. de Arnhemse Scheepsbouw Maatschappij	1961
ZOMER	M 883	N.V. de Arnhemse Scheepsbouw Maatschappij	1962

Displacement, tons: 151 light; 169 full load
Dimensions, feet (metres): 90 pp; 99·3 oa × 18·2 × 5·2 *(27·5; 30·3 × 5·6 × 1·6)*
Gun: 1—20 mm
Main engines: Werkspoor diesels; 2 shafts; 1 100 bhp = 13 knots
Complement: 14

LACOMBLÉ   10/1975, D. Bateman

Eight were built under the offshore procurement programme, with MDAP funds, and the remaining eight were paid for by Netherlands. All ordered in mid-1957. Built of non-magnetic materials. *Alblas*, the first, was laid down on 26 Feb 1958, launched on 29 June 1959, started trials on 15 Jan 1960.

AMPHIBIOUS FORCES

L 9526

Displacement, tons: 20
Dimensions, feet (metres): 50 × 11·8 × 5·8 *(15·3 × 3·6 × 1·8)*
Main engines: 2 Kromhout diesels; 75 bhp = 8 knots
Complement: 3

Now officially rated as LCA Type.
Built by Rijkswerf, Den Helder.

| L 9510 | L 9512 | L 9514 | L 9517 | L 9520 |
| L 9511 | L 9513 | L 9516 | L 9518 | L 9522 |

Displacement, tons: 13·6
Dimensions, feet (metres): 46·2 × 11·5 × 6 *(14·1 × 3·5 × 1·8)*
Main engines: Rolls Royce diesel; Schottel propeller; 200 bhp = 12 knots
Complement: 3

Landing craft made of polyester, all commissioned in 1962-63, except L 9520 in 1964.
Built by Rijkswerf, Den Helder.

SURVEY SHIPS

1 "TYDEMAN" CLASS
(HYDROGRAPHIC/OCEANOGRAPHIC SHIP)

Name	No.	Builders	Commissioned
TYDEMAN	A 906	Scheepswerf En Machine Fabriek "de Merwede"	10 Nov 1976

Displacement, tons: 2 950
Dimensions, feet (metres): 295 × 47·2 × 15·7 *(90 × 14·4 × 4·8)*
Aircraft: 1 helicopter
Main engines: 3 Diesels; 3 690 bhp; electric motor; 2 730 shp
Speed, knots: 15
Complement: 64 plus 15 scientists

Ordered in Oct 1974. Cost £6·7 m. Will be able to operate down to 7 000 m. Fitted with eight laboratories. Supplied with two bow propellers. Laid down 29 Apr 1975, launched 18 Dec 1975.

TYDEMAN   12/1976, Royal Netherlands Navy

2 "BUYSKES" CLASS

Name	No.	Builders	Commissioned
BLOMMENDAL	A 905	Boele's Scheepswerven en Machinefabriek BV, Bolnes	22 May 1973
BUYSKES	A 904	Boele's Scheepswerven en Machinefabriek BV, Bolnes	9 Mar 1973

Displacement, tons: 967 standard; 1 033 full load
Dimensions, feet (metres): 196·6 oa × 36·4 × 12 *(60 × 11·1 × 3·7)*
Main engines: Diesel electric; 3 Diesels; 2 100 hp = 13·5 knots
Complement: 43

Both designed primarily for hydrographic work but have also limited oceanographic and meteorological capability. They will operate mainly in the North Sea. A data logging system is installed as part of the automatic handling of hydrographic data. They carry two 22 ft survey launches capable of 15 knots and two work-boats normally used for sweeping. Both ships can operate two floats, each housing an echo-sounding transducer, one streaming on each beam. This will enable the running of three simultaneous sounding lines 100m. apart.

BLOMMENDAL — 1973, Royal Netherlands Navy

SERVICE FORCES

2 "POOLSTER" CLASS (FAST COMBAT SUPPORT SHIPS)

Name	No.	Builders	Commissioned
POOLSTER	A 835	Rotterdamse Droogdok Mij	10 Sep 1964
ZUIDERKRUIS	A 832	Verolme Shipyards, Albasserdam	27 June 1975

Displacement, tons: 16 800 full load; 16 900 *(Zuiderkruis)*
Measurement, tons: 10 000 deadweight
Dimensions, feet (metres): 515 pp; 556 oa × 66·7 × 27 *(157·1 pp; 169·6 × 20·3 × 8·2)* *(Zuiderkruis 561 oa (171·1))*
Aircraft: Capacity: 5 helicopters
Guns: 2—40 mm
Main engines: 2 Turbines; 22 000 shp = 21 knots *(Poolster)* 2 Werkspoor diesels; 21 000 hp = 21 knots *(Zuiderkruis)*
Complement: 200

Poolster laid down on 18 Sep 1962. Launched on 16 Oct 1963. Trials mid-1964. Helicopter deck aft. Funnel heightened by 4·5 m. *Zuiderkruis* ordered Oct 1972. Laid down 16 July 1973, launched 15 Oct 1974.
Both carry A/S weapons for helicopters.

Radar: Kelvin Hughes navigation set.

Sonar: Hull mounted set.

POOLSTER — 8/1975, Royal Netherlands Navy

ZUIDERKRUIS — 4/1976, J. L. M. van der Burg

TRAINING SHIPS

Name	No.	Builders	Commissioned
ZEEFAKKEL	A 903	J. & K. Smit, Kinderdijk	22 May 1951

Displacement, tons: 355 standard; 384 full load
Dimensions, feet (metres): 149 oa × 24·7 × 6·9 *(45·4 × 7·6 × 2·1)*
Guns: 1—3 in; 1—40 mm
Main engines: 2 Smit/MAN 8 cyl diesels; 2 shafts; 640 bhp = 12 knots
Complement: 29

Laid down Sep 1949, launched 21 July 1950. Former surveying vessel. Now used as local training ship at Den Helder.

Name	No.	Builders	Commissioned
URANIA (ex-*Tromp*)	Y 8050	—	23 April 1938

Displacement, tons: 38
Dimensions, feet (metres): 72 × 16·3 × 10 *(22 × 5 × 3·1)*
Main engines: Diesel; 65 hp
Complement: 15

Schooner used for training in seamanship.

Note: *Gelderland* (ex-destroyer) and *Grypskerk* (ex-minesweeper) are used at Amsterdam as harbour training and accommodation ships for the Technical Training establishment. *Soemba* (ex-sloop) used at Den Oever as harbour training and accommodation ship for divers and underwater-swimmers.

TUGS

Name	No.	Builders	Commissioned
WESTGAT	A 872	Rijkswerf, Willemsoord	10 Jan 1968
WIELINGEN	A 873	Rijkswerf, Willemsoord	4 April 1968

Displacement, tons: 185
Dimensions, feet (metres): 90·6 × 22·7 × 7·7 *(27·6 × 6·9 × 2·3)*
Guns: 2—20 mm
Main engines: Bolnes diesel; 750 bhp = 12 knots

Launched on 22 Aug 1967 and 6 Jan 1968, respectively. Equipped with salvage pumps and fire fighting equipment. Stationed at Den Helder.

Name	No.	Builders	Commissioned
WAMBRAU	A 871	Rijkswerf, Willemsoord	8 Jan 1957

Displacement, tons: 154 standard; 179 full load
Dimensions, feet (metres): 86·5 oa × 20·7 × 7·5 *(26·4 × 6·3 × 2·3)*
Guns: 2—20 mm
Main engines: Werkspoor diesel and Kort nozzle; 500 bhp = 10·8 knots

Launched on 27 Aug 1956. Equipped with salvage pumps and fire fighting equipment. Stationed at Den Helder.

Name	No.	Builders	Commissioned
WAMANDAI	A 870 (ex-*Y 8035*)	Rijkswerf, Willemsoord	1960

Displacement, tons: 159 standard; 201 full load
Dimensions, feet (metres): 89·2 × 21·3 × 7·5 *(27·2 × 6·5 × 2·3)*
Guns: 2—20 mm
Main engines: Diesel; 500 bhp = 11 knots

Launched on 28 May 1960. Equipped with salvage pumps and fire fighting equipment. In the Netherlands Antilles since 1964.

Name	No.	Builders	Commissioned
BERKEL	Y 8037	H. H. Bodewes, Millingen	1956
DINTEL	Y 8038	H. H. Bodewes, Millingen	1956
DOMMEL	Y 8039	H. H. Bodewes, Millingen	1957
IJSSEL	Y 8040	H. H. Bodewes, Millingen	1957

Displacement, tons: 139 standard; 163 full load
Dimensions, feet (metres): 82 oa × 20·5 × 7·3 *(25 × 6·3 × 2·2)*
Main engines: Werkspoor diesel and Kort nozzle; 500 bhp

Harbour tugs specially designed for use at Den Helder.

There are also five small harbour tugs—Y 8014, Y 8016, Y 8017, Y 8022 and Y 8028.

ACCOMMODATION SHIPS

(See note under Training Ships)

Cornelis Drebbel is the name of the "Boatel"—775 tons, length 206·7 feet, beam 38·7 feet, draught 3·6 feet, complement 200, cost 3m guilders. Ordered in 1969 from Scheepswerf Voorwaarts at Hoogezand, launched on 19 Nov 1970 and completed in 1971. Serves as accommodation vessel for crews of ships refitting at private yards in the Rotterdam area. *Snellius* (ex-survey ship) was used for accommodation for R. Neth. N. personnel at the RN Submarine Base, Faslane and returned to Netherlands late 1976.

TENDERS

Name	No.	Builders	Commissioned
VAN BOCHOVE	A 923	Zaanlandse Scheepsbouw Mij, Zaandam	Aug 1962

Displacement, tons: 140
Dimensions, feet (metres): 97·2 × 18·2 × 6 *(29·6 × 5·6 × 1·8)*
Main engines: Kromhout diesel; Schottel propeller; 140 bhp = 8 knots
Complement: 8

Torpedo trials vessel. Ordered Oct 1961. Launched on 20 July 1962.

DREG IV Y 8020

Displacement, tons: 46 standard; 48 full load
Dimensions, feet (metres): 65·7 × 15·1 × 4·9 *(20 × 4·6 × 1·5)*
Main engines: 120 hp = 9·5 knots
Complement: 10

Used for communication duties in Rotterdam area.

4 DIVING TENDERS

Name	No.	Builders	Commissioned
ARGUS	A 847	Rijkswerf, Willemsoord	1939
HYDRA	A 850	Rijkswerf, Willemsoord	20 Apr 1956
NAUTILUS	A 849	Rijkswerf, Willemsoord	20 Apr 1956
TRITON	A 848	Rijkswerf, Willemsoord	4 Apr 1964

Displacement, tons: 44 *(Argus)*; 67 (remainder)
Dimensions, feet (metres): 75·4 × 15·4 × 3·3 *(23 × 4·7 × 1) (Argus)*; 76 × 16·4 × 4·6 *(23·2 × 5 × 1·4)* (remainder)
Main engines: Diesel; 144 hp = 8 knots *(Argus)*
Diesel, 117 hp = 9 knots (remainder)
Complement: 8

NEW ZEALAND

Ministerial

Minister of Defence:
Mr Allan McCready MP

Headquarters Appointments

Chief of Naval Staff:
Rear-Admiral J. F. McKenzie, CBE
Deputy Chief of Naval Staff:
Commodore K. M. Saull

The three New Zealand Service Boards were formally abolished in 1971 as part of the Defence Headquarters reorganisation. The former three Service Headquarters and Defence Office have been reorganised into functional branches and offices.
On 1 June 1970 the command and control of the three New Zealand Services was vested in the Chief of Defence Staff who exercises this authority through the three Service Chiefs of Staff.

Diplomatic Representation

Head of New Zealand Defence Liaison Staff, London and Senior Naval Liaison Officer:
Commodore F. H. Bland, OBE
Deputy Head of New Zealand Defence Staff, Washington and Naval Attaché:
Captain E. R. Ellison

Personnel

(a) January 1974: 2 730 officers and ratings
January 1975: 2 690 officers and ratings
January 1976: 2 800 officers and ratings
January 1977: 2 648 officers and ratings
(b) Voluntary
Reserve; 304 RNZNVR

Base

Auckland (HMNZS *Philomel*)

Prefix to Ships' Names

HMNZS

Mercantile Marine

Lloyd's Register of Shipping:
102 vessels of 164 192 tons gross

Strength of the Fleet

Type	Active	Building
Frigates	4	—
Large Patrol Craft	4	—
Survey Ship	1 (converting)	—
Survey Craft	3	—
Research Vessel	1	—
Tender	1	—
Tug	1	—
Reserve Training HDMLs	4	—

Note: Construction of 10 000 ton Support Ship under discussion.

DELETIONS

Cruiser

Dec 1971   *Black Prince*

Frigate

April 1971   *Blackpool* returned to Royal Navy

Corvettes

Sept 1976   *Inverell, Kiama*

Patrol Craft

1972   *Maroro* (HDML)
1975   *Kahawai, Mako, Parore, Tamure* (HDMLs)

Survey Ships

June 1971   *Endeavour* (ex-US *Namakagon*) returned to USN for transfer to Taiwan (now *Lung Chuan*)

Dec 1974   *Lachlan*

PENNANT LIST

Frigates

F 55	Waikato
F 111	Otago
F 148	Taranaki
F 421	Canterbury

Light Forces

P 3563	Kuparu
P 3564	Koura
P 3565	Haku
P 3567	Manga
P 3568	Pukaki
P 3569	Rotoiti
P 3570	Taupo
P 3571	Hawea

Surveying Vessels

—	Monowai
P 3552	Paea
P 3556	Takapu
P 3566	Tarapunga

Research Vessel

A 2	Tui

MONOWAI

FRIGATES

1 "LEANDER" and 1 "BROAD-BEAMED LEANDER" CLASSES

Name	No.	Builders	Laid down	Launched	Commissioned
CANTERBURY	F 421	Yarrow Ltd, Clyde	12 April1969	6 May 1970	22 Oct 1971
WAIKATO	F 55	Harland & Wolff Ltd, Belfast	10 Jan 1964	18 Feb 1965	16 Sep 1966

Displacement, tons: 2 450 standard; 2 860 full load *Waikato;* 2 470 standard; 2 990 full load *Canterbury*
Length, feet (metres): 360·0 *(109·7)* pp; 372·0 *(113·4)* oa *Waikato;* 370·0 *(112·8)* pp *Canterbury*
Beam, feet (metres): 41·0 *(12·5) Waikato;* 43·0 *(13·1) Canterbury*
Draught, feet (metres): 18 *(5·5)*
Aircraft: 1 Wasp helicopter
Missiles: 1 quadruple Seacat
Guns: 2—4·5 in *(155 mm)* in twin turret; 2—20 mm
A/S weapons: 1 Limbo 3-barrelled DC mortar *Waikato;* 2—Mk 32 Mod 5 A/S torpedo tubes *Canterbury*
Main engines: 2 sets d.r. geared turbines; 2 shafts; 30 000 shp
Boilers: 2 Babcock & Wilcox
Speed, knots: 30 *Waikato;* 28 *Canterbury*
Complement: 248 (14 officers, 234 ratings) *Waikato;* 243 (14 officers, 229 ratings) *Canterbury*

Waikato, ordered on 14 June 1963. Commissioned on 16 Sep 1966, trials in the United Kingdom until spring 1967, arrived in New Zealand waters in May 1967. *Canterbury* was ordered in Aug 1968, arrived in New Zealand in Aug 1972. *Canterbury* has extensions fitted to her funnel uptakes.

Radar: Search: Type 965.
Tactical: Type 993.
Fire Control: MRS 3 System and I Band.

CANTERBURY   *1976, Michael D. J. Lennon*

2 "WHITBY" CLASS (TYPE 12)

Name	No.	Builders	Laid down	Launched	Commissioned
OTAGO (ex-HMS *Hastings)*	F 111	J. I. Thornycroft & Co Ltd, Woolston, Southampton	1957	11 Dec 1958	22 June 1960
TARANAKI	F 148	J. Samuel White & Co Ltd, Isle of Wight	1958	19 Aug 1959	28 Mar 1961

Displacement, tons: 2 144 standard; 2 557 full load
Length, feet (metres): 360·0 *(109·7)* pp; 370·0 *(112·8)* oa
Beam, feet (metres): 41·0 *(12·5)*
Draught, feet (metres): 17·3 *(5·3)*
Missiles: 1 quadruple Seacat
Guns: 2—4·5 in *(115 mm)* in twin turret; 2—20 mm *(Taranaki only)*
A/S weapons: 2 Limbo 3-barrelled DC mortars; 6 (2 triple) Mk 32 Mod 5 A/S torpedo tubes
Main engines: 2 sets d.r. geared turbines; 2 shafts; 30 000 shp
Boilers: 2 Babcock & Wilcox
Speed, knots: 30
Complement: 240 (13 officers, 227 ratings)

Taranaki was ordered direct (announced by J. Samuel White & Co on 22 Feb 1957). For *Otago* New Zealand took over the contract (officially stated on 26 Feb 1957) for *Hastings* originally ordered from John I. Thornycroft & Co in Feb 1956 for the Royal Navy. Both vessels are generally similar to the "Whitby" class in the Royal Navy, but were modified to suit New Zealand conditions and have had the most necessary "Rothesay" class alterations and additions. *Otago* has had enclosed foremast since 1967 refit; *Taranaki* was similarly fitted during 1969.

Radar: Search Type 993 and Type 277.
Fire Control I Band.

Tubes: The original twelve 21 in *(533 mm)* A/S torpedo tubes (8 single and 2 twin) were removed.

OTAGO   *10/1976, Graeme Andrews*

SURVEY VESSELS

MONOWAI (ex-*Moana Roa)*

Measurement, tons: 2 893 gross; 1 318 net
Dimensions, feet (metres): 296·5 oa × 36 × 17 *(90·4 × 11 × 5·2)*
Aircraft: 1 helicopter
Main engines: 2 Sulzer 7-cyl diesels; 3 080 hp = 13·5 knots
Oil fuel, tons: 300
Complement: 120 approx

Previously employed on the Cook Is. service. Taken over 1974—put out to tender in early 1975 for conversion which will include an up-rating of the engines, provision of a helicopter deck and hangar and fitting of cp propellers and a bow thruster. Due for service 1977. Conversion undertaken by Scott Lithgow Drydocks Ltd.
May be used for training when available.

MONOWAI (as *Moana Roa)*   *1975, Graeme Andrews*

3 HDML TYPE

PAEA P 3552 (ex-*Q 1184)*
TAKAPU P 3556 (ex-*Q 1188)*
TARAPUNGA P 3566 (ex-*Q 1387)*

Of similar description as those listed under Light Forces.

LIGHT FORCES

4 "LAKE" CLASS (LARGE PATROL CRAFT)

Name	No.	Builders	Commissioned
HAWEA	P 3571	Brooke Marine, Lowestoft, England	29 July 1975
PUKAKI	P 3568	Brooke Marine, Lowestoft, England	24 Feb 1975
ROTOITI	P 3569	Brooke Marine, Lowestoft, England	24 Feb 1975
TAUPO	P 3570	Brooke Marine, Lowestoft, England	29 July 1975

Displacement, tons: 105 standard; 134 full load
Dimensions, feet (metres): 107 oa × 20 × 11·8 *(32·8 × 6·1 × 3·6)*
Guns: 2—12·7 mm (0·50 cal) M2 MGs (fwd); 1—81 mm mortar/·50 cal MG combination (aft)
Main engines: 2 Paxman 12YJCM Diesels; 3 000 bhp = 25 knots
Complement: 21 (3 officers, 18 ratings)

The first to complete, *Pukaki,* was finished on 20 July 1974. She and *Rotoiti* were shipped to New Zealand in Nov 1974. Launch dates—*Hawea,* 9 Sep 1974; *Pukaki,* 1 March 1974; *Rotoiti,* 8 March 1974; *Taupo,* 25 July 1974.

PUKAKI   *1976, Royal New Zealand Navy*

4 HDML TYPE

HAKU (ex-*Wakefield,* ex-*Q 1197*) P 3565
KOURA (ex-*Toroa,* ex-*Q 1350*) P 3564
KUPARU (ex-*Pegasus,* ex-*Q 1349*) P 3563
MANGA (ex-*Q 1185*) P 3567

Displacement, tons: 46 standard; 54 full load
Dimensions, feet (metres): 72 × 16 × 5·5 *(22 × 4·9 × 1·7)*
Guns: Armament removed
Main engines: Diesel; 2 shafts; 320 bhp = 12 knots
Complement: 9

All built in various yards in the United States and Canada and shipped to New Zealand. All have been converted with lattice masts surmounted by a radar aerial.
Attached to RNZNVR divisions;
   Auckland: *Kuparu.*
   Canterbury: *Haku.*
   Otago: *Koura.*
   Wellington: *Manga.*

HAKU   *1973, Royal New Zealand Navy*

RESEARCH VESSEL

Name	No.	Builders	Commissioned
TUI (ex-USS *Charles H. Davis,* T-AGOR 5)	A 2	Christy Corp, Sturgeon Bay, Wis.	25 Jan 1963

Displacement, tons: 1 200 standard; 1 380 full load
Dimensions, feet (metres): 208·9 × 37·4 × 15·3 *(63·7 × 11·3 × 4·7)*
Main engines: Diesel-electric; 1 shaft; 10 000 hp = 12 knots
Complement: 8 officers, 16 ratings, 15 scientists

Oceanographic research ship. Laid down on 15 June 1961, launched on 30 June 1962. On loan from US since 28 July 1970 for 5 years. Commissioned in the Royal New Zealand Navy on 11 Sep 1970. Announced that she will remain in RNZN until at least 1980. Operates for NZ Defence Research Establishment on acoustic research. Bow propeller 175 hp.

Appearance: Port after gallows removed—new gallows at stern—cable reels on quarterdeck and amidships—light cable-laying gear over bow.

TUI (now has gallows removed—see notes)   *1971, Royal New Zealand Navy*

TUGS

ARATAKI   **MANAWANUI**

Dimensions, feet (metres): Length: 75 *(22·9)*
Main engines: Diesel; 1 shaft; 320 hp

Steel tugs. *Arataki* is used as a dockyard tug and *Manawanui* as a diving tender. Built by Steel Ships Ltd, Auckland in 1947.

MANAWANUI   *Royal New Zealand Navy*

NICARAGUA

Ministerial

Minister of Defence:
Heberto Sanchez

Mercantile Marine

Lloyd's Register of Shipping:
27 vessels of 26 415 tons gross

Personnel

1977: 200 officers and men

All craft operated by Marine Section of the Guardia Naçional

Ports

Carinto, Puerto Cabezas, Puerto Somaza, San Juan del Sur.

PATROL CRAFT

1 SEWART TYPE

Displacement, tons: 60
Dimensions, feet (metres): 85 × 18·8 × 5·9 *(25·9 × 5·6 × 1·8)*
Guns: 3—·50 cal MG
Main engines: 3 GM diesels; 3 shafts; 2 000 shp = 26·5 knots
Range, miles: 1 000 at 20 knots
Complement: 10

Delivered July 1972.

RIO CRUTA

Dimensions, feet (metres): Length: 85 *(25·9)*
Gun: 1—20 mm (bow)
Main engines: Diesels; speed = 9 knots
Complement: 11

Wooden-hulled.

4 90 ft LARGE PATROL CRAFT

Wooden-hulled (27·5 metres).

1 75 ft LARGE PATROL CRAFT

Built in 1925 so present existence doubtful. Was used for training. (22·9 metres).

2 80 ft LARGE PATROL CRAFT

Wooden hulled (24·4 metres)

1 26 ft COASTAL PATROL CRAFT

Armed with a 20 mm gun, capable of 25 knots and with a crew of 6. (7·9 metres).

NIGERIA

Headquarters Appointments

Chief of the Naval Staff:
Rear Admiral Michael Ayinde Adelanwa
Chief of Staff:
Captain Hussaini Abdullahi

Commands

Naval Flotilla:
Captain I. A. Wright
Western Naval Command:
Captain Edwin Kentebe
Eastern Naval Command:
Commander Raheem Adisa Adegbite

Diplomatic Representation

Naval Adviser in Delhi:
Captain Akintunde Aduwo

Personnel

(a) 1977: 260 officers and 2 700 ratings (2 000 reserves)
(b) Voluntary Service

Bases

Apapa—Lagos:
Western Naval Command
Dockyard Training Schools
Calabar:
Eastern Naval Command

Prefix to Ships' Names

NNS.

Mercantile Marine

Lloyd's Register of Shipping:
92 vessels of 181 565 tons gross

Strength of the Fleet

Type	Active	Building
Frigate	1	—
Corvettes	2	2
Large Patrol Craft	12	—
Landing Craft	1	—
Survey Ships	2	—
Supply Ship	1	—
Training Ship	1	—
Tug	1	—
Police Craft	8	—

DELETIONS

Light Forces

1975   3 ex-Soviet "P6" class; *Kaduna, Ibadan II* ("Ford" class)

Survey Ship

1975   *Pathfinder*

NIGERIA

LANA

FRIGATE

Name	No.	Builders	Laid down	Launched	Commissioned
NIGERIA	F 87	Wilton-Fijenoord NV, Netherlands	9 April 1964	12 April 1965	16 Sep 1965

Displacement, tons: 1 724 standard; 2 000 full load
Length, feet (metres): 341·2 *(104·0)* pp; 360·2 *(109·8)* oa
Beam, feet (metres): 37·0 *(11·3)*
Draught, feet (metres): 11·5 *(3·5)*
Guns: 2—4 in *(102 mm)* (1 twin); 3—40 mm (single)
A/S weapons: 1—triple-barrelled Squid mortar
Main engines: 4 MAN Diesels; 2 shafts; 16 000 bhp
Speed, knots: 26
Range, miles: 3 500 at 15 knots
Complement: 216

Cost £3 500 000. Helicopter platform aft.
Refitted at Birkenhead, 1973. Suffered a serious fire on return
from refit.

NIGERIA

7/1976, Wright and Logan

CORVETTES

2 Mk 9 VOSPER THORNYCROFT TYPE

Name	No.	Builders	Commissioned
ERIN'MI	—	Vosper Thornycroft Ltd	1978
—	—	Vosper Thornycroft Ltd	1979

Displacement, tons: 820
Length, feet (metres): 235 *(71·6)*
Missiles: 1 Seacat launcher
Guns: 1—76 mm OTO Melara; 1—40 mm
A/S weapons: 1 Bofors rocket launcher
Main engines: 2 diesels
Speed, knots: 29

Ordered from Vosper Thornycroft in 1975. *Erin'mi* launched Jan 1977.

Radar: Search; Plessey AWS-2.

Vosper Thornycroft Mark 9 Corvette   *1977, Vosper Thornycroft*

2 Mk 3 VOSPER THORNYCROFT TYPE

Name	No.	Builders	Commissioned
DORINA	F 81	Vosper Thornycroft	June 1972
OTOBO	F 82	Vosper Thornycroft	Nov 1972

Displacement, tons: 500 standard; 650 full load
Dimensions, feet (metres): 202 oa × 31 × 11·33 *(61·6 × 9·5 × 3·5)*
Guns: 2—4 in (1 twin) UK Mk 19; 2—40 mm Bofors (single) 2—20 mm
Main engines: 2 MAN diesels; = 23 knots
Range, miles: 3 500 at 14 knots
Complement: 66 (7 officers and 59 ratings)

Ordered on 28 Mar 1968. *Dorina* laid down 26 Jan 1970, launched 16 Sep 1970, *Otobo* laid down 28 Sep 1970, launched 25 May 1971. Both refitted by Vosper Thornycroft 1975.

Radar: Air Search: Plessey AWS-1.
Fire Control: HSA M20.
Navigation: Decca TM626.

DORINA   *9/1976, Wright and Logan*

LIGHT FORCES

4 BROOKE MARINE TYPE (LARGE PATROL CRAFT)

Name	No.	Builders	Commissioned
HADEJIA	P 168	Brooke Marine, Lowestoft	14 Aug 1974
MAKURDI	P 167	Brooke Marine, Lowestoft	14 Aug 1974
—	P 169	Brooke Marine, Lowestoft	1977
—	P 170	Brooke Marine, Lowestoft	1977

Displacement, tons: 115 standard; 143 full load
Dimensions, feet (metres): 107 × 20 × 11·5 *(32·6 × 6·1 × 3·5)*
Guns: 2—40 mm; 2 Rocket flare launchers
Main engines: 2 Ruston Paxman YJCM diesels; 3 000 bhp; 2 shafts = 20·5 knots
Complement: 21

First pair ordered in 1971. Two more ordered 30 Oct 1974, laid down Jan 1975. Launch dates—*Hadejia*, 25 May 1974. *Makurdi*, 21 March 1974.

HADEJIA   *9/1974, C. and S. Taylor*

4 Ex-BRITISH "FORD" CLASS (LARGE PATROL CRAFT)

Name	No.	Builders	Commissioned
BENIN (ex-HMS *Hinksford*)	P 03	Richards, Lowestoft	1955
BONNY (ex-HMS *Gifford*)	P 04	Scarr, Hessle	1954
ENUGU	P 05	Camper & Nicholson's, Gosport	14 Dec 1961
SAPELE (ex-HMS *Dubford*)	P 09	J. Samuel White, Cowes	1953

Displacement, tons: 120 standard; 160 full load
Dimensions, feet (metres): 110 pp; 117·2 oa × 20 × 5 *(33·6; 35·7 × 6·1 × 1·5)*
Guns: 1—40 mm Bofors; 2—20 mm Oerlikon
Main engines: Davey Paxman diesels; Foden engine on centre shaft; 1 100 bhp = 18 knots
Complement: 26

Enugu was the first warship built for the Nigerian Navy. Ordered in 1960. Sailed from Portsmouth for Nigeria on 10 April 1962. Fitted with Vosper roll damping fins. *Hinksford* purchased from Great Britain on 1 July 1966 and transferred at Devonport on 9 Sep 1966. *Dubford* and *Gifford* were purchased from Great Britain during 1967-68.

BENIN   *1970, Nigerian Navy*

4 ABEKING AND RASMUSSEN TYPE (LARGE PATROL CRAFT)

Name	No.	Builders	Commissioned
ARGUNGU	P 165	Abeking & Rasmussen	Aug 1973
YOLA	P 166	Abeking & Rasmussen	Aug 1973
BRAS	—	Abeking & Rasmussen	Mar 1976
EPE	—	Abeking & Rasmussen	Mar 1976

Displacement, tons: 90
Dimensions, feet (metres): 95·1 × 18·0 × 5·2 *(29 × 5·5 × 1·6)*
Guns: 1—40 mm Bofors 60 cal in Mk 3 mtg; 1—20 mm
Main engines: 2 Paxman Diesels; 2 200 hp; 2 shafts = 20 knots
Complement: 25

Launch dates—*Argungu,* 9 July 1973. *Yola,* 12 June 1973. Second pair ordered 1975

YOLA   *10/1974, Michael D. J. Lennon*

SURVEY SHIPS

Name	No.	Builders	Commissioned
LANA	—	Brooke Marine, Lowestoft	Sept 1976

Displacement, tons: 800 standard; 1 100 full load
Dimensions, feet (metres): 189 × 37·5 × 11·2 *(57·8 × 11·4 × 3·5)*
Main engines: 4 diesels; 2 shafts; 3 000 bhp = 16 knots
Range, miles: 4 500 at 12 knots
Complement: 38

Ordered in late 1973, laid down 5 April 1974, launched 4 Mar 1976. Sister to RN "Bulldog" Class.

LANA   *10/1976, Wright and Logan*

Name	No.	Builders	Commissioned
PENELOPE	P 11	Aldous Successors, Brightlingsea	1958

Measurement, tons: 79 gross
Dimensions, feet (metres): 79·5 × 7·8 × 4·5 *(24·2 × 2·4 × 1·4)*
Main engines: 2 Gardner diesels = 10 knots

Used for local survey duties.

SERVICE FORCES

1 Ex-BRITISH LCT (4)

LOKOJA (ex-LCT (4) 1213)

Displacement, tons: 350 standard; 586 full load
Dimensions, feet (metres): 187·5 × 38·8 × 4·5 *(57·2 × 11·8 × 1·4)*
Guns: 2—20 mm
Main engines: 2 Paxman diesels; 920 bhp = 10 knots

Purchased from Great Britain in 1959. Allocated the name *Lokoja* in 1961. Underwent a major refit in 1966-67, including complete replating of the bottom, but currently in poor condition.

1 SUPPLY SHIP

KWA RIVER

1 000-ton ex-Dutch coaster captured while running army stores to the Biafrans.

1 TRAINING SHIP

Name	No.	Builders	Commissioned
RUWAN YARO (ex-*Ogina Brereton*)	A 497	Van Lent, Netherlands	1976

Dimensions, feet (metres): 144·6 × 26·2 × 12·8 *(44·2 × 8 × 3·9)*
Main engines: 2 Deutz diesels

Originally built as a ferry. Used as navigational training vessel.

RUWAN YARO   *12/1976, Michael D. J. Lennon*

TUG

Name	No.	Builders	Commissioned
RIBADU	A 486	Oelkers, Hamburg	19 May 1973

Displacement, tons: 147
Dimensions, feet (metres): 93·5 × 23·6 × 12·1 *(28·5 × 7·2 × 3·7)*
Main engines: Diesel; 800 shp = 12 knots

Fitted for firefighting and salvage work.

POLICE CRAFT

8 VOSPER THORNYCROFT TYPE
(COASTAL PATROL CRAFT)

Displacement, tons: 15
Dimensions, feet (metres): 34 oa × 10 × 2·8 *(10·4 × 3·1 × 0·9)*
Guns: 1 machine gun
Main engines: 2 diesels; 290 hp = 19 knots
Complement: 6

Ordered for Nigerian Police March 1971, completed 1971-72. GRP hulls.

NORWAY

Ministerial

Minister of Defence:
Rolf Hansen

Headquarters Appointments

Inspector General:
Rear-Admiral C. O. Herlotson
Commander Naval Logistics Services:
Rear-Admiral N. A. Owren
Commodore Sea Training:
Commodore Rolf Henningsen

Diplomatic Representation

Defence Attaché in Bonn:
Lt. Colonel L. Tvilde
Defence Attaché in Helsinki:
Lt. Colonel G. J. Jervaas
Defence Attaché in London:
Commander B. Eia
Defence Attaché in Moscow:
Lt. Colonel A. V. W. Lerheim
Defence Attaché in Stockholm:
Captain Paul H. Roest
Defence Attaché in Washington (for USA and Canada):
Lt General Einartufte Johnsen

Training Ship

1974 *Haakon VII*

Personnel

(a)
1974: 8 400 officers and ratings
1975: 8 400 officers and ratings
1976: 8 000 officers and ratings
1977: 8 400 officers and ratings
(All above figures include 1 600 Coast Artillery)

(b)
15 months National Service (5 000)

Naval Bases

Karljohansvern (Horten), Haakonsvern (Bergen),
Ramsund and Ramfjordnes (N. Norway)

Prefix to Ships' Names

KNM

Mercantile Marine

Lloyd's Register of Shipping:
2 759 vessels of 27 943 434 tons gross

Strength of the Fleet

Type	Active	Building
Frigates	5	—
Corvettes	2	—
Submarines—Coastal	15	—
Fast Attack Craft—Missile	26	14
Fast Attack Craft—Torpedo	20	—
Minelayers	3	2
Minesweepers—Coastal	10	—
Minesweepers—Inshore	—	1
LCTs	7	—
Depot Ships	1	1
Tenders	2	—
Royal Yacht	1	—
Research Ship	1	—
Coast Guard Vessels	6	8

DELETIONS

LCT

1975 *Tjeldsund*

Minelayers

1976 *Gor, Tyr*

PENNANT LIST

F (Frigates and Corvettes)		M (Minesweepers)		S (Submarines)		P (Light Forces)		P (Light Forces)		P (Light Forces)		A (Amphibious Forces)	
300	Oslo	315	Ogna	300	Ula	343	Tjeld	387	Lyr	971	Tross	31	Kvalsund
301	Bergen	316	Vosso	301	Utsira	344	Skarv	388	Gribb	972	Hvass	32	Raftsund
302	Trondheim	317	Glomma	302	Utstein	345	Teist	389	Geir	973	Traust	33	Reinsöysund
303	Stavanger	331	Tista	303	Utvaer	346	Jo	390	Erle	974	Brott	34	Söröysund
304	Narvik	332	Kvina	304	Uthaug	347	Lom	960	Storm	975	Odd	35	Maursund
310	Sleipner	334	Utla	305	Sklinna	348	Stegg	961	Blink	976	Pil	36	Rotsund
311	Aeger			306	Skolpen	349	Hauk	962	Glimt	977	Brask	37	Borgsund
				307	Stadt	350	Falk	963	Skjold	978	Rokk		
		N (Minelayers)		308	Stord	357	Ravn	964	Trygg	979	Gnist		
		49	Brage	309	Svenner	380	Skrei	965	Kjekk	980	Snögg	A (Service Forces)	
M (Minesweepers)		50	Uller	315	Kaura	381	Hai	966	Djerv	981	Rapp		
		51	Borgen	316	Kinn	382	Sel	967	Skudd	982	Snar	533	Norge
311	Sauda	52	Vidar	317	Kya	383	Hval	968	Arg	983	Rask	535	Valkyrien
312	Sira	53	Vale	318	Kobben	384	Laks	969	Steil	984	Kvikk		
313	Tana			319	Kunna	385	Knurr	970	Brann	985	Kjapp		
314	Alta					386	Delfin			986-			
										999	New Construction		

SUPPORT SHIP

COASTGUARD VESSEL

SLEIPNER

HORTEN

FRIGATES

5 "OSLO" CLASS

Name	No.	Builders	Laid down	Launched	Commissioned
BERGEN	F 301	Marinens Hovedverft, Horten	1964	23 Aug 1965	15 June 1967
NARVIK	F 304	Marinens Hovedverft, Horten	1964	8 Jan 1965	30 Nov 1966
OSLO	F 300	Marinens Hovedverft, Horten	1963	17 Jan 1964	29 Jan 1966
STAVANGER	F 303	Marinens Hovedverft, Horten	1965	4 Feb 1966	1 Dec 1967
TRONDHEIM	F 302	Marinens Hovedverft, Horten	1963	4 Sep 1964	2 June 1966

Displacement, tons: 1 450 standard; 1 745 full load
Length, feet (metres): 308 *(93·9)* pp; 317 *(96·6)* oa
Beam, feet (metres): 36·7 *(11·2)*
Draught, feet (metres): 17·4 *(5·3)*
Missiles: 6 Penguin, Octuple Seasparrow
Guns: 4—3 in *(76 mm)* (2 twin mounts US Mk 33)
A/S weapons: Terne system; 6 (2 triple) Mk 32 A/S torpedo tubes
Main engines: 1 set De Laval Ljungstrom double reduction geared turbines; 1 shaft; 20 000 shp
Boilers: 2 Babcock & Wilcox
Speed, knots: 25
Complement: 151 (11 officers, 140 ratings)

Built under the five-year naval construction programme approved by the Norwegian *Storting* (Parliament) late in 1960. Although all the ships of this class were constructed in the Norwegian Naval Dockyard, half the cost was borne by Norway and the other half by the United States. The design of these ships is based on that of the "Dealey" class destroyer escorts in the United States Navy, but considerably modified to suit Norwegian requirements.

NARVIK

10/1976, Michael D. J. Lennon

Engineering: The main turbines and auxiliary machinery were all built by De Laval Ljungstrom, Sweden at the company's works in Stockholm-Nacka.

Radar: Search: DRBV 22.
Tactical and Fire Control: HSA M 24 system.

Sonar: 1 Terne III Mk 3; 1 AN/SQS 36.

CORVETTES

Note: An additional ship *Vadso* of 631 tons is also listed.

2 "SLEIPNER" CLASS

Name	No.	Builders	Laid down	Launched	Commissioned
AEGER	F 311	Akers, Oslo	1964	24 Sep 1965	31 Mar 1967
SLEIPNER	F 310	Nylands Verksted Shipyard	1963	9 Nov 1963	29 April 1965

Displacement, tons: 600 standard; 780 full load
Dimensions, feet (metres): 227·8 oa × 26·2 × 8·2 *(69 × 8 × 2·4)*
Guns: 1—3 in *(76 mm)* (US Mk 34 mount); 1—40 mm
A/S weapons: Terne ASW system; 6 (2 triple) Mk 32 A/S torpedo tubes
Main engines: 4 Maybach (MTU) diesels; 2 shafts; 9 000 bhp = over 20 knots
Complement: 62

Under the five-year programme only two instead of the originally planned five new corvettes were built. Temporarily employed as training ships until new construction is available.

Radar and Fire Control: US Mk 63 GFCS with Mk 34 radar.

Sonar: 1 Terne III Mk 3; 1 AN/SQS 36.

SLEIPNER   7/1975, J. L. M. van der Burg

SUBMARINES

TYPE 210

A design contract for a new class of 750 ton patrol submarines has been placed with IKL (Lübeck). This is being carried out in conjunction with the navy of the Federal Republic of Germany.

15 TYPE 207

Name	No.	Builders	Laid down	Launched	Commissioned
KAURA	S 315	Rheinstahl-Nordseewerke, Emden, West Germany	1961	16 Oct 1964	5 Feb 1965
KINN	S 316	Rheinstahl-Nordseewerke, Emden, West Germany	1960	30 Nov 1963	8 April 1964
KOBBEN	S 318	Rheinstahl-Nordseewerke, Emden, West Germany	1961	25 April 1964	17 Aug 1964
KUNNA	S 319	Rheinstahl-Nordseewerke, Emden, West Germany	1961	16 July 1964	1 Oct 1964
KYA	S 317	Rheinstahl-Nordseewerke, Emden, West Germany	1961	20 Feb 1964	15 June 1964
SKLINNA	S 305	Rheinstahl-Nordseewerke, Emden, West Germany	1963	21 Jan 1966	27 May 1966
SKOLPEN	S 306	Rheinstahl-Nordseewerke, Emden, West Germany	1963	24 Mar 1966	17 Aug 1966
STADT	S 307	Rheinstahl-Nordseewerke, Emden, West Germany	1963	10 June 1966	15 Nov 1966
STORD	S 308	Rheinstahl-Nordseewerke, Emden, West Germany	1964	2 Sep 1966	9 Feb 1967
SVENNER	S 309	Rheinstahl-Nordseewerke, Emden, West Germany	1965	27 Jan 1967	1 July 1967
ULA	S 300	Rheinstahl-Nordseewerke, Emden, West Germany	1962	19 Dec 1964	7 May 1965
UTHAUG	S 304	Rheinstahl-Nordseewerke, Emden, West Germany	1962	8 Oct 1965	16 Feb 1966
UTSIRA	S 301	Rheinstahl-Nordseewerke, Emden, West Germany	1963	11 Mar 1965	1 July 1965
UTSTEIN	S 302	Rheinstahl-Nordseewerke, Emden, West Germany	1962	19 May 1965	9 Sep 1965
UTVAER	S 303	Rheinstahl-Nordseewerke, Emden, West Germany	1962	30 June 1965	1 Dec 1965

Displacement, tons: 370 standard; 435 dived
Length, feet (metres): 149 *(45·2)*
Beam, feet (metres): 15 *(4·6)*
Draught, feet (metres): 14 *(4·3)*
Torpedo tubes: 8—21 in *(533 mm)* (bow)
Main machinery: 2 MB 820 Maybach-Mercedes-Benz (MTU) diesels; 1 200 bhp; electric drive; 1 200 hp; 1 shaft
Speed, knots: 10 surfaced; 17 dived
Complement: 18 (5 officers, 13 men)

It was announced in July 1959 that the USA and Norway would share equally the cost of these submarines. These are a development of IKL Type 205 (West German U4-U8) with increased diving depth. *Svenner* has a second periscope for COs training operations—a metre longer.

Names: *Kobben* was the name of the first submarine in the Royal Norwegian Navy. Commissioned on 28 Nov 1909.

SVENNER (with second periscope)   1972, Royal Norwegian Navy

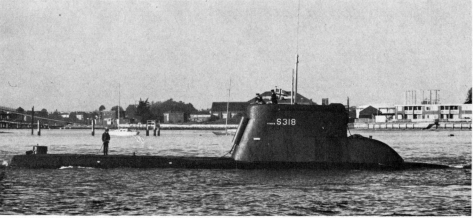

KOBBEN   1976, Michael D. J. Lennon

LIGHT FORCES

Note: Armament varies in "Snögg" and "Storm" classes as Penguin SSM is installed

14 "HAUK" CLASS (FAST ATTACK CRAFT—MISSILE)

P 986-999

Displacement, tons: 120 standard; 150 full load
Dimensions, feet (metres): 119·7 oa × 20·3 × 5·5 *(36·5 × 6·2 × 1·6)*
Missiles: 4—Penguin
Gun: 1—40 mm
Torpedo tubes: 4—21 in *(533 mm)*
Main engines: 2 MTU diesels; 7 000 hp = 34 knots
Range, miles: 440 at 34 knots
Complement: 22

Ordered 12 June 1975—ten from Bergens Mek. Verksteder (Lakesevåg) and four from Wester-möen (Alta). Very similar to "Snögg" class with improved fire control.

Control system: Weapon control by MSI-80S developed by Kongsberg Vappenfabrikk.

Missiles: Of a longer-range version developed in collaboration with the Royal Swedish Navy.

6 "SNÖGG" CLASS (FAST ATTACK CRAFT—MISSILE)

Name	No.	Builders	Commissioned
KJAPP	P 985	Batservice Werft, A/S, Mandal, Norway	1971
KVIKK	P 984	Batservice Werft, A/S, Mandal, Norway	1971
RAPP	P 981	Batservice Werft, A/S, Mandal, Norway	1970
RASK	P 983	Batservice Werft, A/S, Mandal, Norway	1971
SNAR	P 982	Batservice Werft, A/S, Mandal, Norway	1970
SNÖGG (ex-*Lyr*)	P 980	Batservice Werft, A/S, Mandel, Norway	1970

Displacement, tons: 100 standard; 125 full load
Dimensions, feet (metres): 120·0 × 20·5 × 5·0 *(36·5 × 6·2 × 1·3)*
Missile launchers: 4 Penguin
Gun: 1—40 mm
Torpedo tubes: 4—21 in
Main engines: 2 Maybach (MTU) diesels; 2 shafts; 7 200 bhp = 32 knots
Complement: 18

RAPP   *1973, Royal Norwegian Navy*

These steel hulled fast attack craft ordered from Batservice Werft, A/S, Mandal, Norway, started coming into service in 1970. Hulls are similar to those of the "Storm" class gunboats.

20 "STORM" CLASS (FAST ATTACK CRAFT—MISSILE)

Name	No.	Builders	Commissioned	
ARG	P 968	Bergens MV		1966
BLINK	P 961	Bergens MV	18 Dec	1965
BRANN	P 970	Bergens MV		1967
BRASK	P 977	Bergens MV		1967
BROTT	P 974	Bergens MV		1967
DJERV	P 966	Westermoen, Mandal		1966
GLIMT	P 962	Bergens MV		1966
GNIST	P 979	Bergens MV		1968
HVASS	P 972	Westermoen, Mandal		1967
KJEKK	P 965	Bergens MV		1966
ODD	P 975	Westermoen, Mandal		1967
PIL	P 976	Bergens MV		1967
ROKK	P 978	Westermoen, Mandal		1968
SKJOLD	P 963	Westermoen, Mandal		1966
SKUDD	P 967	Bergens MV		1966
STEIL	P 969	Westermoen, Mandal		1967
STORM	P 960	Bergens MV		1968
TRAUST	P 973	Bergens MV		1967
TROSS	P 971	Bergens MV		1967
TRYGG	P 964	Bergens MV		1966

Displacement, tons: 100 standard; 125 full load
Dimensions, feet (metres): 120·0 oa × 20·5 × 5·0 *(36·5 × 6·2 × 1·5)*
Missile launchers: 6 Penguin
Guns: 1—3 in; 1—40 mm
Main engines: 2 Maybach (MTU) diesels; 2 shafts; 7 200 bhp = 32 knots

TRAUST with 6 Penguins fitted   *1971, A/S Kongsbergvappenfabrikk*

The first of 20 (instead of the 23 originally planned) gunboats of a new design built under the five-year programme was *Storm,* launched on 8 Feb 1963, and completed on 31 May 1963, but this prototype was eventually scrapped and replaced by a new series construction boat as the last of the class. The first of the production boats was *Blink,* launched on 28 June 1965 and completed on 18 Dec 1965. The introduction of Penguin surface-to-surface guided missile launchers started in 1970, in addition to originally designed armament.

20 "TJELD" CLASS (FAST ATTACK CRAFT—TORPEDO)

Name	No.	Builders	Commissioned
DELFIN	P 386	Båtservis, Mandal	20 May 1966
ERLE	P 390	Båtservis, Mandal	1966
FALK	P 350	Båtservis, Mandal	1961
GEIR	P 389	Båtservis, Mandal	1965
GRIBB	P 388	Båtservis, Mandal	1965
HAI	P 381	Båtservis, Mandal	1962
HAUK	P 349	Båtservis, Mandal	1961
HVAL	P 383	Båtservis, Mandal	1963
JO	P 346	Båtservis, Mandal	1961
KNURR	P 385	Båtservis, Mandal	1964
LAKS	P 384	Båtservis, Mandal	1964
LOM	P 347	Båtservis, Mandal	1961
LYR	P 387	Båtservis, Mandal	1966
RAVN	P 357	Båtservis, Mandal	1962
SEL	P 382	Båtservis, Mandal	1963
SKARV	P 344	Båtservis, Mandal	1960
SKREI	P 380	Båtservis, Mandal	1962
STEGG	P 348	Båtservis, Mandal	1961
TEIST	P 345	Båtservis, Mandal	1960
TJELD	P 343	Båtservis, Mandal	June 1960

SKARV

1973, Royal Norwegian Navy

Displacement, tons: 70 standard; 82 full load
Dimensions, feet (metres): 80·3 oa × 24·5 × 6·8 *(24·5 × 7·5 × 2·1)*
Guns: 1—40 mm; 1—20 mm
Torpedo tubes: 4—21 in *(533 mm)*
Main engines: 2 Napier Deltic Turboblown diesels; 2 shafts; 6 200 bhp = 45 knots
Range, miles: 450 at 40 knots; 600 at 25 knots
Complement: 18

Built of mahogany to Båtservis design, known generally as "Nasty" class.

Transfers: 2 to Turkey via West Germany, 2 to USA and 6 to Greece.

MINEWARFARE FORCES

2 COASTAL MINELAYERS

Name	No.	Builders	Commissioned
VALE	N 53	Mjellem and Karlsen, Bergen	1977
VIDAR	N 52	Skaaluren Skibsbyggeri, Rosendal	1977

Displacement, tons: 1 673 full load
Dimensions, feet (metres): 212·6 × 39·4 × 29·5 *(64·8 × 12 × 9)*
Guns: 2—40 mm (twin)
Main engines: 2 Wichman 7AX diesels; 4 200 bhp; 2 shafts = 15 knots
Complement: 50

Laid down—*Vale,* 1 Feb 1976; *Vidar,* 1 Mar 1976. One to be used for training duties originally carried out by *Haakon VII* and now by *Sleipner* and *Aeger.*

Mines: To carry 320 on three decks with an automatic lift between. Loaded through hatches forward and aft each served by two cranes.

1 CONTROLLED MINELAYER

Name	No.	Builders	Commissioned
BORGEN	N 51	Marinens Hovedverft, Horten	1961

Displacement, tons: 282 standard
Dimensions, feet (metres): 102·5 ao × 26·2 × 11 *(31·2 × 8 × 3·4)*
Main engines: 2 GM diesels; 2 Voith-Schneider propellers; 330 bhp = 9 knots

Launched 29 April 1960.

BORGEN

1972, Royal Norwegian Navy

2 Ex-US "AUK" CLASS (MINELAYERS—COASTAL)

Name	No.	Builders	Commissioned
BRAGE (ex-USS *Triumph,* MMC 3)	N 49	Associated Shipbuilders	1944
ULLER (ex-USS *Seer,* MMC 5)	N 50	American Shipbuilding Co	1942

Displacement, tons: 890 standard; 1 250 full load
Dimensions, feet (metres): 221·2 oa × 32·2 × 16 *(67 × 9·8 × 3·4)*
Guns: 1—3 in, 50 cal; 4—20 mm (2 twin) *(Brage)*
 1—3 in, 50 cal; 1—40 mm *(Uller)*
A/S weapons: 2 Hedgehogs; 3 DCT *(Brage)*
 Terne ASW system; 1 DCT *(Uller)*
Mines: Laying capability
Main engines: GM diesels; electric drive; 2 shafts; 2 070 bhp = 16 knots
Complement: 83

Former US Coastal Minelayers (MMC) converted from "Auk" class MSOs. *Brage* converted 1960 into coastal minelayer at Charleston Naval Shipyard, but *Uller* was converted in Norway. Both transferred 1959-1960. *Brage* to reserve in 1975—both for deletion in 1977 on completion of *Vale* and *Vidar.*

BRAGE

1972, Royal Norwegian Navy

10 Ex-US "FALCON" CLASS (MSC 60)
(MINESWEEPERS—COASTAL)

Name	No.	Builders	Commissioned
ALTA (ex-*Arlon M 915*, ex-*MSC 104*)	M 314	USA	1954
GLOMMA (ex-*Bastogne*, *M 916*, ex-*MSC 151*)	M 317	USA	1954
KVINA	M 332	Båtservis, Mandal	12 July 1955
OGNA	M 315	Båtservis, Mandal	5 Mar 1955
SAUDA (ex-USS *MSC 102*)	M 311	Hodgeson Bros, Gowdy & Stevens, East Boothbay, Maine	25 Aug 1953
SIRA (ex-USS *MSC 132*)	M 312	Hodgeson Bros, Gowdy & Stevens, East Boothbay, Maine	28 Nov 1955
TANA (ex-*Roeselaere*, *M 914*, ex- *MSC 103*)	M 313	USA	1954
TISTA	M 331	Forende Batbyggeriex, Risör	27 April 1955
UTLA	M 334	Båtservis, Mandal	15 Nov 1955
VOSSO	M 316	Skaaluren Skibsbyggeri, Rosendal	16 Mar 1955

Displacement, tons: 333 standard; 384 full load
Dimensions, feet (metres): 144 × 28 × 8·5 *(44 × 8·1 × 2·6)*
Gun: 1—·50 cal MG
Main engines: GM diesels; 880 bhp = 13·5 knots
Oil fuel, tons: 25
Complement: 38

Hull of wooden construction. Five coastal minesweepers were built in Norway with US engines. *Alta, Glomma* and *Tana* were taken over from the Royal Belgian Navy in May, Sep and Mar 1966, respectively, having been exchanged for two Norwegian ocean minesweepers of the US MSO type, *Lagen* (ex-*MSO 498*) and *Nansen* (ex-*MSO 499*).

TISTA   7/1975, J. L. M. van der Burg

1 SWEDISH "GÄSSTEN" CLASS (MINESWEEPER—INSHORE)

Displacement, tons: 135 full load
Dimensions, feet (metres): 75·5 × 21·7 × 6·5 *(23 × 6·6 × 2)*
Gun: 1—40 mm
Main engines: Diesels = 11 knots

GRP hull. Ordered from Sweden to be used in tests and evaluation.

AMPHIBIOUS FORCES

2 "KVALSUND" CLASS (LCT)

Name	No.	Builders	Commissioned
KVALSUND	A 31	Mjellem & Karlsen, Bergen	1970
RAFTSUNDA	A 32	Mjellem & Karlsen, Bergen	1970

5 "REINØYSUND" CLASS (LCT)

Name	No.	Builders	Commissioned
BORGSUND	A 37	Mjellem & Karlsen, Bergen	1973
MAURSUND	A 35	Mjellem & Karlsen, Bergen	Sep 1972
REINØYSUND	A 33	Mjellem & Karlsen, Bergen	Jan 1972
ROTSUND	A 36	Mjellem & Karlsen, Bergen	1973
SØRØYSUND	A 34	Mjellem & Karlsen, Bergen	June 1972

Displacement, tons: 590 ("Reinøysund" class 596)
Dimensions, feet (metres): 167·3 × 33·5 × 5·9 *(50 × 10·2 × 1·8)*
Guns: 2—20 mm (3 in "Reinøysund" class)
Speed, knots: 11

All capable of carrying 7 tanks. Both classes of same dimensions.

REINØYSUND   1973, Royal Norwegian Navy

DEPOT SHIPS

1 NEW CONSTRUCTION

Name	No.	Builders	Commissioned
HORTEN	—	A/S Horten Verft	April 1978

Displacement, tons: 2 500
Dimensions, feet (metres): 285·5 × 42·6 × 23 *(87 × 13 × 7)*
Aircraft: 1 helicopter on deck
Guns: 2—40 mm
Main engines: 2 Wickmann diesels; 2 shafts = 16·5 knots
Complement: 85

Contract signed 30 Mar 1976. Cost approx £8 mill. To serve both submarines and fast attack craft. Quarters for 60 extra and can cater for 190 extra.

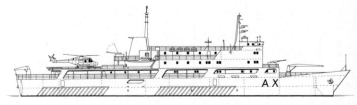

HORTEN   1976, Horten Verft

1 Ex-CANADIAN FRIGATE TYPE

Name	No.	Builders	Commissioned
VALKYRIEN (ex-*Garm*, ex-*Toronto*)	A 535 (ex-*F 315*)	Davie Shipbuilding Co, Lauzon, Port Quebec, Canada	6 May 1944

Displacement, tons: 1 570 standard; 2 240 full load
Dimensions, feet (metres): 301·3 × 36·5 × 16 *(91·9 × 11·1 × 4·9)*
Guns: 2—4 in, 2—40 mm
Main engines: Triple expansion; 2 shafts; 5 500 ihp = 19 knots
Complement: 104

Former Canadian modernised "River" class frigate. Loaned to Norway on 10 Mar 1956 and finally converted as depot ship for Light Forces.

VALKYRIEN   1972, Royal Norwegian Navy

2 DIVING TENDERS

Name	No.	Builders	Commissioned	
DRAUG	—	Nielsen, Harstad	1972	
SARPEN	—	Nielsen, Harstad	1972	Small depot ships of 250 tons for frogmen and divers.

ROYAL YACHT

Name	No.	Builders	Commissioned
NORGE (ex-*Philante*)	A 533	Camper & Nicholson's Ltd, Gosport, England	1937

Measurement, tons: 1 686 *(Thames yacht measurement)*
Dimensions, feet (metres): 263 oa × 28 × 15·2 *(80·2 × 8·5 × 4·6)*
Main engines: 8-cyl diesels; 2 shafts; 3 000 bhp = 17 knots

Built to the order of the late Mr. T. O. M. Sopwith as an escort and store vessel for the yachts *Endeavour I* and *Endeavour II.* Launched on 17 Feb 1937. Served in the Royal Navy as an anti-submarine escort during the Second World War, after which she was purchased by the Norwegian people for King Haakon at a cost of nearly £250,000 and reconditioned as a Royal Yacht at Southampton. Can accommodate about 50 people in addition to crew.

NORGE   *1971, Royal Norwegian Navy*

RESEARCH SHIP

Name	No.	Builders	Commissioned
H. U. SVERDRUP	—	Orens Mekaniske Verkstad, Trondheim	1960

Displacement, tons: 400
Measurement, tons: 295 gross
Dimensions, feet (metres): 127·7 × 25 × 13 *(38·9 × 7·6 × 4)*
Main engines: Wichmann diesel; 600 bhp = 11·5 knots
Oil fuel, tons: 65
Range, miles: 5 000 at 10 knots cruising speed
Complement: 10 crew; 9 scientists

Operates for Norwegian Defence Research Establishment.

COASTGUARD

Set up in 1976 for combined duties of Fishery Protection and Oil Rig Patrol.

Name	No.	Builders	Commissioned
O/S NORNEN	—	Mjellem & Karlsen, Bergen	1963

Measurement, tons: 930 gross
Dimensions, feet (metres): 201·8 × 32·8 × 15·8 *(61·5 × 10 × 4·8)*
Gun: 1—3 in *(76 mm)*
Main engines: 4 diesels; 3 500 bhp = 17 knots
Complement: 32

Launched 20 Aug 1962.

NORNEN   *1970, Royal Norwegian Navy*

Name	No.	Builders	Commissioned
O/S FARM	—	Ankerlokken Verft	1962
O/S HEIMDAL	—	Bolsones Verft, Molde	1962

Measurement, tons: 600 gross
Dimensions, feet (metres): 177 × 26·2 × 16·5 *(54·3 × 8·2 × 4·9)*
Gun: 1—3 in *(76 mm)*
Main engines: 2 diesels; 2 700 bhp = 16 knots
Complement: 29

Farm launched 22 Feb 1962 and *Heimdal* 7 Mar 1962.

Name	No.	Builders	Commissioned
O/S ANDENES	—	Netherlands	1957
O/S NORDKAPP	—	Netherlands	1957
O/S SENJA	—	Netherlands	1957

Measurement, tons: 500 gross
Dimensions, feet (metres): 186 × 31 × 16 *(56·7 × 9·5 × 4·9)*
Gun: 1—3 in *(76 mm)*
Main engines: MAN diesel; 2 300 bhp = 16 knots
Complement: 29

All three built in 1957 as whalers of varying appearance. Acquired by Norway in 1965 and converted into Fishery Protection Ships.

NORDKAPP   *1974, Royal Norwegian Navy, Foto FRO*

7 NEW CONSTRUCTION PATROL VESSELS

Displacement, tons: 1940
Dimensions, feet (metres): 231·2 pp × 37·7 × 16 *(70·5 pp × 11·5 × 4·9)*
Aircraft: 1 helicopter
Guns: 1—76 mm; 2—20 (single)
Main engines: Diesels = 23 knots

Put to tender Nov 1976. Strengthened for ice, some A/S capacity, mention of (possibly) Penguin missiles. To be fitted for fire-fighting, anti-pollution work, diving (recompression chamber) with two motor cutters and a Gemini-type dinghy.

1 NEW CONSTRUCTION SUPPORT SHIP

A new class designed to operate deep-diving vehicles capable of operations at 1 600 feet *(500 metres).*

OMAN, SULTANATE OF

Senior Officers

Commander Sultan of Oman's Navy:
Commodore H. Mucklow
Deputy Commander:
Commander D. M. Connell

Personnel

(a) 1977: 450 officers and men
(b) Voluntary service

Mercantile Marine

5 vessels of 3 149 tons gross

Bases

Qa'Adat Sultan Bin Ahmed Al Bahryya, Muscat (Main base and slipway). Raysut (advanced naval base).

Prefix to Ships' Names

SNV (Sultanate Naval Vessel)

CORVETTES

Name	No.	Builders	Commissioned
AL SAID	—	Brooke Marine, Lowestoft	1971

Displacement, tons: 900
Dimensions, feet (metres): 203·4 × 35·1 × 9·8 *(62 × 10·7 × 3)*
Gun: 1—40 mm
Main engines: 2 Paxman Ventura 12 cyl diesels; 2 shafts; 2 470 bhp
Complement: 32 + 7 staff + 32 troops

Built by Brooke Marine, Lowestoft. Launched 7 Apr 1970 as a yacht for the Sultan of Muscat and Oman, she was converted for a dual purpose role with a gun on her forecastle as flagship of the Sultanate Navy. Carried on board is one Fairey Marine Spear patrol craft. Helicopter deck added in last refit.

Radar: Decca TM 626.

AL SAID — *1971, Brooke Marine*

2 Ex-NETHERLANDS "WILDERVANK" CLASS

Name	No.	Builders	Commissioned
AL NASIRI (ex-*Aalsmeer, M 811*)	P 1	Netherlands	1955
AL SALIHI (ex-*Axel, M 808*)	P 2	Netherlands	1955

Displacement, tons: 373 standard; 417 full load
Dimensions, feet (metres): 149·8 oa × 28 × 6·5 *(46·6 × 8·8 × 2)*
Guns: 3—40 mm
Main engines: 2 Werkspoor diesels; 2 500 bhp
Speed, knots: 16
Range, miles: 2 500 at 10 knots
Complement: 38

Acquired in March 1974 and converted for patrol duties at van der Giessen/de Noord in 1974-75.

Radar: Decca TM 916.

AL SALIHI — *1976, Omani Dept. of Defence*

LIGHT FORCES

7 BROOKE MARINE 37·5 metre TYPE (LARGE PATROL CRAFT)

Name	No.	Builders	Commissioned	
AL BUSHRA	B 1	Brooke Marine, Lowestoft	22 Jan	1973
AL MANSUR	B 2	Brooke Marine, Lowestoft	26 Mar	1973
AL NEJAH	B 3	Brooke Marine, Lowestoft	13 May	1973
AL WAFI	B 4	Brooke Marine, Lowestoft	Mar	1977
AL FULK	B 5	Brooke Marine, Lowestoft	May	1977
AL AUL	B 6	Brooke Marine, Lowestoft	Aug	1977
—	B 7	Brooke Marine, Lowestoft	Aug	1977

Displacement, tons: 135 standard; 153 full load
Dimensions, feet (metres): 123 oa × 22·5 × 5·5 *(37·5 × 6·9 × 1·7)*
Missiles: 2—MM 38 Exocet (see note)
Guns: 2—40 mm (B 1-3); 1—76 mm/62 OTO Melara Compact; 1—20 mm (B 4-7)
Main engines: 2 Paxman Ventura diesels; 4 800 bhp = 29 knots
Range, miles: 3 300 at 15 knots
Complement: 25

First three ordered 5 Jan 1971.
4 more (B 4-7) ordered from Brooke Marine 26 Apr 1974, 2 for delivery Sept 1976 and 2 more in early 1977.

Gunnery: Lawrence-Scott optical director in B 4-7.

Radar: Decca TM 916.

Refits: B 1-3 to be refitted Nov 1977 with addition of twin Exocet.

AL WAFI — *1976, Omani Dept. of Defence*

4 VOSPER THORNYCROFT 75 ft TYPE

HARAS 1-4

Dimensions, feet (metres): 75 × 19·5 × 5 *(22·9 × 6 × 1·5)*
Guns: 2—20 mm
Main engines: 2 Caterpillar diesels
Range, miles: 600 at 20 knots; 1 000 at 11 knots
Complement: 11

Completed 1976-77.

HARAS 4

9/1976, Dr. Giorgio Arra

3 27 ft CHEVERTON TYPE (COASTAL PATROL CRAFT)

W 1   W 2   W 3
Displacement, tons: 3·5
Dimensions, feet (metres): 27 × 9 × 2·8 *(8·2 × 2·7 × 0·8)*
Main engines: Twin diesels = 25 knots

Purchased Apr 1975.

AMPHIBIOUS FORCES

2 60 ft CHEVERTON "LOADMASTERS"

Name	No.	Builders	Commissioned
AL SANSOOR	—	Cheverton's, Cowes	Jan 1975
KINZEER AL BAHR	—	Cheverton's, Cowes	Jan 1975

Measurement, tons: 60 deadweight
Dimensions, feet (metres): 60 oa × 20 × 3·5 *(18·3 × 6·1 × 1·1)*
Main engines: 2 × 120 hp = 8·5 knots

Delivered Jan 1975.

AL SANSOOR

1975, Roger Smith

1 45 ft CHEVERTON "LOADMASTER"

Name	No.	Builders	Commissioned
SULHAFA AL BAHR	—	Cheverton's, Cowes	1975

Measurement, tons: 45
Dimensions, feet (metres): 45 × 15 × 3 *(13·7 × 4·6 × 0·9)*
Main engines: Twin Perkins 4 236 = 8·5 knots

1 LCL

Ordered from Brooke Marine, Lowestoft for delivery mid-1979.

AUXILIARIES

Name	No.	Builders	Commissioned
AL SULTANA	—	Conoship, Gröningen	4 June 1975

Measurement, tons: 1 380 dw
Dimensions, feet (metres): 214·3 oa × 35 × 13·5 *(65·4 × 10·7 × 4·2)*
Main engines: Mirrlees Blackstone diesel; 1 150 bhp = 11 knots
Complement: 12

Launched

AL SULTANA

1975, Dick van der Heijde Jnr.

1 TRAINING SHIP

DHOFAR

Displacement, tons: 1 500 full load
Dimensions, feet (metres): 219 oa × 34 × 13 *(66·8 × 10·4 × 4)*
Main engines: MAK diesel; 1 500 bhp = 10·5 knots
Complement: 22

Ex-Logistic ship now used for new entry training.

DHOFAR

1974, Omani Dept. of Defence

1 CHEVERTON LAUNCH

Of 9 tons, 39 ft and 10 knots—completed April 1975.

PAKISTAN

Ministerial

Minister of Defence:
Zulfiqar Ali Bhutto

Headquarters Appointments

Chief of the Naval Staff:
Admiral M. Shariff HJ
Vice Chief of the Naval Staff:
Rear-Admiral Leslie Norman Mungavin SK

Command Appointment

Commander Pakistan Fleet:
Rear-Admiral K. R. Niazi SJ

Diplomatic Representation

Naval Attaché in London:
Captain T. K. Khan
Naval Attaché in Paris:
Captain Y. H. Malik
Naval Attaché in Teheran:
Captain A. H. Khan
Naval Attaché in Washington:
Captain M. Saeed

Personnel

(a) 1977: 11 000 (950 officers; 10 050 ratings)
(b) Voluntary Service

Naval Bases and Dockyard

Karachi, Kaptai

Naval Air Arm

3 Breguet Atlantic BR 1150
6 Sea King helicopters
4 Alouette III helicopters
2 UH 19 Chickasaw helicopters
2 Cessna

Prefix to Ships' Names

PNS

Mercantile Marine

Lloyd's Register of Shipping:
83 vessels of 483 433 tons gross

Strength of the Fleet

(No building programme announced)

Type	Active	Planned
Cruiser	1	—
Destroyers	4	2
Frigates	2	—
Submarines—Patrol	4	
Submarines—40 tons	6	
Fast Attack Craft—Gun	14	
Fast Attack Craft—Torpedo	6	
Large Patrol Craft	3	
Minesweepers—Coastal	7	
Survey Ship	1	
Tankers	2	
Tugs—Ocean	2	
Tugs—Harbour	2	
Water-boat	1	
Floating Docks	2	

DELETIONS

Destroyer

1971 *Khaibar* (sunk in Indo-Pakistan War Dec 1971)

Submarine

1971 *Ghezi* (ex-US "Tench" class) (sunk in Indo-Pakistan War 4 Dec 1971)

Large Patrol Craft

1971 *Comilla, Jessore* and *Sylhet* (sunk in Indo-Pakistan War Dec 1971)

Minewarfare Forces

1971 *Muhafiz* (ex-US *MSC*) (sunk in Indo-Pakistan War Dec 1971)

PENNANT LIST

C (Cruiser)

84	Babur

D (Destroyers)

160	Alamgir
161	Badr
162	Jahangir
164	Shah Jahan

F (Frigates)

260	Tippu Sultan
261	Tughril

S (Submarines)

131	Hangor
132	Shushuk
133	Mangro
134	Ghazi

M (Minesweepers)

160	Mahmood
161	Momin
162	Murabak
164	Mujahid
165	Mukhtar
166	Munsif
167	Moshal

P (Light Forces)

01-06	"Hu Chwan" Class
140	Rajshahi
141	Lahore
142	Multan
143	Gilgit
144	Sehwan
145	Pishin
146	Kalat
147	Sukkur
148	Quetta
149	Sahiwal
150	Bannu
151	Larkana
152	Bahawalpur
153	Baluchistan
154	—
301-2	"Hai Nan" Class

A (Service Forces)

41	Dacca
42	Madadgar
262	Zulfiquar
298	Attock

YW

15	Zum Zum

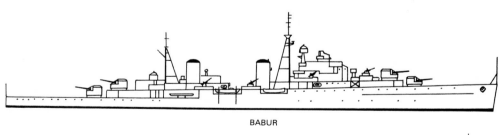

BABUR

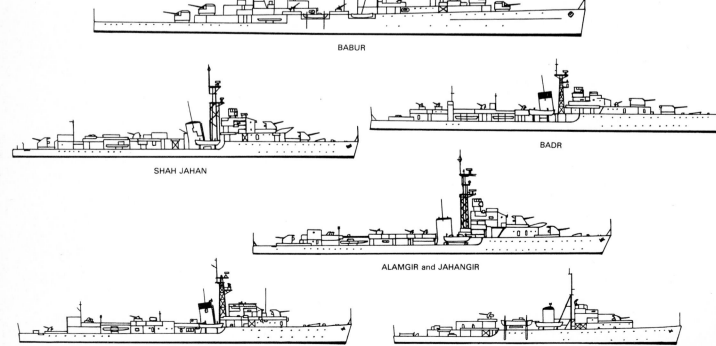

SHAH JAHAN

BADR

ALAMGIR and JAHANGIR

TIPPU SULTAN and TUGHRIL

ZULFIQUAR

CRUISER (Cadet Training Ship)

1 Ex-BRITISH "MODIFIED DIDO" CLASS

Name	No.	Builders	Laid down	Launched	Commissioned
BABUR (ex-HMS *Diadem*)	84	R. & W. Hawthorn Leslie & Co. Ltd., Hebburn-on-Tyne	15 Nov 1939	26 Aug 1942	6 Jan 1944

Displacement, tons: 5 900 standard; 7 560 full load
Length, feet (metres): 485 *(147·9)* pp; 512 *(156·1)* oa
Beam, feet (metres): 52·0 *(15·8)*
Draught, feet (metres): 18·5 *(5·6)*
Guns: 8—5.25 in *(133 mm)* (4 twin); 14—40 mm
Torpedo tubes: 6—21 in *(533 mm)* (2 triple)
Armour: 3 in *(76 mm)* sides; 2 in *(51 mm)* decks and turrets
Main engines: Parsons s.r. geared turbines; 4 shafts;
  62 000 shp
Boilers: 4 Admiralty 3-drum
Speed, knots: 20
Oil fuel, tons: 1 100
Range, miles: 4 000 at 18 knots
Complement: 588

Purchased on 29 Feb 1956. Refitted at HM Dockyard, Portsmouth and there transferred to Pakistan and renamed *Babur* on 5 July, 1957. Adapted as Cadet Training Ship in 1961.

Radar: Search: Type 960, Type 293.
Fire Control: Type 284/285.

BABUR   *1976, Pakistan Navy*

DESTROYERS

2 Ex-US "GEARING" CLASS (FRAM 1)

Name	No.	Builders	Laid down	Launched	Commissioned
– (ex-USS *Wiltsie*, DD 716)	—	Federal SB & DD Co.	1945	31 Aug 1945	12 Jan 1946
– (ex-USS *Epperson*, DD 719)	—	Todd Pacific Shipyards	1944	29 Dec 1944	31 Mar 1945

Displacement, tons: 2 425 standard; 3 500 full load
Length, feet (metres): 390·5 *(119)* oa
Beam, feet (metres): 40·9 *(12·4)*
Draught, feet (metres): 19 *(5·8)*
Guns: 4—5 in *(127 mm)* 38 cal (twin)
A/S weapons: 6 (2 Triple) Mk 32 A/S torpedo tubes; facilities for
  small helicopter
Main engines: 2 geared turbines; 60 000 shp; 2 shafts
Boilers: 4 Babcock and Wilcox
Speed, knots: 30
Complement: 274

Transfer by purchase 1977.

Radar: SPS 10 and 40.
Sonar: SQS 23.

"GEARING" Class (FRAM 1)   *1970, USN*

1 Ex-BRITISH "BATTLE" CLASS

Name	No.	Builders	Laid down	Launched	Commissioned
BADR (ex-HMS *Gabbard*, D 47)	161	Swan, Hunter & Wigham Richardson Ltd, Wallsend-on-Tyne	2 Feb 1944	16 Mar 1945	10 Dec 1946

Displacement, tons: 2 325 standard; 3 361 full load
Length, feet (metres): 355·0 *(108·2)* pp; 379·0 *(115·5)* oa
Beam, feet (metres): 40·2 *(12·3)*
Draught, feet (metres): 17·0 *(5·2)*
Guns: 4—4·5 in *(115 mm)* ; 7—40 mm (2 twin; 3 single)
A/S weapons: Squid triple DC mortar
Torpedo tubes: 8—21 in *(533 mm)* (quadrupled)
Main engines: Parsons geared turbines; 2 shafts; 50 000 shp
Boilers: 2 Admiralty 3-drum type
Speed, knots: 35·75
Oil fuel, tons: 680
Range, miles: 6 000 at 20 knots
Complement: 270

BADR   *1972, Pakistan Navy*

Purchased from Britain on 29 Feb 1956. Modernised with US funds under MDAP. Refitted at Palmers Hebburn, Yarrow, transferred to Pakistan on 24 Jan 1957 and sailed from Portsmouth for Karachi on 17 Feb 1957.

Loss: Sister ship *Khaibar* (ex-HMS *Cadiz*) was sunk during the Indo-Pakistan War in Dec 1971.

Radar: Search: Type 293. One Marconi set.
Fire Control: Type 275.

1 Ex-BRITISH "CH" CLASS

Name	No.	Builders	Laid down	Launched	Commissioned
SHAH JAHAN (ex-HMS *Charity*, D 29)	164	John I. Thornycroft Co Ltd, Woolston	9 July 1943	30 Nov 1944	19 Nov 1945

Displacement, tons: 1 710 standard; 2 545 full load
Length, feet (metres): 350·0 *(106·7)* wl; 362·7 *(110·5)* oa
Beam, feet (metres): 35·7 *(10·9)*
Draught, feet (metres): 17·0 *(5·2)*
Guns: 3—4·5 in *(115 mm)*; 6—40 mm
A/S weapons: 2 Squid triple DC mortars
Torpedo tubes: 4—21 in *(533 mm)* (quadrupled)
Main engines: Parsons geared turbines; 2 shafts; 40 000 shp
Boilers: 2 Admiralty 3-drum type
Speed, knots: 36·75
Range, miles: 5 600 at 20 knots
Complement: 200

Purchased by USA and handed over to Pakistan on 16 Dec 1958, under MDAP, at yard of J. Samuel White & Co Ltd, Cowes, who refitted her. Sister ship *Taimur* (ex-HMS *Chivalrous*) was returned to the Royal Navy and scrapped in 1960-61.

Radar: Search: Type 293.
Fire Control: Type 275.

SHAH JAHAN   *1972, Pakistan Navy*

2 Ex-BRITISH "CR" CLASS

Name	No.	Builders	Laid down	Launched	Commissioned
ALAMGIR (ex-HMS Creole, D 82)	160	J. Samuel White & Co Ltd, Cowes	3 Aug 1944	22 Nov 1945	14 Oct 1946
JAHANGIR (ex-HMS Crispin, ex-Craccher, D 168)	162	J. Samuel White & Co Ltd, Cowes	1 Feb 1944	23 June 1945	10 July 1946

Displacement, tons: 1 730 standard; 2 560 full load
Length, feet (metres): 350·0 (106·7) wl; 362·8 (110·5) oa
Beam, feet (metres): 35·7 (10·9)
Draught, feet (metres): 17·0 (5·2)
Guns: 3—4·5 in (115 mm); 6—40 mm
A/S weapons: 2 Squid triple DC mortars
Torpedo tubes: 4—21 in (533 mm) (quadrupled)
Main engines: Parsons geared turbines; 2 shafts 40 000 shp
Boilers: 2 Admiralty 3-drum type
Speed, knots: 36·75
Oil fuel, tons: 580
Range, miles: 5 600 at 20 knots
Complement: 200

Purchased by Pakistan in Feb 1956. Refitted and modernised in Great Britain by John I. Thornycroft & Co Ltd, Woolston, Southampton, in 1957-58 with US funds under MDAP. Turned over to the Pakistan Navy at Southampton in 1958 (Crispin on 18 Mar and Creole 20 June) and renamed.

Radar: Search: Type 293.
Fire Control: Type 275.

Sonar: Types 170, 174.

ALAMGIR   1973, Pakistan Navy

FRIGATES

2 Ex-BRITISH TYPE 16

Name	No.	Builders	Laid down	Launched	Commissioned
TIPPU SULTAN (ex-HMS Onslow, ex-Pakenham, F 249)	260	John Brown & Co Ltd, Clydebank	1 July 1940	31 Mar 1941	8 Oct 1941
TUGHRIL (ex-HMS Onslaught, ex-Pathfinder, F 204)	261	Fairfield SB & Eng Co Ltd, Glasgow	14 Jan 1941	9 Oct 1941	19 June 1942

Displacement, tons: 1 800 standard; 2 300 full load
Length, feet (metres): 328·7 (100·2) pp; 345·0 (107·2) oa
Beam, feet (metres): 35·0 (10·7)
Draught, feet (metres): 15·7 (4·8)
Guns: 2—4 in (102 mm); 5—40 mm
A/S weapons: 2 Squid triple DC mortars
Torpedo tubes: 4—21 in (533 mm)
Main engines: Parsons geared turbines; 2 shafts; 40 000 shp
Boilers: 2 Admiralty 3-drum type
Speed, knots: 34
Complement: 170

Originally three "O" class destroyers were acquired from Great Britain, Tippu Sultan being handed over on 30 Sep 1949; Tariq on 3 Nov 1949; and Tughril on 6 Mar 1951. An agreement was signed in London between Great Britain and USA for refit and conversion in the United Kingdom of Tippu Sultan and Tughril (announced 29 April 1957) with US funds. All three ships were scheduled for conversion into fast anti-submarine frigates. Tippu Sultan and Tughril were converted at Liverpool by Grayson Rolls & Clover Docks Ltd, Birkenhead, and C. & H. Crighton Ltd, respectively. Tariq disposed of 1959. Tughril employed on training duties.

TUGHRIL   1972, Pakistan Navy

Radar: Type 293 search radar.

SUBMARINES

4 FRENCH "DAPHNE" CLASS

Name	No.
HANGOR	S 131
MANGRO	S 133
SHUSHUK	S 132
GHAZI (ex-Cachalote)	S 134

Builders	Laid down	Launched	Commissioned
Arsenal de Brest	1 Dec 1967	28 June 1969	12 Jan 1970
C. N. Ciotat (Le Trait)	8 July 1968	7 Feb 1970	8 Aug 1970
C. N. Ciotat (Le Trait)	1 Dec 1967	30 July 1969	12 Jan 1970
Dubigeon, Normandie	12 May 1967	23 Sept 1968	1 Oct 1969

Displacement, tons: 700 standard; 869 surfaced; 1 043 dived
Length, feet (metres): 189·6 (57·8)
Beam, feet (metres): 22·3 (6·8)
Draught, feet (metres): 15·1 (4·6)
Torpedo tubes: 12—21 in (550 mm) 8 bow, 4 stern (external)
Main machinery: Diesel electric; 1 300 bhp (surfaced); electric motors 1 600 hp (dived); 2 shafts
Speed, knots: 13 surfaced; 15·5 dived
Complement: 45

Thes first three are the first submarines built for the Pakistan Navy. They are basically of the French "Daphne" class design, but slightly modified internally to suit Pakistan requirements and naval conditions. They are broadly similar to the submarines built in France for Portugal and South Africa and the submarines being constructed to the "Daphne" design in Spain.

Transfer: The Portuguese "Daphne" class Cachalote was bought by Pakistan in Dec 1975.

SHUSHUK   1971, Contre Amiral M. J. Adam

MANGRO   1972

6 "SX 404" CLASS

Displacement, tons: 40
Dimensions, feet (metres): 52·4 × 6·6 × — (16 × 2 × —)
Speed, knots: 11 surfaced; 6·5 dived
Range, miles: 1 200 surfaced; 60 dived
Complement: 4

Purchased 1972-73 from Cosmos, Livorno. With a diving depth of 330 ft (100 metres) and capable of carrying 12 passengers these submarines are valuable craft for clandestine raids, reconnaissance and a multitude of shallow-water tasks.

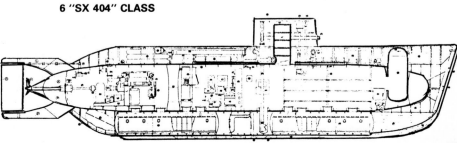

Drawing of "SX 404" Class   1973

LIGHT FORCES

2 Ex-CHINESE "HAI NAN" CLASS
(LARGE PATROL CRAFT)

301, 302

Displacement, tons: 360 standard; 400 full load
Dimensions, feet (metres): 197 × 24 × 6·1 *(60 × 7·4 × 2·1)*
Guns: 2—3 in; 4—25 mm (twins)
A/S weapons: 4—MBU 1 800; 2 DCT; 2 DC Racks
Mines: Rails fitted
Main engines: Diesels; 8 000 shp
Speed, knots: 28
Range, miles: 1 000 at 10 knots
Complement: 60

Transferred mid 1976.

Radar: Pothead

PAKISTAN "HAI NAN" Class   *1976*

14 Ex-CHINESE "SHANGHAI II" CLASS
(FAST ATTACK CRAFT—GUN)

BAHAWALPUR P 152	**LARKANA** P 151	**QUETTA** P 148
BALUCHISTAN P 153	**LAHORE** P 141	**SAHIWAL** P 149
BANNU P 150	**MULTAN** P 142	**SEHWAN** P 144
GILGIT P 143	**PISHIN** P 145	**SUKKUR** P 147
KALAT P 146		**+ 1** (P 154)

Displacement, tons: 120 standard; 155 full load
Dimensions, feet (metres): 128 × 18 × 5·6 *(39·1 × 5·5 × 1·7)*
Guns: 4—37 mm (twin); 4—25 mm (twin)
Mines: Fitted with minerails but for approx 10 mines
Main engines: 4 diesels; 3 000 bhp = 27 knots
Complement: 25

Transferred early 1972 (first eight) next four in 1974 and last pair in 1976.

Radar: Pothead.

PAKISTAN "SHANGHAI" Class   *1973, Pakistan Navy*

6 Ex-CHINESE "HU CHWAN" CLASS
(FAST ATTACK HYDROFOIL—TORPEDO)

HDF 01, 02, 03, 04, 05, 06

Displacement, tons: 45
Dimensions, feet (metres): 70 × 16·5 × 3·1 *(21·4 × 5·0 × 0·9)*
Torpedo tubes: 2—21 inch *(533 mm)*
Guns: 4—14·5 mm (twins)
Main engines: 2—12 cyl diesels; 2 shafts; 2 200 hp = 55 knots (calm)

Hydrofoil craft transferred by China in 1973.

PAKISTAN "HU CHWAN" Class   *1973, Pakistan Navy*

1 "TOWN" CLASS (LARGE PATROL CRAFT)

Name	No.	Builders	Commissioned
RAJSHAHI	P 140	Brooke Marine	1965

Displacement, tons: 115 standard; 143 full load
Dimensions, feet (metres): 107 oa × 20 × 11 *(32·6 × 6·1 × 3·4)*
Guns: 2—40 mm; 70 cal Bofors
Main engines: 2 MTU 12V 538 diesels; 3 400 bhp = 24 knots
Complement: 19

The last survivor of a class of four built by Brooke Marine in 1965 (see "Deletions"). Steel hull and aluminium superstructure.

RAJSHAHI   *1973, Pakistan Navy*

MINE WARFARE FORCES

Note: It is reported that two ex-US "Aggressive" class MSOs were transferred to Pakistan in 1976.

7 US MSC TYPE (MINESWEEPERS—COASTAL)

MAHMOOD (ex-*MSC 267*) M 160
MOMIN (ex-*MSC 293*) M 161
MOSHAL (ex-*MSC 294*) M 167
MURABAK (ex-*MSC 262*) M 162

MUJAHID (ex-*MSC 261*) M 164
MUKHTAR (ex-*MSC 274*) M 165
MUNSIF (ex-*MSC 273*) M 166

Displacement, tons: 335 light; 375 full load
Dimensions, feet (metres): 144 oa × 27 × 8·5 *(43·9 × 8·2 × 2·6)*
Guns: 2—20 mm
Main engines: GM diesels; 2 shafts; 880 bhp = 14 knots
Complement: 39

Transferred to Pakistan by the US under MAP. *Mukhtar* and *Munsif* on 25 June 1959, *Mujahid* in Nov 1956, *Mahmood* in May 1957, *Murabak* in 1957, *Momin* in Aug 1962 and *Moshal* on 13 July 1963.

MUNSIF   *1972, Pakistan Navy*

SURVEY SHIP

Name	No.	Builders	Commissioned
ZULFIQUAR (ex-*Dhanush*, ex-*Deveron F 265*)	262	Smith's Dock Co Ltd, South Bank-on-Tees	2 Mar 1943

Displacement, tons: 1 370 standard; 2 100 full load
Dimensions, feet (metres): 301·5 oa × 36·7 × 12·5 *(91·9 × 11·2 × 3·8)*
Guns: 1—4 in *(102 mm)*; 2—40 mm
Main engines: Triple expansion; 5 500 ihp
Boilers: 2 Admiralty 3-drum type
Speed, knots: 20
Range, miles: 6 000 at 12 knots
Complement: 150

Former British frigate of the "River" class converted into a survey ship, additional charthouse aft. She has strengthened davits and carries survey motor boats. The after 4-inch gun was removed.

TANKERS

1 Ex-US "MISSION" CLASS

DACCA (ex-USNS *Mission Santa Cruz, AO 132*) A 41

Displacement, tons: 5 730 light; 22 380 full load
Dimensions, feet (metres): 523·5 oa × 68 × 30·9 *(159·7 × 20·7 × 9·4)*
Guns: 3—40 mm
Main engines: Turbo-electric; 6 000 shp = 15 knots
Boilers: 2 Babcock & Wilcox
Oil capacity: 20 000 tons
Complement: 160 (15 officers and 145 men)

Transferred on loan to Pakistan under MDAP. Handed over from the US on 17 Jan 1963. Purchased 31 May 1974.

DACCA

1 Ex-US YO TYPE

Name	No.	Builders	Commissioned
ATTOCK (ex-USS *YO 249*)	A 298	Trieste	1960

Displacement, tons: 600 standard; 1 255 full load
Dimensions, feet (metres): 177·2 oa × 32 × 15 *(54 × 9·8 × 4·6)*
Main engines: Direct coupled diesel; speed 8·5 knots
Complement: 26

A harbour oiler of 6 500 barrels capacity built for the Pakistan Navy, under the Mutual Defence Assistance Programme of USA.

RESCUE SHIP

1 Ex-US "CHEROKEE" CLASS

Name	No.	Builders	Commissioned
MADADGAR (ex-USS *Yuma*, *ATF 94*)	A 42	Commercial Iron Works Portland, Oregon	31 Aug 1943

Displacement, tons: 1 235 standard; 1 675 full load
Dimensions, feet (metres): 205 oa × 38·5 × 15·3 *(62·5 × 11·7 × 4·7)*
Main engines: 4 GM diesels; electric drive; 1 shaft; 3 000 bhp = 16·5 knots
Complement: 85

Ocean-going salvage tug. Laid down on 13 Feb 1943. Launched on 17 July 1943. Transferred from the US Navy to the Pakistan Navy on 25 Mar 1959 under MDAP. Fitted with powerful pumps and other salvage equipment.

MADADGAR   *1976*

TUGS

RUSTOM

Dimensions, feet (metres): 105 × 30 × 11 *(32 × 9·1 × 3·3)*
Main engines: Crossley diesel; 1 000 bhp = 9·5 knots
Range, miles: 3 000 at economic speed
Complement: 21

General purpose tug for the Pakistan Navy originally ordered from Werf-Zeeland at Hansweert, Netherlands, in August 1952, but after the liquidation of this yard the order was transferred to Worst & Dutmer at Meppel. Launched on 29 Nov 1955.

Name	No.	Builders	Commissioned
BHOLU (ex-US *YTL 755*)	—	Costaguta-Voltz	Sept 1958
GAMA (ex-US *YTL 754*)	—	Costaguta-Voltz	Sept 1958

Small harbour tugs built under an "off-shore" order.

MISCELLANEOUS

1 WATER CARRIER

ZUM ZUM YW 15

Built in Italy under MDA programme.

2 FLOATING DOCKS

PESHAWAR (ex-US *ARD 6*)

Transferred June 1961. 3 000 tons lift.

FD II

Built 1974. 1 200 tons lift.

PANAMA

Personnel

A Coastguard service split between both coasts.

(a) 1977: approx 100
(b) Voluntary

Mercantile Marine

Lloyd's Register of Shipping:
  2 680 ships of 15 631 180 tons gross

2 VOSPER TYPE (LARGE PATROL CRAFT)

Name	No.	Builders	Commissioned
PANQUIACO	GC 10	Vospers, Porchester, Portsmouth	Mar 1971
LIGIA ELENA	GC 11	Vospers, Porchester, Portsmouth	Mar 1971

Displacement, tons: 96 standard; 123 full load
Dimensions, feet (metres): 90·5 wl; 103·0 oa × 18·9 × 5·8 *(30; 31·4 × 5·8 × 1·8)*
Guns: 2—20 mm
Main engines: 2 Paxman Ventura 12 cyl diesels; 2 800 bhp = 24 knots
Complement: 23

Hull of welded mild steel and upperworks of welded or buck-bolted aluminium alloy. Vosper fin stabiliser equipment. *Panquiaco* was launched on 22 July 1970 and *Ligia Elena* on 25 Aug 1970.

1 Ex-US LFR TYPE

TIBURON (ex-USS *Smokey Hill River*) GN 9

Purchased 14 Mar 1975 from commercial sources.

2 Ex-US CG UTILITY TYPE (COASTAL PATROL CRAFT)

Displacement, tons: 35
Dimensions, feet (metres): 69 × 14 × 5 *(21 × 4·3 × 1·5)*
Gun: 1 MG
Main engines: 400 hp = 13 knots
Complement: 10

Transferred to Panama by the USA at the US Naval Station, Rodman, Canal Zone, in June 1962.

Note: Five additional small craft transferred by USA, three being Coastal Patrol Craft delivered 1965-66, and two handed over in 1947.

4 Ex-US "LCM 8" CLASS

Used for patrol and logistic duties.

PAPUA—NEW GUINEA

The Australian base at Manus in the Admiralty Islands, HMAS *Tarangau* was de-commissioned on 14 Nov 1974 and handed over to the PNG Defence Force. It is now the PNGDF Patrol Boat Base Lombrun. The following ships were handed over to the PNGDF by the RAN.

Senior Officer

Brigadier E. R. Diro OBE (Commander PNGDF)

Bases

Port Moresby (HQ PNGDF); Lombrun.

LIGHT FORCES

5 "ATTACK" CLASS (LARGE PATROL CRAFT)

Name	No.	Builders	Commissioned
AITAPE	84	Walkers Ltd, Maryborough	13 Nov 1967
LADAVA	92	Walkers Ltd, Maryborough	21 Oct 1968
LAE	93	Evans Deakin & Co, Queenborough	3 April 1968
MADANG	94	Evans Deakin & Co, Queenborough	28 Nov 1968
SAMARAI	85	Evans Deakin & Co, Queenborough	1 Mar 1968

Displacement, tons: 146 full load
Dimensions, feet (metres): 107·5 × 20 × 7·3 *(32·8 × 6·1 × 2·2)*
Guns: 1—40 mm; 2 MG
Main engines: 2 Paxman 16 YJCM diesels; 2 shafts; 3 500 bhp = 24 knots
Complement: 18

Steel hulls with aluminium superstructure. Can lay mines.

LAE   *1976, PNGDF*

AMPHIBIOUS FORCES

2 LANDING CRAFT (LCH)

Name	No.	Builders	Commissioned
BUNA	132	Walkers Ltd, Marlborough	1973
SALAMAUA	131	Walkers Ltd, Marlborough	1973

Displacement, tons: 310 light; 503 full load
Dimensions, feet (metres): 146 × 33 × 6·5 *(44·5 × 10·1 × 1·9)*
Guns: 2—0·5 in MG
Main engines: 2 V12 GM diesels; twin screw = 10 knots
Complement: 13

BUNA   *1974, John Mortimer*

PARAGUAY

Ministerial

Minister of National Defence:
 Maj. Gen. Marcial Samaniego

Personnel

1977: 1 900 officers and men including coastguard and 500
 marines

Naval Air Arm (Escuadron de Caza de la Armada)

4 H-13 Sioux helicopters
2 North American T-6 (Trainers)
4 Cessna U-206
2 Cessna 150M

Mercantile Marine

Lloyd's Register of Shipping:
 26 vessels of 21 930 tons gross

Base

Asunciòn/Puerto Sajonia (main base, dockyard with one dry
dock, one floating dock and one slipway)

Strength of the Fleet

2 River Defence Vessels
3 Corvettes
1 Large Patrol Craft
8 Coastal Patrol Craft
3 Tugs
1 Tender
1 Training Ship
2 LCUs
1 Floating Dock
2 Service Craft

RIVER DEFENCE VESSELS

2 "HUMAITA" CLASS

Name	No.	Builders	Commissioned
HUMAITA (ex-*Capitan Cabral*)	C 2	Odero, Genoa	May 1931
PARAGUAY (ex-*Commodor Meza*)	C 1	Odero, Genoa	May 1931

Displacement, tons: 636 standard; 865 full load
Dimensions, feet (metres): 231 × 35 × 5·3 *(70 × 10·7 × 1·7)*
Guns: 4—4·7 in; 3—3 in; 2—40 mm
Mines: 6
Armour: ·5 in side amidships; ·3 in deck; ·8 in CT
Main engines: Parsons geared turbines; 2 shafts; 3 800 shp = 17 knots
Boilers: 2
Oil fuel, tons: 150
Range, miles: 1 700 at 16 knots
Complement: 86

PARAGUAY   *1974, A. J. English*

CORVETTES

3 "BOUCHARD" CLASS

Name	No	Builders	Commissioned
CAPITAN MEZA (ex-*Parker*)	M 11	Sanchez Shipyard, San Fernando	1938
TENIENTE FARINA (ex-*Py*)	—	Rio Santiago Naval Yard	1937
NANAWA (ex-*Bouchard*)	—	Hansen & Puccini, San Fernando	1939

Displacement, tons: 450 standard; 620 normal; 650 full load
Dimensions, feet (metres): 197 oa × 24 × 8·5 *(60 × 7·3 × 2·6)*
Guns: 4—40 mm Bofors; 2 MG
Main engines: 2 sets MAN 2-cycle diesels; 2 000 bhp = 16 knots
Oil fuel, tons: 50
Range, miles: 6 000 at 12 knots
Complement: 70

Former Argentinian minesweepers of the "Bouchard" class.
Launched on 2 May 1937, 20 Mar 1936 and 18 Aug 1938. Can carry mines.
Transferred from the Argentinian Navy to the Paraguayan Navy; *Capitan Meza*, 1967; *Teniente Farina*, 1964; *Nanawa*, 1967.

Deletion: *Hernandez* (ex-*Seaver*) was transferred in 1964 but is believed to have been deleted.

NANAWA   *11/1975, A. J. English*

LIGHT FORCES

1 LARGE PATROL CRAFT

Name	No.	Builders	Commissioned
CAPITAN CABRAL (ex-*Adolfo Riquelme*)	A 1	Werf-Conrad, Haarlem	1908

Displacement, tons: 180 standard; 206 full load
Dimensions, feet (metres): 107·2 oa × 23·5 × 9·8 *(32·7 × 7·2 × 3)*
Guns: 1—3 in Vickers; 2—37 mm Vickers; 4 MG
Main engines: Triple expansion; 1 shaft; 300 ihp = 9 knots
Complement: 47

Former tug. Launched in 1907. Of wooden construction.

2 CG TYPE (COASTAL PATROL CRAFT)

P1 (ex-USCGC 20417) **P2** (ex-USCGC 20418)

Displacement, tons: 16
Dimensions, feet (metres): 45·5 oa × 13·5 × 3·5 *(13·9 × 4·1 × 1·1)*
Guns: 2—20 mm
Main engines: 2 petrol motors; 2 shafts; 190 hp = 20 knots
Complement: 10

Of wooden construction. Built in the United States in 1944. Acquired from the United States Coast Guard in 1944. Existence now doubtful.

6 "701" CLASS (COASTAL PATROL CRAFT)

P 101   **102**   **103**   **104**   **105**   **106**

Patrol craft of 40 ft and 10 tons with 2—20 mm guns transferred by USA—2 in Dec 1967, 3 in Sep 1970 and 1 in Mar 1971.

"701" Class   *11/1975, A. J. English*

TENDER

TENIENTE PRAATS GIL (ex-Argentine *Corrientes*, ex-US *LSM 86*) PH 1

Displacement, tons: 1 095
Guns: 4—40 mm
Speed, knots: 13

Transferred as a gift from Argentina 13 Jan 1972. Light Forces Tender with helicopter deck added aft. Officially classified as "helicopter-carrier" but whether she can carry one or two helicopters is not known—two might be a crowd.

TENIENTE PRAATS GIL   *11/1975, A. J. English*

TUGS

3 Ex-US YTL-YLT TYPE

Name	No.	Builders	Commissioned
— (ex-US *YTL 211*)	A 4	Everett Pacific SB & DD Co, Wash	—
— (ex-US *YTL 567*)	A 5	Everett Pacific SB & DD Co, Wash	—
— (ex-US *YLT 559*)	—	—	—

Dimensions, feet (metres): 66·2 × 17 × 5 *(20·2 × 5·2 × 1·5)*
Main engines: Diesel; 300 bhp

Small harbour tugs transferred to Paraguay by the USA under the Military Aid Programme in May 1963 (YTL 559) and Mar 1967 (YTL 211). YTL 567 loaned April 1974.

MISCELLANEOUS

1 TRANSPORT/TRAINING SHIP

Name	No.	Builders	Commissioned
GUARANI	—	Tomas Ruiz de Valasco, Bilbao	Feb 1968

Measurement, tons: 714 gross; 1 030 dw
Dimensions, feet (metres): 215 × 36 × 12 *(65·6 × 11·9 × 3·7)*
Main engines: Diesel; 1 300 hp = 13 knots

Repaired and refitted 1974 by Ast Olaveaja, Spain.

1 FLOATING DOCK

— (Ex-US *AFDL 26*)

Transferred March 1965, Lift 1 000 tons.

1 DREDGER

TENIENTE O CARRERAS SAGUIER

— (ex-US *YFB 82*)   — (ex-US *YFB 86*)

1 FLOATING WORKSHOP

— (Ex-US *YR 37*)

Transferred March 1965.

1 RIVER TRANSPORT

PTE. STROESNER T 1

2 Ex-US LCUs

Leased by US in June 1970. Used as ferries.

PERU

Headquarters Appointments

Minister of Marine and Chief of Naval Operations:
Vice-Admiral Jorge Parodi Galliani
Chief of Naval Staff:
Vice-Admiral Guillermo Villa Pazos

Command

Commander-in-Chief of the Fleet:
Rear-Admiral Juan Egúsquiza Babilonia

Diplomatic Representation

Naval Attaché in London and Paris:
Rear-Admiral Daniel Masias
Naval Attaché in Washington:
Vice-Admiral Rafael Durán Rey

Personnel

(a) 1977: 14 000 (1 200 officers, 12 800 men) (including Naval Air Arm and 1 000 marines)
(b) 2 years National Service

Bases

Callao—Main naval base; dockyard with ship-building capacity, 1 dry dock, 2 floating docks, 1 floating crane; naval academy; training schools.
Iquitos—River base for Amazon flotilla; small building yard, repair facilities, floating dock.
La Punta, San Lorenzo, Talara

Naval Air Arm

8 Bell AB 212 (on order for "Lupos")
2 Fokker 27 FPA MP aircraft (on order for mid/1977)
2 Alouette III helicopters
10 Bell 206 Jetrangers
2 Bell 47G
20 Bell UH-1D/H
9 Grumman S-2 (ASW)
6 Douglas C-47 (Transport)
1 Piper Aztec C (Liaison)
2 Beech T-34 Mentor (Training)
Following operated in maritime role by Peruvian Air Force.
4 Grumman HU-16B Albatros (ASW/SAR)

Marines

There is one battalion of 1 000 men, additionally armed with vehicle-mounted missiles.

Coast Guard

A separate service set up in 1975 with a number of light forces transferred from the navy.

Prefix to Ships' Names

BAP (Baque Armada Peruana)

Mercantile Marine

Lloyd's Register of Shipping:
681 vessels of 525 137 tons gross

Strength of the Fleet

Type	Active	Building (Planned)
Cruisers	3	1
Destroyers	4	—
Frigates	2	4 (2)
Submarines—Patrol	8	2
River Patrol Craft	3	—
Coastal Patrol Craft	4	—
Lake Patrol Craft	4	—
River Gunboats	5	—
Landing Ships	4	—
Transports	2	—
Tankers	7	1
Survey Vessels	4	1
Floating Docks	3	—
Tugs	5	—
Water Boat	1	—
Floating Workshop	1	—
Hospital Craft	2	2

Coast Guard

	Active	Building
Corvettes	2	—
Large Patrol Craft	14	—

DELETIONS

Frigate

1974 *Aguirre* (target for Exocet tests)

Minewarfare Forces

1974 *Bondy, San Martin* (ex-*YMS*)

Transports

Sept 1972 *Callao*
1973 *Rimac* (transferred to mercantile use on bare bones charter)

Amphibious Forces

1975 3 LCUs, 10 LCAs

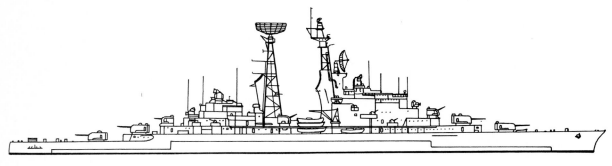

ALMIRANTE GRAU

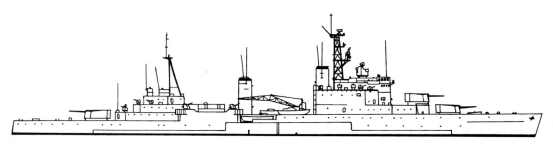

CORONEL BOLOGNESI *(Capitan Quiñones differs)*

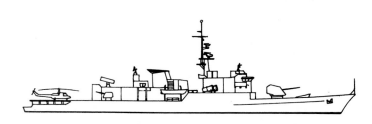

"LUPO" Class

CRUISERS

2 Ex-NETHERLANDS "DE RUYTER" CLASS

Name	No.
ALMIRANTE GRAU (ex-HNLMS *De Ruyter*)	81
— (ex-HNLMS *De Zeven Provincien*)	—

Builders	Laid down	Launched	Commissioned
Wilton-Fijenoord, Schiedam	5 Sep 1939	24 Dec 1944	18 Nov 1953
Rotterdamse Droogdok Maatschappij	19 May 1939	22 Aug 1950	17 Dec 1953

Displacement, tons: 9 529 standard; 11 850 full load
Dimensions, feet (metres): 609 × 56·7 × 22
(187·6 × 17·3 × 6·7)
Guns: 8—6 in (twin turrets); 8—57 mm (twins); 8—40 mm
Main engines: 2 De Schelde-Parsons geared turbines;
85 000 shp; 2 shafts
Boilers: 4 Werkspoor-Yarrow
Speed, knots: 32
Complement: 926

Almirante Grau transferred by purchase 7 March 1973 and *De Zeven Provincien* bought Aug 1976.
Almirante Grau commissioned in Peruvian Navy 23 May 1973 and sailed for Peru 18 June 1973.

Reconstruction: After sale *De Zeven Provincien* was taken in hand by her original builders for conversion to a helicopter carrier. The Terrier missile system has been returned to USA and a helicopter flight deck is to be built from midships to the stern. Completion expected 1977-78.

Radar: Search: LWO 1
Heightfinder: SGR 104.
Tactical: DA 02.
Fire control: HSA M20 for 6 in guns and M45 for secondary battery.

ALMIRANTE GRAU

1973, Peruvian Navy

ALMIRANTE GRAU

1975, Peruvian Navy

2 Ex-BRITISH "CEYLON" CLASS

Name	No.
CAPITAN QUIÑONES	83
(ex-*Almirante Grau*, ex-HMS *Newfoundland*)	
CORONEL BOLOGNESI (ex-HMS *Ceylon*)	82

Builders	Laid down	Launched	Commissioned
Swan, Hunter & Wigham Richardson Ltd, Wallsend-on-Tyne	9 Nov 1939	19 Dec 1941	31 Dec 1942
Alexander Stephen & Sons Ltd, Govan, Glasgow	27 Apr 1939	30 July 1942	13 July 1943

Displacement, tons:
Capitan Quiñones: 8 800 standard; 11 090 full load
Col. Bolognesi: 8 781 standard; 11 110 full load
Length, feet (metres): 538 *(164·0)* pp; 549 *(167·4)* wl; 555·5
(169·3) oa
Beam, feet (metres): 63·6 *(19·4)*
Draught, feet (metres): 20·5 *(6·2)*
Guns: 9—6 in *(152 mm)* (triple turrets); 8—4 in (4 twin)
12—40 mm *Capitan Quiñones*
18—40 mm *Col. Bolognesi*
Armour: 4 in *(102 mm)* sides and CT; 2 in *(51 mm)* turrets and deck
Main engines: Parsons s.r. geared turbines; 72 500 shp;
4 shafts
Boilers: 4 Admiralty 3-drum; 400 psi *(28 km/cm²)*; 720°F *(382°C)*
Speed, knots: 31·5
Oil fuel, tons: 1 620
Range, miles: 6 000 at 13 knots; 2 800 at full power
Complement: *Capitan Quiñones:* 743; *Col. Bolognesi:* 766

83 was transferred as *Almirante Grau* in December 1959, being renamed *Capitan Quiñones* on 15 May 1973. 82 was transferred as *Coronel Bolognesi* on 9 Feb 1960.

Radar: Search: Types 960, 277 and 293.
Fire Control: E band surface, I band AA.

Reconstruction: 83 was reconstructed in 1951-53 at HM Dockyard, Devonport, with two lattice masts, new bridge and improved AA armaments, her torpedo tubes being removed. 82 was modified in 1955-56 with lattice foremast and covered bridge, her torpedo tubes being removed.

CORONEL BOLOGNESI

1975, Peru

CAPITAN QUIÑONES

1975, Peruvian Navy

DESTROYERS

2 Ex-BRITISH "DARING" CLASS

Name	No.
FERRÉ (ex-HMS *Decoy*)	74
PALACIOS (ex-HMS *Diana*)	73

Displacement, tons: 2 800 standard; 3 600 full load
Length, feet (metres): 366 *(111·7)* pp; 375 *(114·3)* wl; 390 *(118·9)* oa
Beam, feet (metres): 43 *(13·1)*
Draught, feet (metres): 18 *(5·5)*
Missiles: 8 MM 38 Exocet launchers abaft after funnel
Guns: 4—4·5 in *(115 mm)*; (2 twin fwd); 2—40 mm
Main engines: English Electric dr geared turbines; 2 shafts
Boilers: 2 Forster Wheeler; Pressure 650 psi *(45·7 kg/cm²)*; Superheat 850°F (454°C)
Oil fuel, tons: 580
Speed, knots: 34
Range, miles: 3 000 at 20 knots
Complement: 297

Purchased by Peru in 1969 and refitted by Cammel Laird (Ship Repairers) Ltd, Birkenhead, for further service.

Reconstruction: This major reconstruction was carried out in 1970-73. The main points of this refit were the reconstructed and enclosed foremast carrying Plessey AWS-1 radar and the Exocet launcher positions in place of the Close Range Blind Fire Director forward of X Turret.
Commissioned after refit—*Palacios* Feb 1973. *Ferré* April 1973. The next major change took place 1975-76 when X 4·5 in turret and the Squid were removed to make way for a helicopter landing deck.

Radar: Fire control; TSF on fore-funnel.
Search; Plessey AWS-1.

Builders	Laid down	Launched	Commissioned
Yarrow Co Ltd, Scotstoun	22 Sep 1946	29 Mar 1949	28 Apr 1953
Yarrow Co Ltd, Scotstoun	3 April 1947	8 May 1952	29 Mar 1954

FERRÉ (before fitting of helicopter deck)   1975, Michael D. J. Lennon

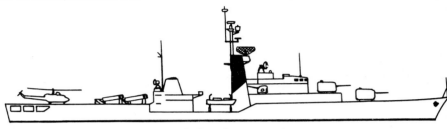

"DARING" Class after reconstruction

PALACIOS   1975, Robert L. Scheina

2 Ex-US "FLETCHER" CLASS

Name	No.
GUISE (ex-USS *Isherwood, DD 520*)	72
VILLAR (ex-USS *Benham, DD 796*)	71

Displacement, tons: 2 120 standard; 2 715 normal; 3 050 full load
Length, feet (metres): 360·2 *(109·8)* pp; 370 *(112·8)* wl; 376·2 *(114·7)* oa
Beam, feet (metres): 39·7 *(12·1)*
Draught, feet (metres): 18 *(5·5)*
Guns: 4—5 in *(127 mm)* 38 cal; (5—5 in *Guise*); 6—3 in *(76 mm)* 50 cal (3 twin)
A/S weapons: 2 fixed Hedgehogs
Torpedo tubes: 5—21 in *(533 mm)* (quintupled)
Torpedo racks: 2 side-launching for A/S torpedoes
Main engines: 2 GE impulse reaction geared turbines; 60 000 shp; 2 shafts
Boilers: 4 Babcock & Wilcox; 600 psi *(42 kg/cm²)*; 850°F *(455°C)*
Speed, knots: 34
Oil fuel, tons: 650
Range, miles: 5 000 at 15 knots; 900 at full power
Complement: 245 (15 officers and 230 men)

Former United States destroyers of the later "Fletcher" class *(Villar)* and "Fletcher" class *(Guise)*.
Two other "Fletcher" class, ex-USS *La Vallette* (DD 448) and *Terry* (DD 513) were transferred for spares in July 1974.

Helicopter: A helicopter deck without hangar or fuelling facilities was fitted on the quarter-deck in 1975-76.

Radar: Search: SPS 6, SPS 10.
Fire Control: GFCS 68 system forward, GFCS 56 system aft.

Transfer: Transferred from the United States Navy to the Peruvian Navy at Boston, Massachusetts, on 15 Dec 1960, and at San Diego, California, on 8 Oct 1961 respectively.

Builders	Laid down	Launched	Commissioned
Bethlehem Steel Co, Staten Island	12 May 1942	24 Nov 1942	10 April 1943
Bethlehem Steel Co, Staten Island	Jan 1943	29 Aug 1943	20 Dec 1943

VILLAR Note helo deck on fantail (GUISE same)   1975, USN

FRIGATES

Note: It is reported that two "Maestrale" ("Improved Lupo") Class have been ordered from CNR.

4 ITALIAN "MODIFIED LUPO" CLASS

Name	No.	Builders	Laid down	Launched	Commissioned
CARVAJAL	—	CNR Riva Trigoso	8 Aug 1974	1977	1978
VILLAVICENCIO	—	CNR Riva Trigoso	Nov 1975	—	1979
—	—	SIM Callao	Nov 1975	—	1979
—	—	SIM Callao	—	—	—

Displacement, tons: 2 208 standard; 2 500 full load
Dimensions, feet (metres): 347·7 × 39·5 × 12 *(106 × 12 × 3·7)*
Aircraft: 1 helicopter
Missiles: 2 Otomat twin-missile launchers; 1 Octuple Albatros (Aspide missiles) launcher for Point Defence
Guns: 1—127 mm OTO Melara; 4 (2 twin) Breda 40 mm L70 Compact
Rocket launchers: 2—105 mm Breda ELSAG multi-purpose 20-barrelled launchers
A/S weapons: 6 (2 triple) Mk 32 A/S torpedo tubes (port and starboard)
Main engines: CODOG with 2 GE Fiat LM 2500 gas turbines; 50 000 hp; 2 Fiat 20 cyl A 230 diesels; 7 800 hp
Speed, knots: 35

The second pair are being built at Servicio Industrial de la Marina at Callao with technical assistance from CNTR. The design is similar to the "Lupo" class of Italy with a major modification in the inclusion of an A/S helicopter at the expense of four surface-to-surface missiles.

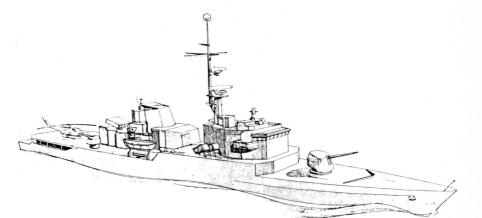

"MODIFIED LUPO" class   *1975, Peruvian Navy*

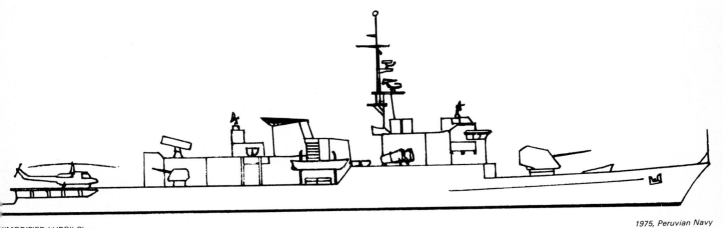

"MODIFIED LUPO" Class   *1975, Peruvian Navy*

2 Ex-US "CANNON" CLASS

Name	No.	Builders	Laid down	Launched	Commissioned
CASTILLA (ex-USS *Bangust*, DE 739)	61	Western Pipe & Steel Co, San Pedro, California	Jan 1943	6 June 1943	30 Oct 1943
RODRIQUEZ (ex-USS *Weaver*, DE 741)	63	Western Pipe & Steel Co, San Pedro, California	Jan 1943	20 June 1943	30 Nov 1943

Displacement, tons: 1 240 standard; 1 900 full load
Dimensions, feet (metres): 306 oa × 36·9 × 14·1 *(93·3 × 11·2 × 4·3)*
Guns: 3—3 in *(76 mm)* 50 cal; 6—40 mm (3 twin); 10—20 mm
A/S weapons: 1 Mk 10 Hedgehog; 8 K mortars; 2 DC racks aft
Main engines: 4 GM diesel-electric sets 6 000 hp; 2 shafts
Speed, knots: 21
Range, miles: 10 500 at 12 knots
Complement: 172 (12 officers and 160 men)

Transferred to Peru on 26 Oct 1951, under the Mutual Defence Assistance Programme. Reconditioned and modernised at Green Cove Springs and Jacksonville, Florida. Arrived in Peru on 24 May 1952.
Castilla now used as a training ship on the Amazon with home port Iquitos and *Rodriquez* as submarine accommodation ship.

RODRIQUEZ   *1975, Peruvian Navy*

SUBMARINES

2 + 2 TYPE 209

Name	No.	Builders	Laid down	Launched	Commissioned
ISLAY	S 45	Howaldtswerke, Kiel	1971	1973	28 Aug 1974
ARICA	S 46	Howaldtswerke, Kiel	1972	17 Apr 1974	21 Jan 1975
—	S 47	Howaldtswerke, Kiel	—	—	—
—	S 48	Howaldtswerke, Kiel	—	—	—

Displacement, tons: 990 surfaced; 1 290 dived
Length, feet (metres): 177·1 *(54·0)*
Beam, feet (metres): 20·3 *(6·2)*
Torpedo tubes: 8—21 in (with reloads)
Main machinery: Diesel Electric; 4 MTU Siemens diesel-generators; 1 Siemens electric motor; 1 shaft
Speed, knots: 10 surfaced; 22 dived
Range: 50 days
Complement: 31

Designed by Ingenieurkontor, Lübeck for construction by Howaldtswerke, Kiel and sale by Ferrostaal Essen all acting as a consortium.
A single-hull design with two ballast tanks and forward and after trim tanks. Fitted with snort and remote machinery control. The single screw is slow revving, very high capacity batteries with GRP lead-acid cells and battery cooling—by Wilh. Hagen and VARTTA. Active and passive sonar, sonar detection equipment, sound ranging gear and underwater telephone. Fitted with two periscopes, radar and Omega reciever. Foreplanes retract.
Islay ran trials in June 1974. *Arica* launched 17 Apr 1974. Two further boats ordered.

ISLAY
1975, Peruvian Navy

2 Ex-US "GUPPY 1A" CLASS

Name	No.	Builders	Laid down	Launched	Commissioned
LA PEDRERA (ex-*Pabellon de Pica*, ex-USS *Sea Poacher SS 406*)	49	Portsmouth Navy Yard	23 Feb 1944	20 May 1944	31 July 1944
PACOCHA (ex-USS *Atule SS 403*)	50	Portsmouth Navy Yard	2 Dec 1943	6 Mar 1944	21 June 1944

Displacement, tons: 1 870 standard; 2 440 dived
Dimensions, feet (metres): 308 oa × 27 × 17 *(93·8 × 8·2 × 5·2)*
Torpedo tubes: 10—21 in; 6 forward 4 aft
Main machinery: 3 diesels; 4 800 hp; 2 electric motors 5 400 shp; 2 shafts
Speed, knots: 18 surfaced; 15 dived
Complement: 85

Modernised under the 1951 Guppy programme. Purchased by Peru—*La Pedrera* on 1 July 1974, *Pacocha* on 31 July 1974. The name of *La Pedrera* was changed a fortnight after purchase. Both became operational in 1975 after refit. Ex-USS *Tench* (SS 417) purchased for spares Sep 1976.

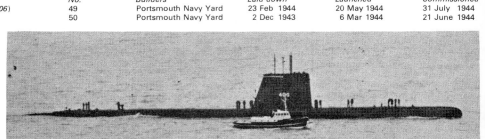

LA PEDRERA (as *Sea Poacher*)
1966, Dr. Giorgio Arra

4 "ABTAO" CLASS

Name	No.	Builders	Laid down	Launched	Commissioned
ABTAO (ex-*Tiburon*)	42	General Dynamics (Electric Boat), Groton, Connecticut	12 May 1952	27 Oct 1953	20 Feb 1954
ANGAMOS (ex-*Atun*)	43	General Dynamics (Electric Boat), Groton, Connecticut	27 Oct 1955	5 Feb 1957	1 July 1957
DOS DE MAYO (ex-*Lobo*)	41	General Dynamics (Electric Boat), Groton, Connecticut	12 May 1952	6 Feb 1954	14 June 1954
IQUIQUE (ex-*Merlin*)	44	General Dynamics (Electric Boat), Groton, Connecticut	27 Oct 1955	5 Feb 1957	1 Oct 1957

Displacement, tons: 825 standard; 1 400 dived
Length, feet (metres): 243 *(74·1)* oa
Beam, feet (metres): 22 *(6·7)*
Draught, feet (metres): 14 *(4·3)*
Guns: 1—5 in *(127 mm)* 25 cal *(Abtao* and *Dos de Mayo)*
Torpedo tubes: 6—21 in *(533 mm);* 4 bow, 2 stern
Main machinery: 2 GM 278A diesels; 2 400 bhp; Electric motors; 2 shafts
Speed, knots: 16 surfaced, 10 dived
Oil fuel, tons: 45
Range, miles: 5 000 at 10 knots (surfaced)
Complement: 40

They are of modified US "Mackerel" class. Refitted at Groton as follows—*Dos de Mayo* and *Abtao* in 1965, other pair in 1968.

IQUIQUE
1975, Peruvian Navy

LIGHT FORCES

2 "MARANON" CLASS (RIVER GUNBOATS)

Name	No.	Builders	Commissioned
MARAÑON	13	John I. Thornycroft & Co Ltd	July 1951
UCAYALI	14	John I. Thornycroft & Co Ltd	June 1951

Displacement, tons: 365 full load
Dimensions, feet (metres): 154·8 wl × 32 × 4 *(47·2 × 9·7 × 1·2)*
Guns: 2—3 in 50 cal; 1—40 mm; 4—20 mm (twins)
Main engines: British Polar M 441 diesels; 800 bhp = 12 knots
Range, miles: 6 000 at 10 knots
Complement: 40

Ordered early in 1950 and both laid down in early 1951. Employed on police duties in Upper Amazon. Superstructure of aluminium alloy. Based at Iquitos.

UCAYALI   *1975, Peruvian Navy*

2 "LORETO" CLASS (RIVER GUNBOATS)

Name	No.	Builders	Commissioned
AMAZONAS	11	Electric Boat Co, Groton	1935
LORETO	12	Electric Boat Co, Groton	1935

Displacement, tons: 250 standard
Dimensions, feet (metres): 145 × 22 × 4 *(44·2 × 6·7 × 1·2)*
Guns: 1—3 in; 2—40 mm; 2—20 mm
Main engines: Diesel; 750 bhp = 15 knots
Range, miles: 4 000 at 10 knots
Complement: 35

Launched in 1934.

LORETO   *1973, Peruvian Navy*

1 RIVER GUNBOAT

Name	No.	Builders	Commissioned
AMERICA	15	Tranmere Bay Development Co Ltd, Birkenhead	1904

Displacement, tons: 240
Dimensions, feet (metres): 133 × 19·5 × 4·5 *(40·6 × 5·9 × 1·4)*
Guns: 2—40 mm; 4—20 mm
Main engines: Triple expansion; 350 ihp = 14 knots
Complement: 26

Built of steel. Converted from coal to oil fuel burning. In the Upper Amazon Flotilla. The river gunboat *Iquitos* was discarded in 1967 and after 92 years service.

AMERICA   *1975, Peruvian Navy*

3 RIVER PATROL CRAFT

Name	No.	Builders	Commissioned
RIO PIURA	252 (ex-*04*)	Viareggio, Italy	5 Sep 1960
RIO TUMBES	251 (ex-*02*)	Viareggio, Italy	5 Sep 1960
RIO ZARUMILLA	250 (ex-*01*)	Viareggio, Italy	5 Sep 1960

Displacement, tons: 37 full load
Dimensions, feet (metres): 65·7 × 17 × 3·2 *(20 × 5·2 × 1)*
Guns: 2—40 mm
Main engines: 2 GM diesels; 2 shafts; 1 200 bhp = 18 knots

Ordered in 1959 as a class of four laid down on 15 July 1959. Stationed at El Salto on Ecuadorian border.

RIO PIURA   *1975, Peruvian Navy*

4 COASTAL PATROL CRAFT

LA PUNTA 230   RÍO CHILLÓN 231
RÍO SANTA 232   RÍO MAJES 233

Of 16 tons with light MGs. Complement 4.

4 LAKE PATROL CRAFT

RÍO RAMIS 290   RÍO LLAVE 291

Of 12 tons with light MGs. Complement 4.

RÍO COATA 292   RÍO HUANCANÉ 293

Of 10 tons with light MGs. Complement 4. All stationed on Lake Titicaca.

Patrol craft on Lake Titicaca   1973, Peruvian Navy

AMPHIBIOUS FORCES

1 Ex-US "LST 1" CLASS

Name	No.	Builders	Commissioned
CHIMBOTE (ex-M/S *Rawhiti,* ex-US *LST 283)*	34	American Bridge Co, Ambridge, Pennsylvania	18 Nov 1943

Displacement, tons: 1 625 standard; 4 050 full load
Dimensions, feet (metres): 328 oa × 50 × 14·1 *(100 × 15·3 × 4·3)*
Gun: 1—3 in
Main engines: GM diesels; 2 shafts; 1 700 bhp = 10 knots
Oil fuel, tons: 600 oil tanks; 1 100 ballast tanks
Range, miles: 9 500 at 9 knots
Complement: Accommodation for 16 officers and 130 men

Laid down on 2 Aug 1943, launched on 10 Oct 1943. Sold to Peru by a British firm in Mar 1947. Served commercially until 1951 when she was transferred to the Peruvian Navy.

1 Ex-US "LST 511" CLASS

Name	No.	Builders	Commissioned
PAITA (ex-USS *Burnett County, LST 512)*	35 (ex-*AT 4)*	Chicago Bridge & Iron Co	8 Jan 1944

Displacement, tons: 1 653 standard; 4 080 full load
Dimensions, feet (metres): 328 oa × 50 × 14·5 *(100 × 15·3 × 4·4)*
Guns: 6—20 mm
Main engines: GM diesels; 2 shafts; 1 700 bhp = 10 knots
Range, miles: 9 500 at 9 knots
Complement: 13 officers, 106 men

Laid down on 29 July 1943. Launched on 10 Dec 1943. Purchased by Peru in Sep 1957. Unique deck-house forward of bridge. Helicopters are operated from upper deck amidships.

PAITA   1972, Peruvian Navy

2 Ex-US "LSM-1" CLASS

Name	No.	Builders	Commissioned
ATICO (ex-US *LSM 554)*	37	Charleston Navy Yard	14 Sep 1945
LOMAS (ex-US *LSM 396)*	36	Charleston Navy Yard	23 Mar 1945

Displacement, tons: 513 standard; 913 full load
Dimensions, feet (metres): 203·5 oa × 34·5 × 7 *(62·1 × 10·5 × 2·1)*
Guns: 2—40 mm; 4—20 mm
Main engines: Diesels; 800 rpm; 2 shafts; 3 600 bhp = 12 knots
Range, miles: 5 000 at 7 knots
Complement: Accommodation for 116 (10 officers and 106 men)

Purchased in 1959.

LOMAS   1975, Peruvian Navy

SURVEY VESSELS

1 NEW CONSTRUCTION OCEANOGRAPHIC SHIP

Of 2 000 tons to be built by SIMAC, Callao.

1 Ex-US "SOTOYOMO" CLASS

Name	No.	Builders	Commissioned
UNANUE (ex-USS *Wateree, ATA 174)*	136	Levingston SB Co, Orange, Texas	20 July 1944

Displacement, tons: 534 standard; 852 full load
Dimensions, feet (metres): 143 oa × 33·9 × 13·2 *(43·6 × 9 × 4)*
Main engines: GM diesel-electric; 1 500 bhp = 13 knots

Former United States auxiliary ocean tug. Laid down on 5 Oct 1943, launched on 18 Nov 1943. Purchased from the USA in Nov 1961 under MAP.

CARDENAS (ex-US *YP 99)*   +2 (ex-US *YP 242* and *243)*

Of 19 tons, launched in 1950, with a complement of 4. Transferred Nov 1958. Last two operated by navy for Instituto del Mar.

1 RESEARCH CRAFT

Of 77 ft *(23·5 metres)* with accommodation for 16 operated on the Amazonas by El Instituto del Mar (Ministry of Marine). Commissioned May 1976.

SERVICE FORCES

1 Ex-US "BELLATRIX" CLASS (TRANSPORT)

Name	No.	Builders	Commissioned
INDEPENDENCIA (ex-USS	31	Tampa Shipbuilding Co,	1941
Bellatrix, AKA 3, ex-Raven, AK 20)	(ex-21)	Tampa, Florida	

Displacement, tons: 6 194 light
Dimensions, feet (metres): 459 oa × 63 × 26·5 *(140 × 19·2 × 8·1)*
Guns: 1—5 in 38 cal; 3—3 in 50 cal; 10—20 mm
Main engines: 1 Nordberg diesel; 1 shaft; 6 000 bhp = 16·5 knots

Former US attack cargo ship. Transferred to Peru at Bremerton, Washington on 20 July 1963 under the Military Aid Programme. Training ship for the Peruvian Naval Academy.

INDEPENDENCIA   1975, Peruvian Navy

1 "ILO" CLASS (TRANSPORT)

Name	No.	Builders	Commissioned
ILO	131	Servicio Industrial de la Marina, Callao	Dec 1971

Displacement, tons: 18 400 full load
Measurement, tons: 13 000 deadweight
Dimensions, feet (metres): 507·7 × 67·3 × 27·2 *(154·8 × 20·5 × 8·3)*
Main engines: Diesels; Speed = 15·6 knots

The *Ilo* is used from time to time for commercial purposes. Her sister ship *Rimac* was launched at the same yard on 12 Dec 1971 and transferred from the navy for commercial use by State Shipping Company (CPV) on "bare-bone charter" in 1973.

ILO   1973, Peruvian Navy

1 + 1 "TALARA" CLASS (REPLENISHMENT TANKERS)

Name	No.	Builders	Commissioned
TALARA	AO 152	Servicio Industrial de la Marina, Callao	Mar 1977
—	—	Servicio Industrial de la Marina, Callao	1978

Measurement, tons: 25 000 dw
Dimensions, feet (metres): 561·5 × 82 × 31·2 *(171·2 × 25 × 9·5)*
Main engines: Diesels; 12 000 hp
Speed, knots: 15·5

Cargo space 35 662 cu metres. *Talara* laid down 1975. Second laid down 9 July 1976 having been originally ordered by Petroperu and transferred to navy while building. A third, *Trompeteros*, of this class has been built for Petroperu.

2 "PARINAS" CLASS (REPLENISHMENT TANKERS)

Name	No.	Builders	Commissioned
PARINAS	155	Servicio Industrial de la Marina, Callao	13 June 1968
PIMENTEL	156	Servicio Industrial de la Marina, Callao	27 June 1969

Displacement, tons: 3 434 light; 13 600 full load
Measurement, tons: 10 000 deadweight
Dimensions, feet (metres): 410·9 × 63·1 × 26 *(125·3 × 19·2 × 7·9)*
Main engines: Burmeister and Wain Type 750 diesel; 5 400 bhp = 14·5 knots

All tankers may be used for commercial purposes if not required for naval use.

PIMENTEL   1975, Peruvian Navy

2 "SECHURA" CLASS (SUPPORT TANKERS)

Name	No.	Builders	Commissioned
LOBITOS	159	Servicio Industrial de la Marina, Callao	1966
ZORRITOS	158	Servicio Industrial de la Marina, Callao	1959

Displacement, tons: 8 700 full load
Measurement, tons: 4 300 gross; 6 000 deadweight
Dimensions, feet (metres): 385·0 oa × 52·0 × 21·2 *(117·4 × 15·9 × 6·4)*
Main engines: Burmeister & Wain diesels; 2 400 bhp = 12 knots
Boilers: 2 Scotch with Thornycroft oil burners for cargo tank cleaning

Zorritos launched 8 Oct 1958, *Lobitos* May 1965.

LOBITOS   *1975, Peruvian Navy*

1 SUPPORT TANKER

Name	No.	Builders	Commissioned
MOLLENDO (ex-*Amalienborg)*	ATP 151	Japan	Sep 1962

Displacement, tons: 6 084 standard; 25 670 full load
Dimensions, feet (metres): 534·8 oa × 72·2 × 30 *(164·3 × 22 × 9·2)*
Main engines: 674-VTFS-160 diesels; 7 500 bhp = 14·5 knots

This Japanese built tanker, completed Sep 1962, was acquired by Peru in Apr 1967. Used in commercial work when not required by navy.

ABA 001

800 ton tanker employed on the Amazon—built in Peru 1972.

ABA 113

300 ton harbour tanker built in Peru 1972.

— (Ex-US *YO 221)*

Transferred to Peru Feb 1975.

MOLLENDO   *1975, Peruvian Navy*

TUGS

1 Ex-US "CHEROKEE" CLASS

Name	No.	Builders	Commissioned
GUARDIAN RIOS (ex-USS *Pinto, ATF 90)*	123	USA	1943

Displacement, tons: 1 235 standard; 1 675 full load
Dimensions, feet (metres): 205 oa × 38·5 × 15·5 *(62·5 × 11·7 × 4·7)*
Main engines: 4 GM diesel electric; 3 000 bhp = 16·5 knots

Launched on 5 Jan 1943. Transferred to Peru in 1960 and delivered in Jan 1961. Fitted with powerful pumps and other salvage equipment.

CONTRAESTRE NAVARRO

50 ton tug for Amazon flotilla built in Peru in 1973.

Name	No.	Builders	Commissioned
OLAYA	—	Ruhrorter, SW, Duisburg	1967
SELENDON	—	Ruhrorter, SW, Duisburg	1967

Measurement, tons: 80 gross
Dimensions, feet (metres): 61·3 × 20·3 × 7·4 *(18·7 × 6·2 × 2·3)*
Main engines: 600 hp = 10 knots

FRANCO (ex-USS *Iwana, YTM2)* ARA 124.
Transferred Mar 1946.

MISCELLANEOUS

1 CONVERTED RIVER GUNBOAT

Name	No.	Builders	Commissioned
NAPO	301	Yarrow Co Ltd, Scotstoun, Glasgow	1921

Displacement, tons: 98
Dimensions, feet (metres): 101·5 oa × 18 × 3 *(31 × 5·5 × 0·9)*
Main engines: Triple expansion; 250 ihp = 12 knots
Boilers: Yarrow
Complement: 22

Launched in 1920. Built of steel. Converted from wood to oil fuel burning. In the Upper Amazon Flotilla. Converted to a Dispensary Vessel in 1968.

NAPO   *1975, Peruvian Navy*

1 + 2 RIVER HOSPITAL CRAFT

Name	No.	Builders	Commissioned
MORONA	—	SIMAI, Iquitos	1976
—	—	SIMAI, Iquitos	1977
—	—	SIMAI, Iquitos	1977

Displacement, tons: 150
Dimensions, feet (metres): 98·4 × 19·6 × 1·5 *(30 × 6 × 0·6)*

For service on Rivers Amazonas, Putumayo and Yavari.

1 FLOATING DOCK

MY20-AOF 112 (ex-US *ARD 8)*

Displacement, tons: 5 200
Dimensions, feet (metres): 492 × 84 × 5·7/33·2 *(150·1 × 25·6 × 1·7/10·1)*

Transferred Feb 1961.

1 FLOATING WORKSHOP

PISCO (ex-US *YR 59)*

Transferred 8 Aug 1961.

1 FLOATING DOCK

ADE 111 (ex-US *AFDL 33)*

Displacement, tons: 1 900
Dimensions, feet (metres): 288 × 64 × 8·2/31·5 *(92·2 × 19·5 × 2·5/9·6)*

Launched in Oct 1944. Transferred July 1959.

1 SMALL FLOATING DOCK

Dimensions, feet (metres): 194 × 61·3 × ? *(59·2 × 18·7 × ?)*
Lift: 600 tons

Built by John I. Thornycroft, Southampton in 1951. Based at Iquitos.

Other names of unidentified types: *Duenas, Noguera, Neptuno, Corrillo.*

WATER CARRIER

Name	No.	Builders	Commissioned
MANTILLA (ex-US *YW 22)*	141	Henry C. Grebe & Co Inc, Chicago, Illinois	1945

Displacement, tons: 1 235 full load
Dimensions, feet (metres): 174 × 32 × — *(52·3 × 9·8 × —)*
Gun: 1 MG forward
Speed, knots: 8
Capacity, gallons: 200 000

Former US water barge. Lent to Peru in July 1963.

COASTGUARD

CORVETTES

2 Ex-US "AUK" CLASS

Name	No.	Builders	Commissioned
DIEZ CANSECO (ex-USS *Shoveller, MSF 382)*	69	Gulf Shipbuilding Corp	28 June 1945
GALVEZ (ex-USS *Ruddy, MSF 380)*	68	Gulf Shipbuilding Corp	28 Apr 1945

Displacement, tons: 890 standard; 1 250 full load
Dimensions, feet (metres): 221·2 oa × 32·2 × 11 *(67·5 oa × 9·8 × 3·4)*
Guns: 1—3 in 50 cal; 2—40 mm
A/S weapons: 1 Hedgehog
Main engines: Diesel electric; 2 shafts; 3 532 bhp = 18 knots
Range, miles: 4 300 at 10 knots
Complement: 100

Recommissioned at San Diego, California, and transferred to the Peruvian Navy under the Mutual Defence Assistance Programme on 1 Nov 1960. Sonar equipment was fitted so that they could be used as patrol vessels. Both purchased by Peru in 1974. Transferred to the Coast Guard Service in 1975. Both still capable of minesweeping.

GALVEZ

1970, Peruvian Navy

6 LARGE PATROL CRAFT

Name	No.	Builders	Commissioned
RIO CANETE	234	SIMA, Peru, Callao	1 Apr 1976
RIO —	235	SIMA, Peru, Callao	1976
RIO —	236	SIMA, Peru, Callao	1976
RIO —	237	SIMA, Peru, Callao	1977
RIO —	238	SIMA, Peru, Callao	1977
RIO —	239	SIMA, Peru, Callao	1977

Displacement, tons: 298 full load
Dimensions, feet (metres): 166·8 × 24·8 × 5·6 *(50·6 × 7·4 × 1·7)*
Guns: 1—40 mm; 1—20 mm
Main engines: 4—MTU diesels; 5 640 hp = 22 knots
Complement: 39

First launched 8 Aug 1974.

6 VOSPER TYPE (LARGE PATROL CRAFT)

Name	No.	Builders	Commissioned
RIO CHICAWA	224	Vosper Ltd, Portsmouth	1965
(ex-*De Los Heros*)	(ex-*23*)		
RIO PATIVILCA	225	Vosper Ltd, Portsmouth	1965
(ex-*Herrera*)	(ex-*24*)		
RIO HUAORA	226	Vosper Ltd, Portsmouth	1965
(ex-*Larrea*)	(ex-*25*)		
RIO LOCUMBA	227	Vosper Ltd, Portsmouth	1965
(ex-*Sanchez Carrion*)	(ex-*26*)		
RIO ICA	228	Vosper Ltd, Portsmouth	1965
(ex-*Santillana*)	(ex-*27*)		
RIO VITOR	229	Vosper Ltd, Portsmouth	1965
(ex-*Velarde*)	(ex-*21*)		

RIO LOCUMBA   *1971, Peruvian Navy*

Displacement, tons: 100 standard; 130 full load
Dimensions, feet (metres): 109·7 oa × 21 × 5·7 *(33·5 oa × 6·4 × 1·7)*
Guns: 2—20 mm
A/S weapons: DC racks
Main engines: 2 Napier Deltic 18 cyl, turbocharged diesels; 6 200 bhp = 30 knots
Range, miles: 1 100 at 15 knots
Complement: 25 (4 officers and 21 ratings)

Of all-welded steel construction with aluminium upperworks. Equipped with Vosper roll damping fins, Decca Type 707 true motion radar, comprehensive radio, up-to-date navigation aids, sonar, and air-conditioning. The first boat, 229, was launched on 10 July 1964, the last, 227, on 18 Feb 1965. Can be armed as gunboat, torpedo boat (four side-launched torpedoes) or minelayer. A twin rocket projector can be fitted forward instead of gun. All transferred to the Coast Guard Service in 1975 and renamed.

2 US "PGM 71" CLASS (LARGE PATROL CRAFT)

Name	No.	Builders	Commissioned
RÍO SAMA (ex-US *PGM 78*)	222 (ex-*PC 11*)	SIMA Callao	Sep 1966
RÍO CHIRA (ex-US *PGM 111*)	223 (ex-*PC 12*)	USA	—

RIO SAMA   *1971, Peruvian Navy*

Displacement, tons: 130 standard; 147 full load
Dimensions, feet (metres): 101 × 21 × 6 *(30·8 × 6·4 × 1·8)*
Guns: 1—40 mm; 4—20 mm; 2—0·5 cal MG
Main engines: 2 diesels; 2 shafts; 1 800 hp = 18·5 knots
Range, miles: 1 500 at 10 knots
Complement: 15

Rio Sama completed Sep 1966 under the US Military Aid Programme. *Rio Chira* transferred by US 30 June 1972. Transferred to the Coast Guard Service in 1975.

PHILIPPINES

Ministerial

Minister of National Defence:
Juan Ponce Enrile

Senior Officers

Flag Officer in Command:
Rear-Admiral Hilario M. Ruiz
Commander, Naval Operating Forces:
Captain Simeon M. Alejandro

Diplomatic Representation

Armed Forces Attaché London:
Captain Artemio A. Tadiar, Jr (Navy)
Naval Attaché Washington:
Commander Ernesto M. Arzaga

Personnel

1977: approx 2 000 officers and 15 000 men

Prefix to Ships' Names

RPS for Republic of Philippines Ship.

Marine Corps

Commandant: Captain Rodolfo Punsalang
Personnel: 500 officers and 5 000 men (organised into a single brigade)

Coast Guard

Commandant: Commodore Ernesto R. Ogbinar
Personnel: 300 officers and 1 700 men

Mercantile Marine

Lloyd's Register of Shipping:
457 vessels of 1 018 065 tons gross

Naval Base

Sangley Point

Strength of the Fleet

	Active	Building
Frigates	10	—
Corvettes	12	—
Large Patrol Craft	10	—
Hydrofoils	4	—
Coastal Patrol Craft	36	?74
Minesweepers (Coastal)	2	—
LSTs	27	—
LSMs	4	—
LSSLs	4	—
LSILs	4	—
Landing Craft	71	—
Repair Ships	2	—
Tankers	7	—
Miscellaneous	15	—
Tugs	8	—
Floating Docks	5	—
Survey Ships	4	—
Coast Guard Craft	33	—

DELETIONS

Corvettes

1976 2 MSO Type 4 (to US for disposal 1977).
(*Davao del Norte, Davao del Sur*)

Light Forces

1976 3 "Swift" Mk 1

Coast and Geodetic Service

1976 *Samar*

FRIGATES

1 Ex-US "SAVAGE" TYPE

Name	No.	Builders	Laid down	Launched	Commissioned
RAJAH LAKANDULA (ex-*Tran Hung Dao*, ex-USS *Camp*, DER 251)	PS 4	Brown SB & Co, Houston	1943	16 Apr 1943	16 Sep 1943

Displacement, tons: 1 590 standard; 1 850 full load
Length, feet (metres): 300 wl; 306 oa (*93·3*)
Beam, feet (metres): 36·6 (*11·2*)
Draught, feet (metres): 14 (*4·3*)
Guns: 2—3 inch (*76 mm*) 50 cal (single)
A/S weapons: 6 (2 triple) Mk 32 torpedo tubes; 1 trainable hedgehog (Mk 15); depth charge rack
Main engines: Diesel (Fairbanks Morse); 6 000 bhp; 2 shafts
Speed, knots: 19
Complement: approx 170

Former US Navy destroyer escort, of the FMR design group. After World War II this ship was extensively converted to radar picket configuration to serve as seaward extension of US aircraft attack warning system; redesignated DER with original DE hull number. Subsequently employed during 1960s in Indochina for coastal patrol and interdiction by US Navy (Operation MARKET TIME). Transferred to South Vietnamese Navy 6 Feb 1971. Acquired by the Philippines in 1975 and formally transferred on 5 Apr 1976.

Fire Control: Mk 63 (forward) SPG 34 on gun mount. Mk 51 (aft).

Radar: SPS-28 and SPS-10 search radars on forward tripod mast. Apparently most electronic warfare equipment was removed prior to transfer. (See Fire Control).

Sonar: SQS 31.

RAJAH LAKANDULA

1971, Vietnamese Navy

6 Ex-US "CASCO" CLASS COAST GUARD CUTTERS

Name	No.	Builders	Laid down	Launched	Commissioned
DIEGO SILANG (ex-*Tran Quang Khai*, ex-USCGC *Bering Strait*, WHEC 382, ex-AVP 34)	PS 9	Lake Washington SY	1943	15 Jan 1944	19 July 1944
— (ex-*Tran Nhat Duat*, ex-USCGC *Yakutat*, WHEC 380, ex-AVP 32)	—	Associated Shipbuilders	1942	2 July 1942	31 Mar 1944
FRANCISCO DAGAHOY (ex-*Tran Binh Trong*, ex-USCGC *Castle Rock*, WHEC 383, ex-AVP 35)	PS 10	Lake Washington SY	1943	11 Mar 1944	8 Oct 1944
— (ex-*Tran Quoc Toan*, ex-USCGC *Cook Inlet*, WHEC 384, ex-AVP 36)	—	Lake Washington SY	1944	13 May 1944	5 Nov 1944
ANDRES BONIFACIO (ex-*Ly Thuong Kiet*, ex-USCGC *Chincoteague*, WHEC 375, ex-AVP 24)	PS 7	Lake Washington SY	1942	15 Apr 1942	12 Apr 1943
GREGORIO DE PILAR (ex-*Ngo Kuyen*, ex-USCGC *McCulloch*, WHEC 386, ex-USS *Wachapreague*, AGP 8, AVP 56)	PS 8	Lake Washington SY	1943	10 July 1943	17 May 1944

Displacement, tons: 1 766 standard; 2 800 full load
Length, feet (metres): 300 wl; 310·75 oa (*94·7*)
Beam, feet (metres): 41·1 (*12·5*)
Draught, feet (metres): 13·5 (*4·1*)
Guns: 1—5 inch (*127 mm*) 38 cal; 1 or 2—81 mm mortars in some ships; most have 2 or 3—40 mm aft; several MG
Main engines: Diesels (Fairbanks Morse); 6 080 bhp; 2 shafts
Speed, knots: approx 18
Complement: approx 200

Built as seaplane tenders of the "Barnegat" class for the US Navy.
All transferred to US Coast Guard in 1946-1948, initially on loan designated WAVP and then on permanent transfer except ex-*McCulloch* transferred outright from US Navy to Coast Guard; subsequently redesignated as high endurance cutters (WHEC).

Appearance: These ships are distinguished from the former US Navy radar picket frigate of similar size by their pole masts forward, open side passages amidships, and radar antenna on second mast. Note combination ·50 cal MG/81 mm mortar forward of bridge in "B" position.

DIEGO SILANG

1971, Vietnamese Navy

Fire Control: Mk 52 with Mk 26 radar for 5 in gun.

Radar: SPN 21 (foremast); SPS 29 (mainmast).

Transfers: Transferred from US Coast Guard to South Vietnamese Navy in 1971-72. Acquired by the Philippines in 1975 and formally transferred on 5 Apr 1976.

3 Ex-US "CANNON" CLASS

Name	No.	Builders	Laid down	Launched	Commissioned
DATU KALANTIAW (ex-USS *Booth*, DE 170)	PS 76	Federal Shipbuilding & Dry Dock Co, Newark, New Jersey	1943	21 June1943	21 July 1943
— (ex-*Asahi*, DE 262, ex-USS *Amick*, DE 168)	—	Federal Shipbuilding & Dry Dock Co, Newark, New Jersey	1943	27 May 1943	26 July 1943
— (ex-*Hatsuhi*, DE 263, ex-USS *Atherton*, DE 169)	—	Federal Shipbuilding & Dry Dock Co, Newark, New Jersey	1943	27 May 1943	29 Aug 1943

Displacement, tons: 1 220 standard; 1 620 full load
Length, feet (metres): 300 *(91·5)* wl; 306 *(93·2)* 0a
Beam, feet (metres): 36·6 *(11·2)*
Draught, feet (metres): 14 *(4·3)*
Guns: 3—3 inch *(76 mm)* 50 cal (single); 6—40 mm (twin); 2—20 mm (single) (6—20 mm in ex-Japanese)
A/S weapons: 1 hedgehog; 6 (2 triple) Mk 32 torpedo tubes; depth charges (PS 76); 1 hedgehog; 6 K-guns; 2 DC racks (ex-Japanese)
Main engines: Diesel-electric drive (General Motors diesels); 6 000 bhp; 2 shafts
Speed, knots: 21
Complement: approx 165

The USS *Booth* was completed by the Norfolk Navy Yard.

Appearance: Ex-Japanese ships have pole foremast.

Fire Control: Mk 52 GFCS with Mk 51 rangefinder and Mk 26 radar for 3 in gun; 3—Mk 51 Mod 2 GFCS for 40 mm.

Radar: The *Datu Kalantiaw* has been refitted with SPS-5 and SPS-6 radars with antennae mounted on tripod mast.

Transfers: PS 76 to Philippines 15 Dec 1967. Ex-Japanese ships *Asahi* and *Hatsuhi* originally transferred 14 June 1955 and were paid off June 1975. Transferred to Philippines 13 Sept 1976.

DATU KALANTIAW — *Philippine Navy*

CORVETTES

2 Ex-US "AUK" CLASS MSF TYPE

Name	No.	Builders	Commissioned
RIZAL (ex-USS *Murrelet*, MSF 372)	PS 69	Savannah Machine & Foundry Co, Georgia	21 Aug 1945
QUEZON (ex-USS *Vigilance*, MSF 324)	PS 70	Associated Shipbuilders, Seattle, Washington	28 Feb 1944

Displacement, tons: 890 standard; 1 250 full load
Dimensions, feet (metres): 215 wl; 221·2 oa × 32·2 × 10·8 *(70·5; 72·5 × 10·5 × 3·5)*
Guns: 2—3 inch *(76 mm)* 50 cal (single); 4—40 mm (twin); 4—20 mm (twin)
A/S weapons: 3 (1 triple) Mk 32 torpedo tubes; 1 hedgehog; depth charges
Main engines: Diesel-electric (General Motors diesels); 3 532 bhp; 2 shafts = 18 knots
Complement: approx 100

Upon transfer the minesweeping gear was removed and a second 3 inch gun fitted aft; additional anti-submarine weapons also fitted. *Quezon* has bulwarks on iron-deck to end of superstructure which *Rizal* does not have.

Radar: SPS 5.

Transfers: PS 69 transferred to the Philippines on 18 June 1965 and PS 70 on 19 Aug 1967.

QUEZON — *1976, Michael D. J. Lennon*

8 Ex-US "PCE 827" CLASS

Name	No.	Builders	Commissioned
CEBU (ex-USS *PCE 881*)	PS 28	Albina E and M Works, Portland, Oregon	1944
NEGROS OCCIDENTAL (ex-USS *PCE 884*)	PS 29	Albina E and M Works, Portland, Oregon	1944
LEYTE (ex-USS *PCE 885*)	PS 30	Albina E and M Works, Portland, Oregon	1945
PANGASINAN (ex-USS *PCE 891*)	PS 31	Willamette Iron & Steel Corp, Portland	1944
ILOILO (ex-USS *PCE 897*)	PS 32	Willamette Iron & Steel Corp, Portland	1944
SULTAN KUDARAT (ex-*Dong Da II* ex-USS *Crestview*, PCE 895)	PS 22	Willamette Iron & Steel Corp, Portland	1943
MIGUEL MALVAR (ex-*Ngoc Hoi* ex-USS *Brattleboro*, EPCER 852)	PS 19	Pullman Standard Car Co, Chicago	1944
DATU MARIKUDO (ex-*Van Kiep II* ex-USS *Amherst*, PCER 853)	PS 23	Pullman Standard Car Co, Chicago	1944

Displacement, tons: 640 standard; 850 full load
Dimensions, feet (metres): 180 wl; 184·5 oa × 33·1 × 9·5 *(59; 60·5 × 10·8 × 3·1)*
Guns: 1—3 inch *(76 mm)* 50 cal; 3 or 6—40 mm (single or twin) (28-32); 2—40 mm (single) (remainder); 4—20 mm (single) (28-32); 8—20 mm (twin) (remainder)
Main engines: Diesels (General Motors); 2 000 bhp; 2 shafts = 15 knots
Complement: approx 90-100

Two originally were fitted as rescue ships (PCER).

Transfers: Five units transferred to the Philippines in July 1948; PS 22 to South Vietnam on 29 Nov 1961, PS 19 on 11 July 1966, and PS 23 in June 1970. PS 19 and 22 to Philippines Nov 1975 and PS 23 in Apr 1976.

CEBU — *Philippine Navy*

2 Ex-US "ADMIRABLE" CLASS

Name	No.	Builders	Commissioned
MAGAT SALAMAT (ex-*Chi Lang II,* ex-USS *Gayety, MSF 239*)	PS 20	Winslow Marine Railway & SB Co, Seattle, Wash	1944
DATU TUPAS (ex-*Chi Linh,* ex-USS *Shelter, MSF 301*)	PS 18	Winslow Marine Railway & SB Co, Seattle, Wash	1944

Displacement, tons: 650 standard; 945 full load
Dimensions, feet (metres): 180 wl; 184·5 oa × 33 × 9·75 *(59; 60·5 × 10·8 × 3·2)*
Guns: 1—3 inch *(76 mm)* 50 cal; 2—40 mm (single); up to 8—20 mm (twin)
Main engines: Diesel (Cooper Bessemer); 1 710 bhp; 2 shafts = 14 knots
Complement: approx 80

Launched 19 Mar 1944 and 14 Nov respectively. Minesweeping equipment has been removed. These ships are believed to have two 20 mm twin mounts at after end of bridge and one or two 20 mm twin mounts on quarterdeck.

Transfers: *Magat Salamat* transferred to South Vietnam in Apr 1962, and *Datu Tupas* Jan 1964. To Philippines Nov 1975.

MAGAT SALAMAT (old name) *1962, Vietnamese Navy*

LIGHT FORCES

5 Ex-US "PC 461" CLASS (LARGE PATROL CRAFT)

Name	No.	Builders	Commissioned
BATANGAS (ex-USS *PC 1134*)	PS 24	Defoe SB Corp	1943
NUEVA ECIJA (ex-USS *PC 1241*)	PS 25	Nashville Bridge Co	1943
CAPIZ (ex-USS *PC 1564*)	PS 27	Leathem D. Smith SB Corp	1944
NUEVA VISCAYA (ex-USAF *Altus*, ex-USS *PC 568*)	PS 80	Brown SB Co	1942
NEGROS ORIENTAL (ex-*E 312,* ex-*L'Inconstant, P 636,* ex-USS *PC 1171*)	PS 29	Leathem D. Smith SB Co	15 May 1943

Displacement, tons: 280 standard; 450 full load
Dimensions, feet (metres): 170 wl; 173·66 oa × 23 × 10·8 *(55·7; 56·9 × 7·5 × 3·5)*
Guns: 1—3 inch *(76 mm)* 50 cal; 1—40 mm; several—20 mm (single or twin)
A/S weapons: depth charges (except *Negros Oriental*)
Main engines: Diesels (General Motors); 2 800 bhp; 2 shafts = 20 knots
Complement: approx 70

Deletion: *Nueva Ecija* due for deletion in FY 1977.

Transfers: PS 24 and 27 transferred July 1948, PS 25 in Oct 1958 and PS 80 (which had served with USAF 1963-68) in Mar 1968. PS 29 to France in 1951, Khmer Republic 1956 and, after transferring to Philippines in 1975 acquired Dec 1976.

CAPIZ *Philippine Navy*

5 100 ft PGM TYPE (LARGE PATROL CRAFT)

Name	No.	Builders	Commissioned
AGUSAN	PG 61	Tacoma Boatbuilding Co, Washington	Mar 1960
CATANDUANES	PG 62	Tacoma Boatbuilding Co, Washington	Mar 1960
ROMBLON	PG 63	Tacoma Boatbuilding Co, Washington	June 1960
PALAWAN	PG 64	Tacoma Boatbuilding Co, Washington	June 1960
BASILAN (ex-*Hon Troc*)	PG 60	Petersen Builders, Wisconsin	—

Displacement, tons: 122 full load
Dimensions, feet (metres): 100·3 × 21·1 × 6·9 *(32·9 × 6·9 × 2·3)*
Guns: 1—40 mm; 4—20 mm (twins); 2—50 cal MG *(Basilan)*; 4—50 cal MGs remainder
Main engines: 2 Mercedes Benz diesels; 1 900 bhp; 2 shafts = 17 knots *(Basilan* 8 GM 6—71 diesels)
Complement: approx 15

Steel-hulled craft built under US military assistance programmes; PG 61-64 for the Philippines, PG 60 for South Vietnam. Assigned US PGM-series numbers while under construction. Transferred upon completion. *Basilan* transferred to South Vietnam in Apr 1967 and acquired by the Philippines Dec 1975.
These craft are lengthened versions of the US Coast Guard 85-foot "Cape" class patrol boat design. Heavier armament is provided in PG 60. No A/S weapons. PG 62 served for a period with the Coastguard and has returned to naval command.

ROMBLON *1968, Philippine Navy*

2 ITALIAN DESIGN (HYDROFOIL PATROL CRAFT)

Name	No.	Builders	Commissioned
CAMIGUIN	HB 77	Cantiere Navaltecnica, Messina	April 1965
SIQUIJOR	HB 76	Cantiere Navaltecnica, Messina	April 1965

Displacement, tons: 28
Dimensions, feet (metres): 15·3 (24·3 over foils) *(4·7 (7·4))* × 3·8 (8·9 foilborne) *(1·2 (2·7))*
Guns: MG
Main engines: Diesel (Mercedes Benz-MTU); 1 250 bhp; 2 shafts = 38 knots
Complement: 9

Laid down on 26 May and 28 Oct 1964. For military and police patrol.

CAMIGUIN *Philippine Navy*

2 HITACHI PT 32 DESIGN (HYDROFOIL PATROL CRAFT)

Name	No.	Builders	Commissioned
BALER	HB 75	Hitachi Zosen, Kanagawa	Dec 1966
BONTOC	HB 74	Hitachi Zosen, Kanagawa	Dec 1966

Displacement, tons: 32 full load
Dimensions, feet (metres): 68·9 × 15·7 (24·6 over foils) *(21 × 4·8, 7·5)*
Guns: MG can be mounted fore and aft; normally unarmed
Main engines: Ikegai-Mercedes Benz (MTU) diesel; 3 200 bhp = 37·8 knots (32 cruising). Also auxiliary engine
Complement: 14

For smuggling prevention. Also used as inter-island ferries. Based on Schertel-Sachsenburg foil system.

BALER on foils   *Philippine Navy*

6 + ? 74 52 ft De HAVILLAND TYPE (COASTAL PATROL CRAFT)

Of 52 ft GRP hulls with 2 diesels of 1 800 hp. Reported capable of 48 (?) knots. First six built by De Havillands, Sydney NSW. In Aug 1975 80 further craft of this design were reported as ordered from Marcelo Yard, Manila to be delivered 1976-78 at the rate of two per month. This total is therefore assumed to include the original 6. Up-to-date this delivery rate is reported as being kept.

15 SWIFT (Mk 1 and 2) TYPE (COASTAL PATROL CRAFT)

PCF 300	PCF 308	PCF 313
PCF 301	PCF 309	PCF 314
PCF 303	PCF 310	PCF 315
PCF 306	PCF 311	PCF 316
PCF 307	PCF 312	PCF 317

Displacement, tons: 22·5 full load
Dimensions, feet (metres): 50 × 13·6 × 4 *(15·2 × 4·5 × 1·3)* (Mk 1 300-303)
51·3 ft *(15·6)* (Mk 2 306-316)
Guns: 2—50 cal MG (twin)
Main engines: 2 geared diesels (General Motors); 860 bhp; 2 shafts = 28 knots

Most built in the United States. PCF 303 served in US Navy prior to transfer to the Philippines; others built for US military assistance programmes. PCF 300 and 301 transferred to Philippines in Mar 1966, PCF 303 in Aug 1966, PCF 306-313 in Feb 1968, PCF 314-316 in July 1970. PCF 317 built in 1970 in the Philippines (ferro concrete) with enlarged superstructure used as yacht for Señora Marcos.

PCF 310   *1969, Philippine Navy*

13 IMPROVED SWIFT TYPE (COASTAL PATROL CRAFT)

PCF 318	PCF 323	PCF 337
PCF 319	PCF 333	PCF 338
PCF 320	PCF 334	PCF 339
PCF 321	PCF 336	PCF 340
PCF 322		

Displacement, tons: 33 full load
Dimensions, feet (metres): 65 oa × 16 × 3·4 *(21·3 × 5·2 × 1·1)*
Guns: 2—50 cal MG (twin); 2—30 cal MG (single)
Main engines: 3 diesels (General Motors); 1 590 bhp; 3 shafts = 25 knots
Complement: 8

Improved Swift type inshore patrol boats built by Sewart for the Philippine Navy. First six delivered Jan-June 1972, 333 and 334 in Apr 1975, 337 and 338 in July 1975, 336 in Nov 1975 and 339 and 340 in Dec 1976.

2 COASTAL PATROL CRAFT

Name	No.
ABRA	FB 83
BUKINDON	FB 84

Displacement, tons: 40 standard
Dimensions, feet (metres): 87·5 oa × 19 × 4·75 *(28·6 × 6·2 × 1·9)*
Guns: 2—20 mm
Main engines: Diesels (Mercedes-Benz/MTU); 2 460 bhp; 2 shafts = approx 25 knots
Complement: 15 (3 officers, 12 men)

Abra built Singapore. Completed 8 Jan 1970. *Bukindon* completed Cavite 1970-71. Wood hulls and aluminium superstructure.

MINEWARFARE FORCES

2 Ex-US MSC TYPE

Name	No.	Builders	Commissioned
ZAMBALES (ex-USS *MSC 218*)	PM 55	Bellingham Shipyard, Washington	7 Mar 1956
ZAMBOANGA DEL NORTE (ex-USS *MSC 219*)	PM 56	Bellingham Shipyard, Washington	23 Apr 1956

Displacement, tons: 320 light; 385 full load
Dimensions, feet (metres): 144 oa × 28 × 8·2 *(47·2 × 9·2 × 2·7)*
Guns: 2—20 mm (twin)
Main engines: 2 diesels; 880 bhp; 2 shafts = 12 knots
Complement: approx 40

Built by the United States specifically for transfer under the military aid programme. Wood hull with non-magnetic metal fittings.

ZAMBALES

AMPHIBIOUS FORCES

27 Ex-US LST TYPE

Name	No.	Commissioned
BULACAN (ex-USS *LST 843*)	LT 38	1945
ALBAY (ex-USS *LST 865*)	LT 39	1945
MISAMIS ORIENTAL (ex-USS *LST 875*)	LT 40	1945
MAQUINDANAO (ex-USS *Caddo Parish, LST 515*)	LT 96	1944
CAGAYAN (ex-USS *Hickman County, LST 825*)	LT 97	1945
ILOCOS NORTE (Ex-USS *Madera County, LST 905*)	LT 98	1945
MINDORO OCCIDENTAL (ex-USNS *T-LST 222*)	LT 93	1944
SURIGAO DEL NORTE (ex-USNS *T-LST 488*)	LT 94	1944
SURIGAO DEL SUR (ex-USNS *T-LST 546*)	LT 95	1942
CAMBOANGA DEL SUR	LT 86	1945
(ex-*Cam Ranh*, ex-USS *Marion County, LST 975*)		
— (ex-*Thi Nai*, ex-USS *Cayuga County, LST 529*)	ex-HQ 502	1944
— (ex-*Nha Trang*, ex-USS *Jerome County, LST 848*)	ex-HQ 505	1943
— (ex-USNS *T-LST 47*)		1943
— (ex-USNS *T-LST 230*)		1944
— (ex-USNS *T-LST 287*)		1944
— (ex-USNS *T-LST 491*)		1943
— (ex-USNS *T-LST 566*)		1944
— (ex-USNS *T-LST 607*)		Mar 1944
— (ex-USNS *Dagger County, T-LST 689*)		1944
— (ex-USNS *Davies County, T-LST 692*)		1944
— (ex-*Can Tho*, ex-USS *Garrett County,*		1944
AGP 786, ex-*LST 786*)		
— (ex-*My Tho*, ex-USS *Harnett County,*		1944
AGP 821, ex-*LST 821*)		
— (ex-USNS *Harris County, T-LST 822*)		1945
— (ex-USNS *Hillsdale County, LST 835*)		1944
— (ex-USNS *Nansemond County, T-LST 1064*)		1945
— (ex-USNS *Orleans Parish, T-LST 1069*, ex-*MSC 6*,		1945
LST 1069)		
— (ex-USNS *T-LST 1072*)		1945

Displacement, tons: 1 620 standard; 2 366 beaching; 4 080 full load
Dimensions, feet (metres): 316 wl; 328 oa × 50 × 14 *(103·6; 107·5 × 19 × 4·9)*
Guns: 7 or 8—40 mm (1 or 2 twin, 4 or 5 single); several 20 mm in former Vietnamese ships; former USNS ships are unarmed
Main engines: Diesels (General Motors); 1 700 bhp; 2 shafts = 11·6 knots
Complement: varies; approx 60 to 110 (depending upon employment)

CAGAYAN   11/1976, Dr. Giorgio Arra

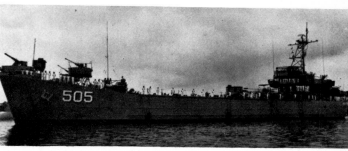

Ex-NHA TRANG (tripod mast)

Cargo capacity 2 100 tons. Many of these ships served as cargo ships in the Western Pacific under the US Military Sealift Command (USNS/T-LST); they were civilian manned by Korean and Japanese crews.
The ex-HQ 505 and some of the later USNS ships have tripod masts; others have pole masts. The USNS ships lack troop accommodations and other amphibious warfare features. Many of these ships are used for general cargo work in Philippine service.

Transfers: LT 38-40 transferred to the Philippines in July 1948; LT 96-98 on 29 Nov 1969; LT 93-95 on 15 July 1972; 502, 505 transferred from US Navy to South Korean Navy in Apr 1962, Dec 1963 and Apr 1970 respectively, and acquired by the Philippines in 1976. Ex-US 689, 835 and 1064 were transferred to Japan in Apr 1961 and thence to Philippines in 1975—remainder transferred from USN in 1976 with exception of ex-*My Tho* and ex-*Can Tho* which were used as light craft repair ships in South Vietnam and have retained amphibious capability (transferred to Vietnam 1970 and to Philippines 1976).

4 Ex-US "LSM-1" CLASS

Name	No.	Commissioned
ISABELA (ex-USS *LSM 463*)	LP 41	1945
ORIENTAL MINDORO (ex-USS *LSM 320*)	LP 68	1944
WESTERN SAMAR	LP 66	1945
(ex-*Hat Giang*, ex-*LSM 9011*, ex-USS *LSM 335*)		
BATANES (ex-*Huong Giang*, ex-USS *Oceanside, LSM 175*)	LP 65	1944

Displacement, tons: 743 beaching; 1 095 full load
Dimensions, feet (metres): 196·5 wl; 203·5 oa × 34·5 × 8·5 *(60·4; 66·7 × 11·3 × 2·7)*
Guns: 2—40 mm (twin); several 20 mm
Main engines: Diesels; 2 800 bhp; 2 shafts = 11·6 knots
Complement: approx 70

LP 41 transferred to the Philippines in Mar 1961 and LP 68 in Apr 1962; LP 66 originally transferred from US Navy to French Navy for use in Indochina in 1954; subsequently transferred to South Vietnam in Dec 1955; LP 65 transferred from US Navy to South Vietnam on 1 Aug 1961. Acquired by the Philippines in Nov 1975.
LP 66 was fitted as hospital ship (LSM-H) for treating casualties retaining her armament. Has deck houses in and above well-deck.

WESTERN SAMAR (Old pennant number)   *Vietnamese Navy*

4 Ex-US "LSSL-1" CLASS

Name	No.	Commissioned
SULU (ex-*LSSL 96*)	LS 49	1944
CAMARINES SUR (ex-*Niguyen Duc Bong*, ex-US *LSSL 129*)	LS 48	1945
— (ex-Japanese, ex-US *LSSL 68*)	—	1944
— (ex-Japanese, ex-US *LSSL 87*)	—	1944

Displacement, tons: 227 standard; 383 full load
Dimensions, feet (metres): 158 oa × 23·7 × 5·7 *(51·8 × 7·8 × 1·8)*
Guns: 1—3 inch; 4—40 mm; 4—20 mm; 4 MG
Main engines: Diesel; 1 600 bhp; 2 shafts = 14 knots
Complement: 60

Former US Navy landing ships support; designed to provide close-in-fire support for amphibious assaults, but suitable for general gunfire missions.
Ex-*Doan Ngoc Tang* (ex-US *LSSL 9*) was transferred to France in 1951 *(Hallebarde* L. 9023) transferred to Japan 1956-1964; returned and transferred to South Vietnam in 1965. Acquired by Philippines for spares 1975 as was ex-*Lulu Phu Tho* (ex-US *LSSL 101*). LS 48 and 49 and ex-US *LSSL 68* transferred 17 Nov 1975. Ex-US *LSSL 87* transferred Sept 1976.

CAMARINES SUR (old pennant number)   *Vietnamese Navy*

4 Ex-US LSIL TYPE

Name	No.	Commissioned
MARINDUQUE (ex-US *LSIL 875*)	LS 36	1944
SERSOGON	LS 37	1944
(ex-*Thien Kich* ex-*L 9038*, ex-US *LSIL 872*)		
CAMARINES NORTE	LF 52	1944
(ex-*Loi Cong* ex-*L 9034*, ex-US *LSIL 699*)		
MISAMIS OCCIDENTAL	LF 53	1944
(ex-*Tam Set* ex-*L 9033*, ex-US *LSIL 871*)		

Displacement, tons: 227 standard; 383 full load
Dimensions, feet (metres): 158 oa × 22·7 × 5·3 *(51·8 × 7·6 × 1·7)*
Guns: 1—3 inch; 1—40 mm; 2—20 mm; 4 MG; and up to 4 army mortars (2—81 mm; 2—60 mm)
Main engines: Diesel; 1 600 bhp; 2 shafts = 14·4 knots
Complement: 55

Designed to carry 200 troops. LF 53 originally transferred to France in 1951 and others in 1953 for use in Indochina; subsequently retransferred in 1956 to South Vietnam. All acquired by the Philippines in Nov 1975. Ex-US *LSIL 476* transferred for spares at same time.

SERSOGON (old pennant number)

11 Ex-US "LCM-8" CLASS

TKM 90-1, TKM 90-2, LCM 257, 258, 260-266.

TKMs transferred Mar 1972, 257 and 258 June 1973, remainder June 1975.

50 Ex-US "LCM-6" CLASS

LCM 224-227, 229, 231-234, 237, 239, 240, 249, 255, 256, 259 + 34

One transferred in 1955, thirteen in 1971-73, twenty-four in Nov 1975, remaining dozen 1973-75.

7 Ex-US "LCVP" CLASS

LCVP 175, 181 + 5

Five to be scrapped or sold in FY 1977. Two transferred in 1955-56, one in 1965, two in 1971 and 175 and 181 in June 1973.

3 Ex-US "LCU" CLASS

Ex US-LCU 1603, 1604, 1606

Transferred from Japan Nov 1 1975.

SERVICE FORCES

2 Ex-US "ACHELOUS" CLASS (REPAIR SHIPS)

Name	No.	Commissioned
KAMAGONG (ex-*Aklan*, ex-USS *Romulus*, ARL 22, ex-*LST 926*)	AR 67	1944
NARRA (ex-USS *Krishna*, ARL, 38, ex-*LST 1149*)	AR 88	1945

Displacement, tons: 4 100 full load
Dimensions, feet (metres): 316 wl; 328 oa × 50 × 14 *(103·6; 107·5 × 16·4 × 4·6)*
Guns: 8—40 mm (2 quad)
Main engines: Diesels (General Motors); 1 700 bhp; 2 shafts = 11·6 knots
Complement: approx 220

Converted during construction. Extensive machine shop, spare parts stowage, supplies, etc.

Transfers: AR 67 transferred to the Philippines in Nov 1961 and AR 88 on 31 Oct 1971.

KAMAGONG   *1968, Philippine Navy*

1 PRESIDENTIAL YACHT

Name	No.	Builders	Commissioned
ANG PANGULO	TP 777	Ishikawajima, Japan	1959
(ex-*The President*, ex-*Roxas*, ex-*Lapu-Lapu*)			

Dimensions, feet (metres): 275 oa × 42·6 × 21 *(90 × 13·9 × 6·9)*
Guns: 2—20 mm
Main engines: Diesels; 5 000 bhp; 2 shafts = 18 knots
Complement: approx 90

Built as war reparation; launched in 1958. Used as presidential yacht and command ship. Originally named *Lapu-Lapu* after the chief who killed Magellan; renamed *Roxas* on 9 Oct 1962 after the late Manuel Roxas, the first President of the Philippines Republic, renamed *The President* in 1957 and *Ang Pangulo* in 1975.

ANG PANGULO   *11/1976, Dr. Giorgio Arra*

1 Ex-US "ADMIRABLE" CLASS (PRESIDENTIAL YACHT)

Name	No.	Builders	Commissioned
MOUNT SAMAT (ex-*Pagasa*,	TK 21	Gulf Shipbuilding Corp	25 Oct 1944
ex-*Santa Maria*, ex-*Pagasa*,			
ex-*APO 21*, ex-USS *Quest*, AM 281)			

Displacement, tons: 650 standard; 945 full load
Dimensions, feet (metres): 190 oa × 33 × 9·8 *(57·9 × 10·8 × 3·2)*
Guns: 2—20 mm
Main engines: Diesels (Cooper Bessemer); 1 710 bhp; 2 shafts = 14·8 knots
Complement: approx 60

Former US Navy minesweeper (AM). Commissioned on 25 Oct 1944. Transferred to the Philippines in July 1948. Used as presidential yacht and command ship.

MOUNT SAMAT   *1971*

1 YACHT

Name	No.	Builders	Commissioned
—	—	Vosper Thornycroft, Singapore	Dec 1975

Dimensions, feet (metres): 212·3 × 38 × 6 *(64·7 × 11·6 × 1·8)*
Main engines: 2 diesels; 7 500 hp = 28·5 knots

1 Ex-US YON TYPE

Ex-US YON 279

Transferred Dec 1975.

6 Ex-US YO/YOG TYPE (TANKERS)

Name	No.	Commissioned
LAKE MAINIT (ex-US YO 118)	YO 35	1943
LAKE NAUJAN (ex-US YO 173)	YO 43	1943
LAKE BUHI (ex-US YOG 73)	YO 78	1944
— (Ex-US YO 115)	—	—
— (Ex-US YO 116)	—	—
— (Ex-US YOG 61)	—	—

Ex-YOG 80   1971, Vietnamese Navy

Displacement, tons: 520 standard; approx 1 400 full load
Dimensions, feet (metres): 174 × 32 × 15 *(57 × 10·5 × 4·9)*
Guns: several 20 mm
Main engines: Diesels; 560 bhp; 1 shaft = 8 knots

Former US Navy harbour oiler (YO) and gasoline tankers (YOG). Cargo capacity 6 570 barrels. YO 43 carries fuel oil and the YO 78 gasoline and diesel oil.

Deletions: Two craft from S. Vietnam ex-*YOG 33* and ex-*YOG 80* accepted for scrapping and spare parts.

Transfers: YO 43 transferred to the Philippines in July 1948 YO 78 in July 1967 and YO 35 in July 1975. Ex-*YO 115, YO 116,* and *YOG 61* transferred from US Navy to the Philippines on 16 July 1975.

4 Ex-US YW TYPE (WATER CARRIERS)

Name	No.
LAKE LANAO (ex-US YW 125)	YW 42
LAKE BULUAN (ex-US YW 111)	YW 33
LAKE PAOAY (ex-US YW 130)	YW 34
— (ex-US YN 103)	—

Displacement, tons: 1 235 full load
Dimensions, feet (metres): 174 oa × 32 × 15 *(57 × 10·5 × 4·9)*
Guns: 2—20 mm
Main engines: Diesel, 560 bhp; 1 shaft = 8 knots

Basically similar to YOG type but adapted to carry fresh water. Cargo capacity 200 000 gallons. *Lake Lanao* transferred to the Philippines in July 1948; others on 16 July 1975.

1 Ex-US COAST GUARD "BALSAM" CLASS (TENDER)

Name	No.	Builders	Commissioned
KALINGA (ex-USCGC Redbud, WLB 398, ex-USNS Redbud, T-AKL 398)	TK 89	Marine Iron & Shipbuilding Co, Duluth	11 Sep 1943

Displacement, tons: 935 standard
Dimensions, feet (metres): 180 oa × 37 × 13 *(59 × 12·1 × 4·3)*
Guns: Unarmed
Main engines: Diesel-electric; 1 200 bhp; 1 shaft = 13 knots

Originally US Coast Guard buoy tender (WAGL 398). Transferred to US Navy on 25 Mar 1949 as AG 398; redesignated AKL 398 on 31 Mar 1949; transferred to Military Sea Transportation Service on 20 Feb 1952 (T-AKL 398); reacquired by Coast Guard on 20 Nov 1970; transferred to Philippines 17 May 1972.

1 Ex-US C1-M-AV1 TYPE (SUPPORT SHIP)

Name	No.	Builders	Commissioned
MACTAN (ex-USCGC Kukui, WAK 186, ex-USS Colquitt, AK 174)	TK 90	Froemming Brothers, Milwaukee	22 Sep 1945

Displacement, tons: 4 900 light; 5 636 full load
Dimensions, feet (metres): 320 wl; 338·5 oa × 50 × 18 *(104·9; 110·9 × 16·4 × 5·9)*
Guns: 2—20 mm
Main engines: Diesel (Nordberg); 1 750 bhp; 1 shaft = 11·5 knots

Commissioned in US Navy on 22 Sep 1945; transferred to the US Coast Guard two days later. Subsequently served as Coast Guard supply ship in Pacific until transferred to Philippines on 1 March 1972. Used to supply military posts and lighthouses in the Philippine archipelago.

1 LIGHTHOUSE TENDER

PEARL BANK (ex-US Army LO 4, ex-Australian MSL)

Displacement, tons: 160 standard; 300 full load
Dimensions, feet (metres): 120 oa × 24·5 × 8 *(39·3 × 8 × 2·6)*
Main engines: Diesels (Fairbanks Morse); 240 bhp; 2 shafts = 7 knots

Originally an Australian motor stores lighter; subsequently transferred to the US Army and then to the Philippines. Employed as a lighthouse tender.

4 Ex-US ARMY FS TYPE (BUOY TENDERS)

Name	No.
BOJEADOR (ex-US Army FS 203)	TK 46
LAUIS LEDGE (ex-US Army FS 185)	TK 45
LIMASAWA (ex-USCGC Nettle WAK 129, ex-US Army FS 169)	TK 79
— (ex-Japanese, ex-US Army FS 408)	—

Displacement, tons: 470 standard; 811 full load
Dimensions, feet (metres): 180 oa × 23 × 10 *(60 × 7 × 3)*
Main engines: Diesels; 1 000 shp; 1 shaft = 11 knots

Former US Army freight and supply ships. Employed as tenders for buoys and lighthouses. Ex-*FS 408* transferred Nov. 1976.

LAUIS LEDGE   1969, Philippine Navy

1 TUG: Ex-US ATR TYPE

Name	No.	Launched
IFUGAO (ex-HMS Emphatic, ex-US ATR 96)	AQ 44	27 Jan 1944

Displacement, tons: 783 full load
Dimensions, feet (metres): 134·6 wl; 143 oa × 33·8 × 13·5 *(44·1; 46·9 × 11 × 4·4)*
Guns: 1—3 inch *(76 mm)* 50 cal; 2—20 mm
Main engines: Diesel; 1 500 bhp; 1 shaft = 13 knots

US-built rescue tug transferred to Royal Navy upon launching; subsequently returned to US Navy and retransferred to the Philippines in July 1948.

IFUGAO

1 TUG: Ex-US ARMY

TIBOLI (ex-US Army *LT 1976*) YQ 58

Transferred Mar 1976.

6 TUGS: Ex-US "YTL 422" CLASS

IGOROT (ex-*YTL 572*) YQ 222   **ILONGOT** (ex-*YTL 427*) YQ 225
TAGBANUA (ex-*YTL 429*) YQ 223   **TASADAY** (ex-*YTL 425*) YG 226
— (ex-*YTL 750*) —   —(ex-*YTL 748*)—

Former US Navy 66-foot harbour tugs.

Ex-748 and 750 transferred from Japan—17 Nov 1975 and 24 Sept 1976 respectively.

5 FLOATING DOCKS

YD 200 (ex-*AFDL 24*)   **YD 203** (ex-*AFDL 3682*)   **YD 205** (ex-*ADFL 44*)
YD 201 (ex-*AFDL 3681*)   **YD 204** (ex-*AFDL 20*)

Floating dry docks built in the United States; three are former US Navy units with YD 200 transferred in July 1948, YD 204 in Oct 1961, and YD 205 in Sep 1969; two other units built specifically for Philippine service were completed in May 1952 and Aug 1955, respectively.

2 FLOATING CRANES

YU 206 (ex-US *YD 163*)   **YU 207** (ex-US *YD 191*)

SURVEY SHIPS

Operated by Coast and Geodetic Service of Ministry of National Defence.

Name	No.	Builders	Commissioned
ATYIMBA	—	Walkers, Maryborough, Australia	1969

Displacement, tons: 611 standard; 686 full load
Dimensions, feet (metres): 161 × 33 × 12 *(49·1 × 10 × 3·7)*
Guns: 2—20 mm
Main engines: 2 Paxman Diesels; 726 bhp = 11 knots
Range, miles: 5 000 at 8 knots
Complement: 54

Similar to HMAS *Flinders* with differences in displacement and use of davits aft instead of cranes.

ATYIMBA   *1976, Dr. Giorgio Arra*

Name	No.	Builders	Commissioned
PATHFINDER	—	—	1909

Displacement, tons: 1 057
Guns: 2—20 mm
Complement: 69

Ex-US Coastguard vessel. Date of transfer unknown.

Name	No.	Builders	Commissioned
ALUNYA	—	Walkers, Maryborough, Australia	1964
ARINYA	—	Walkers, Maryborough, Australia	1962

Displacement, tons: 245 full load
Dimensions, feet (metres): 90 pp × 22 × 10·5 *(27·4 × 6·7 × 3·2)*
Main engines: 2 diesels; 336 bhp = 10 knots

Coaster type with raised quarter deck.

COASTGUARD

The Coast Guard operates 40 ft Coastal Patrol Craft numbered from CGC 100 to CG 132. Of these the majority are of US construction although several come from foreign builders.

POLAND

Headquarters Appointments

Commander-in-Chief of the Polish Navy:
Vice-Admiral Ludwik Janczyszyn

Chief of the Naval Staff:
Rear-Admiral Henryk Pietraszkiewicz

Diplomatic Representation

Naval, Military and Air Attaché in London:
Colonel Henryk Krzeszowski
Naval, Military and Air Attaché in Washington:
Colonel Henryk Nowaczyk
Naval, Military and Air Attaché in Moscow:
Brigadier General Waclaw Jagas
Naval, Military and Air Attaché in Paris:
Colonel Marian Bugaj

Personnel

(a) 1977: 25 000 (2 800 officers and 22 200 men)
(b) 3 years National Service

Bases

Gdynia, Hel, Swinoujscie.

Naval Aviation

There is a Fleet Air Arm of about 50 fixed-wing aircraft (mainly MiG-17 and IL-28) and helicopters.

Prefix to Ships' Names

ORP, standing for *Okrety Polska Rzeczpospolita*

Mercantile Marine

Lloyd's Register of Shipping:
733 vessels of 3 263 206 tons gross

Strength of the Fleet

Including WOP (Coastguard)

Type	Active
Destroyer	1
Submarines—Patrol	4
Fast Attack Craft—Missile	12
Fast Attack Craft—Torpedo	21
	(some as targets)
Large Patrol Craft	26
Coastal Patrol Craft	3
Minesweepers—Ocean	24
Minesweeping Boats	20
LCTs	23
LCPs	15+
Surveying Vessel	1
AGI	1
Training Ships	7
Salvage Ships	2
Tankers	6
TRVs	Several
Tugs	20
DGVs	3
Miscellaneous	40

DELETIONS

Destroyers

1974 *Blyskawica* (museum ship in Gdynia in place of *Burza)*
1975 *Grom* and *Wicher* (ex-"Skory" class) now immobile AA batteries at Gdynia.

Corvettes

1973 *Czuiny, Wytrwaly, Zawziety, Zrezczny, Zwinny, Zwrotny*
1974 *Grozny, Nieugiety* ("Kronshtadt" class)

Fast Attack Craft—Torpedo

1973 3 "P 6" class
1974 6 "P 6" class
1975 4 "P 6" class

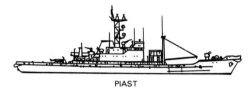

PIAST

DESTROYERS

1 Ex-SOVIET "SAM KOTLIN" CLASS

WARSZAWA (ex-*Spravedlivy*) 275

Displacement, tons: 2 850 standard; 3 885 full load
Length, feet (metres): 415·0 *(126·5)* oa
Beam, feet (metres): 42·3 *(12·9)*
Draught, feet (metres): 16·1 *(4·9)*
Missile launchers: 1 twin SA-N-1 (Goa) aft
Guns: 2—5·1 in (1 twin); 4—45 mm (quad)
A/S weapons: 2—16 barrelled MBU
Torpedo tubes: 5—21 in *(533 mm)* (quin)
Main engines: Geared turbines; 2 shafts; 72 000 shp
Oil fuel, tons: 800
Range, miles: 5 500 at 16 knots
Speed, knots: 36
Complement: 285

Transferred from the USSR to the Polish Navy in 1970.

Radar: Air Search: Head Net A.
Fire Control: Peel Group (SA-N-1), Wasp Head/Sun Visor B (main armament), Hawk Screech.
IFF: High Pole B.

WARSZAWA

5/1975, C. and S. Taylor

SUBMARINES

4 Ex-SOVIET "WHISKEY" CLASS

BIELIK 295	**ORZEL** 292
KONDOR 294	**SOKOL** 293

Displacement, tons: 1 030 surfaced; 1 350 dived
Length, feet (metres): 249·3 *(76)*
Beam, feet (metres): 22 *(6·7)*
Draught, feet (metres): 15 *(4·6)*
Torpedo tubes: 6—21 in *(533 mm)*, (4 bow, 2 stern) 12 torpedoes carried
Mines: 40 mines in lieu of torpedoes
Main machinery: Diesel-electric; 2 diesels; 4 000 hp; 2 shafts; Electric motors; 2 500 hp
Speed, knots: 17 surfaced; 15 dived
Range, miles: 13 000 at 8 knots (surfaced)
Complement: 60

Built in the USSR and transferred to the Polish Navy.

Radar: Snoop Plate.

SOKOL

1971, Polish Navy

KONDOR

1972

LIGHT FORCES

12 Ex-SOVIET "OSA" CLASS
(FAST ATTACK CRAFT—MISSILE)

Displacement, tons: 165 standard; 200 full load
Dimensions, feet (metres): 128·7 × 25·1 × 5·9 *(39·3 × 7·7 × 1·8)*
Missiles: 4 launchers for SS-N-2
Guns: 4—30 mm (2 twin, 1 forward, 1 aft)
Main engines: 3 diesels; 13 000 bhp = 32 knots
Range, miles: 800 at 25 knots
Complement: 25

Most pennant numbers are in the 140-150 series and are carried on side-boards on the bridge

Radar: Search: Square Tie. Fire control: Drum Tilt.

"OSA" Class   1969

15 "WISLA" CLASS (FAST ATTACK CRAFT—TORPEDO)

Displacement, tons: 70 full load
Dimensions, feet (metres): 82·0 × 18·0 × 6·0 *(25 × 5·5 × 1·8)*
Guns: 2—30 mm (twin)
Torpedo tubes: 4—21 in *(533 mm)*
Main engines: Diesels; speed 30 knots

Polish built in a continuing programme since early 1970s. Most pennant numbers in 490 series but include 463.

"WISLA" Class   1975, S. Breyer

6 Ex-SOVIET "P 6" CLASS
(FAST ATTACK CRAFT—TORPEDO)

Displacement, tons: 66 standard; 75 full load
Dimensions, feet (metres): 84·2 × 20 × 6 *(25·7 × 6·1 × 1·8)*
Guns: 4—25 mm; 8 DC
Torpedo tubes: 2—21 in *(533 mm)*
Main engines: 4 diesels; 4 800 bhp = 45 knots
Complement: 25

Acquired from the USSR in 1957-58. Torpedo tubes removed in some. At least two have been converted to target craft with reflectors similar to E. German variant.

Radar: Skin Head surface search.

"P 6" Class   1971, Polish Navy

5 "OBLUZE" CLASS (LARGE PATROL CRAFT)

Name	No.	Builders	Commissioned
—	349	Oksywie Shipyard	1965
—	350	Oksywie Shipyard	1965
—	351	Oksywie Shipyard	1965
—	352	Oksywie Shipyard	1966
—	353	Oksywie Shipyard	1966

Displacement, tons: 170
Dimensions, feet (metres): 143·0 × 19·0 × 7·0 *(42 × 6 × 2·1)*
Guns: 4—30 mm (2 twins)
A/S weapons: 2 internal DC racks
Main engines: 2 diesels = 20 knots

Some belong to WOP (Coastguard).

Sonar: Tamirio RN 231. Drum Tilt (not WOP craft).

"OBLUZE" Class (old number)   1969

8 "MODIFIED OBLUZE" CLASS (LARGE PATROL CRAFT)

301	302	303	304	305	306	307	308

Displacement, tons: 150
Dimensions, feet (metres): 137·8 × 19 × 6·6 *(41 × 6 × 2)*
Guns: 4—30 mm
A/S weapons: 2 internal DC racks
Main engines: 2 diesels = 20 knots

Slightly smaller than original "Obluze" class. Built late 1960s.

Radar: RN 231 search. Drum Tilt.

Modified "OBLUZE" Class   *1972, S. Breyer*

4 "OKSYWIE" CLASS (LARGE PATROL CRAFT)

336	337	338	339

Displacement, tons: 170 standard
Dimensions, feet (metres): 134·5 × 19·0 × 6·9 *(41 × 6 × 2)*
Guns: 2—37 mm; 4—12·7 mm
A/S weapons: 2 DC racks
Main engines: Diesels; speed = 20 knots

This class and the other Polish-built large patrol craft are all based on German R-boat hull design with variations in the superstructure. The first of class was, in fact, an R-boat. Built 1962-64.

Sonar: Tamirio.

"OKSYWIE" Class (old pennant number)   *1972*

"OKSYWIE" Class   *M. Soroka*

9 "GDANSK" CLASS (LARGE PATROL CRAFT)

340-348

Displacement, tons: 120
Dimensions, feet (metres): 124·7 × 19·2 × 5·0 *(35 × 5·8 × 1·5)*
Guns: 2—37 mm; 2—12·7 mm (twin)
A/S weapons: DC rails
Main engines: Diesels = 20 knots

Built in Poland in 1960. Belong to WOP (Coastguard).

Sonar: Tamirio.

"GDANSK" Class (old pennant number)   *1970*

"GDANSK" Class   *M. Soroka*

3 "PILICA" CLASS (COASTAL PATROL CRAFT)

701	702	703

Displacement, tons: 100 (approx)
Guns: 2—25 mm (twin)
Main engines: 2 diesels = 15 knots

Built in Poland in 1973. Belong to WOP (Coastguard).

MINE WARFARE FORCES

12 "KROGULEC" CLASS (MINESWEEPERS—OCEAN)

Name	No.	Builders	Commissioned
ORLIK	643	Stocznia Yard, Gdynia	1964
KROGULEC	644	Stocznia Yard, Gdynia	1963
JASTRAB	645	Stocznia Yard, Gdynia	1964
KORMORAN	646	Stocznia Yard, Gdynia	1963
CZAPLA	647	Stocznia Yard, Gdynia	1964
ALBATROS	648	Stocznia Yard, Gdynia	1965
PELIKAN	649	Stocznia Yard, Gdynia	1965
TUKAN	650	Stocznia Yard, Gdynia	1966
KANIA	651	Stocznia Yard, Gdynia	1966
JASKOLKA	652	Stocznia Yard, Gdynia	1966
ZURAW	653	Stocznia Yard, Gdynia	1967
CZALPA	654	Stocznia Yard, Gdynia	1967

PELIKAN (old pennant number)   5/1975, C. and S. Taylor

Displacement, tons: 500
Dimensions, feet (metres): 190·3 × 24·6 × 8·2 *(58 × 8·4 × 2·5)*
Guns: 6—25 mm (twins)
Main engines: Diesels = 16 knots

12 SOVIET "T 43" CLASS (MINESWEEPERS—OCEAN)

Name	No.	Builders	Commissioned
BIZON	635	Stocznia, Gdynia	1958
BOBR	636	Stocznia, Gydnia	1959
DELFIN	638	Stocznia, Gdynia	1960
DZIK*	634	Stocznia, Gdynia	1958
FOKA	639	Stocznia, Gdynia	1960
LOS*	633	Stocznia, Gdynia	1957
MORS	640	Stocznia, Gdynia	1961
ROSOMAK	637	Stocznia, Gdynia	1959
RYS	641	Stocznia, Gdynia	1961
TUR*	632	Stocznia, Gdynia	1957
ZBIK	642	Stocznia, Gdynia	1962
ZUBR*	631	Stocznia, Gdynia	1957

* 58 metre class.

DELFIN (old pennant number)   1969, Polish Navy

Displacement, tons: 500 standard; 610 full load (*); 630 (remainder)
Dimensions, feet (metres): 190·2 × 28·2 × 6·9 *(58 × 8·6 × 2·1)* (*) 197 ft *(60 m)* (remainder)
Guns: 4—37 mm (twins); 4—25 mm (twins); 4—14·5 mm (twins)
A/S weapons: 2 DC throwers
Minelaying: Can lay mines
Main engines: 2 diesels; 2 shafts; 2 000 hp = 17 knots
Range, miles: 1 600 at 10 knots
Complement: 40

20 "K 8" CLASS (MINESWEEPING BOATS)

Displacement, tons: 40 standard; 60 full load
Dimensions, feet (metres): 55·8 × 11·5 × 4 *(17 × 3·5 × 1·2)*
Guns: 2—25 mm (twin); 2 MG (twin)
Mines: Can lay mines
Main engines: 2 diesels; 2 shafts; 600 hp = 18 knots
Complement: 18

Now obsolescent and due for deletion.

AMPHIBIOUS FORCES

23 "POLNOCNY" CLASS (LCT)

BALAS	**JANOW**	**NARWIK**	
GRUNWALD 811	**LENIN**	**WARTA**	+ 17

Displacement, tons: 780 standard; 1 000 full load
Dimensions, feet (metres): 239·4 × 29·5 × 9·98 *(73 × 9 × 3)*
Guns: 4—30 mm (twin); 2—18 barrelled 140 mm rocket launchers
Main engines: 2 diesels; 5 000 bhp = 18 knots

Polish built in Gdansk, but same as the Soviet "Polnocny" class—can carry six tanks. Of various types including Polish variations. Pennant numbers—811/832 and 882.

Radar: Drum Tilt.

"POLNOCNY" Class (old pennant number)   1971

15 + LCPs

Length, feet (metres): 70 *(21·3)* approx
Gun: 1—30 mm

Pennant numbers in 500 series. Introduced 1975.

LCP   8/1975

SURVEYING VESSEL

1 "MOMA" CLASS

KOPERNIK

Displacement, tons: 1 240 standard; 1 800 full load
Dimensions, feet (metres): 240 × 32·8 × 13·2 *(73·2 × 10 × 4)*
Main engines: Diesels = 16 knots

INTELLIGENCE VESSEL

1 B 10 TYPE

BALTYK

Displacement, tons: 1 200
Measurements, tons: 658 gross; 450 deadweight
Dimensions, feet (metres): 194·3 oa × 29·5 × 14 *(59·2 × 9·0 × 4·3)*
Main engines: Steam; 1 000 hp = 11 knots

Trawler of B-10 type. Built in 1954 in Gdansk. Converted and structure altered.

BALTYK   *1968*

TRAINING SHIPS

2 "WODNIK" CLASS

ELEW   ISKRA

Displacement, tons: 2 000 approx
Dimensions, feet (metres): 239·4 × 39·4 × ?16·4 *(73 × 12 × ?5)*
Guns: 4—30 mm (twin); 2—25 mm (twin)
Speed, knots: 17

Built in early 1970s at Gdynia.

"WODNIK" Class   *9/1976, MOD*

1 "MOMA" CLASS

NAVIGATOR

Details as for *Kopernik* above. Commissioned June 1975. Navigational training ship.

NAVIGATOR   *4/1976, S. Breyer*

3 "BRIZA" CLASS

BRIZA
KADET
PODCHORAZY

Displacement, tons: 150
Dimensions, feet (metres): 98·4 × 9·8 × 6·4 (30 × 7 × 2)
Main engines: Diesels = 10 knots
Complement: 11 plus 26 cadets

Podchorazy commissioned 30 Nov 1974, *Briza* 5 March 1975 and *Kadet* July 1975.

1 SAIL TRAINING SHIP

Name	No.	Builders	Commissioned
— (ex-*Iskra*, ex-*Pigmy*, ex-*Iskra*, ex-*St. Blanc*, ex-*Vlissingen*)	—	Muller, Foxhol, Holland	1917

Displacement, tons: 560
Dimensions, feet (metres): 128 × 25 × 10 (39 × 7·6 × 3·0)
Main engines: Diesels; 250 bhp = 7·5 knots
Complement: 30, plus 40 cadets

A three masted schooner with auxiliary engines. Launched in 1917. Cadet training ship. Now used for harbour training.

— (ex-*Gryf*, ex-*Zetempowiec*, ex-*Opplem*, ex-*Omsk*, ex-*Empire Contees*, ex-*Irene Oldendorf*)

Apart from holding the record in this book for name changes this 1 959 ton ship launched in 1944, is now an alongside—accommodation ship for cadets.

TANKERS

3 "MOSKIT" CLASS

KRAB Z 3	MEDUSA Z 8	SLIMAK Z 9

Displacement, tons: approx 700
Guns: 2—30 mm (Twin)

Z 5	Z 6	Z 7

Lighters of 300 tons gross with diesels, converted into tankers for coastal service.

SALVAGE SHIPS

Name	No.	Builders	Commissioned
PIAST	—	Stocznia, Gdansk	26 Jan 1974
LECH	—	Stocznia, Gdansk	30 Nov 1974

Displacement, tons: 1 560 standard; 1 732 full load
Dimensions, feet (metres): 240 × 32·8 × 13·1 (73·2 × 10 × 4)
Guns: 8—25 mm (twins)
Main engines: 2 ZGODA diesels; 3 800 shp; 2 shafts
Speed, knots: 16·5
Range, miles: 3 000 at 12 knots

Carry a diving bell. Basically a "Moma" class hull.

TORPEDO RECOVERY VESSELS

Some of a new class, including K 11, have been reported.

TUGS

Some 20 of various classes with H pennant numbers.

DEGAUSSING VESSELS

SD 11/13

A new class of d.g.vs of which details are not yet available.

AUXILIARIES

Ex-AGI *Kompas* now used as a barrack ship. Some 18 small diving craft.
Hydrograt and *Kontroller,* of 30 and 80 tons are civilian-operated survey craft.
Icebreaker *Perkun* of 800 is civilian-operated but available for naval use.
Some fifteen other tenders.

PORTUGAL

Headquarters Appointment

Chief of Naval Staff:
Admiral A. S. Silva Cruz

Diplomatic Representation

Naval Attaché in London:
Captain P. M. Guerra Corujo
Naval Attaché in Washington:
Captain Jose L. Ferreira Lamas
Naval Attaché in Paris:
Captain Pedro Azevedo Coutinho

Personnel

(a) 1977: 12 000 including marines
(b) 3 years National Service

Naval Bases

Main Base: Lisbon
Dockyard: Arsenal do Alfeite

Maritime Reconnaissance Aircraft

Whilst there are no aircraft belonging to the Navy, P2V Neptunes of the Portuguese Air Force are placed under naval operational control for specific maritime operations.

Prefix to Ships' Names

NRP

Mercantile Marine

Lloyd's Register of Shipping:
431 vessels of 1 173 710 tons gross

Strength of the Fleet

Type	Active	Building
Frigates	17	—
Submarines (Patrol)	3	—
Large Patrol Craft	10	—
Coastal Patrol Craft	8	—
Minesweepers (Coastal)	4	—
LCT	1	—
LCMs	12	—
LCA	1	—
Survey Ships and Craft	4	—
Replenishment Tanker	1	—
Sail Training Ship	1	—
Ocean Tug	1	—
Harbour Tugs	2	—
Harbour Tanker	1	—

DELETIONS

(See ANGOLA section)

Frigates

1970	Francisco de Almeida, Pacheco Pereira
1971	Alvares Cabral, Vasco da Gama
1975	Pero Escobar

Corvettes

1971	Cacheu
1973	Porto Sante, Fogo, Maio ("Maio" class)
1975	Boavista, Brava, Santa Luzia ("Maio" class)
1976	Sao Nicolau

Submarine

1975	Cachalote ("Daphne" class) (to Pakistan)

Amphibious Forces

1975	Alfanage, Ariete, Cimitarra ("Alfange" class LCTs)
	LDM 401-411, 413-417 ("400" class LCMs)
	LDM 304, 309 ("300" class LCMs)
	LDM 204 ("200" class LCM)
	LDM 101, 102, 105-118 ("100" class LCMs)
	LDP 301-303, 201, 203-217, 107, 108 (21 LCAs)
1976	Bombarda (LDG), Montanee, Bacamarte ("Alfange" class

Survey Ships

1975	Almirante Lacerda, Cavalho Araujo, Cruzeiro do Sul
1976	Pedro Nunes

Service Forces

1975	Sam Bras (Fleet Supply Ship) (now used as accommodation ship), Santo André
1976	São Rafael

Minesweepers

1973	Angra do Heroismo, Ponta Delgada, S. Pedro (MSC), Corvo, Pico, Graciosa, S. Jorge (MSO)
1975	Lajes, Santa Cruz (MSC)
1976	Horta, Velas, Vila do Porto

Light Forces

1975	Cassiopeia, Escorpião, Lira, Orion, Pegaso ("Argos" class)
	Sabre (River patrol craft)
	Albufeira, Aljezur, Alvor ("Alvor" class)
	Aldebaran, Altair, Arcturus, Bellatrix, Espiga, Fomalhaut, Pollux, Procion, Rigel, Sirius and Vega ("Bellatrix" class)
	Jupiter, Marte, Mercurio, Saturno, Urano and Venus ("Jupiter" class)
	Antares (Coastal patrol craft)
	Azevia, Corvina, Dourada ("Azevia" class)
1976	Argos, Centauro, Dragao, Hidra, Sagitario ("Argos" class) (some to Angola)
	Condor ("Albatroz" class), Castor, Regulus, Bicuda ("Azevia" class)

PENNANT LIST

F (Frigates)

F 471	Antonio Enes
F 472	Almirante Pereira Da Silva
F 473	Almirante Gago Coutinho
F 474	Almirante Magalhaes Correia
F 475	João Coutinho
F 476	Jacinto Candido
F 477	Gen. Pereira d'Eca
F 480	Comandante João Belo
F 481	Comandante Hermenegildo Capelo
F 482	Comandante Roberto Ivens
F 483	Comandante Sacadura Cabral
F 484	Augusto de Castilho
F 485	Honorio Barreto
F 486	Baptista de Andrade
F 487	João Roby
F 488	Afonso Cerqueira
F 489	Oliveira Ecarmo

S (Submarines)

S 163	Albacora
S 164	Barracuda
S 166	Delfin

M (Minewarfare Forces)

M 401	Sao Roque
M 402	Ribeira Grande
M 403	Lagoa
M 404	Rosario

LD (Amphibious Forces)

LDG 202	Alabarda
LDM 119-121	
LDM 406	
LDM 414	
LDM 418-424	
LDP 216	

P (Light Forces and Corvettès)

P 370	Rio Minho
P 1140	Cacine
P 1141	Cunene
P 1142	Mandovi
P 1143	Rovuma
P 1144	Cuanza
P 1145	Geba
P 1146	Zaire
P 1147	Zambese
P 1148	Dom Aleixo
P 1149	Dom Jeremias
P 1160	Limpopo
P 1161	Save
P 1162	Albatroz
P 1163	Acor
P 1164	Andorinha
P 1165	Aguia
P 1167	Cisne

A (Service Forces)

A 520	Sagres
A 521	Schultz Xavier
A 526	Afonso de Albuquerque
A 527	Almeida Carvalho
A 5200	Mira
A 5206	São Gabriel

"COMANDANTE JOAO BELO" Class   "ALMIRANTE PEREIRA DA SILVA" Class

"JOAO COUTINHO" Class

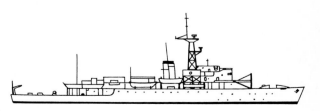

ALFONSO DE ALBUQUERQUE

FRIGATES

4 "COMANDANTE JOÀO BELO" CLASS

Name	No.	Builders	Laid down	Launched	Commissioned
COMANDANTE HERMENEGILDO CAPELO	F 481	At et Ch de Nantes	13 May 1966	29 Nov 1966	26 April 1968
COMANDANTE JOÀO BELO	F 480	At et Ch de Nantes	6 Sep 1965	22 Mar 1966	1 July 1967
COMANDANTE ROBERTO IVENS	F 482	At et Ch de Nantes	13 Dec 1966	8 Aug 1967	23 Nov 1968
COMANDANTE SACADURA CABRAL	F 483	At et Ch de Nantes	18 Aug 1967	15 Mar 1968	25 July 1969

Displacement, tons: 1 990 standard; 2 230 full load
Length, feet (metres): 321·5 *(98)* pp; 338 *(103·0)* oa
Beam, feet (metres): 37·7 *(11·5)*
Draught, feet (metres): 14·5 *(4·42)*
Guns: 3—3·9 in *(100 mm)* single; 2—40 mm
A/S weapons: 1—12 in quadruple mortar
Torpedo tubes: 6—21·7 in *(550 mm)* A/S (triple)
Main engines: SEMT/Pielstick diesels; 2 shafts; 18 760 bhp
Speed, knots: 25
Range, miles: 4 500 at 15 knots; 2 300 at 25 knots
Complement: 200 (14 officers, 186 men)

Construction: The prefabricated construction of these frigates was begun on 1 Oct 1964.

Design: They are similar to the French "Commandant Rivière" class except for the 30 mm guns which were replaced by 40 mm guns.

Radar: Search: DRBV 22A
Tactical: DRBV 50
Fire Control: DRBC 31D
Navigation: Decca RM 316

Sonar: Search: SQS 17A
Attack: DUBA-3A

COMANDANTE ROBERTO IVENS   1970, Portuguese Navy

COMANDANTE SACADURA CABRAL   1972, Portuguese Navy

3 "ALMIRANTE PEREIRA DA SILVA" CLASS

Name	No.	Builders	Laid down	Launched	Commissioned
ALMIRANTE GAGO COUTINHO	F 473 (ex-US *DE 1042*)	Estaleiros Navais (Lisnave), Lisbon	2 Dec 1963	13 Aug 1965	29 Nov 1967
ALMIRANTE MAGALHÃES CORREA	F 474 (ex-US *DE 1046*)	Estaleiros Navais de Viana do Castelo	30 Aug 1965	26 April 1966	4 Nov 1968
ALMIRANTE PEREIRA DA SILVA	F 472 (ex-US *DE 1039*)	Estaleiros Navais (Lisnave), Lisbon	14 June 1962	2 Dec 1963	20 Dec 1966

Displacement, tons: 1 450 standard; 1 914 full load
Length, feet (metres): 314·6 *(95·9)*
Beam, feet (metres): 36·68 *(11·18)*
Draught, feet (metres): 17·5 *(5·33)*
Guns: 4—3 in *(76 mm)* 50 cal
A/S weapons: 2 Bofors 4-barrelled 375 mm rocket launchers;
6 (2 triple) Mk 32 A/S torpedo tubes
Main engines: De Laval dr geared turbines; 1 shaft; 20 000 shp
Boilers: 2 Foster Wheeler, 300 psi, 850°F
Speed, knots: 27
Oil fuel, tons: 400
Range, miles: 3 220 at 15 knots
Complement: 166 (12 officers, 154 men)

Construction: The prefabrication of *Almirante Pereira da Silva* and *Almirante Gago Coutinho* was begun in 1961 at Lisnave (formerly Navais Shipyard, Lisbon) and of *Almirante Magalhães Correa* in 1962.

Design: Similar to the United States destroyer escorts of the "Dealey" class, but modified to suit Portuguese requirements.

Radar: Search: MLA-1b.
Fire control: AN/SPG 34 (on 3 in mounts)
Navigational: Decca RM 316P
Tactical: Type 978.
Extensive EW.

Sonar: Search: AN/SQS 30-32A. AN/SQA 10A (VDS).
Attack: DUBA-3A.

ALMIRANTE GAGO COUTINHO   1976, Michael D. J. Lennon

10 "JOÃO COUTINHO" CLASS

Name	No.	Builders	Laid down	Launched	Commissioned
ALFONSO CERQUEIRA	F 488	Empresa Nacional Bazan, Spain	1973	6 Oct 1973	26 June 1975
ANTONIO ENES	F 471	Empresa Nacional Bazan, Spain	Apr 1968	16 Aug 1969	18 June 1971
AUGUSTO DE CASTILHO	F 484	Empresa Nacional Bazan, Spain	Aug 1968	4 July 1969	14 Nov 1970
BAPTISTA DE ANDRADE	F 486	Empresa Nacional Bazan, Spain	1972	Mar 1973	19 Nov 1974
GENERAL PEREIRA D'ECA	F 477	Blöhm and Voss AG, Hamburg, Germany	Oct 1968	26 July 1969	10 Oct 1970
HONORIO BARRETO	F 485	Empresa Nacional Bazan, Spain	July 1968	11 April 1970	15 April 1971
JACINTO CANDIDO	F 476	Blöhm and Voss AG, Hamburg, Germany	April 1968	16 June 1970	16 June 1970
JOÃO COUTINHO	F 475	Blöhm and Voss AG, Hamburg, Germany	Sep 1968	2 May 1969	7 Mar 1970
JOÃO ROBY	F 487	Empresa Nacional Bazan, Spain	1972	3 June 1973	18 Mar 1975
OLIVEIRA E. CARMO	F 489	Empresa Nacional Bazan, Spain	1972	Feb 1974	Feb 1975

Displacement, tons: 1 203 standard; 1 380 full load
Length, feet (metres): 227·5 *(84·6)*
Beam, feet (metres): 33·8 *(10·3)*
Draught, feet (metres): 11·8 *(3·6)*
Missiles: 2 MM 38 Exocet in 486-489
Guns: 2—3 in *(76 mm)* (twin); 2—40 mm (first six);
1—3·9 in *(100 mm)* 50 cal; 2 Bofors 40 mm (single) (486-489)
A/S weapons: 1 Hedgehog; 2 DC throwers (first six); 2 DC
racks; (2 triple Mk 32 torpedo tubes in 486-489)
Main engines: 2 OEW 12 cyl Pielstick diesels; 10 560 bhp
Speed, knots: 24·4
Range, miles: 5 900 at 18 knots
Complement: 100 (9 officers, 91 men) plus marine detachment
of 34

Fire control: 40 m Mk 51 GFCS (first six)

Radar: In first six:
Air Search: MLA-1B.
Navigation: Decca TM 626.
Main guns: On-mounted radar SPG-34 (Mk 63 GFCS).
In 486-489:
Air Search: Plessey AWS-2.
Navigation: Decca TM 626.
Gun Fire Control: Thomson CSF Pollux.

OLIVEIRA E. CARMO   3/1976, Michael D. J. Lennon

SUBMARINES

3 FRENCH "DAPHNE" CLASS

Name	No.	Builders	Laid down	Launched	Commissioned
ALBACORA	S 163	Dubigeon-Normandie	6 Sep 1965	13 Oct 1966	1 Oct 1967
BARRACUDA	S 164	Dubigeon-Normandie	19 Oct 1965	24 Apr 1967	4 May 1968
DELFIN	S 166	Dubigeon-Normandie	14 May 1967	23 Sep 1968	1 Oct 1969

Displacement, tons: 700 standard; 869 surfaced; 1 043 dived
Length, feet (metres): 189·6 *(57·8)*
Beam, feet (metres): 22·3 *(6·8)*
Draught, feet (metres): 15·1 *(4·6)*
Torpedo tubes: 12—21·7 in *(550 mm);* (8 bow, 4 stern)
Main machinery: SEMT-Pielstick diesels, 1 300 bhp; Electric
motors; 450 kW, 1 600 hp; 2 shafts
Speed, knots: 13·2 surfaced; 16 dived
Oil fuel, tons: 90
Range, miles: 2 710 at 12·5 knots surfaced; 2 130 at 10 knots
snorting
Complement: 50 (5 officers; 45 men)

The prefabricated construction of these submarines was
begun between 1 Oct 1964 and 6 Sep 1965 at the Dubigeon-
Normandie Shipyard. They are basically similar to the French
"Daphne" type, but slightly modified to suit Portuguese
requirements.

Transfer: *Cachalote* transferred to Pakistan as *Ghazi* 1975.

DELFIN   1972, Portuguese Navy

LIGHT FORCES

10 "CACINE" CLASS (LARGE PATROL CRAFT)

Name	No.	Builders	Commissioned
CACINE	P 1140	Arsenal do Alfeite	1969
CUNENE	P 1141	Arsenal do Alfeite	1969
CUANZA	P 1144	Estaleiros Navais do Mendogo	May 1969
GEBA	P 1145	Estaleiros Navais do Mendogo	May 1969
LIMPOPO	P 1160	Arsenal do Alfeite	April 1973
MANDOVI	P 1142	Arsenal do Alfeite	1969
ROVUMA	P 1143	Arsenal do Alfeite	1969
SAVE	P 1161	Arsenal do Alfeite	May 1973
ZAIRE	P 1146	Estaleiros Navais do Mendogo	Nov 1970
ZAMBEZE	P 1147	Estaleiros Navais do Mendogo	1971

Displacement, tons: 292·5 standard; 310 full load
Dimensions, feet (metres): 144·0 oa × 25·2 × 7·1 *(44 × 7·7 × 2·2)*
Guns: 2—40 mm; 1—32 barrelled rocket launcher 37 mm
Main engines: 2 MTU 12V 538 Maybach (MTU) diesels; 4 000 bhp = 20 knots
Range, miles: 4 400 at 12 knots
Complement: 33 (3 officers, 30 men)

Radar: KH 975.

CACINE   1973, Portuguese Navy

2 "DOM ALEIXO" CLASS (COASTAL PATROL CRAFT)

Name	No.	Builders	Commissioned
DOM ALEIXO	P 1148	S. Jacintho Aveiro	7 Dec 1967
DOM JEREMIAS	P 1149	S. Jacintho Aveiro	22 Dec 1967

Displacement, tons: 62·6 standard; 67·7 full load
Dimensions, feet (metres): 82·1 oa × 17·0 × 5·2 (25 × 5·2 × 1·6)
Gun: 1—20 mm
Main engines: 2 Cummins diesels; 1 270 bhp = 16 knots
Complement: 10 (2 officers, 8 men)

Dom Aleixo in use as survey craft.

Radar: Decca 303.

DOM JEREMIAS   1973, Portuguese Navy

5 "ALBATROZ" CLASS (COASTAL PATROL CRAFT)

Name	No.	Builders	Commissioned
ACOR	P 1163	Arsenal do Alfeite	1974
AGUIA	P 1165	Arsenal do Alfeite	1975
ALBATROZ	P 1162	Arsenal do Alfeite	1974
ANDORINHA	P 1164	Arsenal do Alfeite	1975
CISNE	P 1167	Arsenal do Alfeite	1974

Displacement, tons: 45
Dimensions, feet (metres): 72 × 17 × 5 (23·6 × 5·6 × 1·6)
Guns: 1—20 mm; 2—50 cal MGs
Main engines: 2 Cummins diesels; 1 100 hp
Speed, knots: 20
Range, miles: 2 500 at 12 knots
Complement: 8 (1 officer, 7 men)

Radar: Decca RM 316P.

1 COASTAL PATROL CRAFT

Name	No.	Builders	Commissioned
RIO MINHO	P 370	Arsenal do Alfeite	1957

Displacement, tons: 14
Dimensions, feet (metres): 49·2 × 10·5 × 2·3 (15 × 3·2 × 0·7)
Guns: 2 light MG
Main engines: 2 Alfa Romeo diesels; 130 bhp = 9 knots
Complement: 7

Built for the River Minho on the Spanish border.

MINE WARFARE FORCES

4 "SAO ROQUE" CLASS (MINESWEEPERS—COASTAL)

Name	No.	Builders	Commissioned
LAGOA	M 403	CUF Shipyard, Lisbon	10 Aug 1956
RIBEIRA GRANDE	M 402	CUF Shipyard, Lisbon	8 Feb 1957
ROSARIO	M 404	CUF Shipyard, Lisbon	8 Feb 1956
SAO ROQUE	M 401	CUF Shipyard, Lisbon	6 June 1956

Displacement, tons: 394·4 standard; 451·9 full load
Dimensions, feet (metres): 140·0 (42·7) pp; 152·0 oa × 28·8 × 7·0 (46·3 × 8·8 × 2·3)
Guns: 2—20 mm (twin)
Main engines: 2 Mirrlees diesels; 2 shafts; 2 500 bhp = 15 knots
Complement: 47 (4 officers, 43 men)

Similar to British "Ton" class coastal minesweepers, laid down on 7 Sep 1954, under the OSP-MAP. *Lagoa* and *Sao Roque* were financed by USA and other two by Portugal. 40 mm gun removed 1972.

LAGOA (before change of armament)   1972, Portuguese Navy

AMPHIBIOUS FORCES

1 "BOMBARDA" CLASS LDG (LCT)

Name	No.	Builders	Commissioned
ALABARDA	LDG 202	Estaleiros Navais do Mondego	1970

Displacement, tons: 510 standard; 652 full load
Dimensions, feet (metres): 184·3 × 38·7 × 6·2 (56·2 × 11·8 × 1·9)
Main engines: 2 Maybach-Mercedes Benz (MTU) diesels; 910 hp = 9·5 knots
Range, miles: 2 600 at 9·5 knots
Complement: 20 (2 officers, 18 men)

Radar: Decca RM 316.

BOMBARDA (ALABARDA similar)   1972, Portuguese Navy

9 "LDM 400" CLASS (LCM)

LDM 406	LDM 414	LDM 418	LDM 419	LDM 420
LDM 421	LDM 422	LDM 423	LDM 424	

1 "LDP 200" (Ex-LD) CLASS (LCA)

Name	No.	Builders	Commissioned
—	LDP 216	Estaleiros Navais do Mondego	5 Feb 1969

Displacement, tons: 12 light; 18 full load
Dimensions, feet (metres): Length: 46 oa (14)
Main engines: 2 diesels; 187 bhp

3 "LDM 100" CLASS (LCM)

LDM 119	LDM 120	LDM 121

Displacement, tons: 50 full load
Dimensions, feet (metres): Length: 50 (15·25)
Main engines: 2 diesels; 450 bhp

All built at the Estaleiros Navais do Mondego in 1965.

SURVEY SHIPS

1 NEW CONSTRUCTION OCEANOGRAPHIC SHIP

Displacement, tons: 1 140
Dimensions, feet (metres): 196·8 × 39·4 × 15·1 *(60 × 12 × 4·6)*
Main engines: Diesel

Ordered 1976 from Arsenal do Alfeite.

1 Ex-US "KELLAR" CLASS

Name	*No.*	*Builders*	*Commissioned*
ALMEIDA CARVALHO	A 527	Marietta Shipbuilding Co.	31 Jan 1969
(ex-USNS *Kellar*, T-AGS 25)			

Displacement, tons: 1 200 standard; 1 400 full load
Dimensions, feet (metres): 190 oa × 39·0 × 15·0 *(58 × 11·7 × 4·5)*
Main engines: Diesel-electric; 1 shaft; 1 200 hp = 15 knots
Complement: 30 (5 officers, 25 men)

Laid down on 20 Nov 1962, launched on 30 July 1964. On loan from the US Navy since 21 Jan 1972.

Radar: One RCA CRM-N2A-30.
One Decca TM 829.

Name	*No.*	*Builders*	*Commissioned*
ALFONSO DE ALBUQUERQUE	A 526	Wm. Pickersgill & Sons Ltd,	10 Feb 1949
(ex-HMS *Dalrymple*,		Sunderland and	
ex-HMS *Luce Bay*)		HM Dockyard, Devonport	

Displacement, tons: 1 590 standard; 2 230 full load
Length, feet (metres): 286·0 *(87·2)* pp; 307·0 *(93·6)* oa
Beam, feet (metres): 38·5 *(11·7)*
Draught, feet (metres): 14·2 *(4·3)*
Main engines: 4-cylinder triple expansion; 2 shafts; 5 500 ihp
Speed, knots: 19·5
Boilers: 2 Admiralty 3-drum type
Range, miles: 7 055 at 9·1 knots
Complement: 109 (9 officers, 100 men)

Modified "Bay" class frigate. Built by Wm. Pickersgill & Sons Ltd, Sunderland, but completed at HM Dockyard, Devonport. Laid down on 29 April 1944. Launched on 12 April 1945. Purchased from Great Britain in April 1966.

DOM ALEIXO

See Light Forces section for details.

MIRA (ex-*Fomalhaut*, ex-*Arrabida*) A 5200

Displacement, tons: 30 standard
Dimensions, feet (metres): 62·9 × 15·2 × 4 *(19·2 × 4·6 × 1·2)*
Main engines: 3 Perkins diesels; 300 bhp = 15 knots
Range, miles: 650 at 8 knots (economical speed)
Complement: 6 men

Launched 1961. No radar.

SERVICE FORCES

1 REPLENISHMENT TANKER

Name	*No.*	*Builders*	*Commissioned*
SÃO GABRIEL	A 5206	Estaleiros de Viana do Castelo	27 Mar 1963

Displacement, tons: 9 000 standard; 14 200 full load
Measurement, tons: 9 854 gross; 9 000 deadweight
Dimensions, feet (metres): 452·8 pp; 479·0 oa × 59·8 × 26·2 *(138; 146 × 18·2 × 8)*
Main engines: 1 Pametrada-geared turbine; 1 shaft; 9 500 shp = 17 knots
Boilers: 2
Range, miles: 6 000 at 15 knots
Complement: 98 (10 officers, 88 men)

Radar: Search: AN/SPS 6C.
Navigation: KH 975.

SÃO GABRIEL   *1973, Portuguese Navy*

1 TRAINING SHIP

Name	*No.*	*Builders*	*Commissioned*
SAGRES (ex-*Guanabara*,	A 520	Blöhm & Voss, Hamburg	1 Feb 1938
ex-*Albert Leo Schlageter*)			

Displacement, tons: 1 725 standard; 1 869 full load
Dimensions, feet (metres): 293·5 oa × 39·3 × 17·0 *(89·5 × 12 × 4·6)*
Main engines: 2 MAN auxiliary diesels; 1 shaft; 750 bhp = 10 knots
Oil fuel, tons: 52
Range, miles: 3 500 at 6·5 knots
Complement: 153 (10 officers, 143 men)

Former German sail training ship. Built by Blöhm & Voss, Hamburg. Launched in June 1937 and completed on 1 Feb 1938. Sister of US Coast Guard training ship *Eagle* (ex-German *Horst Wessel*) and Soviet *Tovarisch*. Taken by USA as a reparation after the Second World War in 1945 and sold to Brazil in 1948. Purchased from Brazil and commissioned in the Portuguese Navy on 2 Feb 1972 at Rio de Janeiro and renamed *Sagres*.
Sail area 20 793 sq ft. Height of main-mast 142 ft.

SAGRES   *1973, Portuguese Navy*

1 HARBOUR TANKER

BC 3 (ex-US *YO 194*)

Transferred April 1962.

TUGS

1 OCEAN TUG

Name	No.	Builders	Commissioned
SCHULTZ XAVIER	A 521	Alfeite Naval Yard	14 July 1972

Displacement, tons: 900
Main engines: 2 Diesels; 2 shafts; 2 400 hp = 14·5 knots
Range, miles: 3 000 at 12·5 knots

A dual purpose ocean tug and buoy/lighthouse tender ordered late in 1968.

2 HARBOUR TUGS

RB 1 (ex-*ST 1994*)   **RB 2** (ex-*ST 1996*)

Transferred from US Navy—RB 1 Dec 1961, RB 2 March 1962.

QATAR

Now possesses an expanding Marine Police Division of the Qatar Police Force. The geographical position of the state, dividing the Persian Gulf and covering Bahrain, gives this force added importance. The main oil-terminal is at Umm-Said.

Senior Officer

Commander Naval Force:
  Captain K. Lee-White

Mercantile Marine

Lloyd's Register of Shipping:
  13 vessels of 75 747 tons gross

Personnel

(a) 1977: 400 officers and men
(b) Voluntary

Base

Doha

6 VOSPER THORNYCROFT 103 ft TYPE
(LARGE PATROL CRAFT)

Name	No.	Builders	Commissioned	
AL KHATAB	Q 15	Vosper Thornycroft Ltd	22 Jan	1976
AL WUSAAIL	Q 14	Vosper Thornycroft Ltd	28 Oct	1975
BARZAN	Q 11	Vosper Thornycroft Ltd	13 Jan	1975
HWAR	Q 12	Vosper Thornycroft Ltd	30 Apr	1975
TARIQ	Q 16	Vosper Thornycroft Ltd	1 Mar	1976
THAT ASSUARI	Q 13	Vosper Thornycroft Ltd	3 Oct	1975

Displacement, tons: 120
Dimensions, feet (metres): 103·7 pp; 109·7 oa × 21 × 5·5 *(31·1; 32·4 × 6·3 × 1·6)*
Guns: 2—20 mm
Main engines: 2 Diesels; 4 000 hp = 27 knots
Complement: 25

Ordered in 1972-73. All laid down between Sept 1973 and Nov 1974.

AL WUSAAIL   *12/1974, C and S Taylor*

2 75 ft COASTAL PATROL CRAFT

Length, feet (metres): 75 *(22·5)*
Guns: 2—20 mm
Main engines: 2 Diesels; 1 420 hp

Built by Whittingham and Mitchell, Chertsey 1969.

3 KEITH NELSON 45 ft TYPE
(COASTAL PATROL CRAFT)

Displacement, tons: 13
Dimensions, feet (metres): 44 × 12·3 × 3·8 *(13·5 × 3·8 × 1·1)*
Guns: 1—12·7 mm; 2—7·62 mm (singles)
Main engines: 2 Caterpillar diesels; 800 hp = 26 knots
Complement: 6

25 FAIREY MARINE "SPEAR" CLASS
(COASTAL PATROL CRAFT)

Displacement, tons: 4·3
Dimensions, feet (metres): 29·8 × 9 × 2·8 *(9·1 × 2·8 × 0·8)*
Guns: 3—7·62 mm
Main engines: 2 Diesels; 290 hp; 2 shafts = 26 knots
Complement: 4

First seven ordered early 1974. Delivered 19 June 1974, 16 Sept 1974, 18 Sept 1974, 2 Nov 1974, Dec 1974, Jan 1975, Feb 1975. Contract for further five signed December 1975. Third contract for three fulfilled with delivery of two on 30 June 1975 and one on 14 July 1975. Fourth order for ten (4 Mk 1—6 Mk 2) received Oct 1976 and delivery effected Apr 1977.

FAIREY MARINE SPEARS   *1974, Fairey Marine*

2 FAIREY MARINE "INTERCEPTOR" CLASS
(FAST ASSAULT/RESCUE CRAFT)

Displacement, tons: 1¼
Dimensions, feet (metres): 25 × 8 × 2·5 *(7·9 × 2·4 × 0·8)*
Main engines: 2 Johnson outboard motors; 270 bhp = 35 knots
Range, miles: 150 at 30 knots
Complement: 3

In assault role can carry 10 troops. In rescue role carry number of life rafts. GRP catamaran hull. Delivered 28 Nov 1975.

RAS AL KHAIMAH
(See United Arab Emirates)

It is reported that up to five small patrol craft have been acquired.

ROMANIA

Headquarters Appointment

Commander in Chief of the Navy:
Rear Admiral Sebastian Ulmeanu

Diplomatic Representation

Defence Attaché in London:
Colonel C. Popa
Naval, Military and Air Attaché in Washington:
Colonel Nicolae Gheorghe Plesa

Bases

Mangalia, Constanta, Dulcea (Danube base)

Strength of the Fleet

(No details of building programme available)

Type	Active
Corvettes	3
Large Patrol Craft	3
Fast Attack Craft (Missile)	5
Fast Attack Craft (Gun and Patrol)	18
Fast Attack Craft (Torpedo)	22
River Patrol Craft	9
Coastal Patrol Craft	19
Minesweepers (Coastal)	4
Minesweepers (Inshore)	10
MSBs	8
Training Ship	1
Tugs	2

(Other unconfirmed vessels listed at end of section).

Personnel

(a) 1977: 10 000 officers and ratings
(including 2 000 Coastal Defence)
(b) 2 Years National Service

Lloyd's Register of Shipping:
161 vessels of 994 184 tons gross

CORVETTES

3 Ex-SOVIET "POTI" CLASS

V 31   V 32   V 83

Displacement, tons: 550 standard; 600 full load
Dimensions, feet (metres): 193·5 × 26·2 × 9·2 *(59 × 8 × 2·8)*
Guns: 2—57 mm (twin)
Torpedo tubes: 2—21 in *(533 mm)*
A/S weapons: 2—16 barrelled MBU 2 500
Main engines: 2 gas turbines; 2 diesels; 2 shafts; total 20 000 hp = 28 knots
Complement: 50

Transferred from the USSR in 1970.

Radar: Don, Strut Curve, Muff Cob.

"POTI" Class   1971

LIGHT FORCES

3 Ex-SOVIET "KRONSHTADT" CLASS
(LARGE PATROL CRAFT)

V-1   V-2   V-3

Displacement, tons: 310 standard; 380 full load
Dimensions, feet (metres): 170·6 × 21·5 × 9 *(52 × 6·5 × 2·7)*
Guns: 1—3·4 in; 2—37 mm (single); 6—12·7 mm (twins)
A/S weapons: 2 DC throwers; 2 depth charge racks
Main engines: 3 diesels; 3 shafts; 3 300 bhp = 24 knots
Range, miles: 1 500 at 12 knots
Complement: 65

Transferred by USSR in 1956.

Radar: Ball End.

"KRONSHTADT" Class

18 Ex-CHINESE "SHANGHAI" CLASS
(FAST ATTACK CRAFT—GUN and PATROL)

VP 20-29   VS 41-46   + 2

Displacement, tons: 120 standard; 155 full load
Dimensions, feet (metres): 128 × 18 × 5·6 *(39 × 5·5 × 1·7)*
Guns: VP type: 1—57 mm; 2—37 mm (twin). VS type: 1—37 mm; 4—14·5 mm MG
A/S weapons: VS type: 2—5 barrelled RBU 1200; 2 DC racks
Main engines: 4 diesels; 4 800 bhp = 30 knots
Complement: 25

Two variants of the "Shanghai" class of which the VS type (patrol A/S) is a new departure.
Built at Mangalia since 1973 in a continuing programme.

"SHANGHAI" Class—VS Type   8/1974

5 Ex-SOVIET "OSA" CLASS
(FAST ATTACK CRAFT—MISSILE)

194 to 198

Displacement, tons: 165 standard; 200 full load
Dimensions, feet (metres): 128·7 × 25·1 × 5·9 *(39·3 × 7·7 × 1·8)*
Missile launchers: 4 for SS-N-2
Guns: 4—30 mm (2 twin, 1 forward, 1 aft)
Main engines: 3 diesels; 13 000 bhp = 32 knots
Range, miles: 800 at 25 knots
Complement: 30

Transferred by USSR in 1964.

9 CHINESE "HU CHWAN" CLASS
(FAST ATTACK CRAFT—TORPEDO)

VT 51-53 + 6

Displacement, tons: 45
Dimensions, feet (metres): 70 × 16·5 × 3·1 *(21·4 × 5 × 1)*
Guns: 4—14·5 mm (twins)
Torpedo tubes: 2—21 in *(533 mp)*
Main engines: 2 Diesels; 2 200 hp = 55 knots (foilborne in calm conditions)
Range, miles: 500 cruising

Hydrofoils of the same class as the Chinese which were started in 1956.
Three with unknown pennant numbers imported from China. Further three (VT 51-53) locally built in a continuing programme which started 1973-74.

"HU CHWAN" Class   *8/1974*

13 Ex-SOVIET "P 4" CLASS
(FAST ATTACK CRAFT—TORPEDO)

87 to 92 + 7

Displacement, tons: 25
Dimensions, feet (metres): 62·7 × 11·6 × 5·6 *(19·1 × 3·5 × 1·7)*
Guns: 2—14·5 mm (twin)
Torpedo tubes: 2—18 in
Main engines: 2 diesels; 2 200 bhp = 50 knots
Complement: 12

Built in 1955-56. Becoming obsolescent and ready for deletion. One has had guns removed.

9 RIVER PATROL CRAFT

VB 76-82 + 2

Dimensions, feet (metres): 105 × 16 × 3 *(32 × 4·8 × 0·9)*
Guns: 1—85 mm; 1—37 mm; 4—14·5 mm (twins); 2—81 mm mortars
Complement: about 25

Built in Romania from 1973 in continuing programme.

RIVER PATROL CRAFT   *8/1974*

10 "VG" CLASS (COASTAL PATROL CRAFT)

Displacement, tons: 40
Dimensions, feet (metres): 52·5 × 14·4 × 4 *(16 × 4·4 × 1·2)*
Gun: 1—20 mm
Main engines: 2 Diesels; 600 hp = 18 knots
Complement: 10

Steel-hulled craft built at Galata in 1954. Obsolescent.

9 "SM 165" CLASS (COASTAL PATROL CRAFT)

SM 161-169

Locally built from 1954-56.

MINE WARFARE FORCES

4 Ex-GERMAN "M" CLASS (MINESWEEPERS—COASTAL)

DESCATUSARIA DB 13 **DEMOCRATIA** DB 15
DESROBIREA DB 14 **DREPTATEA** DB 16

Displacement, tons: 543 standard; 775 full load
Dimensions, feet (metres): 206·5 oa × 28 × 7·5 *(62·3 × 8·5 × 2·6)*
Guns: 6—37 mm (twin); 3—20 mm (singles)
A/S weapons: 2 DCT
Main engines: Triple expansion; 2 shafts; 2 400 ihp = 17 knots
Boilers: 2 three-drum water tube
Range, miles: 1 200 at 17 knots
Complement: 80

German "M Boote" design—designed as coal-burning minesweepers. Built at Galati. Converted to oil in 1951.

DEMOCRATIA and DREPTATEA *1968*

10 Ex-SOVIET "T 301" CLASS (MINESWEEPERS—INSHORE)

Displacement, tons: 150 standard; 180 full load
Dimensions, feet (metres): 128 × 18 × 4·9 *(39 × 5·5 × 1·5)*
Guns: 2—37 mm; 4—12·7 mm MG (twins)
Main engines: 2 diesels; 1 440 bhp; 2 shafts = 17 knots
Complement: 30

Transferred to Romania by the USSR in 1956-60. Probably half of these are non-operational. Two deleted 1975.

8 Ex-POLISH "TR-40" CLASS (MSBs)

VD-241   VD-242   VD-243   VD-244   VD-245   VD-246   VD-247   VD-248

Displacement, tons: 50 standard; 70 full load
Dimensions, feet (metres): 92 × 13·6 × 2·5 *(28 × 4·1 × 0·7)*
Guns: 2 MG (twin)
Main engines: 2 Diesels; 2 shafts = 14 knots
Complement: 18

Employed on shallow water and river duties. These were originally a Polish class begun in 1955 but completed in Romania in late 1950s.

TUGS

2 "ROSLAVL" CLASS

VITEAZUL RM 101 **VOINICUL** —

Displacement, tons: 450
Dimensions, feet (metres): 135 × 29·3 × 11·8 *(41·2 × 8·9 × 3·6)*
Main engines: Diesels; 1 250 hp = 12·5 knots
Complement: 28

Built in Galata shipyard 1953-54.

TRAINING SHIP

Name	No.	Builders	Commissioned
MIRCEA	—	Blohm & Voss, Hamburg	29 Mar 1939

Displacement, tons: 1 604
Dimensions, feet (metres): 239·5 oa; 267·3 (with bowsprit) × 39·3 × 16·5 *(73; 81·5 × 12 × 5)*
Sail area: 18 830 sq ft
Main engines: Auxiliary MAN 6-cylinder Diesel; 500 bhp = 9·5 knots
Complement: 83 + 140 midshipmen for training

Laid down on 30 April 1938. Launched on 22 Sep 1938. Refitted at Hamburg in 1966.

MIRCEA *1970, Michael D. J. Lennon*

MISCELLANEOUS

Although details are not available the following have been reported—two survey craft, three tankers, ten transports and twelve LCUs.

SABAH

Base

Labuan

2 91 ft PATROL BOATS

Name	No.	Builders	Commissioned
SRI GUMANTONG	—	Vosper Thornycroft Ltd, Singapore	8 April 1970
SRI LABUAN	—	Vosper Thornycroft Ltd, Singapore	6 April 1970

Sri Gumantong launched 18 Aug 1969. On detachment from Royal Malaysian Police (see Malaysian section for details).

1 YACHT

Name	No.	Builders	Commissioned
PUTRI SABAH	—	Vosper Thornycroft Ltd, Singapore	11 July 1971

Displacement, tons: 117
Dimensions, feet (metres): 91 × 19 × 5·5 *(27·8 × 5·8 × 1·7)*
Main engines: 1 diesel = 12 knots
Complement: 22

2 55 ft PATROL BOATS

Name	No.	Builders	Commissioned
SRI SEMPORNA	—	Chevertons, Isle of Wight	Feb 1975
SRI BANGJI	—	Chevertons, Isle of Wight	Feb 1975

Displacement, tons: 50
Dimensions, feet (metres): 55 × 15 × 3 *(16·8 × 4·6 × 0·9)*
Gun: 1—MG
Main engines: Diesels; 1 200 hp = 20 knots
Range, miles: 300 at 15 knots
Complement: 11

ST. KITTS

Senior Appointment

Chief of Police:
O. A. Hector

Mercantile Marine

Lloyd's Register of Shipping: 2 vessels of 405 tons

Base

Basseterre.

1 FAIREY MARINE "SPEAR" CLASS

Displacement, tons: 4·3
Dimensions, feet (metres): 29·8 × 9 × 2·8 *(9·1 × 2·8 × 0·8)*
Guns: Mountings for 2—7·62 mm
Main engines: 2 diesels; 360 hp = 30 knots
Complement: 2

Ordered for the Police in June 1974—delivered 10 Sep 1974.

ST. LUCIA

Mercantile Marine

Lloyd's Register of Shipping: 2 vessels of 904 tons gross

1 BROOKE MARINE PATROL CRAFT

HELEN

Details as *Chatoyer* in St. Vincent section below.

ST. VINCENT

Senior Appointment

Commissioner of Police:
R. J. O'Garro

Mercantile Marine

Lloyd's Register of Shipping: 18 vessels of 5 663 tons gross

Base

Kingstown

1 BROOKE MARINE PATROL CRAFT

CHATOYER

Displacement, tons: 15
Dimensions, feet (metres): 45 × 13 × 3·8 *(13·7 × 4 × 1·2)*
Guns: 3 MG
Main engines: 2 Cummins diesels; 370 hp; 2 shafts = 21 knots

CHATOYER   *1976, St. Vincent Police*

SAUDI ARABIA

Ministeri |

Minister of Defence:
Amir Sultan ibn 'Abd al-'Aziz

Diplomatic Representation

Defence Attaché in London:
Major-Gen Mohammed Sabri

Personnel

(a) 1977: 1 500 officers and men
(b) Voluntary Service

Bases

Jiddah, Al Qatif/Jubail, Ras Tanura, Damman, Yanbo, Ras al-Mishab (under construction).

Coastguard Bases

Haqi, Ash Sharmah, Qizan.

Mercantile Marine

Lloyd's Register of Shipping:
84 vessels of 588 745 tons gross

New Construction

In January 1972 an agreement was signed with the USA for a ten-year programme to provide 6 corvettes, 4 MSC, 2 coastal patrol craft, 4 LCTs, 3 training ships and 2 tugs. The first, second and last of these are listed in this section.
In addition to the above the following are reported under order—nine Tacoma PGM, eight CMN patrol craft (ordered Jan 1976), twelve 50 ft patrol craft from Halter Marine, New Orleans. To man a proportion of these a considerable training programme is under way in the USA.

CORVETTES

0 + 6 NEW CONSTRUCTION

Displacement, tons: 720
Dimensions, feet (metres): 234·5 × 27·6 × 8·8 (71·4 × 8·4 × 2·7)
Missiles: 8 Harpoon SSM
Guns: 1—76 mm OTO Melara; 1—81 mm mortar; 2—40 mm mortars; 2—20 mm
A/S weapons: 6 (2 triple) Mk 32 A/S torpedo tubes
Main engines: CODOG; 1 GE gas turbine, 16 500 hp; 2 diesels; 3 000 hp
Speed, knots: 30 on gas turbines; 20 on diesels
Complement: 53 (5 officers, 48 ratings)

Ordered in USA 1976.

Radar: Surface warning: AN/SPS 60.
Air warning: AN/SPS 40B.
Fire control system: Mk 92.

Sonar: AN/SQS 56.

MINEWARFARE FORCES

4 "MSC 322" CLASS (MINESWEEPERS—COASTAL)

MSC 322, 323, 324, 325

Ordered from Peterson Builders, Sturgeon Bay, Wisconsin on 30 Sept 1975 under the International Logistics Programme. All to be delivered 1978

LIGHT FORCES

6 + ?3 FAST ATTACK CRAFT (MISSILE)

Displacement, tons: 320
Dimensions, feet (metres): 184·4 × 25 × 5·8 (56·2 × 7·6 × 1·8)
Missiles: 2 twin Harpoon launchers
Guns: 1—76 mm OTO Melara; 1—81 mm mortar; 2—40 mm mortars; 2—20 mm
Main engines: CODOG; 1 GE gas turbine, 16 500 hp; 2 diesels; 1 500 hp
Speed, knots: 38 (gas turbine); 18 (diesel)
Complement: 35

Ordered from USA 1976.

Radar: Surface Warning: AN/SPS 60
Air Warning: AN/SPS 40 B
Fire Control: Mk 92 system

3 GERMAN "JAGUAR" CLASS
(FAST ATTACK CRAFT—TORPEDO)

Name	No.	Builders	Commissioned
DAMMAM	—	Lürssen Vegesack	1969
KHABAR	—	Lürssen Vegesack	1969
MACCAH	—	Lürssen Vegesack	1969

Displacement, tons: 160 standard; 190 full load
Dimensions, feet (metres): 139·4 × 23·4 × 7·9 (42·5 × 7 × 2·4)
Guns: 2—40 mm
Torpedo tubes: 4—21 in (533 mm)
Main engines: 4 MTU diesels; 12 000 bhp = 42 knots
Complement: 33 (3 officers, 30 men)

"JAGUAR" Class   1974, Reiner Nerlich

1 USCG TYPE (LARGE PATROL CRAFT)

RYADH

Displacement, tons: 100 standard
Dimensions, feet (metres): 95·0 × 19·0 × 6·0 (29 × 5·8 × 1·9)
Gun: 1—40 mm
Main engines: 4 diesels; 2 shafts; 2 200 bhp = 21 knots
Complement: 15

Steel-hulled patrol boat transferred to Saudi Arabia in 1960.

20 45 ft PATROL BOATS

Built by Whittingham and Mitchell, Chertsey, England. Armed with one ·5 cal MG and powered with two 362 hp diesels.

2 Ex-US 40 ft UTILITY BOATS

Transferred late 1960s.

43 30 ft "C-80" CLASS (COASTAL PATROL CRAFT)

Dimensions, feet (metres): 29·3 oa × 9·3 × 1·5 (8·9 × 2·9 × 0·6)
Main engines: 1 Caterpillar diesel; 210 bhp; Castoldi pump jet unit = 20 knots
Gun: 1 MG

All delivered 1975 to Saudi Coastguard. Built by Northshore Yacht Yards under sub-contract to Planning Associates Ltd (London). Contract 1974.

"C-80" Class   1975, Northshore

10 23 ft "HUNTRESS" PATROL BOATS

Built by Fairey Marine, Hamble, England. Capable of 20 knots with a cruising range of 150 miles and a complement of four.

20 ft PATROL BOATS

Smaller editions of the 45 ft craft above. By the same builder.

8 SRN-6 HOVERCRAFT

Displacement, tons: 10 normal (load 8 200 lbs)
Dimensions, feet (metres): 48·4 × 25·3 × 15·9 (height) *(14·8 × 7·7 × 4·8)*
Main machinery: 1 Gnome model 1050 gas turbine.
Speed, knots: 58

Acquired from British Hovercraft Corporation Ltd, between Feb and Dec 1970.

SRN-6 hovercraft   *1971*

2 AIR SEA-RESCUE LAUNCHES

ASR 1   ASR 2

With two diesels of 1 230 hp and capable of 25 knots. Belong to Ministry of Transportation.

SERVICE FORCES

2 Ex-US LCUs

SA 311   SA 313

Transferred June/July 1976.

SA 311   *7/1976, Stefan Terzibaschitsch*

2 Ex-US YTB TYPE (HARBOUR TUGS)

EN 111 (ex-*YTB 837*)   **EN 112** (ex-*YTB 838*)

Displacement, tons: 350 full load
Dimensions, feet (metres): 109 oa × 30 × 13·8 *(31·1 × 9·8 × 4·5)*
Main engines: 2 Diesels; 2 000 bhp; 2 shafts
Complement: 12

Transferred by USN 15 Oct 1975.

1 ROYAL YACHT

Dimensions, feet (metres): 212 oa × 32 × 10 *(69·5 × 10·5 × 3·3)*
Main engines: 2 Diesels; 6 300 hp = 26 knots
Complement: 26 (accommodation for 18 passengers)

Ordered from "Van Lent" (de Kaag) Netherlands in October 1975.

SENEGAL

Ministerial	Base	Mercantile Marine
Minister of Armed Forces: Amadu Sall	Dakar	*Lloyd's Register of Shipping:* 65 vessels of 26 621 tons gross

Personnel

a) 1977: approx 350 officers and men
b) 2 years conscript service

DELETION

Light Forces

1974 *Sénégal*

LIGHT FORCES

3 "P 48" CLASS (LARGE PATROL CRAFT)

Name	No.	Builders	Commissioned
SAINT LOUIS	—	Ch. Navales Franco-Belges	1 Mar 1971
POPENGUINE	—	Soc. Francais de Constructions Navales	10 Aug 1974
PODOR	—	Soc. Francais de Constructions Navales	Mar 1977

Displacement, tons: 250 full load
Dimensions, feet (metres): 149·3 pp; 156 oa × 23·3 × 8·1 *(45·5; 47·5 × 7·1 × 2·5)*
Missiles: 8—SS 12
Guns: 2—40 mm
Main engines: 2 MGO diesels; 1 shaft; 2 400 bhp = 18·5 knots
Range, miles: 2 000 at 18 knots
Complement: 25

Saint Louis laid down on 20 April 1970, launched on 5 Aug 1970. *Popenguine* laid down in Dec 1973, launched 22 Mar 1974. Sisters to *Malaika* of Malagasy, *Vigilant* of Ivory Coast and "Bizerte" Class of Tunisian Navy. *Podor* ordered Aug 1975, laid down Dec 1975, launched 20 July 1976.

SAINT LOUIS   *1972*

2 Ex-FRENCH VC TYPE

Name	No.	Builders	Commissioned
CASAMANCE (ex-*VC 5, ex-P 755*)	—	Constructions Mécaniques de Normandie, Cherbourg	1958
SINE-SALOUM (ex-*Reine* *N'Galifourou, ex-VC 4, ex-P 754*)	—	Constructions Mécaniques de Normandie, Cherbourg	1958

Displacement, tons: 75 standard; 82 full load
Dimensions, feet (metres): 104·5 × 15·5 × 5·5 *(31·8 × 4·7 × 1·7)*
Guns: 2—20 mm
Main engines: 2 Mercedes-Benz (MTU) diesels; 2 shafts; 2 700 bhp = 28 knots
Complement: 15

Former French patrol craft (Vedettes de Surveillance Côtière). *Casamance* was transferred from France to Senegal in 1963. *Sine-Saloum* was given to Senegal on 24 Aug 1965 after having been returned to France by the Congo in Feb 1965.

SINE-SALOUM   *1967, Senegalese Navy*

1 TRAWLER TYPE

LES ALMADIES

Used previously on fishery protection.

12 VOSPER 45 ft TYPE

Dimensions, feet (metres): 45 × 13·2 × 3·5 *(13·7 × 4 × 1·1)*
Guns: 1—12·7 mm; 2—7·62 mm
Main engines: 2 diesels; 920 hp = 25 knots
Complement: 6

1 FAIREY MARINE "LANCE" CLASS
(COASTAL PATROL CRAFT)

Displacement, tons: 15·7 light
Dimensions, feet (metres): 48·7 × 15·3 × 4·3 *(14·8 × 4·7 × 1·3)*
Guns: 2—7·62 mm
Main engines: 2 GM 8 V 71 T1; 850 hp = 24 volts
Complement: 7

Completed 1976. Has capacity for boarding party of 12. Air conditioned.

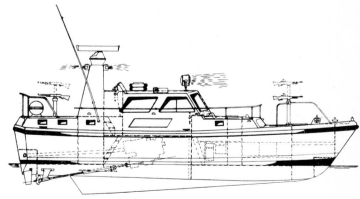

"LANCE" Class   *1977, Fairey Marine*

1 FAIREY MARINE "SPEAR" CLASS
(COASTAL PATROL CRAFT)

Displacement, tons: 4·3
Dimensions, feet (metres): 29·8 × 9 × 2·8 *(9·1 × 2·8 × 0·8)*
Guns: 1—12·7 mm; 2—7·62 mm
Main engines: 2 diesels; 360 hp = 30 knots
Complement: 2

Completed 28 Feb 1974 for Senegal Customs.

2 FAIREY MARINE "HUNTRESS" CLASS
(COASTAL PATROL CRAFT)

Dimensions, feet (metres): 23·2 × 8·8 × 2·8 *(7·1 × 2·7 × 0·8)*
Main engines: 1 diesel; 180 hp; 29 knots
Complement: 2

Completed Mar 1974 for Senegal Customs.

AMPHIBIOUS FORCES

1 Ex-FRENCH EDIC

LA FALENCE (ex-9095) (LCT)

Displacement, tons: 250 standard; 670 full load
Dimensions, feet (metres): 193·5 × 39·2 × 4·5 *(59 × 12 × 1·3)*
Guns: 2—20 mm
Main engines: 2 MGO diesels; 2 shafts; 1 000 bhp = 8 knots
Complement: 6

Launched 7 April 1958. Transferred 1 July 1974.

2 Ex-US "LCM 6" CLASS

DIOU LOULOU (ex-6723)   **DIOMBOS** (ex-6733)

Transferred July 1968. Of 26 tons.

1 TENDER

CRAME JEAN

18 ton fishing boat used as training craft.

SHARJAH

(See United Arab Emirates)

Craft belong to Marine Division of the Sharjah Police Force, which operates under the UAE
Union Border Guard whose main base is at the new harbour in Sharjah.

2 50 ft CHEVERTON TYPE

Name	No.	Builders	Commissioned
AL SHAHEEN	—	Chevertons, Cowes	Feb 1975
AL AQAB	—	Chevertons, Cowes	Feb 1975

Displacement, tons: 20
Dimensions, feet (metres): 50 × 14 × 4·5 *(15·2 × 4·3 × 1·4)*
Gun: 1 MG
Main engines: 2 GM diesels; 2 shafts; 850 bhp = 23 knots
Range, miles: 1 000 at 20 knots
Complement: 8

GRP Hull.

AL SHAHEEN   1975, Roger M. Smith

4 20 ft COASTAL PATROL CRAFT
Ordered 1976.

SIERRA LEONE

Personnel

(a) 1977: 150 officers and men
(b) Voluntary service

Base

Freetown

Mercantile Marine

Lloyd's Register of Shipping:
13 vessels of 17 209 tons gross

3 Ex-CHINESE "SHANGHAI II" CLASS
(FAST ATTACK CRAFT—GUN)

Displacement, tons: 120 standard; 155 full load
Dimensions, feet (metres): 128 × 18 × 5·6 *(39 × 5·5 × 1·7)*
Guns: 4—37 mm; 4—25 mm
A/S weapons: 8 DCs
Mines: Mine rails can be fitted
Main engines: 4 Diesels; 4 800 hp = 30 knots
Complement: 25

Transferred by China June 1973.

Radar: Skin Head.

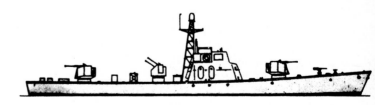

"SHANGHAI II" Class

SINGAPORE

Headquarters Appointments	Personnel	Prefix to Ships' Names
Commander of the Republic of Singapore Navy: Colonel Khoo Eng An	(a) 1977: 3 000 officers and men (b) 2-3 years National Service and regular volunteers	RSS

Mercantile Marine

Lloyd's Register of Shipping: 722 vessels of 5 481 720 tons gross

---

LIGHT FORCES

6 LÜRSSEN VEGESACK "TNC 48" CLASS
(FAST ATTACK CRAFT—MISSILE)

Name	No.	Builders	Commissioned
SEA WOLF	P 76	Lürssen Werft, Vegesack	1972
SEA LION	P 77	Lürssen Werft, Vegesack	1972
SEA TIGER	P 79	Singapore Shipbuilding & Engineering Co	1974
SEA DRAGON	P 78	Singapore Shipbuilding & Engineering Co	1974
SEA HAWK	P 80	Singapore Shipbuilding & Engineering Co	1975
SEA SCORPION	P 81	Singapore Shipbuilding & Engineering Co	1975

Displacement, tons: 230
Dimensions, feet (metres): 158 × 23 × 7·5 *(48 × 7 × 2·3)*
Missiles: 5 Gabriel
Guns: 1—57 mm; 1—40 mm
Main engines: 4 MTU diesels; 4 shafts; 14 400 hp = 34 knots
Complement: 40

Designed by Lürssen Werft who built the first pair, *Sea Wolf* and *Sea Lion,* which arrived Autumn 1972.

SEA SCORPION   *1975, Singapore Navy*

6 VOSPER THORNYCROFT DESIGN
3 "TYPE A" (FAST ATTACK CRAFT—GUN)

Name	No.	Builders	Commissioned
INDEPENDENCE	P 69	Vosper Thornycroft Ltd, UK	8 July 1970
FREEDOM	P 70	Vosper Thornycroft Private Ltd, Singapore	11 Jan 1971
JUSTICE	P 72	Vosper Thornycroft Private Ltd, Singapore	23 Apr 1971

Displacement, tons: 100 standard
Dimensions, feet (metres): 103·6 wl; 109·6 × 21·0 × 5·6 *(31·6; 33·5 × 6·4 × 1·8)*
Guns: 1—40 mm (forward); 1—20 mm (aft)
Main engines: 2 Maybach (MTU 16 V538) diesels; 7 200 bhp = 32 knots
Range, miles: 1 100 at 15 knots
Complement: 19 to 22

On 21 May 1968 the Vosper Thornycroft Group announced the receipt of an order for six of their 110-foot fast patrol boats for the Republic of Singapore. Two sub-types, the first of each *(Independence* and *Sovereignty)* built in UK, the remainder in Singapore. *Independence* was launched 15 July 1969. *Freedom* 18 Nov 1969 and *Justice* 20 June 1970.

INDEPENDENCE   *1971, Vosper Thornycroft*

3 "TYPE B" (FAST ATTACK CRAFT—GUN)

Name	No.	Builders	Commissioned
DARING	P 73	Vosper Thornycroft Private Ltd, Singapore	18 Sep 1971
DAUNTLESS	P 74	Vosper Thornycroft Private Ltd, Singapore	1971
SOVEREIGNTY	P 71	Vosper Thornycroft Ltd, Portsmouth, England	Feb 1971

Displacement, tons: 100 standard; 130 full load
Dimensions, feet (metres): 103·6 wl; 109·6 × 21·0 × 5·6 *(31·6; 33·5 × 6·4 × 1·8)*
Guns: 1—76 mm Bofors; 1—20 mm Oerlikon
Main engines: 2 Maybach (MTU 16 V538) diesels; 7 200 bhp = 32 knots
Range, miles: 1 100 at 15 knots
Complement: 19 (3 officers, 16 ratings)

Sovereignty was launched 25 Nov 1969. *Dauntless* launched 6 May 1971. Steel hulls of round bilge form. Aluminium alloy superstructure.

SOVEREIGNTY   *1971, Vosper Thornycroft*

MINEWARFARE FORCES

2 Ex-US "REDWING" CLASS (MINESWEEPERS—COASTAL)

JUPITER (ex-USS *Thrasher MSC 203*)	M102
MERCURY (ex-USS *Whippoorwill MSC 207*)	—

Displacement, tons: 370 full load
Dimensions, feet (metres): 144 × 28 × 8·2 *(43·9 × 8·5 × 2·5)*
Gun: 1—20 mm
Main engines: 2 GM diesels; 1 760 bhp; 2 shafts = 12 knots
Range, miles: 2 500 at 10 knots
Complement: 39

Transferred by sale 5 Dec 1975.

JUPITER   *1976, Singapore Navy*

TRAINING SHIPS

1 "FORD" CLASS (LARGE PATROL CRAFT)

Name	No.	Builders	Commissioned
PANGLIMA	P 68	United Engineers, Singapore	May 1956

Displacement, tons: 119 standard; 134 full load
Dimensions, feet (metres): 117·0 × 20·0 × 6·0 (35·7 × 6·1 × 1·8)
Guns: 1—40 mm 60 cal; 1—20 mm
Main engines: Paxman YHAXM supercharged B 12 diesels = 14 knots
Oil fuel, tons: 15
Complement: 15 officers and men

Laid down in 1954. Launched on 14 Jan 1956. Similar to the British seaward defence boats of the "Ford" class. Transferred to the Royal Malaysian Navy on the formation of Malaysia. Transferred to the Republic of Singapore in 1967.

PANGLIMA   1975, Singapore Navy

Name	No.	Builders	Commissioned
ENDEAVOUR	P 75	Shiffswarft Oberwinter, Germany	30 Sep 1970

Displacement, tons: 250
Dimensions, feet (metres): 135 × 25 × 8 (40·9 × 7·6 × 2·4)
Guns: 2—20 mm
Main engines: 2 Maybach diesels; 2 600 bhp
Range, miles: 800 at 8 knots
Complement: 24

ENDEAVOUR   1976, Singapore Navy

AMPHIBIOUS FORCES

6 Ex-US "511-1152" CLASS (LSTs)

Name	No.	Builders	Commissioned
ENDURANCE	L 201	American Bridge Co	1944
(ex-USS Holmes County, LST 836)			
INTREPID (ex-US LST 579)	L 203	Chicago Bridge & Iron Co	1944
PERSISTENCE (ex-US LST 613)	L 205	Chicago Bridge & Iron Co	1944
PERSEVERENCE (ex-US LST 623)	L 206	Chicago Bridge & Iron Co	1944
EXCELLENCE (ex-US LST 629)	L 202	Chicago Bridge & Iron Co.	1944
RESOLUTION (ex-US LST 649)	L 204	Chicago Bridge & Iron Co	1944

Displacement, tons: 1 653 light; 4 080 full load
Dimensions, feet (metres): 316·0 wl; 328·0 oa × 50·0 × 14·0 (96·3; 100 × 15·2 × 4·3)
Guns: 8—40 mm (4 twin)
Main engines: GM diesels; 2 shafts; 1 700 bhp = 11·6 knots
Complement: 120

Endurance loaned from the United States Navy on 1 July 1971 and sold on 5 Dec 1975. Remainder transferred 4 June 1976.

Note: 2 other ex-US LSTs transferred for civilian use in Singapore June 1974 (ex-LST 276 and ex-USS *Chase County*, LST 532).

ENDURANCE   7/1975, Singapore Navy

6 LANDING CRAFT

BRANI, BERLAYER + 4

Of 30-50 tons—all ex-Australian.

POLICE PATROL CRAFT

4 VOSPER THORNYCROFT TYPE

Name	No.	Builders	Commissioned
—	PX 10	Vosper Thornycroft Ltd, Portsmouth, England	1969
—	PX 11	Vosper Thornycroft Ltd, Portsmouth, England	1969
—	PX 12	Vosper Thornycroft Ltd, Portsmouth, England	1969
—	PX 13	Vosper Thornycroft Ltd, Portsmouth, England	1969

Displacement, tons: 40 standard
Length, feet (metres): 87·0 (26·5)
Guns: 2—20 mm

Built for marine police duties.

SOMALI REPUBLIC

Personnel

(a) 1977: 350 officers and men
(b) Voluntary service

Bases

Berbera, Mogadishu and Kismayu

Mercantile Marine

Lloyd's Register of Shipping:
   255 vessels of 1 792 900 tons gross

LIGHT FORCES

3 Ex-SOVIET "OSA II" CLASS (FAST ATTACK CRAFT—MISSILE)

Displacement, tons: 165 standard; 200 full load
Dimensions, feet (metres): 128·7 × 25·1 × 5·9 *(39·3 × 7·7 × 1·8)*
Missiles: 4—SS-N-2
Guns: 4—30 mm (twins)
Main engines: 3 diesels; 1 300 bhp = 32 knots
Range, miles: 800 at 25 knots
Complement: 30

Transferred in Dec 1975.

4 Ex-SOVIET "P6" CLASS (FAST ATTACK CRAFT—TORPEDO)

Displacement, tons: 66 standard; 75 full load
Dimensions, feet (metres): 84·2 × 20·0 × 6·0 *(27·6 × 6·5 × 2)*
Guns: 4—25 mm
Torpedo tubes: 2—21 inch
Main engines: 4 diesels; 4 shafts; 4 800 hp = 43 knots
Range, miles: 450 at 30 knots
Complement: 25

Transferred in 1968.

6 Ex-SOVIET "POLUCHAT I" CLASS (LARGE PATROL CRAFT)

Displacement, tons: 100 standard; 120 full load
Dimensions, feet (metres): 98·4 × 20·0 × 5·9 *(32·3 × 6·5 × 1·9)*
Guns: 2—25 mm
Main engines: Diesels = 15 knots

Transferred two in 1965, four in 1966.

AMPHIBIOUS FORCES

4 Ex-SOVIET "T4" CLASS (LCM)

Displacement, tons: 70
Dimensions, feet (metres): 62·3 × 14·1 × 3·3 *(19 × 4·3 × 1)*
Main engines: 2 diesels; 2 shafts = 10 knots

Transferred 1968-69.

SOUTH AFRICA

Ministerial

Minister of Defence:
Mr. P. W. Botha

Headquarters Appointments

Chief of South African Defence Force:
General M. A. de M. Malan, SSA, SM
Chief of the Navy:
Vice-Admiral J. Johnson, SM, DSC
Chief of Naval Staff (Operations):
Rear-Admiral P. A. H. Tomlinson, SM

Diplomatic Representation

Armed Forces Attaché in London:
Maj Gen H. R. Meintjes, SM
Naval Attaché in London:
Captain D. F. Silberbauer
Defence Attaché in Bonn:
Captain P. E. Blitzker
Naval Attaché in Washington:
Captain R. L. Shelver
Naval Attaché in Paris:
Captain J. A. de Kock
Armed Forces Attaché in Buenos Aires:
Captain F. C. Ferris

Personnel

(a) 1974: Total 4 204 (475 officers, 2 329 ratings and 1 400
National Service ratings)
1975: Total 4 250 (475 officers, 2 375 ratings and 1 400
National Service ratings)
1976: Total 4 700 (500 officers, 2 800 ratings and 1 400
National Service ratings)
(b) Voluntary plus 18 months National Service

Naval Bases

HM Dockyard at Simonstown was transferred to the Republic
of South Africa on 2 April 1957. The new submarine base at
Simonstown, SAS *Drommedaris,* incorporating offices,
accommodation and operations centre alongside a Synchrolift
marine elevator, capable of docking all South African ships
except the *Tafelberg,* was opened in July 1972.
A new Maritime Headquarters was opened in March 1973 at
Silvermine on the Cape Peninsula.

Air Sea Rescue Base

The SAAF Maritime Group base at Langebaan was transferred
to the South African Navy on 1 Nov 1969, becoming SAN Sea
Rescue Base (SAS *Flamingo*). The ASR launches were given
Naval Coastal Forces numbers to replace SAAF "R" numbers.

Maritime Air

The SAAF operates an MP group consisting of 18 Piaggio P166s
and 7 Shackleton MR 3. In addition 11 Wasp helicopters are
available for embarkation in the frigates.

Prefix to Ships' Names

SAS (Suid Afrikaanse Skip)

Mercantile Marine

Lloyd's Register of Shipping:
275 vessels of 477 011 tons gross

Strength of the Fleet

Type	Active	Building
Destroyer	1	—
Frigates	3	2
Submarines Patrol	3	2
Fast Attack Craft—Missile	—	6
Large Patrol Craft	4	—
Minesweepers (Coastal)	10	—
Survey Ships	2	—
Fleet Replenishment Ship	1	—
BDV	1	—
TRV	1	—
Training Ship	1	—
Tugs	2	—
SAR Launches	4	—

New Construction

The South African defence budget announced on March 31
1976 showed an increase of 40% over the previous year, resulting in a budget which has nearly doubled in the last two years.
The new frigates, 2 submarines and 6 fast attack craft (missile)
will have a proportion of their costs included in the total of 1·35
billion Rands (£880 mill).

DELETIONS

Destroyer

1976 *Simon van der Stel*

Frigates

1976 *Vrystaat* (sunk as target in April)
Good Hope, Transvaal,
Pietermaritzburg (shore accommodation ship)

Survey Ship

Sep 1972 *Natal* (sunk as target)

Training Ship

1975 HDML 1204

PENNANT LIST

D (Destroyer)

278	Jan Van Riebeeck

F (Frigates)

145	President Pretorius
147	President Steyn
150	President Krüger

S (Submarines)

97	Maria Van Riebeeck
98	Emily Hobhouse
99	Johanna Van der Merwe

M (Minewarfare Forces)

291	Pietermaritzburg
1207	Johannesburg
1210	Kimberley
1212	Port Elizabeth
1213	Mosselbaai
1214	Walvisbaai
1215	East London
1498	Windhoek
1499	Durban

P (Light Forces)

285	Somerset (BDV)
1556	Pretoria
1557	Kaapstad
3105	Gelderland
3120	Nautilus
3125	Reijger
3126	Haerlem
3127	Oosterland
3148	Fleur (TRV)

A (Service Force)

243	Tafelberg
324	Protea

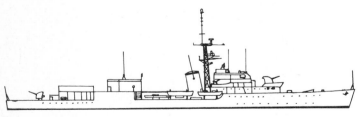

Ex-British "W", Class

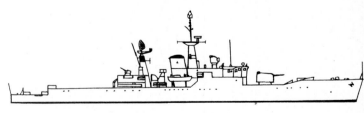

"PRESIDENT" Class

"A69" Class

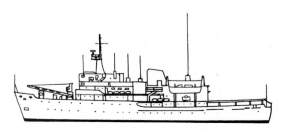

PROTEA

DESTROYERS

1 Ex-BRITISH "W" CLASS

Name	No.	Builders	Laid down	Launched	Commissioned
JAN VAN RIEBEECK (ex-HMS Wessex, ex-Zenith)	D 278	Fairfield SB & Eng Co Ltd, Govan, Glasgow	20 Oct 1942	2 Sep 1943	11 May 1944

Displacement, tons: 2 205 standard; 2 850 full load
Length, feet (metres): 339·5 (103·6) pp; 362·8 (110·6) oa
Beam, feet (metres): 35·7 (10·9)
Draught, feet (metres): 17·1 (5·2)
Aircraft: 2 Westland Wasp helicopters
Guns: 4—4 in (102 mm) (twin); 2—40 mm (single);
  4—3 pdr (saluting)
A/S weapons: 6 (2 triple) Mk 32 torpedo tubes; 2 DCT;
  2 DC racks
Boilers: 2 Admiralty 3-drum type; 300 psi; 670°F
Main engines: 2 Parsons sr geared turbines; 2 shafts;
  40 000 shp
Speed, knots: 36
Range, miles: 3 260 at 14 knots; 1 000 at 30 knots
Oil fuel, tons: 579 (95%)
Complement: 192 (11 officers, 181 men)

JAN VAN RIEBEECK

1973, South African Navy

Purchased from Great Britain. Transferred to South Africa on 29 Mar 1950.

Aircraft: Landing patch on fo'c'sle.

Gunnery: The main armament formerly comprised four 4·7 inch guns.

Modernisation: Modernised in 1964-66.

Radar: Search: Type 293.
Fire Control: I Band (NSG NA 9 system).

FRIGATES

2 Ex-FRENCH "A69" CLASS

Name	No.	Builders	Laid down	Launched	Commissioned
— (ex-Lieutenant de Vaisseau Le Hénaff)	—	Lorient Naval DY	12 Mar 1976	Mar 1977	1977
— (ex-Commandant l'Herminier)	—	Lorient Naval DY	1 Oct 1976	Sept 1977	1978

Displacement, tons: 950 standard; 1 170 full load
Length, feet (metres): 262·5 (80·0) oa
Beam, feet (metres): 33·8 (10·3)
Draught, feet (metres): 9·8 (3·0)
Missiles: 2 MM 38 Exocet
Guns: 1—3·9 in (100 mm); 2—20 mm
A/S weapons: 1—375 mm Mk 54 Rocket launcher; 4 fixed tubes for Mk L3 and L5 torpedoes
Main engines: 2 SEMT-Pielstick PC2V diesels; 2 shafts; controllable pitch propellers; 11 000 bhp
Speed, knots: 24
Range, miles: 4 500 at 15 knots
Endurance, days: 15
Complement: 75 (5 officers, 70 men)

Trials to start Nov 1977 and May 1978. Unconfirmed reports that two more were ordered in Mar 1976.

"A69" CLASS

1976, French Navy

3 "PRESIDENT" CLASS

Name	No.	Builders	Laid down	Launched	Commissioned
PRESIDENT KRUGER	F 150	Yarrow & Co, Scotstoun	6 April 1959	20 Oct 1960	1 Oct 1962
PRESIDENT PRETORIUS	F 145	Yarrow & Co, Scotstoun	21 Nov 1960	28 Sep 1962	4 Mar 1964
PRESIDENT STEYN	F 147	Alex Stephen & Sons, Govan	20 May 1960	23 Nov 1961	25 April 1963

Displacement, tons: 2 250 standard; 2 800 full load
Dimensions, feet (metres): 370 oa × 41·1 × 17·1 (112·8 × 12·5 × 5·2)
Aircraft: 1 Wasp helicopter
Guns: 2—4·5 in (115 mm) (1 twin); 2—40 mm Bofors; 4—3 pdr (saluting)
A/S weapons: 6 (2 triple) Mk 32 torpedo tubes; 1 Limbo 3-barrel DC mortar
Main engines: 2 sets d.r. geared turbines; 2 shafts; 30 000 shp
Boilers: 2 Babcock & Wilcox 550 psi; 850°F
Speed, knots: 30
Oil fuel, tons: 430
Range, miles: 4 500 at 12 knots
Complement: 203 (13 officers, 190 men)

Originally "Rothesay" Type 12 frigates, *President Kruger* arrived in South Africa on 27 Mar 1963.

PRESIDENT STEYN

12/1976, South African Navy

Modernisation: Refitted to carry a Wasp A/S helicopter, with hangar and landing deck. To accommodate this, one Limbo A/S mortar was removed and the two single 40 mm remounted on the hangar roof. *President Kruger* completed refit and recommissioned on 5 Aug 1969, *President Steyn* completed refit in 1971, when *President Pretorius* was taken in hand although delayed to take advantage gained from the previous conversions. The refits were carried out at S.A. Naval Dockyard, Simonstown and included replacement of the lattice foremast by a truncated pyramid tower. *Kruger* retained her original GDS5 director but will later be brought into line with the other pair. Small differences exist between all three ships.

Radar: Surveillance: Thomson CSF Jupiter.
Air/Surface search: Type 293.
Fire control: Elsag NA9C.

PRESIDENT KRUGER

7/1976, USN

SUBMARINES

2 FRENCH "AGOSTA" CLASS

Name	No.	Builders	Laid down	Launched	Commissioned
—	—	Dubigeon—Normandie (Nantes)	15 Sep 1976	—	Nov 1978
—	—	Dubigeon—Normandie (Nantes)	—	—	Aug 1979

Displacement, tons: 1 470 surfaced; 1 790 dived
Dimensions, feet (metres): 221·7 × 22·3 × 17·7 (67·9 × 6·8 × 5·2)
Torpedo tubes: 4—21·7 (550 mm); 20 reload torpedoes
Main machinery: Diesel Electric; 2 SEMT Pielstick diesels; 3 600 bhp; 1 main motor; 4 600 bhp; 1 cruising motor; 1 shaft
Speed, knots: 12 surfaced; 20 dived
Range, miles: 9 000 at 9 knots (surfaced); 350 at 3·5 knots (dived)
Complement: 50

Ordered June 1975. Export licence granted by French Government 1 Oct 1976.

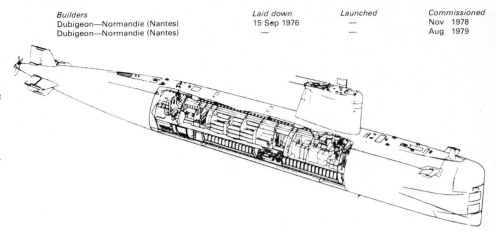

"AGOSTA" Class

3 FRENCH "DAPHNE" CLASS

Name	No.	Builders	Laid down	Launched	Commissioned
EMILY HOBHOUSE	S 98	Dubigeon—Normandie, Nantes-Chantenay	18 Nov 1968	24 Oct 1969	25 Jan 1971
JOHANNA VAN DER MERWE	S 99	Dubigeon—Normandie, Nantes-Chantenay	24 April1969	21 July 1970	21 July 1971
MARIA VAN RIEBEECK	S 97	Dubigeon—Normandie, Nantes-Chantenay	14 Mar 1968	18 Mar 1969	22 June 1970

Displacement, tons: 850 surfaced; 1 040 dived
Length, feet (metres): 190·3 (58)
Beam, feet (metres): 22·3 (6·8)
Draught, feet (metres): 15·4 (4·7)
Torpedo tubes: 12—21·7 in (550 mm) (8 bow, 4 stern)
Main machinery: SEMT-Pielstick diesel electric; 1 300 bhp surfaced; 1 600 hp dived; 2 shafts
Speed, knots: 16 surfaced and dived
Range, miles: 4 500 at 5 knots (snorting)
Complement: 47 (6 officers, 41 men)

First submarines ordered for the South African Navy. They are of the French "Daphne" design, similar to those built in France for that country, Pakistan and Portugal and also built in Spain.

EMILY HOBHOUSE   1973, South African Navy

LIGHT FORCES

6 "RESHEF" CLASS (FAST ATTACK CRAFT—MISSILE)

Displacement, tons: 430 full load
Dimensions, feet (metres): 204 × 25 × 8 (62·2 × 7·8 × 2·4)
Missiles: 4—Gabriel (Selenia control)
Guns: 2—76 mm
Main engines: 4 Maybach diesels; 2 shafts; 5 340 hp = 32 knots
Range, miles: ? 1 500 at 30 knots; 4 000+ at economical speed
Complement: 45

Contract signed with Israel in late 1974; first three under construction at Haifa and three in Durban. Completion of order expected 1978.

"RESHEF" Class   1974, Michael D. J. Lennon

5 BRITISH "FORD" CLASS (LARGE PATROL CRAFT)

Name	No.	Builders	Commissioned
GELDERLAND (ex-Brayford)	P 3105	A. & J. Inglis Ltd, Glasgow	30 Aug 1954
HAERLEM	P 3126	Vosper Ltd, Portsmouth	1959
NAUTILUS (ex-Glassford)	P 3120	Dunston, Thorne	23 Aug 1955
OOSTERLAND	P 3127	Vosper Ltd, Portsmouth	1959
REIJGER	P 3125	Vosper Ltd, Portsmouth	1958

Displacement, tons: 120 standard; 160 full load
Dimensions, feet (metres): 110·0 wl; 117·2 oa × 20·0 × 4·5 (35; 38·4 × 6·5 × 1·3)
Gun: 1—40 mm
A/S weapons: 2 DCT in Oosterland and Reijger
Main engines: 2 Davey Paxman diesels; Foden engine on centre shaft; 1 100 bhp = 18 knots

Gelderland was purchased from Britain, and handed over to South Africa at Portsmouth on 30 Aug 1954. Second ship, Nautilus was handed over 23 Aug 1955, Reijger was launched on 6 Feb 1958, Haerlem on 18 June 1958, Oosterland on 27 Jan 1959. All three of these later ships are fitted with Vosper roll damping fins. Haerlem had a charthouse added aft as an inshore survey craft.

REIJGER   12/1976, South African Navy

MINE WARFARE FORCES

10 BRITISH "TON" CLASS (MINESWEEPERS COASTAL)

Name	No.	Builders	Commissioned
DURBAN	M 1499	Camper & Nicholson, Gosport	1957
EAST LONDON (ex-HMS *Chilton*)	M 1215	Cook Welton and Gemmell	1958
JOHANNESBURG (ex-HMS *Castleton*)	M 1207	White, Southampton	1958
KAAPSTAD (ex-HMS *Hazleton*)	P 1557	Cook Welton and Gemmell	1954
KIMBERLEY (ex-HMS *Stratton*)	M 1210	Dorset Yacht Co	1958
MOSSELBAAI (ex-HMS *Oakington*)	M 1213	Harland & Wolff, Belfast	1959
PORT ELIZABETH (ex-HMS *Dumbleton*)	M 1212	Harland & Wolff, Belfast	1958
PRETORIA (ex-HMS *Dunkerton*)	P 1556	Goole Shipbuilding Co	1954
WALVISBAAI (ex-HMS *Packington*)	M 1214	Harland & Wolff, Belfast	1959
WINDHOEK	M 1498	Thornycroft, Southampton	1959

Displacement, tons: 360 standard; 425 full load
Dimensions, feet (metres): 140·0 pp; 152·0 oa × 28·8 × 8·2 *(45·9; 49·8 × 9·4 × 2·7)*
Guns: 1—40 mm Bofors; 2—20 mm
Main engines: Mirrlees diesels in *Kaapstad* and *Pretoria*, 2 500 bhp; Deltic diesels in remainder; 3 000 bhp = 15 knots
Range, miles: 2 300 at 13 knots

Kaapstad and *Pretoria*, open bridge and lattice mast, were purchased in 1955 and converted with enclosed bridge and lattice mast in 1973. *Windhoek*, enclosed bridge and tripod mast, was launched by Thornycroft, Southampton, on 27 June 1957. *Durban*, enclosed bridge and tripod mast, was launched at Camper & Nicholson, Gosport, on 12 June 1957. *East London* and *Port Elizabeth*, transferred from the Royal Navy at Hythe on 27 Oct 1958, sailed for South Africa in Nov 1958. *Johannesburg*, *Kimberley* and *Mosselbaai* were delivered in 1959. *Walvisbaai* was launched by Harland & Wolff, Belfast on 3 July 1958 and delivered in 1959.
Some now used on patrol duties. (Note change of pennant numbers for *Kaapstad* and *Pretoria*).

JOHANNESBURG   12/1976, South African Navy

SURVEY SHIPS

Name	No.	Builders	Commissioned
PROTEA	A 324	Yarrow (Shipbuilders) Ltd.	23 May 1972

Displacement, tons: 1 930 standard; 2 750 full load
Length, feet (metres): 235 *(71·6)* pp; 260·1 *(79·3)* oa
Beam, feet (metres): 49·1 *(15·0)*
Draught, feet (metres): 15·1 *(4·6)*
Aircraft: 1 helicopter
Main engines: 4 Paxman/Ventura diesels geared to 1 shaft and controllable pitch propeller; 4 880 bhp
Speed, knots: 16
Range, miles: 12 000 at 11 knots
Oil fuel, tons: 560
Complement: Total 121 (10 officers, 104 ratings plus 7 scientists)

An order was placed with Yarrow (Shipbuilders) Ltd, for a "Hecla" class survey ship on 7 Nov 1969. Equipped for hydrographic survey with limited facilities for the collection of oceanographical data and for this purpose fitted with special communications equipment, naval surveying gear, survey launches and facilities for helicopter operations. Hull strengthened for navigation in ice and fitted with a transverse bow thrust unit and passive roll stabilisation system. Laid down 20 July 1970. Launched 14 July 1971.

PROTEA   1973, South African Navy

HAERLEM P 3126

Converted July 1963 from "Ford" class for survey duties. Complement 23. See Light Forces section for details.

FLEET REPLENISHMENT SHIP

Name	No.	Builders	Commissioned
TAFELBERG (ex-*Annam*)	A 243	Nakskovs Skibsvaert, Denmark	1959

Measurement, tons: 12 500 gross; 18 980 deadweight
Dimensions, feet (metres): 559·8 × 72·1 × — *(170·6 × 21·9 × —)*
Main engines: B & W diesels; 8 420 bhp = 15·5 knots
Complement: 100

Built as Danish East Asiatic Co tanker. Launched on 20 June 1958. Purchased by the Navy in 1965. Accommodation rehabilitated by Barens Shipbuilding & Engineering Co, Durban with extra accommodation, air conditioning, re-wiring for additional equipment, new upper RAS (replenishment at sea) deck to contain gantries, re-fuelling pipes. Remainder of conversion by Jowies, Brown & Hamer, Durban. A helicopter flight-deck was added aft during refit in 1975.

TAFELBERG   1973, South African Navy

TORPEDO RECOVERY VESSEL

Name	No.	Builders	Commissioned
FLEUR	P 3148	Dorman Long (Africa) Ltd.	3 Dec 1969

Displacement, tons: 220 standard; 257 full load
Dimensions, feet (metres): 115·0 wl; 121·5 oa × 27·5 × 11·1 *(37·7; 39·8 × 9·0 × 3·6)*
Main engines: 2 Paxman Ventura diesels; 1 400 bhp
Complement: 22 (4 officers, 18 ratings)

Combined Torpedo Recovery Vessel and Diving Tender.

FLEUR   1973, South African Navy

TRAINING VESSEL

Name	No.	Builders	Commissioned
NAVIGATOR	—	Fred Nicholls (Pty) Ltd, Durban	1964

Navigational Training Vessel. 75 tons displacement; 63 × 20 feet; 2 Foden diesels, 200 bhp = 9·5 knots. Based at Naval College, Gordon's Bay. Round bilge fishing boat wooden hull.

BOOM DEFENCE VESSEL

Name	No.	Builders	Commissioned
SOMERSET (ex-HMS *Barcross*)	P 285	Blyth Dry Dock & SB Co Ltd	14 April 1942

Displacement, tons: 750 standard; 960 full load
Dimensions, feet (metres): 150·0 pp; 182·0 oa × 32·2 × 11·5 *(49·2; 59 × 10·5 × 3·8)*
Main engines: Triple expansion; 850 hp = 11 knots
Boilers: 2 single ended
Oil fuel, tons: 186

Originally two in the class. Laid down on 15 April 1941, launched on 21 Oct 1941. Engined by Swan, Hunter & Wigham Richardson Ltd, Tyne.

SOMERSET   12/1976, South African Navy

TUGS

Name	No.	Builders	Commissioned
DE NEYS	—	Globe Engineering Works Ltd, Cape Town	23 July 1969
DE NOORDE	—	Globe Engineering Works Ltd, Cape Town	Dec 1961

Displacement, tons: 180 and 170 respectively
Dimensions, feet (metres): 94·0 × 26·5 × 15·75 and 104·5 × 25·0 × 15·0 *(30·8 × 8·7 × 5·2, 34·2 × 8·2 × 4·9)*
Main engines: 2 Lister Blackstone diesels; 2 shafts; 608 bhp = 9 knots
Complement: 10

De Neys fitted with Voith-Schneider screws.

DE NOORDE   12/1976, South African Navy

AIR SEA RESCUE LAUNCHES

2 FAIREY MARINE "TRACKER" CLASS

Name	No.	Builders	Commissioned
—	P 1554	Groves and Gutteridge, Cowes	1973
—	P 1555	Groves and Gutteridge, Cowes	1973

Displacement, tons: 26
Dimensions, feet (metres): 64 × 16 × 5 *(19·5 × 4·9 × 1·5)*
Main engines: 2 diesels; 1 120 bhp = 28 knots

Built by subsidiary of Fairey Marine.

P 1554   1973, South African Navy

2 KROGERWERFT TYPE

Name	No.	Builders	Commissioned
—	P 1551 (ex-*R 31*)	Krogerwerft, Rendsburg	1962
—	P 1552 (ex-*R 30*)	Krogerwerft, Rendsburg	1961

Displacement, tons: 87
Dimensions, feet (metres): 96 × 19 × 4 *(29·3 × 5·8 × 1·2)*
Main engines: 2 diesels; 4 480 bhp = 30 knots

There are also two 24 ft Tenders.

DEPARTMENT OF TRANSPORT

1 NEW CONSTRUCTION (ANTARCTIC SURVEY AND SUPPLY VESSEL)

Displacement, tons: 1 400
Main engines: Two diesels; one shaft

Tenders invited 1975.

SPAIN

Headquarters Appointments

Minister of the Navy:
Admiral Excmo Sr Don Gabriel Pita da Veiga
Chief of the Naval Staff:
Admiral Excmo Sr Don Carlos Buhigas
Chief of Fleet Support:
Admiral Excmo Sr Don Pedro Durán
Vice Chief of the Naval Staff:
Vice-Admiral Excmo Sr Don Guillermo Mateu

Commands

Commander-in-Chief of the Fleet:
Vice-Admiral Excmo Sr Don Juan C. Muñoz-Delgado
Captain General, Cantabrian Zone:
Admiral Excmo Sr Don Pedro Español Iglesias
Captain General, Straits Zone:
Admiral Excmo Sr Don Vicente Alberto y Lloveres
Captain General, Mediterranean Zone:
Admiral Excmo Sr Don Francisco J de Elizalde
Commandant General, Marines:
Lieut-General Excmo Sr Don Carlos Arriaga

Diplomatic Representation

Naval Attaché in London:
Captain Don Gabino Aranda
Naval Attaché in Washington:
Captain Sr Don Adolfo Gregorio Alvarez

Personnel

(a) 1977: Total 44 799 (4 085 officers, 32 668 ratings, 8 046 civil branch).
Infanteria Marina 10 614 (614 officers, 10 000 marines)
(b) 18 months National Service

Bases

El Ferrol del Caudillo (Cantabrian Zone)
San Fernando, Cádiz (Straits Zone)
Cartagena (Mediterranean Zone)

Naval Air Service

5 Harrier AV-8A (Matador)
2 Harrier TAV-8A
12 Bell 47G helicopters
4 AB 212
4 AB 204B
10 Sikorsky SH-3D
12 Hughes 500 ASW
6 Bell AH-1G ''Hueycobra''
3 Sikorsky S-55 (phasing out)
2 Piper Comanche
2 Twin Comanche

Notes:
Harrier AV-8 aircraft ordered from US Marine Corps in 1973. Initial order of 8 with possible follow-up of 12 and an additional 4.

New Construction

Because of financial considerations the current programme has been cut to the following: eight Corvettes, two ''Agosta'' class submarines, six 400 ton Large Patrol Craft, six 140 ton Large Patrol Craft.
Of the above, 4 corvettes and 2 submarines are building whilst 2 oceanographic vessels and 2 survey vessels are, in addition, under construction. All patrol craft are completed whilst the second 4 corvettes are due to be laid down at Ferrol.
Proposed but not yet approved—1 Sea Control Ship, 3 Frigates (''FFG 7'' class), 2 additional Agosta class submarines and 2 additional Corvettes.

Strength of the Fleet

Type	Active	Building	Proposed
Helicopter Carriers	1	—	?1
Destroyers	13	—	—
Frigates	15	7	?5
Submarines—Patrol	9	4	—
Large Patrol Craft	11	1	—
Coastal Patrol Craft	8	—	—
LSD	1	—	—
Attack Transports	2	—	—
LSTs	3	—	—
LCTs	8	—	—
Minor Landing Craft	79	—	—
Minesweepers—Ocean	10 + 4	—	—
Minesweepers—Coastal	12	—	—
Survey Ships	6	—	—
Transport	1	—	—
Replenishment Tanker	1	—	—
Harbour Tankers	13	—	—
Training Ship	1	—	—
Auxiliary Patrol Craft	7	—	—
Tugs (Ocean, Coastal and Harbour)	25	—	—
Miscellaneous	43	—	—

US Agreement

Under 1976 Agreement US is to provide 4 Minesweepers—Ocean and 1 Repair Ship.

Mercantile Marine

Lloyd's Register of Shipping:
2 792 vessels of 6 027 763 tons gross

DELETIONS

Cruiser

1975 *Canarias* (17 Dec)

Frigates

1971 *Magallanes, Vasco Nunez de Balbao, Hernan Cortes* (''Pizarro'' Class) *Marte* (''Jupiter'' Class)
1972 *Eolo, Triton* (''Elol'' Class), *Neptuno* (''Jupiter'' Class)
1973 *Osado* (''Audaz'' Class)
1974 *Audaz, Furor, Rayo* (''Audaz'' Class), *Jupiter* (''Jupiter'' Class), *Sarmiento de Gamboa* (''Pizarro'' Class)
1975 *Meteoro, Relampago, Temerario,* (''Audaz'' Class)
1977 *Vulcano* (''Jupiter'' Class)

Corvettes

1971 *Descubierta* (''Atrevida'' Class)
1973 *Diana* (''Atrevida'' Class)

Submarines

1971 D 2 (S 21), D 3 (S 22), G 7 (ex-U573 VII C)
Midget submarines SA 41 (F 1), SA 42 (F 2)
1977 SA 51, SA 52 (''Tiburon'' Class)

Minewarfare Forces

1971 *Lerez* (''Bidasoa'' Class)
1972 *Bidasoa, Nervion, Segura, Tambre, Ter* (''Bidasoa'' Class)
1976 *Tinto* (''Guardioro'' Class) (31 Jan)

Amphibious Forces

1974 LSM 3
1976 LSM 1, LSM 2

Light Forces

1971 *Javier Quiroga* (ex-US PC)
1973 *Ciés* (Fishery Protection)
1974 *V 2, V 12, V 13, V 18, Candido Pérez, AR 10* (Coastal Launches)
1977 LT 30, LT 31 (Lürssen Type)

Survey Ships

1971 *Malaspina*
1975 *Tofiño, Juan de la Cosa* (30 Apr)

Service Forces

1974 PP 1, 3, 4, PB 5, 6, 17 (tankers)

LIST OF PENNANT NUMBERS

Helicopter Carrier PH

01	Dédalo

Destroyers D

21	Lepanto
22	Almirante Ferrandiz
23	Almirante Valdes
24	Alcala Galiano
25	Jorge Juan
41	Oquendo
42	Roger de Lauria
43	Marques de la Ensenada
61	Churruca
62	Gravina
63	Mendez Nuñez
64	Langara
65	Blas de Lezo

Frigates D

D 38	Intrépido
51	Liniers
52	Alava

Frigates F

F 31	Descubierta
32	Diana
33	Infanta Elena
34	Infanta Cristina
35	New Construction
36	New Construction
37	New Construction
38	New Construction
41	Vicente Yáñez Pinzon
42	Legazpi
61	Atrevida
62	Princesa
64	Nautilus
65	Villa de Bilbao
71	Baleares
72	Andalucia
73	Cataluña
74	Asturias
75	Extremadura
91-3	Proposed New Construction

Submarines S

31	Almirante Garcia de los Reyes
32	Isaac Peral
33	Narciso Monturiol
34	Cosme Garcia
35	Ex-USS Jallao
61	Delfin
62	Tonina
63	Marsopa
64	Narval
71-72	New Construction
73-74	Proposed New Construction

Light Forces P

P 01	Lazaga
02	Alsedo
03	Cadarso
04	Villamil
05	Bonifaz
06	Recalde
11	Barceló
12	Laya
13	Javier Quiroga
14	Ordóñez
15	Acevedo
16	Candido Pérez
LP 1-5	
LAS 10, 20, 30	
RR 19, 20, 29	
V-1	
V-4	Alcatraz
V-5	
V-22	Cabo Fradera
V-31	
V-32	
W0	Azor
W01	Gaviota
W32	Salvora

Amphibious Forces

TA 11	Aragon
TA 21	Castilla
TA 31	Galicia
L 11	Velasco
L 12	Martin Alvarez
L 13	C. de Venadito
K 1-8	BDK 1-8

Minewarfare Forces M

11	Guadiaro
13	Eume
14	Almanzora
15	Navia
16	Guadalhorce
17	Eo
21	Nalón
22	Llobregat
23	Jucar
24	Ulla
25	Miño
26	Ebro
27	Turia
28	Duero
29	Sil
30	Tajo
31	Genil
32	Odiel
41	Guadalete
42	Guadalmedina
43	Guadalquivir
44	Guadiana

Survey Ships A

21	Castor
22	Pollux
23	Antares
24	Rigel
31	Malaspina
32	Tofiño

Service Forces

A 41	Almirante Lobo
BP 11	Teide

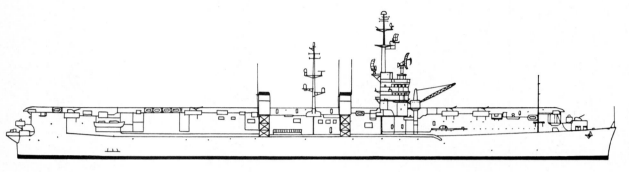

DEDALO

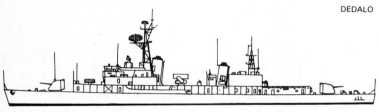

"Ex-US" GEARING ("D 60") Class

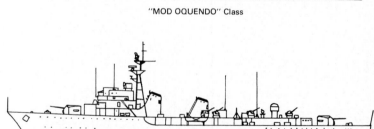

"MOD OQUENDO" Class

ALM. FERRANDIZ, LEPANTO

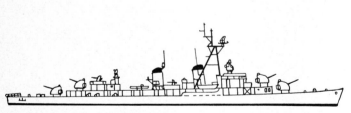

ALCALA GALIANO, JORGE JUAN and VALDES

OQUENDO

"DESCUBIERTA" ("F 30") Class

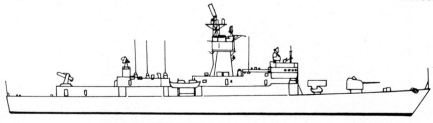

"BALEARES" ("F70") Class

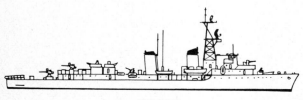

INTREPIDO

"LAZAGA" ("P 00") Class

"BARCELO" ("P 10") Class

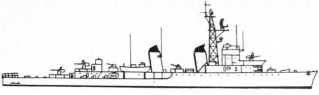

"ALAVA" ("D50") Class

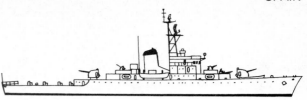

Mod. "PIZARRO" ("F 40") Class

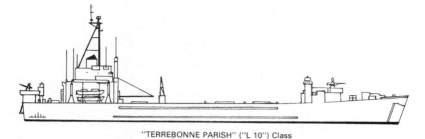

"TERREBONNE PARISH" ("L 10") Class

HELICOPTER CARRIERS

? CANARIAS

The future design of this ship, the eventual successor to *Dedalo*, is still in the planning stage and no definite decision has yet been reached as to her construction although it is reported that she will be built by Bazán Ferrol to the Sea Control ship design obtained from the USA.

1 Ex-US "INDEPENDENCE" CLASS (CVL)

Name	No.	Builders	Laid down	Launched	Commissioned
DÉDALO (ex-USS *Cabot* , AVT 3, ex-CVL 28, ex-*Wilmington, CL 79*)	PH 01	New York Shipbuilding Corporation	16 Aug 1942	4 Apr 1943	24 July 1943

Displacement, tons: 13 000 standard; 16 416 full load
Length, feet (metres): 600·0 *(182·8)* wl; 623·0 *(189·9)* oa
Beam, feet (metres): 71·5 *(21·8)* hull
Width, feet (metres): 109·0 *(33·2)*
Draught, feet (metres): 26·0 *(7·9)*
Aircraft: 7 Harriers (5 AV-8A, 2 TAV-8A) (Matador)
  20 helicopters (ASW/Sea Kings—Combat/Huey Cobras—Landings/specially embarked Bell 212s or 204s)
Guns: 26—40 mm (2 quadruple, 9 twin)
Armour: 2 to 5 in sides; 2 to 3 in deck
Main engines: GE geared turbines; 4 shafts; 100 000 shp
Boilers: 4 Babcock & Wilcox
Speed, knots: 32
Range, miles: 7 200 at 15 knots
Oil fuel, tons: 1 800
Complement: 1 112 (without Air Groups)

Completed as an aircraft carrier from the hull of a "Cleveland" class cruiser. Originally carried over 40 aircraft. Converted with strengthened flight and hangar decks, large port side catapult, revised magazine arrangements, new electronic gear, with stability corrected to offset the added top-weight. Hangar capacity altered to take 20 aircraft. Flight deck: 545 × 108 feet *(166·1 × 32·9 metres)*.
Reactivated and modernised at Philadelphia Naval Shipyard, where she was transferred to Spain on 30 Aug 1967, on loan for five years. Purchased Dec 1973. Fleet flagship.

Aircraft: Hangar capacity—18 Sea Kings. 6 more can be spotted on flight deck.

Gunnery: Reported that Meroka 20 mm system is to be shipped.

Radar: Air search: SPS 6 and SPS 40; SPS 52B
Heightfinder: AN/WLR 1.
Tactical: SPS 10
Fire control: 4 Sets
Tacan

DÉDALO

1974, Michael D. J. Lennon

DÉDALO

1974, Michael D. J. Lennon

DESTROYERS

5 "D 60" CLASS (Ex-US "GEARING" FRAM I CLASS)

Name	No.	Builders	Laid down	Launched	Commissioned
BLAS DE LEZO (ex-USS Noa, DD 841)	D 65	Bath Iron Works Corpn	1945	30 July 1945	2 Nov 1945
CHURRUCA (ex-USS Eugene A. Greene, DD 711)	D 61	Federal SB & DD Co.	1944	18 Mar 1945	8 June 1945
GRAVINA (ex-USS Furse, DD 882)	D 62	Consolidated Steel Corpn	1944	9 Mar 1945	10 July 1945
LANGARA (ex-USS Leary, DD 879)	D 64	Consolidated Steel Corpn	1944	20 Jan 1945	7 May 1945
MENDEZ NUÑEZ (ex-USS O'Hare, DD 889)	D 63	Consolidated Steel Corpn	1945	22 June 1945	29 Nov 1945

Displacement, tons: 2 425 standard; 3 480 full load
Length, feet (metres): 390·5 (119·0) oa
Beam, feet (metres): 40·9 (12·4)
Draught, feet (metres): 19 (5·8)
Aircraft: 1 Hughes 500 helicopter
Guns: 4—5 in (127 mm) 38 cal (twin)
A/S weapons: 1 Asroc launcher; 2 Triple Mk 32 tubes
Main engines: 2 geared turbines (GE or Westinghouse) 60 000 shp; 2 shafts
Boilers: 4 Babcock and Wilcox
Speed, knots: 34
Fuel, tons: 650
Range, miles: 4 800 at 15 knots (economical)
Complement: 274 (17 officers, 257 ratings)

Appearance: Blas de Lezo has two after gun mounts and torpedo tubes by after funnel.

Electronics: ESM; AL/WLRI.

Radar: Air Search: D61 and 62, SPS 40—remainder, SPS 37; Surface Search: SPS 10; Fire Control: Mk 37.

Refits: The first pair were refitted at El Ferrol on transfer. The remainder arrived at El Ferrol on July 23 1974 after refit in the USA.

Sonar: SQS 23 (hull mounted).

Torpedo control: ? Mk 114.

Transfers: D61 and 62—31 Aug 1972; D63-65—31 Oct 1973. (All finally purchased 1975).

LANGARA   1975, Spanish Navy

2 "MODIFIED OQUENDO" CLASS

Name	No.	Builders	Laid down	Launched	Commissioned
MARQUÉS DE LA ENSENADA	D 43	Ferrol	4 Sep 1951	15 July 1959	10 Sep 1970
ROGER DE LAURIA	D 42	Ferrol	4 Sep 1951	12 Nov 1958	30 May 1969

Displacement, tons: 3 012 standard; 3 785 full load
Length, feet (metres): 391·5 (119·3)
Beam, feet (metres): 42·7 (13·0)
Draught, feet (metres): 18·4 (5·6)
Aircraft: 1 Hughes 369 HM ASW helicopter
Guns: 6—5 in (127 mm) 38 cal (3 twin)
A/S weapons: 2 triple Mk 32 tubes for Mk 44 A/S torpedoes
Torpedo tubes: 2—21 in (533 mm) fixed single Mk 25 tubes for Mk 46 torpedoes
Main engines: 2 Rateau-Bretagne geared turbines; 2 shafts; 60 000 shp
Boilers: 3 three-drum type
Speed, knots: 28
Oil fuel, tons: 700
Range, miles: 4 500 at 15 knots
Complement: 318 (20 officers, 298 men)

Ordered in 1948. Originally of the same design as Oquendo. Towed to Cartegena for reconstruction to a new design. Roger de Lauria was re-launched after being lengthened and widened on 29 Aug 1967 and Marqués de la Ensenada on 2 Mar 1968. Weapons and electronics identical to Gearing Fram II.

Electronics: ESM; AL/WLRI. Torpedo control; ? Mk 114.

Fire Control: One Mk 37 director with Mk 25 radar. One Mk 56 director with Mk 35 radar.

Gunnery: To be fitted with Meroka 20 mm system.

MARQUÉS DE LA ENSENADA   1976, Royal Spanish Navy

Radar: Search: SPS 40.
Tactical: SPS 10.

Sonar: One hull mounted, SQS 32C; one VDS, SQA 10.

1 "OQUENDO" CLASS

Name	No.	Builders	Laid down	Launched	Commissioned
OQUENDO	D 41	Ferrol	15 June 1951	5 Sep 1956	13 Sep 1960

Displacement, tons: 2 342 standard; 3 005 full load
Length, feet (metres): 382 (116·4)
Beam, feet (metres): 36·5 (11·1)
Draught, feet (metres): 12·5 (3·8)
Guns: 4—4·7 (120 mm) 50 cal (2 twin NG 53); 6—40 mm, 70 cal (single SP 48)
A/S weapons: 2 Mk 11 Mod 0 hedgehogs; 2 Mk 4 side-launchers with 3 Mk 32 torpedoes each
Main engines: 2 Rateau-Bretagne geared turbines; 2 shafts; 60 000 shp
Boilers: 3 three-drum type
Speed, knots: 32·4
Oil fuel, tons: 659
Range, miles: 5 000 at 15 knots
Complement: 250 (17 officers, 233 men)

Ordered in 1947. Initially completed on 13 Sep 1960. Completed modernisation on 22 April 1963.

Construction: Designed as a conventional destroyer but modified during construction. Seven 21-inch torpedo tubes and two depth charge throwers were replaced by different antisubmarine weapons.

Gunnery: This is the only ship with Spanish-built NG 53 120 mm twin mountings.

OQUENDO   1974, Spanish Navy

Radar: Search: British 293 type.
Air Search: Marconi SNW 10.
Nav: 1 set.
Fire Control: British type 275 on Mark 6 DCT and British Type 262 on CRBFD (or MRS 8).

Sonar: QHB a.

5 "D 20" CLASS (Ex-US "FLETCHER" CLASS)

No.	Builders	Laid down	Launched	Commissioned
D 24	Todd Pacific Shipyards	7 June1943	14 Feb 1944	3 June 1944
D 22	Gulf SB Corpn, Chickasaw, Ala	12 June1941	4 July 1942	18 Sep 1943
D 23	Bath Iron Works Corp, Maine	23 Feb 1942	30 Aug 1942	8 June 1943
D 25	Federal SB & DD Co	May 1943	14 Nov 1943	20 Dec 1943
D 21	Gulf SB Corpn, Chickasaw, Ala.	12 June1941	31 May 1942	23 June 1943

Name
ALCALA GALIANO (ex-USS *Jarvis, DD 799*)
ALMIRANTE FERRANDIZ (ex-USS *David W. Taylor, DD 551*)
ALMIRANTE VALDES (ex-USS *Converse, DD 509*)
JORGE JUAN (ex-USS *McGowan, DD 678*)
LEPANTO (ex-USS *Capps, DD 550*)

Displacement, tons: 2 080 standard; 2 750 normal; 3 050 full load
Length, feet (metres): 376·5 *(114·8)* oa
Beam, feet (metres): 39·5 *(12·0)*
Draught, feet (metres): 18·0 *(5·5)*
Guns: D21, D22: 5—5 in *(127 mm)* 38 cal; Others: 4—5 in *(127 mm)* single
D21, D22: 6—40 mm, 60 cal Mk 1, (3 twin); 6—20 mm, 70 cal Mk 4, (single); Others: 6—3 in *(76 mm)* 50 cal Mk 33, (3 twin)
A/S weapons: 2 Mk 11 Hedgehogs; 6 DCT in D21 and D22, 4 in D23; 2 DC racks in D21, D22, 1 in others
Torpedo tubes: 3—21 in *(533 mm)* in D 23, 24 and 25 only
Torpedo racks: 2 side launching Mk 4 each with 3 Mk 32 A/S torpedoes
Main engines: Geared turbines; Westinghouse in D21, D22, GE in others; 2 shafts; 60 000 shp
Boilers: 4 Babcock & Wilcox
Speed, knots: 35
Oil fuel, tons: 506
Range, miles: 5 000 at 15 knots
Complement: 290 (17 officers, 273 men)

Lepanto, and *Almirante Ferrandiz,* were reconditioned at San Francisco, Cal, and there turned over to the Spanish Navy on 15 May 1957, sailing for Spain on 1 July 1957. *Valdes* was transferred at Philadelphia on 1 July 1959, *Jorge Juan,* was transferred at Barcelona on 1 Dec 1960 and *Alcala Galiano,* at Philadelphia on 3 Nov 1960, both being of the later "Fletcher" class. Modernisation of A/S equipment is planned. All purchased from US on 1 Oct 1972.

Electronics: Torpedo director Mk 5. A/S director Mk 105.

Radar: Search: SPS 6C.
Tactical: SPS 10.
Fire Control: D 23, 24 and 25—Mk 37 and Mk 56, 2 Mk 63 for 3 inch guns; D 21 and 22—Mk 37.

Sonar: One hull mounted set. SQS-29 or SQS-4.

ALMIRANTE VALDES   *1974, Wright and Logan*

FRIGATES

3 "F 90" CLASS (NEW CONSTRUCTION)

This is a projected class of frigates, similar to the USN "Oliver Hazard Perry" class, planned to be built at El Ferrol. Reported as a fully-automated class with possibility of Westinghouse-Canada VDS and of Elettronica-San Giorgio ECM.

4 + 4 + 2 "F 30" CLASS (NEW CONSTRUCTION)

Name	No.	Builders	Laid down	Launched	Commissioned
DESCUBIERTA	F 31	Bazán, Cartagena	16 Nov 1974	8 July 1975	Nov 1977
DIANA	F 32	Bazán, Cartagena	8 July 1975	26 Jan 1976	1978
INFANTA ELENA	F 33	Bazán, Cartagena	26 Jan 1976	14 Sep 1976	1978
INFANTA CRISTINA	F 34	Bazán, Cartagena	26 Jan 1976	14 Sep 1976	1979
—	F 35	Bazán, Ferrol	—	—	1980
—	F 36	Bazán, Ferrol	—	—	—
—	F 37	Bazán, Ferrol	—	—	—
—	F 38	Bazán, Ferrol	—	—	—

Displacement, tons: 1 200 standard; 1 497 full load
Dimensions, feet (metres): 291·3 × 34 × 11·5 *(88·8 × 10·5 × 3·5)*
Missiles: 1 Octuple Seasparrow mounting (16 reloads) (see note)
Guns: 1—3 in *(76 mm)* 62 cal OTO Melara; 2—40 mm 70 cal (singles); 1 or 2 Meroka 20 mm 120 cal (12 barrels non-rotating)
A/S weapons: 1—375 mm Bofors twin-barrelled rocket launcher; 6 (2 triple) Mk 32 for Mk 46 torpedoes
Main engines: 4 MTU-Bazan 16V956 "TB 91" diesels; 16 000 bhp (18 000 bhp supercharged for 2 hours); 2 shafts; cp propellers
Speed, knots: 26
Range, miles: 4 000 cruising
Complement: approx 100

Similar to the Portuguese "João Coutinho" class being built by Bazán with modifications to the armament and main engines. Officially rated as corvettes. Reported as designed to carry 30 marines. *Diana* (tenth of the name) originates with the Armada of 1588. Infanta Elena and Cristina are the daughters of King Juan Carlos. Approval for second 4 ships given on 21 May 1976.

Class: Four were ordered from Bazán, Cartagena in 1973. Approval for four more received whilst two more are planned.

Electronics: ECM probably Elettronica de San Georgio co-produced in Spain.

Missiles: Selenia system (Albatros) for Seasparrow. This will be built partly in Spain. SSMs will be MM 39 or Harpoon with two 4-cell launchers.

Radar: Search and fire control: 1 Hollandse Signaal M 22.
Air Search: 1 Hollandse Signaal LW-04.
Navigation: 1 Hollandse Signaal M25.

Sonar: Possibly Raytheon. VDS possibly Westinghouse (Canada).

"F 30" Class   *1974*

5 "BALEARES (F 70)" CLASS

Name	No.	Builders	Laid down	Launched	Commissioned
ANDALUCIA	F 72	Empresa Nacional Bazán, El Ferrol	2 July 1969	30 Mar 1971	23 May 1974
ASTURIAS	F 74	Empresa Nacional Bazán, El Ferrol	30 Mar 1971	13 May 1972	2 Dec 1975
BALEARES	F 71	Empresa Nacional Bazán, El Ferrol	31 Oct 1968	20 Aug 1970	24 Sep 1973
CATALUÑA	F 73	Empresa Nacional Bazán, El Ferrol	20 Aug 1970	3 Nov 1971	9 Dec 1974
EXTREMADURA	F 75	Empresa Nacional Bazán, El Ferrol	3 Nov 1971	21 Nov 1972	1976

Displacement, tons: 3 015 standard; 4 177 full load
Length, feet (metres): 415·0 *(126·5)* pp; 438·0 *(133·6)* oa
Beam, feet (metres): 46·9 *(14·3)*
Draught, feet (metres): 15·4 *(4·7)*
Missile launchers: 1 single for Tartar/Standard missiles (Lightweight Mk 22)
Gun: 1—5 in *(127 mm)* 54 cal Mk 42 Mod 9
A/S weapons: 1 eight-tube ASROC launcher (8 reloads);
4 Mk 32 for Mk 46 torpedoes;
2 Mk 25 for Mk 37 torpedoes (stern)
Main engines: 1 set Westinghouse geared turbines; 1 shaft; 35 000 shp
Boilers: 2 high pressure V2M type; 1 200 psi *(84·4 kg/cm²)*
Speed, knots: 28
Range: 4 500 miles at 20 knots
Complement: 256 (15 officers, 241 men)

This class resulted from a very close co-operation between Spain and the USA. Programme approved 17 Nov 1964, technical support agreement with USA being signed 31 Mar 1966. USN supplied weapons, sensors, major hull sections—turbines and gearboxes made at El Ferrol, superstructures at Alicante, boilers, distilling plants and propellers at Cadiz.

Anti-submarine: 8 Reloads carried for ASROC.

Design: This class replaced the "Leander" class from Great Britain which order was cancelled in 1962 as the result of political insults in that country. Generally similar to USN "Knox" class although they differ in the missile system, hull sonar, Mk 25 torpedo tubes and lack of helicopter facilities. The last is a cause of criticism along with similar criticisms in USN of low speed, lack of manoeuvrability (1 screw) and inadequate missile stowage.
The anchor arrangement provides for a 2-ton anchor on the port bow and a 4-ton anchor in the keel aft of the sonar dome.

Fire Control: Mk 68 GFCS with SPG-53B radar for guns and missiles; Mk 74 missile control system integrating Mk 73 missile control director and SPG-51C radar. Mk 114 torpedo control system.

Gunnery: 600—5 inch rounds carried.
Meroka system due to be shipped in 1978.

Missile system: Mk 22 launcher with stowage for 16 missiles. Single director with two lines of fire against different targets with MR68 GFCS.

Radar: Search: SPS 52A (3D).
Tactical: SPS 10.
Fire control: SPG-51C continuous wave for missiles; Mk 68 with SPG 53B for guns with continuous wave injection for limited use with missiles.

Torpedoes and tubes: All are fitted fixed internally the Mk 32 being angled at 45°. Total of 41 torpedoes carried.

Sonar: SQS 23 bow mounted; SQS 35V VDS below quarterdeck.

ASTURIAS
7/1976, Arthur D. Baker III

CATALUÑA
9/1975, Dr Giorgio Arra

1 "AUDAZ" CLASS

Name	No.	Builders	Laid down	Launched	Commissioned
INTRÉPIDO	D 38	Ferrol	14 July 1945	15 Feb 1961	25 Mar 1965

Displacement, tons: 1 227 standard; 1 550 full load
Length, feet (metres): 295·2 *(90·0)* pp; 308·2 *(94·0)* oa
Beam, feet (metres): 30·5 *(9·3)*
Draught, feet (metres): 17·1 *(5·2)*
Guns: 2—3 in *(76 mm)* 50 cal US Mk 34; 2—40 mm 70 cal (SP 48)
A/S weapons: 2 Mk 11 hedgehogs; 8 mortars; 2 DC racks;
2 side launching racks for Mk 32 A/S torpedoes (6 torpedoes)
Main engines: 2 Rateau-Bretagne geared turbines; 2 shafts; 28 000 shp (32 500 max)
Boilers: 3 La Seine 3-drum type
Speed, knots: 28
Oil fuel, tons: 290
Range, miles: 3 800 at 14 knots
Complement: 199 (13 officers, 186 men)

Based on the French "Le Fier" design. Allocated D Pennant number in 1961.

Engineering: The boilers are in two compartments separated by the engine rooms.

Radar: Surface search, SPS 5B.
Air search: MLA-1B.
Fire control: one Mk 63.

Sonar: One QHBa hull mounted-set.

INTRÉPIDO
1969, Spanish Navy

2 "ALAVA" CLASS

Name	No.
ALAVA	D 52 (ex-23)
LINIERS	D 51 (ex-21)

Builders	Laid down	Launched	Commissioned
Bazán, Cartagena	21 Dec 1944	19 May 1947	21 Dec 1950
Bazán, Cartagena	1 Jan 1945	1 May 1946	27 Jan 1951

Displacement, tons: 1 842 standard; 2 287 full load
Length, feet (metres): 336·3 (102·5)
Beam, feet (metres): 31·5 (9·6)
Draught, feet (metres): 19·7 (6·0)
Guns: 3—3 in (76 mm) 50 cal, Mk 34; 3—40 mm, 70 cal (SP 48)
A/S weapons: 2 hedgehogs; 8 DC mortars; 2 DC racks;
  2 side launching racks for Mk 32 A/S torpedoes (6 torpedoes)
Main engines: Parsons geared turbines; 2 shafts; 31 500 shp
Boilers: 4 Yarrow 3-drum type
Speed, knots: 29
Oil fuel, tons: 370
Range, miles: 4 100 at 15 knots
Complement: 222 (15 officers, 207 men)

Ordered in 1936, but construction was held up by the Civil War. After being resumed, was again suspended in 1940, but restarted at Empresa Nacional Bazán in 1944. These are the last of the old "Churruca" class of which eighteen were built.

Fire Control: Mk 63 FCS with Mk 34 radar.

Radar: Air search: MLA 1B.
Surface search: SG-6B.
Navigation: Decca TM 626.

Sonar: One SQS 30A hull-mounted set.

ALAVA   1974, Spanish Navy

2 MODERNISED "PIZARRO" CLASS

Name	No.
LEGAZPI	F 42
VICENTE YAÑEZ PINZON	F 41

Builders	Laid down	Launched	Commissioned
Ferrol	Sept 1943	8 Aug 1945	8 Aug 1951
Ferrol	Sept 1943	8 Aug 1945	5 Aug 1949

Displacement, tons: 1 924 standard; 2 228 full load
Length, feet (metres): 279·0 (85·0) pp; 312·5 (95·3) oa
Beam, feet (metres): 39·5 (12·0)
Draught, feet (metres): 17·7 (5·4)
Guns: 2—5 in (127 mm) 38 cal; 4—40 mm, 70 cal (SP 48)
A/S weapons: 2 hedgehogs; 8 mortars; 2 DC racks;
  2 side launching racks for Mk 32 torpedoes (3 torpedoes each)
Main engines: 2 sets Parsons geared turbines; 2 shafts;
  6 000 shp
Boilers: 2 Yarrow type
Speed, knots: 18·5
Range, miles: 3 000 at 15 knots
Oil fuel, tons: 390
Complement: 255 (16 officers, 239 men)

Originally designed to carry 30 mines.

Fire Control: GFCS Mk 52 with Mk 29 radar on one director.

Modernisation: Legazpi completed 14 Jan 1960 and Pinzon 25 Mar 1960.

Radar: Surface search: SPS 5B.
Air Search: MLA-1B.
Navigation: Decca TM 626.

VICENTE YAÑEZ PINZON   1974, Spanish Navy

4 "ATREVIDA - F 60" CLASS

Name	No.
ATREVIDA	F 61
NAUTILUS	F 64
PRINCESA	F 62
VILLA DE BILBAO	F 65

Builders	Laid down	Launched	Commissioned
Bazán, Cartagena	26 June 1950	2 Dec 1952	19 Aug 1954
Bazán, Cadiz	27 July 1953	23 Aug 1956	10 Dec 1959
Bazán, Cartagena	18 Mar 1953	31 Mar 1956	2 Oct 1957
Bazán, Cadiz	18 Mar 1953	19 Feb 1958	2 Sept 1960

Displacement, tons: 1 031 standard; 1 135 full load
Length, feet (metres): 247·8 (75·5) oa
Beam, feet (metres): 33·5 (10·2)
Draught, feet (metres): 9·8 (3·0)
Guns: 1—3 in (76 mm) 50 cal Mk 22; 3—40 mm, 70 cal (SP 48)
A/S weapons: 2 hedgehogs; 8 mortars; 2 DC racks
Mines: 20 can be carried
Main engines: Sulzer diesels; 2 shafts; 3 000 bhp
Speed, knots: 18·5
Oil fuel, tons: 105
Range, miles: 8 000 at 10 knots
Complement: 132 (9 officers, 123 men)

All have been modernised—F 61 in 1959-60, remainder while building. No funnel, the diesel exhaust being on the starboard side waterline. Allocated F pennant numbers in 1961 although still officially classed as corvettes.

Aircraft: Although no deck is fitted helicopters can be refuelled in flight.

Radar: Modified SPS-5B combined air/surface search.

Sonar: One QHBa.

ATREVIDA   1976, Michael D. J. Lennon

SUBMARINES

2 + 2 "S 70" CLASS (FRENCH "AGOSTA" CLASS)

Name	No.	Builders	Laid down	Launched	Commissioned
—	S 71	Bazán, Cartagena	1975	1977	1980
—	S 72	Bazán, Cartagena	1975	1977	1981
—	S 73	Bazán, Cartagena	—	—	—
—	S 74	Bazán, Cartagena	—	—	—

Displacement, tons: 1 450 surfaced; 1 725 dived
Dimensions, feet (metres): 221·7 × 22·3 × 17·7 *(67·6 × 6·8 ×
5·4)*
Torpedo tubes: 4—21·7 in *(550 mm)* (16 reloads)
Main machinery: Diesel-electric; 2 diesels; 3 600 hp; 1 Main
motor; 6 400 hp; 1 cruising motor; 1 shaft
Speed, knots: 12 surfaced; 20 dived
Range, miles: 9 000 at 9 knots (snorting); 350 at 3·5 knots
(dived)
Endurance: 45 days
Complement: 50

Two ordered April 1974. To be built by Bazán Cartagena with
some French advice. Two more orders placed 1976.

Radar: Calypso I Band.

Sonar: Two DUUA active; one DSUV passive.

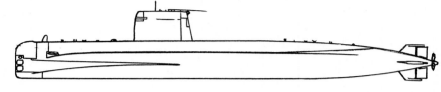

1974

"S 70" Class

4 "S 60" CLASS (FRENCH "DAPHNE" CLASS)

Name	No.	Builders	Laid down	Launched	Commissioned
DELFIN	S 61	E. N. Bazán, Cartagena	13 Aug 1968	25 Mar 1972	3 May 1973
TONINA	S 62	E. N. Bazán, Cartagena	1969	3 Oct 1972	10 July 1973
MARSOPA	S 63	E. N. Bazán, Cartagena	19 Mar 1971	15 Mar 1974	12 April 1975
NARVAL	S 64	E. N. Bazán, Cartagena	1971	14 Dec 1974	22 Nov 1975

Displacement, tons: 870 surfaced; 1 040 dived
Length, feet (metres): 189·6 *(57·8)*
Beam, feet (metres): 22·3 *(6·8)*
Draught, feet (metres): 15·1 *(4·6)*
Torpedo tubes: 12—21·7 in *(550 mm)* (8 bow, 4 stern) (no
reloads — mining capability)
Main machinery: SEMT-Pielstick diesel-electric; 2 600 bhp sur-
faced; 2 700 hp dived; 2 shafts
Speed, knots: 13·2 surfaced; 15·5 dived
Range, miles: 4 500 at 5 knots (snorting); 2 710 at 12·5 knots
(surfaced)
Complement: 47 (6 officers, 41 men)

Identical to the French "Daphne" class and built with extensive
French assistance in the Cartagena Yard. First pair ordered 26
Dec 1966 and second pair in Mar 1970. S 63 cost 1 040 million
pesetas.

Radar: Thompson CSF DRUA-31 plus ECM.

Sonar: Active, DUUA 1; Passive with rangefinding, DSUV.
Goniometer; DUUG-1.

TONINA

6/1975, Dr. Giorgia Arra

4 "S 30" CLASS (Ex-US GUPPY IIA TYPE)

Name	No.	Builders	Laid down	Launched	Commissioned
ISAAC PERAL (ex-USS *Ronquil, SS 396*)	S 32	Portsmouth Navy Yard	9 Sep 1943	27 Jan 1944	22 April 1944
NARCISO MONTURIOL (ex-USS *Picuda, SS 382*)	S 33	Portsmouth Navy Yard	15 Mar 1943	12 July 1943	16 Oct 1943
COSME GARCIA (ex-USS *Bang, SS 385*)	S 34	Portsmouth Navy Yard	30 April 1943	30 Aug 1943	4 Dec 1943
— (ex-USS *Jallao, SS 385*)	S 35	Manitowoc SB Corpn	29 Sep 1943	12 Mar 1944	8 July 1944

Displacement, tons: 1 840 surfaced; 2 445 dived
Length, feet (metres): 306·0 *(93·3)* oa
Beam, feet (metres): 27·0 *(8·2)*
Draught, feet (metres): 17·0 *(5·2)*
Torpedo tubes: 10—21 in *(533 mm)* 6 bow, 4 stern
Main machinery: 3 Fairbanks-Morse diesels; total 4 800 bhp;
2 shafts; 2 Elliot electric motors; 5 400 shp
Speed, knots: 18 surfaced; 14 dived
Oil fuel, tons: 464 (472 in SS 35)
Range, miles: 12 000 at 10 knots
Complement: 74

Transferred to Spain on 1 July 1971 *(Peral)* 1 Oct 1972 *(Garcia
and Monturiol)* and (ex-*Jallao*) 26 June 1974 *Monturiol* and *Garcia* and purchased 18 Nov 1974 the other pair being transferred
by sale. *Narciso Monturiol* had mechanical defects in 1975
which resulted in *Almirante Garcia de los Reyes* being retained
in service with the former's crew. These defects may result in
Narciso Monturiol being paid off.

Appearance: *Monturiol* has stepped section at forward end of
fin, remainder having full fin.

Diving Depth: 450 feet *(140 metres)*.

Electronics: Mk 106 TDC.

Radar: SS 2.

Sonar: BQS, BQR.

COSME GARCIA (PERAL similar)

1973, J. Taibo

NARCISO MONTURIOL

1 Ex-US "BALAO" CLASS

Name	No.	Builders	Laid down	Launched	Commissioned
ALMIRANTE GARCIA DE LOS REYES (ex-USS *Kraken*, SS 370)	S 31	Manitowoc SB Co.	—	30 April 1944	8 Sep 1944

Displacement, tons: 1 816 surfaced; 2 400 dived
Dimensions, feet (metres): 311·5 × 27·2 × 17·2 *(95 × 8·3 × 5·2)*
Torpedo tubes: 10—(6—21 in *(533 mm)* and 4 for A/S torpedoes)
Main machinery: 4 diesels; 6 400 bhp; 2 main motors; 4 600 shp; 2 shafts
Speed, knots: 18·5 surfaced; 10 dived
Oil fuel, tons: 472
Range, miles: 12 000 at 10 knots (surfaced)
Complement: 80

Transferred 24 October 1959 after modernisation at Pearl Harbor. Although due to be paid off in 1975 retained in service (see note under "S 30" class).

ALMIRANTE GARCIA DE LOS REYES

1969, Spanish Navy

LIGHT FORCES

6 "LAZAGA (P-OO)" CLASS (LARGE PATROL CRAFT)

Name	No.	Builders	Commissioned
LAZAGA	P 01	Lürssen Vegesack	18 July 1975
ALSEDO	P 02	Bazán, La Carraca	Dec 1976
CADARSO	P 03	Bazán, La Carraca	July 1976
VILLAMIL	P 04	Bazán, La Carraca	Oct 1976
BONIFAZ	P 05	Bazán, La Carraca	11 Nov 1976
RECALDE	P 06	Bazán, La Carraca	1977

Displacement, tons: 275 standard; 400 full load
Dimensions, feet (metres): 190·2 × 24·9 × 8·5 *(58 × 7·6 × 2·6)*
Guns: 1—3 in 62 cal OTO Melara; 1—40 mm 70 cal Breda-Bofors 350P; 2—20 mm Oerlikon GAM 204
A/S weapons: 2 DC racks; provision for 2 triple Mk 32 torpedo tube mountings
Main engines: 2 MTU-Bazan MA15 TB91 diesels; 8 000 bhp
Speed, knots: 28
Range, miles: 6 100 at 17 knots
Complement: 30 (3 officers, 27 ratings)

Ordered in 1972, primarily for Fishery Protection duties. Although all will be operated by the Navy half the cost is being borne by the Ministry of Commerce. Of similar hull form to Israeli "Reshef" class but with only 2 engines.
Lazaga launched on 30 Sep 1974. She was steamed to Spain in April 1975 for equipping and arming. Laid down dates—01-03, 1974; 04-05, 8 Jan 1975; 06, 1975. Launch dates—02 and 03, 8 Jan 1975; 04 and 05 24 May 1975; 06, 30 Oct 1975.

Fire Control: Optical director CSEE (HSM Mk 22).

Gunnery: All guns built under licence by Bazán.

Missiles: Provision has been made for fitting surface-to-surface missiles (4 Exocet or 8 Harpoon or MM 39), involving a change of gun armament.

Radar: Surface search, Target indication and Navigation; Hollandse Signaal M-20 series; ECM and IFF

Sonar: One hull-mounted set (?ELAC).

CADARSO

12/1976, J. I. Taibo

6 "BARCELO (P 10)" CLASS (LARGE PATROL CRAFT)

Name	No.	Builders	Commissioned
BARCELÓ	P 11	Lürssen Vegesack	20 Mar 1976
LAYA	P 12	Bazán, La Carraca	Dec 1976
JAVIER QUIROGA	P 13	Bazán, La Carraca	1977
ORDÓÑEZ	P 14	Bazán, La Carraca	1977
ACEVEDO	P 15	Bazán, La Carraca	1977
CÁNDIDO PÉREZ	P 16	Bazán, La Carraca	1978

Displacement, tons: 139
Dimensions, feet (metres): 118·7 × 19 × 8·2 *(36·2 × 5·8 × 2·5)*
Guns: 1—40 mm Breda Bofors 350; 2—20 mm Oerlikon GAM 204; 2—12·7 mm
Torpedo tubes: Provision for 2—21 in *(533 mm)*
Main engines: 2 MTU-Bazán MD-16V TB 90 diesels; 6 000 bhp; 2 shafts
Speed, knots: 34; 20 cruising
Range, miles: 1 200 at 17 knots
Complement: 19

Ordered 5 Dec 1973, the prototype, *Barcelo*, being built by Lürssen, Vegesack with MTU engines. Laid down 3 Mar 1975 for launch in Nov 1975. All to be manned by the Navy although the cost is being borne by the Ministry of Commerce.
Launch dates—P 11, Nov 1975, P 12-13, Dec 1975, P 14-15, Sept 76.

BARCELO

3/1976, E. N. Bazán

5 "LP 1" CLASS (COASTAL PATROL CRAFT)

Name	No.	Builders	Commissioned
—	LP 1	Bazan, La Carraca	Feb 1965
—	LP 2	Bazán, La Carraca	Feb 1965
—	LP 3	Bazán, La Carraca	Mar 1965
—	LP 4	Bazán, La Carraca	Mar 1965
—	LP 5	Bazán, La Carraca	Mar 1965

Displacement, tons: 17·2 standard; 25 full load
Dimensions, feet (metres): 46 × 15·4 × 3·3 *(14 × 4·7 × 1)*
Guns: 2—7·62 mm (twin)
Main engines: 2 Gray Marine diesels; 450 hp = 13 knots
Complement: 8

Laid down 1964 by Bazán La Carraca. Wooden-hulled.

LP 3   *1965, Spanish Navy*

3 USCG 83 ft TYPE (COASTAL PATROL CRAFT)

Name	No.	Builders	Commissioned
—	**LAS 10** (ex-*LAS 1*)	E. N. Bazán, Cartagena	26 Apr 1965
—	**LAS 20** (ex-*LAS 2*)	E. N. Bazán, Cartagena	4 May 1965
—	**LAS 30** (ex-*LAS 3*)	E. N. Bazán, Cartagena	3 Sep 1965

Displacement, tons: 49 standard; 63 full load
Dimensions, feet (metres): 78·0 pp; 83·3 oa × 16·1 × 6·6 *(23·8; 25·4 × 4·9 × 2)*
Guns: 1—20 mm; 2—7 mm (single)
A/S weapons: 2 Mousetrap Mk 20 (4 rockets each)
Main engines: 800 bhp; 2 shafts = 15 knots
Complement: 15

Of wooden hull construction. All launched 1964.

Radar: Decca 978.

Sonar: QCU 2.

LAS 30   *1974, Spanish Navy*

1 FISHERY PROTECTION VESSEL

SALVORA (ex-*Virgen de la Almudena*, ex-*Mendi Eder*) W 32

Displacement, tons: 180 standard; 275 full load
Dimensions, feet (metres): 107·0 × 20·5 × 9·0 *(31 × 6·1 × 2·5)*
Gun: 1—20 mm Mk 4 70 cal
Main engines: 1 Sulzer diesel; 1 shaft; 400 bhp = 12 knots
Oil fuel, tons: 25
Complement: 31

Trawler. Built in 1948 by SA Juliana, Gijon. Commissioned 25 Sep 1954. Based in Coruña.

Radar: Decca RM 914.

3 PATROL VESSELS

RR 19	RR 20	RR 29

Displacement, tons: 364 standard; 498 full load
Dimensions, feet (metres): 124·0 × 29·0 × 10·0 *(38 × 8·4 × 3)*
Guns: 1—1·5 in, 85 cal; 1—20 mm
Main engines: Triple expansion; 1 shaft; 800 ihp = 10 knots
Boilers: 1 cylindrical, *(13 kg/cm)*
Fuel, tons: 100 coal
Range, miles: 620 at 10 knots

Former tugs. All launched in 1941-42.

Radar: DK 12.

7 COASTAL/RIVER PATROL LAUNCHES

Name	No.	Builders	Commissioned
GAVIOTA	W 01	Germany	1944
—	V 1	Kiel, Germany	1926
ALCATRAZ	V 4	Egaña, Motrico	10 Apr 1947
—	V 5	Arsenal, Cartagena	13 June1969
CABO FRADERA	V 22	Bazán, La Carraca	25 Feb 1963
—	V 31	Darmstadt, Germany	23 Mar 1974
—	V 32	Barcelona	23 Mar 1974

Gaviota W 01, 104 tons- ex-smuggler; V 1 (ex-*Azor*) 112 tons, 12 knots (Naval School); V 4, 65 tons, 9 knots; V 5, 4·5 tons, 5 knots; *Cabo Fradera* V 22, 28 tons, 1—7·62 mm MG based at Tuy for patrol on R. Miño on Portuguese border; V 31-32, 5 tons, 27 knots.

CABO FRADERA   *1976, Royal Spanish Navy*

AMPHIBIOUS FORCES

1 Ex-US "HASKELL" CLASS (ATTACK TRANSPORT)

Name	No.	Builders	Commissioned
ARAGÓN (ex-USS *Noble, APA 218*)	TA 11	USA	1945

Displacement, tons: 6 720 light; 12 450 full load
Dimensions, feet (metres): 455 oa × 63·5 × 24 *(138·8 × 19·3 × 7·2)*
Guns: 12—40 mm 60 cal (1 quad, 4 twin)
Main engines: 1 Geared turbine; 8 500 shp = 17 knots
Boilers: 2 Babcock & Wilcox
Oil fuel, tons: 1 150
Range, miles: 14 700 at 16 knots
Complement: 357

Former US Attack Transport, transferred at San Francisco on 19 Dec 1964. Can carry 1 190 men and 680 tons cargo (or 11—2½ ton trucks and 49—¾ ton trucks). 24 landing craft. Amphibious forces flagship.

Radar: Air search SPS 6; surface search SPS 4.

ARAGÓN   *1976, Royal Spanish Navy*

1 Ex-US "ANDROMEDA" CLASS

Name	No.	Builders	Commissioned
CASTILLA (ex-USS *Achernar, AKA 53*)	TA 21	USA	1944

Displacement, tons: 7 430 light; 11 416 full load
Dimensions, feet (metres): 457·8 oa × 63 × 24 *(140 × 19·2 × 7·4)*
Guns: 1—5 in 38 cal; 8—40 mm 60 cal (twins) (Mk 1)
Main engines: 1 GE geared turbine; 6 000 shp = 16 knots
Boilers: 2 Foster-Wheeler
Oil fuel, tons: 1 400
Range, miles: 18 500 at 12 knots
Complement: 324

Former US Attack Cargo Ship transferred at New York on 2 Feb 1965. Can carry 98 men, 6 M-48 tanks, 36—2½ ton trucks and 267 Jeeps. 24 landing craft.

Radar: Surface search SPS 10.

CASTILLA   *1976, Royal Spanish Navy*

1 Ex-US "CABILDO" CLASS (LSD)

Name	No.	Builders	Commissioned
GALICIA (ex-USS *San Marcos, LSD 25*)	TA 31	Philadelphia Navy Yard	15 Apr 1945

Displacement, tons: 4 790 standard; 9 375 full load
Dimensions, feet (metres): 475·4 oa × 72·6 × 18·0 *(139 × 21·9 × 4·9)*
Guns: 12—40 mm, 60 cal (2 quadruple, 2 twin)
Main engines: Geared turbines; 2 shafts; 7 000 shp = 15·4 knots
Boilers: 2 3 drum cylindrical
Oil fuel, tons: 1 727
Range, miles: 8 000 at 15 knots
Complement: 301 (18 officers, 283 men)

Transferred to Spain on 1 July 1971 and by sale Aug 1974. Fitted with helicopter platform. Can carry 3 LCUs or 18 LCMs. 1 347 tons of cargo or 100—2½ ton trucks or 27 M-48 tanks or 11 heavy helicopters. Accommodation for 137 troops (overnight) or 500 for short haul.

Fire Control: GFCS with Mk 51 radar.

Radar: SPS 10 and 50.

GALICIA   *1976, Royal Spanish Navy*

3 Ex-US "TERREBONNE PARISH" CLASS (LST)

Name	No.	Builders	Commissioned
CONDE DE VENADITO (ex-USS *Tom Green County, LST 1159*)	L 13	Bath Iron Works	12 Sep 1953
MARTIN ALVAREZ (ex-USS *Wexford County, LST 1168*)	L 12	Christy Corpn	15 June 1954
VELASCO (ex-USS *Terrebonne Parish, LST 1156*)	L 11	Bath Iron Works	21 Nov 1952

Displacement, tons: 2 590 standard; 5 800 full load
Dimensions, feet (metres): 384·0 oa × 55·0 × 17·0 *(117·4 × 16·7 × 3·7)*
Guns: 6—3 in, 50 cal (3 twin, 2 forward, 1 aft)
Main engines: 4 GM diesels; 2 shafts; 6 000 bhp = 15 knots
Range, miles: 15 000 at 9 knots
Complement: 116 (troops 395)

CONDE DE VENADITO   *1974, Spanish Navy*

LST 1156 and 1168 transferred on 29 Oct 1971, LST 1159 on 5 Jan 1972. Can carry 395 men, 10 M-48 tanks or 17 LVTP. 4 landing craft. Purchase approved 5 Aug 1976.

Fire Control: 2 Mk 63 GFCS with Mk 34 radar.

Radar: SPS 10 surface search.

2 Ex-BRITISH LCT (4)

BDK 1   1976, Royal Spanish Navy

BDK 1 K 1   **BDK 2** K 2

Displacement, tons: 440 standard; 868 full load
Dimensions, feet (metres): 185·3 × 38·7 × 6·2 *(56·5 × 11·8 × 1·9)*
Guns: 2—20 mm (single)
Main engines: 2 Paxman diesels; 2 shafts; 920 bhp = 10 knots
Range, miles: 1 100 at 8 knots

Can carry 350 tons or 500 men. Both laid down 1945 and commissioned 11 Nov 1948.

3 SPANISH BUILT LCTs

Name	No.	Builders	Commissioned
BDK 3	K 3	Bazán, El Ferrol	15 June 1959
BDK 4	K 4	Bazán, El Ferrol	15 June 1959
BDK 5	K 5	Bazán, El Ferrol	15 June 1959

BDK 5   1971, Spanish Navy

Displacement, tons: 602 full load
Dimensions, feet (metres): 186 × 38·4 × 6 *(56·6 × 11·6 × 1·7)*
Guns: 2—20 mm (singles)
Main engines: 2 M60 V8 AS diesels; 2 shafts; 1 000 hp = 8½ knots
Range, miles: 1 000 at 7 knots
Complement: Complement 20 (1 officer, 19 men)

All laid down 1958. Can carry 300 tons or 400 men.

3 EDIC TYPE (LCT)

Name	No.	Builders	Commissioned
BDK 6	K 6	Bazán, La Carraca	6 Dec 1966
BDK 7	K 7	Bazán, La Carraca	30 Dec 1966
BDK 8	K 8	Bazán, La Carraca	30 Dec 1966

BDK 6   1976, Royal Spanish Navy

Displacement, tons: 315 standard; 665 full load
Dimensions, feet (metres): 193·5 oa × 39·0 × 5·0 *(59 × 11·9 × 1·3)*
Guns: 1—20 mm; 2—12·7 mm MG
Main engines: 2 diesels; 2 shafts; 1 040 bhp = 9·5 knots
Range, miles: 1 500 at 9 knots
Complement: 17

Landing craft of the French EDIC type built at La Carraca.

2 Ex-US LCUs

LCU 1 (ex-US *YFU 88*, ex-*LCU 1471*)
LCU 2 (ex-US *YFU 95*, ex-*LCU 1491*)

Displacement, tons: 360
Dimensions, feet (metres): 119·7 × 31·5 × 5·2 *(36·5 × 9·6 × 1·6)*
Speed, knots: 7·6
Complement: 13

Transferred June 1972. Sold Aug 1976.

6 US LCM (8)

E 81   **E 82**   **E 83**   **E 84**   **E 85**   **E 86**

Displacement, tons: 115 full load
Dimensions, feet (metres): 74·5 × 21·7 × 5·9 *(22·7 × 6·6 × 1·8)*
Speed, knots: 9
Complement: 5

This new class was ordered from Oxnard, California in 1974. All commissioned in July-Sept 1975.

Note: Total of landing craft (including those attached to *Aragón*, *Castilla*, and LSTs):
16 LCM (6), 43 LCVP, 14 LCP (L).
All of US origin except 8 LCP (L), built at Cartagena.

MINE WARFARE FORCES

4 + 4 Ex-US "AGGRESSIVE" CLASS (MINESWEEPERS—OCEAN)

Name	No.	Builders	Commissioned
GUADALETE	M 41	Colbert BW, Stockton, Calif	15 Dec 1953
(ex-USS *Dynamic*, MSO 432)			
GUADALMEDINA	M 42	Wilmington BW, Calif	12 July 1954
(ex-USS *Pivot*, MSO 463)			
GUADALQUIVIR	M 43	Tacoma, Washington	3 Feb 1956
(ex-USS *Persistant*, MSO 491)			
GUADIANA	M 44	Burgess Boat Co, Manitowoc	8 Nov 1954
(ex-USS *Vigor*, MSO 473)			

Displacement, tons: 665 standard; 750 full load
Dimensions, feet (metres): 165·0 wl; 172·0 oa × 36·0 × 13·6 *(52·3 × 10·4 × 4·2)*
Guns: 2—20 mm (twin)
Main engines: 4 Packard diesels; 2 shafts; controllable pitch propellers; 2 280 bhp = 15·5 knots
Oil fuel, tons: 46
Range, miles: 3 000 at 10 knots
Complement: 74 (6 officers, 68 men)

The first three were transferred and commissioned on 1 July 1971. The fourth unit was delivered 4 April 1972. All purchased Aug 1974. A further four to be provided under the 1976 US Agreement.

GUADALETE   *1973, J. Taibo*

Radar: Surface search: SPS 5C.

Sonar: SQQ 14 (VDS) with mine classification capability.

12 "NALON" (M 20) CLASS (Ex-US MSC TYPE)
(MINESWEEPERS—COASTAL)

Name	No.	Builders	Commissioned
DUERO (ex-*Spoonbill*, MSC 202)	M 28	Tampa Marine Corpn	Jan 1959
EBRO (ex-*MSC 269*)	M 26	Bellingham SY	Dec 1958
GENIL (ex-*MSC 279*)	M 31	Tacoma, Seattle	Sep 1959
JUCAR (ex-*MSC 220*)	M 23	Bellingham SY	June 1956
LLOBREGAT (ex-*MSC 143*)	M 22	S. Coast SY, Calif	Nov 1954
MIÑO (ex-*MSC 266*)	M 25	Adams YY, Mass	Oct 1956
NALÓN (ex-*MSC 139*)	M 21	S. Coast SY, Calif	Feb 1954
ODIEL (ex-*MSC 288*)	M 32	Tampa Marine Corpn	Oct 1959
SIL (ex-*Redwing*, MSC 200)	M 29	Tampa Marine Corpn	Jan 1959
TAJO (ex-*MSC 287*)	M 30	Tampa Marine Corpn	July 1959
TURIA (ex-*MSC 130*)	M 27	Hildebrand DD, NY	Jan 1955
ULLA (ex-*MSC 265*)	M 24	Adams YY, Mass	July 1958

Displacement, tons: 355 standard; 384 full load
Dimensions, feet (metres): 138·0 pp; 144·0 oa × 27·2 × 8·0 *(41·5; 43 × 8 × 2·6)*
Guns: 2—20 mm (1 twin)
Main engines: 2 diesels; 2 shafts; 900 bhp = 14 knots
Oil fuel, tons: 30
Range, miles: 2 700 at 10 knots
Complement: 39

EBRO, Class B, small crane   *1974, Dr. Giorgio Arra*

Wooden-hulled.
Two sub-types: (a) with derrick on mainmast: M 21, 22, 23, 24, 25, 27, 28, 29, (b) with no mainmast but crane abreast the funnel: M 26, 30, 31, 32.

Radar: Decca TM 626 or RM 914.

Sonar: AN/UQS-1.

ULLA, Class A, with mainmast   *1973, Dr. Giorgio Arra*

6 "GUADIARO" CLASS
(MINESWEEPERS—OCEAN AS PATROL VESSELS)

Name	No.	Builders	Commissioned
ALMANZORA	M 14	Cadiz	Nov 1954
EO	M 17	Cadiz	Mar 1955
EUME	M 13	Cadiz	Dec 1953
GUADALHORCE	M 16	Cadiz	Dec 1953
GUADIARO	M 11	Cadiz	Apr 1953
NAVIA	M 15	Cadiz	Mar 1955

Displacement, tons: 671 standard; 770 full load
Dimensions, feet (metres): 203·4 × 27·4 × 8·5 *(62 × 8·5 × 2·6)*
Guns: 2—20 mm
A/S weapons: 2 Mk 20 Mousetrap
Main engines: Triple expansion and exhaust turbines; 2 shafts; 2 400 hp = 13 knots after modernisation
Boilers: 2 Yarrow
Oil fuel, tons: 90
Range, miles: 1 000 at 6 knots
Complement: 68 (as patrol ships)

Modernised in 1959-61. Currently employed on patrol duties. Will be paid off when replaced by "Lazaga" class.

Radar: Decca TM 626 or RM 914.

Sonar: AN/UQS-1.

EUME   *1976, Royal Spanish Navy*

SURVEY SHIPS

4 "CASTOR" (A 20) CLASS

Name	No.	Builders	Commissioned
CASTOR	A 21 (ex-H 4)	E. N. Bazán, La Carraca	10 Nov 1966
POLLUX	A 22 (ex-H 5)	E. N. Bazán, La Carraca	6 Dec 1966
ANTARES	A 23	E. N. Bazán, La Carraca	21 Nov 1974
RIGEL	A 24	E. N. Bazán, La Carraca	21 Nov 1974

Displacement, tons: 327 standard; 383 full load
Dimensions, feet (metres): 111 pp; 125·9 oa × 24·9 × 8·9 *(33·8; 38·4 × 7·6 × 2·8)*
Main engines: 1 Sulzer 4TD-36 diesel; 720 hp = 11·7 knots
Range, miles: 3 620 at 8 knots
Complement: 39 (A 23 and 24) 37 (A 21 and 22)

Antares and *Rigel* ordered summer 1972, launched 1973. Fitted with Raydist, Omega and digital presentation of data. Cost of later ships 105 million pesetas.

Radar: Raytheon.

CASTOR   *1974, Spanish Navy*

2 "MALASPINA" (A 30) CLASS (OCEANOGRAPHIC SHIPS)

Name	No.	Builders	Commissioned
MALASPINA	A 31	E. N. Bazán, La Carraca	21 Feb 1975
TOFIÑO	A 32	E. N. Bazán, La Carraca	23 Apr 1975

Displacement, tons: 820 standard; 1 090 full load
Dimensions, feet (metres): 188·9 × 38·4 × 11·8 *(57·6 × 11·7 × 3·6)*
Guns: 2—20 mm (single)
Main engines: 2 diesels; 3 240 bhp; 2 VP propellers = 15·3 knots
Range, miles: 4 000 at 12 knots; 3 140 at 14·5 knots
Complement: 63 (9 officers, 54 men)

Ordered mid-1972.
Malaspina laid down early 1973, launched 15 Aug 1973. *Tofiño* laid down 15 Aug 1973, launched 22 Dec 1973. Both named after their immediate predecessors. Of similar design to British "Bulldog" class costing 380 million pesetas each.

Equipment: Fitted with Atlas Echograph (4 500 metres), Raydist and Transit, 16 memory computer, active rudder with fixed pitch auxiliary propeller.

TOFIÑO   *1976, Royal Spanish Navy*

SERVICE FORCES

1 TRANSPORT

Name	No.	Builders	Commissioned
ALMIRANTE LOBO (ex-*Torrelaguna*)	A 41	Astilleros Echevarrieta, Cadiz	4 Oct 1954

Displacement, tons: 5 662 standard; 8 038 full load
Dimensions, feet (metres): 362·5 × 48·2 × 25·7 *(103 × 14·6 × 6·8)*
Guns: 2—1·5 in *(37 mm)*, 85 cal Bazan RB
Main engines: 1 triple expansion; 2 000 ihp = 12 knots
Complement: 111

Ex-cargo vessel. Launched Sep 1953. Accommodation 314—plus 620 short haul.

Radar: Navigation: Decca 12.

ALMIRANTE LOBO

1 REPLENISHMENT TANKER

Name	No.	Builders	Commissioned
TEIDE	BP 11	Factoria de Bazán, Cartagena	20 Oct 1956

Displacement, tons: 2 747 light; 8 030 full load
Oil capacity: 5 350 cu m
Dimensions, feet (metres): 385·5 × 48·5 × 20·3 *(117·5 × 14·8 × 6·2)*
Gun: 1—4·1 in (not mounted)
Main engines: 2 diesels; 3 360 bhp = 12 knots
Complement: 98

Ordered in December 1952. Laid down on 11 Nov 1954. Launched on 20 June 1955. Modernised in 1962 with refuelling at sea equipment (300 tons/hr).

Radar: Navigation: Decca TM 707.

TEIDE   *1976, Royal Spanish Navy*

1 HARBOUR TANKER

PP 1

Displacement, tons: 470
Dimensions, feet (metres): 147·5 oa × 25 × 9·5 *(45 × 7·6 × 2·9)*
Main engines: Deutz diesel; 220 bhp = 10 knots
Complement: 12

Built at Santander and launched in 1939.

3 HARBOUR TANKERS

PP 3   PP 4   PP 5

Displacement, tons: 510
Dimensions, feet (metres): 121·4 × 22·3 × 9·8 *(37 × 6·8 × 3)*

9 HARBOUR TANKERS

PB 1, 2, 3, 4, 5, 6, 20, 21, 22

Displacement, tons: 200
Dimensions, feet (metres): 111·5 × 19·7 × 8·9 *(34 × 6 × 2·7)*

Small harbour tankers with capacity between 100 and 300 tons. All built by Bazán between 1960 and 1965.

1 SAIL TRAINING SHIP

Name	No.	Builders	Commissioned
JUAN SEBASTIAN DE ELCANO	—	Echevarrieta Yard, Cadiz	28 Feb 1928

Displacement, tons: 3 420 standard; 3 754 full load
Dimensions, feet (metres): 269·2 pp; 308·5 oa × 43 × 23 *(94·1 × 13·6 × 7)*
Guns: 2—37 mm
Main engines: 1 Sulzer diesel; 1 shaft; 1 500 bhp = 9·5 knots
Oil fuel, tons: 230
Range, miles: 10 000 at 9·5 knots
Complement: 292 + 80 cadets

Four masted top sail schooner—sister of Chilean *Esmeralda*. Named after the first circumnavigator of the world (1519-26) who succeeded to the command of the expedition led by Magellanes after the latter's death. Laid down 24 Nov 1925. Launched on 5 Mar 1927.

Radar: 2 Decca TM 626.

JUAN SEBASTIAN DE ELCANO and friends   *7/1976, US Navy*

1 ROYAL YACHT

Name	No.	Builders	Commissioned
AZOR	W0	E. N. Bazán, El Ferrol	20 July 1949

Displacement, tons: 442 standard; 486 full load
Dimensions, feet (metres): 153·0 × 25·2 × 10·9 *(47 × 7·7 × 3·3)*
Main engines: 2 diesels; 1 200 bhp = 13·3 knots
Range, miles: 4 000
Complement: 47

Built as the Caudillo's yacht. Launched on 9 June 1949. Underwent an extensive refit in 1960, her hull being cut to admit an extension in length. Now painted royal blue with a buff funnel.

Radar: Decca TM 626.

AZOR   *1970, J. I. Taibo*

1 BOOM DEFENCE VESSEL

Name	No.	Builders	Commissioned
—	CR 1 (ex-*G 6*)	Penhoët, France	29 July 1955

Displacement, tons: 630 standard; 831 full load
Dimensions, feet (metres): 165·5 × 34 × 10·5 *(50·5 × 10·2 × 3·2)*
Guns: 1—40 mm; 4—20 mm (single) 70 cal
Main engines: 2 diesels; electric drive; 1 shaft; 1 500 bhp = 12 knots
Oil fuel, tons: 126
Range, miles: 5 200 at 12 knots
Complement: 40

US off-shore order. Launched on 28 Sep 1954. Transferred from the US in 1955 under MDAP. Sister ship of French "Cigale" class. Based at Cartagena.

Radar: One navigation set.

CR 1   *1976, Royal Spanish Navy*

PBP 1, 2 and 3

Dimensions, feet (metres): 73·1 × 28·5 × 2·6 *(22·3 × 8·7 × 0·8)*

Gate Vessels.
Delivered 1959-60.

PR 1-5

Dimensions, feet (metres): 72·2 × 28·5 × 4·3 *(22 × 8·7 × 4·3)*

Net laying barges.
Delivered 1959-60.

PRA 1-8

Dimensions, feet (metres): 91·8 × 27·9 × 2·3 *(28 × 8·5 × 0·7)*

Tugs for PBPs and PRs.
Delivered 1959-60.

2 OCEAN TUGS

Name	No.	Builders	Commissioned
—	RA 1	Bazán, Cartagena	9 July 1955
—	RA 2	Bazán, Cartagena	12 Sep 1955

Displacement, tons: 757 standard; 1 039 full load
Dimensions, feet (metres): 184 × 33·5 × 12 *(56·1 × 10·1 × 3·9)*
Guns: 2—20 mm (singles)
Mines: Can lay 24
Main engines: 2 Sulzer diesels; 3 200 bhp; 1 shaft; cp propeller = 15 knots
Oil fuel, tons: 142
Range, miles: 5 500 at 15 knots
Complement: 49

Originally known as "Valen" class.

Radar: Decca 12.

RA 2   *1974, Reiner Nerlich*

1 OCEAN TUG

Name	No.	Builders	Commissioned
— (ex-*Metinda III*)	RA 3	Wellington, England	1945

Displacement, tons: 762 standard; 1 080 full load
Dimensions, feet (metres): 137 × 33·1 × 15·5 *(41·8 × 10·1 × 4·5)*
Main engines: Triple expansion; 3 200 ihp = 10 knots
Fuel: Coal
Complement: 44

Purchased by Spain 26 May 1961.

RA 3   *1976, Royal Spanish Navy*

3 OCEAN TUGS

Name	No.	Builders	Commissioned
POSEIDÓN	BS 1 (ex-*RA 6*)	Bazán, La Carraca	8 Aug 1964
—	RA 4	Bazán, La Carraca	25 Mar 1964
—	RA 5	Bazán, La Carraca	11 Apr 1964

Displacement, tons: 951 standard; 1 069 full load
Dimensions, feet (metres): 183·5 × 32·8 × 13·1 *(55·9 × 10 × 4)*
Main engines: 2 Sulzer diesels; 3 200 bhp = 15 knots
Range, miles: 4 640
Complement: 49 (*Poseidón* 60)

RA 6 was renumbered BS 1 when she became a frogman support ship, known as *Poseidón*.
She carries a 300 metre/6 hour bathyscope.

Radar: Decca TM 626.

POSEIDÓN   *1973, Dr. Giorgio Arra*

7 COASTAL TUGS

Name	No.	Builders	Commissioned
—	RR 50	Cartagena	1963
—	RR 51	Cartagena	1963
—	RR 52	Cartagena	1963
—	RR 53	Cartagena	1967
—	RR 54	Cartagena	1967
—	RR 55	Cartagena	1967

Displacement, tons: 205 (RR 50-52); 227 (RR 53-55) standard; 320 full load
Dimensions, feet (metres): 91·2 × 23 × 8·2 *(27·8 × 7 × 2·6)*
Main engines: Diesels; 1 shaft; 1 400 bhp (53 to 55), 800 bhp (50 to 52)
Complement: 13

Radar: Pilot 7D 20 in RR 50, 51 and 52.

RR 53   *1975, Dr. Giorgio Arra*

RR 16

81 ft *(27 metres)* long with complement of 10.
Built by Bazán, La Carraca. Commissioned 26 Apr 1962.

14 HARBOUR TUGS

RP 1-12

Dimensions, feet (metres): 60·7 × 15·5 × — *(18·5 × 4·7 × –)*

Of 65 tons and 200 bhp (diesel). Commissioned 1965-67.

RP 40

Dimensions, feet (metres): 69·7 × 19·4 × — *(21·3 × 5·9 × –)*
Complement: 8

Of 150 tons and 600 bhp (diesel). Commissioned 27 Dec 1961.

RP 18

Displacement, tons: 160 standard
Dimensions, feet (metres): 81·0 × 17·7 × 7·9 *(24·7 × 5·4 × 2·4)*
Main engines: Triple expansion; 1 shaft (Kort nozzle)
Fuel: Coal

Laid down 1946 at Cartagena. Commissioned 1952.

Note: 5 tug-launches of less than 50 tons—LR 47, 51, 67, 68, 69.

14 WATER CARRIERS

AB 1, 2, 3, 10, 17, 18

All of less than 400 tons. Harbour water boats with 200 tons (AB 1-3) capacity.

A 1   A 2

Built in 1936. Of 1 785 tons full load with 1 000 tons capacity. Ocean going.

A 6

Displacement, tons: 1 785
Dimensions, feet (metres): 200 × 31·5 × 14·1 *(61 × 9·6 × 4·3)*
Main engines: Triple expansion; 1 shaft; 800 ihp = 9 knots
Complement: 27

Commissioned 30 Jan 1952.

A 7   A 8   A 9   A 10   A 11

Displacement, tons: 610 full load (A 7-8; 706 full load)
Dimensions, feet (metres): 146·9 × 24·9 × 9·8 *(44·8 × 7·6 × 3)*
Main engines: 1 shaft = 9 knots
Range, miles: 1 000
Complement: 16

All built at Bazán, La Carraca. A 7-8 commissioned 1952. A 9-11 24 Jan 1963. All oceangoing.

Radar: Pilot 7 D20 (A 9-11).

A 11   *1973, Spanish Navy*

9 TORPEDO RECOVERY CRAFT

BTM 1-6

Built by Bazán 1961-63 of 60-190 tons. To carry torpedoes and mines and, in emergency, can act as minelayers. Complement 8.

ST 5

Torpedo tracking craft on range at Alcudia, Majorca. 36 ft *(11 metres)* long.

LRT 3 and 4

TRVs built in 1956. 58·2 tons—58·1 × 6·6 × —*(17·7 × 2·2 ×–)*. Can carry 6 torpedoes. Have stern ramp and crane. Based at submarine base, Cartagena.

RESEARCH CRAFT

An unpropelled underwater research base under construction 1976 by Bazán Cartagena. Can accommodate 4: 40·7 × 20·7 *(12·4 × 6·3)*; hull diameter 11·8 *(3·6)*.

6 DIVING CRAFT

BZL 1, 3, 9   NEREIDA (BZL 10)

Small self-propelled craft of less than 50 tons.

BL 10 and 13

Dumb barges for diving.

8 FLOATING CRANES

SANSÓN GRI (100 tons lift)
GR 3, 4 and 5 (30 tons lift)
GR 6, 7, 8, 9 (15 tons lift)

Based at Cartagena, El Ferrol, La Carraca and Mahon.

3 "AGUILUCHO" CLASS (COASTAL PATROL CRAFT)

Name	No.	Builders	Commissioned
AGUILUCHO	—	J. Roberto Rodriguez e Hijos, Vigo	1973
GAVILAN I	—	J. Roberto Rodriguez e Hijos, Vigo	1975
GAVILAN II	—	J. Roberto Rodriguez e Hijos, Vigo	1976

Displacement, tons: 45
Dimensions, feet (metres): 85·5 oa × 16·7 × 4·3 *(26·1 × 5·1 × 1·3)*
Main engines: Diesels; 2 shafts; 2 750 bhp = 30 knots
Range, miles: 750 at 30 knots

Aguilucho launched 19 Feb 1973 for Customs duties. *Gavilan I* launched 22 July 1975.

CUSTOMS SERVICE

There are, in addition to the above, a large number of customs launches of similar size operating off the Spanish coast.

SRI LANKA

Formation

The Royal Ceylon Navy was formed on 9 Dec 1950 when the Navy Act was proclaimed. Called the Sri Lanka Navy since Republic Day 22 May 1972.

Headquarters Appointment

Commander of the Navy:
  Rear-Admiral D. B. Goonesekera

Diplomatic Representation

Services Attaché in London:
  Withdrawn from 1 November 1970

Personnel

(a) 1977: 2 310 (189 officers and 2 121 sailors)
(b) Voluntary Service

Strength of the Fleet

Type	Active	Building
Frigate	1	—
Fast Attack Craft—Gun	6	—
Coastal Patrol Craft	22	—
Survey Craft	4	—

Defence Expenditure and Policy

Since the Indo-Pakistan war visits by US, British, French, Indian and Russian ships have taken place. It is reported that defence spending has been doubled.

DELETIONS

1974 Short hydrofoil and 1 Thornycroft Patrol Craft (101)
1975 Tug *Aliya*

Naval Bases

A Naval Base established at Trincomalee, which was a British base from 1795 until 1957.
Minor bases at Karainagar, Colombo, Welisara, Tangale, Kalpitiya and Talaimannar.

Prefix to Ships' Names

SLNS

Mercantile Marine

Lloyd's Register of Shipping:
  36 vessels of 91 031 tons gross

FRIGATE

1 Ex-CANADIAN "RIVER" CLASS

Name	No.	Builders	Laid down	Launched	Commissioned
GAJABAHU (ex-*Misnak*, ex-HMCS *Hallowell*)	F 232	Canadian Vickers Ltd, Montreal	1944	8 Aug 1944	Jan 1945

Displacement, tons: 1 445 standard; 2 360 full load
Length, feet (metres): 282 *(86·3)* pp; 295·5 *(90·1)* wl; 310·5 *(91·9)* oa
Beam, feet (metres): 36·5 *(11·1)*
Draught, feet (metres): 13·8 *(4·2)*
Guns: 1—4 in *(102 mm)*; 3—40 mm
Main engines: Triple expansion; 5 500 ihp; 2 shafts
Boilers: 2 three-drum type
Speed, knots: 20
Range, miles: 4 200 at 12 knots
Oil fuel, tons: 585
Complement: 160

Acquired from Canada by Israel in 1950 and sold by Israel to Ceylon in 1959. Guns above replaced 3—4·7 inch, 8—20 mm in 1965.

GAJABAHU

1971, Royal Ceylon Navy

LIGHT FORCES

5 "SOORAYA" CLASS (FAST ATTACK CRAFT—GUN)

BALAWATHA	SOORAYA
DAKSAYA	WEERAYA
RAMAKAMI	

Displacement, tons: 120 full load
Dimensions, feet (metres): 130 × 18 × 5·6 *(42·6 × 5·9 × 1·8)*
Guns: 4—37 mm (2 twin); 4—25 mm (2 twin abaft the bridge)
Main engines: 4 Diesels; 5 000 bhp = 30 knots
Complement: 25

All of the "Shanghai II" class.
The first pair was transferred by China in Feb 1972, the second pair in July 1972 and the last in December 1972. In monsoonal conditions off the coast of Sri Lanka these boats are lively and uncomfortable.

Radar: Pot Head.

SOORAYA   *1974, Sri Lanka Navy*

1 Ex-SOVIET "MOL" CLASS (FAST ATTACK CRAFT—GUN)

Name	No.	Builders	Commissioned
SAMUDRA DEVI	—	USSR	31 Dec 1975

Displacement, tons: 205 standard; 245 full load
Dimensions, feet (metres): 126·6 × 25·6 × 9·5 *(38·6 × 7·8 × 2·9)*
Guns: 4—30 mm (twin)
Main engines: 3 M 504 diesels; 15 500 bhp; 2 shafts
Speed, knots: 40
Complement: 25

Built 1975. Has certain variations from standard Soviet craft although the hull is a basic "Osa" type. The after radar pedestal mounts only a Kolonka optical sight and the torpedo tubes have been unshipped although the sponsons remain. An additional section of superstructure has been added abaft the after pedestal.

Radar: Don and High Pole IFF.

SAMUDRA DEVI   *12/1975, Sri Lanka Navy*

20 THORNYCROFT TYPE (COASTAL PATROL CRAFT)

Name	No.	Builders	Commissioned	Name	No.	Builders	Commissioned
—	102	Thornycroft (Malaysia) Ltd, Singapore	1966	—	202	Thornycroft (Malaysia) Ltd, Singapore	1967
—	103	Thornycroft (Malaysia) Ltd, Singapore	1966	—	203	Thornycroft (Malaysia) Ltd, Singapore	1968
—	104	Thornycroft (Malaysia) Ltd, Singapore	1967	—	204	Thornycroft (Malaysia) Ltd, Singapore	1968
—	105	Thornycroft (Malaysia) Ltd, Singapore	1967	—	205	Thornycroft (Malaysia) Ltd, Singapore	1968
—	106	Thornycroft (Malaysia) Ltd, Singapore	1967	—	206	Thornycroft (Malaysia) Ltd, Singapore	1968
—	107	Thornycroft (Malaysia) Ltd, Singapore	1967	—	207	Thornycroft (Malaysia) Ltd, Singapore	1968
—	108	Thornycroft (Malaysia) Ltd, Singapore	1967	—	208	Thornycroft (Malaysia) Ltd, Singapore	1968
—	109	Thornycroft (Malaysia) Ltd, Singapore	1967	—	209	Thornycroft (Malaysia) Ltd, Singapore	1968
—	110	Thornycroft (Malaysia) Ltd, Singapore	1967	—	210	Thornycroft (Malaysia) Ltd, Singapore	1968
—	201	Thornycroft (Malaysia) Ltd, Singapore	1967	—	211	Thornycroft (Malaysia) Ltd, Singapore	1968

Displacement, tons: 15
Dimensions, feet (metres): 45·5 × 12 × 3 *(14·9 × 3·9 × 0·9)*
Main engines: 2 boats: Thornycroft K6SMI engines; 500 bhp; 2 shafts = 25 knots.
7 boats: General Motors 6 71-Series; 500 bhp; 2 shafts = 25 knots

The hulls are of hard chine type with double skin teak planking. Equipped with radar, radio, searchlight etc. Two ordered in 1965. Seven ordered in 1966. 12 more assembled in Sri Lanka and completed by Sep 1968. Originally 21 boats.
They are based, as two squadrons, at Kalpitiya and Karainagar.

2 HARBOUR PATROL LAUNCHES

Name	No.	Builders	Commissioned
DIYAKAWA	—	Italy	1955
KORAWAKKA	—	Italy	1955

Displacement, tons: 13
Dimensions, feet (metres): 46 pp; 48 oa × 12 × 3 *((15; 15·7 × 3·9 × 0·9)*
Main engines: 2 Foden FD 6 diesels; 240 bhp = 15 knots

Built in Italy in 1955.

SURVEY CRAFT

Name	No.	Builders	Commissioned	Name	No.	Builders	Commissioned
HANSAYA	—	Korody Marine Corp, Venice	1956	SERUWA	—	Italy	1955
LIHINIYA	—	Korody Marine Corp, Venice	1956	TARAWA	—	Italy	1955

Displacement, tons: 36
Dimensions, feet (metres): 63·5 pp; 66 oa × 14 × 4 *(20·8; 21·6 × 4·6 × 1·3)*
Main engines: 3 General Motors diesels; 450 bhp = 16 knots

Of similar characteristics to *Diyakawa* and *Korawakka* above.

Originally patrol craft. Employed on Survey duties.

SUDAN

Establishment

The navy was established in 1962 to operate on the Red Sea coast and on the River Nile. The original training staff was from Yugoslavian Navy, but this staff left in 1972.

Personnel

(a) 1977: 600 officers and men
(b) Voluntary service

Diplomatic Representation

Naval, Military and Air Attaché in London:
   Col. A. El-Tayeb El-Mihaina

Mercantile Marine

Lloyd's Register of Shipping: 14 vessels of 45 578 tons gross

Bases

Port Sudan for Red Sea operations with a separate riverine unit on the Nile based at Khartoum.

LIGHT FORCES

2 Ex-YUGOSLAV "KRALJEVICA" CLASS
(LARGE PATROL CRAFT)

Name	No.	Builders	Commissioned
FASHER	PBR 1	Yugoslavia	1954
KHARTOUM	PBR 2	Yugoslavia	1955

Displacement, tons: 190 standard; 245 full load
Dimensions, feet (metres): 134·5 × 20·7 × 7·2 *(41 × 6·3 × 2·2)*
Guns: 2—40 mm; 2—20 mm
Main engines: Diesel; 2 shafts; 3 300 bhp = 20 knots
Range, miles: 1 500 at 12 knots

Transferred from the Yugoslavian Navy during 1969.

6 Ex-YUGOSLAV "101" CLASS
(FAST ATTACK CRAFT—GUN)

Displacement, tons: 55 standard; 60 full load
Dimensions, feet (metres): 78 × 21·3 × 7·8 *(23·8 × 6·5 × 2·4)*
Guns: 2—40 mm; 2—20 mm (single)
Main engines: 3 Packard petrol motors; 3 shafts; 5 000 bhp = 36 knots
Complement: 14

Transferred in this "Gun" version of the class in 1970. Same characteristics as US "Higgins" class.

4 Ex-YUGOSLAV PBR TYPE (LARGE PATROL CRAFT)

Name	No.	Builders	Commissioned
GIHAD	PB 1	Mosor Shipyard, Trogir, Yugoslavia	1961
HORRIYA	PB 2	Mosor Shipyard, Trogir, Yugoslavia	1961
ISTIQLAL	PB 3	Mosor Shipyard, Trogir, Yugoslavia	1962
SHAAB	PB 4	Mosor Shipyard, Trogir, Yugoslavia	1962

Displacement, tons: 100
Dimensions, feet (metres): 115 × 16·5 × 5·2 *(35 × 5 × 1·7)*
Guns: 1—40 mm; 1—20 mm; 2—7·6 mm MG
Main engines: Mercedes-Benz (MTU 12V 493) diesels; 2 shafts; 1 800 bhp = 20 knots
Range, miles: 1 400 at 12 knots
Complement: 20

Of steel construction. First craft acquired by the newly established Sudanese Navy.

HORRIYA   *Sudanese Navy*

3 Ex-IRANIAN COASTAL PATROL CRAFT

Name	No.	Builders	Commissioned
— (ex-*Gohar*)	—	Abeking and Rasmussen	1970
— (ex-*Shahpar*)	—	Abeking and Rasmussen	1970
— (ex-*Shahram*)	—	Abeking and Rasmussen	1970

Displacement, tons: 70
Dimensions, feet (metres): 75·2 × 16·5 × 6 *(22·9 × 5 × 1·8)*
Main engines: 2 diesels; 2 shafts; 2 200 hp = 27 knots
Complement: 19

Built for Iran. Transferred to Iranian Coastguard 1975 and to Sudan later that year. The two classes listed in 1976-77 Edition as transfers were incorrectly reported.

AMPHIBIOUS FORCES

2 Ex-YUGOSLAV "DTK 221" CLASS (LCTs)

SOBAT   DINDER

Displacement, tons: 410
Dimensions, feet (metres): 144·3 × 19·7 × 7 *(44 × 6 × 2·1)*
Guns: 1—20 mm; 2—12·7 mm
Speed, knots: 10
Complement: 15

Transferred during 1969.

3 LCUs

Transferred by Yugoslavia 1970—of 40 tons.

SERVICE FORCES

1 SUPPORT TANKER

FASHODA (ex-PN 17)

Displacement, tons: 420 standard; 650 full load
Dimensions, feet (metres): 141·5 × 22·8 × 13·6 *(43·2 × 7 × 4·2)*
Main engines: 300 bhp = 7 knots

Former Yugoslavian Tanker rehabilitated and transferred to the Sudanese Navy in 1969.

1 SURVEY SHIP

TIENGA

A small vessel, converted into a hydrographic ship, acquired from Yugoslavia in 1969.

1 WATER BOAT

BARAKA (ex-PV 6)

A small water carrier, transferred from Yugoslavia to the Sudanese Navy in 1969.

SURINAM

Formerly Dutch Guyana—granted independence in 1975.

3 PATROL CRAFT

Of unspecified class ordered from Netherlands in 1975.

SWEDEN

Headquarters Appointments

Commander-in-Chief:
Vice-Admiral Bengt Lundvall
Chief of Naval Material Department:
Rear-Admiral Gunnar Grandin
Chief of Naval Staff:
Major-General Bo Varenius (Coastal Artillery)

Senior Command

Commander-in-Chief of Coastal Fleet:
Rear-Admiral Christer Kierkegaard

Diplomatic Representation

Naval Attaché in London:
Captain L. Jedeur-Palmgren
Naval Attaché in Washington:
Captain N. L. Lindgren

Personnel

(a) 1977: 15 100 officers and men of Navy and Coast Artillery made up of 4 500 regulars, 2 900 Reservists and 7 700 National Servicemen. In addition 7 000 conscripts receive annual training.
(b) 9-18 months

Bases

Stockholm, Karlskrona, Göteborg.
Minor base at Härnösand

Composition of the Navy

In addition to seagoing personnel the Navy includes the Coastal Artillery, manning 20 mobile and 45 coastal batteries of both major guns and SSMs. A number of amphibious and patrol craft are also controlled by the Coastal Artillery.

Naval Air Arm

5 Alouette II helicopters (training)
10 Jet Ranger helicopters
10 Vertol 107 (Hkp-4B)

Mercantile Marine

Lloyd's Register of Shipping:
764 vessels of 7 971 246 tons gross

Strength of the Fleet

Type	Active	Building (Planned)
Destroyers	6	—
Frigates	4	—
Submarines—Patrol	18	2
Corvettes—Light Forces	—	(3)
Fast Attack Craft—Missile	1	16
Fast Attack Craft—Torpedo	41	—
Large Patrol Craft	1	—
Coastal Patrol Craft	26	—
Minelayers	3	1
Minelayers—Coastal	9	—
Minelayers—Small	37	—
Minehunters	—	9
Minesweepers—Coastal	18	—
Minesweepers—Inshore	20	—
LCMs	9	—
LCUs	79	(5)
LCAs	54	—
Mine Transports	2	—
Survey Ships	5	(1)
Tanker—Support	1	—
Supply Ship	1	—
Tugs	20	—
Salvage Ship	1	—
Sail Training Ships	2	—
Ice Breakers	8	—
TRVs	3	—
Tenders	5	—
Water Boats	2	—

DELETIONS

Cruiser

1971 *Göta Lejon* to Chile *(Latorre)*

Frigates

1974 *Karlskrona*
1976 *Halsingborg, Kalmar*

Submarines

1975 *Gäddan, Siken* ("Abborren" Class)
1976 *Abborren, Laxen, Makrillen* ("Abborren" Class)

Light Forces

1973 *TV 101-106*
1975 *T 38, 39, 40*

Depot Ship

1972 *Patricia*
1976 *Marieholm*

Surveying Vessels

1972 *Johen Nordenankar, Petter Gedda*
1973 *Anden*
1975 *Lederen*

Miscellaneous

1973 *Gälnan* (water carrier)
1974 *Ymer* (Icebreaker)
1975 *Urd* (experimental ship)

PENNANT LIST

Destroyers

J 18	Halland
J 19	Smaaland
J 20	Ostergotland
J 21	Södermanland
J 22	Gästrikland
J 23	Hälsingland

Frigates

F 11	Visby
F 12	Sundsvall
F 16	Öland
F 17	Uppland

Submarines

Bäv	Bävern
Del	Delfinen
Dra	Draken
Gri	Gripen
Haj	Hajen
Iln	Illern
Näc	Näcken
Naj	Najad
Nep	Neptun
Nor	Nordkaparen
Säl	Sälen
Sbj	Sjöbjörnen
Shu	Sjöhunden
Shä	Sjöhästen
Sle	Sjölejonet
Sor	Sjöormen
Spr	Springaren
Utn	Uttern
Val	Valen
Vgn	Vargen

Light Forces

R 01	Flotilla Leader
R 02	Flotilla Leader
R 03	Flotilla Leader
P 151	Jägaren
P 152-167	"Jägaren" class
T 45-56	"T 42" class
T 102	Plejad
T 103	Polaris
T 104	Pollux
T 105	Regulus
T 106	Rigel
T 107	Aldebaran
T 108	Altair
T 109	Antares
T 110	Arcturus
T 111	Argo
T 112	Astrea
T 121	Spica
T 122	Sirius
T 123	Capella
T 124	Castor
T 125	Vega
T 126	Virgo
T 131	Norrköping
T 132	Nynäshamn
T 133	Norrtälje
T 134	Varberg
T 135	Västerås
T 136	Västervik
T 137	Umea
T 138	Pitea
T 139	Lulea
T 140	Halmstad
T 141	Strömstad
T 142	Ystad
V 01	Skanór
V 02	Smyge
V 03	Arild
V 04	Viken

Amphibious Forces

A 333	Skagul
A 335	Sleipner
L 51-56	LCUs
201-255	LCUs
256-274	LCUs
301-354	LCAs

Minewarfare Forces

M 01	Alvsnabben
M 02	Alvsborg
M 03	Visborg
M 04	New Construction
MUL 11-19	Coastal Minelayers
M 15-16, 21-26	MSI
M 31	Gässten
M 32	Norsten
M 33	Viksten
M 41	Orust
M 42	Tjörn
M 43	Hisingen
M 44	Blackan
M 45	Dämman
M 46	Galten
M 47	Gillöga
M 48	Rödlöga
M 49	Svartlöga
M 51	Hanö
M 52	Tärnö
M 53	Tjurkö
M 54	Sturkö
M 55	Ornö
M 56	Utö
M 57	Arkö
M 58	Spärö
M 59	Karlsö
M 60	Iggö
M 61	Styrsö
M 62	Skaftö
M 63	Aspö
M 64	Hasslö
M 65	Vinö
M 66	Vällö
M 67	Nämdö
M 68	Blidö

Service Forces

S 01	Gladen
S 02	Falken
A 211	Belos
A 216	Unden
A 217	Fryken
A 221	Freja
A 228	Brännaren
A 231	Lommen
A 232	Spoven
A 236	Fällaren
A 237	Minören
A 241	Urd
A 242	Skuld
A 246	Hagern
A 247	Pelikanen
A 248	Pingvinen
A 251	Achilles
A 252	Ajax
A 253	Hermes
A 256	Sigrun
A 321	Hector
A 322	Heros
A 323	Hercules
A 324	Hera
A 326	Hebe
A 327	Passop
A 328	Ran
A 329	Henrik
A 330	Atlas
A 332	Mårsgarn
A 336	Vitsgarn
A 341	ATB 1
A 342	ATB 2
A 343	ATB 3
A 345	Granaten
A 347	Edda
A 349	Gerda

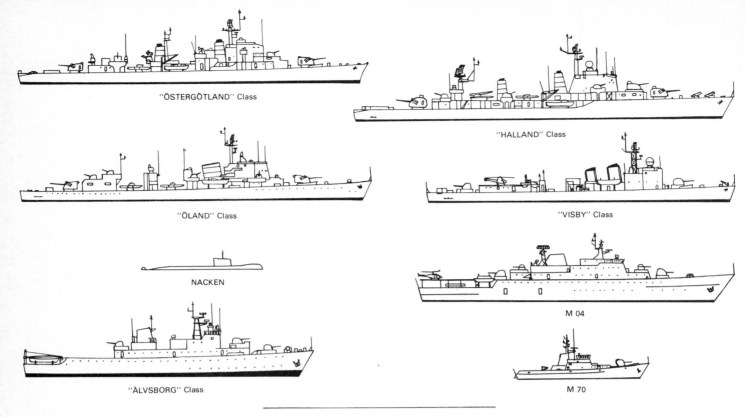

"ÖSTERGÖTLAND" Class

"HALLAND" Class

"ÖLAND" Class

"VISBY" Class

NACKEN

M 04

"ÄLVSBORG" Class

M 70

DESTROYERS

4 "ÖSTERGÖTLAND" CLASS

Name	No.	Builders	Laid down	Launched	Commissioned
GÄSTRIKLAND	J 22	Götaverken, Göteborg	1 Oct 1955	6 June1956	14 Jan 1959
HÄLSINGLAND	J 23	Kockums Mek Verkstads A/B	1 Oct 1955	14 Jan 1957	17 June 1959
ÖSTERGÖTLAND	J 20	Götaverken, Göteborg	1 Sep 1955	8 May 1956	3 Mar 1958
SÖDERMANLAND	J 21	Eriksberg Mekaniska Verkstad	1June 1955	28 May 1956	27 June 1958

Displacement, tons: 2 150 standard; 2 600 full load
Length, feet (metres): 367·5 *(112·0)* oa
Beam, feet (metres): 36·8 *(11·2)*
Draught, feet (metres): 12·0 *(3·7)*
Missile launchers: 1 quadruple Seacat (RB 07) surface-to-air
Guns: 4—4·7 in *(120 mm)*, (2 twin); 4—40 mm (single)
A/S weapons: 1 Squid (triple-barrelled)
Torpedo tubes: 6—21 in *(533 mm)* (1 mount)
Mines: 60 can be carried
Main engines: De Laval turbines; 2 shafts; 47 000 bhp
Boilers: 2 Babcock & Wilcox
Speed, knots: 35
Oil fuel, tons: 330
Range, miles: 2 200 at 20 knots
Complement: 244 (18 officers, 226 men)

Modernisation: *Gästrikland* in 1965, *Södermanland* in 1967, *Hälsingland* in 1968, *Östergötland* in 1969.

Radar: Search and target designator: Thomson CSF Saturn.
Fire control: HSA M 44 for Seacat—M 45 series for guns.

HÄLSINGLAND

1975, Royal Swedish Navy

2 "HALLAND" CLASS

Name	No.	Builders	Laid down	Launched	Commissioned
HALLAND	J 18	Götaverken, Göteborg	1951	16 July 1952	8 June 1955
SMÅLAND	J 19	Eriksberg Mekaniska Verkstad, Göteborg	1951	23 Oct 1952	12 Jan 1956

Displacement, tons: 2 800 standard; 3 400 full load
Length, feet (metres): 380·5 *(116·0)* wl; 397·2 *(121·0)* oa
Beam, feet (metres): 41·3 *(12·6)*
Draught, feet (metres): 14·8 *(4·5)*
Missiles: 1 RB 08A (Mk 20) launcher
Guns: 4—4·7 in *(120 mm)* (2 twin); 2—57 mm (twin); 6—40 mm
A/S weapons: 2 four-barrelled rocket-launcher (Bofors)
Torpedo tubes: 8—21 in *(533 mm)* (2 quad)
Mines: Can be fitted for minelaying
Main engines: De Laval double reduction geared turbines; 2 shafts; 58 000 bhp
Boilers: 2 Penhöet
Speed, knots: 35
Oil fuel, tons: 500
Range, miles: 3 000 at 20 knots
Complement: 290 (18 officers, 272 men)

Both ordered in 1948. The first Swedish destroyers of post-war design. Fully automatic gun turrets forward and aft. Both modernised in 1962.

Radar: Search and target designator: Thomson CSF Saturn (foremast).
Air warning: LW 02/03 (mainmast).
Fire control, search and tracking: M 22 and associated sets (radome).
ECM.

SMÅLAND   *1975, Royal Swedish Navy*

HALLAND   *1973, Wright and Logan*

FRIGATES

2 "ÖLAND" CLASS

Name	No.	Builders	Laid down	Launched	Commissioned
ÖLAND	F 16	Kockums Mek Verkstads A/B, Malmö	1943	15 Dec 1945	5 Dec 1947
UPPLAND	F 17	Karlskrona Dockard	1943	5 Nov 1946	31 Jan 1949

Displacement, tons: 2 000 standard; 2 400 full load
Length, feet (metres): 351 *(107·0)* pp; 367·5 *(112·0)* oa
Beam, feet (metres): 36·8 *(11·2)*
Draught, feet (metres): 11·2 *(3·4)*
Guns: 4—4·7 in *(120 mm)* (2 twin); 6—40 mm (single)
A/S weapon: 1 triple-barrelled Squid mortar
Torpedo tubes: 6—21 in *(533 mm)* (2 triple)
Mines: 60 capacity
Main engines: De Laval geared turbines; 2 shafts; 44 000 bhp
Boilers: 2 Penhöet
Speed, knots: 35
Oil fuel, tons: 300
Range, miles: 2 500 at 20 knots
Complement: 210

Superstructure and machinery spaces lightly armoured. Pennant numbers changed to F superior 1975.

Gunnery: 4·7 inch guns semi-automatic with 80° elevation. 40 mm gun near jackstaff was removed in 1962, and eight 20 mm guns in 1964.

Radar: Search and target designator: Thomson CSF Saturn.
Fire Control: Two M 45 series.
Navigation: One set.

Reconstruction: *Öland* was modernised with new bridge in 1960 and again in 1969; and *Uppland* with new bridge and helicopter platform in 1963.

OLAND (Old pennant number)   *1975, Royal Swedish Navy*

2 "VISBY" CLASS

Name	No.
SUNDSVALL	F 12
VISBY	F 11

Builders	Laid down	Launched	Commissioned
Eriksberg	1941	20 Oct 1942	17 Sep 1943
Götaverken	1941	16 Oct 1942	10 Aug 1943

Displacement, tons: 1 150 standard; 1 320 full load
Length, feet (metres): 310·0 *(94·5)* wl; 321·5 *(98·0)* oa
Beam, feet (metres): 30 *(9·1)*
Draught, feet (metres): 12·5 *(3·8)*
Aircraft: 1 helicopter platform
Guns: 3—4·7 in *(120 mm)*; 2—57 mm; 3—40 mm
A/S weapons: 1—375 mm Bofors 4 tube rocket launcher
Main engines: De Laval geared turbines; 2 shafts; 36 000 shp
Boilers: 3 three-drum type
Speed, knots: 39
Range, miles: 1 600 at 20 knots
Oil fuel, tons: 150
Complement: 140

All of the class of four were originally fitted for minelaying. Will be paid off for disposal in the near future.

Radar: Thompson CSF Saturn S-band long-range search and target designator
M 24 fire control systems with co-mounted radars for search and tracking for guns.

SUNDSVALL

1972, Royal Swedish Navy

SUBMARINES

NEW CONSTRUCTION "A 17" CLASS

In design stage for completion mid 1980s.

3 "NÄCKEN" CLASS (A14)

Name	No.
NÄCKEN	NÄC
NAJAD	NAJ
NEPTUN	NEP

Builders	Laid down	Launched	Commissioned
Kockums, Malmö	Nov 1972	Jan 1975	1977
Karlskrona	Sep 1973	Oct 1975	1978
Kockums, Malmö	Mar 1974	April 1976	1978

Displacement, tons: 980 surfaced; 1 125 dived
Length, feet (metres): 135 *(41)*
Beam, feet (metres): 20·0 *(6·1)*
Draught, feet (metres): 16·7 *(5·1)*
Torpedo tubes: 4—21 in *(533 mm)* (8 reloads)
Main machinery: Diesels; electric motors; 1 shaft with large 5-bladed propeller
Speed, knots: 20 surfaced and dived
Complement: 25

The very high beam to length ratio is notable in this Albacore hull design. Have large bow mounted sonar. Main accommodation space is abaft the control room with machinery spaces right aft.

5 "SJÖORMEN" CLASS (A11B)

Name	No.
SJÖORMEN	SOR
SJÖLEJONET	SLE
SJÖHUNDEN	SHU
SJÖBJÖRNEN	SBJ
SJÖHÄSTEN	SHÄ

Builders	Laid down	Launched	Commissioned
Kockums	1965	25 Jan 1967	31 July 1967
Kockums	1966	29 June 1967	16 Dec 1968
Kockums	1966	21 Mar 1968	25 June 1969
Karlskrona	1967	6 Aug 1968	28 Feb 1969
Karlskrona	1966	9 Jan 1968	15 Sep 1969

Displacement, tons: 1 125 standard; 1 400 dived
Length, feet (metres): 167·3 *(50·5)*
Beam, feet (metres): 20·0 *(6·1)*
Draught, feet (metres): 16·7 *(5·1)*
Torpedo tubes: 4—21 in *(533 mm)* 2 A/S tubes
Main machinery: 2 Pielstick diesels; 1 large 5-bladed propeller; 2 200 bhp; 1 electric motor
Speed, knots: 15 surfaced; 20 dived
Endurance: 3 weeks
Complement: 23

Albacore hull. Twin-decked. Diving depth 500 ft.
Distinctive letters in place of pennant numbers are painted on the conning tower.

SJÖHÄSTEN

5/1976, Reinhard Nerlich

6 "DRAKEN" CLASS (A 11)

Name	No.	Builders	Laid down	Launched	Commissioned
DELFINEN	DEL	Karlskrona	1959	7 Mar 1961	7 June 1962
DRAKEN	DRA	Kockums	1958	1 Apr 1960	4 Apr 1962
GRIPEN	GRI	Karlskrona	1959	31 May 1960	28 Apr 1962
NORDKAPAREN	NOR	Kockums	1959	8 May 1961	4 Apr 1962
SPRINGAREN	SPR	Kockums	1960	31 Aug 1961	7 Nov 1962
VARGEN	VGN	Kockums	1958	20 May 1960	15 Nov 1961

Displacement, tons: 770 standard; 835 surfaced; 1 110 dived
Length, feet (metres): 226·4 (69·0)
Beam, feet (metres): 16·7 (5·1)
Draught, feet (metres): 17·4 (5·3)
Torpedo tubes: 4—21 in (533 mm) bow
Main machinery: 2 Pielstick diesels; 1 660 bhp; 1 large 5-bladed propeller; 1 electric motor
Speed, knots: 17 surfaced; 20 dived
Complement: 36

Distinctive letters are painted on the conning tower in place of pennant numbers.

DRAKEN
5/1976, Reinhard Nerlich

6 "HAJEN" CLASS

Name	No.	Builders	Laid down	Launched	Commissioned
BÄVERN	BAV	Kockums	1956	3 Feb 1958	29 May 1959
HÄJEN	HAJ	Kockums	1953	11 Dec 1954	28 Feb 1957
ILLERN	ILN	Kockums	1956	15 Nov 1957	31 Aug 1959
SÄLEN	SAL	Kockums	1954	3 Oct 1955	8 Apr 1957
UTTERN	UTN	Kockums	1957	14 Nov 1958	15 Mar 1960
VALEN	VAL	Karlskrona	1953	24 Apr 1955	4 Mar 1957

Displacement, tons: 720 standard; 785 surfaced; 1 000 dived
Length, feet (metres): 216·5 (66·0)
Beam, feet (metres): 16·7 (5·1)
Draught, feet (metres): 16·4 (5·0)
Torpedo tubes: 4—21 in (533 mm) bow (8 torpedoes)
Main machinery: 2 SEMT-Pielstick diesels; 1 660 bhp; 2 Electric motors; 2 shafts
Speed, knots: 16 surfaced; 17 dived
Complement: 44

Distinctive letters are painted on the conning tower in place of pennant numbers.

ILLERN (old lettering)
1972, Royal Swedish Navy

LIGHT FORCES

3 PROJECTED FLOTILLA LEADERS

RO 1   RO 2   RO 3

Displacement, tons: 700
Dimensions, feet (metres): 246·0 × 26·2 × 8·0 (80·6 × 8·6 × 2·6)
Missiles: 2 SSM
Guns: 2—57 mm forward
A/S weapons: 1 single barrelled depth charge mortar forward
Main engines: Gas turbines for power; diesels for cruising = 35 knots
Complement: 70

A new type of corvette planned to fill the need for ships to act as flotilla leaders for fast attack craft and for escort duties.

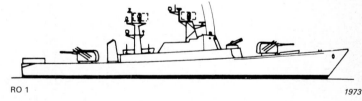
RO 1
1973

1 + 16 "JÄGAREN" CLASS
(FAST ATTACK CRAFT—MISSILE)

Name	No.	Builders	Commissioned
JÄGAREN	P 151	Norway	8 June 1972
—	P 152	Norway	1977
—	P 153	Norway	1977
—	P 154	Norway	—
—	P 155	Norway	—
—	P 156	Norway	—
—	P 157	Norway	—
—	P 158	Norway	—
—	P 159	Norway	—
—	P 160	Norway	—
—	P 161	Norway	—
—	P 162	Norway	—
—	P 163	Norway	—
—	P 164	Norway	—
—	P 165	Norway	—
—	P 166	Norway	—
—	P 167	Norway	—

Displacement, tons: 140
Dimensions, feet (metres): 118 × 20·3 × 4·9 (36 × 6·2 × 1·5)
Missile launchers: 6 Penguin Mark 2
Gun: 1—57 mm Bofors L 70
Torpedo tubes: Fitted for 4—21 inch (533 mm)
Main engines: 2 MTU MB20V 672 TY90 diesels; 2 shafts; 7 000 bhp = 35 knots
Complement: 20

Instead of the motor gunboats projected for several years a choice was made of fast attack craft similar to the Norwegian "Hauk" class armed with Penguin missiles.

JÄGAREN
1976, Royal Swedish Navy

Jägaren underwent extensive trials and, on 15 May 1975, an order for a further eleven was placed with Bergens Mekaniske Verksted, Norway and five from Westermoen. Guns and electronics are being provided from Sweden. Fitted for alternative minelaying capability aft. An extra deck-mounting ring is fitted amidships though now blanked by Penguin mounts.

12 "SPICA T 131" CLASS
(FAST ATTACK CRAFT—TORPEDO)

Name	No.	Builders	Commissioned
HALMSTAD	T 140	Karlskronavarvet AB	1976
LULEA	T 139	Karlskronavarvet AB	1976
NORRKÖPING	T 131	Karlskronavarvet AB	5 Nov 1973
NORRTÄLJE	T 133	Karlskronavarvet AB	1 Feb 1974
NYNÄSHAMN	T 132	Karlskronavarvet AB	Sep 1973
PITEA	T 138	Karlskronavarvet AB	Oct 1975
STRÖMSTAD	T 141	Karlskronavarvet AB	1976
UMEÅ	T 137	Karlskronavarvet AB	June 1975
VARBERG	T 134	Karlskronavarvet AB	13 June 1974
VÄSTERÅS	T 135	Karlskronavarvet AB	25 Oct 1974
VÄSTERVIK	T 136	Karlskronavarvet AB	15 Jan 1975
YSTAD	T 142	Karlskronavarvet AB	1976

Displacement, tons: 230 standard
Dimensions, feet (metres): 134·5 × 23·3 × 5·2 *(41 × 7·1 × 1·6)*
Gun: 1—57 mm Bofors L 70
Rocket launchers: 8 for 103 mm flare rockets
Torpedo tubes: 6—21 in *(533 mm)* for wire-guided torpedoes
Main engines: 3 Rolls Royce Proteus gas turbines; 3 shafts; 12 900 bhp = 40·5 knots

Similar to the original "Spica" class from which they were developed. Guided missiles are not included in the design to date. Launched—*Norrköping* 16 Nov 1972, *Nynäshamn* 24 April 1973, *Norrtalje* 18 Sep 1973, *Varberg* 2 Feb 1974, *Västerås* 15 May 1974, *Västervik* 2 Sep 1974, *Umea* 13 Jan 1975, *Pitea* 12 May 1975. Laid down—*Lulea* 6 Sep 1974, *Halmstad* 7 Feb 1975.

Missiles: Plans exist for the fitting of two twin missile launchers aft post-1978.

Radar: Philips Teleindustrie 9 LV 200-simultaneous air and surface search in I band with tracking in separate band.

VÄSTERVIK   1975, Kapten Goran Frisk

6 "SPICA T 121" CLASS (FAST ATTACK CRAFT—TORPEDO)

Name	No.	Builders	Commissioned
CAPELLA	T 123	Götaverken, Göteborg	1966
CASTOR	T 124	Karlskronavervarvet	1967
SIRIUS	T 122	Götaverken, Göteborg	1966
SPICA	T 121	Götaverken, Göteborg	1966
VEGA	T 125	Karlskronavervarvet	1967
VIRGO	T 126	Karlskronavervarvet	1967

Displacement, tons: 200 standard; 230 full load
Dimensions, feet (metres): 134·5 × 23·3 × 5·2 *(41 × 7·1 × 1·6)*
Gun: 1—57 mm Bofors
Torpedo tubes: 6—21 in *(533 mm)* (single, fixed)
Rocket launchers: 6—57 mm flare rockets; 4—103 mm flare rockets
Main engines: 3 Bristol Siddeley Proteus 1 274 gas turbines; 3 shafts; 12 720 shp = 40 knots
Complement: 28 (7 officers, 21 ratings)

The 57 mm gun is in a power operated turret controlled by a radar equipped director.

Radar: M 22 fire control system with co-mounted radars in radome for guns and torpedoes.

CAPELLA   1976, Royal Swedish Navy

11 "PLEJAD" CLASS (FAST ATTACK CRAFT—TORPEDO)

Name	No.	Builders	Commissioned
ALDEBARAN	T 107	Lurssen, Vegesack	1956
ALTAIR	T 108	Lurssen, Vegesack	1956
ANTARES	T 109	Lurssen, Vegesack	1957
ARCTURUS	T 110	Lurssen, Vegesack	1957
ARGO	T 111	Lurssen, Vegesack	1957
ASTREA	T 112	Lurssen, Vegesack	1956
PLEJAD	T 102	Lurssen, Vegesack	1955
POLARIS	T 103	Lurssen, Vegesack	1955
POLLUX	T 104	Lurssen, Vegesack	1955
REGULUS	T 105	Lurssen, Vegesack	1956
RIGEL	T 106	Lurssen, Vegesack	1956

Displacement, tons: 155 standard; 170 full load
Dimensions, feet (metres): 147·6 × 19 × 5·2 *(45 × 5·8 × 1·6)*
Guns: 2—40 mm Bofors
Rocket launchers: 4—103 mm flare rockets; 1—12 rail 57 mm flare launcher
Torpedo tubes: 6—21 in *(533 mm)*
Main engines: 3 Mercedes-Benz (MTU 20 V 672) diesels; 3 shafts; 9 000 bhp = 37·5 knots
Range, miles: 600 at 30 knots
Complement: 33

ALTAIR   1975, Royal Swedish Navy

Launched between 1954 and 1957.

12 "T 42" CLASS (FAST ATTACK CRAFT—TORPEDO)

Name	No.	Builders	Commissioned
—	T 45	Kockums Mekaniska Verkstads Aktiebolag, Malmo	1957
—	T 46	Kockums Mekaniska Verkstads Aktiebolag, Malmo	1957
—	T 47	Kockums Mekaniska Verkstads Aktiebolag, Malmo	1957
—	T 48	Kockums Mekaniska Verkstads Aktiebolag, Malmo	1957
—	T 49	Kockums Mekaniska Verkstads Aktiebolag, Malmo	1957
—	T 50	Kockums Mekaniska Verkstads Aktiebolag, Malmo	1958
—	T 51	Kockums Mekaniska Verkstads Aktiebolag, Malmo	1958
—	T 52	Kockums Mekaniska Verkstads Aktiebolag, Malmo	1958
—	T 53	Naval Dockyard, Stockholm	1958
—	T 54	Naval Dockyard, Stockholm	1959
—	T 55	Naval Dockyard, Stockholm	1959
—	T 56	Naval Dockyard, Stockholm	1959

Displacement, tons: 40 standard
Dimensions, feet (metres): 75·5 × 19·4 × 4·6 *(23 × 5·9 × 1·4)*
Gun: 1—40 mm Bofors
Rocket launchers: 1—12 rail 57 mm flare launcher
Torpedo tubes: 2—21 in *(533 mm)*
Main engines: 3 Isotta Fraschini Petrol engines; 4 500 bhp = 45 knots

T 56   1975, Royal Swedish Navy

1 LARGE PATROL CRAFT

V 57

Displacement, tons: 115 standard
Dimensions, feet (metres): 98 × 17·3 × 7·5 *(30 × 5·3 × 2·3)*
Gun: 1—20 mm
Main engines: Diesel; 500 bhp = 13·5 knots
Complement: 12

Built at Stockholm. Launched in 1953. Fitted for minelaying. Attached to Coastal Artillery.

5 COASTAL PATROL CRAFT

SVK 1	SVK 2	SVK 3	SVK 4	SVK 5

Displacement, tons: 19 standard
Dimensions, feet (metres): 52·5 × 12·1 × 3·9 *(16 × 3·7 × 1·2)*
Gun: 1—20 mm
Main engines: Diesels; 100 to 135 bhp = 10 knots

Patrol craft of the Sjövarnskarens (RNVR). All launched in 1944.

17 COASTAL PATROL CRAFT

61-77

Displacement, tons: 28 standard
Dimensions, feet (metres): 69 × 15 × 5 *(21 × 4·6 × 1·5)*
Gun: 1—20 mm
Main engines: Diesel; speed = 18 knots

These are attached to the Coastal Artillery. "60" series launched in 1960-61 and "70" series in 1966-67.

Radar: 1 navigation set.

PATROL CRAFT 66   1975, Royal Swedish Navy

4 "V 01" CLASS (COASTAL PATROL CRAFT)

Name	No.	Builders	Commissioned
SKANÖR	V 01	Karlskronavarvet	Dec. 1976
SMYGE	V 02	Karlskronavarvet	1977
ARILD	V 03	Karlskronavarvet	1977
VIKEN	V 04	Karlskronavarvet	1977

Gun: 1—40 mm
Flare launcher: 1—12 rail 57 mm flare launcher

SKÄNOR   1976, Royal Swedish Navy

MINE WARFARE FORCES

2 + 1 "ALVSBORG" CLASS (MINELAYERS)

Name	No.	Builders	Commissioned
ÄLVSBORG	M 02	Karlskrona Naval DY	10 April 1971
VISBORG	M 03	Karlskrona Naval DY	6 Feb 1976
—	M 04	Karlskrona Naval DY	1979

Displacement, tons: 2 700
Length, feet (metres): 301·8 *(92)*
Beam, feet (metres): 48·2 *(14·7)*
Draught, feet (metres): 13·2 *(4·0)*
Aircraft: 1 Helicopter
Guns: 3—40 mm Bofors
Main engines: 2 Nohab-Polar 12 cyl diesels; 1 shaft; 4 200 bhp
Speed, knots: 15
Complement: 95 (accommodation for 205 more)

The *Älvsborg* was ordered in 1968 and launched on 11 Nov 1969. She replaced the submarine depot ship *Patricia* which was sold in 1972.
Visborg, laid down on 16 Oct 1973 and launched 22 Jan 1975 will succeed *Marieholm* as Command Ship for C-in-C Coastal Fleet.

Fire Control: M 20 Series.

M 04

This ship will be slightly larger at 328 ft *(100 m)* length and 3 000 tons. Laid down 1977. When eventually completed is planned to relieve *Alvsnabben* as Cadet Training Ship as well as serving as a minelayer.

ÄLVSBORG   1975, Royal Swedish Navy

1 MINELAYER/TRAINING SHIP

Name	No.	Builders	Commissioned
ÄLVSNABBEN	M 01	Eriksberg Mekaniska Verkstad Göteborg	8 May 1943

Displacement, tons: 4 250 standard
Length, feet (metres): 317·6 *(96·8)* wl; 334·7 *(102·0)* oa
Beam, feet (metres): 44·6 *(13·6)*
Draught, feet (metres): 16·4 *(5·0)*
Guns: 2—6 in *(152 mm)*; 2—57 mm Bofors;
   2—40 mm; 4—37 mm saluting
Main engines: Diesels; 1 shaft; 3 000 bhp
Speed, knots: 14
Complement: 255 (63 cadets)

Built on a mercantile hull. Laid down on 31 Oct 1942, launched on 19 Jan 1943. Employed as a training ship during 1953-58. Relieved the anti-aircraft cruiser *Gotland* as Cadets' Seagoing Training Ship in 1959. Re-armed in 1961. Formerly carried 4—6 inch, 8—40 mm, 6—20 mm.

Radar: Search and Target designator: Thomson CSF Saturn.
Fire control: M45 series.

ÄLVSNABBEN   *7/1976, US Navy*

Note: A new construction coastal minelayer MUL 20 projected.

1 COASTAL MINELAYER

MUL 11

Displacement, tons: 200 full load
Dimensions, feet (metres): 98·8 × 23·7 × 11·8 *(32·4 × 7·8 × 3·9)*
Guns: 2—20 mm
Main engines: 2 Atlas diesels; 300 bhp = 10 knots

Launched in 1946.

Radar: 1 navigation set.

MUL 11   *1976, Royal Swedish Navy*

8 COASTAL MINELAYERS

MUL 12 (1952)	**MUL 14** (1953)	**MUL 16** (1956)	**MUL 18** (1956)
MUL 13 (1952)	**MUL 15** (1953)	**MUL 17** (1956)	**MUL 19** (1956)

Displacement, tons: 245 full load
Dimensions, feet (metres): 95·1 × 24·3 × 10·2 *(29 × 7·4 × 3·1)*
Gun: 1—40 mm
Main engines: 2 Nohab diesel-electric; 460 bhp = 10·5 knots

Launch dates in brackets. All completed in 1957.

Radar: 1 navigation set.

MUL 12   *1975, Royal Swedish Navy*

37 SMALL MINELAYERS

501-537

Ordered in 1969. Of 15 tons and 14 knots with Diesel engines. Mines are laid from single traps on either beam.

Radar: 1 navigation set.

SMALL MINELAYER 502   *1975, Royal Swedish Navy*

9 M 70 MINEHUNTERS

Displacement, tons: 270
Dimensions, feet (metres): 141 × 30 × — (43 × 8·5 × —)
Gun: 1—20 mm
Main engines: 4 Diesels
Complement: 24

Ordered 1976. GRP hulls.

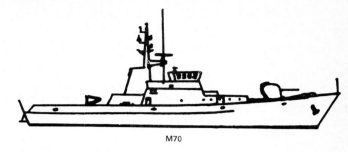

M70

6 "HANÖ" CLASS (MINESWEEPERS—COASTAL)

Name	No.	Builders	Commissioned
HANÖ	M 51	Karlskrona	1954
ORNÖ	M 55	Karlskrona	1954
STURKÖ	M 54	Karlskrona	1954
TÄRNÖ	M 52	Karlskrona	1954
TJURKÖ	M 53	Karlskrona	1954
UTÖ	M 56	Karlskrona	1954

Displacement, tons: 275 standard
Dimensions, feet (metres): 131·2 × 23 × 8 (40 × 7 × 2·4)
Guns: 2—40 mm (except Utö; 1—40mm)
Main engines: 2 Nohab Diesels; 2 shafts; 910 bhp = 14·5 knots

Steel hulls.

TJURKÖ   1975, Royal Swedish Navy

12 "ARKÖ" CLASS (MINESWEEPERS—COASTAL)

Name	No.	Builders	Commissioned
ARKÖ	M 57	Karlskrona	1958
ASPÖ	M 63	Karlskrona	1962
BLIDÖ	M 68	Hälsingborg	1964
HASSLÖ	M 64	Hälsingborg	1962
IGGÖ	M 60	Hälsingborg	1961
KARLSÖ	M 59	Karlskrona	1958
NÄMDÖ	M 67	Karlskrona	1964
SKAFTÖ	M 62	Hälsingborg	1962
SPÄRÖ	M 58	Hälsingborg	1958
STYRSÖ	M 61	Karlskrona	1962
VÄLLÖ	M 66	Hälsingborg	1963
VINÖ	M 65	Karlskrona	1962

Displacement, tons: 285 standard; 300 full load
Dimensions, feet (metres): 131 pp; 144·5 oa × 23 × 8 (42 × 7 × 2·4)
Gun: 1—40 mm
Main engines: 2 Mercedes-Benz (MTU 12V 493) diesels; 2 shafts; 1 600 bhp = 14·5 knots

Of wooden construction. There is a small difference in the deck-line between M 57-59 and M 60-68. Arkö was launched on 21 Jan 1957.

ASPÖ   1975, Royal Swedish Navy

3 "M 47" CLASS (MINESWEEPERS—INSHORE)

GILLÖGA M 47   **RÖDLÖGA** M 48   **SVARTLÖGA** M 49

Details same as "M 44" class. Built in 1964. Trawler type.

RÖDLÖGA   1976, Royal Swedish Navy

3 "M 31" CLASS (MINESWEEPERS—INSHORE)

Name	No.	Builders	Commissioned
GÄSSTEN	M 31	Knippla Skeppsvarv	16 Nov 1973
NORSTEN	M 32	Hellevikstrands Skeppsvarv	12 Oct 1973
VIKSTEN	M 33	Karlskrona	1 July 1974

Displacement, tons: 120 standard; 135 full load
Dimensions, feet (metres): 79 oa × 21·7 × 12·2 *(24 × 6·6 × 3·7)*
Gun: 1—40 mm
Main engines: 1 Diesel, 460 bhp = 11 knots

Ordered 1972. *Viksten* built of glass reinforced plastic as a forerunner to new minehunters to be built at Karlskrona. *Gässten* launched Nov 1972. *Norsten* Apr 1973, *Viksten* Apr 1974.

VIKSTEN   *1975, Royal Swedish Navy*

4 "M 44" CLASS (MINESWEEPERS—INSHORE)

BLACKAN M 44	**GALTEN** M 46
DÄMMAN M 45	**HISINGEN** M 43

Displacement, tons: 140
Dimensions, feet (metres): 72·2 × 21 × 11·2 *(22× 6·4 × 3·4)*
Gun: 1—40 mm
Main engines: 1 Diesel; 380 bhp = 9 knots

Built in 1960. Trawler type.

2 "M 41" CLASS (MINESWEEPERS—INSHORE)

ORUST M 41	**TJÖRN** M 42

Displacement, tons: 110
Dimensions, feet (metres): 62·3 × 19·7 × 8·5 *(19 × 6 × 2·4)*
Gun: 1—20 mm
Main engines: 1 Diesel; 210 bhp = 9 knots

Built in 1948. Trawler type.

8 "M 15" CLASS (MINESWEEPERS—INSHORE)

M 15   M 16   M 21   M 22   M 23   M 24   M 25   M 26

Displacement, tons: 70 standard
Dimensions, feet (metres): 85·3 × 16·5 × 4·5 *(26 × 5 × 1·4)*
Gun: 1—20 mm
Main engines: 2 Diesels; 320-430 bhp = 12-13 knots

All launched in 1941. M 17, M 18 and M 20 of this class were re-rated as tenders and renamed *Lommen, Spoven* and *Skuld* respectively: see later page.

M 25   *1975, Royal Swedish Navy*

2 MINE TRANSPORTS

FÄLLAREN A 236	**MINÖREN** A 237

Displacement, tons: 165 standard
Dimensions, feet (metres): 97 × 19 × 6·7 *(31·8 × 6·2 × 2·2)*
Main engines: 2 Diesels; 1 shaft; 240 bhp = 9 knots

Launched in 1941 and 1940 respectively.

AMPHIBIOUS FORCES

3 LCM

Name	No.	Builders	Commissioned
BORE	—	Åsigeverken	1967
GRIM	—	Åsigeverken	1962
HEIMDAL	—	Åsigeverken	1967

Displacement, tons: 340 full load
Dimensions, feet (metres): 118·1 × 27·9 × 8·5 *(36 × 8·5 × 2·6)*
Guns: 2—20 mm
Main engines: Diesels; 800 bhp = 12 knots

Launched in 1961 *(Grim)* and other two in 1966. Attached to Coastal Artillery.

BORE   *1969, Royal Swedish Navy*

2 LCM

Name	No.	Builders	Commissioned
SKAGUL	A 333	—	1960
SLEIPNER	A 335	—	1960

Displacement, tons: 335 standard
Dimensions, feet (metres): 114·8 × 27·9 × 9·5 *(35 × 8·5 × 2·9)*
Main engines: Diesels; 640 bhp = 10 knots

Sleipner was launched in 1959 and *Skagul* in 1960. Attached to Coastal Artillery.

4 "ANE" CLASS (LCM)

ANE J 324	BALDER J 325	LOKE J 326	RING J 327

Displacement, tons: 135 standard
Dimensions, feet (metres): 91·9 × 26·2 × 6·0 *(28 × 8 × 1·2)*
Guns: 1—20 mm; 1 or 2 MG
Main engines: Speed = 8·5 knots

Built in 1943-45. Attached to Coastal Artillery.

19 + 5 "256" CLASS (LCU)

Nos. 256-274

Of same specifications as the "201" class. Completed 1975. 266-274 laid down 1975 onwards. 275-279 planned.

14 "242" CLASS (LCU)

Nos. 242-255

Of same specifications as the "201" class. Built in 1971-73.

LCU 245 ("242" Class)   1975, Royal Swedish Navy

41 "201" CLASS (LCU)

Nos. 201-241

Displacement, tons: 31
Dimensions, feet (metres): 69 × 13·8 × 4·2 *(20 × 4·2 × 1·3)*
Guns: 2—6·5 mm MG
Main engines: Diesels; 600 hp = 17 knots

Launched 1957-1960.

5 "L 51" CLASS (LCU)

L 51	L 52	L 53	L 54	L 55

Displacement, tons: 32 standard
Dimensions, feet (metres): 50·8 × 16 × 3·2 *(14 × 4·8 × 1)*
Main engines: Diesel; 140 bhp = 7 knots

Launched in 1947-48.

54 LCAs

337-354 of 6 tons and 21 knots. Built 1970-73.
332-336 of 5·4 tons and 25 knots. Built in 1967.
331 of 6 tons and 20 knots. Built in 1965.
301-330 of 4 tons and 9·5 knots. Built in 1956-59.

LCU 227 ("201" Class)   1975, Royal Swedish Navy

SURVEY SHIPS

(Operated by Ministry of Transport)

1 NEW CONSTRUCTION

Projected but not yet laid down.

ANDERS BURE (ex-*Rali*)

Displacement, tons: 54
Dimensions, feet (metres): 82·0 × 19·4 × 6·9 *(25 × 5·9 × 2·1)*
Main engines: Diesels = 15 knots
Complement: 11

Built in 1968 as *Rali*. She was purchased in 1971 and renamed.

RAN

Displacement, tons: 285 standard
Dimensions, feet (metres): 98·4 × 23·0 × 8·5 *(30 × 7 × 2·6)*
Main engines: Diesels; 260 bhp = 9 knots
Complement: 37

Ran was launched in 1945 and commissioned for service in 1946.

ANDERS BURE   1976, Royal Swedish Navy

JOHAN MÅNSSON

Displacement, tons: 977 standard; 1 030 full load
Dimensions, feet (metres): 183·7 × 36·1 × 11·5 (56 × 11 × 3·5)
Main engines: Diesels; 3 300 bhp = 15 knots
Complement: 85

Launched on 14 Jan 1966. Her surveying launches are lowered and recovered over a stern ramp.

JOHAN MÅNSSON   1975, Royal Swedish Navy

GUSTAF AF KLINT

Displacement, tons: 750 standard
Dimensions, feet (metres): 170·6 × 36·2 × 15·4 (52 × 11 × 4·7)
Main engines: Diesels; 640 bhp = 10 knots
Complement: 66

Launched in 1941. Reconstructed in 1963. She formerly displaced 650 tons with a length of 154 feet (47 metres).

GUSTAV AF KLINT   1976, Royal Swedish Navy

NILS STRÖMCRONA

Displacement, tons: 140 standard
Dimensions, feet (metres): 88·6 × 17·0 × 8·2 (27 × 5·2 × 2·5)
Guns: None in peacetime
Main engines: Diesels; 300 bhp = 9 knots
Complement: 14

Launched in 1894, and reconstructed in 1952.

NILS STRÖMCRONA   1976, Royal Swedish Navy

SERVICE FORCES

1 SUPPLY SHIP

Name	No.	Builders	Commissioned
FREJA	A 221	Kroger, Rendsburg	1954

Displacement, tons: 415 standard; 465 full load
Dimensions, feet (metres): 160·8 × 27·9 × 12·1 (49 × 8·5 × 3·7)
Main engines: Diesels; 600 bhp = 11 knots

Launched in 1953. Employed as a provision ship.

1 SUPPORT TANKER

BRÄNNAREN A 228

Displacement, tons: 857
Dimensions, feet (metres): 203·4 × 28·2 × 12·1 (62 × 8·6 × 3·7)
Speed, knots: 11

Ex-German merchant tanker *Indio* purchased early 1972. Built 1965.

1 SALVAGE SHIP

Name	No.	Builders	Commissioned
BELOS	A 211	—	29 May 1963

Displacement, tons: 1 000 standard
Dimensions, feet (metres): 204·4 × 37·0 × 12·0 (58 × 11·2 × 3·8)
Aircraft: 1 helicopter
Main engines: Diesels; 2 shafts; 1 200 bhp = 13 knots

Launched on 15 Nov 1961. Equipped with decompression chamber.

BELOS   1972, Wright & Logan

2 SAIL TRAINING SHIPS

Name	No.	Builders	Commissioned
FALKEN	S 02	—	1948
GLADAN	S 01	—	1947

Displacement, tons: 220 standard
Dimensions, feet (metres): 93 wl; 129·5 oa × 23·5 × 13·5 *(30·5; 42·5 × 7·7 × 4·4)*
Main engines: Auxiliary diesel; 120 bhp

Sail training ships. Two masted schooners. Launched 1947 and 1946 respectively. Sail area 5 511 square feet (512 square metres).

TENDERS

3 TRVs

Name	No.	Builders	Commissioned
PINGVINEN	A 248	Lundevarv-Ooverkstads AB, Kramfors	Mar 1975

Displacement, tons: 191
Dimensions, feet (metres): 108·2 × 20 × 6 *(33 × 6·1 × 1·8)*
Main engines: 2 diesels; 1 100 hp = 13 knots

Ordered 1972. Torpedo recovery and rocket trials ship. Launched 26 Sep 1973.

PINGVINEN
1976, Royal Swedish Navy

Name	No.	Builders	Commissioned
PELIKANEN	A 247	—	26 Sep 1963

Displacement, tons: 130 standard
Dimensions, feet (metres): 108·2 × 19·0 × 6·0 *(33 × 5·8 × 1·8)*
Main engines: 2 Mercedes Benz diesels; 1 040 bhp = 15 knots

Torpedo recovery and rocket trials vessel.

HÄGERN A 246

Displacement, tons: 50 standard
Dimensions, feet (metres): 88·6 × 16·4 × 4·9 *(29 × 5·4 × 1·6)*
Main engines: 2 diesels; 240 bhp = 10 knots

Launched in 1951.

5 TENDERS

SIGRUN A 256

Displacement, tons: 250 standard
Dimensions, feet (metres): 105·0 × 22·3 × 11·8 *(32 × 6·8 × 3·6)*
Main engines: Diesels 320 bhp = 11 knots

Launched in 1961. Laundry ship.

URD (ex-*Capella*) A 241

Displacement, tons: 63 standard; 90 full load
Dimensions, feet (metres): 73·8 × 18·3 × 9·2 *(22 × 5·6 × 2·8)*
Main engines: Diesels; 200 bhp = 8 knots

Experimental vessel added to the official list in 1970. Launched in 1969.

LOMMEN (ex-*M 17*) A 231

Displacement; tons: 70 standard
Dimensions, feet (metres): 85·3 × 16·5 × 4·5 *(26 × 5 × 1·4)*
Main engines: 2 diesels; 410 bhp = 13 knots

SKULD (ex-*M 20*) A 242
SPOVEN (ex-*M 18*) A 232

Former inshore minesweepers of the ''M 15'' Class. All launched in 1941.

TUGS

ACHILLES A 251   **AJAX** A 252

Displacement, tons: 450
Dimensions, feet (metres): 108·2 × 28·9 × 12 *(35·5 × 9·5 × 3·9)*
Main engines: Diesel; 1 650 bhp = 12 knots

Achilles was launched in 1962 and *Ajax* in 1963. Both are icebreaking tugs.

HECTOR A 321   **HERMES** A 253   **HEROS** A 322

Displacement, tons: 185 standard
Dimensions, feet (metres): 75·5 × 22·6 × 11·1 *(24·5 × 7·4 × 3·6)*
Main engines: Diesels; 600 bhp = 11 knots

Launched in 1953-57. Icebreaking tugs.

HERA A 324   **HERCULES** A 323

Displacement, tons: 127 tons
Dimensions, feet (metres): 65·3 × 21·3 × 12·5 *(21·4 × 6·9 × 4·1)*
Main engines: Diesels; 615 bhp = 11·5 knots

Launched 1969 and 1971. Icebreaking Tugs.

AJAX
5/1976, Reinhard Nerlich

Also listed:
ATLAS A330; **HEBE** A326; **HENRIK** A329; **MÄRSGARN** A332; **PASSOP** A327; **RAN** A328; **VITSGARN** A336.

ATB 1 A341; **ATB 2** A342; **ATB 3** A343.

EDDA A347; **GERDA** A349; **GRANATEN** A345.

WATER CARRIERS

FRYKEN A 217

Displacement, tons: 307 standard
Dimensions, feet (metres): 105·0 × 18·7 × 8·9 *(34·4 × 6·1 × 2·9)*
Main engines: Diesels; 370 bhp = 10 knots

A naval construction water carrier. Launched in 1959 and completed in 1960.

UNDEN A 216

Displacement, tons: 540 standard
Dimensions, feet (metres): 121·4 × 23·3 × 9·8 *(39·8 × 7·6 × 3·2)*
Main engines: Steam reciprocating; 225 ihp = 9 knots

Launched in 1946.

FRYKEN   *1976, Royal Swedish Navy*

ICEBREAKERS

3 FINNISH "URHO" CLASS

Name	No.	Builders	Commissioned	
ATLE	—	Wärtsilä, Helsinki	21 Oct	1974
FREJ	—	Wärtsilä, Helsinki	30 Sep	1975
YMER	—	Wärtsilä, Helsinki		1977

Displacement, tons: 7 900
Dimensions, feet (metres): 337·8 × 77·1 × 24·6 *(104·6 × 23·8 × 7·3)*
Aircraft: 1 helicopter
Main engines: 5 Wärtsilä-Pielstick diesels of 25 000 bhp; 4 Stromberg electric motors; 4 shafts (2 for'd, 2 aft); 22 000 shp = 18 knots
Complement: 54 (16 officers, 38 men)

Atle laid down 10 May 1973, launched 27 Nov 1973. *Frej* launched 3 June 1974. *Ymer* ordered 24 Mar 1975. Sister ships of Finnish "Urho" class.

FREJ   *1974, Wärtsilä*

Name	No.	Builders	Commissioned
NJORD	—	Wärtsilä, Finland	Dec 1969

Displacement, tons: 5 150 standard; 5 686 full load
Dimensions, feet (metres): 283·8 oa × 69·6 × 20·3 *(81 × 20·5 × 6·2)*
Main engines: Wärtsilä diesel-electric; 4 shafts, (2 forward, 2 aft); 12 000 hp = 18 knots

Launched on 20 Oct 1968. Near sister ship of *Tor*.
Has deck-rings for 4—40 mm guns.

NJORD   *1971, Royal Swedish Navy*

Name	No.	Builders	Commissioned
TOR	—	Wärtsilä, Crichton-Vulcan Yard, Turku	31 Jan 1964

Displacement, tons: 4 980 standard; 5 290 full load
Dimensions, feet (metres): 283·8 oa × 69·6 × 20·3 *(81 × 20·5 × 6·2)*
Main engines: Wärtsilä-Sulzer diesel-electric; 4 shafts; (2 for'd; 2 aft); 12 000 hp = 18 knots

Launched on 25 May 1963. Towed to Sandvikens Skeppsdocka, Helsingfors, for completion. Larger but generally similar to *Oden,* and a near-sister to *Tarmo* built for Finland. Has deck-rings for 4—40 mm guns

TOR   *1972, Royal Swedish Navy*

Name	No.	Builders	Commissioned
ALE	—	Wärtsilä, Helsinki	19 Dec 1973

Displacement, tons: 1 488
Dimensions, feet (metres): 150·9 × 42·6 × 16·4 *(46 × 13 × 5)*
Main engines: Diesels; 4 750 hp; 2 shafts = 14 knots
Complement: 21

Built for operations on Lake Vänern. Launched 1 June 1973.

Name	No.	Builders	Commissioned
ODEN	—	Sandviken, Helsingfors	1958

Displacement, tons: 4 950 standard; 5 220 full load
Dimensions, feet (metres): 273·5 oa × 63·7 × 22·7 *(78 × 19·4 × 6·9)*
Main engines: Diesel-electric; 4 shafts (2 for'd); 10 500 shp = 16 knots
Oil fuel, tons: 740
Complement: 75

Similar to the Finnish *Voima* and 3 Soviet icebreakers. Launched on 16 Oct 1956.

Name	No.	Builders	Commissioned
THULE	—	Naval Dockyard, Karlskrona	1953

Displacement, tons: 2 200 standard; 2 280 full load
Dimensions, feet (metres): 204·2 oa × 52·8 × 19·4 *(57 × 16·1 × 5·9)*
Main engines: Diesel-electric; 3 shafts (1 for'd); 4 800 bhp = 14 knots
Complement: 43

Launched in Oct 1951.

ODEN   *1972, Royal Swedish Navy*

SWITZERLAND

Diplomatic Representation

Defence Attaché in London: Colonel H. W. Fischer

The Swiss Army operates ten Coastal Patrol Craft on the lakes. These were originally built in 1942 against possible German operations and have been modernised. Fitted with machine guns and radar. New construction would seem imminent. There are also water-transport detachments and other detachments with smaller patrol craft.

Mercantile Marine

Lloyd's Register of Shipping: 28 vessels of 212 526 tons gross

SWISS PATROL CRAFT   *2/1976, Commander Aldo Fraccaroli*

SYRIA

Personnel

(a) 1977: 2 500 officers and men
(b) 2½ years national service

Bases

Latakia, Baniyas

Mercantile Marine

Lloyd's Register of Shipping: 17 vessels of 10 192 tons gross

FRIGATES

2 Ex-SOVIET "PETYA I" CLASS

Displacement, tons: 950 standard; 1 150 full load
Dimensions, feet (metres): 270 × 29·9 × 10·5 *(82·3 × 9·1 × 3·2)*
Guns: 4—3 in *(76 mm)* (twin)
A/S weapons: 4—16 barrelled MBU 2500
Torpedo tubes: 3—21 in *(533 mm)*
Main engines: 1 diesel; 6 000 hp; 2 gas-turbines; 30 000 hp; 3 shafts
Speed, knots: 30
Complement: 100

Transferred by USSR in 1975.

LIGHT FORCES

6 Ex-SOVIET "OSA" CLASS
(FAST ATTACK CRAFT—MISSILE)

Displacement, tons: 165 standard; 200 full load
Dimensions, feet (metres): 128·7 × 25·1 × 5·9 *(42·2 × 8·2 × 1·9)*
Missile launchers: 4, two pairs abreast, for SS-N-2 (Styx)
Guns: 4—30 mm (twins; 1 forward, 1 aft)
Main engines: 3 diesels; 13 000 bhp = 32 knots
Range, miles: 800 at 25 knots
Complement: 25

Original pair sunk in Oct 1973 war. Up to six replacements reported.

Syrian "OSA" Class   *Dec, 1972*

6 Ex-SOVIET "KOMAR" CLASS
(FAST ATTACK CRAFT—MISSILE)

Displacement, tons: 70 standard; 80 full load
Dimensions, feet (metres): 83·7 × 19·8 × 5 *(27·4 × 6·5 × 1·6)*
Missile launchers: 2 for SS-N-2 (Styx)
Guns: 2—25 mm
Main engines: 4 diesels; 4 shafts; 4 800 bhp = 40 knots
Range, miles: 400 at 30 knots

Transferred between 1963 and 1966. Three reported lost in Israeli war October 1973, but were replaced.

"KOMAR" Class

8 Ex-SOVIET "P 4" CLASS
(FAST ATTACK CRAFT—TORPEDO)

"P 4" Class

Displacement, tons: 25 standard
Dimensions, feet (metres): 62·7 × 11·6 × 5·6 (20·5 × 3·8 × 1·8)
Torpedo tubes: 2—18 in
Guns: 2—MG (twin)
Main engines: 2 diesels; 2 200 bhp; 2 shafts = 50 knots

Five torpedo boats were transferred from the USSR at Latakia on 7 Feb 1957, and at least twelve subsequently. One reported lost in Israeli War October 1973. Four transferred to Egypt in 1970. Only eight of the remainder considered operational.

3 Ex-FRENCH CH TYPE (LARGE PATROL CRAFT)

ABABEH IBN NEFEH   **ABDULLAH IBN ARISSI**   **TAREK IBN ZAYED**

Displacement, tons: 107 standard; 131 full load
Dimensions, feet (metres): 116·5 pp; 121·8 oa × 17·5 × 6·5 (38·2; 39·9 × 5·7 × 2·1)
Guns: 2—20 mm
A/S weapons: Depth charges
Main engines: MAN diesels; 2 shafts; 1 130 bhp = 16 knots
Oil fuel, tons: 50
Range, miles: 1 200 at 8 knots; 680 at 13 knots
Complement: 28

All built in France and completed in 1940. Rebuilt in 1955-56 when the funnels were removed. These were transferred in 1962 to form the nucleus of the Syrian Navy. Two of these ships are probably non-operational.

MINE WARFARE FORCES

1 Ex-SOVIET "T 43" CLASS (MINESWEEPER—OCEAN)

YARMOUK

Displacement, tons: 500 standard; 610 full load
Dimensions, feet (metres): 190·2 × 28·1 × 6·9 (58 × 9·2 × 2·3)
Guns: 4—37 mm (twins); 8—12·7 mm (twins)
Main engines: 2 diesels motors; 2 shafts; 2 000 hp = 17 knots
Range, miles: 1 600 at 10 knots
Complement: 40

Reported in 1962 to have been transferred from the Soviet Navy. The second of this class was sunk in the Israeli War October 1973.

2 Ex-SOVIET "VANYA" CLASS (MINESWEEPERS—COASTAL)

Displacement, tons: 225 standard; 250 full load
Dimensions, feet (metres): 130·7 × 24 × 6·9 (39·9 × 7·3 × 2·1)
Guns: 2—30 mm (twin)
Main engines: 2 diesels; 2 200 bhp = 18 knots
Complement: 30

Transferred Dec 1972.

MISCELLANEOUS

1 Ex-SOVIET "NYRYAT" CLASS

Displacement, tons: 145
Main engines: Diesel = 12·5 knots
Complement: 15

Used as divers' base-ship.

TAIWAN

Ministerial

Minister of National Defence:
Kao K'uei-yuan

Senior Flag Officers

Commander-in-Chief:
Admiral Soong Chang-chih
Deputy Commanders-in-Chief:
Vice-Admiral Chih Meng-ping
Vice-Admiral Tsou Chien
Chief of Staff:
Vice-Admiral Chen Tung-hai
Commander, Fleet Command:
Vice-Admiral Li Pei-chou
Commandant of Marine Corps:
Lieutenant-General Kung Lin-cheng

Diplomatic Representation

Naval Attaché in Washington:
Rear-Admiral Chiu Hua-ku

Bases

Tsoying, Makung (Pescadores), Keelung.

Personnel

1977 (a) 7 100 officers and 28 000 men in Navy
3 000 officers and 26 000 men in Marine Corps.
(2 divisions with armour, APCs and heavy artillery)
(b) 2 years conscript service

Naval Aviation

One squadron of Air Force S-2A tracker ASW aircraft is under Navy operational control.
The Marine Corps operates several observation aircraft and helicopters.

Mercantile Marine

Lloyd's Register of Shipping:
438 vessels of 1 483 981 tons gross

Strength of the Fleet

Type	Active	Building
Destroyers	20	—
Frigates	11	
Corvettes	3	—
Submarines (Patrol)	2	—
Fast Attack Craft (missile)	1	14
Fast Attack Craft (Torpedo)	6	—
Coastal Patrol Craft	14	—
Coastal Minesweepers	14	
Minesweeping Boats	8	—
Amphibious Flagship	1	
Landing Ships	28	—
Utility Landing Craft	22	—
Repair Ship	1	—
Transports	2	—
Survey ships	3(?4)	—
Support Tankers	7	—
Cargo Ship	1	—
Tugs	9	—
Floating Docks	5	—
Service Craft	25	—
Customs	5+	—

Pennant Numbers

A major revision of warship pennant numbers was reported to have taken place early in 1976.

DELETIONS

Destroyers

1975 *Lo Yang, Han Yang, Nan Yang* (ex-US "Benson" class)
(all names transferred to later ships)
1976 *Hsien Yang* (sunk for film unit)

Frigates

1972 *Tai Kang*
1972-73 *Tai Cho, Tai Chong, Tai* (ex-US "Cannon" class)
1975 *Tai Hu* (ex-US "Cannon" class)
1976 *Heng Shan, Lung Shan* (APDs)

Submarines

1974-75 3 SX404 small submarines

Repair Ship

1974 *Tien Tai*

Tanker

1972 *Tai Yun*
1975 *Kuichi*

Tugs

1975-76 YTLs 3, 8 and 10

Customs

1974 PC122

DESTROYERS

7 Ex-US "GEARING" CLASS (FRAM I and II)

Name	No.	Builders	Laid down	Launched	Commissioned
DANG YANG (ex-USS *Lloyd Thomas*, DD 764) (FRAM II)	DD 11	Bethlehem Steel (San Francisco)	1945	5 Oct 1945	21 Mar 1947
CHIEN YANG (ex-USS *James E. Kyes*, DD 787)	DD 12	Todd Pacific Shipyards (Seattle, Wash)	1945	4 Aug 1945	8 Feb 1946
HAN YANG (ex-USS *Herbert J. Thomas*, DD 833)	DD 15	Bath Iron Works Corp	1944	25 Mar 1945	29 May 1945
LAO YANG (ex-USS *Shelton*, DD 790)	DD 20	Todd Pacific Shipyards (Seattle, Wash)	1945	8 Mar 1946	21 June 1946
LIAO YANG (ex-USS *Hanson*, DD 832)	DD 21	Bath Iron Works Corp	1944	11 Mar 1945	11 May 1945
—(ex-USS *Richard B. Anderson*, DD 786)	—	Todd Pacific Shipyards (Seattle, Wash)	1945	7 July 1975	26 Oct 1945
— (ex-USS *Rowan* DD 782)	—	Todd Pacific Shipyards (Seattle, Wash)	1944	29 Dec 1944	31 Mar 1945

Displacement, tons: 2 425 standard; approx 3 500 full load
Length, feet (metres): 390·5 *(119·0)* oa
Beam, feet (metres): 40·9 *(12·4)*
Draught, feet (metres): 19 *(5·8)*
Aircraft: 1 helicopter and hangar
Missiles: 3 Gabriel *(Dang Yang)*
Guns: 4—5 inch *(127 mm)* 38 cal (twin) (Mk 38); 4—40 mm (twins) *(Han Yang* only); several ·50 cal MG fitted in some ships
A/S weapons: ASROC 8-tube launcher except in *Dang Yang* and ex-DD 876 and ex-DD 782 which have trainable hedgehog (Mk 15)
6—(2 Triple) Mk 32 A/S torpedo tubes
Main engines: 2 geared turbines (General Electric); 60 000 shp; 2 shafts
Boilers: 4
Speed, knots: 34
Complement: approx 275

The *Dang Yang* was modified to a special anti-submarine configuration and reclassified as an escort destroyer (DDE) in 1950; changed again to "straight" DD upon modernisation in 1962.
Armament listed above was at time of transfer. The *Lao Yang* has twin 5 inch gun mounts in "A" and "B" positions with A/S torpedo tubes alongside second funnel; other ships have the "A" and "Y" gun mounts with torpedo tubes in "B" position except *Dang Yang* has torpedo tubes between funnels.
In 1963-1964 the *Herbert J. Thomas* was modified for protection against biological, chemical, and atomic attack; the ship could be fully "Sealed" with enclosed lookout and control positions, special air-conditioning. Upon transfer to Taiwan the *Herbert J. Thomas* assumed name and pennant number of an

ex-US "Benson" class destroyer in Taiwan service.
Three of the FRAM I ships were initially scheduled for transfer to Spain; however, they were declined by Spain and allocated to Taiwan.

Radar: At time of transfer three of these ships had SPS-37 and SPS-10 search radar antennae on their tripod mast; *Dang Yang* had older SPS-6 and SPS-10 antennae; *Chien Yang* had SPS-40 and SPS-10

Sonar: SQS 23 except *Dang Yang* with SQS 29 series.

Transfers: 11, 12 Oct 1972; 12, 18 April 1973; 15, 6 May 1974; 20, 18 April 1973; 21, 18 April 1973.—ex-DD 786 and 782, March 1977 by sale.

DANG YANG (as USS *Lloyd Thomas*)

LIAO YANG (as USS *Hanson*)   1971, US Navy

1 Ex-US "GEARING" CLASS RADAR PICKET (FRAM II)

Name	No.	Builders	Laid down	Launched	Commissioned
FU YANG (ex-USS *Ernest G. Small, DD 838*)	DD 7	Bath Iron Works Corp	1945	14 June 1945	21 Aug 1945

Displacement, tons: 2 425 standard; approx 3 500 full load
Length, feet (metres): 390·5 *(119·0)* oa
Beam, feet (metres): 40·8 *(12·4)*
Draught, feet (metres): 19 *(5·8)*
Missiles: 3 Gabriels
Guns: 6—5 inch *(127 mm)* 38 calibre (twin) (Mk 38); 8—40 mm (twin); 4—50 cal MG (single)
A/S weapons: 6 (2 triple) torpedo tubes (Mk 32); 2 fixed hedgehogs
Main engines: 2 geared turbines; (General Electric); 60 000 shp; 2 shafts
Boilers: 4 Babcock & Wilcox
Speed, knots: 34
Complement: approx 275

Converted to a radar picket destroyer (DDR) during 1952 and subsequently modernised under the FRAM II programme; redesignated as a "straight" destroyer (DD), but retained specialised electronic equipment. Not fitted with helicopter flight deck or hangar. The 40 mm guns were installed after transfer to Taiwan.

Radar: At time of transfer the *Fu Yang* had SPS-37 and SPS-10 search radars on forward tripod mast, and large TACAN antenna on second tripod mast.

Sonar: SQS-29 (hull-mounted); SQS-10 (VDS)

Transfer: Feb 1971.

FU YANG

8 Ex-US "ALLEN M. SUMNER" CLASS

Name	No.	Builders	Laid down	Launched	Commissioned
HSIANG YANG (ex-USS *Brush, DD 745*)	DD 1	Bethlehem Steel, Staten Island	1943	28 Dec 1943	17 April 1944
HENG YANG (ex-USS *Samuel N. Moore, DD 747*)	DD 2	Bethlehem Steel, Staten Island	1943	23 Feb 1944	24 June 1944
HUA YANG (ex-USS *Bristol, DD 857*)	DD 3	Bethlehem Steel, San Pedro	1944	29 Oct 1944	17 Mar 1945
YUEN YANG (ex-USS *Haynsworth, DD 700*)	DD 5	Federal SB & DD Co	1943	15 April1944	22 June 1944
HUEI YANG (ex-USS *English, DD 696*)	DD 6	Federal SB & DD Co	1943	27 Feb 1944	4 May 1944
PO YANG (ex-USS *Maddox, DD 731*)	DD 10	Bath Iron Works Corp	1943	19 Mar 1944	2 June 1944
LO YANG (ex-USS *Taussig, DD 746*)	DD 14	Bethlehem Steel, Staten Island	1943	25 Jan 1944	20 May 1944
NAN YANG (ex-USS *John W. Thomason, DD 760*)	DD 17	Bethlehem Steel, San Francisco	1944	30 Sep 1944	11 Oct 1945

Displacement, tons: 2 200 standard; 3 320 full load
Length, feet (metres): 376·5 *(114·8)* oa
Beam, feet (metres): 40·9 *(12·4)*
Draught, feet (metres): 19 *(5·8)*
Missiles: 7 Gabriels (1 triple, 2 twin) in DD 1, 3 and 5
Guns: 6—5 inch *(127 mm)* 38 calibre (twin) (Mk 38); 4—3 inch *(76 mm)* 50 calibre (2 twin); some including *Heng Yang* and *Yuen Yang*, have 8—40 mm (1 quad, 2 twin); several ·50 cal MG (single) in most ships
A/S weapons: 6 (2 triple) A/S torpedo tubes (Mk 32); 2 fixed hedgehogs; depth charges in some ships
Main engines: 2 geared turbines (General Electric or Westinghouse); 60 000 shp; 2 shafts
Boilers: 4 Babcock & Wilcox
Speed, knots: 34
Complement: approx 275

These ships have not been modernised under the FRAM programmes, but retain their original configurations with removal of original torpedo tubes, and 40 mm and 20 mm guns, and installation of improved electronic equipment. Secondary gun battery now varies; during the 1950s most of these ships were rearmed with six 3 inch guns (two single alongside forward funnel and two twin amidships); number retained apparently varies from ship to ship, with some ships retaining original 40 mm guns. Tripod mast fitted.
Lo Yang and *Nan Yang* have names and numbers previously assigned to older ex-US destroyers.

Radar: Most ships have SPS-6 and SPS-10 search radars on their tripod mast; *Po Yang* has SPS-40 and SPS-10 while *Nan Yang* has SPS-37 and SPS-10.

Transfers: 1, 9 Dec 1969; 2, Feb 1970; 3, 9 Dec 1969; 5, 12 May 1970; 6, Sep 1970; 10, 6 July 1972; 14, 6 May 1974; 17, 6 May 1974.

HSIANG YANG   *1971, United States Navy*

HENG YANG   *"Ships of the World"*

4 Ex-US "FLETCHER" CLASS

Name	No.	Builders	Laid down	Launched	Commissioned
KWEI YANG (ex-USS *Twining*, DD 540)	DD 8	Bethlehem Steel Co, San Francisco	1943	11 July 1943	1 Dec 1943
CHIANG YANG (ex-USS *Mullany*, DD 528)	DD 9	Bethlehem Steel Co, San Francisco	1942	12 Oct 1942	23 Apr 1943
AN YANG (ex-USS *Kimberly*, DD 521)	DD 18	Bethlehem Steel Co, Staten Island	1942	4 Feb 1943	22 May 1943
KUEN YANG (ex-USS *Yarnall*, DD 541)	DD 19	Bethlehem Steel Co, San Francisco	1943	25 July 1943	30 Dec 1943

Displacement, tons: 2 100 standard; 3 050 full load
Length, feet (metres): 376·5 *(114·7)* oa
Beam, feet (metres): 35·9 *(11·9)*
Draught, feet (metres): 18 *(5·5)*
Missiles: Sea Chaparral launcher (SAM) above "X" 5 in mount
Guns: 5—5 inch *(127 mm)* 38 calibre (single) except 4 guns in *Chiang Yang* (Mk 30); 5—3 inch *(76 mm)* 50 calibre (twin) in *Kwei Yang* and *Chiang Yang*; 6—40 mm (twin) in *An Yang* and *Kuen Yang*
A/S weapons: 6 (2 triple) A/S torpedo tubes (Mk 32) in *Kwei Yang* and *Chiang Yang*; 2 fixed hedgehogs and depth charges in some ships
Torpedo tubes: 5—21 inch *(533mm)* (quintuple) in *Kuen Yang*
Main engines: 2 geared turbines (General Electric in *An Yang*, Allis Chalmers in *Kuen Yang*, Westinghouse in others); 60 000 shp; 2 shafts
Boilers: 4 Babcock & Wilcox
Speed, knots: 36
Complement: approx 250

CHIANG YANG (four guns)

All now have tripod mast. Only *Kuen Yang* retains anti-ship torpedo tubes installed between second funnel and third 5 inch gun mount. Reportedly, the ship has been fitted for minelaying.

Transfers: 8, 6 Oct 1971 (sale); 9, 6 Oct 1971 (sale); 18, 2 June 1967; 19, 10 June 1968. Last pair purchased Jan 1974.

KEUN YANG (five guns and torpedo tubes)

FRIGATES

10 Ex-US "APD 37" and "APD 87" CLASSES

Name	No.	Builders	Laid down	Launched	Commissioned
YU SHAN (ex-USS *Kinzer*, Apd 91/DE 232)	PF 32	Charleston Navy Yard, South Carolina	1943	9 Dec 1943	1 Nov 1944
HWA SHAN (ex-USS *Donald W. Wolf*, APD 129/DE 713)	PF 33	Defoe SB Co, Bay City, Michigan	1944	22 July 1944	13 Apr 1945
WEN SHAN (ex-USS *Gantner*, APD 42/DE 60)	PF 34	Bethlehem SB Co, Higham, Massachusetts	1942	17 Apr 1943	23 July 1943
FU SHAN (ex-USS *Truxton*, APD 98/DE 282)	PF 35	Charleston Navy Yard, South Carolina	1943	9 Mar 1944	9 July 1944
LU SHAN (ex-USS *Bull*, APD 78/DE 693)	PF 36	Defoe SB Co, Bay City, Michigan	1942	25 Mar 1943	12 Aug 1943
SHOA SHAN (ex-USS *Kline*, APD 120/DE 687)	PF 37	Bethlehem, Quincy, Massachusetts	1944	27 June1944	18 Oct 1944
TAI SHAN (ex-USS *Register*, APD 92/DE 233)	PF 38	Charleston Navy Yard, South Carolina	1943	20 Jan 1944	11 Jan 1945
KANG SHAN (ex-USS *G. W. Ingram*, APD 43/DE 62)	PF 42	Bethlehem SB Co, Higham, Massachusetts	1942	8 May 1943	11 Aug 1943
CHUNG SHAN (ex-USS *Blessman*, APD 48/DE 69)	PF 43	Bethlehem SB Co, Higham, Massachusetts	1943	19 June1943	19 Sep 1943
TIEN SHAN (ex-USS *Kleinsmith*, APD 134/DE 718)	APD 215	Defoe SB Co, Bay City, Michigan	1944	27 Jan 1945	12 June1945

Displacement, tons: 1 400 standard; 2 130 full load
Length, feet (metres): 300 *(91·4)* wl; 306 *(93·3)* oa
Beam, feet (metres): 37 *(11·3)*
Draught, feet (metres): 12·6 *(3·2)*
Guns: 2—5 inch *(127 mm)* 38 cal; 6—40 mm (twin); 4—20 mm (single) except *Hwa Shan* and possible others have eight guns (twin mounts)
A/S weapons: 6—12·75 inch *(324 mm)* torpedo tubes (Mk 32 triple) except some have two hedgehogs; depth charges
Main engines: Geared turbines (General Electric) with electric drive; 12 000 shp; 2 shafts
Boilers: 2 Foster Wheeler
Speed, knots: 23·6
Complement: approx 200

35

FU SHAN   *"Ships of the World"*

All begun as destroyer escorts (DE), but converted during construction or after completion to high speed transports carrying 160 troops, commandoes, or frogmen.
The ex-USS *Walter B Cobb* (APD 106/DE 596) transferred to Taiwan in 1966 was lost at sea while under tow to Taiwan; replaced by ex-USS *Bull*.

Appearance: APD 37 class has high bridge; APD 87 class has low bridge. Radars and fire control equipment vary. Davits amidships can hold four LCVP-type landing craft.

Gunnery: All ships are now believed to have been refitted with a second 5 inch gun aft. One twin 40 mm gun mount is forward of bridge and two twin mounts are amidships.

Transfers: PF 32, April 1962; 33, May 1965; 34, May 1966; 35, Mar 1966; 36, Aug 1966; 37, Mar 1966; 38, Oct 1966; 42, July 1967; 43, July 1967; APD 215, June 1967.

1 Ex-US "RUDDEROW" CLASS

Name	No.	Builders	Laid down	Launched	Commissioned
TAI YUAN (ex-USS *Riley*, DE 579)	PF 27	Bethlehem Steel Co, Higham, Massachusetts	1943	29 Dec 1943	13 Mar 1944

Displacement, tons: 1 450 standard; approx 2 000 full load
Length, feet (metres): 300 *(91·4)* wl; 306 *(93·3)* oa
Beam, feet (metres): 37 *(11·3)*
Draught, feet (metres): 14 *(4·3)*
Guns: 2—5 inch *(127 mm)* 38 calibre (single); 4—40 mm (twin); 4—20 mm (single)
A/S weapons: 6—(2 triple) A/S torpedo tubes (Mk 32); 1 hedgehog; depth charges
Main engines: Geared turbines (General Electric) with electric drive; 12 000 shp; 2 shafts
Boilers: 2 Foster Wheeler
Speed, knots: 24
Complement: approx 200

Refitted with tripod mast and platforms before bridge for 20 mm guns. (Hedgehog is on main deck, behind forward 5 inch mount).
Designation changed from DE to PF in 1975.

Radar: SPS 6 and 10.

Transfer: 10 July 1968; sale Mar 1974.

27

TAI YUAN   *Iain G. B. Lovie*

SUBMARINES

2 Ex-US GUPPY II TYPE

Name	No.	Builders	Launched	Commissioned
HAI SHIH (ex-USS *Cutlass*, SS 478)	SS 91	Portsmouth Navy Yard	5 Nov 1944	17 Mar 1945
HAI PAO (ex-USS *Tusk*, SS 426)	SS 92	Federal SB & DD Co, Kearney, New Jersey	8 July 1945	11 April 1946

Displacement, tons: 1 870 standard; 2 420 dived
Length, feet (metres): 307·5 *(93·6)* oa
Beam, feet (metres): 27·2 *(8·3)*
Draught, feet (metres): 18 *(5·5)*
Torpedo tubes: 10—21 inch *(533 mm)*; (6 fwd; 4 aft)
Main machinery: 3 diesels (Fairbanks Morse); 4 800 bhp; 2
   electric motors (Elliot); 5 400 shp; 2 shafts
Speed, knots: 18 surfaced; 15 dived
Complement: 81 (11 officers, 70 ratings)

Originally fleet-type submarines of the US Navy "Tench" class;
extensively modernised under the GUPPY II programme.
These submarines each have four 126-cell electric batteries;
fitted with snorkel.
Taiwan is the only nation in the Western Pacific currently to
operate former US Navy submarines.

Transfers: 91, 12 April 1973; 92, 18 Oct 1973.

HAI SHIH   *1972, United States Navy*

CORVETTES

3 Ex-US "AUK" CLASS

Name	No.	Builders	Commissioned
WU SHENG (ex-USS *Redstart*, MSF 378)	PCE 66	Savannah Machine & Foundry Co, Georgia	4 Apr 1945
CHU YUNG (ex-USS *Waxwing*, MSF 389)	PCE 67	American SB Co, Cleveland, Ohio	6 Aug 1945
MO LING (ex-USS *Steady*, MSF 118)	PCE 70	American SB Co, Cleveland, Ohio	16 Nov 1942

Displacement, tons: 890 standard; 1 250 full load
Dimensions, feet (metres): 215 wl; 221·1 oa × 32·1 × 10·8 *(70·4; 61·4 × 10·5 × 3·5)*
Guns: 2—3 inch *(76 mm)* 50 cal (single); 4—40 mm (twin); 4—20 mm (twin)
A/S weapons: 1 hedgehog; 3—12·75 inch *(324 mm)* torpedo tubes (Mk 32 triple); depth charges
Mines: Minerails fitted in *Chu Yung* (1975).
Main engines: Diesel-electric (General Motors diesels); 3 530 bhp; 2 shafts = 18 knots
Complement: approx 80

Minesweeping equipment removed and second 3 inch gun fitted aft in Taiwan service.

Transfers: 66, July 1965; 67, Nov 1965; 70, Mar 1968.

WU SHENG

LIGHT FORCES

1 + 14 FAST ATTACK CRAFT (MISSILE)

Displacement, tons: 240 standard; 270 full load
Dimensions, feet (metres): 164·5 × 23·9 × 7·5 *(50·2 × 7·3 × 2·3)*
Missiles: 4 Otomat launchers
Guns: 1—76 mm OTO Melara; 2—30 mm (Emerson) (twin); 2—0·50 cal MG
Main engines: CODAG; 3 Avco Lycoming gas turbines 13 800 shp (15 000 max);
   3 Diesels; 2 880 shp; 3 shafts (cp propellers)
Speed, knots: 20 knots (diesels); 40 knots (gas turbines)
Range, miles: 2 700 at 12 knots (1 diesel); 1 900 at 20 knots (3 diesels);
   700 at 40 knots (3 gas turbines)
Complement: 34 (5 officers, 29 ratings)

Ordered from Tacoma Boatbuilding Co. Inc., Washington, USA. The first is being built (1977) at
Tacoma, the remainder to be built in Taiwan. Designated Patrol Ship Multi-Mission Mk 5 (PSMM
Mk 5)

Fire Control: NA 10 Mod 0 GFCS with Selenia RAN 11 L/X and IPN 10. Otomat MFCS.

PSMM Mk 5

---

2 79 ft TYPE (FAST ATTACK CRAFT—TORPEDO)

Name	No.	Builders	Commissioned
FU KWO	—	Hutchins Yacht Corp, Jacksonville, Florida	—
TIAN KWO	—	Hutchins Yacht Corp, Jacksonville, Florida	—

Displacement, tons: 46 light; 53 full load
Dimensions, feet (metres): 79 oa × 23·25 × 5·5 *(25·9 × 7·6 × 1·8)*
Guns: 1—40 mm; 2—50 cal MG (single)
Torpedo launchers: 2
Main engines: 3 petrol engines; 3 shafts = 39 knots max; 32 knots cruising
Complement: 12

Transferred to Taiwan on 1 Sep 1957.

2 71-ft TYPE (FAST ATTACK CRAFT—TORPEDO)

Name	No.	Builders	Commissioned
FAAN KONG	—	Annapolis Yacht Yard, Annapolis, Maryland	—
SAO TANG	—	Annapolis Yacht Yard, Annapolis, Maryland	—

Displacement, tons: 39 light; 46 full load
Dimensions, feet (metres): 71 oa × 19 × 5 *(23·3 × 6·3 × 1·6)*
Guns: 1—20 mm; 4—50 cal MG (twin)
Torpedo launchers: 2 (?)
Main engines: 3 petrol engines; 3 shafts = 42 knots max; 32 knots cruising
Complement: 12

Transferred to Taiwan on 19 Aug 1957 and 1 Nov 1957, respectively.

2 JAPANESE TYPE (FAST ATTACK CRAFT—TORPEDO)

Name	No.	Builders	Commissioned
FUH CHOW	—	Mitsubishi SB Co	—
HSUEH CHIH	—	Mitsubishi SB Co	—

Displacement, tons: 33 light; 40 full load
Dimensions, feet (metres): 69 oa × 19·9 *(22·6 × 6·5)*
Guns: 1—40 mm; 2—20 mm (twin)
Torpedo launchers: 2—18 inch *(457 mm)*
Main engines: 3 petrol engines; 3 shafts = 40 knots max; 27 knots cruising
Complement: 12

Transferred to Taiwan on 1 June 1957 and 6 Nov 1957, respectively.

FUH CHOW (forward 40 mm unshipped)

14 COASTAL PATROL CRAFT

Displacement, tons: approx 30 tons
Gun: 1—40 mm

Small patrol boats designated PB. Constructed in Taiwan with the first of a reported 14 units completed about 1971. These are believed the first warships of indigenous Taiwan construction.

Note: At least three additional fast attack craft (torpedo) are known to be in service; details are not available.

PB 1

MINEWARFARE FORCES

Note: Previously reported transfer of ex-USS *Bold* and *Bulwark* ("Agile" class MSOs) did not take place.

14 US "ADJUTANT" CLASS (MSC)

Name	No.	Builders	Commissioned
YUNG PING (ex-US *MSC 140*)	MSC 155	USA	June 1955
YUNG AN (ex-US *MSC 123*)	MSC 156	USA	June 1955
YUNG NIEN (ex-US *MSC 277*)	MSC 157	USA	Dec 1958
YUNG CHOU (ex-US *MSC 278*)	MSC 158	USA	July 1959
YUNG HSIN (ex-US *MSC 302*)	MSC 159	USA	Mar 1965
YUNG JU (ex-US *MSC 300*)	MSC 160	USA	Apr 1965
YUNG LO (ex-US *MSC 306*)	MSC 161	USA	June 1960
YUNG FU (ex-*Diest*, ex-USS *Macaw MSC 77*)	MSC 162	USA	1953
YUNG CHING (ex-*Eekloo*, ex-US *MSC 101*)	MSC 163	USA	1955
YUNG SHAN (ex-*Lier*, ex-USS *MSC 63*)	MSC 164	USA	1954
YUNG CHENG (ex-*Maaseick*, ex-US *MSC 78*)	MSC 165	USA	1955
YUNG CHI (ex-*Charleroi*, ex-US *MSC 152*)	MSC 166	USA	1955
YUNG JEN (ex-*St Nicholas*, ex-US *MSC 64*)	MSC 167	USA	1953
YUNG SUI (ex-*Diksmude*, ex-US *MSC 65*)	MSC 168	USA	1954

Displacement, tons: approx 380 full load
Dimensions, feet (metres): 144 oa × 28 × 8·5 *(47·2 × 9·2 × 2·8)*
Guns: 2—20 mm (twin)
Main engines: Diesels (General Motors); 2 shafts = 13·5 knots
Complement: 40 to 50

YUNG SHAN (pole mast aft)

Non-magnetic, wood-hulled minesweepers built in the United States specifically for transfer to allied navies. First seven units listed above transferred to Taiwan upon completion: MSC 160 in April 1965, and MSC 161 in June 1966.
All are of similar design; the ex-Belgian ships have a small boom aft on a pole mast. They carried a single 40 mm gun forward in Belgian service.

Transfers: Last seven originally built for Belgium and transferred to Taiwan Nov 1969. *De Panne* (ex-US *MSC 131*) was also transferred but has been stripped for spares.

YUNG CHOU (no pole mast aft)

1 MINESWEEPING BOAT

MSB 12 (ex-US *MSB 4*)

Former US Army minesweeping boat; assigned hull number MSB 4 in US Navy and transferred to Taiwan in Dec 1961.

7 MINESWEEPING LAUNCHES

MSML 1	MSML 5	MSML 7	MSML 11
MSML 3	MSML 6	MSML 8	

Fifty-foot minesweeping launches built in the United States and transferred to Taiwan in March 1961.

AMPHIBIOUS FORCES
1 Ex-US "ASHLAND" CLASS (LSD)

Name	No.	Builders	Commissioned
CHUNG CHENG	LSD 639 (ex-	Moore Dry Dock Co,	2 July 1945
(ex-USS *White Marsh, LSD 8*)	LSD 191)	Oakland, California	

Displacement, tons: 4 790 standard; 8 700 full load
Dimensions, feet (metres): 454 wl; 457·8 oa × 72 × 18 *(148·8; 150 × 23·6 × 5·9)*
Guns: 12—40 mm (2 quad and 2 twin)
Main engines: Skinner Unaflow; 7 400 ihp; 2 shafts = 15 knots
Boilers: 2

Launched on 19 July 1943. Designed to serve as parent ship for landing craft and coastal craft. Transferred from the US Navy to Taiwan on 17 Nov 1960.
Renamed to honour the late President Chiang Kai-Shek on 18 Feb 1976; pennant numbers also changed.

CHUNG CHENG (as LSD 191)

1 Ex-US "CASA GRANDE" CLASS (LSD)

Name	No.	Builders	Commissioned
— (Ex-USS *Comstock, LSD 19*)	—	Newport News SB & DD Co,	2 July 1945
		Newport News, Virginia	

Displacement, tons: 4 790 standard; 9 375 full load
Dimensions, feet (metres): 475·4 oa × 76·2 × 18 *(155·8 × 24·9 × 5·9)*
Guns: 12—40 mm (2 quad and 2 twin)
Main engines: Geared turbines; 7 000 shp; 2 shafts = 15·4 knots
Boilers: 2

Former US Navy dock landing ship. Launched on 28 April 1945 and transferred to Taiwan in 1976.
Docking well is 392 × 44 feet; can accommodate 3 LCUs or 18 LCMs or 32 LVTs (amphibious tractors) in docking well. Fitted with helicopter platform over well (which also can be used for truck parking; see photograph).

COMSTOCK (LSD 19) with LCU   1965, United States Navy

22 Ex-US "LST 1-510" and "511-1152" CLASSES

Name	No. LST
CHUNG HAI (ex-USS *LST 755*)	201
CHUNG TING (ex-USS *LST 537*)	203
CHUNG HSING (ex-USS *LST 557*)	204
CHUNG CHIEN (ex-USS *LST 716*)	205
CHUNG CHI (ex-USS *LST 1017*)	206
CHUNG SHUN (ex-USS *LST 732*)	208
CHUNG LIEN (ex-USS *LST 1050*)	209
CHUNG YUNG (ex-USS *LST 574*)	210
CHUNG KUANG (ex-USS *LST 503*)	216
CHUNG SUO (ex-USS *Bradley County, LST 400*)	217
CHUNG CHIE (ex-USS *Berkley County, LST 279*)	218
CHUNG CHUAN (ex-*LST 1030*)	221
CHUNG SHENG (ex-*LST 211*, ex-USS *LSTH 1033*)	222
CHUNG FU (ex-USS *Iron County, LST 840*)	223
CHUNG CHENG (ex-USS *Lafayette County, LST 859*)	224
CHUNG CHIANG (ex-USS *San Bernadino County, LST 1110*)	225
CHUNG CHIH (ex-USS *Sagadahoc County, LST 1091*)	226
CHUNG MING (ex-USS *Sweetwater County, LST 1152*)	227
CHUNG SHU (ex-USS *LST 520*)	228
CHUNG WAN (ex-USS *LST 535*)	229
CHUNG PANG (ex-USS *LST 578*)	230
CHUNG YEH (ex-USS *Sublette County, LST 1144*)	231

Displacement, tons: 1 653 standard; 4 080 full load
Dimensions, feet (metres): 316 wl; 328 oa × 50 × 14 *(103·6; 107·5 × 16·4 × 4·6)*
Guns: Varies; up to 10—40 mm (2 twin, 6 single) with some modernised ships rearmed with 2—3 inch (single) and 6—40 mm (twin)
  Several 20 mm (twin or single)
Main engines: Diesel (General Motors); 1 700 bhp; 2 shafts = 11·6 knots
Complement: Varies: 100 to 125 in most ships

Constructed during World War II. These ships have been rebuilt in Taiwan.
Hull numbers of LSTs are being changed to 600 series.

Appearance: Some have davits forward and aft.

Transfers: *201-208*, 1946; *209* and *222*, 1947; *228*, 1948; *217, 223-230*, 1958; *210*, 1959; *216* and *218*, 1960; *231*, 1961.

CHUNG CHIE (*Ho Shan* alongside)   1974

CHUNG SHUN

1 Ex-US "LST 511-1152" CLASS (FLAGSHIP)

Name	No.	Builders	Commissioned
KAO HSIUNG (ex-*Chung Hai*, LST 219, ex-USS *Dukes County*, LST 735)	AGC 1	Dravo Corp, Neville Island, Pennsylvania	26 April 1944

Displacement, tons: 1 653 standard; 4 080 full load
Dimensions, feet (metres): 316 wl; 328 oa × 50 × 14 *(103·6; 107·5 × 16·4 × 4·6)*
Guns: Several 40 mm (twin)
Main engines: Diesel (General Motors); 1 700 bhp; 2 shafts = 11·6 knots

Launched on 11 Mar 1944. Transferred to Taiwan in May 1957 for service as an LST. Converted to a flagship for amphibious operations and renamed and redesignated (AGC) in 1964. Purchased Nov 1974.
Note lattice mast atop bridge structure, modified bridge levels, and antenna mountings on main deck.

KAO HSIUNG

4 Ex-US "LSM-1" CLASS

Name	No.
MEI CHIN (ex-USS *LSM 155*)	LSM 341
MEI SUNG (ex-USS *LSM 457*)	LSM 347
MEI PING (ex-USS *LSM 471*)	LSM 353
MEI LO (ex-USS *LSM 362*)	LSM 356

Displacement, tons: 1 095 full load
Dimensions, feet (metres): 196·5 wl; 203·5 oa × 34·5 × 7·3 *(66·4; 66·7 × 11·3 × 2·4)*
Guns: 2—40 mm (twin); 4 or 8—20 mm (4 single or 4 twin)
Main engines: Diesels; 2 800 bhp; 2 shafts = 12·5 knots
Complement: 65 to 75

Constructed during World War II. Originally numbered in the 200-series in Taiwan service. These ships are being rebuilt in Taiwan.

Transfers: *341* and *347* 1946; *353,* 1956; *356,* 1962.

MEI PING

22 Ex-US "LCU 501" and "LCU 1466" CLASSES

Name	No. LCU	Name	No. LCU
HO CHUN (ex-*LCU 892*)	481	HO SHUN (ex-*LCU 1225*)	494
HO TSUNG (ex-*LCU 1213*)	482	HO YUNG (ex-*LCU 1271*)	495
HO CHUNG (ex-*LCU 849*)	484	HO CHIEN (ex-*LCU 1278*)	496
HO CHANG (ex-*LCU 512*)	485	HO CHI (ex-*LCU 1212*)	401
HO CHENG (ex-*LCU 1145*)	486	HO HOEI (ex-*LCU 1218*)	402
HO SHAN (ex-*LCU 1596*)	488	HO YAO (ex-*LCU 1244*)	403
HO CHUAN (ex-*LCU 1597*)	489	HO DENG (ex-*LCU 1367*)	404
HO SENG (ex-*LCU 1598*)	490	HO FENG (ex-*LCU 1397*)	405
HO MENG (ex-*LCU 1599*)	491	HO CHAO (ex-*LCU 1429*)	406
HO MOU (ex-*LCU 1600*)	492	HO TENG (ex-*LCU 1452*)	407
HO SHOU (ex-*LCU 1601*)	493	HO CHIE (ex-*LCU 700*)	SB1

"LCU 501" Class

Displacement, tons: 158 light; 268 full load
Dimensions, feet (metres): 115·1 oa × 32 × 4·2 *(37·7 × 10·5 × 1·4)*
Guns: 2—20 mm (single); some units also may have 2—·50 cal MG
Main engines: 3 diesels; 675 bhp; 3 shafts = 10 knots
Complement: 10 to 25 assigned

HO MOU (LCU 492 ex-*LCU 292*)

"LCU 1466" Class

Displacement, tons: 130 light; 280 full load
Dimensions, feet (metres): 115·1 oa × 34 × 4·1 *(37·7 × 10·5 × 1·4)*
Guns: 3—20 mm (single); some units may also have 2—·50 cal MG
Main engines: 3 diesels; 675 bhp; 3 shafts = 10 knots
Complement: 15 to 25 assigned

The LCU 501 series were built in the United States during World War II; initially designated LCT(6) series. The six of LCU 1466 series built by Ishikawajima Heavy Industries Co, Tokyo, Japan, for transfer to Taiwan; completed in Mar 1955. All originally numbered in 200-series; subsequently changed to 400 series.

Transfers: *401-407;* Nov/Dec 1959. *SB1, 494-496;* Jan/Feb 1958. Remainder; 1946-1948.

SURVEY SHIPS

Note: *Yang Ming* (ex-*Yung Ting;* ex-USS *Lucid* AM 259)—of 650 tons standard; 945 tons full load—a part of US "Admirable" class minesweepers has been reported. Existence now doubtful.

1 Ex-US C1-M-AV1 TYPE

Name	No.	Builders	Commissioned
CHU HWA (ex-USNS *Sgt. George D. Keathley*, T-AGS 35, ex-T-APC 117)	AGS 564	—	—

Displacement, tons: 6 090 tons
Dimensions, feet (metres): 338·8 oa × 50·3 × 17·5 *(111·1 × 16·5 × 5·7)*
Guns: 1—40 mm; 2—20 mm
Main engines: Diesel; 1 750 bhp; 1 shaft = 11·5 knots
Complement: 72

Built in 1945 as merchant ship; subsequently acquired by US Army for use as transport, but assigned to Navy's Military Sea Transportation Service in 1950 and designated as coastal transport (T-APC 117). Refitted for oceanographic survey work in 1966-1967 and redesignated T-AGS 35. Transferred to Taiwan on 29 Mar 1972.

1 Ex-US "LSIL 351" CLASS

Name	No.	Builders	Commissioned
LIEN CHANG (ex-USS *LSIL 1017*)	AGSC 466	Albina Engineering & Machinery Works, Portland, Oregon	12 Apr 1944

Dimensions, feet (metres): 153 wl; 159 oa × 23·6 × 5·6 *(50·2; 52·1 × 7·7 × 1·8)*
Guns: 2—40 mm (twin); several 20 mm
Main engines: Diesel (General Motors); 2 320 bhp; 2 shafts = 14 knots

Launched on 14 Mar 1944. Transferred to Taiwan in Mar 1958. Employed as surveying ship; retains basic LSIL appearance. Existence now doubtful.

1 SURVEY SHIP

WU KANG

Of 907 tons, launched 1943 with complement of 59.

1 Ex-US "SOTOYOMO" CLASS

Name	No.	Builders	Commissioned
CHIU LIEN (ex-USS *Geronimo*, ATA 207)	AGS 563	Gulfport Boiler & Welding Works, Port Arthur, Texas	1 Mar 1945

Displacement, tons: 835
Dimensions, feet (metres): 143 oa × 33·9 × 13·2 *(46·9 × 11·1 × 4·3)*
Main engines: Diesel (General Motors); 1 500 bhp; 1 shaft = 13 knots

Former US Navy auxiliary tug. Launched 4 Jan 1945. Transferred to Taiwan in Feb 1969 and converted to surveying ship. Currently employed as research ship for the Institute of Oceanology. Civilian manned. Painted white.

CHIU LIEN

SERVICE FORCES

1 Ex-US "AMPHION" CLASS (REPAIR SHIP)

Name	No.	Builders	Commissioned
YU TAI (ex-USS *Cadmus*, AR 14)	ARG 521	Tampa Shipbuilding Co, Tampa, Florida	23 Apr 1946

Displacement, tons: 7 826 standard; 14 490 full load
Dimensions, feet (metres): 456 wl; 492 oa × 70 × 27·5 *(149·5; 161 3 × 22·9 × 9)*
Guns: 1—5 inch *(127 mm)* 38 calibre
Main engines: Turbines (Westinghouse); 8 500 shp; 1 shaft = 16·5 knots
Boilers: 2 (Foster Wheeler)

Launched on 5 Aug 1945. Transferred to Taiwan on 15 Jan 1974. A sister ship (ex-USS *Amphion*, AR 13) serves with the Iranian Navy.
Reported in reduced operational status.

1 Ex-US "ACHELOUS" CLASS (TRANSPORT)

Name	No.	Builders	Commissioned
WU TAI (ex-*Sung Shan*, ARL 336, ex-USS *Agenor*, ARL 3, ex-*LST 490*)	AP 520	Kaiser Co, Vancouver, Washington	20 Aug 1943

Displacement, tons: 1 625 light; 4 100 full load
Dimensions, feet (metres): 316 wl; 328 oa × 50 × 11 *(103·6; 107·5 × 16·4 × 3·6)*
Guns: 8—40 mm (quad)
Main engines: Diesels (General Motors); 1 800 bhp; 2 shafts = 11·6 knots
Troops: 600

Begun for the US Navy as an LST completed as a repair ship for landing craft (ARL). Launched on 3 Apr 1943. Transferred to France in 1951 for service in Indochina; subsequently returned to United States and retransferred to Taiwan on 15 Sep 1957
Employed as a repair ship (ARL 336, subsequently ARL 236) until converted in 1973-1974 to troop transport.

WU TAI (as repair ship)

1 TAIWAN TYPE (TRANSPORT)

Name	No.	Builders	Commissioned
LING YUEN	522	Taiwan Shipbuilding Co., Keelung	15 Aug 1975

Measurement, tons: 2 510 DWT; 3 040 gross
Dimensions, feet (metres): 328·7 × 47·9 × 16·4 *(100·2 × 14·6 × 5)*
Guns: 2—20 mm (single); 2—0·5 in MG (single)
Main engines: Diesel 6 cylinder
Complement: 55
Accommodation for Troops: 500

Designed by Chinese First Naval Shipyard at Tsoying.
Launched 27 Jan 1975.

LING YUEN

1975

1 JAPANESE TYPE (SUPPORT TANKER)

Name	No.	Builders	Commissioned
WAN SHOU	AOG 512	Ujina Shipbuilding Co, Hiroshima, Japan	1 Nov 1969

Displacement, tons: 1 049 light; 4 150 full load
Dimensions, feet (metres): 283·8 oa × 54 × 18 *(93·1 × 17·7 × 5·9)*
Guns: 2—40 mm (single); 2—20 mm
Main engines: Diesel; 2 100 bhp; 1 shaft = 13 knots
Complement: 70
Cargo: 73 600 gallons fuel; 62 000 gallons water

Employed in resupply of offshore islands.

WAN SHOU

3 Ex-US "PATAPSCO" CLASS (SUPPORT TANKERS)

Name	No.	Builders	Commissioned
CHANG PEI (ex-USS *Pecatonica* AOG 57)	AOG 507	Cargill, Inc, Savage Minnesota	—
LUNG CHUAN (ex-HMNZS *Endeavour*, ex-USS *Namakagon*, AOG 53)	AOG 515	Cargill, Inc, Savage, Minnesota	—
HSIN LUNG (ex-USS *Elkhorn* AOG 7)	AOG 517	Cargill, Inc, Savage, Minnesota	—

Displacement, tons: 1 850 light; 4 335 full load
Dimensions, feet (metres): 292 wl; 310·75 oa × 48·5 × 15·7 *(95·7; 101·9 × 15·9 × 5·1)*
Main engines: Diesels (General Motors); 3 300 bhp; 2 shafts = 14 knots

The *Chang Pei* was launched on 17 Mar 1945 and transferred to Taiwan on 24 Apr 1961. The ex-USS *Namakagon* was launched on 4 Nov 1944 and transferred to New Zealand on 5 Oct 1962 for use as an Antarctic resupply ship; stengthened for polar operations and renamed *Endeavour*; returned to the US Navy on 29 June 1971 and transferred to Taiwan the same date. The *Hsin Lung* was launched on 15 May 1943 and was transferred to Taiwan on 1 July 1972.

CHANG PEI

1 Ex-US YO TYPE (SUPPORT TANKER)

Name	No.	Builders	Commissioned
SZU MING (ex-US *YO 198*)	AOG 504 (ex-*AOG 304*)	Manitowoc SB Co, Manitowoc, Wisconsin	1945

Displacement, tons: 650 light; 1 595 full load
Dimensions, feet (metres): 174 oa × 32 *(57·1 × 10·5)*
Guns: 1—40 mm; 5—20 mm (single)
Main engines: Diesel (Union); 560 bhp; 1 shaft = 10·5 knots
Complement: approx 65

Transferred to Taiwan in Dec 1949. Reportedly placed in reserve in 1976.

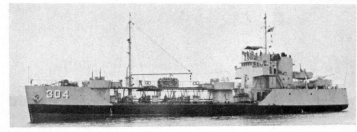

SZU MING (as AOG 304)

2 JAPANESE TYPE (SUPPORT TANKERS)

Also reported to be in service.

1 Ex-US "MARK" CLASS (CARGO SHIP)

Name	No.	Builders	Commissioned
YUNG KANG (ex-USS *Mark, AKL 12*, ex-*AG 143* ex-US Army *FS 214*)	AKL 514	Higgins	1944

Displacement, tons: approx 700
Dimensions, feet (metres): 176·5 oa × 32·8 × 10 *(57·8 × 10·7 × 3·3)*
Guns: 2—20 mm
Main engines: Diesel; 1 000 bhp; 1 shaft = 10 knots

Built as a small cargo ship (freight and supply) for the US Army. Transferred to US Navy on 30 Sep 1947; operated in Indochina area from 1963 until transferred to Taiwan on 1 June 1971.

YUNG KANG

TUGS

2 Ex-US "CHEROKEE" CLASS

Name	No.	Builders	Commissioned
TA TUNG (ex-USS Chickasaw, ATF 83)	ATF 548	United Engineering Co, Alameda, California	4 Feb 1943
TA WAN (ex-USS Apache, ATF 67)	ATF 550	Charleston SB & DD Co, South Carolina	12 Dec 1942

Displacement, tons: 1 235 standard; 1 675 full load
Dimensions, feet (metres): 195 wl; 205 oa × 38·5 × 15·5 *(63·9; 67·2 × 12·6 × 5·1)*
Guns: 1—3 inch *(76 mm)* 50 cal AA; several light AA
Main engines: Diesels (electric drive); 3 000 bhp; 1 shaft = 15 knots

Launched on 23 July 1942 and 8 May 1942 respectively. *Ta Tung* transferred to Taiwan in January 1966 and *Ta Wan* on 30 June 1974.

3 Ex-US "SOTOYOMO" CLASS

Name	No.	Builders	Commissioned
TA SUEH (ex-USS Tonkawa, ATA 176)	ATA 547	Levingston SB Co, Orange, Texas	19 Aug 1944
TA TENG (ex-USS Cahokia, ATA 186)	ATA 550	Levingston SB Co, Orange, Texas	24 Nov 1944
TA PENG (ex-USS Mohopac, ATA 196)	ATA 549	Levingston SB Co, Orange, Texas	21 Dec 1944

Displacement, tons: 435 standard; 835 full load
Dimensions, feet (metres): 134·5 wl; 143 oa × 33·9 × 13 *(44·1; 46·9 × 11·1 × 4·3)*
Guns: 1—3 inch *(76 mm)* 50 cal; several light MG
Main engines: Diesel-electric (General Motors diesels); 1 500 bhp; 1 shaft = 13 knots

Ta Sueh launched on 1 Mar 1944 and transferred to Taiwan in April 1962. *Ta Teng* launched on 18 Sep 1944; assigned briefly to US Air Force in 1971 until transferred to Taiwan on 29 Mar 1972. *Ta Peng* transferred on 1 July 1971. A fourth tug of this class serves as a surveying ship.

TA YU (ex-US *LT 310*) ATA 545

Transferred Apr 1949. Also reported.

1 Ex-US ARMY ST TYPE

YTL 9 (ex-US Army *ST 2004*)

Former US Army 76-foot harbour tug.

3 Ex-US "YLT 422" CLASS

YTL 11 (ex-USN *YTL 454*)   **YTL 14** (ex-USN *YTL 585*)
YTL 12 (ex-USN *YTL 584*)

Former US Navy 66-foot harbour tugs.

SERVICE CRAFT

Approximately 25 non-self-propelled service craft are in use; most are former US Navy service craft.

5 Ex-US FLOATING DRY DOCKS

Name	No.	Builders	Commissioned
HAY TAN (ex-USN AFDL 36)	AFDL 1	—	—
KIM MEN (ex-USN AFDL 5)	AFDL 2	—	—
HAN JIH (ex-USN AFDL 34)	AFDL 3	—	—
FO WU 5 (ex-USN ARD 9)	ARD 5	—	—
FO WU 6 (ex-USS Windsor, ARD 22)	ARD 6	—	—

Former US Navy floating dry docks; see United States section for characteristics.

Transfers: AFDL 1 in Mar 1947, 2 in Jan 1948, 3 in July 1959, 5 in Oct 1967, 6 in June 1971.

CUSTOMS SERVICE

Several small ships and small craft are in service with the Customs Service of Taiwan, an agency of the Ministry of Finance as well as the ships listed below.

2 Ex-US "ADMIRABLE" CLASS

Name	No.	Builders	Commissioned
HUNG HSING (ex-USS Embattle, AM 226)	A 7	American Shipbuilding Co, Lorain, Ohio	25 Apr 1945
— (ex-USS Improve, AM 247)	—	Savannah Machine & Foundry Co, Georgia	29 Feb 1944

Dimensions, feet (metres): 180 wl; 184·5 oa × 33 × 9·75 *(59; 60·5 × 10·8 × 3·2)*
Guns: 2—20 mm
Main engines: Diesel (Cooper Bessemer); 1 710 bhp; 2 shafts = 14 knots

Former US Navy minesweepers (AM). Launched on 17 Sep 1944 and 26 Sep 1943 respectively.

3 Ex-US "PC-461" CLASS

Name	No.	Builders	Commissioned
Ex-Tung Kiang (ex-USS Placerville, PC 1087)	PC 119	—	1943
Ex-Hsi Kiang (ex-USS Susanville, PC 1149)	PC 120	—	1944
—(ex-USS Hanford PC 1142)	—	—	—

Displacement, tons: 450 full load
Dimensions, feet (metres): 173·66 oa × 23 × 10·8 *(56·9 × 7·5 × 3·5)*
Guns: 2—20 mm
Main engines: Diesels (General Motors); 2 880 bhp; 2 shafts = 20 knots

Former US Navy steel-hulled submarine chasers. Originally transferred to Taiwan for naval use; subsequently allocated to the Customs Service. PC 1087 and PC 1149 transferred in July 1957. All sold in May 1976.

TANZANIA

Ministerial

Minister of Defence:
Mr. Rashidi Kawawa

Base

Dar Es Salaam. A new base area built under Chinese supervision.

Mercantile Marine

Lloyd's Register of Shipping: 20 vessels of 34 934 tons gross

Personnel

(a) 1977 700 (approx)
(b) Voluntary service

LIGHT FORCES

6 Ex-CHINESE "SHANGHAI" CLASS
(FAST ATTACK CRAFT—GUN)

JW 9861-6

Displacement, tons: 120 full load
Dimensions, feet (metres): 130 × 18·0 × 5·6 *(42·6 × 5·9 × 1·8)*
Guns: 4—37 mm (twin) 4—25 mm (twins)
Main engines: 4 diesels; 5 000 bhp = 30 knots
Complement: 25

Transferred by the Chinese People's Republic in 1970-71.

"SHANGHAI" Class

4 Ex-CHINESE "HU CHWAN" CLASS
(FAST ATTACK CRAFT—HYDROFOIL (TORPEDO))

Displacement, tons: 45
Dimensions, feet (metres): 70 × 16·5 × 3·1 *(22·9 × 5·4 × 1)*
Guns: 4—12·7 mm (twins)
Torpedo tubes: 2—21 in (533 mm)
Main engines: 2 diesels; 2 200 bhp = 55 knots (calm)
Range, miles: 500 at cruising speed

Transferred 1975.

"HU CHWAN" Class

3 Ex-EAST GERMAN "P6" CLASS
(FAST ATTACK CRAFT—TORPEDO)

Displacement, tons: 75 full load
Dimensions, feet (metres): 84 × 20 × 6 *(25·7 × 6·1 × 1·8)*
Guns: 4—25 mm
Main engines: 4 diesels; 4 shafts; 4 800 bhp = 43 knots
Range, miles: 450 at 30 knots
Complement: 25

Transferred 1974-75.

8 Ex-SOVIET "P4" CLASS
(FAST ATTACK CRAFT—TORPEDO)

Displacement, tons: 22
Dimensions, feet (metres): 62·7 × 11·6 × 5·6 *(19·1 × 3·5 × 1·7)*
Guns: 2—14·5 mm MG (twin)
Torpedo tubes: 2—18 in
Main engines: 2 diesels; 2 shafts; 2 200 bhp = 50 knots
Complement: 12

Transferred 1970-73 (4 from USSR, 4 from Germany).

2 Ex-EAST GERMAN "SCHWALBE" CLASS
(COASTAL PATROL CRAFT)

ARAKA   SALAAM

Displacement, tons: 70 full load
Dimensions, feet (metres): 85·2 × 14·8 × 4·6 *(26 × 4·5 × 1·4)*
Guns: 2—25 mm (twin); 2 MG
Main engines: Diesel; 300 hp = 17 knots

Launched 1955-56. Transferred 1966-67.

"SCHWALBE" Class

2 Ex-WEST GERMAN COASTAL PATROL CRAFT

RAFIKI   UHURU

Displacement, tons: 50
Dimensions, feet (metres): 78·7 × 16·4 × 4·3 *(24 × 5 × 1·3)*
Guns: 1—40 mm; 4 MG

Purchased 1967, via Portugal.

4 Ex-CHINESE "YU LIN" CLASS
(COASTAL PATROL CRAFT)

Displacement, tons: 27
Dimensions, feet (metres): 42·6 × 13 × 4·2 *(13 × 4 × 1·2)*
Gun: 1—12·7 mm MG
Speed, knots: 20
Complement: 10

Transferred late 1966.

2 Ex-CHINESE LCMs

THAILAND

Administration

Commander-in-Chief of the Navy:
Admiral Amorn Sirigaya
Deputy Commander-in-Chief:
Admiral Sontee Boonyachai
Chief of Staff (RTN):
Admiral Ching Chullasukum
Commander-in-Chief, Fleet:
Admiral Satap Keyanon

Diplomatic Representation

Naval Attaché in London:
Captain A. Iamsuro
Naval Attaché in Washington:
Captain Watanapol Saneewong Na Ayudhay

Personnel

(a) 1977: *Navy,* 20 000 (2 000 officers and 18 000 ratings)
including *Marine Corps:* 7 000 (500 officers and 6 500 men)
(b) 2 years National Service

Bases

Bangkok, Sattahip, Songkhla. A new base on the West coast has been reported.

Prefix to Ships' Names

HTMS.

Mercantile Marine

Lloyd's Register of Shipping:
90 vessels of 194 993 tons gross

New Construction

There is a reported interest in further new construction.

Strength of the Fleet

Type	Active
Frigates	6
Fast Attack Craft (missile)	3
Large Patrol Craft	27
Coastal Patrol Craft	20
Coastal Minelayers	2
Coastal Minesweepers	4
MCM Support Ship	1
MSBs	10
LSTs	5
LSMs	3
LCG	1
LSILs	2
LCUs	6
LCMs	26
LCVPs	6
Survey Vessels	4
Support Tankers	2
Harbour Tankers	2
Water Boats	2
Tugs	4
Transports	2
Training Ships	3

DELETIONS

Note: Frigates *Bangpakong, Maeklong* and *Phosamton* transferred to training duties.

Large Patrol Craft

1973 *SC 7*
1976 *Chumporn, Phuket* and *Trad; Kantang* and *Klongyai; CGC 11*

Coastal Patrol Craft

1973 *CGC1* and *11, T 31, 33, 34* and *35*
1976 *T 93*

Harbour Tankers

1975 *Prong* and *Samui*

FRIGATES

1 YARROW TYPE

Name	No.
MAKUT RAJAKUMARN	7

Builders	Laid down	Launched	Commissioned
Yarrow & Co Ltd, Scotstoun	11 Jan 1970	18 Nov 1971	7 May 1973

Displacement, tons: 1 650 standard; 1 900 full load
Length, feet (metres): 305 *(93)* wl; 320·0 *(97·6)* oa
Beam, feet (metres): 36·0 *(11·0)*
Draught, feet (metres): 18·1 *(5·5)*
Missile launchers: 1 quadruple Seacat
Guns: 2—4·5 in Mk 8 *(114 mm)* (single)
2—40 mm 60 cal Bofors (single)
A/S weapons: 1 triple barrelled Limbo mortar; 1 DC rack;
2 depth charge throwers
Main engines: 1 Rolls-Royce Olympus gas turbine; 23 125 shp;
1 Crossley-Pielstick 12 PC2V diesel; 2 shafts; 6 000 bhp
Speed, knots: 26, 18 on diesel
Range, miles: 5 000 at 18 knots (diesel); 1 200 at 26 knots
Complement: 140 (16 officers, 124 ratings)

An order was placed on 21 Aug 1969 for a general purpose frigate. The ship is largely automated with a consequent saving in complement, and has been most successful in service. Fitted as flagship.

Electronics: HSA CIC system. Racal DF.

Radar: Surveillance: one LW 04 (amidships)
Fire Control: one M 20 series (radome)
Seacat Control: one M 44 Series (aft)
Navigation: one Decca Type 626
IFF: UK Mk 10.

Sonar: UK Type 170 and Plessey Type MS 27.

MAKUT RAJAKUMARN

9/1973, Wright and Logan

2 US "PF-103" CLASS

Name	No.
KHIRIRAT	6
TAPI	5

Builders	Laid down	Launched	Commissioned
Norfolk SB & DD Co	18 Feb 1972	2 June 1973	10 Aug 1974
American SB Co, Toledo, Ohio	1 April 1970	17 Oct 1970	1 Nov 1971

Displacement, tons: 900 standard; 1 135 full load
Length, feet (metres): 275 *(83·8)* oa
Beam, feet (metres): 33 *(10·0)*
Draught, feet (metres): 10 *(3·0)*
Guns: 2—3 in *(76'mm)*; 2—40 mm (twin)
A/S weapons: Hedgehogs; 6 (2 triple) Mk 32 A/S torpedo tubes
Main engines: 2 FM Diesels; 6 000 bhp
Speed, knots: 20
Complement: 150

Of similar design to the Iranian ships of the "Bayandor" class. *Tapi* was ordered on June 27 1969. *Khirirat* was ordered on 25 June 1971.

Fire Control: Mk 63 GFCS (SPG 34). Mk 51 GFCS (40 mm).

Radar: Air search: SPS 6.
Fire control: SPG 34.

TAPI

1975, Royal Thai Navy

1 Ex-US "CANNON" CLASS

Name	No.	Builders	Laid down	Launched	Commissioned
PIN KLAO (ex-USS *Hemminger*, DE 746)	3 (ex-1)	Western Pipe & Steel Co.	1943	12 Sep 1943	30 May 1944

Displacement, tons: 1 240 standard; 1 900 full load
Length, feet (metres): 306·0 *(93·3)* oa
Beam, feet (metres): 37·0 *(11·3)*
Draught, feet (metres): 14·1 *(4·3)*
Guns: 3—3 in *(76 mm)* 50 cal; 6—40 mm
A/S weapons: 8 DCT
Torpedo tubes: 6 (2 triple) Mk 32 for A/S torpedoes
Main engines: GM diesels with electric drive; 2 shafts; 6 000 bhp
Speed, knots: 20
Oil fuel, tons: 300
Range, miles: 11 500 at 11 knots
Complement: 220

Transferred from US Navy to Royal Thai Navy at New York Navy Shipyard in July 1959 under MDAP. The 3—21 in torpedo tubes were removed and the 4—20 mm guns were replaced by 4—40 mm. The six A/S torpedo tubes were fitted in 1966. Finally purchased 6 June 1975.

Radar: SPS-5 and SC.

PIN KLAO   1975

2 Ex-US "TACOMA" CLASS

Name	No.	Builders	Laid down	Launched	Commissioned
PRASAE (ex-USS *Gallup*, PF 47)	2	Consolidated Steel Corpn, Los Angeles	18 Aug 1943	17 Sep 1943	29 Feb 1944
TAHCHIN (ex-USS *Glendale*, PF 36)	1	Consolidated Steel Corpn, Los Angeles	6 Apr 1943	28 May 1943	1 Oct 1943

Displacement, tons: 1 430 standard; 2 100 full load
Length, feet (metres): 304·0 *(92·7)* oa
Beam, feet (metres): 37·5 *(11·4)*
Draught, feet (metres): 13·7 *(4·2)*
Guns: 3—3 in *(76 mm)* 50 cal; 2—40 mm; 9—20 mm
A/S weapons: 6 (2 triple) Mk 32 A/S torpedo tubes; 8 DCT
Main engines: Triple expansion; 2 shafts; 5 500 ihp
Boilers: 2 small water tube 3-drum type
Speed, knots: 19
Oil fuel, tons: 685
Range, miles: 7 800 at 12 knots
Complement: 180

Delivered to the Royal Thai Navy on 29 Oct 1951. *Prasae* partially non-operational after collision in Jan 1972 and *Tahchin* may also be non-operational.

PRASAE   8/1976, Dr. Giorgio Arra

LIGHT FORCES

3 LÜRSSEN 45 METRE TYPE (FAST ATTACK CRAFT—MISSILE)

Name	No.	Builders	Commissioned
HANHAK SATTRU	2	Singapore	6 Nov 1976
PRABPARAPAK	1	Singapore	28 July 1976
SUPHAIRIN	3	Singapore	1 Feb 1977

Displacement, tons: 224 standard; 260 full load
Dimensions, feet (metres): 158 × 23 × 7·5 *(48 × 7 × 2·3)*
Missiles: 5 Gabriel launchers (1 triple, 2 single)
Guns: 1—57 mm 70 Bofors (forward); 1—40 mm 70 Bofors (aft)
Main engines: 4 Maybach (MTU) diesels; 14 400 shp = 34 knots
Range: 2 000 cruising
Complement: 41

Ordered June 1973. Launch dates—*Prabparapak* 29 July 1975, *Hanhak Sattru* 28 Oct 1975, *Suphairin* 20 Feb 1976. Unconfirmed report of a fourth ordered.

PRABPARAPAK (model)   1975, Royal Thai Navy

4 "TRAD" CLASS (LARGE PATROL CRAFT)

Name	No.	Builders	Commissioned
CHANDHABURI	22	Cantieri Riuniti dell' Adriatico, Monfalcone	1937
PATTANI	13	Cantieri Riuniti dell' Adriatico, Monfalcone	1937
RAYONG	23	Cantieri Riuniti dell' Adriatico, Monfalcone	1938
SURASDRA	21	Cantieri Riuniti dell' Adriatico, Monfalcone	1937

Displacement, tons: 318 standard; 470 full load
Dimensions, feet (metres): 223 oa × 21 × 7 *(68 × 6·4 × 2·1)*
Guns: 2—3 in; 1—40 mm; 2—20 mm
Torpedo tubes: 4—18 in (2 twin)
Main engines: Parsons geared turbines; 2 shafts; 9 000 hp = 31 knots
Boilers: 2 Yarrow
Oil fuel, tons: 102
Range, miles: 1 700 at 15 knots
Complement: 70

Survivors of class of seven. Armament was supplied by Vickers-Armstrong Ltd. First boat reached 32·34 knots on trials with 10 000 hp. 2 single 18 inch torpedo tubes and the 4—8 mm guns were removed.

"TRAD" Class

7 "LIULOM" CLASS (LARGE PATROL CRAFT)

LIULOM (ex-PC *1253*) PC 7
LONGLOM (ex-PC *570*) PC 8
PHALI (ex-PC *1185*) PC 4
SARASIN (ex-PC *495*) PC 1

SUKRIP (ex-PC *1218*) PC 5
THAYANCHON (ex-PC *575*) PC 2
TONGPLIU (ex-PC *616*) PC 6

Displacement, tons: 280 standard; 400 full load
Dimensions, feet (metres): 174 oa × 23·2 × 6·5 *(53 × 7 × 2)*
Guns: 1—3 in; 1—40 mm; 5—20 mm
A/S weapons: 2 (single) Mk 32 ASW torpedo tubes (except *Sarasin*)
Main engines: Diesel; 2 shafts; 3 600 bhp = 19 knots
Oil fuel, tons: 60
Range, miles: 6 000 at 10 knots
Complement: 62 to 71

Launched in 1941-43 as US PCs. All transferred between Mar 1947 and Dec 1952.

Radar: SPS 25.

PHALI   *8/1976, Dr. Giorgio Arra*

1 "KLONGYAI" CLASS (LARGE PATROL CRAFT)

Name	No.	Builders	Commissioned
SATTAHIP	8	Royal Thai Naval Dockyard, Bangkok	1958

Displacement, tons: 110 standard; 135 full load
Dimensions, feet (metres): 131·5 × 15·5 × 4 *(42 × 4·6 × 1·5)*
Guns: 1—3 in; 1—20 mm
Torpedo tubes: 2—18 in
Main engines: Geared turbines = 2 shafts; 1 000 shp = 19 knots
Boilers: 2 water-tube
Range, miles: 480 at 15 knots
Oil fuel, tons: 18
Complement: 31

Sattahip was laid down on 21 Nov 1956, launched on 28 Oct 1957.

10 Ex-US "PGM 71" CLASS (LARGE PATROL CRAFT)

Name	No.	Builders	Commissioned
—	T 11 (ex-US *PGM 71*)	Peterson Builders Inc	1 Feb 1966
—	T 12 (ex-US *PGM 79*)	Peterson Builders Inc	1967
—	T 13 (ex-US *PGM 107*)	Peterson Builders Inc	28 Aug 1967
—	T 14 (ex-US *PGM 116*)	Peterson Builders Inc	18 Aug 1969
—	T 15 (ex-US *PGM 117*)	Peterson Builders Inc	18 Aug 1969
—	T 16 (ex-US *PGM 115*)	Peterson Builders Inc	12 Feb 1970
—	T 17 (ex-US *PGM 113*)	Peterson Builders Inc	12 Feb 1970
—	T 18 (ex-US *PGM 114*)	Peterson Builders Inc	12 Feb 1970
—	T 19 (ex-US *PGM 123*)	Peterson Builders Inc	25 Dec 1970
—	T 110 (ex-US *PGM 124*)	Peterson Builders Inc	Oct 1970

Displacement, tons: 130 standard; 147 full load
Dimensions, feet (metres): 101·0 oa × 21·0 × 6·0 *(30·8 × 6·4 × 1·9)*
Guns: 1—40 mm; 4—20 mm; 2—·50 cal MG
Main engines: Diesels; 2 shafts; 1 800 bhp = 18·5 knots
Range, miles: 1 500 at 10 knots
Complement: 30

T 11 was launched on 5 May 1965.

T 11   *8/1976, Dr. Giorgio Arra*

1 Ex-US SC TYPE (LARGE PATROL CRAFT)

T 85 (ex-*SC 32*, ex-US *SC 162*)

Displacement, tons: 110 light; 125 full load
Dimensions, feet (metres): 111 × 17 × 6 *(36·4 × 5·5 × 1·9)*
Guns: 1—40 mm; 3—20 mm
A/S weapons: Depth charges, Mousetrap
Main engines: High-speed diesel = 18 knots
Range, miles: 2 000 at 10 knots

Wooden hulled. Non-operational.

4 Ex-US CG "CAPE" CLASS (LARGE PATROL CRAFT)

T 81 (ex-*CG 13*)
T 82 (ex-*CG 14*)

T 83 (ex-*CG 15*)
T 84 (ex-*CG 16*)

Displacement, tons: 95 standard; 105 full load
Dimensions, feet (metres): 95 × 20·2 × 5 *(29 × 5·8 × 1·6)*
Gun: 1—20 mm
A/S weapons: 2 DC racks; 2 Mousetraps
Main engines: 1 500 at 14 knots
Complement: 15

US coastguard cutters transferred in 1954. Similar to those built for USCG by US Coast Guard Yard, Curtis Bay in 1953. Cost £475 000 each.

T 82 (as CG 14)   *Royal Thai Navy*

2 THAI BUILT (COASTAL PATROL CRAFT)

Name	No.	Builders	Commissioned
—	T 91	Royal Thai Naval Dockyard, Bangkok	1971
—	T 92	Royal Thai Naval Dockyard, Bangkok	1971

Displacement, tons: 87·5 standard
Dimensions, feet (metres): 104·3 × 17·5 × 5·5 *(30·8 × 6·4 × 1·9)*
Guns: 1—40 mm; 1—20 mm
Main engines: Diesels; 1 600 bhp = 25 knots
Complement: 21

T 91　　　　　　　　　　　　　　　　　1970, Royal Thai Navy

12 Ex-US "SWIFT" CLASS (COASTAL PATROL CRAFT)

T 21	T 23	T 25	T 27	T 29	T 211
T 22	T 24	T 26	T 28	T 210	T 212

Displacement, tons: 20 standard; 22 full load
Dimensions, feet (metres): 50 × 13 × 3·5 *(15·2 × 4 × 1·1)*
Guns: 2—81 mm mortars; 2—0·50 cal (1 twin)
Main engines: Diesels; 2 shafts; 480 bhp = 25 knots
Complement: 5

"Swift" class patrol craft transferred from USN; T22 in Aug 1968, T23-25 in Feb 1970. T21 in May 1970, T26 in Mar 1970, T27 in Apr 1970, T 28, 29, 210-212 in 1975.

T 21　　　　　　　　　　　　　　　　　8/1976, Dr. Giorgio Arra

6 Ex-US RPC TYPE (COASTAL PATROL CRAFT)

T 31	T 32	T 33	T 34	T 35	T 36

Displacement, tons: 10·4 standard; 13·05 full load
Dimensions, feet (metres): 35 × 10 *(11·5 × 3·2)*
Guns: 2—0·50 cal (1 twin); 2—0·30 cal
Main engines: Diesels; 2 shafts; 225 bhp = 14 knots
Complement: 7

Transferred Mar 1967.

There are reports that a patrol of Riverine Craft is maintained on the Upper Mekong although details are not available.

MINE WARFARE FORCES

Note: Transfer of ex-USS *Prime* and *Reaper* ("Agile" class MSOs) was cancelled.

2 "BANGRACHAN" CLASS (COASTAL MINELAYERS)

Name	No.	Builders	Commissioned
BANGRACHAN	MMC 1	Cantiere dell'Adriatico, Monfalcone	1937
NHONG SARHAI	MMC 2	Cantiere dell'Adriatico, Monfalcone	1936

Displacement, tons: 368 standard; 408 full load
Dimensions, feet (metres): 160·8 × 25·9 × 7·2 *(52·7 × 8·5 × 2·4)*
Guns: 2—3 in; 2—20 mm
Mines: 142
Main engines: Burmeister & Wain diesels; 2 shafts; 540 bhp = 12 knots
Oil fuel, tons: 180
Range, miles: 2 700 at 10 knots
Complement: 55

Launched in 1936.

BANGRACHAN

4 US "BLUEBIRD" CLASS (MINESWEEPERS—COASTAL)

Name	No.	Builders	Commissioned
BANGEKO (ex-USS *MSC 303*)	6	Dorchester SB Corpn, Camden	9 July 1965
DONCHEDI (ex-USS *MSC 313*)	8	Peterson Builders Inc, Sturgeon Bay, Wisc	17 Sep 1965
LADYA (ex-USS *MSC 297*)	5	Peterson Builders Inc, Sturgeon Bay, Wisc	14 Dec 1963
TADINDENG (ex-USS *MSC 301*)	7	Tacoma Boatbuilding Co, Tacoma, Wash	26 Aug 1965

Displacement, tons: 330 standard; 362 full load
Dimensions, feet (metres): 145·3 oa × 27 × 8·5 *(43 × 8 × 2·6)*
Guns: 2—20 mm
Main engines: 4 GM diesels; 2 shafts; 1 000 bhp = 13 knots
Range, miles: 2 500 at 10 knots
Complement: 43 (7 officers, and 36 men)

New construction for Thailand.

BANGEKO　　　　　　　　　　　　　　　　8/1976, Dr. Giorgio Arra

1 MCM SUPPORT SHIP

Name	No.	Builders	Commissioned
RANG KWIEN (ex-*Umihari Maru*)	MSC 11	Mitsubishi Co.	1944

Displacement, tons: 586 standard
Dimensions, feet (metres): 162·3 × 31·2 × 13·0 *(49 × 9·5 × 4)*
Guns: 2—20 mm
Main engines: Triple expansion steam; speed = 10 knots

Originally built as a tug. Acquired by Royal Thai Navy on 6 Sep 1967.

RANG KWIEN   *1969, Royal Thai Navy*

5 MSB

MSML 6-10

Thai built. 50 ft, 30 tons with 2—20 mm guns.

5 MSB

MSML 1-5

Thai built. 40 ft, 25 tons with 2—20 mm guns.

AMPHIBIOUS FORCES

5 Ex-US "1-510" and "511-1152 CLASSES (LST)

Name	No.	Builders	Commissioned
ANGTHONG (ex-USS *LST 294*)	LST 1	USA	1944
CHANG (ex-USS *Lincoln County, LST 898*)	LST 2	Dravo Corp	29 Dec 1944
LANTA (ex-USS *Stone County, LST 1141*)	LST 4	USA	1945
PANGAN (ex-USS *Stark County, LST 1134*)	LST 3	USA	1945
PRATHONG (ex-USS *Dodge County, LST 722*)	LST 5	USA	1944

Displacement, tons: 1 625 standard; 4 080 full load
Dimensions, feet (metres): 328 oa × 50 × 14 *(100 × 15·2 × 4·4)*
Guns: 6—40 mm; 4—20 mm
Main engines: GM diesels; 2 shafts; 1 700 bhp = 11 knots
Range, miles: 9 500 at 9 knots
Complement: 80
Cargo capacity: 2 100 tons

CHANG   *1965, Royal Thai Navy*

Angthong is employed as training ship. *Chang,* transferred to Thailand in 1962, was laid down on 15 Oct 1944. *Pangan* was transferred on 16 May 1966, *Lanta* on 12 Mar 1970 and *Prathong* on 17 Dec 1975.

3 Ex-US "LSM-1" CLASS

Name	No.	Builders	Commissioned
KRAM (ex-USS *LSM 469*)	LSM 3	Brown SB Co, Houston, Tex	17 Mar 1945
KUT (ex-USS *LSM 338*)	LSM 1	USA	1945
PHAI (ex-USS *LSM 333*)	LSM 2	USA	1945

Displacement, tons: 743 standard; 1 095 full load
Dimensions, feet (metres): 203·5 oa × 34·5 × 8·3 *(62 × 10·5 × 2·4)*
Guns: 2—40 mm
Main engines: Diesel direct drive; 2 shafts; 2 800 bhp = 12·5 knots
Range, miles: 2 500 at 12 knots
Complement: 55

Former United States landing ships of the LCM, later LSM (Medium Landing Ship) type. *Kram* was transferred to Thailand under MAP at Seattle, Wash, on 25 May 1962.

2 Ex-US "LSIL" CLASS

PRAB (ex-*LSIL 670*) LSIL 1   **SATAKUT** (ex-*LSIL 739*) LSIL 2

Displacement, tons: 230 standard; 387 full load
Dimensions, feet (metres): 157 × 23 × 6 *(47 × 7 × 1·7)*
Guns: 2—20 mm
Main engines: Diesel; 2 shafts; 1 320 bhp = 14 knots
Complement: 54

Prab non-operational.

1 Ex-US LCG TYPE

NAKHA (ex-USS *LSSL* 102) LSSL 3

Displacement, tons: 233 standard; 287 full load
Dimensions, feet (metres): 158 oa × 23 × 4·25 *(47·5 × 7 × 1·4)*
Guns: 1—3 inch; 4—40 mm; 4—20 mm; 4—81 mm mortars
Main engines: Diesels; 2 shafts; 1 320 bhp = 15 knots
Range, miles: 4 700 at 10 knots

Transferred in 1966. Acquired when Japan returned her to USA.

26 Ex-US LCM 6

14-16, 61-68, 71-78, 81-82, 85-87

First 21 delivered 1969.

6 Ex-US LCVP

LCAs

There is also a large but unknown number of Thai-built LCAs.

6 Ex-US "LCU" CLASS

ARDANG LCU 3	**MATAPHON** LCU 1	**RAWI** LCU 2
KOLUM LCU 5	**PHETRA** LCU 4	**TALIBONG** LCU 6

Displacement, tons: 134 standard; 279 full load
Dimensions, feet (metres): 112 × 32 × 4 *(37 × 9·7 × 1·2)*
Guns: 2—20 mm
Main engines: Diesel; 3 shafts; 675 bhp = 10 knots
Complement: 37

Employed as transport ferries. Originally LCT-6 class.

TRAINING SHIPS

1 Ex-BRITISH "ALGERINE" CLASS

Name	No.	Builders	Commissioned
PHOSAMTON (ex-HMS *Minstrel*)	MSF 1	Redfern Construction Co	1945

Displacement, tons: 1 040 standard; 1 335 full load
Length, feet (metres): 225·0 *(68·6)* oa
Beam, feet (metres): 35·5 *(10·8)*
Draught, feet (metres): 10·5 *(3·2)*
Guns: 1—4 in *(102 mm)* ; 6—20 mm
A/S weapons: 4 DCT
Main engines: Triple expansion; 2 shafts; 2 000 ihp
Boilers: 2 three-drum type
Speed, knots: 16
Oil fuel, tons: 270
Range, miles: 5 000 at 10 knots
Complement: 103

Transferred in Apr 1947. The 20 mm guns were increased from 3 to 6, and the DCTs from 2 to 4 in 1966. Marginally operational—now used for training.

Name	No.	Builders	Commissioned
MAEKLONG	4	Uraga Dock Co, Japan	June 1937

Displacement, tons: 1 400 standard; 2 000 full load
Length, feet (metres): 269·0 *(82·0)*
Beam, feet (metres): 34·0 *(10·4)*
Draught, feet (metres): 10·5 *(3·2)*
Guns: 4—3 in *(76 mm)* 50 cal (singles); 3—40 mm; 3—20 mm
Main engines: Triple expansion; 2 shafts; 2 500 ihp
Boilers: 2 water tube
Speed, knots: 14
Oil fuel, tons: 487
Range, miles: 8 000 at 12 knots
Complement: 155 as training ship

Employed as training ship. The 4—18 inch torpedo tubes were removed.

Armament: 4—4·7 in guns replaced by 3 in guns in 1974.

1 Ex-BRITISH "FLOWER" CLASS

Name	No.	Builders	Commissioned
BANGPAKONG (ex-*Gondwana*, ex- HMS *Burnet*)	P4	Ferguson Bros, Port Glasgow	23 Sep 1943

Displacement, tons: 1 060 standard; 1 350 full load
Dimensions, feet (metres): 203·2 × 33 × 14·5 *(61·9 × 10 × 4·4)*
Guns: 1—3 in *(76 mm)* 50 cal; 1—40 mm; 6—20 mm
A/S weapons: 4 DCT
Main engines: Triple expansion; 2 880 ihp = 16 knots
Boilers: 2 Three-drum type
Range, miles: 4 800 at 12 knots
Complement: 100

Served in Indian Navy before transfer to Thailand 15 May 1947. Now used for training.

SURVEY SHIPS

Name	No.	Builders	Commissioned
CHANDHARA	AGS 11	C. Melchers & Co, Bremen, Germany	1961

Displacement, tons: 870 standard; 996 full load
Dimensions, feet (metres): 229·2 oa × 34·5 × 10 *(71 × 10·5 × 3)*
Gun: 1—20 mm
Main engines: 2 diesels; 2 shafts; 1 000 bhp = 13·25 knots
Range, miles: 10 000 (cruising)
Complement: 72

Laid down on 27 Sep 1960. Launched on 17 Dec 1960.

CHANDHARA   *1962, Royal Thai Navy*

3 OCEANOGRAPHIC CRAFT

Of 90 tons, with a crew of 8 launched in 1955.

SERVICE FORCES

2 SUPPORT TANKERS

CHULA AO 2   **MATRA** AO 3

Displacement, tons: 2 395 standard; 4 744 full load
Dimensions, feet (metres): 328 × 45·2 × 20 *(100 × 14 × 6·1)*
Main engines: Steam turbines

Built in Japan during World War II. Exact sisters *Chula* employed as floating storage, *Matra* as freighting and fleet replenishment tanker and naval stores ship.

CHULA   *1969, Royal Thai Navy*

1 HARBOUR TANKER

Name	No.	Builders	Commissioned
SAMED	YO 11	Royal Thai Naval Dockyard, Bangkok	15 Dec 1970

Displacement, tons: 360 standard; 485 full load
Dimensions, feet (metres): 120 × 20 × 10 *(39 × 6·1 × 3·1)*
Main engines: Diesel; 500 bhp = 9 knots

Launched on 8 July 1966.

1 HARBOUR TANKER

Name	No.	Builders	Commissioned
PROET	YO 9	Royal Thai Naval Dockyard, Bangkok	16 Jan 1970

Displacement, tons: 360
Dimensions, feet (metres): 122·7 × 19·7 × 8·7 *(37·4 × 6 × 2·7)*
Main engines: Diesels; 500 bhp = 9 knots

1 TRANSPORT

Name	No.	Builders	Commissioned
SICHANG	AKL 1	Harima Co, Japan	Jan 1938

Displacement, tons: 815 standard
Dimensions, feet (metres): 160 × 28 × 16 (48·8 × 8·5 × 4·9)
Main engines: Diesel; 2 shafts; 550 bhp = 16 knots
Complement: 30

Sichang was launched on 10 Nov 1937. Completed in Jan 1938.

1 TRANSPORT

KLED KEO AF 7

Displacement, tons: 382 standard; 450 full load
Dimensions, feet (metres): 154·9 × 25·4 × 14 (46 × 7·6 × 4·3)
Guns: 3—20 mm
Main engines: 1 diesel; 600 hp = 12 knots
Complement: 54

Operates with patrol boat squadron.

2 WATER CARRIERS

Name	No.	Builders	Commissioned
CHUANG	YW 8	Royal Thai Naval Dockyard, Bangkok	1965
CHARN	YW 6	Royal Thai Naval Dockyard, Bangkok	1965

Displacement, tons: 305 standard; 485 full load
Dimensions, feet (metres): 136 × 25 × 10 (42 × 7·5 × 3·1)
Main engines: GM diesel; 500 bhp = 11 knots
Complement: 29

Chuang launched on 14 Jan 1965.

TUGS

Name	No.	Builders	Commissioned
SAMAE SAN (ex-*Empire Vincent*)	YTM 1	Cochrane & Sons Ltd, Selby, Yorks, England	—

Displacement, tons: 503 full load
Dimensions, feet (metres): 105·0 × 26·5 × 13·0 (32 × 8·1 × 4)
Main engines: Triple expansion; 850 ihp = 10·5 knots
Complement: 27

3 Ex-US "YTL 422" CLASS

KLUENG BADEN YTL 2
MARN VICHAI YTL 3

RAD (ex-USN *YTL 340*) YTL 4

Displacement, tons: 63 standard (*Rad* 52 standard)
Dimensions, feet (metres): 64·7 × 16·5 × 6·0 (18·6 × 4·5 × 1·8)
  Rad 60·7 × 17·5 × 5·0 (18·3 × 5·3 × 1·5)
Main engines: Diesels; speed = 8 knots (*Rad* 6 knots)

Rad transferred May 1955 from US, the other pair bought from Canada 1953.

RAD

8/1976, Dr. Giorgio Arra

TOGO

Ministerial

Minister of National Defence:
  General Gnassingbe Eyadema (President)

Personnel

a) 1977: 200
b) Voluntary

Base

Lome

Mercantile Marine

Lloyd's Register of Shipping:
  1 vessel of 134 tons gross

2 COASTAL PATROL CRAFT

Name	No.	Builders	Commissioned
MONO	—	Chantiers Navals de l'Esterel	1976
KARA	—	Chantiers Navals de l'Esterel	1976

Displacement, tons: 80
Dimensions, feet (metres): 105 × 19·6 × 5·8 (32 × 5·8 × 1·6)
Missiles: Can carry SS-12
Guns: 2—20 mm
Main engines: 2 MTU diesels; 2 700 bhp = 30 knots
Range, miles: 1 400 at 15 knots
Complement: 17
Radar: One navigation set

Note: Reports of three other patrol craft and a river gunboat are unsubstantiated.

MONO and KARA

1976, Ch. Navals de l'Esterel

TONGA

On 10 Mar 1973 King Taufa 'ahau Tupou IV commissioned the first craft of Tonga's Maritime Force, a necessary service in a Kingdom of seven main groups of islands spread over 270 square miles.

Mercantile Marine

Lloyd's Register of Shipping: 11 vessels of 13 720 tons gross

1 COASTAL PATROL CRAFT

Name	No.	Builders	Commissioned
NGAHAU KOULA	P 101	Brooke Marine, Lowestoft	10 Mar 1973

Displacement, tons: 15
Dimensions, feet (metres): 45 × 13 × 3·8 *(13·7 × 4 × 1·2)*
Gun: 1—50 Browning MG
Main engines: 2 Cummins V8 diesels = 21 knots
Complement: 5

Fitted with Decca Super 100 radar, DF and echo-sounder (Ferrograph). Manned by volunteers from the Royal Guard and Tongan Defence Force.

NGAHAU KOULA   *1973, Statham*

TRINIDAD AND TOBAGO

COAST GUARD

Ministerial

Minister of National Security:
  Mr John Donaldson

Headquarters Appointment

Commanding Officer, T. & T. Coast Guard:
  Commander M. O. Williams, MOM

Personnel

(a) 1977: 264 (28 officers, 236 ratings)
(b) Voluntary

Mercantile Marine

Lloyd's Register of Shipping: 33 vessels of 13 603 tons gross

DELETIONS

1975-76   *Sea Hawk* and *Sea Scout*

2 LATER VOSPER TYPE (LARGE PATROL CRAFT)

Name	No.	Builders	Commissioned
BUCCO REEF	CG 4	Vosper Ltd, Portsmouth	18 Mar 1972
CHAGUARAMUS	CG 3	Vosper Ltd, Portsmouth	18 Mar 1972

Displacement, tons: 100 standard; 125 full load
Dimensions, feet (metres): 103·0 × 19·8 × 5·8 *(31·5 × 5·9 × 1·6)*
Gun: 1—20 mm Hispano Suiza
Main engines: 2 Paxman Ventura diesels; 2 900 bhp = 24 knots
Oil fuel, tons: 20
Range, miles: 2 000 at 13 knots
Complement: 19 (3 officers, 16 ratings)

Chaguaramus was laid down on 1 Feb 1971 and launched on 29 Mar 1971. Fitted with air-conditioning and roll-damping.

CHAGUARAMUS   *1975, Trinidad and Tobago Coast Guard*

2 VOSPER TYPE (LARGE PATROL CRAFT)

Name	No.	Builders	Commissioned
COURLAND BAY	CG 2	Vosper Ltd, Portsmouth	20 Feb 1965
TRINITY	CG 1	Vosper Ltd, Portsmouth	20 Feb 1965

Displacement, tons: 96 standard; 123 full load
Dimensions, feet (metres): 102·6 oa × 19·7 × 5·5 *(31·4 × 5·9 × 1·7)*
Gun: 1—40 mm Bofors
Main engines: 2 12 cyl Paxman Ventura YJCM turbo-charged diesels; 2 910 bhp = 24·5 knots
Oil fuel, tons: 18
Range, miles: 1 800 at 13·5 knots
Complement: 17 (3 officers, 14 ratings)

Designed by Vosper Limited, Portsmouth. Of steel construction with aluminium alloy super-structure. The boats are air-conditioned throughout except the engine room. Vosper roll-damping equipment is fitted. Laid down Oct 1963. *Trinity* was launched on 14 April 1964. *Trinity* is named after Trinity Hills, so named by Columbus on making his landfall in 1498, and *Courland Bay* after a bay in Tobago where a settlement was founded by the Duke of Courland in the 17th century.

TRINITY   *1975, Trinidad and Tobago Coast Guard*

4 COASTAL PATROL CRAFT

CG 6   **CG 7**   **CG 8**   **CG 9**

Three Glastron glass fibre runabouts and one locally built (CG 9), (also of glass fibre). First three capable of 27 knots, are used for inshore patrol work, mainly in the Gulf of Paria. CG 9, 23 ft long with a Caterpillar diesel makes 23 knots.

1 COASTAL PATROL CRAFT

Name	No.	Builders	Commissioned
NAPARIMA	—	Tugs and Lighters, Port of Spain	13 Aug 1976

Dimensions, feet (metres): 50 × 16 × 8 *(164 × 52·5 × 26·2)*
Main engines: 2 GM 8V 71 diesels; 460 bhp
Complement: 5

NAPARIMA   *1976 Trinidad and Tobago Coast Guard*

1 SAIL TRAINING SHIP

HUMMING BIRD II

40 ft cutter-rigged ketch with 3 cyl Lister auxiliary diesel. Built in Trinidad 1966.

TUNISIA

Headquarters Appointment

Chief of Naval Staff:
Capitaine de Fregate Jedidi Bechir

Diplomatic Representation

Defence Ataché in Paris (and for London):
Colonel A. El-Fehri

Personnel

(a) 1977: 2 100 officers and men
(b) 1 year National Service

Mercantile Marine

Lloyd's Register of Shipping:
31 vessels of 62 941 tons gross

Strength of the Fleet

Type	Active	Building
Frigate	1	1
MSC	1	—
Large Patrol Craft	5	1
Coastal Patrol Craft	10	—
Tugs	3	—

FRIGATES

1 Ex-US "SAVAGE" CLASS

Name	No.	Builders	Commissioned
PRÉSIDENT BOURGUIBA (ex-USS *Thomas J. Gary DER 326*, ex-*DE 326*)	E 7	Consolidated Steel Corpn	27 Nov 1943

Displacement, tons: 1 590 standard; 2 100 full load
Dimensions, feet (metres): 306 oa × 36·6 × 14 *(93·3 × 11·1 × 4·3)*
Guns: 2—3 in *(76 mm)* 50 cal; 2—20 mm
A/S weapon: 6 (2 triple) Mk 32 A/S torpedo tubes
Main engines: 4 diesels; 6 000 bhp; 2 shafts = 19 knots
Range, miles: 11 500 at 11 knots
Complement: 169

Completed as "Edsall" class DE. Converted to Radar Picket "Savage" class in 1958. Transferred 27 Oct 1973.

Radar: SPS 29 and SPS 10.

PRÉSIDENT BOURGUIBA   *1974, Wright & Logan*

1 FRENCH A69 TYPE AVISO

Displacement, tons: 950 standard; 1 260 full load
Dimensions, feet (metres): 262·5 oa × 33·8 × 9·8 *(80 × 10·3 × 3)*
Guns: 1—3·9 in *(100 mm)* 1—40 mm; 4—20 mm
A/S weapons: 1 sextuple Mk 64 rocket launcher *(375 mm)* 4 fixed torpedo launchers for homing torpedoes
Main engines: 2 SEMT Pielstick PC2V Diesels; 2 shafts; c-p propellers; 11 000 shp = 24 knots
Range, miles: 4 500 at 15 knots
Complement: 62

Reported as ordered from France in 1972 although this is still not confirmed. Could be equipped with Exocet.

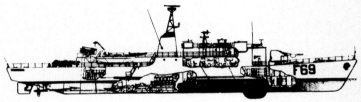

TYPE A69

COASTAL MINESWEEPER

1 Ex-US "ACACIA" CLASS

Name	No.	Builders	Commissioned
HANNIBAL (ex-*Coquelicot*, ex-USN *MSC 84*)	—	USA	1953

Displacement, tons: 320 standard; 372 full load
Dimensions, feet (metres): 141 oa × 26 × 8·3 *(43 × 8 × 2·6)*
Guns: 2—20 mm
Main engines: 2 GM diesels; 2 shafts; 1 200 bhp = 13 knots
Oil fuel, tons: 40
Range, miles: 2 500 at 10 knots
Complement: 38

Built for France under MDAP and delivered in 1953—to Tunisia in 1973.

HANNIBAL   *1974, Tunisian Navy*

LIGHT FORCES

1 Ex-FRENCH "FOUGEUX" CLASS (LARGE PATROL CRAFT)

Name	No.	Builders	Commissioned
SAKIET SIDI YOUSSEF (ex-*UW 12*)	P 303	Dubigeon, Nantes	1956

Displacement, tons: 325 standard; 440 full load
Dimensions, feet (metres): 170 pp × 23 × 6·5 *(53 × 7·3 × 2)*
Guns: 1—40 mm; 2—20 mm
A/S weapons: Mousetrap; 4 DCT; 2 DC racks
Main engines: 4 SEMT-Pielstick diesels; 3 240 bhp = 18·7 knots
Range, miles: 2 000 at 15 knots
Complement: 4 officers, 59 men

Built in France, under US off-shore order. Purchased by Federal Germany in 1957 and served as A/S trials vessel. Transferred to Tunisia in Dec 1969.

SAKIET SIDI YOUSSEF   *1974, Tunisian Navy*

3 "P 48" CLASS (LARGE PATROL CRAFT)

Name	No.	Builders	Commissioned	
BIZERTE	P 301	Ch. Franco-Belges (Villeneuve, la Garenne)	10 July	1970
HORRIA (ex-*Liberté*)	P 302	Ch. Franco-Belges (Villeneuve, la Garenne)	Oct	1970
MONASTIR	P 304	Soc. Francaise Constructions Navale	25 Mar	1975

Displacement, tons: 250
Dimensions, feet (metres): 157·5 × 23·3 × 7 *(48 × 7·1 × 2·3)*
Missiles: 8—SS 12
Guns: 2—40 mm
Main engines: 2 MTU diesels; 4 800 bhp = 20 knots
Range, miles: 2 000 at 16 knots

First pair ordered in 1968. *Bizerte* was launched on 20 Nov 1969. *Horria* launched 12 Feb 1970. *Monastir* ordered in Aug 1973, laid down Jan 1974, launched 25 June 1974, completed 20 Feb 1975 but commissioned on 25 Mar.

HORRIA   1974, Tunisian Navy

2 VOSPER THORNYCROFT 103 ft TYPE
(LARGE PATROL CRAFT)

Name	No.	Builders	Commissioned
MENZEL BOURGUIBA	P205	Vosper Thornycroft	1977
—	P206	Vosper Thornycroft	—

Displacement, tons: 120
Dimensions, feet (metres): 103 × 19·5 × 5·5 *(31·4 × 5·9 × 1·7)*
Guns:
Main engines:
Range, miles: 1 500 cruising
Complement: 24

Ordered in 1974. P205 laid down 23 Mar 1976 and launched 19 July 1976.

4 32-metre COASTAL PATROL CRAFT

Name	No.	Builders	Commissioned	
AL JALA	P 203	Ch. Navals de l'Esterel	Nov	1963
ISTIKLAL (ex-*VC 11, P 761*)	P 201	Ch. Navals de l'Esterel		1957
JOUMHOURIA	P 202	Ch. Navals de l'Esterel	Jan	1969
REMADA	P 204	Ch. Navals de l'Esterel	July	1967

Displacement, tons: 60 standard; 82 full load
Dimensions, feet (metres): 104·5 × 15·5 × 5·6 *(31·5 × 5·8 × 1·7)*
Gun: 1—20 mm
Main engines: 2 MTU 12V 493 (Mercedes Benz) diesels; 2 shafts; 2 700 bhp = 28 knots
Range, miles: 1 400 at 15 knots
Complement: 17

Istiklal transferred from France Mar 1959.

ISTIKLAL   1971, Tunisian Navy

6 25-metre COASTAL PATROL CRAFT

Name	No.	Builders	Commissioned
—	V 101	Ch. Navals de l'Esterel	1961
—	V 102	Ch. Navals de l'Esterel	1961
—	V 103	Ch. Navals de l'Esterel	1962
—	V 104	Ch. Navals de l'Esterel	1962
—	V 105	Ch. Navals de l'Esterel	1963
—	V 106	Ch. Navals de l'Esterel	1963

Displacement, tons: 38
Dimensions, feet (metres): 83 × 15·6 × 4·1 *(25 × 4·8 × 1·3)*
Gun: 1—20 mm
Main engines: 2 twin GM diesels; 2 400 hp = 23 knots
Range, miles: 900 at 16 knots
Complement: 11

V 104   1970, Tunisian Navy

Two further craft of the same design (V 107 and V 108) but unarmed were supplied to the Fisheries Administration in 1971.

V 105   1974, Tunisian Navy

TUGS

Name	No.	Builders	Commissioned	Name	No.	Builders	Commissioned
RAS ADAR (ex-*Zeeland*, ex-*Pan American*, ex-*Ocean Pride*, ex-HMS *Oriana, BAT 1*)	—	Gulfport Boilerworks & Eng Co.	1942	JAOUEL EL BAHR	T 1	Ch. Navals de l'Esterel	—
				SABBACK EL BAHR	T 2	Ch. Navals de l'Esterel	—

Displacement, tons: 540 standard
Dimensions, feet (metres): 144·4 × 33 × 13·5 *(43 × 10 × 4)*

Built in 1942 and lend leased to the Royal Navy in that year as BAT 1 HMS *Oriana*, returned and sold in 1946 as *Ocean Pride*, then *Pan America* in 1947, then *Zeeland* in 1956.

TURKEY

Headquarters Appointment

Commander in Chief, Turkish Naval Forces:
Admiral Hilmi Firat

Senior Command

Fleet Commander:
Vice-Admiral Arif Akdoganlar

Diplomatic Representation

Naval Attaché in Athens:
Captain Y. Günçer
Naval Attaché in Bonn:
Captain T. Özkan
Naval Attaché in Cairo:
Commander Y. Erel
Naval Attaché in London:
Lieut-Cdr. B. Alpkaya
Naval Attaché in Moscow:
Captain R. Maldemir
Naval Attaché in Oslo:
Captain T. Erdinç
Naval Attaché in Rome:
Captain E. Akman
Naval Attaché in Tokyo:
Commander E. Erdilek
Naval Attaché in Washington:
Commander E. Gürsal

Personnel

(a) 1977: 45 000 officers and ratings
(b) 20 months national service

Naval Bases

Headquarters: Ankara
Main Naval Base: Gölçük
Senior Flag Officerş: Istanbul, Izmir
Other Flag Officers: Eregli, Bosphorus,
   Heybeliada (Training), Dardanelles, Iskenderun
Dockyards: Gölçük, Taşkizak (Istanbul)

Naval Air Arm

3 AB-204B Helicopters
16 S2E ASW Aircraft

Mercantile Marine

Lloyd's Register of Shipping:
405 vessels of 1 079 347 tons gross

Strength of the Fleet

Type	Active	Building
Destroyers	12	—
Frigates	2	—
Submarines—Patrol	15	2
Fast Attack Craft—Missile	7	1
Fast Attack Craft—Torpedo	12	—
Large Patrol Craft	41	1
Coastal Patrol Craft	4	—
Minelayer—Large	1	—
Minelayers—Coastal	8	—
Minesweepers—Coastal	21	—
Minesweepers—Inshore	4	—
Minehunting Boats	9	—
LSTs	2	—
LCTs	17	—
LCUs	16	—
LCMs	20	—
Support Tankers	4	—
Harbour Tanker	1	—
Water Tankers	3	—
Repair Ships	3	—
Transports	6	—
Submarine Rescue Ships	3	—
BDVs	4	—
Gate Vessels	3	—
Tug—Ocean	1	—
Tugs—Harbour	7	—
Floating Docks	7	—
Training Ships	2	—
Survey Vessels	4	—
Supply Ships	2	—
Depot Ship	1	—

DELETIONS

Destroyers

1973 *Gaziantep, Giresun*
1974 *Kocatepe* (ex-USS *Harwood*) sunk on 22 July. *Gemlik.*
1976 *Gelibolu*

Corvettes

1973 *Edremit, Eregli* (ex-MSO)
1974 *Çardak, Çesme, Edincik* (ex-MSO)
1975 *Alanya, Ayvalik*

Submarines

(Most replaced by submarines of same name).

1973 *Birinci Inönü, Çanakkale, Çerbe, Ikinci Inönü, Piri Reis*
1974 *Gür* (ex-*Chub*), *Sakarya* (ex-*Boarfish*)

Fast Attack Craft

1973 *Dogan, Marti* ("Nasty" class), *AB 1-4, 6-7*

Support Tanker

1975 *Akar*

Boom Defence Vessels

1975 *AG 2, AG 3, Kaldaray*

Survey Craft

1975 *Mesaha 3* and *4*

Tug

1975 *Önder*

PENNANT LIST

Destroyers

D 340	Istanbul
D 341	Izmir
D 342	Izmit
D 343	Iskenderun
D 344	Içel
D 351	M. Fevzi Çakmak
D 352	Gayret
D 353	Adatepe
D 354	Kocatepe
D 355	Tinaztepe
D 356	Zafer
DM 357	Muavenet

Frigates

D 358	Berk
D 359	Peyk

Submarines

S 333	Ikinci Inönü
S 335	Burak Reis
S 336	Murat Reis
S 337	Oruc Reis
S 338	Uluçali Reis
S 339	Dumlupinar
S 340	Çerbe
S 341	Çanakkale
S 342	Turgut Reis
S 344	Hizir Reis
S 345	Preveze
S 346	Birinci Inönü
S 347	Atilay
S 348	Saldiray

Minewarfare Forces (Sweepers)

M 500	Foça
M 501	Fethiye
M 502	Fatsa
M 503	Finike
M 507	Seymen
M 508	Selcuk
M 509	Seyhan
M 510	Samsun
M 511	Sinop
M 512	Sumene
M 513	Seddulbahir
M 514	Silifke
M 515	Saros
M 516	Sigacik
M 517	Sapanca
M 518	Sariyer
M 520	Karamürsel
M 521	Kerempe
M 522	Kilimli
M 523	Kozlu
M 524	Kuşadasi
M 530	Trabzon
M 531	Terme
M 532	Tirebolu
M 533	Tekirdag

Minewarfare Forces (Layers)

N 101	Mordogan
N 102	Meriç
N 103	Marmaris
N 104	Mersin
N 105	Mürefte
N 110	Nusret
N 115	Mehemedcik

Light Forces

P 111	Sultanhisar
P 112	Demirhisar
P 113	Yarhisar
P 114	Akhisar
P 115	Sivrihisar
P 116	Koçhisar
P 301	AG 1 (BDV)
P 304	AG 4 (BDV)
P 305	AG 5 (BDV)
P 306	AG 6 (BDV)
P 311-4	MTB 1-4
P 316-20	MTB 6-10
P 321	Denizkuzu
P 322	Atmaca
P 323	Sahin
P 324	Kartal
P 325	Melten
P 326	Pelikan
P 327	Albatros
P 328	Şimşek
P 329	Kasirga
P 330	Firtina
P 331	Tufan
P 332	Kiliç
P 333	Mizrak
P 334	Yildiz
P 335	Kalkan
P 336	Karayel
P 338	Yildirim
P 339	Bora
P 340	Dogan
P 341	Marti
P 342	Tayfun
P 343	Volkan
P 1209-12	LS 9-12
P 1221-34	AB 21-34
J 12-30	Large Patrol Craft

Service Forces

A 403	Bayraktar
A 404	Sancaktar
A 571	Yuzbaşi Tolunay
A 572	Albay Hakki Burak
A 573	Binbaşi Saadettin Gürçan
A 574	Akpina
A 575	Savarona
A 579	ex-*Ruhr*
A 581	Onaran
A 582	Başaran
A 583	Donatan
A 584	Kurtaran
A 585	Akin
A 586	Ülkü
A 587	Gazal
A 588	Kanarya
A 591	Erkin
A 593	Çandarli (survey)
A 594	Çarşamba (survey)
L 401	Ertrgul
L 402	Sedar
Y 1081-1087	Floating Docks
Y 1117	Sonduren
Y 1118	Akbas
Y 1119	Kepez
Y 1121	Yedekci
Y 1122	Kuvvet
Y 1123	Öncu
Y 1129	Kudret
Y 1155	Kanaria
Y 1156	Sarköy
Y 1163	Lapseki
Y 1164	Erdek
Y 1166	Kilya
Y 1168	Tuzla
Y 1207	Gölçük
Y 1208	Van
Y 1209	Ulabat
Y 1217	Sogut

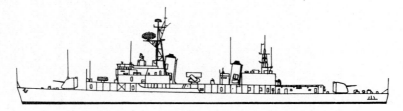

Ex-US "GEARING" Class

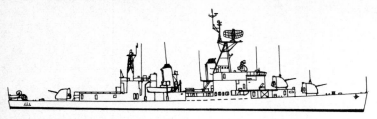

ZAFER

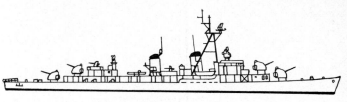

Ex-"FLETCHER" Class

DESTROYERS

5 Ex-US "GEARING" CLASS (FRAM I and II)

Name
ADATEPE (ex-USS *Forrest Royal, DD 872*)
GAYRET (ex-USS *Eversole, DD 789*)
KOCATEPE (ex-USS *Norris, DD 859*)
M. FEVZI ÇAKMAK (ex-USS *Charles H. Roan, DD 853*)
TINAZTEPE (ex-USS *Keppler, DD 765*)

No.	Builders	Laid down	Launched	Commissioned
D 353	Bethlehem (Staten Is.)	1945	17 Jan 1946	28 June 1946
D 352	Todd Pacific Shipyard	1945	8 Jan 1946	10 July 1946
D 354	Bethlehem (San Pedro)	1944	25 Feb 1945	9 June 1945
D 351	Bethlehem Steel Co, Quincy	1944	15 May 1945	12 Sep 1946
D 355	Bethlehem (San Francisco)	1944	24 June 1945	23 May 1947

Displacement, tons: 2 425 standard; 3 500 full load
Length, feet (metres): 390·5 *(119·0)* oa
Beam, feet (metres): 40·9 *(12·5)*
Draught, feet (metres): 19·0 *(5·8)*
Aircraft: Helicopter deck and hangar
Guns: 4—5 in *(127 mm)* 38 cal (2 twin)
A/S weapons: FRAM I; 1 Asroc 8-tube launcher; 2 triple torpedo tubes (Mk 32); FRAM II; 1 Trainable Hedgehog; 2 triple torpedo tubes (Mk 32)
Main engines: 2 geared turbines; 2 shafts; 60 000 shp
Boilers: 4 Babcock & Wilcox
Speed, knots: 34
Oil fuel, tons: 650
Range, miles: 4 800 at 15 knots; 2 400 at 25 knots
Complement: 275 (15 officers, 260 ratings)

Adatepe, Gayret and *Çakmak* FRAM I conversions and *Kocatepe* and *Tinaztepe* FRAM II. They were transferred to Turkey on 27 Mar 1971 *(Adatepe)* 30 June 1972 *(Tinaztepe)* 11 July 1973 *(Gayret)* and 21 Sep 1973 *(Çakmak), Adatepe* purchased 15 Feb 1973 and *Kocatepe* 7 July 1974, commissioned 24 July 1975.

Fire control: GFCS Mk 37 with Mk 25 radar.

Radar: Long range air search: SPS 40 (FRAM I) SPS 6 (FRAM II). Surface search: SPS 10.

Replacement: The previous *Kocatepe* D 354 was sunk 22 July 1974. USS *Norris* had been purchased for spares on 7 July 1974 and has been re-activated to replace *Kocatepe.*

Sonar: FRAM I, SQS 23. FRAM II, SQS 29 series.

ADATEPE

1973, Dr. Giorgio Arra

TINAZTEPE

6/1975, Dr. Giorgio Arra

1 Ex-US "ROBERT H. SMITH" CLASS

Name
MUAVENET (ex-USS *Gwin*, ex-*MMD 33*, ex-*DD 772*)

No.	Builders	Laid down	Launched	Commissioned
DM 357	Bethlehem, San Pedro	1943	9 Apr 1944	30 Sep 1944

Displacement, tons: 2 250 standard; 3 375 full load
Dimensions, feet (metres): 376·5 × 41 × 19 *(114·8 × 12·5 × 5·8)*
Guns: 6—5 in *(127 mm)* 38 cal (twins); 12—40 mm (2 quad, 2 twin); 11—20 mm
Mines: 80
Main engines: Geared turbines; 60 000 shp; 2 shafts
Boilers: 4 Babcock & Wilcox
Speed, knots: 34
Range, miles: 4 600 at 15 knots
Complement: 274

Modified "Allen M. Sumner" class converted for minelaying. After modernisation at Philadelphia she was transferred on 22 Oct 1971.

Fire Control: GFCS director Mk 37 with Mk 28 radar. Mk 34 director for Mk 51 GFCS for a quad 40 mm.

Radar: Air search: SPS 6. Surface search: SPS 10

Sonar: QCU or QHB.

MUAVENET

Godfrey H. Walker

1 Ex-US "ALLEN M. SUMNER (FRAM II)" CLASS

Name	No.	Builders	Laid down	Launched	Commissioned
ZAFER (ex-USS *Hugh Purvis* DD 709)	D 356	Federal SB and DD Co	1944	17 Dec 1944	1 Mar 1945

Displacement, tons: 2 200 standard; 3 320 full load
Length, feet (metres): 376·5 *(114·8)*
Beam, feet (metres): 40·9 *(12·5)*
Draught, feet (metres): 19·0 *(5·8)*
Guns: 6—5 in 38 cal (twins)
A/S weapons: 6 (2 triple) Mk 32 A/S torpedo tubes; 2 Hedgehogs
Main engines: 2 geared turbines; 2 shafts; 60 000 shp
Boilers: 4 Babcock & Wilcox
Speed, knots: 34
Oil fuel, tons: 650
Range, miles: 4 600 at 15 knots
Complement: 275 (15 officers, 260 ratings)

Zafer is of "Allen M. Sumner" class of modified FRAM II having been used as a USN trials ship for planar passive sonar. There is an extra deck-house on the hangar. Purchased 15 Feb 1972.

Radar: Air search: SPS 40.
Surface search: SPS 10.

Sonar: SQS 29 series.

5 Ex-US "FLETCHER" CLASS

Name	No.	Builders	Laid down	Launched	Commissioned
IÇEL (ex-USS *Preston*, DD 795)	D 344	Bethlehem Co, San Pedro	1943	12 Dec 1943	20 Mar 1944
ISKENDERUN (ex-USS *Boyd*, DD 544)	D 343	Bethlehem Co, San Pedro	1942	29 Oct 1942	8 May 1943
ISTANBUL (ex-USS *Clarence K. Bronson*, DD 668)	D 340	Federal SB & DD Co, Newark	1942	18 Apr 1943	11 June 1943
IZMIR (ex-USS *Van Valkenburgh*, DD 656)	D 341	Gulf Shipbuilding Corp	1943	19 Dec 1943	2 Aug 1944
IZMIT (ex-USS *Cogswell*, DD 651)	D 342	Bath Iron Works, Corpn	1942	5 June 1943	17 Aug 1943

Displacement, tons: 2 050 standard; 3 000 full load
Length, feet (metres): 376·5 *(114·8)* oa
Beam, feet (metres): 39·5 *(12·1)*
Draught, feet (metres): 18·0 *(5·5)*
Guns: 4—5 in *(127 mm)* 38 cal; 6—3 in *(76 mm)*
A/S weapons: 2 Hedgehogs
Torpedo tubes: 5—21 in *(533 mm)* (quintuple)
Main engines: GE geared turbines; 2 shafts; 60 000 shp
Boilers: 4 Babcock & Wilcox
Speed, knots: 34
Oil fuel, tons: 650
Range, miles: 5 000 at 15 knots
Complement: 250

Fire Control: Mk 37 GFCS forward with Mk 25 radar. Mk 56 GFCS aft with Mk 35 radar. Two Mk 51 GFCS amidships.

Radar: Search: SPS 6.
Tactical: SPS 10.

Transfers: Transferred as follows: *Istanbul* 14 Jan 1967, *Izmir* 28 Feb 1967, *Iskenderun* and *Izmit* on 1 Oct 1969, and *Içel* on 15 Nov 1969.

ISTANBUL   1975, Turkish Navy

FRIGATES

2 "BERK" CLASS

Name	No.	Builders	Laid down	Launched	Commissioned
BERK	D 358	Gölcük Naval Yard	9 Mar 1967	25 June 1971	12 July 1972
PEYK	D 359	Gölcük Naval Yard	18 Jan 1968	7 June 1972	24 July 1975

Displacement, tons: 1 450 standard; 1 950 full load
Length, feet (metres): 311·7 *(95·0)*
Beam, feet (metres): 38·7 *(11·8)*
Draught, feet (metres): 18·1 *(5·5)*
Aircraft: 1 helicopter
Guns: 4—3 in *(76 mm)* 50 cal (2 twin Mk 33)
A/S weapons: 6 (2 triple) Mk 32 A/S torpedo tubes; 1 DC rack
Main engines: 4 Fiat diesels; 2 shafts; 24 000 bhp
Speed, knots: 25

First major warships built in Turkey, the start of a most important era in the Eastern Mediterranean. Both are named after famous ships of the Ottoman Navy. Of modified US "Claud Jones" design.

Fire Control: Each mounting has GFCS Mk 63.

Radar: SPG 34;
Air search: SPS 40
Surface search: SPS 10

PEYK   7/1976, USN

SUBMARINES

3 + 2 TYPE 209 (HOWALDTSWERKE)

Name	No.	Builders	Laid down	Launched	Commissioned
ATILAY	S 347	Howaldtswerke, Kiel	2 Aug 1972	23 Oct 1974	29 July 1975
SALDIRAY	S 348	Howaldtswerke, Kiel	1973	14 Feb 1975	21 Oct 1975
—	S 349	Howaldtswerke, Kiel	11 June1975	1977	1978

Displacement, tons: 990 surfaced; 1 290 dived
Length, feet (metres): 183·7 *(56·0)*
Beam, feet (metres): 20·3 *(6·2)*
Torpedo tubes: 8—21 inch (with reloads)
Main machinery: Diesel electric; 4 MTU Siemens diesel-generators; 1 Siemens electric motor; 1 shaft
Speed, knots: 10 surfaced; 22 dived
Range: 50 days
Complement: 31

Designed by Ingenieurkontor, Lübeck for construction by Howaldtswerke, Kiel and sale by Ferrostaal, Essen all acting as a consortium.
A single-hull design with two ballast tanks and forward and after trim tanks. Fitted with snort and remote machinery control. The single screw is slow revving. Very high capacity batteries with GRP lead-acid cells and battery cooling—by Wilh. Hagen and VARTA. Active and passive sonar, sonar detection equipment, sound ranging gear and underwater telephone. Fitted with two periscopes, radar and Omega receiver. Foreplanes retract.

Future Construction: Two more of this class are to be built at Gölcük, the first submarines ever built in Turkey. If this class is to replace the ex-USN boats a considerable programme must be planned.

ATILAY   2/1975, Reinhard Nerlich

2 Ex-US "GUPPY III" CLASS

Name	No.	Builders	Laid down	Launched	Commissioned
ÇANAKKALE (ex-USS *Cobbler SS 344*)	S 341	Electric Boat Co	3 Apr 1944	1 Apr 1945	8 Aug 1945
IKINCI INONÜ (ex-USS *Corporal SS 346*)	S 333	Electric Boat Co	27 Apr 1944	10 June1945	9 Nov 1945

Displacement, tons: 1 975 standard; 2 540 dived
Dimensions, feet (metres): 326·5 × 27 × 17 *(99·4 × 8·2 × 5·2)*
Torpedo tubes: 10—21 inch *(533 mm)* 6 bow, 4 stern
Main machinery: 4 diesels; 6 400 shp; 2 electric motors 5 400 bhp; 2 shafts
Speed: 20 surfaced; 15 dived
Complement: 86

Transferred 21 Nov 1973.

Future Additions: When the US Congress imposed an arms embargo on exports to Turkey in 1975 arrangements were well-advanced for the transfer of the two "Guppy III" class, *Clamagore* and *Tiru*. It is reported that these will possibly be transferred in June 1977.

IKINCI INONÜ (ex-US number)   Turkish Navy

1 Ex-US "GUPPY I A" CLASS

Name	No.	Builders	Laid down	Launched	Commissioned
DUMLUPINAR (ex-USS *Caiman, SS 323*)	S 339	Electric Boat Co	—	30 Mar 1944	17 July 1944

Displacement, tons: 1 840 standard; 2 445 dived
Dimensions, feet (metres): 306 × 27 × 17 *(93·2 × 8·2 × 5·2)*
Torpedo tubes: 10—21 in *(533 mm)* (6 bow, 4 stern); 24 torpedoes carried
Main machinery: 3 GM diesels; 4 800 hp; 2 electric motors; 5 400 hp
Speed, knots: 17 surfaced; 15 dived
Range, miles: 12 000 at 10 knots surfaced
Complement: 85

Transferred July 1972. Damaged in collision and later beached 1 Sep 1976. Present condition uncertain.

7 Ex-US "GUPPY II A" CLASS

Name	No.	Builders	Laid down	Launched	Commissioned
BIRINCI INÖNÜ (ex-USS *Threadfin, SS 410*)	S 346	Portsmouth Navy Yard	18 Mar 1944	26 June1944	30 Aug 1944
BURAK REIS (ex-USS *Seafox, SS 402*)	S 335	Portsmouth Navy Yard	2 Nov 1943	28 Mar 1944	13 June 1944
ÇERBE (ex-USS *Trutta, SS 421*)	S 340	Portsmouth Navy Yard	22 May 1944	22 May 1944	16 Nov 1944
MURAT REIS (ex-USS *Razorback, SS 394*)	S 336	Portsmouth Navy Yard	9 Sep 1943	27 Jan 1944	3 Apr 1944
ORUÇ REIS (ex-USS *Pomfret, SS 391*)	S 337	Portsmouth Navy Yard	14 July 1943	27 Oct 1943	19 Feb 1944
PREVEZE (ex-USS *Entemedor, SS 340*)	S 345	Electric Boat Co	3 Feb 1944	17 Dec 1944	6 Apr 1945
ULUÇ ALI REIS (ex-USS *Thornback, SS 418*)	S 338	Portsmouth Navy Yard	5 Apr 1944	7July 1944	13 Oct 1944

Displacement, tons: 1 840 standard; 2 445 dived
Dimensions, feet (metres): 306 × 27 × 17 *(93·2 × 8·2 × 5·2)*
Torpedo tubes: 10—21 in *(533 mm)* (6 bow, 4 stern); 24 torpedoes carried
Main machinery: 3 GM diesels; 4 800 hp; 2 electric motors; 5 400 hp
Speed, knots: 17 surfaced; 15 dived
Range, miles: 12 000 at 10 knots surfaced
Complement: 85

The fact that the same names are used for replacement submarines as for their predecessors can be confusing. eg *"Cerbe"* was used for both ex-USS *Hammerhead* and now for ex-USS *Trutta.*

Transfers: *Burak Reis* Dec 1970, *Murat Reis* 17 Nov 1970, *Oruç Reis* 3 May 1972, *Çerbe,* June 1972, *Preveze, Uluç Ali Reis* 24 Aug 1973, *Birinci Inönü* 15 Aug 1973.

ULUÇ ALI REIS   1975, Turkish Navy

2 Ex-US MODIFIED FLEET TYPE (Ex-"BALAO" CLASS)

Name	No.	Builders	Laid down	Launched	Commissioned
HIZIR REIS (ex-USS *Mero, SS 378*)	S 344	Manitowoc SB Co.	1944	17 Jan 1945	17 Aug 1945
TURGUT REIS (ex-USS *Bergall, SS 320*)	S 342	Electric Boat Co.	1943	16 Feb 1944	12 June 1944

Displacement, tons: 1 562 standard; 1 829 surfaced; 2 424 dived
Dimensions, feet (metres): 311·8 × 27·2 × 13·8 *(95 × 8·3 × 4·2)*
Torpedo tubes: 10—21 inch *(533 mm);* (6 bow, 4 stern) 24 torpedoes carried
Main machinery: 4 GM diesels; 6 400 shp; 2 electric motors; 5 400 shp
Speed, knots: 20 surfaced; 10 dived
Range, miles: 12 000 at 10 knots
Complement: 85

Streamlined boats of "Balao" class. Now becoming obsolescent. *Turgut Reis* purchased 15 Feb 1973 probably for spare parts eventually. *Hizir Reis* purchased Aug 1973.

Transfers: *Hizir Reis,* 20 April 1960; *Turgut Reis,* 17 Oct 1958.

LIGHT FORCES

4 LÜRSSEN TYPE (FAST ATTACK CRAFT—MISSILE)

Name	No.	Builders	Commissioned
DOĞAN	P 340	Lürssen, Vegesack	1976
MARTI	P 341	Taşkizak Yard, Istanbul	1977
TAYFUN	P 342	Taşkizak Yard, Istanbul	1977
VOLKAN	P 343	Taşkizak Yard, Istanbul	—

Displacement, tons: 410
Dimensions, feet (metres): 190·6 × 25 × 8·8 *(58·1 × 7·6 × 2·7)*
Missiles: 8—Harpoon
Gun: 1—76 mm OTO Melara; 2—35 mm (twin)
Main engines: 4—16 cyl MTU diesels; 18 000 hp = 38 knots
Range, miles: 700 at 35 knots

Ordered 3 Aug 1973. *Dogan* laid down 2 June 1975, *Marti* 1 July 1975, *Tayfun* 1 Dec 1975.

9 "KARTAL" CLASS
(FAST ATTACK CRAFT—MISSILE/TORPEDO)

Name	No.	Builders	Commissioned
ALBATROS	P 327 (ex-*P 325*)	Lürssen, Vegesack	1968
ATMACA	P 322 (ex-*P 335*)	Lürssen, Vegesack	1967
DENIZKUSU	P 321 (ex-*P 336*)	Lürssen, Vegesack	1967
KARTAL	P 324 (ex-*P 333*)	Lürssen, Vegesack	1967
KASIRGA	P 329 (ex-*P 338*)	Lürssen, Vegesack	1967
MELTEM	P 325 (ex-*P 330*)	Lürssen, Vegesack	1968
PELIKAN	P 326	Lürssen, Vegesack	1968
SAHIN	P 323 (ex-*P 334*)	Lürssen, Vegesack	1967
ŞIMŞEK	P 328 (ex-*P 332*)	Lürssen, Vegesack	1968

Displacement, tons: 160 standard; 180 full load
Dimensions, feet (metres): 140·5 × 23·5 × 7·2 *(42·8 × 7·1 × 2·2)*
Missiles: (see note)
Guns: 2—40 mm
Torpedo tubes: 4—21 inch
Main engines: 4 MTU 16V 538 (Maybach) diesels; 4 shafts; 12 000 bhp = 42 knots
Complement: 39

DENIZKUSU   *1975, Turkish Navy*

Of the German Jaguar type. Launch dates—*Atmaca* 6 May 1966, *Kartal* 4 Nov 1965, *Meltem* 28 Dec 1966.

Missiles: Harpoon surface-to-surface missiles embarked in *Albatros, Meltem, Pelikan* and *Şimşek* during 1975.

7 Ex-FDR "JAGUAR" CLASS
(FAST ATTACK CRAFT—TORPEDO)

Name	No.	Builders	Commissioned
FIRTINA (ex-*FDR Pelikan, P 6086*)	P 330	Lürssen, Vegesack	1962
KALKAN	P 335	Lürssen, Vegesack	—
KARAYEL	P 336	Lürssen, Vegesack	—
KILIÇ	P 332	Lürssen, Vegesack	—
MIZRAK	P 333	Lürssen, Vegesack	—
TUFAN (ex-*FDR Storch, P 6085*)	P 331	Lürssen, Vegesack	1962
YILDIZ	P 334	Lürssen, Vegesack	—

Displacement, tons: 160 standard; 190 full load
Dimensions, feet (metres): 139·4 × 23·4 × 7·9 *(42·5 × 7·2 × 2·4)*
Guns: 2—40 mm L 70 Bofors (single)
Torpedo tubes: 4—21 inch (2 tubes can be removed to embark 4 mines)
Main engines: 4 Maybach (MTU) diesels; 4 shafts; 12 000 bhp = 42 knots
Complement: 39

In late 1975-early 1976 seven "Jaguar" class were transferred by the FDR to Turkey—*Häher* P 6087, *Löew* P 6065, *Pelikan* P 6086, *Pinguin* P 6090, *Storch* P 6085, *Tiger* P 6063, and *Wolf* P 6062. In addition three more were transferred for spare parts—*Alk* P 6084, *Fuchs* P 6066 and *Reiher* P 6089.

FIRTINA   *1976, Reinhard Nerlich*

? "NASTY" CLASS (FAST ATTACK CRAFT—TORPEDO)

Name	No.	Builders	Commissioned
GIRNE	P—	Taskizak Naval Yard	1975

Displacement, tons: 74·5
Dimensions, feet (metres): 80·4 × 21 × 3·8 *(24·5 × 6·4 × 1·2)*
Guns: 2—40 mm
Torpedo tubes: 4—21 inch *(533 mm)*
Main engines: 2 Deltic diesels; 6 200 hp = 44 knots
Range, miles: 450 at 38 knots
Complement: 20

First of a series currently under construction.

2 Ex-US "ASHEVILLE" CLASS (LARGE PATROL CRAFT)

Name	No.	Builders	Commissioned
BORA (ex-USS *Surprise, PG 97)*	P 339	Petersons, Wisconsin	17 Oct 1969
YILDIRIM (ex-USS *Defiance, PG 95)*	P 338	Petersons, Wisconsin	24 Sep 1969

Displacement, tons: 225 standard; 245 full load
Dimensions, feet (metres): 164·5 oa × 23·8 × 9·5 *(50·1 × 7·3 × 2·9)*
Guns: 1—3 in 50 cal; 1—40 mm; 4—50 cal MG
Main engines: CODAG; 2 Cummins Diesels; 1 450 hp = 16 knots; 1 GE gas turbine; 13 300 shp = 40 knots
Complement: 25

These vessels belong to the largest Patrol Type built by the USN since World War II and the first of that Navy to have gas turbines. Transferred to Turkey on 28th Feb 1973 and 11 June 1973 respectively.

BORA (as *Surprise)*   1975, Turkish Navy

6 Ex-US "PC 173 ft" CLASS (LARGE PATROL CRAFT)

Name	No.	Builders	Commissioned
AKHISAR (ex-PC 1641)	P 114	Gunderson Bros Engineering Co, Portland, Oregon	1943
DEMIRHISAR (ex-PC 1639)	P 112	Gunderson Bros Engineering Co, Portland, Oregon	1943
KOÇHISAR (ex-PC 1643)	P 116	Gölcük Dockyard, Turkey	1965
SIVRIHISAR (ex-PC 1642)	P 115	Gunderson Bros Engineering Co, Portland, Oregon	1943
SULTAN HISAR (ex-PC 1638)	P 111	Gunderson Bros Engineering Co, Portland, Oregon	1943
YARHISAR (ex-PC 1640)	P 113	Gunderson Bros Engineering Co, Portland, Oregon	1943

Displacement, tons: 280 standard; 412 full load
Dimensions, feet (metres): 173·7 oa × 23 × 10·2 *(54 × 7 × 3·1)*
Guns: 1—3 inch; 1—40 mm
A/S weapons: 4 DCT; 1 Hedgehog
Main engines: 2 FM diesels; 2 shafts; 2 800 bhp = 19 knots
Range, miles: 6 000 at 10 knots
Complement: 65 (5 officers, and 60 men)

Transferred on 3 Dec 1964, 22 April 1965, July 1965, June 1965, May 1964 and Sep 1964 respectively.

DEMIRHISAR   1975, Turkish Navy

10 LARGE PATROL CRAFT

Name	No.	Builders	Commissioned
AB 25	P 1225	Taskizak Naval Yard	1967
AB 26	P 1226	Taskizak Naval Yard	1967
AB 27	P 1227	Taskizak Naval Yard	1967
AB 28	P 1228	Taskizak Naval Yard	1968
AB 29	P 1229	Taskizak Naval Yard	1968
AB 30	P 1230	Taskizak Naval Yard	1969
AB 31	P 1231	Taskizak Naval Yard	1969
AB 32	P 1232	Taskizak Naval Yard	1970
AB 33	P 1233	Taskizak Naval Yard	1970
AB 34	P 1234	Taskizak Naval Yard	1970

Displacement, tons: 170
Dimensions, feet (metres): 132 × 21 × 5·5 *(40·2 × 6·4 × 1·7)*
Guns: 2—40 mm
Speed, knots: 22

AB 28 (Old pennant number)   1970, Turkish Navy

First was launched on 9 Mar 1967. Six similar launches are operated by the Gendarmerie.

4 US PGM TYPE (LARGE PATROL CRAFT)

Name	No.	Builders	Commissioned
AB 21 (ex-PGM 104)	P 1221	Peterson, Sturgeon Bay, USA	Dec 1967
AB 22 (ex-PGM 105)	P 1222	Peterson, Sturgeon Bay, USA	Dec 1967
AB 23 (ex-PGM 106)	P 1223	Peterson, Sturgeon Bay, USA	Dec 1967
AB 24 (ex-PGM 108)	P 1224	Peterson, Sturgeon Bay, USA	April 1968

Displacement, tons: 130 standard; 147 full load
Dimensions, feet (metres): 101 × 21 × 7 *(30·8 × 6·4 × 1·9)*
Guns: 1—40 mm; 4—20 mm
Main engines: 2 diesels; 2 shafts; 1 850 hp = 18·5 knots
Range, miles: 1 500 at 10 knots
Complement: 15

AB 23 (Old pennant number)   1970, Turkish Navy

19 LARGE PATROL CRAFT

Name	No.	Builders	Commissioned
—	J 12	Schweers, Bardenfleth	1961
—	J 13	Schweers, Bardenfleth	1961
—	J 14	Schweers, Bardenfleth	1961
—	J 15	Schweers, Bardenfleth	1961
—	J 16	Schweers, Bardenfleth	1962
—	J 17	Schweers, Bardenfleth	1962
—	J 18	Schweers, Bardenfleth	1962
—	J 19	Schweers, Bardenfleth	1962
—	J 20	Schweers, Bardenfleth	1962
—	J 21	Gölcük Navy Yard	1968
—	J 22	Gölcük Navy Yard	1968
—	J 23	Taskizak Naval Yard	1969
—	J 24	Taskizak Naval Yard	1969
—	J 25	Taskizak Naval Yard	1969
—	J 26	Taskizak Naval Yard	1969
—	J 27	Taskizak Naval Yard	1969
—	J 28	Taskizak Naval Yard	1970
—	J 29	Taskizak Naval Yard	1971
—	J 30	Taskizak Naval Yard	1971

J TYPE   1976, Michael D. J. Lennon

Displacement, tons: 150
Dimensions, feet (metres): 129·3 × 20·6 × 4·9 *(39·4 × 6·3 × 1·5)*
Guns: 2—40 mm
Main engines: 4 MTU 12V 493 diesels; 2 shafts; 3 200 bhp = 22 knots

Some operated by Gendarmerie.

1 + 13 SAR 33 TYPE (LARGE PATROL CRAFT)

Dimensions, feet (metres): 108·3 × 28·3 × 9·7 *(33 × 8·6 × 3)*
Main engines: 3 SCAM diesels; 12 000 hp = 40 knots
Range, miles: 450 at 35 knots

Prototype ordered from Abeking and Rasmussen, Lemwerder in May 1976. If successful, remaining 13 will be built in Turkey. Ordered for Gendarmerie.

4 Ex-US COASTGUARD "83 ft" CLASS
(COASTAL PATROL CRAFT)

LS 9 P 1209 (ex-US *A 001*)   **LS 11** P 1211 (ex-US *C 001*)
LS 10 P 1210 (ex-US *B 001*)   **LS 12** P 1212 (ex-US *D 001*)

Displacement, tons: 63 standard
Dimensions, feet (metres): 83·0 × 14·0 × 5·0 *(25·3 × 4·3 × 1·6)*
Gun: 1—20 mm
A/S weapons: 2 Mousetrap
Main engines: 2 Cummins diesels; 1 100 bhp = 20 knots

Transferred on 25 June 1953.

MINE WARFARE FORCES

1 MINELAYER

Name	No.	Builders	Commissioned
NUSRET	N 110 (ex-*N 108*)	Frederikshaven Dockyard, Denmark	16 Sep 1964

Displacement, tons: 1 880 standard
Length, feet (metres): 246 *(75·0)* pp; 252·7 *(77·0)* oa
Beam, feet (metres): 41 *(12·6)*
Draught, feet (metres): 11 *(3·4)*
Guns: 4—3 in *(76 mm)* (2 twin)
Mines: 400
Main engines: GM diesels; 4 800 hp; 2 shafts
Speed, knots: 18
Complement: 146

Laid down in 1962, launched in 1964. Similar to Danish "Falster" class.

Radar: Search: RAN 7S.
Fire Control: I Band.
Navigation Radar.

NUSRET   1975, Turkish Navy

2 Ex-US LST TYPE (COASTAL MINELAYERS)

BAYRAKTAR
(ex-FDR *Bottrop*, ex-USS *Saline County L 1101*) A 403 (ex-N-111, ex-A 579)
SANCAKTAR
(ex-FDR *Bochum*, ex-USS *Rice County L 1089*) A 404 (ex-N-112, ex-A 580)

Displacement, tons: 1 653 standard; 4 080 full load
Dimensions, feet (metres): 328 oa × 50 × 14 *(100 × 15·2 × 4·3)*
Guns: 6—40 mm (2 twin, 2 single)
Main engines: 2 GM diesels; 2 shafts; 1 700 bhp = 11 knots
Range, miles: 15 000 at 9 knots
Complement: 125

Formerly USN LSTs, transferred to West Germany in 1961 and thence to Turkey on 13 Dec 1972. Converted into minelayers in West Germany 1962-64. Present employment uncertain due to double change of pennant numbers to A superior.

BAYRAKTAR (Old pennant number)   1973, Reinhard Nerlich

5 Ex-US LSM TYPE (COASTAL MINELAYERS)

Name	No.	Builders	Commissioned
MARMARIS (ex-US *LSM 481*, ex-*MMC 10*)	N 103	U.S.A.	1945
MERIÇ(ex-US *LSM 490*, ex-*MMC 12*)	N 102	U.S.A.	1945
MERSIN (ex-US *LSM 494*, ex-*MMC 13*)	N 104	U.S.A.	1945
MORDOĞAN (ex-US *LSM 484* ex-*MMC 11*)	N 101	U.S.A.	1945
MÜREFTE (ex-US *LSM 492*, ex-*MMC 14*)	N 105	U.S.A.	1945

Displacement, tons: 743 standard; 1 100 full load
Dimensions, feet (metres): 203·2 oa × 34·5 × 8·5 *(61·9 × 10·5 × 2·4)*
Guns: 2—40 mm; 2—20 mm
Main engines: Diesels; 2 shafts; 2 880 bhp = 12 knots
Oil fuel, tons: 60
Range, miles: 2 500 at 12 knots
Complement: 89

Ex-US Landing Ships Medium. All launched in 1945, converted into coastal minelayers by the US Navy in 1952 and taken over by the Turkish Navy (LSM 481, 484 and 490) and the Norwegian Navy (LSM 492 and 494) in Oct 1952 under MAP. LSM 492 *(Vale)* and LSM 494 *(Vidar)* were retransferred to the Turkish Navy on 1 Nov 1960, at Bergen, Norway.

MERIÇ   *1975, Turkish Navy*

1 Ex-US YMP TYPE (COASTAL MINELAYEER)

Name	No.	Builders	Commissioned
MEHMETCIK (ex-US *YMP 3*)	N 115	Higgins Inc, New Orleans	1958

Displacement, tons: 540 full load
Dimensions, feet (metres): 130 × 35 × 6 *(39·6 × 10·7 × 1·9)*
Main engines: Diesels; 2 shafts; 600 bhp = 10 knots
Complement: 22

Former US motor mine planter. Steel hulled. Transferred under MAP in 1958. For harbour defence.

MEHMETCIK (old pennant number)

12 Ex-US MSC TYPE (MINESWEEPERS—COASTAL)

SAMSUN (ex-USS *MSC 268*)｣M 510   **SEYHAN** (ex-*MSC 142*) M 509
SAPANCA (ex-USS *MSC 312*) M 517   **SEYMEN** (ex-*MSC 131*) M 507
SARIYER (ex-USS *MSC 315*) M 518   **SIGACIK** (ex-USS *MSC 311*) M 516
SAROS (ex-USS *MSC 305*) M 515   **SILIFKE** (ex-USS *MSC 304*) M 514
SEDDULBAHIR (ex-*MSC 272*) M 513   **SINOP** (ex-USS *MSC 270*) M 511
SELCUK (ex-*MSC 124*) M 508   **SURMENE** (ex-USS *MSC 271*) M 512

Displacement, tons: 320 standard; 370 full load
Dimensions, feet (metres): 138·0 pp; 144·0 oa × 28·0 × 9·0 *(41·5; 43 × 8 × 2·6)*
Guns: 2—20 mm
Main engines: 2 diesels; 2 shafts; 1 200 bhp = 14 knots
Oil fuel, tons: 25
Range, miles: 2 500 at 10 knots
Complement: 38 (4 officers, 34 men)

Transferred on 30 Sep 1958, 26 July 1965, 8 Sep 1967, Feb 1966, May 1959, 24 Mar 1970, 24 Mar 1970, 19 Nov 1970, June 1965, Sep 1965, Feb 1959, 27 Mar 1959, respectively. *Selcuk* and *Seyhan* were transferred from France (via USA) and *Seyman* from Belgium (via USA).

SURMENE   *1975, Turkish Navy*

4 Ex-CANADIAN MCB TYPE (MINESWEEPERS—COASTAL)

TIREBOLU (ex-HMCS *Comax*) M 532   **TERME** (ex-HMCS *Trinity*) M 531
TEKIRDAG (ex-HMCS *Ungava*) M 533   **TRABZON** (ex-HMCS *Gaspe*) M 530

Displacement, tons: 390 standard; 412 full load
Dimensions, feet (metres): 152·0 oa × 20·8 × 7·0 *(50 × 9·2 × 2·8)*
Gun: 1—40 mm
Main engines: Diesels; 2 shafts; 2 400 bhp = 16 knots
Oil fuel, tons: 52
Range, miles: 4 500 at 11 knots
Complement: 44

Sailed from Sydney, Nova Scotia, to Turkey on 19 May 1958. Built by Davie SB Co. 1951-53. Of similar type to British "Ton" class.

5 Ex-FDR "VEGESACK" CLASS (MINESWEEPERS—COASTAL)

Name	No.	Builders	Commissioned
KARAMÜRSEL (ex-*Worms M 1253*)	M 520	Cherbourg	1960
KEREMPE (ex-*Detmold M 1252*)	M 521	Cherbourg	1960
KILIMLI (ex-*Siegen M 1254*)	M 522	Cherbourg	1960
KOZLU (ex-*Hameln M 1251*)	M 523	Cherbourg	1960
KUŞADASI (ex-*Vegesack M 1250*)	M 524	Cherbourg	1960

Displacement, tons: 362 standard; 378 full load
Dimensions, feet (metres): 144·3 × 26·2 × 9 *(47·3 × 8·6 × 2·9)*
Guns: 2—20 mm
Main engines: 2 Mercedes Benz (MTU) diesels; 2 shafts; 1 500 bhp = 15 knots (cp propellers)

Of similar class to French *Mercure*. Transferred by FDR to Turkey late 1975-early 1976.

KARAMÜRSEL (*Kerempe* behind)   *8/1975, Reinhard Nerlich*

4 Ex-US MINESWEEPERS—INSHORE

Name	No.	Builders	Commissioned
FATSA (ex-*MSI 17*)	M 502	USA	Sep 1967
FETHIYE (ex-*MSI 16*)	M 501	USA	Aug 1967
FINIKE (ex-*MSI 18*)	M 503	Peterson Builders Inc	8 Nov 1967
FOÇA (ex-*MSI 15*)	M 500	USA	Aug 1967

Displacement, tons: 180 standard; 235 full load
Dimensions, feet (metres): 111·9 × 23·5 × 7·9 *(34× 7·1 × 2·4)*
Gun: 1—·50 cal
Main engines: 4 diesels; 2 shafts; 960 bhp = 13 knots
Complement: 30

Built in USA and transferred under MAP at Boston, Mass, Aug-Dec 1967.

FOÇA   *1970, Turkish Navy*

9 MINEHUNTING BOATS

MTB 1 P 311	MTB 3 P 313	MTB 6 P 316
MTB 2 P 312	MTB 4 P 314	MTB 7 P 317

MTB 8 P 318
MTB 9 P 319
MTB 10 P 320

Displacement, tons: 70 standard
Dimensions, feet (metres): 71·5 × 13·8 × 8·5 *(21·8 × 4·2 × 2·6)*
Main engines: Diesel; 2 000 bhp = 20 knots

All launched in 1942. Now employed as minehunting base ships.

MTB 10   *1972, Turkish Navy*

AMPHIBIOUS FORCES

2 Ex-US LSTs

Name	No.	Builders	Commissioned
ERTUĞRUL	L 401	Christy Corp	1954
(ex-USS *Windham County*, LST 1170)			
SERDAR	L 402	Christy Corp	1954
(ex-USS *Westchester County*, LST 1167)			

Displacement, tons: 2 590 light; 5 800 full load
Dimensions, feet (metres): 384 oa × 55 × 17 *(117·4 × 16·8 × 3·7)*
Guns: 6—3 in 50 cal (twins)
Main engines: 4 GM diesels; 2 shafts (cp propellers); 6 000 bhp = 15 knots
Complement: 116
Troops: 395

Transferred by US June 1973. (L 401) and 27 Aug 1974 (L 402).

ERTUĞRUL   *1975, Turkish Navy*

5 Ex-BRITISH LCTs

C 101 and 103-106

Displacement, tons: 500 light; 700 full load
Dimensions, feet (metres): 180·9 × 27·7 × 5·4 *(55·2 × 8·4 × 1·6)*
Guns: 2—20 mm
Complement: 15

Built in UK in 1942. Transferred 25 Sep 1967.

C 104   *1975, Turkish Navy*

12 TURKISH-BUILT LCTs

C 107-118

Displacement, tons: 400 light; 600 full load
Dimensions, feet (metres): 180·9 × 36·8 × 4·8 *(55·2 × 11·2 × 1·4)*
Guns: 2—20 mm
Speed, knots: 10·5
Complement: 15

Built in Turkey 1966-1973. Of French EDIC type.

12 TURKISH-BUILT LCUs

C 205-216

Displacement, tons: 320 light; 405 full load
Dimensions, feet (metres): 142 × 28 × 5·7 *(43·3 × 8·5 × 1·7)*
Guns: 2—20 mm
Main engines: GM diesels; 2 shafts; 600 bhp = 10 knots

Built in Turkey 1965-66. Of US LCU type.

C 207   *1975, Turkish Navy*

C201-204 (ex-US *LCU 588, 608, 666* and *667)*

Displacement, tons: 160 light; 320 full load
Dimensions, feet (metres): 119 oa × 32·7 × 5 *(36·3 × 10 × 1·5)*
Guns: 2—20 mm
Main engines: 3 diesels; 675 bhp = 10 knots
Complement: 13

Transferred from USA July 1967.

4 Ex-US LCU 501 SERIES

C 204 · 1975, Turkish Navy

20 TURKISH-BUILT LCM 8 TYPE

C 301-320

Displacement, tons: 58 light; 113 full load
Dimensions, feet (metres): 72 × 20·5 × 4·8 *(22 × 6·3 × 1·4)*
Guns: 2—12·7 mm
Main engines: GM diesels; 2 shafts; 660 bhp = 9·5 knots
Complement: 9

Built in Turkey in 1965.

C 302 · 1975, Turkish Navy

SURVEY SHIPS

2 "CANDARLI" CLASS

ÇANDARLI (ex-US *BAM 28)* A 593   **ÇARSAMBA** (ex-US *BAM 32)* A 594

Displacement, tons: 1 125 full load
Dimensions, feet (metres): 221 oa × 32 × 10·8 *(67·4 × 9·8 × 3·3)*
Main engines: Diesel electric; 2 shafts; 3 500 bhp
Speed, knots: 18
Complement: 98 (8 officers, 90 ratings)

Ex-US "Auk" class minesweepers. Both launched in 1942, they are the survivors of a class of seven transferred via UK in 1947.

"CANDARLI" Class

MESAHA 1 and 2

Of 45 tons with a complement of 8—built in 1966.

SERVICE FORCES

1 Ex-FDR DEPOT SHIP

Name	No.	Builders	Commissioned
— (ex-FDR *Ruhr)*	A 579	Schiekerwerft, Hamburg	1963

Displacement, tons: 2 370 standard; 2 540 full load
Dimensions, feet (metres): 323·5 oa × 38·8 × 11·2 *(99 × 11·8 × 3·4)*
Guns: 2—3·9 in *(100 mm)*
Main engines: 6 diesels; 11 400 bhp; 2 shafts
Speed, knots: 20·5
Range, miles: 1 625 at 15 knots
Complement: 110 (accommodation for 200)

Radar: Search: HSA DA 02.
Fire Control: Two HSA M 45.

Transfer: Late 1975.

Ex-*Ruhr* · 12/1976, Roland Wiegran

1 SUPPORT TANKER

Name	No.	Builders	Commissioned
BINBASI SAADETTIN GÜRÇAN	A 573	Taskizak Naval DY, Istanbul	1970

Displacement, tons: 1 505 standard; 4 460 full load
Dimensions, feet (metres): 299 × 39·4 × 18 *(89·7 × 11·8 × 5·4)*
Main engines: Diesels; 4 400 bhp

Launched 1 July 1969.

BINBASI SAADETTIN GÜRÇAN · 9/1976, Michael D. J. Lennon

1 SUPPORT TANKER

ALBAY HAKKI BURAK A 572

Displacement, tons: 3 800 full load
Dimensions, feet (metres): 274·7 oa × 40·2 × 18 *(83·7 × 12·3 × 5·5)*
Main engines: 2 GM diesels; electric drive; 4 400 bhp = 16 knots
Complement: 88

Built in 1964.

ALBAY HAKKI BURAK   *1975, Turkish Navy*

1 SUPPORT TANKER

Name	No.	Builders	Commissioned
YUZBASI TOLUNAY	A 571	Taşkizak, Naval DY, Istanbul	1951

Displacement, tons: 2 500 standard; 3 500 full load
Dimensions, feet (metres): 260 × 41 × 19·5 *(79 × 12·4 × 5·9)*
Main engines: Atlas-Polar diesels; 2 shafts; 1 920 bhp = 14 knots

Launched on 22 Aug 1950.

YUZBASI TOLUNAY   *1975, Turkish Navy*

1 Ex-US SUPPORT TANKER

Name	No.	Builders	Commissioned
AKPINAR (ex-*Chiwankum, AOG 26*)	A 574	East Coast S.Y. Inc, Bayonne	22 July 1944

Displacement, tons: 700 light; 2 700 full load
Measurement, feet (metres): 1 453 deadweight
Dimensions, feet (metres): 212·5 wl; 220·5 oa × 37 × 12·8 *(64·8; 67·3 × 11·3 × 3·9)*
Main engines: Diesel; 800 bhp = 10 knots

Formerly the United States oiler *AOG 26*. Laid down on 2 April 1944. Launched on 5 May 1944. Transferred to Turkey in May 1948.

AKPINAR   *1975, Turkish Navy*

1 Ex-US REPAIR SHIP

DONATAN (ex-USS *Anthedon, AS 24*) A 583

Displacement, tons: 8 100 standard
Dimensions, feet (metres): 492 × 69·5 × 26·5 *(150 × 21·8 × 8·1)*
Main engines: Geared turbines; 1 shaft; 8 500 shp = 14·4 knots
Boilers: 2

Former US submarine tender of the "Aegir" class transferred to Turkey on 7 Feb 1969.

DONATAN   *1972, Turkish Navy*

2 Ex-US REPAIR SHIPS

Name	No.	Builders	Commissioned
BAŞARAN (ex-*Patroclus, ARL 19,* ex-*LST 955*)	A 582	Bethlehem Hingham Shipyard	1945
ONARAN (ex-*Alecto, AGP 14,* ex-*LST 558*)	A 581	Missouri Valley Bridge & Iron Co.	1945

Displacement, tons: 1 625 standard; 4 080 full load
Dimensions, feet (metres): 328 oa × 50 × 14 *(100 × 15·2 × 4·4)*
Guns: 2—40 mm; 8—20 mm
Main engines: Diesel; 2 shafts; 1 700 bhp = 11 knots
Oil fuel, tons: 1 000
Range, miles: 9 000 at 9 knots
Complement: 80

Former US repair ship and MTB tender, respectively of the LST type. *Basaran* was launched on 22 Oct 1944, *Onaran* on 14 April 1944. Acquired from the USA in Nov 1952 and May 1948, respectively.

ONARAN   *1973, Dr. Giorgio Arra*

1 HARBOUR TANKER

Name	No.	Builders	Commissioned
GÖLÇÜK (ex-*A 573*)	Y 1207	Gölcük Dockyard	1954

Displacement, tons: 1 255
Measurement, feet: 750 deadweight
Dimensions, feet (metres): 185 × 31·1 × 10 *(56·4 × 9·5 × 3·1)*
Main engines: B & W diesel; 700 bhp = 12·5 knots

Launched on 4 Nov 1953.

1 SUBMARINE DEPOT SHIP

ERKIN (ex-*Trabzon,* ex-*Imperial*) A 591

Dimensions, feet (metres): 441 × 58·5 × 23 *(133 × 17·5 × 7)*
Guns: 2—40 mm
Speed, knots: 16
Complement: 128

Built in 1938. Purchased in 1968 and placed on the Navy list in 1970.

1 SUBMARINE RESCUE SHIP

KURTARAN (ex-USS *Bluebird, ASR 19,* ex-*Yurak AT 165)* A 584

Displacement, tons: 1 294 standard; 1 675 full load
Dimensions, feet (metres): 205·0 oa × 38·5 × 11·0 *(62·5 × 12·2 × 3·5)*
Guns: 1—3 inch; 2—40 mm
Main engines: Diesel-electric; 3 000 bhp = 16 knots

Former salvage tug adapted as a submarine rescue vessel in 1947. Transferred from the US Navy on 15 Aug 1950.

KURTARAN 9/1976, Michael D. J. Lennon

2 Ex-US "CHANTICLEER" CLASS (SUBMARINE RESCUE SHIPS)

Name	No.	Builders	Commissioned
AKIN (ex-USS *Greenlet, ASR 10)* A585		Moore SB & DD Co.	1942
— (ex-USS *Tringa, ASR 16)*	—	Savannah M & F Co	1947

Displacement, tons: 1 770 standard; 2 321 full load
Dimensions, feet (metres): 251·3 × 42·2 × 14·7 *(75·5 × 12·7 × 4·3)*
Guns: 1—40 mm; 2—20 mm (twin)
Main engines: Diesel-electric; 1 shaft; 3 000 bhp = 15 knots
Complement: 85

Akin transferred 12 June 1970 and purchased 15 Feb 1973. USS *Tringa* transferred 1977.

2 Ex-FDR "ANGELN" CLASS (SUPPLY SHIPS)

Name	No.	Builders	Commissioned
ULKU (ex-*FDR Angeln)*	A 586	A. C. de Bretagne	1955
KANARYA (ex-*FDR Dithmarschen)*	A 588	A. C. de Bretagne	1956

Displacement, tons: 2 600 full load
Dimensions, feet (metres): 296·9 × 43·6 × 20·3 *(90·5 × 13·3 × 6·2)*
Main engines: Pielstick Diesel; 1 shaft; 3 000 bhp = 17 knots
Complement: 57

Ex-cargo ships bought by FDR in 1959. Transferred 22 March 1972 and late 1975.

KANARYA 12/1976, Roland Wiegran

4 TRANSPORTS

ERDEK Y 1164   **KILYA** Y 1166   **LAPSEKI** Y 1163   **TUZLA** Y 1168

Measurement, tons: 700
Dimensions, feet (metres): 183·7 × 37·2 × 8·9 *(56 × 12·2 × 2·7)*
Main engines: Steam; 700 hp = 9·5 knots

Have a minelaying capability. Survivors of a class of eleven car-ferries built in UK. 1940-1942.

2 TRANSPORTS

Y 1204 (ex-US *APL 47)*
Y 1205 (ex-US *APL 53)*

Transferred: Y 1204 on Oct 1972 and Y 1205 on 6 Dec 1974.

2 WATER TANKERS

Name	No.	Builders	Commissioned
ULABAT	Y 1209	Gölcük Dockyard	1969
VAN	Y 1208	Gölcük Dockyard	1970

Displacement, tons: 1 200
Main engines: Designed for a speed of 14·5 knots

Two small tankers for the Turkish Navy built in 1968-70.

1 WATER TANKER

SOGUT (ex-FDR *FW 6)* Y 1217

Measurement, tons: 350 dw
Dimensions, feet (metres): 144·4 × 25·6 × 8·2 *(44·1 × 7·8 × 2·5)*
Main engines: MWM diesels; 230 bhp = 9·5 knots

Transferred by W. Germany late 1975.

SOGUT 9/1976, Michael D. J. Lennon·

BOOM DEFENCE VESSELS

Name	No.	Builders	Commissioned
AG 6 (ex-USS *Butternut, AN 93,* ex-Netherlands *Cerberus, A 895*)	P 306	Bethlehem Steel Co, Staten Island	10 Nov 1952

Displacement, tons: 780 standard; 902 full load
Dimensions, feet (metres): 165·0 × 33·0 × 10·0 *(50·8 × 10·4 × 3·1)*
Guns: 1—3 in; 4—20 mm ·
Main engines: Diesel-electric; 1 shaft; 1 500 bhp = 12·8 knots

Netlayer. Launched in May 1952. Transferred from USA to Netherlands in Dec 1952. Used first as a boom defence vessel and latterly as salvage and diving tender since 1961 but retained her netlaying capacity. Handed back to USN on 17 Sep 1970 but immediately turned over to the Turkish Navy.

AG 6   *1975, Turkish Navy*

Name	No.	Builders	Commissioned
AG 5 (ex-*AN 104*)	P 305	Kröger, Rendsburg	5 Feb 1961

Displacement, tons: 680 standard; 860 full load
Dimensions, feet (metres): 148·7 pp; 173·8 oa × 35·0 × 13·5 *(52·5 × 10·5 × 4·1)*
Guns: 1—40 mm; 3—20 mm
Main engines: 4 MAN diesels; 2 shafts; 1 450 bhp = 12 knots

Netlayer *AN 104* built in US off-shore programme for Turkey. Launched on 20 Oct 1960.

Name	No.	Builders	Commissioned
AG 4 (ex-*Larch*, ex-*AN 21*)	P 304	American SB Co, Cleveland	1941

Displacement, tons: 560 standard; 805 full load
Dimensions, feet (metres): 163·0 oa × 30·5 × 10·5 *(50 × 9·3 × 3·2)*
Gun: 1—3 inch
Main engines: Diesel-electric; 800 bhp = 12 knots

Former US netlayer of the "Aloe" class. Laid down in 1940. Launched on 2 July 1941. Acquired in May 1946.

AG 4   *1969*

1 "BAR" CLASS

Name	No.	Builders	Commissioned
AG 1 (ex-*Barbarian*)	P 301	Blyth SB Co	1938

Displacement, tons: 750 standard; 1 000 full load
Dimensions, feet (metres): 150·0 pp; 173·8 oa × 32·2 × 9·5 *(52·9 × 9·4 × 2·7)*
Gun: 1—3 inch
Main engines: Triple expansion; 850 ihp = 11·5 knots
Boilers: 2 SE

Former British boom defence vessel.

3 GATE VESSELS

KAPI, I, II, III (Y 1201, 1202, 1203)

Displacement, tons: 360
Dimensions, feet (metres): 102·7 × 34 × 4·7 *(30·8 × 10·2 × 1·3)*

These gate vessels were built by US for Turkey under MAP. Transferred Mar 1961.

TUGS

1 OCEAN TUG

GAZAL (ex-USS *Sioux ATF 75*) A 587

Displacement, tons: 1 235 standard; 1 675 full load
Dimensions, feet (metres): 205 oa × 38·5 × 16 *(60·7 × 11·6 × 4·7)*
Gun: 1—3 inch
Main engines: Diesel electric; 3 000 bhp = 16 knots
Complement: 85

Transferred 30 Oct 1972. Purchased 15 Aug 1973.

2 HARBOUR TUGS

AKBAS Y 1118   **KEPEZ** Y 1119

Displacement, tons: 971
Dimensions, feet (metres): 149 × 33·9 × 14 *(44·7 × 10·2 × 4·3)*
Speed, knots: 12

2 Ex-US "YTL" TYPE (HARBOUR TUGS)

SONDUREN (ex-US *YTL 751*) Y 1117   **YEDEKCI** (ex-US *YTL 155*) Y 1121

Transferred July 1957 and Nov. 1954.

1 HARBOUR TUG

ÖNCU Y 1123

Displacement, tons: 500
Speed, knots: 12

US harbour tug ex-*YTL 155*, transferred under MAP.

1 Ex-US HARBOUR TUG

KUVVET (ex-US *ATA*) Y 1122

Displacement, tons: 390
Dimensions, feet (metres): 107 × 26·5 × 12 *(32·1 × 8 × 3·6)*

Transferred Feb 1962.

1 HARBOUR TUG

KUDRET Y 1129

Displacement, tons: 128
Dimensions, feet (metres): 65 × 19·6 × 9 *(21·3 × 6·4 × 2·9)*

FLOATING DOCKS

Y 1081

16 000 tons lift.

Y 1083 (ex-US *AFDL*)

2 500 tons lift.

Y 1085

400 tons lift.

Y 1087 (ex-US *ARD 12*)

3 500 tons lift. Transferred Nov 1971.

Y 1082

12 000 tons lift.

Y 1084

4 500 tons lift.

Y 1086

3 000 tons lift.

MISCELLANEOUS

Note: Others listed but not identified; *Ersen Bayrak* Y 1134, L-1 *Samandira* Y 1148, L-2 *Samandira* Y 1149, *Odev* Y 1228.

1 SMALL TRANSPORT

SARKÖY Y 1156

1 HARBOUR PATROL CRAFT

Y 1223

1 NAVAL DREDGER

TARAK

Of 200 tons.

1 FLOATING CRANE

ALGARNA III Y 1023 (ex-US *YD 185*)

Transferred Sep 1963.

TRAINING SHIPS

Name	No.	Builders	Commissioned
SAVARONA	A 575	Blohm & Voss, Hamburg	1932

Displacement, tons: 5 100
Length, feet (metres): 349·5 *(106·5)* wl; 408·5 *(124·5)* oa
Beam, feet (metres): 53 *(16·2)*
Draught, feet (metres): 20·5 *(6·2)*
Guns: 4—3 in *(76 mm)* 2—40 mm; 2—20 mm
Main engines: 6 geared turbines; 2 shafts; 10 750 shp
Boilers: 4 watertube (400 psi)
Speed, knots: 18
Oil fuel, tons: 2 100
Range, miles: 9 000 at 15 knots
Complement: 132 + 81 midshipmen

Launched on 28 Feb 1931. Formerly probably the most sumptuously fitted yacht afloat. Equipment includes Sperry gyro-stablisers. Converted into a training ship in 1952, the saloons and dining rooms being adapted as classrooms, workshops and libraries for midshipmen.

SAVARONA   8/1976, Wright and Logan

CEZAYIRLI GAZI HASAN PAŞA

General training ship.

UNITED ARAB EMIRATES

This federation of the former Trucial States (Abu Dhabi, Ajman, Dubai, Fujairah, Ras al Khaimah, Sharjah, Umm al Qaiwan) was formed under a provisional constitution in 1971 with a new constitution coming into effect on Dec 2 1976.

A decision of the UAE Supreme Defence Council on 6 May 1976 brought about the unification of the armed forces of the member states with the overall control of land forces exercised by General Headquarters at Abu Dhabi through three regional HQs and a separate Brigade HQ. Abu Dhabi was the only state with a true naval force whilst Dubai, Ras al Khaimah and Sharjah had marine police forces. All UAE marine police forces are now under the control of the Ministry of the Interior, Sharjah. A considerable expansion of this Border Guard force is envisioned although not yet at the stage of definite proposals.

UNITED KINGDOM

Admiralty Board

Secretary of State for Defence (Chairman):
  The Right Honourable Mr F. W. Mulley, PC, MP
Minister of State: Ministry of Defence (Vice-Chairman) and Minister of State for Defence Procurement:
  Dr J. W. Gilbert, MP
Parliamentary Under-Secretary of State for Defence for the Royal Navy:
  Dr Patrick Duffy, MP
Chief of the Naval Staff and First Sea Lord:
  Admiral Sir Terence Lewin, GCB, MVO, DSC
Chief of Naval Personnel and Second Sea Lord:
  Vice-Admiral Sir Gordon Tait, KCB, DSC
Controller of the Navy:
  Vice-Admiral R. P. Clayton
Chief of Fleet Support:
  Vice-Admiral J. H. F. Eberle
Vice-Chief of the Naval Staff:
  Admiral R. D. Lygo
Chief Scientist (Royal Navy): Mr Basil Wilfred Lythall, CB, MA
Deputy Under Secretary of State (Navy): Mr Sydney Redman, CB
Second Permanent Under-Secretary for Administration: Mr J. M. Wilson, CBE
Second Permanent Under-Secretary for Equipment: Sir Martin Flett, KCB

Commanders-in-Chief

Commander-in-Chief, Naval Home Command:
  Admiral Sir David Williams, KCB
Commander-in-Chief, Fleet:
  Admiral Sir Henry Leach, KCB

Defence Staff

Chief of the Defence Staff:
  Admiral of the Fleet Sir Edward Ashmore, GCB, DSC
Vice Chief of the Defence Staff:
  Vice-Admiral A. S. Morton

Flag Officers

Flag Officer, 1st Flotilla:
  Rear-Admiral R. R. Squires
Flag Officer, 2nd Flotilla:
  Rear-Admiral M. La T. Wemyss
Flag Officer, Submarines:
  Rear-Admiral J. D. E. Fieldhouse
Flag Officer, Naval Air Command:
  Vice-Admiral J. O. Roberts
Flag Officer, Carriers and Amphibious Ships:
  Rear-Admiral W. D. M. Staveley
Flag Officer, Sea Training:
  Rear-Admiral G. I. Pritchard
Flag Officer, Gibraltar:
  Rear-Admiral M. A. Higgs
Flag Officer, Malta:
  Rear-Admiral O. N. A. Cecil
Flag Officer, Medway:
  Rear-Admiral C. M. Bevan, ADC
Flag Officer, Plymouth:
  Vice-Admiral J. M. Forbes
Flag Officer, Portsmouth:
  Rear-Admiral: W. J. Graham
Flag Officer, Scotland and Northern Ireland:
  Vice-Admiral C. Rusby, MVO

General Officers, Royal Marines

Commandant-General, Royal Marines:
  Lieutenant-General J. C. C. Richards
Chief of Staff to Commandant-General, Royal Marines:
  Major-General R. P. W. Wall
Major-General Training Group, Royal Marines:
  Major-General P. L. Spurgeon
Major-General Commando Forces, Royal Marines:
  Major-General Ephraums, OBE

Diplomatic Representation

British Naval Attaché in Bonn:
  Captain B. R. Outhwaite
British Naval Attaché in Moscow:
  Captain P. H. Coward
British Naval Attaché in Paris:
  Captain V. M. Howard
British Naval Attaché in Rome:
  Captain M. A. George
British Naval Attaché in Washington:
  Rear-Admiral R. W. Halliday DSC

Personnel (including Royal Marines)

(a) 1973: 77 600 (10 200 officers, 67 400 ratings and ORs) plus 3 600 servicewomen
    1974: 74 700 (10 200 officers, 64 500 ratings and ORs) plus 3 600 servicewomen
    1975: 72 500 (10 000 officers, 62 500 ratings and ORs) plus 3 700 servicewomen
    1976: 72 300 (9 900 officers, 62 300 ratings and ORs) plus 3 900 servicewomen
    1977: 72 200 (9 800 officers, 62 400 ratings and ORs) plus 3 900 servicewomen
(b) Voluntary Service

Mercantile Marine

Lloyd's Register of Shipping: 3 549 vessels of 32 923 308 tons gross

Fleet Air Arm

Aircraft	Role	Deployment	No. of sqdns or flights
Buccaneer 2	Strike	Carrier	1 Sqdn
Gannet 3	AEW	Carrier	1 Sqdn
Gannet 3	AEW	Lossiemouth	1 Sqdn
Phantom FG1	FGA	Carrier	1 Sqdn

Helicopters

Aircraft	Role	Deployment	No. of sqdns or flights
Sea King	ASW	Carrier	1 Sqdn
Sea King	ASW	ASW Carrier	1 Sqdn
Sea King	ASW	Cruisers	2 Sqdns
Sea King	ASW	Prestwick	1 Sqdn
Sea King	Aircrew Training	Culdrose	1 Sqdn
Wasp	ASW	"Leander" Class	
Wasp	ASW	"Rothesay" Class	
Wasp	ASW	"Tribal" Class	40 flights
Wasp	ASW	Type 21	
Wasp	ASW	Type 42	
Wasp	Aircrew Training	Portland	1 Sqdn
Wessex 3	ASW	"County" Class	7 Flights
Wessex 3	Aircrew Training	Portland	1 Sqdn
Wessex 5	Commando Assault	Yeovilton/HMS *Hermes*	2 Sqdns
Wessex 5	Aircrew Training	Yeovilton	1 Sqdn
Wessex 5	Fleet Requirements	Portland	1 Sqdn

Strength of the Fleet

Type	Active	Building (Projected)	Reserve
Aircraft Carrier	1+1 (A/S)	—	—
A/S Carriers (Cruisers)	—	2	—
Helicopter Cruisers	2	—	—
Light Cruisers	8 (2 refit)	—	—
Destroyers	3	6	—
Frigates	56 (13 refit)	6	—
Sonar Trials Ship	1	—	—
SSBNs	4 (1 refit)	—	—
Submarines—Fleet	9 (3 refit)	3 (1)	—
Submarines—Patrol	18 (3 refit)	—	2
Commando Ship	—	—	1
Assault Ships (LPD)	1	—	1
LSLs	6	—	—
LST	1	—	—
LCTs	3	2	—
LCMs	27	—	—
LCVPs	26	—	—
LCPLs	3	—	—
Offshore Patrol Craft	5	—	—
Fast Attack Craft—Patrol	1	—	—
Large Patrol Craft	10	—	—
Fast Training Boats	3	—	—
MCM Support Ship	1 (refit)	—	—
Minehunters	16 (4 refit)	2	—
Minesweepers—Coastal	22	—	—
Minesweepers—Inshore	5	—	—
Maintenance Ships	2	—	—
Submarine Depot Ships	1	—	—
Survey Ships	4 (1 refit)	—	—
Coastal Survey Ships	4	—	—
Inshore Survey Craft	5	—	—
Ice Patrol Ship	1	—	—
Royal Yacht	1	—	—
Hovercraft	5	—	—
Diving Support Ship	1	—	—
Large Fleet Tankers	6	—	—
Support Tankers	4	—	—
Mobile Reserve Tanker	1	—	—
Small Fleet Tankers	6	—	—
Helicopter Support Ship	1	—	—
Stores Support Ships	3	—	—
Fleet Replenishment Ships	4	2	—
Store Carriers	2	1	—
MSBVs	12	—	—
Trials Ships	5	—	—
TRVs	9	—	—
Cable Ship	1	—	—
Armament Carriers	6	—	—
Water Carriers	15	—	—
Ocean Tugs	13	—	—
Harbour Tugs	59	—	—
Tenders	54	—	—
RNXS Craft	10	—	—
DG Vessels	3	—	—
TCVs	6	—	—

DELETIONS

(Note Disposal List following)

Carriers (of all kinds)

1972 *Centaur* and *Albion*

Cruiser

1975 *Lion* (b.u. Inverkeithing 24 April)

Light Cruiser

1976 *Hampshire*

Destroyers

1970 *Aisne, Trafalgar, Camperdown*
1971 *Daring, Delight, Scorpion, Cambrian*
1972 *Crossbow, Defender, Saintes*
1974 *Agincourt* (b.u. Sunderland 27 Oct)
1975 *Corunna* (b.u. Blyth 11 Sep)

Frigates

1970 *Loch Killisport, Loch Fada, Ulysses, Zest, Murray*
1971 *Urania, Relentless, Pellew, Wakeful, Alert, Grafton*
1972 *Verulam, Venus*
1974 *Tenby, Scarborough. Whirlwind* (target 28 Oct)
1975 *Whitby*
1976 *Blackwood, Puma. Llandaff* (to Bangladesh)
1977 *Mermaid* (to Malaysia)

Submarines

1970 *Talent, Thermopylae, Anchorite, Astute*
1971 *Ambush, Alaric, Trump, Taciturn, Auriga*
1972 *Artemis, Acheron, Alderney, Aeneas, Alcide, Alliance*
1976 *Rorqual*

Depot Ship

1977 *Maidstone* to Rosyth for b.u. (Jan)

MCM Vessels

1970 *Dalswinton, Invermoriston, Puncheston, Quainton, Wilkieston*
1974 *Woolaston*
1975 *Boulston, Chawton, Maddiston* (scrapped). *Birdham, Odiham*
1976 *Highburton, Woolaston, Arlingham. Fittleton* (sunk in collision Sep. B.u. after salvage)
1977 *Wiston*

Fast Attack Craft

1976 *Dark Gladiator* (sunk as target—Portland)

Service Forces

1970 *Girdleness* (scrapped)
1973 *Moorsman*
1974 *Wave Chief, Derwentdale* (returned to owners), *Brown Ranger* (Tankers). *Barmond* (MSBV), *Miner III*
1975 *Tidesurge* (Tanker), *Dispenser, Barfoot* (MSBVs), *Reliant,* (Air Stores ship), *Robert Middleton* (Stores Carrier), *Icewhale* (Trials Ship), *Bullfinch* (Cable Ship), *Freshmere* (Water boat), *Bowstring* (Armament Carrier). *Ironbridge, Nordenfeld*
1976 *Tideflow* (to b.u. Bilbao 4 May). *Spalake, Spaburn, Freshpool, Freshpond, Griper*

Survey Ship

1976 *Vidal* (b.u. Cairnryan)

Tugs

1975 *Diver, Driver, Eminent, Empire Ace, Empire Demon, Empire Fred, Empire Rosa, Fidget, Foremost, Freedom, Frisky, Grinder, Handmaid, Impetus, Integrity, (Lilian and May*—existence doubted), *Prompt, Security, Tampeon, Trunnion, Vagrant, Weasel.*
1976 *Reward* (to disposal after salvage 28 Aug)

DISPOSAL LIST

The following ships not on the Active or Reserve list are held in the ports shown pending disposal by sale or scrap.

Aircraft Carrier

Eagle R 05 (Plymouth)

Light Cruiser

Hampshire D 06

Destroyers

Caprice D 01 (Plymouth)
Cavalier D 73 (Museum Ship)
Barrosa D 68 (Portsmouth)

Submarines

1975 *Andrew* S 63
1977 *Narwhal* S 03

Frigates

Blackpool F 77 (Rosyth Target Ship)
Leopard F 14
Grenville F 197 (Portsmouth)
Keppel F 85
Palliser F 94 (Portsmouth)
Rapid F 138 (Milford Haven—Target)
Undaunted F 53 (Gibraltar—Target)
Volage F 41
Whitby F 36

Minesweepers—Coastal

Ashton M 1198 (Rosyth)
Belton M 1199 (Rosyth)
Dufton M 1145 (Portsmouth)

Fast Attack Craft

Brave Borderer (Pembroke Dock)

Fast Attack Craft—*continued*

Brave Swordsman (Pembroke Dock)
Dark Hero (Portsmouth)

LSTs

Lofoten (Rosyth)
Messina (Plymouth)
Stalker (Rosyth)
Zeebrugge (Plymouth)

Immobile Tenders

Diamond D 35. Attached to *Sultan* for engineering training at Portsmouth
Ulster F 83. Accommodation ship at Portsmouth
Russell F 97. Attached to Sultan/Collingwood
Grampus S 04. Harbour Training—Dolphin
Duncan F 80. Attached to Caledonia
Berry Head A 191. Accommodation ship at Devonport

LIST OF PENNANT NUMBERS

Note: Not displayed on Submarines or RMAS craft.. *Disposal List

Aircraft Carriers

R	05	Eagle*
R	08	Bulwark (Reserve)
R	09	Ark Royal
R	12	Hermes

Submarines

S	01	Porpoise
S	03	Narwhal*
S	04	Grampus*
S	05	Finwhale
S	06	Cachalot
S	07	Sealion
S	08	Walrus
S	09	Oberon
S	10	Odin
S	11	Orpheus
S	12	Olympus
S	13	Osiris
S	14	Onslaught
S	15	Otter
S	16	Oracle
S	17	Ocelot
S	18	Otus
S	19	Opossum
S	20	Opportune
S	21	Onyx
S	22	Resolution
S	23	Repulse
S	26	Renown
S	27	Revenge
S	46	Churchill
S	48	Conqueror
S	50	Courageous
S	63	Andrew*
S	101	Dreadnought
S	102	Valiant
S	103	Warspite
S	104	Sceptre

Submarines—*continued*

S	108	Sovereign
S	109	Superb
S	111	Spartan
S	112	Severn
S	113	—
S	126	Swiftsure

Cruisers

C	20	Tiger
C	99	Blake

Light Cruisers and Destroyers

D	01	Caprice*
D	02	Devonshire
D	06	Hampshire*
D	12	Kent
D	16	London
D	18	Antrim
D	19	Glamorgan
D	20	Fife
D	21	Norfolk
D	23	Bristol
D	35	Diamond
D	43	Matapan
D	68	Barrosa*
D	73	Cavalier*
D	80	Sheffield
D	86	Birmingham
D	87	Newcastle
D	88	Glasgow
D	108	Cardiff
D	118	Coventry
D	—	Exeter
D	—	Southampton
D	—	New Construction

Frigates

F	10	Aurora
F	12	Achilles
F	14	Leopard*
F	15	Euryalus
F	16	Diomede
F	18	Galatea
F	27	Lynx
F	28	Cleopatra
F	32	Salisbury
F	37	Jaguar
F	38	Arethusa
F	39	Naiad
F	40	Sirius
F	41	Volage*
F	42	Phoebe
F	43	Torquay
F	45	Minerva
F	47	Danae
F	48	Dundas
F	52	Juno
F	53	Undaunted*
F	54	Hardy
F	56	Argonaut
F	57	Andromeda
F	58	Hermione
F	59	Chichester
F	60	Jupiter
F	69	Bacchante
F	70	Apollo
F	71	Scylla
F	72	Ariadne
F	73	Eastbourne
F	75	Charybdis
F	77	Blackpool*
F	80	Duncan*
F	83	Ulster*
F	84	Exmouth
F	85	Keppel*
F	88	Broadsword
F	—	Battleaxe

Frigates—*continued*

F	—	New construction
F	94	Palliser*
F	97	Russell*
F	99	Lincoln
F	101	Yarmouth
F	103	Lowestoft
F	104	Dido
F	106	Brighton
F	107	Rothesay
F	108	Londonderry
F	109	Leander
F	113	Falmouth
F	114	Ajax
F	115	Berwick
F	117	Ashanti
F	119	Eskimo
F	122	Gurkha
F	124	Zulu
F	125	Mohawk
F	126	Plymouth
F	127	Penelope
F	129	Rhyl
F	131	Nubian
F	133	Tartar
F	138	Rapid*
F	169	Amazon
F	170	Antelope
F	171	Active
F	172	Ambuscade
F	173	Arrow
F	174	Alacrity
F	175	Ardent
F	185	Avenger
F	197	Grenville*

Assault Ships

L	10	Fearless
L	11	Intrepid

List of pennant numbers—*continued*

Logistic Landing Ships and LCTs

L	700-711	LCM 9
L	3004	Sir Bedivere
L	3005	Sir Galahad
L	3027	Sir Geraint
L	3029	Sir Lancelot
L	3036	Sir Percivale
L	3505	Sir Tristram
L	3507-8	LCM 9
L	3513	Empire Gull
L	4001	Ardennes
L	4002	Agheila
L	4041	Abbeville
L	4061	Audemer
—		Arakan

LCMs (RCT)

RPL	01	Avon
RPL	02	Bude
RPL	03	Clyde
RPL	04	Dart
RPL	05	Eden
RPL	06	Forth
RPL	07	Glen
RPL	08	Hamble
RPL	10	Kennet
RPL	11	Loddon
RPL	12	Medway

Helicopter Support Ship

K	08	Engadine

Minelayer

N	21	Abdiel

Support Ships and Auxiliaries

A	00	Britannia
A	70	Echo
A	71	Enterprise
A	72	Egeria
A	75	Tidespring
A	76	Tidepool
A	77	Pearleaf
A	78	Plumleaf
A	80	Orangeleaf
A	82	Cherryleaf
A	85	Faithful
A	86	Forceful
A	87	Favourite
A	88	Agile
A	89	Advice
A	90	Accord
A	93	Dexterous
A	94	Director
A	95	Typhoon
A	96	Tidereach
A	99	Beaulieu
A	100	Beddgelert
A	101	Bembridge
A	102	Airedale
A	103	Bibury
A	104	Blakeney
A	105	Brodick
A	106	Alsatian
A	108	Triumph
A	111	Cyclone
A	113	Alice
A	116	Agatha

Support Ships and Auxiliaries—*continued*

A	117	Audrey
A	121	Agnes
A	122	Olwen
A	123	Olna
A	124	Olmeda
A	126	Cairn
A	127	Torrent
A	128	Torrid
A	129	Dalmatian
A	133	Hecla
A	134	Rame Head
A	137	Hecate
A	138	Herald
A	144	Hydra
A	145	Daisy
A	155	Deerhound
A	162	Elkhound
A	168	Labrador
A	169	Husky
A	171	Endurance
A	176	Bullfinch
A	177	Edith
A	179	Whimbrel
A	180	Mastiff
A	182	Saluki
A	187	Sealyham
A	188	Pointer
A	189	Setter
A	191	Berry Head*
A	201	Spaniel
A	206	Celia
A	210	Charlotte
A	217	Christine
A	218	Clare
A	219	Dewdale
A	220	Loyal Moderator
A	222	Spapool
A	224	Spabrook
A	231	Reclaim
A	232	Kingarth
A	236	Wakefield
A	250	Sheepdog
A	252	Doris
A	259	St. Margarets
A	261	Eddyfirth
A	268	Green Rover
A	269	Grey Rover
A	270	Blue Rover
A	271	Gold Rover
A	273	Black Rover
A	274	Ettrick
A	277	Elsing
A	280	Resurgent
A	281	Kinbrace
A	288	Sea Giant
A	289	Confiance
A	290	Confident
A	310	Invergordon
A	312	Ixworth
A	317	Bulldog
A	319	Beagle
A	320	Fox
A	322	Bridget
A	323	Betty
A	324	Barbara
A	325	Fawn
A	327	Basset
A	328	Collie
A	329	Retainer
A	330	Corgi
A	332	Caldy
A	333	Coll
A	334	Bern
A	335	Brenda
A	336	Lundy
A	338	Skomer
A	339	Lyness
A	340	Graemsay
A	344	Stromness

Support Ships and Auxiliaries—*continued*

A	345	Tarbatness
A	346	Switha
A	352	Epworth
A	353	Elkstone
A	354	Froxfield
A	364	Whitehead
A	367	Newton
A	377	Maxim
A	378	Kinterbury
A	382	Vigilant (ex-*Loyal Factor*)
A	384	Felsted
A	385	Fort Grange
A	386	Fort Austin
A	389	Clovelly
A	393	Dunster
A	397	Boxer
A	404	Bacchus
A	406	Hebe
A	480	Resource
A	482	Kinloss
A	486	Regent
A	502	Rollicker
A	507	Uplifter
A	510	Alert (ex-*Loyal Governor*)
A	1771	Loyal Proctor
A	1772	Holmwood
A	1773	Horning

Auxiliaries

Y	15	Watercourse
Y	16	Waterfowl
Y	17	Waterfall
Y	18	Watershed
Y	19	Waterspout
Y	20	Waterside
Y	21	Oilpress
Y	22	Oilstone
Y	23	Oilwell
Y	24	Oilfield
Y	25	Oilbird
Y	26	Oilman

Boom Defence Vessels

P	190	Laymoor
P	191	Layburn
P	192	Mandarin
P	193	Pintail
P	194	Garganey
P	195	Goldeneye
P	196	Goosander
P	197	Pochard

Light Forces

P	260	Kingfisher
P	261	Cygnet
P	262	Peterel
P	263	Sandpiper
P	271	Scimitar
P	274	Cutlass
P	275	Sabre
P	276	Tenacity
P	295	Jersey
P	297	Guernsey
P	298	Shetland
P	299	Orkney
P	300	Lindisfarne
P	1007	Beachampton
P	1055	Monkton
P	1089	Wasperton
P	1093	Wolverton
P	1096	Yarnton
P	3104	Dee (ex-*Beckford*)
P	3113	Droxford

Coastal Minesweepers

M	1103	Alfriston
M	1109	Bickington
M	1110	Bildeston
M	1113	Brereton
M	1114	Brinton
M	1115	Bronington
M	1116	Wilton
M	1124	Crichton
M	1125	Cuxton
M	1133	Bossington
M	1140	Gavington
M	1141	Glasserton
M	1145	Dufton
M	1146	Hodgeston
M	1147	Hubberston
M	1151	Iveston
M	1153	Kedleston
M	1154	Kellington
M	1157	Kirkliston
M	1158	Laleston
M	1165	Maxton
M	1166	Nurton
M	1167	Repton
M	1173	Pollington
M	1180	Shavington
M	1181	Sheraton
M	1182	Shoulton
M	1187	Upton
M	1188	Walkerton
M	1195	Wotton
M	1198	Ashton*
M	1199	Belton*
M	1200	Soberton
M	1204	Stubbington
M	1208	Lewiston
M	1209	Chawton
M	1216	Crofton

Inshore Minesweepers

M	2002	Aveley
M	2010	Isis (ex-*Cradley*)
M	2611	Bottisham (RAF 5001) R
M	2614	Bucklesham TRV
M	2616	Chelsham (RAF 5000) R
M	2621	Dittisham
M	2622	Downham TRV
M	2626	Everingham TRV
M	2628	Flintham
M	2630	Fritham TRV
M	2635	Haversham TRV
M	2636	Lasham TRV
M	2716	Pagham RNXS
M	2717	Fordham DGV
M	2720	Waterwitch (ex-*Powderham*)
M	2726	Shipham RNXS
M	2733	Thakeham RNXS
M	2735	Tongham RNXS
M	2737	Warmingham DGV
M	2780	Woodlark (ex-*Yaxham*)
M	2781	Portisham RNXS
M	2783	Odiham RNXS
M	2784	Puttenham RNXS
M	2785	Birdham RNXS
M	2790	Thatcham DGV
M	2793	Thornham

DGV	=	*Degaussing Vessels*
RNXS	=	*Royal Naval Auxiliary Service*
TRV	=	*Torpedo Recovery Vessels*
R	=	*Reserve (ex-RAF)*

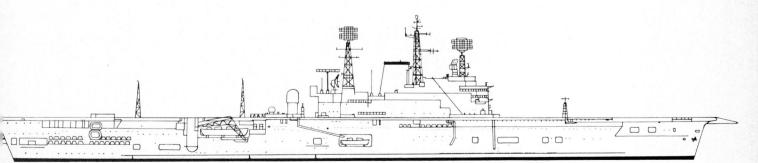

ARK ROYAL (scale = 1:1300)

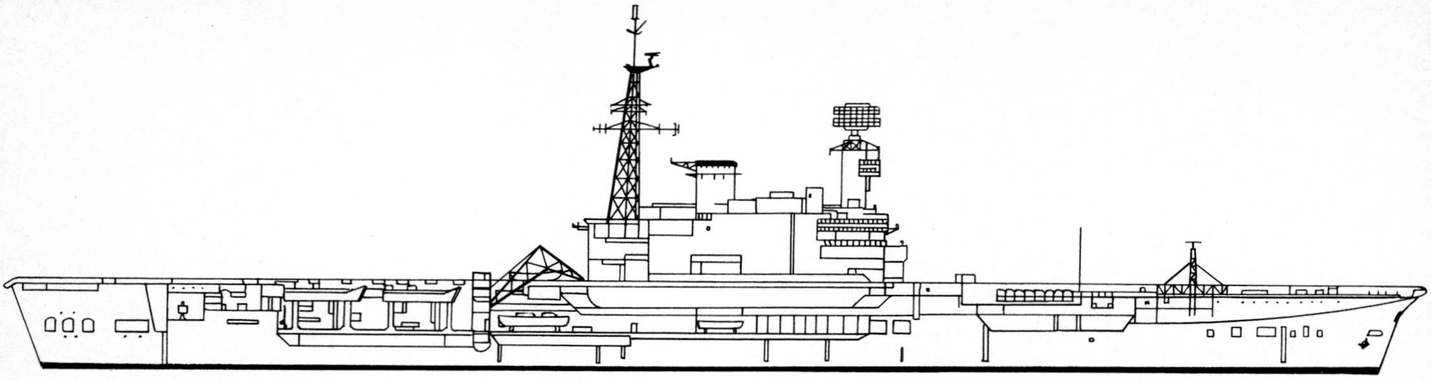

HERMES

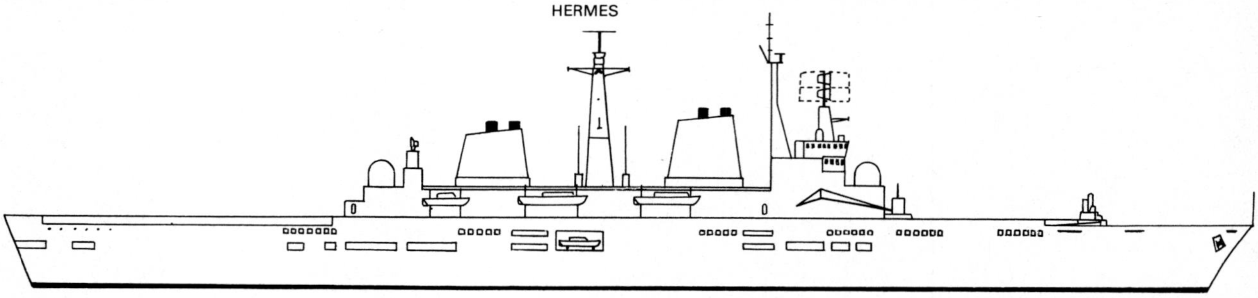

INVINCIBLE

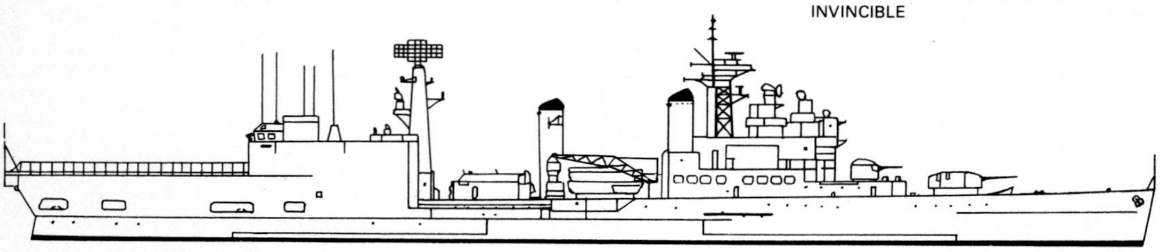

TIGER

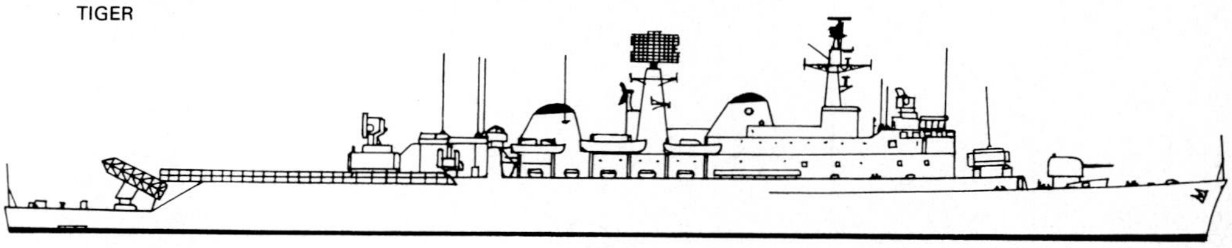

ANTRIM

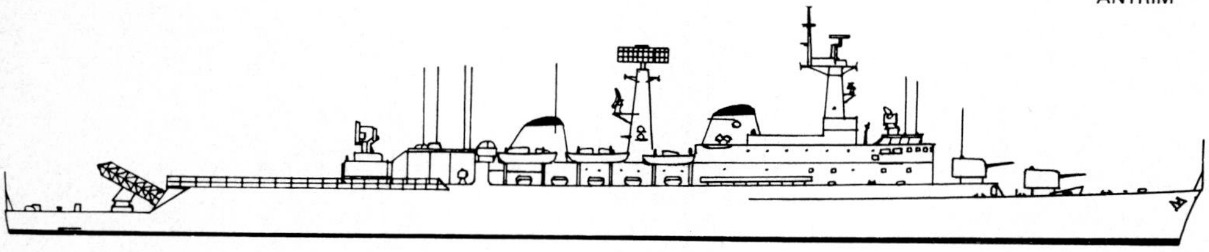

KENT

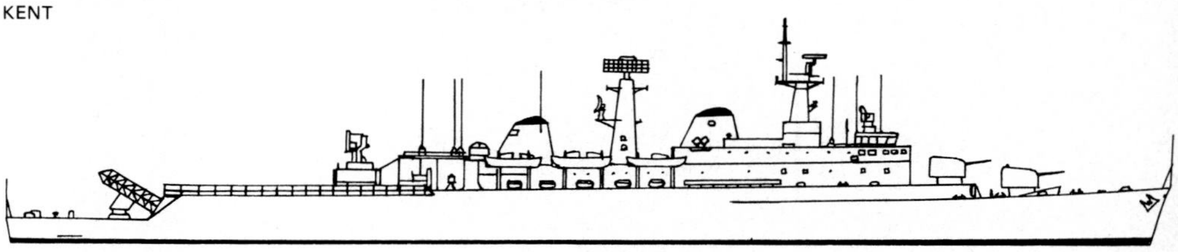

DEVONSHIRE

BRISTOL

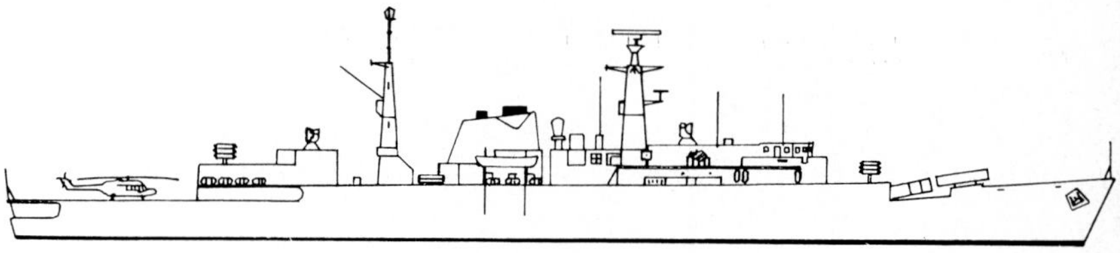

TYPE 22

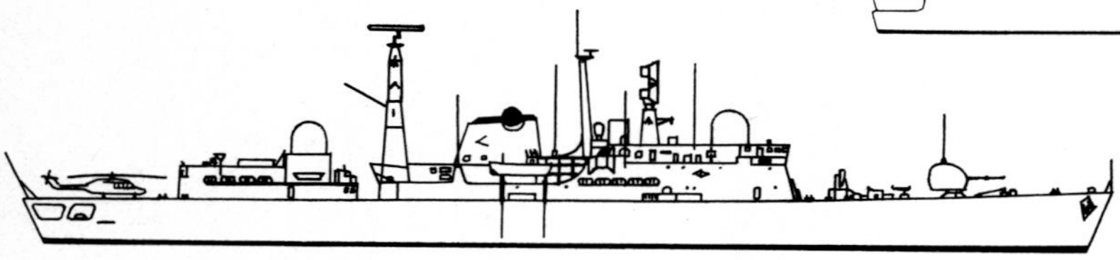

SHEFFIELD

"LEANDER" Class (Ikara)

"LEANDER" Class (Exocet)

"LEANDER A" Class (4-5")

"ROTHESAY" Class

TORQUAY

MATAPAN

AMAZON

"TRIBAL" Class

"LEOPARD" Class

"SALISBURY" Class

"BLACKWOOD" Class

EXMOUTH

SUBMARINES
Nuclear Powered Ballistic Missile Submarines (SSBN)

4 "RESOLUTION" CLASS

Name	No.	Builders	Laid down	Launched	Commissioned
RENOWN	S 26	Cammell Laird & Co Ltd, Birkenhead	25 June1964	25 Feb 1967	15 Nov 1968
REPULSE	S 23	Vickers (Shipbuilding) Ltd, Barrow-in-Furness	12 Mar 1965	4 Nov 1967	28 Sep 1968
RESOLUTION	S 22	Vickers (Shipbuilding) Ltd, Barrow-in-Furness	26 Feb 1964	15 Sep 1966	2 Oct 1967
REVENGE	S 27	Cammell Laird & Co Ltd, Birkenhead	19 May 1965	15 Mar 1968	4 Dec 1969

Displacement, tons: 7 500 surfaced; 8 400 dived
Length, feet (metres): 360 *(109·7)* pp; 425 *(129·5)* oa
Beam, feet (metres): 33 *(10·1)*
Draught, feet (metres): 30 *(9·1)*
Missiles, surface: 16 tubes amidships for Polaris A—3 SLBMs
Torpedo tubes: 6—21 in *(533 mm)* (bow)
Nuclear reactors: 1 pressurised water cooled
Main machinery: Geared steam turbines; 1 shaft
Speed, knots: 20 surfaced; 25 dived
Complement: 143 (13 officers, 130 ratings); 2 crews (see *Personnel*)

In Feb 1963 it was officially stated that it was intended to order four or five 7 000 ton nuclear powered submarines, each to carry 16 Polaris missiles, and it was planned that the first would be on patrol in 1968. Their hulls and machinery would be of British design. As well as building two submarines Vickers (Shipbuilding) would give lead yard service to the builder of the other two. Four Polaris submarines were in fact ordered in May 1963. The plan to build a fifth Polaris submarine was cancelled on 15 Feb 1965. Britain's first SSBN, *Resolution*, put to sea on 22 June 1967 and completed 6 weeks trial in the Firth of Clyde and Atlantic on 17 Aug 1967.

Cost: *Resolution*, £40 240 000; *Renown*, £39 950 000; *Repulse*, £37 500 000; *Revenge*, £38 600 000; completed ships excluding missiles.

Personnel: Each submarine, which has accommodation for 19 officers and 135 ratings, is manned on a two-crew basis, in order to get maximum operational time at sea.

Radar: Search; I-band
Periscope radar.

Sonar: Types 2001 and 2007.

REVENGE at Faslane   3/1976, Wren Veronica Evans (MOD(N))

RENOWN   10/1976, Wright and Logan

REPULSE   11/1976, MOD(N)

1 NEW CONSTRUCTION

Name	No.	Builders	Laid down	Launched	Commissioned
SPLENDID	S 113	Vickers Ltd (Shipbuilding Group), Barrow	1977	—	—

The first of an improved class of Fleet Submarines is planned for 1977.

4 + 2 "SWIFTSURE" CLASS

Name	No.	Builders	Laid down	Launched	Commissioned
SWIFTSURE	S 126	Vickers Ltd (SB Group), Barrow	15 April 1969	7 Sep 1971	17 April 1973
SOVEREIGN	S 108	Vickers Ltd (SB Group), Barrow	17 Sep 1970	17 Feb 1973	11 July 1974
SUPERB	S 109	Vickers Ltd (SB Group), Barrow	16 Mar 1972	30 Nov 1974	13 Nov 1976
SCEPTRE	S 104	Vickers Ltd (SB Group), Barrow	25 Oct 1973	20 Nov 1976	1978
SPARTAN	S 111	Vickers Ltd (SB Group), Barrow	1974	—	—
SEVERN	S 112	Vickers Ltd (SB Group), Barrow	1976	—	—

Displacement, tons: 4 000 light; 4 200 standard; 4 500 dived
Length, feet (metres): 272·0 *(82·9)*
Beam, feet (metres): 32·3 *(9·8)*
Draught, feet (metres): 27 *(8·2)*
Torpedo tubes: 5—21 in *(533 mm)* (20 reloads)
Nuclear reactor: 1 pressurised water-cooled
Main machinery: English Electric geared steam turbines;
   1 shaft
Speed, knots: 30 dived
Complement: 97 (12 officers, 85 men)

Compared with the "Valiant" class submarines these are slightly shorter with a fuller form with the fore-planes set further forward with one less torpedo tube and with a deeper diving depth.
Sovereign visited the North Pole 1976.

Design: The pressure hull in the "Swiftsures" maintains its diameter for much greater length than previously. As a result the fore-planes are mounted even further forward.

Electrical: 112 cell emergency battery.

Engineering: Whilst the basic reactor design remains similar to previous types core-life has probably increased.

Orders: *Swiftsure,* 3 Nov 1967; *Sovereign,* 16 May 1969; *Superb,* 20 May 1970; *Sceptre,* 1 Nov 1971; *Spartan,* 17 Feb 1973; *Severn,* 26 May 1976.

Radar: Search; Type 1003.

Sonar: Type 2001 in "chin" position, Types 2007, 197 and 183.

Torpedoes: Individual reloading in 15 seconds.

SOVEREIGN   *9/1975, John G. Callis*

SOVEREIGN   *9/1975, John G. Callis*

SUPERB   *12/1976, MOD(N)*

Fleet Submarines

5 "VALIANT" CLASS

Name	No.	Builders	Laid down	Launched	Commissioned
VALIANT	S 102	Vickers Ltd (SB Group), Barrow	22 Jan 1962	3 Dec 1963	18 July 1966
WARSPITE	S 103	Vickers Ltd (SB Group), Barrow	10 Dec 1963	25 Sep 1965	18 April 1967
CHURCHILL	S 46	Vickers Ltd (SB Group), Barrow	30 June 1967	20 Dec 1968	15 July 1970
CONQUEROR	S 48	Cammell Laird & Co Ltd, Birkenhead	5 Dec 1967	28 Aug 1969	9 Nov 1971
COURAGEOUS	S 50	Vickers Ltd (SB Group), Barrow	15 May 1968	7 Mar 1970	16 Oct 1971

Displacement, tons: 4 000 light; 4 400 standard; 4 900 dived
Length, feet (metres): 285 (86·9)
Beam, feet (metres): 33·2 (10·1)
Draught, feet (metres): 27 (8·2)
Torpedo tubes: 6—21 in (533 mm) (26 reloads)
Nuclear reactor: 1 pressurised water cooled
Main machinery: English Electric Geared steam turbines; 1 shaft
Speed, knots: 28 dived
Complement: 103 (13 officers, 90 men)

It was announced on 31 Aug 1960 that the contract for a second nuclear powered submarine (Valiant) had been awarded to Vickers Ltd, the principal sub-contractors being Vickers-Armstrong (Engineers) Ltd, for the machinery and its installation, and Rolls Royce and Associates for the nuclear steam raising plant. The class, of which she is the first, is broadly of the same design as that of Dreadnought, but slightly larger. She was originally scheduled to be completed in Sep 1965, but work was held up by the Polaris programme.

Cost: Vary from £24 mill (Warspite) to £30 mill (Conqueror).

Electrical: 112 cell emergency battery.

Endurance: On 25 April 1967 Valiant completed the 12 000-mile homeward voyage from Singapore, the record submerged passage by a British submarine, after 28 days non-stop.

Engineering: Valiant's reactor core was made in Great Britain, with machinery of British design and manufacture similar to the shore prototype installed in the Admiralty Reactor Test Establishment at Dounreay. The main steam turbines and condensers were designed and manufactured by the English Electric Company, Rugby, and the electrical propulsion machinery and control gear by Laurence, Scott & Electromotors Ltd.

Orders: Valiant, 31 Aug 1960—Warspite, 12 Dec 1962—Churchill, 21 Oct 1965—Conqueror, 9 Aug 1966—Courageous, 1 Mar 1967.

Radar: Search; Type 1003.

Sonar: Type 2001 in "chin" position; Types 2007, 197 and 183.

Torpedoes: Individual reloading in 15 seconds.

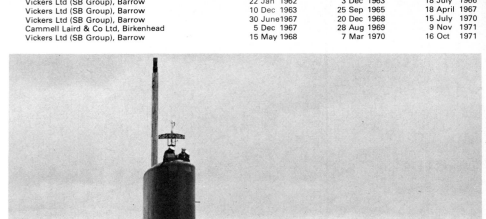

CHURCHILL   3/1976, MOD(N)

CONQUEROR   1976, Michael D. J. Lennon

COURAGEOUS   9/1976, Dr. Giorgio Arra

1 "DREADNOUGHT" CLASS

Name	No.	Builders	Laid down	Launched	Commissioned
DREADNOUGHT	S 101	Vickers-Armstrong, Barrow	12 June 1959	21 Oct 1960	17 April 1963

Displacement, tons: 3 000 standard; 3 500 surfaced; 4 000 dived
Length, feet (metres): 265·8 (81·0)
Beam, feet (metres): 32·2 (9·8)
Draught, feet (metres): 26 (7·9)
Torpedo tubes: 6—21 in (533 mm) (bow)
Nuclear reactor: 1 S5W pressurised water-cooled
Main machinery: Geared steam turbines; 1 shaft
Speed, knots: 28 dived
Complement: 88 (11 officers, 77 men)

As originally planned *Dreadnought* was to have been fitted with a British designed and built nuclear reactor, but in 1958 an agreement was concluded with the United States Government for the purchase of a complete set of propulsion machinery of the type fitted in USS *Skipjack*. This agreement enabled the submarine to be launched far earlier. The supply of this machinery was made under a contract between the Westinghouse Electric Corporation and Rolls-Royce. The latter were also supplied with design and manufacturing details of the reactor and with safety information and set up a factory in this country to manufacture similar cores. *Dreadnought* has a hull of British design both as regards structural strength and hydrodynamic features, although the latter are based on the pioneering work of the US Navy in *Skipjack* and *Albacore*. From about amidships aft, the hull lines closely resemble *Skipjack* to accommodate the propulsion machinery. The forward end is wholly British in concept. In the Control Room and Attack Centre the instruments are fitted into consoles.

The improved water distilling plant for the first time provides unlimited fresh water for shower baths and for washing machines in the fully equipped laundry.

She is fitted with an inertial navigation system and with means of measuring her depth below ice and was the first British submarine to surface at the North Pole, in 1970.

Radar: Search; I-band.

Sonar: Type 2001 in "chin" position; Type 2007.

DREADNOUGHT

11/1976, MOD(N)

DREADNOUGHT

11/1976, MOD(N)

Patrol Submarines

13 "OBERON" CLASS   5 "PORPOISE" CLASS

"OBERON" CLASS

Name	No.	Builders	Laid down	Launched	Commissioned
OBERON	S 09	HM Dockyard, Chatham	28 Nov 1957	18 July 1959	24 Feb 1961
OCELOT	S 17	HM Dockyard, Chatham	17 Nov 1960	5 May 1962	31 Jan 1964
ODIN	S 10	Cammell Laird & Co Ltd, Birkenhead	27 April 1959	4 Nov 1960	3 May 1962
OLYMPUS	S 12	Vickers-Armstrong Ltd, Barrow	4 Mar 1960	14 June 1961	7 July 1962
ONSLAUGHT	S 14	HM Dockyard, Chatham	8 April 1959	24 Sep 1960	14 Aug 1962
ONYX	S 21	Cammell Laird & Co Ltd, Birkenhead	16 Nov 1964	18 Aug 1966	20 Nov 1967
OPOSSUM	S 19	Cammell Laird & Co Ltd, Birkenhead	21 Dec 1961	23 May 1963	5 June 1964
OPPORTUNE	S 20	Scotts SB & Eng Co Ltd, Greenock	26 Oct 1962	14 Feb 1964	29 Dec 1964
ORACLE	S 16	Cammell Laird & Co Ltd, Birkenhead	26 April 1960	26 Sep 1961	14 Feb 1963
ORPHEUS	S 11	Vickers-Armstrong Ltd, Barrow	16 April 1959	17 Nov 1959	25 Nov 1960
OSIRIS	S 13	Vickers-Armstrong Ltd, Barrow	26 Jan 1962	29 Nov 1962	11 Jan 1964
OTTER	S 15	Scotts SB & Eng Co Ltd, Greenock	14 Jan 1960	15 May 1961	20 Aug 1962
OTUS	S 18	Scotts SB & Eng Co Ltd, Greenock	31 May 1961	17 Oct 1962	5 Oct 1963

"PORPOISE" CLASS

Name	No.	Builders	Laid down	Launched	Commissioned
CACHALOT	S 06	Scotts SB & Eng Co Ltd, Greenock	1 Aug 1955	11 Dec 1957	1 Sep 1959
FINWHALE	S 05	Cammell Laird & Co Ltd, Birkenhead	18 Sep 1956	21 July 1959	19 Aug 1960
PORPOISE	S 01	Vickers-Armstrong Ltd, Barrow	15 June 1954	25 April 1956	17 April 1958
SEALION	S 07	Cammell Laird & Co Ltd, Birkenhead	5 June 1958	31 Dec 1959	25 July 1961
WALRUS	S 08	Scotts SB & Eng Co Ltd, Greenock	12 Feb 1958	22 Sep 1959	10 Feb 1961

Displacement, tons: 1 610 standard; 2 030 surfaced; 2 410 dived

Length, feet (metres): 241 *(73·5)* pp; 295·2 *(90·0)* oa

Beam, feet (metres): 26·5 *(8·1)*

Draught, feet (metres): 18 *(5·5)*

Torpedo tubes: 8—21 in *(533 mm)* (6 bow, 2 stern); 24 torpedoes carried

Main machinery: 2 Admiralty Standard Range 1, 16 VMS diesels; 3 680 bhp; 2 electric motors; 6 000 shp; 2 shafts

Speed, knots: 12 surfaced; 17 dived

Complement: 68 (6 officers, 62 men) in "Oberon" class
71 (6 officers, 65 men) in "Porpoise" class

As a result of the 1975 Defence Review the following have been retired some years before the end of hull life:—
Rorqual to disposal 1976
Grampus to reserve 1976
Narwhal to reserve 1977.

Construction: For the first time in British submarines plastic was used in the superstructure construction of the "Oberon" class. Before and abaft the bridge the superstructure is mainly of glass fibre laminate in most units of this class. The superstructure of *Orpheus* is of light alloy aluminium.

Engineering: 3 bladed, 7 foot diameter propellers; 400 rpm.

Gunnery: "O" class submarines serving in the Far East carried a 20 mm Oerlikon gun during Indonesian Confrontation.

Modification: *Oberon* has been modified with deeper casing to house equipment for the initial training of personnel for nuclear powered submarines. Others of this class are currently undergoing modification.

Radar: Search; I-band.

Sonar: Types 186 and 187.

Transfer: The submarine of the "Oberon" class laid down on 27 Sep 1962 at HM Dockyard, Chatham as *Onyx* for the Royal Navy was launched on 29 Feb 1964 as *Ojibwa* for the Royal Canadian Navy. She was replaced by another "Oberon" class submarine named *Onyx* for the Royal Navy built by Cammell Laird, Birkenhead.

OTUS   6/1976, Dr. Giorgio Arra

WALRUS   6/1976, Wright and Logan

ONYX   7/1976, Wright and Logan

AIRCRAFT CARRIERS

Note: *Eagle,* see Disposal List.

1 "ARK ROYAL" CLASS

Name	No.	Builders	Laid down	Launched	Commissioned
ARK ROYAL	R 09	Cammell Laird, Birkenhead	3 May 1943	3 May 1950	25 Feb 1955

Displacement, tons: 43 060 standard; 50 786 full load
Length, feet (metres): 720·0 *(219·5)* pp; 845·0 *(257·6)* oa
Beam, feet (metres): 112·8 *(34·4)* hull
Draught, feet (metres): 36·0 *(11·0)*
Width, feet (metres): 166·0 *(50·6)*
Catapults: 2 improved steam
Aircraft: 30 fixed wing + 9 helicopters
Armour: 4·5 in belt; 4 in flight deck; 2·5 in hangar deck; 1·5 in hangar side
Main engines: Parsons single reduction geared turbines; 4 shafts; 152 000 shp
Boilers: 8 Admiralty 3-drum type; pressure 400 psi *(28·1 kg/cm²)*; superheat 600°F (316°C)
Speed, knots: 31·5
Oil fuel, tons: 5 500 capacity
Complement: 260 officers (as Flagship); 2 380 ratings (with Air Staff)

First British aircraft carrier with steam catapults. Had first side lift in a British aircraft carrier, situated amidships on the port side and serving the upper hangar, but in 1959 this was removed, the deck park provided by the angled deck having obviated its necessity, leaving her with two centre lifts. In 1961, the deck landing projector sight, "Hilo" long range guidance system, and more powerful steam catapults were installed. Ship originally cost £21 428 000.
To be replaced by *Invincible* when *Ark Royal* will probably go into reserve and *Eagle* be scrapped.

Aircraft: Phantom FG1, 892 Squadron (12).
Buccaneer 2, 809 Squadron (14).
Gannet AEW, 849 B Squadron (4).
Sea King ASW, 824 Squadron (7).
Wessex 3, SAR (2).

Corvus: Four 6-tubed Knebworth Corvus launchers for Chaff; single R.F.L. Mk 5 51 mm rocket flare-launcher co-mounted.

Electronics: Fitted with Skynet and Tacan.

Engineering: 5 bladed propellers of 15 ft diameter. 230 rpm.

Modernisation: A three-years "special refit" and modernisation costing £32 500 000, from Mar 1967 to Feb 1970, enables her to operate both Phantom and Buccaneer Mk 2 aircraft. A fully angled deck 8·5 degrees off the centre line was fitted, involving two large extensions to the flight deck and the size of the island was increased. A new waist catapult with an increased launching speed allows her to operate aircraft at almost "nil" wind conditions. A new direct acting gear was installed to enable bigger aircraft to be landed at greater speeds.

Radar: Search: Two Type 965.
Aircraft Direction: One Type 982.
Heightfinder: Two Type 983.
CCA: 1 set.
Navigation: One Type 975.

ARK ROYAL (with two A 7 Corsairs and an A 6 Intruder from USS *John F. Kennedy*)　　6/1976, MOD(N)

ARK ROYAL (at Lisbon—*Stromness* and *Naiad* behind)　　10/1976, MOD(N)

ARK ROYAL　　　　　　　　　　　　　　　　　　　　　　9/1976, MOD(N)

1 HELICOPTER/VSTOL CARRIER

Name	No.	Builders	Laid down	Launched	Commissioned
HERMES	R 12	Vickers-Armstrong Ltd, Barrow-in-Furness	21 June 1944	16 Feb 1953	18 Nov 1959

Displacement, tons: 23 900 standard; 28 700 full load
Length, feet (metres): 650·0 *(198·1)* pp; 744·3 *(226·9)* oa
Beam, feet (metres): 90·0 *(27·4)* hull
Draught, feet (metres): 29·0 *(8·8)*
Width, feet (metres): 160·0 *(48·8)* overall
Aircraft: A squadron of Wessex Sea King, and Wessex V helicopters
Armour: Reinforced flight deck
Missiles: 2 quadruple Seacat launchers either side abaft the after lift
Main engines: Parsons geared turbines; 2 shafts; 76 000 shp
Boilers: 4 Admiralty 3-drum type
Speed, knots: 28
Oil fuel, tons: 3 880 furnace; 320 diesel
Complement: 980. In emergency a Commando can be embarked

Originally name ship of a class including *Albion, Bulwark* and *Centaur,* but design was modified to a more advanced type, incorporating new equipment and improved arrangements, including five post-war developments— angled deck, steam catapult, landing sight, 3-D radar, and deck edge-lift. Air-conditioned. Embarked air squadrons and joined the Fleet summer 1960. Long refit 1964 to 1966, costing £10 000 000.

Conversion: *Hermes* was taken in hand for conversion to a Commando Carrier on 1 Mar 1971, commissioning for this role on 17 Aug 1973. Fixed wing facilities such as catapults and arrester gear were removed. The whole performance cost over £25 million.
In 1976, as a result of the Defence Review and pressure from other NATO countries, *Hermes'* role was altered to that of A/S carrier with the retention of a capability for commando support. As a result she underwent yet another conversion at Devonport which was completed Jan 1977. How long she continues in this role depends on how much extra delay is experienced on the "Invincible" class but it seems likely that she will continue to run until at least 1984-5. When the Harriers are eventually in naval service they will fly from this ship amongst others. The first operational squadron is due for embarkation in *Hermes* in 1980.

Engineering: 15 ft 6 in diameter propellers; 230 rpm.

Flight deck: Angled 6·5 deg off centre line of ship, the biggest angle that could be contrived in an aircraft carrier of this size. Strengthened to take Harrier aircraft.

HERMES (during Harrier trials)   2/1977, MOD(N)

Radar: Surveillance: One Type 965 with single AKE-1 array.
Search: One Type 993.
Navigation: One Type 975.
Fire Control: Two GWS 22.
Tacan beacon.

Turning circle: 800 yds.

HERMES   1/1977, MOD(N)

1 RESERVE HELICOPTER CARRIER

Name	No.	Builders	Laid down	Launched	Commissioned
BULWARK	R 08	Harland & Wolff Ltd, Belfast	10 May 1945	22 June 1948	4 Nov 1954

Displacement, tons: 23 300 standard; 27 705 full load
Length, feet (metres): 650 *(198·1)* pp; 737·8 *(224·9)* oa
Beam, feet (metres): 90 *(27·4)* hull
Draught, feet (metres): 28 *(8·5)*
Width, feet (metres): 123·5 *(37·7)* overall
Aircraft: 20 Wessex and Sioux helicopters
Landing craft: 4 LCVP
Guns: 8—40 mm (twins) Bofors on UK Mk V mountings
Main engines: Parsons geared turbines; 76 000 shp; 2 shafts
Boilers: 4 Admiralty 3 drum
Speed, knots: 28
Oil fuel, tons: 3 880 furnace; 320 diesel
Complement: 980 plus 750 Royal Marine Commando and troops

Former fixed-wing aircraft carrier. Converted into commando ship in Portsmouth Dockyard, Jan 1959 to Jan 1960. Her arrester gear and catapults have been removed but, with a helicopter and VSTOL capability she was placed in reserve in April 1976 as a result of the 1975 Defence Review and will remain in this state until *Illustrious* completes.

BULWARK   7/1973, C. and S. Taylor

0 + 2 ANTI-SUBMARINE CRUISERS

Name	No.	Builders	Laid down	Launched	Commissioned
INVINCIBLE	CAH 1	Vickers Ltd, Barrow	20 July 1973	3 May 1977	?1979
ILLUSTRIOUS	CAH 2	Swan Hunter Ltd, Wallsend	1976	—	?1980

Displacement, tons: 16 000 standard; 19 500 full load
Length, feet (metres): 632 pp *(192·9)*; 677 oa *(206·6)*
Beam, feet (metres): 90 wl *(27·5)*; 104·6 deck *(31·9)*
Draught, feet (metres): ?24 *(7·3)*
Flight deck length, feet (metres): 550 *(167·8)*
Aircraft: Total of 15: 10 Sea King helicopters (also to carry 5 Harriers)
Missile launchers: Twin Sea Dart (see notes)
Main engines: 4 Olympus gas turbines; 112 000 shp; 2 shafts (reversible gear box)
Speed, knots: 28
Range, miles: 5 000 at 18 knots
Complement: 900 (31 officers, 265 senior ratings, 604 junior ratings) (excluding aircrew)

The history of this class is a long and complex one starting almost sixteen years ago. The first of class, the result of many compromises, was ordered from Vickers on 17 April 1973. At that time completion might have been expected in 1977-8 but changes in design and labour problems have delayed this by probably two years. The results of this must be the running-on of the "Tiger" class and *Hermes* to provide the necessary aircraft platforms at sea. The order for the second ship to be named *Illustrious* was placed on 14 May 1976, whilst no decision has yet been reached on the third. Present indications are that *Invincible* will replace *Ark Royal* and *Illustrious* the two "Tiger" class, *Bulwark* being paid off at the same time.
The primary task of this class, apart from providing a command centre for maritime air forces, is the operation of both helicopters and VTOL/STOL aircraft. Provision has been made for sufficiently large lifts and hangars to accommodate the next generation of both these aircraft.
The design allows for an open foc'sle head and a slightly angled deck which will allow the Sea Dart launcher to be set almost amidships.

Cost: Although originally estimated at approximately £60 million the final bill per ship is likely to be nearer £150 million.

Missiles: Original drawing (top) shows four Exocet launchers subsequently apparently deleted.

Radar: Surveillance: One Type 965 with double AKE 1 array.
Search: One Type 992 R.
Fire Control: Two Type 909 for Sea Dart.
Navigation: One Type 1006.

Sonar: Type 184.

INVINCIBLE at launch   5/1977, Vickers Ltd.

1977, Vickers Ltd.

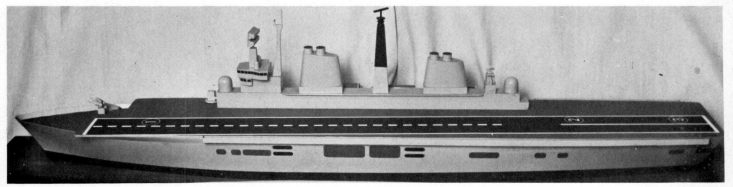

INVINCIBLE model   1973, MOD

CRUISERS

2 "TIGER" CLASS (HELICOPTER CRUISERS)

Name	No.	Builders	Laid down	Launched	Commissioned
BLAKE (ex-*Tiger*, ex-*Blake*)	C 99	Fairfield SB & Eng, Govan	17 Aug 1942	20 Dec 1945	8 Mar 1961
TIGER (ex-*Bellerophon*)	C 20	John Brown, Clydebank	1 Oct 1941	25 Oct 1945	18 Mar 1959

Displacement, tons: 9 500 standard; 12 080 full load
Length, feet (metres): 538·0 *(164·0)* pp; 550·0 *(167·6)* wl; 566·5 *(172·8)* oa
Beam, feet (metres): 64·0 *(19·5)*
Draught, feet (metres): 23·0 *(7·0)*
Aircraft: 4 Sea King helicopters
Missile launchers: 2 quadruple Seacat
Guns: 2—6 in *(152 mm)* (1 twin); 2—3 in *(76 mm)* (twin)
Armour: Belt 3·5 in—3·2 in *(89–83 mm)*; deck 2 in *(51 mm)*; turret 3 in—1 in *(76—25 mm)*
Main engines: 4 Parsons geared turbines; 4 shafts; 80 000 shp
Boilers: 4 Admiralty 3-drum type
Speed, knots: 30
Range, miles: 2 000 at 30 knots; 4 000 at 20 knots; 6 500 at 13 knots
Oil fuel, tons: 1 850
Complement: 85 officers, 800 ratings

This design was originally an improvement on that of *Superb/Swiftsure. Bellerophon* and *Hawke* of a similar design were cancelled in 1945-46 as were the projected ships *Centurion, Edgar, Mars* and *Neptune*. There was much juggling of names between ships; *Blake* was renamed *Tiger* in Dec 1944 and back to *Blake* in Feb 1945. *Defence* was renamed *Lion* in Oct 1957. *Bellerophon* was renamed *Tiger* in Feb 1945. Work on all three of the surviving ships was suspended in July 1946, the decision to complete them being announced on 15 Oct 1954. Subsequent redesign delayed work even further and it was not completed until 1959-61. By this time *Tiger* had cost £13 113 000 and *Blake* £14 940 000. The next stage was conversion to command helicopter cruisers (official title). *Lion* was not converted and was eventually sent for scrap in April 1975. *Blake* was transformed by Portsmouth Dockyard at a cost of £5 500 000 from early 1965 until recommissioning on 23 April 1969. *Tiger* was in hand from 1968 to 1972 at Devonport Dockyard, her cost reaching the staggering sum of £13 250 000.(As a considerable amount of equipment from *Lion* was used in *Tiger's* conversion the latter was unofficially known for a time as "Liger").

Electrical: 4 turbo-generators provide 4 000 kW a/c, the first time this type of power had been used in British cruisers although it was already in use in the "Daring" class destroyers.

Engineering: Main machinery is largely automatic and can be remotely controlled. Steam conditions 400 psi pressure and 640°F. Propellers 11 ft dia, 285 rpm.

Radar: Search: One Type 965 and one Type 993.
Height Finder: One Type 277 or 278.
Fire Control: Four MRS 3 fire control directors.
Navigation: One Type 975.

Turning circle: 800 yds.

BLAKE   5/1976, Wright and Logan

TIGER   6/1975, MOD(N)

BLAKE with friends   4/1976, MOD(N)

LIGHT CRUISERS

1 TYPE 82

Name	No.		Builders		Laid down	Launched	Commissioned
BRISTOL	D 23		Swan Hunter & Tyne Shipbuilders Ltd.		15 Nov 1967	30 June 1969	31 Mar 1973

Displacement, tons: 6 100 standard; 7 100 full load
Length, feet (metres): 490·0 *(149·4)* wl; 507·0 *(154·5)* oa
Beam, feet (metres): 55·0 *(16·8)*
Draught, feet (metres): 16·8 *(5·2)*; 23 *(7)* (sonar dome)
Aircraft: Landing platform for 1 Wasp helicopter
Missile launchers: 1 twin Sea Dart GWS 30 launcher aft
A/S weapons: 1 Ikara single launcher forward; 1 Limbo three-barrelled depth charge mortar (Mark 10) aft
Gun: 1—4·5 in *(115 mm)* Mark 8 forward
Main engines: COSAG arrangement (combined steam and gas turbines) 2 sets Standard Range geared steam turbines, 30 000 shp; 2 Bristol-Siddeley marine Olympus TMIA gas turbines, 56 000 shp; 2 shafts
Boilers: 2
Speed, knots: 30
Fuel, tons: 900
Range, miles: 5 000 at 18 knots
Complement: 407 (29 officers, 378 ratings)

Designed around Sea Dart GWS 30 weapons system. Fully stabilised to present a steady weapon platform. The gas turbines provide emergency power and high speed boost. The machinery is remotely-controlled from a ship control centre. Automatic steering, obviating the need for a quartermaster. Many labour-saving items of equipment fitted to make the most efficient and economical use of manpower resulting in a smaller ship's company for tonnage than any previous warship. Fitted with Action Data Automation Weapon System. Started trials 10 April 1972. Remainder of class cancelled owing to high cost and cancellation of aircraft-carrier building programme for which they were intended as A/A escorts. Officially listed as "destroyer" which is in some measure borne out by her limited fire-power, lack of embarked helicopter, limited ESM, as well as lack of jammers and Knebworth Corvus launchers.

Appearance: Three funnels, one amidships and two aft abreast the mainmast.

A/S weapons: Ikara is GWS 40.

Communications: By GEC-Marconi to include SCOT satellite system compatible with both SKYNET and the US Defence satellites.

Cost: £22 500 000 (£27 000 000 overall). GEC-Marconi equipment for radar, weapons and communications cost over £3 000 000.

Missiles: The Sea Dart ship missile system has a reasonable anti-ship capability.

Radar: Surveillance: One Type 965 with double AKE array and IFF.
Search: One Type 992.
Fire Control: Two Type 909 (Sea Dart)
Navigation: One Type 1006; One Type 978.

Sonar: Types 162, 170, 182, 184, 185, 189.

BRISTOL   4/1975, MOD(N)

BRISTOL   5/1973, John G. Callis

BRISTOL   5/1973, John G. Callis

7 "COUNTY" CLASS

Name	No.
ANTRIM	D 18
DEVONSHIRE	D 02
FIFE	D 20
GLAMORGAN	D 19
KENT	D 12
LONDON	D 16
NORFOLK	D 21

Builders	Laid down	Launched	Commissioned
Fairfield SB & Eng Co Ltd, Govan	20 Jan 1966	19 Oct 1967	14 July 1970
Cammell Laird & Co Ltd, Birkenhead	9 Mar 1959	10 June1960	15 Nov 1962
Fairfield SB & Eng Co Ltd, Govan	1 June1962	9 July 1964	21 June 1966
Vickers-Armstrong Ltd, Newcastle-on-Tyne	13 Sep 1962	9 July 1964	11 Oct 1966
Harland & Wolff Ltd, Belfast	1 Mar 1960	27 Sep 1961	15 Aug 1963
Swan, Hunter & Wigham Richardson, Wallsend	26 Feb 1960	7 Dec 1961	4 Nov 1963
Swan, Hunter & Wigham Richardson, Wallsend	15 Mar 1966	16 Nov 1967	7 Mar 1970

Displacement, tons: 5 440 standard; 6 200 full load
Length, feet (metres): 505·0 *(153·9)* wl; 520·5 *(158·7)* oa
Beam, feet (metres): 54·0 *(16·5)*
Draught, feet (metres): 20·0 *(6·1)*
Aircraft: 1 Wessex helicopter
Missile launchers: 4 Exocet in four ships (see *Missile* note): 1 twin Seaslug aft; 2 quadruple Seacat either side abreast hangar
Guns: 4—4·5 in *(115 mm)*, 2 twin turrets forward; 2—20 mm, (single) (2—4·5 only in ships with Exocet)
Main engines: Combined steam and gas turbines; 2 sets geared steam turbines, 30 000 shp; 4 gas turbines, 30 000 shp; 2 shafts
Boilers: 2 Babcock & Wilcox
Speed, knots: 30
Complement: 471 (33 officers and 438 men)

Fife, Glamorgan, Antrim and *Norfolk* have the more powerful Seaslug II systems. All fitted with stablisers and are fully air-conditioned. Original cost varied from £13·8 million *(Hampshire)* to £16·8 million *(Antrim)*. Officially rated as "destroyers".

Appearance: *Kent* and *London* have mainmast stepped further aft than remainder. The last four of the class have distinctive tubular foremast and twin AKE radar aerial.

Disposal: As a result of the Defence Review *Hampshire* was paid off in April 1976—at least seven years before she might have been expected on the disposal list.

Electrical: Two 1 000 kW turbo-alternators and three gas turbines alternators total 3 750 kW, at 440 V a/c SCOT fitted in *London.*

Engineering: These are the first ships of their size to have COSAG (combined steam and gas turbine machinery). Boilers work at a pressure of 700 psi and a temperature of 950 deg F. The steam and gas turbines are geared to the same shaft. Each shaft set consists of a high pressure and low pressure steam turbine of 15 000 shp combined output plus two G.6 gas turbines each of 7 500 shp. The gas turbines are able to develop their full power from cold within a few minutes, enabling ships lying in harbour without steam to get under way instantly in emergency.

Gunnery: The 4·5 inch guns are radar controlled fully automatic dual-purpose. The 20 mm guns were added for picket duties in S. E. Asia, but have been retained for general close range duties.

Missiles: Four Exocet fitted in *Norfolk, Antrim, Glamorgan* and *Fife.* No reloads carried. *Norfolk* Exocet trials on French missile range (Mediterranean) in April 1974.

Radar: Air Search: One type 965 (double AKE-2 array in *Norfolk, Glamorgan, Antrim* and *Fife*—remainder single AKE-1). Surveillance; One Type 992. Height Finder; One Type 277. Seaslug fire control; One Type 901. Gunnery fire control; MRS 3 (forward). Seacat fire control; GWS 22 in *Kent, Norfolk, Antrim, Fife* and *Glamorgan;* GWS 21 in *Devonshire* and *London.* Navigation; One Type 975.

LONDON
9/1976, C and S Taylor

ANTRIM
6/1976, Michael D. J. Lennon

NORFOLK
10/1976, Wright and Logan

KENT
6/1976, A. D. Baker III

GLAMORGAN
4/1976, C. and S. Taylor

DESTROYERS

4 + 4 + 1 "SHEFFIELD" (TYPE 42) CLASS

Name	No.	Builders	Laid down	Launched	Commissioned
SHEFFIELD	D 80	Vickers Ltd SB Group, Barrow	15 Jan 1970	10 June 1971	16 Feb 1975
BIRMINGHAM	D 86	Cammell Laird & Co Ltd, Birkenhead	28 Mar 1972	30 July 1973	3 Dec 1976
COVENTRY	D 118	Cammell Laird & Co Ltd, Birkenhead	22 Mar 1973	21 June 1974	1978
CARDIFF	D 108	Vickers Ltd SB Group, Barrow (see note)	3 Nov 1972	22 Feb 1974	1978
NEWCASTLE	D 87	Swan Hunter Ltd, Wallsend on Tyne	21 Feb 1973	24 Apr 1975	1977
GLASGOW	D 88	Swan Hunter Ltd, Wallsend on Tyne	7 Mar 1974	14 Apr 1976	1978
EXETER	—	Swan Hunter Ltd, Wallsend on Tyne	1976	—	—
SOUTHAMPTON	—	Vosper Thornycroft Ltd	21 Oct 1976	—	—
	—	Vosper Thornycroft Ltd	—	—	—

Displacement, tons: 3 150 standard; 4 100 full load
Length, feet (metres): 392·0 *(119·5)* wl; 410·0 *(125·0)* oa
Beam, feet (metres): 46 *(14)*
Draught, feet (metres): 14 *(4·3)*
Aircraft: 1 Lynx helicopter (see note)
Missile launchers: 1 twin Sea Dart medium range surface-to-air (surface-to-surface capability) GWS 30 system
Guns: 1—4·5 in automatic, Mark 8, 2—20 mm Oerlikon; 2 saluting
A/S weapons: Helicopter-launched Mk 44 torpedoes; 6 A/S torpedo tubes (triples) for Mk 46 to be fitted at 1st refit in earlier ships and during building for remainder
Main engines: COGOG arrangement of Rolls Royce Olympus gas turbines for full power 50 000 shp; 2 Rolls Royce Tyne gas turbines for cruising 8 000 shp; cp propellers; 2 shafts
Speed, knots: 30
Range: 4 500 miles at 18 knots
Complement: 299 (26 officers, 80 senior rates, 193 junior rates) (accommodation for 312)

This is a class of all gas-turbine ships fitted with four sets of stabilisers and twin rudders. The helicopter will carry the Skua (CK 834) air-to-surface weapon for use against lightly defended surface ship targets such as fast patrol boats. Advantages include ability to reach maximum speed with great rapidity, reduction in space and weight and 25 per cent reduction in technical manpower. Originally to cost approximately £23 000 000 per ship, although this may well be increased by delays and rising costs of raw materials and labour.
Exeter ordered 22 Jan 1976. *Southampton* ordered 18 Mar 1976. Ninth ship ordered in Mar 1977 with further orders planned.
Glasgow damaged by fire whilst fitting out 23 Sep 1976.

Completion: *Cardiff,* whose completion was delayed by lack of man-power at Vickers Ltd, Barrow, was towed to Swan Hunters, Ltd, Wallsend in Feb 1976 for completion in 1978.

Electronics: Twin SCOT Skynet satellite communication aerials; ADAWS 4 for coordination of action information. ECM D/F.

Engineering: Considerable automation has allowed a cut in engine-room staff required, a number of machinery spaces operating unmanned. Propellers by Stone Manganese (Type XX).

Helicopter: First ships provided with Wasp until Lynx becomes available.

Radar: Search; One Type 965 with double AKE-2 array and IFF.
Surveillance and Target indication; One Type 992Q.
Sea Dart fire control and Target; Two Type 909
Navigation, HDWS and helicopter control; One Type 1006

Sonar: Type 184 hull mounted. Type 162 classification.

SHEFFIELD   5/1976, Wright and Logan

SHEFFIELD   5/1976, Wright and Logan

BIRMINGHAM   11/1976, Michael D. J. Lennon

BIRMINGHAM   11/1976, MOD(N)

FRIGATES

7 + 1 "AMAZON" (TYPE 21) CLASS

Name	No.	Builders	Laid down	Launched	Commissioned
AMAZON	F 169	Vosper Thornycroft, Woolston	6 Nov 1969	26 April 1971	11 May 1974
ANTELOPE	F 170	Vosper Thornycroft, Woolston	23 Mar 1971	16 Mar 1972	19 July 1975
ACTIVE	F 171	Vosper Thornycroft, Woolston	23 July 1971	23 Nov 1972	1977
AMBUSCADE	F 172	Yarrow & Co Ltd, Glasgow	1 Sep 1971	18 Jan 1973	5 Sep 1975
ARROW	F 173	Yarrow & Co Ltd, Glasgow	28 Sep 1972	5 Feb 1974	29 July 1976
ALACRITY	F 174	Yarrow & Co Ltd, Glasgow	5 Mar 1973	18 Sep 1974	1977
ARDENT	F 175	Yarrow & Co Ltd, Glasgow	26 Feb 1974	9 May 1975	1977
AVENGER	F 185	Yarrow & Co Ltd, Glasgow	30 Oct 1974	20 Nov 1975	1978

Displacement, tons: 2 750 standard; 3 250 full load
Length, feet (metres): 360·0 *(109·7)* wl; 384·0 *(117·0)* oa
Beam, feet (metres): 41·8 *(12·7)*
Draught, feet (metres): 14·5 *(4·4)*
Aircraft: 1 Lynx helicopter
Missile launchers: 1 quadruple Seacat surface-to-air (later ships planned to have Seawolf; see note); 4 Exocet MM 38
Guns: 1—4·5 in Mk 8; 2—20 mm Oerlikon (singles)
A/S weapons: Helicopter launched torpedoes; 6 (2 triple) torpedo tubes for Mk 46 (to be fitted)
Main engines: COGOG arrangement of 2 Rolls Royce Olympus gas turbines 56 000 bhp; 2 Rolls Royce Tyne gas turbines for cruising 8 500 shp; 2 shafts; controllable pitch, 5-bladed propellers
Speed, knots: 32; 18 on Tyne GTs
Range, miles: 3 500 at 18 knots; 1 200 at 30 knots
Complement: 177 (13 officers, and 164 ratings) (accommodation for 192)

A contract was awarded to Vosper Thornycroft, on 27 Feb 1968 for the design of a patrol frigate to be prepared in full collaboration with Yarrow Ltd. This is the first custom built gas turbine frigate (designed and constructed as such from the keel up, as opposed to conversion) and the first warship designed by commercial firms for many years. All eight were planned for completion by 1978 but the building of some ships has been delayed by lack of technical information and equipment from beyond the shipyards as well as political directives.

Electronics: SCOT satellite communication to be fitted in last four ships, CAAIS fitted.

Helicopter: First ships provided with Wasp until Lynx is available.

Missiles: Although Seawolf was planned for the last four, its fitting is doubtful for some time to come. All now fitted with Exocet.

Radar: Surveillance and Target Indicator: One Type 992Q.
Navigation: One Type 978.
Seacat Control: Two GWS 24.
Gun Fire Control: Orion RTN-10X WSA 4 system.
IFF Interrogator: Cossor Type 1010.
IFF Transponder: Plessey PTR 461.

Sonar: Type 184M hull mounted.
Type 162M classification.

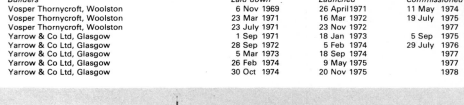

AMBUSCADE   11/1975, Michael D. J. Lennon

AMAZON   5/1975, MOD(N)

ARROW   7/1976, C. and S. Taylor

ANTELOPE   6/1976, C. and S. Taylor

2 + 1 "BROADSWORD" CLASS (TYPE 22)

Name	No.	Builders	Laid down	Launched	Commissioned
BATTLEAXE	—	Yarrow Ltd, Glasgow	1976	18 May 1977	—
BROADSWORD	F 88	Yarrow Ltd, Glasgow	7 Feb 1975	12 May 1976	Late 1978?
BRILLIANT	—	Yarrow Ltd, Glasgow	1977	—	

Displacement, tons: 3 500 standard; 4 000 full load
Dimensions, feet (metres): 430 oa × 48·5 × 14 *(131·2 × 14·8 × 4·3)*
Aircraft: 2 Lynx helicopters with ASM and A/S torpedoes
Missile launchers: 2 Sea Wolf surface-to-air systems; 4 Exocet launchers forward
Guns: 2—40 mm
A/S weapons: 6 (2 triple) Mk 32 torpedo tubes for Mk 46; helicopter carried A/S torpedoes
Main engines: COGOG arrangement of 2 Rolls Royce Olympus gas turbines; 56 000 bhp and 2 Rolls Royce Tyne gas turbines; 8 500 bhp; 2 shafts
Speed, knots: 30+ (18 on Tynes)
Range, miles: 4 500 at 18 knots (on Tynes)
Complement: 250 (approx)

Designed as successors to the "Leander" class, the construction of which ceased with the completion of the scheduled programme of 26 ships. Order for the first of class, *Broadsword,* was placed on 26 Feb 1974, *Battleaxe* ordered 5 Sep 1975. Order for third ship 7 Sep 1976. Fourth to be ordered 1977. This class is primarily designed for A/S operations and is capable of acting as OTC and helicopter control ship. These are the first major ships for the RN which have no main gun armament (apart from the "Blackwood" class.)
It is reported that fourteen of this class are planned.

Radar: Surveillance: Two Type 967/8.
Navigation: One Type 1006.

Sonar: Type 2016.

BROADSWORD model   1974, MOD

16 "LEANDER" CLASS

Name	No.	Builders	Laid down	Launched	Commissioned
AJAX	F 114	Cammell Laird & Co Ltd, Birkenhead	12 Oct 1959	16 Aug 1962	10 Dec 1963
ARETHUSA	F 38	J. Samuel White & Co Ltd, Cowes	7 Sep 1962	5 Nov 1963	24 Nov 1965
ARGONAUT	F 56	Hawthorn Leslie Ltd, Hebburn-on-Tyne	27 Nov 1964	8 Feb 1966	17 Aug 1967
AURORA	F 10	John Brown & Co (Clydebank) Ltd	1 June 1961	28 Nov 1962	9 April 1964
CLEOPATRA	F 28	HM Dockyard, Devonport	19 June 1963	25 Mar 1964	4 Jan 1966
DANAE	F 47	HM Dockyard, Devonport	16 Dec 1964	31 Oct 1965	7 Sep 1967
DIDO	F 104	Yarrow & Co Ltd, Scotstoun, Glasgow	2 Dec 1959	22 Dec 1961	18 Sep 1963
EURYALUS	F 15	Scotts Shipbuilding & Eng Co, Greenock	2 Nov 1961	6 June 1963	16 Sep 1964
GALATEA	F 18	Swan Hunter & Wigham Richardson, Tyne	29 Dec 1961	23 May 1963	25 April 1964
JUNO	F 52	John I. Thornycroft Ltd, Woolston	16 July 1964	24 Nov 1965	18 July 1967
LEANDER	F 109	Harland & Wolff Ltd, Belfast	10 April 1959	28 June 1961	27 Mar 1963
MINERVA	F 45	Vickers-Armstrong Ltd, Tyne	25 July 1963	19 Dec 1964	14 May 1966
NAIAD	F 39	Yarrow & Co Ltd, Scotstoun, Glasgow	30 Oct 1962	4 Nov 1963	15 Mar 1965
PENELOPE	F 127	Vickers-Armstrong Ltd, Tyne	14 Mar 1961	17 Aug 1962	31 Oct 1963
PHOEBE	F 42	Alex Stephen & Sons Ltd, Glasgow	3 June 1963	8 July 1964	15 April 1966
SIRIUS	F 40	HM Dockyard, Portsmouth	9 Aug 1963	22 Sep 1964	15 June 1966

AURORA (with Ikara and SCOT aerials)   6/1976, MOD(N)

10 "BROAD-BEAMED LEANDER" CLASS

Name	No.	Builders	Laid down	Launched	Commissioned
ACHILLES	F 12	Yarrow & Co Ltd, Scotstoun, Glasgow	1 Dec 1967	21 Nov 1968	9 July 1970
ANDROMEDA	F 57	HM Dockyard, Portsmouth	25 May 1966	24 May 1967	2 Dec 1968
APOLLO	F 70	Yarrow & Co Ltd, Scotstoun, Glasgow	1 May 1969	15 Oct 1970	28 May 1972
ARIADNE	F 72	Yarrow & Co Ltd, Scotstoun, Glasgow	1 Nov 1969	10 Sep 1971	10 Feb 1973
BACCHANTE	F 69	Vickers-Armstrong Ltd, Tyne	27 Oct 1966	29 Feb 1968	17 Oct 1969
CHARYBDIS	F 75	Harland & Wolff Ltd, Belfast	27 Jan 1967	28 Feb 1968	2 June 1969
DIOMEDE	F 16	Yarrow & Co Ltd, Scotstoun, Glasgow	30 Jan 1968	15 April 1969	2 April 1971
HERMIONE	F 58	Alex Stephen & Sons Ltd, Glasgow	6 Dec 1965	26 April 1967	11 July 1969
JUPITER	F 60	Yarrow & Co Ltd, Scotstoun, Glasgow	3 Oct 1966	4 Sep 1967	9 Aug 1969
SCYLLA	F 71	HM Dockyard, Devonport	17 May 1967	8 Aug 1968	12 Feb 1970

Displacement, tons: 2 450 standard; 2 860 full load (Leanders) 2 500 standard; 2 962 full load (Broad-beamed)
Length, feet (metres): 360 *(109·7)* wl; 372 *(113·4)* oa
Beam, feet (metres): 41 *(12·5)* (Leanders) 43 *(13·1)* (Broad-beamed)
Draught, feet (metres): 18 *(5·5)*
Aircraft: 1 Wasp helicopter
Missiles: Exocet in some and Seacat (see *Notes*)
Guns: 2—4·5 in *(115 mm)* (twin); 2—40 mm (varies); 2—20 mm (Seacat ships) (see *Notes*)
A/S weapons: Ikara in some (see *Notes*); 1 Limbo 3 barrelled mortar except in Exocet-fitted ships which carry triple A/S torpedo tubes instead
Main engines: 2 double reduction geared turbines; 2 shafts; 30 000 shp (see *Notes*)
Boilers: 2
Speed, knots: 30
Oil fuel, tons: 460
Complement: 251 (Leanders); 260 (Broad-beamed)

This class, whose construction extended over ten years, was an improvement on the Type 12. As originally designed there were several significant improvements—a helicopter, VDS and long-range air warning radar being the most important. Recently a number of conversions have been put in hand (see *Notes* below).

Electrical: 440 volts, 60 cycle AC. 1 900 kw in earlier ships, 2 500 kw in later ones.

Electronics: SCOT satellite communications being fitted at later conversions.

Engineering: The first ten have Y-100 machinery, the remainder of the "Leanders" Y-136. "Broad-beamed Leanders" have Y-160 machinery.

Gunnery: 4·5 in turret removed in Exocet and Ikara conversions and in *Penelope*. 40 mm are not fitted in unconverted ships mounting Seacat. Conversions mount 2 single 40 mm abaft the bridge.

Missiles: A series of rearmament programmes is in progress and some ships have already been completed.
(a) Exocet—Mounted forward in place of 4·5 inch turret.
Cleopatra (Devonport) completed 28 Nov 1975;
Phoebe (Devonport) started Aug 1974, completion Oct 1977;
Sirius (Devonport) started July 1975, completion Oct 1977;
Dido (Devonport) started July 1975, completion Dec 1977;
Argonaut (Devonport) started Nov 1975, completion Oct 1978;
Minerva (Chatham) started Dec 1975, completion Oct 1978;
Juno (Portsmouth) started Oct 1976, completion Oct 1978;
Danae (Devonport) started July 1977, completion Oct 1978;
plus the ten "Broad-beamed" ships.
(b) Ikara—Mounted forward in place of 4·5 inch turret. Radar Type 965 removed.
Leander (Devonport) completed Dec 1972;
Ajax (Devonport) completed Sep 1973;
Galatea (Devonport) completed Sep 1974;
Naiad (Devonport) completed July 1975;
Euryalus (Devonport) completed Mar 1976;
Aurora (Chatham) completed Mar 1976;
Arethusa (Portsmouth) completion Nov 1976;
Penelope on completion of Seawolf trials.
(c) Seacat—Single Seacat first fitted in *Naiad* and subsequently in all but conversions which carry two Seacat mounts in Ikara conversions and three in Exocet conversions.
(d) Seawolf—Subsequent fitting in place of Seacat. Trials in *Penelope* continuing during 1976.

Radar: Air surveillance: One Type 965 with single AKE array (except in Ikara ships)
Combined air/surface warning: One Type 993.
Fire Control: MRS 3/GWS 22.
Navigation: One Type 975.

Sonar: VDS was originally fitted in all but *Diomede*. In some the VDS has been removed leaving the well—in others the well has been plated over to provide extra accommodation for RMs. Can be replaced. Currently all Ikara conversions have VDS.

APOLLO

1976, Michael D. J. Lennon

CLEOPATRA (with Exocet)

8/1976, Wright and Logan

PENELOPE (with Seawolf and VDS)

10/1976, MOD(N)

JUNO

10/1976, C. and S. Taylor

7 "TRIBAL" CLASS (TYPE 81)

Name	No.	Builders	Laid down	Launched	Commissioned
ASHANTI	F 117	Yarrow & Co Ltd, Scotstoun	15 Jan 1958	9 Mar 1959	23 Nov 1961
ESKIMO	F 119	J. Samuel White & Co Ltd, Cowes	22 Oct 1958	20 Mar 1960	21 Feb 1963
GURKHA	F 122	J. I. Thornycroft & Co Ltd, Woolston	3 Nov 1958	11 July 1960	13 Feb 1963
MOHAWK	F 125	Vickers-Armstrong Ltd, Barrow	23 Dec 1960	5 April 1962	29 Nov 1963
NUBIAN	F 131	HM Dockyard, Portsmouth	7 Sep 1959	6 Sep 1960	9 Oct 1962
TARTAR	F 133	HM Dockyard, Devonport	22 Oct 1959	19 Sep 1960	26 Feb 1962
ZULU	F 124	Alex Stephen & Sons Ltd, Govan	13 Dec 1960	3 July 1962	17 April 1964

Displacement, tons: 2 300 standard; 2 700 full load
Length, feet (metres): 350·0 (106·7) wl; 360·0 (109·7) oa
Beam, feet (metres): 42·3 (12·9)
Draught, feet (metres): 17·5 (5·3)
Aircraft: 1 Wasp helicopter
Missile launchers: 2 quadruple Seacats
Guns: 2—4·5 in (singles); 2—20 mm
A/S weapons: 1 Limbo 3-barrelled mortar
Main engines: Combined steam and gas turbine; Metrovick steam turbine; 12 500 shp; Metrovick gas turbine; 7 500 shp; 1 shaft
Boilers: 1 Babcock & Wilcox (plus 1 auxiliary boiler)
Speed, knots: 28
Oil fuel, tons: 400
Complement: 253 (13 officers and 240 ratings)

Ashanti, Eskimo and *Gurkha* were ordered under the 1955-56 estimates, *Nubian* and *Tartar* 1956-57, and *Mohawk* and *Zulu* 1957-58. Designed as self-contained units for service in such areas as the Persian Gulf. *Ashanti* cost £5 220 000. Some still have 4 in flare rocket launchers.

Construction: All-welded prefabrication. Denny Brown stabilisers fitted. Enclosed bridge and twin rudders.

Corvus: Knebworth Corvus Chaff launchers fitted.

Electrical: Generator capacity of 1 500 kW.

Engineering: The gas turbine is used to boost the steam turbines for sustained bursts of high speed and also enables the ship lying in harbour without steam up to get under way instantly in emergency. The machinery is remotely controlled. The main boiler works at a pressure of 550 psi and a temperature of 850 deg F. Five-bladed propeller, 11·75 ft diameter, 280 rpm. The forward funnel serves the boilers, the after one the gas turbine.

Radar: Search: One Type 965 with single AKE 1 array and IFF.
Air and surface warning: One Type 293.
Navigation: One Type 975.
Fire control: MRS 3 system.
Seacat: GWS 21.

Sonar: Types 177, 170 and 162. Type 199. VDS fitted in *Ashanti* and *Gurkha* in 1970.

NUBIAN (off Belize)   1975, MOD(N)

TARTAR   9/1976, Dr. Giorgio Arra

ESKIMO   8/1976, Wright and Logan

9 "ROTHESAY" CLASS (MODIFIED TYPE 12)

Name	No.	Builders	Laid down	Launched	Commissioned
BERWICK	F 115	Harland & Wolff Ltd, Belfast	16 June1958	15 Dec 1959	1 June 1961
BRIGHTON	F 106	Yarrow & Co Ltd, Scotstoun	23 July 1957	30 Oct 1959	28 Sep 1961
FALMOUTH	F 113	Swan Hunter, Wigham Richardson	23 Nov 1957	15 Dec 1959	25 July 1961
LONDONDERRY	F 108	J. Samuel White & Co Ltd, Cowes	15 Nov 1956	20 May 1958	22 July 1960
LOWESTOFT	F 103	Alex Stephen & Sons Ltd, Govan	9 June1958	23 June1960	18 Oct 1961
PLYMOUTH	F 126	HM Dockyard, Devonport	1 July 1958	20 July 1959	11 May 1961
RHYL	F 129	HM Dockyard, Portsmouth	29 Jan 1958	23 Apr 1959	31 Oct 1960
ROTHESAY	F 107	Yarrow & Co Ltd, Scotstoun	6 Nov 1956	9 Dec 1957	23 Apr 1960
YARMOUTH	F 101	John Brown & Co Ltd, Clydebank	29 Nov 1957	23 Mar 1959	26 Mar 1960

Displacement, tons: 2 380 standard; 2 800 full load
Length, feet (metres): 360·0 (109·7) wl; 370·0 (112·8) oa·
Beam, feet (metres): 41·0 (12·5)
Draught, feet (metres): 17·3 (5·3)
Aircraft: 1 Wasp helicopter
Missile launchers: 1 quadruple Seacat
Guns: 2—4·5 in (115 mm) (1 twin); 2—20 mm (single)
A/S weapons: 1 Limbo 3-barrelled DC mortar
Main engines: 2 double reduction geared turbines; 2 shafts; 30 000 shp
Boilers: 2 Babcock & Wilcox
Speed, knots: 30
Oil fuel, tons: 400
Complement: 235 (15 officers and 220 ratings)

Provided under the 1954-55 programme. Originally basically similar to the "Whitby" class but with modifications in layout.

Electrical: Two turbo generators and two diesel generators in all ships. Total 1 140 kW. Alternating current, 440 volts, three phase, 60 cycles per second.

Engineering: Two Admiralty Standard Range turbines each rated at 15 000 shp. Propeller revolutions 220 rpm. Boilers 550 psi (38·7 kg/cm²) pressure and 850°F (450°C) temperature.

Modernisation: The "Rothesay" class was reconstructed and modernised from 1966-72 during which time they were equipped to operate a Wessex Wasp helicopter armed with homing torpedoes. A flight deck and hangar were built on aft, necessitating the removal of one of their anti-submarine mortars. A Seacat replaced the 40 mm gun. A new operations room, new GFCS and full air-conditioning were provided.

Radar: Search; One Type 993
Fire Control; MRS 3
Navigation; One Type 975

Refits: *Londonderry* started refit at Rosyth in Nov 1975 to become trials ship for Admiralty Surface Weapons Establishment.
Rothesay to have similar refit in mid-1977.

Seacat: Optical Director—GWS 20

BRIGHTON   5/1976, Wright and Logan

RHYL   6/1976, C. and S. Taylor

ROTHESAY   4/1976, C. and S. Taylor

LOWESTOFT   1976, Michael D. J. Lennon

3 "SALISBURY" CLASS (TYPE 61)

Name	No.
CHICHESTER	F 59
LINCOLN	F 99
SALISBURY	F 32

Builders	Laid down	Launched	Commissioned
Fairfield SB & Eng Co Ltd, Govan	25 Jan 1953	21 April 1955	16 May 1958
Fairfield SB & Eng Co Ltd, Govan	20 May 1955	6 April 1959	7 July 1960
HM Dockyard, Devonport	23 Jan 1952	25 June 1953	27 Feb 1957

Displacement, tons: 2 170 standard; 2 408 full load
Length, feet (metres): 320·0 *(97·5)* pp; 330·0 *(100·6)* wl; 339·8 *(103·6)* oa
Beam, feet (metres): 40·0 *(12·2)*
Draught, feet (metres): 15·5 *(4·7)*
Missile launchers: 1 quadruple Seacat in *Lincoln* and *Salisbury*
Guns: 2—4·5 in *(115 mm)*; 1—40 mm *(Chichester)*; 2—20 mm (remainder)
A/S weapons: 1 Squid triple-barrelled DC mortar (except *Chichester)*
Main engines: 8 ASR 1 diesels in three engine rooms; 2 shafts; 14 400 bhp; 4 engines geared to each shaft
Speed, knots: 24
Oil fuel, tons: 230
Range, miles: 2 300 at full power; 7 500 at 16 knots
Complement: 237 (14 officers and 223 ratings)

CHICHESTER   7/1976, Wright and Logan

Designed primarily for the direction of carrier-borne and shore-based aircraft. Ordered on 28 June 1951 except *Salisbury*, the prototype ship. Construction was all welded and largely prefabricated. The construction of three other ships *Exeter*, *Gloucester* and *Coventry* cancelled in 1957 being replaced by first three "Leander" class. Fitted with stabilisers (except *Lincoln*). Original lattice masts replaced by tower masts during 1960s. *Lincoln* and *Chichester* in reserve. *Lincoln* was fitted with wooden bow sheathing for Cod War 1976 but has subsequently been returned to reserve.

Corvus: Knebworth Corvus Chaff launchers fitted.

Engineering: Powered by Admiralty Standard Range 1 diesel engines coupled to the propeller shafts through hydraulic couplings and oil operated reverse and reduction gear boxes. *Lincoln* is fitted with controllable pitch propellers, rotating at 200 rpm, which are 12 feet in diameter, manufactured by Stone Marine & Engineering Co Ltd. The fuel tanks are fitted with compensating system.

Fire Control: Seacat control (only *Salisbury* and *Lincoln*): GWS 20 (optical).

Hong Kong Guardship: In 1973 *Chichester* was re-equipped for service as permanent HK Guardship. This involved removal of Type 965. *Chichester* returned to UK early 1976 to reserve.

Radar: Long range surveillance: One Type 965 with double AKE 2 array with IFF (except *Chichester*).·
Combined warning: One Type 993.
Height-finder: One Type 277Q (except *Chichester*).
Target indication: One Type 982 (except *Chichester*).
Fire control: Mk 6M director with Type 275.
Navigation: One Type 975.

Sonar: Types 174 and 170B.

Transfer: *Llandaff* to Bangladesh as *Oomar Farooq* (F 16) on 1 Dec 1976.

LINCOLN (with wooden sheath on bow for Cod War)   5/1976, MOD(N)

2 "LEOPARD" CLASS (TYPE 41)

Name	No.
JAGUAR	F 37
LYNX	F 27

Builders	Laid down	Launched	Commissioned
Wm. Denny & Bros Ltd, Dumbarton	2 Nov 1953	30 July 1957	12 Dec 1959
John Brown & Co Ltd, Clydebank	13 Aug 1953	12 Jan 1955	14 Mar 1957

Displacement, tons: 2 300 standard; 2 520 full load
Length, feet (metres): 320 *(97·5)* pp; 330 *(100·6)* wl; 339·8 *(103·6)* oa
Beam, feet (metres): 40 *(12·2)*
Draught, feet (metres): 16 *(4·9)*
Guns: 4—4·5 in *(115 mm)* (twin turrets); 1—40 mm
A/S weapons: 1 Squid 3-barrelled DC mortar
Main engines: 8 ASR 1 diesels in three engine rooms; 14 400 bhp; 2 shafts; 4 engines geared to each shaft
Speed, knots: 24
Oil fuel, tons: 220
Range, miles: 2 300 at full power; 7 500 at 16 knots
Complement: 235 (15 officers, 220 ratings)

Originally a class of four, a fifth ship having been cancelled for a "Leander" class. Designed primarily for anti-aircraft protection. All welded. *Jaguar* and *Lynx* were ordered on 28 June 1951. Both now in reserve. *Jaguar* having been fitted with wooden bow sheathing and commissioned for Cod War—now back in reserve. Fitted with stabilisers.

Electronics: ECM and D/F.

Engineering: The propelling machinery comprises Admiralty Standard Range 1 diesels coupled to the propeller shafting through hydraulic gear boxes. These diesels are of light weight, about 17 lb/shp. *Jaguar* is the only ship of this class to be fitted with controllable pitch propellers, 12 ft diameter 200 rpm. The fuel tanks have a compensating system, so that sea water replaces oil fuel as it is used.

Radar: Air Search: One Type 965 with single AKE 1 array and IFF.
Fire Control: Mk 6 M I-band. Type 275.
Navigation: One Type 975.

Reconstruction: *Lynx* was extensively refitted in 1963 with new mainmast. *Jaguar* similarly refitted in 1966-7.

Sonar: Types 174 and 170.

Transfer: Another ship of this class, *Panther*, was transferred to India while building and renamed *Brahmaputra*.

JAGUAR (with wooden bow sheathing for Cod War)   7/1976, MOD(N)

LYNX   10/1976, Michael D. J. Lennon

2 "WHITBY" CLASS (TYPE 12)

Name	No.	Builders	Laid down	Launched	Commissioned
EASTBOURNE	F 73	Vickers-Armstrong Ltd, Tyne	13 Jan 1954	29 Dec 1955	9 Jan 1958
TORQUAY	F 43	Harland & Wolff Ltd, Belfast	11 Mar 1953	1 July 1954	10 May 1956

Displacement, tons: 2 150 standard; 2 560 full load
Length, feet (metres): 360·0 *(109·7)* wl; 369·8 *(112·7)* oa
Beam, feet (metres): 41·0 *(12·5)*
Draught, feet (metres): 17 *(5·2)*
Guns: 2—4·5 in *(115 mm)* (twin) (not in *Eastbourne* who has 1—40 mm)
A/S weapons: 1 Limbo 3-barrelled DC mortar (in *Torquay* only)
Main engines: 2 sets d.r. geared turbines; 2 shafts; 30 430 shp
Boilers: 2 Babcock & Wilcox; Pressure 550 psi *(38·7 kg/cm²)*; Temperature 850°F (454°C)
Speed, knots: 31
Oil fuel, tons: 370
Complement: 225 (12 officers, and 213 ratings)

Ordered in 1951. Twin-rudders. They are all-welded.

Class: Originally class of six. *Torquay* used as Navigation/Direction training and trials ship at Portsmouth, having a large deck-house aft and carrying the first CAAIS (Computer Assisted Action Information System) to go to sea. *Eastbourne*, stripped of her 4·5 in guns and A/S armament, is based at Rosyth for engine-room trainees from HMS *Caledonia*. *Blackpool* now in use as target ship.

Electrical: System is alternating current, 440 volts, three phase, 60 cycles per second. Two turbo alternators and two diesel alternators. Total 1 140 kilowatts.

Engineering: Y 100 turbines with double reduction gearing giving low propeller revolutions of 220 rpm at high power.

Radar: Search: One Type 293.
Navigation: Type 975 (*Torquay* Type 978)
Fire Control: Type 275 (Mk 6 MDCT)

Sonar: Types 174, 170 and 162.

TORQUAY   8/1976, Wright and Logan

BLACKPOOL (rigged as target)   3/1976, Michael D. J. Lennon

4 "BLACKWOOD" CLASS (TYPE 14)

TWO ACTIVE SHIPS

Name	No.	Builders	Laid down	Launched	Commissioned
DUNDAS	F 48	J. Samuel White & Co Ltd	17 Oct 1952	25 Sep 1953	16 Mar 1956
HARDY	F 54	Yarrow & Co Ltd	4 Feb 1953	25 Nov 1953	12 Dec 1955

TWO HARBOUR TRAINING SHIPS

Name	No.	Builders	Laid down	Launched	Commissioned
RUSSELL	F 97	Swan Hunter & Wigham Richardson	11 Nov 1953	10 Dec 1954	7 Feb 1957
DUNCAN	F 80	John I. Thornycroft & Co Ltd	17 Dec 1953	30 May 1957	21 Oct 1958

Displacement, tons: 1 180 standard; 1 456 full load
Length, feet (metres): 300 (91·4) wl; 310 (94·5) oa
Beam, feet (metres): 33·0 (10·1)
Draught, feet (metres): 15·5 (4·7)
Guns: 2—40 mm Bofors
A/S weapons: 2 Limbo 3-barrelled DC mortars
Main engines: 1 set geared turbines; 1 shaft; 15 000 shp
Boilers: 2 Babcock & Wilcox; Pressure 550 psi (38·7 kg/cm²);
  Temperature 850°F (454°C)
Speed, knots: 26
Oil fuel, tons: 275
Range, miles: 4 000 at 12 knots
Complement: 140 (8 officers, and 132 ratings)

Originally a class of twelve.

Of comparatively simple construction. Built in prefabricated sections. In 1958-59 their hulls were strengthened to withstand severe and prolonged sea and weather conditions on fishery protection in Icelandic waters.

Class: The first two are currently operational. *Duncan* is at Rosyth for harbour training and *Russell* at Portsmouth for similar duties with HMS *Sultan*. *Hardy* recommissioned Nov 1976.

Engineering: All engined by their builders, except *Russell*, by Wallsend Slipway & Eng Co Ltd. Four-bladed, 12 ft diameter propeller, 220 rpm.

Radar: General search: One Type 978.

Sonar: Types 174, 170 and 162.

Turning circle: 350 yards.

DUNDAS   5/1975, C. and S. Taylor

1 TYPE 14 CONVERSION

Name	No.	Builders	Laid down	Launched	Commissioned
EXMOUTH	F 84	J. Samuel White & Co Ltd	24 Mar 1954	16 Nov 1955	20 Dec 1957

Details of dimensions and armament as for "Blackwood" Class Type 14 above.

Displacement, tons: 1 700 full load
Main engines: 1 Olympus Gas Turbine; 15 000 hp; 2 Proteus Gas Turbines; 6 500 hp; 1 shaft; cp propeller
Speed, knots: 26

The conversion of *Exmouth* to gas-turbine propulsion was completed in Chatham Dockyard on 20 July 1968. She was the first all gas-turbine major warship in the Royal Navy. To reserve Dec 1976.

Engineering: She can be propelled on only one system at a time, either the Olympus or the pair of Proteus engines. Horse power absorbed from Olympus is only 15 000 because:
a) Early version of Olympus.
b) COGOG arrangement.
c) Shafting unchanged.

Radar: General Search: One Type 978.

EXMOUTH   11/1975, Dr Giorgio Arra

TYPE 15

For *Grenville, Rapid, Undaunted* and *Volage* see Disposal List. With *Ulster,* acting as accommodation ship at Portsmouth, these are the sole survivors of the wartime "R", "T", "U", "V", "W", and "Z" classes of destroyers, launched in 1942-43. Of the 48 ships of these classes 33 were converted into Type 15 frigates and 7 ("T" Class) into Type 16 (limited conversion) frigates. A number have been transferred to other navies.

AMPHIBIOUS WARFARE FORCES

2 ASSAULT SHIPS (LPD)

Name	No.	Builders	Laid down	Launched	Commissioned
FEARLESS	L 10 (ex-L 3004)	Harland & Wolff Ltd, Belfast	25 July 1962	19 Dec 1963	25 Nov 1965
INTREPID	L 11 (ex-L 3005)	John Brown & Co (Clydebank) Ltd	19 Dec 1962	25 June 1964	11 Mar 1967

Displacement, tons: 11 060 standard; 12 120 full load; 16 950 ballasted
Length, feet (metres): 500 *(152·4)* wl; 520 *(158·5)* oa
Beam, feet (metres): 80 *(24·4)*
Draught, feet (metres): 20·5 *(6·2)*
Draught, ballasted: 32 *(9·8)* aft; 23 *(7·0)* fwd; 27·5 *(8·4)* mean
Landing craft: 4 LCM(9) in dock; 4 LCVP at davits
Vehicles: Specimen load: 15 tanks, 7 three-ton and 20 quarter-ton trucks
Aircraft: Flight deck facilities for 5 Wessex helicopters
Missiles: 4 Seacat systems
Guns: 2—40 mm Bofors
Main engines: 2 EE turbines; 22 000 shp; 2 shafts
Boilers: 2 Babcock & Wilcox
Speed, knots: 21
Range, miles: 5 000 at 20 knots
Complement: 580 (see Troops note)

They carry landing craft which are floated through the open stern by flooding compartments of the ship and lowering her in the water; are able to deploy tanks, vehicles and men; have seakeeping qualities much superior to those of tank landing ships, and greater speed and range. Capable of operating independently. Another valuable feature is a helicopter platform which is also the deckhead of the dock from which the landing craft are floated out. Officially estimated building cost: *Fearless* £11 250 000; *Intrepid* £10 500 000.
Intrepid to reserve in 1976 for refit in 1978 and to relieve *Fearless* (to reserve) 1979.

Countermeasures: Mount 2 Knebworth Corvus launchers.

Electrical: Power at 440V 60c/s 3-phase a/c is supplied by four 1 000 kW AE1 turbo-alternators.

Electronics: Fitted with CAAIS.

Engineering: The two funnels are staggered across the beam of the ship, indicating that the engines and boilers are arranged *en echelon,* two machinery spaces having one turbine and one boiler installed in each space. The turbines were manufactured by the English Electric Co, Rugby, the gearing by David Brown & Co, Huddersfield. Boilers work at a pressure of 550 lbs per sq in and a temperature of 850 deg F. Two 5-bladed propellers, 12·5 feet diameter, 200 rpm in *Fearless*.

Operational: Each ship is fitted out as a Naval Assault Group/Brigade Headquarters with an Assault Operations Room from which naval and military personnel, can mount and control the progress of an assault operation.

Radar: Air and surface search: One Type 993.
Navigation: One Type 975.

Satellite system: The Royal Navy fitted its first operational satellite communications system in *Intrepid* in 1969, the contract having been awarded to Plessey Radar—now removed.

Training: *Fearless* used for the sea training of officers from the Britannia Royal Naval College, Dartmouth, retaining full amphibious capabilities.

Troops: Each ship can carry 380 to 400 troops at ship's company standards, and an overload of 700 marines and military personnel can be accommodated for short periods.

INTREPID

4/1975, John G. Callis

FEARLESS

8/1975, C. and S. Taylor

INTREPID

3/1976, Wright and Logan

6 LOGISTIC LANDING SHIPS
(RFA MANNED)

Name	No.	Builders	Laid down	Launched	Commissioned
SIR LANCELOT	L 3029	Fairfield	Mar 1962	June1963	Jan 1964
SIR GALAHAD	L 3005	Alex Stephen	Feb 1965	19 April1966	17 Dec 1966
SIR GERAINT	L 3027	Alex Stephen	June 1965	26 Jan 1967	12 July 1967
SIR BEDIVERE	L 3004	Hawthorn Leslie	Oct 1965	20 July 1966	18 May 1967
SIR PERCIVALE	L 3036	Hawthorn Leslie	April 1966	4 Oct 1967	23 Mar 1968
SIR TRISTRAM	L 3505	Hawthorn Leslie	Feb 1966	12 Dec 1966	14 Sep 1967

Displacement, tons: 3 270 light; 5 674 full load (3 370 and 5 550 in *Sir Lancelot*)
Dimensions, feet (metres): 366·3 pp; 412·1 oa × 59·8 × 13·0 *(120; 135·1 × 19·6 × 4·3)*
Guns: Fitted for 2—40 mm—not normally carried
Main engines: 2 Mirrlees Diesels; 9 400 bhp; 2 shafts; (2 Denny/Sulzer diesels; 9 520 bhp in *Sir Lancelot*)
Speed, knots: 17
Oil fuel, tons: 815
Range, miles: 8 000 at 15 knots
Complement: 68 (18 officers, 50 ratings)
Military lift: 340

Sir Lancelot was the prototype of this class which was originally built for the Army but transferred to RFA in Jan and Mar 1970. Fitted for bow and stern loading with drive-through facilities and deck-to-deck ramps. Facilities provided for onboard maintenance of vehicles and for laying out pontoon equipment.

Aircraft: Helicopters can be operated from the well-deck and the after platform by day or night in the later ships. In *Sir Lancelot* well-deck operations are limited to fair weather-day conditions. If required to carry helicopters 11 can be stowed on the Tank Deck and 9 on the Vehicle Deck.

SIR GERAINT   10/1976, C. and S. Taylor

SIR TRISTRAM   6/1976, MOD(N)

14 LCM (9) TYPE

Name	No.	Builders	Commissioned
—	L 700	Brooke Marine Ltd	1964
—	L 701	Brooke Marine Ltd	1964
—	L 702	Brooke Marine Ltd	1965
—	L 703	Brooke Marine Ltd	1965
—	L 704	R. Dunston (Thorne)	1964
—	L 705	R. Dunston (Thorne)	1965
—	L 706	R. Dunston (Thorne)	1965
—	L 707	R. Dunston (Thorne)	1965
—	L 708	R. Dunston (Thorne)	1966
—	L 709	R. Dunston (Thorne)	1966
—	L 710	J. Bolson (Poole)	1965
—	L 711	J. Bolson (Poole)	1965
—	L 3507	Vosper Ltd	1963
—	L 3508	Vosper Ltd	1963

Displacement, tons: 75 light; 176 loaded
Dimensions, feet (metres): 85 oa × 21·5 × 5·5 *(25·7 × 6·5 × 1·7)*
Capacity: 2 tanks or 100 tons of vehicles
Main engines: 2 Paxman 6 cyl YHXAM diesels; 2 shafts; 624 bhp = 10 knots. Screws enclosed in Kort nozzles to improve manoeuvrability

LCM 707 (HMS *Intrepid*)   5/1975, Wright and Logan

LCM (9) 3507 and LCM (9) 3508 were the first operational minor landing craft to be built since the Second World War. Ramped in the traditional manner forward, a completely enclosed radar-fitted wheelhouse is positioned aft. Upon completion they carried out familiarisation trials to perfect the new techniques required in launching and recovering LCMs from the flooded sterns of the parent assault ships. Now operated by RCT. Four each of the 700 Series allocated to assault ships.

LCM 3507 (RCT)   4/1975, John G. Callis

2 LOGISTIC LANDING CRAFT (RCT)

Name	No.	Builders	Commissioned
ARDENNES	L 4001	Brooke Marine, Lowestoft	1977
ARAKAN	L —	Brooke Marine, Lowestoft	—

Displacement, tons: 870 standard; 1 413 full load
Dimensions, feet (metres): 240 oa × 47·5 × 5·8 *(73·1 × 14·4 × 1·8)*
Main engines: 2 diesels; 2 000 bhp = 10·3 knots
Range, miles: 4 000 at 10 knots
Complement: 36 (plus 34 troops)

Ardennes ordered in October 1974, laid down 27 Aug 1975 and launched 29 July 1976.
Arakan laid down 1976 and launched 23 May 1977.

2 LCM (7)

7037   7100

Displacement, tons: 28 light; 63 loaded
Dimensions, feet (metres): 60·2 × 16 × 3·7 *(18·4 × 4·9 × 1·2)*
Main engines: 290 bhp = 9·8 knots

Employed as naval servicing boats and store carriers. Re-engined with Gray Marine diesels.

11 LCM (RCT)

AVON RPL 01
BUDE RPL 02
CLYDE RPL 03
DART RPL 04
EDEN RPL 05
FORTH RPL 06

GLEN RPL 07
HAMBLE RPL 08
KENNET RPL 10
LODDON RPL 11
MEDWAY RPL 12

Diesel-driven LCMs manned by RCT and available for short coastal hauls.

LODDON

1976, Michael D. J. Lennon

3 LCP (L) (3)

LCP (L) (3) 501, 503, 556

Displacement, tons: 6·5 light; 10 loaded
Dimensions, feet (metres): 37 × 11 × 3·2 *(11·3 × 3·4 × 1)*
Main engines: 225 bhp = 12 knots

26 LCVP (1) (2) and (3)

LCVP (1) 102, 112, 118, 120, 123, 127, 128, 134, 136
LCVP (2) 142-149
LCVP (3) 150-158

Displacement, tons: 8·5 light; 13·5 full load
Dimensions, feet (metres): 41·5 (LCVP (2)); 43 (LCVP (3)) × 10 × 2·5 *(12·7; 13·1 × 3·1 × 0·8)*
Main engines: 130 bhp = 8 knots; 2 Foden diesels; 200 bhp = 10 knots (LCVP (2))

LCVP (2)s carried by *Intrepid* and *Fearless* can carry 35 troops or 2 Land Rovers. Crew 4. LCA (2)s were redesignated LCVPs (Landing Craft Vehicle and Personnel) in 1966.
There were also a number of variations and prototypes of about the same length (43 feet).

Note: Raiding Landing Craft, including LCR 5507 and 5508, and Navigational Landing Craft, including LCN 604 (ex-LCR 5505).

LCVP

8/1976, C. and S. Taylor

3 LCT (8) TYPE (RCT)

ABBEVILLE L 4041
AGHEILA L 4002

AUDEMER L 4061

Displacement, tons: 657 light; 895 to 1 017 loaded
Dimensions, feet (metres): 231·2 oa × 39 × 3·2 forward; 5 aft *(70·5 × 11·9 × 1 forward; 1·8 aft)*
   Beaching draughts
Main engines: 4 Paxman engines; 1 840 bhp = 12·6 knots
Complement: 33 to 37

All transferred to the Army's Royal Corps of Transport from the Royal Navy. Originally nine of these ships were operated by the RCT.

ABBEVILLE

8/1976, C. and S. Taylor

1 LST (3) (RFA)

EMPIRE GULL (ex-*Trouncer*) L 3513

Displacement, tons: 2 260 light; 4 960 full load
Dimensions, feet (metres): 347 × 54·1 × 12 *(105·8 × 16·5 × 3·7)*
Main engines: 2 Triple Expansion; 2 shafts; 5 500 shp = 10 knots
Boilers: 2 Water Tube
Oil fuel, tons: 950
Complement: 63 officers and men
Troop accommodation: 8 officers, 72 ORs

Built by Davie Shipbuilding, Quebec. Launched 9 July 1945.

EMPIRE GULL

10/1976, Wright and Logan

HELICOPTER SUPPORT SHIP

Name	No.	Builders	Commissioned
ENGADINE	K 08	Henry Robb Ltd, Leith	15 Dec 1967

Displacement, tons: 8 000 full load
Measurement, tons: 6 384 gross; 2 848 net
Dimensions, feet (metres): 424·0 oa × 58·4 × 22·1 *(129·3 × 17·8 × 6·7)*
Aircraft: 4 Wessex and 2 Wasp or 2 Sea King helicopters
Main engines: 1 Sulzer two stroke, 5 cyl turbocharged 5RD68 diesel; 5 500 bhp = 16 knots
Complement: RFA: 63 (15 officers, 48 men); RN: 14 (2 officers, 12 ratings)
   Accommodation for a further RN 113 (29 officers and 84 ratings)

Projected under the 1964-65 Navy Estimates. Ordered on 18 Aug 1964. Laid down on 9 Aug 1965. Officially named on 15 Sep 1966. Accepted into service on 15 Dec 1967. Largest ship then built by the company. Intended for the training of helicopter crews in deep water operations. She does not carry her own flight but embarks aircraft as necessary. Fitted with Denny Brown stabilisers, the only RFA vessel so equipped. Also fitted with PTA hangar immediately abaft the funnel.

ENGADINE

1976, MOD(N)

MINE WARFARE FORCES

Name	No.	Builders	Commissioned
ABDIEL	N 21	John I. Thornycroft Ltd, Woolston, Southampton	17 Oct 1967

Displacement, tons: 1 375 standard; 1 500 full load
Dimensions, feet (metres): 244·5 pp; 265 oa × 38·5 × 10 *(80·2; 86·8 × 12·6 × 3·3)*
Mines: 44 carried
Main engines: 2 Paxman Ventura 16 cyl pressure charged diesels; 1 250 rpm; 2 690 bhp = 16 knots
Complement: 77

Exercise minelayer ordered in June 1965. Laid down on 23 May 1966. Launched on 27 Jan 1967. Completed on 17 Oct 1967. Main machinery manufactured by Davey Paxman, Colchester. Main gearing supplied by Messrs Wisemans. Her function is to support mine countermeasure forces, maintain these forces when they are operating away from their shore bases and minelaying. Cost £1 500 000.

ABDIEL   1/1977, C. and S. Taylor

0 + 2 "HUNT" CLASS
(MINESWEEPERS/MINEHUNTERS—COASTAL)

Name	No.	Builders	Commissioned
BRECON	—	Vosper Thornycroft Ltd.	1978
EDBURY	—	Vosper Thornycroft Ltd.	—

Displacement, tons: 615 standard; 725 full load
Dimensions, feet (metres): 197 × 32·3 × 7·3 *(60 × 9·9 × 2·2)*
Gun: 1—40 mm
Main engines: 2 Ruston-Paxman Deltic diesels; 3 540 bhp = 17 knots
Complement: 45

A new class of MCM Vessels combining both hunting and sweeping capabilities. Hulls of GRP. The cost of these ships is likely to be in the region of £8 million. Will be equipped with 2 French PAP 104 mine destructor outfits. Second ship ordered 1976. *Brecon* laid down Dec 1975 for launch 1977 (?). It is reported that twelve of this class are planned. Agreement of Mar 1976 provided for Yarrow Ltd equipping their yard to build ships of this class although no order has yet been reported.

Artist's impression of "HUNT" Class   1974, MOD (N)

1 MINESWEEPER/MINEHUNTER (COASTAL)

Name	No.	Builders	Commissioned
WILTON	M 1116	Vosper Thornycroft, Woolston	14 July 1973

Displacement, tons: 450 standard
Dimensions, feet (metres): 153·0 oa × 28·8 × 8·5 *(46·3 × 8·8 × 2·5)*
Gun: 1—40 mm Mark VII
Main engines: 2 English Electric Deltic 18 diesels; 2 shafts; 3 000 bhp = 16 knots
Complement: 37 (5 officers and 32 ratings)

The world's first GRP warship. Contract signed on 11 Feb 1970. Laid down 16 Nov 1970 and launched on 18 Jan 1972. Prototype built of glass reinforced plastic to the existing minehunter design by Vosper Thornycroft at Woolston. Similar to the "Ton" class and fitted with reconditioned machinery and equipment from the scrapped *Derriton*.

WILTON   1976, MOD (N)

32 "TON" CLASS

15 MINEHUNTERS

(* = RNR Training Ship)

Name	No.	Builders	Commissioned
BILDESTON	M 1110	J. S. Doig (Grimsby) Ltd	28 April 1953
BOSSINGTON	M 1133	J. I. Thornycroft & Co, Southampton	11 Dec 1956
BRERETON	M 1113	Richards Ironworks	9 July 1954
BRINTON	M 1114	Cook Welton and Gemmell	4 Mar 1954
BRONINGTON	M 1115	Cook Welton and Gemmell	4 June 1954
GAVINGTON	M 1140	J. S. Doig (Grimsby) Ltd	14 July 1954
HUBBERSTON	M 1147	Fleetlands Shipyards Ltd, London	14 Oct 1955
IVESTON	M 1151	Philip & Sons Ltd, Dartmouth	29 June 1955
*KEDLESTON	M 1153	William Pickersgill & Son	2 July 1955
*KELLINGTON	M 1154	William Pickersgill & Son	4 Nov 1955
KIRKLISTON	M 1157	Harland & Wolff Ltd, Belfast	21 Aug 1954
MAXTON	M 1165	Harland & Wolff Ltd, Belfast	19 Feb 1957
NURTON	M 1166	Harland & Wolff Ltd, Belfast	21 Aug 1957
SHERATON	M 1181	White's Shipyard Ltd, Southampton	24 Aug 1956
SHOULTON	M 1182	Montrose Shipyard Ltd	16 Nov 1955

17 MINESWEEPERS—COASTAL

(* = RNR Training Ship)

Name	No.	Builders	Commissioned
ALFRISTON	M 1103	J. I. Thornycroft & Co., Southampton	16 Mar 1954
BICKINGTON	M 1109	White's Shipyard Ltd, Southampton	27 May 1954
CRICHTON	M 1124	J. S. Doig (Grimsby) Ltd	23 April 1954
*CROFTON	M 1216	J. I. Thornycroft & Co, Southampton	26 Aug 1958
CUXTON	M 1125	Camper and Nicholson Ltd, Gosport	1953
GLASSERTON	M 1141	J. S. Doig (Grimsby) Ltd	31 Dec 1954
*HODGESTON	M 1146	Fleetlands Shipyards Ltd, London	17 Dec 1954
LALESTON	M 1158	Harland and Wolff	1954
LEWISTON	M 1208	Herd & Mackenzie, Buckie, Banff	16 June 1960
POLLINGTON	M 1173	Camper & Nicholson Ltd, Gosport	5 Sep 1958
*REPTON	M 1167	Harland & Wolff Ltd, Belfast	12 Dec 1957
SHAVINGTON	M 1180	White's Shipyard Ltd, Southampton	1 Mar 1956
SOBERTON	M 1200	Fleetlands Shipyards Ltd, Gosport	17 Sep 1957
STUBBINGTON	M 1204	Camper & Nicholson Ltd, Gosport	30 July 1957
*UPTON	M 1187	J. I. Thornycroft & Co, Southampton	24 July 1956
WALKERTON	M 1188	J. I. Thornycroft & Co, Southampton	10 Jan 1958
WOTTON	M 1195	Philip & Sons Ltd, Dartmouth	13 June 1957

Displacement, tons: 360 standard; 425 full load
Dimensions, feet (metres): 140·0 pp; 153·0 oa × 28·8 × 8·2 *(42·7; 46·3 × 8·8 × 2·5)*
Guns: Vary in different ships, some sweepers having no 40 mm, some 1—40 mm whilst hunters have 1 or 2—40 mm; 2—20 mm
Main engines: 2 diesels; 2 shafts; 2 500 bhp (JVSS 12 Mirrlees), 3 000 bhp (18A-7A Deltic)
Speed, knots: 15
Oil fuel, tons: 45
Range, miles: 2 300 at 13 knots
Complement: 29 (38 in minehunters, 5 officers and 33 ratings)

The survivors of a class of 118 built between 1953 and 1960, largely as a result of lessons from the Korean War. John I. Thornycroft & Co Ltd, Southampton were the lead yard for these ships which have double mahogany hull and incorporate a considerable amount of non-magnetic material. Fitted with Vospers stabilisers. The majority has now been fitted with nylon in place of copper sheathing. *Cuxton* commissioned finally in Oct 1975 after 22 years in "moth-balls".

Appearance: Enclosed bridges in *Bildeston, Brereton, Brinton, Crofton, Iveston, Kellington, Kirkliston, Lewiston, Bossington, Bronington, Gavington, Hubberston, Kedleston, Maxton, Repton, Pollington, Nurton, Sheraton, Shoulton, Soberton, Stubbington, Walkerton, Wiston.*

Conversions: *Beachampton, Monkton, Wasperton, Wolverton* and *Yarnton* were converted into coastal patrol vessels late in 1971, (see Light Forces). *Laleston* was converted into diving trials ship in 1966-67. *Walkerton* used by Dartmouth RN College as Navigation Training Ship, to be relieved by *Alfriston* in 1977. *Shoulton* was the original minehunter conversion, fitted with pump-jet and bow thruster.

Engineering: Earlier vessels had Mirrlees diesels, but later units had Napier Deltic lightweight diesels. *Highburton,* the first with Deltic diesels, was accepted on 21 April 1955. All minehunters have Deltics and active rudders. Generators for electrical power are in a separate engine room in Mirrlees, Deltic-conversions and minehunters. Deltic built minesweepers have a generator in the main engine-room and two generators in the generator-room. Mirrlees still fitted in *Glasserton, Laleston, Cuxton* and *Repton.* Three-bladed propellers, 6 ft diameter, 400 rpm. *Shoulton,* refitted 1965-67, has pump-jet propulsion.

Fishery protection: Carried out by *Brereton, Brinton, Highburton, Kedleston, Shavington, Soberton. Cuxton* and *Stubbington* refitting for Fishery Duties.

Osbourne sweep: *Glasserton* is fitted with derricks for Osbourne sweep. *Highburton* used in initial trials.

Royal Naval Reserve: The practice of temporarily renaming ships attached to RNR divisions has been abandoned as the six vessels now operate for various groupings. Other RNR training ships are provided from the "Kingfisher" class (see Light Forces).

Transfers: Argentine (6 in 1968), Australia (6 in 1962), Ghana (1 in 1964), India (4 in 1956), Ireland (3 in 1971), Malaysia (7 in 1960-68), South Africa (10 in 1958-59).

IVESTON   5/1976, C. and S. Taylor

BICKINGTON (Fishery Protection Squadron)   5/1976, Wright and Logan

GLASSERTON (Sweeper—Osbourne and no 40 mm gun)   12/1975, MOD(N)

HUBBERSTON   6/1976, Dr. Giorgio Arra

SHOULTON   1976, Michael D. J. Lennon

LEWISTON   10/1976, C. and S. Taylor

3 "HAM" CLASS (MINESWEEPERS—INSHORE)

Name	No.	Builders	Commissioned
DITTISHAM	M 2621	Fairlie Yacht Slip	1954
FLINTHAM	M 2628	Bolson & Co	1955
THORNHAM (Aberdeen)	M 2793	Taylor, Shoreham	1957

Displacement, tons: 120 standard; 159 full load
Dimensions, feet (metres): 2601 Series: 100 pp; 106·5 oa × 21·2 × 5·5 *(30·5; 32·4 × 6·5 × 1·7)*.
 2793 Series: 100 pp; 107·5 oa × 22 × 5·8 *(30·5; 32·1 × 6·6 × 1·8)*
Gun: 1—20 mm Oerlikon forward
Main engines: 2 Paxman diesels; 1 100 bhp = 14 knots
Oil fuel, tons: 15
Complement: 15 (2 officers, 13 ratings)

The first inshore minesweeper, *Inglesham*, was launched by J. Samuel White & Co Ltd, Cowes, on 23 April 1952. The 2601 series were of composite construction. In all 95 of this class were built.
Thornham attached to Aberdeen University RNU.

Transfers: Australia (3 in 1966-68), France (15 in 1954-55), Ghana (2 in 1959), India (2 in 1955), Libya (2 in 1963), Malaysia (4 in 1958-59), South Yemen (3 in 1967). Ships subsequently returned are not listed.

DITTISHAM _1973, John G. Callis_

2 "LEY" CLASS M 2001 SERIES (MINEHUNTERS—INSHORE)

Name	No.	Builders	Commissioned
AVELEY	M 2002	J. S. White & Co Ltd, Cowes	1953
ISIS (ex-*Cradley*)	M 2010	Saunders Roe Ltd	1955

Displacement, tons: 123 standard; 164 full load
Dimensions, feet (metres): 100 pp; 107 oa × 21·8 × 5·5 *(30·5; 32·3 × 6·5 × 1·7)*
Gun: 1—40 mm *(Isis)*; 1—20 mm *(Aveley)*
Main engines: 2 Paxman diesels; 700 bhp = 13 knots
Complement: 15 (2 officers, 13 ratings)

The "Ley" class, originally of ten ships, differed from the "Ham" class. They were of composite (non-magnetic metal and wooden) construction, instead of all wooden construction. Their superstructure and other features also differed. They had no winch or sweeping gear, as they were minehunters, not sweepers. *Aveley* is attached to Plymouth. *Isis*, renamed in 1963, was transferred to Southampton University RNU on 1 April 1974.

ISIS _9/1976, Dr. Giorgio Arra_

MAINTENANCE SHIPS

Name	No.	Builders	Laid down	Launched	Commissioned
TRIUMPH	A 108 (ex-R 16)	R & W Hawthorn Leslie, Hebburn	27 Jan 1943	2 Oct 1944	9 April 1946

Displacement, tons: 13 500 standard; 17 500 full load
Length, feet (metres): 630·0 *(192·0)* pp; 650·0 *(198·1)* wl; 699·0 *(213·1)* oa
Beam, feet (metres): 80·0 *(24·4)*
Draught, feet (metres): 23·7 *(7·2)*
Width, feet (metres): 112·5 *(34·3)* overall
Aircraft: 3 helicopters in flight deck hangar
Guns: 4—40 mm; 3 saluting (now removed)
Main engines: Parsons geared turbines; 2 shafts; 40 000 shp
Boilers: 4 Admiralty 3-drum type
 Pressure 400 psi *(28·1 kg/cm²)*
 Temperature 700°F *(371°C)*
Speed, knots: 24·25
Oil fuel, tons: 3 000
Range, miles: 10 000 at 14 knots; 5 500 at full speed
Complement: 500 (27 officers, 473 men) plus 285 (15 officers, 270 men) on maintenance staff

TRIUMPH _9/1974, Dr. Giorgio Arra_

Originally an aircraft carrier of the "Colossus" class. Converted for present role at a cost of £10·2 mill. at Portsmouth between 1958 and 1965. Now in reserve at Chatham in preservation.

1 "HEAD" CLASS

Name	No.	Builders	Laid down	Launched	Commissioned
RAME HEAD	A 134	Burrard DD Co, Vancouver	12 July 1944	22 Nov 1944	18 Aug 1945

Displacement, tons: 9 000 standard; 11 270 full load
Length, feet (metres): 416·0 *(126·8)* pp; 441·5 *(134·6)* oa
Beam, feet (metres): 57·5 *(17·5)*
Draught, feet (metres): 22·5 *(6·9)*
Guns: 11—40 mm

Main engines: Triple expansion; 2 500 ihp
Boilers: 2 Foster Wheeler
Speed, knots: 10 approx
Oil fuel, tons: 1 600 capacity
Complement: 425

Escort Maintenance Ship. To reserve in 1972. Accommodation ship at Portsmouth since June 1976. *Berry Head*, sister ship, at Devonport.

ROYAL YACHT

Name	No.	Builders	Laid down	Launched	Commissioned
BRITANNIA	A 00	John Brown & Co Ltd, Clydebank	July 1952	16 April 1953	14 Jan 1954

Displacement, tons: 3 990 light; 4 961 full load
Measurement, tons: 5 769 gross
Dimensions, feet (metres): 360·0 pp; 380·0 wl; 412·2 oa × 55·0 × 17·0 *(109·8; 115·9; 125·7 × 16·8 × 5·2)*
Main engines: Single reduction geared turbines; 2 shafts; 12 000 shp = 21 knots
Boilers: 2
Oil fuel, tons: 330 (490 with auxiliary fuel tanks)
Range, miles: 2 100 at 20 knots; 2 400 at 18 knots; 3 000 at 15 knots
Complement: 270

Designed as a medium sized naval hospital ship for use by Her Majesty The Queen in peacetime as the Royal Yacht. Construction conformed to mercantile practice. Fitted with Denny-Brown single fin stabilisers to reduce roll in bad weather from 20 deg to 6 deg. Cost £2 098 000. To pass under the bridges of the St. Lawrence Seaway when she visited Canada, the top 20 feet of her mainmast and the radio aerial on her foremast were hinged in Nov 1958 so that they could be lowered as required.

BRITANNIA _5/1976, C. and S. Taylor_

SUBMARINE DEPOT SHIP

Name	No.	Builders	Laid down	Launched	Commissioned
FORTH	A187	John Brown, Clydebank	30 June1937	11 Aug 1938	14 May 1939

FORTH   1973, John G. Callis

Displacement, tons: 10 000 standard; 13 000 full load
Length, feet (metres): 497·0 (151·5) pp; 531·0 (161·8) oa
Beam, feet (metres): 73·0 (22·3)
Draught, feet (metres): 21·2 (6·5)
Guns: 5—40 mm Bofors
Main engines: Geared turbines (Brown Curtis); 2 shafts; 7 000 shp
Boilers: 4 Admiralty 3-drum type
Speed, knots: 16
Oil fuel, tons: 2 300
Complement: 695 (45 officers and 650 men)
   Accommodation for 1 159 (119 officers and 1 040 men)

Equipment includes foundry, coppersmiths', plumbers', carpenters'; heavy and light machine, electrical and torpedo repair shops and plant for charging submarine batteries. Designed for maintaining nine operational submarines, and supplying over 140 torpedoes and a similar number of mines. Repair facilities on board for all purposes in attached submarines, and extensive diving and salvage equipment. There are steam laundry, hospital, chapel, two canteens, bakery, barber shops, operating theatre and dental surgery.
In Oct 1969, *Maidstone* was restored and recommissioned as an accommodation ship for 2 000 troops and sent to Belfast.

As the Fleet Maintenance Base, Devonport and parent ship of the 2nd Submarine Squadron *Forth* is the depot ship of HMS *Defiance*.

Reconstruction: *Forth* was modernised and converted into a support ship for nuclear powered submarines in HM Dockyard Chatham, in 1962-66.

ICE PATROL SHIP

Name	No.	Builders	Laid down	Launched	Commissioned
ENDURANCE (ex-*Anita Dan*)	A 171	Krögerwerft, Rendsburg	1955	May 1956	Dec 1956

Displacement, tons: 3 600
Measurement, tons: 2 641 gross
Length, feet (metres): 273·5 (89·7) pp; 300 (91·44) oa; 305 (92·96); including helicopter deck extension
Beam, feet (metres): 46 (14·02)
Draught, feet (metres): 18 (5·5)
Aircraft: 2 Whirlwind Mk IX helicopters
Guns: 2—20 mm
Main engines: 1 B & W 550 VTBF diesel; 3 220 ihp; 1 shaft
Speed, knots: 14·5
Range, miles: 12 000 at 14·5 knots
Complement: 119 (13 officers, 106 men, including a small Royal Marine detachment) plus 12 spare berths for scientists

Purchased from J. Lauritzen Lines, Copenhagen (announced on 20 Feb 1967). Strengthened for operation in ice. Converted by Harland & Wolff, Belfast 1967-68 into an ice patrol ship for southern waters to replace *Protector,* undertaking hydrographic and oceanographic surveys and acting as support ship for the British Antarctic Survey and guard vessel. Original cost £1·8 million.
An unusual feature for one of HM ships is her hull painted a vivid red for easy identification in the ice.

ENDURANCE   3/1975, Dr. Giorgio Arra

HOVERCRAFT

Note: The RN Hovercraft Trials Unit was established at Lee-on-the-Solent in 1974.

2 WINCHESTER (SR.N6) TYPE

Displacement, tons: 10 normal gross weight
Dimensions, feet (metres): 48·4 × 23·0 × 15·0 oa (height); 4·0 (skirt) (14·8 × 7 × 4·6; 1·3)
Main engines: 1 Rolls Royce Gnome gas turbine; 900 shp = 50 knots
Range, miles: 200

Modified with radar and military communications equipment for its primary role of a fast amphibious communication craft to support Royal Marine units.

SR.N6   1975, BHC

1 WELLINGTON (BH.N7) TYPE

Displacement, tons: 50 max weight; 33 light
Dimensions, feet (metres): 78·3 × 45·5 × 34·0 oa (height); 5·5 (skirt) (23·9 × 13 × 10·4; 1·7)
Main engines: 1 Rolls Royce Proteus gas turbine; 4 250 shp = 60 knots
Complement: 14 plus trials crew

Costing about £700 000, delivered to the inter-Service Hovercraft Trials Unit at the Royal Naval Air Station, Lee-on-Solent, in April 1970. She could be used as a missile armed fast patrol craft or amphibious assault craft. Winter trials in Swedish waters in Feb 1972. Records established: longest open sea voyage, furthest north, and sustained speeds of over 55 knots in the Baltic.

BH.N7   7/1976, C. and S. Taylor

1 SR.N5 TYPE

This small hovercraft is used for crew training.

SR.N5   4/1976, C. and S. Taylor

CHARTER

The Vosper Thornycroft VT2 hovercraft was chartered for trials in 1976 by MOD.
An SR.N4 hovercraft was chartered for a short period of trials in 1976.

DIVING SHIP

Name	No.	Builders	Commissioned
RECLAIM (ex-*Salverdant*)	A 231	Wm Simons & Co Ltd, Renfrew	Oct 1948

Displacement, tons: 1 200 standard; 1 800 full load
Dimensions, feet (metres): 200 pp; 217·8 oa × 38 × 15·5 (61; 66·4 × 11·6 × 4·7)
Main engines: Triple expansion; 2 shafts; 1 500 ihp = 12 knots
Oil fuel, tons: 310
Range, miles: 3 000
Complement: 100

Engined by Aitchison Blair Ltd. Laid down on 9 April 1946. Launched on 12 Mar 1948. Construction based on the design of a "King Salvor" class naval ocean salvage vessel. First deep diving and submarine rescue vessel built as such for the Royal Navy. Fitted with sonar, radar, echo-sounding apparatus for detection of sunken wrecks, and equipped for submarine rescue work. Due for replacement although no decision yet made concerning her successor.

RECLAIM   5/1975, C. and S. Taylor

LIGHT FORCES

(See Deletion List for "Dark" and "Brave" Classes).
(See page 527 for "Alert" patrol craft).

5 "ISLAND" CLASS (OFFSHORE PATROL CRAFT)

Name	No.	Builders	Commissioned
GUERNSEY	P 297	Hall Russell & Co Ltd	1977
JERSEY	P 295	Hall Russell & Co Ltd	15 Oct 1976
LINDISFARNE	P 300	Hall Russell & Co Ltd	1977
ORKNEY	P 299	Hall Russell & Co Ltd	1977
SHETLAND	p 298	Hall Russell & Co Ltd	1977

Displacement, tons: 925 standard; 1 250 full load
Dimensions, feet (metres): 195·3 oa × 35·8 × 14 (59·6 × 10·9 × 4·3)
Gun: 1—40 mm
Main engines: 2 diesels; 1 shaft; 4 380 hp = 16 knots
Range, miles: 7 000 at 15 knots
Complement: 24 (accommodation for 40)

Order announced 11 Feb 1975. Order placed 2 July 1975. To be in service 1976-77. *Jersey* launched 18 Mar 1976, *Orkney* 29 June 1976, *Shetland* 22 Oct 1976. Can carry small RM detachment.

JERSEY   11/1976, MOD(N)

4 "BIRD" CLASS (LARGE PATROL CRAFT)

Name	No.	Builders	Commissioned
CYGNET	P 261	R. Dunston Ltd, Hessle	8 July 1976
KINGFISHER	P 260	R. Dunston Ltd, Hessle	8 Oct 1975
PETEREL	P 262	R. Dunston Ltd, Hessle	Aug 1976
SANDPIPER	P 263	R. Dunston Ltd, Hessle	1977

Displacement, tons: 190
Dimensions, feet (metres): 120 oa × 23 × 6·5 *(36·6 × 7·0 × 2)*
Guns: 1—40 mm; 2 MG
Main engines: 2 Paxman 16YJ diesels; 4 800 bhp = 18 knots
Oil fuel, tons: 35
Complement: 24

KINGFISHER   9/1976, C. and S. Taylor

Based on the smaller "Seal" class RAF rescue launches with some improvement to sea-keeping qualities and fitted with stabilisers. *Kingfisher* launched 20 Sep 1974. *Cygnet* laid down June 1975 and launched 6 Oct 1975. *Peterel* was launched 14 May 1976. *Sandpiper* launched 20 Jan 1977.

Design: Comparison of new photographs shows an expected attempt to cut down topweight e.g. radar cross-trees, deletion of scuttles.

Duties: *Kingfisher* and *Cygnet* Fishery Protection Squadron; *Petrel* RNR North Western group; *Sandpiper* RNR Channel group.

3 FAST TRAINING BOATS

Name	No.	Builders	Commissioned
CUTLASS	P 274	Vosper Thornycroft Group, Porchester Shipyard	12 Nov 1970
SABRE	P 275	Vosper Thornycroft Group, Porchester Shipyard	5 Mar 1971
SCIMITAR	P 271	Vosper Thornycroft Group, Porchester Shipyard	19 July 1970

Displacement, tons: 102 full load
Dimensions, feet (metres): 90·0 wl; 100·0 oa × 26·6 × 6·4 *(27·4; 30·5 × 8·1 × 1·9)*
Main engines: 2 Rolls Royce Proteus gas turbines; 9 000 hp = 40 knots (2 Foden diesels for cruising in CODAG arrangement)
Range, miles: 425 at 35 knots; 1 500 at 11·5 knots
Complement: 12 (2 officers, 10 ratings)

SABRE   5/1975, C. and S. Taylor

Hull of glued laminated wood construction. Design developed from that of "Brave" class fast patrol boats. Design permits fitting of third gas-turbine and a gun armament if required. Launch dates:— *Cutlass* 19 Feb 1970, *Sabre* 21 April 1970, *Scimitar* 4 Dec 1969.

1 VOSPER THORNYCROFT (FAST ATTACK CRAFT—PATROL)

Name	No.	Builders	Commissioned
TENACITY	P 276	Vosper Thornycroft Ltd	17 Feb 1973

Displacement, tons: 165 standard; 220 full load
Dimensions, feet (metres): 144·5 oa × 26·6 × 7·8 *(44·1 × 8·1 × 2·4)*
Guns: 2 MGs
Main engines: 3 Rolls Royce Proteus gas turbines; 3 shafts; 12 750 bhp = 40 knots; 2 Paxman Ventura 6 cyl diesels on wing shafts for cruising = 16 knots
Range, miles: 2 500 at 15 knots
Complement: 32 (4 officers, 28 ratings)

TENACITY   1974, Michael D. J. Lennon

Built as a private venture and launched on 18 Feb 1969 at Camber Shipyard, Portsmouth. Steel hull and aluminium alloy superstructure. Purchased by the Ministry of Defence (Navy) on 25 Jan 1972 for approximately £750 000 "as lying" and refitted with minor alterations and additions to meet naval requirements. To be used for exercises and fishery protection. Decca nav, radar.

5 MODIFIED "TON" CLASS

Name	No.	Builders	Commissioned
BEACHAMPTON	P 1007 (ex-M 1107)	Goole SB Co	1953
MONKTON	P 1055 (ex-M 1155)	Herd & Mackenzie, Buckie	1956
WASPERTON	P 1089 (ex-M 1189)	J. Samuel White & Co Ltd	1956
WOLVERTON	P 1093 (ex-M 1193)	Montrose SY Co	1957
YARNTON	P 1096 (ex-M 1196)	Pickersgill	1956

Displacement, tons: 360 standard; 425 full load
Dimensions, feet (metres): 140·0 pp; 153·0 oa × 28·8 × 8·2 *(42·7; 46·3 × 8·8 × 2·5)*
Guns: 2—40 mm Bofors (single, 1 forward, 1 aft)
Main engines: 2 diesels; 2 shafts; 3 000 bhp = 15 knots
Oil fuel, tons: 45
Range, miles: 2 300 at 13 knots
Complement: 30 (5 officers and 25 ratings, but varies)

YARNTON   12/1976, Dr. Giorgio Arra

Former coastal minesweepers of the "Ton" class, refitted at the end of 1971, re-designated as coastal patrol vessels with limited wire-sweeping capability. Fitted with limited armour in bridge area. Form 6th Patrol Squadron Hong Kong.

2 "FORD" CLASS (SDBs)

Name	No.	Builders	Commissioned
DEE (ex-*Beckford*)	P 3104	Wm. Simons, Renfrew	1953
DROXFORD	P 3113	Pimblott, Northwich	1954

Displacement, tons: 120 standard; 142 full load
Dimensions, feet (metres): 110·0 wl; 117·2 oa × 20·0 × 7·0 *(33·6; 35·7 × 6·1 × 2·1)*
A/S weapons: DC rails; large and small DC
Main engines: Davey Paxman diesels. Foden engine on centre shaft. 1 100 bhp = 18 knots
Oil fuel, tons: 23
Complement: 19

Built in 1953-57. Last survivors of a class of 20. *Dee* attached to Liverpool University RNU (administered by RNR Mersey) and *Droxford* to Glasgow University RNU (administered by RNR Clyde). *Dee* renamed 1965, this name having been used for *Droxford* 1955-1965.

DROXFORD   1972, Wright & Logan

SURVEY SHIPS

1 IMPROVED "HECLA" CLASS

Name	No.	Builders	Commissioned
HERALD	A 138	Robb Caledon, Leith	31 Oct 1974

Displacement, tons: 2 000 standard; 2 945 full load
Dimensions, feet (metres): 260·1 oa × 49·1 × 15·6 *(79·3 × 15 × 4·7)*
Aircraft: 1 Wasp helicopter
Main engines: Diesel-electric drive; 1 shaft
Speed, knots: 14
Range, miles: 12 000 at 11 knots
Complement: 128

A later version of the "Hecla" class design. Ordered 1973. Fitted with Hydroplot Satellite navigation system, computerised data logging, gravimeter, magnetometer, sonars, echo-sounders, coring and oceanographic winches, passive stabilisation tank, bow thruster and two surveying motor-boats.
Laid down 9 Nov 1972. Launched by Mrs Mary Hall, wife of the Hydrographer, on 4 Oct 1973.

HERALD

5/1975, C. and S. Taylor

3 "HECLA" CLASS

Name	No.	Builders	Commissioned
HECATE	A 137	Yarrow & Co Ltd, Scotstoun	20 Dec 1965
HECLA	A 133	Yarrow & Co, Blythswood	9 Sep 1965
HYDRA	A 144	Yarrow & Co, Blythswood	5 May 1966

Displacement, tons: 1 915 light; 2 733 full load
Measurement, tons: 2 898 gross
Length, feet (metres): 235 *(71·6)* pp; 260·1 *(79·3)* oa
Beam, feet (metres): 49·1 *(15·0)*
Draught, feet (metres): 15·6 *(4·7)*
Aircraft: 1 Wasp helicopter
Main engines: Diesel-electric drive; 1 shaft; 3 Paxman Ventura 12-cyl Vee turbocharged diesels; 3 840 bhp; 1 electric motor; 2 000 shp
Speed, knots: 14
Oil fuel, tons: 450
Range, miles: 20 000 at 9 knots
Complement: 118 (14 officers, 104 ratings)

The first RN ships to be designed with a combined oceanographical and hydrographic role. Of merchant ship design and similar in many respects to the Royal Research ship *Discovery*. The hull is strengthened for navigation in ice, and a bow thruster is fitted. The fore end of the superstructure incorporates a Landrover garage and the after end a helicopter hangar with adjacent flight deck. Equipped with chartroom, drawing office and photographic studio; two laboratories, dry and wet; electrical, engineering and shipwright workshops, large storerooms and two surveying motor-boats. Air-conditioned throughout.
Average cost £1·25 million. *Hecate* laid down 26 Oct 1964, launched 31 Mar 1965. *Hecla;* 6 May 1964, 21 Dec 1964; *Hydra* 14 May 1964, 14 July 1965.

HYDRA

9/1976, Michael D. J. Lennon

COASTAL SURVEY SHIPS

4 "BULLDOG" CLASS

Name	No.	Builders	Commissioned
BEAGLE	A 319	Brooke Marine Ltd, Lowestoft	9 May 1968
BULLDOG	A 317	Brooke Marine Ltd, Lowestoft	21 Mar 1968
FAWN	A 325	Brooke Marine Ltd, Lowestoft	10 Sep 1968
FOX	A 320	Brooke Marine Ltd, Lowestoft	11 July 1968

Displacement, tons: 800 standard; 1 088 full load
Dimensions, feet (metres): 189 oa × 37·5 × 12 *(60·1 × 11·4 × 3·6)*
Guns: Fitted for 2—20 mm
Main engines: 4 Lister Blackstone ERS8M, 8 cyl, 4 str diesels, coupled to 2 shafts; cp propellers; 2 000 bhp = 15 knots
Range, miles: 4 000 at 12 knots
Complement: 38 (4 officers, 34 ratings)

Originally designed for duty overseas, working in pairs. Launch dates: *Bulldog* on 12 July 1967, *Beagle* on 7 Sep 1967, *Fox* on 6 Nov 1967 and *Fawn* on 29 Feb 1968. Built to commercial standards. Fitted with passive tank stabilizer, precision ranging radar, Decca "Hifix" system, automatic steering. Air-conditioned throughout. Carry 28·5 ft surveying motor-boat.

BULLDOG

1976, Michael D. J. Lennon

INSHORE SURVEY CRAFT

3 "E" CLASS

Name	No.	Builders	Commissioned
ECHO	A 70	J. Samuel White & Co Ltd, Cowes	12 Sep 1958
EGERIA	A 72	Wm. Weatherhead & Sons Ltd, Cockenzie	1959
ENTERPRISE	A 71	M. W. Blackmore & Sons Ltd, Bideford	1959

Displacement, tons: 120 standard; 160 full load
Dimensions, feet (metres): 106·8 oa × 22·0 × 6·8 *(32·6 × 7 × 2·1)*
Gun: Fitted for 1—40 mm
Main engines: 2 Paxman diesels; 2 shafts; controllable pitch propellers; 1 400 bhp = 14 knots
Oil fuel, tons: 15
Range, miles: 1 600 at 10 knots
Complement: 18 (2 officers, 16 ratings); accommodation for 22 (4 officers, 18 ratings)

Echo, the first Inshore Survey Craft, was launched on 1 May 1957. Equipped with two echo sounding machines, sonar, radar, wire sweep gear and surveying motor boat.

Note: *Shipham* M 2726 temporarily employed in place of *Egeria* damaged by fire.

EGERIA

10/1974, C. and S. Taylor

2 "HAM" CLASS

Name	No.	Builders	Commissioned
WATERWITCH (ex-*Powderham*)	M 2720	J. Samuel White & Co Ltd, Cowes	1959
WOODLARK (ex-*Yaxham*)	M 2780	J. Samuel White & Co Ltd, Cowes	1958

Displacement, tons: 120 standard; 160 full load
Dimensions, feet (metres): 107·5 oa × 22 × 5·5 *(32·4 × 6·5 × 1·7)*
Main engines: Diesels; 2 shafts; 1 100 bhp = 14 knots
Endurance, miles: 1 500 at 12 knots
Complement: 18 (2 officers, 16 ratings)

Former inshore minesweepers of the "Ham" class converted to replace the old survey motor launches *Meda* and *Medusa* for operation in inshore waters at home. *Waterwitch,* operated by RMAS.

WATERWITCH

1974, Michael D. J. Lennon

ROYAL FLEET AUXILIARY SERVICE

Note: Many of large RFAs carry two boxed 40 mm guns

LARGE FLEET TANKERS (AOF(L))

3 "OL" CLASS

Name	No.	Builders	Commissioned
OLMEDA (ex-*Oleander*)	A 124	Swan Hunter, Wallsend	18 Oct 1965
OLNA	A 123	Hawthorn Leslie, Hebburn	1 April 1966
OLWEN (ex-*Olynthus*)	A 122	Hawthorn Leslie, Hebburn	21 June 1965

Displacement, tons: 10 890 light; 36 000 full load
Measurement, tons: 25 100 deadweight; 18 600 gross
Dimensions, feet (metres): 611·1 pp; 648·0 oa × 84·0 × 34·0 *(185·9; 197·5 × 25·6 × 10·5)*
Aircraft: 2 Wessex helicopters (can carry 3)
Main engines: Pametrada double reduction geared turbines; 26 500 shp = 19 knots
Boilers: 2 Babcock & Wilcox, (750 psi; 950°F)
Complement: 87 (25 officers and 62 ratings)

Largest and fastest ships when they joined the Royal Fleet Auxiliary Service. *Olmeda* was launched on 19 Nov 1964, while *Olna* and *Olwen* were launched on 28 July 1965 and 10 July 1964, respectively.
Designed for underway replenishment of the Fleet both alongside or by helicopter. Specially strengthened for operations in ice, fully air-conditioned. *Olna* has a transverse bow thrust unit for improved manoeuvrability in confined waters and a new design of replenishment-at-sea systems.

Capacity: Original figures as follows: 18 400 tons FFO; 1 720 tons diesel; 130 tons lub. oil; 3 730 tons Avcat; 280 tons Mogas. The proportions of FFO and diesel may now be changed.

Hangar: On port side of funnel can house 3 helicopters. On starboard side acts as garage for vehicles.

OLNA

9/1976, Dr. Giorgio Arra

---

2 LATER "TIDE" CLASS

Name	No.	Builders	Commissioned
TIDEPOOL	A 76	Hawthorn Leslie, Hebburn	28 June 1963
TIDESPRING	A 75	Hawthorn Leslie, Hebburn	18 Jan 1963

Displacement, tons: 8 531 light; 27 400 full load
Measurement, tons: 18 900 deadweight; 14 130 gross
Dimensions, feet (metres): 550·0 pp; 583·0 oa × 71·0 × 32·0 *(167·7; 177·6 × 21·6 × 9·8)*
Aircraft: 2 Wessex helicopters (can carry 3)
Main engines: Double reduction geared turbines; 15 000 shp = 18·3 knots
Boilers: 2 Babcock & Wilcox
Complement: 110 (30 officers and 80 ratings)

Highly specialised ships for fuelling (13 000 tons cargo fuel) and storing naval vessels at sea. *Tidespring* was laid down on 24 July 1961, launched on 3 May 1962. *Tidepool* was laid down on 4 Dec 1961, launched on 11 Dec 1962.

Hangar: On port side of funnel can house 3 helicopters. On starboard side acts as garage for vehicles.

TIDESPRING

2/1976

---

1 "TIDE" CLASS

Name	No.	Builders	Commissioned
TIDEREACH	A 96	Swan Hunter & Wigham Richardson Ltd, Wallsend-on-Tyne	30 Aug 1955

Displacement, tons: 9 040 light; 27 300 full load
Measurement, tons: 17 900 deadweight; 13 000 gross
Dimensions, feet (metres): 550 pp; 583 oa × 71 × 32 *(167·7; 177·6 × 21·6 × 9·8)*
Main engines: Double reduction geared turbines; 15 000 shp = 19 knots

Tidereach, launched on 2 June 1954, was the first of three Fleet Replenishment Tankers. A fourth ship of this class, *Tide Austral,* built for Australia, was renamed *Supply* on 7 Sep 1962.

TIDEREACH

11/1975, Dr Giorgio Arra

SUPPORT TANKERS (AOS)

Note: Majority under long-term charter

Name	No.	Builders	Commissioned
ORANGELEAF	A 80	Furness Shipbuilding Co Ltd,	June 1955
(ex-M.V. *Southern Satellite*)		Haverton Hill on Tees	

Measurement, tons: 18 222 deadweight; 12 146 gross; 6 800 net
Dimensions, feet (metres): 525 pp; 556·5 oa × 71·7 × 30·5 *(160·1; 169·7 × 21·9 × 9·3)*
Main engines: Doxford 6-cyl diesel; 6 800 bhp = 14 knots
Oil fuel, tons: 1 610

Launched on 8 Feb 1955. Chartered from South Georgia Co Ltd, 25 May 1959. Astern and abeam fuelling.

ORANGELEAF 4/1976

Name	No.	Builders	Commissioned
CHERRYLEAF	A 82	Rheinstahl Nordseewerke	1963
(ex-*Overseas Adventurer*)			

Measurement, tons: 19 700 deadweight; 13 700 gross; 7 648 net
Dimensions, feet (metres): 559 × 72 × 30 *(170·5 × 22 × 9·2)*
Machinery: 7 cyl MAN diesel; 8 400 bhp = 16 knots

Ordered and completed in 1963. Transferred to RFA Mar 1973. No RAS capability.

CHERRYLEAF 8/1975, C. and S. Taylor

Name	No.	Builders	Commissioned
PLUMLEAF	A 78	Blyth DD & Eng Co Ltd	July 1960

Displacement, tons: 26 480 full load
Measurement, tons: 19 430 deadweight; 12 459 gross
Dimensions, feet (metres): 534 pp; 560 oa × 72 × 30 *(162·9; 170·8 × 22 × 9·2)*
Main engines: N.E. Doxford 6-cyl diesels; 9 500 bhp = 15·5 knots

Launched 29 Mar 1960. Astern and abeam fuelling.

PLUMLEAF 4/1976, Dr. Giorgio Arra

Name	No.	Builders	Commissioned
PEARLEAF	A 77	Blythswood Shipbuilding Co Ltd, Scotstoun	Jan 1960

Displacement, tons: 25 790 full load
Measurement, tons: 18 711 deadweight; 12 353 gross; 7 215 net
Dimensions, feet (metres): 535 pp; 568 oa × 71·7 × 30 *(162·7; 173·2 × 21·9 × 9·2)*
Main engines: Rowan Doxford 6-cyl diesels; 8 800 bhp = 16 knots

Chartered from Jacobs and Partners Ltd, London on completion. Launched on 15 Oct 1959. Can carry three different grades of cargo. Astern and abeam fuelling.

PEARLEAF 6/1976, A. D. Baker III

MOBILE RESERVE TANKER (AOM)

Name	No.	Builders	Commissioned
DEWDALE (ex-M.V. *Edenfield*)	A 219	Harland and Wolff, Belfast	1965

Measurement, tons: 63 588 deadweight; 35 640 gross; 24 504 net
Dimensions, feet (metres): 747·0 pp; 774·5 oa × 107·8 × 41·5 *(227·8; 236·2 × 32·9 × 12·7)*
Main engines: B. & W. 9 cyl diesels; 1 shaft; 17 000 bhp = 15 knots
Complement: 51

In July 1967 the Ministry of Defence chartered three large tankers for service East of Suez. After limited modifications the ships operated in the Indian Ocean area. But *Ennerdale* sank on 1 June 1970 after striking a submerged hazard in the Indian Ocean. *Derwentdale* (ex-*Halcyon Breeze*) was returned to owners. *Dewdale* is the largest RFA tanker at present in service. No RAS capability.

DEWDALE 1974, Michael D. J. Lennon

SMALL FLEET TANKERS (AOF(S))

5 "ROVER" CLASS

Name	No.	Builders	Commissioned
BLACK ROVER	A 273	Swan Hunter, Wallsend-on-Tyne	23 Aug 1974
BLUE ROVER	A 270	Swan Hunter, Hebburn-on-Tyne	15 July 1970
GOLD ROVER	A 271	Swan Hunter, Wallsend-on-Tyne	22 Mar 1974
GREEN ROVER	A 268	Swan Hunter, Hebburn-on-Tyne	15 Aug 1969
GREY ROVER	A 269	Swan Hunter, Hebburn-on-Tyne	10 April 1970

Displacement, tons: 4,700 light; 11 522 full load
Measurement, tons: 7 060 deadweight; 7 510 gross; 3 185 net
Dimensions, feet (metres): 461·0 oa × 63·0 × 24·0 *(140·6 × 19·2 × 7·3)*
Main engines: 2 Pielstick 16 cyl diesels; 1 shaft; controllable pitch propeller; 15 300 bhp = 18 knots
Complement: 47 (16 officers and 31 men)

Small fleet tankers designed to replenish HM ships at sea with fuel, fresh water, limited dry cargo and refrigerated stores under all conditions while underway. A helicopter landing platform is provided served by a stores lift, to enable stores to be transferred at sea by "vertical lift". *Green Rover* was launched on 19 Dec 1968, *Grey Rover* on 17 April 1969, *Blue Rover* on 11 Nov 1969. *Gold Rover* on 7 Mar 1973 and *Black Rover* on 30 Oct 1973. The cost of *Black Rover* was £7 mill. an increase of £4 mill. on the price of the original ships. Cargo capacity 6 600 tons fuel.

BLACK ROVER (variation in stern)   9/1975, C. and S. Taylor

GREEN ROVER (variation in stern)   8/1975, Wright and Logan

COASTAL TANKER (AO(H))

1 "EDDY" CLASS

Name	No.	Builders	Commissioned
EDDYFIRTH	A 261	Lobnitz & Co Ltd, Renfrew	10 Feb 1954

Displacement, tons: 1 960 light; 4 160 full load
Measurement, tons: 2 200 deadweight; 2 222 gross
Dimensions, feet (metres): 270 pp; 286 oa × 44 × 17·2 *(82·4; 87·2 × 13·4 × 5·2)*
Main engines: 1 set triple expansion; 1 shaft; 1 750 ihp = 12 knots
Boilers: 2 oil burning cylindrical

The last of a class of eight, all completed 1952-54. Cargo capacity: 1 650 tons oil.

EDDYFIRTH   10/1976, Wright and Logan

FLEET REPLENISHMENT SHIPS (AEFS)

Name	No.	Builders	Commissioned
FORT AUSTIN	A 386	Scott-Lithgow	1978
FORT GRANGE	A 385	Scott-Lithgow	1977

Displacement, tons: 17 200
Measurement, tons: 9 843 dw
Dimensions, feet (metres): 603 × 79 × 29·5 *(183·9 × 24·1 × 9)*
Aircraft: 1 Wessex helicopter
Main engines: Diesel; 23 300 hp single screw = 20 knots

Ordered in Nov 1971. To be fitted with a helicopter flight-deck and hangar, thus allowing not only for vertical replenishment but also a fuelling point for Force A/S helicopters. *Fort Grange* laid down 9 Nov 1973, launched 9 Dec 1976. *Fort Austin* laid down 9 Dec 1975. A/S stores for helicopters carried on board.

FORT GRANGE   1972, MOD (N) Drawing

Name	No.	Builders	Commissioned
REGENT	A 486	Harland & Wolff, Belfast	6 June 1967
RESOURCE	A 480	Scotts Shipbuilding & Eng Co, Greenock	16 May 1967

Displacement, tons: 22 890 full load
Measurements, tons: 18 029 gross
Dimensions, feet (metres): 600·0 pp; 640·0 oa × 77·2 × 26·1 *(182·8; 195·1 × 23·5 × 8)*
Aircraft: 1 Wessex helicopter
Guns: Fitted for 2—40 mm Bofors (single) which are not carried in peacetime
Main engines: AEI steam turbines; 20 000 shp = 21 knots
Complement: 119 R.F.A. officers and ratings; 52 Naval Dept industrial and non-industrial civil servants; 11 Royal Navy (1 officer and 10 ratings) for helicopter flying and maintenance

Ordered on 24 Jan 1963. They have lifts for armaments and stores, and helicopter platforms for transferring loads at sea. Designed from the outset as Fleet Replenishment Ships (previous ships had been converted merchant vessels). Air-conditioned. *Resource* was launched at Greenock on 11 Feb 1966, *Regent* at Belfast on 9 Mar 1966. Official title is Ammunition, Explosives, Food, Stores Ship (AEFS).

RESOURCE   1976, Michael D. J. Lennon

ARMAMENT SUPPORT SHIPS (AE)

Name	No.	Builders	Commissioned
RESURGENT (ex-*Changchow*)	A 280	Scotts Shipbuilding & Engineering Co Ltd, Greenock	1951
RETAINER (ex-*Chungking*).	A 329	Scotts Shipbuilding & Engineering Co Ltd, Greenock	1950

Displacement, tons: 14 400
Measurement, tons: *Resurgent* 9 357 gross; *Retainer* 9 498 gross
Dimensions, feet (metres): 477·2 oa × 62 × 29 *(145·8 × 18·9 × 8·8)*
Main engines: Doxford diesel; 1 shaft; 6 500 bhp = 16 knots
Oil fuel, tons: 925
Complement: 107

RESURGENT   *1976, Michael D. J. Lennon*

Retainer was purchased in 1952 and converted into a naval storeship during autumn 1954-April 1955 by Palmers Hebburn Co Ltd, where further conversion was carried out Mar-Aug 1957 to extend her facilities as a stores ship, including the fitting out of holds to carry naval stores, the installation of lifts for stores, the provision of extra cargo handling gear and new bridge wings. *Resurgent* was taken over on completion.

STORES SUPPORT SHIPS (AVS/AFS)

Name	No.	Builders	Commissioned
LYNESS	A 339	Swan Hunter & Wigham Richardson Ltd, Wallsend-on-Tyne	22 Dec 1966
STROMNESS	A 344	Swan Hunter & Wigham Richardson Ltd, Wallsend-on-Tyne	21 Mar 1967
TARBATNESS	A 345	Swan Hunter & Wigham Richardson Ltd, Wallsend-on-Tyne	10 Aug 1967

Displacement, tons: 9,010 light; 16 792 full load (14 000 normal operating)
Measurement, tons: 7 782 deadweight; 12 359 gross; 4 744 net
Dimensions, feet (metres): 490 pp; 524 oa × 72 × 22 *(149·4; 159·7 × 22 × 6·7)*
Aircraft: Helicopter deck
Main engines: Wallsend-Sulzer 8-cyl RD.76 diesel; 11 520 bhp = 18 knots
Complement: 151 (25 officers, 82 ratings, 44 stores personnel)

TARBATNESS   *6/1976, C. and S. Taylor*

Lifts and mobile appliances provided for handling stores internally, and a new replenishment at sea system and a helicopter landing platform for transferring loads at sea. A novel feature of the ships is the use of close circuit television to monitor the movement of stores. All air-conditioned. *Lyness* was launched on 7 April 1966, *Stromness* on 16 Sep 1966, and *Tarbatness* 22 Feb 1967. *Lyness* is an Air-Stores Support Ship and cost £3·5 million.

STORE CARRIERS (AK)

Name	No.	Builders	Commissioned
BACCHUS	A 404	Henry Robb Ltd, Leith	Sep 1962
HEBE	A 406	Henry Robb Ltd, Leith	May 1962

Displacement, tons: 2 740 light; 8 173 full load
Measurement, tons: 5 312 deadweight; 4 823 gross; 2 441 net
Dimensions, feet (metres): 379 oa × 55 × 22 *(115·6 × 16·8 × 6·4)*
Main engines: Swan Hunter Sulzer diesel; 1 shaft; 5 500 bhp = 15 knots
Oil fuel, tons: 720
Complement: 57

Built for the British India Steam Navigation Co for charter to the Royal Navy on completion. Crew accommodation and engines aft as in tankers. In 1973 both purchased by P and O SN Co, remaining on charter to MOD (N). Boxed 40 mm guns carried on board.

BACCHUS   *1972, C. and S. Taylor*

ROYAL MARITIME AUXILIARY SERVICE

Notes: (a) The Royal Maritime Auxiliary Service and Port Auxiliary Service were combined as RMAS on 1 Oct 1976. (b) To avoid over complication the ships and vessels of the Royal Naval Auxiliary Service and some of the Royal Corps of Transport are included here.

MOORING, SALVAGE AND BOOM VESSELS

Note: *Scarab* ("Insect" Class tender) acts as mooring vessel.

2 "WILD DUCK" CLASS (A)

2 "IMPROVED WILD DUCK" CLASS (B)

2 "LATER WILD DUCK" CLASS (C)

Name		No.	Builders	Commissioned
MANDARIN		P 192	Cammell Laird & Co Ltd, Birkenhead	5 Mar 1964
PINTAIL	A	P 193	Cammell Laird & Co Ltd, Birkenhead	Mar 1964
GARGANEY		P 194	Brooke Marine Ltd, Lowestoft	20 Sep 1966
GOLDENEYE	B	P 195	Brooke Marine Ltd, Lowestoft	21 Dec 1966
GOOSANDER		P 196	Robb Caledon Ltd	10 Sep 1973
POCHARD	C	P 197	Robb Caledon Ltd	11 Dec 1973

Displacement, tons: (A) 941 light; 1 622 full load. (B) 850 light; 1 300 full load. (C) 750 light; 1 200 full load
Dimensions, feet (metres): (A) 197·6 × 40·1 × 13·8 *(60·2 × 12·2 × 4·2)*. (B) 189·8 × 36·6 × 13 *(57·9 × 11·2 × 4)*. (C) 181·8 × 36·6 × 13 *(55·4 × 11·2 × 4)*
Main engines: 1 Davey Paxman 16 cyl diesel; 1 shaft; controllable pitch propeller; 750 (A) 550 (B and C) bhp
Speed, knots: 10·8 (A) 10 (B and C)
Range, miles: 3 260 at 9·5 knots (A); 3 000 at 10 knots (B and C)
Complement: 26

GOLDENEYE   *1976, Michael D. J. Lennon*

Mandarin was the first of a new class of marine service vessels. Launched on 17 Sep 1963. *Pintail* was launched on 3 Dec 1963. *Garganey* and *Goldeneye* were built in 1965-67. *Goosander* and *Pochard* of the later "Later Wild Duck" class were launched 12 April 1973 and 21 June 1973 respectively. Previously their three tasks were separately undertaken by specialist vessels.

Capable of laying out and servicing the heaviest moorings used by the Fleet and also maintaining booms for harbour defence. Heavy lifting equipment enables a wide range of salvage operations to be performed, especially in harbour clearance work. The special heavy winches have an ability for tidal lifts over the apron of 200 tons. Boxed 40 mm guns carried on board.

4 "KIN" CLASS

Name	No.	Builders	Commissioned
KINBRACE	A 281	A. Hall, Aberdeen	1945
KINGARTH	A 232	A. Hall, Aberdeen	1944
KINLOSS	A 482	A. Hall, Aberdeen	1945
UPLIFTER	A 507	Smith's Dock Co Ltd	1944

Displacement, tons: 950 standard; 1 050 full load
Measurement, tons: 262 deadweight; 775 gross
Dimensions, feet (metres): 179·2 oa × 35·2 × 12·0 *(54 × 10·6 × 3·6)*
Main engines: 1 British Polar Atlas M44M diesel; 630 bhp = 9 knots
Complement: 34

Originally classified as Coastal Salvage Vessels, but re-rated Mooring, Salvage and Broom Vessels in 1971. Equipped with horns and heavy rollers. Can lift 200 tons deadweight over the bow. *Kinbrace, Kingarth* and *Uplifter* were refitted with diesel engines in 1966-67, and *Kinloss* in 1963-64.

KINBRACE   *1974, Michael D. J. Lennon*

2 "LAY" CLASS

Name	No.	Builders	Commissioned
LAYBURN	P 191	Wm. Simons & Co Ltd (Simons-Lobnitz Ltd)	7 June 1960
LAYMOOR (RN)	P 190	Wm. Simons & Co Ltd (Simons-Lobnitz Ltd)	9 Dec 1959

Displacement, tons: 800 standard; 1 050 full load
Dimensions, feet (metres): 192·7 oa × 34·5 × 11·5 *(59 × 10·3 × 3·4)*
Main engines: Triple expansion; 1 shaft; 1 300 ihp = 10 knots
Boilers: 2 Foster Wheeler "D" type; 200 psi
Complement: 26 (4 officers; 22 ratings)

Layburn, cost £565 000. Designed for naval or civilian manning. Lifting capacity is greater than that of predecessors; improvement in accommodation enables them to be operated in any climate. Oil-fuelled.

LAYBURN   *1973, John G. Callis*

COASTAL TANKERS
6 "OILPRESS" CLASS

Name	No.	Builders	Commissioned
OILBIRD	Y 25	Appledore Shipbuilders Ltd	1969
OILFIELD	Y 24	Appledore Shipbuilders Ltd	1969
OILMAN	Y 26	Appledore Shipbuilders Ltd	1969
OILPRESS	Y 21	Appledore Shipbuilders Ltd	1969
OILSTONE	Y 22	Appledore Shipbuilders Ltd	1969
OILWELL	Y 23	Appledore Shipbuilders Ltd	1969

Displacement, tons: 280 standard; 530 full load
Dimensions, feet (metres): 130·0 wl; 139·5 oa × 30·0 × 8·3 *(39·6; 41·5 × 9 × 2·5)*
Main engines: 1 Lister Blackstone ES6 diesel; 1 shaft; 405 shp at 900 rpm
Complement: 11 (4 officers and 7 ratings)

Ordered on 10 May 1967. Three are diesel oil carriers and three FFO carriers. Launched:— *Oilbird* 21 Nov 1968, *Oilfield* 5 Sep 1968, *Oilman* 18 Feb 1969, *Oilpress* 10 June 1968, *Oilstone* 11 July 1968, *Oilwell* 20 Jan 1969.

OILFIELD   *9/1976, John G. Callis*

TRIALS SHIPS

Name	No.	Builders	Laid down	Launched	Commissioned
MATAPAN	D 43	John Brown, Clydebank	11 Mar 1944	30 Apr 1945	5 Sep 1947

Displacement, tons: 3 835 full load
Length, feet (metres): 388 *(118·3)* oa
Beam, feet (metres): 40·5 *(12·3)*
Draught, feet (metres): 27 *(8·2)*
Main engines: Parsons geared turbines; 50 000 shp; 2 shafts
Boilers: 2 Admiralty 3-drum; 400 psi *(28·1 kg/cm²)*; 650°F *(343°C)*
Oil fuel, tons: 680
Speed, knots: 31
Range, miles: 1 300 at full power; 3 000 at 20 knots; 4 400 at 12 knots

A former standard "Battle" class destroyer which went into reserve almost immediately after being completed. Attached to the Admiralty Underwater Weapons Establishment at Portland after conversion.

Conversion: Taken in hand at HM Dockyard, Portsmouth in Jan 1971 for conversion into a Sonar Trials Ship. The rebuilding involved a new clipper bow, different bridge, remodelled superstructure, extension of the forecastle deck aft all the way to the counter, thus converting her into a flushdecker, adding a second funnel, and a helicopter landing deck. Commissioned 2 Feb 1973 after a £2½m conversion.

Radar: Search: One Type 978.

MATAPAN   *5/1975, C. and S. Taylor*

Name	No.	Builders	Commissioned
NEWTON	A 367	Scott Lithgow Ltd	1976

Displacement, tons: 3 940
Dimensions, feet (metres): 323·5 × 53 × 15·4 *(98·6 × 16 × 4·7)*
Main engines: Diesel electric; 3 Mirrlees Blackstone diesels; 1 shaft; 4 350 bhp = 15 knots
Range, miles: 5 000 at 13 knots
Complement: 61 (including 12 scientists)

Ordered Nov 1971. Laid down 19 Dec 1973. Launched 25 June 1975. Fitted with bow thruster and Kort nozzle. Propulsion system is very quiet. Passive tank stabilisation. Prime duty sonar propagation trials. Can serve as cable-layer with large cable tanks. Special winch system.

Name	No.	Builders	Commissioned
WHITEHEAD	A 364	Scotts Shipbuilding Co Ltd, Greenock	1971

Displacement, tons: 3 040 full load
Dimensions, feet (metres): 291·0 wl; 319·0 oa × 48·0 × 17·0 *(88·8; 97·3 × 14·6 × 5·2)*
Torpedo tubes: 1—21 inch (bow, submerged); 3—(1 triple) Mk 32 A/S mounting
Main engines: 2 Paxman 12 YLCM diesels; 1 shaft; 3 400 bhp = 15·5 knots
Range, miles: 4 000 at 12 knots
Complement: 10 officers, 32 ratings, 15 trials and scientific staff

WHITEHEAD   1972

Designed to provide mobile preparation, firing and control facilities for weapons and research vehicles. Launched on 5 May 1970. Named after Robert Whitehead, the torpedo development pioneer and engineer. Fitted with equipment for tracking weapons and target and for analysing the results of trials.

Name	No.	Builders	Commissioned
CRYSTAL	RDV 01	HM Dockyard, Devonport	30 Nov 1971

Displacement, tons: 3 040
Dimensions, feet (metres): 413·5 × 56·0 × 5·5 *(126·1 × 17·1 × 1·7)*
Complement: 60, including scientists

Unpowered floating platform for Sonar Research and Development. Ordered in Dec 1969. Launched 22 Mar 1971. A harbour-based laboratory without propulsion machinery or steering which provides the Admiralty Underwater Weapons Establishment at Portland with a stable platform on which to carry out acoustic tests and other research projects. Under Dockyard Control.

CRYSTAL   10/1975, Dr. Giorgio Arra

2 "MINER" CLASS

Name	No.	Builders	Commissioned
BRITANNIC (ex-*Miner V*)	—	Philip & Son Ltd, Dartmouth	26 June 1941
STEADY (ex-*Miner VII*)	—	Philip & Son Ltd, Dartmouth	31 Mar 1944

Displacement, tons: 300 standard; 355 full load
Dimensions, feet (metres): 110·2 × 26·5 × 8·0 *(33·6 × 8·1 × 2·4)*
Main engines: Ruston & Hornsby diesels; 2 shafts; 360 bhp = 10 knots

Last of a class of eight small controlled-minelayers. *Miner V* was converted into a harbour cable-layer and renamed *Britannic* in 1960. *Miner VII* was adapted as a stabilisation trials ship at Portsmouth and renamed *Steady* in 1960 with PAS.

BRITANNIC   8/1976, Wright and Logan

TORPEDO RECOVERY VESSELS

Name	No.	Builders	Commissioned
TORRENT	A 127	Cleland SB Co, Wallsend	10 Sep 1971
TORRID	A 128	Cleland SB Co, Wallsend	Jan 1972

Measurement, tons: 550 gross
Dimensions, feet (metres): 151·0 × 31·5 × 11 *(46·1 × 9·6 × 3·4)*
Main engines: Paxman diesels; 700 bhp = 12 knots
Complement: 19

Torrent was launched on 29 Mar 1971 and *Torrid* on 7 Sep 1971. These ships have a stern ramp for torpedo recovery—can carry 22 torpedoes in hold and 10 on deck.

TORRID   1976, Michael D. J. Lennon

Name	No.	Builders	Commissioned
THOMAS GRANT	—	Charles Hill & Sons Ltd, Bristol	July 1953

Displacement, tons: 209 light; 461 full load
Measurement, tons: 252 deadweight; 218 gross
Dimensions, feet (metres): 113·5 × 25·5 × 8·8 *(34·6 × 7·8 × 2·7)*
Main engines: 2 diesels; Speed = 9 knots

Built as a local store carrier. Launched on 11 May 1953. Converted into torpedo recovery vessel in 1968.

THOMAS GRANT   1969

6 "HAM" CLASS

BUCKLESHAM M 2614   **EVERINGHAM** M 2626   **HAVERSHAM** M 2635
DOWNHAM M 2622   **FRITHAM** M 2630   **LASHAM** M 2636

Details similar to other "Ham" class in Mine Warfare section but converted for TRV in 1964 onwards. Now fitted with stern ramp.

TRV 72 TYPE

A number of this SAR type are still in use.

TRV 72   4/1975, Wright and Logan

EXPERIMENTAL SHIP

WHIMBREL (ex-LCT) A 179

Displacement, tons: 300
Dimensions, feet (metres): 187 × 29·5 × 5 *(57 × 9 × 1·5)*
Main engines: Diesels; 2 shafts

Employed for weapon research by Underwater Weapons Establishment, Portland.

WHIMBREL   1974, Michael D. J. Lennon

CABLE SHIP

Name	No.	Builders	Commissioned
ST. MARGARETS	A 259	Swan Hunter & Wigham Richardson Ltd.	1944

Displacement, tons: 1 300 light; 2 500 full load
Measurement, tons: 1 524 gross; 1 200 deadweight
Dimensions, feet (metres): 228·8 pp; 252 oa × 36·5 × 16·3 *(76 × 10·9 × 4·8)*
Main engines: Triple expansion; 2 shafts; 1 250 ihp = 12 knots

Provision was made for mounting one 4 inch gun and four 20 mm guns but no armament is fitted.

ST. MARGARETS   4/1976, John G. Callis

TARGET SHIP

WAKEFUL (ex-*Dan*, ex-*Heracles*) A 236

Displacement, tons: 492
Dimensions, feet (metres): 145·8 oa × 35 × 15·5 *(44·5 × 10·7 × 4·7)*
Complement: 18

Purchased from Sweden in 1974 at cost of £600 000. Built as a tug and subsequently operated as Submarine Target Ship in the Clyde. Now employed on Fishery Protection duties after undergoing a £1 600 000 refit.

WAKEFUL   12/1976, Michael D. J. Lennon

NEW CONSTRUCTION STORE CARRIER (AK)

Name	No.	Builders	Commissioned
—	—	Cleland SB Co, Wallsend	1977

Measurement, tons: 1 150 dw
Dimensions, feet (metres): 210·9 × 39 × 15 *(64·3 × 11·9 × 4·6)*
Main engines: 2 Mirrlees-Blackstone diesels; 3 000 bhp; 1 shaft = 14 knots

Ordered Dec 1975. To carry armament stores in two holds. Two 5 tonne derricks. Flush deck type to replace *Robert Middleton*.

ARMAMENT CARRIERS

Name	No.	Builders	Commissioned
KINTERBURY	A 378	Philip & Son Ltd	4 Mar 1943
THROSK	—	Philip & Son Ltd	22 Dec 1943

Displacement, tons: 1 490 standard; 1 770 full load
Measurement, tons: 600 deadweight
Dimensions, feet (metres): 199·8 × 34·3 × 13 *(60·9 × 10·2 × 4)*
Main engines: Triple expansion; 1 shaft; 900 ihp = 11 knots
Coal, tons: 154

Launched on 14 Nov 1942 and in 1943, respectively. Rated as naval armament carriers. Converted in 1959 with hold stowage and a derrick for handling guided missiles.

KINTERBURY   *1972, Wright and Logan*

CATAPULT   FLINTLOCK

Of differing displacements and data.

Name	No.	Builders	Commissioned
MAXIM	A 377	Lobnitz & Co Ltd, Renfrew	1944

Displacement, tons: 604
Measurement, tons: 340 deadweight
Dimensions, feet (metres): 144·5 × 25 × 8 *(44·1 × 7·6 × 2·3)*
Main engines: Reciprocating; 500 ihp = 9 knots
Complement: 13

WATER CARRIERS

6 "WATER" CLASS

Name	No.	Builders	Commissioned
WATERFALL	Y 17	Drypool Engineering & Drydock Co, Hull	1967
WATERSHED	Y 18	Drypool Engineering & Drydock Co, Hull	1967
WATERSIDE	Y 20	Drypool Engineering & Drydock Co, Hull	1968
WATERSPOUT	Y 19	Drypool Engineering & Drydock Co, Hull	1967
WATERCOURSE	Y 15	Drypool Engineering & Drydock Co, Hull	1974
WATERFOWL	Y 16	Drypool Engineering & Drydock Co, Hull	25 May 1974

Measurement, tons: 285 gross
Dimensions, feet (metres): 131·5 oa × 24·8 × 8 *(40·1 × 7·5 × 2·3)*
Main engines: 1 Diesel; 1 shaft; 600 bhp = 11 knots
Complement: 11

Launched on 30 Mar 1966, 3 Aug 1966, 20 June 1967 and 29 Dec 1966, respectively and the last pair in 1973. Last pair have after deck-house extended forward.

WATERFOWL   *1976, Michael D. J. Lennon*

2 "SPA" CLASS

Name	No.	Builders	Commissioned
SPAPOOL	A 222	Charles Hill & Sons Ltd, Bristol	1947
SPABROOK	A 224	Philip & Son Ltd, Dartmouth	1945

Displacement, tons: 1 219 full load
Measurement, tons: 630 deadweight; 672 to 719 gross
Dimensions, feet (metres): 172 oa × 30 × 12 *(52·5 × 9·2 × 3·6)*
Main engines: Triple expansion; 675 ihp = 9 knots
Coal, tons: 90

SPAPOOL   *1967, MOD (N)*

3 "FRESH" CLASS

FRESHBURN   **FRESHLAKE**   **FRESHSPRING**

Displacement, tons: 594
Dimensions, feet (metres): 126·2 × 25·5 × 10·8 *(38·5 × 7·8 × 3·3)*
Main engines: Triple expansion; 450 ihp = 9 knots

Freshspring was converted from coal to oil fuel, in 1961.

"FRESH" Class   *1966, Dr. Giorgio Arra*

TUGS

3 OCEAN TUGS

Name	No.	Builders	Commissioned
ROBUST	—	Charles D. Holmes, Beverley Shipyard, Hull	6 April 1974
ROLLICKER	A 502	Charles D. Holmes, Beverley Shipyard, Hull	Feb 1973
ROYSTERER	—	Charles D. Holmes, Beverley Shipyard, Hull	26 April 1972

Displacement, tons: 1 630 full load
Dimensions, feet (metres): 162·0 pp; 179·7 oa × 38·5 × 18·0 *(54 × 11·6 × 5·5)*
Main engines: 2 Mirrlees KMR 6 diesels (by Lister Blackstone Mirrlees Marine Ltd); 2 shafts;
   4 500 bhp at 525 rpm = 15 knots
Range, miles: 13 000 at 12 knots
Complement: 31 (10 officers and 21 ratings) (and able to carry salvage party of 10 RN officers
   and ratings)

These are the biggest and most powerful ocean tugs ever built for the Royal Navy. Bollard
pull—50 tons. Designed principally for salvage and long range towage but can be used for
general harbour duties, which *Robust* now undertakes. Cost well over £2 million apiece.
Ordered Nov 1968 *(Rollicker, Roysterer)* and May 1970 *(Robust)*. Launch dates:— *Robust* 7 Oct
1971, *Rollicker* 29 Jan 1971, *Roysterer* 20 April 1970.

ROLLICKER   *1976, Michael D. J. Lennon*

Name	No.	Builders	Commissioned
TYPHOON	A 95	Henry Robb & Co Ltd, Leith	1960

Displacement, tons: 800 standard; 1 380 full load
Dimensions, feet (metres): 200·0 oa × 40·0 × 13·0 *(60·5 × 12 × 4)*
Main engines: 2 turbocharged vee type 12-cyl diesels; 1 shaft; 2 750 bhp = over 16 knots

Launched on 14 Oct 1958. The machinery arrangement of two diesels geared to a single shaft
was an innovation for naval ocean tugs in the RN. Controllable pitch propeller, 150 rpm. Fitted
for fire fighting, salvage and ocean rescue, with a heavy mainmast and derrick attached. Bollard
pull 32 tons.

TYPHOON   *1976, Michael D. J. Lennon*

5 "CONFIANCE" CLASS

Name	No.	Builders	Commissioned
ACCORD	A 90	A. & J. Inglis Ltd, Glasgow	Sep 1958
ADVICE	A 89	A. & J. Inglis Ltd, Glasgow	Oct 1959
AGILE	A 88	Goole SB Co.	July 1959
CONFIANCE	A 289	A. & J. Inglis Ltd, Glasgow	27 Mar 1956
CONFIDENT	A 290	A. & J. Inglis Ltd, Glasgow	Jan 1956

Displacement, tons: 760 full load
Dimensions, feet (metres): 140·0 pp; 154·8 oa × 35·0 × 11·0 *(42·7; 47·2 × 10·7 × 3·4)*
Main engines: 4 Paxman HAXM diesels; 2 shafts; 1 800 bhp = 13 knots
Complement: 29 plus 13 salvage party

Fitted with 2·50 m diam. Stone Kamewa controllable pitch propellers. *Accord, Advice* and *Agile*,
formerly rated as dockyard tugs were officially added to the "Confiance" class in 1971 as part of
the Royal Maritime Auxiliary Service ocean towing force. Fitted for 1—40 mm gun.

AGILE   *1974, Wright and Logan*

3 "SAMSON" CLASS

Name	No.	Builders	Commissioned
SEA GIANT	A 288	Alexander Hall & Co Ltd, Aberdeen	1955
SUPERMAN	—	Alexander Hall & Co Ltd, Aberdeen	1954
SAMSON	—	Alexander Hall & Co Ltd, Aberdeen	1954

Displacement, tons: 1 200 full load
Measurement, tons: 850 gross
Dimensions, feet (metres): 180 oa × 37 × 14 *(54 × 11·2 × 4·3)*
Main engines: Triple expansion; 2 shafts; 3 000 ihp = 15 knots

Samson was to have been sold to Chile in 1974 but is still laid up in Portsmouth. *Superman* laid
up at Devonport.

SEA GIANT   *6/1976, John G. Callis*

1 "BUSTLER" CLASS

Name	No.	Builders	Commissioned
CYCLONE (ex-Growler)	A 111	Henry Robb Ltd, Leith	Sep 1943

Displacement, tons: 1.118 light; 1 630 full load
Dimensions, feet (metres): 190·0 pp; 205·0 oa × 40·2 × 16·8 (58; 62·5 × 12·3 × 5·1)
Main engines: 2 Atlas Polar 8-cyl diesels; 1 shaft; 4 000 bhp = 16 knots
Oil fuel, tons: 405
Range, miles: 17 000
Complement: 42

Last of class of four. In reserve at Pembroke Dock. Launch date:— 10 Sep 1942.

CYCLONE   1975, Michael D. J. Lennon

6 "DIRECTOR" CLASS

Name	No.	Builders	Commissioned
DEXTEROUS	A 93	Yarrow & Sons Ltd	1957
DIRECTOR	A 94	Yarrow & Sons Ltd	1957
FAITHFUL	A 85	Yarrow & Sons Ltd	1958
FORCEFUL	A 86	Yarrow & Sons Ltd	1958
FAVOURITE	A 87	Ferguson & Co Ltd	1959

Displacement, tons: 710 full load
Dimensions, feet (metres): 157·2 oa × 30 (60 over paddle boxes) × 10 (47·9 × 9·2 (18·4) × 3·1)
Main engines: Paxman diesels and BTH motors; diesel electric; 2 shafts; 2 paddle wheels; 2 000 bhp = 13 knots
Complement: 21

Dexterous at Gibraltar. The only class of paddlers run by any navy in the world.

FORCEFUL   1973, Wright and Logan

19 "DOG" CLASS

AIREDALE A 102	CAIRN A 126	ELKHOUND A 162	SALUKI A 182
ALSATIAN A 106	COLLIE A 328	HUSKY A 169	SEALYHAM A 187
BASSET A 327	CORGI A 330	LABRADOR A 168	SETTER A 189
BOXER A 394	DALMATIAN A 129	MASTIFF A 180	SHEEPDOG A 250
	DEERHOUND A 155	POINTER A 188	SPANIEL A 201

Displacement, tons: 170 full load
Dimensions, feet (metres): 94 × 24·5 × 12 (28·7 × 7·5 × 3·7)
Main engines: Lister Blackstone diesels; 1 320 bhp = 12 knots
Complement: 8

Harbour berthing tugs. *Airedale* and *Sealyham* at Gibraltar. Bollard pull 16 tons. Completed 1962-72.

SEALYHAM   1976, Michael D. J. Lennon

8 "GIRL" CLASS

AGATHA A 116	ALICE A 113	BARBARA A 324	BRENDA A 335
AGNES A 121	AUDREY A 117	BETTY A 323	BRIDGET A 322

The first of four new classes of harbour berthing tugs. Of 40 tons. 495 bhp = 10 knots. "A" names built by P. K. Harris, "B" names by Dunstons. Completed 1962-1972.

AUDREY   11/1975, Michael D. J. Lennon

9 "MODIFIED GIRL" CLASS

CELIA A 206	CHRISTINE A 217	DAISY A 145	DORIS A 252
CHARLOTTE A 210	CLARE A 218	DAPHNE	DOROTHY
			EDITH A 177

Of 38 tons. 495 bhp = 10 knots. *Dorothy* in Hong Kong. *Edith* at Gibraltar.
"C" names built by Pimblott and "D" and "E" names by Dunstons. Completed 1972.

CLARE   12/1976, Dr. Giorgio Arra

12 "TRIDENT" CLASS

IRENE	JOYCE	LESLEY	MYRTLE
ISABEL	KATHLEEN	LILAH	NANCY
JOAN	KITTY	MARY	NORAH

All completed by August 1974 by Dunstons. "Water-tractors" with small wheelhouse and adjoining funnel. 58 ft *(17·7)* and of 107·5 tons. 330 bhp =8 knots.

NANCY *1976, Michael D. J. Lennon*

5 "FELICITY" CLASS

FELICITY	GEORGINA	HELEN
FIONA	GWENDOLINE	

"Water tractors". Of 80 tons. 600 bhp = 10 knots. *Felicity* built by Dunstons and remainder by Hancocks. Completed 1973.

HELEN *6/1976, Michael D. J. Lennon*

FLEET TENDERS

Note: 5 new tenders ordered from Richard Dunston (Hessle) Ltd, Thorn in late 1976.

7 "INSECT" CLASS

Name	No.	Builders	Commissioned
BEE	—	C. D. Holmes Ltd, Beverley, Yorks	1970
CICALA	—	C. D. Holmes Ltd, Beverley, Yorks	1971
COCKCHAFER	—	C. D. Holmes Ltd, Beverley, Yorks	1971
CRICKET	—	C. D. Holmes Ltd, Beverley, Yorks	1972
GNAT	—	C. D. Holmes Ltd, Beverley, Yorks	1972
LADYBIRD	—	C. D. Holmes Ltd, Beverley, Yorks	1973
SCARAB	—	C. D. Holmes Ltd, Beverley, Yorks	1973

Displacement, tons: 450 full load
Dimensions, feet (metres): 111·8 oa × 28 × 11 *(34·1 × 8·5 × 3·4)*
Main engines: Lister-Blackstone Diesels; 1 shaft; 660 bhp = 10·5 knots
Complement: 10

First three built as stores carriers, three as armament carriers and *Scarab,* as mooring vessel capable of lifting 10 tons over the bows.

BEE *9/1976, Dr. Giorgio Arra*

12 "ABERDOVEY" CLASS

Name	No.	Builders	Commissioned
ABERDOVEY	—	Isaac Pimblott & Sons, Northwich	1963
ABINGER	—	Isaac Pimblott & Sons, Northwich	1964
ALNESS	—	Isaac Pimblott & Sons, Northwich	1965
ALNMOUTH	—	Isaac Pimblott & Sons, Northwich	1966
APPLEBY	—	Isaac Pimblott & Sons, Northwich	1967
ASHCOTT	—	Isaac Pimblott & Sons, Northwich	1968
BEAULIEU	A 99	J. S. Doig, Grimsby	1966
BEDDGELERT	A 100	J. S. Doig, Grimsby	1967
BEMBRIDGE	A 101	J. S. Doig, Grimsby	1968
BIBURY	A 103	J. S. Doig, Grimsby	1969
BLAKENEY	A 104	J. S. Doig, Grimsby	1970
BRODICK	A 105	J. S. Doig, Grimsby	1971

Displacement, tons: 117·5 full load
Dimensions, feet (metres): 79·8 oa × 18 × 5·5 *(24 × 5·4 × 2·4)*
Main engines: 1 Lister-Blackstone Diesel; 1 shaft; 225 bhp = 10·5 knots
Complement: 6

Multi-purpose for stores (25 tons), passengers (200 standing) plus a couple of torpedoes. *Ashcott* at Gibraltar. *Alnmouth* operates from Devonport for Sea Cadet Corps training.

ALNMOUTH *5/1976, Michael D. J. Lennon*

4 DIVING TENDERS

Name	No.	Builders	Commissioned
CLOVELLY	A 389	I. Pimblott & Sons, Northwich	1972
ILCHESTER	—	Gregson Ltd, Blyth	1974
INSTOW	—	Gregson Ltd, Blyth	1974
INVERGORDON	A 310	Gregson Ltd, Blyth	1974

Of similar characteristics to "Cartmel" class.

1 DIVING TENDER

Name	No.	Builders	Commissioned
DATCHET	—	Vospers Ltd	1972

Main engines: 2 Gray diesels, 2 shafts, 450 bhp = 12 knots

DATCHET   1976, Michael D. J. Lennon

30 "CARTMEL" CLASS

Name	No.	Builders	Commissioned
CARTMEL	—	I. Pimblott & Sons, Northwich	1971
CAWSAND	—	I. Pimblott & Sons, Northwich	1971
CRICCIETH	—	I. Pimblott & Sons, Northwich	1972
CRICKLADE	—	C. D. Holmes, Beverley	1971
CROMARTY	—	J. Lewis, Aberdeen	1972
DENMEAD	—	C. D. Holmes, Beverley	1972
DORNOCH	—	J. Lewis, Aberdeen	1972
DUNSTER	A 393	R. Dunston, Thorne	1972
ELKSTONE	A 353	J. Cook, Wivenhoe	1971
ELSING	A 277	J. Cook, Wivenhoe	1971
EPWORTH	A 352	J. Cook, Wivenhoe	1972
ETTRICK	A 274	J. Cook, Wivenhoe	1972
FELSTED	A 384	R. Dunston, Thorne	1972
FINTRY	—	J. Lewis, Aberdeen	1972
FOTHERBY	—	R. Dunston, Thorne	1972
FROXFIELD	A 354	R. Dunston, Thorne	1972
FULBECK	—	C. D. Holmes, Beverley	1972
GLENCOVE	—	I. Pimblott & Sons, Northwich	1972
GRASMERE	—	J. Lewis, Aberdeen	1972
HAMBLEDON	—	R. Dunston, Thorne	1973
HARLECH	—	R. Dunston, Thorne	1973
HEADCORN	—	R. Dunston, Thorne	1973
HEVER	—	R. Dunston, Thorne	1973
HOLMWOOD	A 1772	R. Dunston, Thorne	1973
HORNING	A 1773	R. Dunston, Thorne	1973
IXWORTH	A 318	Gregson Ltd, Blyth	Sep 1974
LAMLASH	—	R. Dunston, Thorne	1974
LECHLADE	—	R. Dunston, Thorne	1974
LLANDOVERY	—	R. Dunston, Thorne	1974
LOYAL CHANCELLOR	—	—	—

IXWORTH   11/1976, Wright and Logan

Displacement, tons: 143 full load
Dimensions, feet (metres): 80 oa × 21 × 6·6 *(24·1 × 6·4 × 3)*
Main engines: 1 Lister-Blackstone diesel; 1 shaft; 320 bhp = 10·5 knots
Complement: 6

All fleet tenders as "Aberdovey" class. *Elsing* and *Ettrick* at Gibraltar.
Of three types—A. Cargo only; B. Passengers or cargo; C. Training tenders (complement 12).

4 "LOYAL" CLASS (RNXS)

LOYAL MODERATOR A 220   ALERT (ex-*Loyal Governor*) A 510
LOYAL PROCTOR A 1771   VIGILANT (ex-*Loyal Factor*) A 382

Details as for "Cartmel" class. *Loyal Proctor* employed by RNXS and *Loyal Moderator* used for PAS training. *Alert* and *Vigilant* classified as "Patrol Craft" in the Defence White Paper 1976 as they have, from time to time, carried out patrols off Ulster. (RN manned).

LOYAL MODERATOR   5/1974, John G Callis

6 "HAM" CLASS (RNXS)

PAGHAM M 2716		**SHIPHAM** M 2726	
PORTISHAM M 2781		**THAKEHAM** M 2733	
PUTTENHAM M 2784		**TONGHAM** M 2735	

Details in Minewarfare Section.
Shipham temporarily employed as Inshore Survey Craft in place of *Egeria*.

PORTISHAM   10/1976, Wright and Logan

30 MFV TYPES

A number of MFV types are used in dockyard ports, not necessarily under naval control.

TANK CLEANING VESSELS

7 "ISLES" CLASS

Name	No.	Builders	Commissioned
BERN	A 334	Cook Welton and Gemmell	1942
CALDY	A 332	John Lewis and Sons	1943
COLL	A 333	Ardrossan Dockyard Co	1942
GRAEMSAY	A 340	Ardrossan Dockyard Co	1943
LUNDY	A 336	Cook Welton and Gemmell	1943
SKOMER	A 338	John Lewis and Sons	1943
SWITHA	A 346	A. and J. Inglis Ltd	1942

Displacement, tons: 770 full load
Dimensions, feet (metres): 164 oa × 27·5 × 14 *(49 × 8·4 × 4·2)*
Main engines: Triple expansion; 1 shaft; 850 ihp = 12 knots
Boiler: 1 cylindrical
Coal, tons: 183

Last survivors, in UK service of a class of 145 built for minesweeping and escort duties during the war, most of them were employed on wreck dispersal after the war until conversion to their present role in 1951-57.

BERN   5/1973, Wright and Logan

DEGAUSSING VESSELS

3 "HAM" CLASS

FORDHAM M 2717   **THATCHAM** M 2790   **WARMINGHAM** M 2737

Of the "Ham" class of Inshore Minesweepers. For details see Mine Warfare Section.

WARMINGHAM   10/1974, C. and S. Taylor

SCOTTISH FISHERY PROTECTION VESSELS

2 "JURA" CLASS

Name	No.	Builders	Commissioned
JURA	—	Hall, Russell & Co, Aberdeen	1973
WESTRA	—	Hall, Russell & Co, Aberdeen	1975

Displacement, tons: 778 light; 1 285 full load
Measurement, tons: 942 gross
Dimensions, feet (metres): 195·3 oa × 35 × 14·4 *(59·6 × 10·7 × 4·4)*
Main engines: 2 British Polar SP112VS-F diesels; 4 200 bhp; 1 shaft = 17 knots
Complement: 28

Jura was leased by the Ministry of Defence for oil-rig patrol and armed with 1—40 mm. Returned from RN service Jan 1977. *Westra* was launched on 6 Aug 1974. Three other craft are operated by Scottish Home Dept.

JURA (fitted for North Sea Patrol)   1975, MOD (N)

ROYAL CORPS OF TRANSPORT

As well as the "Avon" class listed in the Amphibious Warfare Section the following craft are operated by the RCT.

1 "HAM" CLASS

R. G. MASTERS (ex-RAF 5012, ex-HMS *Hailsham*)

Details in minewarfare section.

R. G. MASTERS   1976, Michael D. J. Lennon

1 90 ft MFV

YARMOUTH NAVIGATOR

Of 90 ft. *Yarmouth Seaman* sold 1976.

YARMOUTH NAVIGATOR   1976, Michael D. J. Lennon

1 GENERAL SERVICE LAUNCH

TREVOSE

Of 72 ft.

6 GENERAL SERVICE LAUNCHES

JACKSON	**RADDLE**
MARTIN	**SMIKE**
NEWMAN NOGGS	**URIAH HEEP**
OLIVER TWIST	

Of 50 ft.

7 GENERAL DUTIES LAUNCHES

CARP WB 01	**ROACH** WB 05
CHUB WB 02	**PERCH** WB 06
BREAM WB 03	**PIKE** WB 07
BARBEL WB 04	

470 ft work-boats.

6 COMMAND and CONTROL CRAFT

PETREL L 01	**SKUA** L 04
TERN L 02	**SHEARWATER** L 05
FULMAR L 03	**SHELDUCK** L 06

41 ft craft.

PETREL   2/1977, Michael D. J. Lennon

ROYAL AIR FORCE MARINE CRAFT

Officer-in-Charge: Group Captain J. F. Burgess

New Construction: All wooden craft to be replaced by "Seal" class, "Spitfire" class and 27 ft workboats by end 1981.

3 "SEAL" CLASS (LRRSC)

Name	No.	Builders	Commissioned
SEAL	5000	Brooke Marine, Lowestoft	Aug 1967
SEAGULL	5001	Fairmile Construction, Berwick on Tweed	1970
SEA OTTER	5002	Fairmile Construction, Berwick on Tweed	1970

Displacement, tons: 159 full load
Dimensions, feet (metres): 120·3 × 23·5 × 6·5 *(36·6 × 7·2 × 2)*
Main engines: 2 Paxman diesels; 2 200 hp = 21 knots
Complement: 18

All welded steel hulls. Aluminium alloy superstructure.

SEAGULL   *1973, RAF*

4 "SPITFIRE" CLASS (RTTL Mk 3)

Name	No.	Builders	Commissioned
SPITFIRE	4000	James and Stone, Brightlingsea	1972
SUNDERLAND	4001	James and Stone, Brightlingsea	1976
STIRLING	4002	James and Stone, Brightlingsea	1976
HALIFAX	4003	James and Stone, Brightlingsea	1977

Displacement, tons: 70
Dimensions, feet (metres): 77·7 × 18 × 4·9 *(23·7 × 5·5 × 1·5)*
Main engines: 2 Paxman diesels; 2 100 hp = 22 knots
Complement: 9

All welded steel hulls—aluminium alloy superstructure. *Spitfire* has twin funnels, remainder none.

SUNDERLAND   *1976, RAF*

4 RESCUE TARGET TOWING LAUNCHES Mk 2 (RTTL Mk 2)

2752, 2757, 2768, 2771

Displacement, tons: 34·6
Dimensions, feet (metres): 68 × 19 × 6 *(20·7 × 5·8 × 1·8)*
Main engines: 2 Rolls-Royce Sea Griffon; 11 000 bhp = 30 knots
Complement: 9

Hard chine, wooden hulls. Built by Vospers, Saunders Roe and Groves and Gutteridge. To be replaced by RTTL Mk 3.

RTTL Mk 2   *1975, RAF*

10 PINNACES 1300 SERIES

Displacement, tons: 28·3
Dimensions, feet (metres): 63 × 15·5 × 5 *(19·2 × 4·9 × 1·5)*
Main engines: 2 Rolls-Royce C6 diesels; 190 bhp = 13 knots
Complement: 5

Hard chine, wooden hulls. Built by Groves and Gutteridge, Robertsons (Dunoon) and Dorset Yacht Co (Poole). 5 tons cargo capacity.

1300 Series Pinnace   *1975, RAF*

7 RANGE SAFETY LAUNCHES 1600 SERIES

Displacement, tons: 12 full load
Dimensions, feet (metres): 43 × 13 × 4 *(13·1 × 4 × 1·2)*
Main engines: 2 Rolls-Royce C6 diesels; 190 bhp = 16 knots
Complement: 4

Hard chine, wooden double diagonal hulls.

HARBOUR CRAFT

24 ft tenders and Gemini craft in current use. To be replaced by 27 ft Cheverton workboats by 1980-81.

UNITED STATES OF AMERICA

Administration

Secretary of the Navy:
  W. Graham Claytor Jnr

There are one Under Secretary and four Assistant Secretaries.

Principal Flag Officers

Chief of Naval Operations:
  Admiral James Holloway, III
Vice Chief of Naval Operations:
  Admiral Harold E. Shear
Deputy Chief of Naval Operations (Manpower):
  Vice-Admiral James D. Watkins
Deputy Chief of Naval Operations (Submarine Warfare):
  Vice-Admiral Robert L. J. Long
Deputy Chief of Naval Operations (Surface Warfare):
  Vice-Admiral James H. Doyle, Jnr
Deputy Chief of Naval Operations (Air Warfare):
  Vice-Admiral Frederic C. Turner
Deputy Chief of Naval Operations (Logistics):
  Vice-Admiral Edward W. Cooke
Deputy Chief of Naval Operations (Plans, Policy and Operations):
  Vice-Admiral Joseph P. Moorer
***Commander-in-Chief Atlantic and Commander-in-Chief Atlantic Fleet:*
  Admiral Isaac C. Kidd, Jnr
**Commander-in-Chief Pacific:*
  Admiral Maurice F. Weisner
Commander-in-Chief Pacific Fleet:
  Admiral Thomas B. Hayward
Commander Second Fleet (Atlantic):
  Vice-Admiral John J. Shanahan, Jnr
Commander Third Fleet (Eastern Pacific):
  Vice-Admiral Samuel L. Graveley Jnr
Commander Sixth Fleet (Mediterranean) and Commander Strike Force South (NATO):
  Vice-Admiral Harry D. Train, II
Commander Seventh Fleet (Western Pacific):
  Vice-Admiral Robert B. Baldwin
Commander Military Sealift Command:
  Rear-Admiral Sam H. Moore
Chief of Naval Education and Training:
  Vice-Admiral James B. Wilson
Chief of Naval Reserve:
  Vice-Admiral Pierre N. Charbonnet, Jnr

Marine Corps

Commandant:
  General Louis H. Wilson, Jnr
Assistant Commandant:
  General Samuel Jaskilka
Chief of Staff:
  Lieutenant-General L. E. Brown

Materiél

Chief of Naval Material:
  Admiral F. H. Michaelis
Vice Chief of Naval Material:
  Vice-Admiral Vincent A. Lascara
Commander Naval Air Systems Command:
  Vice-Admiral Forrest S. Petersen
Commander Naval Electronic Systems Command:
  Rear-Admiral Earl B. Fowler, Jnr
Commander Naval Facilities Engineering Command:
  Rear-Admiral Albert R. Marschall
****Commander Naval Sea Systems Command:*
  Vice-Admiral Clarence B. Bryan
Commander Naval Supply Systems Command:
  Rear-Admiral Wallace R. Dowd, Jnr

Notes: *Unified Command with the Commander-in-Chief directing all US Army, Navy, and Air Force activities in the area. Only naval officers serving as Unified Commanders-in-Chief are listed. **In addition to Unified Commander, also Supreme Allied Commander Atlantic (NATO position). ***In July 1974 the Naval Ordnance Systems Command and Naval Ship Systems Command were merged into the new Naval Sea Systems Command.

Diplomatic Representation

Defense Attaché and Naval Attaché in London:
  Rear-Admiral Francis T. Brown, USN
Naval Attaché and Naval Attaché for Air in Moscow:
  Captain Ronald J. Kurth, USN
Naval Attaché and Naval Attaché for Air in Paris:
  Captain George N. La Rocque, USN

Personnel

	30 June 1975 (Actual)	30 Sep 1976 (Actual)	30 Sep 1977 (Planned)
Navy			
Officers	65 680	63 176	63 277
Enlisted	466 121	460 231	468 373
Marine Corps			
Officers	18 591	18 581	18 552
Enlisted	177 360	171 204	173 448

Mercantile Marine

Lloyd's Register of Shipping: 4 616 vessels of 14 908 445 tons gross.

US Commerce Department (Vessels over 1 000 tons):
  Active: 588 vessels of 10 535 155 tons gross
  Reserve: 155 vessels of 1 204 419 tons gross

Strength of the Fleet

Number of ships listed in the table are actual as of 1 Feb 1977, based on official tabulations and include ships and craft attached to the Naval Reserve Force (NRF).

Category-Type		Active	Building	Reserve	Conversion
STRATEGIC MISSILE SUBMARINES					
SSBN	Ballistic Missile Submarines	39	4	—	2
SUBMARINES					
SSN	Submarines (nuclear)	65	27	2	—
SS	Attack Submarines (diesel)	10	—	—	—
SSG	Guided Missile Submarines (diesel)	—	—	1	—
AIRCRAFT CARRIERS					
CVN	Aircraft Carriers (nuclear)	2	2	—	—
CV	Aircraft Carriers	11	—	1	—
CVS	Anti-Submarine Carriers	—	—	4	—
CVA	Attack Carrier	—	—	1	—
BATTLESHIPS					
BB	Battleships	—	—	4	—
CRUISERS					
CGN	Guided Missile Cruisers (nuclear)	5	3	—	—
CG	Guided Missile Cruisers	20	—	2	1
CA	Heavy Cruisers	—	—	5	—
DESTROYERS					
DDG	Guided Missile Destroyers	38	—	—	1
DD	Destroyers	53	25	—	—
FRIGATES					
FFG	Guided Missile Frigates	6	10	—	—
FF	Frigates	58	—	—	—
COMMAND SHIPS					
CC	National Command Ships	—	—	2	—
AMPHIBIOUS WARFARE FORCES					
LCC	Amphibious Command Ships	2	—	4	—
LHA	Amphibious Assault Ships (GP)	1	4	—	—
LPH	Amphibious Assault Ships	7	—	—	—
LKA	Amphibious Cargo Ships	6	—	—	—
LPA	Amphibious Transports	2	—	—	—
LPD	Amphibious Transport Docks	14	—	—	—
LSD	Landing Ships Dock	13	—	7	—
LST	Landing Ships Tank	20	—	7	—
LIGHT FORCES					
PHM	Patrol Combatants—Missile (hydrofoil)	—	6	—	—
PCH	Patrol Craft (hydrofoil)	1	—	—	—
PG	Patrol Combatants	8	—	—	—
PTF	Fast Patrol Craft	4	—	—	—
MINE WARFARE FORCES					
MSO	Minesweepers—Ocean	25	—	8	—
SERVICE FORCES (Underway Replenishemnt)					
AE	Ammunition Ships	13	—	—	—
AF	Store Ship	1	—	—	—
AFS	Combat Stores Ships	7	—	—	—
AO	Oilers	8	2	—	—
AOE	Fast Combat Stores Ships	4	—	—	—
AOR	Replenishment Fleet Oilers	7	—	—	—
SERVICE FORCES (Auxiliaries)					
AD	Destroyer Tenders	9	3	1	—
AG	Miscellaneous	3	—	1	—
AGDS	Auxiliary Deep Submergence Support Ship	1	—	—	—
AGEH	Hydrofoil Research Ship	1	—	—	—
AGF	Miscellaneous Command Ship	1	—	—	—
AGFF	Frigate Research Ship	1	—	—	—
AGP	Patrol Craft Tender	1	—	—	—
AGSS	Auxiliary Submarines	2	—	1	—
APB	Self-propelled Barracks Ships	—	—	1	—
AR	Repair Ships	5	—	1	—
ARL	Landing Craft Repair Ships	—	—	4	—
ARS	Salvage Ships	12	—	—	—
AS	Submarine Tenders	11	2	2	—
ASR	Submarine Rescue Ships	8	—	—	—
ATF	Fleet Ocean Tugs	16	—	1	1
ATS	Salvage and Rescue Ships	3	—	—	—
AVM	Guided Missile Ship	1	—	—	—
CVT	Training Aircraft Carrier	1	—	—	—
SERVICE CRAFT					
All Types (Propelled or dumb)		990	7	133	—
MILITARY SEALIFT COMMAND (Nucleus)		62	4	6	1

SPECIAL NOTES

United States Navy ships that are in active commission or are in service are indicated by an asterisk by their names. It should be noted that this marking for active ships applies only to the United States Navy section of *Jane's Fighting Ships*.

SHIPBUILDING/CONVERSION PROGRAMMES

Planned Five Year Shipbuilding/Conversion Programme (FY 1978/1982)

Shipbuilding

8	"OHIO" Class SSBNs
8	"LOS ANGELES" Class SSNs
2	VSTOL/Aircraft Carriers (CVV)
2	Nuclear Powered Strike Cruisers (CSGN)
10	Guided Missile Destroyers (AEGIS) (DDG-47 Class)
56	Guided Missile Frigates (FFG-7 Class)
2	Guided Missile Frigates (FFGX Class)
6	Dock Landing Ships (LSD-41 Class)
19	Mine Countermeasures Ship (MCM)
14	Oilers (AO-177 Class)
1	Fast Combat Suppport Ship (AOE)
2	Destroyer Tenders (AD)
2	Repair Ships (AR)
12	Ocean Surveillance Ships (AGOS)
7	Fleet Ocean Tugs (ATF)
2	Cable Repair Ships (ARC)
4	Submarine Rescue Ships (ASR)

Conversion

2	Carrier Ship Life Extension Programme (SLEP) (For CV/CVN-59/70)
18	Modernisation of "CHARLES F. ADAMS" Class DDGs
1	Patrol Combatant Support Ship (Converted from LST)

Proposed FY 1978 Programme

Shipbuilding

2	"OHIO" Class SSBNs
2	"LOS ANGELES" Class SSNs
1	Guided Missile Destroyers (AEGIS) (DDG-47 Class)
11	Guided Missile Frigates (FFG-7 Class)
4	Oilers (AO-177 Class)
5	Fleet Ocean Tugs (ATF-166 Class)

Long Term Lead Items

1	Nuclear Powered Strike Cruiser (CSGN) (to be requested FY 1979)
1	Carrier Ship Life Extension Programme (SLEP) (to be requested FY 1980)
6	Modernisation of "CHARLES F. ADAMS" Class DDGs (to be requested FY 1980)

Conversion

1	Patrol Combatant Support Ship (Converted from LST)

Approved FY 1977 Programme

Shipbuilding

1	"OHIO" Class SSBN (SSBN-730)
3	"LOS ANGELES" Class SSNs (SSN-716/718)
8	"OLIVER HAZARD PERRY" Class FFGs (FFG-19/24)
1	Destroyer Tender (AD-43)
1	Oiler (AO-179)
1	Submarine Tender (AS-41)

Long Term Lead Items

1	"NIMITZ" Class (CVN) (will not be built)
1	Conversion of "LONG BEACH" (CGN-9) to AEGIS (will not be converted)

Conversion

1	Repair and Modernisation (AEGIS) of *Belknap* (CG-26)

Source: Above data based on Department of Defense Annual Report issued 17 January 1977 by SecDef. Donald H. Rumsfeld.

Naval Aviation

US Naval Aviation currently consists of approx 7 000 aircraft flown by the Navy and Marine Corps. The principal naval aviation organisations are 13 carrier air wings, 24 maritime reconnaissance/patrol squadrons, and three Marine Aircraft Wings. In addition, the Naval Reserve and Marine Corps Reserve operate 7 fighter squadrons, 11 attack squadrons, and 12 patrol squadrons, plus various reconnaissance, electrical warfare, tanker, helicopter and transport units.

Fighter: 26 Navy squadrons with F-4 Phantom and F-14 Tomcat aircraft; 12 Marine squadrons with F-4 Phantoms.

Attack: 39 Navy squadrons with A-6 Intruder and A-7 Corsair aircraft; 13 Marine squadrons with A-4 Skyhawk, A-6 Intruder, AV-8 Harrier aircraft.

Reconnaissance: 10 Navy RA-5C Vigilante and RF-8G Crusader aircraft; 3 Marine squadrons with RF-4B Phantoms.

Airborne Early Warning: 12 Navy squadrons with E-2 Hawkeye aircraft.

Electronic Warfare: 8 Navy squadrons with EA-6B Prowler aircraft (Marines operate EA-6A Intruder aircraft in composite reconnaissance squadrons).

Anti-Submarine: 9 Navy squadrons with S-3 Viking aircraft replacing S-2 Trackers.

Maritime Patrol: 24 Navy squadrons with P-3 Orion aircraft.

Helicopter Anti-Submarine: 16 Navy squadrons with SH-3 Sea King and SH-2 LAMPS helicopters.

Helicopter Mine Countermeasures: 1 Navy squadron with RH-53 Sea Stallion helicopters.

Helicopter Support: 4 Navy squadrons with UH-46 Sea Knight helicopters.

Electronic Reconnaissance: 2 Navy squadrons with EP-3E Orion and EC-121 Warning Star aircraft.

Communications Relay: 2 Navy squadrons with EC-130 Hercules aircraft.

Observation: 3 Marine squadrons with OV-10 Bronco aircraft.

Helicopter Gunship: 3 Marine squadrons with AH-1 Sea Cobra helicopters.

Helicopter Transport: 21 Marine squadrons with UH-1 Iroquois (Huey), CH-46 Sea Knight, and CH-53 Sea Stallion helicopters.

BASES

Naval Air Stations and Air Facilities (44)

NAS Alameda, Calif; NAF China Lake, Calif; NAF El Centro, Calif; NAS Los Alamitos, Calif; NAS Mirimar, Calif; NAS Moffett Field (San Jose), Calif; NAS Point Mugu, Calif; NAS North Island (San Diego), Calif; NAF Andrews, Washington DC; NAS Cecil Field (Pensacola), Fla; NAS Jacksonville, Fla; NAS Key West, Fla; NAS Whiting Field (Milton), Fla; NAS Saufley Field (Pensacola), Fla; NAS Pansacola, Fla; NAS Atlanta (Marietta), Ga; NAS Glenview, Ill; NAS Barbers Point (Oahu), Hawaii; NAS New Orleans, La; NAS Brunswick, Me; NAS Paxtuxent River, Md; NAS South Weymouth, Mass; NAF Detroit, Mich; NAS Meridan, Miss; NAS Fallon, Nev; NAS Lakehurst, NJ; NAF Warminster, Penna; NAS Willow Grove, Penna; NAS Memphis (Millington), Tenn; NAS Chase Field (Beeville), Texas; NAS Corpus Christi, Texas; NAS Dallas, Texas; NAS Kingsville, Texas; NAS Norfolk, Va; NAS Whidbey Island (Oak Harbor), Wash; NAF Lajes, Azores; NAS Bermuda; NAS Guantanamo Bay, Cuba; NAF Naples, Italy; NAF Atsugi, Japan; NAS Agana, Guam; NAF Okinawa; NAS Subic Bay, Philippines; NAF Mildenhall (Suffolk), England.

Naval Amphibious Bases (2)

Coronado (San Diego), Calif; Little Creek (Norfolk), Va.

Naval Stations and Naval Bases (20)

Adak, Alaska; Long Beach, Calif; San Diego, Calif; Treasure Island (San Francisco), Calif; Mayport, Fla; Pearl Harbor, Hawaii; Boston, Mass; Brooklyn, NY; Philadelphia, Pa; Newport, RI; Charleston, SC; Norfolk, Va; Guantanamo Bay, Cuba; Keflavik, Iceland; Agana, Guam; Midway Island; Argentia, Newfoundland; Roosevelt Roads, Puerto Rico; Subic Bay, Philippines; Rota, Spain.

Naval Submarine Bases (2)

New London (Groton), Conn; Pearl Harbor, Hawaii.

Strategic Missile Submarine Anchorages (1)

Holy Loch, Scotland.*

Navy Yards (1)

Washington, DC.**

Naval Ship Repair Facilities (2)

Subic Bay, Philippines; Yokosuka, Japan.

Marine Air Stations and Air Facilities (7)

El Toro (Santa Ana), Calif; Kaneohe Bay (Oahu), Hawaii; Cherry Point, NC; New River (Jacksonville), Fla; Quantico, Va; Iwakuni, Japan; Futema, Okinawa.

Marine Corps Bases (5)

Camp Pendleton, Calif; Twentynine Palms, Calif; Camp H.M. Smith (Oahu), Hawaii; Camp Lejeune, NC; Camp Smedley D. Butler (Kawasaki), Okinawa.

*Polaris/Poseidon submarines also operate from Rota, Spain; Apra harbour, Guam; and Charleston, South Carolina. Trident submarines will be based in Seattle, Washington.
**Primarily administration and historical activities; no ship construction or repair activities.

MAJOR SHIPYARDS

Naval Shipyards

Charleston Naval Shipyard, Charleston, South Carolina
Long Beach Naval Shipyard, Long Beach, California
Mare Island Naval Shipyard, Vallejo, California (formerly a division of the San Francisco Bay Naval Shipyard)
Norfolk Naval Shipyard, Portsmouth, Virginia
Pearl Harbor Naval Shipyard, Pearl Harbor, Hawaii
Philadelphia Naval Shipyard, Philadelphia, Pennsylvania
Portsmouth Naval Shipyard, Portsmouth, New Hampshire (located in Kittery, Maine)
Puget Sound Naval Shipyard, Bremerton, Washington

(Note: None of the above shipyards is now engaged in new construction, but are used for the overhaul and conversion of warships and auxiliaries).

Commercial Shipyards

Avondale Shipyards, Inc, New Orleans, Louisiana
Bath Iron Works Corp, Bath, Maine
Bethlehem Steel Corp, Sparrows Point, Maryland
General Dynamics Corp, Electric Boat Division, Groton, Connecticut (formerly Electric Boat Company)
General Dynamics Corp, Quincy Shipbuilding Division, Quincy, Massachusetts (formerly Bethlehem Steel Corp Yard)
Ingalls Shipbuilding Division (Litton Industries), East Bank Yard, Pasagoula, Mississippi
Ingalls Shipbuilding Division (Litton Industries), West Bank Yard, Pasagoula, Mississippi
Lockheed Shipbuilding & Construction Co, Seattle, Washington
National Steel & Shipbuilding Co, San Diego, California
Newport News Shipbuilding & Dry Dock Co, Newport News, Virginia
Todd Shipyards Corp, San Pedro, California
Todd Shipyards Corp, Seattle, Washington

(Note: All of the above yards have engaged in naval and commercial shipbuilding, overhaul, or modernisation except for the General Dynamics/Electric Boat yard which is engaged only in submarine work).

Notes: (a) Except in special cases these are confined to those after end-1974. (b) Unless otherwise stated ships listed stricken on dates shown.

Submarines

1975 *Tigrone* (stricken as target 30 June, finally sunk 25 Oct 1976).
1976 *Tench* (16 Oct—To Peru for spares)
1977 *Salmon, Sealion* (to be stricken)
Clamagore, Tiru (stricken 1 July 1975, to Turkey? June).
1978-79 *Tang, Trigger, Wahoo* (to Iran)

Aircraft Carrier

1975 *Hancock* (stricken 31 Jan)

Cruisers

1976 *Columbus* (stricken 9 Aug)
Little Rock (stricken 22 Nov—to Boston NY as museum)

Destroyers

"Edsall Class" (all for use as targets)

1974 *Finch, Lansing* (1 Feb), *Durant* (1 April), *Otterstetter, Kirkpatrick, Price, Roy O. Hale, Ramsden, Rhodes* (1 Aug)
1975 *Chambers* (1 Mar), *Falgout, Savage, Vance, Hissem* (1 June)

"Gearing" Class

1975 *Theodore E. Chandler* (1 April), *Ozbourn* (1 June), *Epperson* (1 Dec—to Pakistan), *Rowan, Richard B. Anderson* (18 and 20 Dec—to Taiwan)
1976 *Wiltsey* (23 Jan—to Pakistan), *Gurke* (20 Jan—to Greece), *Stribling* (1 July—target), *New, Richard E. Kraus* (1 July—to S. Korea), *Brownson* (30 Sep), *George K. MacKenzie, Glennon, Holder* (1 Oct), *Leonard F. Mason* (2 Nov—to Colombia), *William M. Wood, Vesole* (1 Dec).
1977 *Bordelon* (1 Feb—to Iran for spares)

"Allen M. Sumner" Class

1977 *Laffey* (29 Mar—target)

"Fletcher" Class

1974 *The Sullivans* (to Buffalo NY as museum)
1975 *Porterfield, Pickings* (1 Mar—targets), *Stoddard* (1 June—target)

Amphibious Forces

"Adirondack" Class LCCs

1976 *Pocono, Taconic* (1 Dec)

"Mt McKinley" Class LCCs

1976 *Mt McKinley, Estes* (30 July)

"Cabildo" Class LSDs

1974 *Fort Marion* (31 Oct—to S. Korea 1977)
1976 *Whetstone* (30 April—to Peru), *Comstock* (30 June—to Taiwan), *Cabildo, Colonial, Tortuga* (15 Oct), *Donner* (1 Nov—to Energy Resources Development Admin.)

"Casa Grande" Class LSDs

1976 *Casa Grande, Rushmore* (1 Nov), *Shadwell* (1 Nov to Energy Resources Development Admin).

"Ashland" Class LSD

1976 *White Marsh* (15 April—on loan to Taiwan since 1960)

"Terrebonne Parish" Class LSTs

1976 *Terrell County, Whitefield County* (15 Aug—to Greece 1977), *Terrebonne Parish, Tom Green County, Wexford County* (1 Nov for sale to Spain—on loan since 1971-72)

"511-1152" Class LSTs (see Military Sealift Command)

1976 *Henry County, Sedgewick County* (7 Oct—to Malaysia), *Summit County* (1 Nov—to Ecuador, 1977), *Duval County* (1 Nov—to Colombia, 1977), *Holmes County* (5 Dec—to Singapore—previously on lease)

"Rankin" Class LKAs

1976 *Seminole, Union, Washburn* (1 Sep)
1977 *Rankin, Vermilion* (1 Jan)

"Andromeda" Class LKAs

1976 *Merrick, Winston* (1 Sep)
1977 *Algol, Capricornus, Muliphen, Thuban, Yancey* (1 Jan)

"Haskell" Class LPAs (laid up before stricken)

1976 *Bexar, Magoffin, Novarro, Pickaway, Talladega* (1 Sep), *Montrail, Sandoval* (1 Dec)

LPRs

1975 *Laning* (1 Mar), *Begor* (15 May), *Balduck* (15 July)

Minewarfare Forces

"Agile", "Aggressive" and "Dash" Classes. MSOs

1975 *Bold, Bulwark, Embattle, Prime, Reaper* (28 Feb), *Aggressive* (28 Feb—to Pakistan, 1977).
1976 *Acme, Advance, Lucid* (15 May), *Nimble* (1 Nov—to Pakistan, 1977)

"Bluebird" Class MSCs

1975 *Peacock, Phoebe* (1 July), *Shrike* (1 July—to Hydrographer 7 Oct), *Thrush* (1 July—leased to Virginia Institute of Marine Sciences), *Thrasher, Whippoorwill* (to Singapore, 5 Dec)
1976 *Woodpecker* (to Fiji—17 June), *Viero, Warbler* (to Fiji—14 Oct)

"Acme" Class MSOs

1976 *Acme, Advance* (15 May)

Light Forces

"Asheville" Class (two possibly to Colombia in 1977)

1975 *Chehalis* (renamed *Athena* to Naval Ship Research Centre—21 Aug)
1976 *Asheville, Cannon, Crockett, Gallup, Marathon*
1977 *Beacon, Green Bay* (to Greece—1 April)

"PTF 17" Class

1976 Six of class (paid off July)

"Nasty" Class

1976 PTF 3, 5, 6, 7, 10, 11, 12 (paid off July)

CPIC

1975 *Prototype* (to S. Korea—1 Aug)

Floating Docks

1974 *AFDB 6* (1 Jan), *White Sands* (ARD 31) (1 April), *AFDL 42* (1 May)
1976 *ARD 9* and *Windsor (ARDS-22)* (15 April—to Taiwan), *AFDLS-26* (18 May—to Paraguay)

Service Forces
Auxiliary Ships:
ADs

1974 *Yellowstone* (12 Sep), *Cascade* (23 Nov)
1976 *Isle Royale* (15 Sep)

ADG

1975 *Surfbird* (21 Feb); *Lodestone, Magnet, Deperm* (21 Feb-targets)

AE

1976 *Firedrake* (15 July), *Wrangell* (1 Oct) "Mount Hood" class, *Mauna Loa* (1 Oct) "Lasseu" class

AF

1976 *Vega* (30 Apr) "Rigel " class. *Denebola* (30 Apr) "Denebola" class, *Aludra, Pictor, Procyon, Zelima* (1 June) "Alstede" class, *Arcturus* (1 Oct) "Bald Eagle" class, *Hyades* (1 Oct) "Hyades" class

AGMR

1975 *Arlington* Converted "Saipan" class (15 Aug)
1976 *Annapolis*. Converted "Commencement Bay" class (15 Oct)

AGP

1977 *Graham County*. Converted "De Soto County" class (1 Mar)

AH

1974 *Constellation* "Haven" class

AO

1975 *Tolavana* (15 Apr), *Guadalupe* (15 May) "Cimarron" class
1976 *Aucilla, Chikaskia,* (1 Dec), "Cimarron" class

AOG

1975 *Chewaucan* (1 July to Colombia), *Noxubee, Nespelen* (1 July) "Patapsco" class

---

AR

1971 *Amphion* (to Iran on lease 1 Oct-1977 for sale), "Amphion" class
1974 *Klondike* "Klondike" class (15 Sept), *Cadmus* (15 Jan-to Taiwan 31 Jan) "Amphion" class
1976 *Markab* "Hamul" class (1 Sep)
1977 *Briarus* (1 Jan) "Delta" class

ARB

1976 *Midas* (15 Apr-to Colombia), *Sarpedon* (15 Apr) "Aristaeus" class

ARL

1977 *Sphinx* (to Spain) "Achelous" class

ARS

1977 *Grapple, Grasp* "Diver" class

ASR

1977 *Tringa* (to Turkey), *Coucal* (commercial sale) "Chanticleer" class

ATA

1975 *Penobscot* (28 Feb) "Sotoyomo" class

ATFs

1975 *Tawasa* (1 Apr), *Luiseno* (1 July-to Argentina) "Cherokee" class
1977-78 *Abnaki, Chowanoc, Cocopa, Cree, Matoco, Molala, Tawakoni* (to be stricken) "Cherokee" class.

YAG

1975 *George Eastman* (1 Dec)

YFB

1975 *Aquidneck* (transferred to State of Washington 23 Dec)

YFRT

1975 YFRT 411 (May)

YPs

1974 YP 584, 585 (1 May), YP 586 (1 Oct)
1976 YP 589, 590 (1 July)

Military Sealift Command

AGs

1975 *Flyer* (17 July) "Kingsport" class
1976 *Pvt. Jose E. Valdez* (15 Aug)

AGOR

1971 *Josiah Willard Gibbs* (leased to Greece 7 Dec—stricken 15 Feb 1977 on sale) "Barnegat" class

AGSs

1975 *Michelson* (15 April) "Bowditch" class
1976 *Coastal Crusader* (30 April)

AK

1975 *Sergeant Moris E. Crane* (1 April)

AOs

1976 *Kennebec* (15 July) "Kennebec" class
Tapahannock (15 July—Taiwan) "Mataponi" class
Sabine (1 Dec) "Cimarron" class

AOGs

1974 *Tonti* (scrapped on return from Colombia)
1977 *Peconic* (possible transfer to Colombia)

LSTs

1975 All following stricken 30 June
LST 579, 613, 623, 629, 649 (to Singapore 4 June 1976)
LST 47, 230, 287, 491, 566, 607, Davies County, Harris County, Orleans Parish, 1072 (to Philippines, 13 Sep 1976)

United States Coast Guard

"Wind" Class WAGB

1976 *Edisto, Staten Island*

"Owasco" Class WHEC

1976 *Chautauqua, Mendota, Minnetonka, Pontchartrain, Winona*

"Cape" Class WPB

1976 *Cape Gull, Cape Hatteras, Cape Higgon, Cape Upright*

"Clematis" Class WLI

1076 *Clematis, Shadbush, Blueberry*

CLASSIFICATION OF NAVAL SHIPS AND SERVICE CRAFT

The following is the official US Navy list of classifications of naval ships and service craft as promulgated by the Secretary of the Navy on 6 Jan 1975.

In actual usage, symbols preceded by the letter "E" indicate that the ship or craft is a prototype in an experimental or developmental status; the prefix "T" indicates that the ship is assigned to the Navy's Military Sealift Command and is civilian manned; and the prefix "F" indicates a ship being constructed by the United States for a foreign government.

The US Navy regularly develops additional ship classifications which do not appear in the official list, primarily to indicate new ship types under consideration. Current non-standard classifications include CSGN for nuclear-propelled strike cruiser, and AGOS for ocean surveillance ship. In addition, the letter "X" is often added to existing classifications to indicate a new class whose characteristics have not yet been decided, as in LX, ARX, and ARSX.

COMBATANT SHIPS

(1) Warships

Aircraft Carriers:
Aircraft Carrier	CV
Attack Aircraft Carrier	CVA
Aircraft Carrier (nuclear propulsion)	CVN
ASW Aircraft Carrier	CVS

Surface Combatants:
Battleship	BB
Heavy Cruiser	CA
Guided Missile Cruiser	CG
Guided Missile Cruiser (nuclear propulsion)	CGN
Destroyer	DD
Guided Missile Destroyer	DDG
Frigate	FF
Guided Missile Frigate	FFG
Radar Picket Frigate	FFR

Patrol Combatants:
Patrol Combatant	PG
Patrol Combatant Missile (hydrofoil)	PHM
Patrol Escort	PCE

Command Ship	CC

Submarines:
Submarine	SS
Submarine (nuclear propulsion)	SSN
Fleet Ballistic Missile Submarine (nuclear propulsion)	SSBN
Guided Missile Submarine	SSG

(2) Amphibious Warfare Ships

Amphibious Command Ship	LCC
Inshore Fire Support Ship	LFR
Amphibious Assault Ship (general purpose)	LHA
Amphibious Cargo Ship	LKA
Amphibious Transport	LPA
Amphibious Transport Dock	LPD
Amphibious Assault Ship	LPH
Amphibious Transport (small)	LPR
Amphibious Transport Submarine	LPSS
Landing Ship Dock	LSD
Landing Ship Tank	LST

(3) Mine Warfare Ships

Mine Countermeasures Ship	MCS
Minesweeper, Coastal (non-magnetic)	MSC
Minesweeper, Ocean (non-magnetic)	MSO

COMBATANT CRAFT

(1) Patrol Craft

Coastal Patrol Boat	CPC
Coastal Patrol and Interdiction Craft	CPIC
Patrol Boat	PB
Patrol Craft (fast)	PCF
Patrol Craft (hydrofoil)	PCH
Patrol Gunboat (hydrofoil)	PGH
Fast Patrol Craft	PTF

(2) Landing Craft

Amphibious Assault Landing Craft	AALC
Landing Craft, Mechanised	LCM
Landing Craft, Personnel, Large	LCPL
Landing Craft, Personnel, Ramped	LCPR
Landing Craft, Utility	LCU
Landing Craft, Vehicle, Personnel	LCVP
Amphibious Warping Tug	LWT

(3) Mine Countermeasures Craft

Minesweeping Boat	MSB
Minesweeper, Drone	MSD
Minesweeper, Inshore	MSI
Minesweeper, River	MSM
Minesweeper, Patrol	MSR

(4) Riverine Warfare Craft

Assault Support Patrol Boat	ASPB
Mini-Armoured Troop Carrier	ATC
River Patrol Boat	PBR
Shallow Water Attack Craft, Medium	SWAM
Shallow Water Attack Craft, Light	SWAL

(5) SEAL Support Craft

Landing Craft Swimmer Reconnaissance	LCSR
Light SEAL Support Craft	LSSC
Medium SEAL Support Craft	MSSC
Swimmer Delivery Vehicle	SDV

(6) Mobile Inshore Undersea Warfare (MIUW) Craft

MIUW Attack Craft	MAC

AUXILIARY SHIPS

Destroyer Tender	AD
Degaussing Ship	ADG
Ammunition Ship	AE
Store Ship	AF
Combat Store Ship	AFS
Miscellaneous	AG
Auxiliary Deep Submergence Support Ship	AGDS
Hydrofoil Research Ship	AGEH
Environmental Research Ship	AGER
Miscellaneous Command Ship	AGF
Frigate Research Ship	AGFF
Patrol Combatant Support Ship	AGHS
Missile Range Instrumentation Ship	AGM
Major Communications Relay Ship	AGMR
Oceanographic Research Ship	AGOR
Patrol Craft Tender	AGP
Surveying Ship	AGS
Auxiliary Submarine	AGSS
Hospital Ship	AH
Cargo Ship	AK
Light Cargo Ship	AKL
Vehicle Cargo Ship	AKR
Net Layer	ANL
Oiler	AO
Fast Combat Support Ship	AOE
Gasoline Tanker	AOG
Replenishment Oiler	AOR
Transport	AP
Self-propelled Barracks Ship	APB
Repair Ship	AR
Battle Damage Repair Ship	ARB
Cable Repairing Ship	ARC
Internal Combustion Engine Repair Ship	ARG
Landing Craft Repair Ship	ARL
Salvage Ship	ARS
Submarine Tender	AS
Submarine Rescue Ship	ASR
Auxiliary Ocean Tug	ATA
Fleet Ocean Tug	ATF
Salvage and Rescue Ship	ATS
Guided Missile Ship	AVM
Training Aircraft Carrier	CVT
Surface Effects Ship	SES

SERVICE CRAFT*

Large Auxiliary Floating Dry Dock	AFDB
Small Auxiliary Floating Dry Dock	AFDL
Medium Auxiliary Floating Dry Dock	AFDM
Barracks Craft (non-self-propelled)	APL
Auxiliary Dry Dock	ARD
Medium Auxiliary Repair Dry Dock	ARDM
Deep Submergence Rescue Vehicle	DSRV
Deep Submergence Vehicle	DSV
Unclassified Miscellaneous	IX
Submersible Research Vehicle (nuclear propulsion)	NR
Miscellaneous Auxiliary (self-propelled)	YAG
Open Lighter	YC
Car Float	YCF
Aircraft Transportation Lighter	YCV
Floating Crane	YD
Diving Tender	YDT
Covered Lighter (self-propelled)	YF
Ferryboat or Launch (self-propelled)	YFB
Yard Floating Dry Dock	YFD
Covered Lighter	YFN
Large Covered Lighter	YFNB
Dry Dock Companion Craft	YFND
Lighter (special purpose)	YFNX
Floating Power Barge	YFP
Refrigerated Covered Lighter (self-propelled)	YFR
Refrigerated Covered Lighter	YFRN
Covered Lighter (Range Tender) (self-propelled)	YFRT
Harbour Utility Craft (self-propelled)	YFU
Garbage Lighter (self-propelled)	YG
Garbage Lighter (non-self-propelled)	YGN
Salvage Lift Craft, Heavy	YHLC
Dredge (self-propelled)	YM
Salvage Lift Craft, Medium	YMLC
Gate Craft	YNG
Fuel Oil Barge (self-propelled)	YO
Gasoline Barge (self-propelled)	YOG
Gasoline Barge	YOGN
Fuel Oil Barge	YON
Oil Storage Barge	YOS
Patrol Craft (self-propelled)	YP
Floating Pile Driver	YPD
Floating Workshop	YR
Repair and Berthing Barge	YRB
Repair, Berthing and Messing Barge	YRBM
Floating Dry Dock Workshop (Hull)	YRDH
Floating Dry Dock Workshop (Machine)	YRDM
Radiology Repair Barge	YRR
Salvage Craft Tender	YRST
Seaplane Wrecking Derrick (self-propelled)	YSD
Sludge Removal Barge	YSR
Large Harbour Tug (self-propelled)	YTB
Small Harbour Tug (self-propelled)	YTL
Medium Harbour Tug (self-propelled)	YTM
Water Barge (self-propelled)	YW
Water Barge	YWN

*Self-propelled barges are indicated in parenthesis. The final letter "N" generally indicates non-self-propelled.

CLASSIFICATION OF MARITIME COMMISSION SHIP DESIGNS

Ships constructed under the jurisdiction of the US Maritime Commission by private shipyards are assigned Maritime Commission design classifications. These classifications consist of three groups of letters and numbers.

First group letter(s) indicate type of ship and number indicates size class. The letters of Maritime Commission ship classifications now on the US Navy List are:

Cargo	C
Passenger	P
Refrigerator	R
Special Purpose	S
Tanker	T
Victory Cargo	VC

Second group letter(s) indicate type of propulsion and number "2" indicates twin shaft ship and "4" quadruple shaft ship.

Motor (diesel)	M
Motor (diesel) Electric	ME
Steam (reciprocating or turbine)	S
Steam Electric	SE

Third group of letters and numbers indicates the design of a particular type of ship, beginning with A1.

ELECTRONIC EQUIPMENT CLASSIFICATION

Major electronic equipment in US Navy ships is identified by the Joint Army-Navy Nomenclature System, with a series of letters indicating the installation, type of equipment, and purpose, with numerals indicating the particular model. This letter-numeral combination is prefixed with the letters AN to indicate that the designation is part of the joint service system. The AN prefix is deleted from the ship electronic listings in the United States section.

The first letter indicates the installation:

Airborne	A
Underwater (submarine)	B
Surface ship	S
Multiple-platform	U
Surface ship and underwater	W

The second letter indicates the type of equipment:

Countermeasures	L
Radar	P
Sonar and underwater sound	Q
Radio	R
Special type (eg, magnetic)	S
Data processing (eg, computer)	Y

The third letter indicates the purpose:

Part of other equipment	A
Fire control	G
Maintenance and test	M
Navigation	N
Special or combination	Q
Receiving/passive detection	R
Detecting	S
Computing	U

STRATEGIC MISSILE SUBMARINES

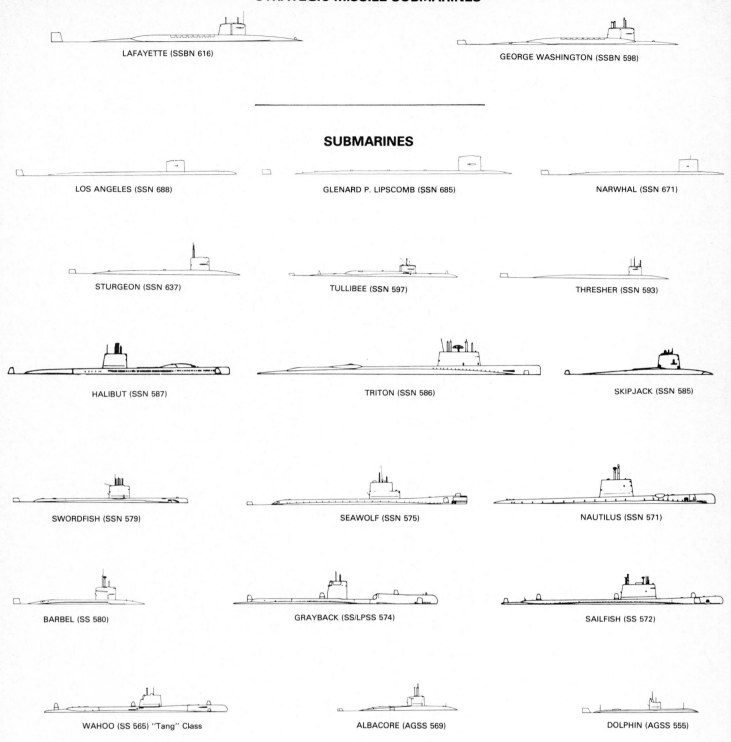

LAFAYETTE (SSBN 616)

GEORGE WASHINGTON (SSBN 598)

SUBMARINES

LOS ANGELES (SSN 688)

GLENARD P. LIPSCOMB (SSN 685)

NARWHAL (SSN 671)

STURGEON (SSN 637)

TULLIBEE (SSN 597)

THRESHER (SSN 593)

HALIBUT (SSN 587)

TRITON (SSN 586)

SKIPJACK (SSN 585)

SWORDFISH (SSN 579)

SEAWOLF (SSN 575)

NAUTILUS (SSN 571)

BARBEL (SS 580)

GRAYBACK (SS/LPSS 574)

SAILFISH (SS 572)

WAHOO (SS 565) "Tang" Class

ALBACORE (AGSS 569)

DOLPHIN (AGSS 555)

AIRCRAFT CARRIERS

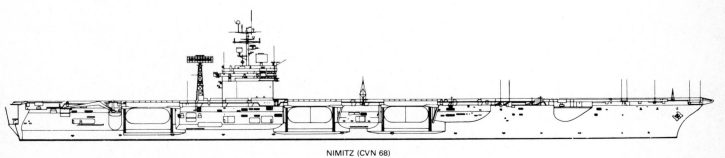

NIMITZ (CVN 68)

Scale: 1 inch = 150 feet (1 : 1 800)
Drawings by A. D. Baker

Aircraft Carriers—*continued*

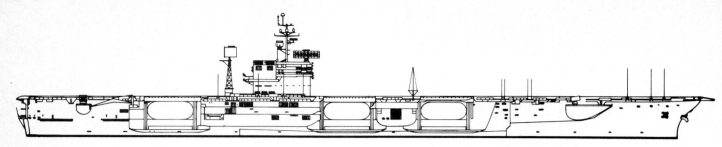

JOHN F. KENNEDY (CV 67)

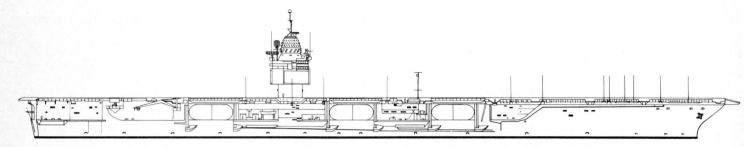

ENTERPRISE (CVN 65)

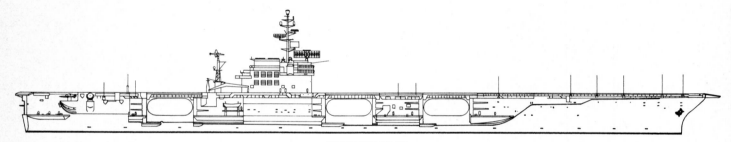

KITTY HAWK (CV 63)

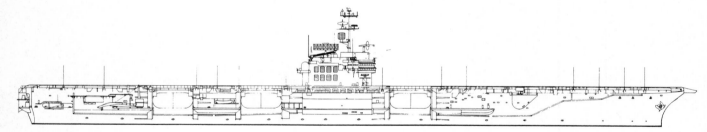

INDEPENDENCE (CV 62)

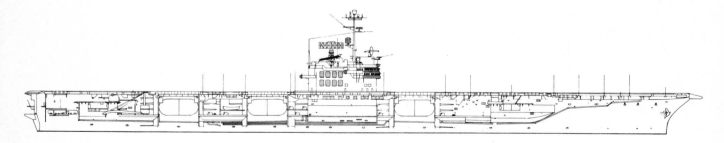

RANGER (CV 61)

SARATOGA (CV 60)

Scale: 1 inch = 150 feet (1 : 1 800)

Aircraft Carriers—*continued*

CORAL SEA (CV 43) "Midway" Class (ROOSEVELT similar)

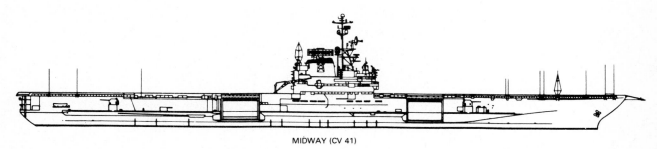

MIDWAY (CV 41)

"HANCOCK" Class

CRUISERS

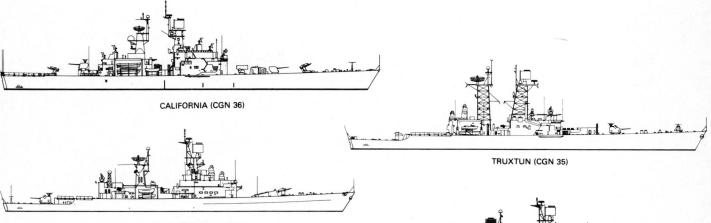

CALIFORNIA (CGN 36)

TRUXTUN (CGN 35)

FOX (CG 33) "Belknap" Class

WAINWRIGHT (CG 28) "Belknap" Class

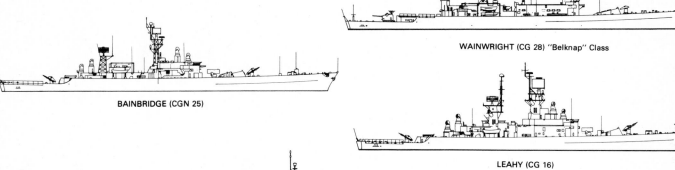

BAINBRIDGE (CGN 25)

LEAHY (CG 16)

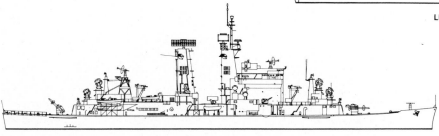

CHICAGO (CG 11) "Albany" Class

Cruisers—*continued*

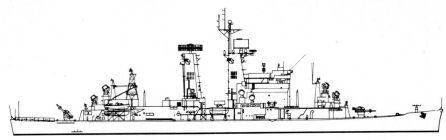

ALBANY (CG 10)

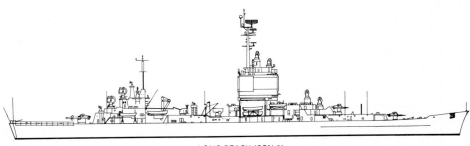

LONG BEACH (CGN 9)

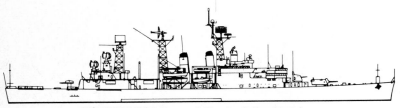

PROVIDENCE (CG 6) Converted "Cleveland" Class (Terrier)

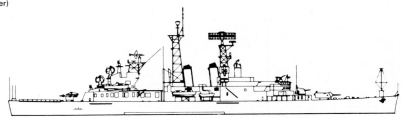

OKLAHOMA CITY (CG 5) Converted "Cleveland" Class (Talos)

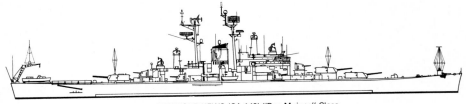

NEWPORT NEWS (CA 148) "Des Moines" Class

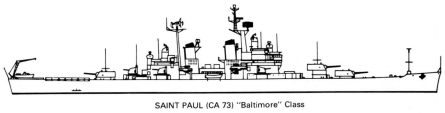

SAINT PAUL (CA 73) "Baltimore" Class

DESTROYERS

MAHAN (DDG 42) "Coontz" Class

FARRAGUT (DDG 37) "Coontz" Class

Destroyers—*continued*

MITSCHER (DDG 35)

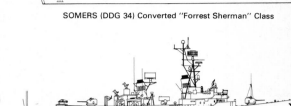

SOMERS (DDG 34) Converted "Forrest Sherman" Class

WADDELL (DDG 24) "Charles F. Adams" Class

BARNEY (DDG 34) Converted "Charles F. Adams" Class

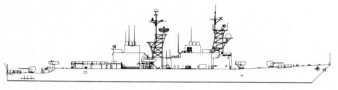

SPRUANCE (DD 963)

MANLEY (DD 940) "Forrest Sherman" Class

JONAS INGRAM (DD 938) "Forrest Sherman" Class (ASW)

BARRY (DD 933) "Forrest Sherman" Class (ASW)

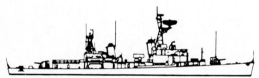

"GEARING" Class FRAM I (guns forward and aft)

"GEARING" Class FRAM I (all guns forward)

ROBERT A. OWENS (DD 827) "Carpenter" Class FRAM I

FRIGATES

BROOKE (FFG 1)

JULIUS A. FURER (FFG 6) "Brooke" Class

"KNOX" Class (improved)

DOWNES (FF 1070) NATO Sea Sparrow

"KNOX" Class

Scale: 1 inch = 150 feet (1 : 1 800)

Frigates—*continued*

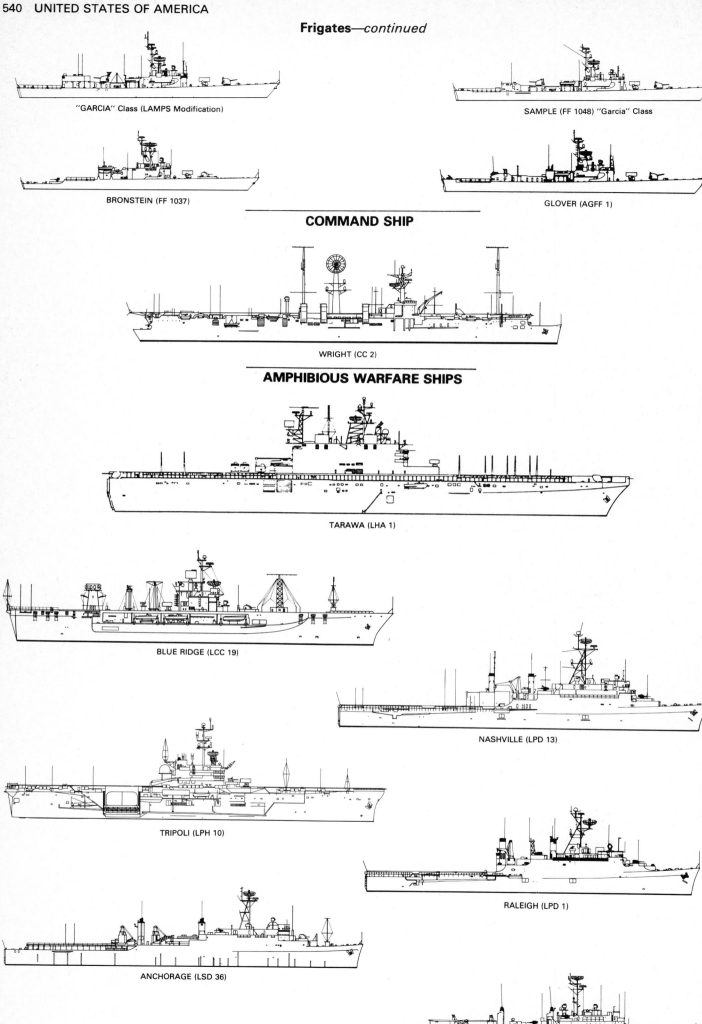

"GARCIA" Class (LAMPS Modification)

SAMPLE (FF 1048) "Garcia" Class

BRONSTEIN (FF 1037)

GLOVER (AGFF 1)

COMMAND SHIP

WRIGHT (CC 2)

AMPHIBIOUS WARFARE SHIPS

TARAWA (LHA 1)

BLUE RIDGE (LCC 19)

NASHVILLE (LPD 13)

TRIPOLI (LPH 10)

RALEIGH (LPD 1)

ANCHORAGE (LSD 36)

HERMITAGE (LSD 34) "Thomaston" Class

Amphibious Warfare Ships—*continued*

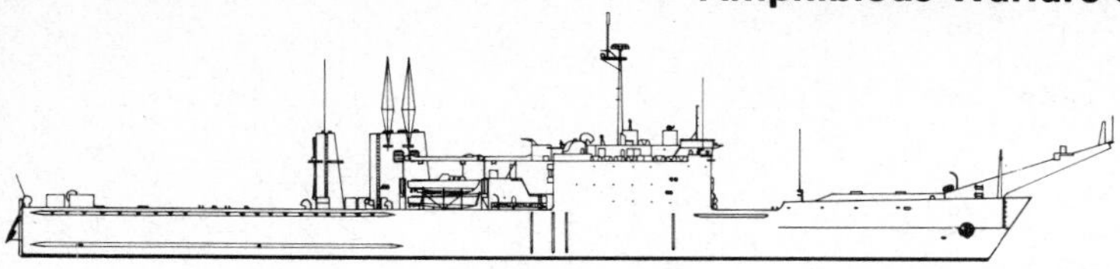

NEWPORT (LST 1179)

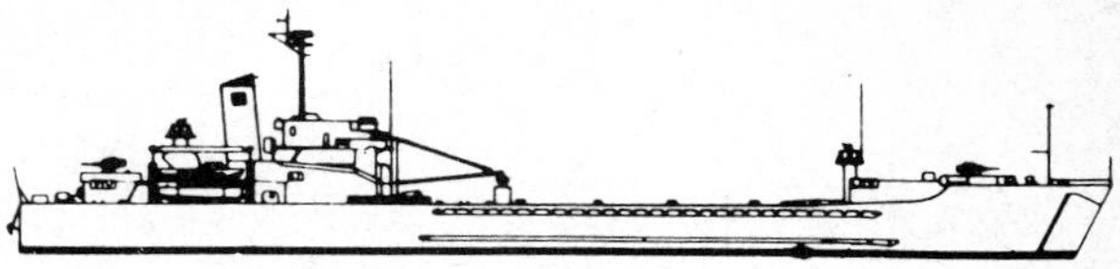

"DE SOTO COUNTY" Class

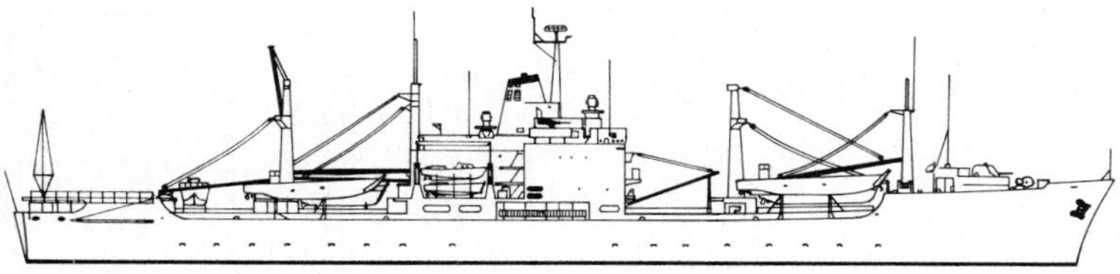

CHARLESTON (LKA 113)

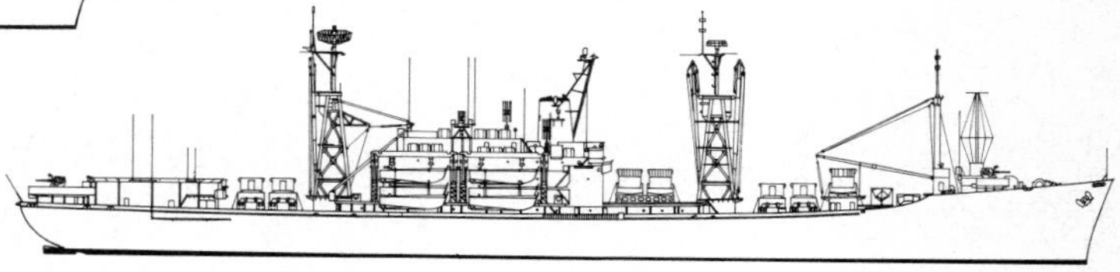

FRANCIS MARION (LPA 249)

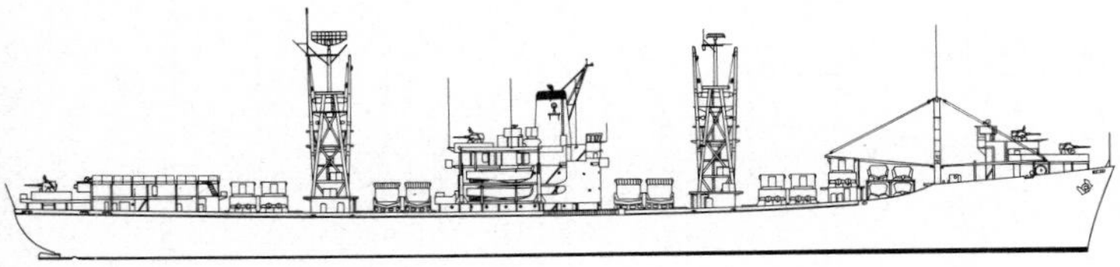

TULARE (LKA 112)

AUXILIARY SHIPS

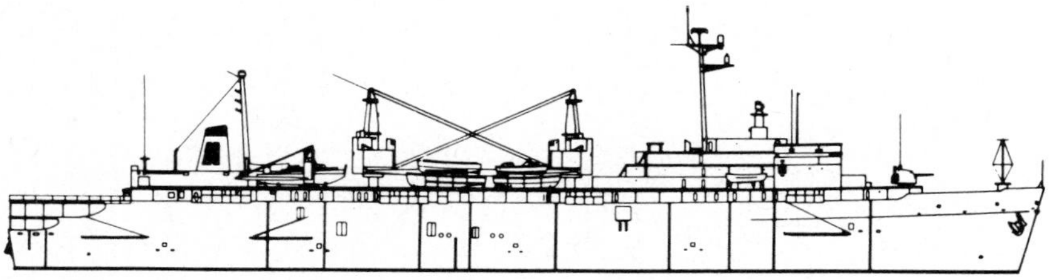

"SAMUEL GOMPERS" Class

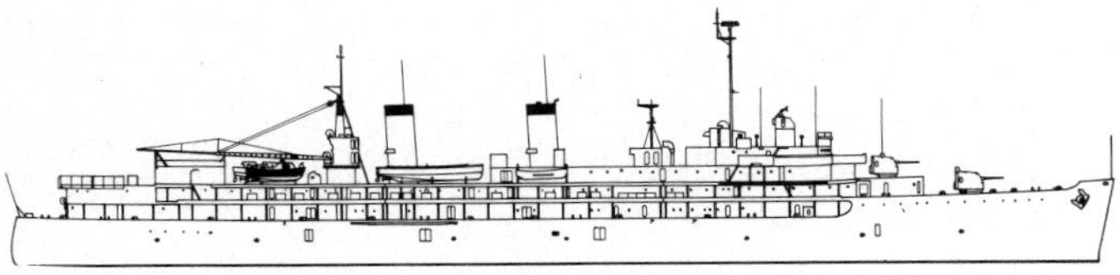

YOSEMITE (AD 19) "Dixie" Class

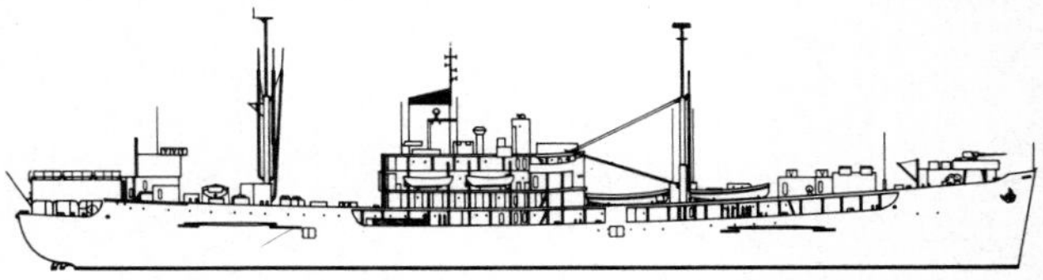

SHENANDOAH (AD 26) "Shenandoah" Class

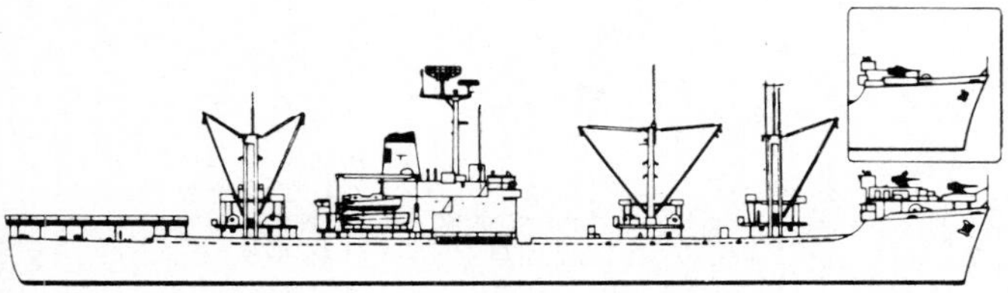

MAUNA KEA (AE 22) "Suribachi" Class
(inset shows gun variation)

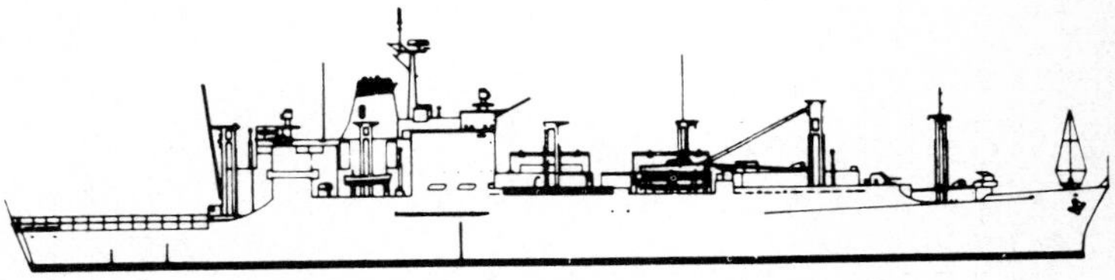

SANTA BARBARA (AE 28) "Kilauea" Class

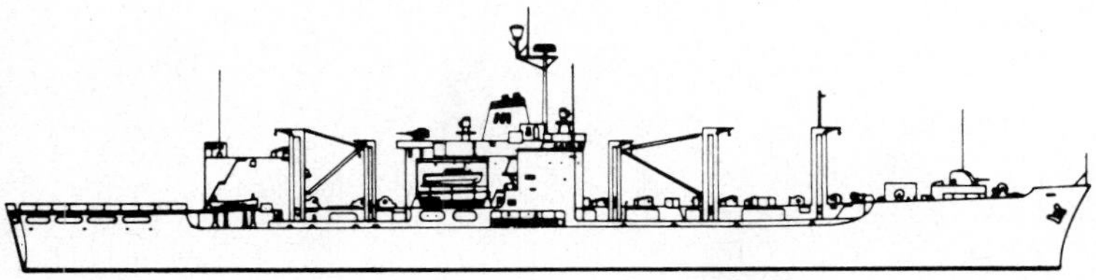

SAN JOSE (AFS 7) "Mars" Class

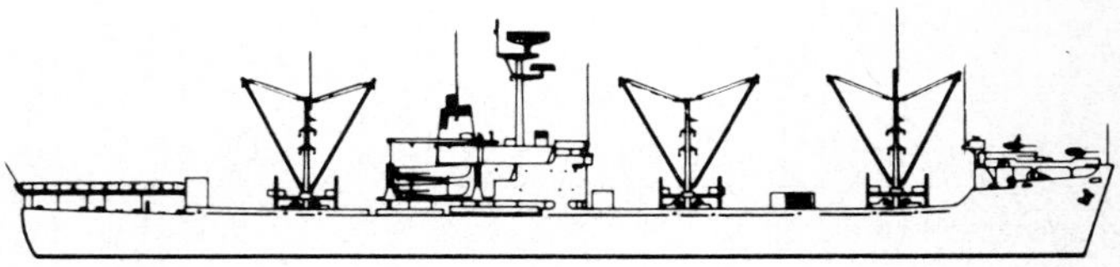

RIGEL (T-AF 58) R3-S-A4 Type

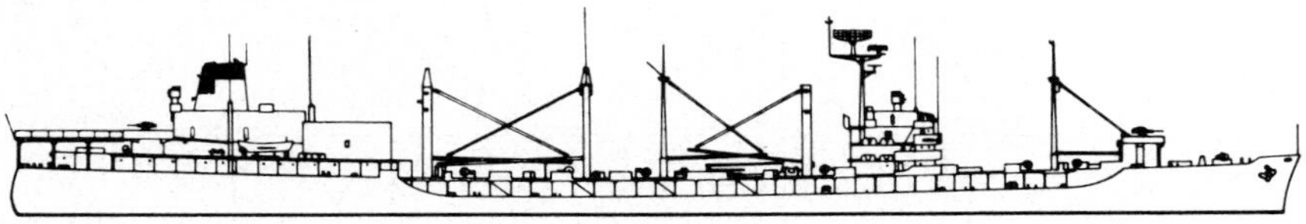

NEOSHO (AO 143)

Auxiliary Ships—continued

MISPILLION (T-AO 105) Jumboised T3-S2-A3

CANISTEO (AO 99) Jumboised T3-S2-A1

"CIMARRON" Class T-AO T3-S2-A1 Type

"SEALIFT" Class (T-AO 168)

WABASH (AOR 5) "Wichita" Class

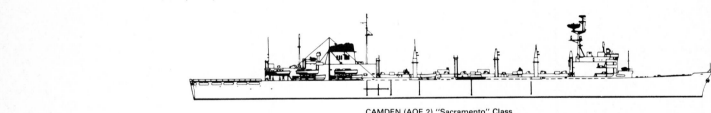

CAMDEN (AOE 2) "Sacramento" Class

VULCAN (AR 5)

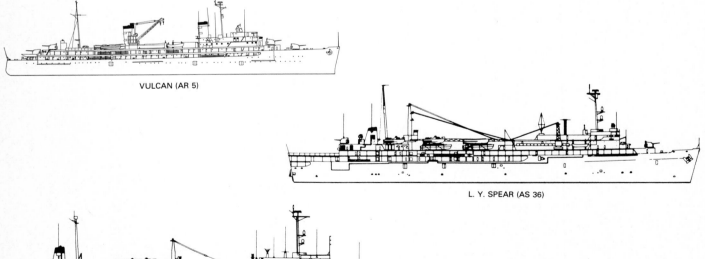

L. Y. SPEAR (AS 36)

CANOPUS (AS 34) "Simon Lake" Class

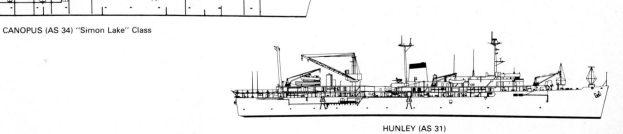

HUNLEY (AS 31)

Scale: 1 inch = 150 feet (1 : 1 800)

Auxiliary Ships—*continued*

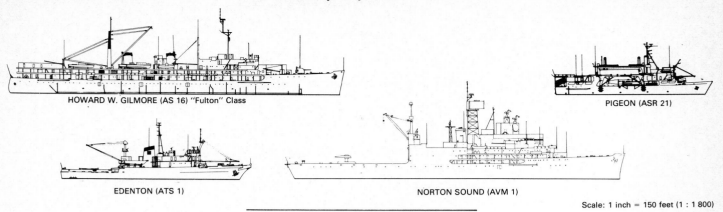

HOWARD W. GILMORE (AS 16) "Fulton" Class

PIGEON (ASR 21)

EDENTON (ATS 1)

NORTON SOUND (AVM 1)

Scale: 1 inch = 150 feet (1 : 1 800)

PATROL SHIPS AND CRAFT

PEGASUS (PHM 1)

ANTELOPE (PG 86) "Asheville" Class

"ASHEVILLE" Class

Scale: 1 inch = 100 feet (1 : 1 200)

UNITED STATES SHIP HULL NUMBERS

(Type designations in order of arrangement within this volume; ships are in numerical sequence)

Strategic Missile Submarines

SSBN—Fleet Ballistic Missile Submarines

"Geo. Washington" Class
598 George Washington
599 Patrick Henry
600 Theodore Roosevelt
601 Robert E. Lee
602 Abraham Lincoln

"Ethan Allen" Class
608 Ethan Allen
609 Sam Houston
610 Thomas A. Edison
611 John Marshall

"Lafayette" Class
616 Lafayette
617 Alexander Hamilton

"Ethan Allen" Class (Cont'd)
618 Thomas Jefferson

"Lafayette" Class (Cont'd)
619 Andrew Jackson
620 John Adams
622 James Monroe
623 Nathan Hale
624 Woodrow Wilson
625 Henry Clay
626 Daniel Webster
627 James Madison
628 Tecumseh
629 Daniel Boone
630 John C. Calhoun
631 Ulysses S. Grant
632 Von Steuben
633 Casimir Pulaski
634 Stonewall Jackson
635 Sam Rayburn
636 Nathanael Greene
640 Benjamin Franklin
641 Simon Bolivar
642 Kamehameha
643 George Bancroft
644 Lewis and Clark
645 James K. Polk
654 George C. Marshall
655 Henry L. Stimson
656 George Washington Carver
657 Francis Scott Key
658 Mariano G. Vallejo
659 Will Rogers

"Ohio" Class
726 Ohio
727 Michigan

Submarines

SS/SSN—Attack Submarines
AGSS—Auxiliary Submarines
LPSS—Amphibious Transport Submarines
SSG—Guided Missile Submarines

"Sealion" Class (LPSS)
315 Sealion

"Dolphin" Class (AGSS)
555 Dolphin

"Tang" Class (SS)
563 Tang (AGSS)
565 Wahoo
566 Trout
567 Gudgeon

"Albacore" Class (AGSS)
569 Albacore

"Nautilus" Class (SSN)
571 Nautilus

"Sailfish" Class (SS)
572 Sailfish
573 Salmon

"Grayback" Class (LPSS)
574 Grayback SS

"Seawolf" Class (SSN)
575 Seawolf

"Darter" Class (SS)
576 Darter

"Grayback" Class (SSG)
577 Growler

"Skate" Class (SSN)
578 Skate
579 Swordfish

"Barbel" Class (SS)
580 Barbel
581 Blueback
582 Bonefish

"Skate" Class (SSN) (Cont'd)
583 Sargo
584 Seadragon

"Skipjack" Class (SSN)
585 Skipjack

"Triton" Class (SSN)
586 Triton

"Halibut" Class (SSN)
587 Halibut

"Skipjack" Class (SSN) (Cont'd)
588 Scamp
590 Sculpin
591 Shark
592 Snook

"Thresher" Class (SSN)
594 Permit
595 Plunger
596 Barb

"Tullibee" Class (SSN)
597 Tullibee

"Thresher" Class (SSN) (Cont'd)
603 Pollack
604 Haddo
605 Jack
606 Tinosa
607 Dace
612 Guardfish
613 Flasher
614 Greenling
615 Gato
621 Haddock

"Sturgeon" Class (SSN)
637 Sturgeon
638 Whale
639 Tautog
646 Grayling
647 Pogy
648 Aspro
649 Sunfish
650 Pargo
651 Queenfish
652 Puffer
653 Ray
660 Sand Lance
661 Lapon
662 Gurnard
663 Hammerhead
664 Sea Devil
665 Guitarro
666 Hawkbill
667 Bergall
668 Spadefish
669 Seahorse
670 Finback

"Narwhal" Class (SSN)
671 Narwhal

"Sturgeon" Class (SSN) (Cont'd)
672 Pintado
673 Flying Fish
674 Trepang
675 Bluefish
676 Billfish
677 Drum
678 Archerfish
679 Silversides
680 William H. Bates
681 Batfish
682 Tunny
683 Parche
684 Cavalla

"Glenard P. Lipscomb" Class (SSN)
685 Glenard P. Lipscomb

"Sturgeon" Class (SSN) (Cont'd)
686 L. Mendel Rivers
687 Richard B. Russell

"Los Angeles" Class (SSN)
688 Los Angeles
689 Baton Rouge
690 Philadelphia
691 Memphis
692 Omaha
693 Cincinnati
694 Groton
695 Birmingham
696 New York City
697 Indianapolis
698 Bremerton
699 Jacksonville
700 Dallas
701 La Jolla
702 Phoenix
703 Boston
704 Baltimore

Aircraft Carriers

CV CVA CVN—Attack Aircraft Carriers
CVS—ASW Aircraft Carriers
CVT—Training Aircraft Carriers

"Intrepid" Class
11 Intrepid (CVS)

"Essex" Class
12 Hornet (CVS)

"Intrepid" Class (Cont'd)
16 Lexington (CVT)

"Essex" Class (Cont'd)
20 Bennington (CVS)

"Hancock" Class
31 Bon Homme Richard (CVA)
34 Oriskany (CV)

"Intrepid" Class (Cont'd)
38 Shangri-La (CVS)

"Midway" Class (CV)
41 Midway
42 Franklin D. Roosevelt
43 Coral Sea

"Forrestal" Class (CV)
59 Forrestal
60 Saratoga
61 Ranger
62 Independence

"Kitty Hawk" Class (CV)
63 Kitty Hawk
64 Constellation

"Enterprise" Class (CVN)
65 Enterprise

"Kitty Hawk" Class (CV) (Cont'd)
66 America

"John F. Kennedy" Class (CV)
67 John F. Kennedy

"Nimitz" Class (CVN)
68 Nimitz
69 Dwight D. Eisenhower
70 Carl Vinson

Battleships

BB—Battleships

"Iowa" Class
61 Iowa
62 New Jersey
63 Missouri
64 Wisconsin

Cruisers

CG/CGN—Guided Missile Cruisers

Converted "Cleveland" Class (CG)
5 Oklahoma City
6 Province
7 Springfield

"Long Beach" Class (CGN)
9 Long Beach

"Albany" Class (CG)
10 Albany
11 Chicago

"Leahy" Class
16 Leahy
17 Harry E. Yarnell
18 Worden
19 Dale
20 Richmond K. Turner
21 Gridley
22 England
23 Halsey
24 Reeves

"Bainbridge" Class (CGN)
25 Bainbridge

"Belknap" Class (CG)
26 Belknap
27 Josephus Daniels
28 Wainwright
29 Jouett
30 Horne
31 Sterett
32 William H. Standley
33 Fox
34 Biddle

"Truxtun" Class (CGN)
35 Truxtun

"California" Class (CGN)
36 California

37 South Carolina

"Virginia" Class (CGN)
38 Virginia
39 Texas
40 Mississippi
41 —

CA—Heavy Cruisers

"Boston" Class
70 Canberra

"Baltimore" Class
73 St. Paul

"Des Moines" Class
134 Des Moines
139 Salem
148 Newport News

Destroyers

DDG—Guided Missile Destroyers

"Charles F. Adams" Class
2 Charles F. Adams
3 John King
4 Lawrence
5 Claude V. Ricketts
6 Barney
7 Henry B. Wilson
8 Lynde McCormack
9 Towers
10 Sampson
11 Sellers
12 Robison
13 Hoel
14 Buchanan
15 Berkeley
16 Joseph Strauss
17 Conyngham
18 Semmes
19 Tattnall
20 Goldsborough
21 Cochrane
22 Benjamin Stoddert
23 Richard E. Byrd
24 Waddell

Converted "Forrest Sherman" Class
31 Decatur
32 John Paul Jones
33 Parsons
34 Somers

Converted "Mitscher" Class
35 Mitscher
36 John S. McCain

"Coontz" Class
37 Farragut
38 Luce
39 MacDonough
40 Coontz
41 King
42 Mahan
43 Dahigren
44 William V. Pratt
45 Dewey
46 Preble

DD—Destroyers

"Gearing" Class
714 William R. Rush
718 Hamner
743 Southerland
763 William C. Lawe
784 McKean
785 Henderson
788 Hollister
806 Higbee
817 Corry
820 Rich
821 Johnston
822 Robert H. McCard
824 Basilone

"Carpenter" Class
825 Carpenter

"Gearing" Class (Cont'd)
826 Agerholm

"Carpenter" Class (Cont'd)
827 Robert A. Owens

"Gearing" Class (Cont'd)
829 Myles C. Fox
835 Charles P. Cecil
837 Sarsfield
839 Power
842 Fiske
845 Bausell
862 Vogelgesang
863 Steinaker
864 Harold J. Ellison
866 Cone

871 Damato
873 Hawkins
876 Rogers
880 Dyess
883 Newman K. Perry
885 John R. Craig
886 Orleck
890 Meredith

"Forrest Sherman" Class
931 Forrest Sherman
933 Barry
937 George F. Davis
938 Jonas Ingram
940 Manley
941 Dupont
942 Bigelow
943 Blandy
944 Mullinnix

"Hull" Class
945 Hull
946 Edson
948 Morton
950 Richard S. Edwards
951 Turner Joy

"Spruance" Class
963 Spruance
964 Paul F. Foster
965 Kinkaid
966 Hewitt
967 Elliot
968 Arthur W. Radford
969 Peterson
970 Caron
971 David R. Ray
972 Oldendorf
973 John Young
974 Comte de Grasse
975 O'Brien
976 Merrill
977 Briscoe
978 Stump
979 Conolly
980 Moosburgger
981 John Hancock
982 Nicholson
983 John Rodgers
984 Leftwich
985 Cushing
986 Harry W. Hill
987 O'Bannon
988 Thorn

Frigates

FFG—Guided Missile Frigates

"Brooke" Class
1 Brooke
2 Ramsey
3 Schofield
4 Talbot
5 Richard L. Page
6 Julius A. Furer

"Oliver Hazard Perry" Class
7 Oliver Hazard Perry

FF—Frigates

"Bronstein" Class
1037 Bronstein
1038 McCloy

"Garcia" Class
1040 Garcia
1041 Bradley
1043 Edward McDonnell
1044 Brumby
1045 Davidson
1047 Voge
1048 Sample
1049 Koelsch
1050 Albert David
1051 O'Callahan

"Knox" Class
1052 Knox
1053 Roark
1054 Gray
1055 Hepburn
1056 Connole
1057 Rathburne
1058 Mayerkord
1059 W. S. Sims
1060 Lang
1061 Patterson
1062 Whipple
1063 Reasoner
1064 Lockwood
1065 Stein
1066 Marvin Shields
1067 Francis Hammond
1068 Vreeland
1069 Bagley
1070 Downes
1071 Badger
1072 Blakely
1073 Robert E. Peary
1074 Harold E. Holt
1075 Trippe

1076 Fanning
1077 Ouellet
1078 Joseph Hewes
1079 Bowen
1080 Paul
1081 Aylwin
1082 Elmer Montgomery
1083 Cook
1084 McCandless
1085 Donald B. Beary
1086 Brewton
1087 Kirk
1088 Barbey
1089 Jesse L. Brown
1090 Ainsworth
1091 Miller
1092 Thomas C. Hart
1093 Capodanno
1094 Pharris
1095 Truett
1096 Valdez
1097 Moinester

Command Ships

CC—Command Ships

1 Northampton
2 Wright

Amphibious Warships

LCC—Amphibious Command Ships (ex-AGC)

"Blue Ridge" Class
19 Blue Ridge
20 Mount Whitney

LHA—Amphibious Assault Ships

"Tarawa" Class
1 Tarawa
2 Saipan
3 Belleau Wood
4 Nassau
5 Da Nang

LPH—Amphibious Assault Ships

"Iwo Jima" Class
2 Iwo Jima
3 Okinawa
7 Guadalcanal
9 Guam
10 Tripoli
11 New Orleans
12 Inchon

LKA—Amphibious Cargo Ships

"Tulare" Class
112 Tulare

"Charleston" Class
113 Charleston
114 Durham
115 Mobile
116 St. Louis
117 El Paso

LPA—Amphibious Transports

"Paul Revere" Class
248 Paul Revere
249 Francis Marion

LPD—Amphibious Transport Docks

"Raleigh" Class
1 Raleigh
2 Vancouver

"Austin" Class
4 Austin
5 Ogden
6 Duluth
7 Cleveland
8 Dubuque
9 Denver
10 Juneau
11 Coronado
12 Shreveport
13 Nashville
14 Trenton
15 Ponce

LSD—Dock Landing Ships

"Thomaston" Class
28 Thomaston
29 Plymouth Rock
30 Fort Snelling
31 Point Defiance
32 Speigel Grove
33 Alamo
34 Hermitage
35 Monticello

"Anchorage" Class
36 Anchorage
37 Portland
38 Pensacola
39 Mt Vernon
40 Fort Fisher

LST—Tank Landing Ships

"De Soto County" Class
1173 Suffolk County
1177 Lorain County
1178 Wood County

"Newport" Class
1179 Newport
1180 Manitowac
1181 Sumter
1182 Fresno
1183 Peroria
1184 Frederick
1185 Schenectady
1186 Cayuga
1187 Tuscaloosa
1188 Saginaw
1189 San Bernardino
1190 Boulder
1191 Racine
1192 Spartanburg County
1193 Fairfax County
1194 La Moure County
1195 Barbour County
1196 Harlan County
1197 Barnstable County
1198 Bristol County

Patrol Ships and Craft

PHM—Patrol Combatants—Missile (Hydrofoil)

"Pegasus" Class
1 Pegasus
2 Hercules

PCH—Hydrofoil Patrol Craft

"High Point" Class
1 High Point

PG—Patrol Combatants

"Asheville" Class
86 Antelope
87 Ready
92 Tacoma
93 Welch
98 Grand Rapids
100 Douglas

Mine Warfare Ships

MSO—Ocean Minesweepers

"Agile" Class
421 Agile

"Aggressive" and "Dash" Classes
427 Constant
428 Dash
429 Detector
430 Direct
431 Dominant
433 Engage
437 Enhance
438 Esteem
439 Excel
440 Exploit
441 Exultant
442 Fearless
443 Fidelity
446 Fortify
448 Illusive
449 Impervious
455 Implicit
456 Inflict
461 Observer
462 Pinnacle
464 Pluck
471 Skill
474 Vital
488 Conquest
489 Gallant
490 Leader
492 Pledge
494 Sturdy
495 Swerve
496 Venture

"Acme" Class
509 Adroit
511 Affray

Service Forces

AE—Ammunition Ships

"Suribachi" Class
21 Suribachi
22 Mauna Kea
23 Nitro
24 Pyro
25 Haleakala

"Kilauea" Class
26 Kilauea
27 Butte
28 Santa Barbara
29 Mount Hood
32 Flint
33 Shasta
34 Mount Baker
35 Kiska

AF—Store Ship

"Rigel" Class
58 Rigel

AFS—Combat Store Ships

"Mars" Class
1 Mars
2 Sylvania
3 Niagara Falls
4 White Plains
5 Concord
6 San Diego
7 San Jose

AO—Oilers

"Jumboised" "Cimarron" Class
51 Ashtabula
98 Caloosahatchee
99 Canisteo

"Neosho" Class
143 Neosho
144 Mississinewa (MSC)
145 Hassayampa
146 Kawishiwi
147 Truckee
148 Ponchatoula

AOE—Fast Combat Support Ships

"Sacramento" Class
1 Sacramento
2 Camden
3 Seattle
4 Detroit

AOR—Replenishment Oilers

"Wichita" Class
1 Wichita
2 Milwaukee
3 Kansas City
4 Savannah
5 Wabash
6 Kalamazoo
7 Roanoke

Auxiliary Ships

AD—Destroyer Tenders

"Dixie" Class
14 Dixie
15 Prairie
17 Piedmont
18 Sierra
19 Yosemite

"Klondike" and "Shenandoah" Classes
24 Everglades
26 Shenandoah
29 Isle Royal
36 Bryce Canyon

"Samuel Gompers" Class
37 Samuel Gompers
38 Puget Sound

AGF—Miscellaneous Flagship
3 La Salle

AGFF—Frigate Research Ship

"Glover" Class
1 Glover

AH—Hospital Ship
17 Sanctuary

APB/IX—Self-Propelled Barracks Ships
504 Echols/IX
502 Mercer/IX
503 Nueces/IX
47 Kingman

AR—Repair Ships

"Vulcan" Class
5 Vulcan
6 Ajax
7 Hector
8 Jason

"Delta" Class
9 Delta

"Markab" Class
23 Markab

"Grand Canyon" Class
28 Grand Canyon

ARL—Landing Craft Repair Ships

"Achelous" Class
8 Egeria
24 Sphinx
31 Bellerophon
37 Indra

ARS—Salvage Ships

"Diver" and "Bolster" Classes
6 Escape
7 Grapple
8 Preserver
23 Deliver
24 Grasp
25 Safeguard
33 Clamp
34 Gear
38 Bolster
39 Conserver
40 Hoist
41 Opportune
42 Reclaimer
43 Recovery

AS—Submarine Tenders

"Fulton" Class
11 Fulton
12 Sperry
15 Bushnell
16 Howard W. Gilmore
17 Nereus
18 Orion

"Proteus" Class
19 Proteus

"Hunley" Class
31 Hunley
32 Holland

"Simon Lake" Class
33 Simon Lake
34 Canopus

"L.Y. Spear" Class
36 L.Y. Spear
37 Dixon

"Emory S. Land" Class
39 Emory S. Land
40 Frank Cable

ASR—Submarine Rescue Ships

"Chanticleer" Class
8 Coucal
9 Florikan
13 Kittiwake
14 Petrel
15 Sunbird
16 Tringa

"Pigeon" Class
21 Pigeon
22 Ortolan

ATA—Auxiliary Tugs

"Sotoyomo' Class
181 Accokeek
190 Samoset
193 Stallion
195 Tatnuck
213 Keywadin

ATF—Fleet Tugs

"Cherokee" and "Abnaki" Classes
- 76 Ute
- 84 Cree
- 85 Lipan
- 86 Mataco
- 91 Seneca
- 96 Abnaki
- 100 Chowanoc
- 101 Cocopa
- 103 Hitchiti
- 105 Moctobi
- 106 Molala
- 110 Quapaw
- 113 Takelma
- 114 Tawakoni
- 149 Atakapa
- 157 Nipmuc
- 158 Mosospelea
- 159 Paiute
- 160 Papago
- 161 Salinan
- 162 Shakori

ATS—Salvage and Rescue Ships

"Edenton" Class
- 1 Edenton
- 2 Beaufort
- 3 Brunswick

Military Sealift Command

Note: All ships of MSC have T prefix.

AG—Hydrographic Research Ship

- 164 Kingsport

AGM—Range Instrumentation Ships

- 8 Wheeling
- 9 General H. H. Arnold
- 10 General Hoyt S. Vandenberg
- 19 Vanguard
- 20 Redstone
- 22 Range Sentinel

AGOR—Oceanographic Research Ships

- 4 James M. Gilliss
- 7 Lynch
- 11 Mizar
- 12 De Steiguer
- 13 Bartlett
- 16 Hayes

AGS—Surveying Ships

- 21 Bowditch
- 22 Dutton
- 26 Silas Bent
- 27 Kane
- 29 Chauvenet
- 32 Harkness
- 33 Wilkes
- 34 Wyman
- 38 H. H. Hess

AK—Cargo Ships

"Greenville Victory" Class
- 237 Greenville Victory
- 240 Pvt. John R. Towle
- 242 Sgt. Andrew Miller
- 254 Sgt. Truman Kimbro

"Private Leonard C. Brostrom" Class
- 255 Pvt. Leonard C. Brostrom

"Eltanin" Class
- 271 Mirfak

"Greenville Victory" Class (Cont'd)
- 274 Lieut. James E. Robinson

"Schuyler Otis Bland" Class
- 277 Schuyler Otis Bland

"Norwalk" Class
- 279 Norwalk
- 280 Furman
- 281 Victoria
- 282 Marshfield

"Wyandot" Class
- 283 Wyandot

AKR—Vehicle Cargo Ships

"Comet" Class
- 7 Comet

"Meteor" Class
- 9 Meteor

AO—Tankers

"Suamico" Class
- 50 Tallulah

"Cimarron" Class
- 57 Marias
- 62 Taluga

"Suamico" Class (Cont'd)
- 73 Millicoma
- 75 Saugatuck
- 76 Schuylkill

"Jumboised Mispillion" Class
- 105 Mispillion
- 106 Navasota
- 107 Pasumpsic
- 108 Pawcatuck
- 109 Waccamaw

"Maumee" Class
- 149 Maumee
- 151 Shoshone
- 152 Yukon

"American Explorer" Class
- 165 American Explorer

"Sealift" Class
- 168 Sealift Pacific
- 169 Sealift Arabian Sea
- 170 Sealift China Sea
- 171 Sealift Indian Ocean
- 172 Sealift Atlantic
- 173 Sealift Mediterranean
- 174 Sealift Caribbean
- 175 Sealift Arctic
- 176 Sealift Antarctic

"Potomac" Class
- 181 Potomac

"Falcon" Class
- 182 Columbia
- 183 Neches
- 184 Hudson
- 185 Susquehanna

AOG—Gasoline Tankers

"Peconic" Class
- 77 Rincon
- 78 Nodaway
- 79 Petaluma

ARC—Cable Ships

- 2 Neptune
- 3 Aeolus
- 4 Thor
- 6 Albert J. Myer

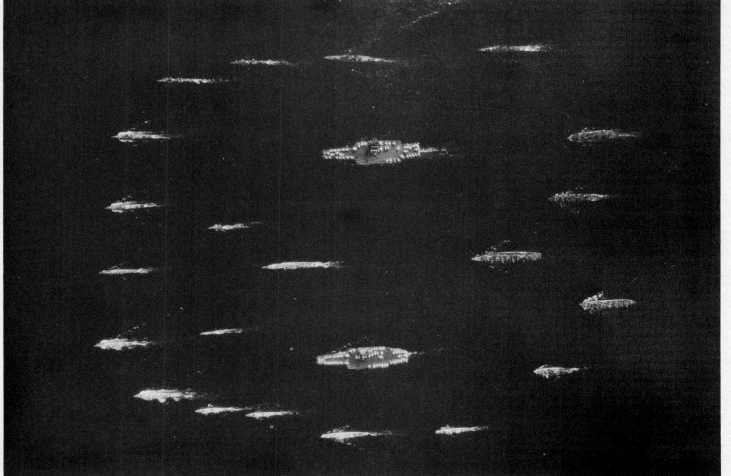

6th Fleet at Sea

SHIPBOARD SYSTEMS

ASROC (Anti-Submarine Rocket) Anti-Submarine missile launched from surface ships with homing torpedo or nuclear depth charge as warhead. Launcher is Mk 10 or Mk 26 combination ASROC/surface-to-air missile launcher or Mk 16 eight-cell "pepper box". Installed in US Navy cruisers, destroyers, and frigates; Japanese, Italian, West German, and Canadian destroyer-type ships.
Weight of missile approximately 1 000 lbs; length 15 ft; diameter 1 ft; span of fins 2·5 ft.
Payload: Mk 44 or Mk 46 acoustic-homing torpedo or nuclear depth charge; range one to six miles.
Designation: RUR-5. Status: Operational.

AEGIS (formerly Advanced Surface Missile System) Advanced surface-to-air missile system intended for use in guided missile destroyers (DDG 47 class) scheduled for construction during the 1980s. To have a capability against high-performance aircraft and air-launched, anti-ship missiles. AEGIS (with combined surface-to-air and surface-to-surface missile capability. AEGIS will have an electronic scanning radar with fixed antenna, and will be capable of controlling friendly aircraft as well as detection. Additional components will include the UYK-7 computer (a component of the Naval Tactical Data System) and SPY-1 radar "illuminators" for missile guidance. Status: Development (radars only; for use with Standard surface-to-air missile). Being evaluated in *Norton Sound* (AVM 1).

BPDMS (Basic Point Defence Missile System) Close-in-air-defence system employing the Sparrow AIM-7E or 7F series missile designated Sea Sparrow and a modified ASROC-type "pepper box" launcher. Installed in aircraft carriers, ocean escorts, and amphibious ships. Status: Operational.

CAPTOR (Encapsulated Torpedo). Mk 46 torpedo inserted in mine casing. Can be launched by aircraft or submarine. Status: Operational.

CIWS (Close-in Weapon System) "Family" of advanced gun and missile systems to provide close-in or "point" defence for ships against anti-ship missiles and aircraft. Specific weapons being developed or evaluated under this programme include the Chaparral, Hybrid launcher, Pintle, Vulcan Air Defence, Phalanx, and OTO Melara 35 mm twin gun mount.

LAMPS (Light Airborne Multi-Purpose System) Ship-launched helicopter intended for anti-submarine and missile-defence missions, with secondary roles of search-and-rescue and utility (e.g., parts and personnel transfer). For use aboard destroyer-type ships with hangars and certain amphibious warfare ships. Sensors include Magnetic Airborne Detection (MAD), and sonobuoys with digital relays to permit control and attack direction by launching ship. Radar provided to extend detection range. Weapons: 2 Mk 46 ASW torpedoes. Crew: pilot and 2 operators.
Status: 105 Kaman Seasprite helicopters being modified to SH-2 configuration as interim LAMPS. Deployed on cruisers, destroyers, and frigates.

LAMPS III Improved Light Airborne Multi-Purpose System based on Army Utility Tactical Transport Aircraft System (UTTAS) helicopter. Status: Development.

MCLWG (Major Calibre Light-Weight Gun). Light-weight 8-inch gun (Mk 71) planned for advanced surface combatants including the strike cruiser (CSGN). Status: Evaluation in destroyer *Hull* (DD 945); see photograph below.

NTDS (Naval Tactical Data System) Combination of digital computers, displays, and transmission links to increase an individual ship commander's capability to assess tactical data and take action by integrating input from various sensors (e.g., radars) and providing display of tactical situation and the defence or offence options available. Data can be transmitted among NTDS-equipped ships. An automatic mode initiates action to respond to greatest threats in a tactical situation. Also can be linked to airborne Tactical Data System (ATDS) in E-2 Hawkeye aircraft. Fitted in US Navy aircraft carriers, missile-armed cruisers, destroyers ("Coontz" class), amphibious command ships, and two frigates *(Voge* [FF 1047] and *Koelsch* [FF 1049]).
Status: Operational.

NATO SEA SPARROW Follow-on to BPDMS with a Target Acquisition System (TAS), powered director, smaller launcher, and control console combined with the Sea Sparrow missile. Planned for US amphibious and auxiliary ships.
Status: Under development; also a NATO co-operative programme with Belgium, Denmark, Italy, Netherlands and Norway. Being evaluated in *Downes* (FF 1070).

QUICKSTRIKE Advanced mine system; details classified. Status: Development.

SINS (Ships' Inertial Navigation System) Navigation system providing exact navigation information without active input from terrestrial sources. Prime components are gyroscopes and accelerometers that relate movement of the ship in all directions, ship speed through water and over ocean floor, and true north to give a continuous report of the ship's position.
Status: Operational.

SIRCS (Shipboard Intermediate Range Combat System). Programme to integrate shipboard self-defence systems (existing and planned). Status: Development.

SUBROC (Submarine Rocket) Anti-submarine missile launched from submarines with nuclear warhead. Launched from 21-inch torpedo tube. Carried in US Navy submarines of "Thresher" and later classes with amidships torpedo tubes, BQQ-2 or BQQ-5 sonar and Mk 113 or later torpedo fire control systems. The missile is fired from the submerged submarine, rises up through the surface, travels through air towards the hostile submarine, and then re-enters the water to detonate.
Weight of missile approximately 4 000 lbs, length 21 ft; diameter 1·75 ft (maximum); estimated range 25 to 30 miles.
Designation: UUM-44A. Status: Operational.

TACTAS (Tactical Towed Array Sonar). Ship-towed long-range acoustic detection system.

PHALANX Rapid-fire, close-in gun system being developed to provide close range defence against anti-ship missiles. Fires 20 mm ammunition from six-barrel "gatling" gun with "dynamic gun aiming" with fire control radar tracking projectiles and target(s). Theoretical rate of fire 3 000 rounds-per-minute. Initially planned for "Spruance" class destroyers, frigates, and some auxiliary ships; tentative programme calls for approx 359 units in 192 ships and three trainers. Status: Development.
Average cost for installation: $100 000 (new construction), $150 000 (retrofitting).

HULL (DD 945) with 8-inch Major Calibre Light-Weight Gun

1975, United States Navy, PH1 Carl R. Begg

NAVAL MISSILES

Type(a)	Designation	Name	Launch Platform (tubes/launchers)	Range n. miles (km)	Length feet (metres)	Weight lbs (kg)	Notes(b)
FBM	UGM-27C	Polaris A-3	"Ethan Allen", "George Washington" submarines (16)	2 500 *(4 625)*	32 *(9·8)*	30 000 *(13 500)*	Thermo-nuclear; MRV warhead
FBM	UGM-73A	Poseidon C-3	"Lafayette" submarines (16)	approx 2 500 *(4 625)*	34 *(10·4)*	65 000 *(29 250)*	Thermo-nuclear; MIRV warhead
FBM	UGM-96A	Trident (I) C-4	"Ohio" submarines (24)	approx 4 000 *(7 400)*	34·1 *(10·4)*	70 000 *(31 500)*	Thermo-nuclear; MIRV and MARV warhead
FBM	UGM	Trident (II) D-5	Trident submarines (24)	approx 6 000 *(11 100)*	45·75 *(13·9)*	126 000 *(56 700)*	Proposed

NAVAL MISSILES—*continued*

Type(a)	Designation	Name	Launch Platform (tubes/launchers)	Range n. miles (km)	Length feet (metres)	Weight lbs (kg)	Notes(b)
SLCM	BGM-109	Tomahawk (c)	Attack submarines (torpedo tubes)	approx 1 500 (2 775)	20·5 (6·3)	2 400-2 700 (10 800-12 150)	Nuclear; under development; tactical 300 mile version proposed
SSM	RGM-66D/E	Standard-ARM	"Asheville" gunboats (4) some surface ships (ASROC launcher)	15 (27·75)	15 (4·6)	1 400 (630)	HE
SSM	RGM-84	Harpoon	Surface ships	50 (80·4)	15 (4·6)	1 425 (641·25)	Operational; HE
SSM	RGM-84	Encapsulated Harpoon	Attack submarines (torpedo tubes)	60 (111)	21 (6·4)		Development; HE
SAM	RIM-2	Terrier	Cruisers (1 or 2 twin); "Coontz" destroyers (1 twin); "Kitty Hawk", "America" carriers (2 twin)	20+ (37)	26·1 (7·9)	3 000 (1 350)	Nuclear or HE
SAM	RIM-7	Sea Sparrow	Surface ships	8 (14·8)	12 (3·7)	380 (171)	HE; Mk 25 or Mk 29 (NATO) multiple launcher; Basic Point Defence Missile System
SAM	RIM-8	Talos	"Albany", "Long Beach" cruisers (2 twin)	65+ (120·2)	31·2 (9·5)	7 000 (3 510)	Nuclear or HE
SAM	RIM-24	Tartar	"Albany" cruisers (2 twin); "Chas. Adams" destroyers (1 twin or single); "Brooke" frigates (1 single); later cruisers	10+ (18·5)	15 (4·6)	1 425 (641·25)	HE
SAM	RIM-66	Standard-MR (SM-1)	Tartar replacement	20+ (37)	14·4 (4·5)	1 200-1 400 (540-630)	HE
SAM	RIM-66C	Standard (SM-2)	Talos replacement	60+ (110+)			Long range with mid-course guidance; development
SAM	RIM-67	Standard-ER (SM-1)	Terrier replacement	35+ (64·7)	26·2 (7·9)	2 900 (1 305)	HE
AAM	AIM-7	Sparrow III	F-4/F-14 fighters	9-16 (16·6-29·6)	12 (3·7)	500 (225)	
AAM	AIM-9C/D	Sidewinder-1B	F-4/F-14 fighters	8-15 (14·8-27·75)	9·5 (2·9)	185 (83·25)	
AAM	AIM-54	Phoenix	F-14 fighter (6)	60+ (14)	13 (3·9)	985 (443·25)	
AAM	AIM-95	Agile	Fighters	2 (3·7)	7·8 (2·4)		Development; close-in missile
ASM	AGM-12B	Bullpup-A	Attack/patrol aircraft	7 (12·9)	10 (3)	571 (156·95)	
ASM	AGM-12C/D	Bullpup-B	Attack/patrol aircraft	10 (18·5)	13·5 (4·1)	1 785 (803·25)	Nuclear or HE
ASM	AGM-45	Shrike	Attack/patrol aircraft	8-10 (14·8-18·5)	10 (3)	390 (175·5)	Anti-radiation
ASM	AGM-53	Condor	Attack/patrol aircraft	40-60 (74-111)	13·8 (4·2)	2 130 (958·5)	Nuclear or HE; production planned
ASM	AGM-62	Walleye	Attack/patrol aircraft	16 (29·6)	11·2 (3·4)	1 100 (495)	Nuclear or HE; larger Walleye II has 35-mile range (2 400 lbs)
ASM	AGM-78	Standard-ARM	Attack/patrol aircraft	35 (64·7)	15 (4·6)		Anti-radiation
ASM	AGM-83	Bulldog	Attack/patrol aircraft	35 (64·7)	9·8 (2·9)	600 (270)	Modified Bullpup
ASM	AGM-84	Harpoon	Attack/patrol aircraft	120 (193·1)	12·6 (3·8)	1 115 (501·75)	Development; HE
ASM	AGM-88	Harm	Attack/patrol aircraft				Development; High-speed Anti-Radiation Missile; larger than Shrike
ASW	RUR-5	ASROC	Cruisers, destroyers, frigates	1-6 (1·8-11·1)	15 (4·6)	1 000 (450)	Nuclear depth charge, Mk 44, or Mk 46 torpedo; multiple launcher in most ships; Mk 26 launcher in later ships; 570 lbs (256·5 kg) with Mk 46
ASW	UUM-44	SUBROC	"Permit" and later attack submarines (torpedo tubes)	25-30 (46·25-55·5)	21 (6·4)	4 000 (1 800)	Nuclear

(a) FBM = Fleet Ballistic Missile; SLCM = Submarine-Launched Cruise Missile; SSM = Surface-to-Surface Missile; SAM = Surface-to-Air Missile; AAM = Air-to-Air Missile; ASM = Air-to-Surface Missile; ASW = Anti-Submarine Warfare.
(b) MRV = Multiple Re-entry Vehicle; MIRV = Multiple Independently targeted Re-entry Vehicle; MaRV = Maneouvering Re-entry Vehicle; HE = High Explosive.
(c) Winner of SLCM competition between General Dynamics Convair BGM-109 and Vought (LTV) BGM-110 configurations.

TORPEDOES

Designation	Launch Platform	Weight lbs (kg)	Length feet (metres)	Diameter, in (mm)	Propulsion	Guidance	Notes
Mk 37 Mod 2	Submarines	1 690 (760·5)	13·4 (4·1)	19 (484·5)	Electric	Wire; active-passive acoustic homing	Anti-submarine
Mk 37 Mod 3	Submarines	1 430 (643·5)	11·25 (3·4)	19 (484·5)	Electric	Active-passive acoustic homing	Anti-submarine
Mk 37C	Submarines				Liquid mono-propellant	Active-passive acoustic homing	Anti-submarine; modified Mk 37-2/3 for allied navies; in production
Mk 44 Mod 1	Surface ships (Mk 32 tubes and ASROC); aircraft	433 (194·8)	8·4 (2·6)	12·75 (323·8)	Electric	Active acoustic homing	Anti-submarine
Mk 45 Mod 1 & Mod 2 (ASTOR)	Submarines	2 213 (995·8)	18·9 (5·7)	19 (484·5)	Electric	Wire	Anti-submarine; nuclear warhead; 10+ mile range; being replaced by Mk 48
Mk 46 Mod 0	Surface ships (Mk 32 tubes and ASROC); aircraft	568 (255·6)	8·5 (2·6)	12·75 (484·5)	Solid-propellant	Active-passive acoustic homing	Anti-submarine; successor to Mk 44
Mk 46 Mod 1 & Mod 2	Surface ships (Mk 32 tubes and ASROC); aircraft	508 (228·6)	8·5 (2·6)	12·75 (484·5)	Liquid mono-propellant	Active-passive acoustic homing	Anti-submarine; successor to Mk 44; Mod 4 used in CAPTOR (Encapsulated Torpedo) mine
Mk 48 Mod 1 & Mod 3	Submarines	3 480 (1 566)	19·1 (5·8)	21 (533·6)	Liquid mono-propellant	Wire/terminal acoustic homing	Anti-submarine and anti-shipping; in production; range approx 20 miles
ALWT	Aircraft; submarines						Advanced Light-Weight Torpedo; to replace Mk 46; in development

STRATEGIC MISSILE SUBMARINES (SSBN)

The current SSBN force will, with the completion of the last Poseidon conversion in 1977, provide over 5 000 separate warheads or "re-entry" vehicles, or about 55 per cent of US strategic warheads. (Each Poseidon missile is believed normally to carry ten separately targetable RVs, while the Polaris A-3 missile delivers three RVs on the same target, thus the latter weapon is considered to deliver only one warhead).

The Trident strategic missile submarine programme has been initiated to replace the older Polaris/Poseidon submarines from about 1980 onwards. All 41 existing submarines will reach their 20th year of active service between 1981 and 1987. The urgency of the original SSBN programme will thus result in block obsolescence at this time causing a substantial decrease in overall SLBM capability in the late 1980s and early 1990s.

Trident Programme: The Trident programme provides for an improved nuclear-propelled submarine and longer-range missiles. The Trident submarine is described below; the Trident I missile now under development will have a nominal range of approximately 4 000 nautical miles. This missile will be installed in the new construction submarines and retrofitted in ten of the Poseidon-armed submarines. The longer range (approx 6 000-mile) Trident II missile is under study. This weapon, which could be available in the mid-1980s, would also have a greater throw weight and accuracy than the Trident I.

When the Trident programme was initiated, the Navy planned to construct the first submarine with Fiscal Year 1974 funding and three submarines each year thereafter for the initial ten-SSBN class. However, in 1974 the Department of Defense slowed the rate to 1-2-2-2-2-1; in 1975 this was again revised to 1-2-1-2-1-2-1, and in 1976 it was further slowed to 1-2-1-1-2-1-2. Also in early 1976, Secretary of Defense Donald H. Rumsfeld announced that for planning purposes additional submarines beyond the ten-submarine force would be procured at the 1-2-1-2 rate continuously consistent with Strategic Arms Limitation Talks (SALT) agreements.

Narwhal Programme: Proposals to develop a type of smaller Trident-carrying submarines from the "Los Angeles" or "Narwhal" class designs have been dropped because of the increased costs which would result.

Strategic Cruise Missiles: The US Navy is in advanced development of a strategic Sea-Launched Cruise Missile (SLCM) (Tomahawk). This is an underwater-launched weapon with ram-jet propulsion which could deliver nuclear warheads to a range of approximately 1 500 nautical miles. A shorter-range (300-mile) version of the weapon with a conventional warhead is planned for use as an over-the-horizon anti-ship weapon.

The strategic cruise missile would have a low-level, terrain following flight path over land, much like that of a manned bomber in contrast to the ballistic trajectory of a Polaris/Poseidon/Trident missile.

Names: US ballistic missile submarines (SSBN) have been named for "distinguished Americans who were known for their devotion to freedom" since 1958 when the Polaris submarine programme was initiated. Included as "Americans" were Latin American and Hawaiian leaders, and several Europeans who supported the American fight for independence. In 1976 the SSBN name source was changed to States of the Union with the first Trident submarine (SSBN 726) being named *Ohio*. This move thoroughly confuses the US ship nomenclature scheme because since 1971 guided missile cruisers have been assigned state names and four state-named battleships of the "Iowa" class remain on the Navy List (in reserve).

WILL ROGERS in Holy Loch, Scotland   *1972, USN*

13 "OHIO" CLASS (FLEET BALLISTIC MISSILE SUBMARINES (SSBN))

Name	No.	Builders	Laid down	Launch	Commission
OHIO	SSBN 726	General Dynamics (Electric Boat)	10 Apr 1976	Late 1977	Early 1979
MICHIGAN	SSBN 727	General Dynamics (Electric Boat)	—	Late 1978	Early 1980
	SSBN 728	General Dynamics (Electric Boat)	—	Mid 1979	Mid 1980
	SSBN 729	General Dynamics (Electric Boat)	—	Early 1980	Mid 1981
	SSBN 730	Approved FY 1977 programme			
	SSBN 731	Proposed FY 1978 programme			
	SSBN 732	Proposed FY 1978 programme			
	SSBN 733	Planned FY 1979 programme			
	SSBN 734	Planned FY 1980 programme			
	SSBN 735	Planned FY 1980 programme			
	SSBN 736	Planned FY 1981 programme			
	SSBN 737	Planned FY 1982 programme			
	SSBN 738	Planned FY 1982 programme			

Displacement, tons: 16 600 surfaced; 18 700 dived
Length, feet (metres): 560 *(170·7)* oa
Beam, feet (metres): 42 *(12·8)*
Draught, feet (metres): 35·5 *(10·8)*
Missiles: 24 tubes for Trident I Submarine-Launched Ballistic Missile (SLBM)
Torpedo tubes: 4—21 inch *(533 mm)* Mk 68 (bow)
Main Machinery: 1 pressurised-water cooled S8G (General Electric) reactor; geared turbines; 1 shaft
Complement: 133 (16 officers, 117 enlisted men)

These submarines will be the largest undersea craft yet constructed, being significantly larger than the Soviet "Delta" class missile submarines which are now the largest afloat. The lead submarine was contracted to the Electric Boat Division of the General Dynamics Corp (Groton, Connecticut) on 25 July 1974. The only other US shipyard currently capable of building submarines of this class is the Newport News SB & DD Co in Virginia.

Design: The size of the Trident submarine is dictated primarily by the larger size missile required for 4 or 6 000-mile range and the larger reactor plant to drive the ship. The submarine will have 24 tubes in a vertical position.

The principle characteristics of the Trident concept as proposed were: (1) long-range missile (eventually of 6 000 miles (Trident II)) to permit targeting the Soviet Union while the submarine cruises in remote areas, making effective ASW virtually impossible for the foreseeable future, (2) extremely quiet submarines, (3) a high at-sea to in-port ratio.

Designation: Initially the hull number SSBN 711 was planned for the first Trident submarine. However, on 21 Feb 1974 the designation SSBN 1 was assigned, confusing the Navy's submarine designation system which goes back to the USS *Holland* (SS 1), commissioned in 1900. Subsequently, the designation was again changed on 10 Apr 1974, with the "block" SSBN 726-735 being reserved for the Trident programme. Three more 736-738 now added.

Electronics: UYK-7 computer is provided to support electronic and weapon systems. Mk 118 digital torpedo fire control system is installed.

Engineering: These submarines will have a nuclear core life of about nine years between refuellings. A prototype of the S8G reactor plant has been constructed at West Milton, New York.

Fiscal: Costs of the first four SSBNs have increased over the initial appropriations. See 1975-1976 edition for initial costs. SSBNs 731 and 732 in Fiscal Year 1978 are funded at $1 969 700 000 for the pair.

Missiles: The Trident submarines will be armed initially with the Trident I missile, scheduled to become operational late in 1978. This missile is expected to have a range of 4 000 nautical miles, a range already exceeded by the SS-N-8 missile in the Soviet "Delta" class submarines. However, the US missile will have a MIRV warhead, which at present is not fitted to SS-N-8, although SS-N-6 (Mod III) has an MRV head.

The Trident missile is expected to carry more than the 10 to 14 re-entry vehicles that the Poseidon can lift. In addition, the Mk 500 MaRV (Manoeuvring Re-entry Vehicle) is under development for the purpose of demonstrating its compatibility with the Trident I missile. This re-entry vehicle intended to evade ABM interceptor missiles and is not terminally guided to increase its accuracy.

Navigation: Each submarine will have two Mk 2 Ships Inertial Navigation Systems; to be fitted with satellite navigation receivers.

Sonar: BQQ-5 (passive only).

31 "BENJAMIN FRANKLIN" and "LAFAYETTE" CLASSES (FLEET BALLISTIC MISSILE SUBMARINES (SSBN))

Name	No.	Builders	Laid down	Launched	Commissioned
*LAFAYETTE	SSBN 616	General Dynamics (Electric Boat Div)	17 Jan 1961	8 May 1962	23 Apr 1963
*ALEXANDER HAMILTON	SSBN 617	General Dynamics (Electric Boat Div)	26 June1961	18 Aug 1962	27 June1963
*ANDREW JACKSON	SSBN 619	Mare Island Naval Shipyard	26 Apr 1961	15 Sep 1962	3 July 1963
*JOHN ADAMS	SSBN 620	Portsmouth Naval Shipyard	19 May 1961	12 Jan 1963	12 May 1964
*JAMES MONROE	SSBN 622	Newport News Shipbuilding & DD Co	31 July 1961	4 Aug 1962	7 Dec 1963
*NATHAN HALE	SSBN 623	General Dynamics (Electric Boat Div)	2 Oct 1961	12 Jan 1963	23 Nov 1963
*WOODROW WILSON	SSBN 624	Mare Island Naval Shipyard	13 Sep 1961	22 Feb 1963	27 Dec 1963
*HENRY CLAY	SSBN 625	Newport News Shipbuilding & DD Co.	23 Oct 1961	30 Nov 1962	20 Feb 1964
*DANIEL WEBSTER	SSBN 626	General Dynamics (Electric Boat Div)	28 Dec 1961	27 Apr 1963	9 Apr 1964
*JAMES MADISON	SSBN 627	Newport News Shipbuilding & DD Co	5 Mar 1962	15 Mar 1963	28 July 1964
*TECUMSEH	SSBN 628	General Dynamics (Electric Boat Div)	1 June1962	22 June1963	29 May 1964
*DANIEL BOONE	SSBN 629	Mare Island Naval Shipyard	6 Feb 1962	22 June1963	23 Apr 1964
*JOHN C. CALHOUN	SSBN 630	Newport News Shipbuilding & DD Co	4 June1962	22 June1963	15 Sep 1964
*ULYSSES S. GRANT	SSBN 631	General Dynamics (Electric Boat Div)	18 Aug 1962	2 Nov 1963	17 July 1964
*VON STEUBEN	SSBN 632	Newport News Shipbuilding & DD Co	4 Sep 1962	18 Oct 1963	30 Sep 1964
*CASIMIR PULASKI	SSBN 633	General Dynamics (Electric Boat Div)	12 Jan 1963	1 Feb 1964	14 Aug 1964
*STONEWALL JACKSON	SSBN 634	Mare Island Naval Shipyard	4 July 1962	30 Nov 1963	26 Aug 1964
*SAM RAYBURN	SSBN 635	Newport News Shipbuilding & DD Co	3 Dec 1962	20 Dec 1963	2 Dec 1964
*NATHANAEL GREENE	SSBN 636	Portsmouth Naval Shipyard	21 May 1962	12 May 1964	19 Dec 1964
*BENJAMIN FRANKLIN	SSBN 640	General Dynamics (Electric Boat Div)	25 May 1963	5 Dec 1964	22 Oct 1965
*SIMON BOLIVAR	SSBN 641	Newport News Shipbuilding & DD Co	17 Apr 1963	22 Aug 1964	29 Oct 1965
*KAMEHAMEHA	SSBN 642	Mare Island Naval Shipyard	2 May 1963	16 Jan 1965	10 Dec 1965
*GEORGE BANCROFT	SSBN 643	General Dynamics (Electric Boat Div)	24 Aug 1963	20 Mar 1965	22 Jan 1966
*LEWIS AND CLARK	SSBN 644	Newport News Shipbuilding & DD Co	29 July 1963	21 Nov 1964	22 Dec 1965
*JAMES K. POLK	SSBN 645	General Dynamics (Electric Boat Div)	23 Nov 1963	22 May 1965	16 Apr 1966
*GEORGE C. MARSHALL	SSBN 654	Newport News Shipbuilding & DD Co	2 Mar 1964	21 May 1965	29 Apr 1966
*HENRY L. STIMSON	SSBN 655	General Dynamics (Electric Boat Div)	4 Apr 1964	13 Nov 1965	20 Aug 1966
*GEORGE WASHINGTON CARVER	SSBN 656	Newport News Shipbuilding & DD Co	24 Aug 1964	14 Aug 1965	15 June1966
*FRANCIS SCOTT KEY	SSBN 657	General Dynamics (Electric Boat Div)	5 Dec 1964	23 Apr 1966	3 Dec 1966
*MARIANO G. VALLEJO	SSBN 658	Mare Island Naval Shipyard	7 July 1964	23 Oct 1965	16 Dec 1966
*WILL ROGERS	SSBN 659	General Dynamics (Electric Boat Div)	20 Mar 1965	21 July 1966	1 Apr 1967

Displacement, tons: 6 650 light surfaced; 7 250 standard surfaced; 8 250 dived
Length, feet (metres): 425 *(129·5)* oa
Beam, feet (metres): 33 *(10·1)*
Draught, feet (metres): 31·5 *(9·6)*
Missile launchers: 16 tubes for Poseidon C-3 SLBM (see *Missile* notes)
Torpedo tubes: 4—21 inch *(533 mm)* Mk 65 (bow)
Main machinery: 1 pressurised-water cooled S5W (Westinghouse) reactor; 2 geared turbines; 15 000 shp; 1 shaft
Speed, knots: 20 surfaced; approx 30 dived
Complement: 168 (20 officers, 148 enlisted men)

These submarines are the largest undersea craft to be completed in the West. The first four submarines (SSBN 616, 617, 619, 620) were authorised in the Fiscal Year 1961 shipbuilding programme with five additional submarines (SSBN 622-626) authorised in a supplemental FY 1961 programme; SSBN 627-636 (ten) in FY 1962, SSBN 640-645 (six) in FY 1963, and SSBN 654-659 (six) in FY 1964. Cost for the earlier ships of this class was approximately $109 500 000 per submarine.

Design: The *Benjamin Franklin* and later submarines are officially considered a separate class; however, differences are minimal (eg, quieter machinery).

Electronics: Fitted with Mk 113 Mod 9 torpedo fire control system.

Engineering: The *Benjamin Franklin* and subsequent submarines of this class have been fitted with quieter machinery. All SSBNs have diesel-electric stand-by machinery, snorts, and "outboard" auxiliary propeller for emergency use.
The nuclear cores inserted in refuelling these submarines during the late 1960s and early 1970s cost approximately $3 500 000 and provide energy for approximately 400 000 miles.

Missiles: The first eight ships of this class were fitted with the Polaris A-2 missile (1 500 nautical mile range) and the 23 later ships with the Polaris A-3 missile (2 500 nautical mile range). The SSBN 620 and SSBN 622-625 (5 ships) were rearmed with the Polaris A-3 missile during overhaul-refuellings from 1968 to 1970. Subsequently, all converted to carry the Poseidon C-3 missile.
The *Andrew Jackson* launched the first Polaris A-3 missile to be fired from a submarine on 26 Oct 1963. The *Daniel Webster* was the first submarine to deploy with the A-3 missile, beginning her first patrol on 28 Sep 1964. The *Daniel Boone* was the first Polaris submarine to deploy to the Pacific, beginning her first patrol with the A-3 missile on 25 Dec 1964. The *James Madison* launched the first Poseidon C-3 missile from a submarine on 3 Aug 1970; the submarine began the first Poseidon deployment on 31 Mar 1971.
The *James Madison* was the first submarine to undergo conversion to carry the Poseidon missile. She began conversion in February 1969 and was completed in June 1970. (See conversion table on following page).
Poseidon conversion, overhaul, and reactor refuelling are conducted simultaneously. In addition to changes in missile tubes to accommodate larger Poseidon, the conversion provides replacement of Mk 84 fire control system with Mk 88 system. The Poseidon conversion programme completed in 1977. This conversion makes no change to the submarines' external appearance.
Current planning provides for the first of ten of these classes of SSBNs to be refitted with the Trident I missile in 1979.

Navigation: These submarines are equipped with an elaborate Ship's Inertial Navigation System (SINS), a system of gyroscopes and accelerometers which relates movement of the ship in all directions, true speed through the water and over the ocean floor, and true north to give a continuous report of the submarine's position. Navigation data produced by SINS can be provided to each missile's guidance package until the instant the missile is fired.
As converted, all Poseidon submarines have three Mk 2 Mod 4 SINS; all fitted with navigational satellite receivers.

SIMON BOLIVAR *9/1976, Dr. Giorgio Arra*

SIMON BOLIVAR *9/1976, Dr. Giorgio Arra*

Personnel: Each submarine is assigned two alternating crews designated "Blue" and "Gold". Each crew mans the submarine during a 60-day patrol and partially assists during the intermediate 28-day refit alongside a Polaris tender.

MARIANO C. VALLEJO

1974, USN

POSEIDON CONVERSION SCHEDULE

No.	Programme	Conversion Yard	Start		Complete	
SSBN 616	FY 1973	General Dynamics Corp (Electric Boat)	Oct	1972	Nov	1974
SSBN 617	FY 1973	Newport News SB & DD Co	Jan	1973	Apr	1975
SSBN 619	FY 1973	General Dynamics Corp (Electric Boat)	Mar	1973	Aug	1975
SSBN 620	FY 1974	Portsmouth Naval Shipyard	Feb	1974	Mar	1975
SSBN 622	FY 1975	Newport News SB & DD Co	Jan	1975	Jan	1977
SSBN 623	FY 1973	Puget Sound Naval Shipyard	June	1973	June	1975
SSBN 624	FY 1974	Newport News SB & DD Co	Oct	1973	Oct	1975
SSBN 625	FY 1975	Portsmouth Naval Shipyard	Apr	1975		1977
SSBN 626	FY 1975	General Dynamics Corp (Electric Boat)	Dec	1975		1977
SSBN 627	FY 1968	General Dynamics Corp (Electric Boat)	Feb	1969	June	1970
SSBN 628	FY 1970	Newport News SB & DD Co	Nov	1969	Feb	1971
SSBN 629	FY 1968	Newport News SB & DD Co	May	1969	Aug	1970
SSBN 630	FY 1969	Mare Island Naval Shipyard	Aug	1969	Feb	1971
SSBN 631	FY 1970	Puget Sound Naval Shipyard	Oct	1969	Dec	1970
SSBN 632	FY 1969	General Dynamics Corp (Electric Boat)	July	1969	Nov	1970
SSBN 633	FY 1970	General Dynamics Corp (Electric Boat)	Jan	1970	Apr	1971
SSBN 634	FY 1971	General Dynamics Corp (Electric Boat)	July	1970	Oct	1971
SSBN 635	FY 1970	Portsmouth Naval Shipyard	Jan	1970	Sep	1971
SSBN 636	FY 1971	Newport News SB & DD Co	July	1970	Sep	1971
SSBN 640	FY 1971	General Dynamics Corp (Electric Boat)	Feb	1971	May	1972
SSBN 641	FY 1971	Newport News SB & DD Co	Feb	1971	May	1972
SSBN 642	FY 1972	General Dynamics Corp (Electric Boat)	July	1971	Oct	1972
SSBN 643	FY 1971	Portsmouth Naval Shipyard	Apr	1971	July	1972
SSBN 644	FY 1971	Puget Sound Naval Shipyard	Apr	1971	July	1972
SSBN 645	FY 1972	Newport News SB & DD Co	July	1971	Nov	1972
SSBN 654	FY 1972	Puget Sound Naval Shipyard	Sep	1971	Feb	1973
SSBN 655	FY 1972	Newport News SB & DD Co	Nov	1971	Mar	1973
SSBN 656	FY 1972	General Dynamics Corp (Electric Boat)	Nov	1971	Apr	1973
SSBN 657	FY 1972	Puget Sound Naval Shipyard	Feb	1972	May	1973
SSBN 658	FY 1973	Newport News SB & DD Co	Aug	1972	Dec	1973
SSBN 659	FY 1973	Portsmouth Naval Shipyard	Oct	1972	Feb	1974

THOMAS A. EDISON in rear, passing FRANCIS SCOTT KEY in Panama Canal

1973, USN

TECUMSEH approaching PROTEUS

USN

5 "ETHAN ALLEN" CLASS (FLEET BALLISTIC MISSILE SUBMARINES (SSBN))

Name	No.	Builders	Laid down	Launched	Commissioned
*ETHAN ALLEN	SSBN 608	General Dynamics (Electric Boat Div, Groton)	14 Sep 1959	22 Nov 1960	8 Aug 1961
*SAM HOUSTON	SSBN 609	Newport News Shipbuilding & DD Co	28 Dec 1959	2 Feb 1961	6 Mar 1962
*THOMAS A. EDISON	SSBN 610	General Dynamics (Electric Boat Div, Groton)	15 Mar 1960	15 June 1961	10 Mar 1962
*JOHN MARSHALL	SSBN 611	Newport News Shipbuilding & DD Co	4 Apr 1960	15 July 1961	21 May 1962
*THOMAS JEFFERSON	SSBN 618	Newport News Shipbuilding & DD Co	3 Feb 1961	24 Feb 1962	4 Jan 1963

Displacement, tons: 6 955 surfaced; 7 880 dived
Length, feet (metres): 410 *(125)* oa
Beam, feet (metres): 33 *(10·1)*
Draught, feet (metres): 32 *(9·8)*
Missile launchers: 16 tubes for Polaris A-3 SLBM
Torpedo tubes: 4—21 inch *(533 mm)* bow
Main machinery: 1 pressurised-water cooled S5W (Westinghouse) reactor; 2 geared turbines (General Electric); 15 000 shp; 1 shaft
Speed, knots: 20 surfaced; approx 30 dived
Complement: 142 (15 officers, 127 enlisted men)

These submarines were designed specifically for the ballistic missile role and are larger and better arranged than the earlier "George Washington" class submarines. The first four ships of this class were authorised in the Fiscal Year 1959 programme; the *Thomas Jefferson* (which is out of numerical sequence) was in the FY 1961 programme. These submarines and the previous "George Washington" class will not be converted to carry the Poseidon missile because of materiel limitations and the age they would be after conversion. Also the "George Washington" class submarines are depth limited compared to the later SSBN classes.

Design: These submarines and the subsequent "Lafayette" class are deep-diving submarines with a depth capability similar to the "Thresher" class attack submarines; pressure hulls of HY-80 steel.

Missiles: These ships were initially armed with the Polaris A-2 missile (1 500 nautical mile range). The *Ethan Allen* launched the first A-2 missile fired from a submarine on 23 Oct 1961. She was the first submarine to deploy with the A-2 missile, beginning her first patrol on 26 June 1962. The *Ethan Allen* fired a Polaris A-2 missile in the Christmas Island Pacific Test Area on 6 May 1962 in what was the first complete US test of a ballistic missile including detonation of the nuclear warhead. All five of these ships have been modified to fire the A-3 missile (2 500 nautical mile range).

Navigation: Fitted with two Mk 2 Mod 3 Ship's Inertial Navigation Systems (SINS) and navigational satellite receiver.

THOMAS JEFFERSON   6/1976, USN

ETHAN ALLEN   1971, USN

ETHAN ALLEN   1971, USN

5 "GEORGE WASHINGTON" CLASS (FLEET BALLISTIC MISSILE SUBMARINES (SSBN))

Name	No.	Builders	Laid down	Launched	Commissioned
*GEORGE WASHINGTON	SSBN 598	General Dynamics (Electric Boat Div, Groton)	1 Nov 1957	9 June1959	30 Dec 1959
*PATRICK HENRY	SSBN 599	General Dynamics (Electric Boat Div, Groton)	27 May 1958	22 Sep 1959	9 Apr 1960
*THEODORE ROOSEVELT	SSBN 600	Mare Island Naval Shipyard	20 May 1958	3 Oct 1959	13 Feb 1961
*ROBERT E. LEE	SSBN 601	Newport News Shipbuilding & DD Co	25 Aug 1958	18 Dec 1959	16 Sep 1960
*ABRAHAM LINCOLN	SSBN 602	Portsmouth Naval Shipyard	1 Nov 1958	14 May 1960	11 Mar 1961

Displacement, tons: 6 019 standard surfaced; 6 888 dived
Length, feet (metres): 381·7 (116·3) oa
Beam, feet (metres): 33 (10·1)
Draught, feet (metres): 29 (8·8)
Missile launchers: 16 tubes for Polaris A-3 SLBM
Torpedo tubes: 6—21 inch (533 mm) Mk 59 (bow)
Main machinery: 1 pressurised-water cooled S5W (Westinghouse) reactor; 2 geared turbines (General Electric); 15 000 shp; 1 shaft
Speed, knots: 20 surfaced; approx 30 dived
Complement: 112 (12 officers, 100 enlisted men)

The *George Washington* was the West's first ship to be armed with ballistic missiles. A supplement to the Fiscal Year 1958 new construction programme signed on 11 Feb 1958 provided for the construction of the first three SSBNs. The Navy ordered the just-begun attack submarine *Scorpion* (SSN 589) to be completed as a missile submarine on 31 Dec 1957. The hull was redesignated SSBN 598 and completed as the *George Washington*. The *Patrick Henry* similarly was re-ordered on the last day of 1957, her materials having originally been intended for the not-yet started SSN 590. These submarines and three sister ships (two authorised in FY 1959) were built to a modified "Skipjack" class design with almost 130 feet being added to the original design to accommodate two rows of eight missile tubes, fore control and navigation equipment, and auxiliary machinery. All are depth limited compared with later designs.

Appearance: Note that "hump" of hull extension for housing missile tubes is more pronounced in these submarines than later classes.

Engineering: The *George Washington* was the first FBM submarine to be overhauled and "refuelled". During her 4½ years of operation on her initial reactor core she carried out 15 submerged missile patrols and steamed more than 100 000 miles.

Missiles: These ships were initially armed with the Polaris A-1 missile (1 200 nautical mile range). The *George Washington* successfully fired two Polaris A-1 missiles while submerged off Cape Canaveral on 20 July 1960 in the first underwater launching of a ballistic missile from a US submarine. She departed on

ABRAHAM LINCOLN   USN

her initial patrol on 15 Nov 1960 and remained submerged for 66 days, 10 hours. All five submarines of this class have been refitted to fire the improved Polaris A-3 missile (2 500 nautical mile range). Missile refit and first reactor refuelling were accomplished simultaneously during overhaul. *George Washington* from 20 June 1964 to 2 Feb 1966, *Patrick Henry* from 4 Jan 1965 to 21 July 1966, *Theodore Roosevelt* from 28 July 1965 to 14 Jan 1967, *Robert E. Lee* from 23 Feb 1965 to 2 July 1966, and *Abraham Lincoln* from 25 Oct 1965 to 3 June 1967, four at Electric Boat yard in Groton, Connecticut, and

Robert E. Lee at Mare Island Naval Shipyard (California). These submarines all have Mk 84 fire control systems and gas-steam missile ejectors (originally fitted with Mk 80 fire control systems and compressed air missile ejectors, changed during A-3 missile refit).

These submarines will not be modified to carry and launch the advanced Poseidon ballistic missile.

Navigation: Fitted with three Mk 2 Mod 4 Ship's Inertial Navigation System (SINS) and navigational satellite receiver.

GEORGE WASHINGTON   USN

ROBERT E. LEE   USN

SUBMARINES (SSN and SS)

The US Navy's submarine forces consist of two principal categories: strategic missile submarines (SSBN), listed in the previous section, and attack submarines (SS and SSN).

The Navy's attack submarine force is almost entirely nuclear. The few remaining diesel-electric submarines are all of post-World War II construction; their age and the demand of foreign transfers to US allies will result in an all-nuclear submarine force by the mid-1980s, if not earlier. At that time the Navy will have some 85 to 90 SSNs ("Skipjack" class and later).

A construction rate of two SSNs per year for the foreseeable future has been proposed by the Department of Defense. Construction of the submarines recently has been slowed by the late delivery of component equipment and problems in the hiring of shipyard workers. Further complicating the situation has been the start-up of the Trident missile submarine programme and the loss of the Litton/Ingalls yard at Pascagoula, Mississippi, which delivered its last nuclear submarine in 1974. This leaves only two shipyards in the United States building nuclear submarines. (No diesel-propelled submarines have been built in the United States since 1959).

In January 1977 Secretary of Defence D. H. Rumsfeld reported "It has been decided to continue the production of the SSN 688 (Los Angeles) class until at least the mid-1980s rather than to introduce a new generation submarine. We plan to procure eight SSN-688s in the five year programme. A faster building rate will be necessary in the 1980s." The initial sea trials of Los Angeles gave an increase over the designed speed and showed improved sound quieting.

Ancillary Programmes: These include development of a wide-aperture array sonar for rapid localization of targets and attack, the retrofitting of BQQ-5 sonar in all submarines of the "Sturgeon" class and deployment of submarine-launched Harpoon.

Anti-ship Missiles: An encapsulated version of the Harpoon anti-ship missile has been developed for launching from submarines. The Harpoon, also capable of surface ship and aircraft launch, is a 15-foot weapon carrying a conventional high-explosive warhead. In the encapsulated version, the Harpoon is launched from a torpedo tube and travels to the surface where the protective capsule is discarded, the missile's fins extend, and the rocket engine ignites. The Harpoon has a range of about 60 nautical miles and will be operational in FY 1978.

Deep Submergence Vehicles: The US Navy's Deep Sub-

mergence Vehicles (DSV), including the nuclear-propelled NR-1, are listed later in the United States Navy section.

Names: US submarines generally have been named for fish and other marine life except that fleet ballistic missile submarines have been named for famous Americans. The tradition of naming "fleet" and "attack" submarines for fish was broken in 1971 when three submarines of the "Sturgeon" class and the one-of-a-kind SSN 685 were named for deceased members of the Congress. Previously US destroyer-type ships have honoured members of the Congress.

Later in 1971 the SSN 688, lead ship for a new class of attack submarines, was named Los Angeles, introducing "city" names to US submarines. This was the third name source applied to US submarines within a year, indicating the considerable confusion in ship nomenclature within the Navy. (Of late, several types of auxiliary ships also have been named for cities, a name source traditionally applied to cruisers in the US Navy).

Transfers: Three of the four remaining "Tang" class submarines (Tang, Wahoo and Trout) are scheduled for transfer to the Imperial Iranian Navy in 1978-79.

31 + 8 "LOS ANGELES" CLASS (SSN)

Name	No.	Builders	Laid down	Launched	Commissioned
*LOS ANGELES	SSN 688	Newport News SB & DD Co	8 Jan 1972	6 Apr 1974	13 Nov 1976
BATON ROUGE	SSN 689	Newport News SB & DD Co	18 Nov 1972	26 Apr 1975	1977
PHILADELPHIA	SSN 690	General Dynamics (Electric Boat)	12 Aug 1972	19 Oct 1974	1977
MEMPHIS	SSN 691	Newport News SB & DD Co	23 June1973	3 Apr 1976	Early 1977
OMAHA	SSN 692	General Dynamics (Electric Boat)	27 Jan 1973	21 Feb 1976	Late 1977
CINCINNATI	SSN 693	Newport News SB & DD Co	6 Apr 1974	1977	1978
GROTON	SSN 694	General Dynamics (Electric Boat)	3 Aug 1973	9 Oct 1976	Late 1977
BIRMINGHAM	SSN 695	Newport News SB & DD Co	26 Apr 1975	1977	1978
NEW YORK CITY	SSN 696	General Dynamics (Electric Boat)	15 Dec 1973	1977	1978
INDIANAPOLIS	SSN 697	General Dynamics (Electric Boat)	19 Oct 1974	1977	1978
BREMERTON	SSN 698	General Dynamics (Electric Boat)	8 May 1976	1977	1978
JACKSONVILLE	SSN 699	General Dynamics (Electric Boat)	21 Feb 1976	1978	1979
DALLAS	SSN 700	General Dynamics (Electric Boat)	9 Oct 1976	1978	1979
LA JOLLA	SSN 701	General Dynamics (Electric Boat)	16 Oct 1976	1978	1979
PHOENIX	SSN 702	General Dynamics (Electric Boat)	1977	1978	1979
BOSTON	SSN 703	General Dynamics (Electric Boat)	1977	1979	1980
BALTIMORE	SSN 704	General Dynamics (Electric Boat)	1978	1979	1980
—	SSN 705	General Dynamics (Electric Boat)	1978	1979	1980
Five submarines	SSN 706-710	General Dynamics (Electric Boat)	1978-1979	1979-1981	1980-1982
Three submarines	SSN 711-713	Newport News SB & DD Co	1977-1979	1979-1980	1980-1982
Two submarines	SSN 714-715	Newport News SB & DD Co			1982-1983
Three submarines	SSN 716-718	Approved FY 1977 programme			1985
Two submarines	SSN 719-720	Proposed FY 1978 programme			
Six submarines	SSN —	Proposed FY 1979-82 programme			

Displacement, tons: 6 000 standard; 6 900 dived
Length, feet (metres): 360 (109·7) oa
Beam, feet (metres): 33 (10·1)
Draught, feet (metres): 32·3 (9·85)
Torpedo tubes: 4—21 inch (533 mm) amidships
Missiles: Tube launched Harpoon (FY 1978)
A/S weapons: SUBROC and Mk 48 A/S torpedoes
Main machinery: 1 pressurised-water cooled S6G (GE) reactor; 2 geared turbines; 1 shaft
Speed, knots: 30+ dived
Complement: 127 (12 officers, 115 enlisted men)

The SSN 688-690 were authorised in the Fiscal Year 1970 new construction programme, SSN 691-694 in FY 1971, SSN 695-699 in FY 1972, SSN 700-705 in FY 1973, SSN 706-710 in FY 1974, SSN 711-713 in FY 1975, and SSN 714-715 in the FY 1976 programme. Additional submarines are planned at the rate of one or two units per year into the early 1980s and then at a faster rate.

Detailed design of the SSN 688 class as well as construction of the lead submarine was contracted to the Newport News Shipbuilding & Dry Dock Company, Newport News, Virginia.

These submarines are considerably behind schedule with the lead ship being completed over two years behind the original schedule. Thus, the Los Angeles is nearly 5 years from keel laying to commissioning.

Design: Every effort has been made to improve sound quieting and the trials of Los Angeles have shown success in this area.

Electronics: UYK-7 computer is installed to assist command and control functions: Mk 113 Mod 10 torpedo fire control system fitted in SSN 688-699; Mk 117 in later submarines.

Engineering: The S6G reactor is reportedly a modified version of the D2G type fitted in the Bainbridge and Truxtun. The D2G reactors each produce approximately 30 000 shp. Reactor core life between refuellings is estimated at ten years.

Fiscal: The costs of these submarines have increased in every fiscal year programme. In FY 1976 an average cost of $221 250 000 per unit was estimated for a 38-submarine class. However, the FY 1977 units are estimated to cost approximately $330 000 000 each.

Radar: BPS-15.

Sonar: BQQ-5 long range acquisition; BQS-15 close range; Towed array fitted.

LOS ANGELES

8/1976, Newport News SB and DD Co

1 "GLENARD P. LIPSCOMB" CLASS (SSN)

Name	No.	Builders	Laid down	Launched	Commissioned
*GLENARD P. LIPSCOMB	SSN 685	General Dynamics (Electric Boat)	5 June 1971	4 Aug 1973	21 Dec 1974

Displacement, tons: 5 813 standard; 6 480 dived
Length, feet (metres): 365 oa *(111·3)*
Beam, feet (metres): 31·7 *(9·7)*
Torpedo tubes: 4—21 inch *(533 mm)* amidships
A/S weapons: SUBROC and A/S torpedoes
Main machinery: 1 pressurised-water cooled S5Wa (Westinghouse) reactor. Turbine-electric drive (General Electric); 1 shaft
Speed, knots: approx 25+ dived
Complement: 120 (12 officers, 108 enlisted men)

Studies of a specifically "quiet" submarine were begun in Oct 1964. After certain setbacks approval for the construction of this submarine was announced on 25 Oct 1968 and the contract awarded to General Dynamics on 14 Oct 1970.

The Turbine-Electric Drive Submarine (TEDS) was constructed to test "a combination of advanced silencing techniques" involving "a new kind of propulsion system, and new and quieter machinery of various kinds", according to the Department of Defense. The TEDS project will permit an at-sea evaluation of improvements in ASW effectiveness due to noise reduction.

No further class of turbine-electric nuclear submarines has been proposed. Rather, quieting features developed in *Glenard P. Lipscomb* which do not detract from speed have been incorporated in the "Los Angeles" design.

Authorised in the Fiscal Year 1968 new construction programme, estimated construction cost was approximately $200 000 000.

Engineering: Turbine-electric drive eliminates the noisy reduction gears of standard steam turbine power plants. The turbine-electric power plant is larger and heavier than comparable steam turbine submarine machinery.

The *Tullibee* (SSN 597) was an earlier effort at noise reduction through a turbine-electric nuclear plant.

GLENARD P. LIPSCOMB   *1974, General Dynamics, Electric Boat Division*

1 "NARWHAL" CLASS (SSN)

Name	No.	Builders	Laid down	Launched	Commissioned
*NARWHAL	SSN 671	General Dynamics (Electric Boat)	17 Jan 1966	9 Sep 1967	12 July 1969

Displacement, tons: 4 450 standard; 5 350 dived
Length, feet (metres): 314·6 *(95·9)* oa
Beam, feet (metres): 43 *(13·1)*
Draught, feet (metres): 27 *(8·2)*
Torpedo tubes: 4—21 inch *(533 mm)* amidships
A/S weapons: SUBROC and A/S torpedoes
Main machinery: 1 pressurised water-cooled S5G (General Electric) reactor. 2 steam turbines; 17 000 shp; 1 shaft
Speed, knots: 20+ surfaced; 30+ dived
Complement: 107 (12 officers, 95 enlisted men)

Authorised in the Fiscal Year 1964 new construction programme.

Design: The *Narwhal* is similar to the "Sturgeon" class submarines in hull design.

Electronics: Mk 113 Mod 6 torpedo fire control system. To be replaced by Mk 117 system.

Engineering: The *Narwhal* is fitted with the prototype seagoing S5G natural circulation reactor plant. According to Admiral H. G. Rickover the natural circulation reactor "offers promise of increased reactor plant reliability, simplicity, and noise reduction due to the elimination of the need for large reactor coolant pumps and associated electrical and control equipment by taking maximum advantage of natural convection to circulate the reactor coolant".

The Atomic Energy Commission's Knolls Atomic Power Laboratory was given prime responsibility for development of the power plant. Construction of a land-based prototype plant began in May 1961 at the National Reactor Testing Station in Idaho. The reactor achieved initial criticality on 12 Sep 1965.

Sonar: BQS-8 upward-looking sonar for under-ice work (photo). BQQ-2 system (BQS-6 active and BQR-7 passive). BQS-6 is fitted in a 15 foot sphere and BQR-7 with conformal hydrophone array forward.

NARWHAL   *2/1974, USN*

37 "STURGEON" CLASS (SSN)

Name	No.	Builders	Laid down	Launched	Commissioned
*STURGEON	SSN 637	General Dynamics (Electric Boat)	10 Aug 1963	26 Feb 1966	3 Mar 1967
*WHALE	SSN 638	General Dynamics (Quincy)	27 May 1964	14 Oct 1966	12 Oct 1968
*TAUTOG	SSN 639	Ingalls Shipbuilding Corp	27 Jan 1964	15 April 1967	17 Aug 1968
*GRAYLING	SSN 646	Portsmouth Naval Shipyard	12 May 1964	22 June 1967	11 Oct 1969
*POGY	SSN 647	Ingalls Shipbuilding Corp	4 May 1964	3 June 1967	15 May 1971
*ASPRO	SSN 648	Ingalls Shipbuilding Corp	23 Nov 1964	29 Nov 1967	20 Feb 1969
*SUNFISH	SSN 649	General Dynamics (Quincy)	15 Jan 1965	14 Oct 1966	15 Mar 1969
*PARGO	SSN 650	General Dynamics (Electric Boat)	3 June 1964	17 Sep 1966	5 Jan 1968
*QUEENFISH	SSN 651	Newport News SB & DD Co	11 May 1965	25 Feb 1966	6 Dec 1966
*PUFFER	SSN 652	Ingalls Shipbuilding Corp	8 Feb 1965	30 Mar 1968	9 Aug 1969
*RAY	SSN 653	Newport News SB & DD Co	1 April 1965	21 June 1966	12 April 1967
*SAND LANCE	SSN 660	Portsmouth Naval Shipyard	15 Jan 1965	11 Nov 1969	25 Sep 1971
*LAPON	SSN 661	Newport News SB & DD Co	26 July 1965	16 Dec 1966	14 Dec 1967
*GURNARD	SSN 662	San Francisco NSY (Mare Island)	22 Dec 1964	20 May 1967	6 Dec 1968
*HAMMERHEAD	SSN 663	Newport News SB & DD Co	29 Nov 1965	14 April 1967	28 June 1968
*SEA DEVIL	SSN 664	Newport News SB & DD Co	12 April 1966	5 Oct 1967	30 Jan 1969
*GUITARRO	SSN 665	San Francisco NSY (Mare Island)	9 Dec 1965	27 July 1968	9 Sep 1972
*HAWKBILL	SSN 666	San Francisco NSY (Mare Island)	12 Sep 1966	12 April 1969	4 Feb 1971
*BERGALL	SSN 667	General Dynamics (Electric Boat)	16 April 1966	17 Feb 1968	13 June 1969
*SPADEFISH	SSN 668	Newport News SB & DD Co	21 Dec 1966	15 May 1968	14 Aug 1969
*SEAHORSE	SSN 669	General Dynamics (Electric Boat)	13 Aug 1966	15 June 1968	19 Sep 1969
*FINBACK	SSN 670	Newport News SB & DD Co	26 June 1967	7 Dec 1968	4 Feb 1970
*PINTADO	SSN 672	San Francisco NSY (Mare Island)	27 Oct 1967	16 Aug 1969	11 Sep 1971
*FLYING FISH	SSN 673	General Dynamics (Electric Boat)	30 June 1967	17 May 1969	29 April 1970
*TREPANG	SSN 674	General Dynamics (Electric Boat)	28 Oct 1967	27 Sep 1969	14 Aug 1970
*BLUEFISH	SSN 675	General Dynamics (Electric Boat)	13 Mar 1968	10 Jan 1970	8 Jan 1971
*BILLFISH	SSN 676	General Dynamics (Electric Boat)	20 Sep 1968	1 May 1970	12 Mar 1971
*DRUM	SSN 677	San Francisco NSY (Mare Island)	20 Aug 1968	23 May 1970	15 April 1972
*ARCHERFISH	SSN 678	General Dynamics (Electric Boat)	19 June 1969	16 Jan 1971	17 Dec 1971
*SILVERSIDES	SSN 679	General Dynamics (Electric Boat)	13 Oct 1969	4 June 1971	5 May 1972
*WILLIAM H. BATES	SSN 680	Ingalls Shipbuilding (Litton)	4 Aug 1969	11 Dec 1971	5 May 1973
*BATFISH	SSN 681	General Dynamics (Electric Boat)	9 Feb 1970	9 Oct 1971	1 Sep 1972
*TUNNY	SSN 682	Ingalls Shipbuilding (Litton)	22 May 1970	10 June 1972	26 Jan 1974
*PARCHE	SSN 683	Ingalls Shipbuilding (Litton)	10 Dec 1970	13 Jan 1973	17 Aug 1974
*CAVALLA	SSN 684	General Dynamics (Electric Boat)	4 June 1970	19 Feb 1972	9 Feb 1973
*L. MENDEL RIVERS	SSN 686	Newport News SB & DD Co	26 June 1971	2 June 1973	1 Feb 1975
*RICHARD B. RUSSELL	SSN 687	Newport News SB & DD Co	19 Oct 1971	12 Jan 1974	16 Aug 1975

Displacement, tons: 3 640 standard; 4 640 dived
Length, feet (metres): 292·2 *(89·0)* oa (see Design notes)
Beam, feet (metres): 31·7 *(9·5)*
Draught, feet (metres): 26 *(7·9)*
Torpedo tubes: 4—21 inch *(533 mm)* Mk 63 amidships
A/S weapons: SUBROC and A/S torpedoes
Main machinery: 1 pressurised-water cooled S5W (Westinghouse) reactor; 2 steam turbines; 15 000 shp; 1 shaft
Speed, knots: 20+ surfaced; 30+ dived
Complement: 107 (12 officers, 95 enlisted men)

The 37 "Sturgeon" class attack submarines comprise the largest US Navy group of nuclear-powered ships built to the same design to date.
They are similar in design to the previous "Thresher" class but are slightly larger. SSN 637-639 were authorised in the Fiscal Year 1962 new construction programme. SSN 646-653 in FY 1963, SSN 660-664 in FY 1964, SSN 665-670 in FY 1965, SSN 672-677 in FY 1966, SSN 678-682 in FY 1967, SSN 683-684 in FY 1968, and SSN 686-687 in FY 1969.

Construction: The *Pogy* was begun by the New York Shipbuilding Corp (Camden, New Jersey), contract with whom was terminated on 5 June 1967; contract for completion awarded to Ingalls Shipbuilding Corp on 7 Dec 1967.
The *Guitarro* sank in 35 feet of water on 15 May 1969 while being fitted out at the San Francisco Bay Naval Shipyard. According to a congressional report, the sinking, caused by Shipyard workers, was "wholly avoidable". Subsequently raised; damage estimated at $25 000 000. Completion delayed more than two years.

Design: These submarines are slightly larger than the previous "Thresher" class and can be identified by their taller sail structure and the lower position of their diving planes on the sail (to improve control at periscope depth). Sail height is 20 feet, 6 inches above deck. Sail-mounted diving planes rotate to vertical for breaking through ice when surfacing in arctic regions. These submarines probably are slightly slower than the previous "Thresher" and "Skipjack" classes because of their increased size with the same propulsion system as in the earlier classes.
SSN 678/684, 686 and 687 are ten feet longer than remainder of class to accommodate extra sonar and electronic gear.

Electronics: Mk 113 torpedo fire control system.

Radar: BPS 14 Search.

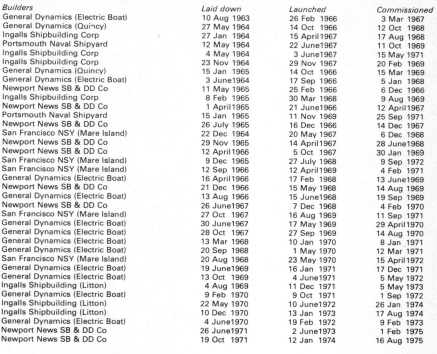

HAWKBILL
2/1977, Dr. Giorgio Arra

RICHARD B. RUSSELL
6/1975, USN

CAVALLA
8/1976, JLM van der Burg

Sonar: BQQ-2 sonar system. Principal components of the BQQ-2 include the BQS-6 active sonar, with transducers mounted in a 15-foot diameter sonar sphere, and BQR-7 passive sonar, with hydrophones in a conformal array on sides of forward hull. The active sonar sphere is fitted in the optimum bow position, requiring placement of torpedo tubes amidships. These submarines also have BQS-8 under-ice sonar and BQS-12 (first 16 units) or BQS-13 active/passive sonars. Transducers for the BQS-8, intended primarily for under-ice navigation, are in two small domes aft of the sail structure.
Sonar suites of the *Guitarro* and *Cavalla* have been modified. All "Sturgeon" class submarines are to be refitted with replacement of the BQQ-2 by BQQ-5 during regular overhauls.

Operational: The *Whale, Pargo,* and older nuclear submarine *Sargo* conducted exercises in the Arctic ice pack during March-April 1969. The *Whale* surfaced at the geographic North Pole on April 6, the 60th anniversary of Rear Admiral Robert E. Peary's reaching the North Pole. This was the first instance of single-screw US nuclear submarines surfacing in the Arctic ice.

Submersibles: The *Hawkbill* has been modified to carry and support the Navy's Deep Submergence Rescue Vehicles (DSRV). See section on Deep Submergence Vehicles for additional DSRV details.

RICHARD B. RUSSELL   *1975, Newport News SB & DD Co*

POGY   *1973, USN*

HAWKBILL with DSRV-1 and fluorescent sail markings to assist DSRV   *1971, USN*

PERMIT ("Thresher" class)   *1970, USN*

13 "THRESHER" CLASS (SSN)

Name	No.	Builders	Laid down	Launched	Commissioned
*PERMIT	SSN 594	Mare Island Naval Shipyard	16 July 1959	1 July 1961	29 May 1962
*PLUNGER	SSN 595	Mare Island Naval Shipyard	2 Mar 1960	9 Dec 1961	21 Nov 1962
*BARB	SSN 596	Ingalls Shipbuilding Corp	9 Nov 1959	12 Feb 1962	24 Aug 1963
*POLLACK	SSN 603	New York Shipbuilding Corp	14 Mar 1960	17 Mar 1962	26 May 1964
*HADDO	SSN 604	New York Shipbuilding Corp	9 Sep 1960	18 Aug 1962	16 Dec 1964
*JACK	SSN 605	Portsmouth Naval Shipyard	16 Sep 1960	24 Apr 1963	31 Mar 1967
*TINOSA	SSN 606	Portsmouth Naval Shipyard	24 Nov 1959	9 Dec 1961	17 Oct 1964
*DACE	SSN 607	Ingalls Shipbuilding Corp	6 June 1960	18 Aug 1962	4 Apr 1964
*GUARDFISH	SSN 612	New York Shipbuilding Corp	28 Feb 1961	15 May 1965	20 Dec 1966
*FLASHER	SSN 613	General Dynamics (Electric Boat)	14 Apr 1961	22 June 1963	22 July 1966
*GREENLING	SSN 614	General Dynamics (Electric Boat)	15 Aug 1961	4 Apr 1964	3 Nov 1967
*GATO	SSN 615	General Dynamics (Electric Boat)	15 Dec 1961	14 May 1964	25 Jan 1968
*HADDOCK	SSN 621	Ingalls Shipbuilding Corp	24 Apr 1961	21 May 1966	22 Dec 1967

Displacement, tons: 3 750 standard; *Flasher, Greenling* and *Gato* 3 800; 4 300 dived except *Jack* 4 470 dived, *Flasher, Greenling* and *Gato* 4 242 dived
Length, feet (metres): 278·5 *(84·9)* oa except *Jack* 297·4 *(90·7), Flasher, Greenling* and *Gato* 292·2 *(89·1)*
Beam, feet (metres): 31·7 *(9·6)*
Draught, feet (metres): 28·4 *(8·7)*
Torpedo tubes: 4—21 inch *(533 mm)* Mk 63 amidships
A/S weapons: SUBROC and A/S torpedoes
Main machinery: 1 pressurised-water cooled S5W (Westinghouse) reactor; 2 steam turbines, 15 000 shp; 1 shaft
Speed, knots: 20+ surfaced; 30+ dived
Complement: 103 (12 officers, 91 enlisted men)

PLUNGER   *12/1976, Dr. Giorgio Arra*

They have a greater depth capability than previous nuclear-powered submarines and are the first to combine the SUBROC anti-submarine missile capability with the advanced BQQ-2 sonar system. The lead ship of the class, the *Thresher* (SSN 593), was authorised in the Fiscal Year 1957 new construction programme, the SSN 594-596 in FY 1958. SSN 603-607 in FY 1959, SSN 612-615 in FY 1960, and SSN 621 in FY 1961.
The *Thresher* (SSN 593) was lost off the coast of New England on 10 Apr 1963 while on post-overhaul trials. She went down with 129 men on board (108 crewmen plus four naval officers and 17 civilians on board for trials).

Construction: *Greenling* and *Gato* were launched by the Electric Boat Division of the General Dynamics Corp (Groton, Connecticut); towed to Quincy Division (Massachusetts) for lengthening and completion.

Design: The *Jack* was built to a modified design to test a modified power plant (see *Engineering* notes).
The *Flasher, Gato* and *Greenling* were modified during construction; fitted with SUBSAFE features, heavier machinery, and larger sail structures.
These submarines have a modified "tear-drop" hull design. Their bows are devoted to sonar and their four torpedo tubes are amidships, angled out, two to port and two to starboard. The sail structure height of these submarines is 13 feet 9 inches to 15 feet above the deck, with later submarines of this class having a sail height of 20 feet.

Electronics: These submarines have the Mk 113 Mod 6 torpedo fire control system.

Engineering: The *Jack* is fitted with two propellers on essentially one shaft (actually a single shaft within a sleeve-like shaft) and a counter-rotating turbine without a reduction gear. Both innovations are designed to reduce operating noises. To accommodate the larger turbine, the engine spaces were

BARB   *1973, USN*

lengthened ten feet and the shaft structure was lengthened seven feet to mount the two propellers. The propellers are of different size and are smaller than in the other submarines of this class. Also eliminated in *Jack* was a clutch and secondary-propulsion electric motor.
The *Jack's* propulsion arrangement provides a ten per cent increase in power efficiency, but no increase in speed.

Names: Names changed during construction: *Plunger* ex-*Pollack; Barb* ex-*Pollack* ex-*Plunger; Pollack* ex-*Barb.*

Sonar: BQQ-2 (BQS-6 active and BQR-7 passive). The positioning of the conformal array for BQR-7 in the bow dictates the use of midships tubes.

1 "TULLIBEE" CLASS (SSN)

Name	No.	Builders	Laid down	Launched	Commissioned
*TULLIBEE	SSN 597	General Dynamics (Electric Boat)	26 May 1958	27 April 1960	9 Nov 1960

Displacement, tons: 2 317 standard; 2 640 dived
Length, feet (metres): 273 *(83·2)* oa
Beam, feet (metres): 23·3 *(7·1)*
Draught, feet (metres): 21 *(6·4)*
Torpedo tubes: 4—21 inch *(533 mm)* Mk 64 amidships
A/S weapons: A/S torpedoes
Main machinery: 1 pressurised-water cooled S2C (Combustion Engineering) reactor; Turbo-electric drive with steam turbine (Westinghouse); 2 500 shp; 1 shaft
Speed, knots: 15 surfaced; 20+ dived
Complement: 56 (6 officers, 50 enlisted men)

The *Tullibee* was designed specifically for anti-submarine operations and was the first US submarine with the optimum bow position devoted entirely to sonar. No additional submarine of this type was constructed because of the success of the larger, more-versatile "Thresher" class. The *Tullibee* was authorised in the Fiscal Year 1958 new construction programme. She is no longer considered a "first line" submarine.

Design: She has a modified, elongated "tear-drop" hull design. Originally she was planned as a 1 000-ton craft, but reactor requirements and other considerations increased her size during design and construction.
Her four amidships torpedo tubes are angled out from the centreline two to port and two to starboard. Not fitted to fire SUBROC.

Electronics: Mk 112 Mod 3 torpedo fire control system.

Engineering: She has a small nuclear power plant designed and developed by the Combustion Engineering Company. The propulsion system features turbo-electric drive rather than conventional steam turbines with reduction gears in an effort to reduce operating noises.

Navigation: Fitted with Ships Inertial Navigation System (SINS).

Sonar: BQQ-2 system (BQS-6 active and BQR-7 passive) the first submarine so fitted.
BQG-4 passive (PUFFS—Passive Underwater Fire Control Feasibility System) with three (originally two) domes on top of hull.

TULLIBEE   *1968, USN*

5 "SKIPJACK" CLASS (SSN)

Name	No.	Builders	Laid down	Launched	Commissioned
*SKIPJACK	SSN 585	General Dynamics (Electric Boat)	29 May 1956	26 May 1958	15 April 1959
*SCAMP	SSN 588	Mare Island Naval Shipyard	23 Jan 1959	8 Oct 1960	5 June 1961
*SCULPIN	SSN 590	Ingalls Shipbuilding Corp	3 Feb 1958	31 Mar 1960	1 June 1961
*SHARK	SSN 591	Newport News SB & DD Co	24 Feb 1958	16 Mar 1960	9 Feb 1961
*SNOOK	SSN 592	Ingalls Shipbuilding Corp	7 April 1958	31 Oct 1960	24 Oct 1961

Displacement, tons: 3 075 surfaced; 3 513 dived
Length, feet (metres): 251·7 (76·7) oa
Beam, feet (metres): 31·5 (9·6)
Draught, feet (metres): 29·4 (8·9)
Torpedo tubes: 6—21 inch (533 mm) bow
A/S weapons: A/S torpedoes
Main machinery: 1 pressurised-water cooled S5W (Westinghouse) reactor; 2 steam turbines (Westinghouse in Skipjack; General Electric in others); 15 000 shp; 1 shaft
Speed, knots: 16 surfaced; 30+ dived
Complement: 93 (8 officers, 85 enlisted men)

Combine the high-speed endurance of nuclear propulsion with the high-speed "tear-drop" "Albacore" hull design. The Skipjack was authorised in the Fiscal Year 1956 new construction programme and the five other submarines of this class were authorised in FY 1957.

These submarines are still considered suitable for "first line" service. Officially described as fastest US nuclear submarines in service.

Each cost approximately $40 000 000.

The Scorpion (SSN 589) of this class was lost some 400 miles southwest of the Azores while en route from the Mediterranean to Norfolk, Virginia, in May 1968. She went down with 99 men on board.

Construction: The Scorpion's keel was laid down twice; the original keel, laid down on 1 Nov 1957, was renumbered SSBN 598 and became the Polaris submarine George Washington; the second SSN 589 keel became the Scorpion. The Scamp's keel laying was delayed when materiel for her was diverted to the SSBN 599. This class introduced the Newport News Shipbuilding and Dry Dock Company and the Ingalls Shipbuilding Corporation to nuclear submarine construction. Newport News had not previously built submarines since before World War I.

Design: The Skipjack was the first US nuclear submarine built to the "tear-drop" design. These submarines have a single propeller shaft (vice two in earlier nuclear submarines) and their diving planes are mounted on sail structures to improve underwater manoeuvrability. No after torpedo tubes are fitted because of their tapering sterns.

Electronics: Skipjack fitted with Mk 101 Mod 20 torpedo fire control system; others with Mk 101 Mod 17.

Engineering: The "Skipjack" class introduced the S5W fast attack submarine propulsion plant which has been employed in all subsequent US attack and ballistic missile submarines except the "Los Angeles" class (SSN 688) Narwhal (SSN 671) and Glenard P. Lipscomb (SSN 685). The plant was developed by the Bettis Atomic Power Laboratory.

Sonar: Modified BQS-4.

SCAMP   12/1976, Dr. Giorgio Arra

SCAMP   12/1976, Dr. Giorgio Arra

SCAMP   12/1976, Dr. Giorgio Arra

1 "HALIBUT" CLASS (SSN)

Name	No.	Builders	Laid down	Launched	Commissioned
HALIBUT	SSN 587 (ex-SSGN 587)	Mare Island Naval Shipyard, Vallejo, Calif.	11 April 1957	9 Jan 1959	4 Jan 1960

Displacement, tons: 3 850 standard; 5 000 dived
Length, feet (metres): 350 (106·6) oa
Beam, feet (metres): 29·5 (8·9)
Draught, feet (metres): 21·5 (6·5)
Torpedo tubes: 6—21 inch (533 mm) 4 bow; 2 stern
Main machinery: 1 pressurised-water cooled S3W (Westinghouse) reactor; 2 steam turbines (Westinghouse); 6 600 shp; 2 shafts
Speed, knots: 15 surfaced; 20+ dived
Complement: 98 (10 officers, 88 enlisted men)

The *Halibut* is believed to have been the first submarine designed and constructed specifically to fire guided missiles. She was originally intended to have diesel-electric propulsion but on 27 Feb 1956 the Navy announced she would have nuclear propulsion. She was the US Navy's only nuclear-powered guided missile submarine (SSGN) to be completed. Authorised in the Fiscal Year 1956 new construction programme and built

for an estimated cost of $45 000 000.
She was reclassified as an attack submarine on 25 July 1965 after the Navy discarded the Regulus submarine-launched missile force. Her missile equipment was removed. Reportedly She has been fitted with a ducted bow thruster to permit precise control and manoeuvring.
She can carry the 50-foot Deep Submergence Rescue Vehicle (DSRV) and other submersibles on her after deck and operate these while dived.
Decommissioned on 30 June 1976. Now in reserve.

Design: Built with a large missile hangar faired into her bow (see photo). Her hull was intended primarily to provide a stable surface launching platform rather than for speed or manoeuvrabilty.

Electronics: Mk 101 Mod 12 torpedo fire control system.

Missiles: Designed to carry two Regulus II surface-to-surface

missiles. The Regulus II was a transonic missile which could carry a nuclear warhead and had a range of 1 000 miles. The Regulus II was cancelled before becoming operational and the *Halibut* operated from 1960 to 1964 carrying five Regulus I missiles, subsonic cruise missiles which could deliver a nuclear warhead on targets 575 nautical miles from launch.
During this period the US Navy operated a maximum of five Regulus guided (cruise) missile submarines, the *Halibut*, the post-war constructed *Grayback* (SSG 574 now LPSS 574) and *Growler* (SSG 577), and the World War II-built *Tunny* (SSG 282 subsequently LPSS 282) and *Barbero* (SSG 317).
As SSGN *Halibut* carried a complement of 11 officers and 108 enlisted men.

Navigation: Fitted with Ship's Inertial Navigation System (SINS).

Sonar: BQS-4.

HALIBUT

1970, USN

1 "TRITON" CLASS (SSN)

Name	No.	Builders	Laid down	Launched	Commissioned
TRITON	SSN 586 (ex-SSRN 586)	General Dynamics (Electric Boat)	29 May 1956	19 Aug 1958	10 Nov 1959

Displacement, tons: 5 940 surfaced; 6 670 dived
Length, feet (metres): 447·5 (136·3) oa
Beam, feet (metres): 37 (11·3)
Draught, feet (metres): 24 (7·3)
Torpedo tubes: 6—21 inch (533 mm) Mk 60 4 bow; 2 stern
Main machinery: 2 pressurised-water cooled S4G (General Electric) reactors; 2 steam turbines (General Electric); 34 000 shp; 2 shafts
Speed, knots: 27+ surfaced; 20+ dived
Complement as SSRN: 170 (14 officers, 156 enlisted men)

The *Triton* was designed and constructed to serve as a radar picket submarine to operate in conjunction with surface carrier task forces.

Authorised in the Fiscal Year 1956 new construction programme and built for an estimated cost of $109 000 000.
The *Triton* circumnavigated the globe in 1960, remaining submerged except when her sail structure broke the surface to enable an ill sailor to be taken off near the Falkland Islands. The 41 500-mile cruise took 83 days and was made at an average speed of 18 knots.
Reclassified as an attack submarine (SSN) on 1 Mar 1961 as the Navy dropped the radar picket submarine programme. She is no longer considered a "first line" submarine and was decommissioned on 3 May 1969 to become the first US nuclear submarine placed in preservation.
There had been proposals to operate the *Triton* as an underwater national command post afloat, but no funds were provided.

Design: *Triton* was fitted with an elaborate combat information centre and large radar antenna which retracted into the sail structure. Until the Trident SSBN programme the *Triton* was the longest US submarine ever constructed.

Electronics: Mk 101 Mod 11 torpedo fire control system.

Engineering: The *Triton* is the only US submarine with two nuclear reactors. The Atomic Energy Commission's Knolls Atomic Power Laboratory was given prime responsibility for development of the power plant. After 2½ years of operation, during which she steamed more than 110 000 miles, the *Triton* was overhauled and refuelled from July 1962 to March 1964.

Sonar: BQS-4.

TRITON

1959, USN

4 "SKATE" CLASS (SSN)

Name	No.	Builders	Laid down	Launched	Commissioned
*SKATE	SSN 578	General Dynamics (Electric Boat)	21 July 1955	16 May 1957	23 Dec 1957
*SWORDFISH	SSN 579	Portsmouth Naval Shipyard	25 Jan 1956	27 Aug 1957	15 Sep 1958
*SARGO	SSN 583	Mare Island Naval Shipyard	21 Feb 1956	10 Oct 1957	1 Oct 1958
*SEADRAGON	SSN 584	Portsmouth Naval Shipyard	20 June 1956	16 Aug 1958	5 Dec 1959

Displacement, tons: 2 570 standard; 2 861 dived
Length, feet (metres): 267·7 (81·5) oa
Beam, feet (metres): 25 (7·6)
Draught, feet (metres): 22 (6·7)
Torpedo tubes: 8—21 inch (533 mm) 6 bow; 2 stern (short)
Main machinery: 1 pressurised-water cooled S3W (Westinghouse) reactor in Skate and Sargo, 1 pressurised-water cooled S4W (Westinghouse) in Swordfish and Seadragon; 2 steam turbines (Westinghouse); approx 6 600 shp; 2 shafts
Speed, knots: 20+ surfaced; 25+ dived
Complement: 95 (8 officers, 87 enlisted men)

The first production model nuclear-powered submarines, similar in design to the Nautilus but smaller. The Skate and Swordfish were authorised in the Fiscal Year 1955 new construction programme and the Sargo and Seadragon in FY 1956.
The Skate was the first submarine to make a completely submerged transatlantic crossing. In 1958 she established a (then) record of 31 days submerged with a sealed atmosphere, on 11 Aug 1958 she passed under the North Pole during a polar cruise, and on 17 Mar 1959 she became the first submarine to surface at the North Pole. The Sargo undertook a polar cruise during January-February 1960 and surfaced at the North Pole on 9 Feb 1960.
The Seadragon sailed from the Atlantic to the Pacific via the Northwest Passage (Lancaster Sound, Barrow and McClure Straits) in August 1960. The Skate, operating from New London, Connecticut and the Seadragon, based at Pearl Harbour, rendezvoused under the North Pole on 2 Aug 1962 and then conducted anti-submarine exercises under the polar ice pack and surfaced together at the North Pole.
The Skate also operated in the Arctic Ocean during April-May 1969, conducting exercises under the Arctic ice pack with the later nuclear-powered attack submarines Pargo and Whale; and again during the spring of 1971 with the nuclear attack submarine Trepang.

Electronics: Skate and Seadragon fitted with Mk 101 Mod 19 torpedo fire control system; Swordfish and Sargo have Mk 101 Mod 15.

Engineering: The reactors for this class were developed by the Atomic Energy Commission's Bettis Atomic Power Laboratory, the new propulsion system was similar to that of the Nautilus but considerably simplified with improved operation and maintenance. The propulsion plant developed under this programme had two arrangements, the S3W configuration in the Skate, Sargo and Halibut and the S4W configuration in the Swordfish and Seadragon. Both arrangements proved satisfactory. The Skate began her first overhaul and refuelling in January 1961 after steaming 120 862 miles on her initial reactor core during three years of operation. The Swordfish began her first overhaul and refuelling in early 1962 after more than three years of operation in which time she steamed 112 000 miles.

Sonar: BQS-4.

SWORDFISH   1970, USN

1 "SEAWOLF" CLASS (SSN)

Name	No.	Builders	Laid down	Launched	Commissioned
*SEAWOLF	SSN 575	General Dynamics (Electric Boat)	15 Sep 1953	21 July 1955	30 Mar 1957

Displacement, tons: 3 765 standard; 4 200 dived
Length, feet (metres): 337·5 (102·9) oa
Beam, feet (metres): 27·7 (8·4)
Draught, feet (metres): 23 (7)
Torpedo tubes: 6—21 inch (533 mm) bow
Main machinery: 1 pressurised-water cooled S2Wa (Westinghouse) reactor; 2 steam turbines (General Electric), 15 000 shp; 2 shafts
Speed, knots: 20+ surfaced; 20+ dived
Complement: 101 (11 officers, 90 enlisted men)

The Seawolf was the world's second nuclear-propelled vehicle; she was constructed almost simultaneously with the Nautilus to test a competitive reactor design. Funds for the Seawolf were authorised in the Fiscal Year 1952 new construction programme.
She is no longer considered a "first line" submarine and has been engaged primarily in research work since 1969.

Design: GUPPY-type hull with stepped sail.

Electronics: Mk 101 Mod 8 torpedo fire control system.

Engineering: Initial work in the development of naval nuclear propulsion plants investigated a number of concepts, two of which were of sufficient interest to warrant full development: the pressurised water and liquid metal (sodium). The Nautilus was provided with a pressurised-water reactor plant and the Seawolf was fitted initially with a liquid-metal reactor. Originally known as the Submarine Intermediate Reactor (SIR), the liquid-metal plant was developed by the Atomic Energy Commission's Knolls Atomic Power Laboratory.
The SIR Mark II/S2G reactor in the Seawolf achieved initial criticality on 25 June 1956. Steam leaks developed during the dockside testing. The plant was shut down and it was determined that the leaks were caused by sodium-potassium alloy which had entered the super-heater steam piping. After repairs and testing the Seawolf began sea trials on 21 Jan 1957. The trials were run at reduced power and after two years of operation the Seawolf entered the Electric Boat yard for removal of her sodium-cooled plant and installation of a pressurised-water plant similar to that installed in the Nautilus (designated S2Wa). When the original Seawolf plant was shut down in December 1958 the submarine had steamed a total of 71 611 miles. She was recommissioned on 30 Sep 1960. The pressurised-water reactor was refuelled for the first time between May 1965 and August 1967, having propelled the Seawolf for more than 161 000 miles on its initial fuel core.

Sonar: BQS-4.

SEAWOLF   1974, William Whalen, Jr.

1 "NAUTILUS" CLASS (SSN)

Name	No.
*NAUTILUS	SSN 571

Displacement, tons: 3 764 surfaced; 4 040 dived
Length, feet (metres): 319·4 *(97·4)*
Beam, feet (metres): 27·6 *(8·4)*
Draught, feet (metres): 22 *(6·7)*
Torpedo tubes: 6—21 inch *(533 mm)* bow
Main machinery: 1 pressurised-water cooled S2W (Westinghouse) reactor; 2 steam turbines (Westinghouse), approx 15 000 shp; 2 shafts
Speed, knots: 20+ surfaced; 20+ dived
Complement: 105 (13 officers, 92 enlisted men)

Builders	Laid down	Launched	Commissioned
General Dynamics (Electric Boat)	14 June 1952	21 Jan 1954	30 Sep 1954

NAUTILUS   *1975, General Dynamics, Electric Boat Division*

The *Nautilus* was the world's first nuclear-propelled vehicle. She predated the first Soviet nuclear-powered submarine by an estimated five years.

The funds for her construction were authorised in the Fiscal Year 1952 budget. She put to sea for the first time on 17 Jan 1955 and signalled the historic message: "Underway on nuclear power".

On her shakedown cruise in May 1955 she steamed submerged from London, Connecticut, to San Juan, Puerto Rico, travelling more than 1 300 miles in 84 hours at an average speed of almost 16 knots; she later steamed submerged from Key West, Florida, to New London, a distance of 1 397 miles, at an average speed of more than 20 knots.

During 1958 she undertook extensive operations under the Arctic ice pack and in August she made history's first polar transit from the Pacific to the Atlantic, steaming from Pearl Harbour to Portland, England. She passed under the geographic North Pole on 3 Aug 1958.

During 1972-74 she underwent a 30-month overhaul and modification at the Electric Boat yard in Groton, Connecticut, where the submarine was built. Modified for submarine communications research. Due to decommission in FY 1979.

Design: She has a GUPPY-type hull.

Electronics: Mk 101 Mod 6 torpedo fire control system.

Engineering: In January 1948 the Department of Defense requested the Atomic Energy Commission to undertake the design, development, and construction of a nuclear reactor for submarine propulsion. Initial research and conceptual design of the Submarine Thermal Reactor (STR) was undertaken by the Argonne National Laboratory. Subsequently the Atomic Energy Commission's Bettis Atomic Power Laboratory, operated by the Westinghouse Electric Corporation, undertook development of the first nuclear propulsion plant.

The *Nautilus* STR Mark II nuclear plant (redesignated S2W) was first operated on 20 Dec 1954 and first developed full power on 3 Jan 1955.

After more than two years of operation, during which she steamed 62 562 miles, she began an overhaul which included refuelling in April 1957. She was again refuelled in 1959 after steaming 91 324 miles on her second fuel core, and again in 1964 after steaming approximately 150 000 miles on her third fuel core.

Sonar: BQS-4.

NAUTILUS   *1975, General Dynamics, Electric Boat Division*

3 "BARBEL" CLASS (SS)

Name	No.
*BARBEL	SS 580
*BLUEBACK	SS 581
*BONEFISH	SS 582

Displacement, tons: 2 146 surfaced; 2 894 dived
Length, feet (metres): 219·5 *(66·8)* oa
Beam, feet (metres): 29 *(8·8)*
Draught, feet (metres): 28 *(8·5)*
Torpedo tubes: 6—21 inch *(533 mm)* Mk 58 bow
Main machinery: 3 diesels; 4 800 bhp (Fairbanks Morse); 2 electric motors (General Electric); 3 150 shp; 1 shaft
Speed, knots: 15 on surfaced; 21 dived
Complement: 77 (8 officers, 69 men)

Builders	Laid down	Launched	Commissioned
Portsmouth Naval Shipyard	18 May 1956	19 July 1958	17 Jan 1959
Ingalls Shipbuilding Corporation	15 April 1957	16 May 1959	15 Oct 1959
New York Shipbuilding Corp	3 June 1957	22 Nov 1958	9 July 1959

These submarines were the last non-nuclear combatant submarines built by the US Navy. All three were authorised in the Fiscal Year 1956 new construction programme.

Construction: The *Blueback* was the first submarine built by the Ingalls Shipbuilding Corp at Pascagoula, Mississippi, and the *Bonefish* was the first constructed at the New York Shipbuilding Corp yard in Camden, New Jersey. None of the three shipyards that built this class is now employed in submarine construction.

Design: These submarines have the "tear drop" hull design which was tested in the experimental submarine *Albacore*. As built, their fore planes were bow-mounted; subsequently moved to the sail.

They introduced a new concept in centralised arrangement of controls in an "attack centre" to increase efficiency; which has been adapted for all later US combat submarines.

Electronics: Mk 101 Mod 20 torpedo fire control system.

Sonar: BQS-4.

BLUEBACK   *1967, USN*

1 "GRAYBACK" CLASS (LPSS/SS)

Name	No.	Builders	Laid down	Launched	Commissioned
*GRAYBACK	SS 574 (ex-LPSS 574, ex-SSG 574)	Mare Island Naval Shipyard	1 July 1954	2 July 1957	7 Mar 1958

Displacement, tons: 2 670 standard; 3 650 dived
Length, feet (metres): 334 (101·8) oa
Beam, feet (metres): 27 (8·2)
Draught, feet (metres): 19 (5·8)
Torpedo tubes: 8—21 inch (533 mm) 6 bow; 2 stern
Main machinery: 3 diesels (Fairbanks Morse); 4 500 bhp;
2 electric motors (Elliott); 5 500 shp; 2 shafts
Speed, knots: 20 surfaced; 16·7 dived
Complement: 88 (10 officers, 78 enlisted men)
Troops: 85 (10 officers, 75 enlisted men)

The Grayback has been fully converted to a transport submarine and is officially classified as an amphibious warfare ship. She was originally intended to be an attack submarine, being authorised in the Fiscal Year 1953 new construction programme, but redesigned in 1956 to provide a Regulus missile launching capability; completed as SSG 574 in 1958, similar in design to the Growler (SSG 577). See Growler listing for basic design notes.

Classification: The Grayback was reclassified as an attack submarine (SS) on 30 June 1975 although she retains her transport configuration and capabilities. The reclassification was an administrative change associated with funding support.

Conversion: She began conversion to a transport submarine at Mare Island in November 1967. The conversion was originally estimated at $15 200 000 but was actually about $30 000 000. She was reclassified from SSG to LPSS on 30 Aug 1968 (never officially designated APSS).
During conversion she was fitted to berth and mess 67 troops and carry their equipment including landing craft or swimmer delivery vehicles (SDV). Her torpedo tubes and hence attack capability are retained. As completed (SSG) she had an overall length of 322 ft 4 in; lengthened 12 ft during LPSS conversion. Conversion was authorised in Fiscal Year 1965 programme and completed with her new commissioning on 9 May 1969; delayed because of higher priorities being allocated to other submarine projects.

Electronics: Mk 106 Mod 12 torpedo fire control system.

Sonar: BQS-2; BQS-4 (PUFFS).

GRAYBACK   1958, USN

1 "GRAYBACK" CLASS (SSG)

Name	No.	Builders	Laid down	Launched	Commissioned
GROWLER	SSG 577	Portsmouth Naval Shipyard	15 Feb 1955	5 April 1958	30 Aug 1958

Displacement, tons: 2 540 standard; 3 515 dived
Length, feet (metres): 317·6 (96·8) oa
Beam, feet (metres): 27·2 (8·2)
Draught, feet (metres): 19 (5·8)
Torpedo tubes: 6—21 inch (533 mm) 4 bow; 2 stern
Main machinery: 3 diesels (Fairbanks Morse); 4 600 bhp;
2 electric motors (Elliott); 5 500 shp; 2 shafts
Speed, knots: 20 surfaced; approx 12 dived
Complement: 87 (9 officers, 78 enlisted men)

The Growler was authorised in the Fiscal Year 1955 new construction programme; completed as a guided missile submarine to fire the Regulus surface-to-surface cruise missile (see Halibut, SSN 587, for Missile notes).

When the Regulus submarine missile programme ended in 1964, the Growler and her near-sister Grayback were withdrawn from service, Growler being decommissioned on 25 May 1964. The Grayback was subsequently converted to an amphibious transport submarine (LPSS). The Growler was scheduled to undergo a similar conversion when the Grayback was completed, but the second conversion was deferred late in 1968 because of rising ship conversion costs.
The Growler is in reserve as an SSG.

Design: The Grayback and Growler were initially designed as attack submarines similar to the Darter. Upon redesign as missile submarines they were cut in half on the building ways and were lengthened approximately 50 feet, two cylindrical han-gars, each 11 feet high and 70 feet long, were superimposed on their bows, a missile launcher was installed between the hangars and sail structure, and elaborate navigation and fire control systems were fitted. The height of the sail structure on the Growler is approximately 30 feet above the deck; the Grayback's lower sail structure was increased during LPSS conversion.

Electronics: Mk 106 Mod 13 torpedo fire control system.

Sonar: BQS-4.

GROWLER   1975, USN

1 "DARTER" CLASS (SS)

Name	No.	Builders	Laid down	Launched	Commissioned
*DARTER	SS 576	General Dynamics (Electric Boat)	10 Nov 1954	28 May 1956	26 Oct 1956

Displacement, tons: 1 720 surfaced; 2 388 dived
Length, feet (metres): 284·5 (86·7)
Beam, feet (metres): 27·2 (8·3)
Draught, feet (metres): 19 (5·8)
Torpedo tubes: 8—21 inch (533 mm) 6 bow; 2 stern
Main machinery: 3 diesels (Fairbanks Morse); 4 500 bhp;
electric motors (Elliott); 5 500 shp; 2 shafts
Speed, knots: 19·5 surfaced; 14 dived
Complement: 85 (10 officers, 75 men)

Designed for high submerged speed with quiet machinery. Planned sister submarines *Growler* and *Grayback* were completed to missile-launching configuration.

Basic design of the *Darter* is similar to the "Tang" class described on a later page.

Authorised in Fiscal Year 1954 shipbuilding programme. No additional submarines of this type were built because of shift to high-speed hull design and nuclear propulsion.

Electronics: Mk 106 Mod 11 torpedo fire control system.

Sonar: BQG-4 (PUFFS).

DARTER   1967, Dr. Giorgio Arra

2 "SAILFISH" CLASS (SS)

Name	No.	Builders	Laid down	Launched	Commissioned
*SAILFISH	SS 572 (ex-SSR 572)	Portsmouth Naval Shipyard	8 Dec 1953	7 Sep 1955	14 April 1956
*SALMON	SS 573 (ex-AGSS 573, ex-SSR 573)	Portsmouth Naval Shipyard	10 Mar 1954	25 Feb 1956	25 Aug 1956

Displacement, tons: 2 625 standard; 3 168 dived
Length, feet (metres): 350·4 (106·8) oa
Beam, feet (metres): 28·4 (8·8)
Draught, feet (metres): 18 (5·5)
Torpedo tubes: 6—21 inch (533 mm) Mk 49 bow
Main machinery: 4 diesels (Fairbanks Morse); 6 000 bhp;
2 electric motors (Elliott); 8 200 shp; 2 shafts
Speed, knots: 19·5 surfaced; 14 submerged
Complement: 108 (12 officers, 96 enlisted men)

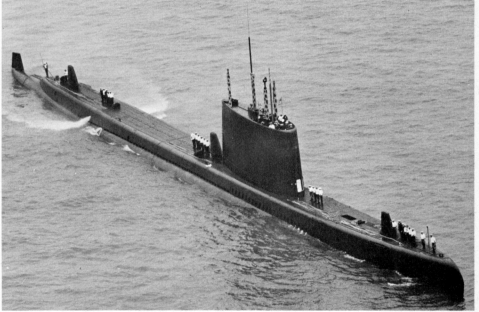

SALMON   1/1977, Dr. Giorgio Arra

The *Sailfish* and *Salmon* were built as radar picket submarines (SSR) with air search radars on their decks and elaborate aircraft control centres. Subsequently modified for "straight" attack operations. They were the largest non-nuclear submarines built by the US Navy since 1930 and are believed to tbe the largest conventional submarines now operated by any navy.

Both authorised in the Fiscal Year 1952 programme; both have been modernised under the FRAM II programme.

Salmon due for disposal in late 1977.

Classification: Reclassified from radar picket submarines (SSR) to SS on 1 Mar 1961; *Salmon* reclassified AGSS on 29 June 1968 to serve as test and evaluation submarine for Navy's Deep Submergence Rescue Vehicle (DSRV). However, the DSRV programme was delayed and the *Salmon* reverted to the SS designation on 30 June 1969.

Electronics: Mk 106 Mod 21 torpedo fire control system.

Sonar: BQG-4 (PUFFS).

SALMON   1/1977, Dr. Giorgio Arra

3 ATTACK SUBMARINES (SS) } "TANG" CLASS
1 AUXILIARY SUBMARINE (AGSS) }

Name	No.	Builders	Laid down	Launched	Commissioned
*TANG	AGSS 563	Portsmouth Naval Shipyard	18 April1949	19 June1951	25 Oct 1951
*WAHOO	SS 565	Portsmouth Naval Shipyard	24 Oct 1949	16 Oct 1951	30 May 1952
*TROUT	SS 566	Electric Boat Co, Groton	1 Dec 1949	21 Aug 1951	27 June1952
*GUDGEON	SS 567	Portsmouth Naval Shipyard	20 May 1950	11 June1952	21 Nov 1952

Displacement, tons: 2 100 standard; 2 700 dived
Length, feet (metres): 287 (87·4) oa
Beam, feet (metres): 27·3 (8·3)
Draught, feet (metres): 19 (6·2)
Torpedo tubes: 8—21 inch (533 mm) 6 bow; 2 stern
Main machinery: 3 diesels (Fairbanks Morse); 4 500 bhp;
  2 electric motors; 5 600 shp; 2 shafts
Speed, knots: 15·5 surfaced; 16 dived
Complement: 86 (11 officers, 75 men)

Six submarines of this class were constructed, incorporating improvements based on German World War II submarine developments. The *Tang* was authorised in the Fiscal Year 1947 new construction programme, *Wahoo* and *Trout* in FY 1948, and *Gudgeon* in FY 1949. The *Gudgeon* was the first US submarine to circumnavigate the world during Sep 1957-Feb 1958. All modernised under FRAM II programme.

Classification: The *Tang* was reclassified as a research submarine (AGSS) on 30 June 1975 for use in acoustic research. She replaces the *Tigrone* (AGSS 419) which had served in that role for two decades. The *Tang* was modified at the Mare Island Naval Shipyard from July 1975 to mid-1976.

Electronics: Mk 106 Mod 18 torpedo fire control system.

Engineering: *Tang, Trout* and *Wahoo* were originally powered by a compact, radial type engine produced after five years of development work, comprising a 16-cylinder 2-cycle plant, mounted vertically with four rows of cylinders radially arranged. These new engines were half the weight and two-thirds the size of the engines previously available for submarines. They proved to be unsatisfactory and were replaced by machinery similar to that in *Gudgeon* which has Fairbanks Morse high speed lightweight engines mounted horizontally.

Reconstruction: All six submarines of this class were built with an overall length of 269 ft 2 in. The units had their original diesel engines replaced during the late 1950s were cut in half and a 9 ft section inserted amidships. All six submarines were modernised during the 1960s with the installation of improved electronics equipment and other features; additional sections were added to give an overall length of 287 ft.

Sonar: BQG-4 (PUFFS).

Transfers: *Trigger* (SS 564) transferred to Italy on 10 July 1973; *Harder* (SS 568) transferred to Italy on 15 Mar 1974. (These were the first US submarines of past-World War II construction to be transferred to foreign navies). *Tang, Wahoo* and *Trout* to be transferred to Iran. When this takes place *Gudgeon* will replace *Tang* and be reclassified AGSS.

"TANG" Class   1974, William Whalen Jr.

GUDGEON   1970, USN

WAHOO   1968, USN

TROUT   3/1976, USN

1 "ALBACORE" CLASS (AGSS)

Name	No.	Builders	Laid down	Launched	Commissioned
ALBACORE	AGSS 569	Portsmouth Naval Shipyard	15 Mar 1952	1 Aug 1953	5 Dec 1953

Displacement, tons: 1 500 standard; 1 850 dived
Length, feet (metres): 210·5 (63·6) oa
Beam, feet (metres): 27·5 (8·4)
Draught, feet (metres): 18·5 (5·6)
Torpedo tubes: None
Main machinery: 2 diesels; radial pancake type (General Motors) electric motor (Westinghouse) 15 000 shp; 1 shaft
Speed, knots: 25 surfaced; 33 dived
Complement: 52 (5 officers, 47 men)

Built as a high-speed experimental submarine to test an advanced hull form. Officially described as a hydrodynamic

test vehicle. Streamlined, whale shaped hull without casing. Decommissioned and placed in reserve on 1 Sep 1972.

Experimental: She has been extensively modified to test advanced submarine design and engineering concepts.
Phase I modifications were made from July 1954 to February 1955 to eliminate the many bugs inherent with completely new construction and equipment.
Phase II modifications from Dec 1955 to Mar 1956 during which conventional propeller-rudder-stern diving plane arrangement was modified; the new design provided for the propeller to be installed aft of the control surfaces. (At this time a small auxiliary rudder on the sail was removed).

A concave bow sonar dome was fitted for tests in 1960. Phase III modifications from Nov 1960 to Aug 1961 during which an entirely new stern was installed featuring the stern planes in an "X" configuration, a system of ten hydraulic operated dive brakes around the hull amidships, a dorsal rudder, and a new bow sonar dome. Phase IV modifications from Dec 1962 to Mar 1965 during which a silver-zinc battery was installed and counter-rotating stern propellers rotating around the same axis were fitted.
The *Albacore* conducted trials with towed sonar arrays from May to July 1966.
All modifications were made at the Portsmouth Naval Shipyard.

ALBACORE   USN

1 "DOLPHIN" CLASS (AGSS)

Name	No.	Builders	Laid down	Launched	Commissioned
*DOLPHIN	AGSS 555	Portsmouth Naval Shipyard	9 Nov 1962	8 June 1968	17 Aug 1968

Displacement, tons: 800 standard; 930 full load
Length, feet (metres): 152 (46·3)
Beam, feet (metres): 19·3 (5·9)
Draught, feet (metres): 18 (5·5) (maximum)
Torpedo tubes: Removed
Main machinery: Diesel/electric (2 Detroit 12 V71 diesels), 1 500 hp; 1 shaft
Speed, knots: 12+ dived
Complement: 24 (3 officers, 21 enlisted men) plus 4 to 7 scientists

Specifically designed for deep-diving operations. Authorised in Fiscal Year 1961 new construction programme but delayed because of changes in mission and equipment coupled with higher priorities being given to other submarine projects. Fitted for deep-ocean sonar and oceanographic research. She is highly automated and has three computer-operated systems, a safety system, hovering system, and one that is classified. The

digital-computer submarine safety system monitors equipment and provides data on closed-circuit television screens; malfunctions in equipment or trends towards potentially dangerous situations set off an alarm and if they are not corrected within the prescribed time the system , unless overridden by an operator, automatically brings the submarine to the surface. There are several research stations for scientists and she is fitted to take water samples down to her operating depth. The single, experimental torpedo tube was removed in 1970. Underwater endurance is limited (endurance and habitability were considered of secondary importance in design). On 24 Nov 1968 she "descended to a depth greater than that recorded by any other operational submarine" according to official statements.
Assigned to Submarine Development Group 1 at San Diego.

Classification: The *Dolphin's* number was taken from a block (551-562) authorised but cancelled late in World War II with no construction being assigned.

Design: Has a constant diameter cylindrical pressure hull approximately 15 feet in outer diameter closed at both ends with hemispherical heads. Pressure hull fabricated of HY-80 steel with aluminium and fibre-glass used in secondary structures to reduce weight. No conventional hydroplanes are mounted, improved rudder design and other features provide manoeuvring control and hovering capability. Access is through a single hatch in the pressure hull (opening into sail structure).

Engineering: Fitted with 330 cell silver zinc battery. Submerged endurance is approximately 24 hours with an at-sea endurance of 14 days.

Status: Completed in early 1969, approximately five years behind official schedule at time of keel laying.

DOLPHIN   USN

1 "SEALION" CLASS (LPSS)

Name	No.	Builders	Laid down	Launched	Commissioned
SEALION	LPSS 315	Electric Boat Company, Groton	25 Feb 1943	31 Oct 1943	8 Mar 1944

Displacement, tons: 2 145 standard; 2 500 dived
Length, feet (metres): 311·5 *(95·0)*
Beam, feet (metres): 27 *(8·2)*
Draught, feet (metres): 17 *(5·2)*
Torpedo tubes: Removed
Guns: Removed
Main machinery: 2 diesels (General Motors), 2 305 bhp;
    4 electric motors (General Electric); 2 shafts
Speed, knots: 13 surfaced; 10 dived
Complement: 74 (6 officers, 68 men)
Troops: 160

Originally a "Balao" class submarine converted to underwater transport for carrying Marines, commandoes or seals. The *Sealion* was to have been replaced by conversion of the *Growler* (SSG 577) to a transport submarine; however, conversion of *Growler* was cancelled.
The *Sealion* is the sole survivor of the US Navy's large World War II submarine construction programme and was decommissioned and placed in reserve in Feb 1970.

Classification: Changed from SS to transport submarine (SSP) in March 1948; changed to auxiliary transport submarine (ASSP) in January 1950; changed to APSS in October 1956; changed again to amphibious transport submarine (LPSS) on 1 Jan 1969.

Conversion: Converted to a transport submarine at the San Francisco Naval Shipyard in 1948. All torpedo tubes and half of her diesel propulsion plant were removed to provide berthing for 160 troops; stowage provided for rubber rafts and other equipment in enlarged superstructure deck aft of conning tower.

Status: In 1960 the *Sealion* was assigned to operational reserve training duties; recommissioned late in 1961 with increase of US conventional warfare capabilities.

SEALION   1965, USN

GUPPY SUBMARINES

All 52 submarines modernised to the GUPPY (Greater Underwater Propulsion Project) configurations have been deleted or transferred to other navies. The last GUPPY submarines to serve with the US Navy were the *Clamagore* (SS 343) deleted on 27 June 1975 and *Tiru* (SS 416) deleted on 1 July 1975. They were not transferred to Turkey, as planned, but are scheduled for transfer in 1977.
Corrections to the comprehensive list of GUPPY submarine disposals and transfers provided in the 1974-1975 edition include: *Blenny* (SS 324) deleted on 15 Aug 1973 (sunk as target); *Sea Poacher* (SS 406) transferred to Peru on 1 July 1974; *Atule* (SS 403) transferred to Peru on 31 July 1974. *Tench* (SS 417) to Peru 16 Sep 1976 for spares.

DEEP SUBMERGENCE VEHICLES

The US Navy's Deep Submergence Vehicles (DSV) are listed in the Service Forces section of the United States Navy portion of this edition.

DIXON with submarines alongside   6/1976, J. L. M. van der Burg

AIRCRAFT CARRIERS

The US Navy currently operates 13 aircraft carriers: ten ships of post-World War II construction (including two nuclear powered) and three "Midway" class ships completed shortly after the war. In addition, an obsolescent "Intrepid" class ship serves as a training carrier.

Two additional nuclear carriers are under construction, the *Dwight D. Eisenhower* (CVN 69), to commission in 1977, and the *Carl Vinson* (CVN 70), to commission in 1981.

With the ever increasing size and costs of aircraft carriers, alternative designs to the "Nimitz" class have been sought to maintain a planned force level of 12 carriers beyond the mid-1980s when the first of the "Forrestal" class nears the end of its service life. Among the alternatives discussed was a concept known as "CVNX". A Navy study group, at the request of the then Secretary of Defense, James R. Schlesinger, was formed and directed to examine the feasibility of constructing "medium" size aircraft carriers of approx 50 000 tons standard displacement as an alternative to the "Nimitz" class. The group submitted its report in January 1976. Known collectively as the "CVNX" concept, it proposed three designs for further development (see the previous edition of Jane's, page 560, bottom for further details). This concept was later discarded. The current planned procurement of a fourth "Nimitz" class (CVN 71), for which long term lead items were requested under FY 1977, has been cancelled. The plan is to proceed as rapidly as possible with the design and construction of VSTOL carriers (CVVs), equipped with catapults (see below for further details on this class), as the successor to the "Nimitz" class design.

Air Wings: Each large aircraft carrier (CV/CVN) normally operates an air wing of some 85 to 95 aircraft: two fighter squadrons of 24 F-4 Phantom or F-14 Tomcats; two light attack squadrons of 24 A-7 Corsairs; one medium attack squadron of 12 A-6 Intruders; one anti-submarine squadron of 10 S-3 Viking aircraft; one A/S squadron of 8 SH-3 Sea King helicopters; and smaller squadrons or detachments of 3 RA-5C Vigilante reconnaissance aircraft, 4 EA-6B Prowler electronic warfare aircraft, 4 KA-6 Intruder tankers, and 4 E-2 Hawkeye early-warning/control aircraft.

The "Midway" class carriers cannot accommodate the full wing described above, and normally would not operate the Vigilante and Viking aircraft.

The carriers generally also embark a Carrier On-board Delivery (COD) aircraft in addition to the air wing.

Classification: From 1972 onward attack aircraft carriers (CVA) were reclassified as aircraft carriers (CV) upon being fitted with anti-submarine control centres and facilities to support A/S aircraft and helicopters (in addition to fighter/attack aircraft). The muti-purpose configuration was dictated by the phasing out of dedicated anti-submarine aircraft carriers (CVS), the last being decommissioned in 1974.

All active ships still classified as attack aircraft carriers (CVA/CVAN) on 30 June 1975 were changed to CV/CVN regardless of their ability to support anti-submarine aircraft.

They will serve past the year 2 000 and eventually replace the big super carriers.

While the new CVVs are being designed and constructed, beginning with the FY 1980 programme, the Carrier Service Life Extension Programme (SLEP) will be initiated. Each carrier, beginning with the *Forrestal* (CV 59), will undergo a two year modernisation and overhaul which is designed to extend each ship's life by 10-15 years. The below listed chart shows the long term implications of the SLEP programme. Also shown are the projected retirement dates of the ships after they have been through the SLEP programme as well as the three "Midway" class ships.

The US Navy's long-range plan provides for 14 or 15 CV/CVN aircraft carriers plus 8 VSTOL support ships. It is considered unlikely that the former force level can be achieved.

Training Carrier: The "Intrepid" class carrier *Lexington* (CVT 16) operates as a training ship and is based at Pensacola, Florida. The ship has no aircraft maintenance or arming capabilities, and is not considered as a combat ship. In an emergency, aircraft could be embarked on a very restricted operational basis.

It is anticipated that the *Coral Sea* (CV 43) will replace the *Lexington* in the training role during the early 1980s.

Names: US aircraft carriers traditionally have been named for American battles and earlier Navy ships. However, during the past few years they have increasingly been named for statesmen and naval leaders.

CARRIER SERVICE LIFE EXTENSION PROGRAMME

(From Annual Defense Department Report FY 1978)

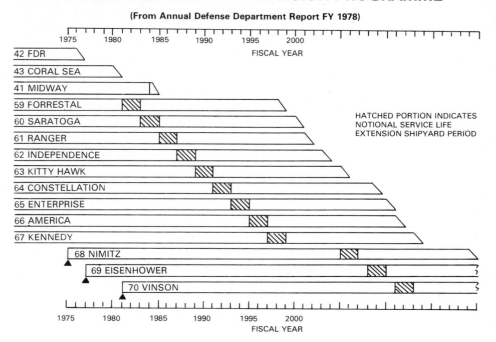

HATCHED PORTION INDICATES NOTIONAL SERVICE LIFE EXTENSION SHIPYARD PERIOD

AIRCRAFT CARRIER, VERTICAL TAKE-OFF (CVV): PLANNED

The Navy seeks to supplement the larger aircraft carriers with a class of "light" aircraft carriers now designated as VSTOL Carriers (CVV). These ships would operate fixed-wing Vertical/Short Take-Off and Landing aircraft and helicopters.

Current plans are for two initial ships, one to be authorized in FY 1979 and one in FY 1981. The first ship would be operational in the mid 1980s. It is expected that the characteristics of the planned 40-50 000 ton CVV will resemble those of the 33 000 ton version listed in the attached table.

Congress refused to fund a VSTOL carrier known as the Sea Control Ship (SCS) that the Navy had planned for the FY 1975 shipbuilding programme. This ship was opposed on the basis of limited size, capability, and speed. Accordingly, the Navy has examined a number of designs that would provide a more flexible employment of sea-based tactical aircraft in a wide range of "low threat" situations as well as being able to conduct anti-submarine operations.

The adjacent table provides the characteristics of the aborted SCS design, and those of a larger ship of some 33 000 tons, which would be able to operate conventional fixed-wing aircraft in limited numbers as well as VSTOL aircraft and helicopters.

The CVV design will be suitable for sea control, amphibious assault, close air support, mine countermeasures, and low-intensity Anti-Air Warfare (AAW) operations. The last would be primarily against long-range reconnaissance and missile guidance aircraft, and not to counter high-performance fighter or attack aircraft. This multi-mission concept overcomes many of the objections which led to Congressional refusal to fund the smaller Sea Control Ship previously proposed by the Navy. In addition, the CVV would have sufficient speed (approximately 28-30 knots) to accompany carrier task forces or fast merchant ships.

The feasibility of the Sea Control Ship/CVV concept was demonstrated from 1972 to 1974 by the amphibious assault ship *Guam* (LPH 9) which operated as an interim SCS. The *Guam* carried AV-8 Harrier VSTOL fighter-attack aircraft, SH-3 Sea King helicopters, and SH-2 LAMPS helicopters during several exercises. She subsequently reverted to the amphibious role.

Aircraft: The VSTOL strike aircraft is the AV-8 Harrier or its successor; the large anti-submarine helicopter is the SH-3 Sea King or SH-53 Sea Stallion (in an A/S configuration); the LAMPS (Light Airborne Multi-Purpose System) is actually a medium-size helicopter primarily configured for A/S search and attack. The current LAMPS helicopter is the SH-2, while a later aircraft based on the Army's Utility Tactical Transport Aircraft System (UTTAS) programme will be developed as the LAMPS III.

A VSTOL carrier over 40 000 tons could operate a small number of conventional fixed-wing aircraft, particularly the S-3 Viking and A-7 Corsair II. These aircraft require catapults and arresting wires. The large CVV design would have two C-13 steam catapults and could operate an air group of 50 or more fixed-wing aircraft and helicopters, the exact number depending upon the type assigned.

Several advanced VSTOL aircraft are under development in the United States for ship-based use, with the more promising candidates being the Hawker Siddeley-McDonnell Douglas AV-16 Advanced Harrier, the Rockwell XFV-12 Thrust-Augmented Wing (TAW) aircraft, and the Grumman "Nutcracker" design.

Gunnery: All of the SCS/CVV designs provide for the installation of at least two Close-In Weapon Systems (CIWS), probably the rapid-fire, multi-barrel 20 mm Phalanx gun system.

Missiles: Harpoon anti-ship missiles in storage/launcher canisters could be fitted in all of these ships.

Propulsion: Despite the Title VIII legislation passed by Congress which encourages nuclear propulsion for surface combatants, all SCS/CVV designs provide for fossil-fuel propulsion because of the high development and procurement costs of nuclear power plants.

Troops: Multi-mission features for the CVV include being able to accommodate 500 troops in the amphibious contingency role for limited periods with minimum modifications.

	Sea Control Ship (SCS) Design	33 000 ton (VSS) Design
Displacement, tons:	14 300 full load	32 800 full load
Length, feet (metres):	640 oa (195·1)	780 oa (237·7)
Beam, feet (metres):	80 (24·4)	100 (30·5)
Draught, feet (metres):	30 (9·1)	25 (7·6)
Aircraft:	3 VSTOL strike aircraft	approx 50+ (see notes)
	14 large A/S helicopters	
	2 LAMPS helicopters	
Catapults:	none	2 C-13 steam
Elevators:	2	2
Guns:	2—20 mm CIWS	2—20 mm CIWS
Main engines:	2 gas turbines; 40 000 shp; 1 shaft	steam turbines; 100 000 shp; 1 shaft
Speed, knots:	approx 26	26+

3 "NIMITZ" CLASS (NUCLEAR POWERED AIRCRAFT CARRIERS (CVN))

Name	No.	Builders	Laid down	Launched	Commissioned
*NIMITZ	CVN 68	Newport News Shipbuilding & Dry Dock Co	22 June1968	13 May 1972	3 May 1975
DWIGHT D. EISENHOWER	CVN 69	Newport News Shipbuilding & Dry Dock Co	15 Aug 1970	11 Oct 1975	1977
CARL VINSON	CVN 70	Newport News Shipbuilding & Dry Dock Co	11 Oct 1975	Mar 1979	1981

Displacement, tons: 81 600 standard; 91 400 full load
Length, feet (metres): 1 040 *(317·0)* wl; 1 092 *(332·0)* oa
Beam, feet (metres): 134 *(40·8)*
Draught, feet (metres): 37 *(11·3)*
Flight deck width, feet (metres): 252 *(76·8)*
Catapults: 4 steam (C13-1)
Aircraft: 90+
Missiles: 3 Basic Point Defence Missile System (BPDMS) launchers with Sea Sparrow missiles (Mk 25)
Main engines: Geared steam turbines; 280 000 shp; 4 shafts
Nuclear reactors: 2 pressurised-water cooled (A4W/A1G)
Speed, knots: 30+
Complement: 3 300 plus 3 000 assigned to air wing for a total of 6 300 per ship

The lead ship for this class and the world's second nuclear-powered aircraft carrier was ordered 9½ years after the first such ship, the USS *Enterprise* (CVN 65). The *Nimitz* was authorised in the Fiscal Year 1967 new construction programme; the *Dwight D. Eisenhower* in the FY 1970 programme; and the *Carl Vinson* in the FY 1974 programme. The builders are the only US shipyard now capable of constructing large, nuclear-propelled warships.

The completion of the first two ships has been delayed almost two years because of delays in the delivery and testing of nuclear plant components. The *Eisenhower* was contracted for delivery to the Navy 21 months after the *Nimitz*. However, the official Navy construction schedule notes that past undermanning by shipbuilder has resulted in slippage beyond contract delivery date.

Classification: *Nimitz* and *Eisenhower* were ordered as attack aircraft carriers (CVAN): reclassified CVN on 30 June 1975. First two ships will be refitted with A/S control centre and facilities for A/S aircraft and helicopters for their new multi-mission role (attack/ASW). The *Vinson* will be completed with these facilities.

Electronics: These ships have the Naval Tactical Data System (NTDS).

Engineering: These carriers have only two nuclear reactors compared to the eight reactors required for the carrier *Enterprise*. The nuclear cores for the reactors in these ships are expected to provide sufficient energy for the ships each to steam for at least 13 years, an estimated 800 000 to 1 million miles between refuelling.

Fiscal: A number of cost growth factors have had an impact on these ships, including delays in schedule. The cost of the *Nimitz* in Fiscal Year 1976 dollars is equivalent to $1·881 billion; the two later ships will cost in excess of $2 billion each in equivalent dollars.

Names: The *Dwight D. Eisenhower* is believed to be the first major US surface warship to be named for an Army officer. The *Carl Vinson* is believed to be the first US naval ship to be named for a living person since the American Revolution. Carl Vinson was a member of the House of Representatives from Georgia from 1914 to 1965; he served as Chairman of the House Naval Affairs Committee and later the House Armed Services Committee.

Radar: 3D Air Search: SPS-48.
Air Search: SPS-43A.
Surface Search: SPS-10.
Navigational: SPS-42, 43 and 44.

Sonar: None.

NIMITZ   9/1976, USN

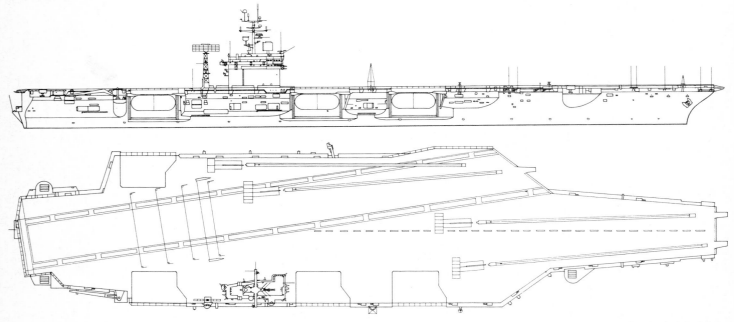

NIMITZ   *Drawing by A. D. Baker*

NIMITZ (with *South Carolina*)   9/1976, USN

NIMITZ   *9/1976, USN*

NIMITZ (with *California* CGN 36 and *South Carolina* CGN 37)   *9/1976, USN*

1 "ENTERPRISE" CLASS (NUCLEAR-POWERED AIRCRAFT CARRIER (CVN))

Name	No.	Builders	Laid down	Launched	Commissioned
*ENTERPRISE	CVN 65	Newport News Shipbuilding & Dry Dock Co.	4 Feb 1958	24 Sep 1960	25 Nov 1961

Displacement, tons: 75 700 standard; 89 600 full load
Length, feet (metres): 1 040 *(317·0)* wl; 1 102 *(335·9)* oa
Beam, feet (metres): 133 *(40·5)*
Draught, feet (metres): 35·8 *(10·8)*
Flight deck width, feet (metres): 252 *(76·8)* maximum
Aircraft: approx 84
Catapults: 4 steam (C 13)
Missile launchers: 2 Basic Point Defence Missile Systems (BPDMS) launchers (Mk 25) with Sea Sparrow missiles
Main engines: 4 geared steam turbines (Westinghouse); approx 280 000 shp; 4 shafts
Nuclear reactors: 8 pressurised-water cooled A2W (Westinghouse)
Speed, knots: approx 35
Complement: 3 100 (162 officers, approx 2 940 enlisted men) plus 2 400 assigned to attack air wing for a total of 5 500)

ENTERPRISE

12/1976, Dr. Giorgio Arra

At the time of her construction, the *Enterprise* was the largest warship ever built and is rivalled in size only by the nuclear-powered "Nimitz" class ships. The *Enterprise* was authorised in the Fiscal Year 1958 new construction programme. She was launched only 19 months after her keel was laid down.
The cost of the *Enterprise* was $451 300 000.
The Fiscal Year 1960 budget provided $35 000 000 to prepare plans and place orders for components of a second nuclear-powered carrier, but the project was cancelled.

Armament: The *Enterprise* was completed without any armament in an effort to hold down construction costs. Space for Terrier missile system was provided. Short-range Sea Sparrow BPDMS subsequently was installed in late 1967.

Classification: Originally classified as CVAN; reclassified as CVN on 30 June 1975.

Design: Built to a modified "Forrestal" class design. The most distinctive feature is the island structure. Nuclear propulsion eliminated requirement for smoke stack and boiler air intakes. Rectangular fixed-array radar antennae ("billboards") are mounted on sides of island; electronic countermeasure (ECM) antennae ring cone-shaped upper levels of island structure. Fixed antennae have increased range and performance (see listing for cruiser *Long Beach*). The *Enterprise* has four deck-edge lifts, two forward of island and one aft on starboard side and one aft on port side.

Electronics: Fitted with the Naval Tactical Data System (NTDS); Tacan.

Engineering: The *Enterprise* was the world's second nuclear-powered warship (the cruiser *Long Beach* was completed a few months earlier). Design of the first nuclear-powered aircraft carrier began in 1950 and work continued until 1953 when the programme was deferred pending further work on the submarine reactor programme. The large ship reactor project was reinstated in 1954 on the basis of technological advancements made in the previous 14 months. The Atomic Energy Commission's Bettis Atomic Power Laboratory was given prime responsibility for developing the nuclear power plant.
The first of the eight reactors installed in the *Enterprise* achieved initial criticality on 2 Dec 1960, shortly after the carrier was launched. After three years of operation during which she steamed more than 207 000 miles, the *Enterprise* was overhauled and refuelled from November 1964 to July 1965. Her second set of cores provided about 300 000 miles steaming. The eight cores initially installed in the *Enterprise* cost $64 000 000; the second set cost about $20 000 000.

The *Enterprise* underwent an extensive overhaul from October 1969 to January 1971, which included installation of a new set of uranium cores in the ship's eight nuclear reactors. The overhaul and refuelling took place at the Newport News shipyard. Estimated cost of the overhaul was approximately $30 000 000, with $13 000 000 being for non-nuclear repairs and alterations, and $17 000 000 being associated with installation of the new nuclear cores (the latter amount being in addition to the $80 000 000 cost of the eight cores). This third set of cores is expected to fuel the ship for 10 to 13 years.
There are two reactors for each of the ship's four shafts. The eight reactors feed 32 heat exchangers. The *Enterprise* developed more horsepower during her propulsion trials than any other ship in history (officially "in excess of 200 000 shaft horsepower"; subsequently, Navy officials stated that she can generate 280 000 shp).

Radar: Search: SPS 32 and 33 ("billboards").
Low Level Search: SPS 58
Search: SPS 10 and 12.
Navigational radars.

ENTERPRISE

12/1976, Dr. Giorgio Arra

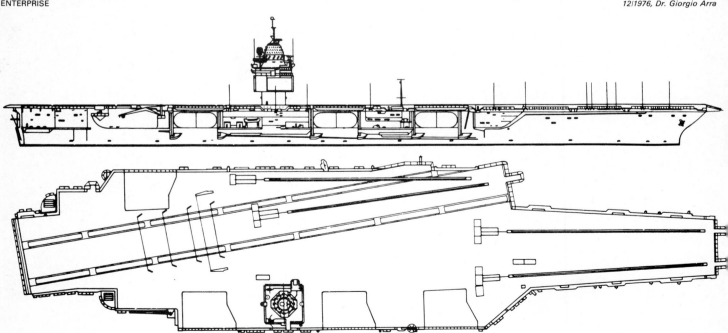

ENTERPRISE

Drawing by A. D. Baker

4 "KITTY HAWK" and "JOHN F. KENNEDY" CLASSES (AIRCRAFT CARRIERS (CV))

Name	No.	Builders	Laid down	Launched	Commissioned
*KITTY HAWK	CV 63	New York Shipbuilding Corp, Camden, NJ	27 Dec 1956	21 May 1960	29 April 1961
*CONSTELLATION	CV 64	New York Naval Shipyard	14 Sep 1957	8 Oct 1960	27 Oct 1961
*AMERICA	CV 66	Newport News Shipbuilding & Dry Dock Co	9 Jan 1961	1 Feb 1964	23 Jan 1965
*JOHN F. KENNEDY	CV 67	Newport News Shipbuilding & Dry Dock Co	22 Oct 1964	27 May 1967	7 Sep 1968

Displacement, tons:
Kitty Hawk: 60 100 standard; 80 800 full load
Constellation: 60 100 standard; 80 800 full load
America: 60 300 standard; 78 500 full load
John F. Kennedy: 61 000 standard; 82 000 full load
Length, feet (metres): 990 *(301·8)* wl
Kitty Hawk and *Constellation:* 1 046 *(318·8)* oa
America: 1 047·5 *(319·3)* oa
J. F. Kennedy: 1 052 *(320·7)* oa
Beam, feet (metres): 130 *(39·6)*
Draught, feet (metres):
J. F. Kennedy: 35·9 *(10·9)*
Remainder: 37 *(11·3)*
Flight deck width, feet (metres): 252 *(76·9)*
Catapults: 4 steam
Aircraft: approx 85
Missile launchers: 2 twin Terrier surface-to-air launchers (Mk 10) in *Constellation, America*
3 Basic Point Defence Missile System (BPDMS) launchers (Mk 25) with Sea Sparrow missiles in *John F. Kennedy*
Kitty Hawk unarmed
Main engines: 4 geared turbines (Westinghouse) 280 000 shp; 4 shafts
Boilers: 8 (Foster Wheeler)
Speed, knots: 30+
Complement: 2 800 (150 officers, approx 2 645 enlisted men) plus approx 2 150 assigned to attack air wing for a total of 4 950 officers and enlisted men per ship

CONSTELLATION

10/1975, USN

These ships were built to an improved "Forrestal" design and are easily recognised by their smaller island structure which is set farther aft than the superstructure in the four "Forrestal" class ships. Lift arrangements also differ (see design notes). The *Kitty Hawk* was authorised in Fiscal Year 1956 new construction programme, the *Constellation* in FY 1957, the *America* in FY 1961, and the *John F. Kennedy* in FY 1963. Completion of the *Constellation* was delayed because of a fire which ravaged her in the New York Naval Shipyard in December 1960. Construction of the *John F. Kennedy* was delayed because of debate over whether to provide her with conventional or nuclear propulsion.

Classification: As completed, all four ships were classified as attack aircraft carriers (CVA); first two changed to multi-mission aircraft carriers (attack and anti-submarine) when modified with A/S command centres and facilities for S-3 Viking fixed-wing aircraft and SH-3 Sea King helicopters. *Kitty Hawk* to CV vice CVA on 29 April 1973; *John F. Kennedy* to CV vice CVA on 1 Dec 1974; *Constellation* and *America* from CVA to CV on 30 June 1975, prior to A/S modifications.

Design: They have two deck-edge lifts forward of the superstructure, a third lift aft of the structure, and the port-side lift on the after quarter. This arrangement considerably improves flight deck operations. Four C13 catapults (with one C13-1 in each of later ships). The *John F. Kennedy* and *America* have stern anchors because of their bow sonar domes (see Sonar notes). All have a small radar mast abaft the island.

Electronics: All four ships of this class have highly sophisticated electronic equipment including the Naval Tactical Data System (NTDS). Tacan in all ships.

Fire Control: 4—Mk 76 MFCS with SPG-55A radars. (*America* and *Constellation*, 3 in *J. F. Kennedy* with SPG-55B.)

Fiscal: Construction costs were $265 200 000 for *Kitty Hawk*, $264 500 000 for *Constellation*, $248 800 000 for *America*, and $277 000 000 for *John F. Kennedy*.

Missiles: The two Terrier-armed ships have a Mk 10 Mod 3 launcher on the starboard quarter and a Mod 4 launcher on the

JOHN F. KENNEDY

9/1975, Reinhard Nerlich

port quarter.
The *America* has updated Terrier launchers and guidance system that can accommodate Standard missiles; the *Constellation* retains older Terrier HT systems which will be replaced by three NATO Sea Sparrow launchers (Mk 29).
Three Sea Sparrow BPDMS launchers were fitted in the *John F. Kennedy* early in 1969.

Names: *Kitty Hawk* honours the site where the Wright brothers made their historic flights.

Radar: 3D Search: SPS 52 (3 ships).
Search: SPS 43.
Search: SPS 30 (3 ships)
Search: SPS 48 and 58 (*J. F. Kennedy*).

Sonar: SQS-23 (*America* only).
This is the only US attack carrier so fitted, although it was planned also for *J. F. Kennedy* but not fitted.

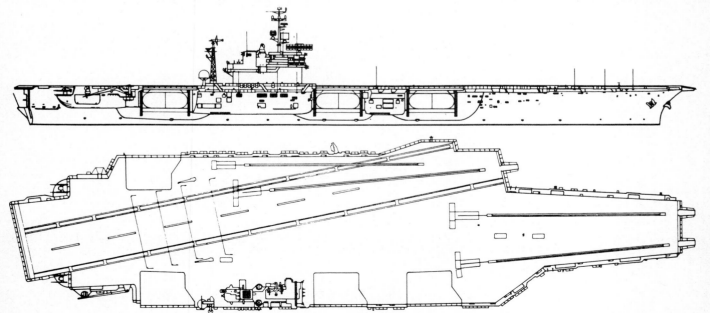

AMERICA

Drawing by A. D. Baker

JOHN F. KENNEDY

10/1976, Michael D. J. Lennon

AMERICA

10/1974, USN

JOHN F. KENNEDY

1974, USN

4 "FORRESTAL" CLASS (AIRCRAFT CARRIERS (CV))

Name	No.	Builders	Laid down	Launched	Commissioned
*FORRESTAL	CV 59	Newport News SB & DD Co	14 July 1952	11 Dec 1954	1 Oct 1955
*SARATOGA	CV 60	New York Naval Shipyard	16 Dec 1952	8 Oct 1955	14 April 1956
*RANGER	CV 61	Newport News SB & DD Co	2 Aug 1954	29 Sep 1956	10 Aug 1957
*INDEPENDENCE	CV 62	New York Naval Shipyard	1 July 1955	6 June1958	10 Jan 1959

Displacement, tons:
Forrestal and Saratoga: 59 060 standard; 75 900 full load
Others: 60 000 standard; 79 300 full load
Length, feet (metres):
Forrestal: 1 086 *(331)* oa
Ranger: 1 071 *(326·4)* oa
Saratoga: 1 063 *(324)* oa
Independence: 1 070 *(326·1)* oa
Beam, feet (metres): 129·5 *(38·5)*
Draught, feet (metres): 37 *(11·3)*
Flight deck width, feet (metres): 252 *(76·8)* maximum
Catapults: 4 steam
Aircraft: Approx 70
Guns: 2—5 inch *(127 mm)* 54 cal (Mk 42) (single) in *Ranger*
Missile launchers: 2 Basic Point Defence Missile Systems (BPDMS) launchers (Mk 25) with Sea Sparrow missiles in all except *Ranger*
Main engines: 4 geared turbines (Westinghouse) 4 shafts; 260 000 shp
Boilers: 8 (Babcock & Wilcox)
Speed, knots:
Forrestal: 33
Others; 34
Complement: 2 790 (145 officers, approx 2 645 enlisted men) plus approx 2 150 assigned to attack air wing for a total of 4 940+ per ship

The *Forrestal* was the world's first aircraft carrier designed and built after World War II. The *Forrestal* design drew heavily from the aircraft carrier *United States* (CVA 58) which was cancelled immediately after being laid down in April 1949. The *Forrestal* was authorised in the Fiscal Year 1952 new construction programme; the *Saratoga* followed in the FY 1953 programme, the *Ranger* in the FY 1954 programme, and the *Independence* in the FY 1955 programme.

Classification: The *Forrestal* and *Saratoga* were initially classified as Large Aircraft Carriers (CVB); reclassified as Attack Aircraft Carriers (CVA) in October 1952 to reflect their purpose rather than size.
Saratoga redesignated CV on 30 June 1972; *Independence* on 28 Feb 1973; *Forrestal* and *Ranger* on 30 June 1975.

Design: The "Forrestal" class ships were the first aircraft carriers designed and built specifically to operate jet-propelled aircraft. The *Forrestal* was redesigned early in construction to incorporate British-developed angled flight deck and steam catapults. These were the first US aircraft carriers built with an enclosed bow area to improve seaworthiness. Four large deck-edge lifts are fitted, one forward of island structure to starboard, two aft of island structure to starboard and one at forward edge of angled flight deck to port. Other features include armoured flight deck and advanced underwater protection and internal compartmentation to reduce effects of conventional and nuclear attack. Mast configurations differ; the *Forrestal* originally had two masts, one of which was removed in 1967.
The first two ships have two C7 and two C11 catapults; the others have four C7.

FORRESTAL

7/1976, A. D. Baker III

Electronics: Naval Tactical Data System (NTDS) and TACAN

Engineering: The *Saratoga* and later ships have an improved steam plant; increased machinery weight of the improved plant is more than compensated for by increased performance and decreased fuel consumption. *Forrestal* boilers are 615 psi *(42·7 kg/cm²)*; 1 200 psi *(83·4 kg/cm²)* in other ships.

Fiscal: Construction costs were $188 900 000 for *Forrestal,* $213 900 000 for *Saratoga,* $173 300 000 for *Ranger,* and $225 300 000 for *Independence.*

Gunnery: All four ships initially mounted 8—5 inch guns (Mk 42) in single mounts, two on each quarter and two on each bow. The forward sponsons carrying the guns interfered with ship operations in rough weather, tending to slow the ships down. The forward sponsons and guns were subsequently removed (except in *Ranger),* reducing armament to four guns per ship. The after guns were removed with installation of BPDMS launchers (see below). *Ranger* now carries only two 5 in which will make way for Sea Sparrow.

Missiles: The four after 5 inch guns were removed from the *Forrestal* late in 1967 and a single BPDMS launcher for Sea Sparrow missiles was installed forward on the starboard side. An additional launcher was provided aft on the port side in 1972. Two BPDMS launchers fitted in *Independence* in 1973, *Saratoga* in 1974; *Forrestal* in 1976. *Ranger* is to be fitted with three launchers in 1977.

Names: The *Forrestal* is named after James V. Forrestal, Secretary of the Navy from 1944 until he was appointed the first US Secretary of Defense in 1947.

Radar: Low angle air search; SPS-58
Search; SPS-30 and 43
Navigation; SPS-10.

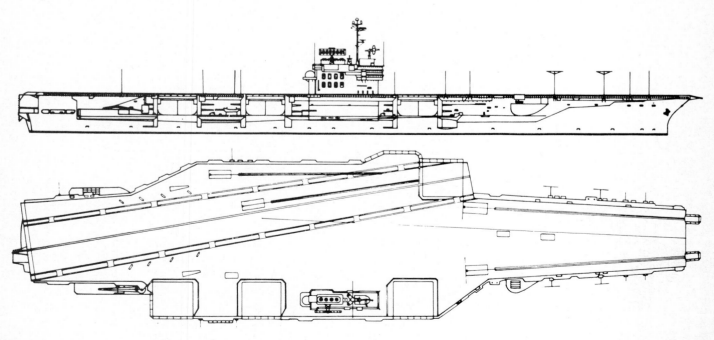

FORRESTAL

Drawing by A. D. Baker III

SARATOGA   1975, USN

INDEPENDENCE   9/1976, Dr. Giorgio Arra

RANGER   2/1976, USN

3 "MIDWAY" CLASS (AIRCRAFT CARRIERS (CV))

Name	No.	Builders	Laid down	Launched	Commissioned
*MIDWAY	CV 41	Newport News SB & DD Co	27 Oct 1943	20 Mar 1945	10 Sep 1945
*FRANKLIN D. ROOSEVELT	CV 42	New York Navy Yard	1 Dec 1943	29 April 1945	27 Oct 1945
*CORAL SEA	CV 43	Newport News SB & DD Co	10 July 1944	2 April 1946	1 Oct 1947

Displacement, tons: *Midway:* 51 000 standard; *F. D. Roosevelt:* 51 000 standard; *Coral Sea:* 52 500 standard; all approx 64 000 full load
Length, feet (metres): 900 *(274·3)* wl; 979 *(298·4)* oa
Beam, feet (metres): 121 *(36·9)*
Draught, feet (metres): 35·3 *(10·8)*
Flight deck width, feet (metres): 238 *(72·5)* maximum
Catapults: 2 steam except 3 in *Coral Sea*
Aircraft: approx 75
Guns: 4—5 inch *(127 mm)* 54 cal (Mk 39) (single) in *F. D. Roosevelt;* (2 inoperative); 3 guns in *Midway* and *Coral Sea* (see *Gunnery* notes)
Main engines: 4 geared turbines (Westinghouse in *Midway* and *Coral Sea;* General Electric in *F. D. Roosevelt);* 212 000 shp; 4 shafts
Boilers: 12 (Babcock & Wilcox)
Speed, knots: 30+
Complement: 2 615 (140 officers, approx 2 475 enlisted men) except *Coral Sea* 2 710 (165 officers, approx 2 545 enlisted men) plus approx 1 800 assigned to attack air wing for a total of 4 400 to 4 500 per ship

These carriers were the largest US warships constructed during World War II. Completed too late for service in that conflict, they were the backbone of US naval strength for the first decade of the Cold War. The entire class has been in active service (except for overhaul and modernisation) since the ships were completed.
The *Midway* was homeported at Yokosuka, Japan, in October 1973; she is the only US aircraft carrier to be based overseas. *Franklin D. Roosevelt* is due to decommission on 15 Dec 1977, and *Coral Sea* in 1981 although she may replace *Lexington* as a training carrier when *Carl Vinson* commissions.
The *Midway* will probably be retained in service until 1985 to provide a 13 carrier force level.

Classification: These ships were initially classified as large Aircraft Carriers (CVB); reclassified as Attack Aircraft Carriers (CVA) in October 1952. All three ships reclassified as Aircraft Carriers (CV) on 30 June 1975.

Design: These ships were built to the same design with a standard displacement of 45 000 tons, full load displacement of 60 100 tons, and an overall length of 968 feet. They have been extensively modified since completion (see notes below). These ships were the first US aircraft carriers with an armoured flight deck and the first US warships with a designed width too large to enable them to pass through the Panama Canal.
The unnamed CVB 44, 56 and 57 of this class were cancelled prior to the start of construction.

Electronics: Naval Tactical Data System (NTDS) in *Midway* and *Coral Sea;* Tacan.

Fire control: One Mk 37 and two or three Mk 56 GFCS.

Fiscal: Construction cost of *Midway* was $85 600 000, *F. D. Roosevelt* $85 700 000, and *Coral Sea* $87 600 000.

Gunnery: As built, these ships mounted 18—5 inch guns (14 in *Coral Sea),* 84—40 mm guns, and 28—20 mm guns. Armament reduced periodically with 3 inch guns replacing lighter weapons. Minimal 5 inch armament remains. The 5 inch guns are 54 calibre Mk 39, essentially modified 5 inch/38 calibre with a longer barrel for greater range; not to be confused with rapid-fire 5 inch/54s of newer US warships.

Missiles: The *Midway* is scheduled to be fitted with three Basic Point Defense Missile launchers (Mk 25) for the Sea Sparrow missile during Fiscal Year 1977.

Modernisation: All have been extensively modernised. Their

MIDWAY   11/1974, USN

main conversion gave them angled flight decks, steam catapults, enclosed bows, new electronics, and new lift arrangement *(Franklin D. Roosevelt* from 1954 to 1956, *Midway* from 1955 to 1957, and *Coral Sea* from 1958 to 1960; all at Puget Sound Naval Shipyard). Lift arrangement was changed in *Franklin D. Roosevelt* and *Midway* to one centreline lift forward, one deck-edge lift aft of island on starboard side, and one deck-edge lift at forward end of angled deck on port side. The *Coral Sea* has one lift forward and one aft of island on starboard side and third lift outboard on port side aft. The *Midway* began another extensive modernisation at the San Francisco Bay Naval Shipyard in February 1966; she was recommissioned on 31 Jan 1970 and went to sea in March 1970.
Her modernisation included provisions for handling newer aircraft, new catapults, new lifts (arranged as in *Coral Sea),* and

new electronics. A similar modernisation planned for the *Franklin D. Roosevelt,* to have begun in Fiscal Year 1970, was cancelled because the *Midway* modernisation took longer and cost more than originally estimated (24 months and $88 000 000 was planned; actual work required approximately 52 months and $202 300 000). The *Franklin D. Roosevelt* completed an austere overhaul in June 1969 which enables her to operate newer aircraft; cost of overhaul was $46 000 000.
The *Midway* is now the most capable of the three ships.
The *Midway* has C13 catapults; C11 catapults in the other ships.

Radar: Low angle air search; SPS 58
Search; SPS-10, 30 and 43
Navigation; SPN-6 and 10

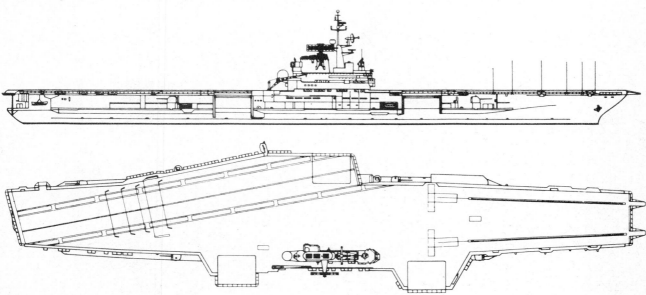

FRANKLIN D. ROOSEVELT   *Drawing by A. D. Baker III*

CORAL SEA   4/1976, USN

MIDWAY   1/1975, USN

FRANKLIN D. ROOSEVELT   6/1971, USN

5 "HANCOCK" and "INTREPID" CLASSES (2CVA/CV, 2CVS, 1CVT)

Name	No.	Builders	Laid down	Launched	Commissioned
INTREPID	CVS 11	Newport News Shipbuilding & Dry Dock Co	1 Dec 1941	26 April 1943	16 Aug 1943
*LEXINGTON	CVT 16	Bethlehem Steel Co, Quincy, Mass	15 July 1941	26 Sep 1942	17 Feb 1943
BON HOMME RICHARD	CVA 31	New York Navy Yard	1 Feb 1943	29 April 1944	26 Nov 1944
ORISKANY	CV 34	New York Navy Yard	1 May 1944	13 Oct 1945	25 Sep 1950
SHANGRI-LA	CVS 38	Norfolk Navy Yard	15 Jan 1943	24 Feb 1944	15 Sep 1944

Displacement, tons: 29 600 light; 41 900 full load. (*Oriskany* 28 200 light; 40 600 full load)

Length, feet (metres): 820 *(249·9)* wl; 899 *(274)* oa *(889 (270·9) Shangri-La, Lexington)*

Beam, feet (metres): 103 *(30·8)* except *Oriskany* 106·5 *(32·5)*

Draught, feet (metres): 31 *(9·4)*

Flight deck width, feet (metres): 172 *(52·4)* except *Lexington* 192 *(58·5)* and *Oriskany* 195 *(59·5)*

Catapults: 2 steam

Aircraft: 70 to 80 for CVA/CV type; approx 45 for CVS type; none assigned to *Lexington*

Guns: 2—5 inch *(127 mm)* 38 cal (Mk 24) (single) in *Oriskany*; 4 guns in other ships except all removed from *Lexington*

Main engines: 4 geared turbines (Westinghouse) 150 000 shp; 4 shafts

Boilers: 8 (Babcock & Wilcox)

Speed, knots: 30+

Complement:
CVA/CV type: 2 090 (110 officers, 1 980 enlisted men); plus approx 1 185 (135 officers, 1 050 enlisted men) in air wing for a total of approx 3 200 per ship
CVS type: 1 615 (115 officers, approx 1 500 enlisted men) plus approx 800 assigned to ASW air group for a total of 2 400 per ship
Lexington: 1 440 (75 officers, 1 365 enlisted men); no air unit assigned

LEXINGTON

5/1975, USN

These ships (formerly six including *Hancock)* originally were "Essex" class aircraft carriers; extensively modernised during 1950s, being provided with enclosed bow, angled flight deck, improved elevators, increased aviation fuel storage, and steam catapults. Construction of *Oriskany* suspended after World War II and she was completed in 1950 to a modified "Essex" design.

Bon Homme Richard decommissioned on 2 July 1971, *Shangri-La* on 30 July 1971, *Intrepid* on 15 March 1974, *Oriskany* on 30 Sep 1976; *Lexington* remains in commission as a training carrier (with no aircraft support capability).

Classification: All "Essex" class ships originally were designated as Aircraft Carriers (CV); reclassified as Attack Aircraft Carriers (CVA) in Oct 1952. *Intrepid* reclassified as ASW Support Aircraft Carrier (CVS) on 31 Mar 1962, *Lexington* on 1 Oct 1962, *Shangri-La* on 30 June 1969. The *Lexington* became the Navy's training aircraft carrier in the Gulf of Mexico on 29 Dec 1962; reclassified CVT on 1 Jan 1969. *Oriskany* redesignated as CV on 30 June 1975 (as was now-stricken *Hancock*).

Electronics: The *Oriskany* conducted the initial sea trials of the Naval Tactical Data System (NTDS) in 1961-1962; Tacan.

Fire control: These ships are generally fitted with one Mk 37 gunfire control system and two Mk 56 GFCS.

Modernisation: These ships have been modernised under

ORISKANY

8/1970, USN

several programmes to increase their ability to operate more-advanced aircraft. The *Oriskany* was completed with some post-war features incorporated. The most prominent difference from their original configuration is angled flight deck and removal of twin 5-inch gun mounts from flight deck forward and aft of island structure. Three elevators fitted; "Pointed" centreline lift forward between catapults, deckedge lift on port side at leading edge of angled deck, and deckedge lift on starboard side aft of island structure. Minimal gun battery retained

(see description of original armament under "Essex" class listings). Remaining guns removed from *Lexington* in 1969; by 1975 the *Oriskany* had only 2—5 inch guns fitted.

Radar: Search; SPS-10, 30 and 43.
Navigation; SPN-10.
Lexington;
Search; SPS-10, 12 and 43.
Navigation; SPN-10.

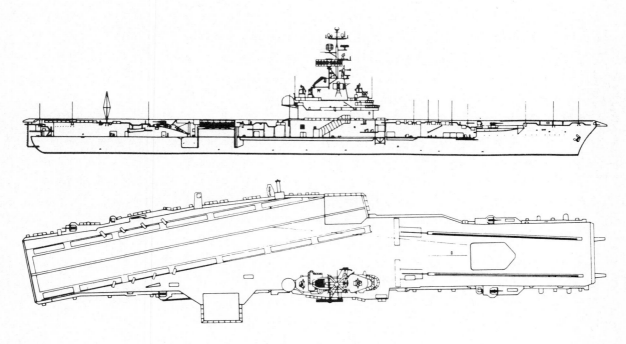

ORISKANY

Drawing by A. D. Baker III

2 MODERNISED "ESSEX" CLASS (ASW AIRCRAFT CARRIERS (CVS))

Name	No.	Builders	Laid down	Launched	Commissioned
HORNET	CVS 12	Newport News Shipbuilding & Dry Dock Co	3 Aug 1942	29 Aug 1943	29 Nov 1943
BENNINGTON	CVS 20	New York Navy Yard	15 Dec 1942	26 Feb 1944	6 Aug 1944

Displacement, tons: approx 33 000 standard; approx 40 600 full load
Length, feet (metres): 820 (249·9) wl; 899 (274) oa
Beam, feet (metres): 101 (30·7)
Draught, feet (metres): 31 (9·4)
Flight deck width, feet (metres): 172 (52·4) maximum
Catapults: 2 hydraulic (H-8)
Aircraft: 45 (including 16 to 18 helicopters)
Guns: 4—5 inch (127 mm) 38 cal (Mk 24) (single)
Main engines: 4 geared turbines (Westinghouse); 150 000 shp; 4 shafts
Boilers: 8 (Babcock & Wilcox)
Speed, knots: 30+
Complement: 1 615 (115 officers, approx 1 500 enlisted men) plus approx 800 assigned to ASW air group for a total of 2 400 per ship

The two above ships and the previously listed "Hancock" and "Intrepid" classes are the survivors of the 24 "Essex" class fleet carriers built during World War II (with one ship, *Oriskany*, not completed until 1950). Both of the above ships were extensively modernised during the 1950s; however, they lack the steam catapults and other features of the "Hancock" and "Intrepid" classes.
The *Bennington* was decommissioned on 15 Jan 1970 and the *Hornet* on 26 June 1970; both ships are in reserve.

Classification: These ships originally were designated as Aircraft Carriers (CV): reclassified as Attack Carriers (CVA) in Oct 1952. Subsequently they became ASW Support Aircraft Carriers (CVS): *Hornet* on 27 June 1958, and *Bennington* on 30 June 1959.

Design: All 24 "Essex" class ships were built to the same basic design except for the delayed *Oriskany*. Standard displacement as built was 27 100 tons, full load displacement was 36 380 tons, and overall length 888 or 972 feet.

Fire control: One Mk 37 and three Mk 56 GFCS.

Electronics: One Mk 37 and three Mk 56 gunfire control systems; Tacan.

Modernisation: These ships have been modernised under several programmes to increase their ability to operate advanced aircraft and to improve sea keeping. Also modernised to improve anti-submarine capabilities under the Fleet Rehabilitation and Modernisation (FRAM II) programme.

Radar: Search; SPS 10, 30 and 43.

Sonar: SQS-23 (bow-mounted).

BENNINGTON (starboard lift raised during replenishment)   *1968, USN*

HORNET   *1968, USN*

BATTLESHIPS

4 "IOWA" CLASS

Name	No.	Builders	Laid down	Launched	Commissioned
IOWA	BB 61	New York Navy Yard	27 June1940	27 Aug 1942	22 Feb 1943
NEW JERSEY	BB 62	Philadelphia Navy Yard	16 Sep 1940	7 Dec 1942	23 May 1943
MISSOURI	BB 63	New York Navy Yard	6 Jan 1941	29 Jan 1944	11 June 1944
WISCONSIN	BB 64	Philadelphia Navy Yard	25 Jan 1941	7 Dec 1943	16 Apr 1944

Displacement, tons: 45 000 standard; 58 000 full load
Length, feet (metres): 860 *(262·1)* wl; 887·2 *(270·4)* oa except *New Jersey* 887·6 *(270·5)*
Beam, feet (metres): 108·2 *(33·0)*
Draught, feet (metres): 38 *(11·6)*
Guns: 9—16 inch *(406 mm)* 50 cal (triple); 20—5 inch *(127 mm)* 38 cal (twin); 20—40 mm guns in *Missouri* only; numerous 20 mm (quad)
Main engines: 4 geared turbines (General Electric in BB 61 and BB 63; Westinghouse in BB 62 and BB 64); 212 000 shp; 4 shafts
Boilers: 8 (Babcock & Wilcox)
Speed, knots: 33 (all may have reached 35 knots in service)
Complement: designed complement varied, averaging 95 officers and 2 270 enlisted men in wartime; *New Jersey* was manned by 70 officers and 1 556 enlisted men (requirements reduced with removal of all light anti-aircraft weapons, floatplanes, and reduced operational requirements) in 1968-1969.

These ships were the largest battleships ever built except for the Japanese *Yamato* and *Musashi* (64 170 tons standard, 863 feet overall, 9—18·1 inch guns). All four "Iowa" class ships were in action in the Pacific during World War II, primarily screening fast carriers and bombarding amphibious invasion objectives. Three were mothballed after the war with the *Missouri* being retained in service as a training ship. All four ships again were in service during the Korean War (1950-1953) as shore-bombardment ships; all mothballed 1954-1958.

The *New Jersey* began reactivation in mid-1967 at a cost of approximately $21 000 000; recommissioned on 6 Apr 1968. The *Iowa* and *Wisconsin* remained in reserve at the Philadelphia Naval Shipyard where the *New Jersey* had been berthed and reactivated; and the mothballed *Missouri* at the Puget Sound Naval Shipyard, Bremerton, Washington.

The *New Jersey* was again decommissioned on 17 Dec 1969 and mothballed at Bremerton with the *Missouri*. Two additional ships of this class were laid down, but never completed: *Illinois* (BB 65), laid down 15 Jan 1945, and *Kentucky* (BB 66), laid down 6 Dec 1944. The *Illinois* was 22 per cent complete when cancelled on 11 Aug 1945. The *Kentucky* was 69·2 per cent complete when construction was suspended late in the war; floated from its building dock on 20 Jan 1950. Conversion to a missile ship (BBG) was proposed but no work was undertaken and she was stricken on 9 June 1958 and broken up for scrap.

Approximate construction cost was $114 485 000 for *Missouri;* other ships cost slightly less.

Aircraft: As built, each ship carried three floatplanes for scouting and gunfire spotting and had two quarterdeck catapults. Catapults removed and helicopters carried during the Korean War.

Armour: These battleships are the most heavily armoured US warships ever constructed, being designed to survive ship-to-ship combat with enemy ships armed with 16 inch guns. The main armour belt consists of Class A steel armour 12·1 inches thick tapering vertically to 1·62 inches; a lower armour belt aft of Turret No. 3 to protect propeller shafts is 13·5 inches; turret faces are 17 inches; turret tops are 7·25 inches; turret backs are 12 inches; barbettes have a maximum of 11·6 inches of armour; second deck armour is 6 inches; and the three-level conning tower sides are 17·3 inches with an armoured roof 7·2b inches (the conning tower levels are pilot house navigation bridge and flag-signal bridge).

Design: These ships carried heavier armament than previous US battleships and had increased protection and larger engines accounting for additional displacement and increased speed.
All fitted as fleet flagships with additional accommodations and bridge level for admiral and staff.

Gunnery: The Mk VII 16 inch guns in these ships fire projectiles weighing up to 2 700 pounds *(1 225 kg)* (armour piercing) a maximum range of 23 miles *(39 km)*. As built, these ships had 80—40 mm and 49 to 60—20 mm anti-aircraft guns (except *Iowa,* only 19 quad 40 mm mounts); all 20 mm guns now removed.
During 1968-1969 the *New Jersey* was fitted with two Mk 34 fire control directors in addition to the two Mk 56 and four Mk 37 previously installed. Mk 48 shore bombardment computer installed when reactivated.

Operational: The *New Jersey* made one deployment to the western Pacific during her third commission (1968-1969). During the deployment she was on the "gun line" off South Vietnam for a total of 120 days with 47 days being the longest sustained period at sea.
While in action *New Jersey* fired 5 688 rounds of ammunition from her 16 inch main battery guns and a total of 6 200 rounds during the commission, the additional firings being for tests and training. While off Vietnam she also fired some 15 000 rounds from her 5 inch secondary battery guns.
(In comparison, during World War II the *New Jersey* fired 771 main battery rounds and during two deployments in the Korean War and midshipmen training cruises she fired 6 671 main battery rounds).

Radar: SPS 6 and 10 (fitted in *New Jersey* 1968-69).

NEW JERSEY (off Vietnam)   4/1969, USN

WISCONSIN   USN

CRUISERS

The US Navy's active cruiser force consists of 27 guided missile ships. Twenty-four of these ships (including six nuclear powered) have been completed during the past 15 years with the three older ships being modernised World War II-built cruisers. All of these ships are oriented primarily toward Anti-Air Warfare (AAW) with the three older ships additionally configured to serve as flagships for the US Navy's numbered fleets. In addi-

tion, the collision-damaged *Belknap* (CG 26) is undergoing a two-year repair/modernisation programme.

Three additional nuclear-propelled missile cruisers are under construction. With these nine nuclear cruisers available by 1980 the Navy could operate two all-nuclear carrier task forces. Future cruiser construction is so much an affair of conjecture that no point is served by discussing it. On February 22 1977

Secretary of Defense Harold Brown announced the cancellation of the nuclear strike cruiser (CSGN) programme preferring the option of two DDG-47 Aegis-equipped destroyers for the price of one CSGN. He promised "study in depth" before "changing the five-year shipbuilding plan" (Details of the proposed CSGN are in *Jane's Fighting Ships* 1976-77).

4 "VIRGINIA" CLASS (NUCLEAR-POWERED GUIDED MISSILE CRUISERS (CGN))

Name	No.	Builders	Laid down	Launched	Commissioned
VIRGINIA	CGN 38 (ex-*DLGN 38*)	Newport News Shipbuilding & Dry Dock Co	19 Aug 1972	14 Dec 1974	11 Sep 1976
TEXAS	CGN 39 (ex-*DLGN 39*)	Newport News Shipbuilding & Dry Dock Co	18 Aug 1973	9 Aug 1975	Aug 1977
MISSISSIPPI	CGN 40 (ex-*DLGN 40*)	Newport News Shipbuilding & Dry Dock Co	22 Feb 1975	31 July 1976	July 1978
—	CGN 41	Newport News Shipbuilding & Dry Dock Co	—	—	May 1980

Displacement, tons: 10 000 full load
Length, feet (metres): 585 *(177·3)* oa
Beam, feet (metres): 63 *(18·9)*
Draught, feet (metres): 29·5 *(9·0)*
Helicopters: 2 (see *Helicopter* notes)
Missile launchers: 2 combination twin Tartar-D/ASROC launchers firing Standard MR surface-to-air missile (Mk 26)
Guns: 2—5 inch *(127 mm)* 54 calibre (Mk 45) (single)
A/S weapons: ASROC *(see above)*; 2 triple torpedo tubes (Mk 32)
Main engines: 2 geared turbines; 2 shafts
Reactors: 2 pressurised-water cooled D2G (General Electric)
Speed, knots: 30+
Complement: 442 (27 officers, 415 enlisted men)

The *Virginia* was authorised in the Fiscal Year 1970 new construction programme, the *Texas* in FY 1971, the *Mississippi* in FY 1972, and CGN 41 in FY 1975.
The CGN 42 was proposed in the FY 1976 new construction programme but was not funded by the Congress.
Construction of this class has been delayed because of a shortage of skilled labour in the shipyard. Newport News SB & DD Co (Virginia) is the only shipyard in the United States now engaged in the construction of nuclear surface ships. The first

three ships of the class are more than one year behind their original construction schedules. Additional delays are anticipated.

Classification: These ships were originally classified as guided missile frigates (DLGN); subsequently reclassified as guided missile cruisers (CGN) on 30 June 1975.

Design: The principal differences between the "Virginia" and "California" classes are the improved anti-air warfare capability, electronic warfare equipment, and anti-submarine fire control system. The deletion of the separate ASROC Mk 16 launcher permitted the "Virginia" class to be ten feet shorter.

Electronics: Naval Tactical Data System (NTDS).

Fiscal: These ships have incurred major cost growth/escalation during their construction. Fiscal data on the earlier ships were in the 1974-1975 and earlier editions.
The CGN 42 was estimated to cost $368 000 000 ($/257 000 000 proposed in FY 1976 and $111 000 000 in FY 1970-1975).

Fire control: Mk 74 missile control directors. Digital Mk 116 ASW FCS.

Gunnery: Mk 86 gunfire control directors. 20 mm CIWS will be fitted in each ship.

Helicopters: A hangar for helicopters is installed beneath the fantail flight-deck with a telescoping hatch cover and an electro-mechanical elevator provided to transport helicopters between the main deck and hangar. These are the first US post-World War II destroyer/cruiser ships with a hull hangar.

Missiles: The initial design for this class provided for a single surface-to-air missile launcher; revised in 1969 to provide two Mk 26 launchers that will fire the Standard-Medium Range (MR) surface-to-air missile and the ASROC anti-submarine missile. "Mixed" Standard/ASROC magazines are planned for each launcher.
Harpoon SSM will be fitted in the immediate future or as new ships complete.

Radar: 3D Search; SPS 48A.
Search; SPS 40B and 55.

Rockets: Mk 76 Chaffroc RBOC (Rapid Bloom Overhead Chaff) to be fitted.

Sonar: SQS-53A (bow-mounted).

VIRGINIA

9/1976, Dr. Giorgio Arra

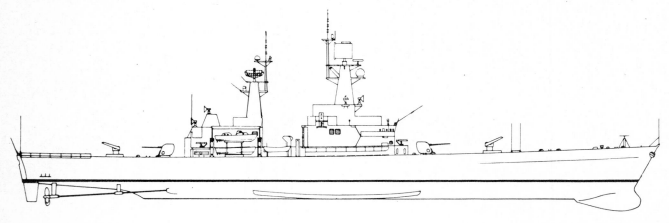

VIRGINIA

Drawing by A. D. Baker III

2 "CALIFORNIA" CLASS (NUCLEAR-POWERED GUIDED MISSILE CRUISERS (CGN))

Name	No.	Builders	Laid down	Launched	Commissioned
*CALIFORNIA	CGN 36	Newport News Shipbuilding & Dry Dock Co	23 Jan 1970	22 Sep 1971	16 Feb 1974
*SOUTH CAROLINA	CGN 37	Newport News Shipbuilding & Dry Dock Co	1 Dec 1970	1 July 1972	25 Jan 1975

Displacement, tons: 9 561 full load
Length, feet (metres): 596 (181·7) oa
Beam, feet (metres): 61 (18·6)
Draught, feet (metres): 31·5 (9·6)
Missile launchers: 2 single Tartar-D surface-to-air launchers firing Standard MR (Mk 13 Mod 3)
Guns: 2—5 inch (127 mm) 54 calibre (Mk 45) (single)
A/S weapons: 4 torpedo tubes (Mk 32); 1 ASROC 8-tube launcher
Main engines: 2 geared turbines; 2 shafts
Nuclear reactors: 2 pressurised-water cooled D2G (General Electric)
Speed, knots: 30+
Complement: 540 (28 officers, 512 enlisted men)

The *California* was authorised in the Fiscal Year 1967 new construction programme and the *South Carolina* in the FY 1968 programme. The construction of a third ship of this class (DLGN 38) was also authorised in FY 1968, but the rising costs of these ships and development of the DXGN/DLGN 38 design (now "Virginia" class) caused the third ship to be deferred.

Classification: These ships were originally classified as guided missile frigates (DLGN); subsequently reclassified as guided missile cruisers (CGN) on 30 June 1975.

Design: These ships have tall, enclosed towers supporting radar antennae in contrast to the open lattice masts of the previous nuclear frigates *Truxtun* and *Bainbridge*.
No helicopter support facilities provided.

Electronics: Fitted with the Naval Tactical Data System (NTDS).

Engineering: Estimated nuclear core life for these ships provides 700 000 miles range; estimated cost is $11 500 000 for the two initial nuclear cores in each ship.

Fire Control: Two Mk 74 Mod 4 MFCS; one Mk 86 Mod 3 GFCS; one Mk 11 Mod 3 Weapons direction system.

Fiscal: Estimated cost is $200 000 000 for *California* and $180 000 000 for *South Carolina*.

Gunnery: 2 Phalanx 20 mm CIWS to be fitted.

Missiles: Reportedly, these ships carry some 80 surface-to-air missiles divided equally between a magazine beneath each launcher.

Radar: 3D Air Search; SPS 48
Search: SPS 10 and 40.
Fire control: SPG 51D, SPG-60 and SPQ-9A.

Rockets: Mk 36 Chaffroc RBOC to be fitted in place of Mk 28 system.

Sonar: SQS-26CX (bow mounted).

SOUTH CAROLINA   9/1975, Wright and Logan

CALIFORNIA   10/1975, J. L. M. van der Burg

SOUTH CAROLINA   9/1976, USN

1 "TRUXTUN" CLASS (NUCLEAR-POWERED GUIDED MISSILE CRUISER (CGN))

Name	No.	Builders	Laid down	Launched	Commissioned
*TRUXTUN	CGN 35	New York Shipbuilding Corp (Camden, New Jersey)	17 June 1963	19 Dec 1964	27 May 1967

Displacement, tons: 8 200 standard; 9 127 full load
Length, feet (metres): 564 *(117·9)* oa
Beam, feet (metres): 58 *(17·7)*
Draught, feet (metres): 31 *(9·4)*
Missile launchers: 1 twin Standard ER/ASROC launcher (Mk 10 Mod 8)
Guns: 1—5 inch *(127 mm)* 54 calibre (Mk 42)
2—3 inch *(76 mm)* 50 calibre (Mk 34) (single)
A/S weapons: ASROC (see above);
4 fixed torpedo tubes (Mk 32);
facilities for helicopter
Main engines: 2 geared turbines; 60 000 shp; 2 shafts
Nuclear reactors: 2 pressurised-water cooled D2G (General Electric)
Speed, knots: 30+
Complement: 492 (36 officers, 456 enlisted men)
Flag accommodations: 18 (6 officers, 12 enlisted men)

The *Truxtun* was the US Navy's fourth nuclear-powered surface warship. The Navy had requested seven oil-burning frigates in the Fiscal Year 1962 shipbuilding programme, the Congress authorised seven ships; but stipulated that one ship must be nuclear-powered.
Although the *Truxtun* design is adapted from the "Belknap" class design, the nuclear ship's gun-missile launcher arrangement is reversed from the non-nuclear ships.
Construction cost was $138 667 000.

Classification: The *Truxtun* was originally classified as a guided missile frigate (DLGN); subsequently reclassified as a guided missile cruiser (CGN) on 30 June 1975.

Electronics: Naval Tactical Data System (NTDS); Tacan.

Fire control: Mk 76 Mod 6 missile control system, one Mk 68 Mod 8 gunfire control system, two Mk 51 Mod 3 gun directors, one Mk 11 Mod 1 weapon direction system, one SPG-53A and two SPG-55B weapon control radars.

Engineering: Power plant is identical to that of the cruiser *Bainbridge*.

Gunnery: 2 Phalanx 20 mm systems to be fitted.

Missiles: The twin missile launcher aft can fire Standard ER anti-aircraft missiles and ASROC anti-submarine rockets.

Name: The *Truxtun* is the fifth ship to be named for Commodore Thomas Truxton *(sic)* who commanded the frigate *Constellation* (38 guns) in her successful encounter with the French frigate *L'Insurgente* (44) in 1799.

Radar: 3D Search; SPS-48.
Search; SPS-10 and 40.

Rockets: Mk 36 Chaffroc RBOC have been fitted.

Sonar: SQS-26 (bow-mounted).

Torpedoes: Fixed Mk 32 tubes are below 3-inch gun mounts, built into superstructure. The two Mk 25 torpedo tubes built into her stern are inoperative.

TRUXTUN   1/1977, Dr. Giorgio Arra

TRUXTUN   1/1977, Dr. Giorgio Arra

TRUXTUN   1/1977, Dr. Giorgio Arra

9 "BELKNAP" CLASS (GUIDED MISSILE CRUISERS (CG))

Name	No.	Builders	Laid down	Launched	Commissioned
BELKNAP	CG 26	Bath Iron Works Corp	5 Feb 1962	20 July 1963	7 Nov 1964
*JOSEPHUS DANIELS	CG 27	Bath Iron Works Corp	23 April 1962	2 Dec 1963	8 May 1965
*WAINWRIGHT	CG 28	Bath Iron Works Corp	2 July 1962	25 April 1964	8 Jan 1966
*JOUETT	CG 29	Puget Sound Naval Shipyard	25 Sep 1962	30 June 1964	3 Dec 1966
*HORNE	CG 30	San Francisco Naval Shipyard	12 Dec 1962	30 Oct 1964	15 Apr 1967
*STERETT	CG 31	Puget Sound Naval Shipyard	25 Sep 1962	30 June 1964	8 Apr 1967
*WILLIAM H. STANDLEY	CG 32	Bath Iron Works Corp	29 July 1963	19 Dec 1964	9 July 1966
*FOX	CG 33	Todd Shipyard Corp	15 Jan 1963	21 Nov 1964	8 May 1966
*BIDDLE	CG 34	Bath Iron Works Corp	9 Dec 1963	2 July 1965	21 Jan 1967

Displacement, tons: 6 570 standard; 7 930 full load
Length, feet (metres): 547 (166·7) oa
Beam, feet (metres): 54·8 (16·7)
Draught, feet (metres): 28·8 (8·7)
Helicopters: 1 SH-2D LAMPS helicopter
Missile launchers: 1 twin Standard ER/ASROC launcher (Mk 10 Mod 7); Harpoon in Sterett (see notes)
Guns: 1—5 inch (127 mm) 54 cal (Mk 42)
2—3 inch (76 mm) 50 cal (Mk 34) (single)
A/S weapons: ASROC (see above); 2 triple torpedo tubes (Mk 32)
Main engines: 2 geared turbines (General Electric in CG 26-28, 32, 34; De Laval in CG 29-31, 33): 85 000 shp; 2 shafts
Boilers: 4 (Babcock & Wilcox in CG 26-28, 32, 34; Combustion Engineering in CG 29-31, 33)
Speed, knots: 34
Complement: 418 (31 officers, 387 enlisted men) including squadron staff
Flag accommodations: 18 (6 officers; 12 enlisted men)

These ships were authorised as guided missile frigates; DLG 26-28 in the Fiscal Year 1961 shipbuilding programme; DLG 29-34 in the FY 1962 programme.
All ships of this class are active except the Belknap, which was severely damaged in a collision with the carrier John F. Kennedy (CV 67) on 22 Nov 1975 near Sicily; the cruiser was towed back to the United States for rebuilding at Philadelphia Naval Shipyard, estimated to take about two years. Placed "Out of Commission—Special" 20 Dec 1975.

Classification: These ships were originally classified as guided missile frigates (DLG); reclassified as guided missile cruisers (CG) on 30 June 1975.

Design: These ships are distinctive by having their single missile launcher forward and 5 inch gun mount aft. This arrangement allowed missile stowage in the larger bow section and provided space aft of the superstructure for a helicopter hangar and platform. The reverse gun-missile arrangement, preferred by some commanding officers, is found in the Truxtun.

Electronics: Naval Tactical Data System (NTDS); Tacan.

Fire control: Two Mk 76 Mod 6 missile control systems, one Mk 68 Mod 8 gunfire control system, two Mk 51 Mod 3 gun directors (removed from Sterett in 1976), one Mk 11 Mod 0 weapon direction system, one SPG-53A and two SPG-55B weapon control radars.

Gunnery: All of this class will be fitted with two Phalanx 20 mm CIWS as will Belknap during rebuilding. One 40 mm mount was removed from Wainwright and two 76 mm 50 from Sterett in 1976 to make way for Harpoon.

Helicopters: These ships are the only conventionally powered US cruisers with a full helicopter support capability. All fitted with the Light Airborne Multi-Purpose System, now the SH-2D helicopter. The Belknap embarked the first operational SH-2D/LAMPS in December 1971.

Missiles: The Truxtun and "Belknap" class ships have a twin Terrier/ASROC Mk 10 missile launcher. A "triple-ring" rotating magazine stocks both Terrier anti-craft missiles and ASROC anti-submarine rockets, feeding either weapon to the launcher's two firing arms. The rate of fire and reliability of the launcher provide a potent AAW/ASW capability to these ships. Sterett had a Harpoon system installed in 1976. The rest of the class will be similarly fitted in the near future.

Radar: 3D Search; SPS 48.
Search; SPS 10 and 37 (26-28) or 40 (remainder).

Rockets: Mk 36 Chaffroc RBOC to be fitted in place of Mk 28.

Sonar: SQS-26 (bow mounted).

Torpedoes: As built, these ships each had two 21 inch tubes for anti-submarine torpedoes installed in the structure immediately forward of the 5 inch mount, one tube angled out to port and one to starboard; subsequently removed.

WILLIAM H. STANDLEY   4/1976, USN

JOSEPHUS DANIELS   1972, Dr. Giorgio Arra

WILLIAM H. STANDLEY   9/1976, Dr. Giorgio Arra

9 "LEAHY" CLASS (GUIDED MISSILE CRUISERS (CG))

Name	No.	Builders	Laid down	Launched	Commissioned
*LEAHY	CG 16	Bath Iron Works Corp	3 Dec 1959	1 July 1961	4 Aug 1962
*HARRY E. YARNELL	CG 17	Bath Iron Works Corp	31 May 1960	9 Dec 1961	2 Feb 1963
*WORDEN	CG 18	Bath Iron Works Corp	19 Sep 1960	2 June1962	3 Aug 1963
*DALE	CG 19	New York SB Corp	6 Sep 1960	28 July 1962	23 Nov 1963
*RICHMOND K. TURNER	CG 20	New York SB Corp	9 Jan 1961	6 Apr 1963	13 June1964
*GRIDLEY	CG 21	Puget Sound Bridge & Dry Dock Co	15 July 1960	31 July 1961	25 May 1963
*ENGLAND	CG 22	Todd Shipyards Corp	4 Oct 1960	6 Mar 1962	7 Dec 1963
*HALSEY	CG 23	San Francisco Naval Shipyard	26 Aug 1960	15 Jan 1962	20 July 1963
*REEVES	CG 24	Puget Sound Naval Shipyard	1 July 1960	12 May 1962	15 May 1964

Displacement, tons: 5 670 standard; 7 800 full load
Length, feet (metres): 533 (162·5) oa
Beam, feet (metres): 54·9 (16·6)
Draught, feet (metres): 26 (7·9)
Missile launchers: 2 twin Standard-ER surface-to-air launchers (Mk 10 Mod 5 and Mod 6)
Guns: 4—3 inch (76 mm) 50 cal (Mk 33) (twin)
A/S weapons: 1 ASROC 8-tube launcher; 2 triple torpedo tubes (Mk 32)
Main engines: 2 geared turbines (see Engineering notes); 85 000 shp; 2 shafts
Boilers: 4 (Babcock & Wilcox in CG 16-20, Foster Wheeler in 21-24)
Speed, knots: 34
Complement: 377 (18 officers, 359 enlisted men) (16, 17, 21, 23); 413 (32 officers, 381 men) (18-20, 22, 24)
Flag accommodations: 18 (6 officers, 12 enlisted men)

These ships are "double-end" missile cruisers especially designed to screen fast carrier task forces. They are limited in only having 3 inch guns. Authorised as DLG 16-18 in the Fiscal Year 1958 new construction programme and DLG 19-24 in the FY 1959 programme.

Classification: These ships were originally classified as guided missile frigates (DLG); reclassified as guided missile cruisers (CG) on 30 June 1975.

Design: These ships are distinctive in having twin missile launchers forward and aft with ASROC launcher between the forward missile launcher and bridge on main deck level.
There is a helicopter landing area aft but only limited support facilities are provided; no hangar.

Electronics: Naval Tactical Data System (NTDS) fitted during AAW modernisation.

Engineering: General Electric turbines in CG 16-18, De Laval turbines in CG 19-22, and Allis-Chalmers turbines in CG 23 and CG 24.

Fire control: Four Mk 76 Mod 5 missile control systems, two Mk 63 Mod 28 gunfire control systems, one Mk 11 Mod 2 weapon direction system, two SPG-50 and four SPG-55 weapon control radars.

Gunnery: 2 Phalanx 20 mm CIWS to be fitted.

Missiles: Reportedly, each ship carries 80 missiles divided between the two magazines. Harpoon to be fitted.

Modernisation: These ships were modernised between 1967 and 1972 to improve their Anti-Air Warfare (AAW) capabilities. Superstructure enlarged to provide space for additional electronic equipment, including NTDS; improved Tacan fitted and improved guidance system for Terrier/Standard missiles installed, and larger ship's service turbo generators provided.
All ships modernised at Bath Iron Works except Leahy at Philadelphia Naval Shipyard.
Cost of Leahy modernisation was $36 100 000.

Radar: 3D Search; SPS 48 (replacing SPS-39 or 52 in some ships)
Search; SPS 10, 37

Rockets: Mk 36 Chaffroc ROBC to be fitted.

Sonar: SQS-23 bow-mounted.

HALSEY   9/1975, USN

HARRY E. YARNELL   1971, USN

LEAHY   1976, Michael D. J. Lennon

1 "BAINBRIDGE" CLASS (NUCLEAR-POWERED GUIDED MISSILE CRUISER (CGN))

Name	No.	Builders	Laid down	Launched	Commissioned
*BAINBRIDGE	CGN 25	Bethlehem Steel Co (Quincy, Mass)	15 May 1959	15 April 1961	6 Oct 1962

Displacement, tons: 7 600 standard; 8 580 full load
Length, feet (metres): 550 *(167·6)* wl; 565 *(172·5)* oa
Beam, feet (metres): 57·9 *(17·6)*
Draught, feet (metres): 31 *(9·5)*
Missile launchers: 2 twin Terrier Standard ER surface-to-air launchers
Guns: 4—3 inch *(76 mm)* 50 calibre (Mk 33) (twin)
A/S weapons: 1 ASROC 8-tube launcher; 2-triple torpedo tubes (Mk 32)
Main engines: 2 geared turbines, approx 60 000 shp; 2 shafts
Nuclear reactors: 2 pressurised-water cooled D2G (General Electric)
Speed, knots: 30+
Complement: 470 (34 officers, 436 enlisted men)
Flag accommodations: 18 (6 officers, 12 enlisted men)

The *Bainbridge* was the US Navy's third nuclear powered surface warship (after the cruiser *Long Beach* and the aircraft carrier *Enterprise).* Authorised in the FY 1956 shipbuilding

programme. Construction cost was $163 610 000.

Classification: The *Bainbridge* was originally classified as a guided missile frigate (DLGN); reclassified as a guided missile cruiser (CGN) on 30 June 1975.

Design: The ship is similar in basic arrangements to the "Leahy" class cruisers.

Engineering: Development of a nuclear power plant suitable for use in a large "destroyer type" warship began in 1957. The Atomic Energy Commission's Knolls Atomic Power Laboratory undertook development of the destroyer power plant (designated D1G/D2G).

Fire control: Two Mk 76 Mod 1 missile control systems, two Mk 63 Mod 28 gunfire control systems, one Mk 7 Mod 0 weapons direction system, two SPG-50 and four SPG-55A weapon control radars.

Missiles: The *Bainbridge* has a Terrier Mk 10 Mod 5 launcher forward and a Mk 10 Mod 6 launcher aft. Reportedly, the ship carries 80 missiles divided between the forward and aft rotating magazines. To be fitted with Harpoon.

Modernisation: The *Bainbridge* underwent an Anti-Air Warfare (AAW) modernisation at the Puget Sound Naval Shipyard from 30 June 1974 to 24 Sep 1976. The ship was fitted with the Naval Tactical Data System (NTDS) and improved guidance capability for missiles. Estimated cost of modernisation $103 000 000.

Radar: 3D Search; SPS-52
Search; SPS-10 and 37

Rockets: Mk 36 Chaffroc ROBC to be fitted.

Sonar: SQS-23 (bow-mounted)

BAINBRIDGE

1 "LONG BEACH" CLASS (NUCLEAR-POWERED GUIDED MISSILE CRUISER (CGN))

Name	No.	Builders	Laid down	Launched	Commissioned
*LONG BEACH	CGN 9 (ex-CGN 160, CLGN 160)	Bethlehem Steel Co, Quincy, Massachusetts	2 Dec 1957	14 July 1959	9 Sep 1961

Displacement, tons: 14 200 standard; 15 540 light; 17 100 full load
Length, feet (metres): 721·2 *(219·8)* oa
Beam, feet (metres): 73·2 *(22·3)*
Draught, feet (metres): 31 *(9·5)*
Missile launchers: 1 twin Talos surface-to-air launcher (Mk 12 Mod 0); 2 twin Terrier Standard-ER surface-to-air launchers (Mk 10 Mod 1 and 2)
Guns: 2—5 inch *(127 mm)* 38 calibre (Mk 30) (single)
A/S weapons: 1 ASROC 8-tube launcher; 2 triple torpedo tubes (Mk 32)
Helicopter: Deck for utility helicopter
Main engines: 2 geared turbines (General Electric); approx 80 000 shp; 2 shafts
Nuclear reactors: 2 pressurised-water cooled C1W (Westinghouse)
Speed, knots: 30
Complement: 1 160 (79 officers, 1 081 enlisted men)
Flag accommodations: 68 (10 officers, 58 enlisted men)

The *Long Beach* was the first ship to be designed as a cruiser for the United States since the end of World War II. She is the world's first nuclear-powered surface warship and the first warship to have a guided missile main battery. She was authorised in the Fiscal Year 1957 new construction program-

me. Estimated construction cost was $332 850 000.

Aegis: Long-lead funding for a scaled-down Aegis system was provided in FY 1977 programme but cancelled in Dec 1976 because of cost. In place of this an improved "Albany" type AAW modernization is planned for early 1980s.

Classification: Ordered as a guided missile light cruiser (CLGN 160) on 15 Oct 1956; reclassified as a guided missile cruiser (CGN 160) early in 1957 and renumbered (CGN 9) on 1 July 1957.

Design: Initially planned at about 7 800 tons (standard) to test the feasibility of a nuclear-powered surface warship. Early in 1956 her displacement was increased to 11 000 tons and a second Terrier missile launcher was added. A Talos missile launcher was also added which, with other features, increased displacement to 14 200 tons.

Electronics: Four Mk 76 Mod 1 missile fire control systems, one Mk 77 Mod 4 missile fire control system, two Mk 56 gunfire control systems, one Mk 6 weapon direction system, two SPG-49B and four SPG-55A weapon-control radars. Naval Tactical Data System (NTDS).

Engineering: The reactors are similar to those of *Enterprise*

(CVN 65). The *Long Beach* first got underway on nuclear power on 5 July 1961. After four years of operation and having steamed more than 167 700 miles she underwent her first overhaul and refuelling at the Newport News Shipbuilding and Dry Dock Company from August 1965 to February 1966.

Gunnery: Completed with an all-missile armament. Two single 5 inch mounts were fitted during 1962-1963. 2 Phalanx 20 mm CIWS to be fitted.

Missiles: The *Long Beach* has two Terrier twin missile launchers stepped forward and one Talos twin missile launcher aft. Reportedly, her magazines hold 120 Terrier missiles and approx 46 Talos missiles. Harpoon to be fitted.

Radar: Long range fixed search; SPS-32
Long range target tracking; SPS-33
(Fixed arrays "billboards" on bridge, SPS 32 horizontal and 33 vertical—both modified in 1970).
Search; SPS 10 and 12

Rockets: Mk 36 Chaffroc to be fitted in place of Mk 28.

Sonar: SQS-23.

LONG BEACH

1968, United States Navy

2 "ALBANY" CLASS (GUIDED MISSILE CRUISERS (CG))

Name	No.	Builders	Laid down	Launched	Commissioned
*ALBANY	CG 10 (ex-CA 123)	Bethlehem Steel Co (Fore River)	6 Mar 1944	30 June 1945	15 June 1946
*CHICAGO	CG 11 (ex-CA 136)	Philadelphia Navy Yard	28 July 1943	20 Aug 1944	10 Jan 1945

Displacement, tons: 13 700 standard; 17 500 full load
Length, feet (metres): 664 *(202·4)* wl; 674 *(205·4)* oa
Beam, feet (metres): 70 *(21·6)*
Draught, feet (metres): 30 *(9·1)*
Missile launchers:
  2 twin Talos surface-to-air launchers (Mk 12 Mod 1)
  2 twin Tartar surface-to-air launchers (Mk 11 Mod 1 and Mod 2)
Guns: 2—5 inch *(127 mm)* 38 calibre (Mk 24) (single)
A/S weapons: 1 ASROC 8-tube launcher; 2 triple torpedo tubes (Mk 32)
Helicopters: Deck for utility helicopters
Main engines: 4 geared turbines (General Electric); 120 000 shp; 4 shafts
Boilers: 4 (Babcock & Wilcox)
Speed, knots: 32
Complement: 1 222 (72 officers, 1 150 enlisted men)
Flag accommodations: 68 (10 officers, 58 enlisted men)

These ships were fully converted from heavy cruisers, the *Albany* having been a unit of the "Oregon City" class and the *Chicago* of the "Baltimore" class. Although the two heavy cruiser classes differed in appearance they had the same hull dimensions and machinery. These ships form a new, homogeneous class.
The cruiser *Fall River* (CA 131) was originally scheduled for missile conversion, but was replaced by the *Columbus* (now deleted). Proposals to convert two additional heavy cruisers (CA 124 and CA 130) to missile ships (CG 13 and CG 14) were dropped, primarily because of high conversion costs and improved capabilities of newer missile-armed frigates.

Conversion: During conversion these ships were stripped down to their main hulls with all cruiser armament and superstructure being removed. New superstructures make extensive use of aluminium to reduce weight and improve stability. The *Albany* was converted at the Boston Naval Shipyard between January 1959 and new commissioning on 3 Nov 1962; *Chicago* at San Francisco Naval Shipyard from July 1959 to new commissioning on 2 May 1964.

Electronics: Naval Tactical Data System (NTDS) is fitted.

Fire control: Two Mk 77 Mod 3 missile fire control systems, four Mk 74 Mod 1 missile fire control systems, two Mk 56 Mod 43 gunfire control systems, one Mk 6 Mod 2 or Mod 3 weapon direction system, four SPG-49B and four SPG-51C weapon control radars.

Gunnery: No guns were fitted when these ships were converted to missile cruisers. Two single open-mount 5 inch guns were fitted subsequently to provide low-level defence. Phalanx 20 mm CIWS to be fitted.

Missiles: One twin Talos launcher is forward and one aft, a twin Tartar launcher is on each side of the main bridge structure. During conversion, space was allocated amidships for installation of eight Polaris missile tubes, but the plan to install ballistic missiles in cruisers was cancelled in mid-1959. Reportedly 92 Talos and 80 Tartar missiles are carried.
Harpoon to be fitted.

Modernisation: The *Albany* underwent an extensive anti-air warfare modernisation at the Boston Naval Shipyard, including installation of NTDS, a digital Talos fire-control system and improved radars. This began in February 1967 and was completed in August 1969. She was formally recommissioned on 9 Nov 1968. The *Chicago* will not have AAW modernisation.

Radar: *Albany*
3D Search; SPS 48
Search; SPS 10, 30 and 43
Chicago
Search; SPS 10, 30, 43 and 52

Rockets: Mk 28 Chaffroc to be fitted.

Sonar: SQS-23 (bow mounted)

ALBANY   8/1975, USN

ALBANY   1976, Michael D. J. Lennon

ALBANY   9/1975, Reinhard Nerlich

3 CONVERTED "CLEVELAND" CLASS (GUIDED MISSILE CRUISERS (CG))

Name	No.	Builders	Laid down	Launched	Commissioned	CLG Comm.
*OKLAHOMA CITY	CG 5 (ex-CLG 5, ex-CL 91)	Cramp Shipbuilding (Philadelphia)	8 Mar 1942	20 Feb 1944	22 Dec 1944	7 Sep 1960
PROVIDENCE	CG 6 (ex-CLG 6, ex-CL 82)	Bethlehem Steel Co. (Quincy)	27 July 1943	28 Dec 1944	15 May 1945	17 Sep 1959
SPRINGFIELD	CG 7 (ex-CLG 7, ex-CL 66)	Bethlehem Steel Co. (Quincy)	13 Feb 1943	9 Mar 1944	9 Sep 1944	2 July 1960

Displacement, tons: 10 670 standard; 14 400 full load
Length, feet (metres): 600 *(182·9)* wl; 610 *(185·9)* oa
Beam, feet (metres): 66·3 *(20·2)*
Draught, feet (metres): 25 *(7·6)*
Missile launchers:
  CG 5: 1 twin Talos surface-to-air launcher (Mk 7 Mod 0)
  CG 6, 7: 1 twin Terrier surface-to-air launcher (Mk 9 Mod 1 or 2)
Guns: 3—6 inch *(152 mm)* 47 cal (triple); 2—5 inch *(127 mm)* 38 cal (Mk 32) (twin)
Helicopters: Utility helicopter carried
Main engines: 4 geared turbines (General Electric); 100 000 shp; 4 shafts
Boilers: 4 (Babcock & Wilcox)
Speed, knots: 31·6 knots
Complement: approx 1 350 (89/92 officers; 1 245/1 288 enlisted men)
Flag accommodations: 216 (50 officers; 166 enlisted men)

Originally a series of six ships converted from light cruisers of the "Cleveland" class; three ships converted to Terrier missile configuration aft and three ships to Talos missile aft, with two ships of each missile type configured to serve as fleet flagships. The surviving ships are all fitted as fleet flagships.
The *Providence* was decommissioned on 31 Aug 1973 and the *Springfield* on 15 June 1974; *Oklahoma City* is flagship of the US Seventh Fleet in the Western Pacific (homeported in Yokosuka, Japan).

Classification: Upon conversion to missile configuration these ships were reclassified as guided missile light cruisers (CLG). On 30 June 1975 the surviving four ships were reclassified as guided missile cruisers (CG).

Conversion: All six of these ships had their two after 6 inch gun turrets replaced by a twin surface-to-air missile launcher, superstructure enlarged to support missile fire control equipment, lattice masts fitted to carry antennae, 5 inch battery reduced from original 12 guns and all 40 mm and 20 mm light anti-aircraft guns removed. The four ships fitted as fleet flagships additionally had their No. 2 turret of 6 inch guns removed and their forward superstructure enlarged to provide command and communications spaces. *Oklahoma City* began conversion at the Bethlehem Steel shipyard in San Francisco in May 1957 and was commissioned on 7 September 1960; *Providence* began conversion at the Boston Naval Shipyard in June 1957 and was commissioned on 17 September 1959; the *Springfield* began conversion at the Bethlehem Steel shipyard in Quincy, Massachusetts, in August 1957, but was moved to the Boston Naval Shipyard in March 1960 for completion and commissioning on 2 July 1960. There is a helicopter landing area on the fantail, but only limited support facilities are provided; no hangar.

Fire control: CG 5 has Mk 77 missile fire control systems and the Terrier ships Mk 73; all had one Mk 34 gun director and one Mk 37 gunfire control system; CG 5 has two Mk 2 weapon direction system and two SPG-49A weapon control radars; Terrier ships one Mk 3 weapon direction system and two SPQ-5A radars.

Gunnery: 2 Phalanx 20 mm CIWS to be fitted in *Oklahoma City*.

Missiles: Reportedly, the cruisers armed with Terrier each carry 120 missiles and the ship armed with Talos carries 46 missiles.

Radar: 3D Search; SPS-52 (6 and 7)
Search; SPS 10, 30 and 43 (5 and 7)
SPS 10, 30 and 37 (6)

Sonar: None.

PROVIDENCE USN

SPRINGFIELD 1973, USN

OKLAHOMA CITY 11/1976, Dr. Giorgio Arra

3 "DES MOINES" CLASS (HEAVY CRUISERS (CA))

Name	No.	Builders	Laid down	Launched	Commissioned
DES MOINES	CA 134	Bethlehem Steel Co (Fore River)	28 May 1945	27 Sep 1946	16 Nov 1948
SALEM	CA 139	Bethlehem Steel Co (Fore River)	4 July 1945	25 Mar 1947	14 May 1949
NEWPORT NEWS	CA 148	Newport News SB & DD Co	1 Oct 1945	6 Mar 1947	29 Jan 1949

Displacement, tons: 17 000 standard; 21 470 full load
Length, feet (metres): 700 *(213·4)* wl; 716·5 *(218·4)* oa
Beam, feet (metres): 76·3 *(23·3)*
Draught, feet (metres): 26 *(7·9)*
Guns: 9—8 inch *(203 mm)* 55 cal (triple) except 6—8 inch guns
in *Newport News* (see *Gunnery* notes); 12—5 inch *(127 mm)*
38 cal (Mk 32) twin; 20—3 inch *(76 mm)* 50 cal (Mk 32) (twin),
2—3 inch *(Newport News)*
Main engines: 4 geared turbines (General Electric); 120 000
shp; 4 shafts
Boilers: 4 (Babcock & Wilcox)
Speed, knots: 33
Complement: 1 803 (116 officers, 1 687 enlisted men) *(Des
Moines)*
1 738 (115 officers, 1 623 enlisted men (remainder)
Flag accommodations: 267 (65 officers, 206 enlisted men) in
Newport News

NEWPORT NEWS   10/1974, USN

These ships were the largest and most powerful 8 inch gun
cruisers ever built. Completed too late for World War II, they
were employed primarily as flagships for the Sixth Fleet in the
Mediterranean and the Second Fleet in the Atlantic. The *Salem*
was decommissioned on 30 Jan 1959 and the *Des Moines* on 14
July 1961. The *Newport News* long served as flagship of the US
Second Fleet in the Atlantic. Her decommissioning was
delayed several times to enable her to provide gunfire support
in Vietnam. Decommissioned on 27 June 1975, the last active
all-gun cruiser of the US Navy.

Aircraft: As completed the *Des Moines* had two stern catapults
and carried four floatplanes; catapults later removed.

Design: These ships are an improved version of the previous
"Oregon City" class. The newer cruisers have automatic main
batteries, larger main turrets, taller fire control towers, and
larger bridges. The *Des Moines* and *Newport News* are fully
air-conditioned.
Additional ships of this class were cancelled: the *Dallas* (CA
140) and the unnamed CA 141-142, CA 149-153.

Electronics: Tacan.

Fire control: Two Mk 56 and two Mk 54 gunfire control directors
(Newport News).

Gunnery: These cruisers were the first ships to be armed with
fully automatic 8 inch guns firing cased ammunition. The guns
can be loaded at any elevation from –5 to +41 degrees; rate of
fire is four times faster than earlier 8 inch guns. Mk XVI 8-inch
guns in these ships; other heavy cruisers remaining on Navy
List have Mk XV guns.

As built, these ships mounted 12—5 inch guns, 24—3 inch guns
(in twin mounts), and 12—20 mm guns (single mounts). The 20
mm guns were removed almost immediately and the 3 inch
battery was reduced gradually as ships were overhauled. With
full armament the designed wartime complement was 1 860.
The No. 2 main gun turret of the *Newport News* was severely
damaged by an accidental explosion in October 1972; not

repaired and centre gun subsequently removed. The turret is
not operable.

Modernisation: The *Newport News* was extensively modified
to provide improved flagship facilities.

Radar: SPS-6, 8, 10 and 37 *(Newport News)*.

NEWPORT NEWS   10/1974, USN

1 "BALTIMORE" CLASS (HEAVY CRUISER (CA))

Name	No.	Builders	Laid down	Launched	Commissioned
SAINT PAUL	CA 73	Bethlehem Steel Co (Fore River)	3 Feb 1943	16 Sep 1944	17 Feb 1945

Displacement, tons: 13 600 standard; 17 750 full load
Length, feet (metres): 664 *(204·4)* wl; 673·5 *(205·3)* oa
Beam, feet (metres): 70·9 *(21·6)*
Draught, feet (metres): 26 *(7·9)*
Guns: 9—8 inch *(203 mm)* 55 cal (triple); 10—5 inch *(127 mm)* 38 cal (Mk 32) (twin); 12—3 inch *(76 mm)* 50 cal (Mk 33) (twin)
Main engines: 4 geared turbines (General Electric); 120 000 shp; 4 shafts
Boilers: 4 (Babcock & Wilcox)
Speed, knots: 33
Complement: 1 777 (106 officers, 1 671 enlisted men)
Flag accommodations: 217 (37 officers, 180 enlisted men)

The *Saint Paul* is the last all-gun cruiser of the "Baltimore" class. Fourteen of these ships were completed 1943-1945. This was the largest class of heavy (8-inch gun) cruisers built by any navy. Two missile ship conversions remain on the Navy List (see *Conversion* notes). The *Saint Paul* was the US Navy's last all-gun cruiser in commission except for the *Newport News;* the former ship was decommissioned 30 April 1971 and placed in reserve.

Aircraft: As completed the "Baltimore" class ships had two stern catapults and carried four floatplanes; catapults removed after World War II. Hangar under fantail.

Conversions: Two ships of this class were converted to partial missile configurations, the *Boston* (CA 69/CAG 1) and *Canberra* (CA 70/CAG 2); and two ships were converted to all-missile configurations, the *Columbus* (CA 74/CG 12) and *Chicago* (CA 136 now CG 11).

Gunnery: As built the "Baltimore" class cruisers were armed with nine 8 inch guns, 12—5 inch guns, 48—40 mm guns, and 23—20 mm guns. After World War II all 20 mm weapons were removed and the 40 mm guns were replaced by 20—3 inch guns. Subsequently the 5 inch twin mount forward of the bridge was removed from the *Saint Paul* and the number of 3 inch twin gun mounts was reduced.

Modernisation: The *Saint Paul* was extensively modified to serve as flagship for the Seventh Fleet in the western Pacific; advanced communications equipment installed and amidships structure built up to provide more office space.

Name: The *Saint Paul* was renamed during construction; ex-*Rochester.*

Radar: (On decommissioning); SPS-8 and 37.

SAINT PAUL

USN

1 "CANBERRA" CLASS (Ex-CAG) (HEAVY CRUISER (CA))

Name	No.	Builders	Laid down	Launched	Commissioned	CAG Comm.
CANBERRA	CA 70 (ex-CAG 2)	Bethlehem Steel Co (Fore River)	3 Sep 1941	19 April 1943	14 Oct 1943	15 June 1956

Displacement, tons: 13 300 standard; 17 750 full load
Length, feet (metres): 664 *(222·3)* wl; 673·5 *(205·3)* oa
Beam, feet (metres): 70·9 *(21·6)*
Draught, feet (metres): 26 *(7·9)*
Missile launchers: 2 twin Terrier surface-to-air launchers
Guns: 6—8 inch *(203 mm)* 55 cal (triple); 10—5 inch *(127 mm)* 38 cal (Mk 32) (twin); 4—3 inch *(76 mm)* 50 cal (Mk 33) (twin)
Main engines: 4 geared turbines (General Electric), 120 000 shp; 4 shafts
Boilers: 4 (Babcock & Wilcox)
Speed, knots: 33
Complement: 1 730 (110 officers; 1 620 enlisted men)
Flag accommodations: 72 (10 officers, 62 enlisted men)

The *Canberra* and her sister ship *Boston* (CA 69 ex-CAG 1) were the US Navy's first guided missile surface ships. They originally were heavy cruisers (CA) of the "Baltimore" class. The *Canberra* was converted 1952-1956 to a combination gun-missile configuration and reclassified CAG 2 on 4 Jan 1952.

Subsequently reverted to original classification of CA 70 on 1 May 1968; as a CA the *Canberra* retained the Terrier missile systems.
Retention of 8 inch guns forward made the *Boston* and *Canberra* valuable in the fire support role during the Vietnam War. The *Canberra* was decommissioned on 16 Feb 1970 and placed in reserve.

Conversion: The *Canberra* was converted to a missile configuration at the New York Shipbuilding Corp, Camden, New Jersey. Conversion included removal of after 8-inch gun turret (143 tons) and after twin 5-inch gun mount; all 40 mm and 20 mm guns replaced by six 3-inch twin mounts (subsequently reduced to two mounts). Original superstructure modified and twin funnels replaced by single large funnel as in "Oregon City" class. Forward pole mast replaced by lattice radar mast and radar platform fitted aft of pole mast. Missile systems include rotating magazine below decks, loading and check-out equipment, two large directors, and two launchers.

Electronics: Tacan.

Fire control: One Mk 37 Mod 91 and four Mk 56 Mod 15 gunfire control systems, one Mk 34 Mod 16 gun director, and one Mk 1 weapon direction system.

Missiles: Reportedly, the *Canberra* can carry 144 Terrier missiles in two rotating magazines. Each launcher can load and fire two missiles every 30 seconds; loading is completely automatic with the missiles sliding up onto the launchers when in the vertical position. Both missile launchers removed prior to decommissioning.

Name: The *Canberra* was originally named *Pittsburgh;* renamed while under construction in commemoration of the Australian cruiser of that name which was sunk at the Battle of Savo Island with several US Navy ships in August 1942. She is the only US warship named for a foreign capital city.

Radar: Search; SPS-30 and 43. Experimental radar removed.

CANBERRA

1968, USN

DESTROYERS

The rapid drop in destroyer numbers began to slow in September 1975 when the first of 30 "Spruance" class destroyers was commissioned. These ships will be completed at regular intervals through 1979. At this time the Navy plans to follow the "Spruance" class with a guided missile destroyer based on the same hull and machinery, but employing the Aegis missile system.

The US Navy destroyer force in early-1977 consisted of 61 ships (including 10 former "frigates") plus 29 ships assigned to the Naval Reserve Force (NRF) and manned partially by reservists.

Increasingly the Navy is using frigates for operations that pre- viously required destroyers. Although the frigates have modern anti-submarine weapons and sensors similar to destroyers, and in some classes superior, the frigates lack the guns, electronics, 30-knot speeds, and in most cases the surface-to-air missiles considered necessary for modern anti-air warfare and surface warfare operations.

Soon after the last of the "Spruance" class ships are completed in 1979, the destroyer force is expected to consist of 69 ships: the 39 missile-armed DDG type and the 30 "Spruance" class non-missile DD type. Most or all of the "Forrest Sherman" class destroyers and the few surviving "Gearing" class ships will probably be assigned to the Naval Reserve Force by that time.

CLASSIFICATION

All guided missile frigates (DLG/DLGN) on the Navy List as of 30 June 1975 were reclassified as guided missile cruisers (CG/CGN) except for the ten ships of the "Coontz" class which were reclassified as guided missile destroyers (DDG).

Previously two all-gun frigates had been reclassified as guided missile destroyers upon conversion to a missile configuration: *Mitscher* DDG 35 (ex-DL 2, ex-DD 927) and *John S. McCain* DDG 36 (ex-DL 3, ex-DD 928).

(10) GUIDED MISSILE DESTROYERS (DDG): AEGIS TYPE

	No.	Programme	Commission
One Ship	**DDG 47**	Proposed Fiscal Year 1978	1982
Three Ships	**DDG**	Planned FY 1980	
Three Ships	**DDG**	Planned FY 1981	
Three Ships	**DDG**	Planned FY 1982	

Displacement, tons: 9 055 full load
Length, feet (metres): approx 563·3 *(171·1)* oa
Beam, feet (metres): 55 *(17·6)*
Missile launchers: 2 twin Standard-MR/ASROC launchers (Mk 26); Harpoon surface-to-surface cannisters
Guns: 2—5 inch *(127 mm)* 54 cal; 2—20 mm Phalanx Close-In Weapon Systems (CIWS)
A/S weapons: 2 LAMPS helicopters; ASROC; torpedo tubes (Mk 32)
Main engines: 4 gas turbines; 80 000 shp; 2 shafts
Speed, knots: 30+
Complement: 316 (27 officers, 289 enlisted men)

The DDG 47 class fulfils the proposal for a non-nuclear Aegis-armed ship as proposed in the early 1970s with the designation DG, but subsequently dropped to avoid conflict with the Navy's nuclear-propelled cruiser programme.

The DDG 47 budget request is for $938 000 000 for the lead ship; follow-on ships are expected to cost slightly less, but still many times that of the late DG proposal. The high cost of these ships and the view that all high-capability Aegis ships should have nuclear propulsion have made the class the target of intensive Congressional criticism. The Navy-Department of Defense five-year plan provides for ten of these ships. A total of 20 to 30 DDG/CSGN Aegis ships is envisioned by the Navy.

Builder: Ingall SB Divn Litton Industries is suggested as a likely builder for the first ships.

Design: The DDG 47 design is a modification of the "Spruance" class (DD 963). The same basic hull will be used, with the same gas turbine propulsion system. The design calls for one-inch steel armour plate to protect the magazines.

Electronics: Aegis is described under "Shipboard Systems". The DDG 47 will have the full Aegis electronics suite.

Fire Control: Aegis Weapons Control System Mk 1 with UYK-7 computers to control radar phasing, Mk 86 gunfire control system, four Mk 99 missile guidance illuminators. Mark 116 Underwater FCS.

Missiles: Two launchers will be provided for the Standard-MR surface-to-air missile. Standard Missile—2 now under trial. The Harpoon surface-to-surface missiles would be carried in two eight-tube deck canisters.

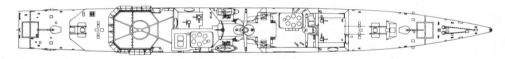

Radar: SPY-1A paired arrays (one forward, one aft)
Search; SPS-49
Weapons; SPQ-9

Sonar: SQS-53 and TACTAS towed array.

DDG 47 Class·   1976, A. D. Baker III

DDG 47 Class   1976, USN Drawing

10 "COONTZ" CLASS (GUIDED MISSILE DESTROYERS (DDG))

Name	No.	Builders	Laid down	Launched	Commissioned
*FARRAGUT	DDG 37 (ex-DLG 6)	Bethlehem Co, Quincy	3 June1957	18 July 1958	10 Dec 1960
*LUCE	DDG 38 (ex-DLG 7)	Bethlehem Co, Quincy	1 Oct 1957	11 Dec 1958	20 May 1961
*MACDONOUGH	DDG 39 (ex-DLG 8)	Bethlehem Co, Quincy	15 April1958	9 July 1959	4 Nov 1961
*COONTZ	DDG 40 (ex-DLG 9)	Puget Sound Naval Shipyard	1 Mar 1957	6 Dec 1958	15 July 1960
*KING	DDG 41 (ex-DLG 10)	Puget Sound Naval Shipyard	1 Mar 1957	6 Dec 1958	17 Nov 1960
*MAHAN	DDG 42 (ex-DLG 11)	San Francisco Naval Shipyard	31 July 1957	7 Oct 1959	25 Aug 1960
*DAHLGREN	DDG 43 (ex-DLG 12)	Philadelphia Naval Shipyard	1 Mar 1958	16 Mar 1960	8 April1961
*WILLIAM V. PRATT	DDG 44 (ex-DLG 13)	Philadelphia Naval Shipyard	1 Mar 1958	16 Mar 1960	4 Nov 1961
*DEWEY	DDG 45 (ex-DLG 14)	Bath Iron Works, Maine	10 Aug 1957	30 Nov 1958	7 Dec 1959
*PREBLE	DDG 46 (ex-DLG 15)	Bath Iron Works, Maine	16 Dec 1957	23 May 1959	9 May 1960

Displacement, tons: 4 700 standard; 5 800 full load
Length, feet (metres): 512·5 (156·2) oa
Beam, feet (metres): 52·5 (15·9)
Draught, feet (metres): 25 (7·6)
Missile launchers: 1 twin Terrier/Standard-ER surface-to-air launcher (Mk 10 Mod 0) (see Missile note)
Gun: 1—5 inch (127 mm) 54 cal (Mk 42) (see Gunnery note)
A/S weapons: 1 ASROC 8-tube launcher; 2 triple torpedo tubes (Mk 32)
Main engines: 2 geared turbines; 85 000 shp; 2 shafts
Boilers: 4 (Foster Wheeler in DDG 37-39; Babcock & Wilcox in DDG 40-46)
Speed, knots: 34
Complement: 377 (21 officers, 356 enlisted men)
Flag accommodations: 19 (7 officers, 12 enlisted men)

These ships are an improvement of the "Mitscher" class (DL/DDG). DDG 37-42 were authorised in the Fiscal Year 1956 programme; DDG 43-46 in FY 1957 programme. Average cost per ship was $52 000 000.
Although now classified as "destroyers", these ships have many of the capabilities of the larger US cruiser classes, including the Terrier/Standard-ER missile system and Naval Tactical Data System (NTDS).

Classification: The *Farragut, Luce* and *MacDonough* were initially classified as frigates (DL 6-8, respectively); changed to guided missile frigate (DLG) 6-8 on 14 Nov 1956. The first ship ordered as a missile frigate was the *Coontz* which became the name ship for the class. All ten ships were classified as guided missile frigates (DLG 6-15) from completion until 30 June 1975 when reclassified as guided missile destroyers (DDG 37-46).

Design: These ships were the only US guided missile "frigates" with separate masts and funnels. They have aluminium superstructures to reduce weight and improve stability. Early designs for this class had a second 5 inch gun mount in the "B" position; design revised when ASROC launcher was developed.
Helicopter landing area on stern, but no hangar and limited support capability.

Electronics: The *King* and *Mahan* along with the aircraft carrier *Oriskany* (CV 34) were the first ships fitted with the Naval Tactical Data System (NTDS), conducting operational evaluation of the equipment in 1961-1962. NTDS now in all ships.

Engineering: De Laval turbines in DDG 37-39 and DDG 46; Allis-Chalmers turbines in DDG 40-45.

Fire Control: Two Mk 76 missile fire control systems, one Mk 68 gunfire control system, one SPG-53A and two SPG-55B weapon control radars.

Gunnery: These ships have a Mk 42 single 5 inch gun forward. The original 4—3 inch 50 cal guns were removed during modernisation.
The *King* was fitted with the 20 mm Phalanx Close-In Weapon System (CIWS) for at-sea evaluation from August 1973 to March 1974. All ships to be fitted with Phalanx in near future.

Missiles: The first five ships of this class were built with Terrier BW-1 beam-riding missile systems; five later ships built with Terrier BT-3 homing missile systems. Reportedly, each ship carries 40 missiles. Harpoon to be fitted in all ships in near future.

Modernisation: These ships have been modernised to improve their Anti-Air Warfare (AAW) capabilities. Superstructure enlarged to provide space for additional electronic equipment, including NTDS (previously fitted in *King* and *Mahan*); improved Tacan installed, first five ships given improved guidance system for Terrier/Standard missiles (SPG-55 fire control radar), and larger ship's service turbo generators fitted. The *Farragut* also had improved ASROC reload capability provided (with additional structure forward of bridge) and second mast increased in height. (Other ships are not believed to carry ASROC reloads).
All ships modernised at Philadelphia Naval Shipyard, except *Mahan* at Bath Iron Works, Bath, Maine, and *King* at Boland Machine & Manufacturing Co, New Orleans, Louisiana between 1969 and 1977.
Cost of modernisation was $39 000 000 per ship in FY 1970 conversion programme.

Names: DDG 38 was to have been named *Dewey;* renamed *Luce* in 1957.

Radar: (After modernisation)
3D Search: SPS-48 (SPS-52 in *King* and *Pratt*)
Search: SPS 10 and 37

Rockets: Mark 36 Chaffroc system to be fitted.

Sonar: SQS-23.

WILLIAM V. PRATT   7/1976, A. D. Baker III

FARRAGUT   9/1976, Dr. Giorgio Arra

COONTZ   7/1976, Wright and Logan

FARRAGUT   9/1976, Dr. Giorgio Arra

2 "MITSCHER" CLASS (GUIDED MISSILE DESTROYERS (DDG))

Name	No.	Builders	Laid down	Launched	Commissioned
*MITSCHER	DDG 35 (ex-DL 2, ex-DD 927)	Bath Iron Works	3 Oct 1949	26 Jan 1952	15 May 1953
*JOHN S. McCAIN	DDG 36 (ex-DL 3, ex-DD 928)	Bath Iron Works	24 Oct 1949	12 July 1952	12 Oct 1953

Displacement, tons: 5 200 full load
Length, feet (metres): 493 (150·3) oa
Beam, feet (metres): 50 (15·2)
Draught, feet (metres): 21 (6·7)
Missile launchers: 1 single Tartar surface-to-air launcher (Mk 13 Mod 2)
Guns: 2—5 inch (127 mm) 54 calibre (Mk 42) (single)
A/S weapons: 1 ASROC 8-tube launcher; 2 triple torpedo tubes (Mk 32)
Main engines: 2 geared turbines (General Electric); 80 000 shp; 2 shafts
Boilers: 4 (Foster Wheeler)
Speed, knots: 33
Complement: 377 (28 officers, 349 enlisted men)

These ships are former "Mitscher" class all-gun frigates which have been converted to a guided missile and improved ASW configuration.

Appearance: Both ships now have the smaller Tacan (Tactical Air Navigation) antenna on the main mast, as shown here in the more recent photo of the *Mitscher*. The Tartar missile launcher is in the vertical position for loading; note the cylindrical structure below the launcher which houses the rotating missile magazine.

Classification: These ships were originally classified as destroyers (DD); reclassified as destroyer leaders (DL) on 9 Feb 1951 while under construction. The DL symbol was changed to "frigate" on 1 Jan 1955. Both ships were changed to DDG on 15 Mar 1967 during Tartar missile conversion.

Conversion: Both ships were converted to DDG at the Philadelphia Naval Shipyard. The *Mitscher* began conversion in March 1966, commissioning on 29 June 1968 and the *John S. McCain* in June 1966, commissioning on 21 June 1969. Superstructure was modified with ASROC launcher installed forward of the bridge in "B" position; two heavy lattice masts fitted; triple Mk 32 torpedo tubes retained amidships; and single Tartar launcher installed aft (system weighs approximately 135 000 pounds).

Fire Control: Mk 74 gun/missile fire control system, Mk 67 gunfire control system, and two SPG-51C missile control radars.

Missiles: Tartar magazine capacity is reported to be 40 missiles.

Radar: 3D Search; SPS-48 Search; SPS-10 and 37

Rockets: Mk 36 Chaffroc to be fitted.

Sonar: SQS 23 (hull mounted)

JOHN S. McCAIN
1975, USN

MITSCHER
1971, USN

MITSCHER
1973, Dr. Giorgio Arra

4 CONVERTED "FORREST SHERMAN" CLASS (GUIDED MISSILE DESTROYERS (DDG))

Name	No.	Builders	Laid down	Launched	Commissioned
*DECATUR	DDG 31 (ex-DD 936)	Bethlehem Steel Co (Quincy)	13 Sep 1954	15 Dec 1955	7 Dec 1956
*JOHN PAUL JONES	DDG 32 (ex-DD 932)	Bath Iron Works	18 Jan 1954	7 May 1955	5 Apr 1956
*PARSONS	DDG 33 (ex-DD 949)	Ingalls Shipbuilding Corp	17 June1957	19 Aug 1958	29 Oct 1959
*SOMERS	DDG 34 (ex-DD 947)	Bath Iron Works	4 Mar 1957	30 May 1958	3 Apr 1959

Displacement, tons: 4 150 full load
Length, feet (metres): 418·4 *(127·5)* oa
Beam, feet (metres): 44 *(13·4)*
Draught, feet (metres): 20 *(6·1)*
Missile launcher: 1 single Tartar surface-to-air launcher (Mk 13 Mod 1)
Gun: 1—5 inch *(127 mm)* 54 calibre (Mk 42)
A/S weapons: 1 ASROC 8-tube launcher; 2 triple torpedo tubes (Mk 32)
Main engines: 2 geared turbines (Westinghouse in *John Paul Jones* and *Decatur*; General Electric in others); 70 000 shp; 2 shafts
Boilers: 4 (Foster Wheeler in *Decatur*; Babcock & Wilcox in *John Paul Jones, Somers* and *Parsons)*
Speed, knots: 32·5 knots
Complement: 337 (22 officers, 315 enlisted men) *(Decatur* and *John Paul Jones)*
364 (25 officers and 339 enlisted men) *(Parsons* and *Somers)*

"Forrest Sherman" class destroyers that have been converted to a guided missile and improved ASW configuration. Plans for additional DDG conversions of this class were dropped. The *Decatur* was reclassified as DDG 31 on 15 Sep 1966; the *John Paul Jones, Somers* and *Parsons* became DDG on 15 Mar 1967. See "Forrest Sherman" class for additional notes.
All ships are active.

Conversion: The *Decatur* began conversion to a DDG at the Boston Naval Shipyard on 15 June 1965, the *John Paul Jones* at the Philadelphia Naval Shipyard on 2 Dec 1965, the *Parsons* at the Long Beach (California) Naval Shipyard on 30 June 1965, and the *Somers* at the San Francisco Bay Naval Shipyard on 30 Mar 1966.
Commissioned as DDGs on 29 Apr 1967, 23 Apr 1967, 3 Nov 1967 and 10 Feb 1968 respectively.
During conversion all existing armament was removed except the forward 5 inch gun; two triple ASW torpedo tubes were installed forward of the bridge; two heavy lattice masts fitted; ASROC launcher mounted aft of second stack; single Tartar Mk 13 launcher installed aft (on 01 level; system weighs approximately 135 000 pounds).
Original DDG conversion plans provided for Drone Anti-Submarine Helicopter (DASH) facilities; however, ASROC was substituted in all four ships as DASH lost favour in the Navy.

Fire Control: Mk 74 gun/missile fire control system, Mk 68 gunfire control system, and SPG-51C and SPG-53B weapon control radars.

Gunnery: These ships and the "Coontz" class are the only US destroyers with one 5 inch gun.

Missiles: Reportedly Tartar magazine capacity is 40 missiles.

Radar: 3D Search; SPS 48.
Search; SPS 10 and 37 (40 in *Somers)*

Rockets: Mk 36 Chaffroc to be fitted.

Sonar: SQS 23 (hull mounted)

PARSONS

12/1976, Dr. Giorgio Arra

DECATUR

1/1977, Dr. Giorgio Arra

DECATUR

1/1977, Dr. Giorgio Arra

23 "CHARLES F. ADAMS" CLASS (GUIDED MISSILE DESTROYERS (DDG))

Name	No.	Builders	Laid down	Launched	Commissioned
*CHARLES F. ADAMS	DDG 2	Bath Iron Works	16 June1958	8 Sep 1959	10 Sep 1960
*JOHN KING	DDG 3	Bath Iron Works	25 Aug 1958	30 Jan 1960	4 Feb 1961
*LAWRENCE	DDG 4	New York Shipbuilding Corp	27 Oct 1958	27 Feb 1960	6 Jan 1962
*CLAUDE V. RICKETTS	DDG 5	New York Shipbuilding Corp	18 May 1959	4 June1960	5 May 1962
*BARNEY	DDG 6	New York Shipbuilding Corp	18 May 1959	10 Dec 1960	11 Aug 1962
*HENRY B. WILSON	DDG 7	Defoe Shipbuilding Co	28 Feb 1958	23 April1959	17 Dec 1960
*LYNDE McCORMICK	DDG 8	Defoe Shipbuilding Co	4 April1958	9 Sep 1960	3 June1961
*TOWERS	DDG 9	Todd Shipyards Inc, Seattle	1 April1958	23 April1959	6 June1961
*SAMPSON	DDG 10	Bath Iron Works	2 Mar 1959	9 Sep 1960	24 June1961
*SELLERS	DDG 11	Bath Iron Works	3 Aug 1959	9 Sep 1960	28 Oct 1961
*ROBISON	DDG 12	Defoe Shipbuilding Co	23 April1959	27 April1960	9 Dec 1961
*HOEL	DDG 13	Defoe Shipbuilding Co	1 June1960	4 Aug 1960	16 June1962
*BUCHANAN	DDG 14	Todd Shipyards Inc, Seattle	23 April1959	11 May 1960	7 Feb 1962
*BERKELEY	DDG 15	New York Shipbuilding Corp	1 June1960	29 July 1961	15 Dec 1962
*JOSEPH STRAUSS	DDG 16	New York Shipbuilding Corp	27 Dec 1960	9 Dec 1961	20 April1963
*CONYNGHAM	DDG 17	New York Shipbuilding Corp	1 May 1961	19 May 1962	13 July 1963
*SEMMES	DDG 18	Avondale Marine Ways Inc	18 Aug 1960	20 May 1961	10 Dec 1962
*TATTNALL	DDG 19	Avondale Marine Ways Inc.	14 Nov 1960	26 Aug 1961	13 April1963
*GOLDSBOROUGH	DDG 20	Puget Sound Bridge & Dry Dock Co	3 Jan 1961	15 Dec 1961	9 Nov 1963
*COCHRANE	DDG 21	Puget Sound Bridge & Dry Dock Co	31 July 1961	18 July 1962	21 Mar 1964
*BENJAMIN STODDERT	DDG 22	Puget Sound Bridge & Dry Dock Co	11 June1962	8 Jan 1963	12 Sep 1964
*RICHARD E. BYRD	DDG 23	Todd Shipyards Inc, Seattle	12 Apr 1961	6 Feb 1962	7 Mar 1964
*WADDELL	DDG 24	Todd Shipyards Inc, Seattle	6 Feb 1962	26 Feb 1963	28 Aug 1964

Displacement, tons: 3 370 standard; 4 500 full load
Length, feet (metres): 437 *(133·2)* oa
Beam, feet (metres): 47 *(14·3)*
Draught, feet (metres): 20 *(6·1)*
Missile launchers: DDG 2-14: 1 twin Tartar surface-to-air launcher (Mk 11 Mod 0)
DDG 15-24: 1 single Tartar surface-to-air launcher (Mk 13 Mod 0) (see Missile note)
Guns: 2—5 inch *(127 mm)* 54 calibre (Mk 42) (single)
A/S weapons: 1 ASROC 8-tube launcher; 2 triple torpedo tubes (Mk 32)
Main engines: 2 geared steam turbines (General Electric in DDG 2, 3, 7, 8, 10-13, 15-22; Westinghouse in DDG 4-6, 9, 14, 23, 24); 70 000 shp; 2 shafts
Boilers: 4 (Babcock & Wilcox in DDG2, 3, 7, 8, 10-13, 20-22; Foster Wheeler in DDG 4-6, 9, 14; Combustion Engineering in DDG 15-19)
Speed, knots: 31+
Complement: 354 (24 officers, 330 enlisted men)

DDG 2-9 were authorised in the Fiscal Year 1957 new construction programme, DDG 10-14 in FY 1958, DDG 15-19 in FY 1959, DDG 20-22 in FY 1960, DDG 23-24 in FY 1961.

Classification: The first eight ships were to be a continuation of "Hull" class DDs and carried hull numbers DD 952-959. Redesigned as Guided Missile Destroyers and assigned DDG numbers. DDG 1 was the *Gyatt* (ex-DD 712), which operated as a missile destroyer from 1956 to 1962 armed with a twin Terrier launcher.

Design: These ships were built to an improved "Forrest Sherman" class design with aluminium superstructures and a high level of habitability including air conditioning in all living spaces. DDG 20-24 have stem anchors because of sonar arrangement.
Several ships have been modified with an extension of the bridge structure on the starboard side on the 02 level.

Fire Control: Mk 68 gunfire control system, Mk 4 weapon control system (except DDG 9, 12, 15 and 21), SPG-51C and SPG-53A weapon control radars.

Missiles: DDG 2-14 have a twin Mk 11 Tartar missile launcher while DDG 15-24 have a single Mk 13 Tartar launcher. Reportedly, their magazine capacities are 42 and 40 missiles, respectively, and ships equipped with either launcher can load, direct, and fire about six missiles per minute. *Lawrence* and *Hoel* fitted in 1972-1973 with multiple launcher for Chaparral (MIM-72A) for operational testing, in addition to their Tartar launcher.
All are being fitted to fire the Standard surface-to-surface missile (launched from Mk 11 or Mk 13 launcher).

Modernisation: This class will be modernised in the late 1970s and early 1980s. The first six ships are due under the FY 1980 programme. Long term lead items requested under FY 1978 ($94·5 million). Standard-ARM and Harpoon missile systems are to be fitted and the main guns and electronics are to be up-dated. Cost per ship (1977 prices) $102·5 million.

Names: DDG 5 was originally named *Biddle*; renamed *Claude V. Ricketts* on 28 July 1964.

Radar: 3D Search; SPS 39 (52 being fitted)
Search; SPS 10 and 37 (2-14)
SPS 10 and 40 (15-24); SPS-39

Rockets: Mk 36 Chaffroc will be fitted shortly.

Sonar: SQS-23 (bow-mounted) (20-24)
SQS-23 (hull-mounted) (remainder)

CHARLES F. ADAMS

1976, Michael D. J. Lennon

LYNDE McCORMICK

1975, A. Burgoyne

HENRY B. WILSON

1/1977, Dr. Giorgio Arra

COCHRANE

10/1976, Dr. Giorgio Arra

TATTNALL

1976, Michael D. J. Lennon

6 + 24 "SPRUANCE" CLASS (DESTROYERS (DD))

Name	No.	Laid down	Launched	Commissioned
*SPRUANCE	DD 963	17 Nov 1972	10 Nov 1973	20 Sep 1975
*PAUL F. FOSTER	DD 964	6 Feb 1973	23 Feb 1974	21 Feb 1976
*KINKAID	DD 965	19 April 1973	25 May 1974	10 July 1976
*HEWITT	DD 966	23 July 1973	24 Aug 1974	25 Sep 1976
*ELLIOTT	DD 967	15 Oct 1973	19 Dec 1974	22 Jan 1976
*ARTHUR W. RADFORD	DD 968	14 Jan 1974	1 Mar 1975	16 April 1977
PETERSON	DD 969	29 April 1974	21 June 1975	1977
CARON	DD 970	1 July 1974	24 June 1975	1977
DAVID R. RAY	DD 971	23 Sep 1974	23 Aug 1975	1977
OLDENDORF	DD 972	27 Dec 1974	21 Oct 1975	1977
JOHN YOUNG	DD 973	17 Feb 1975	7 Feb 1976	1977
COMTE DE GRASSE	DD 974	4 April 1975	26 Mar 1976	1977
O'BRIEN	DD 975	9 May 1975	8 July 1976	1977
MERRILL	DD 976	16 June 1975	1 Sep 1976	1978
BRISCOE	DD 977	21 July 1975	15 Dec 1976	1978
STUMP	DD 978	25 Aug 1975	29 Jan 1977	1978
CONOLLY	DD 979	29 Sep 1975	19 Feb 1977	1978
MOOSBURGGER	DD 980	3 Nov 1975	1977	1978
JOHN HANCOCK	DD 981	16 Jan 1976	1977	1978
NICHOLSON	DD 982	20 Feb 1976	1977	1978
JOHN RODGERS	DD 983	12 Aug 1976	1977	1978
LEFTWICH	DD 984	12 Nov 1976	1977	1978
CUSHING	DD 985	27 Dec 1976	1977	1979
HARRY W. HILL	DD 986	3 Jan 1977	1978	1979
O'BANNON	DD 987	21 Feb 1977	1978	1979
THORN	DD 988	1977	1978	1979
Four ships	**DD 989-992**	1977	1978	1979

Displacement, tons: 7 300 full load
Length, feet (metres): 529 *(161·2)* wl; 563·3 *(171·1)* oa
Beam, feet (metres): 55 *(17·6)*
Draught, feet (metres): 29 *(8·8)*
Guns: 2—5 inch *(127 mm)* 54 calibre (Mk 45) (single)
A/S weapons:
  1 SH-3 Sea King or 2 SH-2D LAMPS helicopters
  1 ASROC 8-tube launcher
  2 triple torpedo tubes (Mk 32)
Main engines: 4 gas turbines (General Electric); 80 000 shp;
  2 shafts
Speed, knots: 30+
Range, miles: 6 000 at 20 knots
Complement: 296 (24 officers, 272 enlisted men)

According to official statements, "the primary mission of these ships is anti-submarine warfare including operations as an integral part of attack carrier task forces."

The Fiscal Year 1969 new construction programme requested funding for the first five ships of this class, although, funds were denied by Congress. In the FY 1970 programme Congress approved funds for five ships, but increasing costs forced the Department of Defense to construct only three ships under the FY 1970 programme (DD 963-965); six ships were authorised in the FY 1971 programme (DD 966-971); seven ships (DD 972-978) in the FY 1972 programme; seven ships (DD 979-985) in the FY 1974 programme, and seven ships (DD 986-992) in the FY 1975 programme.

A/S weapons: The ASROC reload magazine is located under the launcher with the twin-cell launcher nacelles depressing to a vertical position.

Construction: All ships of this class are being built by the Litton Ship Systems Division of Litton Industries in Pascagoula, Mississippi.

Design: Extensive use of the modular concept is used to facilitate initial construction and block modernisation of the ships. The ships are highly automated, resulting in about 20 per cent reduction in personnel over a similar ship with conventional systems.

Engineering: These ships are the first large US warships to employ gas turbine propulsion. Each ship has four General Electric LM2500 marine gas turbine engines, a shaft-power version of the TF39 turbofan aircraft engine, and controllable-pitch propellers, because gas turbine engines cannot use a reversible shaft. Fitted with advanced self-noise reduction features.

Fire Control: Mk 116 digital underwater fire control system and Mk 86 Mod 3 gunfire control system and a Mk 91 missile FCS.

Gunnery: An improved 5 inch 54 calibre Mk 65 gun is being considered for use in later ships of the class. The "Spruance" design can accommodate the 8-inch Major Calibre Light-Weight Gun (MCLWG) (Mk 71). There are now plans to install that weapon in each ship's overhaul beginning 1980.
Two 20 mm Phalanx rapid-fire Close-In Weapon Systems (CIWS) are planned for installation.

Helicopters: Full helicopter facilities are provided to accommodate the Light Airborne Multi-Purpose System (LAMPS), now the SH-2D helicopter. However, the ship can handle the larger SH-3 Sea King series.

Missiles: The NATO Sea Sparrow multiple missile launcher (Mk 29) is planned for installation in these ships (between helicopter deck and after 5 inch gun mount).

Radar: Search; SPS-40
Weapon Control; SPG-60, SPQ-9 (SPS-55 planned)

Rockets: Mk 36 Chaffroc system is to be retrofitted in 1978-79 in DD 963-972 (in place of Mk 33) and in remainder during construction.

Sonar: SQS-53 (bow mounted) (SQS-35 VDS not fitted due to success with SQS-53).

Torpedoes: The triple Mk 32 torpedo tubes are inside the superstructure to facilitate maintenance and reloading; they are fired through side ports.

SPRUANCE   *1974, Litton Industries*

PAUL F. FOSTER   *4/1976, USN*

HEWITT

10/1975, Litton Industries

PAUL F. FOSTER

4/1976, USN

14 "FORREST SHERMAN" and "HULL" CLASSES (DESTROYERS (DD))

Name	No.	Builders	Laid down	Launched	Commissioned
*FORREST SHERMAN	DD 931	Bath Iron Works	27 Oct 1953	5 Feb 1955	9 Nov 1955
*BIGELOW	DD 942	Bath Iron Works	6 July 1955	2 Feb 1957	8 Nov 1957
*MULLINNIX	DD 944	Bethlehem Steel Co, Quincy, Mass	5 April 1956	18 Mar 1957	7 Mar 1958
*HULL	DD 945	Bath Iron Works	12 Sep 1956	10 Aug 1957	3 July 1958
*EDSON (NRF)	DD 946	Bath Iron Works	3 Dec 1956	1 Jan 1958	7 Nov 1958
*TURNER JOY	DD 951	Puget Sound Bridge & Dry Dock Co	30 Sep 1957	5 May 1958	3 Aug 1959

ANTI-SUBMARINE MODERNISATION

Name	No.	Builders	Laid down	Launched	Commissioned
*BARRY	DD 933	Bath Iron Works	15 Mar 1954	1 Oct 1955	31 Aug 1956
*DAVIS	DD 937	Bethlehem Steel Co, Quincy, Mass	1 Feb 1955	28 Mar 1956	28 Feb 1957
*JONAS INGRAM	DD 938	Bethlehem Steel Co, Quincy, Mass	15 June 1955	8 July 1956	19 July 1957
*MANLEY	DD 940	Bath Iron Works	10 Feb 1955	12 April 1956	1 Feb 1957
*DU PONT	DD 941	Bath Iron Works	11 May 1955	8 Sep 1956	1 July 1957
*BLANDY	DD 943	Bethlehem Steel Co, Quincy, Mass	29 Dec 1955	19 Dec 1956	26 Nov 1957
*MORTON	DD 948	Ingalls Shipbuilding Corp	4 Mar 1957	23 May 1958	26 May 1959
*RICHARD S. EDWARDS	DD 950	Puget Sound Bridge & Dry Dock Co	20 Dec 1956	24 Sep 1957	5 Feb 1959

Displacement, tons: approx 2 800 standard; approx 4 050 full load

Length, feet (metres): 418 *(127·4)* oa

Beam, feet (metres): 45 *(13·7)*

Draught, feet (metres): 20 *(6·1)*

Guns A/S Mod: 2—5 inch *(127 mm)* 54 calibre (Mk 42) (single)

Others: 3—5 inch *(127 mm)* 54 calibre (Mk 42) (single); 2—3 inch *(76 mm)* 50 cal (Mk 33) (twin) except *Hull* 1—8 inch *(203 mm)* (Mk 71); 2—5 inch 54 cal (Mk 42) (single) (see "Gunnery" notes)

A/S weapons: 2 triple torpedo tubes (Mk 32); 1 ASROC 8-tube launcher in A/S modified ships

Main engines: 2 geared turbines (Westinghouse in DD 931, 933, and 938; General Electric in others) 70 000 shp; 2 shafts

Boilers: 4 (Babcock & Wilcox in DD 931 and 933, 940-942, 945, 946, 950, 951; Foster Wheeler in others)

Speed, knots: 32·5 knots

Complement: 292 (17 officers, 275 enlisted men) in unmodified ships; 304 in A/S Mod ships (17 officers, 287 enlisted men)

These ships were the first US destroyers of post-World War II design and construction to be completed with the DD designation. Four have been converted to a guided missile configuration and are listed separately. They were authorised in the Fiscal Year 1952-1956 new construction programmes. These ships each cost approximately $26 000 000.

Edson was assigned to the NRF on April 1977 for employment as school ship for officer training at Newport, Rhode Island, and for reservist training.

Armament: As built all 18 ships of this class had three single 5 inch guns, two twin 3 inch mounts, four fixed 21 inch ASW torpedo tubes (amidships); two ASW hedgehogs (forward of bridge), and depth charge racks.

Design: The entire superstructure of these ships is of aluminium to obtain maximum stability with minimum displacement. All living spaces are air conditioned. The *Davis* and later ships have higher bows; the *Hull* and later ships have slightly different bow designs. The *Barry* had her sonar dome moved forward in 1959 and a stem anchor fitted.

Electronics: Several of the unmodified ships have elaborate electronic warfare pods on the main mast.

Gunnery: With original armament of one 5 inch mount forward and two 5 inch mounts aft, these were the first US warships with more firepower aft than forward. Note that *Barry* and later ships have their Mk 68 gunfire control director forward and Mk 56 director aft; positions reversed in earlier ships.

During 1974-1975 the *Hull* was fitted with an 8 inch gun forward to determine feasibility of installing a Major Calibre Light Weight Gun (MCLWG) in destroyer-type ships for shore bombardment. Forward 5 inch gun removed. There are no plans to remove the gun.

Single Phalanx 20 mm CIWS to be installed in *Bigelow*.

Modernisation: Eight ships of this class were extensively modified in 1967-1971 to improve their anti-submarine capabilities: *Barry, Davis, Du Pont* at the Boston Naval Shipyard; *Jonas Ingram, Manley, Blandy* at the Philadelphia Naval Shipyard; and *Morton, Richard S. Edwards* at the Long Beach (California) Naval Shipyard. During modernisation the anti-submarine torpedo tubes installed forward of bridge (on 01 level), deckhouse aft of second funnel extended to full width of ship, ASROC launcher installed in place of after gun mounts on 01 level, and variable depth sonar fitted at stern. Six ships of this class were not modernised because of increased costs.

Radar: Search: SPS 10, 37 or 40.

Sonar: SQS-23 (bow mounted in *Barry*, the first US ship so fitted).

VDS in A/S ships.

HULL with 8 inch gun forward   *4/1975, USN*

DU PONT (ASW modernisation)   *1976, Wright and Logan*

MULLINNIX   *1976, Michael D. J. Lennon*

32 "GEARING" CLASS (FRAM I) (DESTROYERS (DD))

Name	No.	Builders	Laid down	Launched	Commissioned
*WILLIAM R. RUSH (NRF)	DD 714	Federal SB & DD Co	19 Oct 1944	8 July 1945	21 Sep 1945
*HAMNER (NRF)	DD 718	Federal SB & DD Co	23 April 1945	24 Nov 1945	11 July 1946
*SOUTHERLAND (NRF)	DD 743	Bath Iron Works Corp	27 May 1944	5 Oct 1944	22 Dec 1944
*WILLIAM C. LAWE (NRF)	DD 763	Bethlehem (San Francisco)	12 Mar 1944	21 May 1945	18 Dec 1946
*McKEAN (NRF)	DD 784	Todd Pacific Shipyards	15 Sep 1944	31 Mar 1945	9 June 1945
*HENDERSON (NRF)	DD 785	Todd Pacific Shipyards	27 Oct 1944	28 May 1945	4 Aug 1945
*HOLLISTER (NRF)	DD 788	Todd Pacific Shipyards	27 Dec 1944	9 Oct 1945	26 Mar 1946
*HIGBEE (NRF)	DD 806	Bath Iron Works Corp	26 June 1944	12 Nov 1944	27 Jan 1945
*CORRY (NRF)	DD 817	Consolidated Steel Corp	5 April 1945	28 July 1945	26 Feb 1946
*RICH (NRF)	DD 820	Consolidated Steel Corp	16 May 1945	5 Oct 1945	4 July 1946
*JOHNSTON (NRF)	DD 821	Consolidated Steel Corp	6 May 1945	19 Oct 1945	10 Oct 1945
*ROBERT H. McCARD (NRF)	DD 822	Consolidated Steel Corp	20 June 1945	9 Nov 1945	26 Oct 1946
*BASILONE	DD 824	Consolidated Steel Corp	7 July 1945	21 Dec 1945	26 July 1946
*AGERHOLM	DD 826	Bath Iron Works Corp	10 Sep 1945	30 Mar 1946	20 June 1946
*MYLES C. FOX (NRF)	DD 829	Bath Iron Works Corp	14 Aug 1944	13 Jan 1945	20 Mar 1945
*CHARLES P. CECIL (NRF)	DD 835	Bath Iron Works Corp	2 Dec 1944	22 April 1945	29 June 1945
*SARSFIELD	DD 837	Bath Iron Works Corp	15 Jan 1945	27 May 1945	31 July 1945
*POWER (NRF)	DD 839	Bath Iron Works Corp	26 Feb 1945	30 June 1945	13 Sep 1945
*FISKE (NRF)	DD 842	Bath Iron Works Corp	9 April 1945	8 Sep 1945	28 Nov 1945
*BAUSELL	DD 845	Bath Iron Works Corp	28 May 1945	19 Nov 1945	7 Feb 1947
*VOGELGESANG (NRF)	DD 862	Bethlehem (Staten Island)	3 Aug 1944	15 Jan 1945	28 April 1945
*STEINAKER (NRF)	DD 863	Bethlehem (Staten Island)	1 Sep 1944	13 Feb 1945	26 May 1945
*HAROLD J. ELLISON (NRF)	DD 864	Bethlehem (Staten Island)	3 Oct 1944	14 Mar 1945	23 June 1945
*CONE (NRF)	DD 866	Bethlehem (Staten Island)	30 Nov 1944	10 May 1945	18 Aug 1945
*DAMATO (NRF)	DD 871	Bethlehem (Staten Island)	10 May 1945	21 Nov 1945	27 April 1946
*HAWKINS	DD 873	Consolidated Steel Corp	14 May 1944	7 Oct 1944	10 Feb 1945
*ROGERS (NRF)	DD 876	Consolidated Steel Corp	3 June 1944	20 Nov 1944	26 Mar 1945
*DYESS (NRF)	DD 880	Consolidated Steel Corp	17 Aug 1944	26 Jan 1945	21 May 1945
*NEWMAN K. PERRY (NRF)	DD 883	Consolidated Steel Corp	10 Oct 1944	17 Mar 1945	26 July 1945
*JOHN R. CRAIG (NRF)	DD 885	Consolidated Steel Corp	17 Nov 1944	14 April 1945	20 Aug 1945
*ORLECK (NRF)	DD 886	Consolidated Steel Corp	28 Nov 1944	12 May 1945	15 Sep 1945
*MEREDITH (NRF)	DD 890	Consolidated Steel Corp	27 Jan 1945	28 June 1945	31 Dec 1945

Displacement, tons: 2 425 standard; 3 480 to 3 520 full load
Length, feet (metres): 390·5 *(119·0)* oa
Beam, feet (metres): 40·9 *(12·4)*
Draught, feet (metres): 19 *(5·8)*
Guns: 4—5 inch *(127 mm)* 38 calibre (Mk 38) (twin)
A/S weapons: 1 ASROC 8-tube launcher; 2 triple torpedo tubes (Mk 32)
Main engines: 2 geared turbines (General Electric or Westinghouse), 60 000 shp; 2 shafts
Boilers: 4 (Babcock & Wilcox or combination Babcock & Wilcox and Foster-Wheeler)
Speed, knots: 34
Range, miles: 5 800 at 15 knots
Complement: 274 (14 officers, 260 enlisted men); 307 in Naval Reserve training ships (12 officers, 176 enlisted active duty; 7 officers, 112 enlisted reserve)

The USN survivors of the several hundred destroyers constructed in the United States during World War II.
Sarsfield has been used for experimental work (EDD).
The "Gearing" class initially covered hull numbers DD 710-721, 742, 743, 763-769, 782-791, 805-926. Forty-nine of these ships were cancelled in 1945 (DD 768, 796, 809-816, 854-856, and 891-926); four ships were never completed and were scrapped in the 1950s; *Castle* (DD 720), *Woodrow R. Thompson* (DD 721), *Lansdale* (DD 766), and *Seymour D. Owens* (DD 767).
Two similar ships completed to a modified design after World War II are listed separately as the "Carpenter" class.
Twenty-seven ships are assigned to Naval Reserve training and are manned by composite active duty-reserve crews. These ships are noted as NRF (Naval Reserve Force).

Armament-Design: As built, these ships had a pole mast and carried an armament of six 5 inch guns (twin mounts), 12—40 mm guns (2 quad, 2 twin), 11—20 mm guns (single), and 10—21 inch torpedo tubes (quin). After World War II, the after bank of tubes was replaced by an additional quad 40 mm mount. All 40 mm and 20 mm guns were replaced subsequently by six 3 inch guns (2 twin, 2 single) and a tripod mast was installed to support heavier radar antennae. The 3 inch guns and remaining anti-ship torpedo tubes were removed during FRAM modernisation.

Electronics: Electronic warfare equipment fitted to most ships. Single Mk 37 gunfire control system provided.

Engineering: During November 1974 the *Johnston* conducted experiments using liquified coal as fuel in one boiler (Project Seacoal).

Helicopters: Fitted to operate the Drone Anti-Submarine Helicopter (DASH) during FRAM modernisation—no longer carried.

Modernisation: All of these ships underwent extensive modernisation under the Fleet Rehabilitation and Modernisation (FRAM I) programme between 1961 and 1965.
There are two basic FRAM I configurations: *Agerholm,* and *Meredith* have twin 5 inch mounts in "A" and "B" positions and Mk 32 torpedo launchers abaft second funnel; others have twin 5 inch mounts in "A" and "Y" positions and Mk 32 launchers on 01 level in "B" position.

Radar: SPS 10, 37 or 40.

Sonar: SQS 23.

WILLIAM C. LAWE
11/1975, USN

BAUSELL (both 5 inch mounts forward)
2/1977, Dr. Giorgio Arra

HAMNER
3/1976, USN

2 "CARPENTER" CLASS (FRAM I) (DESTROYERS (DD))

Name	No.	Builders	Laid down	Launched	Commissioned
*CARPENTER (NRF)	DD 825	Consolidated Steel Corp (Orange, Texas)	30 July 1945	30 Dec 1945	15 Dec 1949
*ROBERT A. OWENS (NRF)	DD 827	Bath Iron Works Corp	29 Oct 1945	15 July 1946	5 Nov 1949

Displacement, tons: 2 425 standard; 3 540 full load
Length, feet (metres): 390·5 (119·0) oa
Beam, feet (metres): 40·9 (12·4)
Draught, feet (metres): 19 (5·8)
Guns: 2—5 inch (127 mm) 38 calibre (Mk 38) (twin)
A/S weapons: 1 ASROC 8-tube launcher; 2 triple torpedo tubes (Mk 32)
Main engines: 2 geared turbines (General Electric) 60 000 shp; 2 shafts
Boilers: 4 (Babcock & Wilcox)
Speed, knots: 34
Complement: 282 (12 officers, 176 enlisted active duty; 8 officers, 86 enlisted reserve)

These ships were laid down as units of the "Gearing" class. Their construction was suspended after World War II until 1947 when they were towed to the Newport News Shipbuilding and Dry Dock Co for completion as DDK. As specialised ASW ships they mounted 3 inch (76 mm) guns in place of 5 inch mounts and were armed with improved ahead-firing anti-submarine weapons (hedgehogs and Weapon Able/Alfa); special sonar equipment installed. The DDK and DDE classifications were merged in 1950 with both of these ships being designated DDE on 4 March 1950. Upon being modernised to the FRAM I configuration they were reclassified DD on 30 June 1962.
Both of these ships are assigned to Naval Reserve training; they are manned by composite active duty and reserve crews.

Electronics: These ships have electronic warfare "pods" on a smaller tripod mast forward of their second funnel. Fitted with Mk 56 Mod 43 gunfire control system.

Radar: Search: SPS 10 and 40.

Sonar: SQS-23.

CARPENTER

"ALLEN M. SUMNER" (FRAM II) CLASS

All surviving ships of the 70-destroyer "Allen M. Sumner" class have been stricken or transferred to other navies. Between 1943 and 1945, 58 destroyers and 12 minelayers were completed to this design. See 1974-1975 and earlier editions for characteristics.
Ships of this class serve in the navies of Argentina, Brazil, Chile, Colombia, Greece, Iran, South Korea, Taiwan, Turkey and Venezuela.

"FLETCHER" CLASS

The survivors of 175 "Fletcher" class destroyers have been stricken or transferred to other navies. See 1975-1976 and previous editions for characteristics.
Ships of this class serve in the navies of Argentina, Brazil, Chile, Colombia, West Germany, Greece, Italy, Japan, South Korea, Mexico, Peru, Spain, Taiwan and Turkey.

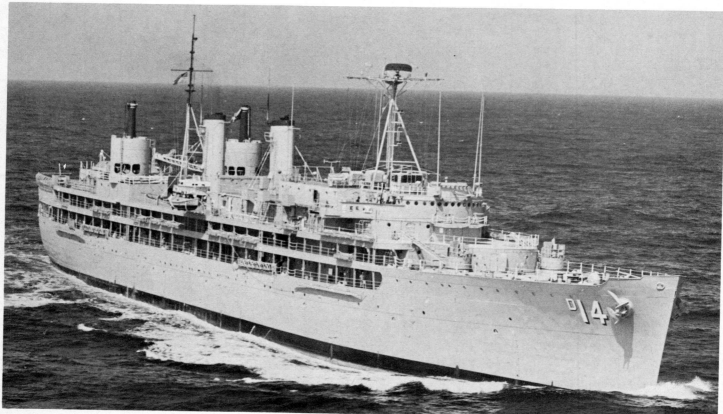

DIXIE (Destroyer Tender and the oldest active ship in continuous service)

1976, CO USS Dixie

FRIGATES

There are 64 frigates (FF/FFG) in commission with another 56 ships planned for construction during the next few years. All ships now in commission have the large SQS-26 sonar, ASROC anti-submarine rockets, and a helicopter capability. However, only six have a surface-to-air missile capability for limited area defence. The hoped-for 74 ships of the "Oliver Hazard Perry" class (FFG 7) will have the smaller SQS-56 sonar. The ASROC will be deleted but the ships will be able to operate two LAMPS (Light Airborne Multi-Purpose System) helicopters and will have a surface-to-air/surface-to-surface missile capability. The

"Perry" class ships will be more versatile than the previous "Knox" class frigates and several other navies have expressed interest in the newer design. The Royal Australian Navy has ordered two of the ships.

The "Perry" class ships could be supplemented in the ocean escort role by the 12 "Hamilton" class high-endurance cutters operated by the Coast Guard. The Coast Guard ships are fitted with sonar and are armed with Mk 32 torpedo tubes (as well as a single 5-inch gun). They also have facilities for operating a large helicopter.

The Coast Guard plans to construct a new class of medium endurance cutters which also will have a limited anti-submarine/escort capability.

Future Programmes: Preliminary studies for a successor class to the "Oliver Hazard Perry" class, currently known as the "FFGX" programme are in hand. At present construction of the first ship is to be requested under the FY 1981 programme with the second scheduled for the FY 1982 programme.

1 + 17 + (56) "OLIVER HAZARD PERRY" CLASS (GUIDED MISSILE FRIGATES (FFG))

Name	No.	Builders	Laid down	Launched	Commission
OLIVER HAZARD PERRY	FFG 7 (ex-PF 109)	Bath Iron Works, Bath, Maine	12 June 1975	25 Sep 1976	28 Oct 1977
	FFG 8	Bath Iron Works, Bath, Maine	1978		1980
	FFG 9	Todd Shipyards Corp, San Pedro, Calif	1977		1980
	FFG 10	Todd Shipyards Corp, Seattle, Wash	1977		1980
	FFG 11	Bath Iron Works, Bath, Maine	1978		1980
	FFG 12	Todd Shipyards Corp, San Pedro, Calif	1978		1980
	FFG 13	Bath Iron Works, Bath, Maine	1978		1980
	FFG 14	Todd Shipyards Corp, San Pedro, Calif	1978		1980
	FFG 15	Bath Iron Works, Bath, Maine	1979		1981
	FFG 16	Bath Iron Works, Bath, Maine	1979		1981
Eight ships	FFG	Approved Fiscal Year 1977 programme			
Eleven ships	FFG	Proposed FY 1978 programme			
Eleven ships	FFG	Planned FY 1979 programme			
Twelve ships	FFG	Planned FY 1980 programme			
Twelve ships	FFG	Planned FY 1981 programme			
Ten ships	FFG	Planned FY 1982 programme			

Displacement, tons: 3 605 full load
Length, feet (metres): 445 (135·6) oa
Beam, feet (metres): 45 (13·7)
Draught, feet (metres): 24·5 (7·5)
Missile launchers: 1 single launcher for Standard/Harpoon missiles (Mk 13 Mod 4)
Guns: 1—76 mm 62 calibre (Mk 75); 1—20 mm Phalanx CIWS (space reserved)
A/S weapons: 2 SH-2 LAMPS helicopters; 2 triple torpedo tubes (Mk 32)
Main engines: 2—LM 2500 gas turbines (General Electric); 41 000 shp; 1 shaft (controllable-pitch propeller)
Speed, knots: 30
Range, miles: 4 500 at 20 knots
Complement: 163 (11 officers, 152 enlisted men)

They are follow-on ships to the large number of frigates (formerly DE) built in the 1960s and early 1970s, with the later ships emphasising anti-ship/aircraft/missile capabilities while the previous classes were oriented primarily against submarines (eg, larger SQS-26 sonar and ASROC).

The lead ship (FFG 7) was authorised in the Fiscal Year 1973 shipbuilding programme; three ships (FFG 8-10) in FY 1975 programme; and six ships (FFG 11-16) in FY 1976 programme. Congress authorised nine ships in FY 1976, but cost escalation permitted the construction of only six ships.

The Navy proposes to build 64 additional ships of this class under the FY 1977-1982 programmes. However, there is strong Congressional opposition to these ships and a reduced number is expected to be procured.

The two additional ships of this class under construction at the Todd-Seattle shipyard for the Royal Australian Navy are assigned US Navy hull numbers FFG 18 and FFG 19 for accounting purposes.

Classification: These ships were originally classified as "patrol frigates" (PF) at a time when the term "frigate" was used in the US Navy for the DL/DLG/DLGN. The *Perry* was designated PF 109 at time of keel laying and designated FFG 7 on 30 June 1975.

Design: These ships are slightly longer but lighter than the preceding "Knox" class. The original single hangar has been changed to two adjacent hangars, each to house SH-2 or follow-on LAMPS helicopters.

Several weapon and sensor systems were evaluated at sea in the guided missile frigate *Talbot* (FFG 4).

Fin stabilisers may be fitted at a later date (space and weight reserved).

Electronics: The Mk 92 Mod 2 weapons control system is installed with a dome-shaped antenna atop the bridge. (The Mk 92 is the Americanised version of the WM-28 system developed by N.V. Hollandse Signaalapparaten).

OLIVER HAZARD PERRY (before launch)   9/1976, USN

Engineering: Two auxiliary retractable propeller pods are provided aft of the sonar dome to provide "get home" power in the event of a casualty to the main engines or propeller shaft. Each pod has a 325 hp engine to provide a ship speed of 3 to 5 knots.

Fiscal: The design-to-cost estimate of $45 700 000 in Fiscal Year 1973 dollars based on a 49-ship programme has increased to $55 300 000 in the same dollars due to design and cost estimating changes. However, adding the estimated inflation and contract escalation factors brings the estimated cost per ship in the FY 1977 programme to $160 375 000. This is approximately $23 100 500 more per ship than estimated one year earlier.

Gunnery: The principal gun on this ship is the single 76 mm

OTO Melara with a 90-round-per-minute firing rate (designated Mk 75 in US service). Space and weight are reserved for the 20 mm Phalanx CIWS.

Missiles: The single-arm Tartar-type missile launcher will be capable of firing both Standard-MR surface-to-air and Harpoon surface-to-surface missiles: "mixed" missile magazines will be provided.

Radar: Long-range search: SPS-49.
Search and navigation: SPS-55.
Weapons control: STIR (modified SPG-60).

Sonar: SQS-56 (hull mounted).
TACTAS (towed passive sonar).

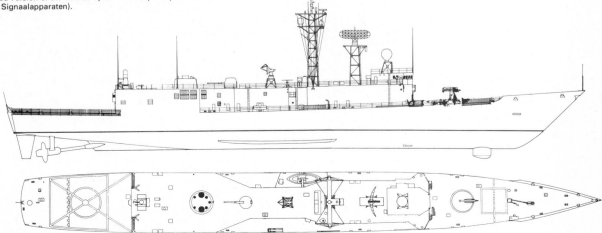

FFG 7   *Drawing by A. D. Baker*

46 "KNOX" CLASS (FRIGATES (FF))

Name	No.	Builders	Laid down	Launched	Commissioned
*KNOX	FF 1052	Todd Shipyards (Seattle)	5 Oct 1965	19 Nov 1966	12 April 1969
*ROARK	FF 1053	Todd Shipyards (Seattle)	2 Feb 1966	24 April 1967	22 Nov 1969
*GRAY	FF 1054	Todd Shipyards (Seattle)	19 Nov 1966	3 Nov 1967	4 April 1970
*HEPBURN	FF 1055	Todd Shipyards (San Pedro)	1 June 1966	25 Mar 1967	3 July 1969
*CONNOLE	FF 1056	Avondale Shipyards	23 Mar 1967	20 July 1968	30 Aug 1969
*RATHBURNE	FF 1057	Lockheed SB & Constn Co	8 Jan 1968	2 May 1969	16 May 1970
*MEYERKORD	FF 1058	Todd Shipyards (San Pedro)	1 Sep 1966	15 July 1967	28 Nov 1969
*W. S. SIMS	FF 1059	Avondale Shipyards	10 Apr 1967	4 Jan 1969	3 Jan 1970
*LANG	FF 1060	Todd Shipyards (San Pedro)	25 Mar 1967	17 Feb 1968	28 Mar 1970
*PATTERSON	FF 1061	Avondale Shipyards	12 Oct 1967	3 May 1969	14 Mar 1970
*WHIPPLE	FF 1062	Todd Shipyards (Seattle)	24 April 1967	12 April 1968	22 Aug 1970
*REASONER	FF 1063	Lockheed SB & Constn Co	6 Jan 1969	1 Aug 1970	31 July 1971
*LOCKWOOD	FF 1064	Todd Shipyards (Seattle)	3 Nov 1967	5 Sep 1964	5 Dec 1970
*STEIN	FF 1065	Lockheed SB & Constn Co	1 June 1970	19 Dec 1970	8 Jan 1972
*MARVIN SHIELDS	FF 1066	Todd Shipyards (Seattle)	12 Apr 1968	23 Oct 1969	10 April 1971
*FRANCIS HAMMOND	FF 1067	Todd Shipyards (San Pedro)	15 July 1967	11 May 1968	25 July 1970
*VREELAND	FF 1068	Avondale Shipyards	20 Mar 1968	14 June 1969	13 June 1970
*BAGLEY	FF 1069	Lockheed SB & Constn Co	22 Sep 1970	24 April 1971	6 May 1972
*DOWNES	FF 1070	Todd Shipyards (Seattle)	5 Sep 1968	13 Dec 1969	28 Aug 1971
*BADGER	FF 1071	Todd Shipyards (Seattle)	17 Feb 1968	7 Dec 1968	1 Dec 1970
*BLAKELY	FF 1072	Avondale Shipyards	3 June 1968	23 Aug 1969	18 July 1970
*ROBERT E. PEARY	FF 1073	Lockheed SB & Constn Co	20 Dec 1970	23 June 1971	23 Sep 1972
*HAROLD E. HOLT	FF 1074	Todd Shipyards (San Pedro)	11 May 1968	3 May 1969	26 Mar 1971
*TRIPPE	FF 1075	Avondale Shipyards	29 July 1968	1 Nov 1969	19 Sep 1970
*FANNING	FF 1076	Todd Shipyards (San Pedro)	7 Dec 1968	24 Jan 1970	23 July 1971
*OUELLET	FF 1077	Avondale Shipyards	15 Jan 1969	17 Jan 1970	12 Dec 1970
*JOSEPH HEWES	FF 1078	Avondale Shipyards	15 May 1969	7 Mar 1970	24 April 1971
*BOWEN	FF 1079	Avondale Shipyards	11 July 1969	2 May 1970	22 May 1971
*PAUL	FF 1080	Avondale Shipyards	12 Sep 1969	20 June 1970	14 Aug 1971
*AYLWIN	FF 1081	Avondale Shipyards	13 Nov 1969	29 Aug 1970	18 Sep 1971
*ELMER MONTGOMERY	FF 1082	Avondale Shipyards	23 Jan 1970	21 Nov 1970	30 Oct 1971
*COOK	FF 1083	Avondale Shipyards	20 Mar 1970	23 Jan 1971	18 Dec 1971
*McCANDLESS	FF 1084	Avondale Shipyards	4 June 1970	20 Mar 1971	18 Mar 1972
*DONALD B. BEARY	FF 1085	Avondale Shipyards	24 July 1970	22 May 1971	22 July 1972
*BREWTON	FF 1086	Avondale Shipyards	2 Oct 1970	24 July 1971	8 July 1972
*KIRK	FF 1087	Avondale Shipyards	4 Dec 1970	25 Sep 1971	9 Sep 1972
*BARBEY	FF 1088	Avondale Shipyards	5 Feb 1971	4 Dec 1971	11 Nov 1972
*JESSE L. BROWN	FF 1089	Avondale Shipyards	8 April 1971	18 Mar 1972	17 Feb 1973
*AINSWORTH	FF 1090	Avondale Shipyards	11 June 1971	15 Apr 1972	31 Mar 1973
*MILLER	FF 1091	Avondale Shipyards	6 Aug 1971	3 June 1972	30 June 1973
*THOMAS C. HART	FF 1092	Avondale Shipyards	8 Oct 1971	12 Aug 1972	28 July 1973
*CAPODANNO	FF 1093	Avondale Shipyards	12 Oct 1971	21 Oct 1972	17 Nov 1973
*PHARRIS	FF 1094	Avondale Shipyards	11 Feb 1972	16 Dec 1972	26 Jan 1974
*TRUETT	FF 1095	Avondale Shipyards	27 Apr 1972	3 Feb 1973	1 June 1974
*VALDEZ	FF 1096	Avondale Shipyards	30 June 1972	24 Mar 1973	27 July 1974
*MOINESTER	FF 1097	Avondale Shipyards	25 Aug 1972	12 May 1973	2 Nov 1974

Displacement, tons: 3 011 standard; 3 877 (1052-1077) 3 963 (remainder) full load
Length, feet (metres): 438 (133·5) oa
Beam, feet (metres): 46·75 (14·25)
Draught, feet (metres): 24·75 (7·55)
Helicopter: 1 SH-2 LAMPS (except 1061 and 1070)
Missile launchers: 1 Sea Sparrow BPDMS multiple launcher (Mk 25) in 1052-1069 and 1071-1083; 1 NATO Sea Sparrow multiple launcher (Mk 29) in Downes; Harpoon in Downes and Ainsworth (see Missile note)
Guns: 1—5 inch (127 mm) 54 calibre (Mk 42)
A/S weapons: 1 ASROC 8-tube launcher; 4 fixed torpedo tubes (Mk 32)
Main engines: 1 geared turbine (Westinghouse) 35 000 shp; 1 shaft
Boilers: 2
Speed, knots: 27+
Complement: 245 (17 officers, 228 enlisted men); increased to 283 (22 officers, 261 enlisted men) with BPDMS and LAMPS installation; (as built 12 ships had accommodation for 2 staff officers)

The 46 frigates of the "Knox" class comprise the largest group of destroyer or frigate type warships built to the same design in the West since World War II. These ships are similar to the previous "Garcia" and "Brooke" classes, but slightly larger because of the use of non-pressure-fired boilers.
Although now classified as frigates they were authorised as DE 1052-1061 (10 ships) in the Fiscal Year 1964 new construction programme, DE 1062-1077 (16 ships) in FY 1965, DE 1078-1087 (10 ships) in FY 1966, DE 1088-1097 (10 ships) in FY 1967, and DE 1098-1107 (10 ships) in FY 1968. However, construction of six ships (DE 1102-1107) was deferred in 1968 as US Navy emphasis shifted to the more versatile and faster DX/DXG ships; three additional ships (DE 1098-1100) were cancelled on 24 Feb 1969 to finance cost overruns of FY 1968 nuclear-powered attack submarines and to comply with a Congressional mandate to reduce expenditures; the last ship of the FY 1968 programme (DE 1101) was cancelled on 9 April 1969. The DEG 7-11 guided missile "frigates" constructed in Spain are similar to this design.

Classification: Originally classified as ocean escorts (DE); reclassified as frigates (FF) on 30 June 1975.

Construction: The ships built at Avondale Shipyards in Westwego, Louisiana, were assembled with mass production techniques. The hulls were built keel-up to permit downhead welding. Prefabricated, inverted hull modules were first assembled on a permanent platen, then lifted by hydraulic units and moved laterally into giant turning rings which rotated the hull into an upright position. Avondale, which also builds the "Hamilton" class cutters for the Coast Guard, side launched these ships.

Design: A 4 000-pound lightweight anchor is fitted on the port side and an 8 000-pound anchor fits into the after section of the sonar dome.

JESSE L. BROWN

1976, Michael D. J. Lennon

LOCKWOOD

2/1977, Dr. Giorgio Arra

Engineering: DE 1101 was to have had gas turbine propulsion; construction of the ship was cancelled when decision was made to provide gas turbine propulsion in the "Spruance" class (DD 963) destroyers.
These ships can steam at 22 knots on one boiler. They have a single 5-blade, 15-foot diameter propeller.

Fire Control: Mk 68 gunfire control with SPG-53A radar. Two directors for NATO Sea Sparrow in Downes.

"KNOX" Class—*continued*

Fiscal: These ships have cost considerably more than originally estimated. Official programme cost for the 46 ships as of January 1974 was $1·424 billion or an average of $30 959 000 per ship not including the LAMPS, Standard missile, VDS, or BPDMS installation.

Helicopters: These ships were designed to operate the now-discarded DASH unmanned helicopter. Beginning in 1972 they were modified to accommodate the Light Airborne Multi-Purpose System, the SH-2D anti-submarine helicopter; hangar and flight deck are enlarged. Cost approximately $1 000 000 per ship for LAMPS modification.

Missiles: Sea Sparrow Basic Point Defence Missile System (BPDMS) launcher installed in 31 ships from 1971-1975 (FF 1052-1069, 1071-1083).
Modified NATO Sea Sparrow installed in *Downes* for evaluation.
In addition, some ships are being fitted with the Standard interim surface-to-surface missile which is fired from the ASROC launcher forward of the bridge. Two of the eight "cells" in the launcher are modified to fire a single Standard.
Cost was approximately $400 000 per ship for BPDMS and $750 000 for Standard missile modification.
The *Downes* and *Lockwood* have been used in at-sea firing tests and shipboard compatability for the Harpoon ship-to-ship missiles.
Harpoon fitted in *Ainsworth* in Aug 1976 (first production model in USN). To be fitted in all other ships in immediate future.

Names: DE 1073 originally was named *Conolly;* changed on 12 May 1971.

Radar: Search: SPS 10 and 40.
(Note: *Downes* has SPS-58 threat detection radar, and Improved Point Defence/Target Acquisition System (IPD/TAS) radar).

Rockets: Mk 36 Chaffroc to be fitted in late 1970s.

Sonar: SQS-26 CX (bow-mounted).
SQS-35 (Independent VDS) (except FF 1053-55, 1057-62, 1072 and 1077).

Torpedoes: Improved ASROC-torpedo reloading capability as in some ships of previous "Garcia" class (note slanting face of bridge structure immediately behind ASROC). Four Mk 32 torpedo tubes are fixed in the amidships structure, two to a side, angled out at 45 degrees. The arrangement provides improved loading capability over exposed triple Mk 32 torpedo tubes.

LANG   *1976, Michael D. J. Lennon*

MEYERKORD   *10/1976, Dr. Giorgio Arra*

RATHBURNE (with LAMPS helicopter)   *1/1977, Dr. Giorgio Arra*

BOWEN   *1976, Michael D. J. Lennon*

6 "BROOKE" CLASS (GUIDED MISSILE FRIGATES (FFG))

Name	No.	Builders	Laid down	Launched	Commissioned
*BROOKE	FFG 1	Lockheed SB & Construction Co	10 Dec 1962	19 July 1963	12 Mar 1966
*RAMSEY	FFG 2	Lockheed SB & Construction Co	4 Feb 1963	15 Oct 1963	3 June 1967
*SCHOFIELD	FFG 3	Lockheed SB & Construction Co	15 April 1963	7 Dec 1963	11 May 1968
*TALBOT	FFG 4	Bath Iron Works Corp	4 May 1964	6 Jan 1966	22 April 1967
*RICHARD L. PAGE	FFG 5	Bath Iron Works Corp	4 Jan 1965	4 April 1966	5 Aug 1967
*JULIUS A. FURER	FFG 6	Bath Iron Works Corp	12 July 1965	22 July 1966	11 Nov 1967

Displacement, tons: 2 640 standard; 3 426 full load
Length, feet (metres): 414·5 (126·3) oa
Beam, feet (metres): 44·2 (13·5)
Draught, feet (metres): 24 (7·3)
Missile launcher: 1 single Tartar/Standard-MR surface-to-air launcher (Mk 22 Mod 0)
Gun: 1—5 inch (127 mm) 38 calibre (Mk 30)
Helicopter: 1 SH-2D LAMPS helicopter
A/S weapons: 1 ASROC 8-tube launcher; 2 triple torpedo tubes (Mk 32)
Main engines: 1 geared turbine (Westinghouse in FFG 1-3, General Electric in others); 35 000 shp; 1 shaft
Boilers: 2 Foster-Wheeler
Speed, knots: 27·2
Complement: 248 (17 officers, 231 enlisted men)

These ships are identical to the "Garcia" class escorts except for the Tartar missile system in lieu of a second 5 inch gun mount and different electronic equipment. Authorised as DEG 1-3 in the Fiscal Year 1962 new construction programme and DEG 4-6 in the FY 1963 programme. Plans for ten additional DEGs in FY 1964 and possibly three more DEGs in a later programme were dropped because of the $11 000 000 additional cost of a DEG over FF. In 1974-1975 the Talbot was reconfigured as test and evaluation ship for systems being developed for the "Oliver Hazard Perry" class (FFG 7) frigates and "Pegasus" class (PHM 7) hydrofoil missile combatants.

Classification: Reclassified as FFG 1-6 on 30 June 1975.

Fire Control: Mk 74 gun/missile fire control system and Mk 56 gunfire control system.

Helicopters: These ships were designed to operate Drone Anti-Submarine Helicopters (DASH), but the programme was cut back before helicopters were provided. They are now fitted to operate the Light Airborne Multi-Purpose System (LAMPS), currently the SH-2D helicopter.

Missiles: These ships have a single Tartar Mk 22 launching system which weighs 92 395 pounds. Reportedly, the system has a rate of fire similar to the larger Mk 11 and Mk 13 systems installed in guided missile destroyers, but the FFG system has a considerably smaller magazine capacity (16 missiles according to unofficial sources).
The FFG 4-6 have automatic ASROC loading system (note angled base of bridge structure aft of ASROC in these ships).

Radar: 3D Search: SPS-52.
Search: SPS-10.
Missile control: SPG-51C.

Sonar: SQS 26 AX (bow-mounted). (SQS-56 evaluated in Talbot).

JULIUS A. FURER (with LAMPS helicopter)　　　　7/1976, A. D. Baker III

RICHARD L. PAGE　　　　2/1976, USN

RAMSEY

1/1977, Dr. Giorgio Arra

10 "GARCIA" CLASS (FRIGATES (FF))

Name	No.	Builders	Laid down	Launched	Commissioned
*GARCIA	FF 1040	Bethlehem Steel (San Francisco)	16 Oct 1962	31 Oct 1963	21 Dec 1964
*BRADLEY	FF 1041	Bethlehem Steel (San Francisco)	17 Jan 1963	26 Mar 1964	15 May 1965
*EDWARD McDONNELL	FF 1043	Avondale Shipyards	1 April 1963	15 Feb 1964	15 Feb 1965
*BRUMBY	FF 1044	Avondale Shipyards	1 Aug 1963	6 June 1964	5 Aug 1965
*DAVIDSON	FF 1045	Avondale Shipyards	20 Sep 1963	2 Oct 1964	7 Dec 1965
*VOGE	FF 1047	Defoe Shipbuilding Co	21 Nov 1963	4 Feb 1965	25 Nov 1966
*SAMPLE	FF 1048	Lockheed SB & Construction Co	19 July 1963	28 Apr 1964	23 Mar 1968
*KOELSCH	FF 1049	Defoe Shipbuilding Co	19 Feb 1964	8 June 1965	10 June 1967
*ALBERT DAVID	FF 1050	Lockheed SB & Construction Co	29 April 1964	19 Dec 1964	19 Oct 1968
*O'CALLAHAN	FF 1051	Defoe Shipbuilding Co	19 Feb 1964	20 Oct 1965	13 July 1968

Displacement, tons: 2 620 standard; 3 403 full load
Length, feet (metres): 414·5 (126·3) oa
Beam, feet (metres): 44·2 (13·5)
Draught, feet (metres): 24 (7·3)
Helicopter: 1 SH-2 LAMPS helicopter (except *Sample* and *Albert David*)
Guns: 2—5 inch (127 mm) 38 calibre (Mk 30) (single)
A/S weapons: 1 ASROC 8-tube launcher; 2 triple torpedo tubes (Mk 32)
Main engines: 1 geared turbine (Westinghouse, 1040, 1041, 1043-1045, remainder, GE); 35 000 shp; 1 shaft
Boilers: 2 (Foster Wheeler)
Speed, knots: 27
Complement: 239 (13 officers, 226 enlisted men (1040, 1041, 1043-1045)
247 (16 officers, 231 enlisted men) (remainder)

These ships exceed some of the world's destroyers in size and ASW capability, but are designated as frigates by virtue of their single propeller shaft and limited speed. The FF 1040 and FF 1041 were authorised in the Fiscal Year 1961 new construction programme, FF 1043-1045 in FY 1962, and FF 1047-1051 in FY 1963.

Classification: Originally classified as ocean escorts (DE); reclassified as frigates (FF) on 30 June 1975. The hull numbers DE 1039, 1042, and 1046 were assigned to frigates built overseas for Portugal to US "Dealey" design.

Design: Anchors are mounted at stem and on portside, just forward of 5 inch gun. Hangar structure of this class modified during the early 1970s to handle LAMPS except in *Sample* and *Albert David*.

Electronics: The *Voge* and *Koelsch* have been fitted with a specialised ASW Naval Tactical Data System (NTDS).

Fire Control: Mk 56 gunfire control system.

Helicopters: The Drone Anti-Submarine Helicopter (DASH) programme was cut back before these ships were provided with helicopters. Reportedly only the *Bradley* actually operated with DASH.
All but two of these ships are fitted to operate the Light Airborne Multi-Purpose System (LAMPS), now the SH-2D helicopter.

Missiles: The *Bradley* was fitted with a Sea Sparrow Basic Point Defense Missile System (BPDMS) in 1967-1968; removed for installation in the carrier *Forrestal* (CV 59).

Radar: Search: SPS 10 and 40.

Sonar: SQS-26 AXR (bow mounted) in FF 1040-1041, 1043-1045.
SQS-26 BR (bow mounted) in FF 1047-1051.

Torpedoes: Most of these ships were built with two Mk 25 torpedo tubes built into their transom for launching wire-guided ASW torpedoes. However, they have been removed from the earlier ships and deleted in the later ships. The *Voge* and later ships have automatic ASROC reload system (note angled base of bridge structure behind ASROC in these ships).

O'CALLAHAN about to refuel from *Kitty Hawk*   1975, USN

GARCIA   1975

EDWARD McDONNELL   3/1975, Wright and Logan

1 "GLOVER" CLASS (FRIGATE RESEARCH SHIP (AGFF))

Name	No.	Builders	Laid down	Launched	Commissioned
*GLOVER	AGFF 1 (ex-AGDE 1, ex-AG 163)	Bath Iron Works	29 July 1963	17 April 1965	13 Nov 1965

Displacement, tons: 2 643 standard; 3 426 full load
Length, feet (metres): 414·5 *(126·3)* oa
Beam, feet (metres): 44·2 *(13·5)*
Draught, feet (metres): 14·5 *(4·3)*
Guns: 1—5 inch *(127 mm)* 38 calibre (Mk 30)
A/S weapons: 1 ASROC 8-tube launcher; 2 triple torpedo tubes (Mk 32)
facilities for small helicopter
Main engines: 1 geared turbine (Westinghouse); 35 000 shp; 1 shaft
Boilers: 2 Foster Wheeler
Speed, knots: 27
Complement: 236 plus 38 civilian technicians

The *Glover* was built to test an advanced hull design and

propulsion system, and has a full combat capability.
The ship was originally authorised in the Fiscal Year 1960 new construction programme, but was postponed and re-introduced in the FY 1961 programme. Estimated construction cost was $29 330 000.

Classification: The *Glover* was originally classified as a miscellaneous auxiliary (AG 163); completed as an escort research ship (AGDE 1). Subsequently changed to frigate research ship on 30 June 1975.

Design: The *Glover* has a massive bow sonar dome integral with her hull and extending well forward underwater.
No reload capability for ASROC because of space requirements for equipment and technical personnel.

Electronics: The ship has a prototype tactical assignment console that integrates signals from the three sonars and radars to present combined and coordinated tactical situation presentations in the Combat Information Centre (CIC). Reportedly, this increases the combat effectiveness of the ship to a considerable extent.

Fire Control: Mk 56 GFCS.

Radar: Search: SPS 10 and 40.

Sonar: Bow-mounted SQS-26 AXR active sonar, hull-mounted SQR-13 Passive/Active Detection and Location (PADLOC) sonar, and SQS-35 Independent Variable Depth Sonar (IVDS) lowered from the stern.

GLOVER

1974, USN

2 "BRONSTEIN" CLASS (FRIGATES (FF))

Name	No.	Builders	Laid down	Launched	Commissioned
*BRONSTEIN	FF 1037	Avondale Shipyards, Westwego, Lousiana	16 May 1961	31 Mar 1962	16 June1963
*McCLOY	FF 1038	Avondale Shipyards, Westwego, Lousiana	15 Sep 1961	9 June1962	21 Oct 1963

Displacement, tons: 2 360 standard; 2 650 full load
Length, feet (metres): 371·5 *(113·2)* oa
Beam, feet (metres): 40·5 *(12·3)*
Draught, feet (metres): 23 *(7·0)*
Guns: 2—3 inch *(76 mm)* 50 calibre (Mk 33) (twin)
A/S weapons: 1 ASROC 8-tube launcher; 2 triple torpedo tubes (Mk 32)
facilities for small helicopter
Main engines: 1 geared turbine (De Laval); 20 000 shp; 1 shaft
Boilers: 2 (Foster Wheeler)
Speed, knots: 26
Complement: 196 (16 officers, 180 enlisted men)

These two ships may be considered the first of the "second generation" of post-World War II frigates which are comparable in size and ASW capabilities to conventional destroyers. The *Bronstein* and *McCloy* have several features such as hull design, large sonar and ASW weapons that subsequently were incorporated into the mass-produced "Garcia", "Brooke", and "Knox" classes.
Both ships were built under the Fiscal Year 1960 new construction programme.

Classification: These ships were originally classified as ocean escorts (DE); reclassified as frigates (FF) on 30 June 1975.

Design: Position of stem anchor and portside anchor (just forward of gun mount) necessitated by large bow sonar dome. As built, a single 3 inch (Mk 34) open mount was aft of the helicopter deck; removed for installation of towed sonar.

Fire Control: Provided with Mk 56 gunfire control system.

Radar: Search: SPS 10 and 40.

Sonar: SQS-26 (bow-mounted).
TASS (Towed Array Surveillance System) installed mid-1970s.
Cable reel on quarterdeck.

BRONSTEIN

7/1975, USN

EXPERIMENTAL SHIPS

1 EXPERIMENTAL SURFACE EFFECT SHIP (SES): AEROJET-GENERAL DESIGN

*SES-100A

Weight, tons: 100 gross
Dimensions, feet (metres): 81·9 oa × 41·9 *(25·0 × 12·8)*
Main/lift engines: 4 gas turbines (Avco-Lycoming) 12 000 hp; three fans for lift and two water-jet
  propulsion systems = 80+ knots (designed)

Surface effect ship developed by Aerojet-General Corp, and built by Tacoma Boatbuilding Co,
Tacoma, Washington, to test feasibility of large SES for naval missions. Christened in July 1971;
underway in mid-1972 in competition with the Bell design described below. Aluminium construction with rigid sidewalls to hold cushion or bubble of air. Cargo capacity ten tons
(instrumentation during evaluation); provision for crew of four and six observers. Fitted with
four TF-35 gas turbine engines, marine version of the T55-L-11A developed for the CH-47C
helicopter. The SES-100A is reported to have reached 76 knots on trials.

SES-100A   *1972, Aerojet General*

1 EXPERIMENTAL SURFACE EFFECT SHIP (SES): BELL AEROSYSTEMS DESIGN

SES-100B

Weight, tons: 100 gross
Dimensions, feet (metres): 78 oa × 35 *(23·8 × 10·7)*
Main engines: 3 gas turbines (Pratt & Whitney); 13 500 hp; 2 semi submerged, super cavitating
  propellers = 80+ knots
Lift engines: 3 gas turbines (United Aircraft of Canada); 1 500 hp; eight lift fans

Surface effect ship developed by Bell Aerospace Division of the Textron Corp; built at Bell
facility in Michoud, Louisiana. Christened on March 6, 1971; underway in Feb 1972 as competi-
tive development platform for Navy.
Aluminium hull with rigid sidewalls to hold cushion or bubble of air. Cargo capacity ten tons
(instrumentation during evaluation); provision for crew of four and six observers.
Fitted with three Pratt & Whitney FT-12 gas turbine engines and three United Aircraft of Canada
ST-6J-70 gas turbine engines.
The SES-100B is credited with having set an SES speed record of 82·3 knots during trials in 1975.

SES-100B   *1974, Bell Aerosystems*

SPECIAL VESSELS

ADVANCED NAVAL VEHICLES
(Not included in US Naval Vessels Register)

The US Navy has applied the term Advanced Naval Vehicles
(ANV) to a number of platforms being considered for future
construction programmes. These include airships, Small
Waterplane Area Twin Hull (SWATH) ships, hydrofoils, Surface
Effect Ships (SES), Air Cushion Vehicles (ACV), and Wing-In-
Ground (WIG) effect machines, among others.
Some of these concepts are relatively old, such as the airship
(which the US Navy discarded in 1962) and hydrofoils; the
latter now being in production for the US Navy after several

years of experimentation. After successful tests of two 100-ton
SES designs the US Navy had planned to construct prototypes
of a 2 000-ton ocean-going SES combatant. Preliminary
characteristics of such an Advanced Naval Vehicle are provided below and the artist's concept is shown on this page.
Navy plans for the 2 000-ton SES were slowed in 1975 by a
Department of Defense decision that the Navy should undertake a comprehensive analysis of all advanced platform concepts, determine their potential roles, and relate estimated

costs. Accordingly, in that year the Navy established the
Advanced Naval Vehicles Concept Evaluation effort which was
expected to complete the analysis in 1977.
The Navy's overall SES programme continues to be the largest
ANV effort in terms of current funding, with $48 000 000 million
requested for Fiscal Year 1977. Still, this is a paltry sum when
compared to research and development efforts in a number of
other areas.

2 000-ton SURFACE EFFECT SHIP (SES)

Weight, tons: 2 000 gross
Length, feet (metres): approx 240 *(73·2)*
Beam, feet (metres): approx 100 *(30·5)*
Helicopters: 2 large (SH-3 Sea King type)
Missile launchers: Harpoon surface-to-surface launchers; Sea
  Sparrow surface-to-air launchers
Main/lift engines: gas turbines
Speed, knots: 80-100

The above characteristics are those of a 2 000-ton national
combat-capable surface effect ship. Contracts were awarded to
the Bell Aerospace Division of Textron and to Rohr Industries to
undertake the development and design of such a ship.
Although the nominal weight of 2 000 tons is in general use, it
has become obvious that the SES will in reality be close to
3 000 tons.
After evaluation of the designs submitted by Rohr and Bell a
contract for design with option to construct was awarded to
Rohr Marine Inc, San Diego. The new administration has
injected an austerity into the design by trimming the value of
the contract.
War games and analysis conducted by the Navy have indicated
that the large SES, with its potential to serve as a highly mobile
sensor carrier and helicopter platform, could play a valuable
role in anti-submarine warfare. In A/S operations the large SES
would employ the sprint-and-drift technique, whereby it would
travel at high speeds—between 60 and 100 knots—to an area,
slow to use its sensors to search the area, and then speed on to
another area.

Classification: During the early 1970s the Navy used the classification DSX for planning purposes to indicate a large SES
employed in destroyer/frigate roles.

Design: The SES concept differs from the Air Cushion Vehicle
(ACV) by having rigid "sidewalls" that pentrate into the water
to provide stability for high-speed operation. Flexible "skirts"
forward and aft trap the air bubble under the hull.

2 000-ton Advanced Naval Vehicle /Surface Effect Ship design   *Bell Aerospace*

AMPHIBIOUS WARFARE FORCES

The relatively large and modern US amphibious warfare force is being improved with deliveries now under way of the five large, "Tarawa" class amphibious assault ships (LHA). These ships are the size (and configuration) of aircraft carriers, and each can embark a reinforced Marine battalion complete with equipment, trucks, landing craft, and helicopters.

The current force of 65 large amphibious ships can simultaneously lift the assault elements of slightly more than one Marine Amphibious Force (MAF) even when one includes a ship non-availability factor of 15 percent for overhauls. An MAF is a division/aircraft wing team and their supporting elements with a total of approximately 30 000 troops.

Upon completion of all five "Tarawa" class assault ships, the amphibious lift will be sufficient for one and one-third division/wing teams (excluding ships in overhaul). When the last LHA is delivered, the amphibious force will have 66 active ships and three Naval Reserve Force (NRF) ships. All are capable of 20-knot or higher sustained speeds and have helicopter facilities.

Although the MAF lift capability is used as measurement

criteria for US Navy amphibious ships by defence officials, a more realistic consideration is the number of reinforced battalions which can be maintained afloat in forward areas, primarily the Mediterranean and the Western Pacific. The US Navy is now able to keep two reinforced battalions continuously afloat in "WesPac" and one in the "Med," albeit one of the former without helicopters because of a shortage of LPH/LHA-type ships. In addition, a reinforced battalion is intermittently deployed in the Atlantic, generally without helicopters. The availability of the five "Tarawa" class LHAs will alleviate the lack of helicopter ships in the deployed forces.

Landing ship (LX): The Navy plans to begin replacement of the "Thomaston" class dock landing ships (LSD) in the mid-1980s as they reach the end of their 30-year service life. Conceptual design work is now under way for a new landing ship, originally designated LX. Now designated LSD 41 class. First unit scheduled for construction under FY 1979 programme, at least six ships being planned. They will be of improved "Anchorage" class design.

V/STOL operations: The *Guam* (LPH 9) operated as an interim sea control ship from 1972 to 1974, during which period she operated AV-8A Harrier V/STOL (Vertical/Short Take-Off and Landing) aircraft in the light attack and intercept role, and SH-3 Sea King helicopters in the anti-submarine role. See 1974-1975 edition for additional data.

The *Guam* has continued to carry 12 Marine-flown Harriers upon return to the LPH role. Increasing V/STOL aircraft operations from the LPH/LHA ships are expected.

Minesweeping Operations: Several LPHs were used to operate RH-53D Sea Stallion helicopters in the mine countermeasures role during the 1973 sweeping of North Vietnamese ports and the 1974 sweeping of the Suez Canal.

Transport submarines: The transport submarine *Grayback* (SS 574, ex-*LPSS 574*) is in active commission and is listed in the Submarine section of this edition.

2 "BLUE RIDGE" CLASS (AMPHIBIOUS COMMAND SHIPS (LCC))

Name	No.	Builders	Laid down	Launched	Commissioned
*BLUE RIDGE	LCC 19	Philadelphia Naval Shipyard	27 Feb 1967	4 Jan 1969	14 Nov 1970
*MOUNT WHITNEY	LCC 20	Newport News Shipbuilding & Dry Dock Co.	8 Jan 1959	8 Jan 1970	16 Jan 1971

Displacement, tons: 17 100 full load
Length, feet (metres): 620 *(188·5)* oa
Beam, feet (metres): 82 *(25·3)*
Main deck width, feet (metres): 102 *(31·1)*
Draught, feet (metres): 27 *(8·2)*
Missile launchers: 2 Basic Point Defence Missile System (BPDMS) launchers for Sea Sparrow missile (Mk 25)
Guns: 4—3 inch *(76 mm)* 50 cal (Mk 33) (twin)
Helicopter: Utility helicopter can be carried
Main engine: 1 geared turbine (General Electric); 22 000 shp; 1 shaft
Boilers: 2 (Foster Wheeler)
Speed, knots: 20
Complement: 720 (40 officers, 680 enlisted men)
Flag accommodations: 700 (200 officers, 500 enlisted men)

These are large amphibious force command ships of post-World War II design. They can provide integrated command and control facilities for sea, air and land commanders in amphibious operations. The *Blue Ridge* was authorised in the Fiscal Year 1965 new construction programme, the *Mount Whitney* in FY 1966. An AGC 21 was planned for the FY 1970 programme but cancelled late in 1968. It was proposed that the last ship combine fleet as well as amphibious force command-control facilities. The phasing out of the converted "Cleveland" class (CG) fleet flagships has fostered discussion of the potential use of these ships in that role. Their capabilities are greater than would be required by a fleet commander while they are considered too slow for striking fleet operations. Both ships are active, *Blue Ridge* in the Pacific and *Mount Whitney* in the Atlantic.

Classification: Originally designated Amphibious Force Flagships (AGC); redesignated Amphibious Command Ships (LCC) on 1 Jan 1969.

Design: General hull design and machinery arrangement are similar to the "Iwo Jima" class assault ships.

Electronics: Tactical Aircraft Navigation (Tacan).
These ships have three computer systems to support their Naval Tactical Data System (NTDS), Amphibious Command Information System (ACIS), and Naval Intelligence Processing System (NIPS).

Fire Control: Each ship has two Mk 56 gunfire control systems.

Gunnery: At one stage of design two additional twin 3 inch mounts were provided on forecastle; subsequently deleted from final designs. Antennae and their supports severely restrict firing arcs of guns.

Missiles: Two BPDMS launchers installed on each ship during 1974 (on antenna deck, aft of superstructure).

Personnel: The ships' complements includes one Marine officer and 12 enlisted men to maintain communications equipment for use by Marine Corps command and staff.

Radar: 3D Search: SPS-48.
Search: SPS 10 and 40.

MOUNT WHITNEY   7/1976, A. D. Baker III

BLUE RIDGE   1/1977, Dr. Giorgio Arra

5 "TARAWA" CLASS (AMPHIBIOUS ASSAULT SHIPS (LHA))

Name	No.	Builders	Erection of First Module	Launched	Commissioned
*TARAWA	LHA 1	Ingalls SB, Litton Industries, Pascagoula, Mississippi	15 Nov 1971	1 Dec 1973	29 May 1976
SAIPAN	LHA 2	Ingalls SB, Litton Industries, Pascagoula, Mississippi	21 July 1972	18 July 1974	Late 1977
BELLEAU WOOD	LHA 3	Ingalls SB, Litton Industries, Pascagoula, Mississippi	5 Mar 1973	Mid 1977	Late 1978
NASSAU	LHA 4	Ingalls SB, Litton Industries, Pascagoula, Mississippi	13 Aug 1973	Early 1978	Mid 1979
DA NANG	LHA 5	Ingalls SB, Litton Industries, Pascagoula, Mississippi	12 Nov 1976	Mid 1979	Early 1980

Displacement, tons: 39 300 full load
Length, feet (metres): 778 *(237·8)* wl; 820 *(250)* oa
Beam, feet (metres): 106 *(32·3)*
Draught, feet (metres): 27·5 *(8·5)*
Aircraft: 16 CH-46, 6 CH-53, 4 UH-IE helicopters or Harrier AV-8 V/STOL aircraft in place of some helicopters
Missile launchers: 2 Basic Point Defence Missile Systems (BPDMS) launchers firing Sea Sparrow missiles (Mk 25)
Guns: 3—5 inch *(127 mm)* 54 cal (Mk 45) (single)
 6—20 mm (Mk 68) (single)
Main engines: 2 Geared turbines (Westinghouse); 140 000 shp; 2 shafts
Boilers: 2 (Combustion Engineering)
Speed, knots: approx 22 sustained; approx 24 maximum
Complement: 902 (90 officers, 812 enlisted men)
Troops: 1 903 (172 officers, 1 731 enlisted men)

The LHA 1 was authorised in the Fiscal Year 1969 new construction programme, the LHA 2 and LHA 3 in FY 1970 and LHA 4 and LHA 5 in FY 1971. The Navy announced on 20 Jan, 1971 that four additional ships of this type previously planned would not be constructed. All ships of this class are under construction at a new ship production facility known as "Ingalls West". The new yard was developed specifically for multi-ship construction of the same design.
Late in 1971, the Navy announced that the LHA design work was behind schedule. Subsequently the Secretary of Defense announced that the ships will be delivered 24-38 months beyond original completion date.

Aircraft: The flight deck can operate a maximum of 9 CH-53 Sea Stallion or 12 CH-46 Sea Knight helicopters; the hangar deck can accommodate 19 CH-53 Sea Stallion or 30 CH-46 Sea Knight helicopters. A mix of these and other helicopters and at times AV-8 Harriers could be embarked.

Contract: These ships were procured by the US Navy with the acquisition processes known as Concept Formulation, Contract Definition, and Total Package Procurement. The proposals of Litton Systems Inc, and two other shipbuilding firms were submitted in response to specific performance criteria. The firms submitted detailed designs and cost estimates for series production of not less than five ships of this type. This procurement process has subsequently been abandoned.

Design: Beneath the full-length flight deck is a half-length hangar deck, the two being connected by an elevator amidships on the port side and a stern lift; beneath the after elevator is a floodable docking well measuring 268 feet in length and 78 feet in width which is capable of accommodating four LCU 1610 type landing craft. Also included is a large garage for trucks and AFVs and troop berthing for a reinforced battalion.
Storage for 10 000 gallons (US) of vehicle petrol and 400 000 gallons (US) of JP-5 helicopter petrol.

TARAWA

1975, Litton Industries

Electronics: Helicopter navigation equipment provided. Each ship also will have an integrated Tactical Amphibious Warfare Data System (ITAWDS) to provide computerised support in control of helicopters and aircraft, shipboard weapons and sensors, navigation, landing craft control, and electronic warfare.

Engineering: A 900 hp fixed bow thruster is provided for holding position while unloading landing craft.

Fire Control: Provided with one Mk 86 gunfire control system in each ship; also one SPG-60 and one SPG-9A weapon control radars.

Fiscal: In early 1974 the estimated total cost to the government of the five LHAs was $1·145 billion or an average of $229 000 000 per ship. A cancellation fee of $109 700 000 was due to the shipyard for cancellation of LHA 6-9.

Medical: These ships are fitted with extensive medical facilities including operating rooms, X-ray room, hospital ward, isolation ward, laboratories, pharmacy, dental operating room and medical store rooms.

Radar: 3D Search: SPS 52.
Search: SPS-10 and 40.
Air/navigation: SPN-35.

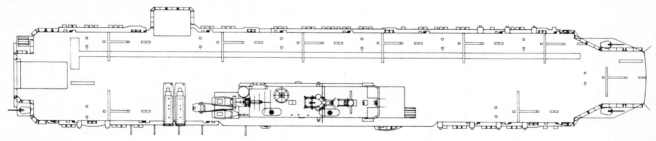

"TARAWA" Class

Drawing by A. D. Baker III

TARAWA

1975, Litton Industries

7 "IWO JIMA" CLASS (AMPHIBIOUS ASSAULT SHIPS (LPH))

Name	No.	Builders	Laid down	Launched	Commissioned
*IWO JIMA	LPH 2	Puget Sound Naval Shipyard	2 Apr 1959	17 Sep 1960	26 Aug 1961
*OKINAWA	LPH 3	Philadelphia Naval Shipyard	1 Apr 1960	14 Aug 1961	14 Apr 1962
*GUADALCANAL	LPH 7	Philadelphia Naval Shipyard	1 Sep 1961	16 Mar 1963	20 July 1963
*GUAM	LPH 9	Philadelphia Naval Shipyard	15 Nov 1962	22 Aug 1964	16 Jan 1965
*TRIPOLI	LPH 10	Ingalls Shipbuilding Corp, Pascagoula, Mississippi	15 June 1964	31 July 1965	6 Aug 1966
*NEW ORLEANS	LPH 11	Philadelphia Naval Shipyard	1 Mar 1966	3 Feb 1968	16 Nov 1968
*INCHON	LPH 12	Ingalls Shipbuilding Corp, Pascagoula, Mississippi	8 Apr 1968	24 May 1969	20 June 1970

Displacement, tons: 17 000 light; 18 000 (2, 3 and 7), 18 300 (9 and 10), 17 706 (11), 17 515 (12) full load
Length, feet (metres): 592 *(180·0)* oa
Beam, feet (metres): 84 *(25·6)*
Draught, feet (metres): 26 *(7·9)*
Flight deck width, feet (metres): 104 *(31·9)* maximum
Aircraft: 20-24 medium (CH-46) helicopters
    4 heavy (CH-53) helicopters
    4 observation (HU-1) helicopters or AV-8 Harriers in place of some troop helicopters
Guns: 4—3 inch *(76 mm)* 50 cal (Mk 33) (twin)
Missile launchers: 2 Basic Point Defence Missile System (BPDMS) launchers firing Sea Sparrow missiles (Mk 25)
Main engines: 1 geared turbine (De Laval—10, GE—12, Westinghouse in others); 22 000 shp; 1 shaft
Boilers: 2 (Combustion Engineering or Babcock & Wilcox (9))
Speed, knots: 23
Complement: 652 (47 officers, 605 enlisted men)
Troops: 1 724 (143 officers, 1 581 enlisted men)

IWO JIMA
1976, Dr. Giorgio Arra

The *Iwo Jima* was the world's first ship designed and constructed specifically to operate helicopters. Each LPH can carry a Marine battalion landing team, its guns, vehicles, and equipment, plus a reinforced squadron of transport helicopters and various support personnel.

The *Iwo Jima* was authorised in the Fiscal Year 1958 new construction programme, the *Okinawa* in FY 1959, *Guadalcanal* in FY 1960, *Guam* in FY 1962, *Tripoli* in FY 1963, *New Orleans* in FY 1965, and *Inchon* in FY 1966.

Estimated cost of the *Iwo Jima* was $40 000 000.

The *Guam* was modified late in 1971 and began operations in January 1972 as an interim sea control ship. She operated Harrier AV-8 V/STOL aircraft and SH-3 Sea King A/S helicopters in convoy escort exercises; she reverted to the amphibious role in 1974 but kept 12 AV-8As on board. Several of these ships operated RH-53 minesweeping helicopters to clear North Vietnamese ports in 1973 and the Suez Canal in 1974.

Aircraft: The flight decks of these ships provide for simultaneous take off or landing of seven CH-46 Sea Knight or four CH-53 Sea Stallion helicopters during normal operations. The hangar decks can accommodate 19 CH-46 Sea Knight or 11 CH-53 Sea Stallion helicopters, or various combinations of helicopters.

Design: Each ship has two deck-edge lifts, one to port opposite the bridge and one to starboard aft of island. Full hangars are provided; no arresting wires or catapults. Two small elevators carry cargo from holds to flight deck. Storage provided for 6 500 gallons (US) of vehicle petrol and 405 000 gallons (US) of JP-5 helicopter petrol.

Electronics: Tacan; advanced electronic warfare equipment fitted.

Fire Control: As rearmed with BPDMS these ships have two Mk 63 gunfire control systems and two SPG-50 weapon control radars. Two Mk 115 missile fire control systems.

Gunnery: As built, each ship had eight 3 inch guns in twin mounts, two forward of the island structure and two at stern. Gun battery reduced by half with substitution of BPDMS launchers (see *Missile* notes).

Medical: These ships are fitted with extensive medical facilities including operating room, X-ray room, hospital ward, isolation ward, laboratory, pharmacy, dental operating room, and medical store rooms.

OKINAWA
1/1977, Dr. Giorgio Arra

Missiles. One Sea Sparrow launcher forward of island structure and one on the port quarter. The *Okinawa* had one BPDMS launcher fitted in 1970 and the second in 1973; *Tripoli* and *Inchon* rearmed in 1972, *Iwo Jima* and *New Orleans* in 1973, *Guam* and *Guadalcanal* in 1974.

Radar: Search: SPS-10 and 40.
Navigation: SPN-10.

OKINAWA
1/1977, Dr. Giorgio Arra

12 "AUSTIN" CLASS (AMPHIBIOUS TRANSPORT DOCKS (LPD))

Name	No.	Builders	Commissioned	
*AUSTIN	LPD 4	New York Naval Shipyard	6 Feb	1965
*OGDEN	LPD 5	New York Naval Shipyard	19 June	1965
*DULUTH	LPD 6	New York Naval Shipyard	18 Dec	1965
*CLEVELAND	LPD 7	Ingalls Shipbuilding Corp.	21 April	1967
*DUBUQUE	LPD 8	Ingalls Shipbuilding Corp.	1 Sep	1967
*DENVER	LPD 9	Lockheed Shipbuilding & Cons	26 Oct	1968
*JUNEAU	LPD 10	Lockheed Shipbuilding & Cons	12 July	1969
*CORONADO	LPD 11	Lockheed Shipbuilding & Cons	23 May	1970
*SHREVEPORT	LPD 12	Lockheed Shipbuilding & Cons	12 Dec	1970
*NASHVILLE	LPD 13	Lockheed Shipbuilding & Cons	14 Feb	1970
*TRENTON	LPD 14	Lockheed Shipbuilding & Cons	6 Mar	1971
*PONCE	LPD 15	Lockheed Shipbuilding & Cons	10 July	1971

NASHVILLE 7/1976, A. D. Baker III

Displacement, tons: 10 000 light; 13 900 (4-6), 16 550 (7-10), 16 900 (11-13), 17 300 (14 and 15) full load
Length, feet (metres): 570 (173·3) oa
Beam, feet (metres): 106·1 (32·4)
Draught, feet (metres): 23 (7·0)
Guns: 8—3 inch (76 mm) 50 cal (Mk 33) (twin)
Helicopters: up to 6 UH-34 or CH-46
Main engines: 2 steam turbines (De Laval); 24 000 shp; 2 shafts = 21 knots
Boilers: 2 (Babcock & Wilcox)
Complement: 473 (27 officers, 446 enlisted men)
Troops: 930 in LPD 4-6 and LPD 14-15; 840 in LPD 7-13
Flag accommodations: Approx 90 in LPD 7-13

These ships are enlarged versions of the previous "Raleigh" class; most notes for the "Raleigh" class apply to these ships. Fitted with one Mk 56 and two Mk 63 gunfire control systems.
The dates of laying down and launching are: *Austin* and *Ogden* 4 Feb 1963 and 27 June 1964; *Duluth* 18 Dec 1963 and 14 Aug 1965; *Cleveland* 30 Nov 1964 and 7 May 1966; *Dubuque* 25 Jan 1965 and 6 Aug 1966; *Denver* 7 Feb 1964 and 23 Jan 1965; *Juneau* 23 Jan 1965 and 12 Feb 1966; *Coronado* 3 May 1965 and 30 July 1966; *Shreveport* 27 Dec 1965 and 25 Oct 1966; *Nashville* 14 Mar 1966 and 7 Oct 1967; *Trenton* 8 Aug 1966 and 3 August 1968; *Ponce* 31 Oct 1966 and 20 May 1970. *Duluth* completed at Philadelphia Naval Shipyard.
The LPD 4-6 were authorised in the Fiscal Year 1962 new construction programme, LPD 7-10 in FY 1963, LPD 11-13 in FY 1964, LPD 14 and LPD 15 in FY 1965, and LPD 16 in FY 1966. LPD 16 was deferred in favour of LHA programme; officially cancelled in Feb 1969.

Rockets: Each ship will be fitted with Mk 36 Chaffroc.

DUBUQUE 1/1977, Dr. Giorgio Arra

2 "RALEIGH" CLASS (AMPHIBIOUS TRANSPORT DOCKS (LPD))

Name	No.	Builders	Commissioned	
*RALEIGH	LPD 1	New York Naval Shipyard	8 Sep	1962
*VANCOUVER	LPD 2	New York Naval Shipyard	11 May	1963

Displacement, tons: 8 040 light; 13 600 full load
Length, feet (metres): 500 (152·0) wl; 521·8 (158·4) oa
Beam, feet (metres): 104 (31·7)
Draught, feet (metres): 22 (6·7)
Guns: 8—3 inch (76 mm) 50 cal (Mk 33) (twin)
Helicopters: up to 6 UH-34 or CH-46
Main engines: 2 steam turbines; (De Laval); 24 000 shp; 2 shafts = 20 knots sustained
Boilers: 2 (Babcock & Wilcox)
Complement: 490 (30 officers, 460 enlisted men)
Troops: 930

The amphibious transport dock was developed from the dock landing ship (LSD) concept but provides more versatility. The LPD replaces the amphibious transport (LPA) and, in part, the amphibious cargo ship (LKA) and dock landing ship. The LPD can carry a "balanced load" of assault troops and their equipment, has a docking well for landing craft, a helicopter deck, cargo holds and vehicle garages. Fitted with one Mk 56 and two Mk 57 directors. The *Raleigh* was authorised in the Fiscal Year 1959 new construction programme, the *Vancouver* in FY 1960. The *Raleigh* was laid down on 23 June 1960 and launched on 17 Mar 1962; the *Vancouver* on 19 Nov 1960 and 15 Sep 1962. Approximate construction cost was $29 000 000 per ship.
A third ship of this class, *La Salle* (LPD 3), was reclassified as a command ship (AGF 3) on 1 July 1972.

Design: These ships resemble dock landing ships (LSD) but have fully enclosed docking well with the roof forming a permanent helicopter platform. The docking well is 168 feet long and 50 feet wide, less than half the length of wells in newer LSDs; the LPD design provides more space for vehicles, cargo and troops. Ramps allow vehicles to be driven between helicopter deck, parking area and docking well, side ports provide roll-on/roll-off capability when docks are available. An overhead monorail in the docking well with six cranes facilitates loading landing craft. The docking well in these ships can hold one LCU and three LCM-6s or four LCM-8s or 20 LVTs (amphibious tractors). In addition, two LCM-6s or four LCPLs are carried on the boat deck which are lowered by crane.

Helicopters: These ships are not normally assigned helicopters because they lack integral hangars and maintenance facilities. It is intended that a nearby amphibious assault ship (LHA or LPH) would provide helicopters during an amphibious operation. Telescoping hangars have been fitted.

Rockets: Mk 36 Chaffroc system to be fitted.

RALEIGH 1/1976, USN

VANCOUVER 1/1977, Dr. Giorgio Arra

5 "ANCHORAGE" CLASS (DOCK LANDING SHIPS (LSD))

Name	No.	Builders	Commissioned
*ANCHORAGE	LSD 36	Ingalls Shipbuilding	15 Mar 1969
*PORTLAND	LSD 37	General Dynamics, Quincy, Mass	3 Oct 1970
*PENSACOLA	LSD 38	General Dynamics, Quincy, Mass	27 Mar 1971
*MOUNT VERNON	LSD 39	General Dynamics, Quincy, Mass	13 May 1972
*FORT FISHER	LSD 40	General Dynamics, Quincy, Mass	9 Dec 1972

Displacement, tons: 8 600 light; 13 600 full load
Dimensions, feet (metres): 553·3 oa × 84 × 18·6 *(168·6 × 25·6 × 5·7)*
Guns: 8—3 inch *(76 mm)* 50 cal (Mk 33) (twin)
Main engines: Steam turbines (De Laval); 24 000 shp; 2 shafts = 20 knots sustained
Boilers: 2 (Foster Wheeler except Combustion Engineering in *Anchorage)*
Complement: 397 (21 officers, 376 enlisted men)
Troops: 376 (28 officers, 348 enlisted men)

These ships are similar in appearance to earlier classes but with a tripod mast. Helicopter platform aft with docking well partially open; helicopter platform can be removed. Fitted with one Mk 56 and two Mk 63 gunfire control systems and 2 AN/SPG 50 gunfire control radars. Docking well approximately 430 × 50 feet can accommodate three LCU-type landing craft. Space on deck for one LCM, and davits for one LCPL and one LCVP. Two 50-ton capacity cranes. LSD 36 was authorised in Fiscal Year 1965 shipbuilding programme; LSD 37-39 in FY 1966 programme; LSD 40 in FY 1967 programme.
Anchorage was laid down on 13 Mar 1967 and launched in 5 May 1968; *Portland* on 21 Sep 1967 and 20 Dec 1969; *Pensacola* on 12 Mar 1969 and 11 July 1970; *Mount Vernon* on 29 Jan 1970 and 17 April 1971; and *Fort Fisher* on 15 July 1970 and 22 April 1972.
Estimated construction cost is $11 500 000 per ship.

PENSACOLA

6/1975, Dr. Giorgio Arra

PENSACOLA

6/1975, Dr. Giorgio Arra

8 "THOMASTON" CLASS (DOCK LANDING SHIPS (LSD))

Name	No.	Builders	Commissioned
*THOMASTON	LSD 28	Ingalls SB Corp, Pascagoula	17 Sep 1954
*PLYMOUTH ROCK	LSD 29	Ingalls SB Corp, Pascagoula	29 Nov 1954
*FORT SNELLING	LSD 30	Ingalls SB Corp, Pascagoula	24 Jan 1955
*POINT DEFIANCE	LSD 31	Ingalls SB Corp, Pascagoula	31 Mar 1955
*SPIEGEL GROVE	LSD 32	Ingalls SB Corp, Pascagoula	8 June 1956
*ALAMO	LSD 33	Ingalls SB Corp, Pascagoula	24 Aug 1956
*HERMITAGE	LSD 34	Ingalls SB Corp, Pascagoula	14 Dec 1956
*MONTICELLO	LSD 35	Ingalls SB Corp, Pascagoula	29 Mar 1957

Displacement, tons: 6 880 light; 11 270 full load
Dimensions, feet (metres): 510 oa × 84 × 19 *(155·5 × 25·6 × 5·8)*
Guns: 12—3 inch *(76 mm)* 50 cal (Mk 33) (twin)
Main engines: Steam turbines (General Electric); 24 000 shp; 2 shafts = 22·5 knots
Boilers: 2 (Babcock & Wilcox)
Complement: 400
Troops: 340

LSD 28-31 launched in 1954 on 9 Feb, 7 May, 16 July and 28 Sep respectively; LSD 32 launched on 10 Nov 1955; LSD 33-35 launched in 1956 on 20 Jan, 12 June and 10 Aug. Fitted with helicopter platform over docking well; two 5-ton capacity cranes; can carry 21 LCM-6 or 3 LCU and 6 LCM landing craft or approximately 50 LVTs (amphibious tractors) in docking well plus 30 LVTs on mezzanine and super decks (with helicopter landing area clear). Welldeck measures 391 × 48 ft.
As built, each ship had 16—3 inch guns; twin mount on each side wall (aft of boats davits) has been removed. Fitted with two Mk 56 and two Mk 63 gunfire control systems and 2 AN/SPG 34 gunfire control radars.
Note pole mast compared to tripod mast of "Anchorage" class which have enclosed 3 inch gun mounts forward of bridge.

MONTICELLO

1/1977, Dr. Giorgio Arra

POINT DEFIANCE

7/1976, Dr. Giorgio Arra

7 "CASA GRANDE" CLASS (DOCK LANDING SHIPS (LSD))

Name	No.	Builders	Commissioned
CASA GRANDE	LSD 13	Newport News SB & DD Co	5 June 1944
RUSHMORE	LSD 14	Newport News SB & DD Co	3 July 1944
SHADWELL	LSD 15	Newport News SB & DD Co	24 July 1944
CABILDO	LSD 16	Newport News SB & DD Co	15 Mar 1945
COLONIAL	LSD 18	Newport News SB & DD Co	15 May 1945
DONNER	LSD 20	Boston Navy Yard	31 July 1945
TORTUGA	LSD 26	Boston Navy Yard	8 June 1945

Displacement, tons: 4 790 standard; 9 375 full load
Dimensions, feet (metres): 475·4 oa × 76·2 × 18 *(144·9 × 23·2 × 5·5)*
Guns: 8— or 12—40 mm (2 quad plus 2 twin in some ships)
Main engines: Geared turbines (Newport News); 2 shafts; 7 000 shp = 15·4 knots
Boilers: 2
Complement: 265 (15 officers, 250 men)

LSD 13-16 launched in 1944 on 11 April, 10 May, 24 May and 28 Dec; LSD 18, 20 and 26 launched in 1945 on 28 Feb, 6 April and 21 Jan.
Originally a class of 15 dock landing ships. *Fort Snelling* LSD 23, and *Point Defiance* LSD 24 cancelled in 1945; former ship completed for merchant service, reacquired by Navy as cargo ship *Taurus*, T-AK 273, T-AKR 8 (stricken in 1968). LSD 9-12 of this class transferred to Britain in 1943-1944.
Docking well is 392 × 44 feet; can carry 3 LCUs or 18 LSMs or 32 LVTs (amphibious tractors) in docking well. All ships are fitted with helicopter platform.
Colonial and *Donner* were modernised under the FRAM II programme in 1960-1962.
All surviving ships of this class are in Navy or Maritime Administration reserve (the latter ships remain on the Navy List).

DONNER

1968, USN

20 "NEWPORT" CLASS (TANK LANDING SHIPS (LST))

Name	No.	Laid down	Launched	Commissioned
**NEWPORT	LST 1179	1 Nov 1966	3 Feb 1968	7 June 1969
*MANITOWOC	LST 1180	1 Feb 1967	4 June 1969	24 Jan 1970
*SUMTER	LST 1181	14 Nov 1967	13 Dec 1969	20 June 1970
*FRESNO	LST 1182	16 Dec 1967	28 Sep 1968	22 Nov 1969
*PEORIA	LST 1183	22 Feb 1968	23 Nov 1968	21 Feb 1970
*FREDERICK	LST 1184	13 April 1968	8 Mar 1969	11 April 1970
*SCHENECTADY	LST 1185	2 Aug 1968	24 May 1969	13 June 1970
*CAYUGA	LST 1186	28 Sep 1968	12 July 1969	8 Aug 1970
*TUSCALOOSA	LST 1187	23 Nov 1968	6 Sep 1969	24 Oct 1970
*SAGINAW	LST 1188	24 May 1969	7 Feb 1970	23 Jan 1971
*SAN BERNARDINO	LST 1189	12 July 1969	28 Mar 1970	27 Mar 1971
*BOULDER	LST 1190	6 Sep 1969	22 May 1970	4 June 1971
*RACINE	LST 1191	13 Dec 1969	15 Aug 1970	9 July 1971
*SPARTANBURG COUNTY	LST 1192	7 Feb 1970	11 Nov 1970	1 Sep 1971
*FAIRFAX COUNTY	LST 1193	28 Mar 1970	19 Dec 1970	16 Oct 1971
*LA MOURE COUNTY	LST 1194	22 May 1970	13 Feb 1971	18 Dec 1971
*BARBOUR COUNTY	LST 1195	15 Aug 1970	15 May 1971	12 Feb 1972
*HARLAN COUNTY	LST 1196	7 Nov 1970	24 July 1971	8 April 1972
*BARNSTABLE COUNTY	LST 1197	19 Dec 1970	2 Oct 1971	27 May 1972
*BRISTOL COUNTY	LST 1198	13 Feb 1971	4 Dec 1971	5 Aug 1972

BARNSTABLE COUNTY   10/1976, Michael D. J. Lennon

Displacement, tons: 8 450 full load
Dimensions, feet (metres): 522·3 hull oa × 69·5 × 17·5 (aft) *(159·2 × 21·2 × 5·3)*
Guns: 4—3 inch *(76 mm)* 50 cal (Mk 33) (twin)
Main engines: 6 diesels (Alco) (GM in 1179-1181); 16 000 bhp, 2 shafts = 20 knots (sustained)
Complement: 196 (12 officers, 174 enlisted men)
Troops: 431 (20 officers, 411 enlisted men)

These ships are of an entirely new design; larger and faster than previous tank landing ships. They operate with 20-knot amphibious squadrons to transport tanks, other heavy vehicles, engineer equipment, and supplies which cannot be readily landed by helicopters or landing craft. These are the only recent construction amphibious ships with a pole mast *vice* tripod-lattice mast. Two Mk 63 gunfire control systems are provided.
The *Newport* was authorised in the Fiscal Year 1965 new construction programme and laid down on 1 Nov 1966. LST 1180-1187 (8 ships) in FY 1966, and LST 1188-1198 (11 ships) in FY 1967. LST 1179-1181 built by Philadelphia Naval Shipyard, LST 1182-1198 built by National Steel & SB Co, San Diego, California. Seven additional ships of this type that were planned for the Fiscal Year 1971 new construction programme were deferred.

SUMTER   6/1975, Dr. Giorgio Arra

Design: These ships are the first LSTs to depart from the bow-door design developed by the British early in World War II. The hull form required to achieve 20 knots would not permit bow doors, thus these ships unload by a 112-foot ramp over their bow. The ramp is supported by twin derrick arms. A ramp just forward of the superstructure connects the lower tank deck with the main deck and a vehicle passage through the superstructure provides access to the parking area amidships. A stern gate to the tank deck permits unloading of amphibious tractors into the water, or unloading of other vehicles into an LCU or onto a pier. Vehicle stowage is rated at 500 tons and 19 000 square feet (5 000 sq ft more than previous LSTs). Length over derrick arms is 562 feet; full load draught is 11·5 feet forward and 17·5 feet aft. Bow thruster fitted to hold position offshore while unloading amphibious tractors.

Gunnery: 2 Phalanx 20 mm CIWS to be fitted.

Rockets: 1 Mk 36 Chaffroc to be fitted.

BOULDER   1976, Dr. Giorgio Arra

3 "DE SOTO COUNTY" CLASS (TANK LANDING SHIPS (LST))

Name	No.	Builders	Commissioned
SUFFOLK COUNTY	LST 1173	Boston Navy Yard	15 Aug 1957
LORAIN COUNTY	LST 1177	American SB Co, Lorrain, Ohio	3 Oct 1959
WOOD COUNTY	LST 1178	American SB Co, Lorrain, Ohio	5 Aug 1969

Displacement, tons: 4 164 light; 7 100 full load
Dimensions, feet (metres): 445 oa × 62 × 17·5 *(138·7 × 18·9 × 5·3)*
Guns: 6—3 inch *(76 mm)* 50 cal (Mk 33) (twin)
Main engines: 6 Diesels (Fairbanks Morse—1173) (Cooper Bessemer—others); 13 700 bhp; 2 shafts; (controllable pitch propellers) = 16·5 knots
Complement: 188 (15 officers, 173 men)
Troops: 634 (30 officers, 604 enlisted men)

Originally a class of seven tank landing ships (LST 1171, 1173-1178 with LST 1172 not built). They were faster and had a greater troop capacity than earlier LSTs; considered the "ultimate" design attainable with the traditional LST bow-door configuration.
Suffolk County launched on 5 Sep 1956, *Lorain County* on 22 June 1957, and *Wood County* on 14 Dec 1957.
The surviving ships were decommissioned in mid-1972 and are in reserve.
The *Graham County* (LST 1176) was converted to a gunboat support ship (AGP); now stricken.

Design: High degree of habitability with all crew and troop living spaces air conditioned. Can carry 23 medium tanks or vehicles up to 75 tons on 288-foot-long (lower) tank deck. Davits for four LCVP-type landing craft. Liquid cargo capacity of 170 000 gallons (US) diesel or jet fuel plus 7 000 gallons (US) of petrol for embarked vehicles; some ships had reduced troop spaces to carry additional 250 000 gallons (US) of aviation petrol for pumping ashore or to other ships.

Conversion: *Wood County* was to have been converted to Patrol Combatant Support Ship (AGHS) under original 1978 FY programme but this has been deleted by the new administration.

SUFFOLK COUNTY   1971, USN

5 "CHARLESTON" CLASS (AMPHIBIOUS CARGO SHIPS (LKA))

Name	No.	Builders	Commissioned	
*CHARLESTON	LKA 113	Newport News SB & DD Co.	14 Dec	1968
*DURHAM	LKA 114	Newport News SB & DD Co.	24 May	1969
*MOBILE	LKA 115	Newport News SB & DD Co.	29 Sep	1969
*ST. LOUIS	LKA 116	Newport News SB & DD Co.	22 Nov	1969
*EL PASO	LKA 117	Newport News SB & DD Co.	17 Jan	1970

Displacement, tons: 18 600 full load
Dimensions, feet (metres): 575·5 oa × 62 × 25·5 *(175·4 × 18·9 × 7·7)*
Guns: 8—3 inch *(76 mm)* 50 cal (Mk 33) (twin)
Main engines: 1 steam turbine (Westinghouse); 22 000 shp; 1 shaft = 20 knots
Boilers: 2 (Combustion Engineering)
Complement: 334 (24 officers, 310 enlisted men)
Troops: 226 (15 officers, 211 enlisted men)

CHARLESTON   10/1976, Michael D. J. Lennon

Charleston laid down 5 Dec 1966, launched 2 Dec 1967; *Durham* laid down 10 July 1967, launched 29 March 1968; *Mobile* laid down 15 Jan 1968, launched 19 October 1968; *St. Louis* 3 April 1968 and 4 Jan 1969 and *El Paso* 22 Oct 1968 and 17 May 1969.
These ships are designed specifically for the attack cargo ship role; can carry nine landing craft (LCM) and supplies for amphibious operations. Design includes two heavy-lift cranes with a 78·4 ton capacity, two 40-ton capacity booms, and eight 15-ton capacity booms; helicopter deck aft; two Mk 56 gunfire control systems.
The LKA 113-116 were authorised in the Fiscal Year 1965 shipbuilding programme; LKA 117 in FY 1966 programme.
Cost of building was approximately $21 000 000 per ship.

Classification: Originally designated Attack Cargo Ship (AKA), *Charleston* redesignated Amphibious Cargo Ship (LKA) on 14 Dec 1968; others to LKA on 1 Jan 1969.

Engineering: These are among the first US Navy ships with a fully automated main propulsion plant; control of plant is from bridge or central machinery space console. This automation permitted a 45-man reduction in complement.

Rockets: 1 Mk 36 Chaffroc to be installed.

DURHAM   1/1977, Dr. Giorgio Arra

1 "TULARE" CLASS (AMPHIBIOUS CARGO SHIP (LKA))

Name	No.	Builders	Commissioned
*TULARE (ex-*Evergreen Mariner*)	LKA 112	Bethlehem, San Francisco	13 Jan 1956

Displacement, tons: 12 000 light; 16 800 full load
Dimensions, feet (metres): 564 oa × 76 × 28 *(171·9 × 23·2 × 8·5)*
Guns: 12—3 inch *(76 mm)* 50 cal (Mk 33) (twin)
Main engines: Steam turbine (De Laval); 22 000 shp; 1 shaft = 23 knots
Boilers: 2 (Combustion Engineering)
Complement: 393 (10 officers, 154 enlisted active duty; 21 officers, 208 enlisted reserve)
Troops: 319 (18 officers, 301 enlisted men)

Laid down on 16 Feb 1953; launched on 22 Dec 1953; acquired by Navy during construction; C4-S-1A type. Has helicopter landing platform and booms capable of lifting 60-ton landing craft. Carries 9 LCM-6 and 11 LCVP landing craft as deck cargo. Fitted with five Mk 63 gunfire control systems. Designation changed from AKA 112 to LKA 112 on 1 Jan 1969.
The *Tulare* was assigned to the Naval Reserve Force on 1 July 1975 and is partially manned by reserve personnel.

Class: Thirty-five "Mariner" design C4-S-1A merchant ships built during the early 1950s; five acquired by Navy, three for conversion to amphibious ships (AKA-APA) and two for support of Polaris-Poseidon programme (designated AG).

TULARE   1969, USN

2 "PAUL REVERE" CLASS (AMPHIBIOUS TRANSPORTS (LPA))

Name	No.	Builders	Commissioned
*PAUL REVERE (ex-*Diamond Mariner*)	LPA 248	New York SB Corp	3 Sep 1958
*FRANCIS MARION (ex-*Prairie Mariner*)	LPA 249	New York SB Corp	6 July 1961

Displacement, tons: 10 709 light; 16 838 full load
Dimensions, feet (metres): 563·5 oa × 76 × 27 *(171·8 × 23·2 × 8·2)*
Guns: 8—3 inch *(76 mm)* 50 cal (Mk 33) (twin)
Main engines: Steam turbine (General Electric); 22 000 shp; 1 shaft = 22 knots
Boilers: 2 (Foster Wheeler)
Complement: 307 (13 officers, 187 enlisted active duty; 15 officers, 237 enlisted reserve)
Troops: 1 657 (96 officers, 1 561 enlisted men)

Paul Revere launched 13 Feb 1954, *Francis Marion* launched 11 April 1953. "Mariner" C4-S-1A merchant ships acquired for conversion to attack transports; *Paul Revere* converted by Todd Shipyard Corp, San Pedro, California, under the Fiscal Year 1957 conversion programme; *Francis Marion* converted by Bethlehem Steel Corp, Key Highway Yard, Baltimore, Maryland, under FY 1959 programme. Helicopter platform fitted aft; 7 LCM-6 and 16 LCVP landing craft carried as deck cargo; each ship has four Mk 63 gunfire control systems. Fitted to serve as force flagships.
Designation of both ships changed from APA to LPA on 1 Jan 1969.
The *Paul Revere* was assigned to the Naval Reserve Force on 1 July 1975 and the *Francis Marion* on 14 Nov 1975; partially manned by reserve personnel.

FRANCIS MARION   1975, Dr. Giorgio Arra

LANDING CRAFT

1 AMPHIBIOUS ASSAULT LANDING CRAFT (AALC):
AEROJET-GENERAL DESIGN (JEFF-A)

Weight, tons: 85·8 empty; 166·4 gross
Dimensions, feet (metres): 96·2 oa × 48 × (height) 23 *(31·5 × 15·7 × 7·5)*
Main engines: 4 gas turbines (Avco-Lycoming T40); 11 200 hp; 4 aircraft type propellers in rotating shrouds for propulsive thrust = approx 50 knots cruising
Lift engines: 2 gas turbines (Avco-Lycoming T40); 5 600 hp; 8 horizontal fans (2 sets) for cushion lift
Complement: 6

AEROJET-GENERAL DESIGN (Model)

This is an Air Cushion Vehicle (ACV) landing craft being developed by the Aerojet-General Corp and being built by Todd Shipyards, Seattle, Washington, under Navy contract. Construction completed in February 1975 with one year of contractor testing before delivery to Navy in February 1976. (Construction shifted from Tacoma Boatbuilding Co).
Above dimensions are for craft on air cushion; when at rest dimensions will be 97 × 44 × 19. Designed to carry 120 000 pound payload at a design speed of 50 knots (same as Jeff-B). Design features include aluminium construction, bow and stern ramps, cargo deck area of 2 100 square feet; two sound-insulated compartments each hold four persons; three engines housed in each side structure; two propellers in rotating shrouds provide horizontal propulsion and steering. Performance parameters include four-hour endurance (200 n mile range), four foot obstacle clearance, and capability to maintain cruise speed in Sea State 2 with 25-knot headwind. Scheduled for delivery in 1976.

Project: Aerojet-General and Bell Aerosystems were awarded contracts in January 1969 to design competitive assault landing craft employing ACV technology. Subsequently, awards were made to both companies in March 1971 to build and test one craft per company.

These are air cushion or bubble craft, supported above the land or water surface by a continuously generated cushion or bubble of air held by flexible "skirts" that surround the base of the vehicle. According to US Navy usage, they differ from surface effect ships (SES) which have rigid sidewalls that penetrate the water surface to help hold the cushion or bubble. Official designation of these craft is Amphibious Assault Landing Craft (AALC), with the Aerojet-General design being referred to as AALC—Jeff(A) and the Bell Aerosystems craft as AALC—Jeff(B).

1 AMPHIBIOUS ASSAULT LANDING CRAFT (AALC):
BELL DESIGN (JEFF-B)

Weight, tons: 162·5 gross
Dimensions, feet (metres): 86·75 oa × 47 × (height) 23·5 *(28·4 × 15·4 × 7·7)*
Main/lift engines: 6 gas turbines (Avco-Lycoming T40); 16 800 hp; interconnected with 2 aircraft-type propellers in rotating shrouds for propulsive thrust and 4 horizontal fans for cushion lift = approx 50 knots cruising
Complement: 6

BELL AEROSYSTEMS DESIGN (Model)

ACV landing craft built by Bell Aerosystems. Completed 1976. Above dimensions are for craft on air cushion; when at rest dimensions are 80 × 43 × 19. Aluminium construction; bow and stern ramps; cargo area of 1 738 square feet; three engines housed in each side structure with raised pilot house on starboard side. Performance parameters similar to Jeff (A).
Distinguished from Aerojet-General craft by having only two shrouded propellers for thrust and steering.

60 UTILITY LANDING CRAFT: LCU 1610 SERIES

LCU 1613	LCU 1627	LCU 1641	LCU 1651	LCU 1661	LCU 1671
LCU 1614	LCU 1628	LCU 1642	LCU 1652	LCU 1662	LCU 1672
LCU 1616	LCU 1629	LCU 1643	LCU 1653	LCU 1663	LCU 1673
LCU 1617	LCU 1630	LCU 1644	LCU 1654	LCU 1664	LCU 1674
LCU 1618	LCU 1631	LCU 1645	LCU 1655	LCU 1665	LCU 1675
LCU 1619	LCU 1632	LCU 1646	LCU 1656	LCU 1666	LCU 1676
LCU 1621	LCU 1633	LCU 1647	LCU 1657	LCU 1667	LCU 1677
LCU 1623	LCU 1634	LCU 1648	LCU 1658	LCU 1668	LCU 1678
LCU 1624	LCU 1635	LCU 1649	LCU 1659	LCU 1669	LCU 1679
LCU 1626	LCU 1637	LCU 1650	LCU 1660	LCU 1670	LCU 1680

Displacement, tons: 200 light; 375 full load
Dimensions, feet (metres): 134·9 oa × 29 × 6·1 *(44·2 × 9·5 × 2)*
Guns: 2—50 cal machine guns
Main engines: 4 diesels (Detroit); 1 000 bhp; 2 shafts (Kort nozzles) = 11 knots
Range, miles: 1 200 at 8 knots
Complement: 12 to 14 (enlisted men)

LCU 1661   *1976, Dr Giorgio Arra*

Improved landing craft, larger than previous series; can carry three M-103 or M-48 tanks (approx 64 tons and 48 tons respectively). Cargo capacity 170 tons.
LCU 1610-1612 built by Christy Corp, Sturgeon Bay, Wisconsin; LCU 1613-1619, 1623, 1624 built by Gunderson Bros Engineering Corp, Portland, Oregon; LCU 1620, 1621, 1625, 1626, 1629, 1630 built by Southern Shipbuilding Corp, Slidell, Louisiana; LCU 1622 built by Weaver Shipyards, Texas; LCU 1627, 1628, 1631-1636 built by General Ship and Engine Works (last six units completed in 1968); LCU 1638-1645 built by Marinette Marine Corp, Marinette, Wisconsin (completed 1969-1970); LCU 1646-1666 built by Defoe Shipbuilding Co, Bay City, Michigan

(completed 1970-1971). The one-of-a-kind aluminium hull, 133·8 ft LCU 1637 built by Pacific Coast Engineering Co, Alameda, California; LCU 1667-1670 built by General Ship & Engine Works, East Boston, in 1973-1974; LCU 1671-1680 built by Marinette Marine Corp, 1974-1976. LCU 1636, 1638, 1639, 1640 reclassified as YFB 88-91 in October 1969 LCU 1620 and 1625 to YFU 92 and 93 respectively, in April 1971; LCU 1611, 1615, 1622 to YFU 97-99 in Feb 1972; LCU 1610, 1612 to YFU 100 and 101 respectively, in Aug 1972.

Engineering: Only two diesels fitted with vertical cycloidal propellers shipped in LCU 1621 and YFUs 92 and 93.

24 UTILITY LANDING CRAFT: LCU 1466 SERIES

LCU 1466	LCU 1470	LCU 1485	LCU 1490	LCU 1537
LCU 1467	LCU 1472	LCU 1486	LCU 1492	LCU 1539
LCU 1468	LCU 1477	LCU 1487	LCU 1525	LCU 1547
LCU 1469	LCU 1482	LCU 1488	LCU 1535	LCU 1548
	LCU 1484	LCU 1489	LCU 1536	LCU 1559

Displacement, tons: 180 light; 360 full load
Dimensions, feet (metres): 115 wl; 119 oa × 34 × 6 *(37·7; 39 × 11·1 × 1·9)*
Guns: 2—20 mm
Main engines: 3 diesels (Gray Marine); 675 bhp; 3 shafts = 18 knots
Complement: 14

These are enlarged versions of the World War II-built LCTs; constructed during the early 1950s. LCU 1608 and 1609 have modified propulsion systems; LCU 1582 and later craft have Kort nozzle propellers. LCU 1496 reclassified as YFU 70 on 1 Mar 1966; LCU 1471 to YFU 88 in May 1968; LCU 1576, 1582 and 1608 to YFU 89-91, respectively, in June 1970; LCU 1488, 1491, and 1609 to YFU 94-96 on 1 June 1971; YFU 94 reverted to LCU 1488 on 1 Feb 1972.

Classification: The earlier craft of this series were initially designated as Utility Landing Ships (LSU); redesignated Utility Landing Craft (LCU) on 15 April 1952 and classified as service craft.

LCU 1488   *1965, USN*

21 UTILITY LANDING CRAFT: LCU 501 SERIES

LCU 539	LCU 660	LCU 768	LCU 1124	LCU 1430
LCU 588	LCU 666	LCU 803	LCU 1241	LCU 1451
LCU 599	LCU 667	LCU 871	LCU 1348	LCU 1462
LCU 608	LCU 674	LCU 893	LCU 1348	
LCU 654	LCU 742	LCU 1045	LCU 1387	

Displacement, tons: 143-160 light; 309 to 320 full load
Dimensions, feet (metres): 105 wl × 119 oa × 32·7 × 5 *(34·6; 39 × 10·7 × 1·6)*
Guns: 2—20 mm
Main engines: Diesels (Gray Marine); 675 bhp; 3 shafts = 10 knots
Complement: 13 (enlisted men)

Formerly LCT(6) 501-1465 series; built in 1943-1944. Can carry four tanks or 200 tons of cargo.

LCU 524, 529, 550, 562, 592, 600, 629, 664, 666, 668, 677, 686, 742, 764, 776, 788, 840, 869, 877, 960, 973, 974, 979, 980, 1056, 1082, 1086, 1124, 1136, 1156, 1159, 1162, 1195, 1224, 1236, 1250, 1283, 1286, 1363, 1376, 1378, 1384, 1386, 1398, 1411, and 1430 reclassified as YFU 1 through 46, respectively, on 18 May 1958; LCU 1040 reclassified YFB 82 on 18 May 1958; LCU 1446 reclassified YFU 53 in 1964; LCU 509, 637, 646, 709, 716, 776, 851, 916, 973, 989, 1126, 1165, 1203, 1232, 1385, and 1388 reclassified as YFU 54 through 69, respectively, on 1 Mar 1966; LCU 780 reclassified as YFU 87. YFU 9 reverted to LCU 666 on 1 Jan 1962; LCU 1459 converted to YLLC 4; LCU 1462 to YFU 102 on 1 Aug 1973. Changes reflect employment as general cargo craft assigned to shore commands (see section on Service Craft).

Classification: Originally rated as Landing Craft, Tank (LCT(6)); redesignated Utility Landing Ships (LSU) in 1949 to reflect varied employment; designation changed to Utility Landing Craft (LCU) on 15 Apr 1952 and classified as service craft.

MECHANISED LANDING CRAFT: LCM 8 TYPE

Displacement, tons: 115 full load (steel) or 105 full load (aluminium)
Dimensions, feet (metres): 75·6 × 73·7 oa or 21 × 5·2 *(24·8 × 24·2 or 6·9 × 1·7)*
Main engines: 2 diesels (Detroit or General Motors); 650 bhp; 2 shafts = 9 knots
Complement: 5 (enlisted men)

Constructed of welded-steel or (later units) aluminium. Can carry one M-48 or M-60 tank (both approx 48 tons) or 60 tons cargo; range is 150 nautical miles at full load. Also operated in large numbers by the US Army.

LCM 8   *1976, Dr. Giorgio Arra*

MECHANISED LANDING CRAFT: LCM 6 TYPE

Displacement, tons: 60 to 62 full load
Dimensions, feet (metres): 56·2 oa × 14 × 3·9 *(18·4 × 4·6 × 1·3)*
Main engines: Diesels; 2 shafts; 450 bhp = 9 knots

Welded-steel construction. Cargo capacity is 34 tons or 80 trops.

LCM 6   *9/1976, Dr. Giorgio Arra*

LANDING CRAFT VEHICLE AND PERSONNEL (LCVP)

Displacement, tons: 13·5 full load
Dimensions, feet (metres): 35·8 oa × 10·5 × 3·5 *(11·7 × 3·4 × 1·1)*
Main engines: Diesel; 325 bhp; 1 shaft = 9 knots

Constructed of wood or fibreglass-reinforced plastic. Fitted with 30-calibre machine guns when in combat areas. Cargo capacity, 8 000 lbs; range, 110 nautical miles at full load.

2 WARPING TUGS (LWT)

LWT 1	LWT 2

Displacement, tons: 61 (hoisting weight)
Dimensions, feet (metres): 85 oa × 22 × 6·75 *(27·9 × 7·2 × 2·2)*
Main engines: 2 diesels (Harbormaster); 420 bhp; 2 steerable shafts = 9 knots
Complement: 6 (enlisted men)

These craft are employed in amphibious landings to handle pontoon causeways. The LWT 1 and 2 are prototypes of an all-aluminium design completed in 1970. A collapsible A-frame is fitted forward to facilitate handling causeway anchors and ship-to-shore fuel lines. They can be "side loaded" on the main deck of an LST 1179 class ship or carried in an LPD/LSD type ship. The propulsion motors are similar to outboard motors, providing both steering and thrust, alleviating the need for rudders.
Built by Campbell Machine, San Diego, California.

LWT 2   *USN*

WARPING TUGS (LWT)

Displacement, tons: approx 120
Dimensions, feet (metres): 92·9 oa × 23 × 6·5 *(30·4 × 7·5 × 2·1)*
Main engines: 2 outboard propulsion units = 6·5 knots

These craft are fabricated from pontoon sections and are assembled by the major amphibious commands as required.

LWT 85   *USN*

COMMAND SHIPS

This section describes the three US command ships configured to support national and regional command requirements. These have different functions from the amphibious command ships, which support Navy or Navy-Marine Corps operations. In reserve are two larger ships configured to serve as National Emergency Command Posts Afloat (NECPA) for the President or other national command authorities. These ships, the converted cruiser *Northampton* and the converted aircraft carrier *Wright*, when operational, steamed off the Atlantic coast of the United States, prepared to receive the President in the event of crisis or nuclear war. In the NECPA configuration the ships were not available for naval command use.

The NECPA programme was phased out in favour of employing underground command centres near Washington, DC, and airborne command posts.

1 CONVERTED "RALEIGH" CLASS (COMMAND SHIP (AGF))

Name	No.	Builders	Laid down	Launched	Commissioned
*LA SALLE	AGF 3 (ex-LPD 3)	New York Naval Shipyards	2 April 1962	3 Aug 1963	22 Feb 1964

Displacement, tons: 8 040 light; 13 900 full load
Length, feet (metres): 500 *(152·0)* wl; 521·8 *(158·4)* oa
Beam, feet (metres): 84 *(25·6)*
Draught, feet (metres): 21 *(6·4)*
Guns: 8—3 inch *(76 mm)* 50 cal (Mk 33) *(twin)*
Main engines: Steam turbines (De Laval); 24 000 shp; 2 shafts
Boilers: 2 (Foster Wheeler)
Speed, knots: 20 sustained; 23 maximum
Complement: 387 (18 officers, 369 enlisted men)
Flag accommodations: 59 (12 officers, 47 enlisted men)

The *La Salle* is a former amphibious transport dock (LPD) of the "Raleigh" class. Authorised in Fiscal Year 1961 new construction programme. The *La Salle* served as an amphibious ship from completion until 1972; the ship retains an amphibious assault capability.

The *La Salle* serves as flagship for the US commander Middle East Force, operating in the Persian Gulf, Arabian Sea, and Indian Ocean; the ship is based at Bahrain. She replaced the *Valcour* (AGF 1) in 1972.

Conversion: Converted in 1972 at Philadelphia Navy Yard. Elaborate command and communications facilities installed; accommodations provided for admiral and staff; additional air-conditioning fitted; painted white to help retard heat of Persian Gulf area. Reclassified as a flagship and designated AGF 3 on 1 July 1972 (the designation AGF 2 not used because of ship's previous "3" hull number).

Fire Control: One Mk 56 and one Mk 70 gunfire control system.

Gunnery: To be fitted with Phalanx 20 mm CIWS.

Radar: Search; SPS 10 and 40.

LA SALLE
8/1975, USN

1 CONVERTED HEAVY CRUISER (COMMAND SHIP (CC))

Name	No.	Builders	Laid down	Launched	Commissioned
NORTHAMPTON	CC 1 (ex-CLC 1, ex-CA 125)	Bethlehem Steel Co Quincy, Mass	31 Aug 1944	27 Jan 1951	7 Mar 1953

Displacement, tons: 14 700 standard; 17 700 full load
Length, feet (metres): 664 *(202·4)* wl; 676 *(206·0)* oa
Beam, feet (metres): 71 *(21·6)*
Draught, feet (metres): 29 *(8·8)*
Gun: 1—5 inch *(127 mm)* 54 cal (Mk 42) (see *Gunnery* notes)
Helicopters: 3 UH/34
Main engines: 4 geared turbines (General Electric); 120 000 shp; 4 shafts
Boilers: 4 (Babcock & Wilcox)
Speed, knots: 33
Complement: 1 191 (68 officers, 1 123 enlisted men)
Flag accommodations: 328 (191 officers, 137 enlisted men)

The *Northampton* was begun as a heavy cruiser of the "Oregon City" class, numbered CA 125. She was cancelled on 11 Aug 1945 when 56·2 per cent complete. She was re-ordered as a command ship on 1 July 1948 and designated CLC 1 (Task Force Command Ship and later Tactical Command Ship). As CLC 1 she was configured for use primarily by fast carrier force commanders and fitted with an elaborate combat information centre (CIC), electronic equipment, and flag accommodations. She was employed as flagship for Commander Sixth Fleet 1954-55 and Commander Second Fleet 1955-61. Her designation was changed to CC (Command Ship) on 15 April 1961 and she was relieved as Second Fleet flagship in October 1961. Decommissioned on 8 April 1970 and placed in reserve.

Design. The *Northampton* is one deck higher than other US heavy cruisers to provide additional office and equipment space. Her foremast is the tallest unsupported mast afloat (125 feet). All living and working spaces are air-conditioned. Helicopter landing area aft with hangar for three UH/34 type.

Electronics: Advanced communications, electronic data processing equipment, and data displays are installed; tropospheric scatter and satellite relay communications facilities.

Gunnery: As built, the *Northampton* mounted 4—5 inch Mark 42 54 calibre and 8—3 inch weapons. When decommissioned, she was armed with only one 5 inch gun aft.

Radar: Search; SPS-8A and 37.

NORTHAMPTON
USN

1 CONVERTED AIRCRAFT CARRIER (COMMAND SHIP (CC))

Name	No.	Builders	Laid down	Launched	CVL Comm	CC Comm
WRIGHT	CC 2 (ex-AVT 7, ex-CVL 49)	New York SB Corp, Camden, NJ	21 Aug 1944	1 Sep 1945	9 Feb 1947	11 May 1963

Displacement, tons: 14 500 standard; 19 750 full load
Length, feet (metres): 664 *(202·4)* wl; 683·6 *(208·4)* oa
Beam, feet (metres): 76·8 *(23·4)*
Draught, feet (metres): 28 *(8·5)*
Flight deck width, feet (metres): 109 *(33·2)*
Helicopters: 3 CH-46, 2 HH-43
Guns: 8—40 mm (twin)
Main engines: 4 geared turbines (General Electric); 120 000 shp; 4 shafts
Boilers: 4 (Babcock & Wilcox)
Speed, knots: 33
Complement: 746
Flag accommodations: 522 (168 officers, 354 enlisted men)

The *Wright* was originally completed as a light aircraft carrier (CVL 49). Although her hull design is that of the "Baltimore" class heavy cruisers, she was ordered as a carrier and not changed during construction as with previous US Light Carriers. She served for a decade as an experimental and training carrier before being decommissioned on 15 Mar 1956. She was converted to a national emergency command ship at the Puget Sound Naval Shipyard, 1962-1963.
She was decommissioned on 27 May 1970 and placed in reserve.

Classification: While in reserve, as a carrier, she was reclassified on 15 May 1959 as an auxiliary aircraft transport (AVT 7). She was reclassified as CC 2 on 1 Sep 1962.

Conversion: She was converted to a command ship under the Fiscal Year 1962 authorisation at a cost of $25 000 000. She is fitted with elaborate communications, data processing, and display facilities for use by national authorities. The command spaces include presentation theatres similar to those at command posts ashore. The *Wright* has the most powerful transmitting antennae ever installed in a ship. They are mounted on plastic-glass masts to reduce interference with electronic transmissions. The tallest mast is 83 feet high and is designed to withstand 100-mph winds.

WRIGHT *1968, USN*

PATROL SHIPS AND CRAFT

The US Navy's programme to construct a series of 30 hydrofoil missile ships has been sharply curtailed, with only six units now planned probably as a result of a 130 per cent increase in estimated unit costs. Designated "patrol combatant missile (hydrofoil)".
Initial problems in the pump, gearbox, and electrical system of the prototype PHM have been overcome.
The six PHMs will be operated as a tactical squadron to develop tactics and gain technical experience with this type of craft. Meanwhile, the Navy has shifted additional units of the conventional-hull "Asheville" class gunboats to the Naval Reserve Force (NRF) and has relegated one of the units to an unarmed research role. Only four of the original 17 "Asheville" class ships remain in first-line Navy although the class has had less than a decade of service.
An earlier hydrofoil craft, the *High Point* (PCH 1) is operated in a test and evaluation status. During 1974-1975 *High Point* was evaluated by the US Coast Guard (subsequently returned to Navy control). Finally, several patrol and riverine warfare craft are operated by the Naval Reserve Force, and two new designs (CPIC and PB) are being developed for US and foreign use. US use of these craft will be minimal; rather they are intended to compete with contemporary small craft built overseas in the foreign sales market.

1 + 5 PATROL COMBATANTS MISSILE (HYDROFOILS)
(see addenda)

Name	No.	Builders	Commissioned
*PEGASUS	PHM 1	Boeing Co, Seattle, Wash	1 July 1976
HERCULES	PHM 2	Boeing Co, Seattle, Wash	—
	PHM 3		1979
	PHM 4		1979
	PHM 5		1979
	PHM 6		1979

Displacement, tons: 239 full load
Dimensions, feet (metres):
foils extended: 131·2 *(40·0)* oa × 28·2 *(8·6)* hull × 23·2 *(7·1)*
foils retracted: 147·5 *(45·0)* oa × 28·2 *(8·6)* hull × 6·2 *(1·9)*
Missile launchers: 8 canisters (quad) for Harpoon surface-to-surface missile
Gun: 1—76 mm 62 calibre (Mk 75) OTO Melara
Main engines: foil borne; 1 gas turbine (General Electric LM 2500); 18 000 shp; waterjet propulsion units = 48 knots
hull borne; 2 diesels (Mercedes-Benz); 1 600 bhp; 2 waterjet propulsion = 12 knots
Complement: 21 (4 officers, 17 enlisted men)

The US Navy plans to construct six ships of this class. The *Pegasus* and *Hercules* were authorised in the Fiscal Year 1973 R and D programme, and four additional ships in the FY 1975 shipbuilding programme. Planning for 24 additional units was halted in 1975. The *Pegasus* was laid down on 10 May 1973 and launched on 9 Nov 1974 and made her first foil-borne trip on 25 Feb 1975. The *Hercules* was laid down on 30 May 1974. *Pegasus* was delayed because of cost escalation while incorrect cost estimates caused a suspension of construction of *Hercules* in August 1975. She will now be completed.
The PHM design was developed in conjunction with the Italian and West German navies in an effort to produce a small combatant that would be universally acceptable to NATO navies with minor modifications. The West German Navy has advised the US government of plans to build up to 12 ships of this design.

Classification: The designation PHM originally was for Patrol Hydrofoil-Missile; reclassified Patrol Combatant Missile (Hydrofoil) on 30 June 1975.

Fire Control: Fitted with the Mk 92 Mod 1 fire control system (Americanised version of the WM-28 radar and weapons control system developed by N. V. Hollandse Signaalapparaten).

Missiles: Each PHM will have two lightweight four-tube cannister launchers. This is double the Harpoon armament originally planned.

Rockets: Mk 36 Chaffroc being fitted.

PEGASUS *10/1975, USN*

6 "ASHEVILLE" CLASS (PATROL COMBATANTS (PG))

Name	No.	Builders	Commissioned
*ANTELOPE	PG 86	Tacoma Boatbuilding	4 Nov 1967
*READY	PG 87	Tacoma Boatbuilding	6 Jan 1968
*TACOMA	PG 92	Tacoma Boatbuilding	14 July 1969
*WELCH	PG 93	Peterson Builders	8 Sep 1969
*GRAND RAPIDS	PG 98	Tacoma Boatbuilding	5 Sep 1970
*DOUGLAS	PG 100	Tacoma Boatbuilding	6 Feb 1971

Displacement, tons: 225 standard; 235 full load
Dimensions, feet (metres): 164·5 oa × 23·8 × 9·5 *(50·1 × 7·3 × 2·9)*
Missile launchers: 2 launchers for Standard Mk 32 surface-to-surface missiles in *Antelope, Ready, Grand Rapids, Douglas*
Guns: 1—3 in *(76 mm)* 50 cal (forward); 1—40 mm (aft); 4—·50 cal MG (twin) except 40 mm gun removed from ships with Standard missile
Main engines: CODAG: 2 diesels (Cummins); 1 450 shp; 2 shafts = 16 knots
1 gas turbine (General Electric LM 2500); 13 300 shp; 2 shafts = 40+ knots
Range, miles: 1 700 at 16 knots; 325 at 37 knots
Complement: 24 (3 officers, 21 enlisted men)

DOUGLAS   7/1976, Dr. Giorgio Arra

Originally a class of 17 patrol gunboats (PG ex-PGM) designed to perform patrol, blockade, surveillance, and support missions. No anti-submarine capability. Requirement for these craft was based on the volatile Cuban situation in the early 1960s.
PG 86 and PG 87 authorised in FY 1964; PG 92, 93, 98 and 100 in FY 1966. *Asheville* was laid down on 15 April 1964 and launched on 1 May 1965; later ships approximately 18 months from keel laying to completion. Cost per ship approximately $5 000 000.
Only the four missile-armed units remain in active US Navy service. The *Tacoma* and *Welch* are at Little Creek, Virginia, involved in training Saudi Arabian naval personnel.
The *Chehalis* (PG 94) was stripped of armament and assigned as a research craft to the Naval Ship Research & Development Center in Annapolis, Maryland, on 21 Aug 1975; renamed *Athena* (no hull number assigned) and civilian manned.

ANTELOPE   6/1973, USN

Classification: These ships were originally classified as motor gunboats (PGM); reclassified as patrol boats (PG) with same hull numbers on 1 April 1967.

Design: All-aluminium hull and aluminium-fibreglass superstructure. Because of the heat-transmitting qualities of the aluminium hull and the amount of waste heat produced by a gas turbine engine the ships are completely air conditioned.

Engineering: The transfer from diesel to gas turbine propulsion (or vice versa) can be accomplished while under way with no loss of speed. From full stop these ships can attain 40 knots in one minute; manoeuvrability is excellent due in part to controllable pitch-propellers.

Fire Control: The *Antelope* and *Ready* have the Mk 87 weapons control system (optical or radar). Other ships have Mk 63 Mod 29 Gunfire Control System with SPG-50 fire control radar.

Gunnery: Mk 34 3 inch gun forward in closed mount with Mk 3 40 mm gun in open mount aft.

Missiles: The *Benicia* (PG 96) was experimentally fitted with a single launcher aft for the Standard interim anti-ship missile in 1971; removed prior to transfer to South Korea later that year.

During the latter part of 1971 the *Antelope* and *Ready* were provided with two Standard missile launchers aft in place of 40 mm gun. A reload is provided in an adjacent magazine for each launcher; subsequently *Grand Rapids* and *Douglas* fitted with missiles.

Transfers: *Benicia* (PG 96) transferred to South Korea on 2 Oct 1971; *Surprise* (PG 97) transferred to Turkey on 28 Feb 1973. *Defiance* (PG 95) transferred to Turkey on 11 June 1973; *Beacon* (PG 99) and *Green Bay* (PG 101) transferred to Greece on 1 April 1977.

1 "HIGH POINT" CLASS (PATROL CRAFT—HYDROFOIL (PCH))

Name	No.	Builders	Commissioned
*HIGH POINT	PCH 1	Boeing, Seattle	3 Sep 1963

Displacement, tons: 110 full load
Dimensions, feet (metres): 115 *(35)* oa × 31 *(9·4)* × 6 *(1·8)* (foils retracted) or 17 *(5·2)* (foils extended)
Guns: removed
A/S weapons: removed
Main engines: foil borne; 2 gas turbines (Bristol Siddeley Marine Proteus); 6 200 shp; 2 paired counter-rotating propellers = 48 knots
hull borne; diesel (Packard); 600 bhp; retractable outdrive with 1 propeller = 12 knots
Complement: 13 (1 officer, 12 enlisted men)

Experimental craft authorised under Fiscal Year 1960 programme. Built at Martinac Boatyard, Tacoma. Laid down 27 Feb 1961, launched 17 Aug 1962. In service 15 Aug 1963. During Mar 1975 the *High Point* was evaluated by the Coast Guard.

Design: The *High Point's* forward foil is supported by a single strut and the after foil by twin struts. Twin underwater nacelles at the junction of the vertical struts and main foil housed contra-rotating, super-cavitating propellers for foil-borne propulsion. After foils modified in 1973 and nacelles repositioned to improve performance in heavy sea states. Also, forward foil strut made steerable to improve manoeuvrability

HIGH POINT   1975, US Coast Guard

Gunnery: A single 40 mm gun was mounted forward in 1968; subsequently removed.

Missiles: During 1973-1974 the *High Point* was employed as a test ship for the lightweight cannister launchers for the Harpoon surface-to-surface missile intended for the PHM.

4 "PTF 23" CLASS (FAST PATROL BOATS (PTF))

*PTF 23   ***PTF 24**   ***PTF 25**   ***PTF 26**

Displacement, tons: 105 full load
Dimensions, feet (metres): 94·7 oa × 23·2 × 7 *(28·8 × 7·1 × 2·1)*
Guns: 1—81 mm mortar; 1—·50 cal MG (mounted over mortar);
1—40 mm (aft); 2—20 mm (single)
Main engines: 2 diesels (Napier-Deltic); 6 200 bhp; 2 shafts = approx 40 knots
Complement: approx 20

PTF 23-26 built by Sewart Seacraft Division of Teledyne Inc of Berwick, Louisiana. First unit completed in 1967, others in 1968. Aluminium hulls. Commercial name is "Osprey".
Two units based at Little Creek (Va) and two at Coronado Amphibious base. One craft fitted with gas turbine for experiments until 1980.

PTF 23   1976, Dr. Giorgio Arra

COASTAL PATROL AND INTERDICTION CRAFT (CPIC)

The US Navy's prototype CPIC was transferred to South Korea on 1 Aug 1975. No additional craft of this type are planned for the US Navy.

5 PATROL BOATS (PB): NEW DESIGN

2 **PB** Mark I series
3 **PB** Mark III series

Displacement, tons:
  Mk I: 26·9 light; 36·3 full load
  Mk III: 31·5 light; 41·25 full load
Dimensions, feet (metres):
  Mk I: 65 oa × 16 × 4·9 *(19·8 × 4·9 × 1·5)*
  Mk III: 65 oa × 18 × 5·9 *(19·8 × 5·5 × 1·8)*
Guns: 6—20 mm or ·50 cal MG (1 twin, 4 single)
Main engines: Diesel (Detroit); 1 635 bhp; 3 shafts = 26 knots

The PB series is being developed as replacements for the "Swift" type inshore patrol craft (PCF). Mk I built by Sewart Seacraft, Berwick, Louisiana; Mk III by Peterson Builders Sturgeon Bay, Wisconsin. Two Mark I prototypes completed in 1972 and delivered to the Navy in 1973 for evaluation; assigned to Naval Reserve Force. Procurement of the PB Mk III for the US Navy is under consideration. (The PB Mark II design was not built.)
The Mk III design has the pilot house offset to starboard to provide space on port side for installation of additional weapons.

PB Mk III   9/1976, Dr. Giorgio Arra

5 "SWIFT" CLASS (PATROL CRAFT (PCF))

5 **PCF** Mark I series

Displacement, tons: 22·5 full load
Dimensions, feet (metres): 50·1 oa × 13 × 3·5 *(15·3 × 4·0 × 1·1)*
Guns: 1—81 mm mortar, 3—·50 cal MG (twin MG mount atop pilot house and single MG mounted over mortar)
Main engines: 2 geared diesels (General Motors); 960 shp; 2 shafts = 28 knots
Complement: 6 (1 officer, 5 enlisted men)

The "Swift" design is adapted from the all-metal crew boat which is used to support off-shore drilling rigs in the Gulf of Mexico. Approximately 125 built since 1965.
Designation changed from Fast Patrol Craft (PCF) to Inshore Patrol Craft (PCF) on 14 Aug 1968.

Transfers: PCF 33, 34, and 83-86 transferred to the Philippines in 1966. Additional PCFs of this type constructed specifically for transfer to Thailand, the Philippines, and South Korea; not assigned US hull numbers in the PCF series; 104 PCFs formerly manned by US Navy personnel transferred to South Vietnam in 1968-1970.

PCF Mk I Type   1969, USN

29 RIVER PATROL BOATS (PBR)

29 **PBR** Mk II series

Displacement, tons: 8
Dimensions, feet (metres): 32 oa × 11 × 2·6 *(9·8 × 3·4 × 0·8)*
Guns: 3—·50 cal MG (twin mount forward; single aft); 1—40 mm grenade launcher; 1—60 mm mortar in some boats
Main engines: 2 geared diesels (General Motors); water jets = 25+ knots
Complement: 4 or 5 (enlisted men)

Fibreglass hull river patrol boats. Approximately 500 built 1967-1973; most transferred to South Vietnam.

PBR Mk II Type   USN

2 ASSAULT SUPPORT PATROL BOATS (ASPB)

Displacement, tons: 36·25 full load
Dimensions, feet (metres): 50 oa × 15·6 × 3·8 *(15·2 × 4·8 × 1·1)*
Guns (varies): 1 or 2—20 mm (with 2—·50 cal MG in boats with one 20 mm); 2—·30 cal MG; 2—40 mm high-velocity grenade launchers
Main engines: 2 diesels (General Motors); 2 shafts = 14 knots sustained
Complement: 6 (enlisted)

The ASPB was designed specifically for riverine operations to escort other river craft, provide mine countermeasures during river operations, and interrupt enemy river traffic. Welded-steel hulls. Armament changed to above configuration in 1968; some boats have twin—·50 cal MG "turret" forward in place of single 20 mm gun.

ASSAULT SUPPORT PATROL BOAT (ASPB)   1968, USN

14 "MINI" ARMOURED TROOP CARRIERS (ATC)

Dimensions, feet (metres): 36 oa × 12·7 × 3·5 *(11·0 × 3·9 × 1·1)*
Main engines: 2 diesels (General Motors); water-jet propulsion = 28 knots except one unit with
gas turbines
Complement: 2
Troops: 15 to 20

A small troop carrier for riverine and swimmer delivery operations; aluminium hull; ceramic
armour. Draft is one foot when underway at high speed.

"MINI" ATC   *1974, USN*

1 COMMAND AND CONTROL BOAT (CCB)

Displacement, tons: 80 full load
Dimensions, feet (metres): 61 oa × 17·5 × 3·4 *(18·6 × 5·3 × 1·0)*
Guns: 3—20 mm; 2—·30 cal MG; 2—40 mm high velocity-grenade launchers
Main engines: 2 diesels (Detroit); 2 shafts = 8·5 knots max (6 knots sustained)
Complement: 11

This craft serves as afloat command post providing command and communications facilities for
ground force and boat group commanders. Heavily armoured. Armament changed to above
configuration in 1968. Converted from LCM-6 landing craft.

COMMAND AND CONTROL BOAT   *USN*

SWIMMER SUPPORT CRAFT

The US Navy operates several specialised craft in support of "frogmen" (combat swimmers)
assigned to SEAL (Sea-Air-Land) teams, Underwater Demolition Teams (UDT), and Explosive
Ordnance Disposal (EOD) teams. Most of the craft listed in previous editions have been discarded and the primary craft in service today is the 36-foot Medium SEAL Support Craft (MSSC).
Several SEAL support craft are operated by the Naval Reserve Force. A new craft for this role will
probably be developed in the near future.

MEDIUM SEAL SUPPORT CRAFT (MSSC)   *USN*

MINEWARFARE FORCES

The US Navy has initiated a programme to construct nineteen
ocean minesweepers especially for deep water operations.
Currently the Navy operates three active and 22 Naval Reserve
Force (NRF) minesweepers. The active ships provide support
to mine research and development activities at the Naval
Coastal Systems Laboratory in Panama City, Florida; the NRF
ships are manned by composite active-reserve crews. In addition, the Navy flies 21 specially equipped RH-53D Sea Stallion
helicopters. These helicopters, which tow mine countermeasure devices, are readily deployable to aircraft carriers or
amphibious ships in overseas areas. They can counter mines
laid in shallow waters but have no capability against deep-
water mines.

The US Navy maintains no surface ships with a minelaying
capability. Rather, the Navy can plant mines by carrier-based
aircraft, land-based maritime patrol aircraft, and attack submarines. The large B-52 Stratofortress bombers of the
Strategic Air Command can also plant sea mines.

(19) MINE COUNTERMEASURE SHIPS (MCM)

One ship	**MCM**	Planned Fiscal Year 1979 programme
Six ships	**MCM**	Planned Fiscal Year 1980 programme
Six ships	**MCM**	Planned Fiscal Year 1981 programme
Six ships	**MCM**	Planned Fiscal Year 1982 programme

Specific characteristics have not yet been developed. Cost approx $61 000 000 per ship.

2 "ACME" CLASS (OCEAN MINESWEEPERS (MSO))

Name	No.	Launched	Commissioned
*ADROIT (NRF)	MSO 509	20 Aug 1955	4 Mar 1957
*AFFRAY (NRF)	MSO 511	18 Dec 1956	8 Dec 1958

Displacement, tons: 720 light; 750 full load
Dimensions, feet (metres): 173 oa × 35 × 14 *(52·7 × 10·7 × 4·3)*
Guns: 1—20 mm or 1—40 mm; 2—·50 cal MG
Main engines: 2 diesels (Packard), 2 280 bhp; 2 shafts (controllable pitch propellers) = 15 knots
Complement: 86 (3 officers, 36 enlisted active duty; 3 officers, 44 enlisted reserve)

This class is different from the "Agile" class but has similar basic particulars. Built by Frank L.
Sample, Jnr, Inc, Boothbay Harbor, Maine. Plans to modernise these ships were cancelled (see
notes under "Agile" class).
Adroit and *Affray* are assigned to Naval Reserve training, manned partially by active and
partially by reserve personnel (see notes under "Agile" class).

AFFRAY   *1969, USN*

31 "AGILE", "AGGRESSIVE" and "DASH" CLASSES
(OCEAN MINESWEEPERS (MSO))

Name	No.	Launched		Commissioned	
AGILE	MSO 421	19 Nov	1955	21 June	1956
*CONSTANT (NRF)	MSO 427	14 Feb	1952	8 Sep	1954
*DASH (NRF)	MSO 428	20 Sep	1952	14 Aug	1953
*DETECTOR (NRF)	MSO 429	5 Dec	1952	26 Jan	1954
*DIRECT (NRF)	MSO 430	27 May	1953	9 July	1954
*DOMINANT (NRF)	MSO 431	5 Nov	1953	8 Nov	1954
*ENGAGE (NRF)	MSO 433	18 June	1953	29 June	1954
*ENHANCE (NRF)	MSO 437	11 Oct	1952	16 Apr	1955
*ESTEEM (NRF)	MSO 438	20 Dec	1952	10 Sep	1955
*EXCEL (NRF)	MSO 439	25 Sep	1953	24 Feb	1955
*EXPLOIT (NRF)	MSO 440	10 Apr	1953	31 Mar	1954
*EXULTANT (NRF)	MSO 441	6 June	1953	22 June	1954
*FEARLESS (NRF)	MSO 442	17 July	1953	22 Sep	1954
*FIDELITY	MSO 443	21 Aug	1953	19 Jan	1955
*FORTIFY (NRF)	MSO 446	14 Feb	1953	16 July	1954
*ILLUSIVE	MSO 448	12 July	1952	14 Nov	1953
*IMPERVIOUS (NRF)	MSO 449	29 Aug	1952	15 July	1954
*IMPLICIT (NRF)	MSO 455	1 Aug	1953	10 Mar	1954
*INFLICT (NRF)	MSO 456	6 Oct	1953	11 May	1954
OBSERVER	MSO 461	19 Oct	1954	31 Aug	1955
PINNACLE	MSO 462	3 Jan	1955	21 Oct	1955
*PLUCK (NRF)	MSO 464	6 Feb	1954	11 Aug	1954
SKILL	MSO 471	23 Apr	1955	7 Nov	1955
VITAL	MSO 474	12 Aug	1953	9 June	1955
*CONQUEST (NRF)	MSO 488	20 May	1954	20 July	1955
*GALLANT (NRF)	MSO 489	4 June	1954	14 Sep	1955
*LEADER	MSO 490	15 Sep	1954	16 Nov	1955
*PLEDGE (NRF)	MSO 492	20 July	1955	20 Apr	1956
STURDY	MSO 494	28 Jan	1956	23 Oct	1957
SWERVE	MSO 495	1 Nov	1955	27 July	1957
VENTURE	MSO 496	27 Nov	1956	3 Feb	1958

Displacement, tons: 665 light; 777 full load
Dimensions, feet (metres): 165 wl; 172 oa × 36 × 13·6 *(52·4 × 11·0 × 4·2)*
Guns: 1—40 mm (MSO 421, 462, 471, 494, 495); 1—20 mm Mk 68 (single) (remainder) some modernised ships are unarmed)
Main engines: 4 diesels (Packard); 2 280 bhp 2 shafts; controllable pitch propellers = 14 knots; *Dash, Detector, Direct* and *Dominant,* have 2 diesels (General Motors); 1 520 bhp (see Modernisation notes)
Range, miles: 2 400 at 10 knots
Complement: 78 (8 officers, 70 enlisted men); 86 in NRF ships (3 officers, 36 enlisted active duty; 3 officers, 44 enlisted reserve) (see Modernisation note)

These ships were built on the basis of mine warfare experience in the Korean War (1950-1953); 58 built for US service and 35 transferred upon completion to NATO navies.(One ship cancelled, MSO 497). They have wooden hulls and non-magnetic engines and other equipment. All surviving ships were built in private shipyards.
Initially designated as minesweepers (AM); reclassified as ocean minesweepers (MSO) in Feb 1955. Originally fitted with UQS-1 mine detecting sonar.
8 ships are laid up in reserve.

Engineering: Diesel engines are fabricated of non-magnetic stainless steel alloy.

Modernisation: The 62 ocean minesweepers in commission during the mid-1960s were all to have been modernised; estimated cost and schedule per ship were $5 000 000 and ten months in shipyard. However, some of the early modernisations took as long as 26 months which, coupled with changes in mine countermeasures techniques, led to cancellation of programme after 13 ships were modernised: MSO 433, 437, 438, 441-443, 445, 446, 448, 449, 456, 488, and 490.
The modernisation provided improvements in mine detection, engines, communications, and habitability: four Waukesha Motor Co diesel engines installed (plus two or three diesel generators for sweep gear), SQQ-14 sonar with mine classification as well as detection capability provided, twin 20 mm in some ships (replacing single 40 mm because of space requirements for sonar hoist mechanism), habitability improved, and advanced communications equipment fitted; bridge structure in modernised ships extended around mast and aft to funnel. Complement in active modernised ships is 6 officers and 70 enlisted men.
Some MSOs have received SQQ-14 sonar but not full modernisation.

Transfers: Ships of this class serve in the navies of Belgium, France, Italy, Netherlands, Norway, Peru, Portugal, Spain, Taiwan, Thailand and Uruguay.

DOMINANT   11/1975, USN

DIRECT   9/1976, Dr. Giorgio Arra

EXPLOIT   9/1976, Dr. Giorgio Arra

COASTAL MINESWEEPERS (MSC): NEW CONSTRUCTION

Four coastal minesweepers are under construction for transfer to Saudi Arabia; designated MSC 322-325 for accounting purposes. Contract awarded 30 Sep 1975 to Peterson Builders, Sturgeon Bay, Wisconsin; scheduled to complete June through October 1978. Hull numbers MSC 320 and MSC 321 assigned to units built in the United States for South Korea.

"ABILITY" CLASS (OCEAN MINESWEEPER (MSO))

The two surviving minesweepers of this class, the *Alacrity* (MSO 520) and *Assurance* (MSO 521), have been allocated to sonar test programmes and redesignated as auxiliary ships AG 520 and AG 521, respectively. See listing under Experimental, Research, and Surveying Ships.

8 MINESWEEPING BOATS (MSB)

*MSB 15	*MSB 25	*MSB 29	*MSB 51
*MSB 16	*MSB 28	*MSB 41	*MSB 52

Displacement, tons: 30 light; 39 full load except MSB 29, 80 full load
Dimensions, feet (metres): 57·2 × 15·5 × 4 except MSB 29, 82 × 19 × 5·5 *(17·4 × 4·7 × 1·2—25 × 5·8 × 1·7)*
Guns: several MG
Main engines: 2 geared diesels (Packard); 600 bhp; 2 shafts = 12 knots
Complement: 6 (enlisted)

Wooden-hull minesweepers intended to be carried to theatre of operations by large assault ships; however, they are too large to be easily handled by cranes and are assigned to sweeping harbours. From 1966 to 1970 they were used extensively in Vietnam for river minesweeping operations.
Of 49 minesweeping boats of this type built only eight remain in active service, all based at Charleston, South Carolina.
MSB 1-4 were ex-Army minesweepers built in 1946 (since discarded), MSB 5-54 (less MSB 24) were completed in 1952-1956. MSB 24 was not built. MSB 29 built to enlarged design by John Trumpy & Sons, Annapolis, Maryland, in an effort to improve seakeeping ability.
Normally commanded by chief petty officer or petty officer first class.

Gunnery: MSBs serving in South Vietnam were fitted with several machineguns and removable fibreglass armour. Note machineguns in tub amidships and on bow of MSB 17, shown here sweeping on the Long Tao river in South Vietnam.

2 "COVE" CLASS (INSHORE MINESWEEPERS (MSI))

The inshore minesweepers *Cove* (MSI 1) and *Cape* (MSI 2) are employed in research activities; see listing under Experimental, Research and Surveying Ships in this edition.

SERVICE FORCES
UNDERWAY REPLENISHMENT SHIPS

Most US Navy replenishment ships are fitted with helicopter platforms to permit helicopters to transfer supplies by vertical replenishment (VERTREP). Helicopters are carried specifically for this purpose by the newer ammunition ships (AE), the combat store ships (AFS), the fast combat support ships (AOE), and some replenishment oilers (AOR). Carrier-based helicopters are sometimes employed in this role.

Planned UNREP ship force levels provide a wartime capability to support deployed carrier and amphibious task groups in up to four or five locations simultaneously. This plan is based on the availability of some storage depots on foreign territory, and the use of Military Sealift Ships to carry fuels, munitions, and the stores from the United States or overseas sources for transfer to UNREP ships in overseas areas.

During peacetime some 16 to 18 UNREP ships normally are forward deployed in the Mediterranean and western Pacific areas in support of the 6th and 7th Fleets, respectively.

The Navy's five-year plan for modernisation of the UNREP forces provides for fourteen fleet oilers (AO) and one fast combat support ship (AOE) in the Fiscal Years 1978-1982 new construction programmes.

Most UNREP ships are Navy manned and armed; however, beginning in 1972, an increasing number of these ships are being operated by the Military Sealift Command (MSC) with civilian crews. The latter ships are not armed and have T-designations.

FLEET SUPPORT SHIPS

Fleet support ships provide primarily maintenance and related towing and salvage services at advanced bases and at ports in the United States. These ships normally do not provide fuel, munitions, or other supplies except when ships are alongside for maintenance.

Most fleet support ships operate from bases in the United States. The five Polaris/Poseidon submarine tenders (AS) are based at Holy Loch, Scotland; Rota, Spain; Charleston, South Carolina; and Apra harbour, Guam, with one ship generally in transit or overhaul. The Rota facility will be disestablished in the next few years. In addition, two support ships (AD/AR/AS type) generally are forward deployed in the Mediterranean and two in the western Pacific.

Fleet support ships are mainly Navy manned and armed; however, an increasing number are being operated by the Military Sealift Command (MSC) with civilian crews. The latter ships are not armed and have T- prefix before their designations.

2 + 5 "AD 41" and "SAMUEL GOMPERS" CLASSES
(DESTROYER TENDERS (AD))

Name	No.	Laid down	Launched	Commissioned
*SAMUEL GOMPERS	AD 37	9 July 1964	14 May 1966	1 July 1967
*PUGET SOUND	AD 38	15 Feb 1965	16 Sep 1966	27 April 1968
	AD 41	Mid 1977	—	Early 1980
	AD 42	Early 1978	—	Mid 1980
	AD 43	Approved FY 1977 programme		Late 1880
	AD 44	Proposed FY 1979 programme		1981
	AD 45	Proposed FY 1980 programme		1982

Displacement, tons: 20 500 full load
Dimensions, feet (metres): 643 oa × 85 × 22·5 *(196·0 × 25·9 × 6·9)*
Guns: 1—5 inch *(127 mm)* 38 cal (Mk 30); 4—20 mm Mk 67 *(Puget Sound* only)
Missile launchers: 1 NATO Sea Sparrow system planned for AD 41 and later ships
Main engines: Steam turbines (De Laval); 20 000 shp; 1 shaft = 20 knots
Boilers: 2 (Combustion Engineering)
Complement: 1 806 (135 officers, 1 671 enlisted men)

SAMUEL GOMPERS   *1/1977, Dr. Giorgio Arra*

These are the first US destroyer tenders of post-World War II design; capable of providing repair and supply services to new destroyer classes. The tenders also have facilities for servicing nuclear power plants. Services can be provided simultaneously to six guided-missile destroyers moored alongside. Basic hull design similar to "L. Y. Spear" and "Simon Lake" submarine tenders. Provided with helicopter platform and hangar; two 7 000-pound capacity cranes. One Mk 56 gunfire control system in *Puget Sound.*

Samuel Gompers authorised in Fiscal Year 1964 new construction programme and *Puget Sound* in FY 1965 programme. Both ships built by Puget Sound Naval Shipyard, Bremerton, Washington; AD 41 and AD 42 to be built by National Steel Shipbuilding Co, San Diego, Calif.

Two sisters of *Samuel Gompers* AD 39 of FY 1969 programme, cancelled—AD 39 on 11 Dec 1965 prior to start of construction to provide funds for overruns in other new ship programmes and AD 40, authorised in FY 1973 new construction programme in 1975. AD 41 in FY 1975 programme and AD 42 in FY 1976 programme with three additional ships planned (AD 41 and later ships of a slightly modified design.)

Estimated cost of AD 43 is $260 400 000 and estimated cost of AD 44 is $289 100 000.

Gunnery: proposed armament of AD 41 and 42 is 2—20 mm Phalanx CIWS, 2—40 mm Mk 64 (singles), 2—20 mm Mk 67 (singles).

Particulars: Apply only to "Samuel Gompers" class.

SAMUEL GOMPERS   *1/1977, Dr. Giorgio Arra*

3 "KLONDIKE" and "SHENANDOAH" CLASSES
(DESTROYER TENDERS (AD))

Name	No.	Launched	Commissioned
EVERGLADES	AD 24	28 Jan 1945	25 May 1951
*SHENANDOAH	AD 26	29 Mar 1945	13 Aug 1945
*BRYCE CANYON	AD 36	7 Mar 1946	15 Sep 1950

Displacement, tons: 8 165 standard; 14 700 full load
Dimensions, feet (metres): 465 wl; 492 oa × 69·5 × 27·2 *(150·0 × 21·2 × 8·3)*
Guns: 1—5 inch *(127 mm)* 38 cal Mk 37 (AD 36)
    2—3 inch *(76 mm)* 50 cal Mk 26 (AD 24)
    4—20 mm Mk 68 (AD 26)
Main engines: Steam turbines (Westinghouse); 8 500 shp 1 shaft = 18·4 knots
Boilers: 2 (Foster-Wheeler)
Complement: 778 to 918

These ships are of modified C-3 design completed as destroyer tenders. Originally class of four. *Shenandoah* built by Todd Shipyards, Los Angeles, Calif; *Bryce Canyon* by Charleston Navy Yard; *Everglades* by Los Angeles SB & DD Co;

Originally 13 ships of two similar designs, the "Klondike" class of AD 22-25 and "Shenandoah" class of AD 26, 27, 28, 29, 30, 31, 33, 35, 36. *Great Lakes* (AD 30), *Canopus* (AD 33, ex-AS 27), *Arrow Head* (AD 35) cancelled before completion; *Klondike* (AD 22) reclassified AR 22; *Grand Canyon* (AD 28) reclassified AR 28 (see under ARs).

Two ships remain in active service with *Everglades* in reserve as accommodation and depot ship at Philadelphia Navy Yard. *Yellowstone* (AD 27) paid off 12 Sep 1974.

Gunnery: Original armament for "Klondike" class was 1—5 in gun, 4—3 in guns, and 4—40 mm guns; for "Shenandoah" class was 2—5 in guns and 8—40 mm guns.

Modernisation: These ships have been modernised under the FRAM II programme to service modernised destroyers fitted with ASROC, improved electronics, helicopters etc.

SHENANDOAH   *9/1976, Dr. Giorgio Arra*

5 "DIXIE" CLASS (DESTROYER TENDERS (AD))

Name	No.	Builders	Commissioned
*DIXIE	AD 14	NY Shipbuilding Corp, NJ	25 April 1940
*PRAIRIE	AD 15	NY Shipbuilding Corp, NJ	5 Aug 1940
*PIEDMONT	AD 17	Tampa Shipbuilding Co, Florida	5 Jan 1944
*SIERRA	AD 18	Tampa Shipbuilding Co, Florida	20 Mar 1944
*YOSEMITE	AD 19	Tampa Shipbuilding Co, Florida	25 Mar 1944

Displacement, tons: 9 450 standard; 17 190 to 18 000 full load
Dimensions, feet (metres): 520 wl; 530·5 oa × 73·3 × 25·5 (161·7 × 22·3 × 7·8)
Guns: 4—20 mm Mk 68 (singles)
Main engines: Steam turbines (New York SB Corp in AD 14 and 15; Allis Chalmers in remainder); 12 000 shp; 2 shafts = 19·6 knots
Boilers: 4 (Babcock & Wilcox)
Complement: 1 131 to 1 271

Launched on 27 May 1939, 9 Dec 1939, 7 Dec 1942, 23 Feb 1943 and 16 May 1943 respectively. All five ships are active with *Dixie* the oldest ship currently in service with the US Navy except for the sail frigate *Constitution*.

Modernisation: All of these ships have been modernised under the FRAM II programme to service destroyers fitted with ASROC, improved electronics, helicopters, etc. Two or three 5 inch guns and eight 40 mm guns removed during modernisation.

DIXIE   4/1976, USN

8 "KILAUEA" CLASS (AMMUNITION SHIPS (AE))

Name	No.	Laid down	Launched	Commissioned
*KILAUEA	AE 26	10 Mar 1966	9 Aug 1967	10 Aug 1968
*BUTTE	AE 27	21 July 1966	9 Aug 1967	14 Dec 1968
*SANTA BARBARA	AE 28	20 Dec 1966	23 Jan 1968	11 July 1970
*MOUNT HOOD	AE 29	8 May 1967	17 July 1968	1 May 1971
*FLINT	AE 32	4 Aug 1969	9 Nov 1970	20 Nov 1971
*SHASTA	AE 33	10 Nov 1969	3 Apr 1971	26 Feb 1972
*MOUNT BAKER	AE 34	10 May 1970	23 Oct 1971	22 July 1972
*KISKA	AE 35	4 Aug 1971	11 Mar 1972	16 Dec 1972

Displacement, tons: 18 088 full load
Dimensions, feet (metres): 564 oa × 81 × 28 (171·9 × 24·7 × 8·5)
Helicopters: 2 UH-46 Sea Knight cargo helicopters normally embarked
Guns: 8—3 inch (76 mm) 50 cal (twin) (Mk 33)
Main engines: Geared turbines (General Electric); 22 000 shp; 1 shaft = 20 knots
Boilers: 3 (Foster Wheeler)
Complement: 401 (28 officers, 373 enlisted men)

Fitted for rapid transfer of missiles and other munitions to ships alongside or with helicopters in vertical replenishment operations (VERTREP). Helicopter platform and hangar aft. AE 26 and 27 authorised in Fiscal Year 1965 new construction programme, AE 28 and 29 in FY 1966, AE 32 and 33 in FY 1967, and AE 34 and 35 in FY 1968. AE 26 and AE 27 built by General Dynamics Corp, Quincy, Massachusetts; AE 28 and 29 Bethlehem Steel Corp, Sparrows Point, Maryland; and AE 32-35 by Ingalls Shipbuilding Corp, Pascagoula, Mississippi.
The 3 inch guns are arranged in twin closed mounts forward and twin open mounts aft, between funnel and after booms. Two Mk 56 gunfire control systems installed.
Each ship will receive one Mk 36 Chaffroc. Plans to instal two NATO Seasparrow cancelled.

KISKA   6/1976, J. L. M. van der Burg

5 "SURIBACHI" and "NITRO" CLASSES
(AMMUNITION SHIPS (AE))

Name	No.	Laid down	Launched	Commissioned
*SURIBACHI	AE 21	31 Jan 1955	2 Nov 1955	17 Nov 1956
*MAUNA KEA	AE 22	16 May 1955	3 May 1956	30 Mar 1957
*NITRO	AE 23	20 May 1957	25 June 1958	1 May 1959
*PYRO	AE 24	21 Oct 1957	5 Nov 1958	24 July 1959
*HALEAKALA	AE 25	10 Mar 1958	17 Feb 1959	3 Nov 1959

Displacement, tons: 7 470 light; 10 000 standard; 15 500 full load (21 and 22), 16 083 (rest)
Dimensions, feet (metres): 512 oa × 72 × 29 (156·1 × 21·9 × 8·8) (21 and 22; 502 oa (153))
Guns: 4—3 inch (76 mm) 50 cal (twin) (Mk 33)
Main engines: Geared turbines (Bethlehem); 16 000 shp; 1 shaft = 20·6 knots
Boilers: 2 (Combustion Engineering)
Complement: 316 (18 officers, 298 enlisted men)

Designed specifically for underwater replenishment. All built by Bethlehem Steel Corp, Sparrows Point, Maryland. A sixth ship of this class to have been built under the FY 1959 programme was cancelled.
All five ships were modernised in 1960s, being fitted with high-speed transfer equipment, three holds configured for stowage of missiles up to and including the 33-foot Talos, and helicopter platform fitted aft (two after twin 3 inch gun mounts removed).

NITRO   9/1975, Dr. Giorgio Arra

Arrangements of twin 3 inch gun mounts differ, some ships have them in tandem and others side-by-side.

Fire Control: 1—Mk 63 director (21 and 22); 2—Mk 51 directors (remainder).

Rockets: Mk 36 Chaffroc to be fitted.

7 "MARS" CLASS (COMBAT STORE SHIPS (AFS))

Name	No.	Laid down	Launched	Commissioned
*MARS	AFS 1	5 May 1962	15 June 1963	21 Dec 1963
*SYLVANIA	AFS 2	18 Aug 1962	15 Aug 1963	11 July 1964
*NIAGARA FALLS	AFS 3	22 May 1965	26 Mar 1966	29 April 1967
*WHITE PLAINS	AFS 4	2 Oct 1965	23 July 1966	23 Nov 1968
*CONCORD	AFS 5	26 Mar 1966	17 Dec 1966	27 Nov 1968
*SAN DIEGO	AFS 6	11 Mar 1965	13 April 1968	24 May 1969
*SAN JOSE	AFS 7	8 Mar 1969	13 Dec 1969	23 Oct 1970

Displacement, tons: 16 500 full load (1-3) 15 900 (remainder)
Dimensions, feet (metres): 581 oa × 79 × 24 (177·1 × 24·1 × 7·3)
Guns: 8—3 inch (76 mm) 50 cal (twin) Mk 33)
Helicopters: 2 UH-46 Sea Knight helicopters normally assigned
Main engines: Steam turbines (De Laval except AFS 6—Westinghouse); 22 000 shp; 1 shaft = 20 knots
Boilers: 3 (Babcock & Wilcox)
Complement: 486 (45 officers, 441 enlisted men)

All built by National Steel & Shipbuilding, San Diego, California. Of a new design with a completely new replenishment at sea system. "M" frames replace conventional king posts and booms, which are equipped with automatic tensioning devices to maintain transfer lines taut between the ship and the warships being replenished despite rolling and yawing. Computers provide up-to-the-minute data on stock status with data displayed by closed-circuit television. Five holds (one refrigerated). Cargo capacity 2 625 tons dry stores and 1 300 tons refrigerated stores (varies with specific loadings).
Automatic propulsion system with full controls on bridge. The large SPS-40 radar fitted in *Mars* and *Sylvania* have been removed; some ships have Tacan (tactical aircraft navigation) radar. Fitted with two Mk 56 gunfire control systems.

WHITE PLAINS   12/1976, Dr. Giorgio Arra

Mars authorised in Fiscal Year 1961 shipbuilding programme, *Sylvania* in FY 1962, *Niagara Falls* in FY 1964, *White Plains* and *Concord* in FY 1965, *San Diego* in FY 1966, *San Jose* in FY 1967. Plans to construct three additional ships of this type in the FY 1977-1978 programmes have been dropped.

Rockets: Mk 36 Chaffroc to be fitted.

1 AUXILIARY DEEP SUBMERGENCE SUPPORT SHIP (AGDS): Ex-DOCK CARGO SHIP

Name	No.	Builders	Commissioned
*POINT LOMA	AGDS 2	Maryland SB & DD Co	28 Feb 1958
(ex-*Point Barrow*)	(ex-AKD 1)		

Displacement, tons: 9 415 standard; 14 094 full load
Dimensions, feet (metres): 475 wl; 492 oa × 78 × 22 *(150·0 × 23·8 × 6·7)*
Guns: None
Main engines: Steam turbines; 6 000 shp; 2 shafts = 18 knots
Boilers: 2
Complement: 160 (Including scientific personnel and submersible operators)

A docking ship designed to carry cargo, vehicles, and landing craft (originally designated AKD). Built for the Military Sea Transportation Service (now Military Sealift Command); launched on 25 May 1957 and delivered to MSTS on 29 May 1958. Maritime Administration S2-ST-23A design; winterised for arctic service. Fitted with internal ramp and garage system.
Subsequently refitted with hangar over docking well and employed in transport of large booster rockets to Cape Kennedy Space Center. Primarily used to carry the second stage of the Saturn V moon rocket and Lunar Modules. Placed out of service in reserve on 1 Jan 1971 with US space programme.
Reactivated in mid-1972 for cargo work; transferred from Military Sealift Command to Navy on 28 Feb 1974 for modification to support deep submergence vehicles, especially the bathyscaph *Trieste II*. Placed in commission "special" on 8 Mar 1974 as the AGDS 2; renamed *Point Loma* for the location of the San Diego submarine base where Submarine Development Group 1 operates most of the Navy's submersibles. The *Point Loma* was placed in commission on 30 April 1975. Aviation gas capacity increased to approximately 100 000 gallons (US) to support *Trieste II* which uses lighter-than-water avgas for flotation.

POINT LOMA   6/1976, J. L. M. van der Burg

Classification: The designation AGDS was established on 3 Jan 1974; technically it is a service craft designation *vice* ship. The AGDS 1 was assigned briefly to the floating dry dock *White Sands* (ARD 20), the previous *Trieste II* support ship.

1 "HAVEN" CLASS (HOSPITAL SHIP (AH))

Name	No.	Builders	Commissioned
SANCTUARY (ex-*Marine Owl*)	AH 17	Sun SB & DD Co, Chester	20 June 1945

Displacement, tons: 11 141 standard; 15 100 full load
Dimensions, feet (metres): 496 wl; 520 oa × 71·5 × 24 *(158·5 × 21·8 × 7·3)*
Guns: None
Main engines: Steam turbines (General Electric); 9 000 shp; 1 shaft = 18·33 knots
Boilers: 2 (Babcock & Wilcox)
Complement: 530 (70 officers, 460 enlisted)

The *Sanctuary* is the survivor of six hospital ships (AH) of the "Haven" class. Built on C4-S-B2 merchant hull and launched on 15 Aug 1944. *Sanctuary* recommissioned from reserve in 1966 for service off Vietnam; decommissioned on 15 Dec 1971 for modification to "dependent support ship" at Hunter's Point Naval Shipyard, San Francisco, California. Subsequently recommissioned on 18 Nov 1972.
As a dependent support ship the *Sanctuary* had special facilities for obstetrics, gynaecology, maternity, and nursery services; fitted as a 74-bed hospital which can be expanded to 300 beds in 72 hours. She was the first US Navy ship with mixed male-female crew (although previously female nurses have been assigned to hospital ships and transports). The medical personnel consisted of 50 officers and approx 120 enlisted including several female nurse officers; the ship's company consisted of 20 officers (including two women) and approx 330 enlisted (including 60 women). The ship was modified to support US dependents of ships homeported in Piraeus, Greece. However, she was not deployed to Greece, but was decommissioned on 28 Mar 1974.

SANCTUARY   1974, USN

3 + 14 "AO 177" CLASS (OILERS)

			Laid down	Commissioned
	AO 177	Fiscal Year 1976 programme	Mid-1978	Early-1980
	AO 178	Fiscal Year 1976 programme	Late-1978	Mid-1980
	AO 179	Authorised FY 1977 programme		
Four ships	AO 186-189	Proposed FY 1978 programme		
Four ships	AO 190-193	Planned FY 1979 programme		
Two ships	AO 194-195	Planned FY 1980 programme		
Two ships	AO 196-197	Planned FY 1981 programme		
Two ships	AO 198-199	Planned FY 1982 programme		

Displacement, tons: 27 500 full load
Dimensions, feet (metres): 588·5 oa × 88 × 35 *(179·4 × 26·8 × 10·7)*
Guns: 2—20 mm Phalanx CIWS
Rockets: 1—Mk 36 Chaffroc
Main engines: 1 Geared turbine; 24 000 shp; 1 shaft = 20 knots
Boilers: 2
Complement: 135

This class of fleet oilers is significantly smaller than the previous built-for-the-purpose AOs of the "Neosho" class; the newer ships are "sized" to provide two complete refuellings of a fossil-fuelled aircraft carrier and six to eight accompanying destroyers. The lead ship was requested in the Fiscal Year 1975 new construction programme but was not approved by Congress. Subsequently, two ships (AO 177 and AO 178) approved in FY 1976.
A contract for the construction of these two ships was awarded to Avondale Shipyards Inc. Westwego, La. on 9 Aug 1976. AO 179 authorised under FY 1977 programme. Fourteen more of this class planned or proposed.
Each ship has a capacity of 120 000 barrels, will have two Phalanx 20 mm CIWS (forward and aft) and a helicopter platform aft.

Classification: The hull numbers AO 168-176 are assigned to the "Sealift" class tankers; AO 180 is USNS *Potomac*; AO 181-185 assigned to "Columbia" class. All listed under Military Sealift Command section.

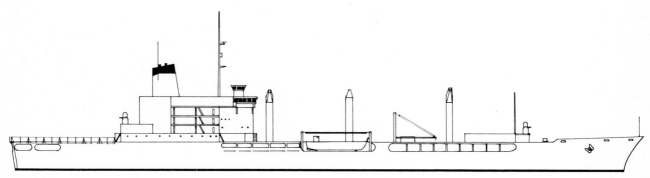

AO 177 DESIGN   *Drawing by A. D. Baker III*

6 "NEOSHO" CLASS (OILERS (AO))

Name	No.	Launched	Commissioned
*NEOSHO	AO 143	10 Nov 1953	24 Sep 1954
*MISSISSINEWA	T-AO 144	12 June 1954	18 Jan 1955
*HASSAYAMPA	AO 145	12 Sep 1954	19 Apr 1955
*KAWISHIWI	AO 146	11 Dec 1954	6 July 1955
*TRUCKEE	AO 147	10 Mar 1955	23 Nov 1955
*PONCHATOULA	AO 148	9 July 1955	12 Jan 1956

Displacement, tons: 11 600 light; 38 000 full load
Dimensions, feet (metres): 640 wl; 655 oa × 86 × 35 (199·6 × 26·2 × 10·7)
Guns: 8—3 inch (76 mm) 50 cal (twin) (Mk 33) (12—3 inch in AO 145 and 146; none in T-AO 144)
Main engines: Geared turbines (General Electric); 28 000 shp; 2 shafts = 20 knots
Boilers: 2 (Babcock & Wilcox)
Complement: 324 (21 officers and 303 enlisted men including staff) when navy manned

Neosho built by Bethlehem Steel Co, Quincy, Massachusetts; others by New York Shipbuilding Corp, Camden, New Jersey. These are the largest "straight" fleet oilers (AO) constructed specifically for the Navy. Cargo capacity is approximately 180 000 barrels of liquid fuels. Original armament was two 5 inch guns and twelve 3 inch guns; former removed in 1969. Two twin 3 inch gun mounts removed from *Neosho, Mississinewa,* and *Truckee* and helicopter platform installed. Those ships also have additional superstructure installed forward of after superstructure. Armed ships have two Mk 56 gunfire control systems. All fitted to carry a service force commander and staff (12 officers).
Mississinewa assigned to Military Sealift Command on 15 Nov 1976 (guns removed; civilian manned); others will follow into MSC operation.

TRUCKEE   8/1975, USN

3 "JUMBOISED CIMARRON" CLASS
("JUMBOISED" T3-S2-A1 TYPE OILERS (AO))

Name	No.	Launched	Commissioned
*ASHTABULA	AO 51	22 May 1943	7 Aug 1943
*CALOOSAHATCHEE	AO 98	2 June 1945	10 Oct 1945
*CANISTEO	AO 99	6 July 1945	3 Dec 1945

Displacement, tons: 34 040 full load
Dimensions, feet (metres): 644 oa × 75 × 35 (196·3 × 22·9 × 10·7)
Guns: 4—3 inch (76 mm) 50 cal (single) (Mk 26)
Main engines: Geared turbines (Bethlehem); 13 500 shp; 2 shafts = 18 knots
Boilers: 4 (Foster Wheeler)
Complement: 300 (13 officers and 287 enlisted men)

All built by Bethlehem Steel Co, Sparrows Point, Maryland. Originally T3-S2-A1 oilers; converted during mid-1960s under "jumbo" programme. Enlarged midsections added to increase cargo capacity to approximately 143 000 barrels plus 175 tons of munitions and 100 tons refrigerated stores. Provided with one Mk 52 gunfire control system. No helicopter platform fitted.
All three ships naval manned.

ASHTABULA   10/1976, Dr. Giorgio Arra

2 "CIMARRON" CLASS (T3-S2-A1 TYPE OILERS (AO))

Name	No.	Launched	Commissioned
*MARIAS	T-AO 57	21 Dec 1943	12 Feb 1944
*TALUGA	T-AO 62	10 July 1944	25 Aug 1944

Displacement, tons: 25 450 full load
Dimensions, feet (metres): 553 oa × 75 × 33 (168·6 × 22·9 × 10·1)
Guns: Unarmed
Main engines: Geared turbines (Bethlehem); 13 500 shp; 2 shafts = 18 knots
Boilers: 4 (Foster Wheeler)
Complement: 274 (14 officers, 260 enlisted men)

These ships are survivors of a large number of twin-screw (S2) fleet oilers built during World War II; some converted to escort carriers. Several ships of this type have been enlarged through the "jumbo" process and are listed separately. All above ships were built by Bethlehem Steel Co, Sparrows Point, Maryland. Original armament consisted of one 5 inch gun, four 3 inch guns and up to eight 40 mm guns. Cargo capacity 145 000 barrels of liquid fuels.
The *Marias* and *Taluga* were assigned to the Military Sealift Command (MSC) on 2 Oct 1973 and 4 May 1972 respectively; manned by civilian crews and guns removed.

MARIAS   10/1976, Michael D. J. Lennon

4 + 1 "SACRAMENTO" CLASS
(FAST COMBAT SUPPORT SHIPS (AOE))

Name	No.	Laid down	Launched	Commissioned
*SACRAMENTO	AOE 1	30 June 1961	14 Sep 1963	14 Mar 1964
*CAMDEN	AOE 2	17 Feb 1964	29 May 1965	1 Apr 1967
*SEATTLE	AOE 3	1 Oct 1965	2 Mar 1968	5 Apr 1969
*DETROIT	AOE 4	29 Nov 1966	21 June 1969	28 Mar 1970
	AOE 5	Planned Fiscal Year 1980 programme		

Displacement, tons: 19 200 light; 53 600 full load
Dimensions, feet (metres): 793 oa × 107 × 39·3 (241·7 × 32·6 × 12·0)
Guns: 8—3 inch (76 mm) 50 cal (twin) (Mk 33)
Helicopters: 2 UH-46 Sea Knight normally assigned
Main engines: Geared turbines (General Electric); 100 000 shp; 2 shafts = 26 knots
Boilers: 4 (Combustion Engineering)
Complement: 600 (33 officers, 567 enlisted men) (AOE 1 and 2);
    680 (33 officers, 647 enlisted men) (AOE 3 and 4)

These ships provide rapid replenishment at sea of petroleum, munitions, provisions, and fleet freight. Fitted with helicopter platform, internal arrangements, and large hangar for vertical replenishment operations (VERTREP). Cargo capacity 177 000 barrels plus 2 150 tons munitions, 500 tons dry stores, 250 tons refrigerated stores (varies with specific loadings). One Mk 56 and one Mk 63 gunfire control systems installed in first two ships; two Mk 56 in second pair. Built by Puget Sound Naval Shipyard except *Camden* by New York Shipbuilding Corp, Camden, New Jersey. *Sacramento* authorised in Fiscal Year 1961 new construction programme; *Camden* in FY 1963, *Seattle* in FY 1965, and *Detroit* in FY 1966. Construction of AOE 5 in FY 1968 was deferred and then cancelled in November 1969. No additional ships of this type were planned because of high cost, the availability of new-construction ammunition ships, and the great success of the smaller "Wichita" class replenishment oilers; however, in 1976 the Department of Defense announced plans to construct another AOE in the Fiscal Year 1980 shipbuilding programme. Approximate cost of the *Camden* was $70 000 000.

Appearance: These ships can be distinguished from the smaller "Wichita" class replenishment oilers by their larger superstructures and funnel, helicopter deck at higher level, and hangar structure aft of funnel.

SEATTLE   9/1976, Dr. Giorgio Arra

Engineering: *Sacramento* and *Camden* have machinery taken from the cancelled battleship *Kentucky* (BB 66).

Gunnery: Two Phalanx 20 mm CIWS to be fitted.

Missiles: NATO Sea Sparrow system with Mark 91 director to be fitted.

7 "WICHITA" CLASS (REPLENISHMENT OILERS (AOR))

Name	No.	Laid down	Launched	Commissioned
*WICHITA	AOR 1	18 June1966	18 Mar 1968	7 June 1969
*MILWAUKEE	AOR 2	29 Nov 1966	17 Jan 1969	1 Nov 1969
*KANSAS CITY	AOR 3	20 Apr 1968	28 June1969	6 June 1970
*SAVANNAH	AOR 4	22 Jan 1969	25 Apr 1970	5 Dec 1970
*WABASH	AOR 5	21 Jan 1970	6 Feb 1971	20 Nov 1971
*KALAMAZOO	AOR 6	28 Oct 1970	11 Nov 1972	11 Aug 1973
*ROANOKE	AOR 7	19 Jan 1974	7 Dec 1974	30 Oct 1976

ROANOKE   7/1976, National Steel and SB Co San Diego

Displacement, tons: 37 360 full load
Dimensions, feet (metres): 659 oa × 96 × 33·3 *(206·9 × 29·3 × 10·2)*
Missile Launchers: 1 NATO Sea Sparrow launcher (Mk 29) in *Roanoke* and *Kansas City*
Guns: 4—3 inch *(76 mm)* 50 cal (twin) (Mk 33) (in AOR 1, 4-6 only)
Helicopters: 2 UH-46 Sea Knight can be embarked
Main engines: Geared turbines (General Electric); 32 000 shp; 2 shafts = 20 knots (18 knots on 2 boilers)
Boilers: 3 (Foster Wheeler)
Complement: 390 (27 officers, 363 enlisted men)

These ships provide rapid replenishment at sea of petroleum and munitions with a limited capacity for provision and fleet freight. Fitted with helicopter platform and internal arrangement for vertical replenishment operations (VERTREP), but no hangar originally provided; some subsequently fitted with hangar. Cargo capacity 175 000 barrels of liquid fuels plus 600 tons munitions, 425 tons dry stores, 150 tons refrigerated stores. Two Mk 56 gunfire control systems in AOR 1-, 4-6; one Mk 91 guided missile control system in *Roanoke* and *Kansas City*.
All built by General Dynamics Corp, Quincy Massachusetts except AOR 7 by National Steel and Shipbuilding Co, San Diego, California. *Wichita* and *Milwaukee* authorised in Fiscal Year 1965 new construction programme, *Kansas City* and *Savannah* in FY 1966, *Wabash* and *Kalamazoo* in FY 1967, and *Roanoke* in FY 1972. Approximate cost of *Milwaukee* was $27 700 000.

4 SELF-PROPELLED BARRACKS SHIPS (APB/IX)

Name	No.	Builders	Commissioned
*ECHOLS	IX 504 (ex-APB 37, ex-APL 37)	Boston Navy Yard	1 Jan 1947
*MERCER	IX 502 (ex-APB 39, ex-APL 39)	Boston Navy Yard	19 Sep 1945
*NUECES	IX 503 (ex-APB 40, ex-APL 40)	Boston Navy Yard	30 Nov 1945
KINGMAN	APB 47 (ex-AKS 18, ex-LST 1113)	Missouri Valley Bridge & Iron Co, Evansville, Indiana	27 June1945

MERCER (as APB 39)   1968, USN

Displacement, tons: 2 189 light; 4 080 full load
Dimensions, feet (metres): 136 wl; 328 oa × 50 × 11 *(100·0 × 15·2 × 3·4)*
Guns: Vary
Main engines: Diesels (General Motors); 1 600 to 1 800 bhp; 2 shafts = 12 knots (APB 47); 10 knots (remainder)
Complement: 193 (13 officers, 180 enlisted men) as APB
Troops: 1 226 (26 officers, 1 200 enlisted men) as APB

Self-propelled barracks ships (APB) built to provide support and accommodations for small craft and riverine forces. Launched on 30 July 1945, 17 Nov 1944, 6 May 1945, 17 April 1945 respectively. *Echols* placed in service *vice* commissioning in Jan 1947. All ex-LST type ships of the same basic characteristics. *Mercer* and *Nueces* recommissioned in 1968 for service in Vietnam; decommissioned in 1969-1971 as US riverine forces in South Vietnam were reduced. Each APB has troop berthing and messing facilities, evaporators which produce up to 40 000 gallons of fresh water per day, a 16-bed hospital, X-ray room, dental room, bacteriological laboratory, pharmacy, laundry, library, and tailor shop; living and most working spaces are air-conditioned.
Mercer and *Nueces* again reactivated in 1975 to serve as barrack ships for ships in overhaul at Puget Sound Naval Shipyard, Bremerton, Washington. *Echols* (in reserve since 1947) reactivated in 1976 to provide berthing for crews of Trident missile submarines being built by General Dynamics Electric Boat Division in Groton, Connecticut. The *Kingman* remains in reserve.

Classification: *Mercer* and *Nueces* reclassified as "unclassified" (IX) on 1 Nov 1975; *Echols* changed to IX on 1 Feb 1976.

1 CONVERTED "SHENANDOAH" CLASS (REPAIR SHIP (AR))

Name	No.	Builders	Commissioned
*GRAND CANYON	AR 28 (ex-AD 28)	Todd Shipyards Corp, Los Angeles	5 Apr 1946

GRAND CANYON   1971, USN

Displacement, tons: 8 165 standard; 17 430 full load
Dimensions, feet (metres): 492 oa × 69·5 × 27·2 *(150·0 × 21·2 × 8·3)*
Guns: 4—20 mm Mk 68 (singles)
Main engines: Steam turbines (Allis-Chalmers); 12 000 shp; 1 shaft = 18·4 knots
Boilers: 2 (Babcock and Wilcox)
Complement: 1 271 (80 officers, 1 191 enlisted men)

The *Grand Canyon* is a modified C-3 cargo ship completed as a destroyer tender and subsequently reclassified as a repair ship; redesignated AR 28 on 10 Mar 1971. Designed armament was 2—5 inch guns and 8—40 mm guns.
Launched on 27 April 1945. Modernised; fitted with helicopter platform and hangar aft. The *Grand Canyon* is active.

1 "MARKAB" CLASS (REPAIR SHIP (AR))

Name	No.	Builders	Commissioned
MARKAB (ex-Mormacpenn)	AR 23 (ex-AD 21, ex-AK 31)	Ingalls SB Co, Pascagoula	15 June 1941

MARKAB   USN

Displacement, tons: 8 560 standard; 14 800 full load
Dimensions, feet (metres): 465 wl; 492·5 oa × 69·8 × 24·8 *(150·1 × 21·3 × 7·6)*
Guns: 4—3 inch *(76 mm)* 50 cal (single)
Main engines: Steam turbines (General Electric); 8 500 shp; 1 shaft = 18·4 knots
Boilers: 2 (Foster-Wheeler)

Launched on 21 Dec 1940. Completed as a destroyer tender; reclassified as repair ship on 15 April 1960 and designation changed from AD to AR. One 5 inch gun and 4—40 mm guns were removed. The *Markab* was decommissioned on 19 Dec 1969 but remains in service in reserve as station ship at Mare Island, California

1 "DELTA" CLASS (REPAIR SHIP (AR))

Name	No.	Builders	Commissioned
DELTA (ex-*Hawaiian Packer*)	AR 9 (ex-AK 29)	Newport News SB & DD Co, Virginia	15 June 1941

Displacement, tons: 8 975 standard; 13 009 full load
Dimensions, feet (metres): 465·5 wl; 490·5 oa × 69·5 × 24·3 *(149·5 × 21·2 × 7·4)*
Guns: 4—3 inch *(76 mm)* 50 cal Mk 26 (single)
Main engines: Steam turbines (Newport News); 8 500 shp; 1 shaft = 16 knots
Boilers: 2 (Babcock & Wilcox)
Complement: 1,003 (46 officers, 957 enlisted men)

C-3 type. Launched in 1941. The 5 inch and 4—40 mm guns originally fitted now removed. *Delta*, decommissioned on 20 June 1970, remains in service in reserve as station ship at Bremerton, Washington.

DELTA   *1969, USN*

4 "VULCAN" CLASS (REPAIR SHIPS (AR))

Name	No.	Builders	Commissioned
*VULCAN	AR 5	New York SB Corp	16 June 1941
*AJAX	AR 6	Los Angeles SB & DD Corp	30 Oct 1942
*HECTOR	AR 7	Los Angeles SB & DD Corp	7 Feb 1944
*JASON	AR 8 (ex-ARH 1)	Los Angeles SB & DD Corp	19 June 1944

Displacement, tons: 9 140 standard; 16 380 full load
Dimensions, feet (metres): 520 wl; 529·3 oa × 73·3 × 23·3 *(161·3 × 22·3 × 7·1)*
Guns: 4—5 inch *(127 mm)* 38 cal (single) (Mk 30) (*Vulcan* only); 4—20 mm (singles) (Mk 67) (remainder)
Main engines: Steam turbines (Allis Chalmers except AR 5—New York SB Corp); 11 000 shp; 2 shafts = 19·2 knots
Boilers: 4 (Babcock & Wilcox)
Complement: 1,336 (63 officers, 1,273 enlisted men)

Vulcan was built under the 1939 programme and the other three under the 1940 programme. Launched on 14 Dec 1940, 22 Aug 1942, 11 Nov 1942 and 3 April 1943 respectively. All carry a most elaborate equipment of machine tools to undertake repairs of every description. *Jason*, originally designated ARH 1 and rated as heavy hull repair ship, was reclassified AR 8 on 9 Sep 1957. Eight 40 mm guns (twin) have been removed; the four 5 inch guns were the standard main battery of large fleet support ships and oilers during World War II.

VULCAN   *9/1975, Dr. Giorgio Arra*

4 "ACHELOUS" CLASS (LANDING CRAFT REPAIR SHIPS (ARL))

Name	No.	Builders	Commissioned
BELLEROPHON	ARL 31 (ex-*LST 1132*)	Chicago Bridge & Iron Co, Seneca, Illinois	19 Mar 1945
EGERIA	ARL 8 (ex-*LST 136*)	Chicago Bridge & Iron Co, Seneca, Illinois	18 Dec 1943
INDRA	ARL 37 (ex-*LST 1147*)	Chicago Bridge & Iron Co, Seneca, Illinois	28 May 1945
SPHINX	ARL 24 (ex-*LST 963*)	Bethlehem Steel Co, Higham, Mass	12 Dec 1944

Displacement, tons: 1 625 light; 4 325 full load
Dimensions, feet (metres): 316 wl; 328 oa × 50 × 11 *(100·0 × 15·2 × 3·4)*
Guns: 8—40 mm (quad); 8—20 mm (Mk 10) (single) (ARL 8 and 31)
Main engines: Diesels (General Motors); 1 800 bhp; 2 shafts = 12 knots
Complement: 266 (18 officers, 248 enlisted men)

Tank landing ships converted during construction to landing craft repair ships (ARL). Launched Feb 1945, 23 Nov 1943, 21 May 1945 and 18 Nov 1944 respectively. Fitted with machine shops, parts storage, lifting gear, etc; 50-ton (ARL 8) and 60-ton (ARL 24 and 37) capacity booms. The ARLs cater for small amphibious, minesweeping, and riverine craft. Pole masts in ARL 8 and 31; tripod mast in ARL 24 and 37. Reactivated during Vietnam War.

SPHINX   *1968, USN*

Transfers: Former US Navy LSTs modified to fleet support ships (AGP-ARB-ARL-ARVE) are operated by the navies of Greece, Indonesia, South Korea, Malaysia, Philippines, Taiwan, Turkey, and Venezuela.
Sphinx due for transfer to Spain late 1977.

14 "DIVER" and "BOLSTER" CLASSES
(SALVAGE SHIPS (ARS))

Note: Plans for new Salvage Ships indefinitely postponed.

Name	No.	Builders	Commissioned
*ESCAPE	ARS 6	Basalt Rock Co, Napa, Calif	20 Nov 1943
*GRAPPLE	ARS 7	Basalt Rock Co, Napa, Calif	16 Dec 1943
*PRESERVER	ARS 8	Basalt Rock Co, Napa, Calif	11 Jan 1944
*DELIVER	ARS 23	Basalt Rock Co, Napa, Calif	18 July 1944
*GRASP	ARS 24	Basalt Rock Co, Napa, Calif	22 Aug 1944
*SAFEGUARD	ARS 25	Basalt Rock Co, Napa, Calif	31 Oct 1944
CLAMP	ARS 33	Basalt Rock Co, Napa, Calif	23 Aug 1943
*GEAR	ARS 34	Basalt Rock Co, Napa, Calif	24 Sep 1943
*BOLSTER	ARS 38	Basalt Rock Co, Napa, Calif	1 May 1945
*CONSERVER	ARS 39	Basalt Rock Co, Napa, Calif	9 June 1945
*HOIST	ARS 40	Basalt Rock Co, Napa, Calif	21 July 1945
*OPPORTUNE	ARS 41	Basalt Rock Co, Napa, Calif	5 Oct 1945
*RECLAIMER	ARS 42	Basalt Rock Co, Napa, Calif	20 Dec 1945
*RECOVERY	ARS 43	Basalt Rock Co, Napa, Calif	15 May 1946

Displacement, tons: 1 530 standard; 1 970 full load (ARS 38-43 2 040)
Dimensions, feet (metres): 207 wl; 213·5 oa × 41 except later ships 44 × 13 *(65·1 × 12·5 or 13·4 × 4·0)*
Guns: 1—40 mm (ARS 39, 41 and 42); 2—20 mm (remainder)
Main engines: Diesel-electric (Cooper Bessemer); 2 440 shp; 2 shafts = 14·8 knots
Complement: 101-151

RECLAIMER   *12/1976, Dr. Giorgio Arra*

These ships are fitted for salvage and towing; equipped with compressed air diving equipment. Launched on 22 Nov 1942, 31 Dec 1942, 1 April 1943, 25 Sep 1943, 31 July 1943, 20 Nov 1943, 24 Oct 1942, 24 Oct 1942, 23 Dec 1944, 27 Jan 1945, 31 Mar 1945, 31 Mar 1945, 25 June 1945 and 4 Aug 1945 respectively. Early ships have 8-ton and 10-ton capacity booms; later ships have 10-ton and 20-ton booms.
ARS 38 and later ships are of a slightly different design, known as the "Bolster" class.

The *Gear* is operated by a commercial firm in support of Navy activities; two additional ships are on loan to private salvage firms, the *Cable* ARS 19 and *Curb* ARS 21, and support naval requirements as needed. The *Clamp* was stricken from the Navy List in 1963 but reacquired in 1973 and is still laid up in Maritime Administration Reserve Fleet.

Conversions: *Chain* ARS 20 and *Snatch* ARS 27 converted to oceanographic research ships, designated AGOR 17 and AGOR 18, respectively. Latter since deleted.

Disposals: *Grapple* and *Grasp* for disposal 1977.

REPAIR SHIPS (ARX): NEW CONSTRUCTION

Current Navy planning provides for the construction of a new class of repair ships. One unit proposed for FY 1979 programme and the second for FY 1982. Will probably replace "Vulcan" class. Characteristics not yet determined.

2 + 3 "EMORY S. LAND" and "L. Y. SPEAR" CLASSES
(SUBMARINE TENDERS (AS))

Name	No.	Builders	Commissioned
*L. Y. SPEAR	AS 36	General Dynamics Corp, Quincy	28 Feb 1970
*DIXON	AS 37	General Dynamics Corp, Quincy	7 Aug 1971
EMORY S. LAND	AS 39	Lockheed SB & Cons Co, Seattle	1978
FRANK CABLE	AS 40	Lockheed SB & Cons Co, Seattle	1979
—	AS 41		1981

L. Y. SPEAR   9/1976, Dr. Giorgio Arra

Displacement, tons: 13 000 standard; 22 640 full load (AS 36 and AS 37); 24 000 (AS 39 and AS 40)
Dimensions, feet (metres): 643·8 oa × 85 × 28·5 (196·2 × 25·9 × 8·7)
Guns: 4—20 mm Mk 67 (single) (AS 36 and 37); 2—40 mm Mk 66 (single) (AS 39-41) (see Gunnery notes)
Missile launchers: NATO Sea Sparrow missile launcher planned for AS 39 and later ships
Main engines: Steam turbines (General Electric); 20 000 shp; 1 shaft = 20 knots
Boilers: 2 (Foster Wheeler)
Complement: 1 348 (96 officers, 1 252 enlisted men) (AS 36 and 37); 1 158 (50 officers, 1 108 enlisted men) (AS 39 and 40)
Flag accommodations: 69 (25 officers, 44 enlisted men)

These ships are the first US submarine tenders designed specifically for servicing nuclear-propelled attack submarines with later ships built to a modified design to support SSN 688 class submarines. Basic hull design similar to "Samuel Gompers" class destroyer tenders. Provided with helicopter deck but no hangar. Each ship can simultaneously provide services to four submarines moored alongside. AS 39 and later ships ("Emory S. Land" class) are especially configured to support SSN 688 class submarines.
L. Y. Spear authorised in the Fiscal Year 1965 shipbuilding programme, laid down 5 May 1966 and launched 7 Sep 1967; Dixon authorised in FY 1966, laid down 7 Sep 1967 and launched 20 June 1970; AS 38 of FY 1969 not built to provide funds for cost increases in other ship programmes. Cancelled 27 Mar 1969. Emory S. Land authorised in FY 1972, and Frank Cable in FY 1973 both laid down on 2 Mar 1976 and launched in 1977. AS 41 proposed in FY 1977 programme with no additional submarine tenders planned through FY 1981.
Estimated cost of AS 41 is $260 900 000.

Gunnery: "Emory S. Land" class to be fitted with one Phalanx 20 mm CIWS.

2 "SIMON LAKE" CLASS (SUBMARINE TENDERS (AS))

Name	No.	Builders	Commissioned
*SIMON LAKE	AS 33	Puget Sound Naval Shipyard	7 Nov 1964
*CANOPUS	AS 34	Ingalls SB Co, Pascagoula	4 Nov 1965

CANOPUS   1966, USN

Displacement, tons: 19 934 full load (AS 33); 21 089 (AS 34)
Dimensions, feet (metres): 643·7 × 85 × 30 (196·2 × 25·9 × 9·1)
Guns: 4—3 inch (76 mm) 50 cal (twin) (Mk 33)
Main engines: Steam turbines (De Laval); 20 000 shp; 1 shaft = 18 knots
Boilers: 2 (Combustion Engineering)
Complement: 1 428 (90 officers, 1 338 men) (AS 33); 1 421 (95 officers, 1 326 enlisted men) (AS 34)

These ships are designed specifically to service fleet ballistic missile submarines (SSBN), with three submarines alongside being supported simultaneously.
The Simon Lake was authorised in the Fiscal Year 1963 new construction programe, laid down on 7 Jan 1963 and launched 8 Feb 1964. The Canopus was authorised in FY 1964, laid down on 2 March 1964 and launched on 12 Feb 1965. AS 35 was authorised in FY 1965 programme, but her construction was deferred 3 Dec 1964.

Conversions: Conversions to permit of Poseidon C-3 missile handling and repairing and support of related systems carried out at Puget Sound Navy yard as follows: Canopus, completed 3 Feb 1970; Simon Lake, completed 9 Mar 1971.

2 "HUNLEY" CLASS (SUBMARINE TENDERS (AS))

Name	No.	Builders	Commissioned
*HUNLEY	AS 31	Newport News SB & DD Co	16 June 1962
*HOLLAND	AS 32	Ingalls SB Co, Pascagoula	7 Sep 1963

HOLLAND   USN

Displacement, tons: 10 500 standard; 19 300 full load
Dimensions, feet (metres): 599 × 83 × 24 (182·6 × 25·3 × 7·3)
Guns: 4—20 mm (singles)
Main engines: Diesel-electric (10 Fairbanks-Morse diesels); 15 000 bhp; 1 shaft = 19 knots
Complement: 2 568 (144 officers, 2 424 enlisted men)

These are the first US submarine tenders of post-World War II construction; they are designed specifically to provide repair and supply services to fleet ballistic missile submarines (SSBN). Provided with 52 separate workshops to provide complete support. Helicopter platform fitted aft but no hangar. Both ships originally fitted with a 32-ton-capacity hammerhead crane; subsequently refitted with two amidships cranes as in "Simon Lake" class.
Hunley authorised in Fiscal Year 1960 shipbuilding programme, laid down on 28 Nov 1960 and launched on 28 Sep 1961; Holland authorised in FY 1962 programme, laid down on 5 Mar 1962 and launched on 19 Jan 1963. Former ship cost $24 359 800.

Conversions: Conversions to permit of Poseidon C-3 missile handling and repairing and support of related systems carried out at Puget Sound Navy Yard as follows: Hunley, completed 22 Jan 1974; Holland, completed 20 June 1975.

7 "FULTON" and "PROTEUS" CLASSES
(SUBMARINE TENDERS (AS))

Name	No.	Builders	Commissioned
*FULTON	AS 11	Mare Island Navy Yard	12 Sep 1941
*SPERRY	AS 12	Moore SB & DD Co, Oakland	1 May 1942
BUSHNELL	AS 15	Mare Island Navy Yard	10 April 1943
*HOWARD W. GILMORE	AS 16	Mare Island Navy Yard	24 May 1944
(ex-*Neptune*)			
NEREUS	AS 17	Mare Island Navy Yard	27 Oct 1945
*ORION	AS 18	Moore SB & DD Co, Oakland	30 Sep 1943
*PROTEUS	AS 19	Moore SB & DD Co, Oakland	31 Jan 1944

Displacement, tons: 9 734 standard; 16 430-19 200 full load
Dimensions, feet (metres): 530·5 oa except *Proteus* 574·5 oa × 73·3 × 25·5 *(161·7 Proteus 175·1 × 22·3 × 7·8)*
Guns: 2—5 inch *(127 mm)* 38 cal in AS 15 and 17; 4—20 mm (Mk 68) (single) in active ships; 2—20 mm (Mk 24) (twin) in AS 17 only
Main engines: Diesel-electric (General Motors); 11 200 bhp; 2 shafts = 15·4 knots
Complement: 1 286-1 937 except *Proteus* 1 300 (86 officers, 1 214 enlisted men)

These venerable ships are contemporaries of the similar-design "Dixie" class destroyer tenders. Launched on 27 Dec 1940, 17 Dec 1941, 14 Sep 1942, 16 Sep 1943, 12 Feb 1945, 14 Oct 1942 and 12 Nov 1942 respectively. As built, they carried the then-standard large auxiliary armament of four 5 inch guns plus 8—40 mm guns (twin). The original 20-ton capacity cylinder cranes have been replaced in the *Howard W. Gilmore*.

Conversion: *Proteus* AS 19 was converted at the Charleston Naval Shipyard, under the Fiscal Year 1959 conversion programme, at a cost of $23 000 000 to service nuclear-powered fleet ballistic missile submarines (SSBN). Conversion was begun on 19 Jan 1959 and she was recommissioned on 8 July 1960. She was lengthened by adding a 44 feet section amidships, and the bare hull weight of this 6-deck high insertion was approximately 500 tons. Three 5 inch guns were removed and her upper decks extended aft to provide additional workshops. Storage tubes for Polaris missiles installed; bridge crane amidships loads and unloads missiles for alongside submarines.

Modernisation: All except *Proteus* have undergone FRAM II modernisation to service nuclear-powered attack submarines. Additional maintenance shops provided to service nuclear plant components and advanced electronic equipment and weapons. After two 5 inch guns and eight 40 mm guns (twin) removed.

HOWARD W. GILMORE   9/1971, USN

2 "PIGEON" CLASS (SUBMARINE RESCUE SHIPS (ASR))

Name	No.	Builders	Commissioned
*PIGEON	ASR 21	Alabama DD & SB Co, Mobile	28 Apr 1973
*ORTOLAN	ASR 22	Alabama DD & SB Co, Mobile	14 July 1973

Displacement, tons: 3 411 full load
Dimensions, feet (metres): 251 oa × 86 (see *Design* notes) × 21·25 *(76·5 × 26·2 × 6·5)*
Guns: 2—20 mm (single)
Main engines: 4 diesels (Alco); 6 000 bhp; 2 shafts = 15 knots
Range, miles: 8 500 at 13 knots
Complement: 115 (6 officers, 109 enlisted men)
Staff accommodation: 14 (4 officers, 10 enlisted men)
Submersible operators: 24 (4 officers, 20 enlisted men)

These are the world's first ships designed specifically for this role, all other ASR designs being adaptations of tug types. The "Pigeon" class ships serve as (1) surface support ships for the Deep Submergence Rescue Vehicles (DSRV), (2) rescue ships employing the existing McCann rescue chamber, (3) major deep-sea diving support ships and (4) operational control ships for salvage operations. Each ASR is capable of transporting, servicing, lowering, and raising two Deep Submergence Rescue Vehicles (DSRV) (see section on Deep Submergence Vehicles). The Navy had planned in the 1960s to replace the 10-ship ASR force with new construction ASRs. However, only two ships were funded, with procurement of others deferred.
Pigeon authorised in Fiscal Year 1967 new construction programme and *Ortolan* in FY 1968 programme. *Pigeon* was laid down on 17 July 1968 and launched on 13 Aug 1969; *Ortolan* was laid down on 22 Aug 1968 and launched on 10 Sep 1969; they were delayed more than two years by a shipyard strike and technical difficulties; additional delays encountered in special equipment installation.

Design: These ships have twin, catamaran hulls, the first ocean-going catamaran ships to be built for the US Navy since Robert Fulton's steam gunboat *Demologus* of 1812. The design provides a large deck working area, facilities for raising and lowering submersibles and under-water equipment, and improved stability when operating equipment at great depths. Each of the twin hulls is 251 feet long and 26 feet wide. The well between the hulls is 34 feet across, giving the ASR a maximum beam of 86 feet. Fitted with helicopter platform and with precision three-dimensional sonar system for tracking submersibles.

Diving: These ships have been fitted with the Mk II Deep Diving System to support conventional or saturation divers operating at depths to 850 feet. The system consists of two decompression chambers, two personnel transfer capsules to transport divers between the ship and ocean floor, and the associated controls, winches, cables, gas supplies etc. Submarine rescue ships are the US Navy's primary diving ships and the only ones fitted for helium-oxygen diving.

Engineering: Space and weight are reserved for future installation of a ducted thruster in each bow to enable the ship to maintain precise position while stopped or at slow speeds. Range is 8 500 miles at 13 knots.

ORTOLAN   9/1976, Dr. Giorgio Arra

ORTOLAN   9/1976, Dr. Giorgio Arra

6 "CHANTICLEER" CLASS (SUBMARINE RESCUE SHIPS (ASR))

Name	No.	Builders	Commissioned
*COUCAL	ASR 8	Moore SB & DD Co, Oakland	23 Jan 1943
*FLORIKAN	ASR 9	Moore SB & DD Co, Oakland	5 Apr 1943
*KITTIWAKE	ASR 13	Savannah Machine & Foundry Co	18 July 1946
*PETREL	ASR 14	Savannah Machine & Foundry Co	24 Sep 1946
*SUNBIRD	ASR 15	Savannah Machine & Foundry Co	28 Jan 1947
*TRINGA	ASR 16	Savannah Machine & Foundry Co	28 Jan 1947

Displacement, tons: 1 653 standard; 2 320 full load
Dimensions, feet (metres): 240 wl; 251·5 oa × 44 × 16 *(76·7 × 13·4 × 4·9)*
Guns: 2—20 mm (single) in some ships
Main engines: Diesel-electric (Alco ARS 8 and 9 General Motors remainder); 3 000 bhp; 1 shaft = 14·9 knots
Complement: 116-221

Large tug-type ships equipped with powerful pumps, heavy air compressors, and rescue chambers for submarine salvage and rescue operations. Launched on 29 May 1942, 14 June 1942, 10 July 1945, 29 Sep 1945, 3 April 1945 and 25 June 1945 respectively.
Fitted for Helium-oxygen diving.
As built, each ship was armed with 2—3 inch guns; removed 1957-1958. Some ships subsequently fitted with two 20 mm guns.

Transfers: Former US Navy submarine rescue ships serve in the navies of Brazil and Turkey—*Tringa* to Turkey late 1977.

SUNBIRD   *9/1975, Dr. Giorgio Arra*

5 "SOTOYOMO" CLASS (AUXILIARY TUGS (ATA))

Name	No.	Builders	Commissioned
ACCOKEEK	ATA 181	Levingston SB Co, Orange, Texas	7 Oct 1944
SAMOSET	ATA 190	Levingston SB Co, Orange, Texas	1 Jan 1945
STALLION	ATA 193	Levingston SB Co, Orange, Texas	26 Feb 1945
TATNUCK	ATA 195	Levingston SB Co, Orange, Texas	1 Feb 1945
KEYWADIN	ATA 213	Gulfport Boiler & Welding Works, Port Arthur, Texas	1 June 1945

Displacement, tons: 534 standard; 860 full load
Dimensions, feet (metres): 134·5 wl; 143 oa × 33·9 × 13 *(43·6 × 10·3 × 4·0)*
Guns: 4—20 mm (twin); all guns removed from some ships
Main engines: Diesel-electric (General Motors diesels); 1 240 bhp; 1 shaft = 13 knots
Complement: 49 (7 officers, 42 enlisted men)

Steel-hulled tugs formerly designated as rescue tugs (ATR); designation changed to ATA in 1944. Launched on 27 July 1944, 26 Oct 1944, 14 Dec 1944, 24 Nov 1944 and 9 April 1945 respectively. During 1948 they were assigned names that had been carried by discarded fleet and yard tugs.
All of the surviving ships were decommissioned in 1969-1971 and placed in reserve. Two ships of this class serve in the Coast Guard.

Transfers: Ships of this class serve with Colombia, Dominican Republic, and Taiwan.

ACCOKEEK   *1970, USN*

21 "CHEROKEE" and "ABNAKI" CLASSES (FLEET TUGS (ATF))

Note: For characteristics of "Powhatan" (ATF 166) Class see Military Sealift Command Section.

Name	No.	Builders	Commissioned
*UTE	T-ATF 76	United Engineering Co, Alameda, Calif	31 Dec 1942
*CREE	ATF 84	United Engineering Co, Alameda, Calif	28 Mar 1943
*LIPAN	T-ATF 85	United Engineering Co, Alameda, Calif	29 Apr 1943
*MATACO	ATF 86	United Engineering Co, Alameda, Calif	29 May 1943
SENECA	ATF 91	Cramp SB Co, Philadelphia	30 Apr 1943
*ABNAKI	ATF 96	Charleston SB & DD Co, SC	15 Nov 1943
*CHOWANOC	ATF 100	Charleston SB & DD Co, SC	21 Feb 1944
*COCOPA	ATF 101	Charleston SB & DD Co, SC	25 Mar 1944
*HITCHITI	ATF 103	Charleston SB & DD Co, SC	27 May 1944
MOCTABI	ATF 105	Charleston SB & DD Co, SC	25 July 1944
*MOLALA	ATF 106	United Engineering Co, Alameda, Calif	29 Sep 1943
QUAPAW	ATF 110	United Engineering Co, Alameda, Calif	6 May 1944
*TAKELMA	ATF 113	United Engineering Co, Alameda, Calif	3 Aug 1944
*TAWAKONI	ATF 114	United Engineering Co, Alameda, Calif	15 Sep 1944
*ATAKAPA	T-ATF 149	Charleston SB & DD Co, SC	8 Dec 1944
*NIPMUC	ATF 157	Charleston SB & DD Co, SC	8 July 1945
*MOSOPELEA	T-ATF 158	Charleston SB & DD Co, SC	28 July 1945
PAIUTE	ATF 159	Charleston SB & DD Co, SC	27 Aug 1945
PAPAGO	ATF 160	Charleston SB & DD Co, SC	3 Oct 1945
*SALINAN	ATF 161	Charleston SB & DD Co, SC	9 Nov 1945
*SHAKORI	ATF 162	Charleston SB & DD Co, SC	20 Dec 1945

Displacement, tons: 1 235 standard; 1 640 full load
Dimensions, feet (metres): 195 wl; 205 oa × 38·5 × 15·5 *(62·5 × 11·7 × 4·7)*
Gun: 1—3 inch *(76 mm)* 50 cal (Mk 22) gun removed from MSC ships
Main engines: Diesel-electric drive; 3 000 bhp; 1 shaft = 15 knots
Complement: 75 (5 officers, 70 enlisted men) navy; 24 civilians plus 6 navy communications personnel in MSC ships.

Large ocean tugs fitted with powerful pumps and other salvage equipment. ATF 96 and later ships ("Abnaki" class) have smaller funnel. As built these ships mounted 2—40 mm guns in addition to 3 inch gun. Launched on 24 June 1942, 17 Aug 1942, 17 Sep 1942, 2 Feb 1943, 22 April 1943, 20 Aug 1943, 5 Oct 1943, 29 Jan 1944, 25 March 1944, 23 Dec 1942, 15 May 1943, 18 Sep 1943, 28 Oct 1943, 11 July 1944, 12 April 1945, 7 March 1945, 4 June 1945, 21 June 1945, 20 July 1945 and 9 August 1945 respectively.
Beginning in 1973 several fleet tugs have been assigned to the Military Sealift Command and provided with civilian crews; these ships are designated T-ATF and are unarmed. ATF 85 and ATF 158 assigned to MSC in July 1973; ATF 76, and ATF 149 to MSC in July-Aug 1974. Three ships of this class serve with the US Coast Guard.

Deletions: Following planned FY 1977/78: *Abnaki, Chowanoc, Cocopa, Cree, Matako, Molala, Tawakoni.*

Military Sealift Command: *Hitchiti* to be transferred FY 1978.

Naval Reserve: Following transferred to Naval Reserve Force:—*Moctobi*, 1 Jan 1977; *Paiute*, 1 Feb 1977; *Papago*, 1 Aug 1977; *Quapaw*, 30 Sep 1977.

Transfers: Ships of this class serve with Argentina, Chile, Dominican Republic, Peru, Turkey, Taiwan, and Venezuela.

PAIUTE   *1976, Michael D. J. Lennon*

CHOWANOC   *1/1977, Dr. Giorgio Arra*

3 "EDENTON" CLASS (SALVAGE AND RESCUE SHIPS (ATS))

Name	No.	Builders	Commissioned
*EDENTON	ATS 1	Brooke Marine, Lowestoft, England	23 Jan 1971
*BEAUFORT	ATS 2	Brooke Marine, Lowestoft, England	22 Jan 1972
*BRUNSWICK	ATS 3	Brooke Marine, Lowestoft, England	19 Dec 1972

Displacement, tons: 2 929 full load
Dimensions, feet (metres): 282·6 oa × 50 × 15·1 (86·1 × 15·2 × 4·6)
Guns: 2—20 mm Mk 68 (single)
Main engines: 4 diesels (Paxman); 6 000 bhp; 2 shafts (controllable-pitch propellers) = 16 knots
Complement: 100 (9 officers and 91 enlisted men)

These ships are designed specifically for salvage operations and are capable of (1) ocean towing, (2) supporting diver operations to depths of 850 feet, (3) lifting submerged objects weighing as much as 600 000 pounds from a depth of 120 feet by static tidal lift or 30 000 pounds by dynamic lift, (4) fighting ship fires, and (5) performing general salvage operations. Fitted with 10-ton capacity crane forward and 20-ton capacity crane aft.
The ATS 1 was authorised in the Fiscal Year 1966 shipbuilding programme; ATS 2 and ATS 3 in the FY 1967 programme. Laid down on 1 April 1967, 19 Feb 1968 and 5 June 1968 respectively; launched on 15 May 1968, 20 Dec 1968 and 14 Oct 1969. In service the British-made components have created severe supply problems with respect to obtaining spare parts.
ATS 4 was authorised in the FY 1972 new construction programme and ATS 5 in the FY 1973 programme, with several additional ships being planned. However, construction of these ships was deferred in 1973 with the smaller modification of a commercial design ATF being substituted in their place.
Classification changed from salvage tug (ATS) to salvage and rescue ship (ATS) on 16 Feb 1971.

Diving: These ships can carry the air-transportable Mk 1 Deep Diving System which can support four divers working in two-man shifts at depths to 850 feet. The system consists of a double-chamber recompression chamber and a personnel transfer capsule to transport divers between the ship and ocean floor. The ships' organic diving capability is compressed air only.

Engineering: Fitted with tunnel bow thruster for precise manoeuvring.

BEAUFORT   8/1974, USN

1 SALVAGE SHIP

— (ex-*Glomar Explorer*) AG 193

Transferred by CIA to naval control 1976. will be in inactive status at Suisun Bay.

1 CONVERTED LSMR (TEST RANGE SUPPORT SHIP (IX))

Name	No.	Builders	Commissioned
*ELK RIVER	IX 501 (ex-LSMR 501)	Brown SB Co, Houston	27 May 1945

Displacement, tons: 1 785 full load
Dimensions, feet (metres): 229·7 oa × 50 × 9·2 (70 × 15·2 × 2·8)
Main engines: Diesels; 1 400 bhp; 2 shafts = 11 knots
Complement: 25 + 20 technical personnel

Elk River is a former rocket landing ship specifically converted to support Navy deep submergence activities on the San Clemente Island Range off the coast of southern California. Launched 21 April 1945.
The ship is capable of supporting (1) deep diving for man-in-the-sea programmes, (2) deep diving for salvage programmes, (3) submersible test and evaluation, (4) underwater equipment testing, and (5) deep mooring operations. Operated by combined Navy-civilian crew.

Conversion: She was withdrawn from the Reserve Fleet and converted to a range support ship in 1967-1968 at Avondale Shipyards Inc, Westwego, Louisiana, and the San Francisco Bay Naval Shipyard.
The basic LSMR hull was lengthened and eight-foot sponsons were added to either side to increase deck working space and stability; superstructure added forward. An open centre well was provided to facilitate lowering and raising equipment; also fitted with 65-ton-capacity gantry crane (on tracks) to handle submersibles and active positioning mooring system to hold ship in precise location without elaborate mooring and permit shifting within the moor. Five anchors including bow anchor. Fitted with prototype Mk 2 Deep Diving System.

ELK RIVER   6/1976, J. L. M. van der Burg

1 CONVERTED "MARK" CLASS AKL (TORPEDO TEST SHIP (IX))

Name	No.
*NEW BEDFORD	IX 308 (ex-AKL 17, ex-FS 289)

Displacement, tons: approx 700
Dimensions, feet (metres): 176·5 oa × 32·8 × 10 (53·8 × 10·0 × 3·1)
Main engines: Diesel; 1 000 bhp; 1 shaft = 10 knots

Former Army cargo ship (freight and supply) acquired by Navy on 1 Mar 1950 for cargo work and subsequently converted to support torpedo testing. Operated since 1963 by Naval Torpedo Station, Keyport, Washington. Employed as Torpedo Test ship.

NEW BEDFORD   1973, USN

1 Ex-BUOY TENDER (INSTRUMENTATION PLATFORM (IX))

Name	No.
*BRIER	IX 307 (ex-WLI 299)

Displacement, tons: 178
Dimensions, feet (metres): 100 × 24 × 5 *(30·1 × 7·3 × 1·5)*
Machinery: Diesel with electric drive; 600 bhp; 2 shafts = 12 knots

Former Coast Guard buoy tender built in 1943; acquired by the Navy on 10 Mar 1969 for use as instrument platform for explosive testing; redesignated IX 307 on 29 Aug 1970.

BRIER (Old pennant number)   *USCG*

1 CONVERTED ARMY SUPPLY SHIP (TORPEDO TEST SHIP (IX))

*IX 306 (ex-FS 221)

Displacement, tons: 906 full load
Dimensions, feet (metres): 179 oa × 33 × 10 *(54·6 × 10·1 × 3·1)*
Main engines: Diesel; 1 shaft = 12 knots

Former Army cargo ship (freight and supply) acquired by the Navy in January 1969 and subsequently converted to a weapon test ship, being placed in service late in 1969. Conducts research for the Naval Underwater Weapons Research and Engineering Station, Newport, Rhode Island; operates in Atlantic Underwater Test and Evaluation Centre (AUTEC) range in Caribbean. Manned by Navy and civilian RCA personnel. Note white hull with blue bow and torpedo tube opening on starboard side just aft of hull number.

IX 306   *1969, USN*

IX 310

A group of barges used by Naval Underwater Sound Laboratory, Newport, Rhode Island. Placed "in service" 1 April 1971. Consists of two barges joined by a deckhouse. Based on Lake Seneca, NY.

1 UNCLASSIFIED MISCELLANEOUS: SAIL FRIGATE

Name	No.	Under Way
*CONSTITUTION	None	23 July 1798

The oldest ship remaining on the Navy List. *Constitution* is one of the six frigates authorised by act of Congress on 27 March 1794. Put to sea date indicated above is probably closer to her commissioning date than the launch date given in previous editions. Has been in full commission since October 1971, haveing been "in commission, special" prior to that date. Serves as Flagship of the First Naval District. Every year she is taken out into Boston Harbor and "turned around" so she will wear evenly on both sides of her masts. Overhauled at the former Boston Naval Shipyard from April 1973 to early 1975 at the cost of $4·2 million to "spruce her up" for the American Bicentennial. The "Unclassified Miscellaneous" classification of IX-21, assigned to her on 8 January 1941 was dropped on 1 September 1975 for some unfathomable reason. With her classification dropped, she is the only USN ship carried on the Naval Vessel Register without a classification. Since a ship in commission can not be on the Naval Register without a classification, her legal status as a naval ship is hazy.

The sailing ship *Constellation,* which survives under private ownership at Baltimore, Maryland, is apparently the last sailing man-of-war built for the US Navy; she was constructed at the Norfolk (Virginia) Navy Yard in 1853-1854, built in part with material from the earlier frigate *Constellation* (launched 1797).

DR-1 (ex-*Guardian,* ex-PT 809) transferred to Fleet Composite Support Squadron 6 at Little Creek, Virginia, in December 1974 for use as recovery boat for aerial targets and control boat surface target drone craft; designated DR-1 in July 1975. Formerly employed as guard boat for presidential yacht. She is the last motor torpedo boat in US Navy service (built in 1950).

DR-1   *9/1976, Dr.Giorgio Arra*

The **Athena** (ex-*Chehalis, PG 94)* stripped of armament and assigned as research craft to Naval Ship Research & Development Center, Annapolis, Maryland; renamed on 21 Aug 1975 (no hull numbers assigned). See "Asheville" class (PG 86) patrol combatants for characteristics and photographs. Civilian manned.

FLOATING DRY DOCKS

The US Navy operates a number of floating dry docks to supplement dry dock facilities at major naval activities, to support fleet ballistic missile submarines (SSBN) at advanced bases, and to provide repair capabilities in forward combat areas.

The larger floating dry docks are made sectional to facilitate movement overseas and to render them self docking. The ARD-type docks have the forward end of their docking well closed by a structure resembling the bow of a ship to facilitate towing. Berthing facilities, repair shops, and machinery are housed in sides of larger docks. None is self-propelled.

Seventeen floating dry docks are in Navy service (including two partial docks), 12 are out of service in reserve (including two partial docks), and 27 are on lease to commercial firms for private use. Several are on loan to other US services and foreign navies (including one partial dock). Asterisks indicate docks in active US service.

The **ARDM 4** is under construction at the Bethlehem Steel Co, Sparrows Point, Maryland. Designed specifically to service "Los Angeles" class (SSN 688) submarines.

Figures in parenthesis indicate the number of sections for sectional docks. Each section of the AFDB docks has a lifting capacity of about 10 000 tons. Four sections of the AFDB 7 form the floating dry dock *Los Alamos* at Holy Loch, Scotland, one section is used at Kwajalein atoll by the US Army in support of the anti-ballistic missile project and two sections are in reserve. (The AFDB sections each are 256 feet long, 80 feet in width, with wing walls 83 feet high; the wing walls, which contain compartments, fold down when the sections are towed).

The *White Sands* (ARD 20) was employed in support of the deep-diving bathyscaph *Trieste II* (see section on Deep Submergence Vehicles). Early in 1969 the *White Sands,* with *Trieste II* on board, was towed to the Azores to support investigation of the remains of the nuclear-powered submarine *Scorpion* (SSN 589). Reclassified as auxiliary deep submergence support vehicle (AGDS 1) on 1 Aug 1973; subsequently stricken. ARD-5 named *Waterford* 1977 and ARD-7 *West Milton* on 18 May 1976.

Transfers: The following floating dry docks are on foreign loan: ARD 23 to Argentina; AFDL 39, ARD 14 to Brazil; ARD 32 to Chile; ARD 28 to Columbia; ARD 13 to Ecuador; AFDL 11 to Khmer Republic (Cambodia); ARD 15, AFDL 28 to Mexico; ARD 6 to Pakistan; AFDL 26 to Paraguay; AFDL 33, ARD 8 to Peru; AFDL 20, AFDL 44 to Philippines; ARD 9, *Windsor* (ARD 22) to Taiwan; ARD 13 to Venezuela; AFDL 22 to South Vietnam; ARD 12 to Turkey; *Arco* (ARD 29) to Iran; ARD 25 to Chile; AFDL 24 to Philippines; ARD 11 to Mexico.

LARGE AUXILIARY FLOATING DRY DOCK (AFDB)

AFDB 1	1943	90 000 tons	Steel (10)	Reserve
AFDB 2	1944	90 000 tons	Steel (10)	Reserve
AFDB 3	1944	81 000 tons	Steel (9)	Reserve
AFDB 4	1944	55 000 tons	Steel (7)	Reserve
AFDB 5	1944	55 000 tons	Steel (7)	Reserve
AFDB 7 (partial)	1944	20 000 tons	Steel (2)	Reserve
***AFDB 7** (partial)	1945	10 000 tons	Steel (1)	US Army
***LOS ALAMOS**				
AFDB 7 (partial)	—	40 000 tons	Steel (4)	Holy Loch, Scotland

MEDIUM AUXILIARY FLOATING DRY DOCK (AFDM)

AFDM 1 (ex-YFD 3)	1942	15 000 tons	Steel (3)	Commercial lease
AFDM 2 (ex-YFD 4)	1942	15 000 tons	Steel (3)	Commercial lease
AFDM 3 (ex-YFD 6)	1943	18 000 tons	Steel (3)	Commercial lease
AFDM 5 (ex-YFD 21)	1943	18 000 tons	Steel (3)	Reserve
***AFDM 6** (ex-YFD 62)	1944	18 000 tons	Steel (3)	Subic Bay, Philippines
***AFDM 7** (ex-YFD 63)	1945	18 000 tons	Steel (3)	Norfolk, Va.
***RICHLAND AFDM 8**				
(ex-YFD 64)	1944	18 000 tons	Steel (3)	Guam, Marianas
AFDM 9 (ex-YFD 65)	1945	18 000 tons	Steel (3)	Commercial lease
AFDM 10	1945	18 000 tons	Steel (3)	Commercial lease

AFDM 6   *1/1977, Dr. Giorgio Arra*

SMALL AUXILIARY FLOATING DRY DOCKS (AFDL)

Name-No.	Completed	Capacity	Construction	Notes
***AFDL 1**	1943	1 000 tons	Steel	Guantanamo Bay, Cuba
AFDL 2	1943	1 000 tons	Steel	Commercial lease
***AFDL 6**	1944	1 000 tons	Steel	Little Creek, Virginia
***AFDL 7**	1944	1 900 tons	Steel	Subic Bay, Philippines
AFDL 8	1943	1 000 tons	Steel	Commercial lease
AFDL 9	1943	1 000 tons	Steel	Commercial lease
AFDL 10	1943	1 000 tons	Steel	Reserve
AFDL 12	1943	1 000 tons	Steel	Commercial lease
AFDL 15	1943	1 000 tons	Steel	Commercial lease
AFDL 16	1943	1 000 tons	Steel	Commercial lease
AFDL 19	1944	1 000 tons	Steel	Commercial lease
AFDL 21	1944	1 000 tons	Steel	Commercial lease
***AFDL 23**	1944	1 900 tons	Steel	Subic Bay, Philippines
AFDL 25	1944	1 000 tons	Steel	Reserve
AFDL 29	1943	1 000 tons	Steel	Commercial lease
AFDL 30	1944	1 000 tons	Steel	Commercial lease
AFDL 35	1944	2 800 tons	Concrete	Commercial lease
AFDL 37	1944	2 800 tons	Concrete	Commercial lease
AFDL 38	1944	2 800 tons	Concrete	Commercial lease
AFDL 40	1944	2 800 tons	Concrete	Commercial lease
AFDL 41	1944	2 800 tons	Concrete	Commercial lease
AFDL 43	1944	2 800 tons	Concrete	Commercial lease
AFDL 45	1944	2 800 tons	Concrete	Commercial lease
AFDL 47	1946	6 500 tons	Steel	Commercial lease
***AFDL 48**	1956	4 000 tons	Concrete	Long Beach Nav Shipyard

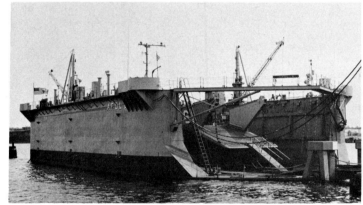

AFDL 6   *9/1976, Dr. Giorgio Arra*

AUXILIARY REPAIR DRY DOCKS and MEDIUM AUXILIARY REPAIR DRY DOCKS (ARD/ARDM)

***WATEFORD** (ARD 5)	1942	3 000 tons	Steel	New London, Connecticut
***WEST MILTON** (ARD 7)	1943	3 000 tons	Steel	New London, Connecticut
ARDM 3 (ex-ARD 18)	1944	3 000 tons	Steel	Reserve
ARDM 4	1978		Steel	Under construction
***OAK RIDGE**				
ARDM 1 (ex-ARD 19)	1944	3 000 tons	Steel	Rota, Spain
ARD 24	1944	3 000 tons	Steel	Reserve
***ALAMAGORDO**				
ARDM 2 (ex-ARD 26)	1944	3 000 tons	Steel	Charleston, South Carolina
***SAN ONOFRE** (ARD 30)	1944	3 000 tons	Steel	Pearl Harbor Nav Shipyard

SAN ONOFRE (ARD 30)   *6/1970, USN*

YARD FLOATING DRY DOCKS (YFD)

YFD 7	1943	18 000 tons	Steel (3)	Commercial lease
YFD 8	1942	20 000 tons	Wood	Commercial lease
YFD 9	1942	16 000 tons	Wood	Commercial lease
YFD 23	1943	10 500 tons	Wood	Commercial lease
YFD 54	1943	5 000 tons	Wood	Commercial lease
YFD 68	1945	14 000 tons	Steel (3)	Commercial lease
YFD 69	1945	14 000 tons	Steel (3)	Commercial lease
YFD 70	1945	14 000 tons	Steel (3)	Commercial lease
***YFD 71**	1945	14 000 tons	Steel (3)	San Diego Naval Base
***YFD 83**				
(ex-AFDL 31)	1943	1 000 tons	Steel	US Coast Guard

SERVICE CRAFT

As of 1 February 1977, the US Navy has 1 130 service craft, primarily small craft, on the US Naval Vessel Register. A majority of them provide services to the fleet in various harbors and ports. Others are ocean going ships such as *Elk River* that provide services to the fleet in the research area. Only the self propelled craft and relics are listed here. The non-self propelled craft, such as floating cranes, dredges are not included. Most of the service craft are rated as "Active, in Service", but a few are rated as "in commission". As of 1 February 1977, 990 are active, 133 are in reserve and 7 are under construction.

1 CONVERTED "YW 83" CLASS (MOBILE LISTENING BARGE (YAG))

MONOB I YAG 61 (ex-IX 309, ex-YW 87)

Displacement, tons: 440 light; 1 390 full load
Dimensions, feet (metres): 174 oa × 33 *(57 × 10·8)*
Main engine: 1 diesel = 7 knots

The *Monob I* is a mobile listening barge converted from a self-propelled water barge. Built in 1943 and completed conversion for acoustic research in May 1969, being placed in service in May 1969. Conducts research for the Naval Ship Research and Development Centre; based at Port Everglades, Florida.
Designation changed from IX 301 to YAG 61 on 1 July 1970.

MONOB I *1969, USN*

2 DIVING TENDERS (YDT)

Tenders used to support shallow-water diving operations. Two self-propelled diving tenders are on the Navy List: *Phoebus* YDT 14 ex-YF 294, and *Suitland* YDT 15 ex-YF 336. (Two non-self-propelled YDTs are in service).

4 COVERED LIGHTERS (YF)

Lighters used to transport materiel in harbours; self-propelled; four are on the Navy List: *Lynnhaven* (YF 328), (YF 862), *Keyport* (YF 885), and *Kodiak* (YF 886).

6 FERRYBOATS (YFB)

Ferryboats used to transport personnel and vehicles in large harbours; self-propelled; YFB 83 and 87-91; all are active. The YFB 88-91 are the former LCU 1636, 1638-1640, all reclassified on 1 Sep 1969. The *Aquidneck* (YFB 14) transferred to State of Washington on 23 Dec 1975.

YFB 88 (ex-LCU 1636) *USN*

1 REFRIGERATED COVERED LIGHTER (YFR)

Lighters used to store and transport food and other materials which require refrigeration. The *YFR 888* remains on the Navy List in reserve.

5 COVERED LIGHTERS (RANGE TENDER (YFRT))

Lighters used for miscellaneous purposes; YFRT 287, 451, 520, and 523 active; YFRT 418 is in reserve. Note Mk 32 torpedo tubes on YFRT 520.
Range Recoverer YFRT 524 (ex-T-AGM 2, ex-T-AG 161, ex-US Army FS 278) stricken on 15 May 1974.

YFRT 520 *1969, USN*

11 HARBOUR UTILITY CRAFT (YFU)

YFU 71	YFU 74	YFU 76	YFU 79	YFU 81
YFU 72	YFU 75	YFU 77	YFU 80	YFU 82
				YFU 83

Dimensions, feet (metres): 125 oa × 36 × 7·5 *(40·9 × 11·8 × 2·4)*
Main engines: Diesels = 8 knots
Guns: 2—50 cal MG

Militarised versions of a commercial lighter design and a single craft *(YFU 83)* built to LCU 1646 design and of similar characteristics. Used for off-loading large ships in harbours and ferrying cargo from one coastal port to another. Built by Pacific Coast Engineering Co, Alameda, California; completed 1967-1968. Can carry more than 300 tons cargo; considerable cruising range.
YFU 71-77 and *YFU 80-82* loaned to US Army in 1970 for use in South Vietnam; returned to Navy control in 1973.

YFU 75 *1968, USN*

Transfer: *YFU 73* transferred to Khmer Republic (Cambodia) on 15 Nov 1973.

11 HARBOUR UTILITY CRAFT (YFU): LCU TYPE

YFU 44 (ex-LCU 1398)	**YFU 91** (ex-LCU 1608)	**YFU 100** (ex-LCU 1610)
YFU 50 (ex-LCU 1486)	**YFU 93** (ex-LCU 1625)	**YFU 101** (ex-LCU 1612)
YFU 55 (ex-LCU 637)	**YFU 97** (ex-LCU 1611)	**YFU 102** (ex-LCU 1462)
YFU 89 (ex-LCU 1576)	**YFU 98** (ex-LCU 1615)	

Former utility landing craft employed primarily as harbour and coastal cargo craft (see section on Landing Craft for basic characteristics). The *YFU 44* has an open centre well for lowering research equipment into the water; assigned to the Naval Undersea Research and Development Centre in Long Beach, California.
Several YFUs were loaned to the US Army in 1970 for use in Vietnam after withdrawal of US Navy riverine and coastal forces.

Classifications: YFU 1-70 and 84-102 were former utility landing craft. Several reverted to LCU designations and three were modified for salvage work: YFU 2, 16, and 33 to YLLC 5, 2, and 3, respectively.

24 FUEL OIL BARGES (YO)

Small liquid fuel carriers intended to fuel ships where no pierside fuelling facilities are available; self-propelled; 24 are on the Navy List. Two named units, *Casing Head* (YO 47) and *Crownlock* (YO 48), are in reserve.

10 GASOLINE BARGES (YOG)

Similar to the fuel barges (YO), but carry gasoline and aviation fuels; self-propelled; 10 are on the Navy List. Named unit *Lieut. Thomas W. Fowler* (YOG 107) stricken on 1 May 1975.

21 SEAMANSHIP TRAINING CRAFT (YP)

YP 587	YP 654	YP 658	YP 662	YP 666	YP 670
YP 591	YP 655	YP 659	YP 663	YP 667	YP 671
	YP 656	YP 660	YP 664	YP 668	YP 672
	YP 657	YP 661	YP 665	YP 669	

YP 584 series:

Displacement, tons: 50
Dimensions, feet (metres): 75 oa × 16 × 4·5 *(24·6 × 5·2 × 1·5)*
Main engines: 2 diesels (Superior); 400 bhp; 2 shafts = 12 knots

YP 654 series:

Displacement, tons: 69·5 full load
Dimensions, feet (metres): 80·4 oa × 18·75 × 5·3 *(26·4 × 6·1 × 1·7)*
Main engines: 4 diesels (General Motors); 660 bhp; 2 shafts = 13·5 knots

YP 669   *1971, Peterson Builders*

These craft are used for instruction in seamanship and navigation at the Naval Academy, Annapolis, Maryland; Naval Officer Candidate School, Newport, Rhode Island; and Surface Warfare Officers School at Newport. Fitted with surface search radar, Fathometer, gyro compass, and UHF and MF radio; the *YP 655* additionally fitted for instruction in oceanographic research at the Naval Academy.
YPs numbered below 654 are older craft of a once-numerous type employed for training and utility work. *YP 654-663* built by Stephens Bros, Inc, Stockton, California; completed in 1958; *YP 664* and *665* built by Elizabeth City Shipbuilders, Inc, Elizabeth City, North Carolina; *YP 666* and *667* built by Stephens Bros; *YP 668* built by Peterson Boatbuilding Co, Tacoma, Washington, completed in 1968; *YP 669-672* built by Peterson completed in 1971-1972.
These craft are of wooden construction with aluminium deck houses.

21 SMALL HARBOUR TUGS (YTL)

Eleven of these craft are on the Navy List; unnamed. Six are active and three in reserve and twelve on loan to private organisations.

72 MEDIUM HARBOUR TUGS (YTM)

HOGA (YTM-146)	**WINGINA** (YTM-395)	**NADLI** (YTM-534)
TOKA (YTM-149)	**YANEGUA** (YTM-397)	**NAHOKE** (YTM-536)
KONOKA (YTM-151)	**NATAHKI** (YTM-398)	**CHEGODEGA** (YTM-542)
JUNALUSKA (YTM-176)	**NUMA** (YTM-399)	**ETAWINA** (YTM-543)
DEKAURY (YTM-178)	**OTOKOMI** (YTM-400)	**YATANOCAS** (YTM-544)
MADOKAWANDO (YTM-180)	**PANAMETA** (YTM-402)	**ACCOHANOC** (YTM-545)
NEPANET (YTM-189)	**PITAMAKAN** (YTM-403)	**TAKOS** (YTM-546)
SASSACUS (YTM-193)	**COSHECTON** (YTM-404)	**YANABA** (YTM-547)
DEKANISORA (YTM-252)	**CUSSETA** (YTM-405)	**MATUNAK** (YTM-548)
HIAWATHA (YTM-265)	**KITTATON** (YTM-406)	**MIGADAN** (YTM-549)
RED CLOUD (YTM-268)	**MINNISKA** (YTM-408)	**ACOMA** (YTM-701)
PAWTUCKET (YTM-359)	**ANAMOSA** (YTM-409)	**ARAWAK** (YTM-702)
SASSABA (YTM-364)	**POROBAGO** (YTM-413)	**MORATOC** (YTM-704)
WAUBANSEE (YTM-366)	**SECOTA** (YTM-415)	**MANKTAO** (YTM-734)
SMOHALLA (YTM-371)	**TACONNET** (YTM-417)	**YUMA** (YTM-748)
CHEPANOC (YTM-381)	**UNNAMED** (YTM-496)	**HACKENSACK** (YTM-750)
COATOPA (YTM-382)	**MAHOA** (YTM-519)	**MASCOUTAH** (YTM-760)
COCHALI (YTM-383)	**NABIGWON** (YTM-521)	**MENASHA** (YTM-761)
WANNALANCET (YTM-385)	**SAGAWAMICK** (YTM-522)	**APOHOLA** (YTM-768)
GANADOGA (YTM-390)	**SENASQUA** (YTM-523)	**MIMAC** (YTM-770)
ITARA (YTM-391)	**TUTAHACO** (YTM-524)	**CHILKAT** (YTM-773)
MECOSTA (YTM-392)	**WAHAKA** (YTM-526)	**HIAMONEE** (YTM-776)
NAKARNA (YTM-393)	**WAHPETON** (YTM-527)	**LELAKA** (YTM-777)
WINAMAC (YTM-394)	**OCMULGEE** (YTM-532)	**POCASSET** (YTM-779)

ETAWINA (YTM 543)   *1975, Dr. Giorgio Arra*

Former YTBs renumbered YTMs in the mid-1960s. Some are former Army Tugboats. About half are in reserve and half active. One unit, *YTM-759* was reclassified *IX-505* on 1 November 1976.

81 LARGE HARBOUR TUGS (YTB)

EDENSHAW	YTB 752	TAMAQUA	YTB 797
MARIN	YTB 753	OPELIKA	YTB 789
PONTIAC	YTB 756	NATCHITOCHES	YTB 799
OSHKOSH	YTB 757	EUFAULA	YTB 800
PADUCAH	YTB 758	PALATKA	YTB 801
BOGALUSA	YTB 759	CHERAW	YTB 802
NATICK	YTB 760	NANTICOKE	YTB 803
OTTUMWA	YTB 761	AHOSKIE	YTB 804
TUSCUMBIA	YTB 762	OCALA	YTB 805
MUSKEGON	YTB 763	TUSKEGEE	YTB 806
MISHAWAKA	YTB 764	MASSAPEQUA	YTB 807
OKMULGEE	YTB 765	WENATCHEE	YTB 808
WAPAKONETA	YTB 766	AGAWAN	YTB 809
APALACHICOLA	YTB 767	ANOKA	YTB 810
ARCATA	YTB 768	HOUMA	YTB 811
CHESANING	YTB 769	ACCONAC	YTB 812
DAHLONEGA	YTB 770	POUGHKEEPSIE	YTB 813
KEOKUK	YTB 771	WAXAHATCHIE	YTB 814
NASHUA	YTB 774	NEODESHA	YTB 815
WAUWATOSA	YTB 775	CAMPTI	YTB 816
WEEHAWKEN	YTB 776	HAYANNIS	YTB 817
NOGALES	YTB 777	MECOSTA	YTB 818
APOPKA	YTB 778	IUKA	YTB 819
MANHATTAN	YTB 779	WANAMASSA	YTB 820
SAUGUS	YTB 780	TONTOGANY	YTB 821
NIANTIC	YTB 781	PAWHUSKA	YTB 822
MANISTEE	YTB 782	CANONCHET	YTB 823
REDWING	YTB 783	SANTAQUIN	YTB 824
KALISPELL	YTB 784	WATHENA	YTB 825
WINNEMUCCA	YTB 785	WASHTUCNA	YTB 826
TONKAWA	YTB 786	CHETEK	YTB 827
KITTANNING	YTB 787	CATAHECASSA	YTB 828
WAPATO	YTB 788	METACOM	YTB 829
TOMAHAWK	YTB 789	PUSHMATHA	YTB 830
MENOMINEE	YTB 790	DEKANAWIDA	YTB 831
MARINETTE	YTB 791	PETALESHARO	YTB 832
ANTIGO	YTB 792	SHABONEE	YTB 833
PIQUA	YTB 793	NEWGAGON	YTB 834
MANDAN	YTB 794	SKENANDOA	YTB 835
KETCHIKAN	YTB 795	POKAGON	YTB 836
SACO	YTB 796		

WATHENA   9/1976, Dr. Giorgio Arra

Displacement, tons: 350 full load
Dimensions, feet (metres): 109 oa × 30 × 13·8 (35·7 × 9·8 × 4·5)
Machinery: 2 diesels; 2 000 bhp; 2 shafts
Complement: 10 to 12 (enlisted)

Large harbour tugs; 81 are in active service. YTB 752 completed in 1959, YTB 753 in 1960, YTB 756-762 in 1961, YTB 763-766 in 1963, YTB 770 and YTB 771 in 1964, YTB 767-769, 776 in 1965, YTB 774, 775, 777-789 in 1966, YTB 790-793 in 1967, YTB 794 and 795 in 1968, YTB 796-803 in 1969, and YTB 804-815 completed in 1970-1972, YTB 816-827 completed 1972-1973, YTB 828-836 completed 1974-1975. YTB 837 and YTB 838 transferred upon completion in late 1975 to Saudi Arabia.

15 WATER BARGES (YW)

Barges modified to carry water to ships in harbour; self-propelled; 15 of these craft are on the Navy List with most·being in reserve.

TORPEDO WEAPONS RETRIEVERS (TWR)

Displacement, tons: 97·4 light; 152 full load
Dimensions, feet (metres): 102 oa × 21 × 7·75 (33·4 × 6·9 × 2·5)
Main engines: 4 diesels; 2 shafts = 18 knots
Range, miles: 1 900 at 10 knots
Complement: 15 (enlisted)

These are the largest of several types of torpedo recovery craft operated by the Navy. They are fitted to recover torpedoes and perform limited torpedo maintenance during exercises. An internal stern ramp facilitates recovery and up to 17 tons of torpedoes can be carried. These large TWRs also perform harbour utility duties. Range is 1 900 miles at 10 knots. Some are numbered—one is given the distinguished Royal Naval name of "Diamond".

TWR   9/1975, Dr. Giorgio Arra

MILITARY SEALIFT COMMAND

(See also under Experimental, Research and Survey Ships)

Sealift ships provide ocean transportation for all components of the Department of Defense. These ships are operated by the Navy's Military Sealift Command (MSC), renamed on 1 Aug 1970 from Military Sea Transportation Service (MSTS). Sealift cargo ships and tankers are not configured to provide underway replenishment (UNREP) of other ships, or land stores over the beach in amphibious landings. Four MSC-operated cargo ships are fitted to carry Submarine-Launched Ballistic Missiles (SLBM) and other supplies for US Polaris/Poseidon submarines.

Most US defence cargo is carried in commercial merchant ships under charter to the government (through the Military Sealift Command).

The Commander, Deputy Commander, and Area Commanders of the MSC (Atlantic, Pacific, and Far East) are flag officers of the Navy on active duty. All ships are civilian manned with most of their crews being Civil Service employees of the Navy. However, the tankers are operated under contract to commercial tanker lines and are manned by merchant seamen.

In addition to the ships listed in this section, the Military Sealift Command also operates a number of underway replenishment (UNREP) ships, fleet support ships, and special projects ships that support other defence-related activities, mostly research, surveying and missile-range support ships (see Experimental,

Research and Surveying Ships listing). Other special projects ships are the cable ships listed in the section on Fleet Support Ships.

Armament: No ship of the Military Sealift Command is armed.

Classification: Military Sealift Command ships are assigned standard US Navy hull designations with the added designation prefix "T". Ships in this category are referred to as "USNS" (United States Naval Ship) *vice* "USS" (United States Ship) which is used for Navy-manned ships.

1 "SCHUYLER OTIS BLAND" CLASS (CARGO SHIP (AK))

Name	No.
SCHUYLER OTIS BLAND	T-AK 277

Displacement, tons: 15 910 full load
Dimensions, feet (metres): 478 oa × 66 × 30 *(145·7 × 20·1 × 9·1)*
Main engines: Geared turbine; 13 750 shp; 1 shaft = 18·5 knots
Boilers: 2

Acquired from the Maritime Administration by the Military Sea Transportation Service in July 1961. The only ship of the type (C3-S-DX1), built in 1961; prototype of the "Mariner" cargo ship design. Laid up in "ready reserve" as of 1 Jan 1977.

SCHUYLER OTIS BLAND   USN

1 "PRIVATE LEONARD C. BROSTROM" CLASS (CARGO SHIP (AK))

Name	No.
*PVT. LEONARD C. BROSTROM (ex-*Marine Eagle*)	T-AK 255

Displacement, tons: 13 865 deadweight
Dimensions, feet (metres): 520 oa × 71·5 × 33 *(158·5 × 21·8 × 10·1)*
Main engines: Geared turbine; 9 000 shp; 1 shaft = 15·8 knots
Boilers: 2
Complement: 57 (14 officers, 43 men)

She is fitted with 150-ton capacity booms, providing the most powerful lift capability of any US ship. C4-S-B1 type built in 1943. Taken over by Military Sealift Command in Aug 1950.

PVT LEONARD C. BROSTROM   USN

1 "ELTANIN" CLASS (CARGO SHIP (AK))

Name	No.	Builders
*MIRFAK	T-AK 271	Avondale Marine Ways, New Orleans

Displacement, tons: 2 036 light; 4 942 full load
Dimensions, feet (metres): 256·8 wl; 262·2 oa × 51·5 × 18·7 *(79·9 × 15·7 × 5·7)*
Main engines: Diesel-electric (ALCO diesels with Westinghouse electric motors); 3 200 bhp; 2 shafts = 13 knots
Complement: 48

Built for Military Sea Transportation Service, Louisiana. Designed for Arctic operation with hull strengthened against ice. C1-M E2-13a type. Launched on 5 Aug 1957. Note icebreaking prow in photo.

Conversion: Two other ships of this class converted for oceanographic research: *Eltanin*, reclassified from T-AK 270 to T-AGOR 8 on 15 Nov 1962 loaned to Argentina as *Islas Orcadas; Mizar* T-AK 272 was reclassified T-AGOR 11 on 15 Apr 1964 (see AGORs "Eltanin" Class).

MIRFAK   USN

4 "NORWALK" CLASS (CARGO SHIPS (AK))

Name	No.
*NORWALK (ex-Norwalk Victory)	T-AK 279
*FURMAN (ex-Furman Victory)	T-AK 280
*VICTORIA (ex-Ethiopia Victory)	T-AK 281
*MARSHFIELD (ex-Marshfield Victory)	T-AK 282

Displacement, tons: 6 700 light; 11 150 full load
Dimensions, feet (metres): 455·25 oa × 62 × 24 (138·8 × 18·9 × 7·3)
Main engines: Geared turbine; 8 500 shp; 1 shaft = 17 knots
Boilers: 2
Complement: 80 to 90 plus Navy detachment

MARSHFIELD   1970, USN

Former merchant ships of the VC2-S-AP3 "Victory" type built during World War II. Extensively converted to supply tenders for Fleet Ballistic Missile (FBM) submarines. Fitted to carry torpedoes, spare parts, packaged petroleum products, bottled gas, black oil and diesel fuel, frozen and dry provisions, and general cargo as well as missiles. No 3 hold converted to carry 16 Polaris missiles in vertical position; tankage provided for 355 000 gallons (US) of diesel oil and 430 000 gallons (US) of fuel oil (for submarine tenders). All subsequently modified to carry Poseidon missiles. All four ships are operated by the Military Sealift Command with civilian operating crews; a small Navy detachment in each ship provides security and technical services.

Conversion: Norwalk converted to FBM cargo ship by Boland Machine & Manufacturing Co, and accepted for service on 30 Dec 1963; Furman converted by American Shipbuilding Co, and accepted on 7 Oct 1964; Victoria converted by Philadelphia Naval Shipyard, and accepted on 15 Oct 1965; and Marshfield converted by Boland Machine & Manufacturing Co, and accepted on 28 May 1970.

5 "GREENVILLE VICTORY" CLASS (CARGO SHIPS (AK))

Name	No.
GREENVILLE VICTORY	T-AK 237
PVT. JOHN R. TOWLE (ex-Appleton Victory)	T-AK 240
SGT. ANDREW MILLER (ex-Radcliffe Victory)	T-AK 242
SGT. TRUMAN KIMBRO	T-AK 254
LT. JAMES E. ROBINSON (ex-T-AG 170, ex-T-AK 274, ex-AKV 3, ex-Czechoslovakia Victory)	T-AK 274

Displacement, tons: 6 700 light; 12 450 full load
Dimensions, feet (metres): 455·5 oa × 62 × 28·5 (138·9 × 18·9 × 8·9)
Main engines: Geared turbine; 8 500 shp; 1 shaft = 17 knots except T-AK 254 15 knots
Boilers: 2

Former merchant ships of the "Victory" type built during World War II. All near sisters. VC2-S-AP3 type capable of 17 knots except T-AK 254 is VC2-S-AP2 type capable of 15 knots. "Victory" type cargo ships configured as Fleet Ballistic Missile (FBM) cargo ships are listed separately.

GREENVILLE VICTORY   USN

Classification: The former Military Sea Transportation Service aircraft cargo and ferry ships Lt. James E. Robinson AKV 3 reclassified as cargo ship on 7 May 1959. Kingsport Victory T-AK 239, was renamed and reclassified Kingsport T-AG 164 in 1962 (see Experimental, Research and Surveying ships).
Lt. James E. Robinson T-AK 274, was to have been transferred to the Maritime Administration, but was modified for special project work and reclassified as T-AG 170 in 1963, and reverted to the original classification T-AK 274 on 1 July 1964. Transferred to Maritime Administration for lay-up at James River. Ship remains on Navy List.
Sgt. Truman Kimbro, Sgt. Andrew Miller and Greenville Victory transferred to Maritime Administration on 6 Mar and 23 Mar 1976 for lay-up at Suisun Bay and James River (last two). Remain on Navy List.

PVT. JOHN R. TOWLE in Antarctic   1961, USN

1 "WYANDOT" CLASS (CARGO SHIP (AK))

Name	No.	Builders	Commissioned
WYANDOT	T-AK 283 (ex-T-AKA 92)	Moore DD Co, Oakland	30 Sep 1944

Displacement, tons: 7 430 light; 14 000 full load
Dimensions, feet (metres): 435 wl; 459·2 oa × 63 × 24 (140·0 × 19·2 × 7·3)
Main engines: Geared turbines (General Electric); 6 000 shp; 1 shaft = 16·5 knots
Boilers: 2 (Combustion Engineering)

Former attack cargo ship (AKA) of the "Andromeda" class; C2-S-B1 type. Launched on 28 June 1944; commissioned as AKA 92. Designation changed to T-AK 283 on 1 Jan 1969. Winterised for arctic service.
On 5 Mar 1976 was transferred to Maritime Administration for lay-up in the fleet at Suisun Bay. Remains on Navy List.

1 "ADMIRAL WM. M. CALLAGHAN" CLASS (VEHICLE CARGO SHIP (AKR))

Name	No.	Builders
ADMIRAL WM. M. CALLAGHAN	—	Sun SB & DD Co, Chester, Pennsylvania

Displacement, tons: 24 500 full load
Dimensions, feet (metres): 694 oa × 92 × 29 (211·5 × 28·0 × 8·8)
Main engines: 2 gas turbines (General Electric); 50 000 shp; 2 shafts = 26 knots
Complement: 33

Roll-on/roll-off vehicle cargo ship built specifically for long-term charter to the Military Sealift Command. Launched on 17 Oct 1967. Internal parking decks and ramps for carrying some 750 vehicles on 167 537 sq ft of parking area; unloading via four side ramps and stern ramp, she can off load and reload full vehicle capacity in 27 hours.

Engineering: She was the first Navy-sponsored all gas-turbine ship; fitted with two GE LM 2500 engines, similar to those of the "Spruance" class destroyers (DD 963) and "Oliver Hazard Perry" class frigates (FFG 7).

ADM. WM. M. CALLAGHAN   USN

1 "COMET" CLASS (VEHICLE CARGO SHIP (AKR))

Name	No.	Builders	Commissioned
*COMET	T-AKR 7 (ex-*T-LSV 7*, ex-*T-AK 269*)	Sun SB & DD Co	27 Jan 1958

Displacement, tons: 7 605 light; 18 150 full load
Dimensions, feet (metres): 465 oa; 499 oa × 78 × 28·8 *(152·1 × 23·8 × 8·8)*
Main engines: Geared turbines (General Electric); 13 200 shp; 2 shafts = 18 knots
Boilers: 2 (Babcock & Wilcox)
Complement: 73

Roll-on/roll-off vehicle carrier built for Military Sea Transportation Service C3-ST-14A type. Laid down on 15 May 1956. Launched on 31 July 1957. Maritime Administration Design includes ramp system for loading and discharging. The hull is strengthened against ice. Can accommodate 700 vehicles in two after holds; the forward holds are for general cargo. Equipped with Denny-Brown stabilisers. Reclassified from T-AK to T-LSV on 1 June 1963, and changed to T-AKR on 1 Jan 1969.

COMET   USN

1 "METEOR" CLASS (VEHICLE CARGO SHIP (AKR))

Name	No.	Builders
*METEOR (ex-*Sea Lift*)	T-AKR 9 (ex-*LSV 9*)	Puget Sound Bridge & DD Co

Displacement, tons: 11 130 light; 16 940 standard; 21 700 full load
Dimensions, feet (metres): 540 oa × 83 × 29 *(164·7 × 25·5 × 8·8)*
Main engines: Geared turbines; 19 400 shp; 2 shafts = 20 knots
Boilers: 2
Complement: 62
Passengers 12

Maritime Administration C4-ST-67a type. Roll-on/roll-off vehicle cargo ship. Cost of $15 895 500. Authorised under the Fiscal Year 1963 programme. Laid down on 19 May 1964 and launched on 18 April 1965. Delivered to Military Sea Transportation Service on 25 April 1967. Designed for point-to-point sea transportation of Department of Defense self-propelled, fully loaded, wheeled, tracked and amphibious vehicles and general cargo. Internal ramps, stern ramp and side openings provide for quick loading and unloading. Designation changed from T-LSV to T-AKR on 1 Jan 1969. Originally authorised as AK-278).

Name: Originally named *Sea Lift*. Renamed *Meteor* on 12 Sep 1975 to avoid confusion with "Sealift" class tankers.

METEOR   1966, Lockheed Shipbuilding

5 "MISPILLION" CLASS
("JUMBOISED" T3-S2-A3 TYPE OILERS (AO))

Name	No.	Launched	Commissioned
*MISPILLION	T-AO 105	10 Aug 1945	29 Dec 1945
*NAVASOTA	T-AO 106	30 Aug 1945	27 Feb 1946
*PASSUMPSIC	T-AO 107	31 Oct 1945	1 April 1946
*PAWCATUCK	T-AO 108	19 Feb 1945	10 May 1946
*WACCAMAW	T-AO 109	30 Mar 1946	25 June 1946

Displacement, tons: 11 000 light; 34 179 full load (33 750 in T-AO 106 and 109)
Dimensions, feet (metres): 646 oa × 75 × 35·5 *(196·9 × 22·9 × 10·8)*
Guns: Removed
Main engines: Geared turbines (Westinghouse); 13 500 shp; 2 shafts = 16 knots
Boilers: 4 (Babcock & Wilcox)
Complement: 290 (16 officers, 274 men) when Navy manned

All built by Sun Shipbuilding & Dry Dock Co, Chester, Pennsylvania. Originally T3-S2-A3 oilers; converted during mid-1960s under "jumbo" programme. Enlarged midsections added to increase cargo capacity to approximately 150 000 barrels. Helicopter platform fitted forward. As "jumboised" these ships had four 3 inch single gun mounts; removed in MSC service.
The *Passumpsic* was assigned to the Military Sealift Command on 24 July 1973 and provided with a civilian crew; subsequently the other ships were assigned to MSC—*Pawcatuck* on 13 Aug 1975.
Appearance: Two funnels in the *Passumpsic*.

NAVASOTA   2/1977, Dr. Giorgio Arra

1 "AMERICAN EXPLORER" CLASS (TANKER (AO))

Name	No.	Builders	Commissioned
*AMERICAN EXPLORER	T-AO 165	Ingalls SB Co, Pascagoula	27 Oct 1959

Displacement, tons: 22 525 deadweight
Dimensions, feet (metres): 615 oa × 80 × 32 *(187·5 × 24·4 × 9·8)*
Main engines: Steam turbines; 22 000 shp; 1 shaft = 20 knots
Complement: 53

T5-S-RM2A type. Laid down on 9 July 1957; launched on 11 Apr 1958. Built for the Maritime Administration, but acquired by Military Sea Transportation Service. Cargo capacity 190 300 barrels.
Operated for Military Sealift Command by commercial firm.

AMERICAN EXPLORER   USN

4 "FALCON" CLASS (TANKERS (AO))

Name	No.	Builders
*COLUMBIA (ex-*Falcon Lady*)	T-AO 182	Ingalls SB Co, Pascagoula
*NECHES (ex-*Falcon Duchess*)	T-AO 183	Ingalls SB Co, Pascagoula
*HUDSON (ex-*Falcon Princess*)	T-AO 184	Ingalls SB Co, Pascagoula
*SUSQUEHANNA (ex-*Falcon Countess*)	T-AO 185	Ingalls SB Co, Pascagoula

Displacement, tons: 37 276 deadweight
Dimensions, feet (metres): 672 oa × 89 × 36 *(204·8 × 27·1 × 11·0)*
Main engines: Geared turbine; 1 shaft = 16·5 knots
Boilers: 2

Former merchant tankers under charter to the Military Sealift Command. *Columbia* and *Neches* built in 1971; *Hudson* and *Susquehanna* in 1972. All four acquired on bareboat charter on 3 May 1974 (182 and 183), 10 Apr 1974 (184) and 17 Apr 1974 (185). Acquired by USN for MSC service on 15 Jan 1976 (182), 11 Feb 1976 (183), 23 Apr 1976 (184) and 11 May 1976 (185). Operated under contract by Mount Shipping Co Ltd. Cargo capacity 310 000 barrels. Civilian manned.

HUDSON (as *Falcon Princess*)

3 "MAUMEE" CLASS (TANKERS (AO))

Name	No.	Builders	Commissioned	
*MAUMEE	T-AO 149	Ingalls SB Co, Pascagoula	Dec	1956
*SHOSHONE	T-AO 151	Sun SB & DD Co, Chester	Apr	1957
*YUKON	T-AO 152	Ingalls SB Co, Pascagoula	May	1957

Displacement, tons: 25 000 deadweight
Dimensions, feet (metres): 591 wl; 620 oa × 83·5 × 32 *(189·0 × 25·5 × 9·8)*
Main engines: Geared turbine; 20 460 shp; 1 shaft = 18 knots
Complement: 62

Yukon laid down 16 May 1955, launched 16 March 1956; *Maumee* laid down 8 Mar 1955, launched 16 Feb 1956; *Shoshone* laid down 15 Aug 1955, launched 17 Jan 1957, T5-S-12A type. *Potomac* T-AO 150 sank after explosion in 1961, but was rebuilt in 1963-1964; see previous listing for *Potomac* (T-AO 181). Cargo capacity 203 216 barrels.
Maumee provided with ice-strengthened bow during 1969-1970 modification at Norfolk SB & DD Co; employed in transporting petroleum products to Antarctica in support of US scientific endeavours.
These ships are operated for the Military Sealift Command by commercial firms.

YUKON

1/1976, Michael D. J. Lennon

4 "SUAMICO" CLASS (TANKERS (AO))

Name	No.	Builders	Commissioned	
TALLULAH (ex-*Valley Forge*)	T-AO 50	Sun SB & DD Co, Chester	5 Sep	1942
MILLICOMA (ex-*Conastoga*, ex-*King's Mountain*)	T-AO 73	Sun SB & DD Co, Chester	5 Mar	1943
SAUGATUCK (ex-*Newton*)	T-AO 75	Sun SB & DD Co, Chester	19 Feb	1943
SCHUYLKILL (ex-*Louisburg*)	T-AO 76	Sun SB & DD Co, Chester	9 April	1943

Displacement, tons: 5 730 light; 22 380 full load
Dimensions, feet (metres): 503 wl; 523·5 oa × 68 × approx 30 *(159·6 × 20·7 × 9·2)*
Main engines: Turbo-electric drive; 6 000 shp; 1 shaft = 15 knots
Boilers: 2 (Babcock & Wilcox)

T2-SE-A1 tankers begun as merchant ships but acquired by Navy and completed as fleet oilers. During the post World War II period, all of these ships were employed in the tanker role, carrying petroleum point-to-point. Launched on 25 June 1942, 21 Jan 1943, 7 Dec 1942, 16 Feb 1943 respectively.
Cargo capacity approximately 134 000 barrels.
Transferred to Maritime Administration for lay-up at James River—T-AO 50, 29 May 1975; T-AO 73, 16 July 1975; T-AO 75, 5 Nov 1974; T-AO 76, 8 Sep 1975. All remain on Navy List—replaced by "Pacific" class AOs.

SCHUYLKILL

USN

1 "POTOMAC" CLASS (TANKER (AO))

Name	No.
*POTOMAC (ex-*Shenandoah*)	T-AO 181

Displacement, tons: 27 467 deadweight
Dimensions, feet (metres): 620 oa × 83·5 × 34 *(189·0 × 25·5 × 10·4)*
Main engines: Geared turbine; 20 460 shp; 1 shaft = 18 knots
Boilers: 2

The merchant tanker *Shenandoah* was built from the stern of the naval tanker *Potomac* (T-AO 150) destroyed by fire on 26 Sep 1961, and new bow and mid-body sections. After being chartered by the Military Sealift Command since 14 Dec 1964 the ship was formally acquired on 12 Jan 1976, assigned the name *Potomac* and placed in MSC service. Cargo capacity 200 000 barrels. Civilian manned.

9 "SEALIFT" CLASS (TANKERS (AO))

Name	No.	Builders	Commissioned
*SEALIFT PACIFIC	T-AO 168	Todd Shipyards	14 Aug 1974
*SEALIFT ARABIAN SEA	T-AO 169	Todd Shipyards	6 May 1975
*SEALIFT CHINA SEA	T-AO 170	Todd Shipyards	9 May 1975
*SEALIFT INDIAN OCEAN	T-AO 171	Todd Shipyards	29 Aug 1975
*SEALIFT ATLANTIC	T-AO 172	Bath Iron Works	26 Aug 1974
*SEALIFT MEDITERRANEAN	T-AO 173	Bath Iron Works	6 Nov 1974
*SEALIFT CARIBBEAN	T-AO 174	Bath Iron Works	10 Feb 1975
*SEALIFT ARCTIC	T-AO 175	Bath Iron Works	22 May 1975
*SEALIFT ANTARCTIC	T-AO 176	Bath Iron Works	1 Aug 1975

Displacement, tons: approx 27 000 deadweight
Dimensions, feet (metres): 587 oa × 84 × 34·4 *(178·9 × 25·6 × 10·5)*
Main engines: 2 Turbo-charged diesels; 14 000 bhp; 1 shaft (controllable-pitch propeller) = 16 knots
Complement: 30 + 2 Maritime Academy cadets

Built specially for long term-charter by the Military Sealift Command. T-AO 168 launched in 1973 on 13 Oct; other launched in 1974 on 26 Jan, 20 April, 27 July, 26 Jan, 9 March, 8 June, 31 Aug and 26 Oct respectively. Operated for MSC by commercial firms with civilian crews.
Fitted with bow thruster to assist docking; automated engine room. Approximately 25 000 tons deadweight; cargo capacity 220 000 barrels. Estimated cost $146 500 000 for the nine-ship class.

SEALIFT ANTARCTIC   1975, USN

3 "PECONIC" CLASS (GASOLINE TANKERS (AOG))

Name	No.	Builders
*RINCON (ex-*Tarland*)	T-AOG 77	Todd Shipyards, Houston
*NODAWAY (ex-*Belridge*)	T-AOG 78	Todd Shipyards, Houston
*PETALUMA (ex-*Raccoon Bend*)	T-AOG 79	Todd Shipyards, Houston

Displacement, tons: 2 060 light; 6 000 full load
Dimensions, feet (metres): 325·2 oa × 48·2 × 19·1 *(99·1 × 14·7 × 5·8)*
Main engines: Diesel; 1 400 bhp; 1 shaft = 10 knots

T1-M-BT2 gasoline tankers. Launched as merchant tankers on 5 Jan 1945, 15 May 1945 and 9 Aug 1945 respectively. All acquired by Navy 1 July 1950 (77) and 7 Sep 1950 (78 and 79) and assigned to Military Sea Transportation Service and employed in point-to-point carrying of petroleum. Cargo capacity approximately 30 000 barrels.
These are the only survivors in US service of a once large number of small gasoline tankers. Several survive in foreign navies.

RINCON   USN

2 "AEOLUS" CLASS (CABLE REPAIR SHIPS (ARC))

Name	No.	Builders	Commissioned
*AEOLUS (ex-*Turandot*)	T-ARC 3 (ex-AKA 47)	Walsh-Kaiser Co, Providence, RI	18 June 1945
THOR (ex-*Vanadis*)	T-ARC 4 (ex-AKA 49)	Walsh-Kaiser Co, Providence, RI	9 July 1945

Displacement, tons: 7 080 full load
Dimensions, feet (metres): 400 wl; 438 oa × 58·2 × 19·25 *(133·5 × 17·7 × 5·9)*
Guns: None
Main engines: Turbo-electric (Westinghouse); 6 600 shp; 2 shafts = 16·9 knots
Boilers: 2 (Wickes)
Complement: 221 (23 officers, 198 enlisted men)

Built as S4-SE2-BE1 attack cargo ships. Transferred to Maritime Administration and laid up in reserve from 1946 until reacquired by Navy for conversion to cable repair ships in 1955-1956 at the Key Highway Plant of Bethlehem Steel Corp, Baltimore, Maryland, being recommissioned on 14 May 1955 and 3 Jan 1956, respectively. Fitted with cable-laying bow sheaves, cable stowage tanks, cable repair facilities, and helicopter platform aft.
Both ships have been employed in hydrographic and cable operations. They were both Navy manned until 1973 when transferred to Military Sealift Command and provided with civilian crews. *Aeolus* is again operational; *Thor* laid up in reserve on 17 July 1975 at Maritime Administration, Suisun Bay.

AEOLUS   USN

2 "NEPTUNE" CLASS (CABLE SHIPS (ARC))

Name	No.	Builders	Commissioned
*NEPTUNE (ex-*William H. G. Bullard*)	T-ARC 2	Pusey & Jones Corp, Wilmington, Del	1 June 1953
*ALBERT J. MEYER	T-ARC 6	Pusey & Jones Corp, Wilmington, Del	13 May 1963

Displacement, tons: 7 080 full load
Dimensions, feet (metres): 322 wl; 370 oa × 47 × 18 *(112·8 × 14·3 × 5·5)*
Guns: Removed
Main engines: Reciprocating (Skinner); 4 800 ihp; 2 shafts = 14 knots
Boilers: 2 (Combustion Engineering)

Built as S3-S2-BP1 type cable ships for Maritime Administration.
Neptune acquired by Navy from Maritime Administration in 1953 and sister ship *Albert J. Meyer* from US Army in 1966, latter ship for operation by Military Sea Transportation Service (now Military Sealift Command). They have been fitted with electric cable handling machinery (in place of steam equipment) and precision navigation equipment; helicopter platform in *Neptune*.
Both ships are operated by the Military Sealift Command with civilian crews; *Neptune* was Navy-manned until 8 Nov 1973 when transferred to MSC.
The USNS *Neptune* (T-ARC 2) should not be confused with the commercial cable ship *Neptun* of the United States Undersea Cable Corp.

NEPTUNE   1975, Dr. Giorgio Arra

4+ 7 "POWHATTON" CLASS (FLEET TUGS (ATF))

Name	No	Builders	Commission
POWHATTON	T-ATF-166	Marinette Marine Corp, Wisconsin	mid-1978
NARRAGANSETT	T-ATF-167	Marinette Marine Corp, Wisconsin	mid-1979
CATAWBA	T-ATF-168	Marinette Marine Corp, Wisconsin	mid-1979
NAVAJO	T-ATF-169	Marinette Marine Corp, Wisconsin	late-1979
Five ships	**T-ATF**	Proposed Fiscal Year 1978 programme	
Two ships	**T-ATF**	Planned Fiscal Year 1979 programme	

Displacement, tons: 2 400 full load
Dimensions, feet (metres): 240 × 48 × 17 *(73·2 × 14·6 × 5·2)*
Guns: See notes
Main engines: 2 Diesels (General Motors); 4 500 bhp; 2 shafts (controllable-pitch propellers) = 15 knots
Complement: 47 (43 civilians, 4 Navy communications ratings)

This is a new class of fleet tugs built to commercial standards successors to "Cherokee" class. The ships will be operated by the Military Sealift Command and manned by civilian crews. Space provided to fit 2—20 mm (single) and 2—·50 cal MG if required. A 300 hp bow thruster will be provided: 10 ton capacity crane.
Estimated cost of the lead ship is $11 500 000; an average of $15 000 000 for the FY 1976 ships and $16 000 000 for FY 1978 ships.

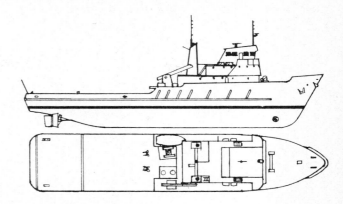

EXPERIMENTAL RESEARCH AND SURVEY SHIPS

2 CONVERTED "ABILITY" CLASS (SONAR RESEARCH SHIPS (AG))

Name	No.	Builders	Commissioned
*ALACRITY	AG 520 (ex-MSO 520)	Peterson Builders Inc, Wisconsin	1 Oct 1958
*ASSURANCE	AG 521 (ex-MSO 521)	Peterson Builders Inc, Wisconsin	21 Nov 1958

Displacement, tons: 810 light; 960 full load
Dimensions, feet (metres): 190 oa × 36 × 12 *(58·0 × 11·0 × 3·7)*
Guns: Removed
Main engines: 2 diesels (General Motors); 2 700 bhp; 2 shafts (controllable pitch propellers) = 15 knots

Former ocean minesweepers. Launched on 8 June 1957 and 31 Aug 1957. Wood-hulled with non-magnetic engines and fittings. Both ships modified for sonar test activities and redesignated as miscellaneous auxiliaries (AG) on 1 June 1973 and 1 Mar 1973, respectively. Fitted with Towed Acoustic Surveillance System (TASS).

ASSURANCE   USN

1 "VICTORY" CLASS (HYDROGRAPHIC RESEARCH SHIP (AG))

Name	No.	Builders
*KINGSPORT (ex-*Kingsport Victory*)	T-AG 164	California SB Corp

Displacement, tons: 7 190 light; 10 680 full load
Dimensions, feet (metres): 455 oa × 62 × 22 *(138·7 × 18·9 × 6·7)*
Main engines: Geared turbines; 8 500 shp; 1 shaft = 15·2 knots
Boilers: 2
Complement: 73 (13 officers, 42 men, 15 technicians)

Maritime Administration type VC2-S-AP3. Employed as cargo ship by Military Sea Transportation Service prior to conversion. Name shortened, ship reclassified and converted in 1961-62 by Willamette Iron & Steel Co, Portland, Oregon, into the world's first satellite communications ship, for Project Advent, involving the promotion of a terminal to meet the required military capability for high capacity, world-wide radio communications using high altitude hovering satellites, and the installation of ship-to-shore communications facilities, additional electric power generating equipment, a helicopter landing platform, aerological facilities, and a 30-foot parabolic communication antenna housed in a 53-ft diameter plastic radome abaft the superstructure. Painted white for operations in the tropics. Protect Advent Syncom satellite relay operations were completed in 1966, and *Kingsport* was reassigned to hydrographic research. Antenna sphere now removed.
Note antenna mast on helicopter platform in photograph; exhaust ducts fitted to funnel.
Operated by Military Sealift Command for Naval Electronic Systems Command; civilian manned.

KINGSPORT   1/1976, Michael D. J. Lennon

1 "MARINER" CLASS (NAVIGATION TRIALS SHIP (AG))

Name	No.	Builders	Commissioned
*COMPASS ISLAND (ex-*Garden Mariner*)	AG 153 (ex-YAG 56)	New York SB Corp, NJ	3 Dec 1956

Displacement, tons: 17 600 full load
Dimensions, feet (metres): 529·5 wl; 563 oa × 76 × 29 *(171·6 × 23·2 × 8·8)*
Main engines: Geared turbines (General Electric); 19 250 shp; 1 shaft = 20 knots
Boilers: 2 (Foster Wheeler)
Complement: 250 (18 officers, 232 enlisted men)

Originally a "Mariner" class merchant ship (C4-S-1A type). Launched on 24 Oct 1953 and acquired by the Navy on 29 Mar 1956.
Converted by New York Naval Shipyard for the development of the Fleet Ballistic Missile guidance and ship navigation systems. Her mission is to assist in the development and valuation of a navigation system independent of shore-based aids. Navy manned.

COMPASS ISLAND   USN

1 "MARINER" CLASS (FBM TEST SHIP (AG))

Name	No.	Builders	Commissioned
OBSERVATION ISLAND	AG 154 (ex-YAG 57)	New York SB Corp, N.J.	5 Dec 1958
(ex-*Empire State Mariner*)			

Displacement, tons: 16 076 full load
Dimensions, feet (metres): 529·5 wl; 563 oa × 76 × 29 *(171·6 × 23·2 × 8·8)*
Main engines: Geared turbines (General Electric); 19 250 shp; 1 shaft = 20 knots
Boilers: 2 (Foster Wheeler)
Complement: 428 (35 officers, 393 enlisted men)

Built as a "Mariner" class merchant ship (C4-S-1A type); launched on 15 Aug 1953; acquired by the Navy on 10 Sep 1956 for use as a Fleet Ballistic Missile (FBM) test ship. Converted at Norfolk Naval Shipyard.
Fitted to test fire Polaris and later Poseidon missiles. Navy manned. Decommissioned on 29 Sep 1972 and placed in Maritime Administration reserve; remains in Navy List.
There are plans to reactivate her as Range Instrumentation Ship (AGM) in which case she will operate as USNS will hull number T-AGM 23.

Missile Testing: The ship is fitted with complete missile testing, servicing and firing systems. She fired the first ship-launched Polaris missile at sea on 27 Aug 1959. Refitted to fire the improved Poseidon missile in 1969 and launched the first Poseidon test missile fired afloat on 16 Dec 1969.

OBSERVATION ISLAND *1971, USN*

1 "PLAINVIEW" CLASS (HYDROFOIL RESEARCH SHIP (AGEH))

Name	No.	Builders	In service
*****PLAINVIEW**	AGEH 1	Lockheed SB & Cons Co, Seattle	1 May 1969

Displacement, tons: 309 full load
Dimensions, feet (metres): 220 oa × 40·5 × 10 (hull borne) or 26 (with foils down) *(67·1 × 12·3 × 3·0 or 7·9)*
A/S weapons: 2 triple torpedo tubes (Mk 32)
Main engines: 2 gas turbines (General Electric Mod J-79); 30 000 hp; 2 diesels (Detroit); 1 200 shp = 50 knots
Complement: 20 (4 officers, 16 men)

Aluminium hull experimental hydrofoil. Three retractable foils, 25 ft in height, each weighing 7 tons, fitted port and starboard and on stern, and used in waves up to 15 feet. Initial maximum speed of about 50 knots, with later modifications designed to raise the speed to 80 knots. Fitted with the largest titanium propellers made. Power plant and transmission designed to permit future investigation of various types of foils. Laid down on 8 May 1964, launched on 28 June 1965. Delayed because of engineering difficulties. In service *vice* being in commission.

PLAINVIEW *1972, USN*

1 CONVERTED "HASKELL" CLASS (MISSILE RANGE INSTRUMENTATION SHIP (AGM))

Name	No.	Builders	Commissioned
*****RANGE SENTINEL**	T-AGM 22	Permanente Metals Corp,	20 Sep 1944
(ex-*Sherburne*)	(ex-*APA 205*)	Richmond, Calif	

Displacement, tons: 11 860 full load
Dimensions, feet (metres): 455 oa × 62 *(138·7 × 18·9)*
Main engines: Turbine (Westinghouse); 8 500 hp; 1 shaft = 17·7 knots
Boilers: 2 (Combustion Engineering)
Complement: 95 (14 officers, 54 men, 27 technical personnel)

Former attack transport (APA) converted specifically to serve as a range instrumentation ship in support of the Poseidon Fleet Ballistic Missile (FBM) programme. Maritime Administration VC2-S-AP5 type. Renamed *Range Sentinel* on 26 April 1971.
Stricken from the Navy List on 1 Oct 1958 and transferred to Maritime Administration reserve fleet; reacquired by the Navy on 22 Oct 1969 for AGM conversion.
Converted from Oct 1969 to Oct 1971; placed in service as T-AGM 22 on 14 Oct 1971. Operated by Military Sealift Command and civilian manned.

RANGE SENTINEL *1973, USN*

2 "CONVERTED" MISSION CLASS (RANGE INSTRUMENTATION SHIPS (AGM))

Name	No.	Builders	Commissioned
*****VANGUARD** (ex-*Muscel Shoals*,	T-AGM 19	Marine Ship Corp,	1944
ex-*Mission San Fernando*)	(ex-*T-AO 122*)	Sausalito, Calif	
*****REDSTONE** (ex-*Johnstown*,	T-AGM 20	Marine Ship Corp,	1944
ex-*Mission de Pala*)	(ex-*T-AO 114*)	Sausalito, Calif	

Displacement, tons: 21 626 full load
Dimensions, feet (metres): 595 oa × 75 × 25 *(181·4 × 22·9 × 7·6)*
Main engines: Turbo-electric; 10 000 shp; 1 shaft = 16 knots
Boilers: 2 (Babcock & Wilcox)
Complement: *Vanguard* 19 officers, 71 enlisted men, 108 technical personnel; *Redstone* 20 officers, 71 enlisted men, 120 technical personnel

Former "Mission" class tankers converted in 1964-1966 to serve as mid-ocean communications and tracking ships in support of the Apollo manned lunar flights. Maritime Administration T2-SE-A2 type.
Converted to range instrumentation ships by General Dynamics Corp, Quincy Division, Massachusetts; each ship was cut in half and a 72-foot mid-section was inserted, increasing length, beam, and displacement; approximately 450 tons of electronic equipment installed for support of lunar flight operations, including communications and tracking systems; balloon hangar and platform fitted aft. Cost of converting the three ships was $90 000 000. Operated by Military Sealift Command for Air Force Eastern Test Range in Atlantic *(Vanguard)* and for NASA Goddard Space Flight Center *(Redstone)*. Civilian crews.
Note different bow structure configurations and deck houses.

REDSTONE *1970, United States Air Force*

VANGUARD *1967, USN*

2 CONVERTED C4-S-A1 TYPE (MISSILE RANGE INSTRUMENTATION SHIPS (AGM))

Name	No.	Builders	Commissioned
*GENERAL H. H. ARNOLD	T-AGM 9	Kaiser Co, Richmond	17 Aug 1944
(ex-USNS *General R. E. Callan*)	(ex-T-AP 139)	California	
*GENERAL HOYT S. VANDENBERG	T-AGM 10	Kaiser Co, Richmond	1 Apr 1944
(ex-USNS *General Harry Taylor*)	(ex-T-AP 145)	California	

Displacement, tons: 16 600 full load
Dimensions, feet (metres): 552·9 oa × 71·5 × 26·3 *(168·5 × 21·8 × 8·0)*
Main engines: Geared turbines (Westinghouse); 9 000 shp; 1 shaft = 16·5 knots
Boilers: 2 (Babcock & Wilcox)
Complement: 205 (21 officers, 71 men, 113 technical personnel)

Former troop transports converted in 1962-1963 for monitoring Air Force missiles firing and satellite launches. Maritime Administration C4-S-A1 type. Upon conversion to range instrumentation ships they were placed in service in 1963 under Air Force operation, however assigned to MSTS for operation on 1 July 1964 *(Arnold)* and 13 July 1964 *(Vandenberg)*.
Both ships are operated by Military Sealift Command for Air Force Eastern Test Range in Atlantic. Civilian manned.

GEN. HOYT S. VANDENBERG   *USN*

1 "VICTORY" CLASS (MISSILE RANGE INSTRUMENTATION SHIP (AGM))

Name	No.	Builders	Commissioned
WHEELING (ex-*Seton Hall Victory*)	T-AGM 8	Oregon SB Corp, Portland	1944

Displacement, tons: 10 680 full load
Dimensions, feet (metres): 455·3 oa × 62·2 *(138·8 × 19·0)*
Main engines: Geared turbines; 8 500 shp; 1 shaft = 17 knots
Boilers: 2
Complement: 107 (13 officers, 46 men, 48 technical personnel)

The *Wheeling* is the only survivor of six "Victory" type military cargo and merchant ships converted to missile range instrumentation ships during the massive US space and military missile programmes of the 1960s. Maritime Administration VC2-S-AP3 type. Assigned to Military Sea Transportation Service on 28 May 1964; operated in support of Pacific Missile Range. Fitted with helicopter hangar and platform aft. Employed to test AWG-9 fire control system for use in the F-14 Tomcat fighter aircraft. Civilian manned. In ready reserve.

WHEELING   *USN*

2 "GYRE" CLASS (OCEANOGRAPHIC RESEARCH SHIPS (AGOR))

Name	No.	Builders	Commissioned
*GYRE	AGOR 21	Halter Marine Service, New Orleans	14 Nov 1973
*MOANA WAVE	AGOR 22	Halter Marine Service, New Orleans	16 Jan 1974

Displacement, tons: 950 full load
Dimensions, feet (metres): 176 oa × 36 × 14·5 *(53·6 × 11·0 × 4·4)*
Main engines: Turbo-charged diesels (Caterpillar); 1 700 bhp; 2 shafts (controllable pitch propellers) = 13 knots maximum; 12 knots cruising
Complement: 21 (10 crew, 11 scientists)

Laid down on 9 Oct 1972 and 10 Oct 1972 respectively; launched on 25 May 1973 and 18 June 1973. They are based on a commercial ship design. Fitted with a 150 hp retractable propeller pod for low-speed or station keeping with main machinery shut down. Open deck aft provides space for equipment vans to permit rapid change of mission capabilities. Each ship cost approximately $1 900 000.
The Navy plans to construct several of these small, utility oceanographic research ships to replace older and obsolescent ships now operated by civilian research and educational institutions in support of Navy programmes. The above ships are assigned for operation to Texas A & M University and the University of Hawaii, respectively.

GYRE   *1973, Halter Marine Services*

1 "HAYES" CLASS (OCEANOGRAPHIC RESEARCH SHIP (AGOR))

Name	No.	Builders	Commissioned
*HAYES	T-AGOR 16	Todd Shipyards, Seattle	21 July 1971

Displacement, tons: 3 080 full load
Dimensions, feet (metres): 220 wl; 246·5 oa × 75 (see *Design* notes) × 18·8 *(75·1 × 22·9 × 5·7)*
Main engines: Geared diesels; 5 400 bhp; 2 shafts (controllable pitch propeller) = 15 knots
Range, miles: 6 000 at 13·5 knots
Complement: 74 (11 officers, 33 men, 30 scientists)

The *Hayes* is one of two classes of modern US naval ships to have a catamaran hull, the other being the ASR 21 class submarine rescue ships. Laid down 12 Nov 1969; launched 2 July 1970. Estimated cost was $15 900 000.
Operated by the Military Sealift Command for the Office of Naval Research under the Technical control of the Oceanographer of the Navy; civilian crew.

Design: Catamaran hull design provides large deck working area, centre well for operating equipment at great depths, and removes laboratory areas from main propulsion machinery. Each hull is 246·5 feet long and 24 feet wide (maximum). There are three 36-inch diameter instrument wells in addition to the main centre well.

Engineering: An auxiliary 165-bhp diesel is fitted in each hull to provide "creeping" speed of 2 to 4 knots. Separation of controllable pitch propellers by catamaran hull separation provides high degree of manoeuvrability eliminating the need for bow thrusters.

HAYES   *1971, Todd Shipyards Corp*

2 "MELVILLE" CLASS (OCEANOGRAPHIC RESEARCH SHIPS (AGOR))

Name	No.	Builders	Commissioned
*MELVILLE	AGOR 14	Defoe SB Co, Bay City, Mich	27 Aug 1969
*KNORR	AGOR 15	Defoe SB Co, Bay City, Mich	14 Jan 1970

Displacement, tons: 1 915 standard; 2 080 full load
Dimensions, feet (metres): 244·9 × 46·3 × 15 *(74·7 × 14·1 × 4·6)*
Main engines: Diesel; 2 500 bhp; 2 cycloidal propellers = 12·5 knots
Range, miles: 10 000 at 12 knots
Complement: 50 (9 officers, 16 men, 25 scientists)

Oceanographic research ships of an advanced design. AGOR 19 and AGOR 20 of this type in FY 1968 programme, but construction of the latter ships was cancelled. These ships are fitted with internal wells for lowering equipment; underwater lights and observation ports. Facilities for handling small research submersibles.
The *Melville* and *Knorr* laid down on 12 July 1967 and 9 Aug 1967 respectively; launched 10 July 1968 and 21 Aug 1968. *Melville* operated by Scripps Institution of Oceanography and *Knorr* by Woods Hole Oceanography Institution for the Office of Naval Research; under technical control of the Oceanographer of the Navy.

Engineering: First US Navy ocean-going ships with cycloidal propellers permitting the ships to turn 360 degrees in their own length. One propeller is fitted at each end of the ship, providing movement in any direction and optimum station keeping without use of thrusters. They have experienced engineering difficulties.

MELVILLE

1969, Defoe Shipbuilding

7 "ROBERT D. CONRAD" CLASS (OCEANOGRAPHIC RESEARCH SHIPS (AGOR))

Name	No.	Builders	Commissioned
*ROBERT D. CONRAD	AGOR 3	Gibbs Corp, Jacksonville	29 Nov 1962
*JAMES M. GILLISS	T-AGOR 4	Christy Corp, Sturgeon Bay	5 Nov 1962
*LYNCH	T-AGOR 7	Marinette Mfg Co, Point Pleasant	27 Mar 1965
*THOMAS G. THOMPSON	AGOR 9	Marinette Marine Corp, Wisc	24 Aug 1965
*THOMAS WASHINGTON	AGOR 10	Marinette Marine Corp, Wisc	27 Sep 1965
*DE STEIGUER	T-AGOR 12	Northwest Marine Iron Works, Portland, Oregon	28 Feb 1969
*BARTLETT	T-AGOR 13	Northwest Marine Iron Works, Portland, Oregon	31 Mar 1969

Displacement, tons: varies; approx 1 200 standard; 1 380 full load
Dimensions, feet (metres): 191·5 wl; 208·9 oa × 37·4 × 15·3 *(63·7 × 11·4 × 4·7)*
Main engines: Diesel-electric (Caterpillar Tractor Co diesels); 10 000 bhp; 1 shaft = 13·5 knots
Range, miles: 12 000 at 12 knots
Complement: 41 (9 officers, 17 men, 15 scientists except *De Steigeur* and *Bartlett,* 8 officers, 18 men)

This is the first class of ships designed and built by the US Navy for oceanographic research. Fitted with instrumentation and laboratories to measure the earth's gravity and magnetic fields, water temperature, sound transmission in water, and the profile of the ocean floor. Special features include 10 ton capacity boom and winches for handling over-the-side equipment; bow thruster propulsion unit for precise manoeuvrability and station keeping; 620 hp gas turbine (housed in funnel structure) for providing "quiet" power when conducting operations in which use of main engines would generate too high a noise level (gas turbine also can drive the ship at 6·5 knots).
Robert D. Conrad laid down on 19 Jan 1961 and launched on 26 May 1962. Operated by Lamont Geological Observatory of Columbia University under technical control of the Oceanographer of the Navy; civilian crew.
James H. Gilliss laid down on 31 May 1961 and launched on 19 May 1962. Operated by the University of Miami (Florida) since 1970 in support of Navy programmes
Lynch laid down on 7 Sep 1962 and launched on 17 Mar 1964. Operated by Military Sealift Command under the technical control of the Oceanographer of the Navy; civilian crew.
Thomas G. Thompson laid down on 12 Sep 1963 and launched on 18 July 1964. Operated by University of Washington (state) under technical control of the Oceanographer of the Navy; civilian crew.
Thomas Washington laid down on 12 Sep 1963 and launched on 1 Aug 1964. Operated by Scripps Institution of Oceanography (University of California) under technical control of the Oceanographer on the Navy; civilian crew.
De Steiguer and *Bartlett* laid down on 12 Nov 1965 and 18 Nov 1965 and launched on 21 Mar 1966 and 24 May 1966. Operated by Military Sealift Command under the technical control of the Oceanographer of the Navy; civilian crew.

Transfers: Ships of this class are in service with Brazil *(Sands)* and New Zealand *(Charles H. Davies).*

JAMES M. GILLISS

USN

LYNCH

1974, Dr. Giorgio Arra

1 "CHAIN" CLASS (OCEANOGRAPHIC RESEARCH SHIP (AGOR))

Name	No.	Builders	Commissioned
*CHAIN	AGOR 17 (ex-ARS 20)	Basalt Rock Co, Napa	31 Mar 1944

Displacement, tons: 2 100 full load
Dimensions, feet (metres): 207 wl; 213·5 oa × 39 × 15 *(65·1 × 11·9 × 4·6)*
Main engines: Diesel-electric (4 Cooper Bessemer diesels); approx 3 000 bhp; 2 shafts = 14 knots
Complement: 29 + 26 scientists

Converted from a salvage ship for oceanographic research. Launched on 3 June 1943. Commission date as ARS. Converted to an oceanographic research ship by Savannah Machine & Foundry in 1958. Fitted with an auxiliary 250 hp outboard propulsion unit for manoeuvering at low speeds (up to 4·5 knots). The *Chain* is operated by the Woods Hole Oceanographic Institution for the Office of Naval Research under the technical control of the Oceanographer of the Navy. Civilian crew.

1 "ELTANIN" CLASS (OCEANOGRAPHIC RESEARCH SHIP (AGOR))

Name	No.	Builders	Commissioned
*MIZAR	T-AGOR 11 (ex-T-AK 272)	Avondale Marine Ways, New Orleans	22 Nov 1957

Displacement, tons: 2 036 light; 4 942 full load
Dimensions, feet (metres): 256·8 wl; 262·2 oa × 51·5 × 22·8 *(79·9 × 15·7 × 7·0)*
Main engines: Diesel-electric (ALCO diesels, Westinghouse electric motors) 3 200 bhp; 2 shafts = 12 knots
Complement: 56 (11 officers, 30 enlisted men, 15 scientists)

Built for Military Sea Transportation Service. Designed for Arctic operation with hull strengthened against ice. C1-ME2-13a type. Delivered as cargo ship to MSTS and subsequently converted to oceanographic research ship.
As research ship the *Mizar* is operated by the Military Sealift Command for Naval Research Laboratory, under technical control of the Oceanographer of the Navy; civilian crew. Transferred to technical control of Naval Electronics Command on 1 July 1975.

Conversion: *Mizar* converted in 1962 into deep sea research ship. Equipped with centre well for lowering oceanographic equipment including towed sensor platforms, fitted with laboratories and elaborate photographic facilities, hydrophone system and computer for seafloor navigation and tracking towed vehicles. *Mizar* had key roles in the searches for the US nuclear submarines *Thresher* and *Scorpion;* the French submarine *Eurydice;* and recovery of the H-bomb lost at sea off Palomares, Spain.

MIZAR

1973, Wright & Logan

OCEANOGRAPHIC RESEARCH CRAFT

The Navy also owns a number of smaller oceanographic research craft that are operated by various educational and research institutions in support of Navy programmes; under technical control of the Oceanographer of the Navy; no Navy hull numbers are assigned; all are 100 feet in length or smaller except for *Lamb,* a converted 136-foot minesweeper (YMS/AMS type) operated by the Lamont Geophysical Laboratory.

(12) OCEAN SURVEILLANCE SHIPS (AGOS)

Three ships	**T-AGOS**	Planned FY 1979 programme
Five ships	**T-AGOS**	Planned FY 1980 programme
Four ships	**T-AGOS**	Planned FY 1981 programme

The Navy plans to construct 12 ocean surveillance ships to operate the new SURTASS (Surface Towed Array Surveillance System). These ships will have a hull design similar to the fleet tugs (T-ATF) now under construction, but will be specially configured for the ocean surveillance mission. They will be operated by the Military Sealift Command, apparently with civilian crews and Navy personnel to operate the classified SURTASS equipment.

1 CONVERTED MERCHANT TYPE (SURVEYING SHIP (AGS))

Name	No.	Builders
*H. H. HESS (ex-*Canada Mail*)	T-AGS 38	National Steel & SB Co.

Displacement, tons: 14 747 deadweight
Dimensions, feet (metres): 564 oa × 76 × 32·7 *(171·9 × 23·2 × 10·0)*
Main engines: Geared turbines; 19 250 shp; 1 shaft = 20 knots
Boilers: 2

Merchant ship acquired by the Navy 9 July 1975 for conversion to replace the "Victory" class surveying ship *Michelson* (T-AGS 23). Above data as merchant ship. As a hydrographic survey ship she will be operated by the Military Sealift Command Pacific Fleet for the Oceanographer of the Navy with a civilian crew from 1 Mar 1977.

H. H. HESS (as *Canada Mail*)

2 "CHAUVENET" CLASS (SURVEYING SHIPS (AGS))

Name	No.	Builders	Delivered	
*CHAUVENET	T-AGS 29	Upper Clyde Shipbuilders, Glasgow	13 Nov	1970
*HARKNESS	T-AGS 32	Upper Clyde Shipbuilders, Glasgow	29 Jan	1971

Displacement, tons: 4 200 full load
Dimensions, feet (metres): 393·2 oa × 54 × 16 *(119·8 × 16·5 × 4·9)*
Main engines: Diesel (Westinghouse); 3 600 bhp; 1 shaft = 15 knots
Complement: 175 (13 officers, approx 150 men and technical personnel, 12 scientists)

Capable of extensive military hydrographic and oceanographic surveys, supporting coastal surveying craft, amphibious survey teams and helicopters. Fitted with two helicopter hangars and platform.
Chauvenet authorised in Fiscal Year 1965 new construction programme; *Harkness* in FY 1966 programme. Laid down on 24 May 1967 and 30 June 1967 respectively; launched on 13 May 1968 and 12 June 1968
These ships are operated by the Military Sealift Command for the Oceanographer of the Navy with Navy detachments on board. Civilian crews.

CHAUVENET   *1971, USN*

4 "SILAS BENT" and "WILKES" CLASSES (SURVEYING SHIPS (AGS))

Name	No.	Builders	Delivered	
*SILAS BENT	T-AGS 26	American SB Co, Lorain	23 July	1965
*KANE	T-AGS 27	Christy Corp, Sturgeon Bay	19 May	1967
WILKES	T-AGS 33	Defoe SB Co, Bay City, Mich	28 June	1971
*WYMAN	T-AGS 34	Defoe SB Co, Bay City, Mich	3 Nov	1971

Displacement, tons: 1 935 standard; *Silas Bent* and *Kane* 2 558 full load; *Wilkes* 2 540 full load; *Wyman* 2 420 full load
Dimensions, feet (metres): 285·3 oa × 48 × 15·1 *(87·0 × 14·6 × 4·6)*
Main engines: Diesel-electric (Westinghouse diesels); 3 600 bhp; 1 shaft = 14 knots
Complement: 77/78 (12 officers, 35 or 36 men, 30 scientists)

These ships were designed specifically for surveying operations. Bow propulsion unit for precise manoeuvrability and station keeping. All four ships operated by Military Sealift Command for the Oceanographer of the Navy; civilian crews.
Laid down on 2 Mar 1964, 19 Dec 1964, 18 July 1968 and 18 July 1968 respectively; launched on 16 May 1964, 20 Nov 1965, 31 July 1969 and 30 Oct 1969.
Wilkes laid up in ready reserve.

WILKES   *6/1971, USN*

2 "BOWDITCH" CLASS (SURVEYING SHIPS (AGS))

Name	No.	Builders
*BOWDITCH (ex-SS *South Bend Victory*)	T-AGS 21	Oregon SB Co.
*DUTTON (ex-SS *Tuskegee Victory*)	T-AGS 22	South Coast Co, Newport Beach

Displacement, tons: 4 512 full load
Dimensions, feet (metres): 455·2 oa × 62·2 × 25 *(138·7 × 19·0 × 7·6)*
Main engines: Geared turbine; 8 500 shp; 1 shaft = 15 knots
Boilers: 2
Complement: 100 to 101 (13 or 14 officers, 47 men, approx 40 technical personnel)

VC2-S-AP3 type ships. Converted to support the Fleet Ballistic Missile Programme, *Dutton* at Philadelphia Naval Shipyard 8 Nov 1957 to 16 Nov 1958 and *Bowditch* at Charleston Naval Shipyard 10 Oct 1957 to 30 Sep 1958.
Designed for general surveying and to record magnetic fields and gravity.
Operated by Military Sealift Command for the Oceanographer of the Navy; civilian crews.

BOWDITCH   *1976, Michael D. J. Lennon*

1 CONVERTED "CURRITUCK" CLASS (GUIDED MISSILE SHIP (AVM))

Name	No.	Builders	Commissioned
*NORTON SOUND	AVM 1	Los Angeles SB & DD Co,	8 Jan 1945
	(ex-AV 11)	San Pedro	

Displacement, tons: 9 106 standard; 15 170 full load
Dimensions, feet (metres): 543·25 oa × 71·6 × 23·5 *(165·6 × 21·8 × 7·2)*
Missile launchers: 1 twin Standard surface-to-air launcher (Mk 26)
Machinery: Geared turbines (Allis-Chalmers); 12 000 shp; 2 shafts = 19 knots
Boilers: 4 (Babcock & Wilcox)
Complement: approx 300

NORTON SOUND

11/1974, USN

Norton Sound is a seagoing laboratory and test centre for advanced weapon systems. Constructed as a seaplane tender (AV 7); laid down 7 Sep 1942, launched 28 Nov 1943. After operating briefly in the Pacific War and afterward as a seaplane tender; in 1948 she was converted to a guided missile test ship.
Subsequently served as test ship for a number of research and weapon programmes, and is currently employed as a test platform for the Aegis advanced fleet defence system.

Classification: Changed from AV 11 to AVM 1 on 8 Aug 1951.

Conversion: *Norton Sound* was initially fitted as a guided missile (test) ship in 1948 during a seven-month conversion at the Philadelphia Naval Shipyard; 30-ton capacity boom removed from fantail (similar boom retained on hangar structure); helicopter deck provided forward; provision for fuelling, checking out, monitoring, and firing rockets and missiles.
Converted from November 1962 to June 1964 at Maryland SB & DD Co, Baltimore, Maryland, to test ship for the Typhon advanced weapons control system (intended for a new class of nuclear-powered guided missile cruisers); Typhon system removed in July 1966.
Modified in 1974 to serve as test ship for the Aegis advanced fleet defence system. SPY-1 paired radar arrays to provide 180° coverage (12 × 12 foot, six-sided "faces") installed atop forward superstructure; Mk 110 radar control system installed (including five UYK-7 computers to control phase steering of radars). The full Aegis system, as planned in warships, would have four radar "Faces" to provide 360° coverage. Twin Standard surface-to-air missile launcher fitted on stern. SPS-52 radar also fitted.

Gunnery: Fitted in 1968 with light-weight 5 inch 54 calibre gun and associated Mk 86 gunfire control system for operational test and evaluation.

Missiles: Missiles and rockets test fired from *Norton Sound* include the Aerobee, Loon (US version of the German V-1), Lark, Regulus, Terrier, Tartar, and Sea Sparrow. During Project Argus in 1958 from a position south of the Falkland Islands she launched three multi-stage missiles carrying low-yield nuclear warheads which were detonated approximately 300 miles above the earth. (The ship was also used to launch high-altitude balloons in Project Skyhook during 1949).

2 Ex-MINESWEEPERS (RESEARCH SHIPS (MSI))

Name	No.	Builders	In service
*COVE	MSI 1	Bethlehem Shipyards Co, Bellingham	20 Nov 1958
*CAPE	MSI 2	Bethlehem Shipyards Co, Bellingham	27 Feb 1959

Displacement, tons: 120 light; 240 full load
Dimensions, feet (metres): 105 × 22 × 10 *(32·0 × 6·7 × 3·0)*
Guns: Removed
Main engines: Diesel (General Motors); 650 bhp; 1 shaft = 12 knots
Complement: 21 (3 officers, 18 men)

CAPE

1968, USN

These ships were prototype inshore minesweepers (MSI) authorised under the Fiscal Year 1956 new construction programme. *Cape* laid down on 1 May 1957 and launched on 5 April 1968; *Cove* laid down 1 Feb 1957 and launched 8 Feb 1958.
Cape is operated by the Naval Undersea Research Development Center, San Diego, California; neither in service nor in commission. *Cove* transferred to Johns Hopkins Applied Physics Laboratory on 31 July 1970; she remains on the Navy List. Both conduct Navy research.

MISCELLANEOUS

1 PRESIDENTIAL YACHT (AG)

Name	No.	Builders
*SEQUOIA	AG 23	Mathias Yacht & SB Co, Camden, NJ

Displacement, tons: approx 110
Dimensions, feet (metres): 99 wl; 104 oa × 18·2 × 4·5 *(31·7 × 5·5 × 1·4)*
Main engines: Diesels (Winton); 400 bhp; 2 shafts = 11·5 knots
Complement: 21 (1 officer, 20 enlisted men; accommodation for only 14 of crew)
Passengers: accommodation for 7 under normal conditions

Small motor yacht built in 1925; acquired by the Navy on 25 Mar 1933. Employed as Presidential Yacht—President Carter, however, does not intend to use her.

SEQUOIA

USN

DEEP SUBMERGENCE VEHICLES

The US Navy operates several deep submergence vehicles for scientific, military research, and operational military missions. The US Navy acquired its first deep submergence vehicle with the purchase of the bathyscaph *Trieste* in 1958. The *Trieste* was designed and constructed by Professor Auguste Piccard. The US Navy sponsored research dives in the Mediterranean Sea with the *Trieste* in 1957 after which the bathyscaph was purchased outright and brought to the United States.

The *Trieste* reached a record depth of 35 800 feet *(10 910 metres)* in the Challenger Deep off the Marianas on 23 Jan 1960, being piloted by Lieutenant Don Walsh, USN, and Jacques Piccard (son of Auguste). Rebuilt and designated *Trieste II*, the craft was subsequently used in the search for wreckage of the nuclear-powered submarine *Thresher* (SSN 593) which was lost in 1963 and the *Scorpion* (SSN 589) lost in 1968.

After the loss of the *Thresher* the US Navy initiated an extensive deep submergence programme that led to construction of two Deep Submergence Rescue Vehicles (DSRV); however, other vehicles proposed in the recommended programme were not built because of a lack of interest, changing opera-

tional concepts, and funding limitations.

Several of these deep submergence vehicles and other craft and support ships are operated by Submarine Development Group One at San Diego, California. The Group is a major operational command that includes advanced diving equipment; divers trained in "saturation" techniques; the DSVs *Trieste II*, *Turtle*, *Sea Cliff*, DSRV-1, DSRV-2; the submarine *Dolphin* (AGSS 555); several submarine rescue ships.

The hull of the original *Trieste* and Krupp sphere are in the Navy Yard in Washington, DC.

NUCLEAR POWERED RESEARCH VEHICLE: PROPOSED

A second nuclear-powered submersible research vehicle has been proposed by Admiral H. G. Rickover, Deputy Commander for Nuclear Propulsion, Naval Sea Systems Command. The craft would have a greater depth capability than the NR-1 (described below) and would employ a nuclear plant similar to that of the earlier craft. The vehicle would have a pressure hull of HY-130 steel.

Reportedly, Admiral Rickover began development of the so-called "NR-2" in 1971. The term HTV for Hull Test Vehicle also has been used for this vehicle, reportedly to avoid critical association with the NR-1 programme.

Estimated construction time would be 2½ years; however, construction has not yet been approved. Current state of programme unknown. Unofficial estimates of construction costs ranged to more than $300 000 000 in Fiscal Year 1975 funding.

1 NUCLEAR POWERED OCEAN ENGINEERING AND RESEARCH VEHICLE

Name	Builders
NR-1	General Dynamics (Electric Boat), Groton

Displacement, tons: 400 submerged
Length, feet (metres): 136·4 oa × 12·4 × 14·6 *(41·6 × 3·8 × 4·5)*
Diameter, feet (metre): 12 *(3·7)*
Machinery: Electric motors; 2 propellers; four ducted thrusters
Reactor: 1 pressurised-water cooled
Complement: 7 (2 officers, 3 enlisted men, 2 scientists)

The NR-1 was built primarily to serve as a test platform for a small nuclear propulsion plant; however, the craft additionally provides an advanced deep submergence ocean engineering and research capability. Vice-Admiral Rickover conceived and initiated the NR-1 in 1964-1965 (the craft was not proposed in a Navy research or shipbuilding budget).

Laid down on 10 June 1967; launched on 25 Jan 1969; placed in service 27 Oct 1969. Commanded by an officer-in-charge vice commanding officer.

Describing the craft Admiral Rickover has stated: "The (NR-1) will be able to perform detailed studies and mapping of the ocean bottom, temperature, currents, and other oceanographic parameters for military, commercial, and scientific use. The submarine (NR-1) will have viewing ports for visual observation of its surroundings and the ocean bottom. In addition, a remote grapple will be installed to permit collection of marine samples and other items. With its depth capability, the NR-1 is expected to be capable of exploring areas of the Continental Shelf.

Construction: Originally costed at $30 000 000 in March 1965. During detailed design of the NR-1 the Navy determined that improved equipment had to be developed and a larger hull than originally planned would be required. Consequently, in July 1967 the Navy obtained Congressional approval to proceed with construction of the NR-1 at an estimated cost of $58 000 300. The final estimated ship construction cost at time of launching was $67 500 000 plus $19 900 000 for oceanographic equipment and sensors, and $11 800 000 for research and development (mainly related to the nuclear propulsion plant), for a total estimated cost of $99 200 000.

Design: The NR-1 is fitted with wheels beneath the hull to permit "bottom crawling". This will obviate the necessity of hovering while exploring the ocean floor. Submarine wheels, a concept proposed as early as the first decade of this century by submarine inventor Simon Lake, were tested in the small submarine *Mackerel* (SST 1).

The NR-1 is fitted with external lights, external television cameras, a remote-controlled manipulator, and various recovery devices. No periscopes, but fixed television mast. Credited with a 30 day endurance, but limited habitability makes missions of only a few days feasible. Reportedly, a surface "mother" ship is required to support the NR-1.

Engineering: The NR-1 reactor plant was designed by the Atomic Energy Commission's Knolls Atomic Power Laboratory. She is propelled by two propellers driven by electric motors outside the pressure hull with power provided by a turbine generator within the pressure hull. Four ducted thrusters, two horizontal and two vertical, are provided for precise manoeuvring.

NR-1   *1969, General Dynamics, Electric Boat*

NR-1   *1969, General Dynamics, Electric Boat*

2 DEEP SUBMERGENCE RESCUE VEHICLES

No.	Builders
DSRV-1	Lockheed Missiles and Space Co
DSRV-2	(Sunnyvale, Calif)

Weight in air, tons: 32
Length, feet (metres): 49·2 oa *(15·0)*
Diameter, feet (metres): 8 *(2·4)*
Propulsion: Electric motors, propeller mounted in control shroud and four ducted thrusters
Speed, knots: 5 (maximum)
Endurance: 12 hours at 3 knots
Operating depth, feet (metres): 5 000 *(1 525)*
Complement: 3 (pilot, co-pilot, rescue sphere operator) +24 rescued men

The Deep Submergence Rescue Vehicle is intended to provided a quick-reaction world-wide, all-weather capability for the rescue of survivors in a disabled submarine. The DSRV will be transportable by road, aircraft (in C-141 and C-5 jet cargo aircraft), surface ship (on "Pigeon" ASR 21 class submarine rescue ships), and specially modified submarines (SSN type).

The operational effectiveness of the craft is limited severely by the lack of large numbers of ships and submarines that air transport and support the craft. They will be used for the forseeable future for evaluation and research.

The carrying submarine will launch and recover the DSRV while submerged and, if necessary, while under ice. A total of six DSRVs were planned, but only two were funded. DSRV-1 was placed in service 7 Aug 1971 and DSRV-2 on 7 Aug 1972.

Cost: The construction cost for the DSRV-1 was $41 000 000 and for the DSRV-2 $23 000 000. The development, construction, test, and support of both vehicles through Fiscal Year 1975 was $220 000 000. This expenditure includes the design and construction, research, spares and training.

Design: The DSRV outer hull is constructed of formed fibreglass. Within this outer hull are three interconnected spheres which form the main pressure capsule. Each sphere is 7·5 feet in diameter and is constructed of HY-140 steel. The forward sphere contains the vehicle's control equipment and is manned by the pilot and co-pilot, the centre and after spheres accommodate 24 passengers and a third crewman. Under the DSRVs centre sphere is a hemispherical protrusion or "skirt" which seals over the disabled submarine's hatch. During the mating operation the skirt is pumped dry to enable personnel to transfer.

Electronics: Elaborate search and navigational sonar, and closed-circuit television (supplemented by optical devices) are installed in the DSRV to determine the exact location of a disabled submarine within a given area and for pinpointing the submarine's escape hatches. Side-looking sonar can be fitted for search missions.

DSRV—*continued*

Engineering: Propulsion and control of the DSRV are achieved by a stern propeller in a movable control shroud and four ducted thrusters, two forward and two aft. These, plus a mercury trim system, permit the DSRV to manoeuvre and hover with great precision and to mate with submarines lying at angles up to 45 degrees from the horizontal. An elaborate Integrated Control and Display (ICAD) system employs computers to present sensor data to the pilots and transmit their commands to the vehicle's control and propulsion system.

DSRV-1 on HAWKBILL (SSN 666)   1971, USN

2 MODIFIED "ALVIN" TYPE (DEEP SUBMERGENCE VEHICLES)

Name	No.	Builders
SEA CLIFF (ex-*Autec I*)	DSV 4	General Dynamics (Electric Boat), Groton, Conn
TURTLE (ex-*Autec II*)	DSV 3	General Dynamics (Electric Boat), Groton, Conn

Weight, tons: 21
Length, feet (metres): 25 oa *(7·6)*
Beam, feet (metres): 8 *(2·4)*
Propulsion: Electric motors, trainable stern propeller; 2 rotating propeller pods
Speed, knots: 2·5
Endurance: 8 hours at 2 knots
Operating depth, feet (metres): 6 500 *(1,980)*
Complement: 2 (pilot, observer)

Intended for deep submergence research and work tasks. Designated *Autec I* and *Autec II* during construction, but assigned above names in dual launching on 11 Dec 1968.
Designated DSV 4 and DSV 3, respectively, on 1 June 1971 when they were placed in service, commissioning Jan 1973.

Construction: Three pressure spheres were fabricated for the *Alvin* submersible programme, one for installation in the *Alvin*, a spare, and one for testing. The second and third spheres subsequently were allocated to these later submersibles.

Design: Twin-arm manipulator fitted to each submersible. Propulsion by stem propeller and two smaller, manoeuvering propeller "pods" on sides of vehicles; no thrusters.

SEA CLIFF   USN

1 "ALVIN" TYPE (DEEP SUBMERGENCE VEHICLE)

Name	No.	Builders
ALVIN	DSV 2	General Mills Inc, Minneapolis, Minn

Weight, tons: 16
Length, feet (metres): 22·5 oa *(6·9)*
Beam, feet (metres): 8·5 *(2·6)*
Propulsion: Electric motors; trainable stern propeller; 2 rotating propeller pods
Speed, knots: 2
Endurance: 8 hours at 1 knot
Operating depth, feet (metres): 12 000 *(3 658)*
Complement: 3 (1 pilot, 2 observers)

The *Alvin* was built for operation by the Woods Hole Oceanographic Institution for the Office of Naval Research. Original configuration had an operating depth of 6 000 feet. Named for Allyn C. Vine of Woods Hole Oceanographic Institution.
The *Alvin* accidentally sank in 5 051 feet of water on 16 Oct 1968; subsequently raised in August 1969; refurbished 1970-71 in essentially original configuration. Placed in service on Navy List 1 June 1971. Subsequently refitted with titanium pressure sphere to provide increased depth capability and again operational in November 1973.

ALVIN   1974

1 "TRIESTE" TYPE (DEEP SUBMERGENCE VEHICLE)

Name	No.
TRIESTE II	DSV 1 (ex-X-2)

Weight, tons: 84
Displacement, tons: 303 submerged
Length, feet (metres): 78·6 *(24·0)*
Beam, feet (metres): 15·3 *(4·7)*
Propulsion: Electric motors, 3 propellers aft, ducted thruster forward (see *Design* notes)
Speed, knots: 2
Endurance: 10-12 hours at 2 knots
Operating depth, feet (metres): 12 000 *(3 658)* (see *Design* notes)
Complement: 3 (2 operators, 1 observer)

The *Trieste II* is the successor to *Trieste I* which the US Navy purchased in 1958 from Professor Auguste Piccard. Several "modernisations" have resulted in the current vehicle being essentially a "new" craft, the third to be named *Trieste*. (The original *Trieste* was built at Castellammare, Italy; launched on 1 Aug 1953.)
The vehicle is operated by Submarine Development Group One at San Diego, California, and is used primarily as a test bed for underwater equipment and to train deep submergence vehicle operators (hydronauts).
Designated as a "submersible craft" and assigned the designation X-2 on 1 Sep 1969; subsequently changed to DSV 1 on 1 June 1971. Placed in commission Jan 1973.
Used in location of wreckage of *Scorpion* and *Thresher*.

Design: The *Trieste II* is essentially a large float with a small pressure sphere attached to the underside. The float, which is filled with aviation petrol, provides buoyancy. Designed operating depth is 20 000 feet but dives have been limited to approximately 12 000 feet. (The record-setting Challenger Deep dive was made with a Krupp sphere which has a virtually unlimited depth capability).
Trieste II was built at the Mare Island Naval Shipyard in Sep 1965-Aug 1966 with a modified float, pressure sphere, propulsion system, and mission equipment being fitted. In the broadside view the sphere is now largely hidden by protective supports to keep the sphere clear of the welldeck when the craft rests in a floating dry dock.
Fitted with external television cameras and mechanical manipulator; computerised digital navigation system installed.

TRIESTE II   1970, USN

Transfers: The 600-foot capability *Nemo* DSV 5 is on loan to the Southwest Research Institute, San Antonio, Texas, since 1974.

COAST GUARD

Senior Officers

Commandant: Admiral Owen W. Siler
Vice Commandant: Vice-Admiral Ellis L. Perry
Chief of Staff: Rear-Admiral James S. Gracey
Commander, Atlantic Area: Vice-Admiral William F. Rea, III
Commander, Pacific Area: Vice-Admiral Austin C. Wagner

Establishment

The United States Coast Guard was established by an Act of Congress approved 28 Jan 1915, which consolidated the Revenue Cutter Service (founded in 1790) and the Life Saving Service (founded in 1878). The act of establishment stated the Coast Guard "shall be a military service and a branch of the armed forces of the United States at all times. The Coast Guard shall be a service in the Treasury Department except when operating as a service in the Navy".
Congress further legislated that in time of national emergency or when the President so directs, the Coast Guard operates as a part of the Navy. The Coast Guard did operate as a part of the Navy during the First and Second World Wars.
The Lighthouse Service (founded in 1789) was transferred to the Coast Guard on 1 July 1939. The Coast Guard was transferred to the newly established Department of Transportation on 1 April 1967.

Missions

The current missions of the Coast Guard are to (1) enforce or assist in the enforcement of applicable Federal laws upon the high seas and waters subject to the jurisdiction of the United States including environmental protection; (2) administer all Federal laws regarding safety of life and property on the high seas and on waters subject to the jurisdiction of the United States, except those laws specifically entrusted to other Federal agencies; (3) develop, establish, maintain, operate, and conduct aids to maritime navigation, ocean stations, icebreaking activities, oceanographic research, and rescue facilities; and (4) maintain a state of readiness to function as a specialised service in the Navy when so directed by the President.

Personnel

Jan 1977: 6 010 officers, 31 466 enlisted men.
An estimated 1 000 personnel were added in 1976-1977 to man an increase in cutter strength to enforce a 200-mile fishing and conservation zone off the US coast.

Aviation

Only the larger "Hamilton" class cutters and certain classes of icebreakers can support helicopters at sea.
As of 30 Sep 1977 the Coast Guard's aviation strength consisted of 64 fixed-wing aircraft and 117 helicopters:

34	HC-130	Hercules
18	HU-16	Albatross
1	VC-4A	Gulfstream I
11	VC-11A	Gulfstream II
38	HH-3F	Pelican
79	HH-52A	Sea Guard

The Coast Guard plans to acquire approximately 40 land-based patrol and rescue aircraft in the period 1979-1983 to replace the long-serving HU-16 Albatross amphibians.

Cutter Strength

All Coast Guard vessels are referred to as "cutters". Cutter names are preceded by USCGC. Cutter serial numbers are prefixed with letter designations similar to the US Navy classification system with the prefix letter "W". The first two digits of serial numbers for cutters less than 100 feet in length indicate their approximate length overall. All Coast Guard cutters are active unless otherwise indicated.
Approximately 600 small rescue and utility craft also are in service.

The following table provides a tabulation of the ship strength of the United States Coast Guard and an index to the ship listings within the Coast Guard section. Ship arrangement is based on function and employment. Numbers of ships listed are actual as of 1 January 1977. Some projections of changes are also included.

Category/Classification		Active*	Reserve	New Construction
Cutters				
WHEC	High Endurance Cutters	18	1	—
WMEC	Medium Endurance Cutters	22	—	2
Icebreakers				
WAGB	Icebreaker	7	—	—
Patrol Craft				
WPGH	Patrol Gunboat (Hydrofoil)	1	—	—
WPB	Large/Small Patrol Craft	75	—	—
Training Cutters				
WIX	Training Cutters	2	—	—
WTR	Reserve Training Cutter	1	—	—
Oceanographic Cutters				
WAGO	Oceanographic Cutters	2	—	—
Buoy Tenders				
WLB	Buoy Tender, Seagoing	31	4	—
WLM	Buoy Tender, Coastal	15	—	—
WLI	Buoy Tender, Inland	14	—	—
WLR	Buoy Tender, River	22	—	—
Construction Tenders				
WLIC	Construction Tender, Inland	12	—	2
Lightships				
WLV	Lightships	2	1	—
Harbour Tugs				
WYTM	Harbor Tugs, Medium	14	—	4
WYTL	Harbor Tugs, Small	15	—	—

Note: *Includes those ships being placed in commission.

Shipbuilding Programmes

Approved FY 1977 Programme

Shipbuilding
2 WMEC (270 ft Class)
1 WLIC (160 ft Class)
3 WYTM (140 ft Class)

Proposed FY 1978 Programme

Shipbuilding
2 WMEC (270 ft Class)
1 WYTM (140 ft Class)

"Campbell" Class

"Reliance" Class

"Hamilton" Class

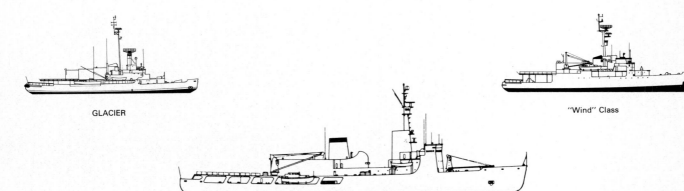

GLACIER

"Wind" Class

POLAR STAR

Scale: 1 inch = 150 feet (1 : 1 800)

Drawings by A. D. Baker III

ICEBREAKERS

2 "POLAR STAR" CLASS (ICEBREAKERS (WAGB))

Name	No.	Builders	Commissioned	
POLAR STAR	WAGB 10	Lockheed Shipbuilding Co, Seattle, Wash	17 Jan	1976
POLAR SEA	WAGB 11	Lockheed Shipbuilding Co, Seattle, Wash	7 Feb	1977

Displacement, tons: 13 190 full load
Dimensions, feet (metres): 399 oa × 83·5 × 28 *(121·6 × 25·5 × 8·5)*
Helicopters: 2 HH-52A
Guns: None
Main engines: Diesel-electric; 6 ALCO diesels; 18 000 shp; 3 gas turbines (Pratt and Whitney FT4A-12); 60 000 shp; 3 shafts (controllable pitch propellers) = 21 knots
Complement: 148 (13 officers, 125 enlisted men) plus 10 scientists

These ships are the first icebreakers built for US service since the *Glacier* was constructed two decades earlier. The programme is intended to replace the World War II-built "Wind" class icebreakers. *Polar Star* authorised in the Fiscal Year 1971 budget of the Department of Transportation; *Polar Sea* in FY 1973 budget. *Polar Star* was laid down on 15 May 1972 and launched on 17 Nov 1973; *Polar Sea* was laid down on 27 Nov 1973 and launched on 24 June 1975. No additional ships are planned for the near future. *Polar Star* based at Seattle.

Design: The "Polar Star" class icebreakers are the largest ships operated by the US Coast Guard. At a continuous speed of 3 knots these ships can break ice 6 ft thick and by riding on the ice they can break 21 ft pack.
These ships have a conventional icebreaker hull form with cutaway bow configuration and well rounded body sections to prevent being trapped in ice. Two 15-ton capacity cranes fitted aft; hangar and flight deck aft; extensive research laboratories provided for arctic and oceanographic research.

Engineering: This CODOG design provides for conventional diesel engines for normal cruising in field ice and gas turbines for heavy icebreaking. The diesel engines drive generators producing AC power; the main propulsion DC motors draw power through rectifiers permitting absolute flexibility in the delivery of power from alternate sources. The use of controllable-pitch propellers on three shafts will permit manoeuvring in heavy ice without the risk to the propeller blades caused by stopping the shaft while going from ahead to astern. The Coast Guard had given consideration to the use of nuclear power for an icebreaker; however, at this time the gas turbine-diesel combination can achieve the desirable power requirements without the added cost and operating restrictions of a nuclear powerplant.

POLAR STAR

6/1976, United States Coastguard

POLAR STAR

6/1976, United States Coastguard

1 "GLACIER" CLASS (ICEBREAKER (WAGB))

Name	No.	Builders	USN Commissioned
GLACIER	WAGB 4 (ex-AGB 4)	Ingalls Shipbuilding Corp, Pascagoula, Mississippi	27 May 1955

Displacement, tons: 8 449 full load
Dimensions, feet (metres): 309·6 oa × 74 × 29 *(94·4 × 6·9 × 8·8)*
Guns: 4—·50 cal MG
Helicopters: 2 helicopters normally embarked
Main engines: Diesel-electric (10 Fairbanks-Morse diesels and 2 Westinghouse electric motors); 21 000 hp; 2 shafts = 17·6 knots
Range, miles: 29 200 at 12 knots; 12 000 at 17·6 knots
Complement: 241 (15 officers, 226 enlisted men)

The largest icebreaker in US service prior to the "Polar Star" class; laid down on 3 Aug 1953 and launched on 27 Aug 1954. Transferred from Navy (AGB 4) to Coast Guard on 30 June 1966. During 1972 the *Glacier* and assigned helicopters were painted red to improve visibility in Arctic regions. All other icebreakers painted red during 1973.

Engineering: When built the *Glacier* had the largest capacity single-armature DC motors ever built and installed in a ship.

Gunnery: As built the *Glacier* was armed with two 5 inch guns (twin), six 3 inch guns (twin), and four 20 mm guns; lighter weapons removed prior to transfer to Coast Guard; 5 inch guns removed in 1969.

GLACIER

1976, John A. Jedrlinic

3 "WIND" CLASS (ICEBREAKER (WAGB))

Name	No.	Builders	Launched
WESTWIND	WAGB 281 (ex-AGB 6)	Western Pipe & Steel Co, San Pedro, California	31 Mar 1943
NORTHWIND	WAGB 282	Western Pipe & Steel Co, San Pedro, California	25 Feb 1945
BURTON ISLAND	WAGB 283 (ex-AGB 1, ex-AG 88)	Western Pipe & Steel Co, San Pedro, California	30 April 1946

Displacement, tons: 3 500 standard; 6 515 full load
Dimensions, feet (metres): 250 wl; 269 oa × 63·5 × 29 (82·0 × 19·4 × 8·8)
Helicopters: 2 helicopters normally embarked (HH 52 A)
Guns: 4—50 cal MG (see Gunnery notes)
Main engines: Diesel-electric; 4 Diesels (Fairbanks-Morse 38D81/8—283, Enterprise—281, 282); 10 000 bhp; 2 shafts = 16 knots
Range, miles: 38 000 at 10·5 knots; 16 000 at 16 knots
Complement: 135

Originally seven ships in this class built. Five ships were delivered to the US Coast Guard during World War II and two to the US Navy in 1946. The *Westwind* served in the Soviet Navy from 1945 to 1951 (named *Severni Polus* in Soviet service). The *Burton Island* was transferred from the US Navy to the Coast Guard on 15 Dec 1966.
The *Westwind* operates on the Great Lakes. The *Burton Island* scheduled to be assigned to Office of Naval Research on Oct 31 1977 for use in Arctic trials. She will remain under Coast-guard control but will cease her ice-breaking duties. Crews of *Northwind* and *Westwind* reduced from 181 to approx 135 during 1975.

Engineering: These ships were built with a bow propeller shaft in addition to the two stern shafts; bow shaft removed from all units because it would continually break in heavy ice. *Westwind* re-engined in 1973-1974, and *Northwind* in 1974-1975.

Gunnery: As built the five Coast Guard ships each mounted four 5 inch guns (one twin mount forward and one twin mount aft on 01 level) and 12 40 mm guns (quad); the two Navy Ships were completed with only forward twin 5 inch mount (as built a catapult and cranes were fitted immediately behind the funnel and one floatplane was carried). Armament reduced after war and helicopter platform eventually installed in all ships.
During the 1960s the *Northwind* carried two 5 inch guns (twin), and the other ships each mounted one 5 inch gun; all primary gun batteries removed in 1969-1970.

WESTWIND · 2/1976, United States Coast Guard

1 "MACKINAW" CLASS (ICEBREAKER (WAGB))

Name	No.	Builders	Commissioned
MACKINAW (ex-*Manitowac*)	WAGB 83	Toledo Shipbuilding Co, Ohio	20 Dec 1944

Displacement, tons: 5 252
Dimensions, feet (metres): 290 oa × 74 × 19 (88·4 × 22·6 × 5·8)
Helicopters: 1 helicopter
Main engines: 2 Diesels (Fairbanks-Morse); with electric drive (Elliot); 3 shafts (1 forward, 2 aft); 10 000 bhp = 18·7 knots
Range, miles: 60 000 at 12 knots; 10 000 at 18·7 knots
Complement: 127 (10 officers, 117 enlisted men)

Laid down on 20 Mar 1943; launched 6 Mar 1944 and completed in January 1945. Specially designed and constructed for service as icebreaker on the Great Lakes. Equipped with two 12-ton capacity cranes. Clear area for helicopter is provided on the quarterdeck.

MACKINAW · United States Coast Guard

1 "STORIS" CLASS
(MEDIUM ENDURANCE CUTTER/ICEBREAKER (WMEC/WAGB))

Name	No.	Builders	Commissioned
STORIS (ex-*Eskimo*)	WMEC 38 (ex-WAGB 38)	Toledo Shipbuilding Co, Ohio	30 Sep 1942

Displacement, tons: 1 715 standard; 1 925 full load
Dimensions, feet (metres): 230 oa × 43 × 15 (70·1 × 13·1 × 4·6)
Guns: 1—3 inch 50 cal (Mk 22); 2—50 cal MG
Main engines: Diesel-electric; 1 shaft; 1 800 bhp = 14 knots
Range, miles: 22 000 at 8 knots; 12 000 at 14 knots
Complement: 106 (10 officers, 96 enlisted men)

Laid down on 14 July 1941; launched on 4 Apr 1942. Ice patrol tender. Strengthened for ice navigation and sometimes employed as icebreaker. Employed in Alaskan service for search, rescue and law enforcement.
Designation changed from WAG to WAGB on 1 May 1966; redesignated as medium endurance cutter (WMEC) on 1 July 1972.

STORIS · 1975, United States Coast Guard

HIGH ENDURANCE CUTTERS

12 "HAMILTON" and "HERO" CLASSES (HIGH ENDURANCE CUTTERS (WHEC))

Name	No.	Builders	Laid down	Launched	Commissioned
HAMILTON	WHEC 715	Avondale Shipyards Inc, New Orleans, Louisiana	Jan 1965	18 Dec 1965	20 Feb 1967
DALLAS	WHEC 716	Avondale Shipyards Inc, New Orleans, Louisiana	7 Feb 1966	1 Oct 1966	1 Oct 1967
MELLON	WHEC 717	Avondale Shipyards Inc, New Orleans, Louisiana	25 July 1966	11 Feb 1967	22 Dec 1967
CHASE	WHEC 718	Avondale Shipyards Inc, New Orleans, Louisiana	15 Oct 1966	20 May 1967	1 Mar 1968
BOUTWELL	WHEC 719	Avondale Shipyards Inc, New Orleans, Louisiana	12 Dec 1966	17 June 1967	14 June 1968
SHERMAN	WHEC 720	Avondale Shipyards Inc, New Orleans, Louisiana	13 Feb 1967	23 Sep 1967	23 Aug 1968
GALLANTIN	WHEC 721	Avondale Shipyards Inc, New Orleans, Louisiana	17 Apr 1967	18 Nov 1967	20 Dec 1968
MORGENTHAU	WHEC 722	Avondale Shipyards Inc, New Orleans, Louisiana	17 July 1967	10 Feb 1968	14 Feb 1969
RUSH	WHEC 723	Avondale Shipyards Inc, New Orleans, Louisiana	23 Oct 1967	16 Nov 1968	3 July 1969
MUNRO	WHEC 724	Avondale Shipyards Inc, New Orleans, Louisiana	18 Feb 1970	5 Dec 1970	10 Sep 1971
JARVIS	WHEC 725	Avondale Shipyards Inc, New Orleans, Louisiana	9 Sep 1970	24 Apr 1971	30 Dec 1971
MIDGETT	WHEC 726	Avondale Shipyards Inc, New Orleans, Louisiana	5 Apr 1971	4 Sep 1971	17 Mar 1972

Displacement, tons: 2 716 standard; 3 050 full load
Length, feet (metres): 350 wl; 378 oa *(115·2)*
Beam, feet (metres): 42·8 *(13·1)*
Draught, feet (metres): 20 *(6·1)*
Guns: 1—5 inch *(127 mm)* 38 cal (Mk 30); 2—20 mm in 716, 718, 720-722; 2—81 mm mortars in remainder; 2—·50 MGs
A/S weapons: 2 triple topedo tubes (Mk 32)
Helicopters: 1 HH-52A or HH-3 helicopter
Main engines: Combined Diesel and Gas turbine (CODAG): 2 diesels (Fairbanks-Morse) 7 000 bhp; 2 gas turbines (Pratt & Whitney FT-4A), 28 000 shp; aggregate 35 000 hp; 2 shafts (controllable-pitch propellers)
Speed, knots: 29
Range, miles: 14 000 at 11 knots (diesels); 2 400 at 29 knots (gas)
Complement: 164 (15 officers, 149 enlisted men)

All active.

Anti-submarine armament: Hedgehog anti-submarine weapons have been removed from earlier ships during overhaul and Mk 309 fire control system for Mk 32 torpedo tubes are installed. Hedgehogs deleted in later ships. *Hamilton* was first to drop hedgehogs and receive Mk 309 during 1970 overhaul.

Design: These ships have clipper bows, twin funnels enclosing a helicopter hangar, helicopter platform aft. All are fitted with oceanographic laboratories, elaborate communications equipment, and meteorological data gathering facilities. Superstructure is largely of aluminium construction. Bridge control of manoeuvring is by aircraft-type joy-stick rather than wheel.

Engineering: The "Hamiltons" were the largest US "military" ships with gas turbine propulsion prior to the Navy's "Spruance" class destroyers. The Fairbanks Morse diesels are 12 cylinder.
Engine and propeller pitch consoles are located in wheelhouse and at bridge wing stations as well as engine room control booth.
A retractable bow propulsion unit is provided for station keeping and precise manoeuvring (unit is located directly forward of bridge, immediately aft of sonar dome).

Gunnery: Planned to ship 2—40 mm guns in all vessels and to replace 2—81 mm mortars by 2—20 mm. Mk 56 GFCS

Radar: Search: SPS 29 and 51.

Sonar: SQS-38.

SHERMAN 5/1975, USN

MORGENTHAU 7/1976, A. D. Baker III

CHASE 1976, Michael D. J. Lennon

6 "CAMPBELL" (327) CLASS (HIGH ENDURANCE CUTTERS (WHEC))

Name	No.	Builders	Laid down	Launched	Commissioned
BIBB (ex-George M. Bibb)	WHEC 31	Charleston Navy Yard	18 May 1935	14 Jan 1937	19 Mar 1937
CAMPBELL (ex-George W. Campbell)	WHEC 32	Philadelpnia Navy Yard	1 May 1935	3 June1936	22 Oct 1936
DUANE (ex-William J. Duane)	WHEC 33	Philadelphia Navy Yard	1 May 1935	3 June1936	16 Oct 1936
INGHAM (ex-Samuel D. Ingham)	WHEC 35	Philadelphia Navy Yard	1 May 1935	3 June1936	6 Nov 1936
SPENCER (ex-John C. Spencer)	WHEC 36	New York Navy Yard	11 Sep 1935	3 Jan 1936	13 May 1937
TANEY (ex-Roger B. Taney)	WHEC 37	Philadelphia Navy Yard	1 May 1935	3 June1936	19 Dec 1936

Displacement, tons: 2 216 standard; 2 656 full load
Length, feet (metres): 308 wl; 327 oa *(99·7)*
Beam, feet (metres): 41 *(12·5)*
Draught, feet (metres): 15 *(4·6)*
Guns: 1—5 inch *(127 mm)* 38 cal (Mk 30); 2—81 mm mortars (except 35) see notes
A/S weapons: Removed
Main engines: Geared turbines (Westinghouse); 6 200 shp; 2 shafts
Boilers: 2 (Babcock & Wilcox)
Speed, knots: 19·8
Range, miles: 4 000 at 20 knots; 8 000 at 10·5 knots
Complement: 144 (13 officers, 131 enlisted men)

These were the Coast Guard's largest cutters until the *Hamilton* was completed in 1967.

The *Duane* served as an amphibious force flagship during the invasion of Southern France in August 1944 and was designated AGC 6 (Coast Guard manned); the other ships of this class, except the lost *Alexander Hamilton* (PG 34), were similarly employed but retained Coast Guard number with WAGC prefix (amidships structure built up and one or two additional masts installed); all reverted to gunboat configuration after war (WPG designation). Redesignated WHEC on 1 May 1966. All of these cutters remain in active service except the *Spencer*, decommissioned on 1 Feb 1974 and placed in reserve at the Coast Guard Yard, Curtis Bay, Maryland. The *Spencer* was scheduled to be recommissioned during 1977.

Taney mans weather station "Hotel" off Norfolk Va. WSR-S1 storm tracking radar in dome.

Anti-submarine armament: During the 1960s these ships each had an ASW armament of one ahead-firing fixed hedgehog and two Mk 32 triple torpedo tube mounts; subsequently removed from all ships.

Gunnery: As built these ships had two 5 inch 51 cal guns (single mounts forward) and several smaller guns; rearmed during World War II with an additional single 5 inch 51 cal gun installed aft plus two or three 3 inch 50 cal anti-aircraft guns, and several 20 mm anti-aircraft guns (depth charge racks installed); *Taney* was experimentally armed with four 5 inch 38 cal guns in single mounts. Present armament fitted after World War II.

Planned to fit all of class with 2—40 mm Mk 64 (single) and 2—20 mm Mk 67 (single) the latter replacing the 2—81 mm mortars. 20 mm shift already done in *Ingham*.

TANEY

1975, United States Coast Guard

INGHAM

6/1976, C. and S. Taylor

1 "CASCO" (311) CLASS (HIGH ENDURANCE CUTTER (WHEC))

Name	No.	Builders	Laid down	Launched	Commissioned
UNIMAK	WHEC 379 (ex-WTR 379, ex-WHEC 379, ex-AVP 31)	Associated Shipbuilders, Seattle, Wash	15 Feb 1942	27 May 1942	31 Dec 1943

Displacement, tons: 1 766 standard; 2 800 full load
Length, feet (metres): 300 wl; 310·75 oa *(94·7)*
Beam, feet (metres): 41 *(12·5)*
Draught, feet (metres): 13·5 *(4·1)*
Guns: 1—5 inch *(127 mm)* 38 cal; 2—81 mm mortars
A/S weapons: Removed
Main engines: Diesels (Fairbanks Morse); 6 080 bhp; 2 shafts
Speed, knots: 18
Range, miles: 8 000 at 18 knots
Complement: 150 (13 officers; 137 enlisted men)

The *Unimak* is the sole survivor of 18 former Navy seaplane tenders (AVP) transferred to the Coast Guard in 1946-1948 (WAVP/WHEC 370-387). The *Unimak* operated as a training cutter (WTR) from 1969 until decommissioned on 30 May 1975 at Baltimore. Replaced by *Reliance* WTR 615. She was slated to be transferred to South Vietnam but with the fall of the Saigon government that year she was retained in reserve. The *Unimak* has been scheduled for commissioning in mid-1977 after repair following serious fire.

Classification: The former Navy AVPs were designated WAVP by the Coast Guard until changed to high endurance cutters (WHEC) on 1 May 1966. The *Unimak* subsequently became a training cutter (WTR) on 28 Nov 1969.

Transfers: Ships of this class (originally "Barnegat" class) serve in the navies of Ethiopia and Italy.

UNIMAK

1970, United States Coast Guard

MEDIUM ENDURANCE CUTTERS

11+ "270-foot" CLASS (MEDIUM ENDURANCE CUTTERS (WMEC))

WMEC 603	Approved FY 1977 Programme
WMEC 631-632	Proposed FY 1977 Programme
WMEC 633-634	Planned FY 1978 Programme
6 more (minimum)	Planned FY 1979-83 Programmes

Displacement, tons: 1 722 full load
Dimensions, feet (metres): 270 oa × 38 × 13·5 *(82·3 × 11·6 × 4·1)*
Helicopters: 1 HH-52A or 1 LAMPS III
Gun: 1—76 mm 62 calibre (Mk 75) OTO-Melara (single)
A/S weapons: See notes
Main engines: Diesels; 7 000 bhp; 2 shafts = 19·5 knots
Complement: 109 (15 officers, 94 enlisted men)

The Coast Guard plans to construct 11 to 25 medium endurance cutters of this class over a seven-year period. They will replace older medium and high endurance cutters when they become operational from about 1980 onwards.

A/S weapons: These ships will have no shipboard A/S weapons, but will rely on helicopters to deliver torpedoes against submarines detected by the ships' towed sonar array.

Design: They will be the only medium endurance cutters with helicopter hangars, and the first cutters with automated command and control centre. Fin stabilisers to be fitted.

Electronics: Fitted with Mk 92 weapons control system, easily identified by radome atop pilot house. These ships will not have hull-mounted sonar, but instead the tactical Towed Array Sonar System (TTASS), capable of providing long-range targeting data for A/S helicopter attack.

Engineering: Diesels were selected over gas turbine propulsion because of the Coast Guard requirement for long on-station time at slow speeds vice high-speed naval operations.

Fiscal: The Coast Guard Fiscal Year 1977 programme provides $49 000 000 for the first two ships of this class.

Gunnery: Weight and space for CIWS.

Helicopters: The design is sized to accommodate the HH-52 Sea Guard helicopter or its Coast Guard successor, or the Navy's planned LAMPS III (Light Airborne Multi-Purpose System) helicopter. The helicopter hangar is extendable. Weight and space reserved for helicopter landing and traversing system.

Missiles: For but not with SSMs.

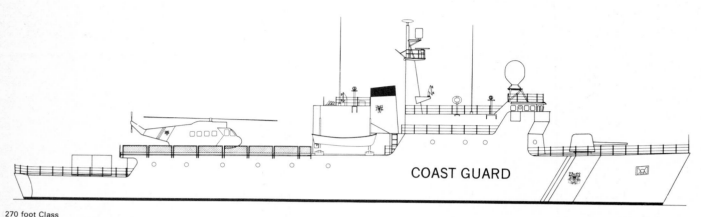

270 foot Class

United States Coast Guard

16 "RELIANCE" (210) CLASS { (15 MEDIUM ENDURANCE CUTTERS (WMEC) 1 RESERVE TRAINING CUTTER (WTR))

Name	No.	Builders	Commissioned	Name	No.	Builders	Commissioned
RELIANCE	WTR 615	Todd Shipyards	20 June 1964	STEADFAST	WMEC 623	American Shipbuilding Co	25 Sep 1968
DILIGENCE	WMEC 616	Todd Shipyards	26 Aug 1964	DAUNTLESS	WMEC 624	American Shipbuilding Co	10 June 1968
VIGILANT	WMEC 617	Todd Shipyards	3 Oct 1964	VENTUROUS	WMEC 625	Coast Guard Yard, Curtis Bay, Baltimore	16 Aug 1968
ACTIVE	WMEC 618	Christy Corp	17 Sep 1966				
CONFIDENCE	WMEC 619	Coast Guard Yard, Curtis Bay, Baltimore	19 Feb 1966	DEPENDABLE	WMEC 626	American Shipbuilding Co	22 Nov 1968
				VIGOROUS	WMEC 627	American Shipbuilding Co	2 May 1969
RESOLUTE	WMEC 620	American Shipbuilding Co	8 Dec 1966	DURABLE	WMEC 628	Coast Guard Yard, Curtis Bay, Baltimore	8 Dec 1967
VALIANT	WMEC 621	American Shipbuilding Co	28 Oct 1967				
COURAGEOUS	WMEC 622	American Shipbuilding Co	10 Apr 1968	DECISIVE	WMEC 629	Coast Guard Yard, Curtis Bay, Baltimore	23 Aug 1968
				ALERT	WMEC 630	American Shipbuilding Co	4 Aug 1969

Displacement, tons: 950 standard; 1 007 full load (except WTR and WMEC 616-619, 970 full load)
Dimensions, feet (metres): 210·5 oa × 34 × 10·5 *(64·2 × 10·4 × 3·2)*
Gun: 1—3 inch *(76 mm)* 50 calibre
Helicopters: 1 HH-52A helicopter embarked for missions
Main engines: 2 turbo-charged diesels (ALCO 251B); 2 shafts; 5 000 bhp = 18 knots; WTR 615 and WMEC 616-619 have 2 Solar gas turbines in addition (4 000 shp); 2 shafts; cp propellers
Range, miles: 6 100 at 13 knots (615-619); 6 100 at 14 knots (remainder)
Complement: 61 (7 officers, 54 enlisted men)

Designed for search and rescue duties. Design features include 360-degree visibility from wheelhouse; helicopter flight deck (no hangar); and engine exhaust vent at stern in place of conventional funnel. Capable of towing ships up to 10 000 tons. Air-conditioned throughout except engine room; high degree of habitability.
Launched, respectively, on the following dates: 25 May 1963, 20 July 1963, 24 Dec 1963, 21 July 1965, 8 May 1965, 30 April 1966, 14 Jan 1967, 18 Mar 1967, 24 June 1967, 21 Oct 1967, 11 Nov 1967, 16 Mar 1968, 4 May 1968, 29 Apr 1967, 14 Dec 1967, 19 Oct 1968.
All these cutters are active. The *Reliance* is the Coast Guard's reserve training cutter based at Yorktown, Virginia, and retains full search, rescue, and patrol capabilities.

Designation: These ships were originally designated as patrol craft (WPC); changed to WMEC on 1 May 1966.

Helicopters: The *Alert* was the first US ship fitted with the Canadian-developed "Beartrap" helicopter hauldown system. No further procurement of this system has been funded.

VIGILANT

9/1976, Dr. Giorgio Arra

1 "FLAGSTAFF" CLASS (HYDROFOIL GUNBOAT (WPGH))

Name	No.	Builders	USN In Service
FLAGSTAFF	WPGH 1	Grumman Aircraft Corp, Stuart, Fla.	14 Sep 1968

Displacement, tons: 56·8 full load
Dimensions, feet (metres): 74·4 oa *(22·7)* × 21·4 *(6·2)* × 4·5 *(1·4)* (foils retracted) or 13·5 *(4·1)* (foils extended)
Guns: 1—81 mm mortar; 2—·50 cal machine guns
Main engines: foil borne: 1 gas turbine (Rolls Royce Tyne Mk 621); 3 620 hp; controllable pitch propeller = 40+ knots
hull borne: 2 diesels (Packard); 300 bhp; water-jet propulsion = 8 knots
Complement: 13 (1 officer, 12 enlisted men)

Flagstaff was a competitive prototype evaluated with the *Tucumcari* (PGH 2). Laid down 15 July 1966 and launched 9 Jan 1968. Construction cost was $3 600 000. She has conducted sea trials with a 152 mm howitzer (see *Gunnery* notes), foil-mounted sonars, and towed shapes representing Variable Depth Sonar (VDS). From 1 Nov 1974 to 20 Dec 1974, She was evaluated by the Coast Guard to determine possible roles for this type of craft was was transferred to the Coast Guard permanently on 29 Sep 1976. After running evaluation tests out of Wood's Hole, Mass, she was commissioned on 2 March 1977 for duty in patrolling the new 200 mile fishing and conservation zone with *Unimak* (WHEC-379).

Design: The *Flagstaff* has a conventional foil arrangement with 70 per cent of the craft's weight supported by the forward set of foils and 30 per cent of the weight supported by the stern foils. Steering is accomplished by movement of the stern strut about its vertical axis. Foil-borne operation is automatically controlled by a wave-height sensing system. The foils are fully retractable for hull-borne operations. Aluminium construction.

Engineering: During foil-borne operation the propeller is driven by a geared transmission system contained in the tail strut, and in the pod located at the strut-foil connection. During hull borne operation two diesel engines drive a water-jet propulsion system. Water enters the pump inlets through openings in the hull and the thrust is exerted by water flow through nozzles in the transome. Steering in the hull-borne mode is by deflection vanes in the water stream.

Gunnery: Originally armed with one 40 mm gun forward, four ·50 cal MG amidships, and an 81 mm mortar aft. Rearmed in 1971 with a 152 mm gun forward. After firing trials in 1971 the gun was removed. As a Coast Guard craft she carries the same armament as a WPB of the "Point" or "Cape" Class.

FLAGSTAFF   *1974, United States Coast Guard*

22 "CAPE" CLASS (PATROL BOATS (WPB))

Name	No.	Builders
"A" Series		
CAPE SMALL	95300	Coast Guard Yard, Curtis Bay, Maryland
CAPE CORAL	95301	Coast Guard Yard, Curtis Bay, Maryland
CAPE GEORGE	95306	Coast Guard Yard, Curtis Bay, Maryland
CAPE CURRENT	95307	Coast Guard Yard, Curtis Bay, Maryland
CAPE STRAIT	95308	Coast Guard Yard, Curtis Bay, Maryland
CAPE CARTER	95309	Coast Guard Yard, Curtis Bay, Maryland
CAPE WASH	95310	Coast Guard Yard, Curtis Bay, Maryland
CAPE HEDGE	95311	Coast Guard Yard, Curtis Bay, Maryland
"B" Series		
CAPE KNOX	95312	Coast Guard Yard, Curtis Bay, Maryland
CAPE MORGAN	95313	Coast Guard Yard, Curtis Bay, Maryland
CAPE FAIRWEATHER	95314	Coast Guard Yard, Curtis Bay, Maryland
CAPE FOX	95316	Coast Guard Yard, Curtis Bay, Maryland
CAPE JELLISON	95317	Coast Guard Yard, Curtis Bay, Maryland
CAPE NEWAGEN	95318	Coast Guard Yard, Curtis Bay, Maryland
CAPE ROMAIN	95319	Coast Guard Yard, Curtis Bay, Maryland
CAPE STARR	95320	Coast Guard Yard, Curtis Bay, Maryland
"C" Series		
CAPE CROSS	95321	Coast Guard Yard, Curtis Bay, Maryland
CAPE HORN	95322	Coast Guard Yard, Curtis Bay, Maryland
CAPE SHOALWATER	95324	Coast Guard Yard, Curtis Bay, Maryland
CAPE CORWIN	95326	Coast Guard Yard, Curtis Bay, Maryland
CAPE HENLOPEN	95328	Coast Guard Yard, Curtis Bay, Maryland
CAPE YORK	95332	Coast Guard Yard, Curtis Bay, Maryland

Displacement, tons: 105
Dimensions, feet (metres): 95 oa × 20 × 6 *(29·0 × 6·1 × 1·8)*
Guns: 1—81 mm mortar and 2—·50 cal MG or 2—·50 cal MG
Main engines: 4 diesels (Cummings); 2 324 bhp; 2 shafts = 20 knots
Range, miles: 2 600 (A series); 3 000 (B series); 2 800 (C series); all at 9 knots
Complement: 14 (1 officer, 13 enlisted men)

CAPE FAIRWEATHER   *7/1976, A. D. Baker III*

Designed for port security, search, and rescue. Steel hulled. A series built in 1953; B series in 1955-1956, and C series in 1958-1959.
Plans to dispose of this class from 1974-1975 onward in favour of new WPB construction have been changed; instead all 22 remaining units will be modernised (see below). Several "Cape" class cutters serve in the South Korean Navy.

Modernisation: All 22 units will be modernised to extend their service life for an estimated ten years. Cost in 1976 was estimated at $500 000 per cutter. They will receive new engines, electronics, and deck equipment; superstructure will be modified or replaced; and habitability will be improved. The programme will begin in July 1977 and complete by 1981. Each unit will take 5 months to modernise.

53 "POINT" CLASS (PATROL BOATS (WPB))

Name	No.	Builders
"A" Series		
POINT HOPE	82302	Coast Guard Yard, Curtis Bay, Maryland
POINT VERDE	82311	Coast Guard Yard, Curtis Bay, Maryland
POINT SWIFT	82312	Coast Guard Yard, Curtis Bay, Maryland
POINT THATCHER	82314	Coast Guard Yard, Curtis Bay, Maryland
"C" Series		
POINT HERRON	82318	Coast Guard Yard, Curtis Bay, Maryland
POINT ROBERTS	82332	Coast Guard Yard, Curtis Bay, Maryland
POINT HIGHLAND	82333	Coast Guard Yard, Curtis Bay, Maryland
POINT LEDGE	82334	Coast Guard Yard, Curtis Bay, Maryland
POINT COUNTESS	82335	Coast Guard Yard, Curtis Bay, Maryland
POINT GLASS	82336	Coast Guard Yard, Curtis Bay, Maryland
POINT DIVIDE	82337	Coast Guard Yard, Curtis Bay, Maryland
POINT BRIDGE	82338	Coast Guard Yard, Curtis Bay, Maryland
POINT CHICO	82339	Coast Guard Yard, Curtis Bay, Maryland
POINT BATAN	82340	Coast Guard Yard, Curtis Bay, Maryland
POINT LOOKOUT	82341	Coast Guard Yard, Curtis Bay, Maryland
POINT BAKER	82342	Coast Guard Yard, Curtis Bay, Maryland
POINT WELLS	82343	Coast Guard Yard, Curtis Bay, Maryland
POINT ESTERO	82344	Coast Guard Yard, Curtis Bay, Maryland
POINT JUDITH	82345	Martinac SB, Tacoma, Washington
POINT ARENA	82346	Martinac SB, Tacoma, Washington
POINT BONITA	82347	Martinac SB, Tacoma, Washington
POINT BARROW	82348	Martinac SB, Tacoma, Washington
POINT SPENCER	82349	Martinac SB, Tacoma, Washington
POINT FRANKLIN	82350	Coast Guard Yard, Curtis Bay, Maryland
POINT BENNETT	82351	Coast Guard Yard, Curtis Bay, Maryland
POINT SAL	82352	Coast Guard Yard, Curtis Bay, Maryland
POINT MONROE	82353	Coast Guard Yard, Curtis Bay, Maryland
POINT EVANS	82354	Coast Guard Yard, Curtis Bay, Maryland
POINT HANNON	82355	Coast Guard Yard, Curtis Bay, Maryland
POINT FRANCIS	82356	Coast Guard Yard, Curtis Bay, Maryland
POINT HURON	82357	Coast Guard Yard, Curtis Bay, Maryland
POINT STUART	82358	Coast Guard Yard, Curtis Bay, Maryland
POINT STEELE	82359	Coast Guard Yard, Curtis Bay, Maryland
POINT WINSLOW	82360	Coast Guard Yard, Curtis Bay, Maryland
POINT CHARLES	82361	Coast Guard Yard, Curtis Bay, Maryland
POINT BROWN	82362	Coast Guard Yard, Curtis Bay, Maryland
POINT NOWELL	82363	Coast Guard Yard, Curtis Bay, Maryland
POINT WHITEHORN	82364	Coast Guard Yard, Curtis Bay, Maryland
POINT TURNER	82365	Coast Guard Yard, Curtis Bay, Maryland
POINT LOBOS	82366	Coast Guard Yard, Curtis Bay, Maryland
POINT KNOLL	82367	Coast Guard Yard, Curtis Bay, Maryland
POINT WARDE	82368	Coast Guard Yard, Curtis Bay, Maryland
POINT HEYER	82369	Coast Guard Yard, Curtis Bay, Maryland
POINT RICHMOND	82370	Coast Guard Yard, Curtis Bay, Maryland
"D" Series		
POINT BARNES	82371	Coast Guard Yard, Curtis Bay, Maryland
POINT BROWER	82372	Coast Guard Yard, Curtis Bay, Maryland
POINT CAMDEN	82373	Coast Guard Yard, Curtis Bay, Maryland
POINT CARREW	82374	Coast Guard Yard, Curtis Bay, Maryland
POINT DORAN	82375	Coast Guard Yard, Curtis Bay, Maryland
POINT HARRIS	82376	Coast Guard Yard, Curtis Bay, Maryland
POINT HOBART	82377	Coast Guard Yard, Curtis Bay, Maryland
POINT JACKSON	82378	Coast Guard Yard, Curtis Bay, Maryland
POINT MARTIN	82379	Coast Guard Yard, Curtis Bay, Maryland

POINT HURON   9/1976, Dr. Giorgio Arra

POINT BRIDGE   1/1977, United States Coast Guard

Displacement, tons: A series 67; C series 66; D series 69
Dimensions, feet (metres): 78·1 wl; 83 oa × 17·2 × 5·8 *(25·3 × 5·2 × 1·8)*
Guns: 1—81 mm mortar and 1—·50 cal MG or 2—·50 cal MG; some boats unarmed
Main engines: 2 diesels; 1 600 bhp; 2 shafts = 23·5 knots except D series 22·6 knots
Range, miles: 1 500 at 8 knots (1 200 D series)
Complement: 8 (1 officer, 7 enlisted men; see notes)

Designed for search, rescue, and patrol. Of survivors, A series built 1960-1961; C series in 1961-1967; and D series in 1970.
Twenty-six cutters of the "A" and "B" series were transferred to South Vietnam in 1969-1970.

Names: WPB 82301-82344 were assigned "Point" names in January 1964.

Personnel: Most of these units now have an officer assigned; a few still operate with an all-enlisted crew.

TRAINING CUTTERS

1 "ACTIVE" CLASS (TRAINING CUTTER (IX))

CUYAHOGA WIX 157 (ex-WMEC 157, ex-WPC 157, ex-WAG 26)

Displacement, tons: 290 full load
Dimensions, feet (metres): 125 oa × 24 × 8 *(38·1 × 7·3 × 2·4)*
Guns: Removed
Main engines: Diesel; 2 shafts; 800 bhp = 13·2 knots
Complement: 11 (1 officer, 10 enlisted men)

Built in 1926 as one of the 33 "Active" class steel patrol boats. The *Cuyahoga* is the only cutter of this type remaining on the Coast Guard list. The *Cuyahoga* is based at Yorktown, Virginia, for the training of officer candidates.

CUYAHOGA   1974, United States Coast Guard

1 "EAGLE" CLASS (SAIL TRAINING CUTTER (IX))

Name	No.	Builders
EAGLE (ex-*Horst Wessel*)	WIX 327	Blohm & Voss, Hamburg

Displacement, tons: 1 784 full load
Dimensions, feet (metres): 231 wl; 295·2 oa × 39·1 × 17 *(90·0 × 11·9 × 5·2)*
Sail area, square feet: 25 351
Height of masts, feet (metres): fore and main 150·3 *(45·8)*; mizzen 132 *(40·2)*
Main engines: Auxiliary diesel (MAN); 728 bhp; 1 shaft = 10·5 knots (as high as 18 knots under full sail alone)
Complement: 245 (19 officers, 46 enlisted men, 180 cadets)

Former German training ship. Launched on 13 June 1936. Taken by the United States as part of reparations after the Second World War for employment in US Coast Guard Practice Squadron. Taken over at Bremerhaven in Jan 1946; arrived at home port of New London, Connecticut, in July 1946.
(Sister ship *Albert Leo Schlageter* was also taken by the United States in 1945 but was sold to Brazil in 1948 and re-sold to Portugal in 1962. Another ship of similar design, the *Gorch Foch*, transferred to the Soviet Union in 1946 and survives as the *Tovarisch*).

Appearance: When the Coast Guard added the orange-and-blue marking stripes to cutters in the 1960s the *Eagle* was exempted because of their affect on her graceful lines; however, in early 1976 the stripes and words "Coast Guard" were added in time for the July 1976 Operation Sail in New York harbour.

EAGLE   7/1976, USN

SEAGOING TENDERS

Note: *Acushnet* WAGO 167 serves as Oceanographic cutter with *Evergreen* WAGO 295 from class below. 167 operates from Gulfport, Miss and *Evergreen* from New London, Conn.

36 "BALSAM" CLASS (BUOY TENDERS (SEAGOING) (WLB)/OCEANOGRAPHIC CUTTER (WAGO))

Name	No.	Launched	Name	No.	Launched
BALSAM*	WLB 62	1942	BITTERSWEET	WLB 389	1944
COWSLIP	WLB 277	1942	BLACTHAW*	WLB 390	1944
GENTIAN	WLB 290	1942	BLACKTHORN	WLB 391	1944
LAUREL	WLB 291	1942	BRAMBLE*	WLB 392	1944
CLOVER	WLB 292	1942	FIREBUSH	WLB 393	1944
EVERGREEN	WAGO 295	1943	HORNBEAM	WLB 394	1944
SORREL*	WLB 296	1943	IRIS	WLB 395	1944
IRONWOOD	WLB 297	1944	MALLOW	WLB 396	1944
CITRUS*	WLB 300	1943	MARIPOSA	WLB 397	1944
CONIFER	WLB 301	1943	SAGEBRUSH	WLB 399	1944
MADRONA	WLB 302	1943	SALVIA	WLB 400	1944
TUPELO	WLB 303	1943	SASSAFRAS	WLB 401	1944
MESQUITE	WLB 305	1943	SEDGE*	WLB 402	1944
BUTTONWOOD	WLB 306	1943	SPAR*	WLB 403	1944
PLANETREE	WLB 307	1943	SUNDEW*	WLB 404	1944
PAPAW	WLB 308	1943	SWEETBRIER	WLB 405	1944
SWEETGUM	WLB 309	1943	ACACIA	WLB 406	1944
BASSWOOD	WLB 388	1944	WOODRUSH	WLB 407	1944

Displacement, tons: 935 standard; 1 025 full load
Dimensions, feet (metres): 180 oa × 37 × 13 *(59 × 12·1 × 4·2)*
Guns: 1—3 inch *(76 mm)* 50 calibre in *Citrus, Cowslip, Hornbeam,* and *Sorrel* (original armament); most others have ·50 calibre MG except *Sedge* has 2—20 mm guns; several ships are unarmed
Main engines: Diesel-electric; 1 000 bhp in tenders numbered WLB 62-303 series, except *Ironwood;* 1 shaft = 12·8 knots; others 1 200 bhp; 1 shaft = 15 knots
Complement: 53 (6 officers, 47 enlisted men)

MARIPOSA   1975, United States Coast Guard

Seagoing buoy tenders. *Ironwood* built by Coast Guard Yard at Curtis Bay, Maryland; others by Marine Iron & Shipbuilding Co, Duluth, Minnesota, or Zeneth Dredge Co, Duluth, Minnesota. Eight ships indicated by asterisks are strengthened for icebreaking. Three ships, *Cowslip, Bittersweet,* and *Hornbeam,* have controllable-pitch, bow-thrust propellers to assist in manoeuvering. All WLBs have 20-capacity booms. The *Evergreen* has been refitted as an oceanographic cutter (WAGO) and is painted white; several ships are laid up in reserve.

COASTAL TENDERS

5 "RED" CLASS (BUOY-TENDERS COASTAL (WLM))

Name	No.	Launched	Name	No.	Launched
RED WOOD	WLM 685	1964	RED CEDAR	WLM 688	1970
RED BEECH	WLM 688	1964	RED OAK	WLM 689	1971
RED BIRCH	WLM 687	1965			

Displacement, tons: 471 standard; 512 full load
Dimensions, feet (metres): 157 oa × 33 × 6 *(51·5 × 10·8 × 1·9)*
Main engines: 2 diesels; 2 shafts; 1 800 hp = 12·8 knots
Range, miles: 3 000 at 11·6 knots
Complement: 31 (4 officers, 27 enlisted men)

All built by Coast Guard Yard, Curtis Bay, Maryland. Fitted with controllable-pitch propellers and bow thrusters; steel hulls strengthened for light icebreaking. Steering and engine controls on each bridge wing as well as in pilot house. Living spaces are air conditioned. Fitted with 10-ton capacity boom.

RED BEECH   1976, Dr. Giorgio Arra

3 "HOLLYHOCK" CLASS (BUOY-TENDERS COASTAL (WLM))

FIR WLM 212   **HOLLYHOCK** WLM 220   **WALNUT** WLM 252

Displacement, tons: 989
Dimensions, feet (metres): 175 × 34 × 12 *(57·4 × 10·9 × 3·9)*
Main engines: Diesel reduction; 2 shafts; 1 350 bhp = 12 knots
Complement: 40 (5 officers, 35 enlisted men)

Launched in 1937 *(Hollyhock)* and 1939 *(Fir* and *Walnut). Walnut* was re-engined by Williamette Iron & Steel Co, Portland, Oregon, in 1958. Redesignated coastal tenders, (WLM), instead of buoy tenders, (WAGL) on 1 Jan 1965. Fitted with 20-ton capacity boom.

WALNUT   1976, John A. Jedrlinic

1 "JUNIPER" CLASS (BUOY-TENDER COASTAL (WLM))

JUNIPER WLM 224

Displacement, tons: 794
Dimensions, feet (metres): 177 × 33 × 9·2 *(58 × 10·8 × 3)*
Main engines: Diesel, with electric drive; 2 shafts; 900 bhp = 10·8 knots
Complement: 38 (4 officers, 34 enlisted men)

Launched on 18 May 1940. Redesignated WLM vice WAGL on 1 Jan 1965. Fitted with 20-ton capacity boom.

JUNIPER (WLM 224)   1971, United States Coast Guard

7 "WHITE SUMAC" CLASS (BUOY-TENDERS COASTAL (WLM))

WHITE BUSH	WLM 542	WHITE PINE	WLM 547
WHITE HEATH	WLM 545	WHITE SAGE	WLM 544
WHITE HOLLY	WLM 543	WHITE SUMAC	WLM 540
WHITE LUPINE	WLM 546		

Displacement, tons: 435 standard; 600 full load
Dimensions, feet (metres): 133 oa × 31 × 9 *(43·6 × 10·1 × 2·9)*
Main engines: Diesel; 2 shafts; 600 bhp = 9·8 knots
Complement: 21 (1 officer, 20 enlisted men)

All launched in 1943. All seven ships are former US Navy YFs, adapted for the Coast Guard. The *White Alder* (WLM 541) was sunk in a collision on 7 Dec 1968. Fitted with 10-ton capacity boom.

WHITE BUSH   *1969, United States Coast Guard*

BUOY-TENDERS (INLAND)

TERN WLI 80801

Displacement, tons: 168 full load
Dimensions, feet (metres): 80 oa × 25 × 5 *(26·2 × 8·2 × 1·6)*
Main engines: Diesels; 2 shafts; 450 hp = 10 knots
Complement: 7 (enlisted men)

The *Tern* is prototype for a new design. A cutaway stern and gantry crane (the first installed in a Coast Guard tender) permit lifting buoys aboard from the stern. The crane moves on rails that extend forward to the deck house. Fitted with 125 hp bow thruster to improve manoeuvrability. Air conditioned.
Built by Coast Guard Yard at Curtis Bay, Baltimore, Maryland. Launched on 15 June 1968 and placed in service on 7 Feb 1969.

TERN   *1969, United States Coast Guard*

AZALEA WLI 641

Displacement, tons: 200 full load
Dimensions, feet (metres): 100 oa × 24 × 5 *(32·8 × 7·8 × 1·6)*
Main engines: Diesels; 2 shafts; 440 bhp = 9 knots
Complement: 14 (1 officer, 13 enlisted men)

Launched in 1958. Fitted with pile driver.

COSMOS	WLI 293	**BLUEBELL**	WLI 313	**PRIMROSE**	WLI 316
RAMBLER	WLI 298	**SMILAX**	WLI 315	**VERBENA**	WLI 317

Displacement, tons: 178 full load
Dimensions, feet (metres): 100 oa × 24 × 5 *(32·8 × 7·8 × 1·6)*
Main engines: Diesels; 2 shafts 600 bhp = 10·5 knots
Complement: 15 (1 officer, 14 enlisted men)

Cosmos launched in 1942, *Bluebell* in 1945, others in 1944. *Verbena* and *Primrose* fitted with pile drivers.

PRIMROSE (with pile driver)   *1976, John A. Jedrlinic*

BUCKTHORN WLI 642

Displacement, tons: 200 full load
Dimensions, feet (metres): 100 oa × 24 × 4 *(32·8 × 7·8 × 1·3)*
Main engines: Diesels; 2 shafts; 600 bhp = 7·3 knots
Complement: 14 (1 officer, 13 enlisted men)

Launched in 1963.

BUCKTHORN   *1975, United States Coast Guard*

BLACKBERRY WLI 65303	**CHOKEBERRY** WLI 65304	**LOGANBERRY** WLI 65305	**BAYBERRY** WLI 65400	**ELDERBERRY** WLI 65401

Displacement, tons: 68 full load
Dimensions, feet (metres): 65 oa × 17 × 4 *(21·3 × 5·6 × 4·6)*
Main engines: Diesels; 1 shaft; 220 hp = 9 knots
Complement: 5 (enlisted men)

Launched in 1946.

Displacement, tons: 68 full load
Dimensions, feet (metres): 65 oa × 17 × 4 *(21·3 × 5·6 × 4·6)*
Main engines: Diesels; 2 shafts; 400 hp = 11·3 knots
Complement: 5 (enlisted men)

Launched in 1954.

BUOY TENDERS (RIVER)

SUMAC WLR 311

Displacement, tons: 404 full load
Dimensions, feet (metres): 115 oa × 30 × 6 *(37·7 × 9·8 × 1·9)*
Main engines: Diesels; 3 shafts; 960 hp = 10·6 knots
Complement: 23 (1 officer, 22 enlisted men)

Built in 1943.

DOGWOOD WLR 259   **FORSYTHIA** WLR 263   **SYCAMORE** WLR 268

Displacement, tons: 230 full load, except *Forsythia* 280
Dimensions, feet (metres): 114 oa × 26 × 4 *(37·4 × 8·5 × 1·3)*
Main engines: Diesels; 2 shafts; 2 800 hp = 11 knots
Complement: 21 (1 officer, 20 enlisted men)

Dogwood and *Sycamore* built in 1940; *Forsythia* in 1943.

FOXGLOVE WLR 285

Displacement, tons: 350 full load
Dimensions, feet (metres): 114 oa × 30 × 6 *(37·4 × 9·8 × 1·9)*
Main engines: Diesels; 3 shafts; 8 500 hp = 13·5 knots
Complement: 21 (1 officer, 20 enlisted men)

Built in 1945.

LANTANA WLR 80310

Displacement, tons: 235 full load
Dimensions, feet (metres): 80 oa × 30 × 6 *(26·2 × 9·8 × 1·9)*
Main engines: Diesels; 3 shafts; 10 000 hp = 10 knots
Complement: 20 (1 officer, 19 enlisted men)

Built in 1943.

GASCONADE	WLR 75401	**CHEYENNE**	WLR 75405
MUSKINGUM	WLR 75402	**KICKAPOO**	WLR 75406
WYACONDA	WLR 75403	**KANAWHA**	WLR 75407
CHIPPEWA	WLR 75404	**PATOKA**	WLR 75408
		CHENA	WLR 75409

Displacement, tons: 145 full load
Dimensions, feet (metres): 75 oa × 22 × 4 *(24·5 × 7·2 × 1·3)*
Main engines: Diesel; 2 shafts; 600 hp = 10·8 knots
Complement: 12 (enlisted men)

Built 1964-1971.

OLEANDER WLR 73264

Displacement, tons: 90 full load
Dimensions, feet (metres): 73 oa × 18 × 5 *(23·9 × 5·9 × 1·6)*
Main engines: Diesel; 2 shafts; 300 hp = 12 knots
Complement: 10 (enlisted men)

Built in 1940.

OUACHITA	WLR 65501	**SCIOTO**	WLR 65504
CIMARRON	WLR 65502	**OSAGE**	WLR 65505
OBION	WLR 65503	**SANGAMON**	WLR 65506

Displacement, tons: 139 full load
Dimensions, feet (metres): 65·6 oa × 21 × 5 *(21·5 × 6·9 × 1·6)*
Main engines: Diesel; 2 shafts; 600 hp = 12·5 knots
Complement: 10 (enlisted men)

Built in 1960-1962.

OSAGE pushing barge   *United States Coast Guard*

CONSTRUCTION TENDERS

PAMLICO	WLIC 800	**HUDSON**	WLIC 801
KENNEBEC	WLIC 803	**SAGINAW**	WLIC 804

Displacement, tons: 413 light
Dimensions, feet (metres): 160·9 × 30 × 4 *(49·1 × 9·1 × 1·2)*
Main engines: 2 Diesels = 11·5 knots
Complement: 15

Built in 1975-1977 at the Coast Guard Yard, Curtis Bay, Maryland.

ANVIL	WLIC 75301	**MALLET**	WLIC 75304	**WEDGE**	WLIC 75307
HAMMER	WLIC 75302	**VISE**	WLIC 75305	**SPIKE**	WLIC 75308
SLEDGE	WLIC 75303	**CLAMP**	WLIC 75306	**HATCHET**	WLIC 75309
				AXE	WLIC 75310

Displacement, tons: 145 full load
Dimensions, feet (metres): 75 oa (WLIC 75306-75310 are 76 oa) × 22 × 4 *(24·6 × 7·2 × 1·3)*
Main engines: Diesels; 2 shafts; 600 hp = 10 knots
Complement: 9 or 10 (1 officer in *Mallet, Sledge* and *Vise;* 9 enlisted men in all)

Launched 1962-1965.

SPIKE pushing barge   *1971, United States Coast Guard*

OCEANGOING TUGS

2 "DIVER" CLASS (1 MEDIUM ENDURANCE CUTTER (WMEC)/1 OCEANOGRAPHIC CUTTER (WAGO))

Name	No.	Builders	USN Comm.
ACUSHNET (ex-USS Shackle)	WAGO 167 (ex-WAT 167, ARS 9)	Basalt Rock Co, Napa, California	5 Feb 1944
YOCONA (ex-USS Seize)	WMEC 168 (ex-WAT 168, ARS 26)	Basalt Rock Co, Napa, California	3 Nov 1944

Displacement, tons: 1 557 standard; 1 745 full load
Dimensions, feet (metres): 213·5 oa × 39 × 15 *(70 × 12·8 × 4·9)*
Guns: Removed
Main engines: Diesels (Cooper Bessemer); 3 000 bhp; 2 shafts = 15·5 knots
Complement: *Acushnet* 64 (7 officers, 57 enlisted men); *Yocona* 72 (7 officers, 65 enlisted men)

Large, steel-hulled salvage ships transferred from the Navy to the Coast Guard after World War II and employed in tug and oceanographic duties. Launched 1 April 1943 and 8 April 1944 respectively. *Acushnet* modified for handling environmental data buoys and reclassified WAGO in 1968; *Yocona* reclassified as WMEC in 1968.

ACUSHNET   8/1975, United States Coast Guard

3 "CHEROKEE" CLASS (MEDIUM ENDURANCE CUTTERS (WMEC))

Name	No.	Builders	USN Comm.
CHILULA	WMEC 153 (ex-WAT 153, ATF 153)	Charleston Shipbuilding & Drydock Co, Charleston, South Carolina	5 April 1945
CHEROKEE	WMEC 165 (ex-WAT 165, ATF 66)	Bethlehem Steel Co, Staten Island, New York	26 April 1940
TAMAROA (ex-Zuni)	WMEC 166 (ex-WAT 166, ATF 95)	Commercial Iron Works, Portland, Oregon	9 Oct 1943

Displacement, tons: 1 731 full load
Dimensions, feet (metres): 205 oa × 38·5 × 17 *(62·5 × 11·7 × 5·2)*
Guns: 1—3 inch 50 calibre; 2—50 cal MG
Main engines: Diesel-electric (General Motors diesel); 3 000 bhp; 1 shaft = 16·2 knots
Complement: 72 (7 officers, 65 enlisted men)

Steel-hulled tugs transferred from the Navy to the Coast Guard on loan in 1946; transferred 1 June 1969. Classification of all three ships changed to WMEC in 1968. Launched on 1 Dec 1944, 10 Nov 1939, and 13 July 1943, respectively.

CHEROKEE   1975, Dr. Giorgio Arra

2 "SOTOYOMO" CLASS
(MEDIUM ENDURANCE CUTTERS (WMEC))

Name	No.	Builders	USN Comm.
MODOC (ex-USS Bagaduce)	WMEC 194 (ex-WATA 194, ATA 194)	Levingston Shipbuilding Co, Orange, Texas	14 Feb 1945
COMANCHE (ex-USS Wampanoag)	WMEC 202 (ex-WATA 202, ATA 202)	Gulfport Boiler & Welding Works, Port Arthur, Texas	8 Dec 1944

Displacement, tons: 534 standard; 860 full load
Dimensions, feet (metres): 143 oa × 33·8 × 14 *(46·8 × 11 × 4·9)*
Armament: 2—·50 cal MG
Main engines: Diesel-electric (General Motors diesel); 1 shaft; 1 500 hp = 13·5 knots
Complement: 47 (5 officers, 42 enlisted men)

Steel-hulled tugs. Launched on 4 Dec 1944 and 10 Oct 1944, respectively. The *Modoc* was stricken from the Navy List after World War II and transferred to Maritime Administration; transferred to Coast Guard on 15 Apr 1959. *Comanche* transferred on loan from Navy to Coast Guard from 25 Feb 1959 until stricken from Navy List on 1 June 1969 and transferred permanently. Both ships reclassified as WMEC in 1968.

MODOC   1977, United States Coast Guard

HARBOUR TUGS

WTM 140 ft CLASS NEW CONSTRUCTION

Displacement, tons: 662 full load
Dimensions, feet (metres): 140 oa × 37·6 × 12 *(42·7 × 11·4 × 3·7)*
Main engines: Diesel-electric; 2 500 bhp; 1 shaft = 14 knots
Range, miles: 4 000 at 12 knots
Complement: 17 (3 officers, 14 enlisted men)

This class is designed to replace 110 ft class. Initial units will be assigned to Great Lakes. Lead ship authorised in 1976 programme. First four built by Tacoma BB Co Inc, Washington—first for delivery Nov 1978. Fifth ship proposed in 1978 FY programme. Class of ten projected.

13 110 ft HARBOUR TUGS (MEDIUM)

MANITOU	WYTM 60	**MOHICAN**	WYTM 73	**CHINOOK**	WYTM 96
KAW	WYTM 61	**ARUNDEL**	WYTM 90	**OBJIBWA**	WYTM 97
APALACHEE	WYTM 71	**MAHONING**	WYTM 91	**SNOHOMISH**	WYTM 98
YANKTON	WYTM 72	**NAUGATUCK**	WYTM 92	**SAUK**	WYTM 99
		RARITAN	WYTM 93		

Displacement, tons: 370 full load
Dimensions, feet (metres): 110 oa × 27 × 11 *(36 × 8·8 × 3·6)*
Main engines: Diesel-electric; 1 shaft; 1 000 hp = 11·2 knots
Complement: 20 (1 officer, 19 enlisted men)

Built in 1943 except WYTM 90-93 built in 1939.

CHINOOK   *1/1977, United States Coast Guard*

1 HARBOUR TUG (MEDIUM)

MESSENGER WYTM 85009

Displacement, tons: 230 full load
Dimensions, feet (metres): 85 oa × 23 × 9 *(27·8 × 7·5 × 2·9)*
Main engines: Diesel; 1 shaft; 700 hp = 9·5 knots
Complement: 10 (enlisted)

Built in 1944.

15 HARBOUR TUGS (SMALL)

CAPSTAN	WYTL 65601	**CATENARY**	WYTL 65606	**LINE**	WYTL 65611
CHOCK	WYTL 65602	**BRIDLE**	WYTL 65607	**WIRE**	WYTL 65612
SWIVEL	WYTL 65603	**PENDANT**	WYTL 65608	**BITT**	WYTL 65613
TACKLE	WYTL 65604	**SHACKLE**	WYTL 65609	**BOLLARD**	WYTL 65614
TOWLINE	WYTL 65605	**HAWSER**	WYTL 65610	**CLEAT**	WYTL 65615

Displacement, tons: 72 full load
Dimensions, feet (metres): 65 oa × 19 × 7 *(21·3 × 6·2 × 2·3)*
Main engines: Diesel; 1 shaft; 400 hp = 9·8 knots except WYTL 65601-65606 10·5 knots
Complement: 10 (enlisted men)

Built from 1961 to 1967.

LINE   *7/1976, A. D. Baker III*

LIGHTSHIPS

LIGHTSHIP COLUMBIA WLV 604   **LIGHTSHIP NANTUCKET** WLV 612
LIGHTSHIP RELIEF WLV 605

Displacement, tons: 617 full load, except WLV 612 and 613 are 607 full load
Dimensions, feet (metres): 128 oa × 30 × 11 *(41·9 × 9·8 × 3·8)*
Main engines: Diesel; 550 bhp; 1 shaft = 10·7 knots , except WLV 612 and 613 = 11 knots

All launched 1950. *Lightship Columbia* assigned to Astoria, Oregon; *Lightship Nantucket* (612) and *Lightship Relief* (605) to Boston, Massachusetts.
Coast Guard lightships exchange names according to assignment; hull numbers remain constant.

NATIONAL OCEANIC AND ATMOSPHERIC ADMINISTRATION

Command

Director, National Ocean Survey:
  Rear-Admiral Allen L. Powell
Associate Director, Office of Fleet Operations:
  Rear-Admiral Herbert R. Lippold, Jnr.
Director, Atlantic Marine Center:
  Rear-Admiral Robert C. Munson
Director, Pacific Marine Center:
  Rear-Admiral Eugene A. Taylor

Establishment

The "Survey of the Coast" was established by an act of Congress on 10 Feb, 1807. Renamed US Coast Survey in 1834 and again renamed Coast and Geodetic Survey in 1878. The commissioned officer corps was established in 1917. The Coast and Geodetic Survey was made a component of the Environmental Science Services Administration on 13 July, 1965, when that agency was established within the Department of Commerce. The Environmental Science Services Administration subsequently became the National Oceanic and Atmospheric Administration in October 1970 with the Coast and Geodetic Survey being renamed National Ocean Survey and its jurisdiction expanded to include the US Lake Survey, formerly a part of the US Army Corps of Engineers; the Coast Guard's national data buoy development project; and the Navy's National Oceanographic Instrumentation Centre.

Missions

The National Ocean Survey operates the ships of the National Oceanic and Atmospheric Administration (NOAA), a federal agency created in 1970. During 1972-1973 the National Marine Fisheries Service (formerly the Bureau of Commercial Fisheries of the Department of Interior) was consolidated into the NOAA fleet which is operated by the National Ocean Survey. Approximately 15 small ships and craft 65 feet or longer are counted in the National Marine Fisheries Service. The former National Marine Fisheries vessels are not described because of the specialised, non-military nature of their work. The National Ocean Survey prepares nautical and aeronautical charts; conducts geodetic, geophysical, oceanographic, and marine surveys; predicts tides and currents; tests, evaluates, and calibrates sensing systems for ocean use; and conducts the development of and eventually will operate a national system of automated ocean buoys for obtaining environmental information.
The National Ocean Survey is a civilian agency that supports national civilian and military requirements. During time of war the ships and officers of NOAA can be expected to operate with the Navy, either as a separate service or integrated into the Navy.

Ships

National Ocean Survey ship designations are: OSS for Ocean Survey Ship, MSS for Medium Survey Ship, CSS for Coastal Survey Ship, and ASV for Auxiliary Survey Vessel. No National Ocean Survey Ships are armed. All ships are believed active in 1976.
Most ships have Maritime Administration design designations.

Personnel

The National Ocean Survey which operates NOAA ships has approximately 225 commissioned officers and 250 officers and 2 250 civil service personnel. In addition, another 125 commissioned officers serve elsewhere in NOAA and several US Navy officers are assigned to NOAA.

Aviation

The National Ocean Survey's Coastal Mapping Division operates two aircraft for aerial photographic missions, a twin-engine de Havilland Canada Buffalo and a twin-engine North American Rockwell Aero Commander. In 1975 NOAA additionally acquired two WP-3D Orion aircraft for weather research.

SURVEY SHIPS

1 "RESEARCHER" CLASS (OCEANOGRAPHIC SURVEY SHIP (OSS))

Name	No.	Builders	Commissioned
RESEARCHER	OSS 03	American Shipbuilding Co, Lorain, Ohio	8 Oct 1970

Displacement, tons: 2 875 light
Dimensions, feet (metres): 278·25 oa × 51 × 16·25 *(84·7 × 15·5 × 4·9)*
Main engines: 2 geared diesels; 3 200 hp; 2 shafts = 16 knots
Range, miles: 13 000 at 14·5 knots
Complement: 11 officers, 55 crewmen
Scientists: 13

The *Researcher* was designed specifically for deep ocean research; she is ice strengthened. Estimated cost $10 000 000. Fitted with 20-ton capacity crane, 5-ton capacity crane, four 2½-ton capacity cranes, and an A-frame with 10-ton lift capacity. Launched on 5 Oct 1968.

Design: Fitted with computerised data acquisition system that automatically samples, processes, and records oceanographic, geophysical, hydrographic, and meteorological data. The 20-ton telescoping crane is designed to handle special sampling equipment and small submersible vehicles as well as small boats. S2-MT-MA74a type.

Engineering: Controllable pitch propellers. A 450-horsepower, 360-degree retractable bow thruster provides sustained low speeds up to seven knots and permits precise positioning.

RESEARCHER   *National Ocean Survey*

2 "OCEANOGRAPHER" CLASS (OCEANOGRAPHIC SURVEY SHIP (OSS))

Name	No.	Builders	Commissioned
OCEANOGRAPHER	OSS 01	Aerojet-General Corp, Jacksonville, Florida	13 July 1966
DISCOVERER	OSS 02	Aerojet-General Corp, Jacksonville, Florida	29 April 1967

Displacement, tons: 3 959 light
Dimensions, feet (metres): 303·3 oa × 52 × 18·5 *(92·4 × 15·8 × 5·6)*
Main engines: 4 diesels with electric drive; 5 000 bhp; 2 shafts = 16+ knots
Range, miles: 15 200 at 16 knots
Complement: 14 officers, 78 crewmen
Scientists: 18

Ice strengthened construction. Fitted with a 5-ton capacity crane and 3½-ton capacity crane. *Oceanographer* launched on 18 April 1964. *Discoverer* launched on 29 Oct 1964, deactivated in 1973 and placed in reserve, but subsequently reactivated.

Design: Fitted with computerised data acquisition system. Centre well 8 × 6 feet provides sheltered access to sea for SCUBA divers and for lowering research equipment. Six ports in submerged bow observation chamber. S2-MET-MA62a type.

Engineering: A 400-horsepower, through-hull thruster provides precise manoeuvring. Not equipped for silent operation.

OCEANOGRAPHER   *National Ocean Survey*

1 "SURVEYOR" CLASS (HYDROGRAPHIC SURVEY SHIP (OSS))

Name	No.	Builders	Commissioned
SURVEYOR	OSS 32	National Steel Co, San Diego, California	30 Apr 1960

Displacement, tons: 3 150 light
Dimensions, feet (metres): 292·3 oa × 46 × 18 *(88·8 × 14·0 × 5·5)*
Main engines: 1 steam turbine (De Laval); 3 520 shp; 1 shaft = 15 + knots
Range, miles: 10 500 at 15 knots
Complement: 14 officers, 106 crewmen
Scientists: 9

Specially designed for marine charting and geophysical surveys. Fitted with helicopter platform aft. Ice strengthened. Twin telescoping 2½-ton capacity cargo booms (forward) and 12½-ton capacity crane. Estimated cost $6 000 000. Launched on 25 Apr 1959. The *Surveyor* was deactivated in 1973 and placed in reserve, but subsequently reactivated.

Design: Large bilge keel (18 inches × 70 feet) permits oceanographic observations to be performed up to Sea State 6. S2-S-RM28a type.

Engineering: Retractable outboard motor mounted to stern for precision manoeuvring.

Disposals: *Pathfinder* OSS 30, ex-US Navy AGS 1 decommissioned in 1972 and stricken.

SURVEYOR   *National Ocean Survey*

3 "FAIRWEATHER" CLASS (HYDROGRAPHIC SURVEY SHIPS (MSS))

Name	No.	Builders	Commissioned
FAIRWEATHER	MSS 20	Aerojet-General Corp, Jacksonville, Florida	2 Oct 1968
RAINIER	MSS 21	Aerojet-General Corp, Jacksonville, Florida	2 Oct 1968
MT. MITCHELL	MSS 22	Aerojet-General Corp, Jacksonville, Florida	23 Mar 1968

Displacement, tons: 1 798 light
Dimensions, feet (metres): 231 oa × 42·07 × 13·9 *(70·2 × 12·8 × 4·2)*
Main engines: 2 diesels; 2 400 bhp; 2 shafts = 13+ knots
Range, miles: 9 000 at 13 knots
Complement: 12 officers, 64 crewmen
Scientists: 2

Ice strengthened. *Fairweather* and *Rainier* launched on 15 March 1967, *Mt. Mitchell* on 29 Nov 1966. S1-MT-MA72a type.

Engineering: Fitted with a 200-horsepower, through-bow thruster for precise manoeuvring. Controllable-pitch propellers.

FAIRWEATHER   *National Ocean Survey*

2 "McARTHUR" CLASS (COASTAL SURVEY SHIPS (CSS))

Name	No.	Builders	Commissioned
McARTHUR	CSS 30	Norfolk SB & DD Co, Norfolk, Virginia	15 Dec 1966
DAVIDSON	CSS 31	Norfolk SB & DD Co, Norfolk, Virginia	10 Mar 1967

Displacement, tons: 995 light
Dimensions, feet (metres): 175 oa × 38 × 11·5 *(53·0 × 11·5 × 3·5)*
Main engines: 2 diesels; 1 600 bhp; 2 shafts = 13·5+ knots
Range, miles: 4 500 at 13·5 knots
Complement: 8 officers, 32 crewmen

Designed for nearshore operations. Ice strengthened. Launched on 15 Nov 1965 and 7 May 1966 respectively. S1-MT-MA70a type.

Engineering: Controllable-pitch propellers.

DAVIDSON *National Ocean Survey*

2 "PEIRCE" CLASS (COASTAL SURVEY SHIP (CSS))

Name	No.	Builders	Commissioned
PEIRCE	CSS 28	Marietta Manufacturing Co, Point Pleasant, West Virginia	6 May 1963
WHITING	CSS 29	Marietta Manufacturing Co, Point Pleasant, West Virginia	8 July 1963

Displacement, tons: 760 light
Dimensions, feet (metres): 164 oa × 33 × 10·1 *(50·0 × 10·0 × 3·1)*
Main engines: 2 diesels; 1 600 bhp; 2 shafts = 12·5+ knots
Range, miles: 4 500 at 12·5 knots
Complement: 8 officers, 32 crewmen

Designed for nearshore operations. Ice strengthened. *Peirce* launched on 15 Oct 1962 and *Whiting* on 20 Nov 1962. S1-MT-59a type.

Engineering: Controllable-pitch propellers.

PEIRCE *National Ocean Survey*

COASTAL VESSELS

2 "RUDE" CLASS (WIRE DRAG VESSELS (ASV))

Name	No.	Builders	Commissioned
RUDE	ASV 90	Jacobson Shipyard Inc, Oyster Bay, New York	29 Mar 1967
HECK	ASV 91	Jacobson Shipyard Inc, Oyster Bay, New York	29 Mar 1967

Displacement, tons: 214 light
Dimensions, feet (metres): 90 oa × 22 × 7 *(27·4 × 6·7 × 2·1)*
Main engines: 2 diesels; 800 bhp; 2 shafts = 11·5+ knots
Range, miles: 740 at 11·5 knots
Endurance: 8 days provisions
Complement: 2 officers, 8 crewmen

Designed to search out underwater navigational hazards along the coast using wire drags. Launched on 17 Aug 1966 and 1 Nov 1966 respectively. S1-MT-MA71a type. A single commanding officer is assigned to both vessels; normally he rides in one ship and the executive officer in the other.

Engineering: Propellers are guarded by shrouds similar to Kort nozzles. Auxiliary propulsion provides 50 horsepower to each propeller for dragging operations.

RUDE *National Ocean Survey*

1 "FERREL" CLASS (CURRENT SURVEY VESSEL (ASV))

Name	No.	Builders	Commissioned
FERREL	ASV 92	Zeigler Shipyard, Jennings, Louisiana	4 June 1968

Displacement, tons: 363 light
Dimensions, feet (metres): 133·25 × 32 × 7 *(40·5 × 9·7 × 2·1)*
Main engines: 2 diesels; 820 bhp; 2 shafts = 10+ knots
Endurance: 15 days provisions
Complement: 3 officers, 13 crewmen

Specially designed to conduct nearshore and estuarine current surveys. Limited surface meteorological observations are also made. Buoy workshop provided in 450-square feet of enclosed deck area with buoy stowage on open after deck. Launched on 4 April 1968. SI-MT-MA83a type.

Engineering: Fitted with 100-horsepower, electric-driven bow thruster. Cruising speed is 10 knots.

FERREL *National Ocean Survey*

UNION OF SOVIET SOCIALIST REPUBLICS

Flag Officers Soviet Navy

Commander-in-Chief of the Soviet Navy and Deputy Minister of Defence:
Admiral of the Fleet of the Soviet Union Sergei Georgiyevich Gorshkov
First Deputy Commander-in-Chief of the Soviet Navy:
Admiral of the Fleet N. I. Smirnov
Assistant Chief of the General Staff of the Armed Forces:
Admiral of the Fleet S. M. Lobov
Deputy Commander-in-Chief:
Admiral N. N. Amelko
Deputy Commander-in-Chief:
Admiral G. A. Bondarenko
Deputy Commander-in-Chief:
Admiral V. V. Mikhaylin
Deputy Commander-in-Chief:
Engineer Admiral P. G. Kotov
Deputy Commander-in-Chief:
Engineer Admiral V. G. Novikov
Commander of Naval Aviation:
Colonel-General A. A. Mironenko
Chief of the Political Directorate:
Admiral V. M. Grishanov
Chief of Rear Services:
Admiral L. Y. Mizin
Chief of Naval Training Establishments:
Vice-Admiral I. M. Kuznetsov
Chief of Main Naval Staff:
Admiral of the Fleet N. D. Sergeyev
1st Deputy Chief of the Main Naval Staff:
Vice-Admiral P. M. Navoytsev
Chief of the Hydrographic Service:
Admiral A. I. Rassokho

Northern Fleet

Commander-in-Chief:
Admiral of the Fleet G. M. Yegorov
1st Deputy Commander-in-Chief:
Vice-Admiral V. S. Kruglyakov
Chief of Staff:
Vice-Admiral V. N. Chernavin
In Command of the Political Department:
Rear-Admiral Y. Padorin

Pacific

Commander-in-Chief:
Admiral V. P. Maslov
1st Deputy Commander-in-Chief:
Vice-Admiral E. N. Spiridonov
Chief of Staff:
Vice-Admiral Ya. M. Kudelkin
In Command of the Political Department:
Rear-Admiral V. D. Sabaneyev

Black Sea

Commander-in-Chief:
Admiral N. I. Khovrin
1st Deputy Commander-in-Chief:
Vice-Admiral V. Samoylov
Chief of Staff:
Rear-Admiral V. Ponikarovsky
In Command of the Political Department:
Vice-Admiral P. N. Medvedev

Baltic

Commander-in-Chief:
Vice-Admiral A. M. Kosov
1st Deputy Commander-in-Chief:
Vice-Admiral V. V. Sidorov
Chief of Staff:
—
In Command of the Political Department:
Vice-Admiral N. I. Shablikov

Caspian Flotilla

Commander-in-Chief:
Rear-Admiral L. D. Ryabtsev
Chief of Staff:
Rear-Admiral V. M. Buynov
In Command of the Political Department:
Rear-Admiral V. N. Sergeyev

Leningrad Naval Base

Commanding Officer:
Admiral V. M. Leonenkov
In Command of the Political Department:
Vice-Admiral A. A. Plekhanov
Head of the Order of Lenin Naval Academy:
Admiral V. S. Sysoyev
Head of Frunze Naval College:
Rear-Admiral V. V. Platonov

Diplomatic Representation

Naval Attaché London: Captain I. Ivanov

Personnel

(a) 1977: Approximately 425 000 officers and ratings (including Naval Infantry)
(b) Approximately 30% Volunteers (officers and senior ratings)—remainder 3 years National Service at sea and 2 if ashore

Mercantile Marine

Lloyd's Register of Shipping: 7 652 vessels of 19 235 973 tons gross

Main Naval Bases

North: Severomorsk (HQ), Archangelsk, Polyarny, Severodvinsk (building).
Baltic: Leningrad (Kronshtadt), Tallinn, Lepaia, Baltiisk (HQ)
Black Sea: Sevastopol (HQ), Tuapse, Poti, Nikolayev (building)
Pacific: Vladivostock (HQ), Nakhodka, Sovetskaia Gavan, Magadan, Petropavlovsk.

Deletions and Conversions

Whilst it is not possible to provide an accurate estimate of total deletions and conversions during the last year the following is a guide to those estimates used in this section.

Cruiser
Deletion of *Zheleznyakov*

Destroyers
"Kashin" class conversions with SSM
1 "Krupny" class conversion to "Kanin" class.
"Kildin" class conversions continue.

Frigates
Conversion of "Petya 1A" class.

Corvettes
Conversion of some "Grisha" class to all-gun ships.

Fast Attack Craft
Deletion of 20 "P6" class and all "P8" and "P10" classes.
Deletion of all "P4" class.

Large Patrol Craft
Deletion of all "Kronshtadt" class

Mine Warfare Forces
Deletion of 5 "T 301" class.

Pennant Numbers

The Soviet Navy has frequent changes of pennant numbers and so these are of little use in identifying individual ships. For that reason such a list has been omitted in this section.
It will be noticed that, in some cases, the same ship has different numbers in different photographs.

Building Programme

The following is an abstract of the programme used in estimating force levels.

Aircraft Carriers
2 "Kiev" class building—continuing programme.

Submarines
Continuing programme for "Delta I", "Delta II", "Charlie", "Charlie II", "Victor", "Victor II" and "Tango" classes.

Cruisers
Continuing programme for "Kara" and "Kresta II" classes

Destroyers
"Krivak" class continues.

Frigates
"Petya" class continues.

Corvettes
"Grisha" and "Nanuchka" classes continue.

Light Forces
"Turya" class hydrofoils continue.
"Zhuk" class coastal patrol craft continues. "Stenka" class continues.

Mine Warfare Forces
"Sonya" class (MSC) and "Natya" class continue.

Amphibious Forces
"Ropucha" class LST continues.

Air Cushion Vehicles
A large programme of unknown size.

Support and Depot Ships
"Amur" and "Ugra" classes continuing.

Service Forces

"Boris Chilikin" class continues.
"Ingul", "Sorum" and "Pamir" class tugs continue.

Subsequent types and classes have been revised from new information, not necessarily as new construction.

Strength of the Fleet

Aircraft Carriers	1 + 2 building	Fast Attack Craft (Patrol)	60+	Survey Ships	73 + 25 (civilian)
Helicopter Cruisers	2	Fast Attack Craft (Hydrofoil)	46	Research Ships	24 (civilian)
Submarines (SSBN)	62 + 6 building	Fast Attack Craft (Torpedo)	90	Space Associated Ships	14 + 9 (civilian)
Submarines (SSB)	22	Large Patrol Craft	60	Fleet Replenishment Ships	6
Submarines (SSGN)	41 + 2 building	River Patrol Craft	130	Tankers	21
Submarines (SSG)	28	Coastal Patrol Craft	25	Harbour Tankers	22
Submarines (SSN)	39 + 2 building	Minesweepers—Ocean	161 + 3 building	Salvage Vessels	20
Submarines (SS)	*130 + 2 building	Minesweepers—Coastal	128 + 3 building	Rescue Ships	15
Cruisers (CG)	22 + 4 building	Minesweepers—Inshore		Lifting Ships	15
Cruisers (Gun)	13	and River	112	Tenders	150 +
Destroyers (DDG)	54 + 4 building	LSTs	22 + 1 building	Icebreakers (Nuclear)	3 + 1 building
Destroyers (Gun)	58	LCTs	60	Icebreakers	39
Frigates	108 (a number in reserve)	LCUs	107	Cable Ships	6 + 3
Corvettes (Missile)	17 + 3 building	LCMs	100 +	Large Tugs	60 +
Corvettes	89 + 2 building	Depot and Repair Ships	65	Transports	10
Fast Attack Craft (Missile)	120	Intelligence Collectors (AGI)	54		

* plus 100 or more in reserve.

SOVIET NAVAL AVIATION

The Soviet Navy operates some 1 200 fixed-wing aircraft and helicopters in *Voyenno Morskaya Aviatsiya*, the world's second largest naval air arm. The primary combat components are
(1) Long range and medium bombers employed in the maritime reconnaissance role.
(2) Medium bombers mostly equipped with air-to-surface missiles in the anti-ship strike role.
(3) Land based patrol aircraft, amphibians and helicopters in the anti-submarine role.
(4) The "Forger" V/STOL aircraft operating from the "Kiev" class.

Bombers: The Soviet naval air arm has about 50 heavy and 550 medium bombers in the anti-shipping, strike, tanker and reconnaissance roles. The main strike force comprises over 300 "Badger" equipped with "Kipper" and "Kelt" air-to-surface missiles as well as the "Backfire" supersonic bombers first introduced in 1974 and the elderly "Blinder" conventional bombers. The reconnaissance aircraft are about 50 "Bear D" (long range recce); 60 "Badger" and a similar number of "Blinders".

ASW Helicopters: Over 220 anti-submarine helicopters are believed to be in the naval air arm, mostly Ka-25 "Hormone" (a twin-turbine craft) and some of the older Mi-4 "Hound" helicopters which are now being replaced for shore-based ASW by the "Haze" helicopters. The "Hormone" anti-submarine helicopters, armed with torpedoes or other ASW weapons operate from the "Kiev" class and *Moskva* and *Leningrad* which can each operate some 15 to 20 helicopters, servicing them in a hangar below the flight deck. They have also been seen in the "Kara", "Kresta I" and "Kresta II" class cruisers which are the first Soviet ships of this type to be fitted with a helicopter hangar. In some of these ships the radar fitted helicopter may also have a

reconnaissance role associated with the surface-to-surface missile system. Other types of helicopter are also used in the transport role ashore. The presence of *Kiev* and, later, her sisters notably increases the seaborne helicopter capability.

ASW Patrol Aircraft: The Soviet Union is the only nation other than Japan maintaining modern military flying boats, about 100 Be-12 "Mail" (turboprop) aircraft of this type being operational. The latter aircraft, an amphibian often-photographed on runways, has an advanced anti-submarine capability evidenced by a radome extending forward, a Magnetic Anomaly Detector (MAD) boom extending aft and a weapons bay in the rear fuselage.
The "May", of which some 60 are in service, is a militarised version of the four-turboprop commercial air freighter (code name "Coot") in wide commercial service. The patrol/anti-submarine version has been lengthened and fitted with a MAD boom as well as other electronic equipment and a weapons capability similar to the US Navy's conversion of the Lockheed Electra into the P-3 "Orion" patrol aircraft. There is also another variant of the "Bear" bomber, the "Bear F" engaged in ASW operations.

Transports/Training Aircraft: There are also about 300 transports, utility, and training fixed-wing aircraft and helicopters under Navy control.

*Aircraft names are NATO code names; "B" names indicate bombers, "H" names for helicopters, and "M" names for miscellaneous aircraft. Single syllable names are propeller driven and two syllable names are jet-propelled.

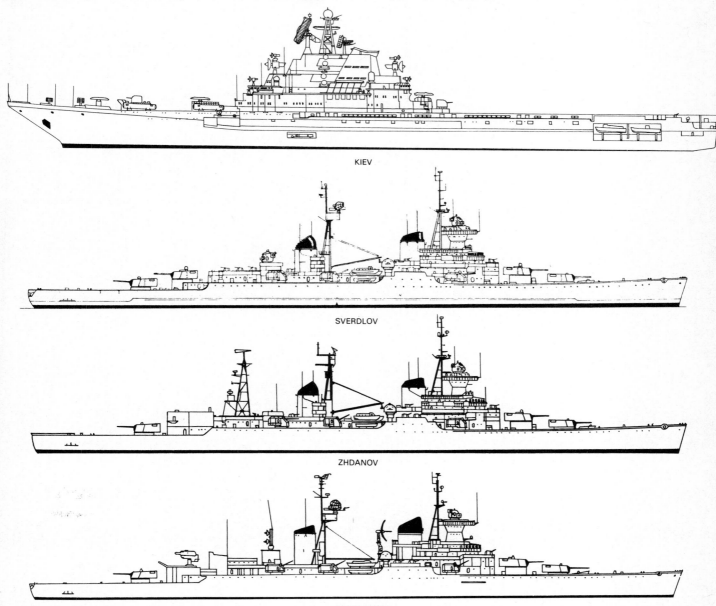

KIEV

SVERDLOV

ZHDANOV

DZERZHINSKI

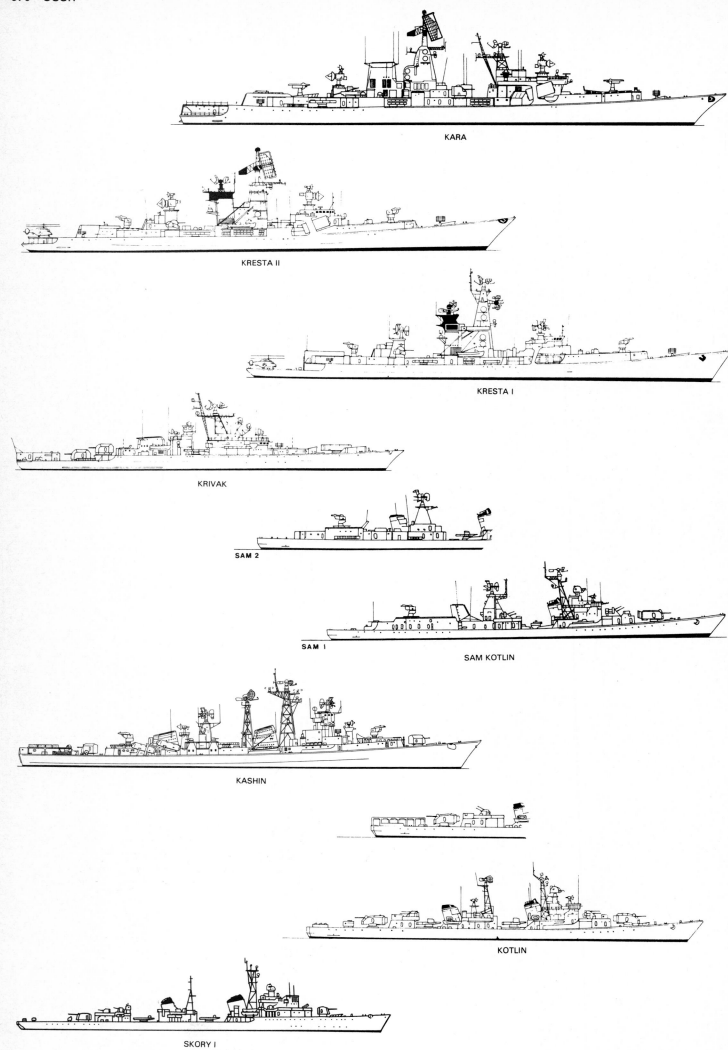

KARA

KRESTA II

KRESTA I

KRIVAK

SAM 2

SAM I

SAM KOTLIN

KASHIN

KOTLIN

SKORY I

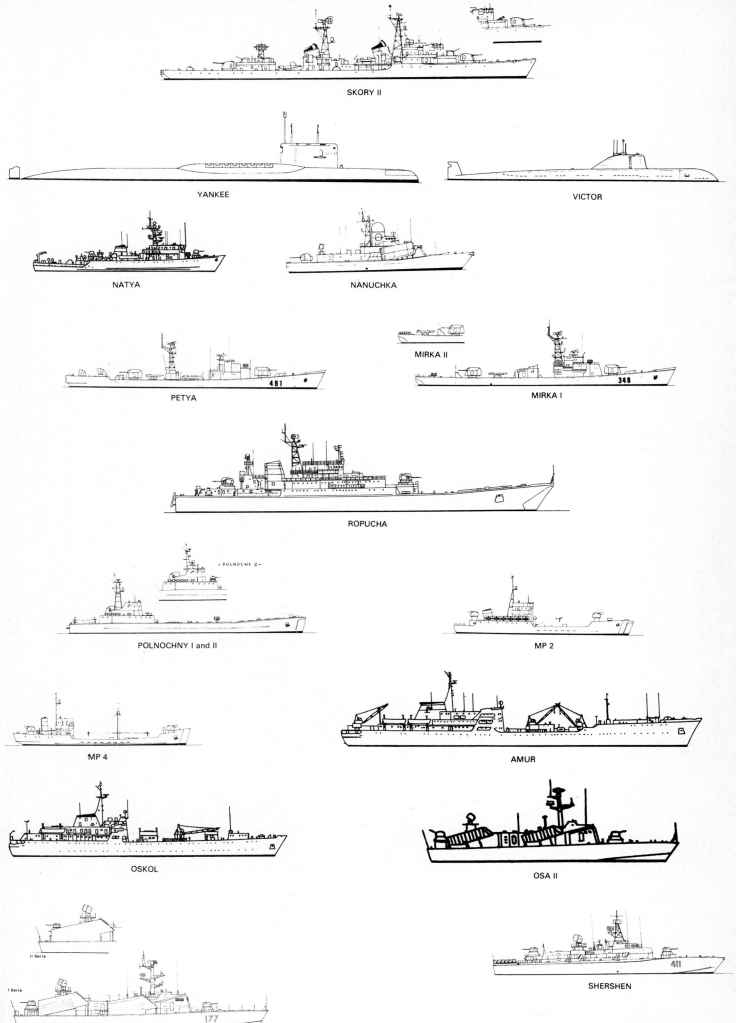

SKORY II

YANKEE

VICTOR

NATYA

NANUCHKA

PETYA

MIRKA II

MIRKA I

ROPUCHA

POLNOCHNY I and II

MP 2

MP 4

AMUR

OSKOL

OSA II

OSA I

SHERSHEN

Note: Line drawings by courtesy of Erminio Bagnasco and Siegfried Breyer. Scale is 1 : 1200 except for Osa I, Osa II and Shershen classes, which are 1 : 600.

SUBMARINES
Ballistic Missile Classes

4 + 3 "DELTA II" CLASS
(BALLISTIC MISSILE SUBMARINES SSBN)

Displacement, tons: 16 000
Dimensions, feet (metres): 500 × 36 × 34 *(152·5 × 11 × 10·4)*
Missiles: 16—SS-N-8 tubes
Torpedo tubes: 6—21 in *(533 mm)*
Main machinery: Nuclear reactors; steam turbines; 2 shafts
Speed, knots: ? 25 dived

The first acknowledgement of this class was made in Nov 1973 by the US Secretary of Defense. Building yard—Severodvinsk. Of the total of twelve submarines per year completing in Soviet yards at least half are probably of the "Delta I and II" classes.

With the limitations of the SALT agreement this programme could result in the deletion of other earlier classes.
It is possible that another variant designed for SS-N-X 18 missiles (approx 5 000 n. miles range) is under construction.

15 + 4 "DELTA I" CLASS
(BALLISTIC MISSILE SUBMARINES SSBN)

Displacement, tons: 9 500 surfaced; 11 000 dived
Length, feet (metres): 426 *(130)*
Beam, feet (metres): 34·8 *(10·6)*
Draught, feet (metres): 32·8 *(10·0)*
Missiles: 12 SS-N-8 tubes
Torpedo tubes: 6—21 in *(533 mm)*
Main machinery: Nuclear reactors; Steam turbine; 2 shafts; 40 000 shp
Speed, knots: 25-30 dived
Complement: About 120

This advance on the "Yankee" class SSBNs was announced at the end of 1972. The missile armament is twelve SS-N-8s with a range of 4 200 nautical miles, at present believed to carry single heads, rather than MRVs. As the SS-N-6 has already been tested with MRV warheads, however, it is not unlikely that these missiles will in due course be similarly armed. The longer-range SS-N-8 missiles are of greater length than the SS-N-6s and, as this length cannot be accommodated below

the keel, they stand several feet proud of the after-casing. At the same time their presumed greater diameter and the need to compensate for the additional top-weight would seem to be the reasons for the reduction to twelve missiles in this class. The total "Delta" class building programme depends on the final outcome of the various Strategic Arms Limitation Talks (SALT).

"DELTA I" Class

"DELTA" Class

1973

Submarines
Ballistic Missile Classes

34 "YANKEE" CLASS
(BALLISTIC MISSILE SUBMARINES SSBN)

Displacement, tons: 8 500 surfaced; 10 000 dived
Length, feet (metres): 426·5 *(130·0)*
Beam, feet (metres): 34·8 *(10·6)*
Draught, feet (metres): 32·8 *(10·0)*
Missile launchers: 16 tubes for SS-N-6 missiles (see note)
Torpedo tubes: 8—21 in
Main machinery: Nuclear reactors; steam turbines; 40 000 shp; 2 shafts
Speed, knots: 30 dived
Complement: About 120

The vertical launching tubes are arranged in two rows of eight, and the SS-N-6 missiles have a range of 1 300/1 600 nautical miles. These missiles have been tested with MRV warheads and these are now operational. At about the time that the USS *George Washington* was laid down (1 Nov 1957) as the world's first SSBN it is likely that the Soviet Navy embarked on its own major SSBN programme. With experience gained from the diesel-propelled "Golf" class and the nuclear-propelled "Hotel" class, the "Yankee" design was completed. The first of the class was delivered late-1967 and the programme then accelerated from 4 boats in 1968 to 8 in 1971, the last of the class being completed in 1975. Construction took place at Severodvinsk and Komsomolsk. The original deployment of this class was to the Eastern seaboard of the US giving a coverage at least as far as the Mississippi. Increase in numbers allowed a Pacific patrol to be established off California extending coverage at least as far as the Rockies.

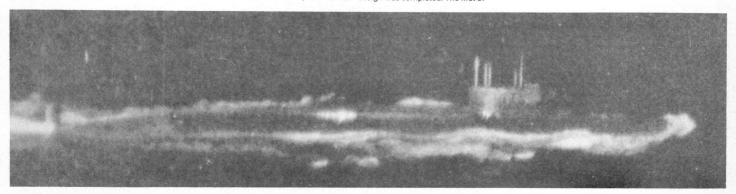

"YANKEE" Class (off Hawaii by night)   *4/1971, USN*

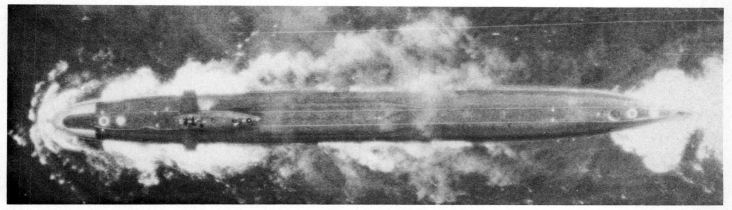

"YANKEE" Class   *1972*

"YANKEE" Class   *1970*

Submarines
Ballistic Missile Classes

1 "HOTEL III" CLASS
8 "HOTEL II" CLASS
(BALLISTIC MISSILE SUBMARINES SSBN)

Displacement, tons: 4 500 surfaced; 5 500 dived
Length, feet (metres): 377·2 *(115·2)*
Beam, feet (metres): 28·2 *(8·6)*
Draught, feet (metres): 25 *(7·6)*
Missile launchers: 3 SS-N-5 tubes
Torpedo tubes: 6—21 in (bow); 4—16 in (stern)
Main machinery: 2 nuclear reactors, steam turbines; 30 000 shp; 2 shafts
Speed, knots: 20 surfaced; 22 dived
Complement: 90

Long range submarines with three vertical ballistic missile tubes in the large fin. All this class was completed between 1958 and 1962. Originally fitted with SS-N-4 system with Sark missiles (300 miles). Between 1963 and 1967 this system was replaced by the SS-N-5 system with Serb missiles capable of 700 mile range. Since then these boats have been deployed off both coasts of the USA and Canada. As the limitations of SALT are felt the "Hotel IIs" will probably be phased-out to allow the maximum number of "Delta" class to be built. The "Hotel III" was a single unit converted for the test firings of the SS-N-8. The earlier boats of this class, which was of a similar hull and reactor design to the "Echo" class, will, by the late 1970s, be reaching their twentieth year in service.

"HOTEL II" Class damaged in North Atlantic   2/1972, USN

"HOTEL II" Class

Submarines
Ballistic Missile Classes

9 "GOLF I" and 13 "GOLF II" CLASS
(BALLISTIC MISSILE SUBMARINES SSB)

Displacement, tons: 2 350 surfaced; 2 800 dived
Length, feet (metres): 295·2 (90)
Beam, feet (metres): 27 (8·2)
Draught, feet (metres): 15·7 (4·8)
Missile launchers: 3 SS-N-4 (G I); 3 SS-N-5 (G II)
Torpedo tubes: 10—21 in (6 bow; 4 stern)
Main machinery: 3 diesels; 3 shafts; 6 000 hp; Electric motors;
  6 000 hp
Speed, knots: 17·6 surfaced; 17 dived
Range, miles: 22 700 surfaced cruising
Complement: 86 (12 officers, 74 men)

This class has a very large fin fitted with three vertically
mounted tubes and hatches for launching ballistic missiles.
Built at Komsomolsk and Severodvinsk. Building started in
1958 and finished in 1961-62. After the missile conversion of
the "Hotel" class was completed in 1967 thirteen of this class
("Golf II") were converted to carry the SS-N-5 system with 700
miles Serb missiles in place of the shorter range (300 mile)
Sarks. One sank in the Pacific in 1968 and was raised by the
USA in 1974.
One of this class has been built by China, although apparently
lacking missiles.

"GOLF II" Class   7/1973

"GOLF II" Class (in the Caribbean)   5/1974, USN

1 "ZULU V" CLASS
(Ex-BALLISTIC MISSILE SUBMARINE SSB)

Displacement, tons: 1 900 surfaced; 2 400 dived
Length, feet (metres): 295 (90)
Beam, feet (metres): 24·1 (7·9)
Draught, feet (metres): 19·0 (4·8)
Missile launchers: 2 tubes for SS-N-4 missiles
Torpedo tubes: 6—21 in (533 mm)
Main machinery: 3 diesels; 3 shafts; 9 000 bhp; 3 electric
  motors; 4 500 hp
Speed, knots: 18 surfaced; 15 dived
Range, miles: 13 000 surfaced cruising
Complement: 85

These were basically of "Zulu" class design but converted in
1955-57 to ballistic missile submarines with larger fins and two
vertical tubes for launching Sark (300 mile) missiles on the
surface. These were the first Soviet ballistic missile submarines, and, in fact, the first in any navy. Of the six converted
only one remains in the list and may be used for research.
Three others have been converted for research duties as *Lira*,
Orion and *Vega* whilst two more may have been converted
back to patrol submarines. Probably in reserve.

"ZULU V" Class   1971

Submarines
Cruise Missile Classes

1 "PAPA" CLASS
(CRUISE MISSILE SUBMARINE SSGN)

Displacement, tons (approx): 4 500 surfaced; 5 200 dived
Dimensions, feet (metres): 318 × 32·8 × 26·3 *(97 × 10 × 8)*
Torpedo tubes: 6—21 in *(533 mm)*

A single member of an SSGN class apparently a development of the "Charlie" class.

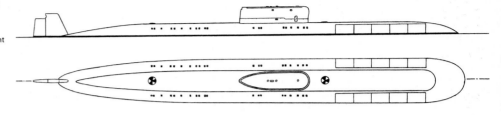

"PAPA" Class

1976, S. Breyer

3 "CHARLIE II" CLASS
(CRUISE MISSILE SUBMARINES SSGN)

An enlarged edition of the "Charlie" class about 25 ft longer.

12 "CHARLIE" CLASS
(CRUISE MISSILE SUBMARINES SSGN)

Displacement, tons: 4 000 surfaced; 5 100 dived
Length, feet (metres): 304·8 *(94)*
Beam, feet (metres): 32·8 *(10·0)*
Draught, feet (metres): 24·6 *(7·5)*
Missile launchers: 8 tubes for SS-N-7 missiles
Torpedo tubes: 8—21 in
Main machinery: 2 nuclear reactors; steam turbines; 25 000-30 000 shp; 3 shafts
Speed, knots: 20 surfaced; 30 approx, dived
Complement: 100

A class of cruise-missile submarines built at Gorky. The first of class was delivered in 1968, representing a very significant advance in the cruise-missile submarine field. With a speed of at least 30 knots and mounting eight missile tubes for the SS-N-7 system (25 n. miles range) which has a dived launch capability, this is a great advance on the "Echo" class. These boats have an improved hull and reactor design and must be assumed to have an organic control for their missile system therefore posing a notable threat to any surface force. Their deployment to the Mediterranean, the area of the US 6th Fleet, is only a part of their general and world-wide operations. Last year's figure has been reassessed in view of the balance between SSBNs, SSNs and patrol submarines now calculated.

"CHARLIE" Class

1974, MOD(N)

"CHARLIE" Class

4/1974

"CHARLIE" Class

1974, MOD(N)

Submarines
Cruise Missile Classes

28 "ECHO II" CLASS
(CRUISE MISSILE SUBMARINES SSGN)

Displacement, tons: 5 000 surfaced; 6 000 dived
Length, feet (metres): 390·7 *(119)*
Beam, feet (metres): 30·2 *(9·2)*
Draught, feet (metres): 25·9 *(7·9)*
Missile launchers: 8 SS-N-3 launching tubes (see note)
Torpedo tubes: 6—21 in (bow); 4—16 in (stern)
Main machinery: 2 nuclear reactors; steam turbines; 22 500 shp; 2 shafts
Speed, knots: 20 surfaced; 22 dived
Complement: 92

The "Echo II" was the natural development of the "Echo I". With a slightly lengthened hull, a fourth pair of launchers was installed and between 1963 and 1967 at least 28 of this class were built. They are now deployed evenly between the Pacific and Northern fleets and still provide a useful group of boats some being deployed to the Mediterranean. Some may be fitted with SS-N-12 missiles.

"ECHO II" Class   6/1973

"ECHO II" Class   1973, MOD(N)

"ECHO II" Class   6/1973

16 "JULIETT" CLASS
(CRUISE MISSILE SUBMARINES SSG)

Displacement, tons: 2 800 surfaced; 3 600 dived
Length, feet (metres): 278·8 *(85)*
Beam, feet (metres): 31·4 *(9·5)*
Draught, feet (metres): 15 *(4·6)*
Missile launchers: 4 SS-N-3 tubes; 2 before and 2 abaft the fin
Torpedo tubes: 6—21 in (bow)
Main machinery: Diesels; 7 000 bhp. Electric motors; 5 000 hp
Speed, knots: 16 surfaced; 16 dived
Range, miles: 15 000 surfaced cruising
Complement: 90

Completed between 1962 and 1967. An unmistakable class with a high casing to house the 4 SS-N-3 launchers, one pair either end of the fin which appears to be comparatively low. This class was the logical continuation of the "Whiskey" class conversions. A number of this class has in the past been deployed to the Mediterranean. Some may be fitted with SS-N-12 missiles.

"JULIETT" Class

6/1973

"JULIETT" Class

1973, MOD(N)

"JULIETT" Class

1973, US Navy

Submarines
Cruise Missile Classes

7 "WHISKEY LONG-BIN" CLASS
(CRUISE MISSILE SUBMARINES SSG)

Displacement, tons: 1 200 surfaced; 1 600 dived
Length, feet (metres): 272·2 *(83)*
Beam, feet (metres): 23·9 *(7·3)*
Draught, feet (metres): 14·1 *(4·3)*
Missile launchers: 4 SS-N-3 tubes
Torpedo tubes: 6—21 in *(533 mm)*
Main machinery: Diesels; 4 000 bhp; Electric motors; 2 500 hp
Speed, knots: 16 surfaced; 14 dived
Range, miles: 13 000 surfaced, cruising
Complement: 75

A more efficient modification of the "Whiskey" class than the "Twin-Cylinder" with four SS-N-3 launchers built into a remodelled fin on a hull lengthened by 33 feet. Converted between 1960-63—no organic guidance and therefore reliance must be made on aircraft or surface-ship cooperation. Must be a very noisy boat when dived.

"WHISKEY LONG BIN" Class

1975

3 "WHISKEY TWIN CYLINDER" CLASS
(CRUISE MISSILE SUBMARINES SSG)

Displacement, tons: 1 100 surfaced; 1 400 dived
Length, feet (metres): 249·3 *(73)*
Beam, feet (metres): 22·0 *(7·3)*
Draught, feet (metres): 15·1 *(4·3)*
Missile launchers: 2 cylinders for SS-N-3
Torpedo tubes: 4—21 in *(533 mm)*
Main machinery: Diesels; 4 000 bhp; Electric motors; 2 500 hp
Speed, knots: 17 surfaced; 15 dived
Range, miles: 13 000, surfaced, cruising
Complement: 70

A 1958-60 modification of the conventional "Whiskey" class designed to test out the SS-N-3 system at sea. Probably never truly operational being a thoroughly messy conversion which must make a noise like a train if proceeding at any speed above dead slow when dived. The modification consisted of fitting a pair of launchers abaft the fin.

"WHISKEY TWIN CYLINDER" Class (Sevastopol Review)

7/1974, Tass

Submarines
Fleet Submarine Classes
2 "ALFA" CLASS
(FLEET SUBMARINES SSN)

Displacement, tons: 3 500 surfaced; 4 500 dived
Dimensions, feet (metres): 265 × 32·8 × 26·2 (81 × 10 × 8)
Torpedo tubes: 6—21 in (533 mm)
Main machinery: 1 nuclear reactor; steam turbine; 25 000 shp
Speed, knots: 16 surfaced; 18 dived

One unit of this class was completed in 1970. A programme which has apparently come to a halt and whose purpose is unclear. Probably no longer operational.

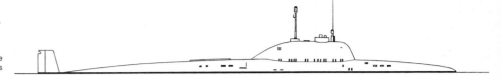

"ALFA" Class   1976, S. Breyer

2 "VICTOR II" CLASS
(FLEET SUBMARINE SSN)

Displacement, tons: 4 700 surfaced; 6 000 dived
Length, feet (metres): 331·3 (101)

An enlargement of the "Victor" class.

18 "VICTOR" CLASS
(FLEET SUBMARINES SSN)

Displacement, tons: 3 600 surfaced; 4 200 dived
Length, feet (metres): 303 (92)
Beam, feet (metres): 32·8 (10·0)
Draught, feet (metres): 26·2 (8·0)
Torpedo tubes: 8—21 in (533 mm)
Main machinery: 2 nuclear reactors; steam turbines;
  25 000-30 000 shp; 3 shafts
Speed, knots: 26 surfaced; 30 plus dived

Designed purely as a torpedo carrying submarine its much increased speed makes it a menace to all but the fastest ships. The first of class entered service in 1967-68 with a subsequent building rate of about two per year, which may now have been superseded by the "Victor II" programme. Some have been built at Admiralty Yard, Leningrad.

The majority is deployed with the Northern Fleet, although some have joined the Pacific Fleet. Reportedly the world's fastest nuclear submarine.

"VICTOR" Class (in S. China Sea)   4/1974, USN

"VICTOR" Class   1974, MOD

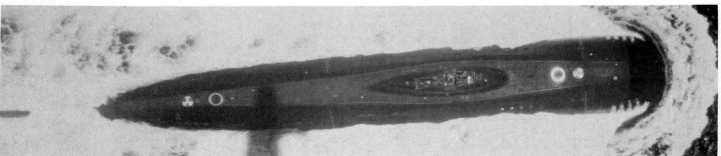

"VICTOR" Class   1974, USN

Submarines
Fleet Submarine Classes

13 "NOVEMBER" CLASS
(FLEET SUBMARINES SSN)

Displacement, tons: 3 500 surfaced; 4 000 dived
Length, feet (metres): 360·9 (110·0)
Beam, feet (metres): 32·1 (9·8)
Draught, feet (metres): 24·3 (7·4)
Torpedo tubes: 10; 6—21 in (533 mm) (bow);
    4—16 in (406 mm) (stern)
Main machinery: 2 nuclear reactors; steam turbines; 32 500
    shp
Speed, knots: 20 surfaced; 25 dived
Complement: 88

The first class of Soviet nuclear submarines which entered service between 1958 and 1963. The hull form with the great number of free-flood holes in the casing suggests a noisy boat and it is surprising that greater efforts have not been made to supersede this class with the "Victors". In April 1970 one of this class sank south-west of the United Kingdom.

Diving Depth: Reported as 1 650 feet (500 metres).

"NOVEMBER" Class   *Tass*

"NOVEMBER" Class (in Gulf of Mexico)   *7/1969, USN*

"NOVEMBER" Class foundering in Atlantic   *April 1970, MOD*

5 "ECHO I" CLASS
(FLEET SUBMARINES SSN)

Displacement, tons: 4 600 surfaced; 5 500 dived
Length, feet (metres): 374·3 (114)
Beam, feet (metres): 31·2 (9·5)
Draught, feet (metres): 25·9 (7·9)
Torpedo tubes: 6—21 in (bow); 4—16 in (stern)
Main machinery: 2 nuclear reactors; steam turbines;
    25 000-30 000 shp
Speed, knots: 20 surfaced; 22 dived
Complement: 92 (12 officers, 80 men)

This class was completed in 1960-62. Originally mounted six SS-N-3 launchers raised from the after casing.
The hull of this class is very similar to the "Hotel"/"November" type and it is probably powered by similar nuclear plant. This class was started at about the same time as the "Juliett" diesel-driven SSGs, and may have been intended as a nuclear prototype using the same SS-N-3 system. Only five "Echo Is" were built, probably an adequate test for a new weapon system, being followed immediately by the "Echo IIs". In 1973-74 the "Echo I" class was converted into fleet submarines with the removal of the missile system.

"ECHO I" Class (as SSN)   *8/1975*

Submarines
Patrol Submarine Classes

5 "TANGO" CLASS
(PATROL SUBMARINES SS)

Displacement, tons: 2 400 surfaced; 3 000 dived
Dimensions, feet (metres): 293 × 30 × 16 (90 × 9·1 × 4·9)
Torpedo tubes: ? 6—21 in (533 mm)
Main machinery: Diesel electric
Complement: 60

This class was first seen at the Sevastopol review in July 1973. Notable features are the rise in the forecasing and a new shape for the snort exhaust. This class, following five years after the "Bravo", shows a continuing commitment to diesel-propelled boats which is of interest in view of the comparatively slow nuclear submarine building programme. If the USSR wishes to maintain a preponderance in numbers as the more elderly patrol submarines are paid off this may be the class chosen for new construction. It would also provide a modern replacement for client nations' navies. Continuing programme of 2 a year.

"TANGO" Class

1973, Tass

"TANGO" Class

1975, MOD

4 "BRAVO" CLASS
(PATROL SUBMARINES SS)

Displacement, tons: 1 100 surfaced; 1 200 dived
Length, feet (metres): 240 (73)
Beam, feet (metres): 30 (9·1)
Draught, feet (metres): 14·8 (4·5)
Torpedo tubes: 6—21 in (533 mm)
Main machinery: Diesel-Electric
Speed, knots: 16 dived

The beam-to-length ratio is larger than normal in a diesel submarine which would account in part for the large displacement for a comparatively short hull.

First completed in 1968. One attached to each of the main fleets, reinforcing the view that these are "padded targets" for torpedo and A/S firings.

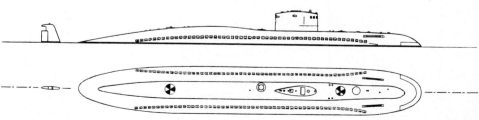

"BRAVO" Class

1976, S. Breyer

60 "FOXTROT" CLASS
(PATROL SUBMARINES SS)

Displacement, tons: 2 100 surfaced; 2 400 dived
Length, feet (metres): 292 *(89)*
Beam, feet (metres): 27·2 *(8·3)*
Draught, feet (metres): 15·7 *(4·8)*
Torpedo tubes: 10—21 in (6 bow, 4 stern) (20 torpedoes carried)
Main machinery: Diesels; 3 shafts; 6 000 bhp; 3 electric motors; 5 000 hp
Speed, knots: 18 surfaced; 17 dived
Range: 20 000 miles surfaced, cruising
Complement: 70

Built since 1958 at Sudomekh and Leningrad although the Soviet naval programme finished in late 1960s. A follow-on of the "Zulu" class with similar propulsion to the "Golf" class. A most successful class which has been deployed world-wide, forming the bulk of the Soviet submarine force in the Mediterranean. Four transferred to India in 1968-69 with a further four new construction following. This is a continuing programme for export, now including Libya—one delivered to that country in 1976 with five more reportedly on order.

"FOXTROT" Class   11/1970, USN

"FOXTROT" Class (Indian Ocean)   5/1974, USN

Frozen "FOXTROT" with bow guard   7/1973

"FOXTROT" Class (Mediterranean—USS *Jonas Ingram* behind)   12/1973, USN

Submarines
Patrol Submarine Classes

19 "ZULU IV" CLASS
(PATROL SUBMARINES SS)

Displacement, tons: 2 000 surfaced; 2 400 dived
Length, feet (metres): 295 *(89·6)*
Beam, feet (metres): 24 *(7·4)*
Draught, feet (metres): 15·7 *(4·8)*
Torpedo tubes: 10—21 in (6 bow, 4 stern); (24 torpedoes carried or 40 mines)
Main machinery: Diesel-electric; 3 shafts; 3 diesels; 8 000 bhp; 3 electric motors; 3 500 hp
Speed, knots: 18 surfaced; 15 dived
Range, miles: 20 000 surfaced, cruising
Complement: 70

"ZULU IV" Class

1969, USN

The first large post-war patrol submarines built by USSR. Completed from late 1951 to 1955. General appearance is streamlined with a complete row of free-flood holes along the casing. Eighteen were built by Sudomekh Shipyard, Leningrad, in 1952-55 and others at Severodvinsk. The general external similarity to the later German U-boats of WW II suggests that this was not an entirely indigenous design. All now appear to be of the "Zulu IV" type. This class, although the majority are probably still operational, is obsolescent and will soon be disposed of.
The "Zulu V" conversions of this class provided the first Soviet ballistic missile submarines with SS-N-4 systems.

"ZULU IV" Class

1974

12 "ROMEO" CLASS
(PATROL SUBMARINES SS)

Displacement, tons: 1 200 surfaced; 1 460 dived
Length, feet (metres): 239·4 *(73)*
Beam, feet (metres): 23 *(7)*
Draught, feet (metres): 14·4 *(4·4)*
Torpedo tubes: 6—21 in *(533 mm)* 18 torpedoes or 36 mines in place of torpedoes
Main machinery: Diesels; 4 000 bhp; Electric motors; 3 000 hp; 2 shafts
Speed, knots: 18 surfaced; 15 dived
Range, miles: 13 000 at 10 knots (surfaced)
Complement: 60

These are an improved "Whiskey" class design with modernised conning tower, and sonar installation. All built in 1958 to 1961. This was presumably an interim class while the "November" class of Fleet Submarines was brought into service—an insurance against failure. Six of this class transferred to Egypt in 1966 and the Chinese and North Koreans are building a considerable force of the same class.

"ROMEO" Class

1974

"ROMEO" Class

1970

Submarines
Patrol Submarine Classes

150 "WHISKEY" CLASS
(PATROL SUBMARINES SS)

Displacement, tons: 1 030 surfaced; 1 350 dived
Length, feet (metres): 249·3 *(76)*
Beam, feet (metres): 22·0 *(6·7)*
Draught, feet (metres): 15·0 *(4·6)*
Torpedo tubes: 6—21 in (4 bow, 2 stern); 18 torpedoes carried
(or 40 mines)
Main machinery: Diesel-electric; 2 shafts
Diesels; 4 000 bhp
Electric motors; 2 500 hp
Speed, knots: 17 surfaced; 15 dived
Range, miles: 13 000 at 8 knots (surfaced)
Complement: 60

This was the first post-war Soviet design for a medium-range submarine. Like its larger contemporary the "Zulu", this class shows considerable German influence. About 240 of the "Whiskeys" were built between 1951 and 1957 at yards throughout the USSR. Built in six types—I and IV had guns forward of the conning tower. II had guns both ends, whilst III and V have no guns. V is the most common variant whilst VA has a diver's exit hatch forward of the conning tower. Possibly 50 operational although very few are now encountered out of area. Remainder in reserve.

Conversions: Two of this class, named *Severyanka* and *Slavyanka,* were converted for oceanographic and fishery research.

Foreign Transfers: Has been the most popular export model; currently in service in Albania (4), Bulgaria (4), China (21), Egypt (6), Indonesia (3), North Korea (4) and Poland (4).

"WHISKEY V" Class   10/1974, MOD

"WHISKEY V" Class   9/1976, MOD

"WHISKEY V" Class   1973

3 "WHISKEY CANVAS BAG" CLASS
(RADAR PICKET SUBMARINES SSR)

Displacement, tons: 1 030 surfaced; 1 350 dived
Length, feet (metres): 249·3 *(76)*
Beam, feet (metres): 22·0 *(6·7)*
Draught, feet (metres): 15·0 *(4·6)*
Torpedo tubes: 6—21 in (4 bow, 2 stern)
Main machinery: Diesels; 4 000 bhp;
   Electric motors; 2 500 hp
Speed, knots: 17 surfaced; 15 dived
Range, miles: 13 000 at 8 knots surfaced
Complement: 65

Basically of same design as the "Whiskey" class but with long-range Boat-Sail radar aerial mounted on the fin. The coy way in which this was covered prompted the title "Canvas Bag". Converted in 1959 to 1963.

"WHISKEY CANVAS BAG" Class (with radar aerial abeam)   *1975*

20 "QUEBEC" CLASS
(PATROL SUBMARINES SS)

Displacement, tons: 470 surfaced; 550 dived
Length, feet (metres): 185·0 *(56·4)*
Beam, feet (metres): 18·0 *(5·5)*
Draught, feet (metres): 13·2 *(4·0)*
Torpedo tubes: 4—21 in *(533 mm)* bow
Main machinery: 1 diesel; 3 shafts; 2 000 bhp; 3 electric
   motors; 2 000 hp
Speed, knots: 18 surfaced; 16 dived
Oil fuel, tons: 50
Range, miles: 7 000 surfaced cruising
Complement: 42

Short range, coastal submarines. Built from 1954 to 1957. Thirteen were constructed in 1955 by Sudomekh Shipyard, Leningrad. The earlier boats of this class of 22 were fitted with what was possibly a closed-cycle propulsion, probably on the third shaft. This was more likely, however, a Kreislof turbine; but, whatever it was, it is believed to have been unsuccessful and was subsequently removed. The majority of this class is now in reserve, some probably paid off—five may be active.

"QUEBEC" Class   *1970*

"QUEBEC" Class   *1970*

AIRCRAFT CARRIERS

1 + 2 "KIEV" CLASS (AIRCRAFT CARRIERS)

Name	No.	Builders	Laid down	Launched	Commissioned
KIEV	—	Nikolayev South	1971	1973	1976
MINSK	—	Nikolayev South	1972	1974	1977
—	—	Nikolayev South	1973	1976	1979

Displacement, tons: 40 000 light (approx); 54 000 full load (estimated)
Length, feet (metres): 934 *(284·8)* oa
Beam, feet (metres): 135 *(41·2)* (hull); 170 *(51·8)* (overall, including flight deck and sponsons)
Aircraft (estimated): 20 fixed wing (V/STOL) or 25 Hormone helicopters
Missile launchers: 8 (4 twin) SS-N-12 SSM launchers; 2 twin SA-N-3; 1 SUW-N A/S launcher; 2 SA-N-4 launchers
Guns: 4—76 mm; 4 Air Defence Gatling mounts
A/S weapons: 2—12 barrelled MBU 2500A launchers forward
Speed, knots: At least 30

After years of argument and indecision the first sign of Soviet acceptance of the need for organic air was the appearance of *Moskva* and *Leningrad* in 1968-69, the first ships built with a flat deck in the post-war years. They carried the embarked helicopter concept a long stage further than the cruisers and destroyers with a single embarked helicopter. It is most probable that a much larger number was projected and the reason for the cancellation of the remainder might by any or all of a number of factors. Two appear to be of considerable importance—the growing Soviet realisation of the important part

their navy could play in overseas affairs and the appearance of the prototype of the first Soviet V/STOL aircraft, the Yakovlev *Freehand.* This first appeared in public in 1967 and its capabilities were known at least a year before that. This was ten years before *Kiev* became operational, a reasonable lead time for Soviet designers and constructors.

The task of this class is probably twofold—an advanced ASW role in wartime and an intervention capability in so-called peacetime. The inclusion of the very considerable SSM capability, A/S weapons as well as sonar equipment, and a gun armament as well as both missile and gun. Point Defence Systems shows a continuation of the Soviet plan for multipurpose ships.

Aircraft: The complement appears to be either 25 *Hormone A* helicopters or a smaller number of *Forger* (Yak 36) V/STOL aircraft—a mixed bag was carried during *Kiev's* initial cruise. The *Forger* comes in two versions—A, a single seater of which about a dozen were embarked in July-August 1976 and B, a twin-seat trainer of which only one was seen.

ECM: A full fit is carried including Side Globe housings.

Flight Deck: 620 feet *(189 m)* long with a 4° angle, 68 feet *(20·7 m)* wide with two lifts, one larger one abaft the island for V/STOL and a smaller one amidships abreast the bridge. Six spots are provided with a seventh at the forward tip of the flight deck. A larger spot amidships aft is apparently for V/STOL.

Missiles: The four twin SSM launchers carry SS-N-12 missiles, an advance on the SS-N-3 with a range of about 250 miles at a speed of mach 2/3.
The SAM armament is standard.
The A/S missile launcher can presumably launch either SS-N-14 or FRAS-1.

Operations: With a relative wind of up to 15 knots fine on the port bow (sometimes requiring a very slow ship's speed) a maximum of two aircraft is normally launched. Take off and landing is normally very cautious, possibly a combination of inexperience and doubt. The inexperience was reflected on the flight-deck where the customary accessories (bulldozer etc) were not visible.

Radar: 3D Search: Top Sail.
Search: Head Net.
Fire control: Head Light (SA-N-3); Pop Group (SA-N-4); Owl Screech *(76 mm).*
In addition two other types of radar, the radome and twin sets aft are fitted.

Sonar: Possibly hull-mounted and VDS.

Soviet Type Name: Protivo Lodochny Kreyser meaning anti-submarine cruiser. This is an interesting designation for a ship of this size, continuing the Soviet practice of calling nearly all major surface units by an ASW title.

KIEV

8/1976, MOD(N)

KIEV (missile launchers)

8/1976, MOD(N)

KIEV

8/1976, USN

KIEV

7/1976, MOD(N)

KIEV

7/1976, USN

KIEV

7/1976, Selçuk Imre

KIEV

10/1976, USN

2 "MOSKVA" CLASS

Name	No.	Builders	Laid down	Launched	Commissioned
MOSKVA	—	Nikolayev South	1962	—	1968
LENINGRAD	—	Nikolayev South	1963	—	1969

Displacement, tons: 14 500 standard; 18 000 full load
Length, feet (metres): 624·8 *(190·5)*; 644·8 oa *(196·6)*
Flight deck, feet (metres): 295·3 *(90·0)* aft of superstructure
Width, feet (metres): 115·0 *(35·0)*
Beam, feet (metres): 75·9 *(23)*
Draught, feet (metres): 24·9 *(7·6)*
Aircraft: 18 Hormone A ASW helicopters
Missile launchers: 4 (2 twin) SA-N-3 systems (180 reloads)
Guns: 4—57 mm (2 twin mountings)
A/S weapons: 1 twin SUWN-1 A/S missile launcher; 2—12 tube MBU 2500A on forecastle
Torpedo tubes: 2 quintuple 21 inch *(533 mm)*
Main engines: Geared turbines; 2 shafts; 100 000 shp
Boilers: 4 watertube
Speed, knots: 30
Complement: 800

This class represented a radical change of thought in the Soviet fleet. The design must have been completed while the "November" class submarines were building and the heavy A/S armament and efficient sensors (helicopters and VDS) suggest an awareness of the problem of dealing with nuclear submarines. Alongside what is apparently a primary A/S role these ships have a capability for A/A warning and self-defence as well as a command function. With a full fit of radar and ECM equipment they clearly represent good value for money. Both ships handle well in heavy weather and are capable of helicopter-operations under adverse conditions. Why only two were built is discussed earlier in the notes on the "Kiev" class aircraft carriers.

Modification: In early 1973 *Moskva* was seen with a landing pad on the after end of the flight deck, probably for flight tests of VTOL aircraft.

Radar: Search: Top Sail 3-D and Head Net C 3-D.
Fire control: Head Light (2). Muff Cob.
Miscellaneous: Electronic warfare equipment.

Sonar: VDS and, probably, hull mounted set. In addition all helicopters have dunking-sonar.

Soviet Type Name: Protivo Lodochny Kreyser meaning Anti-Submarine Cruiser.

MOSKVA ("Hormone" helicopters on deck)   1974, USN

LENINGRAD   11/1974, MOD (N)

MOSKVA   7/1974, USN

CRUISERS

5 + 2 "KARA" CLASS (CG)

NIKOLAYEV	**OCHAKOV**
KERCH	**AZOV**
+1	**+2 building**

Displacement, tons: 8 200 standard; 10 000 full load
Length, feet (metres): 570 *(173·8)*
Beam, feet (metres): 60 *(18·3)*
Draught, feet (metres): 20 *(6·2)*
Aircraft: 1 Hormone A or B helicopter (Hangar aft)
Missile Systems: 8—SS-N-14 (Two mounts abreast bridge)
  4—SA-N-4 (twins either side of mast)
  4—SA-N-3 (twins)
Guns: 4—76 mm (2 twins abaft bridge)
  4—Gatling type close range weapons (abreast funnel) (see *Gunnery* note)
A/S weapons: 2—12 barrelled MBU launchers (forward)
  2—6 barrelled DC throwers
Torpedo tubes: 10—21 in *(533 mm)* (2 quintuple mountings abaft funnel)
Main engines: Gas-turbine; 120 000 hp
Speed, knots: Approximately 34

Apart from the specialised "Moskva" class this is the first class of large cruisers to join the Soviet navy since the "Sverdlovs". *Nikolayev* was first seen in public when she entered the Mediterranean from the Black Sea on 2 March 1973. Clearly capable of prolonged operations overseas.
All built or building at Nikolayev. *Azov* is of a modified design. Continuing programme of about one a year.

ECM: A full oufit appears to be housed on the bridge and mast.

Gunnery: The siting of both main and secondary armament on either beam in the waist follows the precedent of both "Kresta" classes, although the weight of the main armament is increased. The single mountings by the funnel appear to be some form of Gatling and are quite different from the usual twin 30 mm mountings.

Missiles: In addition to the "Kresta II" armament of eight tubes for the SS-N-14 A/S system (possibly with a surface-to-surface capability) and the pair of twin launchers for SA-N-3 system with Goblet missiles, "Kara" mounts the SA-N-4 system in two silos, either side of the mast. The combination of such a number of systems presents a formidable capability, matched by no ship other than *Kiev*.

Radar: Surveillance: Top Sail and Head Net C.
SA-N-3 control: Head Light.
SA-N-4 control: Pop Group.
76 mm gun control: Owl Screech.
Gatling gun control: Drum Tilt.

Sonar and A/S: VDS is mounted below the helicopter pad and is presumably complementary to a hull-mounted set or sets. The presence of the helicopter with dipping-sonar and an A/S weapon load adds to her long-range capability.

Soviet Type Name: Bolshoy Protivolodochny Korabl, meaning Large Anti-Submarine Ship.

KERCH (Hull 3)   *2/1976, MOD*

OCHAKOV (Hull 2) (same pennant number as *Nikolayev* a year earlier)   *3/1975, MOD*

NIKOLAYEV (Hull 1)   *1974, MOD*

9 + 2 "KRESTA II" CLASS (CG)

ADMIRAL ISACHENKOV
ADMIRAL ISAKOV
ADMIRAL MAKAROV
ADMIRAL NAKHIMOV
ADMIRAL OKTYABRSKY
KRONSHTADT
MARSHAL TIMOSHENKO
MARSHAL VOROSHILOV
VASILIY CHAPAEV
+2

Displacement, tons: 6 000 standard; 7 500 full load
Length, feet (metres): 519·9 *(158·5)*
Beam, feet (metres): 55·1 *(16·8)*
Draught, feet (metres): 19·7 *(6·0)*
Aircraft: 1 Hormone A or B helicopter (hangar aft)
Missile launchers: 2 quadruple for SS-N-14; 2 twin for SA-N-3
Guns: 4—57 mm (2 twin); 4—Gatling Close Range Weapons
A/S weapons: 2—12 barrelled MBU (forward);
　2—6 barrelled DC throwers (aft)
Torpedo tubes: 10—21 in *(533 mm)* (two quintuple)
Main engines: 2 Steam turbines; 2 shafts; 100 000 shp
Boilers: 4 watertube
Speed, knots: 35
Range, miles: 5 500 at 18 knots
Complement: 500

The design was developed from that of the "Kresta I" class, but the layout is more up-to-date. The missile armament shows an advance on the "Kresta I" SAM armament and a complete change of practice in the fitting of the SS-N-14 A/S missile system. The fact that it has subsequently been fitted in the "Kara" and "Krivak" classes and that it must have a very limited anti-surface-ship capability indicates a possible change in tactical thought. Built at Leningrad from 1968 onwards. Continuing programme of about one a year.

New construction: Two building at Zhdanov Yard Leningrad (1977).

Radar: 3D Search: Top Sail.
Search: Head Net C.
SA-N-3 control: Head Light.
SA-N-4 control: Pop Group.
57 mm control: Muff Cob.
Gatling control: Bass Tilt.

Soviet Type Name: Bolshoy Protivolodochny Korabl, meaning Large Anti-Submarine Ship.

ADMIRAL MAKAROV　　　　　　　　　　　　　　　　　　　7/1974, USN

MARSHAL TIMOSHENKO　　　　　　　　　　　　　　　9/1976, MOD (N)

ADMIRAL MAKAROV　　　　　　　　　　　　　　　　　　　5/1975, MOD

ADMIRAL OKTYABRSKY　　　　　　　　　　　　　　　　　　1975, MOD

4 "KRESTA I" CLASS (CG)

VICE-ADMIRAL DROZD SEVASTOPOL
ADMIRAL ZOZULYA VLADIVOSTOK

Displacement, tons: 6 140 standard; 7 500 full load
Length, feet (metres): 510 *(155·5)*
Beam, feet (metres): 55·1 *(16·8)*
Draught, feet (metres): 18·0 *(5·5)*
Aircraft: 1 Hormone A and B helicopter with hangar aft
Missile launchers: 2 twin SS-N-3 for Shaddock (no reloads); 2 twin SA-N-1 for Goa
Guns: 4—57 mm (2 twin); 4 Gatling Close Range Weapons (*Drozd* only)
A/S weapons: 2—12 barrelled MBU (60 reloads) (fw'd); 2—6 barrelled DC throwers (aft)
Torpedo tubes: 10 (two quintuple) 21 in
Main engines: Steam turbines; 2 shafts; 100 000 shp
Boilers: 4 watertube
Speed, knots: 35
Range, miles: 5 500 at 18 knots
Complement: 400

Provided with a helicopter landing deck and hangar aft for the first time in a Soviet ship. This gives an enhanced A/S capability and could certainly provide carried-on-board target-location facilities for the 250 mile SS-N-3 system at a lower, possibly optimum, range. The "Kresta I" was therefore the first Soviet missile cruiser free to operate alone and distant from own aircraft.
Built at the Zhdanov Shipyard, Leningrad. The prototype ship was laid down in Sep 1964, launched in 1965 and carried out sea trials in the Baltic in Feb 1967. The second ship was launched in 1966 and the others in 1967-68.

ECM: Full kit.

Radar: Search: Head Net C, Big Net and Plinth Net.
Fire Control: Scoop Pair for Shaddock system and Peel Group (2) for Goa system.
57 mm Control: Muff Cob.
Gatling Control: Bass Tilt (*Drozd* only).

Refit: The first ship undergoing a major refit, *Vice-Admiral Drozd*, was completed in 1975 with new Bass Tilt radar and Gatling guns on a new superstructure between the bridge and the tower mast.

Soviet Type Name: Bolshoy Protivolodochny Korabl, meaning Large Anti-Submarine Ship.

VICE-ADMIRAL DROZD (after 1975 refit with new Bass Tilt radar and Gatling guns)

2/1976, MOD(N)

VLADIVOSTOK

1974, USN

VICE-ADMIRAL DROZD (after 1975 refit—see top picture)

2/1976, MOD(N)

4 "KYNDA" CLASS (CG)

ADMIRAL FOKIN	GROZNY
ADMIRAL GOLOVKO	VARYAG

Displacement, tons: 4 800 standard; 6 000 full load
Length, feet (metres): 465·8 *(142·0)*
Beam, feet (metres): 51·8 *(15·8)*
Draught, feet (metres): 17·4 *(5·3)*
Aircraft: Pad for helicopter on stern
Missile launchers: 2 quadruple mounts, 1 fwd, 1 aft, for SS-N-3 system (1 reload per tube)
  1 twin mount on forecastle for SA-N-1 system (30 reloads)
Guns: 4—3 in *(76 mm)* (2 twin)
A/S weapons: 2—12 barrelled MBUs on forecastle
Torpedo tubes: 6—21 in *(533 mm)* (2 triple amidships)
Main engines: 2 sets geared turbines; 2 shafts; 100 000 shp
Boilers: 4 high pressure
Speed, knots: 35
Complement: 390

The first ship of this class was laid down in June 1960, launched in Apr 1961 at Zhdanov Shipyard, Leningrad, and completed in June 1962. The second ship was launched in Nov 1961 and fitted out in Aug 1962. The others were completed by 1965. Two enclosed towers, instead of masts, are stepped forward of each raked funnel. In this class there is no helicopter embarked, so guidance, for the SS-N-3 system would be more difficult than in later ships. She will therefore be constrained in her operations compared with the later ships with their own helicopters.

Radar: This class showed at an early stage the Soviet ability to match radar availability to weapon capability. The duplicated aerials provide not only a capability for separate target engagement but also provide a reserve in the event of damage.
Search: Head Net A.
Fire Control: Scoop Pair (2) for Shaddock systems, Peel Group for Goa systems and Owl Screech for guns.
Navigation: Don.

Soviet Type Name: Raketny Kreyser meaning Large Rocket Ship.

ADMIRAL GOLOVKO   7/1973, MOD

ADMIRAL GOLOVKO   9/1974, USN

"KYNDA" Class   4/1975, MOD (N)

1 "SVERDLOV" CLASS ((CG)
2 "SVERDLOV" CLASS (CC)
9 "SVERDLOV" CLASS (CA)

ADMIRAL LAZAREV	ALEKSANDR NEVSKI	DZERZHINSKI	OKTYABRSKAYA REVOLUTSIYA
ADMIRAL SENYAVIN	ALEKSANDR SUVOROV	MIKHAIL KUTUSOV	SVERDLOV
ADMIRAL USHAKOV	DMITRI POZHARSKI	MURMANSK	ZHDANOV

Displacement, tons: 16 000 standard; 18 000 full load
Length, feet (metres): 656·2 (200·0) pp; 689·0 (210·0) oa
Beam, feet (metres): 72·2 (22·0)
Draught, feet (metres): 24·5 (7·5)
Aircraft: Helicopter pad in *Zhdanov*. Pad and hangar in *Senyavin*
Armour: Belts 3·9—4·9 in (100—125 mm); fwd and aft 1·6—2 in (40—50 mm); turrets 4·9 in (125 mm); C.T. 5·9 in (150 mm); decks 1—2 in (25—50 mm) and 2—3 in (50—75 mm)
Missile launchers: Twin SA-N-2 aft in *Dzerzhinski*; 2 SA-N-4 in *Zhdanov* and *Senyavin* (twin) (see conversions)
Guns: 12—6 in (152 mm), (4 triple) (9—6 in in *Dzerzhinski* and *Zhdanov*; 6—6 in in *Senyavin*); 12—3·9 in (100 mm), (6 twin), 16—37 mm (twin), 8—30 mm (twin) (*Zhdanov*); 16—30 mm (twins) (*Senyavin*)
Mines: 150 capacity—(except *Zhdanov* and *Senyavin*)
Main engines: Geared turbines; 2 shafts; 110 000 shp
Boilers: 6 watertube
Speed, knots: 30
Oil fuel, tons: 3 800
Range, miles: 8 700 at 18 knots
Complement: 1 000 average

Of the 24 cruisers of this class originally projected, 20 keels were laid and 17 hulls were launched from 1951 onwards, but only 14 ships were completed by 1956. There were two slightly different types. *Sverdlov* and sisters had the 37 mm guns near the fore-funnel one deck higher than in later cruisers. All ships except *Zhdanov* and *Senyavin* are fitted for minelaying. Mine stowage is on the second deck. Two in reserve.

Conversions: *Dzerzhinski* has been fitted with an SA-N-2 launcher aft replacing X-Turret. In 1972 *Admiral Senyavin* returned to service with both X and Y turrets removed and replaced by a helicopter pad and a hangar surmounted by four 30 mm mountings and an SA-N-4 mounting. At about the same time *Zhdanov* had only X-turret removed and replaced by a high deckhouse mounting an SA-N-4.

Flagships: *Admiral Senyavin* is flagship in the Pacific Fleet and *Zhdanov* is flagship in the Black Sea Fleet.

Names: The ship first named *Molotovsk* was renamed *Oktyabrskaya Revolutsiya* in 1957.

Torpedoes: All torpedo tubes removed by 1960.

Radar: Unmodified ships—
Air Search: Big Net or Knife Rest or Top Trough or Hair/Slim Net.
Surface Search: Low or High Sieve.
Target indication: Half Bow.
Fire Control: Top Bow (152 mm); Egg Cup (152 mm turrets); Sun Visor (100 mm).
Navigation: Don.
Dzerzhinski—
Air Search: Big Net; Slim Net.
Surface Search: Low Sieve.
Missile Control: Fan Song E.
Fire Control: As in unmod.
Navigation: Neptun.
Senyavin and *Zhdanov*—
Air Search: Top Trough.
Surface Search, Navigation and Fire Control: As in *Dzerzhinski*.
30 mm Control: Drum Tilt.
SA-N-4 Control: Pop Group.

Soviet Type Name: Kreyser meaning Cruiser.

SVERDLOV   5/1975, MOD(N)

ZHDANOV   4/1975, MOD(N)

SVERDLOV   7/1976, MOD(N)

DZERZHINSKI with twin SA-N-2 launcher in place of X turret

1972

ADMIRAL SENYAVIN

1973

1 "CHAPAEV" CLASS (CA)

KOMSOMOLETS (ex-*Chkalov*)

Displacement, tons: 11 300 standard; 15 000 full load
Length, feet (metres): 659·5 *(201·0)* wl; 665 *(202·8)*
Beam, feet (metres): 62 *(18·9)*
Draught, feet (metres): 24 *(7·3)*
Armour: Side 3 in *(75 mm)*; deck 2 in *(50 mm)*; gunhouses 3·9 in *(100 mm)* CT 3 in *(75 mm)*
Guns: 12—6 in *(152 mm)* 57 cal, (4 triple); 8—3·9 in *(100 mm)*; 70 cal, (4 twin); 24—37 mm (12 twin)
Mines: 200 capacity; 425 ft rails
Main engines: Geared turbines, with diesels for cruising speeds; 4 shafts; 110 000 shp
Boilers: 6 watertube
Speed, knots: 30
Range, miles: 7 000 at 20 knots
Oil fuel, tons: 2 500
Complement: 900

Originally a class of six ships of which one was never completed—shows signs of both Italian and German influence. Laid down in 1939-40. Launched during 1941-47. All work on these ships was stopped during the war, but was resumed in 1946-47. Completed in 1950 in Leningrad. Catapults were removed from all ships of this type. Remaining ship serves as training cruiser.

Gunnery: Turret guns fitting allows independent elevation to 45 degrees.

Radar: Air Search: Slim Net.
Surface Search: Low Sieve.
Fire Control: Top Bow (152 mm), Egg Cup (152 mm turrets), Sun Visor (100 mm).
Navigation: Neptun.

Soviet Type Name: Kreyser meaning Cruiser.

KOMSOMOLETS

1962, MOD(N)

DESTROYERS

15 "KRIVAK" CLASS (DDG)

BDITELNY	DOSTOYNY	RAZYASHCHY	SVIREPY
BODRY	DROZNY	REZVY	ZHARKI
DOBLESTNY	RAZUMNY	SILNY	+ 3
		STOROZHEVOY	

Displacement, tons: 3 300 standard; 3 900 full load
Length, feet (metres): 404·8 *(123·4)*
Beam, feet (metres): 45·9 *(14·0)*
Draught, feet (metres): 16·4 *(5·0)*
Missile launchers: 4 for SS-N-14 system, in A position; (quad-ruple); 4 for SA-N-4 system (twins)
Guns: 4—3 in *(76 mm)* (2 twin) in X and Y positions in earlier ships; 2—100 mm (singles, aft) in later ships
A/S weapons: 2 twelve-barrelled MBU (forward)
Torpedo tubes: 8—21 in *(533 mm)* (2 quads)
Main engines: 4 sets Gas turbines; 2 shafts; 80 000 shp
Speed, knots: 32
Complement: 250

This handsome class, the first ship of which appeared in 1971, appears to be a most successful design incorporating surface and anti-air capability, a VDS with associated MBUs, two banks of tubes, all in a hull designed for both speed and sea-keeping. The use of gas-turbines gives the "Krivak" class a rapid acceleration and availability. Building continues at about 4 per year at Kaliningrad, Kerch and Leningrad.

Missiles: The missiles of the SS-N-14 system continue the A/S trend of the "Kresta II" class and the "Kara" class. The SA-N-4 SAMs are of the same design which is now mounted also in the "Kiev", "Kara", "Nanuchka", "Grisha" and other classes. The launcher retracts into the mounting for stowage and protection, rising to fire and retracting to reload. The two mountings are forward of the bridge and abaft the funnel.

Radar: Search: Head Net C.
Missile Control: Eye Bowl (SS-N-14), Pop Group (SA-N-4).
Gunnery Control: Owl Screech.
Navigation: Don.

Sonar: 1 Hull mounted set in bow; 1 VDS.

Soviet Type Name: Bolshoy Protivolodochny Korabl, meaning Large Anti-Submarine Ship.

STOROZHEVOY   4/1976, MOD(N)

STOROZHEVOY   4/1976, MOD(N)

BODRY   10/1975, USN

STOROZHEVOY   1975, J. A. Verhoog

19 "KASHIN" and "MODIFIED KASHIN" CLASS (DDG)

KOMSOMOLETS UKRAINY	OGNEVOY*	SLAVNY*	SPOSOBNY
KRASNY-KAVKAZ	PROVORNY	SMELY*	STEREGUSHCHY
KRASNY-KRIM	SKORY	SMETLIVY	STROGY
OBRAZTSOVY	RESHITELNY	SMYSHLENY*	STROYNY
ODARENNY	SDERZHANNY*	SOOBRAZITELNY	

(* modified)

Displacement, tons: 3 750 standard; 4 500 full load (4 700 (mod))
Length, feet (metres): 470·9 *(143·3)* or 481 *(146·5)* (mod)
Beam, feet (metres): 52·5 *(15·9)*
Draught, feet (metres): 15·4 *(4·7)*
Missile launchers: 4 (2 twin) SA-N-1 mounted in B and X positions for surface-to-air missiles; 4 SS-N-2 (mod) in mod-class
Guns: 4—3 in *(76 mm)* (2 twin) in A and Y positions; 4—30 mm Gatlings in mod-class
A/S weapons: 2—12 barrelled MBU forward; 2—6 barrelled DC throwers aft (unmodified)
Torpedo tubes: 5—21 in *(533 mm)* quintuple, amidships
Main engines: 4 sets gas turbines; 96 000 hp; 2 shafts
Speed, knots: 35
Complement: 300

The first class of warships in the world to rely entirely on gas-turbine propulsion giving them the quick getaway and acceleration necessary for modern tactics. These ships were delivered from 1962 onwards from the Zhdanov Yard, Leningrad and the Nosenko Yard, Nikolayev.

Conversion: In order to bring this class up-to-date with SSM, new SAM system and VDS a conversion programme was started in 1974. This conversion consists of lengthening the hull by ten feet, shipping 4—SS-N-2 (mod) launchers (SSM), 4 Gatling close range weapons, a VDS under a new stern helicopter platform and removing the DC throwers. By 1977 five had been so converted.

Loss: *Otvazhny* of this class foundered in the Black Sea in September 1974, apparently as the result of an internal explosion followed by a fire which lasted for five hours. Nearly 300 of the ship's company were lost, making this the worst peacetime naval loss for many years.

Radar: Unmodified ships—
Search: Head Net C and Big Net in some ships; Head Net A (2) in others.
Fire control: Peel Group (2) for Goa system and Owl Screech (2) for guns.
Modified ships—
Search: Head Net C and Big Net or 2 Head Net A.
Fire Control: As in unmod plus Bass Tilt for Gatlings.

Sonar: Hull mounted plus VDS in modernised ships.

Soviet Type Name: Bolshoy Protivolodochny Korabl, meaning Large Anti-Submarine Ship.

"KASHIN" Class   7/1974, USN

"KASHIN (MOD)" Class   7/1976, MOD(N)

OBRAZTSOVY at Portsmouth   5/1976, C and S Taylor

SDERZHANNY (modified)   6/1975, MOD(N)

4 "KILDIN" CLASS (DDG)

BEDOVY	NEULOVIMY
NEUDERSIMY	PROZORLIVY

Displacement, tons: 3 000 standatd; 4 000 full load
Length, feet (metres): 414·9 *(126·5)*
Beam, feet (metres): 42·6 *(13·0)*
Draught, feet (metres): 16·1 *(4·9)*
Missile launchers: 1—SS-N-1 (before conversion); 4 for SS-N—2 (mod) system (conversions)
A/S weapons: 2—16 barrelled MBU on forecastle
Guns: 4—76 mm (twins aft); 16—45 mm (after conversion); 16—57 mm (quads—2 forward, 2 between funnels before conversion)
Torpedo tubes: 4—21 in (2 twin)
Main engines: Geared turbines: 2 shafts; 72 000 shp
Boilers: 4 high pressure
Speed, knots: 35
Range, miles: 4 000 at 16 knots
Complement: 300 officers and men

Large destroyers with the "Kotlin" type hull, but redesigned as guided missile armed destroyers.

Conversion: In 1972 *Neulovimy* was taken in hand for modification. This was completed in mid-1973 and consisted of the replacement of the SS-N-1 on the quarterdeck by two superimposed twin 76 mm turrets, the fitting of four SS-N-11 launchers abreast the after funnel and the fitting of new radar. The substitution of the 30 n mile SS-N-11 system (a modified Styx) for the obsolescent SS-N-1 system and the notable increase in gun armament illustrate two trends in Soviet thought. *Bedovy* has now completed this conversion.

Radar: Original ships—
Air Search: Slim Net.
Fire Control: Top Bow; Hawk Screech.

Conversions—
Air Search: Head Net C.
Fire Control: Owl Screech (76 mm); Hawk Screech (45 mm).

"KILDIN" Class (before conversion)

1972

Sonar: Hull mounted.

Soviet Type Name: Bolshoy Protivolodochny Korabl meaning Large Anti-Submarine Ship.

"KILDIN" Class (before conversion)

3/1975, USN

NEULOVIMY after conversion

1974

BEDOVY after conversion

4/1975, MOD(N)

8 "KANIN" CLASS (DDG)

BOYKY	GNEVNY	GREMYASHCHYI	ZHGUCHY
DERZKY	GORDY	UPORNY	ZORKY

Displacement, tons: 3 700 standard; 4 700 full load
Length, feet (metres): 465 *(141)*
Beam, feet (metres): 48·2 *(14·7)*
Draught, feet (metres): 16·4 *(5·0)*
Aircraft: Helicopter platform
Missile launchers: 1 twin SA-N-1 mounted aft
Guns: 8—57 mm (2 quadruple forward); 8—30 mm (twin) (by after funnel)
A/S weapons: Three 12-barrelled MBU
Torpedo tubes: 10—21 in *(533 mm)* A/S (2 quintuple)
Main engines: 2 sets geared steam turbines; 2 shafts; 84 000 shp
Boilers: 4 watertube
Speed, knots: 34
Oil fuel, tons: 900
Range, miles: 4 500 at 16 knots
Complement: 350

All ships of this class have been converted from "Krupnys" at Zhdanov Yard, Leningrad from 1967 onwards, being given a SAM capability instead of the latter's SSM armament.

Appearance: As compared with the "Krupny" class these ships have enlarged bridge, converted bow (probably for a new sonar) and larger helicopter platforms.

Gunnery: The four twin 30 mm abaft the after funnel were a late addition to the armament.

Radar: Search: Head Net C
Fire Control: Peel Group for Goa, Hawk Screech for guns.
Drum Tilt for additional 30 mm guns.
Navigation: Don

Sonar: Hull mounted.

Soviet Type Name: Bolshoy Protivolodochny Korabl, meaning Large Anti-Submarine Ship.

BOYKY with additional 30 mm guns   *10/1973, MOD(N)*

ZHGUCHY   *1976, Michael D. J. Lennon*

"KANIN" Class (off Hawaii)   *9/1974, USN*

8 "SAM KOTLIN I and II" CLASS (DDG)

BRAVY	NASTOYCHIVY	SKROMNY	SOZNATELNY*
NAKHODCHIVY	NESOKRUSHIMY*	SKRYTNY*	VOZBUZHDENNY

* Modified

Displacement, tons: 2 850 standard; 3 800 full load
Length, feet (metres): 414·9 *(126·5)*
Beam, feet (metres): 42·6 *(13·0)*
Draught, feet (metres): 16·1 *(4·9)*
Missile launchers: 1 twin SA-N-1 mounted aft
Guns: 2—5·1 in *(130 mm)* (1 twin); 4—45 mm (1 quadruple or twins); (12—45 mm in *Bravy*); 8—30 mm (twins) in (mods)
Torpedo tubes: 1 quintuple 21 in mounting (not in *Bravy*)
A/S weapons: 2—12 barrelled MBU (2—16 barrelled in *Bravy* and modified ships))
Main engines: Geared turbines; 2 shafts; 72 000 shp
Boilers: 4 high pressure
Speed, knots: 36
Range, miles: 4 000 at 16 knots
Complement: 360

Converted "Kotlin" class destroyers with a surface-to-air missile launcher in place of the main twin turret aft and anti-aircraft guns reduced to one quadruple mounting.
The prototype conversion was completed about 1962 and the others since 1966. One ship transferred to Poland. Three subsequently modified with 30 mm armament and Drum Tilt radar.

Appearance: The prototype "Kotlin" SAM class has a different after funnel and different radar pedestal from those in the standard "Kotlin" SAM class.

Radar: Search: Head Net C or Head Net A.
Fire Control: Peel Group for Goa system, Sun Visor for 130 mm guns, Egg Cup in turret, Hawk Screech for 45 mm guns, Drum Tilt for 30 mm in modified ships.

Soviet Type Name: Esminets meaning Destroyer.

"SAM KOTLIN" Class   10/1975, MOD(N)

"BRAVY"   4/1975, USN

Later "SAM KOTLIN" (with 2 extra Drum Tilt and 8—30 mm by after funnel)   1973

"SAM KOTLIN" Class (with different design of midship radar pedestal and after funnel from the prototype)   1971, MOD

18 "KOTLIN" CLASS (DD)

BESSLEDNY
BLAGORODNY
BLESTYASHCHY
BURLIVY
BYVALY
NAPORISTY

PLAMENNY
SPESHNY
DALNEVOSTOCHNY KOMSOMOLETS
MOSKOVSKY KOMSOMOLETS
SPOKOJNÝ
SVEDUJSCHY

SVETLY
VDOKHNOVENNY
VESKY
VOZMUSHCHENNY
VYDERZHANNY
VYZYVAJUSCHY

Displacement, tons: 2 850 standard; 3 800 full load
Length, feet (metres): 414·9 (126·5)
Beam, feet (metres): 42·6 (13·0)
Draught, feet (metres): 16·1 (4·9)
Guns: 4—5·1 in (130 mm) (2 twin); 16—45 mm (4 quads); 8—25 mm (twin) (in mod "Kotlins"); 4—25 mm (unmod)
A/S weapons: 4—MBU (mod "Kotlins"); 6—DCT (unmod except Svetly)
Torpedo tubes: 5 or 10—21 in (533 mm) (quintuple)
Mines: 80 capacity
Main engines: Geared turbines; 2 shafts; 72 000 shp
Boilers: 4 high pressure
Speed, knots: 36
Range, miles: 4 000 at 16 knots
Complement: 285

Built in 1954-57. The last four hulls laid down were converted to "Kildins".

Modifications: (a) Eight converted to "Sam Kotlins" plus one transferred to Poland. (b) Svetly only ship now provided with helicopter platform on stern. (c) Some had the after torpedo-tubes replaced by a deckhouse. (d) Some ships had two 16-barrelled MBUs fitted. (e) The latest addition in some ships is the fitting of eight 25 mm either side of the after-funnel.

Radar: Search: Slim Net
Fire control: Sun Visor (130 mm), Egg Cup (130 mm turrets), Hawk Screech (45 mm)
Navigation: Don (2) or Neptun.

Sonar: One hull mounted.

Soviet Type Names: Esminets meaning Destroyer.

SVETLY (North Sea)   7/1976, MOD(N)

"KOTLIN" Class (Indian Ocean)   9/1974, USN

"KOTLIN" Class (off Crete)   10/1973, USN

40 "SKORY" CLASS (DD)

BDITELNY	OTCHAYANNY	SOKRUSHITELNY	VAZHNY
BESNERVNY	OTRETOVENNY	SOLIDNY	VDUMCHIVY
BESSMENNY	OTVETSTVENNY	SOVERSHENNY	VERDUSHCHY
BESSMERTNY	OZHESTOCHENNY	SPOSOBNY	VERNY
BEZUPRETCHNY	OZHIVLENNY	STATNY	VIDNY
BEZUKORIZNENNY	SERDITY	STEPENNY	VIKHREVOY
OGNENNY	SERIOZNY	STOJKY	VNESAPNY
OSTERVENELY	SMELY	STREMITELNY	VNIMATELNY
OSTOROZNY	SMOTRYASHCHY	SUROVY	VOLEVOY
OSTROGLAZY	SMYSHLYONY	SVOBODNY	VRAZUMITELNY

Displacement, tons: 2 300 standard; 3 100 full load
Length, feet (metres): 395·2 *(120·5)*
Beam, feet (metres): 38·9 *(11·8)*
Draught, feet (metres): 15·1 *(4·6)*
Guns: 4—5·1 in *(130 mm)*, (2 twin); 2—3·4 in *(86 mm)*, (1 twin);
8—37 mm (4 twin), (see Modernisation Notes)
A/S weapons: 4 DCT
Torpedo tubes: 10—21 in *(533 mm)* (see Modernisation Note)
Mines: 80 can be carried
Main engines: Geared turbines; 2 shafts; 60 000 shp
Boilers: 4 high pressure
Speed, knots: 33
Range, miles: 3 900 at 13 knots
Complement: 280

There were to have been 85 destroyers of this class, but construction beyond 75 units was discontinued in favour of later types of destroyers, and the number has been further reduced to 40 by transfers to other countries, translations to other types and disposals.

Appearance: There were three differing types in this class, the anti-aircraft guns varying with twin and single mountings; and two types of foremast, one vertical with all scanners on top and the other with one scanner on top and one on a platform half way.

Modernisation: At least six ships of the "Skory" class were modified from 1959 onwards including extensive alterations to anti-aircraft armament, electronic equipment and anti-submarine weapons. These now have five 57 mm (single) in place of the 86 mm and 37 mm, five torpedo tubes and two 16-barrelled MBU.

Radar: Slim Net, Hawk Screech and Don (mod); Knife Rest or Cross Bird (unmod).

Reserve: Some 50% of this class now in reserve.

Transfers: Of this class *Skory* and *Smerlivy* were transferred to the Polish Navy in 1957-58, two to the Egyptian Navy in 1956, four to the Indonesian Navy in 1959, and a further two (modernised) to Egypt in 1968.

Soviet Type Name: Esminets meaning Destroyer.

SVOBODNY   1968

"SKORY" Class (unmodified)   10/1971, MOD

OGNENNY (unmodified)   5/1972, MOD(N)

"SKORY" Class Type II (modified)   9/1971, MOD

FRIGATES
20 "MIRKA I and II" CLASS

Displacement, tons: 1 050 standard; 1 200 full load
Length, feet (metres): 272·2 (83)
Beam, feet (metres): 29·9 (9·1)
Draught, feet (metres): 9·8 (3·0)
Guns: 4—3 in (76 mm) (2 twin)
A/S weapons: 4—MBU (2 forward, 2 aft) (I); 2—MBU (forward) (II)
Torpedo tubes: 5—16 in anti-submarine (I); 10—16 in (II)
Main engines: 2 diesels; 12 000 hp; 2 gas-turbines, 30 000 hp; 2 shafts
Speed, knots: 28
Complement: 100

This class of ships was built in 1964-69 as variation on "Petya" class. The difference between the Mark I and II is that the latter have the after MBU rocket launchers removed and an additional quintuple 16-inch torpedo mounting fitted between the bridge and the mast. At least one mounts VDS aft.

Radar: Search: Strut Curve.
Fire Control: Hawk Screech.

Soviet Type Name: Maly Protivolodochny Korabl meaning Small Anti-Submarine Ship.

"MIRKA II" Class (with two torpedo mountings)   4/1975, MOD

"MIRKA I" Class   1975, S. Breyer

14 "PETYA I" CLASS
8 "PETYA I MOD" CLASS
26 "PETYA II" CLASS

Displacement, tons: 950 standard; 1 150 full load
Length, feet (metres): 268·9 (82)
Beam, feet (metres): 29·9 (9·1)
Draught, feet (metres): 10·5 (3·2)
Guns: 4—3 in (76 mm) (2 twins); 2—3 in (76 mm) (I mod)
A/S weapons: 4—MBU (I)
    2—MBU (II)
Torpedo tubes: 5—16 in (406 mm) (I)
    10—16 in (406 mm) (II)
Main engines: 2 diesels, 4 000 hp; 2 gas-turbines; total 36 000 hp; 2 shafts
Speed, knots: 30
Complement: 100

Small freeboard with a low wide funnel. The first ship reported to have been built in 1960-61 at Kaliningrad. Construction continued until about 1964. Fitted with two mine rails. "Petya II" class mount an extra quintuple torpedo-tube in place of after MBUs. Construction probably continuing at a slow rate,

Radar: Search: Strut Curve.
Fire Control: Hawk Screech.

Sonar: 1 hull-mounted (see VDS note)

Soviet Type Name: Maly Protivolodochny Korabl meaning Small Anti-Submarine Ship.

Transfers: Ten to India.

VDS: In six of "Petya I" class a deck-house containing Variable Depth Sonar has replaced the after MBUs and encloses the quarter-deck whilst the prototype has the VDS in the open. This group, part of a continuing programme, is now classified "Petya I Mod" class (originally "Petya III").

"PETYA I" Class (with VDS)   1973, S. Breyer

"PETYA II" Class   10/1974, USN

"PETYA I" Class   3/1975, MOD

BARSUK	KOBCHIK	SAKAL
BUJVOL	LISA	TURMAN
BYK	MEDVED	VOLK
GEPARD	PANTERA	+25
GIENA		

Displacement, tons: 1 200 standard; 1 500 full load
Length, feet (metres): 298·8 *(91·0)*
Beam, feet (metres): 31·2 *(9·5)*
Draught, feet (metres): 11 *(3·4)*
Guns: 3—3·9 in *(100 mm)* (single); 4—37 mm (2 twin); 4—25 mm (twin) in some
A/S weapons: 2—MBU (in some)
Torpedo tubes: 2 or 3—21 in *(533 mm)* in some
Mines: 50
Main engines: Geared turbines; 2 shafts; 20 000 shp
Boilers: 2
Speed, knots: 28
Range, miles: 2 000 at 10 knots
Complement: 150

Built from 1952 to 1959. Successors to the "Kola" class escorts, of which they are lighter and less heavily armed but improved versions. Fitted with mine rails. At least half in reserve.

Anti-submarine: The two 12-barrelled MBU rocket launchers are mounted just before the bridge abreast B gun.

Conversion: A small number of this class has been converted. Some have had the triple torpedo-tube mountings replaced by more modern twin mountings and have a twin 25 mm gun mounting on either side of the funnel.

Radar: Search; Slim Net.
Fire Control; Sun Visor
Navigation; Don

Sonar: 1 hull-mounted.

Soviet Type Name: Storozhevoy Korabl meaning Escort Ship.

Transfers: Bulgaria (2), East Germany (4), Finland (2), Indonesia (6).

37 "RIGA" CLASS

"RIGA" Class

6/1974, MOD

"RIGA" Class

4/1969, USN

3 "KOLA" CLASS

SOVIETSKY AZERBAIDJAN
SOVIETSKY DAGESTAN
SOVIETSKY TURKMENISTAN

Displacement, tons: 1 200 standard; 1 600 full load
Length, feet (metres): 321·4 *(98)*
Beam, feet (metres): 31·2 *(9·5)*
Draught, feet (metres): 10·6 *(3·2)*
Guns: 4—3·9 in *(100 mm)* (single); 4—37 mm
A/S weapons: 4 DC rails
Torpedo tubes: 3—21 in *(533 mm)*
Mines: 30
Main engines: Geared turbines; 2 shafts; 25 000 shp
Boilers: 2
Speed, knots: 30
Range, miles: 3 500 at 12 knots
Complement: 190

Built in 1950-52. In design this class of flushdecked frigates appears to be a combination of the former German "Elbing" class destroyers, with a similar hull form, and of the earlier Soviet "Birds" class escorts. All now serving in the Caspian Sea.

Radar: Surface search; Ball Gun
Air search; Cross Bird
Fire control; Sun Visor (100 mm)
IFF: High Pole

Soviet Type Name: Storozhevoy Korabl meaning Escort Ship.

"KOLA" Class

CORVETTES

18 "GRISHA I", 4 "GRISHA II" and 3 "GRISHA III" CLASSES

Displacement, tons: 1 000 standard; 1 200 full load
Dimensions, feet (metres): 246 × 32·8 × 11 *(75 × 10 × 3·6)*
Missile launchers: SA-N-4 surface-to-air (twin) ("Grisha I" class)
Guns: 2—57 mm (1 twin) (4 in "Grisha II" class); Gatling mount aft ("Grisha III")
Torpedo tubes: 4 (2 twin)—21 in *(533 mm)*
A/S weapons: 2 MBU; DCs
Mines: Fitted for minelaying
Main engines: 1 gas-turbine; 12 000 shp; 2 diesels; 18 000 shp; 3 shafts = 30 knots

Reported to have started series production in the late 1969-70 period. Five built by end of 1972, with a continuing programme of 4 a year. SA-N-4 launcher mounted on the forecastle in "Grisha I" class. This is replaced by a second twin 57 mm in "Grisha II" class some of which may be operated by KGB.

Radar: Air search; Strut Curve.
Fire control; Pop Group (SA-N-4 Grisha I only). Muff Cob (57 mm)
Navigation: Don.

Sonar: 1 hull mounted. Some have a similar VDS to that used in Hormone helicopters.

Soviet Type Name: Maly Protivolodochny Korabl meaning Small Anti-Submarine Ship.

"GRISHA III" Class

1976, S. Breyer "GRISHA II" Class

7/1974, MOD

"GRISHA II" Class

10/1975, MOD(N)

"GRISHA I" Class

7/1974

"GRISHA I" Class

1972

"GRISHA II" Class

7/1974 MOD

17 "NANUCHKA" CLASS
(MISSILE CORVETTE)

Displacement, tons: 750 standard; 850 full load
Length, feet (metres): 196·8 *(60·0)*
Beam, feet (metres): 39·6 *(12·0)*
Draught, feet (metres): 9·9 *(3·0)*
Missile launchers: 6 (2 triple) for SS-N-9; 1—SA-N-4 system
    forward (twin)
Guns: 2—57 mm (1 twin)
Main engines: Diesels; 28 000 shp; 3 shafts
Speed, knots: 32
Complement: 70

Probably mainly intended for deployment in coastal waters
although several have been deployed in the Mediterranean and North Sea. Built from 1969 onwards. Has received many
type designations including "Missile Cutter". Building continues at rate of about 3 a year at Leningrad.

Radar: Fire Control: Muff Cob, Pop Group and SS-N-9 guidance
in radome.
Navigation: Don.

Transfers: Six of a modified version with SS-N-11 missiles are
under construction for India.

"NANUCHKA" Class   7/1976, MOD(N)

"NANUCHKA" Class   7/1976, MOD(N)

64 "POTI" CLASS

Displacement, tons: 400 standard; 500 full load
Dimensions, feet (metres): 193·5 × 26·2 × 8 *(61 × 8 × 2·4)*
Guns: 2—57 mm (1 twin mounting)
Torpedo tubes: 4—16 in *(406 mm)*
A/S weapons: 2 MBU
Main engines: 2 gas turbines 24 000 shp; 2 diesels; 8 000 shp; 2 shafts = 34 knots

This class of ship was under series construction from 1961 to 1968.

Radar: Air Search: Strut Curve.
Fire Control: Muff Cob.
Navigation: Don.

Soviet Type Name: Maly Protivo Lodochny Korabl meaning Small Anti-Submarine Ship.

Transfers: 3 to Bulgaria; 3 to Romania.

"POTI" Class   11/1970, USN

LIGHT FORCES

(**Note**: All "Komars" and "Kronshstadts" now deleted)

120 "OSA I and II" CLASS (70 I and 50 II)
(FAST ATTACK CRAFT—MISSILE)

Displacement, tons: 165 standard; 210 full load
Dimensions, feet (metres): 128·7 × 25·1 × 5·9 *(39·3 × 7·7 × 1·8)*
Missile launchers: 4 in two pairs abreast for SS-N-2
Guns: 4—30 mm; (2 twin, 1 forward, 1 aft)
Main engines: 3 diesels; 12 000 bhp = 32 knots
Range, miles: 800 at 25 knots
Complement: 30

These boats, built since 1959, have a larger hull and four launchers in two pairs as compared with one pair in the "Komar" class. They have a surface-to-surface missile range of up to 23 miles. Later boats have cylindrical missile launchers, comprising the "Osa II" class.

This class was a revolution in naval shipbuilding. Although confined by their size and range to coastal operations the lethality and accuracy of the Styx missile have already been proved by the sinking of the Israeli destroyer *Eilat* on 21 Oct 1967 by an Egyptian "Komar". The operations of the Indian "Osas" in the war with Pakistan in December 1971 were equally successful: they sank *Khaibar* (destroyer) and several merchant vessels by night. These operations surely represent a most important lesson in naval operations and, in light of this, the list of transfers should be noted.

Radar: Square Tie, Drum Tilt.

Transfers: Algeria (4), Bulgaria (4), China (17), Cuba (6), Egypt (12), East Germany (12), India (8), Iraq (5), Korea (N) (4), Poland (12), Romania (5), Somalia (5), Syria (5), Yugoslavia (10).

"OSA II" Class   *1970, Godfrey H. Walker*

"OSA I" Class   *1970*

"OSA I" (right) and "OSA II" Classes   *1973, TASS*

60 "SO I" CLASS (LARGE PATROL CRAFT)

Displacement, tons: 200 light; 225 normal
Dimensions, feet (metres): 138·6 × 20·0 × 7 *(42·3 × 6·1 × 2·1)*
Guns: 4—25 mm (2 twin mountings) see notes
A/S weapons: 4 MBU 1 800; DCT
Torpedo tubes: 2—16 in (some)
Main engines: 3 diesels; 6 000 bhp; 3 shafts = 26 knots
Range, miles: 1 100 at 13 knots
Complement: 40

Built between 1957 and late 1960s—total about 150. Steel hulled. Modernised boats of this class have one 45 mm and two 25 mm guns with two 16 in anti-submarine torpedo tubes. Being phased out of service.

Soviet Type Name: Maly Protivo Lodochny Korabl meaning Small Anti-Submarine Ship.

Transfers: Algeria (6), Bulgaria (6), Cuba (15), Egypt (12), East Germany (12), Iraq (3), Korea (N) (12), Vietnam (2 or 3), Yemen (S) (2).

"SO I" Class   *1970, USN*

60+ "STENKA" ("MOL") CLASS (FAST ATTACK CRAFT—PATROL)

Displacement, tons: 170 standard; 210 full load
Dimensions, feet (metres): 128·7 × 25·1 × 5·9 *(39·3 × 7·7 × 1·8)*
Guns: 4—30 mm (2 twin)
Torpedo tubes: 4—16 in *(406 mm)* anti-submarine
A/S weapons: 2 depth charge racks
Main engines: 3 diesels; 12 000 bhp = 33 knots
Complement: 25

Based on the hull design of the "Osa" class. Built from 1967-68 onwards. Continuing programme of about 5 a year. A variant of this class, the "Mol", is in production apparently for export. (See Sri Lanka.)

Radar: Search: Square Tie. Fire Control: Drum Tilt. Pot Drum.

Sonar: Some have Hormone type dipping sonar.

"STENKA" Class   *11/1970*

25 "TURYA" CLASS (FAST ATTACK CRAFT—PATROL HYDROFOIL)

Displacement, tons: 200 standard; 230 full load
Dimensions, feet (metres): 128·7 × 25·1 × 5·9 *(39·3 × 7·7 × 1·8)*
Guns: 2—57 mm (twin, aft); 2—25 mm (twin, f'd)
Torpedo tubes: 4—21 inch *(533 mm)*
Main engines: Diesels; 14 000 shp
Speed, knots: 40

A new class of hydrofoil with a naval orientation rather than the earlier "Pchela" class. Entered service from 1973—in series production, possibly 4-5 per year. Basically "Osa" hull.

Radar: Pot Drum and Drum Tilt.

Sonar: A form of VDS is fitted on the transom. In view of this the apparent lack of A/S weapons is surprising. Could operate with shore-based helicopters.

"TURYA" Class   *1974, S. Breyer*

1 "SARANCHA" CLASS
(FAST ATTACK CRAFT—MISSILE HYDROFOIL)
An enlarged "Turya" class with two twin SS-N-9 and one twin SA-N-4.

First reported 1976.

20 "PCHELA" CLASS (FAST ATTACK CRAFT—PATROL HYDROFOIL)

Displacement, tons: 70 standard; 80 full load
Dimensions, feet (metres): 88·4 × 18 × 5·2 *(27 × 5·5 × 1·6)*
Guns: 4 MG (2 twin)
Main engines: 2 diesels; 6 000 bhp = 50 knots

This class of hydrofoil is reported to have been built since 1964-65. Also carry depth charges. Used for frontier guard duties by KGB in Baltic and Black Seas.

Radar: Pot Drum.

Sonar: 1 type of VDS.

"PCHELA" Class   *1970*

50 "SHERSHEN" CLASS (FAST ATTACK CRAFT—TORPEDO)

Displacement, tons: 150 standard; 160 full load
Dimensions, feet (metres): 115·5 × 23·1 × 5·0 *(35·2 × 7 × 1·5)*
Guns: 4—30 mm (2 twin)
Torpedo tubes: 4—21 in (single)
A/S weapons: 12 DC
Main engines: Diesels; 3 shafts; 12 000 bhp = 38 knots
Complement: 35

First of class produced in 1963. Programme apparently completed.

Radar: Pot Drum and Drum Tilt. High Pole IFF.

Transfers: Bulgaria (4), East Germany (15), Egypt (6), Korea (N) (4), Vietnam (2), Yugoslavia (13)

"SHERSHEN" Class   *1970*

40 "P 6" CLASS (FAST ATTACK CRAFT—TORPEDO)

Displacement, tons: 66 standard; 75 full load
Dimensions, feet (metres): 84·2 × 20·0 × 6·0 *(25·7 × 6·1 × 1·8)*
Guns: 4—25 mm (twins)
Torpedo tubes: 2—21 in *(533 mm)* (or mines, or depth charges)
Main engines: 4 diesels; 4 shafts; 4 800 bhp = 43 knots
Range, miles: 450 at 30 knots
Complement: 20

The "P 6" class (Soviet Type 184 originally) was of a standard medium sized type running into series production. Launched during 1951 to 1960. Known as "MO VI" class in the patrol craft version. The later versions, known as the "P 8" and "P 10" classes, were powered with gas-turbines, and had different bridge and funnel; "P 8" boats with hydrofoils. The "P 6" class is now being deleted because of old age; some have been converted to radio-controlled target craft. "P 8" and "P 10" classes are reported to have been completely deleted. Originally 250-300 boats of these classes were built.

Radar: Skin Head or Pot Head.

Transfers: Algeria (12), China (80, indigenous construction), Cuba (12), Egypt (24), East Germany (18), Guinea (4), Indonesia (14), Iraq (12), Nigeria (3), Poland (20), North Vietnam (6), Somalia (4).

"P 6" Class

25 "ZUKH" CLASS (COASTAL PATROL CRAFT)

Displacement, tons: 60
Dimensions, feet (metres): 75 × 16 × 6 *(24·6 × 5·2 × 1·9)*
Guns: 2—14·5 mm (twin forward); 1—12·7 mm (aft)
Speed, knots: 28

A new class of patrol craft mainly manned by the KGB. Export versions have twin (over/under) 14·5 mm aft.

Transfers: Angola (1 in 1976), Cuba (5 in 1975), Iraq (4 in 1975).

"ZUKH" Class (on transport)

RIVER PATROL CRAFT

Attached to Black Sea and Pacific Fleets for operations on the Danube, Amur and Usuri Rivers, and to the Caspian Flotilla.

80 "SHMEL" CLASS

Displacement, tons: 80
Dimensions, feet (metres): 92 × 17·7 × 3·3 *(28·1 × 5·4 × 1)*
Guns: 1—76 mm; 2—25 mm (twin)
Main engines: 2 diesels; 2 400 hp; 2 shafts
Speed, knots: 24
Complement: 15

Forward gun mounted in a tank-type turret. Some also mount a ten-barrelled rocket launcher amidships. Built since 1958.

"SHMEL" Class   4/1975, Heinz Stockinger

20 "BK 3" CLASS

Displacement, tons: 120
Guns: 1—100 mm; 1—37 mm; 4 MG (twin mounts)
Speed, knots: 22
Complement: 20

10 "BK 2" CLASS

Displacement, tons: 120
Guns: 1—86 mm; 4—25 mm (twins)
Speed, knots: 20
Complement: 20

20 "BKL 4" CLASS

Displacement, tons: 60
Length, feet (metres): 55 *(16·8)*
Guns: 2—122 mm (mortars); 6 MG
Speed, knots: 28

1 COMMAND SHIP

PS 10

Displacement, tons: 300
Guns: 2—20 mm
Speed, knots: 12

PS 10   4/1975 Heinz Stockinger

MINE WARFARE FORCES

Note: The "Alesha" class (under Support and Depot Ships) probably has a primary minelaying role.

24 "NATYA" CLASS (MINESWEEPERS—OCEAN)

Displacement, tons: 650 standard; 700 full load
Dimensions, feet (metres): 190·2 × 29·5 × 7·2 *(58 × 9 × 2·2)*
Guns: 4—30 mm (2 twin); 4—25 mm (2 twin)
A/S weapons: 2 MBU 1 800
Main engines: 2 diesels; 4 800 bhp; 2 shafts = 18 knots
Complement: 50

First reported in 1971, evidently intended as successors to the "Yurka" class. Building rate of 3 a year.

Radar: Drum Tilt and Don.

"NATYA" Class   2/1975, MOD

47 "YURKA" CLASS (MINESWEEPERS—OCEAN)

Displacement, tons: 500 standard; 550 full load
Dimensions, feet (metres): 164 × 25·3 × 6·5 *(50 × 7·7 × 2)*
Guns: 4—30 mm (2 twin)
Main engines: 2 diesels; 4 000 bhp; 2 shafts = 18 knots
Range, miles: 1 100 at 18 knots
Complement: 50

A class of medium fleet minesweepers with steel hull. Built from 1963 to the late 1960s.

Radar: Drum Tilt and Don.

Transfer: 4 to Egypt.

"YURKA" Class   1975

20 "T 58" CLASS (MINESWEEPERS—OCEAN)

Displacement, tons: 790 standard; 900 full load
Dimensions, feet (metres): 229·9 × 29·5 × 7·9 *(70·1 × 9 × 2·4)*
A/S weapons: 2 MBU 1 800
Guns: 4—57 mm (2 twin)
A/S weapons: 2 MBU 1800; 2 DCT
Main engines: 2 diesels; 2 shafts; 4 000 bhp = 18 knots

Built from 1957 to 1964. Of this class 14 were converted to submarine rescue ships with armament and sweeping gear removed, see later page ("Valdai" class).

Radar: Muff Cob and Neptun.

"T 58" Class (Indian Ocean)   5/1974 USN

70 "T 43" CLASS (MINESWEEPERS—OCEAN)

Displacement, tons: 500 standard; 610 full load
Dimensions, feet (metres): 190·2 × 28·2 × 6·9 *(58 × 8·6 × 2·1)* (older units) (198 *(60 m)* in later ships)
Guns: 2—45 mm (singles); 4—25 mm (2 twin) (not in older units)
Main engines: 2 diesels; 2 shafts; 2 000 bhp = 17 knots
Range, miles: 1 600 at 10 knots
Complement: 40

Built in 1948-57 in shipyards throughout the Soviet Union. A number of this class were converted into radar pickets. The remainder are gradually being replaced by newer types of fleet minesweepers and at least half are probably in reserve.

Radar: Don.

Transfers: Algeria (2), Albania (2), Bulgaria (2), China (20), Egypt (6), Indonesia (6), Poland (12), Syria (2).

"T 43" Class   USN

"T 43" Class   4/1973

5 "T 43/AGR" CLASS

Displacement, tons: 500 standard; 610 full load
Dimensions, feet (metres): 190·2 × 28·2 × 6·9 (58 × 8·6 × 2·1)
Guns: 4—37 mm; 2—25 mm
Main engines: 2 diesels; 2 shafts; 2 000 bhp = 17 knots
Range, miles: 1 600 at 10 knots
Complement: 60

Former fleet minesweepers of the "T 43" class converted into radar pickets with comprehensive electronic equipment. It is reported that there may be a dozen vessels of this type. A large Big Net-like radar is mounted on the mainmast.

"T43-AGR" Class   1973, USN

12 "SONYA" CLASS (MINESWEEPERS—COASTAL)

Displacement, tons: 400
Length, feet (metres): 165 (50)
Guns: 2—30 mm (twin); 2—25 mm (twin)
Main engines: Diesels

Now in series production at about 3/4 a year. First reported 1973.

Radar: Search/Navigation; Don 2.
IFF; Squarehead and High Pole B.

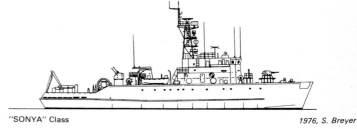

"SONYA" Class   1976, S. Breyer

3 "ZHENYA" CLASS (MINESWEEPERS—COASTAL)

Displacement, tons: 320
Dimensions, feet (metres): 141 × 25 × 7 (43 × 7·6 × 2·1)
Guns: 2—30 mm (twin)
Main engines: 2 diesels; 2 400 shp; 2 shafts = 18 knots

Reported to be a trial class for GRP hulls. First reported 1972.

"ZHENYA" Class   1974, S. Breyer

73 "VANYA" CLASS (MINESWEEPERS—COASTAL)

Displacement, tons: 250 standard; 275 full load
Dimensions, feet (metres): 141 × 24 × 6 (43 × 7·3 × 1·8)
Guns: 2—30 mm (1 twin)
Main engines: 2 diesels; 2 200 bhp = 18 knots
Range, miles: 1 100 at 18 knots
Complement: 30

A coastal class with wooden hulls of a type suitable for series production built from 1961 onwards. Class now believed completed.

"VANYA" Class   1975

40 "SASHA" CLASS (MINESWEEPERS—COASTAL)

Displacement, tons: 250 standard; 280 full load
Dimensions, feet (metres): 150·9 × 20·5 × 6·6 (46 × 6·3 × 2)
Guns: 1—57 mm; 4—25 mm (2 twin)
Main engines: 2 diesels; 2 200 bhp; 2 shafts = 18 knots
Complement: 25

Of steel construction. Built between 1956-60.

"SASHA" Class   1968, S Breyer

8 "EVGENYA" CLASS (MINESWEEPERS—IN SHORE)

Displacement, tons: 90
Dimensions, feet (metres): 85 × 18 × 4·1 *(26 × 5·5 × 1·2)*
Guns: 2—14·7 mm (twin)
Main engines: 2 Diesels = 16 knots

GRP hulls. Production started 1972.

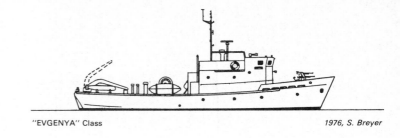

"EVGENYA" Class   *1976, S. Breyer*

4 "ILYUSHA" CLASS (MINESWEEPERS—INSHORE)

Displacement, tons: 75
Dimensions, feet (metres): 78·7 × 16·4 × 4·3 *(24 × 5 × 1·3)*
Guns: 2—14·7 mm (twin)
Main engines: 2 diesels = 15 knots

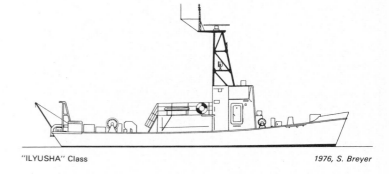

"ILYUSHA" Class   *1976, S. Breyer*

"TR 40" CLASS (MINESWEEPERS—INSHORE)

Displacement, tons: 50 standard; 70 full load
Dimensions, feet (metres): 92·0 × 13·5 × 2·3 *(28 × 4·1 × 0·7)*
Guns: 2 MG (twin)
Main engines: Diesels; 600 bhp = 14 knots

"K 8" CLASS (MINESWEEPERS—RIVER)

Displacement, tons: 40 standard; 60 full load
Dimensions, feet (metres): 55·8 × 11·5 × 4·0 *(17 × 3·5 × 1·2)*
Guns: 2—25 mm (twin); 2 MG (twin)
Main engines: Diesels; speed 18 knots

Auxiliary motor minesweeping boats of the inshore ("TR 40") and river ("K 8") types. A total of about 100 of both classes in service.

"K 8" Class   *1975*

AMPHIBIOUS FORCES

14 "ALLIGATOR" CLASS (LST)

ALEKSANDR TORTSEV   NIKOLAI OEBYEKOV
DONETSKY SHAKHTER   PETR ILICHEV
KRASNAYA PRESNYA   TOMSKY KOMSOMOLETS
KRYMSKY KOMSOMOLETS   VORONEZHSKY KOMSOMOLETS
                                      + 6

Displacement, tons: 4 100 standard; 5 800 full load
Dimensions, feet (metres): 370·7 × 50·9 × 12·1 *(113 × 16 × 4·4)*
Guns: 2—57 mm (twin); 2 rocket launchers; 2—25 mm (some)
Main engines: 4 diesels; 8 000 bhp; 2 shafts = 18 knots

Largest type of landing ship built in the USSR to date. First ship built in 1965-66 and commissioned in 1966. These ships have ramps on the bow and stern. Carrying capacity 1 700 tons. There are three variations of rig. In earlier type two or three cranes are carried—later types have only one crane. In the third type the bridge structure has been raised and the forward deck house has been considerably lengthened.

Radar: Don and Muff Cob (in some).

KRYMSKY KOMSOMOLETS (Type I)   *10/1974, MOD*

"ALLIGATOR" Class   1972

NIKOLAI OEBYEKOV (Type III) (Hull 14)   4/1976, MOD

"ALLIGATOR" Class (Type II)   4/1973, USN

8 + 1 "ROPUCHA" CLASS (LST)

Displacement, tons: 2 500 standard; 3 500 full load
Dimensions, feet (metres): 360 × 49·2 × 11·5 *(110 × 15 × 3·5)*
Guns: 4—57 mm (twins)
Main engines: Diesels; 2 shafts
Speed, knots: 18

Building at Gdansk, Poland at a rate of about 2 a year. Appears to be a "roll-on-roll-off" design.

Armament: Reported to carry SA-N-4 aft.

Radar: Muff Cob, Strut Curve, Don, (presumably Pop Group for those with SA-N-4).

"ROPUCHA" Class   1976, MOD(N)

"ROPUCHA" Class   10/1975

60 "POLNOCNY" CLASS (LCT)

Displacement, tons: 870 standard; 1 000 full load (Type IX 1 300)
Dimensions, feet (metres): 239·4 × 29·5 × 9·8 *(75 × 9 × 3)* (246 ft *(77 m)* in Type VI to VIII)
  (Type IX 285 × 27·7 × 9·8 *(81 × 8·4 × 3)*)
Guns: 2 or 4—30 mm (twin) in all but earliest ships (see note); 2 rocket launchers
Main engines: 2 diesels; 5 000 bhp = 18 knots
Complement: 40 (original)

Carrying capacity 350 tons. Can carry 6 tanks. Up to 9 types of this class have been built. In I to IV the mast and funnel are combined—in V onwards the mast is stepped on the bridge—in VI to VIII there is a redesign of the bow-form—IX is a completely new design of greater length with corresponding increase in tonnage and with 4—30 mm (2 twins). Muff Cob radar.

Missiles: Some reported with SA-7 Grail.

Radar: Don and Drum Tilt (in those with 30 mm)

Transfers: 6 to Egypt, 3 to India, 2 to S. Yemen.

"POLNOCNY" Class with 2—30 mm before bridge and fire control radar on bridge

"POLNOCNY" Class—latest variant with higher funnel   1974, S. Breyer

"POLNOCNY" (Type IX) Class   1973, USN

35 "VYDRA" CLASS (LCU)

Displacement, tons: 300 standard; 475 full load
Dimensions, feet (metres): 157·4 × 24·6 × 7·2 *(48 × 7·5 × 2·2)*
Main engines: 2 diesels; 2 shafts; 400 hp = 10 knots

Built from 1967-1969. No armament. Carrying capacity 250 tons. Fifteen active, fifteen in reserve—rest in auxiliary roles.

Transfers: 10 to Egypt.

"VYDRA" Class   1971

2 "MP 2" CLASS (LCU)

Displacement, tons: 750
Dimensions, feet (metres): 190 × 25 × 8·2 *(58 × 7·6 × 2·5)*
Guns: 6—25 mm (twins)
Main engines: Diesels; 1 200 hp = 10 knots

Built 1956-60. Carrying capacity 200 tons. Phasing out—reserve.

20 "MP 4" CLASS (LCU)

Displacement, tons: 800 full load
Dimensions, feet (metres): 183·7 × 26·2 × 8·9 *(56 × 8 × 2·7)*
Guns: 4—25 mm (2 twin)
Main engines: Diesels; 2 shafts; 1 100 bhp = 10 knots

Built in 1956-58. Of the small freighter type in appearance. Two masts, one abaft the bridge and one in the waist. Gun mountings on poop and forecastle. Can carry 6 to 8 tanks. Several ships now serve as transports.

"MP 4" Class   1973, J. Rowe

10 "MP 10" CLASS (LCU)

Displacement, tons: 200 standard; 420 full load
Dimensions, feet (metres): 157·5 × 21·3 × 6·5 *(48 × 6·5 × 2)*
Main engines: 2 diesels; 2 shafts; 400 hp = 11 knots

A type of landing craft basically similar to the German wartime type in silhouette and layout. Can carry 4 tanks. Loading capacity about 150 tons. Built 1959-66. Probably all in reserve.

"MP 10" Class

1971

40 "SMB 1" CLASS (LCU)

Displacement, tons: 400
Dimensions, feet (metres): 157·4 × 19·6 × 3·2 *(48 × 6 × 2)*
Main engines: 2 diesels; 4 000 hp = 10 knots

Built in 1960-65. Capacity 180 tons.

100+ "T 4" CLASS (LCM)

Displacement, tons: 70
Dimensions, feet (metres): 62·3 × 14·1 × 3·3 *(19 × 4·3 × 1)*
Main engines: 2 diesels; 2 shafts = 10 knots

More than a hundred reported in service (1975).

AIR CUSHION VEHICLES

(Number in service are not accurately known. The following gives an indication of Soviet capability. Fuller details appear in *Jane's Surface Skimmers 1976-77).*

RESEARCH HOVERCRAFT

Operating weight: 15 tons
Dimensions, feet (metres): 70 × 30 *(21·4 × 9·2)*
Propulsion: 2—350 hp aircraft radial engines
Lift: 1—350 hp aircraft radial with centrifugal fan
Speed, knots: 50

In use in the Soviet Navy since 1967 for tests and evaluation.

Research Hovercraft

Jane's Surface Skimmers

25 "GUS" CLASS

Operating weight: 27 tons
Dimensions, feet (metres): 70 × 24 *(21·4 × 7·3)*
Propulsion: 2—780 hp marine gas turbines (VP and reversible propellers)
Lift: 1—780 hp marine gas turbine
Speed, knots: 58
Range, miles: 230 cruising

This is a naval version of a 50-seat passenger carrying design *(Skate).* In production for Naval Infantry.

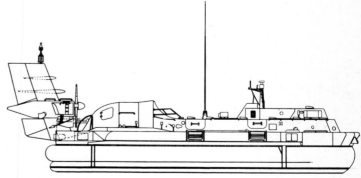

Soviet navy version of the "GUS" class

Jane's Surface Skimmers

5 "AIST" CLASS

Operating weight: 220 tons
Dimensions, feet (metres): 150 × 60 *(45·7 × 18·3)*
Speed, knots: 70 approx

Currently in production at Leningrad for Naval Infantry. Is the first large Soviet hovercraft for naval use. Similar to British SR.N4.

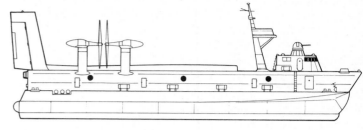

"AIST" Class

Jane's Surface Skimmers

1 AALC TYPE (? "LEBED" CLASS)

Assault hovercraft undergoing evaluation trials. Smaller than "Aist" class though capable of tank transporting.

EKRANOPLAN CRAFT (WIG)

Dimensions, feet (metres): 400 × 125 (approx wing span) *(122 × 38)*
Propulsion: Ten gas turbines (two to assist take-off then eight for cruising)
Speed, knots: 300 approx

An experimental craft, a wing-in-ground-effect machine, with a carrying capacity of about 900 troops and with potential for a number of naval applications such as ASW, minesweeping or patrol. Claimed to be capable of operations in heavy weather as well as crossing marshes, ice and low obstacles. Several other prototypes of unknown characteristics exist.

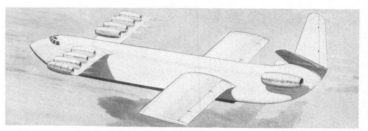

EKRANOPLAN

Jane's Surface Skimmers

SUPPORT AND DEPOT SHIPS

9 "UGRA" CLASS (SUBMARINE DEPOT SHIPS)

BORODINO
GANGUT
IVAN KOLYSHKIN
IVAN KUCHERENKO
IVAN VADREMEEV
TOBOL
VOLGA
+2

Displacement, tons: 6 750 standard; 9 500 full load
Length, feet (metres): 452·6 *(138)*
Beam, feet (metres): 57·6 *(17·6)*
Draught, feet (metres): 19·8 *(6·0)*
Aircraft: 1 helicopter
Guns: 8—57 mm (twin)
Main engines: 4 diesels; 2 shafts; 14 000 bhp = 20 knots
Range, miles: 10 000 at 12 knots
Complement: 300

Improved versions of the "Don" class. Built from 1961 onwards, all in Nikolayev. Equipped with workshops. Provided with a helicopter platform and, in later versions, a hangar. Carries a large derrick to handle torpedoes. Has mooring points in hull about 100 feet apart, and has baggage ports possibly for coastal craft and submarines. The last pair of this class mount a large superstructure from the mainmast to quarter-deck and are used for training.

Radar: Search: Strut Curve.
Fire Control: Muff Cob.
Navigation: Don

Transfer: A tenth ship, *Amba,* which had four 76 mm guns, was transferred to India.

"UGRA" Class

5/1975, MOD

"UGRA" Class

5/1974, MOD

6 "DON" CLASS (SUBMARINE SUPPORT)

DMITRI GALKIN	MIKHAIL TUKAEVSKY
FEDOR VIDYAEV	NIKOLAY STOLBOV
MAGOMED GADZHIEV	VIKTOR KOTELNIKOV

Displacement, tons: 6 700 standard; 9 000 full load
Length, feet (metres): 458·9 *(139·9)*
Beam, feet (metres): 54·1 *(16·5)*
Draught, feet (metres): 22·3 *(6·8)*
Aircraft: Provision for helicopter in two ships
Guns: 4—3·9 in *(100 mm)*; 8—57 mm (4 twin) (see notes)
Main engines: 4 diesels; 14 000 bhp; 2 shafts
Speed, knots: 21
Complement: 300
Range, miles: 10 000 at 12 knots

Support ships, all named after officers lost in WW II. Built in 1957 to 1962. Originally seven ships were built, all in Nikolayev. Quarters for about 450 submariners.

Gunnery: In hull number III only 2—3·9 in. In IV no 3·9 in mounted. In some of class 8—25 mm (twin) are mounted.

Radar: Search: Slim Net and probably Strut Curve in some. Fire Control: Sun Visor.

Transfers: 1 to Indonesia in 1962.

DMITRI GALKIN with HF aerial on mainmast *8/1974, MOD*

6 "LAMA" CLASS (MISSILE SUPPORT)

Displacement, tons: 4 600 full load
Length, feet (metres): 370·0 *(112·8)* oa
Beam, feet (metres): 60·7 *(18·3)*
Draught, feet (metres): 19·0 *(5·8)*
Guns: 8—57 mm, (2 quadruple, 1 on the forecastle; 1 on the break of the quarter deck) (in 2 units); 4—57 mm (quad) (in one unit); 2—57 mm; 4—25 mm (in two units); 2—57 mm (in one unit)
Main engines: Diesels; 2 shafts; 5 000 shp
Speed, knots: 15

The engines are sited aft to allow for a very large and high hangar or hold amidships for carrying missiles or weapons' spares. This is about 12 feet high above the main deck. There are doors at the forward end with rails leading in and a raised turntable gantry or travelling cranes for transferring armaments to combatant ships.
There are mooring points along the hull for ships of low freeboard such as submarines to come alongside. The well deck is about 40 feet long, enough for a missile to fit horizontally before being lifted vertically for loading.

Radar: Search: Slim Net or Strut Curve.

"LAMA" Class *1972, USN*

Fire Control: Hawk Screech, (2) or Muff Cob. Various combinations in different ships.
Navigation: Don

2 "AMGA" CLASS (MISSILE SUPPORT)

Displacement, tons: approx 5 500
Dimensions, feet (metres): 361 × 56 × 19 *(110 × 17 × 5·8)*
Guns: 4—25 mm (twins)
Main engines: Diesels; 10 000 hp = 18 knots

Ships of similar size and duties to the "Lama" class. May be distinguished from those ships by the break at the bridge, giving a lower freeboard than that of the "Lamas". Fitted with a large 50 ton crane forward and thus capable of handling much larger missiles than their predecessors. Probably, therefore, designed for servicing submarines, particularly those armed with SS-N-8 missiles and others of equal size.

Radar: Search; Strut Curve.
Fire control; Hawk Screech.
Navigation; Don.

"AMGA" Class *1974*

14 "AMUR" CLASS (REPAIR SHIPS)

Displacement, tons: 6 500 full load
Dimensions, feet (metres): 377·3 × 57·4 × 18·0 *(115 × 17·5 × 5·5)*
Main engines: Diesels; 2 shafts = 18 knots

General purpose depot ships built since 1969. Successors to the "Oskol" class. In series production.

"AMUR" Class *1/1974*

"AMUR" Class *1973*

1 "URAL" CLASS (? NUCLEAR SUPPORT SHIP)

URAL

Displacement, tons: 4 000 (approx)
Dimensions, feet (metres): 340 × 45 × 20 *(103 × 14 × 6)* (approx)
Main engines: Diesel

Radar: Don.

URAL   7/1973

1 "WILHELM BAUER" CLASS (SUBMARINE TENDER)

PECHORA (ex-*Otto Wünche*)

Displacement, tons: 4 726 standard; 5 600 full load
Dimensions, feet (metres): 446·0 × 52·5 × 14·5 *(136 × 16 × 4·4)*
Main engines: 4 MAN diesels; 2 shafts; 12 400 bhp = 20 knots

Former German ship. Launched in 1939.

3 "ALESHA" CLASS (MINELAYERS)

075   083   +1

Displacement, tons: 3 600 standard; 4 300 full load
Dimensions, feet (metres): 337·9 × 47·6 × 15·7 *(98 × 14·5 × 4·8)*
Guns: 4—57 mm (1 quadruple forward)
Mines: 400
Main engines: 4 diesels; 2 shafts; 8 000 bhp = 20 knots
Range, miles: 8 000 at 14 knots
Complement: 150

In service since 1965. Fitted with four mine tracks to provide stern launchings.
Also have a capability in general support role.

2 "TOMBA" CLASS (REPAIR SHIPS)

Displacement, tons: 3 000
Dimensions, feet (metres): 350 × 50 × 20 *(106 × 15 × 6)* (approx)
Main engines: Diesels

A new type of medium repair ship, first completed 1975. One in Northern Fleet, one in Pacific.

"TOMBA" Class   5/1976, MOD

10 "OSKOL" CLASS (REPAIR SHIPS)

Displacement, tons: 2 500 standard; 3 000 full load
Dimensions, feet (metres): 278·8 × 39·4 × 14·8 *(85 × 12 × 4·5)*
Guns: See notes
Main engines: 2 diesels; 2 shafts; speed = 16 knots

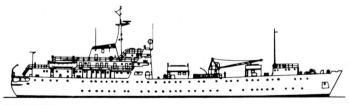

Three series: "Oskol I" class, well-decked hull, no armament; "Oskol II" class, well-decked hull, armed with 2—57 mm guns (1 twin) and 4—25 mm guns (2 twin); "Oskol III" class, flush-decked hull. General purpose tenders and repair ships. Built from 1963 to 1970 in Poland.

Radar: Fire control: Muff Cob (In "II").
Navigation: Don.

"OSKOL III" Class   1973, S. Breyer

6 "ATREK" CLASS (SUBMARINE SUPPORT)

ATREK   AYAT   BAKHMUT   DVINA   MURMATS   OSIPOV

Displacement, tons: 3 500 standard
Measurement, tons: 3 258 gross
Dimensions, feet (metres): 336 × 49 × 20 *(110 × 14·9 × 6·1)*
Main engines: Expansions and exhaust turbines; 1 shaft; 2 450 hp = 13 knots
Boilers: 2 water tube
Range, miles: 3 500 at 13 knots

Built in 1956-58, and converted to naval use from "Kolomna" class freighters. There are six of these vessels employed as submarine tenders and replenishment ships. Some may have up to 6—37 mm (twins).

BAKHMUT   1974

4 "DNEPR" CLASS (SUBMARINE TENDERS)

Displacement, tons: 4 500 standard; 5 250 full load
Dimensions, feet (metres): 370·7 × 54·1 × 14·4 *(113 × 16·5 × 4·4)*
Main engines: Diesels; 2 000 bhp = 12 knots

Bow lift repair ships for S/M support and maintenance. Built in 1957-66 and equipped with workshops and servicing facilities. The last two ships of this class form the "Dnepr II" Class.

"DNEPR II" Class   1974

1 "TOVDA" CLASS (REPAIR SHIP)

TOVDA

Displacement, tons: 2 500 standard; 3 000 full load
Dimensions, feet (metres): 282·1 × 39·4 × 16·0 *(86 × 12 × 4·9)*
Guns: 6—57 mm (3 twin mountings)
Main engines: Triple expansion; 1 300 ihp = 11 knots

Polish built ex-collier converted in 1958.

TOVDA   1959

INTELLIGENCE COLLECTORS (AGIs)

6 "PRIMORYE" CLASS

PRIMORYE	KRYM	ZAPOROZYE
KAVKAZ	ZABAIKALYE	ZAKARPATYE

Displacement, tons: 4 000
Dimensions, feet (metres): 274 × 45 × 26·2 *(83·6 × 13·7 × 8)*
Main engines: Diesels

The most modern intelligence collectors in the world, apparently with built-in processing and possibly, analysis capability. The aerials carried would seem to dispose of the contention that these are fishery research ships.

"PRIMORYE" Class   1972

ZAKARPATYE with friend (compare aerials with 1972 photograph)   3/1976, MOD

2 "NIKOLAI ZUBOV" CLASS

GAVRIL SARYCHEV   KHARITON LAPTEV

Displacement, tons: 3 021 full load
Dimensions, feet (metres): 295·2 × 42·7 × 15 *(90 × 13 × 4·6)*
Main engines: Diesels; 2 shafts = 16·5 knots

Built in Poland.

GAVRIL SARYCHEV   1973, Michael D. J. Lennon

KHARITON LAPTEV   7/1970, USN

GIDROGRAF PELENG

Measurement, tons: 2 000 gross
Dimensions, feet (metres): 256 oa × 42 × 13·5 *(78 × 12·8 × 4·1)*
Main engines: 2—4 stroke diesels; 2 shafts; 4 200 bhp = 17 knots

Built in Sweden 1959-60. Originally salvage tugs.

2 "PAMIR" CLASS

PELENG   4/1970, USN

6 "MOMA" CLASS

ARKHIPELAG	NAKHODKA
ILMEN	PELORUS
JUPITER	SELIGER

Displacement, tons: 1 240 standard; 1 800 full load
Dimensions, feet (metres): 240 × 32·8 × 13·2 *(73·2 × 10 × 4)*
Main engines: Diesels = 16 knots

The modernised version has a new foremast in the fore well-deck.

JUPITER   10/1975, MOD

4 "MIRNY" CLASS

BAKAN	VAL
LOTSMAN	VERTIKAL

Displacement, tons: 850
Dimensions, feet (metres): 208 × 31·2 × 13·8 *(63·4 × 9·5 × 4·2)*
Main engines: Diesel; 1 shaft = 15 knots

Converted from whale-catchers in 1965.

"MIRNY" Class   1972

8 "MAYAK" CLASS

ANEROID	KURSOGRAF
GIRORULEVOY	LADOGA
KHERSONES	GS 239
KURS	GS 242

Measurement, tons: 680 gross; 252 net
Dimensions, feet (metres): 178 × 30·6 × 15·9 *(54·3 × 9·3 × 4·8)*
Main engines: Diesel; 1 shaft; 800 hp = 12 knots

Built in USSR from 1967. Advance on "Okean" class.

GIRORULEVOY (new aerial arrays)   9/1975, MOD(N)

15 "OKEAN" CLASS

ALIDADA	EKHOLOT	REDUKTOR
AMPERMETR	GIDROFON	REPITER
BAROGRAF	KRENOMETR	TEODOLIT
BAROMETR	LINZA	TRAVERZ
DEFLEKTOR	LOTLIN	ZOND

Measurement, tons: 680 gross
Dimensions, feet (metres): 178 × 30·6 × 15·9 *(54·3 × 9·3 × 4·8)*
Main engines: Diesel; 1 shaft; 800 hp = 12 knots

Built in USSR 1965. Have the same variations in the superstructure with the port side closed in and the starboard side open as in the "Mayak" class.

Modified "OKEAN" Class (open starboard side)   *9/1974, MOD*

8 "LENTRA" CLASS

GS 34	GS 43	GS 55
GS 36	GS 46	GS 59
GS 41	GS 47	

Displacement, tons: 250
Measurement, tons: 334 gross; 186 deadweight
Dimensions, feet (metres): 143 × 25 × 12·5 *(43·6 × 7·6 × 3·8)*
Main engines: Diesel; 400 hp = 10·5 knots

All built in USSR and East Germany 1957-63. Now have names in addition to numbers. Two known as *Neringa* and *Izvalta*. Mainly employed in-area.

GS 43   *MOD*

1 "T 58" CLASS

Displacement, tons: 900 full load
Dimensions, feet (metres): 229·9 × 29·5 × 7·9 *(70·1 × 9 × 2·4)*
Main engines: 2 diesels; 2 shafts; 4 000 bhp = 18 knots

Built in USSR 1962.

2 "DNEPR" CLASS

IZMERITEL   PROTRAKTOR

Measurement, tons: 500 gross
Dimensions, feet (metres): 150 × 30 × 8 *(45·8 × 9·2 × 2·4)*
Main engines: Diesel = 11 knots

NAVAL SURVEY SHIPS

9 "NIKOLAI ZUBOV" CLASS

A. CHIRIKOV	F. LITKE	SEJMEN DEZHNEV
A. VILKITSKY	NIKOLAI ZUBOV	T. BELLINSGAUSEN
BORIS DAVIDOV	S. CHELYUSKIN	V. GOLOVNIN

Displacement, tons: 2 674 standard; 3 021 full load
Dimensions, feet (metres): 295·2 × 42·7 × 15 *(90 × 13 × 4·6)*
Main engines: 2 diesels; speed = 16·5 knots
Complement: 108 to 120, including scientists

Oceanographic research ships built at Szczecin Shipyard, Poland in 1964. Also employed on navigational, sonar and radar trials.

ANDREY VILKITSKY   1973, Michael D. J. Lennon

24 "MOMA" CLASS (+6 AGIs)

ALTAIR	ASKOLD	KRILON	PELORUS
ANADIR	BEREZAN	KOLGUEV	RYBACHI
ANDROMEDA	CHELEKEN	LIMAN	SEVER
ANTARES	EKVATOR	MARS	TAYMYR
ANTON KTYDA	ELTON	MORSOVIEC	VEGA
ARTIKA	KILDIN	OKEAN	ZAPOLARA

Displacement, tons: 1 240 standard; 1 800 full load
Dimensions, feet (metres): 240 × 32·8 × 13·2 *(73·2 × 10 × 4)*
Main engines: Diesels; 16 knots

Eight ships of this class were reported to have been built from 1967 to 1970 and the remainder since. Naval manned.

LIMAN   10/1975, MOD

10 "KAMENKA" CLASS
10 "BIYA" CLASS

Displacement, tons: 1 000 full load
Dimensions, feet (metres): 180·5 × 31·2 × 11·5 *(55·1 × 9·5 × 3·5)*
Main engines: Diesels; speed 16 knots

The ships of these classes are not named but have a number with the prefix letters "GS". All reported to have been built since 1967-68. Naval manned.

"KAMENKA" Class   1974, MOD

4 "TELNOVSK" CLASS

AYTADOR	ULYANA GROMOVA	SVIYAGA

Displacement, tons: 1 200 standard
Measurement, tons: 1 217 gross, 448 net
Dimensions, feet (metres): 229·6 × 32·8 × 13·1 *(70 × 10 × 4)*
Main engines: Diesels; speed 10 knots

Formerly coastal freighters. Built in Hungary. Refitted and modernised for naval supply and surveying duties. Naval manned.

AYTADOR   1974, Michael D. J. Lennon

STVOR

Displacement, tons: 1 200 standard
Dimensions, feet (metres): 229·6 × 32·8 × 13·1 *(70 × 10 × 4)*
Main engines: Diesels = 10 knots

Built in Hungary in late 1950s as a survey ship of the "Telnovsk" class. Built with additional accommodation immediately forward of the bridge.
Sivor has additional accommodation forward of the bridge.

STVOR   1972, Michael D. J. Lennon

16 "SAMARA" CLASS

AZIMUT	GLUBOMER	RUMB
DEVIATOR	GORIZONT	TROPIK
GIDROLOG	GRADUS	ZENIT
GIGROMETR	KOMPAS	VAGACH
GLOBUS	PAMYAT MERKURYIA	VOSTOK
		YUG

Displacement, tons: 800 standard; 1 200 full load
Measurement, tons: 1 276 gross; 1 000 net
Dimensions, feet (metres): 198 × 36·3 × 10·8 *(60·4 × 11·1 × 3·3)*
Main engines: Diesels; 3 000 hp; 2 shafts = 16 knots

Built at Gdansk, Poland since 1962 for hydrographic surveying and research. Navy manned.

GIGROMETR   1975, J. A. Verhoog

CIVILIAN MANNED SURVEY SHIPS

IZUMRUD

Measurement, tons: 3 862 gross; 465 net
Main engines: Powered by diesel-electric machinery

A research ship built in 1970. Civilian manned for structural and material tests. Owned by Ministry of Shipping.

IZUMRUD   1972, Michael D. J. Lennon

13 +2 "DMITRI OVTSYN" CLASS

A. SMIRNOV	PROFESSOR BOGOROV
DMITRI LAPTEV	PROFESSOR KURENTSOV
DMITRI OVSTYN	S. KRAKOV*
DMITRI STERLEGOV	STEFAN MALYGIN
E. TOLL	VALERIAN ALBANOV
N. KOLOMEYTSEV	V. SUKHOTSKY*
N. YEVGENOV*	+ 2

Displacement, tons: 1 800 full load
Dimensions, feet (metres): 220 × 39 × 15 *(67·1 × 11·9 × 4·6)*
Main engines: Diesels; 2 000 bhp = 16 knots

Built by Turku, Finland. Civilian manned. Employed largely on geological research and survey in the Arctic. Those marked *, completed Jan-Aug 1974. *P. Bogorov* launched 11 Oct 1975, *P. Kurentsov* 17 Dec 1975. Last pair laid down Oct and Dec 1975. Continuing programme. Owned by Ministry of Merchant Marine.

MIKHAIL LOMONOSOV

Displacement, tons: 5 960 normal
Measurement, tons: 3 897 gross; 1 195 net
Dimensions, feet (metres): 336·0 × 47·2 × 14·0 *(102·5 × 14·4 × 4·3)*
Main engines: Triple expansion; 2 450 ihp = 13 knots

Built by Neptun, Rostock, in 1957 from the hull of a freighter of the "Kolomna" class. Operated by the Academy of Sciences. Equipped with 16 laboratories. Carries a helicopter for survey. Civilian manned.

MIKHAIL LOMONOSOV   1970, Michael D. J. Lennon

AKADEMIK KOVALEVSKY   AKADEMIK VAVILOV

Measurement, tons: 284 gross *(Vavilov 255)*
Dimensions, feet (metres): 126·8 × 23·7 × 11·5 *(38·1 × 7·2 × 3·5)*; *(Vavilov* 119·7 × 24·1 × 11·5 *(36·5 × 7·4 × 3·5)*
Main engines: 1 Diesel = 10 knots

Built in E. Germany in 1949. Civiliain manned oceanographic ships run by Academy of Sciences.

AKADEMIK KOVALEVSKY   1974, Michael D. J. Lennon

AKADEMIK ARKHANGELSKY

Measurement, tons: 416 tons gross
Dimensions, feet (metres): 132·9 × 25 × 13 *(40·5 × 7·6 × 4)*
Main engines: 1 Diesel = 10 knots

Built in USSR in 1963.

AKADEMIK ARKHANGELSKY   *1974, Michael D. J. Lennon*

MGLA

Measurement, tons: 299 gross
Dimensions, feet (metres): 129·5 × 24·3 × 11·8 *(39·5 × 7·4 × 3·6)*
Main engines: 1 diesel = 8·5 knots

Hydromet research ship. Civilian manned.

MGLA   *1974, Michael D. J. Lennon*

ZARYA

Measurement, tons: 333 gross; 71 net

Built in 1952 for geomagnetic survey work. Civilian manned. Run by Academy of Sciences.

ZARYA   *1972, Michael D. J. Lennon*

NEREY   NOVATOR

Measurement, tons: 369 gross
Dimensions, feet (metres): 118·1 × 24·7 × 11·5 *(36 × 7·5 × 3·5)*
Main engines: 2 diesels = 11 knots

Built in USSR in 1956 and 1955. Originally fleet tugs. Converted for seismic research. Civilian manned.
Run by Academy of Sciences.

NEREY   *1972, Michael D. J. Lennon*

PETRODVORETS (ex-*Bore II*)

Measurement, tons: 1 965 gross; 985 net
Dimensions, feet (metres): 254·2 × 39·4 × 24·9 *(77·5 × 12 × 7·6)*
Main engines: Diesel = 13·5 knots

Built at Abo, Finland for Finnish owners in 1938. Sold to USSR in 1950 and renamed.

ZVEZDA

Measurement, tons: 348 gross
Dimensions, feet (metres): 129 × 24·2 × 11·4 *(39·3 × 7·4 × 3·5)*
Main engines: Diesel = 10 knots

Built in East Germany in 1957. Carries winches in the chains on the quarters. Sister ships *Zarnitsa* and *Yug* are used for transporting crews to ships building outside the USSR.

ZVEZDA   *1974, Ian Brooke*

NAVAL RESEARCH SHIPS

3 + 1 "AKADEMIK KRILOV" CLASS

ADMIRAL VLADIMIRSKY   AKADEMIK KRILOV   LEONID SOBOLEV   +1

A new class of research ships, the fourth is building in Stettin (1976). Naval manned.

4 "MODIFIED AKADEMIK KURCHATOV" CLASS

ABKHASIA   ADZHARIYA   BASHKIRIYA   MOLDAVYA

Displacement, tons: 7 500 full load
Dimensions, feet (metres): 409·2 × 56 × 21·1 *(124·8 × 17·1 × 6·4)*
Main engines: 2 Diesels = 20·4 knots
Range, miles: 20 000 at 15 knots
Endurance: 60 days

Fitted with helicopter platform aft. Naval manned. Completed in 1973. Some are hydromet reporting ships.

BASHKIRIYA   *1/1974*

3 "POLYUS" CLASS

BAIKAL   BALKHASH   POLYUS

Displacement, tons: 6 900 standard
Dimensions, feet (metres): 365·8 × 46·2 × 20·7 *(111·6 × 14·1 × 6·3)*
Main engines: Diesel-electric; 3 400 hp = 14 knots

These ships of the "Polyus" class were built in East Germany in 1961-64. Oceanographic research ships. Naval manned.

POLYUS   *1972*

1 "NEVELSKOY" CLASS

NEVELSKOY

Was predecessor to "Zubov" class. Naval manned.

NEVELSKOY   *1970*

CIVILIAN RESEARCH SHIPS

7 "AKADEMIK KURCHATOV" CLASS

AKADEMIK KOROLEV
AKADEMIK KURCHATOV
AKADEMIK SHIRSHOV
AKADEMIK VERNADSKY

DMITRI MENDELEYEV
PROFESSOR ZUBOV
PROFESSOR VIZE

Displacement, tons: 6 681 full load
Measurement, tons: 1 986 deadweight; 5 460 gross; 1 387 net
Dimensions, feet (metres): 400·3 to 406·8 × 56·1 × 15·0 *(122·1 to 124·1 × 17·1 × 4·6)*
Main engines: 2 Halberstadt 6-cylinder diesels; 2 shafts; 8 000 bhp = 18 to 20 knots

All built by Mathias Thesen Werft at Wismar, East Germany between 1965 and 1968. All have a hull of the same design as the "Mikhail Kalinin" class of merchant vessels. There are variations in mast and aerial rig. *Professor Vize* is similar to *A. Shirshov* whilst *A. Kurchatov, A. Vernadsky* and *D. Mendeleyev* are the same. Civilian manned.

AKADEMIK KURCHATOV   *1973, Michael D. J. Lennon*

9 "PASSAT" CLASS

ERNST KRENKEL (ex-*Vikhr*)   MUSSON   PASSAT   PORIV
GEORGI USHAKOV (ex-*Schkval*)   OKEAN   PRIBOI   PRILIV
                                                          VOLNA

Measurement, tons: 3 280 gross
Dimensions, feet (metres): 280 × 43 × 15·5 *(85·4 × 13·1 × 4·7)* (First pair marginally larger)
Main engines: Diesels; 4 800 hp = 16 knots

Hydromet ships built at Szczecin, Poland, since 1968.

GEORGI USHAKOV   *1975, Michael D. J. Lennon*

2 "LEBEDEV" CLASS

PETR LEBEDEV   SERGEI VAVILOV

Measurement, tons: 3 561 gross; 1 180 net
Main engines: Diesels

Research vessels with comprehensive equipment and accommodation. Both built in 1954. Run by Academy of Sciences. Civilian manned.

PETR LEBEDEV   *1975, J. A. Verhoog*

PETR LEBEDEV   *1970, USN*

SERGEI VAVILOV   *1973, Michael D. J. Lennon*

VLADIMIR OBRUCHEV

Measurement, tons: 534 gross
Dimensions, feet (metres): 156·5 × 32·2 × 16·4 *(47·7 × 9·8 × 5)*
Main engines: 2 Diesels; = 11 knots

One of the "Gromovoy" class tugs built in Romania in 1959 and subsequently converted for seismic research duties. Civilian manned.

VLADIMIR OBRUCHEV   *1972, Michael D. J. Lennon*

VITYAZ (ex-*Mars*)

Displacement, tons: 5 700 standard
Dimensions, feet (metres): 357·5 × 48·9 × 15·5 *(109 × 14·9 × 4·7)*
Main engines: Diesels; 3 000 bhp = 14·5 knots
Range, miles: 18 400 at 14 knots
Complement: 137 officers and men including 73 scientists

The first post-war Soviet oceanographic research ship. Formerly a German freighter built at Bremen in 1939. Equipped with 13 laboratories. Has now steamed over 2 million miles. Run by Academy of Sciences.

VITYAZ   *1972, Michael D. J. Lennon*

1 "MODIFIED DOBRINYA NIKITCH" CLASS

VLADIMIR KAVRASKY

Displacement, tons: 2 500 standard
Dimensions, feet (metres): 223·1 × 59·1 × 18·1 *(68 × 18 × 5·5)*
Main engines: 3 shafts = 13·8 knots

One of a numerous class of icebreakers built at Leningrad in the early 1960s—converted for polar research in 1972.

3 "ORBELI" CLASS

AKADEMIK IOSIF ORBELI
PROFESSOR NIKOLAI BARABSKI
AKADEMIK S. VAVILOV

Built in Warnemünde 1969-71. Research ships. Civilian manned.

AKADEMIK S. VAVILOV   *1972, Michael D. J. Lennon*

NAVAL SPACE ASSOCIATED SHIPS

3 "CHAZHMA" CLASS

CHAZHMA (ex-*Dangara*)   **DSHANKOY**   **CHUMIKAN** (ex-*Dolgeschtschelje*)

Displacement, tons: 5 300 light; 14 065 full load
Dimensions, feet (metres): 457·7 × 59·0 × 25·9 *(139·6 × 18 × 7·9)*
Aircraft: 1 helicopter
Main engines: 2—7 cyl diesels = 18 knots

Formerly bulk ore-carriers of the "Dshankoy" class (7 265 tons gross).
Soviet Range Instrumentation Ships (SRIS). Active since 1963. Naval manned.

7 "BASKUNCHAK" (ex-"VOSTOK") CLASS

APSHERON (ex-*Tosnoles*)
BASKUNCHAK (ex-*Vostok 4*)
DAURIYA (ex-*Suzdal*)
DIKSON (ex-*Vagales*)

DONBASS (ex-*Kirishi*)
SEVAN (ex-*Vyborgles*)
TAMAN (ex-*Vostok 3*)

Measurement, tons: 6 450 deadweight; 4 896 gross; 2 215 net
Dimensions, feet (metres): 400·3 × 55·1 × 14·0 *(122·1 × 16·8 × 4·3)*
Main engines: B & W 9-cylinder diesels; speed 15 knots

Standard timber carriers modified with helicopter flight deck. Built at Leningrad between 1963 and 1966. Entirely manned by naval personnel.

TAMAN   *1972, Michael D. J. Lennon*

4 "SIBIR" CLASS

SAKHALIN   **SIBIR**   **SPASSK** (ex-*Chukotka*)   **SUCHAN**

Displacement, tons: 4 000 standard; 5 000 full load
Measurement, tons: 3 767 gross (*Spassk* 3 800, *Suchan* 3 710)
Dimensions, feet (metres): 354 × 49·2 × 20 *(108 × 15 × 6·1)*
Main engines: Triple expansion; 2 shafts; 3 300 ihp = 15 knots
Range, miles: 3 300 at 12 knots

Converted bulk ore carriers employed as Missile Range Ships in the Pacific. *Sakhalin* and *Sibir* have three radomes forward and aft, and carry helicopters. *Suchan* is also equipped with a helicopter flight deck. Launched in 1957-59. Formerly freighters of the Polish B 31 type. Rebuilt in 1958-59 as missile range ships in Leningrad. Naval manned.

CIVILIAN SPACE ASSOCIATED SHIPS

1 "GAGARIN" CLASS

KOSMONAUT YURI GAGARIN

Displacement, tons: 45 000
Measurement, tons: 32 291 gross; 5 247 net
Dimensions, feet (metres): 773·3 oa × 101·7 × 30·0 *(235·9 oa × 31 × 9·2)*
Main engines: 2 geared steam turbines; 1 shaft; 19 000 shp = 17 knots

Design based on the "Sofia" or "Akhtuba" (ex-"Hanoi") class steam tanker. Built at Leningrad in 1970, completed in 1971. Used for investigation into conditions in the upper atmosphere, and the control of space vehicles. She is the largest Soviet research vessel. Has bow and stern thrust units for ease of berthing. With all four aerials vertical and facing forward she experiences a loss in speed of 2 knots.

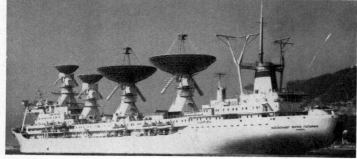

KOSMONAUT YURI GAGARIN   *1972, Michael D. J. Lennon*

KOSMONAUT YURI GAGARIN   *1972, Michael D. J. Lennon*

1 "KOMAROV" CLASS

KOSMONAUT VLADIMIR KOMAROV (ex-*Genichesk*)

Displacement, tons: 17 500 full load
Dimensions, feet (metres): 510·8 × 75·5 × 29·5 *(155·8 × 23 × 9)*
Main engines: Diesels; 2 shafts; 24 000 bhp = 22 knots

She was launched in 1966 at Nikolaev as *Genichesk* and operated as a merchant ship in the Black Sea for about six months. Converted to her present role at Leningrad in 1967. The ship is named in honour of the Soviet astronaut who died when his space craft crashed in 1967.

KOSMONAUT VLADIMIR KOMAROV   *1972, Michael D. J. Lennon*

KOSMONAUT VLADIMIR KOMAROV   *1974, J. van der Woude*
(with new forward aerial)

1 "KOROLEV" CLASS

AKADEMIK SERGEI KOROLEV

Displacement, tons: 21 250
Measurement, tons: 17 114 gross; 2 185 net
Dimensions, feet (metres): 597·1 × 82·0 × 30·0 *(182·1 × 25 × 9·2)*
Main engines: Diesels
Speed, knots: 17

Built at Nikolayev in 1970, completing in 1971. Equipped with the smaller type radome and two "saucers".

| AKADEMIK SERGEI KOROLEV | *1972, Michael D. J. Lennon* | AKADEMIK SERGEI KOROLEV | *1972, Michael D. J. Lennon* |

1 "BEZHITSA" CLASS

BEZHITSA

Measurement, tons: 11 089 gross; 12 727 deadweight
Dimensions, feet (metres): 510·4 × 67·7 × 40·4 *(155·7 × 20·6 × 12·3)*
Main engines: Diesel = 17·5 knots

Former freighter of "Poltava" class launched at Nikolayev in 1964, and subsequently completed as a research ship. The aerial horns were fitted in 1971. Directional aerials similar to those in *Dolinsk* and *Ristna* fitted on crane stowage forward of the bridge.

BEZHITSA   *1972, Michael D. J. Lennon*

4 "MORZHOVETS" (ex-"VOSTOK") CLASS

BOROVICHI (ex-*Svirles*)   **KEGOSTROV** (ex-*Taimyr*)   **MORZHOVETS**   **NEVEL**

Former timber carriers but completely modified with a comprehensive array of tracking, direction finding and directional aerials. Additional laboratories built above the forward holds. Same measurements as the "Baskunchak" class, but tonnage increased to 5 277 gross

NEVEL   *1972, Michael D. J. Lennon*

RISTNA

Measurement, tons: 4 200 gross; 3 724 deadweight; 1 819 net
Dimensions, feet (metres): 347·8 × 47·9 × 14·0 *(106·1 × 14·6 × 4·3)*
Main engines: MAN 6-cylinder diesels; speed = 15 knots

Converted from a timber carrier. Built in East Germany at Rostok by Schiffswerft—Neptun in 1963. Painted white. Fitted with directional aerials on top of bridge wings.
Space tracking ship.

RISTNA   *1970, Michael D. J. Lennon*

CABLE SHIPS

6 + 3 "KLASMA" CLASS

DONETZ   INGUL   KATYN   TSNA   YANA   ZEYA   + 3

Displacement, tons: 6 000 standard; 6 900 full load
Measurement, tons: 3 400 deadweight; 5 786 gross
Dimensions, feet (metres): 427·8 × 52·5 × 19 *(130·5 × 16 × 5·8)*
Main engines: 5 Wärtsila Sulzer diesels; 5 000 shp = 14 knots
Complement: 110

Ingul and *Yana* were built by Wärtsilä, Helsingforsvarvet, Finland, laid down on 10 Oct 1961 and 4 May 1962 and launched on 14 Apr 1962 and 1 Nov 1962 respectively, *Donetz* and *Tsna* were built at the Wärtsilä, Abovarvet, Abo. *Donetz* was launched on 17 Dec 1968 and completed 3 July 1969. *Tsna* was completed in summer 1968. *Zeya* was delivered on 20 Nov 1970. *Donetz*, *Tsna* and *Zeya* are of slightly modified design.
A second group was ordered in 1972/73, the first of the pair, *Katyn*, being launched 20 Mar 1974. Two more were ordered on 16 July 1974.

YANA (Type 1—no gantry aft)   3/1976, MOD

TSNA (Type II—with gantry aft)   *Wärtsilä*

INGUL (Type 1—no gantry aft)   *1973*

LIFTING VESSELS

15 "NEPTUN" CLASS

Displacement, tons: 700 light; 1 230 standard
Dimensions, feet (metres): 170·6 × 36·1 × 12·5 *(52 × 11 × 3·8)*
Main engines: Oil fuelled, speed = 12 knots

Mooring tenders similar to Western boom defence vessels. Built in 1957-60 by Neptun Rostock. Have a crane of 75 tons lifting capacity on the bow. One of this class is now based at Murmansk for the Maritime Fleet. She is acting as a diving vessel for hydrogeologists and construction personnel.

"NEPTUN" Class

COMMUNICATIONS RELAY SHIPS

20 "LIBAU" CLASS

Displacement, tons: 310 standard; 380 full load
Dimensions, feet (metres): 170·6 × 21·5 × 9·0 *(52 × 6·6 × 2·7)*
Main engines: 3 diesels; 2 shafts; 3 300 bhp = 24 knots
Range, miles: 1 500 at 12 knots

Converted "Kronshtadt" class.

SERVICE FORCES

Note: With the Soviet merchant fleet under State control any ships of the merchant service, including tankers, may be diverted to a fleet support role at any time.

5 "BORIS CHILIKIN" CLASS (FLEET REPLENISHMENT SHIPS)

BORIS CHILIKIN
DNESTR

IVAN BUBNOV
VLADIMIR KOLECHITSKY
+ 1

Displacement, tons: 23 000 full load
Dimensions, feet (metres): 531·5 × 70·2 × 28·1 *(162·1 × 21·4 × 8·6)*
Guns: 4—57 mm (2 twin) (except in *Ivan Bubnov*)
Main engines: Diesel; 9 900 hp; 1 shaft = 16·5 knots

Based on the "Veliky Oktyabr" merchant ship tanker design *Boris Chilikin* was built at Leningrad completing in 1971. This is the first Soviet Navy class of purpose built underway fleet replenishment ships for the supply of both liquids and solids, indicating a growing awareness of the need for afloat support for a widely dispersed fleet.
Carry 13 000 tons fuel oil, 400 tons ammunition, 400 tons spares and 400 tons victualling stores.
A continuing programme.

DNESTR   9/1974, MOD

1 "MANYCH" CLASS (FLEET REPLENISHMENT SHIP)

MANYCH

Displacement, tons: 7 500
Dimensions, feet (metres): 377·2 × 52·5 × 19·7 *(115 × 16 × 6)*

Completed 1972, probably in Finland. A smaller edition of the *Boris Chilikin* but showing the new interest in custom-built replenishment ships. The high point on the single gantry is very similar to that on *Boris Chilikin's* third gantry. Reported in use as water-carrier.

MANYCH   2/1973

2 "DUBNA" CLASS (REPLENISHMENT TANKERS)

DUBNA   ERKUT

Measurement, tons: 6 817 deadweight; 6 022 gross: 2 990 net
Dimensions, feet (metres): 416·8 × 65·8 × 23·8 *(136·7 × 21·6 × 7·8)*
Main engines: Diesel; 6 000 hp = 16 knots

Erkut launched Jan 1975, completed Dec 1975 at Rauha/Repola, Finland.

1 "SOFIA" CLASS (REPLENISHMENT TANKER)

AKHTUBA (ex-*Khanoy*)

Measurement, tons: 49 950 deadweight; 32 840 gross, 16 383 net
Dimensions, feet (metres): 757·9 × 101·7 × 32·8 *(231·2 × 31 × 10)*

Built as the merchant tanker *Khanoy* in 1963 at Leningrad, she was taken over by the Navy in 1969 and renamed *Akhtuba*. The hull type was used in the construction of the space associated ship *Kosmonaut Yuri Gagarin*.

AKHTUBA   1971, MOD

3 "KAZBEK" CLASS (REPLENISHMENT TANKERS)

ALATYR   DESNA   VOLKHOV

Displacement, tons: 16 250 full load
Measurement, tons: 12 000 deadweight; 8 230 gross; 3 942 net
Dimensions, feet (metres): 447·4 × 63·0 × 23·0 *(136·5 × 19·2 × 7)*
Main engines: 2 diesels; single shaft

Former "Leningrad" class merchant fleet tankers taken over by the Navy. Built at Leningrad and Nikolaev from 1951 to 1961. Seven others—*Karl Marx, Kazbek, Dzerzhinsk, Grodno, Cheboksary, Liepaya* and *Buguzuslan* have acted in support of naval operations. The original class numbered 64. Radar—Don 2.

"KAZBEK" Class   1973, Michael D. J. Lennon

6 "ALTAY" CLASS (SUPPORT TANKERS)

ALTAY   ELYENYA   IZHORA   KOLA   TARKHANKUT   YEGORLIK

Displacement, tons: 5 500 standard
Dimensions, feet (metres): 344·5 × 49·2 × 19·7 *(105·1 × 15 × 6)*
Main engines: Diesels; speed = 14 knots

Building from 1967 onwards. By early 1975 some 40 of this class had been completed for naval and mercantile use. An improved version of the "Aksay" class.

"ALTAY" Class   1973, Michael D. J. Lennon

6 "UDA" CLASS (SUPPORT TANKERS)

DUNAY   **KOIDA**   **LENA**   **SHEKSNA**   **TEREK**   **VISHERA**

Displacement, tons: 5 500 standard; 7 200 full load
Dimensions, feet (metres): 400·3 × 51·8 × 20·3 *(122·1 × 15·8 × 6·2)*
Main engines: Diesels; 2 shafts; 8 000 bhp = 17 knots

Koida has a beam storing rig on starboard side abaft bridge.
Built since 1961.

LENA   *1/1975, MOD*

3 "AKSAY" CLASS (SUPPORT TANKERS)

IMAN   **OLEKMA**   **ZOLOTOY ROG**

Displacement, tons: 4 000 standard
Measurement, tons: 4 400 deadweight; 3 300 gross: 1 550 net
Dimensions, feet (metres): 344·5 × 47·9 × 20·0 *(105·1 × 14·6 × 6·1)*
Main engines: Diesels; 2 900 bhp = 14 knots

Part of a class of fifty merchant tankers built by Rauma-Repola, Finland between 1961 and 1967.

"PEVEK" Class   *1973, Michael D. J. Lennon*

4 "KONDA" CLASS (SUPPORT TANKERS)

KONDA   **ROSSOSH**   **SOYANNA**   **YAKHROMA**

Displacement, tons: 1 178 standard
Dimensions, feet (metres): 226·4 × 32·8 × 13·8 *(69·1 × 10 × 4·2)*
Main engines: 1 100 bhp = 13 knots

3 "NERCHA" CLASS (SUPPORT TANKERS)

DORA   **IRTYSH**   **IRBIT**

Measurement, tons: 1 300 deadweight; 1 100 gross; 500 net
Built in Finland 1952-55.

15 "KHOBI" CLASS (SUPPORT TANKERS)

CHEREMSHAN	METAN	SEIMA	SOSVA
INDIGA	LOVAT	SHACHA	TUNGUSKA
KHOBI	ORSHA	SHELON	+ 4

Displacement, tons: 800 light; 2 000 approx full load
Speed, knots: 12 to 14

Built from 1957 to 1959.

SALVAGE VESSELS

KARPATY

Displacement, tons: 3 500 light; 5 000 standard
Dimensions, feet (metres): 410·1 × 52·5 × 16·4 *(125·1 × 16 × 5)*
Main engines: Diesels; 2 shafts

Submarine rescue and salvage ship of improved design with a special high stern which extends
out over the water for rescue manoeuvres. *Karpaty* completed 1969.

KARPATY   *1972, A. Nubert*

10 "PRUT" CLASS

ALTAI   **BRESHTAU**   **VLADIMIR TREFOLEV**   **ZHIGUILI**   **+ 6**

Displacement, tons: 2 120 standard; 3 500 full load
Dimensions, feet (metres): 296·0 × 36·1 × 13·1 *(90·3 × 11 × 4)*
Guns: 2—25 m:n
Main engines: Diesels; 4 200 bhp = 18 knots

Large rescue vessels. Built since 1960.

"PRUT" Class   *1970, S. Breyer*

9 "SURA" CLASS

Displacement, tons: 3 150 full load
Dimensions, feet (metres): 285·4 × 48·6 × 16·4 *(87 × 14·8 × 5)*
Main engines: Diesels; 1 770 bhp = 13·2 knots

Heavy lift ships built as mooring and buoy tenders since 1965 in East Germany. Six built by 1972.
Continuing programme.

"SURA" Class   *6/1974*

SUBMARINE RESCUE SHIPS

15 "VALDAY" CLASS (Ex-"T 58" CLASS)

Displacement, tons: 725 standard; 850 full load
Dimensions, feet (metres): 229·9 × 29·5 × 7·9 *(70·1 × 9 × 2·4)*
Main engines: 2 diesels; 2 shafts; 4 000 bhp = 18 knots

Basically of similar design to that of the "T 58" class fleet minesweepers, but they were completed as emergency salvage vessels and submarine rescue ships at Leningrad. Equipped with diving bell, recompression chamber and emergency medical ward. It has been reported that there may be an extra six smaller rescue ships based on the "T 43" hull. One transferred to India *(Nistar)*.

"VALDAY" Class   *1970, S. Breyer*

TRANSPORTS

2 "KAMCHATKA" CLASS

KAMCHATKA   MONGOL

3 COASTAL TYPE

ISHIM   SHILKA   VISHERA

Ishim is Coast Guard transport.

3 "CHULYM" CLASS

CHULYM   INSAR   KUZNETSKY

Displacement, tons: 5 050 full load
Dimensions, feet (metres): 311 × 44·5 × 18·3 *(101·9 × 14·6 × 6)*
Main engines: Compound 4 cyl; 1 650 hp = 14 knots
Range, miles: 5 500 at 11 knots
Complement: 40

Built by Stocznia Szczecinska, Poland from 1953-57. Nineteen others of this class operate with the merchant navy.

1 "BAIKAL" CLASS

OB

Displacement, tons: 12 400 full load
Dimensions, feet (metres): 427 oa × 61·8 × 27 *(140 × 20·3 × 8·9)*
Main engines: Diesel electric; 4 generators; 7 000 shp = 15·5 knots
Range, miles: 13 500 at 15 knots
Complement: 60

Built by Konmij de Scheldt, Flushing. Ice-strengthened. *Ob* is operated by Academy of Sciences as Antarctic Transport/Support ship. Five others of the same class come under the Ministry of Merchant Marine.

OB   *1973, Michael D. J. Lennon*

1 "MIKHAIL KALININ" CLASS

KUBAN (ex-*Nadeshda-Krupskaya*)

Employed under naval command as personnel support ship for the Soviet Mediterranean Squadron.

KUBAN   *9/1976, Michael D. J. Lennon*

TORPEDO RECOVERY/PATROL CRAFT

90 "POLUCHAT I" CLASS

Displacement, tons: 100 standard
Dimensions, feet (metres): 98·4 × 19·7 × 5·9 *(30 × 6 × 1·8)*
Guns: 2 MG (1 twin) (in some)

Employed as specialised or dual purpose torpedo recovery vessels and/or patrol boats. They have a stern slipway. Several exported as patrol craft.

"POLUCHAT I" Class   10/1975, MOD

DIVING TENDERS/PATROL CRAFT

"NYRYAT I" CLASS

Displacement, tons: 145
Dimensions, feet (metres): 93 × 18 × 5·5 *(28·4 × 5·5 × 1·7)*
Gun: 1—12·5 MG (in some)
Main engines: Diesel; 1 shaft; 450 hp = 12·5 knots
Range, miles: 1 500 at 10 knots
Complement: 15

Built from 1955. Can operate as patrol craft.

Transfers: Cuba, Iraq (2), Yemen (North).

FIRE/PATROL CRAFT

"POZHARNY I" CLASS

Displacement, tons: 180
Dimensions, feet (metres): 114·5 × 20 × 6 *(34·9 × 6·1 × 1·8)*
Guns: 4—12·7 mm or 14·5 mm (in some)
Main engines: 2 Diesels; 1 shaft; 1 800 hp = 12·5 knots

Built in USSR in mid 1950s. Harbour fire boats but can be used for patrol duties.

Transfers: Iraq (2), Yemen (North).

WATER CARRIERS

10 "VODA" CLASS

Displacement, tons: 2 100 standard
Dimensions, feet (metres): 267·3 × 37·7 × 14 *(81·5 × 11·5 × 4·3)*
Main engines: Diesels; speed = 12 knots

Built in 1956 onwards. No armament.

DEGAUSSING SHIPS

1 "KHABAROV" CLASS

KHABAROV

Displacement, tons: 500 full load
Dimensions, feet (metres): 150·3 × 26·5 × 8 *(45·8 × 8·1 × 2·4)*
Main engines: Diesel; 1 shaft; 400 bhp = 10·5 knots
Range, miles: 1 130 at 10 knots
Complement: 30

Steel-hulled. Prominent deckhouse and stern anchors. One of class, *Kilat*, transferred to Indonesia 1961—subsequently disposed of.
Several others known to exist.

ICEBREAKERS

Note: The majority of these ships is operated by Ministry of Merchant Marine—only a small number being naval manned. No excuse is offered for including them here as they are an indispensible part of many operations not only in the Baltic, Northern and Pacific Fleet areas but also on rivers, lakes and canals.

1 PROJECTED LARGE NUCLEAR POWERED

Main engines: Nuclear reactors; steam turbines; 80 000 hp

Reported as in the design stage in Oct 1974. Name possibly *Mikhail Somov*—unconfirmed.

2 NUCLEAR POWERED

ARKTIKA   **SIBIR**

Displacement, tons: 19 300 standard; 23 460 full load
Dimensions, feet (metres): 446·1 × 91·8 × 36·1 *(136 × 28 × 11)*
Aircraft: Helicopter with hangar
Main engines: 2 nuclear reactors; steam turbines; 75 000 shp = 21 knots

Building yard—Leningrad. *Arktika* launched summer 1973, started trials on 30 Nov 1974. Fitted with new type of reactor, the development of which may have retarded these ships' completion. *Sibir* on trials Nov 1975. Civilian manned.

ARKTIKA (Sketch)   1967

ARKTIKA   1974

1 NUCLEAR POWERED

LENIN

Displacement, tons: 15 940 standard; 19 240 full load
Dimensions, feet (metres): 406·7 × 87·9 × 34·4 *(124 × 26·8 × 10·5)*
Aircraft: 2 helicopters
Main engines: 3 pressurised water-cooled nuclear reactors, 4 steam turbines;
  3 shafts; 44 000 shp = 19·7 knots
Complement: 230

LENIN   1972

The world's first nuclear powered surface ship to put to sea. Reported to have accommodation for 1 000 personnel. Civilian manned.

Construction: Built at the Admiralty Yard, Leningrad. Launched on 5 Dec 1957. Commissioned on 15 Sep 1959.

Engineering: The original reactors, prototype submarine variety, were replaced during refit at Murmansk 1966-72. The new reactors presumably have a longer core-life than the 18 months of their predecessors. The turbines were manufactured by the Kirov plant in Leningrad. Three propellers aft, but no forward screw.

Operation: Can maintain a speed of 3-4 knots in 8 ft ice, giving a path of some 100 ft.

5 "MOSKVA" CLASS

VLADIVOSTOCK   KIEV   LENINGRAD   MOSKVA   MURMANSK

Displacement, tons: 12 840 standard; 15 360 full load
Dimensions, feet (metres): 368·8 wl; 400·7 oa × 80·3 × 34·5 *(112·5 wl; 122·2 oa × 24·5 × 10·5)*
Aircraft: 2 helicopters
Main engines: 8 Sulzer diesel-electric; 3 shafts; 22 000 shp = 18 knots
Oil fuel, tons: 3 000
Range, miles: 20 000
Complement: 145

Civilian manned.

MOSKVA   1960, Wärtsilä

Construction: Built by Wärtsilä Shipyard, Helsinki. *Moskva* was launched on 10 Jan 1959 and completed in June 1960. *Leningrad* was laid down in Jan 1959. Launched on 24 Oct 1959, and completed in 1962. *Kiev* was completed in 1966. *Murmansk* was launched on 14 July 1967, and *Vladivostock* on 28 May 1968.

Design: Designed to stay at sea for a year without returning to base. The concave embrasure in the ship's stern is a housing for the bow of a following vessel when additional power is required. There is a landing deck for helicopters and hangar space for two machines.

Engineering: Eight generating units of 3 250 bhp each comprising eight main diesels of the Wärtsilä-Sulzer 9 MH 51 type which together have an output of 26 000 hp. Four separate machinery compartments. Two engine rooms, four propulsion units in each. Three propellers aft. No forward propeller. Centre propeller driven by electric motors of 11 000 hp and each of the side propellers by motors of 5 500 hp. Two Wärtsilä-Babcock & Wilcox boilers for heating and donkey work.

Operation: *Moskva* has four pumps which can move 480 metric tons of water from one side to the other in two minutes to rock the icebreaker and wrench her free of thick ice.

3 "JERMAK" CLASS

Name	No.	Builders	Commissioned
ADMIRAL MAKAROV	—	Wärtsilä, Helsinki	2 June 1975
JERMAK	—	Wärtsilä, Helsinki	30 June 1974
KRASIN	—	Wärtsilä, Helsinki	Jan 1976

Displacement, tons: 20 241 full load
Dimensions, feet (metres): 442·8 × 85·3 × 36·1 *(135 × 26 × 11)*
Aircraft: 2 helicopters
Main engines: 9 Wärtsilä-Sulzer 12 cyl 12 ZH 40/48 diesels of 4 600 bhp each (total 41 400 hp) with Stromberg Ab generators feeding three Stromberg electric motors of total 36 000 shp; 3 shafts
Speed, knots: 19·5
Range, miles: 40 000 at 15 knots
Complement: 118 plus 28 spare berths

JERMAK   1974, Wärtsilä

The Soviet Union ordered three large and powerful icebreakers on 29 April 1970 from Wärtsilä Shipyard, Helsinki, for delivery in 1974, 1975 and 1976. Six Wärtsilä auxiliary diesels, 7 200 bhp. Propelling and auxiliary machinery controlled electronically. These are the first vessels to be fitted with Wärtsilä mixed-flow air-bubbling system to decrease friction between hull and ice. *Jermak* launched 7 Sep 1973. *A. Makarov* laid down 10 Sep 1973 and launched 26 April 1974. *Krasin* laid down 9 July 1974, launched 18 April 1975. Civilian manned.

3 SHALLOW WATER TYPE

Name	No.	Builders	Commissioned
KAPITAN M. IZMAYLOV	—	Wärtsilä, Helsinki	15 June 1976
KAPITAN KOSOLAPOV	—	Wärtsilä, Helsinki	14 July 1976
KAPITAN A. RADZABOV	—	Wärtsilä, Helsinki	1 Aug 1976

Displacement, tons: 2 045
Dimensions, feet (metres): 185·3 × 51·5 × 13·8 *(56·5 × 15·7 × 4·2)*
Main engines: Diesel-electric; 3 400 shp; 2 shafts; 2 rudders
Speed, knots: 13

Contract signed with Wärtsilä, Helsinki on 22 Mar 1974 for the building of these three icebreakers for delivery in 1976. All fitted with Wärtsilä air-bubbler system. Machinery by Wärtsilä Vasa. Electrical machinery by Oy Strömberg Ab.
Laid down: *K. Izmaylov* 12 June 1975 (launched 11 Dec 1975), *K. Kosolapov* 19 Aug 1975, *K. Radzabov* 17 June 1975. Civilian manned.

KAPITAN IZMAYLOV   10/1976, Wärtsilä

3 "KAPITAN BELOUSOV" CLASS

Name	Launched	Commissioned
KAPITAN BELOUSOV	1954	1955
KAPITAN MELECHOV	19 Oct 1956	1957
KAPITAN VORONIN	1955	1956

Displacement, tons: 4 375 to 4 415 standard; 5 350 full load
Dimensions, feet (metres): 265 wl; 273 oa × 63·7 × 23 *(80·8 wl; 83·3 oa × 19·4 × 7)*
Main engines: Diesel-electric; 6 Polar 8 cyl; 10 500 bhp = 14·9 knots
Oil fuel, tons: 740
Complement: 120

All built by Wärtsilä Shipyard, Helsinki. The ships have four screws, two forward under the forefoot and two aft. Civilian manned.

KAPITAN BELOUSOV   1970, Michael D. J. Lennon

1 "PURGA" CLASS

Displacement, tons: 2 250 standard; 3 000 full load
Length, feet (metres): 295·2 *(90)*
Beam, feet (metres): 44·3 *(13·5)*
Draught, feet (metres): 17·1 *(5·2)*
Guns: 4—3·9 in *(100 mm)* (singles)
Mines: 50 capacity
Main engines: Diesels
Speed, knots: 18
Complement: 250

Laid down in 1939 in Leningrad and completed in 1948. Equipped as icebreaker. Fitted with director similar to those in the "Riga" class frigates. Modernised in 1958-60.

"PURGA" Class

21 "DOBRINYA NIKITCH" CLASS

AFANASY NIKITIN	IVAN MOSKVITIN	SEMYON DEZHNEV
BURAN	IVAN KRUZENSHTERN	SEMEN CHELYUSHKIN
DOBRINYA NIKITCH	KHARITON LAPTEV	VASILY POYARKOV
EROFFREY KHABAROV	PERESVET	VASILY PRONCHISHCHEV
FEDOR LITKE	PETR PAKHTUSOV	VLADIMIR RUSANOV
GEORGIJ SEDOV	PLUG	YIRIY LISYANSKY
ILYA MUROMETS	SADKO	VYUGA

Displacement, tons: 2 500 standard (average)
Measurements, tons: 2 305 gross (ships vary)
Dimensions, feet (metres): 223·1 × 59·1 × 18·1 *(68 × 18 × 5·5)*
Guns: 2—57 mm; 2—25 mm *(Peresvet* and *Sadko)*
Main engines: 3 shafts; speed = 13·8 knots

All built at Leningrad between 1961 and 1965. Divided between the Baltic, Black Sea and Far East. *Buran, Peresvet* and *Sadko* as well as some others are naval manned although last two only are armed. Remainder civilian manned.

YIRIY LISYANSKY   1972, Michael D. J. Lennon

ARMED ICEBREAKERS

3 "MODIFIED DOBRINYA NIKITCH" CLASS

AISBERG   IVAN SUSANIN   RUSLAN

Of similar major characteristics to "Dobrinya Nikitch" class but lengthened by 80 feet and modified with new bridge structure, twin 76 mm forward, 2—30 mm Gatling guns aft (in all but *Aisberg)* and a helicopter platform. May be operated by KGB.

IVAN SUSANIN   7/1974

TUGS

2 "INGUL" CLASS

PAMIR   MASHUK

Displacement, tons: 3 600
Dimensions, feet (metres): 295 × 52 × 18 *(90 × 16 × 5·5)*

A new class with NATO class-name the same as one of the "Klasma" class cable-ships. Naval manned Arctic salvage and rescue tugs.

PAMIR   4/1975, MOD(N)

2 "PAMIR" CLASS

AGATAN   ALDAN

Measurement, tons: 2 032 gross
Dimensions, feet (metres): 256 oa × 42 × 13·5 *(78 × 12·8 × 4·1)*
Main engines: Two 10 cyl 4 str diesels; 2 shaft; 4 200 bhp = 17 knots

Salvage tugs built at AB Gävie, Varv, Sweden, in 1959-60. Equipped with strong derricks, powerful pumps, air compressors, diving gear, fire fighting apparatus and electric generators.

ALDAN   *4/1975, MOD(N)*

8 "SORUM" CLASS

KAMCHATKA   SAKHALIN   + 6

Displacement, tons: 1 630
Dimensions, feet (metres): 190·2 × 41·3 × 15·1 *(58 × 12·6 × 4·6)*
Guns: 4—30 mm (twins) (in some)
Main engines: Diesels; 2 100 hp

A new class of ocean tugs first seen in 1973. Four are naval manned and at least one, *Sakhalin*, is KGB operated.

KAMCHATKA   *5/1976, MOD*

50 "OKHTENSKY" CLASS

Displacement, tons: 835
Dimensions, feet (metres): 134·5 wl; 143 oa × 34 × 15 *(41 wl; 43·6 × 10·4 × 4·6)*
Guns: 1—3 in; 2—20 mm
Main engines: 2 BM diesels; 2 electric motors; 2 shafts; 1 875 bhp = 14 knots
Oil fuel, tons: 187
Complement: 34

Oceangoing salvage and rescue tugs. Fitted with powerful pumps and other apparatus for salvage. Pennant numbers preceded by MB.

"OKHTENSKY" Class

"OREL" CLASS SALVAGE TUGS

Measurement, tons: 1 070 gross
Dimensions, feet (metres): 201·2 × 39·2 × 18·1 *(61·4 × 12 × 5·5)*
Main engines: 2 Diesels = 14 knots

Class of salvage and rescue tugs normally operated by Ministry of Fisheries with the fishing fleets although at least two are naval manned. Built in Finland in late 1950s and early 1960s.

STREMITELNY—"Orel" Class   *1972, Michael D. J. Lennon*

7 "KATUN" CLASS

Displacement, tons: 950
Length, feet (metres): 210 *(64)*

Built in 1970-71.

FINNISH "530 TON" CLASS

Measurement, tons: 533 gross
Dimensions, feet (metres): 157·1 × 31·3 × 15·5 *(47·9 × 9·5 × 4·7)*
Main engines: Steam = 9·5 knots

Numerous class built in Finland in 1950s.

EAST GERMAN BERTHING TUGS

Measurement, tons: 233 gross
Main engines: Diesels

Numerous class built in 1970 in East Germany.

EAST GERMAN HARBOUR TUGS

Measurement, tons: 132 gross
Dimensions, feet (metres): 94·5 × 21·3 × 9·8 *(28·8 × 6·5 × 3)*
Main engines: 1 Diesel = 10 knots

Very numerous class built in E. Germany in 1964.

There are a large number of other tugs available in commercial service which could be directed to naval use.

URUGUAY

Headquarters Appointment

Commander-in-Chief of the Navy:
  Vice-Admiral Victor González Ibargoyen

Diplomatic Representation

Naval Attaché in Washington:
  Captain Jorge Laborde

Personnel

(a) 1977: Total: 3 500 officers and men (including Naval Infantry)
(b) Voluntary service

Base

Montevideo: Main naval base with a drydock and a slipway

Coast Guard

The Prefectura Maritima operates six coastal patrol craft.

Naval Air Arm

2 CH-34C helicopters
1 Bell 47G
2 Bell CH-13H
3 Grumman S-2A Tracker (ASW)
4 Beech SNB-5 (Training-Transport)
3 North American SNJ (Training)
1 Beech T-34 B Mentor (Training)
2 Piper PA-12 (Liaison)

Prefix to Ships' Names

R.O.U.

Mercantile Marine

Lloyd's Register of Shipping:
  43 vessels of 151 255 tons gross

Strength of the Fleet

	Active	Building
Frigates	3	—
Submarines	—	?2
Corvettes	2	—
Large Patrol Craft	1	—
Coastal Patrol Craft	6	—
Survey Ships	2	—
Salvage Vessel	1	—
Tankers	2	—
Tenders	3	—

Deletion

Frigate

1975 *Montevideo*

FRIGATES

1 Ex-US "DEALEY" CLASS

Name	No.
18 DE JULIO (ex-USS *Dealey*, DE 1006)	DE 3

Builders	Laid down	Launched	Commissioned
Bath Iron Works Corpn	15 Oct 1952	8 Nov 1953	3 June 1954

Displacement, tons: 1 450 standard; 1 900 full load
Length, feet (metres): 314·5 *(95·9)* oa
Beam, feet (metres): 36·8 *(11·2)*
Draught, feet (metres): 13·6 *(4·2)*
Guns: 4—3 in *(76 mm)* (twins)
A/S weapons: 2 triple torpedo tubes (Mk 32)
Main engines: 1 De Laval geared turbine; 20 000 shp; 1 shaft
Boilers: 2 Foster Wheeler
Speed, knots: 25
Complement: 165

Purchased 28 July 1972. *Dealey* was the first US escort ship built after the war.

Fire Control: Mk 63 forward and aft with SPG 34 radar.

Radar: SPS 6, SPS 10.

18 DE JULIO   *1975, Uruguayan Navy*

2 Ex-US "CANNON" CLASS

Name	No.
ARTIGAS (ex-USS *Bronstein*, DE 189)	DE 2
URUGUAY (ex-USS *Baron*, DE 166)	DE 1

Builders	Laid down	Launched	Commissioned
Federal SB & DD Co, Pt Newark	1943	14 Nov 1943	13 Dec 1943
Federal SB & DD Co, Pt Newark	1942	9 May 1943	5 July 1943

Displacement, tons: 1 240 standard; 1 900 full load
Length, feet (metres): 306·0 *(93·3)* oa
Beam, feet (metres): 37·0 *(11·3)*
Draught, feet (metres): 17·1 *(5·2)*
Guns: 3—3 in *(76 mm)* (single); 2—40 mm (see *Gunnery* notes)
A/S weapons: Hedgehog; 8 DCT; 1 DCR (see *Torpedo Tubes* note)
Main engines: Diesel-electric; 2 shafts; 6 000 bhp
Speed, knots: 19
Oil fuel, tons: 315 (95 per cent)
Range, miles: 8 300 at 14 knots
Complement: 160

Appearance: Practically identical, but *Uruguay* can be distinguished by the absence of a mainmast, whereas *Artigas* has a small pole mast aft.

Gunnery: Formerly also mounted ten 20 mm anti-aircraft guns, but these have been removed.

Radar: Search: SPS 6.
Tactical: SPS 10.

Torpedo tubes: The three 21-inch torpedo tubes in a triple mounting, originally carried, were removed.

Transfers: *Uruguay,* May 1952; *Artigas,* Mar 1952.

URUGUAY   *1975, Uruguayan Navy*

SUBMARINES

It is reported, though not confirmed, that two Type 209 submarines (IKL design) are building for this navy.

CORVETTES

1 Ex-US "AUK" CLASS

Name	No.	Builders	Commissioned
COMANDANTE PEDRO CAMPBELL	MS 31	Defoe B & M Works	1942
(ex-USS *Chickadee MSF 59*)	(ex-MSF 1)		

Displacement, tons: 890 standard; 1 250 full load
Dimensions, feet (metres): 221·2 oa × 32·2 × 10·8 *(67·5 × 9·8 × 3·5)*
Guns: 1—3 in, 50 cal; 4—40 mm (twin); 4—20 mm (twin)
Main engines: Diesel electric; 2 shafts; 3 118 bhp = 18 knots
Complement: 105

Former United States fleet minesweeper. Launched on 20 July 1942. Transferred on loan and commissioned at San Diego, Calif. on 18 Aug 1966.

COMANDANTE PEDRO CAMPBELL 1971

1 Ex-US "AGGRESSIVE" CLASS

Name	No.	Builders	Commissioned
MALDONADO	MS 33	USA	1954
(ex-*Bir Hakeim M 614*, ex-USS *MSO 451*)			

Displacement, tons: 700 standard; 795 full load
Dimensions, feet (metres): 171·0 oa × 35·0 × 10·3 *(50·3 × 10·7 × 3·2)*
Gun: 1—40 mm
Main engines: 2 GM diesels; 2 shafts; 1 600 bhp = 13·5 knots
Range, miles: 3 000 at 10 knots
Complement: 54

Former US ocean minesweeper transferred to France in Feb 1954. Returned to the US Navy and transferred to Uruguay in Sept 1970. All sweeping gear removed.

MALDONADO 1975, Uruguayan Navy

LIGHT FORCES

1 Ex-US (FRENCH) "ADJUTANT" CLASS
(LARGE PATROL CRAFT)

Name	No.	Builders	Commissioned
RIO NEGRO	MS 32	USA	1954
(ex-*Marguerite*, ex-USS *MSC 94*)			

Displacement, tons: 370 standard; 405 full load
Dimensions, feet (metres): 141·0 oa × 26·0 × 8·3 *(43 × 8 × 2·6)*
Guns: 2—20 mm
Main engines: 2 GM diesels; 2 shafts; 1 200 bhp = 13 knots
Oil fuel, tons: 40
Range, miles: 2 500 at 10 knots
Complement: 38

Ex-US coastal minesweeper built for France under MDAP. Returned to US in 1969. She was transferred to Uruguay at Toulon on 10 Nov 1969. All sweeping gear removed.

RIO NEGRO 1975, Uruguayan Navy

1 Ex-US 63 ft AVR (COASTAL PATROL CRAFT)

COLONIA PR 10 (ex-*AR 1*)

Displacement, tons: 25 standard; 34 full load
Dimensions, feet (metres): 63 × 15 × 3·8 *(20·6 × 4·9 × 1·2)*
Guns: 4 MGs
Main engines: 2 Hall Scott Defender; 1 260 bhp = 33·5 knots
Range, miles: 600 at 15 knots
Complement: 8

Launched 4 July 1944.

COLONIA 1975, Uruguayan Navy

1 COASTAL PATROL CRAFT

Name	No.	Builders	Commissioned
CARMELO	PR 11	Lürssen, Vegesack	1957

Displacement, tons: 70
Dimensions, feet (metres): 93·0 × 19·0 × 7·0 *(28·7 × 5·9 × 2·1)*
Guns: 1—20 mm
Speed, knots: 25

CARMELO   1975, Uruguayan Navy

1 COASTAL PATROL CRAFT

Name	No.	Builders	Commissioned
PAYSANDU	PR 12	Sewart, USA	1968

Displacement, tons: 60
Dimensions, feet (metres): 83·0 × 18·0 × 6·0 *(26 × 5·6 × 1·6)*
Guns: 3—0·50 cal MG
Main engines: 2 GM diesels; 2 shafts = 22 knots

PAYSANDU   1975, Uruguayan Navy

3 COASTAL PATROL CRAFT

701   702   703

43 ft craft transferred by USN in Feb 1970.

SURVEY SHIPS

Name	No.	Builders	Commissioned
CAPITAN MIRANDA	GS 20 (ex-*GS 10*)	Sociedad Espanola de Construccion Naval, Matagorda, Cadiz	1930

Displacement, tons: 516 standard; 527 full load
Dimensions, feet (metres): 148 pp; 179 oa × 26 × 10·5 *(45; 53 × 8·4 × 3·2)*
Main engines: 1 MAN diesel; 500 bhp = 11 knots
Oil fuel, tons: 37
Complement: 49

Originally a yacht with pronounced clipper bow.

CAPITAN MIRANDA (old pennant number)   1971

Name	No.	Builders	Commissioned
SALTO	GS 24 (ex-*PR 2*)	Cantieri Navali Riuniti, Ancona	1936

Displacement, tons: 150 standard; 180 full load
Dimensions, feet (metres): 137 × 18 × 10 *(42·1 × 5·8 × 3)*
Gun: 1—40 mm
Main engines: 2 Germania-Krupp diesels; 2 shafts; 1 000 bhp = 17 knots
Range, miles: 4 000 at 10 knots
Complement: 26

Now used also as a buoy-tender.

SALTO (old pennant number)   1971

SALVAGE VESSEL

1 Ex-US "COHOES" CLASS

Name	*No.*	*Builders*	*Commissioned*
HURACAN	AM 25	Commercial Ironworks, Portland,	1945
(ex-USS *Nahant AN 83*)		Oregon	

Displacement, tons: 650 standard; 855 full load
Dimensions, feet (metres): 168·5 × 33·8 × 11·7 *(51·4 × 10·2 × 3·3)*
Guns: 3—20 mm (single)
Main engines: Diesel electric; 1 shaft; 1 200 bhp = 11·5 knots
Complement: 48

Former US netlayer, transferred Dec 1968 for salvage services.

HURACAN   1975, Uruguayan Navy

AMPHIBIOUS CRAFT

2 Ex-US "LCM 6" CLASS

LD 40   LD 41

Transferred on lease Oct 1972.

TANKERS

Note: Both *Presidente Oribe* and *P. Rivera* operate under commercial charter when not required for naval purposes.

Name	*No.*	*Builders*	*Commissioned*
PRESIDENTE ORIBE	AO 29 (ex- *AO 9*)	Ishikawajima-Harima Ltd, Japan	22 Mar 1962

Measurement, tons: 18 584 gross; 28 474 deadweight
Dimensions, feet (metres): 620 oa × 84·3 × 33 *(189 × 25·7 × 10·1)*
Main engines: 1 Ishikawajima turbine; 12 500 shp = 16·75 knots
Boilers: 2 Ishikawajima-Harima Foster Wheeler type
Range, miles: 16 100 at 16 knots
Complement: 76

Can carry out alongside replenishment.

PRESIDENTE ORIBE (old pennant number)   1971

Name	*No.*	*Builders*	*Commissioned*
PRESIDENTE RIVERA	AO 28	EN Bazán, Spain	1971

Measurement, tons: 19 686 gross; 31 885 deadweight
Dimensions, feet (metres): 636·3 × 84 × 32 *(194 × 25·6 × 9·8)*
Main engines: 15 300 bhp = 15 knots
Complement: 58

PRESIDENTE RIVERA   1975, Uruguayan Navy

TENDERS

Note: *Tacoma* incorrectly listed last year; is a non-naval prison ship.

VANGUARDIA AM 26 (ex-US YTL 589)

Transferred Sep. 1965.

Following also reported: UA 12 (ex-US) repair ship, *Anapal* No 1, ex-US 20 LH, ex-US 26 MW, *Banco Ingles,* LV 21 (ex-US WLV *Portland*).

VENEZUELA

Administration

Commanding General of the Navy:
Vice-Admiral Felix Mendoza Acosta
Chief of Naval Operations:
Rear-Admiral Magin Lagrave Fry

Diplomatic Representation

Naval Attaché in London:
Captain A. G. Rodriguez-Millán
Naval Attaché in Washington:
Rear-Admiral Rafael Silveira

Personnel

(a) 1977: 7 500 officers and men including 4 000 of the Marine Corps (3 battalions)
(b) 2 years National Service

National Guard

The Fuerzas Armadas de Cooperacion, generally known as the National Guard, is a paramilitary organisation, 10 000 strong. It is concerned, amongst other things, with customs and internal security—the Maritime Wing operates the Coastal Patrol Craft listed under Light Forces, though these nominally belong to the Navy.

Mercantile Marine

Lloyd's Register of Shipping:
165 vessels of 543 446 tons gross

Naval Air Arm

2 Bell 47J helicopters
6 Grumman S-2E Trackers (ASW)
4 Grumman Hu-16A Albatros (SAR)
3 Douglas C-47 (Transports)

Strength of the Fleet

Type	Active	Building
Destroyers	4	—
Frigates	5	6
Submarines, Patrol	5	—
Fast Attack Craft—Missile/Gun	6	—
Large Patrol Craft	10	—
Coastal Patrol Craft	21	—
LST	1	—
LSMs	4	—
Transport Landing Ship	1	—
Transports	3	—
Survey Ships and Craft	3	—
Ocean Tug	1	—
Harbour Tugs	13	—
Floating Dock	1	—
National Guard CPC	16	—

Bases

Caracas: Main HQ.
Puerto Cabello: Main Naval Base (Dockyard, 1 Drydock, 1 synchrolift, 1 floating crane).
La Guaira: Small Naval Base (Naval Academy).
Puerto de Hierro: Naval Supply Base.

DELETIONS

Destroyer

1975 *Aragua*

Frigate

1976 *General José de Austria*

Survey Ships

1975 *Puerto Miranda, Puerto de Nutrius*

NUEVA ESPARTA

FALCON

CARABOBO

"ALMIRANTE CLEMENTE" Class

DESTROYERS

2 "ARAGUA" CLASS

Name	No.	Builders	Laid down	Launched	Commissioned
NUEVA ESPARTA	D 11	Vickers Ltd, Barrow	24 July 1951	19 Nov 1952	8 Dec 1953
ZULIA	D 21	Vickers Ltd, Barrow	24 July 1951	29 June1953	15 Sep 1954

Displacement, tons: 2 600 standard; 3 670 full load
Length, feet (metres): 384·0 *(117·0)* wl; 402·0 *(122·5)* oa
Beam, feet (metres): 43·0 *(13·1)*
Draught, feet (metres): 19·0 *(5·8)*
Missiles: 2 quadruple Seacat in D 11
Guns: 6—4·5 *(114 mm)* (twins); 16—40 mm (twins) in D 21; 4—40 mm (twins) in D 11
A/S weapons: 2 Squids; 2 DCT; 2 DC racks
Main engines: Parsons geared turbines; 2 shafts; 50 000 shp
Boilers: 2 Yarrow
Speed, knots: 34
Range, miles: 5 000 at 10 knots
Complement: 256 (20 officers, 236 men)

Ordered in 1950 as class of three. Air conditioned. Two engine rooms and two boiler rooms served by a single uptake. The 4·5 inch guns are fully automatic.

Fire Control: 2 UK type 276 on DCT for 4·5 in.
2 optical GWS 20 directors for Seacat in D11.

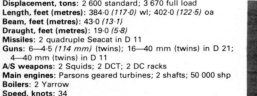

ZULIA

Radar: Search: AWS 2 *(Nueva Esparta)* SPS 6 *(Zulia)*. SPS-12 (both).
Fire Control: I Band.

7/1976, A. D. Baker III

Refits: Both refitted at Palmers Hebburn Works, and Vickers in 1959, and at New York Navy Yard in 1960 to improve anti-submarine and anti-aircraft capabilities. *Nueva Esparta* at Cammell Laird in 1968-69 when Seacat launchers were fitted and some 40 mm and the torpedo tubes removed.

1 Ex- US "ALLEN M. SUMNER (FRAM II)" CLASS

Name
FALCON (ex-USS *Robert K. Huntington* DD 781)

No.	Builders	Laid down	Launched	Commissioned
D 51	Todd Pacific Shipyards	1944	5 Dec 1944	3 Mar 1945

Displacement, tons: 2 200 standard; 3 320 full load
Dimensions, feet (metres): 376·5 × 40·9 × 19 *(114·8 × 12·4 × 5·8)*
Guns: 6—5 in 38 cal (twins)
A/S weapons: 2 Hedgehogs; 2 triple torpedo tubes (Mk 32); facilities for small helicopter
Main engines: 2 geared turbines; 60 000 shp; 2 shafts
Boilers: 4
Speed, knots: 34
Range, miles: 4 600 at 15 knots
Complement: 274

Purchase from USN 31 Oct 1973. Modernised under the FRAM II programme.

Radar: SPS 40 and SPS 10.

Sonar: Hull mounted; SQS 29 series. VDS.

"ALLEN M. SUMNER (FRAM II)" Class   *USN*

1 Ex-US "ALLEN M. SUMNER" CLASS

Name
CARABOBO (ex-USS *Beatty*, DD 756)

No.
D 41

Builders	Laid down	Launched	Commissioned
Bethlehem, Staten Is.	1944	30 Nov 1944	31 Mar 1945

Displacement, tons: 2 200 standard; 3 320 full load
Dimensions, feet (metres): 376·5 × 40·9 × 19·0 *(114·8 × 12·4 × 5·8)*
Guns: 6—5 in (twins)
A/S weapons: 2 fixed Hedgehogs, DCs; 2 triple torpedo tubes (Mk 32)
Main engines: 2 geared turbines; 60 000 shp; 2 shafts
Boilers: 4
Speed, knots: 34
Range, miles: 4 600 at 15 knots
Complement: 274

Transferred from USN 14 July 1972.

Fire Control: Mk 37 GFCS forward with Mk 25 radar; Mk 51 GFCS aft (no radar).

Radar: SPS 6, SPS 10.

CARABOBO (as *Beatty*)   *1965, Dr. Giorgio Arra*

Sonar: SQS 29 series.

FRIGATES

6 "LUPO" CLASS

Displacement, tons: 2 208 standard; 2 500 full load
Dimensions, feet (metres): 366 × 39·4 × 11·8 *(111·6 × 12 × 3·6)*
Aircraft: 1 AB212 helicopter
Missiles: 4 Otomat 2 (singles); 8 cell Albatros SAM system
Guns: 1—5 in *(127 mm)* 54 cal OTO Melara; 4—40 mm 70 cal (singles)
Rocket launchers: 2 SCLAR 4·1 in multi-tube mountings
A/S weapons: 6 for A/S torpedoes (triples)
Main engines: CODAG. 2 Fiat/GELM 2 500 gas turbines; 34 400 bhp; 2 GMT A230/20M diesels; 7 800 hp; 2 shafts
Speed, knots: 35; 21 on diesels
Complement: 185

Letter of intent signed 24 Oct 1975 with Cantiere Navali Riuniti, Riva Trigoso. Delivery of first ship expected Oct 1978.

Radar: Search: Selenia MM/SPS 74.
Navigation: SMA SPQ/2F. Fire Control (guns): Elsag Mark 10 Mod.O Argo.
Fire Control (missiles): EX 77 Mod O.

Sonar: SQS 29.

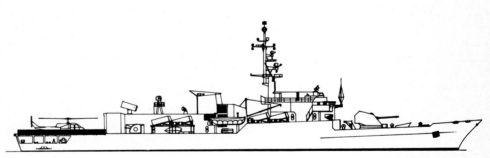

"LUPO" Class   *1976, Italian Navy*

5 "ALMIRANTE CLEMENTE" CLASS

Name	No.	Builders	Laid down	Launched	Commissioned
ALMIRANTE CLEMENTE	D 12	Ansaldo, Leghorn	5 May 1954	12 Dec 1954	1956
ALMIRANTE JOSÉ GARCIA	D 33	Ansaldo, Leghorn	12 Dec 1954	12 Oct 1956	1957
ALMIRANTE BRION	D 23	Ansaldo, Leghorn·	12 Dec 1954	4 Sep 1955	1957
GENERAL JOSÉ TRINIDAD MORAN	D 22	Ansaldo, Leghorn	5 May 1954	12 Dec 1954	1956
GENERAL JUAN JOSÉ FLORES	D 13	Ansaldo, Leghorn	5 May 1954	7 Feb 1955	1956

Displacement, tons: 1 300 standard; 1 500 full load
Length, feet (metres): 325·11 *(99·1)* oa
Length, feet (metres): 35·5 *(10·8)*
Draught, feet (metres): 12·2 *(3·7)*
Guns: 4—4 in *(102 mm)* (2 twin); 4—40 mm; 8—20 mm (modified group 40 mm only) (see note)
A/S weapons: 2 Hedgehogs, 4 DCT and 2 DC racks in original group; 1 A/S Mortar, 4 DCT and 2 DC racks in modified group
Torpedo tubes: 3—21 in *(533 mm)* triple (original group only)
Main engines: 2 sets geared turbines; 2 shafts; 24 000 shp
Boilers: 2 Foster Wheeler
Speed, knots: 32
Oil fuel, tons: 350
Range, miles: 3 500 at 15 knots
Complement: 162 (12 officers, 150 men)

The first three were ordered in 1953. Three more were ordered in 1954. Aluminium alloys were widely employed in the building of all superstructure. All six ships fitted with Denny-Brown fin stabilisers and air conditioned throughout the living and command spaces. D 32 has been deleted.

Gunnery: The 4 inch anti-aircraft guns are fully automatic and radar controlled—replaced by two OTO Melara 76 mm in D 12 and 23.

ALMIRANTE BRION   *1975, Dhr. J. Van der Woude*

Modernisation: *Almirante José Garcia, Almirante Brion* and *General José de Austria* were refitted by Ansaldo, Leghorn, in 1962 to improve their anti-submarine and anti-aircraft capabilities: this group is known as "Modified Almirante Clemente" type. *Almirante Clemente* and *General José Trinidad Moran* were taken in hand for refit by Cammell Laird/-

Plessey group in April 1968. *Almirante Clemente* started her post-refit trials in Feb 1975 and *General Jose Moran* after trials sailed mid-Jan 1976 for Venezuela.

Radar: Search: MLA 1—some, Plessey AWS-1.
Fire Control: I Band

SUBMARINES

2 HOWALDTSWERKE TYPE 209

Name	No.
SABALO	S 21
CONGRIO	S 22

Builders	Laid down	Launched	Commissioned
Howaldtswerke, Kiel	1973	21 Aug 1975	July 1976
Howaldtswerke, Kiel	1973	16 Dec 1975	1977

Displacement, tons: 990 surfaced; 1 350 dived
Dimensions, feet (metres): 177·1 × 20·3 × 18 *(54·0 × 6·2 × 5)*
Torpedo tubes: 8—21 in (with reloads) bow
Main machinery: Diesel-electric; 4 MTU-Siemens diesel generators; 1 Siemens electric motor 5 000 hp; 1 shaft
Speed, knots: 10 surfaced; 22 dived
Range, miles: 50 days
Complement: 31

Type 209, IK81 designed by Ingenieurkontor Lübeck for construction by Howaldtswerke, Kiel and sale by Ferrostaal, Essen, all acting as a consortium.
A single-hull design with two main ballast tanks and forward and after trim tanks. Fitted with snort and remote machinery control. Slow revving single screw. Very high capacity batteries with GRP lead-acid cells and battery-cooling—by W. Hagen and VARTA. Active and passive sonar, sonar detection set, sound-ranging equipment and underwater telephone. Have two periscopes, radar and Omega receiver. Fore-planes retract. Ordered in 1971.

SABALO   *1976, Howaldtswerke*

2 Ex-US "GUPPY II" CLASS

Name	No.
TIBURON (ex-USS *Cubera*, SS 347)	S 12
PICUDA (ex-USS *Grenadier*, SS 525)	S 13

Builders	Laid down	Launched	Commissioned
Electric Boat Co, Groton	11 May 1944	17 June1945	19 Dec 1945
Boston Navy Yard	8 Feb 1944	15 Dec 1944	10 Feb 1951

Displacement, tons: 1 870 surfaced; 2 420 dived
Length, feet (metres): 307·5 *(93·8)*
Beam, feet (metres): 27·0 *(8·2)*
Draught, feet (metres): 18·0 *(5·5)*
Torpedo tubes: 10—21 in *(533 mm)* (6 bow, 4 stern)
Main machinery: 3 diesels; 4 800 shp; 2 electric motors; 5 400 shp; 2 shafts
Speed, knots: 18 surfaced; 15 dived
Range, miles: 12 000 at 10 knots
Oil fuel, tons: 300
Complement: 80

Transferred as follows—*Tiburon* 5 Jan 1972, *Picuda* 15 May 1973.

PICUDA (as GRENADIER)   *US Navy*

1 Ex-US "BALAO" CLASS

Name	No.
CARITE (ex-USS *Tilefish*, SS 307)	S 11

Builders	Laid down	Launched	Commissioned
Mare Island Navy Yard	1943	25 Oct 1943	28 Dec 1943

Displacement, tons: 1 450 standard; 2 400 dived
Dimensions, feet (metres): 312 × 27·2 × 17·2 *(95·1 × 8·3 × 5·3)*
Torpedo tubes: 10—21 in; (6 bow, 4 stern)
Main machinery: 4 diesels; 6 400 hp; 2 electric motors; 5 400 shp; 2 shafts
Range, miles: 12 000 at 10 knots
Speed, knots: 20 surfaced; 10 dived
Complement: 85

Purchased from USN—Transfer 4 May 1960 after 4 month refit. Subsequently refitted with streamlined fin. Now used for training; non-diving.

CARITE   *1969, Venezuelan Navy*

LIGHT FORCES

Note: Also reported 3 ex-US 43 ft PBs transferred Feb 1970

6 VOSPER-THORNYCROFT 121 FT CLASS (FAST ATTACK CRAFT—MISSILE AND GUN)

Name	No.	Builders	Laid down	Launched	Commissioned
CONSITUCION	P 11	Vosper-Thornycroft Ltd	Jan 1973	1 June 1973	16 Aug 1974
FEDERACION	P 12	Vosper-Thornycroft Ltd	Aug 1973	26 Feb 1974	25 Mar 1975
INDEPENDENCIA	P 13	Vosper-Thornycroft Ltd.	Feb 1973	24 July 1973	20 Sep 1974
LIBERTAD	P 14	Vosper-Thornycroft Ltd	Sep 1973	5 Mar 1974	12 June 1975
PATRIA	P 15	Vosper-Thornycroft Ltd	Mar 1973	27 Sep 1973	9 Jan 1975
VICTORIA	P 16	Vosper-Thornycroft Ltd	Mar 1974	3 Sep 1974	22 Sep 1975

Displacement, tons: 150
Dimensions, feet (metres): 121 oa × 23·3 × 5·6 *(36·9 × 7·6 × 1·7)*
Missiles: 2 Otomat and 1—40 mm gun (P 12, 14 and 16)
Gun: 1—76 mm OTO Melara (P 11, 13 and 15)
Main engines: 2 MTU diesels; 7 200 hp; 2 shafts
Speed, knots: 27
Range, miles: 1 350 at 16 knots
Complement: 18

A £6m order the first laid down in Jan 1973. A new design, fitted with Elsag fire-control system NA 10 mod 1 and Selenia radar in 76 mm gun craft. Ten more fast attack craft (missile) projected.

Radar: SPQ-2D.

FEDERACION   4/1975, Vosper Thornycroft

10 Ex-US PC TYPE (LARGE PATROL CRAFT)

Name	No.	Builders	Commissioned
ALBATROS (ex-USS *Lenoir* PC 582)	P 04	—	—
ALCATRAZ (ex-USS *Gilmer* PC 565)	P 03	—	—
CALAMAR (ex-USS *Honesdale* PC 566)	P 02	—	—
*CAMARON (ex-USS *PC 483*)	P 08	—	—
CARACOL (ex-USS *Edenton* PC 1077)	P 06	—	—
*GAVIOTA (ex-USS *PC 619*)	P 10	—	—
*PETREL (ex-USS *PC 1176*)	P 05	—	—
*PULPO (ex-USS *PC 465*)	P 07	—	—
*MEJILLON (ex-USS *PC 487*)	P 01	—	—
*TOGOGO (ex-USS *PC 484*)	P 09	—	—

(* in reserve)

Displacement, tons: 280 standard; 430 full load
Dimensions, feet (metres): 173·7 oa × 23·0 × 10·8 *(53 × 7 × 3·3)*
Guns: 1—3 in; 2—40 mm (1 twin); 2—20 mm
A/S weapons: Provision for 4 DCT
Main engines: 2 Fairbanks-Morse diesels; 2 shafts; 2 800 bhp = 19 knots
Complement: 65

ALBATROS   1972, Venezuelan Navy

Mejillon was refitted and overhauled by Diques y Astilleros Nacionalis, Venezuela, prior to commissioning in the Venezuelan Navy, and from 1962 onwards more ships of this type underwent similar preparation to join the fleet. Altogether twelve of these former United States PCs of the steel-hulled "173-ft" type were purchased from the USA in Oct 1960. *Camaron, Pulpo* and *Gaviota* were placed in reserve 1968-70 and subsequently *Petrel, Mejillon* and *Togogo*.

21 NEW CONSTRUCTION (COASTAL PATROL CRAFT)

Name	No.	Builders	Commissioned
RIO CAPARO	C 89	Inma, La Spezia	1974
RIO ESCALANTE	C 92	Inma, La Spezia	1975
RIO LIMON	C 93	Inma, La Spezia	1975
RIO ORINOCO (?)	C 87	Inma, La Spezia	1974
RIO SAN JUAN	C 94	Inma, La Spezia	1975
RIO TORRES	C 91	Inma, La Spezia	1974
RIO TUCUYO	C 95	Inma, La Spezia	1975
RIO TURBIO	C 96	Inma, La Spezia	1975
RIO VENAMO	C 90	Inma, La Spezia	1974
RIO VENTUARI	C 88	Inma, La Spezia	1974
—	C 128-138	Iadian, Puerto Cabello	—

Displacement, tons: 65
Dimensions, feet (metres): 92·8 × 15·7 × 4·9 *(28·3 × 4·8 × 1·5)*
Main engines: 2 MTU diesels; 2 200 bhp = 25 knots

Ordered in May 1973. Assistance given in overseeing at Puerto Cabello by Inma.

AMPHIBIOUS FORCES

1 Ex-US "TERREBONNE PARISH" CLASS (LST)

Name	No.	Builders	Commissioned
AMAZONAS	T 21	Ingalls Shipbuilding Corpn	1953
(ex-USS *Vernon County LST 1161*)			

Displacement, tons: 2 590 light; 5 800 full load
Dimensions, feet (metres): 384 oa × 55 × 17 *(117·4 × 16·8 × 3·7)*
Guns: 6—3 in 50 cal (twins)
Main engines: 4 GM diesels; 2 shafts; cp propeller; 6 000 bhp = 15 knots
Complement: 116
Troops: 395

Built 1952-53. Carries four LCVP landing craft. Transferred on loan 29 June 1973.

4 Ex-US LSM TYPE

Name	No.	Builders	Commissioned
LOS FRAILES	T 15	Brown Shipbuilding Co, Houston, Texas	1945
(ex-USS *LSM 544*)			
LOS MONJES	T 13	Brown Shipbuilding Co, Houston, Texas	1945
(ex-USS *LSM 548*)			
LOS ROQUES	T 14	Brown Shipbuilding Co, Houston, Texas	1945
(ex-USS *LSM 543*)			
LOS TESTIGOS	T 16	Brown Shipbuilding Co, Houston, Texas	1945
(ex-USS *LSM 545*)			

LOS MONJES   1970, Venezuelan Navy

Displacement, tons: 743 beaching; 1 095 full load
Dimensions, feet (metres): 196·5 wl; 203·5 oa × 34·5 × 8·3 *(59·9; 62·1 × 10·5 × 2·5)*
Guns: 1—40 mm; 4—20 mm
Main engines: Direct drive diesels; 2 shafts; 2 800 bhp = 12 knots
Range, miles: 9 000 at 11 knots
Complement: 59

Transferred to Venezuela under MAP—Feb 1959 (T 13), Sep 1959 (T 14), Dec 1959 (T 15), Jan 1960 (T 16).

1 Ex-US ARL TYPE

Name	No.	Builders	Commissioned
GUYANA	T 18	Chicago Bridge & Iron Co, Seneca, Illinois	1945
(ex-USS *Quirinus, ARL 39*, ex-*LST 1151*)			

Displacement, tons: 1 625 light; 4 100 full load
Dimensions, feet (metres): 316 wl; 328 oa × 50 × 11·2 *(103·6; 107·7 × 16·4 × 3·7)*
Guns: 8—40 mm AA (two quadruple mountings)
Main engines: GM diesels; 2 shafts; 1 800 bhp = 11·6 knots
Complement: 81 (11 officers, 70 men)

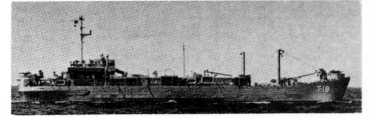

GUYANA   1970, Venezuelan Navy

Former US Navy landing craft repair ship. Laid down on 3 Mar 1945. Loaned to Venezuela in June 1962 and now used as a transport.

TRANSPORTS

1 Ex-US CI-M-AVI TYPE

MARACAIBO

Displacement, tons: 7 450 full load
Dimensions, feet (metres): 338·8 × 50·3 × 21 *(103·3 × 15·3 × 6·4)*
Main engines: Diesel; 1 shaft; 1 750 bhp = 11·5 knots

Built in USA in 1944.

1 JAPANESE TYPE

Name	No.	Builders	Commissioned
PUNTA CABANA	T 17	Uraga Dockyard, Japan	—

Displacement, tons: 3 200
Dimensions, feet (metres): 373·9 × 52·5 × 22·9 *(114 × 16 × 7)*
Main engines: Diesel; 5 500 hp = 17 knots
Range, miles: 6 000 at 15 knots

Name	No.	Builders	Commissioned
LAS AVES (ex-*Dos de Diciembre*)	T 12	Chantiers Dubigeon, Nantes-Chantenay	1955

Displacement, tons: 944
Dimensions, feet (metres): 234·2 × 33·5 × 10 *(71 × 10·2 × 3·1)*
Guns: 4—20 mm (2 twin)
Main engines: 2 diesels; 2 shafts; 1 600 bhp = 15 knots
Radius, miles: 2 600 at 11 knots

Launched in Sep 1954. Light transport for naval personnel. Renamed *Las Aves* in 1961. Can be used as Presidential Yacht.

LAS AVES   1970, Venezuelan Navy

SURVEY SHIPS

1 Ex-US "COHOES" CLASS

Name	No.	Builders	Commissioned
PUERTO SANTO	H 01	Commercial Iron Works,	1945
(ex-USS *Marietta,* AN 82)		Portland, Oregon	

Displacement, tons: 650 standard; 855 full load
Dimensions, feet (metres): 168·5 oa × 33·8 × 11·7 *(51·4 × 10·2 × 3·3)*
Guns: 3—20 mm
Main engines: Bush-Sulzer diesel-electric; 1 shaft; 1 500 bhp = 12 knots
Complement: 46

Puerto Santo loaned from USA in Jan 1961 under MAP and converted into Hydrographic survey vessel and buoy tender by US Coast Guard Yard, Curtis Bay, Maryland, in Feb 1962. Originally carried one 3-inch 50 cal gun.

PUERTO SANTO

1970, Venezuelan Navy

2 SURVEY LAUNCHES

Name	No.	Builders	Commissioned	
GABRIELA	P 119	Abeking and Rasmussen, Lemwerder	5 Feb	1974
LELY	P 121	Abeking and Rasmussen, Lemwerder	7 Feb	1974

Displacement, tons: 90
Dimensions, feet (metres): 88·6 × 18·4 × 4·9 *(27 × 5·6 × 1·5)*
Main engines: 2 diesels; 2 300 hp = 20 knots
Complement: 16

Lely laid down 28 May 1973, launched 12 Dec 1973 and *Gabriela* laid down 10 Mar 1973, launched 29 Nov 1973. Non-naval—civilian manned by Instituto de Canalizaciones.

TUGS

1 OCEAN TUG

Name	No.	Builders	Commissioned
FELIPE LARRAZABAL (ex-USS *Utina,* ATF 163)	R 21	—	—

Displacement, tons: 1 235 standard; 1 675 full load
Dimensions, feet (metres): 205 oa × 38·5 × 15·5 *(61·7 × 11·6 × 4·7)*
Gun: 1—3 in 50 cal
Main engines: Diesel-electric; 3 000 bhp; 1 shaft
Speed, knots: 15
Complement: 85

Transferred 3 Sept 1971. This is the third tug of this name. The first (ex-USS *Discoverer)* was deleted in 1962. The second (ex-USS *Tolowa,* ATF 116) was deleted in 1972 after damage when grounded.

4 HARBOUR TUGS

C 139   **C 140**   **C 141**   **C 142**

Built by IADIAN, Puerto Cabello. 2 Werkspoor diesels; 2 shafts; 1 600 bhp. Ordered in 1973—C 139 launched in 1974 for completion 1975, other three completed 1976.

1 HARBOUR TUG

FERNANDO GOMEZ (ex-USS *Dudley,* YTM 744) R 12

Displacement, tons: 161
Dimensions, feet (metres): 80 × 19 × 8 *(24·5 × 5·8 × 2·5)*
Main engines: Clark diesel; 6-cyl, 315 rpm; 380 bhp = 15 knots
Complement: 10

1 HARBOUR TUG

GENERAL JOSE FELIX RIBAS (ex-USS *Oswegatchie,* YTM 778, ex-YTB 515) R 13

Displacement, tons: 345
Dimensions, feet (metres): 100 × 26 × 9·7 *(30·5 × 7·3 × 2·9)*
Speed, knots: 12
Complement: 10

Transferred in Mar 1965 at San Diego, Calif.

2 Ex-US MEDIUM HARBOUR TUGS

FABRIO GALLIPOLI (ex-USS *Wannalancet* YTM 385) R 14
DIANA III (ex-USS *Sassacus* YTM 193)

Leased to Venezuela in Aug 1965.

5 Ex-US SMALL HARBOUR TUGS

Ex-US YTL 446, 451, 455, 590, 592

80 feet long, leased in Jan 1963.

REPAIR CRAFT

DF 1 (ex-USS *ARD 13)*

Floating dock of 3 000 tons and built of steel. Transferred on loan to Venezuela in Feb 1962.

Ex-US YR 48 (Floating Workshop) transferred 1965.
1 Floating Crane with 40 ton lift.

NATIONAL GUARD

6 COASTAL PATROL CRAFT

RIO META
RIO ORINOCO (?)

RIO PORTUGUESA
RIO URIBANTE
+ 2

Displacement, tons: 45
Dimensions, feet (metres): 88·6 × 16 × 4·9 *(27 × 4·9 × 1·5)*
Guns: 1—20 mm; 1 MG
Main engines: 2 diesels; 3 300 hp = 30 knots
Range, miles: 1 500 at 15 knots
Complement: 12

Built at Chantiers Navals de l'Esterel in 1970-71. Manned by National Guard. 6 more reported as ordered.

8 "RIO" CLASS (COASTAL PATROL CRAFT)

Name	No.	Builders	Commissioned
RIO APURE	—	Chantiers Navals de l'Esterel, Cannes	1954
RIO ARAUCA	—	Chantiers Navals de l'Esterel, Cannes	1954
RIO CABRIALES	—	Chantiers Navals de l'Esterel, Cannes	1954
RIO CARONI	—	Chantiers Navals de l'Esterel, Cannes	1954
RIO GUARICO	—	Chantiers Navals de l'Esterel, Cannes	1954
RIO NEGRO	—	Chantiers Navals de l'Esterel, Cannes	1954
RIO NEVERI	—	Chantiers Navals de l'Esterel, Cannes	1954
RIO TUX	—	Chantiers Navals de l'Esterel, Cannes	1954

Displacement, tons: 38
Dimensions, feet (metres): 82 oa × 15 × 4 *(28 × 4·7 × 1·3)*
Main engines: 2 MTU 12 V 493 diesels; 1 400 rpm; 1 350 bhp = 27 knots

Manned by National Guard.

RIO NEGRO *1972, Venezuelan Navy*

1 COASTAL PATROL CRAFT

GOLFO DE CARIACO

Displacement, tons: 37
Dimensions, feet (metres): 65 × 18 × 9 *(20 × 5·5 × 2·8)*
Main engines: Diesels; speed = 19 knots
Complement: 10

Manned by National Guard.

1 COASTAL PATROL CRAFT

RIO SANTO DOMINGO

Displacement, tons: 40
Dimensions, feet (metres): 70 × 15 × 6 *(22 × 4·6 × 1·9)*
Main engines: 2 GM diesels; 1 250 bhp = 24 knots
Complement: 10

Manned by National Guard.

VIETNAM

Administration

Commander in Chief of the Navy: Rear Admiral Ta Xuan Thu

Strength of the Fleet

It is impossible to give an accurate estimate of this fleet—the details following refer to the known classes in 1975. So far as operational availability is concerned only a very small proportion of this considerable force can be considered fit for sea. Of those that are seaworthy very few can steam any distance due to a chronic lack of fuel oil.

Personnel

1977: ?

FRIGATES

1 Ex-US "BARNEGAT" CLASS

THAM NGU LAO (ex-USCGC *Absecon*, WHEC 374, ex-AVP 23)	HQ 15	Lake Washington SY	8 Mar 1942	28 Jan 1943

Displacement, tons: 1 766 standard; 2 800 full load
Length, feet (metres): 310·75 *(94·7)*
Beam, feet (metres): 41·1 *(12·5)*
Draught, feet (metres): 13·5 *(4·1)*
Guns: 1—5 inch *(127 mm)* .38 cal 1 or 2—81 mm mortars in some ships; several MG
Main engines: Diesels (Fairbanks Morse); 6 080 bhp; 2 shafts
Speed, knots: approx 18
Complement: approx 200

Last of a group built as seaplane tenders for the US Navy. All transferred to US Coast Guard in 1946-1948, initially on loan designated WAVP and then on permanent transfer subsequently redesignated as high endurance cutters (WHEC). Transferred from US Coast Guard to South Vietnamese Navy in 1971-1972.

Ex-US "BARNEGAT" Class *1971, Vietnamese Navy*

1 Ex-US DER TYPE

Name	No.	Builders	Launched	Commissioned
TRAN KHANH DU (ex-USS *Forster*, DER 334)	HQ 04	Consolidated Steel Corp, Orange, Texas	13 Nov 1943	25 Jan 1944

Displacement, tons: 1 590 standard; 1 850 full load
Length, feet (metres): 306 *(93·3)*
Beam, feet (metres): 36·6 *(11·2)*
Draught, feet (metres): 14 *(4·3)*
Guns: 2—3 inch *(76 mm)* 50 cal (single)
A/S weapons: 6 (Mk 32 triple) torpedo tubes; 1 trainable hedgehog (Mk 15); depth charge rack
Main engines: Diesel (Fairbank Morse); 6 000 bhp; 2 shafts
Speed, knots: 21
Complement: approx 170

Former US Navy destroyer escort of the FMR design group.

Employed during 1960s in Indochina for coastal patrol and interdiction by US Navy (Operation MARKET TIME). Transferred to South Vietnamese Navy on 25 September 1971.

Radar: Search; SPS 10 and 28.

TRAN KHANH DU   *1971, Vietnamese Navy*

CORVETTES

2 Ex-US MSF TYPE

Name	No.	Launched
KY HOA (ex-USS *Sentry*, MSF 299)	HQ 09	15 Aug 1943
HA HOI (ex-USS *Prowess*, IX 305, ex-MSF 280)	HQ 13	17 Feb 1944

Displacement, tons: 650 standard; 945 full load
Dimensions, feet (metres): 184·5 × 33 × 9·75 *(56·3 × 10 × 3)*
Guns: 1—3 inch *(76 mm)* 50 cal; 2—40 mm (single); up to 8—20 mm (twin)
A/S weapons: 1 fixed hedgehog; depth charges
Main engines: Diesel (Cooper Bessemer); 1 710 bhp; 2 shafts = 14 knots
Complement: approx 80

Former US Navy minesweepers of the "Admirable" class (originally designated AM). *Ky Hoa* built by Winslow Marine Railway & SB Co, Winslow, Washington, and *Ha Hoi* by Gulf SB Corp, Chicasaw, Alabama.
Ky Hoa transferred in Aug 1962, *Ha Hoi* transferred on 4 June 1970. Minesweeping equipment has been removed and two depth charge racks fitted on fantail; employed in patrol and escort roles.

LIGHT FORCES

1 Ex-US PC TYPE (LARGE PATROL CRAFT)

Name	No.	Launched
VAN DON (ex-USS *Anacortes*, PC 1569)	—	9 Dec 1944

Displacement, tons: 280 standard; 450 full load
Dimensions, feet (metres): 173·7 × 33 × 10·8 *(53 × 10 × 3·3)*
Guns: 1—3 inch *(76 mm)* 50 cal; 1—40 mm; 4—20 mm (single)
A/S weapons: 2 mousetrap launchers; depth charges
Main engines: Diesel; 2 800 bhp; 2 shafts = 19 knots
Complement: approx 50

Built by Leathem D. Smith SB Co. Laid down on 26 Sep 1944 and completed on 14 Mar 1945. Transferred at Seattle, Washington on 23 Nov 1960.

VAN DON   *1971, Vietnamese Navy*

3 Ex-SOVIET "SO 1" CLASS

Displacement, tons: 215 light; 250 normal
Dimensions, feet (metres): 138·6 × 20 × 9·2 *(45·4 × 6·5 × 3)*
Guns: 4—25 mm (2 twin mountings)
A/S weapons: 4—5 barrelled MBU; 2 DCT
Range, miles: 1 100 at 13 knots
Main engines: 3 diesels; 6 000 hp = 29 knots
Complement: 30

Four of Soviet "SO 1" class were originally transferred to North Vietnam, two in 1960-61 and two in 1964-65, but one was sunk by US Navy aircraft on 1 Feb 1966.

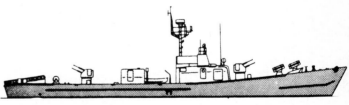

"SO 1" Class

19 100-ft PGM TYPE (LARGE PATROL CRAFT)

Name	No.	Transferred
PHU DU	HQ 600 (PGM 64)	Feb 1963
TIEN MOI	HQ 601 (PGM 65)	Feb 1963
MINH HOA	HQ 602 (PGM 66)	Feb 1963
KIEN VANG	HQ 603 (PGM 67)	Feb 1963
KEO NGUA	HQ 604 (PGM 68)	Feb 1963
KIM QUI	HQ 605 (PGM 60)	May 1963
MAY RUT	HQ 606 (PGM 59)	May 1963
NAM DU	HQ 607 (PGM 61)	May 1963
HOA LU	HQ 608 (PGM 62)	July 1963
TO YEN	HQ 609 (PGM 63)	July 1963
DINH HAI	HQ 610 (PGM 69)	Feb 1964
TRUONG SA	HQ 611 (PGM 70)	Apr 1964
THAI BINH	HQ 612 (PGM 72)	Jan 1966
THI TU	HQ 613 (PGM 73)	Jan 1966
SONG TU	HQ 614 (PGM 74)	Jan 1966
TAT SA	HQ 615 (PGM 80)	Oct 1966
HOANG SA	HQ 616 (PGM 82)	Apr 1967
PHU QUI	HQ 617 (PGM 81)	Apr 1967
THO CHAU	HQ 619 (PGM 91)	Apr 1967

Displacement, tons: 117 full load
Dimensions, feet (metres): 100·3 oa × 21·1 × 6·9 *(30·6 × 6·4 × 2·1)*
Guns: 1—40 mm; 2 or 4—20 mm (twin); 2—MG
Main engines: Diesel; 1 900 bhp; 2 shafts = 17 knots
Complement: approx 15

KIM QUI   *1970, Vietnamese Navy*

Welded-steel patrol gunboats built in the United States specifically for foreign transfer; assigned PGM numbers for contract purposes. Enlarged version of US Coast Guard 95-foot patrol boats with commercial-type machinery and electronic equipment. HQ 600-605 built by J. M. Martinac SB Corp, Tacoma, Washington; HQ 606-610 built by Marinette Marine Corp. Wisconsin.

2 Ex-SOVIET "KOMAR" CLASS

(FAST ATTACK CRAFT—MISSILE)

Displacement, tons: 70 standard; 80 full load
Dimensions, feet (metres): 83·7 × 19·8 × 5·0 *(27·4 × 6·5 × 1·6)*
Missiles: 2—SS-N-2 launchers
Guns: 2—25 mm (twin forward)
Main engines: 4 diesels; 4 shafts; 4 800 hp = 40 knots
Range, miles: 400 at 30 knots

A sister ship was reported sunk on 19 Dec 1972.

6 Ex-CHINESE "P 6" CLASS (FAST ATTACK CRAFT—TORPEDO)

Displacement, tons: 66 standard; 75 full load
Dimensions, feet (metres): 84·1 × 20 × 6 *(27·7 × 6·5 × 1·9)*
Guns: 4—25 mm (2 twin)
Torpedo tubes: 2—21 in (single)
Mines: 4
Main engines: 4 diesels; 4 800 bhp; 4 shafts = 43 knots
Range, miles: 450 at 30 knots
Complement: 25

Built in China and transferred in 1967. Some may have been lost in action.

6 Ex-SOVIET "P 4" CLASS (FAST ATTACK CRAFT—TORPEDO)

Displacement, tons: 25 standard
Dimensions, feet (metres): 62·7 × 11·6 × 5·6 *(20·5 × 3·8 × 1·8)*
Guns: 2 MG (1 twin)
Torpedo tubes: 2—18 in
Main engines: 2 diesels; 2 200 bhp = 50 knots

Approximately a dozen aluminium hulled motor torpedo boats were transferred from the Soviet Union in 1961 and 1964 and some from China. A number have been lost in action.

"P 6" Class

8 Ex-CHINESE "SHANGHAI" CLASS
(FAST ATTACK CRAFT—GUN)

Displacement, tons: 120 full load
Dimensions, feet (metres): 128 × 18 × 5·5 *(39 × 5·5 × 1·7)*
Guns: 4—37 mm (2 twin mountings); 4—25 mm (twins)
Main engines: 4 diesels; 4 800 bhp = 30 knots
Complement: 25

Four were received from the People's Republic of China in May 1966.

"SHANGHAI II" Class   1972, Aviation Fan

14 Ex-CHINESE "SWATOW" CLASS
(FAST ATTACK CRAFT—GUN)

Displacement, tons: 80 full load
Dimensions, feet (metres): 83·5 × 19 × 6·5 *(27·4 × 6·2 × 2·1)*
Guns: 4—37 mm; 2—20 mm
A/S weapons: 8 depth charges
Main engines: 4 diesels; 4 800 bhp = 40 knots
Range, miles: 750 at 15 knots
Complement: 17

Approximately 30 "Swatow" class built in China were transferred in 1958, and 20 were delivered in 1964 to replace those lost in action. Pennant numbers run in a 600 series.

26 Ex-USCG 82-ft "POINT" CLASS
(COASTAL PATROL CRAFT)

Name	No.
LE PHUOC DUI	HQ 700 (ex-*Point Garnet* 82310)
LE VAN NGA	HQ 701 (ex-*Point League* 82304)
HUYNH VAN CU	HQ 702 (ex-*Point Clear* 82315)
NGUYEN DAO	HQ 703 (ex-*Point Gammon* 82328)
DAO THUC	HQ 704 (ex-*Point Comfort* 82317)
LE NGOC THANH	HQ 705 (ex-*Point Ellis* 82330)
NGUYEN NGOC THACH	HQ 706 (ex-*Point Slocum* 82313)
DANG VAN HOANH	HQ 707 (ex-*Point Hudson* 82322)
LE DINH HUNG	HQ 708 (ex-*Point White* 82308)
THUONG TIEN	HQ 709 (ex-*Point Dume* 82325)
PHAM NGOC CHAU	HQ 710 (ex-*Point Arden* 82309)
DAO VAN DANG	HQ 711 (ex-*Point Glover* 82307)
LE DGOC AN	HQ 712 (ex-*Point Jefferson* 82306)
HUYNH VAN NGAN	HQ 713 (ex-*Point Kennedy* 82320)
TRAN LO	HQ 714 (ex-*Point Young* 82303)
BUI VIET THANH	HQ 715 (ex-*Point Patrige* 82305)
NGUYEN AN	HQ 716 (ex-*Point Caution* 82301)
NGUYEN HAN	HQ 717 (ex-*Point Welcome* 82329)
NGO VAN QUYEN	HQ 718 (ex-*Point Banks* 82327)
VAN DIEN	HQ 719 (ex-*Point Lomas* 82321)
HO DANG LA	HQ 720 (ex-*Point Grace* 82323)
DAM THOAI	HQ 721 (ex-*Point Mast* 82316)
HUYNH BO	HQ 722 (ex-*Point Grey* 82324)
NGUYEN KIM HUNG	HQ 723 (ex-*Point Orient* 82319)
HO DUY	HQ 724 (ex-*Point Cypress* 82326)
TROUNG BA	HQ 725 (ex-*Point Maromc* 82331)

"POINT" Class   1970, Vietnamese Navy

Displacement, tons: 64 standard; 67 full load
Dimensions, feet (metres): 83 × 17·2 × 5·8 *(25·3 × 5·2 × 1·8)*
Guns: 1—81 mm/50 cal MG (combination) plus 2 to 4—50 cal MG (single) or 1—20 mm
Main engines: 2 diesels; 1 200 bhp; 2 shafts = 16·8 knots
Complement: 8 to 10

Former US Coast Guard 82-ft patrol boats (designated WPB). All served in Vietnamese waters, manned by US personnel, comprising Coast Guard Squadron One. HQ 700-707 transferred to South Vietnamese Navy in 1969, HQ 708-HQ 725 in 1970.

30 MOTOR LAUNCH TYPES (COASTAL PATROL CRAFT)

Some thirty motor launches were reported to have been incorporated into the North Vietnam Navy before May 1966, but not all are still in service.

AMPHIBIOUS FORCES

3 Ex-US "501-1152" CLASS (LSTs)

Name	No.	Launched
DA NANG (ex-USS *Maricopa County*, LST 938)	HQ 501	15 Aug 1944
VUNG TAU (ex-USS *Cochino County*, LST 603)	HQ 503	14 Mar 1944
QUI NHON (ex-USS *Bullock County*, LST 509)	HQ 504	23 Nov 1943

Displacement, tons: 2 366 beaching; 4 080 full load
Dimensions, feet (metres): 328 oa × 50 × 14 *(100 × 15·2 × 4·6)*
Guns: 7 or 8—40 mm (1 or 2 twin; 4 or 5 single); several 20 mm
Main engines: Diesel (General Motors); 1 700 bhp; 2 shafts = 11 knots
Complement: 110

Former US Navy tank landing ships HQ 501 built by Bethlehem Steel Co, Hingham, Massachusetts; HQ 504 by Jeffersonville B & M Co, Jeffersonville, Indiana; HQ 503 by Chicago Bridge & Iron Co. Illinois. Lattice tripod masts.

QUI NHON   *1971, Vietnamese Navy*

5 Ex-US LSM TYPE

Name	No.	Launched
HAN GIANG (ex-LSM 9012, ex-USS LSM 110)	HQ 401	28 Oct 1944
LAM GIANG (ex-USS LSM 226)	HQ 402	4 Sep 1944
NINH GIANG (ex-USS LSM 85)	HQ 403	15 Sep 1944
TIEN GIANG (ex-USS LSM 313)	HQ 405	24 May 1944
HAU GIANG (ex-USS LSM 276)	HQ 406	20 Sep 1944

Displacement, tons: 743 beaching; 1 095 full load
Dimensions, feet (metres): 203·5 × 34·5 × 8·3 *(62 × 10·5 × 2·5)*
Guns: 2—40 mm; 4—20 mm
Main engines: Diesel; 2 shafts; 2 800 bhp = 12 knots
Complement: 73

First three transferred to French Navy for use in Indo-China, Jan 1954. *Han Giang* transferred to Vietnam Navy, Dec 1955. *Tien Giang* transferred in 1962, *Hau Giang* on 10 June 1965.

LAM GIANG   *Vietnamese Navy*

6 Ex-US LSSL TYPE

Name	No.	Launched
NGUYEN NGOC LONG (ex-USS LSSL 96)	HQ 230	6 Jan 1945

+5

Displacement, tons: 227 standard; 383 full load
Dimensions, feet (metres): 158 × 23·7 × 5·7 *(48·3 × 7·6 × 1·8)*
Guns: 1—3 inch; 4—40 mm; 4—20 mm; 4 MG
Main engines: Diesel; 2 shafts; 1 600 bhp × 14 knots
Complement: 60

Former US Navy landing ships support. Five more from ex-North Vietnamese fleet plus 5 LSIL, 1 LCT(6) and 6 LCT(7). Ex-South Vietnamese ships served in Japanese Navy in 1953 to 1964; retransferred to South Vietnam in 1965 and 1966.

LSSL Type   *Vietnamese Navy*

18 Ex-US LCU TYPE

HQ 533 (ex-US LCU 1479)	**HQ 543** (ex-US LCU 1493)
HQ 534 (ex-US LCU 1480)	**HQ 544** (ex-US LCU 1485)
HQ 535 (ex-US LCU 1221)	**HQ 545** (ex-US LCU 1484)
HQ 536 (ex-US LCU 1595)	**HQ 546** (ex-US YFU 90, ex-LCU 1582)
HQ 537 (ex-US LCU 1501)	**HQ 547** (ex-US LCU 1481)
HQ 538 (ex-US LCU 1594)	**HQ 548** (ex-US LCU 1498)
HQ 539 (ex-US LCU 1502)	**HQ 560** (ex-US YLLC 1, LCU 1348)
HQ 540 (ex-US LCU 1475)	**HQ 561** (ex-US YLLC5, YFU 2, LCU 529)
HQ 542 (ex-US LCU 1494)	**HQ 562** (ex-US YLLC 3, YFU 33, LCU 1195)

LCU 501 series

Displacement, tons: 309 to 320 full load
Dimensions, feet (metres): 119 × 32·7 × 5 *(36·3 × 10 × 1·5)*
Main engines: Diesels (Gray Marine); 675 bhp; 3 shafts = 10 knots

LCU 1466 series

Displacement, tons: 360 full load
Dimensions, feet (metres): 119 × 34 × 5·25 *(36·3 × 10·6 × 1·7)*
Main engines: Diesels (Gray Marine); 675 bhp; 3 shafts = 8 knots

HQ 538   *1971, Vietnamese Navy*

501 series built during World War II with LCT (6) designation; 1466 series built during the early 1950s. Transferred to South Vietnam from 1954 to 1971, with some of the earlier craft serving briefly in French Navy in Indo-China waters.

Most units armed with two 20 mm guns.

RIVERINE CRAFT

The US Navy transferred approximately 700 armed small craft to South Vietnam since 1965. A few former French riverine craft also survive. The exact number of these craft now in service is not known.

In addition to the armed craft grouped here under the category of Riverine (Warfare) Craft, there are numerous small landing craft which are armed.

107 Ex-US "SWIFT" CLASS

Displacement, tons: 22·5 full load
Dimensions, feet (metres): 50 × 13 × 3·5 (15·2 × 3·8 × 1·1)
Guns: 1—81 mm mortar/1—50 cal MG combination mount: 2—·50 cal MG (twin)
Main engines: 2 geared diesels (General Motors); 960 bhp; 2 shafts = 28 knots
Complement: 6

All-metal inshore patrol craft (PCF). Transferred to South Vietnam from 1968 to 1970. Numbered in HQ 3800-3887 and later series.

HQ 3825   *1970, Vietnamese Navy*

293 Ex-US PBR TYPE

Displacement, tons: PBR I series: 7·5; PBR II series: 8
Dimensions, feet (metres): PBR I series: 31 × 10·5 × 2·5 (9·1 × 3·1 × 0·8)
  PBR II series: 32 × 11 × 2·6 (9·3 × 3·2 × 0·8)
Guns: 3—·50 cal MG (twin mount forward; single gun aft)
Main engines: 2 geared diesels; 440 bhp; water-jet propulsion = 25+ knots
Complement: 4 or 5

River patrol boats (PBR) with fibreglass (plastic) hulls. Transferred to South Vietnam from 1968 to 1970. Numbered in HQ 7500-7749 and 7800 series.

PBR Type   *1970, Vietnamese Navy*

27 Ex-US RCP TYPE

Displacement, tons: 15·6
Dimensions, feet (metres): 35·75 × 10·3 × 3·6 (10·9 × 3·1 × 1·2)
Guns: varies: 2—·50 cal MG (twin); 3—·30 cal MG (twin mount aft and single gun at conning station); some units have additional twin ·30 cal mount in place of ·50 cal MH
Main engines: 2 geared diesels; 2 shafts = 14 knots

River patrol craft (RPC); predecessor to PBR type. Welded-steel hulls. Few used by US Navy as minesweepers, but most of the 34 units built were transferred to South Vietnam upon completion in 1965; others in 1968-1969. Numbered HQ 7000-7028.

RCP Type   *1970, Vietnamese Navy*

84 Ex-US ASPB TYPE

Displacement, tons: 36·25 full load
Dimensions, feet (metres): 50 × 15·6 × 3·75 (15·2 × 4·8 × 1·1)
Guns: varies: 1 or 2—20 mm (with 2—·50 cal MG in boats with one 20 mm); 2—·30 cal MG; 2—40 mm grenade launchers
Main engines: 2 geared diesels; 2 shafts = 14 knots sustained
Complement: 6

Assault support patrol boats (ASPB) with welded-steel hulls. Transferred to South Vietnam from 1969 to 1970. Numbered in HQ 5100 series.

ASBP Type   *1970, Vietnamese Navy*

42 Ex-US MONITORS

Displacement, tons: 80 to 90 full load
Dimensions, feet (metres): 60·5 × 17·5 × 3·5 *(18·3 × 5·3 × 1·1)*
Guns: 1—105 mm howitzer; 2—20 mm; 3—·30 cal MG; 2—40 mm grenade launchers
Main engines: 2 geared diesels; 2 shafts = 9 knots
Complement: 11

River monitors (MON). Transferred to South Vietnam in 1969-1970. Numbered in HQ 6500 series.

MONITOR   *1970, Vietnamese Navy*

22 Ex-US LCM MONITORS

Displacement, tons: 75 full load
Dimensions, feet (metres): 60 × 17 × 3·5 *(18·3 × 5·2 × 1·1)*
Guns: varies: 1—81 mm mortar or 2 M10-8 flame throwers; 1—40 mm; 1—20 mm; 2—·50 cal
  MG; possibly 2 to 4—·30 cal MG
Main engines: 2 geared diesels; 2 shafts = 8 knots
Complement: approx 10

Twenty-four LCM-6 landing craft converted to this configuration from 1964 to 1967. Predecessor to the Monitor listed above. Transferred to South Vietnam from 1965 to 1970. Numbered in HQ 1800 series.

LCM MONITOR   *1970, Vietnamese Navy*

100 Ex-US ATC TYPE

Displacement, tons: 66 full load
Dimensions, feet (metres): 65·5 × 17·5 × 3·25 *(20 × 5·4 × 1)*
Guns: varies: 1 or 2—20 mm; 2—·50 cal MG; several ·30 cal MG; 2—40 mm grenade launchers
Main engines: 2 geared diesels; 2 shafts = 8·5 knots (6 knots sustained)

Armoured troop carriers (ATC). Some fitted with steel helicopter platforms for evacuation of wounded. Transferred to South Vietnam in 1969. Numbered in HQ 1200 series.

ATC Type   *1970, Vietnamese Navy*

9 Ex-US CCB TYPE

Displacement, tons: 80 full load
Dimensions, feet (metres): 61 × 17·5 × 3·4 *(18·6 × 5·4 × 1·1)*
Guns: 3—20 mm; 2—·30 cal MG; 2—40 mm grenade launchers
Main engines: 2 geared diesels; 2 shafts = 8·5 knots maximum (6 knots sustained)
Complement: 11

Transferred to South Vietnam in 1969-1970. Numbered HQ6100-6108.

4 Ex-US CSB TYPE

Dimensions, feet (metres): 56 × 18·75 × 6 *(17·1 × 5·7 × 1·7)*
Guns: 4—·50 cal MG (twin)
Main engines: 2 geared diesels; 2 shafts = 6 knots
Complement: 6

Combat salvage boats (CSB) converted from LCM-6 landing craft; configured for river salvage and to support diving operations. Ten-ton capacity "A" frame forward.

Ex-FRENCH CRAFT

The Vietnamese Navy listed 43 ex-French STCAN/FOM and 14 LCM Commandement as being in service. The latter are converted LCM-3 landing craft.

MINESWEEPING LAUNCHES

Before cessation of hostilities 24 minesweeping launches were listed in the S. Vietnamese Navy; ten MLMS 50-foot type transferred in 1963 from US Navy (numbered HQ 150-155, 157-160; HQ 156 and 161 stricken in 1971); eight MSM 56-foot type transferred in 1970 (numbered HQ 1700-1707); six MSR 50-foot type transferred in 1970 (numbered HQ 1900-1905). Other riverine craft had a minesweeping capability.

MLMS   *1971, Vietnamese Navy*

SUPPORT SHIP

1 Ex-US MODIFIED LST TYPE

Name	No.	Launched
VINH LONG (ex-USS *Satyr*, ARL 23, ex-LST 852)	HQ 802	13 Nov 1944

VINH LONG   *Vietnamese Navy*

Displacement, tons: type: 4 100 full load
Dimensions, feet (metres): 328 × 50 × 14 *(100 × 15·2 × 4·3)*
Guns: 8—40 mm (2 quad)
Main engines: Diesels (General Motors); 1 800 bhp; 2 shafts = 11·6 knots

Converted during construction to landing craft repair ship (ARL)

Transferred to S. Vietnam on 15 Oct 1971.

OILERS

4 Ex-US YOG TYPE

HQ 472 (ex-US YOG 67)	HQ 474 (ex-YOG 131)
HQ 473 (ex-US YOG 71)	HQ 475 (ex-YOG 56)

Displacement, tons: 450 light; 1 253 full load
Dimensions, feet (metres): 174·0 × 32·0 × 10·9 *(53 × 9·8 × 3·1)*
Main engines: Diesels; 1 shaft = 10 knots
Cargo Capacity: 6 570 barrels

Former US Navy small gasoline tankers.
Transfers: HQ 472 in July 1967, HQ 473 in Mar 1970; HQ 474 in April 1971, and HQ 475 in June 1972.

WATER CARRIERS

2 Ex-US YW TYPE

HQ 9118 (ex-US YW 152)	HQ 9113 (ex-US YW 153)

Former US Navy self-propelled water carriers. Transferred to South Vietnam in 1956.

HARBOUR TUGS

9 Ex-US YTL TYPE

HQ 9500 (ex-US YTL 152)	HQ 9508 (ex-US YTL 452)
HQ 9501 (ex-US YTL 245)	HQ 9509 (ex-US YTL 456)
HQ 9502 (ex-US YTL)	HQ 9510 (ex-US YTL 586)
HQ 9503 (ex-US YTL 200)	HQ 9511 (ex-US YTL 457)
HQ 9504 (ex-US YTL 206)	

Former US Navy harbour tugs. HQ 9500 transferred to South Vietnam in 1955; HQ 9501, 9503, 9504 in 1956; others from 1968 to 1970.

JUNK FORCE

There were approximately 250 motor-propelled junks in South Vietnamese naval service. The breakdown as of January 1972 included 62 command junks, 31 Kien Giang junks, and 153 Yabuta junks. Some of the Yabuta junks are fabricated of ferrous cement. The Yabuta junk has two ·50 cal MG; some also have a 60 mm mortar.

VIRGIN ISLANDS

An area of some 40 islands, large and small.

Chief of Police:
Rex K. Jones

Base

Road Town

1 BROOKE MARINE PATROL CRAFT

VIRGIN CLIPPER

Displacement, tons: 15
Dimensions, feet (metres): 40 × 12 × 2 *(13·1 × 3·9 × 0·6)*
Gun: 1 MG
Main engines: 2 diesels; 370 hp = 22 knots
Complement: 4

Standard Brooke Marine patrol craft attached to the Royal Virgin Islands Police Force.

VIRGIN CLIPPER   *1975, Virgin Islands Police Force*

YEMEN—NORTH
(Arab Republic of)

Personnel

(a) 1977: 300 officers and men
(b) 3 years National Service

Base

Hodeida

Mercantile Marine

Lloyd's Register of Shipping:
3 vessels of 1 260 tons gross

4 Ex-SOVIET "P 4" CLASS (FAST ATTACK CRAFT—TORPEDO)

Displacement, tons: 25
Dimensions, feet (metres): 62·7 × 11·6 × 5·6 *(20·5 × 3·7 × 1·8)*
Guns: 2 MG
Torpedo tubes: 2—18 in
Main engines: 2 diesels; 2 shafts; 2 200 hp = 50 knots

Transferred by USSR in late 1960s.

4 Ex-SOVIET "POLUCHAT" CLASS (LARGE PATROL CRAFT)

Displacement, tons: 100 standard
Dimensions, feet (metres): 98·4 × 19 × 5·9 *(30 × 5·8 × 1·8)*
Guns: 2—14·5 mm (twin)

Transferred 1970.

Note: In addition a dozen smaller Patrol Craft and two small landing craft have been reported.

YEMEN—SOUTH
(People's Democratic Republic of)

Personnel

(a) 1977: 250 officers and men
(b) 2 years National Service

Bases

Aden, Mukalla

Mercantile Marine

Lloyd's Register of Shipping:
15 vessels of 6 654 tons gross

LIGHT FORCES

2 Ex-SOVIET "SO I" CLASS (LARGE PATROL CRAFT)

Displacement, tons: 215 standard; 250 full load
Dimensions, feet (metres): 138·6 × 20·0 × 9·2 *(42·3 × 6·1 × 2·8)*
Guns: 4—25 mm (twins)
A/S weapons: 2—5 barrelled RBUs; 2 DC racks
Main engines: 3 diesels; 6 000 shp = 29 knots
Range, miles: 1 100 at 13 knots
Complement: 30

Transferred in late 1960 s.

Soviet "SO 1" Class   *USN*

2 Ex-SOVIET "P 6" CLASS

Displacement, tons: 66 standard; 75 full load
Dimensions, feet (metres): 84·2 × 20 × 6·0 *(25·7 × 6·1 × 1·8)*
Guns: 4—25 mm (twins)
Torpedo tubes: 2—21 in
Main engines: 4 diesels; 4 shafts; 4 800 bhp = 43 knots
Range, miles: 450 at 30 knots
Complement: 25

Soviet "P 6" Class   *Novosti*

3 FAIREY MARINE "SPEAR" CLASS

Dimensions, feet (metres): 29·8 × 9·2 × 2·6 *(9·1 × 2·8 × 0·8)*
Guns: 3—7·62 mm MG
Main engines: 2 diesels; 290 hp = 25 knots

Delivered 30 Sep 1975.

1 FAIREY MARINE "INTERCEPTOR" CLASS

Of 25 ft *(7·6 metres)* with a catamaran hull. Can carry eight 25-man liferafts or a platoon of troops. Twin 135 outboard motors = 30 knots. Delivered 27 July 1975.

AMPHIBIOUS FORCES

2 Ex-SOVIET "POLNOCNY" CLASS (LCT)

Displacement, tons: 780 standard; 1 000 full load
Dimensions, feet (metres): 246 × 29·5 × 9·8 *(73 × 9 × 3)*
Guns: 2—25 mm (twin); 2—18 barrelled rocket launchers
Main engines: 2 diesels; 5 000 bhp = 18 knots

Can carry 6 tanks. Transferred in 1973.

Soviet "POLNOCNY" Class

1 "Z" LIGHTER

3 Ex-SOVIET T4 (LCVPs)

Main engines: 3 diesels; 3 shafts; 3 300 bhp = 24 knots
Range, miles: 1 500 at 12 knots

INSHORE MINESWEEPERS

3 Ex-BRITISH "HAM" CLASS

JIBLA   SOCOTRA   ZINGAHAR

Displacement, tons: 120 standard; 160 full load
Dimensions, feet (metres): 106·5 oa × 21·2 × 5·5 *(32·4 × 6·5 × 1·7)*
Gun: 1—20 mm
Main engines: 2 Paxman diesels; 1 100 bhp = 14 knots
Oil fuel, tons: 15
Complement: 15 officers and men

The British inshore minesweepers *Bodenham* (renamed *Al Saqr*), *Blunham* (renamed *Al Dairak*) and *Elsenham* (renamed *Al Ghazala*) were transferred to the South Arabian Navy established by the Federal Government in 1967. All three were renamed after local islands in 1975.

YUGOSLAVIA

Personnel

(a) 1977: 27 000 (2 500 officers and 24 500 men)
(b) 18 months National Service

Ministerial

Secretary of Defence:
  General Nikola Ljubicic
Assistant Secretary of State for National Defence for the Navy:
  Admiral Branko Mamula

Headquarters Appointment

Commander-in-Chief of the Fleet:
  Vice-Admiral Ivo Purisic

Diplomatic Representation

Defence Attaché in London:
  Colonel M. Surlan
Naval, Military and Air Attaché in Moscow:
  Colonel S. Krivokapic
Naval, Military and Air Attaché in Washington:
  Colonel Milan Mavric

Bases

3 Naval Zones with bases at Pula, Sibenik, Zadar and Gulf of Kotor complex. Other minor bases at Split and Dubrovnik.

Naval Air Arm

A number of Soviet-type Hormone helicopters now operate under naval command as well as Mi 8 helicopters.

Mercantile Marine

Lloyd's Register of Shipping:
  423 vessels of 1 943 750 tons gross·

New Construction

As well as the new submarines, fast attack craft and LSTs it is reported that the first of a new class of surface ship, possibly of some 1 500 tons, is now in hand.

Strength of the Fleet

Type	Active	Building
Destroyer	1	—
Corvettes	3	—
Submarines—Patrol	5	?2
Fast Attack Craft—Missile	10	10
Fast Attack Craft—Gun	20	—
Fast Attack Craft—Torpedo	14	—
Large Patrol Craft	23	—
Minesweepers—Coastal	4	—
Minesweepers—Inshore	10	—
River Minesweepers	14	—
LSTs	—	?
LCTs	30+	—
Training Ships	2	—
Survey Ship	1	—
HQ Ship	1	—
Salvage Vessel	1	—
Tankers—Harbour	9	—
Transports	11	—
Tugs	21	—
Water Carriers	8	—
Yacht	1	—

DELETIONS

Destroyers	Frigates	Submarines	Large Patrol Craft
1971 *Kotor* (ex-*Kempenfelt*, ex-*Valentine*) *Pula* (ex-*Wager*)	1971 *Biokovo* (ex-*Aliseo*), *Triglav* (ex-*Indomito*)	1971 *Sava* (ex-*Nautilo*)	1975 2 "Kraljevica" class to Bangladesh, 1 to Ethiopia

DESTROYER

1 "SPLIT" CLASS

Name	No.	Builders	Laid down	Launched	Commissioned
SPLIT (ex-*Spalato*)	R 11	Brodogradiliste, Rijeka (see note)	July 1939	1940	1959 (see note)

Displacement, tons: 2 400 standard; 3 000 full load
Length, feet (metres): 376·3 *(114·7)* pp; 393·7 *(120·0)* oa
Beam, feet (metres): 36·5 *(11·1)*
Draught, feet (metres): 12·3 *(3·8)*
Guns: 4—5 in *(127 mm)*; 12—40 mm
A/S weapons: 2 Hedgehogs; 6 DCT; 2 DC racks
Torpedo tubes: 5—21 in *(533 mm)*
Mines: Capacity 40
Main engines: Geared turbines; 2 shafts; 50 000 shp
Boilers: 2 watertube type
Speed, knots: 31·5
Oil fuel, tons: 590
Complement: 240

Built by Brodogradiliste "3 Maj", Rijeka. The original ship was laid down in July 1939 by Chantieres de Loire, Nantes, in 1939 at Split Shipyard. Completed on 4 July 1958. Ready for operational service in 1959. The original design provided for an armament of 5—5·5 inch guns, 10—40 mm guns and 6—21·7 inch torpedo tubes (tripled), but the plans were subsequently modified.

Fire Control: Mk 37 GFCS forward with Mk 12 and 22 radars; Mk 51 GFCS for 40 mm.

Radar: SC and SG1.

SPLIT   *Commander Aldo Fraccaroli*

CORVETTES

2 "MORNAR" CLASS

Name	No.	Builders	Laid down	Launched	Commissioned
MORNAR	551	Yugoslavia	1957	1958	10 Sep 1959
BORAC	552	Yugoslavia	1964	1965	1965

Displacement, tons: 330 standard; 430 full load
Dimensions, feet (metres): 170 pp; 174·8 × 23 × 6·6 *(51·8; 53·3 × 7 × 2)*
Guns: 4—40 mm (single); 2—20 mm (single)
A/S weapons: 4 MBU-1200; 2 DCT; 2 DC racks
Main engines: 4 SEMT-Pielstick diesels; 2 shafts; 3 240 bhp
Speed, knots: 20
Range, miles: 3 000 at 12 knots; 2 000 at 15 knots
Complement: 60

The design is an improved version of that of *Udarnik*.

BORAC   *Commander Aldo Fraccaroli*

1 FOUGUEUX TYPE

Name	No.
UDARNIK (ex-*P 6*)	581

Displacement, tons: 325 standard; 400 full load
Dimensions, feet (metres): 170 pp; 174·8 oa × 23 × 6·6 *(51·8; 53·3 × 7 × 2)*
Guns: 2—40 mm; 2—20 mm
A/S weapons: 1 Hedgehog; 4 DCT; 2 DC racks
Main engines: 4 SEMT Pielstick diesels; 3 240 bhp = 18·7 knots
Range, miles: 3 000 at 12 knots; 2 000 at 15 knots
Complement: 62

USA offshore procurement.

Builders	Laid down	Launched	Commissioned
F.C. Mediterranee (Le Havre)	1954	1 June 1954	1955

UDARNIK

1972, Yugoslavian Navy

SUBMARINES

2(?) NEW CONSTRUCTION

Displacement, tons: 964 dived
Length, feet (metres): 215·8 *(65·8)*
Torpedo tubes: 6—21 in *(533 mm)* (10 reloads or 20 mines)
Main machinery: Diesel-electric
Speed, knots: 16·1 dived
Complement: 35

A new class of diesel propelled submarine now under construction in Yugoslavia. Diving depth 1 000 ft.

3 "HEROJ" CLASS (PATROL SUBMARINES)

Name	No.
HEROJ	821
JUNAK	822
USKOK	823

Displacement, tons: 1 068 dived
Length, feet (metres): 210·0 *(64)*
Beam, feet (metres): 23·6 *(7·2)*
Draught, feet (metres): 16·4 *(5·0)*
Torpedo tubes: 6—21 in *(533 mm)* (bow)
Main machinery: Diesels; electric motors; 2 400 hp
Speed, knots: 16 surfaced; 10 dived
Complement: 55

Builders	Laid down	Launched	Commissioned
Uljanik Shipyard, Pula	1964	1967	1968
Uljanik Shipyard, Pula	1965	1968	1969
Uljanik Shipyard, Pula	1966	1969	1970

JUNAK

1972, S. and DE. Factory, Split

JUNAK

1972, S. and DE. Factory, Split

JUNAK

1972, S. and DE. Factory, Split

2 "SUTJESKA" CLASS (PATROL SUBMARINES)

Name	No.
NERETVA	812
SUTJESKA	811

Displacement, tons: 820 surfaced; 945 dived
Length, feet (metres): 196·8 *(60·0)*
Beam, feet (metres): 22·3 *(6·8)*
Draught, feet (metres): 16·1 *(4·9)*
Torpedo tubes: 6—21 in *(533 mm)* (bow)
Main machinery: Diesels; electric motors; 1 800 hp
Speed, knots: 14 surfaced; 9 dived
Range, miles: 4 800 at 8 knots
Complement: 38

The first class of submarines to be built in a Yugoslav yard.

Builders	Laid down	Launched	Commissioned
Uljanik Shipyard, Pula	1957	1959	1962
Uljanik Shipyard, Pula	1957	28 Sep 1958	16 Sep 1960

NERETVA

1969, Dr Giorgio Arra

"MALA" CLASS (2 MAN SUBMARINES)

Dimensions, feet (metres): 25 × 6 approx *(8·2 × 1·9 approx)*
Main motors: 1 electric motor; single screw
Complement: 2

This is a free-flood craft with the main motor, battery, navigation-pod and electronic equipment housed in separate watertight cylinders. Constructed of light aluminium it is fitted with fore- and after-hydroplanes, the tail being a conventional cruciform with a single rudder abaft the screw. Large perspex windows give a good all-round view.

"MALA" Class   *1973, S. and DE. Factory, Split*

LIGHT FORCES

10 NEW CONSTRUCTION
(FAST ATTACK CRAFT—MISSILE)

Displacement, tons: 240
Dimensions, feet (metres): 147·6 × 27·6 × 15·4 *(45 × 8·4 × 4·7)*
Missiles: 2 launchers for Exocet
Gun: 1 Bofors 57 mm
Main engines: 2 Rolls-Royce Proteus gas turbines; 11 600 shp; 2 MTU diesels; 7 200 shp
Speed, knots: 40
Complement: 30

Under construction in Yugoslavia. Similar to the Swedish "Spica" class.

Radar: Philips TAB in radome.

10 Ex-SOVIET "OSA" CLASS
(FAST ATTACK CRAFT—MISSILE)

M. ACEV	Z. JOVANOVIC	K. ROJC
V. BAGAT	N. MARTINOVIC	F. ROZMAN
P. DRAPSIN	J. MAZAR	V. SKORPIK
S. FILIPOVIC		

Displacement, tons: 165 standard; 200 full load
Dimensions, feet (metres): 128·7 × 25·1 × 5·9 *(39·3 × 7·7 × 1·8)*
Missile launchers: 4 for SS-N-2 system
Guns: 4—30 mm (2 twin, 1 forward, 1 aft)
Main engines: 3 diesels; 13 000 bhp = 32 knots
Range, miles: 800 at 25 knots
Complement: 25

Acquired between 1965 and 1969. Pennant numbers from 301-310.

"OSA" Class   *1972, Yugoslavian Navy*

"OSA" Class   *1972*

14 Ex-SOVIET "SHERSHEN" CLASS
(FAST ATTACK CRAFT—TORPEDO)

211	213	215	217	219	221	223
212	214	216	218	220	222	224

Displacement, tons: 150 standard; 160 full load
Dimensions, feet (metres): 115·5 × 23·1 × 5·0 *(35·2 × 7 × 1·5)*
Guns: 4—30 mm (2 twin)
Torpedo tubes: 4—21 in (single)
A/S weapons: 12 DC
Main engines: 3 diesels; 3 shafts; 13 000 bhp = 41 knots
Complement: 16

Acquired between 1965 and 1971, some from the USSR whilst the remainder were built in Yugoslavia.

"SHERSHEN" Class   *1972*

20 "101" CLASS (FAST ATTACK CRAFT—GUN)

Displacement, tons: 55 standard; 60 full load
Dimensions, feet (metres): 69 pp; 78 oa × 21·3 × 7·8 *(21; 23·8 × 6·5 × 2·4)*
Guns: 1—40 mm; 4—12·7 mm MG
Torpedo tubes: 2—17·7 in (ex-Italian)
Main engines: 3 Packard motors; 3 shafts; 5 000 bhp = 36 knots
Complement: 14

Of the same class as US "Higgins". Built in Yugoslavia 1951-60. Some have had their torpedo tubes removed. Can be used as FAC-gun when they mount 2—40 mm and either 2 twin 50 cal MG or 2—20 mm (singles). Numbered between 102 and 201.

Transfers: 6 to Sudan in April 1970. 2 to Ethiopia in 1960 (deleted 1969).

"101" Class   *Yugoslavian Navy*

10 TYPE 131 (LARGE PATROL CRAFT)

131	133	135	137	139
132	134	136	138	140

Displacement, tons: 85 standard; 120 full load
Dimensions, feet (metres): 91·9 × 14·8 × 8·3 *(28 × 4·5 × 2·5)*
Guns: 6—20 mm (triple Hispano-Suiza HS 831 mounts)
Main engines: 2 diesels; 900 bhp = 13 knots

Originally used by coastguard until it was absorbed into the navy. Armament varies in individual boats. Built in Yugoslavia 1967-68.
Pennant numbers may be in 300 series.

Type 131   *1968, Yugoslavian Navy*

13 "KRALJEVICA" CLASS (LARGE PATROL CRAFT)

501, 503-4, 506-8, 510-12, 519-21 and 524

Displacement, tons: 195 standard; 250 full load
Dimensions, feet (metres): 134·5 × 20·7 × 7·2 *(41 × 6·3 × 2·1)*
Guns: 1—3 in *(76 mm)* US Mk 22; 1—40 mm; 4—20 mm
A/S weapons: 2 Mousetraps; DCs (some have Hedgehog in place of 3 in gun)
Main engines: Diesels; 2 shafts; 3 300 bhp = 20 knots

Built in 1952-58.

Modernisation: Two RBU 1200 being fitted as elderly 3 in guns are replaced by 40 mm. All export models have this 40 mm shipped.

Transfers: 6 to Indonesia in 1959; 2 to Sudan in 1969; 1 to Ethiopia in 1975; 2 to Bangladesh in 1975.

"KRALJEVICA" Class   *Yugoslavian Navy*

MINE WARFARE FORCES

4 "VUKOVKLANAC" CLASS (MINESWEEPERS—COASTAL)

Name	No.	Builders	Commissioned
BLITVENIC (ex-*Slobodni*)	M 153 (ex-*D 27*)	A. Normand, France	Sep 1957
PODGORA (ex-*Smeli*)	M 152 (ex-*D 26*)	A. Normand, France	Sep 1957
SNAZNI	M 161	Yugoslavia	—
VUKOVKLANAC (ex-*Hrabri*)	M 151 (ex-*D 25*)	A. Normand, France	Sep 1957

Displacement, tons: 365 standard; 424 full load
Dimensions, feet (metres): 140 pp; 152 oa × 28 × 8·2 *(42·7; 46·4 × 8·6 × 2·5)*
Guns: 2—20 mm
Main engines: SIGMA free piston generators; 2 shafts; 2 000 bhp = 15 knots
Oil fuel, tons: 48
Range, miles: 3 000 at 10 knots
Complement: 40

The first three were built as US "off-shore" orders, respectively. *Snazni* was built in Yugoslavia in 1960 with French assistance.

BLITVENIC (ex-*Slobodni*)   *1966, Yugoslavian Navy*

6 "M 117" CLASS (MINESWEEPERS—INSHORE)

M 117	M 118	M 119	M 121	M 122	M 123

Displacement, tons: 120 standard; 131 full load
Dimensions, feet (metres): 98·4 × 18 × 4·9 *(30 × 5·5 × 1·5)*
Guns: 1—40 mm; 2—12·7 mm MG
Main engines: 2 GM diesels; 1 000 bhp = 12 knots

Built in Yugoslav shipyards between 1966 and 1968.

M 121   *1968, Yugoslavian Navy*

4 BRITISH "HAM" CLASS (MINESWEEPERS—INSHORE)

M 141	M 142	M 143	M 144

Displacement, tons: 123 standard; 164 full load
Dimensions, feet (metres): 100 × 21·8 × 5·5 *(32·4 × 6·3 × 1·7)*
Guns: 2—20 mm
Main engines: 2 Paxman diesels; 1 100 bhp = 14 knots
Range, miles: 2 000 at 9 knots
Complement: 22

Built in Yugoslavia 1964-66 under the US Military Aid Programme. Of same design as British "Ham" class.

M 142   *1968, Yugoslavian Navy*

14 "M 301" CLASS (RIVER MINESWEEPERS)

M 301	M 303	M 305	M 307	M 309	M 311	M 313
M 302	M 304	M 306	M 308	M 310	M 312	M 314

Displacement, tons: 38
Gun: 1—20 mm
Main engines: Speed = 12 knots

All launched in 1951-53. Serve on the Danube.

AMPHIBIOUS FORCES

NEW CONSTRUCTION LST

Displacement, tons: 2 980
Dimensions, feet (metres): 334·6 × 46·6 × 10·2 *(102 × 14·2 × 3·1)*
Guns: 2—40 mm D70
Main engines: 2 diesels; 6 800 shp = 8 knots

A new class capable of carrying 6 tanks, a number of LCAs and fitted with a helicopter deck now being built in Yugoslavia.

25 DTK-221-DTM 230 TYPE (LCT)

DTK 221   **DTM 230** onwards

Displacement, tons: 410
Dimensions, feet (metres): 144·3 × 19·7 × 7 *(47·3 × 6·4 × 2·3)*
Guns: 1—20 mm; 2—12·7 mm
Speed, knots: 10
Complement: 15

DTM 230   *B. Hinchcliffe*

Capable of carrying at least two, possibly three of the heaviest tanks. Unlike other tank landing craft in that the centre part of the bow drops to form a ramp down which the tanks go ashore, the vertical section of the bow being articulated to form outer end of ramp. Built in Yugoslavia to German MFP-D3 design.

Transfers: 2 to Sudan in 1969.

2 Ex-ITALIAN MZ TYPE (LCT)

D 206 (ex-*MZ 713*)   **D 219** (ex-*MZ 717*)

Displacement, tons: 225 and 239
Guns: 1—20 mm; 2 MG
Speed, knots: 11

Ex-Italian landing craft. Launched in 1942. Capable of carrying three tanks.

SIEBEL FERRIES

Several ex-German craft are still in use.

CATAMARAN TYPE (LCU)

Displacement, tons: 50 approx

A small craft consisting of two pontoons some feet apart, secured to each other by cross-girders on which stand the bridge and cabins, etc. This vessel appears to be capable of carrying one medium tank or 88 mm guns, to be put ashore by two bridge members which can be seen quite clearly, folded back on the deck. Total number unknown. Can act as minelayers.

Catamaran type   *B. Hinchcliffe*

NEW CONSTRUCTION LCAs

Displacement, tons: 32
Dimensions, feet (metres): 70·2 × 15·1 × 2 *(21·4 × 4·6 × 0·6)*
Gun: 1—20 mm
Main engines: Diesels; 1 125 shp = 22 knots

A programme is under way for the construction of a considerable number of LCAs built of polyester and glass fibre. Probably to be carried in the new class of LSTs.

Note: A number of other amphibious craft of unknown types are also reported.

TRAINING SHIPS

1 "GALEB" CLASS

Name	No.	Builders	Commissioned
GALEB (ex-*Kuchuk*, ex-*Ramb III*)	M 11	Ansaldo, Genoa	1939

Displacement, tons: 5 182 standard
Measurement, tons: 3 667 gross
Length, feet (metres): 384·8 *(117·3)*
Beam, feet (metres): 51·2 *(15·6)*
Draught, feet (metres): 18·4 *(5·6)*
Main engines: 2 diesels; 2 shafts; 7 200 bhp
Speed, knots: 17

Ex-Italian. Launched in 1938. Sunk as an auxiliary cruiser in 1944, refloated and reconstructed in 1952. Now training ship. Also Presidential Yacht. Former armament was four 3·5 inch, four 40 mm and 24—20 mm (six quadruple) guns. The guns were landed. Can act as minelayer.

GALEB   *1972, Yugoslavian Navy*

JADRAN (ex-*Marco Polo*)

Displacement, tons: 720
Dimensions, feet (metres): 190 × 29·2 × 13·8 *(58 × 8·8 × 4·2)*
Sail area, sq ft (m²): 8 600 *(800)*
Main engines: 1 Linke-Hofman Diesel; 375 hp = 8 knots

Topsail schooner. Built in Italy. Launched in 1932. Accommodation for 150 Cadets.

PRESIDENTIAL YACHT

Name	No.	Builders	Commissioned
JADRANKA (ex-*Bjeli Orao*)	—	C. R. dell Adriatico, San Marco, Trieste	Oct 1939

Displacement, tons: 567 standard; 660 full load
Dimensions, feet (metres): 213·2 oa × 26·5 × 9·3 *(60·5 × 7·9 × 2·8)*
Main engines: 2 Sulzer diesels; 1 900 bhp = 18 knots

Launched on 3 June 1939. While in Italian hands was named *Alba*, for some days only, then *Zagaria*.

JADRANKA   *1970, Yugoslavian Navy*

HQ SHIP

VIS

Built in 1956.

SURVEY SHIP

Name	No.	Builders	Commissioned
A. MOHOROVICIC	PH 33	Gdansk Shipyard, Poland	1972

Displacement, tons: 1 475
Dimensions, feet (metres): 240 × 36·3 × 10 *(73·2 × 11·1 × 3·1)*
Main engines: 2 diesels; = 17 knots
Complement: 37

Built in 1971 at the shipyard in Gdansk, Poland, and added to the Yugoslav Navy List in 1972. Of Soviet "Moma" class.

A. MOHOROVICIC   *1972, Yugoslavian Navy*

SALVAGE VESSEL

SPASILAC

New construction to replace ship of same name which was built in Italy in 1929-30—now deleted.

TANKERS

2 PN 24 TYPE (HARBOUR TANKERS)

PN 24   **PN 25**

Built at Split in mid-1950s.

4 PN 13 TYPE (HARBOUR TANKERS)

PN 13 (ex-*Lovcen*)   **PN 14**   **PN 15**   **PN 16**

Displacement, tons: 695 standard
Speed, knots: 8·5

PN 13 (ex-*Lovcen*) was launched in 1932. PN 17 was transferred to the Sudanese Navy in 1969.

1 HARBOUR TANKER

PO 55

Of 600 tons.

2 "KIT" CLASS (HARBOUR TANKERS)

KIT   **ULJESURA**

Of 250 tons.

TRANSPORTS

5 PT 71 TYPE

PT 71—PT 75

Displacement, tons: 310 standard; 428 full load
Dimensions, feet (metres): 141·5 × 22·2 × 16 *(46·4 × 7·2 × 5·2)*
Main engines: 300 bhp = 7 knots

Built at Split and Sibenik in 1953

6 PT 61 TYPE

PT 61—68 (?)

Possibly up to 8 in service. Built at Pula and Sibenik 1951-54.

TUGS

LR 11 (ex-*Basiluzzo*)

Displacement, tons: 108
Main engines: 130 hp = 8 knots

Former Italian tug. Launched in 1915.

PR 51 (ex-*Porto Conte*)

Displacement, tons: 226

Former Italian tug. Launched in 1936.

PR 52 (ex-*San Remo*)

Displacement, tons: 170
Main engines: 350 hp = 9 knots

Former Italian tug and multi-purpose vessel. Launched in 1937.

PR 54 (ex-*Ustrajni*)

Displacement, tons: 160
Main engines: 250 hp = 9 knots

Launched in 1917.

PR 55 (ex-*Snazi*)

Displacement, tons: 100
Main engines: 300 hp = 10 knots

Launched in 1917.

PR 58 (ex-*Molara*)

Displacement, tons: 118
Main engines: 250 hp = 8 knots

Former Italian tug. Launched in 1937.

There are also in service PP1 (ex-*Marljivi*) of 130 tons, LR 67-74 new construction of 130 tons, RRM 11, BM 29, LD 21, LP 21 and RM 27—the last four being small mooring tugs—PR 28 and PR 37.

WATER CARRIERS

| PV 6 | PV 11 | PV 12 |
| PT 12 | PO 54 | +3 |

Of various types and of modern construction.

YACHT

ISTRANKA (ex-*Villa,* ex-*Dalmata*)

Displacement, tons: 260
Dimensions, feet (metres): 132·5 × 16·7 × 6·7 *(40·4 × 5·1 × 2·1)*
Main engines: Diesel; 235 hp = 12 knots

Built in 1896.

ZAIRE

Ministerial

State Commissioner for Defence:
Lieut-Gen Mobuto Sese Seko (President)

Personnel

(a) 1977: 200 officers and men
(b) Voluntary service

Bases

Matadi
Lake Tanganyika

LIGHT FORCES

1 COASTAL PATROL CRAFT

ZAIRE (ex-*President Mobuto,* ex-*General Olsen,* ex-*Congo*)

A 70 ton craft, the first in this naval force.

3 Ex-KOREAN (N) "P 4" CLASS

Displacement, tons: 22
Dimensions, feet (metres): 62·7 × 11·6 × 5·6 *(19·1 × 3·5 × 1·7)*
Guns: 2—14·7 mm MG
Torpedo tubes: 2—18 in
Main engines: 2 diesels; 2 shafts; 2 200 hp = 50 knots
Complement: 12

Transferred 1974.

6 SEWART TYPE (COASTAL PATROL CRAFT)

Displacement, tons: 33
Length, feet (metres): 65 *(19·8)*
Guns: 6 MG
Main engines: 2 GM diesels = 26 knots
Range, miles: 1 000 at 18 knots

Purchased in USA in 1971.

12 COASTAL PATROL CRAFT

Ordered in 1974 in France.

1 COASTAL PATROL CRAFT

Of 18 tons, 25 knots and mounting 3 MG. Purchased in USA in 1968.

3 Ex-US COASTAL PATROL CRAFT

Purchased in 1974. Of same type as Swiftboats.

4 COASTAL PATROL CRAFT

Reported as transferred by China in late 1960s.

ZANZIBAR

Although part of the United Republic of Tanzania, Zanzibar retains a separate Executive and
Legislature, the President of Zanzibar being First Vice-President of Tanzania.

4 VOSPER THORNYCROFT 75 ft TYPE

Displacement, tons: 70
Dimensions, feet (metres): 75 × 19·5 × 8 *(22·9 × 6·0 × 1·5)*
Guns: 2—20 mm
Main engines: 2 diesels; 1 840 hp
Speed, knots: 24·5
Range, miles: 800 at 20 knots
Complement: 11

This was one of the first orders for the new Keith Nelson 75 ft craft. First pair delivered 6 July
1973, second pair 1974.

75 ft Type   *1974, Vosper Thornycroft*

NAVAL AIRCRAFT

NAVAL AIRCRAFT

Notes: (a) For technical details see under country of origin; (b) Class: A Carrier based   B Helicopters   C Land based

Country/ Manufacturer	Strength	Role	Class (See note)	Country of Origin	Max Speed	Service Ceiling	Range	Max Endurance	T/O Weight
ARGENTINA									
McDonnell Douglas Skyhawk (A-4Q)	15	Attack Bomber F/W	A	USA	(a)				
Grumman Tracker (S-2A)	6	Attack A/S, F/W	A	USA					
Grumman Albatross (HU-16B)	3	Amphibian, Search & Rescue, F/W	C	USA					
Aerospatiale Alouette III	4	Helicopter	B	France					
Sikorsky Sea King (S-61D-4)	4	Helicopter	B	USA					
Sikorsky S-61NR	2	Helicopter	B	USA					
Aermacchi MB 326GB	8	Trainer & F/W Light Attack	C	Italy					
Lockheed Neptune (P-2H)	6	Maritime F/W Patrol Bomber	C	USA					
AUSTRALIA									
McDonnell Douglas Skyhawk (A-4G)	14	Attack F/W	A	USA	(Plus 3 TA-4G trainers)				
Lockheed Orion (P-3B)	9	A/S Recce F/W	C	USA	(operated by Air Force)				
Lockheed Neptune (SP-2H)	10	A/S Recce F/W	C	USA	(operated by Air Force; being replaced by P-3Cs)				
Grumman Tracker (S-2E/G)	1	A/S F/W and M.P.	A, C	USA	(12 destroyed by fire 12/1976 being replaced)				
Government Aircraft Factories (GAF) Search Master		F/W Maritime Patrol	C	Australia	168 knots (cruising)	22 500 ft (6 860 m)	730 n. miles at 10 000 ft (3 050 m)		8 500 lb (3 855 kg)
Bell Iroquois (UH-1D)	7	Helicopter	B	USA					
Westland Wessex (HAS.31B)	20	Helicopter	B	UK					
Westland Sea King (HAS 50)	9	Helicopter	B	UK					
BELGIUM									
Aerospatiale Alouette III	3	Coast Guard Helicopter	B	France					
Westland Sea King Mk 48	5	Helicopter	B	UK	(operated by Air Force)				
BRAZIL									
Grumman Tracker (S-2E)	8	A/S F/W	A	USA	(operated by Air Force)				
Bell 47G-2 & 47 J	2	Helicopter	B	USA					
Bell JetRanger II	18	Helicopter	B	USA					
Hughes 269/300	8	Helicopter	B	USA					
Sikorsky Sea King (SH-3D)	5	Helicopter	B	USA					
Westland Wasp	3	A/S Helicopter	B	UK					
Westland Whirlwind	5	Helicopter	B	UK					
Westland Lynx	9	A/S Helicopter	A	UK/ France	Carried on new destroyers and operated by the Air Force				
CANADA									
Sikorsky CHSS-2 Sea King (CH-124)	35	Helicopter	B	USA					
Canadair Argus (CP-107)	31	F/W Maritime Reconnaissance	C	Canada	20 000 ft 274 knots	20 000 ft plus (6 100 m plus)	5 124 n. miles at 194 knots		148 000 lb (67 130 kg)
Canadair CL-215		F/W Amphibian	C	Canada	157 knots (cruising)		1 220 n. miles		Land 43 500 lb (19 731 kg) Sea 37 700 lb (17 100 kg)
Grumman CS2F-3 Tracker (CP-121)	32	F/W A/S	C	USA					
CHILE									
Bell JetRanger	4	Helicopter	B	USA					
Grumman Albatross (HU-16B)	5	Maritime F/W Amphibian	C	USA					
Beech C-45	5	F/W Transport	C	USA					
Douglas C-47	5	F/W Transport	C	USA					
Lockheed Neptune (SP-2E)	4	Maritime Recce F/W	C	USA					

Wing span Rotor diameter	Length	Height	Power Plant	Armament Capacity	Remarks
54 ft 0 in (16·46 m)	41 ft 2·4 in (12·56 m)	18 ft 1½ in (5·52 m)	2 × 400 shp Allison 250-B17B turboprop engines	Provision for underwing stores	Used by Indonesian Navy (Not by Australia)
142 ft 3·5 in (43·38 m)	128 ft 9·5 in (39·25 m)	36 ft 8·5 in (11·19 m)	4 × Wright R-3350 EA-1 turbo-compound radial piston engines 3 700 hp each	15 600 lb of weapons (7 075 kg)	In service with 4 Sqdns. (Nos. 404, 405, 407 and 415)
93 ft 10 in (28·6 m)	65 ft (19·82 m)	29 ft 6 in (8·98 m)	2 × 2 100 hp Pratt & Whitney R-2800 radial piston engines		Used by Greek and Spanish Air Forces for search and rescue (Not by Canada)

Country/Manufacturer	Strength	Role	Class (See note)	Country of Origin	Max Speed	Service Ceiling	Range	Max Endurance	T/O Weight
CHINA (PEOPLE'S REPUBLIC)									
Ilyushin Il-28T	100	Torpedo Bomber	C	USSR (built in China)					
DENMARK									
Aerospatiale Alouette III	8	Helicopter	B	France	Flown from frigates				
FRANCE									
Breguet Br 1050 Alizé	40	A/S F/W	A	France	10 000 ft (3 050 m) 254 knots	26 250 ft (8 000 m)	Normal 1 350 n. miles	7 hrs 40 min	18 100 lb (8 200 kg)
Vought Crusader F-8E(FN)	36	F/W Interceptor	A	USA					
Dassault Etendard IV-M, IV-P	42	F/W Attack Recce	A	France	36 000 ft (11 000 m) Mach 1·02	49 000 ft (15 000 m)	at 442 knots (820 km/h) with ext tanks 1 520 n. miles		22 650 lb (10 275 kg)
Dassault Super Etendard	36 ordered	F/W Fighter	A	France	36 000 ft (11 000 m) above Mach 1		with anti-ship missile 350 n. miles		25 350 lb (11 500 kg)
Aerospatiale Super Frelon SA321G	22	A/S and Minesweeping Helicopter	B	France	at S/L 148 knots	10 325 ft (3 150 m)	at S/L 442 n. miles		28 660 lb (13 000 kg)
Aerospatiale Alouette III	20	Gen-Purpose Helicopter	B	France	At S/L 113 knots	10 500 ft (3 200 m)	290 n. miles		4 840 lb (2 200 kg)
Westland/Aérospatiale Lynx	18 ordered	A/S Helicopter	B	UK/ France					
Breguet Br 1150 Atlantic	38	Long-Range F/W Maritime Patrol	C	France	High Altitude 355 knots	32 800 ft (10 000 m)	4 854 n. miles	At 169 knots 18 hours	95 900 lb (43 500 kg)
Aerospatiale N262	15	F/W Transport	C	France	208 knots	23 500 ft (7 160 m)	With max payload 525 n. miles		23 370 lb (10 600 kg)
Lockheed Neptune (P-2H)	20	F/W Maritime Patrol	C	USA					
GERMANY (FEDERAL REPUBLIC)									
Westland Sea King (HAS Mk 41)	22	Helicopter	B	UK					
Breguet Br 1150 Atlantic	20	F/W Maritime Recce	C	France					
Dornier Do 28D-2 Skyservant	20	F/W Gen Duty	C	Germany	10 000 ft (3 050 m) 175 knots	25 200 ft (7 680 m)	1 090 n. miles		8 470 lb (3 842 kg)
Lockheed Starfighter (F-104G)	120	F/W Fighter	C	USA (Built in Germany)	To be replaced by MRCA				
INDIA									
Ilyushin Il-38 ("May")	3	F/W Maritime Recce	C	USSR					
Breguet Br 1050 Alizé	5	F/W A/S	A	France					
Armstrong Whitworth Sea Hawk	25	F/W Fighter-Bomber	A	UK	Max cruise speed at S/L 512 knots				16 200 lb (7 355 kg)
Aerospatiale Alouette III	18	Helicopter	B	France					
Westland Sea King Mk 42	12	A/S Helicopter	B	UK					
INDONESIA									
Aerospatiale Alouette III	3	Helicopter	B	France					
Grumman Albatross (HU-16A)	5	F/W Maritime Patrol Amphibian	C	USA					
GAF Search Master	6	F/W Maritime Patrol	C	Australia					
IRAN									
Lockheed Orion (P-3F)	6	F/W Maritime Patrol	C	USA	Operated by Air Force				
Sikorsky Sea King (SH-3D)	20	A/S helicopter	B	USA (built in Italy)					
Sikorsky RH-53D	6	Mine Countermeasures	B	USA					
Agusta-Bell 212 ASW	6	Anti-ship Helicopter	B	Italy					
ITALY									
Agusta-Sikorsky SH-3D	24	Helicopter	B	USA (built in Italy)					
Agusta-Bell 204AS	30	A/S Helicopter	B	Italy	At S/L 104 knots	4 500 ft (1 370 m)	340 n. miles		9 500 lb (4 310 kg)
Agusta-Bell 212 ASW	28	A/S Helicopter	B	Italy	At S/L 106 knots		323 n. miles	3 hrs	11 196 lb (5 079 kg)

Wing span Rotor diameter	Length	Height	Power Plant	Armament Capacity	Remarks
51 ft 2 in (15·6 m)	45 ft 6 in (13·86 m)	16 ft 5 in (5·00 m)	1 × 2 100 eshp Rolls-Royce Dart R.Da 21 turboprop	Depth charges, torpedo, rockets, AS.12 missiles	
					Those embarked on *Clemenceau* and *Foch* are fitted to carry 2 Matra R530 missiles each
31 ft 6 in (9·60 m)	47 ft 3 in (14·40 m)	14 ft 1 in (4·30 m)	1 × SNECMA Atar 8B turbojet	2 × 30 mm cannon, 3 000 lb *(1,360 kg)* rockets, bombs, Sidewinder missiles	
31 ft 6 in (9·60 m)	46 ft 11·5 in (14·31 m)	12 ft 8 in (3·85 m)	1 × SNECMA Atar 8K-50 turbojet	2 × 30 mm cannon, rockets, bombs, missiles	Deliveries planned to begin in 1977
62 ft 0 in (18·90 m)	Inc tail rotor 65 ft 10·75 in (20·08 m)	21 ft 10·25 in (6·66 m)	3 × 1 550 shp Turbomeca Turmo III C6 turboshaft engines	Four homing torpedoes, search radar, sonar. Provision for 27 passengers	
36 ft 1·75 in (11·02 m)	42 ft 1·5 in (12·84 m)	9 ft 10 in (3·00 m)	1 × 570 shp Turbomeca Artouste IIIB turboshaft engine	Provision for gun, missiles, torpedoes, MAD equipment	
119 ft 1 in (36·3 m)	104 ft 2 in (31·75 m)	37 ft 2 in (11·33 m)	2 × 6 106 ehp R.R. Tyne R.Ty.20 Mk 21 turboprop engines	Bombs, depth charges, homing torpedoes, rockets or ASMs	
71 ft 10 in (21·90 m)	63 ft 3 in (19·28 m)	20 ft 4 in (6·21 m)	2 × 1 080 hp Turbomeca Bastan VIC turboprop engines	Seating for 29	Used by French Navy as light transports and aircrew trainers
51 ft 0·25 in (15·55 m)	37 ft 5·25 in (11·41 m)	12 ft 9·5 in (3·90 m)	2 × 380 hp Lycoming IGSO-540-A1E piston engines	Seating for 12 or 13	
39 ft (11·89 m)	39 ft 8 in (12·09 m)	8 ft 8 in (2·64 m)	1 × R.R. Nene 103 turbojet	Cannon, bombs or rockets	Operational in carrier *Vikrant*
48 ft (14·63 m)	57 ft (17·37 m)		1 × 1 290 shp General Electric T58-GE-3 turboshaft	2 × Mk 44 torpedoes, dipping sonar	
48 ft (14·63 m)	57 ft 1 in (17·40 m)	14 ft 5 in (4·40 m)	1 × 1 290 shp Pratt & Whitney (Canada) PT6T-3 Turbo Twin Pac twin turboshaft	2 × Mk 44 or Mk 46 torpedoes, depth charges, missiles, dipping sonar	

Country/ Manufacturer	Strength	Role	Class (See note)	Country of Origin	Max Speed	Service Ceiling	Range	Max Endurance	T/O Weight
ITALY—continued									
Breguet Br 1150 Atlantic	18	F/W Long-Range Maritime	C	France	Operated by Air Force				
Grumman Tracker (S-2F)	12	F/W ASW	C	USA					
JAPAN									
Sikorsky Sea King (SH-3A)	80	A/S Helicopter	B	USA (built in Japan)					
Kawasaki-Boeing KV 107/II-3	7	Mine Countermeasures Helicopter	B	Japan USA					
Grumman Tracker (S-2A)	28	F/W A/S	C	USA					
Kawasaki-Lockheed P-2J	82	F/W A/S and Maritime Patrol Bomber	C	Japan	Max cruising 217 knots	30 000 ft (9 150 m)	With max fuel 2 400 n. miles		75 000 lb (34 019 kg)
Lockheed Neptune (P-2H)	40	F/W A/S and Maritime Patrol Bomber	C	USA					
Shin Meiwa PS-1	22	A/S F/W Flying-Boat	C	Japan	Max level at 5 000 ft 295 knots	29 500 ft (9 000 m)	1 169 n. miles	15 hrs	94 800 lb (43 000 kg)
MEXICO									
Grumman Albatross (HU-16A)	4	F/W M.P. Amphibian	C	USA					
Aerospatiale Alouette III	4	Helicopter	B	France					
Catalina PBY-5	5	F/W	C	USA					
NETHERLANDS									
Westland Wasp (HAS Mk 1)	11	Helicopter	B	UK					
Westland Lynx	16	A/S Helicopter	B	UK/France					
Breguet Br 1150 Atlantic	8	F/W A/S	C	France					
Lockheed Neptune (SP-2H)	11	F/W M.P.	C	USA					
Fokker-VFW F.27MPA		M.P. F/W	C	Netherlands	230 knots (cruising)	23 200 ft (7 070 m)	2 215 n. miles		45 000 lb (20 410 kg)
NEW ZEALAND									
Westland Wasp (HAS Mk 1)	2	A/S Helicopter	B	UK					
Lockheed Orion (P-3B)	5	M.P. F/W	C	USA	Operated by R.N.Z.A.F.				
NORWAY									
Westland Sea King (Mk 43)	10	ASR. Helicopter	B	UK	Operated by Norwegian Air Force				
Lockheed Orion (P-3B)	5	M.P. F/W	C	USA	Operated by Norwegian Air Force				
PAKISTAN									
Breguet Br 1150 Atlantic	3	F/W A/S	C	France					
Westland Sea King (Mk 45)	6	A/S Helicopter	B	UK					
PERU									
Grumman Tracker (S-2A/E)	9	F/W A/S	C	USA					
Bell UH-1D/H	13	Helicopter	B	USA					
Bell JetRanger	10	Helicopter	B	USA					
Aerospatiale Alouette III	2	Helicopter	B	France					
Grumman Albatross (HU-16B)	4	MP F/W	C	USA	Operated by Peruvian Air Force				
Fokker-VFW F.27MPA	2	M.P. F/W	C	Netherlands					
POLAND									
Ilyushin Il-28 ("Beagle")	10	F/W Recce & ECM	C	USSR					
PORTUGAL									
Lockheed Neptune (SP-2E)	6	LRMP F/W	C	USA	Operated by Portuguese Air Force				
SOUTH AFRICA									
Westland Wasp (HAS Mk 1)	11	A/S Helicopter	B	UK	Embarked in Destroyers: Jan Van Riebeeck; Simon van der Stel Embarked in Frigates: President Kruger; President Pretorius; President Steyn				
Avro Shackleton MR.3	7	LRMP F/W	C	UK	Operated by S.A.A.F.				
SPAIN									
Hawker Siddeley Matador (Harrier)	5	V/STOL F/W Strike/Recce	A	UK	Supplied via USA for operation from carrier Dedalo (×2 Harrier TAV-8A)				
Agusta-Bell 212 ASW	4	A/S Helicopter	B	Italy					

Wing span Rotor diameter	Length	Height	Power Plant	Armament Capacity	Remarks
97 ft 8·5 in (29·78 m)	95 ft 10·75 in (29·23 m)	29 ft 3·5 in (8·93 m)	2 General Electric T64-IHI-10 turboprop engines and two pod-mounted J3-IHI-7C turbojets	Classified; equipment includes radar smoke detector and MAD	
108 ft 8·75 in (33·14 m)	109 ft 11 in (33·50 m)	31 ft 10·5 in (9·72 m)	4 Ishikawajima-built General Electric T64-IHI-10 turboprop engines each 3 060 ehp	Torpedoes, air-to-surface rockets, bombs, radar, MAD, sonobuoys	Also 3 US-1 search and rescue amphibians
95 ft 2 in (29·00 m)	77 ft 3½ in (23·56 m)	27 ft 11 in (8·50 m)	Two 2 140 shp Rolls-Royce Dart 532-7R turboprop engines	Normally unarmed. Equipment includes underfuselage radome	Used by Peruvian Navy (Not by Netherlands)

Country/ Manufacturer	Strength	Role	Class (See note)	Country of Origin	Max Speed	Service Ceiling	Range	Max Endurance	T/O Weight
SPAIN—continued									
Agusta-Bell 204AS	4	Search & Rescue Helicopter	B	Italy					
Bell AH-1G HueyCobra	20	Armed Helicopter	B	USA					
Sikorsky Sea King (SH-3D)	10	A/S Helicopter	B	USA					
Lockheed Orion (P-3A)	3	M.P. F/W	C	USA	Operated by Spanish Air Force				
Grumman Albatross (HU-16B)	11	F/W M.P. Amphibian	C	USA	Operated by Spanish Air Force				
Hughes 500 M	12	A/S Helicopter	B	USA					
SWEDEN									
Agusta-Bell 206A JetRanger	10	Search and Rescue Helicopter	B	USA					
Boeing Vertol-Kawasaki 107-II	20	A/S & Gen Duty Helicopter	B	USA Japan					
Saab-Scania SH-37 Viggen	15	Maritime Recce F/W	C	Sweden	Mach 2				
SYRIA									
Kamov Ka-25 ("Hormone")	9	A/S Helicopter	B	USSR					
THAILAND									
Grumman Tracker (S-2F)	10	A/S, M.P. F/W	C	USA					
Grumman Albatross (HU.16B)	2	Search and rescue F/W	C	USA					
TURKEY									
Agusta-Bell 205AS	3	A/S Helicopter	B	Italy					
Agusta-Bell 212ASW	3	A/S Helicopter	B	Italy					
Grumman Tracker (S-2A/E)	20	F/W A/S Attack	C	USA					
UNITED KINGDOM									
Hawker Siddeley Buccaneer S Mk 2	16	All weather Strike and Recce F/W	A	UK	at 200 ft Mach 0·85 approx		Tactical radius 1 000 n. miles	9 hours with two flight refuellings	62 000 lb (28 123 kg)
Westland (Fairey) Gannet AEW Mk 3	12	AEW F/W	A	UK	220 knots approx		Approx 695 nm	5-6 hours at 120 knots	
Hawker Siddeley Harrier (AV-8A)	(USMC)	V/STOL F/W Strike & Recce	A	UK	Over 640 knots	over 50 000 ft (15 240 m)	over 3 000 n. miles with one flight refuelling		over 25 000 lb (11 339 kg)
Hawker Siddeley Sea Harrier (FRS.1)	24 ordered	V/STOL Recce Strike Fighter	A	UK					
McDonnell Douglas Phantom F.G.1 (F-4K)	16	Interceptor and Ground Attack F/W	A	USA	Mach 2+		Ferry Range 2 000 n. miles		
Westland/Aerospatiale Gazelle HT.2	29	Helicopter Trainer	B	UK France	At Sea Level 167 knots	16 400 ft (5 000 m)	At S/L with full fuel 361 n. miles		3 970 lb (1 800 kg)
Westland Lynx (HAS.2)	30 ordered	Helicopter Search and Strike	B	UK	148 knots (cruising)		Mission radius 154 n. miles		9 500 lb (4 309 kg)
Westland Sea King (HAS.1 and HAS.2)	69	Helicopter A/S	B	UK	Normal operating 112 knots	10 000 ft (3 050 m)	664 n. miles with normal fuel		21 000 lb (9 525 kg)
Westland Wasp (HAS.1)	80	G/P and A/S Helicopter	B	UK	At S/L 104 knots		approx 234 n. miles		5 600 lb (2 495 kg)
Westland Wessex (HAS.1/3) & (HU.5)	150	A/S, Assault and GP Helicopter	B	UK	At S/L 115 knots	(HAS.1) 14 000 ft (4 300 m)	Max fuel 10% reserve 415 n. miles		13 500 lb (6 120 kg)
Hawker Siddeley Nimrod (MR.1)	46	Long Range Maritime Recce F/W	C	UK	500 knots		Ferry 4 500-5 000 n. miles	12 hrs (typical)	177 500 lb to 192 000 lb (80 510- 87 090 kg)
Avro Shackleton (MR.3)	(SAAF)	L R M Recce AEW F/W	C	UK	Level 152 knots		2 515 n. miles		
Hawker Siddeley (Avro) Shackleton (AEW.2)	12	Airborne Early Warning F/W	C	UK	226 knots			10 hrs	98 000 lb (44 452 kg)
UNITED STATES OF AMERICA									
Rockwell International Bronco OV-10A	114 built	Multi-purpose Counter Insurgency F/W	C	USA	At S/L W/O Weapons 244 knots		Ferry with aux. fuel 1 240 n.m.	Combat radius with max weapon load 198 n. miles	14 466 lb (6 563 kg)
Vought A-7E Corsair II	950 built	Single-seat Attack Aircraft F/W	A	USA	At S/L 600 knots		Ferry 2 800 n. miles		42 000 lb (19 050 kg)
F-8H Crusader	Total all versions 200	Single-seat Fighter F/W	A	USA	F-8A, B, C 868 knots + F-8D, E, H & J nearly Mach 2		F-8A 520 n. miles		34 000 lb (15 420 kg)

Wing span Rotor diameter	Length	Height	Power Plant	Armament Capacity	Remarks
34 ft 9¼ in (10·60 m)	53 ft 5¾ in (16·30 m)	19 ft 0¼ in (5·80 m)	One Volvo Flygmotor RM8A turbojet	Two air-to-air missiles. Provision for attack weapons	
44 ft (13·41 m)	63 ft 5 in (19·33 m)	16 ft 3 in (4·95 m)	Two RR RB 168-1A Spey Mk 101 turbofan engines	Bombs, rockets, air-to-surface missiles—camera. Max load 16 000 lb (7 257 kg)	
54 ft 6 in (16·61 m)	44 ft (13·41 m)	16 ft 10 in (5·13 m)	One Bristol Siddeley Double Mamba 102 turboprop 3 875 ehp	Electronics, early warning for long range ship and aircraft detection	
25 ft 3 in (7·70 m)	45 ft 6 in (13·87 m)	Approx 11 ft 3 in (3·43 m)	One RR Pegasus 103 vectored-thrust turbofan engine	Aden gun pods, bombs, rockets, Sidewinder missiles, flares, camera	In service with USMC and Spain. Total includes 8 TAV-8As
25 ft 3¼ in (7·70 m)	47 ft 7 in (14·50 m)	12 ft 2 in (3·71 m)	One RR Pegasus 104 vectored-thrust turbofan engine	Aden gun pods, bomber, rockets, Sidewinder missiles, air-to-surface missiles, etc	For service from 1979
38 ft 5 in (11·71 m)	62 ft 11·75 in (19·20 m)		Two RR Spey Mk 201 turbofan engines with afterburners	Sparrow III Air-to-air missiles bombs, rockets, etc.	
34 ft 5·75 in (10·50 m)	39 ft 3·25 in (11·97 m)	10 ft 2·25 in (3·15 m)	One 590 shp Turbomeca Astazou IIIA turboshaft engine		
42 ft (12·80 m)	49 ft 9 in (15·16 m)	12 ft 0 in (3·66 m)	Two 900 shp RR BS 360.07.26 Gem turboshaft engines	Two Mk 44 or Mk 46 homing torpedoes, depth charges or missiles	
62 ft 0 in (18·90 m)	72 ft 8 in (22·15 m)	16 ft 10 in (5·13 m)	Two 1 660 shp RR Gnome H 1400-1 turboshaft engines	Dipping sonar type 195 system, radar smoke floats, AD580 doppler navigation, torpedoes, depth charges, machine gun	Data for current Mk 2 version
32 ft 3 in (9·83 m)	40 ft 4 in (12·29 m)	11 ft 8 in (3·56 m)	One RR Bristol Nimbus 503 turboshaft engine, derated to 710 shp	Two Mk 44 homing torpedoes or other stores	
56 ft 0 in (17·07 m)	65 ft 9 in (20·03 m)	16 ft 2 in (4·93 m)	One RR (Bristol) Gnome 112 and one Gnome 113 turboshaft engines, each 1 350 shp	Up to 13 troops or 7 stretchers A/S version (HAS.1) can carry weapons	
114 ft 10 in (35·3 m)	126 ft 9 in (38·63 m)	29 ft 8·5 in (9·08 m)	Four RR RB168 Spey Mk 250 turbofan engines	Bombs, mines, depth charges, MAD, full range ASW detection equipment	Operated by RAF
119 ft 10 in (36·52 m)	87 ft 4 in (26·52 m)	23 ft 4 in (7·11 m)	Four RR Griffon 57A piston engines 2 455 hp each		Operated by SAAF
119 ft 10 in (36·52 m)	92 ft 6 in (28·19 m)	23 ft 4 in (7·11 m)	Four RR Griffon 67 piston engines, 2 450 hp each	Early warning electronics	Operated by RAF
40 ft 0 in (12·19 m)	41 ft 7 in (12·67 m)	15 ft 2 in (4·62 m)	Two 715 ehp Garrett AiResearch T76-G-416/417 turboprops	4 × 0·30 in machine guns, anti-aircraft missiles, bombs, rockets, etc. Max weapon load 3,600 lb (1,633 kg)	
38 ft 9 in (11·80 m)	46 ft 1·5 in (14·06 m)	16 ft 0·75 in (4·90 m)	One Allison TF41-A-2 turbofan	Air-to-air, air-to-surface missiles, guns, rockets, bombs, drop tanks	Total includes A-7A/B/C
35 ft 8 in (10·87 m)	54 ft 6 in (16·61 m)	15 ft 9 in (4·80 m)	One Pratt & Whitney J57-P-20 turbojet	Cannon, rockets, bombs, missiles	Also F-8J/K and RF-8G

Country/ Manufacturer	Strength	Role	Class (See note)	Country of Origin	Max Speed	Service Ceiling	Range	Max Endurance	T/O Weight
UNITED STATES OF AMERICA—*continued*									
Grumman C-2A Greyhound	25	COD Transport F/W	A	USA	At 11 000 ft (3 450 m) 306 knots		At cruising speed and height 1 432 n. miles		54 830 lb (24 870 kg)
Grumman Hawkeye E-2B/C	94	AEW F/W	A	USA	325 knots	30 800 ft (9 390 m)	Ferry 1 394 n. miles		51 569 lb (23 391 kg)
Grumman A-6E Intruder	Total of 546 built	Strike and Recce F/W	A	USA	At S/L 558 knots	46 800 ft (14 265 m)	2 365 n. miles		60 400 lb (27 400 kg)
McDonnell Douglas F-4B Phantom II	Total built 1 189	All Weather Fighter F/W	A	USA	Mach 2·5	Combat 71 000 ft. (21 640 m)	Ferry 1 997 n. miles		54 600 lb (24 765 kg)
McDonnell Douglas A-4M Skyhawk	500	Attack Bomber F/W	A	USA	With 4 000 lb of bombs 561 knots		Ferry 1 740 n. miles		24 500 lb (11 113 kg)
McDonnell Douglas EA-3B Skywarrior	60	Electronic Counter-measure F/W	A	USA	At 10 000 ft 530 knots	45 000 ft (13 780 km)	Normal 2 520 n. miles		73 000 lb (33 112 kg)
Grumman F-14A Tomcat	390 ordered	All Weather Fighter F/W	A	USA	Mach 2·40	Over 56 000 ft (17 070 m)			74 348 lb (33 724 kg)
Grumman E-1B Tracer	88 built	AEW F/W	A	USA	At S/L 230 knots			Endurance at 19 000 ft 156 knots 8 hrs	29 150 lb (13 222 kg)
Grumman S-2E Tracker	180	A/S Attack F/W	A	USA	At S/L 230 knots	21 000 ft (6 400 m)	Ferry 1 128 n. miles	Max endurance 9 hrs	29 150 lb (13 222 kg)
Lockheed S-3A Viking	187 ordered	A/S F/W	A	USA	450 knots	over 35 000 ft (10 670 m)	Ferry 3 000 n. miles+		42 500 lb (19 277 kg)
Rockwell International RA-5C Vigilante	100	Tactical Recce F/W	A	USA	Mach 2·1	64 000 ft (19 500 m)	2 600 n. miles		66 800 lb (30 300 kg)
Sikorsky S-58 Seabat/Seahorse		A/S and GP Helicopter	B	USA	At S/L 107 knots	9 000 ft (2 740 m)	214 n. miles +10% reserve		14 000 lb (6 350 kg)
Bell AH-1J SeaCobra	Total 79	Close Support Helicopter	B	USA	180 knots	10 550 ft (3 215 m)	310 n. miles		10 000 lb (4 535 kg)
Sikorsky SH-3A/D/G Sea King	325	ASW and Transport Helicopter	B	USA	144 knots	14 700 ft (4 480 m)	542 n. miles 10% reserve		18 626 lb (8 450 kg)
Boeing Vertol UH-46D Sea Knight	450 built	Transport and Utility Helicopter	B	USA	144 knots	14 000 ft (4 265 m)	Approx 198 n. miles		Max 23 000 lb (10 433 kg)
Kaman SH-2F Seasprite	100	ASW Helicopter	B	USA	At S/L 143 knots	22 500 ft (6 860 m)	367 n. miles		12 500 lb (5 670 kg)
Sikorsky CH-53A/D Sea Stallion	275	Assault Transport Helicopter	B	USA	170 knots	21 000 ft (6 400 m)	223 n. miles approx.		42 000 lb (19 050 kg)
Sikorsky RH-53D	30	Mine Countermeasures Helicopter	B	USA				over 4 hr	50 000 lb (22 680 kg)
Bell UH-1E	190	Assault Support Helicopter	B	USA	140 knots	21 000 ft (6 400 m)	248 n. miles		9 500 lb (4 309 kg)
Hawker Siddeley AV-8A Harrier	102 built	V/STOL Strike/Recce F/W	A	UK					
Grumman EA-6A/B Prowler	104	ECM/ELINT F/W	A	USA	570 knots at S/L	46 300 ft (14 110 m)	2 182 n. miles with max load		65 000 lb (26 535 kg)
Lockheed C-130 Hercules	117	LR Transport & Recce & Tanker F/W	C	USA	335 knots	33 000 ft (10 060 m)	4 460 n. miles		155 000 lb (70 310 kg)
Lockheed SP-2H Neptune	50	LRMP F/W	C	USA	at 10 000 ft 350 knots	22 000 ft (6 700 m)	3 200 n. miles		79 895 lb (36 240 kg)
Lockheed P-3A/B/C and EP-3E Orion	400	A/S Recce F/W	C	USA	at 15 000 ft 411 knots	28 300 ft (8 625 m)	Mission radius 2 070 n. miles		142 000 lb (64 410 kg)
UNION OF SOVIET SOCIALIST REPUBLICS									
Yakovlev Yak-36 ("Forger-A")	25	VTOL Attack and Reconnaissance	A	USSR	Mach 1·3				22 050 lb (10 000 kg)
Mil ("Haze")		A/S Helicopter	C	USSR					26 455 lb (12 000 kg)
Mil Mi-8 ("Hip")		General Purpose Helicopter	C	USSR	140 knots	14 760 ft (4 500 m)	248 n. miles		26 455 lb (12 000 kg)
Kamov Ka-25 ("Hormone")	200 app.	A/S and Strike Helicopter	B	USSR	119 knots	11 500 ft (3 500 m)	350 n. miles		16 100 lb (7 300 kg)
Tupolev ("Backfire")	30	V/G Recce Bomber F/W	C	USSR	Approx Mach 2·5		Approx 4 775-5 200 n. miles		270 000 lb (122 500 kg)
Tupolev Tu-16 ("Badger")	370	L. Range Bomber Maritime Recce F/W	C	USSR	at 35 000 ft 510 knots	42 650 ft (13 000 m)	With max bomb load 2 605 n. miles		150 000 lb (68 000 kg)
Tupolev Tu-95 ("Bear")	50	L. Range Bomber Maritime Recce F/W	C	USSR	Cruising at 32 000 ft 410 knots		With max load 6 775 n. miles		340 000 lb (154 220 kg)
Tupolev Tu-22 ("Blinder")	60	Recce Bomber F/W	C	USSR	at 40 000 ft Mach 1·4	60 000 ft (18 300 m)	1 215 n. miles		185 000 lb (83 900 kg)
Beriev M-12 ("Mail")	100	A/S Recce Amphibian F/W	C	USSR	329 knots	39 977 ft (12 185 m)	2 160 n. miles		65 035 lb (29 500 kg)

Wing span Rotor diameter	Length	Height	Power Plant	Armament Capacity	Remarks
80 ft 7 in (24·56 m)	56 ft 8 in (17·27 m)	15 ft 11 in (4·85 m)	Two 4 050 ehp Allison T56-A-8A turboprops	10 000 lb freight	
80 ft 7 in (24·56 m)	57 ft 7 in (17·55 m)	18 ft 4 in (5·59 m)	Two 4 910 ehp Allison T56-A-422 turboprops	Early warning and command electronics	Data for E-2C
53 ft 0 in (16·15 m)	54 ft 7 in (16·64 m)	16 ft 2 in (4·93 m)	Two Pratt & Whitney J52-P-8A turbojets	Bombs, missiles and other stores	Total includes A-6A/B/C
38 ft 5 in (11·70 m)	58 ft 0 in (17·76 m)	16 ft 0 in (4·96 m)	Two General Electric J79-GE-8 turbojets with afterburners	Missiles, bombs, rockets	Also F-4J/N and 50 RF-4Bs
27 ft 6 in (8·38 m)	40 ft 4 in (12·27 m)	15 ft 0 in (4·57 m)	One Pratt & Whitney J52-P-408A turbojet	Cannon, bombs, rockets, missiles	Total includes A-4C/E/F/L
72 ft 6 in (22·07 m) Unswept	76 ft 4 in (23·27 m)	22 ft 8 in (6·91 m)	Two Pratt & Whitney J57-P-10 turbojets	Provision for bombs, torpedoes, cannon	Total includes tankers
64 ft 1·5 in (19·54 m)	61 ft 10·5 in (18·89 m)	16 ft 0 in (4·88 m)	Two Pratt & Whitney TF30-P-412A turbofans with afterburners	Guns, missiles, bombs	
72 ft 7 in (22·13 m)	45 ft 4 in (13·82 m)	16 ft 10 in (5·13 m)	Two Wright R.1820-82 piston engines	Early warning and command electronics	
72 ft 7 in (22·13 m)	43 ft 6 in (13·26 m)	16 ft 7 in (5·06 m)	Two 1 525 hp Wright R-1820-82WA piston engines	Depth charges, torpedoes, rockets, sonobuoys	Total includes S-2D/G
68 ft 8 in (20·93 m)	53 ft 4 in (16·26 m)	22 ft 9 in (6·93 m)	Two General Electric TF34-GE-2 turbofan engines	Bombs, depth bombs, rockets, missiles, mines, torpedoes, flares	
53 ft 0 in (16·15 m)	76 ft 7·25 in (23·35 m)	19 ft 5 in (5·92 m)	Two General Electric J79-GE-10 turbojets	Variety of weapons inc. thermo-nuclear bombs	
56 ft 0 in (17·07 m)	56 ft 8·25 in (17·27 m)	15 ft 11 in (4·85 m)	One 1 525 hp Wright R-1820-84B/D piston engine	12 passengers	
44 ft 0 in (13·41 m)	53 ft 4 in (16·26 m)	13 ft 8 in (4·15 m)	One 1 800 shp Pratt & Whitney T400-CP-400 turboshaft	Cannon and rockets	Total includes improved AH-IT
62 ft 0 in (18·90 m)	72 ft 8 in (22·15 m)	16 ft 10 in (5·13 m)	Two 1 400 shp General Electric T58-GE-10 turboshaft	Torpedoes, missiles 840 lb (381 kg) of weapons	Data for SH-3D
51 ft 0 in (15·54 m)	Fuselage 44 ft 10 in (13·66 m) Overall	16 ft 8·5 in (5·09 m)	Two 1 400 shp General Electric T58-GE-10 turboshaft	Up to 10 000 lb load	Total includes CH-46s
44 ft 0 in (13·41 m)	52 ft 7 in (16·03 m)	15 ft 6 in (4·72 m)	Two 1 350 shp GE T58-GE-8F turboshaft	LAMPS equipt. Details in JAWA	
72 ft 3 in (22·02 m)	88 ft 3 in (26·90 m)	24 ft 11 in (7·60 m)	Two 2 850 shp GE T64-GE-6 turboshaft	37 passengers or 24 stretchers with 4 attendants	Data for CH-53D
72 ft 3 in (22·02 m)			Two 4 380 shp GE T64-GE-415 turboshaft	Two machine-guns	
44 ft 0 in (13·41 m)	53 ft 0 in (16·15 m)	12 ft 7·25 in (3·84 m)	One Lycoming T53-L-11 shaft turbine	Machine guns, rockets, 8 passengers or 4 000 lb cargo	Total includes UH-1D/H/L
53 ft 0 in (16·15 m)	59 ft 5 in (18·11 m)		Two Pratt & Whitney J52-P-8A turbojets	Normally unarmed ECM equipment	Data for EA-6B
132 ft 7 in (40·41 m) inc. tip tanks	97 ft 9 in (29·78 m)	38 ft 3 in (11·66 m)	Four 4 508 ehp Allison T56-A-15 turboprop	Cargo up to 26 640 lb (12 080 kg) 92 troops, 64 paras or 74 stretchers	Data for late-model transport
103 ft 10 in (31·65 m)	91 ft 8 in (27·94 m)	29 ft 4 in (8·94 m)	Two 3 500 hp Wright R-3350-32W radial piston + 2 Westinghouse J34 turbojets	8 000 lb (3 630 kg) bombs, torpedoes, depth charges and rockets	
99 ft 8 in (30·37 m)	116 ft 10 in (35·61 m)	33 ft 8½ in (10·29 m)	Four 4 910 ehp Allison T56-A-14 turboprops	Mines, depth bombs, torpedoes	Data for P-3C
23 ft 0 in (7·00 m)	49 ft 3 in (15·00 m)		One conventional turbojet and two lift-jets	Gun pods and rocket pods	Also a two-seat training version ("Forger-B")
69 ft 10¼ in (21·29 m)			Two 1 500 shp Isotov turboshaft		Similar to Mi-8 transport, but with retractable landing gear, undernose radome, towed MAD, boat hull, etc.
69 ft 10¼ in (21·29 m)	82 ft 9¾ in (25·24 m)	18 ft 6½ in (5·65 m)	Two 1 500 shp Isotov TV2-117A turboshaft	Normally unarmed but can carry external stores on outriggers	
51 ft 8 in (15·75 m)	32 ft 0 in (9·75 m)	17 ft 7·5 in (5·37 m)	Two 900 shp Glushenkov GTD-3 turboshaft	A/S torpedoes, flares, small stores	
113 ft (34·45 m)	132 ft (40·23 m)	33 ft (10·06 m)	Possibly two Kuznetsov turbofans	Air-to-surface missiles	
110 ft (33·5 m)	120 ft (36·5 m)	35 ft 6 in (10·8 m)	Two Mikulin AM-3M turbojets	Up to 7 × 23 mm cannon in dorsal, ventral and tail turrets and nose. 19 800 lb (9 000 kg) of bombs or missiles	Total includes flight refuelling tankers
159 ft (48·5 m)	155 ft 10 in (47·5 m)	39 ft 9 in (12·12 m)	Four 14 795 ehp Kuznetsov NK-12MV turboprops	Bombs, missiles, 2 to 6 × 23 mm cannon	
90 ft 10·5 in (27·70 m)	132 ft 11·5 in (40·53 m)	17 ft 0 in (5·18 m)	Two turbojets with afterburners	Cameras. Provision for bombs and missiles	Data for "Blinder-C"
97 ft 6 in (29·70 m)	99 ft (30·20 m)	22 ft 11·5 in (7·00 m)	Two 4 000 shp Ivchenko AI-20D turboprops	Torpedoes, depth charges, sonobuoys, MAD gear, nose radome	

Country/ Manufacturer	Strength	Role	Class (See note)	Country of Origin	Max Speed	Service Ceiling	Range	Max Endurance	T/O Weight
UNION OF SOVIET SOCIALIST REPUBLICS—*continued*									
Ilyushin									
Il-38 ("May")	60	A/S Recce F/W	C	USSR	365 knots	32 800 ft	3 900 n. miles		
URUGUAY									
Bell									
47G-2	2	Helicopter	B	USA					
Grumman									
Tracker (S-2A)	3	A/S Patrol F/W	C	USA					
VENEZUELA									
Bell									
47G	4	Helicopter	B	USA					
Grumman									
Tracker (S-2E)	3	A/S Patrol F/W	C	USA					
YUGOSLAVIA									
Kamov									
Ka-25 ("Hormone")		A/S Helicopter	B	USSR					
Mil									
Mi-8 ("Hip")		Coastal Patrol	B	USSR					

Wing span Rotor diameter	Length	Height	Power Plant	Armament Capacity	Remarks
122 ft 8·5 in (37·4 m)	129 ft 10 in (39·6 m)	33 ft 4 in (10·15 m)	Four 4 250 ehp Ivchenko AI-20 turboprops	A/S weapons, MAD gear, undernose radar	

NAVAL MISSILES

NAVAL MISSILES

(Further details can be found in the current edition of JANE'S WEAPON SYSTEMS)

Country/ Manufacturer	Classifi- cation	Name	No.	Length ft.	Launch Weight, lb.	Powerplant	Guidance	Range n. miles	Mach Speed	Warhead	Remarks
AUSTRALIA Dept of Supply	A/S	Ikara	—	11·3		Solid fuel rocket	Command link	13	—	Torpedo-HE	Acoustic homing torpedo
FRANCE Aerospatiale	SLBM	MSBS	M1	34·1	39 683	Solid fuel rocket 2 stage	Inertial	1 350	—	Nuclear	In "Le Redoubtable" class SSBN
	SLBM	MSBS	M2	35	44 000	as above	Inertial	1 620	—	Nuclear	In production to replace M1
	SLBM	MSBS	M20	35	44 000	as above	Inertial	1 620	—	Thermonuclear MRV	First embarked mid-1976
	SLBM	MSBS	M4	—	—	as above	Inertial	2 000+	—	Thermonuclear with MRV	Production by late 1970s
CNIM	SSM	—	RP14	6·5	118	Solid fuel rocket	Nil	9	—	HE	22 rocket multiple launcher
Matra (with OTO Melara)	SSM	Otomat	—	14·5	1 543	Turbojet	Autopilot Active homer	32	0·9	HE	Sea-skimmer for last 2 miles; can be ASM
Aerospatiale	SSM	Exocet	MM38	17	1 543	2 stage solid fuel rocket	Inertial cruise Active homer	20	1+	220 lb HE	Sea-skimmer throughout flight Variants—AM 38 and 39, air-launched; MM 39, ship-launched version of AM 39; MM 40, improved MM 38 with 40 n. mile range; SM 39, projected submarine launched MM 39
	SSM	—	SS11	3·9	66	2 stage solid fuel rocket	Wire-guided	1·6	330 knots	HE or torpedo	Same characteristics as AS-11 Harpon is very similar with improved guidance
	SSM	—	SS12	6·2	165	2 stage solid fuel rocket	Wire-guided	4·4	—	66 lb HE	Same characteristics as AS-12
Ecan Ruelle	SAM	Masurca	Mk 2	28·2 (with booster)	4 585	2 stage solid fuel rocket	Mod 2 Beam rider. Mod 3. semi active homer	22	2·5 (slant)	105 lbs HE	Mounted in *Colbert, Suffren* and *Duquesne*
	SAM	Hirondelle Super 530	—	—	—	—	—	—	—	—	Project for PDMS for small ships and craft
	SAM	Catulle	—	—	—	—	—	—	—	—	Development. Multi- barrelled rocket system firing salvoes of 40 mm shells
Matra	SAM	Crotale Navale	R440	9·5	176	Solid fuel rocket	Infra-red/ command	5	2·3 (slant)	HE	Being installed (1976) in French Navy
Matra-Hawker Siddeley	ASM	Martel	AS37/ AJ168	12 or 13·2	—	Solid fuel rocket	TV on AJ168 passive radar homing on AS37	30	—	HE	Air-to-surface weapon also in service with RAF
Aerospatiale	ASM	—	AS20	8·5	315	2 stage solid fuel rocket	Radio command	4	—	66 lb HE	In service
	ASM	—	AS30	12·4	1 100	2 stage solid fuel rocket	Radio command	6	1·5	510 lb HE	In service
Matra	AAM	Magic	R550	8·2	176	Solid fuel rocket	Infra-red	4	—	HE	In service 1975
	AAM	—	R530	10·8	430	Solid fuel rocket	Infra-red semi-active radar	9·5	2·7	HE	Proximity fused head
Latecoere	A/S	Malafon Mk 2	—	20·3	3 300	2 stage solid fuel rocket and booster	Radio/acoustic homing	7	450 knots	Torpedo	Torpedo dropped by parachute 875 yards from target
GERMANY Messerschmitt- Bölkow-Blöhm	ASW	Kormoran	—	14·4	1 323	3 stage solid fuel rocket	Active radar	20	0·95	350 lb HE	Suitable for all fixed and rotary-wing aircraft
ISRAEL Israel Aircraft Industries	SSM	Gabriel I and II	—	11·0	882	Two stage solid fuel rocket	Radar or optical with semi-active head	14 26 (Mk 2)	0·7	400 lb HE	Mounted in "Saar" and "Saar IV" classes. Now being exported, eg Singapore, S. Africa
ITALY Sistel	SSM	Sea Killer I (Nettuno)	—	12·3	375	1 stage solid fuel rocket	Beam ride/ radio-command or optical	6+	1·9	77 lb HE	Operational for use in ships or helicopters. Five round launcher in ships
	SSM	Sea Killer II (Vulcano)	—	15·5	661	2 stage solid rocket motor	as above	13	1·9	155 lb HE	
	SSM	Sea Killer III	—	17·4	1 200	1 booster 2 sustainers	Active homer	24	1·9	330 lb HE	Under development
Otomat (with Matra)	SSM	Otomat (see "France")									
Sistel	SAM	Sea Indigo	—	11	266	1 stage solid fuel rocket	Radio command/ beam rider	5·5 (slant)	2·5	46 lb HE	Automatic reloading in ships over 500 tons
	ASM	Airtos	—	12·8	421	1 stage solid fuel rocket	Active radar homing	6	1·5	77 lb HE	All-weather system under development
NORWAY Kongsberg Vaapenfabrikk	SSM	Penguin I and II	—	10	727	2 stage solid fuel rocket	Inertial/infra- red homing	14·5	0·7	264 lb HE	Fitted in frigates and fast attack craft
	A/S	Terne III	—	6·4	298	2 stage solid fuel rocket	Nil	1·5	—	110 lb HE depth charge	Full salvo of six can be fired in 5 seconds Reload time 40 seconds
SWEDEN Saab-Scania	SSM	—	RB 08A	18·8	1 984	Marboré turbo-jet	Radar homing	?100	0·85	HE	For ship and coast artillery use. Entered service 1967
UNITED KINGDOM	SLBM	Polaris A3 (see USA)	—	—	—	—	—	—	—	UK made 3×200 KT Thermo- nuclear MRV	Carried in "Resolution" class
Hawker Siddeley	SAM/ SSM	Sea Dart	CF 299	14·3	1 212	Solid fuel booster Liquid ramjet sustainer	Radar guidance (Type 909) semi-active radar homing	40	—	HE	Fitted in *Bristol* and Type 42 destroyers
	SAM	Sea Slug Mk 1 and 2	—	20	—	4 solid fuel boosters, solid fuel sustainer	Beam-riding (Type 901)	24(Mk 1) (approx)	—	HE Proximity fuse	Surface-to-surface cap- ability. Mk 2 has a longer range and better low-level capability
British Aircraft Corpn.	SAM	Sea Wolf	PX 430	6·5	About 200	Solid fuel rocket	Radio command with TV or radar tracking (Type 910)	—	—	HE	Entire system GWS 25. Lightweight versions for ships smaller than frig- ates are Seawolf Omega and Delta. Normally to be used from 6-barrelled launcher

Country/ Manufacturer	Classifi- cation	Name	No.	Length ft.	Launch Weight, lb.	Powerplant	Guidance	Range n. miles	Mach Speed	Warhead	Remarks
Short Bros and Harland	SAM	Sea Cat	—	4·9	140	2 stage solid fuel rocket	Optical, Radar or TV	1·9	—	HE	Fitted in many systems GWS 20 (visual) GWS 22 and 24 (Radar), M4/3 (Radar), Signaal M40
	ASM	Sea Skua	CL 834	9·2	462	Solid fuel rocket	Radar/radio control radar homing	?5	—	45 lb HE	Developed for use from helicopters
Hawker-Siddeley	AAM	Firestreak	—	10·5	320	Solid fuel rocket	Infra-red homing	4·3	2+	50 lb HE	Being replaced by Red Top (below)
	AAM	Red Top	—	10·8	330	Solid fuel rocket	Infra-red homing	6	3	68 lb HE	A much improved ver- sion of Firestreak
Short Bros and Harland	SAM	Slam (Blow pipe)	—	4·6	40	2 stage solid fuel rocket	Optical with radio guidance	—	—	HE	Privately developed system. Suitable for submarines or surface ships.
USA Lockheed	SLBM	Polaris A3	UGM 27C	32	30 000(3)	2 stage solid fuel rocket	Inertial	2 500	10 at burn-out	Thermonuclear	See USA and UK sec- tions for fitting policy. MRV.
	SLBM	Poseidon (C-3)	UGM 73A	34	65 000	2 stage solid fuel rocket	Inertial	2 500	—	Thermonuclear	As above. Double A3 payload MIRV warhead
	SLBM	Trident I (C-4)	UGM 96A	34·1	70 000	3 stage solid fuel rocket	Inertial	4 000 approx	—	Thermonuclear	MIRV. To replace Poseidon using same tubes
	SLBM	Trident II (D-5)	UGM	45·8	126 000	3 stage solid fuel rocket	Inertial	6 000 approx	—	Thermonuclear	MIRV. For fitting in "Trident" class SSBNs
McDonnell Douglas	SSM	Harpoon	RGM 84	15	1 397	Solid fuel booster Turbojet sustainer	Pre-programmed Active radar homing	50/60 (s/m)	0·9	HE	For general surface-ship fitting. Submarine ver- sion under trial
GDC-Convair	SLCM	Tomahawk	BGM 109	20·5	2 400-2 700	Solid boost- turbofan cruise	TAINS (Strat) Inertial with radar homing (Tact)	1 750 (Strat) 275 (Tact)	475 knots	HE (Tact) Nuclear (Strat)	Under development in both strategic and tactical forms in parallel with ALCM
	ASM	Harpoon	AGM 84	15	1 110	As RGM 84	As RGM 84	60	0·9	HE	
	ASM	Condor	AGM 53	13·8	2 130	1 solid fuel rocket	Radio control TV homing	40-60	1·1	HE (Possible nuclear)	For carrier-borne A/C particularly A6. Production planned
Maxson	ASM	Bullpup A and B	AGM 12B and C	7(A) 10·5(B)	571(A) 1 785(B)	1 liquid fuel rocket	Command	7(A) 10(B)	2	HE 250 lb(A) 1 000 lb(B)	Operational 1959
NASC/NWC	ASM	Shrike	AGM 45	10	390	1 solid fuel rocket	Passive radar homing	8	2	HE	Production 1963
Martin, Marietta	ASM	Walleye	AGM 62	11·2	1 100	Nil	TV guided	35 (Wall- eye II)	—	HE	Details are for Walleye 1 Walleye 2 is larger (2 340 lbs) with 2 000 lb HE head. Glide-bombs
GDC-Pomona	ASM	Standard ARM	AGM 78	15	1 800	Dual-thrust solid fuel rocket	Passive Radar homing	35	2	HE	Production 1968
GDC-Pomona	SAM	Standard-MR (SM-1)	RIM 66	14·4	1 300	Dual thrust solid fuel rocket	Semi-active radar homing	13	—	HE	To be used with AEGIS missile system (MR). Tartar replacement
GDC-Pomona	SAM	Standard (SM-1)	RIM 66C		—	—	—	60+	—	—	Mid-course guidance for long-range Talos replacement
GDC-Pomona	SAM	Standard-E2 (SM-1)	RIM 67	26·2	2 900	2 stage solid fuel rocket	Semi-active radar homing	35+	—	HE	SSM capability. Terrier replacement (ER)
Raytheon	SAM	Seasparrow	RIM 7H	12	380	1 solid fuel rocket	Semi-active radar homing	12(E) 24+(F)	—	HE	Can also be used as SSM. UK version XJ 521. Mk 25 or 29 (NATO) launcher
Bendix A/S	SAM	Talos	RIM 8F, G and H	31·3 (booster)	7 000	Solid fuel booster ram-jet sustainer	Beam rider semi-active radar homing	65+	2·5	HE/ nuclear	SSM capability. RIM H has anti-radiation housing. Replacement by RIM 66C
GDC-Pomona	SAM	Tartar	RIM 24B	15	1 425	Dual-thrust solid fuel rocket	Semi-active radar homing	14	2	HE	Ceiling 40 000 ft Replacement by RIM 66
GDC-Pomona	SAM	Terrier	RIM 2F	26·5 (booster)	3 000	2 stage solid-fuel rocket	Semi-active radar homing	20	2·5	HE	Ceiling 65 000 ft Operational 1963 Replacement by RIM 67
NWC-Hughes	AAM	Agile	AIM 95	8	250	Solid fuel	Infra-red	2	—	HE	Planned replacement for Sidewinder
Hughes	AAM	Phoenix	AIM 54	13	985	1 solid-fuel rocket	Radar homing	69 +	2+	HE	In use in F14 Operational 1973
Raytheon/NWC/ Philco Ford	AAM	Sidewinder-1B	AIM 9G, J H and L	9·5	185	1 solid fuel rocket	Infra-red	9	2	HE	Ceiling 50 000 ft+ First AIM9B entered service 1962
Raytheon	AAM	Sparrow III	AIM 7E and F	12	450(E) 500(F)	1 solid fuel rocket	Semi-active radar homing	12(E) 24+(F)	3·5	HE	For carrier-borne aircraft
Honeywell	A/S	Asroc	RUR 5	15	1 000(Mk 44) 570(Mk 46)	1 solid fuel rocket	Pre-programme	1—6	—	Mk 44 or 46 torpedo or Nuclear D/C	Fired from multi- barrelled launcher. Mk 26 in later ships. 10 mile version under development
Goodyear	A/S or anti- surface- ship	Subroc	UUM 44	21	4 000	2 stage solid fuel rocket	Pre-programme inertial	30	1+	Nuclear	Fired from normal 21 in torpedo tubes
USSR (NATO designa- tions used— further details at head of USSR section)	SLBM	Sark	SS-N-4	37·5	—	?2 stage solid fuel rocket	Inertial	300	—	Nuclear	Operational 1958
	SLBM	Serb	SS-N-5	35	—	2 stage solid fuel rocket	Inertial	700	—	Nuclear megaton	Operational 1963
	SLBM	Sawfly	SS-N-6	42	—	2 stage solid fuel rocket	Inertial	1 300 (1 600)	—	Nuclear (MRV in later versions)	Operational 1967
	SLBM	—	SS-N-8	45 (est)	—	?	Inertial	4 200 5 600 (Mk II)	—	Nuclear (MRV)	Operational 1973 Mark II in 1976-77
	SLBM	—	SS-N-13	—	—	Inertial	350	—	—	Nuclear	Possibly anti-task Force. Status not certain
	SLBM	—	SS-N-17	—	—	?	Inertial	2 400	—	Nuclear	Probably for Yankee class in 1977
	SLBM	—	SS-N-18	45 (est)	—	?	Inertial	4 600	—	Nuclear Probably MRV	Probably operational in Delta II Class 1977
	SSM	Scrubber	SS-N-1	22·5	—	—	Radar Infra-red homing	130	0·9	—	Operational 1958. Soon obsolete
	SSM	Styx	SS-N-2	15	—	2 stage solid fuel rocket	Active radar homing	23	0·9	HE	Operational 1960

Country/ Manufacturer	Classifi-cation	Name	No.	Length ft.	Launch Weight lbs.	Power plant	Guidance	Range n. miles	Mach Speed	Warhead	Remarks
USSR— continued	SSM	Shaddock	SS-N-3	36	—	2 boosters Turbojet sustainer	Radar, mid-course guidance Radar or IR homing	150-250	1·5	HE or nuclear	Operational 1961-62
	SLCM	—	SS-N-7	22	—	—	—	30	1·5	—	Operational 1969-70 Submarine launched from dived
	SSM	—	SS-N-9	30 (est)	—	—	Radar with mid-course guidance	150	1·0+	HE or nuclear	Operational 1968-69. In "Nanuchka" class
	SSM	—	SS-N-12	—	—	—	? Radar—mid course guidance	? 250	—	—	Replacement for Shaddock
	SAM	Goa	SA-N-1	22 (booster)	—	2 stage solid fuel rocket	Beam-rider semi-active radar	17	2	HE	Operational 1961
	SAM	Guideline	SA-N-2	34·7	—	Solid booster liquid sustainer	Radar	25	3·5	HE (290 lb)	
	SAM	Goblet	SA-N-3	20	—	2 stage solid fuel rocket	—	20	—	HE	
	SAM	—	SA-N-4	—	—	—	—	20	—	—	Probably PDMS
	ASM	Kennel	AS-1	27·9	—	1 Turbojet	Command with radar homing	55	0·9	—	Obsolete
	ASM	Kipper	AS-2	31	—	1 Turbojet	Autopilot. Radar homing	115	1·0+	—	Operational 1960
	ASM	Kangaroo	AS-3	49·2	—	1 Turbojet	—	400	1·5+	—	Operational 1961
	ASM	Kitchen	AS-4	37	—	1 stage liquid fuel rocket	? Inertial guidance	185?	2+	—	Operational 1965
	ASM	Kelt	AS-5	30·8	—	1 stage liquid fuel rocket	Active radar homing	120	0·9	—	Operational 1968
	ASM	—	AS-6	—	—	1 stage	—	150	3	—	Operational 1970-71. Badger and Backfire
	A/S	—	FRAS I	—	—	—	?Pre-programme	15	—	?nuclear	Operational 1968 in "Moskva" class on SUWN-1 mounting
	A/S	—	SSN-14	—	—	—	—	25	—	—	Operational 1968 in Kresta II, Kara and Krivak classes
	A/S	—	SSN-15	—	—	—	—	20	—	?nuclear	Operational 1974? for use from submarines in A/S operations

NAVAL RADAR

Country/Number	Type	Transmitter frequency	Transmitter peak power	Range
DENMARK				
Scanter	I Band Navigation Radar	9 375±30 MHz	20 KW± 1dB Measured at output flange	—
FRANCE				
ELI 4	Naval IFF Interrogator	1 030± 0·5 Mcs	Selectable 0·5 or 2 kW	—
ELR 3	IFF Transponder	—	—	—
Triton	G/H band 5 cm air and surface surveillance radar	G/H Band	200 kW	Air target 30 km. Surface horizon
Castor TRS	3200 Band target tracking radar	I/J Band Tunable	36 kW	—
Pollux	I/J Band target tracking radar	I/J Band	200 kW	20 m
Pollux II	Improved version of above	—	—	—
Calypso II	TH D 1030 I Band S/M Radar	I/J Band (variable)	70 kW	—
Calypso III	TRS 3100 I Band S/M Radar	—	—	—
Jupiter	TH D 1077 long range surveillance Radar C Band 2 MW	— D Band 23 cm	— 2 MW	— 200 km
Ramses	TH D 1022 short range nav & surveillance radar	I Band	36 kW	60 nm
Lynx	TH D 1051	—	—	—
Saturne 11-30	TH D 1041. TR5.3043	E/F Band	1 MW	—
Sea Tiger	Surveillance radar	E/F Band	Average 1 kW	60 nm on 2 m² fluctuation target—with P.D 50%
DRBC 32	Gun fire control radar	I/J Band	—	—
DRBI 10	Air surveillance radar	E/F Band	Between 1 and 2 MW	Between 100 and 140 nm
DRBV 13	Air search radar	E/F Band	—	—
DRBV 20	Long range search radar	—	—	—
DRBV 22	Search radar	D Band	—	—
DRBV 23	Air search and surveillance	D Band (23 cm)	—	—
DRBR 51	Tracking and missile guidance	I Band	—	—
DRBI 23	Surveillance and target designator	D Band (23 cm)	—	—
INTERNATIONAL				
EX 77 Mod O	Director for NATO Sea Sparrow	Probably I Band	—	—
ITALY				
Argus 5000	Early warning radar	—	5 MW	—
Orion 250	Fire control radar	I/J Band	—	—
Orion RTN 10X	Fire control radar	I/J Band	—	40 nm
Orion RTN 16X	Monopulse fire control radar	I/J Band	—	—
Orion RTN 20 X	Fire control radar	I/J Band	—	—
Orion RTN 30X	Fire control radar	I/J Band	—	—
RAN 2C	Surveillance radar	G/H Band	—	—
RAN 3L	Early warning radar	D Band	—	Approx 200 nm
RAN 7S	10 cm air and surface search radar	10 cm	—	—
RAN 10S	Air and sea search on small ships	E/F Band	—	—
RAN 11L/X	Air warning and weapons control	D and I/J Band	28 kW D Band, 80 kW I/J Band	—
RAN 13X	Search radar	I/J Band	—	—
RAN 14X	Low altitude and surface search	I/J Band	—	—
Sea Hunter	Search radar	I/J Band	180 kW	—
Sea Hunter	Tracker radar	I/J Band	—	—
SPQ 2D	Search radar	I/J Band	—	—
3 RM	—	—	7 or 20 kW	—
NETHERLANDS				
DA 05	Naval surveillance	E/F Band	—	—
	Naval height finder	—	—	—
LW 02	Air surveillance	D Band 23 cm	500 kW	100 nm
LW 04	Air surveillance	D Band	—	—
ZW 08	Surface warning and navigation	I/J Band	—	—
LW 08	Early warning and weapon detection	D Band	—	145 nm air target
ZW 06	Surface search and navigation	I/J Band	—	—
M 20	Fire control	I/J Band	—	—
3 D MTTR	Multi target tracking radar	No details released	—	—
M 40	Fire control	No details released	—	—
ZW 03	Surface warning & nav radar	I/J	—	—
SWEDEN				
9 GR 600	Transmitter/receiver	I Band	200 kW	—
9 LV 200	Mk 2 Tracking radar	J Band	65 kW	—
SUBFAR	S/M radar	I Band	—	—
UNITED KINGDOM				
	Naval IFF 800 series. Comprising IFF 800-825-825M	—	—	—
MRS 3/GWS 22	Fire control radar	—	—	—
AWS/2/3/4/5	Naval surveillance	E/F Band	—	60 nm
PTR 461	Shipborne IFF transponder	—	—	—
S604 HN	Search radar	D Band	2·3 MW	—
S 810	Surveillance radar	I Band Tunable	200 kW	—
ST 80 1/2	Naval Tracking Radar	I Band	—	—
RN Type 901	Missile guidance for Seaslug	?G/H Band	—	—
RN Type 909	Target tracking for Sea Dart	?G/H Band	—	—
RN Type 910	Target tracking for Sea Wolf	I/J Band	—	—
RN Type 912	Fire control radar	I Band	—	—
RN Type 965	Long range air search	Metric	—	—
RN Type 967	Air surveillance	E/F Band	—	—
RN Type 968	Surface surveillance	D Band	—	—
RN Type 975	Surface warning	I/J Band	50 kW nominal	48 nm
Type 9752W	Mine Hunting & Underwater Detection	I/J Band	—	—
RN Type 978	Navigation radar	I Band 3 cm	—	—
RN Type 992Q	General purpose radar	E/F Band	—	—
RN Type 1006	High definition navigation radar	I Band	—	64 nm

P.R.F.	Manufacturer	Remarks
Short NOM 4000 Hz±200 Hz Long NOM 2000 Hz±200 Hz	TERMA	
—	LMT	Receiver frequency: 1 090 Mc/s
—	LMT	Includes selective identification feature and side lobe suppression
—	Thomson CSF	Used with Castor or Pollux in Vega series; 200 kW
Variable	Thomson CSF	Used in some versions of Vega series fire control system; 20 kW
—	Thomson CSF	Used in some versions of Vega series fire control system; 200 kW
Variable	Thomson CSF	Used for surveillance and navigation; 70 kW
—	Thomson CSF	Improvement of above
—	Thomson CSF	
450 per sec	Thomson CSF	Naval air surveillance radar (long range)
—	Thomson CSF	
—	Thomson CSF	Dual radar. Coastal mine watching system
—	Thomson CSF	Medium range air and surface surveillance radar
—	Thomson CSF	Can be used in Thomson CSF series ship fire control systems
—	Thomson CSF	A, B, C, D, E versions fitted in various classes of French ships
—	Thomson CSF	Robinson scanner
—	Thomson CSF	Pulse doppler air search radar. Multi mode operation
—	Thomson CSF	Operates in metric wave band
—	Thomson CSF	Search radar A.C. and D versions in service on French and other vessels
—	Thomson CSF	Long range naval air search and surveillance radar
—	Thomson CSF	Part of Masurca surface-to-air missile system
—	Thomson CSF	3-Dimensional surveillance-target designator radar. Stacked beam system
—	NATO Consortium	Provides search, target designation tracking and illumination for Sea Sparrow point defence missile system
—	Selenia	High power. Ship's early warning radar
—	Selenia	Used in NA 9. System conical scan; 200 kW
—	Selenia	Fire Control Radar used by R.N.
—	Selenia	
—	Selenia	Used in Dardo system
—	Selenia	Used in Albatros system
—	Selenia	Dual purpose air and surface surveillance radar
—	Selenia	Digital. Signal processing
—	Selenia	Air and surface target warning
—	Selenia	Air and surface surveillance
—	Selenia	D Band air detection, I/J Band surface detection
—	Selenia	Surface and low flying search
—	Selenia	Low altitude and surface search radar
Variable	Contraves	
—	Contraves	
—	SMA	Surface search and short range air search
750-6 000 Hz range	SMA	Series of I Band nav and surface warning radars
—	Signaal	Air surveillance surface warning. Target designation for fire control and weapon direction systems
—	Signaal	Probably similar to SGR 109
—	Signaal	Long range air surveillance
—	Signaal	Long range air surveillance
—	Signaal	
—	Signaal	
—	Signaal	
—	Signaal	
—	—	IFF/SIF secondary radar integrated
—	Signaal	
—	Signaal	Anti sea skimmer radar high power version of WO8
1-3 000 Hz	Philips	
Approx 2 000 Hz	Philips	Frequency agility naval fire control
Variable 250-3 000/sec	Philips	Air and surface search
—	Cossor	
—	Sperry	Control of guns MRS 3 and Seacat missiles GWS/22
400-1000 pps	Plessey	
—	Plessey	Ship identification
—	Marconi	Long range surveillance
1 500 or 4 400 Hz	Marconi	Lightweight surveillance radars
—	Marconi	Target tracking
—	Marconi	
—	Marconi	Target tracking and illuminating services
—	Marconi	Also target designation for guided weapons and IFF Mk 10 facilities
—		Can be combined with Type 968 for medium range to short range defence radar
—	Kelvin Hughes	
—	Kelvin Hughes	U/W version of Type 975
—	Decca	
—	Marconi	
—	Kelvin Hughes	

Country/Number	Type	Transmitter frequency	Transmitter peak power	Range
UNION OF SOVIET SOCIALIST REPUBLICS				
Square Tie	Lightweight search radar	I Band	—	—
Square Head	Naval radar	—	—	—
Pop Group	Fire control radar	? G-J Band	—	—
Head Net B	Air surveillance radar	Probably D or E/F Band	—	—
Drum Tilt	Fire control radar	Probably I Band	—	—
Sun Visor	Fire control radar	Probably I or G/H Band	—	—
Cylinder Head	Fire control radar	—	—	—
Big Net	Search radar	D or E/F Band	—	—
Fan Song E	Naval radar	G/H Band	—	—
Hair Net	Naval radar	—	—	—
Plinth Net	Search radar	—	—	—
Pot Drum	Naval radar	Probably I Band	—	—
Pot Head	Naval radar	Probably I Band	—	—
Scoop Pair	Surface target radar	—	—	—
Hawk Screech	Gun fire control	Probably I Band. Possibly G Band	—	—
Owl Screech	Gun fire control	Probably I Band. Possibly G Band	—	—
High Lune	Naval height finder	Probably E/F Band	—	—
Muff Cob	Fire control radar	G/H or I Band	—	—
Slim Net	Surface warning radar	Probably E/F Band	—	—
Flat Spin	Surveillance radar	D or E/F Band	—	—
Head Net C	Air surveillance radar	—	—	—
Top Sail	3D radar	Probably D Band	—	—
Head Light	Fire control	Probably I and G/H Band	—	—
Strut Curve	Search radar	Probably E/F Band	—	—
Peel Group	Fire control radar	Probably G/H Band	—	—
Head Net A	Air surveillance radar	D or E/F Band	—	—
Boat Sail	Submarine radar	D or E/F Band	—	—
Skin Head	Naval radar	Probably I/J Band	—	—
Top Trough	Surveillance radar	—	—	—
Knife Rest B	Early warning radar	—	—	—
High Sieve	Surface search radar	—	—	—
Top Bow	Gun fire control radar	—	—	—
Seagull	Air search	—	—	—
UNITED STATES OF AMERICA				
RTN 10	Fire control for Sea Sparrow III	I Band	—	—
SPG 49	Guidance for Talos and Terrier. Surface-to-air	Used with SPW 2	—	120 km
SPG 51	Tartar missile guidance	I Band	—	—
SPG 55	Terrier missile guidance radar	G/H Band	Approx 50 kW	50 km
SPG 60	Doppler search and tracking	I/J Band	—	50 nm
SPQ 9	Lockheed MK 86 fire control system	I/J Band	—	20 nm
SPQ 5	Missile guidance	G/H Band	—	—
SPS 6	Air surveillance	D Band	Approx 500 kW	100-200 km
SPS 10	Surface search	G/H Band	—	—
SPS 12	Long range air search	D Band	0·1 and 1·0 MW	—
SPS 30	Long range 3D radar	—	—	—
SPS 32	Air and surface surveillance	—	—	—
SPS 33	Tracking radar	—	—	—
SPS 37	Long range air surveillance	—	—	—
SPS 39	3D radar air surveillance	—	—	200-300 km
SPS 40	Search and surveillance for air targets	?E/F Band	?1 MW	—
SPS 43	High power very long range search radar	? Metric	1-2 MW	—
SPS 48	Air surveillance radar	? E/F Band	—	—
SPS 49	Air search radar	—	—	—
SPS 52	3D air surveillance	?E/F Band	—	—
SPS 55	Surface search and navigation	—	130 kW	—
SPS 58	Pulse Doppler air search and target acquisition radar	D Band	—	—
SPY 1	Multi function array radar	E/F Band	Several MW	—

P.R.F.	Manufacturer	Remarks
—	—	Probably include target detection and tracking for anti-ship missile direction.
—	—	Possible IFF interrogator or directional array for transmission of guidance signals to surface-to-surface missiles
—	—	Associated with Soviet Navy's SAN-4 surface-to-air missile system
—	—	Air search and surveillance and in connection with fire control radars carried for direction of surface-to-air missiles and guns
—	—	
—	—	Believed now obsolete
—	—	Very large long range air surveillance radar
—	—	Shipboard version of Guideline surface-to-air missile control and guidance radar
—	—	Medium range general purpose search and surveillance radar
—	—	Medium range general purpose search radar
—	—	Small surface search radar
—	—	Surface target detection; short range
—	—	Twin radar group for Shaddock SSM
—	—	
—	—	
—	—	Gun fire control
—	—	High definition surface target radar
—	—	Long range air search radar
—	—	Dual V beam 3D installation of Head Net A
—	—	Long range 3D air surveillance radar
—	—	Missile fire control group
—	—	Lightweight search radar
—	—	Missile control group for Goa
—	—	Long range air surveillance radar
—	—	Air search for submarine pickets
—	—	Surface target detection radar for light forces
—	—	High definition surface target radar
—	—	Long wavelength early warning radar
—	—	Target acquisition radar for naval guns
—	—	Long range air search radar
—	Raytheon	
—	Sperry	
—	Raytheon	Part of Mk 73 FCS
—	Sperry	
—	Lockheed	
—	Lockheed	
—	Sperry	Now obsolescent
—	Westinghouse	
—	Sylvania	
—	RCA Moorestown	
—	GEC	
—	Hughes	Companion in use with SPS 33
—	Hughes	
—	Westinghouse	
—	Hughes	
—	Lockheed	
—	Westinghouse	Generally carries IFF antenna
—	ITT-Gilfillan	3D long range air surveillance
—	—	Narrow beam very long range for air search
—	Hughes	
750-2 250 pps	Cordion Electronics	Replacement for SPS 10.
—	Westinghouse	Designed to operate with USN point defence Surface Missile System
—	—	Under development for US Navy Aegis fleet air defence missile system

TORPEDOES

No.	Name	Length	Dia.	Weight	Speed knots	Range	Explosive charge	Guidance	Target/Role	Carrier
FRANCE										
Z 16	Now probably obsolete	7 200 mm	550 mm	1 700 kg	30	10 km	300 kg	Preset plus Pattern	A/S	S/M
E 14	**Acoustic Torpedo**	4 291 mm	550 mm	900 kg	25	5 500 m	200 kg	Acoustic	A/Surface (S/M up to 20 knots)	S/M
E 15	**Acoustic Torpedo**	6 000 mm	550 mm	1 350 kg	25	12 000 m	300 kg	Acoustic	A/Surface 0-20 knots +S/M at shallow depth	S/M
L 3	**Acoustic Torpedo**	4 300 mm	550 mm	910 kg	25	5 500 m	200 kg	Acoustic	A/S 0-20 knots up to 300 m depth	Ship or S/M
L 4	**Acoustic Torpedo**	3 130 mm inc parachute stabiliser	533 mm	540 kg	30			Acoustic	A/S up to 20 knots	Airborne
L 5 Mod 1	**Multi purpose**		533 mm	1 000 kg	35			Direct Attack or Programmed Search		Ship
L 5 Mod 3			533 mm	1 300 kg	35					S/M
FEDERAL REPUBLIC OF GERMANY										
SST 4	**Wire Guided Torpedo**	6 390 mm inc 460 mm wire casket	533 mm					260 kg	Wire Guided Active Passive Sonar Homing	A/Surface	Ship or S/M
	Sea Eel	6 390 mm	533 mm	1 370 kg	35/23	13/28 km		Wire guided, active/ Passive Sonar Homing	A/S	S/M or FPBs
SUT Dual purpose version of Sea Eel not yet in service										
ITALY										
G 6E	**Kangaroo**	6 200 mm	533 mm					Wire guided		
A 184		6 000 mm	533 mm					Wire Guided Active/Passive Sonar	A/S or A/Surface	Ship or S/M
A 244		2 700 mm	324 mm					Homing Course and Depth		Ship or Aircraft
SWEDEN										
Type 41		2 440 mm	400 mm	250 kg				Passive Homing Sonar	Limited A/Surface or A/S	S/M
Type 42		2 440 mm + 180 mm wire section	400 mm	270 kg				Passive Homing Sonar or Wire Guidance	A/S	Ship S/M & Helicopter
Type 61		7 025 mm	533 mm	1 765 kg			250 kg	Wire Guided	A/Surface	Ship or S/M
UNITED KINGDOM										
Mark 8		6 700 mm	533 mm	1 535 kg	45	4 500 m		Pre Set Course Angle & Depth	A/Surface	S/M
	Tigerfish	6 464 mm	533 mm	1 550 kg	Dual high or low			Wire Guided Acoustic Homing	Primarily A/S	S/M
MW 30 Mark 44	**Drill & Practice Torpedo**	2 560 mm	324 mm	233 kg				Active/Acoustic Homing	A/Surface	Aircraft, Ship, Helicopter
UNITED STATES OF AMERICA										
Mark 14	Mod 5	5 250 mm	533 mm	1 780 kg	32·46	46·9 km	230 kg	Preset depth & Course Angles	A/Surface	S/M
Mark 37	Mod 3	3 400 mm	484·5 mm	643 kg	24	—	150 kg H.E.	Free running then Sonar Auto Homing	A/S	S/M
Mark 37	Mod 2	4 090 mm	484·5 mm	760 kg	24	—	150 kg H.E.	Wire Guidance Active/Passive Sonar Homing	A/S	S/M
NT 37 2C Dimensions and warheads as for Mk 37 Mod 2/3 but speed increased by 40%, range by over 100% and wire guided capability in excess of 13 000 yds. Improvements to sonar and homing logic plus additional A/Ship attack modes.									A/Surface, A/S	Ship or S/M
Mark 45	**Mod 1** Astor (Mod 1)	5 760 mm	484·5 mm	995·8 kg		approx 11 km	Nuclear Warhead	Wire Guided	A/S	S/M withdrawn from service
Mark 46	**Mod 0, 1 and 2**	2 670 mm	324 mm	257 kg 229 kg (1 and 2)		—	—	Active/Passive Acoustic Homing	A/S	Ships, (Mk 32 or Asroc), Aircraft, helicopter Mod 1 and 2 have liquid propellant
Mark 46	**Captor Mod 4** Mk 46 inserted in mine casing and sown in narrow seas. See Jane's Weapon Systems 2541.441.									
Mark 48	**Mod 2**	5 800 mm	533 mm	1 566 kg	93 km/h	46 km		Wire Guided and Active/Passive Acoustic Homing	A/Surface A/S	S/M
—	**Freedom Torpedo**	5 720 mm	484·5 cm	1 237 kg	40	10 000 yds	minimum of 295 kg	Wire Guided to hit or free run to intercept followed by pattern run if target missed	A/Surface	Ship or S/M
DEXTOR (Deep EXperimental TORpedo) Mk 48 replacement										
ALWT (Advanced LightWeight Torpedo) Mk 46 replacement										
UNION OF SOVIET SOCIALIST REPUBLICS										
—	—	—	533 mm	—	—	—	—	—	—	Surface ships, submarines and aircraft
—	—	? 16 ft (5 m)	406 mm	—	—	—	—	—	—	

SONAR EQUIPMENT

Country/Designation	Description	Manufacturer	Mounting
AUSTRALIA			
Mulloka	Sonar project for Royal Australian Navy	—	—
Barra	Project Barra is RAAF/RAN project to develop advanced sonobuoy and airborne detection system	Amalgamated Wireless	—
CANADA			
HS 1000	Lightweight search and attack sonar either hull mounted or towed	Canadian Westinghouse	—
SQS 505	Medium search/attack sonar	Canadian Westinghouse	—
SQS 507 (Helen)	Lightweight variable depth towed sonar	Canadian Westinghouse	—
FRANCE			
DUBV/23D	Active surface vessel search/attack sonar	CIT/ALCATEL	Bow mounted
DUBV/43B	Variable depth sonar	CIT/ALCATEL	Towed
DUUX 2A/B/C	Passive sonar. Submarine detection system	CIT/ALCATEL	—
DUBV 24/C	Low frequency panoramic search/attack sonar	CIT/ALCATEL	—
PASCAL Sonar	Surveillance and tracking sonar for small and medium ships	CIT/ALCATEL	—
DUUA 2A	Simultaneous search and attack sonar for modernised "Daphne" class S/M	CIT/ALCATEL	—
HS-71/DUAV-4	Helicopter sonar	CIT/ALCATEL	—
TSM 2 400/DUBA 25	Surface vessel sonar (TARPON). Attack sonar	Thomson CSF	Hull or towed
Diodon (TSM 2314)	Submarine detection, target tracking and attack operations	Thomson CSF	Hull or towed
Piranha (TSM 2140)	Attack sonar	Thomson CSF	Hull
DUBM 41A	Side looking sonar	Thomson CSF	Towed
DUBM 21A IBIS	Mine counter measure sonar	Thomson CSF	Hull mounted
DUBM 40B	Active mine hunting sonar	Thomson CSF	Towed
ITALY			
IP 64 MD 64	Submarine sonars	USEA	—
THE NETHERLANDS			
LWS 30	Passive sonar/intercept system. Omni-directional surveillance against surface or sub-surface targets	Hollandse Signaalpparaten B.V.	—
PSH 32	High performance search and attack sonar	Hollandse Signaalpparaten B.V.	Hull
UNITED KINGDOM			
PMS.26.27	Lightweight search/attack sonar	Plessey	Hull
Type 195	Helicopter sonar	Plessey	Dunking type
PMS 32	Active/passive panoramic sonar	Plessey	Hull
Type 162M	Sideways looking sonar	Kelvin Hughes	Hull
Type 186	Submarine sonar	EMI	Hull
Type 187	Submarine sonar	EMI	Hull
Type 193	RN mine hunting system (Acoustic)	Plessey	Hull
Type 193M	Solid state improved version of type 193 mine hunting sonar	Plessey	Hull
Type 199	Variable depth towed sonar	EMI	Towed
Type 719	Submarine sonar	EMI	Hull
SADE	Sensitive Acoustic Detection Equipment. Intruder detection system	Plessey	Hull
Project 35	Advanced fleet escort sonar in development	Plessey	Hull
UNITED STATES OF AMERICA			
AQS 13	Helicopter sonar	Bendix	Dunking type
BQG 1/4	Submarine passive fire control sonars	Sperry/Raytheon	Hull
BQQ 1	Search and fire control sonars	Raytheon	Hull
BQQ 2	Sonar for Subroc system	Raytheon	Hull
BQQ 5	Nuclear attack submarine sonar	Hughes/GE/IBM	Hull
BQR 2	Submarine passive sonar	Raytheon	Hull
BQR 3	Submarine passive sonar	Raytheon	Hull
BQR 7	Passive sonar. Part of BQQ 2 system	Raytheon	Hull
BQR 15	Towed submarine sonar	Western Electric	Towed
BQR 19	Submarine sonar	Raytheon	Hull
BQR 21	Submarine passive detection and tracking set (DIMUS)	Honeywell	Hull
BQS 6	Active submarine sonar. Part of BQQ-2 system	Raytheon	Hull
BQS 8	Under ice navigation sonar	Hazeltine	Hull
BQS 13	Submarine search sonar. Passive/active	IBM	Hull
SQA 10	Variable depth sonar	Litton	Towed
SQA 13	Variable depth sonar	—	Hull
SQA 14	"Searchlight" sonar	Raytheon	Towed
SQA 16	"Searchlight" sonar	Raytheon	Hull
SQA 19	Variable depth sonar	Litton	Towed
SQG 1	A/S attack sonar	Raytheon	Hull
SQQ 14	Mine hunting and classification sonar	GE	Hull
SQQ 23	Sonar for A/S patrol ships	—	Hull
SQR 14	Surface sonar	—	Hull
SQS 4	Short range active sonar	Sangamo/GE	Hull
SQS 23	Long range active sonar	Sangamo	Hull
SQS 26	Bow mounted "Bottom Bounce" mode sonar to replace SQS 23	EDO/GE	Hull
SQS 29/32	Surface vessel active sonars. Nos relate to differing frequencies	—	—
SQS 35	Variable depth towed sonar	—	Towed
SQS 36	Medium range hull sonar	EDO	Hull
SQS 38	Medium range hull sonar	EDO	Hull
SQS 56	Lightweight sonar under development for USN PF ships	Raytheon	Hull
UQS 2	Mine hunting sonar	GE	Hull
610	Long range hull sonar	EDO	Hull
700 series	Medium range hull and variable depth versions	EDO	Hull and towed

Frequency	Power	Ship Type	Remarks
—	—	—	
—	—	—	
—	—	—	
—	—	—	
4 operating frequencies around 5 kHz, 2 of which are operational	96 kW (2 × 48 kW)	A/S escorts Types T47/T56 "Suffren" class frigates and type C67 and corvettes type C70 of French Navy	
—	—	A/S escorts T47 and T56 also C67 series and C70 series	
4 operating frequencies around 5 kHz, 2 of which are operational	48 kW (2 × 24 kW)	—	
10 and 11·5 kHz	5 kW	—	
8·4 kHz	30 kW	"Daphne" class S/M	
—	—	Helicopter	
—	—	"Aviso" type	
Selectable: 11·12 or 13 kHz	—	ASW small or medium tonnage	
11, 12 or 13 kHz	10 kVa	Small ship	
8, 9 or 10 kHz	5 kVa	Small ship	
100 kHz mod ±10 kHz	—	Mine hunters	
730 kHz	1 kW	Mine hunters	
—	—	Small or medium size S/M	
—	—	—	
—	—	Corvette to frigate size ships	
—	—	Ships and patrol craft over 150 tons	
—	—	Westland Sea King ASW	
—	—	A/S escort ships	
—	—	—	
—	—	Vosper glassfibre 45 metre minehunter	
—	—	Minehunters	
—	—	Submarines	
—	—	Submarines	
—	—	—	
—	—	Shore based	
—	—	—	
—	—	Helicopter	
—	—	S/M	
—	—	—	
—	—	S/M	
—	—	S/M	
—	—	S/M	
—	—	S/M	
—	—	—	
—	—	SSBNs	
—	—	S/M	
—	—	SSBNs and SSNs	
—	—	S/M	
—	—	S/M	
—	—	S/M	
—	—	—	
—	—	—	
—	—	—	
—	—	—	
—	—	MCM	
—	—	—	
—	—	—	
—	—	—	
—	—	—	Re-designated AN/SQS 53. Specified for 30 "Spruance" Class DD 963 destroyers
—	—	—	
—	—	—	
—	—	—	
—	—	—	
—	—	—	

NAVAL STRENGTHS

NAVAL STRENGTHS

	Aircraft Carriers (L=light)	Cruisers and Light Cruisers	Destroyers	Frigates	Corvettes	Ballistic Missile Submarines (N = Nuclear D = Diesel)	Cruise Missile Submarines (N = Nuclear D = Diesel)	Fleet Submarines	Patrol Submarines	FAC Missile	FAC Torpedo	FAC Gun	Patrol Craft	Minelayers
ARGENTINA	1 (L)	2	9 (1)	(6)	12				4 (2)	(2)	2	2	5	
AUSTRALIA	1 (L)		5	6 (2)					4 (2)				12	
BELGIUM				2 (2)									6	
BRAZIL	1 (L)		12 (6)		(?6)				8 (2)				14	
BULGARIA				2	2				2	4	8			
BURMA				2	4								71	
CANADA			4	16					3				13	
CHILE		2	6	5	3				3		4		6	
CHINA			9 (2)	12 (2)	40 (4)	1 (D)		1 (?)	65 (6)	140 (20)	240 (10)	438 (10)	40+	
COLOMBIA			4	3					2+4(small)				25	
CUBA				1 Res						23	24	7	41	
DENMARK				7	3 (3)				6	4 (6)	10		46	5 (2)
DOMINICAN REP				3	7								14	
ECUADOR				3	2				(2)	3	3		7	
EGYPT			5	3					12	16	30		35	
FINLAND				2 (2)	2					4+1 (5)		15	5	1 (1)
FRANCE	2 (L) (1)	2	21 (3)	29 (6+2)		4 (N) 1 (D) (2N)		(11)	22 (1)	5 (6)			34	
GERMANY (DEM)				2						15	65		40	
GERMANY (FED)			11	6 (12)	6				24	30	10			
GREECE			12	4	5				7 (4)	10	19		5	2
INDIA	1 (L)	2		25 (2)	(3)				8	16			8	
INDONESIA				11+3					3	19	5		27	
IRAN			3 (4)	4	4				(3)	(12)			7	
IRAQ										12	12	4	31	
ISRAEL									2 (2)	19 (5)			67	
ITALY		3 (1)	8 (2)	11 (3+8)	13				10 (2+2)	6	4			
JAPAN			31 (3+1)	15 (1)	12				15 (1+1)	5			9	1
KOREA (N)				2					13	18	157	44	51	
KOREA (S)			9	9 (4)	10					8			38 (3)	
MALAYSIA				3						8		6 (4)	22	
MEXICO			2	6	35								36 (9)	
NETHERLANDS			12	6 (8+4)	6				6				5	
NEW ZEALAND				4									8	
NORWAY				5	2				15	26 (14)	20			3 (2)
PAKISTAN		1	4 (2)	2	2				4+6 small		6	14	1	
PERU		3 (1)	4	2 (4+2)					8 (2)				16	
PHILIPPINES				10	12							9	46 (?74)	
POLAND			1						4	12	21		29	
PORTUGAL				17					3				18	
ROMANIA					3					5	22	18	31	
SOUTH AFRICA			1	3 (2)					3 (2)	(6)			3	
SPAIN	1 (L) (1)		13	15 (7+5)					9 (4)		2		26	
SWEDEN			6	4	(3)				18 (2)	1 (16)	41		27	49 (1)
TAIWAN			20	11	3				2	1 (14)	8		14	1
THAILAND				6						3			47	6
TURKEY			12	2					14 (3)	7 (1)	12		45 (1)	9
UNITED KINGDOM	1+1 (L)	10 (2)	3 (6)	56 (6)		4		9 (3+1)	18				19	1
UNITED STATES	13 (2N) +(2N) +6 res	26 (3) (+5 res)	92 (25)	64 (10)		41 (N) (4N)	1 res (D)	65 (27+2 res)	10	1 (1)			12	
USSR	1 (2)	38 (2)	111 (3)	108	112 (6)	61 (6) (N) 23 (D)	41 (2) (N) 28 (D)	39 (2)	230 (2)	120	85	71	180	2
VENEZUELA			4	5 (6)					5		3	3	31	
YUGOSLAVIA			1		3				5 (2?)	10 (10)	14	20	23	

Ocean Mine-sweepers	Coastal Mine-sweepers/ Mine-hunters	Inshore Mine-sweepers	Mine-sweeping Boats	Assault Ships	Landing Ships	Landing Craft	Depot Repair Main-tenance Ships	Survey Research Ships (Large and Small)	Supply Ships	Large Tankers	Small Tankers	Hydrofoils and ACVs	Misc-ellaneous	
	4/2				4 (1)	20		7 (2)		1	2		18 (1)	ARGENTINA
	3					6 (1)	1	4 (1)		1			15	AUSTRALIA
7	4/2	14						2	2				12	BELGIUM
	8 (2)				2		1	17		1	1		11	BRAZIL
2	4	—	24			18							?	BULGARIA
								2					10	BURMA
							2	5	3		2	1	71	CANADA
					4	3	2	1		1 (2)	2		17	CHILE
18	—				36	467	1	11	14 (?12)		10	70	400+	CHINA
								4			1		22	COLOMBIA
					7			6					8	CUBA
	8						1				2		4	DENMARK
					1	2 (1)		5			2		8	DOMINICAN REP
					2			2	1				9 (1)	ECUADOR
10		2				14						3	4	EGYPT
	6 (10)					11							76	FINLAND
8	31/10			2	5	31	9	10	6	5 (1)	5		168 (12)	FRANCE
	52 (3)			8		12		4	4		4		53	GERMANY (DEM)
	40	18				41	14	1	12		11	(10)	504	GERMANY (FED)
	15			1	14	53	2	6			7		26	GREECE
	4	4			1	6	1	3 (1)		21	35		86	INDIA
5	2				9	2	4	4		1	7		5	INDONESIA
	3	2			2 (1)	1	1		2	(1)	1	14	7	IRAN
													3	IRAQ
2		3			3	9							4	ISRAEL
4	30/1 (10)	10			2	59	8	4	1	1 (1)		1 (13)	97 (1)	ITALY
	29 (3+1)		6	6			4	6 (1)			1 (1)		62 (1)	JAPAN
						90							105	KOREA (N)
	10		1		21	1	1	3	6				2	KOREA (S)
	6					3		1	1				28 (3)*	MALAYSIA
17					3			1			2		8	MEXICO
	11/4 (15)	16				11	4	3	2				24	NETHERLANDS
	2							5					2	NEW ZEALAND
	10	1				7	1 (1)	1					9 (2)	NORWAY
	7							1			2		7	PAKISTAN
					4			4 (1)			7 (1)		12 (2)	PERU
	2				39	71	1				7	4	33	PHILIPPINES
24			20			38		1			6		71+1 AGI	POLAND
	4					14		4		1	1		4	PORTUGAL
	4	10	8										?	ROMANIA
	10							2	1				9	SOUTH AFRICA
10/4	12			1	5	87	1 (2)	6		1	13		70	SPAIN
	18 (9)	20				140 (5)		5 (1)	1		1		43	SWEDEN
2	14		8		29	22	1	3			7		42	TAIWAN
	4		10		10	39		4			4		12	THAILAND
	21	4	9 (Hunters)		2	53	4	4	2		5		33	TURKEY
	22/16 (+2)	5		2	7	59 (2)	3	4+9	7 (2)	17	6	5	200	UNITED KINGDOM
25 (8 res)			10 (4) (+4 res)	65 (4) (+18 res)	100		27 (5) (28 res)	40 (5 res)	21	19 (2)		3	50 plus MSC	UNITED STATES
161 (3)	125 (3)	112			22 (2)	142 +100 small	70	130	5	26	18	40	305+ 54 AGIs	USSR
					6			3					18	VENEZUELA
	4	10	14 (river)		(1)	30+		1			9		45	YUGOSLAVIA

* Police
** In addition there are 30 Cargo and Transport Ships (amphib), of which 22 are in reserve.

NAVAL GUNS

Calibre mm	Length in Calibres	Country and Year Introduced	Number of Barrels	Elevation Degrees	Rate of Fire per Barrel (Rounds per Minute)	Weight of Shell kg (Explosive)	Range km (Surface/Height)	AA Slant	Associated Radar/Director
HEAVY									
406	50	US Navy 1936	Single		2	1 235	42 km		Mk 34 Fire Control Director
203	55	US Navy 1971	Single	—5°, +65°, 20°/sec	10-12 rpm	118 kg max.	Estimated over 55 km		Mk 68 fire control system in destroyer *Hull*
203	55	US Navy 1927, 1944	3 Mk XV Mk XVI	30 41	5 10 cased	125	23 km (28)		Mk 34 fire control director with Mk 13 radar
152	53	Bofors, Sweden 1942	Triple and twin	70° 60°	10-15	46	18/10 km (26 max)		
152	50	Vickers, UK 1951	Twin Mk-26	80	20		15 km		MRS-3 F.C.S.
152	50	Vickers, UK, 1934	Triple	45	8	50	23 km max		
152	50	Vickers, UK, 1923	Twin			45			
152	47	US Navy 1933	Triple Mk-16		10	47	23 km max		Mk-33 F.C.S. Mk-34 Director
150	50	USSR 1938	Triple Semi-auto	50	4/10	50	27 km max		26 foot range finder (Built-in)
MEDIUM									
133		UK	Twin						
130	60	USSR 1953	Twin Auto	70	15	27	17/8 (28/13 max)		
130	50	USSR 1936	Twin semi-auto single	40	10	27	24 max 15 opt		
130	58	USSR	Twin semi-auto Dual purpose	50	15	27	28,000 metres max 18,000 opt	13,000 max	Sun Visor, Egg Cup and Wasphead
127	54	US Navy 1969	Single Mk-45	65	20	32			Mk 86 F.C.3 with AN/SPG-60 radar
127	54	OTO Melara, 1968	Single	85	45	32	15/7		
127	54	US Navy 1953	Single Mk-42	85	45	46 (32)	24/14 (max)		Mk-68 Director with AN/SPG-53 radar
127	54	France 1948	Twin semi-auto	80	18	— (32)	18/9 22/13 max		
127	54	US Navy 1944	Single Mk 39	80	15	— (32)	12/8 22/13 max		
127	38	US Navy 1935	Single Mk 30 Twin Mk 38	80	15	37	13/8 17/11		
127	50	US Navy 1923	Single		8	27			
120	50	Bofors, Sweden, 1950	Twin	85	42	24	13/7 (20/12) max		Dutch fire control Director L.A.-01. See note
120	50	San Carlos, Spain, 1950	Twin NG-53	80	15	25	18/11		
120	50	Bofors, Sweden, 1934	Single	70	12	24	20 max		
120	50	Vickers, UK, 1931	Single		8	28	18		
120	50	Ansaldo, Italy, 1926	Twin			23			
120	46	Bofors, Sweden, 1967	Single	80	80	35 (21)	12/8 (19/12)		
120	45	Bofors, Sweden, 1945	Twin	80	20	24	19/13		
114	55	Vickers, UK, 1971	Single Mk-8	53-55	20-25		13/6		
114	50	Vickers, UK, 1946	Twin Mk 6	80	11-25	25	13/6 19		
114	45	Vickers, UK, 1937	Single Mk-5	50 or 85	8, 12, 14	25	11/5 19/3		
105	50	Bofors, Sweden, 1932	Single						
102	60	Vickers, UK, 1955	Single	75	40	16	12/8 18/12		
102	—	Vickers, UK, 1935	Various	80	up to 16	16	19/13		

Remarks

U.S. Navy Reserve Battleships of "Iowa" class.

MCLWG (Major Calibre Lightweight Gun) at present only in destroyer *Hull* for trials. Destined for "Spruance" class if accepted. Intended for surface fire. Digital Mk 86 GECS in new constructions.

Mk XV manually operated fitted to *Saint Paul* and *Canberra*. Mk XVI automatically operated on US cruisers of "Salem" class.

Fitted in cruisers *A. Grau* (Peru) and *A. Latorre* (Chile). *A. Latorre* has the only existing triple mount. Single Bofors 152 mm open shielded mountings in Swedish minelayer *Alvsnabben* are believed to belong to the same general type.

Only on board cruisers HMS *Blake* and *Tiger*. One mounting per ship.

Now only found in British-built cruisers—Indian *Mysore* and Peruvian "Bolognesi" class.

Only aboard Indian Navy cruiser *Delhi*.

Only aboard U.S. cruiser *Cleveland* and "Brooklyn" class owned by Argentina (2) and Chile (1).

Independent-elevating barrels often referred as L.57 long. On "Chapaev" and "Sverdlov" classes of Soviet cruisers.

Dual purpose mounting exists only aboard British built cruiser *Babur* (Pakistan).

"Kotlin" class and variants (USSR and Polish "Warszawa"). Sometimes referred to as 58 calibres long × 50.

"Skory" class destroyers (USSR). "Luta" class Chinese Navy. Single only on Ex-Soviet "Gordy" class of Chinese Navy.

"Skory" (Mod) and "Kotlin" classes.

Ordered by US Navy ("Virginia", "California", "Spruance" and "Tarawa" classes) also Iran "Spruances", Mk-65 improvement, proposed for late "Spruance" class.

In use by Canada (4 "Iroquois" class destroyers) and Italy (2 "Audace" class) ordered for "Lupo" class frigates of Italy, Peru and Venezuela. Probably for Italian "Mastrale" class.

Aboard U.S. carriers, cruisers, destroyers and frigates of post war design. Also in Australia, Federal Germany, Japan and Spain.

Twin gun using American ammunition only remaining aboard four T53 destroyers ("La Bourdonnais" class).

Aboard US carriers of the original "Midway" class and in Japanese "Akizuki" and "Murasame" classes (5 destroyers). Semi-automatic.

Twin Mk-38 aboard U.S.-built destroyers "Gearing" and "Sumner" classes in many navies; Danish, Italian and Spanish built escorts. Single Mk 30 on other wartime escorts; U.S. built in many foreign navies. Cruisers, "Long Beach", "Brooke" and "Garcia" classes of frigates, auxiliaries, and a few Spanish and Yugoslavian built frigates. Both models employ Mk-12 barrel and usually Mk-37 fire control director, sometimes complemented for Mk-56. In austere installations Mk-52 fire control system, including Mk-51 manual director. Other variants of this widely used wartime gun are Mk-32 in several old U.S. cruisers. Single Mk-24 in "Albany" class cruisers also "Hancock"/"Essex" classes of carriers. Open mountings without shield are used in auxiliaries and known as either Mk-37 or Mk-30 Mod 24, both singles.

Single open mountings used (eight per ship) in U.S. built "Brooklyn" class cruisers remaining in Argentine Navy (2) and Chilean Navy (1)

Dutch fire control director LA-01 aboard destroyers of the "Halland" class. (Sweden 2, Columbia 2) and of the Dutch "Tromp", "Holland" and "Friesland" classes.

Data is estimated. Derived from NG-50. NG-53 is semi-automatic. Only in service in Spanish destroyer *Oquendo*.

Only aboard *Halsingborg* and *Kalmar* frigates of the Royal Swedish Navy.

Manually operated. Surface fire only in "R" class destroyers of the Indian Navy (3).

Believed to be used in the two "Paraguay" class gunboats of Paraguayan Navy.

Turret has a 4 mm shield 51 rounds per minute. Private venture only mounted in the two Finnish "Turunma" class escorts. One mounting per ship.

Swedish destroyers of "Öland" and "Östergotland" classes. Semi-automatic light shield. Originally employing Mk-45 fire control.

Developed from the "Abbot" field gun. Aboard British "Amazon", "Bristol" and "Sheffield" classes.

Data is estimated: semi-automatic aboard escorts of Australia (where it is locally built under licence) Chile, India, Netherlands, New Zealand, Peru, South Africa and UK navies. Sometimes referred to as 46 calibres long with automatic version used in "County" class destroyers with rate of fire of 50 r.p.m. per barrel. Dates from 1960.

Fitted to British "Tribal" class, Pakistan "C" class and Malaysian frigate *Rahmat* open turret hand loaded. It is assumed that closed twin turrets in "Battle" class destroyers of Iran and Pakistan navies and Venezuelan "Aragua" class use the same gun but are semi-automatic.

Two Argentinan "Murature" class frigates. 3 guns per ship. Hand loaded. Open shield.

Used exclusively aboard two "Almirante Williams" class destroyers of Chilean Navy. Closed turrets. Four mountings per ship.

These performance figures belong to the pre-war 3·4 ton 4" barrel made by Vickers. This is most widely used in British-built ships in different mountings. All believed to use the above barrel. The single and twin Mk-19 can be found in the navies of Burma, Dominican Republic, Ecuador, Egypt, India, Malaysia, Nigeria, Pakistan, South Africa, Sri Lanka, Thailand. A twin lightweight anti-aircraft British 4" gun is used on Peruvian and Indian cruisers. A modern short barrelled-enclosed mounting, also from Vickers, serves in "Vosper Mk-1" class corvettes owned by Libya and Ghana. Sometimes referred to as the 102 or 100 mm are the twin guns of the Italian-made frigates owned by Venezuela ("A. Clemente" class) and Indonesia ("Surapati" type).

Calibre mm	Length in Calibres	Country and Year Introduced	Number of Barrels	Elevation Degrees	Rate of Fire per Barrel (Rounds per Minute)	Weight of Shell kg (Explosive)	Range km (Surface/Height)	AA Slant	Associated Radar/Director
100	60	USSR, 1942	Twin	80 or 90	15-20	16	11/8 18/12 max		
100	56	China							
100	55	France 1959	Single, various versions	80	60	23·2 (13·4)	13/7 17/11 max		
100	50	USSR	Twin	80	15	16	20,000 m 12,000 m	15,000 max 9,000 Slan	Top Bow/Post Lamp, Egg Cup
100	50	USSR 1947	Single	40 or 80	15	13·5	18/11 16/6	6,000	Sun Visor
85	55	USSR 1943	Single, Twin	70 or 75	10-20	9·5	9/6 14/9	6,000	
76	70	Vickers, UK, 1951	Twin Mk-6	80 or 90	60	7 approx	5 max 17 surface		
76	62	OTO Melara, Italy, 1964	Single	85	85	6	8/5 16/12 max		
76	62	OTO Melara, Italy, 1961	Single	85	60	6	8/5 16/12 max		
76	60	USSR 1961	Twin	85	60	16	15/10	14,000	
76	50	Bofors, Sweden, 1965	Single	30	30	11	7·5/— 13/— max		
76	50	US Navy 1944	See Note	7·5 or 85	45 or 50	6	7/5·5 13/8		
76	50	US Navy 1936	Single Mks 21-22 & 26		20 or 33		12/—		Mk-52
LIGHT 57	80	USSR, about 1965	Twin	85	120	2·7	5/1 12/5 max		Muff Cobb
57	70	USSR 1959	Single, Twin, Quad	85	120	2·8	—/4 9/6 max	6,000	Hawk Screech
57	70	Bofors, Sweden, 1971	Single	75	200	5·9	14/—		Dutch M-20 series
57	60	Bofors, Sweden, 1950	Twin	90	120-130	2·6	—/5 14/9		
45	85	USSR 1953	Quad	90	160-220	1·5	—/4 9/6 max	7,000	Hawk Screech
40	70	Bofors, Sweden, 1946	Single 2·4-3·3 Also Twin	80-90	240-300	2·4	4/— 13/9		
40	60	Bofors, Sweden, 1942	Various	80	120-160	0·89	—12·7 10/4·5 max		
37	80	Krupp, Germany, 1932	Single	85	80	0·745	4/3		
37	63	USSR, 1944	Twin	80	130	0·7	8/5 max	3,000	Eye Shooting
37	63	USSR, 1044	Single	80	130	0·7	8/5 max	3,000	Eye Shooting
35	90	Oerlikon, Switzerland, 1972	Twin	85	550	1·55	6/5 max		
30	75	Oerlikon, Switzerland, 1974	Twin	80-85	650	1 0·36	3 10·2 max		
30	70	Hispano Suiza, France, 1962	Single	83	600	0·42	2·8 8·5 max		
30	65	USSR 1960	Twin	80 or 85	500		2·5 4 max		Drum Tilt

Remarks

Only in Russian cruisers ("Sverdlov" and "Chapaev" class) and "Kotlin" class destroyers. The gunnery of the Chinese "Kiangtung" class could be considered as a local development. Each turret uses its own Egg Cup radar. Fire control is managed with either Top Bow or Post Lamp radars.

Known to exist in Chinese "Kiang-Nan" class. Probably the same as those aboard North Korean frigates of "Najin" class and corvettes of the "Sariwan" and "Tral" classes. The last being Russian built. The guns are thought to be a Chinese refit of a Soviet weapon, possibly the 100/50 1947 model.

Two versions: *Modèle 1953* with analogic fire control and *Modèle 68* associated with digital fire control. Integrating DRBC 32 radar. Aboard two ("Clémenceau") carriers, one "Colbert" cruiser, two "Suffren" frigates, *Jeanne d'Arc* and escorts of the "C 65", "C 70", "A 69", "F 67", "T 47", "ASW", "T 53 ASW", "T 56" and "Commandant Rivière" classes. Total of 36 ships including those under construction in French Navy. Also fitted in Belgian "E 71" class (4); Federal Germany ("Hamburg", "Köln" and "Rhein") classes and *Deutschland,* Portugal ("C. João Belo" and "João Countinho" classes); Tunisia; South Africa (A69 class new Avisos); and Turkish ("Rhein") class. The newest 1976 turret, which is lighter than its predecessors is claimed to reach 90 rounds per minute.

"Sverdlov" and "Chapaev" classes.

"Riga", "Kola", "Don" and "Purga" class ships of Soviet Navy. Semi-automatic.

Twin mounts in "Skory" class. Single mounts in "Kronshtadt" class.

Fully automatic aboard Canadian frigates and HMS *Blake* and *Tiger* cruisers.

Ordered by Argentina, Denmark, Fed. Germany, Iran, Israel, Italy, Libya, Morocco, Netherlands, Nigeria, Oman, Spain, Turkey, Venezuela and USA. The USA has standardised the weapon as the Mk-75 to start its employment in "Pegasus" and "WMEC-630" classes; a variety of fire control systems is used, notably the Dutch M.20 series.

Aboard Italian Navy ships "V Veneto," "A. Doria", "Impavido", "Alpino," "Bergamini", "Centauro" and "De Cristofaro" classes. Sometimes referred to as Brescia model.

"Kiev", "Kara", "Kynda", "Krivak", "Kashin", converted "Kildin", "Mirka", and "Petya" classes.

Surface fire only. Used aboard fast attack craft of Norwegian "Storm" class (20) and Singapore "Type B" Vosper class (3).

Most usual versions are single Mk-34 single mount (weight 7·7 tons). Mk-27 and Mk-33 twin mounts (weight 14·5 tons). In both open and semi-protected versions, the last using a fibre-glass shield. Aboard US-built cruisers, destroyers, frigates and auxiliaries. Extensively used in foreign navies and foreign-built ships; notably Japan. Built under licence (Mk-34) in Spain. Mk-56 and Mk-63 gunfire control systems usually employed.

Semi-automatic; intended for surface fire only; widely used in many obsolete ships of US Navy (auxiliary, amphibious) and abroad including wartime-built escort destroyers. Also Greek "Algerine" class. Many other 76 mm of obsolete types remain in service in small quantities. A single 76/40, probably OTO Melara-built, is used aboard Italian built corvettes ("Albatross" class) owned by Denmark (4) and Indonesia (2). Also a 76/40, probably Vickers' 1914 model is used by the Paraguayan Navy on its "Humaita" and "C. Cabral" classes. These have single mounts. Another 76 mm tank turret 76/41·2 is used by Soviet river patrol launches of "Shmel" and "PB" classes. "Trad" and "Bangrachan" classes of Thai Navy probably use Japanese wartime guns of 76 or 75 mm by 40 or 50 calibres long.

Soviet Navy "Moskva", "Kresta I" and "Kresta II", "Grisha I and II", "Nanuchka", "Poti", "Turya" and "T.58" classes. Amphibious and auxiliary ships sometimes referred to as 73 calibres long. Water cooled.

Only twin mod. has muzzle brake. This and quadruple are aboard Soviet "Kildin", "Kanin" and "Kotlin" classes. Singles are aboard Soviet "Skory" (modified) destroyers and various classes of minesweepers. Also East Germany's amphibious ships. A single Chinese 57 mm gun is used in "Shanghai II" class fast attack craft (including some transferred to Albania) and the new "Luta" class.

Plastic-enclosed turret used by navies of Denmark *(Willemoes)* Malaysia *(Perdana)*; Singapore ("Sea" class); Sweden ("Visby", class frigates and 38 fast attack craft); Thailand's "Prabarapak" class. Single 57 mm guns in Sweden's "Alvsnabben" class are of unidentified model—they have very long barrels.

Current Swedish original turret for this gun weighs 20-24 tons and is aboard Peruvian "A Grau" class and Chilean *A Latorre* Sweden's "Halland" class destroyers use French turret weighing 15 tons with only 80° elevation. Also fitted to French cruiser *Colbert* and escorts of the T47, T53, E50 and E52 classes. Open, unprotected, small and obsolete single 57 mm mountings are operated in 5 patrol vessels of Icelandic Navy. A similar weapon of 47 mm calibre is aboard its 6th fishery protection vessel. Peruvian "Loreto" class (2 ships) also use a similar 47 mm gun but might be of the American 30 calibre long model.

"Kildin" and "Kotlin" classes. Semi-Automatic.

The original 1946 model has appeared in a very wide range of variations built in many western countries. Usually 1958 versions: SP-48 type built in Spain, British Mk-7 and Italian Breda improvements. (106 twin and 107 single) with 32 ready use rounds per barrel; twin type 64 (200 r.p.m./barrel) and type 350P/56H single (144 r.p.m.). Latest improvement is Breda Compatto twin 40/70 using either 736 ready use rounds or 444 r.u. rounds. Ordered for Italy, Peru and Venezuela ("Lupo" class) and Libya. This weapon uses "Dardo" system. Non-Italian models use 20 ready use rounds.

Many local versions have been manufactured from the original system. Most common are the American (twin Mk-1 and quad Mk-2 water-cooled mountings, single Mk-3 aircooled.) Other variants are the British twin Mk-5 weighing 3 tons and a French single.

Single mounting built in Spain around 1950. Derived from standard German twin mounting. Remaining examples aboard 7 Spanish patrol and auxiliary ships. Semi-automatic.

"Sverdlov", "Chapaev", "Skory (modified)" and "Riga" classes. Twin Chinese mountings in "Whampoa", "Shantung" and "Shanghai", "Swatow" classes.

"Skory (unmodified)" "Kronshtadt", "T301" classes.

The original weapon (GDM-A) is only found in Greek "Navsithoi" class fast attack craft, Iranian "Saam" class Libyan *Dat Assawari*, Turkish "Dogan" class and Ecuadorean Lurssen craft. Also possibly in two Japanese "Improved Haruna" class. An Italian mounting variant (Oerlikon OTO) was proposed for Peruvian "Lupo" and Libyan 550 ton corvettes. Probably abandoned in favour of twin Breda 40/70 KDC barrel weighing 120 kg. Has 112 ready use rounds per barrel.

GMC-A muzzle braked barrel KCB, HEX, HS 8, 31SLH. Manufactured in UK and in service. In Abu Dhabi patrol craft and Indonesian "Surapati" class frigates. American Emerlec Mk-74 twin mounting (950 ready use rounds) was first embarked in South Korean "Gireogi" coastal patrol craft.

Mounting (215 ready use rounds) in French "Commandant Rivière" class. "Ouragan" class and single "La Combattante" Fast attack craft. Hispano Suiza system is now owned by Oerlikon.

Water cooled. Small enclosed turret used in Soviet ships of "Kanin" some "Kotlin" and "Sverdlov" (CC version) classes. Also some "Rigas", fast attack craft, minesweepers and amphibious craft. In the German "Hai" class and patrol ships is a 30 mm single mounting which was introduced in the new Polish (series 500) landing craft. This might belong to the same system.

ADDENDA

ADDENDA

JERVIS BAY

ALGERIA

Two "Osa II" class recently acquired (1977). Ten small coastal patrol craft ordered in Italy. Also reported that one "Polnocny" class LCT acquired.

ARGENTINA

New Finnish Icebreaker named *Almirante Isizar*. New Oceanographic Research Ship named *Puerto Deseado*. Heermann (DD-532), *Dortch* (DD-670) and *Stembel* (DD-644) transferred to Argentina by sale on 14 January 1977. Previously on loan.

AUSTRALIA

Two new US-built frigates to be named *Adelaide* and *Canberra*. New Trackers to be collected by *Melbourne*. *Australian Trader* of 7 005 grt built by State Dockyard Newcastle in 1969 taken over for conversion to training ship to be renamed *Jervis Bay*. 75 ft General Purpose Vessel attached as tender to *Cerberus*. Two HDMLs attached for reserve training—one to *Leeuwin* and one to *Lonsdale*.

DENMARK

Names of "KV 72" class corvettes (now known as "Nils Juel" class) as follows—*Nils Juel, Peter Tordenskjold*, and *Olfert Fischer*. Names of "Willemoes" class—for *Huitfelde* read *Huitfeldt*. Minelayer *Møen* acts as midshipmen training ship and flagship of Midshipmen Training Squadron.

ECUADOR

Ex-USS *Summit County* (LST-1146) transferred by sale to Ecuador on 14 February 1977 for service.

FINLAND

New minelayer ordered from Wärtsila, Helsinki early 1977.

FRANCE

Jaureguiberry paid off April 1977. Frigate *Le Bourguignon* (F-769) to be sunk as target in July 1977 in the Western Med. by US 6th Fleet, French and British Naval units.

GERMANY (FDR)

Ex-USS *Ringgold* (DD-500), *Wadsworth* (DD-516), *Dyson* (DD-572) and *Claxton* (DD-571) transferred to Germany (FDR) by sale on 7 March 1977 for further service. Previously on loan. Two tankers. *Rhön* (ex- *Okene*) and *Spessart* (ex-*Okapi*) purchased—conversion by Kröger and MW Bremerhaven started Jan 1977 for completion late 1977.
Photograph at end of section is not *Rosenheim*. *Meerkatze* being replaced by new ship of same name in Fishery Protection service.

GREECE

The next six "La Combattante II" class fast attack craft—missile will be differently armed from the four now in commission. They will have 6 Penguin missiles, 1—76 mm gun and 2—40 mm guns. Ex-USS *Gurke* (DD-783), *Whitfield County* (LST-1169) and *Terrell County* (LST-1157) transferred to Greece by sale on 17 March 1977. Towed to Greece for reactivation and modernization.

HAITI

Jean Jacques Dessalines (ex-USS *Tonawanda*) returned to USN for disposal.

INDIA

Two "Nanuchkas" delivered by USSR. First named *Vijaydurg* (K 71).

INDONESIA

Two new submarines (probably Type 209) ordered from Howaldtswerke, Kiel in Feb 1977.

IRAQ

Two "Polnocny" class delivered from Poland, second in June 1977.

IRELAND

New stern trawler *Le Ferdia* chartered for patrol duties. New Minister of Defence—Mr Oliver J. Flanagan TD.

JAPAN

Shobo (salvage vessel) now YE 41 on auxiliary list. "500 ton" Tenders now ASU 81-85 in place of YAS 101-105. 1978 FY request—one 3 900 ton DDG, two 2 900 ton DD, one 1 200 ton DE/PCE, two or three 440 ton MSC, one 100 ton PHM (possibly Jetfoil type), one 2 700 ton AS.

KOREA, SOUTH

Ex-USS *New* and *Richard E. Kraus* transferred on 23 Feb 1977. *New* (DD-818) now renamed *Taejon* DD 99. *Richard E. Kraus* (DD-849) renumbered DD 100.

VIJAYDURG   *3/1977, MoD*

Iraqui "POLNOCNY" Class   *5/1977, MoD*

MALAYSIA

Revised characteristics for "Spica M" class:—

Displacement, tons: 240
Dimensions, feet (metres): 142·6 × 23·3 ×7·4 *(43·6 × 7·1 × 2·4)*
Missiles: 4 Exocet aft; 1 Blowpipe
Gun: 1—57 mm
Main engines: 3 MTU diesels; 3 shafts; 10 800 hp = 34·5 knots
Range, miles: 1 850 at 14 knots

Bridge further forward than in Swedish class to accommodate Exocet.

MALDIVES

Added from Royal Air Force, Gan in 1976:—one 68 ft Target towing launch, one 63 ft pinnace, four 64 ft Landing Craft General Purpose.

MAURITANIA

Two "Barcelo" class large patrol craft under construction by Bazan, La Carraca.

MOROCCO

Completion dates of three "Batrals"—May 1977, Sept 1977, March 1978.

NETHERLANDS

Callenburgh (F 808) launched 26 March 1977.

NORWAY

Type 207 submarines now fitted with small U/D sonar dome forward.

OMAN

Characteristics of new Brooke Marine LCL:—

Displacement, tons: 2 000+
Dimensions, feet (metres): 276 × 49 × — *(84·1 × 14·9 ×—)*

Fitted with full naval command facilities and helicopter deck. Brooke Marine FAC, B4, completed trials early 1977.

PERU

Pennant number for first "Lupo" class unit, *Carvajal*, is "51".

SAUDI ARABIA

US MSC1322 units' building for this country names and construction data as follows:

Name	Keel laid		Launched
ADDRIYAH (ex-USS MSC-322)	12 May 1976		20 Dec 1976
AL-QUYSUMAH (ex-US MSC-323)	24 Aug 1976		
AL-WADEEAH (ex-US MSC-324)	28 Dec 1976		
SAFWA (ex-US MSC-325)			

Polish ASR LECH *5/1977, MoD*

SPAIN

Commissioning date of *Cataluna* (F73) was 16 Jan 1975 and *Extremadura* (F75) 10 Nov 1976. Name of new helicopter VSTOL carrier apparently remains *Almirante Carrero*. Of 16 000 tons full load probably to be ordered soon from Bazan, Ferrol. Lead time to laying down 18 months with 30 months subsequent building time. *Lepanto* (D21) grounded 16 April 1977 with serious damage. *Infanta Cristina* (F34) correct launch date 25 April 1977. "Lazaga" class to mount 4 SSM. Reported that twelve more "Barcelo" class to be built by Bazan, Ferrol. Reported that a new class of coastal patrol craft to be ordered:

Length: 17·6 metres
Displacement: 36 tons
Guns: 2—20 mm Oerlikon
Range: 500 miles
Horsepower: 1 100
Complement: 7

TURKEY

Also reported that West German AKL *Dithmarschen* (transferred to Turkey December 1976) has been converted to Submarine Tender (AS) in 1977 for German Type 209 units in Turkish Navy. Named *Umurbey*— currently listed as *Kanarya.*

UNITED KINGDOM

Tug *Samson* for sale 1977. TCV *Coll* deleted.

USA

Long Beach (CGN-9) to receive a major overhaul 1978/79 in which ship will get Harpoon and Standard missiles as well as 20 mm Phalanx CIWS system. Electronics are to be modernised. This overhaul replaces the "improved Anti-Aircraft Warfare Modernisation" *Long Beach* was to receive in the early 1980s.
Nuclear Strike Cruiser Programme (CSGN) long term lead items dropped from FY 1978 budget.
Conversion of *Wood County* (LST-1178) to Hydrofoil Support Ship (AGHS) cancelled.

Pegasus (PHM-1) programme cancelled 4/77. PHM-1 will be only unit built. She will serve as High Speed Test Vehicle.
USS *Trout* (SS-566) entered Special Category on 2 January 1977 for overhaul and modernisation prior to being transferred to Iran.
Salmon stricken from the Navy List on 1 October 1977.
Contract for construction of AO-179 awarded to Avondale Shipyards Inc, Westwego, La. on 25 January 1977.
Arthur W. Radford (DD-968) commissioned on 16 April 1977.
Cincinnati (SSN-693) launched on 18 February 1977.
Preliminary characteristics of new CVV design include the following: 2 shafts; max. speed approx 30 knots; conventionally powered; two to three catapults; three to four arresting gear wires; two to three elevators and 60% of aircraft complement on "Nimitz" class. This class will be the successor to the "Nimitz" class.
M/V *Hughes Glomar Explorer* acquired by the US Navy on 30 September 1976.
Marathon (PG-89) transferred to Massachusetts Maritime Academy on 18 April 1977 for use as a training ship.
Crockett (PG-88) transferred to US Environmental Protection Agency on 18 April 1977. Assigned to Great Lakes. Gas Turbine removed. Unarmed.
Douglas (PG-100) to be transferred to Naval Research and Development Center, Annapolis upon decommissioning and strike. Will be unarmed and perform same type of duties as M/V *Athena* (ex-*Chehalis* PG-94).
Arco (ARD-29) struck from Navy List on 15 September 1976.
Amphion was stricken 1 Nov 1976. Both transferred to Iran by sale on 1 March 1977. Both previously on loan.
Towanda (AN-89) struck from Navy List on 15 April 1977. To be returned from loan to Haiti and disposed of.
Panameta (YTM-402) stricken on 15 April 1977. To be disposed of.
Cable (ARS-19) a civilian manned ship, leased to a commercial salvage firm, was returned to USN for disposal. Stricken 15 April 1977.

VENEZUELA

Carite (ex-US *Tilefish* SS-307) decommissioned 28 January 1977 for disposal.

INDEXES

INDEXES

Abbreviations in brackets following the names of the ships indicate the country of origin

AbD	Abu Dhabi	Et	Ethiopia	Ku	Kuwait	Sau	Saudi Arabia
Al	Albania	Fi	Fiji	L	Laos	Sen	Senegal
Alg	Algeria	Fin	Finland	Leb	Lebanon	Sh	Sharjah
A	Argentina	F	France	Li	Liberia	S.L.	Sierra Leone
Ang	Angola	G	Gabon	Lib	Libya	Sin	Singapore
An	Anguila	Gam	Gambia	Ma	Malagasy	Som	Somalia
Aus	Australia	Ger	Germany (Federal Republic)	Ml	Malawi	S.A.	South Africa
Au	Austria	GE	Germany (Democratic Republic)	M	Malaysia	Sp	Spain
B	Bahamas	Gh	Ghana	Mal	Malta	Sri	Sri Lanka
Bah	Bahrain	Gr	Greece	Mau	Mauritania	Su	Sudan
Ba	Bangladesh	Ga	Grenada	Ms	Mauritius	Sw	Sweden
Bar	Barbados	Gu	Guatemala	Mex	Mexico	Sy	Syria
Bel	Belgium	Gui	Guinea	Mo	Montserrat	T	Taiwan
Bze	Belize	GB	Guinea Bissau	Mor	Morocco	Tan	Tanzania
Bo	Bolivia	Guy	Guyana	N	Netherlands	Th	Thailand
Br	Brazil	H	Haiti	N.Z.	New Zealand	To	Togo
Bru	Brunei	Hon	Honduras	Nic	Nicaragua	Ton	Tonga
Bul	Bulgaria	HK	Hong Kong	Nig	Nigeria	T & T	Trinidad & Tobago
Bur	Burma	Hun	Hungary	Nor	Norway	Tu	Tunisia
Cam	Cameroon	Ice	Iceland	O	Oman (Sultanate of)	Tur	Turkey
Can	Canada	In	India	Pak	Pakistan	U.K.	United Kingdom
Chi	Chile	Ind	Indonesia	Pan	Panama	U.S.A.	United States of America
C	China (People's Republic)	Ir	Iran	PNG	Papua-New Guinea	Rus	Union of Soviet Socialist
Col	Colombia	Ira	Iraq	Par	Paraguay		Republics
Co	Congo	Ire	Ireland (Republic of)	P	Peru	U	Uganda
C.R.	Costa Rica	Is	Israel	Ph	Philippines	Ur	Uruguay
Cu	Cuba	I	Italy	Po	Poland	Ven	Venezuela
Cy	Cyprus	I.C.	Ivory Coast	Por	Portugal	V	Vietnam
D	Denmark	Jam	Jamaica	Q	Qatar	V.I.	Virgin Islands
Dom	Dominican Republic	J	Japan	R	Romania	Yem	Yemen
Du	Dubai	Jo	Jordan	S	Sabah	YS	Yemen (South)
Ec	Ecuador	Ka	Kampuchea	St. K	St. Kitts	Y	Yugoslavia
Eg	Egypt	Ke	Kenya	St. L	St. Lucia	Z	Zaire
Eq	Equatorial Guinea	Kor	Korea (Republic of)	St. V	St. Vincent	Zan	Zanzibar
ES	El Salvador	K.N.	Korea (North)				

INDEX OF NAMED SHIPS

ATREVIDA—CAPUCINE

IFUGAO—KONTOURIOTIS

STEADY—UPLIFTER

INDEX OF CLASSES

Printed in England by Netherwood Dalton & Co. Ltd., Huddersfield

RADAR SYSTEMS FOR SHIPS, HELICOPTERS AND GROUND STATIONS - RADARS FOR
NAVIGATION AND AIR-NAVAL SEARCH - DISPLAYS - MISSILE ASSIGNMENT CONSOLLES -
HOMING RADARS - SIGNAL PROCESSING AND DATA HANDLING TECHNIQUES.

SMA
SEGNALAMENTO MARITTIMO ED AEREO

P.O. BOX 200 - FIRENZE (ITALIA) - TELEPHONE: 705651 - TELEX: SMARADAR 57622 - CABLE: SMA FIRENZE